CurrentLaw

YEAR BOOK
1997

VOLUME ONE

Sweet & Maxwell
W Green
Legal Information Resources

AUSTRALIA
LBC Information Services
Brisbane • Sydney • Melbourne • Perth

CANADA
Carswell
Ottawa • Toronto • Calgary • Montreal • Vancouver

Agents:
Steimatzky's Agency Ltd., Tel Aviv
N.M. Tripathi (Private) Ltd., Bombay
Eastern Law House (Private) Ltd., Calcutta
M.P.P. House, Bangalore
Universal Book Traders, Delhi
Aditya Books, Delhi
MacMillan Shupan KK, Tokyo
Pakistan Law House, Karachi, Lahore

Current Law

YEAR
BOOK 1997

Being a Comprehensive Statement of the Law of 1997

LEGAL INFORMATION RESOURCES EDITORIAL TEAM

Shirley Archer	Cherry Dexter	Penny Dickman
Carol Locke	Rachael Lockley	Christine Miskin
Alix Robinson	Mark Scott	Suzanne Warren

LEGAL INFORMATION RESOURCES PRODUCTION TEAM

Hazel Holway   Roger Greenwood

Editors

English and Commonwealth Law

NICHOLAS BAATZ, Q.C., *Barrister*
CHRISTOPHER BLAGG, B.A.
IAN FERRIER, M.A., *Barrister*
SHAUN FERRIS, B.A., *Barrister*
ALASTAIR HUDSON, LL.B., LL.M., *Barrister*
CHARLES JOSEPH, B.A., *Barrister, FCI Arb*
VANESSA MIDDLETON, LL.B., *Solicitor*
ALEXANDRA MILLBROOK, B.A., *Barrister*
NICHOLAS ROSE, LL.B.
WILLIAM VANDYCK, B.A., *Barrister*
GORDON WIGNALL, M.A., *Barrister*

Scotland

MALCOLM THOMSON, Q.C., LL.B.
HEATHER BAILLE, B.A., LL.B., *Solicitor*

Damages Awards

DAVID KEMP, Q.B., B.A., *Barrister*
PETER MANTLE, *Barrister*

The Mode of Citation
of the Current Law Year Book is
[1997] 1 C.L.Y. 1282
The 1997 Year Book is published in two volumes.

Published in 1998 by
Sweet & Maxwell Limited of
100 Avenue Road, Swiss Cottage, London NW3 3PF
Typeset by Legal Information Resources Limited,
Mytholmroyd, Hebden Bridge
Printed by The Bath Press, Bath, Avon.

A CIP catalogue record for this book is available
from the British Library

ISBN: 1997 Yearbook: 0-421-637706
1997 Yearbook and Case Citator: 0-421-637803

No forests were destroyed to make this product;
farmed timber was used and then replanted.

FOREWORD

The 1997 Current Law Yearbook marks the fiftieth anniversary of Current Law. Since 1947 the monthly digests and cumulative annual volumes have consistently and comprehensively recorded developments in the law in England, Northern Ireland, Scotland, Wales and the European Union as it affects the former jurisdictions. Against an ever increasing volume of legal information, Current Law has continued to fulfil its objective to provide an up to date and comprehensive summary of all legal developments, carefully structured and indexed and extensively referenced to ensure that the required information can be found quickly. Current Law has increased its range of source material and has embraced information technology in a multitude of forms in the collection of data, its production techniques and delivery to customers. In the rapidly changing world that is now legal information Current Law Monthly Digest and Yearbook promises to remain a key information source for all our customers.

Barbara Grandage
Product Delivery Director
Sweet & Maxwell

PREFACE

The 1997 Current Law Yearbook supersedes the issues of *Current Law Monthly Digest* for 1997 and covers the law from January 1 to December 31 of that year.

Jurisdiction

The text of the 1997 Current Law Yearbook is divided into three sections respectively; UK, England and Wales and EU, Northern Ireland and Scotland. The European material comprises; cases appearing before the Court of First Instance and European Court of Justice which are published in the reports series and newspapers, and a selection of journal articles and books.

Cases

The 1997 Current Law Yearbook includes digests of 3,587 cases published in over 90 reports series, journals, The Times and Independent newspapers, transcripts and ex relatione contributions from barristers and solicitors. A number of reports edited by David Kemp Q.C. concerning damages awards in personal injury cases in England and Wales appears under the subject heading DAMAGES and are collated in tabular form together with Scottish personal injuries cases at the beginning of Volume 1.

An alphabetical Table of Cases digested in the 1997 Yearbook appears at the beginning of Volume 1. The Current Law Case Citator 1996-1997 appears as a separate bound volume and forms part of the permanent bound volume series for the years 1947-76, 1977-88 and 1989-1995, with separate volumes for Scotland for the years 1948-76 and 1977-88.

The editor thanks those barristers and solicitors who have submitted case reports, many of which demonstrate developments in county court litigation. Whilst all reasonable care is taken in the preparation of the digests it is not possible to guarantee the accuracy of each digest, particularly those cases ex relatione which are not taken from an authorised judgment.

Legislation

All public and private Acts of Parliament published in 1997 are abstracted and indexed. All Statutory Instruments and Statutory Rules of Northern Ireland are abstracted. Cumulative tables of Statutory Instruments arranged alphabetically and by subject are published in Volume 1. A cumulative numerical table of Statutory Rules and Orders for Northern Ireland is also published in Volume 1.

The Current Law Legislation Citators for 1997 appear as a separate bound volume and form part of the series of permanent bound volumes for the years 1989-1995 and 1996.

Articles and Books

A selection of articles appears for the subject headings. A comprehensive guide to articles published in 1997 can be found in Legal Journals Index.

The full title, reference and author of books of interest to the legal profession published in 1997 are arranged by subject heading. A separate list, arranged by author is included in Volume 2.

Index

The subject-matter index in this volume adapts the new, improved format introduced at the beginning of 1991 in the monthly digest. The 30-year Index from 1947-76 may be found in the 1976 *Current Law Year Book*. The Scottish Index for the years 1972-86 may be found in the Scottish 1986 *Year Book*. Scottish material prior to 1972 can be found in the *Scottish Current Law Year Book Master Volumes*, published in 1956, 1961, 1966 and 1971.

May 1997

CONTENTS

THE LAW OF 1997 DIGESTED UNDER TITLES:

Note: Italicised entries refer to Scotland only.

CONTENTS

DIGEST HEADINGS IN USE

Accountancy
Administration of Justice
Administrative Law
Agency
Agriculture
Air Transport
Animals
Arbitration
Armed Forces

Banking

Capital Gains Tax
Capital Taxes
Charities
Children
Civil Evidence
Civil Practice (Scotland)
Civil Procedure
Commercial Law
Company Law
Competition Law
Conflict of Laws
Constitutional Law
Construction Law
Consumer Law
Contracts
Conveyancing
Copyright
Corporation Tax
Criminal Evidence
Criminal Law
Criminal Procedure
Criminal Sentencing
Customs and Excise

Damages
Defamation
Dispute Resolution

Ecclesiastical Law
Economics
Education
Electoral Process
Employment
Energy
Environment
Environmental Health
Equity
European Union
Expenses (Scotland)
Extradition

Family Law
Finance
Financial Services
Food and Drugs
Forestry

Fraud, Misrepresentation and Undue Influence
(Scotland)

Government Administration

Health
Health and Safety at Work
Heritable Property and Conveyancing (Scotland)
Highways and Bridges (Scotland)
Housing
Human Rights

Immigration
Income Tax
Industry
Information Technology
Inheritance Tax
Insolvency
Insurance
Intellectual Property
International Law
International Trade

Jurisdiction (Scotland)
Jurisprudence

Landlord and Tenant
Legal Aid
Legal Methodology
Legal Profession
Legal Systems
Legislation
Leisure Industry
Licensing
Local Government

Media
Medicine
Mental Health

National Health Service
Negligence
Nuisance

Partnerships
Patents
Penology
Pensions
Planning
Police

Rates
Real Property
Registers and Records (Scotland)
Reparation (Scotland)
Restitution (Scotland)
Road Traffic

Sale of Goods

DIGEST HEADINGS IN USE

Science
Shipping
Small Landholder (Scotland)
Social Security
Social Welfare
Succession

Taxation
Telecommunications

Torts
Trade Marks
Trade Unions
Transport
Trusts

Utilities

Value Added Tax

TABLE OF CASES

QUANTUM OF DAMAGES
PERSONAL INJURIES OR DEATH

The table below is a cumulative guide to quantum of damages cases reported in Current Law in 1997.

Injury	Age (at time of injury unless otherwise stated)	Case	Award General £	Award Loss of Earnings Capacity, Family Care £	Reference
Paraplegia	31 (at trial)	L, Re	75,000	177,976	C.L.Y. 1821
Tetraplegia from severe brain injury	14 months	J, Re	80,000	10,000	C.L.Y. 1822
Incomplete tetraplegia	52 (at trial)	Brewer, Re	110,000	27,966	C.L.Y. 1813
Very severe brain damage	27	Sharma (Harshed), Re	150,000	171,413	C.L.Y. 1824
Multiple injuries		Doyle v. Gibbons	375,000		C.L.Y. 1831
	19	Hewlett, Re	35,000	60,200	C.L.Y. 1825
	48	Smith (Brynmor), Re	17,500	7,000	C.L.Y. 1826
	55	Ward v. Lenscrafters EC Corp	13,500		C.L.Y. 1827
	26	Peters v. Robinson	12,500	43,000	C.L.Y. 1828
	38	Wright v. Serco Ltd	10,750		C.L.Y. 1829
	26	Carlin, Re	10,000		C.L.Y. 1830
Head	53	Oxley v. BCH Ltd	1,000		C.L.Y. 1832
Brain and skull	36	Full, Re	90,000	150,000	C.L.Y. 1833
	1 month	Nicholls, Re	85,000	15,000	C.L.Y. 1834
	31	Roberts, Re	70,000	152,370	C.L.Y. 1835
	24 (at trial)	Ives, Re	60,000	60,000	C.L.Y. 1836
	17	John (Mark), Re	25,000	168,997	C.L.Y. 1837
	30	Stoneman, Re	20,000	70,960	C.L.Y. 1838
Epilepsy	43	F, Re	75,000		C.L.Y. 1839
	20	McGuffie, Re	50,000	120,000	C.L.Y. 1840
Psychiatric enuresis	3	G (A Minor) v. Leadstay Ltd	4,000		C.L.Y. 1841
Psychiatric disability after sexual abuse	41	AH, Re	25,000		C.L.Y. 1842
	36	MRR, Re	15,000		C.L.Y. 1843
	20	Jukes v. Radcliffe	5,500	11,111	C.L.Y. 1844
Post traumatic stress	28	Lawson, Re	32,500	56,215	C.L.Y. 1845
	25	ARA, Re	30,000	15,000	C.L.Y. 1847
	35	Gambill (No.1), Re	30,000	119,250	C.L.Y. 1846
	57	Croucher, Re	22,500	24,000	C.L.Y. 1849
	22	Watson v. CICB	22,500		C.L.Y. 1848
		GB, RB, and RP, Re	20,000		C.L.Y. 1850
		M, Re	20,000		C.L.Y. 1851
	12	P, Re	17,500		C.L.Y. 1852
	17 (at trial)	H, Re	15,000		C.L.Y. 1853
		K, Re	13,500		C.L.Y.1854
	49	Jenkins, Re	12,500		C.L.Y. 1856
	28	JW, Re	12,500		C.L.Y. 1855
	34	Zammit v. Stena Offshore Ltd	12,500	246,417	C.L.Y. 1857
	25	Teague v. Camden LBC	11,000	84,103	C.L.Y. 1858

Injury	Age (at time of injury unless otherwise stated)	Case	Award		Reference
			General £	Loss of Earnings Capacity, Family Care £	
Post traumatic stress -*cont.*	7	*O (A Minor), Re*	10,000		C.L.Y. 1865
	16	*MP, Re*	7,500		C.L.Y. 1959
	36	*Smith v. Stickley*	6,000		C.L.Y. 1860
	13	*W (A Minor), Re*	5,000		C.L.Y. 1861
	14	*W (A Minor), Re*	5,000		C.L.Y. 1862
	47	*Lymer v. Henson*	4,500		C.L.Y. 1863
	8	*Collett (A Minor) v. Barlow*	4,250		C.L.Y. 1864
Face	17	*Taylor, Re*	4,500		C.L.Y. 1866
Cheek	9	*G (A Minor) v. Croydon LBC*	1,000		C.L.Y. 1867
Eye	26 (at trial)	*Jackson v. Ikeda Hoover Ltd*	1,250		C.L.Y. 1868
Facial scars	4 1/2	*Gregory (A Minor) v. Millington*	20,000		C.L.Y. 1869
	30	*Burton v. Daxner*	10,000		C.L.Y. 1870
	30 months	*R (A Minor) v. Bradmarr Joiners*	8,500		C.L.Y. 1872
	42	*Cusack, Re*	8,500		C.L.Y. 1871
	17 months	*Waters (A Minor) v. North British Housing Association Ltd*	6,000		C.L.Y. 1873
Teeth	45	*Mitchell (A Minor) v. Burkitt*	6,500		C.L.Y. 1874
Hair	21	*Ramsbottom v. Novacki*	4,000		C.L.Y. 1874
Sight	31	*Kyei v. Utility Tyre Service Ltd*	23,000		C.L.Y. 1876
	25	*Mackel, Re*	17,500		C.L.Y. 1877
Hearing and speech	46 (at trial)	*Earlam v. Hepworth Heating Ltd*	5,500		C.L.Y. 1878
Whiplash type injury	32	*Warburton v. Barrington*	1,400		C.L.Y. 1879
	29	*Hartley v. Postlethwaite*	1,250		C.L.Y. 1880
	21	*Stanley v. Rosewell*	1,200		C.L.Y. 1881
	33	*Rowland v. Matthews*	1,000		C.L.Y. 1882
	24	*Southworth v. Taberner*	1,000	500	C.L.Y. 1885
	48	*Wilson & Wilson v. Seagram Distillers Plc*	1,000		C.L.Y. 1883
	44	*Hajid, Re*	1,000		C.L.Y. 1884
	22	*Hajid, Re*	750		C.L.Y. 1884
		Frost v. Furness	750		C.L.Y. 1886
Neck	36	*J, Re*	30,000	46,165	C.L.Y. 1887
	33	*Camus v. Williams*	13,750	81,737	C.L.Y. 1888
	22	*Jennings v. Cummins & Philips*	13,500	26,400	C.L.Y. 1889
	34	*Macey, Re*	10,000		C.L.Y. 1890
	38	*Edge v. Calderwood*	10,000		C.L.Y. 1891
	48	*Truscott v. Saipe*	7,500	4,000	C.L.Y. 1896
	30	*Beavan v. Derby City Transport*	5,000		C.L.Y. 1892
	19	*Doherty v. Spreadbury*	3,000		C.L.Y. 1893
	18	*Owen v. Prior*	2,600		C.L.Y. 1894
	26	*Hoy v. Coyle*	2,000		C.L.Y. 1895
	28	*Johnson v. Sidaway*	250		C.L.Y. 1897

Injury	Age (at time of injury unless otherwise stated)	Case	Award		Reference
			General £	Loss of Earnings Capacity, Family Care £	
Neck; whiplash type injury	45	Clark v. Commissioner of Police of the Metropolis	17,500		C.L.Y. 1898
	31	Hamilton v. Air Products and Saluveer	8,000		C.L.Y. 1899
	25	Ferguson v. Covel	7,500		C.L.Y. 1900
	36	Hunn v. McFarlane	6,500		C.L.Y. 1901
	51	Rees v. Hooper	6,500		C.L.Y. 1902
	21	Ashton v. Mortlock	5,500		C.L.Y. 1903
	25	Grainger v. Howes	5,000		C.L.Y. 1905
	34	Graham v. Kelly (No.1)	5,000		C.L.Y. 1904
	44	Davis v. Milborrow (No.1)	4,850		C.L.Y. 1906
	49	Hollands v. GK Salter & Associates and O'Neill	4,750		C.L.Y. 1907
	47	Lucas v. Lacey (No.1)	3,500		C.L.Y. 1908
	57	Tree v. Phillips	3,250		C.L.Y. 1909
	14	Miskell (A Minor) v. Bennett (Deceased)	3,000		C.L.Y. 1910
	19	Angell v. Brough	2,800		C.L.Y. 1911
	21	White v. Onions	2,400		C.L.Y. 1912
	37	Ellis v. Soole	1,500		C.L.Y. 1914
	35	Sangster v. Kensington Building Services	1,500		C.L.Y. 1913
	64	Stride (A) v. Lipscombe	1,000		C.L.Y. 1915
	43	Hales v. Clark	750		C.L.Y. 1916
	28	Salmon v. SJT Stafford Ltd	750		C.L.Y. 1917
	14	Hales v. Clark	750		C.L.Y. 1916
		Charnick v. Russell	250		C.L.Y. 1918
Back	36	Waxman v. Scrivens	22,220		C.L.Y. 1919
	27	Watson (Linda), Re	20,000	88,000	C.L.Y. 1921
	35	Jones v. South Galmorgan HA	20,000		C.L.Y. 1920
	17	Treffry v. Smith	17,500	25,000	C.L.Y. 1922
	36	Hodges v. Lambeth LBC	16,000		C.L.Y. 1923
	24	Lill v. Wakefield	16,000	138,806	C.L.Y. 1924
	17	Sollis v. Hughes, Hughes, Colson (t/a Bryon Construction) and Broad	12,500	2,000	C.L.Y. 1925
	27	Garrett v. British Airways	10,000	72,666	C.L.Y. 1927
	38	Vickerage v. Rotherham MBC	10,000	36,995	C.L.Y. 1926
	42	Rogers v. Birmingham City Council	9,250		C.L.Y. 1928
	29	Hibberd (Lesley Ann), Re	9,000		C.L.Y. 1929
	28	O'Boyle v. Lawrence	9,000		C.L.Y. 1930
	32	Warburton v. Halliwell	8,500	3,500	C.L.Y. 1931
	32	Le Gallou v. Malorey	8,000	6,000	C.L.Y. 1932
	31	Bonney v. Radcliffe Infirmary NHS Trust	7,500		C.L.Y. 1934
	55	Downing v. A&P Appledore (Falmouth) Ltd	7,500	4,000	C.L.Y. 1933
	25	Ward v. Batten & Stamford Asphalt Co Ltd	7,500		C.L.Y. 1935
	32	Wray v. Pardey	7,000		C.L.Y. 1936

Injury	Age (at time of injury unless otherwise stated)	Case	Award		Reference
			General £	Loss of Earnings Capacity, Family Care £	
Back -cont.	47	Iqubal v. Amuah	6,500		C.L.Y.1937
	46	Southward v. Peers Recovery	2,000		C.L.Y. 1938
	50	Alldis v. Myer	1,500		C.L.Y. 1939
		Hopper v. Megabyte Ltd	1,000		C.L.Y. 1940
Respiratory organs	48 (at trial)	Tilley v. Tucker	42,000	252,325	C.L.Y. 1941
	49 (at trial)	Smith v. Dicks Eagle Insulation Ltd	27,000	26,949	C.L.Y. 1942
	77 (at trial)	Glendinning v. Powergen Plc	25,000		C.L.Y. 1943
	51	Somerset v. Simpkin Machin & Co Ltd	23,500	8,000	C.L.Y. 1944
	57	Elford v. Ministry of Defence	17,300		C.L.Y. 1945
	69 (at trial)	Barker v. Roberts	14,402		C.L.Y. 1946
	58	Ford v. Clarbeston Ltd	4,750		C.L.Y. 1947
Asthma type illness	51 (at trial)	Sola v. Royal Marsden Hospital	14,000	5,000	C.L.Y. 1948
Digestive Organs	40	Miles v. West Kent HA	60,000	300,000	C.L.Y. 1949
Excretory organs	47	Parkes v. Chester HA	40,000		C.L.Y. 1950
	41	George v. Tower Hamlets HA	30,000		C.L.Y. 1951
	53 (at trial)	Coverdale v. Suffolk HA	20,000		C.L.Y. 1952
Reproductive organs	29	Thurman v. Wiltshire and Bath HA	50,000		C.L.Y. 1953
Hip	30	Betts v. Dolby	22,500		C.L.Y. 1954
	70	Fradgley v. Pontefract Hospitals NHS Trust	20,000		C.L.Y. 1955
Shoulder	49	Rucastle v. Cumberland Motor Services Ltd	5,250	4,250	C.L.Y. 1956
	35	Ullrich v. Carlisle City Council	5,000		C.L.Y. 1957
Shoulder; elbow	50	Lambeth v. Williams	22,500		C.L.Y. 1958
Arm	44	Murtagh, Re	20,000		C.L.Y. 1959
	44	Pritchard v. Cumberland Motor Services Ltd	17,500	120,460	C.L.Y. 1960
	78	Rowland v. Griffin	9,500		C.L.Y. 1961
	10	Mitchell (A Minor) v. Cheshire CC	4,750		C.L.Y. 1962
	21	Hasan v. Boots The Chemist Plc	4,000	4,156	C.L.Y. 1963
Elbow	50	Fahy v. Wolverhampton MBC and Banbury Windows Ltd	18,000	24,550	C.L.Y. 1964
	52 (at trial)	Wright, Willis, Short and Bottomer v. Royal Doulton (UK) Ltd	9,000	11,897	C.L.Y. 1965
	46 (at trial)	Wright, Willis, Short and Bottomer v. Royal Doulton (UK) Ltd	8,000	8,500	C.L.Y. 1965
	29 (at trial)	Wright, Willis, Short and Bottomer v. Royal Doulton (UK) Ltd	8,000	30,000	C.L.Y. 1965

Injury	Age (at time of injury unless otherwise stated)	Case	Award		Reference
			General £	Loss of Earnings Capacity, Family Care £	
Elbow -cont.	58 (at trial)	Wright, Willis, Short and Bottomer v. Royal Doulton (UK) Ltd	7,500	4,000	C.L.Y. 1965
Wrist	26	Lowe v. Haskell	22,500		C.L.Y. 1966
	45	Roberts v. Hunt	7,000		C.L.Y. 1969
	21	Choudhry v. Jhangir	5,500		C.L.Y. 1967
	52	Heden v. BPC Magazines (Leeds) Ltd	5,200		C.L.Y. 1968
Hand	33 (at trial)	Torrance, Re	7,500	25,000	C.L.Y. 1970
	13	Mullett v. East London and City HA	5,750		C.L.Y. 1971
	48	Green v. Northern Foods Plc	4,500	1,500	C.L.Y. 1972
Fingers	44	Marsh v. Ashton Corrugated (Midlands) Ltd	4,500	3,000	C.L.Y. 1973
	12	Hall v. Bolton MBC	4,000		C.L.Y. 1974
	41	Catchpole, Re	3,250		C.L.Y. 1975
		Turner v. British Steel Plc	2,000		C.L.Y. 1976
	50	Murphy v. Gosforth Park Care Homes Ltd	1,250		C.L.Y. 1977
	6	Eason v. Brewster	900		C.L.Y. 1978
Leg	28	Sampson v. Georgiou	25,000	10,000	C.L.Y. 1979
	40	Purkis v. Rehman	16,000	15,000	C.L.Y. 1980
	30	Melling v. Liverpool City Council	3,250		C.L.Y. 1981
Leg; amputated leg	3	Harris v. Harris	42,000		C.L.Y. 1982
Knee	21	Scott v. Gage	26,000	9,000	C.L.Y. 1983
	32	Elder v. Sands	14,000		C.L.Y. 1984
	22	Clements v. Wake	7,500		C.L.Y. 1985
	57	Couch v. Miotla	5,000	806	C.L.Y. 1986
	25	Lowe v. Baron Meats Ltd	3,000		C.L.Y. 1987
Ankle	17	Goodwill v. Jewson Ltd	5,150		C.L.Y. 1988
	39	Wilson (David Michael), Re	3,250		C.L.Y. 1989
	38	Williams v. Smith & Daniels	2,500		C.L.Y. 1990
	21	Reid v. Chowdhury	750		C.L.Y. 1991
	11	Kerr v. Tudor Thomas Construction & Development Ltd	750		C.L.Y. 1992
Foot	12	P (A Minor) v. Meakin	13,500		C.L.Y. 1993
	23	McClean v. Costa	3,848		C.L.Y. 1994
Scars	6	Hobart v. McGiff and Stuart	7,000		C.L.Y. 1995
	30 (at trial)	O'Neill v. Matthew Brown Plc	5,250		C.L.Y. 1996
	30	Leatherland v. Rissman	5,000		C.L.Y. 1997
	11	Dooler, Re	4,500		C.L.Y. 1998
Non-facial scars	12	Khan (Arbab), Re	10,000		C.L.Y. 1999
	16	Escott v. Escott	8,750		C.L.Y. 2000
Burns	8 months	Stocks v. Wadsworth	17,500		C.L.Y. 2001
		Longworth v. Sunbeams Ltd	3,750		C.L.Y. 2002

Injury	Age (at time of injury unless otherwise stated)	Case	Award General £	Loss of Earnings Capacity, Family Care £	Reference
Burns -cont.	49	Barnes v. Kenmore Refrigeration Ltd	2,250		C.L.Y. 2003
	28	Finnigan v. British Steel Plc	700		C.L.Y. 2004
Burns; very severe burns	32	Stokle, Re	70,000		C.L.Y. 2005
Minor injuries	36	Doyle v. Van Bruggen	4,000		C.L.Y. 2006
		Carpenter v. Easton	3,750		C.L.Y. 2008
	14	Parnham (A Minor) v. Metropolitan Housing Trust Ltd	3,750		C.L.Y. 2007
	12	Woodhouse v. Normanton	3,300		C.L.Y. 2009
	26	Hutchinson v. Abdalla	3,000		C.L.Y. 2012
	26	Davis v. Gregg & Co (Knottingley) Ltd	3,000		C.L.Y. 2011
	37	Scourfield and British Gas Plc v. Gammon	3,000		C.L.Y. 2010
	28	Baines (Onkar Singh) v. Sherazia (t/a A&S Autos)	2,700		C.L.Y. 2013
	44	Bourne, Re	2,500		C.L.Y. 2014
	64	Stride (S) v. Lipscombe	1,000		C.L.Y. 2015
	59	Katz v. Sayner	510		C.L.Y. 2016
Miscarriage	21	Dublin, Re	6,000		C.L.Y. 2017
Bruising	25	James v. Watker	2,000		C.L.Y. 2018
	38	Boundy v. Valavanis	1,750		C.L.Y. 2019
	26	Carlisle v. Chapman	500		C.L.Y. 2021
	20	Dooley v. Machin	500		C.L.Y. 2020
Carbon monoxide poisoning	29	Harvey v. Fairscope	5,000		C.L.Y. 2022
Hepatitis		Rubins v. Employment Office	4,250		C.L.Y. 2023
Ringworm	32	Wilcock v. John Mace Ltd	1,200		C.L.Y. 2024
Angina attack	58	Dunn v. Rennoc	2,000		C.L.Y. 2025

Scottish Cases

Injury	Age (at time of injury unless otherwise stated)	Case	Award Solatium £	Total £	Reference
Multiple injuries	29 (at proof)	Lamont v. Cameron's Executrix	10,000	68,050	C.L.Y. 5944
Head	6	Sinclair v. Falkirk DC	17,500	17,500	C.L.Y. 5940
Post traumatic stress		Whyte v. Nestle (UK) Ltd	10,000	56,924	C.L.Y. 5950

Injury	Age (at time of injury unless otherwise stated)	Case	Award		Reference
			Solatium £	Total £	
Post traumatic stress -cont.	54 (at proof)	Lock v. WH Malcolm Ltd	7,000	7,000	C.L.Y. 5951
Face		Airnes v. Chief Constable of Sytrathclyde Police	2,000		C.L.Y. 5938
Neck	16	Akehurst, Re	2,400	2,500	C.L.Y. 5947
Spine below neck		Gartley v. R McCartney (Painters) Ltd	70,000	70,000	C.L.Y. 5957
	50	Taylor v. Marshalls Food Group	500	37,600	C.L.Y. 5958
Whiplash type injury	41 (at proof)	Dingley v. Chief Constable of Strathclyde Police	75,000		C.L.Y. 5959
	49	Stuart v. Lothian and Borders Fire Board	35,000	110,945	C.L.Y. 5960
Back	46	Burns v. HarperCollins Ltd	10,000	14,500	C.L.Y. 5929
	44 (at proof)	Fallan v. Lanarkshire Health Board	8,000	105,650	C.L.Y. 5930
	44 (at proof)	McCarvel v. Strathclyde Fire Board	5,000		C.L.Y. 5932
	53	Hay v. Secretary of State for Scotland	5,000	5,000	C.L.Y. 5931
	43 (at proof)	Fraser v. Greater Glasgow Health Board	3,000	4,250	C.L.Y. 5933
Respiratory organs	58 (at proof)	Kerr v. Newalls Insulation Co Ltd	32,500	51,560	C.L.Y. 5952
	52 (at proof)	Nicol v. Scottish Power Plc	13,500		C.L.Y. 5953
Pelvis		Blackhall v. MacInnes	16,000	18,375	C.L.Y. 5949
Hip	37	George v. Bank of Scotland	15,000	23,597	C.L.Y. 5941
Shoulder		Cullen v. North Lanarkshire Council	5,000	5,000	C.L.Y. 5954
	50	Lennox v. Lanarkshire Health Board	1,500	2,489	C.L.Y. 5955
Elbow	45	Quinn v. Lothian Regional Transport Plc	1,250	1,250	C.L.Y. 5937
	27 (at proof)	Maley v. Daylay Foods Ltd	1,000		C.L.Y. 5956
Wrist	23 (at proof)	Martin v. James S Rennie Slaters & Plasterers Ltd	18,000	75,629	C.L.Y. 5961
	46	Kennedy v. Lees of Scotland	8,000		C.L.Y. 5962
		Blaney v. Post Office	1,000	1,000	C.L.Y. 5963
Leg	57 (at proof)	Kelly v. United Biscuits (UK) Ltd	15,000	15,000	C.L.Y. 5943
Knee		Hutchison v. City of Dundee DC	7,000	7,000	C.L.Y. 5942
Ankle	51 (at proof)	Souter v. Allaburn Holdings Ltd	10,000	96,490	C.L.Y. 5928
Foot	45	Tait v. Fischer	75,000	247,000	C.L.Y. 5939
Burns	43 (at proof)	Swan v. Hope-Dunbar	30,000	35,500	C.L.Y. 5935
	17 (at proof)	Morley v. Campbell	25,000	70,000	C.L.Y. 5934

RETAIL PRICE INDEX

The table below consists of the general index of retail prices (RPI) for 1996/7 (January 1987 = 100).

1996

JAN	150.2	(up 2.9 per cent on Jan 1995)
FEB	150.9	(up 2.7 per cent on Feb 1995)
MAR	151.5	(up 2.7 per cent on Mar 1995)
APR	152.6	(up 2.4 per cent on Apr 1995)
MAY	152.9	(up 2.2 per cent on May 1995)
JUN	153.0	(up 2.1 per cent on June 1995)
JUL	152.4	(up 2.2 per cent on July 1995)
AUG	153.1	(up 2.1 per cent on Aug 1995)
SEPT	153.8	(up 2.1 per cent on Sept 1995)
OCT	153.8	(up 2.7 per cent on Oct 1995)
NOV	153.9	(up 2.7 per cent on Nov 1995)
DEC	154.4	(up 2.5 per cent on Dec 1995)

1997

JAN	154.4	(up 2.8 per cent on Jan 1996)
FEB	155.0	(up 2.7 per cent on Feb 1996)
MAR	155.4	(up 2.6 per cent on Mar 1996)
APR	156.3	(up 2.4 per cent on Apr 1996)
MAY	156.9	(up 2.6 per cent on May 1996)
JUNE	157.5	(up 2.9 per cent on June 1996)
JULY	157.5	(up 3.3 per cent on July 1996)
AUG	158.5	(up 3.5 per cent on Aug 1996)
SEP	159.3	(up 3.6 per cent on Sep 1996)
OCT	159.5	(up 3.7 per cent on Oct 1996)
NOV	159.6	(up 3.7 per cent on Nov 1996)
DEC	160.0	(up 3.6 per cent on Dec 1996)

TAX AND PRICE INDEX

The table below consists of the tax and price index (TPI) for 1996/7 (January 1987 = 100).

1996

JAN	141.6 (up 3.2 per cent on Jan 1995)
FEB	142.3 (up 3.0 per cent on Feb 1995)
MAR	143.0 (up 3.0 per cent on Mar 1995)
APR	141.7 (up 1.0 per cent on Apr 1995)
MAY	142.0 (up 0.7 per cent on May 1995)
JUN	142.1 (up 0.6 per cent on June 1995)
JUL	141.5 (up 0.8 per cent on July 1995)
AUG	142.2 (up 0.6 per cent on Aug 1995)
SEPT	143.0 (up 0.7 per cent on Sept 1995)
OCT	143.0 (up 1.3 per cent on Oct 1995)
NOV	143.1 (up 1.3 per cent on Nov 1995)
DEC	143.6 (up 1.1 per cent on Dec 1995)

1997

JAN	143.6 (up 1.4 per cent on Jan 1996)
FEB	144.2 (up 1.3 per cent on Feb 1996)
MAR	144.6 (up 1.1 per cent on Mar 1996)
APR	143.8 (up 1.5 per cent on Apr 1996)
MAY	144.4 (up 1.7 per cent on May 1996)
JUNE	145.0 (up 2.0 per cent on June 1996)
JULY	145.0 (up 2.5 per cent on July 1996)
AUG	146.0 (up 2.7 per cent on Aug 1996)
SEP	146.9 (up 2.6 per cent on Sep 1996)
OCT	147.1 (up 2.9 per cent on Oct 1996)
NOV	147.2 (up 2.9 per cent on Nov 1996)
DEC	147.6 (up 2.8 per cent on Dec 1996)

ALPHABETICAL TABLE OF STATUTORY INSTRUMENTS 1997

The table below contains a list, in alphabetical order, of 1997 Statutory Instruments digested by Current Law.

C.L.Y.

C.L.Y.

C.L.Y.

C.L.Y.

C.L.Y.

ALPHABETICAL TABLE OF STATUTORY INSTRUMENTS 1997

ALPHABETICAL TABLE OF STATUTORY INSTRUMENTS 1997 (NO. 2)

ELECTORAL PROCESS

EUROPEAN UNION

ROAD TRAFFIC—*cont*

C.L.Y.

NUMERICAL TABLE OF STATUTORY
INSTRUMENTS 1997

1996	C.L.Y.
3105	183
3253	4427

1997	C.L.Y.
1	2065
2	3702
4	4462
5	4431
6	4432
7	196
8	4916
9	4915
10 (S.1)	6338
11	2620
12	4143
13	4144
14	281
15	294
16	296
17	295
18	285
19	4504
21	4446
22	4961
29 (C.1)	800
30	795
31	796
32	2530
33	182
34 (C.2)	3631
35	1303
36 (C.3)	1284
37	4086
38	3956
39	4928
40	3725
41	3746
42	3404
43	3413
45	2705
47 (C.4)	2300
50	4998
51	4999
52	3732
53	3740
54	2064
56	4340
57	4767
58	4323
62 (S.2)	5591
63 (S.3)	5829
64	3909
65	4654
66 (C.5)	2682
71	2746
72	2680
73	2748
74	2679
75	4216
77 (S.4)	6220

1997	C.L.Y.
80	3982
81	4324
82	4299
83	4319
84	4346
87	4423
88	4449
90	4840
91	2053
93 (S.5)	5993
96	4430
97	4326
101	3551
102	4920
119 (S.6)	6328
120 (S.7)	6372
123	4386
124	3474
125	3468
126	3470
127	3438
128	3471
129	3472
130	3451
131 (C.6)	2215
133 (C.8)	4745
134 (C.9)	2208
135	2635
137 (C.10; S.9)	5622
138	2184
139	4404
140	4424
143	3670
150	203
151 (C.19)	6422
152 (C.32)	4527
153	4378
154	4379
155	4377
157	2179
158	4917
165	3550
166	97
167	3574
168	2964
169	284
170	300
171	279
172	286
173	289
174 (S.10)	6268
175	3441
176	3465
177 (L.1)	619
178	1012
179	2182
188	185
189	194
190	3735
191	4315
194	3249

1997	C.L.Y.	1997	C.L.Y.
195	118	286	3944
196	3753	287	225
197 (S.12)	6240	288	2111
198 (S.13)	6239	290	3573
199 (S.14)	6116	291 (S.19)	5642
200	4426	292	4142
201	4398	294	2071
202	4399	302	630
203	4387	304 (C.14)	282
204	4359	305 (C.15)	306
206 (S.11)	5564	306	305
207 (S.15)	5978	307	303
208	4418	308	304
209 (S.16)	6423	309	302
211	966	310	244
212	2981	311	2156
213	4768	312	4019
214	2973	313	4783
215	3502	314	4803
216 (C.11)	4003	315	4828
217 (S.17)	6461	316 (S.20)	6088
218	3977	317 (S.21)	6448
219	4361	318 (S.22)	6453
220	6	319	3430
221	2638	320	4532
224	4202	321	3642
225 (C.12)	2683	322	3641
226	237	323	3211
227	2709	324	3214
228	2710	325	4528
229	2712	326	3673
230	2711	327	3672
231	278	328	2742
232	3527	329	3975
233	4278	330 (S.23)	5584
234	4831	341 (S.24)	6335
235	4809	342 (S.25)	6337
236	4016	343 (S.26)	6336
239	175	346	4541
248	4947	347	4542
249	123	348	4543
250	129	349	4626
251	2364	350 (C.16)	2684
252	3968	351	2363
253	4922	353	4467
254	4017	354	3751
255	5045	355	3733
256	4291	356	4198
257 (S.18)	6021	357	3493
258	4406	358	3988
261	3501	361	40
262	3538	362 (S.27)	6462
263	4300	363 (S.28)	6459
264	4931	364 (S.29)	5991
265	3146	365 (C.17; S.30)	5977
266	199	366	4100
267 (C.13)	4356	367	4673
268	3189	368	2154
269	2403	369	2938
270	2406	371	3990
271	2407	377	2747
272	3227	378 (S.31)	5563
273	3228	379 (S.32)	6000
275	2933	381	3432
278	3195	382	187
279	3229	383	192
280	3230	384	4350
281	3200	389	108
282	3201	390	2075
283	3202	391 (C.18; S.33)	5992
284	3578	393	3492
285	3579	394	4185

1997	C.L.Y.	1997	C.L.Y.
395	3737	504	3611
400	70	506	4573
401	4321	510	4989
402 (C.20)	1280	511	2546
403	216	512 (S.35)	6379
404	3728	513	2051
405	2951	514	2073
406	3483	515	2161
407	2191	526	3676
408	2213	527	3675
409	4829	528	3449
415 (L.2)	780	529	4577
416	3338	530	4307
417	3699	531	4062
418	3695	532	3484
419	3709	533	3460
420	4083	534	1743
421	4963	535	4283
431	2078	536	2204
445	4394	537	2173
446	4389	540	3539
447	3738	541	4275
448	3744	542	98
449	4392	543	4613
450	4391	544	4681
451	2553	545	4619
452 (S.34)	6373	546	4651
453	3727	547	2347
454	4686	548	4448
455	3479	549	4451
456	3549	550	4456
457	3966	553	4934
458	3543	554	4459
459	3542	555	4384
460	3544	558	3661
461	3545	559	3664
463	4390	560	3455
464	4400	561	3456
465	4402	562	4553
466	4403	563	4676
467	4415	564	4330
468	3546	565	4771
469	3548	566	4177
470	4011	567	186
471	1078	568	207
472	2962	569	2734
473	1077	570	2
474	2960	571	833
475	2961	573	2102
476	3547	574	2235
477	4704	575	4620
478	3540	576	4614
479	3541	577	4671
480	4013	578	3972
481	4757	579	290
482	342	580 (L.3)	287
483	2704	581	3698
484	127	582	3716
485	4719	583	3697
486	4722	584	4637
487	4929	585 (S.36)	6269
488	31	586 (S.37)	6365
489	32	587 (S.38)	6366
490	33	589	3530
491	3586	590	4374
492	35	591	4373
493	36	596 (C.21)	2685
494	26	597	2088
495	27	598	3978
496	28	599	2070
497	29	616	209
498	30	617	101

1997	C.L.Y.	1997	C.L.Y.
618 (C.22)	2686	692 (S.52)	5626
619	2728	693 (S.53)	6444
620	2740	694	2601
621	2739	695 (S.54)	6363
622	2737	696 (S.55)	6275
623	2735	697 (S.56)	6274
624	2736	698 (L.4)	1306
625	2738	699 (L.5)	1293
626	2733	700 (L.6)	1295
627	2681	701 (L.7)	1292
628	2651	702 (L.8)	1261
629	2318	703 (L.9)	1307
630	979	704 (L.10)	1351
631	2657	705 (L.11)	1157
632	2329	706 (L.12)	1348
633	2328	707 (L.26)	1352
634	4015	708 (L.13)	1350
635	2982	709 (L.14)	1349
636	2456	710 (L.15)	1346
637	2461	711 (L.16)	1347
638	3639	712	4944
639	257	713	1010
640	3275	714 (S.57)	5641
641 (S.39)	6333	715 (S.58)	5981
642 (S.40)	6334	716 (S.59)	6383
643 (S.41)	6332	717 (S.60)	6382
645	4615	718 (S.61)	6201
646	3674	719 (S.62)	6202
647	4525	720 (S.63)	6247
648	2331	721 (S.64)	6362
649	360	722 (S.65)	5586
650	4288	723	2568
651	2320	724	4005
652	3690	725	3940
653	3127	726 (S.66)	6191
654	4482	727 (S.67)	6195
655	2576	728 (S.68)	6367
656	3491	729 (S.69)	5627
657	3495	730	3680
658	1744	731	4669
659	1731	732	3536
660	5160	733	128
661	2983	734	4708
662	3945	735	4956
663	3994	736	4962
664 (C.23)	4004	737	1297
665	3954	738	1296
666	3989	739	1369
667	227	740	2523
668	4298	741	835
669	4292	742	837
670 (C.24)	948	743	838
671	949	744 (C.27; S.70)	5623
672 (S.42)	6249	745 (S.71)	6059
673 (S.43)	6368	746	3600
674 (S.44)	6256	747	3662
675 (S.45)	5995	748	3761
676 (S.46)	5997	749 (S.72)	6349
677	4909	750 (S.73)	6342
678	2085	751	3358
679	2112	752	3346
680	2090	753	3340
682 (C.25)	1285	754	3350
683 (C.26)	1291	755	2159
684	5181	756 (C.28)	4715
685	2741	757	122
686	3147	758	121
687 (S.47)	6041	759	4709
688 (S.48)	6033	760 (C.29)	4266
689 (S.49)	6197	761	4276
690 (S.50)	6194	762	4277
691 (S.51)	5621	763	4370

1997	C.L.Y.	1997	C.L.Y.
774	5217	850	4360
775	2177	851	4018
776	2183	852	4642
777	2180	853 (S.78)	5629
778	2723	854 (S.79)	5630
779	2176	856	3624
780	2181	857	4636
781	2178	858	4129
782	2174	859	3396
783	2175	860	2092
784	3958	861	915
785	3965	862	3427
786	3986	863	2405
787 (L.17)	613	864	912
788 (L.18)	2465	867	5218
789	3942	868	5219
790	4634	870	3589
791	4679	871	4684
792	4692	872	2707
793	4687	873	2583
794	4002	874	2170
795 (S.74)	5628	875	3694
796 (S.75)	6341	876	3715
797	2656	877	3696
798	307	878	4960
799 (S.76)	6458	879	2169
801	3647	880	2166
802	411	881	224
803	2299	882 (C.31)	1283
805	3637	883	173
806	4630	884	195
807	1236	886	4776
808	3938	887	4781
809	3554	888	4785
810	4666	889	4786
811	4021	890	4787
812	4022	891	4788
813	119	892	4789
814	2557	893	4792
815	4322	894	4793
816	2525	895	4794
817	314	896	4796
818	3757	897	4797
819	3957	898	4799
820	4621	899	4801
821	4082	900	4802
822	4098	901	4821
823	4670	902	4819
824	4631	903	4818
826	4954	904	4816
827	4617	905	4815
828	2575	906	4810
829	2574	907	4812
830 (S.77)	5587	908	4811
831	2628	909	4808
832	3700	910	4814
833	3721	911	4805
834	3701	912	4804
835	3703	913	4806
836	3722	914	4807
837	3704	915	4813
838	3224	916	4779
839	3223	917	4822
840	3225	918	4824
841 (C.30)	514	919	4825
842	4463	920	4826
844	71	921	4834
845	3481	922	4827
846	4293	923	4830
847	4332	924	4832
848	3431	925	4833
849	3555	926	4835

1997	C.L.Y.	1997	C.L.Y.
927	4837	1003 (S.89)	6127
928	4839	1004	4644
929	4841	1005 (C.34)	3585
930	4842	1006	3580
931	169	1007	3215
932	5521	1008	3212
933	2585	1009	4652
934	3462	1010	3351
935	3464	1011	4357
936	7	1012 (S.90)	6284
937	4955	1013 (S.91)	6279
938 (S.80)	6254	1014 (S.92)	6270
939 (S.81)	6255	1015 (C.35)	4746
940 (S.82)	6117	1016	4740
941 (S.83)	6222	1019 (C.36)	1286
942 (S.84)	6223	1033	1290
943 (S.85)	6276	1034	2172
944	4661	1045	4622
945	2729	1046	5216
946	3949	1048 (S.93)	6370
947	3400	1049 (S.94)	5980
948	4576	1050 (S.95)	5657
949	4290	1051 (L.19)	1366
950	3402	1052 (L.20)	1367
954	3976	1053 (L.21)	1368
955	4702	1054 (L.22)	1298
956	2067	1055 (L.23)	1357
957	2234	1056 (L.24)	2462
959	3504	1059	3939
960	4201	1060	2527
961	4190	1071	3399
962	2498	1072	3403
963	2534	1073	3405
964 (S.86)	5608	1074	3398
965 (S.87)	5988	1075	3401
966	3116	1076 (C.37)	1211
967	2167	1077 (C.38)	2458
968	211	1078	3353
969	5215	1079	3339
970	135	1080 (L.25)	2466
971	136	1081	968
972	141	1082 (C.39)	4549
973	138	1083	3730
974	145	1084 (S.96)	5640
975	157	1085	41
976	147	1086	5022
977	2649	1091	4140
978	2650	1092	3454
979 (S.88)	5999	1093	130
980	3665	1095 (S.97)	6218
981	3681	1096	4308
982	4675	1097 (C.40)	4193
983	4677	1098	4297
984	4678	1111	4041
985	3535	1112 (S.98)	6198
986	2494	1113 (S.99)	6192
987	2978	1114	1248
988	2968	1115 (S.100)	6460
989	4946	1116	4368
990	184	1117	4633
991 (C.33)	4748	1118 (S.101)	6045
992	2967	1121	3609
993	2966	1122	4380
994	1742	1133	3414
995	2116	1139 (C.41)	2582
996	2069	1140	2581
997	3356	1142	2117
998	3361	1143 (S.102)	6260
999	3447	1145	189
1000	2724	1148	95
1001	2591	1150	3568
1002	3710	1151 (C.42)	253

1997	C.L.Y.	1997	C.L.Y.
1152	248	1362	2335
1153 (C.43)	2059	1363	2336
1154	2970	1364	2337
1155	2958	1365	4301
1156	4763	1366	4312
1157	4758	1367	4327
1158	2977	1368	2101
1159	1159	1369	4345
1160	2314	1370 (C.49; S.107)	6441
1168	2052	1372	2309
1171	3750	1373 (S.108)	6257
1172	3749	1375	3747
1173	3748	1376	3707
1174	2394	1377 (C.50)	4159
1175	3236	1396	3193
1176	2411	1399	2162
1178	2432	1400	3720
1185	4948	1401	3742
1186	3717	1402	2892
1187	3386	1403	1247
1188	4358	1405	3991
1194 (S.103)	6193	1410	5220
1210	4416	1411 (C.51)	2306
1211	4408	1413	2556
1220	4957	1414	132
1222	4440	1415	191
1223	4412	1418 (C.52)	1238
1224	4435	1420	3485
1225	3705	1421	2310
1236	4376	1427 (C.53)	2521
1237	4375	1428	2584
1257	4414	1429 (S.109)	6360
1260 (S.104)	6036	1430 (C.56; S.110)	6436
1265 (S.105)	6046	1431	4755
1266	4919	1432 (C.54)	4750
1291	3961	1433 (C.55)	4749
1292	4333	1434 (S.111)	6282
1293	4334	1435 (S.112)	6258
1305 (C.44)	1738	1436 (S.113)	6241
1306	161	1437 (S.114)	6243
1307 (C.45)	2520	1438 (S.115)	6238
1308	3752	1439 (S.116)	6236
1313	804	1440	155
1314	77	1441	144
1315 (C.46)	3615	1442	149
1316	1281	1443	150
1317	1543	1444	156
1318	1204	1445	134
1319	3590	1446	137
1320	4578	1447	143
1322 (C.47; S.106)	6020	1448	153
1325	3711	1449	154
1326	3731	1450	133
1328	2889	1451	139
1329	2533	1452	140
1330	4442	1453	142
1331	2365	1454	151
1332	2366	1455	152
1333	3567	1456	148
1334	3221	1457	94
1335	2554	1458	4310
1336	2555	1459	4314
1337	126	1460	2605
1340	4309	1466	73
1341	4579	1468 (C.57)	2060
1342	4341	1469	3638
1349	3640	1472	6426
1350	3626	1473 (S.117)	6277
1354	3587	1474	201
1359	2332	1480	242
1360	2333	1481	176
1361	2334	1482	3712

1997	C.L.Y.	1997	C.L.Y.
1483	3708	1629	170
1484	3352	1630	171
1485	3347	1631 (S.123)	6248
1489	2100	1632	4401
1498 (C.58)	1239	1633	2124
1499	2559	1638 (S.124)	5979
1500	51	1639	2341
1501	4317	1640 (S.125)	5982
1502	4328	1641 (S.126)	5983
1503	4429	1652	426
1504 (C.59)	1287	1653	228
1505 (S.118)	6110	1654	3533
1507	4410	1655	4958
1508	4540	1662	425
1509	4589	1666	3476
1510	4571	1671	4688
1511	4591	1672 (C.69)	928
1513	4458	1673	4914
1514	4441	1674	4545
1515	4436	1675	2151
1523	5040	1676	3391
1524	5031	1677	3392
1525	5023	1678	3663
1526 (S.119)	5830	1679	4325
1527 (S.120)	5658	1680 (S.127)	6384
1528	4598	1681	2954
1529	3606	1682	3570
1530	849	1687	3969
1531	4927	1688	4925
1532	34	1690	914
1533	72	1691	4632
1534	1011	1692	1207
1535 (C.60)	1212	1693	2079
1536 (C.61)	1213	1694	3216
1537	1208	1695 (C.70)	2340
1538	1209	1696 (C.71)	4160
1539 (C.62)	4550	1697	3448
1543	158	1698	3439
1544	4311	1699	3486
1545	4372	1700	3489
1565	180	1701	3463
1572	4732	1702	3450
1573	200	1709	2504
1576	1042	1710	1013
1577 (C.63)	4695	1711	343
1578	3194	1712 (C.72; S.128)	5782
1579	3931	1713	2632
1580 (C.65; S.121)	6414	1714	1734
1581 (C.64)	1490	1715	2971
1584 (S.122)	6024	1716	2547
1585	4153	1717	4599
1588	2985	1718	4600
1603 (C.66)	4751	1719	1192
1604	3406	1720 (S.129)	5659
1607	4417	1721 (S.130)	6225
1608	4411	1723	3610
1611	3222	1724	3691
1612	3971	1725 (C.73)	1186
1613	3973	1726	3500
1614	5024	1727	3625
1615	4971	1728	3619
1616	5043	1729	113
1618	3724	1731	3357
1619	3736	1736	3946
1620	3754	1738	4139
1621	2743	1739	5590
1623 (C.67)	2056	1740	859
1624	2298	1741	2673
1625	2054	1742	2395
1626 (C.68)	2316	1743	3591
1627	4759	1744	2589
1628	5000	1745	297

1997	C.L.Y.	1997	C.L.Y.
1746	231	1858	2544
1747	392	1859	2542
1748	2344	1860	2539
1749	2588	1861	3603
1750	162	1862	2541
1751	3198	1863	2543
1752	3199	1864	2545
1753	3197	1866	315
1755	3561	1869	4574
1756	3562	1870 (S.136)	6329
1757	3563	1871 (S.137)	6345
1759	2416	1872 (S.138)	5719
1760	2421	1873	125
1761	2417	1881	159
1762	2422	1884	3608
1763	2423	1885	3581
1764	2425	1886	4850
1765	2427	1887	797
1766	2428	1888	3981
1767	2424	1889	2046
1768	2426	1890	2045
1769	2430	1891	2044
1770	2326	1892 (C.76)	2459
1771	2327	1893 (L.29)	2463
1773	4583	1894 (L.30)	2495
1775	3932	1895 (L.31)	422
1776	3933	1896 (L.32)	2460
1777	2948	1897 (L.33)	421
1778	4685	1898 (L.34)	2464
1779	311	1899 (L.35)	2467
1780 (C.74)	3685	1900	2564
1781 (S.131)	6375	1901	120
1782 (S.132)	6385	1902	2706
1783	3412	1903	2708
1787 (S.133)	6214	1904	943
1788 (S.134)	5831	1905	103
1789	2160	1906 (C.77)	1219
1790	4623	1907	1217
1791	3726	1908	4182
1820	4559	1909	4680
1821	3669	1910	4567
1824	4453	1911	4544
1827	206	1912	3992
1828	3408	1913	3452
1829	3964	1914	4279
1830	3622	1915	4280
1831	3627	1916 (S.139)	6283
1832	2114	1920 (C.78)	1244
1833	2118	1921	1245
1834 (S.135)	5832	1924	172
1835	3553	1929	3953
1836	5054	1930 (C.79)	4161
1837 (L.27)	618	1931	2093
1838 (L.28)	615	1937	3870
1839	4607	1939 (S.140)	5811
1840	2619	1940	3467
1841	4624	1941	2297
1842	3584	1949	163
1844	4171	1951	4926
1845	4164	1952	6425
1846	4163	1953	6424
1847	4166	1954	2098
1848	4170	1960 (C.80)	1739
1849	4165	1961	188
1850	4169	1962	93
1851 (C.75)	2687	1963	3629
1852	3297	1964	1014
1853	3296	1965	4236
1854	3298	1966	2115
1855	4168	1967	2072
1856	3571	1968	2109
1857	4167	1969	2110

1997	C.L.Y.	1997	C.L.Y.
1970	2120	2174	2074
1972	2150	2175	2068
1974	4638	2176	2097
1975	4639	2177	4777
1976	4602	2178	4790
1977 (C.81)	4267	2179	4791
1978	179	2180	4778
1979 (S.141)	6234	2181	4817
1980 (S.142)	6233	2182	2552
1981 (S.143)	6244	2196	1733
1984	2725	2197	4655
1985	3348	2199 (C.86)	1288
1986	114	2200 (C.87)	1491
1987	3693	2203	2362
1988	4371	2204	75
1990	2091	2205	4612
1991	2385	2206	177
1992	3519	2207	2893
1993	2609	2231	5163
1995 (S.144)	6126	2232	4924
1996	3583	2237	4611
2001	2744	2238	2570
2002	4419	2240	341
2003	4437	2258	2163
2006	2099	2259	3453
2007 (S.145)	6315	2260 (C.88; S.151)	6415
2008 (S.146)	5994	2261 (S.152)	6412
2009	2095	2262	4932
2010	2096	2276	3743
2011	2094	2281	4464
2012	4396	2282	4316
2013	4438	2283	4152
2014	4407	2284	4155
2023	4381	2285	4445
2038	2305	2289	3667
2041	3734	2290	4618
2042	2551	2291	3437
2043	3618	2292	3457
2044	3623	2293	4173
2045	3628	2294	971
2046	2658	2298 (C.91)	2307
2055	4662	2299	4444
2056 (C.82)	4696	2300	4443
2059	3529	2301	4470
2060	2121	2302	2516
2062	5921	2304	4343
2070	4294	2305	4689
2073	110	2306	836
2074	109	2308	408
2078	4344	2309	3963
2079	3409	2310	42
2080	3407	2311	4690
2081 (S.147)	5834	2317 (S.153)	6314
2082 (S.148)	5833	2322 (S.154)	6416
2085 (C.83)	4701	2323 (C.89; S.155)	5779
2092 (S.149)	5593	2326	4460
2095	3552	2327	2730
2111 (C.84)	5166	2328	3469
2132	4469	2329	230
2133	4447	2330	4506
2134	4428	2347	254
2137	3582	2348 (S.157)	6386
2140	2062	2349 (S.158)	6381
2157 (S.150)	5718	2351	1193
2161	301	2352 (C.90)	2057
2162	298	2353	2055
2163	310	2354 (S.156)	6023
2164 (C.85)	283	2364	2122
2169	3445	2365	104
2171 (L.36)	616	2366	4505
2172	2061	2367	4503
2173	2066	2385	4455

1997	C.L.Y.	1997	C.L.Y.
2386	4413	2561	4838
2387	102	2562	3612
2388	4012	2563	2396
2389	215	2564	2119
2390 (C.92)	4162	2565 (C.97)	4913
2391	4154	2566	4565
2392 (C.93)	4753	2567	4561
2393	3762	2568	4560
2394	3354	2569	4572
2395	2076	2570	3231
2400	4348	2571	3203
2401	4439	2572	3232
2402	4382	2573	3233
2403	4468	2574	391
2416	4172	2575	393
2417 (C.94)	4697	2576	2402
2420 (L.37)	1607	2577	2408
2421 (L.38)	1606	2578	4558
2427	4952	2579	4520
2428 (C.95)	4752	2580	4554
2429	4764	2581	4555
2430	4762	2582	4556
2434	4643	2583	4557
2435	4647	2584	4562
2436	4645	2585	4566
2437	5025	2586	4582
2439	4770	2587	4568
2440	2104	2588	4563
2441	198	2589	4569
2452 (S.159)	6145	2590	4570
2453	3739	2591	4593
2454	4383	2592	3239
2455 (S.160)	6285	2593	3240
2456	3446	2594	3234
2457 (C.96)	3686	2595	3235
2458	3475	2596	2415
2464	3237	2598	4564
2465	4933	2599	3241
2466	4930	2600	3242
2467	3974	2601	878
2468	3682	2602	877
2469 (S.161)	6271	2603	2409
2470 (S.162)	6026	2604	4663
2471 (S.163)	6025	2605	3714
2488	3758	2618	3428
2489	4397	2619	4648
2491	2941	2620 (C.98)	3687
2492 (S.164)	6280	2621	4912
2498	4959	2622	178
2499	197	2623	3937
2500	212	2624	2125
2501	3397	2634 (S.167)	5990
2502	3480	2646	2532
2503	4433	2647	3349
2504	4434	2648	3461
2505	2618	2649	3487
2509 (S.165)	5589	2651	3745
2518	3706	2652	3729
2533 (S.166)	5565	2653 (S.168)	5835
2534	4918	2655	4450
2535	4395	2656	4452
2536	4601	2657	4457
2537	2569	2658	2349
2538	4691	2666	221
2539	4575	2667	3970
2540	3478	2668 (C.99)	2522
2542	5046	2669 (C.100)	4698
2543	2529	2670 (L.39)	614
2544	37	2671 (L.40)	2468
2558	4983	2672 (L.41)	53
2559	3985	2673	100
2560	2367	2674	99

1997	C.L.Y.	1997	C.L.Y.
2675	2325	2786	4471
2676	4682	2787	3677
2677	4674	2788	3719
2678	2153	2789	256
2679	2155	2790 (S.175)	5987
2680	1305	2791 (S.176)	6361
2681	6146	2792	4199
2682	4473	2793	4653
2683	4336	2813	4609
2690	3713	2814	4683
2691	3741	2815	3951
2692 (S.169)	5660	2816	2123
2693	2513	2817	3678
2694 (C.101; S.170)	5780	2818	3507
2695	3508	2819	3506
2696	3509	2820	4425
2697	3510	2821	4784
2698	3511	2822	4800
2699	3512	2823	4795
2700	3513	2824 (S.177)	6044
2701	3514	2825 (S.178)	5567
2702	3517	2826 (C.106; S.179)	6369
2703	2629	2827 (S.180)	6374
2704	3125	2840	2514
2705	2957	2841	164
2706	2969	2842	3537
2707	2976	2843 (C.107)	3532
2708 (C.102)	4744	2844	210
2709	2103	2846 (C.108)	2694
2711 (S.171)	5588	2847	2648
2712	96	2848	4465
2713	3220	2849	3115
2714	2518	2850	4466
2732	3442	2851	3962
2733	3466	2852	3993
2734	3458	2862	3522
2735	174	2863	4608
2743	4388	2864	3210
2744	4997	2865	2963
2746	3440	2866	969
2747	3443	2867 (S.181)	6371
2748	3473	2868	146
2749	4420	2869	2515
2750	241	2870	55
2751	240	2876	3632
2752 (C.103)	4194	2877	1079
2756	3444	2878 (C.109; S.182)	6250
2757	167	2879 (S.183)	6245
2758	3213	2880 (S.184)	6246
2759	3217	2884	258
2760	3515	2885	4200
2761	3516	2886	4580
2762	43	2887	5026
2763	3689	2888	3477
2764	2647	2889	3482
2765	4335	2891	168
2766 (C.104)	4699	2892	3643
2767	3718	2893	2565
2768	4782	2894	115
2769	4843	2906	4921
2770	4798	2907	190
2771	4780	2908	3459
2772	4836	2909	4823
2773 (S.172)	5984	2910	4820
2774 (C.105; S.173)	5976	2911	3126
2776	2608	2912	233
2780 (S.174)	5671	2913	4289
2781	3181	2914	970
2782	4422	2915	4295
2783	4421	2916	4284
2784	4393	2917	4282
2785	4454	2918	2086

1997	C.L.Y.
2919	2152
2920	226
2921	4385
2922	4409
2928	3613
2929	3666
2930	4775
2931	4847
2932	4846
2933	4329
2934	4313
2935	4318
2936	4302
2937	229
2938	3692
2939	74
2940 (S.185)	5898
2941 (S.186)	6109
2942 (S.187)	6418
2943 (S.188)	5619
2944	867
2945	866
2946	4141
2947	4281
2948 (S.189)	6278
2949	4529
2950	4331
2951	4369
2954	4217
2959	2558
2960	2330
2961	2084
2962	4531
2963	165
2964	105
2965	106
2966	2321
2967	2323
2968	2322
2969	116
2971	2587
2972	2392
2973	2391
2974	913
2975	3192
2976	1282
2977	1216
2978	2986
2979	2987
2980	1205
2981	2924
2982	76
2985	2949
2986	2950
2987	2952
2988	2953
2989	232
2990	3723

1997	C.L.Y.
2991	2592
3001	3998
3002	239
3003	4196
3004 (C.110; S.190)	5781
3005	3328
3006	4080
3007	3313
3008	3327
3009	2350
3016	4552
3017	4197
3018	2345
3019	3566
3020	202
3021	3668
3022	4526
3023	111
3024	2528
3025	4296
3031	4195
3032	1033
3033	3238
3034	4635
3035	978
3036 (C.111)	1017
3037	1015
3038	3987
3042	4472
3043	2303
3044 (C.112)	2317
3045	4461
3046	2571
3047	5187
3048 (S.192)	6259
3049 (S.193)	6112
3050	3576
3051	3577
3052	3941
3053	4349
3054	166
3055	2311
3056	4339
3057	4342
3058	2343
3059 (S.191)	5661
3060 (S.194)	6339
3061 (S.195)	6340
3062	107
3063	4772
3066	4405
3067	3521
3068 (C.113)	2308
3069 (S.196)	6203
3070 (S.197)	6190
3107 (C.114)	4547
3108 (C.115)	5176
3114 (C.116)	1215

ALPHABETICAL TABLE OF NORTHERN IRELAND STATUTORY RULES AND ORDERS

NORTHERN IRELAND

NUMERICAL TABLE OF STATUTORY RULES AND ORDERS 1997

1997	C.L.Y.
1	5425
2	5462
3	5490
4	5496
5	5461
6	5415
7	5356
8	5364
9	5438
11	5110
12	5471
13	5103
17	5060
18	5302
19	5310
20	5309
22	5510
23	5292
24	5202
25	5457
26	5307
27 (C.1)	5422
28	5418
29	5276
31	5526
32	5173
33	5458
34	5456
35	5130
36 (C.2)	5228
37 (C.3)	5381
38	5380
39	5379
40	5355
41	5122
42	5390
43	5396
45	5232
46	5221
49	5407
50	5416
51	5223
52	5241
53	5087
54	5459
55	5463
56	5369
57	5552
58	5464
61	5061
62	5314
63	5305
65	5557
66	5555
67	5556
68	5558
69	5492

1997	C.L.Y.
70	5067
71	5349
72	5290
73	5419
74 (C.4)	5291
75	5312
76	5304
77	5303
78	5301
79	5282
80	5411
81	5410
82	5414
83	5409
84	5413
85	5465
86	5351
87	5124
89	5100
90	5296
91	5297
92	5295
93	5313
94	5353
95	5357
96	5360
97	5375
98	5359
99	5363
100	5486
101	5343
102	5370
104	5387
105	5361
106	5404
107	5403
108	5089
109	5435
110	5108
111	5322
112	5505
113	5482
114	5524
115	5401
116	5487
117	5342
118	5402
119	5406
120	5229
121	5519
122	5483
123	5497
124	5352
125	5325
126	5484
127	5498
129 (C.5)	5177

1997	C.L.Y.	1997	C.L.Y.
130	5473	218	5255
131	5542	220	5551
132	5332	221	5331
133 (C.6)	5528	222	5330
136 (C.7)	5382	224	5074
137	5319	225	5277
138	5522	226	5125
139	5384	227	5245
140	5368	229	5273
141	5367	230	5077
142	5372	231	5076
143	5376	232	5205
144	5408	234	5274
145	5517	235	5075
146	5460	236	5344
147	5341	240	5111
148	5203	241	5429
149	5271	242	5318
152	5507	243	5107
153	5362	244	5106
154	5099	246	5115
155	5533	247	5553
156	5474	248	5547
157	5518	249	5548
158	5516	250	5423
159	5358	251	5251
160	5385	252	5494
161	5377	253 (C.12)	5454
162	5373	256	5237
163	5488	257	5259
164	5472	258	5136
165	5512	259	5391
166	5062	260	5397
167	5354	261	5398
169	5431	262	5294
170	5499	264	5336
171	5513	265	5068
172	5135	266	5180
173	5132	267 (C.13)	5174
174	5506	268	5172
175	5070	269	5065
177	5247	270	5164
178	5059	271	5371
179	5184	272	5134
180	5489	273 (C.14)	5285
181	5081	275	5246
182 (C.8)	5340	277	5311
183	5529	278	5186
184	5323	279 (C.15)	5449
185	5347	280	5448
186	5329	286 (C.16)	5168
187	5206	295	5063
188 (C.9)	5195	296	5420
190	5335	297	5091
191	5338	298	5093
192 (C.10)	5383	299	5092
193	5279	300	5095
194	5559	301	5094
195	5560	305	5426
197	5469	306	5073
200	5543	307 (C.17)	5196
201	5433	308	5439
203	5204	312	5214
204	5493	313	5145
205	5470	314	5143
206	5466	315	5211
207	5455	316 (C.18)	5535
211	5424	319	5078
212	5437	320	5230
213	5260	321	5231
215 (C.11)	5467	322	5283
217	5345	324	5317

1997	C.L.Y.	1997	C.L.Y.
325	5101	427	5539
326	5123	428	5185
327	5210	429	5479
330	5475	430	5480
331	5511	431	5316
333	5306	432	5256
336 (C.20)	5450	435	5476
338	5262	436	5148
339	5530	437	5531
340	5258	438	5208
341	5207	439	5209
342	5298	440	5348
343	5293	441	5270
344	5446	448	5399
345	5127	449 (C.26)	5536
346	5126	450	5257
349	5222	451	5090
350	5213	452	5502
351	5238	453	5503
352	5131	454	5504
353	5308	455	5275
354	5481	456	5281
355	5491	457 (C.27)	5072
360	5554	458	5339
361	5212	461	5495
362	5393	462	5133
363	5394	463	5102
364	5395	464	5392
365	5468	466	5129
367	5546	468	5436
368	5444	469	5105
369	5445	470	5114
370	5442	471	5112
371	5432	472	5532
372 (C.22)	5451	473	5366
373	5441	474	5549
374	5447	475	5550
375	5434	476	5515
376	5500	477	5086
377	5501	478	5116
378	5096	479	5365
379	5080	480 (C.28)	5537
380	5337	481	5153
381	5333	482	5154
382	5324	483	5525
383	5428	484	5520
384	5443	485	5119
385 (C.23)	5224	486	5104
386	5440	488	5242
387	5280	489	5243
388	5198	492	5263
390	5346	493	5252
391	5269	494	5253
395	5514	495	5254
396	5128	496	5085
397	5109	497	5064
398	5157	499	5265
399	5200	500	5149
400 (C.4)	5541	501	5147
401	5159	504	5225
402	5117	507	5113
403	5190	508 (C.29)	5538
409	5485	509	5098
410 (C.25)	5453	511	5374
412	5509	514	5527
413	5118	515	5508
417	5477	516	5288
421	5266	518	5430
422	5201	519	5178
423	5144	520	5179
425	5097	521	5088
426	5137	522	5315

TABLE OF ABBREVIATIONS

Publishers name follows reports and journals.
(S&M = Sweet & Maxwell; ICLR = Incorporated Council of Law Reporting for England and Wales; LBC = Law Book Company of Australia; OUP = Oxford University Press; Kluwer = Kluwer Law International; Cass = Frank Cass & Co Ltd; CUP = Cambridge University Press; CLP = Central Law Publishing; TSO = The Stationery Office. All other names are in full.)

A. & S.L. = Air and Space Law (*Kluwer*)
A.C. = Appeal Cases (*ICLR*)
A.D.R.L.J. = Arbitration and Dispute Resolution Law Journal (*LLP*)
A.D.R.L.N. = Arbitration & Dispute Resolution Law Newsletter (*LLP*)
A.L.M.D. = Australian Legal Monthly Digest (*LBC*)
A.L.Q. = Arab Law Quarterly (*Kluwer*)
Accountancy = Accountancy (*Institute of Chartered Accountants in England and Wales*)
Ad. & Fos. = Adoption & Fostering (*British Adoption Agency Institute*)
Admin. L.R. = Administrative Law Reports (*Barry Rose*)
Adviser = Adviser (*NACAB*)
All E.R. = All England Law Reports (*Butterworths*)
All E.R. (EC) = All England Law Reports European Cases (*Butterworths*)
All E.R. Rev. = All England Law Reports Annual Review (*Butterworths*)
Anglo-Am. L.R. = Anglo-American Law Review (*Barry Rose*)
Arbitration = Arbitration (*Institute of Arbitrators*)
Arbitration Int. = Arbitration International (*Kluwer*)
Arch. News = Archbold News (*S&M*)

B. News = Business News (*HM Customs & Excise*)
B.C.C. = British Company Cases (*CCH Editions*)
B.C.L.C. = Butterworths Company Law Cases (*Butterworths*)
B.H.R.C. = Butterworths Human Rights Cases (*Butterworths*)
B.I.F.D. = Bulletin for International Fiscal Documentation (*IBFD Publications BV*)
B.J.I.B. & F.L. = Butterworths Journal of International Banking & Financial Law (*Butterworths*)
B.L.E. = Business Law Europe (*Financial Times Finance*)
B.L.R. = Building Law Reports (*Longman Group Ltd*)
B.M.C.R. = Butterworths Merger Control Review (*Butterworths*)
B.M.L.R. = Butterworths Medico-Legal Reports (*Butterworths*)
B.P.I.L.S. = Butterworths Personal Injury Litigation Services (*Butterworths*)
B.P.I.R. = Bankruptcy and Personal Insolvency Reports (*Jordans*)
B.P.L. = British Pension Lawyer (*Keith Wallace*)
B.T.R. = British Tax Review (*S&M*)
B.V.A.T.R. = British Value Added Tax Reporter (*CCH Editions*)
B.Y.B.I.L. = British Year Book of International Law (*OUP*)

Bank. L.R. = Banking Law Reports (*LLP*)
Bracton L.J. = Bracton Law Journal (*University of Exeter*)
Brit. J. Criminol. = British Journal of Criminology (*OUP*)
Build. L.M. = Building Law Monthly (*Monitor Press*)
Bull. J.S.B. = Bulletin of the Judicial Studies Board
Bus. L.B. = Business Law Bulletin (*W. Green*)
Bus. L.R. = Business Law Review (*Kluwer*)
Bus. Risk = Business Risk (*LLP*)

c. = chapter (*of an Act of Parliament*)
C. & E.L. = Construction & Engineering Law (*CLP*)
C. & F.L. = Credit and Finance Law (*Monitor Press*)
C.C.F. = Child Care Forum (*Child Care Forum Ltd*)
C.C.L.R. = Consumer Credit Law Reports (*S&M*)
C.C.M.L.R. = Clifford Chance Media Law Review (*Clifford Chance*)
C.F.L.Q. = Child and Family Law Quarterly (*Jordan*)
C.I.L.L. = Construction Industry Law Letter (*Monitor Press*)
C.I.P.A.J. = Chartered Institute of Patent Agents Journal (*Chartered Institute of Patent Agents*)
C.J.Q. = Civil Justice Quarterly (*S&M*)
C.L. = Current Law Monthly Digest (*S&M*)
C.L. = Commercial Lawyer (*Commercial Lawyer*)
C.L.C. = Commercial Law Cases (*CCH Editions*)
C.L. & P. = Computer Law & Practice (*Tolley*)
C.L. & P.R. = Charity Law and Practice Review (*Key Haven*)
C.L. Pract. = Commercial Law Practitioner (*Round Hall/S&M*)
C.L.B. = Commonwealth Law Bulletin (*Commonwealth Secretariat*)
C.L.C. = Commercial Law Cases (*CCH Editions*)
C.L.C. = Current Law Consolidation (*1947-1951*) (*S&M*)
C.L.J. = Cambridge Law Journal (*CUP*)
C.L.M. = Company Law Monitor (*Monitor Press*)
C.L.P. = Current Legal Problems (*OUP*)
C.L.S.R. = Computer Law & Security Report (*Elsevier Science*)
C.L.W. = Current Law Week (*S&M*)
C.L.Y. = Current Law Yearbook (*S&M*)
C.M. = Compliance Monitor (*CTA Financial Publishing*)
C.M.L. Rev. = Common Market Law Review (*Kluwer*)
C.M.L.R. = Common Market Law Reports (*S&M*)

TABLE OF ABBREVIATIONS

C. McK. Env. L.B. = Cameron McKenna Environmental Law Bulletin
C.O.D. = Crown Office Digest (*S&M*)
C.P.R. = Consumer Policy Review (*Consumer's Association*)
C.S. = case summaries (*in The Independent*)
C.S.R. = Company Secretary's Review (*Tolley*)
C.T.L.R. = Computer and Telecommunications Law Review (*S&M ESC Publishing*)
C.T.P. = Capital Tax Planning (*S&M*)
C.W. = Copyright World (*Intellectual Property*)
CA = Court of Appeal
Cambrian L.R. = Cambrian Law Review (*University of Wales*)
Can. C.L. = Canadian Current Law (*Carswell*)
CCH. T.C. = CCH Tax Cases (*CCH Editions*)
CEC = Customs and Excise Commissioners
CFI = Court of First Instance
Ch. = Chancery (*Law Reports*) (*ICLR*)
Charities M. = Charities Management (*Mitre House*)
Childright = Childright (*Children's Legal Centre*)
Civ. P.B. = Civil Practice Bulletin (*W. Green*)
Clarity = Clarity (*Mark Adler*)
CMAC = Courts Martial Appeal Court
Co. Acc. = Company Accountant (*Institute of Company Accountants*)
Co. Law. = Company Lawyer (*S&M*)
Com. Cas. = Commercial Cases
Com. Jud. J. = Commonwealth Judicial Journal (*Commonwealth Magistrates & Judges Association*)
Comm. Leases = Commercial Leases (*Monitor Press*)
Comms. L. = Communications Law (*Tolley*)
Comp. & Law = Computers & Law (*Society for Computers*)
Co. Acc. = Company Accountant (*Institute of Company Accountants*)
Comp. Law E.C. = Competition Law in the European Communities (*Bryan Harris*)
Con. L.R. = Construction Law Reports (*Butterworths*)
Cons. L. Today = Consumer Law Today (*Monitor Press*)
Cons. Law = Construction Law (*Eclipse*)
Const. L.J. = Construction Law Journal (*S&M*)
Consum. L.J. = Consumer Law Journal (*S&M*)
Conv. = Conveyancer and Property Lawyer (*S&M*)
Corp. Brief. = Corporate Briefing (*Monitor Press*)
Costs L.R. = Costs Law Reports (*CLP*)
Counsel = Counsel (*Butterworths*)
Cox C.C. = Cox's Criminal Cases
Cr. App. R. = Criminal Appeal Reports (*S&M*)
Cr. App. R. (S.) = Criminal Appeal Reports (Sentencing) (*S&M*)
Crim. L.J. = Criminal Law Journal (*LBC*)
Crim. L.B. = Criminal Law Bulletin (*W. Green*)
Crim. L.R. = Criminal Law Review (*S&M*)
Crim. Law. = Criminal Lawyer (*Butterworths*)
Criminologist = Criminologist (*Barry Rose*)

D.L.R. = Dominion Law Reports
Denning L.J. = Denning Law Journal (*University of Buckingham*)
Dir. = Directive

E. & L. = Education and the Law (*Carfax*)
E. & P. = International Journal of Evidence & Proof (*Blackstone Press*)

E.B.L.R. = European Business Law Review (*Kluwer*)
E.C.C. = European Commercial Cases (*S&M*)
E.C.C. = European Community Cases (*CCH Editions*)
E.C.L. = European Corporate Lawyer (*Legalease*)
E.C.R. = European Court Reports (*TSO*)
E.C.L.R. = European Competition Law Review (*S&M*)
E.E.B.L. = East European Business Law (*Financial Times Finance*)
E.E.F.N. = Eastern European Forum Newsletter (*International Bar Association*)
E.E.L.R. = European Environmental Law Review (*Kluwer*)
E.F.S.L. = European Financial Services Law (*Kluwer*)
E.G. = Estates Gazette (*Estates Gazette Ltd*)
E.G.C.S. = Estates Gazette Case Summaries (*Estates Gazette Ltd*)
E.G.L.R. = Estates Gazette Law Reports (*Estates Gazette Ltd*)
E.H.R.L.R. = European Human Rights Law Review (*S&M*)
E.H.R.R. = European Human Rights Reports (*S&M*)
E.I.B. = Environment Information Bulletin (*Eclipse*)
E.I.P.R. = European Intellectual Property Review (*S&M*)
E.I.R.R. = European Industrial Relations Review (*Eclipse*)
E.J.H.L. = European Journal of Health Law (*Kluwer*)
E.J.I.L. = European Journal of International Law (*S&M*)
E.L.B. = Environmental Law Brief (*Monitor Press*)
E.L.J. = European Law Journal (*Blackwell*)
E.L.L.R. = Environmental Liability Law Review (*Kluwer*)
E.L.M. = Environmental Law and Management (*Chancery Law Publishing Ltd*)
E.L.R. = Education Law Reports (*Jordans*)
E.L.R. = European Law Review (*S&M*)
E.M.L.R. = Entertainment and Media Law Reports (*S&M*)
E.O.R. = Equal Opportunities Review (*Eclipse*)
E.O.R. Dig. = Equal Opportunities Review and Discrimination Case Law Digest (*Eclipse*)
E.P.L. = European Public Law (*Kluwer*)
E.P.L.I. = Education, Public Law and the Individual (*John Wiley & Sons Ltd*)
E.P.O.R. = European Patent Office Reports (*S&M*)
E.U. News = European Union News (*S&M*)
E.W.C.B. = European Works Councils Bulletin (*Eclipse*)
EAT = Employment Appeal Tribunal
EC T.J. = EC Tax Journal (*Key Haven*)
Ecc. L.J. = Ecclesiastical Law Journal (*Ecclesiastical Law Society*)
ECJ = European Court of Justice
Eco M. & A. = Eco-Management & Auditing (*John Wiley & Sons Ltd*)
Ed. L.M. = Education Law Monitor (*Monitor Press*)
Emp. L. Brief. = Employment Law Briefing (*S&M*)
Emp. L.B. = Employment Law Bulletin (*W. Green*)

Emp. L.N. = Employment Law Newsletter (*S&M*)
Emp. Lit. = Employment Litigation (*CLP*)
ENDS = ENDS Report (*Environmental Data Services*)
Ent. L.R. = Entertainment Law Review (*S&M*)
Env. L.B. = Environmental Law Bulletin (*W. Green*)
Env. L.M. = Environmental Law Monthly (*Monitor Press*)
Env. L.R. = Environmental Law Reports (*S&M*)
Env. Law = Environmental Law (*S&M*)
Env. Liability = Environmental Liability (*S&M*)
Eu L.R. = European Law Reports (*John Wiley & Sons Ltd*)
Eur. Access = European Access (*Chadwyck Healey*)
Eur. Counsel = European Counsel (*Legal & Commercial Publishing*)
Eur. J. Crime Cr. L. Cr. J. = European Journal of Crime, Criminal Law and Criminal Justice (*Kluwer*)
Euro. Env. = European Environment (*John Wiley & Sons Ltd*)
Euro. L.M. = European Law Monitor (*Monitor Press*)
Expert = Expert (*British Academy*)

F. & D.L.R. = Futures & Derivatives Law Review (*Cavendish*)
F.C.R. = Family Court Reporter (*Justice of the Peace Ltd*)
F.I.T.A.R. = Financial Instruments Tax & Accounting Review (*CTA Financial Publishing*)
F.L.R. = Family Law Reports (*Jordan*)
F.L.T. = Family Law Today (*Monitor Press*)
F.S.B. = Financial Services Brief (*S&M*)
F.S.R. = Fleet Street Reports (*S&M*)
Fam. = Family Division (*Law Reports*) (*ICLR*)
Fam. L.B. = Family Law Bulletin (*W. Green*)
Fam. Law = Family Law (*Jordan*)
Fam. M. = Family Matters (*S&M*)
Fam. Med. = Family Mediation (*National Association of Family Mediation & Conciliation Services*)
Farm T.B. = Farm Tax Brief (*Monitor Press*)
Fem. L.S. = Feminist Legal Studies (*Deborah Charles*)

G.I.L.S.I. = Gazette Incorporated Law Society of Ireland (*The Law Society*)
G.L. & B. = Global Law & Business (*Global Law & Business*)
G.L.J. = Guernsey Law Journal (*Greffier*)
G.W.D. = Green's Weekly Digest (*W. Green*)

H. & S.B. = Health and Safety Bulletin (*Eclipse*)
H. & S.M. = Health & Safety Monitor (*Monitor Press*)
H.K.L.J. = Hong Kong Law Journal (*University of Hong Kong*)
H.L.M. = Housing Law Monitor (*Monitor Press*)
H.L.R. = Housing Law Reports (*S&M*)
H.S. = Hazardous Substances (*Monitor Press*)
HC = House of Commons
Health Law = Health Law (*Monitor Press*)
HL = House of Lords
Hold. L.R. = Holdsworth Law Review (*University of Birmingham*)
Hous. L.R. = Greens Housing Law Reports (*W. Green*)
Howard Journal = Howard Journal of Criminal Justice (*Blackwell*)

I. & C.T.L. = Information & Communications Technology Law (*Carfax*)
I. & N.L. & P. = Immigration & Nationality Law & Practice (*Tolley*)
I. Bull. = Interights Bulletin (*Interights*)
I. Prop. = Intellectual Property (*CLP*)
I.B.F.L. = International Banking and Financial Law (*S&M*)
I.B.L. = International Business Lawyer (*Blackwell*)
I.B.R. = Irish Banking Review (*The Irish Banking Review*)
I.C. Lit. = International Commercial Litigation (*Euromoney*)
I.C.C.L.R. = International Company and Commercial Law Review (*S&M*)
I.C.L.J. = Irish Criminal Law Journal (*Round Hall/S&M*)
I.C.L.Q. = International & Comparative Law Quarterly (*British Institute of International and Comparative Law*)
I.C.L.R. = International Construction Law Review (*LLP*)
I.C.R. = Industrial Cases Reports (*ICLR*)
I.F.L. Rev. = International Financial Law Review (*Euromoney*)
I.H.L. = In-House Lawyer (*Legalease*)
I.I.R. = International Insolvency Review (*Chancery Law*)
I.J.B.L. = International Journal of Biosciences and the Law (*A B Academic*)
I.J.D.L. = International Journal of Discrimination and the Law (*A B Academic*)
I.J.E.L. = Irish Journal of European Law (*Round Hall/S&M*)
I.J.I.L. = International Journal of Insurance Law (*LLP*)
I.J.L & I.T. = International Journal of Law & Information Technology (*OUP*)
I.J.L.P. = International Journal of the Legal Profession (*Carfax*)
I.J.M.C.L. = International Journal of Marine & Coastal Law (*Kluwer*)
I.J.O.S.L. = International Journal of Shipping Law (*LLP*)
I.J.R.L. = International Journal of Refugee Law (*OUP*)
I.J.S.L. = International Journal for the Semiotics of Law (*Deborah Charles*)
I.L. & P. = Insolvency Law & Practice (*Tolley*)
I.L.J. = Industrial Law Journal (*Industrial Law Society*)
I.L.P. = International Legal Practitioner (*International Bar Association*)
I.L.R.M. = Irish Law Reports Monthly (*Round Hall/S&M*)
I.L.T. = Irish Law Times (*Round Hall/S&M*)
I.L.T.R. = Irish Law Times Reports (*Round Hall/S&M*)
I.M.L. = International Media Law (*S&M*)
I.P. News. = Intellectual Property Newsletter (*Monitor Press*)
I.P.D. = Intellectual Property Decisions (*Monitor Press*)
I.P.E.L.J. = Irish Planning and Environmental Law Journal (*Round Hall/S&M*)
I.P.Q. = Intellectual Property Quarterly (*S&M*)
I.R.L.B. = Industrial Relations Law Bulletin (*Eclipse*)
I.R.L.C.T. = International Review of Law Computers & Technology (*Carfax*)

I.R.L.N. = Insurance and Reinsurance Law Newsletter (*LLP*)

I.R.L.R. = Industrial Relations Law Reports (*Eclipse*)

I.R.T.B. = Inland Revenue Tax Bulletin (*Inland Revenue*)

I.R.V. = International Review of Victimology (*A B Academic*)

I.T.P.J. = International Transfer Pricing Journal (*IBFD Publications BV*)

I.T.R. = Industrial Tribunal Reports

I.T.R. = International Tax Review (*Euromoney*)

IALS Bull. = Institute of Advanced Legal Studies Bulletin (*Institute*)

IDS Brief = IDS Brief, Employment Law and Practice (*Income Data Services Ltd*)

IDS Emp. E. = IDS Employment Europe (*Income Data Services Ltd*)

IH = Inner House of the Court of Session

IIC = International Review of Industrial Property and Copyright Law (*John Wiley & Sons*)

Imm. A.R. = Immigration Appeals Reports (*TSO*)

In Comp. = In Competition (*S&M*)

Independent = Independent Law Reports

Info. T.L.R. = Information Technology Law Reports (*Lawtext Publishing*)

Ins. L. & C. = Insurance Law & Claims (*Mitre House*)

Ins. L.M. = Insurance Law Monthly (*Monitor Press*)

Insolv. Int. = Insolvency Intelligence (*S&M*)

Insolv. L. = Insolvency Lawyer (*Chancery Law*)

Insolv. L. & P. = Insolvency Litigation & Practice (*CLP*)

Int. I.L.R. = International Insurance Law Review (*S&M*)

Int. J. Comp. L.L.I.R. = International Journal of Comparative Labour Law and Industrial Relations (*Kluwer*)

Int. J. Law & Fam. = International Journal of Law, Policy and the Family (*OUP*)

Int. J. Soc. L. = International Journal of the Sociology of Law (*Academic Press Ltd*)

Int. M.L. = International Maritime Law (*S&M*)

Int. Rel. = International Relations (*David Davies Memorial Institute*)

Int. T.L.R. = International Trade Law & Regulation (*S&M ESC Publishing*)

Ir. T.R. = Irish Tax Review (*Institute of Taxation in Ireland*)

IT L.T. = IT Law Today (*Monitor Press*)

J. Civ. Lib. = Journal of Civil Liberties (*Northumbria Law Press*)

J. Com. Mar. St. = Journal of Common Market Studies (*Blackwell*)

J. Crim. L. = Journal of Criminal Law (*Pageant*)

J. Env. L. = Journal of Environmental Law (*OUP*)

J. Int. Arb. = Journal of International Arbitration (*Kluwer*)

J. Int. P. = Journal of International Trust and Corporate Planning (*John Wiley*)

J. Law & Soc. = Journal of Law and Society (*Blackwell*)

J. Leg. Hist. = Journal of Legal History (*Cass*)

J. Soc. Wel. & Fam. L. = Journal of Social Welfare and Family Law (*Routledge*)

J.A.L. = Journal of African Law (*OUP*)

J.B.L. = Journal of Business Law (*S&M*)

J.C. = Justiciary Cases

J.E.L.P. = Journal of Employment Law & Practice (*Tolley*)

J.E.R.L. = Journal of Energy & Natural Resources Law (*Kluwer*)

J.F.R. & C. = Journal of Financial Regulation and Compliance (*Henry Stewart*)

J.I.B.L. = Journal of International Banking Law (*S&M*)

J.I.F.D.L. = Journal of International Franchising & Distribution Law (*Tolley*)

J.I.L.T. = Journal of Information, Law & Technology (*http://elj.warwick.ac.uk/jilt*)

J.L.S. = Journal of Legislative Studies (*Cass*)

J.L.S.S. = Journal of the Law Society of Scotland (*Law Society of Scotland*)

J.M.L. & P. = Journal of Media Law & Practice (*Tolley*)

J.P. = Justice of the Peace (*Justice of the Peace Ltd*)

J.P.I.L. = Journal of Personal Injury Litigation (*S&M*)

J.P.L. = Journal of Planning & Environment Law (*S&M*)

J.P.M. = Journal of Pensions Management (*Henry Stewart*)

J.P.N. = Justice of the Peace Reports & Local Government Notes of Cases (*Justice of the Peace Ltd*)

J.P. Rep. = Justice of the Peace and Local Government Law Reports (*Justice of the Peace Ltd*)

J.S.S.L. = Journal of Social Security Law (*S&M*)

Jersey L.R. = Jersey Law Review (*The Jersey Law Review*)

Jur. Rev. = Juridical Review (*W. Green*)

K.B. = Kings Bench (*Law Reports*) (*ICLR*)

K.C.L.J. = Kings College Law Journal (*King's College London*)

K.I.R. = Knights Industrial Reports

L. & T. Review = Landlord & Tenant Law Review (*S&M*)

L. Ex. = Legal Executive (*ILEX*)

L.A.L. = Local Authority Law (*S&M*)

L.E. = Lawyers' Europe (*Butterworths*)

L.G. and L. = Local Government and Law (*Monitor Press*)

L.G. Rev. = Local Government Review (*Barry Rose*)

L.G.C. Law & Admin. = Local Government Chronicle Law & Administration (*Local Government Chronicle Ltd*)

L.M.C.L.Q. = Lloyd's Maritime & Commercial Law Quarterly (*LLP*)

L.P. or L.V.C. = references to denote Lands Tribunal decision (*transcripts available from the Lands Tribunal*)

L.Q.R. = Law Quarterly Review (*S&M*)

L.R.L.R. = Lloyd's Reinsurance Law Reports (*LLP*)

L.S. = Legal Studies (*Butterworths*)

L.S.G. = Law Society Gazette (*The Law Society*)

Law = Law (*The Law*)

Law & Crit. = Law and Critique (*Deborah Charles*)

Law & Just. = Law & Justice (*Plowden*)

Law & Pol. = Law & Policy (*Blackwell*)

Law Lib. = Law Librarian (*S&M*)

Law Teach. = Law Teacher (*S&M*)

Lawyer = Lawyer (*Centaur Communications Group*)
Legal Action = Legal Action (*Legal Action Group*)
Legal Bus. = Legal Business (*Legalease*)
Lit. = Litigation (*Barry Rose*)
Litigator = Litigator (*S&M*)
Liverpool L.R. = Liverpool Law Review (*Deborah Charles*)
Lloyd's Rep. = Lloyd's Law Reports (*LLP*)
Ll. Rep. = Lloyd's List Reports (*LLP*)
LVAC = Land Valuation Appeal Court

M.A.L.Q.R. = Model Arbitration Law Quarterly Review (*Simmons & Hill Publishing Ltd*)
M. Advice = Money Advice (*London Money Advice Support Unit*)
M.C.P. = Magistrates' Courts Practice (*CLP*)
M.E.C.L.R. = Middle East Commercial Law Review (*S&M*)
M.I.P. = Managing Intellectual Property (*Euromoney*)
M.J. = Maastricht Journal of European and Comparative Law (*Roger Bayliss*)
M.L.B. = Manx Law Bulletin (*Central Reference*)
M.L.J.I. = Medico-Legal Journal of Ireland (*Round Hall/S&M*)
M.L.N. = Media Lawyer Newsletter (*Tom Welsh*)
M.L.R. = Modern Law Review (*Blackwell*)
Magistrate = Magistrate (*Magistrate's Association*)
Man. L. = Managerial Law (*MCB University Press Ltd*)
Masons C.L.R. = Masons Computer Law Reports
Med. L. Int. = Medical Law International (*A B Academic Publishing*)
Med. L. Mon. = Medical Law Monitor (*Monitor Press*)
Med. L. Rev. = Medical Law Review (*OUP*)
Med. L.R. = Medical Law Reports (*OUP*)
Med. Leg. J. = Medico-Legal Journal (*Dramrite Printers*)
Med. Sci. Law = Medicine, Science & the Law (*Chiltern*)

N.I.L.Q. = Northern Ireland Legal Quarterly (*SLS Legal Publications*)
N.I.L.R. = Northern Ireland Law Reports (*Butterworths*)
N.L.J. = New Law Journal (*Butterworths*)
N.P.C. = New Property Cases (*New Law Publishing*)
N.Z.L.R. = New Zealand Law Reports
Nott. L.J. = Nottingham Law Journal (*Nottingham Trent University*)

O.D. and I.L. = Ocean Development and International Law (*Taylor & Francis Ltd*)
O.G.L.T.R. = Oil & Gas Law & Taxation Review (*S&M*)
O.J.L.S. = Oxford Journal of Legal Studies (*OUP*)
O.P.L.R. = Occupational Pensions Law Reports (*Eclipse Group*)
O.S.S. Bull. = Office for the Supervision of Solicitors Bulletin (*The Law Society's Gazette*)
O.T.R. = Offshore Taxation Review (*Key Haven*)
Occ. Pen. = Occupational Pensions (*Eclipse*)
OJ = Official Journal of the European Communities

P & I Int. = P & I International (*LLP*)

P. = Probate, Divorce and Admiralty (*Law Reports*)
P. & C.R. = Property, Planning & Compensation Reports (*S&M*)
P. & M.I.L.L. = Personal and Medical Injuries Law Letter (*Monitor Press*)
P. & P. = Practice and Procedure (*S&M*)
P. Injury = Personal Injury (*CLP*)
P.A.D. = Planning Appeal Decisions (*S&M*)
P.C.B. = Private Client Business (*S&M*)
P.C.C. = Palmer's Company Cases (*W. Green*)
P.C.L.B. = Practitioners' Child Law Bulletin (*S&M*)
P.E.L.B. = Planning and Environmental Law Bulletin (*S&M*)
P.I. = Personal Injury (*John Wiley & Sons Ltd*)
P.I.C. = Palmer's In Company (*S&M*)
P.I.Q.R. = Personal Injuries and Quantum Reports (*S&M*)
P.L. = Public Law (*S&M*)
P.L.B. = Property Law Bulletin (*S&M*)
P.L.C. = Practical Law for Companies (*Legal & Commercial Publishing*)
P.L.R. = Planning Law Reports (*Estates Gazette Ltd*)
P.N. = Professional Negligence (*Tolley*)
P.N. & L. = Professional Negligence & Liability (*CLP*)
P.N.L.R. = Professional Negligence and Liability Reports (*S&M*)
P.P.L. = Practical Planning Law (*CLP*)
P.P.L.R. = Public Procurement Law Review (*S&M*)
P.P.M. = Professional Practice Management (*Monitor Press*)
P.S.T. = Pension Scheme Trustee (*S&M*)
P.T. = Pensions Today (*Monitor Press*)
P.T.P.R. = Personal Tax Planning Review (*Key Haven*)
P.W. = Patent World (*Intellectual Property*)
Parl. Aff. = Parliamentary Affairs (*OUP*)
Pen. World = Pensions World (*Tolley*)
Pol. J. = Police Journal (*Barry Rose*)
Policing T. = Policing Today (*Police Review*)
Prison Serv. J. = Prison Service Journal (*HM Prison, Leyhill*)
Probat. J. = Probation Journal (*National Association of Probation Officers*)
Prop. L.B. = Property Law Bulletin (*W. Green*)

Q.A. = Quarterly Account (*Money Advice Association*)
Q.B. = Queen's Bench (*Law Reports*) (*ICLR*)
Q.R. = Quantum Reports (*S&M*)

R.A. = Rating Appeals (*Rating Publishers*)
R.A.D.I.C. = African Journal of International and Comparative Law (*African Society*)
R.A.L.Q. = Receivers, Administrators and Liquidators Quarterly (*Key Haven*)
R.E.C.I.E.L. = Review of European Community and International Environmental Law (*Blackwell*)
R.L.R. = Restitution Law Review (*Mansfield Press*)
R.P.C. = Reports of Patent, Design and Trade Mark Cases (*The Patent Office*)
R.R.L.R. = Rent Review & Lease Renewal (*MCB University Press*)
R.T.I. = Road Traffic Indicator (*S&M*)
R.T.R. = Road Traffic Reports (*S&M*)
R.V.R. = Rating and Valuation Reporter (*Rating Publishers*)

TABLE OF ABBREVIATIONS

Ratio Juris = Ratio Juris (*Blackwell*)
Re L.R. = Reinsurance Law Reports (*LLP*)
Regulator = Regulator & Professional Conduct Quarterly (*Barry Rose*)
Rep. B. = Reparation Bulletin (*W. Green*)
Rep. L.R. Greens Reparation Law Reports (*W. Green*)
Res Publica = Res Publica (*Deborah Charles*)
Res. B. = Home Office Research Bulletin (*Home Office Research and Statistics Department*)
Revenue = Revenue (*S&M*)
ROW Bulletin = Rights of Women Bulletin (*Rights of Women*)
RPC = Restrictive Practices Court

S. & L.S. = Social & Legal Studies (*Sage*)
S. News = Sentencing News (*S&M*)
S.C. = Session Cases (*S&M/W. Green*)
S.C. (*HL*) = Session Cases (*House of Lords*)
S.C.C.R. = Scottish Criminal Case Reports (*The Law Society of Scotland*)
S.C.L.R. = Scottish Civil Law Reports (*The Law Society of Scotland*)
S.C.P. News = Supreme Court Practice News (*S&M*)
S.J. = Solicitors Journal (*S&M*)
S.J.L.B. = Solicitors Journal Law Brief (*S&M*)
S.L.A. & P. = Sports Law Administration & Practice (*Monitor Press*)
S.L.C.R. = Scottish Land Court Reports
S.L.C.R. Apps. = Scottish Land Court Reports (*appendix*)
S.L.G. = Scottish Law Gazette (*Scottish Law Agents Society*)
S.L.L.P. = Scottish Licensing Law & Practice (*Scottish Licensing Services Ltd*)
S.L.P.Q. = Scottish Law & Practice Quarterly (*T & T Clark*)
S.L.R. = Student Law Review (*Cavendish*)
S.L.T. = Scots Law Times (*S&M/W. Green*)
S.L.T. (Land Ct) = Scots Law Times Land Court Reports (*S&M/W. Green*)
S.L.T. (Lands Tr) = Scots Law Times Lands Tribunal Reports (*S&M/W. Green*)
S.L.T. (Lyon Ct) = Scots Law Times Lyon Court Reports (*S&M/W. Green*)
S.L.T. = Scots Law Times News Section (*S&M/ W. Green*)
S.L.T. (Notes) = Scots Law Times Notes of Recent Decisions (*1946-1981*) (*S&M/W. Green*)
S.L.T. (Sh.Ct.) = Scots Law Times Sheriff Court Reports (*S&M/W. Green*)
S.N. = Session Notes
S.P.E.L. = Scottish Planning and Environmental Law (*Planning Exchange*)
S.P.T.L. Reporter = Society of Public Teachers of Law Reporter (*Queen Mary*)
S.T.C. = Simons Tax Cases (*Butterworths*)
S.T.C. (SCD) = Simons Tax Cases: Special Commissioners Decisions (*Butterworths*)
S.W.T.I. = Simon's Weekly Tax Intelligence (*Butterworths*)
SCOLAG = SCOLAG (*Scottish Legal Action Group*)

SI = Statutory Instrument
Soc. L. = Socialist Lawyer (*Haldane Society*)
Stat. L.R. = Statute Law Review (*OUP*)
Sudebnik = Sudebnik (*Simmonds & Hill*)

T. & T. = Trusts & Trustees and International Asset Management (*Gostick Hall*)
T.A.Q. = The Aviation Quarterly (*LLP*)
T.C. or Tax.Cas. = Tax Cases (*TSO*)
T.E.L. & P. = Tolley's Employment Law & Practice (*Tolley*)
T.L.J. = Travel Law Journal (*Travel Law Centre*)
T.L.P. = Transport Law & Policy (*Waterfront Partnership*)
T.N.I.B. = Tolley's National Insurance Brief (*Tolley*)
T.O.C. = Transnational Organized Crime (*Cass*)
T.P.T. = Tolley's Practical Tax (*Tolley*)
T.P.V. = Tolley's Practical VAT (*Tolley*)
T.W. = Trademark World (*Intellectual Property*)
Tax J. = Tax Journal (*Butterworths*)
Tax. = Taxation (*Tolley*)
Tax. P. = Taxation Practitioner (*Chartered Institute of Taxation*)
Tr. & Est. = Trusts & Estates (*Monitor Press*)
Tr. L.R. = Trading Law Reports (*Barry Rose*)
Trans. ref. = Transcript reference number
Tribunals = = Tribunals (*OUP*)
Tru. L.I. = Trust Law International (*Tolley*)
TSO = The Stationery Office
The Times = Times Law Reports

U.L.R. = Utilities Law Review (*Chancery Law Publishing Ltd*)
UCELNET = Universities and Colleges Education Law Network (*University of Stirling*)

V. & D.R. = Value Added Tax and Duties Reports (*TSO*)
V.A.T.T.R. = Value Added Tax Tribunal Reports (*TSO*)
VAT Int. = VAT Intelligence (*Gee Publishing*)
VAT Plan. = VAT Planning (*Butterworths*)

W. Comp. = World Competition (*Werner Publishing*)
W.B. = Welfare Benefits (*CLP*)
W.L. = Water Law (*Chancery Law Publishing Ltd*)
W.L.R. = Weekly Law Reports (*ICLR*)
W.T.R. = World Tax Report (*Financial Times Finance*)
Web J.C.L.I. = Web Journal of Current Legal Issues (*Blackstone*)
Welf. R. Bull. = Welfare Rights Bulletin (*Child Poverty*)
Writ = Writ (*Northern Ireland Law Society*)

Y.E.L. = Yearbook of European Law (*OUP*)
Y.M.E.L. = Yearbook of Media & Entertainment Law (*OUP*)
Yb. Int'l Env. L. = Yearbook of International Environmental Law (*OUP*)

CURRENT LAW
YEAR BOOK 1997

UK, ENGLAND & WALES & EU

ACCOUNTANCY

1. **Accountants–disciplinary procedures–waiver of privilege against self incrimination–delegation of ICAEW power to request information**

   N, a chartered accountant and member of I, audited the accounts of six companies prior to October 1, 1991 when he was not a registered auditor. In 1993 I received a complaint about the accounts of a limited company which had been prepared by N and, in the course of investigating that complaint, the Secretary of the Investigation Committee, P, in March 1994 asked N to provide information about all clients for whom he had been reappointed as auditor since October 1, 1991. In making this request P was acting under a formal delegation of powers given by para.8(a) of Sch.2 to the bylaws of the I. N refused this request on the basis that he was entitled to rely on the privilege against self incrimination. Disciplinary proceedings were then commenced against N, and the complaint that he failed to respond adequately to P's request for information was found proved. N was severely reprimanded and fined. N's appeal to the Appeal Committee of I was dismissed in July 1995. In October 1996 N's application for judicial review of the Appeal Committee decision was dismissed at first instance on the bases that the power to request information had been lawfully delegated to P and that N was not entitled to rely on the privilege against self incrimination in refusing the request to provide information ([1997] P.N.L.R. 433). N appealed.

   Held, dismissing the appeal, that (1) the discretion vested in Committees of I by byLaw 49(b) is a discretion to delegate any of its powers to such person as it thinks fit. Such a discretion introduces the concept of reasonableness as well as relevance, and the power of delegation is constrained by a duty not to exercise it in a manner that is *Wednesbury* unreasonable, *Cinnamond v. British Airports Authority* [1980] 1 W.L.R. 582, [1980] C.L.Y. 121 considered, *Kruse v. Johnson* [1898] 2 Q.B. 91 applied; (2) bylaw 49(b) should not be construed as excessive, but even if it were so, it should be read as modified in accordance with its administrative purpose and obvious rationale so as to permit reasonable delegation, *DPP v. Hutchinson* [1990] 2 A.C. 783, [1991] C.L.Y. 87 applied. In this instance the delegation to P was both reasonable and rational, since the Committee knew they could have trust and confidence in P and delegation to him was of obvious administrative convenience, and (3) upon becoming a chartered accountant the rules of I provide that it shall be the duty of every member to provide such information as the Investigation Committee may consider necessary to discharge its functions. Compliance with that duty necessarily precludes the exercise of any privilege that would excuse the provision of the information and acceptance of the duty necessarily entailed the waiver of the privilege against self incrimination. Moreover, powerful grounds of public policy exist for endorsing the waiver.

R. v. INSTITUTE OF CHARTERED ACCOUNTANTS IN ENGLAND AND WALES, *ex p.* NAWAZ, Trans. Ref: QBCOF 96/1583/D, April 25, 1997, Leggatt, L.J., CA.

2. Accounts—directors—disclosure of emoluments

COMPANY ACCOUNTS (DISCLOSURE OF DIRECTORS' EMOLUMENTS) REGULATIONS 1997, SI 1997 570; made under the Companies Act 1985 s.257. In force: March 31, 1997; £1.95.

These Regulations amend provisions in the Companies Act 1985 Sch.6 Part I relating to the disclosure of directors' emoluments or other benefits in the notes to a company's annual accounts in respect of any financial year. They also make amendments to s.246 as amended by the Companies Act 1985 (Accounts of Small and Medium-Sized Companies and Minor Accounting Amendments) Regulations 1997 (SI 1997 220).

3. Accounts—management accounts—negligent representations—no duty of care owed by vendor's accountant to purchaser

Two actions arose from representations made by S to P regarding the management accounts of a company, ASA. The representations were found to have been falsely and negligently made and to have induced P to purchase all ASA's shares. The first order stated that S, ASA's accountants and auditors, should pay damages to P. The former shareholders in ASA were found, by a second order, not to be liable to pay S the fees claimed for preparation of the management accounts and advice relating to the representations, to the extent that they were found to be false or negligently made. S appealed against both orders. S had prepared a profit and loss account and balance sheet for the 10 months prior to October 1990 when P proposed acquiring ASA. During a pre-completion meeting, P sought an assurance from S as to the accuracy of the accounts which S stated "were right", and later required a warranty to be given. S eventually made a statement as to the reliability of the accounts subject to the qualification that they were not audited. It had not been prepared previously to certify them nor did it believe that they should be warranted. S argued that the judge was wrong to find that it owed a duty of care to P. P had sought assurances from S in order to get a warranty from ASA so that any assumption of responsibility by S was to ASA only and not to P. With regard to the second order, S argued that the accounts should be read together with the disclosure letter and other information given to P.

Held, allowing S's appeal against the first order, that (1) it would not be fair, just or reasonable in the circumstances of the case to impose a duty of care on S to P. P was a qualified accountant, experienced in finance and business. In addition both P and ASA had accountants and solicitors advising them throughout the sale and at the pre-completion meeting. Although S was aware that the accounts were required for P, a prudent purchaser would not rely on such accounts alone without its own advisers checking the figures. This was particularly relevant as P had expressed a low opinion of S's professional qualities and competence, which indicated that P could not be taken to have relied entirely on the accounts prepared by S when contracting to buy all the shares of ASA. Although the judge below had found it relevant that S's statement regarding the accounts was made voluntarily and directly, it did not follow that S was assuming responsibility to P. S made the statement for the benefit and information of its client, ASA, not for P. When P first discovered that the figures were inflated, a claim was made against the vendor and it was not until some months later that the claim was commenced against S; and, dismissing the appeal against the second order, that (2) the management accounts were misleading as found by the judge, and did not give a fair picture of

ASA's trading performance, and this was not rectified by the information provided by the disclosure letter.

PEACH PUBLISHING LTD v. SLATER & CO, Trans. Ref: CHANF 95/1059/B, CHANF 95/1060/B, CHANF 96/1193/B, February 13, 1997, Morritt, L.J., CA.

4. **Accounts–subsidiary companies–accounts to give fair view of financial position of company–profits requiring entry on parent company's balance sheet under Council Directive 78/660 Art.31–European Union**

[Council Directive 78/660 on annual accounts Art.31.]

G held a 100 per cent holding in two subsidiary companies. The accounts of the two subsidiaries showed that profits had been appropriated but not paid to G. G's accounts did not show those profits. T, a shareholder in G, challenged the accounts asserting a failure to comply with Council Directive 78/660 on annual accounts Art.31(1), which required that items shown in annual accounts of certain companies should be valued in accordance with set principles including prudent valuation and the accruals concept. T's action before the regional court was dismissed and the appeal to the federal court decided that the profits owed to a sole shareholder in a subsidiary company were sufficiently certain to be regarded as part of the assets of the parent company and so the debt from the subsidiary company should be included in the parent company's annual accounts. The federal court stayed the proceedings and referred the question of the interpretation of Art.31 (1) to the Court of Justice.

Held, that the national court was entitled to hold that the profits should be entered in the parent company's balance sheet, as Council Directive 78/660 required accounts to give a fair view of the assets and liabilities, financial position and profit or loss of the company concerned. Observance of those requirements was ensured by taking account of all elements which actually related to the year in question. If the subsidiary companies' accounts themselves complied with the principle of the true and fair view it would not be contrary to Art.31 (1) for the national court to decide that the profits in question should be entered in the parent company's balance sheet.

TOMBERGER v. GEBRUDER VON DER WETTERN GmbH (C234/94) [1996] All E.R. (EC) 805, DAO Edward (President), ECJ.

5. **Association of Certified Public Accountants of Britain–whether name misleading**

See COMPANY LAW: Association of Certified Public Accountants of Britain v. Secretary of State for Trade and Industry. §803

6. **Small businesses–accounting provisions**

COMPANIES ACT 1985 (ACCOUNTS OF SMALL AND MEDIUM-SIZED COMPANIES AND MINOR ACCOUNTING AMENDMENTS) REGULATIONS 1997, SI 1997 220; made under the Companies Act 1985 s.257. In force: March 1, 1997; £4.70.

These Regulations amend provisions in the Companies Act 1985 Part VII concerning the accounts of small and medium-sized companies. They also make certain minor consequential amendments to other accounting provisions of Part VII.

7. **Small businesses–audits–exemptions for small businesses**

COMPANIES ACT 1985 (AUDIT EXEMPTION) (AMENDMENT) REGULATIONS 1997, SI 1997 936; made under the Companies Act 1985 s.257. In force: April 15, 1997; £1.10.

These Regulations amend the provisions in the Companies Act 1985 Part VII concerning the exemptions of certain small companies from the requirement to have their annual accounts audited. The amendments are to apply to annual accounts for financial years ending two months or more after coming into force of the Regulations.

8. Articles

ASB issues exposure draft on derivatives disclosures *(Mike Lloyd)*: F.I.T.A.R. 1997, 2(5), 74-77. (FRED 13, Derivatives and Other Financial Instruments: Disclosures, dealing with numerical and discursive type disclosures, with example of disclosures by more complex company).

Accounting and pricing for FRAs *(Mike Lloyd* and *James Rouse)*: F.I.T.A.R. 1997, 2(1), 14-15. (Including reasons for entering into forward rate agreement, dealing or speculative positions, hedging and mark to market valuation, with examples).

Accounting for neutrality—or not? *(Jim Cousins)*: Accountancy 1997, 119(1245), 74-75. (Questions ASB's claim that accounting standards are neutral and argues that ASB should explain economic and social factors underlying standards because of effect of standards in transferring and redistributing wealth).

Cash flow clangers *(Stuart Hastie)*: Accountancy 1997, 120(1250), 117. (Common errors made when completing cash flow statements intended to comply with FRS 1 (Revised)).

Derivatives *(KPMG)*: P.L.C. 1997, 8(5), 74-75. (ASB's FRED 13 Derivatives and Other Financial Instruments: Disclosure on discursive and numerical disclosures).

Earnings per share *(KPMG)*: P.L.C. 1997, 8(7), 58. (Proposals in FRED 16 regarding basis for calculating and presenting earnings per share in company accounts).

FRED 13 supplement: *Derivatives and other Financial Instruments: Disclosures by Banks and Similar Institutions*: Accountancy 1997, 120(1248), 123-129. (Text of supplement to FRED 13, aimed at ensuring that banks and similar institutions provide disclosures that focus on main risks arising from their financial instruments, which may differ from those of other entities).

FRED 13: Derivatives and Other Financial Instruments: Disclosures: Accountancy 1997, 119(1246), 114-135. (Text of exposure draft, including preface, objective, definitions, draft SSAP, explanation and how FRED was developed).

FRED 14: Provisions and Contingencies: June 1997: Accountancy 1997, 120(1247), 114-126. (Text of ASB exposure draft dealing with accounting and reporting of provisions and contingencies, intended to revise SSAP 18).

FRED 15: Impairment of Fixed Assets and Goodwill: June 1997: Accountancy 1997, 120(1247), 126-135. (Text of ASB exposure draft based on April 1996 Discussion Paper and FRED 12).

FRS 1 and beyond *(Sylvia Courtnage)*: C.S.R. 1997, 20(21), 161-162. (Changes resulting from revised FRS 1 on cash flows in financial statements and other recent or proposed changes to accounting standards).

FRS 8-a few months on *(Tony Wedgwood)*: Accountancy 1997, 120(1249), 138-139. (Issues arising from implementation of FRS 8, Related Party Disclosures, including definition of related party, question of materiality and disclosure of controlling parties).

Goodwill - consensus, consultation and certainty *(Kenneth Cleaver* and *Phillip Ormrod)*: Co. Acc. 1997, 136, 28-29. (Protracted and controversial review of accounting for goodwill leading to publication of FRED 12 and extent to which ASB has tried to obtain consensus from interested parties before imposing new standard).

Innovate to renovate R&D treatment *(Richard Letham)*: Accountancy 1997, 120(1248), 90. (ICAS review of SSAP 13 Accounting for Research and Development, disclosing need to change definitions used and methods of accounting adopted).

International proposals *(KPMG)*: P.L.C. 1997, 8(9), 64-65. (IASC's proposed international standards on interim financial reporting, discontinuing operations, intangible assets, business combinations, and provisions, contingent liabilities and contingent assets).

Looking beyond face value *(Anne McGeachin)*: Accountancy 1997, 119(1245), 87. (ASB working paper *Discounting in Financial Reporting* which aims to explain and publicise ASB's approach to discounting when accounting for variety of assets).

Members Handbook Statement 1.401: Financial and accounting responsibilities of directors: Accountancy 1997, 119(1241), 127-139. (Text of ICAEW statement giving guidance for accountants on main accounting and financial duties and responsibilities owed by company directors to company, shareholders and third parties and how duties can best be discharged).

Practice note 13: the audit of small businesses: July 1997: Accountancy 1997, 120(1249), 123-136. (Text of Auditing Practices Board guidance on application of Statements of Auditing Standards to financial statements of small businesses).

Presentation of dividend income: Accountancy 1997, 120(1251), 114. (Text of ASB exposure draft proposing amendments to SSAP 8, The Treatment of Taxation under the Imputation System in the Accounts of Companies, dealing with presentation of dividends from UK and Irish resident companies).

Principles fall on rocky ground *(Michael Davies* and *Paul Davies)*: Accountancy 1997, 120(1249), 95. (Whether ASB's Statement of Principles embracing balance sheet paradigm is suitable model for accounting practice, with particular reference to its use in developing FRED 14 on Provisions and Contingencies).

Professional ethics help sheets: Accountancy 1997, 119(1244), 116-127. (Text of 12 sheets produced by Chartered Accountants Advisory Service on Ethics to help practitioners in applying ICAEW's ethical guidance, including disclosure, use of "chartered accountant", client's money, practice names and complaints).

Taking preliminaries a step further *(Hannah King)*: Accountancy 1997, 120(1251), 86. (Proposed ASB statement of best practice on preliminary announcements, aiming to encourage companies to make timely and full disclosure).

The International Accounting Standards Committee changes its tune *(John Tattersall)*: F.I.T.A.R. 1997, 2(9), 150-151. (Issues raised by IASC concerning need for international accounting standards for multinational companies with shares listed on several stock exchanges).

The international dimension *(Robert Langford)*: Accountancy 1997, 119(1245), 109. (IASC's intention that international accounting standards will be recognised by stock exchanges throughout world by 1998, remaining hurdles to harmonisation and impact on UK).

The price was right: or was it? *(Sarah Perrin)*: Accountancy 1997, 119(1241), 40-41. (Need for accountants to check technical detail of contract to sell or purchase business where consideration is based on completion accounts in order to avoid disputes following sale).

The truth about PFI *(Andy Simmonds)*: Accountancy 1997, 119(1246), 140-141. (Accounting issues arising from private finance initiative contracts, particularly whether SSAP 21 or FRS 5 should be applied, with examples).

Time to put our foot down? *(Mary Keegan)*: Accountancy 1997, 119(1241), 89. (Revision of International Accounting Standard 12, Income Taxes, requiring differed tax liability and assets to be recorded on balance sheet and view that standard should not be adopted by UK).

True, fair and in the open *(Guy Loveday)*: Accountancy 1997, 119(1243), 124-125. (Auditing standards requirement that manner of disclosure of listed company accounts is fair, practice by companies of revealing minimum amount of information and areas where enhanced disclosure would be beneficial, with examples).

UITF prohibits "grossing up"—implications for the leasing industry *(John Williamson)*: F.I.T.A.R. 1997, 2(1), 4-5. (Effects of decision to prevent practice of "grossing up" pre-tax results and ASB exposure draft proposing to amend para.41 of SSAP 21 to remove lessors' option to gross up leases partly financed by tax free grants).

Weightless economy: an issue to treat with gravity *(Tony Tollington* and *Martin Kleyman)*: Accountancy 1997, 120(1249), 94. (Difficulties in applying ASB's definition of asset to intangible assets such as software, brands, intellectual property and human skills).

What to record and what to keep *(Andrew Scott)*: Accountancy 1997, 120(1249), 140. (Advantages and disadvantages of producing and retaining working papers, particularly in audit context, with reference to Statement of Auditing Standards (SAS) 230).

9. Books

Davis, Mike; Paterson, Ron; Wilson, Alister–UK GAAP. Hardback: £55.00. ISBN 0-333-64260-0. Macmillan Press.

Fleck, Richard; Patient, Matthew–Law of Accountancy. Hardback: £120.00. ISBN 0-406-02645-9. Butterworth Law.

Keenen, Denis; Edwards, Martin; Michael, Peter; Woods, David–Butterworths Accountants' Legal Service Set. Unbound/looseleaf: £130.00. ISBN 0-406-99829-9. Butterworth Law.

Taub, Michael; Rapazzini, Adrian–Tolley's Accountancy Litigation Support. Unbound/looseleaf: £165.00. ISBN 1-86012-337-6. Tolley Publishing.

ADMINISTRATION OF JUSTICE

10. Abuse of process–related civil and criminal proceedings–prosecutor acting for plaintiff in civil action

A civil action was brought against A by another company for alleging a connection between their products. Criminal proceedings were also brought against A by the local authority at the instigation of the plaintiff company. Prosecuting counsel in that action was also counsel for the plaintiffs in the civil action. In that capacity, counsel refused to allow A access to documents on the ground that the documents were privileged. A applied for judicial review of the justices' decision to refuse to order disclosure or to stay the criminal proceedings for abuse of process.

Held, allowing the application, that where a party was the defendant in related civil and criminal proceedings, it was an abuse of process for the plaintiff in the civil action to be in effective control of the criminal proceedings by compromising the independence of the prosecution and thereby the integrity of the court. The proceedings would be permanently stayed.

R. v. LEOMINSTER MAGISTRATES COURT, *ex p.* ASTON MANOR BREWERY CO, *The Times*, January 8, 1997, McCowan, L.J., QBD.

11. Access to justice–Supreme Court fees–abolition of concessions for litigants on low income was denial of right to access to a court

[Supreme Court Fees (Amendment) Order 1996 Art.3 (SI 1996 3191); Supreme Court Act 1981 s.130.]

W applied for judicial review of the Supreme Court Fees (Amendment) Order 1996, on the grounds that Art.3 of the Order, which repealed provisions excusing litigants in person in receipt of income support from payment of court fees and allowing the Lord Chancellor to reduce or waive the fee in exceptional cases of undue financial hardship, was ultra vires as it violated his right to access to a court. W, who was on income support, wished to bring proceedings in person for defamation, for which no legal aid was available, and contended that he could not afford the fees imposed under the Order.

Held, allowing the application, that there were clearly numerous situations in which people on low incomes would be denied access to a court absolutely under the Order and where no legal aid would be available to assist them. It was not necessary to refer to the jurisprudence of the European Court of Human Rights, as the common law clearly afforded special protection to a person's right of access to a court as a constitutional right, which meant that the executive could not abrogate that right without express provision to that effect being enacted by Parliament. Under the Supreme Court Act 1981 s.130, there was nothing to suggest that court fees might be imposed in a manner that could deny absolutely a person's access to the court and thus Art.3 of the Order was ultra vires.

R. v. LORD CHANCELLOR, ex p. WITHAM [1997] 2 All E.R. 779, Laws, J, QBD.

12. Bribery–solicitors–agent's acts had to be intended by briber to affect principal's affairs–Hong Kong

[Independent Commission Against Corruption Ordinance s.10B (Hong Kong); Prevention of Bribery Ordinance s.9(1) (Hong Kong).]

P was convicted of conspiracy to defraud and instructed A, a partner in a firm of solicitors, for his appeal. Officers of the Commission obtained a warrant under the Independent Commission Against Corruption Ordinance s.10B authorising them to search S's firm's premises on the basis there was evidence of an offence under the Prevention of Bribery Ordinance s.9. An information sworn in support of the application for the warrant alleged that P provided money to A which he used to bribe R, the former head of a crime unit, to swear a false affidavit to discredit the evidence of L, a chief prosecution witness at P's trial, and that A and R attempted to bribe L. The High Court of Hong Kong granted P judicial review and quashed the warrant for want of jurisdiction, the Court of Appeal dismissed the Commissioner's appeal, and he appealed to the Privy Council.

Held, dismissing the appeal, that the Prevention of Bribery Ordinance s.9(1)(a) applied to corrupt transactions with agents and not dishonest acts by agents, and the agent's act or forbearance had to be intended by the briber to affect the principal's affairs. The Commission's case in the information was that A had offered bribes, not that A had received a benefit from P for rendering services in relation to the firm's affairs; as there was no reason to believe A committed an offence as agent of the firm the magistrate had no jurisdiction to issue the warrant under s.10B, *Morgan v. DPP* [1970] 3 All E.R. 1053, [1971] C.L.Y. 2143 distinguished.

COMMISSIONER OF THE INDEPENDENT COMMISSION AGAINST CORRUPTION v. CH'NG POH [1997] 1 W.L.R. 1175, Lord Lloyd of Berwick, PC.

13. Compensation–miscarriage of justice–compensation for wrongful conviction not payable to company

[Criminal Justice Act 1988 s.133; International Covenant on Civil and Political Rights 1966 Art.14.]

A applied for judicial review of the Secretary of State's decision refusing ex gratia compensation and compensation under the Criminal Justice Act 1988 s.133 for the miscarriage of justice it had suffered on its conviction for being knowingly concerned in the export of prohibited goods, which was subsequently reversed on the grounds of abuse of process by the prosecuting authorities.

Held, dismissing the application, that the wording of s.133 showed that the right to compensation was not intended to apply to companies. The position was supported by the International Covenant on Civil and Political Rights 1966 Art.14.6, which was the precursor to the 1988 Act and was only intended to apply to natural persons. It was also clear that ex gratia payments, made in accordance with a written answer to Parliamentary questions given by the Secretary of State on November 29, 1985, were not intended to apply to companies, only to individuals who had been held in custody.

R. v. SECRETARY OF STATE FOR THE HOME DEPARTMENT, ex p. ATLANTIC COMMERCIAL (UK) LTD [1997] B.C.C. 692, Popplewell, J., QBD.

14. Contempt of court–alleged contemnor could not be remanded in custody before contempt was proved

Held, that, where interference with a prosecution witness was alleged, if a Crown Court judge wished to ensure that an alleged contemnor was not at liberty for the rest of the trial, he must either adjourn the trial and deal with the alleged contempt himself or refer the matter to another judge. Where no contempt had been proved, it was not open to the judge to remand the alleged contemnor in custody pending the decision of the Attorney General.

STEVENS AND HOLNESS, Re, The Independent, June 9, 1997 (C.S.), Pill, L.J., QBD.

15. **Contempt of court—confidential information—disclosure of interviews with alleged perpetrator of sexual abuse**

F applied for contact with his children. It was alleged that he had sexually abused one of the children and the family had attended the special unit at Great Ormond Street Hospital. F sought disclosure of the interviews. The judge ordered that copies of the interviews should only be disclosed to the legal and medical advisers. M was sent copies by her solicitor, who then admitted the breach. Contempt proceedings were brought by the Official Solicitor.

Held, that breach of the order had hindered the administration of justice and the court regarded the disclosure with gravity. The solicitors' firm would be fined £1,000 and ordered to pay the costs on an indemnity basis if not agreed. There would be no penalty imposed on the individual solicitor.

SOLICITOR (DISCLOSURE OF CONFIDENTIAL RECORDS), Re [1997] 1 F.L.R. 101, Johnson, J., Fam Div.

16. **Contempt of court—confidential information—journalist took photographs from counsel's papers**

[Contempt of Court Act 1981 s.4(2).]

In the appeal proceedings by H and B against sentences imposed for contempt of court for failure to give evidence in *R. v. Holt (Sarah)* [1996] 1 C.L.Y. 1349, certain photographs of H with facial injuries, being the property of the Commissioner of the Metropolitan Police, were shown to the court by counsel for the appellants during submissions. The photographs had not been released to the press, despite requests, as they formed part of the evidence of a case due to be tried on November 14, 1996, and a Contempt of Court Act 1981 s.4(2) order was made that no report of *R. v. Holt* should contain matter prejudicial to the fair trial of that case. When the court rose at the completion of submissions, a journalist, G, approached counsel for H and asked whether he could make copies of the photographs. Counsel had apparently indicated where they were, but expressed that he did not give permission to do so. Counsel then left the court leaving the photographs behind with his papers. G took the photographs from the court room, had copies made which were disclosed in television news and newspaper reports. G then replaced them. G was required to appear before the court on the grounds of contempt.

Held, that G's conduct did not amount to contempt. Whilst it was common practice for barristers and solicitors to leave papers in the courtroom during a short adjournment of a hearing, it was essential that the confidentiality of instructions to counsel be respected. The removal of photographs from counsel's papers by a journalist for the purposes of copying them before returning them could, in certain circumstances, constitute a contempt of court. In the present case, however, the attitude of counsel with regard to the reporter's access to the photographs was, on his own admission, "open and unguarded" and as such it was possible that G genuinely believed he had been authorised to take them, and his actions could not amount to contempt of court. The s.4(2) order was lifted and should never have been made.

GRIFFIN (PAUL), Re, The Times, November 6, 1996, Roch, L.J., CA.

17. **Contempt of court—fine in breach of statutory maximum—alleged contemnors should have legal representation to ensure judge is aware of extent of powers**

[Children and Young Persons Act 1933 s.39.]

T were fined £10,000 for contempt of court after the content of a television newsreel was found to have infringed an order made under the Children and Young Persons Act 1933 s.39 protecting the identity of an alleged child victim. T had appeared in the contempt proceedings without legal representation and the judge was unaware that the fine exceeded the maximum permitted in summary proceedings under the Act s.39(2). T appealed.

Held, allowing the appeal, that in order to obtain assistance from counsel or solicitors as to the extent of his powers in any particular case, a judge exercising the contempt jurisdiction should invite, although he could not compel, the alleged contemnor to be legally represented in court. In the instant case, in view of the statutory provisions, the correct approach would have been for the matter to have been reported with a view to possible summary proceedings being brought against T rather than the matter being dealt with by way of contempt.

R. v. TYNE TEES TELEVISION LTD, *The Times*, October 20, 1997, Beldam, L.J., CA (Crim Div).

18. **Contempt of court—jurors unable to reach verdict because of personal beliefs—sentence of imprisonment inappropriate**

[Juries Act 1974 s.9(4).]

Two jurors sentenced for contempt of court after failing to reach a verdict due to their "conscious beliefs" should have been informed of the possibility of being excused on the grounds of conscientious objection. After retiring to consider their verdict, the jury sent the judge a note stating that they were unable to reach a decision due to the conscious beliefs of some of the jurors. The judge asked the jury to clarify what was meant by "conscious beliefs" and after receiving a further note explaining that the affected jurors felt unable to reach a verdict because of their personal beliefs, the judge asked the jury to name the jurors in question and then discharged the whole jury. At a later hearing, the same judge found that the two named jurors, S and B, were in contempt of court and sentenced them to 30 days' imprisonment. S and B appealed.

Held, allowing the appeals, that it was doubtful whether the judge should have asked for written clarification of what was meant by "conscious beliefs", and in any case, he should have asked only for the number of jurors affected and not their names. He should not have automatically discharged the jury, but should have either given a majority direction or discharged S and B alone. The Juries Act 1974 s.9(4) provided for a discretionary power to excuse a juror, and *Practice Direction (Jury Service: Excusal)* (1988) Cr. App. R. 294, [1988] C.L.Y. 1995 allowed a person to be excused on the grounds of conscientious objection, but the jurors were not informed of that possibility. Whilst a juror's refusal to reach a verdict due to a reluctance to judge another could establish the actus reus of contempt, it was still necessary to prove the mens rea, which consisted of an intention to impede or create a real risk of prejudicing the administration of justice. In the light of the evidence given by S and B, and the conduct of the judge, the requisite mens rea had not been established. The judge should not have dealt with the matter of contempt himself, as there was a real danger of bias; the nature of the contempt was not clearly defined, and in any event, a sentence of imprisonment was inappropriate.

R. v. SCHOT (BONNIE BELINDA); R. v. BARCLAY (CAROL ANDREA) (1997) 161 J.P. 473, Rose, L.J., CA (Crim Div).

19. Contempt of court–newspapers–publication of restricted documents–third party liability for minor breach of court order

The Attorney General applied for penalties to be imposed on N for contempt of court relating to the publication in *The Independent* of extracts from two documents in breach of a court order. Disclosure of the documents, which concerned the "Ordtech" appeal against convictions for breach of certain Export of Goods (Control) Orders relating to the export of arms to Iraq, and in respect of which public interest immunity certificates had been signed, had been restricted to those proceedings. The judge had ordered their return at the end of the appeal and indicated that any breach concerning the documents would be referred to the Attorney General. The newspaper, after obtaining the papers from sources other than the Ordtech appellants, carried a report which included facsimiles of extracts from two of the documents cited in the judgment. Relying on *Attorney General v. Newspaper Publishing Plc* [1988] Ch. 33, [1988] C.L.Y. 2773, the Attorney General argued that N, whilst not directly bound by the order, had knowingly acted so as to interfere with the administration of justice.

Held, dismissing the application, that for a third party to be held liable for contempt of court, its actions had to amount to a significant interference with the administration of justice. Whilst it was not necessary to show that the administration of justice in the relevant proceedings was completely frustrated, the actions had to have had a significant and adverse effect thereon. In the instant case, the breaches were too minor.

ATTORNEY GENERAL v. NEWSPAPER PUBLISHING PLC; *sub nom*. R. v. BLACKLEDGE (WILLIAM STUART) [1997] 1 W.L.R. 926, Lord Bingham of Cornhill, L.C.J., CA (Crim Div).

20. Contempt of court–physical assault on Clerk of the Lists

Having received a response to an application made to the court which was not to his satisfaction, D spat in the face of the Clerk of the Lists. Inquiries by the Official Solicitor into D's medical condition established that D was not a person responsible for his actions and should be regarded as being under a disability. It was argued that interference with a court official conducting a purely administrative function did not amount to contempt of court.

Held, that the administration of justice was dependent not only on judges and counsel, but also on the officials of the court who discharged essential functions in ensuring that cases were brought to court. The actus reus of contempt was therefore present where a clerk of the court was physically assaulted and, despite his mental disability, D had acted deliberately and consciously and thus had the required mens rea. In order to provide protection for officials of courts where D might attempt to instigate legal proceedings, an order would be made restraining him from pursuing any proceedings except by a next friend and also restraining him from entering civil court buildings except in response to a subpoena.

DE COURT, *Re, The Times*, November 27, 1997, Sir Richard Scott, V.C., Ch D.

21. Contempt of court–press–article relating to discussions between client and former solicitor–disclosure of source of information not necessary in interests of justice

[Contempt of Court Act 1981 s.10.]

Held, that, balancing the interests of press freedom and legal confidentiality, the interests of justice did not require disclosure of the source of information for an article relating to discussions between a client and his former solicitors in terms of the Contempt of Court Act 1981 s.10.

SAUNDERS v. PUNCH LTD, *The Independent*, November 17, 1997 (C.S.), Lindsay, J., Ch D.

22. **Contempt of court–pretrial publicity–newspaper–report of alleged conspiracy to distribute counterfeit money–pretrial publicity**

[Contempt of Court Act 1981 s.2 (2).]

M, a newspaper journalist, uncovered an alleged conspiracy to distribute counterfeit money. The newspaper informed the police that it intended to publish an article describing M's investigations on September 11, 1994, prompting the police to arrest the suspects the day before. Counsel for the alleged conspirators successfully applied for a stay of proceedings when their case came to trial, on the basis of prejudice caused by the article. The Attorney General contended that the newspaper was in contempt of court in publishing the article as it described the alleged conspiracy as established fact and referred to the defendants' criminal records, thereby creating a substantial risk that subsequent criminal proceedings would be seriously prejudiced.

Held, allowing the application, that publication of the article clearly constituted contempt of court under the strict liability criteria set out in the Contempt of Court Act 1981 s.2(2). The article was designed to create a significant impact on the reader, the portrayal of the defendants as career criminals being a central feature and one which was likely to be remembered by readers. The newspaper must have realised that M was likely to be called as a witness at any trial, and this would increase the likelihood of a juror remembering parts of the article which were inadmissible in evidence. However, it had been unfair during the application for a stay of proceedings for the defence to cross examine M at length, without warning, about his conduct relating to the article, and he should have been warned against self incrimination and offered a chance to obtain legal advice and representation.

ATTORNEY GENERAL v. MORGAN; ATTORNEY GENERAL v. NEWS GROUP NEWSPAPERS LTD, *The Independent*, July 17, 1997, Pill, L.J., QBD.

23. **Contempt of court–pretrial publicity–newspaper publication of defendants' previous convictions and terrorist connections**

[Contempt of Court Act 1981 s.4.]

AN published an article on Belmarsh Prison in one of its newspapers which included photographs and names of three inmates, describing them as IRA terrorists and giving details of the crimes which had led to their imprisonment. The journalist who wrote the article appeared to be unaware that the three men were, at the time the article was published, on trial for offences which included escaping from prison. A previous trial of the men, together with three others, had been abandoned after a different newspaper published details of their convictions, and upon discharging the jury, the judge had made an order under the Contempt of Court Act 1981 s.4 prohibiting publication of the defendants' previous convictions and any indication of their connections with the IRA. Proceedings against the men were permanently stayed and an action for contempt of court was brought against AN.

Held, that, whilst there was no intention to interfere with the trial, AN was in contempt of court in publishing the article. Since the jurors knew at the trial's outset that the defendants were guilty of serious crimes and had been housed in a special secure unit, they could have deduced that they were IRA terrorists, and might also have remembered some of the pretrial publicity. They would, however, have been expected to put aside all that information once they began their deliberations. AN's article was altogether different in that it gave specific information on three of the six defendants while the trial was taking place. It was clear that no judicial warning could have redressed the imbalance created in favour of the prosecution, and there was a substantial risk of serious prejudice as a result of the publication.

ATTORNEY GENERAL v. ASSOCIATED NEWSPAPERS LTD, *The Independent*, November 6, 1997, Kennedy, L.J., QBD.

24. Contempt of court–pretrial publicity–newspaper publication of incriminating material where accused had confessed

[Contempt of Court Act 1981 s.2 (2).]

The respondents, a national and a local newspaper, published articles about a home help, G, stealing money after the victim's son produced a video tape showing two offences taking place. G indicated to reporters that she would not be denying the allegations. At the time of publication, G had been arrested and charged with two offences of theft, but had only admitted the first offence. She subsequently pleaded guilty to both charges. The Attorney General instituted proceedings against the respondents under the Contempt of Court Act 1981 s.2(2), contending that, had G opted for trial by jury, there would have been a substantial risk that the trial would be seriously prejudiced by publication of the articles while proceedings were active.

Held, dismissing the action, that it was important for newspapers to appreciate that the fact that an accused had apparently confessed did not mean that she would plead guilty at trial or was guilty of the offence charged. Reporters should exercise great caution to ensure that publication did not breach the strict liability rule. In the instant case, however, it was clear that G, if convicted by a jury, would not have been granted leave to appeal on the basis of the published articles and therefore the allegation of contempt was not made out.

ATTORNEY GENERAL v. UNGER, *The Independent*, July 8, 1997, Simon Brown, L.J., QBD.

25. Contempt of court–pretrial publicity–newspaper publicity of notorious persons and events–strict liability

[Contempt of Court Act 1981 s.2.]

The Attorney General applied to punish several newspapers for contempt of court allegedly arising from reports surrounding an assault with which K had been charged, and for which the trial judge had stayed criminal proceedings on the ground that pretrial publicity had made a fair trial impossible. K was the longstanding boyfriend of T, a soap opera actress. Prior to the assault charge, K and T had been subject to earlier press coverage stemming from a previous libel case and K's past criminal activities. The Attorney General contended that the reports breached the strict liability rule under the Contempt of Court Act 1981 s.2 in that the publications had created a substantial risk that the course of justice in the proceedings would be impeded or seriously prejudiced.

Held, dismissing the application, that the rule under the 1981 Act s.2 required each publication to be examined separately, with matters being considered as at the time of publication. Earlier publication did not prevent later reports creating a further risk, *Attorney General v. Independent Television News* [1995] 2 All E.R. 370, [1995] 1 C.L.Y. 1012 considered. Substantial risk of impediment or serious prejudice required an assessment of the likelihood of a potential juror having his attention drawn to the publication and the impact it could have both at the time and on a residual basis. Circulation of the publication and the number of copies had to be considered, as did the article's prominence and novelty content. Residual impact requires also the length of time between publication and trial to be examined in the light of the effect both of listening to evidence and of the jury directions, *Attorney General v. News Group Newspapers Ltd* [1987] Q.B. 1, [1986] C.L.Y. 2598 considered. On the facts, the publications had occurred several months before the trial and had to be considered in the context of earlier extensive media coverage of events concerning K and T . As a result it could not be found that the publications had created a substantial risk of serious impediment or prejudice to the course of justice.

Observed, that the present proceedings were not concerned with the decision to stay the criminal proceedings; in the instant case each publication had to be examined separately, whereas the trial judge had correctly been concerned with the publications in total in assessing the risk of prejudice on the minds of the jury.

ATTORNEY GENERAL v. MGN LTD; *sub nom.* MIRROR GROUP NEWSPAPERS, *Re* [1997] 1 All E.R. 456, Schiemann, L.J., QBD.

26. Coroners–boundaries–reorganisation–Bedfordshire

BEDFORDSHIRE (CORONERS) ORDER 1997, SI 1997 494; made under the Local Government Act 1992 s.17, s.26. In force: April 1, 1997; £0.65.

This Order combines the new County of Luton with the County of Bedfordshire to form a single coroner's district.

27. Coroners–boundaries–reorganisation–Buckinghamshire

BUCKINGHAMSHIRE (CORONERS) ORDER 1997, SI 1997 495; made under the Local Government Act 1992 s.17, s.26. In force: April 1, 1997; £0.65.

This Order abolishes the two coroner's districts of South Buckinghamshire and North Buckinghamshire. There will instead be a single coroner for the County of Buckinghamshire.

28. Coroners–boundaries–reorganisation–Derbyshire

DERBYSHIRE (CORONERS) ORDER 1997, SI 1997 496; made under the Local Government Act 1992 s.17, s.26. In force: April 1, 1997; £1.10.

This Order combines the new County of Derby with part of the County of Derbyshire to form a single coroner's district.

29. Coroners–boundaries–reorganisation–Dorset

DORSET (CORONERS) ORDER 1997, SI 1997 497; made under the Local Government Act 1992 s.17, s.26. In force: April 1, 1997; £1.10.

This Order combines the new Counties of Bournemouth and Poole with part of the County of Dorset to form a single coroner's district.

30. Coroners–boundaries–reorganisation–Durham

DURHAM (CORONERS) ORDER 1997, SI 1997 498; made under the Local Government Act 1992 s.17, s.26. In force: April 1, 1997; £0.65.

This Order combines the new County of Darlington with part of the County of Durham to form a single coroner's district.

31. Coroners–boundaries–reorganisation–East Sussex

EAST SUSSEX (CORONERS) ORDER 1997, SI 1997 488; made under the Local Government Act 1992 s.17, s.26. In force: April 1, 1997; £0.65.

This Order abolishes two coroner's districts, Western East Sussex and Eastern East Sussex and provides for a single coroner's district for the County of East Sussex.

32. Coroners–boundaries–reorganisation–Hampshire

HAMPSHIRE (CORONERS) ORDER 1997, SI 1997 489; made under the Local Government Act 1992 s.17, s.26. In force: April 1, 1997; £1.10.

This Order combines the County of Portsmouth with part of the County of Hampshire to form a single coroner's district.

33. Coroners–boundaries–reorganisation–Leicestershire

LEICESTERSHIRE (CORONERS) ORDER 1997, SI 1997 490; made under the Local Government Act 1992 s.17, s.26. In force: April 1, 1997; £1.10.

This Order combines the County of Leicester with part of the County of Leicestershire to form a single coroner's district.

34. Coroners–boundaries–reorganisation–North Yorkshire

NORTH YORKSHIRE (CORONERS' DISTRICTS) ORDER 1997, SI 1997 1532; made under the Coroners'Act 1988 s.4. In force: August 1, 1997; £0.65.

This Order replaces the previous four coroners' districts of the county of North Yorkshire with two new coroners' districts, Eastern (comprising the districts of Hambledon, Ryedale and Scarborough) and Western (comprising the districts of Craven, Harrogate, Richmondshire and Selby).

35. Coroners–boundaries–reorganisation–Staffordshire

STAFFORDSHIRE (CORONERS) ORDER 1997, SI 1997 492; made under the Local Government Act 1992 s.17, s.26. In force: April 1, 1997; £1.10.

This Order combines the new County of Stoke on Trent with part of the County of Staffordshire to form a single coroner's district.

36. Coroners–boundaries–reorganisation–Wiltshire

WILTSHIRE (CORONERS) ORDER 1997, SI 1997 493; made under the Local Government Act 1992 s.17, s.26. In force: April 1, 1997; £0.65.

This Order combines the new County of Thamesdown with the County of Wiltshire to form a single coroner's district.

37. Coroners–fees for copies

CORONERS' RECORDS (FEES FOR COPIES) RULES 1997, SI 1997 2544; made under the Coroners Act 1988 s.24. In force: December 1, 1997; £0.65.

These Rules replace the Coroners' Records (Fees for Copies) Rules 1982 (SI 1982 995 as amended by SI 1990 140).

38. Coroners–inquests–verdict of accidental death where negligence admitted–request to empanel a jury refused

Following an operation to remove his wisdom teeth, W's son died. His medical carers admitted liability for negligence. At the inquest the coroner, who sat with an assessor who both questioned witnesses and gave evidence, refused W's request that a jury be empanelled. A verdict of accidental death was returned. W's application for orders of certiorari and mandamus were refused. W applied for leave to appeal out of time against the decision of the judge.

Held, dismissing the application, that (1) the coroner's refusal to empanel a jury was not a decision that no reasonable coroner could have reached; (2) the fact that negligence had occurred was not a sufficient foundation for a verdict of neglect, or lack of care, both of which were inappropriate in this case, and (3) the judge was right in holding that the coroner could not be criticised for sitting with an assessor, whose evidence did not in any event affect the outcome of the inquest.

R. v. HM CORONER FOR SURREY, *ex p.* WRIGHT (1997) 35 B.M.L.R. 57, Aldous, L.J., CA.

39. Coroners–inquests–verdict of suicide–allegation of inadequate medical treatment

C applied for judicial review and an order quashing the inquest verdict of suicide on his daughter and directing that a fresh inquest be held. C contended that the results of an independent review and the findings of a complaint panel had shown her treatment in hospital for salicylate poisoning to have been grossly inadequate, which might have led to a different verdict in a fresh inquest and it was in the interests of justice that the new facts should be investigated.

Held, dismissing the application, that it was possible that neglect had been a contributory cause of C's daughter's death, but, having regard to the passage of time, it would not be in the interests of justice to order a fresh inquest. It was noted that a number of people had known that the deceased's treatment had not been appropriate, but had not informed the coroner, who had therefore not considered her treatment in arriving at his verdict. It could not be satisfactory for the National Health Service to maintain that their employees had no professional duty to draw the attention of a coroner to relevant matters, *R. v. Southwark Coroner, ex p. Hicks* [1987] W.L.R. 1624, [1987] C.L.Y. 533, *R. v. Portsmouth City Coroner, ex p. Anderson* [1988] 2 All E.R. 604, [1988] C.L.Y. 522, *R. v. HM Coroner for North Humberside and Scunthorpe, ex p. Jamieson* [1995] 1 Q.B. 1, [1994] C.L.Y. 631 and *R. v. HM Coroner for Birmingham and Solihull, ex p. Cotton* (1996) 160 J.P. 123 considered and *R. v. HM Coroner for Surrey, ex p. Wright* [1997] 2 W.L.R. 16, [1996] 1 C.L.Y. 32 distinguished, because in the instant case the deceased had been in hospital care for 12 hours before she died.

R. v. HM CORONER FOR WILTSHIRE, *ex p.* CLEGG; *sub nom.* CLEGG, *Re* (1997) 161 J.P. 521, Phillips, L.J., QBD.

40. County courts–closure

CIVIL COURTS (AMENDMENT) ORDER 1997, SI 1997 361; made under the Supreme Court Act 1981 s.99; and the County Courts Act 1984 s.2. In force: March 27, 1997; £0.65.

This Order amends the Civil Courts Order 1983 (SI 1993 713) so as to close the County Court at Ammanford.

41. County courts–closure

CIVIL COURTS (AMENDMENT) (NO.2) ORDER 1997, SI 1997 1085; made under the County Courts Act 1984 s.2. In force: June 30, 1997; £0.65.

This Order amends the Civil Courts Order 1983 (SI 1983 713) so as to close the County Court at Andover on June 30, 1997.

42. County courts–closure

CIVIL COURTS (AMENDMENT NO.3) ORDER 1997, SI 1997 2310; made under the County Courts Act 1984 s.2; and the Matrimonial and Family Proceedings Act 1984 s.33. In force: Art.3, Art.4(a): December 1, 1997; remainder: November 10, 1997; £0.65.

This Order amends the Civil Courts Order 1983 (SI 1983 713) so as to close the County Courts at Bishop's Stortford and Braintree and to extend divorce jurisdiction to the Brecknock County Court.

43. County courts–closure

CIVIL COURTS (AMENDMENT NO.4) ORDER 1997 1997, SI 1997 2762; made under the County Courts Act 1984 s.2; and the Matrimonial and Family Proceedings Act 1984 s.33. In force: Art.3(b), Art.4(b): December 24, 1997; remainder: December 15, 1997; £1.10.

This Order amends the Civil Courts Order 1983 (SI 1983 713) so as to close the County Courts at Alnwick, Blyth and Bridlington; rename the County Court at Morpeth as the Morpeth and Berwick County Court; and close the County Court at Berwick-upon-Tweed as a separate court as it will become part of the new Morpeth and Berwick County Court.

44. Justices of the Peace Act 1997 (c.25)

This Act consolidates the Justices of the Peace Act 1979 in relation to commissions of the peace and petty session areas, magistrates' courts committees, and appointment, removal and conditions of employment of justices of the peace and justices' clerks. Provisions of the Police and Magistrates' Courts Act 1994 Part IV are also consolidated.

This Act received Royal Assent on March 19, 1997.

45. Law Officers Act 1997 (c.60)

An Act to enable the Solicitor General to exercise functions of the Attorney General and the Attorney General for Northern Ireland.

This Act received Royal Assent on July 31, 1997 and comes into force on September 30, 1997.

46. Litigants in person–chambers hearing–right to McKenzie friend

Held, that, in proceedings for a contact order, it was not inappropriate for a party representing himself in a chambers hearing to have a friend present to listen, take notes and help with advice. Even though the hearing was in chambers, the friend should be permitted to remain, provided he did no more than sit quietly and offer help as a *McKenzie* friend.

H (A MINOR) (CHAMBERS PROCEEDINGS: McKENZIE FRIEND), *Re, The Times*, May 6, 1997, Ward, L.J., CA.

47. Practice directions–Crown Office–procedure for uncontested applications in civil and criminal proceedings

A Practice Direction setting out the procedure for dealing with uncontested applications before the Crown Office in civil and criminal proceedings has been issued. A Practice Direction setting out the procedure for dealing with uncontested applications before the Crown Office and replacing *Practice Direction (Crown Office List: Uncontested Proceedings)* [1982] 1 W.L.R. 979 in respect of civil causes, and *Practice Direction (Crown Office List: Criminal Proceedings)* [1983] 1 W.L.R. 925, [1983] C.L.Y. 597 in respect of criminal matters, has been issued, dealing with: (1) where the terms on which proceedings were to be determined were agreed by the parties, and required a court order to be brought into effect, the parties should lodge a document with the Crown Office setting out the terms of the proposed order, proceedings for which, if approved, would be listed for pronouncement in open court; (2) where the terms on which an interlocutory order would be sought were agreed by the parties, they should lodge a document stating the justification for the order. If the document was approved the order would be sent to the parties without the need for listing of proceedings, and (3) where leave of the court was not required for the withdrawal of proceedings, the party must lodge a notice of withdrawal and serve a copy to the other parties, whereupon the court file would be closed. Where leave was required for withdrawal, a document should be lodged with the Crown Office stating the proposed terms. If the document was approved the order would be sent to the parties without the need for listing of proceedings in open court, and the court file closed.

PRACTICE DIRECTION (CROWN OFFICE LIST: CONSENT ORDERS) [1997] 1 W.L.R. 825, Lord Bingham of Cornhill, L.C.J., QBD.

48. Rights of audience–lay representatives

[Courts and Legal Services Act 1990 s.17, s.28(2).]

The applicant applied to the Court of Appeal for an order under the Courts and Legal Services Act 1990 s.28(2)(c) giving him the right to conduct litigation on behalf of a litigant in person.

Held, refusing the application, that the applicant did not satisfy the criteria in the 1990 Act s.17, nor those in the Solicitors' Accounts Rules, which required, inter alia, that solicitors must be insured. Although the applicant informed those he might represent that he was not insured, it was the duty of the court to have regard to the guidelines laid down by Parliament in s.17 so that the court was bound to reject the application.

CHAUHAN v. CHAUHAN [1997] 2 F.C.R. 206, Neill, L.J., CA.

49. Rights of audience–lay representatives–extent of discretion to grant rights in exceptional circumstances

[Courts and Legal Services Act 1990.]

P sought an order under the Courts and Legal Services Act 1990 for permission to act for D, a litigant in person, in his application for leave to appeal against a decision that D should not enter the home he shared with S and their children pending the result of her application for transfer of the tenancy to herself. P, who had specialist knowledge in the field of fathers' rights and experience of similar cases, argued that he had appeared for D in the court below and that Parliament approved of specialists acting for others in certain family law matters.

Held, refusing the application, that, after reviewing P's reasoned submission and the case of *Chauhan v. Chauhan* [1997] 2 F.C.R. 296, [1997] C.L.Y 48, where P had applied to be allowed to provide legal services and to conduct proceedings on behalf of an appellant in person, there were arguments in support of a relaxation of the law governing this area. However, the question of whether to grant rights of audience was a matter for the court alone, requiring careful consideration, and the wording of the 1990 Act made it plain that the court's discretion to allow a request for rights of audience was to be exercised only where circumstances were exceptional.

D v. S (RIGHTS OF AUDIENCE) [1997] 1 F.L.R. 724, Lord Woolf, M.R., CA.

50. Rights of audience–lay representatives–representative misleading the court–approach to be adopted by courts on each application

[Children Act 1989; Courts and Legal Services Act 1990 s.17(3).]

M applied to rescind an order granting P the right of audience. The court was concerned with applications for contact and maintenance of two children. P, who had no formal legal training and no legal qualifications, had applied for a right of audience and a right to conduct litigation on behalf of F in February 1996 and produced before the district judge a decision where he had been granted leave to represent a housing association of which he was secretary, but he failed to inform the court of an unreported decision of the Court of Appeal, *Chauhan v. Chauhan* [1997] 2 F.C.R. 206, [1997] C.L.Y. 48, in 1994 which had refused to grant him the right to conduct litigation on behalf of a party in matrimonial proceedings. At a subsequent hearing a judge expressed concern as to whether the interests of F and the interests of justice were being advanced by F's representation by P.

Held, granting the application, that the Courts and Legal Services Act 1990 s.17(3) was designed to protect the members of the public by ensuring that a person should only be granted a right of audience and the right to conduct litigation if he was a member of a professional body and legally qualified, which P was not. Considering *Chauhan v. Chauhan* and *D v. S (Rights of Audience)* [1997] 1 F.L.R. 724, [1997] C.L.Y. 49 and he was unable to carry out the duties of a solicitor, and had been guilty of misleading the court by failing to draw its attention to the relevant authority of *Chauhan v. Chauhan*, so that it was not in the interests of justice for F to continue to be represented by P.

Observed, that since the matters before the court involved children, the court was particularly anxious that the parties should be represented by specially experienced representatives, who understood the ethos of the Children Act 1989 that cases should not be carried out under the adversarial system but more discreetly having regard to the overriding interests of the children.

G (A MINOR) (RIGHTS OF AUDIENCE), *Re*; *sub nom.* PELLING (RIGHTS OF AUDIENCE), *Re* [1997] 2 F.L.R. 458, Sir Stephen Brown, Fam Div.

51. Solicitor General – remuneration

SOLICITOR GENERAL'S SALARY ORDER 1997, SI 1997 1500; made under the Ministerial and Other Salaries Act 1975 s.1. In force: June 27, 1997; £0.65.

This Order increases the maximum salary payable to the Solicitor General.

52. Solicitors – anonymity – appeal against removal of legal aid franchise

T, in an application for leave to apply for judicial review, sought anonymity on the basis that if anonymity was not granted their appeal against removal from the franchise scheme for criminal legal aid would be highly damaging to them. T argued that the practice in appeals, as laid down in the Supreme Court Rules, was that solicitors were not named until there was an adverse finding and that the practice of anonymity should be extended for the purposes of this situation.

Held, dismissing the application, that there was no good reason for permitting anonymity in the particular circumstances of this case. The overriding principle was that, save in limited circumstances where it could be demonstrated that justice would be frustrated by the naming of the other person, the proceedings should take place in public.

R. v. LEGAL AID BOARD, *ex p.* T (A FIRM OF SOLICITORS), Trans. Ref: CO-330-97, June 25, 1997, Kay, J., QBD.

53. Supreme Court – fees – exemptions

SUPREME COURT FEES (AMENDMENT) ORDER 1997, SI 1997 2672 (L.41); made under the Supreme Court Act 1981 s.130; the Insolvency Act 1986 s.414, s.415; and the Finance Act 1990 s.128. In force: December 1, 1997; £1.10.

This Order amends the Supreme Court Fees Order 1980 (SI 1980 821) in order to extend the exemption from payment of court fees to those receiving family credit, disability working allowance or income-based jobseekers' allowance. It also sets fees for applications under the Arbitration Act 1996.

54. Supreme Court (Offices) Act 1997 (c.69)

This Act makes provision with respect to the qualification for appointment as, and tenure of office of, Permanent Secretary to the Lord Chancellor and Clerk of the Crown in Chancery.

This Act received Royal Assent on December 17, 1997.

55. Treasury Solicitor – Crown's Nominee Account – holding of monies, securities or property

TREASURY SOLICITOR (CROWN'S NOMINEE) RULES 1997, SI 1997 2870; made under the Treasury Solicitor Act 1876 s.4, s.5. In force: January 1, 1998; £1.10.

These Rules replace and revoke the Treasury Solicitor (Crown's Nominee) Rules 1931 (SR & O 1931 1097). They provide for the Crown's Nominee Account, to which the Treasury Solicitor Act 1876 s.4 requires to be carried all moneys received by the Treasury Solicitor having accrued to the Crown as part of the estate of any deceased person, or under any forfeiture, or otherwise by virtue of the royal prerogative, or which is money arising from property which has so accrued.

56. Trials – adjournment – defendant's choice of counsel unavailable – defendant suffered prejudice as result of mismanagement of counsel's affairs – adjournment should have been permitted

In June 1997, C was advised that A, a barrister, would be available to represent him in an action for possession brought by C's mortgagee, RBS, the trial being fixed for September 24, 1997. The brief was sent to A's chambers on August 20, 1997 and nine days later C was informed that A would not be available after all. C appealed against the county court judge's refusal to adjourn the trial, whilst RBS argued that the court could not interfere with the judge's discretion unless the strict requirements set down in the relevant authorities were met and, as the judge had not erred in principle, his decision should stand.

Held, allowing the appeal, that the case was clearly important as C's home was at risk and some relevant matters had not been referred to by the judge, who had not had all the facts before him. In addition, the judge had failed to ask himself the proper question, namely whether C would suffer prejudice as a result of A being unavailable. Therefore, the court was entitled to come to a different conclusion from that of the judge, but it was a difficult situation as the fault lay neither with C nor RBS. However, C was the innocent victim of the mishandling of A's affairs and would undoubtedly be prejudiced by having to instruct alternative counsel. In those circumstances, the adjournment should have been permitted.

ROYAL BANK OF SCOTLAND PLC v. CRAIG, *The Times*, October 24, 1997, Evans, L.J., CA.

57. **Vexatious litigants–civil proceedings orders–breach of order–old age and ill health justified suspended committal order**

[Supreme Court Act 1981 s.42.]

The Attorney General applied for a committal order against L for deliberately disobeying an all proceedings order made against him under the Supreme Court Act 1981 s.42. L had issued several applications, including witness summonses and committal applications on behalf of his daughter who lived overseas, either in his own name or under certain aliases and in most cases purporting to act under his daughter's power of attorney, in relation to proceedings connected to L's mother's estate. L did not dispute any of the factual matters set out in the Attorney General's evidence. He sought to explain his actions. His daughter had granted a power of attorney in order that her interests in respect of her grandmother's estate be protected. L made clear that he did not intend to continue with any of the proceedings and that he was very concerned about the possibility of being committed because of his age and ill health. The Attorney General, however, expressed scepticism about L's declarations, drawing attention to previous undertakings given when the s.42 order was made.

Held, allowing the application and imposing a committal order of three months suspended indefinitely, that had it not been for L's age and ill health and the fact that his wife was also in ill health and depended on L, the breaches would certainly have resulted in a committal order. In the event of L instituting any further proceedings in breach of the s.42 order the appropriate period of committal would be at least 12 months.

ATTORNEY GENERAL v. LANDAU, Trans. Ref: CO 4321 of 1996, March 13, 1997, Brooke, L.J., QBD.

58. **Vexatious litigants–civil proceedings orders–vexatious litigant continuing to bring proceedings and make applications after bankruptcy for non-payment of costs–order in public interest**

[Supreme Court Act 1981 s.42.]

The Attorney General sought a civil proceedings order under the Supreme Court Act 1981 s.42, on the ground that T had habitually and persistently instituted vexatious proceedings and applications. Following initial proceedings commenced by T on behalf of his brother, he then went on to make a large number of applications concerning supposedly adverse comments about him contained in material revealed in the course of discovery and seeking remedies for alleged professional negligence against his own solicitors. His course of conduct continued in spite of a bankruptcy order, obtained against him for non-payment of costs and as a result of which T commenced an action against a range of defendants, including, inter alia, the Lord Chancellor, Attorney General, Lord Chief Justice, Butler-Sloss L.J. and the Registrar of Civil Appeals.

Held, allowing the application and making the order sought, that the history of T's applications showed he had brought vexatious actions and made vexatious applications since at least 1990 and was undeterred by costs orders made against him. A civil proceedings order was therefore in the legitimate interest of those against whom T sought to litigate and it was also in the public interest that he should not make further applications or bring proceedings without leave of the court.

R. v. ATTORNEY GENERAL, *ex p.* TEJENDRASINGH, Trans. Ref: CO 4113-96, April 10, 1997, McCowan, L.J., QBD.

59. Articles

Caseman: the future of the county court *(Stephen Gerlis)*: Litigator 1997, Jan, 44-47. (Development and operation of computerised case management system for county courts).

From Beeching to Woolf *(Michael Kershaw)*: Liverpool L.R. 1997, 19(1), 47-51. (History of reforms to civil justice system aimed at reducing delay and cost).

Justices' Clerks Society—judicial competence—a partnership checklist: J.P. 1997, 161(17), 403-406. (Paper examining the size of Benches and the maintenance of an effective relationship between justices' clerk and justices in face of financial cutbacks).

Real quality—real justice: the concept of community justice *(Rosie Eagleson)*: J.P. 1997, 161(12), 282-283. (Association of Magisterial Officers consultation document proposing developments towards more accessible justice system and more community involvement, starting with reform of magistrates' courts).

Right to seek judicial review is confirmed, but what is fair? To adjourn or not. To sit or not: M.C.P. 1997, 1(5), 10-12. (Whether defendant can challenge magistrates' decision by way of judicial review on grounds of procedural impropriety, unfairness or bias).

The Attorney General *(Diana Woodhouse)*: Parl. Aff. 1997, 50(1), 97-108. (Constitutional position and responsibilities of Attorney General, with particular reference to situations where is required to act in public interest, and difficulties of accountability).

The behaviour of lay justices of the peace *(Richard Grobler)*: J.P. 1997, 161(34), 813-814. (Expected standards and procedures for dealing with misconduct).

The cost of commercial litigation in England-a European perspective and a look to the future *(Christopher Winder)*: E.R.P.L. 1996, 4(4), 339-349. (Procedural features which make litigation more costly in England than in continental Europe and whether Woolf proposals will improve access and reduce costs).

The judiciary, the community and the media *(Anthony Mason)*: Com. Jud. J. 1997, 12(1), 5-12. (Historical changes that are making judiciary more subject to publicity and criticism, issues arising from proposition that courts are community institutions, role of Attorney General and judicial independence).

The threat to the magistrates' courts service *(David P. Allam)*: J.P. 1997, 161(27), 643-645. (Impact of government spending plans on administration and reorganisation of magistrates' courts).

60. Books

Dorries, Christopher—Coroners Courts. Hardback: £24.95. ISBN 0-471-96721-1. John Wiley and Sons.

McKittrick, N—Handbook for Magistrates. Paperback: £15.95. ISBN 1-85431-456-4. Blackstone Press.

ADMINISTRATIVE LAW

61. Judicial review—application for leave—delay

[Rules of the Supreme Court Ord.53 r.4(1); Supreme Court Act 1981 s.31(6), ; .]

A appealed against the dismissal of her substantive application for judicial review of a decision by CICB on the ground of undue delay in applying for leave to apply under RSC Ord.53 r.4(1), even though the judge had not found that the granting of relief would cause hardship, prejudice or detriment within the meaning of the Supreme Court Act 1981 s.31 (6) (b).

Held, dismissing the appeal, that it was appropriate to treat the application for leave to apply for judicial review and the substantive hearing as two distinct stages. Leave to apply where there had been delay could be refused either if there were no good reason for extending time under Ord.53 r.4(1) or because it was already apparent that the eventual granting of relief was likely to cause hardship, prejudice or detriment under s.31 (6) (a). With regard to the substantive hearing, delay was only relevant to the hardship, prejudice or detriment grounds under s.31 (6) (b). Unless leave was subsequently set aside, once time had been extended by the granting of leave, it could not be cancelled at the substantive hearing unless s.31 (6) (b) applied, *R. v. Tavistock General Commissioners, ex p. Worth* [1985] S.T.C. 564, [1985] C.L.Y. 1744 disapproved. However, A's substantive application would be dismissed on the merits.

R. v. CRIMINAL INJURIES COMPENSATION BOARD, *ex p.* AVRAAM; *sub nom.* R. v. CRIMINAL INJURIES COMPENSATION BOARD, *ex p.* A [1997] 3 All E.R. 745, Simon Brown, L.J., CA.

62. Judicial review–competency–animal exports–locus standi of PAIN

See ANIMALS: R. v. Minister of Agriculture Fisheries and Food, *ex p.* Protesters Animal Information Network Ltd. §238

63. Judicial review–competency–existence of alternative remedy–application not precluded where appeal to Crown Court available

[Magistrates Courts Act 1980 s.108.]

R and another applied for judicial review of the magistrates' refusal to adjourn their trial to allow two defence witnesses to give evidence and of their subsequent convictions on the grounds of unfairness. The question for the court was whether an application for judicial review could be used to challenge decisions of the magistrates' court on the grounds of unfairness, procedural impropriety or bias, where the complainant had a right of appeal to the Crown Court, under the Magistrates Courts Act 1980 s.108, which entitled him to a full retrial on the merits of the case or on a mixed issue of fact and law.

Held, allowing the applications, that, although *R. v. Peterborough Magistrates Court, ex p. Dowler* [1996] 2 Cr. App. R. 561, [1996] 2 C.L.Y. 5087 had been treated as authority for the proposition that judicial review should not be permitted where the complainant had the alternative remedy of an appeal to the Crown Court, it was in fact decided on the narrower ground that there should be no relief where the complainant was seeking to delay proceedings in the hope that the prosecution would be abandoned. The court in *Dowler* had been wrong to suggest that a criminal defendant was not entitled to more than one fair trial, which was demonstrated by the provision in the 1980 Act for appeals to the Crown Court and to the High Court, by way of case stated, as there was a stronger right to fairness in criminal proceedings than before administrative or domestic tribunals, *Calvin v. Carr* [1980] A.C. 574, [1979] C.L.Y. 14 distinguished. The cases relied upon in *Dowler* could not be applied where a defendant had not appealed to the Crown Court, and even if an appeal had been made, it was still a question of discretion whether to allow judicial review. To deny judicial review of a complaint of procedural impropriety, unfairness or bias in the magistrates' court would fetter the Divisional Court's supervisory jurisdiction over the magistrates' courts which ensured that high standards of fairness and impartiality were upheld.

R. v. HEREFORD MAGISTRATES COURT, *ex p.* ROWLANDS; R. v. HEREFORD MAGISTRATES COURT, *ex p.* INGRAM; R. v. HARROW YOUTH COURT, *ex p.* PRUSSIA [1997] 2 W.L.R. 854, Lord Bingham of Cornhill, L.C.J., QBD.

64. **Judicial review–competency–failure to secure foster placement**

   See CHILDREN: R. v. Birmingham City Council, *ex p.* A (A Minor). §423

65. **Judicial review–competency–Federation of Communications Services**

   See TELECOMMUNICATIONS: R. v. Panel of the Federation of Communication Services Ltd, *ex p.* Kubis. §4851

66. **Judicial review–competency–National Trust decision to end deer hunting on Trust land**

   Held, that the court lacked jurisdiction to hear a challenge to a decision of the Council of the National Trust to end deer hunting on Trust land. The decision of the National Trust related to the conduct of its affairs as a charity and had been made by the Trustees in the exercise of their discretionary powers over the management of Trust property. Authorisation from the Charity Commissioners was therefore required before any proceedings could be brought.

   R. v. NATIONAL TRUST FOR PLACES OF HISTORIC INTEREST OR NATURAL BEAUTY, *ex p.* SCOTT, *The Independent*, July 21, 1997 (C.S.), Tucker, J., QBD.

67. **Judicial review–natural justice–ability of mental patient to give evidence to CICB**

   The CICB appealed against a judicial review decision quashing the refusal of M's claim for compensation under the statutory scheme and ordering a rehearing before a differently constituted panel. M had sought compensation having made allegations of rape, buggery and physical assault against her former cohabitee, K. However, medical evidence did not corroborate her allegations of violence with regard to the rape or buggery, and although she stated in her initial application that the cohabitation had ceased, she subsequently admitted that she and K had lived together for a short period after her application. M contended that delays in reporting the matter were due to; (1) not being aware that buggery was an offence, and (2) her being admitted to psychiatric hospital as a result of K's actions toward her. She also contended that she had not misled either the CICB or the police about the resumption of the cohabitation.

   Held, allowing the appeal, that, although the judicial review had found that a failure of communication on the part of the the CICB gave an appearance that M had not received a fair hearing, M had been allowed to give evidence before it and the mere fact that she was a psychiatric patient at that time did not prevent her from giving evidence. The CICB had been justified to decide, on the evidence, that M had concealed matters from the police and given false answers to enquiries about the cohabitation. Evidence from the psychiatrist in charge of M's treatment did not show that she had been unfit to give evidence and it had not been shown that the CICB had failed to take some procedural step which fairness required it to take.

   R. v. CRIMINAL INJURIES COMPENSATION BOARD, *ex p.* MATTISON, Trans. Ref: QBCOF 96/1682/D, April 24, 1997, Stuart-Smith, L.J., CA.

68. **Judicial review–procedure–application to set aside leave on grounds of delay, non disclosure and unarguability**

   [Waste Management Licensing Regulations 1994 (SI 1994 1056); Rules of the Supreme Court Ord.53 r.4.]

   EA applied to set aside leave to seek judicial review on the grounds of delay, non disclosure and that L's application for judicial review was unarguable and bound to fail. L contended that EA's decision to permit the use of a solvent based fuel as a substitute for pet-coke at a lime kiln situated near to his home was based on a misconstruction of the powers conferred by the Waste Management Licensing Regulations 1994 and the need to carry out an environmental impact assessment irrespective of whether the proposed change required planning permission.

Held, refusing the application, that questions of delay in bringing an application for judicial review, where the application was made within the three month period provided under RSC Ord.53 r.4, fell to be considered at the inter partes hearing and there was no evidence to show non disclosure by L which justified setting aside leave. Although L may face great difficulties at the full hearing, that did not justify setting aside leave and applications to do so should not be brought merely on the ground that a respondent had a powerful or even overwhelming case, *R. v. Secretary of State for the Home Department, ex p. Chinoy (Nazir)* (1992) 4 Admin. L.R. 457, [1992] C.L.Y. 2083 applied.

R. v. ENVIRONMENT AGENCY, *ex p.* LEAM; R. v. ENVIRONMENT AGENCY, *ex p.* GIBSON; R. v. LANCASHIRE CC, *ex p.* SELLERS, Trans. Ref: CO-2104/96; CO-3598/96; CO-4216/96, March 18, 1997, Laws, J., QBD.

69. Judicial review–procedure–failure to observe time limits

[Rules of the Supreme Court Ord.53 r.5(5).]

A, an accountant, had been dismissed by his professional body, ICA, for disciplinary reasons. He failed to lodge an appeal against this ruling within the time limits laid down by ICA's rules and then sought permission to appeal out of time. ICA refused to allow him to do this, and A applied successfully to the High Court for leave to move for judicial review of that decision. A was also granted leave to amend his Form 86A by adding to it a damages claim. Having been granted leave, A failed to institute a substantive application for judicial review within the 14 day time limit as required by RSC Ord.53 r.5(3) and r.5(5). A's application for an extension of time was refused and the matter was struck out. A appealed, claiming the delay was due to "lawyer error" and that the more flexible private law principles should apply to the issue of time limits.

Held, dismissing the appeal, that (1) the argument that the more flexible private law rules as to time limits, as stated in *Costellow v. Somerset CC* [1993] 1 W.L.R. 256, [1993] C.L.Y. 3338, should apply, was rejected. On a matter of principle, public law litigation could not be undertaken at the slow pace adopted too often in private law disputes. Further, it was clear from the decision in *Regalbourne Ltd v. East Lindsey DC* (1994) Admin. L.R. 102, [1994] C.L.Y. 3904 that the principle laid out in *Costellow* was not appropriate in a judicial review context, and (2) the submission that the case lacked the importance to justify unyielding application of the rules was also to be rejected. If less important cases were left to proceed at their own relaxed pace that would undoubtedly cause delay and give the wrong impression to court users. It was clear that the judge's decision was right and within his discretion.

R. v. INSTITUTE OF CHARTERED ACCOUNTANTS IN ENGLAND AND WALES, *ex p.* ANDREOU (1996) 8 Admin. L.R. 557, Henry, L.J., CA.

70. Public Record Office–fees

PUBLIC RECORD OFFICE (FEES) REGULATIONS 1997, SI 1997 400; made under the Public Records Act 1958 s.2. In force: April 1, 1997; £1.55.

These Regulations revoke the Public Record Office (Fees) Regulations 1996 (SI 1996 575) and prescribe a new range of fees to be charged for authentication of copies of records and for other services provided by the Public Record Office.

71. Registration–births and deaths–Amendment No.1

REGISTRATION OF BIRTHS AND DEATHS (AMENDMENT) REGULATIONS 1997, SI 1997 844; made under the Births and Deaths Registration Act 1953 s.9, s.21, s.23, s.23A, s.29, s.39. In force: April 1, 1997; £1.55.

These Regulations amend the Registration of Births and Deaths Regulations 1987 (SI 1987 2088) and the Registration of Births and Deaths (Welsh Language) Regulations 1987 (SI 1987 2089). They make provision for the implementation of the Deregulation (Still-Birth and Deaths Registration) Order

1996 (SI 1996 2395), which will allow persons registering a death or still-birth to do so by making a declaration before a person other than the registrar for the sub-district where the death or still-birth occurred.

72. Registration–births and deaths–Amendment No.2

REGISTRATION OF BIRTHS AND DEATHS (AMENDMENT NO.2) REGULATIONS 1997, SI 1997 1533; made under the Births and Deaths Registration Act 1953 s.9, s.10A, s.14, s.29, s.39. In force: July 1, 1997; £1.55.

These Regulations amend the Registration of Births and Deaths Regulations 1987 (SI 1987 2088) and the Registration of Births and Deaths (Welsh Language) Regulations 1987 (SI 1987 2089). They make minor changes to the procedure for re-registration of a birth to add the name of the child's father on legitimation of the child and extend the existing provision for correction of minor clerical errors in re-registered birth entries.

73. Registration–births and deaths–overseas births and deaths

REGISTRATION OF OVERSEAS BIRTHS AND DEATHS (AMENDMENT) REGULATIONS 1997, SI 1997 1466; made under the British Nationality Act 1981 s.41. In force: July 1, 1997; £0.65.

These Regulations amend the Registration of Overseas Births and Deaths Regulations 1982 (SI 1982 1123) by extending the provisions for the registration of births to those born after July 1, 1997 who acquire British Overseas citizenship at birth by virtue of the provisions to reduce statelessness contained in the Hong Kong (British Nationality) Order 1986 (SI 1986 948). They also make provision for the registration of deaths of British National (Overseas) citizens.

74. Registration–births, deaths and marriages–fees

REGISTRATION OF BIRTHS, DEATHS AND MARRIAGES (FEES) ORDER 1997, SI 1997 2939; made under the Public Expenditure and Receipts Act 1968 s.5, Sch.3 para.1, Sch.3 para.2. In force: January 1, 1998; £1.95.

This Order, which revokes the Registration of Births, Deaths and Marriages (Fees) Order 1996 (SI 1996 3152), increases fees payable under Acts relating to the registration of births, deaths and marriages.

75. Registration–marriages

REGISTRATION OF MARRIAGES (AMENDMENT) REGULATIONS 1997, SI 1997 2204; made under the Marriage Act 1949 s.27, s.31, s.32, s.74. In force: October 1, 1997; £3.20.

These Regulations amend the Registration of Marriages Regulations 1986 (SI 1986 1442) and the Registration of Marriages (Welsh Language) Regulations 1986 (SI 1986 1445) by substituting new prescribed forms of notice and certificate of marriage to reflect the provisions of the Deregulation (Validity of Civil Preliminaries to Marriage) Order 1997 (SI 1997 986) which allows most marriages to be solemnized up to 12 months after entry in the marriage notice book. In addition they consolidate amendments made previously relating to the form of instructions for the solemnization of marriage in registered buildings without the presence of a registrar.

76. Time–summer time

SUMMER TIME ORDER 1997, SI 1997 2982; made under the Summer Time Act 1972 s.2. In force: December 31, 1997; £0.65.

This Order, which provides for the periods of summer time in the years 1998, 1999, 2000 and 2001, implements the Council Directive 97/44 ([1997] OJ L206/62) which establishes the start and end dates and times of the periods of summer time for those years in the Member States of the European Community.

77. Visas—fees

CONSULAR FEES ORDER 1997, SI 1997 1314; made under the Consular Fees Act 1980 s.1. In force: June 10, 1997; £1.95.

This Order, which revokes and replaces the Consular Fees Order 1996 (SI 1996 1915), makes changes in respect of visa fees. The fee for the 5 year multiple entry visa is reduced, the fees for settlement and marriage visas are increased, the fee for confirmation of the right of abode is abolished and the cost of a certificate of entitlement is reduced. The overall effect is intended to complete the implementation of full cost recovery for fee-bearing consular services.

78. Articles

Back to basics: reinventing administrative law *(Carol Harlow)*: P.L. 1997, Sum, 245-261. (Extent to which pre-Thatcher consensus politics in administrative law has given way to new public management philosophy with less government growth and more privatisation).

Consistency - a principle of public law? *(Karen Steyn)*: J.R. 1997, 2(1), 22-26. (Whether public bodies have duty to act consistently by giving reasons for decisions and by following previous practice).

Corruption: a Law Commission consultation paper *(John Smith)*: Arch. News 1997, 4, 4-5. (Law Com. No.145 on codification of criminal law, whether to retain distinction between public and other bodies and difficulty of defining potentially corruptive conduct).

Inquiries after Scott: the return of the tribunal of inquiry *(Barry K. Winetrobe)*: P.L. 1997, Spr, 18-31. (Form of inquiries used for the Dunblane tragedy and the North Wales child abuse investigations established under the Tribunals of Inquiry (Evidence) Act 1921).

Members' interests: "Freemasons" *(Colin Crawford)*: L.A.L. 1997, 1, 6-7. (Influence of freemason membership on administrative decision making, following Local Ombudsman's findings of councillors' maladministration in granting planning permission to fellow freemasons).

Public interest immunity *(Ian Leigh)*: Parl. Aff. 1997, 50(1), 55-70. (Constitutional implications of recommendations on public interest immunity in Scott Report on Matrix Churchill trial with particular reference to separation of powers and ministerial responsibility).

Recent developments in public law *(Kate Markus* and *Martin Westgate)*: Legal Action 1997, Nov, 10-14. (Cases on boundaries of public and private law, basis for judicial review and procedural issues).

Requiring reasons at common law *(David Toube)*: J.R. 1997, 2(2), 68-74. (Extent to which there is duty to give reasons in decision making of public bodies).

The collapsing duty: a sideways look at community care and public law *(Luke Clements)*: J.R. 1997, 2(3), 162-165. (Statutory evolution of community care and public law, and effect of cases on public law duties which are being eroded because of resource considerations).

The duty to follow guidance *(Kate Markus)* and *(Martin Westgate)*: J.R. 1997, 2(3), 154-157. (How far existence of self-adopted and received guidance may limit discretion of public law decision maker and extent to which courts will interfere if guidance is not followed).

The waiting game—the Parliamentary Commissioner's response to delay in administrative procedures *(Sheena N. McMurtrie)*: P.L. 1997, Spr, 159-173. (Definition of delay in administrative decision making and circumstances where Ombudsman may seek redress for complainant).

79. Books

Bailey, Stephen; Jones, Brian; Mowbray, Alistair—Cases and Materials on Administrative Law. 3rd Ed. Paperback: £29.95. ISBN 0-421-59770-4. Sweet & Maxwell.

Bradley, A.C.; Ewing, K.D.—Constitutional and Administrative Law. Paperback: £26.99. ISBN 0-582-30817-8. Addison-Wesley Longman Higher Education.

Fordham, Michael–Judicial Review Handbook. Judicial Review. Hardback: £45.00. ISBN 0-471-97022-0. Chancery Wiley Law Publications.

James, Rhoda–Private Ombudsmen and Public Law. Socio-legal Studies. Hardback: £40.00. ISBN 1-85521-769-4. Dartmouth.

Marston, John; Ward, Richard–Cases and Commentary on Constitutional and Administrative Law. Paperback: £23.95. ISBN 0-273-62704-X. Pitman Publishing.

McEldowney, John F.–Public Law. 2nd Ed. Paperback: £28.95. ISBN 0-421-60420-4. Sweet & Maxwell.

Spencer, M.; Spencer, J.–Constitutional and Administrative Law. Nutcases. Paperback: £4.95. ISBN 0-421-60430-1. Sweet & Maxwell.

Stott, David–Administrative Law. Lecture Notes. Paperback: £16.95. ISBN 1-874241-39-2. Cavendish Publishing Ltd.

Supperstone, Michael; Goudie, James–Judicial Review. Hardback: £145.00. ISBN 0-406-99245-2. Butterworth Law.

AGENCY

80. Commercial agency–premature termination–right to recovery

[Commercial Agents (Council Directive) Regulations 1993 (SI 1993 3053) Reg.17; Council Directive 86/653 on self employed commercial agents Art.17.]

P entered into an agency agreement with C to buy and sell commodities. The agreement was to last for four years. After five months C indicated that its South African parent had decided to disinvest in C's operations. P initiated proceedings claiming damages or compensation for repudiation of the agreement. P was refused a Mareva injunction and appealed. It was argued that P had a right to recover damages under the Commercial Agents (Council Directive) Regulations 1993 Reg.17 para.6. The judge concluded that there was no difference between EC and domestic law and took the view that C would have been entitled to operate the contract such that P made no money out of it. As a result, P had no right of recovery as a result of premature termination. The issue was whether C could reduce trading to nil, yet for that to remain "proper performance" of the contract.

Held, allowing the appeal and granting a prior restraint injunction in the sum of £300,000, that P had an arguable case to recover a substantial sum. Council Directive 86/653 Art.17(3) used the equivalent of the word "normal", rather than "proper", in language versions other than English. That could be construed as providing compensation for the lawful termination of an agency contract by providing its own measure of compensation, such that P was entitled to what he might have earned had the contract run its course. There was a clear risk that assets might be dissipated without a Mareva injunction, *Brasserie du Pecheur SA v. Germany (C46/93)* [1996] All E.R. (EC) 301, [1996] 1 C.L.Y. 280 considered.

PAGE v. COMBINED SHIPPING & TRADING CO LTD [1997] 3 All E.R. 656, Staughton, L.J., CA.

81. Consideration–oral variation of agreement–forbearance to sue as consideration

F, a property consultant, appealed against the dismissal of his claim for commission of one per cent on the sale price of property for his introduction of U, a property owner, to Vizcaya Holdings Plc, V, who wished to purchase an investment property. Subsequently, during discussions between V and U about the acquisition of U's entire portfolio by way of the purchase of its issued share capital, F confirmed with U that he would accept a reduced fee of £25,000 plus VAT in the light of the changed transaction. After the take over, V refused to pay F any fee. F contended that the trial judge had erred by deciding that: (1) the second agreement related to the reduction of his fee only and not to the nature of the alternative transaction; (2) no consideration for the second agreement had been provided by F, and (3) F's introduction had not been the effective cause of the later transaction.

Held, allowing the appeal and giving judgment for F in the sum of £29,375, that (1) it was clear that in making the later agreement both parties had in contemplation the sale of U's shares to V; (2) consideration for the later agreement had been provided by F's forbearance from suing on the earlier agreement and this was not past consideration, *Callisher v. Bischoffsheim* (1870) L.R. 5 Q.B. 449 followed. It did not matter that such a claim might later fail, provided that, at the time of the agreement, it was F's bona fide belief that he had such a claim. It was clear that both F and U had accepted F's right to a fee, and (3) it had been accepted by both U and F that there was a special term in the contract such that it was irrelevant whether F was the effective cause of the transaction, *Millar Son & Co v. Radford* [1903] 19 T.L.R. 575 distinguished on its facts.

FREEDMAN (T/A JOHN FREEDMAN & CO) v. UNION GROUP PLC [1997] E.G.C.S. 28, Peter Gibson, L.J., CA.

82. **Estate agents–disqualification orders–conviction in USA–retrospective effect of Estate Agents Act 1979–convictions outside UK relevant consideration**

[Estate Agents Act 1979 s.3.]

A appealed against a decision affirming the Secretary of State's determination that, as A had shown a readiness to commit violence against property, there would be a risk of detriment to the public if he were to undertake estate agency work and therefore he had been properly disqualified from acting as an estate agent under the Estate Agents Act 1979 s.3. A had been convicted of an offence of arson of real estate in Detroit, Michigan, some years before the Act came into force and he contended that the judge had been wrong to hold that the Act had retrospective effect so as to allow this conviction to be taken into account for the purposes of s.3 of the Act.

Held, dismissing the appeal, that, in determining whether a statutory provision had retrospective effect, both the purpose of the legislation and any hardship which might result were important considerations, *L'Office Cherifien des Phosphates v. Yamashita-Shinnihon Steamship Co Ltd (The Boucraa)* [1994] A.C. 486, [1994] C.L.Y. 221 considered. If the power to disqualify was exercisable in respect of past convictions, it could be regarded as severe and capable of causing great hardship, but conviction of a relevant offence was only a precondition to the exercise of the Director General of Fair Trading's powers under the 1979 Act and he still had to go on to determine whether the person concerned was unfit to undertake work as an estate agent. The judge had been correct to hold that "conviction" included a conviction prior to the Act coming into force and a conviction outside the UK.

ANTONELLI v. SECRETARY OF STATE FOR TRADE AND INDUSTRY, *The Times*, October 3, 1997, Beldam, L.J., CA.

83. **Estate agents–restrictive covenants–protection of goodwill**

See PARTNERSHIPS: Espley v. Williams. §3872

84. **Estate agents–sole selling agreement–construction of agreement–sale of fixtures and fittings not triggering payment of fee**

S appealed against the dismissal of his appeal against a judgment for £4,168 in respect of estate agent's fees. S had contracted with D to advertise the sale of a terraced property in which he ran a cafe and newsagent business with living accommodation above. The agreement stipulated that the fees would become due on either the sale of the freehold or the leasehold of the premises under a sole selling agreement. D failed to sell the property or business during the currency of the six months sole selling agreement, but after which time S did not terminate the agreement. Subsequently, S let the shop for 12 years at a full rack rent of £11,440 selling the fixtures and fittings for £1,300 and the stock for £1,700. S contended that, since there had been no sale, he was not liable for the minimum fee of £3,000 plus VAT.

Held, allowing the appeal, that in terms of the agreement, the sale of fixtures and fittings did not trigger the payment of the fee or commission.

DOWLING KERR LTD v. SCOTT (1997) 73 P. & C.R. D29, Morritt, L.J., CA.

85. Estate agents—sole selling rights—no entitlement to commission where client entered private negotiations with purchaser

[Rules of the Supreme Court Ord.14A; Estate Agents (Provision of Information) Regulations 1991 (SI 1991 859).]

An estate agent granted "sole selling rights" during the term of an agency contract is not entitled to commission on the sale of the property where he has taken no part in the negotiations nor introduced the buyer and the sale takes place after expiry of the agency. An estate agent, H, was engaged by S to act with sole selling rights for a minimum period of six months in respect of the sale of a nursing home. S, unhappy with H's performance, decided to give H notice terminating the agency at the end of the period. However, before notice was effected, S responded to a newspaper advertisement from someone seeking a nursing home and entered into negotiations with the advertisers, in which H took no part. Shortly after H's agency was terminated, S sold the home to the advertisers, and H appealed against a decision on his application under RSC Ord.14A that he was not entitled to commission on the sale price of the nursing home.

Held, dismissing the appeal, that the contract between H and S described H as possessing "sole selling rights", the definition of which was taken from the Estate Agents (Provision of Information) Regulations 1991. Interpreting that definition as a client might be expected to, S would only be liable to pay commission where the contracts for the sale of the property were exchanged after the expiry of the agency if either H had introduced the buyer to S, or if the buyer had been introduced to S by another party, but H had negotiated with the buyer on S's behalf. Since neither of those circumstances applied in the instant case, H was not entitled to claim commission.

HARWOOD (T/A RSBS GROUP) v. SMITH, *The Times,* December 8, 1997, Hobhouse, L.J., CA.

86. Solicitors—warranty of authority

See CONVEYANCING: Penn v. Bristol and West Building Society. §1023

87. Articles

Agency agreements under EU competition rules *(John Boyce* and *Anny Tubbs)*: Eur. Counsel 1997, 2(4), 41-46. (Case law on application of Art.85(1) to independent commercial agency agreements which distort competition or restrict agents' operations - includes flowchart).

Agency of car dealer *(Paul Dobson)*: Bus. L.R. 1997, 18(1), 5-7. (Extent to which car dealers act as agents of finance companies when their customers obtain finance from companies with whom the dealers have arrangements).

Commercial Agents Regulations—update: Buyer 1997, 19(4), 3-5. (Provisions of SI 1993 3053 which covers all agency agreements whether made before or after the commencement date of January 1, 1994).

New developments in agency law *(Severine Saintier)*: J.B.L. 1997, Jan, 77-81. (Availability of compensation for termination of agency agreement where principal has ceased trading in UK and assessment of damages for wrongful termination).

AGRICULTURE

88. **Agricultural holdings—alleged shared occupation—partnership acting as agent—activities of agent treated as activities of principal—no breach of covenant**

W, the landlord, appealed against an order dismissing his application contending that there had been an error of law in the arbitrator's finding that W's notice to quit, served on B, the tenant, should not have effect. W alleged that B was in breach of the tenancy agreement as B had failed to cultivate the holding and had parted with possession or shared possession or occupation with a partnership. The partnership, P, was a family operation of a number of agricultural parcels which carried out the farming operations on the holding with B's agreement. The arbitrator found that this did not constitute sharing occupation of the holding in breach of the agreement as there was nothing in the agreement which made it a breach to appoint an agent to manage the farm.

Held, dismissing the appeal, that there was no shared occupation and therefore no breach of covenant. Occupation of a holding by an agent is the occupation of the principal, *Pegler v. Craven* [1952] 2 Q.B. 693, [1952] C.L.Y. 1961 followed and *Hills (Patents) Ltd v. University College Hospital Board of Governors* [1956] 1 Q.B. 90, [1955] C.L.Y. 1513 distinguished. A limited company, as B was, can only operate through its agents and occupation of a holding must therefore be by agents. Where, as here, the holding had no buildings, the activities carried out on the holding must be considered. If an agent's activities are within the scope of his authority they are treated as the activities of the principal as though the agent is an employee. The farming operations carried out by P were as agent for B.

WALLACE v. C BRIAN BARRATT & SON LTD [1997] 31 E.G. 97, Morritt, L.J., CA.

89. **Agricultural holdings—joint tenancies—notice to quit served after one tenant had left—injunction granted to compel other to join in counter notice**

[Agricultural Holdings Act 1986 s.26 (1).]

Two brothers, P and D, were granted an annual agricultural tenancy of a holding in 1974. D ceased to work on the land in 1977 and did not reside there after 1983. In 1991 the family agreed to maintain the status quo so far as D's beneficial interest in the tenancy was concerned. In 1996 the landlord served a notice to quit the tenancy by 1998. P brought an application for a mandatory injunction against D requiring him to join with P in signing a counter notice to the notice to quit under the Agricultural Holdings Act 1986 s.26(1).

Held, allowing the application, that it was arguable that the effect of the family negotiations in 1991 was that P should remain as the occupying farming tenant. It was also arguable that this agreement was effective to vary the prima facie position which was obtained in 1974, namely that either P or D as joint tenants could have served a tenant's notice to quit and declined to serve a counter notice to any notice to quit served by the landlord, *Hammersmith and Fulham LBC v. Monk* [1992] 1 A.C. 478, [1992] C.L.Y. 2684, *Harris v. Black* (1983) 46 P. & C. R. 366, [1984] C.L.Y. 1880, *Sykes v. Land* [1984] 2 E.G.L.R. 8 [1984] C.L.Y. 57, *Featherstone v. Staples* [1986] 1 W.L.R. 861, [1986] C.L.Y. 41, considered. The balance of convenience lay in favour of granting the injunction. P agreed to provide an undertaking to the effect that if at trial D was found not to be compellable to sign a counter notice then P would either concur in effecting a surrender or take such steps as were necessary to bring the tenancy to an end.

CORK v. CORK [1997] 16 E.G. 130, Knox, J., Ch D.

90. Agricultural holdings–notice to quit–meaning of "premises let as a dwelling"

[Protection from Eviction Act 1977 s.5; Agricultural Holdings Act 1986.]

NT appealed against the dismissal of its action for possession of land let on an annual tenancy. Arrears of rent accrued and, in accordance with the Agricultural Holdings Act 1986, NT served first a notice to pay rent and then a notice to quit. K failed to challenge the notice by arbitration under the 1986 Act, and later contended that the notice was defective as it failed to carry the information prescribed by the Protection from Eviction Act 1977 s.5. NT argued that the holding did not constitute "premises let as a dwelling" so as to bring it within the 1977 Act.

Held, allowing the appeal, that premises let as an agricultural holding were not "premises let as a dwelling" for the purpose of the Protection from Eviction Act 1977 s.5. It followed that NT had served a valid notice to quit. The information statutorily required by s.5 did not assist an agricultural tenant since not legal advice but a counter notice within a restricted time scale was required by the 1986 Act and the relevant period of notice was 12 months not four weeks, *Maunsell v. Olins* [1975] A.C. 373, [1975] C.L.Y. 2857 and *Russell v. Booker* [1982] E.G.L.R. 513, [1982] C.L.Y. 29 applied.

NATIONAL TRUST FOR PLACES OF HISTORIC INTEREST OR NATURAL BEAUTY v. KNIPE, *The Times*, June 21, 1997, Pill, L.J., CA.

91. Agricultural holdings–tenancy for term of five years–ministerial consent

[Agricultural Holdings Act 1986 s.3, s.5.]

J was granted a tenancy of agricultural land by O which was expressed as "commencing on the 13th day of November 1991" for five years. Both parties applied jointly to the Secretary of State under the Agricultural Holdings Act 1986 s.5 for approval of the tenancy which would not fall within s.3 of that Act. The tenancy was expressed as ending on November 13, 1996. The Secretary of State granted approval. The tenancy did not commence in fact until February 11, 1992. J applied for a declaration that the tenancy fell within the Agricultural Holdings Act 1986, and was therefore subject to security of tenure, on the basis that the Secretary of State's approval was based on a tenancy due to commence on November 13, 1991, which it did not.

Held, dismissing the application, that the requirements of s.5 had been satisfied. That the parties had made a joint application which indicated that both intended that the tenancy should not fall within the 1986 Act s.3.

JONES v. OWEN [1997] 32 E.G. 85, John Weeks Q.C., Ch D.

92. Agricultural holdings–underleases–subtenancy set up as partnership–sham agreement between landlord and tenant to end subtenancy

[Agricultural Holdings Act 1986.]

In March 1970, E, by a headlease, let over 930 acres of land, including a farm, to himself and his two sons, S and J. In 1976 E died and the freehold in the land passed to S and J. By 1980 the farm had become run down and M entered into possession of part of the land in order to manage the farm. S and J were concerned that at a future date they would be able to sell the farm in order to provide capital for S's children and that accordingly M should not acquire the substantial security of tenure provided under the Agricultural Holdings Act 1986. To ensure this, terms were agreed under which M paid a monthly sum to S and J as a payment under a limited partnership. In 1984 and 1986 the land was severed and that part containing the farm was transferred to B to be held by them on trust for the benefit of S's children. By 1991 S's children indicated that they wished to realise the capital of the farm and to effect this, notice to quit was served under the headlease of 1970. No counter-notice was served by S and J, as would have usually been the case. In 1993 M received notice dissolving the partnership. B brought proceedings claiming possession of the land against M. M resisted the application on the basis that it was a sham designed to avoid the security of tenure conferred by the Agricultural Holdings Act 1986.

Held, dismissing the application, that the facts showed that the landlords acted collusively with the tenants for the purpose of destroying the subtenancy.

In these circumstances the court would act to protect the subtenant from such collusion, *Sparkes v. Smart* [1990] 2 E.G.L.R. 245, [1991] C.L.Y. 115, *Pennell v. Payne* [1995] Q.B. 192, [1995] 1 C.L.Y. 189, applied, *Harrison v. Wing* [1988] 2 E.G.L.R. 4, [1988] C.L.Y. 2047, distinguished.

BARRETT v. MORGAN [1997] 12 E.G. 155, PW Smith Q.C., Ch D.

93. Agricultural holdings—units of production—income

AGRICULTURAL HOLDINGS (UNITS OF PRODUCTION) ORDER 1997, SI 1997 1962; made under the Agricultural Holdings Act 1986 Sch.6 para.4. In force: September 12, 1997; £1.55.

This Order, which revokes and replaces the Agricultural Holdings (Units of Production) Order 1996 (SI 1996 2163), prescribes units of production for the assessment of the productive capacity of agricultural land and sets out the amount which is to be regarded as the net annual income from each such unit for the year September 12, 1997 to September 11, 1998 inclusive.

94. Agricultural policy—environmental protection

AGRICULTURE ACT 1986 (AMENDMENT) REGULATIONS 1997, SI 1997 1457; made under the European Communities Act 1972 s.2. In force: July 1, 1997; £0.65.

These Regulations amend the Agriculture Act 1986 s.18 and form part of the programme to implement Council Regulation 2078/92 ([1992] OJ L215/85) on agricultural production methods compatible with the requirements of protection of the environment and the maintenance of the countryside as last amended by Commission Regulation 2772/95 ([1995] OJ L288/35). They make provision to implement Commission Regulation 746/96 ([1996] OJ L102/19) laying down detailed rules for the application of the Agri-environment Regulation, as now amended by Commission Regulation 435/97 ([1997] OJ L67/2).

95. Agricultural policy—integrated administration and control system

INTEGRATED ADMINISTRATION AND CONTROL SYSTEM (AMENDMENT) REGULATIONS 1997, SI 1997 1148; made under the European Communities Act 1972 s.2. In force: April 29, 1997; £1.55.

These Regulations amend the Integrated Administration and Control Systems Regulations 1993 (SI 1993 1317) which provided for the implementation in part of Council Regulation 3508/92 ([1992] OJ L355/1), as amended, and the Commission Regulation 3887/92 ([1992] OJ L391/36) as amended.

96. Agricultural policy—International Fund for Agricultural Development

INTERNATIONAL FUND FOR AGRICULTURAL DEVELOPMENT (FOURTH REPLENISHMENT) ORDER 1997, SI 1997 2712; made under the Overseas Development and Co-operation Act 1980 s.4. In force: October 15, 1997; £0.65.

This Order provides for the payment of sums not exceeding £13,586,773 into the International Fund for Agricultural Development as representing the contribution of the Government of the United Kingdom to the Fourth Replenishment of the resources of the Fund, and for the redemption of non-interest-bearing and non-negotiable notes issued by the Secretary of State in payment of the contribution.

97. Agricultural policy—organic products

ORGANIC PRODUCTS (AMENDMENT) REGULATIONS 1997, SI 1997 166; made under the European Communities Act 1972 s.2. In force: February 24, 1997; £1.10.

These Regulations further amend the Organic Products Regulations 1992 (SI 1992 2111) by providing for the execution and enforcement of the Council and Commission Regulations amending or supplementing Council Regulation 2092/91 ([1991] OJ L198/1) on organic production of agricultural products and indications referring thereto on agricultural products and foodstuffs.

98. Agricultural policy–wines

COMMON AGRICULTURAL POLICY (WINE) (AMENDMENT) REGULATIONS 1997, SI 1997 542; made under the European Communities Act 1972 s.2. In force: April 1, 1997; £1.55.

These Regulations amend the Common Agricultural Policy (Wine) Regulations 1996 (SI 1996 696) which provide for the enforcement of EC Regulations concerned with the production and marketing of wine and related products. The principal amendment made by these Regulations is to introduce the rules to be observed before a table wine originating in the United Kingdom may be described as "regional wine".

99. Agricultural produce–marketing–grants

FOOD INDUSTRY DEVELOPMENT SCHEME (SPECIFICATION OF ACTIVITIES) ORDER 1997, SI 1997 2674; made under the Agriculture Act 1993 s.50, s.62. In force: December 1, 1997; £0.65.

This Order specifies activities for the purposes of the Agriculture Act 1993 s.50(2)(c) in respect of which payments may be made under the Food Industry Development Scheme 1997 (SI 1997 2672). In addition it amends the Marketing Development Scheme (Specification of Activities) Order 1994 (SI 1994 1404) so that it applies only to payments made under the Marketing Development Scheme 1994 (SI 1994 1403 as amended by SI 1996 2629) para.2(b).

100. Agricultural produce–marketing–grants–fisheries

FOOD INDUSTRY DEVELOPMENT SCHEME 1997, SI 1997 2673; made under the Agriculture Act 1993 s.50. In force: December 1, 1997; £1.95.

This Scheme makes provision for Ministers to pay grants to cover expenditure incurred by persons carrying out proposals for the organisation, promotion, encouragement, development, co-ordination or facilitation of the marketing of the produce of agriculture, fish farming and other activities specified for the purposes of the Agriculture Act 1993 s.50(2).

101. Animal products–diseases and disorders–bovine material

SPECIFIED BOVINE MATERIAL ORDER 1997, SI 1997 617; made under the Animal Health Act 1981 s.1, s.8, s.11. In force: March 28, 1997; £3.70.

This Order revokes and re-makes with amendments the Specified Bovine Material (No.3) Order 1996 (SI 1996 1941). The Order controls specified bovine material, being material which may contain the agent containing bovine spongiform encephalopathy. It implements in part Commission Decision 94/474 ([1994] OJ L194/96) concerning certain protection measures relating to bovine spongiform encephalopathy and the provisions relating to animal waste of Council Directive 90/667 ([1990] OJ L363/51) laying down the veterinary rules for the disposal of animal waste, for its placing on the market and for the prevention of pathogens in feeding stuffs of animal or fish origin. It controls the sale and use of specified bovine material for human and animal consumption and the production of mechanically recovered meat. It regulates the initial treatment of specified bovine material and the rendering of whole carcasses. It prohibits the removal of the brain, eyes and spinal cord from a bovine animal and regulates the importation of specified bovine material from Northern Ireland. The Order regulates the consignment of specified bovine material once it has been removed from the carcass and requires the approval of collection centres, incinerators, rendering plants and other premises that process specified bovine material. It contains provisions on veterinary and laboratory premises, directions, export, sampling, transport, storage and enforcement,

102. Animal products–diseases and disorders–BSE

BOVINE SPONGIFORM ENCEPHALOPATHY (NO.2) (AMENDMENT) ORDER 1997, SI 1997 2387; made under the Animal Health Act 1981 s.1, s.32, s.83. In force: October 24, 1997; £0.65.

This Order amends the Bovine Spongiform Encephalopathy (No.2) Order 1996 (SI 1996 3183) by providing that the Notices in Form F and Form G relating to exposed animals may be served by veterinary inspectors or inspectors, as defined in the Animal Health Act 1981. It continues to implement Commission Decision 96/385 ([1996] OJ L151/39) approving the plan for the eradication of bovine spongiform encephalopathy in the United Kingdom.

103. Animal products–diseases and disorders–BSE

BOVINES AND BOVINE PRODUCTS (DESPATCH PROHIBITION AND PRODUCTION RESTRICTION) REGULATIONS 1997, SI 1997 1905; made under the European Communities Act 1972 s.2. In force: August 1, 1997; £2.80.

These Regulations give effect to Commission Decision 96/239 ([1996] OJ L78/47) on emergency measures to protect against bovine spongiform encephalopathy, as amended by Commission Decision 96/362 ([1996] OJ L139/17), in relation to the despatch to third countries and other member states of bovine animals and embryos and meat and other products from bovine animals.

104. Animal products–diseases and disorders–BSE–compensation

BOVINE SPONGIFORM ENCEPHALOPATHY COMPENSATION (AMENDMENT) ORDER 1997, SI 1997 2365; made under the Animal Health Act 1981 s.32, s.34. In force: October 24, 1997; £1.10.

This Order amends the Bovine Spongiform Encephalopathy Compensation Order 1996 (SI 1996 3184) by limiting its application to herds of 11 or more animals and adding a new definition of "closed herd". It also provides for the appointment of a valuer by the President of the Institute of Auctioneers and Appraisers in Scotland where an exposed animal in Scotland is to be slaughtered and the Minister and the animal's owner have not agreed on the valuation or the appointment of a valuer.

105. Animal products–diseases and disorders–specified risk material

SPECIFIED RISK MATERIAL ORDER 1997, SI 1997 2964; made under the Animal Health Act 1981 s.1, s.10, s.11, s.29, s.35, s.76, s.83, Sch.2 para.1, Sch.2 para.2, Sch.2 para.4, Sch.2 para.5, Sch.2 para.6, Sch.2 para.7, Sch.2 para.8, Sch.2 para.9, Sch.2 para.10, Sch.2 para.11. In force: January 1, 1998; £2.40.

This Order, which revokes the Specified Bovine Materials Order 1997 (SI 1997 617) and the Heads of Sheep and Goats Order 1996 (SI 1996 2264), re-makes the provisions of those Orders prohibiting the use of specified bovine material in feeding stuffs and cosmetic, pharmaceutical and medical products. In addition the Zoonoses Order 1988 (SI 1988 2264), which designated BSE as a disease which constitutes a risk to public health, is amended so as to apply further conditions of the Animal Health Act 1981 to it.

106. Animal products–diseases and disorders–specified risk material

SPECIFIED RISK MATERIAL REGULATIONS 1997, SI 1997 2965; made under the Food Safety Act 1990 s.6, s.16, s.17, s.19, s.26, s.48, Sch.1 para.2, Sch.1 para.3, Sch.1 para.5, Sch.1 para.6. In force: Reg.1, Reg.2, Reg.3, Reg.4, Reg.6, Reg.15(7), Reg.24(2), Sch.1: December 17, 1997; Remainder: January 1, 1998; £4.15.

These Regulations, which control specified risk material in respect of food, continue in force provisions in respect of food up to now contained in the Specified Bovine Material 1997 (SI 1997 617) and the Heads of Sheep and Goats Order 1996 (SI 1996 2264). They implement in part Commission Decision 94/474 ([1996] OJ L194/96) concerning certain protection measures relating to bovine spongiform encephalopathy and provisions of Directive 90/667 ([1990] OJ L363/51) relating to animal waste.

107. Animal products–diseases and disorders–specified risk material

SPECIFIED RISK MATERIAL (AMENDMENT) REGULATIONS 1997, SI 1997 3062; made under the Food Safety Act 1990 s.6, s.16, s.26, s.48, Sch.1 para.2. In force: January 1, 1998; £0.65.

This Order amends the Specified Risk Material Order 1997 (SI 1997 2965) in order to remove burdens relating to carcasses of sheep and goats, and relating to food containing specified risk material derived from animals which were slaughtered or have died outside the UK, which were imposed unintentionally.

108. Animal products–export controls

BOVINE PRODUCTS (PRODUCTION AND DESPATCH) REGULATIONS 1997, SI 1997 389; made under the European Communities Act 1972 s.2. In force: March 15, 1997; £2.40.

These Regulations revoke and remake with amendments the Bovine Products (Despatch to other Member States) Regulations 1996 (SI 1996 2265) which implemented in part Commission Decision 96/239 ([1996] OJ L78/47) on emergency measures to protect against bovine spongiform encephalopathy, as amended by Commission Decision 96/362 ([1996] OJ L139/17) in relation to the despatch to other Member States of meat and other products from bovine animals slaughtered outside the United Kingdom. They also made provision for the Minister to charge fees and contained provisions on enforcement, obstruction, offences and penalties. These Regulations additionally make provision controlling the production from bovine animals of gelatin, tallow and related products, and concerning the export and use of such products. They regulate the consignment of material containing bovine vertebral column to establishments approved under the Regulations.

109. Animal products–hygiene inspections

FRESH MEAT (HYGIENE AND INSPECTION) (AMENDMENT) REGULATIONS 1997, SI 1997 2074; made under the Food Safety Act 1990 s.16, s.19, s.48, Sch.1 para.7. In force: September 21, 1997; £1.10.

These Regulations amend the Fresh Meat (Hygiene and Inspection) Regulations 1995 (SI 1995 539) Reg.7 so that meat from animals slaughtered in a licensed slaughterhouse or farmed game handling facility for consumption by the owners will be treated as if intended for sale and subjected to inspection and health marking requirements contained in the Regulations.

110. Animal products–identification

ANIMAL BY-PRODUCTS (IDENTIFICATION) (AMENDMENT) REGULATIONS 1997, SI 1997 2073; made under the Food Safety Act 1990 s.16, s.48, Sch.1 para.3. In force: September 21, 1997; £1.10.

These Regulations amend the Animal By-Products (Identification) Regulations 1995 (SI 1995 614) Reg.3 by adding to the definition of animal by-product to which the sterilisation and staining requirements of the Regulations apply.

111. Animal products–import and export controls

PRODUCTS OF ANIMAL ORIGIN (IMPORT AND EXPORT) (AMENDMENT) REGULATIONS 1997, SI 1997 3023; made under the European Communities Act 1972 s.2(2). In force: January 1, 1998; £1.95.

These Regulations amend the Products of Animal Origin (Import and Export) Regulations 1996 (SI 1996 3124) in order to implement EC requirements on standard rates of charge for veterinary inspections of imports of products of animal origin from third countries.

112. **Animal products-imports-preclusion of national rules prohibiting import of non heat treated mechanically recovered meat-European Union**

[Council Directive 64/433 on health problems affecting intra-Community trade in fresh meat.]

P imported mechanically recovered meat from Belgium into Germany. The meat arrived frozen and was to be heat treated by P in Germany. The German authorities seized the meat under regulations which required that mechanically recovered meat could not be imported into Germany unless it had been heat treated in its state of origin. P appealed and sought a declaration that the importation of frozen mechanically recovered meat was lawful. The proceedings were stayed and referred to the European Court of Justice for a ruling on questions on the interpretation of Council Directive 64/433 on health problems affecting intra-Community trade in fresh meat Art.6(1).

Held, that the Directive required that mechanically recovered meat should be heat treated as soon as possible after recovery but, if it was not possible for heat treatment to be undertaken at the point of recovery it should be carried out in an appropriate establishment as close as possible to the establishment of origin. The most appropriate establishment might be in an adjoining member state. Accordingly the Directive precluded national regulations that prohibited the importation of mechanically recovered meat that had not been heat treated in the state of origin.

PAUL DAUT GmbH & CO KG v. OBERKREISDIREKTOR DES KREISES GUTERSLOH (C105/95) [1997] All E.R. (EC) 562, CN Kakouris (President), ECJ.

113. **Animal products-residues-examination and limits**

ANIMALS AND ANIMAL PRODUCTS (EXAMINATION FOR RESIDUES AND MAXIMUM RESIDUE LIMITS) REGULATIONS 1997, SI 1997 1729; made under the Food Safety Act 1990 s.6, s.16, s.17, s.26, s.30, s.31, s.45, s.48, Sch.1 para.3, Sch.1 para.7. In force: August 11, 1997; £3.70.

These Regulations revoke and re-enact provisions formerly contained in the Animals, Meat and Meat Products (Examination for Residues and Maximum Residue Limits) Regulations 1991 (SI 1991 2843), the Medicines (Stilbenes and Thyrostatic Substances) Regulations 1982 (SI 1982 626), the Medicines (Hormone Growth Promoters) (Prohibition of Use) Regulations 1988 (SI 1988 705) and the Animals and Fresh Meat (Hormonal Substances) Regulations 1988 (SI 1988 849). They implement Council Directive 96/22 ([1996] OJ L125/3) concerning the prohibition on the use in stockfarming of certain substances having a hormonal or thyrostatic action and of beta-agonists, and repealing Directive 81/602 ([1981] OJ L222/32), Directive 88/146 ([1988] OJ L70/16) and Directive 88/299 ([1988] OJ L128/36). They also implement Council Directive 96/23 ([1996] OJ L125/10) on measures to monitor certain substances and residues thereof in live animals and animal products and repealing Directive 85/358 ([1985] OJ L191/46) and Directive 86/469 ([1986] OJ L275/36) and Decision 89/187 ([1989] OJ L66/37) and Decision 91/664 ([1991] OJ L368/17) and provide for the enforcement and execution of the prohibition in Council Regulation 2377/90 ([1990] OJ L224/1) Art.5 and Art.14.

114. **Animal products-veal-marketing-payments**

VEAL (MARKETING PAYMENT) REGULATIONS 1997, SI 1997 1986; made under the European Communities Act 1972 s.2. In force: August 15, 1997; £1.55.

These Regulations provide for payments by the appropriate Minister to producers in the UK in pursuance of Council Regulation 2443/96 ([1996] OJ L333/2) Art.1 which permits Member States to make additional payments to producers in the beef and veal sector.

115. Animal products−waste disposal

ANIMAL BY-PRODUCTS (AMENDMENT) ORDER 1997, SI 1997 2894; made under the Animal Health Act 1981 s.1, s.8. In force: January 1, 1998; £1.10.

This Order amends the Animal By-Products Order 1992 (SI 1992 3303) by replacing Art.5 and Art.6 which specify the circumstances in which animal by-products are to be buried or burned instead of being rendered or incinerated.

116. Arable land−payments−EC law

ARABLE AREA PAYMENTS (AMENDMENT) REGULATIONS 1997, SI 1997 2969; made under the European Communities Act 1972 s.2. In force: January 15, 1998; £1.55.

These Regulations amend the Arable Area Payments Regulations 1996 (SI 1996 3142) which make provision for the implementation of Council Regulation 1765/92 ([1992] OJ L181/12) which establishes a support system for producers of certain arable crops. The amendments relate to the planting distances in relation to rapeseed, declarations from farmers for non food crops and management requirements for set aside land.

117. Beef−export ban−goods in transit−repayment of export refund

[Council Regulation 565/80 on the advance payment of export refunds in respect of agricultural products; Council Regulation 3665/87 laying down rules for the application of the system of export refunds on agricultural products Art.23.]

Under the terms of the beef export ban imposed by Commission Decision 96/239 Art.1 F were required to repatriate a quantity of beef in transit. F sought judicial review of a decision by the Intervention Board to enforce the repayments of export refunds provided by virtue of Council Regulation 565/80. The Board applied for the leave to be set aside and for the discharge of an injunction granted to prevent enforcement pending outcome of the review.

Held, refusing the application and continuing the injunction with a requirement that F give an undertaking guaranteeing interest accruing under an existing guarantee, that (1) the power to set aside leave was to be sparingly exercised in the absence of deliberate non-disclosure with the court having to decide whether F's case was arguable and not whether MAFF were correct as to their contentions regarding the final outcome, and (2) entitlement to a refund where force majeure had not led to the outright destruction of the beef fell to be dealt with under Council Regulation 3665/87 Art.23 and it was at least arguable that F had a case on this ground. It did not amount to a "knock out blow" with regard to F's application. Leave could not be refused merely because it was thought that the arguments were unlikely to succeed, and F had an arguable case on grounds which on first blush had appeared exceedingly weak.

R. v. MINISTRY OF AGRICULTURE FISHERIES AND FOOD, *ex p.* FIRST CITY TRADING LTD, Trans. Ref: CO 2871-96, March 26, 1997, Collins, J., QBD.

118. Beef−marketing−payments

BEEF (MARKETING PAYMENT) (NO.2) (AMENDMENT) REGULATIONS 1997, SI 1997 195; made under the European Communities Act 1972 s.2. In force: February 4, 1997; £1.10.

These Regulations amend the Beef (Marketing Payment) (No.2) Regulations 1996 (SI 1996 2999) to provide for further payments to be made by the appropriate Minister to beef producers in the United Kingdom in pursuance of Council Regulation 1357/96 ([1996] OJ L175/9) Art.4(b) which permits Member States to make additional payments to producers in the beef and veal sector. The Regulations make provision for such payments to be made in respect of certain bovine animals sold after September 30, 1996 and before November 10, 1996 for slaughter for human consumption, and also in respect of animals slaughtered in the same period by or on behalf of a beef producer for sale for human consumption.

119. Cattle–hides

BOVINE HIDES REGULATIONS 1997, SI 1997 813; made under the European Communities Act 1972 s.2. In force: April 3, 1997; £1.95.

These Regulations make further provision for the enforcement of the requirements of Commission Regulation 716/96 ([1996] OJ L99/14) Art.1 (2) adopting exceptional support measures for the beef market in the United Kingdom, in so far as those requirements relate to the hides of bovine animals aged more than 30 months which do not show any clinical sign of bovine spongiform encephalopathy. They ensure that any untanned parts of hides are treated as controlled waste and destroyed accordingly and provide for the registration of hide dealers and tannery controllers and for the approval of rendering plants.

120. Cattle–identification–enforcement

CATTLE IDENTIFICATION (ENFORCEMENT) REGULATIONS 1997, SI 1997 1901; made under the European Communities Act 1972 s.2. In force: August 22, 1997; £1.55.

These Regulations create offences for breach of certain provisions of Council Regulation 820/97 ([1997] OJ L117/1) establishing a system for the identification and registration of bovine animals and regarding the labelling of beef and beef products. They revoke the Bovine Animals (Identification, Marketing and Breeding Records) Order 1990 (SI 1990 1867), revoke part of the Bovine Animals (Records, Identification and Movement) Order 1995 (SI 1995 12) and amend the Suckler Cow Premium Regulations 1993 (SI 1993 1441) and the Beef Special Premium Regulations 1996 (SI 1996 3241).

121. Cattle–infectious disease control–brucellosis

BRUCELLOSIS ORDER 1997, SI 1997 758; made under the Animal Health Act 1981 s.1, s.6, s.7, s.15, s.28, s.32, s.34, s.35, s.87. In force: April 1, 1997; £2.40.

This Order, which revokes and replaces the Brucellosis (England and Wales) Order 1981 (SI 1981 1455 as amended by SI 1986 2295 and SI 1994 2762) and the Brucellosis (Scotland) Order 1979 (SI 1979 1596 as amended by SI 1980 1673, SI 1987 135 and SI 1994 2770), implements provisions of Council Directive 64/432 ([1964] OJ L121/1977) relating to milk as amended by Council Directive 77/391 ([1977] OJ L145/44) which require the operation of a monitoring and testing programme to maintain the officially brucellosis-free status of Great Britain. The principal changes made to the Regulations relate to the arrangements for testing milk for evidence of brucellosis.

122. Cattle–infectious disease control–enzootic bovine leukosis

ENZOOTIC BOVINE LEUKOSIS ORDER 1997, SI 1997 757; made under the Animal Health Act 1981 s.1, s.6, s.7, s.15, s.28, s.32, s.34, s.35, s.87. In force: April 1, 1997; £1.95.

This Order, which revokes and replaces the Enzootic Bovine Leukosis Order 1980 (SI 1980 79 as amended by SI 1995 13), implements provisions of Council Directive 64/432 ([1964] OJ L121/1977) relating to milk and Council Directive 77/391 ([1977] OJ L145/44) which require the operation of a monitoring and testing programme in order to achieve an officially enzootic bovine leukosis-free status. The principal changes made by this Order relate to the arrangements for testing milk for evidence of enzootic bovine leukosis.

123. Cattle–suckler cow premiums

SUCKLER COW PREMIUM (AMENDMENT) REGULATIONS 1997, SI 1997 249; made under the European Communities Act 1972 s.2. In force: February 28, 1997; £0.65.

These Regulations amend the Suckler Cow Premium Regulations 1993 (SI 1993 1441 as amended by SI 1994 1528, SI 1995 15, SI 1995 1446 and SI 1996 1488), so that where the additional payments provided for by Council Regulation 2443/96 ([1996] OJ L333/2) are made to successful applications for suckler cow premium, those payments are treated as being suckler cow premiums payments for the purposes of the bulk of those provisions of SI 1993 1441, as amended, which relate to financial control and enforcement.

124. Cattle–supply of live cattle–retention of title

See SALE OF GOODS: Chaigley Farms Ltd v. Crawford Kaye & Grayshire Ltd (t/a Leylands). §4478

125. Crops–corn returns

CORN RETURNS REGULATIONS 1997, SI 1997 1873; made under the Corn Returns Act 1882 s.4, s.5, s.14. In force: August 1, 1997; £1.55.

These Regulations, which revoke and replace the Corn Returns Regulations 1976 (SI 1976 1035), the Corn Returns (Scotland) Regulations 1976 (SI 1976 1081), the Corn Returns (Scotland) (Variation) Regulations 1990 (SI 1990 1276) and the Corn Returns (Variation) Regulations 1990 (SI 1990 1351), prescribe the areas from which returns of wholesale purchases of British corn are required to be made under the Corn Returns Act 1882 s.4 and s.5. They provide for the alternative ways of making and submitting a return to the Home-Grown Cereals Authority, subject to a saving for cases where another manner of making the return is agreed between its maker and the Home-Grown Cereals Authority, and set out those items of information that any return must contain.

126. Crops–home-grown cereals–levies–fees

HOME-GROWN CEREALS AUTHORITY (RATE OF LEVY) ORDER 1997, SI 1997 1337; made under the Cereals Marketing Act 1965 s.13, s.23, s.24. In force: July 1, 1997; £1.10.

For the purposes of financing the Home-Grown Cereals Authority's non-trading functions under the Cereals Marketing Act 1965 Part I, for the year beginning July 1, 1997, this Order specifies the rates of dealer levy, grower levy, and processor levies which appear to the Ministers to be sufficient to meet the amount apportioned to certain cereals grown in the United Kingdom. In the case of each of these kinds of cereals, the rate of dealer levy is 51.1125 pence per tonne, the rate of grower levy is 47 pence per tonne, the standard rate of processor levy is 9.69375 pence per tonne and the reduced rate of processor levy is 4.7 pence per tonne and in the case of each of certain oilseeds the rate of levy is 76.375 pence per tonne. Levy will be imposed in accordance with the provisions of the Home-Grown Cereals Authority Cereals Levy Scheme 1987 (SI 1987 691) and the Home-Grown Cereals Authority Oilseeds Levy Scheme 1990 (SI 1990 1317).

127. Crops–sugar beet–research and development

SUGAR BEET (RESEARCH AND EDUCATION) ORDER 1997, SI 1997 484; made under the Food Act 1984 s.68. In force: April 1, 1997; £1.55.

This Order provides for the carrying into effect for the year 1997-98 of the programme of research and education in matters affecting the growing of home-grown beet. It also provides for the assessment of contributions towards the expenditure on this programme and for their collection from the processors and growers of sugar beet in England and Wales. The rates of contributions at 11 pence per adjusted beet tonne are unchanged from the contributions in the Sugar Beet (Research and Education) Order 1996 (SI 1996 679).

128. Dairy produce–agricultural quotas

DAIRY PRODUCE QUOTAS REGULATIONS 1997, SI 1997 733; made under the European Communities Act 1972 s.2. In force: April 1, 1997; £6.10.

These Regulations, which revoke and replace the Dairy Produce Quotas Regulations 1994 (SI 1994 672 as amended by SI 1994 2448, SI 1994 2919, SI 1995 254, SI 1996 2657 and SI 1997 250), implement Council Regulation 3950/92 ([1992] OJ L405/1) establishing an additional levy in the milk and milk products market and Commission Regulation 536/93 ([1993] OJ L57/12) establishing detailed rules for the levy which consolidate earlier legislation relating to the levy. The levy continues to be payable on dairy produce sold by direct sale or by a producer or delivered by him wholesale to a dairy business, unless the sales of deliveries are within a reference quantity described in that legislation. New provisions relate to the variation of the ring fencing of Scottish Islands areas; special quota holders making temporary transfers of quotas; calculating temporary allocation of quota awards; the conversion of quotas from wholesale to direct sales; the powers of authorised officers of the Intervention Board; and the criminal offence of disposing of incorrectly registered quotas.

129. Dairy produce–agricultural quotas

DAIRY PRODUCE QUOTAS (AMENDMENT) REGULATIONS 1997, SI 1997 250; made under the European Communities Act 1972 s.2. In force: February 28, 1997; £1.10.

These Regulations amend the Dairy Produce Quotas Regulations 1994 (SI 1994 672).

130. Dairy produce–agricultural quotas

DAIRY PRODUCE QUOTAS (AMENDMENT) (TIME LIMITS) REGULATIONS 1997, SI 1997 1093; made under the European Communities Act 1972 s.2. In force: April 23, 1997; £0.65.

These Regulations are made in order to correct two defects in the Dairy Produce Quotas Regulations 1997 (SI 1997 733). Regulation 6 is amended to provide that, where a purchaser has had his purchaser quota increased by virtue of any transaction or conversion of quota referred to in Reg.6(2) of the principal Regulations, he shall submit to the Intervention Board, by the latter of May 21, 1997 and the date 28 days after such transaction or conversion, a statement setting out the particulars of the transaction or conversion. Regulation 11(1) is amended to provide that an application for the transfer of quota without transfer of land, within the meaning of Reg.11(1), shall be submitted to the Intervention Board for approval by the latter of May 8, 1997 and the date ten working days before the intended date of such transfer.

131. Dairy produce–agricultural quotas–mortgagee in possession–temporary leases of milk quota–mortgagee entitled to deal and receive income

[Council Regulation 3950/92 establishing an additional levy in the milk and milk products sector Art.7; Dairy Produce Quotas Regulations 1994 (SI 1994 672) Reg.7.]

H appealed against the dismissal of his claim to the sums paid for temporary leases of milk quota and for that part of the sale of a farm attributable to the milk quotas. H granted an "all moneys" legal charge over his dairy farm and subsequently BB appointed a receiver, who sold the herd, and granted temporary leases of the quota, receiving some £349,000 over approximately seven years, until the farm was finally sold for £530,000. H made a second agreement with BB limiting his liability to £797,810, which was the amount of security held. H contended that the quota was not subject to the charge and that he should have been allowed to deal with it or to receive the income from the leases.

Held, dismissing the appeal, that the judge below had correctly decided that after BB went into possession, H could no longer deal with the quota because he could not grant a lease. The benefit of the quota was attached to the land and by Council Regulation 3950/92 establishing an additional levy in the milk and milk products sector Art.7 and Dairy Produce Quotas Regulations 1994 Reg.7 the milk quota had been correctly transferred to the purchasers of the farm.

HARRIES v. BARCLAYS BANK PLC, Trans. Ref: CHANF 96/0087/B, July 16, 1997, Morritt, L.J., CA.

132. Eggs–marketing standards

EGGS (MARKETING STANDARDS) (AMENDMENT) REGULATIONS 1997, SI 1997 1414; made under the Food Safety Act 1990 s.6, s.16, s.17, s.26, s.48. In force: June 30, 1997; £1.10.

These Regulations further amend the Eggs (Marketing Standards) Regulations 1995 (SI 1995 1544) and apply to Great Britain. The Regulations make provision for the enforcement and execution of Commission Regulation 1511/96 ([1996] OJ L189/91) amending Commission Regulation 1274/91 ([1991] OJ L121/11) introducing detailed rules for implementing Council Regulation 1907/90 ([1990] OJ L173/5) on certain marketing standards for eggs. Commission Regulation 1511/96 ([1996] OJ L189/91) is concerned with the grading of eggs by weight, the confidentiality of certain information supplied and the optional use of supplementary indications on egg packs regarding particular characteristics of the type of farming concerned.

133. Environmentally sensitive areas–Avon Valley

ENVIRONMENTALLY SENSITIVE AREAS (AVON VALLEY) DESIGNATION (AMENDMENT) ORDER 1997, SI 1997 1450; made under the Agriculture Act 1986 s.18. In force: July 1, 1997; £1.10.

This Order further amends the Environmentally Sensitive Areas (Avon Valley) Designation Order 1993 (SI 1993 84 amended by SI 1994 927, SI 1995 197 and SI 1996 3104), which designated an area in the Avon Valley as an environmentally sensitive area. Subject to a saving provision, the Order amends the rates of payment to be made by the Minister of Agriculture, Fisheries and Food pursuant to a management agreement made under the Agriculture Act 1986 s.18(3) and adds an option to the operations that may be included in a conservation plan.

134. Environmentally sensitive areas–Breckland

ENVIRONMENTALLY SENSITIVE AREAS (BRECKLAND) DESIGNATION (AMENDMENT) ORDER 1997, SI 1997 1445; made under the Agriculture Act 1986 s.18. In force: July 1, 1997; £1.10.

This Order further amends the Environmentally Sensitive Areas (Breckland) Order 1993 (SI 1993 455 as amended by SI 1994 923, SI 1995 198 and SI 1996 3104), which designated an area in Breckland as an environmentally sensitive area. Subject to a saving provision, the Order amends the rates of payment to be made by the Minister of Agriculture, Fisheries and Food pursuant to a management agreement made under the Agriculture Act 1986 s.18(3) and adds an option to the operations that may be included in a conservation plan.

135. Environmentally sensitive areas–Cambrian Mountains

ENVIRONMENTALLY SENSITIVE AREAS (CAMBRIAN MOUNTAINS) DESIGNATION (AMENDMENT) ORDER 1997, SI 1997 970; made under the Agriculture Act 1986 s.18. In force: May 1, 1997; £1.10.

This Order amends the Environmentally Sensitive Areas (Cambrian Mountains) Designation Order 1986 (SI 1986 2259) which designated an area in the Cambrian Mountains as an environmentally sensitive area. It amends and adds definitions, amends the rates of payments to be made by the Secretary of State, and amends the description of one of the operations that may be included in a conservation plan.

136. Environmentally sensitive areas–Cambrian Mountains–extension

ENVIRONMENTALLY SENSITIVE AREAS (CAMBRIAN MOUNTAINS-EXTENSION) DESIGNATION (AMENDMENT) ORDER 1997, SI 1997 971; made under the Agriculture Act 1986 s.18. In force: May 1, 1997; £1.10.

This Order amends the Environmentally Sensitive Areas (Cambrian Mountains Extension) Designation Order 1987 (SI 1987 2026) which designated an area in the Cambrian Mountains as an environmentally sensitive area. It amends and adds definitions, amends the rates of payments to be made by the Secretary of State, and amends the description of one of the operations that may be included in a conservation plan.

137. Environmentally sensitive areas–Clun

ENVIRONMENTALLY SENSITIVE AREAS (CLUN) DESIGNATION (AMENDMENT) ORDER 1997, SI 1997 1446; made under the Agriculture Act 1986 s.18. In force: July 1, 1997; £1.10.

This Order further amends the Environmentally Sensitive Areas (Clun) Designation Order 1993 (SI 1993 456 amended by SI 1994 921, SI 1995 190 and SI 1996 3104), which designated an area in the vicinity of Clun as an environmentally sensitive area. It amends the rates of payment to be made by the Minister of Agriculture, Fisheries and Food pursuant to a management agreement made under the Agriculture Act 1986 s.18(3) and adds an option to the operations that may be included in a conservation plan.

138. Environmentally sensitive areas–Clwydian Range

ENVIRONMENTALLY SENSITIVE AREAS (CLWYDIAN RANGE) DESIGNATION (AMENDMENT) ORDER 1997, SI 1997 973; made under the Agriculture Act 1986 s.18. In force: May 1, 1997; £1.10.

This Order amends the Environmentally Sensitive Areas (Clwydian Range) Designation Order 1994 (SI 1994 238) which designated an area in the Clwydian Range as an environmentally sensitive area. It amends and adds definitions, amends the rates of payments to be made by the Secretary of State, and amends the description of one of the operations that may be included in a conservation plan.

139. Environmentally sensitive areas–Exmoor

ENVIRONMENTALLY SENSITIVE AREAS (EXMOOR) DESIGNATION (AMENDMENT) ORDER 1997, SI 1997 1451; made under the Agriculture Act 1986 s.18. In force: July 1, 1997; £1.10.

This Order further amends the Environmentally Sensitive Areas (Exmoor) Designation Order 1993 (SI 1993 85 amended by SI 1994 928, SI 1995 195, SI 1995 960 and SI 1996 3104), which designated an area on Exmoor as an environmentally sensitive area. It amends the rates of payment to be made by the Minister of Agriculture, Fisheries and Food pursuant to a management agreement made under the Agriculture Act 1986 s.18(3) and adds an option to the operations that may be included in a conservation plan.

140. Environmentally sensitive areas–Lake District

ENVIRONMENTALLY SENSITIVE AREAS (LAKE DISTRICT) DESIGNATION (AMENDMENT) ORDER 1997, SI 1997 1452; made under the Agriculture Act 1986 s.18. In force: July 1, 1997; £1.10.

This Order further amends the Environmentally Sensitive Areas (Lake District) Designation Order 1993 (SI 1993 85 amended by SI 1994 925, SI 1995 193 and SI 1996 3104), which designated an area in the Lake District as an environmentally sensitive area. Subject to a saving provision, the Order amends the rates of payment to be made by the Minister of Agriculture, Fisheries and Food pursuant to a management agreement made under the Agriculture Act 1986 s.18(3) and adds an option to the operations that may be included in a conservation plan.

141. Environmentally sensitive areas–Lleyn Peninsula

ENVIRONMENTALLY SENSITIVE AREAS (LLEYN PENINSULA) DESIGNATION (AMENDMENT) ORDER 1997, SI 1997 972; made under the Agriculture Act 1986 s.18. In force: May 1, 1997; £1.10.

This Order amends the Environmentally Sensitive Areas (Lleyn Peninsula) Designation Order 1987 (SI 1987 2027) which designated an area in the Lleyn Peninsula as an environmentally sensitive area.It amends and adds definitions, amends the rates of payments to be made by the Secretary of State, and amends the description of one of the operations that may be included in a conservation plan.

142. Environmentally sensitive areas–North Kent Marshes

ENVIRONMENTALLY SENSITIVE AREAS (NORTH KENT MARSHES) DESIGNATION (AMENDMENT) ORDER 1997, SI 1997 1453; made under the Agriculture Act 1986 s.18. In force: July 1, 1997; £0.65.

This Order further amends the Environmentally Sensitive Areas (North Kent Marshes) Designation Order 1993 (SI 1993 82 amended by SI 1994 918, SI 1995 199 and SI 1996 3104) by amending the rates of payment to be made by the Minister of Agriculture, Fisheries and Food pursuant to a management agreement made under the Agriculture Act 1986 s.18(3) and adding an option to the operations that may be included in a conservation plan.

143. Environmentally sensitive areas–North Peak

ENVIRONMENTALLY SENSITIVE AREAS (NORTH PEAK) DESIGNATION (AMENDMENT) ORDER 1997, SI 1997 1447; made under the Agriculture Act 1986 s.18. In force: July 1, 1997; £1.10.

This Order further amends the Environmentally Sensitive Areas (North Peak) Designation Order 1993 (SI 1993 457, amended by SI 1994 922, SI 1995 189 and SI 1996 3104), which designated an area in the North Peak as an environmentally sensitive area. Subject to a saving provision, the Order amends the rates of payment to be made by the Minister of Agriculture, Fisheries and Food pursuant to a management agreement made under the Agriculture Act 1986 s.18(3) and adds an option to the operations that may be included in a conservation plan.

144. Environmentally sensitive areas–Pennine Dales

ENVIRONMENTALLY SENSITIVE AREAS (PENNINE DALES) DESIGNATION ORDER 1997, SI 1997 1441; made under the Agriculture Act 1986 s.18. In force: July 1, 1997; £2.40.

This Order, made pursuant to Council Regulation 2078/92 ([1992] OJ L215/85) as last amended by Commission Regulation 2772/95 ([1995] OJ L288/35), implements in part a zonal programme approved under those Regulations and designates an area in the Pennine Dales as an environmentally sensitive area. The previous designation of an environmentally sensitive area in the Pennine Dales is, in so far as it is made under the Agriculture Act 1986 s.18, revoked, with saving provisions.

145. Environmentally sensitive areas–Preseli

ENVIRONMENTALLY SENSITIVE AREAS (PRESELI) DESIGNATION (AMENDMENT) ORDER 1997, SI 1997 974; made under the Agriculture Act 1986 s.18. In force: May 1, 1997; £1.10.

This Order amends the Environmentally Sensitive Areas (Preseli) Designation Order 1994 (SI 1994 239) which designated an area in the County of Pembrokeshire as an environmentally sensitive area. It amends and adds definitions, amends the rates of payments to be made by the Secretary of State, and amends the description of one of the operations that may be included in a conservation plan.

146. Environmentally sensitive areas–Preseli

ENVIRONMENTALLY SENSITIVE AREAS (PRESELI) DESIGNATION (AMENDMENT NO.2) ORDER 1997, SI 1997 2868; made under the Agriculture Act 1986 s.18. In force: January 5, 1998; £1.10.

This Order further amends the Environmentally Sensitive Areas (Preseli) Designation Order 1994 (SI 1994 239), which designated an area in the County of Pembrokeshire as an environmentally sensitive area, by changing the rates of payments in relation to enclosed partially improved grassland or enclosed unimproved grassland to be made by the Secretary of State pursuant to a management agreement made under the Agriculture Act 1986 s.18(3).

147. Environmentally sensitive areas–Radnor

ENVIRONMENTALLY SENSITIVE AREAS (RADNOR) DESIGNATION (AMENDMENT) ORDER 1997, SI 1997 976; made under the Agriculture Act 1986 s.18. In force: May 1, 1997; £1.10.

This Order amends the Environmentally Sensitive Areas (Radnor) Designation Order 1993 (SI 1993 1211) which designated an area in the County of Powys as an environmentally sensitive area. It amends and adds definitions, amends the rates of payments to be made by the Secretary of State, removes certain additional provisions relating to the management of broadleaved woodland, amends the description of one of the operations that may be included in a conservation plan and adds to the list of such operations.

148. Environmentally sensitive areas–revocation

ENVIRONMENTALLY SENSITIVE AREAS (ENGLAND) DESIGNATION ORDER (REVOCATION OF SPECIFIED PROVISIONS) REGULATIONS 1997, SI 1997 1456; made under the European Communities Act 1972 s.2(2). In force: July 1, 1997; £0.65.

These Regulations revoke, with a saving, certain provisions of specified designation orders made under the Agriculture Act 1986 s.18 designating areas in England as environmentally sensitive areas. The Orders implement in part a zonal programme approved under Council Regulation 2078/92 ([1992] OJ L215/85) on agricultural production methods compatible with the requirements of protection of the environment and the maintenance of the countryside, as last amended by Commission Regulation 2772/95 ([1995] OJ L288/35).

149. Environmentally sensitive areas–Somerset Levels and Moors

ENVIRONMENTALLY SENSITIVE AREAS (SOMERSET LEVELS AND MOORS) DESIGNATION ORDER 1997, SI 1997 1442; made under the Agriculture Act 1986 s.18. In force: July 1, 1997; £2.40.

This Order, made pursuant to Council Regulation 2078/92 ([1992] OJ L215/85) as last amended by Commission Regulation 2772/95 ([1995] OJ L288/35), implements in part a zonal programme approved under those Regulations and designates an area in the Somerset Levels and Moors as an environmentally sensitive area. The previous designation of an environmentally sensitive area in the Somerset Levels and Moors is, in so far as it is made under the Agriculture Act 1986 s.18, revoked, with saving provisions.

150. Environmentally sensitive areas–South Downs

ENVIRONMENTALLY SENSITIVE AREAS (SOUTH DOWNS) DESIGNATION ORDER 1997, SI 1997 1443; made under the Agriculture Act 1986 s.18. In force: July 1, 1997; £2.40.

This Order, which is made pursuant to Council Regulation 2078/92 ([1992] OJ L215/35) as last amended by Commission Regulation 2772/95 ([1995] OJ L288/83) implements in part a zonal programme approved under those Regulations and designates an area in the South Downs as an environmentally sensitive area. The previous designation of the same environmentally sensitive in the South Downs is, in so far as it is made under the Agriculture Act 1986 s.18, revoked, with saving provisions.

151. Environmentally sensitive areas–South Wessex Downs

ENVIRONMENTALLY SENSITIVE AREAS (SOUTH WESSEX DOWNS) DESIGNATION (AMENDMENT) ORDER 1997, SI 1997 1454; made under the Agriculture Act 1986 s.18. In force: July 1, 1997; £0.65.

This Order further amends the Environmentally Sensitive Areas (South Wessex Downs) Designation Order 1993 (SI 1993 86 amended by SI 1994 924, SI 1995 196 and SI 1996 3104) by amending the rates of payment to be made by the Minister of Agriculture, Fisheries and Food pursuant to a management agreement made under the Agriculture Act 1986 s.18(3) and by adding an option to the operations that may be included in a conservation plan.

152. Environmentally sensitive areas–South West Peak

ENVIRONMENTALLY SENSITIVE AREAS (SOUTH WEST PEAK) DESIGNATION (AMENDMENT) ORDER 1997, SI 1997 1455; made under the Agriculture Act 1986 s.18. In force: July 1, 1997; £0.65.

This Order further amends the Environmentally Sensitive Areas (South West Peak) Designation Order 1993 (SI 1993 87 amended by SI 1994 926, SI 1995 192 and SI 1996 3104) by amending the rates of payment to be made by the Minister of Agriculture, Fisheries and Food pursuant to a management agreement made under the Agriculture Act 1986 s.18(3) and by adding an option to the operations that may be included in a conservation plan.

153. Environmentally sensitive areas–Suffolk River Valleys

ENVIRONMENTALLY SENSITIVE AREAS (SUFFOLK RIVER VALLEYS) DESIGNATION (AMENDMENT) REGULATIONS 1997, SI 1997 1448; made under the Agriculture Act 1986 s.18. In force: July 1, 1997; £1.10.

This Order further amends the Environmentally Sensitive Areas (Suffolk River Valleys) Designation Order 1993 (SI 1993 458 amended by SI 1994 920, SI 1995 194 and SI 1996 3104), which designated an area in the Suffolk River Valleys as an environmentally sensitive area. Subject to a saving provision, the Order amends the rates of payment to be made by the Minister of Agriculture, Fisheries and Food pursuant to a management agreement made under the Agriculture Act 1986 s.18(3) and adds an option to the operations that may be included in a conservation plan.

154. Environmentally sensitive areas–Test Valley

ENVIRONMENTALLY SENSITIVE AREAS (TEST VALLEY) DESIGNATION (AMENDMENT) REGULATIONS 1997, SI 1997 1449; made under the Agriculture Act 1986 s.18. In force: July 1, 1997; £1.10.

This Order further amends the Environmentally Sensitive Areas (Test Valley) Designation Order 1993 (SI 1993 459 amended by SI 1994 919, SI 1995 191 and SI 1996 3104), which designated an area in the Test Valley as an environmentally sensitive area. Subject to a saving provision, the Order amends the rates of payment to be made by the Minister of Agriculture, Fisheries and Food pursuant to a management agreement made under the Agriculture Act 1986 s.18(3) and adds further options to the operations that may be included in a conservation plan.

155. Environmentally sensitive areas–The Broads

ENVIRONMENTALLY SENSITIVE AREAS (THE BROADS) DESIGNATION ORDER 1997, SI 1997 1440; made under the Agriculture Act 1986 s.18. In force: July 1, 1997; £2.40.

This Order, made pursuant to Council Regulation 2078/92 ([1992] OJ L215/85), as last amended by Commission Regulation 2772/95 ([1995] OJ L288/35), implements in part a zonal programme approved under those Regulations and designates an area in The Broads as an environmentally sensitive area. The previous designation of an environmentally sensitive area in The Broads is, in so far as it is made under the Agriculture Act 1986 s.18, revoked, with saving provisions.

156. Environmentally sensitive areas–West Penrith

ENVIRONMENTALLY SENSITIVE AREAS (WEST PENWITH) DESIGNATION ORDER 1997, SI 1997 1444; made under the Agriculture Act 1986 s.18. In force: July 1, 1997; £1.95.

This Order, which is made pursuant to Council Regulation 2078/92 ([1986] OJ L215/85) as last amended by Commission Regulation 2772/95 ([1995] OJ L288/35), implements in part a zonal programme approved under those Regulations and designates an area in the West Penwith as an environmentally sensitive area. The previous designation of an environmentally sensitive area in West Penwith is, in so far as it is made under the Agriculture Act 1986 s.18, revoked, with saving provisions.

157. Environmentally sensitive areas–Ynys Mon

ENVIRONMENTALLY SENSITIVE AREAS (YNYS MON) DESIGNATION (AMENDMENT) ORDER 1997, SI 1997 975; made under the Agriculture Act 1986 s.18. In force: May 1, 1997; £1.10.

This Order amends the Environmentally Sensitive Areas (Ynys Mon) Designation Order 1993 (SI 1993 1210) which designated an area comprising the County of the Isle of Anglesey as an environmentally sensitive area. It amends and adds definitions, amends the rates of payments to be made by the Secretary of State, removes certain additional provisions relating to the management of broadleaved woodland, amends the description of one of the operations that may be included in a conservation plan and adds to the list of such operations.

158. Fertilisers

FERTILISERS (AMENDMENT) REGULATIONS 1997, SI 1997 1543; made under the Agriculture Act 1970 s.66, s.68, s.69, s.70, s.74, s.74A, s.84; and the European Communities Act 1972 s.2. In force: July 14, 1997; £1.10.

These Regulations further amend the Fertilisers Regulations 1991 (SI 1991 2197) and implement Commission Directive 96/28 ([1996] OJ L140/30) adapting to technical progress Council Directive 76/116 ([1976] OJ L24/21) on the approximation of the laws of the Member States relating to fertilisers. They amend Sch.1 which relates to prescribed descriptions of material, meanings of names, particulars and information to be contained in the statutory instrument and limits of variation, as regards fertilisers specified in the Table to that Schedule, by specifying additional fertilisers which may, in accordance with Commission Directive 96/28, be designated as "EEC fertilisers".

159. Fish–infectious disease control

FISH HEALTH REGULATIONS 1997, SI 1997 1881; made under the European Communities Act 1972 s.2. In force: August 21, 1997; £5.60.

These Regulations, which revoke and re-enact the Fish Health Regulations 1992 (SI 1992 3300 as amended by SI 1993 2255, SI 1994 1448 and SI 1995 886), implement Council Directive 91/67 ([1991] OJ L46/1) concerning the animal health conditions governing the placing on the market of aquaculture animals and products and Council Directive 95/70 ([1995] OJ L332/33) introducing minimum Community measures for the control of certain diseases affecting bivalve molluscs, in so far as they are not already implemented.

160. Fisheries–agreement to share quota–partnership dissolved–judicial review of allocation–entitlement to increased allocation–New Zealand

[Fisheries Act 1983 s.281 (New Zealand).]

P, a fish processing and packing company, appealed against a decision that it was not entitled to a half share of an increase in the quota for fishing orange roughy, granted after the dissolution of its partnership with M, a fisherman. M was the sole supplier of orange roughy to P and in 1986 P purchased a 50 per cent interest in M's boat and was given an undertaking that half of the orange roughy quota, informally notified to be 447 tonnes, would be transferred forthwith on its allocation. M was later allocated a 447 tonne quota and vigorously pursued an appeal against his allocation which was dismissed. The partnership was dissolved in 1989 and P retained its half interest in the quota. In 1992, at his own expense, M succeeded on a judicial review of the refusal to alter the allocation decision and was granted a declaration increasing his quota of orange roughy by 130 tonnes. P claimed a half share of the increased quota.

Held, allowing the appeal by a majority, that P had a contractual right to a half share of the full quota, which had later been quantified with the addition of a further 130 tonnes. Lord Nolan, in his dissenting speech, opined that judicial review could neither rectify nor give retrospective effect to an executive decision. Lord Nicholls also dissenting, said that P had paid a price that bore relation to a quota of 447 tonnes and it was unreasonable to construe an ambiguously worded contract to give P the benefit of the additional 130 tonnes, worth approximately $400,000.

PENG AUN LIM v. McLEAN, Trans. Ref: No.25 of 1996, March 4, 1997, Lord Clyde, PC.

161. Fisheries–committees

SOUTHERN SEA FISHERIES DISTRICT (CONSTITUTION OF COMMITTEE AND EXPENSES) (VARIATION) ORDER 1997, SI 1997 1306; made under the Sea Fisheries Regulation Act 1966 s.1. In force: May 16, 1997; £1.10.

This Order varies those provisions of the Southern Fisheries District Order 1989 (SI 1989 671) which relate to the constitution of the Committee and the expenses payable by the constituent authorities, in consequence of the changes to the Local Government areas contained in the Isle of Wight (Structural Change) Order 1994 (SI 1994 1210), the Dorset (Boroughs of Poole and Bournemouth) (Structural Change) Order 1995 (SI 1995 1771) and the Hampshire (Cities of Portsmouth & Southampton) (Structural Change) Order 1995 (SI 1995 1775).

162. Fisheries–limits

FISHERY LIMITS ORDER 1997, SI 1997 1750; made under the Fishery Limits Act 1976 s.1. In force: in accordance with Art.1; £1.10.

This Order brings British fishery limits into conformity with the United Nations Convention on the Law of the Sea of December 10, 1982 (Cmnd.8941).

163. Fishing–conservation–enforcement

SEA FISHING (ENFORCEMENT OF COMMUNITY CONSERVATION MEASURES) ORDER 1997, SI 1997 1949; made under the Fisheries Act 1981 s.30. In force: August 12, 1997; £2.40.

This Order, which revokes and replaces the Sea Fishing (Enforcement of Community Conservation Measures) Order 1986 (SI 1986 2090 as amended by SI 1992 1084 and SI 1994 1680), makes provision for the enforcement of certain Community restrictions and obligations concerning technical measures for the conservation of fishery resources contained in Council Regulation 894/97 ([1997] OJ L132/1).

164. Fishing–conservation–enforcement

SEA FISHING (ENFORCEMENT OF COMMUNITY CONSERVATION MEASURES) (AMENDMENT) ORDER 1997, SI 1997 2841; made under the Fisheries Act 1981 s.30. In force: December 22, 1997; £0.65.

This Order extends the protection against civil or criminal proceedings afforded by the Sea Fishing (Enforcement of Community Conservation Measures) Order 1997 (SI 1997 1949) Art.10 to those officers other than British Sea Fishery Officers empowered to enforce aspects of that Order. It also provides that assault, or intentional obstruction, of such officers is an offence.

165. Fishing–conservation–prohibition on fishing

MACKEREL (SPECIFIED SEA AREAS) (PROHIBITION OF FISHING) ORDER 1997, SI 1997 2963; made under the Sea Fish (Conservation) Act 1967 s.5, s.15, s.22. In force: December 17, 1997; £1.55.

This Order prohibits certain British fishing boats from fishing for mackerel in certain ICES areas from December 17, 1997 until immediately before January 1, 1998.

166. Fishing–conservation–prohibition on fishing

SOLE, ETC. (SPECIFIED SEA AREAS) (PROHIBITION OF FISHING) ORDER 1997, SI 1997 3054; made under the Sea Fish (Conservation) Act 1967 s.5, s.15, s.22. In force: January 14, 1998; £1.55.

This Order specifies certain sea areas within which fishing for sole and plaice is prohibited.

167. Fishing–conservation–prohibition on fishing

SOLE, PLAICE, ETC. (SPECIFIED SEA AREAS) (PROHIBITION OF FISHING) ORDER 1997, SI 1997 2757; made under the Sea Fish (Conservation) Act 1967 s.5, s.15, s.22. In force: November 21, 1997; £1.55.

This Order prohibits fishing for sole, plaice, herring and other species in specified sea areas by British fishing boats which do not exceed 10 metres in length or which are used wholly for the purposes of conveying persons wishing to fish for pleasure. The prohibition ceases to have effect immediately before January 1, 1998.

168. Fishing–conservation–prohibition on fishing

SOLE, PLAICE, ETC. (SPECIFIED SEA AREAS) (PROHIBITION OF FISHING) (NO.2) ORDER 1997, SI 1997 2891; made under the Sea Fish (Conservation) Act 1967 s.5, s.15, s.20, s.22. In force: December 10, 1997; £1.55.

This Order, which revokes and replaces the Sole, Plaice, etc. (Specified Sea Areas) (Prohibition of Fishing) Order 1997 (SI 1997 2757), prohibits certain British fishing boats from fishing for sole, plaice, herring and other species in certain ICES areas from December 10, 1997 until immediately before January 1, 1998.

169. Fishing–enforcement of restrictions–Norway and Faroe Islands

THIRD COUNTRY FISHING (ENFORCEMENT) ORDER 1997, SI 1997 931; made under the Fisheries Act 1981 s.30. In force: April 9, 1997; £1.95.

This Order, which revokes and replaces the Third Country Fishing (Enforcement) Order 1996 (SI 1996 1036), provides for the enforcement of certain restrictions and obligations relating to sea fishing set out in Council Regulation 393/97 ([1997] OJ L66/61) and Council Regulation 391/97 ([1997] OJ L66/49) which authorise fishing by vessels of Norway and the Faroe Islands for specified descriptions of fish in specified areas and contain requirements concerning fishing quotas and authorised zones, methods of fishing, the holding of licences and observance of licence conditions, the keeping of log books and the making of radio reports.

170. Fishing—enforcement of restrictions—Norway and Faroe Islands

THIRD COUNTRY FISHING (ENFORCEMENT) (AMENDMENT) ORDER 1997, SI 1997 1629; made under the Fisheries Act 1981 s.30. In force: July 4, 1997; £0.65.

This Order amends the Third Country Fishing (Enforcement) Order 1997 (SI 1997 931) which provides for the enforcement of certain of the enforceable Community restrictions and other obligations relating to sea fishing set out in Council Regulation 391/97 ([1997] OJ L66/49) and Council Regulation 393/97 ([1997] OJ L66/61). The amendments are made in consequence of changes to those Regulations which provide for vessels from Norway and Faroe Islands to fish for herring in ICES division IIa.

171. Fishing—fishing rights—Norway and Faroe Islands

FISHING BOATS (SPECIFIED COUNTRIES) DESIGNATION (VARIATION) ORDER 1997, SI 1997 1630; made under the Fishery Limits Act 1976 s.2, s.6. In force: July 4, 1997; £1.10.

This Order varies the Fishing Boats (Specified Countries) Designation Order 1996 (SI 1996 1035) to enable registered fishing boats from the Faroe Islands and Norway to fish for herring in ICES division IIa and is pursuant to agreements reached between the European Community and these countries on reciprocal fishing rights.

172. Fishing—fishing vessels—decommissioning grants

FISHING VESSELS (DECOMMISSIONING) SCHEME 1997, SI 1997 1924; made under the Fisheries Act 1981 s.15. In force: August 6, 1997; £2.40.

This Scheme provides for the making of grants by the Minister of Agriculture, Fisheries and Food and the Secretaries of State respectively concerned with the sea fish industry in Scotland, Wales and Northern Ireland, in respect of the decommissioning of vessels registered in the United Kingdom. Applications for grants will be considered in respect of vessels meeting specified requirements set out in paragraph 3 of the Scheme.

173. Fishing—quotas—enforcement

SEA FISHING (ENFORCEMENT OF COMMUNITY QUOTA MEASURES) ORDER 1997, SI 1997 883; made under the Fisheries Act 1981 s.30. In force: April 9, 1997; £1.95.

This Order, which revokes the Sea Fishing (Enforcement of Community Quota Measures) Order 1996 (SI 1996 247 as amended by SI 1996 2433), but without prejudice to the application of Art.6 to Art.10 in relation to the enforcement of Art.3, makes provision for the enforcement of certain restrictions and obligations relating to sea fishing set out in Council Regulation 390/97 ([1997] OJ L66/1) which fixes total allowable catches and quotas and lays down conditions under which they may be fished.

174. Food safety—emergency prohibitions—fish—partial revocation

FOOD PROTECTION (EMERGENCY PROHIBITIONS) (OIL AND CHEMICAL POLLUTION OF FISH) ORDER 1997 (PARTIAL REVOCATION) ORDER 1997, SI 1997 2735; made under the Food and Environment Protection Act 1985 s.1, s.24. In force: November 14, 1997; £0.65.

This Order revokes the Food Protection (Emergency Prohibitions) (Oil and Chemical Pollution of Fish) Order 1997 (SI 1997 2509) insofar as it applies to round fish.

175. Food safety—emergency prohibitions—fish and plants—partial revocation No.1 Order

FOOD PROTECTION (EMERGENCY PROHIBITIONS) (OIL AND CHEMICAL POLLUTION OF FISH AND PLANTS) (PARTIAL REVOCATION) ORDER 1997, SI

1997 239; made under the Food and Environment Protection Act 1985 s.1, s.24. In force: February 7, 1997; £1.10.

This Order partially revokes the Food Protection (Emergency Prohibitions) (Oil and Chemical Pollution of Fish and Plants) Order 1996 (SI 1996 448) which contained emergency prohibitions on various activities in order to prevent human consumption of food rendered unsuitable for that purpose by virtue of edible plants, edible seaweed and fish having been affected by oil and other chemical pollutants. This partial revocation provides that the emergency prohibitions contained in the principal Order shall not apply to whelks in a part of the area designated by that Order known as Milford Haven.

176. Food safety−emergency prohibitions−fish and plants−partial revocation No.2 Order

FOOD PROTECTION (EMERGENCY PROHIBITIONS) (OIL AND CHEMICAL POLLUTION OF FISH AND PLANTS) (PARTIAL REVOCATION NO.2) ORDER 1997, SI 1997 1481; made under the Food and Environment Protection Act 1985 s.1, s.24. In force: June 11, 1997; £1.10.

This Order partially revokes the Food Protection (Emergency Prohibitions) (Oil and Chemical Pollution of Fish and Plants) Order 1996 (SI 1996 448) which contained emergency prohibitions on various activities in order to prevent human consumption of food rendered unsuitable for that purpose by virtue of edible plants, edible seaweed and fish having been affected by oil and other chemical pollutants. This partial revocation provides that the emergency prohibitions contained in the principal Order shall not apply in relation to edible plants and edible seaweed.

177. Food safety−emergency prohibitions−fish and plants−revocation

FOOD PROTECTION (EMERGENCY PROHIBITIONS) (OIL AND CHEMICAL POLLUTION OF FISH AND PLANTS) (REVOCATION) ORDER 1997, SI 1997 2206; made under the Food and Environment Protection Act 1985 s.1, s.24. In force: September 12, 1997; £0.65.

This Order revokes the Food Protection (Emergency Prohibitions) (Oil and Chemical Pollution of Fish and Plants) Order 1996 (SI 1996 448) which contained emergency prohibitions to prevent human consumption of food affected by oil and other chemical pollutants.

178. Food safety−emergency prohibitions−nuclear waste

FOOD PROTECTION (EMERGENCY PROHIBITIONS) (DOUNREAY NUCLEAR ESTABLISHMENT) ORDER 1997, SI 1997 2622; made under the Food and Environment Protection Act 1985 s.1, s.24. In force: October 29, 1997; £1.10.

This Order prohibits the movement of all species of demersal and pelagic fish, molluscs and crustaceans out of a designated sea area in order to prevent human consumption of seafood species which may have been contaminated with irradiated nuclear fuel.

179. Food safety−emergency prohibitions−paralytic shellfish poisoning

FOOD PROTECTION (EMERGENCY PROHIBITIONS) (PARALYTIC SHELLFISH POISONING) ORDER 1997 REVOCATION ORDER 1997, SI 1997 1978; made under the Food and Environment Protection Act 1985 s.1, s.24. In force: in accordance with Art.1; £0.65.

This Order revokes the Food Protection (Emergency Prohibitions) (Paralytic Shellfish Poisoning) Order 1997 (SI 1997 1565) in so far as it remains in force, the effect of which is to remove completely the prohibition from fishing for, taking, moving, landing, using in food production and supplying the shellfish affected by that Order, from the designated area.

180. Food safety—emergency prohibitions—paralytic shellfish poisoning

FOOD PROTECTION (EMERGENCY PROHIBITIONS) (PARALYTIC SHELLFISH POISONING) ORDER 1997, SI 1997 1565; made under the Food and Environment Protection Act 1985 s.1, s.24. In force: June 20, 1997 at 8pm; £1.10.

This Order contains emergency prohibitions restricting various activities in order to prevent human consumption of food rendered unsuitable for that purpose by virtue of shellfish having been affected by the toxin which causes paralytic shellfish poisoning in human beings. The Order designates an area of sea within which taking mussels, scallops or razor clams is prohibited and it prohibits the movement of mussels, scallops or razor clams out of that area. Other restrictions are imposed throughout the United Kingdom in relation to the use of any mussels, scallops or razor clams taken from that area.

181. Grants—farm woodland scheme

See FORESTRY §2574, §2575

182. Hill farming—compensation—rates of payment

HILL LIVESTOCK (COMPENSATORY ALLOWANCES) (AMENDMENT) REGULATIONS 1997, SI 1997 33; made under the European Communities Act 1972 s.2. In force: February 4, 1997; £1.10.

These Regulations amend the Hill Livestock (Compensatory Allowances) Regulations 1996 (SI 1996 1500) by setting the rates of payment in respect of the 1997 scheme for the annual compensatory allowance for certain breeding cows and ewes.

183. Nitrate sensitive areas

NITRATE SENSITIVE AREAS (AMENDMENT) REGULATIONS 1996, SI 1996 3105; made under the European Communities Act 1972 s.2. In force: January 1, 1997; £1.55.

These Regulations amend the Nitrate Sensitive Areas Regulations 1994 (SI 1994 1729 as amended) which implemented in part a zonal programme approved under Council Regulation 2078/92 ([1992] OJ L215/85) Art.7. It also makes provision to implement Commission Regulation 746/96 ([1996] OJ L102/19) laying down detailed rules for the application of Council Regulation 2078/92 ([1992] OJ L215/85) on agricultural production methods compatible with the requirements of the protection of the environment and the maintenance of the countryside.

184. Nitrate sensitive areas

NITRATE SENSITIVE AREAS (AMENDMENT) REGULATIONS 1997, SI 1997 990; made under the European Communities Act 1972 s.2. In force: April 11, 1997; £0.65.

These Regulations amend the Nitrate Sensitive Areas Regulations 1994 (SI 1994 1729) by updating a reference to Council Regulation 2078/92 ([1992] OJ L215/85) to take account of an amendment made to that Council Regulation by Commission Regulation 435/97 ([1997] OJ L67/2) and by adjusting the annual rate payable on land set aside which is covered by farmers' undertakings on land management in nitrate sensitive areas from £390 to £388.

185. Pesticides—control of supply, storage and use

CONTROL OF PESTICIDES (AMENDMENT) REGULATIONS 1997, SI 1997 188; made under the Food and Environment Protection Act 1985 s.16, s.24. In force: January 31, 1997; £3.20.

These Regulations amend the Control of Pesticides Regulations 1986 (SI 1986 1510 as amended by SI 1990 2487 and SI 1994 3142) which have been made for the purpose of controlling pesticides in implementation of the Food and Environment Protection Act 1985 Part III and require the advertisement, sale, supply, storage and use in Great Britain of any pesticide product falling within the scope of the principal Regulations to be carried out in accordance with an approval granted by the Minister of Agriculture, Fisheries and Food and the Secretary of State in relation to that product and in accordance with consents made by the Ministers.

186. Pesticides—crops—maximum residue levels

PESTICIDES (MAXIMUM RESIDUE LEVELS IN CROPS, FOOD AND FEEDING STUFFS) (AMENDMENT) REGULATIONS 1997, SI 1997 567; made under the European Communities Act 1972 s.2. In force: April 30, 1997; £3.70.

These Regulations amend the Pesticides (Maximum Residue Levels in Crops, Food and Feeding Stuffs) Regulations 1994 (SI 1994 1985 amended by SI 1995 1483 and SI 1996 1487). They specify maximum levels of pesticide residue which may be left in crops, food and feeding stuffs in implementation of Council Directive 96/32 ([1996] OJ L144/12) and Council Directive 96/33 ([1996] OJ L144/35) which set the Community maximum residue levels for the pesticides concerned for the first time, or replace Community maximum residue levels which have been set previously. In addition, they remove certain maximum levels which were included in the 1994 Regulations by virtue of powers contained in the Food and Environment Protection Act 1985 and which have been replaced by the Community maximum residue levels.

187. Plant breeders rights—renewals—fees

PLANT BREEDERS' RIGHTS (FEES) (AMENDMENT) REGULATIONS 1997, SI 1997 382; made under the Plant Varieties and Seeds Act 1964 s.9, s.36. In force: April 1, 1997; £1.55.

These Regulations amend the Plant Breeders' Rights (Fees) Regulations 1990 (SI 1990 618) by prescribing revised fees in respect of matters arising under the Plant Breeders' Rights Regulations 1978 (SI 1978 294). Application, test, grant and renewal fees have been increased by three per cent, rounded to the nearest £5, except for roses where the increase is £5. The fee for the purchase of a report from a testing authority in another country has been increased to accord with the international charge of 350 Swiss Francs. The remaining fees payable in respect of other matters are unchanged.

188. Plant health—passports—inspections—fees

PLANT PASSPORT (PLANT HEALTH FEES) (ENGLAND AND WALES) (AMENDMENT) REGULATIONS 1997, SI 1997 1961; made under the Finance Act 1973 s.56. In force: September 1, 1997; £1.10.

These Regulations amend the Plant Passport (Plant Health Fees) (England and Wales) Regulations 1993 (SI 1993 1642) in order to increase the level of fees payable in respect of inspections carried out for the purposes of conferring authority to issue plant passports. The fee per quarter of an hour or part thereof spent on site by an inspector is raised to £20.25 and the minimum fee in respect of any visit is raised to £40.50.

189. Plant health—potatoes—imports—Amendment No.1 Order—infectious disease control

PLANT HEALTH (GREAT BRITAIN) (AMENDMENT) ORDER 1997, SI 1997 1145; made under the Plant Health Act 1967 s.2, s.3. In force: May 1, 1997; £0.65.

This Order amends the Plant Health (Great Britain) Order 1993 (SI 1993 1320) so as to implement Commission Directive 97/14 ([1997] OJ L87/17) amending Annex III to Council Directive 77/93 ([1977] OJ L26/20) on protective measures against the introduction into the Community of organisms harmful to plants or plant products and against their spread within the Community. The Order adds Algeria to the list of third countries from which potatoes other than seed potatoes may be imported.

190. Plant health−potatoes−imports−Amendment No.2 Order−potato breeding material

PLANT HEALTH (GREAT BRITAIN) (AMENDMENT) (NO.2) ORDER 1997, SI 1997 2907; made under the Plant Health Act 1967 s.2, s.3. In force: January 1, 1998; £1.10.

This Order amends the Plant Health (Great Britain) Order 1993 (SI 1993 1320) by implementing Commission Directive 97/46 ([1997] OJ L204/43), amending Commission Directive 95/44 ([1995] OJ L184/34) which lays down rules for the import of materials, for trial or scientific purposes and for work on varietal selections, which would otherwise be banned. The amendment incorporates provisions relating to potato breeding materiel.

191. Plant varieties−seeds−fees

SEEDS (FEES) (AMENDMENT) REGULATIONS 1997, SI 1997 1415; made under the Plant Varieties and Seeds Act 1964 s.16, s.36. In force: July 1, 1997; £1.95.

These Regulations amend the Seeds (Fees) Regulations 1985 (SI 1985 581). They prescribe revised fees in respect of matters arising under the Cereal Seeds Regulations 1993 (SI 1993 2005), the Fodder Plant Seeds Regulations 1993 (SI 1993 2009), the Oil and Fibre Plant Seeds Regulations 1993 (SI 1993 2007), the Beet Seeds Regulations 1993 (SI 1993 2006), the Vegetable Seeds Regulations 1993 (SI 1993 2008) and the Seeds (Registration, Licensing and Enforcement) Regulations 1985 (SI 1985 980). A uniform increase of 2.5 per cent has been applied to all fees and has been rounded to the nearest five pence except in the case of the annual fee for Licensed Seed Testing Stations, which has been rounded to the nearest pound.

192. Plant varieties−seeds−fees

SEEDS (NATIONAL LISTS OF VARIETIES) (FEES) (AMENDMENT) REGULATIONS 1997, SI 1997 383; made under the Plant Varieties and Seeds Act 1964 s.16, s.36. In force: April 1, 1997; £1.55.

These Regulations amend the Seeds (National List of Varieties) (Fees) Regulations 1994 (SI 1994 676) so as to prescribe revised fees in respect of matters arising under the Seeds (National Lists of Varieties) Regulations 1982 (SI 1982 844). Application, test, trial, observation plot, award and renewal fees have been increased by three per cent, rounded to the nearest £5. The fee for the purchase of a report from a testing authority in another country has been increased to accord with the international charge of 350 Swiss Francs. Other fees in Sch.5 are unchanged.

193. Plant Varieties Act 1997 (c.66)

This Act makes provision regarding rights in relation to plant varieties, the Plant Varieties and Seeds Tribunal and extends the time limit for institution of proceedings for contravention of seeds regulations.

This Act received Royal Assent on November 27, 1997.

194. Plants−plant protection products−approval for sale

PLANT PROTECTION PRODUCTS (BASIC CONDITIONS) REGULATIONS 1997, SI 1997 189; made under the Food and Environment Protection Act 1985 s.16, s.24. In force: January 31, 1997; £3.20.

These Regulations supplement the Plant Protection Products Regulations 1995 (SI 1995 887 as amended by SI 1996 1940) which implement Council Directive 91/414 ([1991] OJ L230/1) concerning the placing of plant protection products on the market, as amended. The principal Regulations require that plant protection products may not be placed on the market or used within Great Britain unless they have been approved by the Minister of Agriculture, Fisheries and Food and the Secretary of State and make provision concerning the process of application for, evaluation and granting of approvals, which may be given subject to conditions, and the packaging and labelling of approved plant protection products. The Regulations have been made for the purpose of controlling pesticides in implementation of the Food and Environment Protection Act 1985 Part III and apply to all plant protection products which are subject to the principal Regulations and are substances, preparations or micro-organisms prepared or used for destroying pests, protecting plants or plant products from harmful organisms, or rendering harmful creatures harmless, or regulating the growth of plants. Plant protection products to which these Regulations apply are described as prescribed plant protection products.

195. Plants–plant protection products–fees

PLANT PROTECTION PRODUCTS (FEES) (AMENDMENT) REGULATIONS 1997, SI 1997 884; made under the Finance Act 1973 s.56. In force: April 8, 1997; £1.55.

These Regulations, which revoke and replace the Schedule to the Plant Protection Products (Fees) Regulations 1995 (SI 1995 888), prescribe fees to be paid to the Ministry of Agriculture, Fisheries and Food in connection with services provided and approvals granted by the Ministry in pursuance with obligations under Council Directive 91/414 ([1991] OJ L230/1) concerning the placing of plant protection products on the market.

196. Plants–plant protection products–marketing

PLANT PROTECTION PRODUCTS (AMENDMENT) REGULATIONS 1997, SI 1997 7; made under the European Communities Act 1972 s.2. In force: Reg.3(a): March 31, 1997; Reg.3(b): April 30, 1997; remainder: January 31, 1997; £1.10.

These Regulations further amend the Plant Protection Products Regulations 1995 (SI 1995 887 amended by SI 1996 1940) which implement in Great Britain Council Directive 91/414 ([1991] OJ L230/1) concerning the placing of plant protection products on the market. The Regulations amend the definition of the Directive provided in the principal Regulations; make certain modifications to the powers of seizure and disposal and strengthen the enforcement of such powers; extend the disapplication of the Control of Pesticides Regulations 1986 (SI 1986 1510) to plant protection products which are approved under the principal Regulations Reg.9.

197. Plants–plant protection products–marketing

PLANT PROTECTION PRODUCTS (AMENDMENT) (NO.2) REGULATIONS 1997, SI 1997 2499; made under the European Communities Act 1972 s.2. In force: Reg.3(b): November 30, 1997; remainder: November 13, 1997; £1.10.

These Regulations further amend the Plant Protection Products Regulations 1995 (SI 1995 887 amended by SI 1996 1940 and SI 1997 7) which implements Council Directive 91/414 ([1991] OJ L230/1) concerning the placing of plant protection products on the market.

198. Potatoes–imports–infectious disease control–Netherlands

POTATOES ORIGINATING IN THE NETHERLANDS REGULATIONS 1997, SI 1997 2441; made under the European Communities Act 1972 s.2. In force: October 11, 1997; £1.10.

These Regulations, which revoke the Potatoes Originating in the Netherlands Regulations 1996 (SI 1996 2563), impose certain requirements in respect of potatoes grown in the Netherlands during 1997 in accordance with Commission Decision 95/506 ([1995] OJ L291/48) authorising Member States to take additional measures against the dissemination of Pseudomonas solanacearum (Smith) Smith as regards the Kingdom of the Netherlands as last amended by Commission Decision 97/649 ([1997] OJ L274/14).

199. Potatoes–marketing–establishment of British Potato Council

POTATO INDUSTRY DEVELOPMENT COUNCIL ORDER 1997, SI 1997 266; made under the Industrial Organisation and Development Act 1947 s.1, s.2, s.3, s.4, s.5, s.6, s.14, Sch.2. In force: February 11, 1997; £2.40.

This Order establishes a development Council for the potato industry in Great Britain to be known as the British Potato Council.

200. Potatoes–marketing–functions of Potato Marketing Board

POTATO MARKETING BOARD (RESIDUARY FUNCTIONS) REGULATIONS 1997, SI 1997 1573; made under the Agriculture Act 1993 s.38, s.62. In force: June 30, 1997; £1.95.

In accordance with the Agriculture Act 1993 the Minister of Agriculture, Fisheries and Food, the Secretary of State for Scotland and the Secretary of State for Wales have granted an application by the Potato Marketing Board for the approval of a scheme providing for the transfer of its property, rights and liabilities under s.27 on June 30, 1997. As a result of the transfer, s.26 of the Act provides that the Potato Marketing Scheme 1955, which constituted the Board, is also revoked with effect from July 1, 1997 although, under s.37, the Board shall not be deemed to be dissolved by reason of the revocation but shall continue to exist in residuary form and so much of the potato marketing scheme as relates to the winding up of the Board shall continue in force, subject to Regulations which may be made under s.38 of the Act. These Regulations make provision for the purpose of giving effect to so much of the approved scheme as relates to the Board in the period after the transfer and make provision in relation to the constitution of the Board and for the purpose of enabling the Board to wind up its affairs. In accordance with that section the Regulations provide for certain provisions of the potato marketing scheme to continue to have effect, subject to certain modifications, and contain new provisions.

201. Potatoes–packaging

SEED POTATOES (AMENDMENT) REGULATIONS 1997, SI 1997 1474; made under the European Communities Act 1972 s.2. In force: July 1, 1997; £0.65.

These Regulations, which further amend the Seed Potatoes Regulations 1991 (SI 1991 2206), implement Council Directive 96/72 ([1996] OJ L304/10) amending Council Directive 66/400 ([1966] OJ 125/2290), Council Directive 66/401 ([1966] OJ 125/2298), Council Directive 66/402 ([1966] OJ 125/2309), Council Directive 66/403 ([1966] OJ 125/2320), Council Directive 69/208 ([1969] OJ L169/3) and Council Directive 70/458 ([1970] OJ L225/7) on the marketing of beet seed, fodder plant seed, cereal seed, seed potatoes, seed of oil and fibre plants and vegetable seed. They provide for the substitution of the letters EC for the letters EEC on official labels for seed potatoes but provide for remaining stocks of labels bearing the abbreviation EEC to continue to be used until December 31, 2001.

202. Potatoes–Potato Marketing Scheme–revocation

POTATO MARKETING SCHEME (CERTIFICATION OF REVOCATION) ORDER 1997, SI 1997 3020; made under the Agriculture Act 1993 s.26. In force: December 17, 1997; £0.65.

This Order, which applies in Great Britain, certifies the revocation of the Potato Marketing Scheme on July 1, 1997, subject to specified savings.

203. Poultry–diseases and disorders

DISEASES OF POULTRY (AMENDMENT) ORDER 1997, SI 1997 150; made under the Animal Health Act 1981 s.1, s.7, s.8, s.15, s.23, s.25. In force: January 28, 1997; £1.10.

This Order amends the Diseases of Poultry Order (SI 1994 3141) to provide for restrictions to be placed on premises which have in them poultry, racing pigeons or other captive birds which may have been directly or indirectly exposed to the risk of disease.

204. Restrictive trade practices—exclusive purchasing agreements for milk

See COMPETITION LAW: Dale Farm Dairy Group Ltd (t/a Northern Dairies) v. Akram. §865

205. Rights of way—use of agricultural land—forestry operations—use of right to store trees felled elsewhere was excessive usage

J sold to R a farmhouse and land, and granted a right of way over a private roadway and across a causeway. R later purchased a plantation and started felling timber which was transported over the right of way and stored at the farm house. J sought an injunction and damages, contending that R could only use the right of way for access to and from the farmhouse and the other land sold to them by J. J was granted an interim injunction restraining R from using the right of way for access to or egress from the plantation and from removing the timber stored at the farmhouse. It was held that the collection of timber stored at the farmhouse was a purpose connected with the use and enjoyment of the farmhouse as agricultural land which came within the terms of the grant of right of way, but that use of the right of way for access to and egress from the plantation was unlawful. J appealed, despite the timber having already been removed from the farmhouse, his concern being that he would be held liable on his cross-undertaking in damages given when he was granted the interim injunction. J argued that an expressly granted right of way could only be exercised in accordance with the accommodation of the dominant tenement and that removal of the stored timber from the farmhouse was part of the tree felling operation carried out at the plantation and was not use of the farmhouse as agricultural land.

Held, allowing the appeal, that a right of way granted for the benefit of a defined area of land cannot be used for accommodating operations on another area of land, *Harris v. Flower* (1905) 74 L.J. Ch. 27 followed. Storage and removal of the timber was an excessive use of the right of way and not authorised by the terms of the grant. Had the trees been felled at the farmhouse, then the storage thereof would have been use of the farmhouse as agricultural land.

JOBSON v. RECORD (1997) 74 P. & C.R. D16, Morritt, L.J., CA.

206. Rural areas—countryside stewardship

COUNTRYSIDE STEWARDSHIP (AMENDMENT) REGULATIONS 1997, SI 1997 1827; made under the Environment Act 1995 s.98. In force: October 1, 1997; £2.40.

These Regulations amend the Countryside Stewardship Regulations 1996 (SI 1996 695 as amended by SI 1996 1481 and SI 1996 3123) which supplement Council Regulation 2078/92 ([1992] OJ L215/85) on agricultural methods compatible with the requirements of the protection of the environment and the maintenance of the countryside, as last amended by Commission Regulation 2772/95 ([1995] OJ L288/35), as itself rectified by Commission Regulation 1962/96 ([1996] OJ L259/7). They amend the payment rates applicable to certain activities in the 1996 Regulations, revise the payment structure applicable to scrub management and bracken management, and make minor drafting corrections and amendments to the 1996 Regulations.

207. Rural areas—grants—Wales

RURAL DEVELOPMENT GRANTS (AGRICULTURE) (WALES) (AMENDMENT) REGULATIONS 1997, SI 1997 568; made under the European Communities Act 1972 s.2. In force: April 1, 1997; £1.10.

These Regulations amend the Rural Development Grants (Agriculture) (Wales) Regulations 1996 (SI 1996 529) which supplement Council Regulation 2052/88 ([1988] OJ L185/9), Council Regulation 4253/88 ([1988] OJ L374/1), and

Council Regulation 4256/88 ([1988] OJ L374/25), which together provide for assistance from the Guidance section of the European Agriculture Guidance and Guarantee Fund towards operations which promote rural development by facilitating the development and structural adjustment of certain rural areas. The Regulations enable operations falling within the operational programme approved by the Commission of the European Communities to be eligible for grant, amend and add to the references to Community legislation and add a requirement for the Secretary of State to give reasons and allow the beneficiary to make representations before exercising the power of revocation and recovery.

208. Sea Fisheries (Shellfish) (Amendment) Act 1997 (c.3)

The Act amends the Sea Fisheries (Shellfish) Act 1967 s.1 to make provision for fisheries for lobsters and other crustaceans.

This Act received Royal Assent on February 27, 1997 and comes into force on February 27, 1997.

209. Seeds–packaging

SEEDS (MISCELLANEOUS AMENDMENTS) REGULATIONS 1997, SI 1997 616; made under the Plant Varieties and Seeds Act 1964 s.16, s.36. In force: July 1, 1997; £1.10.

These Regulations implement Commission Decision 97/125 ([1997] OJ L48/35) authorising the indelible printing of prescribed information on packages of seed of oil and fibre plants and Council Directive 96/72 ([1996] OJ L304/10) on the marketing of beet seed, fodder plant seed, cereal seed, seed potatoes, seed of oil and fibre plants and vegetable seed. They amend the Oil and Fibre Plant Seed Regulations 1993 (SI 1993 2007) to provide that certain particulars may be printed or stamped on a package of seeds rather than on a label secured to that package and the Fodder Plant Seed Regulations 1993 (SI 1993 2009) so that the provision that certain particulars may be printed or stamped on a package of seeds rather than on a label secured to that package is no longer limited to field beans and field peas.

210. Sheep–cattle–premiums

SHEEP ANNUAL PREMIUM AND SUCKLER COW PREMIUM QUOTAS REGULATIONS 1997, SI 1997 2844; made under the European Communities Act 1972 s.2. In force: December 31, 1997; £3.70.

These Regulations, which consolidate the Sheep Annual Premium and Suckler Cow Premium Regulations 1993 (SI 1993 1626 as amended by SI 1993 3036, SI 1994 2894 and SI 1996 1939), make provision for the administration of the quota system for sheep annual premium established by Council Regulation 3013/89 ([1989] OJ L289/1) Art.5b and the quota system for suckler cow premium established by Council Regulation 805/68 ([1968] OJ L48/24) Art.4(d) and Art.4(f).

211. Sheep–infectious disease control–sheep scab

SHEEP SCAB ORDER 1997, SI 1997 968; made under the Animal Health Act 1981 s.1, s.7, s.8, s.14, s.15, s.23, s.25, s.28, s.83. In force: July 1, 1997; £1.55.

This Order gives a local authority power to serve a notice requiring the temporary clearance from common land of sheep affected with sheep scab. If sheep are not moved in accordance with the notice the local authority may seize them. It prohibits the movement of sheep affected with sheep scab from any premises other than in accordance with this Order or in other specified circumstances, requires a keeper of a sheep affected with sheep scab to treat the animal and all other sheep in the flock, gives local authorities powers to serve notices requiring treatment, enables a veterinary inspector to take samples relating to sheep scab and enables an inspector to mark the sheep.

212. Sheep-premiums

SHEEP ANNUAL PREMIUM (AMENDMENT) REGULATIONS 1997, SI 1997 2500; made under the European Communities Act 1972 s.2. In force: December 4, 1997; £1.10.

These Regulations make amendments to the Sheep Annual Premium Regulations 1992 (SI 1992 2677 as amended by SI 1994 2741, SI 1995 2779 and SI 1996 49) by giving effect to new para.1 (a)(3) of Commission Regulation 2700/93 ([1993] OJ L245/99), on detailed rules for the application of the premium in favour of sheep meat and goat meat producers, inserted by Commission Regulation 1526/96 ([1996] OJ L190/21).

213. Articles

Agricultural property relief: the status of a limited partner *(Matthew Hutton)*: P.C.B. 1997, 2, 67-69. (Steps a limited partner can take in order to qualify for IHT agricultural property relief).

Agricultural relief: wider still and wider *(Roy R. Greenfield)*: C.T.P. 1997, 16(3), 35-36. (Increasingly wide scope of agricultural property IHT relief, legislation to extend relief to wildlife habitats and application to schemes to conserve vulnerable habitats in specific areas).

Disappearing loophole? *(Terry Jordan)*: Tax. 1997, 139(3601), 40-43. (Scope and availability of IHT agricultural property relief including tenanted and settled property situations with reference to case law authorities and potential for future changes).

European Union law *(Angela Sydenham)*: Farm T.B. 1997, 12(1), 7-8. (Implications for farmers of Community institutions' areas of responsibility and legislative functions, CEC's role in formulating CAP and Member States' ability to challenge secondary legislation).

Exchange of joint property interests, private residence exemption and IHT reliefs: Tr. & Est. 1997, 11 (6), 43-45. (IHT and CGT implications where agricultural property and farmhouse formerly held jointly between spouses passes to survivor and child on death of spouse, with worked examples showing available reliefs).

Farming: BSE compensation: I.R.T.B. 1997, 27 (Feb), 396-397. (Tax treatment of BSE compensation payments, herd basis election, replacement of cattle and relevance of payment being under compulsory slaughter programme).

Field of dispute *(Angela Sydenham)*: E.G. 1997, 9740, 138-141. (Agricultural holdings cases on Ministry consent tenancies, notices to quit, subtenancies and covenants against sharing).

IHT agricultural and business reliefs: shortening the qualifying period: Tr. & Est. 1996, 11 (3), 19-21. (Tax planning techniques where donee qualifies for relief and intends eventually to make transfer to his own heirs).

Landowners, farmers and public liability insurance *(Angela Sydenham)*: Farm T.B. 1997, 12(2), 15-16. (Legislation imposing duty of care on owners and occupiers of land towards persons coming onto property, including trespassers, liability on public rights of way and need to obtain effective insurance cover).

"Mad cows and Englishmen"-the institutional consequences of the BSE crisis *(Martin Westlake)*: J. Com. Mar. St. 1997, 35, Supp 1996 11-36. (Institutional aspects and ramifications of BSE crisis and legitimacy of UK's non cooperation policy; includes chronology of events).

Retention of title in contracts of sale: Farm Law 1997, 24, 9-13. (Use of retention of title clauses to protect interests of farmers, particularly livestock farmers, how to avoid creation of legal charge and ingredients for retention of title clause).

Self assessment: farmers' averaging: I.R.T.B. 1997, 27 (Feb), 392-395. (Rules for making, calculating and giving effect to farmers' averaging claims under self assessment with worked examples).

The Nitrate Directive and farming practice in the European Union *(Floor Brouwer* and *Petra Hellegers)*: Euro. Env. 1996, 6(6), 204-209. (Identification of farms and regions likely to be affected by Directive 91/676, and European policy implications of regional variations in Directive's impact).

The option to tax and the agricultural estate owner *(Jeremy De Souza)*: P.C.B. 1997, 1, 61-63. (Effect on country landowners of provisions in force March 1, 1995 concerning development of land, right to waive VAT exemption, construction self supply and agricultural election extension).

Tied cottages: lettings to farm workers *(Angela Sydenham)*: Farm T.B. 1997, 12(4), 31-32. (Changes in force on February 28, 1997 provide for new lettings to be assured agricultural occupancies, assured tenancies or assured shorthold tenancies).

Valuation for tax purposes: Tr. & Est. 1997, 11 (9), 71-72. (Correct method of valuing part of land comprised in estate for council tax and IHT, with particular reference to farm land).

214. Books

Barr, William; Slatter, Michelle; Falkner, James–Farm Tenancies. Hardback: £65.00. ISBN 0-421-60160-4. Sweet & Maxwell.

Davis, Nigel; Smith, Graham; Sydenham, Angela–Agricultural Lawyer's Precedents. Hardback. ISBN 0-85308-386-X. Jordan.

Moss, Joanne–Agricultural Holdings. Property and Conveyancing Library. Hardback: £120.00. ISBN 0-421-44490-8. Sweet & Maxwell.

Rodgers, Christopher P.–Agricultural Law. Paperback: £55.00. ISBN 0-406-00221-5. Butterworth Law.

Smith, Graham–Agricultural Law. Paperback: £30.00. ISBN 1-85811-163-3. CLT Professional Publishing.

Sydenham, Angela–Agricultural Tenancies. Practice Notes. Paperback: £15.95. ISBN 1-85941-308-0. Cavendish Publishing Ltd.

AIR TRANSPORT

215. Airports–groundhandling

AIRPORTS (GROUNDHANDLING) REGULATIONS 1997, SI 1997 2389; made under the European Communities Act 1972 s.2. In force: in accordance with Reg.1; £4.15.

These Regulations implement Council Directive 96/67 ([1996] OJ L272/36) on access to the groundhandling market at Community airports. They set out what is required of managing bodies of airports and suppliers of ground handling services and make provision for the powers of the Civil Aviation Authority in relation to groundhandling.

216. Airports–reference to Monopolies and Mergers Commission–maximum charges

ECONOMIC REGULATION OF AIRPORTS (EXPENSES OF THE MONOPOLIES AND MERGERS COMMISSION) REGULATIONS 1997, SI 1997 403; made under the Airports Act 1986 s.47. In force: April 21, 1997; £1.10.

These Regulations revoke and replace the Economic Regulation of Airports (Expenses of the Monopolies and Mergers Commission) Regulations 1986 (SI 1986 1543). The maximum sum an airport is liable to be charged in respect of a reference to the Monopolies and Mergers Commission relating to the airport of which he is the operator is amended from 0.2 per cent of the annual turnover of the airport business to two per cent of that turnover in the case of airports designated for the purpose of the Airports Act 1986 s.40 and one percent of that turnover for airports not so designated. Provision for sharing among operators that proportion of the expenses of the Monopolies and Mergers Commission that cannot be recovered because the maximum liability of an airport operator is confined to those expenses arising in respect of airports not designated for the purposes of s.40 of the 1986 Act.

217. Cabotage–Civil Aviation Authority–entitlement to prohibit cargo carrying night flight by single engined aircraft

[Air Navigation (No.2) Order 1995 (SI 1995 1970) Art.102; Council Regulation 2407/92 on licensing of air carriers; Council Regulation 2408/92 on access for Community air carrier to intra Community air routes.]

The Civil Aviation Authority is entitled to make an operational rule relating to safety to prohibit night flights of carriage of cargo by light aircraft registered in a Community State. P had a contract to transport cargo at night using a single engined light aircraft. The CAA gave a direction to the captain of the aircraft not to carry out the flight as it would be a breach of the Air Navigation (No.2) Order 1995 Art.102 which prohibited night flights by the aircraft. The flight would have been prohibited if the aircraft was UK registered. P argued that Council Regulation 2407/92 and Council Regulation 2408/92 (the "open skies" Regulations) meant that the prohibition did not apply to flights by aircraft registered in another Community state. P argued that its operating certificate issued in Norway permitted it to fly at night, and therefore it was permitted to fly in the UK under the "open skies" Regulations. The CAA argued that the Norwegian Regulations required P to observe procedures governing aviation laid down by the UK and that the practice that prohibited single engined aircraft carrying cargo for reward was a procedure in the sense that it was a "way of proceeding". P also argued that the prohibition on night flights was an operational rule relating to safety and therefore permitted under the "open skies" Regulations.

Held, that the CAA was entitled to direct that the aircraft should not operate at night for valuable consideration, that Norwegian law permitted flights in a foreign state only if there was compliance with the procedures of that state. There was nothing requiring such procedures to be laid down in writing or published. The practice prohibiting night flights for the carriage of cargo was such a procedure. It followed that P's operating licence did not permit such flights. The restriction was within the scope of an operational rule provided that it was applied to all aircraft without discrimination as to nationality.

H5 AIR SERVICE NORWAY AS v. CIVIL AVIATION AUTHORITY [1997] C.L.C. 1,264, Thomas, J., QBD.

218. Carriage by air–forum conveniens–conflict between Brussels and Warsaw Conventions

See CONFLICT OF LAWS: Deaville v. Aeroflot Russian International Airlines. §879

219. Carriers liabilities–injury to passenger caused by pre-existing medical condition

[Warsaw Convention on International Carriage by Air 1929 Art.17, Art.18.]

Held, that an action against a carrier under the Warsaw Convention 1929 Art.17 was rightly struck out as disclosing no reasonable cause of action where the applicant's pre-existing medical condition caused him to fall and sustain injury. When determining the meaning of the word "accident" under Art.17, the cause rather than the effect had to be considered, "accident" being distinct from "occurrence" under Art.18.

CHAUDHARI v. BRITISH AIRWAYS PLC, *The Times*, May 7, 1997, Leggatt, L.J., CA.

220. Carriers liabilities–Warsaw Convention–sole remedy for claims against carriers to exclusion of domestic law

[Warsaw Convention on International Carriage by Air 1929.]

S and A, passengers on a BA flight who were taken prisoner when the plane landed in Kuwait for refuelling during the Iraqi invasion, appealed against decisions of the Court of Appeal and the Inner House that they were not entitled to damages for negligence, breach of contract or delay as the Warsaw Convention 1929 excluded claims brought under the common law and, by virtue of Art.29, extinguished actions which had not been brought within the two year limitation period.

Held, dismissing the appeals, that the terms of the Convention had to be given a purposive construction, the effect of which was to provide an exhaustive code for the liability of carriers which excluded any claims under domestic law. To allow passengers to sue outside the Convention would distort its operation. It was not intended to provide remedies against carriers for all loss but to set out limits of liability and define the circumstances under which liability could be established.

SIDHU v. BRITISH AIRWAYS PLC; ABNETT (KNOWN AS SYKES) v. BRITISH AIRWAYS PLC [1997] A.C. 430, Lord Hope of Craighead, HL.

221. Dangerous goods–chemical oxygen generators

AIR NAVIGATION (DANGEROUS GOODS) (SECOND AMENDMENT) REGULATIONS 1997, SI 1997 2666; made under the Air Navigation (No.2) Order 1995 Art.52, Art.118. In force: December 1, 1997; £0.65.

These Regulations amend the Air Navigation (Dangerous Goods) Regulations 1994 (SI 1994 3187) by including an Addendum to the 1997/98 edition of the International Civil Aviation's Technical Instructions for the Safe Transport of Goods by Air containing instructions for the carriage of chemical oxygen generators in the definition of "Technical Instructions".

222. Exclusion clauses–standard terms–damage to aircraft at airport

[Unfair Contract Terms Act 1977.]

One of M's aircraft was damaged by loose paving blocks at L's airport. M brought an action for damages in negligence and for breach of statutory duty. L sought to rely on its standard terms of use which excluded liability for damage to aircraft caused by any act, omission, neglect or default. It was argued by M that the clause did not cover negligence by L and that it did not satisfy the test of reasonableness set out in the Unfair Contract Terms Act 1977.

Held, giving judgment for L, that the words "neglect or default" were wide enough to cover negligent acts by L. The clause did satisfy the test of reasonableness. It had been generally accepted in the market, its meaning was clear and both parties could make insurance arrangements on the basis of the clause.

MONARCH AIRLINES LTD v. LONDON LUTON AIRPORT LTD [1997] C.L.C. 698, Clarke, J., QBD (Adm Ct).

223. Fuel–jet aviation fuel supply contract–product quality–meaning of "user"

In 1994 D, as sellers, contracted with P, as buyers, that D would supply P with a quantity of jet aviation fuel. The supply contract contained a term that the product would inter alia meet Directorate of Engineering Research and Development (DERD) specifications' latest issue and that D would make "best endeavours to have ASA 3 or Stadis 450 on board the [shipping] vessel in drums". ASA 3 or Stadis 450 constituted additives, otherwise known as static dissipator additives (SDA), designed to dissipate static electricity in certain handling conditions. At the date of the contract the latest DERD specification (DERD 2494) provided that the limits for electrical conductivity were to be between 50 (minimum) and 450 (maximum) pico-Siemens per metre (pS/m). At the time of shipment no SDA had been added to the fuel and its conductivity was 0 pS/m. After shipment SDA loaded in drums was added to the fuel on board the vessel, but too much was added with the result that the conductivity measured well in excess of 450 pS/m. P commenced proceedings against D claiming damages for breach of contract in that the fuel had not been supplied in accordance with DERD 2494. D raised a number of points of construction by way of preliminary issues, including inter alia whether note 11 to DERD 2494, which stated the conductivity limits "apply at the point, time and temperature of delivery to the user", meant that there was no obligation on a seller to an intermediate buyer of DERD 2494 jet fuel to deliver a product which contains an appropriate admixture of SDA. A related question was whether the reference to "user" in note 11 referred only to end-users such as airlines, or whether it included intermediate buyers in the position of P. The insertion of the word "user" was a recent amendment to note 11; previously it referred to "purchaser".

Held, that D had breached the contract by failing to deliver a product which contained an appropriate admixture of SDA, that (1) the word "user" in note 11 to DERD 2494 could not mean "any purchaser", and did not embrace an intermediate trader in the position of P; (2) the construction adopted by D, although superficially attractive, concentrated too much on note 11 to the exclusion of other important considerations. Such considerations included the mandatory requirement of Clause 4.2.2 of DERD 2494 that "an SDA of a type and at a concentration detailed in Appendix A shall be added to the fuel to impart electrical conductivity in accordance with Serial 20 of Table A". The mandatory requirement to add SDA had to be fulfilled by the time of delivery under any sale incorporating DERD 2494. The conclusion was reinforced by a consideration of the remainder of DERD 2494, which was drafted when note 11 referred to "purchaser", and the reality that SDA was invariably added before the fuel reached the airlines. To construe note 11 as meaning that a seller was under no obligation to add SDA was unrealistic in light of the evidence presented concerning the supply and distribution of fuel.

TRASIMEX HOLDING SA v. ADDAX BV (THE RED SEA) [1997] 1 Lloyd's Rep. 610, Rix, J., QBD (Comm Ct).

224. Navigation

AIR NAVIGATION (GENERAL) (AMENDMENT) REGULATIONS 1997, SI 1997 881; made under the Air Navigation (No.2) Order 1995 Art.42. In force: March 27, 1997; £0.65.

These Regulations amend the Air Navigation (General) Regulations 1993 (SI 1993 1622). The following changes are made: a height keeping performance capability is prescribed; aircraft registered in the United Kingdom flying within airspace prescribed for the purposes of minimum navigation performance and notified for the purpose of reduced vertical separation minima must carry equipment which have the prescribed height keeping performance capability and an amendment is made to the airspace prescribed for the purposes of minimum navigation performance.

225. Navigation

AIR NAVIGATION (SECOND AMENDMENT) ORDER 1997, SI 1997 287; made under the Civil Aviation Act 1982 s.60, s.61, s.102, Sch.13. In force: March 27, 1997; £1.10.

This Order further amends the Air Navigation (No.2) Order 1995 (SI 1995 1970). In addition to minor and drafting amendments the changes relate to public transport aircraft, notified airspace, area traffic control centres and air transport undertakings.

226. Navigation—charges—Amendment No.1

CIVIL AVIATION (ROUTE CHARGES FOR NAVIGATION SERVICES) REGULATIONS 1997, SI 1997 2920; made under the Civil Aviation Act 1982 s.73, s.74, s.102. In force: January 1, 1998; £2.40.

These Regulations, which revoke and replace the Civil Aviation (Route Charges for Navigation Services) Regulations 1995 (SI 1995 3160 as amended by SI 1996 1495, SI 1996 3089 and SI 1997 1653), introduce new unit rates reflecting forecasts of costs and traffic for 1998, and a new method of calculating the distance factor for flight in specified airspace. There are no longer any standard points of entry into and exit from specified airspace nor is there any provision for transatlantic charges.

227. Navigation–charges–Amendment No.2

CIVIL AVIATION (NAVIGATION SERVICES CHARGES) (SECOND AMENDMENT) REGULATIONS 1997, SI 1997 667; made under the Civil Aviation Act 1982 s.73. In force: April 1, 1997; £0.65.

These Regulations amend the Civil Aviation (Navigation Services Charges) Regulations 1995 (SI 1995 497) as follows: they reduce the charges payable to the CAA for navigation services provided in connection with the use of the aerodromes in respect of Heathrow, Gatwick, Stansted, Aberdeen (Dyce), Edinburgh and Glasgow airports; they reduce the charge payable to the CAA by the operator of an aircraft which flies within the Shanwick Oceanic Control Area and in respect of which a flight plan is communicated to the appropriate air traffic control unit; and they increase the charge payable to the CAA by the operator of a helicopter which flies from any place in the United Kingdom to a vessel or an off-shore installation within the area of the Northern North Sea described in Reg.7(2) of the principal Regulations.

228. Navigation–charges–Amendment No.3

CIVIL AVIATION (ROUTE CHARGES FOR NAVIGATION SERVICES) (THIRD AMENDMENT) REGULATIONS 1997, SI 1997 1653; made under the Civil Aviation Act 1982 s.73. In force: August 1, 1997; £1.95.

These Regulations amend the Civil Aviation (Route Charges for Navigation Services) Regulations 1995 (SI 1995 3160) by introducing new unit rates for Hungary and Switzerland. The Hungarian unit rate is reduced from 24.01 to 21.54 ECU. The Swiss unit rate is reduced from 84.87 to 80.39 ECU.

229. Navigation–charges–Denmark–Iceland

CIVIL AVIATION (JOINT FINANCING) REGULATIONS 1997, SI 1997 2937; made under the Civil Aviation Act 1982 s.73, s.74, s.102. In force: January 1, 1998; £1.95.

These Regulations, which revoke and replace the Civil Aviation (Joint Financing) Regulations 1994 (SI 1994 3055), increase the charge payable by operators of aircraft to the CAA in respect of crossings between Europe and North America from £59.25 to £62.88 as a result of increases in charges payable in respect of air navigation services provided by the Governments of Denmark and Iceland.

230. Navigation–equipment–technical specifications

PROCUREMENT OF AIR NAVIGATION EQUIPMENT (TECHNICAL SPECIFICATIONS) REGULATIONS 1997, SI 1997 2329; made under the European Communities Act 1972 s.2. In force: December 1, 1997; £0.65.

These Regulations oblige National Air Traffic Services Ltd to ensure that the specifications for the procurement of air navigation equipment are included in documents or specifications when it purchases or seeks to purchase air traffic management equipment covered by such specifications.

231. Navigation–notified airspace

AIR NAVIGATION (OVERSEAS TERRITORIES) (AMENDMENT) ORDER 1997, SI 1997 1746; made under the Civil Aviation Act 1949 s.8, s.41, s.57, s.58, s.59, s.61. In force: August 22, 1997; £1.10.

This Order amends the Air Navigation (Overseas Territories) Order 1989 (SI 1989 2395) in order to provide that airspace which is prescribed for the purposes of minimum navigation performance may now be notified for the purposes of reduced vertical separation. An aircraft registered in the territory may not fly within such notified airspace unless it carries appropriate equipment and operates in accordance with approved procedures.

232. Security—Guernsey

AVIATION SECURITY (GUERNSEY) ORDER 1997, SI 1997 2989; made under the Tokyo Convention Act 1967 s.8; the Aviation Security Act 1982 s.39; and the Aviation and Maritime Security Act 1990 s.51. In force: January 17, 1998; £2.80.

This Order extends certain provisions of the Aviation Security Act 1982, the Aviation and Maritime Security Act 1990 s.1 and s.50 to the Bailiwick of Guernsey. It also revokes the Tokyo Convention Act 1967 (Guernsey) Order 1969 (SI 1969 596), the Hijacking Act 1971 (Guernsey) Order 1971 (SI 1971 1744) and the Protection of Aircraft Act 1973 (Guernsey) Order 1973 (SI 1973 1760) to the extent that they relate to the extension to the Bailiwick of Guernsey of enactments replaced by the Aviation Security Act 1982.

233. Travel organisers—definition of end users

CIVIL AVIATION (AIR TRAVEL ORGANISERS' LICENSING) (SECOND AMENDMENT) REGULATIONS 1997, SI 1997 2912; made under the Civil Aviation Act 1982 s.71, Sch.13 Part III. In force: December 31, 1997; £1.10.

These Regulations further amend the Civil Aviation (Air Travel Organisers' Licensing) Regulations 1995 (SI 1995 1054) by defining end user as a person who either uses, or provides to another person without charge to use, flight accommodation and by prohibiting ticket providers from supplying tickets to a person unless they have reasonable grounds to believe that that person will be the end user.

234. United Nations—prohibition of flights—Angola

See INTERNATIONAL LAW. §3203

235. Articles

Air carrier liability for exposure of aircrew to cosmic radiation *(Ruwantissa I.R. Abeyratne)*: A. & S.L. 1997, 22(2), 91-97. (Effects of radiation at high altitude, liability for personal injury or death, and safeguards and precautions to be taken by carrier).

Bumpy take-off for liberalised EU air transport market *(Ciaran Walker)*: E.C.L. 1997, 19, 33-35. (Application of EC competition law to deregulated international air transport industry focusing on alliances with US airlines).

Council Directive 96/97 on ground handling: T.A.Q. 1997, 4(Apr), 265-266. (Provisions of Directive adopted October 1996).

Defining the right to fly *(Michael Nott)*: Trans. L. & P. 1997, 1(5), 43-45. (Liberalisation of air routes and who is qualified to take advantage of them, with possible problems of access to airport slots in future as capacity is constrained).

Drunkenness on aircraft *(Alan Davenport)*: T.L.J. 1997, 2, 57-58. (Use of the Air Navigation Order 1989 Art.50 and Art.52 to prosecute drunk passengers).

Enforcement of "authentic" lease instruments in Europe *(Berend J.H. Crans)*: A. & S.L. 1997, 22(2), 77-80. (Use of "authentic instruments" within meaning of Art.50 of Brussels Convention in aircraft leasing transactions in order to facilitate enforcement of lease agreement).

Free trade in air traffic rights and preferential measures for developing countries *(Ruwantissa I.R. Abeyratne)*: Tr. Law 1997, 16(4), 289-305. (Examination of factors preventing introduction of free open skies policy between states and measures taken to ensure trends in commercial air transport do not impede competitiveness of carriers from developing countries).

Ground-handling claims: who pays? does it matter? and to whom? *(Tony Kilbride)*: T.A.Q. 1997, 3(Jan), 179-185. (Liability of carriers and handling companies for injuries to passengers and employees and damage to property occurring when aircraft is on ground; includes text of current Art.8 of IATA Agreement and proposed revisions).

Liberalisation of ground handling services at Community airports *(Wolfgang Deselaers)*: A. & S.L. 1996, 21 (6), 260-266. (Key concepts in Directive and how general competition rules relate to ground handling services).

Recent developments on the ATOL Regulations *(Helen Simpson)*: I.T.L.J. 1997, 3, 113-116. (Implementation of Civil Aviation (Air Travel Organisers' Licensing) Regulations 1995 (SI 1995 1054), problem of underbonding and call for directors' guarantees to make them personally liable for reimbursing Air Travel Trust Fund for expenditure if company fails).

Relaxing airline ownership and investment rules *(Rigas Doganis)*: A. & S.L. 1996, 21 (6), 267-270. (Constraints of bilateral regulatory system on foreign investment in airline industry and pressures for liberalisation).

The Warsaw Convention between dusk and dawn: the IATA Intercarrier Agreements - a requiem for a well-proved liability system *(Ronald Schmid)*: A. & S.L. 1997, 22 (1), 50-55. (Criticism of IATA amendments limiting airlines' liability).

The aerospace plane and its implications for commercial air traffic rights *(Ruwantissa I.R. Abeyratne)*: T.A.Q. 1997, 3 (Jan), 186-193. (Effect of aircraft such as space shuttle on air traffic control).

The destruction of aircraft in flight over Scotland and Niger: the questions of jurisdiction and extradition under international law *(Sami Shubber)*: B.Y.B.I.L. 1995, 66, 239-282. (Offence of aircraft sabotage under Montreal Convention, jurisdiction over offence, extradition arrangements and action of UN Security Council in response to Lockerbie and Niger offences).

The display of airline computer reservation systems on the Internet *(Ruwantissa I.R. Abeyratne)*: T.A.Q. 1997, 6 (Oct), 360-369. (Regulatory framework under ICAO Code of Conduct, US Code and GATS, and legal implications).

The hybrid relationship between computer reservation systems (CRS) and airlines *(Mia Wouters)*: T.A.Q. 1997, 6 (Oct), 346-359. (Development of EC and US codes of conduct aiming to prevent anti competitive practices).

The intercarrier agreements - state of the art: A. & S.L. 1997, 22 (1), 56-57. (EU and US developments in moves to abolish passenger liability limits).

236. Books

Hill, Timothy; Ghaffar, Arshad—EC Air Transport Law. Hardback: £150.00. ISBN 1-85044-969-4. LLP Limited.

ANIMALS

237. Animal conservation—Muntjak deer

WILDLIFE AND COUNTRYSIDE ACT 1981 (VARIATION OF SCHEDULE 9) ORDER 1997, SI 1997 226; made under the Wildlife and Countryside Act 1981 s.22. In force: March 5, 1997; £0.65.

This Order adds the Muntjak Deer to the Wildlife and Countryside Act 1981 Sch.9 Part I, which lists animals which may not be released or allowed to escape into the wild.

238. Animal welfare—live animal export trade

[Animal Health Act 1981; Welfare of Animals During Transport Order 1994 (SI 1994 3249).]

PAIN, a limited company concerned with the welfare of animals in the live export trade, sought judicial review of the way in which MAFF exercised its powers to control the trade, alleging that many sea vessels sailed across the English Channel with live animals on board in conditions that caused the animals unnecessary suffering. PAIN suggested that the relevant regulations, ie. the Animal Health Act 1981 and the Welfare of Animals During Transport Order 1994, were not being properly implemented by the Minister. A policy of non-intervention by MAFF was inferred by a lack of notices pursuant to Art.16 of the 1994 Order being served on the masters of the vessels for failing in their obligation under Art.11 of the Order to consider the welfare of the animals when deciding whether to sail in certain weather conditions. MAFF argued that PAIN had no locus standi to bring the proceedings.

Held, refusing leave to seek judicial review, that (1) there was substantial information regarding the work carried out by the MAFF inspectors to show that there was regular contact between the inspectors and the masters to dispel concerns that the policy was non-interventionist. Had such a policy of non-intervention been found it would have been unlawful. Subjective judgments had to be made as to whether the weather conditions would cause suffering to the animals being transported, and (2) with regard to the issue of locus standi, PAIN was a responsible body, making a serious application which raised issues of concern, establishing a sufficient interest in the issues and therefore had locus standi.

R. v. MINISTER OF AGRICULTURE FISHERIES AND FOOD, *ex p.* PROTESTERS ANIMAL INFORMATION NETWORK LTD, Trans. Ref: CO 1150/96, CO 220/96, December 20, 1996, Latham, J., QBD.

239. Animal welfare—prohibition on keeping mink

MINK KEEPING ORDER 1997, SI 1997 3002; made under the Destructive Imported Animals Act 1932 s.10. In force: January 1, 1998; £1.10.

This Order prohibits the keeping of mink on certain off shore islands of Great Britain and in certain parts of the Highland Region of Scotland and prohibits the keeping of mink in the rest of Great Britain except under licence. It continues the prohibition imposed by the Mink Keeping Order 1992 (SI 1992 3324) which ceases to have effect on January 1, 1998. This Order ceases to have effect on January 1, 2001.

240. Animal welfare—special licences to keep coypus—fees

COYPUS (SPECIAL LICENCE) (FEES) REGULATIONS 1997, SI 1997 2751; made under the Destructive Imported Animals Act 1932 s.2. In force: January 1, 1998; £1.10.

These Regulations prescribe fees for special licences under the Destructive Imported Animals Act 1932 s.8 authorising the keeping of coypus for exhibition, purposes of scientific research or other exceptional purposes. The fee for England and Wales is £185 and for Scotland, £60.

241. Animal welfare—special licences to keep mink—fees

MINK (KEEPING) (AMENDMENT) REGULATIONS 1997, SI 1997 2750; made under the Destructive Imported Animals Act 1932 s.2. In force: January 1, 1998; £0.65.

These Regulations amend the Mink (Keeping) Regulations 1975 (SI 1975 2223) in respect of the fees for licences to keep mink. In the case of special licences to keep mink for exhibition or for purposes of scientific research or other exceptional purposes, granted under the Destructive Imported Animals Act 1932 s.8, they prescribe a fee of £185 in England and Wales and £60 in Scotland. In the case of a licence granted under s.3, which covers all other cases in which licences are granted, they prescribe a fee of £630.

242. Animal welfare—transport

WELFARE OF ANIMALS (TRANSPORT) ORDER 1997, SI 1997 1480; made under the Animal Health Act 1981 s.1, s.7, s.8, s.37, s.38, s.39, s.72, s.83, s.87. In force: July 1, 1997; £5.60.

This Order revokes and re-enacts with modifications the Welfare of Animals during Transport Order 1994 (SI 1994 3249 as amended), and other animal welfare legislation, which implemented Council Directive 91/628 ([1991] OJ

L340/17) on the protection of animals during transport. This Order, which implements that Directive as amended by Council Directive 95/29 ([1995] OJ L18/52), makes general provision for the welfare of animals in transport including provisions as to the means of transport or receptacles used, the amount of space available to each animal, the fitness of the animal to travel and the feeding and watering of animals before and during a journey and on journey times and rest periods.

243. Animal welfare—unfit animal exposed at market—proof of knowledge of unfitness not required

[Welfare of Animals at Market Order 1990 (SI 1990 2628) Art.5, Art.20; Animal Health Act 1981 s.73.]

D appealed by way of case stated against conviction of an offence of permitting an unfit animal to be exposed for sale at market contrary to the Welfare of Animals at Market Order 1990 Art.5 and Art.20(c) and the Animal Health Act 1981 s.73. D had taken the ewe to market where its condition was noticed by HOOF, an animal welfare organisation, who purchased it and had it seen by an RSPCA officer. It was concluded that the ewe was not suffering so much that it should be taken from the market nor should it be seen by a veterinary surgeon. However, it died later and was found to have had a chronic and fatal lung condition. D was convicted on the basis of strict liability. The question for the case stated was whether the offence contrary to Art.5 of the 1990 Order was an absolute offence that did not require that the accused had knowledge of the unfitness of the animal. The prosecution accepted that if the offence was not one of strict liability then it had not shown that D had known that the ewe was unfit, nor that he was wilfully blind to the fact. It was agreed that the prosecution would have to show that D knowingly exposed the ewe for sale in the market by virtue of use of the word "permit" in Art.5, the issue being whether D's knowledge of the animal's state of unfitness had to be shown also, which had to be determined by having regard to Art.5 in the context of the 1990 Order as a whole.

Held, dismissing the appeal, that having regard to the 1990 Order as a whole, the offence contrary to Art.5 was an offence of strict liability. The prosecution did not have to prove that D knew or was wilfully blind to the unfitness of the animal in order to establish the Art.5 offence. To promote the purpose of the 1981 Act and the 1990 Order it was found that to establish an offence under Art.5 it was necessary first to show that the animal was unfit and then that the vendor knowingly exposed the unfit animal for sale. He may have had a defence if he could show that the animal was not unfit or that he had reasonable grounds for believing on the balance of probabilities that the animal was not unfit. If it had to be proved that the vendor knew of the unfitness of the animal to establish the offence, a person with careless disregard of the state of the animal would escape liability from the offence.

DAVIDSON v. STRONG, *The Times*, March 20, 1997, Moses, J., QBD.

244. Bees—imports—infectious disease control

IMPORTATION OF BEES ORDER 1997, SI 1997 310; made under the Bees Act 1980 s.1. In force: March 17, 1997; £1.10.

This Order revokes and re-enacts the Importation of Bees Order 1980 (SI 1980 792 as amended by SI 1987 867 and SI 1993 3249) which prohibited the importation of bees or bee pests except under the authority of a general or specific licence issued by the Minister of Agriculture, Fisheries and Food or the Secretary of State. A specific licence permitted the licensee to import a specified consignment of bees or bee pests from a country named in the general licence issued under that Order. The principal change made by this Order is to provide for the issue of a specific licence which permits the licence holder to import an unlimited number of consignments of bees or bee pests from any specified country. Specific licences are valid for a specified period not exceeding three years. Provision is also made for the procedure to be followed before a specific licence is suspended or revoked.

245. **Birds–cruel ill treatment–caged kestrel harming itself–no deliberate or wilful cruelty**

[Protection of Animals Act 1911 s.1 (1).]

H, a licensed zoo keeper, appealed by way of case stated against the decision dismissing his appeal against conviction under the Protection of Animals Act 1911 s.1 (1) (a) of cruelly ill treating a juvenile male kestrel. H owned a bird sanctuary which was open to the public, with a collection of over 150 birds of prey. The juvenile kestrel had been found with wounds caused by flying repeatedly into the side of its cage, which H was found to have known about, although he was not found to have deliberately mistreated it. The question was whether the court had been correct in finding, as a matter of law, that an offence under s.1 (1) (a) of the 1911 Act could be committed in the absence of deliberate or wilful ill treatment. H contended that he could not be guilty of cruel ill treatment as he had not committed a positive act of deliberate and wilful cruelty.

Held, dismissing the appeal, that had H been charged under the second limb of s.1 (1) (a) that is the doing or omitting to do an act which caused unreasonable suffering, there was no doubt that he would have been found guilty of cruelty. Considering the degree of overlap between the first and second limbs of the section it is apparent that the same conduct can give rise to convictions under each limb. Although the offence in this case would have been better charged under the second limb the charge could also be sustained under the first. H had caused the bird unnecessary suffering and as such was guilty of cruelty, *Bernard v. Evans* [1925] 2 K.B. 794. It was not necessary to establish that H had wilfully brought about the bird's injuries for him to be guilty of cruel ill treatment. He should have taken the bird to another type of aviary with soft netting inside the wire or had it put down rather than keep it in the cage where it continued to harm itself.

HOPSON v. DPP, Trans. Ref: CO/2293/96, March 11, 1997, Simon Brown, L.J., QBD.

246. **Birds (Registration Charges) Act 1997 (c.55)**

The Act amends the Wildlife and Countryside Act 1981 to provide for charges to be imposed for registration of sellers of dead wild birds and of certain captive wild birds.

This Act received Royal Assent on March 21, 1997 and comes into force on March 21, 1997.

247. **Dangerous dogs–attack without prior warning was capable of being conduct giving grounds for reasonable apprehension of injury**

[Dangerous Dogs Act 1991 s.3(1).]

Held, that for the purposes of establishing whether a dog acted in such a way as to give grounds for reasonable apprehension that it would cause injury to someone within the meaning of the Dangerous Dogs Act 1991 s.3(1), it was enough that the dog attacked without prior warning.

RAFIQ v. DPP; *sub nom.* RAFIQ v. FOLKES (1997) 161 J.P. 412, Auld, L.J., QBD.

248. **Dangerous dogs–fees**

DANGEROUS DOGS (FEES) ORDER 1997, SI 1997 1152; made under the Dangerous Dogs (Amendment) Act 1997 s.4. In force: June 8, 1997; £0.65.

The Dangerous Dogs (Amendment) Act 1997 amends the Dangerous Dogs Act 1991 to enable the owners of certain dangerous dogs which were not registered under the Scheme provided for in that Act to be registered if particular conditions are met. The 1991 Scheme specified a fee of £12.50 plus VAT for a certificate of exemption. This Order replaces that fee with one of £20 plus VAT for certificates issued pursuant to the 1997 Act.

249. Dangerous dogs—magistrate's discretion to stay proceedings on grounds of abuse of process—police involved in commission of offence by allowing dog to remain unmuzzled

[Dangerous Dogs Act 1991 s.1, s.4(1).]

S had been charged with an offence of having a pit bull terrier unmuzzled in a public place under the Dangerous Dogs Act 1991 s.1. The charge was dismissed when the expert witness for the prosecution, on the issue of whether the dog was a pit bull terrier, could not attend and the magistrate refused to adjourn the case. The dog was returned to S and a further information was laid against him relating to his being in charge of the unmuzzled dog in a public place on that same day. S applied for a stay of the information on the basis that it was an abuse of process. The application was refused and S applied for judicial review of that decision, contending that the police had been involved in the commission of the alleged offence by allowing him to leave the police station with the dog unmuzzled.

Held, allowing the application, that, although it was not an abuse of process to have brought further proceedings against S as the issue on which the trial rested, ie. whether the dog was a pit bull terrier, had not been resolved, the circumstances in which the information had been laid did amount to an abuse of process. When the dog was returned to S, it was reasonable for him to believe he was entitled to take it into a public place unmuzzled, and he was unaware that the police intended to charge him having observed him leave the police station. As a general principle, courts were not concerned with the decision to prosecute, but rather with the conduct of the trial. Any resulting harshness in that principle could be taken into account in mitigation during sentencing. However, under s.4(1) of the Act, conviction carried with it the mandatory sentence that the dog be destroyed and as such the circumstances in which the offence was committed could have no effect by way of mitigation on the sentence passed. In the light of these considerations, proceeding with the action against S would be unfair and offend against the court's sense of justice.

R. v. LIVERPOOL MAGISTRATES COURT, *ex p.* SLADE, *The Independent*, June 13, 1997, Pill, L.J., QBD.

250. Dangerous dogs—pit bull type—destruction order—abuse of process

[Dangerous Dogs Act 1991 s.5(4).]

C applied for judicial review of the decision by the Metropolitan Police Commissioner to apply for a destruction order of C's dog under the Dangerous Dogs Act 1991 s.5(4), and the finding by the magistrate that the dog was a pit bull terrier and the granting of the destruction order. The dog had been seized, but the CPS decided not to prosecute so the dog remained with the Commissioner who made the s.5(4) application; a civil application for which C could not get legal aid. C wished to have the dog examined by a behaviourist, behavioural characteristics being one of the ways of determining breed, but the police would allow access to the dog for examination only on payment of a £300 fee which he could not afford, so C had no evidence to submit. The burden of proof was on C to show that the dog was not a pit bull. C argued that not to allow free access to the dog for inspection was an abuse of process.

Held, allowing the application, quashing the destruction order and remitting the matter to a different magistrate, that the Commissioner was not wrong in principle to apply for a destruction order in terms of s.5(4), but in view of there being no right of appeal under s.5(4), the absence of entitlement to legal aid and the inordinate fee to allow examination meant that it was all the more important that a party resisting such an application for destruction be ensured a fair trial and given all reasonable opportunity to produce evidence in support of their objections. On the facts it was apparent that C did not receive a fair trial.

R. v. KNIGHTSBRIDGE CROWN COURT, *ex p.* CRABBE, Trans. Ref: CO 3987/95, December 18, 1996, McCowan, L.J., QBD.

251. Dangerous dogs–pit bull type–destruction order–abuse of process–dog entitled to benefit of previous acquittal

[Dangerous Dogs Act 1991 s.1 (2), s.5; Prosecution of Offences Act 1985 s.23.]

C, the owner of the dog, applied for judicial review of a destruction order. B, a friend of C's, who had been seen with the dog by a police officer in 1992, had been charged under the Dangerous Dogs Act 1991 s.1. As B was not the owner, the only issue was whether the dog was a pit bull terrier so as to come within the section. The CPS notified B of their intention not to continue with the matter, but B wished the matter to proceed as was his right under the Prosecution of Offences Act 1985 s.23. The case was subsequently dismissed due to no evidence being offered by the CPS. The dog was, however, not immediately returned, and the police pursued the matter by way of an application made pursuant to s.5 of the 1991 Act on the basis that the dog was after all of the pit bull type. A hearing took place with expert evidence, following which a destruction order was made. The stipendiary magistrate based this decision on factual findings, and refused to state a case when asked to do so. An application for judicial review was granted and it was submitted for C that there had been an abuse of process and a breach of natural justice.

Held, allowing the application, and quashing the order for destruction of the dog, that where a dog had been the subject of a previous charge under the Dangerous Dogs Act 1991 s.1 (2) of which the defendant, who was not the owner, was acquitted, and the dog was still under the same ownership, it was an abuse of process to bring fresh proceedings for an order for the destruction of the dog under s.5 (4). The dismissal of the case by virtue of the CPS offering no evidence in effect amounted to an acquittal, *R. v. Walton Street Justices, ex p. Crothers* [1992] Crim.L.R. 875, [1993] C.L.Y. 939 and *R. v. Walton Street Justices, ex p. Crothers* [1995] C.O.D. 159 considered.

R. v. HARINGEY MAGISTRATES COURT, *ex p.* CRAGG (1997) 161 J.P. 61, Maurice Kay, J., QBD.

252. Dangerous Dogs (Amendment) Act 1997 (c.53)

This Act amends the Dangerous Dogs Act 1991 to give the court discretion not to order the destruction of a dog in certain circumstances.

This Act received Royal Assent on March 21, 1997 and comes into force on June 8, 1997.

253. Dangerous Dogs (Amendment) Act 1997 (c.53)–Commencement Order

DANGEROUS DOGS (AMENDMENT) ACT 1997 (COMMENCEMENT) ORDER 1997, SI 1997 1151 (C.42); made under the Dangerous Dogs (Amendment) Act 1997 s.6. Commencement details: bringing into force various provisions of the Act on June 8, 1997; £0.65.

This Order brings the Dangerous Dogs (Amendment) Act 1997 into force on June 8, 1997.

254. Diseases and disorders–approved disinfectants

DISEASES OF ANIMALS (APPROVED DISINFECTANTS) (AMENDMENT) ORDER 1997, SI 1997 2347; made under the Animal Health Act 1981 s.1, s.7, s.23. In force: October 20, 1997; £2.40.

This Order amends the Diseases of Animals (Approved Disinfectants) Order 1978 (SI 1978 32) by replacing Sch.1, which lists approved disinfectants, and Sch.2, which lists disinfectants no longer approved, although they can continue to be used as approved disinfectants until December 31, 1997. The Diseases of Animals (Approved Disinfectants) (Amendment) Order 1994 (SI 1994 2965) and the Diseases of Animals (Approved Disinfectants) (Amendment) Order 1996 (SI 1996 697) are revoked.

255. Horses—injury caused by motor vehicle—loss of use and enjoyment—damages

See DAMAGES: Farrer-Sowerby v. Stubbs. §1757

256. Horses—passports

HORSE PASSPORTS ORDER 1997, SI 1997 2789; made under the Animal Health Act 1981 s.1, s.8, s.72. In force: January 1, 1998; £3.20.

This Order, which establishes a system of identification documents for horses registered with recognised organisations and born in Great Britain, implements Council Directive 90/427 ([1990 OJ L224/55) Art.8 on the zootechnical and genealogical conditions governing intra-Community trade in equidae and Commission Decision 93/623 ([1993] OJ L298/45) establishing the identification document (passport) accompanying registered equidae. The Order is enforced by the local authority.

257. Imports—fees

ANIMALS (THIRD COUNTRY IMPORTS) (CHARGES) REGULATIONS 1997, SI 1997 639; made under the European Communities Act 1972 s.2. In force: April 1, 1997; £1.10.

These Regulations implement, in Great Britain, Council Directive 96/43 ([1996] OJ L162/3). They relate to the detention and inspection of animals at border inspection posts and other premises and make provision for the payment of charges for veterinary and health inspections which vary according to the species of animal inspected.

258. Veterinary medicines—complementary medicines

MEDICINES (RESTRICTIONS ON THE ADMINISTRATION OF VETERINARY MEDICINAL PRODUCTS) AMENDMENT REGULATIONS 1997, SI 1997 2884; made under the European Communities Act 1972 s.2. In force: February 1, 1998; £1.55.

These Regulations consolidate with amendments the Medicines (Restrictions on the Administration of Veterinary Medicinal Products) Regulations 1994 (SI 1994 2987) Reg.2 to Reg.5 which implemented in part Council Directive 81/851 ([1981] OJ L317/1), as amended by Council Directive 90/676 ([1990] OJ L373/15) and in part Council Directive 92/74 ([1992] OJ L297/12) widening the scope of Council Directive 81/851 and laying down additional provisions on homeopathic veterinary medicinal products. In addition consequential amendments are made to the Marketing Authorisations for Veterinary Medicinal Products Regulations 1994 (SI 1994 3241), the Medicines for Human Use (Marketing Authorisations Etc.) Regulations 1994 (SI 1994 3144) and the Registration of Homeopathic Veterinary Medicinal Products Regulations 1997 (SI 1997 322).

259. Articles

Dangerous Dogs (Amendment) Act 1997: J.P. 1997, 161 (24), 577-578. (Home Office Circular 29/1997 on provisions of Act in force June 8, 1997 allowing limited discretion in sentencing and procedure for obtaining certificates of exemption).

Dogs and the law *(Colette Kase)*: Magistrate 1997, 53(4), 94-95. (Advice for magistrates in dealing with cruelty cases and offences under Dangerous Dogs Act).

Hello Dolly *(G.D. McLeish)*: N.L.J. 1997, 147(6791), 682-683. (Whether cloned sheep is within the definition of "livestock" for which owners are liable under the Animals Act or a "product" under the Consumer Protection Act).

Humane trapping-or how the Community was hoist with its own petard *(Rhiannon Williams)*: E.L.M. 1997, 9(4), 176-178. (Background to EC negotiations on international agreement on humane trapping standards).

Regulating xenotransplantation *(Marie Fox* and *Jean McHale)*: N.L.J. 1997, 147(6777), 139-140. (Report of Advisory Group to Department of Health on ethics of transplanting tissue from animals into humans to alleviate shortage of transplantable organs).

Release of horses-is keeper liable?: Farm Law 1996, 8, 6-7. (Whether keeper of horses was liable for damage to car caused when animals panicked after being maliciously released onto road).

Roots and branches: cruelty to animals-the role of the magistrates' court *(Lynne McGechie)*: Magistrate 1997, 53(8), 221. (Training programme by Magistrates' Association and RSPCA on magistrates sentencing options in animal cruelty cases).

Tempering the draconian elements of the Dangerous Dogs Act 1991: J.P. 1997, 161(40), 934-936. (Criticism of provisions of 1991 Act, amendments made by Dangerous Dogs (Amendment) Act 1997 and clarification of "dangerously out of control and in a public place").

The Birds Directive *(Lara Levis)*: R.E.C.I.E.L. 1997, 6(2), 207-209. (Interpetation of Council Directive 79/409 on the conservation of wild birds Art.9 on derogations from prohibition on capture of birds for breeding purposes).

The pig, the transplant surgeon and the Nuffield Council *(Will Cartwright)*: Med. L. Rev. 1997, 4(3), 250-269. (Nuffield Council on Bioethics' report published in March 1996, examining the ethical questions raised by xenotransplantation).

Validity of Directive 64/433: Euro. L.M. 1997, 5(10), 10. (Whether Directive's requirement that animal inspections should be carried out by veterinary surgeon was unlawful).

260. Books

Love, Mark–Animals and the Law. Paperback: £30.00. ISBN 0-406-04967-X. Butterworth Law.

Soave, Orland A.–Animals, the Law and Veterinary Medicine. Hardback: £59.95. ISBN 1-57292-089-0. Paperback: £43.95. ISBN 1-57292-088-2. Austin and Winfield.

ARBITRATION

261. Appeals–arbitration awards–consent under arbitration agreement to appeal–no requirement to obtain leave to appeal

[Arbitration Act 1979 s.1(3).]

Held, that, where parties had, under the terms of an arbitration agreement governed by the Arbitration Act 1979, consented that an arbitration could be appealed to the High Court, there was no need to obtain leave to appeal. It was immaterial that the parties' "consent" in terms of s.1(3)(a) of the 1979 Act had been obtained before the dispute arose.

POSEIDON SCHIFFAHRT GmbH v. NOMADIC NAVIGATION CO LTD (THE TRADE NOMAD) [1997] C.L.C. 1542, Colman, J., QBD (Comm Ct).

262. Arbitrators–discretion–power to award interest on basis of own findings

[Arbitration Act 1979 s.19A; Supreme Court Act 1981 s.35A.]

Further to an agreement between A and C, A sought arbitration. On appeal from the arbitrator the following issues arose; (1) whether interest could be awarded by an arbitrator under the Arbitration Act 1979 s.19A where he substituted his extension of time for that of the architect and where there was not "wrongful detention of money" and (2) whether head office overheads, due to the employer's default, could be recovered.

Held, that (1) s.19A should not necessarily be construed in the same way as the Supreme Court Act 1981 s.35A. The aim of the 1979 Act was to give the arbitrator absolute discretion to do justice between the parties. Therefore, it could not be right that on the facts the arbitrator should not have been able to compensate the party which had been deprived of its money, and (2) it was for A to establish that lost office overheads had been suffered as a result of breach of duty by the employer. The arbitrator applied a formula for the calculation of the amounts which formula was sustained by the evidence before him. Therefore, there was nothing in the arbitrator's approach which would cause the court to overturn his decision.

AMEC BUILDING LTD v. CADMUS INVESTMENT CO LTD 51 Con. L.R. 105, Michel Kallipetis Q.C., QBD (OR).

263. Arbitrators–GAFTA procedure–dissent between arbitrators–appointment of substitute

See INTERNATIONAL TRADE: Cargill International SA v. Sociedad Iberica de Molturacion SA. §3208

264. Arbitrators–jurisdiction–building and engineering contracts–powers of determination

[Arbitration Act 1950 s.26.]

D appealed against the refusal to allow leave to enforce an award made under the Arbitration Act 1950 s.26 on the ground that the arbitrator had no jurisdiction to make the award he did. A civil engineering contract between D and L contained an arbitration clause which came into effect after agreement could not be reached on the amount of extra payment due when the contractors encountered difficult ground. The arbitrator made an award of £4,000 plus interest and concluded that L should pay D's costs. L submitted that correspondence between the parties narrowed, by agreement, the jurisdiction of the arbitrator.

Held, allowing the appeal, that the initial arbitration clause to which the parties agreed conferred on the arbitrator power to determine conclusively whether the agreement was subsequently varied in the way proposed.

DELTA CIVIL ENGINEERING CO LTD v. LONDON DOCKLANDS DEVELOPMENT CORP 81 B.L.R. 19, Staughton, L.J., CA.

265. Arbitrators–procedural error–request to remove arbitrator and umpire–no grounds for allegation of bias

[Arbitration Act 1950 s.22(1), s.23(1).]

F agreed with E to co-operate in the establishment and operation of a cruise business, subject to an English arbitration clause. The business proceeded in part through a jointly owned company EL. The business failed, and E claimed a balance due from F in respect of its share. The dispute was referred to arbitration. F applied for the removal of the arbitrators and umpire under the Arbitration Act 1950 s.23(1), or that a decision regarding discovery be set aside or remitted to the arbitrators, alleging that the tribunal had misunderstood F's discovery request and failed to give F a fair hearing or reasons, misconduct by overparticipation by the umpire, and bias on the part of one arbitrator, H. At first instance it was held that: (1) the 1950 Act s.22(1) applied to interlocutory proceedings so that a party could complain of procedural unfairness falling short of misconduct so as to put it right before the substantive hearing; (2) it was sensible and desirable for the umpire to have sat and retired with the arbitrators in the absence of any direct objection so that arguments arising did not have to be reargued in front of him; (3) the umpire's interventions did not indicate he was usurping the function of the arbitrators; (4) the arbitrators were not obliged to give reasons on an interlocutory ruling regarding discovery, and (5) there was no evidence of bias on the part of H, notwithstanding that in separate proceedings he had given a witness statement critical of F's solicitor's competence and judgment. F applied for leave to appeal.

Held, dismissing the application, that (1) given that the umpire did not participate in the decision making process, it was far fetched to suggest that the fact he listened to the arguments created a real danger he would have a predilection to take an adverse view of F thereafter, and (2) there was no basis for the allegation of bias against H; H was right not to mention the statement in other proceedings to his fellow arbitrators; F was aware of it and could have objected or changed lawyers, but in any event the fact a tribunal had formed strongly adverse views about a lawyer's competence did not disqualify the tribunal from acting on the grounds of actual or imputed bias.

Observed, that insofar as the judge below relied on s.22(1) as providing the power to review and remit a decision not in the form of an award, it was inconsistent with well established authority.

FLETAMENTOS MARITIMOS SA v. EFFJOHN INTERNATIONAL BV (NO.2) [1997] 2 Lloyd's Rep.302, Waller, L.J., CA.

266. Arbitrators–protracted proceedings–commitment fee–request for interim payment met by only one party

[Arbitration Act 1950 s.23(1).]

An arbitrator was appointed to conduct rent review proceedings which became protracted, leading him to request that each party make an interim payment. T objected, but SBC complied and sent a cheque which the arbitrator cashed, although he returned the money three months later. T's application for an order to have the arbitrator removed for misconduct under the Arbitration Act 1950 s.23(1), and for the appearance of bias, was dismissed. On appeal three points arising in *Norjarl A/S K/S v. Hyundai Heavy Industries Co Ltd* [1992] 1 Q.B. 863, [1991] C.L.Y. 186 were addressed to the effect that (1) a commitment fee could not be implied where it was not specified on appointment, (2) terms of appointment could not be changed unilaterally, and (3) to propose a commitment fee was not capable of amounting to misconduct.

Held, dismissing the appeal, that (1) in protracted proceedings, the arbitrator could not be expected to work for no reward until being reimbursed upon conclusion of the proceedings. On the true construction of the contract and the circumstances prevailing when it was made, there was an implied term that the arbitrator could request an interim payment towards costs for work done, which was quite different from a commitment fee. He was entitled to make a reasonable interim demand and to resign if it was not met, and (2) it was clear from *Norjarl A/S K/S* that an arbitrator could not accept a fee from just a single party after commencement of arbitration, and in such circumstances it was better for the arbitrator to return the fee immediately. However, in the instant case there was no deliberate wrongdoing on the part of the arbitrator to justify removal, the application was made to both parties and there was no private agreement between the arbitrator and SBC.

TURNER v. STEVENAGE BC [1997] 3 W.L.R. 309, Staughton, L.J., CA.

267. Awards–misunderstanding of interim award–no grounds for remission

Arbitrators of a dispute between N and S, having noted that S admitted that if it was in breach of the two contracts at the centre of the dispute it was liable to N for $468,853, made an interim award in favour of N of that amount. S applied for the award to be remitted on the grounds that: (1) neither S nor, at the hearing its representative, T, admitted or intended to admit the same; (2) there was a misunderstanding as to what had been asked by the arbitrators, and (3) it would be inequitable to allow the award to stand.

Held, dismissing the application, that S had not established that any aspect of the dispute had not been dealt with as fully as the parties were entitled to expect; there was every indication that the experienced arbitrators had been careful to ensure that T accepted the position as stated, so there had been no procedural mishap, *King v. Thomas Mckenna Ltd* [1991] 2 Q.B. 480, [1991] C.L.Y. 199 applied; N's undertaking to proceed with all due despatch to a further hearing and to repay any excess in the event of a finding of a lesser sum being due removed any suggestion of inequity.

NAPORANO IRON & METAL CO v. SIVAS IRON & STEELWORKS INC [1997] 2 Lloyd's Rep. 359, Cresswell, J., QBD (Comm Ct).

268. Commercial Court–practice note

[Rules of the Supreme Court Ord.73; Arbitration Act 1996.]

Held, that an entirely new Rules of the Supreme Court Ord.73 came into force on the same day as the Arbitration Act 1996, and both of which applied to applications and arbitrations commenced on or after January 31, 1997. Part I of Ord.73 sets out procedures; Part II dealt with the procedure for arbitrations begun and applications made before January 31, and Part III related to the enforcement of all awards. A multi purpose form of originating and subsidiary process known as an "arbitration application" to be used for all arbitrations save enforcement and a new uniform process including comprehensive directions to apply unless the court otherwise ordered. Applications for leave to appeal on a question of law to be determined without a hearing, unless the court otherwise ordered. Arbitration applications to be heard in chambers and the time limit for applications challenging an award to be 28 days. Where an overseas party was represented by an English solicitor who had been authorised to accept service of notices or documents in the arbitration and whose authority to act in the arbitration had not been determined, there would be no need to obtain leave to serve an arbitration application outside the jurisdiction. The Commercial Court continued to have primary responsibility for monitoring the supervisory jurisdiction over arbitrations and sought to achieve consistency in construction and approach by immediately circulating decisions. Such circulation to be extended to the profession, which was invited to cooperate in facilitating publication of awards in chambers and identifying problems with the new system.

PRACTICE NOTE (ARBITRATION: NEW PROCEDURE); *sub nom.* PRACTICE NOTE (COMMERCIAL COURT: ARBITRATION) [1997] 1 W.L.R. 391, Colman, J., QBD (Comm Ct).

269. Construction–application of FETAC provisional rules–FETAC succeeded by CIETRAC–application of successor's rules

[Arbitration Act 1975 s.5(2)(e).]

C contracted with B to purchase steel. The contract contained an arbitration clause which provided for any disagreements to be submitted to the Foreign Trade Arbitration Commission of the China Council for the Promotion of International Trade, FETAC, in accordance with its provisional rules. By the date of the dispute between the parties FETAC had changed its name to China International Economic and Trade Arbitration Commission, CIETAC. The court below opined that the CIETAC rules applied. B appealed against the refusal to set aside ex parte leave to enforce the arbitration award in the sum of $51,678 and RMB (Chinese Yuan) 385,372 together with RMB 35,350 costs. B claimed that the later arbitration procedure was not in accordance with the agreement of the parties as required by the Arbitration Act 1975 s.5(2)(e), because the arbitration body CIETAC which had taken over from FETAC had different rules and in particular had changed a maximum arbitration fee of one per cent to a sliding scale which allowed a charge of 2.7 per cent in the instant case.

Held, dismissing the appeal, that the true construction of the clause must be that arbitration was to take place under the rules of FETAC or any successor body. Although the court retained a discretion, the effect of the change of rules was to make B liable for an extra £1,500 in fees which was insufficiently prejudicial to justify refusal to enforce the award, *Chen Jen Nan Dar Industrial and Trade United Co Ltd v. FM International Ltd* [1992] 1 Hong Kong Cases 328 followed.

CHINA AGRIBUSINESS DEVELOPMENT CORP v. BALLI TRADING, [1997] C.L.C. 1437, Longmore, J., QBD (Comm Ct).

270. Costs–breach of building contract–rejection of two sealed offers–final award less than rejected offers–costs awarded from time of second offer

C appealed against an arbitrator's final costs award in an arbitration in which A claimed payment for loss and expenses under a contract with C for building work. A was employed by C to carry out building work to which there were delays and disruptions. The arbitrator awarded A costs of £437,356 which was approximately £25,000 less than the amount of C's first sealed offer which A had rejected. A also rejected a second offer which was also for more than the final award. C was awarded its costs only from the date of the second offer. C appealed, contending that it should have been awarded costs from the date of the first offer and that the arbitrator had erred in accepting A's argument that C's first offer should be disregarded because of a late amendment made by C to its defence to A's claim. The amendment concerned an aspect of the building work which was found, as a preliminary point, to have been the subject of a compromise agreement between the parties so that A's claim on that issue was not heard.

Held, dismissing the appeal, that it was not right to speculate whether A would have rejected the first offer regardless of the late amendment and its public stance could not be taken as a true indication of its intentions because it would inevitably wish to appear to be more confident than it actually was about achieving a higher award. The arbitrator, therefore, was justified in finding as he did and he properly directed himself according to *Blexen v. G Percy Trentham* 54 B.L.R. 37, [1991] C.L.Y. 188.

CADMUS INVESTMENT CO LTD v. AMEC BUILDING LTD, Trans. Ref: 1996-Folio 1864, April 17, 1997, Tuckey, J., QBD (Comm Ct).

271. **Experts—decision referred to an independent consultant—appointee to act as an expert not arbiter—stay of proceedings**

B and C alleged a breach of each other's contractual obligations for B's packaging of C's soft drinks. Clause 14 of the agreement, headed "arbitration", provided that any dispute arising from the construction or performance of the agreement be referred for decision by a person appointed by the Director General of the British Soft Drinks Association who "shall be an independent consultant and shall act as an expert and not as an arbiter and his decision shall be final and binding on the parties". B referred the matter to the Director General who appointed F. F had much experience of the soft drinks industry but none of dispute resolution. C commenced proceedings which B sought to stay by reference to cl.14.

Held, refusing the stay, (1) the heading of a contract's clause could not prevail over its express terms nor create ambiguity in them, therefore notwithstanding the heading of cl.14 it was not an arbitration clause, and the appointee was to act as an expert, not an arbitrator, and (2) the court had inherent jurisdiction to stay proceedings arising out of an agreement providing for resolution by an expert, the burden being on the person opposing the clause to show grounds for refusal; there were grounds for refusal as F had no experience of dispute resolution and the clause provided no rules or principles for the dispute resolution, *Channel Tunnel Group Ltd v. Balfour Beatty Construction* [1993] 1 All E.R. 644, [1993] C.L.Y. 151 considered.

COTT UK LTD v. FE BARBER LTD [1997] 3 All E.R. 540, Hegarty Q.C., QBD.

272. **International commercial arbitration—extension of time to set aside award—enforcement of illegal contracts—public policy**

[Arbitration Act 1975 s.3(1)(a); Rules of the Supreme Court Ord.3 r.5.]

N applied for time to set aside an ex parte order giving leave to enforce an award made under the Arbitration Act 1975 s.3(1)(a) in respect of shortages and defects in contracts for the supply of aluminium to S. N contended that there was fresh evidence available from legal experts that the judgment of the Kemerovo arbitration court suggested that the contract and its enforcement was illegal under Russian law and that its enforcement was therefore contrary to public policy. N relied on the decision in *Mortgage Corp Ltd v. Sandoes* [1997] P.N.L.R. 263, [1997] C.L.Y. 783 to contend that the lack of any good reason for its failure to conform to the time limit was not fatal to its application for the exercise of the court's discretion to extend time under RSC Ord.3 r.5.

Held, dismissing the application and refusing a stay of execution, that the matter of illegality had been considered by the arbiters. Notwithstanding the fact that the order had been made ex parte, good reasons would be required for an application outside the 21 day time limit to succeed, *Beachley Property Ltd v. Edgar* [1997] P.N.L.R. 197, [1996] 1 C.L.Y. 943 and *Mortgage Corp Ltd v. Sandoes* distinguished as referring to trial preparation rather than the enforcement of concluded arbitration proceedings, *Industria de Oleos Pacaembu SA v. NV Bunge* [1982] 1 Lloyd's Rep. 490, [1982] C.L.Y. 109 and *International Petroleum Refining & Supply Sdad v. Elpis Finance SA (The Faith)* [1993] 2 Lloyd's Rep. 408, [1994] C.L.Y. 220 considered.

SOINCO SACI v. NOVOKUZNETSK ALUMINIUM PLANT (NO.1), Trans. Ref: 1996-Folio No.1915, February 12, 1997, Colman, J., QBD (Comm Ct).

273. Limitations–notice stating that dispute was to be referred–notice insufficient to commence arbitration

[Hague Rules Art.III r.6; Limitation Act 1980 s.34(3); Arbitration Act 1996 s.12(3).]

T contracted to deliver a consignment of pipes to V, the contract providing that disputes were to be referred to three arbitrators and that each of the parties was to appoint one arbitrator, with the third to be chosen by the two appointees. It was accepted that the contract was subject to the Hague Rules Art.III r.6, such that unless suit was brought within one year of delivery T would be discharged of any liability. On inspection the delivered pipes were found to be damaged and in 1995 V wrote a letter to T stating that the dispute was to be referred to the three arbitrators. In 1997 V appointed an arbitrator and called on T to appoint their arbitrator. T denied that the letter satisfied the conditions necessary to bring suit under the Limitation Act 1980 s.34(3) and V applied for a declaration that the dispute had been validly referred to arbitration in 1995.

Held, dismissing the application, that a notice which merely stated that a dispute was to be referred to arbitration in accordance with a prior agreement was insufficient to commence arbitration under s.34(3). Such a notice did not carry with it an implied request that an arbitrator be appointed by the recipient, *Nea Agrex SA v. Baltic Shipping Co Ltd* [1976] Q.B. 933, [1976] C.L.Y. 2534 not followed. Were it otherwise, the carefully drafted provisions of s.34 spelling out the procedure to be followed if an arbitration was to be treated as validly commenced would be rendered otiose. However, the court was satisfied that the circumstances were outside the reasonable contemplation of both parties when the time limit was agreed and that it would be just to grant V an extension of time for the commencement of proceedings pursuant to the Arbitration Act 1996 s.12(3).

VOSNOC LTD v. TRANSGLOBAL PROJECTS LTD, *The Times*, August 27, 1997, Raymond Jack Q.C., QBD (Comm Ct).

274. Stay of proceedings–statutory discretion to refuse stay–applicable standard of proof

[Arbitration Act 1950 s.4.]

A's trustee in bankruptcy appealed against a decision staying an action against B under the Arbitration Act 1950 s.4 on the ground that the contemplated proceedings related to matters which the parties had agreed to refer to arbitration. In resisting the stay, the trustee contended that if B had not wrongfully terminated the agreement under which A had been employed as a sub-contractor, then it was unlikely he would have become bankrupt and that, whereas legal aid was available for the present action, it was unavailable for arbitration proceedings and that would effectively stifle his claim if the stay remained.

Held, dismissing the appeal, that although the court had discretion under the 1950 Act s.4, the terms of the agreement would stand unless there was sufficient reason to refuse a stay. Poverty of itself was not a sufficient reason, but a breach resulting in an inability to prosecute arbitration proceedings could suffice. The authorities were inconsistent as to the applicable standard of proof, *Fakes v. Taylor Woodrow Construction Ltd* [1973] Q.B. 436, [1973] C.L.Y. 97

and *Goodman v. Winchester and Alton Railway Plc* [1985] 1 W.L.R. 141, [1984] C.L.Y. 125 considered. To adopt a normal civil standard would require a mini trial to establish the prospect for success, which would be wrong in the circumstances, and it would not be appropriate to adopt a test based on the seriousness of the issue to be tried. The correct approach, when deciding whether to exercise discretion under s.4, required the plaintiff to show a reasonable prospect of success. On the facts, even if A had not been bankrupt it was unlikely he would have been able to fund the arbitration. B's actions could not be shown to have caused A's inability to prosecute proceedings and therefore A failed to establish the exceptional circumstances necessary to remove the stay.

TRUSTEE OF THE PROPERTY OF ANDREWS v. BROCK BUILDERS (KESSINGLAND) LTD [1997] 3 W.L.R. 124, Aldous, L.J., CA.

275. Articles

Arbitrate don't litigate *(D. Mark Cato)*: A.D.R.L.J. 1997, 3(Jul), 158-168. (Case studies on how introduction of 1996 Act will improve conduct of arbitration).

Arbitration around the world *(Joseph D. Garon)*: M.I.P. 1996, 61, 41-46. (Advantages and disadvantages of arbitration in Canada, France, Germany, Italy, India, Japan, Korea, Mexico, Sweden, UK and US).

Arbitration on probate *(Philip Rossdale)*: S.J. 1997, 141 (16), 380. (Use of Part I of 1996 Act to resolve probate disputes, and possible methods of enforcing award).

Arbitration under Order 73 *(John H.M. Sims)*: S.J. 1997, 141 (31), 766-767. (Rule by rule guide to revised RSC Ord.73 Part I, in force January 31, 1997, highlighting change in court's role from supervision to support).

Arbitration: interim awards *(Robert Briner)*: I.B.L. 1997, 25(4), 153-155, 160. (Considerations for arbitrator in awarding costs).

Arbitrators get real teeth *(North of England P&I Association)*: P & I Int. 1997, 11 (10), 216-217. (Arbitration Act 1996 in force January 31, 1997 introduces concept of autonomy of parties and extends arbitrators' powers).

Avoiding court intervention in international arbitrations *(Norton Rose)*: I.H.L. 1997, 47(Feb), 71-72. (Whether possible or desirable to bypass courts entirely in international arbitration, mandatory provisions of 1996 Act and extent to which can be avoided by specifying different forum).

Challenging an international arbitration award under the Arbitration Act 1996 - what has changed? *(Norton Rose)*: I.H.L. 1997, 51 (Jun), 76. (Reduction of UK court's powers to intervene in proceedings and limits on parties' abilities under the Arbitration Act 1996 s.66 to s.69 to challenge awards).

Choice of substantive law in international arbitration *(Marc Blessing)*: J. Int. Arb. 1997, 14(2), 39-65. (Extent to which parties are free to choose applicable law, and subjective and objective approaches to determining applicable law where parties have failed to do so).

Costs, fees and security for costs in international arbitrations *(Nigel Rawding)*: Int. T.L.R. 1997, 3(3), 70-75. (Treatment of costs under 1996 Act, including arbitrator's power to award costs and security).

Does business need litigation and arbitration? *(Paul Newman)*: Arbitration 1997, 63(2), Supp 35-54. (Advantages and disadvantages of arbitration, ADR, litigation and mediation in commercial dispute resolution).

Domestic arbitration: practice in continental Europe and its lessons for arbitration in England *(Robert Briner)*: Arbitration Int. 1997, 13(2), 155-166.

Extending time to commence arbitration *(Miranda Karali)*: P & I Int. 1997, 11 (10), 215-216. (Provision to replace test based on undue hardship with more restrictive criterion reducing delay, uncertainty and judicial intervention).

For better or worse? *(Robert Akenhead)*: Legal Bus. 1997, 73(Apr), Supp Con 12-13. (Provisions of 1996 Act focusing on the removal of the discretion on whether to allow stay of proceedings to arbitration and the new powers of arbitrators).

How non-contracting states to the "universal" New York Arbitration Convention enjoy third-party benefits but not third-party rights *(Richard J. Graving)*: J. Int. Arb. 1997, 14(3), 167-183.

Incorporation of arbitration clauses *(Norton Rose)*: I.H.L. 1996/97, 46(Dec/Jan), 76-77. (Common law position that arbitration clauses cannot be incorporated into contract by reference and effect of s.5 of 1996 Act).

International arbitration in England *(Norton Rose)*: P & I Int. 1997, 11(6), 124-126. (How the Arbitration Act 1996 strengthens London's position as centre of international arbitration).

International arbitration: challenging arbitration awards in London under the Arbitration Act 1996 *(Peter J. Rees)*: I.C. Lit. 1997, Oct, 36-38. (Including challenging substantive jurisdiction of tribunal, alleging serious irregularity of arbitrator, or appealing on point of law).

International arbitration: how to choose a forum that is right for you *(Cedric Chao)*: I.C. Lit. 1997, Nov, 30-35. (Procedural considerations).

International commercial arbitration on the Internet: has the future come too early? *(Jasna Arsic)*: J. Int. Arb. 1997, 14(3), 209-221. (Jurisdictional problems, enforcement of awards, forum shopping and possible future changes).

Keep quiet *(Jonathan Gaunt)* and *(Vivien King)*: E.G. 1997, 9735, 82-84. (Enforcement of confidentiality clauses in arbitration proceedings, extent to which clauses can be broken open by order for discovery and subpoena, and requirements imposed by Arbitration Act 1996 for issue of subpoena).

Multiparty disputes and arbitration *(Michael P.F. Furmston)*: Cons. Law 1997, 8(2), 37-38. (Whether court has jurisdiction to stop arbitration in circumstances where one party wants to litigate and other wants to arbitrate).

New Arbitration Act aims to restore London's supremacy *(David Wyld* and *Simon Nurney)*: I.F.L. Rev. 1996, 15(11), 52-55. (Provisions of consolidating and amending legislation, its deviations from UNCITRAL Model Law and its benefits for London as international commercial arbitration centre).

New-look arbitration in England–definitely worth considering *(Dominic Spenser Underhill)*: I.C. Lit. 1997, Mar, 49-51. (New legislation to reduce problems of expense and delay which have restricted effectiveness and popularity of previous arbitration procedures).

Practical issues in drafting international arbitration clauses *(Richard H. Kreindler)*: Arbitration 1997, 63(1), 47-55. (How to draft an arbitration clause, including settling choices such as institution, arbitrators and what wording to leave out or include and whether to use standard clauses or vary them).

Sea-change or beached whale? *(Stewart Patterson)*: Arbitration 1997, 63(2), 135-137. (Power of arbitrators and more flexible arbitration procedures under 1996 Act).

Security for costs *(Peter Bowsher)*: Arbitration 1997, 63(1), 36-40. (Approaches which arbitrators may take in awarding security for costs after implementation of 1996 Act which transfers court's power to award costs to them).

Some private international law aspects of the Arbitration Act 1996 *(Jonathan Hill)*: I.C.L.Q. 1997, 46(2), 274-308. (Effect on jurisdiction of English courts, choice of law questions and enforcement of foreign awards).

The Arbitration Act 1996: implications for drafting commercial contracts and conducting arbitrations *(Ted Greeno* and *Adam Johnson)*: O.G.L.T.R. 1997, 15(1), 3-10. (Framework and scope of Act, choice of law issues, disapplying provisions of Act, consolidation of proceedings and changes effected by Act).

The ICE arbitration procedure *(Paul Newman)*: Cons. Law 1997, 8(7), 224-229. (Powers given to arbitrators under 1983 Procedure and subsequent review to take account of Arbitration Act 1996).

The UNCITRAL model law and the problem of delay in international commercial arbitration *(Andrew I. Okekeifere)*: J. Int. Arb. 1997, 14(1), 125-139. (Sources of delay and extent to which Model Law has helped solve or reduce problem).

The independence of arbitrators in totalitarian states: tackling the tough issues *(Jacques Werner)*: J. Int. Arb. 1997, 14(1), 141-144. (Contradictions in application of Art.2.7 of ICC Arbitration Rules requiring independence).

The trade explosion and some likely effects on international arbitration *(Jacques Werner)*: J. Int. Arb. 1997, 14(2), 5-15. (Growth of arbitration as result of explosion of world trade, covering lack of contractual relationship between parties in dispute, public law issues which private arbitrators will face and case for international appellate arbitral body).

This year's changes at the ICC:

pitfalls for the unwary *(Gary B. Born)*: I.C. Lit. 1997, Nov, 27-29. (Comprehensive revision of International Chamber of Commerce Rules of Arbitration).

UNCITRAL Notes on Organizing Arbitral Proceedings and the conduct of evidence: a new approach to international arbitration *(Roberto Ceccon)*: J. Int. Arb. 1997, 14(2), 67-85. (How evidence is treated in international commercial arbitration and rules given under Notes relating to documentary evidence, witnesses and expert witnesses; includes text of Notes).

When is an arbitration clause unenforceable in an international transaction? *(Norton Rose)*: I.H.L. 1997, 50(May), 84-85. (Courts' jurisdiction to hear matters that within scope of arbitration clause where clause held to be null and void, inoperative or incapable of being performed under Art.11(3) of 1958 Convention).

276. Books

Bernstein, Ronald; Tackaberry, John; Marriott, Arthur—Handbook of Arbitration Practice. Hardback: £110.00. ISBN 0-421-56540-3. Sweet & Maxwell.

Cato, D. Mark—Arbitration Practice and Procedure. 2nd Ed. Hardback: £150.00. ISBN 1-85978-150-0. LLP Limited.

Kendall, John; Sutton, David St John; Gill, Judith—Russell on Arbitration. Hardback: £140.00. ISBN 0-420-48090-0. Sweet & Maxwell.

Salzedo, Simon; Lord, Richard—Arbitration. Practice Notes. Paperback: £15.95. ISBN 1-85941-302-1. Cavendish Publishing Ltd.

Seppala; Bond; Buhler—1997 ICC Rules of Arbitration. Hardback: £48.00. ISBN 0-421-60130-2. Sweet & Maxwell.

ARMED FORCES

277. Air Force—causing annoyance by flying—mens rea required to prove offence

[Air Force Act 1955 s.52.]

Held, that the offence of flying an aircraft so as to cause, or be likely to cause, unnecessary annoyance to any person contrary to the Air Force Act 1955 s.52 was not a strict liability offence. The mens rea required was an intention to fly so as to cause or be likely to cause annoyance, or recklessness as to whether annoyance was or was likely to be caused and, in interpreting recklessness, the approach in *R. v. Kimber* (1983) 77 Cr. App. R. 225, [1983] C.L.Y. 693 was to be preferred to that in *R. v. Caldwell* [1982] A.C. 341, [1981] C.L.Y. 385 and *R. v. Lawrence* [1982] A.C. 510, [1981] C.L.Y. 2382.

R. v. PAINE (NICHOLAS), *The Times*, June 21, 1997, Stuart-Smith, L.J., CMAC.

278. Air Force—conditions of employment

ROYAL AIR FORCE TERMS OF SERVICE (AMENDMENT) REGULATIONS 1997, SI 1997 231; made under the Armed Forces Act 1966 s.2. In force: March 1, 1997; £0.65.

These Regulations further amend the Royal Air Force Terms of Service Regulations 1985 (SI 1985 1820) by revoking Reg.4 which enabled persons between the ages of 16 years and 19 years and seven months to be enlisted for a special term of 12 months or two years service. They also bring into line the position of men and women under Reg.5 of the 1985 Regulations which provides for engagements with the right to transfer to the reserve and amend Reg.5 to enable those who have enlisted on a notice engagement pursuant to that Regulation to be treated as if they had been enlisted on a fixed term engagement pursuant to Reg.3. In addition they amend Sch.1 to update the titles of the office holders who are the competent air force authorities for the purposes of the 1985 Regulations.

279. Air Force–courts martial

COURTS MARTIAL (ROYAL AIR FORCE) RULES 1997, SI 1997 171; made under the Air Force Act 1955 s.75, s.83B, s.84A, s.92, s.93, s.94, s.102, s.103, s.113, s.141, s.143, s.209. In force: April 1, 1997; £6.75.

These rules prescribe the procedure governing the prosecution and trial of offences at courts martial under the Air Forces Act 1995. They generally accord with procedures in the Crown Court. They replace and revoke the Rule of Procedure (Air Force) 1972 (SI 1972 419) and take account of changes in the law and procedure since then, giving effect in particular to the provisions of the Armed Forces Act 1996.

280. Air Force–courts martial–jurisdiction of court–objection to charge

[Air Force Act 1955 s.70(4); Rules of Procedure (Air Force) 1972 (SI 1972 419) r.36, r.37.]

L applied for leave to appeal against his conviction of indecent assault before an RAF court martial. A charge of attempted rape had also been brought, to which L had objected on the grounds that such an offence could not be charged under the Air Force Act 1955 s.70(4).

Held, refusing the application, that the conviction could not be considered unsafe. The court martial had dealt with the objection under the Rules of Procedure (Air Force) 1972 r.36, which covered applications where the court lacked any jurisdiction to try a charge. Since L's objection related to a particular charge it should have been dealt with under r.37(2), which provided that where there was another charge the court could pursue that charge, and it was proper for the court to proceed on the charge of indecent assault. Although it was wrong to deal with L's application under r.36, all parties understood why the application had been brought, and L had not been prejudiced.

R. v. LISLE (GRAHAM DAVID), *The Times*, February 26, 1997, Harrison, J., CMAC.

281. Air Force–criminal procedure

RULES OF PROCEDURE (AIR FORCE) (AMENDMENT NO.2) RULES 1997, SI 1997 14; made under the Air Force Act 1955 s.103, s.209. In force: February 1, 1997; £0.65.

These Rules amend the Rules of Procedure (Air Force) 1972 (SI 1972 419) in consequence of the Criminal Justice and Public Order Act 1994 (Application to the Armed Forces) Order 1997 (SI 1997 16) which applies s.34 to s.38 of the 1994 Act to the Armed Forces. The amendment substitutes a new form of words which an accused is to be asked under r.9(d) when evidence is being taken. The new words will inform the accused that it may harm his defence not to mention something which he later relies on in court.

282. Armed Forces Act 1996 (c.46)–Commencement No.2 Order

ARMED FORCES ACT 1996 (COMMENCEMENT NO.2) ORDER 1997, SI 1997 304 (C.14); made under the Armed Forces Act 1996 s.36. Commencement details: bringing into force various provisions of the Act on April 1, 1997; £1.10.

This Order brings various provisions of the Armed Forces Act 1996 into force.

283. Armed Forces Act 1996 (c.46)–Commencement No.3 Order

ARMED FORCES 1996 (COMMENCEMENT NO.3 AND TRANSITIONAL PROVISIONS) ORDER 1997, SI 1997 2164 (C.85); made under the Armed Forces Act 1996 s.36. Commencement details: bringing into force various provisions of the Act on October 1, 1997; £1.10.

This Order brings into force the Armed Forces Act 1996 s.20 to s.27 which relate to applications for redress of complaints and complaints to industrial tribunals.

284. Army–courts martial

COURTS MARTIAL (ARMY) RULES 1997, SI 1997 169; made under the Army Act 1955 s.75, s.83B, s.84A, s.92, s.93, s.94, s.102, s.103, s.113, s.141, s.143, s.209. In force: April 1, 1997; £6.10.

These Rules prescribe the procedure governing the prosecution and trial offences at courts-martial under the Army Act 1995. They generally accord with procedures in the Crown Court. They replace and revoke the Rules of Procedure (Army) 1972 (SI 1972 316) and take account of changes in the law and procedure since then, giving effect in particular to the provisions of the Armed Forces Act 1996.

285. Army–criminal procedure

RULES OF PROCEDURE (ARMY) (AMENDMENT NO.2) RULES 1997, SI 1997 18; made under the Army Act 1955 s.103, s.209. In force: February 1, 1997; £0.65.

These Rules amend the Rules of Procedure (Army) 1972 (SI 1972 316) in consequence of the Criminal Justice and Public Order Act 1994 (Application to the Armed Forces) Order 1997 (SI 1995 16) which applies s.34 to s.38 of the 1994 Act to the Armed Forces. The amendment substitutes a new form of words which an accused is to be asked under r.9(d) when evidence is being taken. The words will inform the accused that it may harm his defence not to mention something which he later relies on in court.

286. Courts–standing civilian courts

STANDING CIVILIAN COURTS ORDER 1997, SI 1997 172; made under the Armed Forces Act 1976 Sch.3 para.1, para.12. In force: April 1, 1997; £6.10.

This Order makes provision with respect to the prosecution and trial of offences by Standing Civilian Courts, the review of findings and sentences of, and appeals from, such courts. It revokes and replaces the Standing Civilian Courts Order 1977 (SI 1977 88) and give effect to changes to the Armed Forces Act 1976 made by the Armed Forces Act 1996.

287. Courts martial–appeals

COURTS-MARTIAL APPEAL (AMENDMENT) RULES 1997, SI 1997 580 (L.3); made under the Courts-Martial (Appeals) Act 1968 s.49. In force: April 1, 1997; £2.40.

These Rules amend the Courts-Martial Appeal Rules 1968 (SI 1968 1071). They change the time limit for presentation of a petition before the exercise of a right of appeal to 28 days in all cases, consequent on the abolition of the requirement for findings of army and air force courts martial to be confirmed by the appropriate officer. They also make provision for applications under the Criminal Justice Act 1988 s.32(1) (evidence through television links where witness is outside the country where the court is sitting and such evidence is by child witnesses) and s.32A of that Act (video recordings of testimony from child witnesses). Rights of audience in the Courts-Martial Appeal Court have been extended to include all those who have rights of audience in the Criminal Division of the Court of Appeal. Substituted Form 1 and Form 2 reflect the fact that an appeal can now be made by servicemen against sentence as well as conviction and have been generally updated. The new provisions relating to time limits for presenting a petition and the new Form 1 shall not apply to appeals where the conviction has taken place or sentence passed before April 1, 1997.

288. Courts martial–appeals–withdrawal of abandonment of appeal–jurisdiction to grant application

[European Convention on Human Rights 1950 Art.6; Army Act 1955.]

W, convicted at a court martial of wounding with intent, applied for his notice of abandonment to be treated as a nullity. W's application for leave to appeal against conviction was dismissed and W completed a notice of abandonment. W contended that, in view of the decision of the European Court of Human Rights in *Findlay v. United Kingdom* [1997] C.L.Y. 2807, his conviction was flawed and his notice of abandonment should be withdrawn. The European Court upheld the complaint against the United Kingdom under the European Convention on Human Rights 1950 Art.6, ruling that the court martial procedure, under the Army Act 1955, did not give *Findlay* a hearing by an independent and impartial tribunal.

Held, dismissing the application, that the jurisdiction to grant leave to withdraw a notice of abandonment was narrow, there being no discretionary jurisdiction to grant leave due to a subsequent decision of the courts which may be favourable to the appellant, *R. v. Medway* [1976] Q.B. 779, [1975] C.L.Y. 502 considered. As to the jurisdiction which did exist, W had not satisfied the "nullity test". W was aware of the proceedings on which he sought to rely and accordingly, the act of abandonment was obviously his act.

R. v. WIGNALL (PHILLIP GEORGE), Trans. Ref: 96/4954/S2, June 16, 1997, Timothy Walker, J., CMAC.

289. Courts martial–criminal evidence–application of Criminal Justice Act 1967

CRIMINAL JUSTICE ACT 1967 (APPLICATION TO COURTS-MARTIAL) (EVIDENCE) REGULATIONS 1997, SI 1997 173; made under the Army Act 1955 s.99A; the Air Force Act 1995 s.99A; the Naval Discipline Act 1957 s.64B; and the Criminal Justice Act 1967 s.12. In force: April 1, 1997; £1.10.

These Regulations amend the Criminal Justice Act 1976 s.9, s.10 and s.11 in their application to courts-martial. The modifications reflect differences in terminology between civilian courts and courts-martial.

290. Courts martial–prosecution of civilians

COURTS-MARTIAL AND STANDING CIVILIAN COURTS (ARMY AND ROYAL AIR FORCE) (ADDITIONAL POWERS ON TRIAL OF CIVILIANS) REGULATIONS 1997, SI 1997 579; made under the Army Act 1955 Sch.5A para.17; the Air Force Act 1955 Sch.5A para.17; and the Naval Discipline Act 1957 Sch.4A para.17. In force: April 1, 1997; £2.80.

These Regulations revoke the Courts-Martial and Standing Civilian Courts (Additional Powers on Trial of Civilians) Regulations 1977 (SI 1977 87) and the subsequent amending regulations, which were tri-service in application. These Regulations, which principally affect only the prosecution of civilians under the Army Act 1955 and the Air Force Act 1955 make provision for matters which are supplementary and incidental to the additional powers available under Schedule 5A to the 1955 Acts. Those Schedules permit the court to exercise additional powers on sentence if a civilian is convicted under either of the 1955 Acts by a court-martial or by a Standing Civilian Court established under the Armed Forces Act 1976. The Regulations substantially re-enact the 1977 Regulations, but take into account the changes made to the 1955 Acts and the 1976 Act by the Armed Forces Act 1996.

291. Courts martial–right to fair trial–army procedure violated ECHR

See HUMAN RIGHTS: Findlay v. United Kingdom. §2807

292. Courts martial–right to fair trial–RAF procedure violated ECHR

See HUMAN RIGHTS: Coyne v. United Kingdom. §2808

293. Courts martial–sending obscene material through post–sentence of dismissal from service

[Armed Forces Act 1996 s.17.]

A sentence imposed by a court martial, dismissing a staff sergeant in the Royal Military Police and reducing him to the ranks so that he would lose certain pension rights, was too harsh where the offence of sending obscene material through the post would only have attracted a small fine in a civilian court. L, a staff sergeant in the Royal Military Police, appealed against a sentence that he be dismissed from Her Majesty's Service and reduced to the ranks following conviction on two counts of sending obscene material through the post. He had exchanged the material with a male civilian and the correspondence had only been discovered when the civilian's house was searched in connection with other offences. L argued that the sentence was too severe, particularly as dismissal would result in considerable loss of pension rights.

Held, allowing the appeal, that sentences imposed by a court martial were intended both to punish serving officers for their criminal conduct and to discipline them, and the court, in determining an appeal under the Armed Forces Act 1996 s.17, should bear in mind that, in general, a military court was better placed to decide the appropriate penalty necessary to maintain efficiency and discipline. However, as the offence in question was of limited seriousness, did not jeopardise trust and discipline within L's unit and would have attracted only a small fine in a civilian court, the sentence was too harsh, particularly in view of its effect on L's pension rights. The sentence would be quashed and a fine of £200 substituted.

R. v. LOVE (COLIN GILBERT), *The Times*, December 3, 1997, Simon Brown, L.J., CMAC.

294. Criminal evidence–application of PACE

POLICE AND CRIMINAL EVIDENCE ACT 1984 (APPLICATION TO THE ARMED FORCES) ORDER 1997, SI 1997 15; made under the Police and Criminal Evidence Act 1984 s.113. In force: February 1, 1997; £1.95.

This Order applies specified provisions of the Police and Criminal Evidence Act 1984 which concern questioning and treatment of persons by the police, to investigations of offences conducted by the Service police under the Army Act 1955, the Air Force Act 1955 or the Naval Discipline Act 1957 and to persons arrested under any of those Acts. It revokes the Police and Criminal Evidence Act 1984 (Application to Armed Forces) Order 1985 (SI 1985 1882 as amended by SI 1990 1448).

295. Criminal evidence–application of PACE codes of practice

POLICE AND CRIMINAL EVIDENCE ACT 1984 (CODES OF PRACTICE) (ARMED FORCES) ORDER 1997, SI 1997 17; made under the Police and Criminal Evidence Act 1984 s.113. In force: February 1, 1997; £0.65.

This Order appoints February 1, 1997 as the date on which revised codes of practice issued under the Police and Criminal Evidence Act 1984 s.113(3) will come into operation. This Order revokes the Police and Criminal Evidence Act 1984 Codes of Practice (Armed Forces) Order 1986 (SI 1986 307) and the Police and Criminal Evidence Act 1984 Codes of Practice (Armed Forces) Order 1989 (SI 1989 2128) which brought into operation the previous codes.

296. Criminal evidence—rights to silence—application of Criminal Justice and Public Order Act 1994

CRIMINAL JUSTICE AND PUBLIC ORDER ACT 1994 (APPLICATION TO THE ARMED FORCES) ORDER 1997, SI 1997 16; made under the Criminal Justice and Public Order Act 1994 s.39. In force: February 1, 1997; £1.10.

This Order applies specified provisions of the Criminal Justice and Public Order Act 1994 s.34 to s.38 to the Armed Forces. Section 34 makes provision for the effect of an accused's failure to mention facts when questioned or charged. Section 35 makes provision for the effect of an accused's silence at trial. Section 36 makes provision for the effect of accused's failure or refusal to account for objects, substances or marks. Section 37 makes provision for the effect of an accused's failure or refusal to account for his presence at a particular place.

297. Discipline Acts—continuation in force

ARMY, AIR FORCE AND NAVAL DISCIPLINE ACTS (CONTINUATION) ORDER 1997, SI 1997 1745; made under the Armed Forces Act 1996 s.1. In force: July 22, 1997; £0.65.

This Order enables the Army Act 1955, the Air Force Act 1955 and the Naval Discipline Act 1957 to continue in force for a period of 12 months beyond August 31, 1997.

298. Equal pay—industrial tribunals—complaints from armed forces personnel

EQUAL PAY (COMPLAINTS TO INDUSTRIAL TRIBUNALS) (ARMED FORCES) REGULATIONS 1997, SI 1997 2162; made under the Equal Pay Act 1970 s.7A. In force: October 1, 1997; £0.65.

These Regulations specify the circumstances in which a person may present a complaint to an industrial tribunal in respect of his service in the armed forces, notwithstanding that he would otherwise be precluded from making such a complaint by the Equal Pay Act 1970 s.7A(5) which requires a person to go through the service redress procedures before making a complaint to an industrial tribunal.

299. Equal treatment—reference to ECJ on whether protection of Equal Treatment Directive afforded to homosexuals

[Council Directive 76/207 on equal treatment for men and women as regards access to employment Art.2.]

P, who was discharged from the Royal Navy because of his homosexuality, applied for a reference to be made to the ECJ on the question of whether Council Directive 76/207 Art.2 on equal treatment extended protection to homosexuals.

Held, that the following questions should be referred to the ECJ: (1) whether discrimination on the basis of sexual orientation amounted to discrimination on grounds contrary to the Equal Treatment Directive Art.2(1), and (2) whether the armed forces could be considered an occupational activity in which the sex of the worker constituted a determining factor under Art.2(2) such that its blanket policy of discharging any person on grounds of their homosexual orientation could be justified. Clarification was needed as to whether the ECJ's judgment in *P v. S and Cornwall CC (C13/94)* [1996] I.C.R. 795, [1996] 1 C.L.Y. 2536 rendered the Court of Appeal's ruling in *R. v. Secretary of State for Defence, ex p. Smith* [1996] 2 W.L.R. 305, [1996] 1 C.L. 39, that the Directive only related to gender discrimination, too restrictive. The reference should not be stayed pending the ECJ's decision in *Grant v. South West Trains Ltd* subsequently reported at Times, February 23, 1998 since that case might be decided on other grounds and there were already 30 cases relating to discharged servicemen which had been stayed pending the outcome of the instant case.

R. v. SECRETARY OF STATE FOR DEFENCE, *ex p.* PERKINS [1997] I.R.L.R. 297, Lightman, J., QBD.

300. Navy—courts martial

COURTS-MARTIAL (ROYAL NAVY) RULES 1997, SI 1997 170; made under the Naval Discipline Act 1957 s.52I, s.53A, s.58, s.60, s.61, s.70. In force: April 1, 1997; £6.10.

These Rules prescribe the procedure to be followed in court-martial trials under the Naval Discipline Act 1957. They accord in general with procedures in the Crown Court. These rules replace and revoke the Naval Courts-Martial General Orders (Royal Navy) 1991 (SI 1991 2737) and take account of changes in the law and procedure since then, in particular, to give effect to the changes in the way arrangements are made for court-martial trials made by the Armed Forces Act 1996.

301. Race relations—industrial tribunals—complaints from armed forces personnel

RACE RELATIONS (COMPLAINTS TO INDUSTRIAL TRIBUNALS) (ARMED FORCES) REGULATIONS 1997, SI 1997 2161; made under the Race Relations Act 1976 s.75. In force: October 1, 1997; £0.65.

These Regulations specify the circumstances in which a person may present a complaint to an industrial tribunal in respect of his service in the armed forces, notwithstanding that he would otherwise be precluded from making such a complaint by the Race Relations Act 1976 s.75(9) which requires a person to go through the service redress procedures before making a complaint to an industrial tribunal.

302. Reserve forces—call-out and recall for permanent service—compensation of employers

RESERVE FORCES (CALL-OUT AND RECALL) (FINANCIAL ASSISTANCE) REGULATIONS 1997, SI 1997 309; made under the Reserve Forces Act 1996 s.83, s.84. In force: April 1, 1997; £3.20.

These Regulations give effect to a new scheme for providing financial assistance for individuals and employers who suffer financial loss as a result of the call out or recall of individuals for permanent service in the armed forces. A reservist who is self employed or a partner in a firm may claim in the capacity of a reservist, an employer or both.

303. Reserve forces—call-out and recall for permanent service—exemptions

RESERVE FORCES (CALL-OUT AND RECALL) (EXEMPTIONS ETC) REGULATIONS 1997, SI 1997 307; made under the Reserve Forces Act 1996 s.78, s.79. In force: April 1, 1997; £2.80.

These Regulations entitle persons who have been called out or recalled for service in the armed forces, or their employers, to apply for deferral of or exemption from that liability or, in the case of persons already serving, release or discharge from service. Applications are to be determined by an adjudication officer appointed by or in accordance with the directions of the Secretary of State for the Defence Council.

304. Reserve forces—recall for service—provision of information

RESERVE FORCES (PROVISION OF INFORMATION BY PERSONS LIABLE TO BE RECALLED) REGULATIONS 1997, SI 1997 308; made under the Reserve Forces Act 1996 s.75. In force: April 1, 1997; £1.10.

These Regulations require former members of the armed forces who may at some time in the future be recalled for service to provide information of their whereabouts, current occupation, qualifications and fitness for service.

305. Reserve forces-transitional provisions

RESERVE FORCES ACT 1996 (TRANSITIONAL, CONSEQUENTIAL AND SAVING PROVISIONS) REGULATIONS 1997, SI 1997 306; made under the Reserve Forces Act 1996 s.130. In force: April 1, 1997; £1.95.

These Regulations amend the Reserve Forces Act 1980 in consequence of the coming into force of the Reserve Forces Act 1996 to make provision for persons who remain subject to the 1980 Act.

306. Reserve Forces Act 1996 (c.14)-Commencement No.1 Order

RESERVE FORCES ACT 1996 (COMMENCEMENT NO.1) ORDER 1997, SI 1997 305 (C.15); made under the Reserve Forces Act 1996 s.132. Commencement details: bringing into force various provisions of the Act on April 1, 1997; £0.65.

This Order brings into force all of the provisions of the Reserve Forces Act 1996 except for s.121 (2), which came into force on the passing of the Act, and Sch.11 to the extent that it provides for the repeal of the provisions in the Reserve Forces Act 1980. Section 48, s.55, s.130 to s.138, s.140, s.151 and s.156 to s.158 of the 1980 Act are also not repealed by the coming into force of the 1996 Act as they are expressed excluded from repeal by Sch.11.

307. Reserve Forces Appeal Tribunals-establishment and regulation

RESERVE FORCES APPEAL TRIBUNALS RULES 1997, SI 1997 798; made under the Reserve Forces Act 1996 s.93. In force: April 3, 1997; £3.20.

These Rules establish and regulate the Reserve Forces Appeal Tribunals which are subject to the supervision of the Council on Tribunals and these Rules are based on their Model Rules.

308. Sex discrimination-compensation-employees in armed forces terminating pregnancy due to MoD policy

O enlisted in the RAF in 1979 and became pregnant in 1987. If she had continued with her pregnancy her career in the armed forces would have ended under the policy operated by the MoD at that time, and she elected to terminate her pregnancy. This caused grave and lasting problems in her marriage. An industrial tribunal regarded the injury to O's feelings as particularly serious and awarded her £10,000 in her sex discrimination claim. L joined the RNS in 1983 and became pregnant in November 1984. She did not have a continuing relationship with the father of the child and had an abortion in December 1984. At the hearing of L's claim for sex discrimination the tribunal concluded that there was a 75 per cent chance that she would have had an abortion irrespective of the discriminatory policy and awarded her £500 for injury to feelings. The MoD appealed against the quantum of these awards.

Held, dismissing the appeals, that (1) applying the principles laid down in *Ministry of Defence v. Cannock* [1994] I.C.R. 918, [1995] 1 C.L.Y. 2039 and *Ministry of Defence v. Mutton* [1996] I.C.R. 590, [1996] 1 C.L.Y. 2605, and personal injury cases concerning post traumatic stress, *North West Thames RHA v. Noone* [1988] I.C.R. 813, [1989] C.L.Y. 1452, considered, the compensation for the injury to feelings of having to make the decision about an abortion in the context of losing one's job should be in the order of £2,000. The degree of injury to feelings consequent upon having an abortion is more difficult to categorise and any bracket must inevitably be wider. In cases where the injury to feelings consequent upon the decision to have an abortion is relatively transient compensation should be in the order of £1,500 to £3,000. In cases where it was more durable the bracket should be £3,000 to £7,500; (2) the award to O represented the upper limit of an award for injury to feelings consequent upon an abortion and there would have to be the most grave consequences for the total sum to exceed £10,000, and (3) in the case of L, the tribunal, having found that there was a 75 per cent chance that L would have had an abortion in any event, erred in failing to hold that L had failed to not established on the balance of probabilities that the MoD policy was a cause of her decision to seek an abortion. Notwithstanding this misdirection, the tribunal was entitled to award her an amount for injury to feelings, having clearly found that the discriminatory policy was a part of her decision to terminate her pregnancy.

MINISTRY OF DEFENCE v. O'HARE (NO.2); MINISTRY OF DEFENCE v. LOWE (NO.2) [1997] I.C.R. 306, Pugsley, J., EAT.

309. Sex discrimination–compensation–women unlawfully dismissed from armed forces for pregnancy

In calculating compensation for unfair dismissal from the armed forces, the percentage probability of having remained with the forces should be applied to the difference between the amount which the individual would have earned in the forces and their expected earnings in civilian employment. W and D had been unlawfully dismissed from the armed forces upon becoming pregnant and both had found alternative employment after their dismissal, but at a lower rate of pay. MoD appealed and W and D cross appealed against an EAT decision [1996] 1 C.L.Y. 2608 dismissing MoD's appeal against the amount of compensation awarded by the industrial tribunal. MoD contended that the amount of compensation payable should be calculated by reducing the total figure the complainant would have earned had she remained in the armed forces by a percentage discount agreed by the industrial tribunal to reflect the probability that the complainant would have left the armed forces anyway, and then subtracting from that sum the amount the complainant had or should have earned in civilian employment. W and D argued that the correct method was to subtract the sum that the complainant had or should have earned in civilian employment from the amount she would have earned in the forces and only then apply the percentage discount.

Held, dismissing the appeal and the cross appeal, that the method of calculation advocated by W and D was the correct one. Applying the percentage discount to the sum that a complainant would have earned in the forces, as MoD suggested, did not properly reflect the total figure for loss of earnings, as it ignored the fact that if the complainant had remained in the forces, she would not have earned less pay or no pay at all in an alternative employment. Further, when determining the percentage discount to be applied where there were varying probabilities that a complainant would have remained in the forces at different points in her career, those probabilities had to be applied cumulatively, although the tribunal ought to be aware there was not necessarily a diminishing percentage probability that a woman would remain in the armed forces in later periods as compared with earlier periods.

MINISTRY OF DEFENCE v. WHEELER; MINISTRY OF DEFENCE v. DONALD; MINISTRY OF DEFENCE v. NIXON; MINISTRY OF DEFENCE v. JOSLYN, *The Times*, November 19, 1997, Swinton Thomas, L.J., CA.

310. Sex discrimination–industrial tribunals–complaints from armed forces personnel

SEX DISCRIMINATION (COMPLAINTS TO INDUSTRIAL TRIBUNALS) (ARMED FORCES) REGULATIONS 1997, SI 1997 2163; made under the Sex Discrimination Act 1975 s.85. In force: October 1, 1997; £0.65.

These Regulations specify the circumstances in which a person may present a complaint to an industrial tribunal in respect of his service in the armed forces, notwithstanding that he would otherwise be precluded from making such a complaint by the Sex Discrimination Act 1975 s.85(9B) which requires a person to go through the service redress procedures before making a complaint to an industrial tribunal.

311. Visiting forces–application of 1952 Act

VISITING FORCES (DESIGNATION) ORDER 1997, SI 1997 1779; made under the Visiting Forces Act 1952 s.1, s.15. In force: July 22, 1997; £0.65.

This Order designates Albania, Bulgaria, the Czech Republic, Estonia, Hungary, Latvia, Lithuania, Poland, Romania, the Slovak Republic, Slovenia and Sweden as countries to which the provisions of the Visiting Forces Act 1952 apply. It partially implements the obligations imposed on the United Kingdom by the agreement, dated June 19, 1995, made between Member States of the North Atlantic Treaty Organisation (NATO) and those other States which have accepted the invitation to take part in the Partnership for Peace (Miscellaneous No.12 (1996) Cm 3237).

312. Articles

A change for the better *(David Poole)*: S.J. 1997, 141 (19), 456-457. (Act and Rules in force April 1, 1997 altering procedure governing courts martial in response to ECHR ruling that previous practice breached right to fair trial).

Debt in the forces *(Kate Thomas)*: Adviser 1997, 60, 38-40. (Extent to which service personnel and families face special liability and consideration of the policy of armed forces towards employees in debt).

European briefing *(Peter Duffy)*: S.J. 1997, 141 (13), 310. (Whether the armed forces' policy of excluding homosexuals was compatible with Equal Treatment Directive).

In the line of fire: L.S.G. 1997, 94 (38), 18-19. (Views of lawyers who have acted for and against armed forces on workings of court martial system).

New reserve forces legislation: I.R.L.B. 1997, 571, 11-13. (Employment aspects of the Reserve Forces Act 1996 and related regulations in force April 1, 1997).

Surviving the desert storm *(Nina Montagu-Smith)*: I.C. Lit. 1997, Feb, 11-16. (Ill health suffered by veterans of Gulf War, possibly as result of exposure to chemicals, and progress of law suits).

The modern army court-martial system *(Stephen Vowles)*: L. Ex. 1997, Feb, 30-31. (Functions and operation of system and why it is successful).

313. Books

Rant, Judge; Bayliff, Judge–Courts-martial Handbook. Hardback: £45.00. ISBN 0-471-97482-X. Chancery Wiley Law Publications.

BANKING

314. Banking Act 1987–exempt transactions

BANKING ACT 1987 (EXEMPT TRANSACTIONS) REGULATIONS 1997, SI 1997 817; made under the Banking Act 1987 s.4. In force: April 3, 1997; £5.60.

These Regulations, which revoke and replace the Banking Act 1987 (Exempt Transactions) Regulations 1988 (SI 1988 646 as amended by SI 1989 465, SI 1990 20, SI 1990 1018, SI 1990 1529, SI 1991 29 and SI 1991 2168), prescribe certain transactions as ones to which the prohibition on unauthorised deposit-taking imposed by the Banking Act 1987 s.3 does not apply.

315. Banking Act 1987–exempt transactions

BANKING ACT 1987 (EXEMPT TRANSACTIONS) (AMENDMENT) REGULATIONS 1997, SI 1997 1866; made under the Banking Act 1987 s.4. In force: August 21, 1997; £0.65.

These Regulations amend the Banking Act (Exempt Transactions) Regulations 1997 (SI 1997 817) Reg.14 (1) which provided that the acceptance of a deposit involving the issue of shorter term debt securities which were not themselves listed would only be an exempt transaction if a single debt security was issued and the redemption value of each debt security when issued or transferred was not less than £100,000. The amendment gives effect to the intention that these requirements should apply in respect of the issue of any shorter term debt securities, whether listed or not.

316. **Banks–discovery–professional negligence claim against auditors–criminal sanctions for disclosure of information under Banking Act 1987**

[Banking Act 1987 s.82(1); Insolvency Act 1986.]

During the course of a discovery exercise undertaken pursuant to negligence proceedings brought by BCCI against PW, their former auditors, PW's solicitors removed a large number of files on the grounds that their disclosure would expose them and their clients to criminal liability under the Banking Act 1987 s.82(1). BCCI's liquidators brought interlocutory applications against PW to determine the scope and effect of s.82(1), which made it an offence to disclose information received under or for the purposes of the Act relating to the business or other affairs of any person.

Held, that a person, including the Bank of England, would commit a criminal offence if they disclosed information relating to the business affairs of any person contrary to s.82(1), and "any person" had to be construed broadly. The recipient of information must have realised that he had received it under or for the purposes of the Act and if, at the time of receipt, he anticipated that it would be used for some other purpose, disclosure would not breach s.82(1). If the recipient obtained the same information twice, the first time for a purpose covered by s.82(1) and the second for a different purpose, he would be entitled to disclose it after the second receipt, although this would not validate any earlier disclosure. The obligations in s.82(1) were not overridden by the duty to give discovery in unrelated civil proceedings, *Rowell v. Pratt* [1938] A.C. 101 applied. Where the contents of a draft report prepared pursuant to s.41 of the Act had been widely disseminated, they had been made available to the public within the meaning of s.82(2). BCCI could not rely on s.85(1)(d) or (f) to defeat s.82(1), as the action brought against PW was in negligence and not under the 1987 Act or the Insolvency Act 1986.

BANK OF CREDIT AND COMMERCE INTERNATIONAL (OVERSEAS) LTD (IN LIQUIDATION) v. PRICE WATERHOUSE (NO.2) [1997] 6 Bank. L.R. 216, Laddie, J., Ch D.

317. **Cheques–bankers duties–forgery–deductions from accounts–extent of customer's duty–Australia**

M and P were individuals who had effective control of N's customer, H. M allowed a bookkeeper, B, to sign cheques in his name, knowing B was writing cheques for higher amounts than was entered in H's books. M also gave B blank signed cheques so as to obtain cash for himself and B in amounts larger than those recorded. N accepted it was prima facie liable to pay on the presentation of the forged cheques but contended that (1) it was not liable to pay on those cheques B had been authorised to sign by M; (2) H was precluded from denying the regularity of cheques signed in M's name by B as it acquiesced in the practice and did not tell N of it, and (3) H owed N an implied contractual or tortious duty to detect and prevent cheque forgery which they had breached. At first instance N succeeded on (1) but failed on (2) and (3). N appealed.

Held, dismissing the appeal, that (1) the general rule was that a bank's debt to its customer remained unless the latter had authorised the bank to make payments in reduction or was estopped from denying it, and there were only two qualifications, namely that a customer had to (a) take usual and reasonable precautions to prevent a fraudulent alteration of a cheque which might cause loss to the banker, and (b) inform the bank of any forgery as soon as he became aware of it, *Tai Hing Cotton Mill v. Liu Chong Hing Bank* [1986] A.C. 80, [1985] C.L.Y. 150 applied; (2) it was not appropriate to extend the customers' duty further, (a) irrespective of whether there was an estoppel, if the duty was based on estoppel, (b) the suggested obligation would be for large and small customers to take precautions varying in nature and cost; not all forgeries would be prevented, and there was no evidence as to the quantification of the burden on the bank remaining in respect of those not prevented by reasonable means; (c) the bank could charge for their burden, or contract with the customer so as to avoid it, and (3) although no claim could be made for certain forged cheques, there was no general estoppel as there was nothing done or permitted by H to constitute a representation that the cheques remaining in question should be paid.

NATIONAL AUSTRALIA BANK LTD v. HOKIT PTY LTD [1997] 6 Bank. L.R.177, Mahoney, P, CA (NSW).

318. Cheques–forgery–employer failed to notify drawee banks–collecting bank had statutory protection–Canada

[Bills of Exchange Act 1985 s.48 (Canada).]

P's employee forged cheques and cleared them through D, a collecting bank. P discovered the forgery but failed to give notice to D and the other drawee banks within one year as required by the Bills of Exchange Act 1985 s.48 (Canada). The Act provided that a failure to give notice meant that the "cheque shall be held to have been paid in due course with respect to every other party thereto". P sued D and D argued that it was not liable by reason of P's failure to give notice. P argued that the Act was to protect only the drawee.

Held, dismissing the claim, that the provisions of the Act were not to be given the narrow interpretation contended for by P and that the wider interpretation was appropriate, *Bank of Montreal v. Quebec (Attorney General)* [1978] 96 D.L.R. (3d) 586. P's failure to give notice as required by the Act meant that they had no right to recover the amounts in question from D.

ENOCH BAND OF STONY PLAIN INDIAN RESERVE NO.135 v. MORIN [1996] 5 Bank. L.R. 397, Costigan, J., QBD.

319. Cheques–payment after cheque countermanded–unjust enrichment–Canada

C, contractors, performed work for W, subcontracting management of the contract to O. W's subcontractor D accepted a post-dated cheque from C, which C then countermanded. C's bank, B, debited $7.50 for the service of placing a stop payment on the account, but then certified the cheque to the payee and paid it. O paid a cheque to C to cover the overdraft created as a result, without prejudice to C's rights to question the payment by B. At first instance it was held that the payment was inadvertent, and that as C legitimately owed the money covered by the cheque it would amount to unjust enrichment if O were to get the money back. C appealed.

Held, dismissing the appeal, that it was appropriate to apply the principle that a person should not be unjustly enriched by a mistake of fact as here there was enrichment of C, corresponding deprivation of B, and no juristic reason for the enrichment. D had been paid and had no reason to pursue C; as the cheque was certified B could not recover from D; C therefore successfully avoided paying D. Authorities on unjust enrichment following *Barclays Bank v. WJ Simms Son & Cooke (Southern)* [1979] 3 All E.R. 522, [1979] C.L.Y. 157 were not distinguishable by reason of the fact that it was O, not D's debtor C, who had paid the bank, because the payment to the bank had been on the express basis that the issue for determination was B's payment over the countermand to C's debtor, thus O put itself in C's position.

RCL OPERATORS LTD v. NATIONAL BANK OF CANADA [1997] 6 Bank. L.R. 195, Hoyt, C.J.N.B, CA (Brunswick).

320. Electronic funds transfer–fraud–bank accepting transfer in good faith–restitution

SN, the State Bank of New South Wales Ltd, approved a loan to E to be repaid over five years. SN was told that the first repayment was to be made and so faxed its New York office to expect a payment into E's account. A money market deposit ticket was processed in the dealing room at Swiss Bank purporting that SN had agreed to deposit $20 million to be repaid in New York, the repayment to be made to E's account in New York. In fact, the ticket was fraudulently prepared by a Swiss Bank employee. The $20 million was transmitted from Swiss Bank to SN in New York with a direction for payment to be made to E's account. The instruction was executed by a Clearing House Inter Bank Payment System, CHIPS, message. At the same time the bank in New York received a message from SN in Australia indicating that E had advised it that $20 million was to be paid into its account on that day. On receipt of the $20 million from Swiss Bank the New York bank assumed that the money was to be credited to E's account even though the CHIPS message did not refer to E or contain any information to link the money to E. At a later state an executive of E gave instructions for the disbursement of the money which were acted on. Subsequently Swiss Bank discovered that SN did not make any deposit, notified SN of the error and requested repayment. SN replied that the funds had been credited to the account of the bank's customer. The New South Wales Commercial Court found that there was no reason for SN to suspect the validity of the payment and that the New York bank had not been negligent in accepting the payment but that the CHIPS message had not entitled the bank to treat the funds as available for E. It was held that electronic transmissions of money had to be handled strictly in accordance with the terms of the message. By paying away the funds SN failed to act on the faith of the receipt. Swiss Bank was allowed to recover the mistaken payment from SN. SN appealed.

Held, dismissing the appeal, that SN had not shown that it had acted to its detriment on the receipt as the CHIPS message did not authorise the payment of funds to E. SN was not acting on the faith of that message when making the payment to E. It did not matter that SN had no reason to doubt or suspect the CHIPS message.

STATE BANK OF NEW SOUTH WALES LTD v. SWISS BANK CORP [1997] 6 Bank. L.R. 34, Priestley, J.A., CA.

321. **Fraud—tortious liability—employee assisted third party in fraudulent enterprise—employer was not vicariously liable for tort of deceit**

G appealed against a decision dismissing their action against E whose employee, P, had assisted a third party, C, in a fraudulent enterprise by underwriting E's guarantees so that G would make facilities available to C's companies by which G bought forged and worthless bills of exchange. G submitted that P, aware of the deceit which caused substantial losses to G, was a joint tortfeasor with C and therefore liable to G in respect of the losses, and that E was vicariously liable for P's actions as they were done in the course of his employment.

Held, dismissing the appeal, that if P was a joint tortfeasor with C, he would be vicariously liable to G to make good the loss arising out of C's tort as if he had practised the deceit himself, but it did not follow that E would be vicariously liable for P's actions. E was only liable to G if the tort, which in this case was the deceit, had been practised in the course of P's employment, ie. within his actual or ostensible authority. The actions done by P in the course of his employment did not consist of the deceit itself, but rather of assisting C in furthering the fraudulent scheme, and even if P had personally deceived G by promulgating the forged documents as genuine, that would not have been within his actual or ostensible authority. G's action therefore failed.

GENERALE BANK NEDERLAND NV (FORMERLY CREDIT LYONNAIS BANK NEDERLAND NV) v. EXPORT CREDITS GUARANTEE DEPARTMENT, *The Times*, August 4, 1997, Stuart-Smith, L.J., CA.

322. **Guarantees—effect of notice to determine on guarantor's liability**

Notice to determine the guarantee was given by the guarantor. The issue was whether that notice terminated all liability on the part of the guarantor. BCCI argued that the terms of the guarantee were such that the guarantor's liability crystallised at the date upon which the notice period expired and continued until a demand was made. The judge upheld the bank's argument and the guarantor appealed.

Held, dismissing the appeal, that there were no words in the guarantee to the effect that notice determined the guarantee, but it did provide that the expiry of the notice period crystallised the guarantor's obligations. The implication was that the contract remained in force and a demand might thereafter be made.

BANK OF CREDIT AND COMMERCE INTERNATIONAL SA v. SIMJEE [1997] C.L.C.135, Hobhouse, L.J., CA.

323. **Guarantees–guarantor subject to undue influence of debtor–constructive knowledge of creditor**

See REAL PROPERTY: Bank of Scotland v. Bennett. §4232

324. **International banking–loan and swap agreements–capacity of Greek municipality–agreement governed by English law**

[Presidential Decree 323/1989 Art.220 (Greece).]

The municipality of Piraeus, P, borrowed money from a syndicate of banks, including Mitsubishi Bank Ltd acting as agent for M, to finance the construction of car parks. The loan was for $30 million for five years, and if P defaulted under the loan agreement or the swap agreement the banks could terminate the loan. Under the swap agreement the interest rate under the loan agreement was swapped into a fixed quarterly rate of 14.98 per cent payable in drachma at a fixed rate of exchange. P defaulted under the loan agreement and M wrote demanding repayment of the capital sum of $30 million and interest. P's principal contention was that it did not have the capacity to enter into either the swap or loan agreements, its council's decision to do so being ultra vires and contrary to Greek administrative law in the form of the Presidential Decree 323/1989 Art.220(2). P commenced proceedings in a Greek civil court on the basis that there was no default and in subsequent proceedings in England, P was ordered until further notice not to pursue the Greek proceedings as P was specifically excluded in the agreement from taking proceedings in Greece. M applied in relation to both the loan agreement and the swap agreement for (1) summary judgment for the sum due following early termination and default with interest; (2) damages for past breaches of a jurisdiction clause with interest, and for an injunction to prevent future breaches of that clause, and (3) an order striking out the points of defence and counterclaim or parts thereof. P sought leave to substitute an amended defence on the ground of capacity and counterclaimed for restitution of sums paid under the swap agreement.

Held, granting P conditional leave to defend, that English law, which was the law governing the transactions, could only have a limiting effect on capacity, since a legal person could not exercise greater power than that bestowed by the legal system of which it was a creature. Article 220 of the 1989 Decree was concerned with the internal management and not the capacity of the municipality. Under English law there was a fundamental difference between internal management and capacity, and there was nothing to concern the banks about P's internal management. However, the evidence as to Greek law and its effect in terms of P's capacity to enter into the transactions disclosed triable issues which would have to be tested.

MERRILL LYNCH CAPITAL SERVICES INC v. MUNICIPALITY OF PIRAEUS; MITSUBISHI BANK LTD v. MUNICIPALITY OF PIRAEUS, Trans. Ref: 1995 Folio No.2329, March 12, 1997, Cresswell, J., QBD (Comm Ct).

325. **International banking–loan and swap agreements–capacity of Greek municipality**

[Presidential Decree 323/1989 Art.220 (Greece).]

The Municipality of Piraeus, P, resolved by decision 564/93 to borrow $30 million to finance car parks. P's mayor, M, entered into a series of interdependent agreements with the plaintiff banks, including a loan agreement with B and a swap agreement with MLCS. The full amount was drawn down and transferred to a blocked US dollar account. Default was claimed in two actions. B claimed the balance of the loan and MCLS claimed the sum due for early termination of currency swap together with interest. Both claimed an injunction to prevent future breaches of an exclusive jurisdictional clause and the costs of enforcement. P claimed a lack of capacity to make the agreements or of authority on the part of M to enter them.

Held, giving judgment for B and MCLS for every relief sought, that: (1) the loan and swap agreements had to be considered together as they were part of a single transaction or package under their proper law (Greek) and P had the power to conclude them under the Greek Civil Code Art.220, *Britannia Steamship Insurance Association v. Ausonia Assicurazioni* [1984] 2 Lloyd's Rep 98, [1984] C.L.Y. 2669, *Janred Properties v. Ente Nazionale Italiano per il Turismo (No.2)* [1989] 2 All E.R. 444, [1988] C.L.Y. 1372 and *Presentaciones Musicales v. Secunda* [1994] Ch. 271, [1994] C.L.Y. 107 applied; (2) it was not practicable for P to examine and agree every clause, but by decision 564/93 it had done more than enough to satisfy the requirements of Art.220 of determining the terms of the agreement by indicating the amount, currency, duration, security, governing law, expenses and management fees and how the interest and capital repayments were to be made, and (3) M acted within his actual authority in signing the agreements.

MERRILL LYNCH CAPITAL SERVICES INC v. MUNICIPALITY OF PIRAEUS (NO.2); MITSUBISHI BANK LTD v. MUNICIPALITY OF PIRAEUS (NO.2) [1997] 6 Bank L.R. 241, Cresswell, J., QBD (Comm Ct).

326. Letters of credit—assignment of proceeds to suppliers—entitlement of bank to set off proceeds against indebtedness

The second defendant, Mundratech, had a banking relationship with the first defendant, Mashreqbank (M), and was heavily in debt to M to which it had given a debenture and general letter of set off. Mundratech was also heavily in debt to MEM from whom it bought parts used to make engines. The engines were sold to a company that paid for them under a letter of credit. To secure further supplies from MEM Mundratech assigned the proceeds of the letter of credit to MEM and gave notice of assignment to M. Some payments were made but then M applied the proceeds of the sales to reduce Mundratech's debt to M. MEM challenged its right to do so.

Held, dismissing MEM's claim, that although equity permitted notice of an assignment given prior to the existence of the relevant debt being an assignment of actual proceeds as and when collected under the letter of credit, the assignment was subject to M's right at common law to set off the pre-existing debt, *Rother Iron Works Ltd v. Canterbury Precision Engineers Ltd* [1974] Q.B. 1, [1973] C.L.Y. 338 and *Business Computers Ltd v. Anglo African Leasing Ltd* [1977] 1 W.L.R. 578, [1977] C.L.Y. 385 applied. A debt that accrued before the notice of assignment was received could be set off against the assignee.

MARATHON ELECTRICAL MANUFACTURING CORP v. MASHREQBANK PSC [1997] 2 B.C.L.C. 460, Mance, J., QBD (Comm Ct).

327. Letters of credit—discrepancies in documentation—defendant's oral rejection of documents constituted "expeditious means" and was therefore valid

B opened a letter of credit, subject to Uniform Customs and Practice for Documentary Credits ICC No. 400, Art.16 of which provided a refuse for the documents if they did not conform with the terms and conditions of the credit. There were discrepancies in the documentation relating to the letter of credit and the shipment of arms to which it related. B sought to reject the documents orally. S claimed payment from B. The issue arose whether B had orally rejected the documents, whether oral rejection was a valid refusal in terms of Art.16. and whether the rejection had been made in time.

Held, dismissing the claim, that at the meeting between B and S, B's agent communicated the fact of rejection, having drawn discrepancies between the documents and credits to S. Article 16(d) did not require any particular form of words or conduct of rejections, simply that there be notification by "telecommunication or other expeditious means". The oral communication at the meeting would constitute "expeditious means", as would a telephone call. That notice of rejection be given "without delay" in Art.16 meant that rejection had to take place promptly and this would be determined by reference to the time taken between receipt of the documents and their rejection within a reasonable time. The lapse of three months between first presentation and rejection was within a reasonable time. There was no contractual requirement that notice be given in any other form.

SEACONSAR FAR EAST LTD v. BANK MARKAZI JOMHOURI ISLAMI IRAN [1997] 2 Lloyd's Rep. 89, Tuckey, J., QBD (Comm Ct).

328. Letters of credit–documents produced on word processor–criteria for determining whether document complied with credit

MB, at the behest of K, opened a letter of credit, expressed to be subject to the code in Uniform Customs and Practice for Documentary Credits (1993 Revision), payable against documents from the beneficiary, MG. MB rejected an insurance document produced on a word processor on the ground that it was neither original nor marked "original" as required by Art.20(b) of the code. KA, through whom the credit was negotiated, discounted the credit and then applied to the court for reimbursement from MB, whilst K sought an injunction preventing the reimbursement of KA and a declaration that the document did not conform with the credit. KA contended that the document was "marked as original" for the purposes of Art.20(b) as it was printed on the insurers' original paper, it included a clause that the policy was issued in "original and duplicate", and two copies of the document were sent, one of which was a photocopy marked "duplicate".

Held, allowing KA's application and dismissing the application brought by K, that where the requirements of the credit were ambiguous, a banker could adopt a reasonable interpretation of the credit's requirements, having regard to the commercial purpose of the document, with any doubt being resolved in favour of giving effect to the transaction. Any document produced on a word processor was a document produced by a computerised system within Art.20(b) and therefore had to be marked as original, *Glencore International AG v. Bank of China* [1996] 1 Lloyd's Rep. 135, [1996] 1 C.L.Y. 415 applied. However, a document could be regarded as "marked as original" if, either it was expressly marked with the word "original", or if it was a necessary implication of the terms and markings of the document that it was original. In the instant case, the document complied with the latter test and therefore conformed with the credit.

KREDIETBANK ANTWERP v. MIDLAND BANK PLC; KARAGANDA LTD v. MIDLAND BANK PLC, *The Times,* October 31, 1997, Judge Anthony Diamond Q.C., QBD.

329. Mortgages–matrimonial home–discharge of constructive notice of undue influence

See REAL PROPERTY: Turner v. Barclays Bank Plc. §4244

330. Mortgages–matrimonial home–duty of bank's solicitor to ensure wife received independent legal advice

See REAL PROPERTY: Royal Bank of Scotland Plc v. Etridge. §4242

331. Overdrafts–bank terminating facilities–loss to director–no duty of care to director due to lack of proximity

C appealed against an order dismissing his action on the grounds that the statement of claim disclosed no reasonable cause of action. C was a director and shareholder of companies known as the Bass Group, BG, which had overdraft facilities with Barclays Bank, B. In 1988 B made known its intention to cancel the facilities. BG presented B with a deal, the "Broseley deal", but the bank required an independent assessment of BG's financial state. Following the assessment which recommended that an administrator be appointed over BG, B made a formal demand for outstanding debts and obtained administration orders, following which BG went into liquidation. In 1994 C claimed damages against B for breach of contract or collateral warranty between himself and B, and/or damages for breach of duty of care. The claims were dismissed as being unsustainable. B had been aware of an arrangement by which C had the right to acquire all BG's issued shares. C argued that the administration orders had been obtained on the basis of a defective report as the financial report on BG contained inaccuracies and that the orders would not have been made if the report had been accurate and consequently he would not have suffered damage and loss.

Held, dismissing the appeal, that there was no evidence of a contractual relationship between C and B. The original agreement between B and BG was that the facilities were terminable on demand. Beyond that B agreed to consider an independent financial assessment of BG before terminating the facility, an obligation which it fulfilled. The criteria to establish a duty of care following *Caparo Industries Plc v. Dickman* [1990] 2 A.C. 605, [1990] C.L.Y. 3266, being (1) a relationship of proximity; (2) damage was foreseeable, and (3) that it was just, fair and reasonable in the circumstances to impose a duty, were not satisfied as there was no proximity between C and B as C was not B's customer, *Howard & Witchell v. Woodman Matthews & Co* [1983] B.C.L.C. 117, [1983] C.L.Y. 3611 and *Barings Plc (In Administration) v. Coopers & Lybrand* [1996] 1 C.L.Y. 1088 distinguished, *White v. Jones* [1995] 2 W.L.R. 187, [1995] 2 C.L.Y. 3701 considered.

CHAPMAN v. BARCLAYS BANK PLC, [1997] 6 Bank L.R. 315, Otton, L.J., CA.

332. Possession proceedings—pleadings—legal charge induced by misrepresentation—constructive notice of bank

See REAL PROPERTY: Barclays Bank Plc v. Boulter. §4238

333. Subordination agreement—refusal of interlocutory injunction—Western Australia

Three companies, including WT, forming part of the Bell Group were to be wound up. The group reached an agreement with its bankers, including W, relating to the debt position of the group. The group's inter company debt was to be subordinated to the bank debt. The issue arose as to the banks' knowledge that the three companies were close to insolvency at the time when the subordination deed was affected. W sought an interlocutory injunction that until trial the group, their liquidators or their agents, be restrained from taking any action leading to an order being made for the liquidation of the three companies.

Held, denying an injunction, that under the terms of the subordination deed it was a matter for WT and the other companies to establish that the balance of convenience lay with the refusal of the injunction and that there was a serious question to be tried. Convenience dictated that the three companies be parties to the proceedings which were to be taken to avoid the deed of subordination. Therefore, there was a serious question to be tried.

WESTPAC BANKING CORP v. WESTERN TRANSPORT PTY (IN LIQUIDATION) [1996] 5 Bank. L.R. 311, Walsh, J., Sup Ct (WA).

334. Articles

ASB issues FRED 13 supplement for banks *(Mike Lloyd):* F.I.T.A.R. 1997, 2(8), 131-132. (Supplement adapting FRED 13, Derivatives and Other Financial Instruments: Disclosures, to needs of banks and certain similar institutions).

Bank of England liberalises debt issuance regime *(Vincent Keavenay):* C. & F.L. 1997, 9(7), 121-123. (Criteria for unauthorised institutions to issue debt instruments as exempt transactions under Banking Act 1987 (Exempt Transactions) Regulations 1997, types of securities, maturity, denomination and disclosure requirements).

Banking: notification of "close links" *(Denton Hall)*: I.H.L. 1997, 47(Feb), 42. (Practical effects of Regulations implementing Directive which require financial institutions to notify Bank of England of any close links with other institutions, including subsidiary and parent companies, and exceptions to rule).

Basle market risk rules and the CAD *(Philip Gowman)*: F.I.T.A.R. 1996, 1(7), 108-109. (Comparison of Basle rules and Directive 93/6 capital adequacy requirements—includes chart).

Breaking the billion dollar barrier - learning the lessons of BNL, Daiwa, Barings and BCCI *(Thomas C. Baxter)*: J.M.L.C. 1997, 1(1), 15-25. (Four cases of fraudulent conduct in banking, each resulting in large losses, reveal lessons to be learned in detecting unlawful activities and need to act decisively to mitigate losses).

Controlling risks in large value interbank payment systems *(Richard Dale)*: J.I.B.L. 1997, 12(11), 426-434. (Alternative methods of risk control including net settlement safeguards and real time gross settlement and 1996 reforms to UK payment system CHAPS).

Derivatives disclosure by banks and securities firms *(John Tattersall)*: F.I.T.A.R. 1996, 1(2), 26-28. (Recommendations on derivatives disclosure by banking and security institutions from Basle Committee and IOSCO technical committee and Basle activity survey of derivatives trading).

Duty of care and damages in banking cases *(Hans Tjio)*: J.B.L. 1997, Jul, 350-358. (Extent to which banks can be liable for breach of fiduciary duty or duty of care for non disclosure or misrepresentation).

Electronic cash - the regulatory issues *(Trystan C.G. Tether)*: B.J.I.B. & F.L. 1997, 12(5), 202-209. (Development of systems for electronic money, current supervisory and regulatory provisions and policy issues of who should be allowed to issue it, how to control it and how to regulate mechanics of electronic cash systems).

Electronic presentation of cheques *(Denton Hall)*: I.H.L. 1997, 47(Feb), 44-45. (Provisions of SI 1996 2993 deregulating procedure for clearing cheques so as to allow truncation and electronic transfer without presentation of cheque).

Equity and the pursuit of hot money: warning to banks *(Michael Ashe)* and *(Paula Reid)*: C.L. Pract. 1997, 4(8), 188-194. (Banks' liability as constructive trustees for handling proceeds of fraud or breach of trust).

International deposit netting agreement *(Denton Hall)*: I.H.L. 1996, 45(Nov), 52-53. (British Bankers' Association standard form of agreement for set off of counterparty deposits in event of liquidation or default and obligations of defaulting party).

Limitations to free movement of banking services *(Sideek Mohamed)*: J.I.B.L. 1997, 12(2), 67-73.

Mondex: structure of a new payments scheme *(Jane Finlayson-Brown)*: J.I.B.L. 1997, 12(9), 362-366. (Struture of electronic cash system using smart card, associated legal issues, licensing agreements and operating regulations).

New Basle core principles *(Timothy Polglase)*: I.B.F.L. 1997, 16(4), 42-43. (Seven core sections in Basle Committee's banking supervision consultation paper deal with essential measures to create effective supervisory system).

New banking and mortgage lending codes of best practice *(Colin Mercer)*: Corp. Brief. 1997, 11(5), 3-5. (Voluntary codes, effective from July 1, 1997, reflect OFT and Consumer Association pressure on financial institutions to adopt more sympathetic and user friendly attitude towards customers).

News from the Money Advice Liaison Group *(Anthony Sharp)*: Q.A. 1997, 45(Aut), 14. (Main features of 1997 edition of Code of Banking Practice, including evolution from first edition published 1991 and key provisions designed to improve relations with personal customers).

Second Banking Directive: P.L.C. 1997, 8(8), 51. (CEC guidance on interpretation of concepts "freedom to provide services" and "interest of the general good" used in Directive 89/646 on ability of financial institutions to provide banking services in another Member State).

Silent confirmations-a hazardous practice? *(Gayl Russell)*: C. & F.L. 1997, 9(11), 153-155. (Effectiveness of banks' practice of silently confirming letters of credit in order to obtain reimbursement from defaulting issuing bank).

Summary of the Bank of England Banking Act Report 1996/1997: I.F.L. Rev. 1997, 16(7), Supp Ban 126-130. (Progress towards improved banking supervision procedures and competition in banking markets).

The Banking Ombudsman *(David Thomas)*: Adviser 1997, 62, 35-36, 39. (Role of Ombudsman, including jurisdiction in dealing with complaints).

The plight of the unbanked payee *(J.K. Macleod)*: L.Q.R. 1997, 113(Jan), 133-166. (Historical view of legal nature of cheques before and after 1992 Act which allow payment to account payee only and position for individuals without bank accounts).

Trade association profile: British Bankers' Association: Q.A. 1997, 44(Sum), 12. (Aims and objectives of BBA, including membership, customer relations, codes of practice, complaints procedure and publications).

UK banking supervision after the Arthur Andersen report *(Maximilian J.B. Hall)*: B.J.I.B. & F.L. 1996, 11(11), 525-529. (Findings and recommendations of report to Bank of England following collapse of Barings and implications of implementation for banking supervision mechanisms).

Using the Banking Ombudsman Scheme *(Andrew Campbell)*: S.J. 1997, 141 (18), 428-430. (Scheme to deal with unresolved complaints from banking customers, eligibility, procedure and test case provision).

335. Books

Arora, Ann–Practical Banking and Building Society Law. Paperback: £20.00. ISBN 1-85431-628-1. Blackstone Press.

Bueno, Antonio–Byles on Bills of Exchange. Hardback. ISBN 0-421-45600-0. Sweet & Maxwell.

Bueno, Antonio; Hedley, Richard; Stallebrass, Paul–Electronic Transfer of Funds. Hardback: £50.00. ISBN 0-421-52060-4. Sweet & Maxwell.

Cranston, Ross–Principles of Banking Law. Hardback: £45.00. ISBN 0-19-876484-7. Paperback: £19.99. ISBN 0-19-876483-9. Clarendon Press.

Howard, Chris–Butterworth's Money Laundering Manual. Unbound/looseleaf: £135.00. ISBN 0-406-08135-2. Butterworth Law.

Howard, Chris–Butterworths Money Laundering Manual. Unbound/looseleaf: £150.00. ISBN 0-406-08135-2. Butterworth Law.

Malaguti, Maria Chiara–Free Movement of Capital and Payment Systems in the EU. Hardback: £85.00. ISBN 0-421-59430-6. Sweet & Maxwell.

McCracken, Sheelagh–Banker's Remedy of Set-off. Hardback: £95.00. ISBN 0-406-99613-X. Butterworth Law.

Neate; McCormick–Bank Confidentiality. Hardback: £135.00. ISBN 0-406-99991-0. Butterworth Law.

Penn, Graham; Shea, Tony–Law Relating to Domestic Banking. Paperback: £28.00. ISBN 0-421-41380-8. Sweet & Maxwell.

Penn, Graham; Shea, Tony; Haynes, Andrew–Law and Practice of International Banking. Paperback: £38.00. ISBN 0-421-41390-5. Sweet & Maxwell.

Penn, Graham; Shea, Tony–Law Relating to Domestic Banking. Paperback: £40.00. ISBN 0-421-41380-8. Sweet & Maxwell.

Practical Banking and Building Society Law. Paperback: £20.00. ISBN 0-1-85431-628-1. Blackstone Press.

Rider, Barry–Tracing of Assets. Unbound/looseleaf: £295.00. ISBN 0-7520-0412-3. FT Law & Tax.

CAPITAL GAINS TAX

336. Consideration–entitlement of taxpayer to deduct costs incurred in establishing value of asset

[Taxation of Chargeable Gains Act 1992 s.38(2).]

C's administrators contested the value to be attributed to shares in C's estate. The Special Commissioner held that the administrators were entitled to deduct from the tax the cost of the hearing by virtue of Taxation of Chargeable Gains Act 1992 s.38(2). The High Court allowed the Revenue's appeal and the administrators appealed.

Held, dismissing the appeal, that the costs deductible by the taxpayer did not extend to those incurred in negotiating over or contesting his liability to capital gains tax arising out of a disposal, *Smith's Potato Estates Ltd v. Bolland (Inspector of Taxes)* [1948] A.C. 508, [1947-51] C.L.C. 4729 applied.

COUCH (INSPECTOR OF TAXES) v. ADMINISTRATORS OF THE ESTATE OF CATON; *sub nom.* ADMINISTRATORS OF THE ESTATE OF CATON v. COUCH (INSPECTOR OF TAXES) [1997] S.T.C. 970, Morritt, L.J., CA.

337. Exemptions–qualifying corporate bonds–whether exemption extended to previously held shares

[Finance Act 1989 s.139(1).]

J owned shares in PJ Ltd. In 1984 he exchanged them on a takeover for loan notes of MII Ltd. In 1987 he exchanged the loan notes for non voting shares under a share reorganisation. In 1991 to 1993 he disposed of some of his shares. He was assessed to capital gains tax on the disposals. He appealed, contending that under the Finance Act 1989 s.39(1), the shares fell to be treated as qualifying corporate bonds. The Special Commissioner dismissed his appeal.

Held, dismissing the appeal, that the provision should not be construed so as to deem a previous transaction to be a disposal when it was specifically provided not to be a disposal at the time it occurred, *O'Rourke (Inspector of Taxes) v. Binks* [1992] S.T.C. 703, [1992] C.L.Y. 352 applied.

JENKS v. DICKINSON (INSPECTOR OF TAXES) [1997] S.T.C. 853, Neuberger, J., Ch D.

338. Retirement relief–disposal of land by family company shareholder–business purpose requirement

[Finance Act 1985 s.69(2), s.70(6), s.70(7), Sch.20.]

H disposed of land owned by him which was used for the purposes of a family company. The company ceased trading at that time. The Revenue refused H's claim for retirement relief on the disposal on the ground that the land required to be used for the purposes of a business carried on by H himself under the Finance Act 1985 s.69(2)(b). The special commissioner dismissed H's appeal. H's executors appealed.

Held, dismissing the appeal, that on a true construction of s.69(2), the words "a business" denoted any business of the person making the disposal and the situation arising where a person made a disposal of an asset used by another was expressly provided for under s.70(6) and s.70(7) of the 1985 Act. The absence of a specific reference to rent in Sch.20 para.12(2) of the Act was consistent with the interpretation of s.69(2)(b), in that a person making a disposal of an asset used in the business had to be the person carrying on that business. Therefore, the asset disposed of did not qualify for retirement relief, as it had not been used for the purposes of a business by H when he disposed of it.

PLUMBLY (PERSONAL REPRESENTATIVES OF THE ESTATE OF HARBOUR) v. SPENCER (INSPECTOR OF TAXES) [1997] S.T.C. 301, Lightman, J., Ch D.

339. Roll over relief—business property—part disposal of single asset

[Capital Gains Tax Act 1992 s.152.]

T acquired business premises and within one year sold part of them. He was assessed to capital gains tax on the disposal. He appealed, contending that he was entitled to roll over relief under Capital Gains Tax Act 1992 s.152. The Deputy Special Commissioner allowed his appeal. The High Court allowed the Revenue's appeal.

Held, dismissing the appeal, that it was crucial to the application of s.152 that there must be an acquisition of assets other than the assets disposed of.

WATTON (INSPECTOR OF TAXES) v. TIPPETT [1997] S.T.C. 893, Simon Brown, L.J., CA.

340. Articles

A risky shelter? *(Jon Zigmond)*: Tax. 1997, 138(3591), 491-492. (Potential double taxation disadvantages in using treaty protected companies for CGT planning purposes, includes worked example).

A tale of woe *(Stanley Dencher)*: Tax. 1997, 138(3587), 366-367. (CGT treatment of goodwill arising on incorporation of sole trader, with professional negligence implications for incorrect valuation).

Capital distributions from non resident trusts: a tax trap for charities *(Robert Venables)*: C.L. & P.R. 1997, 4(3), 173-178. (Whether UK charity which receives capital payment from trustees of settlement subject to offshore beneficiary provisions and uses it solely for charitable purposes is liable for CGT).

Capital gains tax retirement relief and family companies—proceed with care *(Frank Haskew)*: C.T.P. 1997, 16(9), 104-106. (Planning issues including automatic nature of relief, position of trustees and treatment of non trading assets).

Capital gains tax: authorised unit trust umbrella schemes: I.R.T.B. 1997, 28(April), 419-421. (CGT treatment of schemes permitting switches between sub pools within total umbrella fund, TCGA s.99 requirements and rules applicable to switches between income and accumulation sub funds).

Capital gains tax: holdover relief and SP8/92: I.R.T.B. 1997, 28(April), 417-418. (Statement SP 8/92 on CGT valuation will continue to apply under self assessment and revised claim forms will be issued requiring more information).

Caveat settlor *(Paul Baxendale-Walker)*: Tax J. 1997, 413, 15-16. (Tax planning options for offshore trust reducing CGT liability by replacing chargeable asset with cash in second trust).

Closing in on conversions *(Francesca Lagerberg)*: Tax. 1997, 139(3610), 294-295. (Changes to CGT treatment of QCB qualifying corporate bonds disposed of on or after November 26, 1996).

Don't let CGT spoil the party *(Jan Matthews)*: Tax. P. 1997, Mar, 8-11. (Schemes to minimise CGT for individuals who sell shares including use of UK and offshore trusts, stock dividends, offshore insurance policies and unauthorised unit trusts).

Earn outs reconstructed *(Malcolm Gunn)*: Tax. 1997, 139(3611), 315-317, 319. (CGT anti avoidance provisions introduced to enact ESC D27 as TCGA s.138A, give taxpayer opportunity to opt for earnout tax treatment and define unascertainable consideration).

Hector's house *(Robin Williamson)*: Tax. P. 1997, Sep, 11-13. (Self assessment provisions which leave issues relating to CGT private residence relief previously determined by Inland Revenue for taxpayer to decide).

Hold-over relief via revocable settlements *(Robert Venables)*: P.T.P.R. 1997, 6(1), 59-75. (Use of revocable settlements to acquire CGT holdover relief).

Identifying with CGT *(Daron H. Gunson)*: T.P.T. 1997, 18(23), 177-179. (Rules for identification of share sales after April 6, 1996 with regard to liability for capital gains tax-includes worked examples).

Less tax law needed *(Oliver Stanley)*: Tax J. 1997, 423, 15-17. (Historic CGT development and potential changes in light of consultation exercise announced in August).

Losses on loans to traders and QCBs *(Robin Williamson)*: Tax. P. 1997, Aug, 24. (Enactment of former concessionary relief enabling CGT loss relief claims where qualifying loans have become irrecoverable and effect of alteration of time limits for claims).

Never do today.. *(Terry Jordan)*: Tax. 1997, 139(3619), 540-541. (Process of making gifts and time at which they are perfected for capital tax planning purposes).

New reinvestment rumpus *(Kevin Slevin)*: Tax. 1997, 139(3603), 87-88. (Effect of CGT reinvestment relief rule changes on share acquisitions by subscription including where consideration is based on exchange of assets rather than cash).

Pains that conquer trust *(Colin Masters)*: T. & T. 1996, 3(1), 9-12. (CGT implications of anti avoidance rules applicable to trusts set up outside UK which have either UK resident settlor or UK resident beneficiaries).

Picking up windfalls *(Alastair Hick* and *David Wells)*: T.P.T. 1997, 18(10), 73-75. (CGT implications of demutualisation share issues and cash bonuses with use of PEPs for tax planning purposes).

Principal private residence revisited *(Frank Haskew)*: C.T.P. 1997, 16(12), 138-141. (Rules under Taxation of Chargeable Gains Act 1992 s.222 and s.226 governing CGT relief upon disposal of principal private residence, highlighting practical problems which can arise).

Reducing the trust CGT rate *(Philip Laidlow)*: C.T.P. 1997, 16(10), 118-120. (When to trigger trust disposals for conversion to lower tax rate).

Reinvesting reinvestment *(J.D. McNeile)*: Tax J. 1997, 390, 6-7. (Tax planning opportunities based on proposed reforms to CGT reinvestment relief and introduction of advance clearance scheme).

Reinvestment relief *(David Hughes)*: Tax. P. 1997, Jan, 16-18. (Relationship between CGT reinvestment relief, retirement relief and holdover relief, including examples).

Reinvestment relief and self-investment *(Frank Haskew)*: C.T.P. 1997, 16(5), 55-57. (Conditions of CGT reinvestment relief, qualifying trades for reinvestment company, withdrawal of relief where conditions cease to be fulfilled, anti-avoidance provisions and rules on self-investment).

Reinvestment revisited *(David Whiscombe)*: T.P.T. 1997, 18(12), 89-91, 96. (Changes to CGT reinvestment relief introduced by Finance Act 1997, including permitted uses of reinvested money, treatment of groups of companies and limitation of relief to investment in UK based trades).

Reorganising trusts–the CGT problem: Tr. & Est. 1997, 11(7), 52-54. (CGT treatment where trustees of interest in possession settlement distribute capital to beneficiaries, including application of holdover relief deferring CGT charge).

Section 13 structures *(Lindsay Pentelow)*: Tax J. 1997, 408, 7-9. (Planning opportunities utilising provisions on attribution of offshore company gains to resident participators, residence, corporate structure and close company issues, includes worked examples).

Share shake up *(Peter Rayney)*: T.P.T. 1997, 18(14), 109-112. (CGT treatment of company reorganisations illustrated by case study involving rationalisation of family owned concern with complex shareholding structure).

Taxation of warranty and indemnity payments *(Nick Cronkshaw)* and *(Simon Yates)*: P.L.C. 1997, 8(9), 12-13. (CGT liabilities where seller of company indemnifies buyer against company's historic tax liabilities and payments are regarded by Revenue as proceeds of disposal of chargeable asset, and effect of gross-up clauses in indemnity).

Taxation update: capital gains tax reforms *(Julie Evans)*: S.J. 1997, 141(37), 919-920. (Tax planning opportunities prior to probable reform of CGT in which such opportunities are likely to be restricted).

The RPI and CGT indexation *(Peter Templeton)*: Co. Acc. 1997, 136, 14-15. (Development of CGT indexation since its introduction in 1982 and relationship between Retail Price Index and CGT indexation allowance).

Three indexation solutions *(Malcolm Gunn)*: Tax. 1997, 139(3601), 44-45. (CGT indexation relief calculation methods applicable to active building society accounts on the receipt of demutualisation bonus payments).

Transactions and loss relief for non resident trustees *(Frank Haskew)*: C.T.P. 1997, 16(11), 127-130. (CGT treatment of transactions between non resident trustee and connected persons, and loss relief for non resident trustee).

Trustees, CGT and losses *(Frank Haskew)*: C.T.P. 1997, 16(3), 31-33. (CGT rules applicable to appointment of assets by trustee to beneficiaries and entitlement to loss relief, with example).

Valuing unquoted shares: the allowance for unmarketability *(Roy R. Greenfield)*: C.T.P. 1997, 16(4), 40-43. (Whether decided cases show that traditionally accepted discount percentages are too low).

What your inspector thinks *(Andrew C. Goodhall)*: Tax. 1997, 138(3593), 541-543. (CGT planning advice and guidance on acceptable avoidance measures from Inland Revenue Capital Gains Manual and Independent Taxation Manual available to advisers and clients).

CHARITIES

341. Administration–Clergy Orphan Corporation

CHARITIES (CLERGY ORPHAN CORPORATION) ORDER 1997, SI 1997 2240; made under the Charities Act 1993 s.17. In force: September 29, 1997; £1.55.

This Order gives effect to a Scheme to administer the Clergy Orphan Corporation, a charity currently administered by the Clergy Orphan Corporation Act 1809 and the Clergy Orphan Corporation Act 1958. The Scheme alters the 1809 Act and the 1958 Act by appointing a corporation by the name of the Corporation of the Sons of the Clergy to be the trustee of the charity and modernising its objects and the way in which it is administered.

342. Bequests–Iveagh Bequest

CHARITIES (IVEAGH BEQUEST, KENWOOD) ORDER 1997, SI 1997 482; made under the Charities Act 1993 s.17. In force: March 12, 1997; £1.55.

This Order gives effect to a scheme of the Charity Commissioners for the Charity known as the Iveagh Bequest, which is regulated by the Iveagh Bequest (Kenwood) Act 1929. The Scheme alters some of the statutory provisions governing the Charity and continues the existing trusteeship of English Heritage whilst providing for the removal of the present Custodian Trustee and giving English Heritage the discretion to hold the investments or to appoint a new Custodian Trustee. English Heritage is empowered to delegate its investment management powers and also to acquire and otherwise deal with additional property for display primarily at Kenwood House, Hampstead, London.

343. Funds–Peabody Donation Fund

CHARITIES (THE PEABODY DONATION FUND) ORDER 1997, SI 1997 1711; made under the Charities Act 1993 s.17. In force: July 28, 1997; £2.80.

The Order relates to the Peabody Donation Fund which was founded by George Peabody in 1862 and is currently regulated by the Peabody Donation Fund Act 1948.

344. Jurisdiction–action by Indian religious association operating in England– foreign institution not charity within meaning of Charities Act 1993– Attorney General could not be added as party to proceedings

[Charities Act 1993 s.96(1).]

G, a religious organisation operating in India and London, was registered in India, where it had charitable status, but was not so registered in England. G brought an action against the priest in charge of its London temple and against the trustees of GMST, a registered English charity, and the court ordered that the Attorney General should be added as a party to the proceedings in accordance with the Charities Act

1993. The Attorney General appealed, contending that the Act did not apply to an association such as G.

Held, allowing the appeal, that the crucial issue was whether G was an institution established for charitable purposes and subject to the control of the High Court with respect to charities within the meaning of the 1993 Act s.96(1). There was nothing in the 1993 Act to suggest that it applied to institutions other than those established for charitable purposes in England and Wales, and the detailed provisions of the Act were inappropriate for institutions established in foreign states. The authorities showed that the English courts were unable to control bodies established and administered abroad, and "charity" within the 1993 Act did not include an institution incorporated under the laws of a foreign legal system, *Camille and Henry Dreyfus Foundation Inc v. Inland Revenue Commissioners* [1956] A.C. 39, [1955] C.L.Y. 304 followed. It had to be concluded, therefore, that G was not a charity under the Act, and the Attorney General could not properly be added as a party to G's action.

GAUDIYA MISSION v. BRAHMACHARY, *The Times*, September 24, 1997, Mummery, L.J., CA.

345. Articles

Charitable bequests: post-death problems *(Francesca Quint)*: E.C.A. 1997, 2(4), 21-23. (How to deal with bequests to charities which are unclear or impossible to achieve).

Charitable gifts by will: a choice of approaches *(Francesca Quint)*: E.C.A. 1997, 2(2), 12-13. (Straightforward legacy, gifts for charities selected by trustees, charitable trust or gift to testator's own charity).

Charities, members, accountability and control *(Jean Warburton)*: Conv. 1997, Mar/Apr, 106-118. (Legal position of members of charitable trusts, unincorporated associations and companies limited by guarantee, who are intent on having greater role in controlling the direction and operation of the charity).

Charity landholding: a new beginning *(Christopher Jessel)*: C.L. & P.R. 1997, 4(3), 191-200. (History of charitable land tenure and implications for voluntary organisations of 1996 Act which removes distinction between settlements and trusts).

Charity update *(Douglas G. Cracknell)*: S.J. 1997, 412, Supp Spr, 22, 24, 26, 28-29. (Developments between Winter 1996 and Spring 1997).

Focus on... charities *(Brian Mulholland)*: T.P.T. 1997, 18(17), 136b-136c. (Tax exemption for charities, including concessionary exemption, trading companies, extraction of profits and changes in legislation).

Minimising fundraising problems *(Catherine Allison)*: Charities M. 1997, 18(Sum), 25-26. (Legal requirements for charitable appeals, fund raising events and trading activities).

The insurance needs of charities *(Mark Ingram)*: Charities M. 1997, 18(Sum), 31-33.

The need for a considered approach to appointing charity trustees *(Alec Sandison)*: Charities M. 1997, 17(Spr), 18-20.

You could be liable *(Catherine Allison)*: Charities M. 1997, 17(Spr), 16-17. (Wide scope of charitable trustees' personal liability).

346. Books

Adirondack, Sandy; Taylor, James Sinclair–Voluntary Sector Legal Handbook. Paperback: £50.00. ISBN 1-873860-79-X. Directory of Social Change.

Vincent, Robert–Charity Accounting and Taxation. Paperback: £45.00. ISBN 0-406-02921-0. Butterworth Law.

Warburton, Jean; Morris, Debra–Tudor on Charities: 1st Supplement to the 8th Edition. Property and Conveyancing Library. Paperback. ISBN 0-421-58890-X. Sweet & Maxwell.

CHILDREN

347. **Adoption—adoption register—disclosure of information—application by birth mother—application failing to establish exceptional need to know**

[Adoption Act 1976 s.50(5).]

D's daughter had been placed for adoption in 1960. D, as the birth mother, sought information about her daughter from the adoption files on two occasions and was refused. She issued a summons against the Registrar General, contending that information from his records should be supplied to enable a registered charity to trace her daughter. The judge refused to make the order and D appealed.

Held, dismissing the appeal, that disclosure would only be ordered in exceptional circumstances in accordance with the terms of the Adoption Act 1976 s.50(5), and an applicant would have to establish an exceptional need to know the information of which disclosure was sought.

L (A MINOR) (ADOPTION: DISCLOSURE OF INFORMATION), *Re; sub nom.* D v. REGISTRAR GENERAL [1997] 2 W.L.R. 739, Sir Stephen Brown, CA.

348. **Adoption—application to adopt foreign national—Secretary of State opposing application—balancing welfare of child with public policy—factors to be considered**

[Adoption Act 1976 s.6.]

A and her husband were married in Pakistan but came to England shortly afterwards and became British citizens. They were unable to have children and in 1990 they "adopted" the youngest child of A's brother and his wife, which was not uncommon in their culture. There was no court order. Later that year A's husband suddenly died and she and the child went to live with her brother and his family in Pakistan. In September 1990 A returned to England without the child. In 1992 her brother, his wife and the child sought entry clearance to England. The only reason given was to visit relatives. The application was refused but an appeal was successful two years later. Throughout this time A maintained contact with the child on the basis that he would eventually come to live with her in England. In 1994 the child came to England with his natural parents and it was made known to the entry clearance officer that A intended to adopt the child. It was Home Office policy to refuse entry for adoption unless this involved a genuine transfer of parental responsibility on the grounds of the parents' inability to care and the child would be maintained and cared for without recourse to public funds. In December 1994 A applied to adopt the child, her application being opposed by the Home Office.

Held, dismissing the application, that, although there were factors in favour of an adoption order being made, the child's welfare was the first consideration under the Adoption Act 1976 s.6 but was not paramount and a proper consideration of welfare included public policy, the effect of an adoption order on nationality and the right of abode. When considering an adoption application in respect of a non patrial, the court must adopt a two stage approach. First, it must consider the motive for the application and only if satisfied that the motivation was not to achieve British nationality was the court allowed to proceed to the second stage and carry out the balancing exercise between public policy and the child's welfare. Although the case did not fail at the first stage, the benefits of adoption had to be weighed against countervailing policy considerations. The most important was the deception used to obtain entry to England since the adoption would have conflicted with Home Office policy in that the child could be looked after by his natural parents and secondly A was in receipt of social security benefits. On the facts the welfare of the child was not an overwhelming benefit and was clearly outweighed by public policy considerations.

QS (A MINOR) (ADOPTION: NON PATRIAL), *Re* [1997] 1 F.C.R. 9, Stuart-White, J., Fam Div.

349. Adoption—breach of immigration controls—adoption application supported by genuine parent and child relationship

[Adoption Act 1976 s.6.]

J, a child of parents living in Pakistan, was brought to England at the age of five and left with family members, British citizens who were infertile, to be brought up as their son. J's natural parents, who had been granted entry clearance for a two week holiday, returned to Pakistan and the couple with whom J had been left applied to adopt him. In the lower court, Singer, J., citing *H (A Minor) (Adoption: Non Patrial), Re* [1997] 1 W.L.R. 791, [1996] 1 C.L.Y. 466, decided that it would be contrary to public policy to allow an application where there had been a deliberate breach of immigration regulations and refused to make an adoption order. The adoptive parents appealed.

Held, allowing the appeal, that what had been said in *H, Re* about blatant abuse of the right to apply for adoption was directed towards sham applications and applications of convenience on a par with marriages of convenience. In the instant case, however, the application was based on a genuine parent and child relationship and it was for the court to apply the Adoption Act 1976 s.6, giving due consideration to the guidance in *W (A Minor) (Adoption: Non Patrial), Re* [1986] Fam. 54, [1986] C.L.Y. 2152 on non patrial cases. Orders had only been refused in cases where the child was about to attain the age of majority. Home Office policy, which required that a proposed adoption involve a transfer of parental responsibility based on the fact that the natural parents were unable to care for the child, made no provision for the fact that the family arrangement in issue was a recognised custom in many parts of the world.

J (A MINOR) (ADOPTION: NON PATRIAL), Re, *The Independent*, October 30, 1997, Thorpe, L.J., CA.

350. Adoption—brother and sister placed for adoption—placement of sister breaking down—separation of siblings

Two children, whose mother had had a disturbed childhood and a history of substance abuse and whose father was of a violent nature, were made wards of court. The children were placed with their maternal grandparents and then with foster parents. Following unsuccessful attempts to rehabilitate the children with M, the local authority decided to place them for adoption. The children were placed on three conditions: that they would remain together, that there would be contact with the grandparents and that their paternal roots would be dealt with sensitively. At the freeing proceedings the grandparents applied for contact, because contact had broken down since the placement. No contact order was made as the prospective adopters stated that they would honour the commitment to contact, but they changed their minds having formed the view that the grandparents had betrayed their trust. Eventually the local authority agreed that direct contact should be postponed for two years. The placement for the girl broke down at the same time as the relationship with the local authority and in April 1995 she was placed on a week long respite placement. At the end of the week the adopters refused to have the girl back unless she was psychologically assessed and provided with therapy. As a result of their concern for the welfare of the children the local authority applied to remove the boy and the grandparents applied for leave to make a contact application. M also applied for freeing orders with a view to resuming the care of her children. During the proceedings the adopters applied for an adjournment for mediation and therapy. The local authority, M and the guardian ad litem opposed the order on the grounds that the relationship between the children should continue and that if the boy continued to live with the adopters he would grow up isolated from his natural family which would cause emotional harm and be detrimental to his long term future.

Held, that (1) since there was ample evidence that there was no realistic prospect of rehabilitation of the girl to the prospective adopters, who were temperamentally ill equipped to undergo therapy, it would be an unjustifiable risk to return her to them. Therefore it was right to revoke the freeing order and in the girl's best interests to make an interim care order to enable the local authority to implement the care plan, which should give the girl a chance of a happy and secure childhood, and (2) in refusing the prospective adopters' application to adopt the boy, regard had to be had to all the circumstances. Although he had been with them for two years and had stated that he wished to remain with them, there was strong evidence that the important and consistent relationship with his sister was essential for the boy's long term welfare and emotional health. The distress and long term damage to the boy would be less if he were removed form the adopters and reunited with his sister. Accordingly the boy should be returned within seven days to the care of the local authority, although an emergency protection order would be granted to enable the local authority to remove the boy immediately if the guardian ad litem were satisfied that it would safeguard his welfare. An interim care order would be granted and contact to the grandparents at the discretion of the local authority.

P (MINORS) (BREAKDOWN OF ADOPTION PLACEMENT), *Re* [1996] 3 F.C.R. 657, Stuart-White, J., Fam Div.

351. Adoption–foreign child adopted abroad–adoption order sought in England– applicants separating after adoption application made

[Matrimonial Causes Act 1973; Inheritance (Provision for Family and Dependants) Act 1975; Adoption Act 1976 s.13(3).]

The applicants paid a lawyer £5,000 to arrange the adoption of a child from El Salvador. The mother of the child agreed to the adoption in El Salvador and the applicants then brought him to England and notified the local authority of their intention to adopt. However they separated after making the application with the child continuing to live with the female applicant but having contact with the male applicant.

Held, that the making of the adoption order was in the child's best interests since an order in favour of both parties conferred parental responsibility upon the male applicant and the child would be a child of the family for the purposes of the Matrimonial Causes Act 1973 and the Inheritance (Provision for Family and Dependants) Act 1975, and would enjoy equal status with the applicants' natural child. There was no specific provision which barred the making of a joint adoption order in favour of a couple who had separated, although under the Adoption Act 1976 s.13(3), the court had to be satisfied that the local authority had had sufficient opportunity to see the child with both applicants in the home environment. In the instant case the social worker had been able to do that between the making of the application and the couple's separation.

WM (ADOPTION: NON PATRIAL), *Re* [1997] 1 F.L.R. 132, Johnson, J., Fam Div.

352. Adoption–freeing order–consent of mother unreasonably withheld– indirect contact with sibling

[Children Act 1989 s.1 (5).]

M appealed against an order freeing her children L, seven years old, and C, three years old, for adoption and dispensing with her consent on the basis that she was withholding it unreasonably. E, the eldest daughter, appealed against the decision refusing contact between her and her siblings. The decisions in both cases were supported by the local authority and the guardian ad litem. M had a history of excessive drinking, mood swings and neglectful and abusive behaviour towards the children. L and C were placed with foster parents under interim care orders and claimed they did not wish to return to live with M. M started attending anger and stress management courses and a psychiatrist recommended a referral to the Cassel Hospital, and supported rehabilitation of the children with M. The local authority did not accept that proposal, refusing to fund the Cassel, and a social worker opposed rehabilitation on the basis that M did not have any prospects of improvement. Where evidence of the social workers conflicted with that of the psychiatrist the judge preferred the former, holding that M would be unable to change sufficiently in the appropriate length of time so as to be a responsible carer for L and C. At the time of the hearing the children had been in temporary foster care for over a year and there was great concern regarding the harm any further delay in settling L and C with permanent carers would have on their welfare.

Held, dismissing both appeals, that (1) the judge should have considered the issues of the reasonable prospects of a rehabilitation being successful depending on M's ability to change in the future and the importance of delay in settling the future of the children. In the former, the judge had erred and in the latter, given the ages of the children and the time they had already spent in foster care, any further delay would be detrimental to their welfare, *D (A Minor) (Adoption: Freeing Order), Re* [1991] 1 F.L.R. 48, [1991] C.L.Y. 2499 and *W (An Infant), Re* [1971] A.C. 682, [1971] C.L.Y. 5831 considered. In those circumstances it would be unreasonable for "the reasonable hypothetical mother" to withhold consent to adoption, and (2) with regard to E's appeal, the local authority did not oppose indirect contact but was opposed to the making of an order, following the principle of the Children Act 1989 s.1 (5) that no order should be made unless it were better to do so. E wished to have a contact order so that she would be able to obtain leave to be heard in the adoption proceedings where M would not. The local authority's offer to undertake to continue indirect contact until adoption, to inform E of the date of the adoption hearing and to advise that indirect contact continue if possible following adoption was reasonable and should be accepted.

L AND C (MINORS), *Re,* Trans. Ref: CCFMF 97/0215/F; CCFMF 97/0287/F, April 25, 1997, Butler-Sloss, L.J., CA.

353. Adoption—freeing order—mother killed by father—residence order in favour of paternal grandmother inappropriate

G's paternal grandmother, R, applied for an extension of time to appeal against an order freeing G, who was seven, for adoption and dismissing her residence application. G's mother had been killed by the father who was serving a prison sentence of six years for manslaughter. G was initially placed with his maternal aunt on the recommendation of the Official Solicitor, acting as guardian ad litem, and a child psychiatrist, and G had contact with his paternal grandparents and visited his father in prison. In June 1994 a care order was made in favour of the local authority, but with the aunt retaining residence. However, the aunt was subjected to extreme harassment by the father and members of his family, despite moving twice and changing her name. In February 1995, in the interest of safety, G was placed with foster parents. The local authority applied for a freeing order and to terminate contact with the paternal family.

Held, refusing the application for extension of time, that although R was genuine in her wish and her ability to care for R, even though that would require her to stay away from the rest of her family, the evidence from the Official Solicitor and the child psychiatrists was that it was in G's best interests to be adopted and to have no contact with his paternal family. In following the advice of the experts the judge was not plainly wrong.

R (A MINOR), *Re,* Trans. Ref: FC3 96/5496/F, April 23, 1997, Butler-Sloss, L.J., CA.

354. Adoption—freeing order—proposed adoption by single woman in homosexual relationship—public policy

[Adoption Act 1976 s.15.]

A local authority applied for an order freeing for adoption a child in its care who, two years prior to the application, had been placed with the prospective adopter, a single woman cohabiting with another woman. The order was opposed by the natural mother on the grounds that, under the adoption legislation, a single woman in a homosexual relationship could not apply to adopt a child and the granting of an order would be contrary to public policy.

Held, that nothing in the Adoption Act 1976 s.15 suggested that a single person, whether living alone or cohabiting, should be precluded from adopting a child by reason of his or her sexual orientation. It would be for Parliament, not the courts, to decide whether a gap in the legislation existed. Although the courts must consider the particular circumstances of every case, the welfare of the child was their primary consideration.

W (A MINOR) (ADOPTION: HOMOSEXUAL ADOPTER), *Re* [1997] 3 All E.R. 620, Singer, J., Fam Div.

355. Adoption—freeing order—revocation

[Adoption Act 1976 s.18, s.20(1); Children Act 1989 s.12(3)(aa).]

A freeing order was made in respect of G under the Adoption Act 1976 s.18, the mother's consent to the adoption being dispensed with as being unreasonably withheld. The prospective adoption did not proceed and G became a boarder in a special school for severely emotionally disturbed children. As he had not been placed with adopters within 12 months, M applied for the freeing order to be revoked under s.20 of the 1976 Act. The application was refused on the basis that to do so would vest sole parental responsibility for G in M and care proceedings would need to be brought by the local authority. When the freeing order was made parental responsibility was given to the local authority as the adoption agency and under the Children Act 1989 s.12(3)(aa) the existing care order was discharged and was not automatically revived on the revocation of the freeing order. M appealed to the Court of Appeal, accepting that the local authority would need to apply for a care order, but the appeal was dismissed as the grant to M of unfettered parental responsibility for G was held inappropriate. M appealed.

Held, allowing the appeal, that where a freeing order had been made but no adoption had taken place within 12 months and there was no immediate prospect of adoption, the freeing order might be revoked so that the parent's rights were restored and the child did not have to remain in "adoption limbo". The requirement in s.20(1) for revocation on the ground of resumption of parental responsibility did not stipulate that the parent had to have sole responsibility for the child. Section 20 of the 1970 Act had to be construed in the light of the Children Act 1989 and against the background of the inherent jurisdiction of the court. If the parent was not fit to have unfettered sole parental responsibility the court had jurisdiction to make the order revoking the freeing order conditional upon the making of the appropriate order under the 1989 Act so that the welfare of the child was protected. As M had agreed to consent to a care order there was no justification for not revoking the freeing order.

G (A MINOR) (ADOPTION: FREEING ORDER), *Re* [1997] 2 W.L.R. 747, Lord Browne-Wilkinson, HL.

356. Adoption—non disclosure application—confidential serial number proceedings—test applied—weighting of parents' interests

In adoption proceedings, a prospective adopter made an application to prevent disclosure to the natural mother of certain documents which would reveal a prior conviction for a serious offence. The issues were whether the natural mother should be informed of this application and whether these documents should be disclosed to her.

Held, that in confidential serial number adoption proceedings it was unnecessary to serve notice of such an application. Further, since the mother was unrepresented, the effect of service of the notice would be to disclose the information itself. In adoption proceedings the court must apply the three-stage test laid down in *D (Minors) (Adoption Reports: Confidentiality)*, *Re* [1996] A.C. 593, [1996] 1 C.L.Y. 474 before applying the general principle that parties in children proceedings should have access to all relevant information. The court must determine (a) whether the disclosure involved a real possibility of significant harm to the child; (b) the overall benefit to the child of non disclosure, having regard to the magnitude of risk and gravity of harm that disclosure would cause, and (c) if the child's interests are best served by non disclosure, then the parents' interests in disclosure must be weighed against this. On the facts of the present case the information would not be disclosed.

K (ADOPTION: DISCLOSURE OF INFORMATION), *Re* [1997] 2 F.L.R. 74, Wall, J., Fam Div.

357. **Adoption–removal of child from prospective adopters–local authority duty to consult–inadequate consideration of wishes and feelings of child and proposed adopters**

[Adoption Act 1976 s.1 (4), s.6; Children Act 1989 s.22(1) (b), s.22(4).]

O applied for judicial review of D's decision to serve a notice pursuant to the Adoption Act 1976 s.6 on O that C, who had been living with O for over two years, be returned within seven days. C, aged nine at the time, had had a disturbed childhood, having suffered child abuse and lived with varous different foster carers. He was placed with O in June 1994 and a freeing order was made in January 1995. C's allocated social worker went on extended sick leave from the end of 1995 and was not directly replaced. However, someone was allocated to undertake supervision of C and another social worker was asked to collect information relating to C's needs. The assessment started in September 1996. In November 1996 a strategy meeting was held to discuss concerns about C's future, following which the decision to remove C from O was made. O was not invited to attend the meeting. At that time O had not yet made an application to adopt C, although O stated it was their intention to do so. D was an adoption agency for the purposes of the 1976 Act s.1 (4) and C was a child under D's care within the meaning of the Children Act 1989 s.22(1) (b). O argued that D had failed, in making the decision to remove C, to (1) consult them sufficiently, and (2) take into account all relevant matters.

Held, allowing the application and quashing the decision to remove C from O, that (1) D had failed to consult O and its decision was thereby flawed. Under the 1989 Act s.22(4) O came within the category of persons whose wishes and feelings were relevant, *R. v. Hereford and Worcester CC, ex p. D* [1992] 1 F.L.R. 448, [1992] C.L.Y. 3007 considered. Although D were concerned that, if O was given notice of the meeting, D's plans would have been frustrated by O making an immediate application for adoption, O should have been given the opportunity to answer and discuss D's concerns about C's future. There was no urgent need for C to be removed, and given that C had lived with O for over two years, any decision to remove should have been by planned removal for which C could have been adequately prepared, and (2) D had failed to give adequate consideration to C's wishes and feelings.

R. v. DEVON CC, *ex p.* O (ADOPTION), [1997] 2 F.L.R. 388, Scott Baker, J., QBD.

358. **Adoption–removal of children from prospective adopters–subsequent adoption application–no jurisdiction to intervene after notice for return served**

[Adoption Act 1976 s.30(1) (b), s.25; Children Act 1989.]

H appealed against a decision dismissing his adoption application, made following notice from the local authority that D and L would be removed pursuant to the Adoption Act 1976 s.30(1) (b). H and his wife, prospective adopters of D and L, separated and it had been decided at a local authority meeting that they would be replaced as prospective adoptive parents. The local authority contended that the court did not have jurisdiction to intervene in the planned removal of the children as the notice had been served on H before the issue of H's application, and that s.30(3) of the 1976 Act required H to return the children to the local authority within seven days of receipt of the notice, and refusal to do so was a criminal offence under s.30(7). Accordingly H's adoption application could not succeed as he would not have residence of the children as required by s.13. The judge held that it was for the local authority and not the court to decide whether to remove the children, and rejected the submission for H that the court's discretion under s.25 should be exercised as this was inconsistent with the object of s.30.

Held, dismissing the appeal, that the purpose of s.25, in Part II of the Act, was to give the court additional powers to make an interim order in a substantive hearing where a final adoption order would be inappropriate, compared to an interim order made under the Children Act 1989 whose purpose was to define the interim position of the parties at an early stage before the matter was fully heard. It could not be used to adjourn dismissal of the adoption applications until such time as H qualified as a prospective adopter, *W (A Minor) (Adoption Agency: Wardship), Re* [1990] 2 All E.R. 463, [1990] C.L.Y. 3122 considered.

C AND F (MINORS) (ADOPTION: REMOVAL NOTICE), *Re* [1997] 1 F.L.R. 190, Butler-Sloss, L.J., CA.

359. Adoption—rights of putative father—South Africa

See HUMAN RIGHTS: Fraser v. Children's Court, Pretoria North. §2753

360. Adoption agencies—arrangements for placement and reviews

ADOPTION AGENCIES AND CHILDREN (ARRANGEMENTS FOR PLACEMENT AND REVIEWS) (MISCELLANEOUS AMENDMENTS) REGULATIONS 1997, SI 1997 649; made under the Adoption Act 1976 s.9; and the Children Act 1989 s.23, s.26, s.59, s.104, Sch.2 para.12. In force: Reg.2(4) (part): November 1, 1997; remainder: July 1, 1997; £1.95.

These Regulations amend the Adoption Agencies Regulations 1983 (SI 1983 1964). They make provision for the membership of adoption panels and for the tenure of office of members. They require the agency to send prospective adopters, for their observations, a copy of any assessment of their suitability to be adoptive parents prepared for the panel and establish a new procedure whereby any prospective adopters whom the agency considers not suitable must be notified of the agency's reasons and given an opportunity to make representations before the agency reaches its decision. They also require the agency to notify a child's parents of their intention to place the child for adoption, to make appointments for the regular examination and assessment by a registered medical practitioner of the child's health, to carry out regular reviews of the child's placement until such time as an application for an adoption order is made, and make provision as to the conduct of such reviews and the persons to whom any consequential decisions should be sent. They make provision for information about the child to be given by the agency to the adopters once the adoption order has been made and for the adopters to be advised that the information should be made available to the child no later that his 18th birthday.

361. Care—child accommodated by local authority other than that responsible for care—duty to provide support and advice after age 18 lay with local authority in which applicant lived

[Children Act 1989 s.24.]

C, who was in the care of L, was placed with a foster mother in 1992 after several years of unsuccessful placements. He resided with the foster parent in Kent but was still funded by L until he reached the age of 18, after which time L renounced responsibility for providing C with continuing support and advice under the Children Act 1989 s.24, stating that the duty had passed to the local authority for the area in which C was resident. C applied for judicial review of L's decision.

Held, dismissing the application, that L was no longer responsible for providing support for C after he had reached his 18th birthday and moved out of the foster home. L's sole duty was to inform K, the local authority serving the area in which C was living, of C's presence. K was then under a duty to provide C with the advice, financial assistance and support he required.

R. v. LAMBETH LBC, *ex p.* CADDELL, *The Times*, June 30, 1997, Connell, J., QBD.

362. Care–local authority duty of care owed to children taken into care

B, who was placed in the care of E as a baby, appealed against the striking out of his personal injuries claim in which he alleged that E and its employees were in breach of a common law duty of care owed to him. B argued that the local authority had a duty to act as, and to apply the standard of care of, a responsible parent in relation to protecting him from physical, emotional, psychiatric or psychological harm, providing an appropriate education and home environment, and planning his short and long term future, and that E's social workers owed similar duties. B's specific complaints included that E had failed to arrange for his adoption and had placed him in unsuitable foster placements and community homes while monitoring his case inadequately. Other alleged inadequacies by E related to unsuitable psychiatric treatment and the management of his reintroduction to his mother and half sister.

Held, dismissing the appeal, that the imposition on a local authority of a common law duty of care, to a child placed in its care in respect of decisions which would normally be taken by a parent, was not in the public interest. It would not be just and reasonable to make a local authority directly liable in respect of the use of discretion exercised daily by parents regarding their children's future. Further, the practical effect of imposing a common law duty of care over and above an authority's statutory responsibilities might be to cause local authorities and social workers to adopt a more cautious approach to their work in order to avoid litigation. A complaint to the ombudsman was more appropriate than use of the courts. However, social workers could be held to be negligent at an operational level, in implementing decisions of the authority, and a local authority might then be vicariously liable where the requisite causation of injury or damage was established.

BARRETT v. ENFIELD LBC [1997] 3 W.L.R. 628, Lord Woolf, M.R., CA.

363. Care orders–care plan for disturbed child included no parental contact with view to adoption–court ordered contact

[Children Act 1989 s.34.]

The child, who was born in 1989, was disturbed and was accommodated at the request of his mother, by the local authority in August 1995. M had personality problems and her relationship with the child had always been difficult. The local authority considered that adoption was in his best interests and applied for a care order, proposing that contact should be reduced from twice a week to two meetings a year with indirect contact in the form of letters and cards. The experts and the guardian believed that the child would be difficult to place for adoption because of his behavioural difficulties and that he should have regular contact with M. The justices made a care order but ordered the child to have contact with M for two hours twice a week. The local authority appealed.

Held, dismissing the appeal, that the welfare of the child was the paramount consideration when considering an application for a care order under the Children Act 1989 s.34 and contact could be ordered in the child's interests even if the local authority's plans included the eventual termination of contact. The justices had exercised their discretion properly on the evidence before them at the time and the court would not interfere with their decision. The case had involved complex and delicate issues of psychological harm and it was appropriate therefore that any further applications should be dealt with by a higher court.

BERKSHIRE CC v. B [1997] 1 F.L.R. 171, Hale, J., Fam Div.

364. Care orders–care plans–inconsistency between care plan and adoption order

[Children Act 1989 s.34.]

In making an order under the Children Act 1989 s.34 that contact between a mother and her children be reduced, the judge had a duty to consider the local authority's proposals and the benefits to the children of contact with their mother. A local authority sought care orders for two girls, D and H, following concern that their mother was neglecting them. In its care plan, the local authority aimed to place the children in long term fostering with the mother maintaining contact. The mother did not oppose the making of a care order but was determined to continue contact. The guardian ad litem took the view that the girls should be placed for adoption and contact phased out. The judge made the care order, but considered adoption to be the best course of action, and exercised his power under the Children Act 1989 s.34 to direct that contact be reduced at the discretion of the local authority and terminated after placement. The mother brought an application for leave to appeal, arguing that the order was inconsistent with the care plan, while the local authority submitted that the views of the judge were merely to be taken into account in fulfilling the care plan.

Held, allowing M's application and discharging the judge's order, that (1) the judge clearly had the power to make the order under s.34(2) and s.34(5), but had a duty when making such an order to consider the plans of the local authority, *B (Minors) (Termination of Contact: Paramount Consideration), Re* [1993] Fam. 301, [1993] C.L.Y. 2771 considered. The judge had not assessed the local authority's proposals and had failed to consider the recent improvement in contact between the mother and the children. The serious nature of the order required the judge to deal expressly with the benefits to the children from unhindered contact with their mother, and (2) it was wrong that adoption totally sublimated any consideration of the long term fostering plan, and to avoid inconsistency between the two options the judge should have authorised the local authority to refuse contact by making an order under s.34(4) of the Act, *J (Minors) (Care: Care Plan), Re* [1994] 1 F.L.R. 253, [1995] 2 C.L.Y. 3389 followed.

D AND H (MINORS) (CHILDREN IN CARE: TERMINATION OF CONTACT), *Re* [1997] 1 F.L.R. 841, Cazalet, J., CA.

365. Care orders–interim order–court's power to make direction for residential assessment of parents and child

[Children Act 1989 s.38(6).]

A local authority was granted an interim care order in respect of a child of four months who suffered serious non-accidental injuries which his young parents were unable to explain. The child's guardian ad litem and the social workers involved felt that, despite the parents' inadequacies, the child and parents should be placed at a residential assessment unit to determine whether there was a possibility that the child could eventually be returned to his parents' care. The local authority opposed that course of action, both on the ground of cost and because of the risk to which the child would be exposed if rehabilitated with his parents. The judge made a direction for a residential assessment under the Children Act 1989 s.38(6) which provided for "medical or psychiatric examination or other assessment of the child". The Court of Appeal allowed the local authority's appeal on the ground that it was bound by *M (Minors) (Interim Care Order: Directions), Re* [1996] 3 F.C.R. 137, [1996] 1 C.L.Y. 513, where it was held that an assessment under s.38(6) must be of a similar type to a medical or psychiatric examination and that the court's powers were limited to assessment of the child alone. The parents appealed.

Held, allowing the appeal, that "assessment" in s.38(6) was to be given a broad construction. Whilst there was no specific provision for assessment of the parents, consideration of the relationship between a child and his carers was an essential part of an assessment of the child. Section 38(6) allowed the court to order any assessment involving the child that would provide relevant evidence to enable the court to decide whether a full care order should be granted. The cost of an assessment and the impact on a local authority's resources were relevant considerations in deciding whether to make a direction. In the instant case the judge, in making the direction, had taken account of both these factors and her decision could not be criticised.

C (A MINOR) (INTERIM CARE ORDER: RESIDENTIAL ASSESSMENT), *Re*; *sub nom.* C (A MINOR) (LOCAL AUTHORITY: ASSESSMENT), *Re* [1997] A.C. 489, Lord Browne-Wilkinson, HL.

366. Care orders—interim order—mother and children living in different local authorities—ordinary residence—determination of designated local authority

[Children Act 1989 s.31 (8).]

N applied for a determination as to which local authority was the designated authority in respect of interim care orders on two children. M had been offered temporary accommodation and her two children voluntarily accommodated by N but she was subsequently offered permanent accommodation by B. When N learned that the mother intended to remove the children from voluntary care, they obtained interim care orders.

Held, that N was the designated authority. The court was satisfied that M was ordinarily resident in Brent, having regard to the type of accommodation she had been given and her intentions for the future. Applying *Gateshead MBC v. L* [1996] 3 F.C.R. 582, [1996] 1 C.L.Y. 484, a child subject to an interim care order could have a different ordinary residence to its mother and on the facts the children had no ordinary residence. Thus, the court had to consider in terms of the Children Act 1989 s.31 (8) any circumstances in consequence of which the order was being made. Thus, although M was living in Brent whilst the predominant circumstances arose in Newham, when proceedings were commenced, N still had the care of the children and a substantial involvement in the history of the family so that N was the designated local authority for the purposes of the proceedings.

NEWHAM LBC v. I AND BRENT LBC [1997] 2 F.C.R. 629, Sumner, J., Fam Div.

367. Care orders—judicial decision making—child abuse—use of expert evidence

The local authority, supported by the guardian ad litem, appealed against an order dismissing its application for a care order, making an interim care order and refusing leave to terminate contact with M. B had received non-accidental injuries of a serious nature from F and the judge had disagreed with experts in exonerating M and finding her capable of meeting B's physical and emotional needs. It was contended that the judge erred in not following the unanimous opinion of the consultant paediatrician, the guardian and the social worker, who all advised that adoption was the best way forward.

Held, allowing the appeal in part, that (1) the interim care order be discharged and a residence order in favour of M be set in its place. The interim order was because of a misunderstanding over the local authority's inability to fund foster care pending the return of the child to her mother's care and (2) family judges were assisted by the valuable contribution from experts and must also consider the views of the guardian, but the assessment of their evidence and the final decision was the role of the judge alone. However, if a judge disagreed with an expert he could not merely substitute his own opinion without disclosing his reasons and the evidence he relied on. In this case the judge gave adequate reasons for his disagreement with the experts.

B (CARE: EXPERT WITNESSES), *Re*; *sub nom*. B (A MINOR) (REJECTION OF EXPERT EVIDENCE), *Re* [1996] 1 F.L.R. 667, Ward, L.J., CA.

368. Care orders—jurisdiction—child habitually resident in Scotland

[Children Act 1989 Part IV, Part V.]

Held, that, provided a child was physically present in England at the time applications under the Children Act 1989 Part IV or Part V were made, a court had jurisdiction to determine the applications and to make further orders to implement a proposed care plan, even though the child was habitually resident in Scotland, *R (Care Proceedings: Jurisdiction), Re* [1995] 1 F.L.R. 711, [1996] 1 C.L.Y. 581 considered.

M (A MINOR) (CARE ORDERS: JURISDICTION), *Re* [1997] Fam. 67, Hale, J., Fam Div.

369. Care orders—supervision order rather than care order where family reluctant to cooperate

The parents had six children. Allegations of repeated sexual abuse and excessive physical chastisement were made by the two elder girls. F was charged with indecent assault but failed to turn up for his trial and disappeared. Full care orders were made on the elder two girls who were placed with foster parents. M was granted residence orders in respect of the younger four children with an express order that there should be no contact with F. M also entered into an agreement with the local authority which included a provision that any of the four children could be referred to experts for assessment or protection work and that she would see a psychologist for assistance with her parenting. The case was listed for consideration as to whether care or supervision orders should be made. The guardian argued that care orders were required for the protection of the children who would remain at home with M while the local authority argued that a supervision order was sufficient and would ensure M's continued cooperation.

Held, making a supervision order, that the threshold criteria were satisfied in the light of M's admissions and the court had to determine whether to make no order or a care or supervision order. A care order could be made even though the children remained with M and the local authority sought supervision orders. A care order was a stronger and more serious order to make and should be made only if necessary for the protection of the child, a fundamental difference being that under a care order the local authority was under an obligation to safeguard the welfare of the child whereas with a supervision order the obligation remained with the mother. On the facts a supervision order would be made having regard to the views of the local authority that the powers of a care order were excessive in the circumstances of this case, that there was concern at the way in which the children would react to care orders and that M was likely to be less cooperative if a care order was made. The monitoring of the children's needs and protection work could be undertaken away from the home and could all be achieved within the scope and powers of a supervision order coupled with the agreement scheduled to the residence orders.

B (MINORS) (CARE OR SUPERVISION ORDER), *Re* [1996] 1 F.L.R. 693, Holman, J., Fam Div.

370. Care orders—supervision orders—threshold criteria for care orders met but care orders inappropriate

In the course of care proceedings regarding six children it was conceded that the threshold criteria were met because they had suffered emotional and physical deprivation and a lack of stimulation which had resulted in their developmental delay. However their educational needs were largely met by the parents, there was love and affection within the family and standards within the home were satisfactory. The local authority did not seek to remove the children but applied for supervision orders so that progress in working with the family could be maintained. The guardian ad litem's application for care orders to be made so that the local authority shared parental responsibility with the parents was granted and the parents appealed.

Held, allowing the appeal and substituting supervision orders, that the children's welfare and not their needs was the paramount consideration. The magistrates had not addressed fully the reasons for and against making care orders as opposed to supervision orders. The court could impose a different order than that requested by the local authority, but there should be cogent reasons for doing so. A court should also consider, in accordance with the Children Act 1989 s.1 (5), whether an order should be made at all. The local authority was under a duty to safeguard and promote the welfare of children in its area who were in need and while there was a difference in the duty towards a child who was subject to a care order, as opposed to one who was subject to a supervision order, the 1989 Act placed duties on the local authority to consider the welfare of children whose needs had been identified. The magistrates' reasons for making care orders rather than supervision orders were fundamentally flawed. They had given undue weight to the fact that the parents had not given evidence, although it was clear they had been advised there was no need for them to do so, they had assumed that the care plan being incomplete was due to the parents' lack of cooperation, without considering whether that was material, they had given no reasons for rejecting the social worker's evidence that the local authority would return to court if the supervision order did not work, and they had stated that the parents would build barriers between themselves and the local authority when there was no evidence that this would happen. They had also given insufficient weight to the improvements in the children's condition, the parents' cooperation and the recent intensification of the local authority's effort.

O (MINORS) (CARE OR SUPERVISION ORDER), *Re* [1997] 2 F.C.R. 17, Hale, J., Fam Div.

371. **Care proceedings–allegations of sexual abuse against stepfather highly relevant to mother's application for residence–stepfather able to intervene in proceedings**

M and F were married in 1982 and separated in 1990. They had two children who remained with F. In 1992 M married P. Subsequently there were indications that the children had been sexually abused and F made certain admissions regarding his personal sexual practices after pornographic material was found in his house. The local authority instituted care proceedings and F, denying the allegations, sought the return of the children. M applied for residence and P revealed that there were allegations of sexual abuse against him by his adult niece from a time when he was a teenager and she was a child. The local authority sought to raise those allegations against P as part of its case that M should not have residence, its proposed care plan being that the children go into long term foster care. P applied to become a party to the care proceedings. The judge refused and P appealed.

Held, allowing the appeal and granting leave to intervene (but not to be a party), that although no one wished to call P as a witness, his evidence could be crucial to M's application for residence and the trial judge might wish to know what the position was with regard to the allegations against him. If he were not permitted to intervene, he would be exposed to examination by the local authority without the opportunity to seek help in relation to their enquiries and would not be able to deal effectively with the final outcome of the proceedings where serious findings of fact might be made against him. The consequences for P were very serious and he should be entitled to intervene in the proceedings to the limited extent of his involvement in the case.

S (MINORS) (CARE: RESIDENCE: INTERVENER), *Re*; *sub nom.* S (CHILD CASE: INTERVENER), *Re* [1997] 1 F.L.R. 497, Butler-Sloss, L.J., CA.

372. **Care proceedings–application by mother to discharge care orders and for father to cease to be party to proceedings–father convicted of murder and sexual abuse of stepdaughter**

M had three children, a girl and two boys. F was the natural parent of the two boys. In 1991 the girl was found dead having been grossly abused sexually. F was convicted of her murder and sentenced to life imprisonment, with a recommendation that he should serve at least 18 years. Care orders were made in respect of the two boys. F had no parental responsibility for either child, had never seen the younger, who was born after his imprisonment, and had had nothing to do with M or the children since he was arrested in 1991 and it was unlikely that he would make any contribution to their lives in the future. M applied to discharge the care orders and for an interlocutory order that F cease to be a party to the proceedings.

Held, allowing the application, that although the welfare of the child was important it was not the paramount consideration. This was an extreme case where the court had a discretion to discharge a party. F had no constructive role to play in the proceedings and the guardian ad litem would put his views to the court. Weighing up what had occurred in the past and the impact that further stress would have on M with the welfare of the children and the natural father's rights, the balance indicated that he should be discharged from the proceedings.

W (DISCHARGE OF PARTIES TO PROCEEDINGS), Re [1997] 1 F.L.R. 128, Hogg, J., Fam Div.

373. Care proceedings–change of residence–participation of designated local authority

[Children Act 1989 s.34(11).]

Care proceedings were commenced by one local authority but before they were concluded the mother and children moved to another local authority's area. The first local authority continued with the proceedings and prepared a care plan. At the hearing of the application for a care order both parents, the guardian ad litem and the first local authority accepted that a care order should be made on the understanding that the children would live with their mother with detailed provisions for contact with their father. Although the first local authority notified the second of the hearing the second local authority did not propose to play any part in the proceedings.

Held, that when, during the course of care proceedings, the child concerned became ordinarily resident in the area of another local authority, consideration should always be given to that local authority becoming a party or taking over the conduct of the care proceedings. The appropriateness of such a course of action depended on the facts of each case. Where an order involving the local authority was likely to be made, there should be close liaison between the two authorities at as early a stage as possible; the care plan should be put forward as a joint document and any areas of disagreement clearly identified. Even if the second local authority was not to be present or represented at the care hearing, then a fully informed and appropriately authorised representative of that authority should be present in court to deal with any issues which might arise as to the future of the children and to give assurances to the court and to the parents of the local authority's commitment to the care plan. The care plan was almost meaningless if the local authority in whose area the children lived did not take part in the proceedings since it was essential for the court and the parties to be confident that the actual local authority into whose care the children were to be committed had the financial and practical resources to implement the care plan. This was particularly pertinent in the instant case where the local authority under the care plan was expected to provide supervised contact with the father. Reference to local authority in the Children Act 1989 s.34(11) meant the local authority in whose care the child was to be placed.

L v. BEXLEY LBC [1996] 2 F.L.R. 595, Holman, J., Fam Div.

374. Care proceedings–change of residence whilst proceedings continuing–determination of designated local authority

[Children Act 1989 s.105, s.23(1)(a).]

A dispute arose as to which of two local authorities was the designated authority responsible for ongoing care where children who were the subject of care proceedings had been allowed to live with their mother and moved from one local authority to another while proceedings were continuing.

Held, that the provisions of the Children Act 1989 s.105 did not apply in determining residence, as children living at home were not "accommodated" by the local authority within the meaning of s.23(1)(a) of the Act. Therefore the court had jurisdiction to determine the appropriate authority by using conventional principles regarding residence. As far as the interim orders were concerned, the designated authority was that in which the children were living when proceedings were instituted but, since they were likely to have acquired ordinary residence in the other authority before a final order was made, it was appropriate to join the latter authority as a party to proceedings.

C (MINORS) (CARE ORDER: APPROPRIATE LOCAL AUTHORITY), Re; sub nom. C (MINORS) (CARE PROCEEDINGS: ORDINARY RESIDENCE), RE; HACKNEY LBC v. C [1997] 1 F.L.R. 544, Wall, J., Fam Div.

375. Care proceedings–child of mixed race–threshold criteria–private fostering arrangement–issues relevant to mixed race children

[Children Act 1989 s.31.]

H, foster parents, appealed against a care order made on the application of T, in respect of a baby girl of mixed race. M was involved in prostitution and drug taking and was psychiatrically disturbed. H had befriended M and cared for the baby from the age of three weeks under an informal private fostering arrangement. T commenced care proceedings on the grounds that the child was likely to suffer significant harm for lack of a settled home. M was assessed and found to be unsuitable to have the long term care of her child. H was joined in the proceedings applying for a residence order. H contended that the threshold criteria provided by the Children Act 1989 s.31 had not been met since M had not abandoned the child and there was no evidence that she would peremptorily remove the child.

Held, dismissing the appeal, that at the time of the commencement of care proceedings the child was subject to an informal fostering arrangement, where M could have reclaimed the child at any time and H had not put themselves forward as long term carers or adopters. The justices had correctly concluded that the threshold criteria in terms of s.31 (2) were met. Although H argued that the justices had elevated the child's colour to a point of principle, overriding the factors identified in assessing the placement of black or mixed race children, the justices had in fact used the question of colour in the context of the child's racial and cultural background. The court had been entitled to take into account the importance of the child's race and cultural heritage, taking account of H's dismissal of the need to reinforce that, as well as their age and likely infirmity, and M's unpredictability and possible disruptive effect. The decision could not be said to have been plainly wrong.

H v. TRAFFORD MBC [1997] 3 F.C.R. 113, Wall, J., Fam Div.

376. Care proceedings–direction given for assessment of parents and children–justices proceeding to final hearing without assessment

Care proceedings were commenced in December 1995 in respect of four children following a non-accidental injury to one child, for which M was convicted of assault and placed on probation. The court directed that there be an assessment of M and the stepfather, which recommended that there should be a further assessment of their parenting skills and counselling. In June 1996, at the date fixed for the final hearing, the local authority was not in a position to proceed and the court made further interim care orders, directed a psychological assessment and fixed a directions hearing for two weeks later. The guardian lodged an appeal against the refusal to proceed with the application for care orders but subsequently withdrew her appeal. At the directions hearing the court, having been informed that the assessment could not take place within the three month period laid down by the court, concluded that the welfare of the children should be determined without further delay and directed that the case be set down for hearing one week later. M's application for an adjournment was refused on the grounds that further delay was detrimental to the welfare of the children and that the court was in possession of all the necessary information and evidence despite the absence of the assessment. Full care orders were made. M appealed on the basis that the justices had been wrong to proceed with the case when their colleagues had directed that there should be an assessment and there had been no change in circumstances since that direction had been given.

Held, dismissing the appeal, that the situation had changed in the time between the direction for an assessment and the final hearing. It had become clear that the assessment could not be completed within the three month period contemplated. The balancing exercise had been carried out correctly and the making of the care orders could not be said to be plainly wrong. There should be minimal delay when seeking to achieve a final determination of the future of children and the justices could not be criticised for making care orders, *R (Minors) (Care Proceedings: Care Plan), Re* [1994] 2 F.C.R. 136, [1995] 2 C.L.Y. 3391 referred to.

S (MINORS) (CARE ORDER: DELAY), *Re* [1997] 1 F.C.R. 490, Cazalet, J., Fam Div.

377. Care proceedings–evidence of child abuse–disclosure of confidential information to police–guardian ad litem opposed order to promote family rehabilitation

Following the discovery of a series of non-accidental injuries to a boy aged one year and nine months, responsibility for which was admitted in a statement by the father, the local authority sought an order that the father's statement be disclosed to the police. The application was initially supported by the guardian ad litem, but following therapy undertaken by both parents with a view to rehabilitation and the father leaving the family home, the guardian expressed concerns as to the effect reopening the investigations would have on family rehabilitation. The father appealed against the order disclosing the statement to the police.

Held, allowing the appeal, that pending care proceedings were the only place to evaluate the factors raised by the guardian. Given these circumstances, and having proper regard for the guardian's position, the matter should be referred to the judge in the care proceedings, where the factors set out in *EC (A Minor) (Care Proceedings: Disclosure), Re* [1996] 3 F.C.R. 556, [1996] 1 C.L.Y. 1347 could be given their proper weight in the light of the facts then available.

S (MINORS), *Re*, Trans. Ref: CCFMI 96/1446/F, October 28, 1996, Butler-Sloss, L.J., CA.

378. Care proceedings–evidence of child abuse–disclosure of confidential information to police–scope of the Family Proceedings Rules 1991 r.4.23

[Family Proceedings Rules 1991 (SI 1991 1247) r.4.]

A local authority appealed from a county court decision that the local authority could not disclose to the police information received by a social worker from a parent about a child's injuries. The question at issue was the scope of the Family Proceedings Rules 1991 r.4.23 in relation to information received for the purposes of care proceedings, particularly whether oral admissions made to a social worker and documents coming into existence for the purpose of proceedings could be disclosed without leave of the court.

Held, allowing the appeal, that while information gathered by a guardian ad litem could only be disclosed with leave of the court, the position of social workers was different in that their duties were much wider and not limited to court proceedings, *Oxfordshire CC v. P (A Minor)* [1995] 2 All E.R. 225, [1995] 2 C.L.Y. 3516 approved. Rule 4.23 should be interpreted narrowly so that only documents held by the court in the court file would be covered. There was no justification for extending its scope to oral admissions made to a social worker and recorded in case notes which never became part of the court file.

G (A MINOR) (SOCIAL WORKER: DISCLOSURE), *Re; sub nom.* G (A MINOR) (CARE PROCEEDINGS: DISCLOSURE), RE; G (A MINOR) (CHILD PROTECTION: INVESTIGATIONS), *Re* [1996] 1 W.L.R. 1407, Butler-Sloss, L.J., CA.

379. Care proceedings—evidence of sexual abuse by father disclosed in prior proceedings—disclosure of confidential information to non party local authority

[Children Act 1989 s.17, s.47.]

A local authority involved in care proceedings applied for disclosure of the address of a father found to have committed serious acts of sexual abuse against his children and for leave to disclose that information to the local authority in whose area the father was now resident.

Held, allowing the application, that there was a strong public interest in permitting such disclosure in order to help a local authority to safeguard the welfare of children within its area in accordance with its statutory duties under the Children Act 1989 s.17 and s.47. A judge in chambers had power to control whether facts and findings in particular proceedings should be given to non parties depending on the circumstances and the person or authority in question. To allow disclosure only to specific bodies would restrict the court's discretion which should remain unfettered, particularly where there was a substantial risk of further sexual abuse, *R. v. Chief Constable of North Wales Police, ex p. AB* [1997] C.LY. 4148 considered.

L (MINORS) (SEXUAL ABUSE: DISCLOSURE), *Re, The Times*, October 9, 1997, Bennett, J., Fam Div.

380. Care proceedings—expert evidence—parent granted leave to disclose case papers to psychiatrist—failure to refer case papers within timetable set by court

Care proceedings were brought in respect of five children on the grounds that they would be likely to suffer significant harm attributable to the poor quality of care given by M. Leave was granted to M to disclose the papers of the pending case to a psychiatrist, but she failed to do so in time so that the magistrates subsequently rescinded the leave. M later sought leave to disclose the papers to a psychiatrist which was refused by the magistrates. M appealed.

Held, dismissing the appeal, that while it was important that M had every opportunity of putting her case to the court supported by the witnesses she wished to call, the court had to bear in mind the issue which was the basis of C's application which was M's parenting ability. It was unlikely that the views of the psychiatrist would bear usefully on the matters which the court would have to decide, so that the magistrates were right to refuse leave. Furthermore, when considering the principle that delay was detrimental to the interests of the children, it should be borne in mind that M had not taken the opportunity to instruct a psychiatrist when leave was initially granted, *G (Minors) (Expert Witnesses), Re* [1994] 2 F.C.R. 106, [1995] 2 C.L.Y. 3418 considered.

H v. CAMBRIDGESHIRE CC [1996] 2 F.L.R. 566, Johnson, J., Fam Div.

381. Care proceedings—injunctions—jurisdiction of county court

[Children Act 1989 s.100(3).]

Following the granting of a care order in favour of D, B appealed against the granting of an injunction under the county court's inherent jurisdiction which purported to prevent B from entering the town in which her child was living.

Held, allowing the appeal, that the county court had no inherent jurisdiction relating to the exercise of statutory powers in children cases, *D v. D (County Court Jurisdiction: Injunctions)* [1993] 2 F.L.R. 802, [1994] C.L.Y. 3216 followed. Further, the Children Act 1989 s.100(3) made it clear that a local authority could not make an application for the exercise of the court's inherent jurisdiction in relation to child cases without first obtaining the leave of the High Court, which D had not done.

DEVON CC v. B [1997] 1 F.L.R. 591, Sir Stephen Brown, CA.

382. Care proceedings–jurisdiction–child present but not habitually resident in England

[Children and Young Persons Act 1969 s.1, s.2; Children Act 1989 Sch.2 para.19.]
The parents of a child were habitually resident in Scotland at the time of his birth in 1993. They moved to England and it was in dispute whether M had remained habitually resident in Scotland, had become habitually resident in England or had lost her habitual residence in Scotland but had not yet acquired one in England. Care proceedings were commenced in England, following complaints that F had assaulted the child and a series of interim care orders made. The parents returned to live in Scotland. The local authority was then given approval under the Children Act 1989 Sch.2, para.19 to arrange for the child to live in Scotland with his paternal grandparents. The care plan was for the child to live with the grandparents and have contact with his parents. The issue for the court was whether the care proceedings should continue in England or be transferred to Scotland.
Held, that it would be assumed that M had retained her habitual residence in Scotland. The Children Act 1989 had replaced the provision as to care proceedings under the Children and Young Persons Act 1969 where there had been a clear indication that jurisdiction was assumed on the basis of presence and not habitual residence. Further, the 1989 Act was intended to incorporate the best of the wardship jurisdiction within the statutory framework, which could be exercised over a child who was physically present in the jurisdiction although not necessarily habitually resident. There was nothing in the 1989 Act to suggest that the court could not exercise jurisdiction over a child who was present within the jurisdiction of England and Wales irrespective of whether they were habitually resident abroad or in another part of the UK. The child's presence at the time of the application gave the court jurisdiction to make an emergency protection order and interim care orders. Where the Scottish and English courts had concurrent jurisdiction, the court would decide the most convenient forum. Although the parties and the child were living in Scotland, the evidence relating to the care proceedings was mainly in England and neither the local authority nor the guardian was able to bring proceedings in Scotland. It was important for the two jurisdictions to work in harmony and not in competition with one another. The Scottish court had already indicated that it would be better for the case to be tried in England and the English court would retain jurisdiction until the courts in Scotland decided to assume it.
M (A MINOR) (CARE PROCEEDINGS: JURISDICTION), *Re* [1997] 1 F.C.R. 109, Hale, J., Fam Div.

383. Care proceedings–publicity–disclosure of confidential information to police but not press

[Children Act 1989 s.98.]
Care proceedings were taken in respect of three children, at the conclusion of which a finding was made that one child had been injured while in the care of a child minder. During the course of the proceedings and following inquiries by journalists, injunctions were made preventing the parents disclosing any information relating to the proceedings and prohibiting the publication of any material which might lead to the identification of the children. After the conclusion of the proceedings, the police, who had not been a party, applied for disclosure of some of the evidence and the judgment, to be used by the police in their child protection functions and to formulate their investigations but not to be used in any criminal prosecution. The local authority also sought leave to disclose a document to the police. The parents of one child sought to vary the injunctions. The guardian ad litem took part in the proceedings, but her locus standi was challenged because the care proceedings had terminated.
Held, ordering disclosure to the police but refusing to allow disclosure to the press, that (1) the locus standi of the guardian was not clear but it was desirable that she should continue to represent the children in the present proceedings; (2) the court had jurisdiction to hear an application for disclosure by a non party

and the principles applicable in wardship proceedings applied to applications brought under the Children Act 1989. The discretion whether to order disclosure should be exercised judicially taking into account the interests of the children, the public interest in ensuring frankness in proceedings by preserving confidentiality and the public interest in upholding the law by providing evidence for other proceedings. The welfare of the child was a major factor but not necessarily paramount, and (3) the words "statement" or "admission" in s.98 of the 1989 Act covered statements made in the course of or in connection with court proceedings. Litigation privilege, including the privilege which would normally attach to experts' reports sought by or on the instructions of a party, was inapplicable in proceedings under the 1989 Act. When considering whether leave should be granted to publish information which would otherwise amount to a contempt of court, the welfare of the children, the freedom of the press, the public interest in the confidentiality of children's proceedings and the importance of all those involved in child protection matters performing their duties with candour and frankness without unnecessary public exposure should be weighed up. The welfare of the child was not paramount and no child was entitled to privacy and confidentiality: any right of confidentiality concerning a child belonged to the court and was imposed to protect the proper functioning of the court's jurisdiction. Here the importance of the confidentiality of the care proceedings, coupled with the welfare of the child, outweighed the importance of the freedom of the press.

OXFORDSHIRE CC v. L AND F [1997] 1 F.L.R. 235, Stuart White, J., Fam Div.

384. Care proceedings–witnesses–relevant considerations in deciding whether to issue witness summons against child

M and her partner, P, applied for leave to appeal against a decision refusing to issue a witness summons compelling N, a 12 year old friend of M's daughter, to give oral evidence with regard to an allegation of abuse made against P in proceedings which resulted in a care order being made in respect of M's daughter.

Held, dismissing the application, that the judge had a discretion to decide whether to issue a witness summons against a child and could refuse if to do so would be oppressive, *R. v. B County Council, ex p. P* [1991] 1 W.L.R. 221, [1991] C.L.Y. 2517 followed. In order to succeed, M and P had to show that the judge had made the kind of error identified in *G v. G (Minors: Custody Appeal)* [1985] 1 W.L.R. 647, [1985] C.L.Y. 2594. Although the judge did not use the word "oppressive", she had considered all the factors that were encompassed in that word and had not erred in the way she made her decision. In general, an application to issue a witness summons would be more likely to be granted in the case of an older child. Given the grave harm that could result from compelling a child to give evidence, it was preferable that oral evidence was not required from a child of N's age or younger, whether or not they were a member of the family, even though this might lead to the weakening of the evidence against the adult.

P (A MINOR) (WITNESS SUMMONS), *Re, The Times*, April 18, 1997, Wilson, J., CA.

385. Change of name–unmarried father wishing to change child's registered surname

[Children Act 1989 s.8.]

M appealed against an order made in the county court, on an application under the Children Act 1989 s.8 by an unmarried father that their child, A, be known by F's surname rather than M's, under which he was originally registered. M's surname was that of her former husband and the same as her two children of that marriage who lived with her and A following her separation from F.

Held, allowing the appeal, that it was within the jurisdiction of the county court to make such an order provided no residence order was in force, but the fact of registration under a certain name must be regarded as of major significance in the exercise of the court's discretion. In the instant case the judge had erred by not giving due weight to such considerations as the registration and the fact that, given the family circumstances, M's choice of surname could not be deemed illogical.

DAWSON v. WEARMOUTH, *The Times*, August 22, 1997, Hirst, L.J., CA.

386. **Child abduction—acquiescence—child removed from Australia to England— whether father's conduct constituted acquiescence**

[Children Act 1989; Hague Convention on the Civil Aspects of International Child Abduction 1980 Art.3, Art.13.]

M, who was British, and F, who was Australian, married in 1989 and had a son in 1993. When M announced that the marriage was over and she wished to live with the child in England, F later alleged that M threatened to kill herself and the child if he did not let her go. M contended that she had, in temper, threatened to kill herself on one occasion but had never threatened to harm the child. Subsequently M drafted a document to protect her and F's rights in respect of the child. The agreement, inter alia, stated that M would be able to live with the child in England or elsewhere and that F consented to her taking the child out of Australia. M and F signed the agreement in the presence of a lawyer in the CAB and on the following day M left with the child for England. F took legal advice which he said later was ambiguous. His later communication with M was also ambiguous. In 1996 M filed for divorce in England and sought residence under the Children Act 1989. F responded with a document which stated that M supported the child with help from her parents. F then made an application under the Hague Convention for the summary return of the child to Australia.

Held, dismissing the application, that F had, prima facie, given his consent to the removal of the child when he signed the document at the CAB. His rights of custody had not been breached since the reasons he gave for his consent, to stop M harming the child, were not valid reasons. If it was contended that the consent had been vitiated by deceit or threats, so the consent was not true, then the matter fell within Art.3 of the Hague Convention. If the fact of consent was in issue, then the matter fell within Art.13. The removal was not wrongful and F's application was dismissed on that ground. The only inference that could be drawn from F's conduct, his explanations and the correspondence from his lawyers was that he had acquiesced, post removal, in the child living permanently in England. F's application would be dismissed on the grounds that there was no difference in the suitability of the competing jurisdictions to deal with the child's future, the likely outcome of the proceedings was that M would be the primary carer of the child, the child was likely to have settled in England and an immediate return was likely to upset the child. Given that F had acquiesced so emphatically, there would be no frustration of the underlying philosophy and purpose of the Convention if an order for return were refused.

O (ABDUCTION: CONSENT AND ACQUIESCENCE), *Re* [1997] 1 F.L.R. 924, Bennett, J., Fam Div.

387. **Child abduction—acquiescence—whether religious belief forbidding secular court action without consent constituted acquiescence**

[Hague Convention on the Civil Aspects of International Child Abduction 1980 Art.13; Child Abduction and Custody Act 1985 s.1.]

F appealed against a decision of the Court of Appeal overturning the trial judge that he had acquiesced in the removal to England of his three young children from their home in Israel by M. F and M were strict Orthodox Jews and F was forbidden by his religion to involve the secular courts without the permission of his religious court in Israel. Six months passed, during which time M consistently failed to submit to the religious court, until F was allowed to apply for an order returning the children under the Hague Convention 1980. M contended that F had acquiesced by failing to take immediate legal action for the children's return and by his promise to return them to M if they were allowed to spend Passover with him.

Held, allowing the appeal and ordering the immediate return of the children to Israel, that the Court of Appeal had been wrong to apply the purely English law concepts of active and passive acquiescence within the ambit of international law and the Convention. Article 13 referred to the subjective state of mind of the deprived parent, which was a question of fact and these subjective intentions of the requesting parent should be disregarded only where a clear and unambiguous statement or action showing acquiescence had ensued, *A (Minors) (Abduction: Custody Rights), Re* [1992] Fam. 106, [1992] C.L.Y. 3051, *AZ (A Minor) (Abduction: Acquiescence), Re* [1993] 1 F.L.R. 682, [1994] C.L.Y. 3145, *S (Minors) (Abduction: Acquiescence), Re* [1994] 1 F.L.R. 819, [1995] 2 C.L.Y. 3430 followed; *Wanninger v. Wanninger* (1994) 850 F. Supp. 78, *Friedrich v. Friedrich* (1996) 78 F. 3d 1060 approved.

H v. H (CHILD ABDUCTION: ACQUIESCENCE); *sub nom.* H (MINORS) (ABDUCTION: ACQUIESCENCE), *Re* [1997] 2 W.L.R. 563, Lord Browne-Wilkinson, HL.

388. **Child abduction—consent—child removed from USA to UK—mother claiming father agreed—mother's refusal to return with child not a defence**

B was born in 1991 and was aged five at the date of hearing. The family was habitually resident in Michigan in the USA, F and M having emigrated to the USA in March 1986. On August 24, 1996 M left the USA to return to England with B. M admitted that in early August 1996 she had told F she would be visiting England for three months and that she would be returning in mid November. M admitted that, contrary to what she had told F, she intended to settle permanently in England but because of the circumstances surrounding her departure, F knew that she would not be returning. During a telephone conversation in early September 1996, M told F that they would not be returning and, on September 29, F made an application under the Hague Convention to secure B's return. M argued that, because F consented to her taking B to England when he knew that B and M would not be returning, F had given consent for the purposes of Art.13(a). M argued that (1) F had made impromptu comments suggesting he knew M would not be returning; (2) F had bought M and B one-way tickets to England; (3) M had packed eight suitcases containing almost all of her and B's personal belongings; (4) M had, with F's knowledge arranged to live in rented accommodation as opposed to residing at her parents' home. M also said that if she was ordered to return B, she could not bear to return to the US with him and that returning and living without her would expose B to the grave risk of psychological harm or otherwise put him in an intolerable position because she had always been his primary carer and there was a strong bond between them. M said such facts were sufficient to constitute a defence under Art.13(b).

Held, ordering the return of B, that although M had evidence which suggested that F knew she would not be returning, such evidence was equivocal as F had an explanation for why it did not cause him to believe they would not be returning. In an ordinary case the fact that the plaintiff had bought one way tickets as opposed to return tickets would be very strong evidence of consent. However, F had been able to show that such purchase was a matter of convenience because, contrary to what one would expect, a return ticket on a flight taken by M and B would not have been a financial saving. Therefore, there was no finding that F consented to B's removal for the purposes of the Art.13(a) defence raised by M. M's assertion that she would not return with B if an order was made could not be allowed to stand as something which exposed B to a risk of harm sufficient to satisfy a defence under Art.13(b). If this was the case every mother could refuse to return with a child and thereby prevent a child's return. In any event if M had established an Art.13 defence, there would have to be an order for B to return to the US because the child was to all extents and purposes an American citizen, whose future custody should be decided by the American courts.

B (ARTICLE 13 DEFENCE), *Re*, February 4, 1997, Johnson, J., Fam Div. [*Ex rel.* JS Boora, Barrister, Regent Chambers, Stoke on Trent].

389. Child abduction–consent–evidence of consent–burden and standard of proof

F, a US citizen, and M, a British national, made their home in Texas. They had one daughter. Their relationship broke down and M returned to England with the child. The issue was whether F had consented to or acquiesced in the child's removal.

Held, that on the facts, F had consented to the child's removal to England. Following *C (Minors) (Abduction: Consent), Re* [1996] 1 F.L.R. 414, [1996] 1 C.L.Y. 521, express oral consent was given by F for the child's removal, and that F knew there was only a 50 per cent chance of M returning to the US did not change that fact. His change of mind did not cancel the consent.

K (ABDUCTION: CONSENT), *Re* [1997] 2 F.L.R. 212, Hale, J., Fam Div.

390. Child abduction–contempt of court–removal from jurisdiction by father

F removed four children from the jurisdiction for a six month educational holiday in Bangladesh without the consent of M, in whose favour residence orders had been made, or the leave of the court. He failed to comply with orders given on four separate occasions for the children's return and M applied for his committal. F was also ordered to surrender his passport. At the hearing of the application to commit, the judge returned his passport, accepting F's submission that the only way to secure the children's return was to travel to Bangladesh himself and bring the children back. M appealed and in granting leave to appeal the Court of Appeal directed that F should produce either tickets for the children's air travel or evidence of their purchase and a letter to his family in Bangladesh instructing them to return the children and explaining the arrangements for their return.

Held, allowing the appeal, that while the judge at first instance had considered the risk of F's failure to return to the UK was justified, F's non compliance with the directions of the Court of Appeal placed a different complexion on the case. The evidence revealed a number of serious contempts which indicated that the judge had been wrong to order the return of the passport, and subsequent events merely reinforced that view.

A (RETURN OF PASSPORT), *Re* [1997] 2 F.L.R. 137, Ward, L.J., CA.

391. Child abduction–custody–Cayman Islands

CHILD ABDUCTION AND CUSTODY (CAYMAN ISLANDS) ORDER 1997, SI 1997 2574; made under the Child Abduction and Custody Act 1985 s.28. In force: December 2, 1997; £3.20.

This Order extends certain modified provisions of the Child Abduction and Custody Act 1985 to the Cayman Islands.

392. Child abduction–custody–parties to Conventions–Amendment No.1– Liechtenstein

CHILD ABDUCTION AND CUSTODY (PARTIES TO CONVENTIONS) (AMENDMENT) ORDER 1997, SI 1997 1747; made under the Child Abduction and Custody Act 1985 s.2, s.13. In force: August 1, 1997; £1.10.

This Order amends the Child Abduction and Custody (Parties to Conventions) Order 1986 (SI 1986 1159). It adds Liechtenstein to the list of Contracting States to the European Convention on Recognition and Enforcement of Decisions concerning Custody of Children and on the Restoration of Custody of Children, signed at Luxembourg on May 20, 1980 (Cm. 191).

393. Child abduction–custody–parties to Conventions–Amendment No.2– Georgia and South Africa

CHILD ABDUCTION AND CUSTODY (PARTIES TO CONVENTIONS) (AMENDMENT) (NO.2) ORDER 1997, SI 1997 2575; made under the Child Abduction and Custody Act 1985 s.2, s.13. In force: October 30, 1997; £1.10.

This Order amends the Child Abduction and Custody (Parties to Conventions) Order 1986 (SI 1986 1159) by adding Georgia and South Africa to the list of

Contracting States to the Convention on the Civil Aspects of International Child Abduction, set down at The Hague on October 25, 1980 (Cm.33).

394. Child abduction–directions hearing–application by children to be joined as parties and separately represented–exceptional circumstances under the Hague Convention Art.13

[Hague Convention on the Civil Aspects of International Child Abduction 1980 Art.13.]

The parties moved to New Zealand from the UK with their two children. The marriage broke down and M abducted the children to the UK but they were returned to NZ and an order made preventing their removal. F maintained that he had almost no contact with the children. In 1994 custody was granted to M with interim contact to F following family therapy. In 1995 the mother's application to remove the children from the jurisdiction was refused and they were made wards of the NZ High Court. The children remained in foster care and M went to the UK with her two children from her second marriage. In 1996, when the children were 12 and 14, M returned and took the children to the UK. The children's applications for leave to apply for residence and prohibited steps orders were stayed pending the Hague Convention on the Civil Aspects of International Child Abduction 1980 Art.13 proceedings where the court considered whether they should be joined as parties and have separate representation in the substantive application.

Held, allowing the application, that an unusual feature of the case was that if returned to NZ the children would be returned to foster carers with no prospect of contact with F. There must be exceptional circumstances to justify separate representation for the children. Representation through M was inappropriate since she was in contempt of the NZ High Court and it was found that she had exercised undue influence over the children and her conduct could undermine their objections. The children needed to be able to take independent advice and to present views which might be in conflict with M's views, particularly in the light of their possible objections under Art.13(b). There was evidence that the children were of an age and degree of maturity such that it was appropriate for their views to be taken into account, *M (A Minor) (Child Abduction), Re* [1994] 1 F.L.R. 390, [1995] 2 C.L.Y. 3431 considered.

S (ABDUCTION: CHILDREN: SEPARATE REPRESENTATION), *Re* [1997] 1 F.L.R. 486, Wall, J., Fam Div.

395. Child abduction–habitual residence

[Domicile and Matrimonial Proceedings Act 1973 Sch.1, para.8(1); Family Law Act 1986 s.2A(4), s.5(2); Children Act 1989.]

The parents were married in 1986, had two children and settled in Scotland. In June 1996 M took the children to England without F's knowledge where she instituted divorce proceedings and obtained an ex parte residence order and a prohibited steps order preventing him from removing the children. F had intended to issue a divorce petition in Scotland but the judge in the English proceedings granted an injunction preventing him from doing so. The judge concluded that the children had no habitual place of residence so that there had been no wrongful removal and that welfare considerations required them to remain in England, which was also the forum conveniens for the divorce proceedings. F appealed.

Held, allowing the appeal, that the judge had erred in (1) finding that there had been no habitual residence simply because the family had intended at some point in the future to return to England, and (2) approaching the question of the divorce and the children's future from the point of view of the children's welfare. By virtue of the Domicile and Matrimonial Proceedings Act 1973 Sch.1 para.8(1), an earlier petition presented in another part of the UK should be stayed in favour of a divorce petition presented where the parties had been habitually resident. The English court therefore had no jurisdiction under the Children Act 1989, unless it was required to deal with urgent matters. The judge had failed to have regard to the Family Law Act 1986 s.2A(4) and s.5(2) and to whether he should stay the English proceedings pending the issue of a divorce petition in Scotland.

M (MINORS) (JURISDICTION: HABITUAL RESIDENCE), *Re; sub nom.* M v. M (ABDUCTION: ENGLAND AND SCOTLAND) [1997] 2 F.L.R. 263, Butler-Sloss, L.J., CA.

396. Child abduction–habitual residence–family spending summer in Greece and winter in England–mother refusing to take children to Greece–father applying for return of children to Greece

[Hague Convention on the Civil Aspects of International Child Abduction 1980; Child Abduction and Custody Act 1985.]

M was English and F was Greek. They had two children, aged four and one. F ran a hotel in Corfu and the family lived in a villa attached to the hotel during the summer months. The family spent the winter months in a home in London. F returned to Greece in March 1995, expecting that M and the children would join him in April. Unknown to F, M had taken steps to bring divorce proceedings in England and she concealed her intention not to return. M obtained an interim residence order. F applied for a stay of the proceedings and for the return of the children to Greece under the Child Abduction and Custody Act 1985 and the Hague Convention on the Civil Aspects of International Child Abduction 1980. F contended that the children were habitually resident in both Greece and England and that M had wrongfully retained the children in England. In the alternative, F contended that the children's habitual residence from March 1995 was in Greece and M's deception could not change that.

Held, dismissing the application, that (1) a broad view of the evidence was required in Hague Convention proceedings. Oral evidence and cross-examination should be very limited, *B (Minors) (Abduction) (No.2), Re* [1993] 1 F.L.R. 993, [1994] C.L.Y. 3152 applied; (2) whilst it was possible in other fields for a person to have more than one habitual residence, this idea of concurrent residence did not fit easily into the scheme of the Convention, *Cooper (Surveyor of Taxes) v. Cadwallader* [1904] 5 T.C. 101; *Norris (ex p. Reynolds), Re* (1888) 4 T.L.R. 452; *Pittar v. Richardson* (1917) 87 L.J.K.B. 59 and *V v. B (A Minor) (Abduction)* [1991] 1 F.L.R. 266, [1991] C.L.Y. 2525 considered; (3) on the facts, the children had consecutive habitual residences in England and Greece and they were habitually resident in England at the moment M failed to take them to Greece, *J (A Minor) (Abduction: Custody Rights), Re* [1990] 2 A.C. 562, [1990] C.L.Y. 3151 applied, and (4) although no one parent could alter the children's habitual residence without the consent of the other, F's alternative argument failed. There was never any intention that the children would return to Greece in March. The children were habitually resident in England at the relevant time and the application would be dismissed, *A (A Minor) (Wardship: Jurisdiction), Re* [1995] 1 F.L.R. 767, [1996] 1 C.L.Y. 605 considered.

V (ABDUCTION: HABITUAL RESIDENCE), *Re* [1995] 2 F.L.R. 992, Douglas Brown, J., Fam Div.

397. Child abduction–inherent jurisdiction of High Court to order surrender of father's foreign passport

F, who held an Iranian passport, appealed against an order that his passport should be kept by his solicitors and only released by order of the court or with the mother's consent. This order, together with an order for limited supervised contact in a secure room at the Royal Courts of Justice, was made in response to the mother's anxiety at the possibility that F, who had previously abducted one of their children, might do so again.

Held, dismissing the appeal, that the High Court's inherent jurisdiction to order the surrender of a passport was not limited to UK nationals and, given the circumstances of the case, the court had acted within its discretion, in the interests of the children.

A-K (MINORS) (FOREIGN PASSPORT: JURISDICTION), *Re*; *sub nom.* A-K (MINORS) (CONTACT), *Re* [1997] 2 F.C.R. 563, Sir Stephen Brown, CA.

398. Child abduction–interim care and control under wardship order–determination of habitual residence–removal to Ireland wrongful

[European Convention on Recognition and Enforcement of Decisions Concerning Custody of Children 1980; Hague Convention on the Civil Aspects of International Child Abduction 1980; Family Law Act 1986 s.2(3)(a), s.3(1)(a).]

When S's mother died, his grandmother and aunt removed him to Ireland, where, two days later, an Irish court granted guardianship and care and control to the aunt. On the same day, the English High Court granted an order giving interim care and control of S to his father, who had not been married to the mother, and ordered S's return to England, making him a ward of court. The grandmother and aunt now appealed against the Court of Appeal's decision that their removal of S to Ireland was wrongful within the meaning of the Hague Convention on the Civil Aspects of International Child Abduction 1980 and the European Convention on Recognition and Enforcement of Decisions Concerning Custody of Children 1980. The issue turned on whether S was habitually resident in England at the time his father applied for the order granted to him.

Held, dismissing the appeal, that the removal of S to Ireland by persons without parental rights and the order made by the Irish court did not serve to change S's habitual residence, and the English court had jurisdiction under the Family Law Act 1986 s.2(3)(a) and s.3(1)(a) to make the order granting interim care and control to S's father. Consequently, S's father had acquired rights of custody within the meaning of the Hague Convention Art.3 and Art.5 and the retention of S in Ireland became wrongful on the making of the order. For the purposes of the European Convention, once the High Court made the order giving interim care and control to S's father, S's retention in Ireland and the failure to return him constituted an "improper removal" within Art.1(d) and Art.12. The court therefore had jurisdiction to declare such removal unlawful.

S (A MINOR) (CUSTODY: HABITUAL RESIDENCE), *Re*; *sub nom.* S (A MINOR) (ABDUCTION: EUROPEAN AND HAGUE CONVENTIONS), *Re* [1997] 3 W.L.R. 597, Lord Slynn of Hadley, HL.

399. Child abduction–return of child–application by grandparents–relationship between Hague Convention Art.13 and European Convention Art.10(1)(b)

[European Convention on the Recognition and Enforcement of Decisions Concerning Custody of Children 1980 Art.10; Hague Convention on the Civil Aspects of International Child Abduction 1980 Art.13.]

M and F, from Switzerland, had a daughter, A, aged 10 years. After M and F divorced, M experienced difficulties in caring for A, with the result that the Swiss authorities became involved and A's care was delegated to the paternal grandparents by order of the court. M later abducted A to England. The court dismissed the grandparents' applications to have the Swiss order enforced and A returned to Switzerland under the Hague Convention 1980 Art.13 and European Convention 1980 Art.10 on the grounds that the Swiss order was no longer in the best interests of the child. The grandparents appealed.

Held, dismissing the appeal, that the application under the European Convention could not be determined until the outcome of the Hague Convention proceedings was known. Under Art.10(1)(b) of the European Convention, the circumstances at the time of the original decision should be determined and then the question of a change in circumstances considered, which consideration should include the passage of time but not the improper removal. The changes in circumstances were obvious as M could provide proper care for A, her financial difficulties had abated and enforcement of the original order of the Swiss court would not be in A's interests. In addition, A had expressed the wish to remain with M and her maturity was assessed by a social worker as being such that her views should be taken into account.

R (ABDUCTION: HAGUE AND EUROPEAN CONVENTIONS), *Re* [1997] 1 F.L.R. 673,Ward, L.J., CA.

400. Child abduction–return of child–children objecting to return

[Hague Convention on the Civil Aspects of International Child Abduction 1980 Art.13.]

M was Danish and F was English. After their marriage broke down their two children, now aged 13 and 11, lived with M and her new husband. The elder child became unruly and disturbed and M placed him in a children's home and she suggested that he should go and live permanently with F, although nothing was agreed. Eventually, in April 1996, he was sent on a one-way ticket to F for contact, while his sister followed with a return ticket in July 1996. F then refused to return the children and applied for a residence order. M initiated proceedings under the Hague Convention on the Civil Aspects of International Child Abduction 1980 Art.13. F conceded that his retention of the children was wrongful, but argued that: (1) under Art.13(b) of the Convention the return of the children would expose them to grave risk of physical or psychological harm because of ill treatment at the hands of M and the step-father, and (2) the children objected to returning and were of an age and degree of maturity at which it was appropriate to take their views into account.

Held, that (1) the children's allegations of ill-treatment demonstrated insensitivity and inappropriate chastisement but did not amount to deliberate ill-treatment such as would expose them to grave risk of physical or psychological harm for the purposes of Art.13(b), and (2) the defence under Art.13 should be interpreted independently from Art.13(b) and read literally. Although both children were of an age and maturity at which their views could be taken into account, the girl's objections were not sufficient to outweigh the policy of the Convention, that where children visited another country for the purposes of contact, the parent with whom they live should feel confident that they would be returned. Even though the boy's reasons for not being returned were far stronger, the arguments against separating the siblings should also outweigh his objections and both children should be returned to Denmark with an exhortation to M and the Danish authorities that special consideration should be given to the difficult position in which F and the children presently found themselves.

HB (ABDUCTION: CHILDREN'S OBJECTIONS), *Re* [1997] 1 F.L.R. 392, Hale, J., Fam Div.

401. Child abduction–return of child–custody rights–application by grandparents–joint custody rights in absence of formal agreement

[Hague Convention on the Civil Aspects of International Child Abduction 1980 Art.3.]

O was born in Germany in 1992 and lived there until December 1996 when her German mother and current partner brought her to England. While in Germany, O had lived with her maternal grandparents since mid-1995 and had previously spent long periods with them due to concerns over her mother's parenting ability. After O was taken to England, the grandparents initiated custody proceedings and obtained an interim custody order in Germany. They now sought O's return to Germany under the Hague Convention on the Civil Aspects of International Child Abduction 1980.

Held, ordering O's summary return, that, on the facts, the grandparents had established joint rights of custody within the terms of Art.3 of the Convention, despite the absence of any agreement or court order regarding the child's care. The word "may" in the last paragraph of Art.3 meant that the court, in establishing rights of custody, was not limited to the situations laid down therein, *B (A Minor) (Child Abduction: Consent), Re* [1994] 2 F.L.R. 249, [1995] 2 C.L.Y. 3447 considered, but had to judge whether, on the facts, parental or custodial functions were exercised, albeit in the absence of any official custodial status. Furthermore, the court was entitled to exercise its inherent discretion, following wrongful removal of a child, to require her summary return to the country of habitual residence where it was in the child's best interests for further investigations to be made as to long term welfare. O's connections with Germany were so strong that it was clearly right that she be returned.

O (A MINOR) (CHILD ABDUCTION: CUSTODY RIGHTS), *Re* [1997] 2 F.C.R. 465, Cazalet, J., Fam Div.

402. **Child abduction–return of child–custody rights–father's rights of access did not amount to rights of custody**

[Hague Convention on the Civil Aspects of International Child Abduction 1980 Art.3, Art.12.]

F applied for the summary return of his child under the Hague Convention on the Civil Aspects of International Child Abduction 1980 Art.3 and Art.12, after M had moved to England from Italy with the child. The child was born in Italy and the Italian courts awarded custody to M and access to F. The issue was whether F's rights under Italian law amounted to rights of custody under the Convention.

Held, refusing the application, that F's rights, which were to watch over the child's education and living conditions and to have access twice a week and during holidays, did not amount to rights of custody under Italian law. However, removal could still be considered wrongful under the Convention, and rights of access could change into rights of custody where the interests of the child, which were paramount, so required, *B (A Minor) (Child Abduction: Consent), Re* [1994] 2 F.L.R. 249, [1995] 2 C.L.Y. 3447 and *C v. C (Minor: Abduction: Rights of Custody Abroad)* [1989] 1 W.L.R. 654, [1989] C.L.Y. 2437 considered. However, the Convention clearly distinguished between rights of custody and rights of access and, on the facts of the instant case, M could not be said to have removed the child in breach of F's rights.

S v. H (ABDUCTION: ACCESS RIGHTS) [1997] 1 F.L.R. 971, Hale, J., Fam Div.

403. **Child abduction–return of child–custody rights–parents removing children from Ontario to England–maternal grandmother granted sole custody in Ontario**

[Hague Convention on the Civil Aspects of International Child Abduction 1980 Art.12, Art.13; Child Abduction and Custody Act 1985.]

M was a Canadian citizen and F was British. They married in 1994 and lived in Canada. There were two children aged nine and two. In 1994 a deportation order was made against F. In June 1995 the maternal grandmother applied for visitation rights and later for an injunction to prevent the children being removed from Canada, for disclosure of the father's criminal record and for custody. At the time that the grandmother's applications were heard M and F had left for England with the children. An order was made granting the grandmother sole custody of the children. Since, when the children were removed, the grandmother had no rights of custody, the Ontario court was made the plaintiff in proceedings under the Child Abduction and Custody Act 1985 for the return of the children. A declaration that the removal of the children was wrongful was made under the Hague Convention 1980 Art.13. The parents' appeal against that order was dismissed.

Held, dismissing the originating summons, that on the basis that the Ontario court had found that the children were wrongfully removed, the English court was bound to order the return of the children under Art.12 of the Convention, unless Art.13(b) applied. It was necessary for the court to take into account the elder child's objections to being returned, in circumstances where the child regarded the grandmother's proceedings as an unwarranted intrusion into her life and the grandmother's custody application was based on insubstantial evidence. There was a risk that, if the child were returned to the grandmother whom she disliked, against her will, she would be placed in an intolerable situation within Art.13. There was no submission that the two children should be treated differently and the court would exercise its discretion not to return the children.

ONTARIO COURT v. M AND M (ABDUCTION: CHILDREN'S OBJECTIONS) [1997] 1 F.L.R. 475, Hollis, J., Fam Div.

404. Child abduction–return of child–custody rights–wardship proceedings– putative father had "no rights in custody"

[Hague Convention on the Civil Aspects of International Child Abduction 1980 Art.3, Art.5; Child Abduction and Custody Act 1985 s.8.]

F and M, an unmarried couple, had a relationship which ended in December 1994. In August 1994 a son, J, was born. At all times J lived with M, although F had regular contact with him. At no time did F have any parental responsibility or legal rights of custody or access to J. In February 1997 F, believing that M was not caring properly for J, issued an application for a parental responsibility order. In March 1997 M removed J to Italy, her home state. In April F issued an originating application in wardship seeking a declaration pursuant to the Child Abduction and Custody Act 1985 s.8 that the removal of J was wrongful within the meaning of the Hague Convention 1980 Art.3. The declaration was refused and F appealed.

Held, dismissing the appeal, that the object of the Hague Convention was to ensure the speedy return, without lengthy proceedings or inquiries, of children who had been wrongfully removed from the person having the care of them. On the facts it would be impossible to say that F had "rights of custody" within the meaning of Art.3 of the Convention, *B (A Minor) (Child Abduction: Consent), Re* [1994] 2 F.L.R. 249, [1995] 2 C.L.Y. 3447 distinguished. Similarly no wardship order had been made and in the circumstances it would be wholly inappropriate to make a declaration under Art.3 for a peremptory return of the child, although such an order might be appropriate after an inter partes hearing, *BM (A Minor) (Wardship: Jurisdiction), Re* [1993] 1 F.L.R. 979, [1994] C.L.Y. 3279 distinguished. Where a court makes an interim custody order then it will retain "the right to determine the child's place of residence" for the purposes of Art.5(a) of the Convention, but as no such order was made in the present case no rights of custody were vested either in an English court or in F, *B v. B (Child Abduction: Custody Rights)* [1993] 1 F.L.R. 238, [1993] C.L.Y. 2789 considered. Accordingly, this was not an appropriate case within the Convention for a peremptory order.

B (ABDUCTION) (RIGHTS OF CUSTODY), *Re*, [1997] 2 F.L.R. 594, Swinton Thomas, L.J., CA.

405. Child abduction–return of child–discretion to refuse summary return of child wrongfully removed from country of habitual residence

[Hague Convention on the Civil Aspects of International Child Abduction 1980 Art.12, Art.13.]

S was born in Germany in 1986 to Italian parents who had married in England. In May 1996, her mother, M, removed her to England without her father's knowledge, with a view to settling there permanently, but they returned to Germany for a three day visit in September 1996. In October 1996, the child's father, F, was granted custody of S by the German courts and in June 1997 began proceedings under the Hague Convention 1980 for her summary return. M admitted that S's removal from Germany in May 1996 had been wrongful, but contended that, as S had been settled in England for more than 12 months, the court had a discretion under Art.12 to refuse to order her summary return.

Held, refusing to order summary return, that Art.12 was not applicable as the second removal in September 1996 had to be taken into account and that constituted a separate wrongful removal. However, Art.13 gave the court a discretion to consider the views of abducted children if they were of sufficient maturity. In the instant case, in view of the fact that S had clearly shown that she had rational objections to being returned to Germany, *S (A Minor) (Abduction: Custody Rights), Re* [1993] Fam. 242, [1993] C.L.Y. 2796 applied, and that F had delayed for some time before bringing proceedings under the Convention, the court would exercise its discretion to decline to order S's summary return.

S (A MINOR) (CHILD ABDUCTION: DELAY), *Re, The Times*, November 20, 1997, Wall, J., Fam Div.

406. Child abduction–return of child–return to non Convention country

[Hague Convention on the Civil Aspects of International Child Abduction 1980.]

F appealed against the refusal of his application for the return of his child to the United Arab Emirates, her country of habitual residence. M submitted that the child's welfare was the court's paramount consideration and that it was not open to an English court to order a child's peremptory return to a country which was not a party to the Hague Convention 1980 unless satisfied that the child's welfare would be protected by the foreign court charged with deciding her future.

Held, dismissing the appeal, that, notwithstanding the general principle of international comity, the English court had a duty to ensure the child's welfare, *M (Minors) (Abduction: Peremptory Return Order), Re* [1996] 1 F.L.R. 478, [1995] 2 C.L.Y. 3446 not followed. In the instant case, given the limited powers available to the courts of the United Arab Emirates and medical evidence indicating that M's health, and therefore the child's welfare, might be put at risk if she was forced to remain in that country, it was not appropriate to order the child's return.

A (A MINOR) (ABDUCTION: NON CONVENTION COUNTRY), *Re, The Times*, July 3, 1997, Ward, L.J., CA.

407. Child abduction–return of child–role of police serving ex parte order–solicitors misinformed police as to order's effect

The unmarried parents of three girls separated and the children remained with M. M went to France with the children without F's knowledge or consent. He obtained an ex parte order for the return of the children and interim residence of all three. M returned the elder two girls to England without knowledge of the order and the girls went to live with F. At a subsequent hearing the judge ordered M to return the youngest child to England and for the matter to be restored upon the child's return for further consideration as to her residence. When M returned to England arrangements were made to serve the order upon her. The police were informed that F had an order requiring M to hand the child over to him, that she might not hand the child over easily and problems were anticipated. The police went with the process server to serve M and told her that while she should seek legal advice, she should abide by the terms of the court order. She believed the order required her to hand over the child and did so. After an inter partes hearing concerning the residence of the child, the judge arranged a further hearing at which the police and legal representatives for both sides were present to consider the action taken following the first order of the court.

Held, that, since there was almost always the potential for serious injustice where courts were invited to make orders without hearing both sides of a case, those seeking ex parte orders should behave with scrupulous care in relation to the application and to the implementation of any order made. The order had been designed to procure the return of the child to the jurisdiction and then to preserve the status quo until the matter could be returned to court. F's solicitors had misrepresented the effect of the order to M and to the police with the effect that a small child who had lived with her mother all her life and who was not believed to be at immediate risk of significant harm was taken from her mother's care to her father whom she had not seen for 20 months. The police should always be clear as to whether (1) an order, such as a recovery order, required them to do anything; (2) circumstances required them to do anything such as when a child was taken into police protection; or (3) their presence was required merely to prevent a breach of the peace, such as had been the position here. The police should always take care to understand what the order itself required and, further, should exercise some independent judgment as to whether a breach of the peace was likely. Solicitors had a duty to be scrupulously accurate when describing the terms of any order, especially to the person to whom it was addressed but also to others such as process servers and the police. Counsel should never advise on the terms of an order made in their absence without being completely satisfied that they knew exactly what it said, normally by seeing a copy.

J (MINORS) (EX PARTE ORDERS), *Re* [1997] 1 F.L.R. 606, Hale, J., Fam Div.

408. Child abuse—offenders—prevention from adoption and fostering

CHILDREN (PROTECTION FROM OFFENDERS) (MISCELLANEOUS AMENDMENTS) REGULATIONS 1997, SI 1997 2308; made under the Adoption Act 1976 s.9; and the Children Act 1989 s.23, s.68, Sch.4 para.4, Sch.5 para.7, Sch.5 para.8, Sch.6 para.10, Sch.9 para.2. In force: October 17, 1997; £1.55.

To ensure that those with convictions for serious offences against children or those who have been cautioned in respect of such offences are prevented from adopting or fostering children, these Regulations amend the Adoption Agencies Regulations 1983 (SI 1983 1964), the Foster Placement (Children) Regulations 1991 (SI 1991 910), the Children's Homes Regulations 1991 (SI 1991 1506) and the Disqualification for Caring for Children Regulations 1991 (SI 1991 2094).

409. Child support—declaration of parentage—artificial insemination by donor

[Child Support Act 1991 s.27; Human Fertilisation and Embryology Act 1990.]

The Secretary of State for Social Security applied for declarations of parentage in respect of two children. The issue was whether a husband was a "parent" within the meaning of the Child Support Act 1991 in respect of two children born in 1981 and 1986 by artificial insemination with third party donor sperm. The Secretary of State contended that the husband had consented to the insemination and was therefore estopped from denying that he was a parent within the meaning of the 1991 Act.

Held, that the children were born before the enactment of the Human Fertilisation and Embryology Act 1990 which did not have retrospective effect. Under the law applicable at the time of their births a male parent meant the biological father so the husband was not liable to maintain the children under the 1991 Act.

M (CHILD SUPPORT ACT: PARENTAGE), *Re* [1997] 2 F.L.R. 90, Bracewell, J., Fam Div.

410. Child support—declaration of parentage—putative father refused blood test—inference to be drawn from refusal

[Child Support Act 1991 s.27; Family Law Reform Act 1969 s.23.]

The Secretary of State appealed, by way of case stated, against a decision of the justices that G's refusal to supply a blood test sample for DNA testing to establish the parentage of a child was reasonable, fair and just. Following the mother's claim for income support, the Secretary of State made an application under the Child Support Act 1991 s.27 for a declaration that G was the father of the child. The family proceedings court subsequently made a direction that G should supply a blood test. G refused to comply with the direction. The Family Law Reform Act 1969 s.23 allows a court to draw inferences from a failure to give effect to a direction. However, the justices chose not to draw such inferences and the Secretary of State appealed on the ground that the inference to be drawn from G's refusal was overwhelming and that the justices' formulation of their reasons was not sustainable.

Held, allowing the appeal, that G's refusal to provide a sample of blood for DNA analysis created an almost inescapable inference that he was the father of the child, *A (A Minor) (Paternity: Refusal of Blood Test), Re* [1994] 2 F.L.R. 463, *H (A Minor) (Blood Test: Parental Rights), Re* [1996] 3 W.L.R. 506, [1996] 1 C.L.Y. 597 and *G (Parentage: Blood Sample), Re* [1997] 1 F.L.R. 360, [1997] C.L.Y. 441 applied. In addition, the reasons given by the justices for accepting the validity of G's refusal were unacceptable. It was irrelevant that G had provided a blood test sample in 1981. Furthermore, G's honest belief that the child was not his did not constitute an objective reason for not submitting to a blood test.

R. v. SECRETARY OF STATE FOR SOCIAL SECURITY, *ex p.* G, Trans. Ref: [1997] 3 F.C.R. 728, June 16, 1997, Sir Stephen Brown, QBD.

411. Child Support Commissioners–procedure–Secretary of State's inclusion in proceedings

CHILD SUPPORT COMMISSIONERS (PROCEDURE) (AMENDMENT) REGULATIONS 1997, SI 1997 802; made under the Child Support Act 1991 s.22, s.24. In force: April 14, 1997; £0.65.

These Regulations amend the Child Support Commissioners (Procedure) Regulations 1992 (SI 1992 2640) in relation to the Secretary of State's inclusion as a party to certain proceedings.

412. Contact orders–application by grandparent–approach where person other than parent applies for contact

M and the child's maternal grandmother were not on good terms with each other. The grandmother had extensive contact with the child when he was living with his father, but following a change in residence, contact was stopped by M. The grandmother obtained leave to apply for contact but the substantive application was refused due to the risk that the child would suffer from emotional harm as a result of the hostility between M and the grandmother and that it was desirable for the child to be able to settle with M. The grandmother appealed.

Held, dismissing the appeal, that the justices had decided that there should be no contact for the time being since it was in the child's interests to settle with M and their decision was unassailable. Save in the case of a parent, a person applying for contact had to show grounds for the making of an order once leave had been granted, and once a case for contact had been established a respondent had to demonstrate that there were cogent reasons why there should be no contact.

W (A MINOR) (CONTACT: APPLICATION BY GRANDPARENT), *Re* [1997] 1 F.L.R. 793, Hollis, J., Fam Div.

413. Contact orders–application for leave to apply for contact–magistrates refusing leave but failing to give reasons

[Family Proceedings Courts (Children Act 1989) Rules 1991 (SI 1991 1395) r.21.]

The applicant and the mother of a child, born in August 1991, lived together. The period of cohabitation was in dispute but on the applicant's evidence lasted from the time the child was 10 months until he was two years and eight months. After their separation the applicant had some contact but this was terminated a year later. He applied to the family proceedings court for leave to apply for contact. The magistrates refused and gave no reasons for their decision. The applicant appealed.

Held, allowing the appeal and remitting the case for rehearing, that the Family Proceedings Courts (Children Act 1989) Rules 1991 r.21 (5) and r.21 (6), provided, inter alia, that the justices' clerk should record in writing the reasons for the refusal of an application and the justices should state the reasons for the court's decision and failure to comply with the rules was a serious deficiency. The issue before the court was important and the applicant was entitled to know why his application had been refused. This was not one of those exceptional cases where the court's reasons need not be given.

T v. W (CONTACT: REASONS FOR REFUSING LEAVE) [1996] 2 F.L.R. 473, Connell, J., Fam Div.

414. Contact orders–children's welfare–threats by stepfather to reject child–dismissal of natural father's contact application at directions hearing

F and W separated shortly after the birth of their child, B, and W remarried. When F made an application for contact with B, B's stepfather indicated that in the Asian community it was normal practice after divorce for children to have no contact with the other party, and that if the application were granted B would have to reside with F. No contact order was made and F made a further application which was dismissed at a directions hearing, which F did not attend, after B's stepfather stated that if the proceedings continued he would reject both B and W. F appealed.

Held, dismissing the appeal, that, whilst, as a general principle, the court would seek to maintain contact between a child and his natural parent and would not respond to threats, the court's overriding concern was for the welfare of the child. A court had jurisdiction to dismiss a contact application at a directions hearing, but only if it was satisfied that if it continued with a full hearing on the merits the child would undoubtedly suffer harm. The instant case was such an exceptional case, where B was at risk of being removed from a stable home, and the judge had acted within his discretion in summarily dismissing the application.

B (A MINOR) (CONTACT: STEPFATHER'S OPPOSITION), *Re*; *sub nom*. B (A MINOR) (CONTACT: STEPFATHER'S HOSTILITY), *Re*, *The Times*, July 9, 1997, Lord Woolf, M.R., CA.

415. Contact orders–conditions–county court had no jurisdiction to impose injunctive orders aimed at protecting mother from harassment by father

[Children Act 1989 s.11 (7).]

F appealed against a decision of the county court that a contact order made in respect of his child would be subject to conditions imposed under the Children Act 1989 s.11 (7), with a penal notice attached. Some of the conditions related to contact, but others were aimed at protecting the mother and her relatives from harassment and vindictive acts by F, who contended that these conditions should not have been attached to a contact order as they amounted to injunctions relating to trespass, assault and domestic violence, rather than the arrangements for contact.

Held, allowing the appeal in part, that in contact proceedings it was inappropriate and outside the power of the county court to impose injunctive type conditions under s.11 (7) against a father to protect the mother from harassment. Such orders were more appropriately made by the High Court in the exercise of its inherent jurisdiction and therefore the case would be transferred to the High Court for a review hearing. In the meantime, the orders which related to the protection of the mother without having any direct bearing on the issue of contact would be discharged.

D (A MINOR) (CONTACT ORDERS: CONDITIONS), *Re*, *The Times*, August 5, 1997, Sir Stephen Brown, CA.

416. Contact orders–enforcement–repeated breaches of contact orders–mother committed to six weeks' imprisonment–welfare of child material but not paramount consideration

M and F had a daughter, T, in January 1992 and separated in 1994. When F applied for contact and parental responsibility M objected, alleging that another man was T's father, although DNA testing demonstrated conclusively that F, the applicant, was the natural father. A number of contact orders were made and were breached by M between September 1995 and October 1996. In September 1996 the judge imposed a sentence of six weeks' imprisonment suspended for six months and ordered M to permit contact at a contact centre. M flouted the order and the sentence was activated. M applied for a stay of execution pending appeal which was refused. M appealed against that refusal.

Held, dismissing the appeal, that the welfare of the child was material but not the paramount consideration when considering whether to commit a mother for breach of a contact order, *Churchard v. Churchard* [1984] F.L.R. 635 doubted. The judge had exercised his discretion properly, having been fully aware of the effect of separating the mother and child, but there was a limit to the tolerance of the court when confronted with persistent defiance of its orders, *O (A Minor) (Contact: Imposition of Conditions), Re* [1995] 2 F.L.R. 124, [1995] 2 C.L.Y. 3476 and *F, Re* (Unreported, 1996) applied.

A v. N (COMMITTAL: REFUSAL OF CONTACT); *sub nom.* N (A MINOR), *Re* [1997] 1 F.L.R. 533, Ward, L.J., CA.

417. Contact orders–four year old child–two week holiday with father in Palestine premature and potentially unsafe

M appealed against an order granting F leave to remove their child, A, aged four years, from the jurisdiction to Hebron for a two week holiday, and also against the same judge's refusal to set the order aside on July 10, 1997. M was English and F Palestinian. They were married in 1993 and, after separating in 1995, F exercised supervised contact with A that was increased to occasional overnight stays after a residence order, in favour of M, was made in March 1997. F applied, in June 1997, to take A to Hebron to see his family. M objected to F's application on the grounds that; (1) F would not return A to the jurisdiction, (2) the visit was dangerous for A because of the political situation, and (3) it was premature for A to spend so long away from M, as he had only spent a few nights with his father and was not familiar with him. It was decided at first instance that F, who was a university student with roots in England, was bona fides and that the undertaking he gave to return A was sufficient to ease M's anxieties. Previous overnight contact had gone well and A enjoyed being with F. At the hearing to set aside the order, it was stated that F would bring A home if he was upset by the separation.

Held, allowing the appeal, that (1) whilst it was right that A should visit his family in Palestine, it was too soon for a substantial holiday abroad and to be away from his mother. A had only just started staying overnight with F, and it was likely he would be upset; (2) the judge was entitled to find that F was bona fides, but M was extremely concerned that A would not be returned and it was in the child's interests to ease that concern. The undertaking was not sufficient to achieve that aim and there needed to be "watertight arrangements" in Hebron as well, so that M and the court were satisfied A would be returned. Furthermore, the arrangements should not be made hastily, and (3) even though it might be subjective, notice should have been taken of the political situation which was still too unstable for A to visit safely.

Observed, that the Palestinian National Authority should have a court order registered with them or undertaking by F to return A filed with them, before A was removed from the jurisdiction.

AR (A MINOR), *Re*, Trans. Ref: LTA 97/6593/K, July 31, 1997, Wall, J., CA.

418. Contact orders–supervised contact–need to take account of medium and longer term issues based on benefit to child

F appealed against the dismissal of his application for supervised contact with his two year old daughter. The parents were not married and the relationship broke down two months after the girl was born. Although some supervised contact had taken place and been successful, later unsupervised contact was ended for reasons relating to the care of the child. F's application was refused as the judge found that his drug and alcohol abuse and lack of a permanent home posed a potential risk to his daughter.

Held, allowing the appeal and making an order for one hour's supervised contact per week, that the judge had erred in principle by giving undue weight to short term problems, *O (A Minor) (Contact: Imposition of Conditions), Re* [1995] 2 F.L.R. 124, [1996] 1 C.L.Y. 550 considered, and failing to address medium and longer term issues. F's application was limited strictly to contact at the contact centre, with unsupervised contact being something he had suggested only for the future. It was wrong for the judge to conclude, on the evidence available, that F could never organise his life so as to make unsupervised contact a possibility at some point in the future. The child would undoubtedly benefit from meaningful contact with F, who had in many ways shown himself to be a committed father.

M (A MINOR) (CONTACT: SUPERVISION), Re, The Times, June 10, 1997, Ward, L.J., CA.

419. County courts–jurisdiction–change of name

See CHILDREN: Dawson v. Wearmouth. §385

420. Family assistance orders–parental contact–father in prison–no power to order escort for children's visits

[Children Act 1989 s.16.]

The court has no power to order a local authority to provide an escort for children visiting their father in prison. F, who was serving a prison sentence, applied for parental responsibility and contact orders in respect of his two children and also asked the court to make a family assistance order under the Children Act 1989 s.16 to require the local authority to provide an escort to bring the children to visit him in prison, as he was estranged from the children's mother and all other members of the family refused to undertake the journey.

Held, dismissing the applications on other grounds, that it was not appropriate for the court to make a family assistance order for such a purpose. Whether or not a local authority should provide escorts for children in such circumstances was a question for the authority itself.

S v. P (CONTACT APPLICATION: FAMILY ASSISTANCE ORDER) [1997] 2 F.L.R. 277, Judge Callman, Fam Div.

421. Family proceedings–allocation of proceedings between courts

CHILDREN (ALLOCATION OF PROCEEDINGS) (AMENDMENT) ORDER 1997, SI 1997 1897 (L.33); made under the Children Act 1989 s.92, Sch.11 Part I. In force: Art.2 to Art.4: October 1, 1997; remainder: September 1, 1997; £1.10.

This Order amends the Children (Allocation of Proceedings) Order 1991 (SI 1991 1677) which provides for the allocation of proceedings between the High Court, the county courts and the magistrates' courts of proceedings relating to children. It extends the power of county courts to review the refusal by a magistrates' court of the transfer of proceedings to a county court; extends the power to provide for cases to be transferred from county courts to magistrates' courts; makes Shoreditch County Court one of the particular county courts in which proceedings may be taken; enables the three named county courts to make orders under the Children Act 1989 s.4; nominates Salisbury County Court as a family hearing centre; and provides that the care centre for the Salisbury Petty Sessions Area is Swindon County Court in place of Bournemouth County Court.

422. Family proceedings–magistrates courts

FAMILY PROCEEDINGS COURTS (CHILDREN ACT 1989) (AMENDMENT) RULES 1997, SI 1997 1895 (L.31); made under the Magistrates' Courts Act 1980 s.144. In force: October 1, 1997; £2.40.

These Rules amend the Family Proceedings Courts (Children Act 1989) Rules 1991 (SI 1991 1395) to relax for specified purposes the requirements for confidentiality in respect of the report of a guardian ad litem; to make provision where the court includes an exclusion requirement in an interim care order or an emergency protection order; and to enable magistrates to set an order aside where there has been failure of service.

423. Fostering—delay—statutory complaints procedure—judicial review

[Children Act 1989 s.26.]

A's mother applied by way of judicial review for a declaration that B had erred in law by failing to ensure that an appropriate special foster care placement was found for A, pursuant to the Children Act 1989 s.26, after A's doctor had advised that such a placement was imperative.

Held, dismissing the application, that where neither the facts nor the law were in dispute, relief should have been sought under the complaints procedure in s.26 rather than through judicial review. Delay did not constitute an error in law and a judicial review hearing could not investigate the undisputed delay in the authority performing their duty to provide accommodation under s.20 of the Act.

R. v. BIRMINGHAM CITY COUNCIL, *ex p.* A (A MINOR) [1997] 2 F.C.R. 357, Sir Stephen Brown (President), Fam Div.

424. Fostering—local authority duty of care—child allegedly abused by foster parents

[Children Act 1948; Boarding-Out of Children Regulations 1955 (SI 1955 1377); Child Care Act 1980.]

H applied for leave to appeal against the dismissal of his action in negligence against N. H had been placed with foster parents between the ages of five and 14 and claimed to have been physically and sexually abused. He claimed that N had been negligent in (1) failing to monitor and supervise the foster placement; (2) failing to investigate reports of abuse, and (3) failing to remove him from foster care. The claim was struck out as disclosing no reasonable cause of action on the ground that N owed H no common law duty of care.

Held, dismissing the application, that an appeal would inevitably fail. The question was whether, in all the circumstances, it was just and reasonable to impose a common law duty of care on N, *Caparo Industries Plc v. Dickman* [1990] 2 A.C. 605, [1990] C.L.Y. 3266 followed; (1) the statutory monitoring system, under the Boarding-Out of Children Regulations 1955, the Children Act 1948, as amended, and the Child Care Act 1980, did not preclude other duties owed by the police, educational bodies and doctors. Accordingly, it would be unfair to impose a liability on the local authority alone and the allocation of responsibility would be difficult were it imposed on all relevant bodies, *X (Minors) v. Bedfordshire CC* [1995] 3 W.L.R. 152, [1995] 2 C.L.Y. 3452 followed; (2) although the instant case concerned fostering, the policy considerations identified in the *Bedfordshire* case were comparable and sufficient to override the consideration of remedying a wrong, and (3) it was not possible to infer that a duty of care existed where an injury had been deliberately inflicted, *Surtees v. Kingston upon Thames RBC* [1991] 2 F.L.R. 559, [1992] C.L.Y. 3198 considered. An analogy with school children was unhelpful because school activities were susceptible to a degree of control greater than a local authority could exercise over foster parents.

H v. NORFOLK CC [1997] 1 F.L.R. 384, Simon Brown, L.J., CA.

425. Guardian ad litem—appointment

GUARDIANS AD LITEM AND REPORTING OFFICERS (PANELS) (AMENDMENT) REGULATIONS 1997, SI 1997 1662; made under the Adoption Act 1976 s.65A, s.67; and the Children Act 1989 s.41, s.104. In force: July 29, 1997; £1.55.

These Regulations amend the Guardians Ad Litem and Reporting Officers (Panels) Regulations 1991 (SI 1991 2051) in relation to the extension of membership of guardians ad litem, or reporting officers not re-appointed at the end of their existing appointment; the establishment of joint complaints boards to consider the termination of panel membership; the joint investigation of complaints by more than one local authority; the functions of the panel committee; the reimbursement of expenses; and the membership of complaints boards.

426. Guardian ad litem–contracting out

CONTRACTING OUT (FUNCTIONS IN RELATION TO THE PROVISION OF GUARDIANS AD LITEM AND REPORTING OFFICERS PANELS) ORDER 1997, SI 1997 1652; made under the Deregulation and Contracting Out Act 1994 s.70, s.77. In force: July 1, 1997; £0.65.

This Order makes provision to enable a local authority in England and Wales to authorise another person, or that person's employees, to exercise the authority's functions in relation to the provision of a panel of guardians ad litem and reporting officers for their area. It revokes the Contracting Out (Functions in relation to the Provision of Guardians Ad Litem and Reporting Officers Panels) Order 1996 (SI 1996 858).

427. Human rights–corporal punishment–competence of complaint–stepfather acquitted of assault–reasonable chastisement defence

[European Convention on Human Rights 1950 Art.26.]

The issue arose whether a boy's claim for unreasonable chastisement by his stepfather was admissible before the court.

Held, that the issue of whether the chastisement of the boy had been reasonable had been fully rehearsed at the criminal trial of the stepfather. The stepfather was acquitted on the basis that the prosecution had not proved that the chastisement had been unreasonable. The boy's claim was held to be competent on the basis that he had exhausted all domestic remedies in accordance with the European Convention on Human Rights 1950 Art.26. The Commission was convinced that the case raised serious issues of fact and law and therefore would be admissible, *Costello-Roberts v. United Kingdom* [1994] 1 F.C.R. 65, [1993] C.L.Y. 2118.

A AND B v. UNITED KINGDOM [1996] 3 F.C.R. 569, Judge not specified, ECHR.

428. Medical treatment–children's welfare–court's jurisdiction to order detention for treatment of eating disorder

The court had power to direct that a 16 year old girl could be detained in a specialist clinic until completion of her treatment for anorexia nervosa, as her presence in the clinic was an essential part of her treatment and she would leave if free to do so. A local authority applied for an order that C, a 16 year old girl, be detained at a specialist clinic so that she could be treated for anorexia nervosa. C had already received treatment at the clinic, but had a history of absconding and the medical director, who took the view that C's detention formed an essential part of her treatment, refused to re-admit her without a court order. C argued that she was willing to undergo treatment voluntarily and there was no need for a court order, the only effect of which would be to deprive her of her liberty.

Held, allowing the application, that the court, in exercising its inherent jurisdiction, was bound to treat a child's welfare as the paramount consideration and, having regard to the circumstances of the instant case, the treatment proposed was in C's best interests. Since C's continued presence in the clinic was an essential part of her treatment programme, and she would probably leave the clinic if free to do so, the court had power to direct that she be detained until completion of her treatment or until further order of the court.

C (A MINOR) (MEDICAL TREATMENT: COURT'S JURISDICTION), Re; *sub nom*. C (A MINOR) (DETENTION FOR MEDICAL TREATMENT), Re [1997] 2 F.L.R. 180, Wall, J., Fam Div.

429. Medical treatment–use of reasonable force–competency of minor to refuse consent–hospital ward with restricted access–appropriate authorisation of ward as secure accommodation

[Children Act 1989 s.25.]

B was aged 17 and subject to a deemed care order. She suffered from a cocaine/crack addiction and was pregnant. Complications developed in the pregnancy which were potentially fatal to the patient and to the foetus. However she had a phobia about needles, doctors and any medical treatment and wished to discharge herself from hospital, despite advice that without medical assistance she would endanger her life and the baby's life. The local authority obtained an ex parte order from the High Court that she should undergo such treatment as was necessary in the opinion of the responsible doctor and that reasonable force could be used in the course of that treatment. B accepted treatment and gave birth to a daughter by caesarean section. At the inter partes hearing the local authority applied for the ex parte order to be continued and for leave to place B in secure accommodation under the Children Act 1989 s.25. B argued that (1) the hospital ward was not secure accommodation within the meaning of s.25 and so the local authority's application was misconceived; and (2) the order as to medical treatment should be amended to delete the reasonable force provision.

Held, that (1) although B had a right to refuse to give consent to medical treatment as she was over 16 years, that right could be overriden by the court or a person with parental responsibility for her. Although B's refusal was an important factor it carried little weight as it had been demonstrated that she could neither comprehend and retain information about her treatment, nor believe such information, and was unable to make a reasoned choice about her treatment. The local authority and her mother having parental responsibility could take steps to protect her best interests, which could permit the use of reasonable force in order to administer the correct treatment. An order would be made that the local authority was entitled to administer such treatment as was medically required with the use of reasonable force necessary to prevent her death or serious deterioration of health, and (2) the restriction of liberty was the essential factor in determining whether accommodation could be secure accommodation within the meaning of s.25 of the Act so that secure accommodation did not need to be previously so designated but each case would turn on its facts. There were grounds to detain the patient in secure accommodation given that she had a history of absconding, she had made plain her resistance to remaining in hospital and it had been conceded that if she were in any other accommodation there was a risk of self harm. B was in a maternity ward to which entry was restricted to those with a pass or key so that, having regard to the manner in which B was confined to the ward with staff instructed to prevent her from leaving, the ward could be regarded as secure accommodation within the meaning of s.25.

B (A MINOR) (TREATMENT AND SECURE ACCOMMODATION), *Re* [1997] 1 F.C.R. 618, Cazalet, J., Fam Div.

430. **Ouster orders–child protection–former cohabitees living apart in same house–aggression towards grandchild**

[County Courts Act 1984 s.38; Supreme Court Act 1981 s.37.]

C was a single woman aged 55 who began cohabiting with K as husband and wife: they were joint tenants of their home, a local authority house. However, the relationship broke down in 1993 and the parties lived separately and apart in the house. In 1995 C took on the care of her grandson aged two when his mother was sent to prison. K resented the child occupying the property. He became violent and removed the child's bed from his bedroom and put a lock on the door. C sought a residence order and an ouster order against K.

Held, granting a residence order, adjourning the application for three months and granting interim injunctions against molestation, that the court should interfere with the proprietary rights of individuals only with extreme caution and only where the child was likely to suffer significant harm. The powers under the Supreme Court Act 1981 s.37 and the County Courts Act 1984 s.38 to grant injunctive relief to protect legal and equitable rights, including residence orders, would extend to molestation and ouster injunctions. However, while there was a jurisdiction to make such an order, the court should not do so to vary a proprietary interest and must consider whether such an order was necessary to protect the child from harm and achieve a result which was just.

C v. K (INHERENT POWERS: EXCLUSION ORDER); *sub nom*. C v. K (OUSTER ORDER: NON PARENT) [1996] 2 F.L.R. 506, Wall, J., Fam Div.

431. Parental contact–allegation of sexual abuse–proper procedure for investigation not followed–previous flawed determination of issues in county court

M and F had one child, T, born in 1987. They separated in 1991 and F had contact until 1992 when M terminated all contact because she believed that F had been sexually abusing T. T was examined by a police surgeon who found no evidence to support the suggestion that T may have been sexually abused. However, T was subsequently interviewed by a social worker and police officer who ignored all the guidelines for such cases. F applied for contact and at a directions hearing leave was granted to instruct a paediatrician and a child psychiatrist although no experts were instructed. The court welfare officer interviewed T and stated that he believed that his complaints about F were sincere. A county court judge found that F was guilty of sexual abuse of T but adjourned the issue of contact until advice had been sought from a child psychiatrist. F appealed.

Held, allowing the appeal and remitting the matter for hearing in the High Court, that the evidence suggested that there may have been some inadvertent touching by F, but did not support a finding of sexual abuse. It would appear that T had overheard and picked up the suspicions of the maternal family that F, who was on any view ambivalent about his sexuality, was homosexual. The case had been badly managed by the professionals. The interviews had been badly handled and the report of the police surgeon who had initially examined T largely ignored. Social services had prejudged the issue of sexual abuse and had embarked on a policy which created a belief system in T and his family before there had been any findings by a court as to whether T had been sexually abused by F. The judge had wrongly revoked the leave to instruct experts who could have provided invaluable assistance in assessing T's words and providing advice in the complex field of human sexuality. The court welfare officer had paid no heed to the Cleveland guidelines, which he admitted choosing to ignore, and had conducted a flawed interview with T where he had completely misunderstood his function. Further, he had made findings about the credibility of the parents and T which were a matter for the court alone to decide. The hearing in the county court had been flawed and it would now be difficult for M and her family to entertain the possibility that there had been mistakes in the previous conduct of the case. M was emotionally antagonistic about future contact, which, if it continued, would inflict lasting and irreparable damage to T. A family assistance order would be made to the local authority and supervised contact ordered, with the arrangements and duration to be at their discretion in consultation with the Official Solicitor.

T (A MINOR) (PROCEDURE: ALLEGED SEXUAL ABUSE) (NO.2), *Re* [1997] 2 F.C.R. 55, Thorpe, J., Fam Div.

432. Parental contact–children in care–parental contact terminated when children placed for adoption–placement breaking down–interim contact order inappropriate as contact with mother could only be temporary

Care orders were made in respect of two children on the basis of M's neglect and poor parenting ability. G's plan was to place the children for adoption and contact with M was ordered on a monthly basis until prospective adopters had been identified. Contact was then terminated and the children had a farewell visit with M and their maternal grandmother. The adoptive placement broke down due to the children's disturbed behaviour and they were returned to foster care, although G continued with the adoption plan. M applied to discharge the care orders and for contact. The magistrates made an interim contact order in favour of M and the maternal grandmother on the basis that the resumption of contact would not destabilise the children pending the identification of a second adoption placement. G appealed.

Held, allowing the appeal, that the decision of the magistrates was plainly wrong. There was no advantage to the children in ordering contact pending the determination of M's application. Contact would only distress the children who had already said goodbye to M once and were now being told that they would be seeing her again where there was a possibility that contact would once more cease. The magistrates should have deferred any decision about contact until M's application to discharge the care order had been determined.

GREENWICH LBC v. H [1996] 2 F.L.R. 736, Johnson, J., Fam Div.

433. Parental contact—children unaware of true paternity

S's mother, M, appealed against an order granting F, who was not S's father, contact on alternate Saturdays. S was four years old. M sought a rehearing and it was agreed that the Official Solicitor should be appointed as S's guardian ad litem. M and F were married in 1979 and had two children. M then had four more children by two other men, the youngest of whom was S, born in 1992. Shortly before S's birth M and all six children returned to live with F. In 1993 M formed another relationship with B who moved into the matrimonial home. F left in mid summer 1994 and in July 1994 M had another child, A, of whom B was the father. F continued to have contact with the five elder children, but not with S. In early 1996 F applied for contact with all six children including S. During a conciliation appointment in April 1996 the court welfare officer expressed the view that the children should be told about their paternity, but M and F disagreed. The five elder children all believed that F was their father and that S and A were their half siblings and S believed that B was her father. Because M and F did not agree with the court welfare officer the case proceeded with no report, no assistance from the Official Solicitor and no consultant child psychiatrist. M argued that the judge had not fully considered the effect contact with F would have on S given that she had not seen him for approximately two years and that F was not her biological father. In addition she believed that B was her father and if she was reintroduced to F she would want to know why and that was likely to raise the issue of paternity which would affect all the children.

Held, allowing the appeal, that the issue of paternity was central to the question of whether there should be contact between F and S and as such it had to be resolved before contact was ordered. M and F had agreed that the Official Solicitor should be invited to act as guardian ad litem for S, and following *R (A Minor) (Contact), Re* [1993] 2 F.L.R. 762, [1994] C.L.Y. 3192 and *Practice Note (Official Solicitor: Appointment in Family Proceedings)* [1995] 2 F.L.R. 479 this was an appropriate case in which to direct a rehearing and do as M and F had agreed.

H (MINORS), *Re,* Trans. Ref: CCFMI 96/1643/F, April 14, 1997, Bennett, J., CA.

434. Parental contact—contact order made against advice of court welfare officer—whether departure from court welfare officer's advice sufficiently reasoned

M and F had two children aged five and 10. There were difficulties over contact which eventually resulted in F's committal for 28 days. M then applied to terminate contact. The judge accepted the advice of the court welfare officer that contact should be terminated between F and the elder, disturbed child, but in relation to the younger child, the judge concluded that the arguments were finely balanced, believed that contact should be reintroduced and ordered three meetings over a period of six months to be supervised by the court welfare officer. M appealed on the grounds that the judge had failed to give sufficient reasons for departing from the advice of the court welfare officer.

Held, dismissing the appeal, that the judge had dealt with all matters thoroughly and conscientiously and had provided for the cautious introduction of contact, safeguarded by the supervision of the court welfare officer. There were no grounds upon which the exercise of the judge's discretion could be challenged in an appellate court.

F (MINORS) (CONTACT: APPEAL), *Re* [1997] 1 F.C.R. 523, Thorpe, L.J., CA.

435. Parental contact—disrupted contact—contact application dismissed in directions hearing—extent of judicial discretion

[Children Act 1989 s.91 (14).]

F applied for leave to appeal against an order dismissing his application for contact with S and an order under the Children Act 1989 s.91 (14) made after a history of continually disrupted contact arrangements and domestic violence. The judge making the order was of the opinion that in the unusual circumstances of the case it was no longer for the court to make arrangements but it was open to M and F to make any future arrangements to fulfil their duty that S see both parents. F argued that, as the hearing at which the order was made was a directions hearing, it was not open to the judge to make a conclusive order without a full investigation on oral evidence.

Held, granting the application, allowing the appeal, setting aside the s.91 (14) order and remitting the contact application to the county court, that, although the s.91 (14) order should not have been made, the judge was entitled to make the order he did and it was within his discretion to do so. The court has a very wide power to make the appropriate order in the appropriate circumstances and the firm line taken by the judge was justified in the unusual circumstances of the case. M's argument was not that there should be no contact, but that F was not entitled to contact in the way he had been conducting himself. Accordingly, F could continue with the existing application although he also had the right to issue a fresh application at any time.

S (A MINOR), *Re*, Trans. Ref: LTA 97/5331/F, March 21, 1997, Thorpe, L.J., CA.

436. Parental contact—father's history of violence—contact opposed by mother—judicial discretion

An unmarried couple who never lived together had a child in 1991. F visited several times per week but after the relationship broke down M alleged that he had been violent towards her and terminated contact. In 1993 F applied for parental responsibility and contact orders, but was unsuccessful. On his further application in 1995 the court welfare officer concluded that there were no cogent reasons for allowing contact and his application was refused. F appealed.

Held, dismissing the appeal, that (1) the judge had been entitled to find on the evidence that M's fears of the risk of violence to herself and the child were genuine, and (2) it was not in the child's interests to have contact with his father at that time. The judge had not precluded the possibility of future contact and since clear reasons for his findings had been given, there were no grounds upon which the exercise of his discretion could be challenged.

D (CONTACT: REASONS FOR REFUSAL), *Re* [1997] 2 F.L.R. 48, Hale, J., CA.

437. Parental contact—prohibited steps orders

[Children Act 1989 s.91 (14).]

F appealed against an order that there be no direct contact between him and his three children, together with an order under the Children Act 1989 s.91 (14) preventing any further application by him for residence or contact without leave of the court. The order was granted after M applied to reduce contact and it was clear that the children did not wish to have direct contact with F.

Held, allowing the appeal, that, although a power to make an order for no contact or no direct contact under the 1989 Act existed, it should be exercised only rarely and only when the total exclusion of contact was appropriate. In the instant case, there was an agreement for indirect contact and, had the children been willing for contact to resume, then M would have been amenable to it. The order should have been "no order on the application for direct contact". An order under s.91 (14) should not be made unless applications had repeatedly and unreasonably been made and conduct had been intentionally oppressive or vexatious, *B v. B (Residence Orders: Restricting Applications)* [1997] 1 F.L.R. 139, [1996] 1 C.L.Y. 622 followed.

P (MINORS), *Re*, Trans. Ref: CCFMI 97/0130/F, May 9, 1997, Holman, J., CA.

438. Parental contact–termination of contact–application to discharge order

[Children Act 1989 s.34(4).]

M appealed against the dismissal of her application to discharge an order under the Children Act 1989 s.34(4) authorising the local authority to terminate contact with her two children who were in care.

Held, allowing the appeal in respect of one child, that the s.34(4) order was justifiable at the time it was made, and should not be discharged unless, during the intervening period, some material change of circumstances had occurred. The court had to determine, as interlocking considerations, the extent to which circumstances had changed and, where they had, whether it was desirable to reinvestigate whether the order should remain. The greater the change in circumstances, the more intensively the court should be prepared to reconsider the order.

T (MINORS) (TERMINATION OF CONTACT: DISCHARGE OF ORDER), *Re; sub nom.* T (CHILDREN IN CARE: CONTACT), *Re* [1997] 1 W.L.R. 393, Simon Brown, L.J., CA.

439. Parental responsibility orders–contact orders–separate treatment of applications

Held, that applications for contact and parental responsibility orders made by an unmarried father should be treated separately and it did not follow that a parental responsibility order should be refused because a contact order had been refused. Parental responsibility orders were designed to enable a natural father to have the status of fatherhood he would have had if married to the child's mother, and it was important to appreciate that for a committed father to have that responsibility contributed to a child's welfare in providing a positive image of the absent parent.

C AND V (MINORS) (PARENTAL RESPONSIBILITY ORDER), *Re, The Times*, June 30, 1997, Ward, L.J., CA.

440. Parental responsibility orders–judicial discretion–father's imprisonment and criminal conduct were relevant factors

F, an unmarried father, who was serving two terms of 15 years' imprisonment for robbery, the last offence having been committed while he was on home leave from prison, appealed against the refusal to grant him a parental responsibility order in respect of his two young children. In refusing to make the order, the judge had referred to F's criminal conduct while out of prison as an indication of his lack of commitment to the children.

Held, dismissing the appeal, that, whilst the fact that an applicant was serving a prison sentence was not a conclusive factor in determining whether to grant parental responsibility, the court, in exercising its discretion, was entitled to take into account F's criminal behaviour and the fact that his circumstances necessarily limited his ability to exercise such responsibility.

P (MINORS: PARENTAL RESPONSIBILITY ORDER), *Re, The Times*, April 24, 1997, Ward, L.J., CA.

441. Paternity–blood tests–husband applying for contact–mother asserting that husband not father of child–husband refusing to provide blood samples– inference to be drawn from refusal

[Family Law Reform Act 1969 s.23; Guardianship of Minors Act 1971; Matrimonial Causes Act 1973 s.41.]

M and P began to cohabit in 1985 and a child, S, was conceived in July 1988, when M was having a brief affair with another man. M and P resumed cohabitation and married in 1989. They separated in 1991 and in proceedings brought by M under the Guardianship of Minors Act 1971, M raised the issue of S's paternity, claiming that P was not the father. No blood tests were ordered or obtained. M subsequently sought to curtail contact, which prompted P to issue an application for contact, and M applied for leave to obtain DNA testing. A court direction for tests was made and P indicated his willingness to submit to testing, but refused to give samples, contending that he was almost certain that he was the father but if the test demonstrated that he was not M would use that fact to break the bond between him and S. The judge made a declaration that P was the father, on the basis that he could not be satisfied that there had been no sexual intercourse between M and P at the relevant time, that M had not raised the paternity question for two and a half years and she had appeared to accept that P was the father on the child's birth certificate, in the divorce in which the certificate under the Matrimonial Causes Act 1973 s.41 had described the child as a child of the family and by her demands for maintenance. M appealed.

Held, allowing the appeal, that under the Family Law Reform Act 1969 s.23, the court had a duty to determine what inference should be drawn from the refusal to submit to a direction for a blood test. A forensic inference was the proper inference, *A (A Minor) (Paternity: Refusal of Blood Test), Re* [1994] 2 F.L.R. 463 followed. Since the forensic process was advanced by presenting the truth to the court, P would have the inference drawn against him as he had obstructed the truth. M was willing to have her belief that P was not the father put to the test, while P was not, so the proper inference to be drawn was that P was not the father of the child. The judge had misdirected himself by failing to draw that inference and his declaration would be set aside.

G (PARENTAGE: BLOOD SAMPLE), *Re*; *sub nom.* G (A MINOR) (PATERNITY: BLOOD TESTS), *Re* [1997] 1 F.L.R. 360, Ward, L.J., CA.

442. **Paternity—no appeal against declaration—subsequent probative medical evidence disproving paternity**

[Child Support Act 1991 s.27, s.45(1); Rules of the Supreme Court Ord.15 r.16.]

Held, that in the case of a paternity application, where a declaration had been made, the High Court did not have the power to hear an appeal made under the Child Support Act 1991 s.27 because there was no right of appeal created by that Act either expressly or pursuant to powers granted to the Lord Chancellor under s.45(1)(b). However, if after the court had made a declaration under s.27, there was medical evidence establishing that a person was not the father of a child, the court could make a declaration to that effect under the RSC Ord.15 r.16, where there was no other relief available.

T v. CHILD SUPPORT AGENCY [1997] 4 All E.R. 27, Cazalet, J., Fam Div.

443. **Publicity—proposed documentary on work of CSA—applicant seeking to prevent broadcasting of information relating to his infertility—court's jurisdiction to restrain publication**

[Administration of Justice Act 1960 s.12(1).]

The BBC intended to televise a programme about the operations of the Child Support Agency. M applied for an injunction to prevent the publication of any information concerning his forthcoming case, where he intended to argue that he was not liable to maintain two children born to his former wife during their marriage following donor insemination. M objected to information being broadcast which revealed his infertility, but did not object to the identification of the children.

Held, dismissing the application, that the Administration of Justice Act 1960 s.12(1) defined the limits of permissible publication relating to proceedings held in public. The court's jurisdiction could only be invoked to restrain the publication of information relating to children over whose welfare publicity might jeopardise the operation of the court's jurisdiction. Although the proceedings, which were brought under the Child Support Act 1991, related to their maintenance, an adult could not claim protection from publication of information relating to him and the public interest in the principle of free speech should prevail.

M v. BBC [1997] 1 F.L.R. 51, Hale, J., Fam Div.

444. Residence orders–condition attached to residence order that mother continue to live at specified address

[Children Act 1989 s.8.]

M appealed against a condition imposed on a residence order granted under the Children Act 1989 s.8 that she continue to live at a specified address.

Held, allowing the appeal, that where a parent was considered to be suitable and a court chose to grant a residence order in her favour, attaching a condition to that order was an unjustified interference with that parent's right to choose where to live within the UK and with whom. Where the children would live was one of the relevant factors to be considered if there were cross-applications for residence, but it was not a separate issue.

E (MINORS) (RESIDENCE ORDERS), *Re, The Times*, May 16, 1997, Butler-Sloss, L.J., CA.

445. Residence orders–contested proceedings–costs

See CIVIL PROCEDURE: R (A Minor) (Legal Aid: Costs), *Re*. §530

446. Residence orders–interim orders–father admitted to psychiatric hospital–mother assuming care of children

The father of three children was granted a residence order. When a relationship with a female friend failed, F cut his wrists and was admitted to a psychiatric ward. M applied to the court to vary the residence order, a welfare report was ordered and the matter adjourned for a week. Before the return date M changed the school of the two elder children. When the matter came before the judge he ordered the children to return to their original school and that they should return to F when he was certified by his doctors as fit to care for them. M appealed.

Held, allowing the appeal in part, that the judge had been right to order the children to return to their schools, but wrong to order that the children should return to F after the doctors had certified that he was fit to care for them. Since the parties were agreed that the children should remain with M pending a further hearing, an interim residence order would be granted to M to run alongside the father's residence order.

M (MINORS) (INTERIM RESIDENCE ORDER), *Re* [1997] 2 F.C.R. 28, Butler-Sloss, L.J., CA.

447. Residence orders–no principle or presumption in favour of mother of young child–relevance of UN Declaration of the Rights of the Child

The marriage of F and M, the parents of A, broke down when A was two years old. Each sought a residence order and the court welfare officer recommended that the residence order be made in favour of F. The court, however, despite agreeing with many of the conclusions reached in the report, ruled in favour of M. In giving his judgment the judge stated that he was following a principle found in the UN Declaration of the Rights of the Child 1959 which stated that only in exceptional circumstances should a child of tender years be separated from its mother. F appealed.

Held, allowing the appeal, that (1) the judge was wrong to reject the recommendation of the court welfare officer without any explanation for the basis of that rejection, and (2) there was no principle of law which suggested that a presumption exists giving either parent preference over the other, *A (A Minor: Custody), Re* [1991] 2 F.L.R. 394, [1992] C.L.Y. 3081 and *S (A Minor:*

Custody), Re [1991] 2 F.L.R. 388, [1992] C.L.Y. 3080 applied, and the relevance of the UN Declaration was doubted in light of its age.

A (A MINOR), *Re*, Trans. Ref: LTA 97/5903/F, FC2 97/6404/F, July 16, 1997, Thorpe, L.J., CA.

448. Residence orders–relevance of welfare checklist under Children Act 1989

[Children Act 1989 s.1 (3).]

M appealed against a decision to make a residence order in favour of the father of their six year old son. The recorder, in delivering his judgment, had accepted that it was unnecessary to refer to the welfare checklist in the Children Act 1989 s.1 (3) since the parties had not made complaints against one another.

Held, allowing the appeal and remitting the matter for rehearing, that, in finely balanced cases such as this, it was important that all the reasons for the decision should be clearly set out. The judge had made no error of law when delivering his judgment, but where the reasons for a decision were not so obvious as to be inferred from the judgment, it was impossible for the Court of Appeal to determine whether the decision was right or wrong. Consideration of the checklist in s.1 (3) ensured that all relevant matters were taken into account and could also be useful in helping to clarify the reasons for a decision. The fact that the parties had not made allegations against one another was not a good reason for ignoring the checklist.

B v. B (MINOR: RESIDENCE ORDER), *The Times*, June 6, 1997, Holman, J., CA.

449. Residence orders–specific issue orders–jurisdiction–child living with mother in Sweden

[Family Law Act 1986 s.3(1) (b), s.5(2); Children Act 1989 s.1 (3).]

M and F married and had one child, C, born in 1990. After their divorce M was granted a residence order and leave to remove C permanently out of the jurisdiction to her native Sweden. F appealed unsuccessfully to the Court of Appeal and later applied, when C was present in the jurisdiction on a contact visit, for (1) a shared residence order; (2) a specific issue order in relation to C's religious upbringing, and (3) a variation of the contact order.

Held, dismissing F's application, that under the Family Law Act 1986 s.3(1) (b) the court had jurisdiction to entertain F's applications since C had been present within the jurisdiction but the court had a discretion under s.5(2) of the 1986 Act to stay the proceedings if it considered that the case should more appropriately be determined outside England and Wales, even though M had not applied for a stay. It was relevant that C was habitually resident in Sweden and welfare was an important consideration when determining whether the court should exercise its jurisdiction. The court should apply the welfare check list found in the Children Act 1989 s.1 (3) when considering the merits of F's application. On the facts there was no possibility of F's applications succeeding. A shared residence order should be made only where it would confer a positive benefit on a child and in a case where there were substantial issues between the parties, as in the instant case, such an order would not be appropriate. A specific issue order from the English court would be unenforceable in Sweden so that any such application should be brought in the Swedish courts. Contact would be further defined, but it was not appropriate to consider any long-term variation.

H v. H (A MINOR) (FORUM CONVENIENS) (NO.2) [1997] 1 F.C.R. 603, Bracewell, J., Fam Div.

450. Special educational needs–child seeking injunction to prevent parents from removing him from school–no jurisdiction to grant relief where no justiciable issue between the parties

V, a young man born in 1977, suffered from cerebral palsy, was quadriplegic, had learning difficulties and required help with most everyday tasks. He was subject to a care order but was cared for by his parents, who had, at times in the past, been over protective and had frustrated his attendance at a special school. The young man, acting through a next friend, applied for declaratory and injunctive relief against his parents so that there was some authoritative mechanism to ensure his continued attendance at the special school after his 18th birthday when the care order ceased to have effect. The judge granted injunctions declaring that V had a right to choose where to live and with whom he should associate and granted an injunction against his mother, preventing her from removing him from the special school. The parents appealed.

Held, allowing the appeal, that declaratory relief should be granted when there was a justiciable issue between the parties. Since the parents did not wish to prevent their son from attending the special school, there was no issue immediately affecting his legal rights which would give the judge authority to grant declaratory and injunctive relief.

V (A MINOR) (INJUNCTION: JURISDICTION), *Re*; *sub nom.* V (DECLARATION AGAINST PARENTS), RE; V (HANDICAPPED ADULT: RIGHT TO DECIDE RESIDENCE) [1997] 2 F.C.R. 195, Sir Stephen Brown, CA.

451. Wardship–Bosnian child fostered by English couple–child's family seeking her return–appropriate order to be made

K, a Bosnian Muslim, was born in March 1992. When she was nine weeks old, her mother and other members of her family were massacred by Serbian soldiers, and her father went missing. Her grandfather and uncle were placed in a concentration camp and the child was taken to an orphanage where her plight was discovered by an English couple, who contacted a charity specialising in the casualties of the civil war. The couple agreed to provide foster care if the child came to England for medical treatment. The child was brought to England in November 1992. A guardian was appointed for the child in Bosnia and in January 1993 the couple were informed that the Bosnian authorities had forbidden all adoptions until at least the end of the war. In November 1992 the grandfather went to Switzerland as a refugee and, having learned that the child was alive, made a formal request for her return, K (A Minor) (Adoption: Foreign Child), Re [1997] 2 F.L.R. 221, [1996] 1 C.L.Y. 465. The child's guardian was in contact with the grandfather as well as the English couple. In August 1993 the couple applied to adopt the child and an adoption order was made in the county court in January 1994. The adoption order was subsequently held to be irregular by the Court of Appeal and set aside and a rehearing ordered. Faced with opposition from the grandfather, the local authority and the Official Solicitor, the couple abandoned their application to adopt the child. There remained the question of the appropriate order to be made.

Held, stating that the matter was to be reviewed in 18 months, that since the child had been in the care of the English couple since November 1992, this was the only family she had ever known and they had provided excellent care for her. The child was particularly vulnerable as a result of the injuries she had suffered in the atrocity and the institutional neglect during the first five months of her life in an orphanage. Although the English couple had deliberately avoided enquiries and had not provided full disclosure when making their application to adopt in 1993, they had expressed regret for their actions. The psychiatrist was of the view that separation from her English family would cause the child profound mental suffering and harm, but that it was important to develop strong links with her family. The child would remain a ward of court with the Official Solicitor acting as guardian ad litem. There would be access at least four times a year to her natural family. The husband and wife would also be responsible for ensuring that she was taught the Bosnian language and receive instruction in the Muslim religion.

K (WARDSHIP: FOREIGN CHILD) (NO.2), *Re* [1997] 2 F.L.R. 230, Sir Stephen Brown, Fam Div.

452. Articles

A child's place of residence *(Victor Smith)*: Fam. Law 1997, 27(Aug), 551-554. (Relevance of place of residence in establishing whether court has jurisdiction over child and in designating appropriate local authority where court makes care order, including meaning of residence).

Adoption and confidential information *(Kevin Barnett)*: Fam. Law 1997, 27(Jul), 489-493. (Privilege of confidentiality and sources of information, with procedure for seeking information from Registrar General, adoption agencies and court files and how courts may treat such applications).

Are children seen and heard? Do solicitors see their child clients as a matter of good practice? Are there exceptions? *(Barbara Mitchells)*: Fam. M. 1997, 3, 5-6. (Need for solicitors to give time, attention and respect to child clients of all ages, with reference to guidance published by Law Society and Solicitors' Family Law Association and role of guardian of litem in public law proceedings).

Capital provision for children *(Gareth Miller)*: P.C.B. 1997, 1, 51-59. (Shortcomings of Child Support Act 1991, interaction with orders for capital provision for children of unmarried parents under Children Act 1989 and comparison with situation of married parents).

Change of name *(Chris Bazell)*: Fam. Law 1997, 27(Aug), 569-570. (Law and practice governing right to change child's surname, contrasting position where residence or care order in force with position where no such order exists).

Children Act: legal professional privilege *(Julie Brannan)*: J. Soc. Wel. & Fam. L. 1996, 18(4), 475-481. (Principles governing disclosure of expert's reports in children cases).

Children's rights: judicial ambivalence and social resistance *(Carole Smith)*: Int. J. Law & Fam. 1997, 11(1), 103-139. (Courts' dilemma in attempting to balance children's rights and children's welfare with reference to recent case law).

Children, privacy and the press *(Jaclyn Moriarty)*: C.F.L.Q. 1997, 9(3), 217-242. (Current methods of protecting privacy of children, both inside and outside courtroom, with reference to media self-regulation, statutory regulation and judicial protection).

Cleveland: ten years on *(Peter De Cruz)*: P.C.L.B. 1997, 10(5), 49-50. (Impact of 1987 Report of the Inquiry into Child Abuse in Cleveland, including effect on law and procedure, professional training and medical practice relating to child abuse).

Competing constructions of childhood: children's rights and children's wishes in divorce *(Liz Trinder)*: J. Soc. Wel. & Fam. L. 1997, 19(3), 291-305. (Adult approaches to children and divorce decision-making, including legal constructions and social work constructions drawn from research interviews with court welfare officers).

Delay and timetabling *(Anthony Cleary)*: Fam. Law 1997, 27(Apr), 251-260. (Potential for delay in Children Act cases, both before case comes to court and in court procedures, with reference to public and private law proceedings).

Divorce reform: new child satisfaction arrangements *(David Hodson* and *Gillian Bishop)*: S.J. 1997, 141(5), 116-117. (More stringent provisions requiring arrangements to be made for children before divorce can be granted introduce new criteria to determine whether arrangements are satisfactory).

Evidential privilege in cases involving children *(Colin Tapper)*: C.F.L.Q. 1997, 9(1), 1-16. (Distinction between rules of privilege, immunity and admissibility and disclosure of confidential documents in civil and criminal proceedings involving children).

Forced contact—a child's right or an impossibility? *(Helen L. Conway)*: N.L.J. 1997, 147(6783), 374-375. (Cases and legislation on approach of court where parent refuses to accede to contact order, right of child to parental contact and whether enforcement of order is desirable).

Goodbye doli, must we leave you? *(Paul Cavadino)*: C.F.L.Q. 1997, 9(2), 165-171. (Recent developments relating to rule of doli incapax and case for retaining rule in light of low age of criminal responsibility in UK).

Implacable hostility—seeking a breakthrough *(Helen L. Conway)*: Fam. Law 1997, 27(Feb), 109-111. (Recent cases illustrating court's approach where parent with care is implacably hostile to contact between child and other parent and proposal to create children's officer to provide information about divorce and its consequences).

Inherent jurisdiction and children-complications in the county court *(Christopher Tromans)*: Fam. Law 1997, 27(Sep), 614-617. (Extent to which county court can exercise jurisdiction to grant injunctions or accept undertakings in children cases).

Inherent jurisdiction, ouster orders and children *(Kevin Barnett)*: Fam. Law 1997, 27(Feb), 96-103. (Whether court has inherent jurisdiction to grant injunctive relief, particularly by way of ouster order, to protect children from harm).

Intercountry adoption of unaccompanied refugee children *(Kisch Beevers)*: C.F.L.Q. 1997, 9(2), 131-147. (Issues concerning desirability of intercountry adoption, criticism of 1994 Hague Recommendation to Contracting States to 1993 Convention, and proposal for international residence order as alternative).

Judicial power and local authority discretion-the contested frontier *(Carole R. Smith)*: C.F.L.Q. 1997, 9(3), 243-257. (Tension between courts' and local authorities' powers in relation to care orders and interim care orders, with reference to significant shift in boundary in HL decision dealing with court's powers to order residential assessment).

Juveniles: case study on section 39 orders: M.L.N. 1997, 7, 30-32. (Exercise of court's discretion in banning identification of juvenile offenders and whether justification for order necessary).

Minors' privacy, free speech and the courts *(Ian G. Cram)*: P.L. 1997, Aut, 410-419. (Treatment of children's privacy issues by courts shows occasional failure to probe free speech claims advanced by media).

Offering children confidentiality: law and guidance *(Carolyn Hamilton* and *Lucy Hopegood)*: Childright 1997, 140, Supp 1-8. (Children's right to confidentiality including Gillick ruling on children's capacity and adult involvement in giving consent, examples of legal and moral duty to disclose and remedies for breach).

Putting the paramountcy principle into practice *(Brian Cantwell)*: Fam. Law 1997, 27(May), 350-351. (Practical ways in which family court welfare officers, in working with the court, interviewing parents and working directly with children, can help disengagement from parental conflict).

Re EC and criminal trials *(David Farrer* and *Rachel Langdale)*: Fam. Law 1997, 27(Jul), 480-482. (Advice to be given by solicitors to client suspected of abusing his child where admissions made to social workers will be reported to police).

Representing children with a learning difficulty *(Barbara Mitchels)*: L. Ex. 1997, Nov, 12-13. (Including definitions, rights of children regarding medical treatment and family proceedings, and communicating with such children).

Secure accommodation and welfare *(Jonathan Butler* and *Sue Hardy)*: Fam. Law 1997, 27(Jun), 425-428. (Criteria for making secure accommodation order under s.25 of 1989 Act and additional questions which courts need to address when dealing with applications for orders, particularly issue of restriction of liberty).

Significant changes made to the Children Act 1989 by the Family Law Act 1996 *(Robert Stevens)*: J.P. 1997, 161(14), 327-329. (Attempts to provide greater protection for children at risk of abuse by provision for exclusion requirements as part of interim care orders and emergency protection orders and by allowing court to accept undertakings).

Supervision
or care orders? *(Glenn Brasse)*: Fam. Law 1997, 27(May), 351-354. (Distinction between orders in terms of control over child's care, factors taken into account in deciding which order is appropriate, and need for order lying midway between two).

The blood tie: raised to the status of a presumption *(Ines Weyland)*: J. Soc. Wel. & Fam. L. 1997, 19(2), 173-188. (Whether presumption favouring care of child by natural parents in residence disputes conflicts with application of paramountcy principle in light of checklist in s.1(3) of 1989 Act).

The guardian ad litem's independence *(Pat Walton)*: Fam. Law 1997, 27(Feb), 106-108. (Inherent conflicts in system of administration by local authorities and options for future, including possibility of establishing national independent service).

The new Hague Convention on Children *(Eric Clive)*: Fam. L.B.1997, 25(Jan), 3-5. (Convention awaiting ratification will replace Hague Convention on the Protection of Minors 1961 to provide new framework for child protection).

The return of children to non-Convention countries by the English High Court *(Henry Setright)*: P.C.L.B. 1997, 10(5), 56-58. (Courts' approach to applications for return, including relevance of Convention principles and whether welfare approach remains paramount).

To disclose or not to disclose? *(Michael Batey)*: Fam. Law 1997, 27(Sep), 611-613. (Uncertainty over extent to which reports or other material obtained in children proceedings without leave of court are subject to legal professional privilege).

Violence in the home: the new law and how it will affect children *(Kate Standley)*: Childright 1997, 140, 17-20. (Provisions of Family Law Act 1996 Part IV in force October 1, 1997, concerning domestic violence, including children's right to apply for non molestation and occupation orders, definition of family proceedings and powers of arrest and exclusion).

When did you next see your father? Emigration and the one-parent family *(Chris Barton)*: C.F.L.Q. 1997, 9(1), 73-83. (UK and Canadian courts' approach to application by custodial parent to emigrate with child).

Who should hold the baby? *(Glenn Brasse)*: Fam. Law 1997, 27(Jul), 497-498. (Problems arising in determining child's ordinary residence for purposes of designating local authority in care order).

453. Books

Hale, Hon. Justice–Clarke, Hall and Morrison on Children. Unbound/looseleaf: £195.00. ISBN 0-406-99662-8. Butterworth Law.

Jones, Richard M.–Adoption Act Manual. 2nd Ed. Paperback: £49.50. ISBN 0-421-52010-8. Sweet & Maxwell.

Levy, A.; Josling, J.F.–Adoption of Children. Longman Practitioner Series. Paperback: £25.00. ISBN 0-85121-619-6. FT Law & Tax.

CIVIL EVIDENCE

454. Admissibility–appeals–application to adduce evidence of crime committed by plaintiff under foreign law

Held, that a defendant in legal proceedings was free to adduce evidence that the plaintiff had committed a serious crime under foreign law, but that was a grave allegation which had to be properly pleaded and proved. Where the allegations were made for the first time in the Court of Appeal and the defendant's application amounted to an application to amend the defence, it was hard to imagine circumstances where the application would be allowed.

SHARAB v. SALFITI, *The Times*, February 13, 1997, Waller, L.J., CA.

455. Admissibility–cross examination on previous spent convictions irrelevant to credit–police assault on limbo dancer–measure of damages

[Rehabilitation of Offenders Act 1974 s.7(3).]

Following acquittal on a charge of threatening behaviour, T, a leading limbo dancer, brought an action against the Commissioner for assault, damage to property, false imprisonment and malicious prosecution. At first instance, the jury found for T in respect of the assault and damage to property claim, but against him on the claims for false imprisonment and malicious prosecution. Damages were awarded by the jury for the assault, £15,815 general damages and £16,185 special damages, for damage to property £310, and interest of £4,091, making a total of £36,401 which was less than the sum paid into court by the Commissioner. T appealed, seeking an order for a new trial, contending that the judge erred in permitting cross examination on two spent convictions and that the general damages award was inadequate and irreconcilable with the special damages award.

Held, dismissing the appeal, that (1) the judge erred in law in admitting cross examination of T concerning previous convictions for unlawful wounding in 1980 and criminal damage in 1983 which were rehabilitated under the Rehabilitation of Offenders Act 1974 s.7(3), as the offences were of no probative value in the instant case and not relevant to T's credit; (2) however, a new trial would not be ordered, owing to the minimal mention made of the offences combined with the directions given to the jury and the nature of the verdicts, which showed that the spent convictions had not been detrimental to the jury's view of T's credibility, and (3) as to quantum of damages, the judge had correctly directed the jury on the need to consider the issues affecting T's loss of earnings from limbo dancing, presently and in the future. The special and general damages awards revealed neither perversity nor error of law on the part of the jury.

THOMAS v. COMMISSIONER OF POLICE OF THE METROPOLIS [1997] 2 W.L.R. 593, Sir Richard Scott, V.C., CA.

456. Admissibility–expert evidence–psychiatric illness after witnessing accident–failure to disclose improvement in condition

V claimed damages for psychiatric illness caused by witnessing the death of his two children in an accident caused by B's negligent driving. At the trial, two expert witnesses gave evidence as to V's psychiatric condition and the prognosis for the future and V was awarded £1,332,231 in damages and interest. B's appeal was dismissed, but the amount of damages was reduced. Before a final order was drawn up, B's counsel received copies of a judgment relating to family proceedings between V and his wife, which indicated that the same two expert witnesses had testified that V's mental state had greatly improved since September 1993 and that he was substantially recovered. The evidence in the family proceedings had been given after the hearing but the judgment was handed down before judgment in the tort action and certainly before B's appeal. B successfully applied for a rehearing of the appeal.

Held, that the new evidence as to V's improved mental state would be admitted as it was likely to have a significant impact on the amount of damages awarded, and the later reports by the expert witnesses of V's improved mental health should have been disclosed to B and to the court before judgment was given. The reports, having been obtained in Children Act proceedings, were not subject to litigation privilege, *L (A Minor) (Police Investigation: Privilege), Re* [1996] 2 W.L.R. 395, [1996] 1 C.L.Y. 502 applied. A litigant had a duty not to mislead the court up until the point that judgment was given and this duty was not discharged simply by following counsel's advice. Where there had been a change in material circumstances essential to the case, there was no difference between actively misleading the court and passively allowing it to believe that the earlier state of affairs still existed. If there was a risk that the court would be misled, counsel had a duty to advise his client to disclose the new information and if the advice was rejected, counsel should withdraw from the case. Damages would be reduced to £541,493.

VERNON v. BOSLEY (NO.2) [1997] 1 All E.R. 614, Stuart-Smith, L.J., CA.

457. Admissibility–expert evidence–solicitor's professional negligence– evidence from another solicitor

[Civil Evidence Act 1972 s.3.]

A brought an action for professional negligence against his former solicitor, H concerning their advice and dealings with a mortgage. A sought to adduce expert evidence from a senior solicitor at another firm as to how a reasonably competent solicitor should have approached an enquiry of the type posed byA. A took out the mortgage to assist her brother establish a solicitor's practice. H objected to the evidence on the basis that it usurped the judicial function.

Held, allowing the evidence, that it assisted the court which lacked the relevant experience and was properly admitted in terms of the Civil Evidence Act 1972 s.3.

ARCHER v. HICKMOTTS [1997] P.N.L.R. 318, H.H.J. Brunning, CC (County Court).

458. Admissibility—fresh evidence on appeal—summary judgments—allegation of fraud credible

S appealed against a summary judgment arising from an insurance claim for £700,000 brought by Z in respect of a jet aircraft engine and three helicopter gearboxes damaged by fire while in transit in France. S applied to introduce fresh evidence of three signed statements from an original informant and two others corroborating the fact that the fire had been started deliberately and that there had been no end purchaser.

Held, allowing the appeal and granting unconditional leave to defend, that the three signed statements had not been available at the time of the interlocutory hearing, and would probably have an important influence on the result as they were credible and therefore could be admitted following, *Ladd v. Marshall* [1954] 1 W.L.R. 1489, [1954] C.L.Y. 2507. The strict requirements of *Ladd v. Marshall* might, in certain circumstances, be relaxed in order to set aside a summary judgment, where fraud or dishonesty were involved.

ZINCROFT CIVIL ENGINEERING LTD v. SPHERE DRAKE INSURANCE PLC, *The Times*, December 13, 1996, Potter, L.J., CA.

459. Admissibility—hearsay evidence—applicability of Civil Evidence Act 1995—jurisdiction of Supreme Court Rule Committee

[Supreme Court Act 1981 s.87(3); Civil Evidence Act 1995 s.16(3).]

B appealed against a declaration that the Civil Evidence Act 1995, on the admissibility of hearsay evidence, applied to proceedings commenced before the Act came into force on January 31, 1997. Q contended that the Supreme Court Act 1981 s.87(3) gave the Supreme Court Rule Committee jurisdiction to amend the provisions in s.16(3) of the 1995 Act whereby "the Act shall not apply in relation to proceedings begun before commencement".

Held, allowing the appeal, that the 1995 Act applied to proceedings commenced only after January 31, 1997. In addition, the Supreme Court Rule Committee did not have the jurisdiction to give the Act retroactive effect.

BAIRSTOW v. QUEENS MOAT HOUSES PLC, *The Times*, October 23, 1997, Phillips, L.J., CA.

460. Admissibility—interim payments—evidence of payment into court admissible in interim payment proceedings

[Rules of the Supreme Court Ord.29 r.11, Ord.29 r.18.]

B, a building contractor, sought to recover retention monies from W and intended to make a further claim for additional work. W counterclaimed far greater sums for the cost of remedial works and consequential losses and diminution of value suffered as a result of defective work. B made a payment into court which took into account its own claim for retention monies. On the same date B wrote a Calderbank letter offering to pay the amount of the payment into court plus the amount of the retention monies plus interest on the retention and the costs of the counterclaim. The *Calderbank* letter took the proposed additional work claim into account. W applied for an interim payment pursuant to RSC Ord.29 r.11 and r.18. In support of the application W relied upon the payment into court and offer. B contended that evidence of the payment was inadmissible.

Held, granting an interim payment, that evidence of a payment into court was admissible on an application for an interim payment and that the fact of a payment into court was relevant to the assessment of whether if the action proceeded to trial the applicant would obtain judgment for substantial damages.

BOWMER & KIRKLAND LTD v. WILSON BOWDEN PROPERTIES LTD 80 B.L.R. 131, Judge Hicks Q.C., QBD (OR).

461. Admissibility-without prejudice correspondence-copyright breach not pleaded-issue estoppel

H alleged passing off and trade mark infringement in relation to invalid cushions. On July 7, 1993 H obtained an injunction preventing W from distributing or dealing in the cushions pending the substantive hearing of H's motion for interlocutory relief. H gave the usual cross undertaking in damages. At the substantive hearing W gave an undertaking in the same terms as the original injunction. At trial, H's claim failed and the judge ordered an inquiry as to the damage suffered by W under the cross undertaking. H claimed that no damages should be awarded because W could not lawfully have sold the cushions without infringing copyright. The issue of breach of copyright had come up in correspondence but H had never amended the statement of claim to include it or taken any other action in relation to the claim. W claimed that H was estopped from raising the copyright issue now. H claimed that "without prejudice" correspondence showed that H had held off on the copyright issue solely at W's request and that it would be unjust to deny H the chance to raise it now.

Held, that H was not entitled to raise the copyright issue, that (1) in addition to the public policy reasons for enforcing the rule that "without prejudice" correspondence would not be referred to in proceedings, there was a contractual ground for so doing. Where both these grounds could be relied on, only unconscionability would be sufficient to allow consideration of the "without prejudice" correspondence. Mere inconsistency, in the absence of dishonesty, would not be enough; (2) where one party made a clear and unambiguous statement in "without prejudice" correspondence and that statement was reasonably acted on by the other party, an objection by the first party to the correspondence being put in evidence by the second party in order to justify the step taken by the second party would be plainly unconscionable and would not be upheld by the court. However, in this case W's solicitors merely stated that the copyright issue was not needed to support the interlocutory injunction, which was true. They did not state that there was no need to raise the issue in the substantive proceedings. The "without prejudice" correspondence should be excluded from consideration; (3) the second part of the rule in *Henderson v. Henderson* (1843) 3 Hare 100 that the plea of issue estoppel applied to every point which properly belonged to the subject of earlier litigation and which the parties, exercising reasonable diligence, might have brought forward at the time was not an absolute rule; (4) the copyright issue was not academic. Had it been raised in the proceedings it might have led to H partially winning the action rather than losing it. H could and should have raised the issue in September 1993 by seeking to amend the statement of claim, bringing parallel proceedings or obtaining W's formal agreement to it being raised later. If the point had been raised earlier it was likely that one trial could have dealt with all the issues, *Barrow v. Bankside Agency Ltd* [1996] 1 W.L.R. 257, [1995] 2 C.L.Y. 3894 distinguished, and (5) it was not unjust in the circumstances to allow W to rely on the rule in *Henderson*. H's decision not to pursue the copyright issue was based on considerations which were closely akin to negligence, inadvertence or even accident.

HODGKINSON & CORBY LTD v. WARDS MOBILITY SERVICES LTD [1997] F.S.R. 178, Neuberger, J., Ch D.

462. Admissibility—witness statements—admissibility of late evidence

[Inheritance (Provision for Family and Dependants) Act 1975.]

T appealed against the decision excluding additional witness evidence that T wished to rely on. S was the daughter of the deceased and T was allegedly his cohabitee. When the deceased died intestate, and the letters of administration were issued to his widow, T sought provision under the Inheritance (Provision for Family and Dependants) Act 1975 issuing the originating summons in the Family Division. The widow died and S was designated as the defendant in her place. S contended that T had not been the deceased's cohabitee. A consent order was made providing for the mutual exchange of witness statements and timetabling of the matter. The matter was transferred from the Family Division to the county court with the acquiescence of the parties. T sought leave to rely upon three additional witnesses whose statements had not been served within the agreed timetable. The judge indicated that he would have exercised his discretion to admit the evidence but for the judgment in *Beachley Property Ltd v. Edgar* [1997] P.N.L.R. 197, [1996] 1 C.L.Y. 943. T argued that the judge had exercised his discretion wrongly by giving inadequate consideration to the fact that S had not been prejudiced by T's application.

Held, allowing the appeal, that the witness evidence was potentially important for T's case and S was given prior notice of T's wish to file the statements. Time limits should be adhered to, not merely aimed for, but that need must be balanced against the overriding principle of attaining justice. In deciding whether to exercise its discretion to allow an extension in time for a party who is in default, the court must consider the circumstances of the case, carrying out the necessary balance, *Mortgage Corp Ltd v. Sandoes* [1997] P.N.L.R. 263, [1997] C.L.Y. 783, considered. The proceedings brought under the 1975 Act were essentially inquisitorial and not adversarial in character, and that character should be maintained despite the transfer of the proceedings to the county court.

TABBENOR v. SHAW, Trans. Ref: CCRT1 96/1463/G, January 30, 1997, Thorpe, L.J., CA.

463. Disclosure—plaintiff seeking disclosure of third party's medical records—interest did not outweigh immunity

C appealed from an order of the district judge setting aside a subpoena ad duces tecum (issued at the instance of C) that an official of Wiltshire HA attend at the trial of C's action against the defendant and produce the GP's medical records relating to a former (now deceased) officer for whose acts the defendant accepted vicarious liability. C's claim alleged malicious prosecution and it was stated that the purpose of seeking the disclosure of the medical records was to establish the state of mind of the officer (who later committed suicide) at the time that he was involved in the arrest of and subsequent criminal proceedings against C. Upon service of the subpoena the HA raised the issue of public interest immunity. It also argued that the summons would be tantamount to an application for discovery of information solely relating to the credibility of the witness. C argued that the documents were not covered by public interest immunity and that in any event the needs of C should outweigh the issues of public interest. The defendant argued that C, having obtained the substance of the information sought from other sources, disclosure of the documents now being sought would not progress C beyond her current position.

Held, that as public interest immunity was at issue the HA had a duty to raise it as such. Immunity could not be waived by the HA. The documents were clearly covered by public interest immunity by reason of the importance of patient confidentiality. Therefore, and having inspected the documents, the judge decided that as C had already obtained the substance of the information which was contained within the documents from the other sources C's interest in having access to those documents did not outweigh the desirability of upholding the immunity from production. Further, that the HA should have its costs of raising the issue to be paid by the party seeking production.

COPP v. CHIEF CONSTABLE OF AVON AND SOMERSET POLICE, November 5, 1996, H.H.J. McCarraher, CC (Bristol). [*Ex rel.* Bevan Ashford, Solicitors, 35 Colston Avenue, Bristol].

464. Discovery–action in negligence–sale of company–contract term allowing reasonable access to documents for purpose of litigation

[Rules of the Supreme Court Ord.24 r.3, r.7.]

PW sought discovery against BA under RSC Ord.24 r.3 and r.7. BA and OH, a subsidiary thereof, sued PW in negligence following PW's advice on the purchase of a company, S, by OH. After a breakdown in negotiations for informal discovery, PW made an application for discovery of all documentation generated by S relating to its acquisition by OH and post dating that acquisition until November 1996. In 1996 OH and S had been sold to G, with a term in the contract of sale that S would allow BA reasonable access to all documents as may be reasonably requested in connection with the litigation. This term was subject to the proviso that nothing in that requirement should prevent S from carrying out its business or be contrary to its interests. PW argued that the wide terms of the order sought were within the permitted scope following *Compagnie Financiere du Pacifique v. Peruvian Guano Co* (1882) 11 Q.B.D. 55 and that the documents were within the power of BA by virtue of the terms of the sale agreement.

Held, granting the discovery sought in part, that the *Peruvian Guano* definition of relevance should not be given an excessively wide application, the observations in *O Co v. M Co* [1996] 2 Lloyd's Rep. 347, [1996] 2 C.L.Y. 5330 approved. There was no real evidence that the attempts at voluntary discovery had failed given that there was no evidence that S was refusing to deliver up a manageable class or classes of documents, rather that it was objecting to the degree of the burden being placed upon it. Furthermore, in view of the likely effect of compliance with the proposed order on S's operations it would not voluntarily comply with the order nor could it, under the terms of the sale agreement, be required by BA to do so. Such being the case, the documents were not within the power of BA.

BANK AUSTRIA AG v. PRICE WATERHOUSE, Trans. Ref: 1995-B-7013, April 16, 1997, Neuberger, J., Ch D.

465. Discovery–Anton Piller orders–trade mark action–leave to use documents in unrelated contempt proceedings not granted

C applied for leave to use documents obtained from R's premises on the execution of an Anton Piller order by another company, T. Both C and T had previously obtained undertakings to the court from R in separate proceedings that it would not infringe their rights in respect of golf clubs sold under the mark KING COBRA. T had commenced the Anton Piller proceedings against R because it had discovered that R was in breach of the undertakings in T's action. C also had reason to believe that R was in breach of the undertakings in C's action, but believed that the documents already recovered by T would also cover R's activities relating to C. An order for discovery of these documents in C's favour would therefore eliminate the need for C to issue a separate Anton Piller application. C intended to use the documents in contempt proceedings against R for breach of the undertakings given in C's action.

Held, dismissing the application for leave, that (1) the implied undertaking given by a party receiving discovery of documents not to use those documents for a collateral purpose could be released at the discretion of the court; (2) documents obtained as a result of an Anton Piller order should not be treated any differently from any other discovery documents; (3) the undertaking would be released and the documents permitted to be used in separate proceedings provided that no significant injustice was done to the disclosing party; (4) prima facie, it was not in the interests of justice to allow discovery to be released to support the initiation of contempt proceedings in a separate unrelated action,

Crest Homes Plc v. Marks [1987] A.C. 829, [1987] C.L.Y. 2885 followed and (5) although the decision may have resulted in the wastage of costs by C having to apply for an Anton Piller order to obtain the documents, the decision in Crest Homes meant that, on balance, the court would dismiss the application.

COBRA GOLF INC v. RATA; TAYLOR MADE GOLF CO INC v. RATA & RATA (A FIRM) [1996] F.S.R. 819, Laddie, J., Ch D.

466. Discovery—commercial confidentiality not sufficient reason to justify disclosure

E sought damages against C and D alleging that C, who worked for E, had knowingly sold goods to D in collusion with them at under value. Part of D's defence was that other suppliers sold identical goods to them at similar prices. E sought discovery of all relevant invoices from such suppliers held by D. For reasons of commercial confidentiality, D refused.

Held, refusing discovery of the documents, that commercial confidentiality may be an insufficient reason to bar discovery. However, following *Air Canada v. Secretary of State for Trade (No.2)* [1983] 2 A.C. 394, [1983] C.L.Y. 2936, it was irrelevant that the documents were only likely to assist D. E could not show that they could rebut D's defence or assist E's case or line of enquiry. It was up to D how they chose to present their case.

ELMATIC (CARDIFF) LTD v. COX AND DELTA HEAT LTD, July 2, 1997, District Judge Hendicott, CC (Cardiff). [*Ex rel.* Lee Ingham, Barrister, 32 Park Place, Cardiff].

467. Discovery—disclosure of settlement agreement of third party proceedings

[Rules of the Supreme Court Ord.24 r.7, Ord.24 r.11.]

R appealed against the refusal of an application under RSC Ord.24 r.7 for disclosure of a settlement agreement made between ICL and a former third party, and an application under RSC Ord.24 r.11 (1) (b) for disclosure of draft witness statements prepared by the third party. R claimed damages of £1.8 million for misrepresentation and breach of a contract to supply a computer system and software from ICL, who introduced as a third party to the action the main contractors, Computer Systems for Business, CSB. Both ICL and CSB counterclaimed for losses under the contract. The third party proceedings were compromised and subsequently ICL were granted leave to serve out of time witness statements on behalf of nine of CSB's witnesses while R was refused discovery of both the third party settlement agreement and draft witness statements prepared by CSB for the third party action. R contended that the settlement was relevant in the sense of *Compagnie Financiere du Pacifique v. Peruvian Guano Co* (1882) 11 Q.B.D. 55 in that there was a close relationship between the claims and contentions advanced and the third party proceedings. Further that the document would reveal what ICL and CSB thought of the merits of R's claim. R also stated that the statements were copies produced specifically for use in the main action.

Held, dismissing the applications, that (1) the agreement was not relevant to issues in the main action. The argument as to relevance broke down because the revelation of ICL and CSB's opinion of the strength of R's claim did not advance that claim, and (2) in terms of legal professional privilege, the distinction between originals and photocopies of documents was left undecided. However, policy dictated that the sharing of material by defendants and third parties should be encouraged in order to save costs, *Ventouris v. Mountain (The Italia Express) (1990)* [1991] 1 W.L.R. 607, [1992] C.L.Y. 3479, *Lee v. South West Thames RHA* [1985] 1 W.L.R. 845, [1985] C.L.Y. 2651 and *Cole v. Elders Finance and Investment Co Ltd* [1993] 2 V.R. 356 distinguished on their facts.

ROBERT HITCHINS LTD v. INTERNATIONAL COMPUTERS LTD, Trans. Ref: FC3 96/7693/B, December 10, 1996, Simon Brown, L.J., CA.

468. Discovery—legal professional privilege—partial disclosure of documents—privilege not waived where undisclosed material related to separate issue

Held, that, where a party had made partial disclosure of documents subject to legal professional privilege, he could not later be obliged to waive privilege with regard to the undisclosed documents where the issues to which the disclosed and undisclosed documents related were separate. In some circumstances it was possible to determine before the trial whether the disclosing party was attempting to take unfair advantage of his partial disclosure in the evidence which he deployed in court. In general, there was no distinction between disclosure of a document and deploying it in evidence for the purpose of waiver of privilege over associated documents, and a party was not entitled to show only part of the evidence in his possession. Whether privilege should be waived would depend on whether the privileged material was going to be relied on by the disclosing party at trial. A claim to further and associated discovery might have to be determined at the trial itself if the manner in which a party intended to use the disclosed privileged material was unclear.

R. v. SECRETARY OF STATE FOR TRANSPORT, *ex p.* FACTORTAME (NO.5), *The Times*, May 16, 1997, Auld, L.J., QBD.

469. Discovery—legal professional privilege—proceedings commenced after compromise amounting to implied waiver—no discovery where material disclosed by mistake

In a dispute between H and D over the running of a private company, PD, was compromised by H's solicitors, E, on the basis that D should buy out H's interests. H then sued D, PD and others and sought to upset the compromise relying on alleged misrepresentation, and alleged that E had acted contrary to instructions. Attendance notes of H's new solicitors, F, were inadvertently disclosed by H. D sought discovery of all communications between H, E and F. H resisted the application, and sought to obtain delivery up and restrain the use of the disclosed material, on the ground that the material was privileged.

Held, that (1) D was entitled to discovery of the material insofar as it was relevant to the inducement to compromise, as privilege relating to that was waived by the bringing of proceedings, *Waldrope v. Dunne* [1996] 1 Qd.R.244 followed and (2) no wider discovery was permitted and as disclosure was the result of an obvious mistake, privilege was not waived and H was entitled to the orders sought, *Guinness Peat Properties v. Fitzroy Robinson Partnership* [1987] 1 W.L.R. 1027, [1987] C.L.Y. 3060 followed.

HAYES v. DOWDING [1996] P.N.L.R. 578, Jonathan Parker, J., Ch D.

470. Discovery—legal professional privilege—waiver in respect of one party did not amount to waiver of privilege in respect of whole world

S were custodians of a painting, the ownership of which was to be the subject of a consolidated action in the High Court. C, who claimed to have owned the painting since 1989, appealed against the dismissal of their appeal against an order to disclose various documents to the plaintiff, GC, including a copy of a letter sent from solicitors to C containing legal advice and minutes of a meeting between the two at which legal advice was given. The judge had found that, because the letter had been copied to S and the meeting had been attended by S, there had been a waiver of privilege in relation to the whole world.

Held, allowing the appeal, that, where there was a waiver of privilege in relation to a single party, this did not necessarily amount to a waiver of privilege in respect of the whole world. In the instant case, disclosure of documents to S was apparently intended to be confidential and it would therefore be appropriate to set aside the disputed paragraphs of the order for discovery.

GOTHA CITY v. SOTHEBY'S, *The Times*, July 3, 1997, Staughton, L.J., CA.

471. Discovery–letter of request from Minnesota District Court too wide ranging in its terms

[Evidence (Proceedings in Other Jurisdictions) Act 1975; Rules of Procedure r.26.02 (Minnesota).]

Four former employees of the British American Tobacco group of companies, BAT, appealed against an order, pursuant to the Evidence (Proceedings in Other Jurisdictions) Act 1975, that they attend an examiner to give evidence, following the delivery of a Letter of Request from a Minnesota District Court. The State of Minnesota claimed penal damages from BAT for losses resulting from the concealment of research showing that nicotine was addictive and that cigarettes were lethal. BAT contended that the Request was a "fishing trip" permitted by the wider rules of oral discovery under the US legal system, but not allowed by the English legal system. BAT argued that its terms were too uncertain, extending over a 40 year period, and of imprecise scope. BAT submitted that limits on the time and on the extent of the enquiry that were given in affidavit evidence showed that the Request was outside the parameters of the English system.

Held, allowing the appeal, that the Letter of Request was too wide ranging. Notwithstanding the desire of the English courts to cooperate with those in the US, under English law a witness must be given sufficient indication of the scope of the matters about which he could be lawfully examined. The Letter of Request appeared to incorporate the Rules of Procedure r.26.02 (Minnesota), which allowed evidence to be sought beyond that admissible at trial and it was apparent from affidavit evidence seeking to limit the breadth of the Request, that it was couched in such broad terms that it went beyond the limitations of the 1975 Act, *Westinghouse Electric Corp Uranium Contract Litigation MDL Docket 235* [1978] A.C. 547, [1978] C.L.Y. 1422 and *Radio Corp of America v. Rauland Corp* [1956] 1 Q.B. 618, [1956] C.L.Y. 6731 considered.

MINNESOTA v. PHILIP MORRIS INC, Trans. Ref: QBENI 97/1009/E, July 30, 1997, Lord Woolf, M.R., CA.

472. Discovery–public interest immunity–initial report forms sent by police to CPS–immunity from disclosure in civil action against police

K, who brought an action against C for malicious prosecution, appealed against a decision refusing discovery of initial report documents, used by police investigating an offence, which were subsequently sent to the CPS. The police contended that the forms were privileged against disclosure by public interest immunity.

Held, allowing the appeal, that a judge should, when considering the extent to which public interest immunity applied to certain forms, first decide whether production of the documents was necessary for either the fair disposal of the case or to save costs, *Ventouris v. Mountain (1990)* [1991] 1 W.L.R. 607, [1992] C.L.Y. 3479 and *Taylor v. Anderton* [1995] 1 W.L.R. 447, [1995] 2 C.L.Y. 4123 considered. Following *Wallace Smith Trust Co Ltd (In Liquidation) v. Deloitte Haskins & Sells* [1997] 1 W.L.R. 257, [1996] 1 C.L.Y. 1361 a judge should, after deciding that production of documents was necessary, examine the relevant forms before deciding whether to make an order for production. The judge should then consider whether the forms belonged to a class of documents protected by immunity. The forms in question, on which the police provided the CPS with a summary of the case, did constitute a class subject to public interest immunity, *O'Sullivan v. Commissioner of Police of the Metropolis* (1995) 139 S.J.L.B. 164 considered. Accordingly, the case would be remitted for the judge to apply the test of whether production of the forms was necessary for disposing of the case fairly or for saving costs.

KELLY v. COMMISSIONER OF POLICE OF THE METROPOLIS, *The Times*, August 20, 1997, Kennedy, L.J., CA.

473. Documentary evidence–defendant destroying evidence–reliance on Calderbank offer

[Rules of the Supreme Court Ord.22 r.14, Ord.62 r.9.]

M, an accountant, sought remuneration due for work he carried out for D, also an accountant, for which he was to receive half of the firm's profits from January 1, 1978 when he started, until October 12, 1979 when he left at D's request. An account of the profits for the relevant period was ordered following this. D made a *Calderbank* offer on March 1, 1993, for £10,000 and a further offer on March 25, 1993 of £16,000. D had moved offices in March 1984 and admitted destroying files relating to clients for whom he no longer acted. On hearing evidence of both parties the judge preferred D's evidence, finding that the destruction was not with the intention of destroying the evidence which was relevant to M's claim. D was ordered to pay £735 with interest and M's costs up to March 1, 1993, and M was ordered to pay D's costs thereafter on an indemnity basis. M appealed, claiming that D should pay £21,277 with interest and all of M's costs, on the grounds: (1) that the consequence of D destroying the client files had not been correctly dealt with, and (2) whether D could rely on his *Calderbank* offer when a payment into court could have been made, and whether it was right that M was ordered to pay D's costs on an indemnity basis.

Held, dismissing the appeal, that (1) in the absence of any direct authority on the point, a definitive three part test on how to apply the principle in *Gray v. Haig & Sons* (1855) 20 Beav. 219 was set down: (a) if the destruction was deliberate so as to hinder the proof of the plaintiff's claim, then there would be an inference as to the credibility of the destroyer enabling the court to disregard his evidence; (b) if the court was undecided as to which of the two parties' evidence to accept, then it should decide in favour of the party who had not destroyed the documents, and (c) if the court had a clear view as to the truth, the judge was not bound to follow the principle. In the instant case, not all relevant evidence was destroyed as there remained the ledger, the fees book and the wages sheet from which to obtain information regarding the work carried out by M. It would be inconsistent with the documentary evidence to apply the presumption, following the principle of omnia praesumuntur contra spoliatorem, in order to give credence to evidence otherwise found to be unacceptable, and (2) under RSC Ord.22 r.14 and Ord.62 r.9(1)(d) the rule that a party was unable to rely in his *Calderbank* offer when a payment into court could have been made, did not apply to actions for an account, only to actions for a debt or damages. The judge had not erred in ordering costs on an indemnity basis.

MALHOTRA v. DHAWAN, February 26, 1997, Saville, L.J., CA. [*Ex rel.* Mark Watson-Gandy, Barrister, 3 Paper Buildings, Temple].

474. Documentary evidence–disclosure in criminal proceedings–implied undertaking not to use in different proceedings

[Rules of the Supreme Court Ord.24 r.14A.]

C's former employer, E, made accusations of theft against C in a letter to a subsequent employer which was later disclosed to C under subpoena during criminal proceedings against him for theft. C was acquitted and now appealed against the striking out of an action for libel and malicious falsehood brought against E, based on the content of the letter. E contended that C was bound by an undertaking not to use the letter for purposes other than the criminal proceedings.

Held, dismissing the appeal, that where evidence was obtained under compulsion in Crown Court proceedings, an undertaking was implied that it could not be used in other proceedings without the court's permission, *Derby & Co Ltd v. Weldon* [1988] C.L.Y. 2911 applied. Where evidence was obtained in civil proceedings, the RSC Ord.24 r.14A operated to discharge the undertaking once the evidence had been read out in open court, but this did not apply to evidence obtained in criminal proceedings, *Mahon v. Rahn* (Unreported) followed. Therefore C could not use the letter without first obtaining an order from the court varying the undertaking, and as he had not done so his action would fail as an abuse of process.

CUNNINGHAM v. ESSEX CC, *The Times*, March 31, 1997, Geoffrey Rivlin Q.C., QBD.

475. Documentary evidence–disclosure to defence in criminal proceedings–no implied undertaking to prevent defendant using documents to found libel action

[Criminal Procedure and Investigations Act 1996 s.17; Rules of the Supreme Court Ord.24 r.14A.]

M appealed against a decision striking out his action for libel against R on the ground that the documents relied upon by M had been obtained by disclosure in unsuccessful criminal proceedings brought against him, which constituted an abuse of process. R contended that, by analogy with the rule on implied undertakings which existed in relation to civil proceedings, there was an implied undertaking not to use documents obtained in criminal discovery for other purposes without the permission of the court. Although RSC Ord.24 r.14A discharged the undertaking in relation to civil proceedings after a document had been read in open court, the authorities showed that special restrictions applied to libel cases. R argued that the justification for an implied undertaking was even more compelling in criminal cases because of the need to protect informers and guarantee full disclosure by the prosecuting authorities.

Held, allowing the appeal, that there was no basis upon which an implied undertaking could be applied to criminal proceedings on the grounds of privacy or confidentiality, and that was confirmed by the provisions of the Criminal Procedure and Investigations Act 1996 s.17 which showed that the legislature did not intend to treat material which had been disclosed to the defence and had been or would be adduced in court as confidential. Nor was there anything to suggest that, prior to the 1996 Act, material that had been used in open court was subject to any restriction other than public interest immunity. Section 17 could not be read as preventing documents from a criminal trial being used to found a libel action and, in any case, Ord.24 r.14A had to be construed broadly. Whilst exceptional circumstances could exist with regard to criminal proceedings, they were limited to public interest immunity and absolute privilege, which was sufficient to protect informers. Public policy, the administration of civil justice and abuse of the civil process had no application to criminal proceedings where the rules of disclosure had a different purpose and were embodied in the 1996 Act.

MAHON v. RAHN [1997] 3 All E.R. 687, Otton, L.J., CA.

476. Documents–inspection of documents organised in electronic form– reasonable charge for inspection of copies supplied on CD ROM

A court has jurisdiction to give directions on whether copy documents may be supplied in electronic form for the purpose of discovery and if so to determine a reasonable charge for the service.

Held, that where a party to an action had scanned and organised documents into electronic form and the parties disagreed over the charges for inspection of copies supplied on CD ROM, the court had the power to give directions on whether inspection was to be afforded in electronic or printed form. A party wishing to produce copies of documents in electronic form for the purposes of inspection could apply to the court in advance for an order on the issue, including a determination as to the charges for supplying electronic copies. Reasonable charges for supplying copies of the material on CD ROM would not include the costs of the original process of converting the documents into electronic form, but would be restricted to the costs of copying and supplying the CD ROMs using the data and systems in existence.

GRUPO TORRAS SA v. AL SABAH (NO.3); JAFFAR v. GRUPO TORRAS SA, *The Times*, October 13, 1997, Mance, J., QBD.

477. Expert evidence–judge had no jurisdiction to edit expert's report at interlocutory stage

[Civil Evidence Act 1972 s.3.]

S brought an action to prevent K selling its product as whisky, as it was distilled twice and fell outside the EC definition of whisky. K submitted an expert witness report to which S objected in part, arguing that the expert gave evidence on matters irrelevant to the action. S requested alterations to be made before the report could be submitted as an expert report.

Held, that, as a matter of law, a judge in an interlocutory hearing had no jurisdiction to alter details contained in an expert report. The report was not expert evidence within the Civil Evidence Act 1972 s.3, but was merely information exchanged between the parties regarding intended evidence to be given by an expert in court and could not be edited before the hearing took place, *Sullivan v. West Yorkshire Passenger Transport Executive* [1985] 2 All E.R. 134, [1985] C.L.Y. 1506 applied.

SCOTCH WHISKY ASSOCIATION v. KELLA DISTILLERS LTD, *The Times*, December 27, 1996, Harman, J., Ch D.

478. Expert evidence–medical examinations–substantial claim–not unreasonable to order second MRI scan

D, aged 30, was involved in a road traffic accident on November 8, 1990 in which she suffered personal injuries. Negligence was not in issue. D alleged that she suffered a severe whiplash injury to her cervical spine in the accident which prevented her from resuming to her employment as a health visitor. She retired on the grounds of ill health on October 2, 1992 and claimed special damages in respect of past and future loss of earnings exceeding £250,000. D's medical experts accepted that D had ongoing persistent pain in the neck and restriction of movement. L's medical experts noted that D was claiming extensive disability following the accident in the absence of any good medical explanation for the almost total failure of her symptoms to improve after five years. D underwent an MRI scan of her cervical spine in 1992, which was essentially normal with no evidence of damage to any of the intevertebral discs or to the bony structures. L's medical experts considered that a second MRI scan might be helpful in that comparison with the first scan could reveal positive or negative information which could be of substantial significance in respect of the medico-legal claim, and might demonstrate why D had persistent symptoms which were unexplained or accompanied by inappropriate clinical signs. D refused to undergo a second scan on two grounds: (1) that she would find the experience extremely unpleasant due to claustrophobia, and (2) her medical experts were of the opinion that a further scan would not have any direct medical benefit and would be unnecessarily cruel, in view of her reluctance. In support of her objections, D relied upon *Hill v. West Lancashire HA* (Unreported, 1995). L applied for the proceedings to be stayed unless D consented to a second MRI scan within 14 days.

Held, allowing L's application, that it would not be unreasonable to order the test to go ahead. Following *Hill* there was a threefold test to determine whether the medical examination should be ordered, the judge had to consider whether L's request was reasonable. If he concluded that it was, he then had to consider whether D's refusal was reasonable. If he concluded that both the request and refusal were reasonable, he then had to balance the competing tests of reasonableness. It was decided that both the request and refusal were reasonable, as there was no suggestion that D would suffer any physical harm or risk to health if she underwent a further scan, *Hill* distinguished. Factors taken into account were that modern technology had moved on since 1992 so that the scan would be completed in less than ten minutes; that D would find the scan unpleasant but not impossible; and D's claim for special damages was substantial.

DIGNAM v. LBS POLYTHENE, February 26, 1997, District Judge Fairwood, CC (Leeds). [*Ex rel.* Langleys, Solicitors, Queens House, Micklegate, York].

479. Expert evidence–medical negligence–deletion of parts of consultant's witness statement

[Rules of the Supreme Court Ord.38 r.2A.]

T sued P in respect of her medical treatment. The essence of the case concerned criticisms of the consent/information procedures and the conduct of surgery upon T. T was under the overall care of a consultant who was not involved with the surgery which was carried out by a registrar. Exchange of witness statements of fact and of expert reports took place, both the registrar and the consultant were among the witnesses of fact. The consultant was not served as an expert; the reports of two experts were served. No leave was applied for to rely upon the consultant as a further and third expert. In his witness statement the consultant not only referred to his own involvement with T, but also directly referred to the actions of the registrar in the course of surgery and commented upon those actions and their appropriateness. T applied to delete parts of the statement of the consultant and in particular to delete those parts which concerned the actions of the registrar and which T argued amounted to expert evidence. P argued that (1) questions of admissibility of evidence in statements served pursuant to RSC Ord.38 r.2A were more appropriately dealt with by the trial judge and not by the district judge at an interlocutory stage, and (2) if it was appropriate for the district judge to consider the matter, it was further argued that a consultant in overall charge of the patient was in a position somewhere between a pure witness of fact and independent expert witness and should be entitled to comment, not only upon his own treatment of a patient, but upon another's treatment of a patient, even though he was not being put forward and relied upon by P as an independent expert witness.

Held, that (1) the court had power at an interlocutory stage to delete inadmissible or inappropriate parts of statements of witnesses of fact albeit that such power should be exercised sparingly and cautiously, and (2) it was appropriate to exercise such powers in a medical negligence case where the effect of a statement was to attempt to rely upon a witness of fact as in practical terms an additional medical expert.

TYRIE v. PRESTON AHA, September 4, 1997, District Judge Ashton, Preston District Registry. [*Ex rel.* Christopher Limb, Barrister, Young Street Chambers, 38 Young Street, Manchester, M3 3FT 0161 833 0489].

480. Expert evidence–plaintiff refusing to complete defendants questionnaire on basis it would jeopardise claim

E brought a claim against B in respect of noise induced industrial deafness he alleged he had contracted whilst in their employ. B requested that E be examined by their nominated medical expert. Prior to E's appointment with the expert, the expert sent to E a questionnaire for him to fill in dealing with, inter alia, his employment history and other instances of exposure to loud noise. E refused to fill in parts of the questionnaire and B's expert considered he could not obtain enough information to write a meaningful report, unless E cooperated fully. The appointment was cancelled and B made an application for the proceedings to be stayed unless and until E completed the questionnaire, on the grounds that his refusal was unreasonable, *Starr v. National Coal Board* [1977] 1 W.L.R. 63, [1977] C.L.Y. 2323. E resisted the application on the grounds that to fill in the questionnaire was oppressive, that he had already given B permission to have access to all his medical records and that the questionnaire was interrogative in nature and B was precluded from asking the questions by reason of the decision in *Hall v. Sevalco* [1996] 1 P.I.Q.R. P.344, [1996] C.L.Y. 795.

Held, granting the application and staying the action until E completed the questionnaire, that although the questionnaire was lengthy and repetitive, there was nothing in it which would jeopardise E's chances of a just trial. The questionnaire was not oppressive, since if E was unsure of the answers to any of the questions it asked, he had only to say so. It might be right to say that some of the questions could form the content of interrogatories, but the purpose of the questionnaire was to assist B's medical expert.

EDWARDS v. BRITISH STEEL PLC, January 31, 1997, Deputy District Judge Talbot, CC (Manchester). [*Ex rel.* Andrew Hogan, Barrister, 11 The Ropewalk, Nottingham].

481. Judicial review—discovery and cross examination of witnesses allowed only where jurisdictional fact in dispute or evidence might be misleading or materially incomplete

[Rules of the Supreme Court Ord.24, Ord.38 r.2.]

In judicial review proceedings brought to challenge the decision of the A to refuse W's application for lottery funding, W issued a summons seeking discovery under RSC Ord.24 and leave to cross examine witnesses on their affidavits under RSC Ord.38 r.2(3).

Held, dismissing the summons, that where the existence of a jurisdictional fact was genuinely disputed in a judicial review case, and that fact had to be established before a discretionary power under statute could be exercised lawfully, the court had a duty to resolve such questions. However, there was no such situation in the instant case, and, since it had not been established that A's evidence might be misleading or materially incomplete, the court would not order discovery or cross examination of witnesses.

R. v. ARTS COUNCIL OF ENGLAND, *ex p.* WOMEN'S PLAYHOUSE TRUST, *The Times*, August 20, 1997, Laws, J., QBD.

482. Solicitors—Solicitors Disciplinary Tribunal—applicability of Civil Evidence Acts

See LEGAL PROFESSION: Solicitor (No.976 of 1996), *Re.* §3380

483. Witnesses—personal injuries action—plaintiff attaching conditions on defence access to witness

P, a child who suffered a brain tumour which was treated in hospital, brought a personal injury action against three general practitioners by his father and next friend. In the course of P's illness he was treated at two hospitals by a number of doctors (the treating doctors) and after proceedings were commenced orders were made for the exchange of witness statements, including the statements of the treating doctors. Before statements were exchanged P sought to impose a condition on D's solicitor talking to the treating doctors, namely that P's solicitor be present during the interviewing process. D refused to accept this condition and appealed against an order requiring the service of witness statements.

Held, allowing the appeal, that (1) in bringing a personal injury action a plaintiff waived his right to confidentiality and it was appropriate for the court to insist that evidence as to P's medical condition be brought before it; (2) a plaintiff who sought to bring an action but by his own actions prevented material evidence being obtained by the other side and brought before the court was impeding the process of law. If necessary, courts would entertain an application to stay proceedings if the plaintiff refused to be medically examined or give consent to hospitals or doctors to disclose confidential information; (3) in view of those basic principles it was undesirable for a plaintiff to attach any conditions to any such consent. If the plaintiff sought to attach conditions those conditions had to be justified, and (4) P had demonstrated no sufficient justification for the condition sought to be attached in the instant case. That the condition could not do any harm was not a sufficient justification.

SHAW v. SKEET [1996] 7 Med. L.R. 371, Buckley, J., QBD.

484. Witnesses—witness statements to stand as evidence in chief—oral evidence required in cases of conflict

C appealed against the dismissal of an action for negligence against K, a firm of estate agents, and against a counterclaim for commission of £30,318.02. K conducted negotiations for the sale of some 15 acres of agricultural land to W, a development company, for £1,302,000. W made a back to back contract with Wiggins Homes Group Plc (WHG) to sell the land on for £2,128,410, provided that K should act as sole agents for the sale of all completed houses at 2 per cent commission and with 0.5 per cent per sale paid to C. C contended that the judge below had failed to deal with the evidence satisfactorily.

Held, allowing the appeal and ordering a fresh trial, that C had been deprived of an opportunity to dispute evidence of K's restricted retainer and K's alleged disclosure of WHG's interest in the purchase. Where witness statements revealed no factual dispute, they should stand as evidence in chief, following *Practice Direction (Civil Litigation: Case Management)* [1995] 1 W.L.R. 262. However, the Practice Direction should not be applied too strictly and, in the event of a conflict of fact as in the instant case, a judge had an unfettered discretion to require a witness to give oral evidence, even where pre trial exchange of witness statements had been directed.

COLE v. KIVELLS, *The Times*, May 2, 1997, Mummery, L.J., CA.

485. Articles

A matter of opinion *(Ronnie Conway)*: Rep. B. 1997, 17 (Sep), 1-4. (Whether it is reasonable to rely upon expert witnesses' opinions in personal injuries cases where they may lack objectivity and may stray outside area of competence).

Abolition of hearsay in civil proceedings *(Anthony Beck)*: Corp. Brief. 1997, 11 (4), 16-18. (Interaction with statutes under which evidence remains inadmissible, notice requirements, guidelines on weight of hearsay evidence and right to call witnesses for cross-examination under provisions in force January 1, 1997).

Civil Evidence Act *(Daniel Barnett)*: N.L.J. 1997, 147 (6791), 701-702. (Mechanism provided under Act in force January 31, 1997 for presenting and objecting to hearsay evidence and assessing credibility of witnesses who will not give oral evidence).

Document-making analysis as expert evidence *(L.R.C. Haward)*: Pol. J. 1997, 70 (2), 154-158. (Details of case where expert evidence was required concerning psychological analysis of writing process).

New rules on hearsay notices *(Ian D. Grainger)*: S.J. 1997, 141 (5), 112-113. (Changes to RSC Ord.38, implementing provisions of 1995 Act in force January 31, 1997, focusing on hearsay notices, cross examination of hearsay evidence and challenging credibility of person giving hearsay evidence).

Photography for personal injury and medical negligence claims *(Jeremy Nayler)*: N.L.J. 1997, 147 (6790), 644,646. (Use of medical photographs to complement expert reports and advice on what qualifications, services and photographic medium to look for according to claim being made).

The Civil Evidence Act 1995: a new regime *(Barry Cotter)*: J.P.I.L. 1997, Sep, 170-176. (Major changes to hearsay rule in civil proceedings and likely areas of dispute).

The Civil Evidence Act 1995—new rules of court *(Paula Loughlin)*: S.L.R. 1997, 21 (Sum), 3-4. (Abolition of rule against admission of hearsay evidence in civil proceedings and new rules for High Court and county courts laying down notice procedure for adducing such evidence, in force January 1, 1997).

The Civil Evidence Act 1995 and the admissibility of documents by English notaries *(Jenny Marriott)*: Litigator 1997, Mar, 119-123. (Extent to which English notarial documents are admitted in evidence in English civil courts and potential impact of 1995 Act).

486. Books

Allen, Christopher—Practical Guide to the Law of Evidence. Paperback: £39.95. ISBN 1-85941-316-1. Cavendish Publishing Ltd.

Graham-Hall, Jean; Martin, Douglas–Expert Witness. Hardback: £22.00. ISBN 1-872328-59-8. Barry Rose Law Publishers Ltd.

Style, Christopher; Hollander, Charles–Documentary Evidence. Hardback. ISBN 0-7520-0447-6. FT Law & Tax.

Uglow, Steve–Evidence: Text and Materials. Paperback: £26.95. ISBN 0-421-57130-6. Sweet & Maxwell.

CIVIL PROCEDURE

487. Abuse of process–breach of patent–defence abandoned in previous action–subject matter of a final judicial decision could not ordinarily be relitigated

[Patents Act 1977 s.44.]

C applied to set aside leave to appeal granted ex parte by the Court of Appeal. C was the holder of a patent relating to the Hepatitis C Virus. In a previous action for infringement of the patent O alleged invalidity and counter claimed for revocation, one of the grounds being that at the priority date the invention was not new. O relied upon experiments relating to the Ross River Virus, RRV, to prove anticipation. At the trial O relied partly on experiments which C had not seen. This evidence was ruled inadmissible and O dropped the defence based on RRV. O did not apply for an adjournment and did not reserve its rights to renew this ground of attack later. The trial judge found that most of the patent claims were valid but ruled against C under the Patents Act 1977 s.44 because of restrictive provisions in C's licence agreements. Shortly before judgment C was allowed to delete the invalid claims and O's counter claim was dismissed. C removed the offending provisions from its licence agreements and commenced the instant action against O for infringement of the amended patent. O raised the RRV defence. The trial judge struck out this pleading and O sought leave to appeal from the Court of Appeal. Leave was refused and O renewed its appeal to the full court, which granted leave. C applied to set aside the leave.

Held, setting aside leave to appeal, that (1) once a matter had been the subject of a final judicial decision it could not ordinarily be relitigated as this would not be in the interests of the parties or the public. It was the duty of parties to any action to present their whole case to the court. There might be an exception to that rule where a party was reasonably ignorant of matters which could found a claim or a defence. In such a case, the correct course was to seek an adjournment or ask the judge to try a preliminary issue or reserve argument on certain issues until later and (2) the RRV defence had been abandoned in the first action with the result that the judge upheld the validity of the patent. In those circumstances to raise it again would be an abuse of the process. Alternatively, O was estopped from raising the RRV defence again, *Arnold v. National Westminster Bank Plc* [1991] 2 A.C. 93, [1991] C.L.Y. 1736 applied.

CHIRON CORP v. ORGANON TEKNIKA LTD (NO.14) [1996] F.S.R. 701, Sir Thomas Bingham, M.R., CA.

488. Abuse of process–courts powers to strike out contempt and supervisory proceedings

T appealed against the striking out as an abuse of process of her motion seeking orders of committal and compensation under the court's supervisory jurisdiction against Y, R's solicitor. T alleged that Y had been in contempt of court by aiding and abetting breaches of an order against R and by breaching a personal undertaking to the court. However, the judge found that there had been inordinate and inexcusable delay in issuing proceedings by which Y had been seriously prejudiced. T argued that (1) the court had no power to strike out proceedings as an abuse of process where they were brought under the court's contempt or supervisory jurisdiction; (2) there was no limitation period for bringing such actions, and (3) the proceedings could not be struck out on the grounds of prejudice arising from inordinate and inexcusable delay.

Held, dismissing the appeal, that the court had an inherent discretionary power to strike out as an abuse of process both contempt and supervisory proceedings, notwithstanding the absence of a limitation period. The court's supervisory power over solicitors as officers of the court was a discretionary jurisdiction, unbound by absolute rules, and was to be exercised according to the facts of each case. On a strike out application, the court would consider the prospects of exercising its powers at the substantive hearing to grant disciplinary or compensatory relief. In the instant case, there had been a long and inexcusable delay in bringing the case and, since there was a genuine risk of prejudice to Y and no real prospect of the court exercising its powers to grant the relief sought, it was an abuse of process for the motion to proceed to a substantive hearing. However, it was generally preferable for submissions on delay and prejudice in relation to the court's contempt and supervisory jurisdiction to be made at the substantive hearing rather than during an application to strike out the motion.

TAYLOR v. RIBBY HALL LEISURE LTD, *The Times*, August 6, 1997, Mummery, L.J., CA.

489. Abuse of process–defendant not intending to conclude proceedings

G appealed against the dismissal of his appeal against a decision that his libel writ and statement of claim should be struck out for want of prosecution on the grounds that G had no intention of bringing the litigation to a conclusion. G contended that his conduct did not amount to an abuse of process under the first limb of the test in *Birkett v. James* [1978] A.C. 297, [1977] C.L.Y. 2410 and that, whilst there had been inordinate and inexcusable delay, no serious prejudice had been caused to the defendant so as to satisfy the second limb of the test.

Held, dismissing the appeal, that abuse of process was by itself a ground for striking out or staying proceedings which operated independently of the first limb of the test in *Birkett*. The requirement in the second limb of the test that the delay must cause serious prejudice to the defendant had been the subject of criticism, but until new rules were introduced it might be preferable not to impinge on the principles laid down in *Birkett*. In the meantime, both defendants and the court had the means to deal with delay, through the use of peremptory orders and unless orders. On the facts, the Court of Appeal had been entitled to conclude that the reason for G's inactivity was that he did not intend to pursue the proceedings, and such conduct constituted an abuse of process.

GROVIT v. DOCTOR [1997] 1 W.L.R. 640, Lord Woolf, M.R., HL.

490. Abuse of process–local authority refusing payment of improvement grant–ordinary action to enforce payment

[Housing Act 1985 s.189; Local Government and Housing Act 1989 s.113, s.117(3).]

Following service of a repairs notice upon them, T conducted repair work to render premises fit for human habitation under the Housing Act 1985 s.189. S refused to pay the sums due to T by way of improvement grants, contending that the works had not been completed to their satisfaction as required by the Local Government and Housing Act 1989 s.117(3). T brought an action for payment of the grants under the 1989 Act s.113. S, arguing that it was wrong for T to bring an ordinary action in such circumstances and that the correct procedure was an application for judicial review, appealed against a refusal to strike out T's actions.

Held, dismissing the appeal, that, bearing in mind the principles on which the general rule in *O'Reilly v. Mackman* [1983] 2 A.C. 237, [1982] C.L.Y. 2603 was founded, in cases where it was unclear whether the correct procedure had been adopted a court should consider the practical consequences of the choice of procedure, including the interests of the parties, the public and the court. In the instant case, T's relationship with S, as a public body, whether it was statutorily or contractually based, entitled them to conditional rights to payment of grants under the 1985 and 1989 Acts, so that the launch of an ordinary action to enforce those rights did not amount to an abuse of process. There was no reason why a landlord could not bring an ordinary action to recover sums due as an ordinary debt. It was disproportionate for judicial review to be used as a procedure for enforcing payment of a grant or for debt collecting. Any challenge to S's refusal to express satisfaction for work done required an examination of issues of fact, ideally resolved by the court with the assistance of a surveyor's report, and such issues were more appropriately determined in ordinary proceedings than at judicial review.

TRUSTEES OF THE DENNIS RYE PENSION FUND v. SHEFFIELD CITY COUNCIL, *The Times*, August 20, 1997, Lord Woolf, M.R., CA.

491. Abuse of process—plaintiff unsuccessful against third party—second action brought against defendant

In May 1995 S, Y and M were involved in a road traffic accident in the fast lane of a three carriageway road. It was a "concertina" collision with Y in the front, S in the middle and M in the rear. In the first action S sued M as the sole defendant. By her defence M contended, inter alia, that the accident was wholly the fault of Y who had stopped without reason in the fast lane. S did not join Y as a party to the first action and failed against M, the judge finding the accident was wholly the fault of Y. S then sued Y who joined M seeking an indemnity or contribution. M applied to have the action struck out as an abuse of the process of the court under the wider principle of res judicata. It was contended by M (and supported by Y) that if S was to sue Y then she had to do so in the first action since it was inevitable that if she sued Y subsequently Y would join M who would then be required to litigate the whole matter over again.

Held, striking out the action, that the second action was an abuse of the process, *Yat Tung Investment Co Ltd v. Dao Heng Bank Ltd* [1975] A.C. 581, [1975] C.L.Y. 211 and *Talbot v. Berkshire CC* [1994] Q.B. 290, [1993] C.L.Y. 1851 followed.

SADEKALY v. YUSUFALI AND McLEAN, June 16, 1997, District Judge Madge, CC (West London). [*Ex rel.* Russell Bailey, Barrister, 3 Paper Buildings, Temple].

492. Abuse of process—striking out—identical actions issued in High Court and county court

[County Court Rules 1981 Ord.13 r.5.]

I issued proceedings in the county court seeking damages for trespass, nuisance, unlawful eviction and conversion that related to a restaurant business and premises owned by C and in respect of which the parties had entered into a franchise agreement. Shortly prior to these proceedings I had also issued an action against C in the High Court, which he had served together with a statement of claim identical to the particulars served in this action. I had refused C an extension of time to defend and both actions were defended and subject to counterclaims. I had legal aid for both actions. C applied for the county court action to be struck out on the grounds of an abuse of process pursuant to the County Court Rules 1981 Ord.13 r.5. I submitted that there were no authorities to support the principal argument that the issue of two actions in different courts was an abuse of process. In addition I contended that it had been necessary to issue the High Court action to seek an equitable remedy of relief from forfeiture after the expiration of the statutory six month period and that it had always been I's intention to pursue the county court action and to have a stay of proceedings in the High Court action pending trial in the county court. C submitted that for a litigant to issuing identical process in two different courts was an obvious abuse of process that placed the burden upon I to satisfy the court as to a reasonable explanation for the issue of more than one action where the same relief and remedies were claimed. Furthermore, I had actively pursued both actions and C had been obliged to defend in two courts.

Held, striking out the action and ordering I to pay C's costs and ordering I's solicitors to show why a wasted costs order should not be made, that the issue of two identical proceedings was on the face of it an abuse of process of the court and invited such an application, particularly in circumstances where C's solicitor had written to I's solicitor asking for discontinuance of one of the actions and impliedly seeking an explanation which was not forthcoming. Therefore I should provide an explanation and I's counsel submitted that it had been necessary to issue the High Court action as a protective measure by reason of the High Court's jurisdiction for equitable remedy of relief from forfeiture and that it had always been I's intention to seek a stay of the High Court proceedings and to proceed with the county court action. However, far from being a protective measure, I had actively pursued the High Court action and where the court was considering only the question of the county court proceedings, it was of the view that it should be struck out as an abuse of process.

IANNONE v. CICCANTELLI, December 12, 1996, District Judge Owen, CC (Stratford upon Avon). [*Ex rel.* Blackhams, Solicitors, King Edward House, 135a New Street, Birmingham].

493. Abuse of process–striking out–no admission of liability–premature issue of proceedings would be a matter for costs

Following a road traffic accident on December 5, 1995, a letter before action was sent by F's solicitors to both D and D's insurers, on December 7, 1995, requesting an admission of liability. No admission was made by D. D's insurers replied on December 12, 1995, requesting further information. Again, there was no admission of liability, and a notice of intention to issue proceedings was sent by F's solicitors to D's insurers on January 4, 1996, and the summons and particulars of claim were issued on January 5. The defence, dated January 19, 1996, stated that it was admitted that there was a collision and negligence for the collision, but the loss was disputed. A district judge acceded to D's application to have F's action struck out as an abuse of process for precipitous issue of proceedings. F appealed.

Held, allowing F's appeal, that the timetable of events in this case did not have the characteristics of an abuse of process. There was no admission of liability. The court read the defence as stating that F's claim was denied. Although there were other methods of mediation open to F, the dispute in question was capable of resolution by litigation. If proceedings were issued prematurely, any unnecessary costs incurred would be disallowed by the court.

FREETH v. DRISCOLL, April 23, 1996, H.H.J. George, CC (Bolton). [*Ex rel.* Sherrington & Co, Solicitors, Sherrington House, 66 Chorley St, Bolton].

494. Anonymity–informers–waiver of anonymity–no immunity from disclosure on grounds of public interest

S, a police informer, appealed against the refusal to amend particulars of his claim to recover money which the police had allegedly promised him in return for information leading to the arrest of persons involved in serious offences or to the recovery of property. S wished to waive his anonymity to bring the claim but the Chief Constable asserted that to do so would be contrary to the principle of public interest immunity and interfere with the functions of the police service.

Held, allowing the appeal, that although there was a long established principle that immunity from disclosure could not be waived, *Marks v. Beyfus* (1890) 25 Q.B.D. 494 considered, it was not necessarily applicable in all civil proceedings. If a police informer wished to sacrifice his anonymity he should not automatically be precluded from doing so. In the instant case there was no reason to infer that such disclosure might assist criminals or reveal details of police investigations and S should have been allowed to amend the particulars of claim.

SAVAGE v. CHIEF CONSTABLE OF HAMPSHIRE; *sub nom.* SAVAGE v. HODDINOT [1997] 1 W.L.R. 1061, Judge, L.J., CA.

495. Appeals–application to set aside leave–circumstances in which justified

GC applied to have set aside an order granting R leave to appeal an order granting him leave to defend the action against him, conditional on his paying £30,000 into court. GC, a casino owner, sought to recover sums due on five cheques given by R in exchange for gaming tokens but dishonoured by his bank. R contended that he had an arrangement with his bank whereby certain sums could be transferred to honour such cheques but that the money was held in a fixed monthly deposit and would not be available until the end of the month. It was found that R's factual assertions were not incredible and that they disclosed an arguable case that he had reason to believe that payment would be made on presentation of the cheques for the purposes. R argued that given those findings unconditional leave should have been granted, and that in imposing a condition the judge had erred in law. GC contended that there were material omissions from the note of judgment before the judge who granted R leave and that R had not produced any evidence to the court of any agreement with his bank to substantiate his contentions.

Held, refusing the application, that the test to be satisfied on an application to have conditional leave to defend was high, as the intention was to discourage appeals which were not likely to succeed, *Iran Nabuvat, The* [1990] 1 W.L.R. 1115, [1990] C.L.Y. 3735 and *First Tokyo Index Trust Ltd v. Morgan Stanley Trust Co* [1995] 2 C.L.Y. 3925 followed. The judge who had granted leave had considered all the relevant material and concluded that R had an arguable ground for being granted leave without the condition and it was not possible to say that his appeal would definitely fail. The omissions in the judgment referred to by GC were not important because mention was made of those issues elsewhere in the judgment.

GROSVENOR CLUBS LTD v. RASHED, Trans. Ref: FC2 97/5219/E, March 25, 1997, Nourse, L.J., CA.

496. **Appeals—case stated to High Court—no jurisdiction of Court of Appeal to hear appeal—decision of High Court final**

[Magistrates Courts Act 1980 s.111; Supreme Court Act 1981 s.28A, s.18.]

M appealed against the dismissal of his appeal by way of case stated against the decision to grant the application of MCC to stop up as being unnecessary a number of footpaths. The judge rejected the appeal by way of case stated, made pursuant to the Magistrates Courts Act 1980 s.111, and, rather than sending the case back for amendment pursuant to the Supreme Court Act 1981 s.28A(2), proceeded to deal with it himself. M contended that (1) the case should have been sent back, and (2) that he was prejudiced by the fact that he never received a copy of MCC's skeleton argument. M argued that both matters raised points of law on which he could appeal.

Held, dismissing the appeal, that the court had no jurisdiction to entertain the appeal as the 1981 Act s.28A(4) and s.18 prohibited appeals on points of law as well as appeals on fact. The fact that the 1981 Act s.111 was concerned with stating a case on a question of law or jurisdiction meant that a projected challenge to the decision of a judge on hearing a case stated would almost always raise a point of law.

MAILE v. MANCHESTER CITY COUNCIL, *The Times*, November 26, 1997, Hutchison, L.J., CA.

497. **Appeals—leave to appeal on specified grounds—appropriate practice where appellant seeks to rely on additional grounds**

Held, that, where limited leave to appeal on specified grounds had been granted by a Lord Justice, an appellant was entitled to seek to rely on additional grounds only with leave of the court. He should notify the respondent of any grounds for which leave had not been granted and on which he intended to rely. The court could then decide whether it would be appropriate to grant leave, either before or at the hearing of the appeal.

GREENALLS MANAGEMENT LTD v. CANAVAN, *The Times*, May 19, 1997, Lord Woolf, M.R., CA.

498. Appeals–leave to appeal out of time–striking out–inordinate and inexcusable delay

[County Court Rules 1981 Ord.6 r.5.]

H applied for leave to appeal out of time following an incident in which she tripped and fell on a footpath on which certain work was being carried out by M, the third defendant, at the behest of BT, the second defendant. However the pavement was the responsibility of HFLBC and H applied for leave to issue a summons two days inside the statutory period of limitation although there was no schedule of special damages and no medical report as required by CCR Ord.6 r.5. The application was made on February 15, 1995 with an affidavit giving reasons for the delay in filing the medical report and stating that the summons with particulars of claim and medical report and schedule of special damages should have been filed within four months. Leave to issue summons was granted. Validity of summons for service expired on June 14, 1995 and on July 31, 1995 H served the summons and particulars of claim. HFLBC issued a summons for a declaration that they were invalid at time of service and in December 1995 H's proceedings were struck out. H lodged a notice of appeal at the county court and did nothing further for several months. On making an enquiry from the county court as to when the matter would be listed, H was informed that the appeal was to be dealt with in the Court of Appeal, but H still did nothing further for three months.

Held, refusing the application, that it would not be appropriate given the history of delay to grant leave to appeal out of time. The delay was caused by the error of H's solicitor, but the error persisted for an inordinate length of time and there were other remedies available to H.

HILLIER v. HAMMERSMITH AND FULHAM LBC, Trans. Ref: REG 96/7572, March 14, 1997, Kennedy, L.J., CA.

499. Appeals–no appeal as of right in boundary dispute–leave to appeal injunction

[Rules of the Supreme Court Ord.59 r.1B; County Courts Act 1984 s.77; County Court Appeals Order 1991 (SI 1991 1877) Art.3.]

M and Y had adjoining properties. M erected a hut on the terraced area over the basement at the rear of Y's property. Y applied for an injunction that M remove the hut but did not seek a declaration. The injunction was granted and M was further ordered not to trespass on Y's property. The issue to be determined was whether, on the construction of RSC Ord.59 r.1B (1) (i) and the County Courts Act 1984 s.77, M required leave to appeal against the order.

Held, that leave is required to appeal an injunction made in connection with a boundary dispute by virtue of RSC Ord.59 r.1B. Although the injunction did not specify it was a boundary dispute it was a dispute between neighbours relating to the existence, position and course of the boundary in terms of the rule. Thus, on a purposive construction of the rule such disputes required leave. If the case had not involved a boundary dispute M would have had an appeal as of right following the grant of the injunction against him under the County Court Appeals Order 1991 Art.3. Schiemann, L.J. dissenting, that the principle of the right of appeal against an injunction in the High Court or county court, which exists because of the possibility of imprisonment if an injunction is disobeyed, cannot be defeated by the policy considerations or purposive construction of the rules.

YUI TONG MAN v. MAHMOOD, Trans. Ref: LTA 96/7726/G, December 13, 1996, Leggatt, L.J., CA.

500. Appeals–respondent conceded material ground of appeal–unnecessary for court to hear all other grounds to comply with RSC Ord.55 r.7(5)

[Rules of the Supreme Court Ord.55 r.7(5); Tribunals and Inquiries Act 1992 s.11.]

N appealed under the Tribunals and Inquiries Act 1992 s.11 against L's fair rent determination of N's properties. N submitted that although L had conceded that two of the 13 grounds of appeal had been made out and a decision made to remit the matter to the tribunal, the RSC Ord.55 r.7 (5) obliged the court to hear full argument on all 13 grounds so that the tribunal could have the court's opinion.

Held, allowing the appeal, that the court could decline to hear argument beyond that necessary to determine the appropriate relief as part of the exercise of its inherent jurisdiction to control its own procedures. When exercising such discretion, the wider interests of cost and time savings were to be considered, and the court would be reluctant to allow other grounds of appeal to be pursued unless it was necessary to do so in the interests of justice.

NORTHUMBERLAND AND DURHAM PROPERTY TRUST LTD v. LONDON RENT ASSESSMENT COMMITTEE, *The Times*, June 26, 1997, Latham, J., QBD.

501. Applications–leave to appeal–automatic striking out–leave could be granted where appeal had no realistic prospect of success if legal issues required clarification or a public interest existed

C applied for the setting aside of an order granting S leave to appeal against the striking out of an action against C.

Held, dismissing the application, that leave to appeal would only be refused where the court was satisfied that an applicant had no realistic prospect of success, which was the same as the "no arguable case" test, with "realistic" being adopted to show that a merely fanciful prospect or unrealistic argument was insufficient. Applications could be granted even where the test was not satisfied, for example if matters of public interest required examination, or for clarification of legal issues. Where reasons were given for granting leave, it was a misconception to assume that if only one aspect of the proposed appeal was mentioned no other issues were to be determined, unless the reasons clearly stated this to be the case. A respondent seeking to have leave set aside was under a heavy onus to establish that there was no good reason to grant leave, and should also bear in mind that such applications would not be welcomed where they involved parties in the same expense as determining the appeal itself and would not save court time. Whilst a litigant might feel aggrieved when faced with waiting for an appeal which had no prospect of success, the only consequence of set aside applications having to be heard was to delay the determination of purposeful appeal hearings.

SMITH v. COSWORTH CASTING PROCESSES LTD [1997] P.I.Q.R. P227, Lord Woolf, M.R., CA.

502. Applications–leave to appeal out of time–automatic striking out–extent of judicial discretion

Held, that, on an appeal against the refusal to grant leave to appeal out of time from a decision to automatically strike out an action on the grounds of failure to request a hearing date before the guillotine date, it was open to a judge to refuse to extend time on the basis that there was no material offered on which to exercise his discretion. He was not fettering his discretion by relying on *Savill v. Southend HA* [1995] 1 W.L.R. 1254, [1996] 1 C.L.Y. 676, as the matter before him was not dissimilar to a decision to dismiss a claim for want of prosecution.

SMITH v. COSWORTH CASTING PROCESSES LTD (NO.2), *The Times*, May 15, 1997, Waller, L.J., CA.

503. Automatic directions–contradictory request for hearing date–directions complied with

[County Court Rules 1981 Ord.17 r.11.]

F's solicitors, in a default action to which automatic directions under CCR Ord.17 r.11 applied, sent a letter to the court, within the 15 month period, stating "please treat this letter as our formal request for the matter to be set down for trial in accordance with the automatic directions. However we would request that the matter is not passed to listing as we are hoping to agree to the transfer of the case to Hemel Hempstead County Court". P submitted that such a request was contradictory; that it contained a request not to fix a hearing date and that therefore there had been no proper compliance with Ord.17 r.11 (3) (d).

Held that (1) the obligation upon F was not to set the matter down but simply to "request the proper Officer to fix a day for the hearing"; (2) the letter and the accompanying court fee was a proper request, and (3) the statement within the letter that the matter be passed to listing was a reflection of F's intention to apply to have the matter transferred at a later date to another county court. Accordingly the matter was not struck out and P would pay F's costs of, and incidental to, the application.

FOSTER v. PARKER, December 10, 1996, Deputy District Judge Bradley, CC (Banbury). [*Ex rel.* Philip Goddard, Barrister, 1 Essex Court, Temple].

504. Automatic directions—exchange of witness statements—factors affecting discretion to extend time for service

[County Court Rules 1981 Ord.17 r.11.]

P appealed against a decision granting leave to H to serve and rely on three statements not exchanged in accordance with an order made under CCR Ord.17 r.11. In granting leave to serve out of time, the judge took the view that a trial would be impossible without the statements and P contended that the party seeking an extension must give an acceptable reason or excuse for non compliance.

Held, dismissing the appeal, that when considering an application for an extension of time for the service of witness statements, the court must consider the general principles in *Mortgage Corp Ltd v. Sandoes* (1997) 94(3) L.S.G. 28, [1997] C.L.Y. 783 considered, and look at the circumstances of a case before deciding whether to exercise its discretion, *Beachley Property v. Edgar* [1997] P.N.L.R. 197, [1996] 1 C.L.Y. 943.

HOME ENTERTAINMENTS CORP v. PATEL (T/A RAJ MINI MARKET), Trans. Ref: CCRTI 96/1779/G, April 14, 1997, Swinton Thomas, L.J., CA.

505. Automatic directions—interim payments—write off value of car

C was involved in a road traffic accident on October 27, 1996. Proceedings were issued on January 20, 1997. C claimed for the write off value of her motor vehicle; recovery and storage charges; the cost of hiring an alternative motor vehicle and general damages for personal injuries. N, through his insurers, made an interim payment in relation to the write off value of C's motor vehicle before the issue of proceedings. The proceedings included a pleaded claim for this head of damage notwithstanding that it had been discharged. N applied for the case to be referred to arbitration on the basis that the remaining unpaid damages would be below £3,000.

Held, dismissing N's application, that the rules do not distinguish between interim payments made before the issue of proceedings and those made after. The whole claim arose out of one tortious act, and in those circumstances if N settled part but not all of C's claim before proceedings were issued it did not mean the case should be referred to arbitration. The court was not satisfied that the automatic directions should be rescinded in this matter.

CASEY v. NEAL, February 25, 1997, Deputy District Judge Hamlin, CC (Birkenhead). [*Ex rel.* Michael W Halsall, Solicitors, 2 The Parks, Newton-le-Willows].

506. Automatic directions—interlocutory judgments—no requirement to serve witness statements

[County Court Rules 1981 Ord.17 r.11.]

By a consent order dated September 27, 1996 the defendant's solicitors agreed to A's solicitors having an interlocutory judgment entered against them with damages to be assessed and costs. On April 18, 1997 the defendant issued an application that A serve any witness statement of fact that A intended to rely upon at trial, within 14 days. A's solicitors objected on the grounds that CCR Ord.17 r.11 had been disapplied because of the entry of interlocutory judgment and that there was no formal requirement to serve witness statements of fact or indeed, any authority that the defendant could rely upon to compel a statement to be served.

Held, dismissing the application, that there was no provision in the CCR for the service of witness statements of fact once interlocutory judgment had been entered for the plaintiff. The plaintiff was awarded the costs of, and incidental to the application, in any event.

ANDREWS (BRENDA), *Re*, May 1, 1997, District Judge Richardson, CC (Birkenhead). [*Ex rel.* Michael W Halsall, Solicitors, 2 The Parks, Newton-le-Willows].

507. Automatic directions—issue of notice requiring parties to appear for purposes of CCR Ord.17 r.10—whether automatic directions disapplied

[County Court Rules 1981 Ord.17 r.10.]

Held, that a district judge's direction that a notice in Form N233 be sent to parties to a personal injury action requiring them to appear before him for the purposes specified in CCR Ord.17 r.10 did not, ipso facto, disapply automatic directions.

EDMONDSON v. SCOTTISH AND NEWCASTLE BREWERIES PLC, *The Times*, June 21, 1997, Brooke, L.J., CA.

508. Case management—commercial court—extent of Court of Appeal's jurisdiction

Held, that the Court of Appeal should not interfere with a commercial court judge's decision on applications concerning case management unless there were grounds for concluding that the judge had seriously erred or reached a manifestly unjust decision. Such applications were a matter for the commercial court judge and it was not for the Court of Appeal to oversee or direct another court's case management.

GRUPO TORRAS SA v. AL SABAH (NO.2), *The Times*, April 17, 1997, Saville, L.J., CA.

509. Case management—Lloyd's timetable for outstanding litigation concerning reconstruction and renewal package

Held, ordering *Phillips v. Society of Lloyd's* to be heard in the Commercial Court at the same time as *Society of Lloyd's v. Colfox*, that, for case management purposes, all other Lloyd's Names who wished to commence proceedings relating to the Lloyd's reconstruction and renewal package should do so before May 16, 1997, so that their cases could be joined with *Colfox*. The court also provisionally laid down that any further summonses would be heard during the week of June 9, at which time directions would be given for all matters to be decided together in June.

PHILLIPS v. SOCIETY OF LLOYD'S, *The Times*, May 9, 1997, Colman, J., QBD (Comm Ct).

510. Case stated—magistrates courts—resolution of conflicting evidence a question of fact not a question of law—council should have challenged decision by appeal to Crown Court

[Magistrates Courts Act 1980 s.111 (1).]

The user of a motor cycle racing track appealed against a noise abatement notice served on him by F on the ground that his activities constituted a statutory nuisance. The magistrates, after hearing conflicting evidence, decided to accept the user's evidence and allowed his appeal. F applied to the magistrates to state a case pursuant to the Magistrates Courts Act 1980 s.111 (1), and to pose questions, including whether there was any evidence on which a reasonable bench could have found that the user's activities did not constitute a statutory nuisance. The magistrates dismissed F's application as "frivolous", and F successfully applied for judicial review of their refusal to state a case. The magistrates appealed.

Held, allowing the appeal, that "frivolous" in this context meant that the magistrates considered an application to be futile, misconceived, hopeless or academic. Although it was not a conclusion which magistrates should often or easily reach, they were entitled to do so in appropriate circumstances, and, if they did, it would be helpful if they briefly stated their reasons for doing so. The magistrates' resolution of the conflicting evidence before them was a question of fact and F should have pursued its right of appeal to the Crown Court. The question which F had asked the magistrates to pose when stating the case was clearly inappropriate, as a finding of fact could be reviewed by the High Court as an error of law only where it was obviously perverse and lacked any evidential basis, not simply where the evidence of one party was preferred to that of another, *Bracegirdle v. Oxley* [1947] K.B. 349 distinguished.

R. v. MILDENHALL MAGISTRATES COURT, *ex p.* FOREST HEATH DC (1997) 161 J.P. 401, Lord Bingham of Cornhill, L.C.J., CA.

511. Case stated–statement unnecessarily complex–guidance to magistrates

[Council Tax (Administration and Enforcement) Regulations 1992 (SI 1992 613) Reg.45.]

Magistrates appealed, by way of case stated, to determine whether they had been correct on appeal to refuse to order the return of a car. The vehicle had been seized, pursuant to the Council Tax (Administration and Enforcement) Regulations 1992 Reg.45, from the owner, who owed £1,066 in unpaid council tax. The owner contended that bailiffs had failed to hand him a copy of Reg.45 and Sch.5 as required, and that the vehicle was protected from seizure, under Reg.45(1)(a) as being necessary for his business.

Held, remitting the case to the magistrates, and ordering a restatement of case, that a case should state simply the magistrates' findings of fact relevant to the issues involved; the contentions of the parties, and the questions for which answers were required. The statement of the instant case was unnecessarily complex, involving 18 pages, with 70 pages of documents exhibited, where two pages would have sufficed. Guidance was given on how to express succinctly findings of fact and questions to be answered by the court.

UTTLESFORD DC v. BARNES, Trans. Ref: CO/1500/96, October 25, 1996, Jowitt, J., QBD.

512. Case stated–stipendiary magistrates–costs order could be made against magistrate refusing to state case

Held, that, in exceptional circumstances, it was appropriate to make an order for costs against a stipendiary magistrate who had refused to state a case and had continued to refuse to do so even after the judge, upon granting leave to apply for judicial review, had said that, without a stated case, it would not be possible to determine whether the magistrate had erred in her decision. It made no difference that the magistrate had not appeared before the court either when leave was granted or when the substantive application was heard, and the costs order would run from the date on which proceedings were issued.

R. v. METROPOLITAN STIPENDIARY MAGISTRATE, *ex p.* ALI, *The Independent*, May 12, 1997 (C.S.), Latham, J., QBD.

513. Civil Procedure Act 1997 (c.12)

The Act provides for a unified rule committee, known as the Civil Procedure Rule Committee, to introduce a single set of procedures for all civil litigation in both the High Court and county courts in England and Wales. The Act amends the procedure for making and approval of county court practice directions, and places the courts' jurisdiction to make Anton Piller orders on a statutory footing.

This Act received Royal Assent on February 27, 1997.

514. Civil Procedure Act 1997 (c.12)–Commencement No.1 Order

CIVIL PROCEDURE ACT 1997 (COMMENCEMENT NO.1) ORDER 1997, SI 1997 841 (C.30); made under the Civil Procedure Act 1997 s.11. Commencement details: bringing into force various provisions of the Act on April 27, 1997; £0.65.

This Order brings into force the Civil Procedure Act 1997 s.10 insofar as it relates to Sch.2 para.3(a) to the Act which amends the Matrimonial and Family Proceedings Act 1984 s.40 to allow Family Proceedings Rules to make different provision for different cases or areas. This Order also brings into force, on April 27, 1997, the remaining provisions of the Civil Procedure Act 1997 with the exception of some minor and consequential amendments in Sch.2 to the Act. These amendments, which relate to the Supreme Court Act 1981 and the County Courts Act 1984, cannot take effect until the rules made under those Acts are replaced by the Civil Procedure Rules made under the Civil Procedure Act 1997.

515. Costs–acceptance of payment into court–review of taxation

[County Court Rules 1981 Ord.38.]

H applied for a review of the taxation of costs in a claim for damages for noise-induced hearing loss where H accepted a payment into court of £2,000 and at the original taxation the district judge refused to exercise discretion to exceed Scale 1 costs.

Held, allowing the review application, that the approach on review was set out in the CCR Ord.38 r.9(1) namely whether "the judge is satisfied from the nature of the case or conduct of the proceedings that the costs ... on taxation may be inadequate in the circumstances". The judge and two assessors believed that industrial deafness claims did involve more work for solicitors than many other types of cases. Here substantial work had to be done. The judge did not feel inhibited in exercising discretion in r.9(1) by any reference to the case of *Royer v. Llanelli Radiators Ltd* (Unreported) or the phrase "exceptional complexity" which did not appear in r.9(1). An order for costs made in the sum which H and B had already agreed in the event that the review was allowed. B ordered to pay the costs of the reconsideration on Scale 1 and the costs of the review on Scale 2.

HARPER v. BRITISH STEEL PLC, July 9, 1997, H.H.J. Swanson, CC (Sheffield). [*Ex rel.* Graysons Solicitors, 6 Paradise Square, Sheffield].

516. Costs–agreement for consideration–court barred from exercising its discretion to reconsider costs order where parties had reached agreement as to payment of costs

Held, that where parties to litigation had, following judgment on appeal, reached an enforceable agreement whereby the plaintiffs would pay the defendants' costs in consideration of the defendants not claiming the interest payable on the costs, their agreement for consideration prevented the court from exercising its discretion to re-examine the costs order it had made on the merits so as to remedy an injustice, *National Benzole Co Ltd v. Gooch* [1961] 1 W.L.R. 1489, [1961] C.L.Y. 6755 considered.

NEVILLE v. WILSON (NO.2), *The Times*, July 28, 1997, Nourse, L.J., CA.

517. Costs–appeals–Pensions Ombudsman not present at hearing to defend his determination–inappropriate to order costs against Ombudsman

The court allowed an appeal against a decision of the Pensions Ombudsman who did not appear at the hearing of the appeal although named as a party thereto. The pensioner trustee applied for costs against the Ombudsman.

Held, dismissing the application, that it was not appropriate to order costs where the Ombudsman had not made himself a party to the list by appearing at the hearing to defend his determination. To do so in the instant case would be oppressive. There was no unyielding rule that a successful party could always expect to recover costs from someone.

PROVIDENCE CAPITOL TRUSTEES LTD v. AYRES [1996] 4 All E.R. 760, Chadwick, J., Ch D.

518. Costs–appeals–Pensions Ombudsman only liable to pay costs incurred by his participation

Held, that when determining costs on a successful appeal against a decision of the Pensions Ombudsman, the fact that an appeal was necessary to set aside his findings was not an adequate basis for ordering him to pay costs, *Seifert v. Pensions Ombudsman* [1997] 4 All E.R. 947, [1997] C.L.Y. 3996 followed. The correct principle was to order the Ombudsman to pay the appellant's costs only to the extent that they had been increased by his participation.

ELLIOTT v. PENSIONS OMBUDSMAN, *The Times*, November 20, 1997, Blackburne, J., Ch D.

519. Costs–application for stay of costs order–wide discretion under RSC Ord.47 r.1–no special circumstances despite claim being settled in Idaho courts

[Rules of the Supreme Court Ord.47 r.1.]

R applied under the RSC Ord.47 r.1 (1) for a stay of costs orders made pursuant to first instance proceedings of July 1995, subsequently upheld on appeal in January 1997. R contended that, whereas the Court of Appeal had decided that Idaho was the most suitable jurisdiction for the dispute between the parties, the claims there had been settled by agreement. Furthermore, as G had no assets in England and the defendant, A, in a related action was subject to Chapter 11 bankruptcy proceedings in the USA, there were "special circumstances" rendering it "inexpedient" under RSC Ord.47 r.1 (1) (a) to enforce the costs orders from the original proceedings.

Held, refusing the application save for a limited stay pending the outcome of an application for leave to appeal to the House of Lords, that, following the decisions in *Canada Enterprises Corp Ltd v. MacNab Distilleries Ltd* [1987] 1 W.L.R. 813, [1987] C.L.Y. 3003 and *Burnet v. Francis Industries Plc* [1987] 1 W.L.R. 802, [1987] C.L.Y. 3002, the court had a wide discretion to order a stay of costs, dependent upon the size and respective strengths of the claim, the risk to a party of the fruits of the judgment being removed from the jurisdiction and the delay in bringing the application. On the facts, however, although R could find it difficult, if not impossible, to recover the sums paid under the orders given the respective status of G and A and their locations, the delay in bringing the Ord.47 application meant that there was no overall unfairness to R if the costs orders took their usual course.

ROWLAND v. GULFPAC LTD; INOCO PLC v. GULF USA CORP, Trans. Ref: 1995-R-No.744; 1995-I-No.781, May 12, 1997, Rix, J., QBD.

520. Costs–bankruptcy–trustee in bankruptcy liable for costs of action when solicitors instructed to issue notice of intention to proceed

[Supreme Court Act 1981 s.51.]

A trustee in bankruptcy who has instructed solicitors to issue a notice of intention to proceed may be the subject of an order for costs under the Supreme Court Act 1981 s.51.

Held, that costs could be awarded under the Supreme Court Act 1981 s.51 against a trustee in bankruptcy, in respect of an action which had become vested in him, once he had given solicitors instructions to issue a notice of intention to proceed, as he had, at that point, effectively adopted the proceedings and it would be unjust to permit him to evade liability for costs.

TRUSTEE OF THE PROPERTY OF VICKERY (A BANKRUPT) v. MODERN SECURITY SYSTEMS LTD, *The Independent*, October 27, 1997 (C.S.), Peter Gibson, L.J., CA.

521. Costs–Calderbank letter–solicitors failing to take instructions on offers–case proceeding to trial–no order as to costs made

SW made an application that costs should not be awarded to B and the second plaintiff, S, due to their abuse of the court process. Both claimed damages for personal injuries arising from accidents at work but when further details of the negligence and supporting medical evidence were requested by SW's insurers it was not provided. B and S instead issued proceedings and in both cases a defence was filed admitting negligence and a *Calderbank* letter sent stating that proceedings were issued prematurely. Settlements were offered of £2,500 to B and £1,500 to S which were rejected by their respective solicitors before further instructions were taken. At trial B was awarded £2,250 general damages and interest of £60, £395 special damages and £66 interest, and S was awarded £1,250 general damages and interest of £37. SW submitted that in both cases there was a failure to provide an indication of the extent of the claim and the invitation to discuss a possible settlement was ignored. At the time of the *Calderbank* offers SW could not make a payment into court as this would have given B and S the entitlement to their costs. B and S admitted that no discussions or meetings to attempt to settle the claims had taken place prior to issue of proceedings.

Held, allowing the application, that no order as to costs should be made. The solicitors advising B and S were under an obligation to take instructions on the offers made, and the parties should have tried to settle the matter before issuing proceedings.

BAKER v. SOUTHERN WATER; STURGESS v. SOUTHERN WATER, October 14, 1996, Crawford Lindsay Q.C. sitting as a High Court Judge, Mayors and City of London Court. [*Ex rel.* Robin Churchill, Bunkers Solicitors, 7 The Drive, Hove].

522. Costs–claim paid in full–subsequent defence filed–abuse of process–plaintiff's entitlement to taxed costs

[County Court Rules 1981 Ord.11 r.2, Ord.19, r.3, Ord.38.]

N suffered loss and damage in a road traffic accident, A's liability was not disputed. N issued proceedings claiming general and special damages, which were ascertained at £770, and interest. Three days later A's insurer sent N a cheque for the full claim excluding interest, which was accepted and cashed. N requested payment of her costs, but no agreement was reached. N therefore issued an application for a declaration that she was entitled to costs taxed on Scale 1 as A had paid the claim in full. Before the application was heard, A filed a defence admitting negligence but denying causation and quantum, and stating that the matter should be referred to arbitration. The court referred the matter to arbitration, but at the hearing of the application the district judge granted the declaration sought. A appealed from that order, on the grounds that interest was still theoretically in issue and the matter had been properly referred to arbitration under County Court Rules 1981 Ord.19 r.3, so taxed costs could not be awarded.

Held, dismissing the appeal, that the claim was one for unliquidated damages, not liquidated damages, as it included items such as vehicle hire and loss of use and inconvenience. CCR Ord.11 r.2(2), which limited costs to those on the summons after a prompt payment of the full claim, did not therefore apply. CCR Ord.11 r.2(3) thus allowed taxed costs unless the claim was within the scope of arbitration under CCR Ord.19 r.3. In the instant case, all issues between the parties had been resolved before the filing of the defence, as was made clear by N's application which stated that the claim had been paid in full. The defence was meaningless and an abuse of process as it was an attempt to play the rules and limit liability for costs, and consequently there was no reference to arbitration. It made no difference that an interlocutory judgment had not been entered. There was no basis for the exercise of the discretion under CCR Ord.38 r.1 to limit costs to those recoverable under CCR Ord.19 r.4, as N had not behaved improperly in any way. N was entitled, as of right, to her taxed costs under CCR Ord.38 r.2. If it was undesirable that there should be two regimes for costs in relation to small claims, the remedy was in the hands of defendants and their insurers, who should pay up in full before the issue of proceedings if there was no defence to a claim either as to liability or quantum.

NECREWS v. ARC LTD, March 10, 1997, H.H.J. Graham Jones, CC (Cardiff). [*Ex rel.* Ivor Collett, Barrister, No.1 Serjeant's Inn, Fleet Street, London, EC4Y 1LL].

523. Costs–claim settled–negotiations on costs breaking down–appropriate procedure to claim costs

[Solicitors Act 1974.]

G claimed damages for personal injuries following a road traffic accident. Negotiations resulted in a settlement whereby L was to pay £1,750 damages plus G's legal costs and disbursements. Negotiations on costs were unsuccessful and, as the claim had been settled without proceedings, G was unable to tax. Accordingly, G issued an originating application seeking an order that L pay G reasonable costs, such sum to be taxed pursuant to contract and/or terms of the Solicitors Act 1974 on the standard basis unless otherwise agreed. On appeal to the circuit judge the application was dismissed.

Held, dismissing G's application that the appropriate procedure in these circumstances was to bring a separate action in contract, claiming a fixed amount in respect of the costs or alternatively a reasonable amount to be assessed by the court. Such a procedure would have some parallel to an ordinary taxation but would not be a simple taxation. In the same proceedings, it would be prudent for the plaintiff to include an alternative claim pleading the personal injury default action in the usual way. This would cover the situation in which the court did not consider the pre-proceedings correspondence had produced a binding agreement.

GRIEVE v. LINDSAY, July 31, 1995, H.H.J. Corrie, CC (Northampton). [*Ex rel.* Doug Christie, Solicitor, Thompsons, Congress House, London].

524. Costs–claim settled–subsequent defence filed–abuse of process

M and H were involved in a road traffic accident on June 13, 1995. H emerged too early from a side road into which M was turning. The repair costs for M's vehicle were paid by H's insurers prior to issue of proceedings. M's claim was therefore for uninsured losses. Proceedings were issued on May 21, 1996. M's uninsured losses were paid on June 6, 1996 and H filed a defence on June 25, 1996. M applied to have the defence struck out as an abuse of process.

Held, striking out the defence, that as the defence had been filed after settlement of M's claim, it served no purpose and was an abuse of process. H was ordered to pay M's costs, to be taxed on Scale 1 if not agreed.

McGORIAN v. HUGHES, October 21, 1996, District Judge Lambert, CC (Sheffield). [*Ex rel.* Irwin Mitchell, Solicitors, St Peters House, Hartshead, Sheffield].

525. Costs–claim settled–subsequent defence filed–abuse of process

P's claim arose from a road traffic accident in which it was alleged that D emerged from a side road without stopping and collided with P's car. Following unsuccessful discussions with D's insurers, P's solicitors issued proceedings on February 18, 1997. On February 24, 1997, D's insurers contacted P's solicitors and settlement of P's claim was agreed. A cheque was drawn by D's insurers and sent to P's solicitors on February 25, 1997. After a discussion on costs, a defence was filed by D's solicitors on February 25, 1997. P's solicitors contended that the filing of the defence represented an abuse of the process on the grounds that P's claim had already been agreed and in fact, at the time of filing there were no issues on which to form a defence.

Held, striking out the defence as an abuse of the process and awarding P costs on Scale 1 to be taxed if not agreed.

CHARNWOOD CAR CO v. POMFREIT, May 14, 1997, Deputy District Judge Burstall, CC (Sheffield). [*Ex rel.* Irwin Mitchell Solicitors, St Peters House, Hartshead, Sheffield].

526. Costs–claim settled–subsequent defence filed–plaintiff originally accepting fixed costs

L's claim arose from a road traffic accident which occurred on January 27, 1995. E's car had travelled onto the wrong side of the road around parked cars and collided with L's vehicle. E's insurers had no claim form and proceedings were issued. Payment of L's claim was received from E's insurers on September 18, 1995. E filed a defence on May 17, 1996 following correspondence with his insurers regarding L's costs. L had originally agreed to accept fixed costs which were not paid. L applied to strike out the defence as an abuse of process, arguing that the claim had been paid and the defence was filed purely to have the matter referred to arbitration.

Held, allowing the application, that E had acted unreasonably and therefore L was entitled to costs on Scale 1 from the date that fixed costs were requested.

LACEY v. EVANS, July 29, 1996, District Judge Hill, CC (Sheffield). [*Ex rel.* Irwin Mitchell, Solicitors, St Peters House, Hartshead, Sheffield].

527. Costs–conflicting expert evidence–report not disclosed–whether chargeable to defendant

W was seriously injured in a road traffic accident. A young man of high intelligence, W had had an erratic work record, but six months before the accident he had started manual work on low pay. In the schedule of damage served with the proceedings, W's loss of earnings was based on those rates. Subsequently, for the purpose of calculating figure loss, a report was obtained from an occupational psychologist, to assess W's potential but for the accident. The report was detailed, but was not disclosed. W secured substantial damages and costs. On taxation C challenged the fees as between party and party on the basis that as the report had not been disclosed, and had not been relied upon in the amended schedule of damage served prior to trial, the cost of it should not fall upon C. W's experts presented conflicting evidence concerning W's injuries and C challenged both the solicitors' costs in dealing with this, and the additional fees charged on the basis that they were not disclosed and not relied upon.

Held, that as between party and party the experts' fees and the solicitors' fees incurred in relation to them were reasonable and properly incurred, and therefore chargeable to C.

WOODCOCK v. CURRY, July 22, 1997, District Judge Moon, CC (Exeter). [*Ex rel.* DVH Wheeler, Solicitor, Crosse & Crosse, 14 Southernhay West, Exeter].

528. Costs–consent orders–court retains jurisdiction to resolve dispute concerning interest payable on costs

[Judgments Act 1838.]

Where a consent order was made, staying proceedings and allowing the plaintiff, E, to withdraw payments made into court, the court retained jurisdiction to deal with enforcement proceedings for breach of the consent order. After a consent order was made, staying proceedings by E against F and allowing E to withdraw payments into court made by them, E's solicitors delayed in lodging their bill of costs, with the result that F refused to pay interest on the costs for the whole period beginning when the consent order was made. E appealed against the refusal of an order lifting the stay of proceedings so as to allow enforcement proceedings to be brought against F for breach of the consent order. The judge had held that, once E had leave to withdraw the money paid into court, the court no longer retained any jurisdiction in the matter and issues relating to costs were delegated to the taxing master. F argued that the taxing master did not have jurisdiction to resolve issues about interest payable on costs and therefore E's only remedy was to commence new proceedings.

Held, allowing the appeal, that the court retained jurisdiction to make the order sought by E even after a consent order had been made, and it was not necessary to bring a new action. On the correct construction of the consent order, the interest payable on costs under the Judgments Act 1838 ran from the date the consent order was made and not from the date of the taxing master's certificate, *Hunt v. RM Douglas (Roofing) Ltd* [1990] 1 A.C. 398, [1989] C.L.Y. 2935 considered.

ELECTRICITY SUPPLY NOMINEES LTD v. FARRELL [1997] 1 W.L.R. 1149, Kennedy, L.J., CA.

529. Costs–construction disputes–defendant required to pay third party costs–whether court's discretion exercised correctly

C claimed damages against H, alleging that damage to his yacht had been largely caused by a defective deck lamp, refitted by H under an install and supply contract. H alleged that the third party who had carried out the work had done so negligently. Despite almost every issue being resolved in favour of C, C's claim was dismissed because the defective deck lamp was not the cause of the damage. C was ordered to pay H's costs including H's liability for the third party's costs up to the date of the trial. H was ordered to pay the third party's costs of defending the claim including the costs of the trial. C appealed against the dismissal of the action and H appealed against the order for costs, as it limited the liability of C to pay his costs, including H's liability for the third party's costs up to the date of the trial. Both claims were dismissed by the circuit judge who held that the district judge had applied the correct principles. H appealed.

Held, dismissing the appeal, that the court was not entitled to interfere with the judge's exercise of his discretion unless it was shown that (1) he did not have the material before him on which to exercise his discretion in the way that he did; (2) he made an error of principle or took into account matters not relevant to the exercise of his discretion, or (3) he failed to take account of matters relevant to the exercise of his discretion. There was no such error by the district judge nor in the order he made about third party costs, nor any disregard of relevant or irrelevant matters.

CHARLWOOD v. HOOD SAILMAKERS LTD 52 Con. L.R. 123, Mummery, L.J., CA.

530. Costs–contested residence proceedings–father ordered to pay mother's costs–failure of judge to adjourn consideration of father's ability to pay until ancillary relief proceedings concluded

[Legal Aid Act 1988 s.17(1).]

A judge at the conclusion of a lengthy residence hearing found that F had maintained unreasonable views throughout the hearing and ordered him to pay M's costs out of his share of the equity of the former matrimonial home. The judge did not adjourn the question of F's ability to pay until after the conclusion of the ancillary relief hearing. F appealed.

Held, allowing the appeal in part, that, under the provisions of the Legal Aid Act 1988 s.17(1), the judge should have adjourned the question of F's ability to pay costs until after the conclusion of the ancillary relief proceedings. However, the judge had not erred in principle in ordering F to pay M's costs since it was plain that F had adopted unreasonable views and behaved unreasonably throughout the residence proceedings.

R (A MINOR) (LEGAL AID: COSTS), *Re*; *sub nom*. R v. R (CHILDREN CASES: COSTS) [1997] 2 F.L.R. 95, Hale, J., CA.

531. Costs–counterclaims–interlocutory applications–litigation lasting 10 years

D applied for time and leave to appeal against two orders for costs made within an action for a declaration with regard to fishing rights on the Tyne. The final order was for A to pay the costs of the counterclaim to D, but D claimed that he was also entitled to the costs of earlier interlocutory injunctions in which costs had either been awarded against him or where no order for costs had been made. The litigation between the parties had continued for 10 years.

Held, dismissing the application, that there was no prospect of success in any of the appeals since a large number of the costs orders had been made many years earlier and had not been appealed at the time. Nor was there any prospect of success in D's appeal from the dismissal of his earlier appeal against those costs orders.

DIXON v. ALLGOOD,Trans. Ref: LTA 97/5406-5438/K, May 8,1997, Mummery, L.J., CA.

532. Costs-county courts-appeal against decision on taxation of costs was complete rehearing-circuit judge not bound to follow discretion of district judge

[County Court Rules 1981 Ord.13 r.1.]

Held, that an appeal under CCR Ord.13 r.1 (10) from a district judge to a circuit judge on the taxation of costs in a county court case constituted a complete rehearing and the circuit judge was not bound to follow the district judge on issues of discretion.

VANDERSTEEN (EXECUTOR OF THE ESTATE OF McGUINNES, DECEASED) v. AGIUS; *sub nom.* VANDERSTEEN (EXECUTOR OF THE ESTATE OF MAGINNES, DECEASED) v. AGIUS, *The Times*, November 14, 1997, Staughton, L.J, CA.

533. Costs-damage to motor vehicle-cost of superfluous engineer's report could not be recovered

[County Court Rules 1981 Ord.19 r.4.]

M's vehicle was damaged in a collision with N's vehicle. M made a claim under the small claims procedure and was awarded damages of £888, in respect of car repairs and car hire. M also claimed damages of £60 for the cost of an engineer's report prepared prior to the repairs being carried out. The report was commissioned by M's solicitors on behalf of M's insurers and it dealt with the extent of damage and the cost of repairs required. The engineer did not attend the hearing.

Held, that the cost of a report prepared prior to the repairs for the benefit of the insurers and dealing with the cost of such repairs and the extent of the damage was not recoverable as damages, but could, in an appropriate case, be recovered as costs under the CCR Ord.19 r.4(3)(c). If the extent of damage or cost of repair were in issue, then the cost of preparing an engineer's report would be recoverable. However, in this case there was no real issue. No objection had been taken to the garage repair invoice. An expert's report stating that the repairs were necessary was redundant and, consequently, the costs of preparing the report could not be recovered.

MISTRY v. NE COMPUTING, March 20, 1997, District Judge Sonnex, CC (Slough). [*Ex rel.* Lloyd Sefton-Smith, Barrister, Bridewell Chambers, London].

534. Costs-damages-child settlement to be approved by court-defendant liable for costs of approval

[Rules of the Supreme Court Ord.22 r.3, Ord.62 r.5, Ord.80 r.12.]

R was seriously injured in a road traffic accident in October 1993. Judgment was entered against S in January 1995. R's claim included sums for her past and future care to be held on trust pursuant to the principles of *Hunt v. Severs* [1994] 2 A.C. 350, [1994] C.L.Y. 1530, inter alia, for R's children who WEre minors. S eventually paid £425,000 into court. R did not serve a notice of acceptance of payment in the prescribed form but indicated, by a letter dated April 21, 1997, that she wished to accept the monies in court and stating the view that "the most appropriate way to deal with this is for a comprehensive order to be drawn recording the basis of the payments and for the trial judge to be invited to approve the basis of the proposed order". S contended that gaining formal approval of the settlement insofar as it related to minor beneficiaries was not a matter for their concern and they could not therefore be liable for the costs of obtaining approval. The question before the court was the extent of S's liability to meet the costs of the action incurred subsequent to acceptance of the payment in.

Held, that (1) since an element of the claim related to the provision of past and future care of R by minors and the corresponding damages would be held on trust for the same by R, pursuant to the principles of *Hunt v. Severs*, the provisions of the RSC Ord. 80 r.12(1) made it inescapable for R to obtain the court's approval of the settlement, notwithstanding RSC Ord.22 r.3(4), and (2) since R was required to obtain the court's approval of the settlement, it could not be argued by S that all matters immediately come to an end upon acceptance of the payment into court. Therefore the costs of obtaining the said approval would be recoverable notwithstanding RSC Ord.62 r.5(3).

READ v. SMITH, May 12, 1997, H.H.J. MacDonald, QBD. [*Ex rel.* Peter Mitchell, Barrister, 29 Bedford Row, London].

535. Costs–damages for personal injury–payment into court–amount repayable exceeding damages awarded–plaintiff's entitlement to costs

[Social Security Administration Act 1992; Rules of the Supreme Court Ord.62 r.9; Social Security Act 1989 Sch.4 para.12.]

A plaintiff awarded damages in excess of a payment into court, but not personally receiving them, may still recover costs. In a personal injury action against D, M was awarded damages of £33,560, reduced by one third to £22,373 for contributory negligence. In 1993 D had paid £2,500 into court and, following the judgment, M requested a full costs order on the basis that the damages awarded exceeded D's payment into court. D submitted that, as under the Social Security Administration Act 1992, the entire award must be repaid to the DSS compensation recovery unit (CRU), M had gained nothing through the litigation and was therefore the unsuccessful party. M appealed against a ruling in favour of D.

Held, allowing the appeal and varying the order for costs made below to award the costs to M, that although M had personally failed to recover any money in excess of that paid to the CRU, the situation was similar to a subrogated action and it could hardly be held that D had been successful. Where a defendant considered that a plaintiff would recover less than the amount owed to the CRU and he was therefore prevented from making a payment into court, then he should write a Calderbank letter offering a sum not exceeding that contained in the Certificate of Total Benefit (CTB) and pointing out that, if the offer was accepted, then that sum would be paid to the CRU. Should the offer be rejected and the plaintiff subsequently be awarded a lesser sum in damages, then the defendant could rely on the letter under the Rules of the Supreme Court Ord.62 r.9(d). If the defendant considered that the plaintiff would recover more than the sum in the CTB, even if by less than the exempt £2,500, then he should make a payment into court using form A23 and employing the words "The Defendant has withheld from his payment the sum of ... in accordance with paragraph 12(2)(a)(i) of Schedule 4 of the Social Security Act 1989". Order 62 r.9(d) precluded a defendant from making a payment into court and relying on a Calderbank offer in addition or in the alternative.

McCAFFERY v. DATTA (COSTS) [1997] 1 W.L.R. 870, Stuart-Smith, L.J., CA.

536. Costs–defendant wishing to adjourn case day before trial–wanting plaintiff to be medically examined despite being fully recovered

Following a road traffic accident on November 26, 1996 court proceedings were issued on February 3, 1997 and a defence was filed on February 25, 1997. The court was asked to set the matter down for hearing on April 2, 1997 and a trial date was set for June 3, 1997. S issued an application to be heard on June 2, 1997, to vacate the trial listed for the following day, on the grounds that S wished to have P medically examined, an appointment having been arranged for October 1997, notwithstanding that P had made a full recovery.

Held, dismissing the application, that the district judge felt it was far too late to issue such an application, and failed to see the point of having P medically examined when she was fully recovered in any event. The trial went ahead the next day and S was ordered to pay P's costs.

PIERCE v. STEVENS, June 2, 1997, District Judge Wright, CC (Birkenhead). [*Ex rel.* Michael W Halsall, Solicitors, 2 The Parks, Newton-le-Willows].

537. Costs—discretion of judge to increase Scale 1 costs

The parties' solicitors disagreed on the question of costs in a Scale 1 matter which was settled at £3,000, a couple of days before trial. The matter was to be heard before the trial judge with regard to costs, and the court heard arguments from both solicitors. The plaintiff's solicitors argued for quite substantially more than Scale 1 rates on the basis that the matter raised complex issues of a medical nature (it was a noise induced hearing loss case), in which the plaintiff's solicitors were expert and alternatively that Scale 2 costs would be appropriate. In addition, some months previously the plaintiff's solicitors had served a reverse *Calderbank* letter on the defendants at the figure at which this case subsequently settled and therefore claimed indemnity costs from that date.

Held, refusing the application, that whilst there were medical and engineering reports, the case was not exceptionaly complex. The same principle applied not only to the question of whether Scale 2 costs should be allowed, but also to the question of whether discretion ought to be granted to allow a larger sum to be claimed under Scale 1. In addition, the parties being a union on one side and an insurance company on the other, went into such cases fully aware of the costs consequences. The judge therefore ordered that Scale 1 costs should apply and that discretion should not be used to increase those Scale rates.

POYER v. AUSTIN ROVER GROUP LTD, Date not specified, Judge not specified, CC (Llanelli). [*Ex rel.* Howard Palser Grossman Hermer and Partners, Solicitors, Atlantic Wharf, Cardiff Bay].

538. Costs—fixed costs where action compromised

[County Court Rules 1981 Ord.38 r.24.]

C suffered damages in a road accident caused by F. A final settlement of £275 was agreed in correspondence before action by way of compromise, but F made no payment to C. C's solicitors, issued proceedings for an unliquidated sum less than £400 and for costs to be taxed. F elected not to dispute liability or quantum and did not file a defence. C obtained judgment in default assessed at £310 together with costs to be taxed on Scale 1. C's bill of costs amounting to £1,550 was taxed down to £93 representing fixed costs plus the costs of entering judgment on the basis that C should have proceeded on the compromise. C applied for reconsideration of the taxation under CCR Ord.38 r.24(1) on the grounds that (1) the district judge was wrong to go behind the order for costs taxed on Scale 1; (2) F was obliged to file a defence or set aside the costs order if he sought to avoid taxed costs, and (3) the district judge had failed to consider each individual item in the bill.

Held, affirming the taxation, that (1) the district judge was entitled to make findings regarding the earlier conduct of the parties. F was not obliged to file a defence or set aside the costs order solely to avoid the tax costs regime (although it would often be wise to do so) and the district judge retained his discretion to take all appropriate matters into consideration; (2) C should have issued proceedings to enforce the compromise rather than issue for unliquidated damages. This was an attempt to "play the rules" in order to obtain a disproportionate award of costs. Only fixed costs would be allowed, and (3) once that stage had been reached it was artificial and unnecessary to go through C's bill item by item, *Bevis v. Tarmey* [1994] C.L.Y. 3617 distinguished, *Scarrott v. Stratton* (Unreported, 1989) applied.

CURTIS v. FITZGERALD, June 20, 1997, District Judge Karet, CC (Watford). [*Ex rel.* Lloyd Sefton-Smith, Barrister, Bridewell Chambers, London].

539. Costs—indemnity principle

H's action arose from a road traffic accident on March 14, 1995. Liability was conceded at an early stage. In dispute was the amount of special damages to which H was entitled. H hired a replacement vehicle from a company called Three Arrows. The action was settled by acceptance of a payment into court. Following acceptance solicitors acting for H submitted a bill of costs for taxation. T's solicitors raised as a preliminary issue whether H be reimbursed for costs under the indemnity principle. T submitted that there was no agreement between H and H's solicitors. At the hearing on the preliminary issue the district judge heard evidence from H who was served with a witness summons and had the benefit of examining H's solicitors' file of papers. The district judge accepted that T had a heavy burden of proof to satisfy the court that H was not under a personal obligation to pay the costs. The district judge went on to say that T could discharge the burden not only by direct evidence but from all circumstances surrounding the appointment and subsequent conduct of the solicitors. It would only be in exceptional circumstances that T was likely to have any direct evidence. The district judge therefore felt an examination of H's solicitors' file was essential. Upon examination the district judge noted that H's solicitors received instructions directly from a credit hire company and thereafter some time later received instructions from H himself. The district judge did not consider that even with the later letter from H to H's solicitors were in receipt of proper instructions from H. H's solicitors did not send a client care letter and did not make any effort to contact H other than to carry on with the claim.

Held, that T had discharged the burden of proof by the oral evidence of H's confusing contractual documentation, given the dates of initial instruction from credit hire company which raised sufficient doubts for the district judge to carry out an inspection of H's solicitors' files. H's solicitors were not entitled to receive any part and party costs. T's solicitors to recover costs of taxation on an indemnity basis.

HARRISON v. TINSLEY, November 25, 1996, Judge not specified, CC (Pontefract). [*Ex rel.* Nelson & Co, Solicitors, St Andrew's House, St Andrew's Street, Leeds].

540. Costs—instruction of London rather than local solicitors—restriction of liability of unsuccessful party

In determining liability for costs on taxation, the court must have regard to factors other than the presence of competent local firms in establishing whether the successful party's instruction of a London firm was reasonable; however the existence of competent local firms may make instruction of London firms reasonable only when those firms charge acceptable rates. Two cases before the court raised issues as to costs. In the first F appealed against a decision on a taxation appeal that it was not reasonable for him to have instructed a solicitor from London rather than a local firm in connection with an order for the sale of his property. F was subject to an order, registered in the magistrates court, for periodic payments in favour of his two children. M claimed arrears of £5,156.38 and sought to enforce payment by obtaining a charging order on a house in which F and his second wife lived and by applying for an order for sale. F succeeded in striking out the order on the ground that the magistrates court alone had jurisdiction over any enforcement proceedings and a wasted costs order was made in his favour. However, M succeeded on appeal on taxation, contending that F should have used a firm local either to the court or to his home. In the second, a similar case, W was injured at work and was represented by a London firm instructed by his trade union. The defendants, SFL, settled, and subsequently failed, both on taxation and on appeal, in their objections to the hourly rate charged by the London firm.

Held, allowing the appeals, that in the case of W the decision was remitted, (1) notwithstanding the presumption that any doubt would be resolved in favour of the payer, F had managed to discharge the burden of showing that it had been reasonable for him to instruct City solicitors. The judge below had erred by considering only the differential between solicitors' rates and not such relevant matters as, the importance of the case to F; the complexity of the issues; the locations of his home, his work, the relevant court, and the solicitor's firm; and any advice or recommendations that F had received on who to instruct, and (2) in the case of W, it appeared that the union habitually sent all its work to solicitors in London despite the presence of competent local firms in Leeds or Sheffield. Remitting the decision, it was suggested that it might be found reasonable to instruct London solicitors, but only at the rates acceptable locally in Leeds, *R. v. Dudley Magistrates Court, ex p. Power City Stores Ltd* (1990) 154 J.P. 654, [1990] C.L.Y. 892 and *L v. L (Legal Aid: Taxation)* [1996] 1 F.L.R. 873, [1996] 2 C.L.Y. 3872 considered and *Jones v. Secretary of State for Wales (1996)* [1997] 1 W.L.R. 1008, [1997] C.L.Y. 574 distinguished on its facts.

TRUSCOTT v. TRUSCOTT; WRAITH v. SHEFFIELD FORGEMASTERS LTD, *The Times*, October 15, 1997, Kennedy, L.J., CA.

541. Costs–interest on the costs of taxation ran from date judgment granted

[Rules of the Supreme Court Ord.62 r.27 (1).]

R had obtained judgment with costs against O and the costs were ordered to be taxed. R appealed against a decision that interest on the costs of taxation did not run from the date of the judgment, but from a number of subsequent dates on which the taxing master had made costs orders in favour of R.

Held, allowing the appeal, that the order for costs entitled R to interest on the costs from the date of the judgment and that included the costs of taxation. The original order for costs was not affected by any later orders made in R's favour, *Hunt v. RM Douglas (Roofing) Ltd* [1990] 1 A.C. 398, [1989] C.L.Y. 2935 applied, as there was no requirement under RSC Ord.62 r.27(1) that the taxing master make a separate order to cover the costs of taxation.

ROSS v. OWNERS OF THE BOWBELLE [1997] 1 W.L.R. 1159, Leggatt, L.J., CA.

542. Costs–interlocutory judgment–costs should be fixed only where defence filed

O's claim arose from a road traffic accident on July 26, 1994. K's insurers refused to grant indemnity to their insured and proceedings were issued against K. No defence was filed and on May 10, 1996 interlocutory judgment was entered for damages to be assessed. The assessment duly took place at which only fixed costs were allowed. O appealed on the grounds that no defence had been filed and the matter had not therefore been referred to arbitration. O further argued that the case of *Scarrott v. Stratton* (Unreported, 1989) referred to in the County Court Rules 1981 in relation to the costs of small claims, only applied where there was some suggestion that a party was playing the rules. In addition, the CCR encompass two sets of rules, one of which was applicable when no defence had been filed and one applicable when a defence is filed. The rules relating to the entry of interlocutory judgment refer specifically to costs. The case of *Bevis v. Tarmey* [1994] C.L.Y. 3617 suggested that those costs should not be fixed costs.

Held, accepting O's arguments and allowing the appeal, that costs should be awarded to O on Scale 1.

OSMAN v. KAYUM, July 22, 1996, H.H.J. Bullimore, CC (Sheffield). [*Ex rel.* Irwin Mitchell, Solicitors, St Peters House, Hartshead, Sheffield].

543. Costs–judicial discretion to award fixed costs

Following a road traffic accident T issued proceedings for the cost of hiring a car and loss of use. Liability was never in dispute and the cost of repairs to the motor car had been paid before these proceedings were issued. Certain other costs incurred in respect of hiring a car and loss of use, had not been dealt with, therefore T entered interlocutory judgment against D for damages to be assessed and costs on September 17, 1996. No defence was served. Damages were assessed at £1,400 and the district judge ordered that D should pay fixed costs. T appealed by notice seeking to set aside the costs order stating that the district judge had erred by ordering fixed costs, and costs should have been awarded on Scale 1.

Held, allowing the application, that the district judge had erred in exercising his discretion to award fixed costs. T and his solicitors had acted properly, there had been no attempt to play the rules and no abuse of the process of the court, and the district judge had been wrong to act as though they had been. D was ordered to pay T's costs on Scale 1 to be taxed if not agreed.

TOVEY v. DYSON, April 7, 1997, H.H.J. O'Brien, CC (Bury St Edmunds). [*Ex rel.* Betesh Partnership, Cardinal House, 20 St Mary's Parsonage, Manchester].

544. Costs–legally aided plaintiff–enforcement of costs

See LEGAL AID: Wraith v. Wraith. §3344

545. Costs–liability to costs of party pursuing action pending appeal to have action struck out

Held, that where a party chose to pursue an action pending an appeal to have the action struck out, he should, if the appeal succeeded, expect to bear the costs incurred by the appellant during the time the appeal was pending.

ROYAL BROMPTON HOSPITAL NHS TRUST v. CHETTLE; *sub nom.* BOARD OF GOVERNORS OF THE NATIONAL HEART AND CHEST HOSPITAL v. CHETTLE, *The Independent*, November 10, 1997 (C.S.), Aldous, L.J., CA.

546. Costs–liability to costs where party covered by legal expenses insurance

[County Court Rules 1981 Ord.38.]

B suffered personal injuries in a road traffic accident. They had the benefit of a legal expenses insurance policy designed to assist them to claim losses not covered by their road traffic policy. Proceedings were issued and the claim was settled. A consent order was lodged with the court providing that R would pay the first and second defendants damages and would pay B's costs to be taxed on Scale 2 if not agreed. At the taxation before the deputy district judge R successfully argued that there had been a breach of the "indemnity principle" in that a letter written to B by their solicitors at the outset of the litigation stated that: "Please note that the legal costs of the claim will be met by your legal expenses insurance but should the costs fall outside the ambit of the policy then you will be notified before you are committed to any expenses". As a result B's costs were not taxed. B appealed.

Held, allowing the appeal with costs, that (1) B was proceeding on the basis that they were primarily liable for their solicitors costs but as B had insurance they would be covered for such costs. It was clear that where parties legal costs were covered by insurance the parties were primarily liable for costs to their solicitors and that was the basis on which the legal profession operated. It was also plain from the terms of the letter that B's insurers were not primarily liable: if the insurers did not pay B would be liable, and (2) B was correct to appeal to the circuit judge rather than apply by way of review to the district judge pursuant to the County Court Rules Ord.38.

BAYLES AND WING v. RILEY, June 12, 1997, H.H.J. Paynter-Reece, CC (Romford). [*Ex rel.* Paul Corben, Barrister, 169 Temple Chambers, Temple Avenue].

547. Costs–litigants in person–burden of establishing pecuniary loss–RSC Order 62 r.18(3) not ultra vires

[Rules of the Supreme Court Ord.62 r.18; Litigants In Person (Costs and Expenses) Act 1975; Supreme Court Act 1981 s.84.]

M, a litigant in person, obtained judgment and an order for costs against G. M submitted a bill for £87,000 charging her time at a basic rate of £75 per hour, uplifted to £125 and £200. M lodged a detailed breakdown of the bill and an affidavit in support. The taxing master held that M had not proved her claim for a pecuniary loss and allowed only £9.25 per hour pursuant to the Rules of the

Supreme Court Ord.62 r.18(3). M applied to the judge contending that the provisions of RSC Ord.62 r.18(3) were ultra vires and outside the scope of that authorised by the Supreme Court Act 1981 s.84(1) and s.84(2). The burden of proof M submitted, had been on G who, in the absence of any affidavit evidence, had failed to discharge that burden.

Held, affirming the taxing master's decision, that the provisions of Ord.62 r.18 were matters of practice and procedure to define and regulate a litigant in person's right to costs under the Litigants in Person (Costs and Expenses) Act 1975. The provisions were not ultra vires. The question of a pecuniary loss was one peculiarly within the plaintiff's own knowledge and it would be placing too onerous a burden on G to have the burden of proof on such a question. The burden lay on M and the taxing master was entitled to find that she had not discharged that burden.

MAINWARING v. GOLDTECH INVESTMENTS LTD [1997] 1 All E.R. 467, Robert Walker, J., Ch D.

548. Costs–magistrates courts–party against whom costs order to be made must see bill of costs submitted by other side

Held, that, although a magistrate would normally ensure that a party against whom a costs order might be made was made aware of the other party's bill of costs, counsel for the party against whom the order was to be made was still responsible, where necessary, for making sure that the bill had been inspected. A magistrate also had the responsibility of ensuring that the party who might be liable was given an opportunity to comment on the question of the award of costs.

HUTBER v. GABRIELE, *The Times*, August 19, 1997, Gage, J., QBD.

549. Costs–magistrates courts–refusal of costs application–improper exercise of discretion to depart from normal rule that costs follow event

[Building Act 1984 s.76, s.102; Environmental Protection Act 1990.]

B made application against the refusal of their costs application against New Ages. B served a notice on New Ages, pursuant to the Building Act 1984 s.76, declaring an intention to remedy the defective state of the premises. New Ages appealed against the notice under the 1984 Act s.102. The appeal was rejected and ruled to be misconceived on the basis of an absence of jurisdiction as there was no right to appeal against a s.76 notice, and the application by B for costs was refused. E, for New Ages, contending that the s.76 notice had been inappropriate and it was unreasonable for the B to expect compliance with the notice within the nine days stipulated, argued that the appeal was also under the Environmental Protection Act 1990 s.80, s.81 and s.82.

Held, quashing the refusal of the costs application, that the justices either did not properly exercise discretion, or did not have substantial grounds for exercising it in the way they did. No reason was given as to why the justices decided not to award costs.

R. v. BRENT MAGISTRATES COURT, *ex p.* BRENT LBC, Trans. Ref: CO 857-96, November 4, 1996, Ognall, J., QBD.

550. Costs–patent action–no order as to costs where successful defendant raised number of issues which failed

Held, that where defendants in a patent action were successful overall but wasted substantial sums in raising a number of issues which failed, justice could be achieved, and the need for a complex taxation could be avoided, by making no order as to costs, *Elgindata Ltd (No.2), Re* [1992] 1 W.L.R. 1207, [1993] C.L.Y. 3144 and *Rediffusion Simulation Ltd v. Link-Miles Ltd* [1993] F.S.R. 369, [1994] C.L.Y. 3433 applied.

UNITED WIRE LTD v. SCREEN REPAIR SERVICES (SCOTLAND) (COSTS), *The Times*, August 20, 1997, Robert Walker, J., Ch D.

551. Costs–payment into court–claims and counterclaims–determination of issue between the parties

[Rules of the Supreme Court Ord.62 r.9.]

I entered into a contract hiring two copiers, supplied by C, for five years from P. I alleged that an employee of C, who was also acting as the agent of P, made misrepresentations to I by which they were induced to enter into a further agreement which resulted in more expense to I than the first agreement. I then rescinded the second agreement indicating that they would be willing to honour the first agreement provided that they received credit for the expense they had incurred by reason of the misrepresentation. I continued to use the copiers for another year but made no further payments to P. I sought a declaration that the second agreement was either void or had been rescinded, and also sought damages for negligent misrepresentation from P and C. P counterclaimed on the basis that the second contract had not been rescinded and under that contract I should pay them or alternatively that if that contract had been rescinded I should pay P for their continued use of the copiers. Before the action was to be heard, I made a payment into court of less than £5,000 in satisfaction of P's counterclaim, which was accepted by P. P then served a notice of abandonment. At the hearing an order was made discontinuing the action and it was agreed that no order for costs would be made between I and C. I and P then agreed that the only issue between them was the issue of costs. The judge ruled that, as costs follow the event, the payment into court indicated that P was the successful party and no costs would be awarded in favour of I. I appealed on the basis that the substance of the case was whether the second contract had been rescinded and that was the basis upon which the payment into court had been made and accepted. P argued that the court should not go behind the payment.

Held, allowing the appeal and substituting an order awarding costs to I, except in relation to the alternative part of the counterclaim, that (1) while it was true that costs would follow the result, the judge was incorrect to hold that the issue behind the case was one of who owed what money, but rather the issue was to determine the basis on which money was owed, and so the question of the rescission of the contract lay behind the case; (2) RSC Ord.62 r.9(1) required that not only the amount of a payment into court be considered, but that the basis upon which it was made be taken into account, and (3) the facts of the instant case pointed to the action being concerned with restitutio in integrum following the rescission of a contract, and the payment into court was made in satisfaction of P's claim that if the contract was rescinded I owed them money for the use of the machines.

IBEROTRAVAL LTD v. PALLAS LEASING (NO.32) LTD, Trans. Ref: CHAN 96/0678/B, June 19, 1997, Ward, L.J., CA.

552. Costs–payment into court–defendants sued separately–limits and discretion of court

[Rules of the Supreme Court Ord.22 r.3(1), Ord.65 r.5(4).]

C sued W, an architect, and B, a builder, for breach of contract and negligence arising out of alleged defects in a car showroom designed by W and built by B. On March 15, 1996, B made a payment into court in respect of all causes of action. On April 11, 1996, W made a payment into court in satisfaction of all causes of action. C sought leave to take out of court money paid in by the defendants on terms that the defendants should pay the costs of the proceedings or, alternatively, that W should indemnify C against any order that C should pay the costs of B from March 15, 1996.

Held, granting leave subject to payment of costs, that (1) RSC Ord.65 r.5(4) referred to the "costs of the action" meaning the costs as against only the defendant paying in, *QBE Insurance (UK) Ltd v. Mediterranean Insurance and Reinsurance Co Ltd* [1992] 1 W.L.R. 573, [1992] C.L.Y. 3561 followed, *Hodgson v. Guardall Ltd* [1991] 3 All E.R. 823, [1992] C.L.Y. 3562 not followed; (2) the court had no discretion in relation to costs when the payment in was accepted within time, *QBE Insurance (UK) Ltd v. Mediterranean Insurance and Reinsurance Co Ltd* and *Hodgson v. Guardall Ltd* not followed, *Fell v. Gould*

Grimwade Shirbon Partnership (1995) 36 Con. L.R. 62 followed; (3) there had to be exceptional and compelling reasons why a plaintiff who wished to accept a payment in by a defendant where he had sued more than one should obtain a more advantageous order for costs by application to the court than if he had accepted the payment in by following the provisions of Ord.22 r.3(1), *Fell v. Gould Grimwade Shirbon Partnership* followed, and (4) there were no exceptional or compelling reasons in this case and therefore C should recover costs against W up to April 11, 1996, the date of W's payment in but pay the costs incurred by B since March 15, 1996, the date of B's payment in.

CARRS BURY ST EDMUNDS LTD v. WHITWORTH PARTNERSHIP; CARRS BURY ST EDMUNDS LTD v. BARNES GROUP (1997) 13 Const. L.J. 199, Judge Esyr Lewis Q.C., QBD (OR).

553. Costs–payment into court–judge's discretion–meaning of "special circumstances"

E acted as C's solicitors in an action for damages in 1985 which was dismissed in 1991. C then sought to recover damages for negligence from E. E made a number of substantial payments into court. The judge below concluded that the value of the payment in was $837,368 and awarded damages of $824,103.86. C had claimed a great deal more than the damages awarded. It was directed that costs after the final payment into court should be awarded to E as it was within the court's discretion so to do. The judge also concluded that had C beaten the payment in by a narrow margin she would still have awarded costs to E from the date of the final payment in. C appealed against the decision to make that costs order.

Held, allowing the appeal, that (1) the judge's conclusions concerning the calculation of the value of the damages and payments in were wrong. The figures of $841,070 damages and $822,368 were to be preferred because no award of interest should have been made on that part of the damages equivalent to the amount of the interim payment after the date of receipt; (2) it is an established principle that, in the absence of special circumstances, where an award is made that is greater than the value of a payment into court a defendant cannot argue that he is entitled to recover costs, *Findlay v. Railway Executive* [1950] 2 All E.R. 969, [1950] C.L.Y. 7595 applied; (3) the facts of the case, having regard to the high level of costs involved, the large amount of damages claimed and the narrow margin between the amount of the final judgment and the payments into court, were such that special circumstances might be said to exist, and (4) while it was not open to E to claim their costs, it was a valid exercise of the judge's discretion to order that following the date of payment into court each party bore their own costs.

Observed, that if a de minimis rule applied it was in absolute rather than relative terms so that a few thousand dollars would not be covered by such a rule.

CHARM MARINE INC v. ELBORNE MITCHELL, Trans. Ref: QBENI 96/1125/C, July 22, 1997, Evans, L.J., CA.

554. Costs–payment into court–libel action–defendant should pay costs of plaintiff's application to make unilateral statement in open court

[Rules of the Supreme Court Ord.82 r.5.]

Following an accepted payment into court the defendant was not required to pay the costs of the plaintiff's application to make unilateral statement in open court. C had accepted money paid into court by BCC in satisfaction of a libel action, entitling C to costs up to that point. The parties then entered into discussions about the content of a joint statement to be read out in open court. However, no agreement was reached and BCC indicated that whilst they would not agree to a joint statement, they would not oppose C's application to make a unilateral statement. The question for the court was whether BCC should bear the costs incurred by C in issuing a summons for leave to read the statement pursuant to the RSC Ord.82 r.5.

Held, declining to make an order for costs, that, where a defendant had not agreed to a joint statement, but had paid money into court which had been accepted by the plaintiff, the defendant was no longer an active participant in the proceedings and the plaintiff would have to bear the costs of making a unilateral statement under Ord.82 r.5. If the defendant opposed the terms of the plaintiff's statement, costs might be awarded against him if he failed to obtain a significant amendment to the statement from the judge. In this case, although BCC had entered into discussions about the proposed statement, it would not be right to order them to pay the costs of the application under Ord.82 r.5 when the negotiations had been unsuccessful and they had decided to take no further part in the action.

COFF v. BERKSHIRE CC, *The Independent*, February 6, 1997, Drake, J., QBD.

555. Costs–payment into court–plaintiff beating payment in following supplemental witness statement

In an action for damages H obtained judgment in excess of monies paid into court, but appealed against an order limiting costs up to the date of the payment in, and awarding M costs thereafter. The court found that had it not been for service of a supplemental witness statement 10 days before trial, which went almost exclusively to H's claim for disadvantage on the labour market, H would probably have failed to beat M's payment in. H's claim for disadvantage on the labour market had previously been pleaded, but not particularised. M gave notice of its intention to oppose any application for the statement to be admitted. H sought leave on the first day of trial. The recorder offered M an adjournment, which M declined, on the basis that the amount involved did not warrant it. The trial proceeded, and H was awarded £23,202 beating M's payment into court of £20,000.

Held, dismissing the appeal, that there was nothing in the recorder's reasoning which justified interference with the exercise of his discretion. H's submissions that M had had notice of the nature of the claim from medical reports served, and that the recorder's decision was flawed because he had mistakenly believed M had expressly reserved its position on the question of costs when agreeing the adjournment, were rejected.

HARMER v. MacKENZIE GLASS (EXETER) LTD, June 27, 1997, Potter, L.J., CA. [*Ex rel.* Lyndi Hughes, Solicitor, Bond Pearce, Darwin House, Southernhay Gardens, Exeter].

556. Costs–payment into court–plaintiff under disability–general practice regarding costs still applicable

[Rules of the Supreme Court Ord.80 r.10.]

Held, that where a plaintiff under a disability rejected a payment into court made by the defendant in an action for damages in respect of personal injuries and was subsequently awarded damages amounting to less than the payment in, the general practice of the court to order the plaintiff to pay the defendant's costs from the date of the payment in was still applicable. The only situation in which it would not be appropriate was where the plaintiff's next friend had decided to accept the payment in, but the court, exercising its powers under RSC Ord.80 r.10, had not approved such acceptance.

ABADA v. GRAY, *The Times*, July 9, 1997, Lord Woolf, M.R., CA.

557. Costs–payment into court–refusal of pre-action offer–defendant seeking payment of costs

[County Court Rules 1981 Ord.11 r.3.]

The plaintiffs appealed from an order awarding S his costs of a claim brought against him by the first plaintiff. Liability was admitted. Before action, during negotiations between the parties, S had offered one, or both, of the plaintiffs the sum of £2,500 in settlement of their claim. The first plaintiff claimed that no such offer had been made to her. Proceedings were issued and S paid in £2,500 in settlement of the first plaintiff's claim. The first plaintiff accepted that sum on the day after the payment in was made.

Held, allowing the appeal, that, the first plaintiff had an absolute right under CCR Ord.11 r.3(5) to her costs, *Stafford Knight v. Conway* [1970] C.L.Y. 401 and *Hudson v. Elmbridge BC* [1991] All E.R. 55, [1992] C.L.Y. 3564 followed. Notwithstanding the clear wording of CCR Ord.11 r.3(5), the county court has a jurisdiction to prevent an abuse of process. The correspondence between the parties did, on close inspection, reveal a pre-action offer of £2,500 to the first plaintiff, but it did not protect S against the normal rule as to costs following the acceptance of a payment in, because, inter alia, S's offer was silent as to whether or not it included the plaintiff's "reasonable costs". Leave to appeal to the Court of Appeal was granted to S.

WARMAN & WARMAN v. SMITH, January 3, 1997, H.H.J.Viljoen, CC (Barnet). [*Ex rel.* David McIlroy, Barrister, Chambers of Michael Parroy Q.C., 3 Paper Buildings, Temple].

558. Costs–plaintiff's insistence on unfair statement being read in court

See TORTS: Williamson v. Commissioner of Police of the Metropolis. §4857

559. Costs–premature issue of proceedings

[Rules of the Supreme Court Ord.37 r.2.]

A motor car accident occurred on April 9, 1996 in which W's vehicle was damaged. W claimed the cost of the repairs plus car hire. W's solicitors wrote a pre-action letter to L on May 7, 1996 and proceedings were issued on June 4, 1996, no response having been received save a telephone call on May 24, 1996 from L's insurers asking that proceedings should not be issued. The insurers wrote on June 6 asking for full details of the claim, to which W's solicitors replied on June 13 giving the details requested. On June 14, 1996 the insurers confirmed that liability would not be in issue and again asked for full details of the claim. On June 24, 1996 the insurers' solicitors wrote asking for the case number to file a defence. W's solicitors replied on June 26, 1996 giving them this information and on the same day applied to enter judgment. Judgment in default of defence was entered. Damages were assessed on August 7, 1996 in the sum of £976 and W was awarded costs on Scale 1. The action had been limited to £1,000. On October 8, 1996 the insurers' solicitors applied to the court for costs to be restricted to fixed costs, on the grounds that proceedings had been issued prematurely without allowing the insurers an opportunity to negotiate settlement.

Held, dismissing the application, that this was an appeal "through the back door" against the district judge's order and was not an application to set aside judgment under RSC Ord. 37 r.2. The district judge considered that he did not have the jurisdiction to deal with the matter on the basis of the application, the facts and the terms of the order, but if there was any such jurisdiction, in the instant case there had been no playing of the rules by the plaintiff to obtain an order for costs. Any delays were those of the defendant, evidenced by the fact that there was at least six weeks' delay between the order of August 7, 1996 and the application of October 8, 1996. If an application had been made under Ord.37 r.2 it should have been made forthwith, but the instant application was not made under Ord.37 r.2, but was in effect an appeal against the Scale 1 costs order.

WILLIAMS v. LOWE, December 23, 1996, District Judge Williams, CC (Mold). [*Ex rel.* JC Kelsall, Solicitor, Bartlett & Son, 6 & 16 Nicholas Street, Chester].

560. Costs–proceedings wrongly brought against second defendant–plaintiff aware that first defendant responsible for accident

On October 8, 1995 a car driven by Q collided with a motorcycle driven by K, propelling K into S's car. S's solicitors wrote to K alleging 100 per cent liability on her part for damages to S's car. In November 1995 K's solicitors obtained a copy of the police report from which it was clear that the accident was caused entirely by Q. Q was subsequently convicted of driving with excess alcohol and driving without insurance. K's solicitors wrote to S's solicitors on December 13, 1995 informing them of this and denying liability. Thereafter K issued proceedings against Q in April 1996 and informed S's solicitors of this. In April 1996 S's solicitors again alleged liability on K's part. K's solicitors again referred them to available evidence. In September 1996 S's solicitors issued proceedings against both Q and K alleging negligence. K issued a defence denying all liability. Q issued a defence admitting liability, but disputing quantum. In January 1997 S settled with Q on the basis of 100 per cent liability for a figure of approximately £350 less than claimed. S then indicated an intention to discontinue against K. K refused to discontinue without payment of costs by S. S refused and therefore K made an application on the arbitration hearing for costs. S made a counter-application that any costs awarded against S be paid by Q.

Held, that for K to recover costs, it was necessary to show S had been unreasonable in proceedings against K. S had not disclosed in correspondence any reasonable grounds for proceedings against K. The fact that there had been no evidence to support S's contention that K was liable and that Q had been convicted supported K's application that it was unreasonable to proceed against K. K could therefore recover costs from the date of availability of the police report. On counter-application for S to succeed it must be shown that Q had acted unreasonably. Q had issued a defence which was provided for under the County Court Rules and could not be criticised. S's application must therefore fail and as there had been no reasonable chance of success and as S's application had meant that Q had had to attend despite having settled, S must therefore pay Q's costs of attending the hearing.

SALES v. QUINN AND KYLE, March 17, 1997, District Judge Langley, CC (Central London). [*Ex rel.* Michael Poole, Solicitor, David Levene & Co, David Levene & Co, Ashley House, 235-239 High Road, Wood Green, London].

561. Costs—real property—application for access to neighbouring land—owners acting unreasonably

[Access to Neighbouring Land Act 1992.]

W wished to redevelop part of his property, the Coach House, and sought access via E's property amounting to the construction of scaffolding from which to work. In summer 1995 W and E discussed the proposals for the Coach House and workmen entering E's property, at which time E (especially the first respondent) gave their consent for the work and access. In December 1995 W's architect sent presentation drawings to E indicating that if they sought further information they could contact either the architect or W. E did nothing. E objected to access by a letter dated June 2, 1996. Thereafter W's builder wrote to E on August 8, 1996 indicating the reason for and position of the scaffolding and inviting E to discuss the matter. E wrote refusing their consent. Thereafter W wrote to the respondents on August 15, 16 and 20, 1996 attempting to gain access and his solicitors wrote on September 3, 1996. W also attended at E's home where he was refused an audience and attended the first respondent's offices without success. The correspondence had informed E of the Access to Neighbouring Land Act 1992. An originating application was issued on September 11, 1996 and E replied on November 25, 1996 indicating they were prepared to allow access on strict conditions including that W pay their costs. W's builder replied in a letter of November 28, 1996 indicating almost all of the conditions could be met. Thereafter, E sought to attach further conditions by their solicitor's letter of January 20, 1997 including a payment into court of £2,000 and for E's costs to be paid on County Court Scale 2. W's builder was able to agree the terms sought, save for payment into court and costs. At trial the terms were agreed between the parties, there being no payment into court.

Held, that E had taken an unreasonable attitude and W had done all that was possible and accordingly E was ordered to pay W's costs on Scale 1. E, on a set off basis, was allowed the cost of one consultation with a solicitor to obtain advice.

WILLIAMS v. EDWARDS AND EDWARDS, April 30, 1997, H.H.J. Masterman, CC (Cardiff). [Ex rel. Julian Winn Reed, Barrister, 32 Park Place, Cardiff].

562. Costs–security–action funded by third party–court had no jurisdiction to grant stay of proceedings unless abuse of process existed

[Rules of the Supreme Court Ord.23; Supreme Court Act 1981 s.51 (1).]

A appealed against a decision ordering him to disclose to the fifth and sixth defendants whether his action was being funded by a third party and, if so, the identity of that third party. The court had held that proceedings could be stayed where a plaintiff was being funded by a third party against whom a costs order in favour of a successful defendant might be difficult to enforce.

Held, allowing A's appeal, that, unless an abuse of process existed, there was no jurisdiction to compel a plaintiff to provide security for costs outside the regime specified in RSC Ord.23. To allow the imposition of a stay of proceedings in the absence of such security would be to fetter the individual's right of access to the courts to pursue a bona fide claim and would be to act in opposition to the underlying policy of the legislation. Where a defendant suspected third party funding would make a costs order difficult to enforce, the proper course of action was to apply for a determination under the Supreme Court Act 1981 s. 51 (1) once the action had proceeded to trial.

ABRAHAM v. THOMPSON, *The Times,* August 19, 1997, Potter, L.J., CA.

563. Costs–security–appropriate amount–plaintiff unable to pay costs from own resources–other resources available

G appealed against an order for security for costs totalling £100,000 in an action for an injunction, a declaration and damages in relation to a distribution agreement for M's mobile telephones. M cross-appealed and argued that the sum in security should be £300,000.

Held, dismissing both the appeal and the cross-appeal, that, although G appeared to be unable to provide security for M's costs itself, it had associated companies with substantial assets. M admitted owing at least £70,000 to G and it would be unjust to prevent G from continuing with its claim by ordering the oppressive sum of £300,000; consequently, a figure of £100,000 was appropriate, *Sir Lindsay Parkinson & Co v. Triplan Ltd* [1973] 1 Q.B. 609, [1973] C.L.Y. 2632 and *Keary Developments Ltd v. Tarmac Construction Ltd* [1995] 3 All E.R. 534, [1996] 1 C.L.Y. 724 followed.

GLOBEWIDE COMMUNICATIONS LTD v. MERCURY PERSONAL COMMUNICATIONS LTD, Trans. Ref: 1997-G-134, May 16, 1997, Judge Toulmin Q.C., QBD.

564. Costs–security–burden of proof

[Companies Act 1985 s.726(1).]

E appealed against a master's decision refusing to order security for costs against U in an action not yet set down for trial, concerned with issues of contract and intellectual property. E sought money under the Companies Act 1985 s.726(1) on the basis that there was reason to believe that U would be unable to meet E's further costs. It was accepted by both parties that U would be unable to do so if ordered to pay them immediately, but U argued that there was likely to be sufficient funds at the date of trial to meet any costs. E put in a bill of costs which U criticised on the basis that it over estimated the time to be spent on the case. E submitted that intellectual property proceedings always involved difficult and technical work and any uplift was justified on this basis.

Held, dismissing the appeal, that (1) section 726(1) considered U's position at the date the supposed costs order would be made, not at the date of the application for security. Accordingly, if U would not be able to pay costs at the date of the application but would be able to do so at trial, security for costs would not be ordered. If U was unable to pay immediately, the burden of proof was on them to show that the position would be different at trial; (2) just because the action was concerned with intellectual property law did not justify E inflating its costs in support of its security for costs application. The patent in issue concerned the simplest type of mechanical device and there was no material before the court to suggest that the issues involved were complex and (3) E had failed to show that U would be unable to pay E's further costs at trial, estimated at no more than £30,000, and therefore there was no jurisdiction to order security.

UNI-CONTINENTAL HOLDINGS LTD AND ADLOCK PACKAGING LTD v. EUROBOND ADHESIVES LTD [1996] F.S.R. 834, Laddie, J., Ch D.

565. Costs—security—stay of execution—use of assets subject to charging order for appeal

C claimed that S had fraudulently conspired to divert a substantial amount of C's business and funds to Sun Ltd, a company controlled by S. C obtained a Mareva injunction restraining S from disposing of his assets and an order that S pay $750,000 and costs. S claimed that he had assets of approximately £100,000 and that Sun Ltd had no assets. S gave notice of appeal and sought to use his assets to fund the costs of his appeal. He subsequently sought a stay of execution. C contended that as the process of execution would render S impecunious, he should be required to provide security of costs of the appeal. S argued, in reliance upon *Customs and Excise Commissioners v. Norris* [1991] 2 W.L.R. 962, [1991] C.L.Y. 873, that the process of execution was equated with the Mareva process in that the court should not permit the process of execution to deprive S of the means of funding his appeal any more than a Mareva injunction permitted a defendant to be deprived of the means of funding his defence.

Held, dismissing the application, that (1) a very wide approach to the exercise of discretion in deciding whether or not to grant a stay should be adopted, *Winchester Cigarette Machinery Ltd v. Payne (No.2)* Times, December 15, 1992, [1994] C.L.Y. 3779 applied, and (2) as there was a risk of C suffering irremediable harm should a stay be granted, but no similar detriment to S, it was not in the interest of justice to order a stay of execution, *Customs and Excise Commissioners v. Norris* distinguished. In addition, S's appeal did not have sufficient chance of success so as to justify exposing C to the injustice of having to bear its own costs. Accordingly, a security for costs order was granted.

COMBI (SINGAPORE) PTE LTD v. SRIRAM, July 23, 1997, Phillips, L.J., CA.

566. Costs—security—whether automatic directions displaced

[Companies Act 1985 s.726(1); County Court Rules 1981 Ord.17 r.11.]

On October 28, 1993 H commenced proceedings in respect of an alleged breach of contract on October 7, 1993. On December 5, 1994 H was ordered to provide security for costs pursuant to the Companies Act 1985 s.726(1) in the sum of £10,000. Pending provision of the security the proceedings were stayed. No further steps were taken in the proceedings until August 1996 when H endeavoured to provide security and sought to have the stay removed. PS applied for a declaration that the proceedings should be struck out pursuant to CCR 1981 Ord.17 r.11, or alternatively an order that the proceedings be dismissed for want of prosecution.

Held, that the proceedings were struck out pursuant to CCR Ord.17 r.11. The order for security to be given had not displaced the automatic directions regime, *Downer and Downer Ltd v. Brough* [1996] 1 W.L.R. 575, [1996] 1 C.L.Y. 918 distinguished. The stay did not excuse H from complying with directions, *Whiteley Exerciser Ltd v. Gamage* [1898] 2 Ch. 405 applied. H had taken no steps for 20 months either to comply with or to vary the order of December 5,

1994 and must bear the consequences of their inaction, *Thomas Storey Engineers Ltd v. Wailes Dove Bitumastic Ltd* Times, January 21, 1988 applied.

HAMPSHIRE TECHNOLOGY ORGANISATION LTD v. PEGASUS SOFTWARE LTD, November 21, 1996, District Judge Willis, CC (Southampton). [*Ex rel.* Andrew Bruce, Barrister, 3 Paper Buildings, Temple].

567. Costs–small claims–aggregate of claim exceeded limit–whether costs should be fixed

[County Court Rules 1981 Ord.19 r.3, Ord.19 r.4.]

P applied for an order restricting the plaintiffs' to fixed costs. N was driving KL's lorry in the course of his employment when on May 12, 1995 it was in collision with a motor car driven by P. It was undisputed that the resulting injuries of N were never going to exceed £1,000 in terms of general damages, nor would the loss to KL, ie. the damage to the lorry, exceed £1,000, which at the date of issue was the limit for small claims arbitrations. In the event the action was settled upon N and KL accepting £540 and £790 respectively, which monies were paid into court on August 6, 1996. P argued that, for the purposes of assessing whether or not either or both of the plaintiffs' claims were properly referable for small claims arbitration and so governed by the costs provisions of CCR Ord.19 r.4, each of the two claims must be looked at and evaluated separately. P relied upon the undoubted proposition that where two or more plaintiffs each recover damages the court was not entitled to aggregate the sums recovered for the purposes of determining the appropriate scale of costs, *Haile v. West* [1940] 1 K.B. 250. The argument that each plaintiff's claim should similarly be valued separately when deciding whether Ord.19 applied, found favour in *French, French and French v. Barlow* [1994] C.L.Y. 3566. However in *Wright and Wright v. Holman* [1994] C.L.Y. 3604 where two plaintiffs respectively settled their claims at £525 and £625 it was held that it was enough to avoid Ord.19 to show that the aggregate of the claims exceeded the maximum limit for small claims arbitration. That decision was followed in *Smith and Smith v. Bishop* [1995] 2 C.L.Y. 3973. It was argued on behalf of the plaintiffs that the wording of Ord.19 r.3(1) itself supported this approach: "any proceedings ... in which the sum claimed or amount involved does not exceed £3,000 (leaving out of account the sum claimed or amount involved in any counterclaim) shall stand referred for arbitration".

Held, dismissing the application, that each plaintiff had a separate cause of action, which was properly joined in the same proceedings by reason of the nexus of one accident which caused two losses. Since Ord.19 referred not to "any course of action" but to "any proceedings" it can only have been the intention of the draftsman to take the global approach. The plaintiffs were awarded costs on Scale 1, *Wright and Wright v. Holman* and *Smith and Smith v. Bishop* applied.

NEWTON AND KLUBER LUBRICATIONS v. PRIME, Date not specified, Deputy District Judge Miller. [*Ex rel.* Richard Copnall, Barrister, Pearl Chambers, Leeds].

568. Costs–small claims–claim for general and special damages

[County Court Rules 1981 Ord.19 r.3(1A) (b).]

Q appealed against a decision refusing Q's claim for costs to be taxed on Scale 1 following his acceptance of the sum of £1,059 which was paid into court by B in settlement of a claim for damages arising out of a road traffic accident. B claimed general damages for pain suffering and loss of amenity, loss of use of his motor vehicle and special damages consisting of loss of earnings of £61, travelling expenses at £21, replacement cost of pictures and frames damaged in the accident at £109 and other incidental expenses in the sum of £25. The particulars of claim specifically limited damages to £3,000. B sustained minor injuries in the accident which were resolved in two weeks. Q admitted negligence but specifically averred that B had no reasonable expectation of recovering damages for pain and suffering and loss of amenity in excess of £1,000. On October 26, 1996 Q paid into court the sum of £1,192 of which

£1,059 was in respect of B's claim for damages and interest, and £132 in respect of fixed costs on the summons. On January 31, 1997 B sought the court's leave to accept out of time the sum of £1,059 paid into court and claimed to be entitled to costs to be taxed in default of agreement on a standard basis on Scale 1. B claimed that because the action included a claim for personal injuries and had been settled in B's favour in excess of £1,000 the proceedings fell within CCR Ord.19 r.3 (1A) (b) and were not therefore automatically referred to arbitration. Before the district judge B conceded that the personal injury element of the claim was never anticipated to exceed £1,000 and that both sides agreed the value of the personal injury element at £750. B argued that a logical interpretation of Ord.19 r.3 would take out of the arbitration forum any claim exceeding £1,000 in total which included some element of personal injury. Q argued because Ord.19 r.3, para.1A referred to proceedings which included a claim for damages for personal injuries, the court was constrained to look at the personal injury element alone plus any claims which arose as a direct consequence of the personal injuries.

Held, dismissing the appeal, that it was necessary to construe RSC Ord.19 r.3 to achieve access to justice and an informal forum in which small cases could be disposed of. The judge stated that the interpretation argued for by B would give rise to quixotic results and he contemplated a situation where a case involving a nominal claim for slight personal injury might fall to be tried outside the arbitration jurisdiction simply because the injured plaintiff might have sustained damage to an expensive item of property thereby increasing the overall value of the claim to a sum in excess of £1,000. A claim brought by a similar plaintiff who had escaped personal injury but had sustained the same property damage would remain in the arbitration forum if the total value of the claim were less than £3,000. The judge's order was upheld and B was entitled to recover fixed costs on the summons.

BUNCE v. QUINN, March 5, 1997, H.H.J. Pugsley, CC (Stoke on Trent). [*Ex rel.* Sean Hale, Barrister, St Mary's Chambers, 50 High Pavement, Nottingham].

569. Costs—small claims—default judgments—fixed costs not appropriate where claim not referred to arbitration

In a claim limited to £1,000, judgment was entered in default of a defence, for damages to be assessed and costs. H sought costs on Scale 1, A argued that fixed costs only should be awarded, given the value of the claim.

Held, that the special costs regime only applied to a case referred to arbitration, and not, necessarily, to a case below £1,000. In addition, *Video Box Office v. GST Holdings* [1990] C.L.Y. 3593, clearly demonstrated the court's approach that, whilst apparently unsatisfied with the state of the rules, the court took the view that small claims costs were to be treated differently whether or not they were referred to arbitration. In the present case the entering of the default judgment had the effect that this case was not referred to arbitration and the normal costs rules would apply. Finally, *Afzal v. Ford Motor Co Ltd* [1994] 4 All E.R. 720, [1995] 2 C.L.Y. 3897 clearly encouraged defendants to state the value of the claim in any defence, and this had not been done in this case. Costs were awarded to H on Scale 1.

HALL v. ABU NASSAR, Date not specified, District Judge Henson, CC (Uxbridge). [*Ex rel.* Caspar Glyn, Barrister, 3 Paper Buildings, Temple].

570. Costs—small claims—defendant not admitting liability—plaintiff seeking Scale 1 costs following settling of claim

As the result of a collision in April 1995, liability for which was denied, J suffered damage to his motor vehicle. County court proceedings were commenced in December 1995 seeking £1,111 repair costs and £560 for loss of earnings. Before those proceedings, in September 1995, M's insurers had sent a cheque for the repair costs (with another in October for the VAT element), but marking both payments "without prejudice to liability". When served with particulars of claim M served a defence which admitted liability but put J to strict proof on loss and damage. In subsequent correspondence they admitted the repair costs and offered £180 for the loss of earnings with fixed costs only. J accepted £180 for the balance of the claim but insisted on Scale 1 costs. At the hearing M argued that, following *Eccleston v. DJ Ryan & Sons* [1997] C.L.Y. 726, the bulk of the claim had been settled before proceedings and J therefore had no legitimate expectation of an award exceeding £1,000 (the arbitration limit then in force). J argued that he was both entitled and obliged to pursue a Scale 1 claim as liability had been denied and the repair costs only paid without prejudice to liability, these being fully refundable if M contested the action successfully.

Held, awarding J £1,291 plus Scale 1 costs, that M's insurers could not have it both ways. They could have admitted liability, even for part of the claim, but had not done so. Otherwise J had no option but to sue for the full sum, above the arbitration limit. Payment expressly made conditional on the outcome of liability could not give them protection within *Afzal v. Ford Motor Co* [1994] 4 All E.R. 720, [1995] 2 C.L.Y. 3897 so as to prejudice J.

JAMES v. MALIK, July 17, 1997, District Judge Cernik, CC (Northampton). [*Ex rel.* Adrian Salter, Barrister, 11 Stone Buildings, Lincoln's Inn].

571. Costs–small claims–expert evidence–engineer's report on motor vehicle– experts fees are claimable in small claims arbitration

[County Court Rules 1981 Ord.19 r.4.]

S was involved in a road traffic accident which occurred on June 11, 1996, in which S's vehicle was damaged beyond economical repair with a pre-accident value of £900. An engineer's report stated that the vehicle had a pre-accident value of £1,000, a salvage value of £100 and stated that an equitable settlement would be £900. Liability was denied by B's insurers and court proceedings were commenced on October 29, 1996. A defence was filed by B's insurers, on November 13, 1996 denying that B was involved in the road traffic accident and stating that B had merely stopped following an accident to assist S. On April 7, 1997 the engineer's report was served on B and on April 14 B's insurers replied to S that the engineer's report was agreed subject to liability. This matter proceeded to arbitration hearing at Mold county court on June 30, 1997. The district judge found in favour of S on liability and awarded £1,357. However, he would not allow the engineer's fee of £61 by stating that it was not an expert's report and the fees were therefore not claimable in arbitration. He went on to state that had the authors of the reports been present then these would have been claimable, *Mistry v. NE Computing* [1997] C.L.Y. 533. S appealed against the refusal to allow the engineer's fees.

Held, allowing the appeal, that the fees of an expert included the preparation of a report and attendance at court and such fees were limited to £200 by CCR Ord.19 r.4(3). The judge took the view that the district judge incorrectly applied the rules in concluding that the fees of an expert who did not attend court could not be allowed. He ordered that the arbitration award made by the district judge be set aside only insofar as it failed to conclude the sum of £61 in respect of the engineer's report. B was ordered to pay the costs of the appeal on Scale 1 to be taxed if not agreed.

SMITH v. BOGAN & SONS LTD, August 8, 1997, H.H.J. Davies, CC (Chester). [*Ex rel.* TR Morris, Solicitor, Bartlett & Son, 16 Nicholas Street, Chester].

572. Costs–small claims–limit of claim did not avoid costs

M sought leave to appeal, out of time, against a decision striking out his claim as disclosing no cause of action and ordering him to pay costs. M contended that the order for costs was unjust on the ground that he had sought to avoid the risk of having to pay such costs by limiting his claim to £3,000 so as to bring it within the arbitration jurisdiction of the county court.

Held, dismissing the application, that in the absence of specific pleadings the judge was entitled to strike out the claim as disclosing no cause of action. The judge then had a discretion as to the measure of costs, it being irrelevant that M had limited his claim to the maximum level for arbitration.

MARKS v. AFS LTD, Trans. Ref: LTA 96/7764/G, June 4, 1997, Auld, L.J., CA.

573. Costs—small claims—unreasonable conduct—failure to make realistic offer of settlement—both parties funded by insurers

[County Court Rules 1981 Ord.19 r.4(2).]

C claimed damages arising out of a road traffic accident from N. N accepted that C was established on a roundabout at N's time of entry, that he hit C squarely in the middle of the car with the front of his vehicle, and that he had skidded upon braking to avoid C. Two days before the hearing N offered 50 per cent of the sum claimed in settlement. The offer was rejected. One witness was called for each party. C having succeeded in his claim applied for costs under CCR Ord.19 r.4(2)(c).

Held, that a distinction should to be drawn between cases where parties were funding their cases privately and where insurers were involved on both sides. Public policy decreed that whatever their status, parties should take stock of the strength of their respective cases at an early stage, so that cases could be settled where appropriate. Needless litigation should be discouraged. Where a defendant elected to proceed with a case which was difficult at best and hopeless at worst, it was not improper to characterise the defendant's holding out until the last moment as improper or unreasonable in relation to the proceedings. N ought to have put in a realistic offer to avoid the award of costs.

CHOHAN v. NEWBOLD, September 16, 1997, District Judge Wharton, CC (Loughborough). [*Ex rel.* Wayne Beglan, Barrister, 2-3 Gray's Inn Square, London].

574. Costs—solicitors—market rate—higher hourly rate than local average justified for specialist provincial firm

The Secretary of State applied to review the decision of the taxing master to allow an hourly expense rate of £100 for work done on a planning appeal by a specialist provincial commercial litigation firm.

Held, allowing the application, that a rate of £75 offered by the Secretary of State would be substituted. Whilst it was normal to use local average rates in taxing costs for work done by a provincial firm of solicitors, a taxing master was entitled to exercise his discretion to consider a higher rate where a firm had specialist expertise, provided that the costs were reasonably incurred and the work not such as could reasonably have been handled by other local firms. However, it was unreasonable to accede to the firm's figure without any evidence of the firm's increased overheads. Taxing officers must consider input from local solicitors or law societies and not merely impose a local hourly rate, which may be out of date or unreasonable, *Johnson v. Reed Corrugated Cases Ltd* [1992] 1 All E.R. 169, [1992] C.L.Y. 3447 and *L v. L (Legal Aid: Taxation)* [1996] 1 F.L.R. 873, [1996] 2 C.L.Y. 3872 followed.

JONES v. SECRETARY OF STATE FOR WALES [1997] 1 W.L.R. 1008, Buckley, J., QBD.

575. Costs—solicitors—market rate—non contentious business—complex conveyancing work—relevance of market rate

[Solicitors' (Non-contentious Business) Remuneration Order 1994 (SI 1994 2616).]

Solicitors applied for a review of taxation of costs for conveyancing work arising out of family litigation. The basis for the application was that the approach of the district judge was inconsistent with the provisions of the Solicitors' (Non-contentious Business) Remuneration Order 1994.

Held, that the district judge had erred in taking into account the market rate for conveyancing work, since the 1994 Order Art.3 made no mention of it when setting out the factors to be considered when taxing non contentious business. The work included elements not normally found in straightforward conveyancing. The correct approach was to tax the bill taking into account the criteria in Art.3 and then to decide whether the overall figure was reasonable.

The actual cost in terms of time spent and the hourly rate were matters properly considered within the general discretion of the taxing officer.

C v. C (COSTS: NON-CONTENTIOUS BUSINESS) [1997] 2 F.L.R. 22, King, J., CC (County Court).

576. Costs–solicitors–unknowing representation of undischarged bankrupt in property proceedings–liability for costs

N instructed M, a solicitor, to act for him in proceedings to obtain a Mareva injunction to protect a property without disclosing that he was an undischarged bankrupt. The judge below, although finding M had acted with due diligence, ordered costs on an indemnity basis against M.

Held, allowing the appeal, that a solicitor should not be liable for costs where he unwittingly commenced proceedings relating to property on behalf of an undischarged bankrupt. A bankrupt had the right to bring any legal action except one regarding property and had the capacity to retain a solicitor. The solicitor commencing proceedings warranted only that he had a client, who bore the name of a party to the proceedings, and that this client had instructed him, and did not warrant that his client had a good cause of action.

NELSON v. NELSON [1997] 1 W.L.R. 233, McCowan, L.J., CA.

577. Costs–subpoena served on witness–witness entitled to costs incurred in complying with subpoena

Held, that, where a witness had been served with a subpoena duces tecum, he was entitled not only to conduct money, but also to the costs incurred in complying with the subpoena, which could include the cost of taking legal advice if it was reasonable for the witness to have done so. It was a matter for the judge's discretion as to whether costs should be paid on a standard or indemnity basis and any dispute as to the amount payable could be settled before the taxing master.

JH SHANNON v. COUNTRY CASUALS HOLDINGS PLC, *The Times*, June 16, 1997, Garland, J., QBD.

578. Costs–successful negligence action–damages recovered less than already received from CICB

O brought a successful action in negligence against S, the Chief Constable, following an attack by a remand prisoner. However, the damages he recovered at trial fell below an award he had already received from the Criminal Injuries Compensation Board, CICB, and which therefore had to be repaid to the Board. As O obtained no benefit from the civil action, the trial judge refused to make any order for costs. O appealed.

Held, allowing the appeal, that the fact O had received an award from the CICB did not disentitle him from bringing a civil action; it was in the public interest that he do so, as the CICB could then be repaid by the tortfeasor. O had been wholly successful on liability, and should have been awarded costs.

OLDHAM v. SHARPLES [1997] P.I.Q.R. Q82, Roch, L.J., CA.

579. Costs–taxation–apportionment of costs–solicitor retained by legally aided and non legally aided clients in same action

[Rules of the Supreme Court Ord.62 r.35; Civil Legal Aid (General) Regulations 1989 (SI 1989 339) Reg.32, Reg.107A.]

A solicitor applied under the Rules of the Supreme Court Ord.62 r.35 for review of a taxing master's decision regarding the taxation of costs in an action for damages in which judgment was entered against three defendants. The defendants were on separate retainers and only the first defendant was legally aided. When his legal aid certificate was discharged his costs fell to be taxed in accordance with the Civil Legal Aid (General) Regulations 1989 Reg.107A. The taxing master applied the basic principle of dividing the costs equally between the defendants with an appropriate adjustment where necessary. Whilst the solicitor considered the third defendant responsible for the costs of the action prior to the grant of the legal aid certificate, the first defendant argued that he had been the main protagonist and the third defendant had been a nominal defendant only, such that it was inappropriate to apply pro rata apportionment. In addition, the Legal Aid Board had not required any contribution from the second and third defendants under Reg.32 of the Regulations which implied that it was taking responsibility for all the defence costs.

Held, dismissing the application, that the Legal Aid Board would have taken into consideration the fact that in the course of taxation the apportionment rules would apply to exclude costs attributable to the second and third defendants. Where a solicitor was retained by both legally aided clients and non-legally aided clients, the paramount consideration was that each defendant was to be charged only for costs incurred in his own defence. Costs which were not specifically attributable to the separate defences were to be apportioned pro rata for the purposes of taxation.

BAYLIS v. KELLY, *The Times*, June 6, 1997, Chadwick, J., QBD.

580. **Costs–taxation–assignment of arbitration award to solicitor under costs settlement agreement–agreement not a waiver of right to seek taxation– statutory protection**

[Solicitors Act 1974 s.59, s.61, s.68, s.70.]

As the result of disputed solicitor and client costs arising from a maritime arbitration, C sought an order under the Solicitors Act 1974 s.61 setting aside an apparent costs agreement, an order under s.68 of the Act that S deliver a detailed bill of costs and an order for taxation under either s.61 (5) or s.70. Following negotiations between C and S, C agreed to assign the proceeds of the arbitration award and purported to accept S's previously tendered bills. However, C later assigned the award to D as security for an overdraft facility, without S's knowledge or consent, and S subsequently obtained an injunction restraining further assignment with D agreeing to rank after C. C later brought an originating summons seeking a detailed bill under s.68 and an application under s.61 setting aside the earlier agreement assigning the arbitrator's award to S.

Held, dismissing the application, that the fact that a client enters into a contentious business agreement does not necessarily mean that the solicitor takes a benefit under the agreement, this being a situation dependent on the facts of each case, *Lloyd v. Coote & Ball* [1915] 1 K.B. 242 considered. The matter is completely governed by s.59 and s.61, which provide statutory protection against unfair or unreasonable conduct by a solicitor where the client brings an application within the specified time limit. There was no evidence of improper or unfair conduct on S's part, as, although they had required payment or security in a reasonable amount for their costs, S had not required C to forego their right of taxation in return for continuing to act, and the size of S's bills were not redolent of overcharging.

CELESTE LTD v. STEPHENSON HARWOOD, Trans. Ref: 1996 Folio No.670, May 8, 1997, Toulson, J., QBD (Comm Ct).

581. **Costs–taxation–bills of costs not served on paying party–proceedings continuing in absence–rerun of taxation not in public interest**

[Rules of the Supreme Court Ord.62 r.30.]

In a taxation, following the making of an order for costs against the plaintiffs, M and L, one of the paying parties, L, was not served with a copy of the bill of costs, as required by the RSC Ord.62 r.30(3). Six years had passed between the order for costs and the present application. L applied for a review of the Master's decision that copies of the bills sent in March 1996, should stand as good service and the interest should be deducted from the bills of costs, accruing from March 1, 1990 to May 23, 1996.

Held, ordering the certificate to be amended to take account of deductions, that on the facts, the taxation was not a nullity but was irregular. The taxing master had the power, further to RSC Ord.60 r.30(5), to set aside the taxation either wholly or in part, permanently or temporarily, and substitute whatever order he thought fit. It was not a reasonable exercise of the Chief Taxing Master's discretion to order a rerun of the taxation, given the passage of time. Rather, it was in the public's and the parties' interests bring this process to an end.

MAINWARING v. GOLDTECH INVESTMENTS LTD (NO.2) [1997] 4 All E.R. 16, Robert Walker, J., Ch D.

582. **Costs–taxation–costs certificate issued following provisional taxation–taxing officer had no review powers**

[Rules of the Supreme Court Ord.62 r.31.]

Held, that in a case where a taxing officer had proceeded under RSC Ord.62 r.31 (4) to r.31 (7) and neither party had expressed a wish to be heard on the taxation of costs, the taxing officer's decision was a decision on a provisional taxation in respect of which there was no power of review once a certificate for the costs allowed had been issued. Neither was there a power to set aside a certificate, once issued, to enable an application for review to be made.

BROMSGROVE MEDICAL PRODUCTS LTD (FORMERLY PETERBOROUGH PRESSURE CASTINGS LTD) v. EDGAR VAUGHAN & CO LTD [1997] 1 W.L.R. 1188, Chadwick, J., QBD.

583. **Costs–taxation–extent of jurisdiction to review not determined by status of applicant**

[County Court Rules 1981 Ord.38 r.24; Rules of the Supreme Court Ord.62 r.35.]

K appealed against a decision refusing a review of a district judge's taxation of his costs. The judge stated that he was bound by the decision in *Hart v. Aga Khan Foundation (UK)* [1984] 1 W.L.R. 994, [1984] C.L.Y. 2604 that such a review was limited to *Wednesbury* grounds, finding that, although *Hart* had subsequently been criticised in *Madurasinghe v. Penguin Electronics* [1993] 1 W.L.R. 989, [1993] C.L.Y. 3170 as being in need of revision, it was applicable in K's case due to his status as a litigant in person.

Held, allowing the appeal and remitting the application for a review for reconsideration, that the judge below had erred when finding that his powers were limited to Wednesbury grounds, but that such an error was understandable, given the apparently contradictory nature of the authorities. A judge hearing a taxation review application under either CCR Ord.38 r.24 (6) or RSC Ord.62 r.35 (4) had the jurisdiction to exercise all the powers and discretion of a district judge in relation to the application's subject matter, *Evans v. Bartlam* [1937] A.C. 473 considered. Such powers of review were identical irrespective of whether the taxation of costs was made by a district judge or a taxing officer, and whether the application for review was made by a solicitor or a litigant in person.

KAWARINDRASINGH v. WHITE [1997] 1 All E.R. 714, Brooke, L.J., CA.

584. **Costs–taxation of non contentious business bill–remuneration certificate procedure followed–special circumstances to justify taxation**

[Solicitors Act 1974 s.70; Solicitors (Non-Contentious Business) Remuneration Order 1994 (SI 1994 2616) Art.4, Art.14 (1).]

R used D's services to draft a prospective partnership agreement and received D's bill on February 13, 1996. R then exercised his right under the Solicitors (Non-Contention Business) Remuneration Order 1994 Art.4 (1) requiring D to obtain a remuneration certificate from the Law Society. A provisional assessment upheld the bill on November 8, 1996 and R appealed on December 6, 1997. On February 17, 1997 the provisional assessment was further upheld. R then wrote requiring D to tax their bill. On their refusal R issued an originating summons for taxation. The summons was dismissed as 12 months had expired from the delivery of the bill and there were no special circumstances present as required by the Solicitors Act 1974 s.70(3).

Held, that (1) the lapse of time occurred while the proper remuneration certificate procedure was being gone through; (2) ordinarily the court could be expected to exercise its discretion to order a taxation in favour of the client when there was something to contra-indicate it; (3) this was especially so when the remuneration certificate procedure had been pursued; (4) only "special" not "exceptional" circumstances need be shown, and (5) a timeous and sensible resort to the remuneration certificate route was a special circumstance. The judge further rejected the submission that it would have been proper or sufficient to pay the bill in full whilst reserving the right to tax. This would result in an absolute bar under s.70(4) if the Law Society procedure ran for over 12 months from full payment. The solicitor was in any event protected under the 1994 Order Art.14(1) allowing for the securing of interest on the bill. In addition in the circumstances there was no duty on R to attempt to expedite the Law Society procedure to the detriment of other applicants nor did the outcome of the Law Society procedure mitigate against the exercise of the court's discretion.

RILEY v. DIBB LUPTON ALSOP, June 5, 1997, Sedley, J., QBD. [*Ex rel.* John G Baldwin, Barrister, Oriel Chambers, Liverpool].

585. Costs–third party proceedings–main action settled prior to third party case–defendant seeking contribution from third party for whole costs of action

[Rules of the Supreme Court Ord.16 r.10.]

J employed PA under a JCT minor works contract to design and supervise a third party's construction of a chill-room. When constructed the chill-room was not waterproofed resulting in one of the chill-room's floors breaking up and another becoming sodden and unhygienic. PA commenced third party proceedings, withdrew the proceedings, then re-served them with leave. At the trial PA accepted that it was in breach and the argument devolved upon ascertaining the most appropriate remedial scheme and the extent, if any, to which the third party was responsible for the defect's through poor workmanship. PA and the third party reached a settlement following the third party's contribution offer by facsimile letter pursuant to Rules of the Supreme Court Ord.16 r.10. The offer provided, inter alia, that the third party, which denied liability and contended that the issue was primarily one of design, would "contribute 35 per cent of any damages which may be recovered, whether by judgment, or a reasonable settlement, against PA, and to pay PA's costs of the third party proceedings, to be taxed if not agreed." Shortly afterwards the main action was settled. PA sought an order in the terms of the third party's offer but the third party argued that the settlement of the main action could not be described as "reasonable" and that it should have been compromised earlier, resulting in a substantial reduction in the costs against the third party.

Held, that the damages settlement figure in the main action was reasonable and there was no conclusive evidence to lead the court to the view that a more reasonable settlement could have been achieved at some earlier stage. However, it would not be fair to hold the third party liable to pay any part of the costs of the main action incurred before the third party proceedings were re-served when the bulk of the main action costs had already been incurred. The proper order as to costs was that the third party should pay PA a contribution not exceeding 35 per cent of J's costs incurred after the date when the third party was joined in the proceedings together with a contribution not exceeding 35 per cent of PA's costs in the main action also after that date.

JACK BRAND LTD v. PRIOR ASSOCIATES LTD (1997) 13 Const. L.J. 271, Judge Wilcox, QBD.

586. Costs–Tomlin order–costs of action included costs of implementing order

W commenced proceedings against G in 1994 alleging the negligent survey of a residential property. A settlement was reached at trial. The terms, which included

G's agreement to carry out certain underpinning works to the property, were embodied in a Tomlin order, dated July 7, 1995. These included, inter alia, a provision that G pay W's "costs of the action". W was obliged to expend substantial sums by way of costs in seeking to carry out the works which he had promised to perform. In January 1997 W issued a summons to force the implementation of the order. A dispute arose as to whether G was liable to pay the costs incurred by W arising after the date of the order and before the issue of the summons.

Held, that the "costs of the action" when appearing in a Tomlin order included the costs incurred in its implementation after the date of the order. If it were otherwise, the purpose of the order, namely to settle the dispute without further recourse to the court, would be frustrated, *Krehl v. Park* (1875) L.R. 10 Ch. App. 334 and *Copeland v. Houlton* [1955] 1 W.L.R. 1072, [1955] C.L.Y. 2154 followed.

WALLACE v. BRIAN GALE & ASSOCIATES, March 7, 1997, Humphrey Lloyd Q.C., QBD (OR). [*Ex rel.* Charles H Joseph, Barrister, 4 Paper Buildings, Temple].

587. Costs–unless order–amendment of judgment on counter claim

[Supreme Court Act 1981 s.51; Insolvency Act 1986 s.285; Rules of the Supreme Court Ord.15 r.7 (2), Ord.20 r.11.]

V commenced proceedings against M over fees for security work, and was then adjudged bankrupt. In January 1992 a trustee in bankruptcy, T, was appointed who, by March 1993, had received funds from creditors to cover discovery and a summons for directions, and gave instructions to V's solicitors, S, to proceed with those steps; S served a notice of intention to proceed, and subsequently the list of documents. The summons for directions was adjourned from October 1993 to February 1994, partly so that M could consider an application for security for costs. In the adjournment, M served a proposed amended defence and counterclaim pleading a substantial case beyond its initial bare denial, and T and S investigated the possibility of obtaining legal aid. T requested S to adjourn the February 1994 summons, but the judge refused the application, ordering, inter alia, V to provide further and better particulars of the claim. When they were not provided, in April 1994 M obtained an order that unless they were provided by May 15, 1994 judgment could be entered in default, which it was on the counterclaim on June 14, 1994. M applied to vary the judgment so as to refer to the claim, and for an order that T or S pay the costs under the Supreme Court Act 1981 s.51.

Held, granting the application to amend and making no order on the costs applications, that (1) the unless order insofar as it related to the claim was valid, as leave was not required under the Insolvency Act 1986 s.285, and retrospective leave would be granted for T to carry on the proceedings as was required by the Rules of the Supreme Court Ord.15, r.7 (2); (2) the judgment would be amended under the RSC Ord.20, r.11 and if that was wrong, leave would be given to M to enter a fresh judgment; (3) the effect of the retrospective leave and the amendment rendered T liable for costs, and (4) the material costs were those prior to the February 1994 summons; these were covered by the foregoing, but if not, (a) s.51 of the 1986 Act applied to those who authorised the conduct of proceedings, including a trustee in bankruptcy, and T here had acted improperly, unreasonably and negligently in authorising the resumption of proceedings for the benefit of creditors on terms that he was not going to adopt the same so as to be at risk as to M's costs; (b) whatever S's errors, they had not acted improperly, unreasonably or negligently and in any event the costs prior to February 1994 arose because of the resumption of proceedings by T and, thereafter, were incurred by M to safeguard its interests.

VICKERY v. MODERN SECURITY SYSTEMS LTD [1997] B.P.I.R. 319, Humphrey Lloyd Q.C., QBD.

588. Costs–unreasonable conduct–Calderbank offer rejected

In an action for damage to a car in a motor accident, the particulars of claim contained a claim for loss of use for a period of 56 days. At the arbitration hearing S applied to amend the pleading to include loss of use to the present day. The pre-accident value of the car had been agreed at £400. S had incurred £6 per week in bus fares and some taxi expenses. One week prior to the hearing J made a *Calderbank* offer of £790.

Held, that the application to amend was unsustainable. Loss of use was awarded at £40 per week for 42 days, bringing the total award to £640. In view of the fact that the loss of use claim had not involved any particularly high figures where quantifiable amounts were concerned S had been guilty of unreasonable conduct in rejecting the *Calderbank* offer and was liable for J's costs since the date of the offer.

SCOTCHFORD v. JOANNOU, November 20, 1996, District Judge Southcombe, CC (Clerkenwell). [*Ex rel.* Elaine Strachan, Barrister, Chambers of Michael Parroy Q.C., Oxford].

589. Costs–unreasonable conduct–defence filed–settlement offered at late stage

J's claim arose from a road traffic accident on January 19, 1996. J's vehicle was hit by H as he turned right across traffic at traffic lights. There were two independent witnesses in J's favour. Proceedings were issued and H filed a defence. The matter was referred to arbitration and H offered to settle J's claim eight days prior to the hearing. J applied for unreasonable conduct costs at the hearing.

Held, awarding unreasonable conduct costs against H, that a defence should not have been filed and it was unreasonable to offer settlement at such a late stage having filed a defence.

JANCEY v. HIGGINS, July 31, 1996, District Judge Oldham, CC (Sheffield). [*Ex rel.* Irwin Mitchell, Solicitors, St Peters House, Hartshead, Sheffield].

590. Costs–unreasonable conduct–"dripfeeding"–interim payments–conduct before issue of proceedings relevant–small claims

J and D were involved in a road traffic accident. J claimed for repairs, loss of use of vehicle and incidental expenses. Liability was accepted by D's insurers on July 1, 1995. J asked D to pay the claim on August 7, 1995. By December 13, 1995, J had received two interim payments but no offer in settlement of the remainder of the claim. J therefore issued proceedings. There was further payment by D after issue of proceedings. The claim was referred to arbitration, with D claiming that the two interim payments took the claim below the arbitration limit, relying on *Tatter and Tatter v. Singh* [1995] 2 C.L.Y. 3981. There was further payment by D after issue and the claim was then settled. D was only prepared to pay the fixed costs on the summons, as the case had been referred to arbitration. J sought an unreasonable costs order. J contended that the two interim payments and failure to settle the claim in full amounted to "dripfeeding" following *Kirk-Smith v. Richardson* [1992] C.L.Y. 3434.

Held, that the case was very similar to *Kirk-Smith*, and D's conduct before issue of proceedings was relevant. D was ordered to pay J's costs, to be taxed on Scale 1 if not agreed.

JONES v. DONKER, July 1, 1996, District Judge Hill, CC (Sheffield). [*Ex rel.* Lyons Davidson, Solicitors, Bridge House, Bristol].

591. Costs–unreasonable conduct–"dripfeeding"–offers to settle–failure to prepare case

[County Court Rules 1981 Ord.19 r.4.]

W brought a claim against S for damages arising out of a road traffic accident. A defence was filed and the case was referred to arbitration with a hearing date listed for February 18, 1997. On February 13, S's solicitor offered to pay 50 per cent of W's claim. On February 14, this offer was rejected whereupon S's solicitor offered to pay

80 per cent of W's claim. On February 17, the day before the listed hearing, W's solicitor informed S's solicitor that that offer was also not acceptable whereupon S's solicitor immediately offered to pay the whole of the claim. S's solicitor also advised W's solicitor that he had neither arranged for S or S's witnesses to go to the hearing nor had he instructed any representatives to attend. W claimed entitlement to costs as; (1) the succession of offers of settlement culminating in an offer to pay the whole claim amounted to "dripfeeding" following *Kirksmith v. Richardson* [1992] C.L.Y. 3434, and (2) S's failure to prepare the case for hearing indicated that there had never been any intention to defend the case and both these actions amounted to unreasonable conduct under CCR Ord.19 r.4(2)(a).

Held, that the tactics which S's solicitor had employed in making several offers and then agreeing to pay the whole of the claim were analagous to the facts in *Kirksmith v. Richardson* and together with the fact that S's solicitors were clearly not prepared for the hearing did give rise to the conclusion that S had not been willing to defend the case and had acted unreasonably. S was ordered to pay W's costs on Scale 1, to be taxed if not agreed.

WOODGATE v. STAFANTOS, February 18, 1997, District Judge Wade, CC (Swindon). [*Ex rel.* Susan Chan, Barrister, Chambers of Graeme Williams Q.C., 13 Kings Bench Walk, Temple].

592. **Costs–unreasonable conduct–failure to accept settlement**

See DAMAGES: Ashby v. Wiggins. §1789

593. **Costs–unreasonable conduct–filing untrue defence–whether unreasonable conduct for costs purposes**

[County Court Rules 1981 Ord.19 r.4(2).]

A road traffic accident occurred on February 3, 1996 in which A alleged that R had reversed from a parking place into his stationary car. There was one additional person in R's car, a woman. R got out of the car through the driver's door, and admitted responsibility for the accident and signed a written admission to that effect. A issued proceedings, a defence was filed and the matter was referred to arbitration. In the defence it was alleged that R was in fact the passenger in the car which was driven by the woman and an insurance claim was made by her. Her insurance company conducted an investigation and established that in fact it was R who was the driver. At the arbitration R failed to attend and an application was made for costs for unreasonable conduct under CCR Ord.19 r.4(2)(c).

Held, that it was not unreasonable conduct to file a defence that was untrue. Whilst it may have been true that R was involved in defrauding insurers that does not give A the right to claim his costs. It was clear that A told his solicitor who was driving and on his instructions the solicitor sued the correct defendant. As A identified the correct person from day one there cannot have been any extra costs arising out of R running a defence that was false and untrue. Had an application to amend been necessary that would have wasted costs. Nevertheless, R was dishonest and the judge awarded A the cost of a consultation with a solicitor to obtain advice in bringing a claim and a consultation when the defence was filed. This was taxed at £90 out of a bill of over £600.

ARMSTRONG-JAMES v. RADCLIFFE-SMITH, April 30, 1997, District Judge Cawood, CC (Portsmouth). [*Ex rel.* Richard Case, Barrister, Chambers of Michael Parroy Q.C., 4 St Peter Street, Winchester].

594. **Costs–unreasonable conduct–insurance claim–liability and quantum agreed–delay in payment led to proceedings being issued**

C's claim arose out of a road traffic accident on February 1, 1996 in which her vehicle was hit in the rear as she turned left into her driveway. C's cover was third party, fire and theft. A claim was intimated to B's insurers on February 2, 1996 and and an inspection requested. The engineer's report on C's vehicle was not made available until April 25,1996. B's insurers confirmed that liability was not in dispute at that point. Quantum was agreed. Despite promptings from C, payment was not forthcoming and proceedings were issued. Payment was received by C on June 17, 1996. A defence was filed on July 3,1996 resulting in a reference to arbitration. C applied for unreasonable conduct costs against B.

Held, allowing C's claim, that proceedings need not have been issued and B had behaved unreasonably in delaying payment. B was ordered to pay C unreasonable conduct costs, to be assessed if not agreed.

CALDERBANK v. BURTON, December 24, 1996, District Judge Oldham, CC (Sheffield). [*Ex rel.* Irwin Mitchell, Solicitors, St Peters House, Hartshead, Sheffield].

595. Costs—unreasonable conduct—late settlement

W's claim arose out of a road traffic accident on September 9, 1995. M's bus pulled out from the side of the road into the path of W's vehicle causing a collision. M's insurers admitted that their driver had no knowledge of the incident. Proceedings were issued and a defence was filed citing specific acts of negligence against W. W's claim was paid five days before the arbitration hearing. W argued that M should pay unreasonable conduct costs due to the late settlement of the matter and the fact that a defence was filed when M's driver had no knowledge of the incident.

Held, ordering M to pay W's costs, that M had behaved unreasonably.

WALKER v. MIDLAND FOX LTD, October 21, 1996, Deputy District Judge Vaz, CC (Leicester). [*Ex rel.* Irwin Mitchell, Solicitors, St Peters House, Hartshead, Sheffield].

596. Costs—unreasonable conduct—liability for accident disputed—non-attendance at court by defendant—defence withdrawn

P's claim arose out of a road traffic accident following which P wrote to O in 1995 and O's insurers responded, informing P they had a claim form from their insured disputing liability. P issued proceedings and a defence was filed, resulting in the matter being referred to arbitration. However O refused to attend court to pursue the defence and, after due notice to O by his insurers to which he did not respond, the defence was withdrawn seven days prior to the arbitration hearing. P applied for unreasonable conduct costs on the grounds that O had disputed liability, but was not prepared to follow that through by attending court.

Held, that O had acted unreasonably and therefore costs would be awarded to P on Scale 1, to be taxed if not agreed.

PATHAN v. O'CONNOR, February 21,1997, Deputy District Judge Duchenne, CC (Bedford). [*Ex rel.* Irwin Mitchell, Solicitors, St Peters House, Hartshead, Sheffield].

597. Costs—unreasonable conduct—one party deliberately misleading court

[County Court Rules 1981 Ord.19 r.4.]

P and D were involved in a road traffic accident to which there were no independent witnesses. Each party claimed for the damage to their vehicles. They both gave accounts of the road accident which were wholly impossible to reconcile. On behalf of P it was submitted that the divergence of evidence was such that one party was intentionally misleading the court; that P's account was inherently more probable, and that in the circumstances judgment should be entered for P with costs on the basis of D's unreasonable conduct.

Held, accepting P's submissions, that where a party deliberately misled the court, in this case giving a version of events which simply could not be believed, it was an appropriate case to award costs for unreasonable conduct under CCR Ord.19 r.4(2)(c).

RYLAND v. RUSSELL, February 10, 1997, District Judge Sturdy, CC (Kingston upon Thames). [*Ex rel.* Ben Williams, Barrister].

598. Costs–unreasonable conduct–plaintiff's non attendance at hearing–no notice and no reason given

[County Court Rules 1981 Ord.19 r.4.]

T and S were involved in a road traffic accident. Having pursued his claim for several months T failed to attend the hearing despite having been notified of the date. He gave no warning of his decision not to attend, nor did he contact the court on the day of the hearing with any justification for his non-appearance. S attended the hearing, as did counsel for both sides. The judge refused an adjournment, dismissed the claim and entered judgment for S on the counterclaim. S applied for costs on the basis of T's unreasonable conduct.

Held, awarding costs to S, that where a party initiated proceedings causing another party to be put to the task of defending them and attending a hearing, it was unreasonable conduct for the claimant to fail without warning, to enter an appearance. The judge assessed costs pursuant to CCR Ord.19 r.4(2) accordingly.

TRAVERS v. STYCH, February 26, 1997, District Judge Campbell, CC (Oxford). [*Ex rel.* Ben Williams, Barrister, Chambers of Michael Parroy Q.C., Oxford].

599. Costs–unreasonable conduct–premature issue of proceedings–claim in excess of small claims limit

[County Court Rules Ord.19 r.4, Ord.38 r.2.]

B suffered loss and damage in a road traffic accident in which BG never disputed liability. B issued proceedings 11 days after B's motor insurer wrote to BG asking for payment "by return" of the insured loss and specifying the sum. The letter did not give a deadline for payment or threaten proceedings. No warning of proceedings was given. The total amount recovered by B was £1,066, but £375 of it was admitted in the defence. The small claims limit in force at the time was £1,000.

Held, that (1) B was fixed with constructive knowledge both of matters known to his motor insurer and of matters known to his personal solicitors, where both were dealing with BG to recover the different elements of the loss caused; (2) B acted prematurely in issuing proceedings when he did, without a pre-action letter and this, whilst not a bar to bringing a claim, was a matter of relevance when the court came to exercise its discretion in awarding costs either taxed on Scale 1 or limited to the level of fixed costs which would have been allowed under the small claims procedure, since a pre-action letter would probably have clarified the sum truly in dispute between the parties and (3) even where B had not "played the rules" or artificially inflated his claim, and even where the total amount recovered after issue of proceedings was in excess of £1,000, where it was plain to B or his advisers on or shortly after BG's filing of a defence that the amount actually in dispute, as opposed to the amount claimed in the summons, was clearly less than the arbitration limit, B was not entitled to his taxed costs on Scale 1, but only to fixed costs under CCR Ord.19 r.4. Neither an order for interlocutory judgment and costs, which was an administrative standard form sent out without a hearing, nor CCR Ord.38 r.2 would act as a bar to the exercise of the court's discretion to limit costs in this way, *Scarrott v. Stratton*, (Unreported, 1989) applied.

BURY v. BRITISH GAS PLC, December 10, 1996, H.H.J. Morgan, CC (Staines). [*Ex rel.* Ivor Collett, Barrister, No.1 Sergeants' Inn, Fleet Street].

600. Costs–unreasonable conduct

See DAMAGES: Stonard v. Dunster. §1787

601. Costs–unsuccessful directors disqualification proceedings–award against Secretary of State on indemnity basis

Administrative receivers were appointed after a company creased trading and the Secretary of State sought a disqualification order against its directors. This was supported by a sworn affidavit from one of the receivers, who later admitted that his allegations were groundless and unsound. The directors applied for a court order which awarded costs against the Secretary of State on an indemnity rather than a standard basis.

Held, that the court had power to award costs against the Secretary of State in such proceedings and could order such costs to be taxed on an indemnity or a standard basis. In the present case, where the respondents had never been asked for an explanation of their actions, where the allegations made against them were unfounded and misconceived and where the case against them had not been advanced on a sound basis, an order for indemnity costs against the Secretary of State would be made.

SECRETARY OF STATE FOR TRADE AND INDUSTRY v. BLAKE [1997] B.C.L.C. 728, District Judge Cardinal, Ch D.

602. Costs—wasted costs orders—application to strike out personal injury action not a wasted cost

[Supreme Court Act 1981 s.51 (7); Rules of the Supreme Court Ord.62 r.11.]

Following a successful application to strike out a High Court personal injury action for want of prosecution, T's solicitors applied for an order pursuant to RSC Ord.62 r.11 against G's solicitors that they show cause why they should not pay T's costs of and occasioned by the action personally. The summons was unsupported by any affidavit identifying which precise aspect of the conduct was complained about, nor were any particular "wasted costs" identified by T.

Held, dismissing the application for a wasted costs order, that T's application to strike out the personal injury claim could not be said to be a "wasted" cost. Applying the principles set out by the Court of Appeal in *Ridehalgh v. Horsefield* [1994] 3 All E.R. 848, [1994] C.L.Y. 3623, fairness requires that any respondent lawyer should be very clearly told what he was said to have done wrong and what is claimed. This T had failed to do. Further, citing *Barrister (Wasted Costs Order) (No.1 of 1991), Re* [1992] 3 All E.R. 429, [1992] C.L.Y. 748, the court had jurisdiction to make a wasted costs order only where the improper, unreasonable or negligent conduct complained of had caused a waste of costs and only to the extent of such wasted costs, and that demonstration of a causal link was essential, the court held that T could not argue that the whole costs of the action up to the application to strike out had been "wasted". Accepting the argument advanced on behalf of G's former solicitors, the court held that whereas in the case of automatic strike out in the county court a defendant successfully opposing an application to reinstate had been forced by the plaintiff's solicitor to incur costs in order to preserve the default position (and could hope to recover its "wasted costs" in respect of a totally unnecessary application), in the High Court the position was different. There, the default position was that the action would proceed to trial, forcing the defendant to incur significant costs, which might be irrecoverable against a legally aided plaintiff, unless the defendant made a timely and successful application to strike out (which would produce a significant saving in outlay). The application to strike out in the instant case was a perfectly usual type of application, the costs of which could not be said to have been "wasted" within the meaning of the Supreme Court Act 1981 s.51 (7).

GODDARD v. THOMAS ELLIS ENGINEERING LTD, May 12, 1997, Deputy District Judge Fountain, Colchester District Registry. [*Ex rel.* Graham Sinclair, Barrister, East Anglian Chambers, Norwich].

603. Costs—wasted costs orders—appropriate on clear indication of improper conduct

[Supreme Court Act 1981 s.51.]

W had been legally aided in an unsuccessful action alleging a negligent survey of his house by L, who applied for a wasted costs order against W's professional advisers which was refused. L appealed.

Held, dismissing the appeal and ordering indemnity costs against L, that the wasted costs jurisdiction was a summary remedy only to be used where clearly improper, unreasonable or negligent conduct under the Supreme Court Act

1981 s.51 on the part of professional advisers could be readily established. Any appeal against the refusal of an order by the judge hearing the original action would be unsuccessful unless it could be shown that the approach had been "wholly wrong" on a point of principle.

WALL v. LEFEVER, *The Times*, August 1, 1997, Lord Woolf, M.R., CA.

604. Costs—wasted costs orders—appropriate procedure

As part of a dispute between L, landlords and F, the tenant, F made an application for an injunction requiring L to cause the gas supply to be reconnected so that the central heating in the accommodation would work. At a hearing it became clear that there had been no central heating available in the accommodation when the tenancy had been entered into. The view was taken by the judge that the application should never have been made and a wasted costs order was made against F's solicitors. The solicitors, having had no opportunity to defend themselves, appealed against that decision.

Held, allowing the appeal, that (1) the judge, in not allowing the solicitors an opportunity to show why the order should not be made, did not follow the proper procedure and acted outwith his jurisdiction, and (2) L should be awarded costs arising from the application for injunction.

LIVINGSTONE v. FRASSO, Trans. Ref: CCRTI 96/0377/G, July 9, 1997, Otton, L.J., CA.

605. Costs—wasted costs orders—district judge competent and compellable witness to financial provision agreement

Judges may be called as witnesses in proceedings, but only as a last resort. C, the husband's solicitor in ancillary relief proceedings, appealed against a wasted costs order imposed for his unreasonably subpoenaing the district judge who had suggested the basis for an undertaking in respect of matrimonial property. C submitted that, as the trial judge had indicated that evidence from both counsel was relevant to a dispute as to the interpretation of the undertaking, then the district judge should be compellable as a witness to the making of the undertaking.

Held, allowing the appeal, that although the wasted costs order had been made as the result of disproportionate conduct on both sides, the use of such orders needed control to prevent it becoming a new and costly form of litigation, *Ridehalgh v. Horsefield* [1994] Ch. 205, [1994] C.L.Y. 3623 considered. While a judge was competent as a witness, the authorities showed that judges should only be called as a last resort, with an exception to the principle of compellability being matters related to and resulting from the exercise of a judicial function, *Duke of Buccleuch v. Metropolitan Board of Works* (1872) L.R. 5 H.L. 418 considered. Whereas the conduct of the case had been inappropriate on both sides, C had not been unreasonable in seeking the judge's attendance, given the admitted relevance of counsel's evidence and that the notes provided by the judge in lieu of giving evidence did not show that he could not have given further evidence.

WARREN v. WARREN [1997] Q.B. 488, Lord Woolf, M.R., CA.

606. Costs—wasted costs orders—failure to amend pleadings when partnership dissolved

V instructed solicitors to commence proceedings for allegedly defective products supplied by M to V's farm. At the time the farm was run as a partnership by V and his father. Counsel settled pleadings in the name of the partnership but, before proceedings were commenced the partnership dissolved and V took over the farm on his own. V's solicitor issued proceedings without changing the title reflecting the change in ownership. M applied to strike the action out on account of the misnomer and succeeded although V's appeal was allowed. At the end of the action V and M sought an order that the solicitors should pay the costs of the striking out application and appeal.

Held, granting the application, that the solicitors had been guilty of incompetence and, on the balance of probabilities, the costs of the striking out proceedings had been incurred by that incompetence.

VEASEY v. MILLFEED CO LTD; *sub nom.* VEASEY v. PICKERING KENYON; MILLFEED CO LTD v. PICKERING KENYON [1997] P.N.L.R. 100, Rose, L.J., CA.

607. Costs–wasted costs orders–non-party liability–judicial review proceedings–council officers not personally liable for costs incurred.

[Supreme Court Act 1981 s.51.]

L and two of its housing assessment officers appealed against non-party costs orders made under the Supreme Court Act 1981 s.51 that the officers were personally liable for the cost of judicial review proceedings brought by W.

Held, allowing the appeal, that the judge had failed to take account of L's offer to pay W's costs and had focused instead on the delay and inactivity on L's part. The judge had relied on the decision in *R. v. Lambeth LBC, ex p. Mahmood* [1994] C.L.Y. 3622 as authority for the proposition that council officers might be liable for wasted costs following a last minute decision not to defend judicial review proceedings, but that case related to officers' responsibilities in internal disciplinary proceedings. The costs agreement put the outcome of the appeal beyond doubt, but even in its absence it was difficult to conceive of circumstances, apart from fraud, where a s.51 order against an officer might be appropriate. The order also had to be set aside because of procedural unfairness as the order assumed, without investigation, that there were officers against whom it could be made, but left their identification to the council. The judge himself should have ordered affidavit evidence as to the individual officers' responsibilities to consider whether an order could properly be made against one or more of them. While the judge's criticism of L's conduct was justified, the course taken had merely resulted in a greater waste of costs than those originally incurred.

R. v. LAMBETH LBC, *ex p.* WILSON, *The Times*, March 25, 1997, Nourse, L.J., CA.

608. Costs–wasted costs orders–settlement–statement concerning reputation could be made to court

Held, that, where an application for a wasted costs order was settled between parties before reaching court, counsel and solicitors should be entitled to submit clear and concise written statements to the court clarifying matters relating to their reputation. The statements could then be transmitted to the judiciary previously involved with the order, who would not otherwise have been provided with such information after a settlement had been reached. The practice of laying a statement before the court had the advantages of saving on court time, avoiding the expense of litigation and encouraging settlement, and the statement would only be conveyed to the judiciary where no objection was raised by the other parties.

MANZANILLA LTD v. CORTON PROPERTY AND INVESTMENTS LTD (NO.2), *The Times*, August 4, 1997, Lord Woolf, M.R., CA.

609. Costs–wasted costs orders–solicitor's failure to follow counsel's and liquidator's advice–pursuit of litigation amounted to negligence under Supreme Court Act s.51

[Supreme Court Act 1981 s.51 (7).]

The plaintiff brought proceedings against the liquidator for discovery of documents relating to the insurance of factory premises owned by the company which had been damaged by fire. The liquidator's solicitors wrote to the plaintiff's solicitors indicating that the proposed action against the liquidator was in the company, not the plaintiff. The summons against the liquidator was dismissed as misconceived and the registrar made a wasted costs order against the plaintiff's solicitors to pay the costs of the summons on an indemnity basis. He rejected their argument that they had relied upon counsel's opinion, finding that there had been no such reliance. The solicitors appealed.

Held, dismissing the appeal, that the registrar's finding that there had been no reliance on counsel's opinion could not be supported but that the court would exercise the discretion afresh and, in doing so, would order the solicitors to pay the costs personally. Counsel had indicated that any action in negligence against the liquidator would have to be prosecuted in the company's name and that it became apparent that the proceedings might not be cost effective if the company's financial position was poor. Given that advice, the solicitors' omission to reconsider the viability of the actions amounted to negligence under the Supreme Court Act 1981 s.51(7)(a) in that they had failed to heed the liquidator's advice, that the funds in the litigation had been exhausted. They had also been negligent in failing to consider the manner in which the application was made and the benefit that might have derived to the plaintiff as a result.

D WALTER & CO LTD v. NEVILLE ECKLEY & CO [1997] B.C.C. 331, Sir Richard Scott V.C., Ch D (Companies Court).

610. Costs—wasted costs orders—solicitor's obligation to finance clients to attend court

The parties disputed the amount of contribution made by the respondent husband to the mortgage repayments after the parties separated. The wife's solicitors requested the husband's solicitors to provide up to date figures from the building society before the directions hearing, although the mortgage was in joint names. They were not available for the directions hearing which the respondent, who lived in Hertfordshire, did not attend. At a subsequent hearing the district judge ordered the respondent's solicitors to pay the wife's costs of the directions hearing and disallowed the respondent's solicitors' legal aid taxation of costs. The respondent's solicitors were criticised for failing to lend their client money to attend the hearing.

Held, setting aside the wasted costs order, having regard to the principles enunciated in *Ridehalgh v. Horsefield* [1994] Ch. 205, [1994] C.L.Y. 3623, that of the three bases for a wasted costs order, namely that the solicitor's conduct was improper, unreasonable or negligent, the only possible category into which such failure to advance the costs could fit was that of negligence. As it was probable but not inevitable that such costs would be recovered as a disbursement, failure to advance them could not be characterised as negligent. Solicitors should not be expected to take risks by advancing such costs. To have done so might not have ensured the respondent's attendance at court in Margate in any event. Had the respondent attended, in the absence of the building society's up to date figures, the case could not have been resolved at the hearing, so there was no consequential loss.

MARDELL v. MARDELL, January 9, 1997, H.H.J. Boulton, CC (Thanet). [*Ex rel.* Peter Gibbs, Barrister, 36-38 London Road, Enfield].

611. Counterclaims—time barred claims could not be brought as counterclaims to defeat limitation period

[Limitation Act 1980 s.35(1).]

B was advised by AY in relation to flotations in the period 1987 to 1989. The firm AY merged with EW to form a new partnership called EY. B brought an action against EY in Montana on May 20, 1992 for negligence, fraud and breach of contract; and EY commenced proceedings against B on May 26, 1992 to recover payment for services rendered since the merger. B's action against EY was dismissed in January 1995 for want of jurisdiction. The period for issue of a writ in England had expired by that time. B sought to rely on the Limitation Act 1980 s.35(1) to bring such a claim as a counterclaim to the 1992 action. Consequently EY discontinued its claim against B on February 1, 1996. B issued its counterclaim later the same day.

Held, striking out the counterclaim, that an action could be brought against or defended by any two or more persons as defendants in an action in the name of the firm. An action could not be brought against a firm which did not exist at the time when the matters complained of arose. On the facts, the balance was strongly in favour of disposal of the claim in a separate action. There was limited connection between the main action and the counterclaim. It would be unjust for the counterclaim to be used as a vehicle to defeat the Limitation Act.

ERNST & YOUNG v. BUTTE MINING PLC (NO.2); *sub nom*. BUTTE MINING PLC v. ERNST & YOUNG [1997] 2 All E.R. 471, Lightman, J., Ch D.

612. County courts–automatic directions–transfer of personal injuries action from High Court

D raised an action for damages against his former employers as a result of an injury he suffered at work in 1988. Three years later a High Court writ was issued with the statement that the action exceeded £50,000. The action was then transferred to the county court and D appealed against the transfer. Eventually a notice was issued by the county court informing D that the action had been transferred. D's application for judicial review of the notice was refused. D then renewed the application, maintaining that the county court had no jurisdiction to deal with the case.

Held, refusing the application, that (1) despite the size of the award of damages sought, the High Court was entitled to transfer the case, and the county court had jurisdiction, and (2) as there was no stay on the order to transfer the action, D's attempt to appeal the transfer to the House of Lords and his attempt to raise aspects of the case in the European Court of Human Rights did not affect jurisdiction.

R. v. BASINGSTOKE COUNTY COURT, *ex p.* DE SOUZA, Trans. Ref: FC3 95 6190/D, August 19, 1997, Brooke, L.J., CA.

613. County courts–fees–exemptions–Amendment No.1

COUNTY COURT FEES (AMENDMENT) ORDER 1997, SI 1997 787 (L.17); made under the County Courts Act 1984 s.128. In force: March 13, 1997; £0.65.

This Order amends the County Court Fees Order 1982 (SI 1982 1706 as amended by SI 1994 1936, SI 1995 2627 and SI 1996 3189) so as to restore the provisions governing exemption and remission from payment of court fees to their wording immediately prior to the coming into force of the County Court Fees (Amendment) Order 1996 (SI 1996 3189). It also revokes the relevant article of the 1996 Order.

614. County courts–fees–exemptions–Amendment No.2

COUNTY COURT FEES (AMENDMENT) (NO.2) ORDER 1997, SI 1997 2670 (L.39); made under the County Courts Act 1984 s.128. In force: December 1, 1997; £0.65.

This Order amends the County Court Fees Order 1982 (SI 1982 1706) in order to extend the exemption from payment of court fees to those receiving family credit, disability working allowance or income-based jobseekers' allowance.

615. County courts–forms–Amendment No.1

COUNTY COURT (FORMS) (AMENDMENT) RULES 1997, SI 1997 1838 (L.28); made under the County Court Act 1984 s.75. In force: r.2: October 1, 1997; remainder: September 1, 1997; £6.10.

These Rules amend the County Court (Forms) Rules 1982 (SI 1982 586) so as to substitute new forms to be used under the accelerated possession procedure; amend the defence forms as a result of the change in the way fees for counterclaims are charged; substitute re-designed versions of certain forms;

provide two new forms for use in applications for injunctions against anti-social behaviour; and reflect the change in name of chief clerk.

616. County courts-forms-Amendment No.2

COUNTY COURT (FORMS) (AMENDMENT NO.2) RULES 1997, SI 1997 2171 (L.36); made under the County Court Act 1984 s.75. In force: October 1, 1997; £0.65.

These Rules correct Form N.11B which is a form of reply to application for accelerated possession under the Housing Act 1988 s.21. The form was introduced by the County Court (Forms) (Amendment) Rules 1997 (SI 1997 1838).

617. County courts-jurisdiction-power to hear appeal after transfer of action from High Court

[County Courts Act 1984 s.40(7).]

K appealed against the striking out of its action by a county court judge upon an appeal from a decision of the High Court. The action had been transferred to the county court and K argued that a judge of the county court had no jurisdiction to hear an appeal from an order made by a High Court judge which predated the transfer.

Held, dismissing the appeal, that by the time the appeal was heard the documents in the action had been lodged in the county court so the action had been effectively transferred, *Welply v. Buhl* (1878) 3 Q.B. 253 considered. Once transfer had taken place a county court judge had power to hear an appeal subject to the exceptions in the County Courts Act 1984 s.40(5) and s.40(7).

KINGS QUALITY HOMES LTD v. AJ PAINTS LTD [1997] 3 All E.R. 267, Staughton, L.J., CA.

618. County courts-rules-Amendment No.1

COUNTY COURT (AMENDMENT) RULES 1997, SI 1997 1837 (L.27); made under the County Court Act 1984 s.75. In force: September 1, 1997; £1.10.

These Rules amend the County Court Rules 1981 (SI 1981 1687) to reflect the change in name of chief clerk; to enable the proper officer to take oral examinations and to remove the requirement for that officer to be of a certain grade in the Court Service; to provide a procedure where a question arising in proceedings is transferred to a leasehold valuation tribunal for determination; to amend the accelerated possession procedure following the enactment of the Housing Act 1988 s.19A; to provide the procedure for making an application for an injunction against anti-social behaviour; to enlarge the circumstances in which a summons in a business list action may be served out of England and Wales; and to correct a cross reference in Ord.42 r.5.

619. Court funds

COURT FUNDS (AMENDMENT) RULES 1997, SI 1997 177 (L.1); made under the Administration of Justice Act 1982 s.38. In force: February 21, 1997; £1.10.

These Rules amend the Court Fund Rules 1987 (SI 1987 821) so as to give the Accountant General the option to make the payment of court funds held by him by means of the Bankers' Automated Clearing System, in addition to by cheque. They make other minor amendments where necessary to take account of changes in legislation.

620. Default judgments-setting aside-application to set aside on ground of mistake after substantial delay

[Rules of the Supreme Court Ord.19 r.9.]

B, Lloyd's underwriters, appealed against an order setting aside the judgment in default entered by C against B. B were the insurers of E which provided a film completion guarantee to C who were making a film in South Africa with a budget of SAR 11.2 million. B indemnified C for additional sums incurred as a result of increased cost of working. C obtained a further guarantee from ACIC which undertook to pay if E did not. The film exceeded both the budget and time limit and in 1988 C issued a writ against E, which later went into liquidation. In 1992 C amended its statement of claim to include the primary claim for repayment of SAR 11.2 million and, alternatively, SAR 4.9 million, the approximate amount by which the budget had been exceeded. In 1993 C entered judgment in default against B for SAR 11.2 million, notwithstanding that B told C that the policy did not cover the claim on the proper construction of the policy. C also sought default judgment against ACIC which was refused. C's claim was based on a mistake but they were slow to act on the mistake. In December 1994, 18 months after the judgment had been entered, C took out a summons to set aside their own default judgment. Due to the considerable delay before the mistake was recognised and acted on by C, the judge had to consider whether the delay had resulted in any prejudice to B. The judge, in balancing any possible prejudice to B against any injustice to C in preventing it from making its claims, decided to allow the judgment to be set aside.

Held, allowing the appeal and dismissing C's application to set aside judgment, that the court has jurisdiction to exercise its discretion under RSC Ord.19 r.9 in setting aside a judgment on the ground of a mistake if the applicant has acted diligently, and if the application is made within a reasonable time after the judgment has been acted on, *Cannan v. Reynolds* (1855) 5 El. & Bl. 301 considered. It was of utmost importance that parties were able to rely on the finality of judgments. Whether B were liable under E's guarantee depended on the construction of the insurance policy. The mistake relied on was of C's own doing and it should have acted as soon as the mistake came to its notice. There was a culpable delay and C did not act promptly as a result of which B was prejudiced. Per Ward L.J. dissenting, that the exercise of judicial discretion by the judge should not be interfered in without good reason. The judge was entitled to reach the conclusions he did. The need for the issues between the parties to be resolved on their merits was greater, for the sake of justice, than the principle of procedural expedience.

CRYSTAL EYE MANAGEMENT (PTY) LTD v. ENTERTAINMENT GUARANTEES LTD, Trans. Ref: QBENI 95/1628/E, January 15, 1997, Leggatt, L.J., CA.

621. Default judgments–setting aside–judgment not set aside to allow automatic reference to arbitration

[County Court Rules 1981 Ord.9, Ord.19.]

B's vehicle was written off in an accident and B claimed hire charges of £1,116, incidental telephone and postal expenses of £35, and two weeks loss of use, £150. S's insurers wrote an open letter on January 23, 1997 asking for a reduction in hire charges and offering one week's loss of use and £25 for incidentals. The offer was rejected. B's solicitors issued proceedings on April 4, 1997. No defence was served in time. B's solicitors entered interlocutory judgment on April 30, 1997.

Held, dismissing the application to set aside and referring B's assessment of damages to arbitration, that (1) the draft defence denying all damage was unsustainable in the light of the insurer's letter dated January 23, 1997 and it was thus an abuse of process; (2) it was established law that in non arbitration proceedings, where B could show negligence and at least some resulting damage, then B would be entitled to summary judgment under CCR Ord.9 r.14. The test under r.14 was the same test as that on an application to set aside a default judgment, namely S had to show a triable defence on merits. As B would have been entitled to summary judgment under r.14 in a non arbitration case, it followed, ipso facto, that S could not have a triable defence on merits for the purpose of setting aside B's default judgment; (3) the definition of "defence" in Ord.19 r.3(4) was irrelevant because such definition applied for the purposes of Ord.19 r.3(1) and not for the purposes of determining whether or not S had a triable defence on merits when attempting to set aside a default judgment; (4) it was clear that S's application to set aside judgment was made purely for the purpose of avoiding the risk of inter partes costs but this was not a sufficient reason to set aside judgment; (5) because the court declined to set aside B's interlocutory judgment it followed that the action could not be "automatically" referred to arbitration under r.3 for the reason that S could not serve a valid defence in the proceedings and thus S could not trigger an automatic reference to arbitration; (6) however, the court could refer the assessment of B's damages under the interlocutory judgment to arbitration, ie. pursuant to Ord.19 r.9 there being nothing in r.9 to exclude such a reference to arbitration even after B had obtained interlocutory judgment, and (7) at the final hearing the arbitrator would under r.10 have a full discretion as to costs.

BROOKS v. SMITH, July 1, 1997, District Judge Chapman, CC (Salford). [*Ex rel.* M Walker, Solicitor, Seager & Co, Branker Buildings, Bolton].

622. **Default judgments–setting aside–payment of damages awarded against uninsured driver refused by Motor Insurers Bureau**

[County Court Rules 1981 Ord.37 r.4.]
ON obtained a default judgment against OB, an uninsured driver, following an accident. The Motor Insurers Bureau, MIB, refused to pay the damages awarded on the grounds that they had not been informed of the date when damages were to be assessed, pursuant to the Motor Insurers Bureau (Compensation of Victims of Uninsured Drivers) Agreement 1988. ON successfully applied for the judgment to be set aside under CCR Ord.37 r.4 so that a fresh action could be brought. MIB appealed, arguing that the original judgment was properly decided and could not be set aside.

Held, dismissing the appeal, that the ability to bring applications under Ord.37 r.4 was not confined to defendants and the rule was sufficiently broad to enable the plaintiff or the court to set aside a default judgment. In the instant case, it would be in the interests of justice and of all the parties to set aside the judgment, thus allowing the MIB to make representations on the assessment of damages and preventing any dispute as to MIB's liability.

O'NEILL v. O'BRIEN [1997] P.I.Q.R. P223, Lord Woolf, M.R., CA.

623. **Default judgments–setting aside–res judicata–refusal to set aside was exercise of discretion not decision on merits**

[Rules of the Supreme Court Ord.13 r.9.]
C had obtained summary judgment in default against M with regard to unpaid petrol bills and M had unsuccessfully applied to have the judgment set aside under RSC Ord.13 r.9. M appealed against the striking out of later proceedings against C, in which he alleged that C's contract with him was so unfair as to be unenforceable, on the grounds that the substance of C's claim had already been determined in the earlier proceedings.

Held, allowing the appeal, that a decision not to set aside a default judgment under Ord.13 r.9 was an exercise of discretion and was not a determination based on the merits of the issues involved. M was not estopped, therefore, from taking further action and C could not rely on the doctrine of res judicata. It was difficult to conceive of a situation where an interlocutory hearing might give rise to an estoppel since, even where the court had considered the issues in order to assess the possibility of a defendant's action succeeding, the decision might have been given on at least a partially discretionary basis.

MULLEN v. CONOCO LTD, *The Times*, April 30, 1997, Evans, L.J., CA.

624. **Delay–inordinate and inexcusable delay in prosecuting action–stress and business disruption could amount to prejudice sufficient to strike out action**

[Rules of the Supreme Court Ord.3 r.6.]
A brought a claim of breach of contract and misrepresentation against E, of which N was principal director, in relation to antique candelabra which had been purchased from E in 1987 and 1988. In 1996 N issued a summons to have the action struck out consequent to a breach of the Rules of the Supreme Court

Ord.3 r.6. The judge held that, despite there being an inordinate and inexcusable delay in prosecuting the action, N had failed to show that they had suffered prejudice sufficient to justify striking out. N appealed.

Held, allowing the appeal, that not only prejudice in the actual conduct of proceedings but also prejudice to N's business and reputation, which resulted in stress to N and disruption to the business, were relevant factors for the court's consideration. Having made serious allegations of dishonesty against N, A had a duty to proceed without undue delay.

AL-FAYED v. EMANOUEL ANTIQUES LTD, *The Times*, August 22, 1997, Roch, L.J., CA.

625. Discovery–delay–defendant objecting to discovery–application to extend time limits

L's claim was for unpaid invoices for replacement motors on a bulldozer which it had supplied to S in 1989, dated March 1994. S claimed set off and counterclaimed on the basis that the original motors had only broken down because of design defects, or alternatively that L had negligently advised S that it was safe to continue to use the machine when the defects were discovered. The claim was issued on November 28, 1994. On October 27, 1995 directions were given for the exchange of witness statements within 10 weeks and of expert reports in 12 weeks. Thereafter cross applications were made with regard to discovery and a further direction was given on January 23, 1996 for exchange of expert reports within two months. No further direction was given in respect of witness statements. S only complied with the direction for discovery on April 11, 1996. On May 3, L's solicitors wrote to S's solicitors seeking an agreement for the exchange of witness statements by May 31. On May 22, S's solicitors replied that they did not think it appropriate to exchange as they were still not satisfied that full discovery had been given. On June 3, L filed its factual evidence at court, notified S that it was ready to exchange, and served its expert report. S continued to complain about L's alleged failure to give full discovery. On November 19 and 26, with a trial date fixed for December 6, S served its expert's report and a witness statement which was dated May 30, 1996. The hearing on December 6 was adjourned owing to listing difficulties and the matter came before the court on January 27. On January 17, S had made application to extend time for the service of reports and statements. That application was heard at the trial.

Held, refusing S's application, that the onus was on S to explain the delay and provide reasons for the exercise of the court's discretion. The only reason given, namely S's dissatisfaction at the lack of discovery, was inadequate given that matters of discovery were concluded by early spring 1996 and L's managing director had stated on affidavit on February 28, 1996 that no further documentation was available. No affidavit had been filed explaining the delay or why S's statement of fact had been withheld and it was clear that the whole course of the litigation had been punctuated by S's failure to comply with requests and directions. L had done its best to comply with the directions and had made it clear to S from May onwards that it would object to evidence adduced late. It had been active in seeking to move the case forward and to effect an exchange. Potential prejudice to the opposing party was still a relevant consideration. L would suffer substantial prejudice if the evidence were admitted at this stage, since it would either have to deal with a mass of material at short notice, or seek an adjournment and be kept out of its money for longer than it had been already. Insofar as L also needed leave to adduce its evidence, that leave would be granted. Notwithstanding that the effect of disallowing the application was to deny S a trial of the issues, the time limits would not be extended, *Beachley Property Ltd v. Edgar* [1997] P.N.L.R. 197, [1996] C.L.Y. 943, *Mortgage Corp Ltd v. Sandoes* [1997] P.N.L.R. 263, [1997] C.L.Y. 783 applied, *Letpac Ltd v. Harris* [1997] P.N.L.R. 239, [1997] C.L.Y. 784 distinguished.

LEIHBERR GB LTD v. SIM, January 27, 1997, H.H.J. Sander, CC (Exeter). [*Ex rel.* Andrew Butler, Barrister, Francis Taylor Building, Temple].

626. Foreign judgments-application for leave to appeal against registration unnecessary

[Civil Jurisdiction and Judgments Act 1982; Rules of the Supreme Court Ord.59 r.1B.]

M applied for leave to appeal against a decision dismissing his appeal against an order to register a Belgian debt as a High Court judgment, pursuant to the Civil Jurisdiction and Judgments Act 1982. M contended that leave was not required.

Held, allowing the appeal, that no leave was required because the Brussels Convention 1968 Art.37 para.2, as incorporated in Sch.1 to the 1982 Act, gave an absolute right to a single further appeal on a point of law which was not overruled by RSC Ord.59 r.1B (1) (g).

LANDHURST LEASING PLC v. MARCQ, Trans. Ref: LTA 97/5577/J, June 6, 1997, Auld, L.J., CA.

627. Foreign judgments-registration of Israeli judgment-application by judgment debtor to set aside registration-no jurisdiction to order security for costs against judgment creditor

[Foreign Judgments (Reciprocal Enforcement) Act 1933 s.2, s.4; Reciprocal Enforcement of Foreign Judgments (Israel) Order 1971 (SI 1971 1039); Rules of the Supreme Court Ord.71 r.4.]

S issued proceedings in Israel against T claiming repayment of £44,471 he allegedly paid to T for investment in a business in England. T denied that the money had been paid and a contested trial followed in which T was ordered to pay £29,666 plus interest and costs. S registered the judgment in England. On an application by T an order was made by Judge Batterbury that the court did have jurisdiction to order a payment by S of security for T's costs in challenging the Supreme Court decision, which S complied with. A further order relating to payment of security was made, which was set aside on appeal by Moses Q.C. who stated that had he had the jurisdiction to do so he would have ordered payment of security. T was given leave to appeal that order and S was granted leave ex parte to appeal Judge Batterbury's order out of time so the two decisions, being contrary, could be considered together. There was an arguable case that the original judgment against T had been obtained by fraud. The issue was whether the court had jurisdiction to order security for costs against S, having registered the judgment of a superior court in Israel, on T's application to set aside that registration.

Held, allowing S's appeal and dismissing T's appeal, that there was no jurisdiction for an order for security for costs to be made. The object of registration of judgments was to allow for the process of enforcement and a registered judgment was not enforceable until determination of the set aside application. An application to register a judgment and proceedings to have the judgment set aside were two separate processes under the Foreign Judgments (Reciprocal Enforcement) Act 1933 s.2 and s.4. The words "any person making application for the registration of judgment" in the Reciprocal Enforcement of Foreign Judgments (Israel) Order 1971 identified the person against whom no order for security might be made, in this case the judgment creditor, and did not have the effect of limiting the immunity of a judgment creditor to the mere process of application and excluding immunity in respect of a related but separate process of setting aside registration. The requirement that the person making application for registration was not required to pay security of costs was intended to govern the whole process of the application under the Convention between the UK and Israeli governments contained in the schedule to the 1971 Order, and orders for security could only be made under RSC Ord.71 r.4 subject to the 1971 Order.

TUVYAHU v. SWIGI, Trans. Ref: FC3 97/5187/E, QBENI 96/0296/E, February 7, 1997, Potter, L.J., CA.

628. Group actions–medical negligence–failure to give warnings about addictive properties of medication–actions by remaining applicants struck out as abuse of process

In 1988 a steering committee of solicitors was established to coordinate potential claimants against the drug companies which manufactured benzodiazepines, widely prescribed as tranquillisers in the 1960s. Legal aid was granted to several thousand applicants to pursue claims in negligence against the companies, the central allegation being a failure to exercise reasonable care in not placing on packets sufficient warnings about the addictive properties of the drugs. Actions were commenced in 1991 and 1992, but in mid-1992 the Legal Aid Board instituted an audit of all the pleaded cases and, having assessed the chances of success as minimal, withdrew funding from the applicants. By 1996 only 70 non-legal aid plaintiffs remained, unrepresented or represented on a conditional fee basis. The drug companies successfully applied to have those actions struck out, inter alia, as an abuse of process and AB appealed.

Held, dismissing the appeal, that while access to the courts was a fundamental right and litigants could not have their claims dismissed without good reason, this right was not unfettered, *Hunter v. Chief Constable of the West Midlands Police* [1982] A.C. 529, [1982] C.L.Y. 2382, considered, *Ashmore v. British Coal Corp* [1990] 2 All E.R. 981, [1990] C.L.Y. 3542 followed. Proceedings that were conducted in a way that was vexatious and oppressive to another party could be struck out as an abuse of process. In assessing the viability of AB's claims it was relevant to take into account the fact that legal aid had been withdrawn as the Legal Aid Board had been advised by leading counsel that it would be unreasonable to grant AB representation on the basis that they did not have reasonable grounds for their claims. As regards causation, there was no substantial evidence from general practitioners that AB would not have taken the drugs if the companies had provided more adequate advice and warnings. Without legal aid funding, there was no prospect whatsoever of the remaining cases even being brought to trial, let alone to a successful outcome.

AB v. JOHN WYETH & BROTHER LTD; AB v. ROCHE PRODUCTS LTD [1997] 8 Med. L.R. 57, Stuart-Smith, L.J., CA.

629. Injunctions–disclosure of confidential material stored on computer– whether failure to disclose justified discharge of order

R applied for a notice of motion to discharge Anton Piller orders against him as S had failed to make full and frank disclosure to the court in their application. S were two associated companies which provided consulting services in the field of business information technology. R and others worked for the companies either as employees or independent contractors. The issue was the nature of the duty of fidelity owed to the companies. R retained on a personal computer shared with his wife, a large quantity of material which related either to the internal organisation and working of S's business or to work which S had undertaken or hoped to undertake for clients or prospective clients. There was compelling evidence that, while working out their notice, employees communicated information concerning the internal affairs of S to employees who had already left the company. There was strong evidence of flagrant and repeated breaches of the duty of fidelity. R's evidence was that much of the confidential information stored on the computer related to his wife's work and therefore should not have been taken on the execution of the Anton Piller order.

Held, dismissing the application regarding the Anton Piller orders, that (1) despite S's failure, although not deliberate, to make full disclosure to the court of the fact that the personal computer used by R had information belonging to his wife's clients, that omission was not sufficient to justify any discharge of the ex parte orders, *Dormeuil Freres SA v. Nicolian International (Textiles) Ltd* [1988] 1 W.L.R. 1362, [1988] C.L.Y. 2892 and *Lock International v. Beswick* [1989] 1 W.L.R. 1268, [1990] C.L.Y. 1881 considered, and (2) since damages would be an inadequate remedy in these circumstances, injunctive relief was granted

prohibiting R from soliciting or providing business services, directly or indirectly to clients of S until six months after the execution of the Anton Piller order.
STRATEGICAL SOLUTIONS LTD (T/A CANNON HILL CONSULTING) v. ROBINSON, Trans. Ref: 1997-S-No.602, May 2, 1997, Robert Walker, J., Ch D.

630. Interim relief—jurisdiction

CIVIL JURISDICTION AND JUDGMENTS ACT 1982 (INTERIM RELIEF) ORDER 1997, SI 1997 302; made under the Civil Jurisdiction and Judgments Act 1982 s.25. In force: April 1, 1997; £0.65.

This Order enlarges the power of the High Court in England and Wales or Northern Ireland to grant interim relief in aid of legal proceedings in other countries. At present such relief can only be granted where the principal proceedings are taking place in a country which is a party to the 1968 Brussels Convention or the 1988 Lugano Convention on jurisdiction and the enforcement of judgments in civil and commercial matters and where the proceedings are within the scope of those Conventions. This Order removes those two limitations from the Courts' powers.

631. Interim relief—licensing of medicines—adjournment of judicial review proceedings on ECJ reference—usual principles of interim relief not applicable where competing cases of public interest resting on interpretation of Directive

[Council Directive 65/65 on proprietary medicinal products.]
S, the initiator of the drug Captopril, was licensed to market the drug for myocardial infarction and for diabetic nephropathy and had applied for judicial review of a decision to grant a licence to G to market Captopril for myocardial infarction. G, in turn, had applied for judicial review of a decision refusing it a licence to market Captopril for diabetic nephropathy. The outcome of the litigation rested on three different interpretations by S, G and the licensing authority of an article in Council Directive 65/65, which regulated the granting of licences for the marketing of medicinal products, and a reference was made to the ECJ for a preliminary ruling on the matter. S and G appealed against the refusal of their applications for interim relief.

Held, dismissing the appeals, that this was a highly unusual case and the normal method of assessing the balance of convenience in order to decide whether the court should grant interim relief was not applicable. It was inappropriate for the court to express a view on the correct interpretation of the Directive and each claim was presumed to have an equal probability of success, so that the principles in *American Cyanamid Co v. Ethicon Ltd* [1975] A.C. 396, [1975] C.L.Y. 2640 were not applicable. Similarly, attempting to assess the injustice to each party was problematic, since an incorrect decision to refuse or grant an injunction would deprive the other party of a financial asset which it was in the public interest that they should receive. It was the role of the ECJ to decide which of two competing cases of public interest should succeed at the expense of the other.

R. v. SECRETARY OF STATE FOR HEALTH, *ex p.* GENERICS (UK) LTD; R. v. SECRETARY OF STATE FOR HEALTH, *ex p.* ER SQUIBB & SONS LTD, *The Times*, February 25, 1997, Schiemann, L.J., CA.

632. Interlocutory injunctions—enforcement of undertaking by local authority—exclusion of secure tenant following alleged racist attack

SLBC applied for leave to admit further evidence and appealed against an order discharging an interlocutory injunction and directing an enquiry as to the damages sustained by S as a result of that injunction. After an argument with racist overtones, it was alleged that S had broken into a neighbour's flat and inflicted grievous bodily wounds with a 15 inch knife to the face of one of the occupants. There was considerable publicity and fear amongst both tenants and housing staff, because of the racist connotations of the attack. SLBC sought an ex parte injunction with the usual undertaking in damages, restraining S from (i) returning to the flat, of which he was the secure tenant; (ii) entering the estate on which the flat was situated except to collect his belongings; (iii) causing a nuisance to other tenants or their associates; (iv) assaulting other tenants and (v) entering the local housing office. S was subsequently arrested and put on an identification parade but was released when he was not identified by any of the witnesses. SLBC applied for leave to adduce further evidence of allegations that witnesses had not identified S because of indirect threats that they would be killed. SLBC contended that an enquiry into damages could not be ordered before the determination of the question whether the undertaking should be enforced, and that, although S had been excluded from his home by the injunction for approximately four weeks, damages should be awarded on a contractual basis, and S could have mitigated his loss by an application for the injunction to be lifted, it would be no defence that S was in prison for another offence at the time. The resultant damage claim was so trivial that the court should decline to enforce the injunction.

Held, refusing the application to adduce further evidence and dismissing the appeal, that (1) the additional evidence was inadmissible in an application for enforcement of an undertaking, because it was largely hearsay and in any case could, with due diligence, have been put before the judge below; (2) the judge below had considered the issue of enforcement and even if he had not, then the court would confirm that the undertaking should be enforced, and (3) it was open to SLBC to make a payment into court if it believed that the claim was of little value, *Cheltenham and Gloucester Building Society v. Ricketts* [1993] 1 W.L.R. 1545 [1993] C.L.Y. 3283 considered, *Columbia Picture Industries v. Robinson* [1987] Ch. 38, [1986] C.L.Y. 2564 distinguished as referring to an order which should not have been made on the evidence then before the judge.

SOUTHWARK LBC v. STORRIE, Trans. Ref: QBENI 96/0351/E, December 3, 1996, Sir Ralph Gibson, CA.

633. Interlocutory judgments–personal injuries–quantum only triable issue–whether error of law

[County Court Rules 1981 Ord.9 r.14; Rules of the Supreme Court Ord.27 r.3.]

I issued proceedings for damages for personal injury and other losses sustained as a result of a road traffic accident. A defence was filed admitting liability but disputing quantum and I applied for interlocutory judgment to be entered pursuant to CCR Ord.9 r.14. This was granted by the district judge and B appealed on the grounds that the district judge had misdirected himself in law.

Held, dismissing the appeal, that in exercise of its jurisdiction under CCR Ord.9 r.14 and the High Court equivalent, the court has a wider power to look at the reality of the situation than it would in the strict interpretation of CCR Ord.9 r.6 and its High Court equivalent, RSC Ord.27 r.3. To that end the decision in *Parrott v. Jackson* [1996] P.I.Q.R. p394, [1996] 1 C.L.Y. 904 was distinguished. There was no doubt that B's negligence had caused the accident and the only question which remained was the exact amount of damage suffered. There was a clear distinction in the application of CCR Ord.9 r.6 and Ord.9 r.14 otherwise there would be no need for separate rules. The district judge was entitled on the evidence before him and on the nature of the application to come to the view that no triable issue remained save quantum.

IBBOTSON v. BOND CONFECTIONERS, February 7, 1997, H.H.J. Mahon, CC (Kendal). [*Ex rel.* Ingham Clegg & Crowther, Solicitors, 4/8 Leopold Grove, Blackpool].

634. Interrogatories–measure of damages

[Rules of the Supreme Court Ord.26.]

Proceedings were issued following a road traffic accident on June 7, 1995. The issue of liability conceded. H's claim included claims for (a) cost of repair of motor car; (b) diminution in value of motor car and (c) hire charges. N served interrogatories enquiring as to various aspects of the claim which were set aside.

N appealed on the basis that the interrogatories fell within the provisions of RSC Ord.26. and the information was required in particular to enable a realistic and informed assessment to be made of H's case for the purposes of a payment in.

Held, allowing the appeal in respect of certain of the interrogatories as follows: (a) as to the date of repair of the vehicle as that was relevant to the interest calculation; (b) as to whether the vehicle had been involved in any other accident and if so details as to the repairs, as that was relevant to the claim for diminution in value; (c) as to the date of payment for car hire as that was relevant to the issue of interest; (d) as to whether alternative enquiries were made of other hirers to ascertain terms and rates of hire as that was relevant to issue of reasonableness of H's steps in relation to hire; (e) as to the particular make and model of the vehicle as that was relevant to the claim for diminution in value; (f) as to the date of disposal of the vehicle and details as to the sum paid on disposal and to whom it was disposed as that was relevant to the claim for diminution in value; (g) as to the circumstances in which H obtained two expert's reports in respect of the vehicle as N was entitled to have an explanation as to why this had occurred where the expert's figures differed, and (h) as to the recorded mileage at the date of sale as this was relevant to the issue of diminution in value.

HONEY v. NEWMAN, July 26, 1996, H.H.J. Bernstein, CC (Birkenhead). [*Ex rel.* William Rankin, Barrister, Oriel Chambers, Liverpool].

635. Interrogatories–variation–withdrawal–requirements

[Rules of the Supreme Court Ord.26 r.3.]

M had served interrogatories on S but no replies were received. S indicated in correspondence that they intended to seek variation and withdrawal of the interrogatories, but did not issue a summons within 14 days. M issued a summons to seek an order that the interrogatories be answered, amongst other orders. At the hearing S made an application to have the interrogatories withdrawn.

Held, disallowing the late application, that although RSC Ord.26 r.3 use the permissive word "may", in the instant case it was mandatory that a party wishing to resist interrogatories that had been served on them was required to proceed by summons within 14 days of the date the interrogatories were served.

McGANN v. SHARP FILMS LTD, December 4, 1996, Master Turner. [*Ex rel.* Charles Pugh, Barrister, 1 Verulam Buildings, Gray's Inn].

636. Joinder–director/shareholder as representative of company–rights of audience in High Court

[Misrepresentation Act 1967 s.2; Courts and Legal Services Act 1990 s.17, s.27, s.28; Rules of the Supreme Court Ord.15 r.4, Ord.15 r.6.]

F agreed to carry out earthworks subcontract works on a measure and value basis upon the terms of FCEC subcontract. They brought an action against three defendants successively the main contractors. F purported to assign the benefit of the subcontract to F, the managing director and majority shareholder. The Court of Appeal held that the assignment of the majority of F's claims was invalidated by the prohibition on assignment contained in cl.2(3) of the FCEC subcontract. F applied to be joined as an additional plaintiff under RSC Ord.15 r.4(1) or Ord.15 r.6(2)(b) in order to pursue such claims as were not caught by the prohibition on assignment ie. claims for misrepresentation under the Misrepresentation Act 1967 s.2(1) against S and claims in quasi contract or restitution against MS and MG and in order to be heard in relation to an application for a costs order against him personally. He further applied for leave to represent F both in conducting the litigation and as an advocate on the grounds that the company could not afford representation by both solicitors and counsel.

Held, that (1) since the requirements of RSC Ord.15 r.4(1) were met, the court had no discretion and F should be allowed to be joined as co plaintiff in respect of the restitutionary claims which were independent of the subcontract and, in any event, MS and MG were not parties to the subcontract and so could not have the benefit of cl.2(3); (2) however, Ord.15 r.4(1) did not require the court to permit joinder in relation to causes of action which were bound to fail. The claim under the Misrepresentation Act 1967 was such a claim since it was caught by the prohibition upon assignment contained in cl.2(3) of the FCEC Rules because it was a benefit under the subcontract and could not be saved by the proviso to that clause; (3) in his position as assignee and as the object of the proposed costs order, F had a right to be joined under RSC Ord.15 r.6(2)(b), and (4) there were no exceptional circumstances justifying departure from the normal rules that in the High Court a company must be represented by a solicitor and that the advocate must be a barrister or other qualified advocate and therefore F's application to represent the company would be refused, *Radford v. Samuel* [1994] 1 B.C.L.C. 445, [1994] C.L.Y. 417 applied, *Europa Holdings Ltd v. Circle Industries (UK) Ltd* [1995] C.I.L.L. 1079 considered but not followed. This position had not been altered by any provision of the Courts and Legal Services Act 1990.

Observed, that (1) the Courts and Legal Services Act 1990 recognised and preserved the court's inherent right to decide who should appear before it. It was not concerned with the grant of rights of audience in specific cases such as that raised by the current application. In particular s.27 and s.28 of the Courts and Legal Services Act 1990 did not confer upon the court power to grant the right to conduct litigation or rights of audience upon individuals; (2) further, F did not meet the criteria comprised in the general principle, ie. as to qualifications or membership identified in s.17(3) of the Courts and Legal Services Act 1990 and could not therefore benefit therefrom, and (3) even if the Courts and Legal Services Act 1990 had replaced the common law rule, the principles already laid down in relation to the power at common law remained valid and applicable and the application would be rejected, *Radford v. Samuel* applied.

FLOODS OF QUEENSFERRY LTD v. SHAND CONSTRUCTION LTD 81 B.L.R. 49, Judge Humphrey Lloyd Q.C., QBD (OR).

637. Joinder–joinder of party after expiry of limitation period

[Rules of the Supreme Court Ord.15 r.6(2), Ord.15 r.16(3), Ord.58 r.1(3).]

P fell from a ladder in February 1990. In May 1991 he issued a writ against G and in December 1994 he successfully applied ex parte for leave to join M. No affidavit was sworn, pursuant to the Rules of the Supreme Court Ord.15 r.16(3) and the limitation point not raised. M served defence, and again limitation was not pleaded. M applied unsuccessfully in March 1995 to be dismissed from the action on the grounds that there was no cause of action against him. After some time, following an oversight by solicitors and counsel, the limitation issue was recognised and M issued notice of appeal in January 1996. In February 1996 an application for extension of time was refused.

Held, granting the application for an extension of time, that the district judge had erred in imposing a fetter on the exercise of his discretion under RSC Ord.58 r.1(3). In refusing an extension of time on the sole ground of inexcusable long delay, he failed to view the matter before him in the round and did not make an overall assessment of what was required by the justice of the case. The order joining M in 1994 was made without prior notice and M had no prior opportunity to state his reasons for opposing that order. At the hearing in March 1995 the limitation point was overlooked. It could have been raised on appeal to a judge in chambers. The ex parte order for the joinder of M was made pursuant to RSC Ord.15 r.6(2)(b): "no person shall be added or substituted as a party after the expiry of any relevant period of limitation". The claim against M was already statute barred in December 1994. The order joining M was set aside with P ordered to pay the costs of the action and the appeal.

MARSHALL v. GRADON CONSTRUCTION SERVICES LTD AND MILL, June 27, 1997, Ward, L.J., CA. [*Ex rel.* DVH Wheeler, Solicitor, Crosse & Crosse, 14 Southernhay West, Exeter].

638. Joinder–proper party to proceedings–service outside jurisdiction

[Rules of the Supreme Court Ord.15 r.4(1).]

B claimed under a contract for the sale of propane gas that the propane gas provided to them as buyer was not of the contractually required quality. B sought to join the shippers of the propane as parties to the action on the basis that the quality of the propane may have deteriorated during shipment. The issue arose whether or not the shippers were a proper party to the action and whether this case was a proper one for service out of the jurisdiction.

Held, that the claims which B sought to bring against either party would arise out of the same set of facts. Therefore, because the claims would arise out of the same transaction or series of transactions, under RSC Ord.15 r.4(1)(a), the shippers could be joined as a party to the action. The affidavit joining the parties was defective in that it did not disclose the reason why the shippers were to be joined to the action. There was no agreement that the Saudi courts could not be used. Therefore, there was a real risk of different findings on the same facts if all the litigation were not conducted in one jurisdiction. While it would be inconvenient for the shippers to bring their witnesses from Saudi Arabia to England, they would have been required to do so under arbitration in any event and therefore there was no special hardship caused to them. On these facts, the right course would be to provide an opportunity for an affidavit to be sworn in the correct form before allowing service out of the jurisdiction to preclude extra costs in requiring a further application for leave.

BOREALIS AB v. STARGAS LTD (THE BERGE SISAR) [1997] 1 Lloyd's Rep. 635, Waller, J., QBD (Comm Ct).

639. Judgment debts–enforcement–court had no jurisdiction to order surrender of foreign national's passport

[Supreme Court Act 1981 s.37(1).]

H, a foreign national, had failed to meet a costs order requiring him to pay some of the costs of matrimonial proceedings. It had already been established that H had sufficient assets to meet the debt and W applied under the Supreme Court Act 1981 s.37(1) for an injunction to prevent H leaving the country until he paid the sum owed to her by requiring him to surrender his passport.

Held, dismissing the application, that although s.37(1) had been used to restrain parties from leaving the country where their departure would frustrate the established procedures for the enforcement of judgments, it was usually used where a hearing was pending which would dispose of the proceedings. Such an order could only be used to supplement existing powers and could not be imposed as a free standing order to detain a judgment debtor for an indefinite period. Therefore, the court had no statutory or inherent power to order H to surrender his passport, *B (Child Abduction: Wardship: Power to Detain), Re* [1994] 2 F.L.R. 479, [1994] C.L.Y. 3277 applied.

B v. B (INJUNCTION: RESTRAINT ON LEAVING JURISDICTION); *sub nom.* B v. B (PASSPORT SURRENDER: JURISDICTION) [1997] 3 All E.R. 258, Wilson, J., Fam Div.

640. Judgments and orders–alleged fraud of litigant did not impugn finding of liability in personal injuries action

G appealed against the order for a retrial following dismissal of W's personal injuries claim on the basis that the court was misled into ordering a new trial on the question of liability. The original proceedings were for damages for personal injuries following a road traffic accident in 1988 and after an appeal a new trial, following the hearing of fresh evidence, found that C and W were equally responsible for the accident. G appealed against that finding. At the second trial the judge found that W was lying about whether or not he was working on the day of the accident. G argued that finding constituted a finding of fraud.

Held, dismissing the appeal, that where a judgment was alleged to have been obtained by fraud, the normal course was for a fresh action to be brought making a specific allegation of fraud so that the issue could be fully aired. In certain special circumstances, for instance if the fraud could clearly be established, it might be better to proceed by way of appeal in order to avoid unnecessary additional litigation. However the instant case it was not appropriate to set aside the judgment which W obtained as the judge at the second trial, although expressing doubt as to the truth of the evidence which prompted the decision to order a new trial, did not deal with the question of whether fraud had been practised on the Court of Appeal, *Flower v. Lloyd* (1876) 6 Ch. 297 considered.

WOOD v. GAHLINGS, *The Times*, November 29, 1996, Lord Woolf, M.R., CA.

641. Judgments and orders—setting aside—judgment in absence of defendant—judicial discretion

A appealed against a refusal to set aside judgment for S given in A's absence. S's claim was for the balance unpaid on five invoices for rolls of fabric but A had defended and counterclaimed on the grounds that some of the rolls had been faulty and some had not been delivered.

Held, allowing the appeal and setting aside judgment on the terms of a payment in by A of £10,000 within 14 days, that the judge below had been wrong to decide that A merely wished to delay payment, since he had offered to pay into court the whole of the claim with interest and costs thrown away. S would not be prejudiced by a retrial within a few weeks of exchange of witness statements and the judge below appeared to have failed to consider the likelihood of A's success, which even S conceded was certainly arguable and not weak, *Shocked v. Goldschmidt* [1998] 1 All E.R. 372, [1998] 3 C.L.73, *Grimshaw v. Dunbar* [1953] 1 Q.B. 408, [1953] C.L.Y. 709 and *Hayman v. Rowlands* [1957] 1 All E.R. 321, [1957] C.L.Y. 638 considered.

SHAHTEX LTD v. ABOOBAKER (T/A HIGHLINE CLOTHING CO), Trans. Ref: CCRTI 96/1014/G, February 28, 1997, Morland, J., CA.

642. Judicial decision making—findings of fact—person accused of misrepresentation entitled to primary finding as to truth of allegation

Held, that where a person was accused of misrepresentation during civil litigation, the judge was required to make a primary finding as to whether a representation had been made, whether it was fraudulent and why. In reaching his conclusion, the judge should address all the evidence and give reasons for all significant findings of fact. It was quite wrong for those questions to be determined purely on the basis of whether the recipient of the representation was considered credible.

MOORE v. INNTREPRENEUR ESTATES (GL) LTD, *The Times*, October 10, 1997, Henry, L.J., CA.

643. Limitations—extortionate credit agreements

See CONSUMER LAW: First National Bank Plc v. Ann & Ann. §963, Homestead Finance Ltd v. Warriner and Tasker. §961, Ricketts and Ricketts v. Hurstanger Ltd. §962

644. Limitations—fatal accidents—minor dependents—action dismissed for want of prosecution—no second action

[Fatal Accidents Act 1976 s.1, s.2(3).]

C was a motor cyclist killed in an accident in July 1985 when a taxi driven by Y turned across his path. The deceased left a widow and two children, aged four and one, as his dependents. S, a firm of solicitors, were instructed to prosecute an action against Y. Proceedings under the Fatal Accidents Act 1976 were duly instituted. In January 1991 that action was dismissed for want of prosecution. In the professional negligence action brought by the widow and the children, S pleaded that the infant plaintiffs had sustained no loss as they still had a continuing and independent right of action under the Act s.1 and were not prevented from issuing a new writ against Y.

It was argued that limitation had not run as against the minors. The infant plaintiffs contended that given the dismissal of the original action, which had been properly constituted under the 1976 Act, s.2(3), which precluded a second action and that there was now no machinery whereby they could take proceedings under the 1976 Act.

Held, that the plaintiffs' contentions were correct. The dismissal of the original action for want of prosecution put an end to that action. Accordingly, the 1976 Act s.2(3) precluded a second action against the other driver. Furthermore, in the circumstances, a second action against Y would now be an abuse of process. *Cooper v. Williams* [1963] 2 Q.B. 567, [1963] C.L.Y. 2846 and *Birkett v. James* [1978] A.C. 297, [1977] C.L.Y. 2410 considered.

CROFT v. SHAVIN & CO, November 16, 1995, H.H.J. Prosser, QBD. [*Ex rel.* Basil Yoxall, Barrister].

645. Limitations—insurance broker gave negligent advice on insurance policy— cause of action accrued on payment of premium not when insurer avoided policy

K brought an action against an insurance broker, D, alleging that he had negligently advised them to purchase a voidable policy, which the insurer avoided when K claimed under it. D appealed against a decision refusing to strike out K's action as being time barred, contending that the limitation period started to run from the date when K paid their renewal premium, and not, as K claimed, either when the insurer avoided the policy or when the fire occurred which gave rise to K's claim.

Held, allowing the appeal, that a cause of action accrued once the plaintiff had relied to his detriment on the negligent advice and had failed to obtain what he was entitled to, which in the instant case was when K paid their renewal premium without receiving a binding contract of insurance in exchange. This was not changed by the fact that the seriousness of the effects of D's negligence could only be ascertained later, as future contingencies were only relevant to the quantification of K's loss and not to the fact of loss, even though K was unaware of the deficiency at the time the premium was renewed. Therefore K's claim against D was time barred.

KNAPP v. ECCLESIASTICAL INSURANCE GROUP PLC, *The Times,* November 17, 1997, Hobhouse, L.J., CA.

646. Limitations—negligence—failure   by   plaintiffs   to   show   deliberate concealment

[Limitation Act 1980 s.14B, s.32.]

B contracted with W to install and supply bellows units for a blast furnace. The units were delivered to the site in 1976, but not installed until 1978. Problems occurred with the units both before and after commissioning and an explosion occurred in April 1990. B alleged in a re-amended statement of claim that one of the two defendants entered into a subcontract with what was thought to be a subsidiary company of B, to design, manufacture and supply the bellows. It was now common ground that the subcontract was in fact between one of the defendants and B using a trading name. The action was commenced on the assumption that there was no contract between B and either of the defendants, and the claim was brought in negligence, with a defence of contributory negligence.

Held, giving judgment for the defendants, that (1) the correct defendants were the second defendants, and (2) the action was statute barred because the acts or omissions alleged to constitute negligence and to which damage was alleged to be attributable occurred at the latest in August 1976. B's claim was, therefore, time barred under the Limitation Act 1980 s.14B. B had failed to start the action within the long stop period and had also failed to prove deliberate concealment within s.32 of the 1980 Act.

BRITISH STEEL PLC v. WYVERN STRUCTURES LTD (FORMERLY MUNRO & MILLER LTD) (IN LIQUIDATION) 52 Con. L.R. 67, Judge Bowsher Q.C., QBD (OR).

647. Limitations–negligence–negligent insurance advice–date action accrued

See CIVIL PROCEDURE: Knapp v. Ecclesiastical Insurance Group Plc. §645

648. Limitations–negligence–professional negligence–solicitors–failure to advise client to take independent advice amounted to deliberate concealment

[Limitation Act 1980 s.14(A)(5), s.32(1).]

In 1987 M instructed C in relation to the purchase of a workshop. In 1991 C discovered from a neighbour, BG, that there was a right of way vested in BG through the workshop. C informed M of the right of way but took no further action. M did nothing believing that he had no liability as he had not constructed the workshop. In 1994 M commenced proceedings against C and the question of limitation was taken as a preliminary issue.

Held, that the claim was not statute barred, that M knew nothing of the problem until 1991 and M's knowledge in 1991 did not amount to knowledge that the defect in title might imply negligence by C so as to trigger the three year extended limitation period under the Limitation Act 1980 s.14(A)(5). In any event C's failure to apprise M of the possible claim in negligence against themselves or at least to tell him to seek independent legal advice amounted to deliberate concealment within s.32(1)(b) of the Act and prevented time running against him.

MARKES v. COODES [1997] P.N.L.R. 252, Judge Anthony Thompson Q.C., QBD.

649. Limitations–negligence–professional negligence–solicitors–negligent misstatement–disapplication of limitation period–continuing duty of care

[Limitation Act 1980 s.33.]

C pursued a claim against the Motor Insurer's Bureau and its agent S. When S informed C of the expiry of the limitation period it was suggested that she seek legal advice. C approached F who pursued her case but following S's insistence on the limitation point in a letter of October 3, 1988, F informed C that nothing further could be done in a letter dated October 4, 1988. C raised an action for professional negligence against F. F successfully argued at trial that they ought to have commenced proceedings in June 1988 and made an application to disapply the limitation period in terms of the Limitation Act 1980 s.33 and so C's claim against them was also timed barred. However, the trial judge found F negligent and the letter of October 4 amounted to a negligent misstatement. The judged failed to uphold F's submission that C's claim should not be allowed to proceed as it had not been pleaded. It was also held that had a s.33 application been made H would have had an 80 per cent chance of success. F appealed and C cross appealed.

Held, dismissing the appeal allowing the cross appeal, that (1) F had not been negligent in failing to initiate proceedings under the 1980 Act s.33 before October 3 when it became an issue; (2) the letter from F to C on October 4 amounted to a negligent misstatement of C's position; (3) the judge's decision that amendment of the pleadings was unnecessary was within his discretion; (4) the judge's assessment of C's chance of success was within his discretion and would not be interfered with, and (5) F had been under a continuing duty of care, *Midland Bank Trust Co v. Hett, Stubbs & Kemp* [1979] 1 Ch. 384, [1978] C.L.Y. 2822 considered.

CARLTON v. FULCHERS [1997] P.N.L.R. 337, Henry, L.J., CA.

650. Limitations–personal injurieis–medical negligence–parents acting as plaintiff's agent–knowledge gained when aware of expert's report contents–complexity of care required degree of specificity of actual knowledge

[Limitation Act 1980 s.14.]

O, aged 26, commenced proceedings against D by a writ issued on May 11, 1994, alleging negligence in respect of injuries she claimed to have suffered at her birth. In particular O alleged negligence in the failure of D to deliver her by caesarean section as soon as a diagnosis of cord prolapse was made, which O claimed led to hypoxia and consequent brain damage which left her severely physically disabled and completely reliant on her parents. Neither O nor her parents were aware that there might have been any negligence involved at O's birth until 1985, when they saw a television programme on cerebral palsy. They resolved not to take any action for a further six years, when O attained the age of 21, in the mistaken belief that at this point O would be an adult and could bring the claim in her own right. O's father wrote a letter to D alleging negligence in October 1991 and a writ was issued in May 1994 after an expert's report was obtained in June 1993. D sought to have the action struck out on the basis that it was time barred under the Limitation Act 1980, either because time had started to run when O turned 18, or because O was fixed with actual or constructive knowledge under the 1980 Act s.14 by the end of 1990, one year after the breech delivery of her sister.

Held, that O's claim was not time barred, as (1) since O had understandably left the management of her case to her parents, they were agents to know and their knowledge could be imputed to O for the purposes of s.14 of the 1980 Act, *Atkinson v. Oxford HA* [1993] 4 Med L.R. 18, [1993] C.L.Y. 2605, applied; (2) the letters written by O's father to D did not afford grounds for supposing that O's parents had actual knowledge for the purposes of s.14 before they received the expert's report in June 1993. In a complex case the act or omission constituting negligence has to be known with some degree of specificity, *Hallam-Eames v. Merrett Syndicates* [1996] 7 Med L.R. 122, [1995] 1 C.L.Y. 3169, applied. Although O may have suspected that her injury was due to birth hypoxia, expert confirmation was required before that suspicion could attain the degree of firmness needed to amount to actual knowledge; (3) as to the state of O's parents' knowledge at the time of O's sister's birth, on the evidence nothing said to them by the doctors either endowed them with knowledge for the purposes of s.14(3) or created a new situation which demanded the seeking of expert advice, nor made it unreasonable for O not to do so; (4) the temporal and circumstantial span of reasonable enquiry for the purpose of acquiring constructive knowledge is to be judged on the factual context of the case and the subjective characteristics of the individual plaintiff, *Nash v. Eli Lilly & Co* [1993] 1 W.L.R. 796, [1993] C.L.Y. 2603 followed. In the circumstances of this case, and in particular O's complete reliance on her parents' advice that she should wait until she was 21 before doing anything about her claim, constructive knowledge in O could not be made out, *Forbes v. Wandsworth HA* [1996] 7 Med L.R. 175, [1996] 2 C.L.Y. 4466, distinguished. O first had knowledge for the purposes of s.14 when she became aware of the contents of the expert's report in June 1993.

O'DRISCOLL v. DUDLEY HA [1996] 7 Med. L.R. 408, Poole, J., QBD.

651. Limitations–personal injuries–date action accrued–delay in bringing action justified

[Limitation Act 1980 s.33(3).]

S was a police officer who had worked as a firearms instructor between May 1978 and July 1983. During that period he was exposed to noise from more than one million pistol rounds and approximately 300,000 shotgun rounds. In 1979/80 he became aware of a permanent ringing in his ears which he accepted as part of his job. Although that gradually became a source of constant discomfort, S was concerned about promotion prospects and did not seek legal advice until

January 1994. Court proceedings were issued in January 1996 and an application made for a preliminary hearing on the question of limitation.

Held, that (1) the permanent ringing in the ears constituted a significant injury and in 1980 S attributed the problem to his work which was held to be when the cause of action occurred. The judge held, on the basis of medical evidence which linked deafness and tinnitus to firearms, that S would succeed on causation. In considering S's delay in complaining to his employers, reference was made to *McCarthy v. Metropolitan Police District Receiver* [1977] W.L.R. 1073, [1977] C.L.Y. 999. It was reasonable for a career policeman of many years to decide not to put his future at risk, and (2) in respect of the Limitation Act 1980 s.33(3)(b) the defendants argued it was difficult to investigate the system of work for protective measures taken but failed to produce an affidavit to that effect. The action should be allowed to proceed and costs of the application awarded to S.

SYKES v. CHIEF CONSTABLE OF WEST YORKSHIRE POLICE, January 21, 1997, Deputy District Judge Miller, CC (Leeds). [*Ex rel.* M Farran, Solicitor, Russell Jones and Walker, Solicitors].

652. Limitations–personal injuries–defendant company dissolved–effect of dissolution on limitations

[Limitation Act 1980 s.33; Companies Act 1985 s.651, s.652, s.653.]

I brought proceedings for noise induced deafness arising out of exposure to noise at D's steel works at Llanelli from 1953 to 1980 by summons dated August 25, 1994. D was originally dissolved following a voluntary winding up on May 12, 1990. That dissolution was declared void on November 9, 1992 and the company was restored to the register following an application by an ex employee who wished to bring personal injury proceedings against the company. During the period when the company was restored to the register I issued proceedings. Unknown to I the company was then dissolved again, this time by the Registrar of Companies under the Companies Act 1985 s.652, on February 13, 1996. Subsequently, D was again restored to the register on August 2, 1996 pursuant to powers under the 1985 Act s.651 and s.653 following an application by another ex worker wishing to pursue an industrial injuries claim. D sought an order in I's action that the second dissolution on February 13, 1996 brought to a permanent end I's proceedings and relied on the judgment in *Philip Powis Ltd, Re* [1997] 2 B.C.L.C. 481, [1997] C.L.Y. 834.

Held, allowing the action to proceed having granted a dispensation in terms of the Limitation Act 1980 s.33, that (1) P's action was not brought to a permanent end because the order restoring the company to the register on the second occasion dated August 2, 1996 had the effect of resurrecting P's action as it contained a deeming provision pursuant to the powers contained in the 1985 Act s.653(3), and (2) *Philip Powis Ltd, Re* was thereby to be distinguished as it concerned the restoration of a company to the register pursuant to s.651 but not s.653 and concerned an application to restore a company to the register following a dissolution after a winding up procedure rather than a restoration following an administrative dissolution pursuant to s.652, *Townreach Ltd (No.002081 of 1994), Re* [1995] Ch. 28, [1995] 1 C.L.Y. 571 and *Morris v. Harris* [1927] A.C. 252 considered.

ISAAC v. DUPORT STEELS LTD, September 23, 1997, H.H.J. M Evans Q.C., CC (Llanelli). [*Ex rel.* Frank Burton, Barrister, 12 Kings Bench Walk, Temple].

653. Limitations–personal injuries–disapplication of limitation period–failure of action by inadvertent failure to effect service

[Limitation Act 1980 s.11, s.33.]

F appealed against the refusal of an application for a direction that the Limitation Act 1980 s.11 should not apply to fresh proceedings brought after the limitation period pursuant to s.33. F was injured while travelling as a passenger in a minibus when it collided with a van being driven by the fourth defendant, who was employed by the third defendant company. A writ was issued and served on the fourth defendant by post at an address supplied by the police. Some four and a half years later, the insurers of the third and fourth defendant applied for a ruling that the writ had not been duly served on the fourth defendant and on appeal it was held that service had not been effected.

Held, dismissing the appeal, that where an initial action had been issued within the limitation period, an application under s.33 would not allow a second set of proceedings on the same cause of action. The rule prevailed despite the anomalous position that a defendant would be better off if a writ had been issued but not served, than if the writ had never been issued at all, *Walkley v. Precision Forgings Ltd* [1979] 1 W.L.R. 606, [1979] C.L.Y. 1663 and *Deerness v. Keeble & Son (Brantham)* [1983] 2 Lloyd's Rep. 260, [1983] C.L.Y. 2219 followed, *Firman v. Ellis* [1978] Q.B. 886, [1978] C.L.Y. 1848 distinguished because, though issued within the primary limitation period, the writ had been neither served nor renewed within a year.

FORWARD v. HENDRICKS [1997] 2 All E.R. 395, McCowan, L.J., CA.

654. Limitations–personal injuries–disapplication of limitation period–meaning of "disability"

[Limitation Act 1980 s.33(3)(d), s.38(2); Mental Health Act 1983.]

On July 14, 1984 P suffered serious personal injuries, including a head injury causing epilepsy, in a road traffic accident. D and P were travelling on a motor cycle. D was the owner but was uninsured. There was a dispute as to which of them was the rider and which the pillion passenger. P was prosecuted for careless driving on the basis that she was the rider but the prosecution case collapsed for lack of evidence. The limitation period expired on July 13, 1987. The writ was issued on October 14, 1994, seven years and three months out of time. P's case was that she had not commenced proceedings earlier because of a variety of matters including that (1) until 1992 she did not know of the existence of the Motor Insurers Bureau; (2) the seriousness of her injuries and the resulting disability (although she was not suffering from mental disorder so serious as to make her a patient within the meaning of the Mental Health Act 1983) was such as to make it difficult for her to seek legal advice; (3) until recovery of memory by "flashbacks" in April 1994 she could not remember whether she had been the rider or the passenger although she had never believed that she had been the rider, and (4) she had received no legal advice relating to the possibility of civil action from the solicitors who had the conduct of her defence in the criminal proceedings. The district judge granted P's application to disapply the limitation period pursuant to the Limitation Act 1980 s.33. D appealed.

Held, dismissing D's appeal and allowing P's action to proceed, that a point of legal principle arose as to the true construction of s.33(3)(d) of the 1980 Act and as to the meaning of "disability" for the purpose of that provision; "disability" had been construed for the purposes of s.33(3)(d) as encompassing not only mental disorder within the meaning of the Mental Health Act 1983 as defined in s.38(2) of the 1980 Act but also a wider range of disability, including P's condition which involved serious memory problems, forgetfulness, depression and inability to concentrate, *Bater v. Newbold* (Unreported, 1991) relied on. The Court of Appeal decided that "disability" for this purpose referred only to the concept of a person under disability by reason of mental disorder so as to be a patient within the meaning of the Mental Health Act 1983 and not some lesser mental disability or physical disability however severe. However, such other disability may be relevant under s.33(3)(a) or generally as part of "all the circumstances of the case" for the purposes of s.33(3). In all the circumstances, the misconstruing of s.33(3)(d) had not affected the overall correctness of the exercise of judicial discretion, *Bater v. Newbold* disapproved, the Law Reform Committee 20th report (1994) referred to, *Yates v. Thakeham Tiles Ltd* [1995] P.I.Q.R. 135, [1994] C.L.Y. 3528 (which had not been cited below) considered.

THOMAS v. PLAISTOW, April 23, 1997, Hirst, L.J., CA. [*Ex rel.* Philip A Butler, Barrister, Deans Court Chambers, Manchester].

655. Limitations–personal injuries–industrial deafness–date of knowledge

P, aged 74, was employed by D and its predecessor between 1957 and 1980. He worked in a noisy environment and earplugs were available in 1977, which he wore as part of his routine in his work until 1980. He appreciated that the purpose of the earplugs was to protect his ears which would otherwise be damaged by the noise. In 1980 he moved to quieter work. In about 1983 he began to notice that his hearing was failing and in February 1984 he consulted his GP who referred him to a hospital ENT clinic. Neither the GP nor the hospital inquired about the nature of his previous work and P did not volunteer it. On March 4, 1992, prompted by his brother, P underwent a hearing test by the Sheffield Occupational Health Project and was advised to consult solicitors about the possibility of a claim for "occupational deafness". He did not in fact consult solicitors until March 18, 1993, and a medical report which supported P's case was obtained on August 9, 1993. D was first notified of a claim in September 1993 and proceedings were issued on March 22, 1995. P contended that the limitation period started to run on August 8, 1993 when the medical report was received. D contended that the limitation period ran from March 4, 1992 at the latest but that P had constructive knowledge in February 1984 when he consulted his GP.

Held, applying *Nash v. Eli Lilly & Co* [1993] 1 W.L.R. 782, [1993] C.L.Y. 2603, P had actual knowledge on March 4, 1992 when he was clearly aware of the possibility of a claim. What he then lacked was the will to make a claim. That was not caused by any reluctance to proceed without expert reassurance. P had constructive knowledge in February 1984. At that time he ought reasonably to have had in mind the nature of his employment between 1957 and 1980 and in particular the period from 1977 when he wore earplugs. Those were facts observable by him and in respect of which discussion could and should have taken place with his GP notwithstanding his quieter work after 1980 and the gradual onset of his deafness. The limitation period therefore expired in February 1987. Section 11 would not be disapplied. It was very many years since the exposures complained of. D faced problems in obtaining evidence: an important witness was dead; other witnesses would be difficult to trace and their evidence was likely to be unreliable; the premises no longer existed. The delay between March 1992 and instructing solicitors and the delay thereafter was inexplicable. Account was also taken of the strength and value of the claim, that there had been exposure in other employment and before the likely date of D's responsibility, other contributory causes of P's deafness, his age and his present degree of impairment.

BOYNTON v. BRITISH STEEL PLC, October 8, 1996, Recorder Rudland, CC (Sheffield). [*Ex rel.* Mark Diggle, Barrister, 24 The Ropewalk, Nottingham].

656. Limitations–personal injuries–industrial deafness–date of knowledge

[Limitation Act 1980 s.11, s.14, s.33.]

P brought a claim for damages in 1994 for noise induced deafness caused by his exposure to excessive levels of noise during the course of his employment, between 1968 and 1975, with S and B. S and B contended that the three year limitation period for personal injury negligence action, as prescribed by the Limitation Act 1980 s.11, had expired. P argued that, for the purpose of the date of knowledge under s.14(1) of the 1980 Act he was not aware until 1992 that the injury was significant.

Held, dismissing the claim, that the period of limitation had expired against S in 1976 and against B in 1978. The dates of knowledge, of when the injury became significant to P pursuant to s.14 of the 1980 Act, were 1973 and 1975 respectively. The tests to be applied in relation to the significance of the injury under s.14(2) of the 1980 Act were both objective and subjective, *McCafferty v. Receiver for the Metropolitan Police District* [1977] 1 W.L.R. 1073, [1977] C.L.Y. 999 applied. Applying the subjective test, P should have considered the injury sufficiently serious to justify instituting proceedings for damages between 1970 and 1975. P realised that the injury was significant during that period as he was aware that his work colleagues were also going deaf as a result of the excessive levels of noise. The judge, having considered all the relevant statutory provisions, declined to exercise the discretion conferred upon him by s.33 of the 1980 Act to allow the action to proceed notwithstanding that it was brought outside the primary limitation period. Public policy considerations further prevented the judge from exercising his discretion, *Beattie v. British Steel* (Unreported, 1997) considered.

PIETKOWICZ v. SMETHWICK DROP FORGINGS LTD AND BRITISH & MIDLANDS FORGINGS LTD, May 13, 1997, H.H.J. Hodson, CC (Dudley). [*Ex rel.* Everatt & Co, Solicitors, 104 High Street, Evesham, Worcestershire].

657. Limitations–personal injuries–industrial deafness–date of knowledge

[Limitation Act 1980 s.14, s.33.]

P brought a claim in respect of deafness allegedly caused by his exposure to industrial noise during the course of his employment with B and others. P commenced employment with B in 1960 and became aware of a buzzing in his ears in the 1960s, a problem P attributed to loud machinery. P's wife began to complain about P's hearing loss in the 1980's. In 1990 P made a claim through the NUM before issuing proceedings in November 1995.

Held, dismissing the claim, that P acquired knowledge pursuant to the Limitation Act 1980 s.14 in January 1988 when he was aware that his problem was both significant and attributable to his work. P's claim was therefore time barred. The judge declined to exercise the power of discretion conferred upon him by the Limitation Act 1980 s.33 on the grounds that P failed to offer an adequate explanation for the delay in instituting proceedings and provided insufficient evidence, as regards where he was working at the time and the levels of noise to which he was exposed, to prove his claim. It was therefore impossible for the defendants to make proper enquiries in order to test P's claim.

POPE v. BRITISH COAL CORP, August 27, 1997, H.H.J. Hugh Jones, CC (Bridgend). [*Ex rel.* Caroline Barnes, Nabarro Nathanson, 1 South Quay, Victoria Quays, Wharf Street, Sheffield].

658. Limitations–personal injuries–industrial deafness–failure to explain delay

[Limitation Act 1980 s.14, s.33(1).]

P claimed damages against F for injury to his hearing sustained as a result of exposure to excessive levels of noise during the course of his employment with F between 1967 and 1974. P noticed a deterioration in his hearing in 1988, prompting him to consult solicitors in March of the same year with a view to making a claim against F. In September 1988 P was examined by a consultant surgeon who could not attribute P's hearing loss to exposure to industrial noise and recommended only that P attend a further hearing test six to 12 months later. P failed to have his hearing retested, contending that he was unable to fund his claim privately. In September 1990 P became aware that legal assistance was available from his trade union leading his solicitors to arrange for him to be medically examined in January 1991. Despite a favourable medical report, P did not commence proceedings until January 1994. P gave no explanation for that period of delay. F submitted that the action was time barred under the Limitation Act 1980 s.14. P sought a discretionary extension under s.33(1) for the limitation period to be disapplied.

Held, dismissing the claim, that P had knowledge, for the purposes of the 1980 Act s.14, when he consulted solicitors in March 1988 as he then possessed a sufficiently firm belief that there was a causal connection between the matters of complaint and his injury so as to justify him taking the preliminary steps for proceedings, *Nash v. Eli Lilly & Co* [1993] 1 W.L.R. 782, [1993] C.L.Y. 2603 and *Spargo v. North Essex DHA* [1997] 8 Med. L.R. 125, [1997] C.L.Y. 663 considered. The court chose not to exercise the power of discretion conferred upon it by s.33(1) on the ground that P had not discharged the heavy burden of proof on him to explain the reasons for his delay in pursuing the claim. Whilst the negative medical advice and lack of funds provided an excuse for the delay from September 1988 to January 1991, P failed to discharge the burden for the periods between January 1991 and January 1994. The absence of prejudice suffered by F was not determinate of the issue.

PRUDEN v. FORD MOTOR CO LTD, April 30, 1997, Assistant Recorder Michael Black Q.C., CC (Liverpool). [*Ex rel.* Hill Dickinson, Solicitors, Pearl Assurance House, Derby Square, Liverpool].

659. **Limitations – personal injuries – industrial injuries – disapplication of limitation period – plaintiff responsible for delay**

[Limitation Act 1980 s.33.]

On December 17, 1992 H suffered an accident in the course of his employment. H first consulted solicitors in August 1994 and a claim, in general terms, was intimated to S. Between August 1994 and July 1995 S's solicitors investigated the claim and on July 26, 1995 liability was denied. A medical report was obtained on August 2, 1995 but H's solicitors would not proceed with the action until initial costs had been paid. H, who at the time was saving to buy a house and to get married, failed to pay these costs. Proceedings were finally commenced on April 26, 1996, some four months after the expiry of the limitation period. H sought to rely on the Limitation Act 1980 s.33 to disapply the limitation period.

Held, dismissing the action, that this was not a case where the limitation period should be disapplied. Responsibility for the delay incurred lay solely with H. H was aware that he might possibly have a claim but had failed to take action to pursue it. When he did act H then chose to spend his income on other items rather than pursuing his claim. This was H's choice and S should not be penalised for it; to disapply the limitation period would be prejudicial to S and inequitable.

HODGSON v. STOCKTON CASTING COMPANY LTD, January 15, 1997, H.H.J. Bryant, CC (Teeside). [*Ex rel.* Jacksons, Solicitors, Middlesbrough].

660. **Limitations – personal injuries – industrial injuries – settlement of claims under Iron Trades Union Scheme – disapplication of scheme**

[Limitation Act 1980 s.33(1).]

B, an employee of BSC for periods between 1963 and 1975, claimed damages to compensate him for loss of hearing which he allegedly suffered as a result of his employment. B, previously unaware that he could take legal action against his employer, first contacted his solicitor, A, in July 1990. A attempted to resolve the claim under an alternative dispute resolution scheme created by insurers in response to the numerous claims for loss of hearing made against employers. In August 1993 BSC terminated the alternative dispute resolution scheme and A instituted litigation proceedings which commenced in February 1994. BSC raised the defence of limitation which was rejected by the judge who ruled that BSC had waived any entitlement to rely on any limitation point in claims made under the scheme and that this waiver continued to bind BSC even after the termination of the scheme. The judge disapplied the limitation periods under the Limitation Act 1980 s.33(1). BSC appealed.

Held, allowing the appeal, that BSC were within their rights to terminate the scheme and that such termination entitled those involved in the scheme to litigate unhampered by its terms. The waiver, by BSC, of its right to rely on the Limitation Act 1980 for the purposes of the scheme, did not extend to litigation. In addition, the judge, in exercising his discretion, attached excessive significance to the conduct of BSC within the scheme and its decision to terminate the scheme. The scheme had advantages for both BSC and B and at no time was B misled nor refused any relevant information either before he became involved in the scheme, during its operation or after its termination. The judge regarded the effect of the delay as equally prejudicial to both parties, but in so doing he failed to address the fact that BSC were not required to meet the claim of B, whose hearing loss was not attributed to a single, lengthy period of employment. Consequently, the decision of the judge to disapply the limitation periods under s.33(1) was set aside as being inequitable.

BYTHEWAY v. BRITISH STEEL CORP PLC, Trans. Ref: CCRT1 97/0433/G, June 26, 1997, Judge, L.J., CA.

661. Limitations–personal injuries–medical negligence–date of knowledge

[Limitation Act 1980 s.14.]

S was born in 1967 by way of internal version and breech extraction. During delivery her spine was damaged, resulting in disability. In 1994 S issued proceedings against the consultant obstetrician in charge of her delivery, alleging negligence. It was held at a preliminary hearing that the action was time barred. S appealed.

Held, dismissing the appeal, that by 1985 when S was 18, she had knowledge as defined by the Limitation Act 1980 s.14, and the action was time-barred. She knew that she should have been delivered by caesarean section and that if she had she would not have suffered spinal injury and this amounted to knowledge that the injury was attributable in whole or in part to the act or omission alleged to constitute negligence.

SLEVIN v. SOUTHAMPTON AND SW HAMPSHIRE HA [1997] 8 Med. L.R. 175, Mantell, J., QBD.

662. Limitations–personal injuries–medical negligence–date of knowledge

[Limitation Act 1980 s.33.]

In 1976 D underwent an operation for a suspect rodent ulcer on his nose. A histological report following the operation stated that the ulcer was cancerous and had not been completely removed. D claimed he was not told to return for any follow-up examination. Soon after the operation the mark reappeared on D's nose and in 1978 he had to have his nose removed. In 1992 D received expert advice that G, in failing to recall D following receipt of the 1976 histology report, had been negligent. D brought an action against G, arguing that his date of knowledge for limitation purposes was 1992.

Held, that had D investigated the questions posed by the facts known to him by 1978, he would have been aware of the possible negligence by 1982 at the latest, and so had constructive knowledge from that point. His action was statute-barred but the court would exercise its discretion under the Limitation Act 1980 s.33 and disapply the limitation period as; (1) the delay was in part contributed to by the defendants; (2) it was unlikely that the delay would prejudice the defendants, and (3) once D knew he had a claim he had pursued it promptly and expeditiously.

DRURY v. GRIMSBY HA [1997] 8 Med. L.R. 38, Judge Bentley Q.C., QBD.

663. Limitations–personal injuries–medical negligence–date of knowledge–appropriate test

[Limitation Act 1980 s.11, s.14(1).]

A person not having actual or constructive knowledge could nevertheless be clear in their own mind that their condition was attributable to a medical diagnosis and the court did not have to enquire further whether a rational lay person would have made the causal connection. The health authority appealed against a decision on the trial of a preliminary issue that S's claim for damages for injury resulting from a mistaken medical diagnosis was not statute barred under the Limitation Act 1980 s.11 and s.14. S had been diagnosed as suffering from selective brain damage and was compulsorily detained in hospital from 1975 until 1981. The damages writ was not issued until 1993, although S had first consulted solicitors in 1986, at which time, although not knowing whether she had a case, she was clear in her own mind that her suffering was attributable to a mistaken diagnosis.

Held, allowing the appeal, that, in finding that S did not have actual knowledge under s.14(1) and could not be fixed with constructive knowledge under s.14(3), the judge had substituted the less rigourous attributability test for the more stringent causation test in *Nash v. Eli Lilly & Co* [1993] 1 W.L.R. 782, [1993] C.L.Y. 2603. Whilst in general, a person did not have the requisite knowledge where they thought that their condition was capable of being attributable to a particular cause but realised such belief required medical confirmation, S was clear in her own mind that a connection existed between her suffering and the misdiagnosis when she sought legal advice in 1986. As a result, it was not necessary for the court to enquire further whether a rational lay person would have been willing to say they knew of a possible causal connection between their suffering and the misdiagnosis itself without first obtaining medical confirmation.

SPARGO v. NORTH ESSEX DHA [1997] 8 Med. L.R. 125, Brooke, L.J., CA.

664. Limitations—personal injuries—medical negligence—date of knowledge—cerebral palsy followed breech birth—qualified objective test

[Limitation Act 1980 s.11, s.14(1), s.14(3).]

P, who was born in 1966 severely disabled suffering from cerebral palsy, brought proceedings against C, alleging negligence resulting from carrying out a breech birth rather than a caesarean section. C contended that the action was statute barred by virtue of the Limitation Act 1980 s.11 on the basis that any alleged tort was committed more than three years before the date of the action. P contended that she only became aware of her claim on seeing a television programme which suggested the cause of her disability. She discussed the programme with her mother and then sought legal advice.

Held, ruling that the action was not time barred, that the test was whether a person of P's intelligence knowing of the facts in question would have appreciated that there was a real possibility of the facts in the context of the 1980 Act s.14(1). Following *Nash v. Eli Lilly* [1993] 1 W.L.R. 782, [1993] C.L.Y. 2603, the test was a qualified objective test as to whether or not there was actual knowledge of the s.14(1) facts. Under the 1980 Act s.14(3), the issue was whether the same test should be applied. *Forbes v. Wandsworth HA* [1996] 3 W.L.R. 1108, [1996] 2 C.L.Y. 4466 represented a construction of s.14(3) which accorded more closely with its purpose. The criteria for the application of the test should be exclusively objective. On these facts, P and her mother were not of a level of intelligence substantially different from a person of moderate intelligence. On the basis of the s.14(1) test, it was not established that a person of P's intelligence would have known of the facts before the television programme.

PARRY v. CLWYD HA [1997] 8 Med. L.R. 243, Colman, J., QBD.

665. Limitations—personal injuries—medical negligence—date of knowledge—delay meant inappropriate to exercise discretion to disapply time limit

[Limitation Act 1980 s.14(1)(b), s.33.]

In August 1987 S was prescribed the drug Tagamet by doctors at DHA. He experienced an increase in breast size in July 1988 and in October 1988 he was diagnosed as having right-sided gynaecomastia. His treatment was changed to Ranitidine in December 1988 and his symptoms reduced. In August 1989 he consulted a solicitor with a view to issuing proceedings if advised that he had a cause of action. In August 1991 S received an expert medical report disclosing that his condition was a known side effect of Tagamet, and issued proceedings in May 1993. DHA contended that the action was time-barred, on the basis that S had knowledge that his symptoms were attributable to the act or omission of which he complained under the Limitation Act 1980 s.14(1)(b) in December 1988, when his treatment was changed to Ranitidine.

Held, giving judgment for DHA, that (1) applying s.14(1) knowledge that any act or omission did or did not, as a matter of law, involve negligence, was irrelevant. The crucial knowledge was of the act or omission to which the injury is attributable, not knowledge of a cause of action. S's date of knowledge arose in December 1988 when his treatment was changed and his symptoms reduced, *Bentley v. Bristol & Weston HA* [1991] 3 Med. L.R. 1, [1992] C.L.Y.

3244, considered, and (2) having regard to the delay in bringing proceedings and the fact that evidence would be less cogent eight years or more after the event, this was not an appropriate case in which to exercise the discretion under the Act s.33 to direct that the time limits did not apply.

SIMS v. DARTFORD AND GRAVESHAM HA [1996] 7 Med. L.R. 381, Judge HM Crush, CC (Croydon).

666. **Limitations–personal injuries–medical negligence–date of knowledge–injury sustained during birth of first child–no action taken until after birth of third child**

[Limitation Act 1980 s.14, s.33.]

H was admitted to hospital for the birth of her first child in September 1988. Delivery was difficult and required an episiotomy and the use of forceps. Subsequent to her discharge from hospital H experienced faecal incontinence. She was reassured by her midwife and GP that this would resolve naturally but was eventually referred to a consultant surgeon who diagnosed a defect to her anal sphincter and carried out a repair operation which was not entirely successful. Although by the date of the hearing it was common ground that this defect was a consequence of either a cut or tear sustained during the course of her delivery, she was not told this at the time. She continued to suffer incontinence of both faeces and flatus and had two further children which had to be born by caesarean section due to previous injury. She began to question her treatment in 1988 after the birth of her third child in March 1991 and she first consulted solicitors in June 1991. It was not until May 1993 that a later consultant expressed a preliminary view that the original treatment had been negligent. A writ was issued shortly thereafter. H argued that for the purposes of the Limitation Act 1980 s.14 her date of knowledge was May 1993 when she was first informed by a medical expert that her treatment had been negligent, and certainly no earlier than March 1991 when she first began to question her treatment. On either basis the writ was issued well within the three year limitation period. Alternatively, H sought exercise of the court's discretion to allow the claim to proceed under s.33. Y argued that the date of knowledge was shortly after discharge from hospital, and in any event no later than the time she first saw the consultant who performed the repair operation in March 1989.

Held, on trial of a preliminary issue, that for the purposes of s.14(1)(b) the causally relevant omission to which injury was attributable was the failure to repair the tear to the sphincter immediately after the birth. H had no knowledge of a real possibility that her injury was attributable to that omission, indeed what she had been told was very different. The suggestion that she had the requisite knowledge because she knew enough to make it reasonable for her to investigate whether she had a case against Y entirely ignored the realities of the situation. H did not ignore the problem but rather acted upon the medical advice she was given and was thereby reassured. Simply telling H that she had a defect which required surgery was not the same as imbuing her with knowledge of an omission to rectify it immediately after it occured, *Smith v. West Lancashire HA* [1995] P.I.Q.R. 514, [1995] 1 C.L.Y. 3169 followed. For the purposes of deciding whether H had constructive knowledge, s.14(3) should be interpreted neutrally so that an objective standard applies rather than a "qualified objective" test, *Forbes v. Wandsworth HA* [1997] Q.B. 402, [1996] 2 C.L.Y. 4468 followed. Upon this test H did not have constructive knowledge, she remained under medical care throughout her three pregnancies and that care was precisely appropriate to her problem which she believed had originated naturally from the birth of her first child rather than in consequence of her medical treatment. H's claim was not statute barred and could proceed to a trial of liability and quantum. As an alternative, for the purposes of the application under s.33 the merits of H's case were a relevant factor. Here H had a reasonable prospect of success and the only prejudice to Y was H's dilatoriness in pursuing claim and the unavailability of the doctor who had attended the birth in 1988, who could not now be traced. However, Y had adduced no expert evidence to counter H's evidence and could be criticised for having no adequate system to keep track of doctors who left its employment. The real issue was how easy it was to overlook such an injury, and expert evidence would no doubt be able to deal with that. Thus, in any event, the court would have exercised H's discretion to allow H to proceed under s.33.

HIND v. YORK HA, August 6, 1997, Mitchell, J., QBD. [*Ex rel.* David Rose, Barrister, 6 Park Square, Leeds].

667. **Limitations–personal injuries–medical negligence–disapplication of limitation period–professional medical indemnity insurance–insurer and insured considered as one to determine possible prejudice**

[Limitation Act 1980 s.28, s.33, s.38.]

K, who suffered injuries at birth in 1965, leading to his suffering a severe form of cerebral palsy, sought an order disapplying the limitation provisions under the discretion conferred under the Limitation Act 1980 s.33. The judge at first instance held that, although under s.28 and s.38 of the 1980 Act, the limitation period would have expired in February 1986, some 16 months before K commenced the action, the claim could proceed against the estate of B, the doctor who had delivered K, due to the fact that B had the benefit of medical indemnity insurance. B, the doctor's personal representatives, appealed.

Held, allowing the appeal, that due to the long period that had expired, B should have been entitled to rely on the prejudice such a claim would present, *Donovan v. Gwentoys Ltd* [1990] 1 W.L.R. 472, [1990] C.L.Y. 2960 considered. Such prejudice was not overcome by the fact that the injury was suffered during K's minority and that the limitation period had been extended for reasons of minority. The judge at first instance had erred in his interpretation of *Hartley v. Birmingham City Council* [1992] 1 W.L.R. 968, [1992] C.L.Y. 2811 in finding that the action should proceed, as B's estate itself would not be prejudiced, due to the fact of the insurance. Whereas *Hartley* could permit a claim under the 1980 Act s.33 where a short delay occurred which did not affect the defence and where there had been early notification of the claim, it did not preclude the insurers from relying on any evidential point which demonstrated prejudice affecting their ability to defend the claim. Where a defendant is insured the correct approach is to consider the insured and the insurer as forming a composite whole when considering the effect prejudice may have on the defence, *Davis v. Soltenpur* (1983) 133 N.L.J. 720, [1983] C.L.Y. 2212 approved, with nil weight being accorded to the fact that a defendant was insured in such instances.

KELLY v. BASTIBLE [1997] 8 Med. L.R. 15, Waller, L.J., CA.

668. **Limitations–personal injuries–medical negligence–disapplication of limitation period–whether discretion should be exercised**

[Limitation Act 1980 s.11, s.14, s.33.]

In 1974, J underwent hospital treatment which he subsequently claimed was negligent. In 1976 he had sought a report from an independent surgeon and counsel's opinion was that there was no evidence to support an action for negligence. Having ceased work in 1984, J instructed his present solicitors in 1986 and a writ was issued in 1987 when J was examined by another surgeon. He was examined by a third in 1991. In 1993 there was a trial of preliminary issues. The judge below ruled that J's claim was statute barred by reason of the Limitation Act 1980 s.11 and s.14 finding that J had the requisite knowledge in 1977. The judge refused to give a direction, under s.33, disapplying the effect of s.11. J appealed.

Held, dismissing the appeal, that the judge had applied the correct test under the the 1980 Act s.14. In 1977 J had known the facts which constituted the essence of the present complaint. It was not necessary that he should have had knowledge of a possible cause of action, *Wilkinson v. Ancliff (BLT) Ltd* [1986] 1 W.L.R. 1352, [1987] C.L.Y. 2336, *Davis v. Ministry of Defence* [1985] C.L.Y. 2017, *Nash v. Eli Lilly & Co* [1993] 1 W.L.R. 782, [1993] C.L.Y. 2603, *Halford v. Brookes (1990)* [1991] 1 W.L.R. 428, [1991] C.L.Y. 2848, *Broadley v. Guy Clapham & Co* [1994] 4 All E.R. 439, [1994] C.L.Y. 2907. Having concluded that the relevant period of delay was some ten years, the judge below considered all the factors under s.33(3). He was entitled to conclude that J had not acted promptly and reasonably, had a clear opportunity to seek further and particular advice as to the adequacy of his treatment and that it was no longer equitable between the parties to allow J's action to proceed. It could not be said that these conclusions were wholly wrong.

JONES v. LIVERPOOL HA [1996] P.I.Q.R. P251, Glidewell, L.J., CA.

669. Limitations–personal injuries–medical negligence–impecuniosity of plaintiff

[Limitation Act 1980 s.33.]

K appealed against a decision that S's action for negligence after K's misdiagnosis was not time barred. After an accident at work, S's deceased husband had developed a cancerous growth on his shin, which for nine years had been wrongly diagnosed and treated by K as psoriasis and later as a varicose ulcer. The judge below had held that, because S had been unable to afford a medical expert, he had insufficient knowledge that his injury was attributable to K's act or omission, or, in the alternative, that the discretion allowed by the Limitation Act 1980 s.33 should be exercised.

Held, allowing the appeal, that the lack of expert medical evidence had not prevented the limitation period from commencing and it would be inequitable to disapply the limitation period pursuant to s.33. S had the requisite knowledge by November 1986 and, in such circumstances, his belief was equivalent to his knowledge that the cancer was attributable to K's acts or omissions. S's poverty had made it difficult, but not impossible, for him to have obtained a medical report at an approximate cost of £600 and it was reasonable for him to have sought such evidence. The only difference between the situation in 1988, when S had decided not to proceed, and that in 1993, when the action was begun, was that S's widow was eligible for legal aid, *Nash v. Eli Lilly & Co* [1993] 1 W.L.R. 782, [1993] C.L.Y. 2603, *Jones v. Liverpool HA* [1996] P.I.Q.R. P251, [1997] C.L.Y. 668, and *Halford v. Brookes (1990)* [1991] 1 W.L.R. 421, [1991] C.L.Y. 2848 considered.

SKITT v. KHAN [1997] 8 Med. L.R. 105, Roch, L.J., CA.

670. Limitations–personal injuries–medical negligence–plaintiff chose to ignore advice given over 20 year period–action prevented diagnosis of actual complaint

[Limitation Act 1980 s.14(3), s.33.]

D began to experience bouts of abdominal pain in 1972. In 1973 he was admitted to WC Hospital and underwent several tests. In November 1973 he was diagnosed as suffering from coeliac disease and was re-admitted to WC Hospital in 1974 for further tests. The trial judge found that the diagnosis was, as D knew or ought to have known, provisional, and that in proposing further tests the medical staff were trying to trace the true cause of his complaint. D took a contrary view and discharged himself from the hospital before any of the tests could be carried out. In 1981, D underwent tests at a private hospital which revealed that gallstones were present. His consultant recommended that he be admitted to WC Hospital for further tests. D refused to take this advice on the basis that extensive tests had already been done at WC Hospital. In 1991 D experienced a severe attack of stomach pain and was admitted to KG Hospital, where he was diagnosed as having cholecystitis and gallstones and underwent an operation to have the gallstones removed. He was told that he had never suffered from coeliac disease. D obtained a consultant's opinion that his original treatment in 1973 had been negligent and he commenced proceedings against WC Hospital and its medical staff in 1994. The Hospital claimed that the action was time-barred by virtue of the Limitation Act 1980 s.14(3) on the basis that D could reasonably have been expected to undergo the further tests at WC Hospital in 1975 and that time started running from that point.

Held, that D's claim was statute barred, that (1) D chose to ignore advice and refused further tests in the belief that they would serve no useful purpose. He might reasonably have been expected to acquire the knowledge of his true medical condition from facts which were ascertainable by him with the help of medical advice which it was reasonable for him to seek, within the meaning of s.14(3) and that knowledge ought to have been acquired by D by 1975 at the latest; (2) the proviso to s.14(3) did not assist D since he did not take reasonable steps to obtain medical advice and (3) there would be serious prejudice to RWHA if the action were allowed to continue and accordingly the general discretion under the 1980 Act s.33 would not be exercised in favour of D.

DENFORD v. REDBRIDGE AND WALTHAM FOREST HA [1996] 7 Med. L.R. 376, Tucker, J., QBD.

671. Limitations−personal injuries−medical negligence−service of writ−date of knowledge

[Limitation Act 1980 s.14.]

S requested a termination of her pregnancy on September 24, 1991, but was told by her doctor, M, that the pregnancy was too advanced. After the birth of her child S brought an action against M alleging that he had been negligent in failing to make inquiries which would have revealed that at the time of her request she had been 18 or 19 weeks pregnant and therefore within the statutory time limit for an abortion. S issued a writ in August 1994, but this was not served before the deadline and she obtained an order extending the time for service to April 1995. M's application to set aside the order was granted on the basis that the three year limitation period under the Limitation Act 1980 expired after issue of the writ but before it was served. S appealed, arguing that the limitation period only started in October 1992 after M's notes were received which showed that, at the time of her consultation, S was within the 24 week time limit, and until that time she had been unaware of the negligence of his advice and that she could have had a lawful termination.

Held, dismissing the appeal, that under s.14 the date when knowledge was first acquired was the date when the plaintiff first became aware of relevant facts crucial to the cause of action. The date of the plaintiff's first knowledge that acts or omissions of the defendant actually involved negligence or were actionable was irrelevant. S knew all essential facts on which her cause of action was to be based more than three years before she made her application for an extension and her claim that she was unaware that M's advice was negligent until more than a year after it was given did not have the effect of postponing the limitation period.

SAXBY v. MORGAN [1997] P.I.Q.R. P531, Mummery, L.J., CA.

672. Limitations−personal representative−incorrectly drafted order−expiry of limitation period−request for an extension of time

[County Court Rules 1981 Ord.5 r.8, Ord.13 r.4, Ord.15 r.4, Ord.37 r.5.]

P alleged non repayment of a loan made in 1989 by G, who died in 1991. In July 1994 P issued proceedings against the estate. P applied for an order pursuant to County Court Rules 1981 Ord.5 r.8 that a personal representative be appointed for the purposes of the proceedings. An order was made during the validity of the summons, "the first order", but was incorrectly drafted by P's solicitor to state that the personal representative be appointed for "the purpose of proceedings to be instituted". P's solicitor then sent the summons back to the court to be "re-issued", together with the order for sealing. Proceedings were served in late February 1995, being three months after the expiry of the summons. The limitation period for P's claim expired in May 1995. At trial, P argued that an application under CCR Ord.5 r.8 could be made before proceedings were instituted so that the re-issue and service were valid. Alternatively, P applied for a retrospective order under CCR Ord.5 r.8 and an extension of time to serve the proceedings on the personal representative under CCR Ord.37 r.5 and CCR Ord.13 r.4.

Held, that (1) the first order was ineffective because it looked forward to proceedings being instituted so there was no defence before the court; (2) the court could not make an order under CCR Ord.5 r.8(4)(a), as the application must be made within the four month period of validity of the summons, the "re-issue" and the service were defective; (3) the court could not make a retrospective order under CCR Ord.5 r.8(4)(b) where service was defective, *Foster v. Turnbull* [1990] C.L.Y. 3787 and *Webb v. Personal Representatives of Whatley (Deceased)* [1995] 2 C.L.Y. 4211 considered; (4) the court would not exercise its discretion under CCR Ord.5 r.8(4)(b) because D had a limitation defence, the recollections of the witness would be impaired due to the passage of time and P's solicitors had provided no satisfactory reasons why the first order had been incorrectly drafted, and (5) the court would not grant an extension of time to serve the summons where there was no explanation for the late application, *Lewis v. Harewood* [1997] P.I.Q.R. P58, [1996] 1 C.L.Y. 879, and *Singh (Joginder) v. Duport Harper Foundries Ltd* [1994] 1 W.L.R. 769, [1994] C.L.Y. 3827 considered.

GESEK v. PERSONAL REPRESENTATIVE OF GILLER (DECEASED), July 30, 1997, H.H.J. Simpson, Mayor's and City of London Court. [*Ex rel.* Simon Mills, Barrister, 1 Essex Court, Temple, London].

673. Limitations–plaintiff alleging deliberate concealment–standard of proof

[Rules of the Supreme Court Ord.18 r.12; Limitation Act 1980 s.14A, s.32(1)(b).]

T instructed B, a firm of solicitors, to draft a debenture to be secured against the assets of a company of which he was a director and shareholder. T suffered loss when the company went into administration and commenced proceedings against B in contract and tort after expiry of the primary limitation period pursuant to the Limitation Act 1980 s.14A, alleging that B had deliberately concealed from him their error regarding the debenture. T appealed against an order striking out his amended statement of claim against B, who contended that for T to have an arguable case under s.32(1)(b) of the Act, he had to identify a fact relevant to his cause of action and a course of conduct of concealment, then plead that such concealment was deliberate, identifying the actor and giving particulars as to his state of mind and knowledge.

Held, allowing the appeal, that, following the provisions of RSC Ord.18 r.12, T had to do more than merely assert knowledge of concealment, as particulars of the facts had to be given either in the pleading itself or in separate particulars. On the facts, T alleged that B had had cause to reconsider the debenture and it was likely that a competent solicitor would have realised an error had been made. If at trial, when examining the facts and assisted by oral evidence, the court drew an inference of such realisation, then it was likely also to infer that B had deliberately failed to disclose the error to T. Therefore, T's plea under s.32(1)(b) was not so bad that it should be struck out.

TUNBRIDGE v. BUSS MURTON & CO, *The Times*, April 8, 1997, Laddie, J., Ch D.

674. Magistrates courts–closure–solicitors had no legitimate expectation of consultation

[Justices of the Peace Act 1979 s.56(1).]

T, a local solicitor, applied for leave to seek judicial review of M's decision to close temporarily Clacton Magistrates' Court on the ground that she had a legitimate expectation that she would be consulted.

Held, refusing leave, that while making no finding as to what consultation might be required if permanent closure were envisaged, T had no legitimate expectation to be consulted, in particular since there was a statutory requirement pursuant to the Justices of the Peace Act 1979 s.56(1) to consult only with the local authority responsible for paying.

R. v. MAGISTRATES COURTS COMMITTEE FOR ESSEX, *ex p.* THOMSON, Trans. Ref: CO-246/97, March 19, 1997, Laws, J., QBD.

675. Magistrates courts–procedural impropriety or bias–availability of judicial review

See ADMINISTRATIVE LAW: R. v. Hereford Magistrates Court, *ex p.* Rowlands. §63

676. Mareva injunctions–discovery–sanction for failure of foreign defendant to comply with discovery order

Held, that where a foreign defendant, with no assets in the UK, failed to comply with an order for discovery made by the High Court pursuant to a Mareva injunction, and there was a strong case against that defendant, the only appropriate sanction was to debar him from taking any further action in the litigation and from defending the case, if he failed to adhere to the order within a reasonable time limit. The defendant's claim that the disclosure requirements of the order would compel him to breach the law of another jurisdiction, while a factor to be taken into consideration, did not outweigh the plaintiffs' urgent need for the specified evidence.

CANADA TRUST CO v. STOLZENBERG (MAREVA INJUNCTION), *The Times,* November 10, 1997, Neuberger, J., Ch D.

677. Mareva injunctions–extraterritoriality–fraudulent document–effect of injunction limited to England

[Brussels Convention on Jurisdiction and the Enforcement of Judgments in Civil and Commercial Matters 1968 Art.50; Civil Jurisdiction and Judgments Act 1982 s.25; Rules of the Supreme Court Ord.71 r.27, Ord.71 r.28.]

N gave B, a German company, a formal acknowledgment of debt which entitled B to proceed to enforce payment without suing on the document or prove the underlying debt. N issued proceedings in Germany seeking a declaration that a later document rendered the acknowledgment no longer enforceable against him. B defended these proceedings, counterclaiming for the debt, alleging fraud, and successfully applied ex parte to the English Court under the Civil Jurisdiction and Judgments Act 1982 s.25 and relying on the Brussels Convention 1968 Art.50 (as set out in Sch.1 of the 1982 Act) for a worldwide Mareva injunction. On the inter partes hearing the effect of the injunction was limited to England on the basis that the relief was in support of another jurisdiction and the circumstances were not exceptional. B appealed contending that since the acknowledgment was enforceable in England and registrable under the Rules of the Supreme Court Ord.71 r.27 and r.28 by virtue of Art.50 of the Convention the relief could not be so categorised.

Held, dismissing the appeal, that the purpose of s.25 and Art.50 was to enable rights existing under the laws of one jurisdiction to be enforced in others by the same enforcement procedures. The relief sought therefore was granted in support of another jurisdiction. The court would not therefore make an order extending beyond its own territorial jurisdiction save in an exceptional case, and the evidence of fraud and concealment of assets did not amount to special or exceptional circumstances, *Rosseel NV v. Oriental Commercial and Shipping (UK) Ltd* [1990] 3 All E.R. 545, [1991] C.L.Y. 2919 followed.

S&T BAUTRADING v. NORDLING [1997] 3 All E.R. 718, Saville, L.J., CA.

678. Parties–interveners–disclosure by solicitor of client's identity

I applied for an order requiring a firm of solicitors, RW, to disclose the names and addresses of two clients whom they had represented as interveners in a hearing following the granting of an order appointing a receiver over a wide range of assets in a complex international fraud case. RW argued that the court's inherent jurisdiction to order disclosure by a solicitor of his client's name and address should only be exercised in the rarest circumstances and where it was necessary to make the court's process effective, for example where an order for committal had to be served. In the instant case, whilst disclosure might be desirable from I's point of view, it was far from necessary.

Held, allowing the application, that the power to order disclosure was exceptional and would only be used in the rarest cases. However, in the instant case it had been proved at trial that some of the defendants had committed serious frauds against I and, since this was an exceptional case which involved offshore trusts and companies whose participants were difficult to identify, necessity should not be the deciding factor. There was clear evidence of attempts to defeat the jurisdiction of the court with regard to freezing of assets and evidence that RW's clients were themselves involved in the offshore trusts concerned. It was therefore proper for the court to order disclosure.

INTERNATIONAL CREDIT AND INVESTMENT CO (OVERSEAS) LTD v. ADHAM; *sub nom.* ICIC (OVERSEAS) LTD v. ADHAM, *The Times*, February 10, 1997, Harman, J., Ch D.

679. Parties—summons issued against wrong party—delay in application to substitute correct defendant—leave granted as no confusion or substantial prejudice caused

[County Court Rules 1981 Ord.15 r.1.]

C suffered injuries at work and brought an action against B, an individual and director of A, a limited company. A expressly informed C's solicitors that they had sued the wrong party and informed its own insurers. Following the expiry of the limitation period and 20 months after the defence had been filed C sought leave to substitute A as defendant under CCR Ord.15 r.1. Leave was granted and A appealed.

Held, dismissing the appeal, that the judge was entitled to find that C had made a genuine mistake when suing in the wrong name and that no confusion or substantial prejudice had thereby been caused.

CROOK v. AARON DALE CONSTRUCTION AND ROOFING LTD; CROOK v. PROVINCIAL INSURANCE PLC [1997] P.I.Q.R. P36, Henry, L.J., CA.

680. Payment into court—acceptance—payment in notice not an offer capable of compromising an action

[Rules of the Supreme Court Ord.22; Social Security Administration Act 1992 s.93(2), s.93(3).]

T appealed against a decision that a claim by G, arising from a car collision in which G's wife and youngest child were killed, had not been compromised. G and two children in the car at the time of the accident claimed damages for their injuries, alleging that T caused the accident by his negligence. G also claimed damages as representative for the estates of the deceased. T denied liability but made a payment into court in the total amount of £165,403 to be accepted in satisfaction of G's cause of action, £15,000 of which had already been paid by way of interim payments. T, informing G, withheld the sum of £23,142 in accordance with the Social Security Administration Act 1992 s.93(2) and s.93(3). T wrote an open letter giving a break down of the total payment but the letter did not refer to the £15,000 already paid, nor the social security reduction and was taken as being an amendment of the notice of payment. G responded by letter, accepting four out of the five payments, including his own. However, the approval of the court was required for the payments in respect of the children and of the deceased. T argued that, by his conduct in accepting the amount, G had estopped himself from continuing his action, or alternatively, that G's claim was compromised.

Held, dismissing the appeal, that G was not bound by any compromise where he accepted a notice of payment into court pursuant to the Rules of the Supreme Court Ord.22. Such notice on being accepted could not constitute a contract capable of compromising an action, *Cumper v. Pothecary* [1941] 2 K.B. 58 considered. The formal procedure for acceptance of the payment was not followed as G did not give a notice in Form 24 as required by the Rules of the Supreme Court Ord.22 r.3.

GORSE v. TINKLER, *The Times*, February 20, 1997, Sir Iain Glidewell, CA.

681. Payment into court–concurrent and several claims–court's power to assess part paid claim

[Rules of the Supreme Court Ord.22 r.1.]

In an action for breach of contract between O and R, the first defendant, who acted for O as architect for a restaurant conversion and W, the second defendant, a building company who carried out the work, O accepted money paid into court by R, but continued the action against W. At first instance the judge found that deductions had to be made from damages awarded against W to take into account the sum paid in by R. This was in respect of concurrent claims against R and W. W appealed.

Held, allowing the appeal and reducing the value of O's claim against R in respect of claims solely against R and claims jointly against both R and W, that where no apportionment could be made under the RSC Ord.22 r.1 (5), it was for the plaintiff to provide evidence upon which the court could properly assess the losses due to the defective work. On the facts O had failed to do so, and there was no material upon which an apportionment could be based, *Townsend v. Stone Toms & Partners (No.2)* (1984) 27 B.L.R. 26 [1985] C.L.Y. 2701 considered

OAK TREE LEISURE LTD v. RA FISK AND ASSOCIATES, *The Times*, January 1, 1997, Peter Gibson, L.J., CA.

682. Payment into court–infringement of copyright–election for account of profits in place of damages–application to withdraw payment out of time

[Rules of the Supreme Court Ord.22 r.1, Ord.22 r.3, Ord.22 r.5.]

E admitted infringement of B's copyright relating to a computer game and agreed that B could elect either an assessment as to damages or an account of profits. E subsequently paid £5,000 into court in satisfaction of "all the causes of action" claimed by B. Although initially electing an account of profits instead of damages, B was prepared to accept the money paid into court as settlement but failed to accept the payment within the 21 day limit set down in RSC Ord.22 r.3 and applied to the court to exercise its discretion under Ord.22 r.5 to grant leave to withdraw the payment out of time.

Held, dismissing the application, that under Ord.22 r.1 the payment into court had to be in respect of an action for debt or damages and therefore Ord.22 r.5 could not be invoked once an action for debt or damages had been extinguished by an election to take an account of profits, as Ord.22 r.5 only authorised money to be withdrawn in respect of the cause of action for which it was paid in. Even though the money was paid in to satisfy "all causes of action", Ord.22 r.3 and Ord.22 r.5 could only authorise withdrawal for actions for debt and damages and B's claim for damages disappeared once the election had been made. Even if Ord.22 r.5 could be invoked, the court could only exercise its discretion in favour of B if nothing had occurred since the money was paid in that would affect the sum B was likely to be awarded at trial. The election of an account of profits was an event which altered the amount B was likely to be awarded at trial, as the sum awarded would be different from that awarded in respect of damages. The money would accordingly be returned to E under Ord.22 r.1 (3).

BRABEN v. EMAP IMAGES LTD [1997] 2 All E.R. 544, John Cherryman Q.C., Ch D.

683. Payment into court–personal injuries compensation–deduction of social security benefit

See DAMAGES: Houghton v. British Coal Corp. §1816

684. Payment into court–strike out provisions inapplicable during 21 day period given for acceptance of payment

[County Court Rules 1981 Ord.9 r.10, Ord.11 r.3.]

Held, that where a defendant had made a payment into court under CCR Ord.11 r.3, it was not open to her to apply for the action to be struck out under Ord.9 r.10, on the ground that 12 months had elapsed since service of the summons, before expiry of the 21 day period given by the court to the plaintiff for acceptance of the payment.

HARDING v. CARTWRIGHT, *The Times,* June 9, 1997, Lord Woolf, M.R., CA.

685. Personal injuries–claim including loss of past and future earnings–obligation of plaintiff to be interviewed by employment consultant instructed by defendant

W, a warehouse packer, suffered head and other injuries in a motor car accident for which the deceased defendant was liable. W alleged total inability to work since that accident. For a period of three years ceasing approximately six months before the accident, W had been unemployed. His employer before and after that period was the same. His personal behaviour during that three year period left much to be desired. His inability to work was not accepted by T. W had adduced a report from his own employment consultant who had interviewed him, but refused to be interviewed by an employment consultant instructed by T.

Held, allowing that part of the summons, that on the particular facts of the case it was appropriate for W to make himself available for interview in the presence of his solicitors or a companion, on terms as to venue, within 50 miles of his home, on a date to be mutually agreed, failing which the action be stayed.

WATTS v. THOMAS (DECEASED), April 23, 1997, H.H.J. Dyer, Bristol District Registry. [*Ex rel.* Edward Lewis Solicitors, Verulam Gardens, 70 Grays Inn Road, London].

686. Personal injuries–mode of trial–civil proceedings dealing with criminal issues–identification of issues to be tried by jury

[Supreme Court Act 1981 s.69; Rules of the Supreme Court Ord.33 r.4, Ord.33 r.5.]

P was a burglar who was caught redhanded by W, a farmer, on his land. P had, with others, been removing a large number of slates from the roof of an agricultural building. He was captured by W and before the police arrived on the scene he had received multiple injuries some of which were serious and life threatening. P sued for assault. W denied having caused all the injuries and those injuries that he had caused, or was proven to have caused, were, he contended, inflicted in the course of (a) self defence, (b) protection of property or (c) effecting a citizen's arrest. The action had been set down for trial by judge alone, both as to liability and quantum, pursuant to RSC Ord.33 r.5 and the Supreme Court Act 1981 s.69. At the start of the trial the judge invited counsel to consider the question of trial by jury.

Held, that the court having the power to vary mode of trial under RSC Ord.33 r.4(1) would exercise its discretion to direct that the issue of liability should be tried by a jury where the issue to be considered fell close to the boundary between criminal and civil proceedings (what constituted "reasonable" force as a defence to assault) even though neither party had sought trial by jury and that such a direction would result in delay and further costs because of an inevitable and possibly substantial degree of overlap between the issues on liability and those on quantum and that on a split trial a number of medical witnesses would have to be called twice over. The reason for that was, that (1) the issue of reasonableness was one that had classically been decided by juries in a criminal law forum for generations and (2) more importantly, a judge sitting alone necessarily had to apply the test of reasonableness empathising with the standard of the right thinking citizen. It was more satisfactory in the public interest that the judge, while not abjuring his responsibilities, should not embark on that exercise but rather leave it to a jury, who were by definition a real microcosm of society who must be assumed to reflect the prevailing attitudes of society to issues of general public importance.

PHILLIPS v. WILES, Date not specified, Ognall, J., QBD. [*Ex rel.* Stephen J Glover, Barrister, 37 Park Square, Leeds].

687. Pleadings—amendment—amendment sought after expiry of limitation period—libel claim arising out of same facts could be added

[Limitation Act 1980 s.35; Rules of the Supreme Court Ord.20 r.5.]

L had refused to honour cheques and direct debit agreements charged against R's bank account whilst R had a secured overdraft with the bank. R disputed the level of interest and bank charges and L credited him an amount, blaming computer error, but at the same time issued a writ demanding the full amount with interest. In response to expert evidence suggesting L's charges were unreasonable, L abandoned its interest claim, substantially reducing the sum claimed, which meant that R did not necessarily have inadequate account funds at the time cheques and agreements were dishonoured. R served an amended defence and counterclaim alleging that L had acted wrongfully in dishonouring his cheques and had made false statements that there were inadequate sums to meet his obligations, amounting to breach of contract and libel. R successfully applied for leave to amend his pleadings after the three year limitation period for libel claims had expired, relying on the Limitation Act 1980 s.35 and RSC Ord.20 r.5. L appealed.

Held, dismissing the appeal, that a later pleading of the same facts could operate to support an out of time amendment. The policy of s.35 anticipated the introduction of causes of action that could otherwise be time barred, so that parties could plead any cause of action arising from substantially the same issues of fact which were to be the subject of litigation. Although defamation cases should usually be initiated promptly after the defamatory statement came to the attention of the claimant, this was an unusual case in that R was not in a position to prove whether he had been libelled until the facts relating to the state of his account had been established. L's conduct was to be litigated, and there was no reason why a claim of libel arising from those facts should not be allowed. L's position had not been prejudiced by the passage of time, and the judge had acted correctly in exercising his discretion in R's favour.

LLOYDS BANK PLC v. ROGERS, *The Times*, March 24, 1997, Hobhouse, L.J., CA.

688. Pleadings—amendment—damages for personal injuries—abuse of process—previous action compromised;

R appealed against a decision to stay her action and the dismissal of her application to amend particulars to include a claim for damages for personal injuries. A collision occurred on December 21, 1991 between R's car and E's van in which R received whiplash injuries. Both claimed their vehicles were stationary. On April 2, 1993, three days before an arbitration hearing was due, the first action, which was concerned only with financial loss, was compromised by agreement. E requested that the hearing be vacated. An order was made that arbitration be adjourned but with liberty to restore. On November 3, 1994 R commenced a second action in which the particulars of injury were fully pleaded. Also served with the pleading was a schedule of special damages totalling over £130,000 including a figure of £105,000 for loss of future earnings. E repeated the assertion that R had driven into a parked vehicle and also relied on estoppel, an assertion that the second action was an abuse of process and an assertion that the first action had disposed of all matters in issue between the parties.

Held, allowing the appeal, that there was no foundation to E's claim that the investigation into liability and quantum would be prejudiced by lapse of time, *GL Baker Ltd v. Medway Building and Supplies Ltd* [1958] 1 W.L.R. 1216 followed; *Lambert v. Mainland Market Deliveries Ltd* [1977] 1 W.L.R. 825, [1977] C.L.Y.

446 and *Buckland v. Palmer* [1984] 1 W.L.R. 1109, [1984] C.L.Y. 2549 considered.
ROWLEY v. EMPIRE STORES LTD [1996] P.I.Q.R. P412, Douglas Brown, J., CA.

689. Pleadings–amendments–unlawful act in foreign country–pleas of illegality not hopeless

S, a resident of Commonwealth state, C, sued his English bank, B, over allegedly unauthorised debits from his accounts at B's English high street branch. B relied on S's signed third party mandate to K to operate the bank account. S admitted the document but alleged K, acting on B's behalf, had agreed to operate the mandate only on S's specific instruction, and that K's knowledge that no specific instruction was given should be imputed to B as K was a senior employee of B's at the branch. B averred K acted outside the scope of any actual or implied authority to bind them, then sought to amend to allege that if K bound B, the arrangements between S and K (and thus B) were designed to and did enable S to breach C's exchange control laws and were therefore unenforceable by reason of English public policy ("the illegality plea"), alternatively that there was a conspiracy between S and K to break the exchange control provisions of C which was in serious breach of K's duties to B so that K's activity and state of mind could not be imputed to B ("the imputation plea"). C's control regulations made it unlawful for any person resident in the state to make any payment to or for the credit of any person outside C, or to draw or negotiate any bill or acknowledge any debt, or place any sum, to the credit of any person outside C.

Held, permitting both amendments, that (1) the illegality plea was not hopeless as, although the Bretton Woods agreement could not affect the enforceability of non-exchange contracts, (a) where illegality by reference to the laws of a foreign country was properly in issue, the court was entitled to look beyond the overt contractual obligations to evidence of the parties' wider adventure; (b) where the proper law and the location of performance of a contract were English, mere knowledge of a breach of the laws of a friendly foreign country would not brand the contract as unenforceable at English law; the breach had to be intended by active participation rather than seen as a likely consequence; (c) if an adventure included relevant acts unlawful by reference to a friendly country's laws a court would be able to decline to enforce it and the contracts within it even if the illegal acts were not necessarily to be committed by the parties to the contracts or required by the overt contracts; (d) the apparent requirement of the authorities that for an adventure to be unlawful by reason of English public policy that an illegal act was performed in the friendly country could be satisfied by reference to the whole adventure; (e) if the whole adventure was unlawful, the court would not sever enforceable obligations, but treat the whole as unenforceable: *Foster v. Driscoll* [1929] 1 K.B. 470, *Regazonni v. Sethia (KC) (1944)* [1958] A.C. 301, [1957] C.L.Y. 585 applied; (2) the proposed pleading, by reference to the design of S and K to enable contravention of S's exchange control was sufficient allegation of active participation in the violation of a friendly state's laws for the defence to proceed albeit that particulars would be sought, and (3) neither could the imputation plea be described as hopeless as common sense suggested K would be unlikely to perform his pleaded duty to disclose any conspiracy of his to breach the laws of a foreign country.
S v. A BANK [1997] 6 Bank. L.R. 163, Lindsay, J., Ch D.

690. Pleadings–evidence departing from plaintiff's pleaded case–success of plaintiff's unpleaded claim

P1 and P2 were the parents and parents-in-law, respectively, of the first and second defendants. D1 approached Ps for a loan of £20,000 to carry out building and renovation work to a house that Ds wished to purchase and to which they wished to add a stable block. Ps agreed to advance the monies to Ds, but they were never in fact given over to Ds, save for a single sum of £853, instead D1 retained monies in P2's bank account and agreed to pay for labour and materials when payment of the same became due. It was further agreed that P1 would assist the building contractor employed to carry out the building works as a labourer and that he would be paid for this in order to compensate him for the loss of interest on the monies advanced. After approximately £8,000 worth of labour and materials had been expended, Ps refused to advance any further monies and P1 and the building contractor left the property with the work unfinished. Ps commenced an action for the recovery of the sum of £8,004 and in their particulars of claim pleaded that certain sums of money had been lent to Ds on diverse dates. Ds by their defence and counterclaim denied that any monies had been advanced and pleaded an agreement that P1 would provide £20,000 of his labour and materials. Ds further alleged that the works carried out were defective and that P1 was liable for such defects as Ds had contracted with P1 rather than the building contractor. The evidence at trial revealed that there had never been any loan, save for the £853, but that Ps had paid out the sum of £8,057 in labour and material costs.

Held, that the witness statements produced by Ds indicated that they were aware of the case that they had to meet at trial, namely, the agreement whereby Ps would pay for labour and materials when required albeit that was completely at odds with the pleaded case of a straightforward loan. D submitted that Ps case as revealed by the evidence was a complete departure from the pleaded case and invited the judge to dismiss Ps claim on this basis, relying upon *Waghorn v. George Wimpey & Co Ltd* [1969] 1 W.L.R. 1764, [1969] C.L.Y. 2448. The judge rejected the submission and ruled that whilst there had been a departure from the pleaded case it amounted to a technicality and furthermore that Ds had not been prejudiced by it. Judgment was given for Ps and the judge found that Ds had contracted with the building contractor and that accordingly any counterclaim should have been made against the building contractor. On Ps application for costs a Scale 2 award was made with a direction that the costs of Ps pleadings be disallowed on taxation due to their failure to reflect the case on which Ps had succeeded at trial.

HIRST v. HIRST, July 31, 1997, H.H.J. Charlesworth, CC (Bradford). [*Ex rel.* Nigel S Brockley, Barrister, Bracton Chambers, 95a Chancery Lane, London, WC2A 1DT].

691. Pleadings—possession proceedings—legal charge induced by misrepresentation—constructive notice of bank

See REAL PROPERTY: Barclays Bank Plc v. Boulter. §4238

692. Pleadings—striking out—reasonable cause of action established

[Rules of the Supreme Court Ord.18 r.19.]

C, a former director of J, applied by way of a summons under RSC Ord.18 r.19 for the striking out of H's pleadings on the sole ground that they disclosed no reasonable cause of action against him. H asserted in its pleadings that C had been actively involved in paying company pension scheme funds for the acquisition of the company's main site at an inflated price and without proper valuation or legal advice. H also pleaded that C had been involved in a decision to increase the company chairman's pension provision at the scheme's expense. J was the former sole corporate trustee of the company pension scheme of which the main operating company had gone into receivership. C, the third defendant, was not only a director of J but managing director of the operating company. C contended, in reliance upon *Wilson v. Lord Bury* (1880) 5 Q.B.D. 518 and *Bath v. Standard Land Co* [1911] 1 Ch. 618 that, due to his status as a fiduciary in relation to J, he could only face suit in that capacity.

Held, refusing the application, that (1) the case revealed by the pleadings allowed C to know the case he had to meet was the assertion that he had dishonestly assisted in the breach of trust by the removal of funds from the scheme in favour of the company at a time when he knew its true financial state; (2) following *Bath v. Standard Land Co*, H's pleadings supporting an allegation of breach of direct fiduciary duty were unarguable. There was nothing to disturb the principle that a director of a trust company stands only as a fiduciary to the company; (3) H's pleadings in tort as argued by reference to *Henderson v. Merrett Syndicates Ltd* [1995] 2 A.C. 207, [1994] C.L.Y. 3362 and *White v. Jones* [1995] 2 A.C. 207, [1995] 2 C.L.Y. 3701, had no prospect of success because he had no relationship with the beneficiaries of the scheme. However, the contention based on the concepts of dishonesty and "accessory" liability as given in *Royal Brunei Airlines v. Tan* [1995] 2 A.C. 378, [1995] 1 C.L.Y. 2193 was arguable. Whereas no liability attached to C as a result of his fiduciary capacity or in tort, *Henderson v. Merrett Syndicates Ltd* and *White v. Jones* considered, his acts of knowing assistance incurred liability in the sense referred to in *Royal Brunei Airlines v. Tan.*

HR v. JAPT, Trans. Ref: CH 1995 H No.6588, March 19, 1997, Lindsay, J., Ch D.

693. Practice directions–Commercial Court–abridged procedure for taxation of costs

An abridged procedure for the taxation of costs will be introduced for a trial period of one year from October 1, 1997. If the new procedure is to be used, all parties are required to consent before judgment, with consent embodied in a formal order of the court. A summary bill of costs is to be served on the paying party's solicitors within three months of the order for taxation. If agreement cannot be reached between the parties, the solicitors for the receiving party may begin proceedings for taxation by lodging the requisite documents. A date for the hearing will then be fixed no more than three months ahead and the parties may be required to provide any further information considered necessary for the taxation. The taxation is to be heard by a commercial taxing master or taxing officer on the basis of the material lodged and of any oral submissions made by the parties relevant to that material. The taxing fee is payable within seven days of the abridged taxation.

PRACTICE DIRECTION (COMMERCIAL COURT: ABRIDGED TAXATION OF COSTS PROCEDURE); *sub nom.* PRACTICE DIRECTION (COMMERCIAL COURT: COSTS) [1997] 1 W.L.R. 1198, Colman, J., QBD (Comm Ct).

694. Practice directions–Commercial Court–alterations and additions to Guide to Commercial Court Practice (4th edition)

[Arbitration Act 1996.]

A number of alterations and additions to the Guide to Commercial Court Practice have been approved, particularly to r.5.8, r.5.9, r.6.2, r.6.5, r.7.1, r.8.4, r.8.5, r.9.4, r.11.1, r.17.2, r.20.3, r.21.1 and r.22.1. Significant amendments include: (1) provision for evidence to be exchanged prior to hearing an application for discharge of a Mareva injunction; (2) basic requirements for content and delivery of skeleton arguments; (3) procedure under the new Ord.23 relating to the Arbitration Act 1996; (4) in security for costs applications it is not normally necessary to investigate the merits of a claim; (5) a party obtaining a security for costs order may be required to give an undertaking in damages; (6) applications for further and better particulars or specific discovery are not to be listed prior to a meeting between counsel or solicitors; (7) assignment of longer cases to two judge management teams; (8) a new abridged procedure for taxation of costs from October 1, 1997; (9) suspension of procedural steps pending steps towards resolution of disputes through ADR, with the court having to be informed of steps taken and reasons for any failure, and (10) index of unreported judgments available on disk.

PRACTICE DIRECTION (COMMERCIAL COURT: GUIDE TO COMMERCIAL COURT PRACTICE: FOURTH EDITION) [1997] C.L.C. 1538, Colman, J., QBD (Comm Ct).

695. Practice directions–Commercial Court–summonses–applications for extension of time limits

With respect to the maximum times allocated for summonses in Practice Direction (9) in Appendix 1 of the *Guide to Commercial Court Practice in The*

Supreme Court Practice 1997 (Vol.1 p.1280), where it is expected either before or after the fixing of a date that there is a significant risk that a hearing will exceed the time limit specified, an application for a longer hearing, accompanied by a justification of the extension, should be submitted to the judge responsible for the Commercial Court list; (2) in the absence of such an application, and if it transpires that there has been a material under-estimation of the time required, the judge is free to adjourn proceedings and impose such special costs orders, including those for wasted costs, as appropriate, and (3) a separate time estimate is to be specified for any subsequently issued summons added to a hearing in the same action, unless counsel or solicitors certified that determination of the earlier application will determine the subsequent application or they will not to contest any matters raised in the subsequent summons.

PRACTICE DIRECTION (COMMERCIAL COURT: TIME ESTIMATES FOR SUMMONSES); *sub nom.* PRACTICE NOTE (COMMERCIAL COURT: SUMMONSES) [1997] 1 W.L.R. 955, Colman, J., QBD (Comm Ct).

696. **Practice directions–Court of Appeal–procedures to ensure timeous lodging of skeleton arguments and establish new case management system**

In order to address the problem of late lodgment of skeleton arguments, from November 10, 1997, *Practice Direction (Court of Appeal: Procedure) para.49 and para.50* [1995] 1 W.L.R. 1191, [1996] 1 C.L.Y. 865 is replaced. From that date, applications for extensions of time for lodging skeleton arguments will normally be dealt with by the presiding Lord Justice, except for cases assigned to the Short Warned List, where applications will usually be dealt with by the Registrar of Civil Appeals. Applications should be made personally by the advocate well before the skeleton argument is due to be lodged, setting out the reasons why the timetable cannot be adhered to and the further time required, and (2) a panel of supervising Lord Justices have been appointed to oversee groups of appeals. The supervising Lord Justices will give directions concerning the progress and future conduct of appeals of their own motion, and requests from parties for directions can be made to the Civil Appeals Listing Office. Where hearings are necessary, they will be conducted in chambers, giving solicitors and counsel a right of audience at which they should make their points briefly and without preamble. No detailed judgment will be given, although a shorthand note will be taken.

PRACTICE DIRECTION (COURT OF APPEAL: SKELETON ARGUMENTS AND CASE MANAGEMENT) [1997] 1 W.L.R. 1535, Lord Woolf, M.R., CA.

697. **Practice directions–Court of Appeal–unnecessary documentation in core bundles–new hear by dates**

With effect from June 1, 1997, changes are made to the regime in *Practice Direction (Court of Appeal: Procedure)* [1995] 1 W.L.R. 1191 Part II, [1996] 1 C.L.Y. 865 affecting all appeals and applications where bundles are to be lodged and where the appellant or applicant has representation. The amendments reflect the Court of Appeal's concern over the excessive volume and range of documentation being lodged in some cases, the omission of relevant documents in others, and the unnecessary lodging of multiple sets of trial bundles. In addition, new hear by dates are detailed, reducing the time between the lodging and hearing of appeals. The key amendments are: (a) only core bundles should be lodged, and not trial or other bundles; (b) documents should be included only where it is essential they be pre-read or where they will be referred to at the hearing; (c) the content of core bundles is to be determined on lodging the appeal or application; (d) solicitors must lodge the number of sets of core bundles with the Civil Appeals Office no later than the date of entry of the case in the court's records, and (e) one set of the full trial bundles should be brought to the hearing rather than lodged in advance.

PRACTICE DIRECTION (COURT OF APPEAL: REVISED PROCEDURE); *sub nom.* PRACTICE NOTE (COURT OF APPEAL: PROCEDURAL CHANGES) [1997] 1 W.L.R. 1013, Lord Woolf, M.R., CA.

698. Practice directions–fees–taxation–amounts payable on lodging bill for taxation

The Supreme Court Fees (Amendment) Order 1996 increased the fees payable on taxation from January 15, 1997. In respect of bills lodged earlier, the Supreme Court Taxing Office will continue to have regard to para. 2.2 of *Practice Direction (Taxation: Practice) (No.2 of 1992)* [1993] 1 W.L.R. 12. The lodging of a bill of costs for taxation will be £3.75 for each £100. On a Solicitors Act 1974 taxation where a taxation bill is lodged by the client or chargeable party the lodgment fee is limited to £50, unless the taxing master orders the full fee. On taxation, the fee is £7.50 for each £100 or part £100 of the amount allowed, less any amount paid on lodging the bill. Where a bill lodged on or after January 15, 1997 is withdrawn, no refund of the fee already paid will be made. There is no longer a power to reduce fees in case of hardship. However, following *R. v. Lord Chancellor, ex p. Witham* (1997) 147 N.L.J. 379, [1997] C.L.Y. 11, Art.3 of the 1996 Order is ultra vires, in that it sought to remove the court fee exemption from those in receipt of income support. With reference to *Calderbank* offers, the offer should make it clear whether or not the taxing fee is included.

PRACTICE NOTE (TAXATION: FEES); *sub nom.* PRACTICE DIRECTION (COSTS: TAXATION: FEES) [1997] 1 W.L.R. 218, Judge not applicable, Sup Ct.

699. Practice directions–High Court (Queens Bench) trials on North Eastern Circuit–listing

The practice of listing cases in delimited civil hearing periods will continue for most cases. There will be three civil hearing periods per year in each centre. The practice direction takes effect from November 4, 1996 and covers the following issues: that (1) all proceedings set down in the Queen's Bench Division shall, within seven days of setting down, go before a District Judge, who will either order that the proceedings remain in the High Court or be transferred to the County Court; (2) long and complex cases with an agreed time estimate of 10 days or more will no longer be listed as part of a civil hearing period; (3) cases with an agreed time estimate of five to ten days will normally be warned at least six months in advance of the hearing period in which it is proposed that the hearing will take place; (4) other trials will normally be warned at least four months in advance of the hearing period in which it is proposed that they will be heard; (5) short interlocutory hearings will be warned on a weekly basis at least two weeks in advance; (6) within two weeks after receipt of notice that their case has been warned for hearing, any party may seek an appointment with the civil listing officer to list or fix a case; (7) parties' solicitors must follow good practice, including obtaining firm commitments from witnesses as to dates of availability and ensuring that judicial directions are carried out within the specified period, and (8) once an action has been listed or fixed for hearing, an application to vacate will be heard before the Civil Liaison Judge, the Trial Judge, or a Presiding Judge.

PRACTICE DIRECTION (LISTING OF HIGH COURT (QUEEN'S BENCH) TRIALS), October 1996, Smith, J., QBD.

700. Practice directions–House of Lords–civil appeals–expedited consideration of petitions for leave to appeal

A Practice Direction amending the procedure for leave to appeal in the House of Lords has been issued. In an addendum to Practice Directions Applicable to Civil Appeals to the House of Lords, that in normal circumstances where papers detailed in direction 4.2 had been lodged it would generally take no more than eight sitting weeks before the preliminary procedures specified in directions 4.5 and 4.6 were met. A party could request expedited consideration of petitions for leave to appeal at any point, but such consideration would be granted only in exceptional circumstances. Where the liberty of the citizen, the welfare of children or urgent medical attention were reasons for the request, it would usually be allowed.

Written requests setting out the reasons should be made to the principal clerk, with copies sent to the other parties.

PRACTICE DIRECTION (HOUSE OF LORDS: CIVIL PROCEDURE AMENDMENT) [1997] 1 W.L.R. 167, Judge not specified, HL.

701. Practice directions–judicial review–additional material to be lodged by applicant's solicitor–applicants to list relevant legislative provisions

On lodging an application for leave to apply for judicial review, an applicant's solicitor must lodge material in addition to that stated in *Practice Direction (Crown Office List: Preparation for Hearings)* [1994] 1 W.L.R. 1551. The additional material required will be a paginated indexed bundle of the relevant legislative provisions and statutory instruments required for the proper consideration of the application. Applicants applying in person should seek to comply with this direction to the extent that they were able. In any event, applicants in person should list the legislative provisions and statutory instruments on which they relied.

PRACTICE DIRECTION (CROWN OFFICE LIST: LEGISLATION BUNDLE); *sub nom.* PRACTICE NOTE (JUDICIAL REVIEW: DOCUMENTS TO BE LODGED); PRACTICE DIRECTION (CROWN OFFICE LIST: PROVISION OF RELEVANT COPY LEGISLATION) [1997] 1 W.L.R. 52, Lord Bingham of Cornhill, L.C.J., QBD.

702. Practice directions–Patents Court–modifications to improve efficiency

Patents: Patents Court; practice directions; sittiings

A number of modifications have been made to improve efficiency in the Patents Court, namely: (1) from 1998 the Court will sit in September, with that extra month's sitting initially reserved for trials and applications whose estimated duration was no more than five days; (2) the practice of sitting at 10 am on most days to deal speedily with short applications would continue; (3) a new practice of sitting on Tuesday mornings from 9 am to 11 am will be introduced to deal with more lengthy applications; (4) in relation to any applications referred to in paragraphs (2) and (3) above, the parties should provide the court with all necessary documents and skeleton arguments by no later than 4 pm on the preceding working day, and (5) the court should be provided with accurate estimates of duration so that more than one application could be listed for hearing before 10.30 am wherever possible and, where necessary, guillotines on oral submissions are likely to be imposed to enforce those estimates.

PRACTICE NOTE (PATENTS COURT: SITTINGS); *sub nom.* PRACTICE NOTE: PATENTS COURT [1997] 1 W.L.R. 1421, Laddie, J., Pat Ct.

703. Practice directions–Queen's Bench Division–establishment of mercantile courts in Leeds and Newcastle upon Tyne

[Rules of the Supreme Court Ord.72.]

A Practice Direction establishing two mercantile courts in the North East has been issued. The Lord Chief Justice of England's Court issued the following practice direction on February 4, 1997, to have effect from February 18, 1997, that (1) the District Registries of Leeds and Newcastle upon Tyne would include two new Queen's Bench lists, "The Leeds Mercantile Court List" and "The Newcastle upon Tyne Mercantile Court List"; (2) issues for trial would be of a broadly commercial nature, such as sale of goods, banking and insurance and professional negligence, but excluded those which were more appropriately listed in the Chancery Division or before official referees; (3) subject to the Rules of the Supreme Court and provisions of the present direction, proceedings commenced in either of the courts could subsequently be transferred to the other, so long as relevant documents were clearly marked with the name of the intended court; (4) four judges were to be appointed initially, designated as "Circuit Mercantile Judges", with responsibility for hearing all interlocutory applications, and (5) actions were Queen's Bench actions and therefore subject to the RSC, but RSC Ord.72 was not applicable. The mercantile courts would generally follow Commercial Court practice.

PRACTICE DIRECTION (MERCANTILE COURT LISTS: LEEDS AND NEWCASTLE UPON TYNE) [1997] 1 W.L.R. 219, Lord Bingham of Cornhill, L.C.J., Court not specified.

704. Service of process–Anton Piller orders–courts retrospective power to dispense with service of copy order

[Rules of the Supreme Court Ord.45 r.7.]

The Rules of the Supreme Court Order 45 r.7 (7) could operate, retrospectively, to permit retrospective dispensation of service after an event alleged to breach the order, and the court's power was not limited to being used prospectively or at a particular time. DI were granted an Anton Piller order in respect of the offices of the fourth defendant, V, which required V not to destroy certain documents. The order did not have a penal notice attached as required by the RSC Ord.45 r.7 (4). DI claimed that documents had been destroyed in breach of the order, and brought a notice of motion seeking a sequestration order over V's assets. V's application to strike out the notice of motion was dismissed, and they appealed. Relying on *Lewis v. Lewis* [1991] 1 W.L.R. 235, [1991] C.L.Y. 2481 and *Denman v. Temple* (Unreported, 1991), they contended that the court's power to dispense with service of a copy of an order, conferred by Ord.45 r.7 (7), could only be used prospectively, before the time set aside for compliance with the order expired. DI, relying on *Turner v. Turner* (1978) 122 S.J. 696, [1978] C.L.Y. 370 and *Hill Samuel & Co Ltd v. Littaur (No.2)* [1985] C.L.Y. 2705, argued that the rule also permitted retrospective dispensation of service after occurrence of the events which were alleged to breach the order.

Held, dismissing the appeal, that the authorities on which DI relied, which had not been cited in the later cases, were binding on the court in establishing that r.7 (7) was not limited to having effect prospectively, but could also operate retrospectively. The wording in r.7 (7) was general and the court's power was not restricted to operating at a particular time.

DAVY INTERNATIONAL LTD v. TAZZYMAN; DAVY INTERNATIONAL LTD v. DURNIG [1997] 3 All E.R. 183, Morritt, L.J., CA.

705. Service of process–default judgments–service on dissolved partnership– meaning of "last known address"

[Rules of the Supreme Court Ord.12, Ord.10.]

On January 14, 1994 R commenced an action against B, a partnership of two solicitors, alleging breach of contract and negligence causing R loss and damage. B had been dissolved 10 days earlier, with S, the solicitor who had dealt with R's affairs when R was a client, forming another partnership. The address of practice had changed, and R was aware of the new address, but not of the dissolution. R delivered the writ in person through the letterbox of the new address. B acknowledged service of the writ on January 26, indicating the intention to contest the action. Default judgment was obtained on February 18, and on November 11 it was held that the judgment had been obtained irregularly and an order for costs was made in favour of B. R appealed, the issue of whether the February 18 judgment was regular depended upon whether the writ had been duly served on January 14. R contended that the judgment was regular and that due service was on January 14 as there was proof of the writ coming to the attention of S on that date, or that service would be deemed on January 21, ie. seven days after delivery to the premises. Alternatively R submitted that as B did not make an application under the Rules of the Supreme Court Ord.12 r.8 to set aside service of the writ, or to claim it had not been served, B had waived the irregularity in service.

Held, allowing the appeal, that (1) RSC Ord.10 r.1 (2) (b) provided for service by insertion of the writ through the letter box of the defendant's usual or last known address. It was open for B to show that the writ never came to his notice, *Forward v. West Sussex CC* [1995] 1 W.L.R. 1469, [1996] 1 C.L.Y. 886 applied, and for R to establish that it did come to B's notice prior to the seventh day after service by insertion through the letter box, *Hodgson v. Hart DC* [1986] 1 W.L.R. 317, [1986] C.L.Y. 2727 applied. Giving the rules a purposive construction, the defendant should be notified of the proceedings, thus the deemed date of service may be displaced by proof that the writ came to the defendant's attention at some other date, *Barclays Bank of Swaziland Ltd v. Hahn* [1989] 1 W.L.R. 506, [1989] C.L.Y. 3099 applied and (2) the "last known address" under Ord.10 r.1 could be construed as the business address; in particular, in the case of a solicitor and his client, it was acceptable for that address to be the business address of the solicitor, *R. v. Braithwaite* [1918] 2 K.B. 319, *Price v. West London Building Society Ltd* [1964] 1 W.L.R. 616, [1964] C.L.Y. 2103, *R. v. Southend Magistrates Court, ex p. Kingsway Furniture (West Thurrock) Ltd* (Unreported, 1996) and *Austin Rover Group Ltd v. Crouch Butler Savage Associates* [1986] 3 All E.R. 50, [1986] C.L.Y. 2725 applied, *Marsden v. Kingswell Watts* [1992] 2 All E.R. 239, [1992] C.L.Y. 3596 distinguished.

ROBERTSON v. BANHAM & CO [1997] 1 W.L.R. 446, Roch, L.J., CA.

706. Service of process–dissolved solicitors' partnership–writ duly served where former partner examined document but refused to accept service

[Rules of the Supreme Court Ord.65 r.2, Ord.81 r.3.]

A former partner of a firm accused of professional negligence was duly served if he had knowledge of the writ and had control of it for a time, however short. It was unnecessary for all former partners to be served if the Solicitor's Indemnity Fund had agreed that one would suffice. N claimed damages for professional negligence against P, a solicitors' partnership which had subsequently been dissolved. The Solicitors' Indemnity Fund, which was defending the action, had agreed that N need only serve the writ on one of P's former partners, who was now a partner in another firm. Shortly before the writ was to expire, a process server went to see the former partner, who looked at the writ and saw that the defendant was P but said he could not accept service and told the process server to take the writ away. N appealed against a decision that the writ had not been duly served on P in accordance with RSC Ord.65 r.2, governing personal service, and Ord.81 r.3, pursuant to which, in the event of dissolution of a partnership, the writ must be served on all the individuals alleged to be liable.

Held, allowing the appeal, that the agreement reached with the Solicitors' Indemnity Fund absolved N of having to serve the writ on all P's former partners. Under Ord.65 r.2, personal service was effected by leaving a copy of the writ with the person to be served, and "leave" in that context meant "to cause to or let remain", rather than to "depart without taking". Once the person to be served, having knowledge of the nature of the document, had been given sufficient opportunity to take possession of the writ and have control of it for a period of time, however short, the writ had been left with him within the meaning of Ord.65 r.2 and process was duly served.

NOTTINGHAM BUILDING SOCIETY v. PETER BENNETT & CO, *The Times*, February 26, 1997, Waite, L.J., CA.

707. Service of process–foreign jurisdiction–contract action against succession–writ failed to establish UK jurisdiction

[Rules of the Supreme Court Ord.11.]

E obtained leave to serve a writ outside the jurisdiction on A. E had effected contracts of reinsurance with a state owned Romanian company. The Romanian government subsequently dissolved the state owned company and decreed that all international insurance and reinsurance activities would be taken over by A. The writ was served on A who applied successfully to have it set aside. E appealed.

Held, dismissing the appeal, that before leave to serve outside the jurisdiction could be given the court had to be satisfied that the claim fell within RSC Ord.11. The writ was required to identify the cause or causes of action with sufficient clarity for the defendant to be able to ascertain whether the case fell within the court's jurisdiction. The writ, not the affidavit, would be served on the defendant. In the present case the liability of A could be deduced only from an examination of the affidavit. The writ simply stated that the policies had been made between E and A and failed to set out the steps by which A, although party to the original contracts, was alleged to be liable.

EXCESS INSURANCE CO LTD v. ASTRA SA INSURANCE AND REINSURANCE CO [1996] 5 Re L.R. 471, Neill, L.J., CA.

708. **Service of process–Motor Insurers Bureau–service of evidence of instigation of proceedings–mandatory requirements**

C was injured in a motor accident involving an uninsured driver and sent a letter to the Motor Insurers Bureau, MIB, notifying the instigation of proceedings against it in the county court and enclosing a notice of issue of a default summons. MIB claimed it had not been given notice of the proceedings in the form prescribed by the Motor Insurers' Bureau (Compensation of Victims of Uninsured Drivers) Agreement 1988 cl.5, and they were therefore not liable for any claim. C successfully appealed against a decision that the condition precedent of MIB's liability to satisfy a judgment obtained against an uninsured driver had not been met. MIB appealed and C cross-appealed.

Held, allowing the cross-appeal, that it was a mandatory requirement for MIB to be served with official evidence of the instigation of proceedings, and C's service of the notice of issue complied with that requirement. The requirement in cl.5(1) that the notice of proceedings given to the MIB "shall be accompanied by a copy of the writ, summons or other document initiating the proceedings" was part of the condition precedent as it formed part of the grammatical sense of cl.5(1) as a whole, and the word "shall" was mandatory. The purpose of the requirement was to provide MIB with official proof of the issue of proceedings, and therefore a notice of issue or a copy of an unstamped writ was not enough. For proceedings initiated in the High Court, a copy of the stamped writ should be sent to MIB. In the county court there were two procedures: (1) the court officer would stamp the summons and return it to the plaintiff's solicitor, who would then be in possession of a stamped copy, or (2) service was instigated directly by the court officer, in which case the plaintiff's solicitor was sent a notice of issue but would not have a stamped copy. In that case MIB could not be served with a copy of an officially stamped writ and service of a notice of issue of default summons would suffice as evidence.

CAMBRIDGE v. CALLAGHAN, *The Times*, March 21, 1997, Millett, L.J., CA.

709. **Service of process–service of defence by fax just within time limit–meaning of reasonable time**

[Rules of the Supreme Court Ord.19 r.2, Ord.65 r.5.]

In an action for breach of contract, A served an amended statement of claim seeking £11,991 owing from a total bill of £36,000 for the provision of a function for T's guests at a hotel in England and T was given 21 days to serve an amended defence. Some four months later, while A's clerk was actually in court seeking to enter judgment in default of defence, pursuant to RSC Ord.19 r.2, T began to transmit a fax of the original defence. T applied to set aside judgment and for leave to appeal out of time against the original order.

Held, dismissing both the application and leave to appeal, that the service was too late. A reasonable time must elapse between the arrival of a fax and its communication to a person in the firm with relevant knowledge, which could not be less than half an hour. Therefore service by fax, under the RSC Ord.65 r.5(2)(b), had to be both sensible and workable. This was notwithstanding the fact that a document was taken to be served as soon as the last page was out of the machine.

ANSON v. TRUMP, Trans. Ref: 1994-A-2188, December 12, 1996, Richard Mawrey Q.C., QBD.

710. Service of process–service out of the jurisdiction–application refused

[Rules of the Supreme Court Ord.11.]

The issue arose in connection with a claim by a reinsured under reinsurance policies, whether or not there had been a material omission or other deficiency in the pleadings. E appealed contending that further to RSC Ord.11 r.4, the court was able to look to the affidavit prepared in connection with the writ, to make good any material omission. A submitted that it was not subject to the jurisdiction of the court, the appropriate forum being Romania.

Held, dismissing the appeal, that RSC Ord.11 r.4 provided that an application for leave to serve a writ out of the jurisdiction had to be supported by affidavit and that the affidavit had to state the grounds on which the writ was to be served; (2) however, reading RSC Ord.11 r.4 with Ord.11 r.1, it was clear that the court had to have cognisance to the writ rather than the affidavit in deciding whether or not leave to serve the writ outside the jurisdiction should be allowed. The court would not interfere with the exercise of the judge's discretion as to forum conveniens. The judge correctly held that England was forum conveniens on the basis that the litigation arose out of reinsurance treaties which were broked in London, were governed by English law and had an English arbitration clause.

EXCESS INSURANCE CO LTD v. ASTRA SA INSURANCE & REINSURANCE CO [1996] L.R.L.R. 380, Neill, L.J., CA.

711. Service of process–service out of the jurisdiction–court order that ship be inspected–court lacked capacity to serve proceedings

[Arbitration Act 1950 s.12(6)(g); Rules of the Supreme Court Ord.29 r.7A, Ord.75 r.28.]

The court made an order that F permit U's surveyor to inspect a ship which had been subject to charterparty and that an originating summons be served. The second defendants, C, who were not parties to the arbitration agreement between U and F, contended that the court had no jurisdiction to serve that order. The plaintiffs contended that the court had jurisdiction to make the order under the Arbitration Act 1950 s.12(6)(g), and to order service of proceedings outside the jurisdiction by virtue of RSC Ord.29 r.7A or Ord.75 r.28.

Held, that the purpose of Ord.29 r.7 was that the parties to arbitration were subject to English law by virtue of their arbitration agreement. C were not parties to such an agreement. The court therefore did not have the capacity to give permission for the service of proceedings out of the jurisdiction. The words of Ord.75 r.28 should be given their natural meaning. They could not be relied upon independently to give the courts jurisdiction over persons that they would not otherwise have had jurisdiction over.

UNICARGO v. FLOTEC MARITIME S DE RL (THE CIENVIK) [1996] 2 Lloyd's Rep. 395, Clarke, J., QBD (Adm Ct).

712. Service of process–service out of the jurisdiction–meaning of "constructive trustee" for purposes of service under RSC Ord 11 r.1

[Rules of the Supreme Court Ord 11 r.1.]

G, the plaintiff in a claim for the recovery of stolen bankers drafts, sought leave to serve C and two other defendants out of the jurisdiction with an order restraining them from disposing of any moneys transferred into their bank accounts. G did not assert that the defendants were aware of the theft at the time the money was transferred, but argued that they were constructive trustees within RSC Ord.11 r.1 and that therefore a personal claim could be made against them.

Held, allowing the application, that it was arguable that the defendants became constructive trustees under Ord.11 r.1 once they had knowledge of the injunction and that thereafter they would be prevented from dealing with funds in their accounts. In addition to a personal claim, G also had a proprietary claim against the defendants from the moment the money was received into their accounts, as the fiduciary relationship required for a tracing claim could arise from the theft, *Westdeutsche Landesbank Girozentrale v. Islington LBC* [1996] 2 W.L.R. 802, [1996] 2 C.L.Y. 4149 considered.

GHANA COMMERCIAL BANK v. C, *The Times*, March 3, 1997, Peter Leaver Q.C., QBD.

713. Service of process–service out of the jurisdiction–service of concurrent writ in Tunisia–fraudulent misrepresentation alleged–no loss within Tunisia to justify service

A applied for leave to appeal against an order extending the validity of its writ and setting aside service of a concurrent writ in Tunisia. A claimed damages for fraudulent misrepresentation of bad debts in B's accounts that had induced it to purchase shares in B, contending (1) the accounts had been sent to London, where the misrepresentation had occurred, and (2) the loss was suffered in London where the contract had been induced and accepted.

Held, dismissing the application, that (1) there had been no challenge to affidavit evidence that the accounts, which were the purported inducement, had been handed over in Tunisia, and (2) there was no evidence of loss suffered within the jurisdiction, particularly since A had not even been in existence at the time when money had been paid from a Swiss bank to purchase worthless shares in Tunisia, *Metall und Rohstoff AG v. Donaldson Lufkin & Jenrette Inc* [1990] 1 Q.B. 391, [1989] C.L.Y. 3528 considered, *DW Moore v. Ferrier* [1988] 1 W.L.R. 267, [1988] C.L.Y. 2154 distinguished as being concerned with the date of loss, not the application of Ord.11.

ARAB BUSINESS CONSORTIUM INTERNATIONAL FINANCE & INVESTMENT CO v. BANQUE FRANCO-TUNISIENNE [1997] 1 Lloyd's Rep. 531, Neill, L.J., CA.

714. Service of process–service out of the jurisdiction–validity of service where no other defendant served

[Rules of the Supreme Court Ord.2 r.1, Ord.11 r.1.]

K obtained leave under the Rules of the Supreme Court Ord.11 r.1 (1) (c) to serve a writ on the third defendant, S, outside the jurisdiction and then served the first defendant in the UK and S in Australia a few days later. S applied for leave to be set aside on the grounds that when K had obtained it, no other defendant had been served. The judge held that whilst Ord.11 r.1 (1) (c) required one defendant to be served before leave could be granted to serve another defendant outside the jurisdiction, he would exercise his power under Ord.2 r.1 to validate the service retrospectively. S appealed and K contended that the court had jurisdiction to grant leave to serve outside the jurisdiction under Ord.11 r.1 (1) (c), even though no other defendant had been served at the time of the application.

Held, dismissing the appeal, that it was clear from the wording of the 1983 version of Ord.11 r.1 (1), that it was necessary for a defendant to be served within or out of the jurisdiction before leave could be granted to serve outside the jurisdiction. Further, there had to be good cause or reason to allow retrospective validation of leave in order for the judge to exercise his powers under Ord.2 r.1, *Kleinwort Benson v. Barbrak (The Mytro) (No.3)* [1987] 1 A.C. 597, [1987] C.L.Y. 3125 followed. In the instant case, the judge had approached the issue with great care, finding that K's error in failing to serve the first defendant before applying for leave to serve S was a genuine mistake, which was of little importance and which would not prejudice S. K could still bring proceedings against S in Australia and the judge had thought it preferable that the action should be brought against all the defendants in the same jurisdiction. In the light of those considerations, the judge had not erred in treating K's service of the writ upon S as valid.

KUWAIT OIL TANKER CO SAK v. AL BADER (NO.2) [1997] 2 All E.R. 855, Staughton, L.J., CA.

715. Service of process—service out of the jurisdiction—writ capable of proper service beyond jurisdiction without leave

[Rules of the Supreme Court Ord.11 r.9, Ord.48 r.1.]

L, a Greek national resident in Greece, entered into personal guarantees of loans granted by UBF to a company. The guarantees provided that they were to be governed by English law and, in the event of a dispute, L would submit to the jurisdiction of the English High Court. UBF served notices of default and then a writ for recovery of the sums due on L and his London agent. Judgment in default was obtained and UBF applied for an order under RSC Ord.48 r.1 requiring L to attend before the court in London to be examined as to his assets. The order was granted and served on L in Greece. L applied to set aside the order on the grounds that it was incapable of being served outside the jurisdiction. The master refused the application and the judge dismissed his appeal. L appealed.

Held, dismissing the appeal, that service out of the jurisdiction of orders ancillary to execution after judgment was valid if the proceedings were appropriate for service out of the jurisdiction without leave under the RSC Ord.11 r.9(4). As the writ in the present case was capable of service outside the jurisdiction without leave it followed that the service of the master's order could be served outside the jurisdiction, *Tucker (A Bankrupt), ex p. Tucker, Re* [1988] 1 All E.R. 603, [1988] C.L.Y. 190 not followed.

UNION BANK OF FINLAND LTD v. LELAKIS [1997] 1 W.L.R. 590, Henry, L.J., CA.

716. Service of process—service out of the jurisdiction

See CONFLICT OF LAWS: DR Insurance Co v. Central National Insurance Co of Omaha (In Rehabilitation). §907

717. Service of process—writs—defects in indorsement—postal rules

[Rules of the Supreme Court Ord.5 r.6(2), Ord.6 r.5.]

P entered an agreement with D1, an economic unit of the Republic of Angola with separate legal personality. The commercial attache at the Angolan embassy in London was appointed under the terms of the agreement to accept service of any proceedings. P issued a writ against D1 and also against the Ministry of Commerce and the Republic of Angola. The writ was indorsed that it had been issued by T, a solicitor in the employ of P. In fact T was absent at the time and her solicitors subsequently wrote that the writ had not been issued by her or with her authority or privity. The three writs were all served in the same envelope addressed to D1 at the Angolan embassy. Judgment in default of acknowledgment of service was entered against all defendants. D2 and D3 then sought to set the judgment aside.

Held, setting aside the judgments as irregular, that where a solicitor declared under the Rules of the Supreme Court Ord.6 r.5, that the name indorsed on a writ was not issued by that solicitor or with that solicitor's authority or privity, that was conclusive. It made no difference that T had done so by way of a letter from her solicitors. It followed that the writ had been issued by P as a body corporate otherwise than by a solicitor in breach of RSC Ord.5 r.6(2). To satisfy the rules of postal service the writ had to be in an envelope addressed to the defendant. That had not been the case here. In any event there was no evidence that D2 and D3 had agreed to accept service at the Angolan embassy in the same way as D1. Service of the writs would therefore be set aside.

CRESCENT OIL AND SHIPPING SERVICES LTD v. IMPORTANG UEE [1997] 3 All E.R. 428, Thomas, J., QBD (Comm Ct).

718. Small claims—automatic reference to arbitration—abuse of process—inclusion of costs of repairs already paid

[County Court Rules 1981 Ord.19 r.2.]

G's employee and D were involved in a road traffic accident on June 12, 1994. Correspondence took place between their respective insurers, following which D's insurers made a payment to G of £3,100 to meet the cost of repairs to D's vehicle in or around early January 1997. On February 26, 1997 proceedings were issued by G against D claiming £5,592 together with interest. That sum included a claim for the cost of the repairs which had already been paid, and without which the remaining claim would have been under £3,000. D applied to have the matter automatically referred to small claims arbitration.

Held, the cost of repairs which had already been paid by D prior to the issue of proceedings should not have been included in the particulars of claim. This amounted to an abuse of process in an attempt to inflate the value of the claim in dispute beyond the small claims limit. The matter would be automatically referred to arbitration under CCR Ord.19 r.2, and G would pay D's costs.

GRAYLINE COACHES v. DICKSON, May 22, 1997, District Judge Burgess, CC (Reading). [*Ex rel.* Davies Arnold Cooper, Solicitors, 6-8 Bouverie Street, London].

719. Small claims—automatic reference to arbitration—claim below £3,000 at the time of issue

Following a road traffic accident on September 16, 1996, W sought hire charges of £2,117, the write-off value of the vehicle £1,900, storage/recovery charges £217 and damages for loss of use/inconvenience. On October 17, 1996, W's solicitors asked for interim payment of £2,117, to cover value of vehicle and storage/recovery, and advised that hire was continuing. On or about October 24, 1996, F's insurers sent a cheque in the sum of £2,117 to W's solicitors. W ceased hiring on October 31, 1996. Proceedings were issued on December 12, 1996 and W's schedule of special damages was in the total sum of £4,235, but stated that W would give credit for interim payment received.

Held, that the action be automatically referred to arbitration on the ground that at the time of issue of the summons the amount involved in the proceedings did not exceed £3,000. W was entitled to Scale 1 costs up to October 24, 1996. In addition W was ordered to pay F's costs of, and incidental to, the application, such costs to be set off against W's entitlement to costs.

WORTHINGTON v. FRUISH, March 18, 1997, District Judge Wilby, CC (Bury). [*Ex rel.* Horwich Farrelly, Solicitors, Manchester].

720. Small claims—boundary dispute litigated in county court and small claims arbitration—issue estoppel

[County Courts Act 1984 s.64(3).]

H appealed against a decision striking out his action for trespass arising from a boundary dispute with W. H and W owned adjoining land. The dispute arose when W trimmed trees that had been planted by H and H sued W for trespass. W contended that the trees had been planted on his land and the matter went for a small claims arbitration, where it was found that the hedge of trees was on W's land and W was therefore entitled to do as he liked with them. W subsequently cut the trees down. H brought a fresh action in the county court alleging trespass and damage to a bush and avoiding reference to the hedge. The county court made a declaration as to ownership of the land in direct contradiction to the small claims judgment. H then brought a further action of trespass against W for cutting down the trees, which was struck out on the principle of issue estoppel. H appealed arguing that (1) the small claims order was in relation to costs only and did not make a finding as to the boundary; (2) the small claims proceedings, being an arbitration, were of less authority than those in open court and that the latter should therefore take precedence, and (3) the county court declaration overturned the small claims judgment. H disputed the principle of issue estoppel. W contended that both of the contradictory decisions were made at first instance and that neither set aside or overturned the other.

Held, dismissing the appeal, that (1) the arbitrator in a small claims arbitration was required to inform the parties present of the award he was making and his reasons. H was present when the judge made his finding of fact with regard to the boundary, ie. that the hedge was on W's land and that W had a legal right to cut the hedge, and H could not dispute what had been said; (2) the award given in a small claims arbitration was as binding and effectual as if it had been given in an open court by a judge, as provided by the County Courts Act 1984 s.64(3), and (3) applying the principle of issue estoppel, the issue between the parties in the small claims proceedings was whether or not the hedge was on land owned by W and was conclusive of the action being appealed, *Fidelitas Shipping Co Ltd v. V/O Exportchleb* [1966] 1 Q.B. 630, [1965] C.L.Y. 100 applied. Further, the county court judgment could not affect the small claims finding.

HAMILTON v. WESTON [1997] E.G.C.S. 10, Henry, L.J. Waite, L.J., CA.

721. Small claims–damages for personal injuries–automatic reference to arbitration

[Rules of Supreme Court Ord.80 r.2(3).]

H, aged five years, was a passenger in his father's vehicle at the time of a road traffic accident on February 3, 1996. On January 31, 1997 proceedings were issued on his behalf by solicitors instructed by his mother and next friend. F, in his defence of February 20, 1997 contended that H's claim was worth less than £3,000 and that the personal injury element was worth less than £1,000 and that H had no realistic expectation of exceeding such a sum when proceedings were issued and therefore the matter should be referred to arbitration. On May 1, 1997 the matter came before the deputy district judge. F sought an order that the matter be referred to arbitration for the reasons given in their defence. H contended that the action should not be referred to arbitration on the grounds that H was a minor relying on RSC Ord.80 r.2(3) and the decision in *M (A Minor) v. Liverpool CC* [1994] 2 C.L.Y. 3774. The deputy district judge accepted the argument that H must proceed by way of next friend, and the next friend must proceed by way of solicitor, and stated that automatic directions should be ordered in this case. The reference to arbitration was rescinded. F appealed.

Held, accepting the argument brought by H and upholding the decision in *M (A Minor)*, and that costs be incidental to the appeal by H's in any event.

HUGHES (A MINOR) v. FILIPE, June 26, 1997, H.H.J. Trigger, CC (Birkenhead). [*Ex rel.* Michael W Halsall Solicitors, 2 The Parks, Newton-le-Willows].

722. Small claims–damages for personal injuries–automatic reference to arbitration–aggregation of claims arising from one accident

[County Court Rules 1981 Ord.19 r.4.]

P's vehicle was damaged in a collision with D's vehicle on October 15, 1996. N was driving P's vehicle at the time of the collision. P, who was not in the vehicle at the time of the accident, claimed special damages limited to £3,000. N claimed general damages exceeding £1,000. On attending the pre-trial review it was argued by D's solicitors that P's case should be referred to arbitration as the claim was limited to an amount not exceeding £3,000. They argued that P should not be entitled to Scale 1 costs and the matter should be limited to the costs liable under CCR Ord.19 r.4. P's solicitors stated that the claims in this action could not be separated and accepted that if P's claim was not brought under the same proceedings as N's claim then the matter would be referred to arbitration. Order 19 provided for "any proceedings in which the sum claimed or amount involved does not exceed £3,000 (or £1,000 in the case of personal injuries) to be automatically referred to arbitration when the court receives a defence to the claim". P's solicitors stated that it was clear that in these proceedings the amount claimed did have a claim for personal injury which exceeded £1,000 and the value of N's claim was agreed to be over the £1,000 limit by P's solicitors.

Held, that P's claim should not be referred to arbitration, as to deal with the two matters separately would only increase the costs. Referring P's case to arbitration would lead to two issue fees, two hearings and the possibility of two differing decisions being reached. Where possible like claims should be kept together and go to trial in one hearing.

McHUGH v. McGREEVY, April 23, 1997, Judge not specified, CC (Birkenhead). [*Ex rel.* Michael W Halsall Solicitors, 2 The Parks, Newton-le-Willows].

723. Small claims–damages for personal injuries–automatic reference to arbitration–claim just exceeding £1,000

[County Court Rules 1981 Ord.19 r.3; Rules of the Supreme Court Ord.24 r.7A; Limitation Act 1980 s.11.]

S was involved in a road traffic accident. General damages were agreed at £600 and special damages (specifically loss of earnings) were agreed at £477, producing a total of £1,077. F applied claiming that the figure of £1,000 in the CCR Ord.19 r.3 (1) applied only to general damages for pain, suffering and loss of amenity. S appealed.

Held, allowing the appeal, that followiing a wide interpretation of the term "damage" as evidenced by the Law Reform (Personal Injuries) Act 1948, RSC Ord.24 r.7A and Limitation Act 1980 s.11, the expression "claim for damages which exceeds £1,000" in Ord.19 r.3(1) meant a claim arising out of the personal injury whether it be general or special.

SCHOLEY v. FOSTER, May 21, 1997, H.H.J. Goldstein, CC (Bow). [*Ex rel.* Nicholas A Peacock, Barrister, Ground Floor, 6 Pump Court, Temple].

724. Small claims–damages for personal injuries–automatic reference to arbitration–claim within arbitration limit

[County Court Rules 1981 Ord.19 r.3.]

R and the second plaintiff were involved in a road traffic accident which occurred on February 26, 1996. Proceedings were issued against the defendant for damages for personal injury and consequential losses for both R and the second plaintiff. The second plaintiff was a minor and medical evidence was disclosed which both parties accepted would not attract an award for damages in excess of the arbitration limit of £1,000. J made an application requesting that the second plaintiff's claim be referred to arbitration pursuant to CCR Ord.19 r.3(1), on the grounds that the claim for damages for personal injury would not exceed £1,000. The court of its own volition requested both parties to attend the hearing on January 3, 1997 to consider J's application. The district judge refused to refer the second plaintiff's claim to arbitration and J appealed the decision.

Held, allowing the appeal and referring the second plaintiff's claim to arbitration, that the fact that the second plaintiff was a minor was not on its own a sufficient ground to avoid the claim being referred automatically to arbitration. The claim should have been referred automatically to arbitration pursuant to Ord.19 r.3(1).

ROCHFORD v. JONES, February 19, 1997, H.H.J. Hardy, CC (Oldham). [*Ex rel.* Lace Mawer, Solicitors, King's House, 42 King Street West, Manchester].

725. Small claims–damages for personal injuries–automatic reference to arbitration–reasonable prospect of recovering damages of over £1,000

W was involved in a road traffic accident on December 17, 1996 when her vehicle came into collision with S's vehicle. As a result of the collision, W sustained injuries to her cervical spine which fully settled within 10 days and had intermittent headaches which settled within seven days. Proceedings were issued on April 10, 1997 and S filed a defence on April 28, 1997 stating that W's personal injuries would not exceed £1,000. The court on its own volition on May 9 referred the matter to arbitration. W issued an application to rescind the reference to arbitration.

Held, after hearing evidence the court found that W's claim should never have been referred to arbitration as there was a reasonable prospect that W would have recieved damages exceeding £1,000.

WALKER v. SOVEREIGN DESPATCH, June 19, 1997, Deputy District Judge Fletcher, CC (Birkenhead). [*Ex rel.* Michael W Halsall, Solicitors, 2 The Parks, Newton-le-Willows].

726. Small claims–damages for personal injuries–automatic reference to arbitration–value of claim

[County Court Rules 1981 Ord.19 r.3.]

DJ originally made an application on September 26, 1996 for an order that proceedings be referred to arbitration. The district judge made his decision on the basis of his interpretation of CCR Ord.19 r.3(1)(b) which stated that any claim exceeding £1,000, which included a claim for personal injuries, should not stand referred to arbitration. DJ appealed against the decision and argued that some special damages had been paid prior to the issue of proceedings, but that as the remaining damages fell below £3,000, the case should have been referred automatically to arbitration. The personal injury element of the claim had already been agreed between the parties at £750. DJ argued that, furthermore, the amendment of Ord.19 r.3(1) para.1A provided for proceedings which included a claim for damages which exceed £1,000. DJ stressed that most personal injury claims include other categories of damage and that these were not to be included in the £1,000 limit which related only to quantum of the injuries themselves. E argued that the payments made prior to issue of proceedings should form part of the overall claim and that these would take the value of the entire claim over £3,000. E also argued that Ord.19 r.3(1)(b) meant that where damages for personal injuries and their consequential losses exceeded £1,000, the matter would not stand referred to arbitration.

Held, that monies received prior to issue of proceedings cannot be included in the plaintiff's claim, as a plaintiff can only claim for something which is outstanding and owing to them, and a defendant may very well concede liability for certain aspects of a claim and dispute others. For the purposes of these proceedings, the monies which E had received could not be regarded as interim payments within the rules. The judge held that Ord.19 r.3 para.1A(b) was plain and clearly provided for personal injuries exceeding £1,000 and not other types of claim and that the personal injury element of a claim had to exceed £1,000 before that claim became an exception to r.3(1). The matter was therefore, referred to arbitration and the costs of the original application and of the appeal were awarded to DJ on Scale 2.

ECCLESTON v. DJ RYAN & SONS, November 1, 1996, Judge Hardy, CC (Manchester). [*Ex rel.* Lace Mawer, Solicitors, King's House, 42 King St West, Manchester].

727. Statements of claim–amendment–affecting limitation defence–estoppel

[Limitation Act 1980 s.14A, s.32.]

B engaged, R, the first defendant, as consultant engineers in 1978 on a project to create an artificial lake. Preparatory work had been completed by 1978 and the next step was contract work which included the preparation of a basin to receive an impervious artificial liner, to supply and install the liner and cover it with a stone free soil protection layer. The second defendant, L, was appointed as contractor by a contract under seal on June 17, 1981 and the work was carried out between May and October 1981. B issued a writ on March 24, 1995 alleging concealment of defects by both defendants within the Limitation Act 1980 s.32 and that it was not until some date between May 5, 1992 and October 1994 that B first learned of the material facts for the purposes of s.14A. On November 29, 1996 B applied for leave to amend the statement of claim. This raised questions as to whether R was estopped from relying on limitation defences and whether it was under a continuing duty to inform B about defects in construction of the liner. The present hearing considered whether leave should be given and associated preliminary issues.

Held, that amendments should not be approved which simply consisted of claims for damages for loss suffered from failure to sue in time without setting out the facts relied upon as creating a duty to avert such a loss. In principle estoppel could not be set up so as to exclude the limitation defence without, at least, some allegation that R had represented to B at some relevant time that it was not to worry about losing the right to sue.

BLAENAU GWENT BC v. ROBINSON JONES DESIGN PARTNERSHIP LTD 53 Con. L.R. 31, John Hicks Q.C., QBD (OR).

728. Statements of claim–amendment–causes of action–duty to warn of negligence of fellow professionals

B were members of C's team of professional advisers for the development of a site in London. C sought and B opposed leave to make amendments to the original statement of claim which made allegations of breach of contract and negligence against the 33 professional advisers. The proposed amendments were numerous and complex including many allegations that the relevant defendants failed to advise or warn C that extensions of time granted to the contract were caused by the performance of one or more of the defendants or were likely to be so caused or that an investigation should be carried out to establish that likelihood. Against the project manager and quantity surveyor there were additional allegations of negligently prepared progress reports and financial statements and failure to advise that sums due to the contractor for prolongation, loss and expense were due to the deficiencies of one or more of the defendants. Against the project manager and architect there were also allegations of failure to advise or warn of the need to commence arbitration proceedings against the contractor. Further allegations were made that in addition to duties in contract and tort B were in breach of fiduciary duties.

Held, granting most of the applications, that though much of the factual background sought to be included in the amendments was the same as existing claims, new causes of action would be added. A duty to warn of the negligence of oneself or of other professionals was different from duties such as design, calculation, measurement and management. Though there was some overlap, the factual component of the amended claim was not identical to the original. In particular, the knowledge or means of knowledge of B of actual or potential deficiencies in performance were new. However, allegations of failure to advise of the possibility of commencement of arbitration proceedings or failure to react with due care and skill to the allegedly unmeritorious claims for extensions of time did involve substantially the same facts as existing claims. No basis was shown for a plea of breach of fiduciary duty. In the absence of an express term, it would be necessary to imply a term that the project manager was under a duty under the terms of the contact of engagement to report to C deficiencies in the performance of its codefendants. The architect had no duty to report to C any actual or potential deficiencies in the performance of the project manager: it did, however, have a duty to report deficiencies in the performance of the structural engineer and the quantity surveyor which could be read from the express terms of the contract but in addition would be necessarily implied. On the balance of probabilities, there was no duty on the structural engineer to report on the performance of the other members of the professional team. In the absence of express written terms of appointment of the quantity surveyor, it was not necessary to imply a term imposing a duty to report on the performance of other members of the professional team. Since a duty, as set out above, was a continuing one, if it was held to exist the date of breach for limitation purposes would be when B's engagement ended.

CHESHAM PROPERTIES LTD v. BUCKNALL AUSTIN MANAGEMENT SERVICES LTD 82 B.L.R. 92, John Hicks Q.C., QBD (OR).

729. Statements of claim–amendment–limitations–claims in tort and contract–date from which action accrued

Relying on advice from E, solicitors, T agreed to act as surety for C, a company owned by T, in respect of an underlease of premises from which C operated a pizza restaurant. C had occupied the premises and commenced trading before the lease was executed, and as a result T had been obliged to spend £12,000 on completing dilapidations before the landlord would approve the lease. C subsequently defaulted on the rent and assigned its rights of action to T, who brought claims in tort and contract against E in respect of negligent legal advice given to C, namely failure to advise on the existence of the dilapidations and on the consequences of occupying the premises before the lease was executed. T now appealed against the refusal of an application to amend his statement of claim to the effect that E owed duties in tort and contract to both C and T. E argued that the claim was statute barred as the limitation period had begun to run from the time when the underlease was executed in February 1989, whilst T contended that time did not begin to run against him as guarantor until C had defaulted on the rent some three years later.

Held, dismissing the appeal, that, in regard to the contract claim, time began to run from when the lease was executed and was statute barred as a result. A right of action in tort accrued when T had suffered damage, and he could have succeeded in a claim for more than nominal damages if action had been taken when the lease was executed as the dilapidations had already been completed, thereby making the guarantee more onerous. Further, the judge at first instance had not made a proper comparison of the facts comprised in the original claim and the amendment sought by T. The differences raised by the amendment could not be said to have arisen out of the same or substantially the same facts as those already pleaded and therefore leave to amend the statement of claim could not be granted.

TABARROK v. EDC LORD & CO [1997] P.N.L.R. 491, Aldous, L.J., CA.

730. Statements of claim–amendment–whether trial would be dislocated–costs

G issued a writ against B in June 1992 which related to an accident which had taken place in September 1990. Following a change of counsel, G wished to amend the statement of claim by adding eight further particulars of negligence. G also sought leave to adduce the evidence of a new witness, formal exchange of witness evidence already having taken place. In February 1997 the district judge gave G leave to amend the statement of claim in relation to four particulars, but refused leave to adduce the other four, and refused leave to adduce the witness statement on the basis that witness exchange had already taken place.

Held, allowing the additional amendments, that the relevant issue was the likelihood of late amendments dislocating a trial date, and whether compensation for such dislocation could be awarded in the form of costs, *Mortgage Corp Ltd v. Sandoes* [1997] P.N.L.R. 263, [1997] C.L.Y. 783 and *Letpak Ltd v. Harris* [1997] P.N.L.R. 239, [1997] C.L.Y. 784 applied. The answer to this question was that the trial date would not be dislocated therefore the additional amendments would be allowed, on the basis that G paid all the costs of the amendments, to include re-interviews of witnesses or the taking of statements regarding issues arising out of the amendments. The additional witness statement was admissible, and if B wanted to put forward evidence to deal with that statement, they had leave to do so. B were awarded the costs in the cause of the appeal.

GIBBS v. BRITISH ROAD SERVICES, March 11, 1997, May, J., High Court. [*Ex rel.* Leo Abse & Cohen, Solicitors, Cardiff].

731. Statements of claim–limitations–statement served out of time and after expiry of limitation period

In a claim for damages for negligent advice, W issued a writ on February 2, 1996 and served it on June 21, 1996. Having received notice that H intended to defend the action, W were required to serve the statement of claim within 14 days, but failed to do so and their application for a 28 day extension was refused. The statement of claim was served on August 7 without leave and the action was struck out, but restored on appeal. H appealed against the decision to restore the proceedings, contending that an extension of time beyond the expiry of the limitation period should not be permitted.

Held, dismissing the appeal, that a judge was entitled to exercise his discretion to allow an extension of time for serving a statement of claim. Although the possibility of any prejudice to a defendant must be considered where the limitation period had expired, in the instant case the late service of the writ added only six weeks.

WALKER v. HOWARD, *The Times*, November 13, 1997, Staughton, L.J., CA.

732. Stay of proceedings–further allegations contained in new evidence–no lifting of corporate veil

B applied for leave to appeal and a stay pending appeal from two orders dismissing their applications for a stay and setting aside a default judgment. M was a German company which carried out business as a commercial bank until the insolvency of the parent company caused it to be placed into liquidation. B sought to justify their refusal to pay sums due to M on the basis that third parties had alleged improper transfers between companies in the group and had made competing claims to ownership of the money in the accounts and sought to set off against monies due to M, monies due from the parent company which was indebted to B for more than $15 million. B sought to adduce fresh evidence and submitted that the amounts in certain accounts may not be the property of M and that the interests of a third party claimant, among others, should be considered. The fresh evidence consisted of a letter purporting to confirm that T, a third party, deposited £500,000 with the parent company as security for the performance of certain contractual obligations it had undertaken subject to which the money was to be returned. It was alleged that the £500,000 represented money held by the parent company in trust. It was also argued that the right to trace the money into other accounts existed. B claimed that, prior to M's collapse, its commercial activities were controlled and directed by the parent company to such an extent that the corporate veil should be lifted with the result that M was liable for the obligations of the parent company. B further submitted that New York law was the appropriate law to determine whether the corporate veil should be lifted.

Held, refusing the applications, that the letter contained no allegation, and no evidence to support any allegation, that the money in M's accounts represented money which T deposited with the parent company. There was nothing requiring the court to stay the action on this point and no basis to withhold payment from M. The judge correctly regarded B's conduct in bringing proceedings in New York as forum shopping of the worst kind. There was no basis for alleging that the fact that the parent company placed its ultimate subsidiary into liquidation supported an allegation that the corporate structure was disregarded. Leave to appeal was refused, stay continued until the determination of the application for leave to appeal.

MERIDIEN BIAO BANK GmbH v. BANK OF NEW YORK [1997] 1 Lloyd's Rep. 437, Sir Thomas Bingham, M.R., CA.

733. Stay of proceedings–general stay granted without time limit for service of medical report–automatic strike out provisions inoperative

[County Court Rules 1981 Ord.6 r.1, Ord.9 r.10.]

B appealed against a decision allowing C's appeal against a decision that C's personal injury action had been automatically struck out under CCR Ord.9 r.10. Concerned as to the existence of a limitation point, C commenced proceedings whilst still awaiting receipt of a medical report. Leave was granted in the county court permitting the issue of a summons without the report, with the action being stayed pending service. However, the action was automatically struck out 12 months after the grant of leave and B contended that C could not rely on the statutory stay provided under CCR Ord.6 r.1(6) when in default owing to non production of the medical report.

Held, dismissing the appeal, that the stay provided by Ord.6 r.1(6) effectively prevented further steps being taken in the proceedings and C could validly serve her summons with no further action being required as long as the stay remained in force, as the 12 month period under Ord.9 r.10 only ran from the time when the stay was lifted. In effect, the stay served as an agreement on the part of B not to enter judgment in default, nor to exploit the situation to C's prejudice, notwithstanding the fact that C could have pursued her action with greater diligence. The problems could have been resolved by the requirement for the report to be served within a prescribed time period, as the indefinite period of the general stay under Ord.6 r.1 (6) deprived Ord.9 r.10 of its normal effect, *Heer v. Tutton* [1995] 1 W.L.R. 1336, [1996] 1 C.L.Y. 903 considered.

CASHMORE v. BLUE CIRCLE PLUMBING FIXTURES LTD (T/A QUALCAST BATHROOMS),Trans. Ref: CCRT195/1341/G, July 30,1996, LordWoolf, M.R., CA.

734. Stay of proceedings–professional negligence–protective writs

[Limitation Act 1980.]

W applied to stay proceedings concerning third party claims against a number of solicitors, pending the hearing of a test case in the House of Lords. M applied for a time limit for the delivery by W of a fully particularised statement of claim on pain of dismissal of the actions. A large number of investors had lost money through equity relief schemes in which solicitors, acting for both investor and the building society, might have given inadequate advice during the period 1988 to 1990. Some claims had already been pursued and test cases had ensued, but potential claims against W would not be subject to any time limitation save the doctrine of laches, whereas any claim by W against the solicitors took effect either in contract or negligence and were therefore subject to the six year limitation period under the Limitation Act 1980. W had taken the precaution of issuing protective writs within the limitation period, but had not produced particularised statements of claim.

Held, allowing the application by W and dismissing that of M, that, as a matter of discretion, the prejudice to W that would arise from it being time barred from pursuing third party proceedings outweighed potential prejudice to M arising from the need to incur the costs of correspondence on the progress of the case. The latter costs could in any event be contested at taxation should the cases later be discontinued by W, *Steamship Mutual Underwriting Association v. Trollope & Colls (City)* (1986) 33 Build. L.R. 77, [1984] C.L.Y. 2699 distinguished and *Rediffusion (Hongkong) Ltd v. Attorney General of Hong Kong* [1970] A.C. 1136, [1970] C.L.Y. 185 considered.

WEST BROMWICH BUILDING SOCIETY v. MANDER HADLEY & CO,Trans. Ref: CH-1995-W-No.7967, March 21, 1997, Evans-Lombe, J., Ch D.

735. Striking out–automatic striking out–automatic striking out inappropriate after judgment

[County Court Rules 1981 Ord.17 r.11.]

G had obtained judgment in a personal injury action against C, with damages to be assessed. An order was made to the effect that (1) the automatic directions were to apply; (2) a revised schedule was to be served on C within 28 days, and (3) a counter schedule could then be served by C within 14 days if necessary. G failed to request a hearing within the time limit and C successfully applied to have the assessment of damages part of G's action struck out under CCR Ord.17 r.11 (9) for failure to comply with the automatic directions. G appealed.

Held, allowing the appeal, that the language of CCR Ord.17 r.11 was inconsistent with the proposition that it still applied after final judgment, and it was inappropriate to dismiss an action where judgment for damages had already been obtained. The order did not specifically refer to CCR Ord.17 r.11 (9) so could not be regarded as sufficient to invoke automatic striking out. Similarly, if the judge had wished to impose the harsh penalty of staying proceedings for failing to comply with time limits, express provision to that effect would have had to be made in the order. Whilst damages should be assessed at the earliest convenient time, in maintaining control over the proceedings it was more appropriate for the court to take steps such as reserving the power to fix a hearing date for the assessment of damages or making a specific order that certain consequences would flow if an application to set a date was not made within a defined period.

GOMES v. CLARK [1997] P.I.Q.R. P219, LordWoolf, M.R., CA.

736. Striking out—automatic striking out—Court of Appeal guidance on interpretation of rules

[County Court Rules 1981 Ord.17 r.11.]

In the consideration of 19 appeals and two applications, a large number of unresolved problems relating to the interpretation of automatic directions, particularly the strike out penalty under the CCR Ord.17 r.11, were addressed by the issue of new guidelines.

Held, that it would in the future be unnecessary to refer to any of the earlier authorities, since the principles of law laid down here were intended not only to resolve outstanding issues and litigation, but to constitute a comprehensive restatement of existing authority. The introduction of the automatic strike out penalty had created such significant problems that many courts now preferred to fix a date for a hearing at an early stage, which, when combined with a far firmer attitude to excusing delays, had much to commend it. Guidance was provided on a number of issues, including the consolidation and transfer of actions, third party actions, counterclaims, the identification of a trigger date where service of several defences was involved and the effect of interlocutory and summary judgment. It was clear that many disputes could be avoided if courts or judges would date stamp the documents, especially defences.

BANNISTER v. SGB PLC; *sub nom.* ORDER 17, RULE 11 OF THE COUNTY COURT RULES, *Re* [1997] P.I.Q.R. P165, Saville, L.J., CA.

737. Striking out—automatic striking out—Court of Appeal guidance on interpretation of rules

[County Court Rules 1981 Ord.17 r.11.]

Further guidance was issued on the automatic directions regime, particularly the strike out penalty under the CCR Ord.17 r.11, which was to supersede the court's judgment in *Bannister v. SGB Plc* [1997] C.L.Y 736 where the rulings were incompatible. The guidance in *Bannister* would be amended with regard to (1) computation of time for the delivery of a defence; (2) actions which were to be regarded as constituting a request for a hearing date; (3) ouster of the automatic directions where proceedings were referred to arbitration under Ord.19; (4) ouster of the automatic directions where there was an application for summary or interlocutory judgment, and (5) the practical implications of ouster of the automatic directions.

GREIG MIDDLETON & CO LTD v. DENDEROWICZ (NO.1); *sub nom.* ORDER 17, RULE 11 OF THE COUNTY COURT RULES, *Re, The Times*, July 28, 1997, Saville, L.J., CA.

738. Striking out—automatic striking out—Court of Appeal guidance on interpretation of rules

[County Court Rules 1981 Ord.9 r.3, Ord.17 r.11, Ord.19.]

The final cases in a list of over 100 appeals relating to the automatic striking out provisions pursuant to CCR Ord.17 r.11 were heard under this nomenclature and a revised version of the judgment in *Bannister v. SGB Plc* [1997] P.I.Q.R. P165, [1997] C.L.Y. 736 delivered, which was to appear in any future law report of it and be circulated and placed on the Internet. In the eponymous case G, who were stockbrokers, claimed £10,000 from D, a customer. D made a limited admission on Form N9B and paid £204.50 before filing a fully pleaded defence. Numerous interlocutory hearings ensued until the judge below refused to strike out the action on the basis that G had applied for an extension before the guillotine date. D appealed and G contended that (1) D's partial admission in Form N9B, regarded as the defence when calculating the trigger date, meant that the action was not within Ord.17 r.11, because of the application of r.11 (1) (o), which excepted an action to which Ord.9 r.3(6) applied. Order 9 r.6 concerned an admission of part of a plaintiff's claim; and (2) the action had initially been referred to arbitration under Ord.19 by the court and therefore fell outside Ord.17 r.11.

Held, allowing the appeal, that the judge below had erred in refusing the strike out, (1) Ord.9 r.3(6) was concerned with situations where a plaintiff was not willing to accept an admitted sum in full satisfaction of his claim. Although G had accepted the sum as a payment on account, it had failed to inform the court that the amount did not satisfy the claim and, therefore, Ord.9 r.3(6) did not apply, and (2) where an action was for a sum less than £3,000, the referral to arbitration was automatic and there was no need for an order to be made to that effect. In the instant case, the amount claimed was above the arbitration limit and the referral to arbitration had been a clerical error. The court went on to consider extensions of time for appeals, the computation of time and trigger dates, the ousting of the strike out provisions in various circumstances and reinstatement, *Bannister v. SGB Plc* [1997] P.I.Q.R. P165, [1997] C.L.Y. 736, *Ferreira v. American Embassy Employees Association* [1996] 1 W.L.R. 536 and *Williams v. Globe Coaches* [1996] 1 W.L.R. 553, [1996] 1 C.L.Y. 911 considered.

GREIG MIDDLETON & CO LTD v. DENDEROWICZ (NO.2); OLALEYE-ORUENE v. LONDON GUILDHALL UNIVERSITY, *The Times*, July 28, 1997, Saville, L.J., CA.

739. Striking out—automatic striking out—Court of Appeal guidance on interpretation of rules

[County Court Rules 1981 Ord.17 r.11.]

Following its judgment in *Greig Middleton & Co Ltd v. Denderowicz (No.2)* [1997] C.L.Y. 738, the Court of Appeal gave guidance on how it would exercise its discretion in relation to applications to extend time to appeal in cases involving CCR Ord.17 r.11 where there had been an authoritatively stated change in the law since the judgment under challenge was delivered.

Held, that Ord.17 r.11 had resulted in cases being struck out without trial on the merits, so that the principle that there should be finality in litigation fell to be applied in a quite different context. It was hard to imagine circumstances more special than those which had resulted from the introduction of r.11 (9) in terms of the possibility of more than one legitimate interpretation of the rules. Thus if an applicant could prove he had acted on reasonable advice in relation to Ord.17 r.11, on reliance of which he did not appeal immediately, and he had a strong argument that his appeal would succeed, those facts could form the basis of a successful application for an extension on the grounds of special circumstances. However, an extension would not be granted automatically and certain factors would weigh against the grant of an extension, including (1) inexcusable delay in applying; (2) the respondent could show that a third party might be affected by the re-opening of the case; (3) the respondent could show that he or his insurers had reasonably acted on the basis that the action was at an end and had conducted their affairs accordingly or prejudice had otherwise been suffered; (4) the plaintiff had brought a second action and the respondent had incurred costs in defending it, and (5) the plaintiff was unlikely to win the appeal if an extension of time was granted.

GREIG MIDDLETON & CO LTD v. DENDEROWICZ (NO.3); *sub nom.* ORDER 17, RULE 11 OF THE COUNTY COURT RULES, *Re, The Times*, July 28, 1997, Saville, L.J., CA.

740. Striking out—automatic striking out—damages claim for personal injuries—admission of negligence but not liability for whole claim

[County Court Rules 1981 Ord.9 r.10.]

S appealed against the dismissal of his application for a declaration that P's claim for damages in respect of a road traffic accident be struck out under the provisions of the CCR Ord.9 r.10. P claimed that S was negligent and pleaded a conviction for careless driving. P claimed unliquidated damages: general damages for pain, suffering, loss of amenity, specified damages and damages for loss of earnings. S admitted negligence but did not admit liability for the whole claim. S argued that his pleadings were an admission of P's whole claim and as P had failed to enter default judgment within the 12 month period stipulated in Ord.9 r.10 the matter should have been automatically struck out.

Held, dismissing the appeal, that the pleading which put at issue the heads of damage actually claimed did not amount to an admission of all of P's claim for the purposes of Ord.9 r.6. The narrower definition as given to "admission" in Ord.9 r.2(2) applies to the provisions of Ord.9 r.6, requiring that an admission be made in the appropriate form if judgment was to be entered under Ord.9 r.10, *Watkins v. Toms* (Unreported, 1996) followed, *Parrott v. Jackson* [1996] P.I.Q.R. P394, [1996] 1 C.L.Y. 904 considered.

PERRIN v. SHORT, Trans. Ref: CCRTI 96/1107/G, April 10, 1997, Swinton Thomas, L.J., CA.

741. Striking out—automatic striking out—failure to request hearing date

[County Court Rules 1981 Ord.17 r.11.]

The appellants appealed against the striking out of their respective actions when a request for a hearing date had been received before the 15 months cut off date under CCR Ord.17 r.11, but a request for an extension of time had not been made.

Held, dismissing the appeals, that it was clear that the sanction of striking out was intended to apply to failure to make a request within the 15 months period. The six months period under r.11 (3) (d) was not nugatory, but enabled a defendant to apply to the court for a fixed timetable with costs penalties available, or enabled the court to impose a procedural timetable on the parties. There was no necessity for an extension of time after the six months period and before the 15 months guillotine date.

PERRY v. KANG HO WONG; SAMPSON v. MOON; JONES v. ROE SHOPFITTING LTD [1997] 1 W.L.R. 381, Lord Bingham of Cornhill, L.C.J., CA.

742. Striking out—automatic striking out—failure to request hearing date within period—meaning of "proper officer"

[County Court Rules 1981 Ord.1 r.3.]

K issued proceedings against G in the Aylesbury County Court. A defence was entered and the case was transferred to Oxford County Court. The automatic directions timetable commenced. Before the guillotine date for automatic striking out K wrote to the Chief Clerk at Aylesbury requesting a hearing date. He complied with the necessary formalities and paid the fee. Aylesbury did not revert to K, but banked the cheque, and forwarded the request to Oxford some weeks later. By then the guillotine date had passed, and the Chief Clerk at Oxford said that the case had been struck out.

Held, the case had been automatically struck out. The rules require that a "request" is made to the "proper officer". Although authorities from the Court of Appeal had been liberal in the interpretation of the meaning of "request" there was no scope to be similarly generous in defining "proper officer", as it was a term of art defined by CCR Ord.1 r.3. It could only mean that the district judge or chief clerk (or other officer of the court acting on his behalf) of the court in which the action was proceeding at the material time. As such there had been no valid request for a hearing within the 15 month period.

KENT v. GRANT, May 11, 1997, District Judge Scandrett, CC (Oxford). [*Ex rel.* Benjamin Williams, Barrister, Chambers of Michael Parroy Q.C., Oxford].

743. Striking out—automatic striking out—partial admission by defendant constituted defence

[County Court Rules 1981 Ord.9 r.2, r.3, r.6, r.20.]

On May 18, 1995 S had a collision with a vehicle owned by P1 and driven by P2. P1 incurred losses including car hire charges. P2 suffered personal injury and loss of earnings. P1 and P2 issued proceedings on December 11, 1995. S served a document entitled "defence", para.1 of which admitted "that as a result of the collision, the plaintiffs have suffered some personal loss and damage"; para.2

admitted negligence; para.3 stated: "the alleged personal injury loss and damage are denied".The court issued notice that automatic directions applied. P1 and P2 did not enter judgment. On April 24,1997, P1 and P2 wrote to the court requesting a trial date. S applied to the court for a declaration that the action had been automatically struck out under CCR Ord.9 r.10(ii). P1 and P2 argued, inter alia, that: (1) there had not been a sufficient admission of at least some damage because para.1 of the defence did not specify that both plaintiffs had suffered some loss, and also because para.3 was a bold denial of the loss and damage claimed; (2) S had not served an admission for the purposes of Ord.9 r.10(ii) because Ord.9 r.2(2) defines an "admission" as "the form appended to the summons" but such form had not been used by S, and (3) Ord.9 r.10 would only bite if P1 and P2 were entitled to enter judgment but they had been unable to do so, first because Ord.9 r.6(c) prohibited P1 and P2 entering judgment where S had, as in the instant case, served a defence and second because under Ord.9 r.3(7) following a partial admission P1 and P2 would have no right per se to enter judgment but merely a right to apply for such judgment or order as the court might think fit.

Held, dismissing S's application to strike out, that as S had served a defence disputing quantum, that constituted a defence for the purposes of Ord.9 r.6(c) which therefore prevented P1 and P2 entering any judgment.

PHILIPS AND SIMONS v. STACEY, June 20, 1997, District Judge Duerdon, CC (Bury). [*Ex rel.* M Walker, Solicitor, Seager & Co, Branker Buildings, Bolton].

744. Striking out—automatic striking out—period of delay

[County Court Rules 1981 Ord.17 r.11.]

S applied for leave to appeal out of time against a decision that his case, concerning a dispute over a six inch strip of land, had been struck out by automatic directions under CCR Ord.17 r.11, despite a clear direction that the case should be set down when the plaintiff was ready.

Held, granting leave and allowing the appeal, that the total period of delay was 10 months, which would normally be a maximum, and the reasons for that delay were predominantly unhelpful to S. However, following the decision in *Downer,* the appeal was bound to succeed and the defendant would not be overly prejudiced, because the dispute itself was unresolved and and a fresh action could still be brought within the limitation period, *Downer & Downer Ltd v. Brough* [1996] 1 W.L.R. 575, [1996] 1 C.L.Y. 918 followed.

SEGARAM v. GRANT (1997) 73 P. & C.R. D35, Lord Woolf, M.R., CA.

745. Striking out—automatic striking out—personal injuries claim—reasonable diligence

[County Court Rules 1981 Ord.17 r.11.]

K appealed against an order reinstating D's claim for damages for personal injury after it had been struck out by automatic directions, under CCR Ord.17 r.11. D was struck by a car reversed by K, a taxi driver. He suffered a fractured tibia which confined him to hospital for three days and kept him off work for three months. Proceedings were issued one day within the three year limit and a defence issued shortly afterwards, despite which D sought summary judgment on the basis that K's insurers had admitted liability. Summary judgment was dismissed, but the application to fix a date for trial was not made until six days after the guillotine date. K applied to strike out, but D's application to reinstate the case was successful, a decision which was upheld on appeal and D was subsequently awarded damages without contributory negligence. K contended that (1) D had not demonstrated reasonable diligence since D's list of documents had been inadequate and his medical reports had been disclosed out of time and (2) D had provided no acceptable excuse for his failure.

Held, dismissing the appeal, that (1) there had been difficulties caused by a progressive deterioration in D's condition, the transfer of the file within the solicitor's office, and by the illness of the preferred medical expert so that the judge below had correctly held that the case had been progressed with reasonable diligence, and (2) this was not a case where a solicitor had ignored the deadline and it was likely that an earlier application for postponement of the "guillotine" would have been successful, *Rastin v. British Steel Plc* [1994] 1 W.L.R. 732, [1994] C.L.Y. 3635, *Hoskins v. Wiggins Teape (UK) Ltd* [1994] P.I.Q.R. P377, [1995] 2 C.L.Y. 4082 and *Reville v. Wright* [1996] 1 W.L.R. 592, [1996] 1 C.L.Y. 914 applied.

DOWSE v. KAPPELL, Trans. Ref: CCRT196/1096/G, December 12, 1996, Sir Brian Neill, CA.

746. **Striking out–automatic striking out–plaintiff requesting a hearing date but from wrong county court–request still valid despite expiry of 15 month timetable**

M commenced proceedings in Sheffield County Court on April 21, 1995. The action was one to which automatic directions applied and an N450 notice was issued by the court on June 13, 1995. The 15 month period was to expire on September 27, 1996. On February 19, 1997 the case was transferred from Sheffield to Leicester, and on March 1, 1996 Leicester County Court issued a notice, received by M's solicitors, stating that the case had been transferred. On September 26, 1996 M's solicitors sent a request for a hearing enclosing a time estimate and a court fee but addressed to "The Proper Officer" of Sheffield County Court, not Leicester County Court. The fee was banked by Sheffield County Court. Sheffield then returned the request letter and repayment of the fee on November 5, 1996. On receiving this M's solicitors sent a duplicate of the letter and a further fee to Leicester county court on November 20, 1996. C applied to strike out M's action on the ground that the request of September 26, 1996 was not a proper discharge of M's obligation under CCR Ord.17 r.11 (3) (d).

Held, dismissing C's application and penalising C in costs, that the jurisdiction of the county court was a general one and was not restricted by reference to the particular district in which the county court was held, *Sharma v. Knight* [1986] 1 W.L.R. 757, [1986] C.L.Y. 463 applied. It therefore followed that a request to "the Proper Officer" of the county court one day before the expiry of the 15 month timetable, although addressed to the wrong district was nevertheless a sufficient request for the purposes of Ord.16 r.11 (3) (d) even though it was not received by the proper district until after the expiry of the 15 month timetable.

MOORE v. CITY ELECTRICAL FACTORS, December 23, 1996, District Judge Eaton, Court not specified. [*Ex rel.* Philip Goddard, Barrister, Chambers of Nicholas Jarman Q.C., Temple].

747. **Striking out–automatic striking out–premature request for trial date–expiry of time limits**

[County Court Rules 1981 Ord.17 r.11.]

E applied to the county court for a trial date to be set in an action for breach of contract against W, pursuant to CCR Ord.17 r.11 (3) (d), by which a plaintiff had six months after the close of pleadings to request a hearing date. E made the request more than six months after close of pleadings but before the expiry of the 15 month period laid down in CCR Ord.17 r.11 (9) for automatic striking out, but the judge refused to make an order setting a date because the case was complex and no witness statements had been exchanged. After the 15 month period had expired, W obtained a declaration that E's action had been struck out under the automatic directions for failure to request a trial date. E successfully appealed and obtained a declaration that their action had not been struck out and that their request for a trial date, albeit premature, had been valid. W appealed, contending that either r.11 (9) applied despite the request made by E, or that E's request for a trial date was an abuse of process and a nullity.

Held, dismissing the appeal, that E's request would have been valid had it been made within the six months period and was still valid, even though it was made within the extended period. The obligation to request a trial date was independent of the other requirements in r.11 (3) and simply meant that a request had been made within the time limits laid down. The request was not a nullity just because the court was unable to set a trial date, as there was a difference between an abuse of process and a premature application. There was no indication that the district judge or the parties thought that there was an abuse of process at the time of the request and there was no obligation on E to make another request.

EVER v. WT PARTNERSHIP CONSTRUCTION MANAGEMENT, *The Times*, January 9, 1997, Aldous, L.J., CA.

748. Striking out–automatic striking out–reinstatement–misled as to trigger date

[County Court Rules 1981 Ord.17 r.11.]

A was injured in an accident at work on August 2, 1990. Proceedings were issued on July 30, 1993 and a short denial defence on form N9 was entered on August 11, 1993. No medical report nor schedule of special damages was served with the particulars of claim and on August 3, 1993 the court, of its own motion, made an order that the proceedings be stayed unless, within 42 days of the order, a medical report and schedule of special damages were served. No schedule or medical report were served and accordingly the action was stayed. A was medically examined on January 4, 1994. He applied to remove the stay on May 19, 1994 and disclosed his medical report and schedule of special damages on June 6, 1994. The stay was removed by consent on July 27, 1994. C served a fully pleaded defence and list of documents on September 6, 1994 and an N450, dated September 19, was issued. On October 30, 1995 C applied for a declaration that A's claim had been automatically struck out pursuant to CCR Ord.17 r.11 on November 25, 1994. The judge found that the timetable under Ord.17 did not run during the currency of a stay. He therefore calculated that the 15 months expired on October 8, 1995 and as A had applied to set the matter down on October 5, 1995, the case was not struck out.

Held, granting the application to strike out, that the proceedings were automatically struck out pursuant to Ord.17 r.11. The stay was not a stay for all purposes and so it did not affect the timetable. A's claim was, however, reinstated on the grounds that he had been misled by the date on the N450. The case, therefore, fell within the ambit of *Williams v. Globe Coaches* [1996] 1 W.L.R. 553, [1996] 1 C.L.Y. 911.

ALLAN v. COSTELLO, July 9, 1996, H.H.J. MacDonald, CC (Newcastle). [*Ex rel.* Hay & Kilner, Solicitors, 30 Cloth Market, Newcastle Upon Tyne].

749. Striking out–automatic striking out–reinstatement of action–excusability of oversight

[County Court Rules 1981 Ord.17 r.11.]

Two applications were made for leave to appeal against the reinstatement of actions which had been struck out under CCR Ord.17 r.11 (9) involving the issue of how discretion regarding the automatic strike out provisions should be exercised since *Rastin v. British Steel* [1994] 1 W.L.R. 732, [1994] C.L.Y. 3635. In the first case the automatic timetable established by CCR Ord.17 r.11 (9) had not been adhered to and the matter was struck out. The application to reinstate was granted and on appeal against that decision, the judge considered (1) whether the action had been pursued with reasonable diligence, and (2) whether the default had been excusable. It was argued that the judge could have misdirected himself as there was authority to say that an oversight in itself was not an acceptable excuse for failure to comply with Ord.17 r.11 (9). In the second case the plaintiff's solicitors relied on the date of the form N450 as being the date of delivery of the defence, but the date was incorrect. The timetable would normally run from the actual delivery date, but, following *Williams v. Globe Coaches* [1996] 1 W.L.R. 553, [1996] 1 C.L.Y. 911, where there has been reliance on an incorrect date an application for reinstatement would usually be granted.

It was argued that the present case was distinguishable from *Williams v. Globe Coaches*.

Held, dismissing the applications, that there was no reason for the court to interfere if the judge had directed himself properly according to the guidelines, allowing for the varying facts of each individual case. In the first case the judge had not misdirected himself. Most cases involved an oversight and whether or not that oversight was excusable would depend on the circumstances of the particular case. *Hoskins v. Wiggins Teape (UK) Ltd* [1994] P.I.Q.R. P377, [1995] 2 C.L.Y. 4083 was not authority for the proposition that oversight per se cannot be excusable, but that oversight was not ordinarily excusable. In the second case, although it was well known within the profession that details on the form N450 were often inaccurate, H had relied on the incorrect date and as such the judge had directed himself properly in granting the reinstatement; *Williams v. Globe Coaches* could not be distinguished in this instance.

Observed, that the purpose of the automatic strike out provisions was to prevent lengthy and complicated litigation and therefore litigation pertaining to the provisions should be kept to a minimum.

SAMUELS v. JOHN LAING CONSTRUCTION LTD; HEWARD v. JOHN NIKE LEISURE LTD, Trans. Ref: LTA 95/5636/G, December 16, 1996, Lord Woolf, M.R., CA.

750. Striking out−automatic striking out−reinstatement of actions−categories of cases allowing reinstatement

R appealed against a refusal to reinstate her action for personal injury after her solicitor missed the guillotine deadline as a result of misinterpreting the rules on time limits. R argued that the two categories identified in *Bannister v. SGB Plc* [1997] P.I.Q.R. P165, [1997] C.L.Y. 736 should be extended to include a third category of cases to allow reinstatement where a plaintiff or her advisers had failed to comply with the rules because of reasonable misinterpretation.

Held, allowing the appeal but for other reasons, that in *Bannister* the court had set down a strict requirement that plaintiffs must prosecute their actions with reasonable diligence unless their advisers had been genuinely and reasonably misled. The court had rejected the possibility of creating a third category and R's excuse for missing the deadline was not persuasive enough to dispense with the obligation of having to satisfy the category one test of prosecuting actions diligently.

ROMANO v. CROYDON LBC, *The Times*, June 5, 1997, Brooke, L.J., CA.

751. Striking out−automatic striking out−stay of proceedings−automatic provisions did not apply to stayed proceedings

[County Court Rules 1981 Ord.17 r.11 (9).]

A appealed against a decision that W's action for damages for back injuries had not been automatically struck out under CCR Ord.17 r.11 (9). The 15 month period provided for under Ord.17 r.11 (9) had expired but the "guillotine date" for requesting a hearing date was postponed. The proceedings were then stayed pending an examination of W by A's psychiatrist. A argued that, although a stay prevented any further procedural steps from being taken, it did not prevent Ord.17 r.11 (9) from having the effect of automatically striking out the action on the expiry of the "guillotine date", and, whilst a hearing date could not be requested during the operation of the stay, W should have applied for an extension of time to keep the action going and, as she did not do so, the action should be struck out.

Held, dismissing the appeal, that where an order was made staying proceedings but it did not specify a final date by which a hearing was to be requested, the automatic striking out provisions were inconsistent with the stay order. Accordingly, on the proper construction of the rules, and following *Downer & Downer Ltd v. Brough* [1996] 1 W.L.R. 575, [1996] 1 C.L.Y. 918, the striking out provisions must cease to apply.

WHITEHEAD v. AVON CC [1997] P.I.Q.R. P148, Waller, L.J., CA.

752. Striking out—bare order for discovery not expressed as unless order—striking out defence for failure to comply with bare order

[Rules of the Supreme Court Ord.24 r.16(1).]

SR had installed a refrigeration unit supplied by the third parties, UPO, in SNS's premises. The unit caught fire and UPO contended that the compressor used in the unit, which had been supplied by the fourth party, UH, was responsible. In an action for negligence and breach of contract, judgment was given for UPO after UH's defence to a fourth party was dismissed under the RSC Ord.24 r.16(1) on the ground that an order for discovery, which had not been expressed as an unless order, had not been complied with. UH appealed.

Held, allowing the appeal, that, although Ord.24 r.16(1) gave the court jurisdiction to make an order striking out a defence for breach of a non peremptory order, it was a misuse of that power to do so where the effect would be to prevent a fourth party from submitting an arguable defence and to render it vulnerable in relation to damages flowing from the main action and third party proceedings. In the instant case, UH's failure to comply with the order for discovery did not justify the ultimate sanction of striking out and the proper approach would have been for the judge to have exercised his discretion to grant UH an extension of time in the form of a final or unless order.

STAR NEWS SHOPS v. STAFFORD REFRIGERATION LTD, *The Times*, November 18, 1997, Otton, L.J., CA.

753. Striking out—delay

D applied for leave to appeal against a decision dismissing an action against R for want of prosecution and for an extension of time for service of a statement of claim against the second defendant, a firm of solicitors. The claims arose from the collapse of D's group of companies resulting in litigation in England and the Isle of Man. The writ in the present action was issued in September 1994, but the draft statements of claim were not served on R and the second defendant until February and March 1996 respectively.

Held, refusing the applications, that although the judge at first instance had decided that little or no prejudice had been incurred as the action in the UK reproduced issues already raised in the Manx litigation, a distinction arose between cases where time extensions were sought for delivery of pleadings and those seeking extensions for service of writs or leave to appeal from a final order. Where, as here, there were cross applications to strike out for want of prosecution and for time extensions in which to serve a statement of claim, the principles surrounding adherence to time limits and the denial to a plaintiff of an adjudication on the merits of his case due to procedural default fell to be considered, *Costellow v. Somerset CC* [1993] 1 W.L.R. 256, [1993] C.L.Y. 3338 followed. There had been an inordinate delay prior to the service of the draft statements of claim which meant that prejudice was inevitable given that six years had elapsed since the events forming the basis of the claims.

Observed, that it was not to be assumed that the court would be ready to examine unreported authorities without justification. Unreported cases had been referred to in written submissions and produced at the hearing and the court must protect itself against the mass citation of authorities in reliance upon *Practice Statement (Court of Appeal: Authorities)* [1996] 1 W.L.R. 854, [1996] 1 C.L.Y. 864.

DOUGLAS v. ROYAL BANK OF SCOTLAND PLC, Trans. Ref: LTA 96/7483/E; QBENI 96/1450/E, May 23, 1997, Leggatt, L.J., CA.

754. Striking out—delay—action dismissed for delay even though limitation period was unimpaired

The case concerned a pop group, Paper Lace, who enjoyed their main success in 1974 and 1975. The writ for the action was issued in 1984 and followed the division of the group into two factions who both claimed rights in the name Paper Lace. No statement of claim was served and in 1987 the defendants applied successfully to have the action dismissed. Following the dismissal one of the defendants rejoined the plaintiffs' group. The plaintiffs appealed from the decision to dismiss the action. They admitted inordinate and inexcusable delay but claimed that the defendants had suffered no prejudice. The appeal was rejected. The plaintiffs now appealed from that decision and to protect themselves with regard to the limitation period they issued a second set of proceedings.

Held, dismissing the appeal, that (1) it was for the defendant to establish that the inordinate delay had caused or would cause prejudice if the action was allowed to continue. It was not for the plaintiff to prove that the dismissal could be of no benefit to the defendant; (2) the long period of inaction had caused real prejudice to the defendants. If the application to dismiss had been brought at a time when a second action would have been time barred, it would have been entitled to succeed, *Birkett v. James* [1978] A.C. 297, [1977] C.L.Y. 2410 referred to, and (3) there was no absolute bar to dismissal when the limitation period had not expired but it would be out of the ordinary to stop a first action if a second action could proceed unimpaired. However, there was a real possibility that the defendants would be better off if the order for dismissal was upheld. Firstly, because the composition of the two groups had changed and the second action could be a more effective vehicle for determining the rights of the parties, and secondly, the defendants were entitled to benefit from the possibility that one of the plaintiffs would fail to get legal aid and the second action would not get off the ground.

WRIGHT v. MORRIS [1997] F.S.R. 218, Mustill, L.J., CA.

755. Striking out–delay–action subject to automatic directions could be struck out at an earlier date

[County Court Rules 1981 Ord.17 r.11.]

Held, that a court was entitled to strike out an action for want of prosecution due to inordinate and inexcusable delay before the date upon which the action would be struck out automatically under CCR Ord.17 r.11. The fact that the automatic directions applied did not preclude the court from exercising its discretion to strike out at an earlier date even if the action would not have been struck out under Ord.17 r.11, although appropriate weight should be given to its provisions.

JONES v. BAYFORD MINING CO LTD, *The Times*, June 6, 1997, Lord Woolf, M.R., CA.

756. Striking out–delay–application by codefendants–material considerations

Held, that in a case where codefendants brought an application to strike out a claim for want of prosecution and there were distinct but overlapping periods of delay which might have caused prejudice to a particular defendant, the following considerations were relevant: (1) each defendant could base his claim for inordinate delay on any period where it was considered that the plaintiff had failed to pursue proceedings with the requisite degree of urgency to be expected; (2) the claim should be looked at as part of the total proceedings, and not in isolation from claims made by the other defendants. Where a period of delay to one defendant was excusable it would usually be the case that the same period would also be excusable in relation to the other defendants; (3) however, any prejudice was to be judged in isolation, with respect to the individual position of each defendant and (4) the court was free to exercise its discretion to strike out for delay differently for each defendant.

KINCARDINE FISHERIES LTD v. SUNDERLAND MARINE MUTUAL INSURANCE LTD [1997] C.L.C. 739, Colman, J., QBD.

757. Striking out–delay–application to dismiss inquiry into damages given under cross undertaking for want of prosecution–applicant did not have to show that delay caused prejudice

On an application to dismiss an inquiry into damages for want of prosecution and discharge a cross undertaking in damages, the requirement to show prejudice decreases as the period of delay increases. The Attorney General who had given a cross undertaking in damages pending his appeal against a decision that a Class D (ii) land charge had to be vacated to permit B to develop the site for housing, appealed against a decision refusing to strike out, for want of prosecution or abuse of process, an inquiry as to damages agreed following his unsuccessful appeal.

Held, dismissing the appeal, that the judge below was wrong to conclude that the Attorney General's inability to demonstrate that B's delay had caused prejudice or made a fair trial of the inquiry impossible defeated his application. The principles applying to the exercise of the court's discretion to discharge the cross undertaking for failure to prosecute the inquiry should be the same as those pertaining to the original grant or refusal of the inquiry. Whilst the existence of prejudice was always relevant, there was less need to establish prejudice as the period of delay increased, and where the period of delay was excessive, the court should discharge the cross undertaking and dismiss the inquiry even where no prejudice could be shown. In the instant case, however, the court would exercise its discretion to allow the inquiry to proceed.

BARRATT MANCHESTER LTD v. BOLTON MBC, *The Times*, November 3, 1997, Millett, L.J., CA.

758. Striking out–delay–appropriate to allocate prejudice–sufficient evidence for fair trial

In November 1981 H issued proceedings against S for breach of contract, obtaining final judgment for damages to be assessed in June 1988. However, S disappeared without leaving an address and reappeared in July 1990. He then commenced to appeal out of time and set aside the judgment which finally failed in February 1991. Discovery and directions followed until April 1993 when the trial of a preliminary issue was resolved in S's favour. The judge held that there was no culpable delay by H for the period, November 1987 and April 1993, but that there was for subsequent periods April 1993 to May 1994 and September 1994 to February 1996. He further ruled it would be artificial to allocate prejudice to separate periods, but that H's delay had materially contributed to the most serious prejudice, that of the dimming of the parties' recollection; S also complained of the non-availability of three expert witnesses. H appealed the striking out of her claim for want of prosecution, due to the unjustifiable behaviour of S.

Held, allowing the appeal, the judge had erred in not allocating prejudice to the various periods of delay in this case, given the unusual feature of the initial culpable delay of S, *Roebuck v. Mungovin* [1994] 1 All E.R. 568, [1994] C.L.Y. 3790 distinguished. Re-assessing the facts, the prejudice for which H was responsible was at most marginal; the dimming of recollections would have been most substantial initially, which was during the period of S's delay. Further, it was still possible to have a fair trial, given that much of the evidence was still visible on the premises, covered by expert reports, or documented, including S's affidavit on the crucial issues sworn in 1990.

HUNTER v. SKINGLEY [1997] 3 All E.R. 568, Hirst, L.J., CA.

759. Striking out–delay–claims could not be dismissed where delay had not caused serious prejudice

I appealed against a decision dismissing the claim of the second plaintiff, UM, for £1.6 million and I's counterclaim for £2.6 million, brought in respect of transactions regulated by the EC Common Agricultural Policy. Both parties had been guilty of delay with regard to the proceedings, and whilst the judge thought that UM might be prejudiced at trial by evidential difficulties, he found that I's delay had not caused them serious prejudice. I argued that the judge had erred in law in apparently concluding that, where parties acted with reasonable expedition, the court had a duty to hear the case regardless of any difficulties of proof, but where parties were guilty of inordinate and inexcusable delay, the court could decline jurisdiction.

Held, allowing the appeal, that, as there was no allegation that the parties' conduct constituted an abuse of process, once the judge had established that the delay had not caused serious prejudice to UM, he was bound by *Birkett v. James* [1978] A.C. 297, [1977] C.L.Y. 2410 not to dismiss the claims. Further, even if the delay had prevented IBAP or UM from discharging their respective evidential burdens under the relevant EC regulations, a fair trial would still have been possible.

PURCELL MEATS (SCOTLAND) LTD v. INTERVENTION BOARD FOR AGRICULTURAL PRODUCE; ULSTER MEATS LTD v. INTERVENTION BOARD FOR AGRICULTURAL PRODUCE, *The Times*, June 5, 1997, Henry, L.J., CA.

760. Striking out–delay–judge entitled to draw conclusions from specific instances of delay

S brought an action for damages against W after being injured in a road accident in 1987 for which W admitted liability. Interlocutory judgment was obtained in 1994 for damages to be determined, but in November 1995 W applied to strike out the action for want of prosecution. S subsequently served a financial loss schedule which included details of losses from the short-term employments he had had to abandon. W's application was dismissed and he appealed.

Held, dismissing the appeal with costs, that on established principles it was for a defendant to satisfy the court that the delay had been inordinate and inexcusable, or would be likely to result in serious prejudice. The court would only interfere if the judge had erred in principle or reached a perverse decision and would be slow to dismiss for want of prosecution where liability was not in issue. The judge had not erred by considering memoranda which shed doubt on the reasons for S leaving his employments, and concluding that there was insufficient evidence to sustain a striking out application. *Shtun v. Zalejska* [1996] 1 W.L.R. 1270, [1996] 1 C.L.Y. 898 was authority that there need not necessarily be evidence of instances of delay, with a court being able to draw inferences in the absence of specific evidence, but it was not authority for the converse, and it was not wrong for a judge, as here, to examine specific instances and draw conclusions from them.

SPOONER v. WEBB, *The Times*, April 24, 1997, Hirst, L.J., CA.

761. Striking out–delay–new proceedings after expiry of limitation period

Following the sale of F's half share in a business to K in 1986, two agreements were entered into. The first provided for F's retention as a paid consultant for five years with the second being an indemnity guarantee for payments under the first agreement in case of default by the purchaser. However, payments ceased in April 1987 and F commenced the present proceedings in September 1992, seeking payments under the agreements with interest from the due payment date. K served a defence in November 1992, contending that the agreements had been rescinded for innocent misrepresentation by F over the continuation of certain agreements. F sought a time extension in February 1994 within which to apply for a trial date in the county court, and replies and defences were served in March 1994. An application to dismiss for want of prosecution was allowed on appeal in January 1996, where the judge found that K had shown that they would be unfairly prejudiced in that their defence case relied heavily on the oral evidence of four witnesses in their seventies, who had expressed doubts as to the accuracy of their memories concerning events that had taken place 10 years ago. F appealed, contending, *inter alia*, that the action should be statute barred only if it could be shown that the agreements had been repudiated in April 1987, when the payments ceased and that the prejudice to K had been overstated when placed alongside the issues raised by the pleadings.

Held, dismissing the appeal, that it was at least arguable that the facts showed that F had accepted K's repudiation in April 1987, which meant that any new proceedings would indeed be statute barred and that the delay found by the trial judge was inordinate and inexcusable to the extent that it justified dismissal for want of prosecution, *Birkett v. James* [1978] A.C. 297, [1977]

C.L.Y. 2410 and *Barclays Bank Plc v. Miller* [1990] 1 W.L.R. 343, [1990] C.L.Y. 3644 considered.

FUNNELL v. KAY WELDING SUPPLIES LTD, Trans. Ref: CCRTI 96/0844/G, March 20, 1997, Morritt, L.J., CA.

762. Striking out—delay—no cause or contribution to delay by defendants failing to proof witnesses at beginning of action

Held, that, in determining whether to strike out an action for want of prosecution, the failure of the defendants to take elaborate proofs from possible witnesses at the beginning of the action could not be regarded as a factor causing or contributing to the delay. Prejudice caused by the delay in the form of witnesses being unable to remember things clearly was not caused by the defendants' failure to proof their witnesses, as defendants were not obliged to incur substantial costs at a preliminary stage in an action by taking such proofs.

SHEARING v. CINVEN LTD (FORMERLY CIN VENTURE MANAGEMENT LTD), *The Times*, November 24, 1997, Harman, J., CA.

763. Striking out—delay—personal injuries claim

B appealed against the striking out of his personal injury claim on the ground that B's inordinate and inexcusable delay had caused prejudice to W. B had allegedly suffered personal injuries at work, on October 6, 1989. A letter before action sent on August 29, 1990 referred to the accident, but gave no details. B's solicitors indicated that the accident was reported to W three weeks later, understanding that it would be recorded in the accident book. On October 11, 1990 W responded saying that they had no recollection of the accident. B's account was given to W for the first time on January 11, 1993 when the statement of claim was served, a time at which W could not investigate the accident. In acknowledging the statement of claim W's solicitors indicated that they wished to conduct an examination and an appointment was made but was not kept by B. A writ was served on W in December 1992 and a defence was served in March 1993, at which time further particulars were sought and delivered, nearly 12 months later in February 1994, giving detailed information of the accident for the first time. More evidence was received on April 13, 1994, four and a half years after the event, giving the names of three potential witnesses.

Held, dismissing the appeal, that (1) there had clearly been an inordinate and inexcusable delay in preparing the case for trial before February 1994, as well as subsequently, resulting in prejudice to W in the potential dimming of witnesses' memories. The judge could infer that any substantial delay, whenever it occurred, could lead to further loss of witness recollection, and it was not necessary to show that a witness forgot during the later rather than the earlier of two periods of delay, *Homagold v. Fairclough Building Ltd.* (Unreported). It was not necessary for details of specific prejudice relied upon to be given, *Roebuck v. Mungovin* [1994] 2 A.C. 224, [1994] C.L.Y. 3790 and *Shtun v. Zaljejska* [1996] 1 W.L.R. 1270, [1996] 1 C.L.Y. 898, and (2) there was also the possibility of further prejudice relating to the request for a medical examination by W, in that any doctor asked to conduct an examination five years after an accident would be under a severe disadvantage.

BLACKBURN v. WADKIN PLC, December 12, 1996, H.H.J. Fawcus, CC (Manchester). [*Ex rel.* Hammond Suddards, Solicitors, 2 Park Lane, Leeds].

764. Striking out—delay—requirement to reserve on books sum required to meet contingent loss not financial prejudice

N made a claim under a marine insurance policy three months before the expiry of the limitation period. The defendant insurers, a syndicate of Lloyd's Names, successfully applied to have the claim struck out for inordinate and inexcusable delay in commencing proceedings. The judge accepted that the syndicate suffered financial prejudice because the amount required to satisfy a successful claim had to be kept on the underwriters' books and could not be used to offset losses or be distributed as dividends, causing cash flow difficulties. N appealed.

Held, allowing the appeal, that any commercial organisation faced with a potentially successful legal claim against it had to make provision in its books for a sum sufficient to cover the claim, which would affect the profit and loss account for both the year in which the sum was set aside and the year in which the claim was discharged, and would boost reserves to meet outstanding liabilities as long as it was carried on the books. However, as these were simply accounting entries and it was not necessary to actually set aside the cash provided and enough was available when the claim was settled, cash flow could not be said to be affected. Financial detriment resulted from the claim and not any delay in pursuing it. The only effect of delay was that the amount set aside would remain on the balance sheet longer. The system used by the syndicate meant that delay in bringing the claim would not affect Names in future years, as reserves would have been carried forward from the time the claim was notified, the losses being borne by the Names in the syndicate at that time. Unless there were special circumstances where particular or significant loss had been suffered, the requirement to set aside reserves for contingent losses could not amount to financial prejudice for the purposes of striking out a claim on grounds of delay.

NOVELLI SpA v. WATKINS, *The Times*, December 24, 1996, Potter, L.J., CA.

765. Striking out–delay–transfer of action to Official Referee–no prejudice caused by delay–no abuse of process

[Rules of the Supreme Court Ord.36 r.6.]

C appealed against an order striking out his claim for non compliance with the obligation imposed by RSC Ord.36 r.6(1)(d) to make an application to the Official Referee for directions within 14 days of the date of transfer of the action to his list. C entered into an oral agreement with O to complete building works. C ceased work and started proceedings claiming money due to him for labour and materials. O disputed that the sum was due and counterclaimed for overpayments and for damages for C's failure to complete the work by the contractual date. There followed delays and non-compliance with the rules by C. Eventually a consent order was made transferring the matter to the Official Referee's list, but C did not transfer the action and did not apply for directions within 14 days. There was found to have been a delay of approximately 18 months, with no explanation given for the inactivity. The judge found that the delay was inordinate and inexcusable, but did not find that there was sufficient prejudice to O to justify striking out. He did find, however, that C's failure to apply for directions under RSC Ord.36 r.6 was an abuse of process.

Held, allowing the appeal and restoring the action, that the judge was right to find that there was insufficient prejudice to dismiss the action. The onus of proving that C's delay amounted to an abuse of process was on O and was difficult to prove given that C had given no explanation. There was no indication that C had applied for the transfer to the Official Referee's list with the intention not to comply with the 14 day time limit. The conduct was incompetent and dilatory but not contumelious so as to amount to a deliberate abuse of process, *Teale v. McKay* [1994] P.I.Q.R. P508 considered. That there was no peremptory order was fatal to the judge's decision to strike out. The failure to comply with the 14 day rule did not equate with non-compliance with a peremptory order, *Costellow v. Somerset CC* [1993] 1 W.L.R. 256, [1993] C.L.Y 3338 applied.

CHARLES v. OSMAN, Trans. Ref: QBENI 96/0336/B, March 4, 1997, Henry, L.J., CA.

766. Striking out–estoppel–parallel proceedings–recovery of uninsured losses– default judgment previously granted in favour of insurers

R appealed against the refusal to strike out S's claim for uninsured losses. Judgment was given for S's insurers in relation to her insured losses after a road traffic accident in which R's vehicle hit S's stationary vehicle from the rear. R contended that S was bound by cause of action estoppel which allowed the court no discretion whether to consider her later claim, which included damages for personal injuries. S argued that the court had such a discretion and that there were exceptional circumstances such that the court should allow the action to proceed, namely that (1) the fact that the earlier judgment had been obtained by default; (2) S had originally believed her claim to be hopeless because she had been informed that R's insurers had repudiated liability since he had been driving a milk float with excess alcohol and at a time of day when it was uninsured, and (3) the first application to strike out had been withdrawn.

Held, allowing the appeal, that assuming, without deciding, the existence of a discretion, (1) the fact that there was a judgment in default of defence was because no reasonable defence could be argued in the circumstances in which the accident occurred; (2) the existence of the MIB scheme for such claims should have been known to her solicitors, and (3) R could not be prevented from taking subsequent action because of his earlier withdrawal, *Arnold v. National Westminster Bank Plc* [1991] 2 A.C. 93, [1991] C.L.Y. 1736 followed and *Talbot v. Berkshire CC* [1994] Q.B. 290, [1993] C.L.Y. 1851 considered.

SIDDLE v. REDFERN, Trans. Ref: CCRT1 97/0089/G, July 2, 1997, Pill, L.J., CA.

767. Striking out—failure to adjourn

[County Court Rules 1981 Ord.13 r.3, Ord.17 r.11; Rules of the Supreme Court Ord.34 r.3.]

In 1988 W was knocked down by C's minibus. He sustained serious injuries and was left with residual disabilities and brain damage causing memory loss and reactive depression. An action was commenced in the High Court and a statement of claim was served on July 8, 1991, nearly three years later. C admitted liability in their defence on July 29, 1991. Medical reports were obtained from at least five different specialists and supplied to C's solicitors. In 1992 the action was transferred from the High Court to Middlesbrough County Court, and in 1994 C increased their payment into court to £23,500 which due to W's continuing depression was rejected. On June 19, 1995 W wrote to the court asking for a trial date to be listed. On the application of C, W's action was struck out for delay on the ground that CCR Ord.17 r.11 did not apply as this action was already set down. The question which arose was whether the action had in fact been set down. Although the requirements of the Rules of the Supreme Court Ord.34 r.3 were not complied with, both sets of solicitors treated the action as having been set down. Negotiations continued in an effort to settle the claim, and an unsuccessful further payment into court was made. Following this decision W's solicitors served a notice of appeal out of time on October 4, 1995. C served a cross appeal on October 11, 1995. W claimed that the delay was because in Middlesbrough County Court when a notice of appeal was issued it was for the court to serve the notice, and the delay may have arisen between the lodging of the notice and its service by the court. W's solicitors lodged the appeal on September 15, 1995 nine days after the hearing, some four days out of time. There was then an additional delay by the court's service so that a total delay of over 20 days occurred. Following service of the notice the matter came before the court which declined to extend time and refused leave to appeal. W submitted that the judge erroneously exercised his discretion in refusing to extend time and had failed to take account of the relevant matters.

Held, dismissing the appeal, that the district judge had failed to follow the spirit of Ord.13 r.3(5)(2) in failing to allow an adjournment. Although this was unfair and contrary to natural justice the district judge had exercised his discretion with regard to striking out lawfully. It was unfortunate, but the case was still not ready for trial and W clearly had an unanswerable case against his solicitors in negligence and he should receive justice and a proper award of damages within a short period of time so long as his new solicitors progressed his claim with the expedition that it deserved. This was a case where the plaintiff's solicitors were unable to lodge their appeal in time and this had to be viewed against a history of delay. The explanation proffered by W's solicitors was deemed inadequate and the district judge had been entitled not to rely on it.

WELSH v. COPPINGER AND KELLY (T/A M&P MINIBUS HIRE), February 25, 1997, Butler-Sloss, L.J., CA. [*Ex rel.* Jonathan Holmes, Barrister, Plowden Buildings, Temple].

768. Striking out–failure to comply with unless order–appropriate test to be applied

In the course of an action for breach of contract by HIS, C failed to comply with an order stating that unless it submitted further and better particulars of its defence and counterclaim by a particular date its pleading would be struck out. HIS's application for the pleading to be struck out was allowed and judgment given for the plaintiff in the presence of C's instructing solicitors after C's counsel failed to attend the hearing because she considered that the details had been provided. The judge found that C had shown an intention to flout the order and dismissed an application to set aside the striking out order. C appealed.

Held, dismissing the appeal, that as the striking out order was final and had not been made in C's absence, the judge was correct to refuse to review his decision and C was not entitled to rely on errors made by its legal representatives. An unless order represented a last chance for the defaulter, being made only when there had been previous failures to comply with orders, and failure to comply would normally result in a penalty. Such penalties were necessary for the efficient administration of justice and would apply unless the litigant could show compelling reasons to excuse his failure to comply, which would usually involve circumstances beyond the litigant's control. Each case had to be judged on its own merits and continuing failure to comply with orders through negligence or incompetence could lead to a striking out of pleadings in the same way that an intentional or deliberate disregard of the order would, *Jokai Tea Holdings Ltd, Re* [1992] 1 W.L.R. 1196, [1993] C.L.Y. 3343 considered.

HYTEC INFORMATION SYSTEMS LTD v. COVENTRY CITY COUNCIL, *The Times*, December 31, 1996, Ward, L.J., CA.

769. Striking out–failure to give notice to MIB within time limit

[Council Directive 72/166 relating to insurance against civil liability in respect of the use of motor vehicles Art.3.]

Following an accident in 1992 S's solicitors sent to the court a summons dated October 7, 1994 for issue. The court issued the summons on October 13, 1994 and S's solicitors stated that they did not receive notice from the court until October 22, 1994. S's solicitors did not send the notice of issue to the MIB and their agents until October 28, 1994. The MIB were joined in the action and a defence was served arguing a failure to comply with cl.5(1) of the MIB agreement. S's solicitors did not take up the point and continued with the conduct of the case until such time as an application was made by G. The judge found that S had failed to provide notice of the commencement of the proceedings within seven days and struck out S's claim. S appealed arguing that (1) the notice would have been received by G's agents on October 29, 1994, which was seven days from receipt, by S, of notice from the court; (2) the MIB were estopped from relying on cl.5(1)(a) by the agent's conduct and had waived the reservation, and (3) cl.5(1)(a) was in breach of Council Directive 72/166 relating to insurance against civil liability in respect of the use of motor vehicles Art.3(1) in so far as it was to be interpreted as meaning that compulsory motor insurance must enable third party victims of accidents caused by vehicles to be compensated for all the damage to property and personal injury to them, up to the amount fixed by them in the Second Directive.

Held, dismissing the appeal, that (1) the "bringing of the proceedings" was when the court prepared, issued and sealed the summons for service, which in this case was on October 13, 1994. The words "the commencement of the proceedings" in cl.5(1)(a) of the agreement were to have their ordinary meaning, namely the point in time at which the proceedings commenced; (2) the MIB raised the issue of incorrect notice with S's solicitors and in a letter stated "the MIB may have no liability and we reserve our position". S's solicitors could not fail to understand the meaning of what those words meant. There was no waiver by the MIB and no estoppel could be raised against the MIB, and (3) as to the point of European law, S could not succeed upon it. The structure of the law, including the terms of the MIB agreement, are not such that there had been a failure to comply with the Directive. There was no real difficulty for a competent solicitor, or a layman who paid attention to the language of the agreement and the notes attached to it, to comply with the requirement of cl.5(1)(a).

SILVERTON v. GOODALL AND MOTOR INSURERS BUREAU, March 26, 1997, Sir Ralph Gibson, CA. [*Ex rel.* Linda Atherstone, Solicitor, Cole & Cole, Reading].

770. Striking out—group actions—failure to serve medical report—waiver of confidentiality relating to medical history

The subject matter of the litigation was a claim by up to 5,000 plaintiffs against J and the second defendants, R, concerning the effects of drugs manufactured by J and R. The Legal Aid Board had abandoned its support for the litigation in January 1993. N appealed against an order of the master that his action be struck out for failure to serve a medical report substantiating the causal link between his injury and J and R. J and R sought an order permitting them to approach the plaintiffs' general practitioners to seek comment on their cases.

Held, dismissing the appeal against the master's order as the report did not contain sufficient relevant evidence to sustain N's complaint, J and R's application would be allowed on the basis that a plaintiff in such an action necessarily put in issue his medical history. The order would be made because it would be more economical for J and R to consider the information while an audit of each plaintiff's claim was being conducted.

NUR v. JOHN WYETH & BROTHER LTD [1996] 7 Med. L.R. 300, Ian Kennedy, J., QBD.

771. Striking out—personal injuries claim—partial admission by defendants— plaintiff not applying for judgment within 12 months of admission

[County Court Rules 1981 Ord.9 r.3(7), Ord.9 r.6(1), Ord.9 r.10.]

Following a road traffic accident in March 1991, in which the plaintiffs suffered serious injuries, proceedings were issued in March 1994. A defence was served admitting liability and "some personal injury loss and damage" but denying the extent of such injury. G brought an application to strike out the action pursuant to CCR Ord.9 r.10, claiming that there had been an admission of the plaintiff's claim and therefore that the plaintiffs ought to have entered judgment under CCR Ord.9 r.6(1)(b). The defence contained an allegation of contributory negligence against the second of the three plaintiffs regarding her failure to wear a seatbelt and G argued, inter alia, that this was an argument as to quantum rather than liability and there had, in respect of each of the plaintiffs, been an "admission" and therefore, because judgment had not been entered within the period of 12 months, the action should be struck out. The plaintiffs contended that (1) Ord.9 r.6 was not the appropriate rule but that Ord.9 r.3(7) was "tailor made" for these circumstances, ie. that "the plaintiff may apply for judgment where the action is for unliquidated damages and the defendant delivers an admission of liability for the claim but disputes or does not admit the amount of the plaintiff's damages". Striking out under Ord.9 r.10 occurs where judgment should have been entered under Ord.9 r.6(1) and not where judgment could have been entered under Ord.9 r.3(7); (2) in relation to the second plaintiff, the argument of contributory negligence related to liability and not to quantum. The plaintiffs relied upon the authority of *Murphy v. Culhane* [1976] 3 All E.R. 533, [1976] C.L.Y. 2133. Consequently, the second plaintiff would have been prevented from making an application for judgment pursuant to Ord.9 r.6, and (3) if the second plaintiff's claim was not struck out then the first and third plaintiffs' claims could not be struck out because "the action" referred to in Ord.9 r.10 was the entire action not simply a claim within an action.

Held, dismissing the application to strike out the claim, that the arguments put forward by the plaintiffs were correct and the case should be allowed to proceed.

DEHAVILLAN, LORD AND LORD (A MINOR) v. GREENWOOD, March 21, 1997, H.H.J. Holman, CC (Oldham). [*Ex rel.* Mulderrigg Small, Solicitors, 11 King Street, Oldham].

772. Striking out—premature issue of proceedings

B was injured in a road traffic accident on November 22, 1995. B's solicitors wrote to S on two occasions with no response. On December 18, 1995 contact was established with S's insurers who confirmed on January 17, 1996 that liability "did not appear to be in dispute". On January 19, 1996, B's solicitors indicated that proceedings would be issued shortly and on January 31, 1996 the insurers requested that proceedings be served on S direct. Proceedings were issued on March 1, 1996 and S made an application to strike out or stay the proceedings. The defence admitted negligence only.

Held, dismissing the application, that no admission of liability was given by the insurers either in correspondence or in the defence. By the letter of January 31, 1996, the insurers were leaving the door open for the issue of proceedings, *Greaves v. William Barker* [1995] 2 C.L.Y. 3900 and *Parr v. Bolton* [1996] 1 C.L.Y. 718 followed.

BESWICK AND BESWICK v. STRINGER, August 2, 1996, District Judge Tromans, CC (Plymouth). [*Ex rel.* David Cadin, Barrister, 2 King's Bench Walk, Temple].

773. Striking out—premature issue of proceedings—abuse of process

F was injured on September 27, 1994 when a wallpaper stripper failed causing her to be showered with boiling water. She suffered scalds to her face and arm. F was a model and claimed damages for loss of income, sundry expenses and disadvantage on the labour market in addition to PSLA. F notified RB promptly of her claim which they acknowledged. Admission of liability was sought on May 4, 1995 and was eventually given. On November 1, 1995 F's solicitors sent to RB a medical report and schedule of loss detailing special damages totalling £1,725. They contended for substantial *Smith v. Manchester* damages. On November 24, 1995 RB's solicitor requested facilities for medical examination and sought documentation detailing loss of earnings. Facilities for medical examination were granted and on April 1, 1996 the defendants offered £750 in full and final settlement of F's claim. They also sought access to F's doctor's notes and hospital records and this request was refused. RB warned in advance that they would apply to strike out any proceedings that were issued without disclosure of medical records and income documentation relying on *Mountford v. Evans* [1995] 2 C.L.Y. 3898. In view of the level of the April 9, 1996 offer F took the approach that the parties were a long way apart on general damages and proceedings were issued. The documents in support of special damages were disclosed after issue of proceedings and RB applied for an order striking out F's claim as an abuse of process.

Held, dismissing RB's application, that the district judge was not persuaded that any right existed for a defendant to apply for a strike out or stay where a plaintiff issued proceedings in pursuit of a bona fide claim. The view to be preferred was that expressed by *Baker v. Southern Water* [1996] 1 C.L.Y. 661, namely, that where defendants feel aggrieved on account of premature issue of proceedings their remedy was to seek an appropriate costs order in due time. The district judge was aware of no rule or statute requiring a plaintiff to negotiate for any period of time. That was a choice which a plaintiff could make and at any time the plaintiff had the right to issue. A plaintiff with a cause of action had the right to ask the court to determine it. The rules required a medical report and a schedule to be issued with proceedings. They did not require disclosure of other documentation to be simultaneous with issue. For these reasons alone the application should fail. Even if there was a power to strike out under these circumstances it would not be right to exercise it in this case. RB had a lot of information; a schedule of special damages and F's qualification of the claim together with medical evidence. The fact that RB had asked for but not been given access to the F's doctor's records would not be sufficient to make the issue of proceedings premature and the application would have been refused on that ground also.

FRITH v. ROBERT BOSCH LTD, November 7, 1996, District Judge Cole, CC (Birmingham). [*Ex rel.* Jonathan Peacock, Solicitor, Shoosmiths & Harrison, Bloxam Court, Rugby].

774. Striking out–premature issue of proceedings–costs

S was injured in a road traffic accident on December 7, 1995. On March 11, 1996, S's solicitors wrote to H's insurers requesting, inter alia, that they would indemnify H, admit liability and accept that interest was running on the claim as if proceedings had been issued. H's insurers confirmed that they would indemnify H and requested that proceedings be issued on them. They also requested details of the claim and documentary evidence in support. Despite reminders, no documentary evidence or medical report was sent to H's insurers until proceedings were issued on August 19, 1995. The defence admitted negligence only. H made an application to strike out or stay the proceedings.

Held, refusing the application, that there is no legal or procedural obligation requiring a proposed plaintiff to notify the proposed defendant of his intention to issue proceedings, although in certain cases he may be putting himself at risk so far as costs are concerned if proceedings are issued precipitously. There may be circumstances in which the commencement of proceedings would be regarded by the court as wholly unnecessary or possibly oppressive but this case was not in that category. No useful purpose would be achieved by ordering a stay given that H's insurers now knew the case that they were facing and there were steps which they could take to obtain protection against a costs order being made at the conclusion of the trial. H was ordered to pay one half of S's costs of the application to be taxed if not agreed.

STOKES v. HAWKER, October 7, 1996, District Judge Crosse, CC (Plymouth). [*Ex rel.* David Cadin, Barrister, 2 King's Bench Walk, Temple].

775. Striking out–premature issue of proceedings–costs

T and F were involved in a road traffic accident on April 13, 1995. G's insurers were notified of T's claim on April 25, 1995. On May 10, 1995 G's insurers requested details of negligence and on May 16, 1995 T's solicitors indicated that proceedings would be issued shortly. G's insurers gave an indication that liability would not be in dispute on August 7, 1995. T's solicitors failed to provide further documentary evidence in support of T's claim until proceedings were issued on January 16, 1996 by T's solicitors on behalf of T and F. Defence admitted negligence only. G made an application to strike out or stay proceedings.

Held, dismissing the application, that although the costs of issuing proceedings were unnecessary, T and F ought not to be penalised for issuing proceedings where they had a clear cause of action. There is no rule that a plaintiff must wait to give the defendant the opportunity of settling the case. The plaintiff is entitled to issue proceedings without a letter before action and if he does so he does so on risk as to costs. On the facts, there would be no purpose in staying the proceedings, and G to pay T's costs of the application in any event.

TOY AND FOWLER v. GIBSON, July 16, 1996, Deputy District Judge Norham, CC (Plymouth). [*Ex rel.* David Cadin, Barrister, 2 King's Bench Walk, Temple].

776. Striking out–premature issue of proceedings–issue matter for costs not for striking out

K was injured in a road traffic accident on November 14, 1995. P's insurers were notified on November 16, 1995 and on December 22, 1995 the insurers indicated that liability was not in dispute. On April 17, 1996, K's solicitors requested, inter alia, an admission of liability and confirmation that interest was running on the claim. On May 8, 1996 P's insurers admitted liability and requested details of the claim. On May 10, 1996, K's solicitors stated that proceedings would be issued. Thereafter unsuccessful attempts were made by P's insurers to obtain full details of the medical position. Proceedings were issued on July 31, 1996. P's insurers applied to strike out or to stay the proceedings as an abuse.

Held, dismissing the application, that if the application were for costs, the plaintiff might be in grave difficulties. Premature issue is a matter for costs not for striking out. Further, it cannot be right to stay proceedings which the plaintiff was entitled to issue.

KINSMAN v. PEACOCK, January 24, 1997, District Judge Child, CC (Plymouth). [*Ex rel.* David Cadin, Barrister, 2 King's Bench Walk, Temple].

777. Striking out–recovery of loan–res judicata–public policy–abuse of process

[Rules of the Supreme Court Ord.18 r.19.]

E appealed against the refusal to strike out B's claim for recovery of monies allegedly lent to E. On November 6, 1991 a letter was sent by the solicitors of IB, the proprietor of B, stating that an agreement had been made on April 17, 1989 whereby B loaned £1,200,000 to E, and proceedings would follow against E for failure to repay the monies owed. When the writ was issued in January 1992 it was framed on a different basis, alleging that the loan had been made by IB personally in fulfilment of an agreement made in December 1988. This claim was dismissed on June 23, 1992 as no cause of action was disclosed since the oral contract alleged pre-dated the incorporation of E. Another writ was issued by B in January 1993 in respect of the loan. An amended statement of claim stated that the cause of action was once again the failure to comply with the agreement entered into on April 17, 1989 but claiming that the monies had been lent by B. The various accounts given by IB of what had happened were clearly inconsistent. E sought to rely on the doctrine of res judicata, and B submitted that the doctrine had no application since the earlier proceedings were quite different from the present claim.

Held, dismissing B's appeal and striking out the writ and statement of claim under RSC Ord.18 r.19, that (1) the requirements of the doctrine of res judicata had been satisfied. There was a sufficient identity between B and IB for them to be recognised as privies and create identity of parties for the purposes of res judicata, and there was identity of subject matter, both claims being in relation to what was the same loan transaction; (2) IB decided to pursue a claim in 1992 could have been brought on the present basis. Since B failed to do so the doctrine operated to preclude him from pursuing the action. It was against public policy and an abuse of process for matters which could have been litigated in earlier proceedings to be allowed to proceed on a later occasion and (3) the action could also have been struck as being an abuse of process, without applying the doctrine of res judicata.

BARAKOT LTD v. EPIETTE LTD [1997] 1 B.C.L.C. 303, Deputy Judge D Eady Q.C., QBD.

778. Striking out–vexatious claim–part of claim arguable

[Rules of the Supreme Court Ord.18 r.19.]

M appealed and B cross appealed against the dismissal of B's application under Rules of the Supreme Court Ord.18 r.19 to strike out as vexatious M's claim for damages for breach of contract. In 1994 M provided two specimens of urine to the International Amateur Athletic Federation for testing by a Portuguese laboratory. The results of the first test showed a testosterone:epitestosterone ratio of 40:1 which was above the permitted level. The second sample was also tested by the same laboratory with similar results. M was prevented from competing at the Commonwealth Games in Canada and subsequently suspended from competing. She attended a disciplinary hearing in the UK at which she was found to have committed a doping offence, but this finding was subsequently overthrown by the Independent Appeal Panel. M contended that (1) B had breached its contract by allowing the samples to be tested at different and unaccredited laboratory premises, and (2) that two members of the disciplinary committee showed actual or likely bias against her. B argued that M had waived her right to complain of bias by failing to raise it at the hearing.

Held, allowing B's appeal in part, that M's claim on the accreditation issue was struck out, but that the court should consider the bias and waiver issues. B's appeal against the refusal of the judge below to strike out M's whole claim was dismissed.

MODAHL v. BRITISH ATHLETIC FEDERATION LTD,Trans. Ref: QBEN1 96/1040/E, July 28, 1997, Lord Woolf, M.R., CA.

779. Summons–summons issued by person not qualified as a solicitor–irregularity capable of rectification

[Solicitors Act 1974 s.20.]

In November 1992, C, a passenger in a car driven by Y, was injured in a collision. In December 1992, Y was convicted of driving with excess alcohol and C consulted a Legal Advice Centre, believing that it consisted of solicitors. In October 1995, a county court default summons was issued: it named the centre and gave the centre's address in the box marked "Plaintiff's solicitors' address", and was signed by a person whose name appeared on the letterhead of the centre. At the end of the statement of claim attached appeared that person's name, and the centre's name and address and the words "Legal Practitioners for the Plaintiff". Y's solicitors queried the centre's qualification on November 22, 1995. A solicitor gave notice of acting for C on December 1, 1995. C's action was dismissed by the district judge on the basis of a breach of the Solicitors Act 1974.

Held, allowing C's appeal and reinstating his claim, that proceedings had been issued in breach of the Solicitors Act 1974 s.20, but the court's displeasure should be directed at the person who acted wrongfully, not his innocent victim. The defect was an irregularity capable of ratification which had been ratified.

CHRISTOFOROU v. YAXLEY, March 14, 1996, Assistant Recorder Phillips, CC (Worthing). [*Ex rel.* Paul Ashwell, Barrister, Sussex Chambers, Brighton].

780. Supreme Court–rules

RULES OF THE SUPREME COURT (AMENDMENT) 1997, SI 1997 415 (L.2); made under the Supreme Court Act 1981 s.84, s.85. In force: April 1, 1997; £1.10.

These Rules amend the Rules of the Supreme Court so as to enable service to be effected out of the jurisdiction where the plaintiff claims interim relief in order to prevent the dissipation of assets within the jurisdiction pending the outcome of legal proceedings abroad; amend the definition of a patent; reflect the change in name of chief clerk; and make minor amendments to Ord.73.

781. Time limits–court directions–delay in compliance with procedural acts–directions are to be observed provided that justice is done

Two appeals dealt with the issue of how the court should deal with situations where the parties have delayed in complying with directions of the court, and failed to complete certain acts within the time limits set by the court: (1) K appealed against a decision dismissing applications for an extension of time to obtain expert evidence in proceedings relating to a personal injury claim by O, arising from an accident in which O was seriously injured, and following which K was convicted of driving without due care and attention. Negotiations to settle the claim had failed and after O served his list of documents K delayed before finding psychiatric and accountancy experts and (2) WT appealed against a decision to extend the time in which Hill, who was claiming damages for personal injuries from

WT, his employers, could serve statements. The injury suffered by H was allegedly from exposure to an organophosphate pesticide for which WT had admitted liability, but questions of causation and quantum had yet to be resolved. H considered this to be a test case. H had failed to serve a statement in time, serving the statement on the Monday rather than the previous Friday. That statement was considered to be inadequate necessitating service of a further more detailed statement.

Held, dismissing the appeals, that directions and timetables given by the court are rules to be observed, but the overriding principle is that justice must be done, so that if the strict adherence to a timetable will result in an injustice to one of the parties, the court would have to depart from the rules set down. Departure from directions can be an attempt to prejudice the other party, and will undermine orders given by the court. (1) K had done nothing to find an expert witnesses in time, nor had they made an application to the court for an extension within a reasonable time. The judge had exercised his discretion in deciding that enough was enough correctly; (2) H's failure to serve the statement in time was found not to be a deliberate flouting of the order, but was the result of the solicitor having conduct of the matter being overseas on business at the material time. Although the explanation may not have been satisfactory, an explanation was given. The information provided in the statements was not significantly new information, so that WT was not prejudiced by the delay, *Beachley Property Ltd v. Edgar* [1997] P.N.L.R. 197, [1996] 1 C.L.Y. 943 considered.

OTTO v. KEYS [1997] P.I.Q.R. P120, Lord Woolf, M.R., CA.

782. Time limits—exchange of witness statements—application to extend time for exchange—principles to be applied

In a personal injuries action brought by H against W, where neither party complied with the initial direction concerning exchange of witness statements, a further direction was made that exchange take place by November 1, 1996. H served his statement, which failed to address special damages, three days late. H then prepared a supplementary statement, and on November 21 applied for an extension of time for service, stating that his solicitor had been abroad on November 1. W appealed against the order allowing H an extension of time.

Held, dismissing the appeal, that the judge correctly weighed the nature of the offence committed by H, and the prejudice to the administration of justice thereby caused. An explanation had been provided by H for the non compliance with the order, and the delay in service was limited.

HILL v. WILLIAM TOMKINS LTD [1997] P.I.Q.R. P115, Lord Woolf, M.R., CA.

783. Time limits—exchange of witness statements and expert reports

[Rules of the Supreme Court Ord.38 r.2A, Ord.38 r.36.]

M reapplied for leave to appeal against the refusal of its application for an extension of time for the exchange of witness statements and expert reports, pursuant to RSC Ord.38 r.2A and Ord.38 r.36. M claimed that S had negligently overvalued land at £1 million as a result of which M had advanced £700,000 from which only £365,000 had been realised on its later sale. S had procrastinated in giving details of its expert and had relied on the decision in *Beachley Property Ltd v. Edgar* [1997] P.N.L.R. 197, [1996] 1 C.L.Y. 943 to preclude M from adducing its own expert evidence, because of M's failure to meet time limits, thus effectively preventing trial of the issue.

Held, allowing the appeal, that M were granted leave to adduce the evidence exchanged out of time and S was directed to serve its own witness statements and expert reports by that night. The judge below had erred in dealing with M's application separately from S's applications for leave to call evidence from an additional expert and to vacate the hearing. The failure of M to serve evidence at the proper time, S being unready, was a failure of both parties and the breach of procedural rules should not result in the loss of either M's claim, or of S's defence. Time requirements were not targets but rules to be obeyed, although it remained the overriding consideration that justice must be done. Non-compliance prejudiced other parties and other litigants, particularly if it caused vacation or an adjournment, which would be granted solely as a measure of last resort. The court should normally give effect to any agreed new time limits at trial, removing the need for separate applications, but if no agreement could be reached then prompt application for directions should be made, *Costellow v. Somerset CC* [1993] 1 W.L.R. 256, [1993] C.L.Y. 3338 and *Beachley Property Ltd v. Edgar* considered.

MORTGAGE CORP LTD v. SANDOES [1997] P.N.L.R. 263, Millett, L.J., CA.

784. Time limits—exchange of witness statements and expert reports—failure to adhere to agreed timetable—factors affecting exercise of discretion to extend time limits

[Rules of the Supreme Court Ord.38 r.2A.]

L appealed against a decision refusing a time extension for the exchange of witness statements and expert witness reports in a negligence claim against a solicitor, H, arising from the transfer of assets to L. Under a direction given under RSC Ord.38 r.2A evidence was to be disclosed by January 31, 1996 and witness statements cross served by November 15, 1995, with a trial date of November 11, 1996 being fixed in October 1995. However, a shorter timetable agreed between the parties was not adhered to and the statements were not ready until eight months after the agreed date and only one month before the trial, with the expert evidence report being similarly delayed. A summons for costs by H was met with an indemnity offer from L and both sides issued further summonses, with L seeking a time extension and H an order to strike out the action as an abuse of process or debarring L from giving evidence at the trial.

Held, allowing the appeal and ordering that witness statements be exchanged immediately, but refusing to extend the time for exchange, of expert reports, that L should not be deprived of a trial due to their solicitors' inability to adhere to the time limits. The judge at first instance had erred in finding that the decision in *Beachley Property Ltd v. Edgar* [1997] P.N.L.R. 197 [1996] 1 C.L.Y. 943 had changed the practice established in *Costellow v. Somerset CC* [1993] 1 W.L.R. 256, [1993] C.L.Y. 3338 whereby the discretion to grant time extensions was to be exercised in the light of the requirements of justice, on the facts of each case, and should ordinarily be granted to permit an action to proceed in the overall interests of justice. However, a party in default could not seek the discretion to be exercised in their favour unless such action were justified in all the circumstances. The facts of the case showed that the potential prejudice on the defendant's part was largely due to their solicitor's own inaction and that L had already been put to expense in giving a measure of security, a fact to which the judge may not have given sufficient weight when refusing the time extension at first instance.

LETPAK LTD v. HARRIS [1997] P.N.L.R. 239, Waller, L.J., CA.

785. Time limits—service of schedules of special damage and witness statements—non compliance with time limits—each case to be assessed on own facts

W appealed against an order made on October 28, 1996 refusing leave to serve schedules of special damage and witness statements out of time. W, and others, employees of RD, commenced proceedings on May 24, 1993 claiming they had suffered repetitive strain injuries to their elbows, shoulders and backs, with each claim being limited to £5,000, a limit that was later lifted with RD's consent on the condition that W be ordered to file schedules of special damages. Solicitors for W failed to comply with three subsequent orders for such service, which were finally filed on October 3, 1996. These were rejected by the solicitor for RD as being out of time. W's application for leave to serve the schedules out of time was dismissed on the basis that the continued breaches of the orders had thwarted the conclusion of a speedy and efficient trial, *Beachley Property Ltd v. Edgar* [1997] P.N.L.R. 197, [1996] 1 C.L.Y. 943 considered. However, RD conceded that the delay had not occasioned any prejudice to them or to their ability to have a proper trial, and whilst prejudice was not a precondition of refusing an application, it was a relevant consideration to which the judge below failed to have proper regard.

Held, allowing the appeal, that (1) no peremptory order had been made, which differed from nearly all other cases in which relief to the defaulting partly was refused; (2) RD had conceded the defaults did not result in any prejudice to them, the proceedings to be heard in December would not be prevented and, although the conduct of W's solicitors should not be excused, little had been lost by the failure to provide schedules earlier, and (3) the court must disregard the possibility of compensation for W for the heavy losses they would incur if the order refusing service were to stand, *Birkett v. James* [1978] A.C. 297, [1977] C.L.Y. 2410 applied. It would have been an abuse of process for W to have sought to press its claims in the absence of the required schedules. The gravity of non-compliance depended on the individual circumstances of each case, and had to be considered by the court having regard to the nature of the order, the seriousness of the breach, the explanation for the failure and whether non-compliance had affected the proceedings or disrupted the administration of justice generally.

WILLIS v. ROYAL DOULTON (UK) LTD,Trans. Ref: LTA 96/7367/G, November 4, 1996, Simon Brown, L.J., CA.

786. Trials–conduct of trial–directions as to conduct–no interference by Court of Appeal

P brought a number of actions against a number of solicitors alleging breaches of duty when carrying out loan transactions. The actions were to be tried together by Chadwick J. B was a defendant in a number of the actions. Initially B was indemnified by the Solicitors Indemnity Fund and was represented by solicitors, I. Insurers subsequently repudiated cover and B was represented by different solicitors. B applied for an adjournment of the trials against him on the basis that it would be difficult for him to prepare for the trial and that the trial would subject him to personal hardship. The application was refused and B sought leave to appeal.

Held, refusing leave to appeal, that an appellate court would only rarely interfere with directions given by a trial judge as to the conduct of a trial. In giving such directions the judge had to weigh up the interests of both parties not just the convenience of one side. The judge's decision was correct.

BRISTOL AND WEST BUILDING SOCIETY v. BHADRESA (T/A BHADRESA & CO) [1997] P.N.L.R. 329, Hobhouse, L.J., CA.

787. Trials–vacation of hearing–expert witness unavailable

In a road traffic accident case, the defendant applied for leave to appeal against both an order dismissing their application to vacate a date fixed for trial because their medical expert was unavailable and another order refusing leave to adduce the evidence of an alternative expert.

Held, allowing the application and the appeal, that an agreement had been reached to consider only liability, contributory negligence and causation as preliminary issues on the trial date. The costs of the application to vacate and the costs of the appeal to be in the cause and those of the application to adduce to be the plaintiff's costs.

Observed, that it would be an unfortunate development if subpoenas were issued against experts with conflicting engagements.

STRINGER v. SHARP [1996] P.I.Q.R. P439, Sir Thomas Bingham, M.R., CA.

788. Vexatious litigants–civil proceedings order

[Supreme Court Act 1981 s.42.]

Following a series of civil actions and criminal prosecutions commenced by C against his former solicitor, two building societies and other legal advisers, all of which were struck out as an abuse of process or on the basis of being frivolous or vexatious, the Attorney General applied for an all proceedings order under the Supreme Court Act 1981 s.42.

Held, making the all proceedings order sought, that, due to the interference such orders presented to the rights of an individual, a balance had to be struck between the protection of the object of the litigation and the individual. The history of the litigation and prosecutions commenced by C revealed that he had attempted to deal with matters previously disposed of by way of litigating and re-litigating the same issues, with allegations of negligence turning into fraud as he tried to seek redress. The facts showed that C had habitually and persistently instituted vexatious proceedings and prosecutions without reasonable cause. Following the making of the order C would be perfectly entitled to apply to a High Court judge for leave if he felt there was a specific matter on which he could properly litigate.

ATTORNEY GENERAL v. COLLINS, Trans. Ref: CO 2492/96, December 9, 1996, Collins, J., QBD.

789. Vexatious litigants–civil proceedings order–time limited order

[Supreme Court Act 1981 s.42; European Convention on Human Rights 1950 Art.6; Law Officers Act 1944.]

The Attorney General applied for a civil proceedings order under the Supreme Court Act 1981 s.42 against P for persistently instituting vexatious civil proceedings and making vexatious applications since at least 1990, without any reasonable ground. P had an ongoing dispute with the group of Novell companies. P was a director and holder of all issued shares, except one, in Novell Data Systems Ltd, NDS, and he had the benefit of an exclusive distribution agreement for products manufactured by Novell Inc. Agreement between NDS and Novell was varied in 1984 to a non-exclusive distributorship and in 1986 an English subsidiary started to trade in the UK. P alleged that the agreement had been varied under intimidation or economic duress. He pursued proceedings in NDS's name unsuccessfully. When NDS went into liquidation and the liquidator settled the action, he attempted, again unsuccessfully, to re-litigate the issues in a personal capacity and then to re-open the original action on more than one occasion. P applied for an adjournment of the application on the basis that it was premature given that an action seeking to impeach all adverse judgments on grounds of fraudulent non-disclosure by Novell Inc, as a "final" avenue of appeal, had not yet been heard. As far as the merits were concerned P contended that (1) following *Attorney General v. Williams* [1996] C.O.D. 368, [1996] 1 C.L.Y. 932, the application should not be entertained because there was no evidence to show personal consideration of the merits of the application by the Attorney General; (2) the making of the order sought would constitute a denial of P's right of access to the courts under the European Convention on Human Rights 1950 Art.6(1), and (3) the statutory criteria in any event were not fulfilled.

Held, granting the civil proceedings order but limited to 15 years, that (1) the action attempting to impeach all relevant adverse judgments had no reasonable prospect of success and an adjournment would therefore be refused; (2) the application for the order had been authorised by the Solicitor General under authority properly delegated to him under the Law Officers Act 1944. It was not necessary for the law officers themselves personally to consider every document and taking counsel's advice was a perfectly proper course; (3) Art.6 of the Convention does not confer an unfettered right of access to the courts and the procedure of s.42 conformed with the UK's Convention obligations, *Tolstoy Miloslavsky v. United Kingdom* (1995) 20 E.H.R.R. 442, [1995] 1 C.L.Y. 2647 followed, and (4) P's conduct had been vexatious and the statutory criteria had been, on the evidence before the court, made out. Although a time limited order had never before been made, it was appropriate in this case.

ATTORNEY GENERAL v. PRICE, Trans. Ref: CO 3390/96, March 19, 1997, Brooke, L.J., QBD.

790. Vexatious litigants–injunction pending all proceedings order

[Supreme Court Act 1981 s.42(1).]

The Attorney General applied for an interim injunction preventing F from instituting, taking any further step in, or making any application in civil proceedings without the leave of a judge of the High Court and from laying any information or seeking to prefer any bill of indictment at all, pending the hearing of the substantive application under the Supreme Court Act 1981 s.42(1) to restrain F, as a vexatious litigant, from bringing proceedings without the leave of a High Court judge.

Held, allowing the application, an interim injunction and expedition of the substantive hearing were granted, that to obtain the grant of an injunction in such proceedings was unusual and required the court to be satisfied that there was (1) a very strong case for the substantive order; (2) a probability of delay before it could be heard, caused, for example, by an application for legal aid or a full timetable, and (3) good reason to suppose that the respondent would act in the manner the injunctor wished to restrain. F had brought 10 civil actions, a number of interlocutory proceedings and a number of private prosecutions against the managing director of the Mayfair Hotel and a litigation solicitor who acted for him. Eight of those actions had been struck out or dismissed and F had been found guilty of three offences of sending obscene messages by facsimile. It appeared that F intended to apply for legal aid, and within the past week, F had made two applications, laid an information against the solicitor and issued a summons against the Attorney General and it seemed likely that he would continue to issue proceedings if left unrestrained.

ATTORNEY GENERAL v. FABIAN, Trans. Ref: June 18, 1997, February 11, 1997, Lord Bingham of Cornhill, L.C.J., QBD.

791. Articles

Crime by another name *(Gary Slapper)*: N.L.J. 1997, 147(6783), 398. (Applicability of criminal standard of proof in civil cases brought by victims of crime where suspect has been acquitted in criminal courts).

Double trouble: E.G. 1997, 9718, 115-116, 118. (Legal position where litigant attempts to relitigate a previously determined issue, including questions of double jeopardy and overlap between property and criminal law, cause of action estoppel, issue estoppel and serial litigation).

From Beeching to Woolf *(Michael Kershaw)*: Liverpool L.R. 1997, 19(1), 47-51. (History of reforms to civil procedure aimed at reducing delay and cost).

Is it too early for you? *(Kevin Browne)*: S.J. 1997, 141(37), 916-917. (Case law on extent to which court can impose sanctions on plaintiff who issues court proceedings without first giving defendant adequate opportunity to settle dispute).

Liability of insurers for litigant's cost: S.C.P. News 1997, 8(Oct), 6. (Whether insurance company which funds and influences party to action should be liable to pay costs if action fails).

Listing of substantive applications *(Pat Addis* and *Lynne Knapman)*: J.R. 1997, 2(1), 1-3. (Procedure for fixing date for hearing in Crown Office applications, lodging of skeleton arguments and withdrawal or settlement of cases).

New court fees: guidelines *(Suzanne Burn)*: L.S.G. 1997, 94(4), 27. (Details of increases to civil court fees from January 15, 1997, including Law Society's objections to proposals, exemptions and remissions, and effect on legal aid cases).

Summary judgment in the county court *(David J. Oldham)*: S.J. 1997, 141(23), 578-579. (Procedure for applying under Ord.9 r.14, defendant's response, procedure at hearing and County Court Rules 1981 consequences of summary judgment).

The inherent jurisdiction to regulate civil proceedings *(M.S. Dockray)*: L.Q.R. 1997, 113(Jan), 120-132. (Origins of inherent powers of court, theories of juridical basis and limits to jurisdiction).

The perils of late service *(Colin Passmore)*: N.L.J. 1997, 147(6778), 192-193. (Five 1996 cases concerning CA's approach to extension of procedural time limits).

The reform of document management in civil procedure *(Alistair Kelman)*: J.I.L.T. 1997, 1. (Work in progress article on history of copying documents for discovery and barriers to development of electronic discovery).

Transfer of proceedings between county courts *(David J. Oldham)*: S.J. 1997, 141 (36), 899. (Automatic and non automatic transfer of actions under County Court Rules 1981).

792. Books

Arlidge, Anthony; Eady, David; Smith, A.T.H.–Contempt. Common Law Library. Hardback: £195.00. ISBN 0-421-45910-7. Sweet & Maxwell.

Baldwin, John–Small Claims in the County Courts in England and Wales. Oxford Socio-Legal Studies. Hardback: £35.00. ISBN 0-19-826477-1. Clarendon Press.

Boyle, Alan; Marshall, Philip; Jones, Philip; Kosmin, Leslie; Richards, David; Gillyon, Philip–Practice and Procedure of the Companies Court. Lloyd's Commercial Law Library. Hardback: £110.00. ISBN 1-85044-502-8. LLP Limited.

Cook, Michael–Butterworth's Costs Services. Unbound/looseleaf: £245.00. ISBN 0-406-99644-X. Butterworth Law.

Moore, T.G.–Anthony and Berryman's Magistrates' Court Guide: 1997. Spiral bound: £23.95. ISBN 0-406-89020-X. Butterworth Law.

Oughton, D.W.; Lowry, J.P.–Limitation of Actions. Hardback: £125.00. ISBN 1-85978-128-4. LLP Limited.

Sime, S.–Practical Approach to Civil Procedure. 3rd Ed. GPB 23.00. ISBN 1-85431-654-0. Blackstone Press.

Thurston, John–Powers of Attorney. Paperback: £39.95. ISBN 1-86012-434-8. Tolley Publishing.

COMMERCIAL LAW

793. Indemnities–government contracts–advance performance guarantee–counter indemnity–termination of contract–variation of commission rates

Following termination of a contract by the Kuwaiti government, M notified G by letter that an advance performance guarantee, APG, supplied by G had also terminated and that no payments should be made under it. G contended that the notification amounted to a default of the counter indemnity contract under which the APG had been supplied. At first instance, G succeeded in its claim for a declaration that it was entitled to the full amount of the APG and the right to retain funds deposited by M under the terms of the counter indemnity and also for the right to raise the applicable commission rate unilaterally. G contended that, inter alia, although the counter indemnity contract was governed by English law, it could impose the variation under a pre-existing facilities contract governed by Kuwaiti law and subject to Kuwaiti customary banking practice. M appealed and G cross-appealed.

Held, allowing the appeal and dismissing the cross-appeal, that the letter to G merely contained M's bona fide opinions as to the effect of the termination on the counter indemnity contract and did not constitute a default under the terms of the contract. The judge had erred in finding that a self contained commercial purpose existed underlying the contract, which was wider in operation than the ordinary or usual construction of the actual words used. Although G could not claim a right of set off in respect of the sums deposited under the contract, such powers did exist under the facilities contract, which was entered into prior to the counter indemnity. However, as the only right to commission payments arose under the counter indemnity, G could not claim the right to vary unilaterally the rate existing in Kuwaiti law as the contract itself was subject to English law. Even though it was possible in theory for the later English law contract to be subject to an earlier Kuwaiti law contract no such agreement had been shown to exist, as the facilities contract did not purport to give rights to fix or re-fix charges already set for a specific period under the terms of a bilateral agreement.

MITSUBISHI HEAVY INDUSTRIES LTD v. GULF BANK KSC [1997] 1 Lloyd's Rep. 343, Potter, L.J., CA.

794. Loans–contractual provision excluding set off of claim in damages reasonable

See FINANCE: Skipskredittforeningen v. Emperor Navigation. §2507

795. Pyramid selling

TRADING SCHEMES REGULATIONS 1997, SI 1997 30; made under the Fair Trading Act 1973 s.119. In force: February 6, 1997; £1.95.

These Regulations apply to any pyramid selling or similar trading scheme to which the Fair Trading Act 1973 Part XI as amended by the Trading Schemes Act 1996 applies and which came into existence after the date of coming into force of these Regulations, and to any agreement made under such a trading scheme. The Pyramid Selling Schemes Regulations 1989 (SI 1989 2195) as amended by the Pyramid Selling Schemes (Amendment) Regulations 1990 (SI 1990 150) are disapplied in respect of these trading schemes and agreements.

796. Pyramid selling

TRADING SCHEMES (EXCLUSION) REGULATIONS 1997, SI 1997 31; made under the Fair Trading Act 1973 s.118. In force: February 6, 1997; £1.10.

These Regulations disapply the provisions of the Fair Trading Act 1973 Part XI in respect of certain single tier trading schemes, trading schemes in which the promoter or all the promoters and all participants are registered for value added tax, and chain letters.

797. Pyramid selling

TRADING SCHEMES (EXCLUSION) (AMENDMENT) REGULATIONS 1997, SI 1997 1887; made under the Fair Trading Act 1973 s.118. In force: August 21, 1997; £0.65.

These Regulations amend the Trading Schemes (Exclusion) Regulations 1997 (SI 1997 31) so as to apply the £50 limit on benefits to participants only in respect of horizontal recruitments by participants operating at the level immediately below that of the promoter or single participant operating in the UK; and so that trading schemes in which participants who do not make taxable supplies in the UK are not registered for value added tax can benefit from these Regulations.

798. Sale of business–sale of insurance company–breach of accounts warranties

See INSURANCE: Ken Randall Associates Ltd v. MMI Companies Inc. §3180

799. Set off–equitable defences–payment by direct debit–cancellation of direct debit–application of rules relating to payment by cheque–insufficiently close connection between claim and counter claim

E appealed against a decision dismissing an application for summary judgment against M, who, as licensee of two service stations, cancelled a direct debit mandate for payment of fuel supplied by E. M claimed the defence of set off, arguing that he regarded his business relationship with E to be at an end, in view of E's increasingly stringent financial terms. E contended that set off was not available, as the cancellation of a direct debit was subject to the same strict rules on stays of judgment and scope of defences as applied to dishonoured cheques.

Held, allowing the appeal, that where goods were effectively being sold for cash, the vendor should have the security that accompanied cash payments where the parties had decided to use a common banking service to transfer the cash from one account to another. Treating a direct debit in the same way as a cheque was a natural development of the principle in *Nova (Jersey) Knit Ltd v. Kammgarn Spinnerei GmbH* [1977] 1 W.L.R. 713, [1977] C.L.Y. 195, without extending it. In any case, equitable set off was not available on the facts, as there was not a sufficiently close connection between M's counter claim and the payment for the fuel, which was the subject of E's claim, given that it was not enough that the two claims arose out of the same business relationship.

ESSO PETROLEUM CO LTD v. MILTON [1997] 1 W.L.R. 938, Simon Brown, L.J., CA.

800. Trading Schemes Act 1996 (c.32)–Commencement Order

TRADING SCHEMES ACT 1996 (COMMENCEMENT) ORDER 1997, SI 1997 29 (C.1); made under the Trading Schemes Act 1996 s.5. Commencement details: bringing into force various provisions of the Act on February 6, 1997; £0.65.

This Order brings into force the Trading Schemes Act 1996.

801. Articles

100 practical guidelines for the international expansion of a franchise *(Albrecht Schulz)*: I.B.L. 1997, 25(5), 200-206.

Commercial communications in the internal market–at what price? *(Claire Miskin and Arnold Vahrenwald)*: E.I.P.R. 1996, 18(11), 621-624. (CEC's Green Paper on need for EC action to harmonise laws on commercial communications, such as advertising, which can be shown to hamper cross border activity).

Comparative advertising regulations worldwide: M.I.P. 1996, 64, 37-47. (Survey of position in Australia, Brazil, Canada, European Union, France, Germany, India, Italy, Japan, Korea, Mexico, Sweden, Thailand, UK and US).

Fiduciaries in a changing commercial climate *(Gerard McCormack)*: Co. Law. 1997, 18(2), 38-45. (Criteria for establishing whether particular relationship is fiduciary with particular reference to parties in commercial relationship and approaches in Australia and Canada).

Franchising *(Martin Mendelsohn)*: Uniform L.R. 1996, 1(4), 679-692. (Elements of franchising, its commercial rationale, techniques involved and whether legislation is necessary when franchising activity commences in particular country).

Franchising or pyramid selling? *(Rodney Taylor and Virginia Irons)*: Tax. 1997, 138(3599), 744-745. (Effect of statutory regulation of pyramid selling operations on business format franchises and the use of VAT registration to avoid pyramid selling classification).

International expansion through franchising *(Mark Abell)*: M.I.P. 1997, 68, 35-36. (Opportunities presented by franchising as method of licensing to aid international business expansion, with outline of structures and principal regulatory restrictions).

New controls on trading schemes *(Helen Cavanagh)*: I.C.C.L.R. 1997, 8(8), 296-298. (Provisions of legislation which outlaws money circulation schemes and regulates pyramid selling and multi level marketing schemes, with its impact on franchising and basic distribution schemes).

"This is all right, isn't it?": legal pitfalls of sales promotions *(Duncan Hope)*: C.L. 1997, 16, Supp 22-23. (Advice for in house lawyers on legal requirements and commercial considerations when approving company's promotional material).

Trade association profile: the Mail Order Traders' Association: Q.A. 1997, 45(Aut), 11. (Membership, objectives and complaints procedure of association providing liaison between MOTA members and their customers).

802. Books

Adams, John N.; Jones, K.V. Pritchard–Franchising. Hardback: £95.00. ISBN 0-406-08139-5. Butterworth Law.

Adams, John N.; Pritchard Jones, K.V.–Franchising. Hardback: £95.00. ISBN 0-406-13790-0. Butterworth Law.

Campbell of Alloway, Lord Yaqub, Zahd–Law of Advertising. Hardback: £85.00. ISBN 1-85941-287-4. Cavendish Publishing Ltd.

Christou, Richard–International Agency, Distribution and Licensing. Commercial Series. £55.00. ISBN 0-7520-0445-X. FT Law & Tax.

Davies, Iwan–Law of Equipment and Motor Vehicle Leasing and Hiring. Intellectual Property in Practice. Hardback: £79.00. ISBN 0-421-53500-8. Sweet & Maxwell.

Jenkins, Colin; Dean, Paul–International Timeshare Law and Practice. Hardback: £80.00. ISBN 0-406-89106-0. Butterworth Law.

Sinclair, Neil–Commercial Transaction Checklists on Disk. £75.00. ISBN 0-7520-0525-1. FT Law & Tax.

Sinclair, Neil; Rosenberg, Daniel–Commercial Transactions Checklists. Unbound/looseleaf: £150.00. ISBN 0-7520-0388-7. FT Law & Tax.

Standard Business Contracts. Hardback: £55.00. ISBN 0-421-55080-5. Sweet & Maxwell.

COMPANY LAW

803. Company name–direction to change name on ground that name misleading

[Companies Act 1985 s.32.]

A applied under the Companies Act 1985 s.32 to set aside the Secretary of State's direction that it should change its registered name as it was likely to mislead the public as to the nature of its activities. The case rested upon the use of the word "certified", which the Secretary of State found connoted a higher professional standard of its members than was actually required by the association.

Held, dismissing the application, that a s.32 application was neither an appeal nor judicial review and was to be heard de novo by the court on the evidence put before it. Both sides could submit new evidence which had not been considered by the Secretary of State, and the company was not required to prove that its name was not misleading. Before a change of name was enforced it had to be shown that there was a likelihood of harm to the public and the relevant date for deciding whether the name was misleading was the date of the judgment rather than the date of the original order.

ASSOCIATION OF CERTIFIED PUBLIC ACCOUNTANTS OF BRITAIN v. SECRETARY OF STATE FOR TRADE AND INDUSTRY, *The Times*, June 12, 1997, Jacob, J., Ch D.

804. Company registration–branch officers–Hong Kong

COMPANIES OVERSEAS BRANCH REGISTERS (HONG KONG) ORDER 1997, SI 1997 1313; made under the Hong Kong Act 1985 Sch.para.3. In force: July 1, 1997; £0.65.

This Order amends the Companies Act 1985 Sch.14 Part I, which specifies the countries and territories in which by virtue of s.362 a company may cause to be kept in such country or territory a branch register of members there resident, by inserting a reference to the Hong Kong Special Administrative Region of the People's Republic of China. Schedule 14 Part I will therefore continue to apply to Hong Kong after June 30, 1997 notwithstanding that the Region will not be a part of Her Majesty's dominions. A corresponding amendment to the Companies (Northern Ireland) Order 1986 (SI 1986 1032) Sch.14 Part I is also made.

805. **Company registration–landlord seeking restoration of insolvent sublessee–extent of discretion to restore**

[Companies Act 1985 s.653(2).]

The applicant, a local authority, leased a property to S subject to a rent review. S sublet the property to P, a company. P was struck off the register and later dissolved. Subsequently the local authority served notice of the rent review on S and on P. The local authority applied for P to be restored to the register.

Held, restoring P to the register, that there was a discretion under the Companies Act 1985 s.653(2) to restore the company if it was just to do so. Except in special circumstances, restoration should follow. The exercise of the discretion to restore should be the norm rather than the exception. Any prejudice suffered by S was as a result of the terms of the lease, not the restoration of the company.

PRICELAND LTD, *Re*; *sub nom.* WALTHAM FOREST LBC v. REGISTRAR OF COMPANIES [1997] 1 B.C.L.C. 467, Laddie, J., Ch D.

806. **Directors–disqualification orders–conduct at upper end of range of conduct justifying disqualification**

[Company Directors Disqualification Act 1986 s.6.]

Disqualification orders under Company Directors Disqualification Act 1986 s.6 were made against M and E after the company had gone into liquidation with Crown debts of over £1 million and trade debts of £10,000. Both had been directors of other companies which went into liquidation. The judge disqualified M for eight years and E for four years. The Secretary of State appealed.

Held, allowing the appeals and increasing the length of the orders, that M had operated a policy of not paying creditors who did not press for payment thereby allowing three companies to continue to trade when they had inadequate funds, sold the business of one company on deferred terms without security, misappropriated the assets of one company and failed to cooperate with the receiver. His conduct was at the top end of the scale and a disqualification of 12 years was appropriate. E was equally involved in trading at the risk of creditors, the failure to take security for a debt and some of the misappropriations. His conduct fell into the middle bracket of misconduct meriting a disqualification for six years.

SECRETARY OF STATE FOR TRADE AND INDUSTRY v. McTIGHE (NO.2) [1996] 2 B.C.L.C. 477, Morritt, L.J., CA.

807. **Directors–disqualification orders–insolvent company–recommendations for economies disregarded by other directors–decision not to disqualify**

[Company Directors Disqualification Act 1986 s.6(1).]

T, who was employed as a bookkeeper, was one of three directors and 10 per cent shareholder, of a company in financial difficulties. Following a letter from the company's bank, T made recommendations for economies, which were ignored by the other directors and the company went into voluntary liquidation. On the application of the Secretary of State for Trade and Industry, the district judge disqualified the other two directors but, after hearing from the company's auditor that T's suggested economies might have saved it from liquidation and taking into account T's modest salary, the fact that he stood to gain nothing extra from further trading and that he had little influence, decided not to disqualify T. The Secretary of State appealed.

Held, dismissing the appeal, that the judge had weighed all relevant considerations in deciding whether T was "unfit to be concerned in the management of a company" within the Company Directors Disqualification Act 1986 s.6(1)(b). Generally, if a director no longer had any influence over his colleagues to the extent of being superfluous, and the only reason he remained a member of the board was to receive his director's fees, the court might declare him unfit. However, the judge had not found this to be T's objective in failing to resign his directorship and there was no reason to interfere with his decision.

SECRETARY OF STATE FOR TRADE AND INDUSTRY v. TAYLOR; *sub nom.* CS HOLIDAYS LTD, RE; COMPANY (NO.004803 OF 1996), *Re* [1997] 1 W.L.R. 407, Chadwick, J., Ch D.

808. Directors–disqualification orders–jurisdiction to correct imperfect order

[Company Directors Disqualification Act 1986 s.1, s.13; Rules of the Supreme Court Ord.20 r.11.]

A disqualification order which omitted the capacities in which a director was prevented from acting should be set aside and the omissions could be corrected. H appealed against a decision that the court had jurisdiction under RSC Ord.20 r.11 to correct a disqualification order made against him pursuant to the Company Directors Disqualification Act 1986 s.1, which had omitted the capacities in which he was prevented from acting. H was facing a charge of being a director in contravention of a disqualification order, contrary to s.13, and argued that the court had no jurisdiction to correct the order, and in any case, the court should not exercise its discretion to do so. H contended that the order was not a disqualification order within the meaning of s.1 and s.13, by reason of the omissions of the provisions of s.1 (1) (b) and s.1 (1) (c), such that he would, on application, be entitled to have the order set aside. If the court amended the order to make it valid, this would amount to making H's actions an offence retrospectively.

Held, dismissing the appeal, that it was inconceivable that the order against H would be set aside so as to leave him undisqualified. The judge had clearly and correctly considered H unfit to be concerned in the management of a company and had intended to make a disqualification order fully complying with s.1. Regardless of whether the original order was valid or not, any perceived imperfection caused by the omission of the additional capacities was accidental and could be corrected under Ord.20 r.11.

OFFICIAL RECEIVER v. HANNAN; *sub nom.* CANNONQUEST LTD, *Re* [1997] B.C.C. 644, Morritt, L.J., CA.

809. Directors–disqualification orders–no misconduct by director of liquidated company–permission to act as director of companies with similar names

[Insolvency Act 1986 s.216.]

L was a director of Lightning Electrical Contractors Ltd which was in liquidation. L sought permission to continue to act as a director of a company called Lightning Electrical Construction Ltd and five similar named dormant companies.

Held, granting the application, that the disqualification under the Insolvency Act 1986 s.216 was not imposed because of some misconduct on L's part. On the facts leave would be granted.

LIGHTNING ELECTRICAL CONTRACTORS LTD, *Re* [1996] 2 B.C.L.C. 302, EW Hamilton Q.C., Ch D (Companies Court).

810. Directors–disqualification orders–preferential payments to bank instead of trade creditors–case founded on general conduct

[Company Directors Disqualification Act 1986 s.6; Insolvency Act 1986 s.238, s.239, s.240.]

Held, that, where a director caused a payment to be made to the company's bank in preference to trade creditors, the Secretary of State, when asking the court to find that the director was unfit to be involved in the management of a company under the Company Directors Disqualification Act 1986 s.6, was entitled to found his case on the general conduct of the director rather than solely on an allegation that the conduct constituted a statutory preference liable to be set aside under the Insolvency Act 1986 s.238 to s.240.

SECRETARY OF STATE FOR TRADE AND INDUSTRY v. RICHARDSON, *The Times*, May 16, 1997, Ferris, J., Ch D (Companies Court).

811. **Directors–disqualification orders–purpose of disqualification order being to protect the public–effect of delay in proceedings**

[Company Directors Disqualification Act 1986 s.6.]

The Secretary of State applied for a disqualification order in respect of K, an employee alleged to be a de facto director of a company whose director, T, had been convicted of fraudulent trading after the company went into voluntary liquidation in 1992. T had been sentenced to nine months' imprisonment and disqualified from being a company director for 10 years. The Secretary of State successfully argued that a longer period of disqualification was necessary in the public interest and T then consented to a period of 15 years. Before criminal proceedings were instituted against T, the Secretary of State applied for disqualification orders against T, K and another director but those proceedings were stayed without K's knowledge or consent and separate trials were ordered.

Held, dismissing the application, that the primary purpose of a disqualification order was to protect the public from directors who were unfit to manage companies, and the same standard was to be applied in both civil and criminal courts. The public interest had to be weighed against continuing de facto disqualification proceedings after a long period of delay and the legal costs involved. The Company Directors Disqualification Act 1986 s.6, which provided that proceedings had to be commenced within two years of the company's insolvency, clearly intended that cases should be disposed of quickly. As the delay was not the fault of K and the charges related to events as far back as 1990, the public interest would not be served by making an order when K was not shown to have conducted herself in such a manner as to make her unfit to manage a company.

SECRETARY OF STATE FOR TRADE AND INDUSTRY v. TJOLLE, *The Times*, May 9, 1997, Jacob, J., Ch D.

812. **Directors–disqualification orders–shadow directors–company secretary or employee not acting as de facto director**

[Company Directors Disqualification Act 1986 s.6.]

S applied under the Company Directors Disqualification Act 1986 s.6 seeking the disqualification of three respondents, including C, for unfitness. The question arose whether C, an accountant appointed as company secretary, was a director within the meaning of s.6.

Held, dismissing the application, that C was not a director. For there to be a finding that a person was acting as a de facto director there had to be clear evidence that he was the sole person directing the affairs of the company, or that he had acted on an equal footing with other directors in the company. Here there had been two directors active in the running of the company, and C's role was consistent with acting as company secretary or as an employee.

SECRETARY OF STATE FOR TRADE AND INDUSTRY v. HICKLING [1996] B.C.C. 678, Judge Weeks Q.C., Ch D.

813. **Directors–disqualification orders–stay of proceedings–Secretary of State entitled to continue disqualification proceedings notwithstanding undertakings offered by director**

[Company Directors Disqualification Act 1986.]

S, had brought disqualification proceedings against D, a director of a number of companies, under the Company Directors Disqualification Act 1986 on the basis of allegations of serious misconduct and dishonesty. D disputed the claims, but offered S permanent undertakings that he would not act as a company director or similar office holder, take part in the promotion, formation or management of a company, nor apply to vary or discharge the undertakings. D appealed against the dismissal of his application for a stay of proceedings and for leave to apply for judicial review of S's decision to continue the proceedings and refuse consent to the stays [1997] 8 C.L. 79, contending that it was oppressive, contrary to the public interest and a misuse of process for S to continue the proceedings in the light of the undertakings offered.

Held, dismissing the appeal, that it was open to S to conclude that it was expedient in the public interest to continue with the disqualification proceedings despite the undertakings offered by D. The undertakings, offered as they were without any admission of fact, were not equivalent to a disqualification order made under the Act. There was no provision in the Act for the disposal of proceedings by way of an undertaking without admissions, as the statutory scheme envisaged that an order would have a factual basis, founded on either admissions or findings, which was sufficient to justify the conclusion that an individual was unfit to act as director of a company. That factual basis of a disqualification order served as a deterrent and protected the public from individuals who were unfit to act as company directors.

SECRETARY OF STATE FOR TRADE AND INDUSTRY v. DAVIES (NO.2); ATLANTIC COMPUTER SYSTEMS PLC, RE; SECRETARY OF STATE FOR TRADE AND INDUSTRY v. ASHMAN; *sub nom.* BLACKSPUR GROUP PLC, *Re, The Times*, December 9, 1997, Mummery, L.J., CA.

814. Directors–disqualification orders–three years' disqualification

L were found guilty of trading for 21 months after they knew that the company of which they were directors was insolvent, of making loans on a non commercial basis to an associated company when the company was insolvent, of preferring trade creditors and themselves over Crown debts and of paying themselves excessive remuneration. As to the level of remuneration the question was not how much was the work of the directors worth, but how much could the company afford. In the circumstances the appropriate course would have been for payments to have been suspended.

Held, granting the application, that a period of three years' disqualification was appropriate.

SECRETARY OF STATE FOR TRADE AND INDUSTRY v. LUBRANI; *sub nom.* AMARON LTD, *Re* [1997] 2 B.C.L.C. 115, Deputy Registrar Jaques, Ch D.

815. Directors–disqualification orders–trading when insolvent

L was a director of a company that was operating at a loss. The board decided to seek an investor and M agreed to purchase the issued share capital of the company. M was unable to complete the transaction as it too ran into financial difficulties. G, a foreign company, gained control of M. The purchase of the company's shares by M was not proceeded with and the company was sold. The moneys were paid into the company's bank and the company was put into voluntary liquidation owing the Crown substantial sums. The Secretary of State brought disqualification proceedings against L and two directors of M.

Held, dismissing the proceedings against the directors of M, that there was no evidence that they had acted either as de facto or as shadow directors. As against L it was proved that he had caused the company to trade in the knowledge that it was insolvent, that he had caused the company to retain money owed to the Crown, that he had caused the company to fail to file accounts and had caused the company to prefer the bank and M as creditors to the expense of preferential creditors. Of these the first was the most serious and justified a disqualification.

SECRETARY OF STATE FOR TRADE AND INDUSTRY v. LAING [1996] 2 B.C.L.C. 324, Evans-Lombe, J., Ch D.

816. Directors–disqualification orders–undischarged bankrupt–conduct as director of collateral companies–no statutory requirement that conduct with all companies had to be the same or similar

[Company Directors Disqualification Act 1986 s.6(1).]

The Secretary of State sought a disqualification order against I following the making of a bankruptcy order in relation to C of which I was a director. The

Secretary of State, in reliance upon the Company Directors Disqualification Act 1986 s.6(1)(b), invited the court to consider the conduct of I in relation to his management of four collateral companies which went into voluntary liquidation or were compulsorily wound up. The Secretary of State argued that I's conduct as a director of the collateral companies made him unfit to be concerned in the management of C. I appealed, contending, in reliance upon *Godwin Warren Controls Systems Plc, Re* [1992] B.C.C. 557, [1993] C.L.Y. 361, that the judge was wrong to conclude that there was no statutory requirement that the conduct in relation to the collateral companies had to be the same or similar to the conduct in relation to C.

Held, dismissing the appeal, that while there had to be a nexus between the conduct in relation to the collateral companies and C there was no requirement for a further connection such as similarity of conduct, *Godwin Warren Controls Systems Plc, Re* not followed. The test to be applied in relation to s.6 of the 1986 Act was whether the conduct of I as a director of C made him unfit to be concerned in the management of the company. The conduct relied upon in relation to the collateral companies must have demonstrated such unfitness.

SECRETARY OF STATE FOR TRADE AND INDUSTRY v. IVENS; *sub nom.* COUNTRY FARM INNS LTD, *Re, The Times*, September 24, 1997, Morritt, L.J., CA.

817. Directors–disqualification proceedings–admissibility of compelled evidence obtained by Companies Act investigators–effect of European Convention on Human Rights

[Company Directors Disqualification Act 1986 s.8, s.434(5); European Convention on Human Rights 1950 Art.6.1.]

M applied for certain evidence to be excluded from disqualification proceedings brought against nine company directors under the Company Directors Disqualification Act 1986 s.8 following the collapse of Atlantic Computers Plc and British & Commonwealth Holdings Plc. M was compelled to give evidence under s.434 of the 1986 Act. The issue arose as to what use could be made of the transcripts of the compelled evidence. M contended that they should be excluded from the forthcoming trial to the extent that it could be in contravention of the European Convention on Human Rights 1950 Art.6.1 following *Saunders v. United Kingdom* (1997) 23 E.H.R.R. 313, [1997] C.L.Y. 2816. He denied the intention of wrecking the forthcoming trial.

Held, refusing the application, that s.434(5) of the 1986 Act specifically provided for the admissibility of the compelled evidence. Use could be made of compelled evidence given to Companies Act inspectors in criminal trials, *R. v. Saunders (Earnest) (No.2)* [1996] 1 Cr. App. R. 463, [1995] 1 C.L.Y. 1141 and *R. v. Morrissey (Ian Patrick)* [1997] C.L.Y. 2818 followed. The UK domestic law remained as determined in *R. v. Saunders* and it was not for the court to apply the Convention in determining whether the UK had breached it. The court could not find the admissibility of the evidence to be oppressive given that it was specifically provided for by the 1986 Act.

SECRETARY OF STATE FOR TRADE AND INDUSTRY v. McCORMICK, Trans. Ref: No.1614 of 1995, April 30, 1997, Jacob, J., Ch D.

818. Directors–disqualification proceedings–admissibility of evidence–reliance on alleged hearsay evidence from liquidator in proceedings

[Company Directors Disqualification Act 1986 s.7, s.8.]

The Secretary of State appealed against an order striking out sections of an affidavit sworn by a liquidator in proceedings for disqualification orders against a company's directors under the Company Directors Disqualification Act 1986 s.7, on the grounds that the evidence was hearsay and inadmissible.

Held, allowing the appeal, that it was necessary for the court to be satisfied on the basis of admissible and credible evidence that a director's conduct rendered him unfit to be concerned in the management of a company. Statements obtained by the Secretary of State from an office holder, such as a liquidator, were admissible in relation to disqualification proceedings under s.7 in the same way as under s.8, as there was no significant difference between the two types of case, *Rex Williams Leisure Plc (In Administration), Re* [1994] Ch. 350, [1994] C.L.Y. 401 applied.

SECRETARY OF STATE FOR TRADE AND INDUSTRY v. ASHCROFT [1997] 3 W.L.R. 319, Millett, L.J., CA.

819. Directors—disqualification proceedings—affidavits should distinguish between factual evidence and reasons why director deemed unfit

[Company Directors Disqualification Act 1986; Insolvent Companies (Disqualification of Unfit Directors) Proceedings Rules 1987 (SI 1987 2023) r.6.]

Held, that respondents in proceedings under the Company Directors Disqualification Act 1986 should be encouraged to concentrate on the necessary factual matters when preparing affidavits under the Insolvent Companies (Disqualification of Unfit Directors) Proceedings Rules 1987 r.6, and liquidators should distinguish between submissions which placed the facts before the court and matters upon which allegations of a director's unfitness were based which had been relied upon by the Secretary of State.

SECRETARY OF STATE FOR TRADE AND INDUSTRY v. CARTER, *The Times*, August 14, 1997, Neuberger, J., Ch D.

820. Directors—disqualification proceedings—de facto director acting in that capacity for companies not carrying on same form of business

[Company Directors Disqualification Act 1986 s.6(1).]

S sought the disqualification of I as a company director under the Company Directors Disqualification Act 1986 s.6 on the basis that whilst bankrupt he acted as a de facto director of CFI. S sought to put in evidence I's conduct in relation to four other companies which did not carry on the same form of business as CFI. I argued that within the meaning of s.6(1)(b) of the 1986 Act it was not permissible to do so unless his conduct in respect of them was alleged to be the same or similar to his conduct in respect of CFI. He sought, as a preliminary issue, to have tried whether his conduct as a director of the other companies was "conduct as a director of any other companies" within the meaning of s.6(1)(b).

Held, answering the question in the affirmative, that there was no express or implied requirement in s.6(1)(b) that the conduct had to be the same or similar in the other companies to that alleged in the lead company, *Godwin Warren Control Systems Plc, Re* [1992] B.C.C. 557, [1993] C.L.Y. 361 distinguished.

SECRETARY OF STATE FOR TRADE AND INDUSTRY v. IVENS [1997] B.C.C. 396, Judge Weeks Q.C., Ch D.

821. Directors—disqualification proceedings—delay in disqualification proceedings—no striking out due to contributory fault

N went into liquidation in 1990. Disqualification proceedings were commenced in 1992. Orders were made requiring the director, M, to submit evidence and for evidence in reply to be filed by the official receiver. M's affidavit was served in June 1994. In August 1995 M's solicitors consented to an extension of time within which the official receiver could file his reply. The reply was made within the extended time limit. M sought to have the proceedings struck out on the grounds that there had been inordinate and inexcusable delay, rendering a fair trial impossible.

Held, dismissing the application, that there had been inordinate and inexcusable delay on the part of the official receiver but the court had to consider the fact that M had, to begin with, been partly at fault for the delay. Furthermore, the fact that an extension of time had been granted for the service of the official receiver's reply indicated a readiness on the part of M to proceed at that stage, and M must have been taken as being prepared to excuse the delay. It would require some powerful reason, such as malpractice, before proceedings would be struck out after such an act.

NEW TECHNOLOGY SYSTEMS LTD, *Re* [1996] B.C.C. 694, Judge Rich Q.C., Ch D.

822. **Directors–disqualification proceedings–disclosure of administrators' report to Secretary of State–statutory duty of administrators could not be overridden on grounds of privilege**

[Company Directors Disqualification Act 1986 s.7(3); Rules of the Supreme Court Ord.24 r.11.]

As documents prepared by office holders acting under a statutory duty, administrators' reports to the Secretary of State pursuant to the Company Directors Disqualification Act 1986 s.7(3) were not protected by privilege in the absence of a claim for public interest immunity, and were subject to disclosure. Following the collapse of Barings Bank, a report to the Secretary of State was prepared on behalf of the administrators pursuant to their duty under s.7.(3) proceedings were brought against T and other former directors. T applied under the Rules of the Supreme Court Ord.24 r.11 for disclosure of the report and other documents. The Secretary of State resisted production of the report, contending that every document brought into existence for the purpose of use in litigation was protected by privilege.

Held, allowing the application, that the Secretary of State was not entitled to claim privilege in relation to a report which had been prepared by office holders acting under a statutory duty. The authorities relied upon in support of the claim of privilege involved the maker of the document choosing whether or not to bring it into existence, whereas, in the instant case, the administrators were obliged by statute to make the report. Whether disclosure would be ordered, therefore, depended on whether there existed a public interest requiring protection from disclosure which outweighed the right of a litigant to obtain discovery of relevant documents. In the present case, in the absence of a claim of public interest immunity, there clearly did not.

SECRETARY OF STATE FOR TRADE AND INDUSTRY v. BAKER; *sub nom.* BARINGS PLC, *Re, The Times*, October 23, 1997, Sir Richard Scott, V.C., Ch D.

823. **Directors–disqualification proceedings–extent to which conduct of non lead company director to be taken into account–grounds for amending proceedings by adding lead company**

[Company Directors Disqualification Act 1986 s.6.]

DCS, a computer retailer, ran into financial difficulties and its bankers demanded repayment of its overdraft. DT, whose director and driving force was B, was owed £500,000, partly unsecured, and agreed to supply goods worth £480,000 in exchange for the freehold title to six properties of DCS. M, a newly formed company, purchased DCS's entire undertaking including its interest in the properties for a price equal to its net asset value and agreed to indemnify DCS against its existing and contingent liabilities. B was involved in that transaction, then became a director of M, which then declared it held the properties on trust for DT. DCS and M went into liquidation, and the Official Receiver sought disqualification orders against the managing director of DCS and B under the Company Directors Disqualification Act 1986 s.6 on the basis that the transactions took place when they knew DCS to be insolvent and that the properties had been transferred to put them beyond the reach of DCS's other unsecured creditors. B applied to strike out the proceedings against him as disclosing no reasonable cause of action or being scandalous, frivolous, vexatious or otherwise an abuse of the process of the court. The Official Receiver applied to add DT to the proceedings as B had never been a director of DCS, but did not intend to lead fresh evidence.

Held, dismissing B's striking out application and the Official Receiver's application to amend, that (1) B's involvement as a director of M was capable of constituting conduct which might satisfy a court as to his unfitness to act as a director, so the claim should not be struck out, particularly as it could be taken into account alongside his conduct as a director of DT, and (2) this was not an appropriate case for the amendment of proceedings to add a lead company, as to add DT would alter the fundamental focus and nature of the complaint against B, and the amendment was applied for without setting out fully in evidence the essence of the complaint; whilst the fact that DT and its creditors benefited from the transactions did not preclude a finding that B's conduct merited disqualification, it did require that the criticism should be made with some particularity.

DIAMOND COMPUTER SYSTEMS LTD, *Re; sub nom.* OFFICIAL RECEIVER v. BROWN [1997] 1 B.C.L.C. 174, Jules Sher Q.C., Ch D (Companies Court).

824. Directors–disqualification proceedings–inadmissibility of evidence of good character or good reputation

[Company Directors Disqualification Act 1986 s.6; Rules of the Supreme Court Ord.41 r.6.]

The Secretary of State applied under RSC Ord.41 r.6 for the striking out of affidavits served on behalf of the respondents in disqualification proceedings on the grounds that the material contained in the affidavits was irrelevant or otherwise oppressive. The affidavits contained evidence that the respondents were of good character, skilled in acting as directors and of excellent reputation. The respondents argued that the disqualification proceedings were akin to criminal proceedings in which the defendant was entitled to adduce evidence of good character.

Held, striking out the affidavits, that disqualification proceedings under the Company Directors Disqualification Act 1986 s.6 were civil proceedings in which the general rule excluding evidence of good reputation applied and no departure from the rule was justified on the grounds that the alleged matters involved imputations against the respondent's honesty. The matters contained in the affidavits were not relevant to whether or not the respondents had committed the acts alleged nor were they relevant to any period of disqualification that might be imposed, *Bath Glass Ltd, Re* [1988] 4 B.C.C. 130, [1988] C.L.Y. 313, *Grayan Building Services Ltd (In Liquidation), Re* [1995] B.C.C. 554, [1995] 1 C.L.Y. 582 followed.

DAWES & HENDERSON (AGENCIES) LTD (IN LIQUIDATION), *Re* [1997] 1 B.C.L.C. 329, Blackburne, J., Ch D (Companies Court).

825. Directors–disqualification proceedings–inappropriate to investigate validity of company debenture and guarantee in disqualification proceedings years after receiver appointed

[Company Directors Disqualification Act 1986 s.6.]

A floating charge and guarantee were executed by a company, M, of which J and others were directors. The bank called in the guarantee and, when it was not honoured, appointed an administrative receiver and M was struck off the register of companies. The Secretary of State subsequently issued a summons under the Company Directors Disqualification Act 1986 s.6, seeking the disqualification of M's directors. In the disqualification proceedings, the directors sought to have the validity of the receiver's appointment tried as a preliminary issue on the ground that the debenture and guarantee were conditional upon the provision of an overdraft facility by the bank, and, because that condition had not been met, the appointment of the receiver was invalid. In the Chancery Division the appointment was ruled valid, and the directors appealed.

Held, allowing the appeal, that it was wrong for the court to rule on the validity of the appointment of a receiver or the debenture and guarantee in disqualification proceedings to which neither the company, administrative receiver nor bank were parties. At no time previously had the directors taken steps to challenge the receiver's appointment and the company had subsequently been wound up and the assets distributed. In such circumstances, it was inappropriate for the preliminary issue to have been tried and the correct approach would have been for the disqualification proceedings to be stayed and proceedings brought against the debenture holder.

SECRETARY OF STATE FOR TRADE AND INDUSTRY v. JABBLE, *The Times*, August 5, 1997, Millett, L.J., CA.

826. Directors–disqualification proceedings–liquidator's evidence–expert evidence or opinion

In disqualification proceedings S sought to rely on a report from an accountant which concluded that S had not been responsible for any of the matters about which complaint was made by the Secretary of State. The Secretary of State applied to strike out the affidavit as irrelevant because it did not contain any expert evidence, merely statements of opinion on questions that the court was required to decide.

Held, striking out the affidavit, that there was nothing in the report that could constitute expert opinion. Those preparing and swearing affidavits should be careful to distinguish between facts which could be established by direct evidence, inferences of fact that the court was being invited to draw and matters which were said to amount to unfitness by the respondent.

PINEMOOR LTD, *Re* [1997] B.C.C. 708, Chadwick, J., Ch D (Companies Court).

827. Directors–disqualification proceedings–registered office relocated to liquidator's office in another county court jurisdiction–appropriate jurisdiction to bring disqualification proceedings

[Company Directors Disqualification Act 1986 s.6; Insolvency Act 1986 s.117.]

A resolution was passed for the voluntary winding up of L, whose registered office was within the district of the Walsall County Court. The day after the resolution the registered office was changed to the liquidator's office, in the jurisdiction of the Birmingham County Court, wherein the Secretary of State commenced disqualification proceedings two years later under the Company Directors Disqualification Act 1986 s.6. The district judge rejected the director's argument that, as Walsall County Court had the jurisdiction to wind up, the disqualification proceedings had been brought in the wrong court. The director appealed.

Held, dismissing the appeal, that the words "any court having jurisdiction to wind up the company" in s.6 of the 1986 Act were in the present tense and therefore referred to the court having such jurisdiction at the date the disqualification proceedings were issued. That would have been the Birmingham County Court, given that the company's registered office was within that court's jurisdiction for the six months prior to that date, in the light of the Insolvency Act 1986 s.117.

LICHFIELD FREIGHT TERMINAL LTD [1997] B.C.C. 11, Neuberger, J., Ch D.

828. Directors–disqualification proceedings–restricted line of inferences in Carecraft procedure–standard required for Carecraft statement

[Company Directors Disqualification Act 1986 s.6.]

On an application to disqualify B as a director under the Company Directors Disqualification Act 1986 s.6 and using the summary procedure sanctioned by *Carecraft Construction Ltd, Re* [1993] B.C.C. 336, [1993] C.L.Y. 374, the liquidator alleged that the respondents caused false accounts to be circulated, but the non disputed statement provided that B knew or ought to have known that circulated accounts were materially inaccurate.

Held, allowing the application and disqualifying B for six years, that the court could not draw secondary inferences from agreed primary facts in *Carecraft* statements, which meant that it was important for such statements to leave no room or need for infilling or interpretation. The court could not infer actual knowledge of the inaccuracies and so the admission arising out of the statement had to be limited to one of negligence rather than fraud. Nevertheless the admission remained sufficiently serious to justify disqualification. The parties had agreed that six to eight years was appropriate if there was disqualification and, as other ambiguous admissions had to be interpreted restrictively, B's good conduct in respect of the company and its liquidation had generally been good and the case had been hanging over him for some time, six years was appropriate.

SECRETARY OF STATE FOR TRADE AND INDUSTRY v. BANARSE; *sub nom.* PS BANARSE & CO, *Re* [1997] 1 B.C.L.C. 653, Jules Sher Q.C., Ch D.

829. **Directors–disqualification proceedings–stay of proceedings–undertakings by director rejected–no abuse of process–undertaking not having same force as an order**

[Company Directors Disqualification Act 1986.]

D was a director of a number of companies that went into administrative receivership. The Secretary of State brought proceedings against D to disqualify him. D offered an undertaking never to act as a director of a company again, to be personally responsible for the debts of any company should he act in breach of the undertaking and never to seek to vary the order. D applied for a stay of the disqualification proceedings when the Secretary of State refused to accept the undertakings.

Held, dismissing the application for a stay, that an undertaking did not have the same force as an order under the Company Directors Disqualification Act 1986. It would be wrong for the court to intervene to prevent the Secretary of State from taking proper proceedings on the basis that such an undertaking had been made, *Secretary of State for Trade and Industry v. Rogers* [1996] 1 W.L.R. 1569, [1996] 1 C.L.Y. 978 considered, *Carecraft Construction Co Ltd, Re* [1994] 1 W.L.R. 172, [1993] C.L.Y. 374 distinguished.

BLACKSPUR GROUP PLC, *Re*; ATLANTIC COMPUTER SYSTEMS PLC, *Re* [1997] 1 W.L.R. 710, Rattee, J., Ch D.

830. **Directors–disqualification proceedings–summons brought one day out of time–retrospective leave refused–Secretary of State having not always been diligent–director's undertaking gave same degree of public protection as disqualification order**

[Company Directors Disqualification Act 1986 s.7(2).]

S sought to disqualify C and W from acting as directors on the grounds, inter alia, that they received excessive remuneration and bonus payments from companies of which they were directors when they ought to have been aware that the group was in financial difficulty. The holding company had become insolvent on October 27, 1993, and S issued an originating summons under the Company Directors Disqualification Act 1986 s.7(2) on October 27, 1995, one day out of time. S sought retrospective and prospective leave to issue out of time; C sought to have the proceedings stayed if he gave a perpetual undertaking not to seek appointment as a director in the future, stating that because of his age and medical condition he had been advised not to work again.

Held, refusing leave to pursue W and granting the stay sought by C, that (1) retrospective leave should be refused as it would not be appropriate to extend the period by analogy with cases involving the assertion of private rights in a disqualification case which involved protection of the public by means of an interference with an individual's freedom, *Crestjoy Products, Re* [1990] B.C.L.C. 677, [1990] C.L.Y. 476 applied; (2) as to prospective leave, it was necessary first to examine the nature of the delay which, although slight, showed that S's conduct in the preceding two years had not always been diligent, and he had therefore run the risk of not filing within two years, and a good reason for the delay had not been given, although it was not a bad case; (3) on the facts, although the bonuses and remuneration paid to C and W could go toward findings of unfitness, the case against W was far from strong and did not discharge S's burden of showing good reason why leave should be granted, and (4) there was a stronger case against C, but in the circumstances the court would accept the undertaking as giving the public protection intended by the 1986 Act and would stay proceedings against him.

SECRETARY OF STATE FOR TRADE AND INDUSTRY v. CLELAND; *sub nom.* STORMONT LTD, *Re* [1997] 1 B.C.L.C. 437, Lloyd, J., Ch D (Companies Court).

831. **Directors–disqualification proceedings–undertaking preferred in place of disqualification order–offer refused in absence of statutory provision giving undertaking equal status and effect as order**

[Company Directors Disqualification Act 1986 s.1.]

D sought to stay proceedings brought against him by S under the Company Directors Disqualification Act 1986 on D giving undertakings intended to provide protection to the public for a longer period than a disqualification order and in the alternative for leave to seek judicial review of S's decision to continue the proceedings. D sought to avoid the costs of the proceedings by offering to pay S's costs to date, giving an undertaking to reflect an order under s.1 of the Act, and undertakings to be personally liable for all debts and liabilities of any company if he became involved in its management, never to act as trustee of a charity, and never to apply to vary or discharge the undertakings. S accepted that it was unnecessary to consider the judicial review proceedings separately and that if he had been *Wednesbury* unreasonable in deciding to continue proceedings in light of D's undertakings, the proceedings could be stayed on that ground.

Held, dismissing the applications, that a statutory amendment would be necessary to give an undertaking the same effect as an order, and it was wrong in principle for the court to intervene to stop perfectly proper proceedings against S's wishes on the grounds that something less practically efficacious than an order under the Act was being offered. Whilst such undertakings had been deemed sufficient in cases involving respondents' medical problems, it would not be appropriate to extend such acceptance to a case such as this where there were no factors to render a trial unfairly oppressive. Unless and until amending legislation rendered undertakings as having the same status and effect as an order, S could not be said to be *Wednesbury* unreasonable in pursuing the latter, *Secretary of State for Trade and Industry v. Rogers* [1997] B.C.C. 155, [1996] 1 C.L.Y. 978 considered.

SECRETARY OF STATE FOR TRADE AND INDUSTRY v. DAVIES (NO.2) [1997] B.C.C. 488, Rattee, J., Ch D (Companies Court).

832. **Directors–misrepresentation–personal liability of director for negligent misstatements–duty of care in exceptional circumstances**

M, the managing director of N, appealed against a decision finding him personally liable for negligent misstatements made on N's behalf in pre-agreement negotiations with W in regard to a franchise agreement to lease a health food shop and in projected profits given in a brochure advertising franchising opportunities with N. The projections showed turnover figures of £227,250 and £338,000 in the first and second years of operation, with projected profits of nearly £30,000 over the same period, whereas W's shop closed after 18 months having achieved a turnover of only £248,000 and losses of £38,600.

Held, dismissing the appeal, that, due to N's limited liability status, special circumstances were needed to establish a duty of care between M and W. The facts showed, however, that M had played a considerable, albeit indirect, role in the pre-agreement negotiations and the production of the relevant business projections. The experience and knowledge referred to in the brochure derived solely from M's operation of a shop run in a personal capacity which was completely separate from N and his role as N's managing director, *Trevor Ivory v. Anderson* [1992] 2 N.Z.L.R. 517 and *Fairline Shipping Co v. Adamson* [1975] 1 Q.B. 180, [1974] C.L.Y. 2582 considered.

WILLIAMS v. NATURAL LIFE HEALTH FOODS LTD [1997] 1 B.C.L.C. 131, Hirst, L.J., CA.

833. Directors–reports–statement of payment practice

COMPANIES ACT 1985 (DIRECTORS' REPORT) (STATEMENT OF PAYMENT PRACTICE) REGULATIONS 1997, SI 1997 571; made under the Companies Act 1985 s.257. In force: March 4, 1997; £1.10.

These Regulations amend the Companies Act 1985 by substituting a new Sch.7 Part VI and making amendments to s.234. The new Part VI provides that the directors' report of public companies and large private companies which are subsidiaries of a public company must contain a statement of the company's policy and practice on payment of its suppliers. It re-states existing provisions and adds a new requirement to state the company's practice on payment of its suppliers. The directors' report must state the figure, expressed in days, which bears the same proportion to the number of days in the year as the amount owed to trade creditors at the year end bears to the amount invoiced by suppliers during the year.

834. Dissolution–personal injuries action commenced prior to dissolution–proceedings coming to permanent end on dissolution not going into abeyance–court had no jurisdiction to validate proceedings–dissolution not declared void

[Companies Act 1985 s.651.]

H, a former employee of PP, suffered a back injury in the course of his employment and, three days before the expiry of the relevant limitation period, issued a writ claiming damages against PP for personal injury. PP's insurers, SA, paid £5,000 into court, but PP subsequently went into voluntary liquidation and was later dissolved, fully solvent. H applied for an order under the Companies Act 1985 s.651 declaring that PP's dissolution was void and validating H's action against PP, which had been abated by the dissolution.

Held, dismissing the application, that the court had no jurisdiction to validate proceedings which had commenced before PP was dissolved, as once a company was dissolved all proceedings relating to it came to a permanent end and did not simply go into abeyance. Express statutory authority would be required to permit the court to revive proceedings which had come to a permanent end and to validate actions against a company in spite of its dissolution. Further, the court would not exercise its power to declare PP's dissolution void and restore it to the register so as to allow H to bring fresh proceedings, as any new action would be prima facie statute barred and, in the circumstances of the case, the court would not exercise its discretion to extend the time limit.

PHILIP POWIS LTD, *Re, The Times*, April 30, 1997, Sir John Knox, Ch D.

835. Friendly societies–fees–Commission expenses

FRIENDLY SOCIETIES (GENERAL CHARGE AND FEES) REGULATIONS 1997, SI 1997 741; made under the Friendly Societies Act 1974 s.104; and the Friendly Societies Act 1992 s.2, s.114. In force: April 1, 1997; £1.95.

These Regulations provide for a general charge to be paid by friendly societies towards the expenses of the Friendly Societies Commission.

836. Holding companies–share ownership–dealings in securities–exclusion

COMPANIES (MEMBERSHIP OF HOLDING COMPANY) (DEALERS IN SECURITIES) REGULATIONS 1997, SI 1997 2306; made under the European Communities Act 1972 s.2. In force: October 20, 1997; £1.10.

These Regulations, which further implement Second Council Directive 77/91 ([1977] OJ L26/1) on the co-ordination of safeguards in respect of the formation of public limited liability companies and the maintenance and alteration of their capital, alter the scope of the exemption contained in the Companies Act 1985 s.23(3) which excludes certain kinds of dealings in securities from the prohibition on the ownership by a body corporate of shares in its holding company.

837. Industrial and provident societies—credit unions—fees

INDUSTRIAL AND PROVIDENT SOCIETIES (CREDIT UNIONS) (AMENDMENT OF FEES) REGULATIONS 1997, SI 1997 742; made under the Industrial and Provident Societies Act 1965 s.70, s.71. In force: April 1, 1997; £1.10.

These Regulations supersede the Industrial and Provident Societies (Credit Unions) (Amendment of Fees) Regulations 1996 (SI 1996 612). They generally increase, by an average of three per cent, the fees to be paid for matters to be transacted under the Industrial and Provident Societies Act 1965, the Industrial and Provident Societies Act 1967 and the Credit Unions Act 1979. In addition, the fee for a change of name has been reduced, a new fee has been introduced for the issue of a certificate of approval of the management systems of a credit union which is seeking to take advantage of the greater powers made available under the Deregulation (Credit Unions) Order 1996 (SI 1996 1189) and fees in respect of amendments of rules will be reduced in certain circumstances when changes to membership qualification are made.

838. Industrial and provident societies—fees

INDUSTRIAL AND PROVIDENT SOCIETIES (AMENDMENT OF FEES) REGULATIONS 1997, SI 1997 743; made under the Industrial and Provident Societies Act 1965 s.70, s.71. In force: April 1, 1997; £1.10.

These Regulations supersede the Industrial and Provident Societies (Amendment of Fees) Regulations 1996 (SI 1996 613). They generally increase, by an average of three per cent, the fees to be paid for matters to be transacted under the Industrial and Provident Societies Act 1965 and the Industrial and Provident Societies Act 1967. In order to clarify the fees currently charged for the replacement by a society of one set of model rules for another, the description of the relevant fees for such transactions has been re-worded to provide for separate fees where the new model is used unamended and for cases where further amendments to the new model are made.

839. Practice directions—Companies Court—schemes of arrangement—reduction of capital

Petitions to sanction schemes of arrangement will in future be heard by the Companies Court judge whilst petitions to confirm reductions of capital will, unless otherwise ordered, be heard in open court by the Companies Court registrar every Wednesday after the list of winding up petitions has been completed. Where a hearing during the long vacation is desirable on financial, commercial or economic grounds and the application is one which cannot, with reasonable diligence, have been made and prosecuted before the long vacation began, an informal application should be made in chambers to the court manager so that a timetable might be fixed. Applications to confirm reductions not falling into the above category might still be heard by the registrar on the grounds that an urgent hearing was necessary or that time was available once the urgent petitions had been dealt with. The vacation judge would be available to hear petitions in relation to schemes and reductions which needed to be heard by a judge on certain dates to be arranged in August and September, to be printed in the Daily Cause List.

PRACTICE DIRECTION (COMPANIES COURT: SCHEMES OF ARRANGEMENT AND REDUCTIONS OF CAPITAL) [1997] 1 W.L.R. 1, Sir Richard Scott V.C., Ch D.

840. Share transfers—signature on transfer form disputed—expert evidence—burden of proof

[Companies Act 1985 s.359.]

E, C and H, members of a band called The Hollies which was incorporated in 1963, brought an action to rectify the share register under the Companies Act 1985 s.359, by striking out the name of EH and inserting their names in lieu. E, H and C contended that EH, a former band member, signed a share transfer form in 1970 transferring his single share in the company to them. E, H and C adduced evidence from CW, the company's accountants, that they held a share transfer form, signed by EH and witnessed by an unknown party, in their safe for 15 years before forwarding it to the Controller of Stamps who subsequently lost the form. EH denied that he had ever signed a share transfer form.

Held, dismissing the application, that E, H and C had not discharged the evidential burden upon them as they had failed to prove that EH had signed the share transfer form. The indirect evidence, adduced by E, H and C from CW that EH's signature was on the form, would have been sufficient to discharge the burden of proof had EH not contested the authorship of the signature. Proof of a signature on a share transfer form could only be achieved by evidence of (1) a person who witnessed the signature; (2) a person familiar with the signature who could identify the signature on the form, and (3) a handwriting expert who, having compared the signature on the form with that of the alleged transferor, could confirm that the signature on the form was authentic. E, H and C had, in omitting to call such witnesses, failed to discharge that burden of proof.

ELLIOTT v. THE HOLLIES LTD, July 14, 1997, Deputy Registrar Jaques, Ch D (Companies Court). [*Ex rel.* Mark Watson-Gandy, Barrister, 3 Paper Buildings, Temple].

841. **Shareholders–minority shareholders–unfair prejudice–employee having been promoted to the board–original director reneging on agreements–sale of shares allotted to director of private company**

[Companies Act 1985 s.459.]

O appealed against the dismissal of his petition for relief under the Companies Act 1985 s.459 for undue prejudice caused by the breach of agreements that he was entitled to a half share of the profits of a private company, Pectel Ltd, and applied for an order that shares held by him and his wife should be purchased by P at a fair value. O started as an employee in the company in which P was the sole shareholder and director, but worked his way up to become a director, receiving an emolument in the form of 25 per cent of the issued share capital in the company. It was later agreed orally that O would be entitled to a half share of the profits and, subsequently in a written document, that O would acquire equal equity rights when net assets reached £500,000 and equal voting rights when the net assets reached £1,000,000. Although O received half of the profits for several years, P eventually reneged on both agreements and effectively forced O out of the company.

Held, allowing the appeal and the application, that there had been unfair prejudice to O's interests as a member of the company and that O's shares must be purchased by P at a fair value without discount because it was a minority shareholding. The parties' collaboration showed all the characteristics of a quasi partnership and, in general in such circumstances, it would only be as a member of a company that a party's interests would be unfairly prejudiced. The judge below had erred by attributing undue importance to the fact that O had started as an employee before being promoted to the board, and had not contributed capital, *R&H Electric Ltd v. Haden Bill Electrical Ltd* [1995] 2 B.C.L.C. 280, [1996] 1 C.L.Y. 1025 followed.

O'NEILL v. PHILLIPS, Trans. Ref: CHANF 95/1316/B; FC3 97/5397/B, May 1, 1997, Nourse, L.J., CA.

842. **Shareholders–minority shareholders–unfair prejudice–premature notice of petition–principles governing striking out procedure**

[Companies Act 1985 s.459.]

The petitioner argued that the respondents had been guilty of conduct that was unfairly prejudicial to him and issued a summons under the Companies Act 1985 s.459. The respondents applied to strike the application out as the petitioner had prematurely given notice of the petition before its advertisement and that amounted to an abuse of the process of the court.

Held, dismissing the application to strike out, that it was an abuse of the process of the court to bring to the attention of any person the fact that the petition existed where no direction as to advertisement had been given. In such cases the court had a discretion to make whatever order was fair and just, balancing the need to discourage such conduct against any purpose that would be served in striking out the proceedings. As a general rule the court would be ready to strike out a petition where the breach amounted to a serious abuse such as where there was some improper purpose behind the notification. The same applied where the respondent had suffered prejudice by reason of the abuse. In the present case the abuse was not so serious as to justify striking out the petition.

COMPANY (NO.002015 OF 1996), *Re* [1997] 2 B.C.L.C. 1, Judge Kaye Q.C., Ch D (Companies Court).

843. Shareholders—minority shareholders—unfair prejudice—purchase of minority shareholding—mistaken valuation—transfer of shares set aside

The plaintiffs succeeded in a claim alleging unfair prejudice to themselves as minority shareholders of two family companies. The articles of each company contained a pre-emption clause under which members of the company who wished to sell their shares were obliged to give notice of sale to the company and to offer the shares to other members of the company at a value to be fixed by the company's auditors. The judge ordered the plaintiffs to offer their shares to the other shareholders and ordered the defendant to purchase the shares. In her judgment the judge copied an error in the value of the property owned by the companies as given in evidence and that figure was used by the valuer instructed by the auditor to determine a fair price for the plaintiffs' shares. The defendant accepted the valuation and gave notice of his intention to buy the shares. The plaintiffs requested payment of the money, but issued proceedings to set aside the auditor's valuation and any share transfer based on the valuation. It was contended that the valuation was based on a fundamental mistake, that the auditor had acted with partiality and that he had wrongfully delegated the task of valuing the shares. The defendant argued that the plaintiffs were estopped from disputing the valuation by reason of their representation of their desire to sell the shares and that, by requesting payment, the plaintiffs had affirmed the contract.

Held, setting aside the transfer of the shares, that there had been no representation by the plaintiffs to the defendant to found an estoppel. There was no affirmation if the party making the affirmation did not know that there was a choice and that the making of a choice would be inferred from what he said or did. In the present case the plaintiffs' conduct was not sufficiently clear to amount to an affirmation as they had, at the same time as accepting payment, withheld an undertaking not to continue their action. Although the auditor had been imprudent in his dealings with the defendant's solicitor and with the professional valuers he had not gone so far that it could be said that he had acted with partiality or that he had delegated his valuing function.

MACRO v. THOMPSON (NO.3) [1997] 2 B.C.L.C. 36, Robert Walker, J., Ch D.

844. Shareholders—minority shareholders—unfair prejudice—quasi partnership—legitimate expectation of a role in the running of the company—dismissed and excluded without good reason—rights not restricted to strict rights under constitution—buy out ordered

[Companies Act 1985 s.459.]

Q acquired shares in the company, E, amounting to 15 per cent and was appointed a director at a time when the only other active director was R, the majority shareholder. Three other directors were subsequently appointed each with a shareholding of one share. After more than 20 years working for the company, Q was summarily dismissed and excluded from management. He presented a petition under the Companies Act 1985 s.459 alleging unfair prejudice in the conduct of the company's affairs.

Held, granting the relief sought and ordering the purchase of Q's shares on a pro rata basis, that there had been no justification for Q's dismissal nor for his exclusion from management. He had entered into the share agreement with the legitimate expectation of a role in the running of the company on a quasi partnership basis with R. It followed that Q's rights were not restricted solely to his strict rights under the constitution of the company and his service agreement. His shares would therefore be valued on a pro rata basis taking no account of the fact that he was a minority shareholder.

QUINLAN v. ESSEX HINGE CO LTD [1996] 2 B.C.L.C. 417, EW Hamilton Q.C., Ch D (Companies Court).

845. Shareholders—minority shareholders—unfair prejudice—quasi partnership—shareholders' informal agreement not transferred to restructured company—pre-emption rights

[Companies Act 1985 s.459.]

LU, a football club, was owned by the directors G, S and F who informally made a shareholders' agreement to offer each other their shares first if they decided to sell. The share capital was restructured so that the capital was acquired by L. The majority of the shares in L were registered in the names of three investment companies controlled by G, S and F respectively. Relations between S and F on the one hand and G on the other became strained. Takeover bids for L were made by Caspian and by Conrad. At a board meeting the majority (S and F) decided to accept the Caspian bid and, contrary to G's objection, rejected the Conrad bid. G's company brought a petition seeking the sale of the shares held by S and F's companies on the grounds that the affairs of L had been conducted in a way that was unfairly prejudicial to G's company. G alleged that L was a quasi partnership. S and F sought to strike the petition out for disclosing no cause of action.

Held, striking out the petition, that on the facts there were no grounds for finding any legitimate expectation that S and F would not sell their shares without first giving G an opportunity to buy them. Whatever G's legitimate expectations in relation to the shares held in LU, these could not be transferred to the shares held in L. An expectation that a shareholder would not sell his shares without the consent of the other shareholders was not a matter that related to the conduct of the company and was not a matter that fell within the scope of the Companies Act 1985 s.459.

LEEDS UNITED HOLDINGS PLC, *Re* [1996] 2 B.C.L.C. 545, Rattee, J., Ch D.

846. Shareholders—minority shareholders—unfair prejudice—writ action and unfair prejudice action—circumstance where leave would be required

[Companies Act 1985 s.459; Rules of the Supreme Court Ord.2, r.1, Ord.15, r.1, Ord.15, r.12A.]

P and D held shares in a company. P claimed by a writ action that in breach of an agreement D had caused the company to issue a disproportionate number of shares to them, drew excessive remuneration and diverted company benefits to themselves. P issued a petition under the Companies Act 1985 s.459 making substantially the same factual allegations but seeking wider relief including a court order that D purchase his shares. D applied to have the writ struck out on the basis that P had failed to obtain leave to issue, necessary pursuant to the Rules of the Supreme Court Ord.15, r.1. The district judge decided leave was not required and that in any event he would have exercised his discretion under the RSC Ord.2, r.1 in favour of P. D appealed.

Held, dismissing the appeal, that leave was required where an individual shareholder sought to claim in his personal capacity and as representative for all the shareholders in the company and P could not at this stage rely on the RSC Ord.15 r.12A(11), which might enable the court to dismiss the derivative claim for relief without prejudice to the remainder of P's claim. This was a case where the court could exercise its discretion to cure an irregularity under RSC Ord.2 r.1 if no prejudice flowed from it, which it did not as D would not be deprived of any limitation defence.

COOKE v. COOKE [1997] B.C.C. 17, Chadwick, J., Ch D.

847. Shareholders–remedies–oppressive or prejudicial conduct by company– shareholder could seek alternative remedy to winding up–Bermuda

[Companies Act 1981 s.111 (Bermuda); Companies Act 1985 s.459.]

Held, that in cases involving oppressive or prejudicial conduct by a company, it was open to a shareholder to apply to the court under the Bermuda Companies Act 1981 s.111, corresponding to the UK Companies Act 1985 s.459, for an alternative remedy to winding up, even though the basis of the petition was that the company was conducting business unlawfully.

BERMUDA CABLEVISION LTD v. COLICA TRUST CO LTD [1997] B.C.C. 982, Lord Steyn, PC.

848. Shareholders–voting rights–deadlock between two equal shareholders– court could not use power to call meeting under Companies Act 1985 s.371 to shift balance of power

[Companies Act 1985 s.371.]

T and R were equal 50 per cent shareholders in a company. T appealed against an order made under the Companies Act 1985 s.371 allowing R to outvote T in order to resolve deadlock between them.

Held, allowing the appeal, that the issue turned on whether s.371 was an appropriate means by which to determine a deadlock between two equal shareholders. *Opera Photographic Ltd, Re* [1989] 1 W.L.R. 634, [1989] C.L.Y. 321 and *Sticky Fingers Restaurant Ltd, Re* [1991] B.C.C. 754, [1992] C.L.Y. 380 merely showed that a minority shareholder could not be allowed to use quorum tactics to prevent a majority shareholder exercising his or her rights, and were inapplicable to the instant case. A potential deadlock at company meetings arising from an equal division of shares between two shareholders was taken to have been imposed with consent and for the protection of each shareholder. Section 371 was a procedural section, not one designed to affect shareholder voting rights, and the court accordingly had no jurisdiction under those provisions to make an order to allow R to override the wishes of T.

ROSS v. TELFORD, *The Times*, July 4, 1997, Nourse, L.J., CA.

849. Shares–Unichem Ltd

UNICHEM LIMITED (ALLOTMENT OF SHARES) REVOCATION ORDER 1997, SI 1997 1530; made under the Fair Trading Act 1973 s.90, Sch.8 para.1, Sch.8 para.2; and the Competition Act 1980 s.10. In force: July 17, 1997; £0.65.

This Order revokes the Unichem Limited (Allotment of Shares) Order 1989 (SI 1989 1061) made while Unichem Ltd was a registered industrial and provident society before its conversion to a Companies Act company and flotation.

850. Take overs–pension scheme assets–no breach of fiduciary duty where directors failed to secure undertaking of predator as to status of scheme surplus on takeover

[Companies Act 1985 s.459, s.461.]

P, minority preference shareholders in BH, claimed the company's affairs had been conducted in a manner unfairly prejudicial to their interests and sought relief under the Companies Act 1985 s.459 and s.461. In 1990 BM took over BH by purchasing issued ordinary shares. BH also had three classes of preference share listed on the Stock Exchange. At takeover, BH's two employee pension schemes had a funding surplus in that the actuary calculated that the rate of contribution exceeded that necessary for the scheme to meet its liabilities and BH thus was taking a contributions holiday. From 1991 the BH schemes were treated as if they had merged with the BM scheme and run together as a single fund. In 1994 there was a deed purporting to merge retrospectively the larger BH scheme with the BM scheme; no attempt was made with the smaller BH scheme. P sought relief under s.459 in respect of the purported merger. The BH board then recommended acceptance of BM's offer for all three classes of preference share. P rejected the offer, retained their holdings and petitioned as holders of preference shares. P claimed that BH ought to have recognised the pension funding surplus as an asset and secured BM's undertaking that it would continue to make the benefit available to BH, and that in the absence of such undertaking the transfer was not bona fide in the interests of BH. P claimed a breach of fiduciary duty by BH's directors for failing to question whether the transfer was in BH's interests, and that BM took the benefit of the pension surplus with notice of the breach of duty and was thus constructive trustee of the same. P sought an order under s.459 and s.461 of the 1985 Act that BM purchase the preference shares at a price to be determined by an independent valuer.

Held, dismissing the petition, that (1) BH's directors were in breach of duty to BH in failing properly to consider actuarial advice to merge the pension schemes, but that did not establish unfair prejudice; (2) it was fallacious to treat an actuarial value of the funding surplus as the value of a BH asset, or to argue that the purported merger of the schemes transferred that asset from BH to BM; the issue was whether the merger deprived or bestowed benefits deriving from the funding surplus such that BH ought to have secured some quid pro quo from BM; (3) the value of a contributions holiday was speculative, dependent on changes in investment return, unforeseen liabilities and differing actuarial assumptions, and BM would have refused to provide any undertaking from BM as a condition of merging the pension scheme; there was therefore no cause of action against the directors of BH in that respect worth pursuing, and (4) the only possible transfer of assets was the administrative process of treating the BH schemes as if they were part of, and subject to, the BM scheme, but the purported mergers were ineffective and the beneficial assets had never ceased to be subject to the trusts of the BH schemes.

BLACKWOOD HODGE PLC, *Re* [1997] B.C.C. 434, Parker, J., Ch D (Companies Court).

851. Winding up–foreign company–multi level marketing scheme–winding up of foreign company on public interest grounds–no sufficient connection with the jurisdiction–mere association insufficient

T was a company incorporated in the USA whose purpose was to invest a proportion of funds generated by a money circulation scheme administered by Titan International LLC, LLC. The scheme was a variation of one already ruled illegal under the Lotteries and Amusements Act 1976 s.1, *Senator Hanseatische Verwaltungsgesellschaft GmbH, Re* [1996] 2 B.C.L.C. 562, [1996] 1 C.L.Y. 1010. A successful application was made by the Secretary of State for the just and equitable winding up of LLC on public interest grounds and a provisional liquidator was appointed. A winding up order was, however, refused on the basis that T had no sufficient connection with the jurisdiction in accordance with the principles laid down in *Real Estate Development Co, Re* [1991] B.C.L.C. 210, [1992] C.L.Y. 2579 for an order to be made. The Secretary of State appealed.

Held, dismissing the appeal, that even taking into account further considerations such as the fact that the same solicitors acted for both companies (instructions being received from the same individual), there was no evidence that T was involved in the promotion of the scheme within the jurisdiction, nor even that it had any presence whatsoever in this country. Mere association with LLC was insufficient.

TITAN INTERNATIONAL INC, *Re*, Trans. Ref: CHANI 96/1251/B, March 10, 1997, Peter Gibson, L.J., CA.

852. Articles

Articles of association: valuation issues *(Angela Hennessey)*: S.J. 1997, 141 (19), 460-461. (Importance of clearly drafting clauses explaining how shares are to be valued on transfer, interpretation of fair value and open market value and who should undertake valuation exercise).

Blowing the whistle on fraud *(Keith Gaines)*: C.S.R. 1997, 21(14), 105-106. (Extent to which current law imposes duty on companies to report instances of fraud, and issues that might arise if there was statutory duty to do so).

Board meetings: best practice and new trends *(Harriet Creamer* and *Serena Michie)*: P.L.C. 1997, 8(4), 31-37. (Company law requirements focusing on directors duties and holding of meetings by telephone conference call or video link).

Breaking a deadlocked company *(James Dirks)*: Litigator 1997, July, 251-259. (Attempt to settle company dispute, raising issues over exercise of court's discretion to order that deadlocked company be wound up).

Buying target company shares during a takeover bid *(Lovell White Durrant)*: I.H.L. 1997, 50(May), 63-64. (Shortcomings of City Code in regulating acquisition of shares by bidders pending competition decisions and defensive purchases by advisers to target company).

City Code amendments *(John Bennett)*: C.S.R. 1997, 21(5), 33-34. (Extension of duty of disclosure to derivatives, amendments consequential on CREST, earnings enhancement statements and possible changes under Takeover Directive).

Combating fraud: the enemy within *(Jeremy Cole* and *Paul Natali)*: P.L.C. 1997, 8(6), 21-30. (Steps to be taken by businesses on discovering fraud, including securing assets, preventing further fraud, securing evidence, establishing solvency, notifying external parties and recovering funds).

Company charges *(Jennifer James)*: S.L.R. 1997, 21(Sum), 9-10. (Distinction between fixed and floating charges created by a company as security interest in property, with particular reference to freedom to deal with a charged asset).

Company law and trade in securities *(Takis Tridimas)*: I.C.L.Q. 1997, 46(1), 202-205. (Adoption of 13th Company Law Directive on take overs and recent EC cases).

Company share purchase *(Ian Saunders)*: Tax J. 1997, 426, 21-23. (Extent of statutory restriction on company providing financial assistance for acquisition of own shares and effect of changes proposed following Brady).

Corporate governance–fund managers' statements *(Allen & Overy)*: I.H.L. 1997, 47(Feb), 49-50. (Policy statements by Mercury Asset Management and National Association of Pension Funds advising on good corporate governance and investment management, especially relating to voting rights).

Corporate groups: legal aspects of the management dilemma *(Karen Yeung)*: L.M.C.L.Q. 1997, 2(May), 208-269. (Economic and legal ramifications of managing groups as integrated enterprises and as autonomous operations).

Directors' liability *(Andrew Edgar)*: S.J. 1997, 141(14), 328-330. (Circumstances in which a director rather than the company may incur criminal liability for actions, including product liability, health and safety, environmental liability, corporate killing and impact of EC law).

Directors' share dealings: share schemes and the Model Code *(David Cohen)* and *(David Collins)*: P.L.C. 1997, 8(9), 27-31. (Rules under Stock Exchange's Model Code to be observed by directors and other employees when dealing in shares obtained through employee share schemes).

Focus on company law *(James Dirks)*: C.L.W. 1997, 5(21), 2a-2b. (Remedies available to protect minority interests against unjust treatment in deadlocked companies).

From private to public and back: how to re-register *(Sarah Atkinson)*: P.L.C. 1997, 8(6), 16-20. (Regulatory effect of re-registering as public company, procedural and share capital requirements for private company to re-register as public company and procedure for reregistration back to private company).

Giving private shareholders a right to participate *(Jennifer Payne)*: Co. Law. 1997, 18(3), 90-93. (Fears for the erosion of private shareholders' rights in the face of trend towards increasing number of private shareholders holding shares through custodianship arrangements, as voiced by joint DTI and Treasury Consultation Document).

Hampel Committee preliminary report on corporate governance *(Freshfields)*: I.H.L. 1997, 53(Sep), 68-69. (Report published on August 5, 1997, with particular reference to recommendations on matters arising out of Greenbury Report relating to directors' remuneration and service contracts).

Important new cases regarding wrongful trading and shadow directors: shadow directors *(Denton Hall)*: I.H.L. 1997, 49(Apr), 75-76. (Whether shareholders of company were shadow directors and the distinction between actual and shadow directors).

Liability of parent companies for the actions of the directors of their subsidiaries *(Ross Grantham)*: Co. Law. 1997, 18(5), 138-148. (Conflict between tortious rules of vicarious liability and company law principles which emphasise relationship between company and director).

Listing Rules: Amendment 11 *(Lucian Pollington)*: C.S.R. 1997, 21(11), 81-82. (Amendment 11 in force September 8, 1997, on sponsors' duties, suitability for listing, controlling shareholder arrangements, presentation of financial information and other important changes).

Non-executive directors *(Sheena McCaffrey)*: C.S.R. 1997, 21(8), 57-58. (Selection, appointment, role and remuneration of non executive directors inlight of Hampel Committee report).

Paperless offices? *(Nicholas Hutton)*: C.S.R. 1997, 20(24), 190-191. (Company secretaries' duties where company's statutory and administrative records are stored on computer, the need to retain hard copies and admissibility in civil proceedings).

Paying for the benefits of incorporation *(Jennifer James)*: S.L.R. 1997, 22(Aut), 15-17. (Cases on interpretation of corporate personality and directors' responsibilities).

Statutory procedures: company and business names *(Neil McLean)*: C.S.R. 1997, 21(12), 96. (Legislative restrictions on choice and protection of company and business names).

Statutory procedures: directors *(Steve Martin)*: C.S.R. 1997, 21(10), 80. (Different types of directors of UK companies, role and responsibilities and relationship of shadow directors with board).

Statutory procedures: lost shareholders *(Claire Cranidge)*: C.S.R. 1997, 20(26), 208. (Company liability for unclaimed dividends and untraceable shareholders).

Statutory procedures: purchase of own shares *(Jerry P.L. Lai)*: C.S.R. 1997, 20(24), 192. (Exceptions to general rule under the Companies Act 1985 s.143 prohibiting a company from acquiring its own shares).

Statutory procedures: registered office *(Jerry P.L. Lai)*: C.S.R. 1997, 21(8), 64. (Regulations governing location of registered office, documents to be held there and procedure for change of registered office address).

Takeover timetable: against the clock *(Stephen Cooke)*: P.L.C. 1997, 8(2), 25, 27-30. (The offer timetable to be observed by bidder and target company in take overs of public companies set out in City Code on Take Overs and Mergers).

The Hampel Report: a move away from the "tick box" mentality *(Vanni Treves)*: C.L. 1997, 18, 56-57. (Impact of interim Hampel Report on development of code of corporate governance, including recommendations relating to directors, shareholders and AGMs).

The company and "social responsibility" *(Lilian Miles* and *Rima Abouchedid)*: Bus. L.R. 1997, 18(5), 110-112. (Ways in which company law could be developed to impose duties on directors towards wider community in which company operates).

The section 14 contract: limitation issues *(Katherine Reece-Thomas)*: C.J.Q. 1997, 16(Oct), 318-333. (Uncertainties arising from drafting of Companies Act 1985 concerning limitation periods for claims by company or member).

Two fundamental principles of company law? *(Aisha Yaqoob)*: Co. Law. 1997, 18(1), 14-19. (CA failed to address principles that company must maintain capital and must not make gratuitous dispositions of assets in case on failure to redeem shares).

Unfit to be a director? *(MichaelJames)*: S.J. 1997, 141 (7), 152-153. (Applications to disqualify directors of insolvent companies, including grounds for disqualification, period of disqualification, mitigating factors, procedure and discovery and expert evidence, with case law examples).

Virtue and virtuality: C.M. 1997, 9(11), 148-149. (Concern over regulatory implications of derivatives trading over Internet, including security of transactions and whether Internet is appropriate forum).

853. Books

Atkinson, Nigel; et al—Practitioner's Guide to the Stock Exchange "Yellow Book": 1997. Hardback: £60.00. City and Financial Publishing.

Bendaniel, David; Rosenblum, Arthur H.—International Mergers and Acquisitions. Frontiers in Finance. Hardback: £50.00. ISBN 0-471-16036-9. John Wiley and Sons.

Bertram, David; Maher, Paul—Due Diligence. Paperback: £85.00. ISBN 0-7520-0332-1. FT Law & Tax.

Chamberlain, Colin E.—Tolley's Practical Guide to Employees' Share Schemes. £49.95. ISBN 1-86012-535-2. Tolley Publishing.

Creighton, Brian; Wright, D.—Butterworth's Rights and Duties of Directors. Paperback: £50.00. ISBN 0-406-05342-1. Butterworth Law.

Davenport, Simon; Powell, William Giles—Disqualification of Company Directors. Hardback: £43.00. ISBN 0-421-54690-5. Sweet & Maxwell.

Davies, Paul L.; Prentice, Dan—Gower's Principles of Modern Company Law. 6th Ed. Hardback: £45.00. ISBN 0-421-52470-7. Paperback: £28.00. ISBN 0-421-52480-4. Sweet & Maxwell.

Defriez, Alistair; et al—Practitioner's Guide to the City Code on Takeovers and Mergers: 1997. Hardback: £60.00. City and Financial Publishing.

Dwyer, Maurice—Management Buy Outs. Hardback: £95.00. ISBN 0-421-52670-X. Sweet & Maxwell.

Farrar, John F.; Furey, Nigel; Hannigan, Brenda; Wylie, Philip—Farrar's Company Law. Paperback: £26.95. ISBN 0-406-04800-2. Butterworth Law.

Hatchick, Keith; Collins, David; Smith, Keith—Alternative Investment Market Handbook. Hardback: £40.00. ISBN 0-85308-406-8. Jordan.

Heshon, Dennis—Acquisitions and Group Structures. Legal Practice Course Resource Books. Paperback: £17.50. ISBN 0-85308-359-2. Jordan.

Hewitt, Ian—Joint Ventures. Commercial Series. £75.00. ISBN 0-7520-0448-4. FT Law & Tax.

Hicks, A.; Goo, S.—Cases and Materials on Company Law. 2nd Ed. £24.00. ISBN 1-85431-668-0. Blackstone Press.

Knight, William J.L.—Acquisition of Private Companies and Business Assets. Commercial Law Series. Paperback: £75.00. ISBN 0-7520-0292-9. FT Law & Tax.

Leighton, Gerald; Lowe, Jim—Jordans Company Secretarial Precedents. Hardback: £60.00. ISBN 0-85308-324-X. Jordan.

Maitland-Walker, Julian H.—Guide to European Company Laws. Hardback: £85.00. ISBN 0-421-57900-5. Sweet & Maxwell.

Rapakko, Timo—Unlimited Shareholder Liability in Multinationals. Hardback: £85.00. ISBN 90-411-0997-8. Kluwer Law International.

Ricardo-Campbell, Rita—Resisting Hostile Takeovers. Hardback: £51.95. ISBN 0-275-95830-2. Praeger Publishers.

Shearman, Ian—Shackleton on the Law and Practice of Meetings. Hardback: £68.00. ISBN 0-421-53910-0. Sweet & Maxwell.

Shilling, Helen—Corporate Governance. Paperback: £45.00. ISBN 0-406-04936-X. Butterworth Law.

Sinclair, Neil; Vogel, David; Snowden, Richard—Company Directors: Legal Advisor's Manual. Unbound/looseleaf: £185.00. ISBN 0-7520-0291-0. FT Law & Tax.

COMPETITION LAW

854. Abuse of dominant position—Art.86 applied to conduct on a distinct but associated market by trader which dominated another market—tied sales not objectively justified—proof of predatory pricing—European Union

[Treaty of Rome 1957 Art.86.]

T had 90 to 95 per cent of the market for aseptic carton packaging of liquid and semi liquid foods, and 50 to 55 per cent for non aseptic packaging. The Commission found that T was abusing its dominant position in the aseptic market in breach of the Treaty of Rome 1957 Art.86 by tying in sales of non-aseptic filling machines to carton sales and setting predatory prices for cartons and non-aseptic machines. The CFI dismissed T's action for an annulment of the decision and T appealed to the ECJ on the grounds that the court had erred in law (1) in considering that conduct in a non-dominated market, which was not intended to reinforce the position on the dominated market, was covered by Art.86; (2) in applying Art.86 where there was a natural link between the tied sales in accordance with commercial usage, and (3) in finding predatory pricing without it being established that T had a reasonable prospect of recouping its losses.

Held, dismissing the appeal, that (1) Art.86 presupposed a link between the dominant position and the alleged abusive conduct which was not normally present where conduct in a distinct market had an effect in that distinct market. The application of Art.86 to such conduct could be justified only in special circumstances. Special circumstances existed in the instant case as the potential customers were the same in both markets and T could use its almost complete domination of the aseptic market to act independently of other economic operators in the associated non-aseptic market; (2) Art.86's list of abusive practices was not exhaustive. Tied sales could constitute abuse unless objectively justified. T's tied sales were not justified as other manufacturers could produce cartons for use in T's machines and T could not justify its policy by reference to technical or product liability considerations, protection of public health or commercial reputation, and (3) it was necessary to be able to penalise predatory pricing whenever there was a risk that competitors would be eliminated without waiting for that result. Prices below average variable costs were always to be regarded as predatory as each sale involved a loss without there being any other conceivable economic purpose. Prices below average total costs were to be considered predatory only if an intention to eliminate was shown. In the instant case both categories had been demonstrated and it was not therefore appropriate to require proof that T had a realistic chance of recouping its losses, *Akzo Chemie BV v. Commission of the European Communities (C62/86)* [1991] E.C.R. I-3359, [1991] C.L.Y. 3834 applied.

TETRA PAK INTERNATIONAL SA v. COMMISSION OF THE EUROPEAN COMMUNITIES (C333/94) [1997] All E.R. (EC) 4, ML Sevon (President), ECJ.

855. Abuse of dominant position—complaint to European Commission—High Court jurisdiction to stay domestic proceedings pending decision

[Treaty of Rome 1957 Art.85, Art.86.]

In 1992 MTV complained to the European Commission that various companies which were concerned with broadcasting rights in music videos were parties to a price fixing agreement which had not been notified and had abused a dominant position, thus infringing the Treaty of Rome 1957 Art.85 and Art.86. MTV also sought damages for breaches of Art.85 and Art.86 in the High Court in England. The judge ordered that the action should be stayed temporarily until a specified date, after which preparations for trial could proceed, but accepted an undertaking not to set down for trial in the Chancery Division until the Commission had reached a decision. The defendants appealed against the dismissal of their renewed application for a full stay of proceedings. It was submitted that the judge lacked the jurisdiction to grant a partial stay. It was contended that ECJ case law, binding on national courts, precluded the exercise of any purported discretion in the circumstances of the instant case. It was not enough to pause, unless the answer to the complaint was clear, the national court should order the temporary cessation of all preparations for trial.

Held, dismissing the appeal, that the judge had recognised the risk that a premature judgment might conflict with a later decision of the Commission. The effect of ECJ case law concerned the extreme undesirability of inconsistent decisions of the Commission and of national courts. There was no authority for a submission that the ECJ intended to forbid a national court, in cases where the outcome was unclear, from allowing the preparation of proceedings to go ahead until a point short of decision or any reason why it should seek to intrude in that area. The power of national courts to order their own procedure, so long as no Community interest was adversely affected, had always been respected. It was a matter for national courts to ensure that litigants before them were not unfairly treated. In the instant case, the judge had concluded that the potential injustice to MTV of prolonged delay before damages could be recovered outweighed the potential prejudice to the defendants if they had to do a lot of preparation (for which they would be compensated in costs if successful), *BRT v. SABAM* [1974] E.C.R. 51, *Garden Cottage Foods v. Milk Marketing Board* [1984] A.C. 130, [1983] C.L.Y. 2987, *Delimitis v. Henninger Brau AG (C234/89)* [1991] E.C.R. I-935, [1991] C.L.Y. 3979 and *Gottrup-klim Grovvareforeninger v. Dansk Lanburgs Grovvareselskab AMBA* [1994] E.C.R. I-5641, [1995] 1 C.L.Y. 617 considered.

MTV EUROPE v. BMG RECORD (UK) LTD [1997] Eu L.R. 100, Sir Thomas Bingham, M.R., CA.

856. Advertising–quantitative restrictions–"British meat" logo

See FOOD AND DRUGS: Meat and Livestock Commission v. Manchester Wholesale Meat & Poultry Market Ltd. §2550

857. Free movement of goods–parallel import–trade mark protection prior to accession

See PATENTS: Merck & Co Inc v. Primecrown Ltd (C267/95). §3892

858. Groups of companies–concerted practices–subsidiary not autonomous–applicability of Art.85(1)–European Union

[Treaty of Rome 1957 Art.85(1), Art.86.]

Held, that the Treaty of Rome 1957 Art.85(1), prohibiting agreements between undertakings which had the aim or effect of preventing competition, was not applicable where a company and its subsidiaries formed a single economic unit within which the subsidiaries enjoyed no real autonomy in determining their activities, even though the parent company's policy of dividing national markets between its subsidiaries could affect a third party's competitive position. However, Art.86 could apply to such unilateral conduct if the conditions laid down therein were fulfilled.

VIHO EUROPE BV v. COMMISSION OF THE EUROPEAN COMMUNITIES (PARKER PEN LTD INTERVENING) (C73/95P) [1997] All E.R. (EC) 163, Judge not specified, ECJ.

859. Licensed premises–tied estates–supply of beer

SUPPLY OF BEER (TIED ESTATE) (AMENDMENT) ORDER 1997, SI 1997 1740; made under the Fair Trading Act 1973 s.56, s.90, s.134, Sch.8 para.1, Sch.8 para.2. In force: August 22, 1997; £0.65.

This Order amends the Supply of Beer (Tied Estate) Order 1989 (SI 1989 2390) which provides that brewers and brewery groups owning more than two thousand licensed premises must allow their "tied" premises to sell one brand of draught cask-conditioned beer supplied by someone chosen by the tenant or recipient of the loan. This Order provides that from April 1, 1998, such brewers and brewery groups must also allow their tied premises to sell one brand of bottle-conditioned beer supplied by someone chosen by the tenant or recipient of the loan.

860. Licensed premises–tied house tenancy–applicability of Art.85

[Treaty of Rome 1957 Art.85; Council Regulation 1984/83 on the application of Art.85(3) of the Treaty to categories of exclusive purchasing agreements; Rules of the Supreme Court Ord.14.]

S, a brewery company, claimed summary judgment under RSC Ord.14 against B, a tenant of one of its public houses. B had accepted the obligations of a tied house, but eventually stopped paying rent and obtained supplies of intoxicating liquor from elsewhere. S issued proceedings in respect of rent, trade debts and mesne profits. B claimed that the tied provisions of his tenancy had as their object or effect the prevention, restriction or distortion of competition within the EU, and thereby infringed the Treaty of Rome 1957 Art.85. S refuted that B had raised an arguable defence

Held, awarding summary judgment in S's favour, that B had not raised an arguable defence to S's claim. Article 85 was intended to regulate the position between competitors operating in the same market but not between a particular supplier and customer, *Plessey Co v. General Electric Co, Siemens AG and GEC Siemens* [1990] E.C.C. 384, [1991] C.L.Y. 3821 considered. B was not entitled to rely on Art.85 as a defence against S his landlord, *Inntrepreneur Estates v. Smyth* (Unreported, 1993) and *Inntrepreneur Estates v. Milne* (Unreported, 1993) followed. In addition the agreement between B and S was protected from the operation of Art.85 by Council Regulation 1984/83 on the basis that B agreed to obtain supplies only from S in consideration for special commercial or financial advantages.

SCOTTISH & NEWCASTLE PLC v. BOND, Trans. Ref: 1996-S-No.223, March 25, 1997, Judge Peter Crawford Q.C., QBD.

861. Licensed premises–tied house tenancy–restrictive trade practices– proceedings stayed pending European Commission decision on parent company application

[Treaty of Rome 1957 Art.85.]

H appealed against an order staying proceedings pending the determination of an application to the CEC by MB's parent company, S. At first instance H had contended that the brewery tie provisions in a lease formerly between H and MB for the tenancy of a public house infringed the Treaty of Rome 1957 Art.85(1). However, in the intervening period, S had launched an application and notification with CEC for either a negative clearance or block exemption for the brewery tie clause, and similar applications had also been brought by other breweries.

Held, dismissing the appeal and granting a stay pending a decision by CEC, that given the dual competence of national courts and CEC in Art.85 cases the potential for inconsistent or conflicting decisions was undesirable and to be avoided where possible, *Delimitis v. Henninger Brau AG (C234/89)* [1991] E.C.R. I-935, [1991] C.L.Y. 3979 and *MTV (Europe) v. BMG Records (UK) Ltd* [1997] 1 C.M.L.R. 867, [1997] C.L.Y. 855 considered. A stay was appropriate here, given the absence of a continuing relationship between H and MB, the lack of progress in the proceedings to date and the fact that H was seeking a money judgment, thereby allowing for any delay to be compensated by interest. However, to obviate any risk to H due to undue delay in proceedings before CEC, or if CEC indicated the matter was suitable for resolution by the national courts, H would be entitled to have the stay lifted in the event of a material change of circumstances.

HARRISON v. MATTHEW BROWN PLC, Trans. Ref: CH.1996-H-3184, May 16, 1997, Judge Robert Englehart Q.C., Ch D.

862. Net Book Agreement–application to discharge orders that agreement not contrary to public interest–collapse of NBA undermined basis of previous orders

[Restrictive Trade Practices Act 1976 s.4; Resale Prices Act 1976 s.14, s.17.]

The Director General of Fair Trading applied under the Restrictive Trade Practices Act 1976 s.4 and the Resale Prices Act 1976 s.17 for the discharge of orders previously made by the court that restrictions on the resale price of books under the Net Book Agreement, NBA, were not contrary to the public interest.

Held, allowing the application, that the jurisdiction of the court to review and reverse its own orders was subject to express limitations and applications under the RTPA s.4 and the RPA s.17 involved a two stage process. Firstly, it was necessary to determine whether a material change amounting to a "change in an essential part of the reasoning by which the court reached its previous conclusion" had occurred, *Cement Makers Federation Agreement (No.2), Re* [1974] I.C.R. 445, [1974] C.L.Y. 3810 applied. If there had been a material change, the second stage required consideration of (1) whether the NBA restrictions were in the public interest, and (2) whether books and maps ought to be exempted for the purposes of the RPA s.14. On the facts, the court was satisfied that relevant changes in circumstances had occurred, the most important being the collapse of the NBA itself, with none of the leading publishers publishing at net prices. Collapse of the NBA had undermined the whole basis of the court's previous reasoning and the court was not satisfied that ending the NBA would result in any of the adverse consequences which had founded the basis for the previous orders, such that none of the conditions which would justify continuing retail maintenance under the RPA s.14 was satisfied.

NET BOOK AGREEMENT 1957 (M AND N), *Re, The Times,* March 20, 1997, Ferris, J., RPC.

863. Quantitative restrictions–Member State prohibiting marketing of biocidal product–validity of restriction given nature of hazardous substance– European Union

[Treaty of Rome 1957 Art.30, Art.36.]

B managed a Belgian supermarket which imported and sold a product that contained a dangerous substance. The product was made and sold in the Netherlands by the same supermarket and had been given the appropriate Dutch authorisation although it had not been given the equivalent Belgian authorisation. B was prosecuted. She argued that the requirement that the product have Belgian authorisation was a measure having equivalent effect to a quantitative restriction prohibited under Treaty of Rome 1957 Art.30. The national court stayed the proceedings and referred the matter to the Court of Justice.

Held, that legislation prohibiting the sale of the product without prior authorisation was permissible. Member States were required to bring about a relaxation of intra Community trade restrictions and were therefore required to take account of technical or chemical analyses or tests undertaken in another state. The measure did have an effect equivalent to a quantitative restriction but the product in question was a biocide for which there were no Community harmonisation measures. National legislation prohibiting the marketing of biocidal products without prior authorisation was justified under Art.36 of the Treaty.

CRIMINAL PROCEEDINGS AGAINST BRANDSMA (C293/94) [1996] All E.R. (EC) 837, DAO Edward (President), ECJ.

864. Restrictive trade practices–consent orders–jurisdiction to deliver reasoned judgment

[Restrictive Trade Practices Act 1976.]

The Director General of Fair Trading applied for orders against API and others under the Restrictive Trade Practices Act 1976. All the represented parties had offered to make undertakings equal to the most severe order the court had the power to make and the only unrepresented party had agreed to have a similar order made against it. Even though the applications were unopposed, the Director General asked the court to deliver a reasoned judgment in order to highlight the seriousness of the respondents' conduct, attract publicity, help deal with issues arising out of future agreements, provide greater certainty and aid the court if the respondents applied to have the undertakings discharged. The respondents opposed the request, contending that the court had no jurisdiction to make a judgment where there had been a consent order.

Held, that the court had jurisdiction to deliver a reasoned judgment in the case of a consent order, even though it might not be necessary to do so. However, in this case, it would be wrong to give a reasoned judgment because the Director General wanted the court to make findings of fact that were not admitted by the parties and would not be included in the court orders. It would be wrong to evaluate the extent of a restrictive practice where it would not affect the content of the court order, nor should the court try to solve problems arising from potential future agreements or applications to discharge the undertakings. Although the court might issue a general warning about the legal consequences of particular conduct, this was not appropriate here and publicity should rarely, if ever, be a reason for the court elucidating its decision in a particular manner.

AGREEMENTS RELATING TO THE SUPPLY OF FREIGHT FORWARDING SERVICES BETWEEN THE UNITED KINGDOM AND AUSTRALASIA, *Re, The Times*, January 24, 1997, Ferris, J., RPC.

865. **Restrictive trade practices–exclusive purchasing agreements for milk not registrable–meaning of "to other persons"**

[Restrictive Trade Practices Act 1976 s.28, Sch.3(2).]

A, who was a milkman, appealed against a decision on a preliminary issue that a contract made between him and the predecessor in title of D was not a restrictive agreement registrable under the Restrictive Trade Practices Act 1976. A contended that a restriction preventing him from selling, to customers of the dairy, milk that he had purchased elsewhere, was prima facie registrable and that the fact that s.28 and Sch.3(2)(a) contained the words "to other persons" whereas Sch.3(2)(b) did not, implied that a restriction could only be exempted if it applied to all persons and not to a limited set.

Held, dismissing the appeal, that the words "to other persons" were included for clarity and did not have the effect contended for, *MD Foods Plc (formerly Associated Dairies Ltd) v. Baines* [1997] 2 W.L.R. 364, [1997] C.L.Y. 4477 considered.

DALE FARM DAIRY GROUP LTD (T/A NORTHERN DAIRIES) v. AKRAM, Trans. Ref: CCRTF 95/0693/C, July 17, 1997, Schiemann, L.J., CA.

866. **Restrictive trade practices–non notifiable agreements–sale and purchase, share subscription and franchise agreements**

RESTRICTIVE TRADE PRACTICES (NON-NOTIFIABLE AGREEMENTS) (SALE AND PURCHASE, SHARE SUBSCRIPTION AND FRANCHISE AGREEMENTS) ORDER 1997, SI 1997 2945; made under the Restrictive Trade Practices Act 1976 s.27A. In force: January 9, 1998; £1.10.

This Order specifies descriptions of non-notifiable agreements for the purposes of the Restrictive Trade Practices Act 1976 s.27A.

867. **Restrictive trade practices–non notifiable agreements–turnover threshold**

RESTRICTIVE TRADE PRACTICES (NON-NOTIFIABLE AGREEMENTS) (TURNOVER THRESHOLD) AMENDMENT ORDER 1997, SI 1997 2944; made under the Restrictive Trade Practices Act 1976 s.27A. In force: January 9, 1998; £0.65.

This Order amends the Restrictive Trade Practices (Non-notifiable Agreements) (Turnover Threshold) Order 1996 (SI 1996 348) by increasing the aggregate turnover threshold for parties in respect of non-notifiable agreements to £50 million.

868. **Sporting organisations–membership restrictions–rugby clubs challenging decision that clubs joining Welsh Rugby Union must remain members for 10 years**

[Treaty of Rome 1957 Art.85, Art.86.]

W, on behalf of Cardiff Athletic Club and Cardiff Rugby Football Club, CRFC, and R on behalf of Ebbw Vale Rugby Football Club, EVRFC, applied for injunctions restraining P, on behalf of the Welsh Rugby Union, WRU, from restricting their actions pending the result of litigation. WRU demanded that clubs wishing to join it must remain members for 10 years, whereas the clubs contended that five years was adequate to ensure stability. The clubs alleged that the 10 year rule was a breach of contract, in restraint of trade and in breach of the Treaty of Rome 1957 Art.85 and Art.86 since if they did not join they would be prevented from playing either in Europe or in the Premier League. WRU contended that the court should be slow to intervene in respect of decisions taken by a sporting body.

Held, granting injunctive relief to restrain P from preventing W from entering the Premier League or from playing in Europe for 12 months, that notwithstanding a reluctance to intervene against sporting bodies, there was an arguable case with a real prospect of success and both parties possessed sufficient funds to pay damages if they lost, *American Cyanamid Co v. Ethicon Ltd* [1975] A.C. 396, [1975] C.L.Y. 2640 followed.

WILLIAMS v. PUGH; RUSSELL v. PUGH, Trans. Ref: 1997-W-No.497, 1997-R-No.679, July 23, 1997, Popplewell, J., QBD.

869. **Standard forms of contract–retransmission agreement between cable operators and musical copyright collecting society–negative clearance–jurisdiction of Court of First Instance–European Union**

[Treaty of Rome 1957 Art.85; Council Regulation 17/62 implementing Art.85 and Art.86 of the Treaty Art.3.]

In May 1985 the representatives of cable operators in the Netherlands concluded an agreement with the holders of rights in television and radio programmes, allowing standard form contracts to be entered into on an individual basis between rights holders and cable operators. B, as agent for all holders of Netherlands copyrights, and as the holder of a legal monopoly as the Netherlands organisation for owners of musical copyright, was a party to the standard form contracts. The standard form contracts were notified to the Commission in December 1985 for the purpose of obtaining a negative clearance or an exemption from competition rules under the Treaty of Rome 1957 Art.85(3). The Commission replied that it did not intend to investigate the notified agreements with regard to the competition rules. K, a composer and manager of a photographic agency, began in 1985 to write to the Commission complaining of the de facto monopolies enjoyed by societies such as B and objecting to the standard form agreements. In October 1990 K lodged a complaint concerning those agreements, seeking inter alia, that the Commission's decision not to initiate the investigation procedure in Council Regulation 17/62 Art.3 in respect of the agreements following K's complaints, be declared void. K's complaints were rejected by the Commission, and he applied to the Court for annulment of the decision and compensation.

Held, rejecting K's claims and ordering that he pay costs, that (1) as held in *Koelman v. Commission (T56/92)* [1993] E.C.R. II-1267 and *Viho Europe BV v. Commission (T109/92)* [1995] E.C.R. II-17, [1995] 1 C.L.Y. 649, the Court had no jurisdiction to issue directions to the Community institutions, member states or to natural or legal persons. Accordingly, K's requests that it was for the Court to ensure that authors were free to choose the organisation to manage their works, and that these were given fair access to the market, were inadmissible. Only that part of K's complaint which sought to annul the Commission's decision not to initiate the procedure in Regulation 17/62 Art.3 was admissible; (2) the Commission might reject a complaint made under Regulation 17/62 Art.3 on the ground that the agreements complained of satisfied, in any event, the requirements laid down in the Treaty Art.85(3) for grant of an exemption from prohibition, even though the Commission had not issued a decision to the parties concerned to exempt the agreements or given a definitive decision on the agreements compatibility with the Treaty Art.85(1), and (3) the Commission did not commit a manifest error of appraisal by partly basing its rejection of K's complaint on the fact that the standard agreements satisfy in any event the condition laid down in the Treaty Art.85(3). K adduced no evidence to support his assertion that the agreements did not constitute the most effective and efficient method of ensuring the lawful transmission of programmes by cable and that the Commission's assessments were therefore vitiated by a manifest error of appraisal.

KOELMAN v. COMMISSION OF THE EUROPEAN COMMUNITIES (T575/93) [1996] E.M.L.R. 555, Barrington (President), CFI.

870. Articles

A new approach in competition cases? *(Simon Holmes)*: Eur. Counsel 1997, 2(1), 35-39. (Analysis of Kimberley-Clark merger its effect on cooperation between CEC and national competition authorities).

Access to the case file: B.L.E. 1997, 97(2), 6-7. (CEC Notice on extent to which alleged infringers in competition investigations are entitled to disclosure of documents).

Cartels under the EU competition rules *(Jacques Buhart* and *Stephen O. Spinks)*: Eur. Counsel 1997, 2(8), Supp Com 23-27. (Including enforcement and investigative powers of CEC).

Commercial agreements under the EU competition rules *(John Boyce)*: Eur. Counsel 1997, 2(8), Supp Com 28-33. (Application of EU competition law to different types of commercial agreements, with flow chart on determining whether notification is necessary).

Commitments in phase one merger proceedings: the Commission's power to accept and enforce phase one commitments *(Morten P. Broberg)*: C.M.L. Rev. 1997, 34(4), 845-866.

Competition complaints: complaining to the Commission *(Michael Reynolds* and *Philip Mansfield)*: Eur. Counsel 1997, 2(5), 33-38. (Guidelines for bringing successful complaint to CEC in respect of alleged infringements of Treaty of Rome 1957 Art.85 and Art.86).

Dominant positions and monopolies *(Richard Eccles)*: Eur. Counsel 1997, 2(8), Supp Com 17-22. (Issues relating to product and geographic market definition).

EU competition law: implications of international joint ventures and other common commercial arrangements *(Luan Kane* and *Barbara Linehan)*: C. & E.L. 1997, 2(2), 11-14.

Joint brand advertising: is it allowed? *(Erik R. Vollebregt)*: E.C.L.R. 1997, 18(4), 242-250. (Circumstances in which joint advertising under common brand is permissible under the Treaty of Rome 1957 Art.85, with discussion of CEC and ECJ cases).

New rules on comparative advertising *(John Sipling)*: Paisner E.B. 1997, 13(Aut), 1. (Conditions in Directive 97/55 which comparative advertising must fulfil to prevent it being used in anti competitive or unfair manner).

Non-competition factors and their future relevance under European merger law *(David Banks)*: E.C.L.R. 1997, 18(3), 182-186.

Parallel imports - exploiting EC competition law *(Velia Maria Leone)*: I.H.L. 1997, 50(May), 39-42. (Ways in which manufacturers attempt to prevent parallel imports and extent to which competition law protects parallel trading).

Recent developments in United Kingdom competition law *(Aidan Robertson)*: J.B.L. 1997, Jul, 358-368. (Including attempts to reform law and recent cases and statutory instruments).

Rethinking Walt Wilhelm, or the supremacy of Community competition law over national law *(Robert Walz)*: E.L.R. 1996, 21(6), 449-464. (whether concept of parallel application appropriate basis for relationship between EU and domestic competition law).

Rights of complainants in Community law *(Ignace Maselis* and *Hans M. Gilliams)*: E.L.R. 1997, 22(2), 103-124.

Selective distribution systems *(John Boyce* and *Diane Somborn)*: Eur. Counsel 1997, 2(2), 47-53. (Advice for suppliers of cars, technical products and luxury brands on selecting dealers without breaching EU competition law, (includes flowcharts)).

Subsidiarity in Community antitrust law: setting the right agenda *(Rein Wesseling)*: E.L.R. 1997, 22(1), 35-54. (Evolution of EU competition law, its original purpose, development and whether enforcement powers should be strengthened).

Tetra Pak II—lack of reasoning in Court's judgment *(Valentine Korah)*: E.C.L.R. 1997, 18(2), 98-103. (Whether ECJ should give its reasons rather than just judgments in important competition decisions).

The complainant in competition cases: a progress report *(Christopher S. Kerse)*: C.M.L. Rev. 1997, 34(2), 213-265. (Locus standi to complain of breaches of Art.85 and Art.86, grounds for rejecting complaints, role of national authorities and courts, extent of CEC's competence and complainant's right to information regarding decision to reject).

The demise of resale price maintenance *(Craig Pouncey)*: C.L. 1997, 13, 78. (Approach of UK competition law to resale price maintenance agreements).

The franchise agreements block exemption *(John Boyce* and *Anny Tubbs)*: Eur. Counsel 1997, 2(1), 49-54. (Conditions that must be fulfilled for franchise agreements to benefit from block exemption, including flow chart).

The international dimension of EC competition law: the case of the Europe Agreement *(A.M. Van den Bossche)*: E.C.L.R. 1997, 18(1), 24-37. (With reference to undertakings in agreements between EU and central and eastern European countries).

Unilateral agreements and EC competition law *(Robert Lane)*: Edin. L.R. 1997, 1(4), 494-500. (With reference to parallel imports).

United Kingdom: from notification to approval *(Richard Taylor)*: Eur. Counsel 1997, 2(8), 117-124. (Analysis of competition law and application of EU rules in UK, with contact details, powers of relevant authorities and flow chart of merger notification requirements).

871. Books

Dworkin, Gerald—Unfair Competition Law. Hardback: £55.00. ISBN 0-421-47480-7. Sweet & Maxwell.

Korah, Valentine—Introductory Guide to EC Competition Law and Practice. Paperback: £22.50. ISBN 1-901362-27-2. Hart Publishing.

Whish, Richard—Competition Law. Paperback: £29.95. ISBN 0-406-00266-5. Butterworth Law.

CONFLICT OF LAWS

872. Bills of lading—exclusive jurisdiction clause—time bar

Under a bill of lading, there was a term that all disputes be referred to the courts of South Korea. A salvage service was provided in respect of the vessel for which M disputed the rateable proportion of liability of salvage. The matter was time barred in

South Korea and there was a promptly served English writ. The issue arose whether the choice of jurisdiction clause should be enforced.

Held, the contractual jurisdiction should be enforced unless strong cause was shown by M for not doing so, *El Amria, The* [1981] 2 Lloyds Rep. 119, [1980] C.L.Y. 322. M had shown strong cause on these facts because there was a need to render all of the many claims into one jurisdiction. By the claim proceeding in England and South Korea there would be decisions as to identical facts. Given the small size of the claim, it should be heard in the jurisdiction where it could be most conveniently and cost effectively dealt with. Further, the case would probably be disposed of in South Korea on grounds of cost, which would be unjust. In the circumstances, England was the best jurisdiction to concentrate all of these claims. There was a serious issue to be tried and it was on that basis that a stay would not be enforced solely on the grounds of the existence of the time bar in South Korea.

MAHAVIR MINERALS LTD v. CHO YANG SHIPPING CO LTD (THE MC PEARL) [1997] 1 Lloyd's Rep. 566, Rix, J., QBD (Adm Ct).

873. **Choice of law—insurance contracts—insurance policies centred exclusively on United Kingdom—applicable law English law**

[Insurance Companies Act 1982 Sch.3A Part 1 s.94B; Insurance Companies (Amendment) Regulations 1990 (SI 1990 2890); Second Council Directive 88/357 on coordination of laws relating to direct insurance other than life insurance.]

The issue centred on the choice of law for two policies of insurance which centred exclusively and expressly on the United Kingdom. The plaintiff was a French entity; the defendant was organised in the USA. There was no choice of law clause in either contract. Rather, choice of law was to be determined with reference to the Insurance Companies Act 1982 Sch.3A Part 1 s.94B, as amended by the Insurance Companies (Amendment) Regulations 1990. N appealed contending that French law was the proper law for the claim, by which law a claim by C would be statute barred.

Held, dismissing the appeal, that the presumption that English law was the applicable law had not been rebutted. The office of the policyholder was the London office for the purposes of the policies. This was therefore the significant geographical location within the terms of the Second Council Directive 88/357, and the 1982 Act. Furthermore, the risks related to property and activities to be carried on in the United Kingdom, and the payment of premiums and claims was to be in the United Kingdom.

CREDIT LYONNAIS v. NEW HAMPSHIRE INSURANCE CO [1997] 2 Lloyd's Rep. 1, Hobhouse, L.J., CA.

874. **Foreign judgments—enforcement—natural justice—judgment obtained in contravention of orders of Bermudan court—Bermuda**

Al, a Bermudan company, reinsured risks of N who went into liquidation in New York in 1984, M being appointed liquidator. In 1985 M sought to recover sums said to be due under the treaties. In 1987 the Bermuda court made an order restraining M from taking or continuing proceedings. M commenced contempt proceedings against Al in New York. In 1991 the New York Supreme Court, on M's motion, ordered that Al's answer in the New York proceedings be struck out unless Al posted pre-answer security of over $10 million within 30 days. Al did not, judgment was entered in default, and M applied to the Bermuda court to enforce the final judgment for over $16 million obtained in 1994.

Held, dismissing M's action, that (1) M was in contempt of the Bermuda court as the 1987 order was valid until set aside, and M's continued proceedings were in breach of the same; further the contempt proceedings were an obvious attempt to interfere with the Bermuda proceedings; (2) M's continuing contempt was a complete bar to M seeking the exercise of the Bermuda court's powers, alternatively the same would be refused as a matter of discretion, and (3) it was contrary to natural justice to require a defendant to put up, as a condition of defending, a security he could not meet; the New York courts wrongly regarded as irrelevant the evidence that AI could not meet the sum imposed, on the evidence AI could not meet it, and there could be no issue of estoppel where the New York courts had not decided whether the proceedings against AI in New York conformed with the English ideas of substantial or natural justice, *MV Yorke Motors v. Edwards* [1982] 1 All E.R. 1024, [1982] C.L.Y. 2398 applied.

MUHL v. ARDRA INSURANCE CO LTD [1997] 6 Re L.R. 206, Richard Ground, Sup Ct (Ber).

875. **Foreign judgments–res judicata–barring of claim in rem against ship in England brought when claim in personam against shipowners pending in India**

[Civil Jurisdiction and Judgments Act 1982 s.34.]

An action in rem against a ship must be treated as an action against the shipowners themselves and will be barred by the Civil Jurisdiction and Judgments Act 1982 s.34 following a foreign judgment against them in a claim in personam arising from the same cause of action. The Indian government, IG, had succeeded in an action in personam in India for short delivery of cargo against ISC, owners of a ship, who had jettisoned IG's cargo following a fire. Before the judgment, IG brought an action in rem in England, against a sister ship, for loss of cargo in respect of the same incident. IG appealed against a Court of Appeal ruling ([1997] 1 W.L.R. 538, [1996] 1 C.L.Y. 1105) allowing ISC's appeal against a decision that IG's claim in rem did not fall to be barred under the Civil Jurisdiction and Judgments Act 1982 s.34, as an action in personam and an action in rem fell to be treated as actions between different parties even when they arose from the same cause of action.

Held, dismissing the appeal, that IG's action in rem had to be regarded as an action "brought... between the same parties or their privies" within s.34 as, in an action in rem against a ship, the real defendants were the shipowners, *Compania Naviera Vascongada v. SS Cristina* [1938] A.C. 485 followed. As the policy behind the barring of actions under s.34 was that it was unjust to allow the same matter to be litigated for a second time between the same parties, it was wrong to allow an action in rem to proceed where a foreign judgment in personam had been obtained based on the same cause of action.

REPUBLIC OF INDIA v. INDIA STEAMSHIP CO LTD (INDIAN ENDURANCE AND INDIAN GRACE) (NO.2) [1997] 3 W.L.R. 818, Lord Steyn, HL.

876. **Judgment debts–no satisfaction of judgment debt by garnishee order– Zambian foreign exchange rules–no jurisdiction to enforce foreign public law**

C, a judgment creditor, appealed against a refusal to make absolute a garnishee order nisi against Z, a mining company and the largest foreign currency earner in Zambia. Z were required under Zambian law to give almost half their foreign earnings to B, the judgment debtor, who had given the company written directions indicating the amount of foreign earnings they could retain but much of the remainder was deposited in UK bank accounts. C argued that the foreign exchange which had been paid into Z's own account should be garnished to satisfy the outstanding judgment debt against B and contended that B had a civil cause of action against Z to recover the foreign currency which English courts had jurisdiction to enforce.

Held, dismissing the appeal, that B's directions did not give rise to a civil cause of action because the mechanisms in place for regulating the disposition of foreign money were explicitly criminal. The payment obligations imposed on Z were public law requirements calling for precise compliance and as such did not have the status of civil law debts. Furthermore, English courts had no jurisdiction to enforce C's claim since to do so would constitute the enforcement of a foreign public law and the assertion of authority over another independent

sovereignty, *Government of India v. Taylor* [1955] A.C. 491, [1995] 1 C.L.Y. 377 considered.
CAMDEX INTERNATIONAL LTD v. BANK OF ZAMBIA (NO.3) [1997] 6 Bank. L.R. 44, Simon Brown, L.J., CA.

877. Judgments and orders—reciprocal enforcement—Gibraltar

CIVIL JURISDICTION AND JUDGMENTS ACT 1982 (GIBRALTAR) ORDER 1997, SI 1997 2602; made under the Civil Jurisdiction and Judgments Act 1982 s.39. In force: February 1, 1998; £1.10.
The effect of this Order is to make provision corresponding to the relevant provisions of the Brussels Convention 1968 for the purpose of regulating, as between the United Kingdom and Gibraltar, the jurisdiction of courts and the recognition and enforcement of judgments. For this purpose the Order provides, in effect, that Gibraltar shall be treated as if it were a separate Contracting State.

878. Judgments and orders—reciprocal enforcement—Gibraltar

RECIPROCAL ENFORCEMENT OF JUDGMENTS (ADMINISTRATION OF JUSTICE ACT 1920, PART II) (AMENDMENT) ORDER 1997, SI 1997 2601; made under the Administration of Justice Act 1920 s.14. In force: February 1, 1998; £0.65.
This Order amends the Reciprocal Enforcement of Judgments (Administration of Justice Act 1920, Part II) (Consolidation) Order 1984 (SI 1984 129) by deleting the entry relating to Gibraltar. Relevant judgments given after February 1, 1998, will be enforced in the United Kingdom in accordance with the provisions of the Civil Jurisdiction and Judgments Act 1982 (Gibraltar) Order 1997 (SI 1997 2602).

879. Jurisdiction—actions brought in England and France—English proceedings stayed pending outcome of French litigation

[Brussels Convention on Jurisdiction and Enforcement of Judgments in Civil and Commercial Matters 1968; Civil Jurisdiction and Judgments Act 1982; Warsaw Convention on International Carriage by Air 1929 Art.28.]
An aircraft belonging to A crashed killing a number of passengers while on route to Hong Kong. D were relatives and dependants of the victims of that crash who sought damages against A and the manufacturer of the aircraft in actions brought in France and England. A contended that the matter should be governed by the Warsaw Convention and that the action should be brought in Russia, England or Hong Kong under the terms of Art.28. On that basis A challenged the proceedings in the French courts as being contrary to international law and beyond the jurisdiction of those courts, thus seeking an anti suit injunction. The English proceedings had been commenced in case the French courts were found not to have jurisdiction. D sought to stay proceedings under the inherent jurisdiction of the court further to the Brussels Convention 1968 Art.21 and Art.22. However the Brussels Convention Art.57 provided that it was not to interfere with the terms of any other convention.
Held, allowing the application, that the court had power to stay proceedings in the interests of justice under its inherent jurisdiction, or to stay proceedings under Art.21 and Art.22. The Warsaw Convention fell within the terms of the Brussels Convention Art.57. The Warsaw Convention applied so as to displace Art.21 and Art.22. However, the Warsaw Convention was silent on the situation where the manufacturer was also a defendant to litigation. However, on construction of the Warsaw Convention, it was not possible to bring an action against the defendant airline or the manufacturer in France, *Sidhu v. British Airways Plc* [1997] A.C. 430, [1997] C.L.Y. 220 applied. Dismissing A's applications, it was not appropriate for the English court to impose an anti suit injunction until the French court had ruled on jurisdiction, *Societe Nationale Industrielle Aerospatiale v. Lee Kui Jak* [1987] 1 A.C. 871, [1987] C.L.Y. 3024 applied. It would be contrary to principles of comity to grant the declaratory

relief sought at an interlocutory stage. D's application for a stay would be granted, pending the outcome of the French litigation.

DEAVILLE v. AEROFLOT RUSSIAN INTERNATIONAL AIRLINES [1997] 2 Lloyd's Rep. 67, Geoffrey Brice Q.C., QBD.

880. Jurisdiction—anti suit injunctions—contractual agreement for disputes to be settled in London under English law—proceedings commenced in Algeria

A charterparty provided that all disputes were to be settled by arbitration in London and that the agreement was to be governed by English law. A dispute arose and S commenced proceedings in Algeria, obtained an order of the Algerian court and arrested part of the cargo. I applied to the Algerian court for an order that S recognise the jurisdiction of London arbitration. As part of the pleadings before the Algerian court, I served a document similar to a defence and counterclaim. The English court was required to determine whether I was entitled to an interlocutory injunction restraining S from enforcing the Algerian order and whether I had surrendered to the jurisdiction of the Algerian court.

Held, refusing an injunction, that it was plain that I had always contested the jurisdiction of the Algerian court. There was a dispute as to whether or not I had served something which was equivalent to a defence and counterclaim before the Algerian court, and further whether a counterclaim to obtain the release of goods was a submission to the jurisdiction of the court in any event, *Adams v. Cape Industries Plc* [1990] Ch. 433, [1990] C.L.Y. 3684 considered. Therefore there was a serious issue for trial. However, the court was not persuaded that an interlocutory injunction should be granted, because there was no evidence of prejudice to I. The award of an injunction against the enforcement of the order of a foreign court would be outside the principle in *Aggeliki Charis Compania Maritima SA v. Pagnan SpA (The Angelic Grace)* [1995] 1 Lloyd's Rep. 87, [1994] C.L.Y. 4066.

INDUSTRIAL MARITIME CARRIERS (BAHAMAS) INC v. SINOCA INTERNATIONAL INC (THE EASTERN TRADER) [1996] 2 Lloyd's Rep. 585, Rix, J., QBD (Comm Ct).

881. Jurisdiction—anti suit injunctions—contractual exclusive jurisdiction clause—proceedings commenced elsewhere

W appealed against prior restraint orders made against him in two actions, the Melbourne action and the Estonian action, in proceedings by two ship owning concerns. W appealed also against injunctions ordering W not to continue proceedings commenced against both shipowners in Sierra Leone. In the Melbourne action W claimed a shortage of bales of textiles in a shipment purchased from M, which M disputed. The contract stated that the bill of lading should be subject to English law and jurisdiction. The issue arose as to whether the proceedings commenced by W in Sierra Leone were a breach of contract and whether the jurisdiction of the English courts was intended to be exclusive. In the Estonian action W issued a writ against the shipowners and again the issue was whether he had breached the contract by commencing proceedings in Sierra Leone. W contended that the shipowners had also breached the contract by starting proceedings in England as the contract provided that it be governed by Estonian law. W argued that the injunction proceedings in England should be dismissed on the basis that the shipowners had submitted to the jurisdiction of the Sierra Leone courts and by virtue of the lapse of time. The actions in England differed to the extent that they raised the jurisdiction issues. It was put forward on behalf of the shipowners that there was an alleged claims industry in Sierra Leone with fraudulent claims being made, which evidence was not submitted in the proceedings in Sierra Leone. G, the solicitor who had investigated such claims, asserted that it would be unsafe for him to return to Sierra Leone as a death threat had been made against him.

Held, dismissing the appeal, that (1) in the Melbourne action and Estonian action, exclusive jurisdiction of the English courts was conferred by the agreement. The clause stated that English law would be mandatory if US law did not apply; and the court was of the same opinion as the court below that the shipowners had submitted to the Sierra Leone courts and in the normal course of events, the English injunctions would have been dismissed; (2) although it was assumed that the contract had been breached by the proceedings in England, it was not necessary to stay those proceedings as the English courts did not have to comply, in all circumstances, with a private contract by which they would be deprived of jurisdiction, *Aratra Potato Co v. Egyptian Navigation Co (The El Amria)* [1981] 2 Lloyd's Rep. 119, [1980] C.L.Y. 322 considered, and (3) the evidence of G and other allegations of fraud meant that the judge was justified in restraining W from dealing with his assets and continuing the Sierra Leone proceedings. There was no reason to disbelieve the evidence given by G for the ship owners and as a consequence W's evidence was discredited.

SVENBORG A/S/ D/S/ v. WANSA (T/A MELBORNE ENTERPRISES); ESTONIAN SHIPPING CO LTD v. WANSA (T/A D&M IMPEX) [1997] 2 Lloyd's Rep. 183, Staughton, L.J., CA.

882. Jurisdiction—anti suit injunctions—debt enforcement proceedings in England and Greece

B applied for an interlocutory injunction to restrain W from commencing or continuing proceedings in the Greek courts. B had loaned $19.8 million to W and three other defendants, taking first charges over four ships by way of Liberian mortgages, each loan agreement containing a clause providing for governance by English law. In the agreement B also reserved a right to take proceedings in other competent jurisdictions. B alleged that W had defaulted and began proceedings in England. B then issued in Greece a 905 petition requesting a declaration to establish that the mortgage deed was enforceable, which was defended by W. W subsequently began proceedings against B in the multi member court in Greece to declare the loan agreement contrary to Greek banking law and therefore void.

Held, allowing the application, that an anti suit injunction was granted and directions made for an expedited trial. It was clear that the loan agreement required W to submit any dispute to the jurisdiction of the English courts. B's application to the Greek court was merely a protective measure pending the hearing of the substantive issues in England, which was considered necessary because it was alleged that there were already six arrests of one of the ships by creditors and port charges were rising while the value of that ship was falling. The two sets of proceedings had the same cause of action and the same subject matter and the question of whether W had exceeded the steps necessary to defend the 905 proceedings should be considered at trial, *Continental Bank NA v. Aeakos Compania Naviera SA* [1994] 1 W.L.R. 588, [1994] C.L.Y. 3715 considered.

BANQUE CANTONALE VAUDOISE v. WATERLILY MARITIME INC, Trans. Ref: 1997 Folio No.2, February 26, 1997, Cresswell, J., QBD (Comm Ct).

883. Jurisdiction—anti suit injunctions—failure to refer dispute to arbitration

[Brussels Convention on Jurisdiction and Enforcement of Judgments in Civil and Commercial Matters 1968 Art 1.4; New York Convention on the Recognition and Enforcement of Foreign Arbitral Awards 1958.]

Further to a contract for the sale of soya bean pellets, issues arose as to the condition of the cargo. The contract was governed by arbitration under the GAFTA rules, it was further provided that no court proceedings were to be brought until disputes had been settled by arbitration. S brought two interlocutory matters before the French court before seeking substantive relief before that court. T sought an anti suit injunction before the English court maintaining that any dispute should be brought to arbitration in the first place. S contended further that the English courts had no jurisdiction under the Brussels Convention 1968 because the same issues were already before the French courts.

Held, allowing the application, that (1) the New York Convention 1958 sought to ensure that arbitration agreements were observed. The French proceedings were in contravention of the arbitration agreement. Therefore, Art.1.4 must be held to exclude the dispute, *Marc Rich & Co AG v. Societa Italiana Impianti PA* [1992] 1 Lloyds Rep. 342, [1991] C.L.Y. 3930 applied, and (2) there was no reason why the English courts should give weight to issues such as forum non conveniens when deciding whether or not to issue an anti suit injunction. The French proceedings had not progressed beyond service of pleadings. There was no reason why the injunctive relief sought should not be granted. S had not made its case that there would be conflicting judgments.

TOEPFER INTERNATIONAL GmbH v. SOCIETE CARGILL FRANCE [1997] 2 Lloyd's Rep. 98, Colman, J., QBD (Comm Ct).

884. **Jurisdiction–anti suit proceedings–Australian insured commencing claim in United States–advantage to insurer in seeking injunction and declaratory relief in Australia–New South Wales**

[Sherman Act 1890 (United States).]

In June 1995 CSR commenced proceedings in the District Court of New Jersey against a number of insurance companies, including CIA. The New Jersey action claimed damages and declaratory and injunctive relief with respect to the failure of the insurers to defend and indemnify CSR in the more than 40,000 claims brought against CSR in the US alleging bodily injury as a result of exposure to asbestos fibre sold by CSR. In July 1995 CIA issued proceedings in the New South Wales Supreme Court seeking an anti suit injunction restraining CSR from continuing with the New Jersey proceedings. CSR moved to have the New South Wales proceedings stayed on the basis of forum non conveniens. CSR objected that the bringing of the New South Wales proceedings in response to the New Jersey proceedings offended the principles in which the forum of the United States proceedings was properly to be tested and was accordingly vexatious, oppressive and an abuse of process. The evidentiary, logistic and cost difficulties for CSR if it were required to litigate 40,000 US claims in Australia would be vexatious and oppressive. It was accepted by all parties that, following the decision in *Voth v. Manildra Flour Mills Pty Ltd* (1990) 171 C.L.R. 538, it was for CSR to establish that New South Wales was a clearly inappropriate forum.

Held, refusing to stay the New South Wales proceedings, that (1) under the principles in *Voth*, even if New Jersey were a more appropriate forum, it would not follow that New South Wales was an inappropriate forum, and (2) there was a special juridical advantage to CIA proceeding in New South Wales, namely that a claim under the Sherman Act 1890 could not be brought against CIA.

CIGNA INSURANCE AUSTRALIA LTD v. CSR LTD [1996] 5 Re L.R. 421, Rolfe, J., Sup Ct (NSW).

885. **Jurisdiction–anti suit proceedings–US subscribers to Australian debentures sue US lawyers–Australia**

Seventeen applicants, with one exception substantial American investors, subscribed to senior subordinated debentures issued by LT in October 1988. Some of the applicants had their principal place of business in New York and some were formed under the laws of New York. In 1991 two sets of proceedings were commenced against LT and others in New York on the basis that the applicants were induced to subscribe to the debentures by misleading and deceptive conduct in that they were led to believe that the debentures would not be subject to any senior indebtedness whereas in truth they were. The applicants' preferred forum was the US District Court in New York (NYC) but to safeguard against the possibility of those proceedings being dismissed proceedings were also commenced in 1991 in the Federal Court of Australia (FCA). All defendants to both proceedings were Australian residents and both proceedings were dismissed in 1992 on the ground of forum non conveniens and comity. Appeals were dismissed in 1993. In April 1994 six applicants brought proceedings in NYC against Skadden Arps, S, a New York firm of solicitors with a Sydney office which had provided advice in connection with the original issue of the debentures, seeking damages for fraud pursuant to the common law of New York. Similar proceedings were commenced in NYC against S later in 1994 by the other applicants. Several of the respondents to the Australian proceedings filed cross claims against S in the FCA actions. S filed a motion seeking to have the proceedings dismissed on the ground of forum non conveniens. The motions were dismissed and appeals were dismissed in September 1995. S then filed a notice of motion in the FCA proceedings seeking an "anti-suit injunction" against the applicants to restrain them from taking any further steps in the NYC proceedings.

Held, granting the injunction, that (1) the court had jurisdiction, similar to the broad equitable jurisdiction to restrain the exercise of national legal rights, to restrain actions abroad based on foreign legal rights; *Societe Nationale Industrielle Aerospatiale v. Lee Kui Jak* [1989] 1 A.C. 871, [1987] C.L.Y. 3024 and *National Mutual Holdings Pty Ltd v. Sentry Corp* (1989) 22 F.C.R. 209 followed, and (2) the applicants should have foreseen when they commenced the actions that S might have to defend substantially the same allegations in lengthy proceedings in FCA and NYC and then sue one or more parties for contribution or indemnity and alternatively that the claims and cross claims in the FCA action might be substantially duplicated in NYC. That could have been avoided if they had joined S as an additional respondent. The situation suggested vexatious and oppressive conduct against S. Unless strong countervailing considerations existed which did not apply in the instant case the court would enjoin the foreign action.

ALLSTATE LIFE INSURANCE CO v. AUSTRALIA & NEW ZEALAND BANKING GROUP LTD [1997] 6 Bank. L.R. 92, Lindgren, J., Fed Ct (Aus).

886. Jurisdiction–applicant contending breach of contract and statutory provisions occurred in Australia–Danish respondent failing to show actions oppressive or vexatious forum–Australia

[Trade Practices Act 1974 s.5, s.82, s.85 (Australia).]

The applicant company, B, brought proceedings against the Danish bank, S, alleging breaches of the Trade Practices Act 1974 s.82 and s.87 and breaches of contract. B was an Austrialian company and the proceedings were brought in Australia. B's case rested on representations made to B's employees in Australia. S sought a stay or an order setting aside service of proceedings.

Held, dismissing S's application, that B had shown a prima facie case for the breach of the 1974 Act and for breach of contract. The relevant conduct had arguably occurred in Australia and B was based in Australia. No ministerial consent was required when the conduct occurred in Australia and s.5(1) did not apply. S had not established a case for a stay of the proceedings because it had failed to show that the continuation of the proceedings would be oppressive or vexatious.

BANNERTON HOLDINGS PTY LTD v. SYDBANK SOENDERJYLLAND A/S [1997] 6 Bank. L.R. 19, RD Nicholson, J., Fed Ct (Aus).

887. Jurisdiction–application for production of documents to prove that court had jurisdiction in action–court's power to make order to establish jurisdiction

[Rules of the Supreme Court Ord.38 r.13.]

CT and others, trustees of Canadian pension funds, claimed to have been the victims of a number of large international frauds committed by S. In order to recover the funds, proceedings had also been brought against 36 other parties and, as there was no single natural forum for the action, CT wanted to bring proceedings in England, based on the residence there of S as the first defendant, with other defendants being necessary parties to the proceedings. In order to help prove that S was resident in England at the relevant time, CT applied under the RSC Ord.38 r.13 for orders for the production of documents from banks and other bodies that were likely to provide evidence of S's address. The judge dismissed the application on the grounds that the court would not allow its process to be used to enable a plaintiff to establish the court's jurisdiction. CT appealed.

Held, allowing the appeal, that the High Court had two different kinds of jurisdiction to try the matter which was disputed, and to determine whether it had the jurisdiction to try the matter in dispute. The High Court was a court of unlimited jurisdiction in that it could determine the existence and boundaries of its own jurisdiction, and as such it had an indisputable jurisdiction of the second type to determine whether it had jurisdiction of the first type to hear a substantive action. Therefore allowing CT's application would not have amounted to an assumption that the court had the jurisdiction to try the substantive action or to an exercise of the court's jurisdiction to try a substantive matter, but rather to an exercise of the court's jurisdiction to determine its own jurisdiction. Thus the judge's decision could not be upheld and the matter would be restored for hearing by the judge.

CANADA TRUST CO v. STOLZENBERG, *The Times,* May 1, 1997, Millett, L.J., CA.

888. Jurisdiction–consumer contracts–exclusive jurisdiction clause–person concluding contract for future pursuance of trade or profession not "consumer"–European Union

[Brussels Convention on Jurisdiction and Enforcement of Judgments in Civil and Commercial Matters 1968 Art.13, Art.14.]

A party who contracts to pursue a trade or profession is not a consumer for the purposes of the Brussels Convention 1968 Art.13 and Art.14 and is therefore bound by any contractual jurisdiction clause. B entered into a contract with D to open a franchise in Munich of D's Italian based chain, but B never commenced trading. The contract specified that disputes would be resolved in the Italian courts, but B brought an action in Germany, maintaining that, as he sought to have the entire contract declared void, the jurisdiction clause had no effect. B further argued that, as he had not commenced trading, he should be regarded as a "consumer" under the Brussels Convention 1968 Art.13 and Art.14 and therefore be permitted to bring an action in the country "in which he... is domiciled". The German court made a reference to the ECJ on the correct interpretation of the Convention.

Held, that the concept of a "consumer" within Art.13 and Art.14 had to be construed strictly to mean a private final consumer and did not extend to a person who concluded a contract with the intention of pursuing a trade or profession either at the present time or in the future. In the absence of that protection, the courts of a contracting state named in a valid jurisdiction clause would, under Art.17 of the Convention, be awarded exclusive jurisdiction to hear all matters concerning the contract, including an action to declare the contract void.

BENINCASA v. DENTALKIT SRL (C269/95), *The Times,* October 13, 1997, GF Mancini (President), ECJ.

889. Jurisdiction–determination of jurisdiction by domicile–relevant date

[Lugano Convention on Jurisdiction and Enforcement of Judgments in Civil and Commercial Matters 1988 Art.6; Rules of the Supreme Court Ord.11 r.1.]

The relevant date for determining domicile of a party to an action under the Lugano Convention 1988 Art.6.1 is the date of issue and not date of service of the writ; however, where joinder of foreign defendants domiciled in non Convention States is sought under RSC Ord.11, proceedings must have been served on that party prior to issue of proceedings against the foreign defendants. C brought an action against S, alleging that he was the principal perpetrator of a massive investment fraud, and sought to join as defendants other parties they believed had participated in the fraud. Three of those defendants appealed against a decision that S was domiciled in England and that the court had jurisdiction over them because they were domiciled in a contracting state to the Lugano Convention 1988, and, under Art.6.1 thereof could be sued in the courts where any other defendant to the same action was domiciled. Four other defendants, who were domiciled in non Convention states, appealed against a decision that they were necessary and proper parties to P's claim against a person duly served, whether within or out of England under the RSC Ord.11 r.1 (1) (c). All the defendants contended that S was not domiciled in England at any material time.

Held, dismissing the appeals (Pill, L.J. dissenting in part), that (1) the judge had been correct to conclude that the Convention defendants' application to set aside service could not succeed if C had established a good arguable case that Art.6.1 was satisfied, and there was no evidence that the judge had applied the "good arguable case" test wrongly; (2) the correct date for determining whether S was domiciled in England for the purposes of Art.6.1 was when the writ was issued and not at the date of service of proceedings, and (3) while Ord.11 r.1 (1) (c) expressly required that the defendant domiciled in the state where proceedings had been brought be served before issue or service of the proceedings against the other defendants, there was no such requirement under Art.6.

CANADA TRUST CO v. STOLZENBERG (NO.2), *The Times*, November 10, 1997, Waller, L.J., CA.

890. Jurisdiction–insurance contracts–negative declaration–service of process out of jurisdiction

[Rules of the Supreme Court Ord.12 r.8.]

P appealed against the rejection of its application, pursuant to RSC Ord.12 r.8 to set aside N's application for a negative declaration on liability, on the basis of subsequent events in the alternative forum of fact in Illinois. P took out an insurance policy to cover, inter alia, employee dishonesty. An employee, F, knowingly supplied defective ballast resistors in order to earn fraudulent bonuses and set up a fraudulent travel company to exploit P's travel needs by overcharging P. N applied for a negative declaration that it was not liable under the contract for much of the claimed loss.

Held, dismissing the appeal, that the test for the grant of a negative declaration was that it must be "useful". However, where the plaintiff in the English proceedings was likely to be sued in a foreign jurisdiction, it was incumbent on the court to satisfy itself that the declaration was not merely being sought to obstruct or delay matters elsewhere, *Camilla Cotton Oil Co v. Granadex SA* [1976] 2 Lloyd's Rep.10, [1976] C.L.Y. 99 followed. Although P's advocacy of alternative dispute resolution procedures could not be faulted, the judge below was correct to find a reluctance on P's part to press ahead with the action. N had aroused suspicion by not rejecting the proof of loss, by producing no letter before action, and by filing a writ on the day before P was allowed to commence litigation proceedings in Illinois. However their legitimate aim was to resolve the construction issues under English law. N were justified in taking the procedural steps it did to attempt to resolve preliminary issues. The proceedings in Illinois had been stayed in order for the English proceedings to resolve the construction issues.

NEW HAMPSHIRE INSURANCE CO LTD v. PHILLIPS ELECTRONICS NORTH AMERICA CORP, Trans. Ref: FC3 97/5946/B; QBCMI 96/0894/B, May 16, 1997, Phillips, L.J., CA.

891. Jurisdiction–insurers–Brussels Convention applied to insurer domiciled in non contracting state–no joinder of persons not parties to original action

[Brussels Convention on Jurisdiction and Enforcement of Judgments in Civil and Commercial Matters 1968 Art.11.]

J, an English company which ran a motor racing team, alleged it had agreed to make bonus payments to its employees if it finished in the top six of the Formula 1 world championship, and that it had insured this contingent liability with BIG, a Lithuanian entity, through managing agents in Belgium. Q, an Irish company, claimed that it had agreed to make sponsorship payments to J contingent on J finishing in the top six, again with insurance from BIG. J finished fifth in the championship, but BIG refused to pay J and Q, claiming they and others had conspired to defraud BIG. J brought proceedings in the UK to recover the money it claimed was due under the insurance contract, whilst Q commenced an action in Belgium. In its defence to J's action, BIG counterclaimed damages for conspiracy and fraud against J, Q and two of Q's directors, D and G. BIG appealed against a decision that the court had no jurisdiction to determine BIG's claims against Q, D and G by virtue of the Brussels Convention 1968 Art.11, which provided that an insurer could only bring proceedings in the courts of the contracting state in which the defendant was domiciled.

Held, dismissing the appeal, that (1) the application of Art.11 was not limited to insurers who were domiciled in contracting states, but extended to any insurer who sought to bring proceedings against a defendant in one contracting state, where the defendant was domiciled in another; (2) BIG's right to counterclaim as a defendant insurer did not include the right to join D and G as codefendants where they were not parties to the action brought by J; (3) D and G were entitled to take advantage of the provisions of Art.11, even though they were not policyholders, the insured or beneficiaries, and (4) it was not necessary to make a preliminary reference to the ECJ on the issues raised by the case.

JORDAN GRAND PRIX LTD v. BALTIC INSURANCE GROUP; *sub nom.* BALTIC INSURANCE GROUP v. JORDAN GRAND PRIX LTD, *The Times*, November 14, 1997, Robert Walker, L.J., CA.

892. Jurisdiction—maintenance orders—proceedings brought in domicile of applicant where order yet to come in force—European Union

[Brussels Convention on Jurisdiction and Enforcement of Judgments in Civil and Commercial Matters 1968 Art.2, Art.5.]

M, who was resident in Ireland, sought an order for maintenance in respect of a child against the alleged father, who was resident in Belgium. M contended that the Irish courts had jurisdiction by virtue of the Brussels Convention 1968 Art.5(2), which established that, in matters relating to maintenance, jurisdiction rested with the courts for the place where the maintenance creditor was domiciled or habitually resident. F submitted that Art.5(2) was not applicable since M had not at that time obtained a maintenance order and she could not therefore be deemed to be a maintenance creditor. A reference was made to the ECJ for interpretation of Art.5(2).

Held, that Art.5(2) was a derogation from the normal rule in Art.2 of the Brussels Convention, whereby jurisdiction was conferred on the courts of the contracting state where the defendant was domiciled. It was intended to give an applicant, who was regarded as generally being the weaker party in maintenance proceedings, an alternative jurisdictional basis and this overrode the general need to protect the defendant as the weaker party, which was the purpose of Art.2. Article 5(2) applied to all maintenance actions, including any initial action brought by an applicant seeking maintenance, even where an issue of paternity fell to be determined as a preliminary issue.

FARRELL v. LONG (C295/95) [1997] 3 W.L.R. 613, GF Mancini (President), ECJ.

893. Jurisdiction—Mareva injunctions—order by English court in support of proceedings in Switzerland—English court could grant interim relief against UK resident where Swiss court had no jurisdiction

[Civil Jurisdiction and Judgments Act 1982 s.25(1); Lugano Convention on Jurisdiction and Enforcement of Judgments in Civil and Commercial Matters 1988 Art.24.]

C appealed against a decision refusing to discharge a world wide Mareva injunction and associated disclosure order granted in favour of CS pursuant to the Civil Jurisdiction and Judgments Act 1982 s.25 in support of CS's claim in civil proceedings brought in Switzerland. C was resident and domiciled in England and was believed to have assets in other jurisdictions, but as C was not resident in Switzerland, the Swiss court could not order him to disclose their whereabouts. The court had the jurisdiction to grant interim relief under s.25(1), but could refuse relief under s.25(2) if "the fact the court has no jurisdiction apart from this section in relation to the subject-matter of the proceedings in question makes it inexpedient for the court to grant it".

Held, dismissing the appeal, that there was no reason in principle why the court should not grant a world wide Mareva injunction against a defendant domiciled in England under s.25 in support of proceedings in another country. To do otherwise would be contrary to the policy underlying s.25 and the Lugano Convention 1988 Art.24. Whilst an ancillary jurisdiction should be exercised with caution so as to prevent conflict with orders made by the court seised of the substantive proceedings, interim relief under s.25 was not restricted to remedies which would be available to the foreign court, but extended to all remedies that would be available if the English court was seised of the substantive proceedings itself. When deciding whether to make an order with extraterritorial effect, the court should not ask itself whether there were exceptional circumstances, but simply whether it was inexpedient to do so, *S&T Bautrading v. Nordling* [1997] 3 All E.R. 718, [1997] C.L.Y. 677 not followed. If the foreign court had already refused a similar order to the one requested under s.25, then the court would generally refuse relief, but if the foreign court had no jurisdiction to grant the order requested, it would not necessarily object to the granting of the order.

CREDIT SUISSE FIDES TRUST SA v. CUOGHI [1997] 3 All E.R. 724, Millett, L.J., CA.

894. Jurisdiction–oral contracts in international trade–letter confirming jurisdiction–place of jurisdiction established by conduct–European Union

[Brussels Convention on Jurisdiction and Enforcement of Judgments in Civil and Commercial Matters 1968 Art.5, Art.17.]

Determination of the court to have jurisdiction in a dispute over a contract relating to international trade, was by accepted practice according to the finding of the national court. Where one party specified a particular court and the other party did not object, consensus was deemed to have been reached. Upon a reference from the German Federal Court, the ECJ was asked to rule on the interpretation of the Brussels Convention 1968 Art.5(1) and Art.17 for the purposes of establishing the place of jurisdiction under oral agreements concluded in international trade or commerce between two parties from different contracting states. M, a German company, had orally agreed to charter an inland waterway vessel to a French company, G, and in a letter of confirmation stated that the place of performance was Germany, whose courts would have exclusive jurisdiction in any proceedings which arose from the contract. G made no challenge to the letter and M argued they were therefore entitled to bring proceedings in Germany under Art.17.

Held, that under Art.17, as amended, where one party had specified the court which was to have jurisdiction over disputes arising from a contract relating to international trade or commerce, consensus was deemed to have been reached and the contract concluded if the other party did not object and if the conduct between the parties was consistent with accepted practice in that particular branch of trade or commerce, of which the parties should have been aware. It was for the national court to decide whether a relevant practice existed and whether the parties ought to have been aware of it. Further, if an oral agreement specifying the place of performance was not concerned with where the obligations under the contract were to be carried out, but rather with which courts were to have jurisdiction, it was not governed by Art.5(1), but by Art.17.

MAINSCHIFFAHRTS GENOSSENSCHAFT EG (MSG) v. LES GRAVIERES RHENANES SARL (C106/95) [1997] 3 W.L.R. 179, JL Murray (President), ECJ.

895. Jurisdiction–passing off–place where harmful event occurred

[Brussels Convention on Jurisdiction and the Enforcement of Judgments in Civil and Commercial Matters 1968 Art.5.]

M manufactured and sold butane gas refills for cigarette lighters in Hong Kong and the People's Republic of China. The refill cans had a distinctive get up and M had a substantial reputation and goodwill in those countries. B, a company domiciled in Scotland, exported butane gas refill cans to the same countries in a similar get up. M sued B in England for passing off. Whilst the position was unclear, the evidence suggested that B's cans were manufactured and printed by a subcontractor in England, sent to Scotland where they were filled with gas and then shipped to Hong Kong and China, probably via an English port. B successfully applied to set aside service of the writ on the ground that the English courts did not have jurisdiction. M appealed, arguing that England was the place where the harmful event occurred within the meaning of the Brussels Convention 1968 Art.5(3).

Held, dismissing the appeal and setting aside service of the writ, that (1) the words "place where the harmful event occurred" left it open for a plaintiff to choose between the place of the event giving rise to the damage, or the place where the damage occurred. *Handelswekerij GJ Bier BV and Stichtung Reinwater v. Mines de Potasse d'Alsace SA* (C21/76) [1978] 1 Q.B. 708, [1977] C.L.Y. 1283 referred to; (2) M was wrong to contend that, in a passing off action where it was not alleged that the defendant's goods were of inferior quality, the place where the harmful event occurred was the place where the loss of sales occurred. Both where there was passing off by the defendant of inferior goods and where there was passing off by the defendant of goods of at least the same quality as those of the plaintiff, the place where the damage occurred was the place where the passing off was effected. The place where the damage was suffered was not of itself enough to constitute the place where the damage occurred. Accordingly, England, where M claimed to have suffered loss, was not the place where the harmful event occurred within the meaning of Art.5(3) *Shevill v. Presse-Alliance SA* (C68/93) [1995] 2 A.C.18, [1995] 1 C.L.Y. 3127 referred to, and (3) it was not appropriate to dissect the events relied upon so that if one element could be found as occurring within one jurisdiction, that could be sufficient justification for treating that jurisdiction as within the range of permissible options open to the plaintiff under Art.5(3). In the instant case, the English elements were all subsidiary to the fact that B did what it did in Scotland and it was B's actions that were principally relied upon. The cause of action, if there was one, therefore arose in Scotland.

MODUS VIVENDI LTD v. BRITISH PRODUCTS SANMEX LTD [1996] F.S.R. 790, Knox, J., Ch D.

896. Jurisdiction–patent infringement–claim for breach of foreign intellectual property right in English court

[Civil Jurisdiction and Judgments Act 1982 Sch.1; Private International Law (Miscellaneous Provisions) Act 1995 s.10; Brussels Convention on Jurisdiction and Enforcement of Judgments in Civil and Commercial Matters 1968 Art.16,.]

C owned identical patents in the UK, Germany and Spain for a coin dispensing machine. S manufactured a coin dispensing device and sold it in the UK, Germany and Spain. C brought an action alleging breaches of the patents. S contended that the English courts did not have jurisdiction to hear the claims relating to the Spanish and German claims as the foreign intellectual property rights were not justiciable in England, and because the court was required to decline jurisdiction because of the provisions of the Civil Jurisdiction and Judgments Act 1982 Sch.1. C contended that the rule that foreign intellectual property claims were not justiciable was based on the rule against double actionability which had been abrogated by the Private International Law (Miscellaneous Provisions) Act 1995 s.10, and that the actions for the foreign claims were linked to the actions relating to the breaches in the UK so it was expedient to try them together to avoid the risk of irreconcilable judgments. S applied to strike out the foreign claims.

Held, granting S's applications, that the rule against entertaining an application for breach of a foreign intellectual property right was founded on public policy and not on the rule against double actionability. The rule had not been abrogated. Where an action concerned an attack on the validity of a foreign patent the court was required to decline jurisdiction by virtue of the provisions of the Brussels Convention Art.16 and Art.19 as set out in the 1982 Act Sch.1. This was so even if the claims related to breaches of a UK patent as well as foreign patents.

COIN CONTROLS LTD v. SUZO INTERNATIONAL (UK) LTD [1997] 3 All E.R. 45, Laddie, J., Ch D.

897. Jurisdiction—patent infringement

See PATENTS: European Patent (UK) No.189958 in the Name of Akzo Nobel NV, *Re*. §3898

898. Jurisdiction—place of performance—claims in contract and tort arising from same facts could not be litigated in UK

[Brussels Convention on Jurisdiction and Enforcement of Judgments in Civil and Commercial Matters 1968 Art.5.]

S, a UK company, required a certificate of quality in order to open a letter of credit to pay for goods to be imported from China and Taiwan. S asked TUV, a German company, to examine the goods and prepare a report, but contended that the inspection had been conducted negligently and that the reports were inaccurate, and sued TUV for breach of its contractual duty to exercise reasonable care and skill and for a similar breach of duty in tort. Under the Brussels Convention 1968 Art.5(1), a person resident in one contracting state could be sued in another contracting state "in matters relating to a contract, in the courts for the place of performance of the obligation in question", or under Art.5(3), "in matters relating to tort, in the courts for the place where the harmful event occurred". Service of the writ outside the jurisdiction upon TUV was set aside on the grounds that the English court lacked jurisdiction to hear the claims, and S appealed.

Held, dismissing the appeal, that under Art.5(1), where there had been a breach of more than one contractual obligation, jurisdiction was to be determined with reference to the place of performance of the main obligation, which in the instant case was the inspection of the goods in China and Taiwan, not the presentation of the reports. The meaning of "matters relating to tort" under Art.5(3) was not to be interpreted by reference to national law, but was to be given an EC law or Convention meaning of all actions which seek to establish the liability of a defendant and which are not related to a "contract" within the meaning of Art.5(1), *Kalfelis v. Schroder (C189/87)* [1988] E.C.R. 5565, [1991] C.L.Y. 3936 applied. Those words operated to exclude a claim which could be brought on the same facts under a contract or independently of a contract. Both related to the contract and since S could not bring a contractual claim in the UK under Art.5(1), it was similarly excluded from bringing a claim in tort.

SOURCE LTD v. TUV RHEINLAND HOLDING AG [1997] 3 W.L.R. 365, Staughton, L.J., CA.

899. Jurisdiction—reinsurance contracts—place of performance—duty to make fair presentation of risk amounting to obligations under Lugano Convention Art.5

[Lugano Convention on Jurisdiction and the Enforcement of Judgments in Civil and Commercial Matters 1988 Art.5.]

A, a reinsurer in the London market, entered into a reinsurance contract with L, a Swedish insurance company operating in Stockholm, and pursuant to that contract A wrote reinsurance of L's cover of underwater valves. A then alleged that the reinsurance was induced by a material false representation that the valves were "tried and tested", and issued proceedings in England relying on the Lugano Convention 1988 Art.5(1) which gave jurisdiction to the courts of the place of performance of the contractual obligation. L applied to set aside the writ on the basis that the duty to make a fair presentation of the reinsurance risk could not constitute an "obligation" within the meaning of Art.5(1).

Held, dismissing the application, that the duty to make a fair presentation was an obligation within the meaning of Art.5(1) as it drew no express distinction between obligations arising in the context of negotiations of a contract and obligations arising under or after the contract. *Bauunternehmung (Martin Peters) GmbH v. Zuid Nederlandse Aannemers Vereniging (C34/82)* [1983] E.C.R. 987, [1984] C.L.Y. 1464 applied, *Trade Indemnity Plc v. Forsakringsaktiebolaget Njord* [1995] 1 All E.R. 796, [1994] C.L.Y. 2700 not followed.

AGNEW v. LANSFORSAKRINGSBOLAGENS AB [1996] 4 All E.R. 978, Mance, J., QBD (Comm Ct).

900. Jurisdiction–related actions–action commenced in England after proceedings brought in Spain

[Brussels Convention on Jurisdiction and Enforcement of Judgments in Civil and Commercial Matters 1968 Art.22.]

It is inappropriate to apply a distinction between essential and non essential issues in addressing the question of whether actions begun in different jurisdictions are related actions giving rise to a risk of incompatible judgments for the purposes of the Brussels Convention 1968 Art.22; rather, a broad common sense approach is required. S brought proceedings against K and others in Spain, claiming that K was liable for large sums under an exercised put option given to them in relation to the sale of their special paper business. While that action was pending, S commenced proceedings against K in England, claiming damages for negligent misrepresentation in the negotiations for the sale of the business. K successfully argued that the proceedings in Spain and England were related actions that would give rise to a risk of irreconcilable judgments in the two jurisdictions for the purposes of the Brussels Convention 1968 Art.22 if S were allowed to proceed in England, and that the actions should be heard by the Spanish court as the court first seised of the matter. K now appealed against a Court of Appeal decision [1996] 1 C.L.Y. 1089 allowing S's appeal against the stay of proceedings ordered by the judge.

Held, allowing the appeal, that, given that Art.22 was concerned not with the substantive rights and obligations of the parties but with the ancillary and procedural question as to where those rights should be determined, the issue of whether actions were related for the purposes of Art.22 should be determined using a broad common sense approach. The distinction drawn by the Court of Appeal between essential and non-essential issues was wrong and was not supported by the judgment in *Owners of Cargo Lately Laden on Board Tatry v. Owners of Maciej Rataj (C406/92)* [1995] All E.R. (EC) 229, [1995] 1 C.L.Y. 704. However, due to a change in position by S, the judge's order staying the proceedings would be amended to one declining jurisdiction pursuant to Art.22.

SARRIO SA v. KUWAIT INVESTMENT AUTHORITY [1997] 3 W.L.R. 1143, Lord Saville, HL.

901. Jurisdiction–related actions–action for breach of Dutch copyright–defendant domiciled in UK

[Brussels Convention on Jurisdiction and Enforcement of Judgments in Civil and Commercial Matters 1968 Art.2, Art.6; Private International Law (Miscellaneous Provisions) Act 1995 s.10.]

Held, that, where an action for breach of a Dutch copyright was brought against a defendant domiciled in the UK, the English courts were bound to accept jurisdiction as there was no discretion to decline to hear an action under the terms of the Brussels Convention 1968, and the doctrine of forum conveniens was not applicable. The fact that other defendants were based in the Netherlands could not affect jurisdiction as they could also be sued in England under Art.6(1). Following the enactment of the Private International Law

(Miscellaneous Provisions) Act 1995 s.10, which abolished the double actionability rule, English courts could no longer refuse to accept jurisdiction as to do so would frustrate the fundamental principle laid down in the Brussels Convention Art.2 that a person domiciled in a contracting state could be sued in the courts of that state. The Convention also overrode the rule in *British South Africa Co v. Companhia de Mocambique* [1893] A.C. 602 that an English court should not entertain an action for breach of a foreign statutory intellectual property right.

PEARCE v. OVE ARUP PARTNERSHIP LTD [1997] 2 W.L.R. 779, Lloyd, J., Ch D.

902. Jurisdiction–related actions–passing off action in England–trade mark infringement proceedings commenced in Germany–similarity between causes of action

[Brussels Convention on Jurisdiction and Enforcement of Judgments in Civil and Commercial Matters 1968 Art.5, Art.21.]

D, a German company, had brought proceedings in Germany against M's German licensee for infringement of D's German trade mark registration. M, a United States corporation and its English subsidiary, had brought an action in the English courts alleging that D had committed the tort of passing off in relation to the use of the words "Internet World", causing damage to M in England. D applied to have M's writ set aside, arguing that there could be no goodwill in the words "Internet World" as they were merely descriptive and in any case the court did not have jurisdiction in the matter under the Brussels Convention 1968, either because the harmful event occurred in Germany, making Germany the appropriate forum under Art.5, or because the case arose from the same cause of action as the infringement of D's trade mark and the German courts were already seised of that matter so that Art.21 applied.

Held, dismissing the application, that there was a serious question to be tried in that M clearly had extensive goodwill in the name "Internet World" in England, and D's contention that no goodwill could exist in those words was inconsistent with claiming to have a registered trade mark in Germany consisting of the name and its use in brochures distributed in England. There was also a question as to whether D's conduct would mislead the public and cause damage to M's reputation. M was entitled to sue either in the country where D was domiciled or where the damage took place, and any damage had been to M's goodwill in England, so it did not matter whether D's actions in Germany were lawful under German law. Further, M could not be regarded as the same party as its licensee for the purposes of Art.21 and the passing off claim and the action for trade mark infringement in Germany arose from different causes of actions, so that Art.21 did not apply.

MECKLERMEDIA CORP v. DC CONGRESS GmbH [1997] 3 W.L.R. 479, Jacob, J., Ch D.

903. Jurisdiction–related actions–proceedings commenced in England while proceedings pending in Portugal–European Union

[Brussels Convention on Jurisdiction and Enforcement of Judgments in Civil and Commercial Matters 1968 Art.21; Convention on the Accession of Spain and Portugal to the Convention on Jurisdiction and Enforcement of Judgments 1989 Art.29.]

In August 1991, C, domiciled in the UK, sought a declaration in Portugal that he did not owe V, who was domiciled there, sums she alleged were due upon the sale of shares in a property company. In November 1992, V brought proceedings in England for payment of the sums and C sought a writ that the English court had no jurisdiction to entertain the proceedings. The House of Lords made a reference to the ECJ as to whether V's action ought to be stayed or jurisdiction declined pursuant to the Brussels Convention 1968 Art.21, given that the San Sebastian Convention 1989 brought the 1968 Convention into force between the UK and Portugal on July

1, 1992, which was before V brought her action but after C had brought proceedings in Portugal.

Held, that Art.29(1) of the 1989 Convention did not make it clear whether Art.21 of the 1968 Convention applied where only the second action had been brought after July 1, 1992 or whether both sets of proceedings had to be brought after that date. Both interpretations could give rise to difficulties and thus Art.29(1) had to be interpreted in accordance with the structure and objectives of the two Conventions. In circumstances such as those in the instant case, the court seised of the second action must apply the Brussels Convention Art.21 if the first court had assumed jurisdiction in accordance with a rule which conformed to Title II of the Brussels Convention or a convention which was in force between the two states when the proceedings were brought. If the first court had not yet ruled on whether it had jurisdiction, the second court should apply the Brussels Convention provisionally. However, if the first court had assumed jurisdiction on some other basis, the second court should not apply the Brussels Convention.

VON HORN v. CINNAMOND (C163/95) [1997] All E.R. (EC) 913, H Ragnemalm (President), ECJ.

904. Jurisdiction–restitution–recovery of money paid to local authority under void interest rate swap agreements–jurisdiction determined by domicile

[Civil Jurisdiction and Judgments Act 1982 Sch.4; Brussels Convention on Jurisdiction and Enforcement of Judgments in Civil and Commercial Matters 1968.]

K commenced proceedings in the English High Court for restitution of sums paid to G under interest rate swap agreements which had been found to be ultra vires G and therefore void ab initio. G appealed against a ruling allowing K's appeal against the striking out of its action on the ground that the matter should be heard in Scotland where G was domiciled. K contended that the claim was either (1) a matter relating to a contract under the Civil Jurisdiction and Judgments Act 1982 Sch.4 Art.5(1), which could be heard in the place of performance of the obligation in question, or (2) a matter relating to tort, delict or quasi delict within Art.5(3), which could be heard in the place where the harmful event occurred. The ECJ had declined the Court of Appeal's request to provide an interpretation of the provisions of the Brussels Convention 1968 corresponding to Art.5(1) and Art.5(3) on the grounds that the Convention was not directly applicable.

Held, allowing the appeal (Lord Mustill and Lord Nicholls dissenting as to Art.5(1)), that, even though the ECJ had felt unable to provide guidance on Sch.4, it was still necessary to apply the ECJ's jurisprudence on the relevant parts of the Convention. Those cases showed that "obligation" within Art.5(1) meant the contractual obligation on which the action was based and it was difficult to see how that could apply to a claim for money passed under a contract which in law had never existed. A claim in restitution was based on the principle of unjust enrichment and, as there was no provision for such claims in Art.5, it was fair to infer that they should be heard in the courts where the defendant was domiciled in accordance with the ordinary rule in Sch.4 Art.2. Further, the claim did not fall within Art.5(3), as an action based on unjust enrichment could only exceptionally involve a harmful event or threatened wrong.

KLEINWORT BENSON LTD v. GLASGOW CITY COUNCIL (NO.2) [1997] 3 W.L.R. 923, Lord Goff of Chieveley, HL.

905. Jurisdiction–trespass to land in Northern Cyprus–English court had jurisdiction to hear proceedings

[Civil Jurisdiction and Judgments Act 1982 s.30(1).]

The four applicants owned properties in Northern Cyprus. Following occupation by Turkey in 1974, ownership of immovable property in the Turkish Republic of Northern Cyprus, including land owned by the applicants, was claimed by Turkey. It was claimed by the applicants that, since the appropriation, P, a company now in administration, had trespassed on their property by encouraging its subsidiaries to occupy it without authority. P's administrators sold shareholdings in the companies alleged to have trespassed to a company in Northern Cyprus in order to recover assets. The applicants sought to bring proceedings against P and its administrators, seeking a declaration that the administrators were, in effect, trustees for consideration from those sales and seeking an injunction to prevent the administrators from dealing with the monies recovered. P argued that the court lacked jurisdiction over the matter.

Held, granting leave to bring proceedings, that under the Civil Jurisdiction and Judgments Act 1982 s.30(1) the court had jurisdiction to hear proceedings for trespass to immovable property where the property was located outside the UK, unless the proceedings were mainly concerned with the question of title or the right to possession of the property. Although in any action for trespass it would be necessary for the plaintiff to establish title or right to possession, there were several other important questions raised by the present claim, such as whether P itself committed any acts of trespass or whether the corporate veil could be pierced to make P liable for the acts of its subsidiaries, and therefore the court did have jurisdiction under s.30(1).

POLLY PECK INTERNATIONAL PLC, *Re* [1996] N.P.C. 176, Rattee, J., Ch D.

906. Loans–applicability of Unfair Contract Terms Act 1977reasonable

[Unfair Contract Terms Act 1977 s.13, s.27.]

S, a bank with its registered office in the Cayman Islands being a subsidiary of a French company, applied for summary judgment in respect of three loan agreements entered into in 1991, 1992 and 1993 with O, one-ship companies. The choice of law and jurisdiction clause provided for the loan agreements to be governed by English law. O cross claimed that S had misallocated payments causing O loss and that it had suffered loss because of S's conduct giving rise to rights in delict in French law. S contended that due to the anti set off clause in the agreement, O was unable to make those claims in its defence. O argued that the Unfair Contract Terms Act 1977 applied and that the anti set off term of the agreement was unreasonable.

Held, adjourning the hearing and dealing with preliminary issues, that O was not entitled to rely on the Unfair Contract Terms Act 1977. Although there was a choice of law clause that provided for the agreement to be governed by English law, there was no indication that English law would have been the proper law for the agreements given that they were made outside England and none of the parties were English. Accordingly, the potential application of the 1977 Act was excluded by s.27. Section 13 of the Act would apply if the choice of law clause formed part of S's standard terms of business, *Stewart Gill Ltd v. Horatio Myer & Co Ltd* [1992] Q.B. 600, [1992] C.L.Y. 510 considered. With regard to the issue of whether the terms of the agreement were reasonable for the purposes of the Act, no factual complaint of unreasonableness was made. Commercial organisations should, prima facie, be given freedom of contract and courts should give effect to the terms agreed between parties. It was reasonable that a bank would wish to include an anti set off clause in a loan agreement of this kind.

SURZUR OVERSEAS LTD v. OCEAN RELIANCE SHIPPING CO LTD, Trans. Ref: 1997 F-No.83, April 18, 1997, Toulson, J., QBD (Comm Ct).

907. Service of process–service outside the jurisdiction–concurrent New York proceedings

[Insurance Companies Act 1974; Insurance Companies Act 1982; Rules of the Supreme Court Ord.11 r.1.]

D was the successor in title to reinsurance business originally underwritten by E. E entered contracts of reinsurance with the defendant, C. The business underwritten by E was transferred to D by an "Agreement of Bulk Reinsurance". Claims were made by C against D on the reinsurance agreements. D issued a writ seeking a declaration that the contracts of reinsurance were void and unenforceable as having been effected in contravention of the Insurance Companies Act 1974 and Insurance Companies Act 1982. D obtained leave to serve the writ outside the jurisdiction. C then instituted proceedings in the United States to enforce the contracts and applied to set aside D's leave to serve outside the jurisdiction.

Held, setting aside the order, that (1) the relevant contract was not the agreement of bulk reinsurance but the contract between E and C which had been transferred to D. The expression "contract" in the RSC Ord.11 r.1 was wide enough to cover contractual rights and liabilities vested in one party in that way, *Gulf Bank KSC v. Mitsubishi Heavy Industries Ltd* [1994] 1 Lloyd's Rep. 323, [1994] C.L.Y. 3765 applied, *Finnish Marine Insurance Co Ltd v. Protective National Insurance Co* [1990] 1 Q.B. 1078, [1989] C.L.Y. 3091 not followed; (2) the agreements contained indications that the relevant law was that of England. Where parties entered a particular market to transact business it was a reasonable inference that they intended to be bound by the law of the place in which the market was located. Accordingly the proper law was English law, and (3) the existence of the concurrent New York proceedings, where the same subject matter would be dealt with, was a strong argument for setting aside the order, *Insurance Corp of Ireland v. Strombus International Insurance Co Ltd* [1985] 2 Lloyd's Rep. 139, [1985] C.L.Y. 2743 followed. If the instant action continued there might be a duplication of proceedings. That and the fact that the instant action was founded on an assertion of an illegal act by D's predecessor indicated that it was undesirable to force the parties to contest the issues in England.

DR INSURANCE CO v. CENTRAL NATIONAL INSURANCE CO OF OMAHA (IN REHABILITATION) [1996] 1 Lloyd's Rep. 74, Martin Moor-Bick Q.C., QBD (Comm Ct).

908. **Stay of proceedings–forum non conveniens–availability of legal aid or conditional fee arrangement could be taken into account**

[Legal Aid Act 1988 s.33(1).]

C appealed against a Court of Appeal ruling that his action against RTZ should be stayed on the ground of forum non conveniens. The court had found that the case should be heard in Namibia and it was not possible to take into account C's eligibility for legal aid in the UK when determining the most appropriate forum as this was inconsistent with the Legal Aid Act 1988 s.33(1)(b), which stated that the receipt of legal aid should not affect "the principles on which the discretion of any court or tribunal is normally exercised". RTZ appealed against a subsequent decision of the Court of Appeal to lift the stay after C undertook not to apply for legal aid and his solicitors agreed to continue to act for him under a conditional fee arrangement.

Held, allowing C's appeal but dismissing RTZ's appeal, that s.33(1)(b) was never intended to apply to an application to stay proceedings brought in the UK by a plaintiff on the ground of forum non conveniens, and the correct test was whether "the court was satisfied that there was some other tribunal, having competent jurisdiction in which the case might be tried more suitably for the interests of all the parties and for the ends of justice", *Sim v. Robinow* (1892) 19 R. 665 followed. Where the possibility of either legal aid or a conditional fee arrangement was an issue, the general principle was that if a more appropriate forum had been identified, the stay would not be refused simply because the plaintiff would not have financial assistance available to him overseas which would be available in the UK. However, exceptionally, the question of the availability of financial assistance could be a relevant factor if the plaintiff could show that substantial justice would not be done if he had to proceed in a forum where no assistance was available to him, *Spiliada Maritime Corp v. Cansulex Ltd (The Spiliada)* [1987] A.C. 460, [1987] C.L.Y. 3135 applied.

CONNELLY v. RTZ CORP PLC [1997] 3 W.L.R. 373, Lord Goff of Chieveley, HL.

909. Articles

A rose by any other name–quasi contract and the Judgments Convention *(T.P. Kennedy)*: C.L. Pract. 1997, 4(3), 60-64. (Whether place for quasi contract claims can be determined under Art.5(1) or Art.5(3) of the Brussels Convention).

Anti-suit injunctions *(Julian Wilson)*: J.B.L. 1997, Sep, 424-437. (English courts' jurisdiction to order stay of proceedings in foreign court based on forum conveniens doctrine).

Choice of law issues in international arbitration *(Michael Pryles)*: Arbitration 1997, 63(3), 200-209.

Choice of substantive law in international arbitration *(Marc Blessing)*: J. Int. Arb. 1997, 14(2), 39-65. (Extent to which parties are free to choose applicable law, and subjective and objective approaches to determining applicable law where parties have failed to do so).

Double Dutch *(Julian Outen)*: P.I. 1997, 4(1), 63-65. (Jurisdiction of English court to hear claim in tort where Scottish employee of English firm who was contracted to Dutch company died following industrial accident in Holland, and application of double actionability test).

Enforcing abroad *(Stephen Cromie)*: Adviser 1997, 60, 35-37. (Rules governing enforcement of foreign judgments in UK and of UK debts abroad, with reference to EU, EFTA and non convention countries).

English civil jurisdiction and negative declarations *(Jonathan Leslie)*: I.C. Lit. 1997, Feb, 41-42. (Comparison of cases decided under Brussels Convention and common law rules applicable in non EU cases regarding jurisdiction for declarations that plaintiff is under no liability to defendant).

First to the courtroom door *(Andrew Henshaw)*: Eur. Counsel 1997, 2(6), 17-21. (Strategies for ensuring that dispute is heard in preferred jurisdiction, where contract contains exclusive jurisdiction clause).

Foreign court judgments in Asia: I.C. Lit. 1997, Nov, 17-20. (Enforcement of foreign judgments in India, Myanmar, Philippines, Singapore, Thailand and Vietnam).

Foreign court judgments: I.C. Lit. 1997, Sep, 17-22. (Recognition and enforcement of foreign judgments in Denmark, Hungary, Ireland, Norway, Spain, Portugal, Poland, Turkey and Switzerland).

Foreign torts: jurisdiction and applicable law: P. Injury 1997, 1(3), 3-5. (Where English plaintiff is victim of accidental injury abroad before and after May 1, 1996).

Intellectual property and the Brussels Convention: an English perspective *(Laurence J. Cohen)*: E.I.P.R. 1997, 19(7), 379-382. (Jurisdiction of English courts to hear cases involving foreign intellectual property rights).

International initiatives: United States *(Gordon W. Johnson)*: I.I.R. 1997, 6(Spe), S89-90. (Decision of US Court of Appeals to uphold dismissal of debtor's preference law suit against foreign creditors in deference to English courts, applying principles of international comity).

Public policy and payment obligations *(Charles Proctor)*: B.J.I.B. & F.L. 1997, 12(9), 427-436. (Impact that public policy may have on enforceability of payment obligations under contracts subject to English and foreign law).

Settling down in Jersey *(Tony Pitcher)*: Legal Bus. 1997, 76(Jul/Aug), Supp Tru 30-31. (Implications for practitioners of conflict of law issues affecting settlors domiciled in civil law countries).

910. Books

Campbell, Dennis; Campbell, Christian–Enforcement of Foreign Judgements. Hardback: £137.00. ISBN 1-85978-123-3. LLP Limited.

Dicey and Morris on the Conflict of Laws: 4th Supplement to the 12th Edition. Paperback: £32.00. ISBN 0-421-59970-7. Sweet & Maxwell.

Mayss, Abla J.–Conflict of Laws. Lecture Notes. Paperback: £15.95. ISBN 1-85941-172-X. Cavendish Publishing Ltd.

CONSTITUTIONAL LAW

911. Amnesty—wrongdoing during apartheid era—civil and criminal liability—South Africa

[Promotion of National Unity and Reconciliation Act 34 of 1995 s.20(7) (South Africa); Constitution of the Republic of South Africa Act 200 of 1993.]

In accordance with the "epilogue"of the interim Constitution of South Africa, the Promotion of National Unity and Reconciliation Act 34 of 1995 was passed, to facilitate the granting of amnesty to persons who made full disclosure of the facts relating to acts, omissions and offences associated with political objectives and committed in the course of conflicts during the apartheid era. Section 20(7) of the Act provided that once a person had been granted amnesty he could no longer be held criminally liable for any such deeds for which amnesty had been granted, nor be held civilly liable for any damages sustained by the victim. Furthermore, that should such deeds have been committed during the course and scope of his employment by the state, the state was equally discharged from civil liability which would ordinarily have arisen as a result of such deeds. The constitutionality of s.20(7) was challenged on the grounds that; (1) its consequences were not authorised by the interim Constitution, (2) they were inconsistent with the right to obtain redress in the ordinary courts, laid down in Constitution of South Africa Act 200 of 1993 s.22, (3) even if the Constitution authorised the consequences of s.20(7) it did not authorise as wide an amnesty as that allowed, and (4) since the state was obliged under international law to prosecute those responsible for gross human rights violations, the provisions of s.20(7) authorising amnesty for such offenders constituted a breach of international law. Violation of the right provided by the Constitution s.22 was unlawful under s.33(2), which provided that no law "save as provided for in subsection (1) or any other provision of this Constitution" should limit any right entrenched there. The "epilogue" was determined by Act 200 of 1993 s.232(4) as having "no lesser status than any other provision"of the Constitution.

Held, refusing the application, that (1) the limitation of the right to obtain redress of s.22 of the interim Constitution was in fact authorised by the Constitution, by s.33(2); (2) the epilogue had the same effect as if it had been incorporated as a qualification to the s.22 right; (3) this gave Parliament not only the authority, but, by virtue of the wording of the epilogue, an obligation to enact Act 34 of 1995 s.20(7); (4) an amnesty in respect of both criminal and civil liability was necessary to encourage those responsible of acts normally considered invasions of human rights to admit fully to their actions free from such liability, and this disclosure of the all relevant facts was necessary if they were to be granted amnesty, giving the victims or their relatives the benefit of discovering the truth; (5) an exclusion of the civil liability of the state had to be seen in the light of the fundamental objective of the Constitution, the transition to a new democratic order committed to reconciliation between the people and the reconstruction of society; (6) for such an aim to be achieved it was necessary that the state be able to deploy its limited resources to the benefit of the community as a whole, and not be diverted into settling civil claims of individuals, however justified; (7) under the Constitution Parliament was permitted to legislate for this wider concept of reparation, and on that basis s.20(7) was not unconstitutional; (8) the interim Constitution provided that an Act of Parliament could override any contrary rights or obligations under international agreements entered into before its commencement, and that the rules of international law would only become part of domestic law if they were consistent with the Constitution or an Act of Parliament, and so the contention that s.20(7) breached international law was untenable, since irrelevant, and (9) in enacting the Act 34 of 1995 s.20(7) the legislature had not exceeded any constitutional limitation of its power.

AZANIAN PEOPLES ORGANISATION (AZAPO) v. SOUTH AFRICA (1996) 1 B.H.R.C. 52, Chaskalson (President), Const Ct (SA).

912. Falkland Islands

FALKLAND ISLANDS CONSTITUTION (AMENDMENT) ORDER 1997, SI 1997 864; made under the British Settlements Act 1887; and the British Settlements Act 1945. In force: September 1, 1997; £1.10.

This Order makes a number of amendments to the Constitution of the Falkland Islands following a constitutional review of that territory and the report on that review by a Select Committee of the Legislative Council of the Falkland Islands.

913. Falkland Islands—elections

FALKLAND ISLANDS CONSTITUTION (AMENDMENT) (NO.2) ORDER 1997, SI 1997 2974; made under the British Settlements Act 1887; and the British Settlements Act 1945. In force: February 1, 1998; £1.10.

This Order removes the restriction under the Falklands Islands Constitutuion Order 1985 (SI 1985 444) Sch.1 s.23 that a person standing for election as a member of the Legislative Council must be a registered voter in the constituency in which election is being sought and provides that persons seeking to be elected in respect of one of the two Falkland Island constituencies must be registered as a voter pursuant to Sch.1 s.27 of the Constitution Order.

914. Government of Northern Ireland—temporary provisions—interim period extension

NORTHERN IRELAND ACT 1974 (INTERIM PERIOD EXTENSION) ORDER 1997, SI 1997 1690; made under the Northern Ireland Act 1974 s.1. In force: July 11, 1997; £0.65.

This Order extends until July 16, 1998 the period specified in the Northern Ireland Act 1974 s.1 (4) for the operation of the temporary provisions for the government of Northern Ireland contained in Sch.1 to that Act.

915. House of Commons—disqualification from membership

HOUSE OF COMMONS DISQUALIFICATION ORDER 1997, SI 1997 861; made under the House of Commons Disqualification Act 1975 s.5. In force: March 19, 1997; £1.55.

This Order amends the list of offices which disqualify holders for membership of the House of Commons and which are contained in the House of Commons Disqualification Act 1975 Sch.1.

916. Parliament—judicial review—investigation of MP following allegation of corruption—activities of Parliamentary Commissioner for Standards not subject to judicial review

The Parliamentary Commissioner for Standards, PCS, produced a report in which it concluded that Michael Howard MP had no case to answer in relation to F's allegation that he had received a corrupt payment while in ministerial office. Following the refusal of his application for leave to apply for judicial review of the report, F brought a renewed application for leave, contending that, because of the similarities between the positions of the PCS and the Parliamentary Commissioner for Administration, PCA, the former was subject to judicial review to the same extent as the latter.

Held, allowing the application for leave, but dismissing the substantive application, that the activities of the PCS were not subject to judicial review. There was a critical distinction between the roles of the PCA and the PCS. Whilst the PCA was concerned with the proper administration of the public service outside Parliament, the PCS was an independent person appointed by Parliament to fulfil an investigative function under the supervision of a Standing Committee of the House of Commons and was concerned with activities within

Parliament. It therefore fell to the Standing Committee, and not the courts, to supervise the activities of the PCS.

R. v. PARLIAMENTARY COMMISSIONER FOR STANDARDS, *ex p.* FAYED, *The Times*, November 13, 1997, Lord Woolf, M.R., CA.

917. **Parliamentary privilege–select committee procedure–violation of constitutional right to fair hearing–Zimbabwe**

[Privileges, Immunities and Powers of Parliament Act s.6(1) (Zimbabwe); Constitution of Zimbabwe s.18(2), s.20(1), s.20(2).]

On December 7, 1992 M, at that time a Minister in the Government of Zimbabwe, made a public speech in which he was disparaging about some Members of Parliament and the described Parliament as "meaningless". Shortly afterwards the Parliament passed a motion for the establishment of a Select Committee of Privileges to, inter alia, investigate M's utterances and determine whether such utterances were a contempt of Parliament. When M appeared before the Select Committee he was not allowed to engage legal counsel or to re-examine witnesses who had testified against him. The Select Committee recommended that M be suspended from Parliament for 12 months and on October 12, 1993 he was given a severe reprimand by the Speaker. In January 1994 M commenced judicial review proceedings contending that the proceedings of the Select Committee violated his fundamental right to a fair hearing under the Constitution of Zimbabwe s.18 and that his utterances outside Parliament were protected by his right to enjoyment of freedom of expression conferred by s.20(1) of the Constitution. In response the Speaker produced, in reliance on the Privileges, Immunities and Powers of Parliament Act (Zimbabwe) s.6(1), a certificate to the judge at first instance requiring him to stay the proceedings permanently. The judge duly stayed the proceedings and M appealed.

Held, dismissing the appeal, that provided the certificate issued in terms of s.6(1) mentioned any matter of privilege known to the law, and the proceedings instituted concerned the privilege of Parliament, the presiding judicial officer should immediately stay the proceedings, *Smith v. Mutasa NO* 1990 (3) SA 756 (ZS) applied. In utilising its powers of punishment for contempt under the Privileges, Immunities and Powers of Parliament Act, Parliament was not exercising a criminal or civil jurisdiction. Accordingly the Constitution s.18(2), which guaranteed a right to a fair hearing for every person charged with a criminal offence, did not apply. Parliament had the undoubted privilege to punish a contempt, and its management of its own internal affairs in doing so would only be susceptible of judicial interference where it happened to violate the Declaration of Rights contained in the Constitution. In the instant, case M's words were contemptuous of Parliament. M was not protected by the right to freedom of speech, since s.20(2)(b)(iii) placed a specific limitation on the freedom of expression where there existed a law which provided for the maintenance of the authority and independence of the courts or tribunals or Parliament. The Privileges, Immunities and Powers of Parliament Act constituted such a law.

MUTASA v. MAKOMBE (1997) 2 B.H.R.C. 325, Gubbay, C.J., Sup Ct (Zim).

918. **Privy Council–jurisdiction–power to entertain appeal not wholly prerogative–abolition of right to appeal–New Zealand**

DM and another sought special leave to appeal to the Privy Council against decisions of the New Zealand Court of Appeal, where the relevant legislation provided that the court's determination was to be "final" or "final and conclusive". DM argued that, despite the New Zealand Parliament's increased statutory powers to limit or abolish appeals to the Privy Council, the right of the Crown to entertain such an appeal was still a prerogative power and could only be limited or taken away by express words.

Held, refusing leave to appeal, that the right to entertain appeals to the Privy Council was no longer wholly prerogative, but was regulated by statute and the New Zealand legislature could limit or abolish the right to appeal by either express words or necessary intendment, *British Coal Corp v. King, The* [1935] A.C. 500 followed. In the instant case, the only possible interpretation was that, in making the Court of Appeal's decisions final, the New Zealand Parliament intended to remove the right of appeal by special leave to the Privy Council and therefore the Privy Council had no jurisdiction to hear DM's appeal.

DE MORGAN v. DIRECTOR GENERAL OF SOCIAL WELFARE; SEARS v. ATTORNEY GENERAL OF NEW ZEALAND, *The Times*, November 4, 1997, Lord Browne-Wilkinson, PC.

919. Referendums (Scotland and Wales) Act 1997 (c.61)

This Act makes provision for referendums to be held in Scotland in relation to the creation of a Scottish Parliament, and in Wales in relation to the creation of a Welsh Assembly. It also provides for expenditure in preparation for such bodies.

This Act received Royal Assent on July 31, 1997.

920. State immunity—third party notice against the ruler of Abu Dhabi set aside

[Diplomatic Privileges Act 1964; State Immunity Act 1978.]

Liquidators commenced actions against D, the bank's former auditors. D sought to bring third party proceedings against Abu Dhabi, a constituent territory of the United Arab Emirates. The third party notice was issued against Z, the ruler of Abu Dhabi and president of the UAE. He applied to set aside the notice on the grounds that he was immune from suit. D contended that the proceedings against Z were brought against him in his public capacity as the ruler and embodiment of Abu Dhabi, and the territory was not immune from suit, therefore Z should not be immune from suit.

Held, striking out the proceedings against Z, that a sovereign or head of a recognised state enjoyed immunity from suit when acting in a public capacity under the terms of the State Immunity Act 1978, and he also enjoyed immunity from suit in relation to all other circumstances under the Diplomatic Privileges At 1964.

BANK OF CREDIT AND COMMERCE INTERNATIONAL (OVERSEAS) LTD (IN LIQUIDATION) v. PRICE WATERHOUSE (NO.1) [1997] 4 All E.R. 108, Laddie, J., Ch D.

921. Articles

Acquiring rights—losing power: a case study in ministerial resistance to the impact of European Community law *(Mike Radford* and *Allen Kerr)*: M.L.R. 1997, 60(1), 23-43. (Impact of Acquired Rights Directive on UK Government's attempts to promote competition in provision of public services, with implications for doctrine of parliamentary sovereignty).

Bringing a Francovich claim in English courts *(Thomas De la Mare)*: J.R. 1997, 2(3), 143-149. (Practical advice on bringing state liability claim before English courts, including suitability of judicial review procedure).

Changing state *(David Faulkner)*: Magistrate 1997, 53(2), 45. (Changes to traditional concepts of state and citizenship and relationship between them, and impact on judges and magistrates, particularly regarding independence of judiciary).

European integration and United Kingdom constitutional law *(Patrick Birkinshaw)*: E.P.L. 1997, 3(1), 57-91. (Implications for doctrine of parliamentary sovereignty and increased role of judiciary).

Jeremy Bentham on political corruption: a critique of the first report of the Nolan Committee *(Philip Schofield)*: C.L.P. 1996, 49(2), 395-416. (Criticism of report's assumption that corruption is matter of personal weakness and utility of Bentham's thinking that corruption is essential feature of, not aberration from, representative government).

Parliamentary reform: paving the way for constitutional change *(Katy Donnelly)*: Parl. Aff. 1997, 50(2), 246-262. (Parliamentary procedures for dealing with constitutional Bills and obstacles that the Labour Party reform policies may encounter).

The Attorney General *(Diana Woodhouse)*: Parl. Aff. 1997, 50(1), 97-108. (Constitutional position and responsibilities of Attorney General, with particular reference to situations where is required to act in public interest, and difficulties of accountability).

The referendum: what, when and how? *(Geoffrey Marshall)*: Parl. Aff. 1997, 50(2), 307-313. (Constitutional implications and legislative requirements for referendums in light of increased support for their use).

CONSTRUCTION LAW

922. Arbitration–ICE conditions of contract

[Arbitration Act 1950 s.4.]

F agreed to design and construct a purification process plant for R by a written building contract which included a document headed "(A) AGREEMENT" which was signed by both parties and stated "the following documents.. shall together constitute the contract: (A) Agreement, (B) the General Conditions of Contract, (C) the Special Conditions...". The General Conditions were to be incorporated by reference to the Institute of Chemical Engineers' Model Form of Contract for Process Plant, Lump Sum Contracts, 1981 revision General Conditions, save as amended by the Special Conditions. The Special Conditions contained amendments to the Model Form including that either party could give to the other a written request to "concur in the appointment of an arbitrator under cl.47". H, the second defendant, entered into a contract of guarantee, which did not contain an arbitration agreement, with one or both of the plaintiffs, R and R's agent. Disputes arose and R commenced proceedings against F and H. F applied for a stay to arbitration pursuant to the Arbitration Act 1950 s.4. H applied for a stay under the inherent jurisdiction of the court and offered to undertake to be bound by the findings of the arbitrator in any arbitration between F and the plaintiffs and to pay any sums found by the arbitrator to be due from F. The judge had to decide whether "the Building Contract" contained an arbitration agreement and, if it did, whether the proceedings against H should be stayed pending the outcome of the arbitration between the plaintiffs and F.

Held, granting the stay, that cl.47 of the Model Form was part of the contract, by virtue of document A, or the parties intended to incorporate it; and, subject to H's undertaking, the stay should be granted because the primary contract was the Building Contract and the choice of arbitration in that contract outweighed both the absence of an arbitration agreement in the contract of guarantee and the ability of all parties to join in litigation.

ROCHE PRODUCTS LTD v. FREEMAN PROCESS SYSTEMS LTD; BLACK COUNTRY DEVELOPMENT CORP v. KIER CONSTRUCTION LTD 80 B.L.R. 102, Judge Hicks Q.C., QBD (OR).

923. Arbitration–ICE conditions of contract–failure to comply with arbitration procedure provisions did not render reference invalid

[Arbitration Act 1950 s.27.]

C was employed by B under a contract on the ICE conditions of contract and wished to refer a dispute to arbitration. Clause 66(3) provided for a reference to arbitration and laid down the requirements of the reference. C gave a notice purporting to refer the dispute to arbitration but it failed to comply fully with the requirements set out in the provisions of the contract. C then gave a later notice which fully complied with the requirements. That was more than three months after the relevant engineer's decision. B argued that there had been no effective reference to arbitration. C applied by originating summons for a declaration that a valid notice to refer the dispute to arbitration had been given, that the parties could validly proceed to concur in the appointment of an arbitrator and, further or alternatively, for an order under the Arbitration Act 1950 s.27 extending the time to give notice to refer to arbitration under the contract.

Held, giving judgment for C, that it was natural for a practical person reading cl.66(3) to consider that it told him all that he needed to know concerning the steps necessary to start an arbitration. This judgment was reinforced by the wording of cl.66(3) which referred to the arbitration being "conducted" in accordance with ICE procedure, which naturally meant the carrying on of the arbitration rather than its commencement. Therefore failure to comply with the requirements of the Arbitration Procedure was not fatal to the effective commencement of the arbitration. If this reasoning were found to be wrong it would be appropriate to grant an extension under s.27 of the 1950 Act, since this was not a case of failure to refer and there was no evidence of prejudice to the other party.

CHRISTIANI & NIELSEN LTD v. BIRMINGHAM CITY COUNCIL 52 Con. L.R. 56, Judge Hicks Q.C., QBD (OR).

924. Arbitration—JCT forms of contract—liability of main contractor to subcontractor

[Arbitration Act 1979 s.2.]

B appealed against a decision that it was bound under the terms of an arbitration in a main contract to satisfy a claim for £1.13 million due under a subcontract despite having been found blameless. B was the main contractor and CWS was the subcontractor in a contract, made under standard 1983 JCT terms, for the construction of a shopping centre for CEL. After completion of the contract, claims in arbitration for losses caused by delay and disruption were made by B against CEL in the main contract, and by CWS against B in respect of the subcontract. The arbitrator found that these events were the responsibility of neither B nor CWS and decision was given against CEL in a sum approaching £5 million. CEL went into liquidation avoiding payment and thereupon B contended that it was contractually liable to pay CWS on the subcontract only if an architect's certificate had been issued or if it was shown that CWS had been impeded by B's actions.

Held, dismissing the appeal, that the judge below had correctly determined that the arbitrator's award had replaced the architect's certificate and the main contractor was therefore bound to pay the subcontractor whether or not the award in the main contract had been honoured. Clear and express terms would be required if it was desired to avoid such a consequence, *Northern RHA v. Derek Crouch Construction Co Ltd* [1984] 1 Q.B. 644, [1984] C.L.Y. 117 followed.

COOPERATIVE WHOLESALE SOCIETY LTD (T/A CWS ENGINEERING GROUP) v. BIRSE CONSTRUCTION LIMITED (FORMERLY PETER BIRSE LTD), *The Times*, August 13, 1997, Phillips, L.J., CA.

925. Arbitration—JCT rules of arbitration—interim award—misconduct of arbitrator—test for dismissal

[Arbitration Act 1950 s.22, s.23.]

L employed AW as a subcontractor in respect of certain substructure works. A dispute arose between them which was referred to arbitration. AW as the claimant alleged that it was entitled to be paid certain interim payments. At a first preliminary meeting before the arbitrator, it was agreed that the JCT Arbitration Rules be applied and, in particular, r.5 dealing with "procedure without hearing", and the arbitrator was requested to make an interim award. Rule 12.3 of the JCT Rules provided for the arbitrator to change the procedure if necessary for the just and expeditious determination of the dispute. After receipt of AW's statement of case, at a second preliminary meeting, L raised the point that it was no longer possible to proceed on a documents only basis since the statement of claim raised significant issues of fact and the documents exhibited contained none of the information that would enable the arbitrator to decide on a documents only basis. The arbitrator ordered a further exchange of statements of case and at close of pleadings the arbitrator stated that he was able to determine many of the matters in dispute from the submitted documents. An interim award was issued which ruled against L on several items in the claim and on each of its counterclaims on the basis that L had failed to prove its case as to liability, causation and/or loss. L applied for an order setting aside the interim award and removing the arbitrator under the Arbitration Act 1950 s.23 or alternatively, remitting the matter to the arbitrator for reconsideration under s.22 on the grounds of misconduct of the reference.

Held, setting aside the award and removing the arbitrator. The arbitrator had misconducted the proceedings by failing to ensure that the nature and terms of the preliminary issues were crystallised and communicated to the parties, by purporting to determine by his interim award, a number of issues which no one had previously suggested as fit for determination by interim award, and by deciding so to proceed in the face of L's clear insistence upon the need for further evidence before any preliminary issues were determined. The legal test for removal of an arbitrator was whether a reasonable person would no longer have confidence in the present arbitrator's ability to come to a fair and balanced conclusion on the issues if remitted. The whole interim award should be set aside and the arbitrator should be removed because it would, in the circumstances, be inappropriate to require him to try to re-determine what he had already determined once on the wrong basis.

LOVELL PARTNERSHIPS (NORTHERN) LTD v. AW CONSTRUCTION PLC 81 B.L.R. 83, Mance, J., QBD (Comm Ct).

926. Architects–builders–joint and several liability–apportionment of liability

[Defective Premises Act 1972 s.1.]

M purchased a house which had been built by P, the work having been supervised by architects, DC. Subsequently, floors cracked and expert advice showed that inappropriate construction materials had been used. M instituted proceedings against both P and DC claiming breach of statutory duty under the Defective Premises Act 1972 s.1. DC had accepted P's assurances that the correct materials had been used but had not sought to verify that they had. The judge found that the defendants were jointly and severally responsible and that the proper apportionment was 40 per cent against DC. DC appealed.

Held, dismissing the appeal, that the judge had applied the right tests. He had considered questions of causation and culpability. The apportionment made was within the spectrum of his discretion.

McKENZIE v. POTTS 50 Con. L.R. 40, Russell, L.J., CA.

927. Architects Act 1997 (c.22)

This Act consolidates enactments relating to architects in respect of the Architects Registration Board, professional standards and disciplinary procedures, and persons entitled to use the title "architect".

This Act received Royal Assent on March 19, 1997.

928. Architects Act 1997 (c.22)–Commencement Order

ARCHITECTS ACT 1997 (COMMENCEMENT) ORDER 1997, SI 1997 1672 (C.69); made under the Architects Act 1997 s.28. Commencement details: bringing into force various provisions of the Act on July 21, 1997; £0.65.

This Order brings the Architects Act 1997 into force with the exception of s.28 which came into force on Royal Assent.

929. Building and engineering contracts–defective work–defences–leave to raise further issues

C engaged H to carry out substantial improvements to a council estate and subsequently damp was discovered in a number of houses. Proceedings were commenced against H and the architects involved. The defence did not admit that damp was discovered after the improvements commenced and pleaded that the houses had been built on former marshland, that damp had been a problem since the houses were built and that the damp proof courses and membranes were inadequate. Also expressly pleaded was the fact that C had known of the damp penetration before the improvements commenced and contributory negligence was alleged. After 20 days of hearing, during which all C's witnesses of fact were heard, including the second defendant, the action was adjourned. Prior to commencement of the adjourned hearing H sought leave to raise two new matters; (1) whether or not there was actually any penetrating damp in the houses at any material time after H had carried out the improvements, and (2) whether or not in employing its own direct works department to remedy the alleged defects C had acted ultra vires.

Held, refusing leave to raise those issues, that the amendments concerning the timing of the existence of the damp were not only put forward at a late stage but were also inconsistent with the basis upon which all parties had prepared for trial. They were the type of issue which should have been raised at an early stage to enable all parties to evaluate the position, and obtain further advice if necessary before incurring the heavy costs of preparation for trial. In exercising its discretion to allow an amendment during a trial, the court should be satisfied that a new defence would be supported by firm evidence which was not so in the instant case. C's case was not an action to enforce an ultra vires contract but one to recover damages for defective work and the normal measure of loss was the cost of reinstatement to the condition in which the houses should have been. There was never a suggestion that the work should not have been carried out and therefore there was no defence of ultra vires.

COPELAND BC v. HAYTON BUILDERS LTD (1997) 13 Const. L.J. 253, Judge Gilliland Q.C., QBD.

930. **Building and engineering contracts–disputes–role of superintendent–court had jurisdiction to review supervising officer's decision–New South Wales**

A agreed to construct for W a flood prevention levee on the Hunter River. The contract was a Schedule of Rates Contract on the NPWC Ed. 3 (1981) form. The contract provided for material to be used for zone 1 fill in the levee to be obtained from a designated borrow-pit area. In excavating that area, A encountered significant quantities of material unsuitable for use in zone 1 and consequently there was a deficiency of suitable material. Clause 12 of the Special Conditions provided that if the contractor encountered physical conditions which could not reasonably have been foreseen, notice should be given to the superintendent who could order a variation to the work under the contract, provided the appropriate conditions applied. Clause 45 of the General Conditions provided that disputes be submitted to the superintendent for decision in the first instance. If the contractor was dissatisfied with that decision, it should then be submitted to the principal. If the contractor was dissatisfied with the principal's decision, the matter could then be referred to arbitration; and further, that no proceedings should be instituted unless and until the arbitrator had made his award in respect of that matter. A made a claim under cl.12. W contended that since A had not disputed the superintendent's rejection of the claim within the time stated in cl.45, the court had no jurisdiction to entertain the claim.

Held, upholding the decision of the court referee, that (1) the deficiency of suitable material within the designated borrow-pit area was a physical condition within the meaning of cl.12; (2) A had given notice sufficient for the purposes of cl.12; (3) the superintendent had ordered a variation; (4) even if the superintendent had not ordered a variation, the court was not precluded by the terms of the arbitration clause from finding that a variation should have been ordered because the superintendent's role was to determine questions of fact and not to exercise discretion, *Northern RHA v. Derek Crouch Construction Co Ltd* [1984] Q.B. 644, [1984] C.L.Y. 117 distinguished, and because the contractor had not given notice of arbitration and nothing in cl.45 excluded the

right of the contractor to go to court in such circumstances, and (5) the court would apply the contract by awarding a reasonable rate or price for the work.
ATLANTIC CIVIL PROPRIETARY LTD v. WATER ADMINISTRATION MINISTERIAL CORP (1997) 13 Const. L.J. 184, Giles, J., Sup Ct (NSW).

931. Building and engineering contracts—formation of contract—misunderstanding as to existence of contract—fair value for work performed

D required extensive building work to be carried out at its business premises. The original stripping out works were let to an undischarged bankrupt, V, who engaged others to carry out the work and invoiced D in another name to disguise the fact that he could not trade himself. D then approached V to tender for the main contract works and V approached L. He allowed L to think that he was the authorised representative of D and D to think that he was the agent of L. L duly commenced work and both parties believed there was a contract in place at that time. No discussion or agreement was reached as to how variations would be dealt with and their effect on the completion date. The works took longer than anticipated and there were substantial increases in work, then disputes arose as to who owed what to whom. L issued proceedings and D counterclaimed for losses suffered.

Held, that contrary to both parties' belief at the time, there was no contract concluded and therefore L were entitled to be paid a fair value for the work carried out. As a general rule a fair value for work in these circumstances ought to provide for a reasonable or normal profit margin over and above the costs actually and properly incurred in carrying out the work. The general rule did not, however, apply in all circumstances. When fixing a fair value, the pricing level at which the building contractor had indicated it was prepared to undertake the works should be taken into account, even if that level would inevitably result in the building contractor making an overall loss. What was fair between any two particular parties can only be judged by reference to the particular facts of the case. Both parties had sued upon the basis that a contract existed. Even though the judge had invited the parties to consider an amendment to plead a quantum meruit, since no costs would have been avoided if the alternative plea had been added earlier, it was fair and reasonable to allow the amendment after the draft judgment had been handed down.
LACHHANI v. DESTINATION CANADA (UK) LTD (1997) 13 Const. L.J. 279, Recorder Reese Q.C., QBD.

932. Building and engineering contracts—global claims—power of court to strike out claim—Victoria

J and K entered into a joint venture agreement in connection with works in relation to a floating production storage offloading facility. On behalf of the joint venture J entered into two contracts with a third party which had had a drilling operation in the area. J claimed against K for extra costs alleged to have been incurred in performing one of the contracts. K applied to strike out J's statement of claim as insufficiently particularising the link between breach and damage.

Held, dismissing the application, that the claim objected to was a global claim and a total cost claim in which the causal nexus between breach and damage was inferred rather than demonstrated. However, it was for the relevant party and not the court to determine how its case should be framed and the power of the court to strike out a claim was very limited. It might be exercised where the claim was so evidently unsustainable that it would be a waste of resources to permit that to be demonstrated only after a trial or where the pleading was likely to prejudice, embarrass or delay the fair trial of the action. The question whether in a given case a pleading based on a global claim or even a total cost claim or some variant was likely to or might prejudice, embarrass or delay the fair trial of a proceeding must depend upon an examination of the pleading itself and the claim being made, *British Airways Pension Trustees Ltd v. Sir Robert McAlpine & Sons Ltd* 72 B.L.R. 26, [1996] 1 C.L.Y. 858. However, the court should be assiduous in pressing a plaintiff to set out the causal nexus between breach and loss with sufficient particularity to enable the defendant to know exactly the case it was required to meet and to enable the defendant to direct its discovery and its attention generally to that case and that the issues so arising were defined with sufficient particularity to enable the trial judge to address the issues, to rule on relevance and generally to contain the parties to the issues. J would be given the further opportunity to remedy the defects in its statement of claim by amendment or further particularisation.

JOHN HOLLAND CONSTRUCTION & ENGINEERING PTY LTD v. KVAERNER RJ BROWN PTY LTD 82 B.L.R. 81, Byrne, J, Sup Ct (Vic).

933. Building and engineering contracts–installation of UPVC windows– defective work causing structural damage to property–loss of amenity and inconvenience–harassment and intimidation

B a retired lady who lived alone, entered into a contract with W in 1990 for installation of new UPVC windows to her house at a lump sum price of £3,300 plus VAT. The work involved the manufacture and installation of the window units, and took three days. The work was of appalling standard, the frames were too big and to make the windows fit W cut out part of the structure of the house by removing bricks and gable supports, without the knowledge or consent of B. The house suffered severe structural damage, weakening the strength of the gable end, leaving it to rest directly on the window frame. The windows were delivered with broken glass, and gaps on the outside were left during installation. The windows were fitted at wrong angles, had the wrong finishes and wrong type of wood. The original stained glass was removed and not returned. Birds were able to nest in eaves of the gable end. No dust covers had been used in the house and it was left in a very dirty state after the work was completed. Evidence was that the windows were not re-usable after removal from property. B refused to pay for the work and issued proceedings for damages. Thereafter over a four year period a director of W visited B's house and threatened to remove the windows and demanded payment and there was evidence that someone had removed leading from the windows. B was very intimidated and lost one stone in weight due to worry. The police were involved, and threats were made to B's solicitors by W's director on the telephone.

Held, awarding damages to B, that the judge accepted that the actions of W's director were intended to intimidate B and cause her to withdraw proceedings. The court awarded £11,600 for the costs of repairing damage to house and obtaining replacement windows; £1,500 for loss of amenity and inconvenience over the two year period; aggravated damages of £3,000 to express the court's grave displeasure at the action of the director of W. W's counterclaim for cost of work done was dismissed on the grounds of substantial non performance of lump sum contract, *Bolton v. Mahadeva* [1972] 1 W.L.R. 1009, [1972] C.L.Y. 502 applied.

BROWN v. WEST MIDLANDS PATIO DOORS LTD, February 20, 1997, H.H.J. McEvoy Q.C., CC (Kidderminster). [*Ex rel.* John Stenhouse, Barrister, 6 Fountain Court, Birmingham].

934. Building and engineering contracts–JCT forms of contract–employer failed to insure against risk of fire–contractor not entitled to escape liability for fire caused by own negligence

S was instructed to carry out work in accordance with the JCT standard form of agreement for minor building works (October 1988). Under condition 6.2, S was required to insure against loss caused by its negligence and under condition 6.3B, the employer was to take out insurance against fire in joint names. However, B did not effect the joint insurance cover and later sought to claim against S under condition 6.2 for direct and consequential loss from damage to the building and its contents following a fire caused by the negligence of S's subcontractor. S's submission by way of set off and counterclaim, that much of B's claim under condition 6.2 would have been covered by the insurance obtained pursuant to condition 6.3B and B's failure to insure had therefore deprived it of the protection it would otherwise have had, was rejected and S appealed.

Held, dismissing the appeal, that although in *National Trust for Places of Historic Interest or Natural Beauty v. Haden Young Ltd* 72 B.L.R. 1, [1996] 1 C.L.Y. 1215 it was considered that a general overlap might exist between the provisions of conditions 6.2 and 6.3B, they were concerned with different types of damage. Under condition 6.2 unqualified liability was imposed on a contractor for damage culpably caused by him, but condition 6.3B did not indicate that an employer had to insure against specified perils in a way that included acts due to the contractor's negligence. Most of the risks specified in condition 6.3B were natural phenomena or "acts of God" type risks, and "fire" should be interpreted in that context. Unnecessary expense and duplication of cover would arise if there was an overlap between the conditions and that could not have been the intention of the draftsman. In addition, it could not have been the intention of either the parties or the draftsman for the benefit of employer's insurance under condition 6.3B to be used to allow the contractor to avoid liability imposed under condition 6.2 and at common law.

BARKING AND DAGENHAM LBC v. STAMFORD ASPHALT CO LTD 82 B.L.R. 25, Auld, L.J., CA.

935. Building and engineering contracts—JCT forms of contract—notice of termination—injunction to restrain discharge of notice

P, a developer, engaged W as management contractor under a contract based substantially on the JCT standard form of management contract 1987 edition. The contract administrator served notice of default under cl.7.1 upon W citing alleged failure to carry out works in an economical and expeditious manner. W commenced proceedings against P for an interim and permanent injunction restraining P from serving a notice of determination based on the notice of default. P sought to have the interim injunction set aside.

Held, refusing P's application and granting W a permanent injunction, that the notice of default was invalid. As management contractor, W did not have any duty to carry out the works. W's duties were to carry out the obligations referred to under Art.1 regularly and diligently. The notice required W to provide satisfactory information to answer an unstated complaint, *Hounslow LBC v. Twickenham Garden Developments Ltd* [1971] 1 Ch. 233, [1970] C.L.Y. 2436 distinguished, and gave no indication as to what remedial action WC should take. It expressed an intention to determine the contract regardless of W's future performance. The balance of convenience lay in continuing the injunction. Although P could lawfully determine the contract under the non standard cl.7.10, there were doubts as to whether P would be financially able to compensate W in damages. Since the notice was invalid, there was insufficient documentation to start the contractual procedure for determination of the contract, *Tara Civil Engineering Ltd v. Moorfield Developments Ltd* 46 B.L.R. 72, [1990] C.L.Y. 410 distinguished, and the court was not satisfied that P would determine the contract under cl.7.10.

WILTSHIRE CONSTRUCTION (SOUTH) LTD v. PARKERS DEVELOPMENTS LTD (1997) 13 Const. L.J. 129, Judge Havery Q.C., QBD (OR).

936. Building and engineering contracts—JCT forms of contract—precontract letter a document forming part of contract

By letter dated December 22, 1989, C's architects invited E's tender for work comprising the construction of a sports and social club. The architects supplied E with a number of drawings and an outline specification. E tendered, and on August 30, 1990 the architects wrote that C intended to enter into a contract with E for the works based on the drawings and specifications sent to E. Work started on site in September 1990. On October 30, 1990 E wrote to C's architects making certain alterations to the drawings and other documents to be incorporated into the contract and stating that the letter had also been included in and would form part of the contract documents. The letter and the documents referred to in it were bound up into the contract sent to C for signature and that contract was signed by C on October 31, 1990. The further documents were, insofar as they related to the car park works and electrical works, discrepant with documents which it was common ground were contract documents. The contract incorporated the JCT standard form of building contract private without quantities form 1980 ed. C later contended that since the relevant documents did not fall within the definition of contract documents contained in Condition 1.3 of the Conditions of Contract they were not contract documents. The dispute was referred to arbitration and the award was appealed.

Held, dismissing the appeal, that (1) the further drawings and documents were incorporated into the contract because they were the culmination of months of negotiation and were bound into the contract documents; (2) the discrepancies between the two drawings relating to the car park works and between the specification in relation to the electrical works were to be resolved by the express statement in E's tender letter, dated August 16, 1990, itself a contract document, that the extent of those works was limited by the reference to them in the drawings and on the electrical specification supplied by subcontractor M, identified in E's tender letter, and (3) part of the arbitrator's award in relation to electrical works would be remitted to the arbitrator so that the claim could be properly particularised so that the individual items which were to be valued could be particularised and once identified priced.

CRITTALL WINDOWS LTD v. TJ EVERS LTD 54 Con. L.R. 66, Judge John Lloyd Q.C., QBD (OR).

937. **Building and engineering contracts–labour only subcontracts–personal injuries sustained by employee of subcontractor–construction of indemnity clause**

M, an employee of B, was working on a construction site at which the main contractor was S, under a labour only subcontract between B and S under which the former agreed to supply labour for the latter on the site. The subcontract contained an indemnity clause, requiring B to insure against all employer's liability and third party risks, indemnify S against all claims, and provided further that S would not be liable for any claim arising out of an accident to an employee of B. In 1983 M was seriously injured on the site, and recovered damages in negligence and breach of statutory duty against B. B joined S as third parties claiming a contribution. B's claim against S was dismissed at first instance in 1996 and B appealed, arguing that B's obligation to indemnify S was limited to B's own liabilities; it did not extend to an obligation to indemnify S in respect of S's liabilities.

Held, dismissing the appeal, that in every case concerning the proper construction of an indemnity clause the question whether an indemnity would run or not depended on the construction of the words used, read in the context of the contract as a whole. The approach to be adopted in ascertaining the presumed intention of the parties, where not otherwise apparent from the contract, was in accordance with the test laid down in *Canada Steamship Lines Ltd v. Queen, The* [1952] A.C. 192, [1952] C.L.Y. 610 considered. But where appropriate steps had been taken to allocate risk, and a sensible construction leads to the conclusion that the proferens was indemnified against his own negligence, then no court has shown any inhibition in accepting that result without seeking to resile from it by recourse to *Canada Steamship* test. In the instant case the contract contemplated that a workman who was injured might sue both his own employer and the main contractor, which demonstrated the purpose of the clause that B should maintain insurance and indemnify S against all risks commonly insured against. B's obligation to produce receipts showing payment of premiums could be relevant only if the intention was to relieve S of the obligation to insure, it being specifically contemplated that S would otherwise want to insure against injury to B's employees. The fact that B contended that they would not have entered the contract on the basis that they were to indemnify S in respect of its own negligence was irrelevant. Although there was no express reference to negligence on the part of S in the indemnity clause, the words "all claims", when used in the instant context, necessarily covered S's negligence.

MORRIS v. BREAVEGLEN LTD (T/A ANZAC CONSTRUCTION CO); MORRIS v. SLEEMAN LTD, Trans. Ref: QBENF 96/0501/C, May 9, 1997, Leggatt, L.J., CA.

938. Building and engineering contracts—performance bond—notification of non observance or non performance as condition precedent of bond

[Unfair Contract Terms Act 1977.]

O engaged a contractor to construct halls of residence. The contract was substantially in the terms of a JCT Standard Form of Building Contract with Contractor's Design (1981 edition incorporating amendments 1 to 6 inclusive). The contractor had procured the issue of a bond by A. The bond provided as a condition precedent to A's liability that notification should be made to it by O of any non performance or non observation of the contract by the contractor. The contractor failed to perform in two material respects. First, from August 23, 1994 the contractor was in breach of cl.23.1 of the JCT conditions by reason of its failure to complete the works by August 23, 1994. O failed to notify A of this non performance or non observation of the contract within one month of it coming to its attention. Secondly, the employment of the contractor was automatically determined on October 18, 1994 pursuant to cl.27.2 because of it being placed in the hands of administrative receivers. O did give notice to A within one month of this event. A resisted O's claim to be paid pursuant to the bond on the ground that due notice had not been given. O denied this contending on its true construction the condition precedent required notification of the non performance or non observance which constituted or gave rise to the particular breach in relation to which the call under the bond was made. O further contended that the Unfair Contract Terms Act 1977 applied to the bond and that the condition precedent was unreasonable.

Held, dismissing the claim, that (1) on its true construction the condition precedent to the bond applied to any non performance and non observation of the contractual obligations and since notice had not been given timeously in relation to the first non performance or non observation A was not liable under the bond at all, *Clydebank & District Water Trustees v. Fidelity & Deposit Co of Maryland* 1915 S.C. 69 followed; (2) the Unfair Contract Terms Act 1977 applied to the bond which was a contract made upon A's written terms of business within the meaning of s.3, and (3) the terms of the bond satisfied the requirement of reasonableness since A did not claim to be entitled to render no performance or a substantially different contractual performance from that reasonably to be expected of it.

OVAL (717) LTD v. AEGON INSURANCE CO (UK) LTD 54 Con. L.R. 74, Recorder Colin Reese Q.C., QBD (OR).

939. Building and engineering contracts—referral of dispute to construction manager—statements of claim

B was a landscape contractor awarded a contract by S's predecessor for the construction of a new golf course at a reclaimed landfill site. The contract incorporated some provisions of the ICE conditions of contract 5th ed. Clause 66 was deleted and by a new cl.68 it was provided that the parties should refer their disputes to the construction manager, whose decision should be final and binding until after completion of the works, and English courts should have jurisdiction over any dispute or difference which should arise between the employer or the construction manager on its behalf and the contractor. The progress of the works were dependent upon the progress of an earthworks contractor, and the provision of the site and access to various parts of the site by S. B contended that its progress overall and within every section and area was held up by the various acts and defaults on the part of S. B issued proceedings and served a statement of claim which annexed to it a claim document, but failed to set out in the body of the statement of claim itself any of the terms of the contract, the nature of the breaches of those terms relied upon as founding claims for damages, or the basis upon which claims were advanced under the express terms of the contract. Subsequently, B sought leave to amend its statement of claim. S applied to strike out the existing statement of claim and opposed the application for leave to amend on the grounds that the proposed amended pleading was no better than the original. S also argued that B was obliged to submit the dispute to the construction manager pursuant to cl.68.

Held, allowing certain of the amendments sought, refusing others and making no order on the application to strike out the pleading, that (1) S was prima facie entitled to insist that the dispute be first submitted to the construction manager in accordance with cl.68, *Enco Civil Engineering Ltd v. Zeus International Development Ltd* 56 B.L.R. 43, [1993] C.L.Y. 298 and *Channel Tunnel Group Ltd v. Balfour Beatty Construction Ltd* [1993] A.C 334, [1993] C.L.Y. 151 applied. The proper course, however, was to order the issue to be pleaded out so that B could put forward reasons why prior reference to the construction manager was not required, and (2) a party was entitled to present its case as it thought fit and was not to be directed as to the method by which it was to plead or prove its claim but a defendant was entitled to know the case it had to meet. In order to ensure fairness and observance to the principles of natural justice, a court might require a party to spell out its case with sufficient particularity and, where its case depended upon the causal affect of an interaction of events, to spell out the nexus in an intelligible form. A party would not be entitled to prove at trial a case which it was unable to plead having been given a reasonable opportunity to do so since in that event the other party would be faced at trial with a case which it did not have a reasonable and sufficient opportunity to meet. A cost effective balance had to be struck in assessing the degree of sufficient particularity. In those circumstances, conditions would be attached to the grant of leave to amend so as to limit B's case but not to require it to present a case other than the one which it wished to put forward. B should identify those variations, events or acts and omissions which were relied upon as critical or crucial to the costs claim so that S knew which of the events were said to rely on a notion or critical part and which costs were caused by those key events, *Wharf Properties Ltd v. Eric Cumine Associates (No.2)* 52 B.L.R. 1, [1992] C.L.Y. 3375, *Nauru Phosphate Royalties Trust Ltd v. Matthew Hall Mechanical & Electrical Engineering Pty* [1994] 2 V.R. 386 and *John Holland Construction & Engineering Pty Ltd v. Kvaerner RJ Brown Pty Ltd* 82 B.L.R. 81, [1997] C.L.Y. 932 considered.

BERNHARD'S RUGBY LANDSCAPES LTD v. STOCKLEY PARK CONSORTIUM LTD 82 B.L.R. 39, Humphrey Lloyd Q.C., QBD (OR).

940. Building and engineering contracts–repudiation–VAT payable in addition to the quoted price

T agreed to transfer land to J and undertake certain infrastructure works. The price of the work was agreed to be £800,000 but omitted any reference to VAT. Attempts to negotiate the termination of the contract were made which T contended were successful, but which J denied. T sued for the recovery of the unpaid VAT.

Held, allowing the claim for VAT, that (1) vital terms of an agreement that T might abandon the works were not agreed, but T nevertheless went off site without having achieved such agreement. T therefore repudiated the agreement, and (2) there was a notorious, certain and reasonable custom in the construction industry and between those involved in the construction industry that VAT was payable on top of the quoted price.

TONY COX (DISMANTLERS) LTD v. JIM 5 LTD (1997) 13 Const. L.J. 209, Judge Bowsher Q.C., QBD (OR).

941. Building and engineering contracts–standard forms of contract–construction in face of counter offer–DOM/1

J invited DS to tender. DS submitted a tender and revised tender, then J made an order for DS to carry out subcontract works on a building project. There was a provision in the contact that "No conditions of your quotation which may be additional to, or at variance with, those of this order shall be applicable except as stated below (For standard conditions see reverse)". An agreement in writing was subsequently signed. The project was delayed and the employer deducted sums due to J who then withheld monies from DS. DS issued a specially endorsed writ and applied for summary judgment or an interim payment. J counterclaimed a higher sum by way of set off and DS's claim was dismissed. By summons J then sought declarations from the Official Referee that (1) J's standard terms and conditions were not incorporated in the agreement, and (2) in any event, cl.4 was unenforceable because it was inconsistent with cl.23 of DOM/1. The first argument was dismissed but the second was accepted in part and a declaration made that parts of cl.4 were unenforceable, resulting in J's right to set off being restricted. J appealed in respect of the second argument and DS cross-appealed in respect of the first.

Held, dismissing the appeal and cross appeal, that a counter offer purporting to offer two standard terms was unbusinesslike but that did not necessarily mean one set should be excluded. The court was under a duty to consider the terms of the contract documents and the concluded agreement and if possible to give effect to all the terms of the agreement. J's order form permitted that conditions at variance with the order could apply. J's order referred to DS's tender which incorporated DOM/1 by specific reference and therefore fell within the provision "except as stated below" in the order. Therefore, the standard terms and conditions were ineffective to the extent that they were in conflict with DOM/1.

DRAKE & SCULL ENGINEERING LTD v. J JARVIS & SONS PLC (1997) 13 Const. L.J. 263, Pill, L.J., CA.

942. **Building regulations–breach of building regulations–service of notice where no application for building regulation approval**

[Building Act 1984 s.36; Building Regulations 1991 (SI 1991 2768).]

Held, that a notice under the Building Act 1984 s.36 could be validly served on a person carrying out works who had not made an application for building regulation approval, as there was nothing in s.36 of the 1984 Act which gave rise to an inference that it was necessary for such an application to have been made before a notice could be issued. To give effect to such an inference would be contrary to the purpose of s.36, which was to provide local authorities with a practical means of dealing with works which contravened the Building Regulations 1991.

PARLETT v. KERRIER DC, *The Independent,* October 6, 1997 (C.S.), Scott Baker, J., QBD.

943. **Building regulations–safety**

BUILDING REGULATIONS (AMENDMENT) REGULATIONS 1997, SI 1997 1904; made under the Building Act 1984 s.1, s.3, s.126, Sch.1 para.1, Sch.1 para.2, Sch.1 para.7, Sch.1 para.8, Sch.1 para.10. In force: January 1, 1998; £1.10.

These Regulations amend the Building Regulations 1991 (SI 1991 2768) by extending existing provisions relating to the safety of stairs, ladders and ramps and relating to safety features preventing people from falling, to stairs which give access to levels of buildings for maintenance purposes only. They also incorporate new requirements relating to the protection of people from collision with vehicles in loading bays, the protection of people from collision with open windows, skylights and ventilators, the protection of people from being trapped or hit by sliding doors or gates, the provision of safe means of opening, closing and adjusting windows, skylights and ventilators and for the provision of safe means of access for cleaning windows and skylights.

944. Design and build contracts–binding contract despite failure to agree on terms of performance tests

J, the main contractor for the turnkey construction of a power station, engaged M to design, manufacture and install two generators. It was envisaged that the generators would be performance tested but the parties were unable to agree on the nature of tests. M was anxious for tolerance but J required strict compliance with design requirements and the payment of liquidated damages in the event of failure. The contract was signed by both parties but the clause headed "Performance Tests" was struck out and a marginal annotation "to be discussed and agreed" added. There was evidence to show that, at the time of signature, both J and M expected an agreement about performance testing would soon be reached, but this was not done. M applied for a declaration that no contract came into existance, or, if there was a contract, failure subsequently to agree the outstanding terms rendered the agreement unworkable or void for uncertainty.

Held, refusing the declaration, that (1) the signed document was a binding contract. The objective inference from the language and circumstances was that the parties intended to be bound by the document. Failure to agree on the tests did not render the agreement unworkable or void for uncertainty, and (2) if there had been no contract M had done nothing to waive any defects in the contractual arrangements. However, the parties had acted on the basis that it was a binding contract, with M seeking to obtain payment from J on the basis of the contractual terms, without which no such payment would have been due. M's conduct amounted to estoppel which would preclude M from denying it was a binding contract.

MITSUI BABCOCK ENERGY LTD v. JOHN BROWN ENGINEERING LTD 51 Con. L.R. 129, Esyr Lewis Q.C., QBD (OR).

945. Dispute resolution–ICE conditions of contract–right to challenge engineer's decision

T and E entered into a contract for the construction of a motorway service area based substantially on the ICE conditions of contract (5th ed.), but with significant additions to cl.60 and a major alteration of cl.66 removing the provision for arbitration and providing that matters in dispute were to be "determined by litigation". There were numerous disputes with T requesting decisions by the engineer and the engineer issuing decisions under cl.66. T gave notice to E of dissatisfaction with the decisions and intention to proceed to litigation. E applied to strike out T's claim. E contended that the engineer's decision was final, provided it was given honestly, fairly and reasonably. The function of the court in a reference to litigation under cl.66 was limited to whether or not the reference was valid pursuant to cl.66 and if valid, whether there had been a breach of the contract, a failure by the engineer to act honestly, fairly and reasonably or a failure by the engineer to give a proper decision under cl.66. The final certificate in the sum of £10,819,710 was conclusive as the total amount finally due. In response T contended that the engineer's decision was provisional and not necessarily binding.

Held, refusing to strike out the claim, that the decision in *Northern RHA v. Derek Crouch Construction Co Ltd* [1984] 1 Q.B. 644, [1984] C.L.Y. 117 was concerned with a contract where the parties had agreed either that the decision of a third party was final and binding or that the modification or variation of rights and obligations determined by a third party might be reviewed by another. The decision did not establish a principle capable of overriding or qualifying what otherwise would be the natural interpretation of a contract. Although a contract could be worded so that the final certificate removed the court's dispute adjudication powers, the clarity of language needed to do so was absent here. T had adequately demonstrated dissatisfaction with the final certificate within the requisite time.

TARMAC CONSTRUCTION LTD v. ESSO PETROLEUM CO LTD 51 Con. L.R. 187, Humphrey Lloyd Q.C., QBD (OR).

946. Fire precautions—shopping centres—liability of managing agents

See ENVIRONMENTAL HEALTH: DTZ DebenhamThorpe Ltd v. Shropshire CC. §2376

947. Negligence—economic loss—losses resulting from severance of electricity supply

See NEGLIGENCE: Londonwaste Ltd v. Amec Civil Engineering Ltd. §3776

948. Party Wall etc. Act 1996 (c.40)—Commencement Order

PARTY WALL ETC. ACT 1996 (COMMENCEMENT) ORDER 1997, SI 1997 670 (C.24); made under the Party Wall etc. Act 1996 s.22. Commencement details: bringing into force various provisions of the Act on July 1, 1997; £0.65.

Subject to transitional provisions, this Order brings the provisions of the Party Wall etc. Act 1996 into force.

949. Party walls—repeal of local enactments

PARTY WALL ETC. ACT 1996 (REPEAL OF LOCAL ENACTMENTS) ORDER 1997, SI 1997 671; made under the Party Wall etc. Act 1996 s.21. In force: July 1, 1997; £1.10.

Subject to saving provisions, this Order repeals the London Building Acts (Amendment) Act 1939 Part VI and the Bristol Improvement Act 1847 s.xxvii to s.xxxii due to the coming into force of the Party Wall etc. Act 1996 on July 1, 1997.

950. Subcontracts—standard forms of contract—contractual regulation of equitable set off—defence of abatement unavailable

[Rules of the Supreme Court Ord.14.]

M appealed against the refusal to grant summary judgment for interim payments due from B for work undertaken. M were subcontractors, and B the main contractors, for construction of educational premises. The terms of the subcontract governed by DOM/1 provided by cl.21 for interim payments, in accordance with a timetable, to be paid by B to M, and entitled B to deduct any set off permitted by cl.23 of the agreement, provided that there was advance notice. Payments were due on August 13 and September 13, 1995 and on September 18 B wrote claiming set off for costs incurred as a result of M's delay. M claimed the balance of the payments totalling £10,165. The Official Referee held that, although B could not claim set off under cl.23 because notice was served after the payments were due, B could use the defence of abatement for the costs caused by M's delay. M contended that the defence was limited to loss of value of goods or works supplied.

Held, allowing the appeal, that (1) B was not able to raise the defence of abatement for losses attributable to delay, *Mondel v. Steel* (1841) 8 M. & W. 858 considered. It must be shown that the breach of contract directly affected and reduced the actual value of the work or goods which was not the case here as B's losses related to disruption of their work and that of other subcontractors. A separate action should be brought for losses caused by delay; the established limits of abatement should not be departed from, *Davis v. Hedges* [1871] L.R. 6 Q.B. 687, *Oastler v. Pound* [1863] L.T. 852 applied, and (2) an error in the affidavit in support, claiming an incorrect amount, was an error of procedure rather than substance and the requirements of RSC Ord.14 had been complied with.

MELLOWES ARCHITAL LTD v. BELL PROJECTS LTD, Trans. Ref: QBENI 97/0437/B, October 15, 1997, Buxton, L.J., CA.

CONSTRUCTION LAW

951. Articles

A consulting engineer's view: delegation of duties *(Stephen Rockhill)*: C. & E.L. 1997, 2(2), 6-8. (Contractual position where consulting engineer delegates elements of design process to specialist contractor).

An engineer's view: safety in numbers *(John Wasilewski)*: C. & E.L. 1997, 2(2), 3-5. (Interpretation of terms used in construction contracts such as "factor of safety" and "best endeavours", and practical and legal importance of appreciating how common sense meanings may not coincide with engineer's understanding).

Arbitration: C.I.L.L. 1997, Apr, 1241-1242. (Comparison of new ICE Arbitration Procedure and Construction Industry Model Arbitration Rules following entry into force of Arbitration Act 1996).

Case study: construction *(Shaun Tame)*: Litigator 1997, Mar, 84-105. (Case study of liability for loss and remedial works necessitated by fire in retail development exacerbated by structural defects, giving position of the architect, engineer, contractor and developer).

Compulsory adjudication in construction contracts *(Simmons & Simmons)*: I.H.L. 1997, 51 (Jun), 52-53. (Housing Grants, Construction and Regeneration Act 1996 Part II procedure imposing duties on contractors and whether scope of statutory definition of "construction contracts" could include licences and leases).

Exclusive remedies and liability in respect of pre-contract misrepresentations *(John Little)*: Cons. Law 1997, 8(9), 305-307. (Whether cl.44.4 of Model Form of General Conditions of Contract excludes claims for damages based on breaches of contract or pre-contract misrepresentation).

Expert witnessing in the dock *(Nick Barrett)*: Cons. Law 1997, 8(4), 137-138. (Abuse of expert witness system by experts not giving unbiased opinions and RICS practice statement on professional obligations).

Fit for a change: the position of fitness for purpose in the construction industry *(Paul Buckland)*: Cons. Law 1997, 8(8), 255-259. (Distinctions between fitness for purpose warranty and warranty to exercise reasonable skill and care, illustrated by relevant cases).

Fitness for purpose: the implied design obligation in construction contracts *(Hazel Fleming)*: Const. L.J. 1997, 13(4), 227-242. (Cases in which courts have imposed implied term as to standard of care in traditional construction contracts and design and build contracts).

Formula calculations for the ascertainment of losses *(John Deacon)*: Cons. Law 1997, 8(6), 204-206. (Mathematical formulae for calculating losses arising out of breach of construction contract and whether they are substitute for basic common law principles of ascertaining losses).

How will "pay-when-paid" clauses be affected by the Construction Act? *(Jonathan Hosie)*: Cons. Law 1997, 8(7), 236-240. (Extent to which conditional clauses are prohibited by the Housing Grants, Construction and Regeneration Act 1996).

My bond is my word *(Robert Akenhead)*: C. & E.L. 1997, 2(4/5), 13-14. (Use of on demand bonds and conditional bonds as means of protection from insolvency of party to construction contract).

Partnering: contractual considerations *(Trevor Butcher)*: Cons. Law 1997, 8(3), 79-83. (Legal effect of partnering agreements in construction industry).

Party animals: knocking down the walls *(Mark Watson-Gandy)*: Lit. 1997, 16(7), 267-268. (Extent to which law recognises right of support for buildings and rights of party wall owners under the London Building Acts (Amendment) Act 1939).

Potential side-effects of the CDM regulations *(John Barber)*: Const. L.J. 1997, 13(2), 95-106. (Practical effect of the Construction (Design and Management) Regulations 1994, primarily dealing with health and safety aspects of construction sites, and on relationships between design and construction team).

Recent cases on the Blue Form *(David Gwillim)*: Cons. Law 1997, 8(5), 152-155. (Subcontractor's right to claim against contractor under FCEC standard form of subcontract and extent to which claims under main contract and subcontract are back to back).

Remedies for defective work: drafting practice and policy *(Peter Sheridan and Tom Pemberton)*: Cons. Law 1997, 8(6), 196-199.

Remedies for defective work: principles *(Peter Sheridan and Tom Pemberton)*: Cons. Law 1997, 8(5), 156-160.

Spark of hope for subcontractors: E.G.1997, 9746, 149-151. (Provisions of Housing Grants, Construction and Regeneration Act 1996 Part II relating to payments due under construction contracts).

Stay of proceedings: the new law in construction matters *(Peter Sheridan)*: A.D.R.L.J. 1997, 3(Jul), 208-220. (Disadvantages of the Arbitration Act 1996 for dealing with construction disputes, particularly regarding applications for stay of proceedings).

The Housing Grants Construction and Regeneration Act 1996: unexpected implications for infrastructure agreements *(Martin J. White)*: J.P.L. 1997, Jul, 611-614.

The magic formula *(Rosalind M.M. McInnes)*: S.J. 1997, 141(37), 926-927. (Approach of courts to use of formulae to ascertain loss of overheads and profits sustained by contractor in building project which has overrun).

The proof of excusable delay in building contracts without "as-built" records *(Keith Pickavance)*: Const. L.J. 1997, 13(4), 243-252. (Use of "as planned impacted" critical path analysis as method of establishing effect of variations and other events on contractor's work and liability for delays).

Towards a common law: the difficulty of harmonising international construction *(A. Martin Odams de Zylva)*: Const. L.J. 1997, 13(2), 107-117. (Practical consequences of standardising international construction law to accommodate global marketplace).

Works in occupied premises: some contractual pitfalls *(David Mosey)*: Cons. Law 1997, 8(4), 118-121. (Example of refurbishment of large number of residential units).

952. Books

Campbell, Peter—Construction Disputes. Hardback: £35.00. ISBN 1-870325-07-9. Whittles Publishing Services.

Clarke, H.W.; Higgs, T.A.; Thompson, E.—Knight's Building Regulations. Unbound/looseleaf: £250.00. ISBN 0-85314-737-X. Tolley Publishing.

Cockram, Richard—Manual of Construction Agreements. Unbound/looseleaf: £125.00. ISBN 0-85308-228-6. Jordan.

Fenn, Peter—Mediating Building and Construction Disputes. Paperback: £24.95. ISBN 1-85941-150-9. Cavendish Publishing Ltd.

Gordon, Kate—Adjudication in the Construction Industry. Special Reports. Hardback: £125.00. ISBN 0-7520-0453-0. FT Law & Tax.

Kelleher, Thomas J.—Construction Litigation: Practice Guide with Forms. Construction Law Library. Paperback: £75.00. ISBN 0-471-19729-7. Wiley.

Pickavance, Keith—Delay and Disruption in Construction Contracts. LLP Construction Practice Series. Hardback: £95.00. ISBN 1-85978-148-9. LLP Limited.

Scriven, John—Practical Construction Law. Paperback: £35.00. ISBN 0-421-57950-1. Sweet & Maxwell.

CONSUMER LAW

953. Advertisements—false descriptions—estate agents—prima facie case that the adverts had been placed by the partners—strict liability

[Trade Descriptions Act 1968 s.13, s.14, s.24(1).]

W appealed by way of case stated against a magistrates' decision to dismiss charges alleging breaches of the Trade Descriptions Act 1968 s.13 and s.14 made against R and S, who were partners in an estate agency. An advertisement bearing the partnership name had been placed in a local paper giving details of properties previously sold by the partnership. Out of 22 properties in the advertisement, 19 had been sold for less than the figure shown as the selling price. The magistrates had required the prosecutor, who was the local trading standards officer, to prove that the accused had initiated the placing of these advertisements, which contained false indications and false statements.

Held, allowing the appeal, that the magistrates had erred by stopping the case. The prosecutor had clearly established a prima facie case that the advertisement had been placed by the partners and that was all that was required by s.13. With regard to s.14, that offence was one of strict liability. It was for the defendants either to provide evidence to rebut that case or to establish a defence under s.24(1), *Wings Ltd v. Ellis* [1985] A.C. 272, [1984] C.L.Y. 3122 followed.

WALL v. ROSE, Trans. Ref: CO/4465/96, March 24, 1997, Brooke, J., QBD.

954. Advertisements–misleading claims–expectation of average citizen would be price reduction not free item

[Consumer Credit Act 1974 s.46.]

C advertised the sale of electrical equipment and its willingness to provide credit, stating, "Your purchase absolutely free. If we cannot beat our competitors' prices ask for details." The practice of C's manager was, when presented with evidence of a competitor's lower price, to beat it but not provide a full refund. D laid an information charging C with publishing a misleading advertisement contrary to the Consumer Credit Act 1974 s.46. The magistrates acquitted C on the basis that the advertisement was not misleading as the average citizen would not normally expect a free item, but a price reduction. D appealed by way of case stated.

Held, dismissing the appeal, that the magistrates had applied the correct test in asking themselves whether an ordinary person would be misled and the decision was neither unreasonable nor perverse.

DUDLEY MBC v. COLORVISION PLC [1997] C.C.L.R. 19, Schiemann, L.J., QBD.

955. Advertisements–test to be used when determining false trade description

Held, that the test for determining whether a false trade description had been given in an advertisement in a brochure issued with a specialised computer magazine, should be to consider the document as a whole and the reaction of a reasonable customer wishing to purchase equipment through that medium.

SOUTHWARK LBC v. TIME COMPUTER SYSTEMS LTD, *The Independent*, July 14, 1997 (C.S.), Henry, L.J., QBD.

956. Alcohol–use of term "whiskey" for clear spirit redistilled from blended Scotch whisky–drink did not comply with definition in EC Regulation–trade association had locus standi to seek injunction restraining use of name

[Council Regulation 1576/89 laying down detailed rules on the definition, description and presentation of spirit drinks Art.1.]

S sought an injunction against G restraining it from using the term "whiskey" to describe a clear spirit drink made by the redistillation of blended Scotch whisky which had previously undergone the traditional maturation process.

Held, granting the injunction, that the liquid sold by G could not be described as "whiskey" as it did not meet the standards laid down in the definition of whisky in Council Regulation 1576/89 Art.1(4)(b). The maturation process imparted the traditional colour and contributed to the taste of whisky, whereas the redistilled liquid produced by G was missing certain involatile maturation cogeners which remained in the container from which the mature whisky was redistilled. As the whisky producers' trade association, S had locus standi to bring proceedings to enforce the provisions of the Regulation, *Scotch Whisky Association v. JD Vintners Ltd* (Unreported) followed. The risk of damage to S's goodwill if G were permitted to continue to use the name "whiskey" would be the start of an insidious erosion of traditionally-made whisky's integrity and reputation in the eyes of consumers. For G to sell its drink as whisky was in breach of the Regulation and constituted passing off.

SCOTCH WHISKY ASSOCIATION v. GLEN KELLA DISTILLERS LTD (NO.2), *The Times*, April 1, 1997, Rattee, J., Ch D.

957. Conditional sales—part exchange of car—dealers failing to pay previous finance—car dealers becoming insolvent

I appealed against a decision, overturning the judge at first instance, that CF, as a third party, were not liable to indemnify her against a judgment in the sum of £3,135 including interest. I made a conditional sale agreement with FF to purchase a car and a year later agreed with a car dealer to purchase a newer model. The dealer agreed to take the first car in part exchange and to discharge the balance of £1,992 that was outstanding to FF. A new conditional sale agreement was made with CF for the second car, which involved I paying a deposit of £1,000. The dealer went into liquidation, having failed to pay FF, and the first car disappeared from the dealer's premises. CF argued that the two transactions were entirely separate.

Held, allowing the appeal, that the mere fact that the agreed value for the first car cancelled out the amount still outstanding upon it did not mean that there had been two transactions. Where goods which would be the subject of a debtor, creditor, supplier agreement, were sold or proposed to be sold by a broker, then any negotiations relating to those goods would be deemed to have been made by the negotiator on behalf of the creditor, *Powell v. Lloyds Bowmaker Ltd* [1996] C.C.L.R. 50, [1996] 2 C.L.Y. 6697 disapproved and *UDT v. Whitfield* [1987] C.C.L.R. 60, [1986] C.L.Y. 375 approved.

FORTHRIGHT FINANCE LTD v. INGATE, [1997] 4 All E.R. 99, Staughton, L.J., CA.

958. Consumer credit—car hire charges—enforceability of agreement

[Consumer Credit Act 1974 s.61, s.65.]

D was involved in a road traffic accident in November 1995 in which his car sustained substantial damage. D hired a Porsche from Revaforce Rental Ltd, R, in December 1995 and signed an agreement on a standard form for hire of the car for 15 days. The agreement provided that it was "subject to and included the terms, conditions and limitations of the lessor's insurance policy, a copy of which may be inspected at the office of the lessor". The figure for the rate of hire on the written agreement had not been filled in but left blank. D gave evidence that he had been told orally at the time of hire that the rate was £315 or £320 per day. D also stated that he had asked his insurance company and R at the time whether he would have to pay for the hire of the vehicle and was categorically told that he would not. He gave further evidence that he had never seen the invoice for hire which showed a daily rate of £325. Proceedings were issued claiming hire charges of £5,346. The defendant argued that the hire agreement was unenforceable since R did not have a consumer credit licence. Evidence was produced that they had had one as of April 1997. The defendant further argued that by virtue of the Consumer Credit Act 1974 s.61 (1) (b) and s.65 the agreement was improperly executed and unenforceable without a court order; firstly the rates of hire were not included on the agreement and secondly the document did not embody all the terms of the agreement because of the clause set out above.

Held, dismissing D's claim, that the agreement was improperly executed because of both breaches of the 1974 Act s.61 (1) (b). Further there was no evidence that at the time of hire R had a consumer credit licence. In any event, D would have a sound defence based either on misrepresentation or estoppel to any subsequent proceedings brought by R for recovery of the hire charges on the basis that he was induced to enter into the contract by statements made to him that he would not be liable for any of the hire charges and on that basis too the agreement was unenforceable. The judge noted that it is very common for such statements to be made, *Smerdon v. Ellis* [1997] C.L.Y. 963 cited and approved. D was ordered to pay the defendant's costs of the assessment of damages.

DIXON-VINCENT, *Re*, August 19, 1997, District Judge Karet, CC (Watford). [*Ex rel.* Joel CT Kendall, Barrister, 12 King's Bench Walk, Temple, London, EC4Y 7EL].

959. **Consumer credit–car hire charges–unlicensed hirer–agreement enforceable by consent**

[Consumer Credit Act 1974 s.40, s.65, s.173(3).]

W's vehicle, valued at £1,650, was damaged beyond economical repair in an accident for which F admitted liability. W hired a vehicle from Crash Care Accident Management. At the assessment of damages hearing it was held that the contract of hire was unenforceable against F on the grounds that Crash Care Accident Management did not at the material time have a licence to enter credit agreements. W appealed.

Held, allowing the appeal, that the agreement was enforceable as it fell within the terms of the 1974 Act and the hire charges could be recovered from F. W's reliance on the 1974 Act s.173(3) was properly placed, the effect of which was to override the provisions of s.40 and s.65. Such consent was implicit from the commencement of proceedings to recover the hire charges.

WOTTON v. FLAGG, January 31, 1997, Judge Overend, Exeter District Registry. [*Ex rel.* Stephen Climie, Barrister].

960. **Consumer credit–car hire charges–unlicensed hirer–hirer telling plaintiff that he wouldn't have to pay hire charges–unenforceable hire agreement– no obligation on either party to pay**

[Consumer Credit Act 1974 s.40(2).]

S was involved in a road traffic accident on November 13, 1994 in which his car was rendered uneconomical to repair. S hired a car from Western Car Hire, WCH, on November 17, 1994 at a daily rate of £38. The hire ended on February 11, 1995 after S received £1,025 payment from E's insurers for the car's pre-accident value. The hire agreement, which was on a WCH standard form, signed only by S, sought payment of £3,305 and was addressed to S who gave evidence that he had never received it. Proceedings were commenced against E in November 1995 seeking hire charges of £3,305 and interest. E alleged that the hire agreement was regulated by the Consumer Credit Act 1974 and that WCH was an unlicensed trader and as such the hire agreement was unenforceable against S. S conceded that the hire agreement was regulated by the 1974 Act and averred that WCH had applied for a retrospective credit licence pursuant to s.40(2) which was granted on January 22, 1997. E alleged that there were multiple breaches of the 1974 Act and that as a result the hire agreement was improperly executed and unenforceable and as such S had no liability to repay the hire charges. S gave evidence that as he was very concerned about his liability to pay for the hire he had telephoned WCH regularly seeking confirmation that he would not be liable and that he had been assured that he would not have to pay for the hire charges. On February 12, 1996, WCH wrote to S informing him that he would have no liability to pay the hire charges since he was not at fault for the accident and stating that they would recover all of the hire charges from E's insurers. At trial, S conceded that the hire charges could only be enforced if WCH obtained a court order under the 1974 Act, *Giles v. Thompson* [1994] 1 A.C. 142, [1993] C.L.Y. 1405 considered.

Held, dismissing S's claim, that the agreement was unenforceable as S had been told he would never have to pay for the hire of the car. He had never been sent the invoice or asked to pay it and he would never have been able to pay the amount even if he had been asked. As there was no liability on S to pay the hire charges there could be no liability on E either. Furthermore, inasmuch as S conceded that the hire charges could only be enforced if WCH obtained a court order, having regard to the representations which S had received and the provisions of the Consumer Credit Act 1974, no court would ever grant such an order against S in favour of WCH. S was ordered to pay E's costs of the action and leave to appeal was refused.

SMERDON v. ELLIS, March 17, 1997, H.H.J. Neville, CC (Torquay and Newton Abbot). [*Ex rel.* Hugh Hamill, 12 King's Bench Walk, Temple].

961. Consumer credit—extortionate credit agreements—limitation periods

[Consumer Credit Act 1974 s.139(2); Limitation Act 1980 s.9.]

In 1990 W entered into two Consumer Credit Act 1974 regulated loan agreements with H. In 1997 and following the default of W, H commenced proceedings to enforce the loans. The debtors in their defence alleged, inter alia, that the loans were extortionate credit bargains within the meaning of the Consumer Credit Act 1974 s.138 to s.142. The creditor applied to have that part of the defence struck out, alleging that the debtors were barred from seeking such relief by virtue of a six year limitation period prescribed by the Limitation Act 1980 s.9.

Held, that s.9 of the 1980 Act provided that a six year limitation period applied to actions brought to recover any sum recoverable by virtue of an enactment. Section 139(2) of the 1974 Act provided that if the court was satisfied that a credit bargain was extortionate, and it was just to reopen the agreement, then one of the remedies which the court could grant was to require the creditor to repay a sum. This was not a case where the debtor was seeking only a sum from the creditor (although it was one of the forms of relief sought). Rather, the debtors were seeking a whole range of alternative heads of relief available under s.139(2) of the 1974 Act. In those circumstances, the 1980 Act did not apply. The district judge expressly disagreed with the decision of the judge in *First National Bank v. Ann & Ann* [1997] C.L.Y. 963.

HOMESTEAD FINANCE LTD v. WARRINER AND TASKER, July 21, 1997, District Judge Buchan, CC (Dewsbury). [*Ex rel.* Nicholas Hill, Barrister, 6 Park Square, Leeds].

962. Consumer credit—extortionate credit agreements—limitation periods

[Consumer Credit Act 1974 s.139(4); County Court Rules Ord.37; Limitation Act 1980 s.5, s.9.]

The defendant mortgagee issued proceedings, "the first action", against the plaintiff borrowers in reference to default under a second legal charge and loan agreement dated August 31, 1989, and obtained a suspended order for possession dated December 19, 1991. No substantive defence was raised to the first action. On January 24, 1997, the plaintiffs issued proceedings, "the second action", alleging that the legal charge and loan agreement constituted an extortionate credit bargain within the meaning of the Consumer Credit Act 1974 s.137 to s.139. The defendant applied to strike out the second action as an abuse of process on the grounds that: (1) the action was statute barred, having been issued more than six years after the date of the agreement of August 31, 1989 and, following *First National Bank v. Ann & Ann* [1997] C.L.Y. 963, the cause of action accrued at the date of the agreement and was governed by s.5 and/or s.9 of the Limitation Act 1980; (2) the doctrine of issue estoppel expounded in *Yat Tung Investment v. Dao Heng Bank* [1975] A.C. 581, [1975] C.L.Y. 211 applied, in that the present cause of action was one which the plaintiffs could and should with reasonable diligence have raised and argued in the first action and failed for good reason to do so, and (3) it was an abuse of process to issue an action against a mortgagee without invoking the machinery of County Court Rules Ord.37 by way of a challenge to a prior order for possession.

Held, striking out the action, that (1) all the facts relevant to the issue of extortionate credit bargain were available to the plaintiffs at the date of the agreement and therefore the cause of action under the 1974 Act accrued at the date of the agreement. The matter being governed by s.5 and/or s.9 of the 1980 Act, the action was statute barred and should be struck out; (2) the matter was in any event subject to an issue estoppel, and (3) by virtue of s.139(4) of the 1974 Act, an order reopening an agreement on the basis that it is an extortionate credit bargain, "...shall not alter the effect of any judgment". The relief sought would have impinged upon the order of December 19, 1991 and therefore constituted an abuse of the process of the court.

RICKETTS AND RICKETTS v. HURSTANGER LTD, July 15, 1997, Deputy District Judge Arnold, CC (Aldershot and Farnham). [*Ex rel.* Marc Beaumont, Barrister, Harrow-on-the-Hill Chambers, Harrow].

963. Consumer credit—extortionate credit agreements—whether mortgage an extortionate credit agreement—limitation period runs from date of agreement

[Consumer Credit Act 1974; Limitation Act 1980 s.9.]

A opposed F's claim for possession of A's property for non payment of arrears under a mortgage by contending that the loan agreement was an extortionate credit bargain under the Consumer Credit Act 1974, s.137 to s.139, and should be re-opened. F argued that the Limitation Act 1980 s.9, which stipulates a limitation period of six years, was applicable to actions brought under s.137 to s.139 of the 1974 Act. F submitted that A's application was time barred because it was not commenced within six years from the date of the loan agreement on October 19, 1987 and should be struck out.

Held, striking out the claim, that the 1980 Act s.9, which established a time limit of six years applies to applications to re-open extortionate credit bargains, and that the six year period ran from the date of the loan agreement not from the date of redemption of the loan as submitted by A and consequently the counterclaim was statute-barred.

FIRST NATIONAL BANK PLC v. ANN & ANN, January 25, 1996, District Judge Skerratt, CC (Colchester). [*Ex rel.* Marc Beaumont, Barrister, Harrow-on-the-Hill Chambers, Harrow].

964. Consumer credit—finance agreement for car purchase—payment waiver premium—whether constituted credit—meaning of credit

[Consumer Credit Act 1974 s.8, s.9; Consumer Credit (Total Charge for Credit) Regulations 1980 Reg.4.]

T appealed against an order refusing to set aside a judgment in default in the sum of £4,982 in favour of H. T purchased a car from H with finance supplied by H of £14,497 with an additional £796 for the payment waiver insurance premium. T fell behind in the payments, and H repossessed the car without a court order and, T alleged, without consent. The judge below concluded that the finance agreement was not a regulated agreement because the total sum exceeded £15,000 and therefore T were not entitled to recover sums previously paid. T submitted that the judge below was wrong to conclude that the agreement was not a regulated agreement in terms of the Consumer Credit Act 1974 s.8 and s.9.

Held, allowing the appeal, that (1) the agreement was a regulated agreement, there was an agreement to supply T with credit and provide terms on which payments would be waived in the event of the debtor's death. Thus, there was a distinction between credit and the costs of that credit, £796 was part of the total charge for credit, under the Consumer Credit (Total Charge for Credit) Regulations 1980 Reg.4(1)(b); (2) in terms of s.90 and s.91 of the 1974 Act, repossession of goods in the event of default requires an order of the court, otherwise the agreement should terminate, and the debtor should be entitled to recover all sums paid. That there was no court order and conflict in evidence as to consent to repossession was sufficient for the court to set aside the default document, and (3) although there had been a 14 months' delay before the application to set aside default judgment was made, the court was not prevented from exercising its discretion in the circumstances of the case, *Savill v. Southend HA* [1995] 1 W.L.R. 1254, [1995] 2 C.L.Y. 3932 distinguished, *Atwood v. Chichester* (1878) 3 Q.B. 722 applied. To do so would not prejudice H, whereas not to do so could result in an injustice.

HUMBERCLYDE FINANCE LTD v. THOMPSON (T/A AG THOMPSON) [1997] C.C.L.R. 23, Aldous, L.J., CA.

965. **Consumer credit–mortgage interest rates–calculation of APR–meaning of "certain"–possibility of one per cent base rate so remote that it could be ignored**

[Consumer Credit (Total Charge for Credit) Regulations 1980 Reg.2; Consumer Credit Act 1974.]

Despite receiving an absolute discharge, S appealed by way of case stated against the decision that there was not even a remote possibility that its variable interest rate could fall to one per cent in two years time. H had prosecuted S for the display of an poster advertising discount mortgages from one per cent, at an APR of 1.1 per cent. A leaflet explained that this rate would continue for the first six months, that discounts of two per cent and 0.5 per cent from base rate would be applicable for the following six months and 12 months, respectively. The issue was the proper meaning of "certain" in terms of the Consumer Credit (Total Charge for Credit) Regulations 1980 Reg.2(1)(d) made under the Consumer Credit Act 1974. The Regulation provides for the calculation of APR and the assumptions governing that calculation.

Held, dismissing the appeal, that the stipendiary magistrate had been entitled to exercise his common sense in holding that the possibility of a one per cent base rate was so remote that it could be ignored. Regulation 2(1)(d) was not concerned with the possibility that lenders might grant indulgences to borrowers, *National Westminster Bank v. Devon CC* [1993] C.C.L.R. 69, [1993] C.L.Y. 473 considered.

SCARBOROUGH BUILDING SOCIETY v. HUMBERSIDE TRADING STANDARDS DEPARTMENT [1997] C.C.L.R. 47, Staughton, L.J., QBD.

966. **Consumer credit–quotations–revocation**

CONSUMER CREDIT (QUOTATIONS) (REVOCATION) REGULATIONS 1997, SI 1997 211; made under the Consumer Credit Act 1974 s.52, s.152, s.182, s.189. In force: March 10, 1997; £0.65.

These Regulations revoke the Consumer Credit (Quotations) Regulations 1989 (SI 1989 1126) which prescribed the form and content of documents ("quotations") in which persons, who carry on consumer credit businesses, consumer hire businesses and businesses in the course of which credit is secured on land is provided to individuals, give prospective customers information about the terms on which they are prepared to do business. The 1989 Regulations also applied to quotations and information given by credit-brokers about the business of any person to whom the credit-broker effects introductions, as well as to the giving of quotations and information about his own business.

967. **Consumer protection–holiday lettings–landlord responsible for electrical equipment for tenant's use and liable for defects**

[Consumer Protection Act 1987 s.12(1), s.39, s.46; Low Voltage Electrical Equipment (Safety) Regulations 1989 (SI 1989 728).]

DR appealed against a conviction on each of five informations relating to the supply of equipment which failed to comply with the Low Voltage Electrical Equipment (Safety) Regulations 1989 contrary to the Consumer Protection Act 1987 s.12(1). On appeal DR had not established a defence of due diligence under s.39 of the 1987 Act, and the appeal was dismissed. DR had let a cottage as holiday accommodation. The tenant had complained to the Trading Standards Department about the state of the cottage and defective electrical equipment. It was to be determined whether (1) provision of electrical equipment by a landlord for holiday accommodation came within s.46 of the 1987 Act and (2) non-compliance of that equipment with the 1989 Regulations constituted an offence under s.12 of the 1987 Act.

Held, dismissing the appeal, that (1) goods left on premises for the use of the tenant are being hired out or lent, and therefore come within s.46 and (2) the equipment was defective under the Regulations and consequently the offence under s.12 was committed.

DRUMMOND-REES v. DORSET CC (TRADING STANDARDS DEPARTMENT), Hooper, J., QBD.

968. Consumer protection–time sharing

TIMESHARE REGULATIONS 1997, SI 1997 1081; made under the European Communities Act 1972 s.2. In force: April 29, 1997; £2.80.

These Regulations implement Council Directive 94/47 ([1994] OJ L280/83) which requires Member States to provide measures for the protection of purchasers of timeshare rights in immovable properties. The Regulations provide for a new right in respect of timeshare rights in buildings. The protection of purchasers of timeshare rights in caravans and mobile homes remains unchanged save for some very minor adjustments. To benefit from the new protection a purchaser must be an individual who is not acting in the course of a business. The Timeshare Act 1992 has been amended and extended.

969. Consumer safety–children–prams and pushchairs

WHEELED CHILD CONVEYANCES (SAFETY) REGULATIONS 1997, SI 1997 2866; made under the Consumer Protection Act 1987 s.11. In force: December 29, 1997; £1.10.

These Regulations, which revoke and replace the Perambulators and Pushchairs (Safety) Regulations 1978 (SI 1978 1372), the Perambulators and Pushchairs (Safety) Regulations (Northern Ireland) Order 1978 (SR 1978 329), the Pushchairs (Safety) Regulations 1985 (SI 1985 2047) and the Pushchairs (Safety) Regulations (Northern Ireland) 1986 (SR 1986 37), provide that wheeled child conveyances must conform to British Standards Specification 7409:1996.

970. Cosmetics–safety

COSMETIC PRODUCTS (SAFETY) (AMENDMENT) REGULATIONS 1997, SI 1997 2914; made under the European Communities Act 1972 s.2. In force: in accordance with Reg.1 (2); £1.10.

These Regulations amend the Cosmetic Products (Safety) Regulations 1996 (SI 1996 2925) by changing the date the prohibition on the supply of cosmetic products tested on animals shall come into force from January 1, 1998 to June 30, 2000. They also implement Council Directive 97/18 ([1997] OJ L114/43) and Commission Directive 97/45 ([1997] OJ L196/77) relating to cosmetic products.

971. Explosives–fireworks–safety

FIREWORKS (SAFETY) REGULATIONS 1997, SI 1997 2294; made under the Consumer Protection Act 1987 s.11. In force: Reg.3(2), Reg.4(1)(b)(2)(f), Reg.7: December 31, 1997; remainder: October 15, 1997; £2.80.

These Regulations revoke and re-enact with amendments the provisions of the Fireworks (Safety) Regulations 1996 (SI 1996 3200) and make other provision relating to the safety of fireworks and assemblies which include fireworks.

972. Hire purchase–conditional sales–agreement to pay instalments and exercise option to pay further sum

[Hire Purchase Act 1964 Part III.]

C appealed against a decision that it was liable for £12,943 plus interest for the wrongful conversion of a car belonging to F. Under a purported hire purchase contract, F delivered the car to Senator Motors, S, who in turn supplied it to a customer, G, under a conditional sale agreement made with C. It was not disputed that G had obtained good title under the Hire Purchase Act 1964 Part

III, but C contended that the contract between F and S was a conditional sale and not a hire purchase agreement and that therefore good title had been passed to S. F argued that under a conditional sale the purchaser must pay all the instalments and must take the title in the goods, whereas if he has an option whether or not to acquire the goods then the contract is a hire purchase agreement.

Held, allowing the appeal, that the contract was a conditional sale agreement. S were contractually bound to pay all the instalments at which point, unless they exercised the option not to, they would receive title and this option not to take title did not affect the true nature of the agreement. It was unnecessary to decide whether an agreement having a positive option to pay a nominal payment was a conditional sale agreement, *Helby v. Matthews* [1895] A.C. 471 followed.

FORTHRIGHT FINANCE LTD v. CARLYLE FINANCE LTD, [1997] All E.R. 90, Phillips, L.J., CA.

973. **Price marking–misleading price indication–concession agreement–price indication given in course of retailer's business–statutory interpretation**

[Consumer Protection Act 1987 s.20.]

BR and another company, B, operated a concession in a shop belonging to BR. Although the goods were owned by B, half of the merchandise displayed BR's labels and all of it was paid for at BR's tills. The agreement which established the relationship set pricing parameters, but the exact price of goods was the responsibility of B, and BR had no means of monitoring or controlling those prices. Misleading price tags were displayed in the shop and B pleaded guilty to an offence under the Consumer Protection Act 1987 s.20. BR, however, was acquitted and the trading standards officer appealed by way of case stated, contending that BR was also guilty of the offence, even though the labels had been put in place by an employee of B.

Held, allowing the appeal, that the issue for the court was whether the offence had been committed in the course of BR's business within the meaning of s.20. It was not important to consider who was responsible for fixing the prices or writing the price tags, as the duty created by s.20 was not one which could be delegated. Since the concession was an integral part of BR's business, it was clearly the case that the misleading price indication had been given in the course of BR's business for the purposes of s.20.

DENARD v. BURTON RETAIL LTD; *sub nom.* SURREY CC v. BURTON RETAIL LTD, *The Times*, November 19, 1997, Brooke, L.J., QBD.

974. **Price marking–misleading price indication–items must already be on sale in open market to justify advertisement**

[Consumer Protection Act 1987 s.20(1).]

Held, that, other than in exceptional cases, in order to justify an advertisement offering a £50 watch for £4.99, so as to avoid conviction of an offence of giving a misleading indication as to the price at which goods were available, under the Consumer Protection Act 1987 s.20(1), it was necessary to show that items of that description were already available for sale on the open market so that the requisite price comparison could be carried out.

MGN LTD v. RITTERS; *sub nom.* MGN LTD v. NORTHAMPTONSHIRE CC, *The Times*, July 30, 1997, Simon Brown, L.J., QBD.

975. **Product liability–UK legislation was valid to implement Council Directive 85/374–European Union**

[Consumer Protection Act 1987 s.4(1)(e); Council Directive 85/374 on liability for defective products Art.7.]

Held, that, having regard to the scope of Council Directive 85/374, there was no obvious conflict between the wording of Art.7(e) and that of the Consumer Protection Act 1987 s.4(1)(e) which was intended to implement it in the UK. CEC's allegation that the defence available to producers under s.4(1)(e) was considerably wider than that available under the Directive and that the UK had therefore failed to fulfil its obligations in regard to transposing the Directive was not made out.

COMMISSION OF THE EUROPEAN COMMUNITIES v. UNITED KINGDOM (C300/95) [1997] All E.R. (EC) 481, JC Moitinho de Almeida (President), ECJ.

976. Trade descriptions–supply of goods with false description–fire engine not conforming to specifications when supplied–application of description to future goods

[Trade Descriptions Act 1968 s.1 (1) (b).]

W, a trading standards officer, appealed by way of case stated against a decision to acquit SD on four informations alleging the unlawful supply of goods to which a false trade description had been applied contrary to the Trade Descriptions Act 1968 s.1 (1) (b). Having received a specification for a fire engine, SD tendered for its supply. Following acceptance of the tender, modifications to the original specifications were agreed between the fire service and SD. However, on supply, the engine did not meet the original specifications, nor had it been modified. The stipendiary magistrate held that, although the agreed modifications had not been complied with, the error occurred in the course of the supply and was neither foreseen nor deliberate.

Held, allowing the appeal, that, in the circumstances in which the fire engine was supplied, it was reasonable to infer that SD had applied to the goods the trade description corresponding to the initial request and agreed specifications, and the representation that the goods would conform to the purchaser's requirement was still in force at the time of supply, *Cavendish Woodhouse Ltd v. Wright* (1985) Tr. L.R. 40 considered, so that s.4(3) of the Act applied. Therefore, where the description given proved false in relation to the goods supplied, an offence was committed under s.1 (1) (b). A request for a tender was a request for the purposes of s.4(3), and the time of supply was the relevant time for determining whether a trade description had been applied under s.1 (1) (b).

WALKER v. SIMON DUDLEY LTD; *sub nom.* SHROPSHIRE CC v. SIMON DUDLEY LTD (1997) 16 Tr. L.R. 69, Hooper, J., QBD.

977. Trading standards–inaccurate trade description of car–due diligence–extent and sufficiency of evidence

[Trade Descriptions Act 1968 s.1.]

C appealed by way of case stated against the acquittal of B on two of the three counts with which B was charged in relation to the sale of a car in an auction. B purchased the car from S who had purchased it approximately four weeks earlier from motor traders who had added a disclaimer to the statement of the mileage. B had marked on the auction form that the mileage was correct and that it was under 100,000. The two counts on which he was charged in relation to this information were not found proved and he was acquitted. B argued the defence of having taken all reasonable precautions and exercised all due diligence pursuant to the Trade Descriptions Act 1968 s.1 and he was allowed to run this defence notwithstanding that he had not given notice of his reliance on it to the prosecution. The questions in the case stated were: (1) was there any evidence on which to find that B had taken all reasonable precautions to found the defence of due diligence; (2) was there sufficient evidence on the balance of probabilities so to find, and (3) was the clerk correct to advise the court that the prosecution could not make submissions on the evidence B gave in support of his claim to that effect.

Held, allowing the appeal and remitting the matter to a different bench, that (1) there was no evidence on which the justices could come to that conclusion. B had not made enquiries with the motor traders from whom S had bought the car and if he had done he would have been put on notice that they had sold the car with a disclaimer as to the mileage. In addition B put forward his evidence after he had come out of the witness stand and so was not cross-examined on it, and (2) as B gave evidence having left the stand and that material was new, the prosecution was entitled to make submissions in relation to that evidence, particularly as they had no prior notice of the defence.

COUPE v. BUSH, Trans. Ref: CO 2915-96, January 28, 1997, McCowan, L.J., QBD.

978. Weights and measures—equipment—EC law

NON-AUTOMATIC WEIGHING INSTRUMENTS (EEC REQUIREMENTS) (AMENDMENT) REGULATIONS 1997, SI 1997 3035; made under the European Communities Act 1972 s.2. In force: February 1, 1998; £1.95.

These Regulations amend the Non-automatic Weighing Instruments (EEC Requirements) Regulations 1995 (SI 1995 1907), which implement Council Directive 90/384 ([1990] OJ L258/1) on the harmonisation of the laws of the member States relating to non-automatic weighing instruments.

979. Weights and measures—equipment—fees

MEASURING INSTRUMENTS (EEC REQUIREMENTS) (FEES) (AMENDMENT) REGULATIONS 1997, SI 1997 630; made under the Finance Act 1973 s.56. In force: April 1, 1997; £0.65.

These Regulations amend the fees payable in connection with services undertaken by the Department of Trade and Industry under the Non-Automatic Weighing Instruments (EEC Requirements) Regulation 1992 (SI 1992 1579) and other Regulations relating to instruments for which the Measuring Instruments (EEC Requirements) (Fees) Regulations 1993 (SI 1993 798) provide.

980. Articles

Accidents on holiday: P. Injury 1996, 1 (1), 9-10. (Tour operators' liability when contract may not specifically mention incident).

But which interpretation favours the consumer? Use of Regulation 6 of Unfair Terms in Consumer Contracts Regulations 1994 *(Elizabeth Macdonald* and *Samantha Halliday)*: C. & C.C. 1997, 1 (1), 9-11. (Similarity of 1994 Regulations Reg.6 to contra proferentem rule on construction of ambiguous clauses and dangers of not using interpretation "most favourable to consumer" as envisaged by Council Directive 93/13 on unfair terms in consumer contracts).

Consumer law *(W.H. Thomas)*: C.L.W. 1997, 5(36), 2i-2ii. (How OFT defines unfair clauses in consumer contracts and measures used to remedy unreasonableness).

Consumer protection: references to "worth" or "value" *(Geoffrey H. Holgate)*: J.P. 1997, 161 (36), 856-857. (Statutory provisions and code of guidance prohibiting advertisements which claim that goods are "worth" certain amount or have certain "value" where goods have not been on open market at that price).

Consumers and lawyers *(E. Susan Singleton)*: Cons. L. Today 1997, 20(11), 9-12. (Rights of action and remedies available for consumers against lawyers, including details of official complaints procedures).

Mobile phone companies - unfair terms: Tr. Law 1997, 16(2), 144-146. (Improvements to phone companies' consumer contracts following DGFT warning of legal action).

National models of European contract law: a comparative approach to the concept of unfairness in Council Directive 93/13 on unfair terms in consumer contracts *(Gianluca Sepe)*: Consum. L.J. 1997, 5(4), 115-122. (Differences in concept of fairness in Member States' legal systems and its application to harmonisation of law on unfair contract terms).

Opposites attract: plain English with a European interpretation *(Tracey Reeves)*: N.L.J. 1997, 147(6788), 576-578. (Difficulties in requirement that consumer contracts be written in plain English including need for a change in method of interpretation).

Product liability and consumer guarantees in the European Union: a brief comparison between an old Directive and a new proposal *(Mario Tenreiro)*: Consum. L.J.1997, 5(2), 56-61.

Product liability in the European Community-the "development risks" defence *(Ian Awford)*: T.A.Q. 1997, 6(Oct), 381-387. (Implications of ECJ decision on UK's implementation of Product Liability Directive by Consumer Protection Act 1987 particularly reference to defects which are undetectable because of lack of scientific knowledge).

Promises to the future: goods and services and the Trade Descriptions Act *(Victor Smith)*: J.P. 1997, 161(41), 956-958. (Criminal liability for false assurances relating to future promises including applicability to sale of goods, case law and whether false representations under Trade Descriptions Act 1968 s.4(3) are breach of contract or criminal offence).

The Distance Contracts Directive: direct mail, tele, video and Internet sales *(E. Susan Singleton)*: Cons. L. Today 1997, 20(8), 9-12. (Provisions of Council Directive 97/7 on the protection of consumers in respect of contracts negotiated at a distance, in force June 4, 1997 intended to protect customers of direct sellers, including definition of distance contract, requirement to provide prior information and consumer's right to withdraw).

The European requirements on after-sales product monitoring with regard to the intercompany division of labour *(Brunhilde Steckler)*: Consum. L.J.1997, 5(1), 1-7. (Liability of subcontractors, particularly components producers, for product defects and consequences for production methods such as "just-in-time" delivery where supply of parts is coordinated with manufacturing process).

The applicable law to consumer contracts made over the Internet: consumer protection through private international law? *(Reinhard Schu)*: I.J.L & I.T. 1997, 5(2), 192-229.

The use and abuse of fireworks: legislative and other controls *(Geoffrey H. Holgate)*: Tr. Law 1997, 16(2), 126-135. (DTI review of current legislation on sale of fireworks).

Time for a change *(Tim H.S. Bourne)*: N.L.J. 1997, 147(6789), 594-595. (Provisions of the Timeshare Regulations 1997 implementing Council Directive 94/47 on disclosure of information, structure of agreements, rights of buyers and offences).

Trade Descriptions Act and future goods *(E. Susan Singleton)*: Cons. L. Today 1997, 20(2), 9-11. (Implications of decision that representations as to specifications made before manufacture carried through to time of supply as description of goods).

Trade description, fallible forecasts and statements of existing fact *(Geoffrey Holgate)*: J.P. 1997, 161(26), 626-627. (Whether representations that fire engine would meet certain specifications was trade description at time of supply under the Trade Descriptions Act 1968 s.4(3)).

Travel law update *(Melanie Ross)*: S.J. 1997, 141(20), 493-494. (Potential criminal liability for tour operators whose brochures are misleading, unfair contract terms, disabled customers' rights and 1996-97 damages awards for disappointed tourists).

Unfair terms in consumer contracts - third OFT bulletin *(E. Susan Singleton)*: Cons. L. Today 1997, 20(6), 11-12. (Guidance on application of the Unfair Terms in Consumer Contracts Regulations 1994 and case studies on companies' compliance).

981. Books

Bridge, Michael – Sale of Goods. Hardback: £80.00. ISBN 0-19-825871-2. Oxford University Press.

Miller, C.J.; Mildred, Mark; Morse, C.G.J.– Product Liability and Safety Encyclopaedia. Unbound/looseleaf: £230.00. ISBN 0-406-00758-6. Butterworth Law.

Moore, Roy L.; Farrar, Ronald T.; Collins, Erik L.–Advertising and Public Relations Law. Communication Series. Hardback: £113.50. ISBN 0-8058-1679-8. Lawrence Erlbaum Associates Inc.

Painter, Anthony; Harvey, Brian W.–O'Keefe: the Law of Weights and Measures. Unbound/looseleaf: £230.00. ISBN 0-406-99896-5. Butterworth Law.

Parry, Deborah L.; Rowell, Roland; Harvey, Brian W.; Ervine, Cowan–Butterworths Trading and Consumer Law. Unbound/looseleaf: £230.00. ISBN 0-406-99655-5. Butterworth Law.

Product Liability. Hardback: £49.00. ISBN 1-86058-062-9. Mechanical Engineering Publications.

CONTRACTS

982. Accord and satisfaction–claim for money due under contract–defendant sending cheque for lesser amount saying it was in settlement of account–cashing of cheque–cheque not a binding accord

F agreed to provide D with certain specialist tapes, records and discs in exchange for other specialist items to the wholesale value of £600 to be delivered by a certain date, or D was to pay £1,700 in cash. D only delivered goods and cash to the value of approximately £150, and F sued in the county court. By way of defence and counterclaim, D filled in form N9B stating that he admitted owing the sum of £150 but that he had paid F the outstanding amount. D sent a cheque for £150 to the court with a letter saying that the cheque was in settlement of F's account and that he admitted owing F money, but disputed the amount. F cashed the cheque but, in reply to a letter from D stating that he hoped the cheque would resolve the dispute, F indicated his intention to continue his action. The judge found that D still owed £1,400 but that, although F had not intended to accept the cheque as full settlement, his acceptance gave rise to a binding settlement and accord and he could not continue his claim. F appealed.

Held, allowing the appeal, that the admission made by D on the N9B form that he owed F money was a formal, unqualified admission of liability for the £150 and could not, in the absence of offering F some additional benefit by way of consideration, constitute an offer to compromise in order to settle the claim. The cashing of the cheque did not constitute a binding accord that no further sum was due simply because D had written a letter claiming that it should.

FERGUSON v. DAVIES [1997] 1 All E.R. 315, Henry, L.J., CA.

983. Assignment–computer contracts–no consent given by lessee–assertion of invalidity of assignment not estopped

O, assignees of a lease of computer equipment, appealed against a decision that J, lessees of the equipment, were not estopped from relying on the invalidity of the assignment. A, suppliers of computer equipment, offered their customers long-term leases with a flexibility which enabled them to upgrade their equipment and gave them the right to terminate the lease before its term expired. This was known as the Flex and Walk agreement. If the hirer exercised either of those rights then A would bear the resulting costs or if the lease was assigned to a third party A would indemnify the hirer against any liabilities which might be incurred by the third party assignee. A assigned leases to O without the consent of J. A sent a letter of notice of assignment to J to which they received no response. Following J's subsequent termination of the lease agreement O argued that J's failure to inform O that they had not consented to the assignment, estopped J from claiming that the assignment was invalid and that they were entitled to rely upon their rights under the Flex and Walk agreement. O contended that J knew that O was acting under the mistaken belief that the assignment was valid and that J was therefore under a duty to make known to O their contentions.

Held, dismissing the appeal, that the notice of assignment from A did not place J under a duty to communicate with O. There was no previous relationship or course of dealings between J and O, *Henrik Sif, The* [1982] 1 Lloyd's. Rep. 456, *Spiro v. Lintern* [1973] 1 W.L.R. 1002, [1973] C.L.Y. 399 and *Willmott v. Barber* (1880) 15 Ch. D. 96 distinguished. Estoppel can only be alleged by the person from whom the communication was received. In addition, J's failure to acknowledge the purported assignment could not properly be regarded as a positive representation that they consented to it or that they would not seek to exercise, against O, the rights they had obtained contractually against A. The loss O suffered by reason of the invalidity of the assignment was a result of its own negligence to ensure that J had consented, *Orion Finance Ltd v. Crown Financial Management Ltd* [1994] 2 B.C.L.C. 607, [1995] 2 C.L.Y. 4490 and *Orion Finance Ltd v. Heritable Finance Ltd* (Unreported, 1995) distinguished.

ORION FINANCE LTD v. JD WILLIAMS & CO LTD, Trans. Ref: CHANF 96/0374/B, July 22, 1997, Evans, L.J., CA.

984. Assignment—interpretation of "sum" payable under subcontract—substitution of plaintiff in civil action not allowed

A contractual clause allowing assignment of sums due in an action was only permissible where liability had been established. A contractual clause prevented the subcontractors, FQ, from assigning without consent the benefit of the subcontract except "any sum which is or may become due and payable to him under this subcontract". S appealed against a decision allowing F to be substituted as plaintiff in place of FQ in an action against S.

Held, allowing the appeal, that the "sum" which could be assigned under the clause was a fixed or liquidated amount, which had already been determined and was therefore payable immediately, or would be payable in the future once the quantum had been determined. Similarly, a right to claim additional remuneration could not be assigned, but there could be an assignment of the future right to receive a sum awarded by an arbitrator or court, whilst a claim for damages could not be assigned until the amount due was fixed and the defendant had been found liable. This approach was consistent with the intended commercial purpose of the clause, in that whilst it would make little difference to S whether they paid a sum to a third party assignee rather than to the subcontractor, once the amount payable had been determined, S should not have to deal with a party with whom they had not chosen to contract regarding litigation or arbitration to substantiate a claim and establish the sum due. The identity of the plaintiff would not affect the nature and scope of the proceedings but could affect the prospects of settlement or agreement on particular matters and therefore the substitution could not be allowed.

FLOOD v. SHAND CONSTRUCTION LTD 81 B.L.R. 31, Evans, L.J., CA.

985. Bailment—duty of care of bailee for reward—commercial vehicle at repairers

B left their lorry worth approximately £18,500 with H, the repairers, one evening at 5.00 pm, just as H were finishing work for the day. The lorry had been expected the following day. Overnight the lorry was left in H's compound which was surrounded by a wire mesh fence and barbed wire. The gate was locked with a heavy duty padlock and a thick chain. Inside the compound there was a burglar alarm consisting of movement activated lights, a recorded warning and a siren. At about 8.00 pm thieves broke in by sawing their way through the chain which was not alarmed. They then broke a window in the vehicle, started it and drove it away. They did not obtain the keys to the lorry which were kept in a locked secure cabinet in another compound. The lorry was not recovered.

Held, that H were not liable for not having: (1) immobilised the lorry with a crook lock; (2) surrounded it with other vehicles; (3) taken a wheel off, and (4) placed the lorry in their other compound which had a garage and a more sophisticated alarm system.

BILLINGTON UK LTD v. HITCHIN RECOVERY LTD, December 6, 1996, H.H.J. Sessions, CC (Bromley). [*Ex rel.* John Gallagher, Barrister].

986. Computer contracts—leasing—hire and lease back—collateral agreement—no anticipatory breach of contract

H appealed against an order allowing O to amend its statement of claim to include a claim for the full six years of a lease agreement and making H liable for all O's costs save those of a late amendment. Atlantic Computer Systems Plc, A, arranged for O to purchase H's computer equipment and to return it to A on hire purchase. A then leased it back to H. The lease had a six year term and included a clause entitling the lessor to the return of the equipment and a termination sum should the lessee default. H and A signed a collateral agreement giving H the right to terminate after five years without penalty, on six months' prior notice, and the right to replacement equipment after four years. Subsequently A informed H that it had assigned the lease to O and went into administration. When H applied to O for replacement equipment, O responded that it was not bound by the collateral agreement. H then gave notice to terminate early under the collateral agreement, whereupon O claimed that this was an anticipatory breach of the main contract and claimed a termination sum of £117,339 plus VAT and interest. O applied to amend at a late stage to seek a declaration that the lease was extant and lasted for the full six years.

Held, dismissing the appeal, that the judge below had been correct to hold that (1) H's mistaken reliance on the collateral agreement was not a repudiation of the lease, *Woodar Investment Development Ltd v. Wimpey Construction UK Ltd* [1980] 1 W.L.R. 277, [1980] C.L.Y. 2792 followed; (2) O's claim for money and its assertion that H had terminated the lease had not been accompanied by any threat or action to repossess the equipment and was, despite its terms, not a repudiation, and (3) the judge had not erred in the exercise of his discretion to allow the amendment. However, he had erred in his award of costs which was replaced by an order for no costs save for those against O for the late amendment.

ORION FINANCE LTD v. HERITABLE FINANCE LTD, Trans. Ref: CHANF 95/1142/B, March 10, 1997, Lord Woolf, M.R., CA.

987. Contract terms—agreement concluded by telephone—substitution of subsequent written contract ineffective

A contract was created for the sale of Nigerian gum arabic, with the agreement initially made by telephone. The seller's, T, form of contract provided for "IGPA Spot conditions to apply" but the buyers, J, failed to sign, date and return the form. The only reference to the IGPA terms had been in the written contract, no mention had been made on the telephone. J alleged that the goods were not of sufficient quality. The issue was referred to arbitration and the question arose whether or not T's form of contract was binding on J.

Held, that it could not be said that J intended to accept T's form of contract whatever it provided in spite of the telephone agreements. The written contract was never accepted by J, the contract was concluded orally and it was wrong for T subsequently to attempt to substitute a contract which was fundamentally different. The court would not accept that J had agreed to amend their agreement to accept T's form of contract.

JAYAAR IMPEX LTD v. TOAKEN GROUP LTD (T/A HICKS BROTHERS) [1996] 2 Lloyd's Rep. 437, Rix, J., QBD (Comm Ct).

988. Contract terms—contract excluding right of set off

Contracts between J and W required payment by W of "initial down payments" as a standing charge calculated by reference to the number of J's vehicles set aside for W's use. Further charges were raised based on the use made by W of those vehicles. J went into receivership and the contracts were determined on the sale of J. J then sought to recover sums owed by W. The contracts between the two had provided that the payments by W were to be made in full "without any set off or abatement on any occasion whatsoever". W sought to set off the sums it had paid by way of initial down payments against the sums claimed by J. W argued that there had been a course of dealings in which J had set off initial down payments made for vehicles

CONTRACTS

that had subsequently been withdrawn from service against other charges incurred by W.

Held, allowing the claim, that W had no right to set off, the parties having contracted to exclude the right of a set off in clear and unambiguous terms. The course of dealing did not raise an estoppel against J's reliance on the contract.

JOHN DEE GROUP LTD v. WMH (21) LTD (FORMERLY MAGNET LTD) [1997] B.C.C. 518, Neuberger, J., Ch D.

989. **Contract terms—meaning of consequential loss**

Held, that the contractual term "consequential loss" was to be interpreted as meaning such loss proved by the plaintiff in excess of that which was a direct result of the breach in accordance with the rule in *Hadley v. Baxendale* (1854) 9 Ex. 341.

BRITISH SUGAR PLC v. NEI POWER PROJECTS LTD [1997] C.L.C. 622, Alliott, J., QBD.

990. **Exclusion clauses—standard terms—damage to aircraft at airport**

See AIR TRANSPORT: Monarch Airlines Ltd v. London Luton Airport Ltd. §222

991. **Implied terms—contract for supply of services—express provision that obligation to provide services was to be judged subjectively by service provider excluded statutory implied terms**

[Supply of Goods and Services Act 1982.]

Held, that, where, in a contract for the supply of services falling within the Supply of Goods and Services Act 1982 s.12, there was express provision that the obligation to provide services was to be judged subjectively by the service provider, the implied terms contained in s.13 and s.14 of the Act were excluded by virtue of s.16.

EAGLE STAR LIFE ASSURANCE CO LTD v. GRIGGS, *The Independent*, October 20, 1997 (C.S.), Kennedy, L.J., CA.

992. **Misrepresentation—breach of collateral warranty—milling machine misrepresented as to capability—exclusion clause unenforceable—rescission inequitable**

[Unfair Contract Terms 1977 s.8, s.11 (1).]

M claimed damages for misrepresentation and breach of collateral warranty by Y, the vendor of a milling machine which did not fulfil M's requirements. He further claimed rescission of the agreement and entitlement to reject the machinery. M was the proprietor of an engineering business involved in making, milling and drilling metal engineering components. He was interested in purchasing a machine that had the same accuracy as the machine he already used but with a higher speed of production. Y's salesman, H, visited M at his workshop and discussed M's requirements. He showed M a brochure and they discussed one machine in particular. There was a conflict of evidence between them as to what was said at the meeting. M then attended a demonstration of that machine at Y's premises which was found to be a standard demonstration rather than a special demonstration catered towards M's product as contended by M. M purchased the machine for £82,000. The machine did not fulfil M's requirements because it could not produce the necessary accuracy at an increased speed. There was nothing wrong with the machine as such other than that it was the wrong machine for M's needs. Y contended that had it known of the product and use for which M needed the machine they would not have recommended that particular machine. The agreement between M and Y sought to exclude liability which M argued did not satisfy the requirements of reasonableness under the Unfair Contract Terms 1977 s.8 and s.11 (1).

Held, allowing the claim, that (1) H represented to M that the machine would produce gears as accurately as the machine M then used and that it would do so at a significantly faster rate. M relied on those representations when he decided to purchase the machine. Y, through H, had given a collateral warranty, collateral to and antecedent to M's decision to buy the machinery. Where evidence conflicted, M's evidence was generally preferred to that of H. It was found that H did know of the specific application for which M required the machine and should have concluded that it was not the right machine for his needs. In addition H knew that speed of production was important to M. H did not take reasonable care to ensure that the representations he made were accurate; (2) the exclusion of liability term relied on by Y was not reasonable as it was too wide and excluded all loss in all circumstances. With regard to M's claim that the contract should be rescinded and the machine returned to Y, given that M had the machine for five years and it was still in good working order, it would be inequitable to order rescission of the contract as the consequent loss to Y would be disproportionate. Damages for misrepresentation and breach of warranty were ordered, to be assessed if not agreed.

MILJUS (T/A A&Z ENGINEERING) v. YAMAZAKI MACHINERY UK LTD, Trans. Ref: 1994 Orb. No. 774, May 28, 1996, Recorder Fernyhough Q.C., QBD (OR).

993. Performance bonds—liability to account for bond despite no loss flowing from breach—bond being a guarantee of due performance not estimate of damages potentially to be suffered

C agreed to supply sugar to B. C's offer was accepted subject to the payment of a performance bond by C, to be forfeited in the event of non-compliance with any contract terms or if C were responsible for any loss to B. The contract stipulated that the sugar would be transported in a ship not more than 20 years old and would arrive by a certain date. In fact the ship used was more than 20 years old and the cargo arrived a few days late. B made a call on the bond. C applied to the Commercial Court to restrain B on the basis that B had suffered no loss as a result of C's failure to meet the terms of the contract.

Held, dismissing the application, that the bond was not an estimate of the damages that might flow from a breach of contract but a guarantee of due performance. In the event of a failure by C, B was entitled to call on the full amount of the bond even if it had suffered no loss. It was implicit in the nature of the bond that, unless the contrary was expressly stated, there would at some stage be an accounting and, if B had suffered no loss and had called on the bond, it would be liable to account to C for any amounts received under the bond.

CARGILL INTERNATIONAL SA v. BANGLADESH SUGAR & FOOD INDUSTRIES CORP [1996] 4 All E.R. 563, Morison, J., QBD (Comm Ct).

994. Performance bonds—monies paid—Mareva injunction obtained over monies discharged by reason of culpable delay

[Arbitration Act 1950 s.27.]

C appealed against an order discharging a Mareva injunction granted to C over an amount of £1,887,200, being the amount paid under performance bonds issued by C following C's breach of its contract with S by failing to open letters of credit in favour of S. C obtained an injunction but this was discharged on the basis that C did not have an accrued cause of action. C claimed that S had to account to it for the balance between the monies paid by C and the amount of S's loss arising from C's breach of the contract. After further arbitrations, C obtained the injunction which was the subject of this hearing. Delays occurred and C's application for an extension of time under the Arbitration Act 1950 s.27 was heard in the House of Lords, and granted. S applied for the injunction to be discharged on the ground of delay and the application was granted. C argued that the judge, in exercising his discretion to discharge the injunction (1) was wrong to imply from correspondence that the parties had agreed to "freeze" the proceedings as at January 1994. He should have dealt with the matter as it stood on the date of the application, November 1995, which would have rendered the 19 month period of delay as historic relative to C's previous action on its claim, and (2) had wrongly taken account of the information provided regarding S's financial position in finding that the injunction imposed had the effect of tying up S's capital and stopping it from trading.

Held, dismissing the appeal, that (1) the judge was wrong to infer an agreement between the parties that the position be frozen, but the error made no difference to the outcome as the delay period of 19 months did not become merely historic when taking the position at the later date, and (2) the monies on which the Mareva injunction was imposed had not formed part of S's capital and were, therefore, a windfall as submitted by C, rather than compensation for actual loss. However, as C had not proceeded with its claim with diligence and was responsible for 19 months' culpable delay, the injunction should not have been allowed to continue and the judge was correct to discharge it. A bond is a guarantee of due performance and it is implicit that there would be an "accounting" between the parties to the contract to determine their rights and obligations at some future date so that if the bond were inadequate, the buyer would be liable in damages for the balance, and if it were in excess of the amount of the seller's damages, the buyer would be able to recover that excess, *Cargill International SA v. Bangladesh Sugar and Food Industries Corp* [1996] 2 Lloyd's Rep. 524, [1997] C.L.Y. 993 considered.

COMDEL COMMODITIES LTD v. SIPOREX TRADE SA [1997] 1 Lloyd's Rep. 424, Potter, L.J., CA.

995. Rectification—accounting dispute—guidance given as to when a court will grant rectification

By an agreement W purchased two companies, William Hill and Mecca, from G. The agreement provided for a price reduction by reference to profits shown in the 1989 accounts which were to consist of a pro forma consolidation of the accounts of William Hill and Mecca for a specified period. An accountant, appointed to resolve disputes arising out of the 1989 accounts, obtained advice from leading counsel that the agreement applied to the separate group accounts of William Hill and Mecca but not the 1989 accounts. The result was that the 1989 accounts did not have to comply with GAAP. G argued that the accounts had to be drawn up in accordance with the principles of acquisition accounting complying with GAAP but W argued that the accounts merely had to be aggregated without adjustment. G sought rectification of the agreement to provide that the 1989 accounts had to be prepared on a consolidated basis combining the accounts of William Hill and Mecca.

Held, granting rectification, that the party seeking rectification had to show that there was a continuing common intention in relation to a particular matter that had not been reflected in the written agreement, that the common intention had persisted up to the time of the written agreement and that there was an outward expression of accord. If rectification was granted the court had to be sure that the provisions of the agreement did not conflict. It was not necessary to show the exact words to which the parties had agreed nor that the parties had reached a prior concluded agreement, a common continuing intention was sufficient. In the present case G had satisfied those requirements and on the facts it was clear that the parties had intended that the 1989 accounts would be prepared on a consolidated basis.

GRAND METROPOLITAN PLC v. WILLIAM HILL GROUP LTD [1997] 1 B.C.L.C. 390, Arden, J., Ch D.

996. Rectification—sale of goods—fundamental mistake in contract—parties mistaken as to the real error—rectification not correcting the mistake—contract not binding

Parties to a contract entered into a shipping contract in which they believed that figures had been transposed. In fact, the error related to tonnages. The parties agreed to rectify the contract by reversing the supposed transposition. The issue arose whether the rectification agreement and contract were enforceable.

Held, that where the parties had sought to rectify the mistake, they were both mistaken as to the real error. Therefore, to enforce the rectification

agreement would be contrary to the purpose of that agreement, namely to remove the mistake. The mistake was fundamental. There was no evidence that either party had accepted the risk of such mistake. Therefore, the contract was not binding on the parties.

GRAINS & FOURRAGES SA v. HUYTON [1997] 1 Lloyd's Rep. 628, Mance, J., QBD (Comm Ct).

997. Repudiation—shipbuilding contracts—entitlement to damages—amendment of pleadings to claim acceptance of repudiation

S agreed to design, construct, and deliver six ships to L, on instalment payments. L, in anticipatory repudiatory breach of contract, informed S it would be unable to raise the second instalment. S issued keel-laying notices and, after non-payment, notices of rescission for all six hulls, claiming the second instalment for each. It appeared that only two hulls were ever brought into existence, first numbered 1 and 2, then re-numbered 3 and 4, then 5 and 6. In January 1994 S sued claiming L were in repudiatory breach of all six contracts but did not by the writ accept the breach; S claimed the second instalment for hulls 1 and 2 submitting they were accrued debts and Clarke J. gave summary judgment. S had meanwhile commenced the 1995 action claiming the keel-laying instalments for hulls 3, 4, 5 and 6 and applied for summary judgment, and further applied for judgment for damages to be assessed for the initial wrongful repudiation. S argued it was entitled to recover damages pursuant to contract Art.5.05 in addition to the instalment after it had rescinded the contract for non payment of the instalment. Waller J. gave leave to defend in relation to all six contracts. Both judgments were appealed. The Court of Appeal held that S was not entitled to unpaid keel-laying instalments as accrued debts, but confined to damages recoverable under Art.5.05; no keel-laying instalments could be claimed for hulls 3 to 6 as no keels were laid. Damages were to be assessed. S contended that damages should be assessed as if there had been a repudiatory breach at common law; L contended that the Art.5.05 regime applied alone. Longmore J. ordered the common law particularisation to be struck out as inconsistent with the Art.5.05 regime and the Court of Appeal judgment and order. S sought leave to amend the points of claim in both actions to plead acceptance of repudiation of the contracts which entitled them to common law damages.

Held, refusing leave to amend, the keel-laying notices were unequivocal assertions of the continuing operation of the contract and inconsistent with an intention to treat the contracts as at an end. They were the clearest possible indication to L that if L was to avoid an actual breach they must perform by making the second instalment on time. S was then obliged to permit L to perform. Failure to perform would entitle S then to rescind by reference to Art.5.05 and receive, only, compensation specified by that article. The rescission after the invalid keel-laying notices neither entitled S to treat the contract as terminated by reference to L's earlier anticipatory breach, nor terminated the contract on the grounds of non payment of the keel-laying instalments, but was a wrongful repudiatory termination of the contracts. Further, the service of the 1994 action constituted affirmation of the contract, claiming as they did injunctive relief against other parties inducing L to break the contract. This was not a case where the court should exercise any jurisdiction to grant the amendments, given the overlap between the effect of the anticipatory breach and the breaches relied on in the Court of Appeal with the result that allowing the amendments would effectively re-litigate the substance of the claim decided by the Court of Appeal. Further, the common law claim, so closely related to the Art.5.05 claim, ought to have been raised with the original claims; there was no good reason why this was not done, nor were there special circumstances to take account of to ensure there was no injustice to S. The proposed amendments were thus an abuse of process, *Henderson v. Henderson* (1843) 67 E.R. 313 applied.

STOCZNIA GDANSKA SA v. LATVIAN SHIPPING CO [1997] 2 Lloyd's Rep. 228, Colman, J., QBD (Comm Ct).

CONTRACTS

998. **Sale of business—fraudulent misrepresentation—breach of warranty—accountant failed to disclose full accounts**

W, a family company, appealed against the judge's findings concerning a dispute arising from the sale of one of W's businesses. The judge found claims in fraudulent misrepresentation to be made out and further held that R had made out their claims for breach of warranty against W. R's case was that there existed management accounts which showed the business for sale was making heavy losses, but that the accountant acting for W fraudulently concealed this and produced accounts which erroneously overstated the turnover of the business. It was submitted that W told R that it was not possible to segregate the overheads of the business for sale from those of other businesses owned by them when in fact a specific computerised accounting system could do this. A further misrepresentation was that figures for turnover were correct whereas they were overstated. The third misrepresentation was that the business was profitable whereas it made substantial losses. The judge found each of the alleged misrepresentations was made and was false as pleaded. W submitted that even if the first misrepresentation was made it had no relevant causative effect. W submitted that regarding the second misrepresentation their accountant was not aware of the erroneous figures and challenged the finding that these errors induced R to enter into the agreements. They further challenged the finding that the third misrepresentation was made and that if it was so made it did not induce R into the agreements.

Held, dismissing the appeal, that the evidence supported the first misrepresentation and there was evidence of an agreement between W and the accountant that potential purchasers were not to be given the full accounts for the business for sale. The accountant plainly prepared the accounts with the intention of restricting the information placed before potential purchasers.

RENTALL LTD v. DS WILLCOCK LTD (DECEMBER 1996), Trans. Ref: QBENF 95/0028/C, QBENF 95/0058/C, QBENI 95/0366/C, December 4, 1996, Phillips, L.J., CA.

999. **Termination—construction of terms in main and subcontract**

U obtained a contract from YH to repaint an oil tanker permanently anchored in the Red Sea. M had helped U to prepare the initial bid and subsequently made a subcontract with U which did not pass to M all the obligations undertaken by U under the main contract. The works were delayed and YH terminated the contract for cause, but it was subsequently reinstated by agreement. The terms of the main contract were incorporated into the subcontract between M and U. There were important financial provisions which were the main basis of the claim and counterclaim including cl.5 which provided that if the main contract were terminated by YH for any reason attributable to one party then the other party would undertake to reimburse on demand all costs and expenses incurred as a result of the termination. Clause 7.3 apportioned the costs and profits of the contract price. Clause 7.4 provided that costs incurred by M in preparation for, in anticipation of, or in connection with the completion of the contract, its obligations thereunder, or commencement of work under the contract in excess of those set out in cl.7.3, to the extent that they had been incurred as a result of failure by U in the performance of its obligations under the contract or were otherwise attributable to U would be paid by U. Clause 7.5 was a mirror image of cl.7.4 with U substituted for M and vice versa. Clause 9.1 provided that the parties agreed to bear their own costs. M brought an action against U claiming general damages and an enlargement of damages under cl.5 and cl.7 in the same amounts. U counterclaimed, mirror imaging M's claims though in different amounts and also claimed an indemnity against any damages it might be called to pay under the main contract. U's primary submission was that neither party was at liberty to claim common law damages at large but merely sums specifically provided for by the contract.

Held, giving judgment for M and dismissing the counterclaim, that YH had been entitled to terminate the contract for cause, the substantial causes being faults of U. The contract did not exclude the right to common law damages and there were no express words of the subcontract excluding the common law right to damages. Clause 9.1 did not exclude any right to damages but merely limited the contractual scheme for the apportionment of costs under cl.5 and cl.7, which could be read as giving extra rights. The claim for damages was not excluded because the contract was a loss making one. M's primary claim for common law damages was not a claim to recover contract expenses, and if the contract had been performed, M would have made less of a loss than it in fact made. M was therefore entitled to damages which would put it in a position of making that lesser loss. M's alternative claim for damages at common law for wasted expenditure was not sustainable. M was entitled to sums under cl.5 and cl.7 of the subcontract in addition to general common law damages, since the latter do not include provision for costs incurred before the termination of the contract. On the true construction of cl.5 and cl.7 of the subcontract the division of costs was not only to refer to costs incurred as a result of breaches of the agreement but also to costs thrown away (including pre-contract costs) as a result of blameworthiness, including breach of agreement. The main contract did not exclude vital implied terms such as the term for implied access and because of breach of this term the contract had come to an end.

MILBURN SERVICES LTD v. UNITED TRADING GROUP (UK) LTD 52 Con. L.R. 130, Judge Bowsher Q.C., QBD (OR).

1000. **Unfair contract terms—standard conditions—reasonableness of standard conditions—plaintiff did not need to raise in pleadings issue of reasonableness on which defendant relied**

[Unfair Contract Terms Act 1977.]

S brought an action against P for breach of contract and negligence, and sought leave to file a reply pleading that P's standard conditions were unreasonable under the Unfair Contract Terms Act 1977 and could not operate to exclude or limit its liability. Leave was refused on the grounds that S was obliged to make it clear in pleadings that an attack on the reasonableness of the conditions was to be made. Judgment was given for P, and S appealed, arguing that it was implicit that, where pleadings showed that P intended to rely on standard conditions, P considered its conditions to be reasonable and therefore this would be an issue that P should be prepared to meet at trial if no reply were filed. Alternatively, S submitted that P was obliged to state that the conditions on which it sought to rely were reasonable and it was aware of the need to meet the requirements of the Act. P argued that it was for S to indicate that reasonableness would be put in issue and it was not its role to make express reference to it, as to do so would amount to an invitation to S to object on that basis.

Held, allowing the appeal, that where a plaintiff wished to challenge the reasonableness of contract conditions relied upon by the defendants to exclude liability, it was not necessary for an indication to be given to that effect in the pleadings, as it was implicit that the defendants considered that the conditions met the requirements of the Act. There were also advantages in defendants clearly stating that they regarded the conditions relied upon as reasonable, so that the plaintiff could then say whether this would be an issue, thus giving the defendants the opportunity to gather evidence to prove reasonableness at trial.

SHEFFIELD v. PICKFORDS LTD [1997] C.L.C. 648, Lord Woolf, M.R., CA.

1001. **Articles**

Aspects of frustration: Buyer 1997, 19(7), 6-8. (Expanation of doctrine, including self induced frustration, perishing of goods and effect of force majeure clauses).

Breach of contract and damages for mental distress *(Nelson Enonchong)*: O.J.L.S. 1996, 16(4), 617-640. (Whether compensatory damages for mental distress should be available).

Contract law: fulfilling the reasonable expectations of honest men *(Johan Steyn)*: L.Q.R. 1997, 113(Jul), 433-442. (Application of external standard of reasonableness in contract law).

Contracting across the Internet *(Nick Page)*: I.P. News. 1997, 20(9), IF i-iv. (Issues relating to nature of contract, global implications, IP rights, security and confidentiality, and guidelines for avoiding problems).

How rogues break contracts *(Nigel Boardman* and *Alex Greystoke)*: C.L. 1997, 19, 58-59. (Ways in which parties can seek to avoid their contractual obligations).

Incorporation by course of dealing: Buyer 1997, 19(1), 4-6. (Development of case law on incorporation into contract of conditions through course of dealing and issues involved where contract term is particularly onerous).

Practical reasoning and contract as promise: extending contract-based criteria to decide excuse cases *(Andrew J. Morris)*: C.L.J. 1997, 56(1), 147-174. (How courts apply theories of contractual liability in cases involving impossibility, frustration and mistake).

Sub-bailment on terms: implications of the decision in the Pioneer Container and its application in recent cases *(Paul Bugden)*: I.C.C.L.R. 1997, 8(4), 141-144. (Issues arising from decision that principal bailor is bound by sub-bailment terms where goods have been sub-bailed with his consent).

The effect of an anticipatory breach: Buyer 1997, 19(5), 1-3. (Effect of acceptance of breach, including the right to claim damages and to rescind, and rights on the refusal to accept a breach).

The millennium: legal and management issues *(Richard Stephens)*: I.H.L. 1997, 50(May), 45-48. (Potential problem of software failing to recognise year 2000, possible solutions, contractual liability through implied terms and practical steps to reduce impact).

Threatened breach of contract and refusal to supply as grounds for duress *(Gerard McMeel)*: Nott. L.J. 1997, 5(2), 120-139. (Need to prove that oppressor acted in bad faith or deliberately exploited position of advantage).

1002. Books

Beatson, Jack; Friedman, Daniel–Good Faith and Fault in Contract Law. Paperback: £19.99. ISBN 0-19-826578-6. Clarendon Press.

Furmston, Michael; Poole, Jill; Norisado,Takao–Contract Formation and Letters of Intent. Contract Law Series. Hardback: £65.00. ISBN 0-471-95238-9. Chancery Wiley Law Publications.

Lewison, Kim–Interpretation of Contracts. 2nd Ed. Hardback: £110.00. ISBN 0 421 60830-7. Sweet & Maxwell.

Poole, Jill–Casebook on Contract. 3rd Ed. Paperback: £20.00. ISBN 1-85431-644-3. Blackstone Press.

Quigley, Conor–European Community Contract Law: Vols 1 &2. The Effect of EC Legislation on Contractual Rights: Obligations and Remedies; EC Legislation. Hardback: £156.00. ISBN 90-411-0720-7. Kluwer Law International.

Villiers, Theresa; Wilkin, Sean–Law of Estoppel, Variation and Waiver. Hardback: £65.00. ISBN 0-471-96921-4. John Wiley and Sons.

CONVEYANCING

1003. Contract–assurance plan–mistake–entitlement of vendor to amend plan–five per cent reduction of area was not a substantial reduction

[Rules of the Supreme Court Ord.14A.]

H contracted with L to purchase a house on a development being constructed by L. The contract had annexed to it a plan of the property to be sold which included the passageway between that property, no.25, and the neighbouring property, no.26. H contended that the passageway was not subject to any right of way, without which no.26 would have no access through its kitchen door as it opened onto that passageway. L claimed that the plan had been drawn including the passageway in error, that the passageway should have been cross hatched on the plan to indicate shared private access and that it was entitled to submit an amended plan. The contract provided for the vendor to amend the plan provided that it did not compel the buyer to accept a substantial reduction in the area to be sold. As the passageway constituted approximately five per cent of the total area to be sold, L argued this was not a substantial reduction which H disputed. An injunction restraining L from dealing with the property in a way contrary to H's alleged rights was granted which meant that no.26 could not complete its purchase. H applied for the rights and obligations of both parties to be reviewed as a matter of construction under RSC Ord.14A and for the injunction to be renewed.

Held, making no order, that the starting point for construction was the contract. L had put forward an assurance plan which was not irrevocable but given the terms of the contract it would be able to submit an amended plan to show the passageway as shared, provided it did not substantially reduce the area sold. Given that the passageway was relatively open and passed between the two properties, five per cent of the area in that context did not constitute a substantial reduction.

HAMMOND v. LAING HOMES LTD, Trans. Ref: CH.1997-H-2110, April 28, 1997, Lloyd, J., Ch D.

1004. **Contract–exclusivity agreement–acceptance of higher offer–injunction–damages as the appropriate remedy**

D, as owners of a golf course, entered into negotiations with P for the sale of that property. During the course of those negotiations P offered terms which D accepted. P alleged that those terms included an undertaking of exclusivity, namely that D would not negotiate with another purchaser once they had accepted P's offer. Written heads of agreement were sent by D to P, but those did not include any exclusivity agreement. Subsequently, D received a higher offer from another party, and informed P that they were minded to accept that higher offer. Upon receiving such notification P made an ex parte application for an injunction to restrain D from proceeding with the later offer. The injunction was granted and at the inter partes hearing D contended, inter alia, that P had not demonstrated that the exclusivity agreement was supported by consideration flowing from P, and that in the alternative damages were an appropriate remedy.

Held, dismissing the motion for injunctive relief, that (1) the fact that P required an exclusivity agreement indicated that he had bound himself to complete by a certain date and so to incur expense and cost before that date, and that was capable of constituting consideration, *Pitt v. PHH Asset Management Ltd* [1994] 1 W.L.R. 327, [1994] C.L.Y. 570 applied, and (2) the injunction should not be prolonged as damages were a suitable alternative remedy. An exclusivity agreement conferred on the purchaser no right to require the vendor to sell the land to him; rather it was designed to protect the purchaser from having incurred substantial costs in getting themselves ready to complete and at the last minute losing the property because the vendor elected to sell to someone else. The purchaser could then recover his costs thrown away as damages.

TYE v. HOUSE [1997] 41 E.G. 160, Evans-Lombe, J., Ch D.

1005. **Contract–oral contract for residential development in return for freehold–no claim for damages–estoppel–restitution as amendment to pleadings not permitted**

[Law of Property (Miscellaneous Provisions) Act 1989 s.2.]

G appealed against the striking out of his claim for damages for breach of contract on the ground that it revealed no cause of action. G, a builder, contended that (1) an oral contract he made with M that he would be reimbursed for the purchase of a site, the obtaining of planning permission, the demolition of the existing buildings and the construction of seven houses had been an oral collateral contract amounting to consideration for the transfer of the freehold to M; (2) M were prevented by the doctrine of estoppel by convention from denying the agreement, and (3) his claim for restitution should be allowed as an amendment to the pleadings.

Held, dismissing the appeal, that the claim was void because the contract was not in writing as required by the Law of Property (Miscellaneous Provisions) Act 1989 s.2, (1) it was unrealistic to construct a collateral contract on the facts, *Daulia Ltd v. Four Millbank Nominees Ltd* [1978] 1 Ch. 231, [1978] C.L.Y. 2501 followed and *Tootal Clothing Ltd v. Guinea Properties Management Ltd* (1992) 64 P. & C.R. 452, [1992] C.L.Y. 543 distinguished because, there, two separate contracts were in writing and there was a question of incorporation; (2) an estoppel could not be invoked to validate a transaction that, as here, was void on the grounds of public policy, *Amalgamated Investment & Property Co Ltd v. Texas Commerce International Bank Ltd* [1982] 1 Q.B. 84, [1981] C.L.Y. 1273 considered, and (3) it was clearly inappropriate to raise such a difficult alternative case as restitution as an amendment to pleadings on appeal.

GODDEN v. MERTHYR TYDFIL HOUSING ASSOCIATION (1997) 74 P. & C.R. D1, Simon Brown, L.J., CA.

1006. Contract–specific performance–Hong Kong

C appealed against the decision to grant a decree of specific performance to L in respect of a dispute concerning an agreement to sell property. C agreed to sell her flat to L and signed a receipt for a deposit paid by L. When C failed to complete, L commenced proceedings for specific performance. C submitted that no agreement had been made, the receipt was forged and the payment had been a loan to finance gambling. L asserted that he had advanced C money to invest in a massage parlour and in return he was given six postdated cheques which were dishonoured on presentation. Later, C told L that because she was financially embarrassed she would have to sell her flat.

Held, dismissing the appeal, that there was no evidence that L had persuaded C to sell him the flat. There was no basis on which the agreement for the sale of the flat could be reopened under money lenders legislation.

CHEUNG BING SUM JUANA v. LEO LEE, Trans. Ref: No.47 of 1995, November 26, 1996, Lord Hoffmann, PC.

1007. Contract–specific performance–striking out for inordinate and inexcusable delay–applicability of defence of laches

W appealed after their previous appeal against an order striking out their claim for want of prosecution was dismissed. S purchased a property with an agreement with W whereby W would contribute some money towards the purchase price and owe S a further £24,000 on an interest free loan for an indefinite period. They then carried out extensive renovation work on the property. W issued proceedings seeking specific performance of a contract of sale of the property, claiming that part of the property was held by S on trust for them, subject only to an equitable charge in S's favour to secure repayment of the £24,000. Alternatively, they claimed a beneficial interest in the property. S claimed that the contract of sale was terminated when W informed S that they no longer wished to purchase the property. After various stages in the proceedings and without prejudice negotiations, S died. A few months later W served notice of intention to proceed. On the application of S's personal representatives the proceedings were struck out on the basis that (1) there was inordinate and inexcusable delay; (2) there would be prejudice to S's case, and (3) that W had failed to show that the defence of laches would not bar further proceedings. The principles in *Trill v. Sacher* [1993] 1 W.L.R. 1379, [1993] C.L.Y. 3336 and *Birkett v. James* [1978] A.C. 297, [1977] C.L.Y. 2410 were followed. W argued that (1) the delay was not inordinate and the time taken was relatively short for this type of case; (2) although there were disputes as to the details of the agreement between S and W, S's evidence was not critical as there were other witnesses, and (3) it was futile to strike out the proceedings as the doctrine of laches did not apply. W remained in possession of the property and were equitable owners, with only the perfection of the legal title outstanding. As such they could not lose their rights because of a delay in proceedings. In addition, it was exceptional for a case to be struck out within the limitation period.

Held, dismissing the appeal, that (1) having regard to the history of proceedings the judge was entitled to find that the delay was inordinate, and it was admitted by W that it was inexcusable; (2) S would have been the main witness in the defence against W's claim. There were important disputes about the terms of the agreement and as S was no longer alive and able to give evidence the defence case was prejudiced, and (3) W had failed to show that striking out the proceedings would be futile. There was a dispute as to the basis on which W was in possession of the property and they were not recognised as legal owners. The judge had not erred in principle in concluding that the defence of laches applied, *Joyce v. Joyce* [1978] 1 W.L.R. 1170, [1978] C.L.Y. 2419 and *Wright v. Morris* [1997] F.S.R. 218, [1997] C.L.Y. 754 considered.

WELLS v. STEPHEN, Trans. Ref: CHANI 96/0887/B, February 19, 1997, Mummery, L.J., CA.

1008. Contract–staged payment–interest terminated if no planning permission granted

MH, a property development concern, agreed with M to purchase land over which planning permission was granted. The agreement between the parties provided for the staged payment of the acquisition and development amounts. Under cl.4, failure to obtain planning permission would terminate MH's interest in any part of the land which did not receive planning permission, subject to a notice period or the expiry of a term of 12 years. The issue arose as to MH's interest with reference to the land.

Held, dismissing the appeal, that MH ceased to have any interest in the property on the expiry of the first period of extension to the contractual period. The agreement clearly provided that the interest came to an end at the expiry of the first contract period where there was no planning permission. Even though the agreement provided that it did not come to an end without notice or the expiry of the 12 year period, that could not maintain the interest once it had ceased without obtaining planning permission. There was reason for the judge to believe that the parties had acted as though the agreement was at an end and therefore no estoppel arose in favour of MH.

MITCHEM v. MAGNUS HOMES SOUTH WEST LTD (1997) 74 P. & C.R. 235, Peter Gibson, L.J., CA.

1009. Deposits–solicitor as stakeholder–lien–set-off–freedom of principal to dispose of stake without consent before payment made but after event on which stake to be paid has occurred

[Rules of the Supreme Court Ord.62 r.11.]

The fourth defendant, H, appealed against a decision refusing it leave to appeal against a summary judgment to repay $200,000 paid as deposits by M for land purchases. Both M and the vendors, V, had claimed breach of contract against each other and when V went into administrative receivership, H was joined and applied the deposits, which it had held as stakeholder, in payment of debts owed to them by V under a lien or right of set off. M and V later compromised the action on terms that M was entitled to the return of the deposits, which would be used to pay each party's costs and the balance be divided between them, but concealed the nature of the agreement from the court below.

Held, allowing the appeal, that H had an arguable defence to the claim for the return of the deposits which could not be defeated by a compromise to which it was not a party. If H established that the deposits had been duly forfeited before it had exercised its lien or rights of set off, then it had a complete defence. M's solicitors and counsel had to show cause under RSC Ord.62

r.11 (4) why a wasted costs order should not be made, *Rockeagle v. Alsop Wilkinson* [1992] Ch. 47, [1992] C.L.Y. 4084 considered.

MANZANILLA LTD v. CORTON PROPERTY AND INVESTMENTS LTD (NO.1), Trans. Ref: CHANI 95/1014/B, November 13, 1996, Millett, L.J., CA.

1010. Land registration–conduct of business

LAND REGISTRATION (CONDUCT OF BUSINESS) REGULATIONS 1997, SI 1997 713; made under the Land Registration Act 1925 s.126. In force: April 1, 1997; £1.10.

These Regulations, which revoke and replace the Land Registration (Solicitor to HM Land Registry) Regulations 1990 (SI 1990 2236), make amendments to the acts of the registrar which may be done by a legally qualified registrar, called the Solicitor to HM Land Registry or, during a vacancy in the office of, or in the absence of, the Solicitor to HM Land Registry, by another legally qualified registrar (styled the Acting Solicitor to HM Land Registry). They further provide for those acts to be done by any other legally qualified registrar, for the purpose of hearing matters under the r.220 (hearing of cautioner by registrar) and r.298 (hearings by the registrar) of the Land Registration Rules 1925 (SR & O 1925 1093), and making orders consequent upon such hearings, where such registrar is directed by the Chief Land Registrar to conduct the hearing.

1011. Land registration–district registries

LAND REGISTRATION (DISTRICT REGISTRIES) ORDER 1997, SI 1997 1534; made under the Land Registration Act 1925 s.132. In force: September 1, 1997; £1.55.

This Order, which supersedes the Land Registration (District Registries) Order 1995 (SI 1995 2962), changes the name of the Durham District Land Registry to the Durham (Southfield House) District Land Registry; creates two new district land registries called the Durham (Boldon House) District Land Registry and the District Land Registry for Wales/Cofrestrfa Tir Ddosbarthol Cymru respectively; transfers responsibility for the registration of titles in Cumbria and Surrey from the Durham (Southfield House) District Land Registry (formerly the Durham District Land Registry) to the new Durham (Boldon House) District Land Registry; and transfers responsibility for the registration of titles in all counties and county boroughs in Wales from the Swansea District Land Registry/Cofrestrfa Tir Ddosbarthol Abertawe to the new District Land Registry for Wales/Cofrestrfa Tir Ddosbarthol Cymru. It also takes account of the changes made to administrative areas in England by certain structural change orders made during 1995 and 1996.

1012. Land registration–fees–No.1 Order

LAND REGISTRATION FEES ORDER 1997, SI 1997 178; made under the Public Offices Fees Act 1879 s.2, s.3; the Land Registration Act 1925 s.145; and the Finance Act 1990 s.128. In force: April 1, 1997; £3.20.

This Order, which supersedes the Land Registration Fees Order 1996 and takes effect on April 1, 1997, reduces overall the fees payable in relation to applications made and services provided under the Land Registration Acts 1925 to 1986 and the Rules made under the Land Registration Act 1925.

1013. Land registration–fees–No.2 Order

LAND REGISTRATION FEES (NO.2) ORDER 1997, SI 1997 1710; made under the Public Offices Fees Act 1879 s.2, s.3; the Land Registration Act 1925 s.144; and the Public Officers Fees Act 1990 s.128. In force: October 1, 1997; £2.80.

This Order, which revokes and replaces the Land Registration Fees Order 1997 (SI 1997 178), amends the land registration fee scales.

1014. Land registration–matrimonial home rights

LAND REGISTRATION (MATRIMONIAL HOME RIGHTS) RULES 1997, SI 1997 1964; made under the Land Registration Act 1925 s.144; and the Family Law Act 1996 s.32, Sch.4 para.4. In force: October 1, 1997; £1.95.

These Rules, which replace the Land Registration (Matrimonial Homes) Rules 1990 (SI 1990 1360) prescribe the forms to be used and the evidence to be provided when applying to register a notice, or renew a registration of a notice or caution, in respect of matrimonial home rights under the Family Law Act 1996; prescribe the form of application for an official search in respect of matrimonial home rights by a mortgagee of registered land for the purpose of s.56(3) of the 1996 Act and the form and contents of the official certificate of result of search; and provide that, in certain circumstances, applications for official searches or official certificates of result of search, or information, may be made, issued or given by any other means of communication.

1015. Land registration–rules

LAND REGISTRATION RULES 1997, SI 1997 3037; made under the Land Registration Act 1925 s.13, s.18, s.21, s.33, s.41, s.53, s.87, s.90, s.94, s.99, s.123A, s.144; and the Charities Act 1993 s.37, s.39. In force: April 1, 1998; £6.10.

These Rules amend the Land Registration Rules 1925 (SR & O 1925 1093) in order to implement compulsory registration provisions contained in the Land Registration Act 1997 and the associated amendments to the Charities Act 1993; make provision for new forms of application for first registration, caution against first registration and registration of dealings with whole, new forms of transfer, assent and discharge of whole, new forms of transfer and assent of a registered charge, and a new list of documents form, and make associated amendments to certain existing prescribed forms; introduce common forms for freehold and leasehold dispositions; make new provision for executing discharges; make it unnecessary to enter a description of the registered proprietor on the register; require the entry of a company's registered number on to the register; make fresh provision for the modification of examination of title on first registration and as to the certificate to be provided; remove the registrar's duty to advertise first registration applications; abolish priority notices against first registration and provisional possessory registration; make provision for Welsh language forms and instruments; and to make fresh provision for instruments for which no form is prescribed, for the registration of rentcharges, for exchanges, and for the entry of a restriction on first registration. In addition, r.11, r.33, r.63, r.66, r.71, r.80, r.115, r.118, r.119, r.120, r.142, r.143, r.167, r.194, r.229, r.223, Form 1 to Form 5, Form 7, Form 8, Form 13, Form 17, Form 19, Form 32, Form 33, Form 37 to Form 39, Form 43 to Form 50, Form 54, Form 55, and Form 72 are revoked.

1016. Land Registration Act 1997 (c.2)

This Act amends the Land Registration Act 1925 to strengthen the security provided by registration of title and to speed up the registration of land with unregistered title.

This Act received Royal Assent on February 27, 1997.

1017. Land Registration Act 1997 (c.2)–Commencement Order

LAND REGISTRATION ACT 1997 (COMMENCEMENT) ORDER 1997, SI 1997 3036 (C.111); made under the Land Registration Act 1997 s.5. Commencement details: bringing into force various provisions of the Act on April 1, 1998; £0.65.

This Order brings into force the remaining provisions of the Land Registration Act 1997.

1018. Professional negligence–solicitors–defective advice concerning restrictive covenant

See NEGLIGENCE: Hartle v. Laceys. §3839

1019. Professional negligence–solicitors–extent of duty to mortgagee

See NEGLIGENCE: Birmingham Midshires Mortgage Services Ltd v. George Ide Phillips. §3831

1020. Professional negligence–solicitors–failure to investigate suspicion of boundary dispute

See NEGLIGENCE: McManus Developments Ltd v. Barbridge Properties Ltd and Blandy & Blandy. §3825

1021. Professional negligence–solicitors–instructions taken from one of several clients without express authority

See NEGLIGENCE: Farrer v. Copley Singletons. §3826

1022. Rescission–minor breach of essential time condition–equity would intervene to order specific performance–facts outside the limit of the doctrine

UE entered into an agreement to purchase a flat from GA and paid a deposit, the contract stating that completion had to take place on or before a specified date and time, and that time was to be of the essence. The contract also provided that failure by UE to comply with any of the terms and conditions would lead to forfeiture of the deposit and entitle GA to rescind the agreement. UE tendered the purchase price 10 minutes after the deadline for completion had passed and GA declared that UE's deposit was forfeited and the contract rescinded. UE, whose action for specific performance was dismissed by the High Court and the Court of Appeal of Hong Kong, made a further appeal, contending that the court should exercise its equitable powers to relieve it from the consequences of late completion.

Held, dismissing the appeal, that whilst the extent of the equitable power to grant relief against contractual penalties and forfeitures was not always precise, the court's powers were not unlimited and the facts of the instant case were clearly outside the limits of the doctrine. An undefined power to refuse to enforce provisions of a contract which the parties had expressly agreed would create unacceptable uncertainty in transactions and it was not possible to distinguish between a commercial contract and one concerning land simply because the latter was traditionally subject to the doctrine of equity. Relief from rescission of a contract for the sale of land was different from relief against forfeiture of a deposit or part payment of the purchase price, where the court could provide relief when the sum retained amounted to a penalty. Although the right to rescind UE's contract involved terminating their equitable interest in the land, the purpose was to restore to GA the right to deal with the property how it pleased and to allow GA to exercise those rights with certainty. Thus the court would not grant an order of specific performance where there had been a breach of a time limit where time was said to be of the essence, *Steedman v. Drinkle* [1916] 1 A.C. 275 followed.

UNION EAGLE LTD v. GOLDEN ACHIEVEMENT LTD [1997] A.C. 514, Lord Hoffmann, PC.

1023. Sale of land–mortgage fraud–breach of warranty to building society that solicitor had authority to act for both vendors

[Rules of the Supreme Court 1965 Ord.62 r.3.]

PP and DP, husband and wife, bought a house as beneficial joint tenants with a mortgage from Bradford & Bingley Building Society, B&B. Following financial difficulties PP decided to execute a mortgage fraud with W, whereby PP sold the house to W without DP's knowledge or consent. B, the solicitor acting for PP in the conveyance, wrongly believed that he was acting for both DP and PP and in reliance on that fact G, the solicitors acting for W and Bristol & West Building Society, B&W, arranged with B&W for W to borrow money from B&W by executing a charge over the house. B&W advanced a sum of money which PP used to pay off the existing mortgage with B&B and to discharge his business debts. DP obtained a declaration that the transfer to W and B&W's charge over the house were null and void and obtained damages in negligence against B. It was further held that PP and W were liable in damages to DP and to B&W and that B&W was entitled to succeed against B for breach of warranty of authority. B appealed against the decision questioning the finding that (1) he had warranted to B&W that he had DP's authority to negotiate the sale, and (2) B&W's loss was caused by breach of the warranty, not by PP's dishonest conduct in forging DP's signature. B also appealed against the order that B pay B&W's costs in defending and counterclaiming against DP on an indemnity basis.

Held, dismissing the appeal, that (1) to establish that a warranty of authority had been made there had to be shown to be a contract under which an express or implied promise was made to the promisee for consideration. That consideration could be supplied by the promisee entering into a transaction with a third party, *Rasnoimport V/O v. Guthrie and Co Ltd* [1966] 1 Lloyd's Rep. 1, [1966] C.L.Y. 11164 considered. The promise could be made to one person or to a number of people depending on the circumstances. In the instant case B did represent to G that he was authorised to act for DP, and B knew that G was acting for B&W as well as W and that B&W relied on B's purported authority to act for DP in order to complete the transaction. Thus a warranty by B that he had DP's authority to act was established in favour of B&W, and B&W were entitled to enforce it; (2) it was clear that B&W could establish that the loss it suffered was caused by B not having the authority which he promised he had. If B had obtained instructions from DP then the transaction would never have proceeded and B&W would not have suffered any loss, and (3) on the issue of the costs it would appear to be against the philosophy of RSC Ord.62 r.3(2) to award costs on an indemnity basis where, but for that rule, they would have been recoverable in damages. It is inappropriate for costs to be awarded on an indemnity basis unless there is some additional factor justifying that conclusion. In this instance there was no such additional factor.

PENN v. BRISTOL AND WEST BUILDING SOCIETY [1997] 3 All E.R. 470, Waller, L.J., CA.

1024.   **Sale of land–mortgages–solicitors–misrepresentation to mortgage lender– sums recovered under mortgage indemnity–no credit given for recoverable sums–risk of double jeopardy**

M, solicitors, acted for B, a building society, in connection with a domestic mortgage. The borrower was required to pay a premium, by deduction from the advance, for mortgage indemnity guarantee, which B proposed to take from a third party insurer I. If B exercised its power of sale, I became liable to pay B a sum calculated by reference to the sale proceeds shortfall of the outstanding debt. The court held that B paid the advance to M on the basis of a representation or warranty which M knew, or must be taken to have known, was misleading so that B were entitled to the full amount of its loss. M contended that recoveries under the MIG should be taken into account in assessing the loss; B contended they should not, being in the nature of insurance proceeds.

Held, that the treatment, as between B and I, of sums recovered other than from the borrower depended on the basis on which they were recovered. Damages from solicitors or valuers who had acted for the society should accrue to the benefit of the person who had suffered the loss in respect of which the damages had been awarded. Thus the rule against double recovery had no application as B would not make a double recovery. Thus in calculating the loss for which M were liable, B was not required to give credit for sums recoverable under the MIG. However, as M might be exposed to double jeopardy if required to pay B's claim before obtaining a discharge from I, M should be given an opportunity to join I in the proceedings before an order for payment to B was made, *Hussain v. New Taplow Paper Mills* [1988] 1 All E.R. 541, [1988] C.L.Y. 1070, *Hunt v. Severs* [1994] 2 All E.R. 385, [1994] C.L.Y. 1350 considered.

BRISTOL AND WEST BUILDING SOCIETY v. MAY MAY & MERRIMANS (NO.2) [1997] 3 All E.R. 206, Chadwick, J., Ch D.

1025. Sale of land–registered title–status of conveyance under Chinese customary law as against registered owner–enforceability of contract against purchaser's successor and lessee's descendant–Hong Kong

[New Territories Ordinance 1910 s.17 (Hong Kong); Conveyancing and Property Ordinance s.3 (Hong Kong).]

A lease of land in the New Territories was granted to the father, who was registered as the owner. On his death (under customary Chinese law of succession) the land passed to his son who never registered as successor under the New Territories Ordinance 1910 s.17. The son agreed to sell the land in 1934 and a document binding under Chinese law was executed, but it was not signed by the son in accordance with the Conveyancing and Property Ordinance s.3(1). The purchaser took possession. The son died, and his own son succeeded to the estate of the father and grandfather, but he was registered under s.17 of the 1910 Ordinance as his father's successor only. On the grandson's death, the defendant was registered as his successor under s.17. In 1991 the purchaser died whilst still in possession of the land or in receipt of rents from the land, leaving the plaintiff as his successor. The defendant sought to recover the land from the plaintiff who themselves commenced proceedings claiming a declaration of beneficial ownership. The judge granted the declaration, holding that the 1934 document was a valid conveyance with the defendant holding the legal title in trust for the plaintiff. The Court of Appeal of Hong Kong reversed that decision and the plaintiff appealed.

Held, allowing the appeal, that (1) the transfer of land in the New Territories was governed by the general law of Hong Kong, not customary Chinese law. As the son had never been registered as successor, he could not have transferred title to the purchaser; therefore title vested in the grandson, the defendant, by reason of s.17 of the 1910 Ordinance, (2) however, the son had contracted to sell to the purchaser, and the plaintiff was not precluded from relying on the contract by s.3(1) as in accordance with s.3(2) the son had partly performed the contract by receiving the purchase price and permitting possession. In any event, a devisee of land in an unadministered estate, such as the son was, could make a binding contract to sell it, so that at his death the contract between the son and the purchaser was specifically enforceable by the purchaser, notwithstanding the son's registration as successor. The son and the plaintiff's entitlement to the land arose through succession to the son and were subject to all rights then specifically enforceable against the land; the purchaser and the plaintiff, as his successor, had an equitable interest in the land enforceable against any subsequent holder except a bona fide purchaser for value, and the defendant was a volunteer. The defendant was therefore ordered to vest the land in the plaintiff forthwith, *Lord Sudeley v. Attorney-General* [1897] A.C. 11 distinguished.

WU KOON TAI v. WU YAU LOI [1997] A.C. 179, Lord Browne-Wilkinson, PC.

1026. Sale of land–transfer of registered land–transfer of title from third party to vendor–limit of time on request to make title

[Land Registration Act 1925 s.37, s.110(5).]

S appealed against an order declaring that S's contract with U to purchase a property had been effectively rescinded and that U was entitled to forfeit the deposit, and that the caution registered by S against the title of the property be vacated. A condition of the contract was that title was to be deduced in accordance with the Land Registration Act 1925 s.110(5). At the time the contract was entered into another party was the registered proprietor of the property and on completion of its purchase from that party, on January 9, 1995, U wrote informing S of that fact. In addition U sent S answers to the requisitions and the approved draft transfer, giving S notice pursuant to National Condition 22, requiring completion on January 25, 1995 as agreed. U applied to be registered as proprietor of the property on January 19, 1995 at which time S had not submitted his observations on U's answers to the requisitions as required under National Condition 9. S failed to complete and an extension of time was agreed which expired on February 3,

1995. On February 1, 1995 S informed U that he was unable to complete as U was not the registered proprietor and U subsequently wrote to S claiming that the contract had been rescinded and the deposit forfeited. The caution applied for by S was registered and notice given to U. It was held that S had accepted U's title not later than January 24, 1995 and that the letter from S on February 1, 1995 was a request under s.110(5) of the 1925 Act. The issue arose as to whether a contractual provision requiring S to make his request within a limited time under s.110(5) of the 1925 Act was "a stipulation to the contrary" so as not to be effective.

Held, dismissing the appeal, that the notice to complete served by U on January 10, 1995 was valid notwithstanding that U was not yet registered as proprietor, so it was unable to comply with a requirement of s.110(5) of the 1925 Act because at that time S had not made a request for completion in accordance with s.110(5), *Lee v. Olancastle* (Unreported) distinguished. S was deemed to have accepted U's title on January 25, 1995, when the notice originally expired and the request made by S on February 1, 1995 was of no effect and U had been ready and willing to fulfil its outstanding obligations by completing in accordance with s.37(2) of the 1925 Act on February 3, 1995. Accordingly U was entitled to rescind the contract and forfeit the deposit under National Condition 22.

Observed, that a condition requesting that completion under s.110(5) of the 1925 Act be made within a certain time before completion was not "a stipulation to the contrary" within that provision.

URBAN MANOR LTD v. SADIQ [1997] 1 W.L.R. 1016, Morritt, L.J., CA.

1027. Title to land–undertakings–solicitors–effect of undertaking given to mortgagee–good marketable title

L, a firm of solicitors, acted for the purchasers in the acquisition of unregistered freehold land, for which B provided the finance. L gave an undertaking to B that any sums received would be applied solely for acquiring a good marketable title. £157,817 was remitted to L as a secured advance to enable the purchasers to complete and was used by L for that purpose. B advanced further sums thereafter. Subsequently it emerged that the purchasers had acquired no right of way to the land.

Held, determining preliminary issues, that the undertaking was a binding contract, because B gave consideration by providing L's clients with facilities for the purchase. L's obligation under the undertaking was to apply the money to acquire a good marketable title and not merely to take reasonable care or to use their best endeavours. The purchasers had not acquired a good marketable title, ie. one that an unwilling purchaser under open contract would be obliged to accept. Good marketable title could be acquired if there was evidence of a good root of title and uninterrupted passage of title with nothing to cast doubt on the chain of title or to suggest an undisclosed encumbrance. The fact that the purchasers had not acquired a right of way was not of itself decisive, because knowledge acquired after completion was not of itself relevant to the existence of a good marketable title. However, the evidence showed it was not in fact good marketable title at completion.

BARCLAYS BANK PLC v. LOUGHER 51 Con. L.R. 75, John Hicks Q.C., QBD (OR).

1028. Articles

A return to scale fees and conflicts of interest? *(D.G. Barnsley)*: S.J. 1997, 141 (39), 969, 971. (Evidence that charging of low fees for conveyancing as result of competitive pressures leads to reduced level of service to client, and benefits of reintroducing scale fees for such work).

Commercial conveyancing practice *(Phillip H. Kenny)*: Conv. 1997, Sep/Oct, 330-332. (Criticism of new code of practice for streamlining commercial property transactions published by Investment Property Forum)).

Common record *(Alec Samuels)*: S.J. 1997, 141(38), 954. (Value to conveyancers and environmental lawyers of recorded decisions of Commons Commissioners made under Commons Registration Act 1965, covering period 1965 to 1990).

Conveyancing liens *(D.G. Barnsley)*: Conv. 1997, Sep/Oct, 336-361. (Issues raised by recent CA decisions relating to how vendor's lien for unpaid purchase money and purchaser's lien for deposit can arise and how they can be enforced).

Conveyancing solutions... when speed is of the essence *(Grant Whiskin)*: L. Ex. 1997, Sep, 33-34. (Use of insurance policies covering local searches and title to land as means of speeding up property transactions).

Implications for conveyancing practice of the Land Registration Act 1997 *(John E. Adams)*: Conv. 1997, May/Jun, 180-181.

Matrimonial conveyancing *(Justin Shale* and *Timothy G.C. Becker)*: Fam. Law 1997, 27(Apr), 269-270. (Whether costs of conveyancing which give effect to an order of court in ancillary relief proceedings, could be met under a legal aid certificate and be taxed by the court).

Property selling and conveyancing *(Penny Butler)*: L.S.G. 1997, 94(41), 30-31. (Changes introduced under Solicitors' Practice (Joint Property Selling) Amendment Rule 1997 to deregulate jointly owned conveyancing practices; includes text of new r.6 and flow chart showing effect on solicitors).

The cautioner in person *(Phillip H. Kenny)*: Conv. 1997, Jul/Aug, 246-247. (Land Registry statement on entering cautions against registered land by firms which are not limited or unlimited companies).

Time for reflection! *(Peter Ashby)*: L. Ex. 1997, Sep, 36. (Difficulties facing conveyancing solicitors in providing quality service for clients, stressing importance of investigating title carefully and advantages of having professional indemnity insurance).

1029. Books

Aldridge, Trevor M.–Practical Conveyancing Precedents on CD-ROM. ISBN 0-7520-0558-8. FT Law & Tax.

COPYRIGHT

1030. Circuit diagrams–literary copyright–small amounts copied regularly–design right–"must fit" exception applied to component parts

[Copyright, Designs and Patents Act 1988 s.16.]

E and C were in competition as manufacturers of transformers. E commenced proceedings against C claiming infringement of copyright in E's data sheets, which contained detailed technical descriptions as well as circuit diagrams. E also claimed design right infringement in respect of the shape and configuration of its transformers. E applied for summary judgment and an order to strike out parts of C's defence relating to the design right claim. E had produced a number of data sheets over the years and claimed that C had systematically copied small parts from each of those sheets, which when taken as a whole amounted to substantial copying. As a defence to the design right claim, C sought to rely on the "must fit" exception in respect of component parts of E's transformers. E contended that the "must fit" exception applied only to the whole of an article and not to parts of an article.

Held, dismissing the applications, that (1) whilst the wording of the Copyright, Designs and Patents Act 1988 s.16 did not suggest that the issue of whether work had been copied should be determined by the behaviour of the infringer, such behaviour had previously been taken into account, *Cate v. Devon and Exeter Constitutional Newspaper Co Ltd* (1889) 40 Ch. D. 500 considered. A possible interpretation was that copying of small amounts which did not amount to infringing acts at the time may later amount to infringing acts when considered with subsequent further copying of small but regular amounts. However, even if C's behaviour was considered, it was not possible at that stage to say that there was no prospect of C's non-infringing argument succeeding at trial; (2) the borderline between whether a particular work fell within one category or another might be difficult to define, but that did not justify giving protection in more than one category. The proper category was that which most nearly suited the characteristics of the work at issue; (3) the decision in *Anacon Co Ltd v. Environmental Research Technology Ltd* [1994] F.S.R. 659, [1995] 1 C.L.Y. 852 went no further than to confirm that literary copyright subsisted in the list of notations included on the circuit diagram. It did not decide that literary copyright also covered the graphics which connected the individual components on that list. Accordingly, since the diagrams in question amounted to a list of five or six components, C had a significant defence that they were too unsubstantial to qualify for copyright; (4) the design right provisions were concerned with protecting certain types of designs, not particular articles, and (5) the "must fit" exception under the 1988 Act might copy to two interfitting articles carrying interface features despite the fact that when they were fitted together they form the whole or part of another larger article.

ELECTRONIC TECHNIQUES (ANGLIA) LTD v. CRITCHLEY COMPONENTS LTD [1997] F.S.R. 401, Laddie, J., Ch D.

1031. Damages–account of profits–election of remedy–declaration at interlocutory judgment stage appropriate

[Copyright, Designs and Patents Act 1988 s.96(1).]

W, owners of copyright in respect of film rights, applied for a declaration that they were, at an interlocutory judgment stage, entitled to elect for either damages or an account of profits for infringement of copyright. V contended that if W were entitled to postpone their decision to elect until they learned how much they were likely to recover from an account of profits, V was equally entitled to examine the figures before deciding whether to oppose the right of W to elect. It was further argued that W should not be permitted to elect for an account of profits where W would receive a windfall sum in excess of that likely to be recovered as damages, and where V were innocent infringers of the copyright.

Held, granting the declaration, that following *Island Records Ltd v. Tring International Plc* [1996] 1 W.L.R. 1256, [1995] 1 C.L.Y. 849 W did not have to elect between damages and an account of profits until they had all the information they required. It was unnecessary for V to be given equivalent rights of discovery since it was to be assumed that W would elect for an account of profits where it was more profitable for them to do so. In addition, the Copyright, Designs and Patents Act 1988 s.96(1) gave W the right to seek any remedy against V as an infringer. The Act also had the effect of making an innocent infringer liable for an account of profits but not liable for damages. V was a knowing infringer and was therefore liable for either damages or an account of profits.

WIENERWORLD LTD v. VISION VIDEO LTD, Trans. Ref: CH.1996-W-No.476, July 24, 1997, MJ Burton Q.C., Ch D.

1032. Damages–secondary loss–cash flow problems arising from infringement–secondary loss

[Copyright, Designs and Patents Act 1988 s.96(2).]

C brought proceedings against H for infringement of copyright and/or design right in its drawings and designs for metalwork. C sought compensatory damages under the Copyright, Designs and Patents Act 1988 s.96(2) in respect of loss of profit resulting from the infringement and secondary losses to compensate for damage done to C's cash flow which forced C to offer early payment discounts in relation to past work, reduce prices of future work and increase its overdraft facility. H submitted to judgment but challenged C's right to recover damages in respect of the secondary losses claimed. H applied for a preliminary determination of C's legal entitlement to recover the damages. The master held that the secondary losses were recoverable and dismissed H's summons. D appealed.

Held, allowing the appeal, that (1) the general principle in tort, as in contract, was that damages should put a successful claimant in the same position as he would have been in if he had not sustained the wrong. Consequential damages were recoverable in the same way as normal damages provided they arose directly and naturally from the tort, *General Tire & Rubber Co Ltd v. Firestone Tyre & Rubber Co Ltd* [1975] 1 W.L.R. 819, [1975] C.L.Y. 2503 referred to; (2) in tort, it was not necessarily sufficient for a plaintiff to establish a causal link between the wrong and the damage. The damage must still not be too remote. The doctrine of remoteness was no less applicable because copyright infringement was a tort of strict liability, *Cambridge Water Co v. Eastern Counties Leather Plc* [1994] 2 A.C. 264, [1994] C.L.Y. 3410 considered; (3) it was not alleged that H knew anything of relevance concerning C's finances. The remoteness issues were purely legal and did not necessitate a factual inquiry; (4) it could not sensibly be argued that the parties could reasonably have contemplated that a cash flow crisis of the type which beset C's business would be the likely result of H's breach. The fact that in their reasonable contemplation such a crisis might conceivably result was insufficient to allow recovery of the secondary losses. A merely conceivable result could not be deemed to be reasonably foreseeable so as to give C more redress than that available for an analogous wrong sounding in contract, and (5) the remedy was specifically intended to protect the exclusive statutory licensing rights of the copyright owner, and compensate the owner for infringement of those rights. To allow C to recover the secondary losses would be an unwarranted extension of this statutory protection, *Paterson Zochonis & Co Ltd v. Merfarken Packaging Ltd* [1986] 3 All E.R. 522, [1987] C.L.Y. 523 applied and *Gerber Garment Technology Inc v. Lectra Systems Ltd* [1995] R.P.C. 383, [1995] 2 C.L.Y. 3780 distinguished.

CLAYDON ARCHITECTURAL METALWORK LTD v. DJ HIGGINS & SONS LTD [1997] F.S.R. 475, Martin Mann Q.C., Ch D.

1033. Database systems

COPYRIGHT AND RIGHTS IN DATABASES REGULATIONS 1997, SI 1997 3032; made under the European Communities Act 1972 s.2. In force: January 1, 1998; £3.20.

These Regulations implement the provisions of Council Directive 96/9 ([1996] OJ L77/20) on the legal protection of databases and apply to databases made before and after January 1, 1998. They make amendments to the Copyright, Designs and Patents Act 1988, which made no specific provision for databases, and introduce a new right to prevent extraction and re-utilisation of the contents of databases.

1034. Designs–design right–copying surface design on furniture–concept of design right does not include surface decoration

[Copyright, Designs and Patents Act 1988 s.51 (3), s.213(2), s.226.]

Held, that since surface decoration was expressly excluded from the definition of a design under the Copyright, Designs and Patents Act 1988 s.51 (3) and s.213(2) (c), the copying of surface decoration on an original design could not amount to the infringement of a design right under s.226 of the Act.

MARK WILKINSON FURNITURE LTD v. WOODCRAFT DESIGNS (RADCLIFFE) LTD, *The Times*, October 13, 1997, Jonathan Parker, J., Ch D.

1035. Designs–design right–infringement–appropriate test where alleged infringement refers to part of article design

[Copyright, Designs and Patents Act 1988 s.213(3), s.213(4).]

P designed a range of leather cases to fit individual models of mobile phone. For several years P's products were manufactured by D1. Subsequently P started to manufacture its own products and dispensed with D1's services. D1 later started to manufacture its own mobile phone cases. P claimed that D1's cases infringed their design right. D claimed that P did not have design right in the phone cases. D argued that many of the features were found on industry standard phone cases and were therefore commonplace. In addition, D relied on the "must fit" exception contained in Copyright, Designs and Patents Act 1988 s.213(3)(b)(I).

Held, finding some aspects of the mobile phone cases to be protected by design right and infringed, that (1) where design of part of an article was reproduced in part of an allegedly infringing article, it was necessary to determine what by way of comparative design would be suggested to the interested observer, in the light of the entirety of the allegedly infringing article, not just by confining attention to the corresponding parts, *C & H Engineering v. F Klucznik & Sons Ltd* [1992] F.S.R. 421, [1993] C.L.Y. 3023 followed; (2) aspects of the design which were found in industry standard cases were commonplace and thus excluded from design right; (3) aspects of the design which enabled the cases to be placed around telephones so that either the telephones or the cases could perform their functions were excluded from any design right even if there was more than one way of permitting a particular function to be performed. Such an approach accorded with the natural and ordinary meaning of the words of the 1988 Act s.213(3)(b)(I), *Amoena (UK) Ltd v. Trulife* (1996) 19(1) I.P.D. 12 referred to and *Ocular Sciences Ltd v. Aspect Vision Care Ltd (No.2)* [1997] R.P.C. 289, [1997] C.L.Y. 3894 followed; (4) design right subsisted in some aspects of the phone cases including the holes in the diamond shaped configuration on the front of one case, the leather pinches at the top of one case, the flap design of some cases, the configuration of leather and elastic on the side of some cases and the zip on some cases, and (5) D had copied particular aspects of the phone cases which attracted design right protection. The overall similarities between the respective cases were such that a potential customer would conclude that D's cases were produced substantially to the same design as P's cases.

PARKER (T/A PJ INTERNATIONAL EXCLUSIVE LEATHERCRAFTS) v. TIDBALL (T/A SATCHEL); PARKER (T/A P J INTERNATIONAL EXCLUSIVE LEATHERCRAFTS) v. AXESS INTERNATIONAL; PARKER (T/A P J INTERNATIONAL EXCLUSIVE LEATHERCRAFTS) v. BATCHELOR (1997) 20(3) I.P.D. 20027, Robert Englehart Q.C., Ch D.

1036. Designs—reverse engineering—agricultural machinery—copy by former employee—causal connection between drawings and infringement

[Copyright, Designs and Patents Act 1988 Sch.1; Copyright Act 1956.]

M sought injunctions against C in respect of two automatic bag handling machines manufactured and sold by M, claiming that C was in breach of his duty of fidelity to M that existed during employment, and that C infringed M's copyright in drawings of the two machines, a fixed head stitcher and a stitcher automator. C was employed by M as a sales manager and, having given notice, left the employment on July 31, 1995. A company, P, of which C was managing director, was set up on July 11, 1995. P sold machines which, it was accepted, were copied from M's two machines. However, they were not found to be copied from M's drawings of the machines so it was a case of reverse engineering. C decided not to give evidence and not to cross examine M's witnesses. Invoices came to light which revealed that C had been carrying out work on his own behalf several weeks before his employment with M terminated and prior to the incorporation of P. On the basis that the invoices were dated prior to C's departure he was found to have started the reverse engineering before the end of July 1995. M claimed copyright protection over drawings of the machines which were existing works for the purposes of the transitional provisions of the Copyright, Designs and Patents Act 1988 Sch.1, and subject to the Copyright Act 1956 as they had been made before the 1988 Act came into force.

Held, granting the injunction sought in relation to the stitch automator but not the fixed head stitcher, that (1) to claim copyright infringement in a reverse engineering case it had to be shown that there was a causal connection between the drawing in respect of which M claimed copyright and the machine produced by P; and that M's machine copied by P derived from M's drawings, *Billhofer Maschinenfabrik GmbH v. TH Dixon & Co Ltd* [1990] F.S.R. 105 applied. The drawings of the stitcher automator were used for the production of that machine and were part of the process of its design and so a causal connection was shown. The drawings of the fixed head stitcher were sketches used for the manufacture of the prototype. There were then drawings made in 1989 of the machine, but these were found not to be part of the continuous design process, as they were merely a record of the design of the machine that had been in production for some time. As no causal connection was shown, M's copyright claim in respect of that machine failed; (2) the drawings of the fixed head stitcher, a two dimensional copy of a three dimensional object, could have the requisite degree of originality, but in this instance, they could not attract copyright because the drawings could not be regarded as part of the same design process with the owner still having copyright protection, *LA Gear Inc v. Hi-Tec Sports* [1992] F.S.R. 121, [1992] C.L.Y. 577 considered, *Interlego AG v. Tyco Industries* [1989] 1 A.C. 217, [1988] C.L.Y. 502 distinguished, and (3) C was personally involved in the infringement of M's copyright in the stitcher automator, even prior to P being set up and there was no evidence of anyone else's involvement. As such C had breached his duty of fidelity and was liable as a joint tortfeasor with P in respect of the infringement of the stitcher automator.

WJ MORRAY ENGINEERING LTD v. CESARE, Trans. Ref: CH.1996-M-No.1976, April 25, 1997, Sir John Knox, Ch D.

1037. **Infringement–abuse of process for want of prosecution–infringement action kept alive merely to damage defendant and warn off competitors**

F brought an action against R for copyright infringement and breach of confidence. There was found to be a serious issue to be tried but F failed to obtain an interlocutory injunction, ([1996] F.S.R. 935). R then applied to have F's statement of claim struck out and the action dismissed on the grounds that R's continuation and exploitation of the action was an abuse of process and for want of prosecution. In particular, R argued that F had kept the proceedings alive simply to draw them to the attention of third parties and to damage R.

Held, dismissing the motion, that (1) it was clear that striking out as an abuse of process could succeed only where the defendants had demonstrated the abuse shortly and conclusively. It was acceptable for a litigant to obtain a collateral advantage which was reasonably related to the main grievance. On the evidence it was not possible to conclude that F had kept the action alive to further their own interests in such a way as to constitute an abuse of process, *Lonrho Plc v. Fayed (No.2)* [1992] 1 W.L.R. 1, [1992] C.L.Y. 3375, and *Majory, Re* [1955] Ch. 600, [1955] C.L.Y. 167 referred to, and (2) although F were guilty of inordinate and inexcusable delay in prosecuting the action, there was a difficulty over the question of limitation. F had made it clear that they intended to issue a fresh writ claiming the same relief if the present action were dismissed. Accordingly, a dismissal would be futile. There would have to be exceptional circumstances before it would be appropriate to strike out the first action where the limitation period had not expired. There were no such circumstances in the instant case, *Birkett v. James* [1978] A.C. 297, [1977] C.L.Y. 2410 and *Wright v. Morris* [1997] F.S.R. 218, [1997] C.L.Y. 754 referred to.

FLOGATES LTD v. REFCO LTD (1997) 20(1) I.P.D. 20002, Blackburne, J., Ch D.

1038. **Infringement–industrial drawings–pipettes–exclusive licences–significant changes to copies of drawings–rendered drawings as originals– reproduction of substantial parts constituted breach**

[Treaty of Rome 1957 Art.30, Art.36; Copyright, Designs and Patents Act 1988; Copyright Act 1956 s.3.]

L brought an action for infringement of copyright in drawings of parts of pipettes, claiming that they were the owners of copyright in those drawings and exclusive licensees. L alleged that their copyright had been infringed by, inter alia, the importation and sale of pipettes by B. The judge ruled that B had copied a substantial part of the drawings in which copyright subsisted, there had been infringement of that copyright, L were exclusive licensees and B had no defence under the Treaty of Rome 1957 Art.30 and Art.36. B appealed on the grounds that (1) copyright did not subsist in the drawings as they were not originals but copies from earlier drawings; (2) the amount copied by them had not been established to be a substantial part of the relevant drawings in accordance with the Copyright, Designs and Patents Act 1988 s.16(3)(a). B contended that, as some of the drawings were not originals but copies of another pipette, certain elements of the drawings were not original and therefore should be disregarded when deciding whether a substantial part had been copied; (3) L were not exclusive licensees for the purposes of the 1988 Act s.92 and therefore had no right of action. B submitted, in reliance upon *Avel Pty Ltd v. Multicom Amusements Pty Ltd* (1990) 18 I.P.R. 443 and *Broderband Software Inc v. Computermate (Australia) Pty Ltd* (1991) I.P.R. 215, that the licence granted to L was not a licence to exercise the exclusive right given by s.16 and was therefore not an exclusive licence within s.92. At best it was an exclusive licence to do acts which would otherwise be an infringement pursuant to s.22 and s.23, and (4) the alleged infringements were not within the specific subject matter of copyright as applied in the jurisprudence of the European Court. B argued that the enforcement of copyright against the imported parts could not be justified for the protection of the copyright within the meaning of the Treaty of Rome 1957 Art.36 and amounted to a disguised restriction on trade between member states.

Held, dismissing the appeal, that (1) copyright subsisted in the drawings as they included significant changes which made them originals for the purposes of the Copyright Act 1956 s.3; (2) B's pipettes were reproductions of a substantial part of the drawings. Industrial drawings often consisted of shapes copied from earlier drawings combined with original, new shapes. To decide whether copyright subsisted, the drawing as a whole had to be dissected rather than the component parts, *Ladbroke (Football) Ltd v. William Hill (Football) Ltd* [1964] 1 W.L.R. 273, [1964] C.L.Y. 611 applied. B's approach was therefore wrong; (3) s.92 should not be restricted to the exclusive right given in s.16. Section 92 was concerned with any right which could be exercised exclusively by the copyright owner. The copyright owner had, pursuant to s.96, the right to bring an action for infringement of his copyright and to the appropriate relief. The construction advanced by B was contrary to commercial sense in that if the licence referred to in s.96 was limited to a licence to do the acts referred to in s.16, then the exclusive licensee would never be able to bring proceedings to prevent acts falling within s.22 and s.23, and (4) UK law provided an intellectual property right which prevented copying of industrial drawings and the enforcement of that right fell within the specific subject matter of copyright as applied in the jurisprudence of the European Court, *British Leyland Motor Corp Ltd v. Armstrong Patents Co Ltd* [1984] F.S.R. 591, [1984] C.L.Y. 1362 considered.

BIOTRADING & FINANCING OY v. BIOHIT LTD, Trans. Ref: CHANF 95/1691/B, CHANF 95/1692/B, CHANI 96/0407/B, CHANI 96/0408/B, October 7, 1997, Aldous, L.J., CA.

1039. Infringement—prior art

P applied to strike out D's particulars of objection in a case involving infringement of copyright, design right and registered design on two grounds. First, that they failed to give particulars of sale relating to alleged prior art; and secondly, that D had indiscriminately pleaded a large amount of prior art, some of which P considered to be irrelevant.

Held, dismissing the strike out application, that (1) D had done enough to meet the required level of particularity. The design involved was an inexpensive children's Halloween mask and if the required level of particularity was set too high, certain designs which had been available in the UK would not satisfy this required level. Also the prior art in this kind of case tended to originate in the Far East and was sold in locations where the required documentation would be patchy, and (2) D was justified in pleading 10 or 15 pieces of prior art because they were relevant for restricting the scope of P's registered design, and for showing whether or not P's design was commonplace.

LONE STAR TOYS LTD v. JM ENTERPRISES OF WETHERBY LTD [1996] F.S.R. 857, Laddie, J., Pat Ct.

1040. Infringement–toner cartridges–competitor making similar product–toner cartridges did not fall within spare parts exception

A company infringing a copyright in drawings for replacement toner cartridges was not entitled to continue to manufacture the cartridge under the spare parts exception. C manufactured printers and photocopiers, but a substantial amount of its revenue was generated from the sale of replacement toner cartridges for the machines. G also manufactured replacement toner cartridges and C appealed against a ruling of the Court of Appeal of Hong Kong ([1996] F.S.R. 874) allowing G's appeal against the granting of an injunction restraining G from infringing C's copyright in drawings from which a number of parts for G's cartridges had been made. It was accepted that C owned the artistic copyright in the drawings and the issue was whether the exception for spare parts identified in *British Leyland Motor Corp Ltd v. Armstrong Patents Co Ltd* [1986] A.C. 577, [1986] C.L.Y. 432 applied to entitle G to infringe C's copyright.

Held, allowing the appeal, that the decision in *British Leyland* was founded on unfairness to the customer and abuse of monopoly power. However, where these features were not obvious, the jurisprudential and economic basis for the doctrine was greatly undermined. In the instant case, the analogy with the sort of repair that a person who bought an item would assume he could do for himself without infringing the manufacturer's rights was much weaker, as when the cartridge was replaced nothing in the machine would need to be repaired. Equally, the competition argument was far less compelling in that the cost of replacement toner cartridges was significant and it could not be assumed that customers did not take account of such costs when choosing a machine, which did introduce an element of competitiveness to the aftermarket as well as into the market for photocopiers and printers itself. Further, there was competition as between the manufacturers of replacement cartridges and those who refilled existing cartridges, such that it could not be said without proof that C's use of its intellectual property rights had allowed it to obtain a dominant position in the market, much less to abuse that position.

CANON KABUSHIKI KAISHA v. GREEN CARTRIDGE CO (HONG KONG) LTD [1997] 3 W.L.R. 13, Lord Hoffmann, PC.

1041. Infringement–unauthorised photographs of album cover shoot–publication by newspaper was breach of confidence

[Copyright, Designs and Patents Act 1988 s.4(1).]

C, a record company, sought an interlocutory injunction restraining N from further publication of unauthorised photographs which had already been published in The Sun newspaper on the grounds of breach of copyright or breach of confidence. The Sun had booked a photographer into the hotel where a photo shoot was taking place for the cover of Oasis's forthcoming album and photographs were taken during the shoot, one of which was very similar to the official one chosen by the group for the album cover. The Sun had published this photograph on two occasions and had made an offer inviting readers to purchase a poster version of the photograph.

Held, granting the injunction as damages were an inadequate remedy, that, although C's case alleging breach of copyright was not sufficiently arguable to grant an injunction, C did have an arguable case that the unauthorised photograph had been taken in breach of confidence. The process of arranging objects and members of the group to form the scene comprised in the photograph could not be considered a sculpture or collage under the Copyright,

Designs and Patents Act 1988 s.4(1)(a) or a work of artistic craftsmanship under s.4(1)(c). The unauthorised photograph could not be regarded as a copy of the official photograph and the person who arranged the scene did not own the copyright in the unauthorised photograph. However, although the Sun's photographer was lawfully at the scene, the nature of the operation and the imposition of security measures made it arguable that the shoot was intended to be confidential. It could be argued that he had behaved surreptitiously, knowing he would not be allowed to take photographs and was only entitled to remain on the basis that he refrained from doing so.

CREATION RECORDS LTD v. NEWS GROUP NEWSPAPERS LTD, *The Times*, April 29, 1997, Lloyd, J., Ch D.

1042. Libraries—public lending right

PUBLIC LENDING RIGHT SCHEME 1982 (COMMENCEMENT OF VARIATIONS) ORDER 1997, SI 1997 1576; made under the Public Lending Right Act 1979 s.3. In force: July 15, 1997; £1.10.

This Order amends the Public Lending Right Scheme 1982 (SI 1982 719). Provisions relating to the calculation of an illustrator's or co-author's share of Public Lending Right in respect of a book are modified. Where an illustrator's or co-author's share in Public Lending Right in respect of which there is more than one authors (disregarding a translator, editor or compiler) exceeds 50 per cent, the Registrar will need to be satisfied that it is reasonable in relation to that author's contribution to the book. The duration of the Public Lending Right in respect of any book and the period during which the right may be transferred is extended to seventy years. The minimum eligibility for payment due in respect of Public Lending Right for each financial year is increased to £5.

1043. Licences of right—term of protection for unregistered design right—UK law supplemented TRIPs protection—TRIPs did not have direct effect

[Copyright, Designs and Patents Act 1988 s.237, s.247; Council Decision 94/800; Registered Designs Act 1949; Agreement on Trade-Related Aspects of Intellectual Property Rights including Trade in Counterfeit Goods (TRIPs) Art.25, Art.26.]

A applied under the Copyright, Designs and Patents Act 1988 s.247 to settle the terms of a licence of right in respect of certain designs. The rights holder, Meccano SA, M, filed an opposition, contending that the 1988 Act was in conflict with the Agreement on Trade-Related Aspects of Intellectual Property Rights including Trade in Counterfeit Goods (TRIPs). M argued that there were circumstances when the period of protection under the 1988 Act would be less than 10 years, in conflict with Art.26(3) of TRIPs, which set the minimum duration of protection at 10 years. Section 237 of the 1988 Act allowed anyone to apply for a licence of right in the last five years of the design right term, which M contended deprived the owner of full protection for 10 years. In addition, the need for eye appeal under UK registered design legislation meant that the UK fell below the minimum requirements of Art.25 of TRIPs.

Held, that (1) as far as TRIPs was concerned, competence was shared between the Community and the Member States. However, the provisions of UK law relevant to these proceedings did not correspond to a part of TRIPs in which the Community had competence. There was no question of the UK provisions being over ridden by TRIPs. A plain reading of Council Decision 94/800 concerning the conclusion on behalf of the Community, as regards matters within its competence, of the agreements reached in the *Uruguay Round Treaties* multilateral negotiations would not leave it open to M to invoke TRIPs in these proceedings. This conclusion was consistent with three cases concerning the old GATT, in which the ECJ concluded that several articles of the old GATT were not directly applicable and could not be invoked by individuals in national courts, *International Fruit Co NV v. Produktschap voor Groenten en Fruit* (No.3) (C21/72) [1972] E.C.R. 1219, [1975] C.L.Y. 1267, *Schluter v. Hauptzollamt Lorrach* (C9/73) [1973] E.C.R. 1135, [1974] C.L.Y. 1376 and *Amministrazione delle Finanze dello Stato v. Societa Petrolifera Italiana SpA* (C267/81) [1983] E.C.R. 801, [1984] C.L.Y. 1419 referred to; (2) the ECJ referred to different procedures and voting arrangements to achieve harmonisation. A was right to say that the ECJ had rejected the use of TRIPs as an indirect means of harmonisation, *Uruguay Round Treaties, Re* (1/94) [1995] 1 C.M.L.R. 205 referred to; (3) in the event that TRIPs was directly applicable in UK law, the Registered Designs Act 1949 fully met the obligations of Art.25 and exceeded the requirements of Art.26(1) by enabling a rights owner to prevent the use of any infringing design, whether a copy or not. The 1949 Act also gave 25 years' protection. The UK's unregistered design right provisions were additional to the requirements of TRIPs, and (4) it was not clear that a reference to the ECJ would be conclusive.

AZRAK-HAMWAY INTERNATIONAL INC'S LICENCE OF RIGHT APPLICATION, *Re* [1997] R.P.C. 134, S Dennehey, PO.

1044. Licences of right—wrenches—design rights—reasonable royalty terms

[Copyright, Designs and Patents Act 1988.]

B applied to settle the terms of a licence of right of a copyright protected design for impact wrenches. B gave an undertaking to take a licence of right to settle infringement proceedings brought by A. A sought a royalty rate in excess of 10 per cent based on a manufacturing agreement in 1981 which provided for a 10 per cent royalty rate in certain circumstances. B considered that the rate of five to seven per cent customarily used in the patent field was an appropriate figure. The parties agreed that the royalty rate should be that which would be agreed between a willing licensor and licensee and that it would be based on the price of the complete wrench units as listed on A's 1992 price list, less the cost of the motors, which were not protected by A's copyright.

Held, granting the licence of right, that (1) the 1988 Act did not permit the Comptroller to withhold a licence from B, but it was incumbent on the Comptroller to settle terms which protected the interests of the parties in a manner which was fair and reasonable; (2) the Comptroller was not in a position to resolve the issue of title to the copyright, so the application had to proceed on the basis that A owned and was entitled to enforce the copyright; (3) a comparison with the 10 per cent royalty rate in the 1981 agreement was not helpful. The parties did not have copyright in mind when that figure was negotiated. The 10 per cent rate was included in the agreement as an in terrorem provision and therefore could represent only an absolute maximum figure; (4) there was no clear justification for accepting the five to seven per cent figure as a suitable starting point. However, a calculation of the profit available to B gave a profit percentage of about 10 per cent. If profit were shared equally a royalty rate at the bottom end of the five to seven per cent range would be suggested. A suitable starting point was therefore five per cent; (5) although the fact that the product was successful justified an uplift of two per cent on the five per cent figure, an element of uplift equal to two per cent had already been included in the 1992 price list. The appropriate royalty rate should therefore be reduced back to five per cent and (6) because the spare parts business was particularly profitable, it was appropriate that the royalty rate for spare parts be 6.75 per cent.

BANCE LTD'S LICENCE OF RIGHT (COPYRIGHT) APPLICATION, *Re* [1996] R.P.C. 667, GM Bridges, PO.

1045. Musical works—assignment of copyright—breach of warranty—measure of damages

L and Nosebag Music Ltd, NM, purported to assign to P from Geoffrey Downes, D, a songwriter and player member of the pop groups Buggles, Yes, and Asia, D's share of the copyrights and rights to income from certain compositions. It was common ground that an agreement assigning D's copyrights to Island Music, IM, had not expired, but L and NM counterclaimed that a second agreement had been substituted for the one they intended to sign and that the contract was void for fraud, and common mistake. L was allowed to amend his counterclaim to include a defence of non est factum.

Held, giving judgment for P, that L and NM had been in breach of warranties to the effect that the agreement with IM had expired so that all rights and titles in the compositions had reverted to D and those warranties had induced P to contract. The counterclaim was dismissed largely on the basis of the preferred evidence of P's solicitor. Damages were based on IM's receipts from the compositions in question and, in the case of the Asia compositions, extrapolated to cover the period until the agreement with IM actually terminated. This figure was then decreased by an estimated four per cent for subpublishing costs abroad to give an estimated loss of income of £21,509. The copyrights in the Buggles compositions remained with IM and estimated damages for the loss of both the publisher's share and the writer's share, based on historical earnings over a three year period, were put at £130,267 making a total of £150,915.

PALAN MUSIC PUBLISHING LTD v. LANE, Trans. Ref: Ch.1995-P-No.6500, April 8, 1997, Judge Gloster Q.C., Ch D.

1046. Musical works–copyright agreement–US standard form of agreement– copyright assignable by author on expiry of statutory period prescribed by US federal law–continued exploitation by assignee on reversion an infringement

[Copyright Act 1956 s.36(2)(c); Civil Jurisdiction and Judgments Act 1982 s.2(1).]

Under the terms of a 1958 agreement on American Guild of Authors and Composers standard terms, copyright in the song "To know him is to love him" passed from the author, S to W, a publisher, who assigned it to B, an English company by an agreement dated October 17, 1958, which operated as a licence to exploit copyright in this jurisdiction. By a 1965 agreement, W assigned all its copyright to V, subject to B's licence. The copyright term under US federal law was 28 years, and during this time S restated his interest in the song in a series of trust instruments and assignments. Following the end of the copyright period, S sought unsuccessfully to persuade B to account for the proceeds of the song and for an acknowledgement that ownership lay with S or MB. The present proceedings were commenced in 1989, with MB claiming injunctive relief against B as an infringer of MB's worldwide copyright, a declaration that B had no rights in the song from the end of the copyright period and an order that B vest all title in MB.

Held, giving judgment for MB, that the UK copyright in the song remained vested in S under the 1958 agreement, subject to the 28 year statutory period, and on expiry of that period reverted to S without the need for a transfer or "revesting", as contended for by B. Alternatively, were re-vesting required before S could re-assign to MB, this was adequately provided for by the terms of the assignment to MB by S dated December 1988, notwithstanding the fact that six months' notice, as required by cl.8 of the 1958 agreement, had not been served. Exploitation of the song by B in the UK since 1987 was an infringement of copyright remediable by an award of damages, but this could not extend to other countries where B had exploited its interest by way of sub-licences in the intervening period, due to an inability to decide how the terms of those licences were to be determined by reference to the 1958 agreement and the Copyright Act 1956 s.36(2)(c).

Observed, that further argument was to be invited prior to the making of a precise order following the decision in *Pearce v. Ove Arup Partnership Ltd* [1997] 2 W.L.R. 779, [1997] C.L.Y. 901 as to the applicability of the Civil Jurisdiction and Judgments Act 1982 s.2(1) in actions brought in this jurisdiction for infringement of foreign copyright.

MOTHER BERTHA MUSIC LTD v. BOURNE MUSIC LTD, Trans. Ref: CH 1989 No.5846, March 21, 1997, Ferris, J., Ch D.

1047. Musical works–copyright agreement–US standard form of agreement–infringement in UK–entitlement to account for profits for infringement elsewhere

[Brussels Convention on Jurisdiction and Enforcement of Judgments in Civil and Commercial Matters 1968; Lugano Convention on Jurisdiction and Enforcement of Judgments in Civil and Commercial Matters 1988.]

S wrote a song in 1958 and entered into a publishing agreement with W. The agreement provided that S assigned the right to secure copyright throughout the world for the original term of the United States copyright or for 28 years whichever was the shorter. The agreement also provided that all rights in the song throughout the world would revert to S after the expiry of 28 years and that W would execute all necessary documents to revest such rights in S provided that if S assigned or sold his rights in the United States renewal copyright for the period after the 28 years to someone other than the publisher then, unless six months notice was given to the publisher, the publisher would not be obliged to assign to S the rights in countries other than the United States and Canada. In such a case the contract was to continue to determine the rights in countries other than the United States and Canada. W subsequently gave B a licence to exploit the copyright in the song. S established a trust in 1970 to which he transferred all his right, title and interest including "writer's rights" (not "copyright") in the song. At the end of the 28 year period S claimed all rights in the song and an assignment was made in 1987. S assigned the copyright in the song to M in 1988. B had continued to exploit the song after 1986 and refused to account to M for the revenue received. M brought proceedings against B and sought an account of profits made by B throughout the world excluding the United States and Canada. The issues were whether M had good title to the UK copyright, the nature of the effect of the 1958 publishing agreement and M's entitlement to an account in respect of worldwide receipts by B.

Held, giving judgment for M, that (1) the trust set up by S did not contain an assignment of the sort referred to in the 1958 agreement. S had assigned his contractual right to be paid royalties not his residual copyright interest in the song. The 28 year term provided for by the contract applied to the period for which the UK copyright was to run and without clear and express terms copyright would revert without specific acts or words of revesting or transfer at the end of that period; (2) the 1988 assignment to M could not operate retrospectively and so M had title only from 1988. However S owned the copyright before 1988 and B would be liable to S as an infringer. The 1988 assignment was effective to transfer to M S's causes of action against B; (3) the proviso to the 1958 agreement did not apply to any assignment made by S after the expiry of the 28 year period but only to assignments made during the initial 28 year period, and (4) B would be ordered to account for profits made in the UK but not in other countries outside the UK in view of M's concession that it would only seek adjudication on UK infringements. To assume that all the copyright law of all signatories to the Brussels and Lugano Conventions was so similar as to English law and allow M to pursue claims in the English courts was unsustainable, *University of Glasgow v. Economist Ltd* [1997] E.M.L.R. 495, [1997] C.L.Y. 2034 distinguished. Furthermore M was not entitled to withdraw its concession in view of the state of their pleadings and potential prejudice to B, *Gale v. Superdrug Stores Plc* [1996] 1 W.L.R. 1089, [1996] 1 C.L.Y. 759 considered and *Welsh Development Agency v. Redpath Dorman Ltd Ltd* [1994] 1 W.L.R. 1409, [1995] 2 C.L.Y. 4191 applied.

MOTHER BERTHA MUSIC LTD v. BOURNE MUSIC LTD (NO.2) [1997] E.M.L.R. 457, Ferris, J., Ch D.

1048. Musical works–infringement–arrangement not cover of original song–state of knowledge

[Copyright, Designs and Patents Act 1988 s.23.]

LP, trading as Pinnacle Records, the sixth defendant, appealed against an order restraining them from infringing under the Copyright, Designs and Patents Act

1988 s.23, ZYX's copyright in the arrangement of the song "Please Don't Go", originally written in 1979. Z composed the arrangement prior to January 1992, and it was recorded by a band called Double You. Z agreed with ZYX that they would distribute the recording in the UK and Germany and it was released in the UK on April 21, 1992. KWS, the first three defendants, made their recording, substantially a copy of the Double You recording, with Network Records and this was distributed by LP on April 13, 1992. The test of infringement was whether LP had actual knowledge or reason to believe that its recording was an infringing copy, both of which tests were found proved on the basis that it was obvious when listening to the recordings that the recordings were arrangements and not covers of the original, LP had knowledge of articles published in the Daily Mirror regarding ZYX's anger at the production of the KWS version of the song, and of an interlocutory injunction granted in Cologne for ZYX against LP's subsidiary company. LP argued that (1) it was wrong of the judge to find that it had actual knowledge of infringement on the basis of obviousness because ZYX had not pleaded obviousness as part of its claim and which matter had only been raised following judicial intervention, giving LP no opportunity to challenge the point, thereby denying it natural justice; (2) the material on which the judge found LP had reason to believe that the copy was an infringing copy amounted to mere allegations over which there could be dispute, relying on *Hutchinson Personal Communications v. Hook Advertising* [1995] F.S.R. 365, [1995] 1 C.L.Y. 860, and (3) the copyright of the original song was found to be vested in EMI who had granted a licence to ZYX to exploit the Double You recording in Germany but not in the UK and as the record's release in the UK was a technical infringement of EMI's copyright, ZYX were precluded from enforcing any copyright against LP.

Held, dismissing the appeal, that (1) the judge was right to conclude that LP had actual knowledge that the two 1992 versions were arrangements and not covers of the original, at the release date. If this was not so then LP was deliberately blind to the issue. Whilst it would have been better had obviousness been specifically pleaded, there was no denial of natural justice as the issue arose and was dealt with at length during an exchange between the judge and counsel for LP. It had to be shown that the difference between the original and the arrangements was obvious to LP as a result of a comparison made by it at the relevant time and there was evidence of such; (2) the reasonable distributor with LP's earlier acquired knowledge, having read the Daily Mirror articles would have the reasonable belief to alert him to ZYX's objection to the KWS recording. Any fact communicated to LP must be evaluated in light of all other facts known, so as to amount to obviousness, *LA Gear Inc v. Hi-Tech Sports Plc* [1992] F.S.R. 121, [1992] 1 C.L.Y 577 applied and *Hutchinson* distinguished on the facts, and (3) EMI were found to have acquiesced in ZYX's release of the record in the UK so that ZYX were not precluded from taking action against LP. LP's infringement of ZYX's copyright was flagrant and it had financially benefited substantially from the release of the KWS recording.

ZYX MUSIC GmbH v. KING [1997] 2 All E.R. 129, Hirst, L.J., CA.

1049. Musical works–recordings–injunction restraining unlicensed playing– purpose was to protect rights of copyright holder

Held, that the aim of granting injunctions to the holder of the copyright in certain recordings, restraining the respondents from unlicensed playing of the recordings, was to protect the copyright holder's rights in relation to future unlicensed playing, and not to provide it with a means of recovering payments for past unlicensed playing.

PHONOGRAPHIC PERFORMANCE LTD v. MAITRA [1997] 3 All E.R. 673, Chadwick, J., Ch D.

1050. Musical works–summary judgments

[Rules of the Supreme Court Ord.14.]

DE applied for summary judgment under RSC Ord.14 for F's alleged breach of copyright of 26 recordings in respect of which DE was entitled to copyright. In earlier proceedings F resisted the summary judgment application in reliance upon licences which he claimed entitled him to sell copies of the recordings. F subsequently sought leave to defend, at a late stage, on the ground that no evidence had been adduced to prove that F's allegedly infringing copies of recordings were in fact copies of recordings in respect of which DE had copyright. F contended that the recordings were made by artists who could have made recordings for other companies, DE having no copyright in respect of such recordings.

Held, allowing the application, that the submission made by F at a late stage was insufficient to justify the granting of leave to defend. As a professional within the record making industry F had the knowledge to make him capable of raising the defence at an earlier stage. In addition, F's argument was unsupported by expert evidence and therefore had no more substance than a mere possibility that the recordings were copies in respect of which DE had no copyright. Accordingly, DE was entitled to summary judgment and a permanent injunction was granted in relation to the 26 recordings.

DOMINION ENTERTAINMENT INC v. FLUTE INTERNATIONAL LTD, Trans. Ref: Ch.1996-D-6873, June 30, 1997, Sir Richard Scott V.C., Ch D.

1051. Photographs–publication of newspaper photographs before licence granted

Held, that, whilst it was common practice in the newspaper world to publish a copyright photograph which had previously been published in another newspaper without waiting for the copyright owner to grant a licence, on the presumption that the licence fee could be paid retrospectively, the practice was both unjustified and unlawful.

BANIER v. NEWS GROUP NEWSPAPERS LTD; BANIER v. TIMES NEWSPAPERS LTD, *The Times*, June 21, 1997, Lightman, J., Ch D.

1052. Sentencing–distributing infringing articles via computer bulletin board

[Copyright, Designs and Patents Act 1988 s.107 (1).]

L appealed against a sentence of 27 months' imprisonment, having pleaded guilty to 10 specimen counts of distributing infringing articles contrary to the Copyright, Designs and Patents Act 1988 s.107(1)(d)(iv). He operated a computer bulletin board which was used to exchange copyright computer games without the copyright owner's licence. Callers could download computer games onto L's computer system, and upload games from that system. Over a period of three months 934 games were downloaded and 592 were uploaded. The value of each game to the copyright owner was about £40.

Held, allowing the appeal and reducing the sentence to 12 months' imprisonment, concurrent on each count, that while an immediate prison sentence was necessary and appropriate, 27 months was longer than required, having regard to L's plea and good character.

R. v. LEWIS (CHRISTOPHER) [1997] 1 Cr. App. R. (S.) 208, Judge Crawford Q.C., CA (Crim Div).

1053. Sentencing–making infringing copy of computer program

L was convicted of six counts of making an infringing article and was sentenced to 12 months' imprisonment on each count concurrent. L made compact discs containing counterfeit copies of computer programs. Sixty one discs were found at L's home.

Held, allowing the appeal, that given that the maximum sentence for the offence was two years' imprisonment, the sentencer had taken too high a starting point; a sentence of six months' imprisonment would be substituted, *R.*

v. Kemp (Paul Geoffrey) (1995) 16 Cr. App. R. (S.) 941 and *R. v. Gross (Neville Emmanuel)* [1996] 2 Cr. App. R. (S.) 189, [1996] 1 C.L.Y. 2100 considered.

R. v. LLOYD (GRANT OATEN) [1997] 2 Cr. App. R. (S.) 151, Ebsworth, J., CA (Crim Div).

1054. Software–loading unlicensed software onto PCs for sale to customers–summary judgments

[Copyright, Designs and Patents Act 1988 s.17, s.18.]

E were an original equipment manufacturer who built personal computers to their own specification and sold them to the public after loading them with appropriate software. M, the proprietor of a range of computer software, claimed that E were in breach of M's copyright by making unlicensed copies of its software and loading it onto their PCs before selling them to their customers. M sought summary judgment against E for injunctions restraining them from further infringing their copyright, orders for delivery up of offending materials and various types of disclosure on affidavit, and an inquiry as to damages for infringement. In asserting a fair probability of having a bona fide defence, E claimed that (1) there was doubt as to whether they had infringed the Copyright, Designs and Patents Act 1988 s.17 and s.18 and that in any case s.18 excluded liability for an isolated act of issue; (2) there was doubt as to whether M owned any copyright that might exist in the disputed software, and (3) they did not have the facilities to make illicit copies of M's software and had never done so.

Held, granting summary judgment, that the court had to take care when being asked to remove the opportunity for a defendant to have his evidence tested at trial, but if, after examining all the circumstances of the case, the court found that the defence presented was clearly not credible, it had to act accordingly. Even if E were correct about the interpretation of s.18, it was clear from other evidence that their sales policy did not involve an isolated act of issuing software and one of E's customers had provided convincing evidence that non-authentic software had been supplied with one of their PCs. Further, it was unlikely that a company of M's size would not take the necessary steps to ensure that it owned the copyright in its major products and E's argument that they could contest M's claim that it owned the copyright was not a defence, merely a forlorn hope.

MICROSOFT CORP v. ELECTRO-WIDE LTD [1997] F.S.R. 580, Laddie, J., Ch D.

1055. Software–sound card–reverse engineering by disassembly–fair dealing–Singapore

[Copyright Act s.30 (Singapore), s.35(1) (Singapore).]

C counterclaimed that A had reverse engineered through disassembly and copied a substantial portion of the firmware housed in the microprocessor of their sound card and had infringed their copyright in the software of the ancillary program supplied with it. A denied disassembly but admitted copying the ancillary software on the basis that it was fair dealing for the purpose of research or private study under Copyright Act (Singapore) s.35(1). The Judicial Commissioner held that A had not been shown to have had access to the firmware by means of disassembly and that they had not infringed copyright in the firmware. He also held that A's copying of the software did constitute fair dealing and was lawful use of copyright software for a reasonable purpose as implied by licence pursuant to the principle in *Betts v. Wilmott* (1871) 6 Ch. 239. C appealed.

Held, allowing the appeal, that (1) the Judicial Commissioner had failed to address the cumulative weight and significance of all the similarities of the parties' firmware. A had the means, motive and opportunity to disassemble C's firmware. There was no reasonable explanation of development absent copying through disassembly; (2) in terms of literal copyright infringement, A's software code did not amount to a substantial part of C's firmware. This did not prejudice the finding of infringement by disassembly, which involved a degree of reproduction and adaptation having a greater impact in terms of revealing the ideas and interfaces of C's software; (3) the burden of proof remained with the party bringing the claim to prove copying and access to his work. Once this was established, the burden shifted to the other party to rebut that inference by way of evidence. A had failed to rebut the inference, *IBCOS Computers v. Barclays Mercantile Highland Finance* [1994] F.S.R. 275, [1995] 1 C.L.Y. 854 referred to; (4) on the plain ordinary meaning of Copyright Act (Singapore) s.35 private study for commercial purposes was not fair dealing, *University of London Press Ltd v. University Tutorial Press Ltd* [1916] 2 Ch. 601 and *Sillitoe v. McGraw-Hill Book Co Ltd* [1983] F.S.R. 545 considered; (5) the principle of an implied term of "unfettered use" in *Betts* did not apply to copyright law. Terms would be implied only to the extent that they lent business efficacy to the contract. There was no implied term that C consented to the copying of its ancillary software in order to discover its functionality in order to make a competing product, *Time-life International (Nederlands) BV v. Interstate Parcel Express Co Pty Ltd* [1978] F.S.R. 251, [1978] C.L.Y. 346 and *Betts* applied; (6) the principle of non-derogation from grant in *British Leyland v. Armstrong* [1986] 1 A.C. 577, [1986] C.L.Y. 432 was a separate principle to that advanced in *Betts*, and (7) copying by A of C's ancillary software was not part of an essential step in the utilisation of the software program. Accordingly, A's conduct was not protected by Copyright Act (Singapore) s.30, *Vault Corp v. Quaid Software Ltd* (1988) 847 F.2d 255 distinguished and *Sega Enterprises Ltd v. Accolade Inc* (1992) 977 F.2d 1510 followed.

AZTECH SYSTEMS PTE LTD v. CREATIVE TECHNOLOGY LTD; *sub nom.* CREATIVE TECHNOLOGY LTD v. AZTECH SYSTEMS PTE LTD [1997] F.S.R. 491, Karthigesu, J.A., CA (Singapore).

1056. **Television–satellite transmission–films broadcast beyond stipulated area– copyright infringement and breach of contract–defence of acquiescence**

F, a Liberian company with copyright or licence rights in films intended for adult viewing, brought an action against H alleging copyright infringement and breach of contract. Under the terms of a licence agreement between the two parties, H was licensed to exhibit films within the United Kingdom. However, the satellite system used for transmission had a footprint capable of covering most of Europe and, when H became aware that the films were being viewed there by use of either pirated cards or genuine cards sold beyond the licence area, they began selling decoder cards permitting reception of their transmissions throughout Europe. H denied breach of the licence agreement and contended that F acquiesced in the arrangement by which films were received by viewers in Europe.

Held, dismissing the action, that the defence of acquiescence was made out as the facts showed that F had been aware for some time that films were being exhibited beyond the licence area and had made no complaint to H. The principle established in *Taylor Fashions Ltd v. Liverpool Victoria Friendly Society* [1982] 1 Q.B. 133, [1979] C.L.Y. 1619 meant that it would be unconscionable for F to be permitted to deny that which they had allowed or encouraged H to assume to their detriment.

FILM INVESTORS OVERSEAS SERVICES SA v. HOME VIDEO CHANNEL LTD (T/A THE ADULT CHANNEL) [1997] E.M.L.R. 347, Carnwath, J., Ch D.

1057. **Television–unauthorised inclusion of interview clip in television programme– fair dealing defence not available–liability for additional damages absolved by laudable motives**

[Copyright, Designs and Patents Act 1988 s.30(1), s.30(2), s.97(2).]

P, a German television company, had been granted the exclusive right to exploit a filmed interview with a pregnant woman who was found to be carrying eight live embryos and included the interview in two satellite programmes. C, a UK television company, commissioned a series of current affairs programmes, one of which incorporated a short clip of the interview from one of P's programmes without P's prior knowledge. P sued C for infringement of copyright and the issues before the court were: (1) whether C could rely on the defence of fair dealing for the purposes of criticism or review under the Copyright, Designs and Patents Act

1988 s.30(1) or for the purpose of reporting current events under s.30(2), and (2) if not, whether additional damages could be awarded under s.97(2).

Held, giving judgment for P, that (1) C's use of the clip had not been accompanied by sufficient acknowledgement of its source as required by s.30(1) of the 1988 Act and, furthermore, it seemed that any criticism contained in C's programme was not directed towards the interview contained in P's film, but rather to P's decision to pay for it. It was not clear that C saw the clip as newsworthy at all and the use made of it could not be deemed fair under s.30(2) of the 1988 Act, and (2) C clearly believed that their use of the clip was permissible and for the public good, and that their programme was not intended to compete with P's programme or to devalue it. Whilst those laudable motives provided no defence, they were effective in absolving C from paying additional damages under s.97(2) of the 1988 Act.

PRO SIEBEN MEDIA AG v. CARLTON UK TELEVISION LTD, *The Times,* September 24, 1997, Laddie, J., Ch D.

1058. Video recordings—royalty contract—construction

VP, a licensing body, appealed on behalf of its members against a declaration in respect of a royalty contract. VV produced an hour long television programme containing music videos under a licence granted by VP at a rate of £675,000 per annum, but which provided for reductions to be made pro rata where the total quantity of the music video amounted to less than 48 minutes. A dispute arose over the terms of the 1993 licence, which was compromised before the Copyright Tribunal by an agreement that the annual fee would be £390,000. Subsequently, a further dispute was resolved when the judge below determined that the original pro rata reduction in the annual fee had survived in the new agreement. VP appealed.

Held, dismissing the appeal, that VP wished to take the benefit of the original agreement in order to restrict VV from making more than 52 programmes annually and it was therefore fair that it should be bound to the rebate system contained therein. In addition, were the new agreement to replace the old entirely, then VV would have no way of avoiding a contractual duty to pay the monthly royalty instalments even if its programme were cancelled by the television company and that could not have been the intention of the parties.

VIDEO PERFORMANCE LTD v. VIDEO VISUALS LTD, Trans. Ref: CHANI 96/ 0109/B, April 9, 1997, Simon Brown, L.J., CA.

1059. Articles

Controlling the aftermarket: new UK regulations give added powers to copyright owners *(Justin Watts* and *Brian Cordery)*: C.W. 1997, 68, 33-36. (Reforms of copyright law introduced by SI 1996 2967, including extending distribution right, providing that subsistence of copyright can affect subsequent dealings in original work, extending rental rights and new publication right).

Copyright and electronic publishing *(Paul Sampson)*: C.W. 1997, 75, 22-26. (Issues relating to ownership, enforcement, licensing, hypertext links, international aspects and pricing, databases and restrictions on access to information).

Copyright and public lending in the United Kingdom *(Jonathan Griffiths)*: E.I.P.R. 1997, 19(9), 499-503. (Changes made under the Copyright and Related Rights Regulations 1996).

Copyright implications in the paperless office *(Brian Slack)*: Comms. L. 1997, 2(3), 119-121. (Including problem of definition of "computer program" with regard to making back up copies, and data protection issues).

Copyright in character merchandising *(John N. Adams)*: C.W. 1997, 66, 29-35.

Copyright in the cyberspace era *(Antonio Mille)*: E.I.P.R. 1997, 19(10), 570-577.

Databases: the EC Directive *(Peter J. Groves)*: Bus. L.R. 1997, 18(3), 59-61. (Council Directive 96/9 on the legal protection of databases will harmonise copyright law in Member States and enable operators to control extraction and reutilisation of material).

Developments in the law of copyright and public access to information *(Anthony Mason)*: E.I.P.R. 1997, 19(11), 636-643. (Provisions of Copyright Treaty 1996 (WIPO) on scope of copyright, computer programs, and rights of reproduction and communication, but leaving national jurisdictions to resolve problems concerning fair dealing and Internet regulation).

Discotheques and the copyright exemption for charities and near charities *(Hubert Picarda)*: C.L. & P.R. 1997, 4(3), 153-172. (Criteria for exemption from infringement under the Copyright, Designs and Patents Act 1988 s.67 and whether "near charities" such as clubs and students unions profit unfairly at expense of copyright holders).

Fair is not always fair: media monitors and copyright *(Michael Sinclair)*: E.I.P.R. 1997, 19(4), 188-191. (Whether press cuttings agencies and similar information services are protected by provisions of 1988 Act regarding copying for research, criticism and news reporting purposes).

First step protection - the internationalisation of systems for civil inaudita altera parte search procedures *(Gunnar W.G. Karnell)*: C.W. 1997, 71, 34-38. (Provisions in TRIPs for ex parte procedure enabling rights owners to obtain orders to search for illegally copied software programs and comparison with procedures in EU countries).

Frustrated windfall: rental rights, lending rights and equitable remuneration *(Greg Sweeting)*: I.M.L. 1997, 15(6), 44-48. (Effect of SI 1996 2967, in force December 1, 1996, which implements Directive 92/100 by introducing right for authors to receive remuneration for exploitation of lending or rental rights).

Leppard changes its spot: recent changes to the approach of courts in England and Wales to issues of jurisdiction in copyright claims *(Adam Wolanski)*: Ent. L.R. 1997, 8(4), 143-145.

Look before you leap: copyright warranties of title *(Jonathan Radcliffe and Peter Price)*: Ent. L.R. 1997, 8(3), 83-88.

New rules for our global village *(Peter Wand)*: Ent. L.R. 1997, 8(5), 176-180. (Provisions of WIPO Copyright and Performances and Phonograms Treaties with table comparing provisions, and summary of CEC Green Paper on copyright).

Parallel imports and copyright-books and the Internet: IT L.T. 1997, 5(10), 1-3. (Whether importation of US editions of books bought over Internet can be prevented by publishers as copyright infringement or whether EC exhaustion of rights principle applies).

Solicitors in breach of copyright *(Roderick Ramage)*: N.L.J. 1997, 147(6780), 250-251. (Whether law firms need to obtain CLA licence to avoid liability for photocopying from books and journals outside scope of fair use exemption).

The advertising world and intellectual property *(Iain C. Baillie)*: C.W. 1997, 66, 24-28. (Practical advice on how to avoid copyright conflicts when commissioning creative work).

The effect of the Council Directive 96/9 on the legal protection of databases on United Kingdom copyright law in relation to databases: a comparison of features *(Simon Chalton)*: E.I.P.R. 1997, 19(6), 278-288.

The life and terms of UK copyright in original works *(Anthony Robinson)*: Ent. L.R. 1997, 8(2), 60-70. (Rationale behind copyright duration for creator and assignee, legislative history of copyright duration, extension of term through implementation of Directive 93/98 and effect of the Duration of Copyright and Rights in Performances Regulations 1995 relating to revived copyright).

The multimedia maze: an illustration of the legal rights in multimedia products *(Mitzi Gilligan)*: Comms. L. 1997, 2(2), 49-56. (Fictional case studies on copyright implications for producers, publishers, creators, contributors and users of multimedia products).

The new publication right: how will it affect museums and galleries? *(Helen Simpson and David Booton)*: A.A. & L. 1997, 2(3), 283-291. (Potential problems for museums and art galleries in managing their collections as result of new property right under Copyright and Related Rights Regulations 1996 (SI 1996 2967) Reg.16).

The valuation of copyright *(Mark Bezant* and *Kevin Brown)*: C.W. 1997, 70, 17-20. (Cost-based, market-based and economic-based approaches).

To sample or not to sample? *(Stephen Bate)* and *(Lawrence Abramson)*: Ent. L.R. 1997, 8(6), 193-196. (Copyright issues involved in sampling sound recordings and remedies).

1060. Books

Flint, Michael F.–User's Guide to Copyright. Hardback: £30.00. ISBN 0-406-04608-5. Butterworth Law.

Phillips, Jeremy; Durie, Robyn; Karet, Ian–Whale on Copyright. Intellectual Property Guides. Paperback: £35.00. ISBN 0-421-59380-6. Sweet & Maxwell.

Phillips, Jeremy; Durie, Robyn; Karet, Ian–Whale on Copyright. 2nd Ed. Intellectual Property Guides. Paperback: £38.00. ISBN 0-421-59380-6. Sweet & Maxwell.

CORPORATION TAX

1061. Advance corporation tax–company ceasing to trade–absence of income source meant company no longer within charge to corporation tax–ACT carry back unavailable

[Income and Corporation Taxes Act 1988 s.12, s.239, s.832(1).]

C was a subsidiary of WB. In 1992 it transferred its assets and business by contract to a fellow subsidiary, but continued the business as an agent without remuneration. In April 1993 it declared a dividend of £2.1m, on which it paid ACT of £695,000. In September 1993 it opened an interest bearing bank account which earned interest of £8 in the next quarter. In December 1993 it paid a further dividend of £915,000 on which the ACT was £265,000. C claimed to carry back the ACT paid during 1993 to the two preceding years under the Income and Corporation Taxes Act 1988 s.239. The Revenue allowed the claim in respect of the second dividend but refused it in respect of the first on the ground that, under s.12 of the 1988 Act, C ceased to be within the charge to corporation tax since it had no source of income after transferring its business. C appealed, contending that under the tailpiece to s.832(1) a potential source of income brought it within the charge. The special commissioner allowed the appeal. The Revenue appealed.

Held, allowing the appeal, that on the true construction of the tailpiece it was necessary to have an actual source of income within the charge to corporation tax. The facts showed that, following the transfer of assets and liabilities, C had ceased to be within the charge to corporation tax due to its lack of income source and no new accounting period had begun, so that C's claim to carry back ACT failed.

WALKER (INSPECTOR OF TAXES) v. CENTAUR CLOTHES GROUP LTD [1997] S.T.C. 72, Sir John Vinelott, Ch D.

1062. Business expenses–groups of companies–payment to terminate contractual liability of one company was deductible

[Income and Corporation Taxes Act 1988 s.74.]

V appealed against a ruling that a payment to a US company to terminate a contract which required V to make annual payments for technical support and know how was not tax deductible. V incorporated into a joint venture company the activities of two subsidiaries, one selling mobile telephones and the other running a telephone network, in order to comply with DTI licensing requirements. The court upheld the special commissioners' ruling that the payment was revenue not capital in nature and was not wholly and exclusively expended for the purpose of V's trade within the meaning of the Income and

Corporation Taxes Act 1988 s.74, as it was made to benefit the trade of all three companies and not V alone. The Crown cross-appealed.

Held, allowing the appeal and dismissing the cross-appeal, that (1) the payment was revenue in nature because it terminated a contractual liability to make revenue payments and did not secure an enduring benefit for V's trade, and (2) the issue of whether the money was expended wholly and exclusively for V's trade was a question of fact for the special commissioners. However, their finding that in the context of the contract V's directors regarded the three companies as a single trading entity, did not reasonably support their conclusion that the directors intended to benefit all three companies rather than just one. The question to consider was what purpose the directors intended to achieve by the payment, which was to relieve V of a trading liability to which V alone was subject under the contract and therefore the payment was expended wholly and exclusively for the purposes of V's trade.

VODAFONE CELLULAR LTD v. SHAW (INSPECTOR OF TAXES) [1997] S.T.C. 734, Millett, L.J., CA.

1063. Business expenses–interest–property development–interest incurred on borrowing to finance acquisition–use amounting to capital purpose–Hong Kong

[Inland Revenue Ordinance s.16, s.17 (Hong Kong).]

W, a property development company, appealed against a decision refusing the deduction of interest payments for the purpose of calculating taxable profits under the Inland Revenue Ordinance s.16(1) (Hong Kong). The interest had been incurred on sums borrowed to finance the acquisition of a former tram depot which W redeveloped into a commercial complex.

Held, dismissing the appeal, that although interest incurred for the purpose of earning taxable profits was deductible under s.16(1)(a), the allowable expenditure provisions of s.16 fell to be considered alongside the prohibited categories found in s.17, with both sections exhaustively providing the permitted deductions, *Hong Kong Inland Revenue Commissioner v. Mutual Investment Co Ltd* [1967] A.C. 587, [1966] C.L.Y. 870 considered. Under s.17 no deduction was permitted for expenditure of a capital nature, and the facts showed that the interest payments for the period in question were made for a capital purpose, as they amounted to consideration for the use of money needed for the acquisition of the depot pending its conversion into an interest earning asset. Income from licence fees during this period formed an adventitious benefit unconnected with the larger project and had been more than adequately provided for by being treated as a subsidiary purpose for which a deduction equivalent to the amount of interest concerned had been allowed.

WHARF PROPERTIES LTD v. INLAND REVENUE COMMISSIONER [1997] A.C. 505, Lord Hoffmann, PC.

1064. Business expenses–redundancy payments–whether made wholly and exclusively for purposes of company's trade

C, a Hong Kong company, ceased business and made redundancy payments to its employees. The Commissioner disallowed them for tax purposes. The Hong Kong courts allowed C's appeal. The Commissioner appealed.

Held, dismissing the appeal, that the payments had been incurred as a necessary condition of retaining the services of the employees concerned, *Godden (Inspector of Taxes) v. A Wilson's Stores (Holdings) Ltd* [1962] T.R. 19, [1962] C.L.Y. 1510 followed.

COSMOTRON MANUFACTURING CO LTD v. INLAND REVENUE COMMISSIONER [1997] 1 W.L.R. 1288, Lord Nolan, PC.

1065. Capital allowances—groups of companies—distribution depot not used for purpose "ancillary to purposes of a retail shop"

[Capital Allowances Act 1968 s.7(3).]

The Crown appealed against a decision that the members of a retail group, DG, were entitled to initial and writing-down allowances under the Capital Allowances Act 1968 in relation to expenditure on a warehouse development used as a storage and distribution depot by one member of the group, DGD. Whilst the warehouse was an industrial building or structure within the meaning of s.7(1) of the Act, the Crown contended that DG was prevented from obtaining the allowances by s.7(3), which excluded buildings used for any purpose "ancillary to the purposes of a retail shop".

Held, dismissing the appeal, that (1) s.7(3) was not a freestanding provision but was rather concerned with excluding from s.7(1) certain uses of buildings which would otherwise have qualified for allowances under that subsection and (2) in order for a building to be used for a purpose ancillary to the purposes of a retail shop, it had to be subservient and subordinate to retail selling and its activities had to be confined to furthering the purposes of the shop. In the instant case, whilst the services provided by the warehouse were needed by DG's shops, it was not used for a purpose ancillary to the running of the shops, as the warehouse was used by DGD for the purpose of carrying on its own separate and independent trade.

SARSFIELD (INSPECTOR OF TAXES) v. DIXONS GROUP PLC [1997] S.T.C. 283, Lightman, J., Ch D.

1066. Capital allowances—industrial buildings allowance—whether site value of land to be excluded—whether developer's profit to be apportioned between land and building

[Capital Allowances Act 1990 s.21(1).]

B and other investors bought an industrial building for £1.1 million. The land value was £200,000 and the cost of the building was £333,000, the balance representing the developer's profit. The inspector contended that the land value should be excluded from the industrial buildings allowance and the developer's profit should be apportioned between land and buildings. The Special Commissioners dismissed the investor's appeal. B and some other investors appealed.

Held, dismissing the appeal, that (1) land was excluded from allowances under the terms of the Capital Allowances Act 1990 s.21(1), and (2) the only just way of arriving at a fair apportionment was to attribute the developer's profit rateably between the land value and the cost of construction.

BOSTOCK v. TOTHAM (INSPECTOR OF TAXES) [1997] S.T.C. 764, Sir John Vinelott, Ch D.

1067. Capital allowances—plant—neither car wash site nor wash hall single items of plant

[Capital Allowances Act 1990 s.22.]

A operated car washing facilities at 78 sites throughout the UK. It claimed that each site constituted a single unit of plant. The Revenue assessed A to tax on the basis that only 19 of the 48 component parts of the car wash facilities qualified as plant. The Special Commissioners decided in principle that the sites were generally single units of plant but the High Court allowed the Revenue's appeal, [1996] S.T.C. 110, [1996] 2 C.L.Y. 5564. A appealed.

Held, dismissing the appeal, that the car wash site which allowed for cars to pass through the system and the wash hall functioned as premises on which the car wash business operated. Neither the entire site nor the wash hall constituted a single unit of plant within the Capital Allowances Act 1990 s.22,

Benson (Inspector of Taxes) v. Yard Arm Club Ltd [1979] S.T.C. 266, [1979] C.L.Y. 1441.
ATTWOOD (INSPECTOR OF TAXES) v. ANDUFF CAR WASH LTD [1997] S.T.C. 1167, Beldam, L.J., CA.

1068. Capital gains–rental purchase transaction requiring payment by instalments in foreign currency–fluctuation in exchange rate–whether gave rise to adjustment in assessment

[Capital Gains Tax Act 1979 s.24, s.40(2).]
The Crown appealed against a special commissioners' decision allowing an adjustment to a corporation tax assessment in respect of capital gains made on the disposal by L of four oil rigs for consideration of $38,610,000, payable by instalments over a nine year period. L, a non resident company specialising in oil rig supply through a branch or agency, entered into a rental purchase agreement, whereby the rigs were leased with a purchase option at a pre-determined price. The Crown contended that the gain exceeded £6.7 million, based on the sterling equivalent of the reference price, with the exchange rate varying between $1.06 and $1.98 over the repayment period. However, the spot exchange rate, applied on a monthly basis, showed L had made an allowable loss of £2.7 million.
Held, allowing the appeal, that the Capital Gains Tax Act 1979 s.40(2) did not apply to exchange rate changes or other changes in valuation occurring after the date of valuation of the consideration, which was the date of the transaction under s.24 of the Act. The words "subsequently shown... to be irrecovable" in s.40(2) covered the risk that part of the consideration might be irrecovable due to a debtor's default or where the right to receive part of it was contingent on an unfulfilled contingency. Under s.40(2) the fact that the right to receive the consideration was postponed had to be ignored and no discount was allowable as a consequence. Sterling remained the applicable currency throughout and no calculation in dollars was permissible for capital gains computation purposes. On the facts, L had received the full consideration expected under the agreement and no part of it had proved to be irrecovable.
LOFFLAND BROTHERS NORTH SEA INC v. GOODBRAND (INSPECTOR OF TAXES); *sub nom.* GOODBRAND (INSPECTOR OF TAXES) v. LOFFLAND BROTHERS NORTH SEA INC [1997] S.T.C. 102, Lloyd, J., Ch D.

1069. Capital losses–associated companies–sale of shares in group member at undervalue–interaction between depreciatory transaction provisions and indexation rules

[Income and Corporation Taxes Act 1970 s.280; Finance Act 1982 s.86(4).]
T owned the shares in THL, a holding company, which had increased in value appreciably since 1982. THL owned the shares in TSL, which in turn owned the goodwill and assets of the trade conducted under the name "Tesco". THL sold TSL to T at a considerable undervalue, which made it a depreciatory transaction under the Income and Corporation Taxes Act 1970 s.280 and substantially reduced the value of THL's shares to well below the 1982 value. T then sold THL to BAT in an arm's length transaction. T sought to extinguish chargeable gains made on certain currency transactions by reference to the loss on the disposal of THL. T appealed against a special commissioners' determination that s.280 eliminated the allowable loss.
Held, dismissing the appeal, that s.280 was intended to prevent depreciatory transactions between associated companies being used to create artificial allowable losses. The Finance Act 1982 s.86 normally provided for indexation to increase the amount of any allowable loss and, under s.86(4), the allowable loss would be produced by the application of the indexation allowance to the unindexed loss. Therefore, s.280 fell to be applied to the indexed allowable loss, if there was one. There was no justification for breaking up the indexed allowable loss, subtracting indexation allowance and then applying s.280 to the remaining allowable loss. Section 280 prohibited the use of indexation to

create an allowable loss in relation to the value of T's assets which could be attributed to the depreciatory transaction.

TESCO PLC v. CRIMMIN (INSPECTOR OF TAXES) [1997] S.T.C. 981, Sir Richard Scott V.C., Ch D.

1070. Consideration–option to purchase land–value of consideration–cost of procuring release of restrictive covenants was deductible from chargeable gain

[Capital Gains Tax Act 1979 s.32; .]

The grant of an option was the disposal of an asset but the transaction had to be considered as a whole to establish the consideration received. P granted MG an option to purchase its shares in development land for consideration of £399,750. The option agreement contained a term requiring P to procure release from certain restrictive covenants relating to the land or refund the purchase price. The Crown appealed against a decision that, under the Capital Gains Tax Act 1979 s.32, P was entitled to deduct the £90,000 it had spent securing the release from the amount of the chargeable gain, although it was not specified what part of s.32 applied.

Held, dismissing the appeal, that the grant of an option was a disposal of an asset and the Act implied that where a disposal was at arm's length for monetary consideration, such consideration formed the starting point for calculating the gain. However, it was necessary to consider the transaction as a whole to establish what consideration P actually received. The facts in this case did not fit any of the categories in s.32, as the asset was provided before the expenditure was incurred so that the £90,000 was spent pursuant to the option, but not in its provision. The correct approach was to identify the consideration by reference to the onerous obligation incurred under the agreement to secure the releases, the value of which was the sum of £90,000, *Randall v. Plumb* [1975] 1 W.L.R. 633, [1975] C.L.Y. 1642 applied. It would be wrong to take into account only the consideration stated in the agreement without having regard to other matters which materially affected the consideration's value to P. Thus, the value of the consideration was not £399,750, as P's entitlement to that amount was dependent on being able to secure the release, and, assuming this had occurred, the net consideration received would be the sum stated in the agreement less the amount incurred in securing the release.

GARNER (INSPECTOR OF TAXES) v. POUNDS SHIPOWNERS AND SHIPBREAKERS LTD; *sub nom.* GARNER (INSPECTOR OF TAXES) v. POUNDS [1997] S.T.C. 551, Carnwath, J., Ch D.

1071. Consideration–sale of business–capital gains–obligation to discharge debt formed part of consideration

SI sold an American subsidiary SIH to ABI. Prior to the sale SIH paid a dividend of $20 million to SI which was funded by a bank loan secured by a deposit of the monies. The consideration for the shares was expressed to be $20,001,000. On completion, ABI repaid the loan of $20 million to the bank, and paid $1,000 to SI. The Revenue assessed SI to corporation tax on the basis that the consideration for the shares was $20,001,000. SI appealed, contending that the consideration was $1,000. The special commissioners dismissed the appeal. SI appealed.

Held, dismissing the appeal, that on the true construction of the sale agreements and taking account of business sense and reality the discharge of the debt was part of the consideration for the sale, *Aberdeen Construction Group Ltd v. Inland Revenue Commissioners* [1978] 1 All E.R. 962, [1979] C.L.Y. 371 considered. The critical issue was to identify the consideration allocated to the common stock disposal. Although the agreement did not state to whom the purchase price was payable, it clearly identified a purchase price for all assets at $23 million, with a common stock purchase price of $20,001,000, and the fact that ABI was obliged to deliver evidence of payment supported the view that the payment obligation formed part of the payment price.

SPECTROS INTERNATIONAL PLC (IN VOLUNTARY LIQUIDATION) v. MADDEN (INSPECTOR OF TAXES) [1997] S.T.C. 114, Lightman, J., Ch D.

1072. Controlled foreign companies–interest paid–no exemption from charge by double taxation agreement

[Income and Corporation Taxes Act 1988 s.747, Sch.24(B) para.1; Double Taxation Relief (Taxes on Income) (Netherlands) Order 1980 (SI 1980 1961) Art.11.]

B had a subsidiary S, incorporated and resident in the Netherlands. S lent funds to B on which it paid interest. The Revenue assessed B to tax on S's chargeable profits including the interest sourced in the UK under the Income and Corporation Taxes Act 1988 s.747. B appealed, contending that the interest was exempt from tax by virtue of Double Taxation Relief (Taxes on Income) (Netherlands) Order 1980 Art 11. The Special Commissioners dismissed B's appeal. B appealed.

Held, dismissing the appeal, that (1) on a purposive construction of Sch.24(B) para.1 of the 1988 Act the interest was not to be excluded in computing S's chargeable profits as those profits were measured by reference to S's total income inclusive of UK sourced interest, and (2) the interest was not included in the sum apportioned to B but provided a measure by which a notional sum was calculated and tax charged, *Ostime (Inspector of Taxes) v. Australian Mutual Provident Society* (1957) 38 T.C. 492, [1959] C.L.Y. 1533 applied.

BRICOM HOLDINGS LTD v. INLAND REVENUE COMMISSIONERS [1997] S.T.C. 1179, Beldam, L.J., CA.

1073. Debts–exchange losses on secured intra-group–debt on a security

[Capital Gains Tax Act 1979 s.82(3)(b), s.134(1).]

A loan made by a company to its subsidiary, secured by promissory notes, was not equivalent to a market investment, and exchange losses made by the company when converting the repaid US dollars into sterling were not allowable for capital gains tax purposes. TCI made a loan in US dollars to its wholly owned US subsidiary to finance the purchase of development property. The loan was secured by promissory notes encumbering the property and was to be repayable on demand, with interest payable on the debt. During its 1992 accounting period, TCI made exchange losses upon converting repaid dollars into sterling and now appealed against a decision that the losses were not allowable for capital gains tax purposes on the grounds that TCI's right to repayment of the loan was not a "debt on a security" within the meaning of the Capital Gains Tax Act 1979 s.134(1). TCI contended, relying on *WT Ramsay Ltd v. Inland Revenue Commissioners* [1979] 1 W.L.R. 974, [1981] C.L.Y. 1385 and *Aberdeen Construction Group Ltd v. Inland Revenue Commissioners* [1978] A.C. 885, [1979] C.L.Y. 371, that "security" within s.134(1) meant any proprietary security. The Crown argued that as the definition of "security" laid down in s.82(3)(b) of the Act was to be applied to s.134(1), Parliament could not have intended that all debts backed by proprietary security were to be included in s.134(1) and "security" was limited to loan stocks or similar items.

Held, dismissing the appeal, that the decisions in *Ramsay* and *Aberdeen Construction* did not support the proposition that a "debt on a security" could include a debt backed by proprietary security that was not similar to a market investment. Although the debt was assignable and had documentary title, it was unlikely to be of interest to an external investor. The terms and context of the debt, as a secure, interest bearing loan to fund a particular project within a group of companies meant that it was unlikely that the benefit of repayment would be marketed or dealt in. It was also significant that the debt had no fixed term and the creditor or debtor could demand repayment at any time, and therefore lacked a structure of permanence.

TAYLOR CLARK INTERNATIONAL LTD v. LEWIS (INSPECTOR OF TAXES) [1997] S.T.C. 499, Robert Walker, J., Ch D.

1074. Dividends–withholding tax exemption–Member State not entitled to set conditions–companies entitled to rely directly on Directive 90/435–no compensation for incorrect transposition–European Union

[Council Directive 90/435 on the common system of taxation applicable in the case of parent companies and their subsidiaries of different Member States.]

Under Council Directive 90/435 on the common system of taxation applicable in the case of parent companies and their subsidiaries of different Member States, dividends paid by subsidiaries to parent companies were exempt from withholding tax, subject to conditions laid down by Member States. Germany purported to impose conditions on the availability of the exemption by requiring that the qualifying shareholding be held for at least 12 months. Three companies appealed and the matter was referred to the European Court of Justice for a preliminary ruling.

Held, that (1) it was not permissible to impose as a condition a minimum holding period which had to be complied with before the exemption could be granted, but the company was not entitled to claim the exemption immediately giving only a unilateral undertaking; (2) companies were entitled to rely directly on the Directive and (3) in the circumstances it was not appropriate to award compensation for loss, because no previous decisions had interpreted the Directive and the breach could not be treated as sufficiently serious.

DENKAVIT INTERNATIONAL BV v. BUNDESAMT FUR FINANZEN (C283/94) [1996] S.T.C. 1445, Moitinho de Almeida (President), ECJ.

1075. Double taxation–foreign banks–bank cannot carry forward losses–statutory interpretation

[United Kingdom-United States Double Taxation Agreement 1946 Art.15; United Kingdom-United States Double Taxation Agreement 1975; Finance Act 1976 s.50(1).]

BdB appealed against a decision reversing a special commissioner's finding that the Finance Act 1976 s.50(1) prevented BdB, as a non-resident bank, from carrying forward losses from 1974 and 1975 as provided for under the United Kingdom-United States Double Taxation Agreement 1946 Art.15, to set against profits arising after 15 April, 1976, the publication date of the Finance Bill 1976. BdB contended that the interpretation given to s.50(1) was retrospective in effect, and that such a construction was contrary to Parliament's intention in the absence of any contra-indication.

Held, dismissing the appeal, that s.50(1) was not fully retrospective as it only applied to profits arising on or after 15 April, 1976, and was therefore of only intermediate retrospectivity, *L'Office Cherifien des Phosphates Unitramp SA v. Yamashita-Shinnihon Steamship Co Ltd* [1994] 1 A.C. 486, [1994] C.L.Y. 221 considered. As such, the purpose of the legislation and any potential hardship was particularly important when determining the proper construction. The purpose of s.50(1) was to limit the effect of Art.15 of the 1946 Agreement prior to ratification of the United Kingdom-United States Double Taxation Agreement 1975, which removed the exemption from March 1976. Difficulties arose in interpreting s.50(1), as it was unclear how to determine issues of fairness contained in a revenue provision, given the annual nature of corporation tax and the attendant rate, relief and exemption alterations. An interpretation of such provisions had to take account of Parliament's intention and any retrospective effect that the section could produce in the interim.

BOOTE (INSPECTOR OF TAXES) v. BANCO DO BRASIL SA [1997] S.T.C. 327, Morritt, L.J., CA.

1076. Freedom of establishment–legality of Luxembourg conditions imposed for carrying forward of business losses by non resident company–European Union

[Treaty of Rome 1957 Art.52.]

S was the Luxembourg branch of a French resident company, F. When determining S's liability to revenue tax for the year 1986, F sought to offset losses made between 1981 and 1985 on an apportionment basis under the law applicable to non resident companies which had not kept separate accounts for their activities in Luxembourg for the relevant period. The set off was refused on the grounds that a non-resident taxpayer could only carry forward losses where (1) the losses were economically related to income earned in Luxembourg, and (2) the taxpayer had kept and held accounts in Luxembourg, relating to his activities there, which complied with national rules. In appeal proceedings, F contended that failure to allow the carry forward of the losses breached the right to freedom of establishment under the Treaty of Rome 1957 Art.52 and the matter was referred to the ECJ for a preliminary ruling.

Held, that provided resident taxpayers did not receive more favourable treatment, Art.52 did not prevent a Member State imposing a condition that previous losses must be economically related to income earned by the taxpayer in that state in order for them to be carried forward at the request of a non resident taxpayer with a branch in that state. However, Art.52 did prohibit the imposition of a condition that the taxpayer must have held accounts for the relevant year which complied with local rules within the Member State. It was, however, open to the Member State to require the taxpayer to show clearly and precisely that the amount of losses claimed to have been incurred corresponded to the amount actually incurred under the domestic rules of the state on the calculation of income and losses applicable in the relevant year.

FUTURA PARTICIPATIONS SA v. ADMINISTRATION DES CONTRIBUTIONS (C250/95), *The Times*, June 23, 1997, GC Rodriguez Iglesias (President), ECJ.

1077. Friendly societies

FRIENDLY SOCIETIES (MODIFICATION OF THE CORPORATION TAX ACTS) REGULATIONS 1997, SI 1997 473; made under the Income and Corporation Taxes Act 1988 s.463. In force: March 20, 1997; £3.70.

These Regulations re-enact the Friendly Societies (Modification of the Corporation Tax Acts) Regulations 1992 (SI 1992 1655, amended by SI 1993 3111, SI 1995 1916 and SI 1997 471) for accounting periods beginning on or after January 1, 1995; they also re-enact the Friendly Societies (Taxation of Transfers of Business) Regulations 1995 (SI 1995 171, amended by SI 1997 472) in relation to transfers of the whole or part of a friendly society's business and to amalgamations and conversions of friendly societies taking place on or after January 1, 1995. New Regulations provide for the ambit of enactments in the Corporation Tax Acts to be confined to the taxable business of friendly societies, make additional provision for computing profits arising from pension business in the cases of those friendly societies which are non-directive societies, make provision for computing the profits arising from overseas life assurance business carried on by friendly societies, and make changes to the Taxes Acts consequential upon the division of the basic life and general annuity business carried on by friendly societies into taxable and tax exempt business.

1078. Friendly societies–Amendment No.1

FRIENDLY SOCIETIES (MODIFICATION OF THE CORPORATION TAX ACTS) (AMENDMENT) REGULATIONS 1997, SI 1997 471; made under the Income and Corporation Taxes Act 1988 s.463. In force: March 19, 1997; £1.10.

These Regulations amend the Friendly Societies (Modification of the Corporation Tax Acts) Regulations 1992 (SI 1992 1655).

1079. Friendly societies—Amendment No.2

FRIENDLY SOCIETIES (MODIFICATION OF THE CORPORATION TAX ACTS) (AMENDMENT NO.2) REGULATIONS 1997, SI 1997 2877; made under the Income and Corporation Taxes Act 1988 s.463. In force: December 31, 1997; £0.65.

These Regulations amend the Friendly Societies (Modification of the Corporation Tax Acts) Regulations 1997 (SI 1997 473) by omitting Reg.16 and Reg.21 (2) and inserting a new Reg.53A which amends the Finance Act 1977 Sch.12 para.18.

1080. Groups of companies—validity of indirect tax charge on company granting interest free loan to subsidiary—European Union

[Council Directive 69/335 concerning indirect taxes on the raising of capital Art.4, Art.10.]

R made an interest free loan to a subsidiary. The Danish tax authority levied tax on R on the basis of interest on the average value of the loan. On appeal, the Danish court referred the questions whether Council Directive 69/335 Art.4(2)(b) applied to the amount of interest saved by the subsidiary and whether Art.10 precluded the levying of income tax on such a loan.

Held, that (1) Art.4(2)(b) of the Directive applied to an interest free loan the amount of interest received where a company benefited from such a loan, *Trave Schiffahrts GmbH & Co KG v. Finanzamt Kiel Nord* (C249/89) [1991] E.C.R. I-257 applied. As the Directive was intended to abolish indirect taxes, the harmonisation provided for by it did not extend to direct taxes, therefore Art.10 could not preclude the levying of income tax on an interest free loan granted to a subsidiary by a parent.

RICHARD FREDERIKSEN & CO A/S v. SKATTEMINISTERIET (C287/94) [1997] S.T.C. 264, CN Kakouris, ECJ.

1081. Investment companies—industrial and provident society—management of council housing stock—investment company for corporation tax purposes

[Income and Corporation Taxes Act 1988 s.130.]

An industrial and provident society which managed a council's housing stock was an investment company as the intention involved was to realise profit. The Crown appealed against a special commissioner's ruling that M, an industrial and provident society established to purchase and run the council's housing stock, was an investment company within the meaning of the Income and Corporation Taxes Act 1988 s.130 which was entitled to carry forward management expenses against income for corporation tax. M obtained private loans to purchase the stock and efficiency savings were made with a view to paying off all loans over 19 years and running at a profit thereafter. The issue for corporation tax purposes was whether M's business in running the properties with a view to making a profit was that of making investments.

Held, dismissing the appeal, that M was an investment company within s.130 although it was not a commercial company. The housing amounted to an investment because it was run with the intention of realising a profit. The object of providing social housing at affordable rents was not incompatible with the intention of making profits. Whether a company's business was that of an investment company within s.130 depended on the quality, purpose and nature of the company. The company's current activities were relevant but so were the circumstances in which its assets were obtained, the objects set out in the formal documents and the company's future plans. The issue was whether the company held assets to make profit from the business which it carried on or whether they were merely incidental to carrying on another business.

COOK (INSPECTOR OF TAXES) v. MEDWAY HOUSING SOCIETY LTD [1997] S.T.C. 90, Lightman, J., Ch D.

1082. Investment companies–profit arising on share disposals–no liability to tax where nature of business unchanged–New Zealand

R was an investment company. It was assessed to income tax on certain transactions on the footing that it had changed the nature of its business. At first instance, the evidence of R's chairman was accepted that it had not changed its general policy, but his decision was reversed by the Court of Appeal in New Zealand. R appealed.

Held, allowing the appeal, that the question was one of fact on which the judge was entitled to reach the conclusion he did on the evidence before him, *Californian Copper Syndicate Ltd v. Harris (Surveyor of Taxes)* (1904) 5 T.C. 159 applied.

RANGATIRA LTD v. INLAND REVENUE COMMISSIONER [1997] S.T.C. 47, Lord Nolan, PC.

1083. Mergers–jurisdiction of ECJ–Directive transposed as national law–interpretation by ECJ–validity of anti avoidance provisions–European Union

[Council Directive 90/434 on the common system of taxation applicable to mergers concerning companies of different Member States.]

L carried out a number of share transactions which she asked the Netherlands tax authorities to treat as a merger by exchange of shares thereby giving her a tax advantage. She appealed against the refusal of her application. The Netherlands court referred to the European Court of Justice for a preliminary ruling the questions whether the ECJ had jurisdiction to consider legislation applying to a local Netherlands situation which was aligned with Community law under Council Directive 90/434, and if so whether the operations in question constituted a merger by exchange of shares and whether provisions in the Netherlands law to counter tax evasion were valid.

Held, that (1) the ECJ had jurisdiction to interpret Community law at the request of the national court, although Community law did not directly apply to the instant case, where a Member State had chosen in implementing EC law to apply it to purely internal situations, *Kleinwort Benson Ltd v. Glasgow City Council (C346/93)* [1996] Q.B. 57, [1995] 2 C.L.Y. 4337 distinguished, and (2) anti-avoidance provisions must observe the principle of proportionality and must not undermine the aim pursued by the Directive. Article 2 did not limit the benefits of the Directive to mergers where from a financial and economic point of view the business of two companies was merged permanently into a single unit. Article 11 permitted anti-avoidance rules, but the rules should be applied by the national authorities upon examination of each individual case. A rule establishing a presumption of avoidance if the purpose of the transaction was not for valid commercial reasons would be permitted. However, a rule that excluded relief whenever the sole director of the acquired companies became sole director of the acquiring company, whether or not tax avoidance was in fact present, would contravene the principle of proportionality.

LEUR-BLOEM v. INSPECTEUR DER BELASTINGDIENST/ONDERNEMINGEN AMSTERDAM 2 (C28/95) [1997] All E.R. (EC) 738, GC Rodriguez Iglesias (President), ECJ.

1084. Profits–company profits

O, a Cayman Islands company, lent money through a company in the same group to borrowers in Hong Kong. It was assessed to tax on the basis that its profits were derived from Hong Kong. The Board of Review and the Court Appeal upheld O's appeal. The Commissioner appealed.

Held, allowing the appeal, that the only reasonable conclusion from the facts was that the profits of O arose from business transacted in Hong Kong through its associated company, *Inland Revenue Commissioner v. Hang Seng Bank Ltd* [1991] 1 A.C. 306, [1991] C.L.Y. 596 considered.

INLAND REVENUE COMMISSIONER v. ORION CARIBBEAN LTD (IN VOLUNTARY LIQUIDATION) [1997] S.T.C. 923, Lord Nolan, PC.

1085. Articles

ACT - a wasting asset? *(Hugh S.A. Macnair)*: Co. Acc. 1997, 136, 19-21. (Operation of advance corporation tax).

Basing tax on consolidated accounts *(Ian Barlow)*: Tax J. 1997, 400, 21-22. (Viability of use of consolidated accounts for determining group corporation tax liability where accounts fail to follow accepted taxation criteria and legal status of companies).

Company residence *(Lindsay Pentelow)*: Tax. P. 1997, Apr, 23-25. (Criteria for determination of residence for corporation tax purposes).

Corporate and government debt: more developments *(John Lindsay.)*: F.I.T.A.R. 1996, 1(11), 157-159. (Including tax relief for incidental costs of obtaining loan, borrowing by non-resident companies, interest falling out of charge to tax, stock lending and repos, double tax relief and interpretation of pre-trading interest).

Corporate debt - the rules for loss relief *(John Lindsay)*: F.I.T.A.R. 1997, 2(4), 66-68.

Corporate debt: Inland Revenue interpretations *(John Lindsay)*: F.I.T.A.R. 1997, 2(3), 51-52. (Corporate control issues arising on reorganisation following rule changes on tax treatment of corporate debt, scope of connected party measures, implications for breweries and conflict with ICTA s.417(9) loan provisions).

Corporate debt rules: one year on *(Simon Court)*: I.H.L. 1997, 47(Feb), 36-37. (Taxation regime created by 1996 Act as it affects funding of company acquisitions, tax avoidance issues and areas which Inland Revenue have clarified or amended).

Debt contracts: the interaction of FA1994 and FA1996 *(Roger Muray and Richard Williams)*: F.I.T.A.R. 1997, 2(2), 21-23. (Relationship between corporation tax provisions on forex, financial instruments and loan relationships, double tax rules and accounting on accruals or mark to market basis).

Get back *(Peter Rayney)*: Accountancy 1997, 120(1250), 80-81. (Changes introduced by the Finance (No.2) Act 1997 to tax loss reliefs for single companies, including restriction of loss carry back period to one year and transitional provisions).

Hybrid entities and financing structures: a view from the United Kingdom *(Jonathan S. Schwarz)*: B.I.F.D. 1997, 51(6), 265-270. (Domestic rules on classification of resident and non resident corporate entities and unincorporated associations, double tax provisions and tax treatment of dividends).

Interest discharged by the void? *(Robert Grierson)*: Tax. 1997, 138(3596), 654-655. (Liability to interest on unpaid tax where loans by close company to participators are repaid after end of accounting period and whether includes payments in breach of s.151 CA 1985).

Interesting times for treasury tax *(Duncan Whitecross)*: Tax J. 1997, 399, 11-13. (Effect of forex, financial instrument and corporate debt taxation rule changes on corporate investment, financing and cross-border transactions).

Intra group transfers *(Tony Foley)*: Tax J. 1997, 404, 9-10. (Interaction between TCGA s.171(2) and s.122(5) on post liquidation asset transfers within groups and capital reduction tax planning opportunities).

Investment companies: "tax privileges should not be taken for granted" *(Hugh S.A. Macnair)*: Co. Acc. 1997, 139, 23-24. (Corporation tax treatment of investment companies, including cases on test for determining whether business is investment company, relief for expenses and capital allowances).

New relationships *(Tim Palmer)*: T.P.T. 1997, 18(8), 57-59. (Corporation tax rules on loan relationships applicable to accounting periods ending after March 31, 1996).

Own shares or special dividends *(Adrian Rudd)*: Tax J. 1997, 392, 5, 7. (ACT treatment of intra group dividend payments following proposed Sch.7 rule change raises practical difficulties posed by foreign income dividend deeming provisions).

Schedule 7 Finance Act 1997: I.R.T.B. 1997, 29 (Jun), 429-434. (Inland Revenue guidance on deemed foreign income dividend rules which withdraw tax credits for certain purchases of own shares and special dividends, with examples).

Schedule 7, share buy-backs and special dividends *(Howard Nolan)*: Tax J. 1997, 398, 14-16. (Effect of foreign income deeming provisions on repurchases and dividend payments, with capital payment and share dividend planning options).

Special dividends: practical problems *(Robert Turnbull* and *Catherine Ghosh)*: Tax J. 1997, 389, 14-15. (Disproportionate effect of proposed special dividend rule changes for certain investors and companies, with alternatives based on purposive nature of dividend payments).

The taxation treatment of forward contracts and currency swaps *(John Lindsay)*: F.I.T.A.R. 1997, 2(2), 32-35. (Treatment of forward contracts and currency swaps as currency contracts under financial instruments and forex legislation, taking effect from start of first accounting period ending on or after March 23, 1995).

Trading status: does it matter? *(Daron H. Gunson)*: T.P.T. 1997, 18(13), 101-103. (Problems in determining whether company is trading company, investment company or inactive for purposes of completing corporation tax return and why correct categorisation is important).

What scope for tax planning? *(Brenda Coleman)*: Tax J. 1997, 403, 14-16. (Courts' approach to determining whether taxpayers entered transactions for purpose of avoidance and implications for application of FA 1996 Sch.9 Para.13 corporation tax rules on loan relationships).

Where credits are due *(Anne Redston)*: T.P.T. 1997, 18(17), 129-131. (How changes to withdraw tax credit repayments on dividends in force April 6, 1999 will affect individuals, including discretionary trusts, overseas residents and investors in pensions, unit trusts and PEPS).

CRIMINAL EVIDENCE

1086. Admissibility–appeals–fresh evidence–child witness–delay in lodging appeal

In March 1995 O was convicted of offences including buggery and indecent assault on a boy aged four years, and in May 1995 was sentenced to serve 12 months' detention in a young offender institution. The victim of the alleged crimes gave video evidence which included, inter alia, a statement that a young girl, N, was present on some of the occasions when the incidents were said to have taken place. N was not called to give evidence at the trial and the prosecution told the defence that, although she recalled being present at the relevant time and place, she could not remember anything happening. The defence did not seek to adjourn the trial so that N could be traced. O's parents obtained new solicitors and obtained an affidavit from N refuting any suggestion that she witnessed any indecent incidents. On July 24, 1995 N completed the appropriate appeal form, and this was sent together with N's affidavit to counsel with instructions to lodge an appeal. Despite requests for information nothing further occurred until a conference was held with O's mother in September 1995 and grounds of appeal were settled. Counsel stated that the appeal documents would be submitted to the court in the usual way. By December 1995 O had completed his sentence and counsel had not advised on the progress of the appeal. In January 1996 O's solicitors wrote asking for advice as to whether the appeal papers had been lodged. No information was forthcoming, despite numerous requests, until July 1, 1996, when the solicitors wrote threatening to remove all work from the chambers in question. The appeal papers were finally lodged on July 9, 1996.

Held, allowing the appeal, that N's evidence was plainly admissible evidence. Although she should have been called as a defence witness, it was understandable that she was not. Having heard her evidence, the Court of

Appeal was not prepared to reject it, and it might well have had a significant effect on the outcome of the trial. N's evidence would have undermined the prosecution case, in that it would have demonstrated that the evidence for the complainant might in a significant respect have been unreliable. Having regard to all the evidence available to the jury and N's evidence, the convictions could not be regarded as safe. Further, having regard to the delay and the length of time that had passed since the events were alleged to have taken place, and the age of the main witnesses to those events, it was not possible for the court to order a retrial.

R. v. O (A JUVENILE),Trans. Ref: 9604716 X3, May 1, 1997, Judge, L.J., CA (Crim Div).

1087. **Admissibility–appeals–fresh evidence–details given by prosecution witness to victim support counsellor–different version given in evidence**

[Criminal Procedure Act 1865 s.4; Criminal Appeal Act 1968 s.23.]

S applied for leave to adduce fresh evidence in an appeal against conviction of attempting to cause grievous bodily harm with intent, affray and making off without payment, for which he was given concurrent sentences of two years', nine months' and 28 days' imprisonment respectively, all suspended for two years. The convictions followed an incident involving S and F, a taxi driver, early on July 14, 1995, and in respect of which F made a police statement later the same day. Ten days later, F gave a different version of events to R in the course of a victim support counselling session, and S sought leave for R's evidence to be admitted under the Criminal Appeal Act 1968 s.23 and the Criminal Procedure Act 1865 s.4, on the ground that the new evidence rebutted F's prosecution evidence by contradicting F's evidence in chief given at the trial.

Held, allowing the application to adduce fresh evidence but dismissing the appeal, that although the new evidence was admissible as being capable of belief under the 1968 Act s.23, it could not be shown to be evidence that would have led the jury to return a not guilty verdict. Whereas the new evidence tended to support that given by S, the jury had shown that they believed F, which followed the details given in his police statement. The account given by F to R occurred in the course of a counselling session in circumstances where accuracy and detail were not a primary concern. In addition, R had not approached S's solicitor until some months after the counselling session, during which time he could have confused the details given by F with newspaper reports, conversations with other people or even local gossip. These factors led to the conclusion that a jury would have felt there was a large question mark over the accuracy of R's evidence which would not have led them to cease being satisfied that F had told the truth.

R. v. SARICH (PHILIP),Trans. Ref: 96 03728 W4, December 16, 1996, Evans, L.J., CA (Crim Div).

1088. **Admissibility–appeals–fresh evidence–diminished responsibility**

[Homicide Act 1957 s.2; Criminal Appeal Act 1968 s.23; Mental Health Act 1983 s.37, s.41.]

A had been convicted of murder. She was later diagnosed by a consultant forensic psychiatrist as having been suffering from a depressive illness prior to the commission of the crimes for which she had been convicted, and therefore that she should have been detained under the Mental Health Act 1983 s.37 and s.41. That report was subsequently used as a basis for an application to appeal against conviction. An application was made under the Criminal Appeal Act 1968 s.23 for expert psychiatric evidence.

Held, dismissing the appeal, that A had not tendered any evidence herself, and that raised the questions whether the necessary factual basis for the provisions of expert psychiatric evidence had been laid, and why no defence of diminished responsibility had been raised at the trial. Whether there was any abnormality of mind, within the Homicide Act 1957 s.2, at the material time of the commission of the offence was a matter of fact for the jury. At that time, there were no such facts on which the jury could have relied. Parties to a civil or a criminal trial must raise their case at trial and not raise alternative grounds in an appellate court. No evidence had been placed before the court as to why the defence of diminished responsibility had not been raised at trial. No factual basis had been provided for an argument based on amnesia. The court could find no basis for treating the jury's verdict as having been unsafe.

R. v. ARNOLD (1996) 31 B.M.L.R. 24, Hobhouse, L.J., CA (Crim Div).

1089. **Admissibility—appeals—fresh evidence—discrepancy between expert witness statement and evidence given at trial not material non disclosure**

[Criminal Appeal Act 1968 s.23(2)(d).]

S appealed against conviction of murder on the grounds that he had acted in either self defence or provocation or otherwise lacked the requisite mens rea for murder. S and his victim, M, had fallen asleep after drinking alcohol. S stated that he killed M having woken up to find M attacking him. Evidence showed that, although M had a drink problem, he was not aggressive when drunk and was difficult to wake after drinking. S contended that he had stabbed M in the throat, eyes and ear, and forensic evidence showed that a time interval had elapsed between the first stab wounds to M's body and the fatal wound to his head. Expert evidence for the Crown was that the interval between the first and last blows was "some minutes", but this was given as "approximately 10 minutes" during the evidence in chief. However, the Crown's expert was not cross examined as to the validity of the 10 minutes estimate, and S submitted that this should now be tested on appeal, as the revision amounted to a material non disclosure.

Held, dismissing the appeal, that acceptance of the less precise, "some minutes" by defence counsel was reasonable, given the fact that a shorter time period between wounds was beneficial to S. There was no material non disclosure by the Crown. The evidence could not be admitted as fresh evidence on appeal under the Criminal Appeal Act 1968 s.23(2)(d), given the obligation on S to advance his entire case before the jury at first instance.

R. v. SHARMA (ACHRU RAM), Trans. Ref: 9508015/Y4, October 11, 1996, McCowan, L.J., CA (Crim Div).

1090. **Admissibility—appeals—fresh evidence—murder—diminished responsibility—psychiatric evidence of battered woman's syndrome**

[Homicide Act 1957 s.2; Criminal Appeal Act 1968 s.23.]

H appealed against her conviction for murder after she admitted stabbing her abusive and alcoholic partner to death in the course of an argument. H sought to admit in evidence, under the Criminal Appeal Act 1968 s.23, two psychiatrists' reports obtained since her trial in 1992 stating that at the time of the killing H was suffering from battered woman's syndrome, which could form the basis of a defence of diminished responsibility under the Homicide Act 1957 s.2. H submitted that it was not until 1994 that battered woman's syndrome was added to the standard British classification of mental diseases and at the time of her trial it was not widely recognised. The Crown relied on another psychiatrist's report to the effect that, whilst H might have been suffering from battered woman's syndrome, her symptoms were not severe enough to support a claim of diminished responsibility. The Crown further argued that H's evidence breached the 1968 Act s.23(2)(d) in that no reasonable explanation had been given for failure to adduce the evidence at trial.

Held, allowing the appeal, that it was right to admit, in evidence, the doctors' reports submitted by both H and the Crown. Consideration of the material submitted led to the conclusion that the fact that battered woman's syndrome was not included in the British classification until 1994 was of some significance, although at the time of H's trial the condition was certainly not unknown. The conviction would therefore be quashed and a retrial ordered.

R. v. HOBSON (KATHLEEN), *The Times*, June 25, 1997, Rose, L.J., CA (Crim Div).

1091. Admissibility—audio tape recordings—murder—victim's emergency telephone call—tape played to jury after retirement

H appealed against conviction of murder on the grounds that the jury having retired should not have been allowed to hear a tape which had not been played in evidence. H's defences were self defence, lack of intent and provocation. The prosecution adduced evidence of a taped emergency telephone call made by the victim. The tape was not played to the jury but an agreed transcript was used instead. In giving evidence, an expert testified that he thought there was a second voice on the tape saying the words "come on". Those words were not included in the transcript of the call. The jury retired and asked to hear the tape.

Held, dismissing the appeal, that in general there could be no objection to a jury hearing a tape to establish tone of voice. It was a matter for the judge whether or not it was fair for the tape to be played after the jury retired. On the facts, where the prosecution had agreed to the use of a transcript, the jurors should not have been allowed to form their own view on hearing the tape after they retired. However, it was inconceivable that the jury's consideration of the contents of the tape could have made any difference to the verdict.

R. v. HAGAN (SEAN) [1997] 1 Cr. App. R. 464, Pill, L.J., CA (Crim Div).

1092. Admissibility—bank accounts—supply of drugs

E appealed against conviction of possession with intent to supply of 6.61 grammes of heroin for which he was given a custodial sentence of four years. E contended that the admission of evidence that he had over £6,000 in a bank account was wrong and that the trial judge had confounded matters in his summing up and by replying to a jury question that they could not see the bank books.

Held, allowing the appeal, that the conviction was unsafe and was quashed and a conviction of possession simple substituted, for which a custodial term of six months was appropriate. The authorities showed that money held either as cash sums or in accounts could be relevant to whether drugs were intended for supply to others, but in the instant case the evidence was not admitted to counter an explanation for E's possession of large sums of cash, and, if relevant at all, it could only be evidence of past drug dealing and not present active dealing, *R. v. Grant (Stephen)* [1996] 1 Cr. App. R. 73, [1996] 1 C.L.Y. 1367 followed and *R. v. Gordon (Stafford George)* [1995] 2 Cr. App. R. 61, [1996] 1 C.L.Y. 1396 considered.

R. v. EVANS (MARTIN PAUL),Trans. Ref: 97/0754/Z5, July 11,1997, Brooke, L.J., CA (Crim Div).

1093. Admissibility—breath tests—intoximeter statement—computer clock displaying wrong time

[Police and Criminal Evidence Act 1984 s.69(1).]

A malfunction of an intoximeter was relevant only where it was material to the accuracy of the statement to be adduced in court on a drink driving charge, and the malfunctioning of the computer clock was insufficient to render the evidence inadmissible. The DPP appealed against a decision quashing M's conviction for driving with excessive alcohol on the grounds that the computer clock in the intoximeter used at the police station had been displaying the wrong time and therefore the statement produced by the computer was inadmissible under the Police and Criminal Evidence Act 1984 s.69(1).

Held, allowing the appeal, that (1) if it was accepted that the intoximeter's computer was not operating properly within the meaning of s.69, the question was whether the malfunction was "such as to affect the production of the document or the accuracy of its contents". Section 69 was only concerned with the proper operation and function of a computer and not the accuracy of the information supplied to the computer or the truth of the statement it produced. In order for a statement to be admissible under s.69, all that was required was that the computer had correctly processed, stored and retrieved the information it was given and malfunctions which did not affect these processes were not relevant. Even if a relevant malfunction was established, a statement would only be inadmissible if there were reasonable grounds for believing that the error was material to the accuracy of the statement to be adduced in court, and (2) in any case, it was doubtful whether the malfunctioning of the computer clock could be said to prevent the computer operating properly or whether the computer's clock could be said to form part of the computer for the purposes of s.69.

DPP v. McKEOWN (SHARON); DPP v. JONES (CHRISTOPHER) [1997] 1 W.L.R. 295, Lord Hoffmann, HL.

1094. Admissibility–confessions–allegation of police mistreatment at time of disputed oral confession

Held, that the principles laid down in *Ajodha v. Trinidad and Tobago* [1982] A.C. 204, [1981] C.L.Y. 415 in relation to written statements applied equally to oral admissions. Thus, where the prosecution claimed that a defendant had made an oral admission, but the defendant disputed that such an admission had been made and complained of police mistreatment either before or at the time of the alleged admission, two issues, which were not mutually exclusive, arose; (1) whether, assuming that the admission was made, the evidence was inadmissible on the grounds of being involuntary, which was a question for the judge, and (2) whether, if the judge ruled the evidence was admissible, the admission had actually been made, which was a question for the jury.

THONGJAI v. THE QUEEN; LEE CHUN-KONG v. QUEEN, THE, *The Times*, August 5, 1997, Lord Hutton, PC.

1095. Admissibility–confessions–failure to record incriminating statement in custody record

H appealed against conviction for murder on the ground that the Police and Criminal Evidence Act 1984 Code C was breached by not entering in the custody record a comment he made, admitting stabbing the victim. The police officer recorded the comment in his notebook which H signed.

Held, dismissing the appeal, that there was no specific requirement that comments such as those made by H should be entered in the custody record, and his conviction was not unsafe.

R. v. HESLOP [1996] Crim. L.R. 730, Hutchison, L.J., CA (Crim Div).

1096. Admissibility–confessions–mentally disabled defendant–appropriate adult absent from police interview

[Police and Criminal Evidence Act 1984 s.76(2)(b).]

Held, that the court should hear evidence of what happened at a police interview and who was present when determining whether a confession made by a mentally disabled defendant in the absence of an appropriate adult was reliable. Such evidence should not be excluded as it was relevant to the issue of admissibility. On hearing the evidence, a court would be in a position to determine, under the Police and Criminal Evidence Act 1984 s.76(2)(b), whether the absence of an appropriate adult rendered the confession unreliable.

DPP v. CORNISH, *The Times*, January 27, 1997, Kennedy, L.J., QBD.

1097. Admissibility–confessions–pattern of police misconduct in West Midlands Serious Crime Squad

C appealed against convictions of conspiracy to rob, taking a vehicle without lawful authority and handling stolen goods. The case against him was dependent on admissions made in the course of police interviews which C submitted could not be relied upon in view of the background of discreditable behaviour and practices employed by the West Midlands Serious Crime Squad which had investigated the offences.

Held, allowing the appeals, that (1) it was unnecessary for the court to hear similar fact evidence of the pattern of discreditable behaviour of officers of the West Midlands Serious Crime Squad, and (2) having regard to the circumstances of this case, there was material which could properly have been put to certain of the police officers involved in the matter. In view of the fact that the case against C was based on his admissions alone and the doubts which had been cast on the honesty of the police investigation the convictions were unsafe.

R. v. CLANCY (THOMAS) [1997] Crim. L.R. 290, Pill, L.J., CA (Crim Div).

1098. Admissibility–cross examination–evidence suggesting dishonest disposition–no application for leave to admit such evidence

[Criminal Evidence Act 1898 s.1 (f).]

C appealed against conviction on five counts of obtaining property by deception, for which he was sentenced to concurrent eight months' imprisonment on each count. During the trial prosecuting counsel questioned C on collateral matters which the defence challenged on the basis that there was a suggestion of criminality. The prosecution did not seek leave to question C in terms of the Criminal Evidence Act 1898 s.1. Defence counsel eventually intervened, claiming that the line of questioning suggested criminality and that the jury should be discharged. The recorder allowed the questioning to stand, and stated, in his summing up, that all witnesses are equal prior to questioning, and that it was for them to ascertain credibility of witnesses following crossexamination. The question was whether the cross examination was permissible and whether the convictions against C could stand.

Held, allowing the appeal, that (1) cross examination of a defendant designed to show a dishonest disposition, which did not arise naturally from the evidence before the jury, came within s.1 (f) of the 1898 Act; (2) the leave of the court is required before such cross examination takes place, and may only be given if the provisions of s.1 (f) are satisfied and (3) where leave is granted, the judge and prosecutor must use discretion in limiting the questioning so as not to make unfair suggestions of propensity, or to inquire, at length, into matters of little relevance. The court cannot accept irregular questioning where leave has not been sought on the basis that, if sought, leave would have been granted. The cross examination had little relevance, and was likely to discredit C, so it did not come within permissible questioning, *R. v. Wilson* [1991] 2 N.Z.L.R. 707, [1991] C.L.Y. 669, *R. v. Funderburk* (1990) 90 Cr. App. R. 466, [1990] C.L.Y. 794 and *R. v. McLeod (Hartgeald)* [1995] 1 Cr. App. R. 591, [1995] 1 C.L.Y. 1026 considered. The recorder had failed in his summing up to instruct the jury that the cross examination should not be treated by them as evidence of propensity.

R. v. CARTER (COLIN MARK) (1997) 161 J.P. 207, Sedley, J., CA (Crim Div).

1099. Admissibility–cross examination–previous convictions–codefendants–test for determining whether defendant had given evidence against codefendant

[Criminal Evidence Act 1898 s.1.]

C appealed against her conviction of robbery, in respect of which her codefendant, A, was also convicted. The victim alleged that she had been robbed jointly by C, A and L, but C gave evidence to the effect that, whilst she had been in the company of A and L, she was not present at the time of the robbery, but had seen A and L emerge from where the robbery took place. A stated in evidence that she had been a mere bystander and the robbery was carried out by C and L alone. The issue was whether the judge had been correct to allow cross examination of C about her previous convictions under the Criminal Evidence Act 1898 s.1 (f) (iii) on the grounds that C had given evidence against another person charged with the same offence.

Held, dismissing the appeal, that in determining whether C had "given evidence against any other person charged with the same offence" within the meaning of s.1 (f) (iii), the crucial question was whether the defendant's evidence, if accepted, damaged in a significant way the defence of the codefendant. If there was no issue between the Crown and the codefendant with regard to any factual matter, the defendant's evidence would not damage the codefendant's defence if it was to the same effect. Equally, if the defendant's evidence supported the Crown with regard to a noncontentious issue, the evidence was not material for the purposes of s.1 (f) (iii). However, if the defendant's evidence supported the Crown on a disputed issue between the Crown and the codefendant with regard to proof of the commission of the offence, such evidence would be damaging to the codefendant's defence so as to satisfy the statutory provision, *Murdoch v. Taylor* [1965] A.C. 574, [1965] C.L.Y. 788, *R. v. Bruce (Steven)* [1975] 1 W.L.R. 1252, [1975] C.L.Y. 558 and *R. v. Varley* [1982] 2 All E.R. 519, [1982] C.L.Y. 556 considered.

R. v. CRAWFORD (CHARISSE), *The Times*, June 10, 1997, Lord Bingham of Cornhill, L.C.J., CA (Crim Div).

1100. Admissibility–cross examination–previous convictions improperly admitted

[Criminal Evidence Act 1898 s.1 (A) (ii).]

S appealed against conviction of possessing an offensive weapon on the ground that the judge erred in exercising his discretion under the Criminal Evidence Act 1898 s.1 (A) (ii) allowing cross-examination of S's previous convictions, which involved other offences concerning offensive weapons.

Held, allowing the appeal, that the judge failed to weigh up the prejudicial effect on S of admitting evidence of his particular convictions, and failed to properly direct the jury regarding the evidential value of previous convictions.

R. v. SHOWERS [1996] Crim. L.R. 739, Swinton Thomas, L.J., CA (Crim Div).

1101. Admissibility–documentary evidence–computer output

[Police and Criminal Evidence Act 1984 s.69; Computer Misuse Act 1990 s.1.]

Y appealed by way of case stated against the decision of a metropolitan stipendiary magistrate to allow the prosecution to reopen its case in order to adduce certificates evidencing the proper functioning of certain computers for the purposes of the Police and Criminal Evidence Act 1984 s.69. Y was charged with securing unauthorised access to computer files comprising security software from a computer belonging to Marks & Spencer and disseminating that confidential information, contrary to the Computer Misuse Act 1990 s.1. The prosecution produced documentary evidence from computers, the admissibility of which was not challenged by Y during the course of the prosecution case. However, Y made a submission of no case to answer on the basis that the computer evidence was inadmissible because the prosecution had not produced certificates as required by s.69 and Sch.3 Part II of the 1984 Act. The magistrate allowed an application to reopen and adduce a certificate in existence but omitted from the evidence through oversight and, at an adjourned hearing, certificates not in existence at the time of the original submission in relation to other computers.

Held, dismissing the appeal, that although there was no duty incumbent upon counsel to raise the question of admissibility during the course of the prosecution case, such a tactic as was used here was not to be encouraged. The magistrate had been entitled to exercise his discretion as he did and counsel's failure to raise the issue at an earlier stage was a matter which might properly result in any discretion being exercised against him. The test was whether the magistrate had exercised his discretion unreasonably so as to create a real risk of injustice, *R. v. Francis (Peter Robert)* (1990) 91 Cr. App. R. 271, [1991] C.L.Y. 634 and *R. v. Munnery (Vincent)* (1992) 94 Cr. App. R. 164, [1993] C.L.Y. 898 applied. Re-admission of the certificates did not affect the overall fairness of the trial and an adjournment to challenge the recently obtained certificates had been offered to, and refused by, the defence.

YEARLY v. CROWN PROSECUTION SERVICE, Trans. Ref: CO-3328-96, March 21, 1997, Blofeld, J., QBD.

1102. Admissibility—doli incapax—evidence of previous incident to rebut presumption

[Sexual Offences Act 1956 s.14(1).]

Held, that evidence that a child of 12 had previously been involved in an incident which constituted an indecent assault, but for which no prosecution had been brought, could be admitted where a charge was brought against the child under the Sexual Offences Act 1956 s.14(1) in order to rebut the presumption of doli incapax by demonstrating that the child knew that such conduct was wrong.

G (A MINOR) v. DPP, *The Times*, November 27, 1997, Gage, J., QBD.

1103. Admissibility—drug offences—coded accounts admitted as course of dealing—specimen counts

[Criminal Justice Act 1991 s.2(2), s.31(2).]

Following B's arrest for drug offences, a large number of pieces of paper were found at premises connected to B upon which he had written coded notes. A police officer, H, gave evidence at B's trial that his interpretation of the notes suggested that B had been involved in the supply of drugs on hundreds of occasions. Counts one to three in the indictment were specimen counts covering the whole course of B's supply of drugs. B sought leave to appeal on the ground that the evidence of offences other than those charged in the indictment could not, following the enactment of the Criminal Justice Act 1991 s.2(2)(a) and s.31(2), be adduced as evidence of specimen counts. It was further argued that the evidence given by H did not constitute expert evidence and should not have been admitted since it went to the issue the jury had to try. B also sought leave to appeal against sentence on the ground that he should only have been sentenced in respect of offences specified in the indictment and of which he was convicted.

Held, dismissing the applications, that (1) the 1991 Act did not preclude the use of specimen counts. The inclusion in the indictment of counts one to three as specimen counts, followed by the admission of evidence of documents in support of the prosecution case, adhered to well established practice and in no way produced any unfairness to B; (2) it was proper that the jury were given assistance, by someone with a knowledge of drug trafficking, on the interpretation of the notes to prevent speculation. H, as a police officer with substantial experience in investigating drug offences, had the expertise to give the evidence he did. It was correct that the judge, who gave an appropriate direction to the jury, admitted the evidence of H, and (3) the sentence imposed by the trial judge was not manifestly excessive.

Observed, disapproving of *R. v. Clark (Raymond Dennis)* [1996] 2 Cr. App. R. 282, [1996] 1 C.L.Y. 1944 that the 1991 Act s.2(2)(a) and s.31(2) references to offences and associated offences included specimen counts and it was therefore strongly arguable that the court should adhere to previous practice of sentencing on specimen counts.

R. v. BARRY (JOHN JAMES), Trans. Ref: 95/7817/W2, July 30, 1996, Jowitt, J., CA (Crim Div).

1104. Admissibility—drug offences—drugs paraphernalia and money—evidence of intention to supply

W and F pleaded guilty to possession of drugs and were found guilty of possession with intent to supply for which they received sentences of five years' imprisonment. A police raid on a flat occupied by W and F found, among other paraphernalia concerned with the use of drugs, a number of empty plastic bags, a plastic bag containing 0.18 grammes of heroin, a bag containing 4.4 grammes of heroin, a pager, a mobile phone and a small quantity of money totalling £135. The Crown contended that these items provided evidence of drug dealing, and they were admitted as evidence. W and F appealed, arguing that the money, plastic bags, pager and mobile phone should not have been admitted, and that, having admitted them, the judge did not properly direct the jury that evidence indicating past dealing should have been distinguished from evidence demonstrating ongoing dealing.

Held, dismissing the appeal, that (1) the pager, mobile phone and plastic bags were clearly admissible as part of the paraphernalia of drug dealing; (2) although in admitting such a small sum of money the judge was acting at the limit of his discretion, the money was admissible in the context of the prosecution case which was based around the defendant's intentions and past actions with respect to a larger consignment of drugs; (3) in accordance with *R. v. Grant (Stephen)* [1996] 1 Cr. App. R. 73, [1996] 1 C.L.Y. 1367 the judge had directed that evidence of past dealing was not probative, and (4) in excluding prior dealing in the same consignment of drugs from the concept of past dealing the judge had not erred as the jury were entitled to take the view that such evidence amounted to evidence of a current intention to supply.

R. v. WILKINSON; R. v. FRASER, Trans. Ref: 9700349W2, 9700870W2, August 7, 1997, Potter, L.J., CA (Crim Div).

1105. Admissibility–drugs paraphernalia–jury directions

Held, that, where a sheet of jottings was admitted in evidence as drugs paraphernalia at the trial of a defendant charged with possessing drugs with intent to supply, the trial judge should have taken particular care to direct the jury to consider whether the material was relevant to a future intention to supply as well as to past incidents of drug dealing. The failure to direct the jury on how they should deal with the documentary evidence was a material non direction.

R. v. LOVELOCK (WILLIAM), *The Times*, June 5, 1997, Ognall, J., CA (Crim Div).

1106. Admissibility–evidence of interview by headteacher investigating assault on pupil was admissible even though PACE Codes of Practice had not been adhered to

[Police and Criminal Evidence Act 1984 s.67(9).]

Held, that, since a headteacher who investigated an assault on a pupil was not a person "charged with the duty of investigating offences or charging offenders" under the Police and Criminal Evidence Act 1984 s.67(9), evidence of an interview conducted by the headteacher was admissible even though the Codes of Practice had not been adhered to.

DPP v. G (DUTY TO INVESTIGATE), *The Times*, November 24, 1997, Gage, J., QBD.

1107. Admissibility–evidence of previous acquittal

[Drug Trafficking Act 1994 s.42, s.43.]

In 1991 T had been charged with involvement in the importation of Class B drugs, but the case was dismissed when the prosecution offered no evidence against him. In 1995, T was stopped by Customs and Excise officers at Luton airport whilst boarding a plane to Spain, and was found to be carrying £12,500 cash. The money was seized under the Drug Trafficking Act 1994 s.42, and forfeiture proceedings followed, for which C sought to lead evidence of the 1991 charge under s.43 of the 1994 Act. The evidence was ruled to be inadmissible and a differently constituted bench dismissed the forfeiture proceedings. By way of stated case the court was asked to decide whether the finding regarding the admissibility of the evidence had been correct.

Held, that the evidence of the previous incident was admissible. Whilst a person cannot be retried on a charge for which he has been acquitted, C were not precluded from relying on evidence from the 1991 incident by virtue of the fact that T had been acquitted of the charge. No estoppel arose from the acquittal. The standard of proof required in the forfeiture proceedings was civil, *DPP v. Humphrys* [1977] A.C. 1, [1976] C.L.Y. 488 and *Hunter v. Chief Constable of the West Midlands Police* [1982] A.C. 529, [1982] C.L.Y. 2382 followed.

CUSTOMS AND EXCISE COMMISSIONERS v. T, Staughton, L.J., QBD.

1108. Admissibility—guilty pleas

[Police and Criminal Evidence Act 1984 s.74, s.78.]

KM and NM appealed against convictions of the rape of a 16 year old girl, who had been unable to consent by reason of being affected by drink. M contended that the trial judge had erred in admitting, under the Police and Criminal Evidence Act 1984 s.74 and s.78, evidence that L, a third coaccused, had admitted his own rape of the girl between the two alleged rapes, during the same evening.

Held, allowing the appeal, quashing the convictions and ordering retrials, that the trial judge had erred by admitting the evidence and holding that it was relevant to the issue of consent, since it was highly prejudicial and the basis of L's plea had not been revealed. There were several possibilities: that L had known the victim had not consented, that he had been reckless as to her consent, that he had known that she was so intoxicated that she was incapable of consenting, or that he had known she had withheld consent to him alone. It was noted that the sexual intercourse with NM had taken place before L's rape and about an hour had elapsed between the first and last acts of intercourse, *R. v. Robertson (Malcolm)* (1987) 85 Cr. App. R. 304, [1987] C.L.Y. 562 and *R. v. Boyson* [1991] Crim. L.R. 274, [1991] C.L.Y. 750 followed, *R. v. Skinner* [1995] Crim. L.R. 805, [1996] 1 C.L.Y. 1319 considered.

R. v. MANZUR (NANAH); R. v. MAHMOOD (KHALID) [1997] 1 Cr. App. R. 414, Bracewell, J., CA (Crim Div).

1109. Admissibility—guilty pleas—conspiracy—exclusion of evidence as unfairly prejudicial

[Police and Criminal Evidence Act 1984 s.74, s.78.]

B was charged with conspiracy to burgle along with codefendants C, D and E. Prior to trial C, D and E pleaded guilty. The prosecution applied to use the guilty pleas of the co-defendants in opening the case before the jury. The defendant argued that following *R. v. Manzur (Nanah)* [1997] 1 Cr. App. R. 414, [1997] C.L.Y. 1108, the judge must apply a two stage test when considering such an application: (1) he must determine that the codefendants' pleas were relevant to an issue in the proceedings, and (2) if they were, to consider the effect of their admission on the fairness of the proceedings under the Police and Criminal Evidence Act 1984 s.78. It was submitted by the Crown, and accepted by the defence, that the guilty pleas were prima facie admissible under s.74, as relevant to an issue in the proceedings, ie. the existence of a conspiracy. But it was argued that the fact that all codefendants had pleaded guilty would drive the jury to the conclusion that this last remaining defendant must also be guilty of conspiracy and thereby deprive the defendant of a fair trial.

Held, refusing the Crown's application and ruling the pleas inadmissible, this was not a case which could be brought within the ratio decidendi of *R. v. O'Connor* (1987) 85 Cr. App. R. 298, [1988] C.L.Y. 549 in which the guilty plea to conspiracy of one defendant was inadmissible against the other. A guilty plea to conspiracy in those circumstances was excluded under s.78, because the jury would otherwise be presented with the logical necessity that the defendant had also to be a party to the agreement, since the first defendant must have conspired with somebody. However, where all co-defendants but one had pleaded guilty to a charge involving conspiracy, then the prejudicial effect of those pleas upon the remaining defendant outweighed their probative value and ought to be excluded under s.78.

R. v. BANFORD (TERENCE), July 11, 1997, Judge not specified, Crown Court (Chester). [*Ex rel.* Royston Harlow Delaney, Barrister, Young Street Chambers, Manchester].

1110. Admissibility—handling stolen goods—evidence of further items not proven as stolen

I appealed against conviction of handling stolen goods that were found in a cellar beneath the public house of which he was manager. I contended that the admission of a list of 29 further items found in the cellar, but not proven to be stolen, was highly prejudicial and should not have been admitted.

Held, allowing the appeal, that the conviction was unsafe. Although the evidence was strictly admissible, it had little probative value. On the other hand, it had a highly prejudicial effect, which was not palliated by the directions given in the summing up.

R. v. IRWIN (THOMAS), Trans. Ref: 9606357 X2, October 29, 1996, Roch, L.J., CA (Crim Div).

1111. Admissibility–hearsay evidence–admissibility of computer printouts in extradition proceedings

See EXTRADITION: R. v. Governor of Brixton Prison, *ex p.* Levin. §2418

1112. Admissibility–hearsay evidence–codefendant's actions and declarations given in evidence against appellant

AM, GM and S were convicted of drug related offences in 1995. Appealing against their conviction, it was contended, inter alia, that the judge had wrongly exercised his discretion in admitting evidence of actions and conversations of a co-accused, which had not occurred in AM's presence. Furthermore, the co-accused had absconded before trial and could not be cross examined.

Held, dismissing the appeals, that the acts and declarations were in the course and pursuance of the common purpose and since there was independent evidence which proved the existence of a conspiracy or a joint enterprise, then the evidence was properly admitted, *R. v. Gray (David John)* [1995] 2 Cr. App. R. 100, [1994] C.L.Y. 673 considered.

Observed, R. v. Gray was authority primarily for the proposition that the common law exception to the hearsay rule could not be applied to cases where individual defendants are charged with separate substantive offences and terms of a common enterprise are not proved or were ill defined. It did not narrow the common law exception to the hearsay rule.

R. v. MURRAY (ANTHONY JOHN LEE); R. v. MORGAN (GERALD PATRICK); R. v. SHERIDAN (PAUL JAMES) [1997] 2 Cr. App. R. 136, Otton, L.J., CA (Crim Div).

1113. Admissibility–hearsay evidence–confessions–codefendant's unofficial confession to police was admissible at instance of defendant

M appealed against the dismissal of her appeal against conviction of the murder of H in a joint trial in which her accomplice, Q, was convicted of manslaughter. At the trial, M claimed that it was Q who had murdered H, but before the trial M had allegedly made voluntary statements to police officers to the effect that it was her and not Q who had committed the murder. The circumstances in which the statements were made meant that they were inadmissible as evidence for the Crown, but the trial judge had allowed Q to adduce the evidence in support of his defence. The question for the court was whether admission of such evidence contravened the rule against hearsay.

Held, dismissing the appeal, that a defendant should be permitted to cross-examine a co-accused about a previous inconsistent confession provided that the confession was relevant to the defendant's own defence. The defendant should also be able to cross-examine the witnesses to whom the confession was made provided that the material affected his defence and was given voluntarily. If the statements were relevant to either the facts in issue or to credibility, then they were admissible at the instance of the defendant, as a defendant had an absolute right to lead all relevant evidence in his defence and the court had no discretion to exclude such evidence on the grounds that it might incriminate a co-defendant or because it had been obtained by unfair or improper means.

R. v. MYERS (MELANIE) [1997] 3 W.L.R. 552, Lord Slynn of Hadley, HL.

1114. Admissibility—hearsay evidence—witness statements—no cross examination of witness abroad—unfairness to the accused

[Criminal Justice Act 1987 s.9(11); Criminal Justice Act 1988 s.23, s.26; European Convention on Human Rights 1950 Art.6(3).]

G controlled companies which, as a result of false documents, were lent far greater sums by a bank than the regulatory authorities would otherwise have permitted. He was charged with conspiracy to account falsely and defraud. G denied the allegations and asserted that any wrongdoing by officers of the companies or the bank was outside his knowledge and done without his consent. At a preparatory hearing the prosecution sought to adduce, pursuant to the Criminal Justice Act 1988 s.23 and s.26, the statement of the applicant's brother in law, C, who claimed to have acted as the applicant's general assistant. C was outside the UK and was unwilling to return to give evidence in person. The defence argued that C was to be regarded as an accomplice whose evidence was unreliable and should not be admitted where it could not be tested in cross examination. The judge concluded that the admission of C's statement would not result in unfairness to the accused and ruled it admissible. G applied under the Criminal Justice Act 1987 s.9(11) for leave to appeal against that ruling on the grounds, inter alia, that although the trial judge was bound by *R. v. Cole* (1990) 90 Cr. App. R. 478, [1990] C.L.Y. 836, the Court of Appeal was not so bound and should overrule that decision because of its effect on the privilege against self incrimination.

Held, refusing the application, that the language of s.26(ii) was plain and its purpose clear, that (1) in considering the interests of justice regard was to be had to the risk of unfairness to the accused; (2) the possibilities of controversion were wide, including cross examining or calling other witnesses or by putting the statement maker's credibility in issue, and was not limited to the accused himself giving evidence, and (3) the right to silence was not abrogated even though it might be more difficult to exercise. Further, there was no breach of the European Convention on Human Rights Art.6(3)d.

R. v. GOKAL (ABBAS); *sub nom.* R. v. GOKAL (ABAS) [1997] 2 Cr. App. R. 266, Ward, L.J., CA (Crim Div).

1115. Admissibility—hearsay evidence—witness statements—witness in state of fear—statement not whole truth

[Magistrates Courts Act 1980 s.6(1); Criminal Justice Act 1988 s.23, s.26;]

H applied for an order of certiorari to quash an order by the justices committing him for trial at the Crown Court under the Magistrates Courts Act 1980 s.6(1). Following an armed robbery H was charged with conspiracy to rob. A, whose car had been used in the commission of the offences, made a written statement to the police that he had allowed his car to be used because he was in fear of H. On the day of the committal hearing A, who was the subject of a warrant compelling him to attend, was seen by a custody officer to be in a state of fear at the thought of having to give evidence. At that time A mentioned that his statement was not the whole truth. The CPS subsequently made a successful application to the justices to read A's statement at the hearing in terms of the Criminal Justice Act 1988 s.23. H contended that the justices were wrong to admit the statement without investigating the condition of A. In addition it was argued that in light of A's admission that his statement was not the whole truth the justices should not have exercised their discretion in terms of s.26 without assessing the quality of the statement.

Held, dismissing the application, that the justices properly admitted the statement in terms of s.23. The justices were entitled to have regard to the reported observation made of A when he mentioned that the statement was not the whole truth. At that time A was in a state of considerable anxiety making any further investigation impossible. The justices adequately considered the matter and were right to be impressed by the plausibility of the statement. Accordingly, H was correctly committed for trial.

R. v. AMERSHAM MAGISTRATES COURT, *ex p.* HUSSAIN, Trans. Ref: CO/ 0124/97, July 7, 1997, Lord Bingham of Cornhill, L.C.J., QBD.

1116. Admissibility–hearsay evidence–witness statements–witness in state of fear–whether failure to continue with oral evidence rendered statement inadmissible

[Criminal Justice Act 1988 s.23(3)(b).]

W appealed against his conviction for wounding with intent to cause grievous bodily harm on the grounds that a written statement, made by the victim at the time of the attack, identifying W as one of his attackers, had been improperly admitted in evidence. The victim had received threats that his life and that of his family would be in danger if he continued to support W's prosecution and, although he gave evidence in court, the victim said he could not identify his attackers. As a result, the prosecution successfully applied for the written statement to be admitted under the Criminal Justice Act 1988 s.23(1), on the grounds that the witness was unable to give oral evidence through fear under s.23(3)(b).

Held, dismissing the appeal, that, on one reading of s.23(3)(b), the words "does not give oral evidence" did not apply where the witness had been present in court and had given evidence. However, where the witness had given only partial evidence and there was additional evidence which he had been expected to give, but he then claimed he could not remember the relevant details, if the prosecution could show to the criminal standard of proof that the witness had been prevented from giving further oral evidence due to fear, then s.23(3)(b) applied, *R. v. Ashford Justices, ex p. Hilden* [1993] Q.B. 555, [1993] C.L.Y. 681 considered.

R. v. WATERS (SCOTT MARTIN) (1997) 161 J.P. 249, Kennedy, L.J., CA (Crim Div).

1117. Admissibility–hearsay evidence–witness statements–witness not found

[Criminal Justice Act 1988 s.23(2), s.23(3), s.26.]

W applied for judicial review of a decision to admit prejudicial written hearsay evidence at his committal for robbery. The evidence was adduced pursuant to the Criminal Justice Act 1988 s.23(2)(c) and s.23(3) and W contended that the witnesses, who were themselves the subject of police theft investigations, were unreliable and that the magistrates had wrongly used their discretion under s.26 by admitting the evidence.

Held, dismissing the application, that the magistrates had correctly determined that the matter should go to trial, where the admissibility of the evidence in question could be properly assessed by the judge, *R. v. Bedwellty Justices, ex p. Williams* [1996] 3 W.L.R. 361, [1996] 1 C.L.Y. 1558 followed.

R. v. TUNBRIDGE WELLS JUSTICES, *ex p.* WEBB, Trans. Ref: CO 4046/96, January 14, 1997, Mance, J., QBD.

1118. Admissibility–hearsay evidence–witness statements–witness unable to attend committal proceedings–defence counsel's admission need not be made in writing

[Criminal Justice Act 1967 s.10; Criminal Justice Act 1988 s.23(2); Magistrates Courts Rules 1981 r.71.]

Held, that where, in committal proceedings, a letter had been submitted by a doctor to the effect that a witness was unable to attend court to give evidence and defence counsel had not challenged that letter, the magistrate had not erred in permitting the witness statement to be read out pursuant to the Criminal Justice Act 1988 s.23(2)(a). Although the Magistrates Courts Rules 1981 r.71 demanded that an admission by counsel be made in writing, this defect was cured by the Criminal Justice Act 1967 s.10, which provided that an admission by counsel need not be made in writing where it had been made orally in open court.

R. v. HORSEFERRY ROAD MAGISTRATES COURT, *ex p.* BROWN, *The Independent*, October 6, 1997 (C.S.), Rose, L.J., QBD.

1119. Admissibility–heavy goods vehicles–weight restrictions–hearsay evidence–no printed result of test and no evidence of operator–presumption of accuracy rebutted

[Road Vehicles (Construction and Use) Regulations 1986 (SI 1986 1078) Reg.80; Road Traffic Act 1988 s.41; Road Traffic Offenders Act 1988 Sch.2; Police and Criminal Evidence Act 1984 s.69.]

M appealed by way of case stated following conviction of exceeding the maximum permitted rear axle weight for a two axle Bedford HGV vehicle, contrary to the Road Vehicles (Construction and Use) Regulations 1986 Reg.80(1)(a), the Road Traffic Act 1988 s.41(b) and the Road Traffic Offenders Act 1988 Sch.2. M contended that the admissibility of a police officer's evidence as to tests conducted at a private weighbridge, in the absence of either the weighbridge operator or the printed card showing the readings taken, amounted to hearsay evidence and that no evidence had been adduced as to the accuracy of the weighbridge itself.

Held, allowing the appeal and quashing the conviction, that given that the weighbridge was of private and not public operation, and that the weight readings revealed inconsistencies between the overall weight of the vehicle when set against individual readings for the front and rear axles, the justices were not entitled to base their decision on a presumption that the weighbridge was operating correctly. Given the absence of the police officer from the room when the card was produced, that the card had not been adduced in evidence nor the weighbridge operator called as a witness, the police officer's evidence on these matters amounted to hearsay. The failure to produce the card could have been overcome if secondary evidence of its contents had been given. In the absence of specific findings as to the card's contents, the best evidence of the operator was required, but this evidence had not been given. The hearsay evidence of the officer was not admissible in the absence of evidence as to the weighbridge's accuracy. The evidence given was insufficient to satisfy the requirements of the Police and Criminal Evidence Act 1984 s.69.

MURRAY v. DPP, Trans. Ref: CO/1135/96, October 21, 1996, Blofeld, J., QBD.

1120. Admissibility–heavy goods vehicles–weight restrictions–reliability of computer printouts

[Road Vehicles (Construction and Use) Regulations 1986 (SI 1986 1078) Part IV; Road Traffic Act 1988 s.41(b); Police and Criminal Evidence Act 1984 s.69.]

An information was preferred against E that they used a motor goods lorry to which the Road Vehicles (Construction and Use) Regulations 1986 Part IV applied and that the vehicle was overweight (the plated weight of the first axle being 7,530 kilogrammes against the permitted maximum of 6,500, 15.85 per cent over) contrary to Reg.80(1)(b) and the Road Traffic Act 1988 s.41(b). The question was whether E could be convicted when there was no evidence that the computer generating the weight tickets from the weighbridge was working properly. The justices had concluded that the Police and Criminal Evidence Act 1984 s.69 did not apply. They assumed that in the absence of evidence to the contrary that the weighbridge was working properly. E appealed by way of case stated.

Held, allowing the appeal and quashing the conviction, that following *R. v. Shephard* [1993] A.C. 380, [1992] C.L.Y. 722, s.69(1) of the 1984 Act applied to the weighing machine, because s.69 was of general application to documents produced by a computer and the conclusion of the justices flew in the face of that principle, *Connolly v. Lancashire CC* [1994] R.T.R. 79, [1994] C.L.Y. 675

applied. It was unlikely that the justices would have decided as they did had *R. v. Shephard* been brought to their attention.

EAST WEST TRANSPORT LTD v. DPP [1996] R.T.R. 184, Rose, L.J., QBD.

1121. Admissibility – indecent assault – admissibility of pornographic magazines

B was convicted on eight counts of indecently assaulting his two grandsons and sentenced to three years' imprisonment in 1996. He denied any indecency claiming that his grandsons and their mother fabricated the allegations as part of a conspiracy against him. B appealed against his conviction, contending that the judge was wrong to admit evidence of pornographic magazines found in his possession and to permit cross-examination about the magazines and B's sexual proclivities.

Held, allowing the appeal, and quashing the convictions, that the magazines and B's answers to related questions had no probative value except to propensity and evidence of them should not have been admitted, *R. v. Wright* (1990) 90 Cr. App. R. 325, [1990] C.L.Y. 963 applied.

R. v. BURRAGE (RA); *sub nom.* R. v. B (EVIDENCE: PROPENSITY) [1997] 2 Cr. App. R. 88, Rose, L.J., CA (Crim Div).

1122. Admissibility – police interviews – claim in interview that acted in self defence – self serving statements – mixed statements

[Public Order Act 1986 s.4(1).]

W, aged 16 at the time of the offence, appealed by way of case stated against his conviction under the Public Order Act 1986 s.4(1), arising from a fight with another youth. W was cautioned and interviewed by the police. W claimed that he had acted in self defence. At trial W chose not to give evidence, and argued that the prosecution had to disprove self defence. The magistrates were advised that, to be able to raise self defence, the onus was on W to adduce some evidence in support, and that the statement he made in the police interview was self serving and inadmissible. The case stated asked whether the court was correct in determining that the self serving statement was inadmissible as evidence to support the assertions made therein and, therefore, incapable of raising the issue of self defence. W asserted that the statement was not self-serving but mixed and was, therefore, admissible. The prosecution argued that, although the statement contained admissions as well as excuses, the admissions were not relied on by the prosecution, because it had sufficient evidence from witnesses about the fight, so the entire statement should be regarded as self serving and inadmissible.

Held, allowing the appeal and quashing the conviction, that the magistrates were wrong to conclude that W's interview was a self-serving statement. Where a statement is "mixed", including both inculpatory and exculpatory parts, the latter constitute evidence in support of the assertions made in the statement, *R. v. Duncan* (1981) 73 Cr. App. R. 359, [1981] C.L.Y. 437 and *R. v. Sharp* (1988) 86 Cr. App. R. 274, [1988] C.L.Y. 547 considered. There was nothing to suggest that the prosecution did not rely on the admissions in W's statement. If, however, the statement had been entirely self serving, then the answer to the case stated may have been in the affirmative.

WESTERN v. DPP [1997] 1 Cr. App. R. 474, Butterfield, J., QBD.

1123. Admissibility – police interviews – note of cell interview never read to appellant – breach of PACE codes of practice

[Police and Criminal Evidence Act 1984.]

The appellants were convicted of conspiracy to murder. On appeal, it was contended by the second appellant that the judge was wrong to admit evidence of cell interviews which, at the appellant's insistence, were neither contemporaneously noted nor tape recorded, but which were subsequently noted although never read to him to allow him to comment at the time on their accuracy, in breach of the Codes of Practice issued under the Police and Criminal Evidence Act 1984.

Held, dismissing all the appeals, that the correct approach to the exercise of the judge's discretion in admitting the evidence of the cell interviews was that identified in *R. v. Quinn* [1995] 1 Cr. App. R. 480, [1994] C.L.Y. 916: that before reaching the conclusion that the judge was wrong the court would have to be satisfied that no reasonable judge, having heard the evidence could have reached the conclusion that he did. That statement of principle represented the practice of the court, *R. v. Middlebrook and Caygill* (Unreported, 1994) not followed. Accordingly, since it could not be said that the judge's decision to admit the evidence of the cell interviews was perverse and that his subsequent direction to the jury was adequate, the appeal failed.

R. v. DURES (THOMAS); R. v.WILLIAMS (FLORENCE ELIZABETH); R. v. DURES (STEVEN) [1997] 2 Cr. App. R. 247, Rose, L.J., CA (Crim Div).

1124. Admissibility – police interviews – oral evidence taken in interview on another matter admissible

[Road Traffic Act 1988 s.103; Police and Criminal Evidence Act 1984 s.78.]

C was charged with driving a motor vehicle whilst disqualified from holding or obtaining a driving licence contrary to the Road Traffic Act 1988 s.103(b). A police constable gave evidence about an interview under caution he had had with C on another matter and part of that taped interview, in which C admitted being disqualified, was submitted as evidence. The police constable also submitted a memorandum of conviction from October 1994 but did not seek to rely on that alone. The magistrate found that to admit the evidence of the interview would be manifestly unfair to C as he was not given a clear warning when interviewed that what he said might be used against him in future proceedings. The DPP appealed by way of case stated against the magistrates' finding that the evidence of the police constable should have been excluded. The magistrates' question was whether he had properly exercised his discretion under the Police and Criminal Evidence Act 1984 s.78 in not allowing evidence which related to other proceedings in which C admitted to being disqualified from driving for a period of 12 months in October 1994.

Held, allowing the appeal and remitting the matter to the magistrates' court for the case to continue, that the evidence should have been admitted and the magistrate fell into error in exercising his discretion. The memorandum of conviction alone would have been insufficient evidence, but oral evidence confirming the conviction would render the evidence sufficient, *R. v. Derwentside Magistrates Court, ex p. Swift* [1997] R.T.R. 89, [1997] C.L.Y 1150 considered.

DPP v. CLARKSON, Trans. Ref: CO 1245/96, March 18, 1997, Blofeld, J., QBD.

1125. Admissibility – police powers – eavesdropping on police cell

[Police and Criminal Evidence Act 1984 s.78.]

R was arrested on suspicion of robbery along with C. R remained silent during interviews. C denied any armed robbery but was identified by two witnesses as being involved in one and was charged. C asked to be put in a cell with R in order to get him to admit the robbery and to exculpate C. The Assistant Chief Constable gave permission for the cell to be bugged, and R made unequivocal detailed admissions as to three armed robberies. C was not prosecuted, having established a satisfactory alibi. At trial, R unsuccessfully sought to exclude the cell conversations pursuant to the Police and Criminal Evidence Act 1984 s.78. R appealed against conviction on the grounds that the police had failed, in breach of the PACE codes of practice, to ask C to confirm and sign contemporaneous notes and that the deliberate introduction of a person into the presence of a suspect to obtain admissions went beyond permissible eavesdropping.

Held, dismissing the appeal, that the codes were not to protect one suspect against breaches of the codes in respect of another, and there being no causal link between the breaches of the codes and R's admissions, the judge was right to regard such breaches as insignificant to R. Cases of this kind were to be decided on their own facts and the test was whether the conduct of the police had wittingly or unwittingly led to unfairness or injustice. The trial judge was the proper adjudicator for this question and on the facts of the instant case his discretion could not be faulted.

R. v. ROBERTS (STEPHEN PAUL) [1997] 1 Cr. App. R. 217, Hirst, L.J., CA (Crim Div).

1126. **Admissibility—police suspicions as to supply of drugs inadmissible—summing up factually inaccurate containing information not part of evidence**

[Criminal Justice Act 1967 s.10.]

C appealed against conviction of possessing heroin with intent to supply. The police deposed he was seen leaving the house of a "known drug user" and, on being searched, found to be in possession of 4.31 grammes of heroin of 28 per cent purity, in 13 foil wrapped packages. C claimed the heroin was for his own use. The only issue before the jury was whether the heroin was for C's personal use or to be supplied to others. The judge below was not prepared to admit evidence from the Crown that the house C was seen to leave was the residence of a person the police suspected of supplying drugs. C argued that the judge had erred in so doing as the police were competent to make an admission of their suspicions or that the suspicions could be proven, and that the admission should not be subject to the hearsay rule. C further argued that the judge had been wrong to refuse an adjournment for him to find a way of presenting that information in an admissible form. A further ground of appeal was that the judge, in his summing up, appeared to present to the jury evidence which was not part of the evidence given when discussing ways in which a heroin addict might obtain money to pay for the heroin used.

Held, allowing the appeal, that (1) the Crown's admission could only have been made under the Criminal Justice Act 1967 s.10 and the statement could only be admissible if the fact it purported to determine was admissible. A matter which was suspected was not admissible and as such the statement regarding the suspicion was not admissible. There was nothing admissible as evidence that the person known to be a drug user was also a drug dealer and accordingly the judge was right not to allow an adjournment for the purpose sought, and (2) in the summing up, the judge used information which had not been adduced in evidence and had used some inaccurate information, so that it did not amount to a fair summary of the facts of the case.

R. v. COULSON (JASON LEE), Trans. Ref: 96/7255/Y5, March 26, 1997, Ebsworth, J., CA (Crim Div).

1127. **Admissibility—provocation—medical evidence of chronic alcoholism**

P appealed against conviction of murder after stabbing his neighbour in a fit of anger. P sought to raise the defence of provocation, in support of which he adduced medical evidence that he was a chronic alcoholic with damage to the left temporal lobe of his brain which amounted to a special disability rendering him more susceptible to provocation. Following the Privy Council decision in *Luc Thiet Thuan v. Queen, The* [1996] 3 W.L.R. 45, [1996] 1 C.L.Y. 1456, the evidence sought to be adduced was found to be inadmissible. P submitted that the dissenting judgment of Lord Steyn in that case should have been followed. The Crown contended that the Court of Appeal was entitled to follow the Privy Council decision rather than previous decisions of the Court of Appeal.

Held, allowing the appeal, quashing the conviction and ordering a retrial, that (1) previous Court of Appeal decisions, until overruled, were binding and the Privy Council decision was not, *R. v. Campbell (Colin Frederick)* [1997] 1 Cr. App. R. 199, [1997] C.L.Y. 1194 applied. Accordingly, the Recorder's decision could not stand, and (2) having regard to the authorities identified by Lord Steyn in *Luc Thiet Thuan v. Queen, The* and applying Smith and Hogan Criminal Law (8th ed) evidence of mental infirmity was relevant to the question of capacity of the defendant to self control. As the medical reports had only been available a few days before the trial, were not considered by the Court of Appeal and only 19 months had elapsed from the date of the incident, a retrial was appropriate.

R. v. PARKER (PHILIP),Trans. Ref: 96/5529/Y2, February 25,1997, Otton, L.J., CA (Crim Div).

1128. Admissibility–similar fact evidence–several offences

GO and GA appealed against conviction for 18 armed robberies and one attempted robbery of public houses, for which they received custodial terms of 18 and 14 years respectively. GO claimed that the evidence in relation to only three of the counts had directly implicated him. He contended that the jury should have been directed to consider the evidence against him on each specific count and, if none, then he should have been acquitted regardless of any similarities with other offences, and that evidence that the same two persons committed all the offences should have been ruled inadmissible.

Held, dismissing the appeals, that the jury should consider each defendant and count separately, and then only convict if convinced that the defendant committed that specific offence, taking into consideration all the relevant and admissible evidence. Similar fact evidence from another offence was admissible, either in support of prosecution on a similar charge or where evidence existed that the same person or persons had committed both offences. In the instant case, it would have been contrary to common sense for the jury to have been directed to disregard the evidence, *DPP v. P* [1991] 2 A.C. 447, [1991] C.L.Y. 676, *R. v. Downey (James)* [1995] 1 Cr. App. R. 547, [1994] C.L.Y. 928 and *R. v. Barnes (Anthony)* [1995] 2 Cr. App. R. 491 considered and *R. v. Wain* (Unreported, 1995) distinguished on its facts.

R. v. GOURDE (AARON PAUL); R. GARLAND (JASON JAMES), Trans. Ref: 9605746 X5, 9605787 X5, July 31,1997, Evans, L.J., CA (Crim Div).

1129. Admissibility–telephone tapping–evidence obtained by consensual interception not prevented by Interception of Communications Act 1985 s.9

[Interception of Communications Act 1985 s.1, s.9(1).]

R and C appealed against their convictions of conspiracy to supply drugs on the ground that evidence obtained from the interception of telephone calls to which one party had consented was not admissible pursuant to the Interception of Communications Act 1985 s.9(1)(a), *R. v. Preston* [1994] 2 A.C. 130, [1994] C.L.Y. 864 relied on.

Held, dismissing C's appeal but allowing R's appeal on other grounds, that s.9 stated that no evidence could be adduced which suggested that an offence under s.1 had been committed by the person receiving the communication or that a warrant authorising the interception had been issued to them. However, the Court of Appeal in *R. v. Effik* (1992) 95 Cr. App. R. 427, [1994] C.L.Y. 685 had laid down the principle that the section did not prevent the admission of a telephone intercept and *Preston* had modified that rule only in regard to warranted interceptions. The purpose of s.9 was to regulate the manner in which intercepted information was obtained rather than protect the evidence produced and could not be applied by itself to prevent the admission of evidence from a consensual interception.

R. v. RASOOL (SHAFQAT); R. v. CHOUDHARY (NASSIR) [1997] 1 W.L.R.1092, Stuart-Smith, L.J., CA (Crim Div).

1130. Admissibility–telephone tapping–evidence obtained in foreign jurisdiction– exclusion of evidence not an abuse of process

[European Convention on Human Rights 1950 Art.8; Interception of Communications Act 1985; Police and Criminal Evidence Act 1984 s.78.]

At A's trial on a charge of conspiracy to bring illegal immigrants into the UK, the judge ruled that evidence of a telephone conversation between A in the UK and someone in the Netherlands, which had been lawfully intercepted by the

Netherlands authorities, was admissible. A sought leave to appeal against the judge's ruling, arguing that the evidence should have been excluded under the Police and Criminal Evidence Act 1984 s.78 as its admission was against the spirit of the Interception of Communications Act 1985 and contrary to the European Convention on Human Rights 1950 Art.8, or that proceedings should have been stayed as an abuse of process.

Held, granting leave but dismissing the appeal, that the 1985 Act did not prohibit the use in UK proceedings of material gained through the tapping of telephone communications abroad and the circumstances did not constitute a breach of Art.8 of the 1950 Convention. The judge acted within his discretion when deciding not to exclude the evidence under the 1984 Act s.78 and there was no abuse of process.

R. v. AUJLA (AJIT SINGH); R. v. AUJLA (HARBANS KAUR); R. v. AUJLA (INDERPAL SINGH), *The Times*, November 24, 1997, Roch, L.J., CA (Crim Div).

1131. Admissibility–video recordings–evidence of child witness excluded on basis of age

[Criminal Justice Act 1988 s.33A(2A).]

M was convicted of an offence of indecently assaulting a girl, aged four. At his appeal to the Crown Court M sought to render inadmissible the evidence of the girl. The court refused to view video tapes of the girl's interviews or to see and assess the girl. The prosecution appealed by way of case stated.

Held, allowing the appeal, that the court had been wrong to refuse to admit the evidence by reason of the witness's age alone. The court should receive a child's evidence unless it appeared that the child was incapable of giving intelligible testimony, in terms of the Criminal Justice Act 1988 s.33A(2A). To reach that judgment the court should look at any video tapes of the interviews with the witness and ask various general questions of the child to assess his or her ability to give intelligible evidence. The court had failed to consider the question properly, *R. v. Z* [1990] 2 All E.R. 972, [1990] C.L.Y. 834 and *R. v. Hampshire (David Peter)* [1995] 2 All E. R. 1019, [1995] 1 C.L.Y. 908 considered.

DPP v. M [1997] 2 All E.R. 749, Phillips, L.J., QBD.

1132. Admissibility–witness statements–whether omission of age on statement invalidated proceedings

[Criminal Attempts Act 1981 s.9; Magistrates Courts Rules 1981 r.70; Magistrates Courts Forms Rules 1981 (SI 1981 553) r.2.]

M was charged with interfering with a motor vehicle contrary to the Criminal Attempts Act 1981 s.9. The only witness was the owner of the car, whose statement, served on M's solicitors, with no notice of objection given by them, had no entry made in the space reserved for the age of the witness. On that basis the statement was held to be inadmissible as it did not comply with the Criminal Justice Act 1967 s.9, Magistrates Courts Rules 1981 r.70(1) and Magistrates Courts Forms Rules 1981 r.2(1), and the charge was dismissed. The DPP appealed.

Held, allowing the appeal, that admissibility under s.9(1) of the 1967 Act depended on satisfaction of the conditions set out in s.9(2) thereof. The age of the witness is dealt with in s.9(3) which requires the age to be given if the person making the statement is under 21. This is directory and not mandatory. The witness was not under 21, and there was strictly no non compliance, so the proceedings were valid, *R. v. Carey* (1983) 76 Cr. App. R. 152, [1983] C.L.Y. 2308 applied, *Paterson v. DPP* [1990] R.T.R. 329, [1991] C.L.Y. 3109 distinguished.

DPP v. MANSBRIDGE, Trans. Ref: CO/568/96, October 18, 1996, Simon Brown, L.J., QBD.

1133. Children–unsworn evidence–breach of statutory requirement

See CRIMINAL PROCEDURE: R. v. Jackson (Paul Maitland). §1370

1134. Confessions–sufficiency–supergrass evidence tainted

T appealed against conviction based on the evidence of two supergrass accomplices, a written confession said to have been made voluntarily to the police, and evidence of expenditure of cash which the judge allowed as corroboration. The Crown submitted that the evidence of the two supergrasses was sufficient to sustain T's convictions despite the ruling that T was denied access to a solicitor and was assaulted by four police officers whilst in custody.

Held, allowing the appeal, that T's confession could not be relied on by the Crown and the evidence of the two supergrasses was manifestly tainted. The convictions were quashed.

R. v. TREADAWAY (DEREK JOHN), Trans. Ref: 9502720/X2, November 18, 1996, Rose, L.J., CA (Crim Div).

1135. Corroboration–rape–uncorroborated evidence of rape victim–retraction of allegation

W appealed against two convictions of rape of an 11 year old girl. There was medical evidence of sexual intercourse. W contended that the trial judge erred in not referring to the victim's letter of retraction, addressed to the police, stating that she had lied in order to be reunited with her natural father, or her later retraction of that letter.

Held, allowing the appeal, that the conviction was quashed. The summing up contained no reference to either retraction, nor did it contain any guidance to the jury on how to approach the victim's uncorroborated evidence. The question of a special warning in such circumstances should be resolved by discussion with counsel, *Makanjuola v. Commissioner of Police of the Metropolis* [1992] 3 All E.R. 617, [1992] C.L.Y. 2068 followed.

R. v. WALKER (HAUGHTON ALFONSO) [1996] Crim. L.R. 742, Ebsworth, J., CA (Crim Div).

1136. Criminal Evidence (Amendment) Act 1997 (c.17)

This Act amends the Police and Criminal Evidence Act 1984 s.63 to extend the categories of person from whom non-intimate body samples may be taken without consent to persons imprisoned or detained by virtue of pre-existing conviction for sexual offence and persons detained following acquittal on grounds of insanity or finding of unfitness to plead. A further time limit is added to those operating for the purposes of s.63A(4)(a) of the 1984 Act.

This Act received Royal Assent on March 19, 1997 and comes into force on March 19, 1997.

1137. Dangerous driving–identification of driver–hire car

A appealed against his conviction of dangerous driving. One of three independent witnesses, who observed a car being driven in a dangerous manner, made a mental note of the car's registration number. This was subsequently communicated to a police officer who ascertained that the car, a rental vehicle, was in the possession of A on the day in question. A contended that whilst he was in possession of the car there was no evidence that it was the vehicle which had been driven dangerously. The witness made no written note of the registration number, gave no evidence as to the number he had relayed to the police officer and did not refresh his memory from the note made by the police officer.

Held, allowing the appeal, that while there was evidence that a car of the same model as that of A's hire vehicle was being driven dangerously at the relevant place on the relevant date, as well as evidence that a similar car was in A's possession at that time, there was no evidence to identify the car hired by A as the vehicle in question, *Jones v. Metcalfe* [1967] 3 All E.R. 205, [1967] C.L.Y. 751, *R. v. McLean (John)* (1968) 52 Cr. App. R. 80 and *Cattermole v. Millar* [1978] R.T.R 258, [1978] C.L.Y. 2548 considered. Accordingly, A's conviction was quashed.

AHMED v. DPP, Trans. Ref: CO/0636/97, June 25, 1997, Lord Bingham of Cornhill, L.C.J., QBD.

1138. Disclosure–credibility of defence witnesses–extent of principle of fairness

B appealed against his conviction of wounding with intent to do grievous bodily harm on the ground that his conviction was rendered unsafe by a material irregularity brought about by the Crown's failure to disclose information relating to the credibility of two defence witnesses. The appeal was dismissed by the Court of Appeal and B appealed.

Held, dismissing the appeal, that (1) as questions as to a witness's credibility were often entirely irrelevant to the question of the defendant's guilt, it was reasonable to distinguish material relating to witness credibility from material that might assist the defence case, the withholding of which would be contrary to the principle of open justice, and (2) the requirements of a fair trial did not demand that defence witnesses should be exempt from challenges to their credibility. The existing duty of disclosure on the prosecution was sufficient to ensure that the defence were in possession of all relevant information to conduct the defence and to decide which witnesses to call. It was unnecessary to extend the duty to disclosure of material relevant only to witnesses' credibility.

R. v. BROWN (WINSTON) [1997] 3 W.L.R. 447, Lord Hope of Craighead, HL.

1139. Disclosure–informers–fair trial–firearms offeces

A appealed against conviction of robbery and possession of a firearm on the grounds that his activities as a police informant should not have been disclosed, but in that event, ought to have been given in camera.

Held, allowing A's appeal, that he did not get a fair trial and the convictions could not stand. A retrial was ordered as judicial discretion had not been exercised, *R. v. Turner (Paul David)* [1995] 2 Cr. App. R. 94, [1995] 1 C.L.Y. 1102 considered.

R. v. ADAMS (PETER); R. v. ROBINSON (MICHAEL) [1997] Crim. L.R. 292, Brooke, L.J., CA (Crim Div).

1140. Disclosure–witness statements–whether failure by prosecution to disclose a material irregularity rendering convictions unsafe

M and P appealed against the dismissal of their appeals against conviction of murder, contending that the prosecution had been under a duty to disclose to the defence copies of statements made by J, who had witnessed acts of violence in respect of which M and P had been charged, but who, in the prosecution's opinion, was not a truthful witness. At the trial, J had not been called by either the prosecution or the defence, but had spoken to the defence solicitor. M and P argued that the rule in *R. v. Bryant (Horace Henry)* (1946) 31 Cr. App. R. 146, which made a distinction between disclosing the statement of a credible witness to the defence and informing the defence about a witness considered to be untruthful, could no longer be sustained, as it conflicted with Court of Appeal decisions made since M and P's trial in 1990, which emphasised the importance of full disclosure by the Crown. The Crown argued that its duty in respect of witnesses such as J extended only to providing the defence with the witness's name and address.

Held, dismissing the appeal, that in some circumstances the rule in *Bryant* could result in an injustice in the trial leading to an unsafe conviction and should not be retained as part of the common law unless there was strong argument to do so. The risk that disclosure could help the defence to tailor its evidence was outweighed by the risk of injustice and the rule did not conform with the principles of disclosure enunciated since 1990. Therefore, the rule should no longer be applied and the failure to disclose J's statement represented a material irregularity in the course of the trial. However, the convictions could not be regarded as unsafe as the defence had been aware of the nature of the information given by J and of the dangers of calling him as a defence witness, so any prejudice was largely eliminated. Further, having seen and heard J give evidence, the court had been entitled to conclude that, even if J had appeared as a witness for the defence, M and P would still have been convicted.

R. v. MILLS (GARY); R. v. POOLE (ANTHONY KEITH) [1997] 3 W.L.R. 458, Lord Hutton, HL.

1141. DNA profiling–expert evidence–statistical evaluation–application of mathematical formula confusing for jurors

Held, that whilst the prosecution could properly rely upon a DNA sample supported by statistical evidence as to the random occurrence ratio of the DNA match, in the absence of special circumstances the defence should not be permitted to adduce expert evidence based on Bayes Theorem to encourage the jury to attach mathematical probabilities to non scientific evidence called at the trial with a view to comparing the probabilities with those from the DNA evidence. While Bayes Theorem was methodologically sound and reliable in certain circumstances, it was not appropriate to use it in a jury trial as it was apt to lead to confusion, misunderstanding and misjudgment and was unlikely to assist the jury in their task, *R. v. Doheny (Alan James)* [1997] 1 Cr. App. R. 369, [1996] 1 C.L.Y. 1364 considered.

R. v. ADAMS (DENIS JOHN) (NO.2), *The Times*, November 3, 1997, Lord Bingham of Cornhill, L.C.J., CA (Crim Div).

1142. DNA profiling–expert evidence–statistical evaluation–procedure for adducing evidence

D and another, A, appealed against conviction for offences in which the prosecution relied on the comparison of DNA profiles obtained from a sample of blood provided by each appellant. The grounds of appeal were that the verdicts were unsafe due to the misleading and inaccurate manner in which forensic evidence was presented, in particular the way in which the random occurrence ratio, the frequency with which the matching characteristics were likely to be found in the population at large, was expressed. D was convicted of rape and buggery after a 65 year old widow was attacked at her home. The expert witness for the prosecution used two different test methods to examine samples and his results were undermined by fresh expert evidence on appeal. The issue was whether it was legitimate for the prosecution's expert to multiply the result of one test with the results of the other. The second appellant, A, was convicted of buggery and sentenced to five years' imprisonment which he served after a 32 year old woman was attacked in her home by a man she claimed to have spoken to on the telephone when she rang the Samaritans. A was a volunteer worker for the Samaritans and a chair cushion found at the complainant's home bore traces of semen which, after A provided a blood sample, which showed a DNA match. A's grounds of appeal were that the DNA evidence presented to the jury was inappropriate and erroneous, the jury should have been directed that he may have visited the complainant's home to participate in a sexual activity other than buggery, the judge misdirected the jury on corroboration and alibi and should have given a direction on lies following *R. v. Lucas* (1981) 73 Cr. App. R. 159, [1981] C.L.Y. 400.

Held, allowing D's appeal but dismissing A's, that (1) in D's case the approach demonstrated by the prosecution's expert was not legitimate and the conviction was unsafe and was quashed. In A's case the complainant's identification of him was considered as well as the DNA evidence and the judge was under no duty to put before the jury the possibility of facts which were at odds with the evidence adduced by both the prosecution and defence; it was desirable that a corroboration direction should have been given but it was not necessary that the jury should have been directed that there should be corroboration of every element of the complainant's evidence and (2) when adducing DNA evidence in a criminal trial the expert should also provide his calculations of the random occurrence ratio and the prosecution should provide the defence with the means of calculation to allow adequate scrutiny of the results. The expert should explain the match between the DNA samples, but should not give his opinion on the chances of the defendant having left the crime stain. The trial judge should make clear to the jury other evidence which either pointed to or away from the defendant being responsible for the crime stain in the context of the random occurrence ratio and direct them that it was their task to decide, on all the evidence, whether they were satisfied that it was the defendant who left the crime stain.

R. v. DOHENY (ALAN JAMES); R. v. ADAMS (GARY ANDREW) [1997] 1 Cr. App. R. 369, Phillips, L.J., Jowitt, J., CA (Crim Div).

1143. Documentary evidence–production of complainant's counselling record sought by witness summons–record not "material evidence"

[Criminal Procedure (Attendance of Witnesses) Act 1965 s.2; Magistrates Court Act 1980 s.97; Criminal Justice Act 1988 s.24.]

A, a GP, was charged with indecent assault on one of his patients. The incident was alleged to have taken place on December 14, 1995 and in her statement to the police on December 20, 1995, the complainant stated that she attended for counselling on December 15 after reporting the matter to the police. Prior to the trial A issued a witness summons addressed to the clinical director of the counselling centre requiring that person's attendance to give evidence and to produce the original medical and counselling records and any other documents generated as a result of the complainant's attendance on December 15, 1995. On return of the summons the clinical director applied for it to be set aside.

Held, setting the summons aside, that the central principles to be derived from the authorities under the Criminal Procedure (Attendance of Witnesses) Act 1965 s.2 and the Magistrates Court Act 1980 s.97 are, that (1) to be material evidence, documents must not only be relevant to the issues arising in the criminal proceedings but also documents admissible as such in evidence, and (2) documents which are desired merely for the purpose of possible cross-examination are not admissible in evidence, and thus, are not material for the purposes of either s.97 of the 1980 Act nor s.2 of the 1965 Act, *R. v. Derby Justices, ex p. B* [1995] 4 All E.R. 526, [1995] 1 C.L.Y. 1104, applied; *R. v. Clowes* (1992) 95 Cr. App. R. 440, [1992] C.L.Y. 819 distinguished, and (2) the Criminal Justice Act 1988 s.24 was available if necessary for the purpose of getting before the jury any material which the defence found in the transcripts which positively advanced the defence case, *R. v. Clowes* considered. In the instant case A's principal reason for seeking disclosure of the counselling records was to equip himself with material for cross-examination. It was little more than fanciful to suppose that the document positively advanced the defence case and this was confirmed after an examination of the document in question. Accordingly the counselling centre could not produce any document "likely to be material evidence" within the meaning of s.2 and so the summons was set aside.

R. v. AZMY [1996] 7 Med. L.R. 415, Mitchell, J., Crown Ct.

1144. Documentary evidence–production sought by witness summons–purpose of summons–procedure

[Criminal Procedure (Attendance of Witnesses) Act 1965 s.2.]

Held, that the only legitimate purpose of a summons under the Criminal Procedure (Attendance of Witnesses) Act 1965 s.2 to procure documents was to procure those likely to prove themselves to be material evidence, not merely documents likely to afford or assist a relevant line of inquiry or challenge. Material which might simply be useful in cross examination could not be extracted from third parties by use of a witness summons. Where a witness summons was followed by an application to set it aside, there would ordinarily be no good reason for the parties not to consent to a private consideration of the documents and written submissions by the parties, unless oral argument was clearly necessary or requested by the judge. Such a procedure should not be regarded as affording a free adjudication wherever a third party withheld documents; a speculative challenge to such a refusal might well amount to an "improper, unreasonable or negligent act" capable of attracting a wasted costs order.

H (L), *Re* [1997] 1 Cr. App. R. 176, Sedley, J., Crown Ct.

1145. Drink driving offences–blood tests–admissibility–certificate of service

[Road Traffic Offenders Act 1988 s.16.]

L was convicted of drink driving. Following a breath test L provided a blood sample. On appeal by way of case stated it was submitted, inter alia, that the blood sample analysed was not necessarily the sample taken from L. The question was whether the analyst's certificate was admissible in evidence. There was no signature to the certificate of service. Thus the provisions of the Road Traffic Offenders Act 1988 s.16 were not fulfilled thereby rendering the certificate inadmissible, *Tobi v. Nicholas* [1988] R.T.R. 343, [1988] C.L.Y. 552 relied upon.

Held, dismissing the appeal, that all that was in issue here was the certificate of service and not service itself, *Tobi v. Nicholas* distinguished.

LOUIS v. DPP, *The Times*, July 21, 1997, Owen, J., QBD.

1146. Drink driving offences–breath tests–intoximeter reading–certificate recording time as GMT–effect of British Summer Time

[Police and Criminal Evidence Act 1984 s.69.]

The DPP appealed by way of case stated against a decision of magistrates to acquit S of driving with excess alcohol. The breath test was supplied at 23.30 GMT on July 6 but took place during British Summer Time and the date recorded on the certificate by a police officer, as required by the Police and Criminal Evidence Act 1984 s.69, was the following day. The defence contended that the machine was faulty and that the certificate did not adequately prove the print out since it bore the wrong date, which showed that the arresting officer had not fully understood the meaning and purpose of the certificate.

Held, allowing the appeal, that the justices had been entitled to reject S's claim to have taken only two pints of beer and to find the breathalyser machine to have been working satisfactorily, but had erred in acquitting since the arresting officer had given oral evidence that was sufficient to confirm that the machine was working correctly and the safeguards of the 1984 Act were satisfied. In addition, in the absence of contrary evidence, there was no reason to believe that the machine was not functioning correctly, *Parker v. DPP* [1993] R.T.R. 283, [1993] C.L.Y. 3505 approved.

DPP v. SCHON, Trans. Ref: CO 481-97, June 27, 1997, Henry, L.J., QBD.

1147. Drink driving offences–breath tests–intoximeter reading–time of test–discrepancy with police record

H was arrested by the police for drink driving. Having provided a sample of her breath at the roadside she was taken to the police station. H agreed to provide two further samples of breath for analysis. The first of these was recorded by a police sergeant in attendance as being given at 23.52 BST, but the Lion Intoximeter 3000 print out stated the time as 22.54 GMT. The magistrates hearing the case concluded that this evidence was inadmissible on the basis of the rule in *DPP v. McKeown (Sharon)* [1997] 1 W.L.R. 295, [1997] C.L.Y. 1093 which considered such evidence. Although the accuracy of the machine was unchallenged, the discrepancy in the times was thought enough to render its evidence inadmissible.

Held, allowing the appeal, that in the case of *DPP v. McKeown* it was ruled that the relevancy of any malfunction in a machine must be considered. Malfunctions which did not affect any material aspect of the document produced could not be considered as rendering that document inadmissible as evidence.

DPP v. HORSWILL, Trans. Ref: CO/2879/96, July 2, 1997, Gage, J., QBD.

1148. Drink driving offences–police evidence defective–prosecution denied opportunity to present evidence

[Road Traffic Act 1988 s.5(1)(a); Magistrates Courts Act 1980 s.9(2).]

The DPP applied for judicial review of a decision of a stipendiary magistrate to summarily dismiss a case against O. O was stopped by two officers, given a breath test which proved positive and later charged with driving with excess alcohol contrary to the Road Traffic Act 1988 s.5(1)(a). In the course of cross-examination by O, who was unrepresented, a police officer admitted that she had not recorded a contemporary statement, made by O, denying that he had been driving and the stipendiary summarily dismissed the case. The DPP contended that the stipendiary magistrate had erred by dismissing the case forthwith, without hearing further prosecution evidence and without allowing the prosecutor to respond to her misgivings.

Held, allowing the application and declaring the proceedings null and ordering mandamus, that the case should be remitted. It was clear that the magistrate had made a grave error by disregarding the provisions of the Magistrates Courts Act 1980 s.9(2) and dismissing the case without permitting the prosecution to address the court, *Harrington, Re* [1984] A.C. 743, [1984] C.L.Y. 490 and *R. v. Barking and Dagenham Justices, ex p. DPP* (1995) 159 J.P. 373, [1994] C.L.Y 945 followed.

R. v. HORSEFERRY ROAD MAGISTRATES COURT, *ex p.* DPP (1996); *sub nom.* OKIYA, *Re*, Trans. Ref: CO 644-96, October 30, 1996, Maurice Kay, J., QBD.

1149. Expert evidence–actual bodily harm–psychiatric harm resulting from non physical assault

M appealed against conviction of assault occasioning actual bodily harm. No actual physical contact had taken place between M and the victim who gave unchallenged evidence that she suffered nervousness, anxiety, a change in personality and certain physical symptoms as a result of M's stalking of her over a period of time. Evidence of those symptoms was also accepted from the victim's GP who was not, however, qualified in psychiatry. Prior to the trial, both parties had applied to the judge for an adjournment to allow expert evidence relating to the psychiatric harm suffered by the victim to be obtained. The judge rejected the application on the basis that such evidence was unnecessary.

Held, allowing the appeal and ordering a retrial, that, following *R. v. Chan-Fook* [1994] 1 W.L.R. 689, [1994] C.L.Y. 1076, the question of whether the symptoms complained of by the victim constituted psychological illness or injury which had been brought about by M assaulting her in a manner which was not physical, should not have been left to be determined by the jury without expert evidence from a witness who was qualified in psychiatry.

R. v. MORRIS (CLARENCE BARRINGTON), *The Times*, November 13, 1997, Potter, L.J., CA (Crim Div).

1150. Identification–driving whilst disqualified

S and B appealed against convictions for driving whilst disqualified. They claimed that it had not been proved that they were the same people as the S and B named as disqualified.

Held, dismissing the appeals, that there was sufficient evidence that the applicants were the same men who had previously been disqualified, *Ellis v. Jones* [1973] 2 All E.R. 893, [1973] C.L.Y. 1418 followed.

R. v. DERWENTSIDE MAGISTRATES COURT, *ex p.* SWIFT; R. v. SUNDERLAND JUSTICES, *ex p.* BATE; *sub nom.* R. v. DERWENTSIDE

JUSTICES, *ex p.* SWIFT; R. v. DERWENTSIDE MAGISTRATES COURT, *ex p.* BATE [1997] R.T.R. 89, Rougier, J., QBD.

1151. Identification–jury directions–no evidence of joint enterprise

M appealed against conviction of attempted murder for which he received a custodial sentence of 10 years. M together with three friends drove to the victim's house, whereupon three of them entered and beat the victim with a stick. Of the four, only M, who was of Asian appearance, appeared to have a motive for the attack, since the victim was living with M's former girlfriend, the mother of his two children. The trial judge ruled that there was no evidence of a joint enterprise of attempted murder. It was common ground that one man had remained in the car and the evidence of two key eye witnesses was that three white men had run out of the house. M contended that, although the trial judge had been correct to give a *Turnbull* warning in relation to the identification evidence, because it implicated the white accomplice who had claimed he had remained in the car, he had been obliged to give a further direction, since casting doubt on the identification evidence would directly implicate M.

Held, allowing the appeal, that the conviction was unsafe and a retrial was ordered. It was impossible to disregard the possibility that the jury had felt obliged by common sense to convict one of the four even though they had not been certain of the guilt of any single one.

R. v. McCOLL (TREVOR), Staughton, L.J., CA (Crim Div).

1152. Identification–jury directions–poor quality of evidence–witness having sincere and obvious belief in identification–danger of false confidence in minds of jury

D appealed against conviction of robbery for which he was sentenced to seven years' imprisonment. Following the armed robbery of S's shop, during which the two robbers wore ski masks, D, whom S had known for eight years as a regular customer, was picked out by S at an identity parade at which all the participants wore ski masks. S contended that he recognised D by reference to his height, build and the way he spoke "money, money" during the robbery. D contended that the trial judge should have withdrawn the case from the jury as the identification evidence was not such as could safely sustain a conviction, as it did not add any weight to the poor identification at the scene.

Held, allowing the appeal and quashing the conviction, that the trial judge should have acceded to the submission that the evidence was poor, *R. v. Turnbull* [1977] Q.B. 224, [1976] C.L.Y. 451 applied, and that the matter actually depended on the accuracy of S's voice identification. The risk of the jury making a genuine mistake due to S's sincerity as a witness and his obvious belief that he was right was too great. The reliance on similarity in general body shape and height could just as easily have reinforced an incorrect identification as confirmed a correct one. Where evidence is of a poor quality, the judge has a special responsibility as he knows the danger inherent in identification cases, where there is the risk that the assurance and honesty of an identifying witness may create a confidence in the minds of the jury that an objective appreciation and analysis of the facts shows they should not feel.

R. v. DEVLIN (GYLL WESLEY), Trans. Ref: 9605547 W3, March 14, 1997, Hutchison, L.J., CA (Crim Div).

1153. Identification–jury directions–similar fact evidence–adequacy of Turnbull direction in respect of possible mistakes by honest witnesses

G was convicted on six counts of burglary and was sentenced to six years' imprisonment on each count concurrent. He appealed against conviction and sentence. The offences were committed against elderly persons. Identification evidence on five counts followed identification parades. On one count, however, the victim was shown a jacket G had been wearing, which she identified, but she had failed to identify G at an identification parade and this was not disclosed to the jury. The judge had in fact told the jury there had been no parade and the judge had not been corrected.

Held, dismissing the appeals, that (1) in the light of the authorities the judge was entitled, if not obliged, to sum up on the basis that the identification evidence of each victim could support the others, in a similar fact case, even though the jury might have doubts as to any particular identification, *R. v. McGranaghan* [1995] Crim. L.R. 430, [1992] C.L.Y. 661 distinguished, *R. v. Downey* [1995] 1 Cr. App. R. 547, [1994] C.L.Y. 928 and *R. v. Barnes* [1995] 2 Cr. App. R. 491 followed. A reasonable jury would have concluded that all the instant offences had been committed by the same person, and that the identification evidence pointed at G, even had they been correctly informed on the matter of one of the identification parades; (2) although commenting broadly on the dangers of convicting on the basis of identification evidence alone, the judge failed to give the conventional direction that an honest witness may be mistaken as to identification, *R. v. Turnbull* [1977] Q.B. 224, [1976] C.L.Y. 451 and *R. v. Weeder* (1980) 71 Cr. App. R. 228, [1980] C.L.Y. 482 considered. The judge had erred but the weight of the similar fact evidence and the strength of some of the identifications made it improbable that the jury could have been right on five of the counts yet wrong on the sixth, and (3) G had an appalling record of like offences and the sentence was entirely appropriate.

R. v. GRANT (RICHARD FRANCIS) [1996] 2 Cr. App. R. 272, Laws, J., CA (Crim Div).

1154. Identification–magistrates' discretion to allow dock identification of defendant in absence of identity parade

Held, that magistrates had a discretion to allow the identification of a defendant in court where there had been no identity parade. Although this appeared contrary to the 1997 edition of Archbold: Criminal Pleading, Evidence and Practice, it had long been the practice in magistrates' courts to allow dock identification, and to insist on an identity parade in every case where identification was at issue would severely impair the process of justice.

BARNES v. DPP; *sub nom.* BARNES v. CHIEF CONSTABLE OF DURHAM, *The Times*, May 6, 1997, McCowan, L.J., QBD.

1155. Identification–murder–witnessed by police officers–identification by officer accepted notwithstanding that there was no identification parade

In January 1990 two armed men on board a minibus in Jamaica shot dead one of the passengers following a struggle. The incident was witnessed by C and L, two off-duty policemen who were on the bus. The following day C accompanied a team of officers to an address, where C identified W as one of the armed robbers. W was arrested and charged with murder. At trial L identified W in the dock as one of the armed robbers. The case against W was based entirely on the identification evidence of C and L. In summing up the trial judge warned the jury not to accept the identification evidence without caution, and gave appropriate directions in accordance with *R. v. Turnbull* [1977] Q.B. 224, [1976] C.L.Y. 451. W was convicted of murder and appealed unsuccessfully to the Court of Appeal. W then appealed to the Privy Council arguing, inter alia, that since the correct practice was for an identification parade to have been held and there was no explanation as to why that was not done, C's evidence was so tainted that it should have been held to be inadmissible.

Held, dismissing the appeal, that (1) in cases where the witness did not know the suspect previously, the proper course was for an identification parade to be conducted. Confrontation should be confined to exceptional circumstances, *R. v. Hassock* (1977) 15 J.L.R. 135 approved. In the instant case, it was appropriate that C, as a serving police officer, should attend the arrest of W and there was nothing underhand or pernicious in his identifying W at the time of the arrest. It would have been wholly impractical for C's evidence to have been excluded from consideration by the jury and the judge provided ample directions as to how C's evidence should be treated, and (2) although the dock identification of W by L was undesirable, since it was volunteered not prompted it could not have been prevented and the judge dealt with the matter appropriately in his summing up.

WILLIAMS (NOEL) v. QUEEN, THE [1997] 1 W.L.R. 548, Lord Hope of Craighead, PC.

1156. Identification—note should be made of witness's description prior to ad hoc confrontation identification

Held, that, prior to an ad hoc confrontation identification, a note should be made of the witness's description of the offender. The note should then be made available for examination at trial to act as a safeguard against the risk of auto-suggestion.

R. v. VAUGHAN (MATTHEW), *The Independent*, May 12, 1997 (C.S.), McCowan, L.J., CA (Crim Div).

1157. Magistrates' courts—expert evidence—mutual disclosure

MAGISTRATES' COURTS (ADVANCE NOTICE OF EXPERT EVIDENCE) RULES 1997, SI 1997 705 (L.11); made under the Magistrates' Courts Act 1980 s.144; and the Criminal Procedure and Investigations Act 1996 s.20. In force: April 1, 1997; £0.65.

These Rules provide for mutual disclosure of expert evidence between parties to proceedings for the summary trial of an offence where the person charged with the offence pleads not guilty.

1158. Manslaughter—disputed cause of death—consistency of verdict with cause of death

T appealed against a sentence of six years' imprisonment for manslaughter on a murder indictment, with the sentence being on the basis that T had not intended to kill or cause really serious bodily harm. T's wife died as a result of head injuries sustained during a violent fight, during which both parties also suffered various superficial injuries. The police were initially called at 1.30 pm by a neighbour, but T declined to speak to them and they had not realised another person was involved. T later called the police himself at 5.30 pm and the body was discovered at 7.30 pm. In evidence for the prosecution a pathologist stated that the head injury was consistent with being struck by a blunt object, and that the remaining injuries were consistent with a fight. T submitted that the trial judge had been wrong to describe the assault as vicious, owing to the superficiality of the injuries. T also submitted that the jury's decision was inconsistent with the pathologist's evidence, of a deliberate strike causing the head injury which caused death. T argued that his actions amounted to self-defence, as his wife had attacked him with a pair of scissors.

Held, dismissing the appeal, that (1) on the evidence the trial judge had been fully entitled to describe the assault as vicious and that he had correctly taken account of T's behaviour after the incident as it was so obviously closely related to it, and (2) based on the pathologist's evidence as to the cause of death it was possible that the jury could have concluded that T intended some harm, albeit not serious, and that the verdict was not decided on the basis that the death occurred as a result of excessive self defence, *R. v. Walker (Colin Frederick)* (1992) 13 Cr. App. R. (S.) 474, [1993] C.L.Y. 1219 and *R. v. Morgan (Matthew)* (1993) 14 Cr. App. R. (S.) 734, [1994] C.L.Y. 1305 distinguished.

R. v. TZAMBAZLES (CHRISTOS) [1997] 1 Cr. App. R. (S.) 87, Harrison, J., CA (Crim Div).

1159. PACE codes of practice

POLICE AND CRIMINAL EVIDENCE ACT 1984 (CODES OF PRACTICE NO.4) ORDER 1997, SI 1997 1159; made under the Police and Criminal Evidence Act 1984 s.67. In force: May 15, 1997; £0.65.

This Order appoints May 15, 1997 as the date on which a revised code of practice under the Police and Criminal Evidence Act 1984 s.66(a) will come into operation. It supersedes the code which has been in operation since April 10, 1995.

1160. Pornography—possessing indecent photograph of child under 16—expert evidence did not have to be adduced as to age of child

[Protection of Children Act 1978 s.1, s.2.]

L appealed against conviction on two counts of possessing indecent photographs of a child with a view to their being distributed or shown contrary to the Protection of Children Act 1978 s.1(1)(c). The offences related to photographs in two video cassettes depicting young adolescent males and no direct evidence had been adduced about the identity of those involved or their ages. L contended that: (1) the judge should have directed the jury that, in order to convict, it had to be proved that he not only possessed a photograph that was indecent, but that he knew that the person depicted in it was under 16, and (2) expert paediatric evidence should have been adduced to demonstrate to the jury that puberty could begin in adolescent males at different times and that variations existed between adolescents of different racial groups.

Held, dismissing the appeal, that (1) the statutory defence in s.1(4) to a charge under s.1(1)(c) was limited to those who were in possession of indecent material for a legitimate purpose or who did not know and had no reason to believe they were in possession of indecent items. A brief look at the material would show whether it did or might depict a person under 16 and prosecution could then be avoided by disposing of the material forthwith, and (2) s.2(3) emphasised that it was a question of fact, based on inference, whether a person was a child for the purposes of the Act and there was no need for formal proof. Paediatric or other expert evidence was not required in order for the jury to decide that the person depicted in a photograph was under 16, as the jury was just as able as an expert to determine whether the Crown had made out its case on the issue of age.

R. v. LAND (MICHAEL), *The Times*, November 4, 1997, Judge, L.J., CA (Crim Div).

1161. Right to silence—jury directions—no adverse inference to be drawn

F was convicted of the indecent assault of an eight year old girl. At his trial F did not give evidence. F appealed on the basis, inter alia, that the directions given to the jury did not make it clear to the jury that no adverse inference should be drawn from F's failure to give evidence. The judge had earlier agreed with F's counsel that such a direction should be made, but despite mentioning F's good character and statement made to the police no specific direction was given.

Held, allowing appeal, that the judge's observation concerning character and denial was insufficient for the purposes of making it clear to the jury that no inference as to guilt should be drawn.

R. v. FRENCH (JOHN CHARLES), Trans. Ref: 97/2278/Z5, July 18, 1997, Judge Peter Crawford Q.C., CA (Crim Div).

1162. Right to silence—juvenile offenders—14 year old with mental age of nine—no automatic immunity from adverse comment

[Family Law Reform Act 1969 s.9; Criminal Justice and Public Order Act 1994 s.35.]

F, aged 14 at the time of the offence, appealed against a conviction of murder. During a voir dire held to establish F's mental capacity, a clinical psychologist gave evidence that F had an IQ of 63 and a low mental age, but that he was less suggestible than the average person. F contended that (1) although it was accepted he was fit to plead, that his mental age was nine entitled him to immunity from adverse comment for failing to give evidence as provided by the Criminal Justice and Public Order Act 1994 s.35. In addition, the trial judge had exercised his discretion unreasonably by giving undue weight to F's police interview and the allegation that F had gone to dispose of the murder weapon; (2) the trial judge had placed undue emphasis on alleged lies in the police interview and, although he had given a *Lucas* direction, it was separated from the summing up on the evidence relating to F, and (3) two members of the jury, who had been openly wearing favours in support of the private prosecution of the murderers of Stephen Lawrence, should have been discharged.

Held, dismissing the appeal, that (1) there was no correct test laid down as to the exercise of judicial discretion in terms of s.35 of the 1994 Act; however it was apparent that the trial judge considered all relevant factors, including the psychiatric assessment and opinion as to whether F could do himself justice as a witness. Nothing in the section allows for the conclusion that because the accused has a lower mental than physical age he should be entitled to immunity. In most cases an accused would be found unfit to plead if he could not comprehend the process and there was no reason to deviate from the definition of age contained in the Family Law Reform Act 1969 s.9; (2) the *Lucas* direction had been clearly and correctly included in the directions on the law rather than during the analysis of the evidence, and (3) the trial judge properly applied the appropriate test of whether there was real danger of bias and, in the light of the fact that the Lawrence case was substantially different to that before them, was justified in concluding there was no bias and had been correct to refuse the application to discharge the jurors distinguishing Lawrence on the basis that it appeared to have been racially motivated.

R. v. FRIEND (BILLY-JOE) [1997] 2 All E.R. 1012, Otton, L.J., CA (Crim Div).

1163. Right to silence–police interviews–six conditions to be met before jury could draw inferences from failure to mention fact relied on in defence

[Criminal Justice and Public Order Act 1994 s.34(2).]

A appealed against conviction and sentence of 10 years' imprisonment for manslaughter having been indicted for murder. Following his arrest after an anonymous call to the police, he declined to answer questions in police interviews on legal advice. The trial judge declined to admit police evidence of a first interview, but admitted the second on the ground that it had been preceded by a positive identification. A contended that the judge had erred when directing the jury that it was open to them to draw an inference from A's silence.

Held, dismissing the appeal against conviction and sentence, that (1) before a jury could draw "such inferences ..... as appear proper", in terms of the Criminal Justice and Public Order Act 1994 s.34(2)(d), from an accused's failure to mention during police questioning any fact which he subsequently relied on in his defence, six conditions had to be fulfilled. As well as the requirement for proceedings to have been instituted, the alleged failure, which must have taken place before the defendant was charged, had to have occurred while the accused was undergoing questioning under caution, the objective of which was to establish whether or by whom the alleged offence was committed. In addition, the alleged failure had to be to mention any fact which the defendant relied on in his defence, and it was for the jury to decide, as questions of fact, whether there was some fact so relied on and whether the defendant failed to mention such fact when being questioned. Finally, the relevant fact had to be one which, in the circumstances, the defendant could reasonably have been expected to mention, taking account of that particular defendant's characteristics, such as age, health and mental capacity, and legal advice as relevant circumstances. Whilst the issue requires appropriate jury directions, the matter should then be left for the jury to decide and it would only rarely be the case that a judge should direct a jury that they should or should not draw the appropriate inference and (2) with regard to sentence for an offence of manslaughter with use of a knife, *Attorney General's Reference (No.33 of 1996) (R. v. Latham), Re* [1997] 2 Cr. App. R. 10, [1997] C.L.Y. 1622 applied. Seven blows with the knife were inflicted on the victim, there was no provocation, guilty plea or excuse, and in those circumstances the sentence was appropriate.

R. v. ARGENT (BRIAN) [1997] 2 Cr. App. R. 27, Lord Bingham of Cornhill, L.C.J., CA (Crim Div).

1164. Road traffic offences–careless driving–case stated–evidence given insufficient consideration by magistrates

[Road Traffic Act 1988 s.3.]

DPP appealed by way of case stated against a decision by magistrates that there was no case to answer in a charge against S of driving without due care and attention contrary to the Road Traffic Act 1988 s.3. S, when driving his car, had turned into a street and a cyclist, colliding with the near side of his car, sustained fatal injuries.

Held, allowing the appeal and remitting the case for trial by a different bench, that (1) the magistrates did not adequately apply themselves to the issue of whether there was sufficient evidence to show that S's driving was below the degree of care and attention to be exercised by a reasonable and careful driver, and (2) following Practice Direction (Submission of No Case) [1962] 1 All E.R. 448, [1962] C.L.Y. 1876 and *R. v. Galbraith* [1981] 1 W.L.R. 1039, [1981] C.L.Y. 513, a no case to answer submission may be made where an essential element of the alleged offence was not proved or where the prosecution evidence was discredited or was manifestly unreliable so that no reasonable tribunal could safely convict on it. The magistrates did not refer specifically to the grounds they relied on or the eye witness evidence they rejected and their findings were not set out sufficiently clearly. The local knowledge claimed by the magistrates was not of a general nature because it related to a specific junction. The magistrates' conclusion was flawed, particularly as there was evidence from three witnesses stating that the street into which S was turning was visible and the cyclist should have been seen by S.

DPP v. SPICER, Trans. Ref: CO 3862 of 1996, March 13, 1997, Blofeld, J., QBD.

1165. Road traffic offences–driving under influence of drugs–blood tests–evidence of advice from doctor

[Road Traffic Act 1988 s.7(3).]

B was seen driving in an erratic manner and was stopped by police. The police officers suspected that he was under the influence of drugs and recovered a quantity of speed from B's car. B subsequently admitted that he took speed on most days. A doctor was called upon to examine B and signed a form indicating his suspicion that B was impaired through drugs. A police officer then obtained a blood sample which revealed a significant level of amphetamine. The doctor was not called to give evidence. B submitted that the requirements of the Road Traffic Act 1988 s.7(3)(c) had not been complied with, rendering the blood sample inadmissible. In the absence of any challenge to the evidence of the police officer who dealt with the case the evidence was admitted. B appealed by way of case stated against the justices' decision.

Held, dismissing the appeal, that, although the doctor's signing of the form was hearsay evidence and could not in itself be relied upon, the circumstances in which the officer completed the form could be taken to indicate that the doctor had in fact advised the officer that B's condition might have been due to a drug.

BELL v. DPP, Trans. Ref: CO 2950-95, July 30, 1997, Rose, L.J., QBD.

1166. Road traffic offences–speeding–motorways–rebuttal of presumption that speed enforcement system was functioning properly

Held, that, whilst there was a presumption that the speed enforcement system on the M25 was functioning correctly, in exceptional cases that presumption could be rebutted. Such an exceptional case arose where a driver with an untarnished record contended that the speed limit had not been displayed at the time his car had been photographed by the automatic cameras and the witness giving evidence as to the removal of the film could provide no information as to how the system worked.

DPP v. UNDERWOOD, *The Independent*, June 23, 1997 (C.S.), Simon Brown, L.J., QBD.

1167. **Search and seizure–judicial review–person alleging excessive seizure should pursue private law remedy rather than bring application for judicial review**

[Police and Criminal Evidence Act 1984 s.16.]

Held, that a person alleging excessive seizure contrary to the Police and Criminal Evidence Act 1984 s.16(8) should pursue his private law remedy rather than make an application for judicial review, as the latter procedure was not a fact finding exercise and therefore was an extremely unsatisfactory means of establishing whether there had been a seizure of material not authorised by a search warrant, except in the clearest cases. In contrast, the court in a private law action could hear evidence and make findings of fact unrestricted by Wednesbury principles of reasonableness and could grant speedy interlocutory relief where appropriate.

R. v. CHIEF CONSTABLE OF WARWICKSHIRE, *ex p.* FITZPATRICK; *sub nom.* R. v. CHIEF CONSTABLE OF WARWICKSHIRE, *ex p.* F, *The Times*, November 26, 1997, Rose, L.J., QBD.

1168. **Self incrimination–refusal to testify–witness risked criminal sanctions under law of foreign country–privilege against self incrimination inapplicable–New Zealand**

B worked in the Cook Islands tax haven as accountants for a New Zealand company and were required to give evidence before a New Zealand commission of inquiry established to investigate tax fraud allegations involving the company. They refused to testify, arguing that the evidence that they were required to give would leave them liable to prosecution in the Cook Islands for violating financial secrecy laws. The commissioner dismissed their objection and a High Court order was made requiring them to give evidence which was upheld in the New Zealand Court of Appeal. B appealed to the Privy Council.

Held, dismissing the appeal, that the privilege against self incrimination was not applicable where there was the risk that the witness could face criminal sanctions under the law of a foreign country in respect of prior conduct or the giving of evidence.

BRANNIGAN v. DAVISON [1997] A.C. 238, Lord Nicholls of Birkenhead, PC.

1169. **Trials–fresh evidence discovered after jury retired–trial to continue at defence counsel's invitation**

At K's trial for possession of cannabis with intent to supply, fresh evidence was discovered by the jury after retiring, but counsel invited the judge to permit the trial to continue. K was convicted and appealed.

Held, allowing the appeal, that the introduction of additional material after a jury had retired would normally result in the jury being discharged. In the instant case, defence counsel's decision not to apply for the jury to be discharged was an indication that they waived the right to examine the fresh evidence. However, as the introduction of the evidence in question, which was clearly relevant, warranted re-examination of certain matters, K's conviction could not be regarded as safe.

R. v. KAUL (NATASHA); R. v. COLLIN (PETER JOHN), *The Times*, November 10, 1997, Evans, L.J., CA (Crim Div).

1170. Verdicts–inconsistent verdicts–conspiracy to rob

W and his two co-accused appealed against convictions of conspiracy to rob a post office for which they received custodial sentences of seven years each. W contended that a verdict of not guilty to possessing firearms with intent was inconsistent with the prosecution case.

Held, allowing the appeals and quashing the convictions, that the prosecution had been founded upon an armed robbery of the post office and the verdicts were inconsistent, *R. v. McCluskey (Kevin)* (1994) 98 Cr. App. R. 216, [1994] C.L.Y. 872 distinguished on the basis that the alleged second offence in the present case was a very serious crime carrying a maximum life sentence and not merely affray.

R. v.WARD (PAUL); R. v. DEAN (GARY); R. v. GERALD (CADMAN THOMAS), Trans. Ref: 96/4367/X4, 96/4522/X4, 96/4915/X5, July 8, 1997, Brooke, L.J., CA (Crim Div).

1171. Victims–oral evidence–public order offences–use of threatening words or behaviour–no need for victim to give evidence in court

[Public Order Act 1986 s.4(1).]

A victim's belief that violence would follow threatening words or behaviour could be inferred from witness evidence, it was not necessary for the victim to give evidence to that effect in court. S appealed by way of case stated against his conviction for using threatening, abusive or insulting words or behaviour with intent to cause another to believe that immediate and unlawful violence would be caused, contrary to the Public Order Act 1986 s.4(1), on the grounds that the victim had not given evidence before the magistrates.

Held, dismissing the appeal, that whilst the offence required that the victim must have been present to perceive the offending words or behaviour, it was not necessary for him to give evidence in court to prove that he did perceive the words or behaviour, *Atkin v. DPP* (1989) 89 Cr. App. R. 199, [1990] C.L.Y. 1156 distinguished. The magistrates could rely solely on evidence given by another witness and infer from that evidence that the victim did perceive S's words and behaviour. In addition, any admissible evidence could be used to prove that S acted with intent and there was no need to hear evidence from the victim as to his actual belief.

SWANSTON v. DPP (1997) 161 J.P. 203, McCowan, L.J., QBD.

1172. Video recordings–duty to disclose and preserve relevant material–abuse of process

R appealed against conviction on one count of robbery and two counts of unlawful wounding, for which he was sentenced to 18 months' detention on each count. He was acquitted of another assault alleged to have taken place on the previous day, March 18, 1996, against one of the victims. R entered a chemist's shop from which he had previously been banned. He was seen to put stock into a bag and J confronted him. A fracas followed during which R stabbed N with a knife, and J threw acetic acid at R. It was found by the jury that R had the knife in his hand and had stabbed N before J threw the acid at him. On a voir dire R's application to stay proceedings due to the absence of a video film of the shop taken at the relevant time, was refused on the basis that the police constable investigating the matter had stated the video contained nothing of relevance. R alleged abuse of process, complaining that (1) by the absence of the video film, relevant material had not been preserved, and (2) he had not been informed about a letter written by N to his MP complaining about the police officers who attended the chemist after the incident on March 18, alleging that they had joked about crime and that N and J should deal with the matter themselves whilst ensuring they had no witnesses.

Held, dismissing the appeal, that (1) a breach of the duty to preserve relevant material may constitute an abuse of process if the defendant would be unable to have a fair trial, *R. v. Birmingham* [1992] Crim. L.R. 117, [1992] C.L.Y. 623 and *R. v. Beckford* [1996] 1 Cr. App. R. 94, [1995] 1 C.L.Y. 1109 considered. In determining whether the absence of the video rendered the conviction unsafe, it was necessary to assess whether its absence was unfair. The constable concluded that the video did not contain any relevant material, and the judge hearing evidence from the constable and J determined that the absence of the video was not unfair, and (2) the letter should have been disclosed. Its disclosure was ordered but, in error, the wrong letter was disclosed. Whilst this was unfortunate, it did not make the conviction unsafe.

R. v. REID (HAINSLEY),Trans. Ref: 9605572 Y3, March 10, 1997, Owen, J., CA (Crim Div).

1173. Witnesses–children–competence of child witness–admissibility of video recordings–admissibility of expert evidence to determine competence

[Criminal Justice Act 1988 s.32A(3), s.33A(2A); Police and Criminal Evidence Act 1984 s.78.]

G appealed by way of case stated against conviction of two offences of indecent assault for which he was sentenced to a two year supervision order.The issues were (1) whether the child witnesses were competent; (2) whether expert evidence should have been admitted to assist in determining the question of competence; (3) whether video recordings of children's evidence should have been admitted, and (4) whether the way in which the interviews had been conducted complied with the Cleveland Guidelines and Home Office and Department of Health Memorandum of Good Practice.

Held, dismissing the appeal, that (1) the court had been correct in determining the competence of the children by following the test set out in *R. v. Hampshire (David Peter)* [1995] 2 All E.R. 1019, [1995] 1 C.L.Y. 908. To be admissible the evidence had to be "intelligible testimony" for the purposes of the Criminal Justice Act 1988 s.33A(2A) ie. capable of being understood; (2) it does not require expert evidence to determine whether a child is capable of giving intelligible evidence and the court was correct to decline to hear expert evidence; (3) video taped interviews should not be admitted if to do so would be contrary to the interests of justice as provided in s.32A(3)(c) of the 1988 Act and the Police and Criminal Evidence Act 1984 s.78. The court was right to exercise its discretion in deciding not to hear the expert evidence on the issue of whether to admit the video interviews of the children. If a child suffered a particular abnormality then it was right for there to be expert assistance, otherwise, it was for the jury or the judge to assess the reliability of the evidence, *R. v. D (Criminal Evidence: Child Witnesses)* [1996] 2 W.L.R. 1, [1995] 1 C.L.Y. 909 followed, and (4) following the Cleveland Enquiry it was of the utmost importance that interviews of young children were conducted in accordance with the Guidelines and the Memorandum of Good Practice. Minor breaches could be disregarded but significant breaches could lead to unreliable evidence and injustice. However, it was also necessary to consider the evidence to which the breaches related and how other evidence was affected. The breaches would have to be extreme to conclude that admitting the video evidence was *Wednesbury* unreasonable as submitted by the applicant and here that was not the case.

GIBSON v. DPP [1997] 2 All E.R. 755, Phillips, L.J., QBD.

1174. Witnesses–children–jury directions–repetition of evidence given on video by way of transcript–duty to warn jury about attaching disproportionate weight to repeated evidence

Held, that, where a judge declined to exercise his discretion to accede to a request from the jury to replay a video recording of a child complainant's evidence-in-chief, but rather decided to read out large parts of the transcript of the video evidence verbatim, the judge was obliged to advise the jury to have regard to all the other evidence in the case and not to attach disproportionate weight to the complainant's evidence just because it had been heard a second time, long after all the other evidence had been presented. The judge had a particular duty to use his notes to remind the jury of the complainant's cross-examination and re-examination, and of any part of the defendant's own evidence which might be relevant.

R. v. McQUISTON (JAMES WALLACE), *The Times*, October 10, 1997, Otton, L.J., CA (Crim Div).

1175. Witnesses—television link with foreign country—procedure available even where no extradition treaty

[Perjury Act 1911; Criminal Justice Act 1988 s.32(3).]

Held, that a judge was wrong to rule that he had no power to permit a witness to give evidence from outside the UK by means of a television link on the ground that there was no extradition treaty in force with the country concerned and the sanction under the Criminal Justice Act 1988 s.32(3), whereby evidence given in this way was deemed to have been given in court and was therefore subject to the Perjury Act 1911, would not be available. Notwithstanding that there were many foreign countries in which that sanction could not be invoked, Parliament had placed no limits on the countries in which the television link procedure was to be available.

R. v. FORSYTH (ELIZABETH) [1997] 2 Cr. App. R. 299, Beldam, L.J., CA (Crim Div).

1176. Articles

Admitting irregularly or illegally obtained evidence from abroad into criminal proceedings-a common law approach *(Mark Mackarel)* and *(Christopher H.W. Gane)*: Crim. L.R. 1997, Oct, 720-729. (Review of cases).

An inference of guilt? *(Kevin Browne)*: S.J. 1997, 141(9), 202-203. (Circumstances in which jury may draw adverse inferences from defendant's failure to mention facts during police questioning, to testify or to answer questions at trial).

Corroboration in distress *(Fraser P. Davidson)*: S.L.P.Q. 1997, 2(1), 30-40. (Whether principle of corroboration by evidence of victim's distress has been extended beyond its rational scope).

Criminal Procedure and Investigations Act 1996: committals and magistrates' courts *(Neil O'May)*: Legal Action 1997, Jun, 14-16.

Evidence obtained by use of a covert listening device *(P.B. Carter)*: L.Q.R. 1997, 113(Jul), 468-480. (Whether such evidence is admissible or should be excluded on human rights grounds and legislation providing authorisation system for police use of listening devices).

Fairness and the exclusion of evidence under section 78(1) of the Police and Criminal Evidence Act *(Katharine Grevling)*: L.Q.R. 1997, 113(Oct), 667-685.

Hearsay in criminal cases: an overview of Law Commission Report No. 245 *(Colin Tapper)*: Crim. L.R. 1997, Nov, 771-784. (Why hearsay rule as applied in criminal cases is imperfect and extent to which Law Commission proposals are likely to remedy problems).

Maximising disclosure: Part 1 *(David Corker)*: N.L.J. 1997, 147(6796), 885-886. (Opportunities for criminal defence lawyers using Code of Practice to hold police to account for failure to record, retain and report to CPS relevant information from investigations).

Maximising disclosure: Part 2 *(David Corker)*: N.L.J. 1997, 147(6798), 961-962. (Duties of primary and secondary prosecution disclosure and defence disclosure under the Criminal Procedure and Investigations Act 1996, advantages and disadvantages of non-disclosure, challenges and public interest immunity).

More Crown Court advocacy *(Jeffrey Gordon)*: N.L.J. 1997, 147(6811), 1473. (Prosecutors' inadequacies in investigating information provided by defence under disclosure requirements).

More on proving conspiracy *(John C. Smith)*: Crim. L.R. 1997, May, 333-338. (Admissibility of hearsay evidence in proving conspiracy or joint enterprise and appropriate jury directions).

New techniques and new devices *(Philip Plowden)*: N.L.J. 1997, 147(6786), 502-504. (Status of video evidence as criminal evidence, ways of improving its credibility by regulating enhancement procedures, how evidence is used in court and principles of evidence applied).

Prosecution and privilege *(Colin Tapper)*: E. & P. 1996, 1(1), 5-24. (Whether placing of legal professional privilege above accused's need to have access to evidence unjustifiable in principle and on authority).

Prosecution disclosure, crime and human rights *(John Wadham)*: N.L.J. 1997, 147(6791), 697-698. (Whether provisions allowing prosecution to restrict disclosure on grounds of public interest immunity violate the right to a fair trial under the ECHR).

Proving computer crime *(Peter Sommer)*: Comp. & Law 1997, 8(3), 29-30. (Admissibility of computer printouts in criminal proceedings and need for guidelines and standard procedures for computer-derived exhibits).

The sharp end of the wedge: use of mixed statements by the defence *(Diane J. Birch)*: Crim. L.R. 1997, Jun, 416-431.

The significance of compellability in the prosecution of domestic assault *(Antonia Cretney* and *Gwynn Davis)*: Brit. J. Criminol. 1997, 37(1), 75-89.

Two mysteries appertaining to the documentary evidence provisions of the Criminal Justice Act 1988: part-heard testimony and the exercise of judicial discretion under the statute *(Roderick Munday)*: J.P. 1997, 161 (29), 691-696.

Who qualifies as a "witness" for the purpose of imputations made under the Criminal Evidence Act 1898 section 1(f)(ii) *(Roderick Munday)*: J.P. 1997, 161(16), 379-382.

1177. Books

Andrews, John A.; Hirst, Michael–Criminal Evidence. 3rd Ed. Criminal Law Library. Hardback: £99.00. ISBN 0-421-56820-8. Sweet & Maxwell.

CRIMINAL LAW

1178. Administration of justice offences–intimidation of witnesses–spitting did not constitute "harm"

[Criminal Justice and Public Order Act 1994 s.51(2), s.51(4).]

N appealed against conviction of intimidation of a witness, contrary to the Criminal Justice and Public Order Act 1994 s.51(2), for which he received a custodial sentence of 12 months. N uttered abuse and threatened the victim and spat in her face. N accepted that there had been an assault and battery, but contended that the trial judge had erred by ruling that spitting in a person's face was sufficient to satisfy the definition of "harm" contained within s.51(2).

Held, allowing the appeal, that despite the extension of the term "harm" by s.51(4) to cover "financial harm" and "damage to property", there was no reason to extend it beyond its ordinary meaning of physical harm given that there was no evidence of physical injury either threatened to, or sustained by, the victim.

R. v. NORMANTON (LEE), Trans. Ref: 96/7917/X4, August 14, 1997, Hutchison, L.J., CA (Crim Div).

1179. Affray–conduct not continuous but fell into separate sequences–jury directions

[Public Order Act 1986 s.3(1).]

S was convicted of affray contrary to the Public Order Act 1986 s.3(1). The offence was committed during a party and, although the prosecution initially relied on events which took place outside the house to found the count of affray, the Recorder referred to incidents both inside and outside the house in his summing-up. S appealed against conviction on the ground that the Recorder had misdirected the jury in failing to direct them that they had to be satisfied that either the events inside the house or those outside the house constituted the offence, leading to the possibility that, although the jury's verdict was unanimous, it had been reached on different factual bases.

Held, allowing the appeal, that the nature of the offence of affray typically involved a continuous course of conduct. The criminal character of that conduct depended on its general nature and effect and not on particular incidents and events. Where the Crown relied on such a continuous course of conduct it was unnecessary to identify and prove particular incidents. To require such proof would be to deprive s.3(1) of the 1986 Act of its intended effect. Where, however, the conduct relied on by the Crown was not continuous but fell into separate sequences, different considerations might apply. The character of the conduct in each sequence and its effect on those present at the scene might be quite different. The jury might not all be persuaded that the same sequence amounted to an affray, the result being that there was no unanimous verdict in support of a conviction based on any one sequence. Since there was a possibility that that had happened in the instant case, the conviction was quashed, *R. v. Brown (Kevin)* (1984) 79 Cr. App. R. 115, [1984] C.L.Y. 624 and *R. v. Houlden (Melissa Ann)* (1994) 99 Cr. App. R. 244, [1995] 1 C.L.Y. 1091 applied. *R. v. Keeton (Geoffrey Wayne)* [1995] 2 Cr. App. R. 241, [1994] C.L.Y. 814 considered.

R. v. SMITH (CHRISTOPHER FLOYD) [1997] 1 Cr. App. R. 14, Lord Bingham of Cornhill, L.C.J., CA (Crim Div).

1180. Arrest–driving whilst disqualified–meaning of "driving"

[Police Act 1964 s.51 (3); Road Traffic Act 1988 s.103.]

J and C appealed by way of case stated against a conviction of wilfully obstructing a police officer in the execution of his duty contrary to the Police Act 1964 s.51 (3). The police officer had seen J driving with the owner of the car, G, as the passenger. He followed them as he recognised the owner as someone who was disqualified. When J stopped to converse with C in his front garden, the officer questioned him as to his identity and discovered that he was a disqualified driver. The officer told J he was arresting him for driving whilst disqualified. J ran away, and when the officer attempted to follow him, C stood in his way. The issue was whether the officer had been acting in the execution of his duty, which depended on whether J was driving a motor vehicle on the road at the time of arrest. There was no question that the other conditions under the Road Traffic Act 1988 s.103 for lawful arrest in these circumstances were satisfied, namely that the officer suspected J of being disqualified and had reasonable cause for that suspicion.

Held, allowing the appeal and quashing the convictions, that an interpretation of s.103(3) to read "driving or having driven", thereby conferring wider powers of arrest than the legislation intended, was unsustainable. The issue was whether J's reason for ceasing to drive was sufficiently connected with the actual driving of the vehicle and that was a matter of fact and degree, the appropriate test to apply being laid down in *Stevens v. Thornborrow* [1969] 3 All E.R. 1487, [1970] C.L.Y. 2516 and *Edkins v. Knowles* [1972] 2 All E.R. 503, [1973] C.L.Y. 2925. There were circumstances in which a person may still be driving although the car had stopped and the engine was switched off, but the present case was not one of them.

JAMES v. DPP, Trans. Ref: CO/3543/96, February 12, 1997, Moses, J., QBD.

1181. Assault–actual bodily harm–harassment–fear of violence at some time sufficient to prove assault

C appealed against his conviction for assault occasioning actual bodily harm, contending that his conduct, which had involved stalking the victim over a prolonged period, did not amount to assault as the victim could not have feared immediate and unlawful personal violence because no physical harm had occurred.

Held, dismissing the appeal, that if the prosecution could prove that the victim had a fear of violence at some time, not excluding the immediate future, this was enough to make out the offence of assault which could be committed solely by words.

R. v. CONSTANZA (GAETANO), *The Times*, March 31, 1997, Schiemann, L.J., CA (Crim Div).

1182. Assault—actual bodily harm—malicious telephone calls—psychiatric injury to victim

[Offences against the Person Act 1861 s.47.]

I was convicted of assault occasioning actual bodily harm contrary to the Offences against the Person Act 1861 s.47 after pleading guilty to making malicious telephone calls to women. He appealed against the dismissal of his appeal against conviction.

Held, dismissing the appeal, that a recognisable psychiatric illness suffered by a victim of malicious telephone calls amounted to "bodily harm" within the meaning of the Act, *R. v. Chan-Fook* [1994] 1 W.L.R. 689, [1994] C.L.Y. 1076 followed. Given that harassment of women by malicious calls was a significant social problem against which the law should be able to provide protection, the Act should be construed in the light of the scientific knowledge current at the time of the offence, notwithstanding the fact that psychiatric illness was not considered to be bodily harm during the original drafting of the Act. An assault was committed under s.47 if the victim was caused to apprehend imminent personal violence and the question whether a malicious telephone caller was guilty of assault would thus be a question of fact in each case.

R. v. IRELAND (ROBERT MATTHEW); R. v. BURSTOW (ANTHONY CHRISTOPHER) [1997] 3 W.L.R. 534, Lord Steyn, HL.

1183. Assault—grievous bodily harm—harassment—"inflict" not given restrictive meaning

[Offences Against the Person Act 1861 s.20.]

B was charged with inflicting grievous bodily harm under the Offences Against the Person Act 1861 s.20. It was alleged that he had stalked the victim and subjected her to a catalogue of harassment, including silent telephone calls and theft of washing, which resulted in her suffering severe depression. B argued that it was an abuse of process for the case to proceed on the basis of s.20.

Held, rejecting defence submissions, that there was no reason for "inflict" to be given a restrictive meaning. B then changed his plea to guilty and was sentenced to three years' imprisonment on s.20, with 18 months concurrent for theft.

R. v. BURSTOW [1996] Crim. L.R. 331, Judge Lait, Crown Ct.

1184. Computer crime—police officers' access to Police National Computer for unauthorised purpose

[Computer Misuse Act 1990 s.1, s.17(2), s.17(5); Data Protection Act 1984 s.5(2)(B).]

Police officers with authorised access to computer information were not convicted under the Computer Misuse Act 1990 for unauthorised use of that information as the Act was concerned only with preventing unauthorised access. Unauthorised use should be dealt with under the Data Protection Act 1984. The DPP appealed by way of case stated against the overturning of the respondent police officers' convictions of offences under the Computer Misuse Act 1990 s.1. The respondents had, for private purposes, obtained details relating to two motor cars from the Police National Computer. The DPP maintained that the Commissioner of Police, who controlled access to the computer, gave authority to police officers to access information only for police purposes and the respondents' use of the computer to gain material for non-police purposes was therefore unauthorised. The respondents distinguished between the gaining of access, which was said to be authorised, and the admittedly unauthorised purpose of their excursion.

Held, dismissing the appeal, that the Act was concerned with the protection of computer systems and criminalised the "hacking" or unauthorised access to computer material. It was not designed to protect the integrity of information stored on computers, which was the purpose behind the Data Protection Act 1984. Whether or not the Commissioner alone was entitled to control access to the computer, the respondents' access was not unauthorised in terms of s.17(5) or s.17(2) and they were not therefore in breach of s.1. There was not a gap in the law since police officers were open to prosecution for use of the computer for improper purposes under s.5(2)(b) of the 1984 Act.

DPP v. BIGNALL, *The Times*, June 6, 1997, Astill, J., QBD.

1185. Confiscation of Alcohol (Young Persons) Act 1997 (c.33)

This Act allows a constable to confiscate intoxicating liquor held by, or for use by, a young person in a public place or a place to which the young person has unlawfully gained access.

This Act received Royal Assent on March 21, 1997.

1186. Confiscation of Alcohol (Young Persons) Act 1997 (c.33)–Commencement Order

CONFISCATION OF ALCOHOL (YOUNG PERSONS) ACT 1997 (COMMENCEMENT) ORDER 1997, SI 1997 1725 (C.73); made under the Confiscation of Alcohol (Young Persons) Act 1997 s.2. Commencement details: bringing into force various provisions of the Act on August 1, 1997; £0.65.

This Order brings into force the Confiscation of Alcohol (Young Persons) Act 1997 s.1

1187. Conspiracy–conspiracy to defraud–characteristics of offence–jury directions

F and M appealed against their conviction of conspiracy to defraud. F was director and shareholder of two public limited companies, PMH and MP. M was an accountant and stockbroker. PMH wished to sell business premises. F invented a purchaser, C, and forged powers of attorney, which M signed, empowering him to purchase and mortgage the property. The sale was completed and C sold the property to BPL who sold it on to a subsidiary of MP. F subsequently extracted the surplus funds from the sale. F and M contended that the judge misdirected the jury on the offence of conspiracy to defraud when he told them that, although the particulars of offence alleged a conspiracy to defraud PMH and MP, they could convict if they were agreed that only one company had been defrauded. F and M submitted that following the judge's direction they were at risk of being convicted of three conspiracies. It was argued, in reliance upon *R. v. Greenfield* [1973] 1 W.L.R. 1151, [1973] C.L.Y. 492, that a count for conspiracy was bad for duplicity if it charged more than one conspiracy.

Held, dismissing the appeal, that the judge had not misdirected the jury on the offence. Following *Adams v. Queen, the* [1995] 1 W.L.R. 52, [1995] 1 C.L.Y. 1241 where a person was charged with conspiracy to defraud based on economic loss it was necessary to show that the victim had a right or interest which was capable of being prejudiced. A defendant who dishonestly concealed information which he was under a duty to disclose was guilty of fraud. Since a company was entitled to recover secret profits made by its directors at its expense, a dishonest agreement by directors to prevent a company exercising its right of recovery constituted a conspiracy to defraud. On the facts, there was sufficient evidence that F and M's conduct, designed to achieve and conceal a profit, resulted in economic loss to PMH. In addition, there was evidence of conspiracy to defraud MP as there was an agreement which embraced a right or interest of MP capable of being prejudiced. The judge was entitled to direct the jury that they had to be satisfied that only one company was defrauded, *R. v. Brown (Kevin)* (1984) 79 Cr. App. R. 115, [1984] C.L.Y. 624 and *R. v. Hancock (Paul)* [1996] 2 Cr. App. R. 554, [1996] 1 C.L.Y. 1563 considered. The contention that F and M were at risk of being convicted of three conspiracies was therefore rejected.

R. v. FUSSELL (SIMON ANTHONY); R. v. ASSIZ DE MENDONCA (RUDOLPH), Trans. Ref: 96/4236/X4, 96/4238/X4, July 9, 1997, Otton, L.J., CA (Crim Div).

1188. Criminal damage—defences—whether duress of circumstances could extend to the fear of psychological harm

[Criminal Law Act 1967 s.3; Child Abduction Act 1984 s.2; Criminal Damage Act 1971 s.5(2)(b).]

B and her husband, W, appealed against convictions of criminal damage to the front door of a house, where the father of B's daughter was holding the child having refused to return her after a contact visit. B contended that (1) the defence of necessity had been widened in *R. v. Pommell* [1995] 2 Cr. App. R. 607, [1995] 1 C.L.Y. 1258 and could include circumstances other than those where there was an immediate fear of death or serious injury; (2) under the Criminal Law Act 1967 s.3 the force was lawful because it was used in the prevention of the crimes of kidnapping, child abduction or false imprisonment; and (3) the Criminal Damage Act 1971 s.5(2)(b) provided a defence where such force was used to protect the property of an accused from damage and a fortiori would be a defence where the child of an accused was at risk.

Held, dismissing the appeals, that (1) duress of circumstances could not be extended to circumstances where the defendant had feared serious psychological injury. There was a pressing need for Parliament to codify the defences of duress in line with the recommendations of the Law Commission to prevent such cases clogging the system; (2) no criminal act had been committed by the father because he had a defence under the Child Abduction Act 1989 s.2(3)(i)(a) or s.2(3)(i)(b) and (3) the child clearly did not represent property within the meaning of s.5(2)(b) of the 1971 Act, *R. v. Pommell* distinguished as merely accepting that necessity might be extended from driving cases to other charges except murder, attempted murder and treason.

R. v. BAKER (JANET); R. v. WILKINS (CARL) [1997] Crim L.R. 497, Brooke, L.J., CA (Crim Div).

1189. Criminal injuries compensation—grave injury to infant—calculation of future loss

C applied for judicial review to quash an award of £628,872 compensation for criminal injuries. C contended that the CICB had erred in its assessment of future loss having reduced the award by some £250,000 and having failed to afford C the opportunity to address it on either the facts or the law.

Held, allowing the application and granting certiorari to quash the decision and mandamus for the CICB to reconsider the claim, that the CICB had failed to allow C an opportunity to address it before making such substantial reductions from his claim. However, it was important to recognise that this case turned on its own facts.

R. v. CRIMINAL INJURIES COMPENSATION BOARD, *ex p.* CATTERALL [1997] P.I.Q.R. P128, Ognall, J., QBD.

1190. Criminal injuries compensation—rape—standard of proof required as to consent

SD sought judicial review of a decision of the CICB refusing her claim for compensation on the ground that the Board was not satisfied SD had not consented to sexual intercourse with three men she alleged had raped her when she was drunk. SD contended that in dealing with a rape complaint CICB should not take account of the characteristic of rape that required the prosecution to prove that the defendant knew the victim, did not consent or was reckless as to whether she consented or not, and that by failing to give due weight to the evidence the decision was *Wednesbury* unreasonable.

Held, refusing the application, that by ignoring the criminal element necessary in rape, the CICB could, if finding other facts in an applicant's favour, make a compensation award even if no crime had occurred. The CICB heard the application as a tribunal of fact and considered evidence from SD and other witnesses so that the court could not conclude that the CICB had been *Wednesbury* unreasonable in finding that SD was not so drunk that she could not have consented to intercourse.

R. v. CRIMINAL INJURIES COMPENSATION BOARD, *ex p.* SD, Trans. Ref: CO/201/96, June 4, 1997, Laws, J., QBD.

1191. Criminal injuries compensation—unlawful sexual intercourse—offence not a violent crime—use of force not probative of violence

P sought judicial review of a decision of the CICB refusing her claim for compensation under the 1990 CICB Scheme following L's conviction for having unlawful sexual intercourse with her. By virtue of para.4(a) of the scheme an ex gratia payment application would be entertained from a victim of a crime of violence. Although L's not guilty plea to a charge of rape was accepted, P, who was 12 at the time of the incident, contended that she had not consented to intercourse and that medical evidence showed that force had been used.

Held, refusing the application, that although consent by a female under 16 to sexual intercourse or indecent touching was not recognised by law, it did not follow that the commission of either offence involved violence. P had sustained a bruise which could have resulted from the use of force, but that force was not necessarily violent. L's admission that intercourse had taken place did not amount to an admission of violence towards P. Each case had to be decided on its own facts.

R. v. CRIMINAL INJURIES COMPENSATION BOARD, *ex p.* P, Trans. Ref: CO/399/96, April 14, 1997, McCullough, J., QBD.

1192. Cultural property—unlawful removal

RETURN OF CULTURAL OBJECTS (AMENDMENT) REGULATIONS 1997, SI 1997 1719; made under the European Communities Act 1972 s.2. In force: September 1, 1997; £0.65.

These Regulations implement Council Directive 96/100 ([1996] OJ L60/59) which amends the Annex to the Council Directive 93/7 ([1993] OJ L74/74) on the return of cultural objects unlawfully removed from the territory of a Member State, which in turn was implemented by the Return of Cultural Objects Regulations 1994 (SI 1994 501). They amend the definition of "the Directive" in the 1994 Regulations so that it includes a reference to Directive 96/100 and introduce an additional category of objects which may constitute a national treasure for the purposes of the 1994 Regulations provided the monetary value of any such object is above the specified financial threshold.

1193. Curfew orders—responsible officers

CURFEW ORDER (RESPONSIBLE OFFICER) ORDER 1997, SI 1997 2351; made under the Criminal Justice Act 1991 s.12, s.30. In force: October 1, 1997; £0.65.

This Order describes the persons who are to be made responsible, by a curfew order relating to a place of curfew in Berkshire, Cambridgeshire, Greater Manchester, the London Borough of Barnet, Brent, Ealing, Enfield, Haringey, Harrow, Hillingdon or Hounslow, Norfolk, Suffolk, or West Yorkshire, for monitoring an offender's whereabouts during the curfew periods. The Curfew Order (Responsible Officer) (Berkshire, Greater Manchester and Norfolk) Order 1995 (SI 1995 2840) is revoked.

1194. Defences–diminished responsibility–epilepsy capable of resulting in diminished responsibility–jury directions on provocation

[Criminal Appeal Act 1968 s.17(1)(a).]

C pleaded guilty to manslaughter by reason of provocation, but was convicted of murder in 1985. He contended that, in the light of psychiatric evidence given at trial, the jury should also have been directed on diminished responsibility but his appeal failed. Although C suffered from epilepsy the jury was directed that this was not a characteristic they could take into account in determining whether the provocation was enough to make a reasonable man do as he had done. The Home Secretary referred the case under the Criminal Appeal Act 1968 s.17(1)(a). The victim accepted a lift from C and when she refused his sexual advances by hitting him in the face he punched her. He then claimed to have panicked and strangled her. The evidence of two psychiatrists was that C suffered from epilepsy and frontal lobe damage which affected his functions of judgment, control of emotions and control of impulses and that he also suffered from absence seizures which led to a change in intellect and a reduction of his ability to appreciate the circumstances surrounding him. Both doctors were of the opinion that at the time of the killing C was suffering from an abnormality of mind of such significance as seriously to diminish his responsibility for the act. C argued that a verdict of manslaughter, on the grounds of diminished responsibility, should be substituted and that the interests of justice did not demand a retrial. C also sought to challenge the direction on provocation given to the jury as the law had changed since his trial.

Held, allowing the appeal, that a defence of diminished responsibility should be put before a jury and it was ordered that C be retried. If provocation was raised as an issue at the retrial then the judge would apply the law as it then stood.

R. v. CAMPBELL (COLIN FREDERICK) [1997] 1 Cr. App. R. 199, Lord Bingham of Cornhill, L.C.J., CA (Crim Div).

1195. Defences–duress of necessity–defence not available where causation of offence not extraneous to offender

Held, that duress of necessity was only available as a defence where the offender acted as he did in response to an objective danger and could not be relied upon where the defendant had absconded from prison due to thoughts of suicide, since a subjective element was thereby introduced.

R. v. RODGER (ANDREW), *The Times*, July 30, 1997, Sir Patrick Russell, CA (Crim Div).

1196. Defences–self defence–jury directions–recording of summing up

[Criminal Appeal Rules 1968 (SI 1968 1262) r.18.]

R appealed against conviction of causing grievous bodily harm with intent for which he was sentenced to three and a half years' imprisonment. The grounds of appeal were that the judge failed to direct the jury fully as to self defence. The transcript of the summing up did not contain the directions of law as the recording machinery was not working and neither counsel was informed. An incident occurred in the early hours, between R and four men who had been out drinking, and was filmed on closed circuit television which was watched by the jury. Three of the four men were off duty police officers. R claimed that he was provoked by racist remarks and tried to defend himself from attack by the man he was convicted of assaulting. R delivered a blow to the victim who suffered a fractured skull. He argued that the video evidence conflicted with the victim's assertion that he tried to defuse the situation.

Held, allowing the appeal, that (1) the direction on self defence was incomplete as the two limbed rule was not applied. The jury should have been directed to firstly consider the position as the accused honestly, if unreasonably, believed it to be, and then secondly to consider objectively whether it was reasonable for him, holding that belief, to behave in the way he did and, if it was reasonable for him to use force, whether the amount of force used was reasonable, and (2) there was a clear breach of the Criminal Appeal Rules 1968 r.18 in not recording the summation.

R. v. RICHARDS (JASON) [1997] Crim. L.R. 48, Brooke, L.J., CA (Crim Div).

1197. **Doli incapax–12 year old child with mental age of six or seven–presumption of doli incapax rebutted**

[Mental Health Act 1983.]

D appealed against a conviction of actual bodily harm committed when he was 12 years old. A submission of incapacity to plead had been rejected, and the issues were whether D could plead self defence, and it was found he could not, and whether D was doli incapax. Reports from a chartered psychologist and from a consultant psychiatrist were submitted, and both concluded that D was unfit to plead or to appear as a witness. The latter gave evidence, adding that D's condition did not come within the provisions of the Mental Health Act 1983. The issue before the court was whether the magistrates were justified in their findings of fact that D knew, when committing the offence, that it was wrong.

Held, dismissing the appeal, that there were no errors of law and the magistrates had made findings of fact having correctly directed themselves in law. D had the mental age of six or seven, which leads to a presumption of incapacity which is rebuttable. The difficulty in rebutting that presumption had been adequately taken into account below, *L (A Minor) v. DPP* [1996] 2 Cr. App. R. 501, [1996] 1 C.L.Y. 1398 and *C (A Minor) v. DPP* [1996] 1 A.C. 1, [1995] 1 C.L.Y. 1108 considered.

D (A JUVENILE) v. CROWN PROSECUTION SERVICE, Trans. Ref: CO 3281-96, November 11, 1996, Schiemann, L.J., QBD.

1198. **Drink driving offences–blood tests–urine tests–refusal of blood test did not exclude subsequent request**

[Road Traffic Act 1988 s.7.]

The DPP appealed by way of case stated against a decision of a stipendiary magistrate to dismiss the case against a motorist who had refused to give both a specimen of blood and one of urine. T refused to give a sample of breath and was taken to a police station. The intoximeter was unavailable and the custody sergeant asked for a specimen of blood, which T refused to provide on unspecified medical grounds. T was subsequently asked to provide a specimen of urine which he also refused and was then charged with failing to provide a urine specimen. T contended that, when he had initially refused to provide a blood sample, either a doctor's opinion should have been requested or he should have been charged forthwith, and that the officer was prevented from asking for a specimen of urine.

Held, allowing the appeal and remitting the matter with a direction to convict, that, under the Road Traffic Act 1988 s.7, the refusal of one type of specimen did not exclude a subsequent request for another type, *DPP v. Garrett* [1995] R.T.R. 302, *Barnes v. DPP* [1997] 2 Cr. App. R. 505, [1997] C.L.Y. 1154 and *R. v. Paduch (Jan)* (1973) 57 Cr. App. R. 676, [1973] C.L.Y. 2898 considered.

DPP v. TAYLOR, *The Independent*, July 28, 1997 (C.S.), Garland, J., QBD.

1199. **Drink driving offences–mens rea–defence of insanity unavailable for strict liability offence**

[Road Traffic Act 1988 s.5(1)(A).]

The DPP appealed by way of case stated against a decision of magistrates to acquit H of a charge of driving with excess alcohol contrary to the Road Traffic Act 1988 s.5(1)(A). H conceded that he had driven with a blood alcohol level over the legal limit but claimed a defence of insanity, by reason of a manic depressive psychosis for which he was being treated. The DPP contended that although the defence of insanity was available in a magistrates court, it was only available in relation to an offence requiring a mental element.

Held, allowing the appeal and remitting the case with a direction to convict, that the offence of driving with excess alcohol was a strict liability offence and therefore no defence of insanity was available. Where the offence did require an element of mens rea, the burden was on the accused to establish insanity on the balance of probabilities, *R. v. Horseferry Road Magistrates Court, ex p. K* (1996) 160 J.P. 441, [1996] 1 C.L.Y. 1642 approved.

DPP v. HARPER; *sub nom.* DPP v. H, *The Times*, May 2, 1997, McCowan, L.J., QBD.

1200. Drug offences–drug trafficking–attempts

[Customs and Excise Management Act 1979 s.170(2).]

Q was convicted of being knowingly concerned in the attempted fraudulent evasion of the prohibition on exportation of 12.31 kilogrammes of heroin contrary to the Customs and Excise Management Act 1979 s.170(2). Q's defence was that he was involved in the offence at the direction of his uncle who persuaded him that he was assisting the authorities in the apprehension of M, a convicted drug smuggler, and would therefore be immune from prosecution. Q subsequently worked for M, storing the drugs before handing them to his cousin who offered them for sale. Q appealed on the ground that as there was no real evidence as to how far M, as the principal in the attempt, proceeded in the commission of the offence, there was no evidence as to whether or not the actus reus of any attempt in which Q was knowingly concerned was sufficiently established. Q contended that the judge should have directed the jury that there was insufficient actus reus to constitute the offence. Q argued that his acts constituted merely preparatory acts to the substantive offence alleged to have been attempted and not to the commission of the offence itself.

Held, dismissing the appeal, that in order to establish the actus reus of the offence the Crown had to prove that there was a fraudulent evasion and that Q was knowingly concerned therein, it being unnecessary to distinguish between those concerned in the offence in terms of principal and accessories. The terms of s.170(2) create a "compendious provision" which includes all concerned with an evasion or attempted evasion. In addition, it was open to the jury to regard the transporting and handing over of the drugs as being more than merely preparatory acts.

R. v. QADIR (MANZOOR), Trans. Ref: 96/2311/X4, 96/2312/X4, July 25, 1997, Potter, L.J., CA (Crim Div).

1201. Drug offences–incitement to commit an offence contrary to the Misuse of Drugs Act 1971–publication of book

[Misuse of Drugs Act 1971 s.18, s.19; Criminal Attempts Act 1981 Sch.1.]

M appealed against conviction of incitement to commit an offence contrary to the Misuse of Drugs Act 1971 s.19 and applied for leave to appeal against three concurrent custodial sentences of 12 months each for that offence and for production and possession of cannabis. M wrote and published a book on the cultivation and production of cannabis which sold approximately 500 copies. M contended that, (1) the trial judge had misled the jury by directing that the offence would be made out if the book "may" have encouraged readers and the test was too low, and (2) no evidence had been brought that M had incited anyone to commit an offence under the Misuse of Drugs Act 1971 s.18 and that s.19 applied only to s.18 and not other offences under the 1971 Act because of the amending procedure of the Criminal Attempts Act 1981 Sch.1.

Held, allowing the appeal against sentence for production and possession of cannabis, that the sentences were excessive and terms of six months were substituted, that (1) although the inclusion of the word "may" was regrettable, the direction itself was clear and the jury had not been misled, and (2) it was apparent that any anomaly resulted from a draftsman's error and the construction of the 1981 Act was clearly not intended to restrict the offence of incitement to s.18 alone, but to cover the offences set out in other sections of the 1971 Act.

R. v. MARLOW (MICHAEL DAVID), Trans. Ref: 96/2436/W4, July 14, 1997, Potter, L.J., CA (Crim Div).

1202. **Drug offences–occupier of premises knowingly permitting the smoking of cannabis–meaning of "occupier"**

[Misuse of Drugs Act 1971 s.8.]

R appealed by way of case stated against his conviction of being the occupier of premises in which he knowingly permitted the smoking of cannabis contrary to the Misuse of Drugs Act 1971 s.8(d). R contended that he was not the occupier of the property as the tenancy of the council house was in the name of his girlfriend, R having no proprietary interest.

Held, dismissing the appeal, that R was the occupier of the property for the purposes of the 1971 Act since he had possession of the premises so as to enable him to exclude those who wished to smoke cannabis there, *R. v. Ben Nien Tao* (1976) 63 Crim. App. R. 163, [1976] C.L.Y. 512 and *R. v. Campbell* [1982] Crim. L.R. 595, [1982] C.L.Y. 643 considered. It was unrealistic not to regard R as a joint occupier of the property after nine years of cohabitation.

READ (KEITH PAUL) v. DPP, Trans. Ref: CO-442/97, June 20, 1997, Simon Brown, L.J., QBD.

1203. **Drug offences–smuggling–customs officers–job titles**

See CUSTOMS AND EXCISE. §5921

1204. **Drug trafficking–foreign jurisdictions**

DRUG TRAFFICKING ACT 1994 (DESIGNATED COUNTRIES AND TERRITORIES) (AMENDMENT) ORDER 1997, SI 1997 1318; made under the Drug Trafficking Act 1994 s.39. In force: July 1, 1997; £0.65.

This Order amends the Drug Trafficking Act 1994 (Designated Countries and Territories) Order 1996 (SI 1996 2880) by adding Ireland to the list of designated countries, inserting an appropriate authority for Antigua and Barbuda and amending the appropriate authority for Colombia. The Appendix to the 1996 Order is also amended so as to add the point at which proceedings are instituted in both Antigua and Barbuda and Colombia.

1205. **Drug trafficking–foreign jurisdictions**

DRUG TRAFFICKING ACT 1994 (DESIGNATED COUNTRIES AND TERRITORIES) (AMENDMENT) (NO.2) ORDER 1997, SI 1997 2980; made under the Drug Trafficking Act 1994 s.39. In force: February 1, 1998; £1.10.

This Order amends the Drug Trafficking Act 1994 (Designated Countries and Territories) Order 1996 (SI 1996 2880) in order to add Austria, Benin, Botswana, Hungary, Kazakhstan, Tonga and the United Republic of Tanzania to this list of countries designated for the purposes of recovering payments or other rewards received in connection with drug trafficking. Various other minor amendments are made.

1206. **False imprisonment–requirements of offence–victim of assault too frightened to escape**

J, having pleaded guilty to assault occasioning actual bodily harm, was also convicted of false imprisonment. In response to a request by the jury to clarify what was required to convict and whether the fact that the victim was too frightened to move was sufficient, the trial judge had merely reiterated the facts and allowed counsel to submit their alternative definitions of the offence. J appealed against conviction.

Held, allowing the appeal, that (1) the requirements of the offence of false imprisonment were that an act of restraint was committed without legal authority and that the accused intended both to commit the act in question and that the act should restrain the victim, and (2) the trial judge erred in not giving a clear direction to the jury that the fear occasioned in the victim had to arise from an act intended to frighten her.

R. v. JAMES (ANTHONY DAVID), *The Times*, October 2, 1997, Potter, L.J., CA (Crim Div).

1207. Firearms–licences–museums

FIREARMS (MUSEUMS) ORDER 1997, SI 1997 1692; made under the Firearms (Amendment) Act 1988 Sch.para.5. In force: July 28, 1997; £0.65.

This Order specifies museums and similar institutions which are registered with the Museums and Galleries Commission for the purpose of making them eligible for a museum firearms licence under the Firearms (Amendment) Act 1988. Such a licence exempts a museum or similar institution from the need to hold a firearm certificate and an authority from the Secretary of State in respect of firearms which form part of its collection.

1208. Firearms–prohibition–exemptions–historic interest

FIREARMS (AMENDMENT) ACT 1997 (FIREARMS OF HISTORIC INTEREST) ORDER 1997, SI 1997 1537; made under the Firearms (Amendment) Act 1997 s.7. In force: July 1, 1997; £0.65.

This Order specifies the description of firearms, the possession, purchase, acquisition, sale or transfer of which is, if the firearm was manufactured before January 1, 1919, and is held by virtue of a firearm certificate subject to a condition requiring the firearm to be held as part of a collection, exempt from the prohibition of large-calibre handguns by the Firearms (Amendment) Act 1997 s.1.

1209. Firearms–prohibition–exemptions–historic interest–transitional provisions

FIREARMS (AMENDMENT) ACT 1997 (TRANSITIONAL PROVISIONS AND SAVINGS) REGULATIONS 1997, SI 1997 1538; made under the Firearms (Amendment) Act 1997 s.51. In force: July 1, 1997; £0.65.

These Regulations limit, for a certain period, the effect of one of the exemptions from the prohibition of large-calibre hand guns by the Firearms (Amendment) Act 1997. The exemption in question is that which enables holders of firearm certificates for certain handguns of historic interest to possess, purchase, acquire, sell or transfer such guns without the authority of the Secretary of State if their certificates are subject to a condition requiring such guns to be kept and used only at a place designated by the Secretary of State.

1210. Firearms (Amendment) Act 1997 (c.5)

The Firearms Acts 1968 to 1992 are amended by this Act, which prohibits all handguns above .22 calibre, with those of a lower calibre having to be kept at registered gun clubs. It will be an offence to have a small calibre pistol outside a licensed club. Special permits from the police must be obtained when handguns are removed from clubs. Prohibited handguns and ammunition are to be handed in at designated police stations. Compensation will be paid to handgun owners and dealers who surrender prohibited handguns, ammunition or equipment on or before the due date. The Act also provides for the licensing of pistol clubs and for their regulation.

This Act received Royal Assent on February 27, 1997.

1211. Firearms (Amendment) Act 1997 (c.5)–Commencement No.1 Order

FIREARMS (AMENDMENT) ACT 1997 (COMMENCEMENT) (NO.1) ORDER 1997, SI 1997 1076 (C.37); made under the Firearms (Amendment) Act 1997 s.53. Commencement details: bringing into force various provisions of the Act on March 17, 1997; £0.65.

This Order brings the Firearms (Amendment) Act 1997 s.16, s.17 and s.18 into force on March 17, 1997 for the purposes of making a compensation scheme. Under s.16 the Secretary of State is to make a compensation scheme for persons who will effectively be deprived of their firearms or ammunition by virtue of the 1997 Act. Under s.17 any scheme made by the Secretary of State is to provide compensation for persons whose ancillary equipment for such firearms has no practicable use in relation to any other firearm. Section 18 provides that a compensation scheme cannot be made unless a draft of it has been laid before Parliament and approved by each House.

1212. Firearms (Amendment) Act 1997 (c.5)–Commencement No.2 Order

FIREARMS (AMENDMENT) ACT 1997 (COMMENCEMENT) (NO.2) ORDER 1997, SI 1997 1535 (C.60); made under the Firearms (Amendment) Act 1997 s.53. Commencement details: bringing into force various provisions of the Act on June 10, 1997, July 1, 1997 and October 1, 1997; £1.10.

This Order brings into force various provisions of the Firearms (Amendment) Act 1997.

1213. Firearms (Amendment) Act 1997 (c.5)–Commencement No.2 Order– Amendment

FIREARMS (AMENDMENT) ACT 1997 (COMMENCEMENT) (NO.2) (AMENDMENT) ORDER 1997, SI 1997 1536 (C.61); made under the Firearms (Amendment) Act 1997 s.53. In force: in accordance with Art.2; £0.65.

This Order amends the Firearms (Amendment) Act 1997 (Commencement) (No.2) Order 1997 (SI 1997 1535) by substituting, for Art.4, a new Art.4 and a new Art.4A with the effect that, in addition to the provision made by the existing Art.4, the prohibition of firearms by s.1 (2) of the 1997 Act is not to have effect until October 1, 1997 in relation to the acquisition or purchase of a firearm by a registered firearms dealer.

1214. Firearms (Amendment) (No.2) Act 1997 (c.64)

This Act extends the class of prohibited weapons under the Firearms Act 1968 to include small calibre pistols.

This Act received Royal Assent on November 27, 1997.

1215. Firearms (Amendment) (No.2) Act 1997 (c.64)–Commencement Order

FIREARMS (AMENDMENT) (NO.2) ACT 1997 (COMMENCEMENT) ORDER 1997, SI 1997 3114 (C.116); made under the Firearms (Amendment) (No.2) Act 1997 s.3. Commencement details: bringing into force various provisions of the Act on December 17, 1997 and February 1, 1998.; £1.10.

This Order brings various provisions of the Firearms (Amendment) (No.2) Act 1997 Sch. Part I and Sch. Part II into force on December 17, 1997 and February 1, 1998. These provisions do not have effect until March 1, 1998 in relation to certain certificate or permit holders and registered firearms dealers.

1216. Forfeiture–reciprocal enforcement

CRIMINAL JUSTICE (INTERNATIONAL CO-OPERATION) ACT 1990 (ENFORCEMENT OF OVERSEAS FORFEITURE ORDERS) (AMENDMENT)

(NO.2) ORDER 1997, SI 1997 2977; made under the Criminal Justice (International Co-operation) Act 1990 s.9. In force: February 1, 1998; £1.10.

This Order amends the Criminal Justice (International Co-operation) Act 1990 (Enforcement of Overseas Forfeiture Orders) Order 1991 (SI 1991 1463) and the Criminal Justice (International Co-operation) Act 1990 (Enforcement of Overseas Forfeiture Orders) (Northern Ireland) Order 1991 (SI 1991 1464) by substituting a revised point at which proceedings are instituted in Australia, by changing the list of countries designated for drug trafficking offences to include Austria, Benin, Botswana, Hungary, Kazakhstan, Tonga and the United Republic of Tanzania and by adding Australia and Austria to the list of countries designated for other offences.

1217. Knives–forfeited property–disposal by police authorities

KNIVES (FORFEITED PROPERTY) REGULATIONS 1997, SI 1997 1907; made under the Knives Act 1997 s.7. In force: September 1, 1997; £1.10.

These Regulations provide for the disposal of knives subject to a forfeiture order under the Knives Act 1997 s.6 by the relevant police authority and for the application of any proceeds of such disposals.

1218. Knives Act 1997 (c.21)

This Act creates new criminal offences in relation to the possession or marketing of knives or publications relating to knives. Supplementary powers of entry, seizure and retention are conferred on the police in relation to knives or offensive weapons and provision is made in respect of offences by bodies corporate.

This Act received Royal Assent on March 19, 1997.

1219. Knives Act 1997 (c.21)–Commencement No.1 Order

KNIVES ACT 1997 (COMMENCEMENT) (NO.1) ORDER 1997, SI 1997 1906 (C.77); made under the Knives Act 1997 s.11. Commencement details: bringing into force various provisions of the Act on September 1, 1997; £0.65.

This Order brings into force the Knives Act 1997 s.1 to s.7, s.9 and s.10.

1220. Murder–joint enterprise–mens rea required to found conviction of murder by secondary party

To establish the requisite mens rea for murder against a secondary party to a joint enterprise, it must be proven that the secondary party contemplated the type of act actually committed by the principal. Where death is caused by a weapon more dangerous than that known to be in the possession of the principal, foresight of its use to kill or to cause serious injury will be difficult to prove. P and D appealed against the dismissal of their appeals against conviction of the murder of a drug dealer, who had been shot by one of a group of three men, although the Crown could not prove who had actually fired the gun. The Crown contended that it was enough for a conviction of murder that each man knew that the third man was carrying a gun and that he might use it to kill with intent to do so or to cause serious harm to the victim, even though they might not have intended that the act be carried out. E appealed against the dismissal of his appeal against conviction of the murder of a police sergeant who had been stabbed by W with a knife while both E and W were attacking the victim with wooden posts. The judge had directed the jury that, even if E did not know W had a knife, they still had to consider whether E realised that W might cause serious injury with the wooden post. E contended that, to sustain a conviction, he would have had to have foreseen an act of the type actually carried out and that the use of the knife was fundamentally different from the use of a wooden post.

Held, dismissing P and D's appeals, but allowing the appeal by E, that (1) where there was a joint enterprise to commit a crime, it was enough to found a conviction for murder that the secondary party contemplated that the primary party might kill with intent to do so or to cause really serious injury, even though this meant imposing a lower level of mens rea in relation to a secondary party than would have to be proved in relation to a principal, and (2) if, however, the secondary party did not foresee that the principal might commit an act which was fundamentally different from that which they jointly contemplated, he could not be guilty of murder or manslaughter unless the weapon used was just as dangerous as that which was contemplated.

R. v. POWELL (ANTHONY GLASSFORD); R. v. DANIELS (ANTONIO EVAL); R. v. ENGLISH (PHILIP) [1997] 3 W.L.R. 959, Lord Hutton, HL.

1221. Murder—manslaughter—jury directions

B, aged 25, applied for an extension of time in which to renew his application for leave to appeal against conviction. Both B and his codefendant, T, were convicted of the murder of J and sentenced to life imprisonment. The two men had allegedly gone to the victim's flat to rob his flatmate. The result was that J was badly beaten about the face and had a broken nose, consistent with being hit with a sawn off shotgun. The cause of death was a shotgun wound to J's thigh. T had fired the gun. B submitted that, although he was present and knew a gun was being carried, he had no idea until it was fired that it was loaded. The grounds of appeal related to the judge's directions to the jury that they should convict B of murder if the gun was used to cause grievous bodily harm; a broken nose was enough. This had effectively withdrawn B's case that he was properly guilty of manslaughter not murder, *Chang Wing-siu v. The Queen* (1985) 80 Cr. App. R. 117 cited.

Held, dismissing the application, that it made no real difference what form of really serious harm was contemplated by B and T. Even if the jury had not rejected B's case, had B known that really serious harm was going to be inflicted with the gun, and went on with the enterprise, as he did, then he would be properly convicted of murder. It was unreal, in the circumstances, to think that B and T did not know what might happen. This was plainly a case of murder not manslaughter.

R. v. BAMBOROUGH (ARRON) [1996] Crim. L.R. 744, Staughton, L.J., CA (Crim Div).

1222. Murder—mens rea—wounding of pregnant woman—child born alive then dying—mens rea insufficient for murder but sufficient for manslaughter

[Criminal Justice Act 1972 s.36.]

B stabbed a pregnant woman, who later gave birth to a premature child, S, who died after 121 days. Although S had been wounded in the stabbing, it could not be proved that the wound contributed to her death. B, convicted of wounding the mother with intent, was, after S's death, charged with her murder, but his acquittal was ordered after it was held that he could not in law be convicted of murder or manslaughter, even if causation was proved. A reference was made by the Attorney General under the Criminal Justice Act 1972 s.36 for a ruling on whether (1) murder or manslaughter could be committed where unlawful injury was deliberately inflicted on a mother carrying a child in utero, where the child was born alive but subsequently died and the injuries inflicted caused or contributed to death, and (2) liability for murder or manslaughter could be negatived where death was caused solely as a result of injury to the mother, as opposed to direct injury to the foetus.

Held, that B could be convicted of manslaughter but not of murder. An intention to harm the mother could not be equivalent to intent to harm the foetus, since they were two distinct organisms living symbiotically. There was no basis for extending the doctrine of transferred malice to a case where there had been no intention to injure the foetus. The mens rea for murder was not, therefore, present. However, B could be guilty of manslaughter resulting from an unlawful and dangerous act, for which it was unnecessary for the act to have been directed against the person who died as a result of it or for B to have known that his act was likely to injure that person. All that was needed was proof that B intentionally stabbed the mother, that the act caused the death, and that reasonable people would have appreciated the risk that some harm would result. Although the foetus was not a living person at the time, it was not unreasonable on grounds of public policy to regard S, when she became a living person, as within the scope of B's mens rea when he stabbed her mother, and the actus reus for manslaughter was completed when S died.

ATTORNEY GENERAL'S REFERENCE (NO.3 OF 1994), Re [1997] 3 W.L.R. 421, Lord Mustill, HL.

1223. **Obscenity–possession of indecent photographs of a child–requirements of possession**

[Protection of Children Act 1978 s.1 (1), s.1 (4).]

M was employed as an assistant in a sex shop. Police officers with a warrant raided the shop and took possession of a number of video cassettes. M was found guilty in relation to a charge of possessing indecent photographs of a child contrary to the Protection of Children Act 1978 s.1 (1) (c) in relation to one video. He was sentenced to 12 months' imprisonment. M appealed against conviction on two grounds, firstly that the judge had made an error in law regarding the requirements of possession by equating it with mere physical control, and, secondly, that his counsel had been in serious error in not putting forward a defence under s.1 (4) of the 1978 Act. M also sought leave to appeal against sentence.

Held, dismissing the appeal against conviction and refusing leave to appeal against sentence, that (1) no error had been made by the judge on the matter of possession. M was clearly in possession of the video and as it was in a shop the possession was clearly for the purpose of distribution. In the circumstances, knowledge of the contents of the video was not required although it may have been relevant to a defence under s.1 (4), *R. v. McNamara (James)* (1988) 87 Cr. App. R. 246, [1988] C.L.Y. 779 considered; (2) it was not sufficient for the purposes of establishing a defence under s.1 (4) that a defendant had no knowledge that indecent images of children were contained in the relevant material, but rather that a defendant had no knowledge that the material concerned contained any indecent images; (3) the actions of M's counsel did not render the verdict unsafe, *R. v. Clinton (Dean)* (1993) 97 Cr. App. R. 320, [1993] C.L.Y. 751 applied, and (4) in light of a previous conviction for a similar offence the sentence imposed on M was not excessive.

R. v. MATRIX (BILLY), Trans. Ref: 9703175 Y5, August 4, 1997, SwintonThomas, L.J., CA (Crim Div).

1224. **Obtaining by deception–mortgage fraud–building society cheque a "valuable security"–telegraphic transfer amounting to "service"– substitution of alternative verdicts**

[Criminal Appeal Act 1968 s.3(1); Theft Act 1968 s.15, s.17, s.20(2); Theft Act 1978 s.1 (1).]

C appealed out of time against conviction on three counts of obtaining property by deception under the Theft Act 1968 s.15, for which he received three concurrent two year sentences. The offences arose from a series of mortgage applications in which C acted deliberately or recklessly by deceiving building societies into making advances for the purchase of residential property. The sums advanced were instead used to finance a company involved in short term flat lettings and property development. The Crown conceded that the convictions under s.15 could not be sustained in the light of the decision in *R. v. Preddy (John Crawford)* [1996] A.C. 815, [1996] 1 C.L.Y. 1530, submitting instead that alternative offences under either the Theft Act 1978 s.1 or s.17(1)(b) and s.20(2) of the 1968 Act be substituted.

Held, substituting a verdict of procuring the execution of a valuable security by deception contrary to s.20(2) of the 1968 Act and a verdict of obtaining services by deception under s.1 (1) of the 1978 Act and confirming the original sentence, that (1) the substitution of verdicts of offences contrary to s.17(1)(b) of the 1968 Act (supplying false information) was precluded by the withdrawal of such counts at first instance and the fact that the second requirement of the Criminal Appeal Act 1968 s.3(1) had not been fulfilled in that the counts under s.15 did not refer to matters required under s.17, *R v. Graham (Hemamali Krishna)* [1997] 1 Cr. App. R. 302, [1996] 1 C.L.Y. 1532 considered; (2) allowing substitution of a verdict under s.20(2) in that a crossed building society cheque could amount to a valuable security, given the wide definitions contained in s.20(3). Where, by fraud or deception, a defendant procures the handing over of a cheque made out in his favour, the allegation of "obtaining" includes both the procurement of the cheque's execution and its delivery. On the facts, therefore, the jury must have been satisfied that C would have been guilty under s.20(2), thereby allowing the substitution of verdicts, and (3) although s.20(2) was unavailable where an advance was obtained by telegraphic transfer as opposed to a cheque, an alternative verdict of obtaining services by deception under s.1 of the 1978 could be used, *R. v. Graham (Hemamali Krishna)* supra followed, given the similarity in wording between s.15(1) of the 1968 Act and s.1 (2) of the 1978 Act.

R. v. COOKE (DAVID) [1997] Crim.L.R. 436, Potter, L.J., CA (Crim Div).

1225. Obtaining by deception–mortgage fraud–substitution of alternative verdicts

[Criminal Appeal Act 1968 s.3.]

P was convicted of obtaining property by deception, but appealed when the cases of *R. v. Preddy (John Crawford)* [1996] 3 W.L.R. 255, [1996] 1 C.L.Y. 1530 and *R. v. Graham (Hemamali Krishna)* [1996] 1 C.L.Y. 1532 made it clear that convictions in respect of mortgage fraud where the advance had been made by cheque or electronic transfer were no longer sustainable. The prosecution asked that the court exercise its discretion under the Criminal Appeal Act 1968 s.3 to substitute the jury's verdict with a verdict of guilty of the alternative offence of procuring the execution of a valuable security by deception. P argued that no other verdict should be substituted as an act of mercy or mitigation, given the grave effect of the conviction on his career.

Held, granting leave to appeal but substituting a verdict of guilty of the alternative offence, that the court's apparently unrestricted discretion under s.3 of the Act had to be exercised having regard to the procedural and evidential history of the case and therefore P's argument could not succeed.

R. v. PETERSON (ANDREW DUNCAN) [1997] Crim. L.R. 339, Potter, L.J., CA (Crim Div).

1226. Obtaining by deception–mortgage fraud–substitution of alternative verdicts

[Theft Act 1968 s.15(1), s.17(1)(b); Criminal Appeal Act 1968 s.3.]

O appealed against a conviction of obtaining property by deception contrary to the Theft Act 1968 s.15(1) after falsely representing the income and work record of an applicant for a mortgage advance of £56,955 from the Alliance and Leicester Building Society. O contended (1) that no "property" was appropriated and (2) the trial judge had misled the jury over the concepts of dishonesty and of recklessness to be applied to the deception. The prosecution conceded that, following the case of *R. v. Preddy (John Crawford)* [1996] 3 W.L.R. 255, [1996] 1 C.L.Y. 1530, it could not show that "property" had been obtained, but that, pursuant to the Criminal Appeal Act 1968 s.3, an offence of providing an accounting reference with a view to obtaining a gain for another or with intent to cause loss under s.17(1)(b) could be properly substituted.

Held, allowing the appeal, that (1) the substituted verdict was neither available nor appropriate since the evidence at trial went only to show that the society had relied on O's statement to make an advance and not for any accounting purpose and (2) it was therefore unnecessary to consider the summing up, *R. v. Preddy (John Crawford)* [1996] 3 W.L.R. 255, [1996] 1 C.L.Y. 1530, *R. v. Graham (Hemamali Krishna)* [1997] 1 Cr. App. R. 302, [1996] 1 C.L.Y. 1532 followed and *R. v. Wilson (Clarence)* [1984] A.C. 242, [1983] C.L.Y. 686 and *R. v. Mallett* [1978] 1 W.L.R. 820, [1978] C.L.Y. 507 considered

R. v. OKANTA (KWASI) [1997] Crim. L.R. 451, Potter, L.J., CA (Crim Div).

1227. Obtaining by deception–mortgage fraud–substitution of alternative verdicts–admissibility of fresh evidence on appeal

[Criminal Appeal Act 1968 s.3, s.23(1), s.23(2); Criminal Appeal Act 1995 s.41; Theft Act 1968 s.15; Criminal Law Act 1967 s.6; Criminal Justice Act 1987 s.12(1).]

G applied to adduce fresh expert evidence on appeal against his conviction of conspiracy to obtain property by deception for which he was sentenced to two years' imprisonment. G was the solicitor acting for W in various conveyancing transactions in which W had induced building societies to lend him money for property at a domestic rate when he was letting the properties and should have been charged at a commercial rate. G's defence was that he had been unaware of W's actions, had been overworked at the time and unable to give much attention to detail. The prosecution conceded that, applying *R. v. Preddy (John Crawford)* [1996] 3 W.L.R. 255, [1996] 1 C.L.Y. 1530, a charge under the Theft Act 1968 s.15 could not stand where a defendant obtained a mortgage advance by telegraphic transfer or cheque because the bank account of the defendant or his solicitor is credited and the defendant does not obtain the lender's chose in action. However, the Crown argued that the conviction should be substituted with one for common law conspiracy to defraud in terms of the Criminal Appeal Act 1968 s.3.

Held, dismissing the application, that (1) having regard to the Criminal Appeal Act 1968 s.23(1) and s.23(2) as amended by the Criminal Appeal Act 1995 s.41 the evidence of G's expert witness was not admissible. Late applications for expert evidence were of two kinds: either they related to expert forensic or scientific evidence which may have been omitted because certain scientific developments or discoveries had not yet come to light, so a delay would be justified, or they related to professional duty and practice which were regulated by codes and guidelines, for which a delay would be less likely to be justified. The reason G's expert evidence had not been submitted earlier was that G had previously been unable to find a witness who disagreed with the prosecution witness; (2) with regard to the substitution of the conviction, the Criminal Appeal Act 1968 s.3 did allow for a substituted conviction provided that the jury, if satisfied on the facts, would have found the defendant guilty on the substituted charge, *R. v. Graham (Hemamali Krishna)* [1997] 1 Cr. App. R. 302, [1996] 1 C.L.Y. 1532 considered. That the jury was not directed on the alternative charge does not preclude the court exercising its discretion to substitute, but the absence of direction is relevant if the court decides to proceed. Also, the court has to have regard to the Criminal Law Act 1967 s.6. In this case it was accepted that the jury would have convicted G on the common law offence, and (3) with regard to the submission relying on *R. v. Ayres* (1984) 78 Cr. App. R. 232, [1984] C.L.Y. 538, that prior to July 20, 1987 when s.12(1) of the Criminal Justice Act 1987 came into force the conviction could not be substituted was rejected on the basis that the offending transactions had continued and even increased in number after that date, so that the jury would have found G guilty for the offence of conspiracy to defraud for the overall period.

R. v. GARNER (DAVID), Trans. Ref: 94/00071/W5, December 20, 1996, Potter, L.J., CA (Crim Div).

1228. Obtaining by deception–substitution of alternative verdicts

[Theft Act 1968 s.15(1).]

A had been employed at the Probate Registry. While working there he had discovered details of the estate of a deceased man, T. A attempted to obtain that estate by representing himself as, D, T's nephew, and supported his claim with forged documents. Included amongst the documents were an affidavit which purported to identify D as being entitled to T's estate under Greek law and an oath of administration purporting to be made by T and witnessed by a Californian notary. A also represented himself as C, a person authorised by D to obtain letters of administration. A firm of solicitors, M, was persuaded to obtain letters of administration and subsequently £399,188 was transferred to M's client account with Barclays Bank. The only offence put before a jury was of obtaining property by deception under the Theft Act 1968 s.15(1). A was convicted and sentenced to five years' imprisonment. A appealed against conviction and the Crown conceded that in light of the decision in *R. v. Preddy (John Crawford)* [1996] A.C. 815, [1996] 1 C.L.Y. 1530 the conviction must be quashed and submitted three alternative offences which could be substituted, namely procuring execution of a valuable security and two offences concerned with the forged documents.

Held, allowing the appeal, that (1) the Crown was correct to concede that the conviction must be quashed; (2) on the principles in *R. v. Graham (Hemamali Krishna)* [1997] 1 Cr. App. R. 302, [1996] 1 C.L.Y. 1532 it was necessary for the charge in respect of which A was originally convicted to contain elements of the offence which the Crown sought to substitute. In this case there was nothing to suggest the alternative offences, and (3) in determining whether to substitute alternative offences the court could have no regard to the facts of the case, as reference should be made to the pleaded case alone.

R. v. ADEBAYO (OLUSEGUN), Trans. Ref: 9700865 W2, July 7, 1997, Hutchison, L.J., CA (Crim Div).

1229. Obtaining by deception–substitution of alternative verdicts

[Theft Act 1968 s.15(1), s.17(1).]

A was the owner of a company employing L, an optician. A was charged with false accounting and obtaining by deception contrary to the Theft Act 1968 s.15(1). It was alleged that forms submitted to a local authority in relation to payment for sight tests contained false statements. The payments in question amounted to nearly £30,000. On two different occasions A's counsel and solicitors withdrew shortly before his trial. On the second occasion the case proceeded to trial with A representing himself. It was alleged that patients mentioned in the forms did not exist and the signature of L had been forged by A. A defended himself on the basis that no false statements had been made, that the patients did exist and evidence relating to his forgery of L's signature had been fabricated by police. A was convicted and sentenced to four years' imprisonment. A appealed on the grounds, inter alia, that the judge had misdirected the jury and should not have seen A's counsel in private to hear why they sought to withdraw from the case. In relation to the charges of obtaining by deception it was conceded that the facts proved by the Crown did not constitute the offence, following *R. v. Preddy (John Crawford)* [1996] A.C. 815, [1996] 1 C.L.Y. 1530 and the Crown sought to substitute an offence of furnishing false information.

Held, allowing the appeal against conviction of contravention of s.15 of the 1968 Act and substituting a conviction under s.17(1)(b), and allowing appeal against sentence and substituting sentence of three years, that (1) the jury must have been satisfied of the facts necessary for a conviction under s.17(1)(b) of the 1968 Act in light of their findings on the s.15 and false accounting charges, thus satisfying the conditions for substitution outlined in *R. v. Graham (Hemamali Krishna)* [1997] 1 Cr. App. R. 302, [1996] 1 C.L.Y. 1532; (2) although some of the trial judge's directions were questionable or ill advised, the summing up in its entirety did not prejudice A; (3) the trial judge was not wrong in failing to offer an adjournment to A when he found himself to be unrepresented, having considered the whole circumstances of the case. A had previously departed from representation on the eve of trial and was aware he would face his trial unrepresented; (4) meetings between counsel and judges in private are not desirable, but, while the presence of a shorthand writer at such meetings was to be hoped for, the conviction in this case was not rendered unsafe because this had not happened, and (5) considering that less than £30,000 was involved, the sentence was above the level normally imposed.

R. v. ANKA-LUFFORD (JOSEPH), Trans. Ref: 9604381 W5, July 11, 1997, Hutchison, L.J., CA (Crim Div).

1230. Obtaining by deception–substitution of alternative verdicts–court had no power where appellant pleaded guilty to original offence

[Theft Act 1968 s.15(1), s.20(2); Criminal Appeal Act 1968 s.2(1), s.3; Criminal Appeal Act 1995.]

H appealed against conviction on two counts of obtaining property by deception on a guilty plea under the Theft Act 1968 s.15(1) for offences involving the obtaining of cheques. Following the House of Lords decision in *R. v. Preddy (John Crawford)* [1996] A C 815, [1996] 1 C.L.Y. 1530, his application for an extension of time in which to apply for leave to appeal had been granted.

Held, allowing the appeal and quashing the conviction, that although H was guilty of serious dishonesty and an application to amend the indictment to contain counts of procuring a valuable security by deception contrary to s.20(2) of the Act would have succeeded, there was no power to substitute a verdict of guilty to another offence under the Criminal Appeal Act 1968 s.3 where an appellant had pleaded guilty. The court's powers flowed only from statute and, however anomalous, the power to substitute only applied to a verdict from a jury and could not be construed in any other way. Prior to the Criminal Appeal Act 1995, which amended the 1968 Act s.2(1), the court had merely applied the proviso contained in s.2(1) where an appellant had pleaded guilty to an offence not known to law but was clearly guilty of some offence. The effect of the change introduced by the 1995 Act was demonstrated by the decision in *R. v. Graham (Hemamali Krishna)* [1997] 1 Cr. App. R. 302, [1996] 1 C.L.Y. 1532, which also established that where the particulars of an offence given in the indictment could not support a conviction for the offence charged, the conviction was to be considered unsafe.

R. v. HORSMAN (RICHARD DAVID) [1997] 3 All E.R. 385, Waller, L.J., CA (Crim Div).

1231. Obtaining by deception–substitution of verdicts–whether property actually obtained

[Theft Act 1968 s.15; Theft Act 1978 s.1.]

N appealed against conviction of obtaining property by deception contrary to the Theft Act 1986 s.15(1) for which he was sentenced to three years' imprisonment, but was then released on bail. It was alleged that N's co-accused, S, who was later acquitted, obtained, by a false representation, a loan for £1.5 million with which he intended to purchase a property. N was S's solicitor acting in the transaction. The money was transferred by telegraphic transfer to N's client account and N undertook not to do anything with the money until after exchange of contracts. However, he transferred monies before the exchange in breach of the undertaking. N argued that, as the money had been passed telegraphically, no property had passed and, following *R. v. Preddy (John Crawford)* [1996] A.C. 815, [1996] 1 C.L.Y. 1530, he could not be guilty of obtaining property by deception. The Crown argued that, as N had obtained control of the monies acquiring legal ownership thereof as a trustee and had then appropriated it in breach of his undertaking, s.15 ought to have effect; further, that the chose in action remained the property of the bank until exchange of contracts and N had obtained legal ownership and control of it before it ceased being the bank's property.

Held, allowing the appeal, quashing the conviction under s.15 of the 1968 Act and substituting a conviction under s.1 of the 1978 Act, that following *Preddy* the conviction under s.15 was unsafe. The property obtained by N had never been the property of the bank and no identifiable property had passed. Accordingly it did not constitute obtaining property belonging to another. A conviction of an alternative offence could be substituted only where (1) the jury, on the indictment, would have returned a guilty verdict for that offence, and (2) the court is satisfied that the jury, on returning that verdict, were not in any doubt about the facts on which they based that verdict, *R. v. Graham (Hemamali Krishna)* [1997] 1 Cr. App. R. 302, [1996] 1 C.L.Y. 1532 referred to. Although s.1 of the 1978 Act made no reference to obtaining money for another, unlike s.15 of the 1968 Act, there was no suggestion that a person must have obtained a service for himself in order to be guilty. Further, N was a joint venturer in the plan and was deriving a personal benefit, *R. v. Cooke (David)* [1997] Crim. L.R. 436, [1997] 4 C.L. 181 considered.

R. v. NATHAN (RONALD STEPHEN), Trans. Ref: 96/6899/Z4, April 14, 1997, Lord Bingham of Cornhill, L.C.J., CA (Crim Div).

1232. Offences–carrying knives–knife carried for purpose of heroin use–good reason defence not established

[Carrying of Knives etc. (Scotland) Act 1993 (c.13) s.1 (4).]

F was found carrying a knife in a public place. The reason which he gave for being in possession of the knife was that its use formed part of the process involved in preparing heroin for injection. The Carrying of Knives etc. (Scotland) Act 1993 creating the offence provides, in s.1 (4) that having a good reason is a defence. The sheriff, following a concession by the procurator fiscal depute, found that F did have a good reason. The Crown appealed.

Held, allowing the appeal, that (1) the concession by the procurator fiscal depute was a concession in law which could not bind the advocate depute especially as F had not been prejudiced, *HM Advocate v. Bennett* 1996 S.L.T. 662, [1996] 2 C.L.Y. 6835 distinguished, and (2) where a general prohibition had been established by Parliament the court would not be justified in accepting as a good reason, forming an exception to that general prohibition, a reason which was bound up in the committal of an unlawful act. Opinion of the Court per Lord Rodger, Lord Justice-General.

BROWN v. FARREL 1997 J.C. 205, Lord Rodger L.J.G., Lord Kirkwood, Lord McCluskey, HCJ Appeal.

1233. Offences against the person–causing bodily harm by wanton or furious driving–jury directions

[Offences against the Person Act 1861 s.35.]

O appealed against conviction of causing bodily harm by wanton or furious driving contrary to the Offences against the Person Act 1861 s.35 after acquittal of unlawful wounding. O was a minicab driver, who had an altercation with a passenger over the fare and drove off with him hanging or hooked onto the door of his vehicle, causing injuries which required the victim to spend three days in hospital. O, relying on *R. v. Mohan* [1976] Q.B. 1, [1975] C.L.Y. 510, contended that the trial judge had erred: (1) in his direction on the ingredients of the offence by suggesting that it was objective (*Caldwell/Lawrence*), rather than subjective (*Cunningham*), recklessness that fell to be proved. The Crown, however, submitted that, following *R. v. Cooke (Philip)* [1971] Crim. L.R. 44, [1971] C.L.Y. 10400, it was only necessary to show (a) misconduct in that O's driving fell below the necessary standard; (b) that he wilfully drove in that manner; and (c) that such behaviour was the substantial cause of the injury.

Held, dismissing the appeal, that it was unnecessary to consider the construction of s.35 since the trial judge had clearly warned the jury to be sure that O was fully cognisant of the risk to his passenger before they could convict him, *R. v. Cooke* and *R. v. Mohan, R. v. Caldwell (James)* [1982] A.C. 341, [1981] C.L.Y. 385, *R. v. Lawrence (Stephen)* [1981] 2 W.L.R. 524, [1981] C.L.Y. 2382 and *R. v. Cunningham (Roy)* [1957] 2 Q.B. 396, [1957] C.L.Y. 780 considered.

R. v. OKOSI (FELIX) [1997] R.T.R. 450, Simon Brown, L.J., CA (Crim Div).

1234. Offensive weapons–pickaxe handle–whether adapted for causing injury

[Prevention of Crime Act 1953 s.1 (1).]

W appealed by way of case stated from a conviction under the Prevention of Crime Act 1953 s.1 (1) of having an offensive weapon, namely a pickaxe handle in a public place. W was convicted on the basis that the pickaxe handle was an article adapted for use of causing injury to the person. W submitted that in the absence of any finding by the justices that the pickaxe handle was deliberately detached so as to make it a useful weapon, their conclusion was defective.

Held, allowing the appeal, that it was not possible to sustain the conclusion that the pickaxe handle when detached from the rest of the implement was adapted for use for violent ends. There was no finding that the handle was deliberately detached from its head.

WARNE v. DPP, Trans. Ref: CO/1100/97, June 3, 1997, Simon Brown, L.J., QBD.

1235. Offensive weapons—possession of butterfly knife at airport—whether made or adapted for causing injury

[Aviation Security Act 1982 s.4(4); Criminal Justice Act 1988 s.141; Criminal Justice Act 1988 (Offensive Weapons) Order 1988 (SI 1988 2019).]

H was charged with having an article made or adapted for causing injury contrary to the Aviation Security Act 1982 s.4(4) after being found in possession of a butterfly knife at Heathrow Airport. The DPP appealed by way of case stated against the magistrates' decision that simply because the Criminal Justice Act 1988 s.141 prohibited the sale, hire or lending of butterfly knives it did not necessarily imply that such a knife would constitute a dangerous article made for causing injury within the meaning of s.4 of the 1982 Act.

Held, allowing the appeal, that a butterfly knife was similar to a flick knife which constituted an offensive weapon per se, and fitted the description in the Schedule to the Criminal Justice Act 1988 (Offensive Weapons) Order 1988, both weapons possessing similar characteristics in that they could be easily concealed and produced quickly and without warning to the victim, *Gibson v. Wales* (1983) 76 Cr. App. R. 60, [1983] C.L.Y. 730 and *R. v. Simpson (Calvin)* (1984) 78 Cr. App. R. 114, [1984] C.L.Y. 679 considered. It followed that the magistrate should have concluded that a butterfly knife was necessarily made for the purpose of causing injury to the person.

DPP v. HYNDE, *The Times*, July 18, 1997, Henry, L.J., QBD.

1236. Prevention of Terrorism (Temporary Provisions) Act 1989—continuance

PREVENTION OF TERRORISM (TEMPORARY PROVISIONS) ACT 1989 (CONTINUANCE) ORDER 1997, SI 1997 807; made under the Prevention of Terrorism (Temporary Provisions) Act 1989 s.27. In force: March 22, 1997; £0.65.

This Order continues in force for a period of 12 months from March 22, 1997, the Prevention of Terrorism (Temporary Provisions) Act 1989 Part I to Part V and s.27(6)(c).

1237. Protection from Harassment Act 1997 (c.40)

This Act makes it an offence for a person to pursue a course of conduct amounting to harassment of another person and introduces a civil remedy for the offence of harassment.

This Act received Royal Assent on March 21, 1997.

1238. Protection from Harassment Act 1997 (c.40)—Commencement No.1 Order

PROTECTION FROM HARASSMENT ACT 1997 (COMMENCEMENT) (NO.1) ORDER 1997, SI 1997 1418 (C.52); made under the Protection from Harassment Act 1997 s.15. Commencement details: bringing into force various provisions of the Act on June 16, 1997; £0.65.

This Order brings into force the Protection from Harassment Act 1997 s.1, s.2, s.4, s.5, s.7, s.8, s.9, s.10, s.11 and s.12.

1239. Protection from Harassment Act 1997 (c.40)—Commencement No.2 Order

PROTECTION FROM HARASSMENT ACT 1997 (COMMENCEMENT) (NO.2) ORDER 1997, SI 1997 1498 (C.58); made under the Protection from Harassment

Act 1997 s.15. Commencement details: bringing into force various provisions of the Act on June 16, 1997; £0.65.

This Order brings into force the Protection from Harassment Act 1997 s.3(1)(2) and s.6.

1240. Public order offences—offensive behaviour—meaning of "immediate unlawful violence"

[Public Order Act 1986 s.4.]

V appealed by way of case stated against his conviction for threatening behaviour contrary to the Public Order Act 1986 s.4. V made threats to his neighbours that next time the husband was on duty he would burn the house down. The question for the case stated was whether the word "immediate" in s.4 of the 1986 Act could mean in a short time rather than instantaneous. In addition, V contended that, before any violence could be feared, the "intervening occurrence" of the husband going on duty was required and the threat could not, therefore, be said to be immediate.

Held, dismissing the appeal, that "immediate" did not necessarily mean instantaneous and could mean within a short time, *R. v. Horseferry Road Magistrates Court, ex p. Siadatan* [1990] 3 W.L.R. 1006, [1991] C.L.Y. 973 followed. There was a sufficient factual basis from which to conclude that D believed there would be immediate unlawful violence as threatened.

VALENTINE v. DPP, Trans. Ref: CO 3729/96, March 24, 1997, Simon Brown, L.J., QBD.

1241. Public order offences—unlawful assembly—trespassory assembly—no right of peaceful assembly on public highway

[Public Order Act 1986 s.14.]

J and another were involved in a peaceful demonstration on part of the highway near Stonehenge. As the area was subject to an order under the Public Order Act 1986 s.14A they were arrested and convicted of trespassory assembly under s.14B(2). Their appeal against conviction was allowed by the Crown Court, which accepted their argument that a peaceful and non-obstructive assembly was not unlawful. The prosecution appealed by way of case stated.

Held, allowing the appeal and restoring the convictions, that although there was a right of passage over the public highway which also covered anything incidental, an assembly of more than 20 people was not incidental and exceeded reasonable rights of access allowed by law. Demonstrations were not associated with rights of passage and there was no legal authority allowing a right of assembly on the public highway.

DPP v. JONES (MARGARET) [1997] 2 W.L.R. 578, McCowan, L.J., QBD.

1242. Road traffic offences—dangerous driving—death—knowledge that vehicle dangerous—negligence did not impute knowledge of dangerousness—jury directions

[Road Traffic Act 1991 s.2A.]

R and another, G, appealed against conviction of causing death by dangerous driving, under the Road Traffic Act 1991 s.2A(2) and s.2A(3), after the rear wheel of a lorry, driven by G, became detached and hit an oncoming car, killing the driver. R, the owner of a haulage business and G's employer, contended that the trial judge had misdirected the jury on the mental element necessary for G's conviction and therefore his own conviction of procuring the offence was unsafe. R submitted that the trial judge effectively directed the jury that if they found negligence in the system of vehicle maintenance operated by him and G then they were entitled to convict.

Held, allowing the appeal, that G's conviction was unsafe as a consequence of a misdirection that if the jury considered that there had been negligence in the system of maintenance, they could convict G. It was for the jury to decide whether G had carried out a visual check of the vehicle and, if so, if he had carried out that check in the manner of a careful and competent driver. Thus, the jury would have been able to decide whether or not the loose wheel bolt was "obvious" to G, *R. v. Strong* [1995] Crim. L.R. 428 considered. R's conviction was automatically quashed, and in addition, custodial sentences for five counts of fraud in relation to vehicle excise licences were quashed and absolute discharges substituted.

R. v. ROBERTS (DAVID GERAINT); R. v. GEORGE (GRAHAM HAROLD) [1997] Crim. L.R. 209, Collins, J., CA (Crim Div).

1243. Sex Offenders Act 1997 (c.51)

This Act requires sex offenders to notify the police of any change of name or address, and provides that a British citizen or UK resident who commits a sexual offence in another jurisdiction shall be deemed to have committed that sexual offence under UK law.

This Act received Royal Assent on March 21, 1997.

1244. Sex Offenders Act 1997 (c.51)–Commencement Order

SEX OFFENDERS ACT 1997 (COMMENCEMENT) ORDER 1997, SI 1997 1920 (C.78); made under the Sex Offenders Act 1997 s.10. Commencement details: bringing into force various provisions of the Act on September 1, 1997; £0.65.

This Order brings into force the Sex Offenders Act 1997.

1245. Sexual offences–caution of offenders–form of certificate

SEX OFFENDERS (CERTIFICATE OF CAUTION) ORDER 1997, SI 1997 1921; made under the Sex Offenders Act 1997 s.5. In force: September 1, 1997; £0.65.

This Order prescribes the form to be used by a constable to certify that a person has been cautioned for an offence to which the Sex Offenders Act 1997 Part I applies and that the person has been so informed.

1246. Taxis–driver misbehaviour–Hackney carriages

[London Hackney Carriage Act 1843 s.28.]

R was charged with being the driver of a hackney carriage who during his employment misbehaved contrary to London Hackney Carriage Act 1843 s.28. It was alleged that he had pulled up his empty cab in Mayfair, got out and urinated into the road. The fact of urinating was in any event denied.

Held, that the case be dismissed on submission of no case to answer.

R. v. REISMAN, October 31, 1996, H.H.J. Zucker, Middlesex Crown Court. [*Ex rel.* Gabriel Buttimore, Barrister].

1247. Terrorism–emergency provisions

NORTHERN IRELAND (EMERGENCY PROVISIONS) ACT 1996 (AMENDMENT) ORDER 1997, SI 1997 1403; made under the Northern Ireland (Emergency Provisions) Act 1996 s.30. In force: June 4, 1997; £0.65.

This Order adds The Loyalist Volunteer Force and The Continuity Army Council to the list of proscribed organisations contained in the Northern Ireland (Emergency Provisions) Act 1996 Sch.2, with effect from June 4, 1997.

1248. Terrorism–emergency provisions–extension

NORTHERN IRELAND (EMERGENCY AND PREVENTION OF TERRORISM PROVISIONS) (CONTINUANCE) ORDER 1997, SI 1997 1114; made under the Prevention of Terrorism (Temporary Provisions) Act 1989 s.27; and the Northern Ireland (Emergency Provisions) Act 1996 s.62. In force: June 16, 1997; £0.65.

This Order continues in force, with exceptions, the temporary provisions of the Northern Ireland (Emergency Provisions) Act 1996 for a period of 12 months beginning with June 16, 1997. The exceptions are s.36 and Sch.3 which relate to the detention of terrorists and which are not in force. This Order also continues in force for the same period the provisions referred to in the Prevention of Terrorism (Temporary Provisions) Act 1989 s.27 (11).

1249. Theft–appropriation–electronic funds transfer–instructions to bank to make payment–instructions amounted to appropriation

[Theft Act 1968 s.3 (1).]

H appealed against conviction and sentence on three counts of theft, amended to read "stole a credit balance", and for which he was sentenced to two years' imprisonment concurrent on each count. H was a charity chairman who caused three separate sums of money to be transferred from the charity's bank account in settlement of his own personal obligations. One transfer had been effected without a second signature, making it one on which the bank was neither obliged nor entitled to act. H contended that, following *R. v. Preddy (John Crawford)* [1996] A.C. 815, [1996] 1 C.L.Y. 1530 and *R. v. Graham (Hemamali Krishna)* [1997] 1 Cr. App. R. 302, [1996] 1 C.L.Y. 1532, his actions had not amounted to an "appropriation" for the purposes of the Theft Act 1968 s.3(1), in that the electronic transfer of funds, brought about by direct instructions to the bank in the absence of a cheque or other form of valuable security, were acts not brought about by H himself.

Held, dismissing the appeal against conviction but suspending the portion of the sentence still to be served, that an appropriation occurred where the defendant assumed the rights of an owner over the account balance by causing a transfer out of the account, with his instructions to make the transfer as the key to set the process in motion, *R. v. Wille (Bryan)* (1988) 86 Cr. App. R. 296, [1988] C.L.Y. 839 considered and that the reasoning in *Preddy* should not be taken so far as to concentrate solely on the legal obligation owed by a bank to the customer. The law governing this type of offence remained as stated in *R. v. Kohn* (1979) 69 Cr. App R. 395, [1980] C.L.Y. 591 unimpaired by the decision in *Graham*, in that the theft of a chose in action could occur where a dishonest appropriation had the effect of permanently depriving the owner of it and such reasoning was entirely consistent with the decision in *Preddy*.

R. v. HILTON (PETER ARNOLD) (1997) 161 J.P. 459, Evans, L.J., CA (Crim Div).

1250. Theft–appropriation–theft of credit balance–cheques presented for payment in Scotland and England as part of joint enterprise–place of appropriation

[Theft Act 1968 s.3.]

When N opened a bank account, the allocated account number had previously been used for a debt collection agency and cheques intended for the agency were paid into the account by mistake. N signed a number of blank cheques and sent them to her sister in Scotland, who knew about the mistaken payments. N's sister presented two of the cheques for payment in Scotland and one for payment in England. N was charged with stealing the agency's credit balance. N's argument at trial that there was no case to answer since no offence had been committed in England was rejected, and it was held that there had been a joint enterprise between the sisters, with the appropriation under the Theft Act 1968 s.3 of the rights of the agency having taken place in England where the account, the credit balance and the paying bank were all located. N now appealed against conviction on three counts of theft, the first two relating to cheques presented in Scotland and the third to the cheque presented in England.

Held, allowing the appeal in part and quashing the conviction on the first two counts, that the central question was whether there was an act within the jurisdiction which could amount to an assumption by N of the rights of the agency. The act of theft was the presentation of the cheque which drew upon the agency's credit balance. N's signing of the cheques was merely preparatory and did not amount to the assumption of any rights against the bank, but by supplying the signed blank cheques which she knew were to be used to steal from the agency, she aided and abetted the substantive offence of theft committed in Scotland and would be liable to be convicted as a principal.

However, the joint enterprise was effectuated in Scotland and the fact that her part in the theft took place in England was insufficient to give the English courts jurisdiction. There could be no offence under English law when the cheques were presented in Scotland, but an offence was committed when the third cheque was presented for payment in England.

R. v. NGAN (SUI SOI), *The Times*, July 24, 1997, Leggatt, L.J., CA (Crim Div).

1251. Trespass—obstruction of tree felling—breach of health and safety regulations

[Criminal Justice and Public Order Act 1994 s.68(1), s.68(3); Health and Safety at Work etc. Act 1974 s.2, s.3; Management of Health and Safety at Work Regulations 1992 (SI 1992 2051) Reg.12.]

H appealed by way of case stated against a conviction of having obstructed a lawful activity while trespassing in the open air, contrary to the Criminal Justice and Public Order Act 1994 s.68(1) and s.68(3). H had refused to leave his position in a tree in order to obstruct a chain saw operator from felling it in the course of land clearance by the highways authority (Newbury bypass). H contended that the fact that the operator was using his chain saw without gloves or a visor and felling trees too close to other protestors meant he had breached the requirement of the Health and Safety at Work etc. Act 1974 s.2 to comply with the Management of Health and Safety at Work Regulations 1992 Reg.12 and made his activity unlawful. H claimed that s.2 and s.3 of the 1974 Act provided that it was an offence for an employer to contravene any health and safety regulations.

Held, dismissing the appeal, that the activity in question was the clearance of land and the felling of trees which had been properly authorised and was lawful. The fact that a breach of the regulations had occurred did not make the activity as a whole unlawful.

HIBBERD v. DPP, Trans. Ref: CO 2614/96, November 27, 1996, Tucker, J., QBD.

1252. Trespass—removal orders—magistrate had no discretion to assess reasonableness of local authority

[Criminal Justice and Public Order Act 1994 s.77, s.78.]

S issued a notice under the Criminal Justice and Public Order Act 1994 s.77 directing W to leave the land he occupied. On W's failure to comply, S applied to the magistrate for an order under s.78 requiring W to leave. The application was refused on the grounds that it was unreasonable. S appealed by way of case stated.

Held, allowing the appeal, that the word "may" in s.78 was not sufficiently explicit to grant a discretion to refuse to make the order on grounds of reasonableness. Whilst a magistrate had a strictly limited discretion to decline to make an order in certain special circumstances, eg. where an occupier had undertaken to leave by a certain date, thus rendering an order unnecessary, the issue of reasonableness was one for the council to determine when it made the removal direction under s.77.

SHROPSHIRE CC v. WYNNE, *The Times*, July 22, 1997, Henry, L.J., QBD.

1253. Articles

Can psychiatric injury amount to bodily harm? *(Adrian Clarke)*: S.J. 1997, 141 (41), 1020-1021. (Whether defendant who causes psychiatric injury by making silent or abusive phone calls can be guilty of offence under Offences against the Person Act 1861).

Criminal attempts and provocation *(Alan Reed)*: Crim. Law. 1996, 68, 1-3. (Demarcation between preparatory acts and acts amounting to attempt and relevant characteristics attributable to reasonable man for defence of provocation).

HIV/AIDS, sex and the criminal law *(Helen Power)*: J. Soc. Wel. & Fam. L. 1997, 19(3), 343-351. (Whether criminalisation of HIV/AIDS transmission or of sexual conduct risking transmission is appropriate response to spread of HIV/AIDS and likely impact of criminalisation on persons with AIDS and on gay community).

Insanity defences in summary trials *(Stephen White* and *Paul Bowen)*: J. Crim. L. 1997, 61 (2), 198-208. (Whether defence is available in summary trials, magisterial attitudes to insanity defence and issues regarding burden of proof and foreclosing defences).

Intention thus far *(A.P. Simester)* and *(Winnie Chan)*: Crim. L.R. 1997, Oct, 704-719. (Extent to which HL cases have clarified understanding of intention and how law allows scope for findings of intention which are morally rather than conceptually driven).

Magistrates, insanity and the common law *(Tony Ward)*: Crim. L.R. 1997, Nov, 796-804. (Historical and practical issues surrounding availability of insanity defence in magistrates courts, particularly differences between common law and statutory defence and fact that defence is not available for strict liability offences).

Making sense of self-defence *(James Slater)*: Nott. L.J. 1997, 5(2), 140-167. (Concepts of reasonable, necessary and proportionate force and interaction with concepts of justification and excuse).

Paedophiles, privacy and protecting the public *(Bill Hebenton)* and *(Terry Thomas)*: Crim. Law. 1997, 75, 7-8. (Extent to which information on convicted sex offenders should be disclosed to public by police).

The Protection from Harassment Act 1997: injunctions and restraining orders *(Neil Addison* and *Timothy Lawson-Cruttenden)*: Crim. Law. 1997, 73, 5-6. (Implications of provisions which make breach of civil injunction a criminal offence, and potential role of restraining orders).

The irrelevance of a low intelligence quotient to a claim of duress *(Alan Reed)*: Crim. Law. 1996, 67, 1-3. (Whether defence of duress needs re-evaluation regarding relevant characteristics of accused and whether it could legitimately be extended to murder).

The meaning of "intention" *(Alan Reed)*: Crim. Law. 1997, 70, 1-3. (CA decisions raising concerns over adequate jury directions relating to intention in murder cases and failure to apply golden rule in *R. v Moloney*).

1254. Books

Allen, Michael J.–Elliott and Wood's Casebook on Criminal Law. 7th Ed. Paperback: £26.95. ISBN 0-421-59930-8. Sweet & Maxwell.

Carter, Peter; Harrison, Ruth–Offences of Violence. Criminal Law Library. Hardback: £90.00. ISBN 0-421-53770-1. Sweet & Maxwell.

Curzon, Leslie B.–Criminal Law. Paperback: £15.99. ISBN 0-7121-0873-4. Pitman Publishing.

Hill, Barry; Fletcher-Rogers, Karen–Sexually Related Offences. Criminal Practice Series. Hardback: £45.00. ISBN 0-421-58370-3. Sweet & Maxwell.

Jones, Alun–Conspiracy, Attempt and Incitement. Criminal Law Library. Hardback: £99.00. ISBN 0-421-54130-X. Sweet & Maxwell.

Kirk, David N.; Woodcock, Anthony J.J.–Serious Fraud: Investigation and Trial. Hardback: £120.00. ISBN 0-406-05690-0. Butterworth Law.

Lawson-Crutteneden, Timothy; Addison, Neil–Guide to Protection from Harassment Act 1997. £14.95. ISBN 1-85431-695-8. Blackstone Press.

Passmore, Colin–Privilege. Hardback: £76.00. ISBN 1-85811-078-5. CLT Professional Publishing.

Rook, Peter; Ward, Robert–Rook and Ward on Sexual Offences. 2nd Ed. Criminal Law Library. Hardback: £99.00. ISBN 0-421-53920-8. Sweet & Maxwell.

Stone, Richard–Offences Against the Person. Paperback: £18.95. ISBN 1-874241-13-9. Cavendish Publishing Ltd.

CRIMINAL PROCEDURE

1255. Abuse of process—continuance of case despite prosecuting counsel not intending to offer evidence

B was charged with possession of a Class A controlled drug. At a plea and directions hearing prosecuting counsel indicated to the defence that the Crown wished to offer no evidence because it was accepted that B had been the victim of a set-up. Owing to the presence in court of certain people it would have been embarrassing to the police and prosecution if no evidence had been offered that day so counsel spoke to the judge in his room. An order was then made in open court to adjourn the case and relist it "for mention". The CPS arranged a conference with new prosecuting counsel and informed the defence that there had been a change of plan and the Crown intended to continue the prosecution. An application at the trial to stay the proceedings as an abuse of process failed. B pleaded guilty and was sentenced to three months' imprisonment. B appealed against conviction on the question of (1) whether it was an abuse of process for the Crown to revoke a decision to offer no evidence which had been communicated to the defendant and the court and, if it could be an abuse of process, whether (2) it made any difference if prosecuting counsel had made that decision and communicated it to the defendant and the court without authority.

Held, allowing the appeal, that (1) whether or not there was prejudice to B, it would bring the administration of justice into disrepute to allow the Crown to revoke the original decision without any reason being given as to what was wrong with it, particularly as it was made in the presence of the judge and (2) neither the court nor B could be expected to enquire whether prosecuting counsel had authority to conduct a case in court in any particular way and they were therefore entitled to assume in ordinary circumstances that counsel did have such authority, *R. v. Croydon Justices, ex p. Dean* [1993] Q.B. 769, [1994] C.L.Y. 663 applied.

R. v. BLOOMFIELD (MARK ANDREW) [1997] 1 Cr. App. R.135, Staughton, L.J., CA (Crim Div).

1256. Abuse of process—dismissal on ground of abuse of process inappropriate

A rugby player was charged with assault occasioning actual bodily harm following an incident six months earlier in which he allegedly injured another player. He appeared before magistrates and proceedings were adjourned for two weeks for papers to be served on the defence. After a further adjournment the case again came before magistrates without the papers having been served. Following the defendant's submission that he had suffered prejudice as a result of the delay the justices dismissed the prosecution as an abuse of process. The DPP sought judicial review of the decision.

Held, allowing the application, that it was inappropriate for the justices to dismiss the prosecution on the ground of abuse of process without a proper evaluation of the allegations of prejudice by delay, *R. v. Beckford (Ian Anthony)* [1996] 1 Cr. App. R. 94, [1995] 1 C.L.Y. 1109 and *R. v. Horseferry Road Magistrates Court, ex p. Bennett* [1994] 1 A.C. 42, [1993] C.L.Y. 1867 considered. The fairness of the defendant's trial had not been affected and accordingly, the decision of the justices was quashed.

R. v. HAVERFORDWEST JUSTICES, *ex p.* DPP, Trans. Ref: CO-3814/96, June 9, 1997, Owen, J., QBD.

1257. Abuse of process—issue of abuse of process to be tried before plea entered

A, aged 16, was found in possession of amphetamine and cannabis resin but denied intention to supply drugs. It was allegedly intimated to A's legal representative that if A cooperated in the police interview he would be cautioned and not charged. However the interviewing officer denied making the offer. A made admissions and was charged following which he applied for a stay of proceedings on the grounds that they amounted to an abuse of process, and that was an issue which should be determined before A was required to enter a plea. It was suggested at a hearing fixed for determination of the preliminary issue that it be considered during the substantive hearing. The justices decided they could not rule on the issue before the trial, and the issue could only be raised during the summary trial either by way of no case to answer or in closing submissions. Further, that the type of abuse of process alleged would not directly affect A's trial in particular and was not the type described as delay or unfair manipulation of court proceedings under *R. v. Horseferry Road Magistrates' Court, ex p. Bennett* [1994] 1 A.C. 42, [1995] 1 C.L.Y. 2282.

Held, allowing the application, quashing the ruling and remitting the matter to a differently constituted bench, that as a matter of principle A should not be required to enter a plea before making his application for a stay. The type of abuse of process alleged directly affected A's trial in particular, and the justices' ruling was misconceived. As the application to stay was an application to prevent the trial from commencing it was not appropriate to consider the issue within the trial itself, *R. v. Telford Justices, ex p. Badham* [1991] 2 Q.B. 78, [1991] C.L.Y. 605 considered.

R. v. ALDERSHOT YOUTH COURT, *ex p.* A, Trans. Ref: CO/1911/96, February 19, 1997, Stuart White, J., QBD.

1258. Abuse of process–three year delay between offence and trial

The DPP applied for judicial review of a decision of magistrates, who stayed a prosecution and acquitted M, of driving with excess alcohol. M failed to answer bail in 1993 and a warrant for his arrest was issued. M subsequently moved away and was arrested in 1996. At trial, M claimed that his trial would be an abuse of process because of the delay.

Held, allowing the application, quashing the decision of the magistrates and remitting the case to them with an instruction to continue, that it was clear that a stay should only be applied in the most exceptional case, whereas M's own actions had contributed to the delay and he should not be granted a stay. In the instant case, it was difficult to see where prejudice to M would arise since his identification was not in dispute and the evidence against him was largely documentary, consisting of custody records and the readout from the Lion intoximeter together with the evidence of the arresting officer, who possessed his contemporaneous notes, *R. v. Derby Crown Court, ex p. Brooks* (1985) 80 Cr. App. R. 164, [1985] C.L.Y. 2126 followed, *R. v. Oxford City Justices, ex p. Smith* (1982) 75 Cr. App. R. 200, [1982] C.L.Y. 1979 and *R. v. Watford Justices, ex p. Outrim* [1983] R.T.R. 26, [1983] C.L.Y. 2361 distinguished because the defendants had not known whether charges were to be pressed.

R. v. BISHOP'S STORTFORD JUSTICES, *ex p.* DPP, Trans. Ref: CO 3169/96, April 17, 1997, Brian Smedley, J., QBD.

1259. Acquittals–plea in bar of autrefois acquit–conviction for more serious offence–acquittal on lesser count after no evidence proffered by the Crown

K pleaded not guilty to charges of dangerous driving and driving without reasonable consideration for other road users. The Crown offered no evidence on the lesser alternate count and K was acquitted. The justices then convicted K of dangerous driving. K successfully appealed to the Crown Court on the basis of a plea in bar of autrefois acquit. The DPP appealed by way of case stated. The Crown Court concluded that the proof of facts was the same for both offences and that the position had not been affected when no evidence was offered on the lesser count. It was K's case that, having been acquitted of the lesser offence, he should be acquitted of the greater offence.

Held, allowing the appeal, and remitting the case to the Crown Court, that the defence had been under no misapprehension that the Crown intended to proceed with only the more serious charge and, at the time of acquittal on the lesser charge, the justices had not considered the merits of the charge, *R. v. Brookes* [1995] Crim. L.R. 630 followed. There was some theoretical validity in a submission that K suffered prejudice because he could no longer be convicted on the lesser alternative count. It could be assumed, however, that the Crown Court would only convict were it satisfied that the more serious offence had been made out.

DPP v. KHAN (NASIM) [1997] R.T.R. 82, Schiemann, L.J., QBD.

1260. Appeals—abandonment—withdrawal of abandonment following change in law

N, convicted on November 14, 1991 of obtaining property by deception and attempting to obtain property by deception, applied for his notice of abandonment to be treated as a nullity. N's application for leave to appeal against conviction was refused and N completed a notice of abandonment on February 1, 1992. N submitted that, by virtue of *R. v. Preddy (John Crawford)* [1996] A.C. 815, [1996] 1 C.L.Y. 1530 the law had changed since his conviction. N contended, in reliance upon *R. v. Medway* [1976] Q.B. 779, [1975] C.L.Y. 502 that the court had jurisdiction to grant leave to withdraw a notice of abandonment where the abandonment could be treated as a nullity and where the abandonment was not the result of a deliberate and informed decision.

Held, dismissing the application, that there was no jurisdiction to grant leave to appeal to withdraw the notice of abandonment and, even if there was, it would be inappropriate when no substantial injustice had been done to N and an extensive period of time had elapsed since conviction, *R. v. Hawkins (Paul Nigel)* [1997] 1 Cr. App. R. 234, [1996] 1 C.L.Y. 1548 and *R. v. Medway* followed.

R. v. NICHOLLS (THOMAS BENJAMIN),Trans. Ref: 916452Z4, June 10, 1997, Sir Patrick Russell, CA (Crim Div).

1261. Appeals—committal proceedings

CRIMINAL APPEAL (AMENDMENT) RULES 1997, SI 1997 702 (L.8); made under the Criminal Appeal Act 1968 s.23; and the Supreme Court Act 1981 s.84, s.86. In force: April 1, 1997; £0.65.

These Rules amend the Criminal Appeals Rules 1968 (SI 1968 1262) to take account of the provisions of the Criminal Procedure and Investigations Act 1996 relating to magistrates' courts procedure at committal proceedings and a court order restricting publication of a derogatory assertion made against another person in the course of mitigation by or on behalf of a person convicted of an offence. They remove a reference in r.9(2) of the 1968 Rules to evidence being taken before an examiner in the same way as depositions are taken at committal proceedings, since witnesses will no longer appear at committal proceedings.

1262. Appeals—contempt of court—assault on bailiff as officer of the court—jurisdiction of county court and Court of Appeal to hear appeal

[Administration of Justice Act 1960 s.13; County Courts Act 1984 s.14; Legal Aid Act 1988 s.29; County Court Rules 1981 Ord.34 r.1.]

K appealed against conviction of assault on two court bailiffs for which he received, from the district judge, consecutive custodial sentences of three months each, pursuant to the County Courts Act 1984 s.14. K had reversed his car towards K causing him to jump to safety and had struck a female bailiff several times. R argued that the appeal should have been to a judge in accordance with the Administration of Justice Act 1960 s.13. K contended that (1) as form N90 had been used, instead of form N78 to secure his attendance before the court, the wrong form had been used; (2) the trial judge had refused to allow an adjournment for K to produce three witnesses, and (3) the wrong form N91 had been used for his committal, since it did not contain a statement that the contemnor could apply for his discharge and also referred to County Court Rules 1981 Ord.34 r.1 (2), a rule which no longer existed.

Held, discharging the committal orders, that (1) the failure to inform K of his right to legal aid was a material irregularity in the circumstances; (2) a rehearing was not necessary because K had already served the majority of his term. There were two alternative routes for appealing from the decision of a district judge, either to the Court of Appeal or internally to a county court judge. The latter was the normal route, because it was quicker and yet it would also leave the possibility of a further appeal to the Court of Appeal on a point of law. The Court of Appeal would not normally consider an appeal where an internal appeal had not been made, *Director General of Fair Trading v. Stuart* [1991] 1 All E.R. 129, [1991] C.L.Y. 2786 considered; (3) the correct form to secure attendance at court was in fact N90; (4) it was likely that the trial judge had been unfamiliar with the Legal Aid Act 1988 s.29, an obscure provision, which allowed him to grant legal aid without evidence of means in the case of a committal for contempt. He had been under an obligation in such circumstances to advise K of his right to free legal advice, and (5) N91 was the correct form for the committal of the defendant as it contained all the relevant information despite its reference to an obsolete rule. However the court was of the opinion that it should be amended to include reference to the contemnor's right to apply for his discharge.

READ v. KING, Trans. Ref: FC3 96/7342/G, November 18, 1996, Lord Woolf, M.R., CA.

1263. Appeals–conviction of rape on uncorroborated evidence of victims–safe and satisfactory verdict–appropriate test–Hong Kong

[Criminal Procedure Ordinance s.83 (Hong Kong).]
K appealed from a judgment of the Hong Kong Court of Appeal dismissing his application for leave to appeal against two convictions of rape. The Crown's case was based on the uncorroborated evidence of two sisters which contained discrepancies and contradictions. The defence case was never put. It was submitted that the majority judgment erred in not applying the test of lurking doubt enunciated in *R. v. Cooper (Sean)* [1969] 1 Q.B. 267, [1969] C.L.Y. 818.

Held, dismissing the appeal, that the statutory test provided by the Criminal Procedure Ordinance s.83 was invoked by the grounds of appeal. Given the state of the evidence, the terms of the summing up and the verdicts of the jury, there was no reason to doubt that the convictions were safe and satisfactory. There was nothing to support the contention that the appellate court did not properly question whether the conviction was unsafe and unsatisfactory.

KWONG KIN-HUNG v. QUEEN, THE, Trans. Ref: No.38 of 1996, November 11, 1996, Lord Steyn, PC.

1264. Appeals–extension of time limits–theft–obtaining by deception–appeal against sentence following change in law

[Theft Act 1968 s.15(1), s.20; Theft Act 1978 s.1; .]
W appealed against sentence having pleaded guilty to 15 counts of obtaining property by deception contrary to the Theft Act 1968 s.15(1) for which he was sentenced to a total of five years' imprisonment. In addition W sought leave to extend time in order to appeal against conviction following *R. v. Preddy (John Crawford)* [1996] A.C. 815, [1996] 1 C.L.Y. 1530. W controlled a group of companies in the motor business, two of which were vehicle hire companies. Following financial difficulties W dishonestly raised finance over vehicles in relation to which some money was transferred telegraphically and some by cheque. W argued that he would suffer a substantial injustice if he were not allowed an extension and the opportunity to appeal against conviction. The maximum sentence for an offence under s.15 of the 1968 Act was 10 years, whereas the maximum sentence for conviction for alternative verdicts was seven and five years respectively.

Held, refusing the application for leave to appeal out of time and dismissing the appeal against sentence, that a change in the law was not per se a ground for extending time for appealing and in exercising the discretion as to whether to extend time all the relevant circumstances of the case must be taken into consideration. It was relevant that W had pleaded guilty and that the extension of time required was 18 months, the application having been made nine months after *Preddy* was decided, *R. v. Smith* (Unreported, 1997) considered. The sentence was not likely to have been less because of the different maximum sentence for the substituted conviction as the judge had taken into account W's overall criminality. In respect of the appeal against sentence the judge below had taken into account all mitigating circumstances argued and the sentence was not excessive.

R. v. WHITTAKER (CHARLES GEOFFREY), Trans. Ref: 96/1437/Y4, April 10, 1997, Rose, L.J., CA (Crim Div).

1265. Appeals–grounds for appeal–inadequate legal representation

D and M were convicted of murder, causing grievous bodily harm with intent and robbery. For the offence of murder both appellants were sentenced to life imprisonment. D received concurrent sentences of six years' and four years' imprisonment for causing grievous bodily harm with intent and robbery, and M received four and three years' imprisonment concurrent. They appealed on a number of grounds, including criticism of M's counsel.

Held, dismissing the appeals, that (1) the grounds of appeal, were unfounded; (2) criticism of trial counsel was also unfounded, and (3) the court condemned the increasing practice of criticism of trial counsel as a ground of appeal and reiterated guidance given by the Bar Council as approved by the Lord Chief Justice on appropriate procedure. Criticism as a ground of appeal should not be advanced unless it could be shown that no reasonably competent counsel would have sensibly conducted the trial in such a manner. That such cases would by their very nature be extremely rare and should only be pursued if the criticism were reasonable and had some prospect of success.

R. v. DOHERTY (MICHAEL PATRICK); R. v. McGREGOR (SUSAN) [1997] 2 Cr. App. R. 218, Judge, L.J., CA (Crim Div).

1266. Appeals–grounds for appeal–miscarriage of justice proviso no longer applicable under English law

[Criminal Appeal Act 1968 s.2(1); Criminal Appeal Act 1995 s.2(1).]

Held, that the proviso in the Criminal Appeal Act 1968 s.2(1), that, even where the issue raised by the appellant ought to be decided in his favour, the Court of Appeal could still dismiss an appeal if it considered that no miscarriage of justice had occurred, no longer formed part of English law. It had been replaced by the Criminal Appeal Act 1995 s.2(1), which substituted the requirement that the Court of Appeal must consider the conviction unsafe in order to allow the appeal. Practitioners should not be under the misconception that the proviso still applied.

R. v. FOLEY (SHAUN); R. v. MELVILLE (CARL McKENZIE),*TheTimes*, March 17, 1997, Dyson, J., CA (Crim Div).

1267. Appeals–indecent assault–widow's right to pursue appeal on behalf of deceased husband

[Criminal Appeal Act 1968 s.44A.]

Held, that, under the Criminal Appeal Act 1968 s.44A, a widow was entitled to continue her deceased husband's appeal against conviction for indecent assault on his daughter. In the interests of justice, where only death prevented the husband from pursuing the appeal himself, the appeal should be heard and, if upheld, the husband's name cleared.

R. v. W (CRIME: PURSUING DECEASED'S APPEAL), *The Times*, January 8, 1997, Lord Bingham of Cornhill, L.C.J., CA (Crim Div).

1268. Appeals–magisterial duty to give reasons–Mauritius

[District and Intermediate Courts (Criminal Jurisdiction) Act 1888 s.96(2) (Mauritius).]

The Director of Public Prosecutions of Mauritius appealed against the quashing of S's conviction of six offences of possession and supply of drugs and one offence of possession of ammunition, based largely upon the evidence of an accomplice. The Supreme Court found that magistrates had misdirected themselves with regard to their acceptance of such evidence.

Held, dismissing the appeal, that the Supreme Court was acting within its powers. The District and Intermediate Courts (Criminal Jurisdiction) Act 1888 s.96(2) gave the Supreme Court a full right of appeal by rehearing and its power to affirm a conviction made that decision its own. If the Supreme Court was not satisfied that the prosecution had fully discharged the criminal burden of doubt, then it must allow the appeal. Unlike the English system in which a jury was prevented from giving its reasons, magistrates in Mauritius were obliged to do so and the appeal process was completely different, *Boyjonauth v. Queen, The* [1961] M.R. 171 and *R. v. Duma* [1945] A.D. 410 considered.

DPP v. SABAPATHEE [1997] 1 W.L.R. 483, Lord Hoffmann, PC.

1269. Appeals–time limits–need for practitioners to observe time limit for lodging application for leave to appeal against conviction

[Criminal Appeal Act 1968 s.18(2).]

Held, that practitioners should note the need to comply with the Criminal Appeal Act 1968 s.18(2) requiring applications for leave to appeal against conviction to be lodged within 28 days of the conviction. Notwithstanding any practical difficulties which might arise in view of the fact that there was often a delay between conviction and sentence, there was no ambiguity in the statutory rule and time ran from the date of conviction.

R. v. LONG (LEONARD), *The Times,* October 24, 1997, Lord Bingham of Cornhill, L.C.J., CA (Crim Div).

1270. Bail–failure to surrender–solicitor miscalculated date–reasonableness of excuse

[Bail Act 1976 s.6(1).]

Held, that, in deciding whether to initiate proceedings pursuant to the Bail Act 1976 s.6(1), it was necessary for the magistrates to consider whether a solicitor's miscalculation of the date on which his client was due to attend court was, in all the circumstances, a reasonable excuse for the defendant's failure to surrender to bail.

R. v. LIVERPOOL CITY JUSTICES, *ex p.* SANTOS; *sub nom.* R. v. LIVERPOOL STIPENDIARY MAGISTRATES, *ex p.* SANTOS, *The Times,* January 23, 1997, Staughton, L.J., QBD.

1271. Bail–surety and security–forfeiture–surety's liability ended when defendant surrendered to custody at arraignment–security condition continued on new bail order

[Magistrates Courts Act 1980 s.6(3)(b).]

The magistrates' court had committed a defendant to the Crown Court on bail until the case was disposed of, with conditions of security and surety. J had acted as surety for £5,000 and had paid £5,000 security on behalf of the defendant. On arraignment at the Crown Court, the judge had ordered "bail as heretofore" without considering afresh whether the security and surety conditions were suitable. J applied for judicial review of a decision ordering forfeiture of the £5,000 security paid into court and of a decision ordering forfeiture of £3,000 of J's surety.

Held, allowing the second application but refusing the first, that the words "for trial" in the Magistrates Courts Act 1980 s.6(3)(b) were to be interpreted as meaning "for the purposes of trial" and any bail granted by the magistrates ended if the defendant surrendered himself into custody at arraignment or at any other hearing before the Crown Court, *R. v. Central Criminal Court, ex p. Guney* [1996] A.C. 616, [1996] 1 C.L.Y. 1554 applied. Use of the words "bail as heretofore" amounted to the making of a new bail order, which meant that the judge was obliged to consider a surety's position before imposing conditions. As he had failed to do so, J's obligation as a surety ceased at the arraignment, making forfeiture of the £3,000 unlawful. However, ordering "bail as heretofore" meant that security was included as a condition and there was no obligation for the judge to do more than invite representations from the defendant, which he had done. There was no obligation to make inquiries as to the ability of a third party to pay the security, as this obligation belonged solely to the defendant.

R. v. MAIDSTONE CROWN COURT, *ex p.* JODKA; *sub nom.* R. v. KENT CROWN COURT, *ex p.* JODKA, *The Times*, June 13, 1997, Astill, J., QBD.

1272. Binding over—acquittals—relevant considerations

Held, that, when deciding to make a binding over order following an acquittal, a judge had to be satisfied beyond reasonable doubt that the defendant was a violent man and a potential threat to others.

R. v. MIDDLESEX CROWN COURT, *ex p.* KHAN (1997) 161 J.P. 240, McCowan, L.J., QBD.

1273. Binding over—conditions—consent not required where opportunity to make representations regarding proposed order given

[Justices of the Peace Act 1361; Justices of the Peace Act 1968.]

J applied for judicial review of an order binding him over in the sum of £500. J had pleaded not guilty to a charge of affray but the trial could not take place as certain prosecution witnesses were unavailable. On indicating that he intended to bind J over to keep the peace, the judge gave J the opportunity to make submissions regarding the proposed order, but he did not obtain J's consent to the order, which J argued was a requirement of making it.

Held, allowing the application on a different ground, that in making a binding over order against a person in circumstances which required that that person be given the opportunity to make representations regarding the order, it was not also necessary for the court to obtain that person's consent. Although *R. v. South Molton Justices, ex p. Ankerson* [1989] 1 W.L.R. 40 stated that consent was one of several conditions precedent to a binding over order, consent was not mentioned in the provisions conferring the power to make such an order in the Justices of the Peace Acts 1361 or 1968. It was illogical that the power to make an order with the purpose of keeping the peace was conditional on obtaining the consent of the person against whom the order was being made. Further, there was little point in providing a defendant with the opportunity to make submissions against the order if it could not, in any case, be made without his consent. *Ankerson* was an untypical binding over case and should be distinguished on that basis and the requirement that consent be obtained and that warning of the proposed binding over order be given should have been spoken of disjunctively rather than conjunctively, *R. v. Woking Justices, ex p. Gossage* [1973] 1 Q.B. 448, [1973] C.L.Y. 2069 considered.

R. v. LINCOLN CROWN COURT, *ex p.* JUDE [1997] 3 All E.R. 737, Auld, L.J., QBD.

1274. Cautions—confessions—inducement to confess—police powers to administer caution

[Public Order Act 1986 s.5.]

T applied for judicial review of a decision to administer a formal caution and not to withdraw that caution. The issue was whether a caution administered following an inducement to confess by way of a bargain made with the police should be quashed. T had been accused of driving whilst under the influence of alcohol or drugs, but when he was breathalysed the results were negative. However, his objections to the accusation resulted in a charge under the Public Order Act

1986 s.5 of using abusive and insulting language. T argued that he had been induced to make the confession by being told that he would not be taken to court. He was later charged with another offence and the issue of his caution arose.

Held, allowing the application and granting certiorari to delete the caution, that as a confession is a precondition to a decision to administer a caution, the defendant should confess before the decision to administer a caution is made, and a confession should not be sought as part of the cautioning process. The consequences of a caution were serious, potentially affecting any future claim of good character. The offence with which T was charged was classified in the Case Disposal Manual of the Metropolitan Police as a "pivotal" offence for which all aggravating and mitigating factors of the offence and offender had to be considered before a decision was made as to whether to issue a caution or to prosecute. In this case it was considered appropriate to administer a caution, which can only be done if the defendant admits his guilt. If T had been induced to make the confession, evidence of that confession could not be included in any criminal proceedings as it would not be reliable.

R. v. COMMISSIONER OF POLICE OF THE METROPOLIS, *ex p.* THOMPSON [1997] 2 Cr. App. R. 49, Schiemann, L.J., QBD.

1275. **Committal orders—failure to pay fines—requirements for issue of warrant of commitment**

[Magistrates Courts Act 1980 s.82.]

C and K, both over 21, had warrants of commitment issued against them by the magistrates' court following their failure to pay fines imposed in respect of criminal offences. C appealed by way of case stated against a refusal by the magistrates to review the issuing of the warrants, whilst K applied for judicial review of the decision to commit her.

Held, dismissing C's appeal and allowing K's application, that under the Magistrates Courts Act 1980 s.82(6), the only statutory requirement for issuing a warrant in respect of an adult over 21 was that the magistrates had to satisfy themselves that one of the conditions listed in s.82(4) of the Act was satisfied and enter that ground on the warrant. The conditions listed in s.82(4) were that either the offender appeared to be able to pay the outstanding sum forthwith or that failure to pay was due to the offender's wilful refusal or culpable neglect, and all other methods of enforcing payment had been tried or considered and had been found to be unsuccessful or inappropriate. However, where an offender was under 21, the court also had to specify in the warrant why it was satisfied that a money payment supervision order was undesirable or impracticable and state in open court why no other method of dealing with the offender was appropriate and have the reason entered in the register. On the facts, the magistrates had not acted unlawfully in refusing to review the issuing of the warrants in respect of C, but the magistrates dealing with K had acted illogically in rejecting a fines supervision order as an alternative method of dealing with her.

R. v. STOCKPORT JUSTICES, *ex p.* CONLON; R. v. NEWARK AND SOUTHWELL JUSTICES, *ex p.* KEENAGHAN [1997] 2 All E.R. 204, Staughton, L.J., QBD.

1276. **Committals—abuse of process—investigation lasting four years before committal—no prejudice to defendants**

H and others applied for judicial review of the decision of the acting stipendiary magistrate refusing to stay committal proceedings against them as an abuse of process. The applicants were alleged to have deceived and exploited elderly members of the public by inducing them to part with savings and make investments in return for promised rewards which did not materialise. The applicants argued that the delay in prosecution amounted to an abuse of the process of the court. The inquiry into the activities of the applicants began in 1991 and in 1993 one of the applicants was struck off the roll of solicitors though it was not until 1995 that the applicants were charged. The prosecution argued that there were good reasons for the delay including that the local constabulary were investigating a much wider range of offences than those with which the applicants were eventually charged and they were following up leads which were time consuming. The prosecution also argued that a lack of resources meant that the case took longer to investigate and prepare than they desired. The applicants maintained that they suffered prejudice as the Solicitors Disciplinary Tribunal preceded the criminal proceedings and that two of those charged were not aware that the investigation was continuing.

Held, dismissing the applications, that there were no grounds on which it could succeed as many of the points raised by the applicants could be raised at the pre-trial hearing. There were no exceptional circumstances to justify a stay, *Attorney General's Reference (No.1 of 1990), Re* (1992) 95 Cr. App. R. 296, [1992] C.L.Y. 615 considered. The delay did not cause the applicants serious prejudice and the charges against the applicants were not such that they could not fairly defend themselves.

R. v. CARDIFF MAGISTRATES COURT, *ex p.* HOLE; R. v. CARDIFF MAGISTRATES' COURT, *ex p.* LEWIS (KEITH); R. v. CARDIFF MAGISTRATES' COURT, *ex p.* LEWIS (ELLIOT); R. v. CARDIFF MAGISTRATES' COURT, *ex p.* HOWARD (PETER JOHN) [1997] C.O.D. 84, Lord Bingham of Cornhill, L.C.J., QBD.

1277. Committals–adjournment–CPS ignoring court order and failing to warn principal witness to attend hearing

O applied for judicial review of a magistrate's decision to grant an adjournment of committal proceedings. The original request by the CPS for an adjournment on the ground that their preparation was incomplete had been refused but, despite a court order that the date should stand and O should attend, the CPS failed to advise O of the hearing date. When she failed to appear, the magistrate felt compelled to order an adjournment in the interests of justice and sought an explanation from the CPS as to why they decided not to warn O to attend. The CPS made no apology for defying the court's order but pointed to the recommendations of the Working Group Report on Pre-Trial Issues (November 1990) which specified a longer preparation period than was available to the prosecution in the instant case.

Held, dismissing the application, that reliance on the Working Group recommendations could not justify the breach of a court order which resulted in the absence of the principal witness at the hearing. The explanation given by the CPS contained no apology nor any acknowledgement that they were wrong to disregard the court order. If the CPS felt that the order should not have been made, it was open to them to apply to have the order set aside or to appeal against it; non compliance was not an option.

R. v. HIGHBURY CORNER MAGISTRATES COURT, *ex p.* O'DONOGHUE (1997) 161 J.P. 161, Lord Bingham of Cornhill, L.C.J., QBD.

1278. Committals–objection to admission of witness statement–no duty to restate objection after other submissions made

[Magistrates Courts Act 1980 s.102.]

Held, that after other submissions had been made at the request of the magistrate during committal proceedings, nothing in the Magistrates Courts Act 1980 imposed a legal duty to restate an objection to the admission of a witness statement under s.102.

R. v. HIGHBURY CORNER MAGISTRATES COURT, *ex p.* ANTONELLI, *The Independent,* May 12, 1997 (C.S.), Pill, L.J., QBD.

1279. Costs–preparation for criminal trial–reasonable hourly rate for solicitor

G applied for judicial review of the Birmingham Magistrates' Court's taxation of a bill of costs arising out of the representation of a client, A, prosecuted for the offences of driving with excess alcohol and failing to exchange particulars following an accident. At trial the prosecution offered no evidence on the excess alcohol summons and A pleaded guilty to the lesser offence. The areas of concern were (1) the reasonable hourly rate for a Grade A solicitor; (2) the appropriate grade of fee earner for the work undertaken, and (3) the appropriate percentage of uplift for care and conduct.

Held, allowing the application, that (1) the reasonable hourly rate was £90 having regard to all the circumstances of the case and prevailing rates locally and nationally; (2) the case was a summary matter triable only in the magistrates' courts and did not involve a complex question of law, therefore a Grade A solicitor was inappropriate, *Randall v. Motor Insurers' Bureau* [1969] 1 All E.R. 21, [1968] C.L.Y. 3475 considered, and (3) the decision as to uplift could not stand and there should be a reconsideration of this point.

R. v. BIRMINGHAM MAGISTRATES COURT, *ex p.* ADSHEAD, Trans. Ref: CO/3018/96, June 4, 1997, Simon Brown, L.J., QBD.

1280. Criminal Appeal Act 1995 (c.35)–Commencement No.4 Order

CRIMINAL APPEAL ACT 1995 (COMMENCEMENT NO.4 AND TRANSITIONAL PROVISIONS) ORDER 1997, SI 1997 402 (C.20); made under the Criminal Appeal Act 1995 s.32. Commencement details: bringing into force various provisions of the Act on March 31, 1997; £0.65.

This Order brings into force on March 31, 1997 all the provisions of the Criminal Appeal Act 1995 not already in force. These concern mainly the powers of the Criminal Cases Review Commission, established under s.8 of that Act, to consider claims of miscarriages of justice.

1281. Criminal Justice Act 1988–designated countries and territories

CRIMINAL JUSTICE ACT 1988 (DESIGNATED COUNTRIES AND TERRITORIES) (AMENDMENT) ORDER 1997, SI 1997 1316; made under the Criminal Justice Act 1988 s.96. In force: July 1, 1997; £0.65.

This Order amends the Criminal Justice Act 1988 (Designated Countries and Territories) Order 1991 (SI 1991 2873) which provides that, subject to certain modifications, the Criminal Justice Act 1988 Part VI applies to an order made by a court in a designated country or territory for the purpose of recovery of property obtained as a result of or in connection with an offence to which Part VI applies, recovering the value of property so obtained or depriving a person of a pecuniary advantage so obtained. The list of countries to which the 1991 Order applies is extended by the addition of Antigua and Barbuda, Colombia, Cyprus, Czech Republic, Denmark, France and Ireland. The points of institution of proceedings for Antigua and Barbuda and Colombia are also added.

1282. Criminal Justice Act 1988–designated countries and territories–Amendment No.2

CRIMINAL JUSTICE ACT 1988 (DESIGNATED COUNTRIES AND TERRITORIES) (AMENDMENT) (NO.2) ORDER 1997, SI 1997 2976; made under the Criminal Justice Act 1988 s.96. In force: February 1, 1998; £1.10.

This Order amends the Criminal Justice Act 1988 (Designated Countries and Territories) Order 1991 (SI 1991 2873) by adding Australia and Austria to the list of countries to which the Order applies and by changing the point of institution of proceedings in relation to Australia and the Isle of Man.

1283. Criminal Justice and Public Order Act 1994 (c.33)–Commencement No.11 Order

CRIMINAL JUSTICE AND PUBLIC ORDER ACT 1994 (COMMENCEMENT NO.11 AND TRANSITIONAL PROVISION) ORDER 1997, SI 1997 882 (C.31); made under the Criminal Justice and Public Order Act 1994 s.172. Commencement details: bringing into force various provisions of the Act on April 1, 1997; £0.65.

This Order brings into force on April 1, 1997 the Criminal Justice and Public Order Act 1994 s.158(2), s.158(5), s.158(6), s.158(7) and s.158(8) and s.159(5). These make amendments to the procedures to be followed at committal hearings under the Extradition Act 1989 and before a magistrates' court under the Backing of Warrants (Republic of Ireland) Act 1965. By virtue of Art.3(2) of this Order, the amendments to s.9 of the 1989 Act and to Sch.1 para.6 and Sch.1 para.7 to that Act will only apply when the extradition request or, as the case may be, requisition, is received by the Secretary of State after April 1, 1997.

1284. Criminal Procedure and Investigations Act 1996 (c.25)–Appointed Day No.2 Order

CRIMINAL PROCEDURE AND INVESTIGATIONS ACT 1996 (APPOINTED DAY NO.2) ORDER 1997, SI 1997 36 (C.3); made under the Criminal Procedure and Investigations Act 1996 s.52, s.77. In force: appoints February 1, 1997 for certain purposes under the Act; £0.65.

This Order appoints February 1, 1997 for the purposes of the Criminal Procedure and Investigations Act 1996 s.52 which applies where the offence with which the person being remanded is charged is alleged to be committed on or after that date.

1285. Criminal Procedure and Investigations Act 1996 (c.25)–Appointed Day No.3 Order

CRIMINAL PROCEDURE AND INVESTIGATIONS ACT 1996 (APPOINTED DAY NO.3) ORDER 1997, SI 1997 682 (C.25); made under the Criminal Procedure and Investigations Act 1996 s.1, s.51, s.61, s.63, s.69. In force: appoints April 1, 1997 for certain purposes under the Act; £0.65.

This Order provides that the appointed day for the purposes of the Criminal Procedure and Investigations Act 1996 Part I, s.51, s.61, s.63 and s.69 is April 1, 1997.

1286. Criminal Procedure and Investigations Act 1996 (c.25)–Appointed Day No.4 Order

CRIMINAL PROCEDURE AND INVESTIGATIONS ACT 1996 (APPOINTED DAY NO.4) ORDER 1997, SI 1997 1019 (C.36); made under the Criminal Procedure and Investigations Act 1996 s.28, s.54, Sch.3 para.8. In force: appoints April 15, 1997 for certain purposes under the Act; £0.65.

This Order appoints April 15, 1997 for the purposes of the Criminal Procedure and Investigations Act 1996 s.28, s.54 and Sch.3. The provisions specified in this Order apply in the case of s.28 (which relates to the application of Part III and concerns preparatory hearings), in relation to an offence if any of the events mentioned in s.28(1) occur in respect of that offence on or after April 15, 1997; in the case of s.54 (tainted acquittals), in relation to acquittals in respect of offences alleged to be committed on or after April 15, 1997; and in the case of Sch.3 (fraud), in relation to an offence if any of the events mentioned in Sch.3 para.8(1) occur in respect of that offence on or after April 15, 1997.

1287. Criminal Procedure and Investigations Act 1996 (c.25)–Appointed Day No.5 Order

CRIMINAL PROCEDURE AND INVESTIGATIONS ACT 1996 (APPOINTED DAY NO.5) ORDER 1997, SI 1997 1504 (C.59); made under the Criminal Procedure and Investigations Act 1996 s.54, s.61. In force: appoints June 30, 1997 for certain purposes under the Act; £0.65.

This Order appoints June 30, 1997 for the purposes of the Criminal Procedure and Investigations Act 1996 s.54, relating to tainted acquittals, and s.61, relating to the application of s.58 and the reporting of derogatory assertions.

1288. Criminal Procedure and Investigations Act 1996 (c.25)–Appointed Day No.6 Order

CRIMINAL PROCEDURE AND INVESTIGATIONS ACT 1996 (APPOINTED DAY NO.6) ORDER 1997, SI 1997 2199 (C.86); made under the Criminal Procedure and Investigations Act 1996 s.49, s.77. Commencement details: bringing into force various provisions of the Act on October 1, 1997; £0.65.

This Order appoints October 1, 1997, for the purposes of the Criminal Procedure and Investigations Act 1996 s.49 which relates to the accused's intention to plea to either way offences.

1289. Criminal Procedure and Investigations Act 1996 (c.25)–Appointed Day No.7 Order

See Northern Ireland: CRIMINAL PROCEDURE. §5176

1290. Criminal Procedure and Investigations Act 1996 (c.25)–codes of practice

CRIMINAL PROCEDURE AND INVESTIGATIONS ACT 1996 (CODE OF PRACTICE) (NO.2) ORDER 1997, SI 1997 1033; made under the Criminal Procedure and Investigations Act 1996 s.25. In force: in accordance with Art.1 (1); £0.65.

This Order revokes and replaces the Criminal Procedures and Investigations Act 1996 (Codes of Practice) (No.1) Order 1997 (SI 1997 Un-numbered). It appoints, as the day on which the codes of practice prepared under the Criminal Procedure and Investigations Act 1996 s.23 and laid before Parliament on February 27, 1997 are brought into operation in England and Wales, the day which shall be appointed for the purposes of Part I of the 1996 Act (disclosure). The code, which contains provisions relating to the conduct of criminal investigations, applies by virtue of s.25(3) of the 1996 Act in relation to suspected or alleged offences into which no criminal investigation has begun before the day on which the code comes into operation.

1291. Criminal Procedure and Investigations Act 1996 (c.25)–Commencement Order

CRIMINAL PROCEDURE AND INVESTIGATIONS ACT 1996 (COMMENCEMENT) (SECTION 65 AND SCHEDULE 1 AND 2) ORDER 1997, SI 1997 683 (C.26); made under the Criminal Procedure and Investigations Act 1996 s.65, Sch.1 para.39, Sch.2 para.7. Commencement details: bringing into force various provisions of the Act on March 8, 1997; £0.65.

This Order provides that the Criminal Procedure and Investigations Act 1996 s.65, Sch.1 and Sch.2 are to have effect in relation to any alleged offence in relation to which Part I of that Act applies, that is to say any alleged offence into which no criminal investigation has begun before the day appointed for the purposes of that part by the Secretary of State.

1292. Crown Court–committal proceedings–consequential amendments

CROWN COURT (AMENDMENT) RULES 1997, SI 1997 701 (L.7); made under the Supreme Court Act 1981 s.77, s.84, s.86, s.87. In force: April 1, 1997; £0.65.

These Rules amend the Crown Court Rules 1982 (SI 1982 1109) to take account of the changes in the procedure at committal proceedings effected by the Criminal Procedure and Investigations Act 1996. They indicate how and when a person who is committed for trial at the Crown Court is to exercise his right to object to a statement or deposition being read out at the trial without oral evidence being given by the person who made the statement or deposition.

1293. Crown Court–contempt of court

CROWN COURT (CRIMINAL PROCEDURE AND INVESTIGATIONS ACT 1996) (CONFIDENTIALITY) RULES 1997, SI 1997 699 (L.5); made under the Supreme

Court Act 1981 s.84, s.86; and the Criminal Procedure and Investigations Act 1996 s.19. In force: April 1, 1997; £1.10.

These Rules provide for the practice and procedure to be followed in the Crown Court in relation to proceedings to deal with a contempt of court under the Criminal Procedure and Investigations Act 1996 s.18; applications under s.17(4) and s.18(6) of the 1996 Act; and orders under s.17(4) and s.18(4) and s.18(7) of the 1996 Act.

1294. Crown Court—defence disclosure

See CRIMINAL PROCEDURE. §1306

1295. Crown Court—expert evidence—advance notice

CROWN COURT (ADVANCE NOTICE OF EXPERT EVIDENCE) (AMENDMENT) RULES 1997, SI 1997 700 (L.6); made under the Supreme Court Act 1981 s.84, s.86; and the Police and Criminal Evidence Act 1984 s.81. In force: April 1, 1997; £0.65.

These Rules amend the Crown Court (Advance Notice of Expert Evidence) Rules 1987 (SI 1987 716) with effect from April 1, 1997 in relation to proceedings for offences into which no criminal investigation has begun before that date. They insert references to the transfer of proceedings for trial to the Crown Court under the Criminal Justice Act 1987 s.4 or Criminal Justice Act 1991 s.53; and the preferment of a bill of indictment under the Administration of Justice (Miscellaneous Provisions) Act 1933 s.2(2)(b). The provisions of the 1987 Rules concerning mutual disclosure of expert evidence between the parties to criminal proceedings in the Crown Court following committal or an an order for retrial are thereby extended to apply also to such proceedings following a notice of transfer of the preferment of a bill of indictment.

1296. Crown Court—notice of transfer—children cases

CRIMINAL JUSTICE ACT 1991 (NOTICE OF TRANSFER) (AMENDMENT) REGULATIONS 1997, SI 1997 738; made under the Criminal Justice Act 1991 s.53, Sch.6 para.4. In force: April 1, 1997; £0.65.

These Regulations amend the Criminal Justice Act 1991 (Notice of Transfer) Regulations 1992 (SI 1992 1670) concerning the special procedures for the transfer to the Crown Court of certain cases involving children. They make changes to the form of notice of transfer and the form of notice to the defendant to take account of the abolition of witness orders following amendments to the general nature of committal proceedings.

1297. Crown Court—notice of transfer—notice of transfer

CRIMINAL JUSTICE ACT 1987 (NOTICE OF TRANSFER) (AMENDMENT) REGULATIONS 1997, SI 1997 737; made under the Criminal Justice Act 1987 s.5. In force: in accordance with Reg.1; £0.65.

These Regulations amend the Criminal Justice Act 1987 (Notice of Transfer) Regulations 1988 (SI 1988 1691) concerning the special procedures for the transfer to the Crown Court of certain cases involving serious or complex fraud. They make changes to the form of notice of transfer and the form of notice to the defendant to take account of the abolition of witness orders, following amendments to the general nature of committal proceedings, and of the incorporation into the general arrangements for compulsory disclosure by accused persons of particulars of any alibi defence.

1298. Crown Court–tainted acquittals–applications to High Court

CROWN COURT (CRIMINAL PROCEDURE AND INVESTIGATIONS ACT 1996) (TAINTED ACQUITTALS) RULES 1997, SI 1997 1054 (L.22); made under the Supreme Court Act 1981 s.84, s.86. In force: April 15, 1997; £1.55.

These Rules are made in connection with the provision made by the Criminal Procedure and Investigations Act 1996 s.54 and s.55 for applications to be made to the High Court for orders quashing acquittals of offences. They provide for when certification by crown courts shall be made; for the Form in which certification is to be drawn up; for the persons on whom the Form is to be served and the manner of service; for the making of entries in the courts registers; and for the public display of copies of Forms by courts making certification orders.

1299. Custody–remand–expiry of time limits–false imprisonment–breach of statutory duty

[Prosecution of Offences (Custody Time Limits) Regulations 1987 (SI 1981 299) Reg.6.]

O, who had been remanded in custody pending trial for a period exceeding the statutory time limit, brought actions against the Secretary of State for damages for false imprisonment by the prison governor and against the CPS for breach of their statutory duty, under the Prosecution of Offences (Custody Time Limits) Regulations 1987 Reg.6, to bring her before the court so she could apply for bail. The judge struck out O's claim against the Secretary of State but refused to strike out the claim against the CPS. O and CPS appealed.

Held, dismissing O's appeal and allowing the appeal by the CPS, that O could only have been released from custody by order of the court. Once the statutory time limit had expired, the court would have been obliged to order O's release, although her release would have been on bail, which could have included certain conditions. Although O's detention became unlawful once the time limit had expired, this did not mean that failure to obtain an order for her release made the prison governor liable for false imprisonment, as he was neither obliged nor empowered to release her. Whether the CPS's breach of its public duty under Reg.6 should also give rise to a private law remedy in damages depended on the intention of Parliament in enacting the relevant legislation and the Secretary of State in making the 1987 Regulations. The object of the Regulations was to expedite the prosecution of offenders whilst ensuring individuals were not remanded in custody for excessive periods. There was no intention to create a private law cause of action.

OLOTU v. HOME OFFICE; *sub nom.* OLOTU v. CROWN PROSECUTION SERVICE [1997] 1 W.L.R. 328, Lord Bingham of Cornhill, L.C.J., CA.

1300. Custody–remand–extension of time limits–copy of audio tape recordings requested by defence–no lack of due expedition on part of CPS

[Prosecution of Offences Act 1985 s.22(3); Prosecution of Offences (Custody Time Limits) Regulations 1987 (SI 1987 299) Reg.4.]

W, one of a number of co-accused charged with conspiracy to import and supply drugs, sought judicial review of a decision dismissing his appeal against a stipendiary magistrate's decision extending the custody time limits as set out in the Prosecution of Offences Act 1985 s.22(3) and the Prosecution of Offences (Custody Time Limits) Regulations 1987 Reg.4(4) by 88 days. The time extension was granted to permit the copying of a series of covert tape recordings made in the course of police investigations which had been requested by some of the accused. W contended that the delay was exacerbated by a lack of due expedition on the part of the CPS in arranging for the copying to be carried out and that there was no good and sufficient cause to extend the time limit under s.22(3) of the 1985 Act.

Held, refusing the application, that the decision to dismiss the appeal did not disclose any elements of *Wednesbury* unreasonableness on the part of the judge when considering the difficulties involved in copying 792 hours of taped conversations. The machines needed to carry out the task were rare and had to be hired, and the defence were not deprived of transcripts of the recordings. The judge considered the relevant points of law and carefully weighed the criticisms made of the CPS before finding that the Crown had acted with due expedition and that there was good and sufficient cause to increase the time limit.

R. v. MERTHYR TYDFIL CROWN COURT, *ex p.* WEST; R. v. MERTHYR TYDFIL CROWN COURT, *ex p.* EVANS; R. v. MERTHYR TYDFIL CROWN COURT, *ex p.* ALLEN, Trans. Ref: CO-4481/96; CO-455/97; CO-619/97; CO-886/97, March 25, 1997, Curtis, J., QBD.

1301. Custody–remand–extension of time limits–public and witness safety justified extension of time

[Prosecution of Offences Act 1985 s.22(3).]

D applied for judicial review of the decision, pursuant to the Prosecution of Offences Act 1985 s.22(3), to extend custody time limits for 94 days and applied for habeus corpus. D had been arrested for wounding with intent after stabbing a man in a street and was remanded in custody on the basis of witness and public safety. The trial was delayed in order to secure the attendance of a key witness. D contended that the unavailability of a judge or court was not necessarily a sufficient reason for extending the limit and that in the instant case the judge below had relied entirely on the protection of witnesses and the public to allow the extension.

Held, dismissing the applications, that the judge below had considered all the circumstances. The prosecutor had acted with due expedition and the court was not at fault and, although the plain intention of Parliament was to avoid excessive custody for remanded prisoners, in the interest of public safety such long extensions might be necessary, *R. v. Central Criminal Court, ex p. Abu-Wardeh* [1997] 1 All E.R. 159, [1996] 1 C.L.Y. 1585 considered and *R. v. Birmingham Crown Court, ex p. Bell* (1997) 161 J.P. 345, [1997] C.L.Y. 1302 approved.

R. v. LEWES CROWN COURT, *ex p.* DRISCOLL, June 19, 1997, Simon Brown, L.J., QBD.

1302. Custody–remand–extension of time limits–whether prosecution had acted with due expedition and showed sufficient cause for extension

[Prosecution of Offences Act 1985 s.22.]

B was charged with a number of serious offences and remanded in custody. The prosecution successfully applied for an extension to the custody time limits, but a second extension was refused on the grounds that the prosecution had not shown due expedition and B was released on bail. The prosecution then made a successful ex parte application for a voluntary bill of indictment and bail was revoked. B applied for judicial review of a decision to extend the custody time limit arising from the signing of the voluntary bill to the date set for trial, arguing that the prosecution had not shown all due expedition. B contended that the judge should have considered the whole of the prosecution's conduct and not just events occurring after the voluntary bill, and that upon making the ex parte application for the voluntary bill of indictment the prosecution should have disclosed that B was on bail as a result of the earlier refusal to extend the custody time limits.

Held, dismissing the application, that in deciding whether the prosecution had satisfied the criteria under the Prosecution of Offences Act 1985 s.22, a judge should limit himself to the particular stage to which that time limit related, which in the instant case was the period since the granting of the voluntary bill. It was not essential to consider the prosecution's failure to show due expedition at a previous point in the process when determining whether the criteria were met at a subsequent stage. Whilst the prosecution should have disclosed the earlier refusal, it was not clear that the judge would have reached a different conclusion if it had. With regard to what constituted good and sufficient cause under s.22, while protection of the public per se might not be enough to justify an extension, protection of prosecution witnesses allied with other factors might fulfil the requirement.

R. v. BIRMINGHAM CROWN COURT, *ex p.* BELL; R. v. BIRMINGHAM CROWN COURT, *ex p.* BROWN; R. v. BIRMINGHAM CROWN COURT, *ex p.* FRANCIS (1997) 161 J.P. 345, Rose, L.J., QBD.

1303. Custody–remand–magistrates courts

MAGISTRATES' COURTS (REMANDS IN CUSTODY) (AMENDMENT) ORDER 1997, SI 1997 35; made under the Magistrates' Courts Act 1980 s.128A. In force: February 1, 1997; £0.65.

This Order amends the Magistrates' Courts (Remands in Custody) Order 1989 (SI 1989 970) and the Magistrates' Courts (Remands in Custody) Order 1991 (SI 1991 2667) by removing references to accused persons having attained the age of 17. These amendments are made in consequence of the amendment to the Magistrates' Courts Act 1980 s.128A by the Criminal Procedure and Investigations Act 1996 s.52(2) which removed a similar reference in s.128A itself. As a result, the provision in s.128A (remands in custody for more than eight days) applies to all accused persons, whatever their age.

1304. Deception–obtaining by deception–summing up–substitution of verdicts

[Criminal Appeal Act 1968 s.3; Theft Act 1968 s.15(1), s.20(2).]

N appealed against conviction on six counts of obtaining property by deception contrary to the Theft Act 1968 s.15(1) for which he received concurrent sentences of eight months on each count. N took deposits in the form of cheques from customers for double glazing and falsely represented that customers were protected by a deposit protection scheme. It was accepted that, in view of the decision in *R. v. Graham (Hemamali Krishna)* [1997] 1 Cr. App. R. 302, [1996] 1 C.L.Y. 1532, the convictions were unsafe and must be quashed and that convictions for the corresponding offences under s.20(2) of the 1968 Act should be substituted. But N contended that the trial judge had erred; (1) in allowing evidence from customers that the work had not been done, that they had had difficulty contacting N and that they never had their deposits returned; (2) in refusing a submission of no case, and (3) by summing up inappropriately.

Held, dismissing the appeal, that the convictions were quashed and verdicts of guilty under s.20(2) of the 1968 Act substituted, that (1) although there had been irregularities by the prosecution who had referred to evidence that was not part of their case, N had been able to deal with it and it had not caused unfairness; (2) the trial judge had correctly ruled that there was a case to go to the jury, and (3) the summing up was clear and fair, save only that it had misdirected on the law in relation to cheques as property consequent to the decision in *R. v. Preddy (John Crawford)* [1996] A.C. 815, [1996] 1 C.L.Y. 1530 and *R. v. Graham* decided very recently.

R. v. NOBLE (PETER), Hobhouse, L.J., CA (Crim Div).

1305. Disclosure–defence disclosure–time limits

CRIMINAL PROCEDURE AND INVESTIGATIONS ACT 1996 (DEFENCE DISCLOSURE TIME LIMITS) REGULATIONS 1997, SI 1997 684; made under the Criminal Procedure and Investigations Act 1996 s.12, s.77. In force: April 1, 1997; £1.10.

These Regulations prescribe the relevant period for the Criminal Procedure and Investigations Act 1996 s.5 and s.6 which relate respectively to compulsory and voluntary disclosure by the accused in criminal proceedings.

1306. Disclosure–defence disclosure in the Crown Court

CROWN COURT (CRIMINAL PROCEDURE AND INVESTIGATIONS ACT 1996) (DISCLOSURE) RULES 1997, SI 1997 698 (L.4); made under the Supreme Court

Act 1981 s.84, s.86; and the Criminal Procedure and Investigations Act 1996 s.19. In force: April 1, 1997; £1.55.

These Rules provide for the practice and procedure to be followed in the Crown Court in relation to applications under the Criminal Procedure and Investigations Act 1996 s.3(6), s.7(5), s.8(2), s.8(5), s.9(8), s.15(4) and s.16(b); applications and orders under the Criminal Procedure and Investigations Act 1996 (Defence Disclosure Time Limits) Regulations 1997 (SI 1997 684); orders under s.3(6), s.7(5), s.8(5) and s.9(8) of the 1996 Act; and orders under s.15(5) of the 1996 Act.

1307. Disclosure–defence disclosure in the magistrates courts

MAGISTRATES' COURTS (CRIMINAL PROCEDURE AND INVESTIGATIONS ACT 1996) (DISCLOSURE) RULES 1997, SI 1997 703 (L.9); made under the Magistrates' Courts Act 1980 s.144; and the Criminal Procedure and Investigations Act 1996 s.19. In force: April 1, 1997; £1.55.

These Rules provide for the practice and procedure to be followed in magistrates' courts in relation to applications under the Criminal Procedure and Investigations Act 1996 s.3(6), s.7(5), s.8(2), s.8(5), s.9(8), s.14(2) and s.16(b); applications under the Criminal Procedure and Investigations Act 1996 (Defence Disclosure Time Limits) Regulations 1997 s.8 (SI 1997 684); orders under s.3(6), s.7(5), s.8(2) and s.8(5) and s.9(8) of the 1996 Act; orders under s.14(3) of the 1996 Act; and orders under the 1997 Regulations.

1308. Drink driving offences–blood tests–appropriate procedure–fear of needles not a medical reason for refusal

[Road Traffic Act 1988 s.7(6).]

J appealed by way of case stated against his conviction of failing to provide a specimen of blood without reasonable excuse contrary to the Road Traffic Act 1988 s.7(6) during the course of an investigation into driving while unfit to do so through drink or drugs. Following his detention at a police station J, who had refused to give a sample of blood, was asked by a police officer whether there were any medical reasons why a specimen could not be taken to which J replied that he did not like needles. J argued, in reliance upon *DPP v. Warren* [1993] A.C. 319, [1992] C.L.Y. 3788, that the police officer failed to follow the correct procedure by informing J that only medical reasons would be considered as justification for not providing a sample of blood. In addition, J contended that his statement that he did not like needles raised a medical reason which warranted further investigation by the police officer or referral to a doctor.

Held, allowing the appeal, that (1) the police officer had failed to follow the necessary procedure. Following *DPP v. Warren* the police officer was required to ask J whether there were any reasons why a specimen of blood should not be taken by a doctor. In limiting J's right to object to medical reasons the officer had detracted from the formula as laid down in *DPP v. Warren*, and *DPP v. Donnelly (Ronald Francis)* [1997] C.L.Y 1311 considered. Accordingly, J's conviction was quashed. J's argument that his statement as to his dislike of needles raised a medical objection such as to place the police under a duty to investigate further or refer the matter to a doctor failed. Following *Johnson v. West Yorkshire Metropolitan Police* [1986] R.T.R. 167, [1986] C.L.Y. 2891 a medical ground must be recognised by medical science. In addition, there was no duty on the police officer as, even if the statement had created an obligation, by the time the exchanges reached the medical stage J had already made it clear that he would not provide a specimen. Any recourse to a doctor would therefore have been purposeless.

JACKSON v. DPP, Trans. Ref: CO/1290/97, July 10, 1997, Buxton, J., QBD.

1309. Drink driving offences–blood tests–procedure

[Road Traffic Act 1988 s.7, s.8.]

The DPP appealed by way of case stated against the Crown Court's decision that the procedure laid down by Lord Bridge of Harwich in *DPP v. Warren* [1993] A.C.

319, [1992] C.L.Y. 3788 had not been properly followed. The case related to the Road Traffic Act 1988 s.7 and s.8 and the purpose of the procedure was to ensure that the driver was made aware of the conditions for exercising the option for a blood test and then what the option involved and possible consequences of its exercise. The second question before the Court was, if the Crown Court was held to be justified, whether it was obliged to exclude evidence of the result of the analysis of the blood specimen and so allow the respondent's appeal.

Held, allowing the appeal, that as a matter of principle and applying the purpose of the procedure, there was no difficulty in this particular case. A review of the authorities did not raise further problems. The procedure was followed sufficiently and the second question before the court did not therefore arise.

DPP v. HILL BROOKES [1996] R.T.R. 279, Balcombe, L.J., QBD.

1310. Drink driving offences—blood tests—urine tests—extent of duty to inform of option to provide blood or urine specimen

[Road Traffic Act 1988 s.8(2).]

C appealed by way of case stated against the dismissal of his appeal against conviction of an offence of driving with excess alcohol in his blood. The issues were the proper application of the Road Traffic Act 1988 s.8(2) given the conditions laid down in *DPP v. Warren* [1993] A.C. 319, [1992] C.L.Y. 3788. C, a Frenchman, was found by police on the verge of a motorway asleep in his car with the engine running. A roadside breath test was positive and C was arrested and the results of breath specimens provided at the police station triggered the driver's option under s.8(2). C disputed that he was given the driver's option, but contended that, even if he was, it did not satisfy the requirements of *Warren.* The question was whether the magistrates were entitled to hold that C had been fully informed of the option offered to him to supply a replacement sample. C contended that he was not informed that he was over the limit, which specimen he could give, that blood would be taken by a doctor or that he could only object on medical grounds determined by a doctor.

Held, allowing the appeal, that C may have exercised his option differently if he had been given the full facts. Although it was evident to C that he exceeded the statutory limit, the failure to inform him that this was the case would not render the procedure unlawful, *DPP v. Ormsby* [1996] 2 C.L.Y. 5065 considered. That C was not informed of which specimen to give or that he could only refuse on a doctor's determination was also of no consequence.

CHATELARD v. DPP, [1997] R.T.R. 362, Simon Brown, L.J., QBD.

1311. Drink driving offences—blood tests—urine tests—failure to provide specimen—duty to inform driver blood specimen to be taken by doctor

[Road Traffic Act 1988 s.7.]

The DPP appealed, by way of case stated, against the dismissal of the case against D who was charged with failure to provide a specimen of blood or urine pursuant to the Road Traffic Act 1988 s.7. Following D's arrest for being drunk in charge of a motor vehicle he was taken to a police station where he agreed to provide a specimen of breath. However, the intoximeter was found to be inoperative and D was therefore asked by a police officer to provide a specimen of blood or urine. D refused and was subsequently charged. The magistrate found that the police officer's failure to inform D that any sample of blood would be taken by a doctor had invalidated the statutory procedure. The DPP appealed on the ground that the wording used by the police officer followed precisely the words used by Lord Bridge in *DPP v. Warren* [1993] A.C. 319, [1992] C.L.Y. 3788 who went further than was required by statute.

Held, allowing the appeal, that the police officer acted correctly within the law in using the wording he did when he requested a specimen of blood or urine from D. Applying *Fraser v. DPP* [1997] R.T.R. 373, [1997] C.L.Y. 1313 there was no requirement in either driver option cases under s.8 or obligatory cases in terms of s.7 that a driver should be told that a doctor would take the blood sample.

DPP v. DONNELLY (RONALD FRANCIS), Trans. Ref: CO 3331/96, March 10, 1997, Blofeld, J., QBD.

1312. Drink driving offences—blood tests—urine tests—no duty to ask driver if valid reason why blood cannot be taken or to inform that doctor will perform blood test

The Crown appealed by way of case stated against the stipendiary magistrate's decision to acquit D of failing, without reasonable excuse, to provide a specimen of blood or urine. The acquittal was made on the grounds that, prior to D's refusal to provide a specimen, the custody officer did not inform D that any blood sample would be taken by a doctor and he had not asked D if there was any reason, medical or otherwise, why a blood sample could not be taken.

Held, allowing the appeal, that an officer was under no duty to inform a driver that a blood test would be carried out by a doctor or to enquire whether there were any reasons why a blood sample should not be taken, *Fraser v. DPP* [1997] R.T.R. 373, [1997] C.L.Y. 1313 applied.

R. v. CHESHIRE STIPENDIARY MAGISTRATE, *ex p.* DPP, *The Times*, March 13, 1997, Blofeld, J, QBD.

1313. Drink driving offences—blood tests—urine tests—right to replace breath sample with sample of blood or urine—no duty to inform driver that blood sample would be taken by doctor

[Road Traffic Act 1988 s.7(4), s.8(2).]

There was no mandatory requirement to inform a driver, being given the option of replacing a breath sample with a blood or urine sample, that the blood sample would be taken by a doctor. F appealed by way of case stated against his conviction for drink driving on the grounds that, when offered the opportunity, at the police station, to replace the breath sample he had given with one of blood or urine, pursuant to the Road Traffic Act 1988 s.8(2), F had not been informed that any blood sample would be taken by a doctor and therefore the statutory procedure had been invalidated.

Held, dismissing the appeal, that the language of s.7(4) and s.8(2) of the Act expressed no requirement that a driver should be told that a doctor would take the replacement blood specimen. In *DPP v. Warren* [1993] A.C. 319, [1992] C.L.Y. 3788, Lord Bridge of Harwich was only providing guidance when he said that one of the things a driver should be told at the outset was that a blood sample would be taken by a doctor, and his judgment could not be construed as laying down a mandatory requirement to that effect. Although the driver had to consent to blood being taken by a doctor before the event, it was not necessary to inform the driver at the outset that a doctor would take the sample.

FRASER v. DPP; *sub nom.* FRASER v. CROWN PROSECUTION SERVICE, *The Times*, March 13, 1997, Lord Bingham of Cornhill, L.C.J., QBD.

1314. Drink driving offences—breath tests—defendant not entitled to legal advice before making decision concerning blood or urine specimen

[Police and Criminal Evidence Act 1984 s.58; Road Traffic Act 1988 s.7, s.8(2).]

W, who was 17, was arrested and taken to a police station. The level of alcohol in his breath specimen was in the 35 to 50 microgrammes range. He was therefore informed of his right under the Road Traffic Act 1988 s.8(2) to opt for a replacement specimen to be taken of either blood or urine. W asked for a solicitor. It was contended on W's behalf that legal advice could have been given on the telephone. W, who was in some confusion, came to the conclusion that giving a replacement specimen would make his situation worse. The justices excluded the original specimen on the grounds that in the absence of legal advice it was unfair to allow the prosecution to rely on the original specimen. The prosecution appealed by way of case stated.

Held, allowing the appeal and remitting the case with a direction to convict, that in *DPP v. Billington* [1988] 1 W.L.R. 535, [1988] C.L.Y. 3094 the court held that the right to legal advice in the Police and Criminal Evidence Act 1984 s.58 did not apply to breath testing procedures under s.7 of the 1988 Act and this reasoning was equally applicable to s.8(2). Parliament had evinced no intention that legal advice was required for this simple choice. The requirements of fairness entitled a suspect to know of his option but that did not necessarily entitle him to have legal advice as to the consequence of exercising it. Where a suspect did not understand that the option existed, through a breakdown in communication, then the requirement might not have been met.

DPP v. WARD (JACK), *The Times,* March 24, 1997, Brooke, L.J., QBD.

1315. Drink driving offences—breath tests—failure of police to make written record

[Road Traffic Act 1988 s.7.]

D appealed against conviction for drink driving on the basis that the prescribed procedure for the taking of an intoximeter sample had not been carried out in accordance with the Road Traffic Act 1988 s.7. The police officer taking the samples had failed to complete the approved internal form used to record the time that the defendant was delivered to the custody of the Intoximeter Officer and, more importantly, the giving of the warning, as required by s.7(7), that a failure to provide a specimen may render the defendant liable to prosecution. In the instant case the officer had completed the "delivery" section and had signed the form but had not recorded the time of giving the caution or any answers to the form's questions. The officer gave oral evidence that he had given the caution but that he had simply overlooked completing the form. He sought to remedy his oversight by making a statement, some six months after the event, confirming that he had complied with the format of the internal form, albeit that he had not made a written record. It transpired that the later statement was made from memory. It is clear law that the strict requirements of the 1988 Act, in that a caution about the failure to give a specimen, must be followed, *Howard v. Hallett* [1984] R.T.R. 353, [1985] C.L.Y. 2992, *R. v. Fox* [1986] 1 A.C. 281, [1985] C.L.Y. 2986 applied. Whilst the judge in the instant case acknowledged the case law he questioned whether the failure to complete an internal form not specified as part of the prescribed procedure could be held to be a failure to comply with the statutory procedures. The Act makes no reference to making a written record and the officer had given oral evidence as to the fact that the correct procedure had been undertaken. The judge also pointed out that D had given specimens of breath of his own free will and therefore had not objected to the giving of specimens and the warning only applied where a defendant refused to give a specimen. D argued that the failure to record the answers to the questions was prima facie evidence that the requirements of the Act had not been followed.

Held, allowing the appeal, that it is of crucial importance that there be a record of the giving of the warning and the questions as to consumption. It was impossible to accept that the intoximeter officer could recollect this defendant after a delay of six months. The failure to complete the internal form meant that the court could not be certain that the proper procedure had been followed and therefore it would be improper to admit the intoximeter printout upon which the conviction was based.

R. v. DAVIES, October 17, 1996, Recorder Gilchrist, Crown Court (Manchester). [*Ex rel.* David McHugh, Barrister].

1316. Drink driving offences—breath tests—failure to provide specimen—insufficient sample to achieve objective of test

[Road Traffic Act 1972 s.12; Road Traffic Act 1988 s.5(1), s.6(4; .]

The DPP appealed against the dismissal of a charge of failing to provide a specimen of breath pursuant to the Road Traffic Act 1988 s.6(4). H was stopped and asked to give a breath sample into an Alcometer. On two attempts H failed to illuminate either of the lights on the device and on a further two attempts only succeeded in illuminating light "A". On none of these occasions did the arresting officer press the "Read" button on the machine. H was arrested for failing to provide a specimen and it was inferred that on reaching the police station further samples proved positive because she was also charged with driving with excess alcohol contrary to the Road Traffic Act 1988 s.5 (1) (a). The magistrate determined that had the "Read" button been pressed when light "A" was lit, then a positive reading would have been reliable although a negative reading would not and considered that H had sufficiently complied to make the arrest unlawful and consequently subsequent evidence obtained was inadmissible.

Held, allowing the appeal and remitting the case to the magistrate, that amendments to the Road Traffic Act 1972 s.12 had cast doubt on the subjective approach taken in *Walker v. Lovell* [1975] R.T.R. 377, [1975] C.L.Y. 2961 and it was clear from the speech of Lord Mackay, reported in Hansard October 14, 1982, that the question should be whether the defendant had provided a sufficient sample of breath in such a way as to reliably establish whether it tested positive or not. In the instant case she had not. If the arresting officer had pressed the "Read" button and received an unreliable negative result, it would have been difficult for her to justify arresting H, *Walker v. Lovell* distinguished as referring to the situation under the 1972 Act, *Fawcett v. Tebb* (1984) 148 J.P. 303, [1984] C.L.Y. 3005 considered.

DPP v. HEYWOOD, Trans. Ref: CO/1182/97, July 8, 1997, Lord Bingham of Cornhill, L.C.J., QBD.

1317. **Indictments–autrefois convict–second indictment charging offence of manslaughter based upon same facts–exercise of discretion to stay proceedings**

[Health and Safety at Work etc. Act 1974; Housing Act 1985.]

B, a landlord, appealed against his conviction of manslaughter following the death of a tenant from carbon monoxide poisoning caused by a defective gas heater. B had previously pleaded guilty to offences under the Health and Safety at Work etc. Act 1974 and the Housing Act 1985 in respect of the same incident, but at trial his plea of autrefois convict was rejected by the trial judge after consideration of *Connelly v. DPP* [1964] A.C. 1254, [1964] C.L.Y. 665. B argued that the judge had been wrong to reject his plea on the basis that it could only have been accepted if both offences bore the same legal characteristics, and had erred in exercising his discretion by refusing to stay the indictment.

Held, allowing the appeal and quashing the conviction, that the majority of the House of Lords in *Connelly* had identified the narrow principle of autrefois convict which applied only where the same offence was alleged in the second indictment as in the first and had ruled that it was for the judge to exercise discretion in other appropriate cases. Although the trial judge in the instant case had analysed the issues in *Connelly* correctly, he had exercised his discretion wrongly by failing to consider whether any special circumstances existed, by carrying out a balancing exercise which was inappropriate and by taking into account the possibility of a fair trial. A stay of proceedings would have been the appropriate course as the manslaughter indictment arose from the same facts as the earlier prosecutions. Furthermore, the continuance of the trial offended the principle that there should be no sequential prosecutions for offences of greater gravity, *R. v. Elrington* (1861) 1 B. & S. 688 followed.

R. v. BEEDIE (THOMAS SIM) [1997] 2 Cr. App. R. 167, Rose, L.J., CA (Crim Div).

1318. **Indictments–criminal charges–particulars of offence–specimen counts– inadequate identification of incidents**

R was charged on seven counts alleging rape and indecent assault, all save for one count of rape, being specimen counts. It was alleged that R had carried out a sustained course of sexual misconduct against two of his stepdaughters during the period 1984 to 1993. During cross examination of one of the victims, defence counsel applied for identification of the incidents cited in the specimen counts. The judge took the view that because the defence was that the complaints were entirely contrived, there was no prejudice to R and that the matter would be reconsidered at the end of the prosecution case. A further application was made at that stage but the judge did not order any particularisation. R was convicted on all seven counts and sentenced to a total of 10 years' imprisonment. He appealed on the ground, inter alia, that the judge was wrong not to direct identification of the incidents relied on in the specimen counts.

Held, allowing the appeal in relation to the specimen counts, that (1) an indictment had to be drafted in such a way as to enable a defendant to know, with as much particularity as the circumstances would admit, what case he had to meet; (2) in the event of a conviction, a judge needed to know precisely what the jury had found proved; (3) the reservations in *R. v. Shore* (1989) 89 Cr. App. R. 32, [1990] C.L.Y. 967 meant no more than that if a defendant chose to meet general charges without objection he could not then easily raise want of particularity on appeal, and (4) it was necessary to settle an indictment which steered a safe course between prejudicial uncertainty and overloading. In the instant case, the judge erred in failing to accede to the request for clearer identification of the facts relied upon in the specimen counts.

R. v. RACKHAM (TERRANCE JOHN) [1997] 2 Cr. App. R. 222, Ian Kennedy, J., CA (Crim Div).

1319. Indictments–formalities–failure to sign fresh indictments did not render them invalid

Held, that where a judge had ordered a re-arraignment on two fresh indictments after deciding there was no justification for joinder of counts in a three count indictment, the failure of the proper officer to sign the fresh indictments as directed did not render them invalid. The judge had exercised his separate jurisdiction in respect of the procedures and the court officer's signature was a mere clerical formality, *R. v. Morais (Carlton)* (1988) 87 Cr. App. R. 9, [1988] C.L.Y. 654 distinguished.

R. v. JACKSON (ANDREW DAVID); R. v. BRADY (MICHAEL WAYNE); R. v. PACKER (THOMAS JAMES); R. v. POWELL (DAVID); R. v. KEARNS (PATRICK JOSEPH), *The Times*, June 9, 1997, Judge, L.J., CA (Crim Div).

1320. Indictments–joinder–counts neither founded on same facts nor part of series of offences

[Indictment Rules 1971 (SI 1971 1253) r.9; Criminal Justice and Public Order Act 1994 s.34.]

L and S, a codefendant, appealed against convictions of conspiracy to commit burglary and S also appealed against a separate conviction of dangerous driving. They contended that the two counts were incorrectly joined in that the Indictment Rules 1971 r.9 had not been satisfied as the dangerous driving count was not founded on the same facts as the conspiracy count, nor did the counts form part of a series of offences with the same or a similar character. S also submitted that the summing up dealing with his decision not to give evidence failed adequately to direct the jury in accordance with the Criminal Justice and Public Order Act 1994 s.34.

Held, allowing the appeal in respect of the misjoinder, but dismissing the challenge to the adequacy of the summing up, that (1) the offences had been incorrectly joined in that the dangerous driving charge arose from the defective nature of the vehicle, not as a result of the manner of or reason for the driving. It was a charge which could have been made against S without reference to the facts of the conspiracy. However, the misjoinder was not such as to nullify the entire indictment as no prejudice had been caused to either L or S, *R. v. Bell (Peter)* (1984) 78 Cr. App. R. 305, [1984] C.L.Y. 696 and *R. v. Smith (Brian Peter)*, [1997] 2 W.L.R. 588, [1997] C.L.Y. 1321 considered, and (2) although the summing up did not cover all the essential points laid down in *R. v. Cowan (Donald)* [1996] 1 Cr. App. R. 1, [1996] 1 C.L.Y. 1511 any deficiencies were not prejudicial to S, given the fact that L and another co-defendant had been convicted on the same evidence.

R. v. LOCKLEY (SIMON MALCOLM); R. v. SAINSBURY (GLEN JEREMY) [1997] Crim. L.R. 455, Forbes, J., CA (Crim Div).

1321. Indictments–joinder–criminal charges–joinder of road traffic offences of similar nature

[Theft Act 1968; Road Traffic Act 1988.]

S applied for leave to appeal against conviction on the basis that the indictment contained counts which were improperly joined. Counsel for the Crown argued that the counts were properly joined as they all related to offences concerning motor vehicles, were committed within a period of six weeks in the same locality and S was on bail for the offences in the first two counts when he committed the offences in the second two counts. The offences were driving a conveyance taken without authority contrary to the Theft Act 1968 (count 1) two offences of driving whilst disqualified (counts 2 and 4) and dangerous driving contrary to the Road Traffic Act 1988 (count 3).

Held, allowing the appeal, that driving a conveyance without authority and driving a motor vehicle whilst disqualified were not offences of a similar character and were improperly joined to the indictment. The proceedings were not a nullity but the convictions on counts 1 and 2 were quashed, *R. v. Callaghan (Terence Alan)* (1992) 94 Cr. App. R. 226, [1993] C.L.Y. 832 followed, *R. v. Lewis (Hopton)* (1991) 95 Cr. App. R. 131, [1992] C.L.Y. 872 considered.

R. v. SMITH (BRIAN PETER) [1997] 2 W.L.R. 588, Henry, L.J., CA (Crim Div).

1322. Judges–allegation that judge asleep during evidence–prejudice not to be automatically assumed

Held, that a complaint that a trial judge was asleep during the hearing of evidence should be made at the time and be specific, pinpointing which parts of the evidence the judge was alleged to have missed. It was not to be automatically assumed that the defendant had suffered prejudice.

R. v. MORINGIELLO (THOMAS GUY), *The Times*, July 25, 1997, McCowan, L.J., CA (Crim Div).

1323. Judges–bias–comments on right to silence

B, who was charged with several criminal offences, remained silent during police interview on her solicitor's advice. Before the start of the case, the judge remarked that he thought the exercise of the right to silence never helped the innocent and was merely a charter for the dishonest, and that it could not be lawful for a solicitor to advise a client to say "no comment" to every police question. The judge refused an application to disqualify himself from trying the case. B was convicted and appealed on the basis of the judge's remarks.

Held, dismissing the appeal, that the fact that a judge's personal views might be touched upon in a case was insufficient to disqualify him. The judge in question, who was very experienced in criminal cases, had concluded that his views would not prevent him from conducting the case fairly and without bias. The judge was entitled to come to that conclusion, and the fact that B had in fact received a fair and unbiased trial provided proof that he was right.

R. v. BROWNE (NICOLE NATALIE), *The Times*, August 23, 1997, McCowan, L.J., CA (Crim Div).

1324. Judicial decision making–judge not obliged to give reasons for procedural ruling in criminal trial

W appealed against conviction for murder. The sole prosecution evidence at trial had been statements made under caution, which W alleged had not been given voluntarily and which were admitted following a voir dire. W argued that the judge should have given reasons why the evidence was admitted, and it was inadequate merely to say that they had been made voluntarily.

Held, dismissing the appeal, that whether a judge should give reasons for a procedural ruling in a criminal trial depended on the circumstances, there being no rule that reasons should always be given.

WALLACE v. THE QUEEN; FULLER v. QUEEN, THE, December 3, 1996, Lord Mustill, PC.

1325. Juries–alleged bribery of juror–whether judge should have discharged whole jury

W and I appealed against their convictions of conspiracy to deliver counterfeit currency notes with intent, on the ground that the whole jury should have been discharged following information made available to the judge that one of the jurors might have been bribed. The juror was discharged and the trial continued.

Held, allowing the appeal and quashing the convictions, that the jury should have been discharged as the judge had taken into account irrelevant considerations concerning the length of the trial, *R. v. Spencer* (1986) 83 Cr. App. R. 277, [1986] C.L.Y. 561 followed.

R. v. WALKER (REGINALD DOUGLAS); R. v. IVENS (DEREK) [1996] Crim. L.R. 752, Latham, J., CA (Crim Div).

1326. Juries–bias–suspicion of irregular communication–duty of judge to investigate and rectify

O appealed against his conviction on the ground that the judge had failed to rectify an irregularity that occurred during the course of his trial. The husband of one of the jurors was privy to a conversation in court between counsel and the judge held in the absence of the jury. The discussions related to evidence which was subsequently ruled inadmissible. The judge questioned the juror as to her relationship with the man before concluding that no improper communication had occurred between them. O contended, in reliance upon *R. v. Blackwell (Jody Ann)* [1996] Crim. L.R. 428, [1995] 1 C.L.Y. 2949, that in failing to pursue the matter further the judge had neglected his duty to ascertain all facts relevant to the exercise of his discretion.

Held, dismissing the appeal, that a real danger of bias had not occurred during the course of O's trial, *R. v. Gough (Robert)* [1993] A.C. 646, [1993] C.L.Y. 849 applied. A court was entitled to assume that jurors would adhere to the instructions given to them not to discuss the case with anyone else. While the judge could have investigated the matter further it was clear from statements subsequently provided by the juror and her husband that there was no ground for supposing that any impermissible communication took place. A court should only make further investigations of a juror when there is an indication that improper discussions have occurred.

R. v. OKE (OYEBOLA OLAJUNBOJUN), Trans. Ref: 96/5347/Z3, July 8, 1997, Rougier, J., CA (Crim Div).

1327. Juries–contempt of court–juror's statement alleging prejudice

[Contempt of Court Act 1981 s.8 (1).]

M and his co-accused, A, appealed against conviction of violent disorder and M against a conviction of conspiracy to inflict grievous bodily harm and murder. They also sought leave to appeal against sentence. A argued that the court should investigate a statement obtained from a juror alleging prejudice on the part of the other jurors, provided that consideration of such evidence would not contravene the Contempt of Court Act 1981 s.8 (1). M contended that the trial judge had erred by allowing joinder and by giving inadequate directions on lies and good character. M conceded that the trial judge's direction on joint enterprise in relation to murder was in line with the authorities, but contended that the hearing should be adjourned awaiting the outcome of the appeal to the House of Lords in the case of *R. v. Powell (Anthony) and Daniels (Antonio)* [1996] 1 Cr. App. R. 14, [1995] 1 C.L.Y. 1278.

A contended that the trial judge had failed to sum up adequately in relation to the inconsistencies of identifying witnesses.

Held, dismissing the appeals and applications, that (1) from submissions made to the court it was apparent that the defendants were under a misconception that the court should consider any evidence provided that no offence under s.8(1) had been committed to obtain it. An investigation into the juror's statements would not be contrary to s.8 but to a long line of authority, *Straker v. Graham* (1839) 4 M. & W. 721, *R. v. Thompson* (1962) 46 Cr. App. R. 72, [1962] C.L.Y. 673 and *Ellis v. Deer* [1922] 2 K.B. 113 followed, *R. v. Young (Stephen)* [1995] 2 Cr. App. R. 379, [1995] 1 C.L.Y. 2953 distinguished, because it related to a period when the jury had not been deliberating; (2) joinder of charges was justified because the series of offences concerned different victims and different aspects of the events; (3) it was advisable for judges to avoid the use of the word "entitled", where the jury were required to take evidence into account, but there was no set formula for directions and those that the trial judge had given were adequate; (4) an adjournment and leave to appeal were refused, but an identical point to that in *Powell* was certified, *R. v. Powell (Anthony) and Daniels (Antonio)* [1996] 1 Cr. App. R. 14, [1995] 1 C.L.Y. 1278 considered, and (5) the transcript showed that the trial judge had dealt appropriately with the inconsistencies in his summing up.

R. v. MIAH (BADRUL); R. v. AKHBAR (SHOWKAT) [1997] 2 Cr. App. R. 12, Kennedy, L.J., CA.

1328. Juries–discharge–juror unwell–provision of information to counsel

C and G appealed against conviction of kidnapping, causing grievous bodily harm with intent, and false imprisonment for which they received custodial terms of nine and eight years respectively. During the trial, extensive details of the unpleasant offences and of previous violent clashes between two rival gangs in Newcastle were heard. One lady juror was discharged after a panic attack and another passed a note stating that she was unwell, together with a medical report from her GP to the judge. This note was not shown to counsel. The judge told her to reflect over the weekend and she returned on the Monday and served until that Friday, when she was discharged. C and G contended that their convictions were unsafe because the jury should have been discharged as it had ceased to be impartial.

Held, dismissing the appeal, that the convictions were based on strong evidence and nebulous defences and therefore were not unsafe. The trial judge had correctly exercised his discretion in not discharging the jury. The fact that a note had been passed to a judge should be made known to counsel, although the contents of the note should never be made known if they refer to voting figures, and may not be if they refer to the domestic problems of a juror or to administrative problems. However, where the contents refer to evidence in, or conduct of, the case then they must be made known to counsel, *R. v. Gough (Robert)* [1993] A.C. 646, [1993] C.L.Y. 849 and *R. v. Dempsey* [1991] C.L.Y. 826 followed.

R. v. CONROY (PATRICK WILLIAM); R. v. GLOVER (DAVID WILLIAM) [1997] 2 Cr. App. R. 285, Evans, L.J., CA (Crim Div).

1329. Juries–discharge of juror–judge acted within discretion in continuing with 11 jurors

Q appealed against conviction of handling stolen goods on the basis that a material irregularity occurred when the judge continued the trial with 11 jurors at an early stage in the proceedings.

Held, dismissing the appeal, that the issues raised were matters for the discretion of the judge and there was no basis on which it could be said that the judge did not exercise proper judgment. The options open to the judge were to discharge the jury or carry on with 11 jurors, and as the trial was clearly going to be a short one either option was tenable.

R. v. QUINN (PHILLIP CRAIG) [1996] Crim. L.R. 516, Ebsworth, J., CA (Crim Div).

1330. Juries–invitation to reach verdict without retiring permissible

R appealed against conviction of unlawful wounding on the ground that the judge was wrong to invite the jury to consider its verdict without retiring. R contended, in reliance upon *R. v. Trickett and Trickett* [1991] Crim. L.R. 59, [1991] C.L.Y. 837 that it was no longer permissible for a judge to ask a jury if it wished to reach a verdict in court.

Held, allowing the appeal on a different ground, that as a matter of law it was permissible for a judge to ask a jury if it wished to consider its verdict without retiring. A court should only intervene where a jury was placed under pressure to reach its verdict. Accordingly, R's appeal failed on that ground. However, the appeal was allowed on the basis that there was insufficient identification evidence to convict R.

R. v. RANKINE (ELLISTON),Trans. Ref: 97/3144/Z3, June 27,1997, Brooke, L.J., CA (Crim Div).

1331. Juries–jury members visiting scene of crime contrary to trial judge's instructions

M appealed against conviction for arson. M was arrested having been observed near a church subsequently damaged by a fire started in an external boiler room. At first instance a police officer stated that he had seen M enter the boiler room, although M denied this and a defence witness asserted that the boiler room could not be seen from the point where the police officer had been standing. It was later discovered that, contrary to instructions from the trial judge, two jurors had made independent visits to the site.

Held, allowing the appeal, quashing the conviction and ordering a retrial, that whereas the effect of such conduct by jurors on the safety of a conviction was a question of fact and degree in each case, here it created a probability verging on a certainty that the conclusions reached by the two jurors had formed part of the material used in reaching the verdict. The jurors had departed from their role as judges of fact and become, in effect, witnesses whose evidence was unknown to the defence and could not therefore be tested under cross-examination. There was also a substantial risk that the jurors had erred in where they had performed their respective observations, which added to the conclusion that the conviction was unsafe.

R. v. MORRISON (JOHN WILLIAM); R. v. SUTTON (RICHARD),Trans. Ref: 96/2990/X4, January 30,1997, Butterfield, J., CA (Crim Div).

1332. Juries–jury protection–withholding of jurors' names did not render trial a nullity

[Juries Act 1974 s.12(3).]

Shortly after the commencement of C's trial for attempting to possess a Class A drug with intent to supply, the Crown made a public interest immunity application to the trial judge who, after hearing sworn evidence, discharged the jury. Prior to the start of the second trial, the Crown, offering no reasons and calling no evidence, applied for police protection of the jury. The defence objected to the application, but the judge allowed it and ruled that the jurors' names should not be read out in open court and they should instead be referred to by number. C was convicted and appealed, contending that the judge had erred in ordering protection of the jury without requiring supporting evidence and that the failure to name the jurors rendered the trial a nullity as the Juries Act 1974 s.12(3) required that names be called in open court.

Held, dismissing the appeal, that it was important that, where attempts to approach or communicate unlawfully with a jury were suspected, jurors should be afforded the necessary protection and, whilst providing such protection carried its own dangers, C's conviction could not be regarded as unsafe as a result of the judge's order. The procedure adopted by the judge, whereby the jury were not named, represented a departure from usual practice, but did not render the trial a nullity as it did not breach C's legal rights or cause unfairness, given that C had not been denied his right to challenge the jurors.

R. v. COMERFORD (THOMAS ANTHONY), *The Times*, November 3, 1997, Lord Bingham of Cornhill, L.C.J., CA (Crim Div).

1333. Juries–jury sent away for weekend–irregular directions from judge–verdict returned in three minutes

B was charged with a number of counts of arson and attempted arson. B's trial began on a Monday and on Friday of that same week the jury retired to consider their verdicts. When, on Friday afternoon, the jury intimated that they were unable to reach a majority verdict, the judge called them back into court whereupon he asked them to return on Monday. On that day, three minutes after the jury had entered the jury room, and before the jury bailiffs were sworn in, the jury sent a note to the judge indicating that a verdict had been reached. The judge brought the jury into court and asked them to retire formally. Shortly afterwards the jury returned and delivered verdicts of guilty in respect of three charges. B appealed on the ground that the directions given by the judge when sending the jury away for the weekend were irregular and that the manner in which the verdict was returned by the jury rendered it unsafe.

Held, dismissing the appeal, that the fact that the jury were not told that they should not speak of the case to each other over the weekend was an irregularity. However, there was no formula for the form of words which had to be strictly complied with and there was no evidence that members of the jury had in fact contacted each other over the weekend. Thus, there was nothing which rendered the conviction unsafe.

R. v. BROOKER (TINA JOY), Trans. Ref: 9607700/Y3, July 24, 1997, Swinton Thomas, L.J., CA (Crim Div).

1334. Jury directions–alibis–Crown witnesses identifying accused–alibi defence rejected–Lucas direction unnecessary

H was convicted of assault occasioning actual bodily harm and sentenced to one year's imprisonment. He appealed against conviction. Witnesses for the Crown gave evidence that H had glassed the complainant. H had run the defence of alibi which was supported by defence witnesses. Complaint was made as to the jury direction on alibi, specifically, that if the jury rejected the alibi evidence this was not probative of guilt since there were other reasons why an alibi might be fabricated.

Held, dismissing the appeal, that there was nothing unsafe about the conviction. There had been a straightforward conflict of evidence between the defendant and two Crown witnesses. This was not a case where, the jury having rejected H's evidence of alibi, they would see that as evidence supportive of H's guilt of the offence charged. Their decision would not have been affected were they to have been told that a false alibi might be used to bolster an honest defence, *Broadhurst v. R.* [1964] A.C. 441, [1964] C.L.Y. 905, *R. v. Goodway* (1994) 98 Cr. App. R. 11, [1994] C.L.Y. 826 and *R. v. Dehar* [1969] N.Z.L.R. 763 considered. A direction to that effect would have been merely confusing. Since the issue was whether the Crown witnesses were truthful, the question of whether they had made a mistaken identification did not arise, *R. v. Lesley (Leroy Owen)* [1995] Crim. L.R. 946, [1996] 1 C.L.Y. 1634 distinguished. Had the Crown witnesses lied it would have been a deliberately false identification. Whether H had lied was not part of the Crown's case and, accordingly, was not an issue to which the jury had to give separate consideration making a *Lucas* direction necessary, *R. v. House and Meadows* [1994] Crim. L.R. 682, [1995] 1 C.L.Y. 1077 followed and *R. v. Landon* [1995] Crim. L.R. 338 distinguished.

R. v. HARRON (ROBERT DAVID GEORGE) [1996] 2 Cr. App. R. 457, Beldam, L.J., CA (Crim Div).

1335. Jury directions–murder–judge's duty to leave issue of provocation to jury

[Homicide Act 1957 s.3.]

K appealed against conviction for murder on the ground that the judge erred in not leaving the issue of provocation to the jury. K and the deceased belonged to feuding gangs. It was alleged that K had deliberately driven his van over the deceased. K claimed that he had been threatened and attacked in his van, whilst driving, and had not realised that he had run over anyone. Prior to summing up the judge asked counsel for advice as to whether he should leave the issue of provocation to the jury. Neither counsel thought it necessary and consequently the judge did not direct the jury on that issue.

Held, allowing the appeal, quashing conviction and substituting a manslaughter charge, that judge had been wrong not to follow his first inclination that there was sufficient evidence to leave the issue of provocation to the jury. This failure was a misdirection and therefore the court had to decide whether the conviction was unsafe. The appropriate test to consider was the Homicide Act 1957 s.3, whether the provocation was sufficient to make a reasonable man do as the accused had done. As the court could not be sure that the majority of the jury would have been sure of K's guilt, the conviction was quashed as unsafe, *R. v. Cambridge (David John)* [1994] 1 W.L.R. 971, [1994] C.L.Y. 847 applied.

Observed, It was submitted on appeal that the court take into consideration comments, regarding sentence, made by the trial judge to the Home Secretary. The Home Office had disclosed these comments to the appellant and the court was concerned that indiscriminate use of such material, used out of context, was an unacceptable practice, *R. v. Secretary of State for the Home Department, ex p. Doody* [1994] 1 A.C. 531, [1993] C.L.Y. 1213 and *R. v. Jones* (Unreported, 1996) applied.

R. v. DHILLON (KULJIT SINGH) [1997] 2 Cr. App. R. 104, Ward, L.J., CA (Crim Div).

1336. Jury directions–murder–principle of common design–Jamaica

[Jamaica (Constitution) Order in Council 1962 (SI 1962 1550) s.110, Sch.2; Offences Against the Person (Amendment) Act 1992 s.3B, s.7 (Jamaica).]

W and B were convicted in March 1992 of the murder of a man and his mother during the course of a robbery and sentenced to death. Their convictions were based on statements made by each of them to the police, which were ruled admissible after a voir dire hearing. It was not alleged that W committed any violence against either of the victims. The judge directed the jury that if they accepted the truth of the written statement then W was guilty of the murders under the principle of common design. W applied for leave to appeal on the basis that the judge erred in removing from the jury the function of deciding whether he was guilty under the principle of common design. In December 1991 H was convicted of two murders on the basis of identification evidence given by two witnesses. H applied for leave to appeal on the basis of the judge's directions as to the reliability of aspects of the identification evidence. Following the enactment of the Offences Against the Person (Amendment) Act 1992 (Jamaica) the Court of Appeal reviewed the death sentences at the same time as the applications for leave to appeal were heard. In respect of W, H and a fourth man, L, who had been convicted in April 1990 of a double murder though he had not committed violence against the victims, the Court of Appeal held that although the murders were classified as "non-capital" because none of the defendants had used violence, the sentences of death were to be confirmed under s.7 of the 1992 Act because in each case the two murders were done on the same occasion. W, H and L appealed to the Privy Council.

Held, dismissing the appeals, that (1) although the trial judge erred in directing the jury that if they accepted that W's statement was true the proper verdict would be murder, on the evidence it was inevitable that a reasonable jury, properly directed, would have convicted W of the murders, *DPP v. Stonehouse* [1978] A.C. 55, [1977] C.L.Y. 1450 and *Gayle v. Queen, The* [1996] 1 C.L.Y. 1660 considered. The misdirection was a technical one which did not cause any injustice to W; (2) the requirement that notice be given of a previous conviction under s.3B(5)(a) of the 1992 Act applied only in respect of a conviction at a previous trial. Where two non-capital murders were the subject of a single trial no such notice was required before the person convicted on the two non-capital murders could be sentenced to death. The double murder rule applied, *Simpson v. Queen, The* [1997] A.C. 1, [1996] 1 C.L.Y. 1645 applied; (3) whether or not the Court of Appeal carrying out the classification procedure under s.7(4) of the 1992 Act constituted the Court of Appeal of Jamaica, the Privy Council did not have jurisdiction under the Jamaica (Constitution) Order in Council 1962 Sch.2 s.110(3) to grant special leave to appeal from a decision of the Court of Appeal in respect of the classification of a murder unless that decision was itself "on appeal from a court of Jamaica". The single judge of the Court of Appeal carrying out a review under s.7(2) of the 1992 Act could not be regarded as a "court of Jamaica" within the meaning of s.110(5) of the Order in Council of 1962, because he did not conduct any form of hearing, *Simpson v. Queen, The* distinguished, *Huntley v. Attorney General of Jamaica* [1995] 2 A.C. 1, [1995] 1 C.L.Y. 1314 applied. Accordingly the Privy Council did not have jurisdiction to hear an appeal against a classification by the three judges of the Court of Appeal.

WILLIAMS (KERVIN) v. QUEEN, THE; HAMILTON v. QUEEN, THE; LESLIE v. QUEEN, THE [1997] 2 W.L.R. 910, Lord Hutton, PC.

1337. Jury directions—murder—provocation—need for evidence of provoking words or conduct before issue of provocation left to jury

[Homicide Act 1957 s.3.]

A appealed against the dismissal of his appeal against conviction for the murder of his mother on the grounds that the judge had not left the issue of provocation to the jury, pursuant to the Homicide Act 1957 s.3. Although A had denied killing his mother at his trial, he argued that the issue of provocation had been raised by the Crown, who, during cross-examination, had repeatedly suggested that A had lost his self control and attacked his mother because of the way she treated him. Further, the injuries sustained by the victim indicated that there had been a frenzied attack, which suggested a loss of self control, reinforced by factors such as the defendant's unemployment, his mother's treatment of him and his propensity to bad moods and heavy drinking.

Held, dismissing the appeal, that it was the role of the judge to determine whether there was sufficient evidence for a jury to find that there was a reasonable possibility of specific provoking words or conduct which caused the defendant to lose his self control. If the judge found sufficient evidence, the issue of provocation had to be left to the jury, regardless of the source of the evidence and whether or not the defendant had relied on it at trial. However, if, even taking the position most favourable to the defendant, the judge considered there was not sufficient evidence, no issue of provocation arose which could be put to the jury. Whether or not there was sufficient evidence of provocation was a question of fact to be decided by the judge, taking into account all the circumstances of the case. As A had claimed that he enjoyed a good relationship with his mother, the cross-examination had not resulted in any evidence of provoking conduct or loss of self control and the suggestions put to A by the Crown could not by themselves raise an issue of provocation. It was not enough that it might be possible to infer from the victim's injuries that there had been a loss of self control and that A had attacked her in anger; there had to be evidence of specific provoking conduct. Further, it was mere speculation that A might have lost his self control as a result of provocation, and in such circumstances it would be wrong for the judge to direct the jury on the issue of provocation.

R. v. ACOTT (BRIAN GORDON) [1997] 1 W.L.R. 306, Lord Steyn, HL.

1338. Jury directions–robbery–use of force in order to steal

J appealed against conviction of robbery of a taxi driver. During an attack on the driver by his co-defendant, who had pleaded guilty to punching the driver in the head and taking £200 and other property, J had held the driver in a headlock. J contended that his conviction was unsafe because the jury had not been given an adequate direction on the elements of robbery.

Held, allowing the appeal, that the conviction was unsafe because the trial judge had omitted to direct the jury that the force employed in robbery must be used in order to steal. A conviction of theft was substituted and the custodial sentence of three years and nine months commuted to three years, *R. v. Dawson (Anthony Mark)* (1977) 64 Cr. App. R. 170, [1979] C.L.Y. 545 approved.

R. v. JAMES (DEAN ANDREW), Trans. Ref: 9605747 Y2, March 13, 1997, Morland, J., CA (Crim Div).

1339. Jury directions–submission of no case to answer–handling stolen goods–failure to add alternative theft charges

[Theft Act 1968 s.22(1).]

S faced an indictment containing two counts of handling stolen goods contrary to the Theft Act 1968 s.22(1) in relation to two separate motor vehicles which had allegedly been "rung" (with no alternative counts for theft). At the conclusion of the Crown's case, counsel for S made a submission of no case to answer based on the case of *R. v. Cash* [1985] Q.B. 801, [1985] C.L.Y. 609.

Held, upholding the submission, the court stated that "if the prosecution have been unable to show that this defendant did not steal these two cars, why then, the jury must acquit, and if at this stage I am satisfied under the test in *R. v. Galbraith* (1981) 73 Cr. App. R. 124, [1981] C.L.Y. 513 that there is evidence before the court upon which the court is bound to come to the conclusion that any jury properly directed could not properly convict because they would be left in a state of doubt as to whether the defendant was the thief or was the handler, why, then, I must remove the case from them at this stage, pursuant to my duty under the case of *Galbraith*... In these circumstances, it follows that the jury would not be satisfied beyond reasonable doubt that the defendant received the two cars ... otherwise than in the course of stealing ... I am forced to a conclusion that the submission made under *Galbraith* is made out at this stage, and for these reasons... with marked reluctance I do accede to it."

R. v. SUTER (MATTHEW), March 12, 1997, H.H.J. Bull, Crown Court (Guildford). [*Ex rel.* Stephen Field, Barrister, 10-11 Gray's Inn Square, Gray's Inn].

1340. Jury directions–verdicts–departure from Watson direction did not place undue pressure on jury

Held, that, although it was stressed in *R. v. Buono* (1992) 95 Cr. App. R. 338, [1993] C.L.Y. 798 that a trial judge should follow the terms of the direction given in *R. v. Watson* [1988] 1 Q.B. 690, [1988] C.L.Y. 652 when directing a jury on the need to reach a verdict, added comments by the trial judge would not necessarily be fatal to the conviction. In the instant case, although the facts showed that the judge had departed from the *Watson* direction, his words had not been such as to place undue pressure on the jury.

R. v. MORGAN (OLIVER), *The Times*, April 18, 1997, Rose, L.J., CA (Crim Div).

1341. Magistrates–bias–apparent acceptance of police evidence

R sought judicial review to quash his conviction for driving whilst disqualified and driving without insurance. It was claimed that justices disclosed a real danger of bias within the test in *R. v. Gough (Robert)* [1993] A.C. 646, [1993] C.L.Y. 849. The case turned solely on the conflict of evidence as between R and a police witness as to whether R was actually driving at the time of the alleged offence. Under cross examination by defence counsel the police officer said: "Are you calling me a liar?" to which counsel replied, "Yes". The chair of the bench intervened to say that it was not the practice of the court to describe police officers as liars.

Held, allowing the application and remitting the case for rehearing before a different bench that, had the chair told the officer that it was his duty to answer counsel's questions and not to question counsel himself, this episode would not have arisen. It was difficult to see how the chair's intervention could reasonably have been interpreted other than as a strong instinctive reaction in favour of the police when direct conflict arose in evidence with that of the accused. The statement was one of apparently unqualified effect indicating a general readiness to accept police evidence which showed a real possibility that there was not a wholly impartial adjudication of the matter before the bench, a more receptive and open minded attitude was called for, *R. v. Fisher* [1983] Crim. L.R. 486, [1983] C.L.Y. 938, *R. v. Inner West London Coroner, ex p. Dallaglio* [1994] 4 All E.R. 139, [1995] 1 C.L.Y. 872 and *R. v. Gough* followed.

R. v. HIGHGATE JUSTICES, *ex p.* RILEY [1996] R.T.R. 150, Simon Brown, L.J., QBD.

1342. Magistrates–bias–whether magistrate who heard an ex parte application relating to non-disclosure of unused material should have disqualified himself from conducting trial

Tsought judicial review of a decision of a stipendiary magistrate that he was not disqualified from conducting the trial of T after being involved in an inter partes non disclosure application hearing. The hearing was instituted in ex parte proceedings by the Crown prosecutor who sought the non disclosure of unused material relating to an informant. The magistrate ruled, in the presence of T's solicitor but to the exclusion of T, that the prosecution was under no obligation to disclose the relevant material to the defence. The magistrate subsequently decided that he should not disqualify himself from conducting the trial of T. T contended that there was a real danger of bias in relation to the trial such that the magistrate should have disqualified himself. It was argued that the magistrate's decision should be quashed on the grounds that something may have been said at the ex parte hearing which disparaged, in the eyes of the magistrate, the credibility of a witness and that T should not have been excluded from the non disclosure hearing.

Held, dismissing the application, that the magistrate was correct in deciding not to disqualify himself from conducting the trial of T. Following *R. v. Gough (Robert)* [1993] A.C. 646, [1993] C.L.Y. 849 the test, which the magistrate correctly applied, was whether there was a real danger of bias occurring such as to prevent there being a fair trial. At no time was material presented to the magistrate which would have resulted in a real danger of bias. In criminal trials on indictment, when hearing public interest immunity applications, there was a duty on the prosecution to disclose material. However, they were not required to do so unless an order for disclosure was made. Information that an ex parte application had been made may even be denied to the defence, but such cases would be the exception and only used to ascertain whether the public interest justified non disclosure. Where non disclosure was allowed, it was desirable that the judge who heard the application conducted the trial unless the material was so highly prejudicial as to prevent a fair trial, *R. v. Davis (Michael)* [1993] 1 W.L.R. 613, [1994] C.L.Y. 878, *R. v. Keane (Stephen John)* [1994] 1 W.L.R. 746, [1994] C.L.Y. 876 applied and *R. v. South Worcester Magistrates, ex p. Lilley* [1995] 1 W.L.R. 1595, [1996] 1 C.L.Y. 1576 considered. These rules applied equally to summary trials, and to lay and stipendiary magistrates following *R. v. Bromley Magistrates, ex p. Smith and Wilkins* [1995] 1 W.L.R. 944, [1995] 1 C.L.Y. 1168. On the facts the magistrate made all attempts to disclose as much information to T and his solicitor as possible. He applied the proper test and adhered to the principle that the court which ruled on disclosure should conduct the subsequent trial, and the case did not come within the exception as envisaged in *R. v. South Worcester Magistrates, ex p. Lilley.*

R. v. STIPENDIARY MAGISTRATE FOR NORFOLK, *ex p.* TAYLOR, Trans. Ref: CO/0135/97, July 1, 1997, Lord Bingham of Cornhill, L.C.J., QBD.

1343. Magistrates–failure to give full attention to evidence–judicial review of conviction

D applied for judicial review of her conviction for failing to provide a breath specimen without reasonable excuse on the grounds that she had not received a fair trial before the magistrates' court, as one member of the bench had failed to give full attention to D's evidence and had been reading material unconnected with the trial.

Held, allowing the application, that whilst a magistrate was not obliged to look at a witness at all times or to take notes, it was necessary that the bench was able to judge the credibility of the person giving evidence. It was important that all members of the bench gave and appeared to give the matter before them their full attention and should not be engaged for any significant period in an activity unconnected with the evidence being given.

R. v. SOUTH WORCESTERSHIRE JUSTICES, *ex p.* DANIELS; *sub nom.* R. v. WORCESTER JUSTICES, *ex p.* DANIELS (1997) 161 J.P. 121, Tucker, J., QBD.

1344. Magistrates courts–defence disclosure

See CRIMINAL PROCEDURE. §1307

1345. Magistrates courts–remands in custody

See CRIMINAL PROCEDURE. §1303

1346. Magistrates' clerks

JUSTICES' CLERKS (AMENDMENT) RULES 1997, SI 1997 710 (L.15); made under the Magistrates' Courts Act 1980 s.144. In force: April 1, 1997; £0.65.

These Rules amend the Justices' Clerks Rules 1970 (SI 1970 231) r.4(1)(b), r.4(1)(c) and Sch. para.4A(2)

1347. Magistrates' courts–committals

INDICTMENTS (PROCEDURE) (AMENDMENT) RULES 1997, SI 1997 711 (L.16); made under the Administration of Justice (Miscellaneous Provisions) Act 1933 s.2. In force: April 1, 1997; £0.65.

These Rules make consequential amendments to the Indictments (Procedure) Rules 1971 (SI 1971 2084), as a result of the changes to procedure at committal proceedings effected by amendments to the Magistrates' Courts Act 1980 made by the Criminal Procedure and Investigations Act 1996.

1348. Magistrates' courts–committals

MAGISTRATES' COURTS (AMENDMENT) RULES 1997, SI 1997 706 (L.12); made under the Magistrates' Court Act 1980 s.144. In force: April 1, 1997; £1.55.

These Rules amend the Magistrates' Courts Rules 1981 (SI 1981 552) to take account of the changes in magistrates' courts' procedures in respect of committal for trial in the Crown Court effected by the Criminal Procedure and Investigations Act 1996.

1349. Magistrates' courts–committals–abolition of witness orders–children's evidence

MAGISTRATES' COURTS (NOTICE OF TRANSFER) (CHILDREN'S EVIDENCE) (AMENDMENT) RULES 1997, SI 1997 709 (L.14); made under the Magistrates' Courts Act 1980 s.144. In force: April 1, 1997; £0.65.

These Rules amend the Magistrates' Courts (Notice of Transfer) (Children's Evidence) Rules 1992 (SI 1992 2070) to take account of changes made in the procedures at committal proceedings by the Criminal Procedure and Investigations Act 1996 and the abolition of witness orders by that Act. They remove references in the 1992 Rules to witnesses' appearance at such proceedings and to the court's making witness orders.

1350. Magistrates' courts–committals– abolition of witness orders – consequential amendments

MAGISTRATES' COURTS (NOTICES OF TRANSFER) (AMENDMENT) RULES 1997, SI 1997 708 (L.13); made under the Magistrates' Court Act 1980 s.144. In force: April 1, 1997; £0,65.

These Rules amend the Magistrates' Courts (Notice of Transfer) Rules 1988 (SI 1988 1701) to take account of the abolition of witness orders by the Criminal Procedure and Investigations Act 1996. They remove references to the making of witness orders by the magistrates' courts.

1351. Magistrates' courts–contempt of court

MAGISTRATES' COURTS (CRIMINAL PROCEDURE AND INVESTIGATIONS ACT 1996) (CONFIDENTIALITY) RULES 1997, SI 1997 704 (L.10); made under the Magistrates' Courts Act 1980 s.144; and the Criminal Procedure and Investigations Act 1996 s.19. In force: April 1, 1997; £1.10.

These Rules provide for the practice and procedure to be followed in magistrates' courts in relation to proceedings to deal with a contempt of court under the Criminal Procedure and Investigations Act 1996 s.18; applications under s.17(4), s.17(6)(b) and s.18(6) of the 1996 Act; and orders under s.17(4) and s.18(4) and s.18(7) of the 1996 Act.

1352. Magistrates' courts–forms–Amendment No.1–committals

MAGISTRATES' COURTS (FORMS) (AMENDMENT) RULES 1997, SI 1997 707 (L.26); made under the Magistrates' Courts Act 1980 s.144. In force: April 1, 1997; £1.55.

These Rules amend the Magistrates' Courts (Forms) Rules 1981 (SI 1981 553) to take account of the changes effected by the Criminal Procedure and Investigations Act 1996 in magistrates' courts procedures including, in particular, those in respect of committal or trial in the Crown Court. These Rules amend, omit or substitute certain forms used in relation to committal proceedings as a consequence of those changes. In particular, they insert a new form which indicates the nature of the notice to be given by the prosecutor to the accused of his right to object to witness statements and depositions being read out at the trial in the Crown Court without oral evidence being given by the witnesses who made the statements and depositions.

1353. Magistrates' courts–forms–Amendment No.2–consent to community sentences

See CRIMINAL SENTENCING. §1606

1354. Magistrates' courts–mode of trial–supply of drugs–magistrates court perverse to accept jurisdiction

[Magistates' Courts Act 1980 s.19(3).]

The DPP sought judicial review of a decision by the justices to assume jurisdiction in relation to an either way offence. The charge was for possession of a Class A drug (Ecstasy tablets) with intent to supply, an offence that would usually attract a sentence of between two to five years' imprisonment, whereas the justices' power is limited to imposing a maximum custodial sentence of six months. It was contended that no reasonable bench could have reached the decision to assume jurisdiction, and that they must have paid no, or inadequate, regard to the Magistrates' Courts Act 1980 s.19(3) and to the *Mode of Trial Guidelines* re-issued in 1995.

Held, dismissing the appeal, that the justices decision to accept jurisdiction was perverse, and that they should not have done so. Justices should have close regard to the Guidelines in conjunction with s.19(3), when considering their jurisdiction in relation to either way offences. It was concluded, however, that it was inappropriate for the court to exercise its discretion to remit the matter to the justices for possible referral to the Crown Court, for several reasons, including that the prosecution did not bring the Guidelines to the justices attention, did not immediately apply for an adjournment on the announcement that the justices assumed jurisdiction, and only made known its intention to seek judicial review over one month after the justices' decision. In addition, the defendant had pleaded guilty, been sentenced, and had paid the fine ordered.

R. v. HORSEFERRY ROAD MAGISTRATES COURT, *ex p.* DPP [1997] C.O.D. 89, Rose, L.J., QBD.

1355. Magistrates' courts–offences committed outside commission area–court had no jurisdiction where there were no connected proceedings within jurisdiction

[Magistrates Courts Act 1980 s.2(6).]

Held, that, a magistrates' court could extend its jurisdiction to try summonses alleging summary offences committed outside its commission area pursuant to the Magistrates Courts Act 1980 s.2(6) only where the defendant was also being tried for an offence committed within its own jurisdiction.

R. v. CROYDON MAGISTRATES COURT, *ex p.* MORGAN, *The Independent*, June 30, 1997 (C.S.), Simon Brown, L.J., QBD.

1356. Magistrates' courts–store detectives–stipendiary could not dismiss case as means of punishing detective for inappropriate conduct

[Magistrates Courts Act 1980 s.10(1).]

Held, that, where a stipendiary magistrate disapproved of the prosecution's conduct, it was possible to send for a senior member of the CPS, so that the stipendiary's criticisms could be presented to him in open court and the prosecution could then be penalised by way of costs. However, where the stipendiary disapproved of the conduct of a store detective, it was not open to the magistrate to dismiss the case as a way of punishing the detective and encouraging other store detectives to conduct themselves more appropriately in the future. The correct course was to adjourn the case under the Magistrates Courts Act 1980 s.10(1) for a rehearing by a different bench.

R. v. HORSEFERRY ROAD MAGISTRATES COURT, *ex p.* DPP, *The Independent*, June 23, 1997 (C.S.), Simon Brown, L.J., QBD.

1357. Magistrates' courts–tainted acquittals–applications to High Court

MAGISTRATES' COURTS (CRIMINAL PROCEDURE AND INVESTIGATIONS ACT 1996) (TAINTED ACQUITTALS) RULES 1997, SI 1997 1055 (L.23); made under the Magistrates' Court Act 1980 s.144. In force: April 15, 1997; £1.55.

These Rules are made in connection with the provision made by the Criminal Procedure and Investigations Act 1996 s.54 and s.55 for applications to be made to the High Court for orders quashing acquittals of offences. They provide for when certification by magistrates' courts shall be made; for the form in which certification is to be drawn up; for the persons on whom the form is to be served and the manner of service; for the making of entries in the courts' registers; and for the public display of copies of forms by courts making certification orders.

1358. Police powers–arrest–obstruction of police–arrest without warrant–no substitution of reason to validate arrest

[Police and Criminal Evidence Act 1984 s.25.]

During an incident outside a public house M was arrested by S, a police officer, for obstruction. At M's trial for obstructing and assaulting the police officer in the execution of her duty, M contended that the police officer had acted unlawfully in arresting M, but M was convicted. On appeal it was submitted on behalf of M that (1) there was no common law power to arrest without warrant for obstruction, and (2) the Police and Criminal Evidence Act 1984 s.25, allowing arrest without warrant, did not apply in this case. The DPP submitted that (1) S had been entitled to arrest M for breach of the peace, or (2) s.25(3)(a) of the 1984 Act applied.

Held, allowing the appeal, that where a police officer has given a reason for an arrest another reason cannot be substituted, whether that involves the substitution of another offence or the inference that s.25(3)(a) of the 1984 Act was satisfied, *Edwards v. DPP* (1993) 97 Cr. App. R. 301, [1994] C.L.Y. 728 applied.

MULLADY v. DPP, Trans. Ref: CO/1610/97, July 3, 1997, Gage, J., QBD.

1359. Police powers–arrest–wrongful arrest–extent of police officer's discretion

[Police and Criminal Evidence Act 1984 s.24.]

C appealed against a decision awarding L damages for wrongful arrest and false imprisonment. An investigation following a robbery led two police officers, K and A, to L's house with the intention of arresting and interviewing him. K and A found that L was not at the house, but, his friend I was. Following A's disclosure that L was wanted in connection with a robbery, I told K and A that L could not have been involved as he was with I at the time. L was subsequently arrested and he instituted proceedings on the ground that K and A's discretionary decision to exercise their power of arrest under the Police and Criminal Evidence Act 1984 s.24 was flawed by their failure to consider the evidence of I. L contended that K and A's decision to arrest was based on suspicions that L was guilty of the offence which, in light of I's evidence, were not reasonably held. It was argued that this constituted a breach of the *Wednesbury* principle and the arrest was therefore unlawful. This was accepted by the judge. C appealed on the ground that the judge's decision could not be supported.

Held, allowing the appeal, that the judge had erred in upholding the contention that K and A's discretionary decision to exercise their power of arrest was flawed by their failure to consider I's evidence. K and A, suspecting L of being guilty of the offence and having reasonable cause for that suspicion, had the power to arrest L in accordance with s.24. K and A's decision to exercise their discretion was appropriate as I's evidence did not undermine their reasonably held suspicions and was not material to the exercise of discretion, *Castorina v. Chief Constable of Surrey* (1996) 160 L.G. Rev. 241 applied. It was therefore not *Wednesbury* unreasonable for K and A to decide to arrest L.

LYONS v. CHIEF CONSTABLE OF WEST YORKSHIRE, Trans. Ref: CCRTF 96/1379/C, April 24, 1997, Hutchison, L.J., CA.

1360. Police powers–search and seizure–confessions–confession made during search in absence of caution

[Police and Criminal Evidence Act 1984 s.30.]

R, aged 16, appealed against conviction on one count of possessing cannabis with intent to supply and four other counts of possession for which he was sentenced to a combination order comprising two years' probation and 100 hours' community service. A search warrant had been obtained and a search carried out of the flat where R resided with his family. His brother had previous convictions for drug offences. R's father was the appropriate adult present during most of the search and R made various admissions regarding some of the cannabis and drug paraphernalia found. R contended that the confession should be excluded as the codes of practice made under the Police and Criminal Evidence Act 1984 had been breached by the officers conducting the search. When the first exhibit, some cannabis, was found, R admitted it was his, but this occurred without him first being cautioned. R argued that this was in breach of Code of Practice C:10.1. The trial judge held, as a matter of fact, that a caution had not been required as the police suspected that an offence had been committed and that R had committed it. As each item was found an entry was made in the record book with R's comment and he was arrested and cautioned in the presence of the appropriate adult. R argued that he had been coerced into cooperating with the police, and further, that he had not been taken to a police station as soon as practicable in accordance with s.30 of the 1984 Act.

Held, dismissing the appeal, that investigations into alleged offences by juveniles had to be conducted with extreme fairness. The trial judge's finding of fact regarding the caution was one that could be made on the evidence. Breaches of the codes of practice are a question of fact and degree and to be determined in each case. The fact that R made no comment regarding some of the exhibits indicated that he was able to decide whether or not to answer. It would have been impracticable to take R to the police station sooner as it was correct that R should have remained at the house and been questioned there until completion of the search, *R. v. Park (Randy Alyan)* (1994) 99 Cr. App. R. 270, [1994] C.L.Y. 967 and *R. v. Cox (Rodney William)* (1993) 96 Cr. App. R. 464, [1993] C.L.Y. 843 considered.

R. v. R (A JUVENILE), Trans. Ref: 96/7406/W2, March 14, 1997, Judge Colston Q.C., CA (Crim Div).

1361. **Police powers–search and seizure–powers of entry–no written record of grounds for search or nature of evidence–lawfulness of search**

[Police and Criminal Evidence Act 1984 s.18(1), s.30.]

K appealed by way of case stated against a decision upholding his conviction of assaulting a police officer in the execution of his duty. K's son, A, had been arrested on suspicion of handling stolen property. A did not live with K although he did sometimes visit his flat; however, he had not been to K's flat for two months. A gave the police the addresses of both his own flat and his father's flat. The police officers decided to search both addresses, but K refused them entry into his flat. Accordingly they obtained written authority to enter, as required under the Police and Criminal Evidence Act 1984 s.18(1), but the acting inspector who signed the form did not make any further record in writing regarding the grounds of the search and the nature of the evidence sought. K continued to refuse them entry and kicked the sergeant causing him a slight injury. No evidence was found and A was released. K argued that the failure to make a record of details when the written authorisation was given was a breach of s.30 of the 1984 Act and that as such the entry was unlawful. The DPP argued that the requirement to make a record was not mandatory and that the failure to do so did not prejudice or disadvantage K.

Held, dismissing the appeal, that in the particular circumstances of this case, the requirements of s.18 of the 1984 Act should be regarded as directory rather than mandatory so that the search of K's flat was not invalidated. However, the provisions do have to be fully complied with. K chose not to read the written authority which set out his rights when he refused the officers entry but written authority had been given.

KROHN v. DPP, Trans. Ref: CO 3920-96, March 18, 1997, Brooke, L.J., QBD.

1362. Police powers—search and seizure—search warrants failed to state statutory authority—warrant correctly issued—Jamaica

[Customs Act (Jamaica) s.203; Constitution of Jamaica s.18, s.19(1).]

W was being investigated by the Jamaican Ministry of Finance in connection with fraudulent importing. An officer obtained a search warrant pursuant to the Customs Act s.203. The warrant did not refer to that power, but stated that the justice had been satisfied on evidence on oath that uncustomed goods or books, documents "or instruments relating thereto" and authorised seizure of "all such goods and other articles". As well as documents, items such as a cellular phone case, keys and a pocket calculator were seized. C sought a declaration that the warrant was invalid and the search illegal and contrary to the Constitution of Jamaica s.18 and s.19(1). The Jamaican Court of Appeal held the searches illegal and the Attorney General appealed.

Held, allowing the appeal, the justice's statement on the face of the warrant was prima facie to be accepted and in the absence of any evidence to rebut the justice's statement the warrant was correctly issued not undermined by the failure to mention the statutory power under which it was issued. The legality of the search and seizure of documents would not be vitiated by the trivial excess of power involved in the wrongful taking of the above named items, *R. v. Inland Revenue Commissioners, ex p. Rossminster* [1980] A.C. 952 [1980] C.L.Y. 2278 applied.

ATTORNEY GENERAL OF JAMAICA v. WILLIAMS [1997] 3 W.L.R. 389, Lord Hoffmann, PC.

1363. Police powers—search and seizure—warrant must specify premises to be searched

[Police and Criminal Evidence Act 1984 s.15(6).]

C sought to quash a search warrant and a declaration that entry and searches conducted on premises occupied by her were unlawful. The warrant was issued in connection with an alleged offence of conspiracy to commit fraud, the address having been given by a suspect. The address was to premises in multiple occupation, but by the time of the search was a self contained flat occupied by C. C claimed that the Police and Criminal Evidence Act 1984 s.15 should be strictly construed and was not followed as the warrant did not specify the premises or identify the person sought. The police contended that they only wished to search the common parts of the building and it was sufficient to specify a particular building.

Held, allowing the application, that the premises should have been sufficiently specified and it ought to have been made clear that the warrant was only desired to search a particular part of the building and the common parts. Any warrant which omitted to specify the particular premises to be searched was unlawful due to its failure to comply with the Police and Criminal Evidence Act 1984 s.15(6), which applied to warrants to search for property as well as persons.

R. v. SOUTH WESTERN MAGISTRATES COURT, *ex p.* COFIE [1997] 1 W.L.R. 885, Beldam, L.J.: Smith, J., QBD.

1364. Police powers—stop and search—drug offences—reasonable grounds for suspicion

[Police Act 1964 s.51 (3); Misuse of Drugs Act 1971 s.23.]

F appealed against a conviction of obstructing a police officer in the execution of his duty, contrary to the Police Act 1964 s.51 (3). Officer A received a radio message about a person suspected of dealing in drugs, and on arriving at the scene encountered F being questioned by two female officers. F was detained by Officer A on suspicion of drug dealing at the request of the female officers and taken to the police station where he was strip-searched by Officer K and nothing was found. After the search something was seen in F's mouth which he swallowed before it could be identified, claiming it had been chewing gum. The magistrates found, by inference, that the item was a prohibited drug. The issue was whether the search undertaken was lawful, and whether the officer carrying out the search was acting in the execution of his duty. The circumstances in which a police officer is permitted to carry out a search for drugs were considered. It was accepted that F had been stopped and searched under the Misuse of Drugs Act 1971 s.23, which provides that the police officer must have reasonable grounds to suspect possession of drugs.

Held, allowing the appeal, that if the detaining officer had formed reasonable grounds to suspect F was in possession of a prohibited drug, the search was in the execution of duty and, therefore lawful. It was found that the female officers who had originally stopped F were at the beginning of the chain, and they were relevant in determining the reasonableness of the grounds for suspicion. As they had not been called by the Crown, it could not be established that the subsequent search was lawful, nor that the obstruction was unlawful.

FRENCH v. DPP, Trans. Ref: CO 2507-96, November 27, 1996, Butterfield, J., QBD.

1365. Practice directions–Crown Courts–magistrates courts–provision of information from Police National Computer on previous convictions and cautions

New arrangements for providing police national computer details of previous convictions to Crown and magistrates courts have superceded those contained in Practice Direction (Crime: Anticendents) [1993].

Held, that new arrangements designed to assist the prosecution in the Crown Court and magistrates' courts by allowing the provision of information from the Police National Computer on the previous convictions and cautions of offenders would apply immediately, replacing those in *Practice Direction (Crime: Antecedents)* [1993] 1 W.L.R. 1459. In the Crown Court, details of the circumstances of the last three similar convictions and/or convictions likely to be of interest to the court were to be provided by the police, in addition to the circumstances of any offence leading to the making of a community order which was still in force. The police were to prepare the antecedents using standard formats within 21 days of committal proceedings or transfer and were to check the record of convictions seven days before the hearing date, providing details of additional convictions or outstanding cases. In the magistrates' courts, the police were to prepare the antecedents using standard formats and submit them to the CPS with the case file. Where antecedents were provided to the court some time before a hearing, the CPS could request that the police check the record of convictions and provide details of additional convictions and outstanding cases.

PRACTICE DIRECTION (CRIME: ANTECEDENTS) [1997] 1 W.L.R. 1482, Lord Bingham of Cornhill, L.C.J., CA (Crim Div).

1366. Preparatory hearings

CRIMINAL JUSTICE ACT 1987 (PREPARATORY HEARINGS) RULES 1997, SI 1997 1051 (L.19); made under the Supreme Court Act 1981 s.84, s.86; and the Criminal Justice Act 1987 s.9. In force: April 15, 1997; £2.40.

These Rules, which revoke and replace the Criminal Justice Act 1987 (Preparatory Hearings) Rules 1988 (SI 1988 1699), reflect amendments to the Criminal Justice Act 1987 by the Criminal Procedure and Investigations Act 1996 and make minor amendments relating to the making of an application for an order for a preparatory hearing, and the making of orders for disclosure by the prosecution or the accused.

1367. Preparatory hearings

CRIMINAL PROCEDURE AND INVESTIGATIONS ACT 1996 (PREPARATORY HEARINGS) RULES 1997, SI 1997 1052 (L.20); made under the Supreme Court

Act 1981 s.84, s.86; and the Criminal Procedure and Investigations Act 1996 s.33. In force: April 15, 1997; £2.40.

These Rules are made for the purposes of the holding, by Crown Court judges, of preparatory hearings under the Criminal Procedure and Investigations Act 1996 in long or complex cases. They apply in relation to an offence where, on or after the day appointed under s.29(2) of the 1996 Act in respect of the Crown Court sitting at the place concerned, the accused is committed for trial for the offence, proceedings for the trial on the charge concerned are transferred to the Crown Court, or a bill of indictment relating to the offence is preferred by direction of the Court of Appeal or by direction or with the consent of a judge. Provision is made for the regulation of the making of applications for preparatory hearings; for a time limit for the making of representation to the Crown Court by a party service with a copy of another party's notice of application; for representations to be made concerning applications; for the determination of applications; for the determination of orders for preparatory hearings and for the disclosure and service of documents.

1368. Preparatory hearings—appeals

CRIMINAL PROCEDURE AND INVESTIGATIONS ACT 1996 (PREPARATORY HEARINGS) (INTERLOCUTORY APPEALS) RULES 1997, SI 1997 1053 (L.21); made under the Supreme Court Act 1981 s.84, s.86, s.87. In force: April 15, 1997; £3.20.

These Rules make provision for regulating the practice and procedure of the Criminal Division of the Court of Appeal for the purposes of appeals against rulings as to the admissibility of evidence or as to questions of law, made at preparatory hearings in cases which are complex or involve a lengthy trial, under the Criminal Procedure and Investigations Act 1996 s.31.

1369. Prosecutions

PROSECUTION OF OFFENCES (REVOCATION) REGULATIONS 1997, SI 1997 739; made under the Prosecution of Offences Act 1985 s.7, s.8. In force: April 1, 1997; £0.65.

These Regulations revoke the Prosecution of Offences Regulations 1978 (SI 1978 1357) which made provision with respect to certain functions of the Director of Public Prosecutions and the furnishing to him by chief officers of the police, magistrates and clerks of magistrates' courts of information about criminal offences and proceedings.

1370. Prosecutions—buggery—valid consent for prosecution inferred from evidence of Crown prosecutor

[Sexual Offences Act 1967 s.8; Prosecution of Offences Act 1985 s.1 (6); Criminal Justice Act 1988 s.33A.]

J appealed against conviction and applied for leave to appeal against sentence for buggery, attempted buggery, indecency with a child and indecent assaults on a group of nine children, for which he was sentenced to two concurrent life sentences and 13 other concurrent terms of between 18 months' and eight years' imprisonment. J contended that as the DPP's consent had not been obtained as required by the Sexual Offences Act 1967 s.8 in relation to charges of alleged buggery and attempted buggery, the proceedings in relation to those charges were a nullity. As the requisite consent could be given on the DPP's behalf by a Crown prosecutor under the Prosecution of Offences Act 1985 s.1 (6), without the need for an express direction by the DPP, the question arose as to whether the consent had been given by the time J was committed for trial. Although J conceded that the Crown prosecutor had shown he had noticed the consent requirement when considering the evidence prior to taking the decision to prosecute, it was contended that there had to be something, either verbally or in writing, from which consent could be discerned. J also submitted that, as the complainant on the buggery and attempted buggery charges had been sworn prior to giving evidence, the conviction could not be regarded as safe under the Criminal Justice Act 1988 s.33A.

Held, dismissing the appeal and the application, that (1) as there was no requirement for the consent to be in writing it could be inferred from the evidence that the prosecutor had given valid consent for the prosecution when considering the material submitted to him; (2) although a breach of the mandatory statutory requirement regarding children's unsworn evidence had occurred, this had been addressed in the summing up and the convictions on the buggery counts could not be seen as unsafe due to the breach and (3) the sentence was correct given the circumstances of the offences.

R. v. JACKSON (PAUL MAITLAND) [1997] Crim. L.R. 293, Rose, L.J., CA (Crim Div).

1371. Prosecutions—High Court awarded damages for assault by police officers—judicial review of DPP's decision not to prosecute

T applied for judicial review of the DPP's decision not to prosecute five police officers for an assault on T in respect of which he had been awarded damages by the High Court.

Held, allowing the application, that, whilst the civil court's finding was not binding on the DPP and a court would not normally interfere with his decision, the High Court judge in the instant case had set out detailed findings and firm conclusions which required very careful analysis if the DPP was not to institute proceedings.

R. v. DPP, *ex p.* TREADAWAY, *The Times*, October 31, 1997, Rose, L.J., QBD.

1372. Prosecutions—indecent assault—discontinuance and reinstatement of prosecution of alleged sexual offence—reinstatement reasonable on consideration of facts and public interest

[Sexual Offences Act 1956 s.15.]

B applied for judicial review of a CPS decision to reinstate criminal proceedings following the issue of a notice of discontinuance of a charge of indecent assault under the Sexual Offences Act 1956 s.15. In a video recorded interview with the police the complainant described sexual offences alleged to have been perpetrated by B when the complainant was 13 years old. Although B admitted to something short of the allegations having taken place, a decision was taken not to continue with the prosecution on the basis that the evidential test, as set out in the Code of Guidance for Crown Prosecutors 1994, had not been satisfied. The notice of discontinuance was issued citing insufficient evidence as the reason, notwithstanding that the Branch Crown Prosecutor had concluded that the wrong decision had been made. The complainant's mother was dissatisfied with that decision, and the matter was referred to the DPP, who decided to reinstate the prosecution. It was argued for B that there were material considerations that the DPP had failed properly to regard, including the evidential relevance of B's good character, and the time lapse between the issue of the notice and the decision to reinstate. Further, the standard letter that had been sent to B to inform him of the discontinuance had given rise to a legitimate expectation that the prosecution would not be recommenced.

Held, dismissing the application, that (1) the DPP had discretion to form her own view on the facts before her, for which it was necessary to consider what was in the public interest. The DPP rightly concluded that the decision to discontinue was "clearly wrong". That decision was in accordance with policy of the criminal justice system as pertaining to prosecutions. It was not necessary for there to be special circumstances in addition to the fact that the decision was clearly wrong before the DPP could exercise her discretion to reinstate and (2) the decision to reinstate was not *Wednesbury* unreasonable, subject to the question of legitimate expectation. It could not be said that the standard letter sent to B that the prosecution was to be discontinued would justifiably have led

B to believe he was free of jeopardy, *R. v. DPP, ex p. C* [1995] 1 Cr. App. R. 136, [1995] 1 C.L.Y. 29 considered.

R. v. DPP, *ex p.* BURKE, Trans. Ref: CO/2286/96, December 12, 1996, Phillips, L.J., QBD.

1373. Prosecutions–private prosecutions–motive relevant to determine whether prosecution properly brought

H and S applied to set aside leave to move for judicial review and a stay of criminal proceedings. X instituted a private prosecution alleging breaches of the Companies Act by S in which company H had substantial interest. X were members of the constituency party for which H was the prospective parliamentary candidate. X alleged that H was not fit for that role. X contended that the court did not have power to set aside a criminal prosecution in the magistrates court in respect of which there was a prima facie case, whatever the motive of those instigating or instituting it. S submitted that the case here was one of deliberate and mala fide attempt to use the court process to embarrass H and was a misuse of the criminal process as a public platform to cause political disadvantage to him.

Held, refusing the application, that, having considered the authorities, it was arguable that improper motive is a relevant matter when considering whether a prosecution is properly brought and if there was an abuse of process.

SERIF SYSTEMS LTD, *Re*, Trans. Ref: CO/724/97, April 15, 1997, Auld, L.J., QBD.

1374. Prosecutions–private prosecutions–summonses alleging actual bodily harm–abuse of process

S applied for judicial review of a decision of B refusing to dismiss summonses for assault brought against him and his colleague, H, as private prosecutions by K. It was contended by S that the summonses were oppressive and vexatious and an abuse of process, because they were brought for an improper motive, and there was no evidence against H.

Held, allowing the applications in part, and staying the summons against H, that (1) there was no evidence to suggest that the summonses were brought for an improper motive and (2) however, it was clear that there was no evidence against H and the summons against him should have been stayed.

R. v. BOW STREET MAGISTRATES COURT, *ex p.* SAKASHITA, Trans. Ref: CO 3670-95, October 15, 1996, Gage, J., QBD.

1375. Prosecutions–unlawful tree felling–abuse of process–oral assurances not to prosecute insufficient to support abuse of process allegation

[Forestry Act 1967 s.17(1).]

K, the owner of woodland subject to Forestry Commission supervision under a Woodland Grant Scheme which limited his right to fell timber, sought the quashing of an information brought under the Forestry Act 1967 s.17(1) on the grounds of abuse of process. K's application for planning permission for a golf course on the land was supported by the Commission, but they laid the information against him when he commenced felling prior to the grant of permission. K contended that the Commission had previously given oral assurances that he would not be prosecuted, so that the subsequent prosecution was an abuse of process.

Held, refusing the application, that the jurisdiction to stay a prosecution on the grounds of abuse of process was to be exercised exceptionally, in line with the principles established in *R. v. Derby Crown Court, ex p. Brooks* (1985) 80 Cr. App. R. 164, [1985] C.L.Y. 2126 and *R. v. Horseferry Road Magistrates Court, ex p. Bennett* [1994] 1 A.C. 42, [1993] C.L.Y. 1867. On the facts, there was nothing to show that an assurance had been given which justified a finding that the laying of the information amounted to an abuse of process.

R. v. AYLESBURY JUSTICES, *ex p.* KITCHING, Trans. Ref: CO-2434/96, May 9, 1997, Pill, L.J., QBD.

1376. Recognisances–surety–legally aided applicant with nil contribution–magistrates entitled to require recognisance with surety attached to ensure prompt prosecution of appeal

[Magistrates' Courts Act 1980 s.120(3).]

M, a legally aided applicant with a nil contribution, applied for judicial review of the magistrates' decision to refuse to state a case unless he entered a recognisance of £1,000 with a surety attached to ensure that he prosecute his appeal promptly.

Held, dismissing the application, that the fact that an applicant had no disposable assets did not preclude a court from requiring the provision of a surety, as capital could be raised from friends, family or business contacts, *MV Yorke Motors v. Edwards* [1982] 1 W.L.R. 444, [1982] C.L.Y. 2398 considered. The magistrates also had a power under the Magistrates Courts Act 1980 s.120(3) to deal with those who forfeited their recognisance according to individual circumstances and it was for the applicant to show that he lacked the requisite means.

R. v. CROYDON JUSTICES, *ex p.* MORGAN; *sub nom.* R. v. CROYDON MAGISTRATES COURT, *ex p.* MORGAN (1997) 161 J.P. 169, Schiemann, L.J., QBD.

1377. Reporting restrictions–local newspaper in breach of no reporting order

Held, allowing an appeal against conviction of three offences of indecent assault against women, that the convictions were unsafe and a retrial was ordered. Despite an order for no reporting, a local newspaper had run a piece on the trial of M, stating that he was a local police officer and containing the dates of the offences.

R. v. McCOUBREY (ALAN ALEXANDER),Trans. Ref: 9605412/Z5, January 14, 1997, Astill, J., CA (Crim Div).

1378. Right to fair trial–trial within reasonable time–Trinidad and Tobago

See HUMAN RIGHTS: Sookermany v. DPP of Trinidad and Tobago. §2814

1379. Search and seizure–seizure of computers–automatic transfer of information–meaning of downloading

On Friday, December 6, officers of the Serious Fraud Office seized G's computers and sent them to A for the downloading of information covered by a search warrant. G obtained an ex parte injunction providing that no further downloading take place and any downloaded computers be returned by 11 am on Monday, December 9. SFO officers faxed A, but the transfer of information was then continuing automatically and the fax was not seen until Monday morning when S, the SFO director, also learnt of the injunction. On December 10, G obtained a consent order for the return of the computers on the completion of downloading. G later applied to commit S and four SFO officers for contempt, contending the downloading had in fact been completed by midnight on December 6, the information having been transferred. S contended that the writing of the image to disk for the purpose of securing it was part of the downloading so that the process was not completed by that time.

Held, dismissing the application, whilst "download" meant "transfer from one storage device to another", this did not require writing onto disk, so the respondents were in breach of the order. The SFO were not in contempt as the order had not been directed to or served on them personally, the items being too ambiguous. It was stated that the SFO acts as a government department and notice of an injunction must be served properly which may be by telephone, followed by a fax.

R. v. CITY OF LONDON MAGISTRATES COURT, *ex p.* GREEN; *sub nom.* GREEN v. STAPLES [1997] 3 All E.R. 551, Scott Baker, J, QBD.

1380. Sexual Offences (Protected Material) Act 1997 (c.39)

This Act regulates access by defendants and other persons to certain material in relation to proceedings for sexual offences. The protected material includes victims' statements, photographs of victims and medical reports relating to victims.

This Act received Royal Assent on March 21, 1997.

1381. Summary offences—time limit on information—whether information within time limit

[Dangerous Dogs Act 1991; Magistrates' Courts Act 1980 s.1, s.127.]

C was arrested but not charged in connection with an offence under the Dangerous Dogs Act 1991 while on leave from prison on June 2, 1993. An officer laid an information for C's arrest once he had returned to prison on December 1, 1993. C was arrested and charged with assault. Later the assault charge was altered to assault occasioning actual bodily harm and C was acquitted. C was then charged with an offence under the Dangerous Dogs Act 1991. C applied for judicial review contending that under the Magistrates' Courts Act 1980 s.127, C had not been charged within six months of the offence.

Held, dismissing the application, that an information laid under the Magistrates' Courts Act 1980 s.1 for the arrest of a defendant in respect of a summary offence had the effect of commencing the prosecution and accordingly, if it was laid within six months of the alleged offence it satisfied the requirements of s.127 of that Act.

R. v. ENFIELD MAGISTRATES COURT, *ex p.* CALDWELL (1997) 161 J.P. 336, Butterfield, J., QBD.

1382. Summary trial—Crown offered no evidence on information charging either way offence—defendant could be acquitted at summary trial and plead autrefois acquit to subsequent charges

Held, that, where the Crown had submitted no evidence on an information charging an offence triable either way, and no plea had been made nor any decision reached as to the mode of trial, a defendant was entitled to consent to summary trial, plead not guilty and have the case against him dismissed. If fresh informations were then laid charging the same offences, it would be open to the defendant to plead autrefois acquit.

R. v. BRADFORD MAGISTRATES COURT, *ex p.* DANIEL, *The Independent*, June 16, 1997 (C.S.), Simon Brown, L.J., QBD.

1383. Verdicts—acquittals—defendants acquitted of actual bodily harm but convicted of violent disorder—inconsistency of verdicts

The appellants, convicted of violent disorder but acquitted of assault occasioning actual bodily harm, appealed on the basis that their convictions were wholly inconsistent with the acquittals. D appealed further that the judge erred by introducing a questionnaire from the pleas and directions hearing to make a point against D and then failing to discharge the jury or to give directions.

Held, allowing the appeals, that the test was whether the verdicts were so inconsistent as to demand interference by the court. On these facts the court considered that criteria were satisfied. While questionnaires of the sort used were not usually used at trial, being for the efficient disposal of business at earlier stages, they could be used provided counsel had adequate opportunity to address the judge in the absence of the jury as to whether or not they should be permitted. Here the judge introduced the questionnaire under a misapprehension as to the facts and without warning.

R. v. DIEDRICH (ROY VERNON); R. v. ALDRIDGE (NOLAN JOHN) [1997] 1 Cr. App. R. 361, Hutchison, L.J., CA (Crim Div).

1384. Verdicts—failure to leave alternative offence

B and C appealed against convictions of wounding with intent to do grievous bodily harm to a 16 year old on the ground that their convictions were unsafe. B was sentenced to three years' detention and C to four years' detention. Both claimed that the jury should have been told that they could return alternative verdicts of unlawful wounding. The victim received severe injuries during the incident and suffered several stab wounds. B submitted that he acted in self defence, and that the recorder erred in refusing to leave to the jury the lesser alternative of unlawful wounding. B also claimed that the jury should have received a *Lucas* direction in respect of an alleged lie told by him. C submitted that his conviction was unsafe as the jury was not properly directed regarding intention.

Held, dismissing the appeals, that although the alternative offence of unlawful wounding should have been left to the jury to consider that did not render the convictions unsafe, an incorrect refusal to leave an alternative offence would not automatically result in a conviction being overturned. In B's case a *Lucas* direction was not necessary. C's sentence was reduced to three years detention. *R. v. Maxwell* (1990) 91 Cr. App. R. 61, *R. v. Fairbanks* (1986) 83 Cr. App. R. 251 considered.

R. v. BERGMAN (WAYNE ROBERT); R. v. COLLINS (STEPHEN GEORGE) [1996] 2 Cr. App. R. 399, Huchison, J., CA.

1385. Verdicts—manslaughter—jury not required to give basis of verdict

C appealed against a sentence of four years' imprisonment following a conviction of manslaughter on an indictment for murder. C was a childminder and was convicted after a child in her care suffered injuries and later died. C argued that sentence should have been considered on the basis of the version of the verdict most favourable to her.

Held, dismissing the appeal, that whether or not the judge asked the jury to indicate the basis of the verdict was a matter for the judge's discretion. In the instant case the judge was right not to ask the jury to indicate the basis of their verdict, and he was not obliged to warn them in advance that he would do so. The judge was entitled to sentence C on the basis of the facts, which he had heard in evidence, as they appeared to him.

R. v. CAWTHORNE (SUSAN EILEEN) [1996] 2 Cr. App. R. (S.) 445, Swinton Thomas, L.J., CA (Crim Div).

1386. Verdicts—time limit for giving majority verdict

[Juries Act 1974 s.17.]

S appealed against conviction of the burglary of a chronic alcoholic as being unsafe because of an irregularity. The jury were erroneously told that a majority verdict was acceptable after only one hour and 47 minutes, whereas the statutory period under the Juries Act 1974 s.17 was two hours. As soon as the error was realised, they were brought back and told that such a verdict was not available for an unspecified time. S contended that (1) that the error could not be remedied and the jury should have been discharged, and (2) the summing up had been defective on the question of joint enterprise.

Held, dismissing the appeal, that (1) although there was undoubtedly an error, no verdict was given in breach of the s.17 duty. There had been a breach of the Practice Direction but that had been cured by the exercise of his discretion by the trial judge and the verdict was not unsafe, and (2) although it might have been better had the trial judge included a reference to the fact that mere presence at the scene of a crime did not amount to joint enterprise, in fact the direction given was clear and adequate, *Practice Direction (Crime: Majority Verdict)* [1970] 1 W.L.R. 916 and *R. v. Pigg* [1983] 1 W.L.R. 6, [1983] C.L.Y. 2047 considered.

R. v. S (A JUVENILE), Trans. Ref: 96/6329/Y4, February 10, 1997, Otton, L.J., CA (Crim Div).

1387. Wasted costs orders–barrister's failure to attend criminal appeal–liability for clerk's failure

When considering whether to make a wasted costs order against counsel the court will hold him vicariously liable for any act or default by his clerk. D's appeal was listed for hearing. His counsel, S, had telephoned his clerk on the day before the listed date and was told that the appeal had not been listed. S did not attend and the appeal was adjourned with an order for counsel to show cause why a wasted costs order should not be made against him in respect of the wasted costs.

Held, making a wasted costs order against S, that, like solicitors, barristers were vicariously liable for the acts of their clerks.

R. v. RODNEY (ROGER) [1997] P.N.L.R. 489, Potter, L.J., CA (Crim Div).

1388. Wasted costs orders–solicitor's request for committal to see if witness would attend court–no justification for wasted costs order

[Magistrates Courts Act 1980 s.6(1).]

N was a solicitor representing a client charged with indecent assault. It was believed that the complainant would not attend court, and N requested that the court hold a committal under the Magistrates Courts Act 1980 s.6(1) to see if she would do so. Without the testimony of the complainant there was no case. When she subsequently appeared it was agreed by N that a committal on paper would suffice and no evidence need be given in court. N appealed by way of case stated against the justices' decision to make a wasted costs order against him.

Held, allowing the appeal, that N was required to act in his client's best interests, and the test for making a wasted costs order was whether there was a reasonable explanation for the action, *Ridehalgh v. Horsefield* [1994] Ch. 205, [1994] C.L.Y. 3623 considered. N was trying to establish that there was no case to answer, and this was reasonable action in the circumstances, though it was necessary that solicitors should be hesitant in such cases and seek clear instructions in writing from the client.

NEILL v. CROWN PROSECUTION SERVICE; *sub nom.* NEILL v. DPP (1997) 161 J.P. 153, McCowan, L.J., QBD.

1389. Witnesses–children–witness summons–child witness to incident of domestic violence–magistrate's discretion to issue summons

[Magistrates Courts Act 1980 s.97(1).]

P applied for judicial review of the decision refusing to issue a witness summons to secure the attendance at court of his daughter, F, who had allegedly witnessed an incident involving violence between P and his wife, W. F was aged seven at the time. P was charged with common assault and W refused to let F make a statement or go to court. W later allowed F to make a statement to P's solicitors but withdrew consent before the proceedings. P asked for a witness summons to be issued under the Magistrates' Courts Act 1980 s.97(1) which was refused on the grounds that s.97 was not intended to apply to a child of that age, it was within the magistrate's discretion to refuse and it was not in the interests of justice for a seven year old child to give evidence for one of her parents on a grave charge.

Held, allowing the application, that (1) a witness summons, even for a child, had to be issued where, in terms of s.97(1) of the 1980 Act, the person in question was "likely to be able to give material evidence" and that person "would not voluntarily attend as a witness", *R. v. Highbury Corner Magistrates Court, ex p. Deering* [1997] 1 F.L.R. 683, [1996] 1 C.L.Y. 13 followed. Both conditions were satisfied. The terms of s.97(1) were imperative. F could not attend court of her own free will and the magistrate had misdirected himself in deciding not to issue the summons. The decision of how best to balance the interests of justice against the interests of the child should be made at trial by the court, rather than at the stage of issuing a summons, *R. v. B County Council, ex p. P* [1991] 1 W.L.R. 221, [1991] C.L.Y. 2517 considered.

Observed, repeating and reinforcing observations made in *R. v. B County Council, ex p. P*, that as such cases between parents were becoming more prevalent, it was desirable that children should be removed from s.97.

R. v. LIVERPOOL CITY MAGISTRATES COURT, *ex p.* P, Trans. Ref: CO-3474/96, March 14, 1997, Curtis, J., QBD.

1390. Articles

A brief guide to Part I of the Criminal Procedure and Investigations Act 1996 *(Nicholas Purnell)*: Arch. News 1997, 1, 4-7. (Disclosure process governing defence and prosecution duties and comparison with common law duties imposed on prosecution).

Another fine mess they've got us into: M.L.N. 1997, 10, 18-20. (Power of courts to ban reporting of derogatory statements against victims made in mitigation).

Award of costs against the accused *(Alec Samuels)*: Crim. Law. 1997, 75, 4-5. (Principles governing court's discretion).

Child witnesses *(Joyce Plotnikoff* and *Richard Woolfson)*: Magistrate 1997, 53(7), 176-177. (Suggestions to help magistrates courts in cases involving children including use of fast track schemes, screening in courtrooms and use of best practice video entitled *A case for balance* issued in January 1997).

Committed to committals? *(Ian D. Brownlee* and *Clare Furniss)*: Crim. L.R. 1997, Jan, 3-16. (Reasons behind abandonment of transfer for trial system, nature of modified committals procedure under the Criminal Procedure and Investigations Act 1996 and how tension between justice and efficiency raises dangers for quality of justice in pre trial process).

Criminal Procedure and Investigations Act 1996 *(Andrew Mimmack)*: M.C.P. 1997, 1 (4), 3-7. (Main provisions of Act and added complexity caused by its piecemeal introduction and plethora of associated rules and regulations).

Criminal Procedure and Investigations Act 1996, s.49: S. News 1997, 3 (Oct), 6-11. (Effect of s.49 which alters procedure for determining mode of trial in relation to either way offences and s.51 which gives magistrates power to commit defendant for either way offence if committed for trial for related offences).

Criminal Procedure and Investigations Act 1996: S. News 1997, 1 (Feb), 6-8. (Effect of s.17A whereby defendant on either way charge who indicates will plead guilty if proceeds to trial will be sentenced by magistrates court and power to ban derogatory assertions as to character of defendant).

Criminal law: plea before venue *(Anthony Edwards)*: L.S.G. 1997, 94 (39), 40-41. (New procedures relating to either-way offences where defendant pleads guilty when making first court appearance on or after October 1, 1997; includes flowchart summarising procedures).

Custody time limits *(Alec Samuels)*: Crim. L.R. 1997, Apr, 260-268. (Prosecution's duty to comply with time limits so that a case progresses to trial without delay, the procedure for an extension of time and the duty of defence).

Explaining the verdict *(Julian Gibbons)*: N.L.J. 1997, 147(6811), 1454-1455. (Merits of requiring juries to give reasoning behind verdicts, especially where inferences may have been drawn from defendant's silence).

Guide to proceedings in the Court of Appeal, Criminal Division *(Julian Gibbons)*: [1997] 2 Cr. App. R. 459. (Guidance for solicitors and counsel in the preparation of proceedings. Revised edition February 1997).

Home Office circular: Criminal Procedure and Investigations Act 1996: J.P. 1997, 161 (19), 457, 469. (Provisions in force April 15, 1997 on procedure for preparatory hearings, tainted acquittals and fraud cases).

Judicial review of magistrates' court decisions *(Anthony Akiwumi)*: S.J. 1997, 141 (21), 520-521. (Use of judicial review to challenge conviction on grounds of procedural unfairness rather than appeal to crown court or to QBD by case stated).

Juries-judge finding jurors to be in contempt of court by refusing to enter verdict: Crim. L.R. 1997, Nov, 827-829. (Whether jurors were guilty of contempt of court by refusing to enter verdict for personal reasons and whether judge followed correct procedure in dealing with matter).

No case to answer: the judge must stop the case *(Alec Samuels)*: Archbold News 1996, 9(Nov), 6-8. (Whether judges in practice are shifting away from applying the rule in "Galbraith" and whether the rule is still sound in distinguishing between the role of judge and jury).

Plea bargaining and its repercussions on the theory of criminal procedure *(Heike Jung)*: Eur. J. Crime Cr. L. Cr. J. 1997, 5(2), 112-122. (Reasons for development of plea bargaining, implications for structure of criminal procedure and assessment of compatibility with human rights guarantees).

Procedural "rights" of victims of crime: public or private ordering of the criminal justice process? *(Helen Fenwick)*: M.L.R. 1997, 60(3), 317-333. (Extent to which victims have opportunity to influence decisions during criminal process through consultation or participation).

Stacking the odds against the defence *(Michael Grieve)*: Lawyer 1997, 11 (17), 16. (Criticism of defence's duty to disclose evidence imposed by the Criminal Procedure and Investigations Act 1996).

Tainted acquittals *(Franklin Sinclair)*: S.J. 1997, 141(22), 538-539. (Criminal Procedure and Investigations Act 1996 s.54 to s.57, in force April 15, 1997, allowing defendant's acquittal to be quashed where any person has been convicted of relevant offence involving interfering with or intimidating juror, witness or potential witness).

The acceleration of criminal proceedings and the rights of the accused: comparative observations as to the reform of criminal procedure in Europe *(Albin Eser)*: M.J. 1996, 3(4), 341-369. (Whether measures to reduce delay in criminal trials compromise rights of accused and defence counsel).

The press, illnesses and section 11 of the Contempt of Court Act 1981 *(John Marston)*: J.P. 1997, 161(16), 383-384. (Powers to restrict reporting of withheld information in criminal cases and case law giving judicial reasoning behind restrictions).

The right of silence, legal privilege and the decision in Condron *(J.N. Spencer)*: J.P. 1996, 160(52), 1167-1168. (Cases highlighting problems of directing juries regarding right of silence, especially where defendants follow legal advice, and confusion over procedure).

The trial of the facts and unfitness to plead *(R.D. Mackay)* and *(Gerry Kearns)*: Crim. L.R. 1997, Sep, 644-652. (Case study illustrating difficulties courts face in providing for "trial of the facts" under Criminal Procedure (Insanity and Unfitness to Plead) Act 1991 s.2 where defendant has been held to be unfit to plead).

Vulnerable suspects and the appropriate adult *(Jacqueline Hodgson)*: Crim. L.R. 1997, Nov, 785-795. (Research into provision of appropriate adults for juvenile or mentally disabled offenders during police interviews and problems of implementing scheme in practice).

1391. Books

Enright, Sean; Grant, Gary–Bail. Paperback: £27.50. ISBN 0-406-00250-9. Butterworth Law.

Murphy, P.–Blackstone's Criminal Practice 1997. Paperback: £99.00. ISBN 1-85431-600-1. Blackstone Press.

CRIMINAL SENTENCING

1392. Affray–racially motivated disturbance

W pleaded guilty to affray and was sentenced to 21 months' imprisonment. W was one of a group of about 35 men who were involved in an incident in the course of which bottles were thrown in the vicinity of a corner shop in the early hours of the morning. When the group was asked to disperse, W made threatening and racist remarks about the occupants of the shop and was arrested.

Held, allowing the appeal, that the maximum sentence for the offence was three years. W was a man of good character who had pleaded guilty at the first opportunity. The offence was aggravated by the fact that W had offered violence to a police officer and the racial motive for the disturbance. The sentence of 21 months was too long, and a sentence of 12 months was substituted, *R. v. Whalley and Vincent* (1989) 11 Cr. App. R. (S.) 405 considered.

R. v. WILLIAMS (CHRISTOPHER JOHN) [1997] 2 Cr. App. R. (S.) 97, Ebsworth, J., CA (Crim Div).

1393. Aggravated vehicle taking–committal for sentence–powers of Crown Court

[Criminal Justice Act 1967 s.56; Powers of Criminal Courts Act 1973 s.42(1); Magistrates Courts Act 1980 s.38.]

W appeared before a magistrates court for aggravated vehicle taking and a number of summary offences connected with cars. He was committed to the Crown Court for sentence under the Magistrates Courts Act 1980 s.38 in respect of the aggravated vehicle taking and under the Criminal Justice Act 1967 s.56 in respect of the other offences. He was stopped on three occasions by the police whilst driving a car which had been taken without authority. On the third occasion, he drove away in a dangerous manner. W was sentenced to 21 months' imprisonment for aggravated vehicle taking, with a total of nine months' imprisonment consecutive for the various summary offences.

Held, allowing the appeal in part, that for the aggravated vehicle taking, for which W was committed for sentence under the 1980 Act, by virtue of the Powers of Criminal Courts Act 1973 s.42(1) the Crown Court had the same powers of sentence as if W had been convicted on indictment. For the summary offences for which W was committed under the 1967 Act, the powers of the Crown Court were limited to those of the magistrates' court. It followed that the Crown Court had no power to impose sentences for the summary offences which amounted in aggregate to a total of more than six months. The sentences totalling nine months were adjusted so as to amount in all to six months. This provision did not restrict the Crown Court in any way in respect of the offence of aggravated vehicle taking and the sentence of 21 months' imprisonment was lawful, *R. v. Whitlock (Nicholas Anthony)* (1992) 13 Cr. App. R. (S.) 157, [1992] C.L.Y. 1188 and *R. v. Penfold (Paul William)* (1995) 16 Cr. App. R. (S.) 1016 cited.

R. v. WOOLLEY (DARREN JOHN) [1997] 1 Cr. App. R. (S.) 99, Otton, L.J., CA.

1394. Air law–being drunk on an aircraft

V and two others appealed against sentences of six months' imprisonment after pleading guilty to being drunk on an aircraft. The facts of the case were that the three appellants were part of a group of nine who boarded a flight after having consumed a substantial amount of alcohol. The captain decided to discharge the group before take off as he was concerned for the overall safety of the aircraft. The appellants submitted that the sentences were too high given their guilty pleas, age (all were in their twenties), inaccurate media coverage, their remorse and the fact that they did not appreciate that being drunk on an aircraft was an offence.

Held, dismissing the appeals, that the sentences passed on each of the appellants were fully deserved.

R. v. VINCENT (PHILIP LEE); R. v. LEWIS (IAN WILLIAM); R. v. LUNDEN (EDWARD), Trans. Ref: 97/2217/X2, 97/2316/X2, 97/2318/X2, May 13, 1997, Blofeld, J., CA (Crim Div).

1395. Appeals–Crown Court must carry out rehearing of issues not review magistrates' decision

Held, that, where a defendant appealed against a sentence imposed by a magistrates court, the Crown Court should not review the decision reached by the magistrates but should carry out a complete rehearing of the issues and form an independent view, on all the evidence, as to the correct sentence.

R. v. SWINDON CROWN COURT, *ex p.* MURRAY, *The Times*, September 24, 1997, Henry, L.J., QBD.

1396. Appeals–jurisdiction–leave to abandon appeal against sentence granted–Crown Court judge had no power to increase sentence

[Supreme Court Act 1981 s.48.]

Held, that where a Crown Court judge had properly granted leave to abandon an appeal against sentence, he had no jurisdiction under the Supreme Court Act 1981 s.48 to review and increase the sentence previously imposed, as the s.48 power only arose upon the termination of the hearing of the appeal itself.

R. v. GLOUCESTER CROWN COURT, *ex p.* BETTERIDGE, *The Times*, August 4, 1997, Henry, L.J., QBD.

1397. Arson–attempts–long sentence justified by influence of alcohol on defendant

[Criminal Justice Act 1991 s.2(2), s.31(1).]

G appealed against a sentence of six years' imprisonment imposed in respect of attempted arson and 12 months' imprisonment to run concurrently for criminal damage. G held the nozzle of a smashed petrol pump in one hand and a lighted cigarette in the other and threatened to start a fire when approached by police. G submitted that attempted arson was not a "violent offence" for the purposes of the Criminal Justice Act 1991 s.31(1).

Held, dismissing the appeal, that the judge was entitled to take into account the fact that as long as G was unable to control his intake of alcohol he represented a serious danger to the public, and a longer than usual sentence was justified under the Criminal Justice Act 1991 s.2(2)(b).

R. v. GUIRKE (THOMAS JOHN) [1997] 1 Cr. App. R. (S.) 170, Lord Bingham of Cornhill, L.C.J., CA (Crim Div).

1398. Arson–being reckless that life might be endangered–setting fire to public house

P pleaded guilty to arson, being reckless that life might be endangered, threatening to kill, false imprisonment and theft. He quarrelled with his wife, who threw a cup of coffee over him, and then threatened her with a knife. Later that night P was found in the cellar of the public house of which his wife was the licensee, emptying beer barrels onto the floor. When his wife and mother in law rushed into the cellar, he ran out and shut them in. They were able to escape after about six hours. Later P's wife found that £900 had been stolen from the safe and that further damage had been done in the bar. Some days later an attempt was made to set fire to the public house in the early hours of the morning by placing pieces of burning newspaper through delivery doors, petrol had been sprayed into various parts of the premises. P was sentenced to five years' imprisonment for arson, being reckless that life might be endangered, with one year, to run consecutively, for threatening to kill, false imprisonment and theft, giving a total of six years' imprisonment. P appealed.

Held, dismissing the appeal, that the sentence for arson was not too long for a carefully planned offence which might have led to the destruction of the public house and serious injury, and the other sentences were very light. The total sentence was not excessive.

R. v. POTTS (RONALD GORDON) [1996] 2 Cr. App. R. (S.) 291, McKinnon, J., CA (Crim Div).

1399. Arson–criminal damage–cruelty to animals–12 months' probation unduly lenient

[Criminal Justice Act 1988 s.36; Criminal Damage Act 1971 s.1 (1), s.1 (2), s.1 (3); Protection of Animals Act 1911 s.1.]

The Attorney General applied for a sentence to be referred under the Criminal Justice Act 1988 s.36 on the ground that it was unduly lenient. M, aged 48, pleaded guilty to arson, being reckless as to whether life was endangered contrary to the Criminal Damage Act 1971 s.1 (2) and s.1 (3), an offence of cruelty to an animal contrary to the Protection of Animals Act 1911 s.1 (a) and criminal damage contrary to s.1 (1) of the 1971 Act. He was sentenced to 12 months' probation. M, in a jealous rage, had damaged property in his girlfriend's flat, set fire to his girlfriend's clothes and attacked her dog with a sledgehammer. The fire spread causing extensive damage and the dog had to be put down. The property was in a terrace, and although the fire had been extinguished before spreading to the neighbouring properties, M admitted that he had not thought about the risk of endangering life. M served four months in custody before being sentenced.

Held, allowing the reference, that the 12 month probation sentence failed to reflect the gravity of the offence and the element of endangering life. The trial judge erred in expressing the view that the appropriate sentence for an offence of this kind would be nine months' imprisonment, *R. v. Gannon* (1990) 12 Cr. App. R. (S.) 545, [1992] C.L.Y. 1139 and *Attorney General's Reference (No.5 of 1993), Re* (1994) 15 Cr. App. R. (S.) 201 considered. After taking into account the element of double jeopardy the court substituted a sentence of two years' imprisonment.

R. v. McGREGOR (THOMAS HUNTER), Trans. Ref: 9608338 R2, March 11, 1997, Rose, L.J., CA (Crim Div).

1400. Arson–life imprisonment–appropriate specified period

[Criminal Justice Act 1991 s.34.]

P pleaded guilty to two counts of arson, being reckless whether life would thereby be endangered. She moved with her five children to a small bed and breakfast hotel. During one night she started a fire in a lavatory and returned to bed; the fire burned itself out. The following evening she set fire to a cloth in a linen basket in another room. The fire was discovered and extinguished before much damage had been done. On each occasion there were a number of people in the hotel. P had 10 previous convictions, and had previously been sentenced to imprisonment for offences of arson committed in similar circumstances. She was described as extremely immature and inadequate with a severe personality disorder. She was expected to light further fires if at liberty. P was sentenced to life imprisonment, with a period of five years specified for the purposes of the Criminal Justice Act 1991 s.34.

Held, allowing the appeal, that the sentence of life imprisonment was not challenged, but it was argued that the specified period was too long. Section 34 required the court to decide what determinate sentence would have been passed if the case had not justified a life sentence, and by what proportion that term should be reduced to arrive at the actual term which would be served. The court had started with a notional determinate sentence of 10 years, and halved it to produce a specified period of five years. The court was satisfied that a determinate sentence would not have been as long as 10 years; five years would have been appropriate and the court reduced the specified period to two and a half years.

R. v. PARKER (CAROL MARGARET) [1997] 1 Cr. App. R. (S.) 259, McCullough, J., CA (Crim Div).

1401. Arson–two years' probation and 100 hours' community service unduly lenient

[Criminal Justice Act 1988 s.36.]

The Attorney General applied for a sentence to be referred under the Criminal Justice Act 1988 s.36 on the ground that it was unduly lenient. H pleaded guilty to arson, being reckless as to whether life would thereby be endangered. Following a number of letters from his landlord due to rent arrears, H started a fire by placing a mattress across an electric fire. The fire was quickly discovered but about £2,000 worth of damage was caused. H was sentenced to a combination order involving two years' probation and 100 hours' community service.

Held, allowing the reference, that the authorities indicated that a sentence of the order of three years would have been appropriate when H appeared for sentence. He had now completed the 100 hours' community service. The sentence was unduly lenient and bearing in mind the element of double jeopardy a sentence of 18 months' imprisonment was substituted, *R. v. Gannon* (1990) 12 Cr. App. R. (S.) 545, [1992] C.L.Y. 1139, *Attorney General's Reference (No.5 of 1993)* (1993) 15 Cr. App. R. (S.) 201, *R. v. Parkes* (1995) 16 Cr. App. R. (S.) 74, [1996] 1 C.L.Y. 1721, *R. v. Hosker* (1982) 4 Cr. App. R. (S.) 189, [1983] C.L.Y. 767, *R. v. Wilkey* (1982) 4 Cr. App. R. (S.) 100, [1983] C.L.Y. 769 and *R. v. Downey* (1986) 8 Cr. App. R. (S.) 168, [1987] C.L.Y. 865 considered.

ATTORNEY GENERAL'S REFERENCE (NO.35 OF 1996), *Re; sub nom.* R. v. HOYLE (DAMIEN JAMES) [1997] 1 Cr. App. R. (S.) 350, Rose, L.J., CA (Crim Div).

1402. Arson—two years' probation unduly lenient

[Criminal Justice Act 1988 s.36.]

The Attorney General applied for leave under the Criminal Justice Act 1988 s.36 to refer on the grounds of undue leniency, a sentence of two years' probation with a 60 day condition of training for an offence of arson being reckless whether life would be endangered. The Attorney General conceded that W had voluntarily gone to the police and admitted the offence and had later pleaded guilty, but contended that the sentence was too lenient since W had deliberately set fire to a settee and a quilt knowing that the tenant of the flat had been drinking and was probably asleep. W had then gone to a public house without attempting to rouse the tenant or to contact the fire brigade.

Held, allowing the appeal, that the appropriate custodial sentence of six years would be substituted, but reduced to four and a half years on the basis of double jeopardy and W's efforts to curb his alcohol abuse. *R. v. Sparkes (John Louis)* (1995) 16 Cr. App. R. (S.) 393 was distinguished on the basis that there the fire had not been set deliberately.

R. v. WHEELER (IAN), Trans. Ref: 97/0297/R2, April 29, 1997, McCowan, L.J., CA (Crim Div).

1403. Assault—actual bodily harm—driver spraying another driver with de-icing fluid

H appealed against a sentence of 15 months' imprisonment, having pleaded guilty to administering a noxious thing with intent to injure, aggrieve or annoy and assault occasioning actual bodily harm. Following a minor driving incident, he reversed his car towards another vehicle. An altercation took place which led to a struggle, in the course of which H sprayed the other driver with de-icing fluid, some of which got into his eyes and into the eyes of the driver's daughter.

Held, allowing the appeal, reducing the sentence to nine months' imprisonment, that the offence involved the use of a weapon and an element of deterrence was necessary, but the original sentence was too high, *R. v. Hassan and Schuller* (1989) 11 Cr. App. R. (S.) 8, [1989] C.L.Y. 927, *R. v. Ord and Ord* (1990) 12 Cr. App. R. (S.) 12, [1991] C.L.Y. 1008 and *R. v. Remblance* (1991) 13 Cr. App. R. (S.) 388, [1993] C.L.Y. 1175 considered.

R. v. HUNT (NIGEL JOHN) [1997] 1 Cr. App. R. (S.) 414, Hidden, J., CA (Crim Div).

1404. Assault—actual bodily harm—false accusation of racial prejudice—conduct of defence irrelevant to sentence length

B appealed against her conviction for assault occasioning actual bodily harm and against the sentence of 12 months' imprisonment. Before pronouncing sentence, the judge had commented that B had cynically and dishonestly accused her victim of subjecting her to racial abuse prior to the attack and that, on the evidence, this accusation was clearly unfounded and the jury had rejected it accordingly. B contended that the judge had given the impression that her sentence had been increased as a result of the manner in which her defence had been conducted and this was plainly objectionable.

Held, dismissing B's appeal against conviction, but reducing the sentence to six months' imprisonment, that defendants ought to be sentenced on the basis of the offence committed and not on the basis of the arguments raised in defence. A defendant who pleaded not guilty would not obtain the benefit of the discount which was usually given for a guilty plea, but at the same time, did not risk having his sentence increased as a result of the plea. In the same way, false accusations of racial prejudice should not lead to a sentence being increased. Whilst it seemed that the judge did not intend to give the impression that he had increased B's sentence as a result of her conduct, and in fact had not done so, it was important that the court acted to remove any suggestion that this had been the case.

R. v. BLAIZE (DEBBIE), *The Times*, June 12, 1997, Lord Bingham of Cornhill, L.C.J., CA (Crim Div).

1405. Bankruptcy—concealment of assets—custodial sentence appropriate

[Insolvency Act 1986 s.357(3).]

While serving in the army, M failed to make repayments on a loan for the purchase of a car and a judgment debt of £18,337 was entered against him. Following a statutory demand for repayment by the loan company, M was made bankrupt. However, he had, on leaving the army a short time before the bankruptcy order was made, received a gratuity of £31,000 in addition to his pension, but this was concealed from the courts and judgment creditor and used to pay off personal debts. M now appealed against a sentence of two months' imprisonment imposed after he pleaded guilty to fraudulent disposal of property contrary to the Insolvency Act 1986 s.357(3).

Held, dismissing the appeal, that, where a debtor deliberately concealed assets in order to benefit from being declared bankrupt, a custodial sentence was deserved despite evidence that he was of previous good character.

R. v. MUNGROO (IVAN KIMBLE), *The Times*, July 3, 1997, Ognall, J., CA (Crim Div).

1406. Bankruptcy—obtaining credit whilst bankrupt—custodial sentence inappropriate in absence of dishonesty and presence of good character

D appealed against a sentence of three months' imprisonment, having pleaded guilty to three indictments of obtaining credit while bankrupt. He was adjudged bankrupt in the county court in 1991 and in the High Court in 1993. D worked as a specialist carpenter undertaking work for the British Rail Property Board and was made the leading site contractor, with responsibility for receiving payments from the Board and paying the sub-contractors. He failed to pay one sub-contractor £2,357, obtained kitchen units worth £360 and obtained work from a plumber, without disclosing that he was bankrupt.

Held, allowing the appeal, substituting the custodial term with an 80 hour community service order, a custodial sentence could be avoided where the offence was not aggravated by personal profit in fraud of creditors, or by previous similar offences, *R. v. Theivendran* (1992) 13 Cr App. R. (S.) 601, [1993] C.L.Y. 1017 followed. While D had abused the trust of other small businessmen, there was no dishonesty so that his offending, mitigated by his plea and previous good character, did not cross the custody threshold.

R. v. DAWES (RUSSELL) [1997] 1 Cr. App. R. (S.) 149, Judge Beaumont Q.C., CA (Crim Div).

1407. **Bigamy–marriage contracted for money to enable women to evade immigration control**

C appealed against sentence of 15 months' imprisonment after pleading guilty to bigamy. He married a Zimbabwean national in Liverpool and a few weeks later went through a ceremony of marriage with a Nigerian national in London. Both marriages were contracted for payment, in order to allow the women concerned to evade immigration control.

Held, allowing the appeal, that a custodial sentence was inevitable, but 15 months was too long and therefore a sentence of nine months' imprisonment was substituted.

R. v. CAIRNS (EDWARD) [1997] 1 Cr. App. R. (S.) 118, Nelson, J., CA (Crim Div).

1408. **Binding over–prohibition on return to jurisdiction–consent of accused validly given–sentence not contrary to ECHR**

[Mental Health Act 1983; European Convention on Human Rights 1950.]

G, a Spanish national, committed an assault. G was then admitted to a psychiatric hospital where a psychiatrist decided that G had been suffering from paranoid psychosis at the time of the offence and would benefit from transfer to a hospital in Spain as he only spoke Spanish. G showed no symptoms of any illness but the psychiatrist was of the opinion that symptoms could recur at any time. The psychiatrist also said that had G not been Spanish detention under the Mental Health Act 1983 would have been appropriate. Following a plea of guilty the judge made a common law order binding G over not to return to the jurisdiction for five years. To make such an order consent was required, which was given by G. In an application for leave to appeal it was submitted on behalf of G that the consent given by G was not valid and that such an order contravened European law.

Held, refusing leave to appeal, that (1) there was no submission that G was not fit to plead, and if he was fit to plead he was able to consent, and (2) consent having been given to a sentence which was within the power of the court and with no sense of grievance being felt on G's part, no ground of appeal was raised by considerations of the European Convention on Human Rights 1950.

R. v. GONZALEZ-BAILON (PABLO), Trans. Ref: 9701699 Z5, July 11, 1997, Steel, J., CA (Crim Div).

1409. **Blackmail–demanding money from clergyman–untrue allegation of homosexuality**

R appealed against a sentence of three years imprisonment for blackmail. He wrote to a clergyman demanding £7,000 in the form of a loan, and threatened to make allegations of homosexuality against him, which were not true. He sent two subsequent letters and met the clergyman by arrangement; he was arrested when he picked up a bag supposed to contain money sent for him.

Held, allowing the appeal, that the sentence was manifestly excessive and a sentence of 21 months was substituted, *R. v. Christie (Paul Andrew)* (1990) 12 Cr. App. R. (S.) 540, [1992] C.L.Y. 1160 and *R. v. Smith (Jonathan David)* (1993) 14 Cr. App. R. (S.) 786, [1994] C.L.Y. 1175 considered.

R. v. READ (DAVID JONATHAN) [1996] 2 Cr. App. R. (S.) 240, Hutchison, J., CA (Crim Div).

1410. **Blackmail–threats of contamination with AIDS virus to supermarket goods**

R appealed against concurrent sentences of imprisonment of eight years for each of two offences of blackmail and a confiscation order for £1,740. R made telephoned threats to a supermarket alleging that food had been contaminated with the AIDS virus and threatened to inform the press. R obtained a credit card which he used on 73 occasions to obtain £7,500.

Held, allowing the appeal in part, that the offences appeared to have originated from a form of mental derangement rather than greed as was usual, *R. v. Darling (Michael)* (1994) 15 Cr. App. R. (S.) 855, [1995] 1 C.L.Y. 1308 and *R. v. Telford (Robert George)* (1992) 13 Cr. App. R. (S.) 676, [1993] C.L.Y. 1021 considered. Accordingly a term of six years was substituted.

R. v. RIOLFO (FRANK) [1997] 1 Cr. App. R. (S.) 57, Kennedy, L.J., CA (Crim Div).

1411. Blackmail—threats of damage to retail store and goods

B pleaded guilty to three counts of blackmail and was sentenced to eight years' imprisonment on each count concurrent. B made a series of demands by letter and telephone to the proprietor of a large department store requiring payment of £5 million, under the threat either to damage the building or to sabotage merchandise which was on sale.

Held, allowing the appeal, that these were grave offences and those who were susceptible to blackmail in this form were entitled to protection. In view of highly unusual personal mitigating factors, including the guilty plea, good character at age 42, remorse and mental health problems, the sentences would be reduced to five years on each count concurrent.

R. v. BANOT (LYDIE) [1997] 2 Cr. App. R. (S.) 50, Rose, L.J., CA (Crim Div).

1412. Buggery—buggery of wife

T appealed against two concurrent sentences of nine years' imprisonment on conviction of two counts of rape by buggery, and pleaded guilty to making a false declaration with reference to marriage for which he received a consecutive 12 month term. He met the complainant in a club and they were married a few weeks later. The complainant alleged that during their wedding night he tied her up and buggered her against her will on five occasions. The complainant made allegations that he had also buggered her before the marriage, and after the first night, but he was found not guilty on counts alleging rape in the form of buggery without consent on those other occasions.

Held, allowing the appeal, reducing the concurrent terms from nine to six years, that the sentences for rape by buggery were excessive and the reduction gave a total sentence to seven years.

R. v. TARLING (LESLIE DAVID) [1997] 1 Cr. App. R. (S.) 196, Ian Kennedy, J., CA (Crim Div).

1413. Buggery—jury directed that consent was irrelevant consideration—defendant could not be sentenced for rape where jury had not determined issue of consent.

D appealed against sentences of four years' detention in a young offender institution imposed on conviction on one count of buggery and 21 days' detention concurrent on each of three counts of unlawful sexual intercourse with the same girl. The trial judge had directed the jury that, in relation to the buggery count, the question of the girl's consent was not a material consideration, but then passed sentence on the basis that she had not consented.

Held, allowing the appeal, that it was inappropriate to sentence D on the premise that the victim had been buggered against her will when the matter of consent had not been determined by a jury. A sentence reflecting lack of consent could only be imposed where a defendant had been charged with and convicted of rape.

R. v. DAVIES (TARIAN JOHN), *The Times*, October 22, 1997, Judge, L.J., CA (Crim Div).

1414. Burglary–aggravated burglary–attack in victim's home in presence of children–offender recruiting others to assist–15 months' imprisonment unduly lenient

[Theft Act 1968 s.10(1); Criminal Justice Act 1988 s.36.]

The Attorney General applied for a sentence to be referred under the Criminal Justice Act 1988 s.36 on the ground that it was unduly lenient, and was sentenced to 15 months' imprisonment. M was convicted of aggravated burglary contrary to the Theft Act 1968 s.10(1). The offender, a self-employed mechanic, had £25,000 worth of tools stolen and believed W was responsible. Along with four other men he went to W's house and forced his way inside. Although the tools were not found, W was beaten unconscious and needed hospital treatment for an occidental skull fracture. The Attorney General conceded the offender's previous good character and the effect the theft had on his business, but submitted that the sentence was unduly lenient given the fact that four others had been recruited by the offender, that they had forced their way into the house knowing W's children were there and given the seriousness of W's injuries.

Held, allowing the reference, quashing the original sentence and substituting one of four years' imprisonment, that the sentence was unduly lenient given the aggravating features of the burglary, the offender entered the home of the victim, armed with a baseball bat and with others inflicted grievous bodily harm.

ATTORNEY GENERAL'S REFERENCE (NO.10 OF 1996), *Re*; *sub nom*. R. v. MOORE (JOHN MICHAEL) [1997] 1 Cr. App. R. (S.) 76, Rose, L.J., CA (Crim Div).

1415. Burglary–aggravated burglary–elderly victim

One appellant was convicted and the other appellants pleaded guilty to aggravated burglary and sentenced to 15 years' imprisonment, seven years' imprisonment, and 12 years' imprisonment respectively. The appellants argued that the sentences were excessive by comparison with comparable cases. The first two appellants broke into a house occupied by a widow aged 82 who lived alone. The third appellant, who had provided the information relating to her situation, remained outside. The widow woke when she saw torches in her bedroom; one of the appellants struck her on the shoulder and threatened her. The appellants then ransacked the house. When the widow tried to get off her bed, they pushed her down again and tied her hands and her feet. Her hands were tied to a bedpost and she was gagged. One of the appellants threatened to set fire to the house if she did not say where her money was. The appellants took two rings from her finger and left the house leaving her tied up. The police were called the following morning and she was released.

Held, dismissing the appeals, that the sentences passed in the Crown Court were consistent with the principles laid down in *R. v. O'Driscoll (James)* (1986) 8 Cr. App. R. (S.) 121, [1987] C.L.Y. 1042 and properly reflected current judicial thinking about the instant type of case where an elderly victim living alone had been subjected to torture. Furthermore, the cases before the court were each decided on their own facts and did not create a precedent binding on other courts. The sentences were not manifestly excessive, and the distinctions drawn between the appellants were appropriate to their differing criminality.

R. v. EASTAP (ROBERT LESLIE); R. v. CURT (ANTHONY); R. v. THOMPSON (JOHN WILLIAM) [1997] 2 Cr. App. R. (S.) 55, Judge, L.J., CA (Crim Div).

1416. Burglary–aggravated burglary–grievous bodily harm–ringleader of violent revenge attack with baseball bats–three years' imprisonment unduly lenient

[Criminal Justice Act 1988 s.36.]

The Attorney General applied for a sentence to be referred under the Criminal Justice Act 1988 s.36 on the ground that it was unduly lenient. C, aged 22, was convicted of an offence of aggravated burglary and inflicting grievous bodily harm and pleaded guilty to an offence of violent disorder arising from the same incident.

He was sentenced to a total of three years' imprisonment. C, with 15 others, went to the victim's property, having been evicted from a party held there the previous night, broke in by smashing windows and attacked the victim and the property with baseball bats. The victim sustained a laceration to the scalp requiring 15 stitches, abrasion to the forehead, a cut elbow requiring stitches, substantial bruising to the lower torso and a recurrence of psychiatric problems which had resulted from seeing comrades killed while a serving army officer. The Attorney General argued that C had been the ringleader and organiser of the revenge attack and had participated directly in the violence. C had several good character references, but he also had previous convictions for burglary.

Held, allowing the reference, that C had been the ringleader of a group of men in a very serious attack. The attack was during the night and he had been armed. The sentence was unduly lenient in those circumstances, *Attorney General's Reference (No.1 of 1995), Re* [1996] 1 Cr. App. R. (S.) 11, [1996] 1 C.L.Y. 1692 considered, and an appropriate sentence in usual circumstances would be between six and seven years. After taking into account personal mitigation and the element of double jeopardy, the court increased the sentence to five years' imprisonment.

ATTORNEY GENERAL'S REFERENCE (NO.54 OF 1996), *Re; sub nom.* R. v. CROME (DUANE WILLIAM), [1997] 21 Cr. App. R. (S.) 245, February 11, 1997, Rose, L.J., CA (Crim Div).

1417. Burglary–aggravated burglary–offender losing eye during course of burglary–two years' probation and 100 hours' community service unduly lenient despite exceptional circumstances

[Criminal Justice Act 1988 s.36.]

The Attorney General applied for a sentence to be referred under the Criminal Justice Act 1988 s.36 on the ground that it was unduly lenient. R pleaded guilty to aggravated burglary. He forced an entry into a house, wearing a balaclava helmet and armed with a Stanley knife. He threatened the occupier and two visitors, and tied up the occupier. While he was doing so, one of the visitors found an air pistol and shot R in the face. R fled the house and was arrested at a hospital where he was taken for treatment. He lost the sight of an eye. R was sentenced to a combination order involving two years' probation and 100 hours' community service.

Held, allowing the reference, that the sentencer had indicated that in normal circumstances he would have passed a sentence of between five and six years' imprisonment, but was taking an exceptional course because R had lost the sight of his eye. Despite the guilty plea and the loss an eye, the sentence was unduly lenient; allowing for the mitigating factors and the element of double jeopardy, a sentence of three years' imprisonment was substituted, *R. v. Edwards (Anthony Paul)* [1996] 1 C.L.Y. 1750, *Attorney General's Reference (Nos.19 and 20 of 1990), Re* (1990) 12 Cr. App. R. (S.) 490, [1991] C.L.Y. 1027, and *Attorney General's Reference (No.16 of 1994), Re* (1994) 16 Cr. App. R. (S.) 629, [1996] 1 C.L.Y. 1737 considered.

ATTORNEY GENERAL'S REFERENCE (NO.42 OF 1996), *Re; sub nom.* R. v. WOOD (TREVOR) [1997] 1 Cr. App. R. (S.) 352, Rose, L.J., CA (Crim Div).

1418. Burglary–aggravated burglary–two years' imprisonment unduly lenient

[Criminal Justice Act 1988 s.36.]

The Attorney General applied for a sentence to be referred under the Criminal Justice Act 1988 s.36 on the ground that it was unduly lenient. T, masked and armed with a metre long metal bar, together with two other masked men had gained entry to the flat of a woman as part of a planned attack in which he had struck her and demanded money.

Held, allowing the reference, that the sentence was manifestly too lenient. The appropriate sentence on a guilty plea was 54 months, which would be reduced in consequence of the double jeopardy and a sentence of imprisonment of four years made consecutive to a six month term for firearms offences was substituted, *Attorney General's Reference (No.16 of 1994), Re* (1995) 16 Cr. App.

R. (S.) 629, [1996] 1 C.L.Y. 1737, *Attorney General's Reference (No.1 of 1995), Re* [1996] 1 Cr. App. R. (S.) 11, [1996] 1 C.L.Y. 1692 and *Attorney General's Reference (No.42 of 1996), Re* [1997] 1 Cr. App. R. (S.) 352, [1997] C.L.Y 1417 considered.

R. v. TURNER (MARK ANTHONY), Trans. Ref: 97/1960/R2, June 5, 1997, Lord Bingham of Cornhill, L.C.J., CA (Crim Div).

1419. Burglary—aggravated burglary—violent attack on elderly victim at night with use of knife—four years' imprisonment unduly lenient

[Criminal Justice Act 1988 s.36.]

The Attorney General applied for a sentence to be referred under the Criminal Justice Act 1988 s.36 on the ground that it was unduly lenient. U was convicted of aggravated burglary and sentenced to four years' imprisonment after carrying out the premeditated burglary of a 73 year old man, at night, using a large carving knife, with which he had slashed and stabbed the victim. The sentences of two co-defendants had been increased on appeal, *Attorney General's Reference (Nos.32 and 33 of 1995), Re* [1996] 2 Cr. App. R. (S). 346.

Held, allowing the reference, that although the defendant was younger than his co-defendants and had a less extensive criminal record, he had been the instigator and had refused to stop the violence even when begged to do so by a co-defendant. The appropriate sentence of 10 years' imprisonment was substituted.

ATTORNEY GENERAL'S REFERENCE (NO.31 OF 1995), *Re; sub nom.* R. v. UNDERHILL (NEIL ALAN) [1997] 1 Cr. App. R. (S.) 391, Blofeld, J., CA (Crim Div).

1420. Burglary—aggravated burglary—violent attack on elderly victim in own home

S appealed against a sentence of seven years imprisonment for burglary. He accosted a man aged 77 as the man returned to his flat, put his hand round the man's throat and threatened him, claiming to have a knife. The victim was blindfolded with his own scarf and manhandled into his flat. S ransacked the flat and took about £350 and various items of sentimental value.

Held, dismissing the appeal, that the offence was aggravated by the fact that the victim was an elderly person and that violence had been used. The sentence was severe and fell at the top of the bracket which was appropriate for this offence, but there was no mitigation. The sentence was not manifestly excessive and was justified by the facts of the case, *R. v. Tams (Robert)* (1990) 12 Cr. App. R. (S.) 591, [1992] C.L.Y. 1172, *R. v. Mincher* (1990) 12 Cr. App. R. (S.) 592, [1992] C.L.Y. 1170, *R. v. Funnell* (1986) 8 Cr. App. R. (S.) 143, [1987] C.L.Y. 860 and *Attorney-General's Reference (Nos.19 and 20 of 1990), Re* [1991] Crim. L.R. 306, [1991] C.L.Y. 1027 considered.

R. v. STEWART (TREVOR MATHEW) [1996] 2 Cr. App. R. (S.) 302, Schiemann, L.J., CA (Crim Div).

1421. Burglary—aggravated burglary—violent attack on elderly victim in own home—four and seven years' imprisonment unduly lenient

[Criminal Justice Act 1988 s.36.]

The Attorney General applied for a sentence to be referred under the Criminal Justice Act 1988 s.36 on the ground that it was unduly lenient. P pleaded guilty to aggravated burglary and M was convicted of aggravated burglary and attempted robbery. Together with a third man they broke into the home of a man aged 73 in the early hours of the morning wearing balaclava helmets. The victim was punched and kicked by the third man, a pillow was placed on his head, a knife was used to wound him in the head, arms and legs and he was threatened with death. The victim was unable to summon help for five hours and he was later found to be suffering from numerous injuries. P was sentenced to two years' detention in a young offender institution consecutive to two years' detention in a young offender institution for other burglaries, and M was sentenced to seven years' imprisonment concurrent for aggravated burglary and robbery.

Held, allowing the reference, that the sentences did not indicate the length of sentence which would have been appropriate in the first instance. Attacks on elderly people in their homes were particularly despicable and would be regarded as deserving severe punishment. Bearing in mind the element of double jeopardy, the court substituted a sentence of four years' detention and three years for the other burglaries (total seven years) in the case of P. In the case of M the court substituted a sentence of 10 years' imprisonment.

ATTORNEY GENERAL'S REFERENCE (NOS.32 AND 33 OF 1995), *Re*; R. v. PEGG (SHANE ROBIN); R. v. MARTIN (MARK ANTHONY) [1996] 2 Cr. App. R. (S.) 346, Lord Taylor of Gosforth, C.J., CA (Crim Div).

1422. Burglary–disparate sentences–defendant pleaded guilty after absconding and remaining at large for 19 months–absconding undermined discount attached to plea

B pleaded guilty to burglary and was committed for trial with two co-accused. The co-accused were tried and convicted by a jury and sentenced to five years' imprisonment each. B failed to surrender to bail and remained at large for 19 months before being arrested. He then appeared before the Crown Court where he was sentenced to five years' imprisonment on a guilty plea. B reapplied for leave to appeal, arguing that he should have received a substantial discount for his plea, and it was wrong to deprive him of the discount because he had absconded.

Held, refusing the application, that discount was given for a plea because that plea was seen as a cogent token of remorse, the offender gave up his chance of an acquittal, saved public expense, and indicated that he accepted the justification for his punishment. By absconding, B had undermined the basis of the discount; going on the run balanced out the discount that would otherwise have attached to his plea.

R. v. BYRNE (EAMONN PATRICK) [1997] 1 Cr. App. R. (S.) 165, Ognall, J., CA (Crim Div).

1423. Burglary–guidance for determining custodial sentences for domestic burglary

On an appeal by B and others against custodial sentences imposed following guilty pleas to offences of domestic burglary, the Court of Appeal reviewed the authorities on sentencing for the offence.

Held, that domestic burglary was considered a very serious offence in view of the effect it had on the victim, but its seriousness could vary a great deal from case to case and it was possible that, in some circumstances, a non-custodial sentence could be justified. In determining whether a custodial sentence should be imposed, and, if so, the length of the sentence, the court would have regard to the aggravating or mitigating features of the offence and, to a lesser degree, the personal circumstances of the offender. Certain factors would increase the seriousness of a domestic burglary: if the offence was committed at night in an occupied house, was professional and organised in nature, was targeted at the elderly or infirm, involved vandalism or injury to the victim, or was committed by a persistent offender. A guilty plea, particularly at an early stage, would mitigate the seriousness of the offence, as would evidence of genuine regret and remorse, but a defendant could not, in general, rely on self induced drug addition to reduce his sentence.

R. v. BREWSTER (ALEX EDWARD); R. v. THORPE (TERENCE); R. v. ISHMAEL (MARK); R. v. BLANCHARD (WAYNE); R. v. WOODHOUSE (MICHAEL CHARLES); R. v. H (R), *The Times*, July 4, 1997, Lord Bingham of Cornhill, L.C.J., CA (Crim Div).

1424. Burglary–judge exceeding maximum sentence–duty of counsel to correct error of judge in passing unlawful sentence–duty to inform court on extent of sentencing powers

[Criminal Justice Act 1991 s.40(4).]

M pleaded guilty in the Crown Court to an indictment charging burglary and taking a conveyance without authority. He was committed for sentence for attempted burglary, aggravated vehicle taking, and for driving whilst disqualified. On a second indictment he pleaded guilty to two counts of burglary and one of taking a conveyance without authority. The offences were committed while M was subject to a sentence of detention in a young offender institution passed in 1995 and from which he had been released in 1995. Sentenced to two years' imprisonment for the burglary in the first indictment, with nine months' concurrent for taking a conveyance without authority; 18 months' imprisonment for the attempted burglary; 12 months' imprisonment for the aggravated vehicle taking and four months for the driving whilst disqualified for which he had been committed for sentence; three years' imprisonment for each of the burglaries in the second indictment; and 12 months' imprisonment for taking a conveyance without authority on that indictment; all the sentences to be concurrent (total three years), and ordered to be returned to custody for 121 days under the Criminal Justice Act 1991 consecutively.

Held, allowing the appeal in respect of the unlawful sentences, M had been released from a sentence of three years' detention in a young offender institution in April 1995, and committed the first of the current offences in May 1995, when the original sentence had about 16 months still to run. While the sentencer had probably intended to order M to be returned to custody for the full available period he had expressed himself in a way which meant that the period for which M was returned was 121 days, as opposed to 16 months, and the court would not direct any correction of the record. The power to order M to return to custody was subject to the Criminal Justice Act 1991 s.40(4)(b), which provided that the period for which a person was ordered to be returned to custody may, either be served before and be followed by, or be served concurrently with, the sentence imposed for the new offence as the court directed. It followed that the period of 121 days should be served first and the sentence of three years' imprisonment consecutively to it. The sentences of nine months' imprisonment and 12 months' imprisonment for taking a conveyance without authority were each in excess of the maximum sentence for the offence, which was six months, and they were reduced to six months in each case. In relation to the offence of aggravated vehicle taking, there was no assertion that the damage occasioned to the vehicle was more than £5,000, and it followed that the maximum sentence for the offence was six months' instead of 12 months. The sentence was reduced accordingly. The correction of the unlawful sentences had no effect on the overall sentence of three years. The case underlined once again the importance of counsel carrying out their duty of informing the court of its sentencing powers. That was particularly important where either way offences were involved, in view of the complexity of the legislation.

R. v. McDONNELL (ANTHONY JOHN) [1997] 1 Cr. App. R. (S.) 317, Latham, J., CA (Crim Div).

1425. Burglary–juvenile offenders

[Children and Young Persons Act 1933 s.53(2).]

T, aged 16, pleaded guilty to four offences of burglary. He broke into or gained access to four houses, all occupied by elderly persons. The second two offences were committed while he was on bail in respect of the first two. He was sentenced to four years' detention under the Children and Young Persons Act 1933 s.53(2), with two years' detention in a young offender institution concurrent in respect of one of the offences. T appealed.

Held, allowing the appeal in part, that the sentence was severe, but not manifestly excessive. The sentence of two years' detention in a young offender institution was varied to two years' detention under s.53(2).

R. v. TUCKER (PATRICK) [1997] 1 Cr. App. R. (S.) 337, Steel, J., CA (Crim Div).

1426. Burglary–life imprisonment–offender suffering untreatable psychopathic disorder–history of sexual offences

[Mental health Act 1983; Criminal Justice Act 1991 s.2(2), s.31.]

R appealed against a sentence of life imprisonment, having pleaded guilty to having an imitation firearm with intent to commit burglary. He was found not guilty on another charge of attempted burglary with intent to rape. R had an extensive record of sexual offences, theft and burglary. Psychiatrists giving evidence found that R was suffering from a psychopathic disorder and continued to pose a threat to women, and that the condition was not psychiatrically treatable, although he might benefit from therapy.

Held, allowing the appeal and substituting a sentence of five years' imprisonment, that the sentence imposed had to be commensurate with the gravity of the offence under the Criminal Justice Act 1991 s.2(2)(a). The actual offence for which R was being sentenced was not a violent or sexual offence within s.31, and the judge had no jurisdiction to exercise his powers under s.2(2)(b) in imposing a longer than normal sentence. However a longer than normal sentence, possibly life imprisonment, would have been appropriate if the offence had been violent or sexual. The offence was not sufficiently serious to warrant a discretionary life sentence under s.2(2)(a), notwithstanding the medical evidence, and the judge was right to reject a disposal under the Mental Health Act 1983. The judge was not entitled to conclude that R had been contemplating a sexual attack, nor to take into account an unreported attack on a therapist with whom R had previously had a relationship, as it was not a circumstance relating to the offence for which R had pleaded guilty.

R. v. ROBINSON (WILLIAM) [1997] 2 Cr. App. R. (S.) 35, Otton, L.J., CA (Crim Div).

1427. Burglary–previous criminal record

B and S pleaded guilty to burglary. They were seen entering a block of flats. Police officers who were called arrested S in a garden and B inside the flat which had been entered. They were sentenced to four years imprisonment in each case. B and S appealed.

Held, dismissing the appeals, that B and S had substantial records. Burglary was an offence which caused distress, concern and inconvenience and in many cases real fear. The sentences were severe but could not be faulted for experienced burglars.

R. v. BROWN (MARK) AND SAMUELS (ANTHONY JAMES) [1996] 2 Cr. App. R. (S.) 319, Mitchell, J., CA (Crim Div).

1428. Child abduction–attempts–violent offence

[Criminal Justice Act 1991 s.2(2), s.31(1).]

N appealed against a custodial sentence of six years, extended pursuant to the Criminal Justice Act 1991 s.2(2)(b), for attempted abduction of a child. N, aged 43, had pursued and caught a nine year old girl by one wrist and an arm, but had let her go when she screamed and kicked him. N admitted that he had intended to drag his victim down to the river bank and indecently assault her there, but contended that the offence was not a violent offence within the meaning of the Criminal Justice Act 1991 s.31(1).

Held, allowing the appeal in part and reducing the sentence to five years, that although there was no clear evidence of actual physical injury from the grabbing of the victim, it was settled law that false imprisonment might amount to a violent offence. The commission of another offence should not be considered, but the court had a responsibility to determine whether it was likely that physical injury would have resulted from dragging the victim down to the river bank and that positive finding endorsed the view of the trial judge that this was a violent offence. However, insufficient allowance had been made for the guilty plea, the frank admissions and the fact that the victim had suffered no actual harm, *R. v. Watford (Stuart Philip)* [1994] Crim. L.R. 462, [1995] 1 C.L.Y. 1423, *R. v. Cochrane (Robert Brian)* (1994) 15 Cr. App. R. (S.) 708, [1995] 1 C.L.Y. 1425 considered, *R. v. Wrench (Peter)* [1996] 1 Cr. App. R. (S.) 145, [1996] 1 C.L.Y. 1566 distinguished because the judge had not sentenced on the basis that it was a violent offence.

R. v. NEWSOME (PETER ALAN) [1997] 2 Cr. App. R. (S.) 69, Nelson, J., CA (Crim Div).

1429. Child abduction–breach of residence order–deterrent sentence

DH pleaded guilty to two offences of abducting a child and one offence of theft, and asked for a further offence of theft to be taken into consideration. DH had married her first husband in 1982 and they had two children. They separated and subsequently divorced, and DH remarried. Following court proceedings, DH was granted a residence order for the children subject to a prohibition on removing the children from the jurisdiction without the consent of their father. DH made arrangements to move with her second husband to Canada, and eventually did so, taking the children with her, without informing their father. Following proceedings in Canada the children were returned to England, having been away for 21 months. DH subsequently returned with her second husband. DH was sentenced to nine months' imprisonment concurrent for each offence of child abduction and one month concurrent for theft.

Held, allowing the appeal, that the sentencer had correctly referred to the need for a deterrent element in the sentence, and there was nothing wrong with the sentence of nine months' imprisonment imposed for the offence However, there was evidence that the imprisonment of the mother was damaging the children, and for that reason the sentence would be reduced to four months.

R. v. DRYDEN-HALL (JULIE ANN) [1997] 2 Cr. App. R. (S.) 235, Scott Baker, J., CA (Crim Div).

1430. Child abduction–planned offence–child removed from jurisdiction

[Child Abduction Act 1984 s.1 (1).]

T appealed against a sentence of four months' imprisonment, having pleaded guilty to abducting her child under the Child Abduction Act 1984 s.1 (1). She had lived with the father of her child for some time but they separated and a residence order was made by a magistrates' court as a result of which the child lived with her father but T had contact. T removed the child to her home in the Canary Islands and kept the child there for about six months until a Spanish court ordered her to return the child. She immediately complied with this order.

Held, dismissing the appeal, that T had taken the law into her own hands by committing a planned offence whereby the child had been taken out of the jurisdiction. There was nothing wrong with the sentence.

R. v. TAYLOR (YANA DAWN) [1997] 1 Cr. App. R. (S.) 329, Judge Van Der Werff, CA (Crim Div).

1431. Child abduction–spontaneous abduction of boy aged 10 following incident relating to car–case put into wrong bracket of seriousness

R and P appealed against sentences of three years' imprisonment, having pleaded guilty to taking a child without authority and, in the case of R, driving with excess alcohol and without insurance. They were drinking at a public house when two boys took R's car and drove it round a nearby rally circuit. Two other boys, both aged 10 years, who had witnessed the incident told the two men what had happened. When the boys who had taken the car ran away, R and P grabbed one of the 10 year old boys, put him in the boot of the car and drove for a distance of about three miles before releasing him. The boy's mother attempted to stop them driving away, but they drove off forcing her to let go of the car door.

Held, allowing the appeal and reducing the sentences of both R and P to 12 months' imprisonment, that the judge had put the case into the wrong bracket of seriousness. This was a spontaneous offence, committed in anger, without any pre-planning or any of the sinister overtones commonly found in such cases.

R. v. ROWLANDS (JOHN MELVILLE); R. v. PARCELL (STEVEN JOHN) [1997] 1 Cr. App. R. (S.) 152, Mckinnon, J., CA (Crim Div).

1432. **Child abuse–buggery–10 year old female victim–attempts–attitude of child victim in forgiving offender irrelevant to sentence–two years' imprisonment unduly lenient**

[Criminal Justice Act 1988 s.36.]

The Attorney General applied for a sentence to be referred under the Criminal Justice Act 1988 s.36 on the ground that the it was unduly lenient. W was convicted of four counts of attempted rape and two of indecent assault. He lived with a woman who had a daughter aged 10. The child eventually complained that the offender had attempted to bugger her on four occasions and had inserted his finger into her anus on one occasion. W denied all the allegations. The child indicated that she forgave him. W was sentenced to a total of two years' imprisonment.

Held, allowing the reference and substituting sentences of five years in total, that it was an error to treat a child's attitude as a decisive matter when sentencing. A child of 10 was not in a position to make a reliable judgment on the seriousness of the offences and it was important to indicate to the public at large the total unacceptability of such conduct towards children, *R. v. Roberts* (1982) 4 Cr. App. R. (S.) 8, *R. v. Billam* [1986] 8 Cr. App. R. (S.) 48, [1986] C.L.Y. 868, *Attorney General's Reference (No.25 of 1994), Re* (1995) 16 Cr. App. R. (S.) 562 and *R. v. Robinson* (1990) 12 Cr. App. R. (S.) 542, [1992] C.L.Y. 1308 considered.

ATTORNEY GENERAL'S REFERENCE (NO.75 OF 1995), *Re*; *sub nom.* R. v. WILLEY (PHILLIP HENRY) [1997] 1 Cr. App. R. (S.) 198, Lord Bingham of Cornhill, L.C.J., CA (Crim Div).

1433. **Child abuse–buggery–12 and 15 year old male victims–seven years' imprisonment unduly lenient**

[Criminal Justice Act 1988 s.36; Criminal Justice Act 1991 s.2(2)(b).]

The Attorney General applied for a sentence to be referred under the Criminal Justice Act 1988 s.36 on the ground that it was unduly lenient. F, aged 19 when the offences began and 29 at the appeal, was convicted of a number of offences of buggery and indecency in relation to boys aged 12 to 15. He was sentenced to a total of seven years' imprisonment. The Attorney General contended that (1) the Criminal Justice Act 1991 s.2(2)(b) should have been applied, and (2) ggravating factors, such as F's occupation of a position of trust, the vulnerability and age of the victims, intimidation of the victims, the involvement of other adults and the absence of remorse on the part of F were present. F argued that his age and the absence of any previous convictions provided him with mitigation.

Held, allowing the reference and substituting concurrent sentences of nine years, that (1) the judge was not unduly lenient in not applying s.2(2)(b) of the 1991 Act in light of F's youth and clean record and the absence of any psychiatric evidence suggesting the necessity of a longer than normal sentence for the purposes of protecting the public, but (2) the aggravating factors indicated that a sentence of seven years' imprisonment was unduly lenient.

ATTORNEY GENERAL'S REFERENCE (NO.7 OF 1995), *Re*; *sub nom.* R. v. FEARON (ROBERT), Trans. Ref: 95/7587/R2, 95/7689/R2, July 14, 1997, Lord Bingham of Cornhill, L.C.J., CA (Crim Div).

1434. Child abuse–buggery–13 year old male victim–defendant paying child–two years' imprisonment unduly lenient

[Criminal Justice Act 1988 s36; Criminal Justice Act 1991 s.44.]

The Attorney General applied for a sentence to be referred under the Criminal Justice Act 1988 s.36 on the ground that it was unduly lenient. G pleaded guilty to one count of buggery with a boy aged 13. A count of rape was not proceeded with. He met the boy who was truanting from school and invited him to his house. When the boy arrived he took him to a bedroom and buggered him. He gave the boy £10. G was sentenced to two years' imprisonment with an order under the Criminal Justice Act 1991 s.44.

Held, allowing the reference, that the boy had been buggered by G for a payment of £10. The sentence was unduly lenient; allowing for the element of double jeopardy, a sentence of three and a half years' imprisonment was substituted, *R. v. Willis* (1974) 60 Cr. App. R. 146, [1975] C.L.Y. 714 considered.

ATTORNEY GENERAL'S REFERENCE (NO.31 OF 1996), *Re*; *sub nom.* R. v. GOLDS (MICHAEL DAVID) [1997] 1 Cr. App. R. (S.) 308, Rose, L.J., CA (Crim Div).

1435. Child abuse–buggery–14 year old male victim–eight years' imprisonment not unduly lenient–longer than normal sentence appropriate

[Criminal Justice Act 1991 s.2(2), s.36.]

The Attorney General applied for a sentence to be referred under the Criminal Justice Act 1988 s.36 on the ground that it was unduly lenient. J pleaded guilty to one count of buggery against a boy aged 14 and three counts of indecent assault on a boy aged 10, a girl aged 12 and a boy aged nine. He was released from a sentence of four years' imprisonment for buggery and indecent assault and established contact with a woman whom he had known some years earlier. J showed pornographic literature to the 10 year old son of the woman and masturbated him. A few weeks later he met a boy aged 14 in a park and persuaded him to work in his garden. He buggered the boy. He continued to entertain children at his flat and indecently assaulted a girl aged 12 after persuading her to drink cider. He later performed oral sex on a boy aged nine. J was sentenced to eight years' imprisonment for buggery with four years concurrent on each count of indecent assault.

Held, allowing the reference, that while the sentence was not unduly lenient, a longer than normal sentence, under the Criminal Justice Act 1991 s.2(2)(b), was appropriate. J had been sentenced to a substantial period of imprisonment on a previous occasion for similar offences, he had committed the instant offences while still on licence and persisted despite warnings from those responsible for one of the victims. The sentencer should have exercised the powers under s.2(2)(b) in respect of the offence of buggery. The Court substituted a sentence of 11 years, taking account of the element of double jeopardy, *R. v. Hutchison* (1988) 10 Cr. App. R. (S.) 50, [1990] C.L.Y 1217, *R. v. Riddle* (1985) 7 Cr. App. R. (S.) 59, *Attorney General's Reference (No.17 of 1990), Re* (1991) 12 Cr. App. R. (S.) 572, [1991] C.L.Y. 1219, *R. v. McMorrow* (1993) 14 Cr. App. R. (S.) 330, [1994] C.L.Y. 1183, *R. v. Pearce* (1988) 10 Cr. App. R. (S.) 331, and *Attorney General's Reference (No.43 of 1994), Re* (1995) 16 Cr. App. R. (S.) 815, [1996] 1 C.L.Y. 1734 cited.

ATTORNEY GENERAL'S REFERENCE (NO.9 OF 1996), *Re*; *sub nom.* R. v. JOHNSON (JOHN MICHAEL) [1997] 1 Cr. App. R. (S.) 113, Rose, L.J., CA (Crim Div).

1436. Child abuse–buggery–indecent assault–15 year old male victim–degree of authority over victim arising from work relationship

M appealed against concurrent sentences of seven and three years' imprisonment on conviction of buggery and indecent assault on a boy aged 15. M and the victim worked at a cafe where the victim was nominally under M's control. M offered to give the victim a lift home and took him to a car park where he indecently assaulted and then buggered the victim.

Held, allowing the appeal by reducing the term for buggery from seven to five years, that M had taken advantage of the relationship with the boy and had not pleaded guilty or shown any remorse. This was a single incident where there was abuse of authority arising from the work relationship, although the victim was not in M's care, and the indecent assault amounted to an aggravating feature, *R. v. Willis* (1974) 60 Cr. App. R. 146, [1975] C.L.Y. 714 considered.

R. v. MALLOY (JOSEPH) [1997] 1 Cr. App. R. (S.) 189, Leggatt, L.J., CA (Crim Div).

1437.   Child abuse–buggery–indecent assault–young male victims–indecent assault–consecutive sentences–breach of trust–use of charitable organisation as cover–prolonged history of offending–five years' imprisonment unduly lenient

[Criminal Justice Act 1988 s.36.]

The Attorney General applied for a sentence to be referred under the Criminal Justice Act 1988 s.36 on the ground that it was unduly lenient. Following concurrent sentences of imprisonment totalling five years on conviction of two counts of buggery, four counts of indecent assault and one count of indecency with a child. H had enlisted four boys to a youth organisation he ran, having met them through his work at a local radio station. The offences continued over a prolonged time, and involved the victims being tied up and blindfolded.

Held, allowing the reference and increasing the sentence to eight years in total, that H's conduct, using a charitable organisation as a cover for his activities, along with the protracted period over which the offences took place and the fact that he was in a position of trust over his victims, meant that the sentences were unduly lenient. Whereas the correct sentence would have been one of 10 years' imprisonment, this would be reduced taking account of the element of double jeopardy, with two consecutive four year terms for the buggery offences and the other sentences running concurrently.

ATTORNEY GENERAL'S REFERENCE (NO.4 OF 1997), *Re; sub nom.* R. v. HETHERINGTON (PETER), Trans. Ref: 9700376/R2, May 8, 1997, McCowan, L.J., CA (Crim Div).

1438.   Child abuse–cruelty by mother to seven month old female–unexplained hairline fracture

L appealed against sentence of 15 months' imprisonment for cruelty to a child. She and her boyfriend attended a hospital bringing their seven month old daughter, who was found to have a large hairline fracture of the right parietal bone. She claimed that the child had rolled off a bed, but medical witnesses gave evidence that this could not account for the injuries. Between the incident and the trial she gave birth to a second child.

Held, dismissing the appeal, that it could not be said that the sentence was wrong in principle for a very grave attack on a very young child, and it was the least sentence that could have been passed in the circumstances

R. v. LEWIS (AMANDA LOUISE) [1996] 2 Cr. App. R. (S.) 431, Hidden, J., CA (Crim Div).

1439.   Child abuse–cruelty by mother to two year old female

L pleaded guilty to wilfully ill treating a child and wilfully neglecting a child and was sentenced to 16 months' imprisonment with six months' concurrent and two terms each of one month consecutive for failing to surrender to bail (total 18 months). L was the mother of a girl aged two and a half. The child was found to be suffering from a scald extending from her shoulder to her elbow. L admitted holding the child's arm under scalding water. L failed to obtain medical treatment for the scald until a neighbour intervened the following day.

Held, dismissing the appeal, that L had been subject to violence and abuse as a child. This was however a case of apparently deliberate cruelty to a child which necessarily called for a custodial sentence. The judge had not erred in the sentence he had imposed.

R. v. LAVELL (DEBORAH) [1997] 2 Cr. App. R. (S.) 91, Potter, L.J., CA (Crim Div).

1440. Child abuse–cruelty by parents to 15 year old son

B appealed against a sentence of three years' imprisonment, having pleaded guilty to cruelty to his 15 year old son, whose behaviour annoyed B and his wife over a substantial period of time. One evening they forced him into a van and drove him to a lock up garage. B then pushed a cigarette into the boy's mouth, poked him with a metal bar and poured paint thinners over him. A rope was put round his neck and over a girder, and he was made to stand on a crate and eat two cigarettes. He was then left alone, with his wrists chained to the wall, until he was rescued by the police.

Held, allowing the appeal and reducing the sentence to 18 months' imprisonment, that the sentence was excessive, regard being had to the substantial personal mitigation available to B, although the gravity of the offence precluded the substitution of suspended sentence.

R. v. BACON (NIGEL) [1997] 1 Cr. App. R. (S.) 335, Moses, J., CA (Crim Div).

1441. Child abuse–grievous bodily harm–single attack on two year old female

B appealed against sentence of seven years' imprisonment for causing grievous bodily harm with intent to the two year old daughter of his girlfriend. The child suffered a series of blows to the head and a kick to the stomach which caused perforation of the bowel. B, aged 27, did not plead guilty or show signs of remorse.

Held, allowing the appeal, that the incident was an isolated one and B's age, good work record and the fact that he sought help for the child as soon as the injuries were inflicted were taken in mitigation, *R. v. Mason* (1994) 15 Cr. App. R. (S.) 745, [1995] 1 C.L.Y. 1392 considered. The judge incorrectly took as a starting point cases of manslaughter following a period of cruelty and the sentence was reduced to one of five years' imprisonment.

R. v. BRICKLEBANK (SCOTT NORMAN) [1996] 2 Cr. App. R. (S.) 410, Roch, L.J., CA (Crim Div).

1442. Child abuse–grievous bodily harm–six month old child–suspended sentence justified

G pleaded guilty to inflicting grievous bodily harm. G was the father of a child aged six or seven months who was admitted to hospital. The child was found to have subdural haematomas of different ages, and injuries to the legs, arms, spine and ribs, which were also of different ages. G eventually admitted handling the child heavily at times of great stress and tiredness. He appealed against sentence of two and a half years' imprisonment.

Held, considering *R. v. Durkin* (1989) 11 Cr. App. R. (S.) 313, [1990] C.L.Y. 1444 and *R. v. Cameron (John McDougal)* (1993) 14 Cr. App. R. (S.) 801, [1994] C.L.Y. 1358 in view of changes in the family circumstance whereby the family had become reunited and G had successfully been allowed unsupervised daily access, it was desirable to allow G to rejoin the family. The sentence was therefore reduced to two years on the ground of exceptional circumstances and suspended.

R. v. GRAHAM (ROBERT) [1997] 2 Cr. App. R. (S.) 264, Schiemann, L.J., CA (Crim Div).

1443. Child abuse–incest–14 year old daughter becoming pregnant

C pleaded guilty to a single act of incest with his daughter, then aged 14, as a result of which she became pregnant. The offence was not disclosed to the police until six years later. He was sentenced to five years' imprisonment and appealed.

Held, allowing the appeal, that the sentencer had expressly passed sentence on the basis that there had been one single offence, but that sentence was out of line with the authorities, *Attorney General's Reference (No.1 of 1989), Re* [1989] 1 W.L.R. 1117, [1991] C.L.Y. 1138, *R. v. Green* (1990) 12 Cr. App. R. (S.) 114, *R. v. M (Alfred John)* (1993) 14 Cr. App. R. (S.) 286, [1994] C.L.Y. 1272 and *R. v. Cunnah (Derek John)* [1996] 1 Cr. App. R. (S.) 393, [1996] 1 C.L.Y. 1783 considered. A sentence of three years would be substituted.

R. v. C (ALAN CHARLES) [1997] 2 Cr. App. R. (S.) 85, David Clarke Q.C., CA (Crim Div).

1444. Child abuse–incest–rape–13 year old female victim–incidents over six year period

B was convicted of two counts of rape and one of indecent assault on a female. The victim of all the offences was his daughter. B separated from his wife when the daughter was about 18 months old, and did not see her frequently until she was about nine. When she was about 13, the victim began to stay with B and B had intercourse with her while she was asleep. Later the victim ran away from home and was put into foster care; during this period she saw B regularly and sexual intercourse took place frequently. Subsequently, the victim was placed in a children's home and further sexual activity took place. The victim complained to the police five years later. B was sentenced to a total of 11 years' imprisonment and applied for leave to appeal against the sentence.

Held, refusing the application, these were incestuous rapes of a child in gross breach of trust. The sentences could not be regarded as manifestly excessive, *R. v. Baker (Graham David)* (1989) 11 Cr. App. R. (S.) 513, [1991] C.L.Y. 1197, *R. v. Lewis (Terence William)* (1989) 11 Cr. App. R. (S.) 457, [1991] C.L.Y. 1193 and *Attorney General's Reference (No.8 of 1991), Re* (1992) 13 Cr. App. R. (S.) 360, [1993] C.L.Y. 1265 considered.

R. v. B (ALAN GERALD) [1997] 2 Cr. App. R. (S.) 126, Poole, J., CA (Crim Div).

1445. Child abuse–indecent assault–10 year old female victim–isolated incident

D was convicted of indecent assault on a female, aged 10 and was sentenced to two years' imprisonment. D, a trainee priest, met the mother of the victim through working in a charitable organisation. One night the child was left in a flat in his care. The child complained that D had got into her bed naked and pressed her vagina with his hand; the child then got out of the bed and left the flat. D denied the offence.

Held, allowing the appeal, that previous cases showed that there was an established tariff of sentencing for this type of offence. On a plea of guilty for repeated indecent assaults where there had been a breach of trust, sentences of between nine and 12 months' imprisonment had been approved. It followed that in the present case, which involved a trial, the sentence would have been in the region of 13 to 18 months. The case involved a gross breach of trust, but only one isolated act. The sentence of two years' imprisonment was excessive; a sentence of 18 months' imprisonment would be substituted, *R. v. Vinson* (1981) 3 Cr. App. R. (S.) 315, [1982] C.L.Y. 684, *R. v. Smith (Frederick William)* (1986) 8 Cr. App. R. (S.) 325, [1988] C.L.Y. 932, *R. v. Moghal (Adil Farooq* (1993) 14 Cr. App. R. (S.) 125, [1993] C.L.Y. 1191 and *R. v. Aston (Gary)* (1993) 14 Cr. App. R. (S.) 779, [1994] C.L.Y. 1288 considered.

R. v. DEMEL (GEM DELANTHA) [1997] 2 Cr. App. R. (S.) 5, McKinnon, J., CA (Crim Div).

1446. Child abuse—indecent assault—11 year old female victim—adopted daughter of offender—less serious form of assault

C, aged 51, appealed against a sentence of two years' imprisonment on three counts of indecent assault on his adopted daughter. P assaulted his daughter who was aged 11 at the time the abuse began, over a period of two years.

Held, allowing the appeal and substituting a sentence of 15 months, that this was not the gravest form of indecent assault known to the courts, but was a form of conduct which persisted over a period of many months, upon a victim whom P should have been protecting. The appeal was allowed because there were relevant previous decisions of the Court of Appeal which indicated that the sentence passed was inappropriate and those decisions were not drawn to the attention of the sentencer at the time. It was the duty of counsel to cite relevant authorities which indicated the acceptable level of sentencing in respect of the relevant offence, *R. v. Hessey* (1987) 9 Cr. App. R. (S.) 268 and *R. v. Robinson (James)* (1990) 12 Cr. App. R. (S.) 542, [1992] C.L.Y. 1308 considered.

R. v. C (PETER) [1996] 2 Cr. App. R. (S.) 200, Butterfield, J., CA (Crim Div).

1447. Child abuse—indecent assault—seven year old female victim—sexual assault of daughter by father

W appealed against sentence on conviction on a single count of indecent assault against a female for which he was sentenced to three years' imprisonment. W was married and had four children including a seven year old daughter. W had a row with his wife who left the house for a few days. On return his wife noticed a change in her daughter and two days later W confessed to the abuse which took the form of, at least, simulated intercourse, although there was confusion as to whether penetration was penile or digital. The abuse took place during the course of a single night while his wife was away. W later denied the abuse and a trial had to take place.

Held, dismissing the appeal, that the sentence was not excessive in view of the aggravating factors and the judge was justified in viewing the case as seriously as he did, *R. v. Garnett (Leslie)* (1989) 11 Cr. App. R. (S.) 327 distinguished.

R. v. WEATHERLY (PETER); *sub nom.* R. v. W (PETER) [1997] 1 Cr. App. R. (S.) 95, Hobhouse, L.J., CA (Crim Div).

1448. Child abuse—indecent assault—unlawful sexual intercourse—gross indecency—nine year old female victim

C appealed against a sentence totalling four years' imprisonment. C was convicted of having unlawful sexual intercourse with a girl under 13 and was sentenced to four years. He was however acquitted of rape and of attempted buggery which were said to arise out of the same circumstances. Concurrent sentences of 12, nine, and 15 months' imprisonment were passed after C pleaded guilty to one indecent assault and to gross indecency and was convicted of a further indecent assault. The victim was C's nine year old niece. Three episodes were involved over five to six months. C was of previous good character and of limited intellectual ability.

Held, allowing the appeal, to the extent of substituting a sentence of 30 months for that of four years, all other concurrent sentences to stand, that too little weight was given to C's psychological profile which, whilst not excusing his conduct, did provide some powerful mitigation.

R. v. CANTWELL (CLIVE); *sub nom.* R. v. C (CLIVE) [1996] 2 Cr. App. R. (S.) 379, Ognall, J., CA (Crim Div).

1449. Child abuse—indecent assault—unlawful sexual intercourse with a 14 year old girl with consent

B was convicted of indecent assault on a woman. B was tried on an indictment containing counts charging rape, buggery and indecent assault. In the course of the trial, the judge invited the prosecution to amend the indictment by including counts charging unlawful sexual intercourse as alternative counts to the counts charging rape. The prosecution concluded that this was not possible as the time limit for prosecutions for unlawful sexual intercourse had by then expired, but applied instead to amend the indictment by adding counts of indecent assault as alternative counts to the counts charging rape. B was convicted of indecent assault on the basis that he had had sexual intercourse with a girl aged 14 with her consent and sentenced to four years' imprisonment.

Held, allowing the appeal, that considering *R. v. Hinton (Roy)* (1995) 16 Cr. App. R. (S.) 523, the maximum sentence for indecent assault was 10 years' imprisonment, but the maximum sentence for unlawful sexual intercourse with a girl aged 14 was two years. The court had previously drawn attention to the anomaly. B had a justifiable sense of grievance in that he had been sentenced to twice the term of imprisonment permitted by Parliament for the offence of unlawful sexual intercourse. The sentence would be reduced to two years' imprisonment.

R. v. BROUGH (DAVID); *sub nom.* R. v. B [1997] 2 Cr. App. R. (S.) 202, Rose, L.J., CA (Crim Div).

1450. Child abuse–indecent assault–young boy victims

[Criminal Justice Act 1988 s.36.]

The Attorney General applied for a sentence to be referred under the Criminal Justice Act 1988 s.36 on the ground that it was unduly lenient. Concurrent sentences, suspended for two years, of 18 months' imprisonment were imposed following R's plea of guilty to six counts of indecent assault on young boys. R had been in a position of trust and the assaults had been repeated over a substantial period of time.

Held, allowing the application, that, although there were mitigating circumstances insofar as the offender had suffered abuse as a child and had voluntarily sought psychiatric treatment, there were no exceptional circumstances which justified suspending the sentence. Serious indecent assaults provoked strong public condemnation and sentences for such offences should contain a distinct punitive element, so as to afford effective protection to the parents of young children. In the circumstances, a sentence of 15 months' immediate imprisonment was appropriate.

ATTORNEY GENERAL'S REFERENCE (NO.34 OF 1997), *Re; sub nom.* R. v. REED (PETER DAVID), *The Times*, November 20, 1997, Lord Bingham of Cornhill, L.C.J., CA (Crim Div).

1451. Child abuse–indecent assault–young male victims–assault by sports coach

C pleaded guilty to five counts of indecent assault on males and was sentenced to three years' imprisonment. He was the manager of a squash and tennis club and was in charge of training. He indecently assaulted three boys aged between 11 and 15, who had joined the club and were being coached by him. The indecent assaults consisted of masturbating the boys or touching the penis.

Held, dismissing the appeal, that although C was a man of 59 of previous good character, the offences were persistent and involved boys in respect of whom C was in a position of trust. The sentence properly reflected the relevant considerations.

R. v. CLARKE (MALCOLM DAVID) [1997] 2 Cr. App. R. (S.) 53, Latham, J., CA (Crim Div).

1452. Child abuse–rape–12 and 13 year old female victims–offence committed on stepdaughters on many occasions–totality of sentence

M appealed against sentence totalling 28 years after being convicted of various offences of rape of his two stepdaughters on numerous occasions when they were between the ages of 12 and 22 in one case and 13 and 19 in the other. Sentenced to 15 years' imprisonment in respect of the offences against the first stepdaughter, and

13 years' imprisonment in respect of the offences against the second stepdaughter, to run consecutively.

Held, allowing the appeal in part, that the total criminality involved in the case deserved a total period of 18 years' imprisonment, and the individual sentences were adjusted accordingly, *R. v. D (David John)* (1993) 14 Cr. App. R. (S.) 639, [1994] C.L.Y. 1330, *R. v. Billam* [1986] 1 W.L.R. 349, [1986] C.L.Y. 868, *R. v. R (Peter John)* (1993) 14 Cr. App. R. (S.) 328, [1994] C.L.Y. 1334 and *R. v. C (John Francis)* (1993) 14 Cr. App. R. (S.) 562, [1994] C.L.Y. 1255 considered.

R. v. M (ADRIAN ALEXANDER) [1996] 2 Cr. App. R. (S.) 286, Schiemann, L.J., CA (Crim Div).

1453. Child abuse–rape–eight year old female victim–offence aggravated by youth of victim

S appealed against a sentence of imprisonment of six years on conviction of rape of an eight year old child. S, aged 33, contended that there was only one incident and no evidence of undue suffering by the child.

Held, dismissing the appeal, that the offence was aggravated by the age of the child and the sentence was appropriate, *Attorney General's Reference (No.3 of 1995), Re* [1996] 1 Cr. App. R. (S.) 26, [1996] 1 C.L.Y. 1775 considered.

R. v. SANDHII (BALRAJ); *sub nom.* R. v. S (BALRAJ) [1997] 1 Cr. App. R. (S.) 123, Swinton Thomas, L.J., CA (Crim Div).

1454. Child abuse–rape–indecent assault–10 year old female victim–three years' imprisonment unduly lenient

[Criminal Justice Act 1988 s.36.]

The Attorney General applied for a sentence to be referred under the Criminal Justice Act 1988 s.36 on the ground that it was unduly lenient. D was sentenced to three years on each of two attempted rapes, two years for indecent assault and two years for each of two counts of indecency with a child. The offences were committed over 11 months and D gave money to the child. D pleaded guilty and frankly admitted that the offences were committed for his own sexual gratification and that he disliked the child.

Held, allowing the reference in part, that terms of four and a half years for each rape and three years for the indecent assault be substituted. The other terms were left unchanged. There was no doubt that the sentences were too lenient. The offences were an appalling catalogue of abuse of a young girl from a person in a position of trust over a long period. D was given credit for his guilty plea and the element of double jeopardy, *R. v. Billam* [1986] 1 W.L.R. 349, [1986] C.L.Y. 868, *Attorney General's Reference (No.32 of 1992), Re* (1994) 15 Cr. App. R. (S.) 149, *Attorney General's Reference (No.3 of 1994), Re* (1995) 16 Cr. App. R. (S.) 176, [1995] 1 C.L.Y. 1275 and *Attorney General's Reference (No.1 of 1989), Re* (1989) 11 Cr. App. R. (S.) 409, [1991] C.L.Y. 1138 considered.

ATTORNEY GENERAL'S REFERENCE (NO.5 OF 1996), *Re*; *sub nom.* R. v. DODD (CARL); R. v. D (CARL) [1996] 2 Cr. App. R. (S.) 434, Swinton Thomas, L.J., CA (Crim Div).

1455. Child abuse–unlawful sexual intercourse with 12 and 13 year old females

[Criminal Justice Act 1991 s.44.]

D appealed against sentence of three years' imprisonment and an order under the Criminal Justice Act 1991 s.44 after pleading guilty to two counts of unlawful sexual intercourse. He was a friend of the brother of a girl aged 12, and lived with her family. When aged 18, he had intercourse with the girl on one occasion. He left the home and went to live with another family, which included three children. He formed a relationship with a girl aged 13 and had sexual intercourse with her several times.

There was a delay of about 18 months between the committal for trial and the imposition of sentence.

Held, dismissing the appeal, that the sentences were not manifestly excessive.

R. v. DAVIS (NEIL MARTIN) [1997] 1 Cr. App. R. (S.) 74, Ebsworth, J., CA.

1456. Child abuse—unlawful sexual intercourse with 12 year old female—intercourse at victim's instigation

P, aged 45, appealed against a sentence of three and a half years' imprisonment, having pleaded guilty to unlawful sexual intercourse with a girl under the age of 13. The victim, aged 12, absconded with another girl from a children's home where she was living and spent the night at P's flat. After both the girls and P had consumed alcohol, he had intercourse with the victim at her instigation.

Held, allowing the appeal, reducing the sentence to two and a half years, that P was a man of average to low intelligence but he was not a danger to young women, *R. v. Oakley* (1990) 12 Cr. App. R. (S.) 215, [1992] C.L.Y. 1420 considered.

R. v. POLLEY (CHRISTOPHER JAMES) [1997] 1 Cr. App. R. (S.) 144, Astill, J., CA (Crim Div).

1457. Child abuse—unlawful sexual intercourse with 12 year old female—man aged 22 of limited intelligence

B appealed against sentence of two years' imprisonment after pleading guilty to unlawful sexual intercourse with a girl under the age of 13. The complainant was living in a local authority home and had intercourse with B, then aged 22, on three occasions. She became pregnant as a result.

Held, allowing the appeal, that B had a mental age of 11 years and an IQ at the lower end of the normal range. A sentence of imprisonment was justified but a sentence of 15 months was more appropriate, *R. v. B (James Walter)* (1993) 14 Cr. App. R. (S.) 482, [1994] C.L.Y. 1376 and *R. v. Bulmer (Henry Victor)* (1989) 11 Cr. App. R. (S.) 586, [1991] C.L.Y. 1233 cited.

R. v. BROUGH (PHILIP IAN) [1997] 1 Cr. App. R. (S.) 55, Harrison, J., CA.

1458. Child abuse—unlawful sexual intercourse with 14 year old female

H, aged 34, pleaded guilty to unlawful sexual intercourse with a girl aged 14 and was sentenced to nine months' imprisonment against which he appealed. H met the girl at a fairground where he was employed and arranged to visit her the same evening at an address where she was babysitting. Three friends of the girl said that they had told H that the girl was 14, but H denied this. H later had sexual intercourse with the girl with her consent. In an interview following his arrest he said he had no reason to believe the girl was not 16.

Held, allowing the appeal, that the sentencer had passed sentence on the basis that he did not accept that H believed that the girl was 16, but that at best he was reckless as to her age. H was not in breach of trust towards the girl and had pleaded guilty. A sentence of six months' imprisonment would have been appropriate.

R. v. HILL (GRAHAM) [1997] 2 Cr. App. R. (S.) 243, Harrison, J., CA (Crim Div).

1459. Child abuse—unlawful sexual intercourse with 14 year old female—appropriate sentence for single and less serious offence

C appealed against a sentence of 15 months' imprisonment, having pleaded guilty to unlawful sexual intercourse with a girl under 16. C, aged 32, met a girl aged 14 who lived near to his home and they had sexual intercourse on one occasion with her consent. The girl became pregnant and a child was born. C claimed that he did not know the girl's age. Following the discovery of the offence, C's wife left him.

Held, allowing the appeal, and substituting a sentence of six months' imprisonment, that the sentence of 15 months for a single offence was manifestly excessive given that the offence was very much toward the least serious of this type of case.

R. v. CARTER (JAHROY) [1997] 1 Cr. App. R. (S.) 434, McKinnon, J., CA (Crim Div).

1460. Child abuse—wilful neglect

C applied for leave to appeal against sentence and conviction of four offences of cruelty to a child for which she was sentenced to 18 months' imprisonment on each offence after pleading guilty. C also committed a number of shoplifting offences in respect of which she received three months' imprisonment for each offence. C and her husband wilfully neglected each of their four children in a manner likely to cause him or her unnecessary suffering or injury to health during the first half of 1994. H and W were heroin addicts and led a feckless nomadic existence. H was a Schedule 1 sex offender. Three of the children sustained superficial injuries which looked like burn marks. C contended that the judge failed to give sufficient consideration to the fact that she pleaded guilty, that she had never been in prison, that hers was a case of neglect and not cruelty, also that the husband's record made them vulnerable to hostility and that despite the neglect the children were happy and in good health.

Held, allowing the appeal in part, that (1) there was a need to balance the seriousness of the offences with the family's living circumstances and the inadequacy of C as a parent and her past offences and (2) following *R. v. Camille and Partridge* (1993) 14 Cr. App. R. (S.) 296, [1994] C.L.Y. 1225 and *R. v. McIntyre and McIntyre* (1993) 14 Cr. App. R. (S.) 308, [1994] C.L.Y. 1224 sentences of nine months' imprisonment on each count of neglect were appropriate.

R. v. CRANK (KERRY ANN) [1996] 2 Cr. App. R. (S.) 363, Auld, L.J., CA (Crim Div).

1461. Community service orders—breach of order

[Criminal Justice Act 1991 Sch.2 para.4.]

C appealed against a sentence of 15 months' imprisonment imposed in substitution for a community service order that he had breached. C had been charged with supplying a quantity of cannabis resin and of MDMA (Ecstasy) and had changed his plea of not guilty to guilty on four counts. He breached the community service order and committed other drug-related offences and burglary offences. The sentencing judge took the view that he could not sentence him as though the offence had only just taken place and was influenced by C's persistent offending and further breaches of community service orders.

Held, allowing the appeal and reducing the sentence from 15 months to eight months' imprisonment, that when substituting the original sentence with a new one, the court should take into account any part performance of the original sentence. Under the Criminal Justice Act 1991 Sch.2 para.4 non-compliance did not have the effect of aggravating the original offence thereby meriting an increased sentence and the judge had erred in taking that approach.

Observed, that when determining sentence on breach of a community service order it was important for the court to have before it all relevant information about the defendant, the offence, and any co-defendants and the sentences they received. It was the responsibility of the probation service to obtain this information from the CPS in order to supply the court with it.

R. v. CLARKE (DAVID) [1997] 2 Cr. App. R. (S.) 163, Toulson, J., CA (Crim Div).

1462. Community service orders–breach of order by reason of ill health

[Criminal Justice Act 1991 s.1; Criminal Justice Act 1991 Part III.]

C was sentenced to 200 hours' community service for an offence of handling a stolen motor car. Approximately three weeks after he completed one eight hour period of community service C fell from a balcony sustaining back injuries. He later admitted breaching the community service order and was ordered to serve a further 25 hours which he did not do. There followed an application for the revocation of the community service order on the grounds that C was unable to comply due to ill health. C was sentenced to nine months' imprisonment. C appealed arguing that: (1) the court should not have passed a custodial sentence following an application made for the community service order to be revoked on the grounds of inability to comply due to ill health; (2) the court should not exercise its power to revoke and re-sentence where revocation was sought due to a matter amounting to breach, unless that matter was established, and (3) in imposing a custodial sentence where the breach of the order was not properly established, and in the absence of a further sentence the judge erred contrary to the Criminal Justice Act 1991 s.1.

Held, allowing the appeal, that the judge did have jurisdiction to consider revocation of the community service order and re-sentencing C for the original offence under Part III of the 1991 Act but he had not laid the proper evidential basis for doing so and the custodial sentence was substituted by a community service order of 80 hours.

R. v. COLLINS (SHAWN), Trans. Ref: 96/8444/W3, January 28, 1997, Mance, J., CA (Crim Div).

1463. Community service orders–breach of order by reason of ill health

[Powers of Criminal Courts Act 1973 s.16, s.17.]

B appealed against the revocation of a community service order of 100 hours and the substitution of concurrent custodial sentences of four months each for handling stolen goods. B did not appear for work as required by probation officers, but claimed to suffer from asthma, arthritis and blackouts and produced a doctor's certificate to say that he should not work for six months because of arthritis. The judge below considered that B had misled the court by initially agreeing to community service and passed the custodial sentences. B contended that proper evidence had not been brought and his counsel had been prejudiced.

Held, allowing the appeal and substituting a probation order for 12 months, that it was more appropriate for such proceedings to be brought under the Powers of Criminal Courts Act 1973 s.16 as a breach of requirements rather than s.17, *R. v. Jackson (Kimberley)* (1984) 6 Cr. App. R. (S.) 202, [1985] C.L.Y. 564 approved.

R. v. BOOTH (BARRY), Trans. Ref: 9703128 W2, June 3, 1997, Bennett, J., CA (Crim Div).

1464. Community service orders–offence committed prior to making of order– power of Crown Court to revoke community order–whether further sentence for original offence appropriate

[Criminal Justice Act 1991 Sch.2 para.8(2).]

S and P pleaded guilty to assault occasioning actual bodily harm. They were concerned in an incident in November 1994 in the course of which a man was assaulted. Before appearing in the Crown Court in respect of this offence, each was sentenced to a community order (a probation order in the case of one appellant and a community service order in the case of the other) for an offence committed in April 1994. S and P were sentenced to six months' imprisonment and six months' detention in a young offender institution respectively for the later offence, with the community order revoked in each case and a term of three months' imprisonment or detention in a young offender institution consecutive in place of the community order.

Held, allowing the appeals, that by virtue of the Criminal Justice Act 1991 Sch.2 para.8(2) it was open to the Crown Court to revoke the community service order and the probation order, but it was argued that as the later offence was committed before the community order was imposed, it was wrong to impose a further sentence in place of the community order. In the circumstances, a custodial sentence was inappropriate; the consecutive terms were quashed, *R. v. Cawley (William Boy)* (1994) 15 Cr. App. R. (S.) 209 approved.

R. v. SAPHIER (PAUL ANTHONY); R. v. PEARSALL (BENJAMIN PAUL) [1997] 1 Cr. App. R. (S.) 235, Connell, J., CA (Crim Div).

1465. Compensation orders–income support–appropriate level of deduction from benefit

G appealed, by way of case stated, against a compensation order of £2,000, to be paid at £20 per week, made on her conviction on guilty pleas of dishonestly obtaining credit and theft of a vehicle. G had obtained £3,725 by representing that she was a teacher in full time education, in order to purchase a car on hire purchase, which she later sold to a relative for £1,200. Magistrates conducted a means enquiry which appeared to show that her family income was £166 per week and her outgoings only £38.50. G contended that, although she did receive £166 it was made up of income support and child benefit and she had five children and a husband to support so that her actual share of that income was about £37. She relied on *R. v. Olliver (Richard)* (1989) 11 Cr. App. R. (S.) 10, [1990] C.L.Y. 1317 and *R. v. Charalambous (Anne Elizabeth)* (1984) 6 Cr. App. R. (S.) 389, [1985] C.L.Y. 796 to claim that the magistrates had erred in an astonishing way.

Held, allowing the appeal, quashing the decision and substituting an order of £250 payable at £5 per week, that (1) the appropriate test for an error of law in the sentencing court was now "that it fell clearly outside the broad area of the lower court's sentencing discretion", *R. v. Truro Crown Court, ex p. Adair* (Unreported, 1997) followed; (2) the size of a financial order and the length of time over which it was payable should not be such that default was likely. In addition, it was important that fines should not be so high that an offender's family were fined, *R. v. Olliver (Richard)* and *R. v. Charalambous (Anne Elizabeth)* applied, *R. v. Felixstowe, Ipswich and Woodbridge Magistrates Court and Ipswich BC, ex p. Herridge* [1993] R.A. 83, [1993] C.L.Y. 2632 distinguished, *R. v. Stockport Justices, ex p. Conlon* [1997] 2 All E.R. 204, [1997] C.L.Y. 1275 considered, and (3) although it was appropriate to bring this case before the Court of Appeal, such cases were more properly referred to the Crown Court.

GRAY v. SHARPLES, Trans. Ref: CO-4497-96, March 21, 1997, Brooke, L.J., QBD.

1466. Compensation orders–payment period of over three years inappropriate

Y pleaded guilty to two counts of obtaining by deception and one of attempting to obtain by deception and was sentenced to 240 hours' community service and ordered to pay £9,110 in compensation and £250 prosecution costs. He asked for 35 other offences to be taken into consideration. Over a period of about 15 months Y obtained sums amounting to more than £9,000 from the Department of Social Security by claiming income support in the names of other people.

Held, allowing the appeal, that the sentencer had indicated that he expected that it would take the appellant more than two years to pay the compensation ordered. The court had said in *R. v. Bagga* (1989) 11 Cr. App. R. (S.) 497, [1991] C.L.Y. 1050 that a compensation order should not be made if there was no prospect of payment within the foreseeable future, and in *R. v. Bradburn* (1973) 57 Cr. App. R. 948, [1974] C.L.Y. 539 it was made clear that a compensation order should not be stretched out. In *R. v. Hewitt (Raymond Frederick)* (1990) 12 Cr. App. R. (S.) 466, [1992] C.L.Y. 1201 it was said that a compensation order should be made only if there was a realistic ability to pay. In *R. v. Olliver (Richard)* (1989) 11 Cr. App. R. (S.) 10, [1990] C.L.Y. 1317 the court had held that a compensation order might be made on the basis of payment over three years. The evidence about Y's means indicated that he could pay £25 per week, and it followed that he could pay a total of £3,900 over three years. The order requiring payment of £9,110 would be quashed and an order for payment of £3,900 would be substituted.

R. v. YEHOU (IGNACE ERIC) [1997] 2 Cr. App. R. (S.) 48, Hidden, J., CA (Crim Div).

1467.   Confiscation orders—costs orders—relevance of defendant's mortgage debts

[Criminal Justice Act 1988 Part VI.]

Held, that a court could not take into account the mortgage debts of a defendant when determining his realisable property upon imposing a confiscation order under the Criminal Justice Act 1988 Part VI. However, those debts were relevant in deciding whether to make an order that the defendant pay prosecution costs.

R. v. GHADAMI (MOHAMMED REZA), *The Times*, May 21, 1997, Kennedy, L.J., CA (Crim Div).

1468.   Confiscation orders—drug offences—supply of cannabis—determination of realisable amount where property jointly held

[Drug Trafficking Act 1994.]

B appealed against a confiscation order in the amount of £18,406, with 12 months' imprisonment in default, having pleaded guilty to five counts of conspiring to supply cannabis, conspiring to supply cannabis resin, and other offences relating to the supply of cannabis. He and another were involved in the supply of cannabis over a period of about 14 months to about 30 dealers. It was estimated that B had supplied cannabis with a total value of approximately £180,000.

Held, allowing the appeal, reducing the order by £4,300, that B's proceeds had been assessed at £51,000 and the amount that might be realised at £18,406. B's sole asset was a mobile home held jointly with his wife and purchased for £21,750. This was sold in 1996 for £18,406 and the sum held in a joint account subject to a restraint order. The sentencer had rejected evidence that B's wife had contributed £4,500 toward the cash element of the original purchase price and was entitled to find that a cash contribution by B toward the purchase price was a gift to the wife caught by the scheme of the Drug Trafficking Act 1994. The appropriate course of starting from the prima facie position as to where the beneficial interests lay before going on to determine whether there were any gifts capable of increasing the joint property's realisable value under s.6 had not been followed. No finding had been made as to whether money held in a joint account and used to purchase the mobile home represented a gift caught by the Act, so that the wife was entitled to maintain that half of the £10,500 sum that was not caught by the Act. As the sale proceeds were only 85 per cent of purchase price, the amount fell to be deducted by £4,300, being 85 per cent of half the proceeds from the joint account used to purchase the property.

R. v. BUCKMAN (ANDREW) [1997] 1 Cr. App. R. (S.) 325, Brooke, L.J., CA (Crim Div).

1469.   Confiscation orders—drug trafficking—assessment of drug trafficking proceeds—forfeiture of confiscated drugs

[Drug Trafficking Act 1994 s.2, s.4; Misuse of Drugs Act 1971 s.27.]

D appealed against a confiscation order in the sum of £17,600, made pursuant to the Drug Trafficking Act 1994 s.2 following his guilty plea to being concerned in supplying cocaine and possessing cocaine with intent to supply. D was arrested in possession of cocaine, for which it was inferred he had paid £10,800. D contended that: (1) the drugs had already been forfeited under the Misuse of Drugs Act 1971 s.27 and therefore it was double jeopardy to include their value in the calculation of the proceeds of his trafficking, or (2) the trial judge had wrongly exercised his discretion by including their purchase price in his assessment of the proceeds of drug trafficking under s.4(4)(b) of the 1994 Act, with the consequence that D was forced to sell his legitimately acquired home to satisfy the confiscation order.

Held, dismissing the appeal and certifying the following question as a point of law of public importance, "If the sum a defendant has expended on the purchase of drugs found in his possession is properly assumed, under s.4(3)(b) of the Drug Trafficking Act 1994, to have been met by him out of payments received by him in connection with drug trafficking carried on by him, may such sum be properly included in the total sum ordered to be paid under a confiscation order when the drugs themselves are ordered to be forfeited?", that (1) the statutory procedure under s.2(5)(b) of the 1994 Act required that forfeiture was subordinate to confiscation, so that already confiscated drugs could not later be forfeited, and (2) the court had no discretion to mitigate the intended severe consequences of confiscation orders, *R. v. Satchell* [1996] Crim. L.R. 351, [1996] 1 C.L.Y. 1597 and *R. v. Thacker* (1995) 16 Cr. App. R. (S.) 461 not followed, *R. v. Stuart (Augustus)* (1989) 11 Cr. App. R. (S.) 89 approved.

R. v. DORE (ANTHONY) [1997] 2 Cr. App. R. (S.) 152, Lord Bingham of Cornhill, L.C.J., CA (Crim Div).

1470. Confiscation orders–drug trafficking–defendants could appeal against confiscation orders to which they had agreed

[Drug Trafficking Offences Act 1986 s.3(1).]

BE and ME were convicted of offences relating to a scheme to import four metric tonnes of cannabis resin into the UK. As well as imposing prison sentences, the judge, with the agreement of defence counsel, made confiscation orders under the Drug Trafficking Offences Act 1986 against BE and ME. The Crown appealed against a Court of Appeal decision quashing the confiscation orders, contending that, whilst an appeal could be made against a confiscation order as part of the sentence, a general right of appeal against such orders was excluded by s.3(1), because, by agreeing to the making of the orders, BE and ME had accepted an allegation in a statement submitted by the Crown, relating to the assessment of the proceeds of their drug trafficking, which the court had acted upon, and their acceptance of such a statement was "conclusive" for all purposes.

Held, allowing the appeal, that s.3(1) was a procedural provision designed to establish proof that an accused had benefited from drug trafficking and to determine the amount by which he had benefited. Therefore, the provision that the defendant's acceptance of a Crown statement could be regarded as "conclusive" meant only that the defendant might be regarded as having accepted the statement as proof of the matters to which it related. There was no express or implied ouster of the Court of Appeal's jurisdiction to entertain appeals against confiscation orders, *R. v. Tredwen (Ronald)* (1994) 99 Cr. App. R. 154, [1994] C.L.Y. 757 not followed. A defendant was entitled to argue that his acceptance of a prosecution statement was based on a mistake of fact or law, but the burden on the defendant to show that he, and not his counsel, had made a material and causatively relevant mistake might be difficult to discharge. The Court of Appeal could dismiss the appeal if they found that the confiscation order would still have been made notwithstanding a material mistake, as on a global view, no injustice would arise. In the instant case, it had not been proved that BE and ME had agreed to the confiscation orders as a result of a mistake of law and the evidence supported the making of the orders.

R. v. EMMETT (BRIAN); R. v. EMMETT (MICHAEL) [1997] 3 W.L.R. 1119, Lord Steyn, HL.

1471. Confiscation orders–drug trafficking–"proceeds" as the gross receipts

[Drug Trafficking Offences Act 1986; Drug Trafficking Act 1994.]

B pleaded guilty to conspiring to supply cannabis, cannabis resin and amphetamine and was sentenced to seven years' imprisonment with a confiscation order under the Drug Trafficking Act 1994 in the amount of £37,000 with 12 months' imprisonment in default. B sought leave to appeal against the confiscation order. The value of B's proceeds of drug trafficking were assessed at £200,000 and his realisable property at £37,000. B claimed that his profits from drug trafficking were less than £37,000. It was argued that the sentencer was wrong to assess the value of the applicant's proceeds of drug trafficking on the basis of his gross receipts as opposed to his actual profits.

Held, refusing the application, that (1) s.2, s.3 and s.5 of the 1994 Act directed attention to gross payments; (2) following *R. v. Osei* (1988) 10 Cr. App. R. (S.) 289, [1989] C.L.Y. 988, *R. v. Smith* [1989] 1 W.L.R. 765, [1989] C.L.Y. 987, *R. v. Comiskey* (1990) 12 Cr. App. R. (S.) 562, [1992] C.L.Y. 1241 and *R. v. Simons* (1994) 15 Cr. App. R. (S.) 126, [1993] C.L.Y. 1080 "proceeds" was not profit but sale price; (3) the provisions of the 1994 Act regarding "proceeds" re-enacted provisions of the Drug Trafficking Offences Act 1986 without amendment and the court must proceed on the assumption that Parliament were aware of the decisions supra and that they should be given effect, and (4) s.49, s.50 and s.51 of the 1994 Act which referred to money laundering used "proceeds" in the sense of "product" and not profits. That meaning must be intended to be consistent throughout the Act.

R. v. BANKS (DAVID MALCOLM) [1997] 2 Cr. App. R. (S.) 110, Lord Bingham of Cornhill, L.C.J., CA (Crim Div).

1472. Confiscation orders–drug trafficking–production of amphetamine–determining assets acquired through drug trafficking–statutory assumptions

[Criminal Law Act 1977 s.1 (1); Drug Trafficking Offences Act 1986 s.2 (3).]

C and B applied for leave to appeal against sentence after pleading guilty on re-arraignment to a charge under the Criminal Law Act 1977 s.1 (1) of conspiracy to produce a controlled class B drug, amphetamine. Following a *Newton* hearing into the basis of the plea, an inquiry under the Drug Trafficking Offences Act 1986 and the trial, C was sentenced to seven years' imprisonment with a confiscation order in the amount of £83,189 with a further sentence of two years in default. B was sentenced to 12 years imprisonment and a confiscation order for £3,139,599 with a default sentence of seven years. It was argued that the judge had erred in exercising his discretion to make the statutory assumptions and in giving the sentences imposed.

Held, refusing the applications, that in deciding what assets had been acquired through drug trafficking for the purpose of making a confiscation order under the Drug Trafficking Offences Act 1986, a court, after determining whether the defendant appeared to be sentenced for a drug trafficking offence and had benefited from such, had a discretion as to whether to make the statutory assumptions in s.2(3) of the Act, *R. v. Redbourne* [1992] 1 W.L.R. 1182, [1993] C.L.Y. 1073 considered. If it did, it then had to consider, firstly, whether the defendant appeared to have held the property since conviction or since the start of the relevant six year period for the making of the statutory assumptions and, secondly, what expenditure within that period had been met out of payments by the defendant. It then had to consider what payments received by the defendant were related to drug trafficking and assess the precise benefit gained. The court would then be in a position to make an order in the amount to be recovered. The purpose of the 1986 Act was to strip drug traffickers of the benefits gained by them through the illegal trafficking. The conclusion made by the court below to exercise its discretion and to make the statutory assumptions was entirely appropriate in the circumstance, and no fault was found with the sentences imposed.

R. v. CLARK (PAUL JOHN); R. v. BENTHAM (JOHN PRESTON) [1997] 1 W.L.R. 557, Lord Bingham of Cornhill, L.C.J., CA (Crim Div).

1473. Confiscation orders—drug trafficking—standard of proof—statutory assumptions

[Drug Trafficking Offences Act 1986 s.2(3).]

B, convicted of drug offences, appealed against the imposition of a confiscation order made under the Drug Trafficking Offences Act 1986 for the sum of £29,514. The judge found that two sums, £7,500 and £12,690, were payments received by B in connection with drug trafficking. In the alternative the judge made the assumption, under s.2(3)(a)(i) of the 1986 Act, that £12,960 was properly held by B "at any time since his conviction" and, under s.2(3)(a)(ii), that £7,500 had been transferred to him since the beginning of the period of six years ending when the proceedings were instituted against him. In 1986 B was arrested in Holland in possession of a quantity of drugs and £7,500 which was returned to him in 1990. Following B's arrest in 1994 £12,960 was found in his house in addition to drugs and drugs paraphernalia. B argued that £12,690 was a sum found upon him following his arrest in France in 1987. This sum was forwarded to B's brother in 1988 who returned it to B in 1993. B contended that (1) no reasonable tribunal could have been satisfied to the criminal standard of proof that the sums constituted proceeds of drug trafficking, and (2) the assumptions under s.2(3)(a) were incorrectly made as both sums fell outside the six year time limit.

Held, dismissing the appeal, that (1) given the overwhelming evidence against B the court was entitled to find that the sums represented proceeds of drug trafficking, and (2) the judge had not made incorrect assumptions under s.2(3)(a). Following *R. v. Chrastny* [1991] 1 W.L.R. 1381, [1992] C.L.Y. 1046, s.2(3)(a)(i) applied to payments received by B at any time in his life and which he continued to hold since his conviction. Accordingly, the confiscation order would stand.

R. v. BRETT (TERENCE DAVID), *The Times*, October 13, 1997, Nelson, J., CA (Crim Div).

1474. Confiscation orders—reassessment of realisable property an abuse of process

[Criminal Justice Act 1988 s.71, s.80.]

The CPS appealed against an order dismissing its application, made jointly with a receiver, for directions on an issue as to whether C had an interest in a certain property, "the premises". C was convicted of fraudulently obtaining a mortgage in relation to the premises and a confiscation order was made under the Criminal Justice Act 1988 s.71. C failed to make any payment under the order and the CPS applied to appoint a receiver in respect of C's realisable property. However, it was found that the realisable property did not cover the amount of the confiscation order and the CPS considered whether there was other realisable property to which a receiver could be appointed by virtue of s.80 of the 1988 Act. The CPS argued that the premises should be accounted for as realisable property. C argued that, as the premises had not been taken into account in the assessment in the Crown Court of C's realisable property, the CPS could not now consider C's interest in it.

Held, dismissing the appeal, that although the High Court hd jurisdiction to make an order such as that sought by the CPS, it would be inappropriate to do so in this case. When the confiscation order was made and consideration given to the extent to which C benefited from the offence and the amount of realisable property, no account was taken of the premises. The CPS conceded in the Crown Court that C had no interest in the premises and it was not in the public interest to allow the CPS to seek to relitigate that issue so as to reverse the findings. To allow the CPS to do so would be an abuse of process.

CROWN PROSECUTION SERVICE v. CRUDDAS, Trans. Ref: QBENI 96/0673/D, January 24, 1997, Leggatt, L.J., CA.

1475. Consecutive sentences–additional sentence converted offender from short term to long term prisoner

C pleaded guilty to being knowingly concerned in the fraudulent evasion of the prohibition on the importation of a controlled drug, cannabis resin. He was involved in the importation of 36 kilogrammes of cannabis concealed in a motor car. A few weeks after his arrest he was granted bail and absconded to Spain. He remained at large for almost two years. C was sentenced to 42 months' imprisonment for the cannabis offence, with six months, to run consecutively, for the bail offence. It was argued that the effect of making the sentence for the bail offence run consecutively to the principal sentence was to make C a "long term prisoner" and thus subject to the possibility of serving a larger proportion of the sentence in custody.

Held, substituting a three month sentence for the bail offence. *R. v. Waite (Glen Anthony)* (1992) 13 Cr. App. R. (S.) 26, [1992] C.L.Y. 1157 illustrated the principle that it might be unjust to impose a short consecutive sentence, if the effect would be to place an offender in a different category so that he would have to serve a sentence out of all proportion to the additional short sentence. The effect of the consecutive sentence for breach of bail was to subject C to the possibility of serving an additional 11 months in custody. If the judge's attention had been drawn to *Waite*, he might have taken a different view, even though the six months was otherwise unobjectionable.

R. v. COZENS (ALAN WILLIAM) [1996] 2 Cr. App. R. (S.) 321, Hyam, J., CA (Crim Div).

1476. Consecutive sentences–calculation of non parole release date–aggregation of sentences

[Criminal Justice Act 1991 s.33, s.51 (2).]

F, sentenced in 1993 to consecutive terms totalling 19 months' imprisonment and in 1994 to two more terms of four years, to run concurrently inter se but consecutively with the original sentence, applied for judicial review to challenge the assessment of his non parole release date by the prison authorities. The question at issue was whether the imposition of the consecutive sentence of four years had the effect of increasing the time F was required to serve under the original sentence, and specifically whether, for the purposes of the Criminal Justice Act 1991 s.33, F remained a short term prisoner, ie. one serving less than four years, so that he was only required to serve half of the original sentence, or whether s.51 (2) of the Act rendered the original sentence part of a long term sentence, so that he was required to serve two thirds of the cumulative sentence.

Held, refusing the application, that s.51 (2) required consecutive terms to be treated as a single term, regardless of whether they were imposed by a different court on a different occasion, *R. v. Governor of Brockhill Prison, ex p. Evans* [1997] Q.B. 443, [1996] 1 C.L.Y. 1740 applied. There was no justification for the contention that the conclusion in *Brockhill* was obiter or that s.51 (2) referred only to sentences imposed on the same occasion.

R. v. SECRETARY OF STATE FOR THE HOME DEPARTMENT, *ex p.* FRANCOIS; *sub nom.* R. v. GOVERNOR OF SWALEDALE PRISON, *ex p.* FRANCOIS, *The Times*, April 30, 1997, Simon Brown, L.J., QBD.

1477. Consecutive sentences–new offence committed while on licence– reactivated part of original sentence and sentence imposed in respect of new offence formed single term of imprisonment

[Criminal Justice Act 1991 s.40 (4), s.51 (2).]

W was convicted of burglary while on licence from a previous sentence and was ordered to return to prison for 16 months of his unserved sentence pursuant to the Criminal Justice Act 1991 s.40, to be followed by a sentence of three years and 11 months' imprisonment for the burglary. W applied for judicial review of the Secretary of State's decision to treat him as a long term prisoner on the grounds that s.51 (2) of the Act, which stated that consecutive sentences were to be treated as a single term, did not apply to s.40, as there was no provision in the latter to order a reactivated sentence to run consecutively to a new sentence. W argued that each sentence had to be viewed separately and thus he fell to be treated as a short term prisoner with regard to each term.

Held, dismissing the application, that as s.40(4)(a) stated that an order made under s.40 was a sentence of imprisonment for the purposes of Part II of the Act, which included s.51(2), an order for return formed a single term with the new sentence regardless of whether it was to be served prior to or concurrently with the new sentence.

R. v. SECRETARY OF STATE FOR THE HOME DEPARTMENT, *ex p.* WALKER, *The Times*, September 2, 1997, Rose, L.J., QBD.

1478. Consecutive sentences–overlapping sentences–calculation of release date for short term prisoner

[Supreme Court Act 1981 s.47(2); Criminal Justice Act 1991.]

D was due for release from prison, after having served almost half of a nine months sentence for dangerous driving, when he was sentenced to a further 10 months' imprisonment for burglary. However, D was released from prison the following day on the ground that he had already served 72 days in custody and a further 32 days on remand. The judge subsequently resentenced D under the Supreme Court Act 1981 s.47(2) to eight months' imprisonment so as to give effect to his original intention of imposing a consecutive sentence. D appealed.

Held, allowing the appeal, that the failure of the judge to state that the 10 month sentence was to be consecutive to the nine month sentence meant that D was correctly released after having spent 104 days in custody. Sentences imposed concurrently should, for the purposes of determining a prisoner's release under the Criminal Justice Act 1991, be treated as a single term subject to any period already served, *R. v. Governor of Brockhill Prison, ex p. Evans* [1997] Q.B. 443, [1996] 1 C.L.Y. 1740 and *R. v. Secretary of State for the Home Department, ex p. Francois* [1997] C.L.Y 1476 considered. The judge was wrong to increase D's sentence merely because he felt his original sentence to be inadequate. Accordingly, the eight month sentence was reduced to seven months to allow for the immediate release of D.

R. v. DAVIES (GWYN GEORGE), Trans. Ref: 97/3781/Y3, July 10, 1997, Collins, J., CA (Crim Div).

1479. Consecutive sentences–parole–consecutive sentences and unexpired licence period

[Criminal Justice Act 1991 s.40.]

SP, aged 30, appealed against conviction of arson and applied for leave to appeal against sentence of 12 months' imprisonment. It was ordered that he serve six months' imprisonment for the arson offence, consecutive to 12 months, as the unexpired portion of an earlier parole licence period. The incident occurred after SP and his former wife visited a public house where there was a confrontation between SP and another customer. SP's wife, who divorced him before the trial, gave evidence for the Crown that he had later set fire to the publican's car, but SP claimed that his wife was responsible for the arson attack. The grounds of appeal were that there was no direct evidence of arson and the jury should not have been directed that they could convict on the basis of joint venture.

Held, dismissing the appeal against conviction, but allowing the application for leave to appeal against sentence, that (1) the circumstantial evidence was sufficient for the jury to convict SP as the arsonist. The jury was correctly directed on the matter of joint enterprise and clearly warned about the implication of the wife giving evidence and (2) with regard to sentence, the Criminal Justice Act 1991 s.40 provided that the unexpired portion of the parole licence term must be expressed as preceding and being followed consecutively by the sentence for the index offence. It cannot be expressed to run consecutively to the sentence for the index offence. In this case, the error as to form can be remedied by expressing the sentence in terms that the six months representing the unexpired parole licence period should be served first and followed by 12 months for the arson offence.

R. v. ST PIERRE (SHANE),Trans. Ref: 9602502/W4, October 11, 1996, Ognall, J., CA (Crim Div).

1480. Consecutive sentences–totality–handling stolen goods–ringing motor cars

S pleaded guilty to conspiring to handle stolen motor cars and was sentenced to two and a half years' imprisonment, consecutive to a sentence of two years imposed a few months earlier for similar offences. S was concerned in ringing seven cars and helping them to be resold.

Held, allowing the appeal, that considering *R. v. Millen* (1980) 2 Cr. App. R. (S.) 357, which illustrated the principle that while it might be appropriate to pass a sentence to run consecutively to an existing sentence, particularly when the second offence had been committed while the offender was on bail in respect of the first offence, the sentencer must have regard to the totality of the sentence which the offender would have to serve. If the two matters had been dealt with on the same occasion, it was unlikely that a total sentence of four and a half years' imprisonment would have been imposed. Although the sentence of two and a half years was fully justified for the conspiracy, the totality was disproportionate and excessive. The appropriate total sentence for the two matters would have been three and a half years. The sentence would be reduced to 18 months, to run consecutively to the earlier sentence.

R. v. STEVENS (ALAN) [1997] 2 Cr. App. R. (S.) 180, Hobhouse, L.J., CA (Crim Div).

1481. Conspiracy–assisting prisoners to escape–smuggling pistol into prison

B was convicted of conspiracy to assist prisoners to escape. He was serving a sentence of imprisonment, from which he had escaped on two previous occasions. Three persons who were not prisoners conspired to smuggle into the prison a double barrelled pistol and ammunition, for the use of B and another prisoner. B was sentenced to seven years' imprisonment, consecutive to terms totalling 14 and a half years which he was already serving.

Held, dismissing the appeal, that it was difficult to imagine a graver example of this particular crime, and a sentence closer to the maximum term of 10 years would have been justified. Smuggling into prison a lethal weapon with a view to freeing two dangerous and resourceful criminals was a grave offence. The sentence of seven years was not excessive and had to be imposed consecutively to the other sentences.

R. v. BOWMAN (SIMON JOHN) [1997] 1 Cr. App. R. (S.) 282, Simon Brown, L.J., CA (Crim Div).

1482. Conspiracy–assisting prisoners to escape–smuggling pistol into prison–suspended sentence in exceptional circumstances

[Criminal Justice Act 1991 s.5(1).]

A was sentenced to 12 months' imprisonment after pleading guilty to conspiring to assist prisoners to escape. He conspired with two others to smuggle a handgun into prison, to facilitate the escape of two prisoners serving long sentences. He agreed to join in the conspiracy only after his life was threatened. He smuggled the barrels of a pistol into a prison, and handed them over to one of the prisoners. He avoided taking part in a second visit, in the course of which the other conspirators were arrested. The parts of the gun were found following a search of the prison. A subsequently admitted his part in the conspiracy and gave evidence for the prosecution against the other conspirators (one of whom pleaded guilty).

Held, allowing the appeal and suspending the sentence, that the court accepted that A had not been a willing participant in the conspiracy and that he had given evidence and maintained in the face of cross-examination, a true account of the conspiracy, and as such he had placed himself at great risk. The court was in no doubt that the case was "exceptional" for the purposes of the Criminal Justice Act 1991 s.5(1). He could be compared to a supergrass, but unlike most supergrasses had committed one isolated offence under intimidation.

R. v. ARMSTRONG (DAVID CURTIS) [1997] 1 Cr. App. R. (S.) 255, Simon Brown, L.J., CA (Crim Div).

1483. Conspiracy–attempted large scale fraud–account taken of degree of involvement–discount for late guilty plea

K and his codefendants M and H appealed against sentence. K was sentenced to five years, M to five years and H to two years suspended for two years and a fine of £50,000 with £10,000 costs. The conspiracy involved the bribery of British Telecom employees in order to obtain access to telephone lines passing from bank cash machines to the banks' mainframe computers. The lines were tapped and information relating to customers' cards downloaded to a computer to be transferred onto blank plastic cards. K contended that he had been wrongly considered as a principal, that he had no technical expertise and had not been involved in the suborning of the British Telecom staff. K further claimed that he should be entitled to a substantial discount for his guilty plea despite the fact that it had been received late and only after the failure of his attempt to deny admission of the evidence of a serving prisoner turned paid informant. M contended that the totality of his sentence, made consecutive to a term of three years for a similar offence, was too high. H appealed against the scale of the fine.

Held, allowing the appeals in part, reducing the custodial terms of five years to four years in each case, but not reducing the fine, that the scale of financial penalty was entirely appropriate given the scale of the offence and H's means. It appeared the trial judge had misinterpreted K's position in the hierarchy of the conspiracy, but there had been plenty of opportunity for K to plead guilty. M had been on bail for a similar offence when he committed the offence, but in view of the totality a reduction was appropriate, *R. v. Buffrey (Paul Edward)* (1993) 14 Cr. App. R. (S.) 511, [1994] C.L.Y. 1267 considered.

R. v. KIDD (PAUL ANTHONY); R. v. MOORE (GRAHAM HARRY); R. v. HAWARD (WILLIAM ALFRED), Trans. Ref: 9700234 Y4, 9700314 Y4, 9700397 Y4, July 3, 1997, Mance, J., CA (Crim Div).

1484. Contempt of court–witnesses–refusal to give evidence

C was sentenced to four months' imprisonment after admitting contempt of court. Whilst serving a sentence of imprisonment for an unrelated matter, he was called as a prosecution witness at the trial of three men charged with affray and in one case intimidation of a witness. He went into the witness box but declined to give any evidence, saying that threats had been made against his life and his family. The jury was discharged, and eventually the three men pleaded guilty to using threatening words and behaviour. C's sentence was consecutive to the sentence he was already serving.

Held, dismissing the appeal, that although there was other evidence available in the case, C's evidence was important in relation to the gravity of the offence being tried, a serious and potentially dangerous incident involving the use of a firearm. C's failure to give evidence resulted in the discharge of the jury. He was in a vulnerable position as he was in prison, but this was a serious contempt in the course of an important trial on a serious matter, and it had a terminal effect on the trial. The sentence of four months' imprisonment was entirely appropriate, *R. v. Montgomery (James)* [1995] 2 All E.R. 28, [1995] 2 C.L.Y. 3961 cited.

R. v. COLE (ANTHONY) [1997] 1 Cr. App. R. (S.) 228, Maurice Kay, J., CA (Crim Div).

1485. Contempt of court–witnesses–threatening witness

S appealed against a sentence of 12 months' imprisonment, on conviction for contempt of court. He was due to stand trial in the Crown Court for theft from a supermarket. The only prosecution witness was the manager of the supermarket. S spoke to the witness in the court waiting room and referred to damage which had been done to the witness's car, and said, "that was just a warning", and "I'll do you when I see you".

Held, dismissing the appeal, that the problem of protecting witnesses had become more severe in recent years and the sentence of 12 months' imprisonment was entirely appropriate, *R. v. Maloney* (1986) 8 Cr. App. R. (S.) 123, [1987] C.L.Y. 902 and *R. v. Bashir and Azam* (1988) 10 Cr. App. R. (S.) 76, [1990] C.L.Y. 1265 considered.

R. v. STREDDER (NICHOLAS MICHAEL) [1997] 1 Cr. App. R. (S.) 209, Maurice Kay, J., CA (Crim Div).

1486. Copyright offences—distributing infringing articles

See COPYRIGHT: R. v. Lewis (Christopher). §1052

1487. Copyright offences—making infringing copy of computer programs

See COPYRIGHT: R. v. Lloyd (Grant Oaten). §1053

1488. Corruption—police officer disclosed confidential information and destroyed surveillance logs for payment

D pleaded guilty to four counts of corruption. D was a detective constable serving in a Regional Crime Squad. He accepted various sums from a man who was the subject of criminal proceedings to disclose confidential information about the inquiry and to destroy surveillance logs. D had agreed to accept about £50,000 and had actually received about £18,500. He sought leave to appeal against sentence of a total of 11 years' imprisonment.

Held, refusing the application, that the sentence was severe but not manifestly excessive.

R. v. DONALD (JOHN ANDREW) [1997] 2 Cr. App. R. (S.) 272, Lord Bingham of Cornhill, L.C.J., CA (Crim Div).

1489. Crime (Sentences) Act 1997 (c.43)

This Act introduces a mandatory life sentence for a person convicted of a second serious offence unless there are exceptional circumstances. A person convicted of a third class A drug trafficking offence shall be sentenced to a minimum of seven years, and a person convicted of a third domestic burglary shall be sentenced to a minimum of three years unless there are exceptional circumstances. Provision is also made in relation to early release, additional days, supervision after release and release of life prisoners on licence.

This Act received Royal Assent on March 21, 1997.

1490. Crime (Sentences) Act 1997 (c.43)—Commencement No.1 Order

CRIME (SENTENCES) ACT 1997 (COMMENCEMENT) (NO.1) ORDER 1997, SI 1997 1581 (C.64); made under the Crime (Sentences) Act 1997 s.57. Commencement details: bringing into force various provisions of the Act on June 25, 1997; £0.65.

This Order brings into force the Crime (Sentences) Act 1997 Sch.1 para.14 and Sch.1 para.19.

1491. Crime (Sentences) Act 1997 (c.43)—Commencement No.2 Order

CRIME (SENTENCES) ACT 1997 (COMMENCEMENT NO.2 AND TRANSITIONAL PROVISIONS) ORDER 1997, SI 1997 2200 (C.87); made under the Crime (Sentences) Act 1997 s.57. Commencement details: bringing into force various provisions of the Act on October 1, 1997, January 1, 1998 and March 1, 1998; £1.10.

This Order brings into force various provisions of the Crime (Sentences) Act 1997.

1492. Criminal charges–specimen charges–court only empowered to sentence on indicted offences

[Criminal Justice Act 1991 s.1, s.2.]

The appeals of C, K and S were heard together since they raised a common question, namely, where conviction was obtained on the basis of specimen charges, whether it was legitimate to pass an increased sentence to take into account other offences that had not been admitted nor taken into consideration and were not the subject of charges in the indictment. C was charged with damaging property, intimidating a witness, two offences of assault occasioning actual bodily harm and wounding with intent. C had conducted a campaign of harassment in order to prevent his victims from giving evidence against an acquaintance, who was on trial for armed robbery of the victims' shop. C contended that not only was the sentence of 12 months for damage to property unlawful, but that he had also been sentenced on the express basis that he had repeatedly gone to the shop. K was a primary school headmaster who appealed against conviction on four specimen counts of indecent assault of pupils and against custodial sentences of 15 months and three concurrent terms of 12 months each. S, aged 73, was convicted on eight specimen counts of indecent assault involving six victims aged from five to 14, for which he was sentenced to a total of eight years and one specimen rape for which he received a concurrent term of 12 years and appealed against sentence.

Held, allowing the appeals against sentence, that the practice of sentencing for offences that had neither been admitted nor proved by verdict was incorrect, contrary to fundamental principle, and inconsistent with the Criminal Justice Act 1991 s.1 and s.2, *R. v. Clark (Raymond Dennis)* [1996] 2 Cr. App. R. (S.) 351, [1996] 1 C.L.Y. 1944 approved *R. v. Bradshaw (Neil)* [1997] 2 Cr. App. (S) 128, [1997] C.L.Y 1493, *R. v. Barry (John James)* (Unreported, 1996) disapproved, and *R. v. Hutchison* [1972] 1 W.L.R. 398, [1972] C.L.Y. 636 followed. C's submissions were well founded. The sentence for damage to property would be reduced to three months and that for intimidating a witness to 12 months. The grounds for K's appeal against conviction were dismissed, but, notwithstanding the fact that the trial judge had erred by treating the counts as specimen charges, the sentence of 15 months was appropriate considering K's abuse of his position of trust and authority. In the case of S, the trial judge had correctly sentenced for the single offences on the basis of *Clark*, but, considering the circumstances of the offences and S's pitiful medical condition, the sentence for rape was excessive and a term of eight years was substituted.

R. v. KIDD (PHILIP RICHARD); R. v. CANAVAN (DARREN ANTHONY); R. v. SHAW (DENNIS), *The Times*, July 21, 1997, Lord Bingham of Cornhill, L.C.J., CA (Crim Div).

1493. Criminal charges–specimen charges–theft

[Criminal Justice Act 1991 s.2 (2), s.3 (3).]

B was convicted of five counts of theft and sentenced to a total of six years' imprisonment and disqualified as a director for 10 years. B set up an investment company in 1982. The company solicited funds from the public for investment in real property through another company which was a wholly owned subsidiary of a company of which B was a director. The prosecution case was that the money received from investors was not fully secured or invested, but passed through other companies and used for the benefit of B and his family, or to repay maturing bonds of other investors. Eventually one of the companies ceased to trade owing more than £3 million to over 400 investors. B was extradited from the USA on two charges of conspiracy and 138 individual charges of theft. It was later found that the extradition on the conspiracy charges was invalid and B was tried on five counts of theft, separately from his accomplices, who were tried for conspiracy. The charges on which B was convicted each involved a specific sum received from a specific investor. The total amount involved in all of the counts was £97,000. B did not give evidence. B argued that the sentencer was not entitled to pass sentence on the basis that the offences formed part of a fraud involving £3 million; even though the five counts were said to be specimen counts, the sentencer's powers were confined to sentencing for the theft of £97,000 at the appropriate scale. If the prosecution had chosen to "under prosecute" by charging five thefts instead of 138, the sentencer could not make up that deficiency.

Held, appeal allowed in part, that (1) the counts as presented in the indictment were plainly specimen counts and evidence of the other investors and their losses was put before the court, *R. v. Clark (Raymond Dennis)* [1996] 2 Cr. App. R. (S.) 351, [1996] 1 C.L.Y. 1944 distinguished; (2) the court was not required to limit sentence to the five transactions in view of the provisions of the Criminal Justice Act 1991 s.2(2) for the sentence to be commensurate with the seriousness of the offence and offences associated with it. The five offences were associated offences and s.3(3)(a) required the court to take into account all information about the circumstances of the offence and associated offences to determine seriousness. In this case the scale of offending was apparent from its presentation and the verdicts and the court was entitled to sentence on the basis that the offences were part of a fraud committed against many victims who lost a large sum of money in total. Thus, six years was appropriate in this case, and (3) sentence would be reduced by six months to take into account time spent in custody in the USA awaiting extradition.

R. v. BRADSHAW (NEIL) [1997] 2 Cr. App. R. (S.) 128, Pill, L.J., CA (Crim Div).

1494. Criminal damage—recklessness as to endanger life—dangerous driving—car driven into magistrates court building

D, aged 31, pleaded guilty to damaging property being reckless as to whether life was endangered and to dangerous driving. He was sentenced to four years' and six months' imprisonment concurrent and was disqualified from driving for five years. He appealed against sentence. The instant offences arose after D had pleaded guilty to four motoring offences and justices had imposed an interim period of disqualification. D drove his car through the glass fronted doors of the court building, at a speed estimated as up to 40 mph, demolishing the reception desk. £34,000 damage was caused. A psychiatric report indicated that D had a significant personality difficulty when interacting with those in authority and there was a danger of similar incidents in the future.

Held, dismissing the appeal, that the sentence was entirely justified. The judge was entitled to conclude that D was a danger when behind the wheel of a car, given that he had never passed a driving test yet drove unsupervised. Lives had been put at risk and this was an attack directed at an institution of justice. In the circumstances there could be little discount for a plea of guilty.

R. v. DODD (DAVID JOHN) [1997] 1 Cr. App. R. (S.) 127, Judge Beaumont Q.C., CA (Crim Div).

1495. Death penalty—non capital murder—Jamaica

See CRIMINAL PROCEDURE: Williams (Kervin) v. Queen, The. §1336

1496. Deception—goods supplied by mail order with false description—course of conduct over two and a half years—fraud against public involving low value goods

B appealed against a sentence of nine months' imprisonment concurrent for four counts of applying false trade descriptions to goods and four counts of supplying goods to which false trade descriptions applied. Over a two and a half year period B had supplied vehicle entry tools via mail order. These were described as "skeleton keys", but in reality were items known as "slim jims", the value of which had been reduced due to increasingly sophisticated car locks. The items were sold for £50 and B's total proceeds amounted to £54,000. The goods were advertised with a guarantee and prospective purchasers were assured they were skeleton keys and not slim jims. B contended that the sentence was manifestly excessive, that too much weight had been given to the low price of the items and that insufficient credit had been given for his guilty plea and previous good character.

Held, dismissing the appeal, that a custodial sentence was appropriate for this type of offence against the public, with the sentence to be determined on grounds of gravity, scale and the level of persistence involved. On the facts, a sentence of nine months' imprisonment was not excessive, based on the two and a half years course of conduct and the fact that B had continued with the offences in spite of the complaints received.

R. v. BOOTH (MALCOLM ALFRED) [1997] 1 Cr. App. R. (S.) 103, Ebsworth, J., CA (Crim Div).

1497. Deception—making misleading statements—forgery—disparate sentences

L appealed against sentences received after his conviction for two offences of knowingly making a misleading statement, two offences of recklessly making a statement and forgery for which he was sentenced to 15 months, nine months and six months respectively, the first two sentences to run concurrently and the third to run consecutively. The case concerned land close to Disneyworld in Florida for which a prospectus was issued in which the statements were made. L forged letters from banks which falsely set out the financial standing of the companies involved. The sentences of two co-defendants were reduced on appeal.

Held, allowing the appeal, that the sentences were excessive given L's guilty plea, the sentence of a co defendant and L's good character. The sentences were quashed and substituted with ones of six months' imprisonment for knowingly making a misleading statement and recklessly making a statement, to run concurrently. The sentence for forgery was substituted with one of three months to run consecutively making a total of 12 months.

R. v. LENNON (PETER CHARLES CARLTON),Trans. Ref: 97/0720/W5, May 22, 1997, Blofeld, J., CA (Crim Div).

1498. Deception—obtaining goods and services by deception—undischarged bankrupt obtaining credit and mortgage

D appealed against sentence of seven years' imprisonment, having been sentenced to six years concurrent on six counts of obtaining property by deception, one year concurrent for obtaining services by deception, and one year concurrent inter se, but consecutive to the other counts, for being a bankrupt obtaining credit. The six counts of obtaining property by deception were sample counts and referred to a series of 34 fraudulent commercial refrigeration equipment lease agreement applications with a total value of £1.3 million. The charge of obtaining services by deception referred to a mortgage taken out by D and his wife while D was a bankrupt, a fact not declared on the mortgage application. The count of obtaining credit as a bankrupt referred to two successful credit card applications, with credit limits of £750 and £500 respectively, obtained while D was an undischarged bankrupt with which he subsequently exceeded the limits imposed by the bank. D admitted the fraudulent finance deals, but said they were the result of his being in debt and denied any knowledge of the credit card restrictions. He contended that the sentence of six years' imprisonment was excessive, given the type of fraud and lack of aggravating features. D had pleaded guilty and paid back half the fraud proceeds.

Held, allowing the appeal and substituting concurrent four year sentences in place of the six year term, that the large scale nature of the fraud, leading to the loss of £560,000 by the lenders, called for a substantial prison sentence. However, while accepting the excessive nature of the six year sentence, the consecutive nature of the concurrent inter se sentence for the credit card offences was correct, *R. v. Devol (John)* (1993) 14 Cr. App. R. (S.) 407, [1994]

C.L.Y. 1316 and *R. v. Richardson (Roger Stuart)* (1993) 14 Cr. App. R. (S.) 654, [1994] C.L.Y. 1268 considered.

R. v. DE BEER (EUGENE GARRICK) [1997] 1 Cr. App. R. (S.) 97, Harrison, J., CA (Crim Div).

1499. Drug offences—drug trafficking—importation of cannabis

R and P reapplied for leave to appeal against sentences of six and 13 years' imprisonment respectively, having pleaded guilty to being knowingly concerned in the fraudulent evasion of the prohibition on the importation of cannabis resin. P bought a yacht which was then sailed to Portugal, later tracked by Customs vessels until it berthed, when it was found to contain 1,609 kilogrammes of cannabis resin, estimated to be worth in excess of £5.5 million.

Held, refusing the reapplications, that in P's case the facts were as serious as any that could be imagined. P had little scope to contest the charge as he was caught in possession of a large quantity of cannabis and the maximum reductions for a guilty plea had been given at first instance. The appropriate discount had also been given for R's more limited role and his acceptance of responsibility, *R. v. Richardson* (1994) 15 Cr. App. R. (S.) 876, [1995] 1 C.L.Y. 1363 considered.

R. v. ROYLE (GARY); R. v. POLLITT (STEPHEN) [1997] 1 Cr. App. R. (S.) 184, Lord Bingham of Cornhill, L.C.J., CA (Crim Div).

1500. Drug offences—drug trafficking—importation of cannabis—drugs for personal use

A pleaded guilty before a magistrates court to importing 1,100 grammes of herbal cannabis and 20 grammes of cannabis resin and was committed to the Crown Court for sentence. A's car was searched in connection with other matters and the cannabis was found. It was accepted that the cannabis was intended solely for personal use. He was sentenced to nine months' imprisonment.

Held, allowing the appeal, that the length of the sentence was excessive; a sentence of three months' imprisonment would be substituted, *R. v. Elder (Howard Alfred) and Pyle (Terry Christopher)* (1994) 15 Cr. App. R. (S.) 514, [1995] 1 C.L.Y. 1360 considered.

R. v. ASTBURY (MICHAEL) [1997] 2 Cr. App. R. (S.) 93, Judge Martin Tucker Q.C., CA (Crim Div).

1501. Drug offences—drug trafficking—importation of cannabis—offenders not at top of criminal organisation

F and others appealed against sentence after being found guilty to being knowingly concerned in the fraudulent evasion of the prohibition on the importation of a controlled drug, cannabis resin. They were concerned in the importation of four metric tonnes of cannabis in a fishing boat to which the cannabis had been transferred at sea from another vessel. The value of the cannabis was approximately £13 million. Four offenders who were found to have been involved in the organisation of the scheme were sentenced to 12 and a half years' imprisonment and F who was the owner of the fishing boat was sentenced to seven years.

Held, dismissing F's appeal but allowing the others, that the court had to start with the maximum penalty established by Parliament for the offence, 14 years, which was reserved for the very worst examples of the crime. The present offence was close to that, but it had to be assumed that the offenders were not at the very top of the organisation. A sentence of 14 years was not the proper starting point for these offenders, a proper starting point would have been in the region of 10 to 12 years. They were also entitled to a substantial discount for their pleas, even though the evidence against them was strong. The sentences of 12 and a half years were reduced to nine years in each case. The judge had given F too great a discount in his original sentence and his sentence was not reduced.

R. v. FISHLEIGH (RICHARD) [1996] 2 Cr. App. R. (S.) 283, Schiemann, L.J., CA (Crim Div).

1502. Drug offences–drug trafficking–importation of Ecstasy

M and J, appealed against sentences of 24 years' imprisonment imposed in respect of offences concerning importation and supply of over 295 kilogrammes of Ecstasy, in excess of 1.3 million tablets, and confiscation orders of £313,817. The appellants submitted that the sentence was excessive given the particular circumstances of the case and the health of J.

Held, dismissing the appeals, that the sentences of 24 years properly reflected the responsibility of the two appellants in the conspiracy and there was no justification for interfering with the sentence. Although J was not in good health his condition was being properly treated in prison.

R. v. MAIN (RONALD ALAN); R. v. JOHNSON (RONALD WILLIAM) [1997] 2 Cr. App. R. (S.) 63, Latham, J., CA (Crim Div).

1503. Drug offences–drug trafficking–importation of heroin–entrapment

T, the second defendant, pleaded guilty to two counts of being knowingly concerned in the fraudulent evasion of the prohibition on the exportation of heroin and one count of conspiring fraudulently to evade the prohibition on the importation of heroin. M was convicted of conspiring fraudulently to evade the prohibition on the importation of heroin. M was involved in an arrangement by which heroin would be exported to the United States in exchange for cocaine. Two small samples of heroin were sent by post to an American who was an informant of the Drug Enforcement Agency. Subsequently, T arranged for a large quantity of heroin to be imported into the UK. M arrived by car ferry driving a vehicle towing a horse box which was found to contain approximately 90 kilogrammes of 65 per cent heroin. He denied any knowledge of the contents of the horse box. T was sentenced to a total of 25 years' imprisonment, with five years for the exportation offences and 20 years consecutive for importation and a confiscation order in the amount of £3,458,806, with 10 years' imprisonment in default, and M was sentenced to 20 years' imprisonment.

Held, allowing the appeals, that in a genuine case of entrapment the court would make some reduction in the sentence for that feature, and the reduction would be greater if the entrapment had made the offender commit an offence out of the category that he would otherwise have committed. In the case of international drug trafficking, however, the reduction would be very small. A reduction of one year was made in the sentences passed on T on the counts relating to exportation of heroin. In relation to the sentence of 20 years for the importation of heroin, T had been acting at a very high level, but in the light of *R. v. Richardson* (1994) 15 Cr. App. R. (S.) 876, [1995] 1 C.L.Y. 1367 the sentence of 20 years was manifestly excessive and a sentence of 18 years was substituted. In relation to the default term of 10 years, the sentencer should exercise his discretion to fix a default term within the maximum allowed, but a 10 year term in default was too high and a term of eight years was substituted. The sentence on M, who had played a lesser part, was reduced to 16 years, *R. v. Beaumont* (1987) 9 Cr. App. R. (S.) 342, [1989] C.L.Y. 993, *R. v. Chapman and Denton* (1989) 11 Cr. App. R. (S.) 222, [1991] C.L.Y. 1112, *R. v. Bigley* (1993) 14 Cr. App. R. (S.) 201, [1994] C.L.Y. 1251, *R. v. Smurthwaite and Gill* (1994) 98 Cr. App. R. (S.) 43, [1994] C.L.Y. 669, *R. v. Latif and Shazhad* (1994) 15 Cr. App. R. (S.) 864, [1995] 1 C.L.Y. 1362, and *R. v. French* (1995) 16 Cr. App. R. (S.) 841, [1996] 1 C.L.Y. 1868 considered.

R. v. MIDDELKOOP (MARTIN); R. v. TELLI (DAVID) [1997] 1 Cr. App. R. (S.) 423, Gage, J., CA (Crim Div).

1504. Drug offences–drug trafficking–lenient sentence in country of destination irrelevant

[Misuse of Drugs Act 1971; Criminal Justice (International Co-operation) Act 1990 s.19(2).]

M appealed against a sentence of imprisonment of nine years on conviction of being knowingly concerned in the carrying of a Class B drug on a ship contrary to the Criminal Justice (International Co-operation) Act 1990 s.19(2). M, aged 53 and of previous good character, had been arrested in international waters off Newcastle upon Tyne, bound for Holland, carrying 1,850 kilogrammes of cannabis resin, with an estimated street value in the UK of £5.5 million. M contended that the offence was different from that charged under the Misuse of Drugs Act 1971, and the English court should have had regard to the fact that the maximum sentence of imprisonment in Holland was only four years.

Held, dismissing the appeal, that the sentence was appropriate. The trial judge had been correct to ignore the likely sentence in Holland. Although it was accepted, for sentencing purposes, that the destination of the drugs was Holland, it could not be certain, *R. v. Faulkner* (1976) 63 Cr. App. R. 295, [1977] C.L.Y. 651 and *R. v. Lillie (Gavin)* (1995) 16 Cr. App. R. (S.) 534, [1994] C.L.Y. 1253 considered.

R. v. MAGUIRE (BRIAN MICHAEL) [1997] 1 Cr. App. R. (S.) 130, Swinton Thomas, L.J., CA (Crim Div).

1505. Drug offences–non commercial production and supply of cannabis

B pleaded guilty to one offence of obtaining cannabis with intent to supply and two of producing cannabis. Police officers searching a house to which B had access found an elaborate arrangement for the production of cannabis, with 67 plants growing. A further eight cannabis plants were found at B's own address. B appealed against sentence of two years' imprisonment.

Held, allowing the appeal, that it was accepted that B intended to supply the cannabis, although not on a commercial basis, and that he had a previous conviction for possessing cannabis with intent to supply, *R. v. Proud* (1987) 9 Cr. App. R. (S.) 119, [1989] C.L.Y. 971 and *R. v. Marsland (Anthony John)* (1994) 15 Cr. App. R. (S.) 665, [1995] 1 C.L.Y. 1359 distinguished. However, the sentence of two years was too long and a sentence of 12 months would be substituted.

R. v. BLACKHAM (BRIAN FRANCIS) [1997] 2 Cr. App. R. (S.) 275, Mitchell, J., CA (Crim Div).

1506. Drug offences–permitting premises to be used for supply of Class A drug–no profit from use of premises

B, aged 44, appealed against concurrent sentences of imprisonment of four years for permitting premises to be used for the supplying of a Class A drug, namely crack cocaine, six months for simple possession of crack cocaine, and three months for permitting his flat to be used for the purposes of habitual prostitution.

Held, allowing the appeal in part, that a two year sentence was substituted for the four year sentence which was excessive considering that it was based solely on B's unspecific admissions, *R. v. Gregory (Jack Robert)* (1993) 14 Cr. App. R. (S.) 403, [1994] C.L.Y. 1239 applied, and that B was doing nothing to corrupt or encourage those using his property or profiting thereby.

R. v. BRADLEY (ANDREW) [1997] 1 Cr. App. R. (S.) 59, Holland, J., CA (Crim Div).

1507. Drug offences–possession of amphetamines with intent to supply–suspended sentence justified by ill health

[Powers of Criminal Courts Act 1973 s.22(3); Criminal Justice Act 1991 s.5.]

O appealed against a sentence of imprisonment of 18 months on a guilty plea to possession, with intent to supply, of 209.6 grammes of amphetamine sulphate of eight per cent purity. O contended that considering that he was suffering from a life threatening medical condition as a result of a bullet having lodged in his neck after he had been shot six times, he had no previous drug convictions and offered no risk to the public, a suspended sentence was appropriate.

Held, allowing the appeal, that the term was suspended for two years. The medical condition was just sufficiently exceptional to justify the suspension of the sentence, pursuant to the Powers of Criminal Courts Act 1973 s.22(3) as substituted by the Criminal Justice Act 1991 s.5.

R. v. OLIVER (DEAN) [1997] 1 Cr. App. R. (S.) 125, Judge Beaumont Q.C., CA (Crim Div).

1508. Drug offences–possession of LSD with intent to supply–sentencing guidelines for cases involving LSD

[Misuse of Drugs Act 1971 s.4(1).]

H pleaded guilty to possession of a Class A drug, LSD, with intent to supply contrary to the Misuse of Drugs Act 1971 s.4(1). The total estimated value of the drug was in excess of £1,000,000 and the LSD impregnated sheets were divisible into 280,000 units, each with an average LSD content of 31 micrograms. H appealed against a sentence of 14 years' imprisonment and the Court of Appeal was requested to give sentencing guidelines for cases involving LSD.

Held, allowing the appeal, that a sentence of 10 years or more would be correct in cases involving 25,000 or more units of LSD, whereas a sentence of 14 years or more would ordinarily be appropriate for cases involving 250,000 or more units, assuming that each unit contained approximately 50 micrograms of pure LSD. However, the guidelines were not intended to be applied rigidly and a degree of variability would be afforded in individual cases where good reason was given or where the LSD content varied significantly from 50 micrograms per unit. In the instant case, a sentence of 12 or 13 years' imprisonment would normally have been appropriate, but as H had pleaded guilty, a sentence of 10 years' imprisonment would be substituted.

R. v. HURLEY (JOSEPH ROBERT), *The Times*, August 5, 1997, Lord Bingham of Cornhill, L.C.J., CA (Crim Div).

1509. Drug offences–possession with intent to supply–non commercial "cooperative"

C appealed against sentence of three and a half years' imprisonment on conviction on three counts of possession with intent to supply 28 Ecstasy tablets, 82 milligrammes of paste with an amphetamine content of 14 per cent and 3.51 grammes of powder with an amphetamine purity of 4 per cent. C's guilty plea was entered on the basis that he was part of a "cooperative", involved in the purchase and distribution of drugs for no commercial gain. C contended that the sentence was manifestly excessive given his guilty plea and that the term imposed was more consistent with a commercial, as opposed to a social, supply.

Held, allowing the appeal and reducing the term from three and a half to two and a half years' imprisonment, that taking account of C's previous record, which although it did not contain any drug offences was not good, there was a clear distinction between the type of bulk buying for friends in the circumstances in which C had been arrested and where drugs were smuggled into discotheques by a "minder" on behalf of others, *R. v. Byrne* [1996] 2 Cr. App. R.(S.) 34, [1996] 1 C.L.Y. 1849, *R. v. Spalding* (1995) 16 Cr. App. R. (S.) 803, [1996] 1 C.L.Y. 1856 and *R. v. Paparella* [1996] 2 Cr. App. R. (S.) 165, [1996] 1 C.L.Y. 1859 considered.

R. v. COX (SHAUN CARL), Trans. Ref: 96/7674/X3, April 28, 1997, Judge Beaumont Q.C., CA (Crim Div).

1510. Drug offences–possession with intent to supply cannabis

N was convicted of possessing cannabis with intent to supply and was sentenced to seven years' imprisonment. N was stopped while driving his car, which was found to contain 94 kilogrammes of cannabis resin in 24 packages. It was accepted that N was acting as a courier.

Held, allowing the appeal, that the sentence of seven years' imprisonment was too high; a sentence of five years would be substituted, *R. v. Aramah* (1982) 4 Cr. App. R. (S.) 407, [1983] C.L.Y. 764 considered.

R. v. NETTS (ALAN FRANK) [1997] 2 Cr. App. R. (S.) 117, Keene, J., CA (Crim Div).

1511. Drug offences–possession with intent to supply cocaine–disparate sentences

F appealed against concurrent sentences of imprisonment of seven years and three years on conviction of possession with intent to supply, of 44 grammes of crack cocaine, with an estimated street value of £4,500, and 210.7 grammes of cannabis resin, with an estimated street value of £1,500. F contended that the total sentence was excessive for the unsophisticated nature of the offences and that the sentences were disparate to those received by P, his co-accused girlfriend, who had received only half his sentence, despite her previous conviction for a similar offence.

Held, allowing the appeal in part, that a term of five years was substituted for the seven year term. The terms were appropriate, but the allowance for P's family responsibilities had been too great and, therefore, F was justified in a feeling of grievance at the disparity, *R. v. Fawcett* (1983) 5 Cr. App. R. (S.) 158, [1984] C.L.Y. 836 considered.

R. v. FRANKSON (ANDREW); *sub nom.* R. v. McCOLLINS (ANDREW) [1996] 2 Cr. App. R. (S.) 366, Auld, L.J., CA (Crim Div).

1512. Drug offences–production of cannabis–intent to supply on non commercial basis–disparate sentences

C, aged 46, appealed against sentences of five years' imprisonment for producing a Class B controlled drug, namely cannabis plants (count 1); two months' imprisonment concurrent for possession of cannabis plants (count 2) and five years' imprisonment concurrent for possession of a controlled Class B drug with intent to supply (count 3). Of the two co-accused, one was fined £1,000 for being concerned in the production of, and allowing premises to be used for producing, a controlled drug and the other fined £500 for allowing premises to be used. C was a lodger at the home of a married couple, the two co-accused. An agreement was reached between C and H that cannabis plants would be cultivated and the profits shared for personal use. W acquiesced. The grounds of appeal were that the sentence was too high as the possession with intent to supply was on a non-commercial basis and that there was disparity between C's sentence and that of his co-accused.

Held, allowing the appeal, that the correct sentence was two years' imprisonment concurrent for counts 1 and 3, and the sentence of five years would be quashed, *R. v. Aramah* (1982) 4 Cr. App. R. (S.) 407, [1983] C.L.Y. 764 followed; *R. v. Stearn* (1982) 4 Cr. App. R. (S.) 195, [1983] C.L.Y. 783 considered and *R. v. Snow* (1988) 10 Cr. App. R. (S.) 93, [1990] C.L.Y. 1296 considered.

R. v. CHALLIS (BARRY) [1996] 2 Cr. App. R. (S.) 425, Bennett, J., CA (Crim Div).

1513. Drug offences–production of cannabis on a commercial scale

M and H were sentenced to four years' imprisonment after pleading guilty to cultivating and possessing cannabis with intent to supply. They grew cannabis at three addresses: at one address 320 grammes of cannabis was found; at another, 800 grammes of fruiting tops were found, and at the third 19 plants and just less than one kilogramme of harvested fruiting tops were found. They admitted that they had spent about £4,000 on the equipment used in the process. The court determined, after a *Newton* hearing, that they had grown the cannabis with a view to supplying others.

Held, allowing the appeals, substituting sentences of three years, that M and H intended to produce a considerable quantity of cannabis on a commercial scale; they had lost much of the credit for their pleas by contesting a *Newton* hearing, and having regard to sentences passed in comparable cases, the sentences were too high.

R. v. MINEHAM (KEVIN); R. v. HENDERSON (STEVEN) [1997] 1 Cr. App. R. (S.) 268, McCullough, J., CA (Crim Div).

1514. Drug offences–production of cannabis on commercial scale

B and O appealed against sentences of eight years' imprisonment on conviction of conspiring to produce cannabis and conspiring to possess cannabis with intent to supply. B pleaded guilty to possessing a firearm without a certificate and possessing a firearm. Police officers searching a cottage found 534 cannabis plants being cultivated by the hydroponic system. O had lived at the cottage for about two years before the search took place. He claimed that he had bought the hydroponic equipment for an innocent purpose and that all the cannabis plants had been grown after he had left the cottage. B claimed that he had tended the plants but did not know what they were.

Held, allowing the appeals, that sentence had been passed on the basis that B and O were involved in producing cannabis on a large scale, with potential sales of half a million pounds. The production was on a large scale, but comparison with cases of importation of cannabis suggested that the sentences were too high. The appropriate sentence for O would have been six years; B had played a lesser role so his sentence should be shorter, but sentences for the firearms offences were correctly made consecutive. The sentences were reduced to a total of six years in each case, *R. v. Wright* (1993) 14 Cr. App. R. (S.) 584, *R. v. Lee* (1986) 8 Cr. App. R. (S.) 469, [1986] C.L.Y. 656, *R. v. Jeffries* (1987) 9 Cr. App. R. (S.) 497, [1990] C.L.Y. 1385, *R. v. Lyal* (1994) 16 Cr. App. R. (S.) 600, *R. v. Mitchell* (1986) 8 Cr. App. R. (S.) 472, [1988] C.L.Y. 872, *R. v. Rescorl* (1993) 14 Cr. App. R. (S.) 522, [1994] C.L.Y. 1238, *R. v. Sturt* (1992) 14 Cr. App. R. (S.) 440, [1994] C.L.Y. 1237 and *R. v. Dundas and Marshall* (1987) 9 Cr. App. R. (S.) 473, [1990] C.L.Y. 1291 considered.

R. v. BLAKE (RICHARD JOHN); R. v. OWEN (RICHARD CHARLES) [1997] 1 Cr. App. R. (S.) 394, Brooke, L.J., CA (Crim Div).

1515. Drug offences–production of cannabis on commercial scale

B pleaded guilty to producing a controlled drug, cannabis, possessing cannabis with intent to supply, and abstracting electricity and was sentenced to four years' imprisonment on each count concurrent. B acquired a substantial house and converted part of the accommodation for the production of cannabis using the hydroponic method. It was calculated that the arrangements would produce between eight and 12 kilogrammes of cannabis each year.

Held, allowing the appeal in part, that B had established a factory for the commercial production of cannabis. The sentence was a proper sentence for a sophisticated operation, *R. v. Lyall (Javinder Singh)* (1994) 16 Cr. App. R. (S.) 600 considered. The sentence for abstracting electricity would be reduced to 12 months.

R. v. BOOTH (RONALD GEORGE) [1997] 2 Cr. App. R. (S.) 67, Sir Lawrence Verney, CA (Crim Div).

1516. Drug offences–production of cannabis on commercial scale–management of premises

Held, that a sentence of four and a half years' imprisonment following a plea of guilty to being concerned in the management of premises used for the production of a Class B drug was not too long, and the offence was to be considered analogous to that of importing drugs. Due to the difficulties of importation, the cultivation of cannabis had become increasingly prevalent and deterrent sentences were required.

R. v. CHAMBERLAIN, *The Independent*, May 12, 1997 (C.S.), Stuart-Smith, L.J., CA (Crim Div).

1517. Drug offences—supply and possession of cannabis—alternative non custodial sentences rejected by defendant

[Misuse of Drugs Act 1971.]

D appealed against concurrent sentences of 12 months' imprisonment for producing a Class B controlled drug (cannabis) and possessing a Class B controlled drug (cannabis), six months for supplying a Class B controlled drug (cannabis) to another and six months for possessing a Class B controlled drug (cannabis) for which he was sentenced to six months' concurrent after pleading guilty. An order was made for the forfeiture and destruction of the drugs under the Misuse of Drugs Act 1971. D's house was searched by the police who found seeds, 13 cannabis plants and equipment for the propagation thereof. In the garden there were another 19 cannabis plants. D was searched and found to be in possession of £590. D claimed that the money belonged to his cohabitee. In all, the police recovered 360 grammes of usable cannabis plus 256 grammes in the form of fruiting tops. D said the drugs were mostly for his own use although he gave some away to friends. He refused to be put on a probation order or to be made the subject of a community service order.

Held, dismissing the appeal, that the sentence passed was not excessive bearing in mind D's reaction to alternative methods of dealing with the offence, *R. v. Aramah* (1982) 4 Cr. App. R. (S.) 407 considered.

R. v. DAVY (LEONARD FRANCIS) [1997] 1 Cr. App. R. (S.) 17, Bennett, J., CA (Crim Div).

1518. Drug offences—supply of cannabis resin to serving prisoner

F, aged 33, pleaded guilty to possessing a Class B drug, cannabis resin, with intent to supply. F went to a prison to visit an inmate and was found to be in possession of 5.5 grammes of cannabis resin. He was sentenced to 21 months' imprisonment against which he appealed.

Held, allowing the appeal, that considering *R. v. Aramah (John Uzu)* (1982) 4 Cr. App. R. (S.) 407, [1983] C.L.Y. 764 and *R. v. Savage (Jefferson Scott)* (1993) 14 Cr. App. R. (S.) 409, [1994] C.L.Y. 1250, having regard to the need for deterrence and F's bad character, his plea of guilty and serious disability (severe leg injury causing pain and restricted mobility), the appropriate sentence was 15 months.

R. v. FREEMAN (JOHN) [1997] 2 Cr. App. R. (S.) 224, Dyson, J., CA (Crim Div).

1519. Drug offences—supply of cannabis to serving prisoner

B appealed against a sentence of 30 months' imprisonment on conviction of supplying 7.2 grammes of cannabis to a serving prisoner.

Held, allowing the appeal and reducing the sentence to 15 months, that despite the gravity of supplying drugs to prisoners, the sentence was out of line with the range of sentences indicated in *R. v. Savage* (1993) 14 Cr. App. R. (S.) 409, [1994] C.L.Y. 1250. B was a man in full employment with six children to whom he had regular access and supported financially.

R. v. BARTON (ERROL ANGUSTUS) [1997] 1 Cr. App. R. (S.) 140, Newman, J., CA (Crim Div).

1520. Drug offences—supply of crack cocaine

H appealed against a sentence of five years' imprisonment, with forfeiture orders in respect of two motorcars from which the cocaine was sold. H pleaded guilty to four counts of supplying crack cocaine. On four occasions over a period of about two weeks he supplied an undercover police officer with crack cocaine at a cost of £50 on each occasion.

Held, allowing the appeal, that the sentence of five years was manifestly excessive in the light of the particular circumstances of the case, in view of the plea of guilty and H's previous good character. A sentence of four years' imprisonment would be substituted. The forfeiture order in respect of one of the motorcars, which did not belong to him, would be quashed, *R. v. Mitchell (Yvonne Jennifer)* (1989) 11 Cr. App. R. (S.) 562, [1991] C.L.Y. 1108, *R. v. Samuels* (1990) 12 Cr. App. R. (S.) 118 and *R. v. Edwards (Sean Karl)* (1992) 13 Cr. App. R. (S.) 356, [1993] C.L.Y. 1139 considered.

R. v. HOWARD (BARRINGTON) [1996] 2 Cr. App. R. (S.) 273, Otton, L.J., CA (Crim Div).

1521. Drug offences—supply of crack cocaine

V appealed against a sentence of five years' imprisonment with a recommendation for deportation. He pleaded guilty to one count of supplying a Class A drug, crack cocaine, to an undercover police officer. V was of previous good character.

Held, allowing the appeal, that the sentence would be reduced to four years, *R. v. Edwards (Sean Karl)* (1992) 13 Cr. App R. (S.) 356, [1993] C.L.Y. 1139 distinguished. V should be given credit for his guilty plea. His plea was entered on the basis that this was a one off offence made when he was approached; he was not touting for business.

R. v. VIRGO (DEVON) [1996] 2 Cr. App. R. (S.) 443, Bennett, J., CA (Crim Div).

1522. Drug offences—supply of drugs—conspiracy to supply heroin

R and A appealed against sentences of 10 years' imprisonment for conspiracy to supply a Class A controlled drug, heroin, after they attempted to supply 0.5 kilogrammes of the drug to two undercover police officers.

Held, allowing the appeal, that the weight of the drugs at 100 per cent purity (169.2 grammes) did not warrant the sentences given. The sentences were quashed and substituted with seven and a half years' imprisonment in respect of each appellant, *R. v. Aroyewumi* (1995) 16 Cr. App. R. (S.) 211, [1995] 1 C.L.Y. 1364 followed, *R. v. Aramah* (1982) 4 Cr. App. R. (S.) 407, [1983] C.L.Y. 764 considered.

R. v. ROBB (ABDUR) AND AKRAM (MOHAMMED) [1996] 2 Cr. App. R. (S.) 414, Swinton Thomas, L.J., CA (Crim Div).

1523. Drug offences—supply of Ecstasy

K pleaded guilty to possessing and offering to supply a Class A controlled drug, Ecstasy, and possessing a Class B controlled drug, cannabis resin. He was sentenced to 12 months' detention in a young offender institution for offering to supply a Class A drug, with concurrent sentences on the other counts. K was seen in a nightclub apparently dealing in drugs and when searched was found to be in possession of 34 white tablets which he said were Ecstasy tablets. On analysis the 34 tablets were found not to be Ecstasy, but one Ecstasy tablet was found at his flat, together with 3.43 grammes of cannabis resin. K claimed that he had bought 40 tablets on behalf of fellow students and their friends, and that he intended to sell the drugs to them at their cost price to him in most cases, with a small increase in other cases.

Held, dismissing the appeal, that K was a young man of exemplary character. It ought to have been obvious to him that taking Ecstasy tablets involved enormous risk. Having considered authorities, *R. v. Allery (John David)* (1993) 14 Cr. App. R. (S.) 699, [1994] C.L.Y. 1242 in particular, in which the court pointed out the dangers of taking Ecstasy, it was apparent that the sentences for possessing Ecstasy with intent, even in small quantities, were between two and five years. The sentencer had taken account of the mitigation and the sentence was not unjust or manifestly excessive.

R. v. KRAMER (EDWARD NICHOLAS) [1997] 2 Cr. App. R. (S.) 81, Douglas Brown, J., CA (Crim Div).

1524. Drug offences–supply of Ecstasy

M, aged 20, appealed against a sentence of three years' detention in a young offender institution for possession of a Class A drug with intent to supply (Ecstasy). Two police officers at Victoria coach station in London had been informed by a member of the public that a man, not M, but matching his description, was offering cannabis for sale. Police officers approached M who admitted he had 25 Ecstasy tablets in his possession for himself and friends. M's grounds of appeal were that insufficient credit was given for his guilty plea and his good character.

Held, dismissing the appeal, that mitigating factors were considered and the sentence followed similar cases, *R. v. Asquith (Martin Arthur)* (1995) 16 Cr. App. R. (S.) 453 followed.

R. v. MITCHELL (JAMIE) [1996] 2 Cr. App. R. (S.) 369, Saville, L.J., CA (Crim Div).

1525. Drug offences–supply of Ecstasy

T, aged 20, pleaded guilty to supplying a Class A drug, Ecstasy and was sentenced to five years' detention in a young offender institution against which he appealed. T sold a total of four Ecstasy tablets to two undercover police officers at a nightclub for £10 per tablet. On arrest he was found to have £495 in his possession.

Held, allowing the appeal, that the sentencer had indicated that he had taken a term of more than five years as a starting point, and had given T a discount for his guilty plea from that sentence to reach the sentence of five years. The court had indicated in the past that there was no basis for distinguishing between different kinds of Class A drugs, and there were no particular aggravating features about the present case. The sentencer had taken the wrong starting point by considering Ecstasy as more serious than other Class A offences; a sentence of four years' detention in a young offender institution was substituted.

R. v. THOMPSON (DEAN JOHN) [1997] 2 Cr. App. R. (S.) 223, Dyson, J., CA (Crim Div).

1526. Drug offences–supply of Ecstasy–disparate sentences

S, aged 22, appealed against sentence of two years' imprisonment for attempting to supply a Class A drug (Ecstasy) on the ground that there was a disparity in sentencing between the co-accused and herself. Both received a similar sentence despite the fact that the role of the co-accused was more active and more serious. S went to a nightclub with the co-accused who had 50 tablets in her possession and planned to sell them. S agreed to help sell the tablets believing that they were Ecstasy tablets although analysis showed they did not contain any dangerous drug.

Held, dismissing the appeal, that allowance was made for S's age, her previous good character, her guilty plea and the remorse she felt, but the sentence was warranted. There was no foundation in the disparity argument as the co-accused was sentenced upon a lesser basis than that put forward by the prosecution.

R. v. SKIDMORE (LOUISE) [1997] 1 Cr. App. R. (S.) 15, Jowitt, J., CA (Crim Div).

1527. Drug offences–supply of Ecstasy and amphetamines

F pleaded guilty to supplying a Class A drug, Ecstasy, supplying a Class B drug, amphetamine sulphate, and possessing a prohibited weapon, a CS gas canister.

Following a search of F's home, he admitted selling between 20 and 30 Ecstasy tablets, and selling 15 to 20 wraps of amphetamine, to total value of £4,000. F was sentenced to seven years' imprisonment for supplying a Class A drug, with concurrent sentences for the other offences, together with a confiscation order in the amount of £13,115 with nine months' imprisonment in default.

Held, allowing the appeal, that it was now recognised that the tariff for sentencing for offences involving Ecstasy was at substantially the same level as for other Class A drugs. The sentence of seven years was excessive, in view of F's good character, his comparative youth, the scale of the dealing and his plea, *R. v. Burton (Brian O'Neill)* (1993) 14 Cr. App. R. (S.) 716, [1994] C.L.Y. 1245 and *R. v. Catterall (Darren Joseph)* (1993) 14 Cr. App. R. (S.) 724, [1994] C.L.Y. 1311 cited. Accordingly, a sentence of five years' imprisonment was substituted.

R. v. FOGGARTY (RYAN NEAL) [1997] 1 Cr. App. R. (S.) 238, Connell, J., CA (Crim Div).

1528. Drug offences–supply of Ecstasy and amphetamines–entrapment

Over a number of days two police officers visited a public house in plain clothes, held themselves out as drug users and asked S whether he could supply them with Ecstasy and amphetamines. In response to their requests S did in fact obtain and sell what he described as Ecstasy tablets, but which later were discovered to contain no drug of any sort, and amphetamines to the police officers on a number of occasions. The total quantity of pure amphetamines supplied was slightly more than half a gram of 100 per cent purity. There was no evidence that S had supplied drugs to anyone else. S was subsequently arrested and convicted of offering to supply Ecstasy and supplying amphetamines. He was sentenced to 18 months' imprisonment on each count. S appealed, arguing that the sentence should be reduced to reflect the conduct of the officers which S contended amounted to entrapment.

Held, allowing the appeal and reducing the sentence to 12 months on each count to be served concurrently, that having regard to the very small quantity of pure amphetamine supplied, that no Class A drugs were in fact supplied and that S's willingness to supply was only on the basis of persistent approaches by the police officers, the criminality of S's conduct would be sufficiently marked by a reduction in the sentence on each count from 18 months to 12 months.

R. v. SHARPE (TONY); R. v. HODGES (DAVID ALAN), Trans. Ref: 9607221 Y2; 9607222 Y2, May 1, 1997, Longmore, J., CA (Crim Div).

1529. Environmental protection–harmful disposal of waste–discount for guilty plea

See ENVIRONMENT: R. v. Garrett (Terence William). §2354

1530. False accounting–benefit fraud

O pleaded guilty to five counts of false accounting and asked for 68 similar offences to be taken into consideration. O made false applications over a period of three years to the Department of Social Security for benefit, stating that he had no other source of income when he was at one stage in receipt of a student grant and subsequently employed on a part time basis. O obtained a total of £18,105 to which he was not entitled. He appealed against sentence of 18 months' imprisonment.

Held, dismissing the appeal, that considering *R. v. Stewart (Livingstone)* 1987) 9 Cr. App. R. (S.) 135, [1987] C.L.Y. 1015 and *R. v. Olusoji (Michael)* (1994) 15 Cr. App. R. (S.) 356, in view of the facts that the offences continued over a substantial time and involved a substantial sum the sentence was severe but not manifestly excessive.

R. v. OYEDIRAN (OYETOKUNBO) [1997] 2 Cr. App. R. (S.) 277, Lord Bingham of Cornhill, L.C.J., CA (Crim Div).

1531. False imprisonment–unlawful wounding–juvenile offenders–detention under Children and Young Persons Act 1933 s.53(2)

[Children and Young Persons Act 1933 s.53(2).]

The appellants, all girls aged 14 or 15, pleaded guilty to false imprisonment and unlawful wounding. They attacked another girl aged 14 who was playing truant from school. The victim was pushed into a stream, her jewellery was snatched from her, she was forced to bite a dead bird and struck about the head and body with wooden sticks. When she tried to escape she was caught and forced to take her clothes off and run around in circles. She was allowed to put some clothes back on and then made to sit in a ditch where she was forced to drink muddy water and suck a baby's dummy. Her arm was cut with a piece of broken glass. The appellants then ran off. The episode lasted for several hours. The victim was found and taken to hospital, but made a good recovery. The appellants were sentenced to three years' and 11 months' detention under the Children and Young Persons Act 1933 s.53(2) and two appellants who had spent time in secure accommodation on remand although technically on bail were sentenced to three years and seven months and three years and six months respectively. It was argued that it was wrong to impose a sentence of detention under the 1933 Act s.53(2) when the real gravity of the offence lay in the offence of unlawful wounding, for which that sentence was not available.

Held, allowing the appeals, that (1) all the appellants had pleaded guilty to a charge of unlawful wounding, which was subject to a maximum sentence in the case of an adult of five years' imprisonment, and accordingly the maximum sentence in the case of those appellants aged 15 was two years' detention in a young offender institution, and in the case of those under 15 no custodial sentence was available. The victim had been subjected, in addition to her injuries, to an appalling and humiliating experience in which she was degraded and abused for a period of several hours. The court had said in *R. v. Fairhurst (Jonathan)* (1986) 1 W.L.R. 1374, [1987] C.L.Y. 1079 that it was wrong to pass a sentence under s.53(2) for an offence which did not warrant such a sentence to compensate for the inability to pass such a sentence for an offence which justified a longer term of detention, but for which no such term was available. *Fairhurst* did permit the use of s.53(2) where the offence for which that type of detention was not available formed "part and parcel" of the events giving rise to the offence for which detention under s.53(2) was available. That was the situation in the instant case. The two offences were so inextricably bound up together that it was perfectly right for the sentencer to resort to s.53(2). The sentencer was wrong to refer to the long term effects of the offence on the victim, as there was no evidence of the likely long term effects. A deterrent sentence was inappropriate. The court accepted that a custodial sentence was necessary, but taking into account all the relevant material, including the reports on the appellants, took the view that an appropriate starting point would have been two years' detention in a young offender institution for those aged 15 and two years' detention under Children and Young Persons Act 1933 s.53(2) for those under 15. As there were no appropriate young offender institutions for girls of 15, the court would pass sentences of the same length of detention under the 1933 Act s.53(2) in respect of all the appellants.

R. v. W (A JUVENILE) [1997] 2 Cr. App. R. (S.) 210, Brian Smedley, J., CA (Crim Div).

1532. Fines–attachment of earnings–order could still be made where defendant's earnings fluctuated

[Attachment of Earnings Act 1971 s.1 (3), Sch.3.]

Held, that a defendant with outstanding fines and costs, which had not been paid due to culpable neglect, was still eligible to pay the sums owed by way of an attachment of earnings order under the Attachment of Earnings Act 1971 s.1 (3), even though her earnings fluctuated from week to week. Schedule 3 para.5 to the Act took account of such fluctuations by preventing a deduction being made on a particular pay day if the amount earned that day fell below the amount of protected earnings specified in the order.

R. v. YORK MAGISTRATES COURT, *ex p.* GRIMES, *The Times*, June 27, 1997, Astill, J., QBD.

1533. Fines–income support–partner's refusal to allow benefit to be used to pay off outstanding sums

Held, that it was not open to an appellant to argue that she was unable to pay her fines on the ground that her partner would not allow her to use their income support, for which he was the signed claimant, for that purpose, as the benefit received was intended to support both of them and the appellant could use the share to which she was entitled to pay off the outstanding sums.

ALCOTT v. DPP (1997) 161 J.P. 53, Tucker, J., QBD.

1534. Firearms offences–importation of pistol and pump action shot gun

K, a Belgian citizen returning to the UK after some years in Argentina, appealed against sentence of 18 months' imprisonment following his plea of guilty to the knowing fraudulent evasion of the prohibition on the importation of two guns and ammunition. The guns, a pistol and a pump action shotgun, had been purchased in Argentina and Belgium for the protection of K and his family. On arrival in the UK, K failed to declare the weapons on a Customs Declaration Form and they were later discovered when his luggage was unpacked at his new home.

Held, allowing the appeal in part by quashing the original sentence and imposing a term of eight months' imprisonment, that K's actions fully justified a custodial sentence given the need for control on the importation of such weapons. K had failed to pack the weapons correctly or to ensure they were unloaded and the shotgun was of a class of weapon for which no licence could be granted.

R. v. KLEIN (CHRISTIAN LOUIS), Trans. Ref: 96/5429/W3, September 23, 1996, Butterfield, J., CA (Crim Div).

1535. Firearms offences–possession of handgun and ammunition–possession by tourist

H pleaded guilty to possessing a firearm without a certificate, possessing ammunition without a certificate, and possessing a prohibited weapon, a CS gas cylinder. He was sentenced to 12 months' imprisonment with nine months concurrent for possessing ammunition and three months concurrent for possessing a CS gas cylinder. H, a German national, was spending a week in the UK when his car was stopped as a result of his driving. Police officers found a loaded handgun, 152 rounds of ammunitiion, and a CS gas cylinder. H claimed that he did not require a licence for the gun in Germany, and that it was lawful there to possess a CS gas cylinder. The gun was a target pistol for use in sporting events.

Held, allowing the appeal, that possession of a loaded firearm required an immediate custodial sentence, even where the firearm had been acquired legally in a country where it was lawful to possess one. The sentence would be reduced to six months (three months concurrent substituted for the ammunition offence).

R. v. HORN (MICHAEL) [1997] 2 Cr. App. R. (S.) 172, Butterfield, J., CA (Crim Div).

1536. Firearms offences–possession of imitation firearm

Held, that, although a judge had adopted the correct approach in sentencing following a guilty plea to possessing an imitation firearm with intent to commit an offence, the sentence failed to adequately reflect mitigating factors and accordingly a custodial sentence of three years would be reduced to one of two years.

R. v. LARD (GURDIAL SINGH), *The Independent*, May 19, 1997 (C.S.), Lord Bingham of Cornhill, L.C.J., CA (Crim Div).

1537. Firearms offences—possession of machine gun and ammunition—discount for guilty plea

D pleaded guilty to two counts of possessing a prohibited weapon, two counts of possessing ammunition without a certificate, two counts of possessing a shortened shotgun without a certificate, and one of possessing cannabis with intent to supply. He was sentenced to a total of eight years' imprisonment for firearms offences with two years' imprisonment consecutive for possessing cannabis with intent to supply. D was stopped while driving his car and found to be in possession of a loaded submachine gun with ammunition. A search of his home revealed two sawn off shotguns and various other weapons and ammunition, and 2.3 kilogrammes of cannabis resin. D had previous convictions for offences related to firearms.

Held, dismissing the appeal, that the sentencer was entitled to take the maximum sentence of 10 years as the starting point for possessing a prohibited weapon, and allow a discount of two years for the plea. That discount was sufficient in the circumstances and the total sentence was not excessive.

R. v. DICKINS (WESLEY HEATH) [1997] 2 Cr. App. R. (S.) 134, Owen, J., CA (Crim Div).

1538. Firearms offences—possession of revolver for friend

K, aged 36, appealed against sentence of five years' imprisonment for possessing a prohibited weapon (a smooth barrelled revolver). K submitted that he was looking after the gun for someone who had previously given him protection and had not known that it was the same weapon he had sold to them a year previously. K denied reactivating the weapon.

Held, allowing the appeal, that a sentence of five years was half the prevailing maximum and not excessive, but insufficient weight had been attached to the circumstances in which K had possession of the revolver. The sentence was quashed and substituted with one of four years' imprisonment, *R. v. Ecclestone (Paul)* (1995) 16 Cr. App. R. (S.) 8, [1996] 1 C.L.Y. 1894 considered, *R. v. Yates (Neil Albert)* (1994) 15 Cr. App. R. (S.) 400 followed.

R. v. KENT (ANTHONY) [1996] 2 Cr. App. R. (S.) 381, Ognall, J., CA (Crim Div).

1539. Firearms offences—possession of sawn off shotgun

[Firearms Act 1968.]

R pleaded guilty to possession of a shortened shotgun without a certificate, and other firearm offences. Police officers searching R's home found a sawn-off shotgun, a double barrelled shotgun and a .22 rifle. The sawn-off shotgun was not capable of being fired in the normal way. R claimed that he had bought the guns with a view to selling them. R was sentenced to two and a half years' imprisonment for possessing a shortened shotgun without a certificate, with 12 months' imprisonment concurrent for each of the other offences and a forfeiture order under the Firearms Act 1968.

Held, dismissing the appeal, that the court had been referred to *R. v. Ecclestone (Paul)* (1995) 16 Cr. App. R. (S.) 9, [1996] 1 C.L.Y. 1894, but since that case was decided the maximum sentence for possessing a shortened shotgun had been increased from five years to seven years, plainly indicating to the courts the seriousness of the offence. The court must make some response in the level of sentences that were passed. The court bore in mind that the shotgun was not capable of being fired, but R intended to sell it and it was capable of being used to threaten people in robberies. The sentence of two and a half years on a plea of guilty was not out of line with the type of sentence which could now be expected, and could not be considered manifestly excessive.

R. v. ROBB (JOHN GEORGE TATE) [1997] 1 Cr. App. R. (S.) 212, Judge Crane, CA (Crim Div).

1540. Firearms offences—possession of sawn off shotgun—false imprisonment— indication of sentence length given by trial judge before plea entered

[Criminal Justice Act 1988 s.36.]

The Attorney General applied for a sentence to be referred under the Criminal Justice Act 1988 s.36 on the ground that it was unduly lenient. R pleaded guilty to two counts of assault occasioning actual bodily harm, one of false imprisonment and one of having a firearm with intent to commit an indictable offence. His girlfriend, with whom he had a child, left him and some weeks later on her way to work he assaulted her. He continued to telephone her and eventually, while she was staying with her parents, he came in through the back door of their house, carrying a shortened shotgun. He pointed the gun at the girlfriend and demanded the return of a ring he had given her. The girlfriend's mother escaped from the house with the child and called the police. When the police arrived, R threatened to shoot the girlfriend if they tried to break down the door. Eventually he let her leave and surrendered to the police, after a siege lasting 26 hours. R was subject to a suspended sentence passed in 1992 for possessing a shotgun without a certificate. In 1990 he had been put on probation following an incident in which he fired a shotgun in the direction of the mother of a previous girlfriend. R was sentenced to four years' imprisonment for the current offences, with the suspended sentence activated consecutively.

Held, dismissing the reference, that R had been in custody for two and a half years before the matter came before the Crown Court. The delay was caused by R dismissing his legal advisers on two occasions. Counsel had asked the judge for an indication as to the level of sentence which could be expected, following an intimation from another judge who dealt with a bail application. Prosecuting counsel was present when counsel saw the judge and the discussion was fully recorded. The judge indicated that the sentence would be about five years subject to reports. There was a further meeting at which the judge indicated that he would sentence R there and then to five years, without waiting for reports. In the light of that indication, R pleaded guilty. The case illustrated the undesirability of such meetings, on which the court had commented in the past, but in addition it illustrated a new source of mischief. It was submitted on behalf of R that the sentence should not be increased, even if it was considered unduly lenient, since to do so would contradict the indication given by the trial judge, on the basis of which R had pleaded guilty. While the court wished to make plain its extreme distaste for what had taken place, it was appropriate to approach the case on the basis that what had happened in the Crown Court was relevant to the exercise of the court's discretion. Viewed in the light of previous authorities, the sentence was unduly lenient; an appropriate sentence would have been seven years for the false imprisonment with the suspended sentence activated consecutively. However, bearing in mind the element of double jeopardy involved in such references, and the indication given by the trial judge, the sentence which otherwise would have been substituted for the sentence passed at the Crown Court was reduced to five years for false imprisonment, with the suspended sentence activated consecutively, *R. v. Spence and Thomas* (1983) 5 Cr. App. R. (S.) 413, [1984] C.L.Y. 876 and *R. v. Whitehead* (1984) 6 Cr. App. R. (S.) 72, [1985] C.L.Y. 812 considered.

ATTORNEY GENERAL'S REFERENCE (NO.40 OF 1996), *Re*; *sub nom*. R. v. ROBINSON (MARK LESLIE) [1997] 1 Cr. App. R. (S.) 357, Lord Bingham of Cornhill, C.J., CA (Crim Div).

1541. Firearms offences—possession with intent to cause person to believe unlawful violence would be used

[Firearms Act 1968 s.16A.]

M was convicted of possession of a firearm with intent to cause a person to believe that unlawful violence would be used contrary to the Firearms Act 1968 s.16A. B went into a probation office and asked to see a particular probation officer. When she was told that the probation officer was not available, she produced an imitation gun and pointed it at the receptionist. M was sentenced to five years' imprisonment with an order for the destruction of the firearm.

Held, allowing the appeal, that a custodial sentence was necessary, but five years was too long in view of there being no violence offered and that M knew the weapon to be an imitation. A sentence of 12 months' imprisonment was substituted.

R. v. MERCREDI (BARBARA) [1997] 2 Cr. App. R. (S.) 204, Hidden, J., CA (Crim Div).

1542. Firearms offences—possession with intent to cause person to believe unlawful violence would be used

[Firearms Act 1968 s.16A.]

T, aged 31, pleaded guilty to possessing a firearm with intent to cause a person to believe that unlawful violence would be used contrary to the Firearms Act 1968 s.16A. T's flat was burgled and he came to believe that the burglary had been committed by a particular person. He obtained possession of an old air pistol belonging to his brother and went to find the person who had committed the burglary. Together with another man, he went to the home of an aunt of the burglar in the early hours of the morning, and following a conversation in the course of which the aunt said that if anything happened to the burglar his family would retaliate, T produced the airgun and pointed it at her. T was sentenced to three years' imprisonment.

Held, allowing the appeal, that the air pistol was in poor condition and any pellets would have been discharged at greatly reduced velocity. T had taken the law into his own hands after a burglary, and had used the airgun so as to put an innocent person into a state of fear. A custodial sentence was the only appropriate sentence, but taking into account his early plea, the nature of the firearm and the effect on his personal life and career the sentence of three years was excessive; a sentence of two years was substituted.

R. v. THOMPSON (STEVEN) [1997] 2 Cr. App. R. (S.) 188, Judge, L.J., CA.

1543. Forfeiture—reciprocal enforcement

CRIMINAL JUSTICE (INTERNATIONAL CO-OPERATION) ACT 1990 (ENFORCEMENT OF OVERSEAS FORFEITURE ORDERS) (AMENDMENT) ORDER 1997, SI 1997 1317; made under the Criminal Justice (International Co-operation) Act 1990 s.9. In force: July 1, 1997; £1.10.

This Order amends the Criminal Justice (International Co-operation) Act 1990 (Enforcement of Overseas Forfeiture Orders) Order 1991 (SI 1991 1463) and the Criminal Justice (International Co-operation) Act 1990 (Enforcement of Overseas Forfeiture Orders) (Northern Ireland) Order 1991 (SI 1991 1464). The definition of "drug trafficking" is amended in both Orders and a new definition of "offence to which this Order applies" is added to the Northern Ireland Order. The list of countries designated for drug trafficking offences is amended by the addition of Antigua and Barbuda, Colombia, Cyprus, Czech Republic, Denmark, France and Ireland.

1544. Forgery—theft—separate indictments—concurrent sentences inappropriate

T, a 38 year old self employed insolvency consultant, had financial difficulties. He dishonestly obtained funds amounting to £7,000 from a client. He also sold a car which he held as part of a leasing agreement but was owned by a leasing company. T was charged on two indictments with forgery and theft respectively. T pleaded guilty to forgery at which point the judge indicated that a concurrent sentence of 21 months' imprisonment would be imposed whether T pleaded guilty or was found guilty on the second indictment. T then entered a guilty plea to that indictment.

Held, allowing the appeal and substituting sentences of 18 months and 12 months concurrent, that (1) as the case involved a breach of trust the length of the sentence was not inappropriate despite the fact the sum involved was less than £10,000 in terms of the *Barrick* guidelines as updated, and (2) the case was not one in which the imposition of concurrent sentences was appropriate, and had it been open to the court, consecutive sentences totalling 21 months would have been imposed. However, the court was obliged to pass concurrent sentences and the period of imprisonment must be reduced.

R. v. TIGHE (DECLAN PATRICK), Trans. Ref: 9701862 X5, July 22, 1997, Alliott, J., CA (Crim Div).

1545. Fraud—benefit fraud

A was sentenced to four years' imprisonment after being convicted of 10 offences of theft and five offences of obtaining services by deception. Over a period of four years she made false claims for child benefit, income support and housing benefit. Claims were made in her own name and in other names. A total of more than £100,000 was obtained.

Held, dismissing the appeal, that a sentence of four years' imprisonment was fully justified, *R. v. Stewart* (1986) 83 Cr. App. R. 327, [1987] C.L.Y. 625 cited.

R. v. ADEWUYI (STELLA BEATRICE) [1997] 1 Cr. App. R. (S.) 254, Toulson, J., CA (Crim Div).

1546. Fraud—benefit fraud—loss of £300,000

N and others pleaded guilty to conspiracy to defraud the Department of Social Security by making false claims for benefit. Over a period of 21 months a total of 59 claims for benefit were made, and payments in excess of £300,000 were obtained. Information was obtained from the Department of Social Security computer by one of the appellants, who was an employee of the department, and used to facilitate the fraud. Two appellants, one regarded as an organising principal and the other was an employee of the Department were sentenced to six years' imprisonment and the third sentenced to four years' imprisonment.

Held, allowing the appeals, that this was carefully planned, carefully prepared and carefully executed plot to secure very large sums of money, involving, in the case of one appellant, a gross breach of trust. The question for the court was which category of case the case fell into, and whether there was a reasonably close parallel with other cases. Comparing the case with other examples of serious fraud, it seemed that a proper sentence on a plea of guilty would be in the region of three and a half to four years. The sentences of six years would be reduced to four years, and the sentence of four years to two and a half years.

R. v. NWOGA (NICHOLAS) [1997] 2 Cr. App. R. (S.) 1, McKinnon, J., CA (Crim Div).

1547. Fraud—conspiracy to defraud—creation of false share markets to influence takeovers—community service orders unduly lenient

[Criminal Justice Act 1988 s.36.]

The Attorney General applied for a sentence be referred under the Criminal Justice Act 1988 s.36 on the ground that it was unduly lenient. W, JH and GH were convicted of conspiracy to defraud, with W and JH also convicted of theft, arising from their involvement in the creation of false share markets intended to affect the outcome of takeovers. W and JH were each sentenced to concurrent community service orders of 220 hours, and GH was given a 12 month conditional discharge on a plea of guilty.

Held, allowing the reference, that the sentences were unduly lenient and would be substituted by custodial sentences of two years for W, 15 months for JH and 12 months, suspended for two years, for GH. The creation of false share markets was a serious offence which could lead to the defrauding of shareholders and damage to the City of London. Notwithstanding evidence of the offenders' good character and the effect on their families, community service orders were inappropriate. Sentences had to include a deterrent element, serving to warn those taking part in such activities that, if apprehended, imprisonment was very likely.

ATTORNEY GENERAL'S REFERENCE (NOS.14, 15 AND 16 OF 1995), *Re; sub nom.* R. v. WARD (MICHAEL GRAINGER); R. v. HOWARTH (JEREMY JOHN ALAN); R. v. HENDRY (GEORGE), *The Times*, April 10, 1997, McCowan, L.J., CA (Crim Div).

1548. Fraud—conspiracy to defraud—telephone services

A appealed against sentence of six months' imprisonment for conspiracy to defraud British Telecom. A had participated in a scheme to get telephone equipment installed and then to connect callers in Lancashire to Pakistan at a reduced cost. The loss to British Telecom was estimated at between £6,000 and £10,000. A's submission was that he played a minor role and that his co-operation with the police warranted a non-custodial sentence.

Held, allowing the appeal and quashing the sentence of six months' imprisonment and substituting it with one of three months' imprisonment, that a custodial sentence was necessary but mitigating factors meant it could be reduced.

R. v. ASLAM (TAHIR) [1996] 2 Cr. App. R. (S.) 377, Ognall, J., CA (Crim Div).

1549. Fraud—solicitor in breach of trust

C, a former solicitor, appealed against the sentence of six years' imprisonment following his plea of guilty to theft and forgery of £579,376. C submitted that insufficient account had been taken of the mitigation, namely that he had admitted his dishonesty immediately and cooperated fully with the police, and that the sentence was out of scale for an offence of dishonesty involving an amount of approximately half a million pounds by someone in a position of trust.

Held, dismissing the appeal, that an offence of dishonesty on a major scale by someone in a position of trust would usually attract a sentence from about four to seven years dependent upon mitigation and aggravating factors. Notwithstanding the mitigation, there was substantial aggravation, being that C had failed to take heed of a warning he had received from the Solicitors' Disciplinary Tribunal in 1991 following various complaints from clients. Since then C's conduct actually became worse with his dishonesty escalating until he was finally discovered in 1994, *R. v. Barrick* (1985) 7 Cr. App. R. (S.) 142, [1985] C.L.Y. 765 considered.

R. v. CURTIN (RAYMOND PETER), Trans. Ref: 96/06921/Z3, November 21, 1996, Judge, L.J., CA (Crim Div).

1550. Fraudulent trading—creation of false invoices to maintain funding

[Company Directors Disqualification Act 1986.]

S and P pleaded guilty to fraudulent trading, and S also pleaded guilty to being concerned in the management of a company while an undischarged bankrupt. S and P sought to expand the company's activities and various loan facilities were negotiated which were made subject to the condition that outstanding debts to the company should at all times be equal to at least 60 per cent of the amount of the loan. S and P supplied accounts to the lender which included misleading lists of debtors, and false invoices were created to support these accounts. The company eventually went into liquidation with an overall deficit of £520,000. S and P were each sentenced to three years' imprisonment and disqualified for five years under the Company Directors Disqualification Act 1986.

Held, allowing the appeals, that the sentencer accepted that the business began honestly and later became fraudulent, and that the offence had been committed six years before the appellants appeared in the Crown Court.

Offences of fraudulent trading covered a wide spectrum of offences. At one extreme there may have been deliberate reckless trading on a large scale aimed at a rapid return, with no genuine intention to discharge the company's debts. On the other extreme, there may have been a properly funded business which ran into financial difficulties out of which the directors attempt to trade themselves in order to save their own and their employees' jobs, but reach a point where they become reckless as to the reality. In broad terms, a charge of fraudulent trading resulting in a deficiency of a given amount was less serious than a specific charge of theft or fraud to an equivalent amount. The court was satisfied that the sentence of three years was too high. The case lay at the lower end of the scale in terms of criminality. Its serious aspect lay in the creation of false invoices to maintain the funding of the company. The appellants had not attempted to loot the assets of the company and had assisted the receiver and the liquidator to preserve the assets. The sentences would be reduced to 18 months' imprisonment in each case.

R. v. SMITH (COLIN JOHN); R. v. PALK (ANTHONY MALCOLM) [1997] 2 Cr. App. R. (S.) 167, Potter, L.J., CA (Crim Div).

1551. Grievous bodily harm—community service not unduly lenient

[Offences against the Person Act 1861 s.18; Criminal Justice Act 1988 s.36.]

The Attorney General applied for a sentence to be referred under the Criminal Justice Act 1988 s.36 on the ground it was unduly lenient. M was sentenced to 240 hours' community service for grievous bodily harm pursuant to the Offences against the Person Act 1861 s.18. M and his codefendant were involved in a fight, late at night, with two other men in the street. All the parties had been drinking and there was evidence of provocation by the victims. M struck one of the victims in the face, who fell on to the pavement and was struck again by M, rendering the victim unconscious. M then continued to stamp and kick the victim's head several times, even after passers by had administered first aid. The victim suffered cuts and bruising.

Held, dismissing the application, that although the offence was serious the facts and circumstances justified an exceptional course, *Attorney General's Reference (No.10 of 1992), Re* (1994) 15 Cr. App. R. (S.) 1 and *R. v. Gibson (Nicholas)* [1997] 1 Cr. App. R. (S.) 182, [1997] C.L.Y. 1560 considered. A community service order was unduly lenient where there had been serious violence and an appropriate sentence would be 12 to 15 months, of which M would only be required to serve half. However, to impose such a sentence would be harsh as M had completed his community service and started full time employment. It would not be in the public interest to impose a custodial sentence.

ATTORNEY GENERAL'S REFERENCE (NO.33 OF 1997), *Re*; *sub nom.* R. v. McGINN (PHILLIP LEE), Trans. Ref: 97/4654/R2, October 2, 1997, Lord Bingham of Cornhill, L.C.J., CA (Crim Div).

1552. Grievous bodily harm—community service order not unduly lenient

[Criminal Justice Act 1988 s.36.]

The Attorney General applied for a sentence to be referred under the Criminal Justice Act 1988 s.36 on the ground that its was unduly lenient. The two offenders, aged 22 and 17, were sentenced to two concurrent sentences of 180 hours' community service and a two year supervision order, respectively. Each was convicted on charges of wounding with intent to cause grievous bodily harm and affray with the younger offender also convicted of common assault. During a fight early in the morning of New Year's Day between two groups of youths, the offenders had armed themselves with a golf club and a mop handle and had inflicted wounds to the heads and bodies of their victims. Both offenders had previous convictions for violent offences.

Held, dismissing the reference, that custodial sentences of between 12 and 15 months were appropriate for these offences, especially having regard to their deterrent effect. However, it was apparent that both offenders had completed their sentences in exemplary fashion and had now resolved to lead lawful lives. The need for deterrence was outweighed by the element of double jeopardy, the personal mitigation of the offenders and the recognition that the public interest would not be served by the imposition of custodial sentences, *Attorney General's Reference (No.41 of 1994), Re* (1995) 16 Cr. App. R. (S.) 792, [1996] 1 C.L.Y. 1919, *R. v. Johal (Harbinder)* (1991) 12 Cr. App. R. (S.) 695, [1992] C.L.Y. 1483, *Attorney General's Reference (No.34 of 1995), Re* [1996] 1 Cr. App. R. (S.) 386, [1996] 1 C.L.Y. 1923 considered.

ATTORNEY GENERAL'S REFERENCE (NOS.56 AND 57 OF 1996), *Re*; *sub nom.* R. v. E (A JUVENILE); R. v. E (STEVEN GEOFFREY), February 27, 1997, Lord Bingham of Cornhill, L.C.J., CA (Crim Div).

1553. **Grievous bodily harm—disparate sentences—identical sentences passed on two offenders—appropriateness of sentence given that one offender had instigated offence**

P, the second appellant, pleaded guilty to assault occasioning actual bodily harm, and both B and P pleaded guilty to false imprisonment and causing grievous bodily harm with intent. P called at the home of another young woman and attacked her by banging her head against a wall, punching her in the face and kneeing her in the nose. Some months later both B and P were involved in an incident in the course of which a 16 year-old girl was made to go to the house of one of them, where she was kicked about the face and head and made to get into a bath full of cold water. Her head was forced under the water repeatedly and she was later stabbed in the back and cut under the eye. Both offenders were sentenced to five and a half years' imprisonment.

Held, allowing B's appeal and dismissing P's, that the court took the view that P had taken the lead and a larger part in the violence. The court ought to have made some distinction between B and P, particularly as P was being sentenced in addition for another offence. This was an extremely grave case involving a prolonged ordeal and humiliation of a young woman. The sentence on P was wholly appropriate, bearing in mind her role in the affair, but there should be a distinction in favour of B, on the basis of her participation in the offence and because she was not involved in the earlier offence. B's sentence was reduced to four and a half years.

R. v. BELTON (AMANDA JANE); R. v. PETROW (CLAIRE MARIE) [1997] 1 Cr. App. R. (S.) 215, Maurice Kay, J., CA (Crim Div).

1554. **Grievous bodily harm—inflicting serious injury by single blow—no intention to injure**

[Offences against the Person Act 1861 s.18, s.20.]

A appealed against a sentence of three and a half years' imprisonment having pleaded guilty to maliciously inflicting grievous bodily harm contrary to the Offences Against the Person Act 1861 s.20. He was acquitted of causing grievous bodily harm with intent contrary to s.18. A had been molested sexually by the victim some years before the offence and his girlfriend had complained that the victim committed a sexual offence against her some years earlier. A and a friend encountered the victim by chance in a public house and the victim blew him a kiss. A went to the victim and struck him a single blow to the face. The victim fell from his chair and in falling struck his head on a metal bar and then on the floor. The victim suffered multiple cerebral haemorrhage and was still in a state from which it was uncertain whether he would recover.

Held, allowing the appeal, that the sentence was inconsistent with those passed in other cases. A sentence of 18 months' imprisonment was substituted, *R. v. Coleman* (1992) 13 Cr. App. R. (S.) 508, [1992] C.L.Y. 1338 considered.

R. v. AMBROSE (GARY PAUL) [1997] 1 Cr. App. R. (S.) 404, Rougier, J., CA (Crim Div).

1555. Grievous bodily harm—intent to prevent apprehension—driver recklessly colliding with police car

B appealed against sentence after having pleaded guilty to causing grievous bodily harm with intent to prevent apprehension, and to other offences. He was a disqualified driver and was seen by police officers driving a car. When the officers followed a high speed chase developed, in the course of which B drove dangerously. Eventually he drove right round a roundabout and collided with one of the pursuing police cars. B's plea was accepted on the basis that he had not deliberately collided with the police car, but had done so recklessly with intent to escape arrest. The police officer driving the car suffered grave injuries and was permanently disabled as a result. A second police officer suffered multiple injuries. B was sentenced to nine years' imprisonment for causing grievous bodily harm with intent to prevent apprehension, and concurrent terms for other offences.

Held, allowing the appeal, that the court accepted that there was public anxiety about young men driving high performance cars at high speeds to avoid apprehension, but a comparison with the maximum sentence for causing death by dangerous driving was not helpful or appropriate. The judge had taken 12 years as a starting point, and discounted the sentence by one quarter to allow for the guilty plea. In the court's view the starting point was too high, and a sentence of seven and a half years' imprisonment was substituted.

R. v. BOULTER (ANDREW PAUL) [1996] 2 Cr. App. R. (S.) 428, Judge Gibbon Q.C., CA (Crim Div).

1556. Grievous bodily harm—intention—unduly lenient sentence

[Criminal Justice Act 1988 s.36.]

The Attorney General applied for a sentence to be referred under the Criminal Justice Act 1988 s.36 on the ground tha tis was unduly lenient. J pleaded guilty to causing grievous bodily harm with intent. He became involved in a dispute with a fellow worker at his place of work and struck the victim on the back of the head with a crowbar. The victim suffered a fracture of the skull and an extradural haematoma, which required an emergency craniotomy. He had various physical and psychological after effects. J was sentenced to 12 months' imprisonment.

Held, allowing the reference, that although the sentencer was right to refer to the provocation which J had received, and to a psychiatric condition which resulted from being stabbed, the sentence was unduly lenient. At the time of sentence, the proper sentence would have been at least four years' imprisonment but in view of the element of double jeopardy a sentence of three years' imprisonment would be substituted, *Attorney General's Reference (No.47 of 1994), Re* (1995) 16 Cr. App. R. (S.) 865, [1996] 1 C.L.Y. 1910 considered.

ATTORNEY GENERAL'S REFERENCE (NO.36 OF 1996), *Re; sub nom.* R. v. JOHNSON (JASON LEON) [1997] 1 Cr. App. R. (S.) 363, Lord Bingham of Cornhill, C.J., CA (Crim Div).

1557. Grievous bodily harm—juvenile offender—serious unprovoked attack—12 months' detention unduly lenient

[Criminal Justice Act 1988 s.36; Children and Young Persons Act 1933 s.53 (2).]

The Attorney General applied for a sentence to be referred under the Criminal Justice Act 1988 s.36 on the ground that it was unduly lenient. G, aged 17, was sentenced to 12 months' detention on guilty pleas to wounding with intent to cause grievous bodily harm and six months concurrent for robbery. G had thrown a brick at the back of the victim's head, pursued him twice, and assaulted him with a beer bottle. He was found to have stamped on the victim's head six or seven times while the victim was lying on the ground, having lost consciousness. A ring belonging to the victim had been taken. The victim required stitches to lacerations on his scalp and eyelid and suffered bruising and grazing to his face. The attack was unprovoked and, as G admitted, was for no particular reason. The Attorney General argued that the judge should have exercised his powers under the Children and Young Persons Act 1933 s.53(2) in passing a longer than normal sentence.

Held, allowing the reference, that the sentence was unduly lenient and failed to reflect the gravity of the offence and the public concern that others were deterred from carrying out offences of this kind, *R. v. Curry* (1989) 11 Cr. App. R. (S.) 395 and *R. v. Wainfur (Mark Andrew)* [1997] 1 Cr. App. R. (S.) 43, [1997] C.L.Y. 1603 considered. A sentence of four years would have been appropriate at trial, but the court decided a sentence of three years' detention under s.53(2) of the 1933 Act would be substituted.

ATTORNEY GENERAL'S REFERENCE (NO.51 OF 1996), *Re; sub nom.* R. v. G (A JUVENILE), [1997] 2 Cr. App. R.(S.) 248, February 11, 1997, Rose, L.J., CA (Crim Div).

1558. Grievous bodily harm—juvenile offenders—long term detention

[Children and Young Persons Act 1933 s.53(2).]

B, aged 15 at the time of the offence, pleaded guilty to wounding with intent to cause grievous bodily harm. B and his friends were refused admission to a party to which they had not been invited. They subsequently attacked a girl who had left the party. Police were called and took B home. B then taped a kitchen knife with a seven centimetre blade to his arm and went out again. He accosted a youth who was carrying drink in a bag. When the youth refused to give him a can of beer B threatened him with a knife and then stabbed him in the chest in the course of a scuffle. The victim was found to have a deep wound in the chest wall and a collapsed lung. B was sentenced to five years' detention under the Children and Young Persons Act 1933, s.53(2).

Held, allowing the appeal, that considering *R. v. Storey* (1984) 6 Cr. App. R. (s.) 104, [1985] C.L.Y. 810, B had committed an appalling crime, but in view of his youth, his plea, and changes in his behaviour since the sentence was passed, the sentence was reduced to four years' detention.

R. v. B (A JUVENILE) (FEBRUARY 17, 1997) [1997] 2 Cr. App. R. (S.) 260, Hidden, J., CA (Crim Div).

1559. Grievous bodily harm—kicking victim about head—repeated kicking

[Offences Against the Person Act 1861 s.78.]

C pleaded guilty to causing grievous bodily harm with intent and was sentenced to six years' imprisonment. C knocked a man to the ground and kicked him repeatedly about the head. The attack occurred in the early hours of the morning. The victim suffered bruises, abrasions and lacerations, and a cerebral oedema which could have proved fatal, but was released from hospital after three days with no permanent injury.

Held, allowing the appeal, that the court endorsed the comment that an attacker who used his shod feet was using a weapon just as much as someone who wielded an object held in his hand. In such cases, the victim was usually lying helpless on the ground at the time of the attack. Such cases where the attacker put the boot in, either to the victim's head or to some other vulnerable part of the body, were not to be treated more leniently than other Offences Against the Person Act 1861 s.18 cases where a weapon was held in the hand. C was entitled to credit for his plea, and the fact that the attack had not resulted in permanent injury should be reflected in the sentence. In the court's view the appropriate sentence was five years' imprisonment, *Attorney General's Reference (No.40 of 1994), Re* (1995) 16 Cr. App. R. (S.) 862, [1996] 1 C.L.Y. 1907 and *Attorney General's Reference (No.47 of 1994), Re* (1995) 16 Cr. App. R. (S.) 865, [1996] 1 C.L.Y. 1910 considered.

R. v. COLES (BARRIE) [1997] 2 Cr. App. R. (S.) 95, Keene, J., CA (Crim Div).

1560. Grievous bodily harm–kicking victim about head–serious injury caused– appropriate sentence where remorse shown

G appealed a sentence of six years' imprisonment on conviction of causing grievous bodily harm with intent. He visited the home of a woman he knew and knocked the victim to the ground and kicked him about the face and head when he asked G to leave. The victim suffered fractures of the eye socket and cheek bone which required surgery.

Held, allowing the appeal, reducing the sentence to four and a half years, that a long sentence was merited for an attack of this severity where a man was kicked when on the ground, but G had demonstrated remorse for the injuries to the victim, *R. v. Ivory* (1981) 3 Cr. App. R. (S.) 185 cited.

R. v. GIBSON (NICHOLAS) [1997] 1 Cr. App. R. (S.) 182, Hidden, J., CA (Crim Div).

1561. Grievous bodily harm–kicking victim about head–victim suffering brain damage

T was convicted of causing grievous bodily harm with intent and was sentenced to 10 years' detention in a young offender institution. T was involved with others in an incident in which a man queuing at a burger bar was attacked without warning or provocation. The first victim was knocked to the ground and kicked by T and an accomplice. The accomplice then punched a friend of the first victim who attempted to intervene. As the second victim lay on the ground, T and others kicked him on the side and the back, and stamped on him. The second victim suffered facial injuries and brain damage which left him disabled and unable to work.

Held, dismissing the appeal, that it had been submitted that a sentence of the order of six years would have been appropriate for the offence. The court did not accept that submission. This was a case of violence for its own sake involving kicking and stamping on a man lying unconscious on the ground and resulting in extremely grave consequences for the victim and his family. The court endorsed the clear message sent out by the judge that those who went out in a group and took part in violence of that kind must expect to receive heavy sentences for the protection of the public and to mark the gravity of the offence and deter others, *R. v. Ivey* (1981) 3 Cr. App. R. (S.) 185, [1981] C.L.Y. 525, *R. v. Legge* (1988) 10 Cr. App. R. (S.) 208 and *Attorney General's (No.47 of 1994), Re* (1995) 16 Cr. App. R. (S.) 865, [1996] 1 C.L.Y. 1910 considered.

R. v. THOMAS (DEAN ROBERT) [1997] 2 Cr. App. R. (S.) 148, Toulson, J., CA (Crim Div).

1562. Grievous bodily harm–kicking victim when on ground–attempts

R pleaded guilty to attempting to cause grievous bodily harm with intent and was sentenced to three years' imprisonment. R approached a man in a public house who had made a nuisance of himself towards R's wife and asked him to go outside. A fight started, and R was seen kicking the other man's head as he lay on the ground. R left the victim, but R's brother then approached him and kicked him twice on the head. The victim was taken to hospital but was released after two days with no lasting injuries.

Held, allowing the appeal, that the appropriate sentence for the completed offence even on a plea of guilty would have been in excess of four years and might have approached five years, *Attorney General's Reference (Nos. 17 and 18 of 1994), Re* (1995) 16 Cr. App. R. (S.) 418, *Attorney General's Reference (No.47 of 1994), Re* (1995) 16 Cr. App. R. (S.) 865, [1996] 1 C.L.Y. 1910 and *Attorney General's Reference (No.34 of 1995), Re* [1996] 1 Cr. App. R. (S.) 386, [1996] 1 C.L.Y. 1923 considered. The offence was charged as attempt, and it followed that the court had to regard it as an unsuccessful attempt to cause injury. An appropriate sentence for the offence would have been three years, before personal mitigation was taken into account. In the light of the personal mitigation, the sentence would be reduced to 30 months' imprisonment.

R. v. REYNOLDS (SCOTT) [1997] 2 Cr. App. R. (S.) 118, Evans, L.J., CA (Crim Div).

1563. Grievous bodily harm—longer than normal sentence inappropriate

[Criminal Justice Act 1991 s.2(2).]

A appealed against a custodial sentence of 12 years, made pursuant to the Criminal Justice Act 1991 s.2(2)(b), for wounding with intent to cause grievous bodily harm. A had asked for directions from a group of three inebriated men, one of whom had thought that A was an undercover policeman. He punched A in the face and grabbed him, whereupon A retaliated by stabbing the victim about 10 times, leaving a four inch knife blade broken off in the victim's back. A contended that the trial judge had erred in passing such a sentence without the benefit of presentence and psychiatric reports and also that he had been misled by an error in the antecedents.

Held, allowing the appeal and reducing the sentence to six years' imprisonment, made consecutive to the balance of 320 days from a previous 44 months term, that it was clear that the trial judge had been misled into believing that A had been released from custody only days, rather than some 10 months, before the attack. In addition, had the trial judge received the subsequent report from the psychiatrist finding that A had no undue propensity to violence, then it was unlikely that he would have invoked s.2(2)(b) of the 1991 Act.

R. v. AGBEGAH (DEAN), Trans. Ref: 96/6898/Z2, May 12, 1997, Stuart Smith, L.J., CA (Crim Div).

1564. Grievous bodily harm—minor assault resulting in serious injury

[Offences Against the Person Act 1861 s.20.]

B appealed against a sentence of four years imprisonment after being convicted of inflicting grievous bodily harm. He was aged 47 and lived with his brother and both were alcoholics. Following an argument, he kicked his brother once in the bottom of the back as he was going upstairs. The kick caused the brother to fall head first down the stairs, causing an upper lumbar spine injury and a crushed fracture of the vertebrae. As a result the brother was severely disabled.

Held, allowing the appeal in part, that the sentence of four years was out of line with cases where an assault which would have been an offence under the Offences Against the Person Act 1861 s.20 had resulted in death. Some guidance could be obtained from cases of manslaughter. The sentence of four years was manifestly excessive and a sentence of two and a half years was substituted, *R. v. Ruby* (1988) 86 Cr. App. R. 186, [1988] C.L.Y. 952, *R. v. Hughes* (1988) 10 Cr. App. R. (S.) 169, [1989] C.L.Y. 1073, *R. v. Edwards (Martin John)* (1990) 12 Cr. App. R (S.) 199, [1991] C.L.Y. 1163 and *R. v. Gunn* (1992) 13 Cr. App. R. (S.) 544, [1993] C.L.Y. 1220 considered.

R. v. BARR (RAYMOND) [1996] 2 Cr. App. R. (S.) 294, Schiemann, L.J., CA (Crim Div).

1565. Grievous bodily harm—minor assault resulting in serious injury—victim accepted that his injuries were the result of an accident

C appealed against a sentence of 18 months imprisonment for inflicting grievous bodily harm. He and the victim were friends, both had been drinking at a public house and C was asked to leave. He waited outside the public house and when the victim came out at closing time he punched the victim twice and attempted to do so a third time. The victim stepped back to avoid the punch and fell into the path of a lorry, suffering serious injuries as a result.

Held, allowing the appeal and substituting a sentence of ten months. The court found some guidance in cases of manslaughter where death had resulted from what would otherwise have been a minor assault, and the fact that the victim had forgiven C for his part in causing his injuries and accepted that his injuries were the result of an accident was also taken into consideration.

R. v. COLLYER (COLIN) [1996] 2 Cr. App. R. (S.) 238, Laws, J., CA (Crim Div).

1566. Grievous bodily harm—severe and sustained attack—weapons used—four years' imprisonment unduly lenient

[Offences against the Person Act 1861 s.18, s.20; Criminal Justice Act 1988 s.36.]
The Attorney General applied for sentences to be referred under the Criminal Justice Act 1988 s.36 on the ground that they were unduly lenient. AJ and NJ had received consecutive sentences of three years' and one year's imprisonment on conviction of two charges under the Offences against the Person Act 1861 s.18 and s.20 respectively. AJ and NJ assaulted AP and MP, the brothers of NJ's cohabitee, with AP sustaining a severe head injury in a severe and sustained attack in which he was repeatedly kicked to the head and body and attacked with a bar stool and a pick axe handle and his head brought into contact with a fixed metal post. MP was assaulted when he tried to assist AP and received scars to his forehead and lip and lost five teeth.

Held, allowing the reference, that the sentences were unduly lenient given the nature of the assaults and the defendants' previous records for violence. On a guilty plea, the assistant recorder should have passed total sentences of eight and a half years' imprisonment, made up of seven years for the s.18 offence and one and a half years for the s.20 offence. However, taking account of double jeopardy, the terms would be reduced to six years for the s.18 offence and one year consecutive for the s.20 offence, giving a total of seven years.

Observed, that listing officers should pay particular care not to put very serious cases or cases deserving of very severe sentences before assistant recorders.

ATTORNEY GENERAL'S REFERENCES (NOS.8 AND 9 OF 1997), *Re; sub nom.* R. v. JEWITT (ANDREW MARK); R. v. JEWITT (NICHOLAS IAN), Trans. Ref: 9700773/R2; 9700774/R2, May 12, 1997, McCowan, L.J., CA (Crim Div).

1567. Grievous bodily harm—six months' imprisonment unduly lenient

Held, that a sentence of six months was unduly lenient for the offence of assault occasioning actual bodily harm and wounding with intent to cause grievous bodily harm, where the defendant had attacked a motorist and his passenger after a confrontation. In the offender's favour was that, although he had reacted very aggressively, he had not initiated the quarrel nor was the violence entirely gratuitous. While the court should have regard to personal factors relating to the offender, it should not be unduly influenced by them, and it was a matter of public concern that such attacks were seen to be severely punished. A sentence of two years was substituted.

ATTORNEY GENERAL'S REFERENCE (NO.60 OF 1996), *Re; sub nom.* R. v. HARTNETT (MICHAEL CHRISTOPHER), *The Times*, January 27, 1997, Lord Bingham of Cornhill, L.C.J., CA (Crim Div).

1568. Grievous bodily harm—suspended sentence unduly lenient

[Offences against the Person Act 1861 s.18; Criminal Justice Act 1988 s.36.]
The Attorney General applied for a sentence to be referred under the Criminal Justice Act 1988 s.36 on the ground that it was unduly lenient. H received a custodial sentence of two years' suspended for two years and compensation in the sum of £2,000 with £1,200 towards prosecution costs for an offence of grievous bodily harm with intent, contrary to the Offences against the Person Act 1861 s.18. While drunk, H had knocked the victim unconscious, then picked him up and dropped him on the pavement causing him a haemorrhage to the brain and a fractured skull. The Attorney General contended that the starting point for offences of this nature was four years.

Held, allowing the reference, that the sentence was unduly lenient and a custodial term of two years was substituted. Although H was young, of good character and was unlikely to reoffend, it was in the public interest that serious offences of this nature received an appropriate disposal, *Attorney General's Reference (Nos.17 and 18 of 1994), Re* (1995) 16 Cr. App. R. (S.) 418 followed. The circumstances were not sufficiently exceptional to justify suspension of the term, *R. v. Okinikan* (1993) 14 Cr. App. R. (S.) 453, [1993] C.L.Y. 1100 followed.

ATTORNEY GENERAL'S REFERENCE (NO.45 OF 1996), *Re; sub nom.* R. v. HUMPHRIES (JULIAN) [1997] 1 Cr. App. R. (S.) 429, Kennedy, L.J., CA (Crim Div).

1569. **Grievous bodily harm–trapping and reversing over police officer with a car**

[Offences Against the Person Act 1861 s.18, s.20.]

H appealed against concurrent sentences of imprisonment of 12 years on conviction of causing grievous bodily harm with intent, 18 months for aggravated vehicle taking and six months for driving while disqualified. He also received two concurrent sentences of six months each for breach of a two year probation order for handling and burglary. After a police chase, H crashed the stolen car he was driving, but, as a woman police officer approached the car, H reversed into her and trapped her. Although he was warned that she was underneath the car, H accelerated hard and drove over her, fracturing several vertebrae. H contended that the necessary intent which intensified the Offences Against the Person Act 1861 s.20 offence (with a maximum term of five years) into a s.18 offence must have been formed in a very short time and the sentence was excessive.

Held, dismissing the application, that the sentences were appropriate considering the serious assault on a police officer and H's lack of mitigation.

R. v. HALL (DARREN DAVID) [1997] 1 Cr. App. R. (S.) 62, Sachs, J., CA (Crim Div).

1570. **Grievous bodily harm–trial judge indicating neither defendant nor co-accused would be subject to custodial sentences–defendant entering plea on that basis**

[Criminal Justice Act 1988 s.36.]

The Attorney General applied for a sentence to be referred under the Criminal Justice Act 1988 s.36 on the ground that it was unduly lenient. B pleaded guilty to wounding with intent to cause grievous bodily harm. His girlfriend complained that she had been raped by a man and threatened with death if she told anybody. Subsequently the girl repeated the story to her stepfather, M, and B who went to find the man, who was a bus driver. They found him driving his bus, and M punched him, knocking him to the ground. The man admitted that he had had intercourse with the girl, and B punched and kicked him on the floor until M intervened. B kicked the driver again after he had stood up. He admitted the attack to the police. B was sentenced to a probation order for two years.

Held, refusing the reference, that M had been charged with assault occasioning actual bodily harm and the trial judge had given an indication that he would not send either M or B to prison. B pleaded guilty to wounding with intent to cause grievous bodily harm in the light of that indication. The court had indicated the seriousness of attacks involving kicking a man on the ground and of revenge attacks and could not countenance acts of private vengeance. Conduct such as had occurred in this case must ordinarily earn an immediate custodial sentence. The judge should not have been asked whether it would make a difference whether B were convicted of wounding with intent to cause grievous bodily harm, unlawful wounding or assault occasioning actual bodily harm. It was unfortunate that the judge indicated that he had no intention of imposing a prison sentence on either defendant. The sentence imposed on B was unduly lenient, but B had pleaded guilty to wounding with intent to cause grievous bodily harm on the basis that he would be dealt with in a certain way. It was not possible to predict the outcome if B had chosen to contest the issue whether he intended to cause grievous bodily harm, therefore the court would exercise its discretion not to increase the sentence, *Attorney General's Reference (No.10 of 1992), Re* (1994) 15 Cr. App. (S.) 1 and *Attorney General's*

References (Nos.17 and 18 of 1994), Re (1995) 16 Cr. App. R. (S.) 418 considered.

ATTORNEY GENERAL'S REFERENCE (NO.22 OF 1996), *Re; sub nom.* R. v. BROWN (LEE CHARLES) [1997] 1 Cr. App. R. (S.) 191, Lord Bingham of Cornhill, C.J., CA (Crim Div).

1571. Grievous bodily harm–unprovoked attack–combination order unduly lenient

[Offences Against the Person Act 1861 s.18; Criminal Justice Act 1988 s.36.]

The Attorney General applied for a sentence to be referred under the Criminal Justice Act 1988 s.36 on the ground that it was unduly lenient. G, aged 20, was sentenced to combination order, comprising 100 hours' community service and a probation order for two years, after pleading guilty to causing grievous bodily harm with intent, contrary to the Offences Against the Person Act 1861 s.18. G had attacked a man in the street. The victim suffered amnesia, a suspected fracture of the skull, swelling around the eyes, bruising to the side of his face and superficial injuries to his back and knees. The victim was in hospital for several days. Aggravating features were that the victim was a stranger, the attack was unprovoked, consisting of kicks and stamping to the head while the victim was on the ground, the attack was ended only because of the intervention of a third party and G had previous convictions of assault occasioning actual bodily harm. However, G had pleaded guilty at the earliest opportunity and showed remorse for the attack.

Held, allowing the reference, that the combination order was unduly lenient and the interference of the court was justified. The aggravating features of the offence had not been sufficiently taken into consideration. A non-custodial sentence for an offence of this kind was inappropriate, *R. v. Ivey* (1981) 3 Cr. App. R. (S.) 185, [1981] C.L.Y 525 and *Attorney General's Reference (No.10 of 1992), Re* (1993) 15 Cr. App. R. (S.) 1 considered. Taking into account the element of double jeopardy, the six months spent in custody awaiting sentence and the 100 hours' community service completed by G, the court substituted a sentence of three and a half years' detention.

ATTORNEY GENERAL'S REFERENCE (NO.59 OF 1996), *Re; sub nom.* R. v. GRAINGER (TERENCE), [1997] 2 Cr. App. R.(S.) 250, February 11, 1997, Rose, L.J., CA (Crim Div).

1572. Grievous bodily harm–unprovoked attack by man with record of violence– probation order unduly lenient

[Criminal Justice Act 1988 s.36.]

The Attorney General applied for a sentence to be referred under the Criminal Justice Act 1988 s.36 on the ground that it was unduly lenient. F was sentenced to a probation order for two years after being convicted of wounding with intent to cause grievous bodily harm. He lived near the victim and there had been ill feeling between their two families for some time. He attacked the victim as he was walking home from a public house, striking him with a hollow metal tube and causing lacerations to his scalp. The Attorney General asked the court to review the sentence on the ground that it was unduly lenient.

Held, allowing the reference, that this was a serious unprovoked attack with a weapon by a man with a record of violence who was subject to two existing community sentences at the time of the offence. The probation order was unduly lenient. Bearing in mind the element of double jeopardy, the court substituted a sentence of 21 months' imprisonment.

ATTORNEY GENERAL'S REFERENCE (NO.65 OF 1995), *Re; sub nom.* R. v. FERRIS (VERNON) [1996] 2 Cr. App. R. (S.) 209, Lord Taylor of Gosforth, C.J., CA (Crim Div).

1573. Grievous bodily harm–violent disorder–racial violence where victim permanently disabled–sentences unduly lenient

[Criminal Justice Act 1988 s.36; Offences against the Person Act 1861 s.18; Public Order Act 1986 s.2(1).]

The Attorney General applied for a sentence to be referred under the Criminal Justice Act 1988 s.36 on the ground that it was unduly lenient. SA, aged 47 years, and JA and W, both aged 20 years, were convicted of causing grievous bodily harm with intent, contrary to the Offences against the Person Act 1861 s.18, and of violent disorder, contrary to the Public Order Act 1986 s.2(1). SA was sentenced to five years' and two years' imprisonment concurrent, JA to three and a half years' and two years' detention in a young offender institution concurrent and W to four years' and two years' detention in a young offender institution concurrent. The accused had been involved in the operation of a fairground when violence with racialist overtones erupted. A victim had been beaten senseless with a weapon and, after a year, was still hospitalised and incapable of speech or voluntary movement having suffered severe brain damage, with no likelihood of an improvement in his condition. Three other victims suffered lesser injuries. The instant offences were revenge attacks for violence earlier the same evening. SA and W had pleaded not guilty and JA made a late plea of guilty. W's appeal against conviction had been dismissed.

Held, allowing the reference, that the sentences must be increased. The racial element was an aggravating feature, *Attorney General's References (Nos.29, 30 and 31 of 1994), Re* (1995) 16 Cr. App. R. (S.) 698, [1996] 1 C.L.Y. 1917 followed. Notwithstanding that it had not been proved who had struck the blow against the principal victim, that there had been no preplanning, the delay and the element of double jeopardy, these were grave offences which would be dealt with severely. The following sentences would be substituted: SA, seven and four years' imprisonment concurrent, W, five and a half years' and four years' detention concurrent; and JA, five years' and three years' detention concurrent.

ATTORNEY GENERAL'S REFERENCE (NOS.25, 29 AND 27 OF 1995), *Re*; *sub nom.* R. v. WILSON (WILLIAM ROBERT); R. v. APPLETON (STEVEN); R. v. APPLETON (JASON STEVEN) [1996] 2 Cr. App. R. (S.) 390, Lord Taylor of Gosforth, C.J., CA (Crim Div).

1574. Grievous bodily harm–wounding with intent–indication of sentence by judge–three and a half years' imprisonment unduly lenient

[Criminal Justice Act 1988 s.36; Criminal Justice Act 1991 s.2(2)(b).]

The Attorney General applied for a sentence to be referred under the Criminal Justice Act 1988 s.36 on the ground that it was unduly lenient. T was convicted of wounding with intent to cause grievous bodily harm and pleaded guilty to affray. He attacked a man with whom he had previously had an argument, striking him across the back of the head with a pool cue. The victim suffered a five centimetre laceration which required eight stitches. On an earlier occasion T attacked a man in a dispute over a debt. He headbutted the man and kicked and punched him. The victim was found to have a swollen left eye, a nose bleed, a loose tooth and cuts. T was sentenced to 18 months' imprisonment for wounding with intent to cause grievous bodily harm and two years' consecutive for affray.

Held, allowing the reference, that T had been sentenced for both offences by the judge before whom he had pleaded guilty to the affray. The trial for wounding with intent to cause grievous bodily harm had been conducted by another judge, who had commented that he would have imposed a sentence of 18 months for the wounding with intent to cause grievous bodily harm, but transferred the case so that he could be sentenced for both matters by the same judge. The judge who eventually sentenced T for both offences indicated that he would have passed a sentence of five years' imprisonment under the Criminal Justice Act 1991 s.2(2)(b), but considered himself constrained by the comments of the first judge. It was not clear why the judge who had tried T for wounding with intent to cause grievous bodily harm had not passed sentence, but if a judge for good reason decided not to pass sentence, it was appropriate for him to express his view as to the appropriate sentence at least in broad terms. The judge who eventually sentenced T would not necessarily be bound by this view, but if expectations of a particular form or length of sentence were raised it might give him a justifiable sense of grievance to disappoint them. The sentence of 18 months was unduly lenient and the sentence for wounding with intent to cause grievous bodily harm would be increased to four years, consecutive to the sentence for the affray, *Attorney General's Reference (No.41 of 1994), Re* (1995) 16 Cr. App. R. (S.) 792, [1996] 1 C.L.Y. 1919, *Attorney General's Reference (No.47 of 1994), Re* (1995) 16 Cr. App. R. (S.) 865, [1996] 1 C.L.Y. 1910, *Attorney General's Reference (No.30 of 1993), Re* (1995) 16 Cr. App. R. (S.) 318 and *R. v. Utip* (1993) 14 Cr. App. R. (S.), [1994] C.L.Y. 1382 referred to.

ATTORNEY GENERAL'S REFERENCE (NO.38 OF 1996), *Re; sub nom.* R. v. TORGERSON (EDWIN CARL PETER) [1997] 1 Cr. App. R. (S.) 383, Rose, L.J., CA (Crim Div).

1575. Grievous bodily harm—wounding with intent—three years' imprisonment not unduly lenient

[Criminal Justice Act 1988 s.36.]

The Attorney General applied for a sentence to be referred under the Criminal Justice Act 1998 s.36 on the ground that it was unduly lenient. H pleaded guilty to wounding with intent to cause grievous bodily harm and affray. He broke into the house of his former girlfriend and struck her two blows with a pair of scissors. He also attacked the woman's boyfriend and a neighbour who came to their assistance. The former girlfriend suffered a deep laceration which caused a loss of blood and damage to a facial nerve which would give rise to permanent disability. H was sentenced to three years' imprisonment for wounding with intent to cause grievous bodily harm and one year concurrent for affray.

Held, refusing the reference, that the sentencer had passed sentence on the basis that H had gone to the victim's house to seek a reconciliation; although the sentence appeared lenient, it could not be considered unduly lenient in the light of the basis on which the plea had been accepted, *R. v. Ghuman* (1985) 7 Cr. App. R. (S.) 114, [1986] C.L.Y 905, *Attorney General's Reference (No. 39 of 1994), Re* (1994) 16 Cr. App. R. (S.) 763, [1996] 1 C.L.Y. 1911, *R. v. Swain* (1994) 15 Cr. App. R. (S.) 765, [1995] 1 C.L.Y. 1421 and *R. v. Hashi* (1994) 16 Cr. App. R. (S.) 121, [1995] 1 C.L.Y. 1429 considered.

ATTORNEY GENERAL'S REFERENCE (NO.37 OF 1996), *Re; sub nom.* R. v. HOBDAY (DAVID THOMAS) [1997] 1 Cr. App. R. (S.) 304, Rose, L.J., CA (Crim Div).

1576. Handling stolen goods—mitigation for good behaviour unconnected with offence

A pleaded guilty to three counts of handling stolen cars and was sentenced to 15 months' imprisonment. He ran a small car breaking yard in which three stolen cars, all of relatively low value, were found.

Held, allowing the appeal, that on an earlier occasion A had assisted in the apprehension of some men who were carrying out a robbery, and had given evidence against them; he had received a reward by order of the trial judge. A was entitled to expect credit for such behaviour if he was himself in trouble before the courts. The sentencer should have given greater credit for this factor. While the case called for a sentence which would be a deterrent to receivers of stolen motor vehicles, the sentence would be reduced to nine months.

R. v. ALEXANDER (ADRIAN STEPHEN) [1997] 2 Cr. App. R. (S.) 74, Douglas Brown, J., CA (Crim Div).

1577. Handling stolen goods—proceeds of robbery of security van

S and a coaccused, L, sought leave to appeal against sentences of eight and seven years' imprisonment respectively on conviction of handling stolen goods with S also pleading guilty to conspiracy to steal and aggravated vehicle taking.

S and L had both received large sums of foreign money as the result of a security vehicle robbery, but were not charged in respect of the robbery itself.

Held, refusing the application, that the sentencer was entitled to refer to the circumstances of the robbery as the background of the subsequent handling. Those who assisted in the disposal of the proceeds of major crime could only expect severe sentences. A sentence of seven years for handling the stolen money (some £150,000) was a proper sentence notwithstanding that S and L had not commissioned the robbery and were not professional receivers of stolen goods, *R. v. Patel* (1986) 6 Cr. App. R. (S.) 191, [1986] C.L.Y. 831, *R. v. Reader* (1988) 10 Cr. App. R. (S.) 210, *R. v. Bendon* (1983) 5 Cr. App. R. (S.) 328, [1984] C.L.Y. 864, *R. v. Byrne* (1994) 15 Cr. App. R. (S.) 34, *R. v. Hutchings* (1994) 15 Cr. App. R. (S.) 498, [1995] 1 C.L.Y. 1400 and *R. v. Amlani and Smith* (1995) 16 Cr. App. R. (S.) 339 cited.

R. v. SHEARER (IAN PAUL); R. v. LYNCH (KARL PHILLIP) [1997] 1 Cr. App. R. (S.) 159, McKinnon, J., CA (Crim Div).

1578. Harassment–judge could dissent from psychiatric report in determining whether stalker represented continuing threat to victim

S appealed against a sentence of 30 months' imprisonment imposed upon conviction for assault occasioning actual bodily harm, following an obsessive pursuit of the victim from 1992-96, causing injury to the victim's physical and mental health. Whilst accepting that a custodial sentence was merited, S contended that the judge had been wrong to dissent from psychiatric reports indicating that S, if at liberty, would not represent a continuing threat to the victim.

Held, allowing the appeal and reducing the sentence to 21 months, that, whilst in general a judge would be reluctant to dissent from expert medical opinion on technical issues, where the question was whether S was likely to represent a continuing threat to the victim, the judge was justified in concluding that he was better placed to determine the issue than the doctors. A custodial sentence took into account both the need to punish S for his conduct and to protect the victim from future harm. A significant custodial sentence was appropriate, but the gravity of the offence was mitigated somewhat by S's apparent inability to control his obsession with the victim and, in determining the period of protection to be afforded to the victim, it had to be borne in mind that this was S's first custodial sentence, *R. v. Burstow* [1997] 1 Cr. App. R. 144, [1996] 1 C.L.Y. 1438 distinguished.

R. v. SMITH (LEONARD), *The Times*, June 26, 1997, Lord Bingham of Cornhill, L.C.J., CA (Crim Div).

1579. Illegal entrants–facilitating illegal entry

[Immigration Act 1971 s.25.]

B appealed against a sentence of seven years' imprisonment on a conviction for facilitating illegal entry contrary to the Immigration Act 1971 s.25. S and his girlfriend arrived in the country in a lorry driven by S. S claimed that the vehicle contained furniture, but on being searched it was found to contain 19 illegal entrants. B was 22 years old and of previous good character. He claimed that he had no knowledge of the illegal entrants and that he had been paid £450 by a German business colleague to drive the lorry.

Held, allowing the appeal in part, that although the offence was a bad one, bearing in mind the appellant's age and previous good character, the sentence passed was too long and would be reduced to five years' imprisonment.

R. v. BROWN (NICHOLAS ALEXANDER) [1997] 1 Cr. App. R. (S.) 112, Longmore, J., CA (Crim Div).

1580. Illegal entrants–facilitating illegal entry of refugee for humanitarian reasons

G was sentenced to nine months' imprisonment after pleading guilty to facilitating an illegal entry. He was stopped at Dover driving a car with a female passenger and her child. It became apparent that both were refugees from

Bosnia. The woman was the wife of a male refugee who had been brought into the UK legally. She had become separated from him and their sons. When she was traced, an application was made for her to be brought into the UK, but it was not approved. Her husband then arranged to collect her and her daughter by car.

Held, dismissing the appeal, that it was accepted that G had acted for humanitarian reasons and not for financial gain. The offence of facilitating illegal entry was serious and would often merit custodial sentences running into years. G knew that his passengers had been refused permission to enter the country and he had set out deliberately to break the law. A custodial sentence was justified and the sentence of nine months allowed for mitigation and was not manifestly excessive.

R. v. GOFORTH (BARRIE IAN) [1997] 1 Cr. App. R. (S.) 234, Keene, J., CA (Crim Div).

1581. Indecent assault–breach of trust–disabled female victims

T appealed against concurrent sentences of four years' imprisonment on four counts of indecent assault on a female to which he pleaded guilty. T was a voluntary Red Cross worker. His duties included escorting disabled women from one station in London to another. It was during these occasions that T assaulted the women. At the time of the offences T was 45 years old and was of previous good character.

Held, dismissing the appeal, that the judge gave full weight to the mitigating factors and the totality of the sentence passed was not manifestly excessive in view of the breach of trust and the fact that there were four separate assaults on women who were unable to escape from T since they were wheelchair bound, *R. v. Prokop* (1995) 16 Cr. App. R. (S.) 598 and *R. v. Cubitt* (1989) 11 Cr. App. R. (S.) 380 distinguished, *R. v. Pike (Colin)* [1996] 1 Cr. App. R. (S.) 4 affirmed.

R. v. TAYLOR (ANTHONY) [1997] 1 Cr. App. R. (S.) 36, Otton, L.J., CA (Crim Div).

1582. Indecent assault–breach of trust–disabled male victim

B, aged 63, appealed against a sentence of four years' imprisonment having been convicted of indecently assaulting a male. The offence occurred when B, as a Red Cross volunteer driver, took the complainant, a 38 year old severely physically disabled man, to the airport. B's defence was that the complainant had consented to the sexual activity. B had two previous convictions, one for an assault on a male in 1988.

Held, allowing the appeal to the extent of reducing the sentence to 30 months' imprisonment, that there were serious features to this case. It was a gross breach of trust and B could not use his record in mitigation. However, particularly given B's age and the fact that this was his first custodial sentence, a reduction would be made.

R. v. BAYFIELD (RICHARD MELVIN) [1996] 2 Cr. App. R. (S.) 441, Bennett, J., CA (Crim Div).

1583. Indecent assault–breach of trust–fine unduly lenient sentence

[Criminal Justice Act 1988 s.36.]

The Attorney General applied for a sentence to be referred under the Criminal Justice Act 1988 s.36 on the ground that it was unduly lenient. W was fined £250 for two convictions of indecent assault. The victim was a 15 year old girl, and the incidents occurred during a work placement in W's pet shop. W, aged 64 years, repeatedly touched the girl on her breasts, bottom and vagina, over her clothes. The girl objected and attempted to move away from him but he persisted. She was afraid to report him as she believed she might lose her job. After the events she was withdrawn and attempted to cut herself. W, who had a previous conviction for a sexual offence, denied the assaults and alleged the girl was lying and on drugs.

Held, allowing the appeal and substituing a sentence of eight months' imprisonment, that fines, for such an offence, were unduly lenient. The only mitigating factor was his age, but he showed no remorse for his actions. Double jeopardy was taken into account, W had to face the prospect of a custodial sentence for the second time and had lost his business and living accommodation as a result of the proceedings.

ATTORNEY GENERAL'S REFERENCE (NO.25 OF 1997), *Re*; *sub nom*. R. v. WILLIAMS (GWILYN LLOYD), Trans. Ref: 9703780/R2, July 22, 1997, McCowan, L.J., CA (Crim Div).

1584. Indecent assault–Crown Court committal on breach of conditional discharge–persistent offender

R, aged 30, appealed against a sentence of 15 months' imprisonment for indecent assault after he had entered the home of a woman he knew and assaulted her while she pretended to sleep. R pleaded guilty in the magistrates' court to a charge of threatening behaviour and being in breach of two conditional discharges. He was committed to the Crown Court for sentencing and was sentenced for the indecent assault and received consecutive terms in respect of the other offences, resulting in a total of 21 months.

Held, dismissing the appeal, that both the psychological report and the probation report considered there was a high·risk of reoffending and R had a history of persistent behaviour of this sort.

R. v. ROBINSON (PHILIP), Trans. Ref: 9606270 W3, December 4, 1996, Ebsworth, J., CA (Crim Div).

1585. Indecent assault–longer than normal sentence–further consecutive sentence for burglary inappropriate

[Criminal Justice Act 1991 s.2(2).]

W pleaded guilty to indecent assault, attempted burglary and criminal damage and was sentenced to eight years' imprisonment for indecent assault, passed as a longer than normal sentence under the Criminal Justice Act 1991 s.2(2)(b), with two years' imprisonment consecutive for the attempted burglary. W attempted to break into a house; when he was unsuccessful he broke into the home of a lady aged 76 and indecently assaulted her as she lay in her bed. When he was arrested and taken to the police station, he damaged a window. W was described as suffering from a severe personality disorder with borderline schizotypal and paranoid traits; he was a danger to the public but treatment was unlikely to alleviate his condition.

Held, allowing the appeal, that the sentencer was obliged to pass a longer than normal sentence under the 1991 Act s.2(2)(b), and the sentence of eight years for indecent assault was correct. It was wrong to impose a further consecutive sentence for the attempted burglary. Once the sentencer had assessed the term required for the protection of the public, a further period of imprisonment would not be justified for that purpose. The consecutive sentence would be ordered to run concurrently, *R. v. King (Samuel Nathaniel)* (1995) 16 Cr. App. R. (S.) 987, [1996] 1 C.L.Y. 2065 considered.

R. v. WALTERS (DESMOND ARTHUR) [1997] 2 Cr. App. R. (S.) 87, Curtis, J., CA (Crim Div).

1586. Indecent assault–offence committed on female walking home at night–10 months' imprisonment unduly lenient

[Criminal Justice Act 1988 s.36.]

The Attorney General applied for a sentence to be referred under the Criminal Justice Act 1988 s.36 on the ground that it was unduly lenient. W pleaded guilty to threatening to kill, indecent assault and theft. He accosted a young woman as she was walking home from work late at night, seized her from behind and applied pressure to her throat. He told her she was going to die, and grabbed her between the legs through her trousers. He then made off with her purse containing a small sum of money. He absconded and remained at large for over three years until he surrendered. During this time he met a woman with a family and went to live with them, providing support during the woman's illness. W was sentenced to 10 months' imprisonment on each count concurrently.

Held, allowing the reference and substituting 18 months' imprisonment for the original 10 month term, that the case illustrated the difficulty of achieving a balance between the victims of serious offences and an offender's personal circumstances. If the matter had been dealt with when the offence was committed, the sentence would have been at least four years. The sentence had now to be discounted, partly because of the element of double jeopardy and partly due to W's changed life style since absconding, *R. v. Currie* (1988) 10 Cr. App. R. (S.) 85, [1990] C.L.Y. 1334, *R. v. Emery-Barker* (1990) 12 Cr. App. R. (S.) 794, *R. v. Knibbs* (1991) 12 Cr. App. R. (S.) 655, [1992] C.L.Y. 1317, *R. v. Rackley* (1994) 15 Cr. App. R. (S.) 794, [1995] 1 C.L.Y. 1410, *R. v. Bird* (1987) 9 Cr. App. R. (S.) 77, [1989] C.L.Y. 910 and *R. v. Hull* (1991) 13 Cr. App. R. (S.) 223, [1993] C.L.Y. 1298 considered.

ATTORNEY GENERAL'S REFERENCE (NO.34 OF 1996), *Re; sub nom.* R. v. WEST (STEPHEN ANDREW) [1997] 1 Cr. App. R. (S.) 343, Rose, L.J., CA (Crim Div).

1587. **Informers—information provided against accomplices in drug trafficking conspiracy—sentence reduction to reflect value of assistance given**

S appealed against a sentence of seven years' imprisonment and a confiscation order in the amount of £1,371 having pleaded guilty to conspiring to import cannabis resin by boat from France. After a number of successful importations, S was arrested with others in possession of 600 kilogrammes of cannabis resin which had just been imported by inflatable boat. He made full admissions, and gave details of earlier importation, identifying the origin of the cannabis, the purchase price and the precise involvement of each conspirator. S gave evidence for the prosecution which made a substantial contribution to the prosecution case.

Held, allowing the appeal, reducing the term of imprisonment to four and a half years, that S had played a substantial part in the conspiracy and the starting point for his sentence would have been in the region of 10 years. The sentence of seven years did not sufficiently reflect the value of his assistance to the prosecuting authority, and a sentence of four and a half years' imprisonment was substituted, *R. v. Sinfield* (1981) 3 Cr. App. R. (S.) 258 and *R. v. King* (1986) 82 Cr. App. R. 120, [1986] C.L.Y. 861 followed.

R. v. SAGGAR (SUNIL); R. v. PERKS (RAYMOND) [1997] 1 Cr. App. R. (S.) 167, Otton, L.J., CA (Crim Div).

1588. **Informers—offender giving evidence against accomplice—discount entitlement**

W appealed against a sentence of seven years' imprisonment, having pleaded guilty to attempted murder and conspiracy to assault. A woman persuaded two men, separately, that she would marry each of them. The first man paid £30,000 into a bank account in their joint names, from which the woman withdrew £27,000, and both men made wills in her favour. W owed money to the woman, who had also threatened to accuse him of breaking into her car. The woman persuaded him to attack both men. He attacked one man and stabbed him in the back with a screwdriver four times. The other man was attacked with a piece of lead sheet and then thrown into a dock from which he was lucky to be rescued. The woman, who was convicted by the jury of the same offences was sentenced to 10 years' imprisonment. W gave evidence against her and it was accepted that she would not have been convicted without his evidence.

Held, allowing the appeal and reducing the sentence to five years, that the starting point was the benchmark of 10 years set by the sentence on the woman. W's plea was adequately reflected in his sentence of seven years, but it was argued that he was entitled to a further discount for giving evidence. The Court accepted that there should be a discount where the accomplice had given truthful evidence; the discount should reflect the seriousness of the offence, the importance of the evidence, and the effect of giving the evidence on the future circumstances of the witness. The Court was satisfied that there was room for a further discount of two years in respect of the fact that he had given information and eventually evidence.

R. v. WOOD (ROBERT) [1997] 1 Cr. App. R. (S.) 347, Mantell, J., CA (Crim Div).

1589. Juvenile offenders—arson—relevant date for determining age for purposes of Criminal Justice Act 1982 s.18—duty of counsel to monitor lawfulness of sentence

[Criminal Justice Act 1982 s.18; Supreme Court Act 1981 s.47.]

B appealed against a sentence of 42 months' detention in a young offender institution imposed on conviction of attempted arson being reckless as to whether life would be endangered thereby. He threw a petrol bomb, consisting of a milk bottle filled with petrol, at the window of a house where his mother and stepfather lived. The bomb struck the window but failed to ignite. B was in care at the time of the offence and had absconded from a semi-secure unit. He was aged 17 on the date of conviction, but had attained the age of 18 by the date of sentence.

Held, allowing the appeal and substituting a term of two years' detention instead, that as B had reached his 18th birthday by the date on which sentence was imposed, it had been assumed that for sentencing purposes he was to be treated as over 18 years and was accordingly liable to a sentence of detention in a young offender institution which would not be subject to the limitations in the Criminal Justice Act 1982 s.18. It was now well settled that the relevant date for the purpose of determining age for this purpose was the date of conviction, *R. v. Robinson* (1992) 14 Cr. App. R. (S.) 448, [1993] C.L.Y. 979 followed. Had this error been noticed promptly, the sentence could have been varied within 28 days in accordance with the Supreme Court Act 1981 s.47, but that did not happen. Accordingly, by virtue of s.18(5) of the 1982 Act, so much of the term as exceeded two years was to be treated as remitted, *R. v. Anderson* (1991) 13 Cr. App. R. (S.) 325, [1993] C.L.Y. 979 and *R. v. Egdell* (1993) 15 Cr. App. R. (S.) 509, [1995] 1 C.L.Y. 1503 applied. It was unfortunate that in a case where a sentence of the length imposed by the judge was plainly called for, the oversight on his and counsel's part necessitated the declarations that the sentence would take effect as one of two years' detention in a young offender institution. It was to be emphasised that it was the duty of judge and counsel to ensure that errors or omissions in sentencing were not made. In cases where young offenders were involved, it was appropriate for counsel to satisfy themselves in advance what the sentencer's powers were. There was no distinction between counsel for the defence and the prosecution in this regard.

R. v. BRULEY (SHANE KEITH); *sub nom.* R. v. B (A JUVENILE) [1997] 1 Cr. App. R. (S.) 339, Hutchison, L.J., CA (Crim Div).

1590. Juvenile offenders—manslaughter—deterrent sentence—offender threatened with violence by victim

S pleaded guilty to manslaughter and possessing a firearm with intent to endanger life and was sentenced to 12 years' detention in a young offender institution, with six years' detention concurrent respectively. S was thought to have been involved in a robbery at a post office in the course of which a substantial sum was stolen. The deceased and another man went to see S and demanded money from him. During the course of this incident the deceased or his companion threatened S with a gun and shortly afterwards S shot him in the chest. S claimed that he had acted in self defence when the deceased had entered a house where he was; he had not intended to kill him.

Held, allowing the appeal, that although S was only 17, he had acquired the gun and a bullet proof vest before the incident. The use of firearms was a matter of great public concern in the locality. While the court accepted the need to pass a deterrent sentence, the sentencer had given inadequate weight to the fact that S had fired when he was followed to his house by men who had already been violent and who might have been armed. The sentence would be reduced to nine years' detetion in a young offender institution.

R. v. SWATSON (LEIGH MARLOW) [1997] 2 Cr. App. R. (S.) 140, Potter, L.J., CA (Crim Div).

1591. Juvenile offenders—manslaughter—lenient sentence justified by young age, guilty plea, good character and remorse—two years' imprisonment not unduly lenient

[Criminal Justice Act 1988 s.36.]

The Attorney General applied for a sentence to be referred under the Criminal Justice Act 1988 s.36 on the ground that it was unduly lenient. Two girls, aged 13 and 12, received custodial sentences of two years each for manslaughter. The victim, a 13 year old girl, had attempted to stop a fight between her friend and another girl and was pulled to the ground by the offenders who kicked her in the head. The trial judge found in a Newton hearing that the victim had died from subarachnoid haemorrhage caused by a single kick behind the jaw and below the ear. The Attorney General contended that the fact that the attack arose during deliberate fighting, was unprovoked, and involved the kicking of a defenceless victim while on the ground, meant that the sentences were altogether too lenient.

Held, allowing the reference, but refusing to increase the sentence, that the sentences were undoubtedly lenient but not unduly so. The trial judge had correctly weighed the young ages of the offenders, their previous good character, their remorse, their guilty pleas and the likely effect of prolonged incarceration upon them against the need to punish and reflect public disapproval and to provide a deterrent sentence, *R. v. James* (1986) 8 Cr. App. R. (S.) 281, [1987] C.L.Y. 976, *Attorney General's Reference (No.24 of 1991), Re* (1992) 13 Cr. App. R. (S.) 724, [1993] C.L.Y. 1331, *R. v. Silver* (1982) 4 Cr. App. R. (S.) 48, [1983] C.L.Y. 848 and *R. v. Eaton* (1989) 11 Cr. App. R. (S.) 475, [1991] C.L.Y. 1166 considered.

ATTORNEY GENERAL'S REFERENCE (NO.69 OF 1996), *Re; sub nom.* R. v. L (A JUVENILE); R. v. H (A JUVENILE), February 25, 1997, Lord Bingham of Cornhill, L.C.J., CA (Crim Div).

1592. Juvenile offenders—manslaughter—provocation

[Children and Young Persons Act 1933 s.53(2).]

M, aged 15 at the time of the offence, was sentenced to six years' detention under the Children and Young Persons Act 1933 s.53(2), after being convicted of manslaughter by reason of provocation on an indictment charging murder. The deceased was another boy who was known to M. The deceased met M and started to push him around; M took a bottle from a shop and threatened the deceased with it. The deceased left but returned with a stick and began to attack M with the stick. The fight was broken up by police officers. Later M and the deceased arranged to fight and a group of young people gathered to watch the fight. The deceased approached M and was immediately stabbed in the chest.

Held, dismissing the appeal that the sentence was not excessive, as in light of the circumstances M had had ample opportunity to resist the pressures of that particular day and not become involved. Also M, at the time, was on bail for further offences involving offensive weapons.

R. v. McNEIL (MARK) [1997] 1 Cr. App. R. (S.) 266, Cresswell, J., CA (Crim Div).

1593. Juvenile offenders—manslaughter—Secretary of State fixing minimum tariff—legality of applying same principles as used for adults

[Children and Young Persons Act 1933 s.53(2); Criminal Justice Act 1991 s.34.]

F, a juvenile, sought judicial review of the tariff element of a discretionary sentence of detention for life passed under the Children and Young Persons Act 1933 s.53(2). F had pleaded guilty to manslaughter on the grounds of diminished responsibility. The Secretary of State certified that the Criminal Justice Act 1991 s.34 should apply and, following recommendations from the judge and the Lord Chief Justice, imposed a minimum term of nine years' detention to meet the requirements of punishment and deterrence. Following F's initial challenge, the Secretary of State reduced the tariff period to seven years. F challenged that period as being excessive.

Held, allowing the application, that the principles applicable when fixing a specified tariff for adult offenders could not be applied to juveniles when setting the minimum term of a discretionary sentence under s.53(2), *R. v. Secretary of State for the Home Department, ex p. Venables* [1997] 3 W.L.R. 23, [1996] 1 C.L.Y. 1975 applied. The approach should be the same as in cases of murder under s.53(1) and the offender's welfare fell to be considered. In imposing a sentence under s.34 of the 1991 Act, the judge had to specify a tariff based on half to two-thirds of the determinate sentence which would have been appropriate had it not been necessary to impose a life sentence. Following *Venables* however, in the case of juveniles the Court of Appeal's approach in *R. v. Carr (Sharon Louise)* [1996] 1 Cr. App. R. (S.) 191, [1996] 1 C.L.Y. 1971 should be applied to s.53(2) cases such that the specified minimum period should be fixed at half of the relevant determinate sentence. Accordingly, seven years was excessive in F's case, the appropriate tariff not exceeding the six years she had already served.

R. v. SECRETARY OF STATE FOR THE HOME DEPARTMENT, *ex p.* FURBER, *The Times*, July 11, 1997, Simon Brown, L.J., QBD.

1594. Juvenile offenders—murder—boy aged 14 convicted of attempted murder—detention for life—reduction of period specified

[Children and Young Persons Act 1933 s.53(2); Criminal Justice Act 1991 s.34.]

S, aged 14, appealed against sentence after having been convicted of attempted murder. He persuaded a 10 year old girl, his cousin, to walk down a lane with him; he tripped her so that she fell to the ground and applied pressure to her neck so that she became unconscious. While she was unconscious, he interfered with her sexually. S denied all responsibility for the attack. S was sentenced to detention for life under the Children and Young Persons Act 1933 s.53(2), with a period of five years specified for the purposes of the Criminal Justice Act 1991 s.34.

Held, allowing the appeal in part, that although there was no evidence of mental illness, the medical witnesses agreed that S represented a risk which could not be assessed while he continued to deny responsibility for the attack. The totality of the evidence required an indeterminate sentence. The period specified under the Criminal Justice Act 1991 s.34 was reduced to four years.

R. v. SHELDON (LESLIE MAXWELL) (SENTENCING) [1996] 2 Cr. App. R. (S.) 397, Simon Brown, L.J., CA (Crim Div).

1595. Juvenile offenders—murder—Secretary of State fixing minimum tariff—legality of applying some principles as used for adults—public opinion irrelevant

[Children and Young Persons Act 1933 s.53(1); Criminal Justice Act 1991.]

The Secretary of State appealed against a Court of Appeal ruling dismissing his appeal against an earlier ruling that his decision to fix a tariff period of 15 years for the detention at Her Majesty's pleasure of V and T following their conviction for murder at the age of 10 was unlawful. In reaching that conclusion he had applied the same principles applicable to adult offenders and taken into account the public's concern about the case, as evidenced by petitions and letters supporting a period of detention for life. V and T cross-appealed.

Held, allowing the cross-appeals and dismissing the appeal (Lord Goff and Lord Lloyd dissenting), that a term of detention at Her Majesty's pleasure passed under the Children and Young Persons Act 1933 s.53(1) was not to be equated with a sentence of mandatory life imprisonment passed on an adult offender and different considerations applied. In fixing the tariff period the Secretary of State could only have regard to circumstances existing at the time the offence was committed and not events which occurred subsequently. He had been given powers analogous to those of a sentencing judge and was subject to the same constraints. It therefore followed that petitions by the public and public opinion expressed by the media were irrelevant. The Secretary of State had a duty to consider at intervals whether continued detention was justified and to take into account the children's welfare and the possibility of their reintegration into society, depending upon their progress during detention. As the Criminal Justice Act 1991 had not altered the position, the policy applied by the Secretary of State was unlawful.

R. v. SECRETARY OF STATE FOR THE HOME DEPARTMENT, *ex p.* VENABLES; R. v. SECRETARY OF STATE FOR THE HOME DEPARTMENT, *ex p.* THOMPSON [1997] 3 W.L.R. 23, Lord Goff of Chieveley, HL.

1596. Juvenile offenders–robbery–21 months' imprisonment unduly lenient

[Criminal Justice Act 1988 s.36; Children and Young Persons Act 1933 s.53 (2).]

The Attorney General applied for a sentence to be referred under the Criminal Justice Act 1988 s.36 on the ground that it was unduly lenient. R, aged 17, was convicted of robbery. He and a co-defendant stole two bottles of champagne and a quantity of cash from an off licence. The store owner was struck with a bottle and sustained injuries which required stitches. R was sentenced to 21 months' detention in a young offender institution.

Held, allowing the reference, that R was on bail for robbery at the time of the offence. It would normally be appropriate to pass a shorter sentence on a young offender than would be passed on an adult for the same offence, but the court should strike a balance between the youth of R and the need to deter others from offending in a similar manner. The sentence of 21 months' detention in a young offender institution was unduly lenient: a sentence of three and a half years' detention under the Children and Young Persons Act 1933 s.53 (2) was substituted, *Attorney General's Reference (No.9 of 1989), Re* (1990) 12 Cr. App. R. (S.) 71, [1991] C.L.Y. 1214, *R. v. Tidiman* (1990) 12 Cr. App. R. (S.) 702, [1992] C.L.Y. 1155, *R. v. Hollingsworth* (1993) 14 Cr. App. R. (S.) 96, [1993] C.L.Y. 1274, *Attorney General's Reference (No.3 of 1994), Re* (1995) 16 Cr. App. R. (S.) 176, [1995] 1 C.L.Y. 1275 and *R. v. Marriott and Shepherd* (1995) 16 Cr. App. R. (S.) 428 considered.

ATTORNEY GENERAL'S REFERENCE (NO.41 OF 1996), *Re; sub nom.* R. v. RICHARDSON (REUBEN) [1997] 1 Cr. App. R. (S.) 388, Cresswell, J., CA (Crim Div).

1597. Juvenile offenders–robbery–attempts–long term detention

[Children and Young Persons Act 1933 s.53(2), s.53(3).]

C and two others, aged 14, 13 and 15 at the time of the offence, pleaded guilty to attempted robbery. They were sentenced to two years' detention under the Children and Young Persons Act 1933 s.53(2) and s.53(3), or two years' detention in a young offender institution, for the attempted robbery, concurrent with three years' detention under the 1933 Act s.53(2) and s.53(3) in the case of the second appellant for the robbery. They attempted to rob a person working at a newsagent's shop. One appellant jumped over the counter and held and pushed the assistant, while another appellant and a codefendant attempted to open the till. The second appellant pleaded guilty to a further robbery in which he and another attacked the proprietor of an off licence and demanded money. The proprietor was threatened with a knife and struck with a pole, and £140 was stolen.

Held, dismissing the appeals, that the sentencer was dealing with a serious crime which called for a custodial sentence to mark the gravity of the offence and for the protection of the public. The sentencer had taken proper account of each of the appellant's circumstances, and their plea.

R. v. COURTNEY (JULIAN); R. v. AMEWODE (STEPHEN); R. v. EL-WHABE (SHARIFE) [1997] 2 Cr. App. R. (S.) 121, Potter, L.J., CA (Crim Div).

1598. Juvenile offenders–robbery–elderly victim threatened with violence–eight months' detention unduly lenient

[Children and Young Persons Act 1933 s.53(2); Criminal Justice Act 1988 s.36.]

The Attorney General applied for a sentence to be referred under the Criminal Justice Act 1988 s.36 on the ground it was unduly lenient. C was sentenced to eight months' detention in a young offender institution for robbery consecutive to four months' detention for aggravated vehicle taking. C, aged 16 years, and his accomplice forced entry through a window of a flat belonging to an 85 year old woman late at night. They were both wearing masks and one of them threatened the victim that she would be killed if she did not hand over a key. One of the intruders grabbed her and pushed her on to the floor, then put his foot on her chest and stood on her. The victim suffered pain and bruising. The identity of the attacker was not established. C originally pleaded not guilty, then at a later hearing changed his plea. C had previous convictions for robbery and violent offences, and committed the offence whilst on bail. The Attorney General contended that the sentence length did not reflect the aggravatiing features of the case, that there was a need for a deterent sentence and this was an appropriate case for the court to exercise its power under the Children and Young Persons Act 1933 s.53(2).

Held, allowing the application, that the sentence was too lenient and a sentence of three years' detention under s.53(2) would be substituted. Some discount was appropriate for the trauma of facing the sentencing process for the second time.

ATTORNEY GENERAL'S REFERENCE (NO.30 OF 1997), *Re; sub nom*. R. v. C (A JUVENILE), Trans. Ref: 97/4296/R2, October 2, 1997, Lord Bingham of Cornhill, L.C.J., CA (Crim Div).

1599. Juvenile offenders–robbery–long term detention to adult maximum–meaning of "not more than 17 years"

[Children and Young Persons Act 1933 s.53(2); Criminal Justice and Public Order Act 1994 s.16.]

D and S appealed against respective custodial sentences of four years and 42 months for robbery made concurrent, in each case, with terms of 12 months for burglary. D contended that his sentence was ultra vires, because the trial judge purported to make it pursuant to the Children and Young Persons Act 1933 s.53(2), as amended by the Criminal Justice and Public Order Act 1994 s.16. The latter section applied where the defendant was at least 10 and not more than 17 years of age, whereas both he and S were 17 years and one month of age at the time of their convictions. The question for the court was the meaning of "not more than 17 years" in terms of s.16 of the 1994 Act.

Held, dismissing the appeal, that it was clear that Parliament had intended to revise the 1933 Act by amendment in the 1994 Act, in order to include children below the age of 14 but above the age of 10 years. There had been no intention to provide a loophole for those over 17, but less than 18 years old. The sentence was therefore lawful as age at conviction was the relevant age.

R. v. D (A JUVENILE), Trans. Ref: 96/2815/Z5, 96/3136/Z5, October 8, 1996, Judge Van Der Werff, CA (Crim Div).

1600. Juvenile offenders–robbery–possession of imitation firearms–four and a half years' imprisonment unduly lenient

[Criminal Justice Act 1988 s.36.]

The Attorney General applied for a sentence to be referred under the Criminal Justice Act 1988 s.36 on the ground that it was unduly lenient. N and A pleaded guilty to three counts of robbery, three counts of possessing an imitation firearm with intent, and one count of conspiracy to rob. They were involved in two robberies at building society branches during which a female customer was held hostage and threatened with an imitation firearm. They were arrested near a sub-post office planning a further robbery. Both were sentenced to four and a half years' detention in a young offender institution.

Held, allowing the reference and increasing the sentences, that the offences were planned and well executed, realistic firearms were used and members of the public were taken hostage and terrorised to induce cashiers to hand over money. Sentences of seven and a half years' detention in a young offender institution would be substituted, *R. v. Dawkins (Michael)* (1995) 16 Cr. App. R. (S.) 456 cited.

ATTORNEY GENERAL'S REFERENCE (NOS.26 AND 27 OF 1996), *Re; sub nom.* R. v. NAZIR (JANGEER); R. v. AHMED (NAVEED) [1997] 1 Cr. App. R. (S.) 243, Lord Bingham of Cornhill, C.J., CA (Crim Div).

1601.   Juvenile offenders—robbery—possession of imitation firearms—four years' detention unduly lenient

[Children and Young Persons Act 1933 s.53(2); Criminal Justice Act 1988 s.36.]

The Attorney General applied for a sentence to be referred under the Criminal Justice Act 1988 s.36 on the ground that it was unduly lenient. C, aged 20, pleaded guilty to five counts of robbery, five counts of attempted robbery, and eight counts of possessing an imitation firearm. He was concerned in a series of robberies in which small shops were attacked and the assistants threatened with a knife and in one case an imitation firearm. K, aged 16, pleaded guilty to one count of robbery, two counts of attempted robbery and one of possessing an imitation firearm. He was concerned in a similar series of robberies or attempted robberies, one of which was committed with C. C was sentenced to four years' detention in a young offender institution and K to two years' detention under the Children and Young Persons Act 1933 s.53(2).

Held, allowing the references, that it was common knowledge that small business premises were extremely vulnerable and that the public interest in protecting people working in them overrode any personal features which might otherwise weigh in favour of a defendant. Sentences of nine, 10 or 11 years had been passed in similar cases and despite the unusual circumstances of the offenders, the sentences were unduly lenient. The sentences were increased to six years' detention in a young offender institution and three years' detention under s.53(2) respectively.

ATTORNEY GENERAL'S REFERENCE (NOS.23 AND 24 OF 1996), *Re; sub nom.* R. v. CAMPBELL (SCOTT TROY); R. v. KERHARD (ANDREW JEROME) [1997] 1 Cr. App. R. (S.) 174, Lord Bingham of Cornhill, L.C.J., CA (Crim Div).

1602.   Juvenile offenders—robbery—probation order unduly lenient

[Criminal Justice Act 1988 s.36; Criminal Justice and Public Order Act 1994 s.51.]

The Attorney General applied for a sentence to be referred under the Criminal Justice Act 1988 s.36 on the ground that it was unduly lenient. Following conviction for two robberies, blackmail, actual bodily harm and intimidating witnesses contrary to the Criminal Justice and Public Order Act 1994 s.51, W, a juvenile offender, was sentenced to concurrent sentences of two years' probation by an assistant recorder in the Crown Court. The Attorney General submitted that the use of a gun along with threats to kill in one robbery amounted to aggravating features and that the sentence was outside the discretion available to a sentencing judge.

Held, allowing the reference, that such offences committed by juvenile offenders against younger victims were not ordinarily appropriate for community penalties. Although the court always had to be aware of an offender's personal interests, it must also be mindful of the public interest and the indignation that such offences occasioned. In light of the authorities and the number of offences committed, along with the fact that the later offences occurred while W was on bail, the original sentence was unduly lenient and would be substituted for one of nine months' detention in respect of the robbery involving the gun and the threat to kill with no separate penalty imposed for the other offences.

ATTORNEY GENERAL'S REFERENCE (NO.47 OF 1996), *Re*; *sub nom*. R. v. W (A JUVENILE), [1997] 2 Cr. App. R.(S.) 194, January 16, 1997, Lord Bingham of Cornhill, L.C.J., CA (Crim Div).

1603. Juvenile offenders—theft and robbery—sentence for robbery under the Children and Young Persons Act 1933 s.53 unlawful

[Children and Young Persons Act 1933 s.53(2).]

W, aged 16, was involved in a number of incidents in which younger boys were forced to part with property, in some cases as a result of threats or menacing behaviour. W was sentenced to three years' detention under the Children and Young Persons Act, 1933 s.53(2) for the offences of robbery, and two years' detention for each of the theft offences, all to run concurrently, giving a total of three years' detention under s.53(2) of the Act. He appealed on the basis that a sentence under s.53(2) of the Act should only be passed if a custodial sentence of four years or more was merited after allowing for mitigation following *Fairhurst, Re* (1986) 8 Cr. App. R. (S.) 346.

Held, allowing the appeal in part, that the sentence of two years' detention for theft was unlawful and was quashed, leaving a total sentence of three years' detention under s.53(2) of the Act.

R. v. WAINFUR (MARK ANDREW) [1997] 1 Cr. App. R. (S.) 43, Swinton Thomas, L.J., CA (Crim Div).

1604. Kidnapping—conspiracy—van driver with no part in actual kidnap or interrogation of victim

M appealed against a sentence of 10 years' imprisonment for conspiracy to kidnap, with a concurrent sentence of seven years for false imprisonment. M had acted as the driver for the kidnap and transport of B from High Wycombe to Stoke-on-Trent and then to London, where he was arrested for his part in the offences. M was of previous good character and there was no evidence to connect him with the actual kidnap or interrogation of B.

Held, allowing the appeal, that even though M had pleaded not guilty and had not taken part in the kidnap, the sentence of 10 years was excessive and was reduced to eight years, with the concurrent sentence left intact, *R. v. Spence and Thomas* (1983) 5 Cr. App. R. (S.) 413, [1984] C.L.Y. 876 followed.

R. v. MOHEUDDIN (ASHIQ) [1997] 1 Cr. App. R. (S.) 85, Garland, J., CA (Crim Div).

1605. Magistrates' courts—forms—Amendment No.1—committal proceedings

See CRIMINAL PROCEDURE. §1352

1606. Magistrates' courts—forms—Amendment No.2—consent to community sentences

MAGISTRATES' COURTS (FORMS) (AMENDMENT) (NO.2) RULES 1997, SI 1997 2421 (L.38); made under the Magistrates' Court Act 1980 s.144. In force: November 1, 1997; £1.10.

These Rules amend the Magistrates' Courts (Forms) Rules 1981 (SI 1981 553) by amending certain forms used in criminal proceedings to take account of the changes effected by, and consequential upon, the Crime (Sentences) Act 1997 s.38, which removes the requirements for the accused to consent to the making of various community sentences and, in most cases, to indicate his willingness to comply with the requirements of such sentences.

1607. Magistrates' courts–young offenders–forms

MAGISTRATES' COURTS (CHILDREN AND YOUNG PERSONS) (AMENDMENT) RULES 1997, SI 1997 2420 (L.37); made under the Magistrates' Court Act 1980 s.144. In force: November 1, 1997; £1.10.

These Rules amend the Magistrates' Courts (Children and Young Persons) Rules 1992 (SI 1992 2071) by amending certain forms used in relation to criminal proceedings involving young offenders to take account of the changes effected by, and consequential upon, the Crime (Sentences) Act 1997 s.38, which removes the requirement for the accused to consent to the making of various community sentences and, in most cases, to indicate his willingness to comply with the requirements of such sentences.

1608. Manslaughter–aggravated vehicle taking–death caused to owner during course of theft–four and a half years' imprisonment unduly lenient

[Criminal Justice Act 1988 s.36.]

The Attorney General applied for a sentence to be referred under the Criminal Justice Act 1988 s.36 on the ground that it was unduly lenient. D, aged 21 years, was convicted of aggravated vehicle taking and manslaughter. He was sentenced respectively to two years' and four and a half years' detention in a young offender institution concurrent. He had pleaded guilty to causing death by dangerous driving, but was allowed to vacate that plea and plead guilty to manslaughter after a submission of no case had been upheld on a charge of murder. The victim had been killed as D tried to steal his car. At the time of the offence D was disqualified from driving and subject to a probation order.

Held, allowing the reference, that given the aggravating circumstances of the case the least sentence which could be imposed would be six years' imprisonment notwithstanding the mitigation of a guilty plea.

ATTORNEY GENERAL'S REFERENCE (NO.68 OF 1995), *Re*; *sub nom*. R. v. DAWES (PAUL THOMAS) [1996] 2 Cr. App. R. (S.) 358, Lord Taylor of Gosforth, C.J., CA (Crim Div).

1609. Manslaughter–diminished responsibility–internal injury to baby by shaking–psychiatric illness

H appealed against a sentence of four and a half years' imprisonment on conviction of manslaughter on an indictment for murder, apparently on the basis of diminished responsibility. Following a long period of persistent crying he picked up his six week old daughter and shook her so that she suffered severe internal injuries from which she died. He called an ambulance shortly afterwards. At trial the defences were provocation and diminished responsibility, but the jury did not indicate the basis of their verdict. H was sentenced to four and a half years' imprisonment.

Held, dismissing the appeal, that H had killed the child while depressed, suffering from lack of sleep and frustration, and while still affected by the earlier death of another child. The offence called for a determinate sentence with length being dependent on the sentencer's assessment of H's residual responsibility for the killing (it was not suggested that he would remain a danger to the public). The sentencer had not adopted too high a tariff in fixing the sentence of four and a half years' imprisonment and the sentence was not manifestly excessive, *R. v. Williams* (1984) 6 Cr. App. R. (S.) 298, [1986] C.L.Y. 851, *R. v. Wainfor* (1985) 7 Cr. App. R. (S.) 231, [1987] C.L.Y. 1004, *R. v. Horscroft* (1985) 7 Cr. App. R. (S.) 254, [1987] C.L.Y. 1007, *R. v. Yeomans* (1988) 10 Cr. App. R. (S.) 63, [1990] C.L.Y. 1363, *R. v. Bashford* (1988) 10 Cr. App. R. (S.) 359, [1990] C.L.Y. 1360, *R. v. Brannan* (1995) 16 Cr. App. R. (S.) 766, [1996] 1 C.L.Y. 2019 and *R. v. Staynor* [1996] 1 Cr. App. R. (S.) 376, [1996] 1 C.L.Y. 1998 considered.

R. v. HALL (ANTHONY CLIFFORD) [1997] 1 Cr. App. R. (S.) 406, Auld, L.J., CA (Crim Div).

1610. Manslaughter–diminished responsibility–life imprisonment inappropriate for schizophrenic

[Criminal Justice Act 1991 s.34; Mental Health Act 1983 s.37, s.41.]

H was convicted of attempted murder, two counts of manslaughter by reason of diminished responsibility, and three counts of wounding with intent to cause grievous bodily harm. He was sentenced to life imprisonment with an order under the Criminal Justice Act 1991 s.34, specifying 14 years as the minimum period of detention. H attacked a number of people over a period of a week. One man was shot dead with a sawn off shotgun and a woman was stabbed to death. Three other persons were attacked, either with a knife or a shotgun. Some of the victims were strangers to him. H was described in medical reports as very dangerous and suffering from schizophrenia. It was considered that he was liable to relapse if he failed to take medication or used cannabis. A bed was available at a special hospital.

Held, allowing the appeal, that on the authorities it was clear that the appropriate course was for the sentence of life imprisonment to be quashed and a hospital order with a restriction order under the Mental Health Act 1983 s.37 and s.41 to be substituted, *R. v. Mitchell (Jason John)* [1997] 1 Cr. App. R. (S.) 90, [1996] 1 C.L.Y. 2008 considered.

R. v. HUTCHINSON (WAYNE) [1997] 2 Cr. App. R. (S.) 60, Rose, L.J., CA (Crim Div).

1611. Manslaughter–diminished responsibility–wife killing husband after long period of abuse and following discovery of his infidelity–custodial sentence substituted by three years' probation

S appealed against a sentence of 18 months' imprisonment having pleaded guilty to the manslaughter of her husband by reason of diminished responsibility. She had been married for about 22 years when her husband began a relationship with another woman, who eventually became pregnant by him. S took an overdose and later discharged herself from hospital and the following day she attacked her husband, inflicting a wound which penetrated the lower sternum and entered the liver which led to his death some days later. While waiting for her husband to be taken to hospital, she stabbed herself in the stomach with a carving knife, inflicting a minor wound. She had suffered mental and physical cruelty and abuse over a period of 20 years and had made five suicide attempts. Medical opinion was that at the time of the incident she was suffering from depressive illness and was subject to acute stress reaction.

Held, allowing the appeal by substituting the custodial term, of which S had served five months, with a three year probation order, that against the background of intolerable treatment over many years the onslaught of acute stress reaction must have impaired S's judgment and self control to such an extent that she thought of ending her own life.

R. v. SANGHA (BAKHSHISH KAUR) [1997] 1 Cr. App. R. (S.) 202, Leggatt, L.J., CA (Crim Div).

1612. Manslaughter–doing an act to pervert the course of justice

B, aged 52, was convicted of manslaughter and doing an act tending to pervert the course of justice. B owned a plot of land which was bought for development; when the plot was excavated the body of a young man was found wrapped in plastic and tied with a rope. The exact circumstances of his death, some 10 years before the discovery of the body, were not established, but it was assumed for the purposes of sentence that the verdict implied that the young man had died in the course of posing for bondage photographs taken by B, and that B had buried his body. B was sentenced to seven years' imprisonment for manslaughter and five years' consecutive for doing an act tending to pervert the course of justice (total sentence, 12 years' imprisonment).

Held, allowing the appeal, that the sentence had to be imposed on the basis that B was indulging in an unlawful act and was responsible for the death of the

19 year old victim. On its facts the case was properly distinguished from *Attorney General's Reference (No.19 of 1993), Re* (1994) 15 Cr. App. R. (S.) 760, [1995] 1 C.L.Y. 1448. The sentence for manslaughter was too long; a sentence of five years was substituted. The sentence for doing an act tending to pervert the course of justice was properly made consecutive, but was reduced to three years, (total sentence, eight years).

R. v. BLAKEMORE (BRIAN) [1997] 2 Cr. App. R. (S.) 255, Beldam, L.J., CA (Crim Div).

1613. Manslaughter–life imprisonment–tariff sentence

[Mental Health Act 1983; Criminal Justice Act 1991 s.34.]

I, aged 23, pleaded guilty to manslaughter and was sentenced to life imprisonment with a period of eight years specified for the purpose of the Criminal Justice Act 1991 s.34. I was working as a shelf filler at a supermarket when he suddenly attacked 11 people with two knives. One of the persons whom he attacked was stabbed in the stomach and died as a result of complications following medical treatment. I pleaded guilty to manslaughter, on an indictment charging murder, on the basis that he did not intend to cause grievous bodily harm. Medical witnesses gave evidence that I was suffering from a schizoid personality disorder which was not a mental illness within the meaning of the Mental Health Act 1983.

Held, allowing the appeal, that (1) the Criminal Justice Act 1991 s.34 required a judge who imposed a sentence of life imprisonment to fix a period which would be considered appropriate for the offence for punishment and any deterrent part of the sentence; the court had to consider what would be the appropriate sentence apart from the element of risk to the public, *R. v. Willsher (David)* (1995) 16 Cr. App. R. (S.) 147, [1996] 1 C.L.Y. 1984 and *R v. Hutchinson (Wayne Anthony)* [1997] 2 Cr. App. R. (S.) 60, [1997] C.L.Y. 1610 considered. The period of eight years chosen for the purpose of s.34 implied that the sentencer would have imposed a term of 12 years' imprisonment for manslaughter, to which I had pleaded guilty on the basis that he had not intended to cause grievous bodily harm. Twelve years would be too long a sentence for such an offence of manslaughter. A sentence of nine years would have been merited, and it followed that the appropriate period to specify for the purposes of s.34 was six years.

R. v. IQBAL (SHAHID) [1997] 2 Cr. App. R. (S.) 226, Beldam, L.J., CA (Crim Div).

1614. Manslaughter–manslaughter by gross neglect of child

S was convicted of manslaughter and false imprisonment and was sentenced to six years' imprisonment and three years' imprisonment concurrent respectively. S, a man of Nigerian origin, formed the belief that his fiancee was possessed by the devil. He accordingly shut her in a room and kept her without food and drink so that she died from starvation and neglect. Her body was not found until almost 10 months after her death.

Held, dismissing the appeal, that the case had to be treated as one of manslaughter by gross neglect, but it involved cruel and inhuman conduct over a lengthy period, together with false imprisonment. It was impossible to say that the sentence was manifestly excessive, *R. v. Stone* [1977] 2 All E.R. 341, [1977] C.L.Y. 507, *R. v. Williamson (Stuart)* (1994) 15 Cr. App. R. (S.) 364, [1993] C.L.Y. 1218 and *R. v. Patel (Rabiya)* (1995) 16 Cr. App. R. (S.) 827, [1996] 1 C.L.Y. 1997 considered.

R. v. SOGUNRO (NICHOLAS NARIDEEN) [1997] 2 Cr. App. R. (S.) 89, Curtis, J., CA (Crim Div).

1615. Manslaughter–mitigating factors–fight started by the deceased

K appealed against sentence on a conviction for manslaughter for which he was sentenced to eight years' imprisonment after pleading guilty. K and L were friends and during the course of a drunken brawl K stabbed L in the neck. K contended that the judge had not taken sufficient account of mitigating factors, namely (1) K's plea of guilty; (2) the lack of any intent to harm; (3) the fact that the deceased initiated the violence; and (4) his remorse.

Held, allowing the appeal in part, that in all the circumstances, the sentence was out of line with that in reported cases and would be reduced to one of five years' imprisonment.

R. v. KNIGHT (MARK ALAN) [1996] 2 Cr. App. R. (S.) 384, Simon Brown, L.J., CA (Crim Div).

1616. Manslaughter—offender unable to form intent through drunkenness

H appealed against a sentence of 10 years' imprisonment, having pleaded guilty to manslaughter on an indictment charging murder. He left a public house apparently drunk and went to the block of flats where he lived. A few minutes later his next door neighbour, C, was found in the hallway of his flat, bleeding from the head. The victim said he had been slapped and punched, but not kicked. H admitted assaulting him, but could not remember the incident clearly. He was later found to have a blood alcohol level of 230 milligrammes of alcohol per 100 millilitres of blood. C, who was found to have a blood alcohol level of more than 200 milligrammes of alcohol per 100 millilitres of blood, underwent an operation to remove a blood clot from his brain, but died some time later. He was found to have multiple areas of bruising to the brain which were attributed to a large number of blows or kicks.

Held, allowing the appeal and reducing the sentence to five years' imprisonment, that no one case was an absolute guide as to the appropriate sentence in another, but the similarities between *R. v. Gunn* and the present case, and the general tenor of the authorities cited, indicated that the trial judge had erred, *R. v. Silver* (1994) 15 Cr App. R. (S.) 837, [1995] 1 C.L.Y. 1431, *R. v. Gunn* (1992) 13 Cr. App. R. (S.) 544, [1993] C.L.Y. 1220 and *R. v. Murphy* (1992) 13 Cr. App. R. (S.) 717, [1993] C.L.Y. 1221 cited.

R. v. HODGKINSON (WALTER SIDNEY) [1997] 1 Cr. App. R. (S.) 146, Hutchison, L.J., CA (Crim Div).

1617. Manslaughter—provocation

M was convicted of manslaughter by reason of provocation and sentenced to 10 years' imprisonment against which he appealed. Following an incident in a nightclub, the deceased was ejected and M was required to leave. The deceased attacked M and a fight began, in the course of which M kicked the victim in the head, causing a fracture of the skull which resulted in a haemorrhage from which he died.

Held, dismissing the appeal, that the sentence was longer than those commonly passed for manslaughter by reason of provcation, but the sentencer was entitled to pass the sentence for a serious offence of the highest order having in view M's record of convictions which included wounding a man by punching and kicking causing a fractured jaw, misuse of karate skill and easy loss of self control.

R. v. McMINN (JOHN) [1997] 2 Cr. App. R. (S.) 219, Staughton, L.J., CA (Crim Div).

1618. Manslaughter—provocation—battered woman syndrome

H, aged 47, appealed against a custodial sentence of six years for the manslaughter of her husband by shooting him while he was attacking her. H claimed that, having suffered abuse in previous relationships and at the hands of the victim, her behaviour manifested aspects of "battered woman syndrome" which explained her failure to withdraw from the scene.

Held, allowing the appeal and substituting a sentence of 42 months, that the trial judge had erred by overemphasising H's failure to withdraw or escape from the provocation of her attacker. It was also the case that the gun and ammunition had been readily accessible to her and she had not gone to find them, *R. v. Naylor (George Stuart)* (1987) 9 Cr. App. R. (S.) 302, [1989] C.L.Y. 1071, *R. v. Boyer* (1981) 3 Cr. App. R. (S.) 35, *R. v. Degville* (1988) 10 Cr. App. R. (S.) 488, [1991] C.L.Y. 1238 and *R. v. Thornton (Sara Elizabeth) (No.2)* [1996] 2 Cr. App. R. 108, [1996] 1 C.L.Y. 1501 considered.

R. v. HOWELL (PATRICIA ANN), Trans. Ref: 97/1014/W4, July 4, 1997, Brooke, L.J., CA (Crim Div).

1619. Manslaughter–provocation–battered woman syndrome–wife stabbing husband to death–long period of physical and mental abuse

G appealed against a sentence of three years' imprisonment, having pleaded guilty to manslaughter by reason of provocation on an indictment for murder. She married the victim in 1992. Their relationship was volatile and both indulged in excessive drinking. One day they went to a club and later to a public house; when they returned home that afternoon the deceased threw a jar of mint sauce at the wall and raised his fist as if to strike G, but did not do so. The deceased and G later went out separately and both returned home affected by drink. When the deceased returned he was chanting slogans in support of a football team which was not the team which G favoured. He behaved bizarrely, attacking the walls and furniture. The deceased then brought a knife from the kitchen, stabbed himself superficially several times in the area of the chest, and then offered the knife to G. She then brought a carving knife from the kitchen and stabbed the deceased in the chest. The precise circumstances of the incident were disputed by G.

Held, dismissing the appeal, that G had been subject to a long period of physical and mental abuse but was not mentally ill. The prosecution accepted that she had intended to cause serious bodily harm but not to kill, as a result of provocation. This was not a case which could be dealt with by means of a probation order, a sentence of imprisonment was required for the deliberate stabbing and the sentence imposed was not manifestly excessive, *R. v. Higgins* [1996] 1 Cr. App. R. (S.) 271, [1996] 1 C.L.Y. 2018 and *R. v. Gardner* (1993) 14 Cr. App. R. (S.) 364, [1994] C.L.Y. 1309 considered.

R. v. GRAINGER (DAWN TRACEY) [1997] 1 Cr. App. R. (S.) 369, Hutchison, L.J., CA (Crim Div).

1620. Manslaughter–self defence–fight leading to fatal fall

W appealed against sentence of four years' imprisonment after being convicted of manslaughter. He and his co-defendant lived in a house which was shared by others including the deceased. The deceased returned to the house one evening drunk and was unable to open the front door. W and his co-defendant went to the front door to let him in and an argument followed. The deceased threatened to "sort out" the codefendant. W intervened and a fight started on the landing. Eventually W struck the deceased a blow which caused him to fall to the floor of the hall below, suffering fatal injuries. W claimed that he had acted in self defence.

Held, dismissing the appeal, that the offence of manslaughter covered a wide range of offences. This was not a case of an accidental injury resulting in death, but a case of grave violence inflicted in circumstances which were grossly reckless. Notwithstanding W's previous good character the sentence was appropriate, *R. v. Coleman (Anthony Neville)* (1992) 95 Cr. App. R. 159, [1992] C.L.Y. 1338 and *R. v. Ruby (Kenneth)* (1987) 9 Cr. App. R. (S.) 305 cited.

R. v. LLOYD-WILLIAMS (TOMOS) [1997] 1 Cr. App. R. (S.) 41, Hobhouse, L.J., CA (Crim Div).

1621. Manslaughter–self defence–offender shooting victim when attacked with knife–history of animosity between parties

[Criminal Justice Act 1988 s.36.]

The Attorney General applied for a sentence to be referred under the Criminal Justice Act 1988 s.36 on the ground that its was unduly lenient. H was sentenced to seven years' imprisonment following conviction of manslaughter by reason of provocation after originally being charged with murder. H shot E twice when E attacked H with a knife at the culmination of a long period of ill feeling between them. Although H contended that he had acted in self defence this was rejected by the jury and the Attorney General submitted that the sentence failed to reflect the aggravating circumstances involved, provide a necessary deterrent and reflect public concern regarding this type of offence. The Attorney General contended, in reliance upon *Attorney General's Reference (No.33 of 1996), Re* [1997] Crim. L. R. 140, [1997] C.L.Y. 1622, that an appropriate sentence should be in the region of 10 to 12 years, with a more severe sentence to reflect the use of a firearm as opposed to a knife.

Held, allowing the reference and increasing the sentence to nine years, that whatever the history of animosity between H and E, H had voluntarily gone to E's house with the gun and had used the weapon in circumstances that did not amount to self defence. Following *Attorney General's Reference (No.33 of 1996), Re* the use of a firearm may be of greater seriousness than a knife, but never less. On the facts, the lowest sentence was one of 10 years' imprisonment, with a 12 month discount for the inevitable stress and anxiety involved in facing the sentencing process for a second time.

ATTORNEY GENERAL'S REFERENCE (NO.6 OF 1997), *Re; sub nom.* R. v. HOFFMAN (NEVILLE ANTHONY), Trans. Ref: 97/0342/R2, April 17, 1997, Lord Bingham of Cornhill, L.C.J., CA (Crim Div).

1622.   Manslaughter-tariff sentence-deliberate carrying of a knife and its uses

[Offences against the Person Act 1861 s.18, s.20; Criminal Justice Act 1988 s.36; Offensive Weapons Act 1996.]

The Attorney General applied for a sentence to be referred under the Criminal Justice Act 1988 s.36 on the ground that it was unduly lenient. L, aged 22, had been charged with murder and wounding with intent to cause grievous bodily harm contrary to the Offences against the Person Act 1861 s.18. In a violent incident with eight others in a nightclub car park L stabbed four people, one of whom died. He carried a butterfly knife with a four inch blade. After discussions in chambers between counsel and the judge, L pleaded guilty to manslaughter on the ground of provocation and three charges of wounding under s.20 of the 1861 Act, for which he was sentenced to five years' imprisonment, and concurrent terms of 18 months' imprisonment respectively. It was argued for the Attorney General that the tariff sentence of about seven years for a case of manslaughter on the ground of provocation where there was no previous relationship between the victim and the offender, and where a knife had been carried and later used, was inappropriate as being out of line with public expectations and other sentences, and that the tariff should be reviewed.

Held, dismissing the reference, that (1) the court can only increase the sentence if it concludes in terms of the Criminal Justice Act 1988 s.36 that it was unduly lenient, ie. if it falls outside what a judge, having regard to all relevant factors, would reasonably have imposed, *Attorney General's Reference (No.4 of 1989), Re* (1989) 11 Cr. App. R. (S.) 517, [1990] C.L.Y. 1207 applied, *R. v. Pittendrigh (Graeme Richard)* [1996] 1 Cr. App. R. (S.) 65, [1996] 1 C.L.Y. 2017 considered; (2) the court has jurisdiction to review the tariff sentence, such review not being precluded by the 1988 Act, and being in the interests of public policy; (3) the court found that the tariff of seven years for offences of manslaughter with the use of a knife and where there was provocation was too low, *R. v. Walsh* (1983) 5 Cr. App. R. (S.) 222, *R. v. Norman* (1994) 15 Cr. App. R. (S.) 165, *Attorney General's Reference (No.9 of 1993), Re* (1994) 15 Cr. App. R. (S.) 637, [1995] 1 C.L.Y. 1436, and *R. v. Davies (David Patrick)* [1996] 1 Cr. App. R. (S.) 28, considered. However, considering the sentences imposed for similar offences of manslaughter, offences of wounding with intent, the average sentence for murder of 14 years and the provisions of the Offensive Weapons Act 1996, the appropriate tariff should be greater. The appropriate tariff for offences where the offender deliberately carries a knife which is used as a weapon and which is used to cause death, even in provocative circumstances should be 10 to 12 years' imprisonment where the case is contested, and (4) it was against public policy and the good administration of justice to increase the sentence when reconsidering the tariff where that sentence had been properly imposed and the offender had been properly advised of the sentence he was likely to receive. In this case, having regard to the aggravating and mitigating factors and in view of the guilty plea even where there was an arguable defence of self defence, the sentence was not unduly lenient.

ATTORNEY GENERAL'S REFERENCE (NO.33 OF 1996), Re; sub nom. R. v. LATHAM (DANIEL GEORGE) [1997] 2 Cr. App. R. (S.) 10, Kennedy, L.J., CA (Crim Div).

1623. Manslaughter—use of knife outside house

Held, that a sentence of seven years' imprisonment for manslaughter on the grounds of provocation was appropriate where a defendant had armed himself with a knife on leaving his house to confront a rowdy group outside in order to protect himself and his family. Although the offence of carrying a knife in a public place should be regarded severely, the sentencing judge should not have allowed himself to be too influenced by the decision in *Attorney General's Reference (No.33 of 1996), Re* [1997] 2 Cr. App. R.(S.) 10, [1997] C.L.Y. 1622.

R. v. PITT (ANTHONY JOHN), *The Times*, May 6, 1997, McCowan, L.J., CA (Crim Div).

1624. Manslaughter—verdict not based on provocation

Having been charged with murder, K, aged 35, was convicted of manslaughter and sentenced to 10 years' imprisonment. He appealed against sentence. K had stabbed a neighbour following a dispute. The verdict had not been on the basis of provocation. Accordingly, the jury could not have been sure that K had intended to kill the deceased or to cause him grievous bodily harm.

Held, dismissing the appeal, that the verdict of the jury did not mean that they had accepted K's defence that the death had been accidental. The stabbing had taken place in front of the deceased's children and offences involving knives would be severely punished. The sentence was not manifestly excessive.

R. v. KELLY (ALAN ERIC) [1996] 2 Cr. App. R. (S.) 452, Bennett, J., CA (Crim Div).

1625. Murder—attempts—guilty plea

M appealed against a sentence of 10 years' imprisonment, having pleaded guilty to attempted murder. He formed a relationship with the victim. M later told her that he intended to take his own life and showed her a makeshift gallows in the loft of his house. When she told him she wanted to end the relationship he attacked the woman with a chloroform-soaked handkerchief and she found herself standing with M on the hatchway of the loft, both with ropes round their necks. M attempted to kick her feet off the steps but she managed to escape.

Held, allowing the appeal, reducing the sentence to eight years' imprisonment, that it was unusual for a defendant to plead guilty to attempted murder. This was a planned attempt, but insufficient weight had been given to M's guilty plea, *R. v. Donnelly* (1983) 5 Cr. App. R. (S.) 70, [1984] C.L.Y. 821 and *R. v. Drinkald* (1988) 10 Cr. App. R. (S.) 380, [1990] C.L.Y. 1202 considered.

R. v. MORTIBOYS (DERRICK GODFREY) [1997] 1 Cr. App. R (S.) 141, Hutchison, L.J., CA (Crim Div).

1626. Murder—life imprisonment—tariff sentence—extent of Secretary of State's discretion to determine tariff

[Criminal Justice Act 1991 s.35.]

C appealed against the dismissal of his application for judicial review of a decision of the Secretary of State to fix his tariff at 18 years. C and his co-accused, P, were found guilty of murder, while D, a co-accused woman, was found guilty of manslaughter. D's conviction was later quashed by the Court of Appeal on the ground of a misdirection by the trial judge. C contended that, in setting his tariff, the Secretary of State had relied on the trial judge's opinion that the jury's verdict on D had been perverse and that C and P were contract killers hired by D.

Held, dismissing the appeal, that the Secretary of State had an unqualified discretion, in relation to the Criminal Justice Act 1991 s.35, to determine the tariff of a mandatory life sentence, although he could not act arbitrarily and ignore either the jury's verdict or the advice of the judiciary, *R. v. Secretary of State for the Home Department, ex p. Doody* [1994] 1 A.C. 531, [1993] C.L.Y. 1213 followed and *R. v. Secretary of State for the Home Department, ex p. Parker* [1993] C.O.D. 78, [1994] C.L.Y. 3831 considered.

R. v. SECRETARY OF STATE FOR THE HOME DEPARTMENT, *ex p.* CAUSABON-VINCENT, Trans. Ref: QBCOF 96/1114/D, December 19, 1996, Lord Woolf, M.R., CA.

1627. **Murder—life imprisonment—tariff sentence—tariff period cannot be increased where fixed previously**

P had been convicted of the double murder of his parents. The Secretary of State decided to increase the minimum period to be served for the purposes of retribution and deterrence recommended by the trial judge and the Lord Chief Justice from 15 to 20 years on the ground that the killings were a double, premeditated act. Following representations to the Home Office by P, the subsequent Secretary of State accepted that the aggravating factors had been taken into account in error but stated that the offence nevertheless warranted a term of 20 years' imprisonment. Although this constituted an increase in the tariff period since the original tariff had been fixed on the basis of the aggravating factors, the Court of Appeal held that the Secretary of State had the power to use his discretion to review upwards the decision of a predecessor if necessary. P appealed.

Held, allowing the appeal that the Secretary of State was not entitled to increase the tariff previously set as a minimum term for a life sentence prisoner. The terms of the 1993 policy statement issued by the Secretary of State reserving the power to review upwards his own initial view of the penal element rendered it inapplicable where the tariff period had been fixed by a previous Secretary of State, and to increase a tariff so fixed was contrary to the fundamental principle of not retrospectively increasing lawful sentences. A tariff could only be increased in an exceptional situation and, this not being the case in the present circumstances, the decision to reaffirm the 20 year sentence should be quashed.

R. v. SECRETARY OF STATE FOR THE HOME DEPARTMENT, *ex p.* PIERSON; *sub nom.* PIERSON v. SECRETARY OF STATE FOR THE HOME DEPARTMENT [1997] 3 W.L.R. 492, Lord Goff of Chieveley, HL.

1628. **Murder—soliciting—suspended sentence unduly lenient**

[Criminal Justice Act 1988 s.36.]

The Attorney General applied for a sentence to be referred under the Criminal Justice Act 1988 s.36 on the ground that it was unduly lenient. C was convicted of two counts of soliciting to murder. She was subject to a civil judgment by an Italian court requiring payment of £17,000 and proceedings to enforce it were instituted in this jurisdiction. C approached a man with a criminal record and indicated that she wanted the plaintiff shot. The man reported the matter to the police, and an undercover police officer was introduced to the offender. She offered the officer £8,000 to kill the plaintiff. C was sentenced to two years' imprisonment, suspended for two years.

Held, allowing the reference, that the authorities indicated that the minimum starting point for the offence, following a trial, was five to six years. A sentence of two years, even if not suspended, was manifestly unduly lenient. Bearing in mind the element of double jeopardy, a sentence of four years' imprisonment would be substituted, *R. v. Raw* (1983) 5 Cr. App. R. (S.) 229, [1984] C.L.Y. 917,

R. v. Houseley and Kibble (1994) 15 Cr. App. R. (S.) 155 and *R. v. Adamthwaite* (1993) 15 Cr. App. R. (S.) 241, [1995] 1 C.L.Y. 1474 considered.

ATTORNEY GENERAL'S REFERENCE (NO.43 OF 1996), *Re; sub nom.* R. v. COSTAINE (BEATRICE SHEELAGH) [1997] 1 Cr. App. R. (S.) 378, Rose, L.J., CA (Crim Div).

1629. Nuisance–abatement notices–fines applicable for continuing failure to comply–magistrates' discretion to mitigate penalty

[Environmental Protection Act1990 s.80; Magistrates Courts Act1980 s.34(1).]

C appealed by way of case stated against the justices' decision to impose fines of £80 in respect of three offences under the Environmental Protection Act1990 s.80, following conviction for failure to comply with statutory nuisance abatement notices. Relying on the decision in *Osborn v. Wood Brothers* [1897] 1 Q.B. 197, C contended that the justices were obliged, under s.80(5) of the 1990 Act, to impose fines equal to one tenth of Level 5 on the standard scale for each day the offence continued after conviction.

Held, dismissing the appeal, that whereas s.80(5) of the 1990 Act provided for fines at one tenth of Level 5 for continuing failure to comply, the justices had discretion to impose a lesser penalty, as s.80 did not expressly restrict their powers to mitigate penalties under the Magistrates Courts Act 1980 s.34(1), *Osborn v. Wood Brothers* distinguished.

CANTERBURY CITY COUNCIL v. FERRIS [1997] Env. L.R. D14, Simon Brown, L.J., QBD.

1630. Obtaining by deception–obtaining benefits by deception

A pleaded guilty to conspiring to obtaining by deception. The appellants were concerned in a conspiracy to obtain money from the Department of Social Security by obtaining and using stolen benefit books. One appellant admitted obtaining a total of £1,300 and the other appellant £809. Each appellant was sentenced to 18 months' imprisonment and A appealed.

Held, dismissing the appeals, that considering *R. v. Stewart (Livingstone)* (1987) 9 Cr. App. R. (S.) 135, [1987] C.L.Y. 1015, *R. v. Browne (Brendan John)* (1993) 14 C. App. R. (S.) 491, [1994] C.L.Y. 1317 and *R. v. Bolarin (Olusoji Olugbo)* (1990) 12 Cr. App. R. (S.) 543, [1992] C.L.Y. 1351 against the background of increasing prevalence of such frauds, the court was bound to take a more serious view of these offences. The appellants had pleaded guilty to conspiracy and the sentencer was entitled to take the view that there was a degree of organisation and sophistication about the offences. The sentences were not wrong in principle or out of line with authority.

R. v. ARMOUR (JOHN AUSTIN); R. v. SHERLOCK (BERNARD) [1997] 2 Cr. App. R. (S.) 240, Newman, J., CA (Crim Div).

1631. Obtaining by deception–obtaining property by deception

[Magistrates Courts Act 1980 s.38.]

M pleaded guilty before a magistrates court to two charges of obtaining by deception and was committed to the Crown Court for sentence under the Magistrates Courts Act 1980 s.38 where 21 months' imprisonment was imposed. M, who was a prostitute, approached a tourist and offered sex for £20. The tourist agreed, and paid her £20 in cash. He was then asked to pay a further £870 as a returnable deposit, which he did. He was then told to go to a hotel, but was unable to find the hotel. The following day the tourist returned to the area, and found M. He was told that if he paid a further £480, his deposit of £870 would be returned, and he did so. The tourist was then asked for a further £480, and he paid that sum. He was then told to wait at a restaurant but no one came to meet him. M had numerous previous convictions for prostitution and dishonesty.

Held, allowing the appeal, that in view of personal mitigating factors including previous drug addition, having problems and the fact her son was in

Broadmoor, the sentence was in excess of what was justified; a sentence of 12 months would be substituted.

R. v. MUNDLE (ARLENE) [1997] 2 Cr. App. R. (S.) 160, Ebsworth, J., CA (Crim Div).

1632. Parole–new offences committed while released on licence–guidelines for sentencing

[Criminal Justice Act 1991 s.40.]

Held, that, when exercising the power conferred upon it by the Criminal Justice Act 1991 s.40 to sentence an offender convicted of committing an offence whilst on licence, the court should first have regard to the appropriate sentence for the new offence without considering whether to reactivate the original sentence, and then, when considering reactivation, examine the nature and gravity of the new offence, the extent of any progress made by the offender since release, the totality of the sentences and the period of time between the offender's release and the commission of the new offence.

R. v. TAYLOR (ADRIAN EDWARD), *The Times*, August 11, 1997, Rose, L.J., CA (Crim Div).

1633. Parole–new offences committed while released on licence–order for return to prison and sentence for new offences exceeded six months–statutory limits on sentence length did not apply

[Magistrates Courts Act 1980 s.133; Criminal Justice Act 1991 s.40; .]

V committed new offences while released on licence and the magistrates ordered that he be returned to prison for 128 days in respect of his original sentence pursuant to the Criminal Justice Act 1991 s.40, and sentenced him to six months' imprisonment in respect of the new offences, the maximum permissible under the Magistrates Courts Act 1980 s.133, to be served consecutively. V applied for judicial review of the magistrates' decision, contending that the aggregate of the period of return and the sentence imposed for the new offences could not exceed the six month limit set down in s.133. V argued that (1) the period of return amounted to the imposition of a sentence of imprisonment under s.133, and (2) that s.40 could not be regarded as derogating from the maximum period laid down in s.133 in the absence of an express provision to that effect.

Held, dismissing the application, that (1) s.40 of the 1991 Act made it clear that an order returning an offender to prison was not a sentence of imprisonment within the meaning of s.133 of the 1980 Act. The order merely reactivated the original sentence from which the prisoner had been prematurely released, and (2) it followed that as an order under s.40 was not a sentence within s.133, there was no need for the draftsman to provide a derogation from the provisions of the latter section. As s.133 had no special or entrenched status and s.40 was a later provision, the court had to read them together so as to give effect to Parliament's intentions. It was clear that Parliament considered an order for return to be quite distinct from a new sentence, as the period of return was to be ignored when determining the length of the new sentence, which would be contrary to accepted sentencing principles.

R. v. WORTHING AND DISTRICT JUSTICES, *ex p.* VARLEY, *The Times*, July 21, 1997, Lord Bingham of Cornhill, L.C.J., QBD.

1634. Parole–new offences committed while released on licence–sentencing powers of magistrates and Crown Court–summary offences

[Criminal Justice Act 1991 s.40(3)(b).]

S applied for judicial review of the justices' decision to sentence him to six months' imprisonment for offences committed whilst on release from prison on licence and to commit him to the Crown Court for consideration of the revocation of his licence and return to prison. The justices took the view that the Criminal Justice Act 1991 s.40(3)(b) did not allow them to commit a defendant to the Crown Court for sentencing for a summary offence and that, if a defendant were so committed, the Crown Court would have no power to sentence him for the new offences.

Held, allowing the application and quashing the committal order but declining to prohibit the Crown Court from dealing with the committal, that on a true construction of s.40(3)(b) the justices should either have dealt with both the issues of sentencing for the new offences and the return to prison, or committed both issues to the Crown Court for determination, *R. v. Harrow Justices, ex p. Jordan* [1997] 1 W.L.R. 84, [1997] C.L.Y 1635 followed.

R. v. BURTON ON TRENT JUSTICES, *ex p.* SMITH, *The Times*, July 15, 1997, Lord Bingham of Cornhill, L.C.J., QBD.

1635. Parole–new offences committed while released on licence–sentencing powers of magistrates court–summary offences

[Criminal Justice Act 1991 s.40.]

J sought to quash a decision to commit him to the Crown Court for consideration of his return to prison following conviction for an offence prior to the expiry of licence for a previous conviction. The application raised the issue of the proper construction and application of the Criminal Justice Act 1991 s.40. The justices were under the impression that, as the offence of common assault was a summary offence, they could not commit that charge to the Crown Court for sentence and so sentenced J to three months' imprisonment and on his release committed him in custody to the Crown Court for consideration of return. The issue was whether the justices were entitled to do this.

Held, allowing the application, that s.40(3)(b) suggested that the justices should either have dealt with sentence and return or committed both the question of sentence and the question of return to the Crown Court. The order referring the question of return to the Crown Court was quashed.

R. v. HARROW JUSTICES, *ex p.* JORDAN [1997] 1 W.L.R. 84, Lord Bingham of Cornhill, L.C.J., QBD.

1636. Pleas–guilty pleas–appellant pleading guilty prior to contested trial of accomplices–effect on sentence where evidence at contested trial used to assess involvement of appellant pleading guilty–disparate sentences

TW, C and PW, together with two others, appeared in the Crown Court charged with conspiracy to cause grievous bodily harm. C pleaded guilty, on the basis that he had not personally used any violence to the victim. The other codefendants pleaded not guilty but were convicted after a trial lasting 22 days. The prosecution alleged that one codefendant formed the view that the victim had stolen some tools from his shed. That defendant arranged for a group of men to visit the alleged thief and attack him. The five men travelled some distance to the victim's home, gained access and attacked him with a baseball bat. Two defendants were sentenced to eight years' imprisonment; the rest to six years. C appealed contending that he had not received credit for his plea, and that the sentencer had ignored the basis on which his plea was tendered and accepted.

Held, allowing the appeal, that this was an appalling case of a team of men taking the law into their own hands. The offence involved five men attacking one man with a baseball bat, and serious head injuries had been inflicted on the victim endangering his life and causing permanent brain damage. The problem of an offender who pleaded guilty to an offence in respect of which others were tried by jury had been considered previously. It was clear that a sentencer dealing with an offender who had pleaded guilty could take into account evidence given at the contested trial of his accomplices, but he must bear in mind that the evidence at the trial had not been tested by cross-examination on behalf of C, who should have been given the opportunity to give evidence of his version of the incident. In these circumstances C had a genuine grievance that he had not been sentenced on the basis on which he had pleaded, and his sentence was reduced for that reason to five years' imprisonment. TW and PW had pleaded not guilty and claimed that they had dissociated themselves from the eventual violence. In order to ensure that justice was done between appellants, their sentences were also reduced to five years, *R. v. Michaels and Skoblo* (1981) 3 Cr. App. R. (S.) 188, [1981] C.L.Y. 525, *R. v. Smith* (1988) 10 Cr. App. R. (S.) 393, [1989] C.L.Y. 1006 and *R. v. Mahoney* (1993) 14 Cr. App. R. (S.) 291, [1994] C.L.Y. 1261 considered.

R. v. WINTER (TERENCE PETER SCOTT); R. v. COLK (BRETT ANTHONY); R. v. WILSON (PAUL) [1997] 1 Cr. App. R. (S.) 331, Judge Rivlin Q.C., CA (Crim Div).

1637. Pleas—pleas and directions hearing—possibility of extra charges—codefendant wrongly advised to plead not guilty

K, a codefendant, had intended to plead guilty to six counts of obtaining property by deception, but at the pleas and directions hearing he was advised to plead not guilty as the prosecution were considering adding a further charge. He was subsequently convicted and now appealed against his sentence of 18 months' imprisonment.

Held, allowing the appeal and reducing the sentence to 15 months, that as the judge had been unaware of what had taken place at the pleas and directions hearing, K had not been given the extra credit usual for an early guilty plea. K had been badly advised and it was unfair that he had been persuaded to make a plea which he was told would not adversely affect him, when in reality it had.

R. v. KHERBOUCHE (ZOHIR), *The Times*, January 2, 1997, Lord Bingham of Cornhill, L.C.J., CA (Crim Div).

1638. Pornography—importation of books containing indecent photographs of girls under 16

T appealed against concurrent sentences of imprisonment of six months on each count of being knowingly involved in the importation of books containing indecent photographs and drawings of girls under 16. T, aged 38, claimed that the sentence was excessive and out of line with the authorities.

Held, allowing the appeal in part, that a term of three months was substituted. It was clear that anyone commercially involved with such material would receive a custodial sentence. Fines had been imposed where a single indecent item had been imported, or where photographs were solely of naked children with no sexual activity or corruption involved. In the instant case a custodial sentence was appropriate, because the material involved adults and animals and T had a previous conviction for a similar offence, *R. v. Holloway* (1982) 4 Cr. App. R. (S.) 128, [1982] C.L.Y. 700, *R. v. Littleford* (1984) 6 Cr. App. R. (S.) 272, [1985] C.L.Y. 820 and *R. v. Holt (Howard)* (1995) 16 Cr. App. R. (S.) 510 distinguished.

R. v. TRAVELL (RICHARD JOHN) [1997] 1 Cr. App. R. (S.) 52, Ebsworth, J., CA (Crim Div).

1639. Prisons—escape—factors to be considered when determining sentence

Held, that prison breaking was a serious offence for which a significant term of imprisonment should always be expected. If the prisoner had been serving a determinate sentence, the sentence for prison breaking should usually run consecutively, but where a prisoner had been serving a life sentence, the new sentence should run concurrently. Whilst the same length of sentence should be imposed regardless of whether a determinate or life sentence was being served, other factors would be taken into account, including the original crime for which the offender had been imprisoned, his behaviour whilst in prison, the circumstances of his escape and whether he surrendered and pleaded guilty to the escape.

R. v. COUGHTREY (ANTHONY), *The Times*, April 1, 1997, McCowan, L.J., CA (Crim Div).

1640. Prosecutors–warning against attempt to influence level of sentence

M appealed against concurrent sentences of seven years each for conspiracy to rob and possessing a firearm when prohibited made consecutive to concurrent terms of two years for theft, 14 years each for possessing a firearm with intent and for robbery and five years for possession of a firearm when prohibited. M entered a store in London with a sawn off shotgun and a revolver with which he threatened a guard but ran off. Subsequently, in Grimsby, M stole a car and, while robbing a jeweller's shop, threatened a pregnant woman with a pistol and fired shots near the proprietor. M gave himself up shortly afterwards and the question arose of where to hold the trial. The Principal Crown Prosecutor wrote to the trial judge plainly attempting to influence a decision in favour of Grimsby, where the sentence was likely to be higher, but the letter was disclosed to the defence by the trial judge and the trial transferred to London.

Held, allowing the appeal, that the sentences were appropriate but were reduced by one year on each indictment to a total of 19 years in order to reassure M that the letter had not affected his sentence. Any such attempt to influence sentence was totally improper. Prosecution staff had been warned and a copy of the judgment was directed to be sent to the Attorney General, to the head of the CPS and to Glidewell L.J. who was investigating the CPS.

R. v. McSHANE (BRIAN), Trans. Ref: 97/0482/X3, July 11, 1997, Garland, J., CA.

1641. Public order offences–intimidation of witnesses

[Criminal Justice and Public Order Act 1994 s.51 (2).]

W pleaded guilty to threatening a witness contrary to the Criminal Justice and Public Order Act 1994 s.51 (2). W was convicted of falsely imprisoning a woman and unlawfully wounding her; he was acquitted of raping her and threatening to kill her. He was sentenced to five years' imprisonment, subsequently reduced to three years, for those offences. Shortly after arriving in prison W wrote a letter to the woman, in an assumed name, in which he threatened her with violence. He was sentenced to two years' imprisonment, consecutive to the sentence he was then serving and appealed.

Held, dismissing the appeal, that the offence of threatening witnesses was to be viewed extremely seriously; Parliament had imposed a maximum sentence of five years for the offence. The sentence was not excessive and it was right to order it to be served consecutively to the existing sentence.

R. v. WILLIAMS (MARK) [1997] 2 Cr. App. R. (S.) 221, Harrison, J., CA (Crim Div).

1642. Rape–discretionary life imprisonment–length of specified period

[Criminal Justice Act 1991 s.34.]

B appealed against the recommendation that he serve a minimum of 15 years in prison under the Criminal Justice Act 1991 s.34. B was sentenced to life imprisonment for three separate rapes and medical evidence indicated that criteria were filled for the imposition of a discretionary life sentence. It was submitted that the trial judge did not follow the procedure and identify the period of a fixed sentence and then apply it to the notional level for remission and good behaviour and therefore started at too high a level when considering the appropriate period under the Criminal Justice Act 1991 s.34.

Held, allowing the appeal, that the correct sentence if a finite sentence was appropriate was 15 years' imprisonment. The period under the Criminal Justice Act 1991 s.34 would be reduced to 10 years' imprisonment, *R. v. Meak* (1995) 16 Cr. App. R. (S.) 1003 followed.

R. v. BRANDY (PAUL) [1997] 1 Cr. App. R. (S.) 38, Otton, L.J., CA (Crim Div).

1643. Rape–discretionary life imprisonment–length of specified period

[Criminal Justice Act 1991 s.34.]

R was convicted of one count of rape and pleaded guilty to a second count of rape, also to one count each of abducting a woman by force and assault occasioning actual bodily harm, and to two counts of false imprisonment. He formed a relationship with a woman which deteriorated and the woman indicated that she wanted it to end. The woman agreed to see R and allowed him into her home. He subsequently refused to leave when asked, threatened her with a knife, forced her to take part in various sexual acts, and had sexual intercourse with her three times. He later accosted the woman in the street, attacked her and threatened her with a knife, and forced her to go with him to a car park before allowing her to leave. On another occasion he attacked a young couple in their home, holding them captive for a day and raping the young woman. He had various previous convictions, including one for rape, and others involving the use of knives. R appealed against a sentence of life imprisonment with a period of 17 years specified for the purpose of the Criminal Justice Act 1991 s.34.

Held, allowing the appeal and reducing the specified period to 10 years, that the facts showed the conditions for a life sentence had been met and that this was an appropriate case for such a sentence. However, the specified period of 17 years showed that the judge had in mind a determinate sentence of 25 years, which was too long in the circumstances. In the absence of a life sentence, the correct determinate sentence would have been around 16 years, giving an appropriate specified period of 10 years, *R. v. Birch* (1988) 9 Cr. App. R. (S.) 509, [1990] C.L.Y. 1351 considered.

R. v. RAZZAQUE (DAVID MILNE) [1997] 1 Cr. App. R. (S.) 154, Hutchison, L.J., CA (Crim Div).

1644. **Rape–discretionary life imprisonment–offender suffering from mental illness–substitution of hospital order and restriction order**

[Criminal Justice Act 1991 s.34; Mental Health Act 1983.]

M was convicted of rape and possessing an imitation firearm. He obtained access to a hairdressing boutique while it was closed and persuaded a young woman to enter a bathroom by a pretext. He then locked her in, threatened her with the imitation firearm and forced her to submit to intercourse. He suffered from schizophrenia and was also mentally impaired. A hospital order was recommended. M was sentenced to life imprisonment, with a period of nine years specified under the Criminal Justice Act 1991 s.34 for rape; no separate penalty was given for possessing an imitation firearm.

Held, allowing the appeal, that this was a case where the conditions for a hospital order under the Mental Health Act 1983 were satisfied, and such an order was appropriate, in preference to a sentence of life imprisonment. A hospital order, together with a restriction order with no limit of time, were substituted, *R. v. Howell* (1985) Cr. App. R. (S.) 360, [1987] C.L.Y. 913 and *R. v. Mbatha* (1985) Cr. App. R. (S.) 373, [1987] C.L.Y. 992 considered.

R. v. MOSES (ANTHONY) [1996] 2 Cr. App R. (S.) 407, Stuart-Smith, L.J., CA (Crim Div).

1645. **Rape–discretionary life imprisonment–series of aggravating features–gravity of offence and previous convictions of similar nature–nine years' imprisonment unduly lenient**

[Criminal Justice Act 1988 s.36; Criminal Justice Act 1991 s.34(3).]

The Attorney General applied for a sentence to be referred under the Criminal Justice Act 1988 s.36 on the ground that it was unduly lenient. The offender was sentenced to nine years' imprisonment for rape, with four years concurrent for false imprisonment. He had taken the victim to an ex-offenders' hostel where he was staying and where consensual sexual acts took place. However, when the victim attempted to leave the next morning, the offender threatened to throw her out of a window and subjected her to repeated rapes and sexual assaults. The offences were committed shortly after his release from prison. The offender had previous convictions for assault, rape and false imprisonment.

Held, allowing the reference, that the threats and the repeated nature of the rape combined with the other sexual indignities involved amounted to a series of aggravating features which showed the undue leniency of the original sentence, *R. v. Billam* (1986) 8 Cr. App. R. (S.) 48, [1986] C.L.Y. 868 followed. The sentence of nine years' imprisonment was quashed and a sentence of life imprisonment substituted, as the criteria in *R. v. Hodgson* (1968) 52 Cr. App. R. 113, [1968] C.L.Y. 848 were fulfilled, in that the offences were grave enough to require a long sentence and the offender's character revealed the likelihood of similar future offences of an injurious nature. A period of 10 years was identified as the relevant part of the sentence for the purposes of the Criminal Justice Act 1991 s.34(3).

ATTORNEY GENERAL'S REFERENCE (NO.76 OF 1995), *Re; sub nom.* R. v. BAKER (ORLANDO) [1997] 1 Cr. App. R. (S.) 81, Rose, L.J., CA (Crim Div).

1646. **Rape–false imprisonment–juvenile offenders–revenge attack for theft of purse–three and a half years' imprisonment unduly lenient**

[Children and Young Persons Act 1933 s.53(2); Criminal Justice Act 1988 s.36.]

The Attorney General applied for a sentence to be referred under the Criminal Justice Act 1988 s.36 on the ground that it was unduly lenient. W, the first offender, aged 17 at the time of the offences, pleaded guilty to assault occasioning actual bodily harm and false imprisonment, and was convicted of two counts of aiding and abetting rape and one of indecent assault. The second and third offenders were each convicted of rape, aiding and abetting rape and false imprisonment. The victim, a 16-year-old girl, stole a purse from the house of one of the offenders, and spent £130 which she took from the purse. The offenders later went to her home and forced her into a bedroom. The girl was then taken by taxi to a flat where she was attacked by W and another woman. She was made to undress and subjected to various indignities. A lighted cigarette was pushed into her face. The victim was then taken to another house where she was again assaulted and threatened with a knife. One of the offenders attempted to rape her and the other did so. The victim then managed to escape. W was sentenced to three and a half years' detention under the Children and Young Persons Act 1933 s.53(2) and three years' detention in a young offender institution in the case of the second and third offenders.

Held, allowing the reference, that despite giving full weight to the youth and previous good character of the offenders, the sentences for rape and aiding and abetting rape were unduly lenient. W's sentence was increased to six years' detention and the sentences on the second and third offenders to five years' detention in a young offender institution, *R. v. Billam* (1986) 82 Cr. App. R. 347, [1986] C.L.Y. 868 cited.

ATTORNEY GENERAL'S REFERENCE (NOS.53, 54 & 55 OF 1995), *Re; sub nom.* R. v. WILSON (NICOLA JOY) [1997] 1 Cr. App. R. (S.) 219, Lord Bingham of Cornhill, L.C.J., CA (Crim Div).

1647. **Rape–husband raping estranged wife–breach of injunction**

K was sentenced to eight years' imprisonment after being convicted of the rape of his estranged wife. The victim had left K as a result of violence and eventually found a new home. She obtained an injunction restraining K from visiting her or communicating with her. He entered the house while she was out and when she went to bed he confronted her, threatened her with a knife, and wrapped a scarf around her neck. Some time later he removed her jeans and raped her.

Held, dismissing the appeal, that the offence involved a number of aggravating features, including the breach of an injunction, the use of a weapon, and the use of physical violence over and above the force necessary to commit the rape. It was planned and K had previous convictions for other violent offences. The sentence was plainly justified, *R. v. W (Stephen)* (1993) 14 Cr. App. R. (S.) 256, [1994] C.L.Y. 1337 cited.

R. v. K (EDWARD JAMES); *sub nom.* R. v. KEARNEY (EDWARD JAMES) [1997] 1 Cr. App. R. (S.) 251, Cresswell, J., CA (Crim Div).

1648. Rape–indecent assault–offender gaining access to victim's home–seven and a half years' imprisonment not unduly lenient

[Criminal Justice Act 1988 s.36.]

The Attorney General applied for a sentence to be referred under the Criminal Justice Act 1988 s.36 on the ground that it was unduly lenient. F pleaded guilty to one count of rape and three counts of indecent assault. Each count related to a different victim. He gained access to the flat occupied by the victim of the rape by a stratagem, and subsequently threatened her with a knife before raping her twice. On a later occasion he attacked two women who were walking in the street in the early hours, grabbing one of them by the buttock and grabbing the other by the breasts. A few minutes later he entered a women's refuge by climbing through a window and attacked a woman who was asleep in her bedroom with two of her children. He pulled her nightshirt open, squeezed her throat, punched her face and bit her arm and was sentenced to five years' imprisonment for rape and a total of two and a half years consecutive for the indecent assaults.

Held, dismissing the reference, that the sentencer had indicated that he had reduced the individual sentences in order to ensure that the total sentence was not excessive, and that he gave credit for the offender's pleas. In the view of the court, the sentences were unduly lenient. An appropriate total sentence would have been 10 years' imprisonment. In view of the element of double jeopardy, the court would have been forced to substitute a sentence of less than 10 years and the difference between the sentence which would have been substituted and the sentence of seven and a half years was not sufficient to cause the court in the exercise of its discretion to interfere, *R. v. Billam* (1986) 82 Cr. App. R. 347, [1986] C.L.Y. 868, *R. v. Higgins* (1988) 10 Cr. App. R. (S.) 262 and *R. v. Furlong (Sean)* (1993) 14 Cr. App. R. (S.) 222, [1994] C.L.Y. 1185 cited.

ATTORNEY GENERAL'S REFERENCE (NO.29 OF 1996), *Re; sub nom*. R. v. FRIDYE (CARL JUNIOR) [1997] 1 Cr. App. R. (S.) 224, Lord Bingham of Cornhill, L.C.J., CA (Crim Div).

1649. Rape–prostitutes–unprotected sexual intercourse–prostitutes equally entitled to legal protection

[Criminal Justice Act 1991 s.44.]

M pleaded guilty to rape and false imprisonment and was sentenced to nine years' imprisonment and four years' imprisonment concurrent respectively, with an order under the Criminal Justice Act 1991 s.44. M encountered a girl of 16 who was soliciting as a prostitute. She agreed to permit intercourse for £30. She entered M's car and he drove to a car park, where he attacked the girl, placing his fingers on her throat and striking her face. M punched her several times so that she lost consciousness, and then had intercourse against her will without using a condom. The girl was later forced to masturbate M and perform oral sex on him. The girl was released after being detained in the car for about four hours.

Held, dismissing the appeal, that it was for the courts to protect prostitutes. The sentence was not manifestly excessive, *R. v. Cole (Gary Lee)* (1993) 14 Cr. App. R. (S.) 764, [1994] C.L.Y. 1336 considered.

R. v. MASOOD (ASIF) [1997] 2 Cr. App. R. (S.) 137, Judge Martin Tucker Q.C., CA (Crim Div).

1650. Rape–prostitutes–unprotected sexual intercourse–prostitutes equally entitled to legal protection–four years' imprisonment unduly lenient

[Criminal Justice Act 1988 s.36.]

The Attorney General applied for a sentence to be referred under the Criminal Justice Act 1988 s.36 on the ground that it was unduly lenient. S was convicted on five counts of rape after he forced a number of prostitutes to have unprotected sexual intercourse with him, deliberately causing fear of infection and threatening one with death. He was sentenced to four years' imprisonment on each count, the judge considering that the trauma suffered by prostitutes was less than that suffered by other victims as they were used to sexual intercourse with strangers.

Held, allowing the reference, that it was rape for a man to insist on having unprotected sexual intercourse without a prostitute's consent and to use force. Prostitutes had the same entitlement to legal protection as other women, and indeed were more exposed to disease where clients were promiscuous. In view of the aggravating factors which included the deliberate infliction of fear of infection, the threat of force, the fact that the offending continued over a number of years and S's failure to plead guilty, the sentence was unduly lenient and one of six years would be substituted.

R. v. SHAW (GRENVILLE), *The Times*, January 27, 1997, Lord Bingham of Cornhill, L.C.J., CA (Crim Div).

1651. Rape–sentence passed under the Criminal Justice Act 1991 s.2(2)(b)

[Criminal Justice Act 1991 s.2(2)(b).]

H was convicted of rape. He rang the doorbell of a flat in the early afternoon and forced his way in when the door was opened. He threatened the occupant, a woman aged 38, with a knife, removed her clothes and raped her. He left the flat, but returned twice, once to collect his knife and once to ask whether the victim had complained to the police. On the second occasion he was detained by the victim's father. H had been convicted on four occasions of a total of seven indecent assaults. H was sentenced to 18 years' imprisonment, passed as a longer than normal sentence under the Criminal Justice Act 1991 s.2(2)(b).

Held, allowing the appeal and substituting a sentence of 15 years, that it was accepted that this was a case to which s.2(2)(b) applied. In a case of this nature, the court had to consider what sentence would have been appropriate but for the previous convictions and also taking account of those previous convictions. The court had then to decide what additional element there should be in order to provide for the protection of the public. The application of s.2(2)(b) should not result in a sentence which was out of all proportion to the sentence which would have been imposed but for that provision. The court was persuaded that a sentence of 18 years was too long because it was out of proportion to the sentence which would have been imposed but for the statutory provision.

R. v. HOWATT (GARY) [1997] 1 Cr. App. R. (S.) 232, Jowitt, J., CA (Crim Div).

1652. Remand–breach of community order–relevance of time in custody on remand to custodial sentence

[Criminal Justice Act 1967 s.67.]

H, aged 35 pleaded guilty to two offences of assault occasioning actual bodily harm and theft of a motor vehicle. H assaulted a taxi driver by biting him on the cheek. After being released on bail for that offence, he assaulted the licensee of a public house again by biting. H was remanded in custody and eventually appeared in the Crown Court seven months later, when a probation order was made. Two weeks later H stole a car and was arrested for that offence. Sentence was deferred by the magistrates' court, and he left the country in breach of a requirement of the probation order that he should attend an alcohol education unit. He failed to appear for the deferred sentence to be dealt with. When he was arrested, he was committed to the Crown Court to be dealt with in respect of the breach of the requirement of the probation orders, and for sentence in respect of the theft of the car. H was sentenced to nine months' imprisonment, 15 months' imprisonment and four months' imprisonment consecutively (total 28 months), and disqualified from driving for three years (for other road traffic offences). It was argued that H had not been given appropriate credit for the period of seven months spent in custody on remand before the original probation order was made.

Held, dismissing the appeal, that considering *R. v. Wiltshire (Mark)* (1992) 13 Cr. App. R. (S.) 642, [1993] C.L.Y. 1061, *R. v. McDonald (Andrew James McKay)* (1988) 10 Cr. App. R. (S.) 458, [1991] C.L.Y. 1190 and *R. v. Needham* (1989) 11 Cr. App. R. (S.) 506, [1991] C.L.Y. 1187, it was clearly established that it was appropriate to take into account time spent in custody prior to the making of a community order, whether a probation order or a community service order, when sentencing for the original offence on proof of a breach. The reason was that the Criminal Justice Act 1967, s.67 did not allow such time to count against any sentence passed for the original offence following a breach. The extent to which the ultimate sentence should be reduced to reflect the time spent in custody was less clear, although in *R. v. Wiltshire* it was emphasised that it was a matter for judicial discretion. In some cases the court had simply reduced the sentence by the amount of time spent in custody, in others the court had allowed for the effect of remission. In the court's view it would be highly desirable for the sentencing court, if it decided to take into account time spent in custody before a community order was made, to state that fact when passing sentence and to indicate the extent to which the matter was taken into account. On the facts of the case it was not necessary to decide between the two approaches. The appropriate starting point for the two assaults after credit had been given for a plea, would have been three years, and the sentence for theft of a car was properly made consecutive. The sentences passed made appropriate allowance for the time spent in custody before the original order was made.

R. v. HENDERSON (DAVID GEORGE) [1997] 2 Cr. App. R. (S.) 266, Stuart White, J., CA (Crim Div).

1653. **Remand–calculation of release date–credit for time spent on remand for related offences subsequently tried and sentenced separately**

[Criminal Justice Act 1991 s.33.]

M was remanded in custody for 105 days in respect of two sets of related offences which were later tried and sentenced separately. For the first set of offences, the magistrates imposed a sentence of 120 days' imprisonment. Under the Criminal Justice Act 1991 s.33, M was entitled to unconditional release after half that period, 60 days, and was thus immediately released. M was later sentenced by the Crown Court to 457 days' imprisonment for the second set of offences, with s.33 of the 1991 Act allowing him to be released after 229 days. M contended that he was entitled to a further reduction of 45 days, being the unused balance of time spent on remand before the initial trial. The prison governor argued that the 45 days were used up in reducing to 15 days the period for which M remained at risk of being returned to prison to serve the remainder of his initial sentence should he reoffend.

Held, granting a writ of habeas corpus, that the purpose of s.33 of the 1991 Act was to produce a suspended sentence during which an offender was at risk of being returned to prison should he reoffend. It was therefore not appropriate to use the unused remand days to reduce this period artificially, and M was entitled to have his second term of imprisonment reduced by the 45 days in question. Related offences should not be the subject of split sentencing since this was capable of creating injustice to defendants as well as increasing public expenditure. In the instant case the problem could have been avoided if the justices had referred the initial offences to the Crown Court for sentence along with trial of the remaining charges.

R. v. GOVERNOR OF HAVERIGG PRISON, *ex p.* MCMAHON, *The Times*, September 24, 1997, Sedley, J., QBD.

1654. **Remand–time spent in custody before sentence–relevant sentence for determining whether long term or short term prisoner**

[Criminal Justice Act 1967 s.67; Criminal Justice Act 1991 s.33.]

The relevant sentence for determining whether an individual is a long term or short term prisoner under the Criminal Justice Act 1991 s.33(5) is the sentence imposed by the court and not that sentence reduced by (any) time spent on remand. P, sentenced to four years' imprisonment after spending 261 days on remand in custody, applied for judicial review of the Secretary of State's decision to treat him as a long term prisoner for the purposes of determining the appropriate arrangements for his release. P contended that, in determining whether a prisoner was a short term or long term prisoner in terms of the Criminal Justice Act 1991 s.33(5), the relevant sentence was the term pronounced by the court reduced by the time spent on remand.

Held, dismissing the application, that the provisions of the 1991 Act s.33(5) fell to be construed in the light of the Criminal Justice Act 1967 s.67(4) that any statutory reference to a sentence of imprisonment was to be interpreted as a reference to the sentence imposed by the court and not the sentence as reduced by time spent in custody.

R. v. SECRETARY OF STATE FOR THE HOME DEPARTMENT, *ex p.* PROBYN, *The Times*, October 30, 1997, Rose, L.J., QBD.

1655. Road traffic offences–careless driving–death–excess alcohol

[Road Traffic Act 1988 s.3A.]

A, having consumed seven single whiskies, drove his car at 50 mph into a lane of oncoming traffic. He collided with a car and killed the elderly passenger. A's breath test revealed 57 microgrammes of alcohol in 100 millilitres of breath. A was 64 and of previous good character. He pleaded guilty to causing death by careless driving whilst driving under the influence of alcohol contrary to the Road Traffic Act 1988 s.3A and was sentenced to three years' imprisonment and disqualified from driving for five years. A appealed.

Held, allowing the appeal, that a sentence of three years' imprisonment was entirely appropriate on the facts. However, due to A's health and age, the sentence would be reduced to two years.

R. v. ADAMES (DONALD GEORGE) [1997] R.T.R. 110, Astill, J., CA (Crim Div).

1656. Road traffic offences–careless driving–death–excess alcohol–driver failing to see inadequately lit cyclist

L appealed against a sentence of six years' imprisonment, having pleaded guilty to causing death by careless driving. He collided with a cyclist who was travelling in the same direction. The cyclist was wearing dark clothing and had no rear light on his bicycle. L was subsequently found to have a breath alcohol level of about 87 microgrammes per 100 millilitres of breath. He had a previous conviction for driving with excess alcohol.

Held, allowing the appeal and substituting a four year term, that the sentence of six years was longer than was required and did not adequately reflect the guilty plea, *R. v. Corcoran (Terence)* [1996] 1 Cr. App. R. (S.) 416, [1996] 1 C.L.Y. 1768 considered.

R. v. LILL (JAMES ALFRED PIERCY) [1997] 1 Cr. App. R. (S.) 366, Stuart-Smith, L.J., CA (Crim Div).

1657. Road traffic offences–careless driving–death–excess alcohol–mental health–exceptional circumstances justifying release on compassionate grounds

[Criminal Justice Act 1991 s.36.]

P, aged 69, appealed against concurrent custodial sentences of three years each for two offences of causing death by careless driving while unfit through drink, together with a disqualification from driving for six years on the basis of the deterioration in his health and his psychiatric condition. P contended that he suffered paranoid delusions, was fearful of other inmates and was so mentally confused that he regularly missed mealtimes.

Held, allowing the appeal and substituting concurrent sentences of two years each, that the appropriate procedure in such cases was to make an application to the Secretary of State under the Criminal Justice Act 1991 s.36 contending that there existed exceptional circumstances which would justify release on compassionate grounds. However, as P's earliest date of release was imminent and it was unlikely that the Secretary of State would be able to intervene in time, P should not be made to suffer for the fact that his advisors had chosen the wrong procedure, *R. v. Bernard (Basil Mortimer)* [1997] 1 Cr. App. R. (S.) 135, [1996] 1 C.L.Y. 1877 approved.

R. v. PATHE (PETER MICHAEL),Trans. Ref: 9702196 W2, May 15, 1997, Keene, J., CA (Crim Div).

1658. Road traffic offences–dangerous driving–administration of justice offences–serious injury to pedestrian–suspended sentence unduly lenient

[Criminal Justice Act 1988 s.36, s.41.]

The Attorney General applied for a sentence to be referred under the Criminal Justice Act 1988 s.36 on the ground that it was unduly lenient. All four defendants pleaded guilty to an offence of doing acts to pervert the course of justice having dishonestly reported a car to be stolen and then set fire to it. S, with M as passenger, was driving at speeds between 38 and 47 mph in a 30 mile zone and collided with a pedestrian who suffered, inter alia, serious head injuries, fractures and lacerations on her head and face requiring surgery. S did not stop and did not report the accident but abandoned the car and went to the house of B and J, where all four defendants agreed to report the car had been stolen some time before. S also pleaded guilty to dangerous driving, failing to stop and failing to report the accident under the Criminal Justice Act 1988 s.41. S received a suspended sentence of six months' imprisonment and M, B and J were conditionally discharged. The aggravating features were the excessive speed, the serious injury caused, the failure to stop and the subsequent deception. In mitigation were the guilty pleas, entered at the earliest opportunity, the personal circumstances particularly of M and B, the fact that the driving had been on the borderline between dangerous and careless, the delay between the incident and the passing of sentence and the remorse expressed.

Held, allowing the reference, that no exceptional circumstances existed justifying a suspended sentence in the case of S, *R. v. Okinikan* (1993) 14 Cr. App. R. (S.) 453, [1993] C.L.Y. 1100 considered. However, such circumstances did exist for M and B. After taking into account all the aggravating and mitigating factors and the element of double jeopardy the court substituted a six month custodial term for S, a two month term for J and one month suspended sentences in respect of M and B. In addition S was disqualified for 12 months.

R. v. SAMUEL (MICHAEL ANDREW); R. v. BERESFORD (AMANDA ELIZABETH); R. v. JONES (JASON ROBERT); R. v. MURPHY (KAREN AMANDA), Trans. Ref: 9608487 R2, 9608488 R2, 96084889 R2, 9608390 R2, April 11, 1997, Rose, L.J., CA (Crim Div).

1659. Road traffic offences–dangerous driving–death–12 months' imprisonment unduly lenient

[Criminal Justice Act 1988 s.36.]

The Attorney General applied for a sentence to be referred under the Criminal Justice Act 1988 s.36 on the ground that it was unduly lenient. B, aged 28, convicted of causing death by dangerous driving, was sentenced to 12 months' imprisonment and disqualified from driving for four years. B collided with a car killing two out of four of the occupants and seriously injuring the remaining passengers. B was driving in daylight in dry weather at a considerable speed over a long distance. On an expert reconstruction it seemed that the deceased was trying to negotiate a U-turn through a gap in the central reservation and B struck the offside of the deceased's vehicle head on. At a speed of between 96 and 106 miles an hour B's brakes locked and he skidded. When he collided with the deceased's car he was still travelling at about 85 miles an hour.

Held, allowing the reference, that given the speed at which B was travelling and the ensuing tragedy, killing two people, the sentence was unduly lenient, *R. v. Boswell (James Thomas)* (1984) 6 Cr. App. R. (S.) 257, [1984] C.L.Y. 831 followed. After taking into account the personal mitigation of B's good character and the element of double jeopardy the court substituted a sentence of 24 months' imprisonment.

R. v. BRAMLEY (SEAN LESLIE), Trans. Ref: AG/3/97 9700347 R2, March 14, 1997, Rose, L.J., CA (Crim Div).

1660. Road traffic offences–dangerous driving–death–accident caused by driver reading map while driving

M aged 37, pleaded guilty to causing death by dangerous driving. M, a parcel delivery driver, was driving at between 55 and 60 mph on a main road when he briefly looked at a map on his dashboard. As a result he failed to see that traffic ahead of him was stationary, and collided with the vehicle ahead of him, the driver of which died from her injuries. M was sentenced to six months' imprisonment and appealed.

Held, allowing the appeal, that considering *R. v. Boswell (James Thomas)* (1984) 6 Cr. App. R. (S.) 257, [1984] C.L.Y. 831, it was open to the judge to find that the offence was so serious that only a custodial sentence could be justified. M admitted dangerous driving; he failed to pay proper attention to the road ahead. The sentencer was entitled to pass a custodial sentence, but by reason of the nature of the driving, M's record, the lack of any aggravating features, his immediate guilty plea, genuine remorse and personal circumstances, six months was too long; a sentence of two months was substituted.

R. v. MOORE (IAN JOHN) [1997] 2 Cr. App. R. (S.) 239, Judge Martin Stephens Q.C., CA (Crim Div).

1661. Road traffic offences–dangerous driving–death–accident caused by drivers racing on public road

[Criminal Justice Act 1988 s.36.]

The Attorney General applied for a sentence to be referred under the Criminal Justice Act 1988 s.36 on the ground that it was unduly lenient. O was convicted of causing death by dangerous driving and pleaded guilty to dangerous driving. He was driving his car with two passengers along a dual carriageway which was subject to a 30 mph speed restriction, in convoy with another car driven by a person who it was alleged was known to him. The two cars were estimated to be racing at speeds of up to 100 mph. They stopped at traffic lights and when the lights changed both cars set off at high speed. They overtook two other cars in a dangerous manner and continued to race each other over some distance. Eventually the other car struck a pedestrian who was crossing the road, killing her instantly. Neither car stopped. O was sentenced to three years' imprisonment and disqualified from driving for five years.

Held, refusing the reference, that the offence was aggravated by driving at a grossly excessive speed and racing another vehicle. For O, it was said that he had accepted responsibility for the death of the pedestrian and that he was of previous good character. There had been a delay of over two years between the commission of the offence and the trial, as a result of the disappearance of the other driver. In the view of the court, the judge might properly have reflected the mitigating factors by reducing the sentence to four years' imprisonment. As any sentence substituted by the court would be reduced to reflect the element of double jeopardy, the difference between the sentence imposed and the sentence which would be substituted would be insufficient to justify interfering with the sentence, *R. v. Boswell (James Thomas)* [1984] 1 W.L.R. 1047, [1984] C.L.Y. 831 and *Attorney General's Reference (Nos.14 and 24 of 1993), Re* [1984] 1 W.L.R. 530, [1994] C.L.Y. 1193 cited.

ATTORNEY GENERAL'S REFERENCE (NO.20 OF 1996), Re; sub nom. R. v. OMER (SALIM ABDULLA) [1997] 1 Cr. App. R. (S.) 285, Lord Bingham of Cornhill, C.J., CA (Crim Div).

1662. Road traffic offences–dangerous driving–death–aggravated vehicle taking–five years' imprisonment unduly lenient

[Criminal Justice Act 1988 s.36.]

The Attorney General applied for a sentence to be referred under the Criminal Justice Act 1988 s.36 on the ground that it was unduly lenient. L, aged 21 years, was convicted of causing death by dangerous driving and had pleaded guilty to aggravated vehicle taking. He was sentenced to five years' and three years' imprisonment concurrent and was disqualified from driving for seven years.

Held, allowing the reference, that the sentence was unduly lenient and seven years' imprisonment would be substituted. There were many aggravating features to the case: two cars had been racing for a considerable distance; two other drivers had been forced to take evasive action; a vehicle had been taken without consent; L had been uninsured; he had made good his escape knowing there were likely to have been serious injuries; he had an antecedent history of motoring offences; the offence had been committed whilst he was on bail for aggravated vehicle taking; and he had contested the case, *Attorney General's Reference (Nos.14 and 24 of 1993), Re* (1994) 15 Cr. App. R. (S.) 640, [1994] C.L.Y. 1193 considered.

ATTORNEY GENERAL'S REFERENCE (NO.67 OF 1995), *Re; sub nom.* R. v. LLOYD (DAVID RUSSELL) [1996] 2 Cr. App. R. (S.) 373, Lord Taylor of Gosforth, C.J., CA (Crim Div).

1663. Road traffic offences–dangerous driving–death–deliberately hostile driving manner was aggravating feature

Held, that where a driver used his vehicle in a deliberately hostile manner by swerving violently towards a cyclist after an argument at traffic lights and the cyclist then fell, sustaining fatal injuries, the driver's actions were to be taken as a serious aggravating feature, meriting a sentence of three and a half years' imprisonment upon conviction of causing death by dangerous driving, notwithstanding that he may have been provoked and that other mitigating factors existed.

R. v. DICKINSON (ANTHONY), *The Times*, March 13, 1997, Nelson, J, CA (Crim Div).

1664. Road traffic offences–dangerous driving–death–driving towards group of people who had previously attacked car

R appealed against a sentence of five years' imprisonment on conviction of causing death by dangerous driving. He had spent an evening at a nightclub when a fight broke out between his girlfriend and another woman. Following a further incident outside the club, a group of people attacked R's car as he attempted to start it. He drove off, and then turned round and drove towards the group, accelerating. K stood in the road, shouting and R's car swerved towards him, striking him with its nearside wing. R then left the scene. At first instance the judge held that R had not deliberately driven at the group with the intention of causing harm, but had driven dangerously and with indifference towards the safety of people on the road.

Held, allowing the appeal, reducing the sentence from five to four years, that although this was a bad case of dangerous driving, R was entitled to be sentenced on the basis that he had acted in a panic in the course of an incident not of his making.

R. v. ROWBOTHAM (KEVIN) [1997] 1 Cr. App. R. (S.) 187, Laws, L.J., CA (Crim Div).

1665. Road traffic offences–dangerous driving–death–excess alcohol

B appealed against sentence of six years' imprisonment after pleading guilty to causing death by dangerous driving and driving whilst disqualified. B was seen driving a car belonging to a friend at a high speed in a built-up area, swerving from lane to lane and overtaking vehicles on both sides. The car hit a kerb, went out of control and collided with a wall. A boy standing near the wall was killed and a girl was injured. A blood sample taken one and a half hours after the accident showed that B had at that time 60 milligrammes of alcohol per 100 millilitres of blood (below the legal limit) but back calculations indicated that he would have been over the limit at the time of the accident.

Held, allowing the appeal, that this was a serious case involving an element of drink, but an appropriate sentence following a plea of guilty was five years' imprisonment *Attorney General's Reference (Nos.14 and 24 of 1993) (R v. Shepherd), Re* [1994] 1 W.L.R. 530, [1994] C.L.Y. 1193, *R. v. Burns (Michael)* [1996] 1 Cr. App. R. (S.) 821 [1996] 1 C.L.Y. 1822 and *Attorney General's Reference (No.46 of 1994), Re* (1995) 16 Cr. App. R. (S.) 914, [1996] 1 C.L.Y. 1827 cited.

R. v. BARBER (SIMON) [1997] 1 Cr. App. R. (S.) 65, Otton, L.J., CA (Crim Div).

1666. **Road traffic offences–dangerous driving–death–excess alcohol–driver three times over prescribed limit–two years' imprisonment and two years' disqualification unduly lenient**

[Criminal Justice Act 1988 s.36.]

The Attorney General applied for a sentence to be referred under the Criminal Justice Act 1988 s.36 on the ground that it was unduly lenient. S was sentence of two years' imprisonment, disqualification for two years and an order to take an extended driving test following a guilty plea to causing death by dangerous driving. S was found to be three times over the permitted limit for consumption of alcohol when his car was struck by another vehicle while he was attempting to turn right across a dual carriageway. The Attorney General contended that the sentence failed to reflect the aggravating features present, given the amount of alcohol consumed and the fact that S had undertaken a five mile journey when he knew he was over the limit to drive and he was carrying five passengers.

Held, allowing the reference, quashing the sentence and substituting four years' imprisonment and increasing the disqualification period to five years, that the sentence passed was unduly lenient. Taking account of the mitigation available to S for his guilty plea, good character and genuine remorse, S had made a serious misjudgment due to the alcohol he had consumed. The original sentence did not reflect the gravity of the offence, that six people were injured and one person fatally injured, and the quantity of alcohol consumed in the knowledge that S would be driving later, *Attorney General's Reference (Nos.24 and 45 of 1994), Re* (1995) 16 Cr. App. R. (S.) 583 considered.

ATTORNEY GENERAL'S REFERENCE (NO.48 OF 1996), Re; *sub nom.* R. v. SWAIN (PAUL) [1997] 2 Cr. App. R. (S.) 76, Rose, L.J., CA (Crim Div).

1667. **Road traffic offences–dangerous driving–death–excessive speed–12 months' imprisonment unduly lenient**

The Attorney General applied for a sentence to be referred under the Criminal Justice Act 1988 s.36 on the ground that it was unduly lenient. I was convicted of and W pleaded guilty to causing death by dangerous driving. They were not known to each other and were driving in separate cars when they stopped at traffic lights. When the lights changed, I set off at high speed closely followed by W. They continued to drive in this way for about one third of a mile. A pedestrian began to cross the road; I managed to avoid her but W collided with her causing fatal injuries. It was estimated that both vehicles had been travelling at about 60 mph in an area subject to a 30 mph speed restriction. They denied that they had been racing or indulging in competitive driving. They were sentenced to 12 months' imprisonment and nine months' imprisonment respectively, and disqualified from driving for four years in each case.

Held, refusing the reference, that the offences involved driving at a grossly excessive speed in a built up area and driving too close together, and the appropriate sentence indicated by the relevant authorities was five years' imprisonment. The court had to be mindful of the widespread public concern regarding the offence of causing death by dangerous driving which had led to an increase in the maximum sentence for the offence and guidance from the Court of Appeal indicating that much higher sentences should be passed. The offenders were both young men of previous good character, there was no suggestion of the consumption of alcohol and the court accepted that they were not racing or driving competitively. However, the court had no alternative but to impose a custodial sentence, the lowest appropriate sentences being 21 months and 15 months respectively. The sentences were therefore unduly lenient, but in view of the element of double jeopardy, they would not be increased, *R. v. Boswell (James Thomas)* (1986) 82 Cr. App. R. 347, [1986] C.L.Y. 868, *Attorney General's Reference (Nos.14 and 24 of 1993), Re* [1994] 1 W.L.R. 530, [1994] C.L.Y. 1193, *Attorney General's Reference (No.38 of 1994), Re* (1995) 16 Cr. App. R. (S.) 714, [1996] 1 C.L.Y 1835, *R. v. Shaw (Bradley)* (1995) 16 Cr. App. R. (S.) 960, [1996] 1 C.L.Y. 1829, *R. v. Gooch (Shaun Lee)* (1994) 15 Cr. App. R. (S.) 390 and *Attorney General's Reference (No.69 of 1995), Re* [1996] 2 Cr. App. R. (S.) 360, [1997] C.L.Y. 1678 cited.

ATTORNEY GENERAL'S REFERENCE (NOS.17 AND 18 OF 1996), *Re; sub nom.* R. v. ISETON (MARK ANDREW); R. v. WARDLE (LEE) [1997] 1 Cr. App. R. (S.) 247, Lord Bingham of Cornhill, C.J., CA (Crim Div).

1668. Road traffic offences–dangerous driving–death–excessive speed–excess alcohol

M, aged 22, pleaded guilty to causing death by dangerous driving. M while driving his car failed to negotiate a bend and struck a pedestrian guard rail and a street lighting post. The car somersaulted and eventually came to rest on its roof. A passenger was killed instantly. M had drunk six pints of beer in a period of several hours before the accident, and a back calculation of his breath alcohol level indicated a probable level of 52 microgrammes per 100 millilitres of breath. There was evidence that M had driven at high speed shortly before the accident. He appealed against sentence of four years' imprisonment.

Held, dismissing the appeal, that considering *R. v. Boswell (James Thomas)* (1984) 6 Cr. App. R. (S.) 257, [1984] C.L.Y. 831 and *Attorney General's Reference (Nos.14 and 24 of 1993), Re* (1994) 15 Cr. App. R. (S.) 640, [1994] C.L.Y. 1193, although M was young and of previous good character, had pleaded guilty and was impressed with guilt for the death of his best friend, the sentence was not excessive. The aggravating features were excess alcohol, excessive speed, refusal to take a blood sample and initial denial that he was the driver of the car.

R. v. MORRIS (TIMOTHY ANDREW) [1997] 2 Cr. App. R. (S.) 258, Staughton, L.J., CA (Crim Div).

1669. Road traffic offences–dangerous driving–death–excessive speed–excess alcohol–juvenile driver

[Children and Young Persons Act 1933 s.53(2), s.53(3).]

B pleaded guilty to causing death by dangerous driving. B aged 16 at the time of the offence, obtained a car. B consumed some alcohol and then set out in the car with a friend. He drove at speeds estimated at 60 to 70 mph down a winding country lane and lost control of the car, which collided with a cyclist who was killed. T was found to have a blood alcohol level of 90 milligrammes of alcohol per 100 millilitres of blood. B was sentenced to five years' detention under the Children and Young Persons Act 1933 s.53(2) and (3), and disqualified from driving for eight years.

Held, allowing the appeal, that considering *R. v. Boswell (James Thomas)* (1984) 6 Cr. App. R. (S.) 257, [1984] C.L.Y. 831 and *Attorney General's Reference (Nos.14 and 24 of 1993), Re* (1994) 15 Cr. App. R. (S.) 640, [1994] C.L.Y. 1193, Parliament had increased the maximum sentence for causing death by dangerous driving from five years' imprisonment to 10 to reflect public concern. The factor of youth carried less weight than in other areas. B had pleaded guilty and there were personal mitigating factors of a good work record and good character. The court would substitute a sentence of three and a half years' detention under the 1933 Act s.53(2) and (3) and the period of disqualification was reduced to four years.

R. v. B (A JUVENILE) (JANUARY 14, 1997) [1997] 2 Cr. App. R. (S.) 184, Holland, J., CA (Crim Div).

1670. Road traffic offences–dangerous driving–death–heavy goods vehicle–lorry driver falling asleep–failure to take prescribed rest

M was convicted of causing death by dangerous driving and appealed against sentence of three years' imprisonment and disqualification from driving for three years. He was driving a lorry in the course of his employment and was seen driving in an erratic manner over a distance of about eight miles. He eventually collided with a motorcyclist who was killed. He had had only five hours' rest in the previous 24 hours.

Held, dismissing the appeal, that this was a prolonged, persistent and deliberate piece of bad driving. M had a sufficient period to realise that he ought to stop. The maximum sentence for causing death by dangerous driving had been increased and it was clear that Parliament intended the courts to review their sentencing in this category of case. The fact that M was under pressure from his employer to complete the journey was not sufficient mitigation to reduce the burden that rested on him not to drive when he knew he was falling asleep. *R. v. Goodman (Ian Peter)* (1988) 10 Cr. App. R. (S.) 438, [1991] C.L.Y. 1035 and *R. v. Beeby* (1983) 5 Cr. App. R. (S.) 56 cited.

R. v. DE MEERSMAN (EDDY LOUIS) [1997] 1 Cr. App. R. (S.) 106, Ward, L.J., CA (Crim Div).

1671. Road traffic offences–dangerous driving–death–heavy goods vehicle driven at excessive speed in foggy conditions

T, aged 27, pleaded guilty three counts of causing death by dangerous driving. T drove an articulated lorry with a load of 38 tonnes down a hill in foggy conditions at a speed of 62 mph, the limit being 40 mph. He came up behind another lorry and realised that he would be unable to stop in time to avoid colliding with it. He accordingly pulled to the offside and collided head on with an oncoming car. Three persons in the car were killed. T was sentenced to four years' imprisonment and disqualified from driving for six years.

Held, allowing the appeal, that (1) considering *R. v. Boswell (James Thomas)* (1984) 6 Cr. App. R. (S.) 257, [1984] C.L.Y. 831, *Attorney General's References (Nos.14 and 24 of 1993), Re* (1994) 15 Cr. App. R. (S.) 640, [1994] C.L.Y. 1193 and *R. v. Frisby* (Unreported, 1995) and *R. v. Le Mouel* [1996] 1 Cr App. R. (S.) 42, [1996] 1 C.L.Y. 1831 distinguished, the sentence was too long. T had a good driving record and good work record, was remorseful and traumatised by the accident. But having in mind a custodial sentence was inevitable and that the sentence had to reflect the fact that three deaths were caused, the appropriate sentence was three years' imprisonment, three years disqualification and the requirement for an extended driving test was imposed.

R. v. TOOMBS (DAREN) [1997] 2 Cr. App. R. (S.) 217, Brian Smedley, J., CA (Crim Div).

1672. Road traffic offences–dangerous driving–death–heavy goods vehicle driven with knowledge of defective brakes

K appealed against sentence of 30 months' imprisonment and four years' disqualification, having pleaded guilty to causing death by dangerous driving. He was driving an articulated heavy goods vehicle down a steep hill when the brakes failed. The vehicle went out of control and eventually overturned, crushing a stationary car and killing the driver. An examination of the vehicle showed that its brakes were seriously defective. K admitted that he had been advised that the brakes required attention but that remedial work had been put off until the vehicle's annual MOT. He pleaded guilty on the basis that it was his duty to inspect the braking system and that he had failed to do so.

Held, dismissing the appeal, that those who operated heavy goods vehicles frequently allowed commercial considerations to keep vehicles on the road at the expense of regular maintenance, and the risk of potentially catastrophic consequences was enhanced by defective maintenance. Sentences in cases of this kind must contain an element of deterrence and the sentence was not manifestly excessive. The disqualification was wholly warranted.

R. v. KANG (BALVINDER SINGH) [1997] 1 Cr. App. R. (S.) 306, Ognall, J., CA (Crim Div).

1673. **Road traffic offences–dangerous driving–death–juvenile offender–15 months' imprisonment unduly lenient**

[Criminal Justice Act 1988 s.36.]

The Attorney General applied for a sentence to be referred under the Criminal Justice Act 1988 s.36 on the ground that it was unduly lenient. F was convicted of causing death by dangerous driving. He was driving his car along a single carriageway subject to a 40 mph hour limit when he overtook another car and accelerated to a speed estimated by witnesses to be between 70 and 80 mph. His car collided with a youth riding a moped in the opposite direction, who had moved to the centre of the road to turn right. The youth was killed instantly. F was sentenced to 15 months' detention in a young offender institution and disqualified from driving for four years. The Attorney General sought to refer the sentence on grounds of undue leniency.

Held, allowing the reference, that it was submitted for F that he was an inexperienced driver and there was no evidence of persistent bad driving over a long period and he was extremely remorseful. The disastrous consequences of the offence and the public's concern had to be borne in mind and the court was guided by previous decisions which indicated the range of sentences thought appropriate in this kind of case. F did not have the mitigation of a plea of guilty or a good character in driving matters. The sentence of 15 months' detention in a young offender institution was unduly lenient and a sentence of three and a half years detention in a young offender institution was substituted, *R. v. Boswell (James Thomas)* (1984) 6 Cr. App. R. (S.) 257, [1984] C.L.Y. 831, *Attorney General's Reference (Nos.14 and 24 of 1993), Re* (1993) 15 Cr. App. R. (S.) 640, [1994] C.L.Y. 1193, *R. v. Pritchard* (1994) 16 Cr. App. R. (S.) 666, [1996] 1 C.L.Y. 1833, *Attorney General's Reference (No.37 of 1994), Re* (1995) 16 Cr. App. R. (S.) 760, [1996] 1 C.L.Y. 1821, *R. v. Shaw* (1995) 16 Cr. App. R. (S.) 960, [1996] 1 C.L.Y. 1829, *R. v. Mallone (Patrick)* [1996] 1 Cr. App. R. (S.) 221, *R. v. Robbins* [1996] 1 Cr. App. R. (S.) 312, [1996] 1 C.L.Y. 1965, *Attorney General's Reference (No.30 of 1995), Re* [1996] 1 Cr. App. R. (S.) 364, [1996] 1 C.L.Y. 1826 considered.

ATTORNEY GENERAL'S REFERENCE (NO.44 OF 1996), Re; *sub nom.* R. v. FRENCH (RICHARD) [1997] 1 Cr. App. R. (S.) 375, Rose, L.J., CA (Crim Div).

1674. **Road traffic offences–dangerous driving–death–nine months' imprisonment unduly lenient**

[Criminal Justice Act 1988 s.36.]

The Attorney General applied for a sentence to be referred under the Criminal Justice Act 1988 s.36 on the ground that is was unduly lenient. K was convicted of causing death by dangerous driving and was sentenced to nine months' imprisonment. K hit and killed one of a group of people crossing a dual carriageway at a pelican crossing. The crossing had not been activated, as no traffic was in evidence when they began to cross. The offender stated his speed to have been approximately 45 mph, but a police officer who conducted a series of tests estimated a speed of between 60 and 70 mph. The offender failed to stop, but surrendered to the police the following day. In interview he stated he was distracted having been involved in an argument with his girlfriend. The offender contended that his failure to stop was mitigated by his actions the next day and that the criminality involved was at the lower end of the scale for this type of offence.

Held, allowing the reference, quashing the sentence of nine months and substituting a sentence of 21 months' imprisonment, that taking account of the features of the case and the element of double jeopardy present in such references, the sentence was unduly lenient. Public concern regarding loss of life had to be balanced against the circumstances of the instant case and the particular offender concerned.

ATTORNEY GENERAL'S REFERENCE (NO.6 OF 1996), *Re*; *sub nom*. R. v. KOUSOUROUS (ADAM) [1997] 1 Cr. App. R. (S.) 79, Rose, L.J., CA (Crim Div).

1675. Road traffic offences–dangerous driving–death–overtaking on brow of hill

P appealed against a sentence of 18 months' imprisonment and four years disqualification, having pleaded guilty to causing death by dangerous driving. He was driving his car along a straight narrow road towards the brow of a hill. As the car reached the brow of the hill he attempted to overtake the car ahead of him which was being driven by a friend and crossed a solid white line in order to do so. P's car collided head on with a car coming in the opposite direction which was concealed by the brow of the hill. This car burst into flames and the driver died from his injuries. It was not suggested that he had been drinking alcohol. P claimed that he had thought that the road ahead was clear.

Held, allowing the appeal in respect of the disqualification period, that it could not be accepted that this was a case of a momentary reckless error of judgment, nor that the increase in the maximum sentence for the offence from five years to 10 had not affected the custody threshold or the length of sentence. In recent years public attention had focused more on the offence and the intention of courts had been rigorously to apply a proper sentencing process to such offences to seek to deter and seek to control what happened on the roads. This was not a case of momentary inattention. The manner of driving and the nature of the incident indicated that this was a serious case which passed the custody threshold. The sentence of imprisonment was correct in length and took account of the mitigating factors. The period of disqualification was excessive and a period of two years' disqualification from driving was substituted, *R. v. Boswell (James Thomas)* (1984) 6 Cr. App. R. (S.) 257, [1984] C.L.Y. 831, *Attorney General's Reference (No.34 of 1994), Re* (1995) 16 Cr. App. R. (S.) 785, [1995] 1 C.L.Y. 1343 and *R. v. Le Mouel* [1996] 1 Cr. App. R. (S.) 42, [1996] 1 C.L.Y. 1831 considered.

R. v. PRATT (STUART TERENCE) [1997] 1 Cr. App. R. (S.) 419, Hidden, J., CA (Crim Div).

1676. Road traffic offences–dangerous driving–death–overtaking on brow of hill–good character of offender

L appealed against a sentence of three years' imprisonment for causing death by dangerous driving. He was driving at night behind another car which was travelling at about 58 miles per hour. After following this car for some time, he attempted to overtake it at a point where the road rose to a slight crest. His car collided with an oncoming car which caught fire and a baby in the rear of the car was killed. L claimed that as he was overtaking one car, he saw the oncoming car which braked and swerved across the road, whilst he attempted to regain the correct side of the road. L had driven for 43 years without any convictions. It was accepted that he had simply overtaken at a time when he should not have done so.

Held, allowing the appeal, that although there was great public and private distress when people were killed in road accidents, this was a case without many of the common aggravating features. It was a case of misjudgment, but the act of overtaking on approaching the crest of a hill was a deliberate one and the results were disastrous. Balancing L's character with all the other factors in the case, the sentence of three years was manifestly excessive and a sentence of 18 months' imprisonment was substituted, *R. v. Boswell (James Thomas)*

(1984) 6 Cr. App. R. (S.) 257, [1984] C.L.Y. 831, *R. v. Bevan* [1996] 1 Cr. App. R. (S.) 14 and *R. v. Bailey* [1996] 1 Cr. App. R. (S.) 129 considered.

R. v. LOWRY (THOMAS GORDON) [1996] 2 Cr. App. R. (S.) 416, Waterhouse, J., CA (Crim Div).

1677. **Road traffic offences–dangerous driving–death–six months' imprisonment unduly lenient**

[Criminal Justice Act 1988 s.36.]

The Attorney General applied for a sentence to be referred under the Criminal Justice Act 1988 s.36 on the ground that it was unduly lenient. H, aged 18, was sentenced to six months' detention in a young offender institution after pleading guilty to causing death by dangerous driving. He was also disqualified from driving for three years and ordered to take the extended driving test. It was submitted that the following aggravating factors necessitated a longer sentence: (1) excessive speed in an obviously dangerous manoeuvre; (2) acquiescing to the lie told to police about the identity of the driver; (3) knowing that he was driving while uninsured, and (4) a previous conviction for dangerous driving. It was acknowledged that mitigating factors were H's guilty plea and the fact that the victim was his friend.

Held, allowing the reference, that the sentence was too lenient and a sentence of three years' detention was substituted.

ATTORNEY GENERAL'S REFERENCE (NO.28 OF 1996), *Re; sub nom.* R. v. HYSIAK (MARK DOUGLAS) [1997] 2 Cr. App. R. (S.) 79, Rose, L.J., CA (Crim Div).

1678. **Road traffic offences–dangerous driving–death–three years' imprisonment unduly lenient**

[Criminal Justice Act 1988 s.36.]

The Attorney General applied for a sentence to be referred under the Criminal Justice Act 1988 s.36 on the ground that it was unduly lenient. J was convicted of causing death by dangerous driving and was sentenced to three years' imprisonment. The Attorney General contended that J, aged 24, had driven at speed against a no entry sign up a narrow lane, had not been licensed or insured to drive, and had failed to stop after fatally injuring a pedestrian and failed to report the accident. In addition he had a bad record for motoring convictions. J urged his guilty plea, his remorse and the absence of drink.

Held, allowing the reference, that the aggravating features and J's consistent flouting of the law rendered the offence extremely serious and the sentence was too moderate, *R. v. Boswell (James Thomas)* (1984) 6 Cr. App. R. (S.) 257, [1984] C.L.Y. 831 and *Attorney General's Reference (Nos.14 and 24 of 1994), Re* (1993) 15 Cr. App. R. (S.) 640, [1994] C.L.Y. 1193 followed. Accordingly, a sentence of five years' imprisonment was substituted.

ATTORNEY GENERAL'S REFERENCE (NO.69 OF 1995), *Re; sub nom.* R. v. JACKSON (ANTHONY PAUL) [1996] 2 Cr. App. R. (S.) 360, Lord Taylor of Gosforth, C.J., CA (Crim Div).

1679. **Road traffic offences–dangerous driving–death–trailer becoming detached as a result of being inadequately secured**

W pleaded guilty to causing death by dangerous driving. He was driving a goods vehicle towing a trailer loaded with a tar boiler containing molten tar and a gas cylinder. As his vehicle passed over an uneven patch of road surface, the trailer became detached and careered onto the footpath, where it collided with a pedestrian who was propelled into a brick wall which collapsed on top of her. The victim was covered with molten tar and died from her injuries. The cause of the trailer becoming detached was the absence of a proper securing pin for the tow hitch. W was aware that there was no pin and had improvised a connection with a bolt which was pushed up from below and secured with a nut which was not adequately tightened. He had also failed to attach a device which would have caused the trailer's brakes to operate when it became detached. The lid of the tar boiler was inadequately secured. W was sentenced to two years and three months' imprisonment and disqualified from driving for five years.

Held, allowing the sentence of imprisonment to stand but reducing the period of disqualification to two and a half years, *R. v. Rogers* (Unreported, 1994) considered. The sentence must reflect both the mitigating factor, of W's contrition, and the condemnation of his grossly reckless behaviour. The sentence properly balanced these factors and it was not manifestly excessive or wrong in principle.

R. v. WALTON (STEPHEN) [1996] 2 Cr. App. R. (S.) 220, Butterfield, J., CA (Crim Div).

1680. Road traffic offences–dangerous driving–death–unpredictable event at slow speed

[Children and Young Persons Act 1933 s.53(2).]

M aged 15 and 19 were convicted of causing death by dangerous driving and violent disorder, and were sentenced to six years' detention under the Children and Young Persons Act 1933 s.53(2) and eight years' detention in a young offender institution respectively, and disqualified from driving for 10 years in each case. They had attended a party at which about 300 people were present, in the course of which the second appellant was assaulted. M got into their van and drove it through the car park, which was crowded with people. One appellant operated the clutch and gears, and the other steered. The van was driven slowly through the crowd, and collided with two girls who were talking to each other. One of the girls was pulled underneath the van and dragged for about 30 yards. She suffered injuries from which she died. M claimed that they had not seen the girl and did not realise that people banging on the side of the van were trying to attract their attention to the girl.

Held, allowing the appeals, that the offence had caused a tragic loss of life, but the events were unpredictable and had happened when the van was being driven at five miles per hour, *Attorney General's References (Nos. 24 and 45 of 1994), Re* (1995) 16 Cr. App. R. (S.) 583, [1995] 1 C.L.Y. 1344 considered. The sentence of eight years' detention in a young offender institution would be reduced to six years, and the sentence of six years' detention would be reduced to three years, (allowing for nine months which would not count against the sentence). The disqualification would be reduced to five years in each case.

R. v. MOON (PAUL); R. v. MOON (DAVID) [1997] 2 Cr. App. R. (S.) 44, Henry, L.J., CA (Crim Div).

1681. Road traffic offences–dangerous driving–intimidation following minor incident

B pleaded guilty to dangerous driving. B pulled his car up alongside another car which he believed had been driven carelessly and shouted at the driver. B then followed the other car for a distance of six or seven miles, driving close behind the other car and keeping his headlights full on. On two occasions B overtook the other car, driving closely alongside it, and on the second occasion stopped in front of it. The other driver got out of the car and hid in a garden. B was sentenced to six months' imprisonment and disqualified from driving for three years.

Held, allowing the appeal in part, reducing the period of qualification to two years, that the sentence had to reflect a dreadful exhibition of driving which was intended to terrify. The manifestation of road rage required a custodial sentence. The sentence imposed was entirely appropriate, despite the personal mitigation.

R. v. BULL (ASHLEY EDMUND) [1997] 2 Cr. App. R. (S.) 178, Judge, L.J., CA (Crim Div).

1682. Road traffic offences–dangerous driving–intimidation of women drivers

T pleaded guilty to four counts of dangerous driving and four counts of threatening behaviour. On four occasions over a period of 11 months T drove behind women who were driving alone on country roads, following their cars closely with his headlights on. On three occasions T pulled alongside the woman's car and switched on the interior light of his car, so that the woman concerned would see that he was naked and apparently masturbating. On the fourth occasion T forced the woman to stop and began to remove his clothing. The women concerned were frightened and drove at dangerous speeds in attempting to escape. T was sentenced to two terms of 21 months' imprisonment, consecutive, for dangerous driving and five months' imprisonment, concurrent, for using threatening behaviour (total sentence, three years and six months' imprisonment).

Held, dismissing the appeal, that T committed deliberate and serious acts of dangerous driving which were designed to cause grave danger to women driving on their own. Despite T's plea and good work record the sentences were not excessive.

R. v. TAFT (CHRISTOPHER) [1997] 2 Cr. App. R. (S.) 182, Moses, J., CA (Crim Div).

1683. Road traffic offences–drink driving offences–disqualification–special reason for non disqualification–contaminated drinks–judicial discretion to disqualify

D appealed by way of case stated against her disqualification from driving for 12 months for driving with excess alcohol. The justices had accepted expert evidence that the two pints of bitter shandy which D had consumed would not have produced the reading of 46 micrograms and that two non-alcoholic drinks bought for her by a stranger must have been contaminated with alcohol. D suffered from multiple sclerosis which meant that she could not taste the alcohol. She claimed that the justices had wrongly applied their undoubted discretion to disqualify her.

Held, allowing the appeal and quashing the order, that the justices had correctly considered that D should have taken special care about the content of drinks she accepted from a stranger, because of her inability to taste alcohol, but their decision was unsafe because it appeared that they had taken an irrelevant factor, namely the absence of evidence from the stranger, into account, *R. v. Newton (David)* [1974] R.T.R. 451, [1974] C.L.Y. 3265 distinguished.

DIXON-WATMOUGH v. PRESTON JUSTICES, Trans. Ref: CO/2474/96, November 22, 1996, Staughton, L.J., QBD.

1684. Road traffic offences–drink driving offences–disqualification–special reason for non disqualification–objective test

[Road Traffic Act 1988 s.5(1); Road Traffic Offenders Act 1988 s.34(1).]

The DPP appealed against a decision allowing B's plea of special reasons against disqualification after pleading guilty to a charge of driving with excess alcohol contrary to the Road Traffic Act 1988 s.5(1)(a). B had reacted to news that his daughter and a friend had been indecently assaulted and were being held against their will, driving immediately to the address he had been given. This was found to constitute a special reason under the Road Traffic Offenders Act 1988 s.34(1), and he was not disqualified.

Held, allowing the appeal and remitting the case, that (1) a special reason must be special to the facts of the case, which must be viewed objectively, and it is the defendant's burden to prove those facts on the balance of probabilities; (2) if proven, the special reason provides the court with a discretion as to whether or not to disqualify, or alternatively, to disqualify for a period less than the obligatory 12 months and the discretion should be exercised only in compelling circumstances, *Taylor v. Rajan* [1974] 1 All E.R. 1087, [1974] C.L.Y.

3268 followed. Regard must be given to: (a) how much the defendant had had to drink; (b) what threat would he pose driving in that condition, considering also the condition of the vehicle and the roads, and the distance he would drive; (c) how acute was the emergency, and (d) any alternatives open to the defendant to deal with the emergency. The court should ask itself what a sober, reasonable and responsible friend, himself unable to drive, would have advised in the circumstances. B was over twice the permitted limit and there were reasonable alternatives open to him, in those circumstances the court's discretion should not have been exercised.

DPP v. BRISTOW (1997) 161 J.P. 35, Simon Brown, L.J., QBD.

1685. Road traffic offences–drink driving offences–disqualification–special reasons for non disqualification–jeweller called to business premises

[Road Traffic Act 1988 s.5(1).]

T was convicted of driving with excess alcohol contrary to the Road Traffic Act 1988 s.5(1)(a), but was not disqualified as special reasons were found. The DPP appealed. T had driven to the premises of the jewellery business he ran when contacted by the alarm company at 1.30 am after the alarm had been activated. He was required by his insurers to attend within approximately 20 minutes as the alarm would then deactivate, leaving the shop, which carried highly valuable stock, unsecured. He tried without success to contact other key holders, his wife was pregnant and they had two small children who could not be left. It was found that T had considered all alternatives to driving himself, none of which was feasible.

Held, dismissing the appeal, that (1) the circumstances justified a finding of special reasons, and (2) the justices were justified in exercising their discretion as they did, taking into account all the necessary factors. Asking the question of what a sober, reasonable and responsible friend, himself unable to drive, would have advised in the circumstances, *DPP v. Bristow* [1997] C.L.Y. 1684; considered, the court found T's pregnant wife fulfilled this role, and had not prevented him from driving, *Taylor v. Rajan* [1974] R.T.R. 304, [1974] C.L.Y. 3268 considered.

DPP v. TUCKER, Trans. Ref: C0/1572/96, November 6, 1996, Rose, L.J., QBD.

1686. Road traffic offences–driving while disqualified

M had an appalling record for driving whilst disqualified and was sentenced to a combined aggregate of six months' imprisonment for four such offences. He was also liable to disqualification for a minimum period of two years under the totting up procedure, in view of the number of previous disqualifications imposed, but in fact the justices disqualified him for a further three years.

Held, allowing the appeal, that the disqualification period was excessive and was reduced to 18 months, thus affirming the decision in *R. v. Thomas* [1983] 3 All E.R. 756, [1983] C.L.Y. 3250. The court also confirmed that someone imprisoned for offences of driving whilst disqualified should not also receive a lengthy disqualification and that the term of imprisonment in itself constituted a mitigating circumstance for imposing less than the minimum totting up disqualification that would normally be required.

R. v. MEW, January 24, 1997, Recorder Whelon, Crown Court (Taunton). [*Ex rel.* Poole & Co, Solicitors].

1687. Road traffic offences–driving while disqualified–no suspension of disqualification order pending appeal against conviction–conviction of driving while disqualified should stand even though original conviction quashed

[Road Traffic Act 1988 s.103(1).]

L was convicted of road traffic offences for which he was disqualified from driving for 12 months. He appealed against conviction, but did not lodge an application to suspend the disqualification. Although the appeal was successful, he was subsequently convicted of driving while disqualified contrary to the Road

Traffic Act 1988 s.103(1). L applied for judicial review of the magistrate's refusal to permit an appeal by way of case stated, contending that he should not have been convicted in relation to the disqualification when the original conviction had been quashed.

Held, dismissing the application, that L's conviction would stand as the disqualification order was still lawfully in force on the date L was found driving, *R. v. Lynn (Frederick John)* [1971] R.T.R. 369, [1971] C.L.Y. 10287 followed. The fact that the original conviction had been quashed did not mean that L was wrongly convicted of driving while disqualified. To set aside the magistrate's decision would be contrary to the interests of justice.

R. v. THAMES MAGISTRATES COURT, *ex p.* LEVY; *sub nom.* R. v. METROPOLITAN STIPENDIARY MAGISTRATES, *ex p.* LEVY, *The Times,* July 17, 1997, Simon Brown, L.J., QBD.

1688. Road traffic offences–driving without due care–death

J appealed against a sentence of six years' imprisonment on a single count of causing death by driving without due care and attention whilst unfit to drive through drink or drugs. During the course of an evening J visited a number of public houses. J's friend took his car keys and suggested that he should stay the night at a friend's house since he thought J had drunk too much. Despite this J visited another public house and demanded that his friend hand over his car keys. J drove away at speed along country roads with sharp bends. His friend asked him to slow down but he failed to do so. When they came to part of the road with no footpath, J moved to one side but hit and injured pedestrians. One later died of his injuries. J drove off despite being told not to do so by his friend. After giving himself up to police, J showed signs of shock and expressed remorse for what he had done.

Held, dismissing the application, that there was nothing wrong with the sentence in principle nor could it be said to be manifestly excessive, *R. v. Locke (Geoffrey)* (1995) 16 Cr. App. R. (S.) 795, [1996] 1 C.L.Y. 1757 distinguished.

R. v. JACKSON (DAVID) [1997] 1 Cr. App. R. (S.) 34, Latham, J., CA (Crim Div).

1689. Road traffic offences–driving without due care–death–concurrent terms of three years' imprisonment not unduly lenient

[Criminal Justice Act 1988 s.36.]

The Attorney General applied for a sentence to be referred under the Criminal Justice Act 1988 s.36 on the ground that it was unduly lenient. S was convicted on two counts of causing death by driving without due care and attention and having consumed alcohol above the prescribed limit and was sentenced to two concurrent three year terms of imprisonment, five years' disqualification and an order to retake a driving test. S, who was found to be three times over the legal limit, admitted he had been driving and said that he had lost his grip while driving too fast for the wet road conditions. The Attorney General drew the attention of the court to the amount of alcohol consumed, S's excessive speed and relative inexperience as a driver and the deaths of his two passengers. S, who pleaded guilty at the first opportunity, had expressed remorse for the deaths and had accepted his total responsibility for the accident and had not intended to drive having consumed alcohol.

Held, refusing the application, that taking account of the aggravating circumstances and the mitigating features, the sentences were at the lower end of the appropriate bracket. Although properly described as lenient and merciful, they were not unduly lenient such as would require the court to consider increasing them, *Attorney General's Reference (Nos.24 and 45 of 1994), Re* (1995) 16 Cr. App. R. (S.) 583, [1995] 1 C.L.Y. 1344 considered.

ATTORNEY GENERAL'S REFERENCE (NO.66 OF 1996), *Re; sub nom.* R. v. SPENCER (SIMON), Trans. Ref: 96/8597/R2, April 16, 1997, Lord Bingham of Cornhill, L.C.J., CA (Crim Div).

1690. Road traffic offences—driving without due care—death—excess alcohol—15 months' imprisonment unduly lenient

[Criminal Justice Act 1988 s.36.]

The Attorney General applied for a sentence to be referred under the Criminal Justice Act 1988 s.36 on the ground that it was unduly lenient. W, aged 37, pleaded guilty to causing death by driving without due care and attention, having consumed alcohol above the prescribed limit. He was sentenced to 15 months' imprisonment and disqualified from driving for three years. Whilst driving home from New Year's Eve festivities with the deceased, his partner, W lost control of the car and struck the concrete parapet of a bridge. The deceased died instantly from severe head injuries. W immediately left the scene and when he was later arrested, he had consumed more alcohol. A backtracking calculation estimated him to have been at approximately twice the legal limit at the time of driving. The Attorney General argued that too much account had been given to the plea of guilty, W's remorse, the fact that he was greatly affected by the loss of his partner and that he had sustained injuries.

Held, allowing the reference, that driving after consuming substantial amounts of alcohol was very serious and put all other road users in extreme danger. The level of W's alcohol consumption, the fact that he left the scene and had previous motoring convictions were aggravating features. A sentence of three and a half years' imprisonment and five years' disqualification were substituted.

ATTORNEY GENERAL'S REFERENCE (NO.50 OF 1996), *Re; sub nom*. R. v. WILLIAMS (STEVEN JOHN), [1997] 2 Cr. App. R.(S.) 252, Rose, L.J., CA (Crim Div).

1691. Road traffic offences—driving without due care—death—two years' probation unduly lenient

[Criminal Justice Act 1988 s.36.]

S, aged 17 at the time of the incident, was sentenced to two years' probation after conviction of causing death by driving without due care and attention when unfit to drive through drink and aggravated vehicle taking. S first broke into a car with two friends and stole items from it. He later returned to take the car and was seen travelling at excessive speed. S lost control of the car and a passenger later died. There was evidence that S received a head injury which affected his personality and caused him to have short-lived outbursts of anger and aggression. It was submitted that the aggravating factors were that the offences were planned and the accident was the culmination of a spell of driving at excessive speed. Factors pleaded in mitigation were the offender's guilty plea, his age and that he had suffered injuries too.

Held, allowing the reference, that the case justified a sentence of three to four years' detention. Allowing for the mitigating factors the sentence was quashed and substituted with a sentence of 12 months' detention.

R. v. S (A JUVENILE), Trans. Ref: 97/1957/R2, June 12, 1997, Lord Bingham of Cornhill, L.C.J., CA (Crim Div).

1692. Robbery—150 hours' community service unduly lenient

[Criminal Justice Act 1988 s.36.]

The Attorney General applied for a sentence to be referred under the Criminal Justice Act 1988 s.36 on the ground that it was unduly lenient. S was convicted of robbery. He and his co-defendant encountered a youth who was riding a mountain bicycle. S seized the youth's bicycle, kicked the youth off the bicycle and punched and kicked him several times. S was sentenced to 150 hours' community service.

Held, allowing the reference, that the case called for a custodial sentence of more than nominal length and a sentence of 12 months' imprisonment was substituted, *Attorney General's Reference (No.6 of 1994), Re* (1995) 16 Cr. App. R. (S.) 343 considered.

ATTORNEY GENERAL'S REFERENCE (NO.39 OF 1996), *Re; sub nom*. R. v. SEARLE (WAYNE THOMAS) [1997] 1 Cr. App. R. (S.) 355, Lord Bingham of Cornhill, C.J., CA (Crim Div).

1693. Robbery–aggravated vehicle taking–kidnapping–unduly lenient sentence

[Criminal Justice Act 1988 s.36.]

The Attorney General applied for a sentence to be referred under the Criminal Justice Act 1988 s.36 on the ground that it was unduly lenient. JMB pleaded guilty to two counts of robbery, one of kidnapping, one of theft and one of aggravated vehicle taking. RJB was convicted of aggravated vehicle taking, two counts of robbery, one of theft and one of kidnapping. Together with another man, they drove in a car which had been taken without consent to a supermarket car park. They approached a woman who was loading shopping into her car and demanded her bag; when she refused to hand it over, JMB snatched it from her, punched her in the face and ran back to the car. The car was then driven away and collided head on with another car. The offenders and the other man then abandoned the car. B and B got into another car at a petrol station, which was occupied by a woman passenger. They drove away in this car, taking the woman with them and after stealing her bag pushed her out of the car. They were sentenced to 27 months' and three years' imprisonment respectively.

Held, allowing the reference, that the sentences were unduly lenient. The sentences were increased to four and a half years' and six years' imprisonment respectively. Taking account of the fact that JMB had been released, his sentence would run from the time that he surrendered into custody, and the term reflected the time previously spent in custody, *Attorney-General's Reference (Nos. 20 and 21 of 1992), Re* (1993) 15 Cr. App. R. (S.) 152, *R. v. Byfield* (1994) 15 Cr. App. R. (S.) 674, [1995] 1 C.L.Y. 1471, *R. v. Thomas* (1994) 15 Cr. App. R. (S.) 848, [1995] 1 C.L.Y. 1466, *R. v. Perez-Pinto* [1996] 1 Cr. App. R. (S.) 22 and *R. v. Brown* (1985) 7 Cr. App. R. (S.) 15, [1986] C.L.Y. 842 considered.

ATTORNEY GENERAL'S REFERENCE (NOS.1 AND 2 OF 1996), *Re; sub nom*. R. v. BERESFORD (MICHAEL JAMES); R. v. BERESFORD (ROGER JOHN); ATTORNEY GENERAL'S REFERENCE (NO.19 OF 1996), *Re* [1997] 1 Cr. App. R. (S.) 313, Rose, L.J., CA (Crim Div).

1694. Robbery–assault–robbery from video rental shop–deterrent sentence–public protection–combination order unduly lenient

[Criminal Justice Act 1988 s.36.]

The Attorney General applied for a sentence to be referred under the Criminal Justice Act 1988 s.36 on the ground that it was unduly lenient. C, aged 26, pleaded guilty to robbery and common assault. He was sentenced to a combination order of 90 hours' community service and two years' probation with a requirement that he attend a violent offender programme for up to 60 days. In reliance upon *R. v. Wilson (Edward John)* (1992) 13 Cr. App. R. (S.) 397, [1993] C.L.Y. 1275 and *Attorney General's Reference (No.2 of 1994), Re* (1995) 16 Cr. App. R. (S.) 117, [1996] C.L.Y. 2070, the Attorney General asked the court to review the sentence. C, his head and face covered with some sort of cloth, entered a shop and punched a 15 year old youth before demanding that the 19 year old youth in sole charge of the premises open the till and safe. £731 was stolen of which £618 was recovered. The 19 year old youth was also assaulted.

Held, allowing the reference, that, despite favourable reports, the sentence passed was unduly lenient. When passing sentence the court should consider the deterrent effect of the sentence and the need to protect staff of such premises from offenders such as C. In this case the personal mitigation did not outweigh the public element, the proper sentence for this type of case being three years if a trial was contested and two years if a guilty plea tendered.

Accordingly, the combination order was quashed and a one year sentence substituted.

ATTORNEY GENERAL'S REFERENCE (NO.18 OF 1997), *Re; sub nom.* R. v. CUTLER (SAUL ROLAND), Trans. Ref: 97/1966/R2, June 12, 1997, Lord Bingham of Cornhill, L.C.J., CA (Crim Div).

1695. **Robbery–attempts–juvenile offenders–two years' supervision orders unduly lenient**

[Criminal Justice Act 1988 s.36.]

The Attorney General applied for a sentence to be referred under the Criminal Justice Act 1988 s.36 on the ground that it was unduly lenient. W and C were sentenced to two years' supervision orders for offences of attempted robbery. An air pistol was used to attempt to rob a couple walking home at night and to attempt to rob a taxi driver. It was submitted that the aggravating factors were using an imitation firearm and that the taxi driver was a vulnerable person. C carried out the offences in breach of two supervision orders and an order of conditional discharge. In favour of W and C it was submitted that they both pleaded guilty and were only 17 and 16 years old respectively.

Held, allowing the reference, that the sentences imposed were unduly lenient. The applicants were each sentenced to two years' detention.

ATTORNEY GENERAL'S REFERENCE (NOS.13 AND 14 OF 1997), *Re,* Trans. Ref: 97/1751/R2, 97/1752/R2, June 6, 1997, Kennedy, L.J., CA (Crim Div).

1696. **Robbery–attempts–robbery of fish and chip shop–probation orders unduly lenient**

[Criminal Justice Act 1988 s.36.]

The Attorney General applied for two sentences to be referred under the Criminal Justice Act 1988 s.36 on the ground that they were unduly lenient. S and C pleaded guilty to attempted robbery. They entered a fish and chip shop and demanded money from the till. The proprietor of the shop was threatened with shooting and was punched and kicked. They then left the shop. S and C were sentenced to a probation order for three years in each case.

Held, allowing the reference, that the range of sentences shown by previous decisions of the court in similar cases indicated that the range of sentences was a custodial sentence of between three and seven years. A probation order was well out of scale and would require remarkable mitigating circumstances. An appropriate sentence at first instance would have been something in excess of three years. Bearing in mind that S and C had been carrying out the requirements of the probation order and the element of double jeopardy, the court substituted sentences of two and a half years' imprisonment in each case. These sentences should not be treated as guidelines for the proper level of sentencing in this class of case.

ATTORNEY GENERAL'S REFERENCE (NOS.60 AND 61 OF 1995), *Re; sub nom.* R. v. SUNDERLAND (KEVIN THOMAS); R. v. COLLIER (MICHAEL ANTHONY) [1996] 2 Cr. App. R. (S.) 243, Lord Taylor of Gosforth, C.J., CA (Crim Div).

1697. **Robbery–combination order unduly lenient**

[Criminal Justice Act 1988 s.36.]

The Attorney General applied for a sentence to be referred under the Criminal Justice Act 1988 s.36 on the ground that it was unduly lenient. H was sentenced to a combination order and 100 hours' community service for robbery. H, now aged 20, and his coaccused R, had worn overalls and balaclavas and assaulted and robbed a workmate, aged 17, of his wages of £85, a bank card and some tobacco.

Held, allowing the reference, .0; in part, that a term of 12 months' detention be substituted. Despite the mitigation advanced on H's behalf, a custodial sentence was appropriate, although it was reduced to reflect his guilty plea, the double jeopardy and the fact that he had already completed 65 hours' community service.

ATTORNEY GENERAL'S REFERENCE (NO.74 OF 1995), *Re; sub nom.* R. v. HEATH (PAUL ELVIS) [1996] 2 Cr. App. R. (S.) 436, Swinton Thomas, L.J., CA (Crim Div).

1698. Robbery—elderly victim threatened with knife in own home

[Criminal Justice Act 1988 s.36.]

The Attorney General applied for sentences to be referred under the Criminal Justice Act 1988 s.36 on the ground that they were unduly lenient. H, aged 28 and T, aged 22, were sentenced to two years and 18 months respectively, on two counts of robbery. The Attorney General contended that the sentences were too lenient considering the aggravating features of an attack at night on two elderly and vulnerable people involving violence and threats to kill and in which valuable property including diamond rings and watches and £1,000 in cash were taken. The defendants contended that in the absence of an indication from the trial judge on the basis of sentence, the defence version of events in which no threats or knife was used should be preferred. Both defendants refused a *Newton* hearing.

Held, allowing the reference in part, that terms of six years and five years, respectively, were substituted. Although the trial judge had failed to indicate, as he should have, that the defence version was untenable, the court had no hesitation in finding the defence version false, *R. v. Gardener* (1994) 15 Cr. App. R. (S.) 667, [1995] 1 C.L.Y. 1376 and *R. v. Cunnah* [1996] 1 Cr. App. R. (S.) 393, [1996] 1 C.L.Y. 1783 considered, *R. v. Brown (Walter Thomas)* (1981) 3 Cr. App. R. (S.) 250 and *R. v. McFarlane (Kenrick)* (1995) 16 Cr. App. R. (S.) 315 distinguished on their facts, *R. v. Hawkins* (1985) 7 Cr. App. R. (S.) 351, [1987] C.L.Y. 1548 and *R. v. Walton* (1987) 9 Cr. App. R. (S.) 107, [1987] C.L.Y. 938 followed.

ATTORNEY GENERAL'S REFERENCE (NOS.3 AND 4 OF 1996), *Re; sub nom.* R. v. HEALY (ALAN ANTHONY); R. v. TAYLOR (ROBERT WILLIAM) [1997] 1 Cr. App. R. (S.) 29, Swinton Thomas, L.J., CA (Crim Div).

1699. Robbery—elderly victims in vulnerable premises—18 months' imprisonment unduly lenient

[Criminal Justice Act 1988 s.36.]

The Attorney General applied for a sentenced to be referred under the Criminal Justice Act 1988 s.36 on the ground that it was unduly lenient. J was sentenced to 18 months for attempted robbery which was made consecutive to five concurrent sentences of three months each for four counts of shoplifting and one count of possession simple of a Class B drug, namely cannabis resin. J and his codefendant had demanded money from the elderly owners of an off licence. When they refused, J had produced a brick from his jacket but had been disarmed, while his co-accused attempted to take the till. The Attorney General contended that the incident had involved an armed attack on an elderly couple running a vulnerable premises and an assault causing slight injury. In addition J had been released on licence only three days earlier from a custodial sentence for theft and and an assault on a police officer. J had several previous convictions for theft, assault and criminal damage.

Held, allowing the reference, that the sentence was too lenient and a sentence of 42 months was substituted, made consecutive to the unchanged three months term, *Attorney General's Reference (No.9 of 1989), Re* (1990) 12 Cr. App. R. (S.) 7, [1991] C.L.Y. 1214, *Attorney General's Reference (No.3 of 1994), Re* (1994) 16 Cr. App. R. (S.) 176, [1995] 1 C.L.Y. 1275 and *Attorney General's Reference (Nos.60 and 61 of 1995), Re* [1996] 2 Cr. App. R. (S.) 243, [1997] C.L.Y. 1696 followed.

R. v. JONES (KARL DAVID), Trans. Ref: 9607819 R2, February 10, 1997, Rose, L.J., CA (Crim Div).

1700. Robbery—longer than normal sentence

[Criminal Justice Act 1991 s.2(2).]

G pleaded guilty to robbery and was convicted of wounding with intent to resist apprehension. B was convicted of three counts of robbery and one of assault with intent to resist apprehension. B committed three robberies attacking people in their own homes whilst wearing a mask and carrying a weapon. On the first occasion, a mother of young children and her friend were forced to give him jewellery. On the second occasion he entered a house occupied by a family during the evening, stole a handbag and demanded a wallet. The householder was pushed so as to fall to the floor while carrying the baby. On the third occasion G and B entered a house occupied by a couple in their sixties and a man aged 82. There was a fight in the course of which B got on top of the husband threatened him with a screwdriver. The man aged 82 was knocked down and held on the ground. The wife was forced to open a safe and jewellery and about £5,000 in cash was stolen. G had numerous previous convictions for burglary, but none involving violence. B had numerous convictions for burglary, including two for aggravated burglary in 1990 for which he was sentenced to six years' imprisonment. G was sentenced to 16 years' imprisonment for robbery with 12 months' consecutive for wounding with intent to resist apprehension and B to 21 years, 22 years and 27 years' imprisonment respectively on the counts charging robbery, with six months for assault, all concurrent.

Held, allowing the appeals, that (1) having reviewed the authorities the sentences were excesive; (2) domestic burglaries which involved the use of force and cause physical or psychological trauma were rightly regarded as serious crimes; (3) with regard to G, having considered *R. v. O'Driscoll (James)* (1986) 8 Cr. App. R. (S.) 121, [1987] C.L.Y. 1042 taking into account the absence of torture, guilty plea and criminal record for offences of dishonesty the appropriate sentence would have been 12 years for the robbery but with discount for the plea the correct sentence was nine years and this was consistent with *Attorney General's Reference (Nos.32 and 33 of 1995), Re* [1996] 2 Cr. App. R. (S.) 345, [1997] C.L.Y. 1421; (4) with regard to B a longer than normal sentence in terms of the Criminal Justice Act 1991 s.2(2)(b) was properly imposed having in mind his previous convictions and that the offences were violent invasions of domestic dwellings with B carrying a jemmy or wrecking bar. It was necessary to balance considerations of protection of the public and totality of sentence, *R. v. Manzell (Craig John)* (1994) 15 Cr. App. R. (S.) 771, [1995] 1 C.L.Y. 1417 applied. Having considered *R. v. Schultz (Karl)* [1996] 1 Cr. App. R. (S.) 451, [1996] 1 C.L.Y. 2059 and *R. v. Chapman (Ernest Edward)* (1994) 15 Cr. App. R. (S.) 844, [1995] 1 C.L.Y. 1428, taking the robbery offences in isolation the appropriate sentence would be 15 years taking into account that they were committed while on bail with s.2(2)(b) enhancement the appropriate sentence was 20 years.

R. v. GABBIDON (ANTHONY BERNARD); R. v. BRAMBLE (KEITH) [1997] 2 Cr. App. R. (S.) 19, Henry, L.J., CA (Crim Div).

1701. Robbery—possession of firearms—11 years' imprisonment not unduly lenient

[Criminal Justice Act 1988 s.36.]

The Attorney General applied for a sentence to be referred under the Criminal Justice Act 1988 s.36 on the ground that it was unduly lenient. Following concurrent 11 year sentences on conviction of three associated counts of possessing a firearm with intent to rob, the Attorney General contended that the starting point of 16 years' imprisonment was too low and that the five year discount for guilty pleas was too high. The robberies involved a high degree of planning and had been undertaken by B and S as part of a gang in which the proceeds totalled £140,000. B and S had previous convictions for a robbery offence committed together in which firearms had featured.

Held, dismissing the reference, that the sentences were lenient, but not unduly so. The range of starting points for robbery without abnormal features was in the range of 15 to 18 years and it could not be said that a starting point of 16 years was unduly lenient. The plea had been late, and was entered on the basis that a further conspiracy count, where a firearm had been discharged in the course of a robbery on a supermarket, would not be proceeded with. Whereas a discount of three or four years could have been expected on a late plea, the five years allowed by the trial judge, although lenient, was not unduly lenient.

R. v. BRENNAN (RICHARD); R. v. SMITH (RICARDO JAMES), Trans. Ref: 9700769 R2; 970771 R2, May 8, 1997, McCowan, L.J., CA (Crim Div).

1702. Robbery–possession of firearms–violence–discount for guilty plea

D and C, a codefendant, appealed against sentences of 10 years' imprisonment for armed robbery. Together they had used air weapons to hold up a security guard in order to take £40,000 in cash from a supermarket strong room delivery chute. The guard was later struck with one of the guns when he refused to lie down as D and C made their getaway. They were apprehended following a chase in a car fitted with false number plates and during the robbery had worn crash helmets to disguise their identities. Both were of previous good character and pleaded guilty, with D stating that the offence had been committed when he was under severe financial stress. D, who also adduced psychiatric evidence of probable clinical depression at the time of the offence, contended that the sentence was manifestly excessive.

Held, dismissing the appeals, that the robbery had been planned, with the vehicle and air weapons being purchased for the occasion. Following *R. v. Turner (Bryan James)* (1975) 61 Cr. App. R. 67, [1975] C.L.Y. 559, a starting point for the most serious types of armed robbery would have been 15 years. However, the trial judge had used a 12 year starting point, reduced to 10 taking account of the mitigating features of guilty pleas and previous good character. On the facts, the sentences were not manifestly excessive nor wrong in any way.

R. v. DEVLIN (EDWARD JOHN); R. v. COTTER (JAMES McMURRAY) [1997] 1 Cr. App. R. (S.) 68, Ebsworth, J., CA (Crim Div).

1703. Robbery–possession of imitation firearm–previous conviction for similar offence

C and T appealed against sentences of nine and seven years' imprisonment respectively, having pleaded guilty to robbery and possessing an imitation firearm with intent to commit an indictable offence. They went into a small subpost office wearing balaclavas and carrying imitation firearms, in one case with a cucumber concealed in a plastic bag and in the other with a toy gun. They threatened the owner and a cashier. They were given £6,500. Two police officers who were in the shop arrested them. Both had several previous convictions. C had a previous conviction for robbery and having an imitation firearm with intent to commit an indictable offence. T had previous convictions for robbery.

Held, dismissing the appeals, that those who ran small sub-post offices were entitled to protection from the courts. The seriousness of the matter was compounded by the previous convictions for robbery. The sentences were not manifestly excessive.

R. v. CURRY (DAVID PAUL); R. v. TAYLOR (KIERON THOMAS) [1997] 1 Cr. App. R. (S.) 417, Judge Ann Goddard Q.C., CA (Crim Div).

1704. Robbery–possession of imitation firearms–good character and guilty plea

L was sentenced to 12 years' imprisonment after pleading guilty to 11 counts of robbery, one count of attempted robbery and one count of having an imitation firearm with intent, and asked for five further offences to be taken into consideration. He committed a series of robberies at banks and building societies. On each occasion he entered the premises alone undisguised, except by wearing a cagoule with the hood pulled up, and usually carrying an imitation firearm.

Held, dismissing the appeal, that L was responsible for a large number of robberies over a period of two years. Despite his previous good character and guilty pleas, the sentence was not manifestly excessive, *R. v. Daley* (1981) 3 Cr.

App. R.(S.) 340, *R. v. Clarkson* (1990) 12 Cr. App. R. (S.) 119 and *R. v. Mitty (Lee)* (1991) 12 Cr. App. R. (S.) 619, [1992] C.L.Y. 1390 cited.

R. v. LOUGHLIN (MATHEW) [1997] 1 Cr. App. R. (S.) 277, Keene, J., CA (Crim Div).

1705. Robbery—subpost office—imitation air pistol—good character and guilty plea

L pleaded guilty to robbery and was sentenced to eight years' imprisonment against which he appealed. L planned a robbery in a town some distance from where he lived. He obtained a realistic imitation air pistol and put false number plates on a hire car. He then entered a subpost office, which he had visited earlier, seized one of three people there and demanded money. He was handed a bag containing £905, but was arrested shortly afterwards.

Held, allowing the appeal, that L was a man of good character who had resorted to crime because of substantial debts. Bearing in mind the plea of guilty the sentence was too long and a sentence of six years' imprisonment would be substituted.

R. v. LEA (MICHAEL JOHN) [1997] 2 Cr. App. R. (S.) 215, Brian Smedley, J., CA (Crim Div).

1706. Robbery—threatening to kill former partner—three months' and nine months' imprisonment consecutive unduly lenient

[Criminal Justice Act 1988 s.36.]

The Attorney General applied for a sentence to be referred under the Criminal Justice Act 1988 s.36 on the ground that it was unduly lenient. W, aged 24 years, was convicted of robbery and of threatening to kill and was sentenced to three months' and nine months' imprisonment consecutive. Whilst serving a custodial sentence for robbery, W had written threatening letters to his former partner. W had been arrested on release and had subsequently committed other offences for which he had served custodial penalties.

Held, allowing the reference, that the sentences were unduly lenient and twelve months' and three years' imprisonment consecutive would be substituted, that (1) the robbery of persons using cash dispensers was becoming too frequent and W had committed the offence when released on licence after a previous conviction for robbery and had also been on bail, and (2) the victim had been put in great fear as a result of W's threats, following previous episodes of domestic violence, and W had an antecedent history of violent offences, *R. v. Scott (Michael Richard)* (1993) 14 Cr. App. R. (S.) 701, [1994] C.L.Y. 1373 considered.

ATTORNEY GENERAL'S REFERENCE (NO.66 OF 1995), *Re; sub nom.* R. v. WARD (ADRIAN JOHN) [1996] 2 Cr. App. R. (S.) 371, Lord Taylor of Gosforth, C.J., CA (Crim Div).

1707. Sexual offences—child abuse—life imprisonment

See CRIMINAL PROCEDURE: R. v. Jackson (Paul Maitland). §1370

1708. Sexual offences—sentence imposed longer than maximum permitted at time offence was committed—counsel's duty to advise judge of statutory powers

[Sexual Offences Act 1956 s.14(1); Sexual Offences Act 1985.]

S appealed against sentences imposed after pleading guilty to four counts under the Sexual Offences Act 1956 s.14(1), on the grounds that the sentences exceeded the legal maximum for offences committed before the Sexual Offences Act 1985 raised the maximum terms permissible. The fact that these offences had been committed before the 1985 Act came into force was not drawn to the attention of the judge when passing sentence.

Held, allowing the appeal and varying the sentences, that it should be emphasised that counsel for both the Crown and the defence had a duty to ascertain the court's relevant sentencing powers and to advise the judge accordingly, notably where a sentence imposed did not take account of maximum penalty permitted by statute. The task of unravelling sentencing powers was made all the harder by their being spread across so many statutes, and any attempt to consolidate the provisions into one comprehensive statute would be welcomed.

R. v. STREET (ARTHUR) [1997] Crim. L.R. 364, Lord Bingham of Cornhill, L.C.J., CA (Crim Div).

1709. Tax evasion–VAT

C, an accountant, and three associates were indicted on various counts of cheating the public revenue. The offences involved the fraudulent diversion of monies to offshore companies. The defendants were convicted and sentenced to terms of imprisonment ranging from five years down. They appealed against conviction and sentence. They asserted that the transactions were undertaken without dishonest intention as part of a legitimate tax planning scheme.

Held, dismissing the appeals against conviction, that there was ample evidence and the judge's rulings during the trial were correct. However, in all the circumstances, the sentences were excessive and were reduced to three and a half years in the case of C, with proportional reductions in the other sentences.

R. v. CHARLTON [1996] S.T.C. 1418, Farquharson, L.J., CA (Crim Div).

1710. Tax evasion–VAT–confiscation order–sentence of imprisonment reduced in light of confiscation order

[Criminal Justice Act 1988.]

A was convicted of conspiring to cheat the public revenue and offences relating to VAT. He was involved in a family haulage business which concerned a number of companies. Over a period of nearly three years he operated a large scale fraud which resulted in the evasion of income tax and VAT. A total of £300,000 in income tax was lost, a total of £91,000 was falsely reclaimed from the Customs and Excise, and £144,000 in VAT was unpaid. The total benefit to A was assessed at £550,000 and the amount that might be realised (the value of his assets) was assessed at £543,000. A was sentenced to five years' imprisonment and a confiscation order was made under the Criminal Justice Act 1988 in the amount of £543,000, with four years' imprisonment in default.

Held, allowing the appeal and reducing the sentence to three and a half years, that A would have gained little by his frauds, and would have no assets on his release from prison. The fraud had not been directed primarily towards personal wealth but to maintaining the business during a serious economic depression. The sentence was too long, particularly as most of the money would be recovered under the confiscation order.

R. v. ANDREWS (DANIEL THOMAS) [1997] 1 Cr. App. R. (S.) 279, Scott Baker, J., CA (Crim Div).

1711. Tax evasion–VAT–prosecution costs order–confiscation order

A and another were convicted of being knowingly concerned in the fraudulent evasion of VAT through a scheme which charged VAT to customers but was not paid over to the Customs and Excise. A total of £428,000 was lost to the Revenue as a result, and the sentencer determined that the appellants jointly had benefited in this amount. They were each sentenced to two years' imprisonment and disqualified from acting as directors of a company for 10 years, with confiscation orders of £54,000 and £43,000 respectively, and ordered to pay £10,000 prosecution costs in each case.

Held, allowing the appeal in part, that there was no appeal against the sentences of imprisonment or the disqualifications. The confiscation order would be reduced in one case to take account of a mortgage on one of the appellant's properties. The order for the payment of prosecution costs would be quashed in each case; as the sentencer had assessed the amount that might be realised in each case, he could not have been satisfied that further sums were available to satisfy the order for the payment of prosecution costs, *R. v. Hopes* (1989) 11 Cr. App. R. (S.) 38, [1990] C.L.Y. 1268 considered.

R. v. AHMED (NOOR); R. v. CHOUDHURY (RAFIQUE) [1997] 2 Cr. App. R. (S.) 8, Timothy Walker, J., CA (Crim Div).

1712. Tax evasion—VAT—whether custodial sentence appropriate

Held, that, where a defendant omitted to charge value added tax with the intention of avoiding quarantine regulations on the importation of live birds, a custodial sentence of 12 months' imprisonment reduced from 18 months, on a guilty plea was appropriate. Payment of value added tax by traders was a duty not an option and imprisonment for any form of fraudulent evasion of tax would act as a necessary deterrent.

R. v. HAMMOND (BRETT MARTIN), *The Times*, July 15, 1997, Kay, J., CA (Crim Div).

1713. Telecommunications—communicating false information—several previous convictions—appellant with personality disorder

[Criminal Law Act 1977 s.51.]

H pleaded guilty to communicating false information contrary to the Criminal Law Act 1977 s.51 and was sentenced to four years' imprisonment. H made a series of telephone calls to a theatre to the effect that a bomb had been planted by terrorists near the theatre. He had various previous convictions, including several for giving false information relating to bombs and one relating to a false alarm to the fire service. H was said to be suffering from a personality disorder but not mental illness.

Held, dismissing the appeal, that the offence involved danger to the public in that emergency services were diverted from their proper duties and there was a risk of panic or hurried mass movements of people if it became known that a bomb hoax had been given. The only answer to the problem was to contain H for ever longer periods of time, if he continued to commit such offences. The sentence was severe but not manifestly long, *R. v. Rung-Ruangap (Caroline)* (1994) 15 Cr. App. R. (S.) 326 considered.

R. v. HARRISON (CHRISTOPHER ARTHUR) [1997] 2 Cr. App. R. (S.) 174, Judge Tucker Q.C., CA (Crim Div).

1714. Theft—attempting to steal contents of bag

S and R appealed against sentences of 18 months' imprisonment imposed on conviction of attempted theft. They were seen by police officers following two women in a crowded street. One of them was seen to place his hand in a bag which one of the women was carrying, while the other bumped into them. They were arrested shortly afterwards.

Held, allowing the appeals, that although offences of this kind were unpleasant and prevalent the sentences imposed were too long, *R. v. Chebout* (1990) 12 Cr. App. R. (S.) 324, [1992] C.L.Y. 1441 and *R. v. Masagh* (1990) 12 Cr. App. R. (S.) 568, [1992] C.L.Y. 1413 considered.

R. v. SMITH (PATRICK THOMAS); R. v. READ (MICHAEL) [1997] 1 Cr. App. R. (S.) 342, Judge Van Der Werff, CA (Crim Div).

1715. Theft—compensation order—victim died before sentence passed—payment of compensation appropriate

[Powers of Criminal Courts Act 1973 s.35.]

H was involved in stealing £1,900 from a lady who died before sentence was passed. The youth court held that as the person who had suffered the loss was dead, it would be inappropriate to order H to pay compensation.

Held, that the youth court had power to order payment of compensation, notwithstanding the death of the victim, *R. v. Inwood* (1974) 60 Cr. App. R. 70 considered. The youth court was wrong to regard the Powers of Criminal Courts

Act 1973 s.35 as creating a personal right which did not survive the victim. It was true that compensation orders should be made only in simple and straightforward cases, but the circumstances of the present case were straightforward and the death of the victim in no way complicated matters.

HOLT v. DPP [1996] 2 Cr. App. R. (S.) 314, Saville, L.J., QBD.

1716. Theft–conspiracy to steal–disparate sentences

S, aged 47, appealed against sentences of four years and three months' imprisonment after pleading guilty to conspiracy to steal and doing an act tending and intending to pervert the course of justice. He was sentenced to four years and to three months consecutive respectively. The conspiracy involved S and three or four others, who dishonestly deprived an elderly lady of nearly £14,000. S gave a false name and false alibi evidence for nearly seven months prior to trial.

Held, dismissing the appeal, that notwithstanding the authorities, four years was not excessive given S's active role in the conspiracy. There was no question of objectionable disparity with a co-accused's 12 months' sentence given the specific factors involved there and S's appalling criminal record. The consecutive term was appropriate bearing in mind S's three previous convictions for the offence and the persistence of his deception.

R. v. STEWART (DONALD) [1997] 1 Cr. App. R. (S.) 71, Sachs, J., CA (Crim Div).

1717. Theft–going equipped to steal from telephone boxes

F and W pleaded guilty to going equipped for theft, and in one case to attempted theft and each was sentenced to 12 months' imprisonment for going equipped, with six months consecutive in the case of the one for attempted theft. F and W were found in a car near a telephone box which had been damaged. They were in possession of a cordless drill and other tools, and a map indicating the location of other telephone boxes.

Held, allowing the appeal in F's case but dismissing that of W, that the offences involved a sustained enterprise to break into telephone boxes in rural areas, and could not be compared with a single attack on a telephone box in an urban area. The sentences totalling 18 months' imprisonment imposed on W would be upheld; but F had played a lesser role and his sentence would be reduced to six months, *R. v. Arslan* (1994) 15 Cr. App. R. (S.) 90 and *R. v. Costello (Gary William)* (1994) 15 Cr. App. R. (S.) 240, [1995] 1 C.L.Y. 1480 considered.

R. v. FERRY (STEPHEN ROBIN); R. v. WYNN (SHAUN) [1997] 2 Cr. App. R. (S.) 42, Sedley, J., CA (Crim Div).

1718. Threatening to kill–18 months' imprisonment unduly lenient

A was convicted of two counts of threatening to kill and one count of assault occasioning actual bodily harm. A lived with a woman for some years and they had a son. The woman left the offender after he used violence to her and obtained an injunction restraining him from molesting her. Following a meeting between them near her home, A assaulted the woman and forced her and their son to get into her car, which A then drove towards a river, threatening to drive the car into the river and kill the woman and their son. A drove to the river bank and stopped; he later drove them home after stopping near the river bank a second time. A was sentenced to 18 months' imprisonment on each count concurrent, and the Attorney General asked the court to review the sentence on the ground that it was unduly lenient.

Held, considering *R. v. Mason (Mark Anthony)* (1995) 16 Cr. App. R. (S.) 804, [1996] 1 C.L.Y. 1714, *R. v. Walker (Darryl Keith)* [1996] 1 Cr. App. R. (S.) 180, [1996] 1 C.L.Y. 2098 and *R. v. Bowden (David Charles)* (1986) 8 Cr. App. R. (S.) 155, [1987] C.L.Y. 1067, the offence was comparatively serious within the range of offences of its kind. Sentences of six years and more following a trial might be appropriate for the offences committed in the domestic context. The gravity of the matter lay in the apparent seriousness of the threats, in that the oral threat was underlined by driving the woman to the river, knowing the woman could not swim and because of a like threat to an 11 year old child who was a weak swimmer and in the context of a non-molestation order. A sentence of three and a half years was substituted.

ATTORNEY-GENERAL'S REFERENCE (NO.52 OF 1996), *Re; sub nom.* R. v. ANDERSON (STEVEN JOHN) [1997] 2 Cr. App. R. (S.) 230, Rose, L.J., CA (Crim Div).

1719. Threatening to kill–domestic violence–vendetta–threat with pen knife

H appealed against a custodial sentence of five years on a guilty plea to threatening to kill L, his former partner. Since their separation, H had visited L's property at night on a number of occasions shouting abuse and had slashed the tyres of her car and thrown eggs over it. Following an attempted arson attack on her home, L fitted a security light and a panic alarm. H had severed wires running to the telephone and an outside light before entering L's house through an upstairs window. He had hidden under the bed before running downstairs brandishing a penknife and threatening to kill her and himself. H, aged 53, had one previous conviction for the assault of one of L's friends and a conviction for the criminal damage of L's car. H contended that his age, his early plea and his depression following the breakdown of his 10 year long relationship with L had not been sufficiently considered. H also argued that he had not intended to carry out the single threat since he had handed the knife to L immediately afterwards.

Held, allowing the appeal and substituting a sentence of three years, that although H had been guilty of the most unpleasant and terrifying harassment amounting to a vendetta against a woman, the sentence was excessive and out of line with the authorities, *R. v. Bowden* (1986) 8 Cr. App. R. (S.) 155, [1987] C.L.Y. 1067, *R. v. Perry* (1986) 8 Cr. App. R. (S.) 133, [1987] C.L.Y. 1068, *R. v. Munroe (John Eugene)* (1987) 9 Cr. App. R. (S.) 408, [1990] C.L.Y. 431, *R. v. Hull (Graham Brian)* (1992) 13 Cr. App. R. (S.) 223, [1993] C.L.Y. 1298 and *R. v. Brown (Stephen Graham)* (1992) 13 Cr. App. R. (S.) 239, [1993] C.L.Y. 1296 considered.

R. v. HEALY (JOHN), Trans. Ref: 96/7239/Z4, May 13, 1997, Judge Beaumont Q.C., CA (Crim Div).

1720. Threatening to kill–potentially dangerous offender–order under Mental Health Act 1983 unavailable–appropriateness of sentence

[Mental Health Act 1983.]

M pleaded guilty to three counts of threatening to kill. He was serving sentences totalling three and a half years' imprisonment for theft when he took part in a prison riot, as a result of which he was sentenced to a further five years' imprisonment consecutively for attempting to cause grievous bodily harm. While serving this sentence, he wrote a letter to a police chief inspector, in which he threatened to kill his own ex-wife and her boyfriend. A few days later he wrote a second letter in which he threatened to shoot a detective constable who had been the arresting officer when he was last brought before a court. He admitted that he intended the threats when he made them and continued in the intention to carry them out if he ever got the opportunity. M had 23 previous appearances for a variety of offences, mainly of dishonesty. Psychiatric reports indicated that he had a persistent compulsion to kill his wife and children. He himself wished to remain in prison to prevent this happening. He was considered extremely dangerous towards his wife and children. M appealed against sentences of seven years' imprisonment on each count, imposed to run consecutively with the sentence he was serving at the time.

Held, dismissing the appeal, that the sentencer indicated that the sentence was passed partly to punish M and partly to protect his ex-wife and the others who had been threatened. A long prison sentence was inevitable, having regard to M's professed intention to do serious harm, possibly fatal harm, to his ex-wife and children. Given that a hospital order under the Mental Health Act 1983 could not be made, the only thing that the judge could do for the protection of those persons was to mark the gravity of M's conduct with a very substantial sentence of imprisonment. In the circumstances, the sentence was not manifestly excessive.

R. v. MORTIMER (ANTHONY TIMOTHY) [1997] 1 Cr. App. R. (S.) 311, Ognall, J., CA (Crim Div).

1721. Threatening to kill—threats by telephone

M pleaded guilty one count of threatening to destroy or damage property and three counts of threatening to kill and was sentenced to five years' imprisonment concurrent on each charge. M had a relationship with a woman which ended after about 18 months. When the woman ended the relationship, M made frequent telephone calls to her home, in the course of which he threatened to kill her, and her brother and her mother, and to burn the house down. As a result of these calls, the woman moved out of her home and her brother and mother hired private security guards to stay at the house at night. Some days later he visited the house and was arrested. M had previous convictions for offences including robbery, causing grievous bodily harm, assault occasioning actual bodily harm and criminal damage.

Held, allowing the appeal, that these were serious offences which had caused the woman to leave her home. M had pleaded guilty, although at a late stage, and a starting point of six or seven years on a conviction would have been too high. The sentence would be reduced to four years.

R. v. McNALLY (BRIAN FRANCIS) [1997] 2 Cr. App. R. (S.) 30, Auld, L.J., CA (Crim Div).

1722. Trade descriptions—conspiracy—maximum sentence inappropriate—inadequate reasons for recommending deportation

F, aged 34, was convicted of conspiracy to supply goods to which a false trade description had been applied. He was sentenced to two years' imprisonment and was recommended for deportation. F appealed against sentence. The conspiracy involved what purported to be a dieting aid marketed as "the Deakin Diet" utilising "guar gum". In 1988 trading standards officers searched a co-conspirator's, D's, residence, but F had left the country and failed to appear for trial. In 1990 D was convicted and sentenced to six months' imprisonment suspended for two years and fined £250. On F's return in 1994, the investigation resumed and F was committed for trial. He was convicted and fined £21,000 with £8,000 costs for other similar offences. It was submitted that the instant sentence was inappropriate being the maximum, because F had matured in the intervening years having learned his lesson, had suffered financial ruin and the offence had not been of the worst kind.

Held, allowing the appeal in part, that a sentence of one and a half years' imprisonment would be substituted and the deportation order quashed. The aggravating features of the instant offence were that D, a young and relatively vulnerable individual, had been embroiled in a deception where the claims made were wholly untrue and had been committed when F had been summonsed for the similar offences for which he was eventually fined. This was not a case, however, where the maximum sentence was appropriate. The judge should have informed counsel that he was considering deportation and did not give a sufficient statement of his reasons, in the sentencing remarks, for making the recommendation.

R. v. FOSTER (PETER) [1996] 2 Cr. App. R. (S.) 394, Mitchell, J., CA (Crim Div).

1723. Violent disorder—revenge attack by armed men

The appellants were convicted of violent disorder and criminal damage (one appellant pleaded guilty to criminal damage). The appellants took part in a revenge attack on the home of a man who was believed to have assaulted a relative of two of the appellants. When the door was opened, two men who were in the house were attacked, one with a baseball bat, and windows in the front door were broken. A car parked outside the house was damaged. The appellants got into a car which failed to stop when required to do so by police. A police officer was assaulted when one of the occupants of the car was arrested. The appellants were sentenced to three years' imprisonment (in the case of the first) and four years (in the case of the second and third) for violent disorder, with 12 or nine months' imprisonment concurrent for criminal damage.

Held, dismissing the appeals, that (1) the sentences for criminal damage were unlawful; as the damage done did not exceed £5,000, the maximum sentence was three months' imprisonment. The sentences for criminal damage would be reduced to three months in each case, to run concurrently with the sentence for violent disorder, and (2) the sentences for violent disorder were not excessive, notwithstanding that the maximum sentence for violent disorder was five years' imprisonment. This was mob violence involving a planned attack by a group of men, all with criminal records, who had armed themselves with weapons.

R. v. GREEN (STEPHEN EDWARD); R. v. GREEN (DENNIS PAUL); R. v. WELSH (JAMES PETER) [1997] 2 Cr. App. R. (S.) 191, Judge, L.J., CA (Crim Div).

1724. Wounding with intent–custodial sentence appropriate–150 hours' community service unduly lenient

[Criminal Justice Act 1988 s.36.]

The Attorney General applied for a sentence to be referred under the Criminal Justice Act 1988 s.36 on the ground that it was unduly lenient. C was sentenced to 150 hours' community service and a compensation order of £500 on a guilty plea to wounding with intent. In an unprovoked attack from behind, L struck a youth on the back of the head with an unbroken beer bottle, causing him a broken finger and a laceration on the head requiring five stitches, and then punched and kicked his victim while on the ground. L also threatened, with the bottle, a friend of the victim who tried to intervene. The Attorney General drew attention to L's previous convictions for violent offences of actual bodily harm and affray.

Held, allowing the reference, that notwithstanding L's remorse and his achievement in holding down a job, acquiring a house and having a stable relationship, an appropriate custodial sentence of nine months would be substituted, *Attorney General's Reference (No.30 of 1993), Re* (1995) 16 Cr. App. R. (S.) 318, *Attorney General's Reference (No.41 of 1994), Re* (1994) 16 Cr. App. R. (S.) 792, [1996] 1 C.L.Y. 1919, and *Attorney General's Reference (No.34 of 1995), Re* (1996) 1 Cr. App. R. (S.) 386, [1996] 1 C.L.Y. 1923 distinguished either because of the extent of violence or the lack of a guilty plea.

ATTORNEY GENERAL'S REFERENCE (NO.49 OF 1996), *Re*; *sub nom.* R. v. LOASBY (ANDREW WILLIAM) [1997] 2 Cr. App. R. (S.) 144, Lord Bingham of Cornhill, L.C.J., CA (Crim Div).

1725. Articles

Community penalties under new review *(Andrew Rutherford)*: N.L.J. 1997, 147(6803), 1159-1160. (Sentencing trends towards greater use of imprisonment and failure of previous governments to reduce prison numbers by introducing non custodial penalties).

Computer judge *(John Rawlings)*: Magistrate 1997, 53(8), 213. (Public concern over sentencing discrepancies in magistrates courts and suggestion for computer database that would allow unbiased consistency).

Doing time for the community–the sentence of tomorrow in action today *(Malcolm J. Bryant)*: J.P. 1997, 161 (10), 233-235. (Advantages of community service orders in light of public expectations of criminal sentencing system and need to re-evaluate and promote community service).

Home Office Circular 54/1997 October 1, 1997: implementation of Crime (Sentences) Act 1997: J.P. 1997, 161 (42), 977-980. (Text of guidance on implementation of 1997 Act, in force October 1, 1997, and January 1 and March 1, 1998).

Honesty in sentencing: S. News 1997, 1 (Feb), 11-12. (Introduction of proposed honest sentencing scheme, involving sentences equivalent to two thirds of term imposed at present, and compounding of confusion by transitional period provisions).

Justice, "global sentencing" and strict interpretation—further postscript *(J.A. Davis)*: J.P. 1997, 161 (10), 232-233. (Updates article at J.P. 1996, 160 (46), 1012-1015 arguing that single sentence should be imposed for multiple crimes, thus avoiding complications in deducting remand time from concurrent sentences and compensation payments to criminals).

Let's insist on consistent defendants *(Eric Crowther)*: J.P. 1997, 161 (23), 567-568. (Criticism of comprehensive Sentencing Guidelines for magistrates on grounds that some benches interpreted previous guidelines on road traffic fines inflexibly).

Life sentence sentencing - calls for reform *(J.N. Spencer)*: J.P. 1997, 161 (20), 475-476. (Anomalies between discretionary and mandatory life sentences when determining minimum period of detention).

Mad or bad? Child-killers, gender and the courts *(Ania Wilczynski)*: Brit. J. Criminol. 1997, 37 (3), 419-436. (Research findings of project on child killing by parents showing that criminal justice system reacts differently to men and women guilty of infanticide).

Mentally disordered offenders *(Judith M. Laing)*: N.L.J. 1997, 147 (6807), 1313-1314. (Effect on mentally disordered patients of courts' powers to make hospital direction combining imprisonment with admission to hospital).

Pre-sentence reports: the effects of legislation and national standards *(Michael Cavadino)*: Brit. J. Criminol. 1997, 37 (4), 529-548. (Study assessing effects of replacement of social inquiry reports with pre sentencing reports in 1992).

Protective sentences: ethics, rights and sentencing policy *(Ralph Henham)*: Int. J. Soc. L. 1997, 25 (1), 45-63. (History of protective sentencing legislation and extent to which ethical concerns reflected in policy have diminished rights of dangerous offenders).

Racial disparity in sentencing: reflections on the Hood study *(Andrew Von Hirsch* and *Julian V. Roberts)*: Howard Journal 1997, 36 (3), 227-236. (Whether criticism of methodological basis of Roger Hood's 1992 study of race and sentencing is justified and how minority overrepresentation in prisons should be addressed).

Revenge and the law *(Leslie James)*: J.P. 1997, 161 (29), 697. (Human desire to seek revenge and its application to criminal justice system).

Sentencing guidelines revisited *(P.G. Hawker* and *F.G. Davies)*: J.P. 1997, 161 (3), 55-56. (Research into operation of Magistrates' Association Sentencing Guidelines compared with CA guideline judgments, measuring their effectiveness and frequency of use by magistrates).

Sentencing in the magistrates' court: assault-when is imprisonment appropriate? *(Paul R. Farmer)*: M.C.P. 1997, 1 (7), 9-11. (Approach to sentencing in cases of unprovoked or domestic assault, assault on public officials or police, road rage and assault on sports field, with relevant case law).

Sentencing in the youth court—the effect of the Criminal Justice Act 1991 *(Christopher Stanley)*: J.P. 1997, 161 (28), 670-672. (NACRO monitoring of 1991 Act over two year period, analysing how juvenile offenders have been affected by changes in sentencing laws).

Sentencing legislation - the case for consolidation *(David A. Thomas)*: Crim. L.R. 1997, Jun, 406-415. (Difficulties created by piecemeal growth of sentencing legislation resulting in need for consolidation and simplification to aid identification and application of law).

Sentencing the informer *(Alec Samuels)*: J.P. 1997, 161 (4), 80-81. (Relevant factors in assessing discounts and correct procedure).

Specimen counts and sentencing: a principled approach and the proper procedure *(Matthew Chapman)*: J. Crim. L. 1997, 61 (3), 315-323. (Extent to which principles of sentencing on specimen counts are endorsed by prosecutors and sentencers, case law and proper procedures to be followed).

The maximum penalty for dangerous driving *(J.N. Spencer)*: J.P. 1997, 161 (13), 303. (Criticising the anomalous failure to increase the maximum sentences for dangerous driving and aggravated vehicle taking to correspond with the increased maximum for causing death by dangerous driving).

The role of the prosecution in the sentencing process *(Alec Samuels)*: J.P. 1997, 161 (12), 280-282. (Circumstances affecting severity of sentence, process for review and procedure prosecution should follow in setting out arguments).

Viewpoint: S. News 1997, 2(Jun), 9-12. (Arguments against introduction of automatic life sentences under the Crime (Sentences) Act 1997 s.2 where defendant has been convicted of serious offence for second time).

1726. Books

Hungerford-Welch, Peter–Criminal Litigation and Sentencing. Paperback: £29.95. ISBN 1-85941-315-3. Cavendish Publishing Ltd.

CUSTOMS AND EXCISE

1727. Customs duty–additional duty–recoverability–reliance on erroneous information supplied by Customs

[Council Regulation 2913/92 implementing the Community Customs Code Art.220(2)(b).]

Customs appealed against decisions of the Value Added Tax and Duties Tribunal that it was not, by reason of Council Regulation 2913/92 Art.220(2)(b), entitled to recover import duty otherwise payable under the relevant Community legislation in the form of additional duty. The respondents, each importers of a product subject to additional duties, were cleared through customs without the levy of additional duty due to their reliance on information supplied, inaccurately, by the customs authorities. Customs sought to recover the additional duty in accordance with Council Regulation 2913/92, but was prevented from doing so by the tribunal which accepted the respondent's argument that Art.220(2)(b) afforded them protection against the provisions of Council Regulation 2913/92, the respondents having taken all reasonable steps to ensure they complied with the Regulation.

Held, allowing the appeal in each case, that the tribunal had misdirected itself in law, misapplying Art.220(2)(b). Article 220(2)(b) was not satisfied as the error on the part of the customs authorities could reasonably have been detected by the respondents. The test is one of whether steps were available to the trader to bring the error to his attention, not whether the trader acted reasonably in not taking steps which would have brought the error to his attention. A trader can detect any error by reference to the Official Journal which contains the provisions of Community law, deriving understanding on the level of an attentive reader. Accordingly, the respondents were not entitled to a waiver of the recovery of the additional duties.

CUSTOMS AND EXCISE COMMISSIONERS v. INVICTA POULTRY LTD; CUSTOMS AND EXCISE COMMISSIONERS v. DIRECT BARGAIN SUPPLIES LTD, *The Times*, July 29, 1997, Lightman, J., QBD.

1728. Customs duty–costs of three year warranty to be included in value of imported cars

[Council Regulation 2913/92 establishing the Community Customs Code Art.293.]

D imported motor cars from Japan. Of the invoiced amount, 2.23 per cent was expressed to be in respect of a three year warranty. Customs decided that warranty costs should not be excluded from the value of imported cars for the purposes of customs duty. D appealed.

Held, dismissing the appeal, that the warranty was provided as a condition of sale within Council Regulation 2913/92 establishing the Community

Customs Code Art.293(a) and as such was included, under Art.29(1) of the Code, in the customs value.

DAIHATSU (UK) LTD v. CUSTOMS AND EXCISE COMMISSIONERS [1996] V. & D.R. 192, Paul de Voil (Chairman), V & DT.

1729. Customs duty—errors in origin and tariff code of goods—post clearance demand appealable—error "could not reasonably have been detected"

[Council Regulation 92/2913 establishing the Community Customs Code Art.220(3)(b).]

D imported kitchen knives from the USA. Customs made a post clearance demand for duty on the grounds that the goods had been erroneously represented to be from Brazil and that the wrong tariff code had been used. D appealed.

Held, allowing the appeal in part, that (1) the factual error in the goods origin was appealable only to the Revenue Adjudicator, and (2) the tariff code could not be altered since the error was made by the Customs and Council Regulation 92/2913 Art.220(3)(b) applied.

DIRECT BARGAIN SUPPLIES LTD v. CUSTOMS AND EXCISE COMMISSIONERS [1996] V. & D.R. 287, JF Avery Jones, London Tribunal.

1730. Dock dues—repayments—charge levied in breach of Community law—no reimbursement where to do so would constitute unjust enrichment—European Union

S claimed repayment of dock dues levied in breach of community law on goods imported into Guadeloupe. The French court referred to the ECJ for a preliminary ruling the question of whether repayment could be resisted where there was a requirement to incorporate the charge in the price of goods sold.

Held, that a repayment may be refused where the charge had been borne by another person so that reimbursement to the trader would constitute unjust enrichment.

SOCIETE COMATEB v. DIRECTEUR GENERAL DES DOUANES ET DROITS INDIRECTS [1997] S.T.C. 1006, GC Rodriguez Iglesias (President), ECJ.

1731. Excise duty—cider and perry

CIDER AND PERRY (AMENDMENT) REGULATIONS 1997, SI 1997 659; made under the Alcoholic Liquor Duties Act 1979 s.56, s.62; and the Finance (No.2) Act 1992 s.1. In force: April 1, 1997; £0.65.

These Regulations amend the Cider and Perry Regulations 1989 (SI 1989 1355 as amended by SI 1996 2287) by adding an excise duty point viz the time that any cider is consumed on cider premises.

1732. Excise duty—diesel fuel oil—penalty for misuse

[Hydrocarbon Oil Duties Act 1979 s.13.]

B filled his car with gas oil and used it on 10 subsequent occasions until caught. The Customs officers seized the car and imposed a penalty of £1,000 for its release under the Hydrocarbon Oil Duties Act 1979 s.13. The maximum penalty was £2,750. B appealed.

Held, dismissing the appeal, that in the circumstances the sum required was not excessive.

BELL v. CUSTOMS AND EXCISE COMMISSIONERS [1996] V. & D.R. 300, AW Simpson TD (Chairman), Manchester Tribunal.

1733. Excise duty–gambling–administration of gaming duty

GAMING DUTY REGULATIONS 1997, SI 1997 2196; made under the Finance Act 1997 s.11, s.12, s.14, Sch.1 para.11. In force: October 1, 1997; £1.10.

These Regulations provide arrangements for the administration of gaming duty. They oblige those liable to pay gaming duty to make payments after the first three months of an accounting period; provide for the method of calculation; provide for different methods of calculating the amount payable when gaming does not take place throughout the whole of an accounting period; provide for the apportionment of the liability for duty where the provider of premises changes during an accounting period; and set out the manner in which the Commissioners of Customs and Excise must give directions as to the making of returns and concerning premises.

1734. Excise duty–gambling–prize limit increase–exemption from bingo duty

BETTING AND GAMING DUTIES ACT 1981 (BINGO PRIZE LIMIT) ORDER 1997, SI 1997 1714; made under the Betting and Gaming Duties Act 1981 Sch.3 para.7. In force: August 11, 1997; £0.65.

This Order increases the money prize limit for bingo played on a small scale by way of commercial amusement to qualify for exemption from bingo duty. It increases the maximum amount permitted to be distributed as a money prize from £1 to £5.

1735. Excise duty–hydrocarbon oil–statutory right of relief did not preclude common law right of restitution for duty wrongly paid–determination of "approved person" status

[Hydrocarbon Oil Duties Act 1979 s.9(4); Hydrocarbon Oil Regulations 1973 (SI 1973 1311) Reg.37.]

B appealed against a decision that a claim for repayment of duty charged on hydrocarbon oil used in its blast furnaces could only be made under the Hydrocarbon Oil Duties Act 1979 s.9(4), and that a complaint by B that it had not been given relief from such duty, as provided for by s.9(4), could only be pursued by seeking judicial review. B contended that it should qualify for relief as the oil was used as a reduction and extraction agent in its furnaces and not as a fuel, as provided under s.9(2). Customs disputed this claim, further submitting that, even if the use contended for was correct, B's claim could not succeed, as it had never had "approved person" status under s.9(4), and was thereby precluded from claiming relief.

Held, allowing the appeal, that (1) if B could show that the demands for duty to be paid were unlawful, due to an error on Customs's part as to the use to which the oil was put, B would have a right to restitution at common law, *Woolwich Equitable Building Society v. Inland Revenue Commissioners* [1993] A.C. 70, [1992] C.L.Y. 2508 followed; (2) under s.6 of the 1979 Act, duty was payable to secure release of the oil from bond, with a right of relief by virtue of s.9(1) if it were used for a qualifying purpose, and (3) "approved person" status could be conferred under the Hydrocarbon Oil Regulations 1973 Reg.37, without the need for formal application. However, that would only apply in respect of prospective relief, and would not cover applications for repayments of duty previously paid. Although B could have challenged the decision to refuse relief by way of judicial review, private law proceedings in restitution were permissible, if they could show both that the demand for payment was unlawful and that the remedy sought was not excluded under the statutory relief scheme.

BRITISH STEEL PLC v. CUSTOMS AND EXCISE COMMISSIONERS [1997] 2 All E.R. 366, Sir Richard Scott, V.C., CA.

1736. **Excise duty–smuggling–tobacco products–prosecution required to prove goods were imported for commercial purposes without any presumption flowing from quantities**

[Customs and Excise Management Act 1979 s.170(2); Excise Duties (Personal Reliefs) Order 1992 (SI 1992 3155) Art.5.]

Held, that when establishing whether goods were dutiable in a prosecution for fraudulent evasion of excise duty under the Customs and Excise Management Act 1979 s.170(2), the Crown was not required to establish that the defendant intended to import goods in excess of the quantities laid out in the schedule to the Excise Duties (Personal Reliefs) Order 1992 Art.5(3), or to establish that Customs were not satisfied that the goods were for personal use. The prosecution should instead seek to establish beyond reasonable doubt that the goods were being imported for commercial purposes, disregarding any presumption raised by quantities.

R. v. TRAVERS (KELVIN), *The Times*, August 13, 1997, Waller, L.J., CA (Crim Div).

1737. **Excise duty–smuggling–tobacco products–right of appeal restricted by irrefutable presumption in favour of Customs denying judicial control on question of fact**

[Finance Act 1994 s.9; Excise Duties (Personal Reliefs) Order 1992 Art.5; Council Directive 92/12 Art.92.]

H appealed against a penalty of £250 imposed under the Finance Act 1994 s.9, having failed to satisfy Customs officers at Luton Airport that 11.2kg of hand rolling tobacco and 400 cigarettes imported by H had not been imported for a commercial purpose. H contended that the tobacco was intended for his own use and was not for resale. Customs submitted that H had no right of appeal on the merits of the case because the interpretation given to the Excise Duties (Personal Reliefs) Order 1992 Art.5 by *Customs and Excise Commissioners v. Carrier* [1995] 4 All E. R. 38, [1994] C.L.Y. 1429, meant that the determination of whether the tobacco was for H's own use lay with Customs alone.

Held, allowing the appeal, that H was entitled to bring tobacco purchased in another Member State into the UK without paying further duty under Council Directive 92/12 and that the interpretation given to Art.5(3) of the 1992 Order in *Carrier* was incompatible with Art.9.2 of the Directive in that it set up an irrefutable presumption based on Customs' decision. Precluding an appeal on the merits under Art.5(3) amounted to a condition less favourable than those applying to other excise appeals and as such infringed the requirement of judicial control by making Customs' decision a conclusive question of fact that was not susceptible to judicial review.

HODGSON v. CUSTOMS AND EXCISE COMMISSIONERS [1996] V. & D.R. 200, Stephen Oliver Q.C., V & DT.

1738. **Finance Act 1997 (c.16)–Appointed Day Order**

FINANCE ACT 1997, SCHEDULE 6, PARAGRAPH 7, (APPOINTED DAY) ORDER 1997, SI 1997 1305 (C.44); made under the Finance Act 1997 Sch.6 para.7. Commencement details: bringing into force various provisions of the Act on June 1, 1997; £1.10.

This Order appoints June 1, 1997 as the day on which the Finance Act 1997 Sch.6 comes into force.

1739. **Finance Act 1997 (c.16)–Appointed Day Order**

FINANCE ACT 1997, SECTION 7(10), (APPOINTED DAY) ORDER 1997, SI 1997 1960 (C.80); made under the Finance Act 1997 s.7. Commencement details: bringing into force various provisions of the Act on August 15, 1997; £0.65.

This Order brings the Finance Act 1997 s.7, which introduces a new category of heavy oil for excise duty purposes into the Hydrocarbon Oil Duties Act 1979, into force on August 15, 1997.

1740. Forfeiture–artifacts seized by Customs could still be ordered to be condemned on appeal even though they were outside jurisdiction

Held, that where magistrates had declined to make an order for condemnation of artifacts seized by Customs as having been imported without licence or other authority, condemnation could still be ordered on appeal, even though the relevant items were now outside the jurisdiction, as long as the items had been properly seized on the date of the forfeiture proceedings in the magistrates court.

HASHWANI v. CUSTOMS AND EXCISE COMMISSIONERS, *The Independent*, November 3, 1997 (C.S.), Kennedy, L.J., QBD.

1741. Forfeiture–pornography–material found with items liable to forfeiture could itself be liable to forfeiture

[Customs and Excise Management Act 1979 s.141 (1).]

Customs officers entered T's flat and seized 16 books which were deemed to be indecent or obscene, but also seized a number of other books which were found with the indecent material. T appealed by way of case stated against a Crown Court decision that all the items were liable to forfeiture pursuant to the Customs and Excise Management Act 1979 s.141 (1).

Held, dismissing the appeal, that the Crown Court had been correct to conclude that s.141 (1) (a) and s.141 (1) (b) had to be read disjunctively so that anything mixed, packed or found with material liable to forfeiture could itself be liable to forfeiture, although Customs had a discretion not to require such forfeiture. Therefore, all the items seized at T's flat and not just the 16 indecent or obscene books could be condemned by the court.

TRAVELL v. CUSTOMS AND EXCISE COMMISSIONERS, *The Independent*, November 4, 1997, Brooke, L.J., QBD.

1742. Free zones–responsible authority–substitution of Port of Sheerness Ltd

FREE ZONE (PORT OF SHEERNESS) (SUBSTITUTION OF RESPONSIBLE AUTHORITY) ORDER 1997, SI 1997 994; made under the Customs and Excise Management Act 1979 s.100A. In force: April 1, 1997; £0.65.

This Order amends the Free Zone (Port of Sheerness) Designation Order 1994 (SI 1994 2898) by substituting Port of Sheerness Ltd as the responsible authority for the free zone in place of Medway Ports Ltd who were appointed by the previous Order.

1743. VAT and Duties Tribunal–reviews and appeals

CUSTOMS REVIEWS AND APPEALS (TARIFF AND ORIGIN) REGULATIONS 1997, SI 1997 534; made under the Finance Act 1994 s.14. In force: March 24, 1997; £1.10.

These Regulations, which revoke the Customs Review and Appeals (Binding Tariff Information) Regulations 1995 (SI 1995 2351), make provision for reviews and appeals to the VAT and Duties Tribunals from decisions of the Commissioners of Customs and Excise relating to the issue of binding tariff and binding origin information. They also make other decisions in relation to origin which are made by the Commissioners for the purposes of preferential tariff measures subject to review and appeal. They are made in consequence of the coming into force of Council Regulation 82/97 ([1997] OJ L17/1) and Commission Regulation 12/97 ([1997] OJ L9/1) which amend provisions relating to binding tariff information contained in Council Regulation 2913/92 ([1992] OJ L302/1) establishing the Community Customs Code and Commission Regulation 2454/93 laying down provisions for the implementation of Council Regulation 2913/92 ([1992] OJ L302/1) establishing the Community Customs Code.

1744. Wines—excise duty point

WINE AND MADE-WINE (AMENDMENT) REGULATIONS 1997, SI 1997 658; made under the Alcoholic Liquor Duties Act 1979 s.56, s.62; and the Finance (No.2) Act 1992 s.1. In force: April 1, 1997; £0.65.

These Regulations amend the Wine and Made-Wine Regulations 1989 (SI 1989 1356 as amended by SI 1996 2752) by adding an excise duty point, viz the time that any wine, or made-wine, is consumed at a winery.

1745. Articles

Breaking and entering *(Titmuss Sainer Dechert)*: I.H.L. 1996/97, 46 (Dec/Jan), 63. (Extension of Customs and Excise powers of investigation and extent to which courts control such operations with particular reference to searches of premises).

"Bumping" cars: a question of valuation *(Frank Hartley)*: T.P.V. 1997, 11 (3), 17-19. (Action by Customs to combat motor dealers' practice of overvaluing trade-ins or offering cashbacks so that customers can provide minimum deposit needed to obtain finance whilst adding shortfall to total price).

Concealments and searches—some thoughts and words *(C. Burke)*: J.P. 1997, 161 (2), 36-37. (Methods of smuggling drugs inside body, Customs officers' powers, recourse to magistrates' courts to order strip or intimate searches and detainees' right not to consent).

Condemnation procedure explained *(Gavin McFarlane)*: Tax J. 1997, 424, 18-19. (Use of condemnation proceedings to challenge Customs' determination that item seized is liable to forfeiture and implications of procedure for title to seized goods).

Excise duty fraud: could your clients be liable? *(Linda Adelson)*: De Voil I.T.I. 1997, 9, 17-19. (Liability of innocent traders for false export frauds of alcohol and tobacco products involving use of fraudulent adminstrative accompanying documents).

False origin certificates: German importers application for remission of duty demands rejected by the European Commission *(Andrew Hart)*: De Voil I.T.I. 1997, 10, 19-21. (Reasons for and implications of decision by CEC to refuse remission of customs duty on televisions imported from Turkey where importers had in good faith presented invalid origin certificates issued by Turkish authorities).

Fighting bankruptcy *(John D. Brooks)*: Tax. 1997, 138 (3598), 716-717. (Use of bankruptcy proceedings by Customs to collect unpaid VAT and right of appeal against VAT assessment in hardship cases).

Out of time *(Titmuss Sainer Dechert)*: I.H.L. 1997, 49 (Apr), 63. (VAT and Duties Tribunal decision on strict application of time limits imposed on duty rates, where registration of declaration day later than due meant importers were liable to pay duty).

Post-clearance recovery - another fine mess *(Titmuss Sainer Dechert)*: I.H.L. 1997, 51 (Jun), 60-62. (Importers' liability for back duty where misled by customs authorities and defence of "official error" under EC law).

Test results *(Francesca Lagerberg)*: Tax. 1997, 138 (3592), 515. (Customs and Inland Revenue audited annual accounts for 1995/96, with table showing percentage of enforcement actions commenced by regions).

DAMAGES

1746. Breach of contract—damage to underground electricity cable—reasonable costs for repair works

D damaged S's underground electricity cable following which S carried out repair works using its own direct labour force. S claimed as damages: (1) the cost of labour used in effecting the repairs; (2) the cost of materials used in effecting the repairs; (3) on costs mark up amounting to 71 per cent of the labour costs reflecting "direct costs and action taken not reported directly". Evidence was given that these covered six heads of cost: (i) engineering resource to locate the fault and decide action required; (ii) supervisory resource to arrange availability of staff to effect the repair, frequently out of normal hours; (iii) costs of transporting people and materials to site; (iv) clerical resource to take customer enquiries relating to the loss of electricity supply; (v) clerical resource to record the incident, coordinate action and process resulting accounting and billing transaction; (vi) staff to issue materials from stores; (4) a second on cost mark up amounting to 141 per cent of the marked up labour costs ie. 141 per cent of 71 per cent of the labour costs. That further mark up which brought the overall mark up to 366 per cent was said to be to cover "activities support costs" including: (i) clerical resources to pursue outstanding suppliers' accounts, to purchase materials to replace those used, to finance the legal and accounting support and advice services of the Board; (ii) the computer systems of the electricity company; (iii) property costs of the electricity company ie. their ordinary offices, stores, depots etc; (iv) "corporate costs" such as finance, secretarial and executive costs, and (v) cost of finance, including finance costs of maintaining stock levels and funding of debtor balances.

Held, that in addition to the cost of labour and materials S was entitled to recover reasonable overhead costs attributable to the repair works. The percentage on costs mark up claimed by S was not reasonable. The judge held that it was certainly possible to construe the evidence of the witness for the electricity company as implying that there was a very material difference between the first uplift of 71 per cent and the second uplift of 141 per cent. The judge was satisfied that the uplift should be no more than 100 per cent, *London Transport Executive v. Foy Morgan & Co* [1995] 1 C.L.Y. 743, and *London Electricity Board v. Bromley LBC* [1993] C.L.Y 1600 followed.

SOUTH WALES ELECTRICITY PLC v. DMR LTD, January 29, 1996, Recorder Farmer Q.C., CC (Cardiff). [*Ex rel.* Michael LN Jones, Solicitor, Arlbee House, Greyfriars Road, Cardiff].

1747. Breach of contract—house repairs—failure to fit suitable electric equipment— damages for inconvenience

P employed H to organise the refurbishment of her house. In particular, P wished to have low voltage miniature lighting fitted. This required the installation of a number of transformers, which H purchased from a reputable supplier. The transformers proved to be faulty and the lights would flash on and off. Eventually, the lights stopped working altogether. In total, the transformers failed in four rooms, in particular the study and children's bedrooms. These failures continued over approximately the next eighteen months causing much inconvenience to P and her family. P was a publisher and therefore had to complete vast quantities of reading. P's children needed good lighting in their rooms for reading, and P's partner needed lighting in the study since he ran his own business from the house. P claimed, inter alia, for damages for inconvenience caused by the breach of contract.

Held, awarding £200 for inconvenience, that P and her family had suffered much inconvenience over a long period of time and they were entitled to be compensated.

PIATKUS v. HARRIS, June 5, 1997, H.H.J. Maher, CC (Willesden). [*Ex rel.* Tim Kevan, Barrister, 1 Temple Gardens].

1748. Breach of contract—wedding celebrations—hotel failing to fulfil contract— damages for distress and disappointment

B contracted with M to provide a hotel banqueting suite for the wedding of M's daughter. The hotel, for which B was legally liable at the time of the hearing, was to provide the hall, round tables, a stage for a band and a dance floor at a cost of £1,500. There were 120 guests at the wedding and M had entered into separate contractual arrangements with a caterer, and with a band which was to play until 11.30 pm. The banqueting suite was booked until midnight. During the evening, as guests were dancing, M and his family noticed cracks appearing in the dance floor which had been constructed on top of the carpet. The bride caught her heel in one such crack and fell. Other female guests found their heels being caught in the gaps in the dance floor. Both M and his daughter made numerous attempts during the course of the wedding celebration to contact hotel staff to resolve the problem. No member of hotel staff came into the hall until after most of the guests had left, and even then the floor was not repaired. As a result of the problems with the dance floor, M's guests ceased dancing, the atmosphere was affected and the entire celebrations ended prematurely. M and his family suffered extreme distress, embarrassment and upset at the wedding celebrations of M's only daughter having been ruined.

Held, that a wedding was a most important occasion for the families involved. There had been a clear breach of contract by B. Ordinarily, damages are not recoverable for distress or disappointment, per se, however the "holiday cases" provide the exception to this rule. A contract for the supply of arrangements for a wedding is in a higher class calling for a higher level of damages than the "holiday cases". Such a contract goes further than the mere supply of food and drink, for example, when eating at a restaurant. It is something exceptional and damages whould be assessed accordingly, *Cole v. Rana (t/a Advanced Automobiles)* [1993] C.L.Y. 1364 confirmed. £750 was awarded for breach of contract and general damages of £2,000.

MORRIS v. BRITANNIA HOTELS LTD, April 30, 1997, District Judge Southcombe, CC (Willesden). [*Ex rel.* Tanya Callman, Barrister, 2 King's Bench Walk, Temple].

1749. Breach of contract – wedding dress damaged – damages for anguish, distress and disappointment leading up to and immediately prior to wedding

L, well known makers of wedding dresses, took a £895 order in February 1996 for a wedding taking place on September 1, 1996. After unsatisfactory fittings L decided to remake the dress from scratch on July 20, 1996, requiring additional weekly fittings until Friday, August 30, 1996, 48 hours before the wedding, when the dress was finally pressed and sealed for protection. When the dress was removed from the sealed pack that evening for hanging it was not fit to be worn, mainly due to a dirt stain engrained on the bodice. L agreed to collect the dress the next morning for immediate attention and returned it in the afternoon, but when the pack was removed the stain was still visible and the dress was generally in a worse condition. L sent fitters to the house in the evening to chemical/steam clean and press the dress and the fitters finally left at 9 pm. During the wedding the skirt of the dress stood out due to faulty netting. L denied responsibility throughout, saying that sending fitters to the house on the eve of the wedding was a goodwill gesture. Only during the hearing did they concede that a dirty iron might have been used on the bodice.

Held, awarding general damages of £650 and special damages of £25, that breach of contract and negligence in this case had given rise to distress. A wedding was a special occasion and a contract to make a wedding dress was of a nature that a significant breach gives rise to general damages as well as special. H must have been "boiling" during the fitting process and at the end, and suffered considerable anxiety. It was fortunate that the dress was unpacked on the Friday, but the last hours were very anxious.

HARDY v. LOSNER FORMALS, June 13, 1997, District Judge Silverman, CC (Shoreditch). [*Ex rel.* MA Lassman, Barrister, 99 Woodlands, London].

1750. Compensatory damages – UK breach of EC law – compensatory not exemplary damages recoverable

See EUROPEAN UNION: R. v. Secretary of State for Transport, *ex p.* Factortame Ltd (No.5). §2393

1751. Consequential loss—limit of liability

N appealed from the determination that words seeking to place a limitation on liability for damages in relation to consequential loss did not apply to loss flowing directly and naturally from a breach. B claimed damages for increased production costs and loss of profits following the installation and subsequent failure of poorly designed electrical equipment. Following negotiations after the conclusion of the contract, damages were limited only so far as consequential losses were concerned. N contended, in reliance upon MacGregor on Damages (15th ed), that in the context of a commercial contract it was important to ascertain what a reasonable businessman would have intended, placed in the situation of the parties. It was argued that any reasonable businessman would understand that loss of profits, for example, would be consequential. B submitted, in reliance upon *Millar's Machinery Co v. David Way & Son* (1934) 40 Com. Cas. 204 and *Croudace Construction Ltd v. Cawoods Concrete Products Ltd* (1978) 2 Lloyd's Rep. 55, [1978] C.L.Y. 313, that the judge's construction of the contract was correct.

Held, dismissing the appeal, that the judge was right to conclude that the contractual term "consequential loss" was to be interpreted as meaning the loss proved by B in excess of that which was a direct result of the breach. On a true construction of the contract the parties simply agreed to limit N's liability for loss and damage not directly and naturally resulting from the breach to an amount equal to the value of the contract.

BRITISH SUGAR PLC v. NEI POWER PROJECTS LTD, Trans. Ref: QBENF 97/0233/C, October 8, 1997, Waller, L.J., CA.

1752. Damage to property—radioactive contamination—physical damage to neighbouring land—reduction in value and saleability of land—principles governing award of damages

[Nuclear Installations Act 1965 s.7.]

B owned an estate adjoining Aldermaston Atomic Weapons Establishment, AWE, which produced nuclear devices for the MoD. Heavy rain caused water from AWE's land to flow onto B's estate, which AWE later found to be contaminated with amounts of radioactive material above the level permitted by regulation. The contamination was not disclosed to B until some time later when B were negotiating to sell the estate. The prospective purchasers declined to buy the property, which then remained unsold. AWE paid for a substantial operation to remove the contaminated material but now resisted B's claim under the Nuclear Installations Act 1965 for compensation for the resulting reduction in the value and saleability of the estate.

Held, allowing the claim and awarding damages in excess of £5 million that B had not merely suffered pure economic loss. There had also been physical damage to the property which consequently rendered it less valuable, *Merlin v. British Nuclear Fuels Plc* [1990] 2 Q.B. 557, [1991] C.L.Y. 2662, *Murphy v. Brentwood DC* [1991] 1 A.C. 398, [1991] C.L.Y. 2661 and *Invercargill City Council v. Hamlin* [1996] 2 W.L.R. 367, [1996] 2 C.L.Y. 4438 distinguished. This physical damage was evidenced by the extensive clean up operation required to remove the contaminated material and the restrictions on use of the land whilst it was contaminated. It made no difference that the levels of radioactivity present posed no threat to health or that the permitted levels of radioactivity were not mentioned in the Act. The radioactive material had been the cause of the damage within the meaning of the 1965 Act s.7(1), and the fact that the contamination had taken place on a remote part of B's estate could only affect the quantity of damages and not AWE's basic liability. The measure of damages would be assessed in accordance with ordinary common law rules and should put B in the position it would have been in had the contamination not occurred, with some reduction to reflect the possibility that the estate might not have been sold even if the contamination had not occurred.

BLUE CIRCLE INDUSTRIES PLC v. MINISTRY OF DEFENCE [1997] Env. L.R. 341, Carnwath, J., Ch D.

1753. Defective premises—measure of damages

G and her teenage daughter occupied a part modernised cottage in a rural area from May 1988 to June 1994. There was a registered rent of £26. At the outset of the tenancy there were the following defects: the WC bowl was cracked; the floorboards around the WC were in an unsanitary condition; there were rotten floorboards in both bedrooms; the kitchen units were disintegrating; the immersion heater was not working; a wall in the kitchen was damp. Notice of disrepair was given at the outset. During the first six months G installed a new kitchen and bathroom at her own expense, and mended the immersion heater. The landlord replaced one floorboard.

Held, that G be awarded the following sums, for diminution in value: 20 per cent for the first six months and 15 per cent thereafter: £1,148. For discomfort, inconvenience and distress: £2,000. For the costs of the works carried out by the tenant: £1,729. Inconvenience, discomfort and distress for each plaintiff up to August 1993: £1,000 and for each plaintiff for the remainder of the tenancy: £759. Value of decorations and minor repairs carried out by the tenant: £3,000. Special damages to property: £400. Personal injury damages for exacerbation of asthma for two of the plaintiffs: £150 and £500. Total damages awarded (excluding interest): £15,093.

GETHING v. EVANS, March 21, 1996, District Judge Moore, CC (Skegness). [*Ex rel.* Sarah Greenan, Barrister].

1754. Defective premises—plumbing—leaks causing considerable damage—liability of landlord

B reported a leak from under the bath penetrating into the pantry cupboard off the kitchen which was severely damaged with damp stained plaster. B kept a bucket in one corner which he checked daily. On three occasions the bucket overflowed during the night. Plumbers attended on behalf of I. The bath panel was removed and not replaced and the tiling in the toilet was smashed in order to examine the toilet. In November 1995 I's expert examined the premises and concluded the defect was due to the manner in which B had installed the toilet in 1993. B's expert took the view that the leaks were due to the faulty trap under the bath and a defective overflow pipe from the main water tank. B and his wife were in the premises more than usual as B's wife suffered from multiple sclerosis and B was her registered carer. B became increasingly upset by the failure to remedy the problem and the fact that I blamed him for the problems.

Held, that I was liable for the leak and consequent damage and as a result I undertook to effect works within eight weeks. B was awarded judgment in the sum of £4,009 assessed as follows: diminution in value based on rent of £60 per week: £1,508. Cost of new shelves: £15. Damages: £2,250. Interest: £236. The considerable inconvenience that would be present whilst the works were carried out was taken into account in assessing the general damages.

BRYDON v. ISLINGTON LBC, February 27, 1997, H.H.J. Gibson, CC (Clerkenwell). [*Ex rel.* Tracey Bloom, Barrister, 1 Pump Court, Temple].

1755. False imprisonment—false accusation of shoplifting—measure of damages

See TORTS: Evans v. Governor of Brockhill Prison. §4856

1756. Heads of claim—loss of use of vehicle—inconvenience of litigation

See DAMAGES: O'Brien-King v. Phillips. §1814

1757. Horses—injury caused by motor vehicle—damages for loss of use and enjoyment of horse

F's horse was the last in a string of five horses being exercised on a country lane in Staffordshire when S came came up behind it in her car. She followed the horses for some 100 yards or so until the horses came across a gateway with a mini layby in front of it. The horses were intending to take up a position in the layby to enable S's car to pass. The horses in front of F's horse were going into the layby when F's horse suddenly took two paces backwards and then sought to go forward. S was driving too close to the horse and collided with its hindleg causing damage to the hock and the tendon. S was held solely to blame. F, a single working woman, was devoted to her horses which were "her life". She was a keen rider who competed at local shows, both indoor and outdoor, and hunted occasionally. She had bought the horse as an unbroken youngster and was bringing it on. It was unfit for use other than for light hacking and as a companion.

Held, awarding damages of £6,075 including £2,150 for diminution in value, £480 for loss of use being £20 per week for the 24 weeks, and the balance was in respect of veterinary fees and additional stabling costs during the recoupment period, together with some £10 interest. The interesting aspect of the case was the award of £20 per week for 24 weeks by way of loss of use and enjoyment of her horse.

FARRER-SOWERBY v. STUBBS, June 5, 1997, Recorder Coates, CC (Stoke on Trent). [*Ex rel.* Keith Thomas, Barrister, 5 John Dalton Street, Manchester].

1758. **Industrial diseases–death–measure of damages–concurrent tortfeasors– executors could claim for loss of dependency where deceased had already accepted settlement from one tortfeasor**

[Fatal Accidents Act 1976; Civil Liability (Contribution) Act 1978 s.1.]

The defence of accord and satisfaction did not release a concurrent tortfeasor from liability in a claim for damages. The defence of satisfaction could only protect a concurrent tortfeasor where the plaintiff had been fully compensated for the damage suffered. Shortly before his death from an asbestos related disease, J accepted £80,000 in "full and final settlement" of his claim for negligence and breach of statutory duty against his former employer, B, for exposing him to asbestos, although the sum was substantially less than the full value of J's claim. After his death, J's executors brought an action for loss of dependency under the Fatal Accidents Act 1976 against C, on whose premises J had carried out work on behalf of B, based on a similar, but not identical claim of negligence and breach of statutory duty. C appealed against a decision finding for the executors on the preliminary issues, contending that J's settlement with B had satisfied his claim, which prevented J's executors from bringing a further claim against C as concurrent tortfeasor. B appealed against a decision that if the executors succeeded against C, C would be entitled to a contribution from B under the Civil Liability (Contribution) Act 1978, arguing that they could not be said to be "liable in respect of the same damage" as C within the meaning of s.1 of the 1978 Act, as the damage in a claim brought under the 1976 Act was not that suffered by J before he died, but that suffered by his dependents after, and as a result of, his death.

Held, dismissing both appeals, that (1) the defence of accord and satisfaction did not operate to release a concurrent tortfeasor from liability as it did in the case of a joint tortfeasor, unless the amount paid by one of the tortfeasors was sufficient to satisfy the full value of the claim, as, unlike a joint tortfeasor, a concurrent tortfeasor was potentially a defendant to a separate action; (2) the defence of satisfaction, as distinct from accord and satisfaction, could only protect a concurrent tortfeasor from liability where the plaintiff had been fully compensated for the damage he had suffered, even where a settlement was expressed to be in full and final settlement of the claim. In this case, the judge had been entitled to conclude that £80,000 did not represent the full value of J's claim and was not bound to find that a sum agreeable to both parties, taking into account the uncertainties of litigation, amounted to full satisfaction of the claim, and (3) damage within the meaning of s.1 of the 1978 Act meant the event which allegedly caused J's injury and subsequent death and the claim brought by J's executors was a derivative one, in respect of the same damage, thereby entitling C to a contribution from B.

JAMESON v. CENTRAL ELECTRICITY GENERATING BOARD [1997] 3 W.L.R. 151, Auld, L.J., CA.

1759. Interim payments—medical negligence—child injured at birth

[Rules of the Supreme Court Ord.29 r.11.]

H sustained serious brain injuries when she was born, for which E admitted negligence. The injuries being such as to require permanent care, rehousing and special equipment, the cost of which was not agreed. E appealed against an order for an interim payment of £400,000, contending that that sum was excessive given the uncertainties of H's life expectancy, the actual quantity and cost of future health care and rehousing. E argued that H might not ultimately recover as much as £400,000. E introduced further evidence in support of its submission that no order should be made because it did not have the means and resources to enable it to make the interim payment for the purposes of Rules of the Supreme Court Ord.29 r.11 (2) (c). The way in which the budget of the NHS Trust which administered E operated, meant that the payment of £400,000 would have come out of the budget for patient health care and the sum would not be recoverable for many months. E also contended that it was not a public authority, whilst H argued it was. E argued further that an interim payment should not be made as it would preclude a structured settlement being made and that interim payments should be confined to the amount needed by H for maintenance and expenses pending the full hearing.

Held, dismissing the appeal, that after considering the probabilities in terms of life expectancy and the uncertainties referred to by E, an interim payment of £400,000 was not an unreasonable proportion of the total damages likely to be recovered. The claim was likely to be worth £750,000, although it was always possible for the claim to be unexpectedly less than that. E was found to have the resources to enable it to make the interim payment. If the system for funding litigation set up by the NHS Trust was contended by E, then it was not very effective and should be reconsidered by the Trust, *British & Commonwealth Holdings Plc v. Quadrex Holdings Inc* [1989] 3 W.L.R. 723, [1990] C.L.Y. 3804 not followed. The submissions regarding whether E was a public authority were not elaborated and as such could not be dealt with. It was H's choice and not for E to decide that no interim payment should be made as that would preclude a structured settlement being decided once the full award of damages was known. As H wished to purchase a new house and to equip it according to her needs, that justified payment of a substantial sum, *Stringman v. McArdle* [1994] 1 W.L.R. 1653, [1994] C.L.Y. 1482 considered.

HUGGAIR v. EASTBOURNE HOSPITALS NHS TRUST, Trans. Ref: 1996-H-No.244, April 29, 1997, S Goldblatt Q.C., QBD.

1760. Interim payments—motor vehicles—loss of use—interim payment for write off value—referral to arbitration preferred procedure

I was involved in a road traffic accident. Proceedings were issued as I claimed for the write off value of the vehicle, storage charges and the cost of hiring an alternative vehicle. M made an interim payment through his insurers in relation to the write off value of the vehicle before the issue of proceedings. M applied for the case to be referred to arbitration on the basis that the remaining unpaid damages would be below £3,000. I relied on the authority of *Casey v. Neal* [1997] C.L.Y. 505 and asserted the argument that if such matters were referred to arbitration it would encourage litigation at the expense of negotiation, as plaintiffs would issue court proceedings as soon as they were able (without it being an abuse of court process) to protect their position as to costs rather than pursue the avenue of negotiation fully.

Held, dismissing M's application, I's argument was accepted and the authority of *Casey v. Neal* followed. The matter should not be referred to arbitration.

IQBAL v. MIDLAND RED WEST LTD, September 1, 1997, Deputy District Judge Sutton, CC (Birmingham). [*Ex rel.* Andrew Leach, Solicitor, Amery Parkes Solicitors, 169 Edmund Street, Birmingham].

1761. Interim payments–uninsured driver–MIB refusing to make interim payment of damages

[Rules of the Supreme Court Ord.29 r.11.]

In December 1993 C was involved in a road traffic accident, and sued for damages for personal injuries sustained as a result. Liability was not in dispute. C suffered bodily injuries and injuries to his memory and cognitive abilities and as a result he was forced to give up his employment with the RAC and enter into less well paid employment. C applied for an award of interim damages in the sum of £20,000. It was conceded that the figure of £20,000 would be appropriate if an award of interim damages was permitted by the rules. However the point was taken on behalf of M that the provisions of RSC Ord.29 r.11 did not apply. M was not insured at the time of the accident nor was there any policy in force relating to her vehicle. The claim was therefore pursued against the MIB under the terms of the Memorandum of Agreement made on December 21, 1988. The MIB claimed that as M's car had never had a valid policy relating to it, there was no power to award an interim payment.

Held, allowing the application and the interim payment, that the MIB could not avoid liability for making an interim payment under the Uninsured Drivers Agreement. To construe the rules any other way would defeat the purpose of the regulations. Leave to appeal to the Court of Appeal refused.

CRISP v. MARSHALL, May 12, 1997, H.H.J. David Smith Q.C., Bristol District Registry. [*Ex rel.* Clarke Willmott & Clarke, Solicitors, Bristol].

1762. Loss of amenity–horsewoman deprived of ability to pursue lifetime hobby–whiplash type injury

See DAMAGES: Hunn v. McFarlane. §1901

1763. Measure of damages–assault by police officer–damage to property

See EVIDENCE: Thomas v. Commissioner of Police of the Metropolis. §455

1764. Measure of damages–business tenancies–solicitor's negligence causing termination of lease

See LANDLORD AND TENANT: Herbie Frogg Ltd v. Lee Barnett Needleman. §3267

1765. Measure of damages–civil actions against the police–guidelines for jury directions as to appropriate level of award

Guidelines were set down for directions for juries as to the appropriate level of damages to be awarded in civil actions against the police. Upon appeal by the Commissioner against awards of £50,000 and £220,000, the Court of Appeal laid down guidelines for directions to be given to juries as to the appropriate level of damages to be awarded to successful plaintiffs in civil actions against the police.

Held, that it was necessary to establish a correlation between awards for personal injuries and damages for wrongful arrest, false imprisonment or assault against the police where large sums of exemplary damages had been awarded by juries. It should be emphasised that juries were entitled to award ordinary and aggravated damages and the circumstances in which they were appropriate. The judge should also state a suitable bracket as a starting point and suggest a ceiling figure. Where a plaintiff had been wrongfully arrested a likely figure would be £500 for the first hour of detention and £3,000 for 24 hours. For malicious prosecution £2,000-£10,000 was appropriate, depending on the length of time distress was caused to the plaintiff. The guidelines should not be applied rigidly. Aggravating features should be explained and if a jury decided to award aggravated damages they should be made aware that such damages were compensatory, not punitive, and set out a different category in addition to the basic award so that the breakdown of damages could be defined more easily. It was important that a judge explain to the jury that exemplary damages should be awarded only in exceptional cases where the basic and aggravated damages were not sufficient punishment. The amount should be no more than necessary to show the jury's disapproval of arbitrary or oppressive conduct and should not exceed £50,000, the higher awards to be made only in actions involving high ranking police officers.

THOMPSON v. COMMISSIONER OF POLICE OF THE METROPOLIS; HSU v. COMMISSIONER OF POLICE OF THE METROPOLIS [1997] 3 W.L.R. 403, Lord Woolf, M.R., CA.

1766. Measure of damages–fatal accidents–loss of spouse's services

[Law Reform (Miscellaneous Provisions) Act 1934; Fatal Accidents Act 1976.]

D appealed against part of a decision giving judgment against him for £21,253 following a road traffic accident in which P, driving with his wife, W, collided with a van driven by D. P and W were aged 72 and W was killed. D admitted liability and an action was commenced under the Fatal Accidents Act 1976 and the Law Reform (Miscellaneous Provisions) Act 1934. Special damages were agreed and the multiplicand and multiplier were then assessed to take into account the loss to P of W's housekeeping services. This was considered on the basis of commercial loss applied at an hourly rate of £4.29 for 28 hours per week with a multiplicand of four years Thus, the total figure was £24,984, adjusted by an agreed dependency figure giving £7,628. £2,000 for loss of personal care and attention and £1,248 as enhanced food expenditure. D contended that the commercial rate of £4.29 should have been discounted for the notional services to approximately £3.

Held, allowing the appeal in part, that there was ambiguity as to whether there had been agreement between the parties as to the rate of £4.29 and that the assessment should be on an hourly rate basis. The judge below did not fall into error of law or fact in applying the multiplicand to the undiscounted hourly rate. However, the award for enhanced food expenditure resulted in a double compensation because the hours for help allowed included food preparation. Therefore the need for specially pre-cooked food was eliminated and the award was reduced by £1,248, the amount of the enhanced food expenditure.

OSBORNE v. OETEGENN, Trans. Ref: 95/1520/C, April 10, 1997, Otton, L.J., CA.

1767. Measure of damages–harassment–silent telephone calls

See TORTS: Perharic v. Hennessey. §4859

1768. Measure of damages–libel–damages to be proportionate

[Courts and Legal Services Act 1990 s.8(2); Rules of the Supreme Court Ord.59 r.11.]

The editor, the proprietor of the Sunday Mirror, and the co-author of an article that appeared in the paper appealed, pursuant to the Courts and Legal Services Act 1990 s.8(2) and the RSC Ord.59 r.11 (4), against an award of £100,000 general damages for libel contained in two articles about J. The articles alleged that J was a pimp who conspired with the KGB to blackmail foreign businessmen in Moscow. The only defence was justification.

Held, allowing the appeal, that the award for general damages would be reduced to £40,000. It was clear that the jury had found significant justification, but the allegations were serious and the aggravation derived from the plea of justification grave. However, the award for general damages was excessive because it was clear that, since *John*, libel awards should be proportionate and take into consideration the scale of damages for personal injuries, *Pamplin v. Express Newspapers Ltd* [1988] 1 W.L.R. 116, *Rantzen v. Mirror Group Newspapers (1986) Ltd* [1994] Q.B. 670, [1993] C.L.Y. 2579 and *John v. MGN Ltd* [1996] 3 W.L.R. 593, [1996] C.L.Y. 5673 applied.

JONES v. POLLARD [1997] E.M.L.R. 233, Hirst, L.J., CA.

1769. Measure of damages–loss of earnings–burden of proof–future employment prospects

In 1989, G, aged 39 years, was injured in a fall from a ladder, during his employment with T as a roofer, suffering lasting spinal injuries. G was awarded £12,000 general damages, £38,958 special damages for loss of earnings and £30,000 for loss of future earning capacity. T appealed contending that G would have been made redundant in 1990 and by 1993 was fit for light work. It was submitted that the judge had reversed the burden of proof in concluding that, notwithstanding that T had gone out of business in 1990, G could have found work elsewhere.

Held, dismissing the appeal, having sustained a substantial permanent disability, it could not be said that G had been overcompensated. If anything, the total award of damages was on the low side. The judge had been entitled to adopt the approach he had, in rejecting the multiplier/multiplicand approach, when there were so many imponderable factors as to G's future employment prospects. The burden of proof had remained with G throughout. The judge had made primary and secondary findings of fact which were reflected in the quantum of the award, *Blamire v. South Cumbria HA* [1993] 2 P.I.Q.R. Q1, [1993] C.L.Y. 1403 followed.

GOLDBOROUGH v. THOMPSON AND CROWTHER [1996] P.I.Q.R. Q86, Millett, L.J., CA.

1770. Measure of damages–medical negligence–quantification of future care and therapy–seven year old quadriplegic with cerebral palsy and athetosis–life expectancy of 25 years

S was born at DHA in May 1988 in traumatic circumstances which left him severely handicapped and suffering from quadriplegia with the complication of athetosis. This meant that S would be fully dependent on an adult for all his care needs throughout his life. His life expectancy was 25 years. DHA admitted liability for his injuries and agreed damages under several heads in excess of £500,000. The principal areas of dispute as to damages concerned the future care and therapy package that would be reasonable and the appropriate multiplier to be applied to the many items of continuing expense.

Held, that the appropriate multiplier was 12 and that: (1) the question of the appropriate multiplier should be approached by starting from the figure arrived at (the remaining life expectancy) using a discount rate of 4.5 per cent. In the instant case this produced a multiplier of 12.2. No further discount for mortality was appropriate in this case, the estimated life expectancy of 25 years having already taken such matters into account. Making a small discount for life's contingencies the appropriate multiplier was 12, *Hunt v. Severs* [1994] 2 A.C. 350, [1994] C.L.Y. 1530, applied, and (2) a care and therapy package which removes the main burden of the physical handling and routine attention from S's parents was reasonable. Specific night care attendance from the age of 15 was reasonable. The fact that S's parents would spend considerable time with him did not justify any reduction in the amount of care required, and his parent's attention should not be viewed as part of the care regime.

STEPHENS v. DONCASTER HA [1996] 7 Med. L.R. 357, Buxton, J., QBD.

1771. Measure of damages–package holidays–accommodation not available on arrival

G booked a holiday through Thomas Cook with Sovereign Travel (subsequently First Choice Holidays) for two weeks in Gran Canaria at the most expensive hotel that was offered. The cost was £2,159. Two days before departure F knew but did not tell G that their accommodation was not available. On arrival in Gran Canaria G were told that there was no accommodation for them and they were offered alternatives in Tenerife and Lanzarote, which they declined asking to return home. As that was not possible, they were sent to two hotels, the second of which was a five star hotel for businessmen in the port area of the island, 80 kilometres from their desired destination and where the weather was less good. G remained there for five nights until their travel agent obtained a booking in their original hotel for six nights. They moved into that hotel and were told by F that they should be able to stay there for the rest of their holiday. After six nights the hotel was unable to accommodate them any longer, and they returned to their five star businessman's hotel with none of the usual holiday facilities for the balance of their stay. After eight days they were offered a flight home via Fuerteventura with no positive promise of a flight from Fuerteventura. G were supplied with a hire car by F for the whole of their stay in Gran Canaria, although the hire company tried to repossess it after 10 days, and were given £200 in cash towards their expenses. On return to the UK F refunded the holiday cost in full.

Held, that damages would be awarded in respect of G's disappointment in the sum of £500 each and their claim for the cost of a night at Forte Crest at Gatwick and two weeks car parking would also be allowed. G argued that they should be put back in the position they would have been had they not had the holiday at all, but the district judge rejected their claims for repayment of the insurance premium, and the increase in the cost of food consumed over that which they would have eaten at home.

GRAHAM v. FIRST CHOICE HOLIDAYS & FLIGHTS LTD, Date not specified, CC (Bournemouth). [*Ex rel.* Penningtons, Solicitors, Clifton Hall, Bunnion Place, Basingstoke].

1772. Measure of damages–package holidays–holiday not up to expectations of plaintiff

[PackageTravel, Package Holidays and PackageTours Regulations 1992 (SI 1992 3288) Reg.6.]

M brought a claim against C for breach of contract. M booked a two week holiday for July 1995 at a campsite in LaTranche-sur-Mer, France. The holiday was selected from C's brochure entitled "Luxury Beach Holidays" at a cost of £1,180. M was accompanied by his wife, daughter, son-in-law and grandchild who were all to be accommodated in a "luxury holiday home" on the aforesaid site. M relied upon numerous descriptions in the brochure which were said to constitute implied warranties by virtue of the Package Travel, Package Holidays & Package Tours Regulations 1992 Reg.6. A variety of complaints were made relating to both the holiday home and site, which M claimed fell short of his expectations of "luxury". It was alleged, inter alia, that the campsite and home were dirty, inadequate accessories were provided with the home, the site was overcrowded and there was noise from a local amusement park into the early hours of the morning.

Held that, some of the complaints were of a minor nature, and overall the holiday was not completely ruined. However, the brochure itself was slightly misleading insofar as it gave the impression that the homes were spread out and not on top of one another. The sum of £250 was awarded to compensate M for the diminution in the value of the holiday. No award was made for distress and inconvenience.

MORRIS v. CARISMA HOLIDAYS LTD, February 5, 1997, District Judge Van Emden, CC (Watford). [*Ex rel.* Arun Katyar, Barrister, 2 King's Bench Walk, Temple].

1773. Measure of damages–package holidays–misrepresentation and breach of contract

L and G booked a holiday to Spain for two weeks at a cost of £296 per person in a self catering apartment. L and G specifically requested to be placed in three star accommodation where safety standards and standards in general, were high. They were informed by A that A's own 3A rating equated to the three star standard. In fact, the apartment was only a two star rating. In addition: the reception area smelled strongly of sewerage; graffiti had been cut into all the leather furnishings in the reception; the communal toilet areas were filthy; spillages in the reception area and on the landings were left unattended; the kitchen utensils provided were soiled; all the sliding doors in the room failed to work; rubbish had been allowed to accumulate above the crawl space of the beds; sockets were hanging out of the walls, exposing live wiring; the bathroom door could not be opened without the aid of a paperclip; and a communal fire escape failed to reach the ground and ended in an enclosed "cage". Despite daily complaints to the local representative and head office in the resort, A failed to put right any of the problems. There were numerous complaints of a similar nature from other guests. L and G demanded to be moved to alternative accommodation but were told that they would have to make additional payments.

Held, that while it could not be said there was a total failure of consideration, and L and G were not therefore entitled to a repayment of the contract price, there had been a misrepresentation, and a breach of contract, and general damages were awarded. L and G were awarded £750 each in respect of the diminution in value of the holiday, discomfort, inconvenience, loss of enjoyment, frustration and depression, and also to take account of the added expenses incurred, *Clarke and Greenwood v. Airtours* [1995] 1 C.L.Y. 1603 applied.

LYNES AND GRAHAM v. AIRTOURS, April 25, 1996, District Judge Banks, CC (Barnet). [*Ex rel.* Adena Graham, Barrister].

1774. Measure of damages–personal injuries–distinction between past and future loss of earnings on assessment

P had not worked since 1986, when he gave up his job as a fireman due to a bad back. In 1988 he had an accident, for which D was responsible, and suffered further injuries. In an action in damages for personal injury, P claimed that had the accident not occurred he would have been able to find light industrial work. It was held that P had a residual capacity for work before 1988, but that the injuries in 1988 had substantially impaired this. A broad brush approach was applied in assessing damages at £73,157 for loss of earnings, based on P's claimed annual losses over the previous eight years, but making no separate award for future loss of earnings. D appealed, arguing that the multiplier/multiplicand approach for past and future earnings should have been adopted, with separate assessments being made to distinguish between awards of special and general damages.

Held, allowing the appeal and substituting damages of £18,114, that it was wrong to amalgamate past and future loss of earnings in an award without indicating a means to identify specific figures for each. Past and future losses should be treated separately, because past losses were more readily assessable and it was necessary to know their size to calculate the award of interest on special damages. Past losses could be assessed by reference to the earning potential during the period of loss if the injury had not occurred, with uncertainties assessed by a percentage discount. A broad based method, rather than the multiplier/multiplicand approach, should only be considered where the uncertainties were so great as to render a reasoned calculation artificial. In the instant case there was no such uncertainty, there being a clearly identified period of past loss, evidence of what the plaintiff could have earned in the sort of job he claimed he could have performed but for the accident and also medical evidence of his pre-existing disability.

COATES v. CURRY, *The Times*, August 22, 1997, Auld, L.J., CA.

1775. Measure of damages–trespass–scaffolding placed on neighbour's property

A had been instructed by R's neighbour to build an extension to his house right up to the edge of his land. The extension was built immediately abutting R's property, in particular the garage and kitchen extension which were flatroofed extensions and only one storey high. The building works took approximately three months during the summer of 1994. R went on holiday and returned to find that A had constructed scaffolding, without their consent, on their kitchen and garage roofs. Despite being asked to take it down immediately, A delayed matters for a further four days. Further, throughout the period of the building works builders would be on R's kitchen and garage roofs, without consent, attending to the construction of the neighbour's extension.

Held, that the judge accepted the submissions that damages for trespass should be assessed upon the wayleave principles and the Court of Appeal decision in *Whitwham v. Westminster Brymbo Coal and Coke Co* [1896] 2 Ch. 538 was relied upon by the judge. In essence, the measure of damages was assessed by reference to what hypothetically might have been agreed as a charge for the use of R's land. In particular, the judge found that he should take account of what would have been R's extremely strong bargaining position given that A had already contracted to build the extension for the neighbour. The judge awarded £125 per day for the period the scaffolding was on the roof, which was a total of 21 days, and £20 per day for the period the rest of the building work was continuing and the roof being used daily by the builders, a total of 60 days. The total figure amounted of £3,825 upon which interest at six per cent was awarded for a period of two years. Added to this were various items of special damages bringing the total up to £4,728.

RYAN & RYAN v. AL HARWOOD BUILDING SERVICES, November 22, 1996, H.H.J. Dean, CC (Central London). [*Ex rel.* Gabriel Buttimore, Barrister, 11 Old Square, Lincoln's Inn].

1776. Measure of damages—unlawful eviction

See LANDLORD AND TENANT: Burchett and Strugnell v. Vine. §, King v. Jackson (t/a Jackson Flower Co). §, Richardson v. Holowkiewicz. §3284

1777. Motor vehicles—damage to car while in hands of bailee—bailee able to recover losses on behalf of bailor

DR lawfully borrowed JR's car for the day. There was a road traffic accident for which T admitted liability. DR sued T for the cost of repairs, loss of use of the vehicle on behalf of JR, hire charges and telephone calls made by JR related to the accident. T argued that as DR was a mere bailee he could only claim for repairs and his own personal loss of use, if any.

Held, that following the reasoning of *O'Sullivan v. Williams* [1992] 3 All E.R. 385, [1992] C.L.Y. 1521, a bailee can recover all losses arising from damage to a chattel whilst in his hands. This was to avoid duplication of claims. It was for the bailee to account to the bailor.

RICHARDS v. THOMAS, April 16, 1997, H.H.J. Price, CC (Cardiff). [*Ex rel.* Lee Ingham, Barrister, 32 Park Place, Cardiff].

1778. Motor vehicles—damage to vehicle whilst in hands of bailee—bailee unable to recover losses

S lawfully borrowed her husband's car. There was a road traffic accident in which the vehicle was damaged. S sued the third party, T, for the policy excess and hire charges expended by her husband as a result of the accident.

Held, that T was liable for the accident but that S's claim would be dismissed as she had personally sustained no loss as a result of the accident.

SARKAR v. SCOTT, July 18, 1997, District Judge Rogers, CC (Crewe). [*Ex rel.* Rebecca Bensted, Barrister, Bracton Chambers, 95a Chancery Lane, London].

1779. Motor vehicles—loss of use

As a result of a road traffic accident which occurred on February 11, 1993, M's vehicle was damaged beyond economical repair, and she could not afford to replace her vehicle. M was receiving unemployment benefit and continued to do so up to the date of the trial.

Held, awarding judgment against PF, that M recovered the sum of £390 for the net pre-accident value of her vehicle together with the sum of £2,730 for the loss of use and inconvenience of 78 weeks at £35 per week. Interest was awarded on special damages of £85 and general damages of £54. S sustained a whiplash type injury in the accident, with symptoms for approximately a two year period. S was awarded the sum of £2,066.

MILNER AND SHARPE v. PARCEL FORCE, November 22, 1995, H.H.J. Kamil, CC (Leeds). [*Ex rel.* Ison Harrison & Co, Solicitors, Duke House, 54 Wellington Street, Leeds].

1780. Motor vehicles—loss of use

C was involved in a road traffic accident on March 1, 1996 when her vehicle came into collision with R's vehicle. As a result of the collision, C, whose vehicle was worth £370, suffered loss of use of her vehicle for a period of 43 weeks.

CONNOLLY v. ROTHWELL, April 9, 1997, H.H.J. Morgan, CC (Birkenhead). [*Ex rel.* Michael W Halsall, Solicitors, 2 The Parks, Newton-le-Willows].

1781. Motor vehicles—loss of use

D was involved in a road traffic accident on March 9, 1995, in which his vehicle, a C registration Ford Granada, sustained substantial damage. The repairs were estimated at £1,476, which D could not afford to pay. The driver's door had been damaged and could not be opened, and D kept the vehicle off the road for 15 weeks, after which he took the vehicle to a garage to have the door freed. The vehicle was driveable thereafter. D needed his car for work and was forced to ask for lifts from his neighbours. In addition, he was unable to take his disabled 12 year old stepson on weekend trips or on a planned two week holiday to Scotland. V did not contest the proceedings.

Held, that £85 per week damages for loss of use and inconvenience be paid for the full period of 15 weeks.

DORRICOTT v. VILLIERS, March 22, 1996, District Judge Millward, CC (Bromley). [*Ex rel.* Alexander Williams, Barrister, 14 King's Bench Walk, Temple].

1782. Motor vehicles—loss of use

D's car was damaged beyond economical repair. He was unable to replace it for almost fifteen weeks. During this time he had the use of a company car from his works' pool. He was able to use the company car most weekends and occasionally on weekday evenings. There was no other car in the family, and when the company car was not available, D had to rely on friends and taxis for lifts. He would often walk to work, a six mile round trip. The period of loss of use was in the winter months. The net pre-accident value of D's car was £450.

Held, that there was a "going rate" in these cases of about £50 per week. Higher or lower rates would be awarded on the particular facts of a case. Here D's case was ameliorated by the company car, but aggravated by the long walk to and from work when it was not available. It was considered that the two factors cancelled each other out, and loss of use was awarded at £50 per week. D was awarded a total of £735 with additional special damages for the taxi fares.

DURBIN v. LEWIS, August 7, 1996, District Judge Sonnex, CC (Reading). [*Ex rel.* Benjamin Williams, Barrister, Chambers of Michael Parroy Q.C., Oxford Chambers, 1 Alfred Street, Oxford].

1783. Motor vehicles—loss of use

H was involved in a road traffic accident on October 15, 1996 when his vehicle was in collision with T's vehicle. As a result of the collision H, whose vehicle was valued at £1,500, suffered loss of use of his vehicle for a total period of 42 weeks.

Held, that H was awarded loss of use for 25 weeks at £70 and 17 weeks at £50. H was awarded in total £2,600 for the loss of use of his vehicle, and in addition H was awarded £1,500 for the write off value of his vehicle, miscellaneous expenses of £35 and interest on special damages of £99.

HUGHES v. TAYLOR, August 6, 1997, H.H.J. Morgan, CC (Birkenhead). [*Ex rel.* Michael W Halsall Solicitors, 2 The Parks, Newton-le-Willows].

1784. Motor vehicles—loss of use

H was involved in a road traffic accident with A's vehicle on December 1995. As a result of the collision, H suffered loss of use of her vehicle for a period of two weeks. Court proceedings were issued on March 27, 1997. As no defence was filed, interlocutory judgment was entered on April 14, 1997. An assessment of damages hearing was applied for on May 20, 1997 and set for June 12, 1997.

Held, that H was awarded £80 per week, making a total of £160. In addition H was awarded £100 for her insurance excess, with £5 interest together with the outlay for her insurance company amounting to £564 with interest of £58.

HEWITT v. AFGHAR, June 12, 1997, District Judge Wright, CC (Birkenhead). [*Ex rel.* Michael W Halsall, Solicitors, 2 The Parks, Newton-le-Willows].

1785. Motor vehicles—loss of use

T had suffered the loss of use of his Ford Escort motor car for nine weeks. T was a retired gentleman, resident in Uxbridge, who used his car to ferry his wife to work and for general social, domestic and pleasure purposes on a daily basis. T was able to make some use of cars which belonged to his children before his car was repaired although he could not use their cars during the daytime when his children were at work. T's wife had to rely upon lifts from friends and taxis to get to work while the T's car was off the road.

Held, that damages for loss of use would be awarded at the rate of £10 per week for the nine week period.

TWIGG v. HARROW AND HILLINGDON HEALTH CARE, November 20, 1996, Judge Wainwright, CC (Uxbridge). [*Ex rel.* David Barr, Barrister, 1 Temple Gardens].

1786. Motor vehicles—loss of use

W was involved in a road traffic accident which occurred on July 28, 1996 when his vehicle came into collision with F's vehicle. As a result of the collision W whose vehicle was valued at £1,500 suffered loss of use of his vehicle for a total period of 54 weeks.

Held, that W was awarded loss of use at £50 per week for the 54 week period. This gave a total of £2,700 for loss of use. In addition W was awarded compensation for personal injuries in the sum of £1,500, recovery and storage charges for £470, miscellaneous expenses of £10 and interest of £170 thereon.

WEIR v. FIELD, August 13, 1997, H.H.J. Morgan, CC (Birkenhead). [*Ex rel.* Michael W Halsall Solicitors, 2 The Parks, Newton-le-Willows].

1787. Motor vehicles—loss of use—credit hire charges

[County Court Rules 1981 Ord.19 r.4.]

S issued proceedings claiming, amongst other things, credit hire charges equating to £57 per day over a three day period. The case was referred to arbitration and D obtained evidence to show that S could have hired an equivalent vehicle for £26 per day over the same period. D offered to pay a total of £90 in respect of the hire charges and referred S to the House of Lords' decision in *Giles v. Thompson* [1994] 1 A.C. 142, [1993] C.L.Y. 1405. S rejected the offer and D applied for his costs claiming that S had acted unreasonably within the definition of the CCR Ord.19 r.4(2)C.

Held, that S should recover £26 per day in respect of hire charges and that D should recover costs, S having acted unreasonably.

STONARD v. DUNSTER, August 30, 1996, District Judge Enzer, CC (Guildford). [*Ex rel.* Tom Holroyd, BKJ Lewis, Solicitors, Quality House, Chancery Lane].

1788. Motor vehicles—loss of use—credit hire charges—income support claimant—claim had to be within plaintiff's means

A road traffic accident occurred on August 12, 1994, in which S's vehicle was written off. S claimed damages limited to £5,000, consisting of the value of the vehicle net of salvage, £320; postage, telephone and travel costs, £35; hire of alternative transport, £1,110; and public transport costs, £100. M had already settled the vehicle claim before proceedings were commenced. The main argument related to the hire of an alternative vehicle. A car was supplied on a credit hire basis to S for a period of 27 days from August 24 to September 19, 1994. S was on a training scheme, on income support, without savings and with family responsibilities. There was no possibility of his being able to pay for car hire at that time.

Held, that the claim for hire charges would be disallowed. The claim had to be within a plaintiff's means. Income support gave S no room for such luxuries. S admitted that he had not paid the charges, had never had an invoice, and had never been requested to pay. He said that he could not believe that he would have been expected to pay anything, despite the fact that on the back of the hire agreement it stated that it was a credit hire agreement. Left to himself, S would have travelled on the bus and claimed the inconvenience of that. S was awarded £225 for loss of use, £50 for travel costs and £25 for out of pocket expenses, a total of £300. Other than the sum of £30 in respect of the court fee, S's solicitors were not awarded any costs.

SHORE v. MAINLINE GROUP, January 18, 1996, District Judge Peters, CC (Sheffield). [*Ex rel.* Lace Mawer, Solicitors, Castle Chambers, 43 Castle Street, Liverpool].

1789. Motor vehicles–loss of use–credit hire charges–mitigation of loss

A claimed damages for uninsured losses including the cost of car hire following a road traffic accident. A had hired a car at £29 per day for a period of seven days. He subsequently hired another car on "credit hire" for 12 days at a rate of £54 per day.

Held, that (1) damages of £833 were awarded. The credit hire element of the claim was disallowed and substituted by an award at the rate of £35 per day. A had known nothing of the hire rate for the credit hire period but had relied on the advice of his legal expense insurer, and (2) costs for unreasonable conduct were awarded to W, who had made a settlement offer of £850. An objective test had to be applied, *Bloomfield v. Roberts* [1989] C.L.Y. 2948 considered. A, who was not represented at the hearing should not have been left to argue the case on inadequate evidence regarding mitigation of loss. A wasted costs order was not made but on the evidence before the district judge, he expected the costs to be met by A's solicitors or legal expense insurer as A himself appeared to have done nothing wrong.

ASHBY v. WIGGINS, August 26, 1997, District Judge Polden, CC (Tunbridge Wells). [*Ex rel.* Nicholas Moss, Barrister, 1 Temple Gardens, Temple].

1790. Motor vehicles–loss of use–credit hire charges–mitigation of loss

Following an accident L was provided with a car on credit hire terms between June 12, 1996 and July 1, 1996, incurring an account for £445. L was employed as a bank clerk and needed a car to travel to and from work, but between June 21, 1996 and August 1, 1996 L was off work due to injuries she had sustained and she had used the hired car to visit her doctor and the hospital where she was having physiotherapy, both of which were within easy walking distance of L's home.

Held, disallowing the claim that L had hired the car because it was made easy for her do so by her solicitors. L had a duty to mitigate her losses and the judge found it was not reasonable for her to hire a car for any period.

LISA v. EDWARDS, June 19, 1997, H.H.J. Trigger, CC (Birkenhead). [*Ex rel.* Hill Dickinson Solicitors, Pearl Assurance House, Derby Square, Liverpool].

1791. Motor vehicles–loss of use–credit hire charges–mitigation of loss

R sustained a soft tissue injury to her neck in February 1995 when her car was struck from behind when stationary. She was initially shocked, shaken and upset but did not seek medical advice. Later that day a headache and tightness of her neck developed and she took paracetamol. That night she got little sleep. R did not see her doctor but was off work for three days, took paracetamol for ten to 14 days, and experienced a tight "clicky" feeling in her neck and, initially regular, occipital headaches. She also experienced nervousness in motor cars and did not attempt to drive for three weeks. The symptoms decreased over time and within about 14 months of the accident the headaches and nervousness in motor cars had resolved completely. The neck symptoms although much abated were still present at date of trial but a virtually full recovery was expected within about 21 months of the accident. However some vulnerability to future trauma in the neck would remain. R had hired a motor car from a company which deferred any liability for payment until the completion of proceedings. The weekly charge including VAT and insurance was £240 as opposed to what was agreed to be the market rate in the locality £180 per week. A argued (1) that R had failed to mitigate her losses and (2) the hire charges were unenforceable because the hirer did not have a consumer credit licence.

Held, that (1) R was not unreasonable, per se, in entering into a hire agreement which charged a higher rate in order to secure deferrment of liability until resolution of her claim and the court was entitled to have regard to the fact that no interest had accrued in respect of the hire charges whereas had she had to pay at once for the hire she would have incurred bank or credit card charges, which it was taken would have been in the region of 15 per cent. She was not awarded the full hire charges claimed of £1,883 for a 54 day hiring, but £1,715 which was the market rate uplifted by interest at 15 per cent to the date of the trial and (2) it was assumed that the hirer had required a consumer credit licence so that the hire agreement could not be enforced without leave of the Director of Fair Trading, however "it would be wrong for the Plaintiff to be forced to rely on a technicality in respect of something which was morally due for the benefit of the defendant tortfeasor". Therefore R was entitled to recover the reasonable amount of the hire charges.

ROGERS v. AUSTIN, October 2, 1996, District Judge Child, CC (Plymouth). [*Ex rel.* Rawdon Crozier, Barrister, 2 King's Bench Walk, Temple].

1792. Motor vehicles–loss of use–credit hire charges–plaintiff's impecuniosity

L claimed damages from M pursuant to a road traffic accident which occurred on March 24, 1997, when M drove into the rear of L's parked and unattended vehicle. As a result of the collision L's vehicle was an economical write-off. L required a vehicle to get her children to school and also to travel to her mother's to assist in looking after her handicapped sister. L was unemployed and was receiving income support. L sought to recover hire charges incurred following the accident. The hire was on a credit hire basis. M's solicitors made an application to the district judge that the claim for hire charges be disallowed, relying on *Shore v. Mainline Group* [1997] C.L.Y. 1788 which held that a trainee in receipt of income support was not entitled to claim credit hire charges for an alternative vehicle and for which he made no payments. L's solicitors objected strongly stating that L's impecuniosity was no ground to disallow her from hiring a vehicle as L was entitled to be put in a position she was prior to the accident taking place.

Held, allowing the claim in full, following L's contention an award of £1,044 was made.

LLEWYLLN v. McCABE, September 15, 1997, District Judge Frost, CC (Birkenhead). [*Ex rel.* Michael W Halsall, Solicitors, 2 The Parks, Newton-le-Willows].

1793. Motor vehicles–loss of use–credit hire charges–reasonableness

M was involved in a road traffic accident for which she was blameless. Her car was not roadworthy following the accident. She needed a car to fulfil her business and social commitments. The repair garage had no courtesy cars available and she was unable to afford to pay for a hire vehicle. The only way she could satisfy her need for a replacement vehicle was to hire from a credit hire company. She was recommended 1st Automotive by the repair garage proprietor. M hired, a similar sized vehicle to her own, from 1st Automotive for a period of 26 days at a rate of

£36 per day inclusive of collision damage waiver, a delivery charge and VAT. The total hire invoice amounted to £958. M was unfamiliar with the procedure for hiring vehicles and simply followed the advice from the garage proprietor. She made no enquiries whatsoever as to the rates of other hire companies, whether traditional hire or credit hire. F's insurance company produced rates from local traditional hire companies to M as comparisons to show that the credit hire rate was unreasonable. F submitted that a reasonable rate would be the average of the local traditional hire companies. No comparisons with other credit hire companies were proffered by F. The only credit hire comparables were produced by M.

Held, that despite the fact that M did not enquire as to local rates as being pointless as she could only satisfy her need for a replacement vehicle through hiring from a credit hire company, the judge stated that, having looked at the evidence on rates, on a comparison of "like for like" the rate of 1st Automotive was reasonable and favourable. It was the role of the judge to decide the extent to which M was to be compensated and not to protect insurance companies from other commercial companies. The test was reasonableness and M's reasonableness had to be assessed in the light of M's circumstances. Hire charges awarded in full in the sum of £958, for the whole period of 26 days. Costs awarded to M on county court Scale 1.

MARPLES v. FRENCH, June 11, 1997, District Judge Shannon, CC (Manchester). [*Ex rel.* Colemans Solicitors, Elisabeth House, 16 St Peters Square, Manchester].

1794. Motor vehicles—loss of use—credit hire charges—reasonableness

The managing director of H was involved in a road traffic accident in which his car was damaged. The company needed to hire a replacement vehicle and his solicitors informed him that F's insurers would be responsible for the hire invoice, even though it was made out to H. The director signed the credit hire agreement which did not include details of the rates of hire. He never requested details of the rates and never made enquiries of any alternative car hire firms. Hire charges of £13,389 were incurred at £275 per day. F tendered evidence that reasonable vehicles might have been available more cheaply elsewhere if H had made enquiries.

Held, that the hire charges were unreasonable. A reasonable plaintiff would have asked for rates and would not have relied on his solicitor's assurance that everything was fine. Moreover, H could not establish that suitable alternative vehicles were not available at the relevant time from other car hire firms. The sum of £4,300 was awarded.

HL PALLET SERVICES v. FAIRCLOUGH AND IRON TRADES INSURANCE GROUP, September 2, 1996, H.H.J. Urquart, CC (Wigan). [*Ex rel.* Lace Mawer, Solicitors, 43 Castle Street, Liverpool].

1795. Motor vehicles—loss of use—credit hire charges—reasonableness

T's car, valued at £400, was damaged beyond economic repair in an accident for which D admitted liability at the scene and was found 100 per cent to blame. T needed a car and the evidence showed that she was unable to buy or borrow a replacement. She therefore hired a car under a credit hire agreement. D's insurers were invited to make an interim payment to cover the pre-accident value of the car, but failed to do so until after five reminder letters over a period of three months. D contended that the rate, £42 per day plus £9.50 collision damage waiver (CDW) plus VAT, was excessive and that the overall sum, £7,200, was excessive when compared to the value of the car. D called no evidence as to hire rates.

Held, that the test was whether T had acted reasonably. The pre-accident value of her car was not relevant. In the circumstances, it was reasonable for her to enter into a credit hire agreement. D's insurers were not in a position to criticise the period of hire. In the absence of evidence as to what other credit hire companies might charge, D had failed to show that the rate was unreasonable. T was entitled to recover the full amount of £7,200.

THORNE v. DENBY, February 19, 1997, Recorder Donne Q.C., CC (Barnstaple). [*Ex rel.* Andrew Glennie, Barrister, 13 King's Bench Walk, Temple].

1796. Motor vehicles—loss of use—credit hire charges—reasonableness

T was involved in a road traffic accident caused by the negligence of S on August 6, 1995, in which his vehicle was written off. T hired a vehicle similar to his own in order to continue to be able to get to work. T requested inspection of his vehicle via his solicitors on August 16, 1995 and a net valuation of £225 was confirmed in writing on September 14, 1995, following three reminders from his solicitors on August 25, August 30 and September 15, 1995 that T was hiring a vehicle on a credit hire basis. The cheque was received by T on or about September 25, 1995 and the hire vehicle returned. Hire charges amounted to £1,935 and a payment into court was made on July 11, 1996 in the sum of £500. T stated that he had never received the hire invoices but that he had signed some form of document. A copy of the hire agreement was not adduced as evidence.

Held, that T had fully mitigated his losses and had been entirely reasonable in hiring an alternative vehicle on a credit hire basis. The period of hire was entirely reasonable in view of the reminders sent by T's solicitors to S's insurers to make payment in respect of T's vehicle losses as T was continuing to hire on a credit hire basis. T was liable to pay credit hire charges although he had never actually received the hire invoices, as his name was on the invoices and he had signed a rental agreement/delivery note which was adduced as evidence. It was implied from this signed document that there would be a charge for the vehicle for which T would ultimately be responsible. Car hire was payable in full in the sum of £1,935. T was also awarded £75 for loss of use and general inconvenience.

THOMPSON v. STONE, February 27, 1997, H.H.J. Elystan Morgan, CC (Macclesfield). [*Ex rel.* Thorneycroft & Co, Solicitors, 27 Park Street, Macclesfield].

1797. Motor vehicles—loss of use—credit hire charges—mitigation of loss—charges incurred by taxi driver

On December 2, 1995 N's taxi, whilst carrying W, was written off in a road traffic accident caused by the negligence of F. N hired a plated credit hire vehicle in order to continue his employment as a taxi driver. N requested an interim payment for the write off value of his vehicle on January 20, 1996. Legal proceedings were commenced on February 14, 1996. F did not file a defence and interlocutory judgment was obtained on March 15, 1996. The assessment of damages was listed for April 25, 1996. F did not make an interim payment for N's vehicle and hire charges continued up to the date of assessment. F's solicitors made a payment into court but failed to attend the assessment of damages hearing and N was awarded £900 for the write off value of his vehicle, storage and recovery charges of £602, general inconvenience of £200 and credit hire charges to the date of assessment of £6,850 plus an additional sum of £1,100 to allow for payment by insurers. The total award for special damages including interest was £9,676. W sustained a whiplash type injury. He was examined on December 14, 1995 and the report indicated a full recovery would be made between six and nine months from the date of examination. Damages were assessed at £2,000 with interest at £7. On April 26, 1996 F's solicitors issued an application to set aside the award made on April 25, 1996 due to their nonattendance. N requested that an interim payment be made for the write off value of the vehicle as N continued to hire. On June 17, 1996, F was successful in having the respective awards set aside. It was also ordered that F make an interim payment to N for the value of his vehicle. The interim payment was received on July 2, 1996 for the value of N's vehicle and the hire finished on July 5, 1996. The hire charges had increased to a figure of £10,800. The case was relisted for hearing on September 23, 1996.

Held, that N had a duty to mitigate his loss and replace his vehicle if he had the money available. He had hired a plated vehicle instead of facing enforced unemployment for him and the second plaintiff. F had made no payment for the vehicle except under order. F's insurers had the power to bring the hire to an end but instead of making a payment, they attempted to have the case reheard which resulted in more hiring and more costs that insurers knew about. Car hire was payable in full at £10,800. Storage and recovery charges at £602. Total loss value of vehicle of £900. General inconvenience of £100. Total award for N of £12,427 including interest. W's claim was assessed at £2,000 with interest of £23.

NICHOLSON & WARD v. FLEMING, September 23, 1996, District Judge Duerden, CC (Bury). [*Ex rel.* Carl Chapman & Co, Solicitors, 20/22 Bowkers Row, Nelson Square, Bolton].

1798. Motor vehicles—loss of use—credit hire charges—recoverability

R claimed £2,082 being the credit hire charges for a replacement vehicle incurred following an accident on September 2, 1996. R hired a replacement vehicle for a total of 47 days, split into two periods around R's holiday. K contended that the period of hire was too long, that the car should have been hired at a weekly rate rather than a daily rate of £36 and that the full amount of the car hire should not be awarded because it was out of proportion to the value of R's vehicle which was only worth £900.

Held, allowing R's claim, that K's argument should be rejected on all three submissions. In particular, R had indicated her concern about the cost of the hire to K's insurers, who had failed to inspect her vehicle promptly but had instead "dithered", *Allen v. Allanson* [1996] 1 C.L.Y. 2147, *Whyte v. Brown* [1996] 1 C.L.Y. 2152, *Powell v. Linch* [1996] 1 C.L.Y. 2153, *Jones v. Ward* [1996] 1 C.L.Y. 2144, *Zubair v. Younis* [1995] 1 C.L.Y. 1625, *Squires v. Automobile Assurance* [1994] C.L.Y. 1497, *Kalinowski v. Foxon* [1994] C.L.Y. 1498 considered.

RICHARDSON v. KELLY, January 27, 1997, District Judge Tilbury, CC (Wandsworth). [*Ex rel.* David McIlroy, Barrister, Chambers of Michael Parroy Q.C., 3 Paper Buildings, Temple].

1799. Motor vehicles—loss of use—heads of claim

As a result of a road traffic accident P's convertible Volkswagen car was written off. P brought an action seeking to recover: the value of the car as agreed with her insurers, the additional value of that car on the open market, the insurance policy excess, the cost of hiring a replacement vehicle for the month before she was able to identify and purchase an equivalent car to the one written off, the loss of the benefit of part of her road fund licence on the car written off, the cost of petrol expended in going to garages to see cars with a view to purchasing them, the cost of taxi fares during a period when she had neither a hire car or a new car, the cost of an RAC inspection on the car that she eventually bought, and the cost of fitting an alarm to the new vehicle, and miscellaneous expenses, such as telephone calls and postage.

Held, allowing P's claim that all the heads of claim were reasonable, with the exception of the additional value of the car on the open market, which failed for want of an independent engineer's report or a letter from a garage indicating that an equivalent vehicle could not be purchased for less than the amount claimed. The hire charges of £30 per day plus £4 CDW plus VAT were not unreasonable charges, on a credit hire basis, for a medium sized hire car. The RAC inspection fee was recoverable given that P had had the security of buying her original car from a main dealer whereas the replacement car was not so bought. The cost of the new alarm was also reasonable given that the original car had had an alarm and it was a term of her insurance policy that the car should have an alarm. Damages were assessed at £6,682, plus interest of £341.

PALMER v. DUESTER, June 19, 1997, District Judge Goodridge, CC (Kingston-upon-Thames). [*Ex rel.* David McIlroy, Barrister, Chambers of Michael Parroy Q.C., 3 Paper Buildings, Temple].

1800. Motor vehicles—loss of use—hire charges

Following a road traffic accident on February 14, 1996 a valuation was received on February 20, 1996 but no cheque was forthcoming from H's insurance company. Proceedings were issued on April 9, 1996 and a defence was filed on April 18, 1996. The matter proceeded to trial and B was awarded damages. B's claim was for pre-accident value of the motor vehicle of £1,200, hire of an alternative vehicle of

£1,340 together with a miscellaneous expenses claim. B also claimed for loss of use of his vehicle for 34 weeks and two days.

Held, that inconvenience and loss of use would be awarded at the rate of £50 per week. The total award for the loss of use and inconvenience was £1,700 together with pre-accident value, hire and miscellaneous expenses.

BATES v. HORTON, November 8, 1996, Deputy District Judge Frost, CC (Birkenhead). [*Ex rel.* Michael W Halsall, Solicitors, 2 The Parks, Newton-le-Willows].

1801. Motor vehicles–loss of use–hire charges

On November 10, 1995 B and M were involved in a road traffic accident as a result of which B's car was unusable. B was able to hire a car from November 14, 1995 until December 8, 1995. Thereafter B was without a car until January 16, 1996 when his car was repaired and returned to him.

Held, that (1) B was a particularly unfortunate plaintiff from M's point of view in that B's children were asthmatic. The children had suffered from and were susceptible to terrifying attacks. Such attacks could occur at any time. Had such an attack occurred, taxis or other transport might not have been available. Although no such incident actually occurred in the period; B and his wife were extremely anxious; (2) B usually visited his mother and family several times a week. There was no direct bus route. Consequently, he made visits less frequently than usual, and (3) B was greatly inconvenienced in shopping generally and in Christmas shopping particularly. The judge held that the claim for loss of use of the car should be considered for three periods: (1) On November 11, 1995 B moved house. He did so without the assistance of professional removal men. Rather, he hired a van for that day and received assistance from his brother who also made his car available. The accident could not have occurred at a more inconvenient time. Even with professional assistance, any person moving is in desperate need of a car. That day should be treated as an isolated matter, general damages of £100 were awarded; (2) from November 12 until November 14, 1995. It was inevitable that immediately after moving, the need for a car was great, general damages of £15 per day making a total of £45 were awarded, and (3) from December 8, 1995 until January 16, 1996, the judge awarded damages at the rate of £90 per week. The period was treated as one of five weeks.

BROWNLEE v. MOORE, November 27, 1996, District Judge Evans, CC (Hull). [*Ex rel.* Nicholas Hill, Barrister, 6 Park Square, Leeds].

1802. Motor vehicles–loss of use–hire charges

The claim for damages arose out of a road traffic accident that occurred on December 10, 1995. Interlocutory judgment for damages to be assessed and costs was entered on August 16, 1996. The vehicle concerned was written off and the first plaintiff was given judgment in the sum of £1,825 representing the pre-accident value less salvage. The first plaintiff was insured under a third party only policy and gave evidence that impecuniosity had prevented him from replacing the vehicle. The family had another vehicle but it was unreliable and was only used in emergencies. The first plaintiff suffered from osteoarthritis and needed a vehicle for shopping, going to the doctors, taking his son to his shiftwork and for getting about generally as public transport was not available where they lived. The second plaintiff had suffered a flexion/extension injury to the neck and an associated sending sprain to the lower spinal anatomy. He was absent from work for five weeks as a result of the injury. His neck was sore, stiff and painful and he was treated with physiotherapy. He had recovered completely seven months after the accident.

Held, that the first plaintiff be awarded £40 a week loss of use up to the end of the month in which interlocutory judgment was entered. He was awarded £1,360 loss of use; 31 weeks at £40 a week. He was also awarded £906 for hire charges incurred over a three week and four day period immediately after the accident. The second plaintiff was awarded £1,250 for his injuries, a figure agreed between counsel which the judge endorsed as having been the figure he had noted down, and £327 for loss of earnings.

WHEELAN & WHEELAN v. HUGHES, November 14, 1996, District Judge Harris, CC (Liverpool). [*Ex rel.* Rebecca Bensted, Barrister, Bracton Chambers, 95a Chancery Lane].

1803. **Motor vehicles–loss of use–hire charges–car hire offered by insurance company–no evidence that plaintiff had any residual liability–costs of hire recoverable**

Following a road traffic accident which rendered his car unusable, P was offered a car through his brokers. The car was made available by a company called 3 Arrows Hire. A copy of a document headed "car rental agreement" was before the court, but although that document referred to terms and conditions overleaf, those terms and conditions were not available at the hearing. K applied to have the award set aside on the ground that there was not sufficient evidence at the arbitration to establish whether or not P would have to pay the car hire charges if K's insurers did not.

Held, setting aside the award, that the court had to look at the commercial reality of the situation. It was overwhelmingly clear that the car rental agreement was one for which a charge was to be levied. The judge obtained little assistance from *Hanna v. Prophet* [1995] 1 C.L.Y. 1617 but felt that, although the remarks of the Court of Appeal in *Giles v. Thompson* [1993] 3 All E.R. 321, [1993] C.L.Y. 1405 were obiter, it was a powerful court, and he ought to pay great attention to them, notwithstanding Lord Mustill's reluctance to become involved in this issue on the appeal to the House of Lords. K was arguing that in the absence of positive proof that P was personally liable on a car hire agreement then K could escape liability. This was exactly the sort of windfall which the Master of the Rolls had in mind. Following *Giles v. Thompson*, even in the absence of evidence as to whether P would have to pay if K did not, P was still entitled to recover the car hire charges.

PETROU v. KUTI, April 8, 1997, H.H.J. Reynolds, CC (Central London). [*Ex rel.* Lana Wood, Barrister, 3 Paper Buildings, Temple].

1804. **Motor vehicles–loss of use–hire charges–delay by insurers–reasonable period of time for hire charges**

B was involved in an accident on December 14, 1995 in which his car was written off. He was comprehensively insured. N admitted liability. B could not afford to repair his vehicle until the settlement arrived. B needed a vehicle for work and hired a replacement. His insurers made an offer which B claimed was too low. There followed an exchange of correspondence which resulted in the insurer agreeing with B's valuation and increasing their offer by £400. B received his settlement cheque on February 16, 1996, nine weeks after the accident.

Held, that nine weeks was an excessively long period of time for the insurance company to settle the claim and that N was not liable for all the hire charges. The district judge added that six weeks was a reasonable period for the insurance company to settle the claim and he added a further week because of the Christmas break.

BUTLER v. NORTON, July 8, 1997, District Judge Wade, CC (Gloucester). [*Ex rel.* Lyons Davidson Solicitors, Bridge House, 48-52 Baldwin Street, Bristol].

1805. **Motor vehicles–loss of use–hire charges–delay to repairs caused by plaintiff's insurers**

C was involved in a road traffic accident with D on November 16, 1996, which rendered his vehicle undriveable. Liability was not disputed by D. C contacted his own insurance company, P, to advise them that his vehicle was available for inspection under his positive comprehensive insurance, at his local garage, in whom he had confidence and five years of satisfactory experience, and forwarded an estimate. He required an alternative for the period of repairs and hired a car at a daily rate of £37 including VAT upon a credit hire basis. C was then telephoned by P, who advised of the availability of an authorised repairer in his area, and requested that he remove his vehicle to that repairer as soon as possible at which time he would be given a replacement vehicle for the period of repairs. He did not want his vehicle repaired by any other garage. C refused to move his vehicle, P eventually carried out an inspection at C's local garage, repairs were approved, and carried out straight away. Hire charges of £1,386 were then submitted to D's representatives, who refused to satisfy them upon the basis that the work had been unreasonably delayed and a courtesy car offered for the period of repairs. P refused to admit any responsibility for the delay in repairs.

Held, that C had taken all reasonable steps to inform P of the whereabouts of his vehicle for inspection. There was no contract between C and P requiring him or obliging him to use their authorised repairer. The fact that an alternative vehicle might have been available from the authorised repairer did not mean C's hire charge claim was invalid. C had an obligation to a hire at a reasonable commercial rate, and to have his vehicle repaired at a garage which he trusted. C had not been advised by P that the offer of a courtesy car would in anyway prejudice his claim for those hire charges. Accordingly he was awarded hire charges in full against both D and P's jointly and severally, in the sum of £1,386 together with travel expenses of £135 and fixed costs. P was also ordered to pay the sum of £150 for further costs to C.

COCKBURN v. DAVIES AND PROVIDENT INSURANCE PLC, August 14, 1997, District Judge Tynes, CC (Macclesfield). [*Ex rel.* M Coghlan, Solicitor, Thorneycroft & Co, 27 Park Street, Macclesfield].

1806. Motor vehicles–loss of use–hire charges–reasonableness

A's van was written off as the result of a collision with a stationary vehicle, caused by the negligent driving of H. The van was valued at £950. The third party insurers did not inspect the van at an early stage. A worked as an electrical contractor, a job involving a considerable amount of travelling, and had to hire another vehicle. The hire period lasted for five months, and hire charges of £4,582 were incurred. A's business subsequently failed. The third party insurers suggested that A should have purchased alternative transport and not incurred hire charges of over four times the value of his vehicle, which were way out of proportion given the value of the vehicle and the length of hire. A submitted that he did not have the financial resources to buy another vehicle.

Held, allowing A's claim, that (1) H must take A as he found him. Evidence showed that A could not afford to buy another van, and he could not afford to borrow the money due to a county court judgment against him; (2) the length of hire could be attributed in part to the failure of H to inspect the vehicle and (3) despite the high hire charges it was reasonable in the circumstances to award damages to cover the full hire costs of £4,582, together with £950 as the value of the vehicle, storage charges of £1,287 and £480 loss of earnings in the aftermath of the accident.

ATTRILL v. HOLLEY, July 1, 1996, Deputy District Judge Carr, CC (Hertford). [*Ex rel.* Betesh Partnership, Solicitors, Cardinal House, 20 St Mary's Parsonage, Manchester].

1807. Motor vehicles–loss of use–hire charges–reasonableness

D's claim arose out of a road traffic accident on January 26, 1996. J's insurers arranged for an engineer to examine D's car on January 29, 1996. The engineer deemed the car to be beyond economic repair and valued the loss at £725. On March 5, 1996 J's insurers admitted liability and made a written offer of £725 in full settlement. This offer was accepted on D's behalf by letter dated March 28, 1996. A cheque in settlement was sent to D's solicitors early in April. D was provided with a hire car as her own car was not drivable. The period of hire was from January 31, 1996 until April 15, 1996, the date that D claimed to have received J's cheque in settlement from her solicitors, at a daily cost of £28 plus VAT. Total charges amounted to £2,523 for the 76 days of hire. Proceedings were commenced for the recovery of this sum. D was an unemployed single mother of a five year old child who needed a car to take her child to school, shopping and visiting friends. J conceded that D was entitled to be compensated for the loss of use of her motor car for the period between the date of the road traffic accident and the settlement of the total loss claim. However, J argued that a plaintiff must show that the hire of a replacement car was reasonable in all the circumstances. J referred to a number of reported cases in *Current Law* in which impecunious plaintiffs were awarded damages for loss of use of their car and to the fact that some of the reported cases stated that the plaintiff used their car for business. There was also evidence that D had managed without a car from the time that she returned the hire car in April until she purchased a replacement vehicle in August 1996.

Held, that a plaintiff must show that it was reasonable to hire a car to meet a genuine need. The plaintiff in the instant case had failed to do so. She was awarded £770, being 11 weeks' loss of use at a weekly rate of £70, which the judge declined to reduce in spite of the modest value of the car as he thought that D had suffered additional inconvenience in view of having a young child. J was awarded costs of the hearing as the plaintiff had failed to beat a payment into court in respect of the disputed hire charges.

DEAN v. JOANNA TRADING CO LTD, September 25, 1996, Deputy District Judge Lunt, CC (Weymouth). [*Ex rel.* David McHugh, Barrister, Bracton Chambers, Chancery Lane].

1808. Motor vehicles–loss of use–hire charges–reasonableness

E's taxi was involved in a collision with R's vehicle on September 5, 1995. E hired a plated private hire vehicle, for a period of 202 days from September 6, 1995 to March 25, 1996 at a cost of £49 per day, totalling £9,898. R argued that this was unreasonable given R's insurers had authorised repairs to E's vehicle in the sum of £1,086 on November 22, 1995 following receipt of E's engineer's reports, and E had taken no steps to have his vehicle repaired following receipt of that notification. E's evidence was that he could not be sure of the rate of hire, or whether it had been explained to him, and he was not sure who would be discharging the hire invoice. He had not taken any steps to research the possibility of a loan to repair his vehicle. E had purchased his original vehicle on credit at a cost of £50 per week and had subsequently purchased a further vehicle once the hire vehicle was retracted on March 25, 1996, also on credit.

Held, allowing only three months hire at £49 per day, that the course taken by E was not that of a prudent person nor was the hire reasonable, *British Westinghouse v. Underground Electric Railways* [1912] A.C. 6783 considered. Whilst the court accepted that E had attempted to borrow alternative vehicles without success, he had not considered buying a further vehicle on instalments as he had previously done and it was only when the hire car had been taken back that that was done. An initial hire period was reasonable, but E's failure to ascertain the rate of hire, to consider liability, to consider who was to pay for the hire charges when first hiring, and only giving thought to who was to pay after the hire vehicle was retracted, were all examples of E's failure to act in the matter in which a prudent person in his position would have done. To allow hire charges to accrue of nearly £10,000 was not the reasonable act of a prudent person. Once it was clear to E that money was not forthcoming, E ought to have taken steps to make some enquiries to purchase an alternative vehicle by instalments as he had done previously. E was awarded a total of £5,664 and as he had failed to beat R's payment in, costs were awarded accordingly.

EAST v. WALTER RUSSELL LTD, June 19, 1997, Assistant Recorder Storey, CC (Bury). [*Ex rel.* AS Hughes, Solicitor, Peter Rickson & Partners, 4 Norfolk Street, Manchester].

1809. Motor vehicles–loss of use–hire charges–reasonableness

S claimed £1,317 as credit hire charges for a replacement vehicle incurred following an accident on March 13, 1996. M contended that: (1) the rate of hire was excessive and produced comparable tables of other hire companies to prove this; (2) S should have hired at a weekly rather than daily rate, and (3) S could have afforded an alternative to credit hire.

Held, allowing S's claim in full, that (1) the fact that S could have afforded an alternative does not preclude him from taking advantage of credit hire; (2) there was no evidence to suggest that S knew how long it would take for his car to be repaired and there was therefore no basis to suggest that S should have hired on a weekly rather than daily basis; (3) although the hire charges were at the top of the range for credit hire, they were not so excessive to say that they are not within a commercial rate, and (4) it was for M to show that S had failed to mitigate his loss and M had failed to discharge this burden.

SAVILLE v. MUSTAQ, May 16, 1997, District Judge Ackroyd, CC (Oldham). [*Ex rel.* Graham Leigh Pfeffer & Co, Solicitors, Prestwich, Manchester].

1810. Motor vehicles–loss of use–hire charges–reasonableness

On July 14, 1995 a Mercedes 250D motor vehicle belonging to V was being driven by an employee, the 17 year old son of a director. There was an accident. Thereafter V hired for the same director a BMW 325 for the use of the son in the course of his employment for 12 weeks at £120 per week. Invoices had passed between the companies but there was no evidence of payment.

Held, the first question was reasonable need. The district judge accepted that the company needed to keep a high profile amongst customers and did that by using a prestige car. A broadly equivalent vehicle such as this was reasonable. The comparative quotes supplied by V for prestige vehicles showed the rate charged to be reasonable. Further, the district judge accepted the transaction was genuine. Regardless of payment a liability had accrued between companies.

VAUGHAN TRANSPORT SYSTEMS v. FACKRELL, June 10, 1997, District Judge RL Thomas, CC (Cardiff). [*Ex rel.* Thomas Crowther, Barrister, 30 Park Place, Cardiff].

1811. Motor vehicles–loss of use–mitigation of loss–hire charges–reasonableness

C's Vitara 1.6 vehicle was damaged in a road traffic accident, and taken for repair. C hired an Escort 1.4 as an alternative motor vehicle, incurring a daily charge of £36 plus VAT over a period of 26 days. The hire was conducted and approved by C's insurers under the terms of a pre-existing aftercare agreement. Evidence was heard from C showing that she required the use of the car to take her son to school, to shop and to assist in the running of her business. Evidence was also heard from an expert establishing that the prevailing market price for a hire car of equal standard varied from £18 plus VAT to £30 plus VAT, per day.

Held, that C was not entitled to recover the full cost of hire. C and/or her agents had a duty to mitigate her loss, and were therefore under a duty to hire a vehicle at a competitive market price.

COUCH v. HAINES, April 11, 1996, Recorder Flather Q.C., CC (Milton Keynes). [*Ex rel.* Ben Gow, Pupil Barrister].

1812. Motor vehicles–loss of use–mitigation of loss–impecuniosity of plaintiff

M was involved in a road accident on January 13, 1996 in which M's vehicle sustained substantial damage. The vehicle was repairable at a cost agreed by W's motor engineer of about £2,500. However, M could not afford to pay those charges nor was he in a position to pay them at the date of the trial, 78 weeks afterwards. Evidence was given from M that he needed his vehicle for work and had to rely upon friends and taxis for lifts which often caused him to arrive late and lose a day's earnings. M believed his lack of punctuality lead to his losing his job 30 weeks after the accident. M attended hospital for weekly tests and made weekly visits to see his two children by relying on friends and public transport, the amount of time he could spend with them was substantially reduced. In addition, the loss of use of his car significantly curtailed his social activities; he was unable to visit friends, drive his children to the seaside for weekend trips and do shopping by himself. W argued that M had not mitigated his loss sufficiently either by saving up for another car during the period of 30 weeks when he was still in full time employment, or by obtaining a loan with which to purchase another car. W further submitted that any damages awarded for loss of use and inconvenience should reflect the periods when M was in and out of work, because during the 48 weeks of unemployment he would not have been able to afford to use his car anyway.

Held, that (1) in view of the impecunious circumstances of M, it was unreasonable to suggest that he should have mitigated his loss by obtaining a loan with high interest rates to buy another car or to pay for the repairs; (2) there was no reason why M should have saved up and bought a second car when he already owned a car which was waiting to be repaired; there was a limit to the lengths to which the plaintiff should go to mitigate his loss; (3) M was entitled to damages for inconvenience and loss of use for the full period of 78 weeks, and (4) account was taken of the savings made in the general running costs of the car which amounted to £35 to £40 per week and it was decided that since M would not have used the car as much when he was unemployed, different rates of damages should apply for the periods before and after he became unemployed. The following award was made: £1,600 for the 30 weeks when M was working (approximately £53 per week average). £1,600 for the 48 weeks when M was out of work (approximately £33 per week). Total award: £5,806 including repair costs and interest.

ROBSON & MacGREGOR v. WARREN, July 11, 1997, H.H.J. Hutchinson, CC (Bradford). [*Ex rel.* Last & Company, 128 Sunbridge Road, Bradford].

1813. **Motor vehicles—loss of use—mitigation of loss—reasonable not to use student grant or overdraft facility to purchase car**

B's car was involved in a road traffic accident in July 1996. At the time of the accident B was a full time student on a dentistry course in London which lasted for 46 weeks of the year. After she completed her course in June 1997 she obtained employment and received her first monthly salary in September 1997. B was unable to replace the car. It was deemed an economic write off, its pre-accident value being £900 less the salvage value of £75. B had used the car daily for travelling into college, as well as travelling to visit her parents at weekends, and for her social activities. Following the accident B's social life was restricted in the evenings since she was reluctant to use public transport at night in London. B claimed for 57.4 weeks' loss of use and inconvenience at £70 per week, continuing to the date of the hearing for assessment of damages. It was argued on behalf of R that B had failed to mitigate her loss since her bank statements revealed payment of a student grant in January 1997 which had brought her into credit. B having an overdraft facility on her account. Alternatively, it was argued that she could have increased her overdraft and purchased a replacement car before the date of the hearing. B gave evidence that she had not done so because she had not wanted to start her first job in debt.

Held, that general damages were awarded at £60 per week for 57.4 weeks (to the date of the hearing). No future loss was awarded. It was reasonable that B had not used her grant to purchase a replacement car, and B's explanation for not negotiating an increase on her overdraft facility was accepted. The total award was £4,314, including the pre-accident value of the car less salvage, £10 for postage and telephone calls, and interest on the damages for loss of use at 2 per cent. No interest was payable on the damages awarded in respect of the pre-accident value of the car.

BUTTAR v. RAI, September 8, 1997, H.H.J. Butter Q.C., CC (Central London). [*Ex rel.* Emma Smith, Barrister, Old Square Chambers, 1 Verulam Buildings, Gray's Inn].

1814.   Motor vehicles—non pecuniary loss—damages for inconvenience—time spent writing letters to solicitors no matter for damages

P's motor car was damaged by the negligence of D. Liability and quantum were admitted save for general damages as to inconvenience.

Held, that it was possible to distinguish between the aggravation inevitably involved in litigation and other matters. Time spent in writing letters and attending solicitors was not a matter for damages; it was a matter for costs. However, the inconvenience of having to use public transport and the loss of income from taking a day of leave to obtain repair estimates were recoverable in damages. General damages of £50 was awarded for these two heads, *Buckland v. Watts* [1969] 2 All E.R. 985, [1969] C.L.Y. 2820 and *Marley v. Novak* [1996] C.L.Y. 2112 considered; *Taylor v. Browne* [1995] 1 C.L.Y. 1842 distinguished.

O'BRIEN-KING v. PHILLIPS, April 15, 1996, District Judge Moran, CC (Bury). [*Ex rel.* Paul Higgins, Pupil Barrister, Old Colony Hall, Manchester].

1815.   Motor vehicles—repairs to damaged vehicle—compensation for diminution in value—date of assessment

W's employee and B were involved in a car collision. Liability was admitted by V. W's vehicle was a luxury BMW, about one year old, and valued at the time of the accident at £42,000. W asserted, and it was accepted, that despite satisfactory repair, the value of the car had been diminished, by virtue of it being a repaired vehicle, following *Payton v. Brooks* [1974] 1 Lloyd's Rep. 241, [1974] C.L.Y. 841. Further, it was contended that, the incidence of this damage was at the date of the accident, and interest on any damages awarded under this head should run from then, as special damages. B sought to rely on *Brightmore v. Eaton* (Unreported, 1986), and argued that the damages under this head should be assessed at the time of the future sale of the car, and that there ought to be a discount on the award for advance payment.

Held, that notwithstanding the fact that a repair could return the vehicle to substantially the same condition as before, the fact that a vehicle had been repaired as a result of the accident would reduce its value in the marketplace, and this diminished value should be compensated for in damages. Assessment of the effect on the value of the vehicle should take place at the date of the accident, since it was at that time that it became an accident-damaged vehicle, and interest was to be paid from that date as special damages.

WARWICK MOTOR AUCTIONS v. BENNETT, October 14, 1996, Charles Harris Q.C., CC (Warwick). [*Ex rel.* Anthony Verduyn, Barrister, Priory Chambers, 2 Fountain Court, Steelhouse Lane, Birmingham].

1816.   Payment into court—personal injuries compensation—deduction of social security benefit—power to set aside where misunderstanding as to total payment

[Social Security Administration Act 1992 s.93(3)(b).]

B appealed against a decision setting aside an order upholding H's acceptance of their payment into court in satisfaction of damages for personal injury. The DSS had certified £9,200 as the total benefit to be deducted from a payment of compensation under the Social Security Administration Act 1992 s.93(2)(a)(i). B gave notice to H of payment into court of £25,000, with £9,200 certified as withheld under s.93(2)(a)(i), intending to convey to H that a net payment of £15,800 had been paid in, representing £25,000 less the withheld payment. H's solicitors understood this to mean that a total payment of £34,200 would be made, with £25,000 as the net sum paid in, and advised H to accept the payment.

Held, allowing the appeal, that where a compensator opted to obtain a certificate of total benefit before making payment into court, and then withheld the amount certified pursuant to s.93(2)(a)(i), s.93(3)(b) enabled the amount paid into court to be treated as increased by the amount certified. A plaintiff who had been informed of this was deemed to have notice that the payment had been arrived at pursuant to s.93(3)(b) by adding the amount of the certificate to the sum paid into court. Although the court had the power to set aside a payment in where there had been a misunderstanding as to amount, the power would only be exercised sparingly and was limited to occurrences such as typing errors or misconduct, which did not feature in the instant case, *Lambert v. Mainland Market Deliveries Ltd* [1977] 1 W.L.R. 825, [1977] C.L.Y. 446 distinguished.

HOUGHTON v. BRITISH COAL CORP (1997) 35 B.M.L.R. 33, Waite, L.J., CA.

1817. Payment into court—recoupment of benefits

M suffered a whiplash type injury to her neck and back in a road traffic accident on April 14, 1994. Liability was in issue. M was unable to work due to her injuries yet CRU certified "nil" recoupment to May 1996 when her last certificate expired. An interim payment of £10,000 was made in February 1996, and a further payment of £30,000 were both covered by nil certificates. The trial was due to take place on February 10 and 11, 1997. Twenty one days before the trial W paid a further sum of £35,000 into court, which was not covered by any certificate. Meanwhile, settlement was negotiated at £82,500 with no reference to the CRU or the most recent payment in. The subsequent certificate showed benefits of £12,750, accrued since July 1994 to be recouped.

Held, the agreed settlement would be partly satisfied by payment to the Benefits Agency of the amount due to them under the latest certificate. The agreement was silent as to the recoupment of benefits and was made before the last notice of payment into court was received, *Rees v. West Glamorgan CC* [1994] P.I.Q.R. P37, [1993] C.L.Y. 1594 applied.

HI-GROUP PLC AND MALLINSON v. WRIGHT, February 10, 1997, H.H.J. Brunning, CC (Nottingham). [*Ex rel.* Browne Jacobson, Solicitors, 44 Castle Gate, Nottingham].

1818. Personal injuries—holiday booking—loss of enjoyment

G, two days after a road traffic accident, was due to take his wife and six year old daughter for a one week holiday in Tenerife. He decided to go so as not to disappoint his family. He was unable to carry luggage or his daughter as was his custom when she got tired. G and his family considered the holiday to be completely ruined in that he was unable to swim with his daughter and was obliged to spend most of the time on a bed in order to rest his neck. G claimed damages for disappointment and inconvenience as a result of the spoilt holiday. The judge considered the matter firstly as to the diminution in value of the holiday which cost £871 and secondly on the grounds of loss of enjoyment without regard to the cost of the holiday. He stated that if G had cancelled the holiday K would have been liable for its cost irrespective of whether G had travel insurance; in that whilst G had a duty to mitigate his loss he did not have an obligation to claim on an insurance policy.

Held, that the result was much the same whether G cancelled or went on the holiday and that G had received no value from the holiday. *General Damages* in respect of the spoilt holiday were assessed at £1,250, adding interest at two per cent, to reflect the cost of the holiday and the loss of enjoyment by G and his family.

GRAHAM v. KELLY & EAST SURREY NHS TRUST (NO.2), September 18, 1997, Deputy District Judge Arnold, CC (Aldershot & Farnham). [*Ex rel.* David McHugh, Barrister, Bracton Chambers, 95A Chancery Lane, London].

1819. Special damages—mother seriously injured in road accident—no duty of care to child not to injure mother

F appealed against a decision to dismiss his application for B's claim for special damages to be struck out. B, aged two at the date of the accident and seven at the date of the trial, was a passenger in a car involved in a road accident. B's mother, M, who was driving the car at the time, and F collided, both denying liability for the accident. M was seriously injured, and remained in a persistent vegetative state. B issued proceedings claiming damages against F for pain and suffering for his own minor injuries. In addition B claimed special damages arising out of his mother's injuries, in respect of the care provided to B by his paternal grandparents of £30,000, travelling expenses of £1,200 incurred by visiting the mother in hospital and £100 for telephone calls to the hospitals, doctors and solicitors.

Held, allowing the appeal and striking out B's claim, that B was unable to recover the various heads of special damage pleaded. Whilst M would be able to recover the special damages herself in a suit against F, provided she could establish liability against F and subject to any contributory negligence being taken into account to claim for costs incurred for B's care, M would have to show that B's need for care resulted from her injuries. Whilst F owed B and M a duty of care individually not to cause them injury, he did not owe B a duty of care not to cause M injury.

BUCKLEY v. FARROW [1997] P.I.Q.R. Q78, Simon Brown, L.J., CA.

1820. **Special damages—recoupment of benefits from compensation payment— whether loss of non-recoupable benefits paid before accident could be claimed as special damages**

[Social Security Administration Act 1992 s.81 (5), s.82.]

N was involved in a road accident with B in which N sustained personal injuries. At the time N was already in receipt of benefits in respect of a pre-existing back injury. Under the Social Security Administration Act 1992 s.82, the Secretary of State was entitled to recover from the compensation payment made by B a sum equivalent to the benefits paid to N in respect of the accident and, in order to avoid the possibility that the whole of the general damages awarded to him would thus be extinguished, N contended, relying on *Hassall v. Secretary of State for Social Security* [1995] 1 W.L.R. 812, [1995] 1 C.L.Y. 1645, that he could claim as special damages the loss of non recoupable benefits he was receiving before the accident which, but for the accident, he would have continued to receive. That contention was rejected on the basis that it was precluded by s.81 (5), which required the court to disregard any relevant benefits "paid or likely to be paid", and N appealed.

Held, allowing the appeal, that since it was in the "assessment of damages in respect of an accident" that the relevant benefits were to be disregarded, s.81 (5) could not refer to benefits paid to N before the accident and there was no reason why their loss could not be claimed as special damages.

NEAL v. BINGLE, *The Times*, July 24, 1997, Beldam, L.J., CA.

Personal Injuries or Death—Quantum

Details have been received of the following cases in which damages for personal injuries or death were awarded. The classification and sequence of the classified awards follows that adopted in Kemp and Kemp. *The Quantum of Damages*, Vol. 2. Unless there is some statement to the contrary, the age of the applicant is his age at the time of the court hearing. Unless specified the damages are stated on the basis of full liability, *ie.* ignoring any deduction made for contributory negligence. The sum is the total amount of the damages awarded unless otherwise stated. For a cumulative guide to *quantum* of damages cases reported in Current Law during 1997, see the *Quantum* of Damages table. We must stress that we are entirely dependent on the contributor for the accuracy of his or her report; it is impracticable for us independently to check the facts stated to us. We welcome contributions and are most grateful for all the reports received. We would appreciate reports of any alterations to awards noted here, either in, or in anticipation of, appeal.

Paraplegia

1821. Male, aged 31 at the date of the hearing, was injured in 1992 on his way home from a "stag night". A gang of youths started to fight outside a fast food restaurant. L was not involved but as he walked through the crowd he was stabbed and subsequently collapsed. He suffered a severe injury to his spinal cord but not total severance of it. He was left with weakness in both legs due to partial paraparesis with sensory distortion. His right leg was extremely spastic and there was a sensory level at D7. Walking was difficult and running impossible. There was a substantial deprivation and alteration of sensation in both legs, with severe involvement of urinary, bladder, bowel and sexual functions and severe pain in both legs, particularly on the right side. L was and remained profoundly depressed. After being discharged from a spinal unit in 1993, relying on elbow crutches, L's physical mobility had deteriorated due to increased pain and depression and by the date of hearing he had come to spend most of the time using a wheelchair. It was submitted that L was comparable to a paraplegic as although there was not a complete severance of the spinal cord L had many of the physical problems, such as bladder management, associated with paraplegia, similar immobility but in addition considerable pain. L's marriage had broken down and, at the hearing date, he was receiving care from a friend. The Board accepted that L would not work again. The Board approached the award for future nursing care by reference to three periods. It was assumed that the friend would continue to provide care for six years and the multiplicand was based on two-thirds of the commercial rate for that period. For a second six year period the commercial cost of a non-resident carer was allowed and for a final period the multiplicand reflected the cost of a live-in carer. A multiplier of 17 was applied to future losses for life. *General Damages*: £75,000. Past loss of earnings: £43,806. Past nursing care: £20,000. Future loss of earnings; £134,170. Future nursing care: £183,220 (Multiplier of 14). Future cost of occupational aids and equipment: £48,190. Total award (net of benefits): £389,257.

L, *Re*, January 30, 1997, Lord Carlisle, CICB (Manchester). [*Ex rel.* Catherine Leech, Solicitor, Pannone & Partners, Manchester].

Tetraplegia from severe head injury

1822. J was born on March 23, 1984. On May 9, 1984 J sustained a catastrophic head injury. An initial CT scan showed gross cerebral odema and a later scan showed bilateral cerebral infarct and the possibility of a major venous sinus thrombosis. As well as the head injury a skeletal survey showed resolving fractures of the left humerus, the vertex of the skull, seventh and eighth ribs on the left, eighth rib on the right and a new rib fracture on the right. J was treated after initial resuscitation in the Neurosurgical Centre at Addenbrooke's Hospital, Cambridge. The child's natural father was prosecuted for causing the injuries. J was subsequently taken into care and then adopted. As a consequence of his injuries J has significant neurological disability. He is microcephalic (abnormally small head) with severe spastic quadriplegia and gross mental retardation. He is unable to achieve purposeful movement and has a tendency towards epilepsy and hypothermia. In 1988 J had bilateral abductor tenotomies, psosa tenotomies, capsulotomy and anterior obturator neurectomy for dislocated hips. He also had scoliosis. The medical evidence was that there was no reason to suppose that J would not have developed as a normal child had he not sustained the head injuries. Medical evidence suggested that J had a 50 per cent chance of surviving for 10 years from the date of hearing and a 10 per cent chance of surviving for 20 years. On that basis a life expectancy of eight years was contended for and the Board adopted a lifetime multiplier of 6.5. *General Damages*: £80,000 (for pain, suffering and loss of amenity). Past nursing care: £96,000 (provided by the applicant's adopted mother). Future nursing care: £170,400. Physiotherapy: £9,000. Future loss of earnings: £10,000. Accommodation: £20,000. Heating: £8,100. Specialist equipment: £39,541. Miscellaneous: £4,170. Court of Protection fees: £4,120. Total award: £446,821.

J, *Re*, November 11, 1996, Beryl Cooper Q.C. (Chair), CICB. [*Ex rel.* Philip Reeve, Solicitor, The Guildyard, 51 Colegate, Norwich].

Incomplete tetraplegia

1823.   Female, aged 52 at date of assessment, suffered C5/6 fracture dislocation of the spine, with C5 motor complete and sensory incomplete tetraplegia when she was the victim of a mugging and was dragged along some distance by the assailant's car. Life expectancy was 17 to 18 years from date of assessment. The applicant had been employed in a part-time capacity as a school dinner lady and would have worked until 64 years old, but for her injuries. The majority of care up to the date of assessment had been provided by the applicant's husband. Due to his failing health, commercial care was required in the future. The applicant and her husband, who had two adult children, lived together in the family home. The applicant needed re-housing in suitable accommodation. The applicant had been assessed successfully for driving and claimed the future costs of a converted Chrysler Voyager. Note: multipliers were calculated on the basis of 4.5 per cent discount rates. *General Damages*: £110,000. Special damages (net of benefits): £95,825. Awards for future loss and expenses: care: £484,968; accommodation: £67,289; transport: £100,000; private medical treatment: £43,440; earning loss: £27,966. Other future losses (net of benefits deducted): £60,285. Total award: £989,773 (per contributor).

BREWER, *Re*, Date not specified, Judge not applicable, CICB. [*Ex rel.* Bryan Neill, Solicitor, Prince Evans Solicitors, 77 Uxbridge Road, London].

Very severe brain damage

1824.   Male, aged 27 at the date of the accident and aged 30 at the hearing, was attacked and sustained very severe head injuries that resulted in his being totally blind and severely brain damaged. He required 24 hour care but was able to follow basic commands. He had a degree of insight, but was unable to walk and was doubly incontinent. Apart from weekends and holidays S lived in hospital. It was S's family's intention to purchase a large house, pay for 24 hour care and use their energies for provision of love, affection and stimulation. S has a near normal life expectancy. The Board made an interim award. The Board refused to make any award in respect of future care, inviting the applicant to set up his care regime and then re-apply to the Board. The award for Court of Protection costs was also reserved. The Board intimated that consideration was being given to the payment of costs of future care and pension loss through the use of a trust to be set up by the Board. *General Damages*: £150,000. Past loss of earnings: £22,838. Loss of future earnings: £148,575. Award for loss of pension: £20,000. Cost of past care: £38,748. Award for aids and equipment: £48,353. Award for housing costs: £29,000. Special Damages: £15,000. Award for future DIY loss and heating: £18,900. Award for future physiotherapy: £7,650. Total Damages: £498,974.

SHARMA (HARSHED), *Re*, February 12, 1997, Judge not specified, CICB (Birmingham). [*Ex rel.* Richard Langton, Solicitor, Russell Jones & Walker, Birmingham].

Multiple injuries

1825.   Male, aged 19 at the time of the assault and aged 25 at the hearing, was violently attacked sustaining serious head injuries. He suffered a fractured skull, extradural haematoma, intracerebral with generalised brain swelling and post traumatic amnesia lasting approximately four weeks. He was admitted to hospital and required treatment on a ventilator. Further disability included a very short term memory, continual headaches, labyrinthine systems, dizziness and loss of positional joint signs affecting his left hand side. He also started to suffer symptoms of photophobia and developed a peculiar gait requiring physiotherapy treatment. The prognosis was that he would be left with permanently impaired balance and slight weakness to his left side and with a tendency to suffer from recurrent severe headaches. He also had a 15 per cent risk of post traumatic epilepsy and would suffer from agoraphobia causing panic attacks which in turn would disturb his speech and balance. At the time of the assault H was employed as a trainee manager for a cash and carry store. As a result of his injuries H was unable to return to work and was subsequently made redundant. Three years after the accident the applicant was fit to return to gainful employment and found employment as an administration clerk for the Benefits Agency. He had limited prospects with the Agency due to permanent injuries. On appeal the CICB's initial award was increased as follows. *General Damages*: £35,000. Loss of earnings to date: £20,000. Future loss of earnings (multiplicand of £2,200, multiplier of 16): £35,200. *Smith v. Manchester* award: £5,000. No account was taken in the award of the 15 per cent risk of epilepsy and the file was marked to be kept open so that a further application could heard if epilepsy occurred.

HEWLETT, *Re*, January 16, 1997, Judge not specified, CICB. [*Ex rel.* Hodgkinsons, Solicitors, 14 Lumley Avenue, Skegness].

Multiple injuries

1826.   Male, aged 48 at date of assault and 55 at date of hearing, was assaulted in May 1990 whilst celebrating his first job in two years. He was knocked unconscious and suffered pre and post traumatic amnesia. S sustained loss of all eight of his upper, front teeth, suffered three broken ribs, a broken and deformed nose, a five inch scar to his forehead, a two and a half inch scar to his cheek with associated swelling. Permanent numbness ensued in areas immediately surrounding the scars. He also suffered permanent short-term memory loss and a slight reduction in his mental abilities. He occasionally suffered from severe headaches associated with his injuries which were likely to recur for the rest of his life. He underwent significant dental surgery over a 14 month period and had operations to repair his nose and reduce the swelling to his cheek using liposuction to remove fatty tissue. S attempted to return to work on three occasions but found that his memory loss and mental impairment made working almost impossible. This was confirmed by a psychiatrist who assessed him as being virtually unemployable as a result of his continuing symptoms. *General Damages*: £17,500. Award for handicap on the labour market: £7,000 (this award was lower than it otherwise would have been because S had been diagnosed as suffering from unrelated inoperable lung cancer in January 1997). Award for necessary dental surgery: £5,500. Total award: £30,000.

SMITH (BRYNMOR), *Re*, August 19, 1997, D Hollis Q.C., CICB (Birmingham). [*Ex rel.* Glyn R Samuel, Barrister, No.7 Fountain Court, Birmingham].

Multiple injuries

1827.   Female, W, aged 55 at the date of the accident in December 1992 and aged 59 at the date of trial, fell heavily after being directed to sit on a stool with castors when her eyesight was affected by newly fitted contact lenses. W had suffered severe rheumatoid arthritis and had undergone many operations including joint replacements of her right ankle, knees and fingers. She was originally right hand dominant but had become left hand dominant because of her disability. W suffered a strain to her lower back causing painful symptoms and limiting her ability to bend. She wore a corset for 18 months after the accident. She suffered a rotator cuff injury to her left shoulder causing painful symptoms and stiffness. The back and shoulder symptoms were found to be permanent. She continued to have injections of steroids and anaesthetic for these symptoms from time to time. W also suffered a bruising injury to her left shin which ulcerated. The wound was dressed at her GP's twice a week until twenty months after the accident when she underwent a skin graft. The operation was partially successful but another ulcer appeared and she was admitted to hospital for 15 days to give the ulcer an opportunity to heal. The wound eventually healed in March 1996, three years four months after the accident, but the site of the injury remained permanently vulnerable. The wound, ulceration and treatment left unsightly scars on the lower third of W's left leg. W's hobby of gardening and her ability to do housework was limited by the accident. The judge found that W's pre-existng condition made the injuries more significant for her and attracted a higher award than would otherwise be the case. *General Damages*: £13,500 for pain, suffering and loss of amenity. Award for past unpaid care provided by husband: £6,380. Award for future unpaid care: £11,680. Total award: £38,718.

WARD v. LENSCRAFTERS EC CORP, May 8, 1997, H.H.J. Lloyd, CC (Brighton). [*Ex rel.* Gordon Dawes, Barrister, Goldsmith Building, Temple].

Multiple injuries

1828. Male, aged 26 at the time of the road traffic accident and aged 33 at the date of the trial, was a pillion passenger on a motorcycle which went out of control. He sustained multiple injuries which included injuries to right ankle with an avulsion fracture from lateral border of right talus and severe soft tissue injuries; fractures of proximal and distal phalanges of right big toe involving interphalangeal joint; compound fracture of proximal phalanx of right ring finger; laceration of right forearm leaving defect in deep fascia causing muscle to bulge; laceration over hypothenar eminence of right hand. He was in hospital for 12 days. Kirschnir wire was used to immobilise the fracture of right ring finger and was removed after a month. It was not until two months after the accident that the avulsion fracture of the right talus was discovered and walking plaster was applied to the right lower leg for a further month. He was unable to return to work as a heavy goods vehicle driver for six months. The award for future loss of earnings reflected likely periods of time off work due to continuing pain in the right ankle. It was based on a multiplicand of £3,000 rising to £5,000. *General Damages*: £12,500. Special Damages: £6,719. Award for future loss of earnings (multiplicand of £3,000 per annum, multiplier of 11 and multiplicand of £5,000, multiplier of 2) (taking discount of 4.5 per cent and additional discount in accordance with Court of Appeal decisions in *Thomas v. Brighton HA* and *Page v. Sheerness Steel*): £43,000. Additional award for general disadvantage on labour market: £5,000.

PETERS v. ROBINSON, January 27, 1997, Smith, J., QBD. [*Ex rel.* Frank R Moat, Barrister, 3 Pump Court, Temple].

Multiple injuries

1829. Male, Royal Air Force bomb disposal instructor, right handed, aged 38 at date of accident and 43 at date of trial, was travelling over a firing range in the back of a lorry when it encountered soft sand pocket and stopped abruptly. W was thrown against back of cab. He suffered immediate pain in chest and shoulder and breathing difficulty. Taken to hospital by ambulance, during which Oxygen administered. W suffered a fracture to distal third of right clavicle, with disruption of acromio-clavicular joint, torn shoulder muscles, minor head injury, lateral whiplash, bruised and swollen ankle, shoulder injury caused severe initial pain with 80 per cent movement restriction, with the right arm in a sling for eight weeks. Recovered almost full range of movement after four months but with continuing pain. Unsatisfactory healing of clavicle interfered with rotator cuff muscles. Sleep was disturbed two to three times per week for up to four years after accident at which time W underwent remedial surgery. Post-operatively, his arm was in a sling for four weeks, with a further two months pain and soreness. However, the operation allowed almost total recovery. The chest injury resulted in bruising and constant severe pain for about four days and breathing returned to normal in about three weeks. Head, bruised mastoid bone, which subsided after about one month with likelihood of some permanent residual tenderness. The neck resulted in the acceleration, by five years a pre-existing latent cervical spondylosis.W walked with a limp for five to six weeks and some minor discomfort was likely to persist indefinitely. W exhibited significant symptoms of depression for two years after the accident, some anxiety and shortness of temper persisting to date of trial. He left the Royal Air Force voluntarily and obtained employment as a security patrol guard but discontinued when the introduction of static duties caused aches and pains to surface. *General Damages*: £10,750 (for pain and loss of amenity). Award for handicap on the labour market: £2,000. Agreed special damages: £2,150. Total award: £14,900.

WRIGHT v. SERCO LTD, October 14, 1996, H.H. Judge Cottle. [*Ex rel.* Steven Ball, Barrister, 11 Old Square, Lincolns Inn].

Multiple injuries

1830. Male, aged 26 at the time of the incident and aged 29 at the time of the hearing, was stabbed with a 17 centimetre kebab skewer in the back which went through the skin causing a pneumothorax, through the left kidney, behind the pancreas, through the left renal artery, through the posterior wall of the aorta which it virtually transected and through the medial posterior aspect of the interior vena cava. A total of 44 units of blood was given. Post operatively C had a difficult and slow recovery phase which was characterised by sepsis, coagulopathy, chest infections, and renal failure which required dialysis. He also required assisted ventilation and suffered two Grand Mal epileptic fits. He was also diagnosed as suffering from post traumatic stress disorder, the prognosis for which was guarded. By the date of the hearing C had made a full recovery and was left with some discomfort when bending or lifting. His psychiatric condition had continued although with some slight improvement. *General Damages*: £10,000.

CARLIN, *Re*, November 6, 1996, R Macdonald Q.C., CICB (London). [*Ex rel.* Philip Martin, Barrister].

Multiple injuries

1831. On October 29, 1989 D sustained a catastrophic head injury as a pedestrian when struck by G's vehicle. D had no recollection of the accident and was incapable of giving instructions. The police report was extremely brief and did not even identify the exact scene of the accident. Solicitors were instructed in 1989 and legal aid was initially refused because of lack of reasonable prospects of success. A limited certificate was eventually granted to investigate the matter and a writ issued in June 1990. In response to interrogatories, G admitted he did not see D before the collision. Thereafter an offer to settle liability was received on a 50:50 per cent basis accepted and approved by the court in December 1992. The case was then prepared on quantum. D, aged 34 at the date of trial, sustained a very severe head injury and required 24 hour care which was provided by a residential home specialising in rehabilitation of patients with head injury. D had very limited needs outside the care provided by the home. Significant heads of claim were: past loss of earnings: £47,171. Past care: nil. Future care: £992,370. Future loss of earnings: £165,543. Court of Protection fees: £69,300. G's counter schedule put D to strict proof concerning past loss of earnings alleging that D was employed in the building trade as a casual labourer, upon which basis G sought to reduce the multiplier and multiplicand. With regard to future care, the counter schedule contended that D should use his damages to establish a trust, to preserve his entitlement to be maintained at the residential home at public expense, pursuant to the Income Support (General) Regulations 1987. Further, that this argument was particularly forceful because of the reduction by 50 per cent for contributory negligence in respect of the final award. In that event the future care claim was extinguished. This latter argument was not accepted by D's advisers. A round table conference took place in the matter in October 1994 in an attempt to settle the matter and an offer of £375,000 was rejected. The money was subsequently paid into court.

On February 5, 1995 the court approved a settlement of £425,000. D had very modest needs outside the residential care. D's advisers harboured concerns as to his long term security in the residential home at a future date when his fund would be exhausted, estimated to be within 10 years. The balance of the settlement monies were paid into court and the matter adjourned to investigate the possibilities of a structured settlement and/or a special needs trust. D's residential care costs were met approximately 25 per cent from income support, the balance of 75 per cent from the local authority, who in turn recouped half from the Health Authority. The position was clear under the Income Support Regulations. Negotiations were entered into with the local authority by which agreement was reached that provided the income from the structured settlement was paid to the local authority, they would continue to support D in the residential home for the duration of his life. In April 1996 the detailed financial arrangements were approved by the court whereby £375,000 was placed in a structured settlement and the balance of £35,000 in a special needs trust.

DOYLE v. GIBBONS, Date not specified, Judge not specified. [*Ex rel.* Carol Jackson, Solicitor, Pannone & Partners, Solicitors, 123 Deansgate, Manchester].

Head

1832.   O, aged 53 at the time of the accident, sustained an injury in the course of his employment when a heavy metal plate struck him above his left eye. BCH were found to be liable and general damages of £4,400 were awarded, total award £4,400 O. B appealed on the issue of quantum.

Held, allowing the appeal, that as the judge took the view that O had recovered from all physical symptoms five months after the accident at the very latest, an award of £4,000 was excessive. *General Damages*: £1000.

OXLEY v. BCH LTD, Trans. Ref: CCRTF 96/1084 C, July 10, 1997, Swinton Thomas, L.J., CA.

Brain and skull

1833.   F, aged 36 at the date of the assault in October 1991 and 41 at the date of the hearing, was violently attacked with an iron bar, sustaining serious head injuries and a fracture to the right elbow. He suffered a fractured skull, developing a massive blood clot which required evacuation, and remained unconscious for two weeks. F suffered weakness, incoordination and spasms of all four limbs, poor balance, severely limited mobility. The fracture to his right elbow was fixed in flexion surgery, but he was rendered unable to carry anything. Further disabilities included deafness in the right ear, frequency and urgency of micturition, inability to ejaculate properly, slurred and slow speech, regular and persistent headaches, severe pain in his lower back and right arm, and scarring from the initial injury and surgery. F also suffered a severe personality change and behavioural problems, permanent reduction in intellectual level and markedly reduced powers of concentration, such that he required supervision for the daily acts of living. He was however, capable of managing his own affairs. F has an ongoing chance of developing epilepsy assessed at six per cent. Multipliers of 10 (earnings) and 14 (lifetime) were assessed on a conventional basis following the decision of the Court of Appeal in *Wells v. Wells* [1996] C.L.Y. 2125 and an annual sum was claimed for the cost of future investment advice. The award was as follows: *General Damages*: £90,000. Awards for past losses: care: £3,000; aids and equipment: £3,410; loss of earnings £40,000; (net state benefits of £10,177 and ordinary living expenses assessed at £15,000 were deducted from these figures). Awards for future losses: earnings (multiplier 10): £110,000; care: 1st year £10,000; care: years following (multiplicand £36,500, multiplier 13) £474,500; accommodation: £72,718; aids and equipment: £20,000; annual depreciation: £29,150; maintenance of equipment (14 x 250): £3,500; cost of motor vehicle: (lump sum) £40,000; holidays (multiplicand £3,000, multiplier 14): £42,000; medical expenses: £4,500; investment advice: £10,000; Total Award: £927,601.

FULL, *Re*, October 31, 1996, J Crowley Q.C., CICB (Sale). [*Ex rel.* Hugh Potter, Solicitor, Perkins & Company, 1 King Street, Manchester].

Brain and skull

1834. Female baby, aged one month at date of assault and 11 1/4 years at date of hearing, suffered an assault by her mother causing skull fractures and severe brain damage, fractured right humerus and left radius. N was subsequently put into foster care and then adopted at age 20 months. N claimed damages including the cost of care by her adoptive parents for life. Profound mental handicap and severe physical handicaps. No voluntary trunk control so unable to stand, sit unaided or crawl. Unable to feed or toilet herself. Doubly incontinent. Mental age of 1-2 at date of hearing. Could say yes and no but little more. Suffered from epilepsy, partially controlled by drugs, but many minor fits each day. Vision partially reduced and hearing substantially impaired. Sleep disturbed frequently each night. Hypothermic. Required 24 hour care. Adoptive parents living in cramped accommodation and seeking to move to specially adapted accommodation in warmer part of the country. Life expectancy reduced to perhaps age 22. *General Damages*: £85,000 for pain, suffering and loss of amenity. Past care: £45,350 (net of deduction for adoption allowance). Other special damage: £24,868. Future care: £90,000 (multiplier 6 split parental care 1.5, mixed care 3.5, paid care (1)). Future loss of earnings: £15,000 (from age 19, multiplier, 1.5). Future cost of accommodation: £40,000 (split between (1) alterations not increasing capital value and (2) alterations increasing capital value awarded on *Roberts v. Johnson* basis). Future cost of therapy and education: £20,100. Future domestic expenses: £14,828. Future cost of transport and holidays: £18,920. Total award (after deduction for benefits): £308,746.

NICHOLLS, *Re*, September 20, 1996, Judge not specified, CICB (London). [*Ex rel.* Andrew Ritchie, Barrister, Goldsmith Building, Temple].

Brain and skull

1835. Male, aged 31 at the date of assault and aged 37 at the date of the hearing, suffered a severe blow to the head. He lost consciousness for about 10 minutes and was subsequently taken to hospital where he remained for five days until he discharged himself. Friends and family noticed that he had suffered a behavioural change and was uncharacteristically aggressive; a condition of acquired anti-social personality. R was unable to recollect anything about the assault and suffered post traumatic amnesia for between one and two weeks. He suffered a permanent loss to his sense of smell and retained only an elemental sense of taste. R continued to suffer from headaches which lasted for 80 per cent of the day and displayed some features consistent with a psychogenic pain disorder and suffered from a depression of some severity, was tense, miserable and angry. He also suffered from an intellectual impairment as a result of the injury and was unable to return to his previous employment as an electrician. *General Damages*: £70,000. Past loss of earnings: £53,370. Future loss of earnings (multiplier 11): £99,000. Future care (multiplier 15): £15,000. Total award: £227,870.

ROBERTS, *Re*, February 27, 1997, M Churchouse, CICB (London). [*Ex rel.* Hefin Rees, Barrister, 4 Kings Bench Walk, Temple].

Brain and skull

1836. Male, aged 24 at the date of the hearing, was the victim of an attack outside a nightclub in Sheffield following which he fell approximately 15 feet over a subway bridge onto the pavement below. A was admitted to hospital with a severe skull fracture and contusion of the brain. He went on to make a remarkable recovery surprising his treating doctors. However, A was rendered permanently deaf in his right ear and suffered from tinnitus, a full loss of smell and partial loss of taste. A returned to work for the Royal Bank of Scotland part time in April 1994 and full time in July 1994. He was paid by his employer throughout the time he was absent from work. A claimed that as a result of his injuries he would be unable to achieve the seniority which he would have attained at work but for the assault. A neuropsychological report commented that A presented very well on superficial contact and that many people meeting A would believe that he had nothing wrong with him at all. Despite having been able to return to work at his pre-accident level, A had suffered various subtle neurological deficits causing an impairment of his memory and personality changes. *General Damages*: £60,000. *Smith v. Manchester* award: £60,000. Special Damages: £10,000. Total award: £130,000.

IVES, *Re*, December 10, 1996, Judge not specified, CICB (London). [*Ex rel.* Evill and Coleman, Solicitors, London].

Brain and skull

1837.　　Male soldier, aged 17 at the date of the attack and aged 25 at the date of the trial, sustained a serious head injury and moderate brain damage after being struck on the head with a heavy object. J maintained consciousness throughout the attack. He suffered a depressed fracture to the skull, dural tear and lacerations to the head and lip. During the course of an operation the depressed fracture was elevated, the dural tear repaired and the lacerations sutured. He spent a number of weeks in hospital and was invalided out of the army six months later. He suffered continuing symptoms of post concussional syndrome including headaches, bouts of vertigo and dizziness with occasional blackouts. There were more permanent effects to concentration and memory impairment, with a small risk of development of epilepsy. J came from a service family with grandfather, father and uncle all having done life service in the forces. If J had completed his period of service in the Royal Engineers he would have left the army in his late twenties with a skill or trade. However, the attack left him able to undertake only semi-skilled or manual employment. The board ordered that the papers were not to be destroyed to cater for the possibility of the onset of epilepsy. *General Damages*: £25,000. Past loss of earnings: £48,997. Future loss of earnings: £120,000. Total award: £193,997.

JOHN (MARK), *Re*, February 18, 1997, Judge not specified, CICB (London). [*Ex rel.* J David Cook, Barrister, Lamb Building, Temple].

Brain and skull

1838.　　Male, aged 30 at date of assault and aged 36 at date of award, was the victim of an unprovoked assault outside a public house in May 1991. Upon admission to hospital he was aggressive and irritable. He sustained bruising around the right eyelid, bilateral black eyes and subconjunctival haemorrhages, a fractured nose, a split upper lip and a fracture of the left temporal parietal bone. An emergency CT scan indicated a left temporal subdural haematoma and also right temporal lobe contusion. S was placed on a ventilator and remained in hospital for some time after the assault and after initially settling became very agitated and noisy and also disorientated in time and space. He was subsequently transferred to the care of a consultant psychiatrist. S suffered a degree of brain damage affecting his personality, cognitive function and behaviour but otherwise made a good recovery from his physical injuries. S became intolerant of noise, could not cope with interference from others whilst he was performing a task and had difficulty in retaining information and concentrating. S suffered from extremely short temper which affected his relationship with his wife and children. Eventually the relationship between S and his wife broke down. S was unable to go outside on his own for some time and although eventually passed fit to drive a car, he had chosen not to do so since the accident. S has been unable to resume his pre-assault hobby of playing golf. *General Damages*: £20,000. Past loss of earnings: £18,000. Future loss of earnings (a multiplier of 10): £52,960. Total damages: £90,960.

STONEMAN, *Re*, February 25, 1997, E Gee (Chairman), CICB (Cardiff). [*Ex rel.* Richard Miller, Barrister, Newport Chambers, Newport].

Epilepsy

1839. Male, aged 43 at the time of the assault and aged 52 at the date of the hearing, suffered a hammer attack to his skull which caused three fractures. He sustained significant dysphasia which left him almost incapable of speech. In addition he developed grand mal epilepsy which was not completely controlled by drugs and led to a major fit approximately once a month. There was also a right sided weakness particularly in the arm. He was able to live independently and could go out unsupervised. He was able to garden, go to the shops and attend a football match. He had no prospect of re-employment having been a successful engineer. It was accepted that there was a need for a care case manager at a relatively low level of input for the future together with care on a basis of approximately four hours a day predominantly in the form of supervision and domestic assistance. *General Damages*: £75,000. Award for future loss of earnings: £168,591 (multiplier 8). Award for past care: £25,000 (by relatives was assessed at approximately two hours per day). Award for cost of future care: £123,500 (multiplicand £9,500, multiplier 13). Award for loss of pension: £45,000. Award for Court of Protection costs: £28,500. Total award: £610,591.

F, *Re*, May 1, 1997, John Cherry Q.C., CICB (London). [*Ex rel.* Frank Burton, Barrister, 12 Kings Bench Walk, Temple].

Epilepsy

1840. Male, aged 20 at the date of the assault and aged 31 at the time of assessment, was assaulted on November 14, 1985 sustaining a depressed left tempero-parietal fracture with epileptic seizures at the time of his admission to hospital. In the acute period following the injury M was unable to speak, could not walk without assistance and required a high level of care. There was gradual improvement with time. By the date of the assessment M was able to talk with only a slight slur in his speech and his epilepsy was well controlled with drugs. M was assessed in 1996 as having very poor problem solving and decision making abilities, impaired abstract thinking, poor ability to make rational interpretations and realistic decisions. His verbal memory was found to be impaired, achieving scores around the bottom five per cent of the population, his ability to suppress distraction from competing stimuli was very poor and his attention span was in the bottom nine per cent of the population. M had no earning capacity save the possibility of therapeutic earnings, but was well supported by his co-habitee in terms of his needs for care. M's epilepsy was well managed and M could manage most of his daily routine tasks if given a modest amount of supervision. Prior to the assault M had had a negligible work history and had only been in employment for a total period of eight months, after leaving school at 16. However, M's family all had reasonable employment records and because of the assessment of M's personality prior to his injuries compensation was awarded for both past and future loss of earnings. *General Damages*: £50,000. Future loss of earnings: £80,000. Past loss of earnings: £40,000. Award for past care: £20,000. Award for future care: £40,000. Past rehabilitation costs: £9,520. Total award (per contributor): £232,520.

McGUFFIE, *Re*, January 14, 1997, Judge not specified, CICB (Liverpool). [*Ex rel.* Gerard Martin, Barrister, Exchange Chambers, Pearl Assurance House, Derby Square, Liverpool].

Psychiatric enuresis

1841. Infant male, aged three and a half at the time of the accident and six and a half at the trial, fell 20 feet from an unguarded window to concrete below. He sustained a chest injury causing bruising and swelling on the right side of the rib cage (with a possible rib fracture). His chest was sore for five days and the swelling and bruising resolved within one week to 10 days. After two weeks G, who had previously controlled his bladder from the age of two, began suffering from nocturnal secondary enuresis, which involved his wetting the bed two or three times every night. His mother suffered post traumatic stress disorder as a result of the accident which significantly reduced her ability to care for him and bring him up. As a result, G began exhibiting an oppositional disorder at home, involving temper tantrums and aggression to his mother and brother. At trial, three years after the accident, the enuresis had diminished to twice per night three or four times per week, but the oppositional disorder had not improved. The prognosis for the enuresis was that improvement would occur as a result of treatment which was due to commence when G was seven years old, and as G grew up. *General Damages*: £4,000.

G (A MINOR) v. LEADSTAY LTD, August 29, 1997, District Judge Stockton, CC (Oldham). [*Ex rel.* Andrew Clark, Barrister, Manchester House Chambers, 18-20 Bridge Street, Manchester, M3 3BZ].

Psychiatric disability after sexual abuse

1842. Male, aged 41 at the date of the hearing had been severely sexually abused between the ages of six years and 12 years by six abusers (masters and headmasters) at three different children's homes. The acts of abuse included indecent assaults regularly over the first few months, then oral sex and masturbation about twice weekly for 18 months and thereafter indecent assaults once every two weeks, oral sex and masturbation and buggery twice a week for two and a half years. He was also physically abused and subjected to emotional and psychological manipulation. The immediate effects included nightmares and poor sleep, guilt, shame, powerlessness, confusion over sexual identity, depression and isolation. After leaving care, AH embarked on a criminal career, the most serious offence leading to nine months' imprisonment. Long term effects included difficulty maintaining relationships. His last relationship broke down after the police came to interview him about the abuse, this resulted in heavy drinking, panic, an assault on his partner, withdrawal from sexual contact and a referral to a psychiatrist at the suggestion of the police. He discharged himself from hospital as he could not tolerate being in a male ward. At the date of the hearing he was experiencing mood swings, guilt and low self-esteem, anxiety, depression, feelings of suicide and distance in family relationships. He had become very dependent on others. He had difficulty dealing with men in authority which had affected his employment record. Psychological evaluation included a diagnosis of severe/chronic post traumatic stress disorder. *General Damages*: £25,000. (AH's award was then reduced by 50 per cent under para.6(c) of the Scheme due to his current and ongoing criminal record).

AH, *Re*, August 13, 1996, Lord Carlisle Q.C., CICB (Liverpool). [*Ex rel.* Aswini Weereratne, Barrister, Doughty Street Chambers, London].

Psychiatric disability after sexual abuse

1843. A female, aged 36 years, was a chronic schizophrenic with a moderate degree of learning disability and suffered from mental health problems. She was systematically raped by a fellow patient in a psychiatric institution. She had developed extreme anxiety, her disturbed behaviour had escalated and she had become incontinent. She had become more antisocial and aggressive. Her psychoanalytic psychotherapist concluded that her mental stability had decreased dramatically as a result of traumatization by the rapes and sexual assaults. She was continually distressed especially when speaking about the incidents in lucid moments. Despite admissions by the assailant, the single member concluded that the applicant had not "suffered personal injury directly attributable to a crime of violence", but she was successful before the full board. *General Damages*: £15,000.

MRR, *Re* (1997) 97(4) Q.R. 5, Judge not applicable, CICB (Manchester).

Psychiatric disability after sexual abuse

1844.   Male, aged 20 at date of assault, a senior aircraftsman in the RAF, was sexually assaulted by a male sergeant. The assault consisted of the assailant taking hold of the victim's arm, attempting to kiss him, putting his hand down the front of the victim's trousers and attempting to put the victim's hand into the assailant's trousers, at which point the victim got away. There was no genital contact. The victim was greatly distressed by the incident. He had suffered from childhood asthma. Two days after the assault and as the probable result of it he had a severe but isolated asthma attack. As a consequence he was downgraded in his military service which had a profound effect on his career prospects. He became depressed and drank excessively. Following a drug overdose he was admitted to hospital and suffered delirium tremens on withdrawing from alcohol. He demonstrated many of the symptoms of post traumatic stress disorder, the symptoms being exacerbated following his being interviewed about the incident by military police on two occasions. There was no evidence as to his likely career prospects had the assault not occurred. There was psychiatric evidence that two and a half years after the assault he had still not got over it completely. *General Damages* (for the assault and its immediate effects including aggravated damages): £2,500. For the psychological consequences: £3,000. Award for loss of career in the RAF: £1,000. Past loss of earnings: £10,111.

JUKES v. RATCLIFF, April 16, 1997, H.H.J. Peppitt Q.C., CC (Canterbury). [*Ex rel.* Giles Eyre, Barrister, 2 Grays Inn Square].

Post traumatic stress

1845.   Female police officer, aged 28 at the date of assault and 34 at the date of assessment was on duty at Wood Green Shopping Centre in 1991 when she was involved in an incident during which she was stabbed several times around the area of her breast. She suffered greatly from symptoms of post traumatic stress disorder which compromised her work performance and her personal life. She had permanent scarring to an area of her body which she regarded as sensitive and very personal, of which she was acutely conscious. She was originally off work and on restricted duties for a period of 11 months. Following her return to full duties she was caught up in the aftermath of an IRA bomb which had gone off several yards from the location where she had been stabbed. The second incident exacerbated her previous symptoms of post traumatic stress disorder. She was unable to cope with her duties as a police officer and was eventually retired on medical grounds due to her post traumatic stress disorder. Prior to the two incidents, she had an excellent work record and had fully intended to complete 30 years of service. By the time of the assessment, her symptoms of post traumatic stress disorder had lessened although she was still anxious about strangers and fearful when travelling in Central London. The prognosis was that she would continue to feel vulnerable and unsafe for the foreseeable future although she was not psychologically impaired from returning to general forms of employment. At the time of assessment, she had taken on part time employment as a childminder, but it was recognised that her earning capacity had been reduced. *General Damages*: £32,500 (including award for loss of congenial employment). Loss of earnings: £16,215. Future loss of earnings: £40,000. Loss of pension: £16,230. Total award: £104,945.

LAWSON, *Re*, February 26, 1997, Judge not specified, CICB. [*Ex rel.* Russell Jones & Walker, Solicitors, 324 Grays Inn Road, London].

Post traumatic stress

1846.   Male, aged 35 at the date of assault and 39 at the date of hearing was a public house manager assaulted with glasses and a bar stool during an affray at his public house. He sustained severe head injuries comprising a compound depressed left frontal fracture, a comminuted fracture of the roof of the left orbit, and a non-displaced fracture of the floor of the left orbit. He also suffered a fracture to the anterior wall of the left and right maxilla. He spent 12 days in hospital and underwent a craniotomy to elevate and reconstruct the depressed fracture. Several permanent plates were inserted. There was marked discolouration and haematoma of the left eye which was closed. He suffered constant headaches, two to three weeks double vision, and severe post traumatic stress for which he underwent six months intensive counselling. There was a 20 per cent risk of epilepsy. He was left with significant cosmetic deformity comprising a permanent four inch scar over the left eyebrow, and a large permanent scar running sideways along the top of his head. This caused his hair to grow in unsightly clumps, making him adopt a completely shaven hairstyle which caused embarrassment. At the time of hearing he continued to suffer headaches almost daily and depression, the latter exacerbated by the breakdown of his marriage. He was previously a successful manager of a large public house but had been unable to work since the assault and was medically retired by his employers. He had undergone a considerable personality change from a confident outgoing person to one who was introverted, nervous, and easily irritable. He had been forced to lead a limited routinely organised lifestyle to minimise stress and social contact. Prior to the hearing his psychologist described him as "still considerably psychologically disabled", and his GP deemed him unlikely to make a full recovery. There was no evidence of brain damage causing any intellectual or memory impairment. *General Damages*: £30,000. Special Damages: £16,700. Future loss of earnings: £119,250 (based on multiplier of 8). Total award: £166,000.

GAMBILL (NO.1), *Re*, August 12, 1997, Lord Carlisle, Q.C., CICB (Liverpool). [*Ex rel.* Christopher J Buckley, Barrister, First National Chambers, 24 Fenwick Street, Liverpool].

Post traumatic stress

1847.   Female, aged 25 at the date of the injury and aged 29 at the date of the hearing, was subject to a violent attack by her estranged husband. She sustained multiple wounds including stab wounds to the head, the back of neck and scalp, lower back, front of the neck, right cheek, right upper breast, several on the abdominal wall, the front and inner aspects of the right thigh, the right forearm, the back of the left hand over the main knuckle joint of the index finger, the flexor aspect of the wrist and a very large laceration on the left forearm shaped like a "Y". A underwent surgery under general anaesthetic which included a laparotomy. A suffered damage to the left ulnar nerve resulting in numbness in the left ring and little fingers causing her left hand to be significantly weaker and clumsier than it was before. A had to be very careful with her left hand because she could burn or cut herself without actually feeling it. Weakness due to the paralysis of the ulnar nerve innervated muscles would not improve significantly. The appearance of the scars troubled A but no further cosmetic surgery was anticipated. After the assault, during which she was certain that she was about to be killed, and which led to the conviction of her husband for attempted murder, she developed post traumatic stress disorder of a severe nature. A had suffered recurring thoughts, nightmares, profound anxiety and social avoidance. Subsequently A developed a moderate depressive illness requiring anti-depressive medication which she was taking at the date of the hearing. She was also taking painkillers for the continuing discomfort in the left arm and wrist. It was doubted whether A would ever recover completely from the trauma and it would take many years before she achieved any resemblance of normality or regain social confidence. Although A was in receipt of benefits at the time of the attack, she had run a guest house with her husband and had performed a range of manual tasks. The injury to her left hand prevented her from performing a number of manual tasks, in consequence of which she had been unable to find work. She was likely to remain permanently at a disadvantage in the open labour market. *General Damages*: £30,000. *Smith v. Manchester* award: £15,000. Total award: £45,000.

ARA, *Re*, February 18, 1997, Judge not specified, CICB (Manchester). [*Ex rel.* Peter E Buckley, Barrister, 5 John Dalton Street, Manchester].

Post traumatic stress

1848. Female, aged 22 at date of incident and 28 at the date of the hearing, was attacked by another woman outside a public house, sustaining stab wounds to the neck, right breast, sternum, lower left rib cage and abdomen, leaving her critically ill. A laporotomy was performed revealing penetrations to liver, spleen and diaphragm which required suturing. Internal bleeding required a chest drain. Post-operative development of collection around spleen was drained percutaneously. W was an in-patient for 23 days; she made a good physical recovery, save for a stitch abscess developing some 15 months later, which was removed under general anaesthetic. Residual symptoms comprised some discomfort on stretching (due to adhesions of scar tissue), breathlessness and a sensation of pins and needles and numbness around the thoracic wound. The stab wound scars were one centimetre in length save that on the abdomen which was long and obvious, stretching vertically from sternum to three to four centimetres below her naval. W was highly conscious of and embarrassed about her scars and felt unable ever again to wear a bikini. Severe psychological effects included constant feelings of apprehension of impending personal harm and, later on, irrational preoccupation about her son dying. W was scared of all public places and, initially, of being left alone in the house. She encountered problems sleeping and awoke from nightmares, sweating and shaking, three or four times each week. Vivid and constant daily flashbacks of the event were triggered by the slightest reminder such as Christmas (the time of the assault) or a fork being stuck into meat. Bouts of deep depression drove her to an overdose suicide attempt. Resultant low self-esteem led to a series of failed relationships, leaving her a single mother of two young children. Post traumatic stress disorder was diagnosed. Improvement would not occur without therapy, which she felt unable to undergo as this involved further recollection of the event. *General Damages*: £22,500.

WATSON v. CICB, January 20, 1997, Judge not specified, CICB (Birmingham). [*Ex rel.* Rupert Boswell, Barrister, No.8 Chambers, Fountain Court, Steelhouse Lane, Birmingham].

Post traumatic stress

1849. Male, aged 57 at the date of the incident in September 1991 and 62 at the date of the assessment, was employed as an estate cleaner with Hackney LBC with an expected retirement date in July, 1999. The incident involved a street mugging in which he sustained minor physical injuries including a cut lip. Two psychiatric reports (one prepared a year after the incident and the other three years after the incident, but two years before the date of assessment) found that C was suffering from post traumatic stress disorder and clinical depression (the depression having worsened in the time between the two reports). The prognosis was poor and the report concluded that even with treatment C was likely to remain anxious and wary, and subject to feelings of depression for the remainder of his life. The report also suggested that C might benefit from cognitive behaviour therapy with an estimated cost of £2,500. The ongoing effect of C's illness included being unusually nervous when outdoors and being reluctant to use public transport. At the date of the hearing, when at home, he continued to suffer occasional sleep disturbance and a severe startled reaction to calls at his door etc. He had been medically retired from work in 1992 and was not likely to work again. He has been assessed by the DSS as being 10 per cent disabled for life due to emotional difficulties resulting from the incident. *General Damages*: £22,500 (for pain, suffering and loss of amenity, including an element for psychiatric treatment if he chose to use the money in that way). Loss of earnings: £24,000.

CROUCHER, *Re*, October 29, 1996, Judge not specified, CICB (London). [*Ex rel.* Barry Smith, Solicitor, OH Parsons & Partners, Sovereign House, 212-224 Shaftesbury Avenue, London].

Post traumatic stress

1850.   Three applicants had been sexually abused whilst living in care in residential homes in the 1970's. They were abused by one master in particular. GB was aged between 13 years and 15 years at the time of the abuse and 32 at the hearing date. He was subjected to acts of indecency, mutual masturbation, oral sex, digital anal penetration, buggery, physical assaults, drugging and psychological and emotional manipulation once or twice a week for three years. Following release from the home, he went through a period of drug and alcohol abuse and committed a number of minor offences. He suffered nightmares, intrusive thoughts, anxiety, depression and suicidal thoughts. GB had suffered difficulty forming relationships with women and had not held down permanent employment since leaving care. RB who was aged 29 at the hearing date, was aged between 10 and 12 when abused three to five times a week over three years. Abuse included buggery, anal penetration using objects, oral sex, masturbation, physical abuse and psychological and emotional manipulation. Since leaving care he had committed a number of offences, the most serious leading to six months in prison. The last offence had occurred more than six years previously. RB complained of dissociation, impotence, flashbacks during sex, difficulties with relationships, panic attacks, short temper and that he had difficulty cooperating with men in authority and in his relationships with his sons. RP was aged 31 at the hearing date and between 13 and 16 when abused. He suffered assault, fondling, masturbation, buggery and oral sex. He had a number of convictions, including buggery and arson, and had served eight years in prison since leaving care. He had suffered nightmares, sexual problems, drug and alcohol abuse, depression and flashbacks and had developed anti-authoritarian attitudes and felt violently towards sex offenders. Since police interviews in 1994 regarding prosecution of the perpetrators, the victims had all suffered exacerbation of mood swings, depression and anxiety. Psychological reports confirmed that all were suffering from severe/chronic post traumatic stress disorder. The effect of the sexual, physical and emotional abuse would be a life long vulnerability. The Board accepted expert psychological evidence that those subjected to sexual abuse were less likely to form stabilising relationships in their early twenties and they were more likely to continue committing petty crime. *General Damages*: £20,000 (each victim). (RP's award was then reduced by 50 per cent under para.6(c) of the Scheme due to his current criminal record).

GB, RB AND RP, *Re* (1997) 97(1) Q.R. 2, Lord Carlisle Q.C., CICB (Liverpool).

Post traumatic stress

1851.   M was regularly sexually, emotionally and physically abused by her father between the ages of 11 and 21. The sexual abuse included repeated incidents of rape. M missed some schooling and was removed from her college course by her father. Whilst suffering from a sense of insecurity and an inability to make reliable predictions about the motives and trustworthiness of others in subsequent relationships, M managed to survive by the psychological mechanism of disassociation. However, she continued to suffer from nightmares involving her father. At the date of the hearing she was in a stable relationship, but she was considered to be at continued risk of post traumatic stress disorder and also vulnerable to later severe depressive illness. It was possible that as a result of her abuse she might require long term intensive psycho-analytic psychotherapy in later life. *General Damages*: £20,000 (for pain, suffering and loss of amenity).

M, *Re*, April 21, 1997, Judge not specified, CICB (Torquay). [*Ex rel.* Sally King, Solicitor, Rudlings & Wakelam, 1 Woolhall Street, Bury St Edmonds].

Post traumatic stress

1852.   Female, aged 32 at the date of the award, was subject to sexual abuse between the age of 12 and 18 by her stepfather. The abuse initially was limited to kissing followed by fondling her breasts and thereafter to general touching above her nightclothes. The stepfather then started getting into bed naked with her and by the time she was 14 they were having full intercourse three to four times per week. The stepfather had also been abusing P's sister and subsequently, in 1996, was convicted of indecent assault and received five years imprisonment. P had difficulty coming to terms with the abuse and turned to alcohol. She underwent counselling for the alcohol abuse, but continued to suffer nightmares and depressive mood swings. *General Damages*: £17,500.

P, *Re*, July 3, 1997, Judge not specified, Court not specified. [*Ex rel.* Atkinson Cave and Stuart, Solicitors, 45 Springfield Road, Blackpool].

Post traumatic stress

1853.   Male, aged 17 at the date of the hearing, was subjected to sexual abuse and exploitation by an adult female neighbour. The abuse took place over two years on an almost daily basis between the age of 11 and 13. The sexual abuse included indecent touching, oral sex and full sexual intercourse. H was encouraged to adopt the pseudo maturity of boyfriend and father. There was no suggestion of physical violence towards him. H gave evidence in criminal proceedings aged 14. Wide media coverage accompanied the trial which destroyed any protective anonymity. The abuser was convicted of indecent assault and sentenced to 18 months' imprisonment. Upon release the abuser returned to the geographical area and continued to harass H. H suffered distress, anger, guilt and confusion. H's education was interrupted by absenteeism, behavioural problems and an inability to concentrate, resulting in continuing literacy difficulties. H remained frightened of women and found the mother/son relationship difficult. He suffered phobic problems about being left alone and was afraid of going anywhere unless accompanied by his father. H experienced humiliation within the community, found it awkward to make friends and continued to live in fear of his abuser. There had been some regression in his behaviour; he was unable to have normal adolescent experiences and further counselling was required. *General Damages*: £15,000.

H, *Re*, March 18, 1997, Judge not specified, CICB (Nottingham). [*Ex rel.* Claire Knighton, Solicitor, The Smith Partnership, Derby].

Post traumatic stress

1854.   K was raped on three occasions in February 1992 by her ex boyfriend. Subsequently on February 22, 1992 he assaulted her, causing a displacement of the nose, swelling of the left eye, a brief period of unconsciousness and swelling of the forehead. The injury to the nose was partially improved by a full septorhinoplasty operation in February 1993, but the nose remained slightly deviated to the left with some obstruction of the left side and tenderness of the tip. K was diagnosed as suffering from post traumatic stress disorder. She suffered from nightmares and flashbacks, and felt uncomfortable in the presence of men. She had been uncomfortable within intimate relationships since the events. There were also associated symptoms of depression, anxiety, diminished concentration, interrupted sleep and irritability. A further consequence was abuse of and dependence on methadone and alcohol, but that had been brought under control. At the time of the hearing in June 1997 K was still suffering from nightmares and a continuing fear in relation to her ex boyfriend's imminent release from prison. However, she was expected to regain self confidence and self esteem and recover from the majority of her symptoms within the following 3-5 years. *General Damages*: £13,500 (for pain, suffering and loss of amenity).

K, *Re*, June 10, 1997, Judge not specified, CICB (London). [*Ex rel.* Sally King, Solicitor, Rudlings & Wakelam, 1 Woolhall Street, Bury St Edmunds].

Post traumatic stress

1855.   Male, aged 28 at the date of the incident and 30 at the date of the hearing, was employed as a nursing auxiliary and in his part time was a disc jockey. In the grounds of the hospital at which he worked JW was robbed at knifepoint and then kidnapped and taken to a deserted urban area where he was subjected to buggery. JW developed all the symptoms of post traumatic stress disorder, became withdrawn and suffered impotence. He was prone to bursting into tears and was unable to sustain a physical and emotional relationship with his former partner. By the hearing date, the prognosis was cautiously optimistic, JW having entered into a new relationship and having resumed working as a DJ shortly before the hearing. *General Damages*: £12,500.

JW, *Re*, December 12, 1995, Judge not specified, CICB (Manchester). [*Ex rel.* Peter E Buckley, Barrister, 5 John Dalton Street, Manchester].

Post traumatic stress

1856.   Male, aged 49 at date of assault and aged 54 at date of hearing, was working as a publican when he was pushed by a youth and fell striking his face on a wall and sustaining a blow to the side of his face. He suffered considerable facial bruising and had three teeth knocked out. He immediately became very distressed and subsequently suffered serious psychological problems which forced him to give up the tenancy of the public house. He became increasingly irritable, over-sensitive and aggressive. He was unable to cope with any stress, his sleep pattern was totally disturbed, and he frequently broken down crying. He avoided social situations and was unable to carry on his former hobby of running a pigeon club. At the time of the hearing he was still undergoing psychiatric treatment. His condition had improved and was continuing to improve. A further gradual spontaneous improvement was expected, leading to an excellent recovery, with further significant reduction of symptoms in the six to 12 months following the hearing. *General Damages*: £12,500.

JENKINS, *Re*, February 26, 1997, Judge not specified, CICB (Cardiff). [*Ex rel.* Michael Jenkins, Solicitor, Leo Abse & Cohen, Cardiff].

Post traumatic stress

1857.   Male, aged 34 at the date of injury, was a commercial diver employed by S to carry out saturation dives in the North Sea oil fields. In January 1992, after an extremely long and exhausting dive, he was unable to get back to the diving bell. He was left stranded, dangling on the end of an umbilical line 85 metres below the surface of the North Sea for 40 minutes before being rescued. He did not believe that he would survive. He was rescued, but as a result of the experience, suffered psychiatric injury and his medical clearance for diving was withdrawn. The parties agreed that he had suffered post traumatic stress disorder within the definition in DSM3, but there was an argument at trial as to whether or not it could be diagnosed under DSM4. The judge found that Z was suffering from moderate post traumatic stress disorder with depression, which was treatable with medication, and continuing phobic disorders. In addition he found that Z had suffered an event involving a threat to his physical integrity, notwithstanding that he was fully supplied with breathing gases, heat, light and communications throughout. S's argument that injury was not foreseeable was not accepted. Z had commenced working again, but because of his phobias could not work offshore and in particular could not dive. *General*

Damages: £12,500. Past and future loss of earnings: £246,417 (Calculated up to Z's 42nd birthday. The judge felt that diving careers were too uncertain beyond that age for him to make any higher award).

ZAMMIT v. STENA OFFSHORE LTD, March 20, 1997, Garland, J., QBD. [*Ex rel.* Penningtons Solicitors, Basingstoke].

Post traumatic stress

1858.   Male, aged 25 at the date of the accident and aged 30 at the date of trial, was a skilled carpenter who was exposed to high levels of the solvents toluene, e-hexane and ethyl acetate over two days in June 1991 while glueing skirting board in premises where there was little or no ventilation. As a result he experienced hallucinations, temporary blindness, and feared that he was going to die. He suffered a psychiatric injury, which was diagnosed as post traumatic stress disorder, and physical symptoms including headaches, sore throat and sore eyes. He also suffered depression which prevented him from overcoming difficulties in life. It was held that as a result of T's post traumatic stress disorder and its permanent consequences, principal among which was his inability to work with adhesives because they continue to be a disturbing reminder of the incident, T could no longer work as a carpenter. *General Damages*: £11,000 (apportioned £4,000 for physical injuries and £7,000 for psychiatric injury). Award for past loss of earnings: £40,399. Award for future loss of earnings: £84,103 (multiplier 14, multiplicand £5,106 for continuing diminution in earnings, plus one year's total loss at £12,619). Total award: £146,561 (including interest).

TEAGUE v. CAMDEN LBC, November 7, 1996, H.H.J. Quentin Edwards Q.C., CC (Central London). [*Ex rel.* Stuart Gillings, Bolt Burdon, Solicitors, 1 Providence Place, Islington, London].

Post traumatic stress

1859.   Male, aged 16 at the time of the abuse and 32 at the date of the hearing was sexually abused whilst in a children's residential care home by one of the masters. There was only one act of buggery recorded after he had been given a drugged milky drink. The immediate effects included pain and anal bleeding, fear and poor sleep. He felt dirty, questioned his sexuality and developed a fear of being stigmatised and bullied by others if they found out. Subsequently he became involved in crime and was in and out of court for the following six months. Thereafter he was depressed and suicidal, experienced severe sleep disturbance, could not hold down a relationship, was uncomfortable with sex, had problems dealing with men in authority, suffered flashbacks and drank heavily. Since being contacted by the police investigating the abuse he had felt depressed, angry and irritable. He assaulted his girlfriend when she told family and friends of his abuse. He had been diagnosed as suffering from post traumatic stress disorder. *General Damages*: £7,500

MP, *Re*, August 13, 1996, Lord Carlisle Q.C., CICB (Liverpool). [*Ex rel.* Aswini Weereratne, Barrister, Doughty Street Chambers, London].

Post traumatic stress

1860.   Male police officer, aged 36 at the date of the accident and aged 39 at the date of the trial, was injured when a motor vehicle being driven by S drove into a police vehicle at a speed in excess of 50 mph. He sustained modest physical injuries to his neck, chest and right knee which he had recovered from after approximately 18 months from the date of the accident. However, he also developed a psychological condition known as phobic travel anxiety, which meant that although he could drive normally he became a very anxious passenger, anticipating everything that could go wrong. He found that he was putting his foot down on an imaginary brake throughout journeys, gripping the seat and feeling tense. More importantly, as a police traffic officer he was required to undertake high pursuit duties driving in excess of 100 mph and felt that following his accident his "bottle" had gone. Consequently he applied for a transfer and had been moved to the Force Communications Centre taking control /administrative work. He claimed in addition to general damages that he should be compensated for loss of congenial duties. *General Damages* (excluding award for loss of congenial duties): £6,000. Award for loss of congenial duties: £2,500.

SMITH v. STICKLEY, August 4, 1997, Recorder Michael Brent Q.C., CC (Birmingham). [*Ex rel.* Russell Jones & Walker, 16 Waterloo Street, Birmingham].

Post traumatic stress

1861.   Female, aged 13 at the date of the assault and aged 18 at the date of the hearing, was indecently assaulted during a tent party in a field close to her home. The assault had happened over a period of approximately 30 minutes whilst others were present and W had given evidence that she was unable to bring the assault to an end as she was frightened of what the assailant might do if she tried to stop him. The assailant was aged 18 years and about 15 stone whereas W was only slight. W had suffered depression, loss of confidence and low esteem. There had been a number of attempts at self harm following the incident. She had undergone counselling with little effect. She had difficulties in making successful long term relationships and was likely to experience adverse feelings on and off throughout her adult life. *General Damages*: £5,000.

W (A MINOR), *Re*, February 19, 1997, M Shorrock Q.C. (Chairman), CICB (Bath). [*Ex rel.* Bartlett Gooding & Weelan, Solicitors, 57 High Street, Shepton Mallet, Somerset].

Post traumatic stress

1862.   Male, aged 14 was sexually harassed from November 1993 to July 1994 on a daily basis. The attacker was a woman of 39. She followed the applicant, attempted to kiss him, trap him in a corner and touch his private parts without consent. In May 1994, she "got him drunk" and made him watch her having sexual intercourse with another man. The applicant was put under emotional and psychological pressure from the woman who was living at his home and was entrusted from time to time to her by his mother. The woman told the applicant that he was gay and that any boy his age who was normal would want to have the attention of a woman of her age to "show them what to do". The woman gave the applicant money to stay away from school. She told his schoolmates she was going out with him. He was "hassled" by children at his school. The applicant stayed away from school. He was confronted about this but was unable to tell his mother about the problem with the woman, The abuse continued. On one occasion the woman entered the applicant's bedroom, flung him onto his bed, pulled down his boxer shorts and attempted to masturbate him. The applicant flung her off. The applicant was diagnosed as suffering from post traumatic stress disorder. He was left feeling uncomfortable and threatened by women, including his mother, except for his godmother with whom he lived. He had a difficult relationship with his mother whom he blamed. He had begun to re-assemble his social, emotional and family life. At the date of the assessment, some three years after the abuse, he was being prescribed anti-depressant medication. A psychiatric report anticipated that he would continue to be troubled by unbidden recollections of abuse. He had experienced for more than 18 months a "profound depressive reaction in the context of his post traumatic stress disorder" associated with an experience of panic symptoms. The prolonged and systematic abuse had had a profound effect on the applicant who at one stage attempted suicide, and it continued to have a significant impact on all areas of his life. The initial award of £3,000 was increased. *General Damages*: £5,000.

W (A MINOR), *Re*, May 27, 1997, Judge not specified, CICB (Durham). [*Ex rel.* Robert Gilbert, Barrister, Fountain Chambers, Cleveland Business Centre, 1 Watson Street, Middlesbrough].

Post traumatic stress

1863. Female, L, aged 47 at date of the road traffic accident and 50 at date of the trial, was injured when her car was run into from behind by a van. L suffered a minor whiplash injury which caused pain in the left side of the neck radiating into her shoulder. L underwent a course of physiotherapy which alleviated the symptoms but some slight pain was left. The major injury was the exacerbation of L's pre-accident phobic anxiety state. L had been receiving psychological treatment for over 10 years. Before the accident her condition was under control and she had not suffered an attack for some years. After the accident panic attacks featured dizziness, an apparent loss of control of the feet and a fear of falling began again. L was unable to walk to work as she did before the accident because of her fear of an attack and used taxis to work. L also suffered from the occasional headache. The court found that the whiplash type injury had resolved itself within six months of the accident, and that the ongoing symptoms at trial of pain in the neck and shoulder which L experienced at frequent but irregular intervals were not caused by the accident. The court found that the accident was the cause of the recurrence of the panic attacks. It was expected that the panic attacks would be under control again within three years of the accident. An award was made of £1,500 for the whiplash injury and £3,000 for the exacerbation of the psychological condition. *General Damages*: £4,500. Special damages: £1,197. Total award: £5,972.

LYMER v. HENSON, December 16, 1996, District Judge Ilsley, CC (Stoke on Trent). [*Ex rel.* Frederick H Brown, Barrister, Regent Chambers, 29 Regent Road, Hanley].

Post traumatic stress

1864. Boy aged 8 at date of injury and 10 at date of trial was attacked by defendant's alsatian dog. He suffered a large gaping wound to the lateral aspect of his left thigh and three further superficial wounds above. He was taken to hospital where the wounds were cleaned and steristripped and he was given a course of antibiotics. He attended hospital on a further five occasions for further dressings, removal of steristrips and review. The wounds took a month to heal. He was off school for four days, but unable to do any sport for two weeks or swim for a month. He was left with three noticeable hypertrophic scars on his left thigh; one measuring 3.5 centimetres by one centimetres, and two scars measuring 0.5 centimetre by 0.5 centimetre. The scars would be permanent and were described as "quite ugly". He was self conscious about the scars and in addition had sustained post traumatic stress disorder described by the Clinical Psychologist in evidence as of a "high degree of severity". This was manifested by a fear of medium/large sized dogs in the presence of which he would freeze and/or remain physically close to his parent until the dog was out of sight; avoidance behaviour; he would rarely go out alone and if he did would return if he saw a dog; hypersensitivity to the sound of dogs. The incident pervaded his thoughts and he experienced nightmares. The prognosis was that with a course of approximately eight sessions of psychotherapy he would fully regain his previous level of psychological functioning. *General Damages*: £4,250. Other Damages: £468 (including £440 for cost of private psychotherapy treatment).

COLLETT (A MINOR) v. BARLOW, April 10, 1997, McKenzie, J., CC (Redditch). [*Ex rel.* Stephen J Murray, Barrister, 8 Fountain Court, Birmingham].

Post traumatic stress

1865. Female, aged 12 at the date of the hearing and aged seven at the time of abuse, was subject to prolonged sexual abuse. Over a period of approximately one year full sexual intercourse took place on many occasions with her father during access visits, in addition there were signs that anal penetration also took place. She suffered post traumatic stress disorder. Three and a half years later she was functioning on the border line ability range of intelligence, whereas it was reasonable to believe that if she had not been abused she would have been within the low average ability range. She was still indicating symptoms of post traumatic stress disorder. A psychologist advised that she should receive counselling at various stages of her life. At the rates which were current at the time of the report the cost of that counselling, if provided privately, was £5,760 plus VAT. She had suffered significant physical, psychological, social and emotional damage, her early life had been chaotic and this meant that she was already vulnerable and open to exploitation. The Board was concerned that many of her symptoms might be attributable to that early home life rather than the abuse. The Board increased the single member's award of £6,000 to £10,000.

O (A MINOR), *Re*, April 4, 1997, Judge not specified, CICB (Nottingham). [*Ex rel.* PA Carlin, Irvings Solicitors, 10 Iron Gate, Derby].

Face

1866.   Male, aged 17 at the date of the incident and aged 20 at the date of the hearing, was attacked by a number of youths, one of whom punched him to the left side of the face. He suffered considerable bruising around the left eye and orbit together with a fracture of the floor of the orbit. He was treated under general anaesthetic when the floor of the orbit was explored through an incision in the lower eyelid and was reconstructed using a sheet of silastic. The incision left a scar. He was away from school for two weeks but had subsequently returned to pre-injury activities including rugby. He continued to experience some dyplopia with upward gaze, some aching around the eye in cold weather, pain when blowing nose and slight reddening of the scar in cold weather. *General Damages*: £4,500.

TAYLOR, *Re*, April 21, 1997, J Archer Q.C., CICB. [*Ex rel.* Harding Evans, Solicitors, Newport, Wales].

Cheek

1867.   Infant male, aged nine at the date of the accident and 12 at the date of the hearing, slipped and fell on tiles at a swimming pool. He fell forward, landing on his left cheek. The cheek was grazed and bruised, but there was no obvious laceration, although it was bleeding freely. He was badly shaken by the experience and was in pain for about a week after the accident during which time he also suffered headaches but from which he had recovered completely. On very close examination at trial a fine scar remained visible, which was more noticeable in cold weather or when G was suntanned. G's medical expert was of the opinion that the scar, which was very hard to see, would disappear completely in the fullness of time. *General Damages*: £1,000.

G (A MINOR) v. CROYDON LBC, August 7, 1997, District Judge Keogh, CC (Epsom). [*Ex rel.* Copley Clark & Bennett, Solicitors, 36 Grove Road, Sutton, Surrey, SM1 1BS].

Eye

1868.   Male, aged 26 at the date of the trial, was struck in the right eye by a screw whilst at work. He attended hospital the next day, eye drops were applied and it was noted that his cornea was scratched. He wore an eye pad for a week and suffered pain for a similar period of time. He took no time off work, carrying out light duties for approximately seven days. He sustained a superficial scar to his cornea and his eyesight in the right eye was imperceptibly reduced compared to the left. In any event, he had normal vision in both eyes and had to all intents and purposes made a full recovery within a week. There was no likelihood of his sight deteriorating at a later date as a result of the injury. *General Damages*: £1,250.

JACKSON v. IKEDA HOOVER LTD, December 11, 1996, District Judge Nuttall, CC (Durham). [*Ex rel.* Rowley Ashworth Solicitors, Suite 1B, Joseph's Well, Hanover Walk, Leeds].

Facial scars

1869.   Infant male, aged four and a half years at the date of the attack in July 1994 and aged seven years at the date of hearing, was attacked and bitten on the face by a Japanese Akito dog. Initially in hospital for 23 days, he underwent two skin grafts and stitch removal procedure under general anaesthetic. Treatment included the application of surgical leeches. There was further surgery to revise scarring in April 1995. He had very extensive scarring to the right side of the face below the right eye over an area of four centimetres in height and five centimetres in width from the side of the nose to the mid cheek. This area comprised multiple lines, some of which were red, some sunken and others raised. The major scarring commenced on the medial aspect of the right lower eyelid and travelled across and below the eye for approximately five centimetres and then dropped vertically for four centimetres down the cheek before returning across the cheek to a point adjacent to the right nostril. Beneath the chin were two scars, one 16 millimetres by eight millimetres and the other two millimetres by eight millimetres. There were two skin graft donor sites; one on the right buttock four centimetres by three centimetres and one on the groin, two centimetres by one centimetre, the scarring was described by the judge as being "particularly severe". Further improvements would be quite minimal and slow to develop. He had developed behavioural problems, both at home and school, being difficult, aggressive and lacking concentration. These had been well handled by his parents and the school and had resolved within a year of the attack. He was a happy cheerful outgoing child of considerable psychological robustness, but would face stresses due to his disfigurement in future years. *General Damages*: £20,000 (for pain, suffering and loss of amenity). Award for nursing care by mother: £1,000.

GREGORY (A MINOR) v. MILLINGTON, March 12, 1997, District Judge Wilby, CC (Tameside). [*Ex rel.* Michael Goldwater, Barrister, Hollins Chambers, Manchester].

Facial scars

1870.   Male, aged 30 at the date of the incident and aged 32 at the trial of the trial, was struck in the face with a glass by D in the course of a quarrel in a public house. B suffered lacerations extending to the outer corner of his right eye, across his right cheek and towards the lower border of his jaw on the right side. The lacerations were deep enough to sever the branches of the facial nerves supplying the muscles of the cheek, lower eyelid and lips on the right side. The resultant scarring was well healed but visible at conversational distances and constitutes a moderate cosmetic blemish. B is embarrassed at the appearance of the scars which he believes give him a slightly "thuggish" appearance. The damaged nerves have regrown, but imperfectly, so that the nerves originally supplying the right side of the mouth supply the right eye and vice versa. As a result B is afflicted by constant and involuntary spasms of the muscles of the right cheek and right eye. If he blinks or closes his eyes, the right side of his mouth twitches upwards and if he smiles, his right eye winks. There is some right sided facial muscle weakness and asymmetry. The right eye has a tendency to water. The muscle spasms are permanent and B is distressed and embarrassed by them. However, B was receiving palliative treatment which involved the facial muscles being injected at intervals with botulinum toxin. The injections, which are into the right lower eyelid, are painful and cause temporary swelling and bruising around the eye, but within about a week they induce a temporary partial paralysis which subdues the muscle spasm for abut three months. *General Damages*: £10,000.

BURTON v. DAXNER, March 11, 1997, H.H.J. Stretton, CC (Mansfield). [*Ex rel.* Richard Burns, Barrister, 24 The Ropewalk, Nottingham].

Facial scars

1871. Male, aged 42 at the date of the incident, was the landlord of a public house who had a broken beer glass thrust into his face in the area of his left eye and cheekbone. Significant lacerations were caused requiring a large number of stitches. There was permanent and extensive scarring in an area measuring approximately three inches by two inches. It changed colour and tightened giving a pulling sensation around the eye, particularly in hot weather. Since the incident he had lost confidence and become anxious and depressed. He had withdrawn from social interaction, and relationships within his family became strained. He had ceased working at the public house and lost the motivation to find new employment. *General Damages*: £8,500 (for pain and suffering), plus £1,000 for the cost of future psychotherapy.

CUSACK, *Re*, July 15, 1997, T Preston Q.C., CICB (Birmingham). [*Ex rel.* Andrew Wallace, Barrister, 3 Fountain Court Chambers, Birmingham].

Facial scars

1872. Female, aged two and a half at the date of the accident, fell through an internal glass door receiving injuries to her nose and forehead. She was left with a scar between the eyebrow and hairline 23 millimetres long and two to three millimetres at its widest part, and a C shaped scar over the bridge of the nose approximately 25 millimetres in length and three millimetres wide at its widest, the latter being reddened and quite obvious. The nasal scarring had become swollen due to "trap door deformity", the prognosis for which was spontaneous improvement within two years of injury with a possibility of surgical intervention by z-plasty if it did not otherwise recover. Minor psychiatric effects had caused R to be reluctant to be photographed or examined by doctors, but those effects had disappeared by the date of the hearing. *General Damages*: £8,500 (including an undefined element for the likelihood of a pretty girl becoming self-conscious of the scarring in adolescence).

R (A MINOR) v. BRADMARR JOINERS, June 23, 1997, H.H.J. Brown, CC (Workington). [*Ex rel.* Marcus Nickson, Solicitor, KJ Commons & Co, 2 Upper Jane Street, Workington].

Facial scars

1873. Infant female, aged 17 months at the date of the accident, fell in a large pothole at the edge of her garden, causing her to fall into a neighbour's garden on a lower level. She sustained a 1.5 centimetre laceration just beneath her right nostril. She was treated with steristrips and antibiotics were prescribed. At the time of hearing, she was left with a horizontal, slightly curved linear scar 1.3 centremetre long extending from just inside the base of the right nostril. The scar becomes more noticeable when she smiles and it takes on a bluish or reddish tinge in very cold or very not weather. The scar will always remain visible but could be improved by surgery. In assessing quantum, consideration was given to the fact that she was likely to become more conscious of the scar in her teenage years and the possibility that remedial surgery might be necessary at that stage. *General Damages*: £6,000.

WATERS (A MINOR) v. NORTH BRITISH HOUSING ASSOCIATION LTD, April 21, 1997, District Judge Beale, CC (Nottingham). [*Ex rel.* Nelsons Solicitors, Pennine House, 8 Stanford Street, Nottingham].

Teeth

1874. Male, aged 45 at the date of the incident and aged 51 at the date of the trial, suffered the loss of both upper central incisor teeth as a result of the negligence of a dental surgeon. The teeth were removed prior to proposed bridge work which was not in fact feasible. M would not have consented to the removal of the two teeth if he had been told that he would have to wear a denture. In fact, the only available treatment for him on the NHS was the provision of a denture. Substantial restorative dental treatment including the provision of titanium implants to support two crowns to replace the teeth together with associated dental work requiring onlays and inlays on seven posterior teeth was the appropriate form of treatment to return M as near as possible to the pre-negligence situation but such extensive treatment could only be provided privately and M was unable to fund it until the conclusion of the litigation. The two teeth had been removed in August 1991. Between August 1991 and January 1993 M had been provided with a denture which was reasonably comfortable but not a perfect fit and caused difficulty when eating. M had tolerated it because he believed until January 1993 that the originally proposed bridge work would be possible. In January 1993 the original denture broke and it was at that time M was advised by B that the proposed course of treatment would not be possible. M transferred to another dentist who provided a replacement denture but this denture was uncomfortable and unsatisfactory because when tight it caused pain in M's jaw but when loosened it was not secure and caused difficulty both with eating and speaking. M accordingly avoided wearing the denture as much as possible except on social occasions when he was embarrassed by the cosmetic disfigurement of the missing teeth. It was agreed at trial that the necessary restorative dental treatment would cost £7,500 and would take approximately 12 months to complete, involving about 20 one hour dental sessions. Thereafter it was agreed that two cycles of replacement at 10-12 year intervals would be required in respect of the crowns and the onlays/inlays at an agreed cost of £4,500. *General Damages*: £6,500. Cost of future dental treatment (agreed): £12,000. Total damages (including interest): £19,684.

MITCHELL v. BURKITT, July 9, 1997, Judge Swift, CC (Salford). [*Ex rel.* Philip Butler, Barrister, Deans Court Chambers, Crown Square, Manchester].

Hair

1875.	Female, aged 21 at date of incident and 22 at date of trial, went to N's salon for hair straightening treatment by chemical process. As a result of the process, immediately after she returned home, hair started falling out in clumps and there were areas of breakage throughout, which were almost to scalp level at the front. Before the treatment her hair was 14 inches from centre top to tips and the prognosis was that it would take some 28 months from the date of the incident for the hair to regain its lost length and condition. R was deeply distressed and had to have the rest of her hair cut short following which she became depressed and was in a traumatised state for several weeks, exhibiting symptoms of weeping, nightmares, depression, shame and embarrassment and obsession with how she looked. She suffered a traumatic response to a very distressing experience and a phobia developed. The prognosis was that there would be no long term psychological distress. However, at the date of hearing, some 18 months after the incident, R was still distressed by the incident. *General Damages*: £4,000.

RAMSBOTTOM v. NOVACKI, January 2, 1997, H.H.J. James, CC (Manchester). [*Ex rel.* Carolyn Bland, Barrister, Kenworthy's Chambers, 83 Bridge Street, Manchester].

Sight

1876.	Male, aged 31 at the time of the accident and aged 36 at the date of the hearing, was employed as a tyre remoulder and whilst using a portable grinder, a piece of wire measuring about five millimetres broke loose from a tyre and penetrated his left eye. K suffered permanent loss of vision in the left eye. The right eye was normal. He had to give up a number of his pre-accident hobbies and felt socially embarrassed especially when in the company of women. *General Damages*: £23,000. Special damages: £2,650.

KYEI v. UTILITY TYRE SERVICES LTD, July 1, 1997, H.H.J. Quentin Edwards Q.C., Court not specified. [*Ex rel.* Edmund Cofie, Barrister, Somersett Chambers, 52 Bedford Row, London].

Sight

1877. Male, aged 25 at the time of the assault and aged 30 at the time of the assessment, was assaulted sustaining a fracture of the left cheek bone and serious injuries to the left eye. He was, and despite his injuries, continues to be employed as a fitter working on public services vehicles. He held a PSV licence which would expire in 2012. M required a PSV licence in order to carry on with his present job. New Regulations had introduced a higher vision requirement as a result of which, when M was required to renew his licence he would no longer qualify. M was left with two small scars to his face, some loss of sensation to his left cheek bone area in cold weather and permanent damage to the sight in his left eye. This consisted of firstly a loss in his temporal visual field, ie his left eye had "blind spots", and a loss of visual acuity in his left eye which was reduced to 6/18. *General Damages*: £17,500.

MACKEL, *Re*, April 16, 1997, Judge not specified, CICB (Durham). [*Ex rel.* Ben Hoare & Co, Solicitors, 2/3 South Terrace, Southwick, Sunderland].

Hearing and speech

1878. Male, aged 46 at the date of the trial, had suffered significant hearing loss for four to five years attributable to exposure to loud noise in the course of his employment. He suffered no tinnitus. E gave evidence that he sometimes missed his wife calling to him. At home he had to have the television turned up to a volume too loud for other people. When E went out with his wife or family for a meal he would have to sit in the middle of the table to try and hear what was being said. He had bought a second telephone extension because he was having difficulty in hearing the instrument ring. E felt somewhat embarrassed about his handicap and received a certain amount of badinage from his family. Otherwise E's handicap did not interfere with any hobbies or particular pastimes. With time the ageing process would inevitably add to his disability. The audiogram showing E's hearing loss revealed the following hearing losses: at 1 kHz the loss in the right ear (air conduction) was 10 db; at 2 kHz the air conduction loss in the right ear was 20 db and in the left ear 15 db; at 3 kHz the air conduction and bone conduction figures for the right ear were 45/40 respectively and in the left ear 45 for both air conduction and bone conduction; at 4 kHz the figures were 50/35 and 55/50 respectively for air conduction and bone conduction; at 6 kHz the air conduction and bone conduction losses were 50 db in each ear. On the basis of the medical evidence the judge thought there was a 50 per cent chance that E would need a hearing aid at an age earlier than a person who did not suffer from noise induced deafness. *General Damages*: £5,500. Award for cost of hearing aid (discounted by 75 per cent to reflect probability of necessity and accelerated payment): £1,330.

EARLAM v. HEPWORTH HEATING LTD, June 25, 1996, H.H.J. Pugsley, CC (Burton on Trent). [*Ex rel.* Paul Bleasdale, Barrister, 5 Fountain Court, Steelhouse Lane, Birmingham].

Whiplash type injury

1879. Male, aged 32 at the date of the accident and 36 at the date of the assessment, suffered a neck strain in a road traffic accident for which he received a cervical collar which he wore for seven weeks. He required pain killers for the first few days and suffered with headaches following the accident. The symptoms in his neck appeared to settle after three months. However, he remained wary about his neck and thus did not partake in any activities which might have strained it. He made a full recovery six months post accident. He had also developed pain in his lower back two days post accident, causing him difficulties in walking but the lower back symptoms completely settled after one week. He was shaken for a while following the accident and was initially apprehensive when driving. He was off work for a total of eight weeks following the accident. There was also some initial sleep disturbance. *General Damages*: £1,400.

WARBURTON v. BARRINGTON, August 22, 1997, District Judge Geddes, CC (Blackburn). [*Ex rel.* James Hurd, Barrister, St James's Chambers, 68 Quay Street, Manchester].

Whiplash type injury

1880. Male, aged 29 at the date of the incident and 30 at the date of the trial, suffered a minor whiplash injury to his neck, with pain spreading across the top of the left shoulder, and bruising to the chest when the vehicle he was driving was struck from behind whilst stationary. The pain was acute for five days after which he made a gradual recovery over one month from the physical injuries and was symptom free after two months. H lost no time from work although his social life was affected considerably. He did not seek any medical treatment. *General Damages*: £1,250.

HARTLEY v. POSTLETHWAITE, August 19, 1997, District Judge Flanagan, CC (Leeds). [*Ex rel.* Gary Warriner, Russell House, 15 St Pauls Street, Leeds, LS1 2LZ].

Whiplash type injury

1881. Female, aged 21 at the date of a road traffic accident and 23 at the date of trial, was the driver of a car that was stationary when it was hit from behind by another vehicle. Immediately after the accident, the plaintiff reported being shocked but otherwise unaware of any injury. The following morning, she awoke with a stiff neck and a limited range of neck movement. She did not go into her work as an administrative assistant. The pain became worse over the course of three days and she developed shooting pains down the top of her right, dominant, arm. Around seven days after the accident she visited her GP who diagnosed whiplash and prescribed analgesics which she took for two weeks. Three weeks after the accident the most severe pain had diminished and she was left with occasional twinges until about three months after the accident by which time a full recovery had been made. In addition, the plaintiff developed bad eczema around one week after the accident which lasted for two months and which she ascribed to the stress of the accident. The plaintiff gave up sport (aerobics and swimming four times per week) for a period of six months. *General Damages*: £1,200. Award for loss of use of car: £520 (13 weeks use of her mother's car which she used for 40 per cent of the time).

STANLEY v. ROSEWELL, September 5, 1997, District Judge Sturdy, CC (Staines). [*Ex rel.* Richard Case, Barrister, 3 Paper Buildings, Temple].

Whiplash type injury

1882. Male, aged 33 at the time of the accident and 34 at the date of the hearing suffered a minor whiplash type injury to his neck and right upper shoulder whilst driving a vehicle which was struck from behind while stationary. He had pain and stiffness in his neck and right shoulder for a period of five days, during which he wore a cervical collar. After this period he was symptom free. *General Damages*: £1,000. Special damages: £222.

ROWLAND v. MATTHEWS, January 2, 1997, District Judge Gregory, CC (Stockport). [*Ex rel.* Andrew Leach, Amery Parkes Solicitors, Livery House, 169 Edmund House, Birmingham].

Whiplash type injury

1883.   Female, aged 48 at the time of the accident and aged 50 at the time of the assessment, was the driver of a vehicle which was struck from behind whilst stationary. She sustained a minor whiplash type injury which caused pain and stiffness in the neck for a period of three weeks. She also suffered from headaches which lasted for approximately five days. She did not see a doctor and there was no medical report at the hearing. *General Damages*: £1,000.

WILSON & WILSON v. SEAGRAM DISTILLERS PLC, January 27, 1997, District Judge Newman, CC (Chester). [*Ex rel.* Sandra Subacchi, Clement Jones, Solicitors, Holywell House, Parkway Business Centre, Deeside Park, Flintshire].

Whiplash type injury

1884.   Two plaintiffs, female aged 44 and male aged 22 at date of trial, were involved in a road traffic accident and suffered minor multiple soft tissue injuries. The first plaintiff was shocked, distressed and upset. She developed pain in her neck, back and shoulders and wore a collar for two weeks. She took paracetamol tablets and rubbed on "deep heat". She was hesitant and apprehensive when travelling by car for a period of six months. She had to sleep downstairs for a few months, had difficulty with carrying shopping and housework. She continued to suffer neck pain during bouts of cold weather. Restricting rotation of neck was reduced by 30 per cent. Full recovery within six to 12 months post accident. The second plaintiff was dizzy and shaken, suffered bruising to right shoulder and whiplash to neck. Minor soft tissue injury to right leg. Some effusion and restriction in flexion of the right knee. Full recovery within nine months post accident. *General Damages*: £1,000 (first plaintiff); *General Damages*: £750 (Second plaintiff).

HAJID, *Re*, May 15, 1997, H.H.J. Proctor, CC (Preston). [*Ex rel.* Yasmin Ebrahim-Wright, Barrister, New Bailey Chambers, Preston].

Whiplash type injury

1885.   Male, aged 24 at the date of accident and 27 at the date of trial sustained a minor whiplash injury to his neck. His GP provided him with Ibruprofen and a cervical collar. His neck was very painful for ten days. He resumed work as an electrician after two weeks only because he was self-employed. There was some continuing pain in the mornings but he had fully recovered within six months. *General Damages*: £1,000. Loss of earnings: £500.

SOUTHWORTH v. TABERNER, November 21, 1996, District Judge Jeffreys, CC (Chorley). [*Ex rel.* Keith Thomas, Barrister, 5 John Dalton Street, Manchester].

Whiplash type injury

1886.   P developed pain and stiffness in his neck two days after a road traffic accident. The symptoms persisted for ten days before rapidly settling. The only medical treatment that P received was four days after the accident when his GP advised him on medication. The medical report found that P had suffered a soft tissue whiplash injury to the cervical spine from which he made a total recovery. *General Damages*: £750.

FROST v. FURNESS, July 14, 1997, District Judge Sparrow, CC (Reading). [*Ex rel.* David McHugh, Barrister, Bracton Chambers, Chancery Lane].

Neck

1887.   Female police officer, aged 36 at the date of assault and aged 42 at the date of assessment, was on duty when she was viciously assaulted during a sustained attack which resulted in considerable physical injury including stab wounds, an injured wrist and very significant soft tissue injuries in her spinal region especially in the cervical region with extensive resulting symptoms. Despite numerous varieties of medical treatment, her symptoms had not eased at all since the assault. J suffered continuous pains in the neck which frequently woke her during the night and were worsened by any type of activity. The pains were so severe that she was frequently unable to hold her head up unaided. She has constant headaches caused by the neck ache radiating into her orbital area. She has constant low back pain. A number of her most significant symptoms continued to limit her life severely at the date of hearing. As a result of her symptoms she had retired from the Cambridgeshire Constabulary prematurely on medical grounds, with a full injury award. At the time of the assault, she had been a sergeant with a glowing record and had been expected to achieve at least the rank of Chief Inspector prior to normal retirement age. The severe physical symptoms had left her in constant extreme discomfort and had caused her to suffer from a reactive depression which had in the past been so severe that she had contemplated suicide. At the time of the assessment she was still very depressed about her extreme discomfort, loss of career and the limitations that she was now facing in her social and private life. She had taken on part time employment as a beautician, but it was recognised that her earning capacity was very limited. *General Damages*: £30,000. Award for loss of congenial employment: £5,000. Loss of earnings to date of assessment: £7,659. Loss of future earnings (including £17,500 for loss of promotion prospects): £46,165. Total award: £88,824.

J, *Re*, July 31, 1997, Sir Crawford Lindsay Q.C., CICB. [*Ex rel.* Russell Jones & Walker, Solicitors, 324 Gray's Inn Road, London].

Neck

1888.　Female, aged about 33 at the date of the accident and 41 at trial, was involved in a road traffic accident in February 1988 when she sustained a severe whiplash type injury. Prior to the accident she had spent her life working in, and subsequently, running a nursery school. The accident caused a soft tissue injury to her neck. There was also some minor dental injury. She lost her voice temporarily. She returned to work part-time within two months, but only out of necessity. Symptoms in her neck continued despite pain killers and physiotherapy. The school became subject to a Compulsory Purchase Order in March 1990. The judge found as a fact that if it had not been for her injuries and symptoms she would have moved to another school and run it. An attempt to run a public house with her partner failed. She subsequently undertook part-time work doing essentially administrative work in the nursing field. She missed her work with children enormously. She continued to need treatment in a variety of ways. By the time of trial she continued to suffer pain in her neck requiring use of a TENS machine and pain killers. She was restricted in her domestic tasks and recreations, having good days and bad days but was still able to work part time. The judge found that her symptoms were caused by the accident and were likely to continue in the future. The judge rejected the defendants' argument that the plaintiff had failed to mitigate her loss. He found as a fact that she would be able to find better paid employment in time but that her earning capacity was unlikely to catch up completely with the expanding earnings likely to have become available in the nursery business. *General Damages*: £13,750. Damages for loss of congenial employment: £4,250. Past loss of earnings: £40,906. Future loss of earnings (calculated at 1.5 years of partial loss as at date of trial, five further years at a reduced partial loss and £12,500 representing a further 10 years potential loss): £36,581. Sundry awards were made in relation to dental treatment, hairdressing expenses, cleaning, gardening and pain killers and batteries for the TENS machine: Total award including interest £113,739.

CAMUS v. WILLIAMS, July 18, 1996, H.H.J. Perrett Q.C., HC. [*Ex rel.* Robert Holdsworth, Barrister, 5 Fountain Court, Steelhouse Lane, Birmingham].

Neck

1889.   Male, 22 at date of the road traffic accident in 1990 and 28 at date of hearing, was a front seat passenger, seatbelted, in a head-on collision, in which he suffered soft tissue injuries to his neck and spine. The following day he suffered discomfort to the back of his neck and to his back and he called his doctor two days later. He was unable to return to his work as a cellarman. He had sustained very serious injuries in a previous road traffic accident in 1988 but had no residual symptoms to his neck or back at the time of his accident in 1990. He progressively developed chronic but moderately severe fibro-myalgia, described by his medical expert as reactive fibro-myalgia, which prevented him from working. He underwent training as a plumber and obtained qualifications but was unfit to take employment in the field. He managed to obtain light manual work for a 12 month period from February 1995 but had to give it up because of cumulative pain. The judge found that at the date of trial he was fit but only fit for light or semi-sedentary work provided he had an opportunity to move around because of his functional restrictions. He would not be fit for work as a plumber. Although physically fit and mobile with a full range of movement and no degenerative changes his symptoms were characterised by severe pain for the day or days following physical activity. *General Damages*: £13,500. Special damages: £6,427. Future loss of earnings: £26,400. Award for handicap on the labour market £9,000. Total award £57,750.

JENNINGS v. CUMMINS & PHILLIPS, September 25, 1996, Recorder Axtell, CC (Bournemouth). [*Ex rel.* Richards & Morgan, Solicitors].

Neck

1890.   Male police constable, aged 34 at date of assault and 42 at the date of assessment, was jumped on by assailant thereby causing musculo-ligamentous damage to the neck and more permanent damage to the intrevertebral discs. He felt immediate neck pain and could not move his neck that evening. He was off work for three days before returning for two months on normal duties after which his symptoms deteriorated severely. After being off work for four months he returned to light duties for six months. He was discharged from the police force, as a result of the injury 12 months after the assault. At the assessment he was still suffering from pain down the right side of his neck radiating to the top of his shoulder. The pain was a constant ache with occasional sharp spasms. His neck was always stiff. Sometimes he woke in the mornings when his neck was particularly painful and was forced to wear a collar for several days and take analgesic tablets. He found it difficult to lift or carry anything heavy. He could not decorate his home, move heavy furniture or garden. He could not drive a car for any distance. The prognosis was that his symptoms would be permanent. *General Damages*: £10,000.

MACEY, *Re*, October 23, 1996, Judge not specified, CICB. [*Ex rel.* John Tughan, Barrister, 9 Gough Square, London].

Neck

1891.   Male, aged 38 at the time of the accident and 41 at the date of the trial, suffered a wrenching injury to the neck when the car which he was driving was struck from the side. E was told by a police officer at the scene that he was lucky to have survived the accident. He subsequently suffered pain in the neck radiating into the left shoulder. He attended hospital, where he was provided with a soft collar which he wore for three weeks. At the time of the accident, E was unable to work because of a pre-existing back injury which was not affected by the accident. However, he suffered constant aching in the neck as a result of the accident and, at the date of trial, some three and a half years after the accident, it was anticipated that those symptoms would remain indefinitely. E also suffered headaches as a result of the accident. Again no improvement was anticipated. As a result of what he was told by the police officer immediately after the accident, E took the decision not to return to driving. He had still not returned to driving at the time of the trial and indicated an intention never to do so. He feared that he might be killed in a further accident. He described symptoms of arousal, flashbacks and anxiety which amounted to a post traumatic stress disorder. The medical evidence was to the effect that E's psychological symptoms were severe for 12 months after the accident, but that thereafter he could reasonably have sought treatment for his phobia of driving which would probably have resolved within 12 to 18 months of seeking such treatment. E was only awarded damages for the psychiatric symptoms and the phobia of driving for a period of two to two and a half years from the date of the accident. This was classified as a "minor" case of post traumatic stress disorder within the Judicial Studies Board Guidelines. *General Damages*: £10,000 (for pain, suffering and loss of amenity, attributed £7,500 to the neck injury and £2,500 to the psychiatric damage).

EDGE v. CALDERWOOD, September 17, 1996, District Judge McGrath. [*Ex rel.* Richard Pearce, Barrister, Peel Court Chambers, 45 Hardman Street, Manchester].

Neck

1892.   Male, aged 30 at the date of the incident, in July 1986, and 41 at the date of the trial, sustained a soft tissue injury to his neck whilst driving a bus with heavy steering. Even though his symptoms were present at the date of trial, some 10 years later, it was held that only five years of his symptoms from the date of the accident could be attributed to the initial incident and all further symptoms were due to a pre-existing degenerative condition. B sustained two further accidents due to heavy steering in April 1987 and May 1988 which aggravated his initial injury. B was absent from work for a total of 140 days and underwent physiotherapy. *General Damages*: £5,000. Special damages (agreed): £560.

BEAVAN v. DERBY CITY TRANSPORT, November 29, 1996, H.H.J. Styler, CC (Derby). [*Ex rel.* Z Bashir, Solicitor, Royal Oak House, Market Place, Derby].

Neck

1893.   Female, aged 19 at the date of the accident and aged 22 at the date of assessment, was involved in a road traffic accident. She developed pain in her neck immediately and was taken by ambulance to hospital. When she left hospital on the same day she was given advice on home exercise. The pain became worse the following day and during the subsequent week she visited her GP. She had one week off work following the accident and during that time she suffered from nausea. The plaintiff found that during the two months after the accident she had difficulty sleeping and lifting heavy objects in the course of her job as a shop assistant. On examination 17 months after the accident the plaintiff was still aware of discomfort over her neck, particularly in the evening and when carrying books. She also felt discomfort over her right shoulder on rotation and lateral flexion to the right and on full forward flexion. All the symptoms had resolved 20 to 21 months after the accident. *General Damages*: £3,000.

DOHERTY v. SPREADBURY, May 7, 1997, District Judge Mildred, CC (Reading). [*Ex rel.* Richard Case, Barrister, Chambers of Michael Parroy Q.C., Winchester].

Neck

1894.   Male, aged 18 at the date of the accident and aged 19 at the date of the hearing, was injured in a road traffic accident, suffering an acute neck sprain and soft tissue injuries to the dorsal spine, upper limb girdle and lumbosacral spine. Within hours he developed pains in the neck radiating to the shoulders. A cervical collar was provided and analgaesics prescribed. He was employed as a trainee garage mechanic and took three weeks off following the accident. Thereafter he suffered recurrent neck pains which radiated into the shoulders and which were aggravated by the nature of his employment. At the date of the hearing, almost 12 months after the accident, the only remaining symptoms were infrequent aches and pains, together with a feeling of nervousness when travelling by car. It was anticipated a full recovery would be achieved within 16 months from the date of the accident. *General Damages*: £2,600.

OWEN v. PRIOR, May 28, 1997, District Judge Law, CC (Wigan). [*Ex rel.* Karim Sabry, Barrister, Manchester House Chambers, Manchester].

Neck

1895.   Male, aged 26 at the date of the accident and aged 29 at the date of the trial, was injured falling off his motorcycle as a result of a road traffic accident. He was taken to hospital complaining of pain in the left side of his back, in his left shoulder and to the right side of his neck. There were no fractures. He suffered two weeks of severe pain following which the pain in the shoulder and neck settled. He underwent a month of physiotherapy which alleviated the back pain. His symptoms resolved within a year from the accident, although on examination towards the end of that period he had described difficulty in sleeping on his left side and an ache in the left side of his back at the thoraco-lumbar level on picking up his young daughter, on bending and lifting, and when playing snooker and pool. *General Damages*: £2,000. Other damages: £1,495.

HOY v. COLE, April 23, 1997, H.H.J. Groves, CC (Chelmsford). [*Ex rel.* David McIlroy, Barrister, Chambers of Michael Parroy Q.C., 3 Paper Buildings, Temple].

Neck

1896.   Female, T, aged 48 at the date of injury and 52 at the date of assessment, slipped and fell on a defective stair carpet whilst engaged in the course of her employment as a home carer. The fall exacerbated pre-existing degenerative change in her neck and caused painful symptoms in her lumbar spine. She was absent from work for a period of four months. She underwent a period of physiotherapy but was substantially disabled until her return to work. T's symptoms gradually improved until she was left with difficulties in relation to carrying her shopping, lifting of anything other than light weights and discomfort in her neck and shoulder with any excessive use of her arms, particularly above shoulder height. Her condition interfered with her ability to carry out her duties as a home carer and with her home and social life. She was unable to carry out as much of her gardening as she had previously. The symptoms in the lower back resolved by the time of her return to work. However, the significant exacerbation of her previous degenerative condition was permanent, leaving her to continue indefinitely with intermittent discomfort by way of aching sensations after moderate exertions, together with an enhanced vulnerability to muscle strains in the neck and shoulder. But for the injury T would have experienced an increase in the symptoms from her pre-existing degenerative condition in any event, but only a relatively small increase. The judge accepted that T's injuries had affected her ability to work and that given her age, the permanency of her condition, and her limited employment experience other than as a home carer, she was at risk on the open labour market as there was a real risk of being unable to continue with her employment. *General Damages* were reduced by £500 to reflect that she would have suffered some degree of exacerbation of the pre-existing degenerative condition in any event. *General Damages*: £7,500. *Smith v. Manchester* award: £4,000 (one year's net loss of earnings). Special Damages: £1,444. Total award: £13,649.

TRUSCOTT v. SAIPE, September 18, 1997, District Judge Fairwood, CC (Leeds). [*Ex rel.* Paul G Kirtley, Barrister, 37 Park Square, Leeds].

Neck

1897.   Male, aged 28 at the date of a road traffic accident which caused some stiffness and mild discomfort in his neck a few hours later. All symptoms had resolved within

24 hours of the accident. He took no time off work, no cervical collar and no pain killers were necessary. No sequelae were expected. *General Damages*: £250.

JOHNSON v. SIDAWAY, May 13, 1997, Deputy District Judge Torrane, CC (Gloucester). [*Ex rel.* Benjamin Williams, Barrister, Chambers of Michael Parroy Q.C., Oxford].

Neck–whiplash type injury

1898.	Female, aged 45 at the date of the accident and aged 50 at the date of the hearing, sustained a whiplash type injury to the cervical spine in a road traffic accident. C was immediately aware of pain in the neck radiating into the right shoulder and developed a restriction of neck movement. C also sustained bruising of the left knee which resolved over two months, bruising of the chest giving rise to discomfort for a year and a minor back strain. C was given a soft cervical collar and analgesia and underwent physiotherapy, although she was unable to attend as often as advised. C's neck failed to show any significant improvement and at the hearing she was continuing to wear her collar at night, suffered from pain in the neck on a daily basis and intermittent headaches. There was significant restriction of neck movements and abduction and flexion of the right shoulder was only 50 per cent of the expected range. The contention that a pre-existing degenerative change would have become symptomatic by C's mid 50s was rejected. C was unable to carry shopping and all aspects of her domestic chores were affected. She could not return to jogging, aerobics and keep fit and her sleep was disturbed. The judge accepted that C needed six hours' domestic assistance a week. C suffered from a moderate post traumatic stress disorder for a year and mild to moderate post traumatic stress for a further two years. C had nightmares, intrusive thoughts and was tearful. She was unable to pass the scene of the accident without becoming upset. It was held that thereafter her residual symptoms could not be distinguished from anxiety and depression caused as a result of her constant pain. In assessing general damages the judge derived some assistance from *Trotter v. Black* Kemp & Kemp E2-012/1 although he regarded C's pain as being more severe. *General Damages*: £17,500. Comprising £12,500 in respect of the whiplash injury with a separate award of £5,000 for post traumatic stress. Award for domestic assistance: £20,592 (multiplier of 12). Special damages: £555. Total damages (per contributor): £39,609 (including interest).

CLARK v. COMMISSIONER OF POLICE OF THE METROPOLIS, January 10, 1997, H.H.J. Platt, CC (Ilford). [*Ex rel.* Katherine Gough, Barrister, Lamb Chambers, Lamb Building, Temple].

Neck–whiplash type injury

1899.	Female, aged 31 at the date of the accident and aged 33 at the date of the trial, suffered a whiplash type injury to her neck following a road traffic accident. She also complained of headaches and seatbelt bruising. She was prescribed pain killers and anti-inflammatories, and was referred for physiotherapy, initially attending three times a week, reducing to once or twice a week by 11 months after the accident, and continuing intermittently up to the date of the trial, some two years and five months after the accident. She had also had reflexology treatment and massage, although the judge disallowed the costs of such treatment as not being reasonably necessary. She continued to suffer from daily pain, which varied with the strenuousness of her activity, and she was aware of her neck "cracking". She required pain killers and a special pillow. She also suffered from daily headaches and pain sometimes radiated into the right side of her face and down her right arm. She was unable to lift shopping, do the cleaning or gardening, or walk her dogs. Her pre-accident hobby of sewing was restricted to 20 minutes. She had had a baby, and had difficulty in caring for her child, since lifting aggravated her symptoms. She had a full range of movement in her neck, but some pain and tenderness on certain movements. She had had symptoms lower down her spine before the accident, but all her ongoing symptoms were attributable to the accident. The prognosis was that symptoms would be permanent with no improvement in the future but with no prospect of deterioration. *General Damages*: £8,000.

HAMILTON v. AIR PRODUCTS AND SALUVEER, June 23, 1997, H.H.J. Maher, CC (Willesden). [*Ex rel.* Amanda Buckley-Clarke, Barrister, Chambers of Michael Parroy Q.C., Temple].

Neck—whiplash type injury

1900.   Female, age 25 at the date of accident and 29 at the date of trial, was involved in a road traffic accident. She developed pain from a whiplash type injury in her neck almost immediately and, within two weeks, pain in her lumbar spine. She wore a soft collar day and night for two weeks, and then for days only for a further week. She was absent from work for five weeks and required at least eleven sessions of physiotherapy. Her neck pain improved, but back pain continued and had reached a plateau when, eight months after the accident, she was involved in a second road accident for which no one was at fault. This caused her to return to physiotherapy for a short period and have one day off work. The symptoms that resulted from this accident completely resolved after two weeks. Her original neck symptoms had completely resolved by trial, but a moderate back injury persisted. Pain was always to some degree present. She took prescribed pain killers as necessary for two and a half years, and then proprietary pain killers occasionally. She modified her lifestyle to avoid carrying heavy objects. She ceased aerobics and golf, and lost enjoyment from gardening. Her injury had affected her domestic life and made her work with computers uncomfortable. The injuries were purely soft tissue and the prognosis was that the continuing pain was unlikely to improve significantly. *General Damages*: £7,500.

FERGUSON v. COVEL, November 11, 1996, Assistant Recorder Corbett, CC (Birmingham). [*Ex rel.* Anthony Verduyn, Barrister, Priory Chambers, 2 Fountain Court, Steelhouse Lane, Birmingham].

Neck—whiplash type injury

1901.   Female, aged 36 at the date of the accident and aged 38 at the date of trial, sustained a whiplash type injury to her neck when she was in a stationary motor vehicle which suffered a rear impact collision. H who was employed as an accountant, was also a well known local horsewoman who prior to the accident had competed in local show jumping and dressage events. She owned two horses which she was bringing on to competition level. As a result of the accident she was unable to exercise the horses herself or to compete in events for a period of 18 months. For a year of that time she was unable to undertake the hard work of looking after the horses including mucking out, giving them bedding, feeding them and excercising them on a lunge rein. This work was undertaken by H's mother without payment. The judge accepted that there was a serious loss of amenity to H who had been deprived of the ability to pursue a hobby that had been a lifetime interest. The judge concluded that a whiplash injury would normally merit an award of £3,500, coming within the Judicial Studies Board Guidelines, Chapter 6(A)(f), but considered that the loss of amenity warranted the award of a further sum of £3,000. *General Damages*: £6,500.

HUNN v. McFARLANE, June 1996, H.H.J. Previte Q.C., CC (West London). [*Ex rel.* Peter W Keer-Keer, Solicitor, Keer-Keer & Co, Hemel Hempstead].

Neck—whiplash type injury

1902.   R, aged 51 years at the date of the accident was concussed and lost consciousness for a few seconds when when a car collided with the rear of his stationary car. He also sustained a whiplash injury to his neck, bruising to his chest (lasting for about five weeks) and bruising to his knee (lasting about 10 days). R developed headaches shortly after the accident and had difficulty sleeping. He worked as a sales manager which involved driving about 50,000 miles a year. R did not take any time off work, did very little during the first week after the accident but started driving again the following week. R went on a two week canoeing holiday with his wife on their silver wedding anniversary which was marred by his injuries. He underwent a course of physiotherapy for one month three months after the accident after which his symptoms were somewhat improved. Thereafter symptoms persisted at a lower level. Fourteen months after the accident, R was still experiencing neck discomfort every day, made worse by driving, sleeping difficulties most nights and headaches every 10 days or so. The medical evidence was that R's symptoms could be expected to improve over the following 10 months but that it was too early to tell whether he would be one of the 22 per cent of people who continued to suffer symptoms beyond two years. *General Damages*: £6,500.

REES v. HOOPER, September 22, 1997, H.H.J. Paul Clark, CC (Oxford). [*Ex rel.* Rob Weir, Barrister, 3 Paper Buildings, Temple].

Neck – whiplash type injury

1903.　Female, aged 21 at the date of accident and aged 25 at the date of trial, suffered a whiplash type injury in a road traffic accident. A did not wear a surgical collar but took three weeks off work immediately following the accident and one year later, another four weeks off work. The neck pain was constant for nearly a year and it was then reduced to a manageable level by A giving up entirely her horse riding and nightclubbing. She attended 52 physiotherapy sessions over two years. Her symptoms dramatically improved in the third year after she had been treated by a chiropractor. The neck injury was expected to have permanent effects. A would continue to suffer intermittent episodes of pain especially when lifting heavy weights but also from sitting still for long periods of time. There was no risk of deterioration, but she would be vulnerable to further trauma and giving birth to and carrying children would cause neck pain. At the date of trial A was a student. She had previously worked as a gardener and was fit to continue with that occupation. *General Damages*: £5,500. Total Damages; £7,838.

ASHTON v. MORTLOCK, April 28, 1997, H.H.J. Previte Q.C., CC (Plymouth). [*Ex rel.* Peter Telford, Barrister, Devon Chambers, Plymouth].

Neck – whiplash type injury

1904.　G, male police sergeant, aged 34 at the date of the accident and 37 at the date of the hearing, suffered a moderate whiplash injury to his neck as a result of his stationary vehicle being shunted some 10 yards forward. He wore a cervical collar for about a week during which he also took Ibuprofen to counter any inflammation. He was off work for a total of four weeks. He also took painkillers and had a course of physiotherapy consisting of 19 sessions during the ensuing 10 months. The prognosis some three years after the accident was that G would make a full recovery and was unlikely to suffer any late complications. At the date of the assessment of damages G gave evidence that he was still suffering muscle tightness/spasms in his neck two to three times per month. The symptoms usually responded to painkillers but often took two or three days to resolve. G had not consulted his GP or physiotherapist for some two years but the judge deemed him to be a stoic man who was "toughing it out". *General Damages*: £5,000.

GRAHAM v. KELLY (NO.1), September 18, 1997, Deputy District Judge Arnold, CC (Aldershot & Farnham). [*Ex rel.* David McHugh, Barrister, Bracton Chambers, 95A Chancery Lane, London].

Neck – whiplash type injury

1905.　G, female, aged 25 at the time of accident and 29 at the date of hearing, was in her car when it was struck violently from behind by another vehicle. She was not in immediate pain, but was very shaken. The next morning she had severe headache, neck and back pain and attended hospital. Later she attended her GP. She took two days off work. She wore a cervical collar day and night for three weeks. By the end of this period her back pain had cleared up and her neck pain was intermittent (about half a day a week). Three months after the accident there was an episode of serious pain, which was constant for 10 days. Since then she had suffered pain on average on one day per month, associated with exertion or static posture. There was some loss of lumbar lordosis. The diagnosis was of a "chronic whiplash syndrome", and the residual effects were expected to be permanent at the same level. G had undergone numerous sessions of physiotherapy and acupuncture. She had also received an epidural injection. Although the continuing symptoms were extremely minor, the judge found that this was as a result of the adjustments she had made to her lifestyle. She had changed her work pattern and reduced her aerobics and other activities. In addition, she was nervous on driving, and at increased vulnerability to further trauma. The judge described this injury as at the upper end of bracket (e) of the JSB guidelines. *General Damages*: £5,000.

GRAINGER v. HOWES, September 30, 1997, District Judge Davidson, CC (Reading). [*Ex rel.* Benjamin Williams, Barrister, 3 Paper Buildings, Temple].

Neck–whiplash type injury

1906.   D male, aged 44 at the date of the accident and 47 at the date of the trial, was involved in a road traffic accident as a result of which he sustained injuries. The most serious was a whiplash type injury to the neck. He also suffered injuries to the left knee and left arm. At the date of the preparation of the medical report nearly a year after the accident the prognosis was that the neck injury would resolve itself within six months to a year, the arm would settle within one year. His knee was demonstrating symptoms of mild traumatic chondromalacia. D's sleep was initially disturbed but that improved following D's treatment with with anti-inflammatory tablets and two sessions with a chiropractor. He was able to go on a skiing holiday some nine months after the accident, however his enjoyment was curtailed. Pain in the left arm was experienced when changing gear, operating a computer or gardening whilst the leg ached after walking for a couple of miles. D suffered some discomfort in carrying out household activities. D's injuries had substantially resolved at the date of the hearing. *General Damages*: £4,850. Special Damages: £3,363.

DAVIS v. MILBORROW (NO.1), June 24, 1997, H.H.J. Hargrove Q.C., CC (Tunbridge Wells). [*Ex rel.* Nigel S Brockley, Barrister, Bracton Chambers, 95A Chancery Lane].

Neck–whiplash type injury

1907.   Female, aged 49 at the date of the accident in May 1991, and aged 55 at the date of the trial, was employed as a Disablement Resettlement Officer. Following the accident she suffered an exacerbation of an existing neck injury with discomfort, radiating into the muscles on the left hand side of her neck. She also suffered minor seat belt bruising and anxiety. She received physiotherapy treatment. She had been involved in a previous road traffic accident in 1989 in which she had suffered a whiplash injury. It was contended by H and accepted at the trial that by the time of the accident in May 1991 she had 95 per cent recovered from the effects of the previous accident. Bearing in mind pre-accident degeneration, it was concluded that the accident had accelerated/exacerbated symptoms by three years. As a result of the accident, H required some assistance with domestic, household and gardening tasks, she had not required such assistance before the 1991 accident. *General Damages*: £4,750. Special damages: £3,122 (including paid domestic assistance and physiotherapy treatment). Total award (including interest): £8,157.

HOLLANDS v. GK SALTER & ASSOCIATES AND O'NEILL, August 5, 1997, H.H.J. Coombe, CC (Maidstone). [*Ex rel.* Andrew Roberts, Solicitor, Amery Parkes, 12a London Street, Basingstoke].

Neck–whiplash type injury

1908.　　L, the defendant, a nurse, aged 47 at the date of injury and aged 49 at the date of trial, counterclaimed for injuries suffered in a road traffic accident. She suffered a whiplash injury to the neck, wore a cervical collar for two to three weeks and was prescribed muscle relaxant and pain relieving medication. She was off work for a week. The medical evidence anticipated a full recovery within a period of 19 to 25 months from the date of the accident. At the hearing, nearly 27 months after the accident D was still suffering. She was taking analgesics up to four times a day and the district judge accepted that D's symptoms were still extant. D did not return to her pre-accident hobby of aerobics and felt unable to tend her balcony garden as she had done previously. The district judge found that D's injuries came just within band (f) of the Judicial Studies Board Guidelines. *General Damages*: £3,500. Special damages: £713. Total award (including interest): £4,401.

LUCAS v. LACEY (NO.1), March 24, 1997, District Judge Schroeder, CC (Wandsworth). [*Ex rel.* Nigel S Brockley, Barrister, Bracton Chambers, 95A Chancery Lane].

Neck–whiplash type injury

1909.　　Male driving instructor, aged 57 at the date of the accident and aged 58 at the date of the trial, was a passenger in a vehicle that was struck from behind in December 1995. He sustained whiplash type injuries to his neck with some initial lower back symptoms. The back symptoms improved within a week of the incident but the neck symptoms persisted. He was able to return to his job although symptoms were provoked by repetitive twisting of his neck to look to the rear or by sudden jolting movements, eg. when a learner driver braked sharply. In addition, symptoms were provoked by reading for a period of 15 to 20 minutes and he suffered occasional sleep discomfort. One year after the accident, the neck symptoms were described as varying between 40 and 80 per cent of their initial severity. At the time of trial, 18 months after the accident, he had made a full recovery. The judge praised the victim's frankness and indicated that the appropriate award was at the bottom of bracket (f) of the JSB Guidelines (3rd Edition). He noted that this was a case of real inconvenience and suffering with symptoms gradually diminishing over the 19 month period. *General Damages*: £3,250. Special Damages (agreed): £360.

TREE v. PHILLIPS, June 9, 1997, District Judge Thomas, CC (Cardiff). [*Ex rel.* Christopher Taylor, Barrister, All Saints Chambers, 9-11 Broad Street, Bristol].

Neck–whiplash type injury

1910.　　Female, aged 14 at the time of the accident and aged 16 at the date of the hearing, was injured when the car in which she was a passenger was struck by B's vehicle which veered at speed after B had suffered a heart attack. M sustained a wrenching injury to the acromio-clavicular joint of the shoulder, a minor wrenching injury to the cervical spine, an abrasion to the left shoulder and anterior chest area as a result of seat belt restraint and bruising to the right leg and over the lateral aspect of the lower end of the right thigh. M also suffered psychological sequelae. For a year following the accident she suffered from nightmares at the frequency of three per week for six to eight months, thereafter reducing in frequency and severity. She was fearful and nervous when travelling in motor vehicles and was anxious if she thought the vehicle was travelling too fast. She had recovered from her physical injuries within a period of about six months but they were enough to make her give up her hobby of swimming. She was away from school for one week. It was anticipated that M would make a full recovery from the psychological effects of the accident within two years but at the time of the hearing there were minor ongoing psychological problems. *General Damages*: £3,000.

MISKELL (A MINOR) v. BENNETT (DECEASED), March 25, 1997, District Judge Needham, CC (Manchester). [*Ex rel.* Linda Norman, Pannone & Partners, Manchester].

Neck–whiplash type injury

1911. Male, aged 19 at date of the road traffic accident and 22 at date of the hearing suffered a soft tissue flexion/extension injury to neck, "whiplash", and pain in chest occasioned by contact with seatbelt in road traffic accident. Chest pains resolved within a few days. Neck continued to be painful for three weeks. Off work for one week. After three weeks mobility returned. Thereafter intermittent symptoms of stiffness and discomfort on heavy lifting during work as a welder. Neck also stiff on following morning if involved in heavy lifting on previous day involved heavy lifting. By date of medical report, some 18 months after accident, symptoms largely resolved save for lingering tendency of neck ache brought on by heavy lifting. Symptoms almost entirely resolved by two years from date of accident. *General Damages*: £2,800 (for pain, suffering and loss of amenity). Special damages: £80.

ANGELL v. BROUGH, November 29, 1996, District Judge Gavin, CC (Leeds). [*Ex rel.* David N Jones, Barrister, Broadway House, 9 Bank Street, Bradford].

Neck–whiplash type injury

1912. Female, student nurse, W, aged 21 at the date of the road traffic accident and 22 at the date of the hearing, suffered a whiplash type injury to her neck when a vehicle behind collided with hers when attempting to overtake as she was making a right hand turn. She experienced immediate pain in her neck and attended hospital soon after the accident when she was issued with a collar and recommended to take analgesics. She wore the collar every day for two weeks and attended physiotherapy sessions two or three times a week for several weeks. At the date of the hearing she still found it necessary to continue with daily exercises. She used painkillers for about a month after the accident. W owned horses which she had ridden every day before the accident. She was unable to ride at all until two to three months after the accident due to pain in her back. She had to suspend her hobby of running for about four months and she felt unable to resume her hobby of martial arts until 10 months after the accident. Her studying was also affected since she experienced discomfort if her neck was kept in a fixed position for any length of time. Eleven months after the accident she still suffered from pain in her neck and back if she kept her neck in a fixed position for more than 30 minutes. *General Damages*: £2,400. Award for loss of use of vehicle (for 6 weeks): £300. Special damages: £696. Total award (inclusive of interest): £3,463.

WHITE v. ONIONS, November 26, 1996, Deputy District Judge Healey, CC (Exeter). [*Ex rel.* Thomas Garnham, Barrister, Lorne Park Chambers, 20 Lorne Park Road, Bournemouth].

Neck–whiplash type injury

1913. Male, aged 35 at the date of the accident and aged 36 at the date of the trial, was injured in a road traffic accident in January 1996, suffering a whiplash type injury to his neck. The pain in his neck commenced on the day of the accident, and worsened over the next few days. S was prescribed a soft collar which he wore intermittently for three days. He suffered severe pain and stiffness in his neck. He had headaches for two to three weeks. Initially he was anxious and apprehensive about driving. S was off work for two days and then performed light duties for three weeks. When he returned to his usual work he found that his symptoms were exacerbated. He was unable to play football for around two months. His symptoms had resolved completely six months after the accident. *General Damages*: £1,500.

SANGSTER v. KENSINGTON BUILDING SERVICES, February 4, 1997, H.H.J. Trigger, CC (Birkenhead). [*Ex rel.* Matthew Dunford, Barrister, King Street Chambers, 40 King Street, Chester].

Neck–whiplash type injury

1914.   Female, aged 37 at the date of the accident and 38 at the date of the assessment of damages hearing was involved in a road traffic accident and sustained a whiplash type injury. She continued to work that day, woke with a painful neck the following day and attended her GP two days later when she was advised to take painkillers. No collar was worn and no time was taken off work although judge commented that it was apparent that she could have done with some time off. Symptoms impeded typing and lifting notes at work and reversing a car for two months during which time she regularly used painkillers. Occasional stiffness for further a five months, although able to join low impact aerobics class after three months. Virtually fully recovered seven months. District Judge observed that there are two different lines of authorities and he preferred the line of *Crowson v. Evans* Kemp & Kemp E2-034. *General Damages*: £1,500. Special damages: £15. Total damages: £1,515.

ELLIS v. SOOLE, November 20, 1996, District Judge Moon, CC (Exeter). [*Ex rel.* Mary McCarthy, Barrister, Walnut House, 63 St Davids Hill, Exeter].

Neck–whiplash type injury

1915.   Male, aged 64 at the date of the accident and aged 66 at the date of the hearing, was the driver of a motor car involved in a collision when a vehicle pulled out from a minor road on the left hand side into the vehicle which he was driving, causing it to hit a parked vehicle and spin round into a lamp post and brick wall. He sustained strain to his neck and was taken by ambulance to hospital where he was not X-rayed but was given a collar to wear as a precaution. He wore this on and off for the next week and took occasional pain killers to ease the discomfort he was feeling. He visited a chiropractor two days after the accident and his pain and suffering resolved over the following two weeks. He suffered no recurrence of symptoms thereafter. *General Damages*: £1,000. Award for loss of use of car (37 days): £215. Special damages: £4,370. Total award (including interest): £5,856.

STRIDE (A) v. LIPSCOMBE, July 1, 1997, District Judge Langley, CC (Central London). [*Ex rel.* Douglas Silas, Solicitor, David Levene & Co, 235-239 High Road, Wood Green, London].

Neck–whiplash type injury

1916.   P1, aged 43 years, and P2, her daughter, aged 14 years, sustained whiplash type injuries when their car was struck from the rear by another vehicle. Both were extremely distressed; the daughter who had never been involved in an accident before, was showered with glass and screamed for some time. This, and the fact that they were travelling to visit a very sick relative in hospital, caused additional upset to the mother. Approximately half an hour after the collision they both developed pain in their necks the daughter also suffered from a headache which lasted for 24 hours. The neck pain for each plaintiff was severe for the first two to three days and then became moderate. They did not attend a hospital or their GP's surgery. The mother was a teacher but neither she nor her daughter were absent from school as a result of the accident although the daughter was unable to participate in PE, netball or ballet for the first week. Within two weeks both of them ceased to suffer from pain, but they continued to experience "twinges" on certain movements for six to eight weeks. There were no longer term sequelae.

General Damages: £750 (per plaintiff). Each award included £100 for emotional distress.

HALES v. CLARK, April 16, 1997, H.H.J. Wilson, CC (Oxford). [*Ex rel.* Elaine Strachan, Barrister, Chambers of Michael Parroy Q.C., Temple].

Neck–whiplash type injury

1917. Male, aged 28 at the date of the road traffic accident and aged 29 at the date of the hearing, was the driver of a car which was hit from behind whilst stationary. He was shocked and shaken. His neck and lower back ached and became stiff shortly after the accident. He did not seek medical attention but took oral analgesics. He suffered pain and stiffness in his neck and lower back for one week following the accident but thereafter was symptom free. He suffered inconvenience in his day to day activities for one week. He did not miss any time off work as a factory operative although this was due to pressure of work. He was diagnosed as having suffered an acute whiplash to his cervical spine that produced tearing of the posterior cervical muscles and a jarring of his lumbar sacral spine which produced an acute sprain of the lumbar sacral muscle and ligamentous structures. *General Damages*: £750 (for pain suffering and loss of amenity). Loss of use of vehicle for one week (agreed): £50. Special damages (agreed): £607.

SALMON v. SJT STAFFORD LTD, May 21, 1997, District Judge Gregory, CC (Altrincham). [*Ex rel.* Paul Treble, Barrister, 58 King St Chambers, Manchester].

Neck–whiplash type injury

1918. R suffered a whiplash type injury to his neck when his car was hit from the side by C's vehicle. R's neck became stiff within an hour of the collision. He attended hospital on the day of the accident where a 25 per cent loss of rotation was noted together with tender neck muscles. Pain killers were prescribed but R did not take them. R was unable to work for two days as a result of his injury. He suffered no other loss of amenity and his symptoms had completely disappeared within one week. *General Damages*: £250 (for pain, suffering and loss of amenity).

CHARNICK v. RUSSELL, May 13, 1997, District Judge Hall, CC (Tunbridge Wells). [*Ex rel.* David Barr, Barrister, 1 Temple Gardens, Temple].

Back

1919. Female, aged 36 at the date of the accident and aged 40 at the date of the trial, was involved in a road traffic accident and suffered soft tissue injuries to the cervical spine and to the right temporal region, interolateral aspect of the chest and right arm, hip and knees. She was diagnosed as suffering from disc degeneration, disc prolapse and lumbar segmental instability and underwent a lower lumbosacral spinal fusion from L4 to S1. She was left with intermittent lower backache with radiation into the right leg. Medical opinion was that she did not have a pristine back and that the accident had only exacerbated existing low backache and right sided sciatica but had also caused the disc prolapse. She was left with a 40 per cent chance of future spinal instability occurring about 10 years after the date of the operation. She also suffered post traumatic stress disorder which resolved spontaneously over a period of five months from the accident, but leaving her with minor residual symptoms including a phobia of driving and travelling by car. At the time of the accident she was a self employed caterer but due to the spinal injuries she was unable to continue and had to cease trading. Her injuries prevented her from lifting and carrying heavy objects and participating in her hobby of skiing. She also had to employ a cleaner. The multiplier for future loss of business profit and cleaning expenses was discounted from 12 to 9 to take into account that the plaintiff's back had not been asymptomatic prior to the accident. *General Damages*: £22,220 (including £3,250 on account of post traumatic stress). Past loss of profits: £8,481. Future loss of profits: £27,000. Past cleaning expenses:

£4,000. Future cleaning expenses: £11,232. Other Special Damages (agreed): £1,680.

WAXMAN v. SCRIVENS, April 4, 1997, Judge not specified, CC (Lincoln). [*Ex rel.* Hodgkinsons, Solicitors, 14 Lumley Avenue, Skegness].

Back

1920. Female, aged 35 at date of the accident and 46 at date of trial was employed as an auxiliary nurse by the defendants. She sustained an injury to her back as she attempted to lift a patient at the patient's home. She did not seek treatment immediately but drove to visit her next patient. On attempting to get out of the car, she felt in severe pain. She was visited by a general practitioner who diagnosed a prolapsed inter vertebral disc. A subsequent medical examination revealed that in fact there was a soft tissue injury at the dorso lumbar junctions. She was initially unable to work for 10 days after the injury, and subsequently did not return to work. She suffered intermittent back pain lasting three days at a time and occurring every week or every other week. Over the next 10 years the pain became progressively worse. The pain was located in the middle of the back and extended down to the right buttock. She suffered numbness in her lower part of her right leg and in the last three toes of her right foot. Various treatments including physiotherapy had proved ineffective. During the trial evidence was heard concerning back injuries which she had sustained prior to the accident. There was a conflict of medical evidence at the trial as to whether the accident which occurred in 1984 exacerbated a pre-existing back problem or whether the present symptoms originated solely from the accident. The judge accepted that there had not been any pre-accident constitutional back pain and that the accident had resulted in a disabling injury for which an award would be made. *General Damages*: £20,000. Special damages (agreed): £155,000. Total award: £175,000.

JONES v. SOUTH GLAMORGAN HA, April 19, 1996, McKinnon, J., Cardiff District Registry. [*Ex rel.* Bryan Thomas, Barrister, Gower Chambers, Swansea].

Back

1921. Female, aged about 27 at the date of the incident and 38 at date of assessment, sustained injuries to her coccyx and lower spine in an incident during her work as a police officer in September, 1986. W was absent from work for six and a half months. Thereafter she worked light duties for eight weeks. She had to return to light duties about 15 months after the incident and was unable to continue her work after June 1988, some 21 months after the accident and was medically retired in May 1989. Medical experts accepted that the injury had caused W chronic coccydynia but disagreed as to whether it had caused persistent and severe lower back pain as W claimed. A number of experts identified inappropriate illness behaviour signs and considered that there was an element of functional overlay. Nevertheless all experts and the Board treated W's symptoms as genuine. W could not drive for longer than 25 minutes and was uncomfortable and fidgety when sitting for any length of time. She was limited in her ability to carry out domestic chores. She required a gardener to perform heavy lifting and mow her lawn. W had employed a cleaner who ironed, hoovered and brought her washing in. The Board considered that W was able to clean for herself at the date of the hearing. W had enjoyed her job, considered herself a "career woman" and had intended to work in the police force until she was 55 years old. Since the incident she was no longer able to play squash and badminton. She had received various treatments including acupuncture, hydrotherapy, cortisone injections, extensive physiotherapy, manipulation of the coccyx under general anaesthetic and an exploratory operation of the spine. *General Damages*: £20,000. Award for loss of congenial employment: £5,000. Part loss of earnings: £22,000. Future loss of earnings: £66,000 (multiplier of 11). Award for part cost of past and future gardener and past cost of cleaner: £11,600. Total award (per contributor): £126,774.

WATSON (LINDA), *Re*, January 29, 1997, Judge not specified, CICB (Durham). [*Ex rel.* Corin John Furness, Barrister, Park Lane Chambers, Park Lane House, 19 Westgate, Leeds].

Back

1922. T, aged 17 at the date of the accident and 20 at the date of the trial, was a rear seat passenger in a vehicle involved in a road traffic accident. She suffered compressed fractures to 12th dorsal and 2nd lumbar vertebra, fractures to 10th and 11th ribs on the right hand side, an undisplaced fracture to 4th metacarpal and injury to her right (non-dominant) elbow later considered to be fracture. She was in hospital for three weeks, treated conservatively with bed rest, and then mobilised using a surgical corset. Eight weeks after the accident she was still in considerable pain, but thereafter made a "remarkable recovery". At the date of trial she was suffering pain and discomfort on a weekly basis particularly when tired. Pain was relieved by rest. Her back would always be vulnerable, sitting, bending, lifting and standing placed a strain on it. Osteoarthritis was almost a certainty in middle age. Arthritic changes were likely at the radial side of her right elbow. There was also a less than 50 per cent chance that a bone or cartilage fragment might become loose and require surgery to remove it at a cost of £2,000. She was in her first year of a degree in textile design at the date of the trial. Her career prospects were uncertain due to the nature of the trade and her age. If unable to undertake her chosen career she would be at a significant disadvantage on the labour market. A wide range of activities were expected to be closed to her and/or would put her back under strain. *General Damages*: £17,500. Special damages: £4,823. Award for costs of future operation: £600. *Smith v. Manchester* Award: £25,000.

TREFFRY v. SMITH, October 15, 1996, District Judge Vincent, CC (Bodmin). [*Ex rel.* Anne Studd, Barrister, 5 Essex Court, Temple].

Back

1923. Female, aged 36 at the date of accident in 1991 and aged 42 at the date of trial, suffered a prolapsed disc in her lower spine as a result of lifting a disabled child up the steps of a coach. She had undergone extensive physiotherapy and osteopathy but had not returned to her employment as a teacher's assistant working with disabled children. She obtained work in a restaurant some 18 months after the accident but gave this up because of the lifting and bending involved. She failed to complete a course in information technology because of the amount of sitting required. Over four years after the accident she commenced a Theology diploma. She successfully completed the first year and was likely to be ordained within the Church of England on completion of the course in 1997. At the date of trial H suffered from a weak back causing frequent pain and disability. H suffered associated pain in her neck and could not drive for more than 40 minutes without experiencing painful symptoms. She could not stand or sit for any length of time without moving about. Her capacity for housework and gardening was restricted and her studies had been interrupted from time to time by her symptoms. She could not sit to enjoy the theatre or cinema, had suffered depression and was physically vulnerable. The judge was satisfied that she had suffered and continued to suffer a good deal of pain and that this suffering affected the ordinary quality of her life. She protected her back and limited her activities but nevertheless experienced back symptoms every four to six weeks and more frequently if she exceeded her limited capacity. H's condition was permanent. Degenerative changes were likely which might either stabilise her spine and decrease symptoms, or possibly, lead to worse symptoms and the need for surgery. *General Damages*: £16,000. Total award: £72,150.

HODGES v. LAMBETH LBC, January 9, 1997, H.H.J. Quentin Edwards Q.C., CC (Central London). [*Ex rel.* Gordon Dawes, Barrister, Goldsmith Building, Temple].

Back

1924.   Male, L, coalminer, aged 24 at the time of the accident and 32 at the date of the trial, was injured when he fell on an area of defective pavement. He suffered an injury to his back in the form of a disc prolapse. There was no evidence of degeneration or back problems prior to the accident. He made efforts to return to work in the mining industry but was unable to continue. L experienced episodes of increased back symptoms and although there had been improvement he remained vulnerable to further periods of pain. He was still taking analgesics at the date of trial. L had also suffered depression and mood swings, mainly due to his inability to work. Those symptoms were diagnosed as "Adjustment Disorder, with mixed disturbance of emotions and conduct" by L's experts and "Prolonged Depressive reaction" by the defendant's expert. L first saw his GP in November 1996, and was prescribed anti-depressants from that date. Both psychiatric reports agreed that this medication might have a continuing role for six to 18 months following the date of trial. L was unable to return to heavy work, but he was able to do some form of lighter work and had made reasonable efforts to obtain further work. L was awarded loss of earnings up to the date of trial, based on earnings in mining industry, and future loss of earnings on that basis for the first 18 months following trial and thereafter based on mining industry earnings less average earnings for lighter work. *General Damages*: £16,000. Part loss of earnings: £80,164. Future loss of earnings £58,642 (multiplier of 9).

LILL v. WAKEFIELD MDC, September 12, 1997, H.H.J. Robert Taylor, CC (Pontefract). [*Ex rel.* Christopher JG Noble, Hartley & Worstenholme, Solicitors, Bank Street, Hemsworth].

Back

1925.   Female, aged 17 at the time of the accident and aged 22 at the date of the trial, sustained a whiplash type injury to the neck which affected her for a period of approximately 18 months. She also sustained an injury to her lower back which had continued to produce symptoms, which appeared to be permanent. As a result she was unable to stand for long periods or sit for long periods. She was only fit for work in which she could move around. She had had to replace her bed with a futon. She was unable to travel in a car for more than three-quarters of an hour to an hour without pain. Although painkillers diminished the pain, they did not relieve it totally. S was not in work at the time of the accident and therefore had not lost any time off work. She had commenced work a month after the accident in the travel agency business, which enabled her to move around frequently, alleviating her symptoms. S had ABTA qualifications and other travel agency qualifications, and by the date of trial had some five years' experience in travel agency. She was shortly to be made redundant, however, and alternative employment with another travel agent was not going to be so financially rewarding. S had had to change her career plans as a result of the accident. She had not been able to pursue her intended career of teaching horse riding. Her main hobby had been riding and she had been forced to give it up. *General Damages*: £12,500. *Smith v. Manchester* award: £2,000. (Note: contributory negligence was alleged and assessed at 100 per cent).

SOLLIS v. HUGHES, HUGHES, COLSON (T/A BYRON CONSTRUCTION) AND BROAD, December 18, 1996, H.H.J. Huw Jones, CC (Pontypridd). [*Ex rel.* Mark Allen, Barrister, 30 Park Place, Cardiff].

Back

1926.   Female, part time care assistant, aged 38 at the date of the accident and 43 at the date of trial, sustained a back injury when, assisted by another employee, she lifted an elderly patient from her chair using the drag lift or underarm technique. There were significant issues between the parties in respect of the injuries sustained. R's consultant orthopaedic surgeon contended that if the accident had occurred, V would have sustained soft tissue injuries which would have lasted no longer than three to four weeks. V's consultant orthopaedic surgeon contended that the accident related soft tissue injuries would have caused symptoms for six to 12 months. V also relied on evidence from a consultant in pain management and a psychologist that V's ongoing back pain and disability were attributable to a chronic pain-type psychological reaction in a woman with a vulnerable personality who had previous psychological difficulties. The judge accepted that the accident had initially caused a relatively minor soft tissue injury and that according to both orthopaedic experts the continuing level of symptoms ordinarily be expected and that V was suffering from a "conversion hysteria" where V unconsciously converted psychological problems to physical complaints. The judge held that it was the accident which was the precipitating cause of her ongoing condition. V had been unable to return to her employment after the accident. She had been attending a pain clinic and her symptoms had been rapidly improving to the extent that the pain clinician expected her to be fit to return to part-time paid employment within 12 months from the date of trial. *General Damages*: £10,000. Past loss of earnings: £26,660. Future loss of earnings: £10,335. Award for past care: £4,000. Award for future care: £2,000. Other special damages: £972. Total award: £57,364 (including interest).

VICKERAGE v. ROTHERHAM MBC, February 27, 1997, H.H.J. Barber, CC (Sheffield). [*Ex rel.* Clive Garner, Solicitor, Irwin Mitchell, Sheffield].

Back

1927. Male coach driver, aged 27 at the date of the accident and aged 31 at the date of trial, suffered a back injury when lifting an excessively heavy suitcase from a coach. He had relatively minor, pre-accident, symptomless degenerative changes in his back which were unusual for a man in his 20s but the accident accelerated the symptoms by about 15 years according to G's medical expert, or six years according to B's medical expert. G received a facet joint injection to which he had a good initial response, but he had a more limited response to three further injections. He was unable to return to his pre-accident work due to continuing symptoms resulting from severe lower back strain and soft tissue injury. G had attempted to return to his pre-accident job for two weeks in February 1994 but was unable to continue and remained off work until returning to light duties in November 1995. He was medically retired on ill health grounds in January 1997 as a result of the back injury. It was possible that a "pain block" nerve root operation would be advised which would, if successful, eliminate the pain, but would render G vulnerable to the extent that he would not notice how vulnerable his back really was. The trial judge took both experts opinions into account in awarding damages. *General Damages*: £10,000. Past loss of earnings: £21,666. Other special damages: £1,732. Future loss of earnings (multiplicand £6,000, multiplier of 6): £36,000. *Smith v. Manchester* award: £15,000. Future cost of extra swimming (multiplier of 6): £2,100. Total award: £89,893.

GARRETT v. BRITISH AIRWAYS, March 12, 1997, H.H.J. Collins, CC (Wandsworth). [*Ex rel.* Rowley Ashworth, Solicitors, 247 The Broadway, Wimbledon, London].

Back

1928. Male, aged 42 at the time of accident and 45 years at date of trial, was employed by the defendant as a painter and decorator and was injured whilst painting a derelict property. He was standing on a paint tin due to the unavailability of ladders. As he stretched he suffered an injury to his lumbar spine. He was unable to return to work following the accident and was medically retired on the grounds of ill health on November 25, 1994. Agreed medical evidence indicated that R had sustained a prolapse of an already degenerate lumbar disc. It was agreed that the accident had accelerated the effects of that pre-existing degenerate condition by a factor of five years. R experienced sporadic pain in his lumbar spine from the date of the accident to the date of trial and his mobility was restricted. His employment prospects were affected as he was only fit for light work. *General Damages*: £9,250. Special Damages: £79,464 (agreed).

ROGERS v. BIRMINGHAM CITY COUNCIL, January 14, 1997, H.H.J. Alton, CC (Birmingham). [*Ex rel.* Thompsons, Solicitors, The McLaren Building, 35 Dale End, Birmingham].

Back

1929.   Female police constable, aged 29 at the date of the assault, suffered an injury to her lower back by falling onto the edge of the kerb whilst attempting to restrain a drunken youth. She was not off work immediately but increasing symptoms of back pain over the next three months led to a total of 28 weeks' absence over the following two and a half years. By this time intensive physiotherapy had prompted an almost complete recovery of low back symptoms. Pre-existing asymptomatic spondylolithesis was eliminated as being relevant to her symptoms. The onset of increasing symptoms to her right thigh also developed and EMGs showed nerve root entrapment. She had difficulty sleeping, bending or standing for long periods of time and her ability to carry out housework was affected. Nerve blocks failed to relieve pain and surgical decompression of the cutenous nerve was carried out four years post incident. There was a further period of six weeks absence from work and then light duties for six weeks. Surgery has greatly improved symptoms and H is now back on full police duties. She has not yet returned to playing squash and is unable to run at pre-incident levels. There are some permanent symptoms. *General Damages*: £9,000. Special Damages: £2,124.

HIBBERD (LESLEY ANN), *Re*, March 11, 1997, Peter Weizman Q.C., CICB (London). [*Ex rel.* Warren Collins, Solicitor, Russell Jones & Walker, London].

Back

1930.   Male, self-employed music promoter, aged 28 at the time of the accident and 31 at the date of trial, was injured in September 1993 whilst motorcycling. He collided with, and was thrown over, the top of a car which turned across his path. He landed heavily on his back and head and initially suffered bilateral groin pain and neck/back stiffness. At hospital X-rays revealed no bony injury and he was discharged home with painkillers the same day wearing a right (dominant) arm sling on account of shoulder pain. He was bedridden for two weeks and off work for eight weeks returning whilst still suffering significant neck/spinal symptoms. The groin bruising settled in six weeks, and the low back/thoracic tenderness and shoulder injury mostly settled after four months. Neck manipulation was given by his GP in the days after the accident, he received physiotherapy three times weekly for 15 weeks and 27 private osteopathic treatments over the next three years, including several on account of an acute but brief relapse in his neck/back condition six months prior to the trial. Over the period up to trial flattened spinal lordosis, neck/trapezius spasm and a 30 per cent reduction in neck mobility largely settled leaving a continuing tenderness of the neck and upper back. Symptoms were exacerbated by activities causing flexion or twisting of the neck, prolonged standing and the position adopted whilst using a VDU, which all caused pain. His condition was expected to be permanent. He had had to delegate or hire extra help for physical aspects of his job such as carrying and checking stage equipment and cables. He had performed domestic DIY activities prior to the accident but his symptoms had greatly restricted DIY thereafter. His first child had been born shortly after the accident and he had experienced difficulty in carrying and playing with her. He had been a county level rugby player and occasional golf player. Both sports had become impossible as a result of his injuries, as had fox hunting and riding, at which he had previously excelled. He was only able to swim for exercise. He no longer rode a motorcycle on account of the physical demands and the loss of confidence in his safety which had arisen from the circumstances of the accident. *General Damages*: £9,000. Special damages: £7,554.

O'BOYLE v. LAWRENCE, May 12, 1997, Judge Platt Q.C., CC (Ilford). [*Ex rel.* James Candlin, Barrister, Chambers of Geoffrey Hawker].

Back

1931. Male, training manager, aged 32 at the date of accident and 36 at the date of trial, was driving his motor vehicle when he was involved in a relatively minor rear end shunt. He experienced no pain at the time and continued on his way to work. Shortly thereafter he began to suffer headaches and after three or four days developed symptoms of pain and stiffness in his lower back. He had no previous history of back pain. W did not drive for two weeks. W continued to complain of fairly constant discomfort with episodes of more acute suffering. W was prescribed painkillers which caused drowsiness. W also complained of stiffness and cramp in the mornings which was not assisted by the amount of driving which he did in the course of his employment. As a result of his back problem W had given up his hobbies of squash and football. W's sleep was disturbed by pain and he described himself as more impatient and more irritable than he otherwise might have been. There had been some pre-accident degenerative change in the spine which would, on the balance of probabilities have become symptomatic at age 50 to 55 and affected W's ability to lift and bend at age 55 to 60. The judge found that as a result of the accident there was a disc protrusion at L5/S1 and radial tear at L4/L5. There was no prospect of improvement in W's symptoms. There was a two to five per cent risk that the disc prolapse would increase and cause further compression to nerve roots. If that complication did ensue there would be an 80 per cent chance that surgery would be required. W's employers described him as a valued employee and gave evidence that they would continue to employ him but he would be vulnerable to redundancy, and in that event he would be at a disadvantage on the labour market as a result of his condition. If the disc did prolapse at a later date then it would be difficult to establish causation, ie that the prolapse was due to the relevant accident rather than simply being a feature of further constitutional degeneration caused by subsequent trauma. *General Damages*: £8,500. Special Damages (agreed): £4,500. *Smith v. Manchester* award (representing three months' wages): £3,500. Total award (including interest): £16,120.

WARBURTON v. HALLIWELL, October 3, 1996, Judge Robertshaw, CC (Sheffield). [*Ex rel.* John Pickering, Solicitor].

Back

1932. Male, aged 32 at the date of injury, was a window cleaner who fell 20 feet from an inadequately footed ladder whilst at work. He suffered soft tissue injuries to the lefthand side of his body including elbow, wrist, leg, jaw and bridge of his nose. He also suffered neuro-praxia to the medio aspect of the right knee and sustained a lower back injury shown to be more muscular and ligamentous than skeletal. L remained symptomatic at trial from both his knee and lower back and was diagnosed as being likely to become a chronic back sufferer with permanent back pain. He was seen at hospital and given pain killing injections and discharged. He continued to be in great pain and was referred to physiotherapy where he was treated with infra-red pulsation by electric waves, manipulation and calisthenics. Physiotherapy lasted for approximately a year. During all of that time he was under the care of his GP who signed him off in periods of one month at a time. L gave evidence that he did not feel able to carry out manual work during the year that he was off work and that he would have been prepared to undertake office work but that he was not qualified for any such occupation, having been a manual labourer since leaving school at the age of 16. Also he still had periods of no sensation in the knee and he had been incontinent for some three weeks after the accident. He had been unable to have sexual intercourse with his wife for some three months and could not play with his children as he once had. He was no longer able to play pool or darts and his handicap at golf had risen. The court accepted L's current employer's evidence that he could not guarantee L's continued employment in light of his continued back pain and stated that it would be absolutely clear that L would suffer a considerable handicap in the labour market because of this. *General Damages*: £8,000. Loss of earnings: £9,192. Taxi fares: £30. Compensation for damaged clothing: £70. *Smith and Manchester* award: £6,000. Total award: £23,292.

LE GALLOU v. MALOREY, Date not specified, Sir Philip Baihache (Bailiff), Court not specified. [*Ex rel.* Ogier & Le Masurier, Advocates & Solicitors, P.O. Box 404, Pirouet House, Union Street, St Helier, Jersey].

Back

1933. Male, aged 55 at the date of the accident and aged 60 at the date of the trial, suffered a soft tissue injury to the lumbar spine whilst operating a high pressure water hose which he was untrained to do. He was thrown 12 to 15 feet by the pressure of water along the floor of a dry dock. The next day D saw his doctor and was prescribed painkillers. Although in substantial pain he attempted to return to work, working for four weeks during 1991 and two weeks during early 1992. But he was unable to return to any heavy work. Since the accident he had been in constant lumbar pain taking painkillers, which continued until trial and would continue. His hobbies of swimming, diving, dancing, fishing, gardening and boating had ceased. He could manage light housework but could not lift any heavy objects. He could drive a car for 15 minutes and walk with a stick for up to half a mile. He had pre-existing degenerative lumbar spondylosis which was made symptomatic by the accident. Medical opinion agreed that this would have become symptomatic in any event between five and seven years following the accident. Further, three years after the accident D experienced tightness in his chest which was diagnosed as angina and it was agreed that three years after the accident he would have been unfit for heavy manual labour in any event. *General Damages*: £7,500. *Smith v. Manchester* award: £4,000. Total award: £31,040 (including interest).

DOWNING v. A&P APPLEDORE (FALMOUTH) LTD (1997) 97(1) Q.R. 5, John Turner (Assistant Recorder), CC (Truro).

Back

1934. Female nurse, aged 31 at the time of the accident and aged 35 at the date of the trial, suffered a muscular tear to the right lumbar sacral area when she had to lift a heavy patient during the course of her employment. As a result she was off work for two months and was limited to part time work for a further six weeks. She was treated with manipulation and physiotherapy but found these of little use, the best treatment being simple rest and painkillers, which she had continued to take up to the time of trial. Despite suffering pain at work quite often, B was able to do her job satisfactorily, and even gained promotion, but she received help in lifting from her colleagues and had to guard her back. She frequently required rest after work. B took no further time off work as a result of her back injury until May 1996, some three or more years after the accident, since when she had taken five days off work with back pain during a period of six months. The medical evidence was that B would continue to suffer from intermittent low back pain indefinitely, and had a vulnerable back: heavy lifting was likely to lead to injury. B found that she was unable to do certain things such as step aerobics, carrying heavy shopping, doing heavy gardening, carrying the hoover upstairs and walking long distances. *General Damages*: £7,500 (for pain, suffering and loss of amenity). Damages for disadvantage on labour market: £2,500.

BONNEY v. RADCLIFFE INFIRMARY NHS TRUST, February 3, 1997, H.H.J. Collins, CC (Wandsworth). [*Ex rel.* Anthony Snelson and Carolina Guiloff, Barristers, Thomas More Chambers, 51/52 Carey Street, Lincoln's Inn].

Back

1935. Female, aged 25 years at the date of road traffic accident, and aged 30 at the date of assessment, suffered an injury to her lower back with associated pain to her left hip. She had pre-existing asymptomatic degenerative changes which were exacerbated by a factor of 10 years. W had physiotherapy and chiropractic treatment. W's medical expert gave evidence that W would be left with mild continual pain, which would be exacerbated from time to time by performing certain activities. W could not guard against the aggravation of the pain and would require an average of eight to 10 treatments per year, in the form of two or three intensive bouts of physiotherapy. W was unable to do heavy household work and employed her mother to do this work. At the time of the accident W was a dental nurse and was six months pregnant, and B argued that some of her problems were due to back pain from the pregnancy. However, W had suffered no previous back pain with the birth of her first child, and W's medical expert felt that it was unlikely she would have suffered problems in the second pregnancy but for the accident. W gave evidence that she would have difficulty in returning to work as a dental nurse due to the bending which would be necessary, but she had obtained a job as the manager of a shop. *General Damages*: £7,500. Special damages: £3,323 (inclusive of interest). Award for future costs of chiropractic treatment and domestic help: £4,000. Total award: £15,123.

WARD v. BATTEN & STAMFORD ASPHALT CO LTD, June 13, 1997, District Judge Fuller, CC (Basingstoke). [*Ex rel.* Mark Gayler, Amery-Parkes Solicitors, Bristol].

Back

1936. Female, primary school teacher, aged 32 at the date of the accident in 1993 and aged 36 at the date of the trial was the driver of a stationary motor car in which her two year old son was passenger. The car was shunted from the rear. W suffered initial shock and concern about the condition of her son, and was taken to hospital but not detained. She sustained classical whiplash type injuries; hyperextension and hyperflexion injuries to neck, right sacroiliac strain to lower back. She had 15 sessions of physiotherapy in 1993 and 12 further sessions in 1995, which, however, gave only short term relief. Treatment did not involve the use of a collar. She needed to employ a cleaner and childminder for three months. She was left with permanent tenderness in her back from C4 to T9, some crepitus 15 per cent restriction on neck rotation to the left, and 25 per cent restriction of extension and lateral flexion. The cumulative effect of the 1993 accident and a previous accident in 1986 was a slightly increased risk of cervical degenerative arthritis. The principal continuing symptom suffered by N was aching pain in the back of the neck radiating into the interscapular area, considerably aggravated by lifting, heavy housework, dealing with her own small children and the physical demands of her job. Because of possible risk to her ability to carry on in her employment she had had "to grin and bear it". She also suffered some back pain about twice a week, adding to discomfort of subsequent pregnancies. Sleep was not disturbed. She gave up driving long distances and had not returned to pre-accident activities of riding and hill walking, but accepted this was primarily through lack of time. *General Damages*: £7,000. Special Damages: £1,070.

WRAY v. PARDEY, July 1, 1997, H.H.J. Bond, CC (Newport, IOW). [*Ex rel.* Jonathan Sharp, Barrister, 2 King's Bench Walk, Temple].

Back

1937. Male, aged 47 at date of accident in 1993 and 50 at date of trial, suffered an injury to his lumbar spine in a road traffic accident. He went to hospital where he was not detained. He had suffered significant symptoms in the lumbar spine before the accident and had significant degenerative changes at L4/5. The accident caused an acute exacerbation of his pre-accident condition which persisted for three and a half years. For that period this back pain was constant with significant periods of exacerbation which were worse than any pain he had suffered before the accident. As a result of the pain he could no longer go cycling, carry out DIY around his house or do as much gardening as before the accident. He had to be careful when lifting at work and there were some loads that he no longer lifted. His sex life had been affected. The judge accepted medical evidence that, after three and a half years, the condition of his back was at the level that it would have deteriorated to even if there had been no accident and that the affects of the accident had subsided. The plaintiff had also suffered some depression and anxiety about the accident for a short period from which he had almost completely recovered by the time of trial. He was left with a feeling of tension when driving past the scene of the accident. This was expected to resolve within one year. *General Damages*: £6,500.

IQUBAL v. AMUAH, October 16, 1996, H.H.J. Goodman, CC (Croydon). [*Ex rel.* Shaun Ferris, Barrister, 1 Paper Buildings, Temple].

Back

1938.   Male, aged 46 at the date of a road traffic accident, a result of which S sustained injury to his cervical and lumbar spine. S spent a night in hospital and was absent from work for 10 weeks. S experienced pain and suffering for 12 months following the accident both to his cervical and lumbar spine. *General Damages*: £2,000. Special damages: £3,184.

SOUTHWARD v. PEERS RECOVERY, June 12, 1997, District Judge Wright, CC (Birkenhead). [*Ex rel.* Michael W Halsall, Solicitors, 2 The Parks, Newton-le-Willows].

Back

1939.   Male factory worker, A, aged 50 at the date of the accident and 53 at the date of trial, was involved in a slipping accident on a gangway at work. A slipped on a piece of wood causing him to jar his back. A sustained a soft tissue strain of the lumbar spine. The accident happened on a Friday. A reported it on the following Monday to the occuptional health nurse and went home. On Tuesday he saw his GP, complaining that he had jarred his back and of pain radiating to the right of his lumbar spine. A returned to work after about six weeks and was reviewed by his GP about nine weeks after the accident, when he was still suffering backache, with pain in the right calf. A was periodically limping, and was therefore referred to a consultant rheumatologist, whom he saw six months after the accident. On examination he had a very stiff lumbar spine with marked tenderness to the right. His back was manipulated and he was given an injection. His condition was reviewed after about nine months when he received further manipulation and an injection and was discharged back to the care of his GP. A had pre-existing back problems dating back to 1976. It was held that exacerbation caused by the accident had lasted for nine months. *General Damages*: £1,500. Special Damages: £330.

ALLDIS v. MYER, June 20, 1997, Green, J., CC (Central London). [*Ex rel.* Rod Dutton, OH Parsons & Partners, Sovereign House, 212-224 Shaftesbury Avenue, London].

Back

1940.   H was involved in a road traffic accident on November 5, 1994 in which he was thrown forward, restrained by his seatbelt and hit his head on the head restraint. There was shock, but no loss of consciousness with no immediate pain. Pain developed in the lower back within two to three hours and H attended hospital and was advised to take paracetamol. He was off work for two weeks. He suffered occasional twinges of pain in his back after any prolonged sitting in any one position. His sleep was disturbed for three weeks and there was a complete recovery within three to four weeks. *General Damages*: £1,000.

HOPPER v. MEGABYTE LTD, Date not specified, District Judge Cockcroft, CC (Leeds). [*Ex rel.* Ison Harrison & Co, Solicitors, Duke House, 54 Wellington Street, Leeds].

Respiratory organs

1941.   Male aged 48 at the date of the trial was exposed to asbestos in 1963 during an apprenticeship as a carpenter and joiner which lasted until June 1967. During that time he was occasionally engaged in removing old asbestos roofing sheets and replacing them, which entailed cutting and shaping with a disc cutter, drilling and attaching the new sheets. He developed a respiratory disability in the order of 50 per cent due to pleural thickening but also had mild asbestosis. He had two cancer scares and continued to have risks of developing cancer in the order of five per cent with respect to mesothelioma and a two per cent risk of developing lung cancer. He also had significant pain associated with his pleural disease and was unable to work, and was likely to suffer increasingly severe disablement. The defendants were held to be in breach of statutory duty and negligent in exposing the plaintiff to asbestos dust without protection. *General Damages*: £42,000. Past loss of earnings £61,975. Future loss of earnings: £190,350. Award for past care (by wife): £3,401. Award for future care: £19,171. Special Damages for golf trolley (so that he could continue the only hobby he was able to continue): £2,225. Other Special Damages: £1,094. Other future loss (including expenses and equipment such as stairlift and ride-on motor mower): £34,920. Total award: £364,919.

TILLEY v. TUCKER, June 19, 1996, H.H.J. Young, Leicester Crown Court. [*Ex rel.* Frank Burton, Barrister, 12 King's Bench Walk, Temple].

Respiratory organs

1942.   Male, aged 49 at trial, was exposed to asbestos whilst working in the thermal insulation industry. He developed benighn symptomless bilateral pleural thickening. His fitness for work was compromised by breathlessness due to unrelated asthma and obesity. The risk of progression of pleural thickening to the point of causing disability due to asbestos was 20 per cent; the risk of development of asbestosis was five per cent; the risk of development of mesothelioma was ten per cent; the risk of development of lung cancer was 30 per cent. Communication of the nature and causation of illness had caused the development of an obsessive compulsive disorder and acute phobic anxiety about working in emvironments in which further exposure to asbestos might occur, as a result of which he lost the opportunity to undertake work in the thermal insulation industry for a two year period. The prognosis was that the phobia could be successfully treated in four to six months. *General Damages*: £27,000. Past loss of earnings: £19,100. Future losses associated with the malignant risks (discounted for acceleration of receipt and for the fact that those losses might not occur): £7,849. Total award: (including interest) £59,894.

SMITH v. DICKS EAGLE INSULATION LTD, July 11, 1997, Recorder Riza Q.C., CC (Central London). [*Ex rel.* Allan Gore, Barrister, 12 Kings Bench Walk, Temple].

Respiratory organs

1943.   Male, aged 77 years and 9 months at date of hearing, was exposed to asbestos dust between 1946-76. He had retired at age 65 in 1984. G developed breathlessness in 1992 when aged 73. Up to that date G had enjoyed an active retirement, swimming 27 lengths three times per week and working two large vegetable gardens. By date of trial G was diagnosed as suffering from 40 per cent respiratory disability by reason of pleural thickening. There was no radiological evidence of asbestosis. Walking distance was restricted to 40 yards before stopping and resting; had to treat all stairs with respect; could not climb hills or walk any distance on uneven ground. G could not work his garden, go swimming or do DIY about the house and could not help his disabled wife in the performance of routine household tasks. The prognosis was that there was a five per cent risk of further pleural thickening causing increased disablement, a three per cent risk of asbestosis causing increased disablement; a risk of up to ten per cent of suffering lung cancer by reason of asbestos exposure, and a risk of up to ten per cent of mesothelioma by reason of asbestos exposure. G's life expectancy had been reduced by two years from the normal eight by reason of an unrelated heart condition. *General Damages*: £25,000.

GLENDINNING v. POWERGEN PLC, January 15, 1997, Moreland, J., QBD. [*Ex rel.* DJB Trotter, Barrister, 2 Plowden Buildings, Temple].

Respiratory organs

1944.   Male, S, aged 51 at the date of diagnosis and 56 at the date of trial in June 1997, was employed by the defendant companies between 1957 and 1979 as an insulation installer. In 1992 S had a routine x-ray which disclosed pleural changes consistent with asbestosis. A diagnosis of asbestosis was made following a thoracotomy. This operation was an extremely painful and traumatic experience for him. As a result of the operation, it was found that S had widespread fibrosis and (unrelated) mild emphysema. He was diagnosed as having a 25 per cent loss of breathing function which meant that he became out of breath when climbing hills or stairs. He was also not able to continue doing DIY or playing golf and found it difficult to play with his grandchildren. Liability having been admitted, the trial was only concerned with quantum. It was agreed that there was a reduced life expectancy of between two to three years and that S would find it difficult to fight off infection. S had great anxiety about the possibility of developing a malignant condition and the knowledge of the risk of a malignancy developing made him obsessive, withdrawn and introverted. The judge stated, however that he had had five years to come to terms with this fact, and the outlook was not as bleak as it was for him in 1992, when he underwent an open lung biopsy, at which time he genuinely feared for his life. Damages for pain, suffering and loss of amenity were awarded on the basis that S would not develop mesothelioma or bronchial carcinoma, the award being £20,000. A further £3,500 was awarded to reflect the pain and anxiety of the operative procedure and resultant scar. The judge dismissed a claim for future loss of earnings, stating that the plaintiff had intended to retire at 60. The judge concluded that S was overly optimistic in believing that his employment was secure, since he was employed on a year to year contract, as a leak detection engineer and made a *Smith v. Manchester* award. It was quite possible for him to be thrown back onto the open labour market. *General Damages*: £23,500. *Smith v. Manchester* award: £8,000. Total award (including interest): £32,453.

SOMERSET v. SIMPKIN MACHIN & CO LTD, June 11, 1997, Bartfield, J., CC (Sheffield). [*Ex rel.* Irwin Mitchell, Solicitors, St Peter's House, Hartshead, Sheffield].

Respiratory organs

1945.   Male, aged 57 at the date of trial, was exposed to asbestos in the Portsmouth Naval Dockyard from approximately 1970-1995. In 1994, when aged about 54, E was diagnosed as having symptomless pleural plaques. He experienced anxiety about his future health, particularly as he knew of colleagues who had contracted significant asbestos related diseases and living in Portsmouth, which has a high rate of asbestos induced illness. E had been a heavy smoker until 1994. He had risks of developing asbestosis of 1-2 per cent, asbestos bilateral pleural thickening in the order of 1-2 per cent, a risk of contracting mesothelioma of five per cent, a risk of contracting laryngeal cancer in the order of 1-2 per cent and an approximately 23 per cent risk of contracting lung cancer. The lung cancer risk, according to medical evidence was likely to decline at approximately 0.75 per cent per annum to a level of approximately five per cent in 20 years' time. At the date of trial E was earning £14,200 net per annum and had an expectation of a pension in the order of £8,925 per annum. He was awarded £17,300 on a final basis expressed to be £3,500 for the pleural plaques and anxiety and £13,800 for the future risks of ill health and the risks of loss of earnings and pension. *General Damages*: £17,300.

ELFORD v. MINISTRY OF DEFENCE, April 24, 1997, H.H.J. Wroath, CC (Portsmouth). [*Ex rel.* Frank Burton, Barrister, 12 Kings Bench Walk, Temple].

Respiratory organs

1946. Between 1951 and 1953, B, who was aged 69 at the date of the trial, was exposed to asbestos during the course of his employment with the defendants. In early 1994 he developed a cough. A CT scan in June 1994 revealed large pleural plaques and extensive pleural disease with relatively mild fibrotic changes was diagnosed. By November 1995, B was complaining of breathlessness on exertion, particularly when walking up hills but had unlimited exercise tolerance when walking on the flat and no breathlessness at rest or at night. He had stopped smoking in June 1994. It was agreed that he had a very mild respiratory disability which was assessed at 10 per cent. The disability was equally attributable to smoking and asbestosis. The prognosis was: that there was a less than five per cent risk of progression of pleural disease; a slow progression of asbestosis but unlikely to produce severe breathlessness; that there was a five to 10 per cent risk of mesothelioma. Save for the risk of malignant tumours, B had a normal life expectancy. Provisional damages were originally claimed but the prayer was subsequently amended to claim a final award of damages. A claim was presented for the future cost of nursing care on the basis that if B were to develop cancer, his wife would be unable to look after him by reason of a heart condition and that therefore he would require institutional care. The claim was rejected as being too remote and, in any event, not susceptible to quantification. *General Damages*: £14,402.

BARKER v. ROBERTS, March 20, 1997, H.H.J. Carter, CC (Oldham). [*Ex rel.* Jeremy Freedman, Barrister, New Court Chambers, Newcastle upon Tyne].

Respiratory organs

1947. F, male, aged 58 at the date of trial in May 1997, was employed on pipe laying works for a water company by the first defendants from 1972 to 1983 and on similar work for the second defendants from 1983 to 1989 in the course of which he was exposed to significant amounts of asbestos dust. As a result F developed bilateral pleural plaques which gave rise to some anxiety on his part. There was a two per cent risk of F developing a malignant mesothelioma of the pleura in future. Provisional damages were awarded. F would be able to return at any time in the future for a further award in his lifetime should he develop mesothelioma. *General Damages* (provisional): £4,750.

FORD v. CLARBESTON LTD, May 23, 1997, H.H.J. Butterbury, CC (Bristol). [*Ex rel.* Andrew Herbert, Thompsons Solicitors, 18 Lawford Street, Bristol].

Asthma type illness

1948. Female nurse, S, aged 51 at the date of the trial in June 1997, was exposed to gluteraldehyde (in the form of "Cidex") over a period in the course of her duties as a full time theatre sister, which she commenced in September 1989, causing her to develop symptoms of breathlessness and lethargy. In November 1991 and January 1992 she suffered acute attacks, and occupational asthma was later diagnosed. In April 1992 she was redeployed to work in the Nuclear Medicine Department on a part time basis without the remainder of her duties being defined. She was also downgraded. Contrary to expectations the Nuclear Medicine Department was not gluteraldehyde free. It was also situated near to an ambulance bay. S therefore continued to be exposed to fumes that triggered her asthma leading to further absences from work due to ill health. In addition S was not given sufficient supervision or training in Nuclear Medicine. She experienced difficulty in coping with the stress of attending to patients many of whom were in the process of being diagnosed as suffering from cancer. She was not given any opportunity to offload these stresses. As a consequence of her asthma, the loss of her career as a theatre sister, uncertainty about her future employment, and the stresses of working in Nuclear Medicine, S became clinically depressed in September 1992 and went off sick in October 1992. She remained depressed as a consequence of these events for approximately six months. She was also diagnosed as suffering from "nursing burnout" or "compassion fatigue". She no longer felt able to professionally care for others. She was retired on the grounds of ill health in August 1993. S only suffered from asthmatic symptoms if she had contact with gluteraldehyde, which with care she is generally able to avoid. She carried an inhaler at all times, but only rarely has to use it. *General Damages*: £14,000. Award for loss of congenial employment: £5,000.

SOLA v. ROYAL MARSDEN HOSPITAL, June 5, 1997, Recorder Russell, CC (Clerkenwell). [*Ex rel.* Ian Mulkis, Solicitor, Douglas-Mann & Co, 33 Furnival Street, London].

Digestive organs

1949. M underwent keyhole surgery to remove her gall bladder. Due to W's negligence during the operation M's bile duct was clamped and cut in two places. This was not remedied for 11 days, by which time M was jaundiced and suffering from infections. She required a repair operation which caused a major upheaval to her digestive system, and left her suffering from wound pain, irritable bowel syndrome and changed personality.

Held, finding for M on causation, that the repair operation led to M's current complaints. *General Damages*: £60,000, Loss of earnings, past and future: £300,000.

MILES v. WEST KENT HA [1997] 8 Med. L.R. 191, Owen, J., QBD.

Excretory organs

1950. Female, aged 47 at the date of surgery and aged 55 at the date of assessment, underwent what was purported to be a Lord's procedure or anal stretch at the same time as she underwent a hysterectomy. The consultant gynaecologist concerned carried out the anal stretch at the specific request of the plaintiff's GP without assessing the position himself after clinical examination. The risks were never explained to the plaintiff, and it was questionable as to whether the procedure was either necessary or appropriate. The plaintiff sustained internal anal sphincter damage and although undergoing two anterior sphincter repair procedures, was left with faecal incontinence which will not improve over time and would tend to worsen. It was recommended that she should have a permanent colostomy but the plaintiff found the prospect of this too horrific to contemplate. Whilst accepting that she would inevitably require a colostomy in five years' time, she preferred to put up with the daily inconvenience associated with faecal incontinence for the time being. She was a lady who had enjoyed dancing and an active social life, which she was unable to pursue, and she could not plan from one day to the next. Some days were worse than others, but on average, on two days per week, she would be in substantial pain and be unable to leave the house by reason of leakage. She was unable to return to her previous employment as a part-time shop assistant. The cost of future medical treatment was discounted by 10 per cent to take account of advance payment and other eventualities, with a multiplier of seven for future loss of earnings and 11 for ongoing annual expenditure. *General Damages*: £40,000. Total award (including interest): £84,455.

PARKES v. CHESTER HA, April 22, 1997, District Judge Newman, CC (Chester). [*Ex rel.* David Rudd, Solicitor, Walker Smith & Way, Wrexham].

Excretory organs

1951. Female, aged 41 at the date of the incident and 47 at the date of trial, underwent a total abdominal hysterectomy. Eleven days after the operation, her operation wound split open; 12 days post operatively she became incontinent and a VVF was confirmed at cystoscopy. A successful repair operation was carried out three weeks post operatively but she was left with gross urge and stress incontinence. She underwent two Stamey colposuspensions in June 1991 and April 1992 but still had stress and urge incontinence. Burch colposuspension was carried out in August 1993 and afterwards the stress incontinence was much improved. The final prognosis was that there would be no further improvement in remaining urinary symptoms, she would continue to need to wear incontinence pads, she would continue to suffer significant drain of energy, would have a poor sleep pattern and a repression of sexual function. G was considered to have suffered from a depressive syndrome; she had been taking anti-depressants and attending regular counselling; she was advised to undergo cognitive behavioural therapy for three to four months, attending half day sessions once a week. The psychiatric prognosis was that the conclusion of proceedings would assist G's recovery with an improvement in her mental state in the region of 30 per cent, but that even with successful treatment, it would take at least two years before she regained an adequate measure of self-confidence to allow a normal range of activities and normal life style. She was expected to remain vulnerable to further episodes of depression. A supervening arthritic shoulder condition restricted her loss of earnings claim and loss of earnings was agreed up to the date of trial. Other special damages consisted of claims for domestic/nursing assistance and the supply of incontinence wear. Future loss was also awarded for these items and for the cost of therapy. *General Damages*: £30,000 (agreed). Total damages: £90,581 (agreed).

GEORGE v. TOWER HAMLETS HA, March 26, 1996, Scott Baker, J., QBD. [*Ex rel.* Nicola Mooney, Solicitor, Hodge Jones & Allen, London].

Excretory organs

1952. Female, aged 53 at the date of trial, had undergone a successful hysterectomy from which she would have recovered completely but for the accident. A lifting accident resulted in the prolapse of her vaginal wall and she became severely incontinent for one year until she underwent an RAZ Colposuspension operation. That repair operation over-corrected the incontinence resulting in the need permanently to self-catheterise and, consequentially, regular urinary tract infections. In addition she suffered a rectocele, which required her to evacuate her bowels manually, and also a cystocele. Besides the RAZ operation, she underwent posterior and anterior vaginal repair operations, an examination under anaesthetic and a further repair to the posterior vaginal wall to deal with the rectocele. C's ability to have sexual intercourse was reduced because of the psychological effects of the injuries and operations she had sustained. The judge, having considered the cases of *Hendy v. Milton Keynes HA* [1992] C.L.Y. 2824 and *Stanton v. St Helens & Knowsley HA* [1993] C.L.Y. 1509, declined to regard *Hendy* as persuasive. As to *Stanton*, it was unclear from the report whether self-catheterisation was permanent. The award fell between categories B and C of "Bladder" in the JSB Guidelines, the judge holding that neither category was entirely correct for this case. *General Damages*: £20,000.

COVERDALE v. SUFFOLK HA, November 25, 1996, H.H.J. Barham, CC (Norwich). [*Ex rel.* Charles Pugh, Barrister, Old Square Chambers, 1 Verulam Buildings, Gray's Inn].

Reproductive organs

1953. Female, aged 29 at the date of radical surgery and 33 at date of trial, claimed damages for personal injuries as a result of failure to diagnose cervical cancer.

Negligence was admitted. T underwent a routine smear in 1988 which was negligently reported as clear when there were severe dyksaryotic cells. In 1990 T had her first child. In January 1991 she started to notice more heavy and frequent vaginal bleeding and was referred for a D&C in April 1991. Thereafter T was reassured that there was nothing to worry about and was later informed that the histology results had been clear despite the presence of dysplastic squamous epithelium. She intended to have another child and so ceased contraception in June 1991. In August 1991 she moved back to New Zealand. From January 1992 T noticed some vaginal blood loss on rare occasions but was not unduly worried about this, and in May 1992 a second pregnancy was confirmed. However the blood loss became heavier and T consulted a gynaecologist in June 1992. The diagnosis following colposcopy and biopsy was a cervix "almost completely destroyed by a tumour". T underwent a termination of her pregnancy, a Wertheims hysterectomy, followed by a six week course for radiotherapy and a 20 hour implant of caesium into the vagina. T was left with scarring, a need for hormone replacement therapy and was left unable to have children. T's marriage broke down after the treatment but she had since found a new partner. Otherwise the prognosis was good. In considering quantum the following factors were taken into account: (1) development of invasive cancer necessitating radical surgery, (2) abortion of the foetus; (3) the loss of reproductive function in circumstances when the family was not complete and T's new partner had no children of his own; (4) the loss of natural hormones so that T had to have HRT; (5) abdominal scarring which was permanent and significant; (6) a deformed and shortened vagina which interferes with T's enjoyment of intercourse, and (7) psychological suffering. It was accepted that T had made a remarkable recovery. T sought a provisional award on the assumption that her cancer had been completely cured with a right to re-apply in the event of recurrence of secondary cancer, osteoporosis or interference to urinary function secondary to radiotherapy. *General Damages*: £50,000. Special damages: £9,000. Total award: £60,305.

THURMAN v. WILTSHIRE AND BATH HA, February 4, 1997, H.H.J. Hedley, QBD. [*Ex rel.* Evill and Coleman, Solicitors, London].

Hip

1954.   Male, aged 30 at the date of the accident and 35 at the date of the trial, was involved in a road traffic accident in August 1991 where he sustained a severe fracture of his left hip joint which resulted in displacement of fragments involving the socket of the acetabulum. This required an operation to reduce and hold the main fragments using plates and screws. B remained in hospital for 22 days and was then allowed home with non weight bearing crutches. He suffered further lesser injuries; a puncture wound to his left buttock requiring stitches, abrasions to his arms, a laceration to his head, a chipped molar and a soft tissue injury to his left shoulder lasting six to eight months. He was off work for six months and underwent physiotherapy. The fractures united well but 18 months after the accident X-rays indicated the presence of early osteoarthritic change. His hip remained painful and stiff. Prior to the injury B had been a fit and athletic man regularly enjoying football, badminton, golf and skiing. He had only been able to return to the last two activities and even then very infrequently due to pain which he suffered when taking part. He has been prevented from continuing to carry out DIY tasks. His play activities with his children were restricted and his sexual relations have been inhibited. The judge found that B would require a hip replacement in eight to nine years and revision surgery 13 to 14 years thereafter. *General Damages*: £22,500.

BETTS v. DOLBY, November 6, 1996, H.H.J. De Ville, CC (Nottingham). [*Ex rel.* Sebastian Reid, Barrister, Second Floor, Francis Taylor Building, Temple].

Hip

1955.   Female, aged 70 at the date of the operation and aged 74 at the date of the hearing was admitted to hospital for a primary hip replacement operation. During

DAMAGES

surgery the prosthesis was caused to penetrate through the side of the femur. The situation was not corrected or revised either immediately or subsequently, despite post-operative X-rays showing the prosthesis to be at an angle of some 20 to 30 degrees to the femur. F was mobilised and discharged from hospital after seven days. Two weeks after her discharge from hospital the head of the femur fractured causing the prosthesis to separate completely from the femur. She was in agony and could not move. Arrangements were made for her immediate re-admission to hospital. On arrival at hospital she was X-rayed, a procedure which caused her severe distress and pain necessitating her being restrained by her son. Four days later she underwent a revision operation. In the interim, she endured considerable pain relieved only in part by traction and strong analgesia. The revision operation was more complicated than the first as the head of the femur had now fractured and the lesser trochanter had broken off. A 300 millimetre prosthesis was used, together with circlage wire to retain the fractured fragments of bone. Following the operation F was detained in hospital for three weeks. During this period she developed a deep vein thrombosis due to the negligent failure to use anti-coagulants prior to either operation. This required weekly visits to the hospital for a period of six months after the second operation for blood tests and Warfarin treatment. She then underwent a period of convalescence at her son's house before returning to her own home. During this period of immobility F, who had a pre-existing tendency to obsessional behaviour, developed a phobia about spiders. This was precipitated by her anxiety over the failure of the first operation and her having to undergo the second operation.

F's post-operative condition and prognosis were markedly different from that which she could reasonably have expected had the primary hip replacement been successful. She had a continuing nagging ache in her hip and groin area. This increased with activity and tended to be worse at the end of the day and at night. She could walk only limited distances. She had a restricted range of movement in her hip. Scar tissue had decreased the range of movement by some 30 per cent more than might have been expected having regard to her age and the gradual progression of her osteoarthritis. There was a 50 to 75 per cent chance that she would require a further revision operation in four to seven years' time necessitating a further period in hospital and of convalescence. The prospects for this surgery were not good owing to loss of bone at the head of the femur. If the surgery were not a success, she would have to endure increased pain, discomfort and restriction of movement, perhaps even confinement in a wheelchair. *General Damages*: £20,000.

FRADGLEY v. PONTEFRACT HOSPITALS NHS TRUST, May 14, 1997, H.H.J. Kent-Jones, CC (Leeds). [*Ex rel.* Simon Jackson, Barrister, Park Court Chambers, Leeds].

Shoulder

1956. Male, aged 49 at date of accident and 53 at date of trial, was working within C's bus plant and was in the process of manoeuvring some heavy plywood when he hit a stack of tyres obstructing his work area. R sustained a bruising injury to his left shoulder causing pain. He continued working. Thereafter, he saw his GP who prescribed antiflammatory drugs and also referred him for physiotherapy. Pre-existing osteoarthritic changes were rendered symptomatic by the injury and had been accelerated. R would be disadvantaged on the labour market if he lost his existing employment but the judge found that that present employment carried only a small degree of insecurity. *General Damages*: £5,250. *Smith v. Manchester* award: £4,250. Loss of DIY/decorating: £1,500 (multiplier of 10). Total award after deduction of 25 per cent contributory negligence and including interest: £8,447.

RUCASTLE v. CUMBERLAND MOTOR SERVICES LTD, July 26, 1996, H.H.J. Brown, CC (Carlisle). [*Ex rel.* Andrew Kirkpatrick, Solicitor, Hough, Halton & Soal, Solicitors, 32 Abbey Street, Carlisle].

Shoulder

1957. Male, aged 35 at date of accident and 38 at the date of the trial, was a labourer required to straighten a damaged five metre high steel lamp. When he and another labourer manhandled the lamp standard, it fell striking U on the right shoulder. U had four to five weeks off work, having sustained damage to the capsule of the acromioclavicular joint. Bruising to this joint was severe extending to the underlying deltoid muscle and rotator cuff. At the date of the trial, there were some residual symptoms attributable to the accident and it was accepted that these symptoms would continue at the then present level indefinitely. Nonetheless, U had full range of movement in his shoulder with no restriction in movement or power. The judge found there was little insecurity of employment. He considered U's counsel's submission that there would be a disadvantage on the open labour market if U lost his employment and had to admit the previous industrial injury to a potential employer. However the judge found the risk to be negligible and made no *Smith v. Manchester* award. *General Damages*: £5,000. Past loss of earnings: £589. Out of pocket expenses: £96. Award for spoilt holiday: £200. Total award (inclusive of interest): £6,060.

ULLRICH v. CARLISLE CITY COUNCIL, July 26, 1996, H.H.J. Brown, CC (Carlisle). [*Ex rel.* Andrew Kirkpatrick, Solicitor, Hough, Halton & Soal, Solicitors, 32 Abbey Street, Carlisle].

Shoulder–elbow

1958. Male, L aged 59 at trial and 50 years at the date of the accident on December 10, 1987 when he fell off a roof whilst working as a roofer. He was admitted to hospital and underwent lengthy surgery when an open reduction of the left elbow was carried out. The residue of the injuries constituted a considerable deformity of the left upper limb with a 22 centimetre scar with a three centimetre shortening of the humerus. L was no longer capable of heavy work and his prospects on the open labour market were poor. He had no educational qualifications. Prior to the accident, L was a vigorous active man who took a pride in his physical fitness but post accident was only capable of gentle swimming. The issue arose as to the appropriate level of deduction to be made as a result of income support received following the accident. The judge previously held that L would have had to retire on unconnected medical grounds on his 56th birthday in June 1993. W contended income support should be deducted until judgment and L's special damages be extinguished. However, following *Hodgson v. Trapp* [1989] A.C. 807, [1989] C.L.Y. 1285, "income support he was paid was not attributable to the accident. It would be unjust to deduct that which he would have received in any event". *General Damages*: £22,500. Total award: £25,500 to include special damages plus interest reduced by one third for contributory negligence.

LAMBETH v. WILLIAMS (1997) 97(4) Q.R. 7, Connell, J., HC.

Arm

1959. Male, 44 at the date of the incident and 48 at the date of assessment, sustained a comminuted fracture of the distal end of the shaft of his right, dominant humerous when he was assaulted. Initially the injury was treated by a plaster of Paris backslab and a sling; however the fracture did not unite. Almost a year after the accident he underwent an open reduction and fixation operation together with a bone graft. M was left with a permanent loss of extension of approximately 30 degrees and flexion of the elbow was limited to 90 degrees. There was also a permanent loss of both pronation and supination of the right forearm. M, who was formerly a painter and decorator was unable to carry on that work or any form of heavy manual work. He had a permanent restriction in his ability to undertake DIY activities and could not pursue golf, snooker and darts. *General Damages*: £20,000.

MURTAGH, *Re*, March 11, 1997, Lord Carlisle Q.C., CICB (Carlisle). [*Ex rel.* Roger B Cooper, Barrister, Trinity Chambers, Newcastle Upon Tyne].

Arm

1960.   Female, aged 44 at date of accident and 48 at date of trial, was employed as a driver of a minibus when she slipped and fell heavily upon the floor of the bus depot. As a result, P sustained a serious injury to her right dominant arm leaving her permanently unable to continue her employment as a bus driver or any work involving heavy manual duties. P had physiotherapy and underwent an operation to excise the head of the radius which was unsuccessful. She was left with a residual scar. It was unlikely that there would be any material improvement in her range of movement or in her power of grip. She lost her PSV licence to drive passenger vehicles in an area of high unemployment. She was under a permanent disadvantage on the open labour market because of the disability to her dominant arm although she was fit for sedentary work such as receptionist or clerical work. *General Damages*: £17,500. Loss of congenial employment: £3,000. Past loss of earnings: £36,480. Future loss of earnings (multiplier of 8.5): £83,980. Out-of-pocket expenses: £234. Award for loss of housekeeping capacity: £15,000. Award for loss of window cleaning capacity: £600. Award for loss of DIY/decorating capacity: £3,000. Loss of pension (agreed): £15,000. Total award: £176,055.

   PRITCHARD v. CUMBERLAND MOTOR SERVICES LTD, August 2, 1996, H.H.J. Brown, CC (Carlisle). [*Ex rel.* Andrew Kirkpatrick, Solicitor, Hough, Halton & Soal, Solicitors, 32 Abbey Street, Carlisle].

Arm

1961.   Female, aged 78 years at the time of the accident and aged 80 at the date of the trial, was knocked over by a car. She suffered a comminuted fracture of the upper left humerus, a fractured pubic ramus, extensive bruising and deep shock. She was hospitalised for a month following the accident and subsequentlly underwent outpatient care, including extensive physiotherapy. She was able to walk again six weeks after the accident but had difficuilty climbing stairs thereafter. She required the assistance of a carer for the first few weeks after returning home from hospital. Intrusive memories of the accident were still continuing to disturb her sleep at the time of the trial. She was left with a serious and permanent restriction of movement in her left shoulder, although this restriction was only 50 per cent attributable to the accident, the joint was arthritic and she had suffered a second injury to her left arm. She could not brush her hair or put on a bra in the normal way. Described as a very serious and disabling accident which would affect the rest of her life. *General Damages*: £9,500.

   ROWLAND v. GRIFFIN, July 2, 1997, H.H.J. Quentin Edwards Q.C., CC (Central London). [*Ex rel.* David Barr, Barrister, 1 Temple Gardens, Temple].

Arm

1962.   Male, aged 10 at the time of the accident and aged 12 at the date of the trial, suffered personal injury whilst on the school property owned by the defendants. M entered the school grounds as a short cut, entering through the open main entrance. He reached the pedestrian entrance gate and, finding this gate to be locked, climbed over the railings. M caught his left armpit on the pointed ends on one of the vertical bars suffering a wound to the left axillary area penetrating some one to two inches into the axillary fold. He was admitted to hospital where he underwent an operation that day under general anaesthetic. He was left with a V shaped scar measuring six centimetres by four centimetres which was hypertrophic and keloid. There was some slight numbness to the upper arm which might be permanent. M also had restricted movement in the left shoulder which might require further surgery. *General Damages*: £4,750. Special Damages: £75.

   MITCHELL (A MINOR) v. CHESHIRE CC, January 22, 1997, H.H.J. Trigger, CC (Liverpool). [*Ex rel.* Laurence Daniels, Solicitor, Forster Dean Solicitors, 32/34 Widnes Road, Widnes, Cheshire].

Arm

1963.   Female, H, aged 21 at the date of the accident and 25 at the date of trial, was working as a sales assistant when the leading edge of a shelf fell about five feet onto her right (dominant) forearm, causing a soft tissue injury. H suffered immediate pain and visited her local hospital after work. She was given a tubigrip for her arm which she wore for two years. She attempted to return to work after two weeks but was unable to continue because of pain in her arm and nausea. H had difficulty in dressing and in carrying out many household tasks. She saw a number of consultants over the following two years and underwent physiotherapy. About a year after the accident she obtained a place on a part time teacher training access course, though her attendance was erratic due to pain from her arm and she found it difficult to write for any long period of time causing difficulties in exams. At trial, some four years after the accident, her arm was much improved, though she had occasional twinges every few months which would incapacitate her for a couple of days. At trial the experts agreed that she had suffered a significant soft tissue injury which had produced painful symptoms, albeit H had a lower pain threshold than most people. It was held that H had suffered significant pain for a period of 18 months, and she was awarded lost earnings for just under one year, on the basis that by the time she had gained a place on her course she had abandoned any intention of returning to work as a sales assistant. *General Damages*: £4,000. Special Damages: £4,156 (including 50 weeks lost earnings). Total award: £8,887.

HASAN v. BOOTS THE CHEMIST PLC, September 5, 1997, H.H.J. Cooke, CC (Central London). [*Ex rel.* Nicholas A Peacock, Barrister, 6 Pump Court, Temple].

Elbow

1964.   Female, aged 50 at date of accident, was injured when she fell whilst attempting to close a window. She was taken to hospital where X-rays revealed a severe fracture, dislocation to the left elbow, a comminuted fracture of the radius and a fracture of the humerus with vascular injury presenting a significant threat to her left arm. A lengthy operation with a vein graft from her right leg was undertaken. She was in hospital for 12 days and had an external fixator fitted. She had extensive out-patient treatment and physiotherapy. There was stiffness in the left shoulder as a result of disuse, which itself required manipulation and an injection under general anaesthetic. She was left with extensive scarring in the region of her elbow with scars measuring seven centimetres, 11 centimetres and eight centimetres, which whilst pale were still obvious. There was also scarring to the donor grafting site on the inside of her right thigh. She continued to suffer considerable limitation in movement and by the date of trial could move her elbow only between 75 degrees and 110 degrees. She also had only half of relevant supination movement, movement of her left shoulder remained restricted with abduction to 120 degrees and flexion to 110 degrees. Although in little pain she had some continuing discomfort and occasionally took paracetamol towards the end of the day. Prior to the accident she had had two part time jobs, both of which she had had to give up. She had also enjoyed gardening, knitting and sewing and the independence of driving a motor car. She had been responsible for the majority of the domestic chores and had shared the decorating with her husband. As a consequence of her injuries her sleep was occasionally disturbed. She had to kneel in a bath and needed help washing her hair, doing up top buttons and belts, cutting up food and was unable to drive, carry heavy weights, iron or vacuum to any extent. Her husband now undertook all the gardening and decorating and a friend also provided considerable assistance to her.

She was assessed at 36 per cent disabled by D.S.S. The prognosis was for osteo-arthritic changes resulting from her injuries to start at about 60 with no real prospect of any operation to assist her, given the vascular damage. *General Damages*: £18,000. Award for additional decorating costs: £3,000. Part loss of earnings: £9,480. Future loss of earnings (agreed multiplier of 4.25): £14,970. Award for care and attendance (multiplier 12, 14 hours per week at £3.75 per hour): 43,760. Total award: £90,79.

FAHY v. WOLVERHAMPTON MBC AND BANBURY WINDOWS LTD, September 17, 1996, Assistant Recorder Warner, CC (Birmingham). [*Ex rel.* Robert Holdsworth, Barrister, 5 Fountain Court, Steelhouse Lane, Birmingham].

Elbow

1965.   Claims by four male plaintiffs, employed as casting machine operators at R's Crown Derby factory, all developed recognised upper limb disorders as a result of their employment between 1990 and July 1992. Liability was established and the following awards were made. B, aged 46 at the date of the trial developed a partial tear of the common flexor origin (golfer's elbow) in the right elbow. At trial he had constant pain in both elbows and shoulders and could not grip anything with his right hand. He was described by the judge as being "of stoical disposition" and since August 1993 he had been employed in a job which did not entail any heavy lifting, bending or twisting. He had had time off during that employment because of continuing symptoms. *General Damages*: £8,000. Agreed special damages: £577. Future disadvantage on the open labour market: £8,500 (equivalent to one year's net wage loss). Total award (including agreed interest): £17,808. W1, aged 58 at the date of the trial, had developed partial tears of the common flexor origins of both elbows (golfer's elbow), as well as neck pain which was the result of pre-existing degenerative spondylosis being rendered symptomatic by his work, but which might have become symptomatic in time for reasons unassociated with work. The elbow problems gave rise to pain which was likely to be permanent. Any heavy repetitive work produced a great deal of pain, particularly in his right elbow, but also in his back and neck. He continued to work for R but in a different capacity, as a ware inspector, which did not involve any heavy or repetitive work. *General Damages*: £7,500. Future disadvantage on the open labour market: £4,000. Total award (including agreed interest): £12,100. W2, aged 52 at the date of the trial, had developed partial tears in the common flexor origins of both elbows (golfer's elbow), worse in the right arm. Any return to heavy work would have lead to a rapid return of similar symptoms and he was thus disadvantaged on the labour market. He also had an attack of tenosynovitis in his right wrist in April 1991. Since then his wrist had tended to swell up on any degree of activity such as gardening or even writing. He had been unemployed since he was made redundant in May 1993. *General Damages*: £9,000. Special damages (including past loss of earnings): £7,000. Future disadvantage on the open labour market: £11,897 (based on a multiplicand of £3,965 and a multiplier of three, the judge deciding that W2 had a residual earning capacity of £4,000 per annum). Total award (including agreed interest): £29,727. S, aged 29 at the date of the trial, experienced pain in his wrists, elbows, shoulders and back in the course of his employment. He was diagnosed as having tenosynovitis in his left wrist, which caused him to have eight weeks off work whilst still employed by R, and then to be in receipt of invalidity benefit for nearly two years following his redundancy in May 1993. He then worked in a heavy job in a tyre factory, but lost that employment during the course of the trial because of a recurrence of tenosynovitis and its symptoms in his left wrist. He was unable to play with his children properly, garden or do moto-cross, a previous hobby. *General Damages*: £8,000. Future disadvantage on the open labour market: £30,000 (equivalent to three and three quarter years wages). Total award (including agreed interest): £38,640.

WRIGHT, WILLIS, SHORT AND BOTTOMER v. ROYAL DOULTON (UK) LTD, May 16, 1997, H.H.J. David Pugsley, CC (Derby). [*Ex rel.* Richard Toombs, Barrister, King Charles House Chambers, Nottingham].

Wrist

1966.   Male, aged 26 at date of accident and aged 31 at date of trial, was a right handed, non-graduate product engineer employed in interactive multi-media applications by BT for whom he had worked for 13 years. L suffered fractures to his femur and to the radius and ulna of both arms. The judge found that he was an able and well regarded employee whose future looked extremely bright. Whilst his position at the date of trial involved highly skilled manual work, it was likely that in the reasonably near future he would move into a managerial position. The judge further described L as intelligent, determined and resourceful, the sort of plaintiff who would triumph over adversity. Whilst the injuries to his femur and left wrist had almost entirely recovered, there was a permanent significant diminution of stamina and flexibility in the right wrist. The agreed medical evidence was that there was a 70 per cent probability of osteoarthritis developing and a very high likelihood that in around 15 years would be unable to continue with the kind of work he did at trial. Net annual income at the date of trial was £17,500. *General Damages*: £22,500 (agreed). Special Damages: £9,000. Award for handicap on the labour market: £15,000.

LOWE v. HASKELL, March 12, 1997, H.H.J. Beddard, CC (Colchester). [*Ex rel.* Michael Lane, Barrister, East Anglian Chambers, 52 North Hill, Colchester,].

Wrist

1967.   Male, aged 21 at the date of the injury and aged 24 at the date of the trial, was involved in a road traffic accident. He sustained a comminuted fracture of the distal end of the right (non-dominant) radius with an avulsion of the tip of the ulnar styloid. His arm was placed in a full elbow plaster cast for seven weeks and he underwent physiotherapy. During the period the plaster was in place, as a single man living alone, the plaintiff had difficulty bathing, cooking and shopping. Although he made a good recovery and was discharged from treatment five months after the accident, he was referred back to the hospital eight months after the accident as he still lacked the normal range of palmar flexion at the right wrist. At the date of trial (three years after the accident), the plaintiff continued to suffer sporadic, excruciating but short periods of pain every few months. The prognosis was that he would continue to suffer some minor permanent restriction of wrist joint movement with a 10 per cent probability of his developing arthritis within the next 10 to 20 years. If arthritis did develop, then that would result in a slight further reduction of movement and a recurrence of pain and swelling. Prior to the accident, the plaintiff's main hobbies had been keeping fit, martial arts and weightlifting which he pursued to a high standard. As a result of the accident, the plaintiff had been unable to follow those hobbies for two years and at the date of trial he had not managed to return to his pre-accident standard. *General Damages*: £5,500.

CHOUDHRY v. JHANGIR, September 24, 1997, Judge not specified, CC (Leeds). [*Ex rel.* Nicholas Hill, Barrister, 6 Park Square, Leeds].

Wrist

1968.   Male, left-handed, aged 52 at the date of the accident and aged 53 at the date of the trial, fell at work sustaining a fracture to his right radius and laceration to his left knee. Treatment comprised suturing of knee laceration; immobilisation of the wrist in plaster for nearly seven weeks; use of a wrist support for three to four weeks and physiotherapy sessions. H was unfit for work for 17 weeks. Examination six months post accident revealed scarring to the knee (broad, purplish, five centimetres in length) and a fully functional wrist which was subject to short-lived intermittent aching provoked, in particular, by cold. At trial the aching continued but to a lesser degree. *General Damages*: £5,200 (apportioned wrist £4,700; scarring £500). Special Damages: £3,037. Total award: £8,661 (including interest).

HEDEN v. BPC MAGAZINES (LEEDS) LTD, March 20, 1997, H.H.J. Hutchinson, CC (Bradford). [*Ex rel.* Henry Witcomb, Barrister, 199 Strand, London].

Wrist

1969. Female, aged 45 at the date of the accident and 50 at the date of the trial, was thrown from a friend's horse. On admission to hospital X-rays revealed a fracture dislocation of her left radio-carpal joint, taking the form of a fracture of the radial styloid, and dorsal dislocation of the carpus. Dysfunction occurred in median nerve of left wrist and hand. Under general anaesthetic an incision was made on the radial side of the wrist fracture and the radial styloid reduced and fixed with a single percutaneous K wire. The arm was supported in a plaster back slab. R was discharged from hospital three days after the accident. Removal of K wire and plaster nine weeks after the accident revealed a five centimetre scar on the radial aspect of left wrist. Physiotherapy over the following nine months proved successful and rendered the dislocation stable. Six months after accident there was still stiffness in left shoulder due to upper rotator cuff tear, which improved over following five months. At the date of trial R continued to have discomfort due to a neuroma within the scar on radial side of wrist, and dorsiflexed at two-thirds normal range ie. 60 degrees and palmar flexed two-thirds normal range at 50 degrees. The prognosis was that the discomfort in the wrist would be permanent and degenerative changes were likely over the next 20 to 30 years, due to irregularity in the joint surface. R was unable to continue her pre-accident job as a chicken processor but remained capable of light semi-sedentary work. R experienced difficulty lifting objects and dressing. These limitations have had an adverse effect on her hobbies of knitting and gardening as they now prove too uncomfortable. Her horseriding was restricted and she only rode occasionally. R's symptoms were exacerbated in cold and damp weather. The judge found against R on the issue of liability but indicated his award of general damages for pain suffering and loss of amenity would have been £7,000.

ROBERTS v. HUNT, January 8, 1997, H.H.J. Barham, CC (Norwich). [*Ex rel.* Anthony Bate, Barrister, East Anglian Chambers, 57 London Street, Norwich].

Hand

1970. Male, aged 33 at the date of the hearing, was injured when attacked by an unknown assailant with a glass, sustaining damage to both flexor tendons of the ring finger of his right, dominant hand. Initially repaired and treated with Kleinert dynamic splintage. A fortnight later the finger was accidentally knocked and extended. One of the tendons ruptured and the other lengthened, resulting in re-admission to hospital and operative re-repair of the damage, with a passive exercise regime thereafter. The hand was placed in anterior and posterior plaster of paris slabs. Four months later the finger had healed with fixed flexion contracture of 50 degrees at the proximal interphalangal joint and 20 degrees at the distal joint which subsequently improved to 20 degrees and 15 degrees respectively. That degree of contractum was expected to be permanent. There had been some discussion about amputation of the finger as it frequentlly "caught" when being used in different tasks, but the applicant was reluctant. He was a trained painter and decorator, but despite medical evidence that he could adapt to and do that work again, he had made several unsuccessful job applications both for painting and decorating and general labouring work and had in fact been continuously unemployed from the accident to the date of the hearing. The Board rejected making a specific award for either past or future wage loss in the circumstances of the case, preferring a broad brush approach to compensating him for the employment difficultues resulting from this injury. *General Damages*: £7,500. Award for past and future disadvantage of the open labour market: £25,000.

TORRANCE, *Re*, July 24, 1997, M Park, CBE Chairman, CICB (Nottingham). [*Ex rel.* Richard Toombs, Barrister].

Hand

1971. M, female aged 13 awoke one Sunday morning in March 1987 with severe pain in the left dominant hand. She had played hockey the previous day but could not recall any injury to the hand. The left hand was exceedingly painful over the dorsum, which was swollen, and movements were restricted. She was taken to Homerton Hospital A&E department where she was examined by a senior house officer who confirmed the presence of swelling of the first and second metacarpo-phalangeal joints were tender. A diagnosis of tenosynovitis of the tendons overlying the joints was made and M was given anti-inflammatory agents and a wrist splint. She was referred to the hand clinic for review a week later when it was reported that the effects of the splint and anti-inflammatory agent had produced no alleviation of her symptoms. It was wrongly thought prudent to inject the powerful steroid Lederspan and a local anaesthetic into the region of the extensor tendon above but not into any joint. The dosage of the Lederspan was not recorded. The judge held that this injection was performed negligently by a junior doctor. Further, he held that the injection had negligently been made subcutaneously, with the wrong intention of injecting subcutaneously instead of deep into the extensor retinaculum underneath the wrist joint into a protective synovial sheath. By reason of the negligent administration of the injection, M's hand immediately swelled excessively. Within four or five hours of the anaesthetic wearing off, M experienced excruciating pain on the back of her left hand. Despite analgesia being taken by M, the pain persisted and she returned to the hand clinic one week after the injection. By this time the area around the hand was mottled in colour and reddish and looked like a bruise. The symptoms persisted. Three months later M still had a painful left hand, with the pain being localised to the region of the second metacarpal line and between there and the first metacarpal within the soft tissue of the hand. Within the blueish bruising there had appeared a couple of small central plaque-like lesions on the superficial dermis. The area remained exquisitely tender.

By eight months after the initial treatment M had also begun to suffer from wasting of the tissue around the area, thinning of the skin and the presence of broken blood vessels. The hand was sensitive to changes in temperature. The condition of the hand was interfering with her ability to go to school and the pain remained exquisite. She was referred to a consultant anaesthetist specialising in pain management. She found wasting of the intraosseous and lumbrical muscles of the left hand with hyper-sensitivity. There was an area of discolouration which was bluish in colour with a white centre on the left hand. There was no other gross muscle weakness. A diagnosis was made of causalgia due to the trivial injury suffered prior to the injection of the steroid and local anaesthetic and a series of guanethidine blocks were performed. The results were very satisfactory and M became virtually pain free. However, by reason of the negligently administered injection M continued to suffer from general discolouration and unsightly appearance of the lesions. She was referred to a plastic surgeon who advised that the lesions appeared typical of skin atrophy with minor calcification and would be amenable to excision and skin grafting. In June 1991, some four years after the incident, plastic surgery was performed on the left hand. Surgery revealed deposited calcified lumps underneath the fascia which were presumed to be the products of precipitated steroid. This was intermingled with the nerves, but as much as possible was removed. A skin graft was then taken from the left thigh. The results of this surgery were considered to be successful and M subsequently made good progress. The scar on her left hand healed well. It was not as obvious as prior to skin graft but was still visible and concerned M greatly. At an examination one of M's medical experts described the skin graft as "unsightly". M remained self-conscious regarding the appearance of her hand. She was disappointed with the outcome of the skin graft, feeling that the cosmetic appearance was not more improved. M was required to wear factor 21 sun cream and a glove in summer as the lesions continued to be very sensitive to sunlight and easily burned. *General Damages*: £5,750. Special damages (agreed): £1,300. Total award (including interest): £7,418.

MULLETT v. EAST LONDON AND CITY HA, May 16, 1997, H.H.J. Wakefield, CC (Central London). [*Ex rel.* Colin Mendoza, Barrister, Lamb Chambers, Temple].

Hand

1972. Female sandwich maker, aged 48 at the date of the accident and 51 at the date of the trial, sustained crush injuries to fingers of her right, non-dominant hand when it was drawn between the rollers of a conveyor which was started as she was cleaning it. Her hand was trapped for approximately 10 to 15 minutes as colleagues attempted to free it. As colleagues attempted to pull G free she sustained traction type injuries to right elbow and right shoulder. Her hand was released when belt tension slackened. G suffered soft tissue injuries with severe pain, swelling and bruising to the fingers of her right hand. There was no bony damage. She initially attempted to return to work after one month, but found herself unable to cope. She attended 12 sessions of physiotherapy treatment in a five month period following the accident, and attempted to return to work again seven months after the accident, again without success. She returned to light duties 11 months after the accident and to full duties 13 months after the accident, although she indicated that she remained unable to complete heavier aspects of her duties, requiring the assistance of colleagues. Pain, discomfort and stiffness in right elbow and shoulder settled within approximately six months of the accident. G suffered continuing permanent dysfunction in the index and middle fingers of her right hand, and was unable to make a tight fist with her right hand, tips of those fingers only reaching to within two centimetres of palm of hand. She took analgesics to cover pain and to enable her to continue at work. The court accepted that G had sustained a permanent injury, which would cause her some significant interference and disability, both at work and home. It was also accepted that G would be at a disadvantage on the open labour market, but such disadvantage was weighed against the reasonable security of her employment, her age and her general health. She had suffered previous episodes of depression, being a chronic asthmatic and suffering from pre-existing Raynaud's disease to both hands. Further deterioration in the condition of the fingers of her right hand was unlikely. *General Damages*: £4,500. *Smith v. Manchester* award: £1,500. Special Damages: £2,775. Total award: £8,815.

GREEN v. NORTHERN FOODS PLC, February 27, 1997, H.H.J. Bowers, CC (Sheffield). [*Ex rel.* Jonathan Devlin, Barrister, Park Court Chambers, Leeds].

Fingers

1973. Male, aged 44 at the date of the accident at work and aged 50 at the date of the hearing, was employed as a machine worker. He suffered a crush injury to the left non-dominant ring finger comprising a fracture of the top of the terminal phalanx with traumatic amputation of the fingertip. Initially the bone was trimmed and the wound sutured. The injury continued to be troublesome and the wound tended to split open. The end of the digit became white and painful with some loss of feeling. He underwent further surgery when revision of the stump was carried out. The finger end became more stable but whiteness, numbness and some cold intolerance continued. He was initially absent from work for 13 weeks, with a further six weeks absence following the further surgery. At the time of the trial he was still suffering from a degree of cold intolerance and a small reduction in grip strength assessed as approximately 10 per cent. He was able to do a normal job but in cold weather had to regularly warm the injured finger with the use of a hand dryer. He was conscious of the cosmetic disability when out socially. It was accepted that there was an element of uncertainty regarding M's job even though his length of service was over 25 years and that M was suffering from a continuing disability which could affect his future job prospects. The judge regarded the appropriate *Smith v. Manchester* award to be relatively modest, to be "expressed in months rather than years". The award under this head of loss represented approximately three and a half months' net loss of earnings. *General Damages*: £4,500. *Smith v. Manchester* Award: £3,000. Special Damages (including interest): £1,850.

MARSH v. ASHTON CORRUGATED (MIDLANDS) LTD, June 9, 1997, Assistant Recorder Miller, CC (Leeds). [*Ex rel.* Whittles Solicitors, Josephs Well, Leeds].

Fingers

1974. Female, right handed, aged 12 at date of accident and 21 at date of hearing, fell off a swing because ground below was in an unsafe condition. H sustained fractures to the distal part of the proximal phalanx of the left ring finger, the base of the distal phalanx of the middle finger and the distal phalanx of the right middle finger. H also suffered abrasions to the face which healed leaving no scarring. Injury to the left ring finger was the most severe and this required surgery to reduce the fracture and to fix the condyle by means of the insertion of two Kirschner wires. H remained in hospital for two days and returned three months later, as a day case, when the wires were removed under general anaesthetic. At the hearing date H had swelling of the joint which made it impossible for her to wear a ladies' wedding ring. She continued to suffer pain in the finger in cold weather or when her hand was immersed in water. There was slight loss of movement in the finger, such that she could not make a tight fist and the finger would not fully straighten. Future improvement was unlikely. H was conscious of the cosmetic deformity of the hand and tended to conceal it from view. *General Damages*: £4,000. Special Damages: £15. Total award: £4,015.

HALL v. BOLTON MBC, January 13, 1997, District Judge Wilby, CC (Bolton). [*Ex rel.* Timothy White, Barrister, 15 Winckley Square, Preston].

Fingers

1975. Male police constable, aged 41 at time of assault in June 1992, sustained injury to both hands whilst apprehending burglar. He dislocated the interphalangeal joint of his left little finger. At hospital the finger was placed in a plastic Mallet splint. Next day he returned to hospital with a painful swelling of the ring finger of the right dominant hand. A large splint was placed on that finger, and three fingers of the left hand were strapped. The left hand was strapped for six weeks and the splint remained on right hand for a further two months; over three months in total. During the first month he was dependent upon assistance from his wife after going to the toilet. Although the fingers were painful and swollen he returned to work after three months. He had some physiotherapy, and resumed full duties within a month of returning. The right ring finger was left with a deformity giving it a "Z" shape. Otherwise movements of that finger were full. A mallet deformity of approximately ten degrees of distal interphalangeal joint of left little finger also remained, but there was no tenderness in either finger. Power and pinch grips were unaffected. There was little, if any, residual disability and no increased risk of osteoarthritis in either joint. *General Damages*: £3,250.

CATCHPOLE, *Re*, August 14, 1996, CICB; London. [*Ex rel.* James Laughland, Barrister, 1 Temple Gardens].

Fingers

1976. T, male, aged in his thirties, employed as a steel worker, suffered a compound fracture of the terminal phalanx of his right little finger when it was crushed between the sling of a crane and a skip. T attended hospital where the injured finger was strapped to the ring finger. T suffered intense pain and discomfort in the immediate aftermath of the accident but returned to work after one week's absence. Gradually, the fingernail withered and fell off and thereafter the wound healed uneventfully and the fingernail grew. T continued to suffer residual aching and discomfort in the injured finger when carrying out activities such as digging the garden or lifting. He tended to desist from such activities after a period of approximately 20 minutes in order to avoid the development of discomfort. His symptoms tended to be worse in cold weather. Overall the symptoms amounted to no more than a nuisance but they were expected to be permanent. *General Damages*: £2,000 for pain, suffering and loss of amenity.

TURNER v. BRITISH STEEL PLC, December 11, 1996, District Judge Thomas, CC (Cardiff). [*Ex rel.* Jonathan Walters, Barrister, 33 Park Place, Cardiff].

Fingers

1977. Female, aged 50 at the date of the accident, and 54 at the date of the trial, sustained a transverse laceration to the base of her left, non-dominant, index finger on the palmar aspect. The wound was deep and she suffered arterial bleeding. Her hand had to be elevated for 20 minutes to stop the bleeding. The wound was sutured both internally and externally, it was tender for a few months following the accident and the scar was prominent and ached in cold weather for about ten months. She was left with a non-adherent scar. Sensation and grip strength were normal. The scar was of no cosmetic significance. *General Damages*: £1,250. Special Damages: £180. Total award: (inclusive of interest) £1,491.

MURPHY v. GOSFORTH PARK CARE HOMES LTD, July 25, 1997, Depute District Judge Loomba, CC (Newcastle upon Tyne). [*Ex rel.* Roger B Cooper, Barrister, Trinity Chambers, Quayside, Newcastle upon Tyne].

Fingers

1978. Female aged six at the time of the accident and eight at the date of trial. Whilst visiting a public house she placed her hand on a chair and came into contact with a piece of broken glass. She sustained a small laceration to the middle third of her right little finger. The wound bled profusely and E attended hospital where the laceration was closed with steristrips. For three to four days after the accident she was unable to dress herself or cut up her own food and her enjoyment of the school summer holidays was disrupted. The wound took approximately six weeks to heal fully. She suffered some aching in cold weather for approximately 18 months after the accident and at the date of trial complained that she suffered some aching if she had to write for any length of time. The wound left a faint scar approximately 0.5 centimetres long which the District Judge described as of cosmetic significance only. *General Damages* £900, Special damages £62.

EASON v. BREWSTER, November 8, 1996, District Judge Slim, CC (Halifax). [*Ex rel.* Rhodes Thain & Collinson, Solicitors, 27 Harrison Road, Halifax].

Leg

1979. Male, aged 28 at the time of the accident and aged 34 at the time of the hearing, was in collision with G's vehicle whilst riding his motorcycle. S's most severe injury was a comminuted fracture of the tibia and fibula above the right ankle joint with a laceration to the leg. Under general anaesthetic an external fixator was applied. The fracture became angulated and had to be remanipulated. Subsequently the fixator was removed under general anaesthetic but the fracture did not unite. Just short of two years after the accident S underwent a bone graft taken from the hip and internal fixation. Over four years after the accident he developed an infection over the site of the scarring on the leg and this was resolved by the use of antibiotics. Four and a half years after the accident the plate and screws used for internal fixation were removed. S's right knee had slight laxity creating an unstable feeling. S used a walking stick. There was three to four inches shortening of the right leg. S developed back pain due to the leg shortening but the judge held that pain to be minimal. Raised shoes were recommended. His right hindfoot had slightly limited movements causing discomfort when walking on uneven surfaces. The site of the scarring remained more vulnerable to infections. S had undergone a prolonged period of pain and suffering which had restricted his activities and created intense frustration. He was not psychologically well equipped to deal with his injuries. He took substantial quantities of painkillers as a result of his injuries which led to substance intoxication. S also overdosed on several occasions, but the judge held that overdoses were the result of domestic problems and had not been caused by the accident. *General Damages*: £25,000. *Smith v. Manchester* award: £10,000. Total award: £62,996.

SAMPSON v. GEORGIOU, April 22, 1997, H.H.J. David Clarke Q.C.. [*Ex rel.* Antonis Georges, The Coach House, Little Sutton, Cheshire].

Leg

1980.　Male, P, aged 40 at the time of the accident and 43 at the date of the trial, was in a collision with R's car when riding his pedal cycle. He suffered a compound comminuted fracture of the right lower tibia involving the articular surface of the ankle joint and a comminuted fracture in the lower third of the right fibula, just above the ankle. After three months the fractures had united, but degenerative changes were apparent in the ankle joint. P returned to his work as a train driver eight months after the accident. He was left with permanent residual symptoms. His ankle was stiff in the mornings and swollen by the end of the day. He was unable to walk further than two miles and, through apprehension, was no longer able to cycle, leading to a significant increase in weight. There were significant restrictions in movements of the ankle; dorsiflexion to neutral, plantar flexion to 20 degrees and no inversion or eversion of the subtalar joint. The osteoarthritic changes were expected to continue to cause increasing pain and stiffness, but the extent and rate of deterioration was unpredictable. It was agreed that there was a 30 per cent risk that P would be unable to continue in his lifelong work to planned retirement at age 65 by reason of increased symptoms. *General Damages*: £16,000. *Smith v. Manchester* award: £15,000 (one year's loss of net pay). Special Damages (agreed): £9,598.

PURKIS v. REHMAN, September 25, 1997, H.H.J. Davies, CC (Hull). [*Ex rel.* Paul Miller, Barrister, Wilberforce Chambers, Bishop Lane, Kingston Upon Hull].

Leg

1981.　Male, aged 30 at the time of the incident and aged 31 at the time of the hearing, suffered a fracture of the left fibula well above the ankle whilst out running. His foot went into a hole causing him to fall forward. The leg had been placed in tubigrip not plaster and there was no risk of arthritis at the ankle joint. He resumed sports after about three months and the judge held that he had made a full recovery after four months. *General Damages* for pain and suffering and loss of amenity: £3,250.

MELLING v. LIVERPOOL CITY COUNCIL, April 25, 1997, Recorder Wrigglesworth. [*Ex rel.* Antonis Georges, The Coach House, Little Sutton, Cheshire].

Leg–amputated leg

1982.　Male, aged three years and four months at the date of the accident, and nine years and four months at the date of the trial, was riding on a tractor mowing machine operated by his father when he lost balance, fell from the machine and the blade passed over his left leg. He received a subtotal amputation through the mid-lower leg, segmental loss of the tibia, and a length of the fibula which was found at the scene of the accident, cleansed and sterilised and put into the gap in the tibial bone. The right latissimus dorsi muscle was harvested from the right side of the back and transferred to the lower left leg. Satisfactory healing did not occur and four months after the accident the left leg was amputated below the knee (120 mm distal to the tibial tuberosity). He was fitted with his first artificial limb the following month. The NHS artificial limb was not successful as he could not walk properly and running was very difficult. In 1993 he was fitted with "flex-foot", an American prosthesis which mimics a real limb by simulating ankle motion, and was the first UK child to be fitted with the flex-foot. Future costs of prosthesis supplies were awarded on a multiplier multiplicand basis (based on a lifetime multiplier of 28 and a three per cent discount rate). *General Damages*: £42,000. Past cost of care: £9,567. Cost of "flex-foot": £8,983. Other Special Damages: £8,894. Future prosthesis costs (for basic, ski and swim): £149,696. Future loss of earning (due to attendance at limb fitting centre): £10,000. Other future loss: £23,819.

HARRIS v. HARRIS, July 12, 1996, Morland, J., HC. [*Ex rel.* Simon Wheatley, Barrister, 9 Bedford Row, London].

Knee

1983.   Female, S, aged 21 at the date of the accident and 25 at the date of the trial was employed as a machine operator. In December 1992 she was involved in a head on collision on a motorcyele. The most serious injury was to her left knee; a split compression fracture of lateral tibial plateau, rupture of posterior cruciate ligament and damage to meniscus. S also suffered: lacerations to the face requiring stitches; fracture of her front upper incisor with substantial loss of tooth, requiring crown and possible bridgework or implant in 30 years; severe ligamentous rupture of right (non-dominant) thumb. She was detained in hospital for 11 days with her leg on a passive motion machine. She was then allowed home on crutches with her knee in a brace. The right arm was in plaster for six weeks, the thumb subsequently requiring two separate operations in which the ligament was first repaired (unsuccessfully) and then a tendon grafted from the forearm. S started weight bearing at three and a half months, but her knee kept giving way. S underwent arthroscopy in October 1993 and then, in March 1994, an operation for reconstruction of the ligament. She had to spend five days in hospital, her knee was in a brace and she was unable to bear weight on her left leg for a further two months. Subsequent arthroscopy revealed the possible need for further operative treatment. S declined further treatment. She obtained work with the Post Office in April 1996. S was left with permanent symptoms of laxity in the thumb, loss of grip and scars but risk of osteoarthritis in the thumb was not great. There was a permanent valgus deformity in the left knee, laxity, pain and stiffness on exertion and in cold and wet weather and there was also significant scarring to the leg about which S was self conscious. There was a likelihood of degenerative change, but the risk of knee replacement was put at not greater than 50 per cent after 20 years. There was also minor facial scarring to the chin and top lip. *General Damages*: £26,000 (awarded as follows: tooth, £1,500; thumb, £6,000; knee, £18,000; and scarring £3,500; discounted on account of overlap to overall figure of £26,000). Award for handicap on labour market: £9,000 (one and a half times annual net income at date of accident). Award for cost of future operations: £1,600.

SCOTT v. GAGE, September 16, 1997, District Judge Mitchell, CC (Colchester). [*Ex rel.* John Brooke-Smith, Barrister, East Anglian Chambers, 52 North Hill, Colchester, CO1 1PY].

Knee

1984.   Female, aged 32 at the date of the accident and aged 38 at the date of the trial, was hit by a car and thrown some 25 feet. E sustained widespread bruising and superficial grazing, and an injury to her right knee which was swollen and from which 20 millilitres of blood were aspirated. E had to use crutches for six weeks, was unable to drive for three months and underwent physiotherapy for five months. She recovered completely from all injuries except that to her right knee within two months. The knee remained stiff and painful. E had difficulty with stairs and could not kneel. The knee occasionally gave way. E was unable to resume pre-accident sports. In April 1994, an arthroscopy revealed articular cartilage damage in all compartments. Her symptoms were likely to persist indefinitely. It was likely that E would develop osteoarthritis as a result of the accident within five to 10 years of the trial. There was a risk that total knee joint replacement would be required at age 60 to 70. *General Damages*: £14,000. Award for cost of future operation: £2,500.

ELDER v. SANDS, February 2, 1997, H.H.J. Groves, CC (Chelmsford). [*Ex rel.* John Brooke-Smith, Barrister, East Anglian Chambers, 52 North Hill, Colchester].

Knee

1985. Female, aged 22 at the date of accident and 25 at the date of the trial, was employed as a care assistant at a residential home. In December 1993, C entered the lift at the home with an elderly resident when it was at the second floor of the premises, the lift suddenly dropped approximately three feet coming to rest between the first and second floor. C was badly shocked by the accident and was left crying and in pain. She was immediately aware of severe pain in her left knee and her right foot. She was driven to hospital where she was examined. No X-rays were taken and she was discharged home. C returned to the residential home to carry on working. She remained in a lot of pain. Her foot was swollen, her knee was painful and she could hardly take any weight on her foot. She was forced to take one week off work, and on returning to work, she experienced great difficulty in carrying out her duties. Owing to the continuing pain in her foot she attended her GP. X-rays were taken which confirmed fractures of the heads of the fourth and fifth metatarsal bones of the right foot. She was advised that the fractures would heal in time and that it was not necessary for the foot to be placed in plaster. C was off work for a further week as a result. At an examination some seven months after the accident, she complained of continuing pain in the right foot. She could crouch and squat but only with discomfort in the left knee. Examination of the left knee revealed some deficiency of the posterior cruciate ligament. C's medical expert reported that she had suffered a strain injury to the left knee which would leave her with a permanent slight instability and a slightly increased risk of arthritic change in later years. Following the accident, C continued to suffer from shock. She had nightmares about the accident and recurring dreams about the lift falling down to the bottom of the liftshaft and of being killed. She cried a lot and had panic attacks in which she would become sweaty, frightened and shivering. C was unable to enjoy dancing at nightclubs or to return to wearing high heeled shoes and had given up playing golf. It was estimated that any future knee joint degeneration would not set in for about 20 to 25 years, at which time C would be around 45 to 50 years of age. Any symptoms which resulted from this degeneration were unlikely to interfere with her work although she might suffer some discomfort and stiffness on strenuous physical activities. C's psychological symptoms were consistent with the development of a relatively mild post traumatic stress disorder which persisted for under one year. Thereafter she still had residual problems which left her fearful and avoidant in relation to lifts. It was accepted that she would need treatment for this condition consisting of cognitive behavioural therapy, comprising six to 10 sessions with a clinical psychologist. *General Damages*: £7,500. Special damages: £194. Award for cost of future therapy: £500. Total award (per contributor): £8,541.

CLEMENTS v. WAKE, February 10, 1997, H.H.J. Peppitt Q.C., CC (Canterbury). [*Ex rel.* Colin Mendoza, Barrister, Lamb Chambers, Lamb Building, Temple].

Knee

1986. Male, aged 57 at date of accident and aged 60 at the date of the trial, was injured in a road traffic accident. C suffered soft tissue injuries to both knees, the right knee being worst affected, and bruising to the right lower leg. No hospital treatment was required. He had had an osteotomy to the left knee nine months before the accident, from which he had only partially recovered. He was unable to work for a month after the accident but had not taken any time off his work in a quarry after that. He suffered an aching pain in both knees after a day at work. He had had to give up his hobby of boating and although he was able to continue cliff walking and house maintenance he experienced similar pain after those activities. C's knees were frequently swollen and stiff. He tried to avoid tasks involving twisting or kneeling. He underwent physiotherapy for three years. It was unlikely there would be any significant change in his condition in the future. However, natural degeneration would probably have caused similar problems in the left knee by the time of trial in any event. The judge commented that the lasting injuries were of a mild degree but that the award reflected their permanence. *General Damages*: £5,000. Past loss of earnings: £806. Other damages: £1,135.

COUCH v. MIOTLA, February 4, 1997, H.H.J. Collins, CC (Wandsworth). [*Ex rel.* Lee Ingham, Barrister, 33 Park Place, Cardiff].

Knee

1987. Male, aged 25 at the date of the accident and aged 30 at the date of trial, suffered an accident at work on November 16, 1992. He was employed as a factory operative in a meat processing plant. Whilst carrying a bin of waste across the floor he slipped. He did not fall to the ground but in retaining his balance twisted his right knee severely. He sustained what was subsequently diagnosed as a sprain injury. This caused his knee to become immediately painful. He did not suffer any fracture or damage to ligaments or meniscus. Following initial treatment he returned to work 14 days later. On December 8, 1992, as he walked across the factory floor his knee buckled beneath him. He was unable to put any weight on his right leg and was unable to continue working. Subsequently he was retired from work on medical grounds with effect from March 2, 1993. He was referred to an orthopedic clinic and on June 8, 1993 he underwent an arthroscopy with excision of plica. After three months recuperation following the operation (ie. some 10 months after the initial injury) he was sufficiently fit and mobile to attend a training course and to start actively seeking alternative employment. There was an argument between medical experts called at trial as to whether or not he was suffering from the condition known as "plica syndrome". The judge found as a matter of fact that he sustained a strain of the soft tissues of the right knee which was significantly aggravated by the incident on December 8, 1992. *General Damages*: £3,000.

LOWE v. BARON MEATS LTD, April 18, 1997, Assistant Recorder Grant, CC (Nottingham). [*Ex rel.* Ward Gethin, Solicitors, King's Lynn, Norfolk].

Ankle

1988. Male timber yard trainee, aged 17 at the date of accident and aged 20 at the date of trial, sustained a bi-malleolar fracture of his left ankle when a stick of timber fell on his leg. Injury involved fractures of the distal tibia and fibula. Internal fixation was achieved with screws and plates under general anaesthetic and he was detained in hospital for one week. The metal work was removed after six weeks. A plaster cast was required for one further month. G then attended physiotherapy for four months and subsequently underwent a further course of physiotherapy treatment. He was discharged from hospital care and was fit to return to work 12 months after the accident but was left with an eight centimetre scar at the operation site. A sound bony union was achieved in excellent position without disruption of the ankle mortice; there was no osteoarthritis in the ankle and no long term problems were anticipated. *General Damages*: £5,150. Special damages: £5,000.

GOODWILL v. JEWSON LTD, April 4, 1997, District Judge Bailey, CC (Darlington). [*Ex rel.* David J Cole and Co, Solicitors, Northallerton, North Yorkshire].

Ankle

1989. Male, firefighter, aged 39 at the date of the accident and 43 at the time of the hearing, sustained a fracture to his ankle when he slipped on the metal end of a hose whilst firefighting. The fire was caused by a burning cigarette setting alight to a sofa chair. It was accepted by the Board that it was not an accidental fire, but deliberate arson and as such the claim came within the CICB scheme. The applicant was off work for approximately ten weeks and returned for four weeks on light duties. *General Damages*: £3,250. Past loss of overtime: £230.

WILSON (DAVID MICHAEL), *Re*, October 29, 1996, Judge not specified, CICB. [*Ex rel.* Thompsons, Solicitors, Congress House, Great Russell Street, London].

Ankle

1990. Male, aged 38 at the time of the accident and aged 39 at the date of the hearing, sustained damage to his left ankle comprising both medial and lateral ligamentous strain with probable chip fracture of the medial malleolous of the ankle when he trod on a brick embedded beneath undergrowth on waste land. His left ankle was immobilised in plaster for 20 days and he used crutches for about eight weeks. He was able to return to work eight and a half weeks after the accident. Residual aching and stiffness had almost completely resolved by the date of the hearing 15 months after the accident. *General Damages*: £2,500.

WILLIAMS v. SMITH & DANIELS, June 17, 1997, H.H.J. Appleton, CC (Blackpool). [*Ex rel.* Douglas R Green, Solicitor, Blackburn & Co, 7 The Crescent, Thornton-Cleveleys, Lancashire, FY5 3LN].

Ankle

1991. Female, aged 21 at the date of the accident and aged 23 at the date of assessment damages, suffered a wrenching inversion sprain to the soft tissues of the right ankle, with the brunt of the injury being to the lateral ligament complex, after tripping on an unlit weather board at the entrance to an Indian restaurant. She was treated with a support bandage which she wore for four weeks and was prescribed anti-inflammatory medication. She had to use crutches to get around for the first week and a half, with a noticeable limp for the following week and a half. The pain was most severe for the first eight to nine days. After that the pain decreased although there was pain and swelling after prolonged time on her feet when walking or standing. She had to have two weeks away from her job as a shop assistant following the accident. She was also restricted in her ability to carry out domestic chores such as housework and shopping. She was unable to drive for three weeks and could not participate in her hobby of aerobics for four to six weeks. There was also some initial sleep disturbance. She made a full recovery after six to eight weeks. *General Damages*: £750. Award for loss of earnings: £189.

REID v. CHOWDHURY, May 12, 1997, H.H.J. Lachs, CC (Liverpool). [*Ex rel.* James Hurd, Barrister, St James's Chambers, Manchester].

Ankle

1992. Infant male, aged 11 at the time of the accident and aged 14 at the date of the trial, was caught under a brick wall that collapsed on top of him. He was examined the same day and was found to have bruising over the lower third of the right tibia and swelling and bruising over the outer aspect of his right ankle. There was acute tenderness over the lateral malleolus and all movement of the ankle was painfully restricted. There was no bony injury. A plaster of paris back slab was applied and he was discharged from hospital. The back slab was removed after one week. At that time the plaintiff complained of chest pain and there was an area of bruising to the chest wall. He underwent six sessions of physiotherapy on the ankle. The plaintiff was off school for one month and was unable to do physical education or ride his bike for five weeks. *General Damages*: £750. Total award: £765.

KERR v. TUDOR THOMAS CONSTRUCTION & DEVELOPMENT LTD, September 15, 1997, District Judge Ray Singh, CC (Aberdare). [*Ex rel.* Philip Harris Jenkins, Barrister, Angel Chambers, Walter Road, Swansea].

Foot

1993.   Female, aged 12 at the date of the accident and 16 at date of the hearing, a keen horserider, received riding lessons at M's stables and sometimes assisted with work around the stables in return for free rides. Whilst riding at M's indoor facility, P's horse slipped and fell to the side trapping P's left leg and crushing her left foot when it attempted to rise. P contended that the slip was caused by the surface of the indoor facility, which was composed of flint and chalk and was totally unsuitable for horse-riding, particularly when wet as it was on the day in question. M did not dispute liability.

Her principal injury was a crush injury to the left foot, with fractures to four metatarsals, the fracture of the second metatarsal being displaced, and a dislocation of the first metatarsal. P also sustained an undisplaced "greenstick" fracture to the left collarbone which left her with only occasional minor discomfort by the date of the assessment of damages hearing. She suffered great pain during a protracted period before she was taken to hospital and before receiving proper treatment. P was hospitalised for seven days, having two operations under general anaesthetic and her left leg was in plaster for six weeks. The second metatarsal remained displaced and the second toe was raised above the others. P suffered from persistent pain in the foot and just over two years after the accident she had a third operation under general anaesthetic to excise the joint, realign the displaced metatarsal and fuse the joint. This relieved some of the pain. At the time of the assessment of damages hearing P still suffered from stiffness and periodic pain in the arch of the left foot and left big toe. The second toe was raised above the others and there was noticeable bony prominence on the bridge of the foot. These disabilities would be permanent. She had managed a summer job as a waitress but had found the foot painful at the end of the day. She had been able, with some effort, to resume some riding activities from three months after the accident but was no longer able to participate in athletics. Playing tennis caused some pain. There was no risk of osteoarthritis. P was quite conscious of the appearance of her foot particularly when swimming, and found it very difficult to buy court shoes. *General Damages*: £13,500. Special Damages: £1,494. Total award (including interest): £15,567.

P (A MINOR) v. MEAKIN, November 13, 1996, District Judge Davidson, CC (Slough). [*Ex rel.* Paul Stagg, Barrister, No.1 Serjeant's Inn, Fleet Street].

Foot

1994.   Male, aged 23 at the date of the accident and 25 at the date of trial was a trainee floor tiler, who had just opened the passenger door of a parked car and set foot on the ground when he became aware of a car reversing toward him at moderate speed to park in a nearby space. He was unable to escape being stuck on account of his position relative to the oncoming car and his part open door. He cringed to protect himself and raised the sole of his right foot which was caught by the bumper of the reversing car and forced against the tip of the car door thereby hyper-extending his toes and ripping the door from its hinges. He was saved from very serious damage by his heavy working boots, however he suffered immediate and painful swelling of the toes (which necessitated the removal of his boot by cutting) and minor cuts to the shin. He required tubigrip bandage, analgesics and crutches for three weeks and subsequently a stick for four weeks. He was given several sessions of physiotherapy over a period of four months. A keen martial artist and amateur footballer he had had to give up these activities and could no longer walk beyond one mile without some aching. His work which involved much squatting was made more uncomfortable by foot aching. Upon pre-trial medical examination it transpired that he had had a congenital Hallux Valgus deformity of the great toe which restricted the flexibility of his toe/foot. The hyper-extension injury had advanced by 10 years the likely onset of arthritic changes related to the condition which would in any event have necessitated an operation. *General Damages*: £3,848. Special Damages: £276.

McCLEAN v. COSTA, January 9, 1997, Recorder Jarvis Q.C., CC (Brentford). [*Ex rel.* James R Candlin, Barrister, 46/48 Essex Street, London].

Scars

1995. Male, aged six at the time of the incident and aged 14 at the date of trial, sustained injuries while he was on holiday in Portugal. H was sitting on a pouffe with his back to a large wall hanging mirror when he leaned backwards against the mirror and it fell. The mirror hit the floor and then broke about the middle so that the upper half fell onto H's right shoulder and right elbow causing lacerations. There was considerable bleeding and it was necessary for the wound to be closed with a towel to stop the bleeding. H was taken to a small hospital where the right arm was stitched under local anaesthetic but the shoulder wound was considered too severe and it was strapped after an injection of local anaesthetic. H was transferred to Faro hospital where the wound was injected and opened and sutured in at least two layers. After the operation H returned to the villa for a further seven days before returning to the UK. The scar on the right shoulder was irritable for some time after the accident, tended to break down when rubbed by rough material, and blistered on exposure to the sun. H was left with two permanent scars. Firstly, a scar on the outer side of his right elbow measuring seven by one centimetres. It was not tender, although it was thin and pale in colour. Secondly, the shoulder scar measured ten by two centimetres. It was placed obliquely across the shoulder so that it was subject to the maximum tension when the arm was held by the side. The scar was white in colour, thin with multiple small stitch marks. That scar could be improved if H underwent plastic surgery when he was older. H had suffered a degree of embarrassment from the scarring when he was younger but had learned to live with it and embarrassment was expected to diminish as he grew up. *General Damages*: £7,000. Agreed award for future cost of plastic surgery: £1,740.

HOBART v. McGIFF AND STUART, May 19, 1997, H.H.J. Roger Cooke, CC (Central London). [*Ex rel.* Colin Mendoza, Barrister, Lamb Chambers, Temple].

Scars

1996. Male, aged 30 at date of hearing, one and a half years after the accident, suffered severe lacerations to underside of his left, non-dominant forearm. The L-shaped scar extended 14 centimetres along the axis of his arm and three centimetres across the wrist. Following the accident, he had to be admitted to hospital and underwent an operation under anaesthetic to close the wound, with approximately 20 to 25 stitches. He was unable to use his injured arm for about four weeks following the accident due to the risk of rupturing the stitches. He had to have certain food cut for him and could not lift heavy items. He was unable to work as a bricklayer for 10 weeks following the accident. The scar remained painful and itched at the date of trial as well as changing colour in cold weather. In sunny weather it was extremely painful if sun burnt and had to be kept covered. The scar was also especially painful if accidentally knocked. The appearance of the scar was obvious although it had faded somewhat since the accident. The judge found that the plaintiff minimised his embarrassment at the appearance of the scar. Except for the above-mentioned problems associated with the scar, a full recovery had been made. *General Damages*: £5,250. Total award: £8,000.

O'NEILL v. MATTHEW BROWN PLC, October 22, 1996, District Judge Geddes, CC (Accrington). [*Ex rel.* Abigail Holt, Barrister, 24a St John Street, Manchester].

Scars

1997. Male, aged 30 at the date of the accident and aged 32 at the date of the hearing, was hit from behind by a motorcycle whilst riding his pedal cycle. He suffered extensive soft tissue lacerations to the back of his right upper arm and left elbow, friction burns/abrasions to the right buttock and right forearm, and bruising to his right lower leg. He was hospitalised for two days. L's injuries were treated by means of surgical exploration of the laceration to the right arm, and surgical dressings were applied. He took five weeks off work as a result of the injuries, but was then able to return to his normal duties. The injuries healed leaving a hypertrophic "F" shaped scar on the back of the right upper arm measuring 10 centimetres in length and two centimetres at its widest point, and a hypertrophic scar to the left elbow measuring three centimetres by one centimetre. L was left with residual symptoms of tenderness and discomfort to the scarred areas when pressure was applied. He also experienced diminished skin sensation in the affected areas of his right arm. The prognosis was that while the scarring would not diminish in size, its appearance would improve within 19 months of the accident date, becoming paler, flatter, less tender and with a reduction in the area of diminished sensation. *General Damages*: £5,000.

LEATHERLAND v. RISSMAN, February 7, 1997, H.H.J. Mellor, CC (Norwich). [*Ex rel.* Maria Nolan, Solicitor, Ward Gethin Solicitors, Kings Lynn, Norfolk].

Scars

1998. Female, aged 11 at the date of the accident and aged 14 at the date of the trial, was dragged under a runaway car and became trapped underneath. She sustained gravel lacerations to her right shoulder which left a purple, soft circular scar over the point of the right shoulder measuring four and a half centimetres in diameter. The scar had a slight concave contour deformity due to loss of fat thereunder, and there was reduced pinprick sensation to the scar. The scar was felt unsuitable for scar revision surgery. She was embarrassed and self conscious of the scar but had not suffered any psychological sequelae as a result. *General Damages*: £4,500.

DOOLER, *Re*, April 2, 1997, District Judge Foster, CC (Doncaster). [*Ex rel.* Frank Allen Pennington, Solicitors, Doncaster].

Non-facial scars

1999. Male, aged 12 at the date of the accident and 14 at the date of the trial was attacked by a rottweiler. He sustained serious injuries to his right arm, right leg and left leg. He was taken to casualty and subsequently transferred to a plastic surgery unit where he remained for seven days. During the first few months he also suffered from nightmares, waking up in a cold sweat and shouting. After his discharge from hospital he attended his GP for dressings on a regular basis. Initially this was daily, subsequently he attended about two/three times per week. This dressing continued for a total of four weeks after his discharge from hospital. He was left with permanent scarring, a large inverted "V" scar on the anterolateral aspect of his right arm, measuring five centimetres and seven centimetres with a degree of hypo and hyperpigmentation. On the lower third of the right leg and ankle are a series of 30 or more scars measuring between approximately two to three centimetres in diameter to small punctures, on the left leg there are between five to ten slightly hyperpigmented scars round the ankle. All the scars were very unsightly and would be visible at a distance. *General Damages*: £10,000.

KHAN (ARBAB), *Re*, November 14, 1996, Michael Parker (Chairman), CICB (York). [*Ex rel.* Reads, Solicitors, Ivebridge House, 59 Market Street, Bradford].

Non-facial scars

2000. Female, aged 16 at date of accident and 26 at date of trial, was a passenger in a motor vehicle being driven by the defendant when the defendant lost control of the vehicle with the result that it overturned and rolled down an embankment. The plaintiff was thrown out of the vehicle. She was rendered unconscious by the impact but had regained consciousness by the time of her arrival at hospital. She suffered superficial grazes and bruising to her head, face, left wrist and right thigh. The grazing to her left wrist caused minor and insignificant blemishes. The minor head injury produced no ill effects. However she also suffered a four inch long laceration on the prosterior medial surface of the left calf and a second transverse laceration immediately above it. The wounds extended deep into the facia of the muscle. Under general anaesthetic the wounds were cleaned, debrided and sutured. She remained in hospital for five days. The wounds subsequently became infected and she required regular treatment in the form of dressings and further removal of debris by her GP. The wounds healed after about five months. She required crutches to mobilise for about two months and she underwent a course of physiotherapy in order to correct a fixed flexion deformity in the knee. The treatment was successful. The plaintiff had suffered and continued to suffer considerable embarrassment at the scarring on her leg which remained an obvious, considerable and permanent cosmetic defect. She avoided wearing clothing which might reveal the scarring and on holidays she tended to cover her legs when not swimming. She continued to suffer an occasional cramp like sensation at the site of the scarring and there was a slight loss of sensation between the two scars. There was no prospect of further improvement in her condition. Minor grazing to the left wrist had caused minor and insignificant blemishes. *General Damages*: £8,750 for pain, suffering and loss of amenity.

ESCOTT v. ESCOTT, November 20, 1996, H.H.J. Glyn Morgan, CC (Newport). [*Ex rel.* Jonathan Walters, Barrister, 33 Park Place, Cardiff].

Burns

2001.　S, infant female, aged eight months at the time of the accident and three years at the time of the hearing, was scalded whilst at a private day nursery when scalding gravy was spilt onto her scalp, lower face, neck, upper chest and arm. She suffered burns to an area of five to six per cent of her body surface. Two and a half years after the accident she was left with a soft pale scarred area just above the left elbow of four centimetres by four centimetres and an area on the point of the elbow of three centimetres by two centimetres. She also had an area of white soft scarring along the line of the left clavicle approximately 10 centimetres by three centimetres. On the left side of the neck was an inconspicuous area approximately six centimetres by two centimetres of pale, flat streaky scarring. Below the chin was a seven centimetres by three centimetres area of scarring which was mildly indurated and pink. There was also a triangular area approximately three centimetres wide of pale inconspicuous texture change on the left thigh. It was thought that there would be no further improvement and that surgery was unlikely. *General Damages*: £17,500. Special Damages: £1,600.

STOCKS v. WADSWORTH, September 24, 1997, District Judge Slim, CC (Halifax). [*Ex rel.* Allan Western, Rhodes Thain & Collinson, Solicitors, 27 Harrison Road, Halifax].

Burns

2002.　L hired a sunbed from S, which she used for two short periods. The sunbed was defective and caused the following injuries through excessive UVB radiation: (1) severe superficial burns to approximately 80 per cent of the dorsal surface of both calves causing soreness of both calves with immediate erythema (reddening) progressing to swelling and marked blistering, and (2) soreness over the back which settled fully within two days. She was treated in hospital with flamazine dressings, aspiration of the blisters and analgesia. During the next two weeks she returned to the hospital every second day for aspiration of the blisters and to have the dressings changed. L was off work for eight days and in severe pain for two weeks, especially when having the dressings changed. She was unable to drive or walk any distance during this period. At the date of the hearing, three years after the accident, L still suffered some pain, particularly when her legs were knocked or she had been standing for over 30 minutes. She also no longer wore tights or leggings as they would rub against the sensitive skin. She took one dose of non-prescription pain killers every day and no longer rode a bicycle, did aerobics or played as actively with her three young children; all of which she had previously enjoyed. L was reluctant to wear a short skirt as she was embarrassed by the residual red mark on her right calf which was desribed as being about the size of a matchbox, but was invisible when L had a sun tan. There was considered to be only about one per cent increase in the risk of skin ageing and skin cancer in the area due to the fact that L had had frequent exposure to sunbeds in the past and continued to use sunbeds at the date of the hearing. *General Damages*: £3,750.

LONGWORTH v. SUNBEAMS LTD, June 20, 1997, Assistant Recorder Warren Q.C., CC (Reading). [*Ex rel.* Justin Levinson, Barrister, 1 Dr Johnson's Buildings, Temple].

Burns

2003.   Male, aged 49 at the date of the accident and aged 51 at the date of assessment, sustained injuries in an accident at work. He suffered burns to the inside of his right arm resulting in permanent scarring. B attended the works first aid room where his burns were treated with ointment and a bandage applied. He attended the works first aid room on a further three occasions for further dressing to be applied. He then wore a crepe bandage for a further six to seven weeks in an attempt to keep the affected area clean. The scabbing on his arm ceased two months after his accident. During this period he suffered a considerable amount of stinging pain in the affected area particularly upon contact with water. B was left with a "y" shaped scar, the two arms of which measured 10 centimetres and eight centimetres. Upon medical examination some 12 months after his accident the scars were found to be darkish in colour but non tender and not depressed. Symptoms at the date of trial included a tingling sensation of the affected area when exposed to cold conditions and reddening when exposed to the sun. B liked to take two foreign holidays each year and he was conscious of the scars whilst sunbathing. It was anticipated that the scarring would not improve significantly with the passing of time. He had no time off work. *General Damages*: £2,250. Total award: £2,270.

BARNES v. KENMORE REFRIGERATION LTD, May 15, 1997, District Judge Giles, CC (Leeds). [*Ex rel.* Rowley Ashworth Solicitors, Leeds].

Burns

2004.   Male, aged 28 at the time of the accident and aged 31 at the date of the trial, sustained an injury at work when a piece of hot coke fell into his glove, burning the skin of the first webbed space of the back of the left non-dominant hand. F felt immediate discomfort and immersed the burned area in cold water. After attending the work's medical centre, where the burn was cleansed and dressed, he returned to work. Discomfort was experienced for some two days after the accident. The burn had healed fully a week after the accident. There had been no physical difficulties and the residual scar had faded and was well integrated into the background skin tone. F took no time off work. The residual scar measured 1.5 centimetres by 1.0 centimetres with no neurological deficit or vascular innervation. The scar caused no cosmetic embarrassment and did not inhibit any of F's leisure activities. *General Damages*: £700.

FINNIGAN v. BRITISH STEEL PLC, March 4, 1997, District Judge Mainwaring-Taylor, CC (Middlesbrough). [*Ex rel.* John F Harrison, Barrister, St Paul's Chambers, Leeds].

Burns – very severe burns

2005. Male, S, was aged 32 at the date of the assault in November 1991 and 38 at the date of hearing. A former girlfriend caused him and his female partner to be abducted, hit over the head with a car jack, placed into a car which was set aflame and then pushed off a hillside. S and his partner had a miraculous escape, but S was seriously injured. He was detained in intensive care for eight weeks; unconscious for the first six days. Thereafter, he was in extreme pain. He suffered full thickness burns to 40 per cent of his upper body surface including face, neck, upper limbs and especially his right dominant hand. He had eight episodes of surgery from November 1991 to November 1994 incorporating skin grafts, scar revision and release of contractures. At the date of the hearing he was still hampered by lack of pliability in his forearms and right hand; further surgery, possibly by way of "re-lining", was expected, with continuing use of tea tree oils to assist the skin. The assault with the car jack caused a soft tissue whiplash type injury, resulting in chronic and apparently permanent low back pain exacerbated in part by contracting tissue in the neck. He continued to receive osteopathic treatment to ease the pain. He was left with breathlessness and hoarseness due to smoke inhalation and hearing loss in the right ear. S subsequently married his co-victim. S had been a capable sportsman before the attack but was unable to pursue his activities. His ability to carry out domestic chores was handicapped by delicacy of skin on hands, which was prone to blistering, and to overheating as a result of the destruction of sweat glands. Damaged and treated skin had to be protected from sunlight. The use of his right hand was limited. S had attempted to return to work but was forced to retire because of his injuries. The Board accepted that it was unrealistic to expect the victim to work in the future. *General Damages*: £70,000. Total award: £194,531 (including loss of earnings together with past and future costs of osteopathy and aromatherapy).

STOKLE, *Re*, August 28, 1997, Judge not specified, CICB (London). [*Ex rel.* Alex Ralton, Barrister, Albion Chambers, Broad Street, Bristol, BS1 1DR].

Minor injuries

2006. Male, casino inspector, aged 36 at the date of the accident and aged 38 at the date of trial, was involved in a road traffic accident following a rear end impact. He sustained shock and a minor soft tissue injury to his cervical spine, swelling to the right wrist and ulnar nerve entrapment affecting the right elbow, forearm and hand. He was off work for one day. He was seen by his GP following the accident and at an Accident and Emergency department the day after that. He complained of a whiplash type injury to his neck, pain in his right arm with intermittent pins and needles, and the occasional numbness along the ulnar border extending to the right ring and little fingers. Three months following the accident, he was still complaining of pain and tingling in his right arm and was referred for physiotherapy. He had eight sessions of physiotherapy where it was noted he had a swollen and very tender right elbow and pain in his ring and little fingers. There was some loss of dexterity in the right arm and sensory changes in forearm. By October 1995 it was thought that the sensory changes and symptoms in the right elbow were clearing. The accident partially affected his work as a casino inspector when he was called upon to shuffle cards and handle chips. He was examined 10 months after the accident and noted to have a very sore elbow with numbness affecting the ring and little fingers. On examination 18 months after the accident there was a general improvement in manual dexterity although he could not sleep on his right side due to pain in his elbow. By May 1997 there was 95 per cent recovery with no long term problems other than residual symptoms of ulnar nerve contusion. *General Damages*: £4,000. Special Damages: £728. Total award: £4,728.

DOYLE v. VAN BRUGGEN, May 6, 1997, H.H.J. Zucker Q.C., CC (Central London). [*Ex rel.* OH Parsons & Partners, Sovereign House, 212-224 Shaftsbury Avenue, London].

Minor injuries

2007. Male, aged 14 years at the date of the accident, fell on a broken step close to his home. As a result he sustained an avulsion fracture of a small fragment of bone from his right fibula, together with a partial tear of the lateral colateral ligament of his right ankle. He was required to wear a below knee walking plaster for five weeks and was absent from school during this period. He was left with pain over the outer aspect of his right ankle on walking and was also subject to swelling of the right ankle. He had particular difficulty walking on inclined surfaces and going up and down stairs. He was unable to take part in any sports at school for seven months. Twelve months after the accident, the symptoms had improved to the extent that he was left with only slight occasional swelling. He had regained a full range of movements and the ankle no longer caused him any pain. There was no risk of any long term consequences from the injury. *General Damages*: £3,750.

PARNHAM (A MINOR) v. METROPOLITAN HOUSING TRUST LTD, July 18, 1997, District Judge Millard, CC (Nottingham). [*Ex rel.* Nelsons, Solicitors, Pennine House, 8 Stanford Street, Nottingham].

Minor injuries

2008. C and her three young children were involved in a road traffic accident involving a near head on collision between her vehicle and a car which was overtaking on a busy urban road. The collision only consisted of a scraping contact on the offside of C's car which caused some minor damage. Neither C nor her children were physically injured. At the date of the accident C had been rather depressed as a result of her domestic situation. She was unemployed and was living in a bedsit, having divorced from her husband who had custody of the children. Following the accident C suffered poor sleep for about a month. She had nightmares for about two months and flashbacks for about a year. C became a very nervous driver and passenger and generally avoided travel by car although she had re-commenced driving a week after the accident. C did not consult her GP until three months later when he prescribed Prozak for depression which she took for some two months. C neither sought or received any other treatment for psychiatric problems suffered as a result of the accident. C was diagnosed as having suffered depression for a period of about eight months and post traumatic stress disorder for about 12 months as a result of the accident. She was also diagnosed as suffering from ongoing Phobic Anxiety Neurosis in that she could not travel comfortably by road. The prognosis was that the condition would persist but that cognitive behavioural therapy could possibly help settle the symptoms. The court took note of the Judicial Studies Board Guidelines and accepted that the case was in the "minor" band of £1,600 to £3,250. However, it was held that the Phobic Anxiety Neurosis brought C within the "Moderate Psychiatric Damage" band of £3,250 and £8,000. It was held that the symptoms were genuine and might persist, but that some help could be sought with the possibility of resolving the symptoms. *General Damages*: £3,750.

CARPENTER v. EASTON, July 18, 1997, H.H.J. Lorriston, CC (Weymouth). [*Ex rel.* David McHugh, Barrister, Bracton Chambers, Chancery Lane].

Minor injuries

2009. Male, aged 12 at the date of the accident and 14 at the date of settlement, was struck by a vehicle when walking along the pavement. Following the accident he was unconscious for approximately 30 minutes and was observed to have extensive abrasions over the left side of his head and bruising around the upper part of the left thigh and both knees. He remained in hospital for two nights for observation. At the time of the accident he was on holiday but was able to return to his school when term commenced 13 days later. He was unable to play games for about four weeks after the accident. He made a full recovery from his head injury. Initially he was assessed as having an increased risk of developing epilepsy which was put at five per cent, but two and a half years after the accident he was at no greater risk than any other child. Eighteen months after the accident he continued to have some problems with his left knee which tended to click after 25 minutes of walking. He was also left with a small bald patch on the left side of the scalp that was the size of a 20 pence piece. It was expected that the bald spot would be permanent but it was of no great concern to the plaintiff. A settlement was approved by the court. *General Damages*: £3,300. Special Damages: £200. Total award: £3,500.

WOODHOUSE v. NORMANTON, September 24, 1997, District Judge Slim, CC (Halifax). [*Ex rel.* Allan Western, Rhodes Thain & Collinson Solicitors, 27 Harrison Road, Halifax].

Minor injuries

2010. Female, aged 37 at date of accident, suffered short lived pain to lower lumbar spine immediately after a road traffic accident. Some hours after the accident S sought her GP's assistance. Some discomfort developed in her left shoulder. S had bed rest for four days and underwent a course of physiotherapy. Five months after the accident S was referred to a specialist as she was suffering some radiating pain to her left leg. Manipulation under anaesthetic and an injection to lower spine achieved minimal improvement. S was diagnosed as suffering from facet arthrosis syndrome. Various levels of lumbar ache continued up to trial affecting sitting or standing after long periods but not enough to interfere with employment. No long term complications were expected. It was held that pain and symptoms suffered for 18 months were attributable to the accident. *General Damages*: £3,000. Special Damages: £2,700.

SCOURFIELD AND BRITISH GAS PLC v. GAMMON, December 3, 1996, District Judge McWilkinson, CC (Haverfordwest). [*Ex rel.* Dominic Boothroyd, Barrister, Gower Chambers, 57 Walter Road, Swansea].

Minor injuries

2011. Male, aged 26 at the date of the accident and aged 29 at the date of the trial, slipped into a hole in a metal walkway at his place of work. He managed to avoid falling completely into the hole: had he done so he would have fallen into some bottle grinding equipment. He sustained severe chest wall bruising, particularly on the front left side, a 10 centimetres by 0.5 centimetres linear abrasion down the right shin and a 1.5 centimetres by 1 centimetre burn injury to the left forearm. There was no bony injury. The chest caused severe pain for five weeks which disturbed his sleep and prevented sexual relations; the latter causing some friction with his wife. Thereafter the chest was occasionally painful when D had to lift heavy objects or stretch out. Such pain had resolved by the date of trial. The right shin had a flat, irregular, permanent but painless scar which was visible up to ten feet away. It itched in hot weather, would not tan but was of only limited embarrassment. D was absent from work for five weeks, could not play snooker for six weeks and was unable to play cricket as a fast bowler for eight months. *General Damages*: £3,000.

DAVIS v. GREGG & CO (KNOTTINGLEY) LTD, January 9, 1997, District Judge Garside, CC (Bradford). [*Ex rel.* Michael Smith, Barrister, 6 Park Square, Leeds].

Minor injuries

2012. Male, aged 57 at the date of the accident and 59 at trial, suffered personal injuries as a result of a collision with an alsation dog which ran out into the road and hit his motorcycle. He suffered fractures to his third and sixth ribs, a fractured left shoulder blade and a fractured left clavicle. He was hospitalised for seven days and was unable to carry out his hobbies of walking his dog and gardening for six weeks, nor pistol shooting for three months. H had been medically retired five years before the accident. H recovered fully within 12 to 14 months of the accident and the prognosis was that future degenerative changes as a result of the accident were unlikely. *General Damages*: £3,000. Special damages: £215. *Blanche v. Brown* [1995] 1 C.L.Y. 1724 considered.

HUTCHINSON v. ABDALLA, November 11, 1996, Recorder Rose, CC (Central London). [*Ex rel.* David McIlroy, Barrister].

Minor injuries

2013.   Male, aged 28 at the date of the accident and 30 at the date of the trial, was involved in an accident on October 2, 1995, when working on a motor car which was suspended above him by a forklift truck. The hydraulics on the forklift truck failed and the vehicle fell onto the plaintiff. O suffered injury to the head and right leg. He suffered bruising to the top of his head which took seven to 10 days to subside. Resultant headaches settled within three weeks. O also suffered significant soft tissue injury with extensive contusion/bruising to the lower right thigh. He experienced severe pain for two or three weeks followed by continuing aching and discomfort for between two and three months post accident. The symptoms largely settled thereafter save for residual intermittent discomfort after the plaintiff had been driving for a lengthy period or in cold weather. The residual symptoms were not expected to improve. *General Damages* for pain, suffering and loss of amenity: £2,700.

BAINES (ONKAR SINGH) v. SHERAZIA T/A A&S AUTOS, August 26, 1997, District Judge Lingard, CC (Keighley). [*Ex rel.* David N Jones, Barrister, Broadway House Chambers, 9 Bank Street, Bradford].

Minor injuries

2014.   Female, aged 44 at the date of the incidents in 1993 and aged 47 at the date of the hearing, was employed at the Leeds Permanent Building Society. She was present at the building society in September and October 1993 when two armed robberies occurred. B had also been present during three other incidents which had taken place in 1988 and 1989. B was able to return to her employment on the next day after each raid. Following the incidents in 1988 and 1989 she had been aware of heightened anxiety at work if there was a sudden noise or if a customer entered the premises wearing a crash helmet. Those feelings heightened after the raids in 1993. B became apprehensive if she heard a loud noise in the building society or in its vicinity. She also became upset when reminded of the raids, for example, when she saw persons wearing balaclavas on television. B was diagnosed as suffering from very mild post traumatic anxiety state. *General Damages*: £2,500.

BOURNE, *Re*, May 23, 1997, Judge not specified, CICB (Birmingham). [*Ex rel.* J Zindani, Solicitor, Russell Jones and Walker, 16 Waterloo Street, Birmingham].

Minor injuries

2015.   Female, aged 67 at the date of the accident and aged 68 at the time of the hearing, was the front seat passenger of a motor vehicle involved in a collision when a vehicle pulled out from a minor road on the left hand side into the vehicle in which she was being carried, causing it to hit a parked vehicle and spin round into a lamp post and brick wall. She immediately felt discomfort in the back of her neck and across her chest and was taken to hospital by ambulance, where she was X-rayed but no broken bones were revealed. She was prescribed a support collar which she continued to wear on and off for a month. She attended a chiropractor for treatment two days after the accident and again five weeks after the accident. Her pain and suffering continued for a total of three months and during this period she took pain killers, when she considered it necessary. She also suffered some bruising under her right arm. S stated that she had felt nervous when travelling in a car after the accident for a period of two months, especially as a passenger. *General Damages*: £1,600.

STRIDE (S) v. LIPSCOMBE, July 1, 1997, District Judge Langley, CC (Central London). [*Ex rel.* Douglas Silas, Solicitor, David Levene & Co, 235-239 High Road, Wood Green, London].

Minor injuries

2016. Male, 59 years old at the date of the accident, suffered a whiplash injury caused by a car collision. The plaintiff, from Israel, was two days into a two week long touring holiday of Great Britain when the accident happened. Throughout the remainder of the holiday he felt tense and lethargic, slept badly, suffered headaches, back and neck pain. An afternoon visit to York was abandoned whilst his hired car was replaced. Whilst the remainder of the holiday itinerary went largely unchanged, the daily amount of time spent sightseeing was significantly reduced. The intended leisurely vacation was spoilt. *General Damages*: £510 for loss of enjoyment of holiday (including interest).

KATZ v. SAYNER, August 22, 1997, H.H.J. Bowers, CC (Doncaster). [*Ex rel.* Gordon Stables, Barrister, 26 Paradise Square Chambers, Sheffield].

Miscarriage

2017. Female, aged 21 at the time of the incident and 25 at the time of the hearing, was knocked to the ground and struck in the face several times with a stiletto. She suffered a one centimetre laceration above the lateral aspect of her right eyebrow which was closed with four sutures, she also suffered a one centimetre laceration over the inner aspect of her right cheek which was closed with four sutures and two superficial lacerations over her left cheek which required no specific treatment. As a result of the assault D suffered a miscarriage. It had been a planned pregnancy and D had tried unsuccessfully since the incident to conceive another child. The impact was therefore greater on the applicant than on a woman who had already established a family. *General Damages*: £6,000.

DUBLIN, *Re* (1997) 97(1) Q.R. 3, R Macdonald Q.C., CICB (London).

Bruising

2018. Male, 25 at the date of road traffic accident and 27 at the date of trial, was riding a motorcycle when the defendant's car turned directly into his path. He fell off his motorcycle and slid along the road. Within two days he developed marked bruising over his back, both arms and both legs. The worst of the bruising was on his right thigh. In addition, he suffered superficial grazes on both thighs, his left elbow and multiple cuts on both hands. The bruising and grazing were completely resolved in about three weeks. However the graze on his left elbow left a permanent scar which measured two and a half centimetres by one centimetre. The award, however, did not reflect any cosmetic disability. He also developed headaches and neck pain after the accident. These persisted for about a month before partially resolving, but he made a full recovery from these injuries after six months. Although he damaged the joint capsule in his right hip in his fall, he made a full recovery from this injury nine months after the accident. He was obliged to refrain from sporting activities for those nine months. He also lost the use of his motorcycle for 64 weeks, although he was able to travel by car whenever necessary. *General Damages*: £2,000. Award for loss of use of motorcycle: £640. Total award: £6,266.

JAMES v. WATKER, September 20, 1996, H.H.J. Walker. [*Ex rel.* Ian McLauchlan, Barrister, 12 Paradise Square, Sheffield].

Bruising

2019. Male, aged 38 at the date of the accident and 40 at the date of the trial was involved in a road traffic accident. He attended hospital the following day and was prescribed oral analgesia and advised to rest. He sustained soft-issue trauma to the left and right mandibular joints, a hyper extension flexion injury of the spine, jarring and jolting to the upper and lower back and bruising trauma to the right ankle. He did not take any time off work. His jaw pain settled within eight months whilst his neck became symptom free within 11 months. *General Damages*: £1,750. Special damages: £865. Total award (including interest): £2,842.

BOUNDY v. VALAVANIS, September 19, 1996, Assistant Recorder Johnson, CC (Birkenhead). [*Ex rel.* Weightmans, Solicitors, Richmond House, 1 Rumford Place, Liverpool].

Bruising

2020. Female, aged 20 at the date of the accident, was involved in a road traffic accident in which she received bruising to her right hip. She became anxious about driving as a consequence of the accident. The bruising to her hip settled in three weeks and her anxiety of driving lasted about three months. *General Damages*: £500. Special damages: £718.

DOOLEY v. MACHIN, April 22, 1997, District Judge McCullagh, CC (Birkenhead). [*Ex rel.* Michael W. Hallsall, Solicitors, 2 The Parks, Newton-le-Willows].

Bruising

2021. Male, aged 26 at the date of the accident, was thrown from his motorcycle and suffered a soft tissue injury to his right big toe and bruising to his right leg and the right side of his body. The plaintiff was unemployed at the time of the accident. No medical treatment was sought other than the plaintiff taking paracetamol. The plaintiff had a limp for one week, and the foot was painful for ten days to two weeks. The bruising lasted two weeks. There were no after effects that lasted more than two weeks after the accident. *General Damages*: £500.

CARLISLE v. CHAPMAN, November 11, 1996, District Judge Daniels, CC (Medway). [*Ex rel.* Neelima Mehendale, Barrister, Stour Chambers, Barton Mill House, Barton Mill Road, Canterbury].

Carbon monoxide poisoning

2022. Female, aged 29 to 30 during the period of exposure to carbon monoxide and 31 at the date of trial, had a combination gas boiler installed in her home in January 1995. It was fitted negligently and discharged carbon monoxide into her kitchen. She suffered headaches almost immediately thereafter. They increased in intensity with almost constant headaches, frequent migraines and with pins and needles and numbness on one or other side. She suffered nausea and general lethargy, giving up sporting activities. The symptoms reduced during summer as the central heating was not operating. The symptoms resumed with full intensity when the heating was turned on again in the autumn. The defect was discovered and corrected after 10 months, in October 1995. Her symptoms resolved fully three months after the boiler defect was corrected. *General Damages*: £5,000. Special Damages: £1,540.

HARVEY v. FAIRSCOPE, September 3, 1997, Mr Recorder Powles Q.C., CC (Kingston). [*Ex rel.* Simon Cavender, Barrister, Phoenix Chambers, 47a Bedford Row, London, WC1R 4LR].

Hepatitis

2023. In early January 1992, R was working at an unemployment office when a man coming in to sign on vomited on her desk, computer and papers. The office contained no cleaning equipment or materials, and R had to clear up the vomit using toilet tissue. A fortnight later R displayed symptoms of hepatitis, with jaundice, weakness and exhaustion. In February 1992, R was told that she probably had infectious Hepatitis A, but more tests were required to be sure. The second test results were communicated to R in March 1992 when she was admitted to hospital. R remained an inpatient for two months. On discharge, she was weak and listless and had to be cared for by her parents. She continued to lose weight and she was re-admitted in August 1992 for anorexia. She was put on a drip, various tests were conducted with negative results, and was discharged after a further three and a half weeks. The medical evidence was that within six months of the original admission she was fully recovered, with no long term sequelae. *General Damages*: £4,250. Claim for *Smith v. Manchester* award rejected on the evidence.

RUBINS v. EMPLOYMENT OFFICE, June 24, 1997, H.H.J. Peppitt, CC (Canterbury). [*Ex rel.* Simon Michael, Barrister, Bedford Chambers, 27 Rectory Lane, Bedford].

Ringworm

2024. Female, aged 32 at the time of the incident and aged 35 at the time of trial, purchased a kitten from J's petshop which proved to be infected with ringworm, a fungal infection. She was 7 months pregnant and had a young child at the time. She contracted ringworm from the kitten and so did her infant son. She developed spots and patches all over her body. She was prescribed treatment in the forms of creams which had to be applied on a daily basis. It was not possible for her to take oral medication as this may have proved detrimental to the health of her unborn child, and she had to continue treating herself with the creams for a period of six weeks. She suffered considerable anxiety and worry for the health of her son and her unborn child. She had to cancel a holiday which she had booked and felt gravely embarrassed by the spots and blemishes which appeared on her face and upper body. She avoided going out and meeting people she knew whilst she had the condition. She was advised to disinfect her furnishings and clean her house on a daily basis to purge it of the ringworm infection. She also suffered the further distress of having the kitten in question put down. *General Damages*: £1,200. Total award: £1,574.

WILCOCK v. JOHN MACE LTD, May 15, 1997, District Judge Peters, CC (Sheffield). [*Ex rel.* Andrew Hogan, Barrister, Ropewalk Chambers, Nottingham].

Angina attack

2025. Male, aged 58 at the date of the accident and 59 at the date of trial, when the car which he was driving was struck from behind by a HGV in an urban area. He was known to suffer from angina and almost immediately after the impact, whilst still in his car, he began to experience severe pains in his chest and breathlessness. He used his normal inhaler and angina medication but these had no effect. The judge accepted D's evidence that he had thought that he was suffering a heart attack and was going to die. In fact the symptoms were of a severe angina attack which lasted one and a half hours. D was admitted to hospital and detained for observation for three days. In addition, he suffered a mild whiplash injury which caused discomfort and stiffness over his neck, shoulders and upper back for approximately five weeks. The judge stated that it had been a very frightening experience for D. *General*

Damages: £2,000. (The judge indicated that for the whiplash injury alone he would have been awarded general damages of about £700).

DUNN v. RENNOC, September 5, 1997, Belcher, J., CC (Blackburn). [*Ex rel.* Tim Grover, Barrister, Martins Building, 4 Water Street, Liverpool, L2 3SP].

2026. Articles

Assessment of damages in motor vehicle cases *(Alexander Pelling)*: S.J. 1997, 141 (22), 548-549. (Claims for hire charges, including situation where plaintiff has to use hire car for extended period because he is unable to pay repair costs, loss of use claims and awards for diminution in value).

Contingency factors in personal injury multipliers *(Charles Foster* and *Mark Bennet)*: S.J. 1997, 141 (9), 212-214. (Discounts to be applied to multipliers in personal injury cases, including use of Ogden tables, contingencies to be taken into account in addition to death and how they should be assessed and use of fixed period multipliers).

Damage limitation *(David Hamilton)*: Policing T. 1997, 3(1), 44-45. (Implications of CA guidelines for jury directions on appropriate level of damages for successful litigants in civil actions against the police, including a likely reduction in lottery type compensation awards).

Damages for breach of contract: a cause for distress? *(Paula Giliker)*: S.J. 1997, 141 (40), 998-999. (Scope of claims for damages for mental distress).

Damages for personal injury: changes in the assessment of future losses *(Richard Vallance)*: I.I.L.R. 1997, 5(4), 114-115. (Whether damages for future losses should be calculated on basis of ordinary investor willing to take some risk or of victim requiring secure fund).

Damages for spoilt holidays *(Mark Pawlowski)*: Lit. 1997, 16(8), 311-328. (Collection of 36 cases, with special reference to amounts awarded for diminution in value of holiday, disappointment and mental distress).

Duxbury, multipliers and personal injury claims *(Andrew Grantham)*: J.P.I.L. 1997, Jun, 81-86.

Interim payments, split trials and provisional damages: P. Injury 1996, 1 (1), 6-8.

Interim payments: a necessity, not an option *(Bill Braithwaite)*: S.J. 1997, 141 (43), 1074-1075. (How system of interim damages works including limitations under Rules of the Supreme Court, scenarios such as more than one defendant and contributory negligence, and why lawyers should always claim immediately).

Law Commission recommend tortfeasors recompense NHS: Med. L. Mon. 1997, 4(1), 5-6. (Consultation Paper Law Com. No.144 *Damages for Personal Injury* on whether defendants who cause injuries should pay cost of NHS medical care as part of damages).

Loss and liability *(Tony Dugdale)*: P.N. 1997, 13(1), 5-8. (Assessment of damages for negligent valuation where the lender was contributed negligence and confusion over claim for interest on damages, showing the difficulties of applying HL ruling in *South Australia* case).

Mental health law: settlement of personal injury awards *(Penny Letts)*: L.S.G. 1997, 94(5), 31. (Court of Protection Practice Note giving guidance on suitability of settlement into trust for plaintiffs with mental disability in view of DSS policy to disregard such funds for benefit purposes).

Off the road – claiming for loss of use and inconvenience in road traffic accident cases *(Malcolm Johnson)*: Lit. 1997, 16(3), 94-102.

PI litigation: benefits recovery: Writ 1997, 83(Sep), 2-3. (Criticisms of law on recoupment of social security benefits from personal injuries damages, cases on scheme and reforms made by the Social Security Act 1997).

Personal injury: interest calculation *(Rodney Nelson-Jones)*: L.S.G. 1997, 94(36), 47. (Tables of interest rates on special damages awarded in personal injuries cases since 1965 to assist practitioners in calculating applicable interest).

Remedies for defective work: principles *(Peter Sheridan* and *Tom Pemberton)*: Cons. Law 1997, 8(5), 156-160. (Reinstatement or dimunition in value as standard measure of loss and four other means of assessing quantum).

State liability: Factortame in the Divisional Court and other recent developments *(John Tillotson)*: S.L.R. 1997, 22(Aut), 44-45. (Whether 1988 Act was sufficiently serious breach of EC law to warrant claim for damages and how such damages should be assessed).

Structured settlements: P. & M.I.L.L. 1997, 13(4), 31-32. (Judicial dicta on use of structured settlements for personal injury plaintiffs).

Structured settlements: a current perspective *(Robin Hall)*: S.J. 1997, 141(26), 648-649. (Benefits of structured settlements for plaintiffs and defendants in personal injury cases, measures to guard against future economic contingencies, Inland Revenue approval and role of advisers).

Sufficient detail for opportunity to negotiate *(Robin Churchill)*: P. & M.I.L.L. 1997, 13(1), 1-2. (Whether plaintiffs' failure to provide quantum information prior to court proceedings was oppressive or vexatious).

The great deceivers: E.G. 1997, 9734, 82-84. (Differences between measure of damages for fraudulent misrepresentation and for negligent misrepresentation).

The normal expectancies measure in tort damages *(Jane Stapleton)*: L.Q.R. 1997, 113(Apr), 257-293. (Classification of tort compensatory damages into "normal expectancies" and "entitled result" measures of damages, reasons why "normal expectancies" measure is to be preferred and how it applies in particular situations).

The taxation of damages and compensation *(Jason Ellis)*: Litigator 1997, Mar, 132-136.

What price the life of a child? *(Janice Kersey)* and *(Philip De Voil)*: S.J. 1997, 141(36), Supp 17-18. (Accountants' views on appropriate measure of damages in wrongful birth cases arising from failed sterilisation or failure to detect abnormalities during pregnancy where termination would have been possible).

2027. Books

Andrews, Peter, QC; Lee, Terry—Catastrophic Injuries: a Practical Guide to Compensation. Hardback: £70.00. ISBN 0-421-58340-1. Sweet & Maxwell.

Association of Personal Injury Lawyers—Personal Injury: Practice and Procedure in Europe. Paperback: £38.00. ISBN 1-85941-179-7. Sweet & Maxwell.

Barnes, Michael; Braithwaite, Bill; Ward, Anthony B.—Medical Aspects of Personal Injury Litigation. Hardback: £49.50. ISBN 0-632-04176-5. Blackwell Science (UK).

Brennan, Dan; Curran, Patrick—Personal Injury Handbook: 1997. Paperback: £55.00. ISBN 0-421-60040-3. Sweet & Maxwell.

Collett, Philip—Eye Injuries Litigation. Hardback: £65.00. ISBN 0-421-52900-8. Sweet & Maxwell.

Facts and Figures: Tables for the Calculation of Damages 1997. Paperback: £24.95. ISBN 0-421-57590-5. Sweet & Maxwell.

Goldrein, Iain S.; de Haas, Margaret R.—Structured Settlements: a Practical Guide. Hardback: £45.00. Butterworth Law.

Johnson, David—Head Injuries Litigation. Hardback: £60.00. ISBN 0-421-48350-4. Sweet & Maxwell.

Solomon, Nicola; Pritchard, John—Personal Injury Litigation. Practitioner Series. Paperback: £50.00. ISBN 0-7520-0446-8. FT Law & Tax.

Unger, Andy—Know-how for Personal Injury Lawyers. Know-how Series. Paperback: £47.00. ISBN 0-7520-0325-9. FT Law & Tax.

DEFAMATION

2028. Libel—documentary evidence—disclosure in criminal proceedings as basis for action

See EVIDENCE: Mahon v. Rahn. §475

2029. Libel—measure of damages—proportionality

See DAMAGES: Jones v. Pollard. §1768

2030. Libel—mode of trial—action concerning fitness of prominent public figure to hold office could be tried by judge alone

[Supreme Court Act 1981 s.69(1).]

The defendants to two libel actions appealed against a decision that trial of the actions would require prolonged examination of documents which could not conveniently be made with a jury and that, accordingly, they should be tried by a judge alone, pursuant to the Supreme Court Act 1981 s.69(1). The defendants contended that the criteria in s.69(1) were not satisfied and, in any case, where a trial concerned the plaintiff's fitness to hold public office, the public perception was that jury trial was to be preferred and the public interest in allowing trial by jury should have been a weighty, if not conclusive, factor in the judge's decision, particularly where the defendants were major organs of the news media.

Held, dismissing the appeal, that s.69(3) indicated that the emphasis was now against jury trial and this should be taken into account by the court when exercising its discretion under s.69(1), although the fact that a case concerned a prominent public figure and issues of national interest was a factor in favour of jury trial. The fact that the case concerned issues of credibility and an attack on A's honour and integrity should be taken into account, but was not an overriding consideration in support of jury trial, and the need to obtain a reasoned judgment was also relevant. The judge had been entitled to conclude that the criteria in s.69(1) were fulfilled and the public perception that jury trial was to be preferred could not necessarily be considered a reliable guide. It was for the court to decide what mode of trial would best serve the interests of justice with regard to both the parties and the public, and in view of the complex and controversial nature of the instant case, a trial before a judge alone would be more appropriate.

AITKEN v. PRESTON; AITKEN v. GRANADA TELEVISION LTD, *The Times*, May 21, 1997, Lord Bingham of Cornhill, L.C.J., CA.

2031. Libel—mode of trial—delay caused by long vacation

A, the defendant in a libel action brought by M, unsuccessfully sought to have the case heard before a jury. A appealed against refusal to grant leave to appeal out of time, the delay having been caused primarily by the intervention of the long vacation.

Held, allowing the appeal and directing the trial to be heard before a judge and jury, that (1) the exception to the basic rule that a libel case should be held before a jury could not be invoked as no evidence had been led that the case would involve the prolonged examination of documents or accounts, and (2) the delay involved in this case was not very serious when the vacation was taken into account.

MEGHRAJ BANK LTD v. ARSIWALLA, Trans. Ref: QBENI 97/0411/E, July 7, 1997, Hirst, L.J., CA.

2032. Libel—natural and ordinary meaning—words outside possible range of meanings

E, and another, served two writs claiming damages for libel in respect of a passage from Andrew Sinclair's biography of the artist Francis Bacon, part of which was also published in the Sunday Times. E was the brother of FB's long time companion and heir. At preliminary trial it was held that the words did not have the defamatory meaning complained of. Subsequently, E sought to amend and substitute similar natural and ordinary meanings to the words complained of. The amendment was allowed. T appealed.

Held, allowing the appeal, that the basis on which to assess whether the words could have the meaning complained of was a matter of impression of the ordinary reader. The range of possible meanings of the words should be set down and any meanings outside that range ruled out, *Aiken v. Police Review Publishing Co Ltd* (Unreported, 1995) considered.

EDWARDS v. TIMES NEWSPAPERS LTD, Trans. Ref: QBENI 96/0647/E, QBENI 96/0654/E, QBENI 96/0654/E, March 6, 1997, Hirst, L.J., CA.

2033. **Libel—newspapers—cross examination of police officers as to cause of distress and credibility—subsequent events irrelevant to damage caused by publication of defamatory article**

B and others brought an action for libel against G in respect of an article published whilst they were serving police officers, claiming damages for distress arising out of the publication, which resulted in loss of reputation. G appealed against a decision refusing to allow cross examination of the plaintiffs as to the cause of the damage and credibility, and refusing leave to amend G's defence to include an issue of causation where G had sought to introduce events occurring between publication of the article and the commencement of the action.

Held, dismissing the appeal, that (1) the judge was correct to prevent cross examination of the plaintiffs, as the material on which G sought to rely was not relevant to the distress caused to B and the others, which arose solely from the loss of reputation resulting from the article's publication, *Associated Newspapers Ltd v. Dingle* [1964] A.C. 371 applied. Further, refusal to allow cross examination in the circumstances was in accordance with the general principle that a witness should not be subject to cross examination as to credibility on the basis of suspicion, rumour or complaint alone, where no attempt was made to justify the suspicion, *R. v. Edwards* [1991] 1 W.L.R. 207, [1991] C.L.Y. 732 applied, and (2) the judge was also correct to refuse to allow G to amend its defence in order to put causation at issue, as the pleading of a bare denial was defective if the purpose behind it was to raise a positive case that the plaintiffs' distress flowed from another source. Even if the pleading was not defective, the judge could exercise his discretion to permit the amendment at the relevant stage in the proceedings.

BENNETT v. GUARDIAN NEWSPAPERS LTD [1997] E.M.L.R. 301, Otton, L.J., CA.

2034. **Libel—pleadings—presumption that foreign law the same as English law**

U sought to amend its claim for libel to include a complaint of publication in a number of countries outside the UK. No particulars of foreign law were given. U argued that there was a presumption that the laws of those countries were the same as English law.

Held, allowing the amendment, that if the evidence as to foreign law was insufficient or non existent then the courts would apply English law, *Ertel Bieber & Co v. Rio Tinto Co Ltd* [1918] A.C. 260, *Arbitration between Tank of Oslo and Agence Maritime L Strauss of France, Re* [1940] 1 All E.R. 40 and *Szechter v. Szechter* [1971] P. 286, [1971] C.L.Y. 3603 applied. All that the plaintiff had to do was assert that the tort was actionable in the other country. It was for the defendant to show that the law of that country was different, the plaintiff did not have to set out what the law of that country was.

UNIVERSITY OF GLASGOW v. ECONOMIST LTD; UNIVERSITY OF EDINBURGH v. ECONOMIST LTD [1997] E.M.L.R. 495, Popplewell, J., QBD.

2035. **Libel—political parties—public interest prevented political party suing in libel**

B applied to strike out a statement of claim for damages and an injunction for libel brought by the second plaintiff, a company limited by guarantee. B contended that, as a political party could not sue for libel, RP's pleadings disclosed no reasonable cause of action.

Held, allowing the application, that the principle established in *Derbyshire CC v. Times Newspapers Ltd* [1993] A.C. 534, [1993] C.L.Y. 2581, preventing central and local government institutions bringing actions in defamation at common law on the ground that those holding office must remain open to criticism, extended also to political parties. Preventing actions on public interest grounds required caution, but could be justified by the public interest in freedom of speech in a democratic society.

GOLDSMITH v. BHOYRUL, *The Times*, June 20, 1997, Buckley, J., QBD.

2036. Libel—qualified privilege—no duty to publish allegations of racism of public official whether true or not

[Rules of the Supreme Court Ord.18 r.19.]

G, publishers and author of two articles in a newspaper which Y alleged accused him of racism and which he considered to be defamatory, pleaded the defences of fair comment and qualified privilege. G sought relief under RSC Ord.18 r.19 striking out the paragraphs of the defence relating to the defences. G submitted that they had a duty to publish the allegations contained within the articles to the general public irrespective of their truth or falsity. Y submitted that, since there was nothing pleaded to show why there was a duty to make the accusations of racism against him, the plea of qualified privilege was fatally flawed and should be struck out. G submitted that the categories of qualified privilege were not closed.

Held, allowing the application, that there was no public interest in the promulgation of inaccurate allegations and the defence of unqualified privilege was unarguable. The defence of fair comment was capable of affording a partial defence, *Blackshaw v. Lord* [1984] 1 Q.B. 1, [1983] C.L.Y. 2204, *Linghans v. Austria* [1986] E.H.R.R. 407, *Derbyshire CC v. Times Newspapers Ltd* [1993] A.C. 534, [1993] C.L.Y. 2581 considered.

YOUNGERWOOD v. GUARDIAN NEWSPAPERS LTD, Trans. Ref: No.1996-Y-528, June 13, 1997, Eady, J., QBD.

2037. Libel—statement clarifying article written by freelance journalist—natural and ordinary meaning of words

[Rules of the Supreme Court Ord.82 r.3.]

S, a freelance journalist, issued writs in two separate actions claiming damages for libel against the publishers of "Jane's Defence Weekly". The actions related to two articles written by S and printed in the journal. In both cases certain representations were made in relation to concerns about the content of the articles, which resulted in further articles, in the form of a publisher's statement and editor's note, being published in order to clarify the issues raised about S's articles. S claimed that the wording in the articles implied by its ordinary meaning or by innuendo that S had misquoted an interviewee, and had been negligent or careless or had deceived H in relation to the interview, giving particulars in support of that claim pursuant to RSC Ord.82 r.3(1). S claimed that his reputation had been damaged by the two publications. As a preliminary issue, it was considered whether the words complained of were capable of being defamatory, or of having the meaning S claimed they had, having regard to the natural and ordinary meaning of the words and the innuendo meaning or possible innuendo meaning. The judge found that no criticism of S could be inferred from the articles. S appealed. He submitted that there was or may have been an element of bias by the judge which was illustrated by comments to the effect that the judge had been the subject of libel but had never taken any action. S argued that the comments implied that the judge had not approached S's case seriously.

Held, dismissing the appeal, that in their ordinary meaning, the words in the clarification articles were not capable of being defamatory of S. The articles were merely an explanation that there had been a misunderstanding for which no one was to blame. The innuendo meaning did not go any further than the natural ordinary meaning, and there were no special facts known to a special group of people which would give the words a special meaning which would mean the words constituted a defamation. The comments made by the judge, complained of by S, were unfortunate but did not imply that the judge had not considered S's case on its merits. In any case the issue tried was a matter of law and the

Court of Appeal was therefore able to reconsider the issue afresh and reach its own determination, which it had done.

SHANSON v. HOWARD, Trans. Ref: QBENF 95/0844/C, January 30, 1997, Sir Brian Neill, CA.

2038. Libel—whether words complained of capable of bearing defamatory meaning—range of possible defamatory meanings to be delimited by judge

[Rules of the Supreme Court Ord.82 r.3A.]

N appealed against the dismissal of their summons under RSC Ord.82 r.3A to determine whether words complained of in a newspaper article concerning the suicide of a police sergeant were capable of bearing the defamatory meaning pleaded. M had asserted in his statement of claim that the article strongly implied that he and other police officers had been involved in drug dealing and bribery, but N contended that the reasonably fair minded reader would not infer guilt from the words used.

Held, allowing the appeal, that under RSC Ord.82 r.3A it was for the judge to determine whether the words complained of were capable of bearing the defamatory meaning alleged in the statement of claim and set down limits to the possible range of meanings which could be inferred by the reader, in the light of established principles, *Slim v. Daily Telegraph* [1968] 2 Q.B. 157, [1968] C.L.Y. 2231 and *Lewis v. Daily Telegraph* [1964] 2 Q.B. 601, [1964] C.L.Y. 2130 considered. The jury had then to decide the actual meaning from the range determined by the judge. By pre determining the scope of permissible meanings, the court was better able to evaluate defences raised and the degree of harm to the complainant's reputation. As the words in issue could be interpreted in a number of different ways, they could not impute actual guilt.

MAPP v. NEWS GROUP NEWSPAPERS LTD; GILLAN v. NEWS GROUP NEWSPAPERS LTD; GOSCOMB v. NEWS GROUP NEWSPAPERS LTD; WATTON v. NEWS GROUP NEWSPAPERS LTD, *The Times*, March 10, 1997, Hirst, L.J., CA.

2039. Privilege—legal proceedings—contribution towards fostering costs—information requested by solicitor of the case to be relied upon—absolute privilege attached

In 1992 serious problems developed in the relationship between J and his adoptive parents, W. In December 1992 J was placed with a foster family by S and in the course of correspondence between the solicitor acting for W and the S's solicitor, the latter stated that Mrs W had "threatened to lock [J] in his room if he was not removed". Mrs W claimed that these words were defamatory and commenced proceedings for damages against S. S sought to have the writ and statement of claim struck out on the ground that they disclosed no cause of action since the communication in question was covered by the defence of absolute privilege.

Held, striking out the writ and statement of claim, that the privilege from suit for those engaged in the preparation for or conduct of litigation of whatever nature was far reaching, *Marrinan v. Vibart* [1962] 3 All E.R. 380, [1962] C.L.Y. 1759 and *Watson v. M'Ewan, Watson v. Jones* [1905] A.C. 480 applied. Although the circumstances of the instant case had not been the subject matter of a decision, the principle must apply to the answer given by the solicitor in response to a request by the other side for information on which the case would be advanced. The letter in the instant case was written on an occasion of absolute privilege.

WAPLE v. SURREY CC [1997] 2 All E.R. 836, French, J., QBD.

2040. Privilege—qualified privilege—daily brief carried in electronic form to subscribers

O, an information and research provider, produced a daily brief, carried in electronic form to subscribers, which alleged corruption among powerful

Bulgarian business groups that had survived the downfall of the communist regime and named M. Pleas of qualified privilege were struck out below. O appealed and also applied to amend its defence to plead justification.

Held, dismissing both the appeal and the application, that a defence of qualified privilege would be available where a defendant could show a duty to publish the offending article, but in the instant case O's motive was mere commercial self-interest. The Lucas Box meanings that O selected were insufficiently defamatory to support a defence of justification, *Attorney General v. Guardian Newspapers (No.2)* [1990] 1 A.C. 109, [1988] C.L.Y. 2862 and *Derbyshire CC v. Times Newspapers* [1993] A.C. 534, [1993] C.L.Y. 2581 followed.

MULTIGROUP BULGARIA HOLDINGS LTD v. OXFORD ANALYTICA LTD, Trans. Ref: 1995-M-2141, April 25, 1997, Eady, J., QBD.

2041. Articles

Defamation over the Internet *(Simon Jones)*: Corp. Brief. 1997, 11 (4), 8-10. (Liability of service providers, US cases, defence for non-publishers under 1996 Act, statutory definition of publishers and checklist of precautions).

Freedom of speech defences in defamation *(Richard Potter)*: I.M.L. 1997, 15(8), 57-60. (Whether freedom of speech defence available for media in defamation proceedings concerning political matters, comparing defamation law of Australia with other common law jurisdictions).

Hidden dangers of e-mail *(Cameron McKenna)*: I.H.L. 1997, 54(Oct), 83-84. (Importance of companies taking steps to minimise chances of defamatory Emails circulating in internal systems illustrated by settlement of libel action brought by Western Provident Association against Norwich Union).

Liability of service providers for defamation in cyberspace *(John Middleton)*: E.B.L.R. 1997, 8(4), 108-111. (Liability of authors and service providers for defamatory material on Internet, definition of publication, choice of forum and jurisdiction of UK courts, operation of the Defamation Act 1996 and limits of liability).

Libel - latest developments *(Julie A. Scott-Bayfield)*: Comms. L. 1997, 2(3), 116-118. (Significant libel cases in 1996 and 1997).

Libel actions: Channel 4 victory in £2m case: M.L.N. 1997, 9, 12-14. (Settlement of action brought by doctor claiming that TV programme's allegations had damaged his professional reputation will mean that plaintiff will have to pay most of defendant's costs).

Libel by Email: risks for companies *(Rupert Battcock)*: Corp. Brief. 1997, 11 (8), 10-12. (Liability of employers for defamatory statements made by employees in Email messages in light of settled Norwich Union case and advice for companies in defining policy on use of Email).

Libel damages: huge awards "increasingly unlikely": M.L.N. 1997, 11, 15. (Decreasing awards made in libel cases due to power of court under Courts and Legal Services Act 1990 s.8 to reduce jury awards, likely breach of Art.10 ECHR as restriction on freedom of expression and comparison with personal injuries awards).

Libel law *(Alan Williams)*: I.M.L. 1997, 15(7), 52-55. (Whether 1996 Act will overcome problems of existing libel law, particularly those associated with defences, damages and MPs' privilege).

"Only flattery is safe": political speech and the Defamation Act 1996 *(Kevin Williams)*: M.L.R. 1997, 60(3), 388-393. (Criticism of amendment which allows MPs to waive parliamentary privilege to facilitate libel actions against critics of their conduct in House of Commons).

Public libels and qualified privilege: a British solution to a British problem *(Ian Loveland)*: P.L. 1997, Aut, 428-436. (Argues that libel law should be reformed following collapse of Hamilton and Aitken libel actions in order to reflect differences between private individual actions and those relating to alleged political malpractice).

Reforming libel law: the public law dimension *(Ian Loveland)*: I.C.L.Q. 1997, 46(3), 561-585. (Judicial reforms affecting heads and quantum of damages, and constitutional implications of US, ECHR and Australian decisions involving journalists accused of publishing defamatory political stories).

Response strategy: E-mail: coping with the new legal minefield *(Robin Bynoe)*: C.L.1997,18, Supp 18-21. (Legal implications for corporate Email users in light of recent libel action between Norwich Union and Western Provident including discovery, copyright and unintended contracts).

The Defamation Act 1996 and political libels *(Andrew Sharland* and *Ian Loveland)*: P.L.1997, Spr, 113-124. (Influence of New Zealand case on political libel cases in UK and subsequent parliamentary debate on s.13 of 1996 Act which removes automatic parliamentary privilege for libel proceedings).

UK: Defamation Act 1996 *(Taylor Joynson Garrett)*: I.L.P. 1997, 22(3), 84-86. (Provisions on responsibility for publication, offer of amends, reduction in limitation period and summary disposal of claims).

2042. Books

Carter-Ruck, Peter F.; Elliott, Rupert—Carter-Ruck on Libel and Slander. Hardback: £105.00. ISBN 0-406-99248-7. Butterworth Law.

Clarke-Williams—Defamation Law: a Practical Guide. £45.00. ISBN 0-406-08132-8. Butterworth Law.

Price, David—Defamation: Law, Procedure and Practice. Paperback: £48.00. ISBN 0-421-60200-7. Sweet & Maxwell.

Rampton, Richard; Sharp, Victoria; Neill, Sir Brian, Q.C.—Duncan and Neill on Defamation. Hardback: £85.00. ISBN 0-406-17831-3. Butterworth Law.

DISPUTE RESOLUTION

2043. Articles

ADR is (not) for wimps *(Tom Coates)*: I.C. Lit. 1997, Mar, 46-48. (Definitions of alternative dispute resolution, judicial initiatives to encourage use and view of changing litigation landscape in Woolf Report).

ADR-the viable alternative to costly litigation *(John Hull)*: P.P.M. 1997, 15(11), 164-165. (Benefits of ADR, when not to use it and encouragement of use by courts).

ADR—how to solve disputes *(Vivien King* and *David Shapiro)*: C.S.R. 1997, 20(22), 174-175. (Whether mediation is effective alternative to litigation in settlement of commercial disputes).

Alternative dispute resolution-a refreshing outbreak of common sense *(Christine Kynaston)*: Health Law 1997, Sep, 3-4. (Analysis of ADR options including conciliation, arbitration, and mediation, with addresses of organisations providing ADR services).

Anatomy of a computer contract dispute: an ounce of prevention is worth a ton of cure *(Harry Small)*: Comp. & Law 1997, 8(3), 9-11. (Possible reasons for increase in computer contract disputes and main aggravating factors, including implied terms, exclusion and limitation clauses, and methods of dispute resolution).

Anatomy of a computer contract dispute: computer contract disputes *(Michael Turner)*: Comp. & Law 1997, 8(3),12-15. (Case law on computer contracts and fictional case study, focusing on role of expert witnesses and methods of resolving disputes).

Commercial ADR: implications for legal practice *(Bryan Clark)*: S.L.G. 1997, 65(3), 120-122. (Scope for involvement of lawyers in alternative dispute resolution whether representing parties or acting as mediators).

Dispute resolution simplified *(Chris Austin)*: S.J. 1997, 141(18), 441. (Joint initiative by Royal Institution of Chartered Surveyors, Institute of Surveyors, Valuers and Auctioneers and DoE relating to rent reviews for small business premises).

Dispute theory: will cyberspace use cybercourts? *(Richard Hill)*: I.C. Lit. 1997, Oct, 33-35. (Organisations' needs from dispute resolution in cyberspace and telecommunications fields, methods that could be tried, online dispute resolution projects and future for industry specific mechanisms).

Expert determination: informal resolution of technical disputes *(Paul Mitchard)*: P.L.C. 1997, 8(7), 21-25. (When to use expert determination, its advantages and disadvantages, list of appointing authorities, main drafting issues and comparison of expert determination and arbitration).

Get the right bang for your buck *(Steven D. Wood)*: I.C. Lit. 1997, Nov, 39-41. (How principles of project management can help in resolution of complex multinational disputes).

Is expert determination a "final and binding" alternative? *(Douglas S. Jones)*: Arbitration 1997, 63(3), 213-226. (Use of expert determination as method of dispute resolution, its disadvantages and comparison with arbitration).

Mediation *(Denise Masters)*: C.I.P.A.J. 1997, 26(4), 266-267. (Advantages in offering fast, confidential and cost effective means of alternative dispute resolution).

Mediation: a state of mind *(Ian Pears)*: S.J. 1997, 141 (32), 799. (Advantages of mediation as means of resolving medical negligence cases, why take up of mediation has been slow and possible limitations of method).

Mediation? No thanks I negotiate anyway *(Tim Wallis)*: P. & M.I.L.L. 1997, 13(6), 47-48. (Advantages of using mediation and other forms of ADR in medical negligence cases).

Nominet domain name dispute resolution services: IT L.T. 1997, 5(6), 4-5. (Procedure used by national registry for Internet domain names ending in.uk).

Planning for dispute resolution in international franchising relationships *(Franklin C. Jesse* and *Andrew P. Loewinger)*: I.B.L. 1997, 25(5), 221-226. (Minimising damage by including options for resolving disputes by mediation, arbitration or litigation and choice of law and forum in master franchising agreements).

Presumptions and burden of proof in world trade law *(Rutsel Silvestre J. Martha)*: J. Int. Arb. 1997, 14(1), 67-98. (Responsibilities of Dispute Settlement Body of WTO with respect to burden of proof, presumptions involved and general burden of proof rules as applied to violation of WTO obligations and nullification or impairment of benefits).

Rapid century for dispute settlement *(Gavin McFarlane)*: Tax J. 1997, 425, 22-24. (Reasons behind growing recourse to WTO dispute settlement procedure, including how procedure operates and most active participants, with particular reference to disputes between US and EU).

The challenge of ADR *(Paul Newman)*: L. Ex. 1997, Nov, 30-31. (Encouragement of use of ADR by courts through Practice Statements and other initiatives in county courts).

The mediation of neighbour disputes *(John Baldwin)*: C.J.Q. 1997, 16(Oct), 299-301. (Research by Centre for Criminological and Legal Research, Sheffield University, on cost effectiveness of mediation and other strategies for resolving neighbour disputes, and role of local authorities and community services).

The need for due process in WTO proceedings *(David M. Palmeter)*: J.W.T. 1997, 31 (1), 51-57. (Lack of openness in WTO proceedings and lack of right to representation by outside counsel may amount to unfairness for small and developing countries).

The need for due process in WTO proceedings *(J.C. Thomas)*: J.W.T. 1997, 31 (1), 45-49. (Procedural fairness and use of negotiating history in GATT and WTO dispute settlement proceedings).

Use of ADR in professional negligence claims *(Helen Ager)*: S.J. 1997, 141 (11), 255-256. (Whether lawyers should stop perceiving ADR as threat to business and take advantage of opportunities).

Valid settlements in industrial tribunals proceedings *(Barry Phillips)*: Legal Action 1996, Dec, 22-23. (Different means of setting employment cases by agreement between applicant and respondent, namely ACAS agreements, orders by consent and compromise agreements).

Winning ways with mediation *(Vivien King* and *David Shapiro)*: E.G. 1997, 9710, 140-141. (Principles, rules and changing attitude of courts towards alternative dispute resolution and advantages for property market of using mediation).

ECCLESIASTICAL LAW

2044. Fees—baptisms, marriages and burials

PAROCHIAL FEES ORDER 1997, SI 1997 1891; made under the Ecclesiastical Fees Measure 1986 s.1. In force: January 1, 1998; £1.55.

In substitution for fees prescribed by the Parochial Fees Order 1996 (SI 1996 1994), this Order establishes a new table of fees payable for certain matters in connection with baptisms, marriages and burials, for the erection of monuments in churchyards and for other miscellaneous matters.

2045. Fees—diocesan registrars

LEGAL OFFICERS (ANNUAL FEES) ORDER 1997, SI 1997 1890; made under the Ecclesiastical Fees Measure 1986 s.5. In force: January 1, 1998; £1.95.

This Order increases the annual fees for diocesan registrars fixed by the Legal Officers (Annual Fees) Order 1996 (SI 1996 3084) and fixes new annual fees for the provincial registrars.

2046. Fees—faculty proceedings

ECCLESIASTICAL JUDGES AND LEGAL OFFICERS (FEES) ORDER 1997, SI 1997 1889; made under the Ecclesiastical Fees Measure 1986 s.6. In force: January 1, 1998; £1.95.

This Order increases the fees fixed by the Ecclesiastical Judges and Legal Officers (Fees) Order 1996 (SI 1996 3085) in relation to faculty proceedings for injunctions or restoration orders under the Care of Churches and Ecclesiastical Jurisdiction Measure 1991 s.13(4)(5), proceedings under the Care of Cathedrals (Supplementary Provisions) Measure 1994, proceedings in respect of ecclesiastical offences under the Ecclesiastical Jurisdiction Measure 1963, appeals and taxation of costs.

2047. Occupational pensions—Church of England

See PENSIONS. §3953

2048. Articles

Conduct unbecoming *(G.R. Evans)*: Law & Just. 1996, 130/131, 66-83. (Restrictions on clergy's behaviour under ecclesiastical law, different treatment of laity, conduct which would be condemned, treatment of scandal regardless of guilt and change in public expectations of clergy).

On holy ground *(James Hall)*: E.G. 1997, 9739, 169-171. (Idiosyncrasies of property transactions involving Church of England land and buildings).

Outrageous behaviour—a postscript *(T. Hughie Jones)*: Ecc. L.J. 1997, 4(20), 664-666. (Whether protesters' disruption of church service amounted to indecent behaviour).

Response to "Under Authority": Ecc. L.J. 1997, 4(21), 746-751. (Report of Ecclesiastical Law Society Working Party on Clergy Discipline and Ecclesiastical Courts in response to General Synod report).

St. Deniol's Residential Library: a haven of peace in North Wales, United Kingdom *(P.J. Jagger)*: Ecc. L.J. 1997, 4(20), 655-658. (History of library founded by Gladstone and details of its ecclesiastical law collection).

2049. Books

Leeder, Lynne–Ecclesiastical Law Handbook. Hardback: £55.00. ISBN 0-421-57720-7. Sweet & Maxwell.

ECONOMICS

2050. Books

Posner, Richard A.; Parisi, Francis–Law and Economics. The International Library of Critical Writings in Economics Series. Hardback: £395.00. ISBN 1-85278-972-7. Edward Elgar.

EDUCATION

2051. Colleges–dissolution–South Park Sixth Form

SOUTH PARK SIXTH FORM COLLEGE, MIDDLESBROUGH (DISSOLUTION) ORDER 1997, SI 1997 513; made under the Further and Higher Education Act 1992 s.27. In force: August 1, 1997; £0.65.

This Order dissolves the further education corporation established to conduct South Park Sixth Form College, Middlesbrough. It provides that its property, rights and liabilities transfer to Prior Pursglove College, Guisborough, Cleveland and secures the rights of its employees by applying the Further and Higher Education Act 1992 s.26(2) to s.26(4).

2052. Colleges–dissolution–Worcester College of Agriculture

WORCESTER COLLEGE OF AGRICULTURE (DISSOLUTION) ORDER 1997, SI 1997 1168; made under the Further and Higher Education Act 1992 s.27. In force: May 10, 1997; £0.65.

This Order dissolves the further education corporation established to conduct Worcester College of Agriculture. It provides that its property, rights and liabilities are transferred to Pershore College of Horticulture, Worcester, and secures the rights of its employees by applying the Further and Higher Education Act 1992 s.26(2) to s.26(4).

2053. Colleges–transfer to higher education sector–Cumbria College of Art

CUMBRIA COLLEGE OF ART AND DESIGN FURTHER EDUCATION CORPORATION (TRANSFER TO THE HIGHER EDUCATION SECTOR) ORDER 1997, SI 1997 91; made under the Education Reform Act 1988 s.122A. In force: August 1, 1997; £0.65.

This Order makes provision for the transfer of Cumbria College of Art and Design Further Education Corporation to the higher education sector. On August 1, 1997 that corporation became a higher education corporation.

2054. Disabled persons–disability statements for local education authorities

EDUCATION (DISABILITY STATEMENTS FOR LOCAL EDUCATION AUTHORITIES) (ENGLAND) REGULATIONS 1997, SI 1997 1625; made under the Education Act 1996 s.528, s.569. In force: August 1, 1997; £1.10.

These Regulations prescribe the information which must be contained in a disability statement published by every local education authority under the Education Act 1996 s.529, and the intervals at which such statements should be published.

2055. Disabled persons–disability statements for local education authorities–Wales

EDUCATION (DISABILITY STATEMENTS FOR LOCAL EDUCATION AUTHORITIES) (WALES) REGULATIONS 1997, SI 1997 2353; made under the Education Act 1996 s.528, s.569. In force: October 30, 1997; £1.10.

These Regulations, which apply only in relation to Wales, prescribe information which must be contained in disability statements and the intervals at which such statements should be published.

2056. Education Act 1996 (c.56)–Commencement No.2 Order

EDUCATION ACT 1996 (COMMENCEMENT NO.2 AND APPOINTED DAY) ORDER 1997, SI 1997 1623 (C.67); made under the Education Act 1996 s.517, s.583. Commencement details: bringing into force various provisions of the Act on August 1, 1997 and September 1, 1997; £0.65.

This Order brings into force the Education Act 1996 s.528, which provides for a duty on local education authorities to publish disability statements relating to further education in its application to England on August 1, 1997, and s.8 and s.348 which relate respectively to compulsory school age and to the provision of special education at schools which are not maintained schools together with associated consequential amendments and repeals on September 1, 1997. It also appoints September 1, 1997 as the day on which s.517, relating to payment of fees at schools not maintained by a local education authority, has effect with certain modifications.

2057. Education Act 1996 (c.56)–Commencement No.3 Order

EDUCATION ACT 1996 (COMMENCEMENT NO.3) ORDER 1997, SI 1997 2352 (C.90); made under the Education Act 1996 s.583. Commencement details: bringing into force various provisions of the Act on October 30, 1997; £0.65.

This Order brings into force, in its application to Wales, the Education Act 1996 s.528, under which education authorities are placed under a duty to publish disability statements relating to further education.

2058. Education Act 1997 (c.44)

This Act amends the Education Act 1996 in relation to school discipline. Provision is made for baseline assessments and targets for pupils' performance, inspection of LEAs and schools, careers guidance and education and the establishment of a Qualifications and Curriculum Authority to supervise curriculum for schools and external vocational and academic qualifications. The National Council for Vocational Qualifications and the School Curriculum and Assessment Authority are dissolved.

This Act received Royal Assent on March 21, 1997.

2059. Education Act 1997 (c.44)–Commencement No.1 Order

EDUCATION ACT 1997 (COMMENCEMENT NO.1) ORDER 1997, SI 1997 1153 (C.43); made under the Education Act 1997 s.54, s.58. Commencement details: bringing into force various provisions of the Act on April 4, 1997; £0.65.

This Order brings the Education Act 1997 s.1 (which provides for the extension of the assisted places scheme to schools providing only primary education) and an associated repeal into force on April 4, 1997.

2060. Education Act 1997 (c.44)–Commencement No.2 Order

EDUCATION ACT 1997 (COMMENCEMENT NO.2 AND TRANSITIONAL PROVISIONS) ORDER 1997, SI 1997 1468 (C.57); made under the Education Act 1997 s.54, s.58. Commencement details: bringing into force various provisions of the Act on June 14, 1997, September 1, 1997, October 1, 1997, November 1, 1997 and December 1, 1997; £1.55.

This Order brings certain provisions of the Education Act 1997 into force.

2061. Education authorities–Qualifications, Curriculum and Assessment Authority for Wales–transfer of assets

EDUCATION (QUALIFICATIONS AND CURRICULUM AUTHORITY AND QUALIFICATIONS, CURRICULUM AND ASSESSMENT AUTHORITY FOR WALES) (TRANSFER OF PROPERTY AND DESIGNATION OF STAFF) ORDER 1997, SI 1997 2172; made under the Education Act 1997 s.34, s.35, s.54. In force: October 1, 1997; £1.55.

This Order transfers property and certain rights and liabilities from the National Council for Vocational Qualifications and the School Curriculum and Assessment Authority to the Qualifications and Curriculum Authority and the Awdurdod Cymwysterau, Cwricwlwm ac Asesu Cymru, which is otherwise known as the Qualifications, Curriculum and Assessment Authority for Wales. It also designates persons employed by the National Council for Vocational Qualifications of the School Curriculum and Assessment Authority for transfer to the Qualifications and Curriculum Authority or the Awdurdod Cymwysterau, Cwricwlwm ac Asesu Cymru.

2062. Education authorities–Qualifications, Curriculum and Assessment Authority for Wales–transfer of functions

EDUCATION (QUALIFICATIONS, CURRICULUM AND ASSESSMENT AUTHORITY FOR WALES) (CONFERMENT OF FUNCTIONS) ORDER 1997, SI 1997 2140; made under the Education Act 1997 s.30. In force: October 1, 1997; £0.65.

This Order confers on Awdurdod Cymwysterau, Cwricwlwm ac Asesu Cymru, or the Qualifications, Curriculum and Assessment Authority for Wales, certain functions with respect to all external academic and vocational qualifications in Wales except National Vocational Qualifications which are conferred solely on ACCAC. This Order also confers on ACCAC certain more limited functions with respect to NVQs in Wales.

2063. Education (Schools) Act 1997 (c.59)

An Act making provision for the abolition of the assisted places scheme in England, Wales and Scotland.

This Act received Royal Assent on July 31, 1997.

2064. Educational institutions–educational awards–recognised bodies

EDUCATION (LISTED BODIES) ORDER 1997, SI 1997 54; made under the Education Reform Act 1988 s.216. In force: February 5, 1997; £1.95.

This Order lists the name of each body which is not a recognised body within the Education Reform Act 1988 but which either provides any course which is in preparation for a degree to be granted by such a recognised body and is approved by or on behalf of that body, or is a constituent college, school, hall or other institution of a university which is such a recognised body.

2065. Educational institutions–educational awards–recognised bodies

EDUCATION (RECOGNISED BODIES) ORDER 1997, SI 1997 1; made under the Education Reform Act 1988 s.216. In force: February 5, 1997; £1.10.

This Order lists all those bodies which appear to the Secretary of State to be recognised bodies within the Education Reform Act 1988 s.214(2)(a)(a). These are universities, colleges or other bodies which are authorised by Royal Charter or under Act of Parliament to grant degrees.

2066. Further education–information–occupations of former students

EDUCATION (FURTHER EDUCATION INSTITUTIONS INFORMATION) (ENGLAND) (AMENDMENT) REGULATIONS 1997, SI 1997 2173; made under the Further and Higher Education Act 1992 s.50, s.89. In force: October 1, 1997; £0.65.

These Regulations amend the Education (Further Education Institutions Information) (England) Regulations 1995 (SI 1995 2065) which concern the publication of information by institutions within the further education sector in England only. The amendments allow institutions to choose whether to publish information about the occupation of students in relation to the preceding academic year as at present, or to publish the information in relation to the same academic year in respect of which the other information is published.

2067. Grant maintained schools–grants–determination

EDUCATION (NEW GRANT-MAINTAINED SCHOOLS) (FINANCE) REGULATIONS 1997, SI 1997 956; made under the Education Act 1996 s.244, s.245, s.246, s.247, s.257, s.569. In force: April 1, 1997; £4.15.

These Regulations provide for the determination and redetermination of the amount of maintenance grant to be paid to the governing bodies of new grant maintained schools situated in England established pursuant to proposals from the Funding Agency for Schools under the Education Act 1996. They also make provision for capital grants, special purpose grants and the recovery of amounts in respect of maintenance grant from a local education authority.

2068. Grant maintained schools–special schools

EDUCATION (GRANT-MAINTAINED SPECIAL SCHOOLS) (AMENDMENT) REGULATIONS 1997, SI 1997 2175; made under the Education Act 1996 s.344, s.569, Sch.28 para.14. In force: October 1, 1997; £0.65.

These Regulations amend the Education (Grant-Maintained Special Schools) Regulations 1994 (SI 1994 653) by substituting for Reg.41, which applied the Education Act 1993 s.245 in relation to a grant maintained special school not established in a hospital, a new regulation which applies the Education Act 1997 s.23 and s.29 in relation to such a school.

2069. Grant maintained schools–special schools–grants–determination

EDUCATION (GRANT-MAINTAINED AND GRANT-MAINTAINED SPECIAL SCHOOLS) (FINANCE) REGULATIONS 1997, SI 1997 996; made under the Education Act 1996 s.244, s.245, s.246, s.247, s.257, s.569, Sch.28 para.14. In force: April 1, 1997; £8.70.

These Regulations, which revoke and replace the Education (Grant-maintained and Grant-maintained Special Schools) (Finance) Regulations 1996 (SI 1996 889), apply to grant maintained schools and grant-maintained special schools situated in England but not to completely new grant maintained schools. They provide for the determination and redetermination of the amount of maintenance grant to be paid to the governing bodies of schools in respect of which the Regulations apply. They also provide for the payment of capital grants and special purpose grants and the recovery of amounts in respect of maintenance grant from a local education authority.

2070. Grant maintained schools–special schools–grants–determination–Wales

EDUCATION (GRANT-MAINTAINED AND GRANT-MAINTAINED SPECIAL SCHOOLS) (FINANCE) (WALES) REGULATIONS 1997, SI 1997 599; made under the Education Act 1996 s.244, s.245, s.246, s.251, s.252, s.253, s.257, s.569. In force: April 1, 1997; £3.70.

These Regulations, which apply only to grant-maintained schools and grant-maintained special schools situated in Wales, replace with modifications the Education (Grant-Maintained and Grant-Maintained Special Schools) (Finance)

(Wales) Regulations 1996 (SI 1996 537), which are revoked. The present Regulations extend to newly established grant maintained schools and to grant-maintained special schools, as well as to former county and voluntary schools which have acquired grant maintained status. Part II of the Regulations provides for the determination and redetermination of the amount of maintenance grant to be paid to governing bodies of grant maintained schools and grant-maintained special schools on a similar basis to that provided for under Part II of the 1996 Regulations, save that there is now provision for deducting from the amount determined under Reg.4 in respect if maintenance grant amounts representing, respectively, excessive unspent maintenance grant received in respect of earlier financial years and excessive severance payments made on or after January 1, 1997. They also include a new category of special purpose grant to cover expenditure incurred under a contract for the provision of property and services to, or for purposes of, a school, where the provision of the services is linked to and dependent upon the provision of the property.

2071. Grant maintained schools–transfer of functions

EDUCATION (TRANSFER OF FUNCTIONS RELATING TO GRANT-MAINTAINED SCHOOLS) ORDER 1997, SI 1997 294; made under the Education Act 1996 s.568, Sch.3 para.1. In force: March 5, 1997; £0.65.

This Order replaces the Education (Transfer of Functions Relating to Grant-maintained Schools) Order 1996 (SI 1996 2247) which is revoked because of a drafting error. It transfers to the Funding Agency for Schools the Secretary of State's power, in relation to England, to consent to borrowing by grant maintained schools under the Education Act 1996 s.231 (6).

2072. Grants–aided pupils–eligibility–music, ballet and choir schools

EDUCATION (GRANTS) (MUSIC, BALLET AND CHOIR SCHOOLS) (AMENDMENT) REGULATIONS 1997, SI 1997 1967; made under the Education Act 1996 s.485, s.489, s.569. In force: September 1, 1997; £1.10.

These Regulations amend the Education (Grants) (Music, Ballet and Choir Schools) Regulations 1995 (SI 1995 2018) Sch.1 which establishes the aided pupil scheme, sets out conditions of eligibility for aided places, and provides for remission of fees, payment of grant and administrative provisions.

2073. Grants–education support and training

EDUCATION (GRANTS FOR EDUCATION SUPPORT AND TRAINING) (ENGLAND) REGULATIONS 1997, SI 1997 514; made under the Education Act 1996 s.484, s.489, s.569. In force: April 1, 1997; £1.95.

These Regulations revoke and replace the Education (Grants for Education and Training) (England) Regulations 1996 (SI 1996 734 as amended by SI 1996 3066). There are some minor and drafting amendments to the Regulations and the purposes for or in connection with which grants are payable set out in the Schedule have been been revised. The Regulations also make a minor amendment to the Education (Grants for Education Support and Training: Nursery Education) (England) Regulations 1996 (SI 1996 235).

2074. Grants–education support and training

EDUCATION (GRANTS FOR EDUCATION SUPPORT AND TRAINING) (ENGLAND) (AMENDMENT) REGULATIONS 1997, SI 1997 2174; made under the Education Act 1996 s.484, s.569. In force: October 1, 1997; £1.10.

· These Regulations amend the Education (Grants for Education Support and Training) (England) Regulations 1997 (SI 1997 514) by adding three new purposes for which grant is payable at a rate of 100 per cent of approved expenditure and remove the restriction that the immediate payment of grant on the last period of the financial year cannot exceed 75 per cent of the grant applied for.

2075. Grants–education support and training–Wales

EDUCATION (GRANTS FOR EDUCATION SUPPORT AND TRAINING) (WALES) REGULATIONS 1997, SI 1997 390; made under the Education Act 1996 s.484, s.489, s.569. In force: April 1, 1997; £1.95.

These Regulations, which apply only in Wales, supersede the Education (Grants for Education Support and Training) (Wales) Regulations 1996 (SI 1996 334) which are revoked. Apart from minor or drafting changes, there are some changes to the purposes for which a grant is payable and one purpose (projects encouraging the integration of pupils with special educational needs into mainstream schools) has been omitted.

2076. Grants–education support and training–Wales

EDUCATION (GRANTS FOR EDUCATION SUPPORT AND TRAINING) (WALES) (AMENDMENT) REGULATIONS 1997, SI 1997 2395; made under the Education Act 1996 s.484, s.569. In force: November 5, 1997; £0.65.

These Regulations, which amend the Education (Grants for Education Support and Training) (Wales) Regulations 1997 (SI 1997 390), add a new purpose for which grant is payable at 100 per cent of approved expenditure, and in relation to such expenditure, remove the restriction that the immediate payment of grant in the last period of the financial year cannot exceed 75 per cent of the grant applied for.

2077. Grants–higher education–discretionary award–previous mandatory award–reasonable expectation of award

[Education Act 1962 s.1, s.2; Education (Mandatory Awards) Regulations 1994 (SI 1994 3044) Reg.7, Reg.11, Reg.12.]

J sought judicial review of a decision by S refusing his application for a discretionary grant for years two and three of his degree course. J had earlier withdrawn from a previous course in 1983, due to his mother's terminal illness, recommencing his studies in 1994 having been informed that funding would be available for the final two years by way of a major discretionary award under S's discretionary awards policy. However, his application for funding in 1995 was refused owing to the introduction of new criteria. The decision was subsequently criticised by the Secretary of State, who found that, as J was on a designated course, the Education Act 1962 s.2 prevented a discretionary award being made, and that his application should have been considered under s.1 (6) of the 1962 Act.

Held, allowing the application and quashing the decision, that under the 1962 Act s.1 and the Education (Mandatory Awards) Regulations 1994 Reg.7 a full award had to be made for a designated course. J had accepted the decision limiting any award to the final two years, but he had commenced the course and financed the first year himself in reliance on the earlier policy provision. Under the 1962 Act s.1 (6) and the 1994 Regulations Reg.11 and Reg.12 his previous education record should have been taken into account, and S had been incorrect in deciding that J's withdrawal from his earlier degree course was immaterial, as the reasons behind the termination were relevant from the point of view of S's own policy criteria. The 1994 policy had created an understanding that J could expect a grant for years two and three, which meant that J, as a student at the time the new policy was adopted, had a reasonable expectation that he would receive a grant which S had unreasonably refused. The 1995 policy had been too rigidly applied which meant that the desirability that those commencing courses should be able to complete them was not given sufficient weight in the decision making process.

R. v. SHROPSHIRE CC, *ex p.* JONES [1997] C.O.D. 116, Carnwath, J., QBD.

2078. Grants—mandatory awards

EDUCATION (MANDATORY AWARDS) REGULATIONS 1997, SI 1997 431; made under the Education Act 1962 s.1, s.4, Sch.1 para.3, Sch.1 para.4; and the Education Act 1973 s.3. In force: September 1, 1997; £6.10.

These Regulations revoke and replace the Education (Mandatory Awards) Regulations 1995 (SI 1995 3321 as amended by SI 1996 2068).

2079. Grants—mandatory awards

EDUCATION (MANDATORY AWARDS) (AMENDMENT) REGULATIONS 1997, SI 1997 1693; made under the Education Act 1962 s.1, s.4. In force: September 1, 1997; £1.10.

These Regulations amend the Education (Mandatory Awards) Regulations 1997 (SI 1997 431). The amendments ensure that a course for the initial training of teachers which involves full time attendance for the purposes of study or teaching practice for 30 weeks a year continues to be a designated course under Reg.10(1)(d) of the principal Regulations, even if the course involves less than 19 weeks of full time study as provided for in the revised definition of sandwich course in Sch.5 para.1 (1) to the principal Regulations.

2080. Imperial College Act 1997 (c.ii)

This Act unites the Charing Cross and Westminster Medical School and the Royal Postgraduate Medical School with the Imperial College of Science, Technology and Medicine. It transfers all rights, properties, assets and liabilities connected with the medical schools and also makes provision for the merger of the National Heart and Lung Institute with the Imperial College.

This Act received Royal Assent on July 15, 1997 and comes into force on July 15, 1997.

2081. Independent schools—change of ownership—notice given to parents—fees payable in lieu of notice to new owner

[Business Names Act 1985 s.4, s.5.]

P enrolled her daughter at a school in 1992. The school at that time was owned and run by C. In February 1995, C sold the school to CN and, at the same time, wrote to parents informing them of the change of ownership. The managing director of CN also wrote to parents twice in three days, the second time inviting them to one of two meetings at which the change of ownership would be explained. P claimed not to have received either of the letters, but went to part of one of the meetings because a friend had told her about it (but not its purpose). P continued to send her daughter to the school the next term and then withdrew her, alleging that she was dissatisfied with the way the school was being run. CN issued proceedings for one term's fees in lieu of notice. The invoice and the school's letterhead were in the same format as that previously used when C owned the school.

Held, giving judgment for CN, that (1) it was inconceivable that P did not know of the change of ownership and her conduct in the light of that knowledge, in sending her daughter back to the school, amounted to acceptance of the change of ownership; (2) CN provided education in the same manner as C had done; (3) the new contract was on the same terms as the old one, including the provision for fees in lieu of notice printed on the original registration form; (4) there was insufficient evidence to support the allegation of breach of duty in the way P's daughter was taught by CN, and (5) there was no financial loss suffered by P as a result of CN's breach of the Business Names Act 1985 s.4 and so s.5 did not apply.

CAREERNATURE LTD v. PAYNTER, November 7, 1996, District Judge Daniel, CC (Bristol). [*Ex rel.* Alison Castrey, Solicitor, Veale Wasbrough Solicitors, Bristol].

2082. Independent schools–fees–removal of child from school–school seeking fees in lieu of notice–no fundamental breach of contract

On January 6, 1996 the parents, who are US citizens, wrote to T withdrawing their 15 year old son with immediate effect. The school sought the spring term's fees in lieu of notice. The parents refused to pay and T issued proceedings. The main element of W's defence alleged that the school had provided inadequate pastoral care because the pupil did not achieve good academic results and the parents were not told about that until the end of term, and when wishing to discuss the matter with the headmaster the parents were referred instead to the house master.

Held, allowing the school's claim for fees in lieu of notice, that (1) it was a feature of independent schools that house masters are the first point of contact with parents; only if the house master failed to satisfy the parents' enquiries would direct access to the headmaster be expected. It would be impossible for the headmaster to run the school properly if he dealt with every enquiry from a parent, and (2) even if the parents' complaints were entirely true, the facts were very far from the fundamental breach of contract required in order to avoid the contractual obligation to pay fees in lieu of notice.

TAUNTON SCHOOL v. WRIGHT, May 22, 1997, District Judge Mule, CC (Yeovil). [*Ex rel.* Alison Castrey, Solicitor, Veale Wasbrough Solicitors, Bristol].

2083. Independent schools–fees–removal of child from school–school seeking fees in lieu of notice–parent failing to establish alleged bullying

G withdrew her 14 year old daughter from F without notice on the grounds that there had been repetition of bullying by "name calling" which had occurred in the previous term. G sued for the return of fees. The school counterclaimed for the summer term's fees in lieu of notice. G defended the counterclaim by saying that in the previous term the headmaster had agreed, on an open ended basis, that if there was any repetition of name calling the pupil could be withdrawn without notice or a charge to fees in lieu of notice. The headmaster said he had only agreed that for the autumn term.

Held, allowing the school's counterclaim of £2,490, that (1) the claim for return of fees would have been bound to fail in the absence of expert evidence showing harm suffered by the pupil. In any event the claim had been struck out for breach of an unless order, and (2) an agreement that the pupil could be withdrawn without penalty at any time in the future would have been wholly unusual, and the headmaster would have had no authority to make such an agreement. The parent had failed to prove an agreement in those terms.

GREGORY v. FRENSHAM HEIGHTS EDUCATIONAL TRUST, April 16, 1997, District Judge Davies, CC (Chichester). [*Ex rel.* Alison Castrey, Solicitor, Veale Wasbrough Solicitors, Bristol].

2084. Independent schools–grants to assess teachers

EDUCATION (GRANT) (AMENDMENT) (NO.2) REGULATIONS 1997, SI 1997 2961; made under the Education Act 1996 s.485, s.489, s.569. In force: February 1, 1998; £0.65.

These Regulations amend the Education (Grant) Regulations 1990 (SI 1990 1989) so as to enable the Secretary of State to pay grants to persons, other than local education authorities, in respect of assessments carried out under the Education (Teachers) Regulations 1993 (SI 1993 543) Sch.3 para.10 to determine whether the standard of qualified teacher status has been attained. The new provision only applies where persons being assessed have completed teacher training programmes at independent schools in Wales.

2085. Independent schools–grants to proprietors

EDUCATION (GRANT) (AMENDMENT) REGULATIONS 1997, SI 1997 678; made under the Education Act 1996 s.485, s.489. In force: April 1, 1997; £1.10.

These Regulations amend the Education (Grant) Regulations 1990 (SI 1990 1989) so as to enable the Secretary of State to pay grants to the proprietors of independent schools in respect of education provided to certain five year old children. Such grants are to be subject to an additional requirement to secure that no child in respect of whose education grant is made is given corporal punishment.

2086. Independent schools–registration–provision of information

EDUCATION (PARTICULARS OF INDEPENDENT SCHOOLS) REGULATIONS 1997, SI 1997 2918; made under the Education Act 1996 s.465, s.467, s.569, s.579. In force: January 1, 1998; £1.95.

These Regulations, which revoke and replace the Education (Particulars of Independent Schools) Regulations 1982 (SI 1982 1730 as amended by SI 1991 1034 and SI 1994 537), relate to applications for registration of independent schools under the Education Act 1996 s.465 and the provision of information by such registered schools pursuant to s.467

2087. King's College London Act 1997 (c.iii)

This Act unites the United Medical and Dental Schools of Guy's and St.Thomas's Hospitals and King's College London and makes provision for the transfer of all rights, properties and liabilities from those Schools to the College.

This Act received Royal Assent on July 31, 1997.

2088. Local education authorities–boundaries

EDUCATION (AREAS TO WHICH PUPILS AND STUDENTS BELONG) (AMENDMENT) REGULATIONS 1997, SI 1997 597; made under the Education Act 1996 s.569, s.579. In force: April 1, 1997; £0.65.

These Regulations amend the Education (Areas to which Pupils and Students Belong) Regulations 1996 (SI 1996 615) so that a further education student is only treated as belonging to the area of a local education authority if the student is ordinarily resident in the area of that authority.

2089. Local education authorities–duty to provide suitable education–child unable to attend school through illness–resources relevant to provision of "suitable education"

[Education Act 1993 s.298.]

T, a child who was unable to attend school due to ill health, received five hours of home tuition per week, but in 1996 ESCC, in the light of financial constraints, took the decision to set three hours as a new norm for home tuition and reduced T's hours accordingly. T successfully challenged that decision, [1997] 6 C.L. 235, and ESCC appealed against the ruling that, in making arrangements for "suitable education" under the Education Act 1993 s.298, it must determine what was suitable using an objective test focusing on the needs of the child and not one that varied according to the local authority's financial resources.

Held, allowing the appeal (Staughton L.J. dissenting), that s.298 was wide enough to allow a local authority to take available resources into account. The provisions of s.298 specifically referred to the making of arrangements for provision to sick children. Thus, cost became a relevant consideration. An authority was required to have regard to the needs of the individual, but was entitled to balance those against the cost of making arrangements for that individual, and ESCC had not acted unlawfully in formulating a policy which provided a norm, *R. v. Gloucestershire CC, ex p. Barry* [1997] 2 W.L.R. 459, [1997] C.L.Y. 4714 applied.

R. v. EAST SUSSEX CC, *ex p.* TANDY; *sub nom.* R. v. EAST SUSSEX CC, *ex p.* T [1997] 3 W.L.R. 884, Ward, L.J., CA.

2090. Local education authorities–pupils–allocation of funds

EDUCATION (AMOUNT TO FOLLOW PERMANENTLY EXCLUDED PUPIL) REGULATIONS 1997, SI 1997 680; made under the Education Act 1996 s.494, s.569. In force: April 1, 1997; £1.10.

These Regulations revoke and replace the Education (Amount to Follow Permanently Excluded Pupil) Regulations 1994 (SI 1994 1697). The changes from the 1994 Regulations relate to the determining the relevant local education authority where a grant-maintained school straddles two or more areas or where the former maintaining authority of a grant-maintained special school has been subject to reorganisation; and the determination of appropriate amounts of funding where no amount is attributable in accordance with the allocation formula under the authority's scheme for the local management of schools.

2091. Local education authorities–transfer of assets

EDUCATION (LONDON RESIDUARY BODY) (SUSPENSE ACCOUNT PROPERTIES) ORDER 1997, SI 1997 1990; made under the Education Reform Act 1988 s.187, s.231, s.232. In force: August 31, 1997; £1.55.

This Order provides for certain councils or bodies to which property has been transferred under the Education Reform Act 1988 to pay the cost of repairs and maintenance incurred by the London Residuary Body prior to transfer to the council of the Royal Borough of Kensington and Chelsea. It also amends the effect of the Education (London Residuary Body) (Property Transfer) Order 1992 (SI 1992 587).

2092. Local education authorities–transfer of assets–Inner London Education Authority

EDUCATION (INNER LONDON EDUCATION AUTHORITY) (PROPERTY TRANSFER) (MODIFICATION AND AMENDMENT) ORDER 1997, SI 1997 860; made under the Education Reform Act 1988 s.187, s.231, s.232. In force: March 31, 1997; £1.10.

This Order modifies the effect of the Education (Inner London Education Authority) (Property Transfer) Order 1990 (SI 1990 124). The transfer of certain land to the councils of Inner London boroughs under that Order was made subject to conditions. Condition A ceases to apply except in so far as required for the continued operation of Condition C. Condition B ceases to apply altogether. Condition C ceases to apply except in relation to certain named playing fields and sports centres. In cases where the proceeds for sale have already been distributed to the Inner London councils, this Order operates to compensate the councils concerned by amending the Education (London Residuary Body) (Property Transfer) Order 1992 (SI 1992 587). The Council of the Royal London Borough of Kensington and Chelsea is obliged to distribute the capital receipts from the disposal of certain former property of the Inner London Education Authority on the basis set out in that Order. The amendment requires that council, before making any such payments on or after March 31, 1997, to first make the payments to each of the Inner London councils set out in the new Sch.4 which is inserted in that Order.

2093. National curriculum–assessment arrangements–Key Stage 1

EDUCATION (NATIONAL CURRICULUM) (ASSESSMENT ARRANGEMENTS FOR THE CORE SUBJECTS) (KEY STAGE 1) (ENGLAND) (AMENDMENT) ORDER 1997, SI 1997 1931; made under the Education Act 1996 s.356, s.568. In force: August 8, 1997; £0.65.

This Order amends the Education (National Curriculum) (Assessment Arrangements for the Core Subjects) (Key Stage 1) (England) Order 1995 (SI 1995 2071) in relation to the 1997-8 school year and succeeding school years. It requires the assigned authorities to verify the standard task assessments in at least 25 per cent of such schools in any school year. The verifying authority must carry out further checks in any such school the following year where, in its opinion, it is necessary. The results of standard task assessments in every maintained, grant-maintained and grant-maintained special school must be verified once in every four years.

2094. National curriculum–assessment arrangements–Key Stage 1–Wales

EDUCATION (NATIONAL CURRICULUM) (ASSESSMENT ARRANGEMENTS FOR ENGLISH, WELSH, MATHEMATICS AND SCIENCE) (KEY STAGE 1) (WALES) ORDER 1997, SI 1997 2011; made under the Education Act 1996 s.356, s.568. In force: August 31, 1997; £1.55.

This Order, which applies only to schools in Wales, consolidates the Education (National Curriculum) (Assessment Arrangements for English, Welsh, Mathematics and Science) (Key Stage 1) (Wales) Order 1995 (SI 1995 2207). It specifies assessment arrangements for pupils studying mathematics, science and, in relation to schools and classes which are Welsh speaking, Welsh, or, in relation to schools and classes which are not Welsh speaking, English, in the final year of the first key stage.

2095. National curriculum–assessment arrangements–Key Stage 2–Wales

EDUCATION (NATIONAL CURRICULUM) (ASSESSMENT ARRANGEMENTS FOR ENGLISH, WELSH, MATHEMATICS AND SCIENCE) (KEY STAGE 2) (WALES) ORDER 1997, SI 1997 2009; made under the Education Act 1996 s.356, s.568. In force: August 31, 1997; £1.55.

This Order, which applies only to schools in Wales, revokes and replaces the Education (National Curriculum) (Assessment Arrangements for English, Welsh, Mathematics and Science) (Key Stage 2) (Wales) Order 1995 (SI 1995 2208). It specifies the assessment arrangements for pupils studying English, Welsh, mathematics and science in the final year of the second key stage.

2096. National curriculum–assessment arrangements–Key Stage 3–Wales

EDUCATION (NATIONAL CURRICULUM) (KEY STAGE 3 ASSESSMENT ARRANGEMENTS) (WALES) ORDER 1997, SI 1997 2010; made under the Education Act 1996 s.356, s.568. In force: August 31, 1997; £1.55.

This Order, which applies only to schools in Wales, revokes and replaces the Education (National Curriculum) (Assessment Arrangements for English, Welsh, Mathematics and Science) (Key Stage 3) (Wales) Order 1996 (SI 1996 2337). It specifies the assessment arrangements for pupils in the final year of the third key stage.

2097. National curriculum–assessment arrangements–Key Stages 1, 2 and 3

EDUCATION (NATIONAL CURRICULUM) (ASSESSMENT ARRANGEMENTS FOR KEY STAGES 1, 2 AND 3) (ENGLAND) (AMENDMENT) ORDER 1997, SI 1997 2176; made under the Education Act 1996 s.356, s.568. In force: October 1, 1997; £1.10.

This Order substitutes the Qualifications and Curriculum Authority established under the Education Act 1997 s.21, for the School Curriculum and Assessment Authority for the purposes of the Education (National Curriculum) (Assessment Arrangements for the Core Subjects) (Key Stage 1) (England) Order 1995 (SI 1995 2071), the Education (National Curriculum) (Assessment Arrangements for the Core Subjects) (Key Stage 2) (England) Order 1995 (SI 1995 2072) and the Education (National Curriculum) (Key Stage 3 Assessment Arrangements) (England) Order 1996 (SI 1996 2116).

2098. Nursery education–determination of grants to local authorities–Amendment No.1

NURSERY EDUCATION (AMENDMENT) REGULATIONS 1997, SI 1997 1954; made under the Nursery Education and Grant-maintained Schools Act 1996 s.1, s.8. In force: August 29, 1997; £0.65.

These Regulations amend the Nursery Education Regulations 1996 (SI 1996 2086) by inserting a new Reg.4A which provides for the method of determining grants to local authorities in Wales in respect of nursery education provided by them during the period September 1, 1997, to March 31, 1998, and amending Reg.4 so that that regulation ceases to apply in relation to nursery education provided by such local authorities after August 31, 1997.

2099. Nursery education–determination of grants to local authorities–Amendment No.2

NURSERY EDUCATION (AMENDMENT) (NO.2) REGULATIONS 1997, SI 1997 2006; made under the Nursery Education and Grant Maintained Schools Act 1996 s.1, s.8, Sch.1 para.13. In force: Reg.2 (1): August 21, 1997; remainder: September 1, 1997; £1.55.

These Regulations revoke and replace without substantive change the Nursery Education (Amendment) Regulations 1997 (SI 1997 1971) which was not published. They do so in order to remove the possibility of confusion arising from the existence of another set of Regulations of the same title (SI 1997 1954) regarding nursery education in Wales. The effect of the Regulations is to amend, in relation to England, the Nursery Education Regulations 1996 (SI 1996 2086 as amended by SI 1996 3117) in order to make separate provision for the determination of grants in respect of nursery provisions in England and to make different provision for the determination of grants as between providers of nursery education dependent on whether the child resides in specified local government areas.

2100. Pupils–educational achievements–information

EDUCATION (INDIVIDUAL PERFORMANCE INFORMATION) (IDENTIFICATION OF INDIVIDUAL PUPILS) REGULATIONS 1997, SI 1997 1489; made under the Education Act 1996 s.537A. In force: June 14, 1997; £0.65.

These Regulations prescribe the manner of identification of the individual pupil in respect of whom any individual performance information is provided in accordance with the Education Act 1996 s.537A(2).

2101. Pupils–educational achievements–information

EDUCATION (INDIVIDUAL PUPILS' ACHIEVEMENTS) (INFORMATION) REGULATIONS 1997, SI 1997 1368; made under the Education Act 1996 s.408, s.569. In force: June 20, 1997; £2.80.

These Regulations, which revoke and replace the Education (Individual Pupils' Achievements) (Information) Regulations 1993 (SI 1993 3182 as amended by SI 1995 924 and SI 1996 1146), reflect changes in the assessment arrangements for Key Stages 2 and 3.

2102. Pupils–educational achievements–information–Wales

EDUCATION (INDIVIDUAL PUPILS' ACHIEVEMENTS) (INFORMATION) (WALES) REGULATIONS 1997, SI 1997 573; made under the Education Act 1996 s.408, s.569. In force: April 1, 1997; £2.80.

These Regulations revoke and replace the Education (Individual Pupils' Achievements) (Information) (Wales) Regulations 1996 (SI 1996 382). Apart from drafting and other minor changes, changes from the earlier Regulations reflect changes in the assessment arrangements for Key Stage 3 introduced last year by the Education (National Curriculum) (Key Stage 3 Assessment Arrangements) (Wales) Order 1996 (SI 1996 2337) which require teacher assessment at Key Stage 3 to be carried out in respect of all foundation subjects, not just in English, Welsh, mathematics and science as previously.

2103. Pupils–educational achievements–information–Wales–Amendment

EDUCATION (INDIVIDUAL PUPILS' ACHIEVEMENTS) (INFORMATION) (WALES) (AMENDMENT) REGULATIONS 1997, SI 1997 2709; made under the Education Act 1996 s.408, s.569. In force: January 6, 1998; £1.10.

These Regulations amend the Education (Individual Pupils' Achievements) (Information) (Wales) Regulations 1997 (SI 1997 573) which apply to grant maintained schools. The main amendments reflect changes in assessment arrangements at Key Stages 1, 2 and 3 and relate to the information to be included in the head teacher's report to parents of pupils at those stages.

2104. Pupils–performance–information–provision to certain bodies and persons

EDUCATION (INDIVIDUAL PERFORMANCE INFORMATION) (PRESCRIBED BODIES AND PERSONS) REGULATIONS 1997, SI 1997 2440; made under the Education Act 1996 s.537A, s.569. In force: October 31, 1997; £1.10.

These Regulations prescribe which bodies and persons may be provided with information about the performance of individual pupils under the Education Act 1996 s.537A(3)(4)(b). They also prescribe which individual performance information may be provided by those bodies which are responsible for collating or checking information relating to the performance of pupils.

2105. Schools–admissions–allocation of secondary school places–parental preference–legality of policy of allocation on basis of catchment area

[Education Act 1996 s.411.]

A local authority had not complied with its duties by permitting parents automatically allocated places not to respond to the offer and by not enabling them to give reasons. RMBC appealed against a decision that its admissions policy in relation to the allocation of secondary school places was unlawful. RMBC had a policy of automatically allocating places to pupils living within the catchment area of a particular school and wrote to parents informing them of the school to which their child had been allocated and stating that if they were happy with the allocation they need take no action. Under the Education Act 1996 s.411 a local authority was obliged to allow parents to express a preference for a school and give reasons for their preference and to give effect to parental choice, except where, under s.411 (3)(a), to do so would prejudice the provision of efficient education and use of resources.

Held, dismissing the appeal (Buxton, L.J. dissenting), that failure to give effect to the preference of a parent whose child had been denied a place at the school of his choice in favour of a child living within the catchment area whose parent had made no response to the offer of an automatic place did not fall within the exception in s.411 (3)(a). An expression of preference within s.411 meant a positive act and RMBC had not complied with its duties under s.411 by permitting parents automatically allocated places not to respond to the offer and by not enabling such parents to give reasons for their choice.

R. v. ROTHERHAM MBC, *ex p.* CLARK, *The Times*, December 4, 1997, Morritt, L.J., CA.

2106. Schools–admissions–pupil outside catchment area–oversubscription–special circumstances justifying entry

[Education Act 1980 s.5, s.6(3).]

J sought judicial review of a statutory appeal committee decision upholding E's refusal of J's application for his twin children, B and Z, to attend the same secondary school as their older sisters. J was divorced from the children's mother with both living approximately one mile outside the school's designated catchment area, and J chose the school on grounds of convenience, as B and Z spent time at both addresses. In reaching the decision, E stated that the standard number for admissions purposes had been reached by first preference choices from within the catchment area and that, had places been left over, allocation would have been by reference to, inter alia, siblings already in attendance, home to school distance and exceptional medical reasons. The committee decision referred to the prejudicial effect B and Z's admission would have on the efficient provision of education in an already oversubscribed school, whereas J submitted that places had been allocated to children living outside the catchment area with no siblings already in attendance.

Held, allowing the application and quashing the decision, that the appeal committee had to undertake a two stage process under the Education Act 1980 s.5(a) and s.6(3)(a). The first part of the process required the committee to decide whether allowing the appeal would prejudice the efficient provision of education, the second required the committee to decide whether special circumstances existed to outweigh the prejudice. The second point required consideration of all the relevant circumstances, and by concentrating principally on the mother's address, which was outside the LEA area, and effectively discounting the fact that the elder sibling attending the school benefited from its convenient location to both parents' addresses, the committee had failed to take account of a relevant matter. The evidence also showed that the committee had taken into account that the matter could be resolved by moving the elder sibling from the school so that all three children would then be able to attend one school within the catchment area of the maternal home; that amounted to an irrelevant consideration and an improper method of approaching the question of how the elder sibling attending the chosen school weighed in J's favour.

R. v. ESSEX CC, *ex p.* JACOBS [1997] E.L.R. 190, Collins, J., QBD.

2107. Schools–admissions–pupil outside county–admissions policy–reason for refusal of admission

[Education Act 1980 s.6(5).]

R applied for judicial review of W's schools' admission policy, which stated that where a school was oversubscribed, children who lived within the catchment area had priority over children from outside the area who had access to another school. R lived in Somerset on the border with Wiltshire and outside the catchment area of his preferred school. As R had priority at another school in Somerset, his application to W fell to be decided on other criteria, where no weight was to be given to his place of residence. He argued that W's admission policy was in conflict with the Education Act 1980, s.6(5)(a) and *R. v. Greenwich LBC, ex p. Governors of John Ball Primary School* (1990) 154 L.G. Rev. 678, [1990] C.L.Y. 1772, and *R. v. Bromley LBC, ex p. C* [1992] 1 F.L.R. 174, [1992] C.L.Y. 1857. The judge at first instance rejected the claim [1996] E.L.R. 200, [1996] 1 C.L.Y. 2381, on the grounds that R could be refused a place at his preferred school even if he lived in Wiltshire and that the situation was not governed by either of the two cases. On appeal, it was argued that it was unlawful to fix the school catchment areas to be coterminous with the county boundaries, which would give first priority status to county residents and reduce children living in adjacent counties to category B status.

Held, dismissing the appeal, that it was clear that W had adopted reasonable criteria to determine admissions to an oversubscribed school and there had been no discrimination, on the facts, against children resident outside the county. In at least four areas the Wiltshire catchment area stopped short of the county boundary and did not encroach into the adjacent county.

R. v. WILTSHIRE CC, *ex p.* RAZAZAN [1997] E.L.R. 370, Thorpe, L.J., CA.

2108. Schools–admissions–refusal–error in approach taken by appeal committee–provisions of two stage test

The applicants applied for judicial review of the decision of the independent appeal committee of Brighouse High School to dismiss their appeals against the school's decision not to admit them. The applicants submitted that the appeal committee wrongly approached the two stage test as laid down in *R. v. Commissioner for Local Administration, ex p. Croydon LBC* [1989] 1 All E.R. 1033, [1988] C.L.Y. 38. It should have asked whether the admission of each child would prejudice the provision of efficient education or the use of resources, and then the appeal committee should have asked whether the school had made a case out to that effect. The second stage was whether the child's case outweighed the prejudice to the school which matter should have been considered independently.

Held, allowing the applications, that there had been an error of law in the approach of the appeal committee to the test. By limiting its considerations to the school's admissions policy and numbers, it had fettered its judgment when making its decision.

R. v. APPEAL COMMITTEE OF BRIGHOUSE SCHOOL, *ex p.* G AND B [1997] E.L.R. 39, Sedley, J., QBD.

2109. Schools—assisted places—eligibility

EDUCATION (ASSISTED PLACES) REGULATIONS 1997, SI 1997 1968; made under the Education (Schools) Act 1997 s.3. In force: September 1, 1997; £3.70.

These Regulations prescribe arrangements for pupils who are eligible to continue to hold assisted places at independent schools in England and Wales by virtue of the Education (Schools) Act 1997 s.2, notwithstanding the abolition of the assisted places scheme by s.1 of that Act.

2110. Schools—assisted places—incidental expenses

EDUCATION (ASSISTED PLACES) (INCIDENTAL EXPENSES) REGULATIONS 1997, SI 1997 1969; made under the Education (Schools) Act 1997 s.3. In force: September 1, 1997; £1.95.

These Regulations provide for schools to pay grants as regards incidental expenses, and to remit incidental charges, incurred in respect of pupils who are eligible to continue to hold assisted places at independent schools in England and Wales by virtue of the Education (Schools) Act 1997 s.2, notwithstanding the abolition of the assisted places scheme by s.1 of that Act; and the Secretary of State to reimburse schools in respect of grants paid and charges remitted in accordance with the Regulations.

2111. Schools—Chief Inspector of Schools in Wales

EDUCATION (CHIEF INSPECTOR OF SCHOOLS IN WALES) ORDER 1997, SI 1997 288; made under the School Inspections Act 1996 s.4. In force: June 1, 1997; £0.65.

This Order appoints Miss Susan Lewis to be Her Majesty's Chief Inspector of Schools in Wales for a period of five years from June 1, 1997.

2112. Schools—functions—consequential provisions

LOCAL GOVERNMENT CHANGES FOR ENGLAND (EDUCATION) (MISCELLANEOUS PROVISIONS) ORDER 1997, SI 1997 679; made under the Local Government Act 1992 s.17, s.26. In force: April 1, 1997; £1.10.

This Order provides for the exercise on and after April 1, 1997 of functions in respect of specified schools in consequence of the transfer of certain local authority functions from the Hampshire County Council to the Southampton City Council and from the Staffordshire County Council to the Stoke-on-Trent City Council.

2113. Schools—grant maintained status—validity of ballots

W applied for judicial review of decisions of the Secretary of State that (1) a ballot on grant maintained status for two schools was valid, and (2) the publication of the proposals for the acquisition of grant maintained status by those schools was approved. It was common ground that the heads of both schools had circulated misleading letters stating that without grant maintained status there would be staff losses and financial problems and encouraging parents to vote for it. W contended that the Secretary of State had misdirected herself by considering whether voting was in fact influenced, rather than likely to be influenced, by the information. The Secretary of State had conceded that the misleading material would have influenced parents but for the fact that parents already knew about the reorganisation of the schools leading to staff losses, and they had received contrary information from a councillor and generally.

Held, allowing the review, and granting certiorari to quash and remit the Secretary of State's decision, that (1) her decision was *Wednesbury* unreasonable because it expected parents to realise that the projected staff losses were due to reorganisation and would not be prevented by acquiring grant maintained status. In addition the information from the councillor and other sources was not sufficient to dispel the misleading information from the trusted source of the respective school heads, and (2) there had been substantial and sufficient compliance with the statutory regulations governing the display of the proposals.

R. v. SECRETARY OF STATE FOR EDUCATION, *ex p.* WARWICKSHIRE CC, Trans. Ref: CO/2861/96, December 11, 1996, Dyson, J., QBD.

2114. Schools−information−Wales

EDUCATION (SCHOOL INFORMATION) (WALES) REGULATIONS 1997, SI 1997 1832; made under the Education Act 1996 s.408, s.414, s.509, s.537, s.539, s.569, Sch.1 para.3. In force: August 25, 1997; £3.20.

These Regulations consolidate the Education (School Information) (Wales) Regulations 1994 (SI 1994 2330 amended by SI 1995 2070 and SI 1996 1936) which are revoked. There are no changes of substance.

2115. Schools−inspections

EDUCATION (SCHOOL INSPECTION) REGULATIONS 1997, SI 1997 1966; made under the School Inspections Act 1996 s.10, s.15, s.16, s.17, s.18, s.20, s.21, s.23, s.24, s.45, Sch.3 para.6, Sch.4 para.2, Sch.4 para.3; and the Education Act 1996 s.569, Sch.1 para.3. In force: September 1, 1997; £2.40.

These Regulations consolidate, with amendments, the Education (School Inspection) (No.2) Regulations 1993 (SI 1993 1986 as amended by SI 1993 2973, SI 1996 1737 and SI 1997 995). They also amend the Education (Pupil Referral Units) (Application of Enactments) Regulations 1994 (SI 1994 2103) to update the statutory references.

2116. Schools−inspections

EDUCATION (SCHOOL INSPECTION) (NO.2) (AMENDMENT) REGULATIONS 1997, SI 1997 995; made under the Schools Inspections Act 1996 s.10, s.45. In force: April 10, 1997; £1.10.

These Regulations substitute a new Education (School Inspection) (No.2) Regulations 1993 (SI 1993 1986) Reg.4. The effect is to extend by two years the period within which the Chief Inspector is to secure the second and subsequent inspections of a school by a registered inspector. Secondly it provides that, in the case of schools to which the inspection provisions contained in the Schools Inspections Act 1996 s.10 apply for the first time after the periods set out in Reg.4(2), the Chief Inspector is to secure their inspection by a registered inspector within six years from the end of the school year in which that section first applies and following that inspection within six school years from the end of the school year in which the last inspection took place.

2117. Schools–inspections–information–statement of action

DEREGULATION (PROVISION OF SCHOOL ACTION PLANS) ORDER 1997, SI 1997 1142; made under the Deregulation and Contracting Out Act 1994 s.1. In force: April 4, 1997; £1.10.

This Order amends the School Inspections Act 1996 s.17 and s.21 so as to reduce a burden on the appropriate authority for a school to take reasonably practicable steps to secure that every parent of a pupil at the school receives a copy of the authority's statement of action following an inspection of the school under that Act.

2118. Schools–inspections–information–Wales

EDUCATION (SCHOOL INSPECTION) (WALES) (NO.2) (AMENDMENT) REGULATIONS 1997, SI 1997 1833; made under the School Inspections Act 1996 s.16, s.20, s.45. In force: September 1, 1997; £0.65.

These Regulations amend the Education (School Inspection) (Wales) (No.2) Regulations 1993 (SI 1993 1982) by inserting a new provision specifying 10 days as the period within which the appropriate authority is required under the School Inspections Act 1996 to take reasonably practicable steps to provide parents with copies of the summary of the inspection report following its receipt by them.

2119. Schools–inspectors–appointments

EDUCATION (INSPECTORS OF SCHOOLS IN ENGLAND) ORDER 1997, SI 1997 2564; made under the School Inspections Act 1996 s.1. In force: December 5, 1997; £1.10.

This Order makes appointments to Her Majesty's Inspectors of Schools in England.

2120. Schools–leaving date–persons ceasing to be of compulsory school age

EDUCATION (SCHOOL LEAVING DATE) ORDER 1997, SI 1997 1970; made under the Education Act 1996 s.8. In force: September 1, 1997; £0.65.

This Order provides for the school leaving date for 1998 and successive years to be the last Friday in June. This date applies for the purpose of determining, in accordance with the Education Act 1996 s.8(3), when a person ceases to be of compulsory school age.

2121. Schools–performance–information–Amendment No.1 Order

EDUCATION (SCHOOL PERFORMANCE INFORMATION) (ENGLAND) (AMENDMENT) REGULATIONS 1997, SI 1997 2060; made under the Education Act 1996 s.537, s.537A, s.569. In force: September 17, 1997; £1.10.

These Regulations amend the Education (School Performance Information) (England) Regulations 1996 (SI 1996 2577). They add requirements as to the information to be provided to the Secretary of State by schools relating to pupils aged 15. The information about General National Vocational Qualifications is now particularised and relates to information about a Part One GNVQ, an Intermediate GNVQ, a Foundation GNVQ, and a GNVQ Language Unit. They also require the provision of individual performance information to the Secretary of State.

2122. Schools–performance–information–Amendment No.2 Order

EDUCATION (SCHOOL PERFORMANCE INFORMATION) (ENGLAND) (AMENDMENT) (NO.2) REGULATIONS 1997, SI 1997 2364; made under the Education Act 1996 s.537, s.537A, s.569. In force: October 22, 1997; £1.10.

These Regulations amend the Education (School Performance Information) (England) Regulations 1996 (SI 1996 2577) by replacing existing required information in relation to the additional information about second key stage assessment results which must be provided to the Secretary of State on his written request. The required information now relates to the number of pupils at or near the end of the final year of the second key stage who have achieved level four or above of the National Curriculum level scale, failed to achieve a level or were exempted from National Curriculum tests or teacher assessment. The requirements also relate to the provision of individual performance information within the meaning of the Education Act 1996 s.537A(2).

2123. Schools–performance–information–Amendment No.3 Order

EDUCATION (SCHOOL PERFORMANCE INFORMATION) (ENGLAND) (AMENDMENT) (NO.3) REGULATIONS 1997, SI 1997 2816; made under the Education Act 1996 s.537, s.569. In force: December 17, 1997; £1.55.

These Regulations amend the Education (School Performance Information) (England) Regulations 1996 (SI 1996 2577) by adding a new Reg.13 and Sch.7 which provide for the publication of performance information about primary schools by local authorities.

2124. Schools–performance–information–Wales

EDUCATION (SCHOOL PERFORMANCE INFORMATION) (WALES) REGULATIONS 1997, SI 1997 1633; made under the Education Act 1996 s.408, s.414, s.537, s.539, s.569. In force: August 1, 1997; £2.80.

These Regulations, which relate to the provision of school performance information to the Secretary of State and parents, apply in relation to schools and local education authorities in Wales. They replace, with amendments, the Education (School Performance Information) (Wales) Regulations 1995 (SI 1995 1904 as amended by SI 1996 1665). The main changes are that the categories of information specified in Sch.1 Part 1 in respect of GCSE examinations now extend to equivalent GCSE short course examinations and, in two cases, equivalent GNVQ and NVQ qualifications.

2125. Schools–pupils–attendance registers

EDUCATION (PUPIL REGISTRATION) (AMENDMENT) REGULATIONS 1997, SI 1997 2624; made under the Education Act 1996 s.434, s.551. In force: January 1, 1998; £1.10.

These Regulations amend the Education (Pupil Registration) Regulations 1995 (SI 1995 2089) so that when a pupil is attending an approved educational activity outside the school premises the school's attendance register must be marked accordingly, along with the nature of that activity. They also remove work experience in the last year of compulsory schooling from the categories of employment requiring leave of absence and provide that the names of pupils may be deleted from the admission register when they have been continuously absent for four weeks and are detained under a final court order or an order of recall. In addition, an amendment is made so that the children of traveller families can be registered both at a base school which they normally attend and at another school for the time being.

2126. Schools–statistics–publication of performance tables–inclusion of special educational needs classes

[Education (Schools) Act 1992 s.16.]

The governing body of a primary school, G, and the National Association of Head Teachers, NAHT, applied for leave to apply for judicial review of the decision by the Secretary of State to publish in March 1997 the first primary school performance tables for maintained schools in a form set out in Circular 15/96. G and NAHT argued that the way in which the information was presented in the tables would frustrate the intentions of Parliament and was *Wednesbury* unreasonable. The Secretary of State intended to include the information relating to special units or classes for children with special educational needs, being part of the mainstream schools, but to exclude special schools. G submitted that the inclusion of special classes would result in the tables providing misleading information as to the standards in schools as the performance in special classes was lower than in mainstream classes and their primary school had a large proportion of pupils with special educational needs. It was further submitted that pupils who were absent or disapplied when the tests were taken would be treated as failures, thus affecting the results. The Secretary of State pointed out that it was intended that the number of special educational needs pupils would be included in the tables and that individual schools publish information relating to the percentage of absent or disapplied pupils.

Held, refusing the application, that the Secretary of State was given a wide discretion as to the manner in which information in the performance tables was published under the Education (Schools) Act 1992 s.16. G had not shown that in exercising the discretion as she did, the Secretary of State had acted unreasonably or perversely such that the court should interfere. The Secretary of State considered the objections made during the consultation exercise and made some amendments to her proposals accordingly. In addition, other sources of information relating to schools were available. As some special educational needs pupils were included in mainstream classes, and special classes were "wholly or mainly" for such pupils, there was considerable difficulty in determining exclusions. Excluding the special classes might result in discrimination whereas the objective was to achieve uniformity. The purpose in excluding special schools was for administrative simplicity on the first occasion of publishing tables, and it was intended that they would be included thereafter.

R. v. SECRETARY OF STATE FOR EDUCATION AND EMPLOYMENT, *ex p.* GOVERNING BODY OF WEST HORNDON COUNTY PRIMARY SCHOOL, Trans. Ref: CO-4502-96, January 21, 1997, Harrison, J., QBD.

2127. Schools–transport–unsafe route–decision not to provide free transport– challenging local education authority by judicial review inappropriate

[Education Act 1996 s.496, s.497.]

B applied for leave to apply for judicial review of E's decision not to provide free transport to school where the parents contended that the route used to measure walking distance was unsafe, on the grounds that (1) the decision was *Wednesbury* unreasonable; (2) the head teacher had not been consulted at an early stage, and (3) relevant evidence had not been put before the education committee.

Held, refusing the application, that although the application had merit, B had not availed himself of his statutory remedy to make a complaint to the Secretary of State under the Education Act 1996, s.496 and s.497. The question of whether the route was safe and whether relevant evidence had been before the committee could be more properly investigated and judged by the Secretary of State than the court, while the question of whether the head teacher had been informed at a sufficiently early stage had little bearing on the issue to be determined.

R. v. ESSEX CC, *ex p.* BULLIMORE; *sub nom.* R. v. ESSEX CC, *ex p.* EB [1997] E.L.R. 327, McCullough, J., QBD.

2128. Special educational needs–adjournment of Special Educational Needs Tribunal hearing–inadequate notice–expert evidence

[Special Educational Needs Tribunal Regulations 1995 (SI 1995 3113) Reg.8.]

J, a four year old autistic boy was the subject of a special educational needs statement issued by K, the local education authority. J's mother, L, appealed to the tribunal contending that J should receive intensive one to one tuition based on the Lovaas approach and proposed to call expert evidence. One week's notice was given of the hearing and as a result L did not have sufficient time to secure the attendance of a witness, nor submit any further evidence on the merits of the Lovaas approach. She applied for an adjournment to allow a witness to be called. The application was refused on the grounds that a decision should be reached as soon as possible in J's interests and that two other parents were already giving evidence in support of the Lovaas approach. L then applied for leave under the Special Educational Needs Tribunal Regulations 1995 Reg.8(5) to serve written evidence, namely professional articles about the Lovaas approach. The application was refused on the basis that there were no "exceptional circumstances" justifying the grant of leave as required under Reg.8(5). L appealed on the grounds that the tribunal erred in failing to grant an adjournment.

Held, allowing the appeal, that (1) the proper test was not to ask whether the decision by the tribunal could be challenged on *Wednesbury* grounds but rather to decide whether fairness required an adjournment, due regard being had to the views of the tribunal, *R. v. Cheshire CC, ex p. Cherrih* [1996] 1 C.L.Y. 2490, considered. In the instant case the need for an adjournment was not of L's making; it was due to the fact that the hearing was brought forward at very short notice. The virtues of the Lovaas approach lay at the heart of the appeal. The tribunal accorded less weight to the parents' evidence than it would have done to that of the expert, and fairness demanded that an adjournment be granted to allow the expert to be called. The tribunal erred in failing to grant an adjournment, and (2) the tribunal was entitled to take the view that "exceptional circumstances" did not exist so as to permit the granting of leave under the 1995 Regulations Reg.8(5) to serve further written evidence.

L v. KENSINGTON AND CHELSEA RLBC; *sub nom.* LUCY v. KENSINGTON AND CHELSEA RLBC [1997] E.L.R. 155, Dyson, J., QBD.

2129. Special educational needs – admissibility of evidence to Special Educational Needs Tribunal

[Special Educational Needs Tribunal Regulations 1995 (SI 1995 3113) Reg.29.]

D sought judicial review of a decision by the Special Educational Needs Tribunal which refused D's appeal against BCC's decision not to make a statement of special educational needs. D submitted that the decision was flawed because the tribunal failed to admit a speech therapy report which was particularly pertinent to D. D argued that (1) the proviso to the Special Educational Needs Tribunal Regulations 1995 Reg.29 was ultra vires; (2) the refusal by the tribunal to treat the case as exceptional under the 1995 Regulations Reg.8(5) was *Wednesbury* unreasonable, and (3) the tribunal's decision was illogical because it dealt substantively with the question of speech and language therapy without having regard to the report.

Held, refusing the application, that (1) where powers provided by subordinate legislation purported to interfere with common law or statutory rights then, unless that interference was expressly provided for or implied, that legislation was ultra vires. Regulation 29(2) regulated the way an appeal could be presented to a tribunal by placing restrictions on the evidence that might be adduced, with the objective of conducting appeals efficiently. Written statements submitted out of time can be accepted if the case was considered to be exceptional, for example if there had been a change in the child's circumstances prior to the hearing which was relevant to the hearing. If there was no such "safety net" then the proviso would be considered ultra vires, but as it stood that submission was rejected; (2) the decision not to treat D's case as exceptional and not to admit the report because there was no adequate explanation given for its late submission was harsh, but not *Wednesbury* unreasonable, and (3) the tribunal was entitled not to overturn the decision not to make a statement and instead to issue a Note in Lieu of a Statement on its findings having heard the oral and written evidence before it. It was justified in its conclusion that although the child had communications problems these being dealt with adequately in mainstream school.

DUNCAN v. BEDFORDSHIRE CC, Trans. Ref: CO 3062/96, December 13, 1996, Dyson, J., QBD.

2130. Special educational needs – amendment of statement – occupational therapy and physiotherapy as non educational provision

B appealed against a decision of the Special Educational Needs Tribunal dismissing her appeal against the special needs statement produced by IWC for

A, her daughter. B contended that the statement should have included specific allowances for occupational therapy and physiotherapy in Part III, under special educational provision, rather than Part IV, under additional non educational provision.

Held, dismissing the appeal, that the tribunal had not been *Wednesbury* unreasonable in deciding that the statement did not require amendment. Although both parties concurred in allowing that occupational therapy and physiotherapy would assist A to benefit from educational provision, that did not make the provision of those therapies educational rather than non educational.

B v. ISLE OF WIGHT COUNCIL, [1997] E.L.R. 279, McCullough, J., QBD.

2131. Special educational needs–appeal against statement–case stated–inappropriate route of appeal against final decision of Special Educational Needs Tribunal

[Tribunals and Inquiries Act 1992 s.11 (3).]

The application, by way of case stated, raised questions arising under the Education Act 1992 and concerned the jurisdiction of the Special Educational Needs Tribunal. The appellants were parents of a severely disabled child in respect of whom the local authority was required to provide a statement of special educational needs. When they did so it was appealed against and a further statement was issued. The parents' attempt to appeal against the second statement was struck out on the grounds that the tribunal had no jurisdiction to deal with it, and that it was frivolous and vexatious.

Held, refusing the application, that the case stated procedure was only available for the type of matters contemplated by the Tribunals and Inquiries Act 1992 s.11 (3), *R. v. Special Educational Needs Tribunal, ex p. Brophy* [1996] C.O.D. 372 applied.

ALLTON-EVANS v. LEICESTER LEA [1997] C.O.D. 113, Carnwath, J., QBD.

2132. Special educational needs–appeal for extension of time–delay not constituting special circumstances

[Special Educational Needs Tribunal Regulations 1995 (SI 1995 3113) Reg.7, Reg.41.]

J, a 13 year old boy, was the subject of a special educational needs statement issued by MBD, the local education authority, on December 18, 1995. It was received by J's mother on January 11, 1996. J's mother disagreed with the contents of the statement and notified MBD of her wish to appeal to the tribunal. She entrusted the lodging of the appeal notice to D, a parental advocate. When she had heard nothing by the end of February 1996 J's mother contacted solicitors, who then lodged the notice of appeal on March 14, 1996, together with a request for extension of time which was two days outside the two month time limit prescribed by the Special Educational Needs Tribunal Regulations 1995 Reg.7. The request for extension of time was refused. J sought judicial review of the refusal by the tribunal to exercise its discretion under the 1995 Regulations Reg.41, on the basis that the dilatoriness of D constituted "special circumstances" justifying an extension of time.

Held, refusing the application for judicial review, that while the circumstances in the instant case were regrettable they could not be described as "exceptional". While there might be cases where factors pertaining to an applicant's representative, such as accident or illness, might be regarded as exceptional and justify an extension of time, the tribunal made no error of law in not regarding the facts in the instant case as "exceptional", *Regalbourne Ltd v. East Lindsey DC* [1994] R.A. 1, [1994] C.L.Y. 3904, applied.

R. v. SPECIAL EDUCATIONAL NEEDS TRIBUNAL, *ex p.* J [1997] E.L.R. 237, Tucker, J., QBD.

2133. Special educational needs–appeals–choice of secondary school–adverse effect on education if stay of proceedings granted

R, who suffered from cerebral palsy, had a statement of her special educational needs drawn up in 1988. In January 1992 she was placed in a residential primary school, T, in Plymouth. The responsible authority, C, proposed that she should undertake her secondary schooling at a school, J, in Camden. Her parents wanted her to attend a boarding school, D, in Devon and appealed against C's decision to the Special Educational Needs Tribunal. The tribunal decided that R should attend D, on the basis that she needed the kind of care that only a boarding school could provide. The annual cost of D was more than four times greater than the cost of J. C put in a notice of appeal and sought a stay of the tribunal's order pending the hearing of the appeal, on the basis that if C succeeded in the appeal then R would suffer the upheaval on being removed from D and placed in J. If the appeal succeeded the matter would have to be sent back for reconsideration before a fresh tribunal.

Held, dismissing the application for a stay, that a stay should not be granted unless there were good reasons to do so. Although there was a risk that if R went to D that could pre-empt the decision of a new tribunal if C won its appeal, on balance, that was less of a danger than the danger that if R had now to remain at T that may adversely affect her educational achievement, because all parties accepted that T was not where R should stay. On balance, it was in R's best interests for her to start at D and a period there should pre-empt the decision in due course.

CAMDEN LBC v. HODIN AND WHITE [1996] E.L.R. 430, Collins, J., QBD.

2134. Special educational needs–appeals–educational needs could be met by other forms of education, but alternative choice of school could not meet needs sufficiently–no inconsistency in tribunal's reasons

In June 1995 S produced a statement of special educational needs in respect of H, a child born in 1991 who suffered from cerebral palsy, which condition primarily affected her mobility. H's parents, J, believed that conductive education was essential for H, and before S had produced the statement, they had sent her to a private school, B, which specialised in such education. S decided that H required a structured programme for whole body movement, and that she should be sent to a nursery, G, largely on the basis that B would be more expensive. J appealed to the Special Educational Needs Tribunal on the grounds that they wished H to remain at B, that H would move into mainstream education faster if she attended B, and that this would result in a considerable saving of cost overall. On the basis that H had made considerable progress with the assistance of conductive education, and that G could not meet H's mobility needs sufficiently, the tribunal ruled that H should stay at B with a view to entering mainstream education as quickly as possible. The tribunal did note, however, that H's educational needs could be met by other forms of education. S appealed, on the grounds, inter alia, that the tribunal acted inconsistently in stating that the amendment should be made to nominate B but not accepting H's parents' contention that her needs could only be met by conductive education, and that the findings that G was a good choice and that conductive education was not the only way to meet H's needs indicated that G was an appropriate school for H.

Held, dismissing the appeal, that (1) there was no inconsistency in the tribunal's reasons as suggested by S. The tribunal clearly indicated that although it was not satisfied that H's needs could only be met by conductive education the particular regime she was undergoing was one that was beneficial to her, and (2) the finding that G could not meet H's mobility needs sufficiently was wholly fatal to the appeal. Furthermore, the tribunal's finding that B would offer H a better chance of achieving mainstream education meant that the tribunal found that the financial arguments put forward by S were outweighed by the mobility point and the parents' contention that getting H into mainstream education more quickly was itself likely to be a better use of resources.

STAFFORDSHIRE CC v. J AND J [1996] E.L.R. 418, Collins, J., QBD.

2135. Special educational needs–appeals–parent substituted as appellant–extension of time limits

[Tribunals and Inquiries Act 1992 s.11 (1); Rules of the Supreme Court Ord.55 r.4.]

JC, a child, appealed to the High Court against a decision of the Special Educational Needs Tribunal within the 28 day time limit prescribed in the Tribunals and Inquiries Act 1992 s.11 (1) and the RSC 1965 Ord.55 r.4 (2). Shortly afterwards in *S (A Minor) v. Special Educational Needs Tribunal and Westminster City Council* [1996] E.L.R. 102, [1995] 1 C.L.Y. 1937, the QBD held that since a child's parents were a party to the appeal before the tribunal they could also appeal against any decision of the tribunal. When JC's representatives became aware of that decision they applied to substitute JC's mother, MC, as appellant. The tribunal, which had been named as a respondent to the original appeal, made an application that it should not be so named since it was not a proper party to the appeal. In a separate appeal, LS, a child, presented an application for leave to appeal out of time, after a request for a review by the representatives of LS's mother had been refused. The two appeals were heard together.

Held, allowing both appeals, that (1) with MC's agreement and consent, leave was given to withdraw the original appeal and for counsel acting on behalf of MC to enter an appeal in her name within 14 days on similar grounds notwithstanding the time limit having expired. The application by the tribunal that it should not be named as a respondent was refused. The chairman should also be one of the respondents, but could not be required to submit evidence, *S (A Minor) v. Special Educational Needs Tribunal and Westminster City Council* applied, and (2) mistakes by legal advisers or persons who held themselves out as competent to advise and act for a person in the field could not per se be reasons for extending the time limit for entering an appeal, *Regalbourne Ltd v. East Lindsey DC* [1994] R.A. 1, [1994] C.L.Y. 3904, applied. Regard must be had to the fact that the procedures for appeal in the new jurisdiction had not by the relevant time become settled either by practice or by decision, and that, unlike other decisions from other tribunals, no note was attached to the decision setting out clearly the form of an appropriate appeal and the relevant time limits. Bearing those factors in mind it was possible that the importance of time limits might not have been fully brought home to those advising and accordingly the time limits would be extended reluctantly and exceptionally in the case of LS. As in MC's case, leave would be given for LS's appeal to be withdrawn and a new appeal lodged with LS's mother named as appellant.

S AND C v. SPECIAL EDUCATIONAL NEEDS TRIBUNAL; *sub nom.* CARTER AND SMALL v. SPECIAL EDUCATIONAL NEEDS TRIBUNAL [1997] E.L.R. 242, Latham, J., QBD.

2136. Special educational needs–appeals–review only required where SENT decision reached on radically flawed basis of fact

[Education Act 1993; Special Educational Needs Tribunal Regulations 1994 (SI 1994 1910) Reg.32.]

M had severe specific learning difficulties and S made an assessment of his special educational needs. In August 1994 S proposed that M be educated at a mainstream school, C, supported by a resource centre for children with specific learning difficulties. M's parents wanted him to go to a boarding school in Somerset, R, which was a school specifically designed for boys with particular learning difficulties. They made their own arrangements to place him at R while the dispute with S was continuing. S concluded that although both R and C had advantages and disadvantages, R would be significantly more expensive and accordingly affirmed their decision that M should attend C. M's parents appealed successfully to the Special Educational Needs Tribunal, which found that the advantages of attending C would be outweighed by the disadvantages, and that M's needs should be addressed by his going to a small specialist school with small classes designed to provide education for children with severe specific learning difficulties. S appealed, on the basis, inter alia, that the tribunal applied the wrong statutory test in concluding that there would no benefits arising from a placement at C which would not be outweighed by the disadvantages.

Held, dismissing the appeal, that (1) the tribunal fulfilled their statutory duty by determining that the provision made by S would not meet M's needs. The central question was how M's needs would be best addressed, and the tribunal answered this question directly, and (2) as held in *R. v. London Residuary Body, ex p. Inner London Education Authority* [1987] C.L.Y. 31, a mistake as to fact could only vitiate a decision where the fact was a condition precedent to the exercise of jurisdiction, or where the fact was the only evidential basis for a decision, or where the fact was in relation to a matter which expressly or impliedly had to be taken into account. Accordingly, in the context of the Education Act 1993 and the Special Educational Needs Tribunal Regulations 1994, a matter should not be remitted to the tribunal for a rehearing merely for a clarification of reasons when the final decision was clearly expressed. Decisions reached in other statutory contexts were not applicable in the context of determining the educational needs of a disadvantaged child, which process should be done as quickly as possible. Only where a decision had been reached on a radically flawed basis of fact would a review be required under the Regulations Reg.32. In the instant case, there were no grounds for interfering with the tribunal's decision.

SOUTH GLAMORGAN CC v. L AND M; *sub nom.* SOUTH GLAMORGAN CC v. LONG [1996] E.L.R. 400, Carnwath, J., QBD.

2137. Special educational needs–appeals–time limits to be strictly observed

P was dissatisfied with the outcome of an appeal to the Special Educational Needs Tribunal concerning educational provision for her child and applied for an extension of the 28 day period in which to give notice of appeal. The application was opposed by the local authority and the tribunal on the ground that the time limits should be strictly observed even though the application was received four days after the expiry of the 28 day period.

Held, dismissing the application, that the facts offered nothing amounting to an excuse or worthwhile explanation of the delay which occurred and demonstrated a series of derelictions of duty, *Regalbourne v. East Lindsey DC* [1994] R.A. 1, [1994] C.L.Y. 3904 and *Savill v. Southend HA* [1995] 1 W.L.R. 1254, [1995] 2 C.L.Y. 3932 considered.

PHILLIPS v. DERBYSHIRE CC [1997] C.O.D. 130, Sedley, J., QBD.

2138. Special educational needs–breach of amended statement–failure by local education authority to comply with requirement to provide an experienced teacher

M was a minor with autism whose parents were concerned with the suitability of the school which came within W's jurisdiction. There were no schools specialising in autism within the borough and the parents sought a referral. The decision of the tribunal was that the school was appropriate to meet M's needs but that the statement should be amended to include for the provision of a "teacher who is experienced in working with pupils who have significant learning difficulties and autism/communication disorders". W employed a teacher whose experience was questioned by the parents as being insufficient and failing to meet the description set by the Special Educational Needs Tribunal. Leave for judicial review was granted and evidence was provided as to the qualification of the teacher and what was considered to be an "experienced" teacher as per the amended statement. It transpired that the teacher concerned was an overseas qualified teacher and was not actually employed by W or by the school's governors, but was supplied by an agency. The teacher had obtained a Higher Diploma in Education, which included a module called "remedial education", of which one element dealt with autism. The teacher's first employment involved attendance at another maintained special school as a float teacher, from which there was contact with some children with autism. In the next school year, the teacher moved to M's school and was assigned control of his class. Consideration was given to the National Autistic

Society and the requirements for their own teachers. The ordinary meaning and interpretation of the word "experience" and "experienced" was also considered. The court felt that the appropriate time to consider the teacher's experience was the date on which leave was granted, and that as such, experience is not a finite definition, but is a continuing test. The court warned that a teacher who is not experienced today may be an experienced teacher tomorrow. The court felt that to be experienced meant to have "a real and sufficient fund of experience and not merely having encountered in practice a particular subject or topic. In relation to teaching children with autistic disorders it must mean having a substantial trade record of teaching and working with such children".

Held, that W had failed in their duty to comply with the amended statement and that the need to comply with the statement was a continuing duty upon the director of education and was something that must be continually reviewed and considered.

R. v. WANDSWORTH LBC, *ex p.* M, August 12, 1997, Sedley, J., QBD. [*Ex rel.* Evill & Coleman, Solicitors, 113 Upper Richmond Road, Putney, London].

2139. Special educational needs–child attained 16 years–LEA ceased to maintain statement–whether LEA was liable to maintain statement pending appeal

[Education Act 1981 s.7; Further and Higher Education Act 1992; Education Act 1993 Sch.10.]

R had a mental disability and a statement of special educational needs had been made under the Education Act 1981 s.7. The local education authority purported to determine that the statement should cease, R having reached the age of 16 years and the Further Education Funding Council having powers under the Further and Higher Education Act 1992 which O considered apt to displace its own obligations. R appealed to the Special Educational Needs Tribunal, but O refused to reverse its decision pending the appeal. R sought judicial review. The question was whether O had acted lawfully on a true construction of the Education Act 1993 Sch.10 para.11.

Held, dismissing the application, that it was clear that if a local education authority chose to amend a statement there could be no stay, under Sch.10 para.10, pending an appeal. An authority could only cease to maintain a statement if it was no longer necessary to maintain it and only if it did so within the prescribed period under para.11 (4). There was no reason to imply a stay pending appeal in order to make para.11 work. The appeal process itself provided the necessary safeguard. It would be an unfortunate result, moreover, if a hopelessly misconceived appeal could prevent an authority from ceasing to maintain a statement until the disposal of the appeal. It was not necessary to give a strained meaning to para.11 (4), or to supply by implication words which Parliament could easily have added.

R. v. OXFORDSHIRE CC, *ex p.* ROAST [1996] E.L.R. 381, Dyson, J., CA.

2140. Special educational needs–child seeking to prevent parents removing him from school

See CHILDREN: V (A Minor) (Injunction: Jurisdiction), *Re.* §450

2141. Special educational needs–decision on suitability of school

[Education Act 1993 s.160(2).]

Held, that, under the Education Act 1993 s.160(2)(a), the question of the suitability of a particular school for a child with special educational needs should be determined as one of fact rather than fairness. However, when determining an efficient use of resources under s.160(2)(c), a local authority should balance additional expenditure likely to be incurred against parental preference.

CRANE v. LANCASHIRE CC, *The Times*, May 16, 1997, Popplewell, J., QBD.

2142. Special educational needs—duty of care—educational psychologist's failure to diagnose dyslexic pupil—vicarious liability of local authority

In 1985 at the age of 12, P, having shown poor levels of performance in school, was referred to M, an educational psychologist employed by HLBC. M's report stated that no specific learning difficulty or weakness was evident and attributed P's poor performance to emotional problems. During the remaining period of her schooling, P made little progress and assessments made after 1990 found that P suffered from severe dyslexia and that she would have been dyslexic at the age of 12. P brought an action for damages against HLBC for its failure to identify her dyslexia and take the remedial steps appropriate to the condition.

Held, allowing the claim, that (1) following *X (Minors) v. Bedfordshire CC* [1995] 2 A.C. 633, [1995] 2 C.L.Y. 3452, a local authority could be vicariously liable to a child through its parents for the failure of an educational psychologist to discharge her common law duty of care, the appropriate standard of care being the ordinary skill of the competent psychologist, *Bolam v. Friern Hospital Management Committee* [1957] 1 W.L.R. 582, [1957] C.L.Y. 2431 followed; (2) M failed to exercise the appropriate degree of skill and care in making a diagnosis of P's condition when faced with the unusual difficulties which P demonstrated, in particular the discrepancy between her predicted and actual reading ages, and (3) whilst, in the absence of a diagnosis of dyslexia, P's school could not be blamed for failing to provide the remedial teaching appropriate to her needs, HLBC, as employer, was vicariously liable for M's negligence and damages would be awarded.

PHELPS v. HILLINGDON LBC [1997] 3 F.C.R. 621, Garland, J., QBD.

2143. Special educational needs—local authority duty to name school—duty to pay for school

[Education Act 1996 s.348.]

The parents of SW, DW, R and F, who all suffered from autism, wished their children to attend a specific non maintained school in the US. R and F had already been placed at the school by their parents, the fees being met partly by the parents and partly by charitable fund raising. All the children had lodged appeals with the Special Educational Needs Tribunal in respect of the content of statements issued by their education authorities as to how their special educational needs should be met. With regard to R, the tribunal had substituted a statement that he should attend a non residential special school. In SW and DW's cases, the tribunal deleted the reference to a particular school and substituted a description of the type of school which was suitable for their needs. In respect of F, the tribunal determined that the US school met his special educational needs and should be named in the statement, and that F's education authority, SMBC, was responsible for the fees. SW, DW, R and SMBC appealed, the children contending that the tribunal was under a duty to name a specific school.

Held, dismissing the appeals, that there was no absolute duty imposed on either an education authority or the tribunal to name a maintained or non maintained school in a statement of special needs, although there was a power to do so. The tribunal's determination that SMBC must pay F's fees was ultra vires as there was no statutory provision which gave the tribunal power to rule on funding obligations. Under the Education Act 1996 s.348, which was about to come into force, there was a duty to arrange special educational provision if the parents had not made suitable arrangements and the duty to pay for the provision would arise if the name of the school was specified in the statement or if the education authority was satisfied that it was in the child's interests that provision should be made for him in a non maintained school. The decision as to whether the parents had made suitable arrangements was one for the education authority alone and, in F's case, an authority acting reasonably would have come to the same conclusion as the tribunal.

WHITE v. EALING LBC; RICHARDSON v. SOLIHULL MBC; SOLIHULL MBC v. FINN, *The Times,* August 1, 1997, Dyson, J., QBD.

2144. Special educational needs–school transport–compliance with special educational needs statement

[Education Act 1996 s.444(7), s.509(1).]

Where a special educational needs statement has provided for a child's attendance at a special school outside the area, it is irrelevant that the local education authority which is requested to help with transport costs believes that the child could be educated locally. K's son, who was severely dyslexic, was the subject of a special educational needs statement which provided that he should attend a specified school in Kent as a weekly boarder and that K was responsible for the costs of transport to school. HLBC opposed the statement, adopting the view that schools in its own area could adequately meet the boy's needs. When K became unable to provide transport, she looked to HLBC for help, but the local authority refused to make provision on the basis that the statement made K responsible for transport. K applied to the school attendance panel, whose view was that HLBC was not obliged to provide transport because the boy could be educated locally. K applied for judicial review of the panel's refusal to provide financial assistance.

Held, allowing the application and remitting the case, that the statement was not conditional on K providing transport and consequently remained effective. Although lack of transport might amount to an "unavoidable cause" preventing attendance under the Education Act 1996 s.444(7), in the instant case the fact that K found it impossible to comply with the transport requirement had only a secondary affect on the child, and therefore s.509(1) did not require HLBC to provide transport. However, HLBC was not entitled to base its decision to refuse assistance on its belief that the child could be educated locally as this was an extraneous consideration and therefore its decision would be quashed.

R. v. HAVERING LBC, *ex p.* K, *The Times*, November 18, 1997, Sedley, J., QBD.

2145. Special educational needs–statement required National Curriculum to be followed–pupil referral unit

[Education Reform Act 1988 s.18.]

L, a 14 year old girl with emotional instability, was the subject of a special educational needs statement. Part 3 of the statement said that there should be "no disapplication of the National Curriculum". L's mother, R, disagreed with the school specified in Part 4. R's appeal to the Special Educational Needs Tribunal was rejected and R appealed to the High Court, arguing that the school named in the statement, FO, was inappropriate because it could not offer the full national curriculum and it was unrealistic to suggest that L was ever likely to be integrated back into a mainstream school. The tribunal, in concluding that FO was an appropriate school for L, relied on evidence submitted by the local education authority that the facilities offered by FO were meeting L's needs and in particular her emotional needs, as set out in the statement.

Held, allowing the appeal, quashing Part 4 of the statement and remitting the matter to a differently constituted tribunal, that the issue for the tribunal was whether the school named by the local education authority was appropriate for the child. If it was not they must consider whether the school named by the parents was appropriate. The phrase "no disapplication of the National Curriculum" clearly derived from a consideration of the Education Reform Act 1988 s.18 and reflected the authority's assessment that L "needed to have access to the National Curriculum". Nothing in the remainder of the statement or any of the other documents suggested that for a period L would not need all the national curriculum. In a case where the powers under s.18 were not used, there was nothing in principle unlawful in specifying a pupil referral unit in which the full national curriculum was not taught, provided that arrangements were made for subjects not taught in the school itself to be taken at another school. Such arrangements could not at the material time be made for L because of her emotional and behavioural problems. FO was not an appropriate school for L because she could not be taught the entire national curriculum there, and because her emotional condition precluded her, for a time, from being taught the balance in a mainstream school.

R. v. KINGSTON UPON THAMES RLBC [1997] E.L.R. 223, McCullough, J., QBD.

2146. Special educational needs–statements of special educational need–scope of duty to make provision to meet need

[Education Act 1993 s.168(5).]

Q, a grant maintained school, applied for judicial review of a decision by H's education committee adopting a formula for calculating the cost of special education needs provision in respect of pupils with statements of special educational need, which had resulted in a 62 per cent reduction in the sum expected by Q for such purposes.

Held, allowing the application, that although budgetary constraints had no part to play in the assessment of special educational needs, consideration could be given to such constraints in deciding how to meet the needs. However, the non delegable duty fixed on an LEA under the Education Act 1993 s.168(5)(a)(i) meant that special educational needs always had to be met. That could be achieved by either providing the minimum requisite funding, by making the necessary provision itself or by arranging that the provision would be met by the school or a third party. Given that the duty was owed to each child on a personal basis, it would usually be necessary for the LEA to consult the school on how best the provision could be made, and the LEA need not provide funds to a greater extent than the minimum requirement. Where a formula based approach was used, it had to produce a sum sufficient for the child's needs and if the sum provided was insufficient, the LEA had to make up the shortfall and could not require the school to use its own funds to do so. Fairness required that the school should be notified of any proposed reduction in funding and permitted to make representations where a reduction in special needs funding was likely to have a significant effect on a school's total budget.

R. v. HILLINGDON LBC, *ex p.* GOVERNING BODY OF QUEENSMEAD SCHOOL, *The Times*, January 9, 1997, Collins, J., QBD.

2147. Special educational needs–test to be applied to determine whether special needs assessment required–no miscarriage of justice

[Education Act 1993 s.167; Rules of the Supreme Court Ord.55 r.7(7).]

K appealed against a decision of the Special Education Needs Tribunal to dismiss an appeal against D's decision not to carry out an assessment under the Education Act 1993 s.167 of R, K's son, who suffered from dyslexia. The request for assessment was initiated by K. K argued that the tribunal had not properly considered the questions to be addressed under s.167 in determining that R did not require assessment for special needs. If it was held that the tribunal had misdirected itself as to the tests to be applied, a further issue for determination was whether there had been a substantial wrong or miscarriage of justice as a result of that misdirection under the RSC Ord.55 r.7(7).

Held, dismissing the appeal, that (1) the local education authority, when determining whether to make an assessment, must ask itself whether a child fell, or probably fell, within the 1993 Act s.167(2), ie. had special educational needs and required special educational provision for those needs, both elements of which requirement had to be satisfied. The tribunal had misdirected itself by failing to address specifically the legal test to be determined. They had not properly addressed the issue of assessment to determine whether R had a significantly greater difficulty in learning than the majority of children of the same age, and (2) it was likely that the tribunal would have reached the same conclusion had they adopted the correct approach. Accordingly, there was no miscarriage of justice.

KNIGHT v. DORSET CC, Trans. Ref: CO 1110-96, December 20, 1996, Tucker, J., QBD.

2148. **Sports–gymnastics–teacher's duty of care to pupils**

See NEGLIGENCE: Hampshire CC v. Jones. §3850

2149. **Students–exclusion from students union not amenable to judicial review**

[Education Act 1994 Part II; Education (No.2) Act 1986 s.43.]

O applied for leave to review a decision of T excluding him from its premises as a result of his behaviour in being verbally abusive and refusing to comply with a lawful order. O contended that the Education Act 1994 Pt II and the Education (No.2) Act 1986 s.43 gave a public law dimension to the actions of students' unions.

Held, dismissing the application, that the action of T was not amenable to judicial review, which was solely a public law remedy and the legislation did not assist O.

R. v. THAMES VALLEY UNIVERSITY STUDENTS UNION, *ex p.* OGILVY, Trans. Ref: CO 1069/97, April 4, 1997, Sedley, J., QBD.

2150. **Students–fees and maintenance awards–discrimination**

EDUCATION (FEES AND AWARDS) REGULATIONS 1997, SI 1997 1972; made under the Education (Fees and Awards) Act 1993 s.1, s.2. In force: September 1, 1997; £2.40.

These Regulations revoke and replace the Education (Fees and Awards) Regulations 1994 (SI 1994 3042 as amended by SI 1995 1241 and SI 1996 1640). They relate to fees awards and maintenance awards to students and provide that in certain cases it shall be lawful to differentiate between specified persons and anyone else in the granting of such awards. Such differentiation might otherwise be unlawful under the Race Relations Act 1976.

2151. **Students–loans–eligibility**

EDUCATION (STUDENT LOANS) REGULATIONS 1997, SI 1997 1675; made under the Education (Student Loans) Act 1990 s.1, Sch.2 para.1, Sch.2 para.2, Sch.2 para.3. In force: August 1, 1997; £2.80.

These Regulations revoke and replace the Education (Student Loans) Regulations 1996 (SI 1996 1812). They make provision in relation to eligibility for loans, amounts awarded, interest charged, the time and manner of payments, repayment of loans by disabled borrowers and duties of governing bodies.

2152. **Students–loans–eligibility**

EDUCATION (STUDENT LOANS) (AMENDMENT) REGULATIONS 1997, SI 1997 2919; made under the Education (Student Loans) Act 1990 s.1. In force: January 1, 1998; £0.65.

These Regulations amend the Education (Student Loans) Regulations 1997 (SI 1997 1675) in order to provide that the new condition of eligibility for student loans that students are required to be settled in the UK shall not apply to students who began their courses before August 1, 1997.

2153. **Teacher Training Agency–additional functions**

TEACHER TRAINING AGENCY (ADDITIONAL FUNCTIONS) ORDER 1997, SI 1997 2678; made under the Education Act 1994 s.16, s.23. In force: December 1, 1997; £0.65.

This Order confers on the Teacher Training Agency additional functions with regard to the licensing or otherwise authorising of unqualified teachers to be employed as teachers at any school maintained by a local education authority, any special school not so maintained or any grant maintained school; considering and approving the training programme of persons who seek to become qualified teachers and who are not employed at such schools during their training; and approving persons for the purpose of assessing candidates who seek to become qualified teachers.

2154. Teachers–Amendment No.1–ill health retirement pension–employment–suitability of such teachers

EDUCATION (TEACHERS) (AMENDMENT) REGULATIONS 1997, SI 1997 368; made under the Education Reform Act 1988 s.218, s.232. In force: Reg.3: September 1, 1997; remainder: April 1, 1997; £1.10.

These Regulations amend the Education (Teachers) Regulations 1993 (SI 1993 453) Reg.8 by providing that a person in receipt of an ill-health retirement pension under the Teachers' Superannuation (Consolidation) Regulations 1988 (SI 1988 1652) is not, with one exception, to be regarded as having the health and physical capacity to be appointed to relevant employment or to be engaged to provide his services as a teacher at a school or further education institution otherwise than under a contract of employment.

2155. Teachers–Amendment No.2–graduate teacher and registered teacher programmes

EDUCATION (TEACHERS) (AMENDMENT) (NO.2) REGULATIONS 1997, SI 1997 2679; made under the Education Reform Act 1988 s.218, s.232; and the Education Act 1996 Sch.1 para.3. In force: December 1, 1997; £3.20.

These Regulations replace licensed, overseas trained and registered teacher schemes with new programmes to be known as graduate teacher and registered teacher programmes. The new programmes will enable persons who are not qualified teachers to teach at certain schools maintained by local authorities. They amend the Education (Teachers) Regulations 1993 (SI 1993 543), the Education (Teachers) (Amendment) Regulations 1994 (SI 1994 222), the Education (Pupil Referral Units) (Application of Enactments) Regulations 1994 (SI 1994 2103) and the Education (Teachers) (Amendment) Regulations 1997 (SI 1997 368) and revoke the Education (Teachers) (Amendment) Regulations 1995 (SI 1995 602) and the Education (Teachers) (Amendment) Regulations 1996 (SI 1996 1603).

2156. Teachers–compensation for retirement and redundancy

TEACHERS (COMPENSATION FOR REDUNDANCY AND PREMATURE RETIREMENT) REGULATIONS 1997, SI 1997 311; made under the Superannuation Act 1972 s.24, Sch.3 para.9, Sch.3 para.13. In force: April 1, 1997; £4.15.

These Regulations revoke and replace the Teachers (Compensation for Redundancy and Premature Retirement) Regulations 1989 (SI 1989 298 as amended by SI 1994 1059 and SI 1996 2777). Part II adds new provision regarding discretionary compensation for redundancy. Part III adds new provisions regarding discretionary compensation for termination of employment. Part IV adds new provisions regarding mandatory compensation for premature retirement. Parts V and VI retain the provisions regarding compensation for premature retirement.

2157. Teachers–early retirement on health grounds–superannuation regulations lawful

[Teachers' Superannuation (Amendment) Regulations 1997 (SI 1997 312) Reg.7; Teachers' (Compensation for Redundancy and Premature Retirement) Regulations 1997 Reg.7; Education (Teachers) (Amendment) Regulations 1997 (SI 1997 368) Reg.2(b).]

NATFHE applied for a declaration (1) that the Teachers' Superannuation (Amendment) Regulations 1997 Reg.7 and Reg.8 and the Teachers' (Compensation for Redundancy and Premature Retirement) Regulations 1997 Reg.7 were ultra vires the enabling legislation, and (2) that the Education (Teachers) (Amendment) Regulations 1997 Reg.2(b) was also ultra vires. NATFHE contended that teachers in receipt of ill health pensions would be prohibited from working either part time or if they recovered from an illness for which a pension was payable.

Held, dismissing the application, that the exercise of the powers was intra vires the respective legislation, that (1) in 1989 demographic changes had made it necessary temporarily to reduce the number of national teaching staff, but, although the position had subsequently changed, local authorities were continuing to grant early retirement to teachers. The acknowledged intention of the Regulations for Redundancy and Premature Retirement was to discourage the grant of early retirement by making the local authority responsible for a substantial part of the financial burden of pensions and compensation and the Secretary of State was within his powers so to do, and (2) the 1988 Regulations para.E13 made it clear that a teacher who recovered and was no longer incapacitated would no longer be entitled to an ill health pension and thus would not be further prevented from working by the provision.

R. v. SECRETARY OF STATE FOR EDUCATION AND EMPLOYMENT, *ex p.* NATIONAL ASSOCIATION OF TEACHERS IN FURTHER AND HIGHER EDUCATION, Trans. Ref: CO 2744-96, August 28, 1997, Ognall, J., QBD.

2158. Teachers–occupational pensions

See PENSIONS. §4019

2159. Teachers–remuneration–No.1 Order

EDUCATION (SCHOOL TEACHERS' PAY AND CONDITIONS) ORDER 1997, SI 1997 755; made under the School Teachers' Pay and Conditions Act 1991 s.2, s.5. In force: April 4, 1997; £1.95.

This Order amends the School Teachers' Pay and Conditions Document 1996 by uprating the amounts of salary and certain allowances.

2160. Teachers–remuneration–No.2 Order

EDUCATION (SCHOOL TEACHERS' PAY AND CONDITIONS) (NO.2) ORDER 1997, SI 1997 1789; made under the Schools Teachers' Pay and Conditions Act 1991 s.2, s.5. In force: September 1, 1997; £0.65.

This Order directs that the provisions of the School Teachers' Pay and Conditions Document 1997 shall have effect from September 1, 1997. The Education (School Teachers' Pay and Conditions) (No.2) Order 1996 (SI 1996 1816) and the Education (School Teachers' Pay and Conditions) Order 1997 (SI 1997 755) are revoked.

2161. Teachers–training–institutions eligible for funding–Designation No.1

EDUCATION (FUNDING FOR TEACHER TRAINING) DESIGNATION ORDER 1997, SI 1997 515; made under the Education Act 1994 s.4. In force: March 28, 1997; £0.65.

This Order designates Titan Partnership, Solihull Metropolitan Borough Council and Essex County Council as institutions eligible for funding under the Education Act 1994 Part 1. Titan Partnership is a charitable unincorporated association, established on July 2, 1996, having the registered charity number 1058051. Solihull Metropolitan Borough Council and Essex County Council are a Metropolitan District Council and a County Council respectively.

2162. Teachers–training–institutions eligible for funding–Designation No.2

EDUCATION (FUNDING FOR TEACHER TRAINING) DESIGNATION (NO.2) ORDER 1997, SI 1997 1399; made under the Education Act 1994 s.4. In force: August 4, 1997; £0.65.

This Order designates Bedfordshire, Devon, Gloucestershire and Kent County Councils and Headteachers Into Industry as institutions eligible for funding under the Education Act 1994 Part I. Headteachers Into Industry is a company limited by guarantee established to encourage secondments of senior education staff into industry. As a result of this Order, the Teacher Training Agency may make grants, loans or other payments in respect of expenditure incurred or to be incurred by the Institutions for the purposes of the provision of teacher training and the provision of facilities, and the carrying on of other activities which the Institutions consider it necessary or desirable to provide or carry on the purpose of or in connection with the provision of teacher training.

2163. **Teachers–training–institutions eligible for funding–Designation No.3 Order**
EDUCATION (FUNDING FOR TEACHER TRAINING) DESIGNATION (NO.3) ORDER 1997, SI 1997 2258; made under the Education Act 1994 s.4. In force: October 8, 1997; £0.65.

This Order designates Bournemouth, Cambridgeshire, Dudley, Enfield, Essex, Kent, Northamptonshire, Shropshire, Somerset, Suffolk, Sunderland, Wiltshire and Wolverhampton Councils as institutions eligible for funding under the Education Act 1994 Part 1, thus enabling the Teacher Training Agency to make grants and loans in respect of expenditure incurred by those institutions for the purposes of providing teacher training and related facilities.

2164. **Articles**
"A partnership of effort": reducing violence in schools *(Jackie Le Poidevin)*: H. & S.B. 1997, 257, 11-14. (Recommendations of working group on school security, guidance from Department for Education and Employment on security measures and role of safety legislation in dealing with classroom violence).

Attendance requirements at schools *(Anwar N. Khan)*: E. & L. 1997, 9(1), 29-39. (Parental duty to ensure child receives efficient full time education, enforcement measures of school attendance orders and education supervision orders, and modern attitudes to truancy).

Damages for academic under-performance: pupils as plaintiffs *(Jonathan Robinson)*: E. & L. 1997, 9(2), 93-108. (Teachers' duty and standard of care under common law and significance of departmental circulars).

Diverse world of tribunals: education appeal committees: Tribunals 1997, 4(2), 17. (Jurisdiction and functions of tribunals hearing appeals against school admission or exclusion decisions).

Education JR: 20 essential cases *(Tanya Callman)*: J.R. 1997, 2(1), 45-48. (Decisions on special needs, exclusions, discrimination, funding and school closure).

Education and judicial review-an overview *(Neville Harris)*: E.P.L.I. 1997, 2(2), 24-27. (Increase in applications for judicial review brought in relation to education, justiciability of decisions by particular bodies, cases concerning access to education and impact of judicial review in specific areas).

Further education, learning difficulties and the law *(Stephen Hocking)*: E. & L. 1997, 9(1), 13-22. (Law governing education after 16 and after 19 for those with learning difficulties focusing on division of responsibilities between local education authorities and further education councils).

Governors at risk: the legal responsibilities of the governing body *(Richard Gold)*: E.P.L.I. 1997, 2(1), 5-7. (Suggestion for reforming the governing bodies of schools in order to make legal requirements more realistic and assistance more effective).

Physical restraint of children: a new sanction for schools *(Carolyn Hamilton)*: Childright 1997, 138, 14-16. (Concern about introduction of power in Education Act 1996 s.550A to physically restrain children, with reference to definition of "reasonable force" and relationship between corporal punishment and provisions on physical restraint).

Schools, LEAs and damages *(Jonathan Robinson)*: S.J. 1997, 141(4), 80-81. (Liability in damages of school for poor academic performance of pupil due to school's negligence, focusing on particular problems of special educational needs and bullying).

Sex wars: conflict in, and reform of, sex education in maintained secondary schools *(Clare Furniss* and *Ann Blair)*: J. Soc. Wel. & Fam. L. 1997, 19(2), 189-202. (Need for reform, in interests of child, of parental right to withdraw child from sex education lessons).

Student and staff discipline—similarities or differences? *(Ivan Walker* and *Rachel Woolf)*: E.P.L.I. 1997, 2(1), 13-16. (Comparison of university and college disciplinary procedures for teachers, which are based on employment law, and those for students based on administrative law).

2165. Books

Gilliat, Jacqui; Blaker, Gary—Law for Primary and Secondary Schools. Paperback: £30.00. ISBN 1-85941-390-0. Cavendish Publishing Ltd.

Liell, Peter; Coleman, John; Poole, Keneth—Butterworth's Education Law. Paperback: £45.00. ISBN 0-406-02647-5. Butterworth Law.

Liell, Peter; Coleman, John; Poole, Kenneth; Grainger, Joanna—Law of Education. Unbound/looseleaf: £295.00. ISBN 0-406-99895-7. Butterworth Law.

Palfreyman, David; Warner, David—Higher Education and the Law. Hardback: £60.00. ISBN 0-335-19876-7. Open University Press.

ELECTORAL PROCESS

2166. Elections—absent votes

REPRESENTATION OF THE PEOPLE (AMENDMENT) REGULATIONS 1997, SI 1997 880; made under the Representation of the People Act 1983 s.53, s.201, Sch.2 para.3, Sch.2 para.5A; and the Representation of the People Act 1985 s.6, s.7, s.8, s.9. In force: in accordance with Reg.2; £1.10.

These Regulations amend the Representation of the People Regulations 1986 (SI 1986 1081) Reg.64 which sets out the additional requirements which apply where a person applies for an absent vote for an indefinite period on the grounds of physical incapacity and makes provision for the attestation of such applications. These Regulations amend Reg.64(2) to allow any registered nurse to attest such an application (instead of a first level nurse). They amend the provisions in Reg.64 in respect of attestation by registered medical practitioners, registered nurses and Christian Science practitioners. They also extend the deadline in respect of most applications relating to absent voting from noon on the thirteenth working day before the day of the poll to 5 pm on the eleventh working day before the day of the poll. In the case of applications falling within Reg.66(2) (late applications for an absent vote at a particular election because of unforeseen circumstances relating to the applicant's health) the deadline is extended from noon on the sixth working day before the day of the poll to five pm on that sixth day.

2167. Elections—absent votes

REPRESENTATION OF THE PEOPLE (NORTHERN IRELAND) (AMENDMENT) REGULATIONS 1997, SI 1997 967; made under the Representation of the People Act 1983 s.53, s.201, Sch.2 para.3, Sch.2 para.5A; and the Representation of the People Act 1985 s.6, s.7, s.8, s.9. In force: March 24, 1997; £0.65.

These Regulations, which extend to Northern Ireland only, amend the Representation of the People (Northern Ireland) Regulations 1986 (SI 1986 1091) Reg.64 which sets out the additional requirements which apply where a person applies for an absent vote for an indefinite period on the grounds of physical incapacity. Regulation 64(2) makes provision for the attestation of such applications. These Regulations amend Reg.64(2) to allow any registered nurse to attest such an application (instead of a first level nurse). It also amends that Regulation to take account of changes to the law about residential care homes and nursing homes in Northern Ireland made by the Registered Homes (Northern Ireland) Order 1992 (SI 1992 3204 (NI.20)). These Regulations extend the deadline in respect of most applications relating to absent voting from noon on the 13th working day before the day of the poll to 5 pm on the 11th working day of the poll. In the case of applications falling within Reg.66(6) (late applications for an absent vote at a particular election because of unforeseen circumstances relating to the applicant's health) the deadline is extended from noon on the sixth working day before the day of the poll to 5.00 pm on the sixth day.

2168. Elections–allocation of party political broadcasts

See MEDIA: R. v. BBC, *ex p.* Referendum Party. §3565

2169. Elections–candidates–expenses–variation of limits

REPRESENTATION OF THE PEOPLE (VARIATION OF LIMITS OF CANDIDATES' ELECTION EXPENSES) ORDER 1997, SI 1997 879; made under the Representation of the People Act 1983 s.76A, s.197. In force: March 17, 1997; £1.10.

This Order increases the maximum amounts of candidates' election expenses at parliamentary elections in the United Kingdom, local government elections in Great Britain and ward elections and elections by liverymen in common hall in the City of London.

2170. Elections–European Parliament

EUROPEAN PARLIAMENTARY ELECTIONS (AMENDMENT) REGULATIONS 1997, SI 1997 874; made under the European Parliamentary Elections Act 1978 Sch.1 para.2. In force: March 24, 1997; £0.65.

The European Parliamentary Elections Regulations 1986 (SI 1986 2209) Reg.5 applied the provisions in primary and subordinate legislation which were listed in Sch.1 and Sch.2 of those Regulations for the purposes of European Parliamentary elections. These Regulations revoke the specific provisions made by Reg.5(1) and Reg.5(2). Regulation 5(7)(b) of the 1986 Regulations converts references in the primary and subordinate legislation applied by Sch.1 and Sch.2 to those Regulations to parliamentary constituencies into references to European Parliamentary constituencies. This conversion is subject to an exception. Regulation 2(4) of these Regulations creates another exception so that references to a parliamentary constituency in the Representation of the People Act 1985 s.6(2A) are not converted.

2171. Elections–failure to appoint a boundary commission–whether election invalid–St. Vincent

[Constitution of Saint Vincent and the Grenadines s.33, s.96(1).]

R, an unsuccessful candidate in the 1994 general election in Saint Vincent and the Grenadines applied to the High Court for declaratory and other relief under the Constitution of Saint Vincent and the Grenadines s.96(1) on the grounds that the failure to appoint a boundary commission after the 1991 census and before the election breached s.33 of the Constitution. The application being dismissed by the judge and local Court of Appeal, R applied to the Judicial Committee of the Privy Council.

Held, dismissing the appeal, under the Constitution s.33(3)(a), a Constituency Boundaries Commission had to be appointed within a reasonable time after a census, but the appointment was not a condition precedent to a valid election. If a Commission was not appointed within a reasonable time, the court could grant relief, but after an election such relief would be of a discretionary declaratory nature. In this case no relief would be granted as R had failed to demonstrate an infringement of s.33(3).

RUSSELL v. ATTORNEY GENERAL FOR ST VINCENT AND THE GRENADINES [1997] 1 W.L.R. 1134, Lord Mustill, PC.

2172. Elections–returning officers–expenses

PARLIAMENTARY ELECTIONS (RETURNING OFFICERS' CHARGES) ORDER 1997, SI 1997 1034; made under the Representation of the People Act 1983 s.29. In force: April 8, 1997; £1.55.

This Order, which revokes and replaces the Parliamentary Elections (Returning Officers' Charges) Order 1994 (SI 1994 1044), specifies the kinds of services rendered by returning officers for or in connection with a parliamentary election in respect of which they are entitled to recover their charges, together with the maximum recoverable amounts in respect of those services.

2173. Elections–returning officers–parliamentary constituencies–change of name

RETURNING OFFICERS (PARLIAMENTARY CONSTITUENCIES) (ENGLAND) (AMENDMENT) ORDER 1997, SI 1997 537; made under the Representation of the People Act 1983 s.24. In force: April 1, 1997; £0.65.

This Order amends the Returning Officers (Parliamentary Constituencies) (England) Order 1995 (SI 1995 2061) to substitute the name of the District of Brighton and Hove, which is created by the East Sussex (Boroughs of Brighton and Hove) (Structural Change) Order 1995 (SI 1995 1770), for the name of the District of Brighton. The 1995 Order is also amended in consequence of the creation of the County of Rutland by the Leicestershire (City of Leicester and Rutland) (Structural Change) Order 1996 (SI 1996 507).

2174. Local elections–Borough of Blackburn

BOROUGH OF BLACKBURN (PARISHES AND ELECTORAL CHANGES) ORDER 1997, SI 1997 782; made under the Local Government Act 1992 s.17, s.26. In force: in accordance with Art.1; £1.55.

This Order gives effect to recommendations by the Local Government Commission for England for boundary and electoral changes in the borough of Blackburn. It makes changes to the boundaries of the parishes of Eccleshill, Yate and Pickup Bank, Livesey and Tockholes; abolishes all of the existing wards of the borough and provides for the creation of 22 new wards; makes provision for a whole council election in Blackburn in 1997 and for reversion to elections by thirds in subsequent years.

2175. Local elections–Borough of Blackpool

BOROUGH OF BLACKPOOL (ELECTORAL CHANGES) ORDER 1997, SI 1997 783; made under the Local Government Act 1992 s.17, s.26. In force: in accordance with Art.1 (1); £1.10.

This Order gives effect to recommendations by the Local Government Commission for England for electoral changes in the borough of Blackpool. All of the existing wards of the borough are abolished and 22 new wards are created.

2176. Local elections–Borough of Halton

BOROUGH OF HALTON (ELECTORAL CHANGES) ORDER 1997, SI 1997 779; made under the Local Government Act 1992 s.17, s.26. In force: in accordance with Art.1 (1); £1.55.

This Order gives effect to recommendations by the Local Government Commission for England for electoral changes in the borough of Halton. All the existing wards of the borough are abolished and 21 new wards are created. It makes provision for a whole council election in Halton in 1997 and for reversion to elections by thirds in subsequent years; and makes provision regarding elections of parish councils in the Daresbury and Hale district wards of Halton.

2177. Local elections–Borough of Thurrock

BOROUGH OF THURROCK (ELECTORAL CHANGES) ORDER 1997, SI 1997 775; made under the Local Government Act 1992 s.17, s.26. In force: in accordance with Art.1; £1.10.

This Order gives effect to recommendations by the Local Government Commission for England for electoral changes in the borough of Thurrock. All of the existing wards of the borough are abolished and 20 new wards are created.

2178. Local elections–Borough of Warrington

BOROUGH OF WARRINGTON (PARISHES AND ELECTORAL CHANGES) ORDER 1997, SI 1997 781; made under the Local Government Act 1992 s.17, s.26. In force: in accordance with Art.1; £1.95.

This Order gives effect to recommendations by the Local Government Commission for England for boundary and electoral changes in the borough of Warrington. It makes changes to the boundaries of the parishes of Appleton and Stretton; abolishes all the existing wards of the borough and provides for the creation of 24 new wards; makes provision for a whole new council election in Warrington in 1997 and for elections by thirds in subsequent years and makes electoral changes in respect of the parishes of Great Sankey, Winwick and Burtonwood in the borough of Warrington.

2179. Local elections–City of Gloucester

CITY OF GLOUCESTER (ELECTORAL CHANGES) ORDER 1997, SI 1997 157; made under the Local Government Act 1992 s.17, s.26. In force: February 10, 1997; May 7, 1998; £1.10.

This Order gives effect to recommendations by the Local Government Commission for England for electoral changes in the City of Gloucester. Two of the existing wards of the City of Gloucester are abolished and in their place three new wards are created.

2180. Local elections–City of Peterborough

CITY OF PETERBOROUGH (PARISHES AND ELECTORAL CHANGES) ORDER 1997, SI 1997 777; made under the Local Government Act 1992 s.17, s.26. In force: in accordance with Art.1; £1.95.

This Order gives effect to recommendations by the Local Government Commission for England for boundary and electoral changes in the City of Peterborough. It makes changes to the boundaries of the parishes of Peakirk, Castor and Bretton and abolishes all the existing wards of the city. It also provides for the creation of 24 new wards. The Order also abolishes the existing wards of the parish of Bretton and provides for the creation of two new parish wards for the division of the parishes of Orton and Longueville and Orton Waterville into two and five parish wards respectively. It amends the Cambridgeshire (City of Peterborough) (Structural, Boundary and Electoral Changes) Order 1996 (SI 1996 1878).

2181. Local elections–District of the Wrekin

DISTRICT OF THE WREKIN (PARISHES AND ELECTORAL CHANGES) ORDER 1997, SI 1997 780; made under the Local Government Act 1992 s.17, s.26. In force: in accordance with Art.1; £1.55.

This Order gives effect to recommendations by the Local Government Commission for England for boundary and electoral changes in the district of the Wrekin. It makes changes to the boundaries of a number of parishes in the district, abolishes all the existing wards of the district and provides for the creation of 34 new wards. This Order makes electoral changes in respect of the parishes of Stirchley and Brookside, Lilleshall and Donnington, Wellington, Newport, Hadley, and Oakengates in the district.

2182. Local elections–Forest of Dean

FOREST OF DEAN (PARISHES AND ELECTORAL CHANGES) ORDER 1997, SI 1997 179; made under the Local Government Act 1992 s.17, s.26. In force: in accordance with Art.1 (2); £1.10.

This Order makes changes to the boundary between the parishes of West Dean and Coleford in the district of Forest of Dean in the county of Gloucestershire and to the boundaries of parish and district wards and county electoral divisions. Provision is also made for changes in the number of councillors of the district council with effect from the ordinary elections in 1999.

2183. Local elections–Medway Towns

DISTRICT OF THE MEDWAY TOWNS (PARISHES AND ELECTORAL CHANGES) ORDER 1997, SI 1997 776; made under the Local Government Act 1992 s.17, s.26. In force: in accordance with Art.1; £1.55.

This Order gives effect to recommendations by the Local Government Commission for England for boundary and electoral changes in the district of the Medway Towns. It makes changes to the boundaries of the parishes of Cliffe, Frindsbury Extra, Stoke and St Mary Hoo, and renames the first parish of Cliffe and Cliffe Woods; abolishes the existing wards of the district and provides for the creation of 35 new wards; and makes provision regarding elections of parish councils in the district of the Medway Towns.

2184. Local elections–reorganisation

LOCAL GOVERNMENT REORGANISATION (REPRESENTATION OF THE PEOPLE) REGULATIONS 1997, SI 1997 138; made under the Local Government Act 1992 s.19, s.26. In force: March 1, 1997; £0.65.

These Regulations amend the Representation of the People Act 1985 s.6(2A) and s.9(5) to make provision for non-metropolitan counties in England which do not have a county council.

2185. Parliamentary candidates–court's power to restrain breach of electoral process

[Representation of the People Act 1983 s.115(2); Treaty of Rome 1957 Art.8C.]

S sought an interlocutory injunction to restrain a threatened breach of the Representation of the People Act 1983 s.115(2)(b) by H, a fellow candidate in a Parliamentary election. H contended that the alleged breach constituted a criminal act, which meant that the court had no jurisdiction to entertain the application.

Held, dismissing the application, that, despite being a public right, the common law right, confirmed by the Treaty of Rome 1957 Art.8A and Art.8C, as amended, of all persons to stand as Parliamentary candidates, untainted by corrupt practice, could be invoked by individual candidates. Even if this were wrong, and the rights conferred by s.115(2)(b) were purely public, S might be able to show that he would suffer damage from an intended interference with those rights by H. Accordingly, the rights concerned were within the exception to the general rule established in *Gouriet v. Union of Post Office Workers* [1978] A.C. 435, [1977] C.L.Y. 690, and there was a strong prima facie case that the court had jurisdiction to entertain such applications.

SPENCER v. HUGGETT, *The Times*, June 12, 1997, Longmore, J., QBD.

2186. Articles

Another Mr Bell–but no white suit *(Julian Malins)*: Counsel 1997, Jul/Aug, 24,26. (Need for law reform to prevent election candidates from using similar party name to that of main political parties in order to gain votes by confusing voters).

Citizenship and the right to vote *(Heather Lardy)*: O.J.L.S. 1997, 17(1), 75-100. (Concept of citizenship in political theory and relationship with electoral law).

Putting out the writs *(Oonagh Gay)* and *(Barry K. Winetrobe)*: P.L. 1997, Aut, 385-393. (Rules for determining last possible date in Parliamentary term for general election).

EMPLOYMENT

2187. Collective agreements–constitution by letter–new terms incorporated into contract

[Transfer of Undertakings (Protection of Employment) Regulations 1981 (SI 1981 1794); Wages Act 1986.]

B was employed by L as a domestic worker. Until April 1993 her terms and conditions were covered by the national NHS collective agreement. In 1992 the department in which B worked was the subject of a competitive tendering process. As part of the preparation of an in house bid, the employees' representatives agreed to a reduction of the existing terms and conditions of staff. During negotiations, which included correspondence, in December 1992 they sought to reserve their position with regard to the possible impact of the Transfer of Undertakings (Protection of Employment) Regulations 1981 and contractual claims. From April 1, 1993 the new conditions were introduced, with the effect that B and others suffered a reduction in pay. In May 1993 they complained of an unlawful deduction from their wages contrary to the Wages Act 1986. The tribunal rejected their claims, holding that the collective agreement negotiated in December 1992 had the effect of incorporating new terms and conditions into the employees' contracts. B appealed on the grounds, inter alia, that the relevant letters in December 1992 were incapable of constituting a collective agreement because those letters did not contain the language of offer and acceptance and that the agreement was not incorporated into the terms and conditions.

Held, dismissing the appeal, that (1) the letters constituted a collective agreement which the trade union and L intended to be binding; to be a binding agreement there need not be intention in the contractual sense, it was sufficient that there was a mutual intention to enter a collective bargain, the effect of which modified the employees' contracts, and (2) the collective agreement incorporated new terms and conditions into the employees' contracts. There was scope for local agreement to be made between the employer and the relevant unions, and it would be difficult to imagine a position in which either the employer or the unions would wish to say that any such collective agreement was not incorporated into the employees' terms and conditions of employment.

BURKE v. ROYAL LIVERPOOL UNIVERSITY HOSPITAL NHS TRUST [1997] I.C.R. 730, Morison, J., EAT.

2188. Collective agreements–transfer of undertakings–effect of transferree's decision to withdraw from collective agreement–terms of collective agreement incorporated into individual contracts of employment

[Transfer of Undertakings (Protection of Employment) Regulations 1981 (SI 1981 1794); Employment Protection (Consolidation) Act 1978 s.1, s.11; Wages Act 1986 s.5.]

Until April 11, 1994 W was employed by Brent LBC, on terms which included a provision that his rate of remuneration, overtime payments and other matters would be in accordance with the relevant local authorities' collective agreement, the NJC agreement. On April 11, 1994 the activities carried out by W and his colleagues were transferred to T. It was common ground that the transfer was covered by the Transfer of Undertakings (Protection of Employment) Regulations 1981. On April 21, 1994 T wrote to W and his colleagues informing them that the relevant unions had been de-recognised and that "any collective agreements or related arrangements will no longer have any effect and will be regarded as having terminated with immediate effect". At no stage did T seek to vary the individual contracts of employment. Subsequently W and his colleagues claimed that they were entitled to a pay rise in accordance with the revised terms of the NJC agreement. When T refused to pay the amount claimed, W applied to an industrial tribunal seeking a declaration under the Employment Protection (Consolidation) Act 1978 s.11 as to the contents of the written statement of particulars under s.1 of the Act and claiming that T had made an unlawful deduction from his wages contrary to the Wages Act 1986 s.5. The tribunal found in favour of T and W appealed.

Held, allowing the appeal, that the terms of a collective agreement can be incorporated into and become legally binding terms of individual contracts of employment, and unilateral abrogation of or withdrawal from the collective agreement does not affect the latter, *Robertson v. British Gas Corp* [1983] I.R.L.R. 302, [1983] C.L.Y. 1213, considered. While T was entitled to opt out of the collective agreement machinery, the outcome of the annual negotiation of the NJC agreement plainly went to W's substantive rights and not to T's participation in the collective apparatus. Remuneration must be treated as a term in a collective agreement fit for incorporation into an individual's contract of employment, *National Coal Board v. National Union of Mineworkers* [1986] I.R.L.R. 439, [1987] C.L.Y. 3762, applied. The effect of so holding is not that an employer would be bound ad infinitum by a collective bargaining process to which he is not a party, because the employer will always have the option of giving notice to the individuals concerned or negotiating a variation in the relevant contracts.

WHENT v. T CARTLEDGE LTD [1997] I.R.L.R. 153, Judge Hicks Q.C., EAT.

2189. Collective bargaining–construction of agreement–staff employees–hourly rated employees–local agreements

V appealed against a decision that a letter recording an agreement between management and a representative of the staff union, MSF, should be construed to award to H, a staff grade worker, a single payment which had been made to encourage hourly paid manual workers to sign a local agreement. Staff workers had already signed a local pay agreement and were concerned that during protracted negotiations between V and manual workers other significant benefits would be conceded. A letter confirmed that any such benefits would also be awarded to staff workers. V finally offered H a single lump sum of £200. H contended that the payment was a benefit of the kind included in the letter.

Held, allowing the appeal and reversing the judge below, that the letter referred to changes in terms and conditions and not the single payment. It could not have been intended by V to apply to the staff workers who had already signed the local agreement, *Reardon Smith Line v. Hansen-Tangen* [1976] 1 W.L.R. 989, [1976] C.L.Y. 2582 approved.

HOUGHTON v. VAUXHALL MOTORS LTD, Trans. Ref: CCRTF 96/1289/C, April 23, 1997, Peter Gibson, L.J., CA.

2190. Compensation–complaint of action short of dismissal following failure to shortlist for management post–compensation for injury to feelings

[Trade Union and Labour Relations (Consolidation) Act 1992 s.149(2).]

C appealed against an industrial tribunal decision to award B compensation. This award included an award for injury to feelings on his complaint of action short of dismissal following C's failure to shortlist him for a management post, which, B alleged, was because of his trade union activities. The tribunal judged the complaint to be well founded and awarded compensation on the basis of B's loss of chance of promotion. C argued that, in view of *Addis v. Gramophone Co Ltd* [1909] A.C. 488 and *Norton Tool Co Ltd v. Tewson* [1972] I.C.R. 501, [1973] C.L.Y. 1136, the tribunal had no power to make an award for injury to feelings.

Held, dismissing the appeal, that the tribunal acted within its jurisdiction. The words "having regard to the infringement complained of" in the Trade Union and Labour Relations (Consolidation) Act 1992 s.149(2) allowed it to make an award which extended beyond simple pecuniary loss, and the tribunal was entitled to find that B's situation was caused solely by C's unlawful action.

CLEVELAND AMBULANCE NHS TRUST v. BLANE [1997] I.R.L.R. 332, Judge Peter Clark, EAT.

2191. Construction Industry Training Board—levy on employers

INDUSTRIAL TRAINING LEVY (CONSTRUCTION BOARD) ORDER 1997, SI 1997 407; made under the Industrial Training Act 1982 s.11, s.12. In force: February 19, 1997; £1.55.

This Order gives effect to proposals of the Construction Industry Training Board for the imposition of a levy on employers in the construction industry for the purpose of raising money towards meeting the expenses of the Board.

2192. Contract of employment—breach of implied term—employees could recover damages for injury to reputation caused by employer's dishonesty

M and another, both former employees of BCCI, appealed against the dismissal of their appeal against a preliminary decision that they were not entitled to recover damages for injury to their reputation, and consequent difficulties in finding new employment, allegedly caused by BCCI conducting a dishonest or corrupt business. BCCI's liquidators argued that injury to reputation was protected by defamation and a claim should not be allowed in contract that would not succeed in tort, and that, in any case, the claims for damages to the employees' existing reputations were barred by *Withers v. General Theatre Corp Ltd* [1933] 2 K.B. 536.

Held, allowing the appeal, that BCCI was under an implied obligation not to conduct a corrupt and dishonest business, being one aspect of a general implied contractual obligation not to engage in conduct likely to undermine the relationship of confidence and trust between employer and employee. Where the loss suffered by an employee as a result of a breach of this implied term did not simply consist of premature termination losses, for example where the breach adversely affected future employment prospects, such continuing financial losses were, in principle, recoverable, subject to questions of foreseeability, remoteness and mitigation. To limit recovery to premature termination losses was an unacceptably narrow interpretation of the trust and confidence term and employers had a duty not do acts that would damage employees' future employment prospects, *Addis v. Gramophone Co Ltd* [1909] A.C. 488 distinguished. Further, the fact that the loss might be recoverable in defamation did not preclude it being recovered as damages for breach of contract. The ruling in *Marbe v. George Edwardes (Daly's Theatre) Ltd* [1928] 1 K.B. 269, that damages for loss to existing reputation could be recovered, was to be preferred to the judgment in *Withers*.

MALIK v. BANK OF CREDIT AND COMMERCE INTERNATIONAL SA (IN LIQUIDATION); *sub nom.* MAHMUD v. BANK OF CREDIT AND COMMERCE INTERNATIONAL SA (IN LIQUIDATION) [1997] 3 W.L.R. 95, Lord Nicholls of Birkenhead, HL.

2193. Contract of employment—company sick pay scheme—termination of scheme—meaning of "without prior notice"

B appealed against a decision dismissing his claim for breach of contract arising from C's refusal to make disability payments under its company sick pay scheme. B developed dermatitis from exposure to glue used at work and was unable to return to work after November 1985. His contract of employment stated that B was covered by C's sick pay schemes: one covering periods of up to six months, and the other covering longer periods. The rules of the schemes gave C the right to terminate them "without prior notice". B, who received payments under the schemes until being made redundant in March 1993, contended that the failure to make payments after that date breached the terms of his contract of employment. However, C submitted that the long term scheme had ended in March 1982, when C ceased paying the insurance premium.

Held, allowing the appeal, that the judge had wrongly interpreted the contract of employment in holding that no notice of termination was necessary. Although C reserved the right to amend or terminate the schemes "without prior notice", those words were to be construed as meaning without advance notice. The facts showed that C had not informed trade union representatives of the termination until November 1985 and B had not known of the change until his redundancy. Whilst the termination clause operated to put B on notice that the scheme might not be permanent, his rights under the contract continued until he was given notice of variation and C's obligation to make payments did not end when payment of the premiums ceased.

BAINBRIDGE v. CIRCUIT FOIL UK LTD [1997] I.C.R. 541, Aldous, L.J., CA.

2194. Contract of employment–disciplinary measures–transfer in lieu of dismissal–successful appeal–compensatory damages

Held, that an employee who had been transferred as an alternative to dismissal after a ruling of misconduct, but whose appeal against the ruling was successful, was entitled to compensatory damages for breach of contract when his employer refused to allow him to return to his original workplace. Once the appeal was successful the circumstances surrounding the transfer no longer existed and therefore the employer had no contractual right to insist that the employee remain at his place of transfer.

HAILSTONES v. STAFFORDSHIRE CC, *The Times,* August 11, 1997, Roch, L.J., CA.

2195. Contract of employment–employment status of temporary worker engaged by employment agency–entitlement to unpaid wages on liquidation

[Conduct of Employment Agencies and Employment Businesses Regulations 1976 (SI 1976 715) Reg.9; Employment Agencies Act 1973 s.5; Income and Corporation Taxes Act 1988 s.134.]

The Secretary of State for Employment appealed against a decision of the EAT reversing the industrial tribunal and allowing that M could recover from the Redundancy Fund his unpaid earnings of £105 owed by a liquidated employment agency. The Secretary of State argued that M was not eligible for payment because he was not an employee of the agency. M had been on the books of Noel Employment Ltd, N, for just less than one year, and, at the date that N went into creditor's voluntary liquidation, had been working for a catering firm for four days. The Conduct of Employment Agencies and Employment Businesses Regulations 1976 Reg.9(6)(a), enacted under the Employment Agencies Act 1973 s.5, made it a statutory requirement to produce a written statement of the conditions of service, which, in the instant case, included a specific denial of a contract of service, a reservation by N of the right to place work elsewhere, the lack of any obligation on M to accept offered employment, and the acknowledgement that there would be periods when no work was available. However, N also agreed to pay weekly wages subject to statutory deductions, reserved the powers of instant dismissal and summary termination of an assignment without giving reason, and offered review and grievance procedures. M contended that the Inland Revenue had confirmed his status as an employed person.

Held, dismissing the appeal, that it was necessary for both the general and the specific engagement to be considered, although the standard terms and conditions might need to be interpreted differently in each context, *Pertemps Group v. Nixon* (Unreported) not followed. In the instant case, the express statement that M was self employed was overborne by the reservation to N of the powers of summary dismissal for misconduct, and of summary termination of an assignment, the provision of grievance and review procedures, and an hourly pay rate subject to deductions for unsatisfactory time keeping, attitude, work or misconduct. Since M was an employee of N by virtue of the specific engagement, his status under the general engagement did not need to be considered. There was no single decisive factor in differentiating between a contract for services and a contract of service and it was especially difficult in the case of temporary workers because they had both a specific engagement which began and ended with one task, and a general engagement in which tasks were performed sporadically. The fact that the Inland Revenue treated M as an employed person was not significant because it was as a result of the deeming provision of the Income and Corporation Taxes Act 1988 s.134, *O'Kelly v. Trusthouse Forte* [1984] 1 Q.B. 90, [1983] C.L.Y. 1225, *Nethermere (St Neots) Ltd v. Taverna* [1984] I.R.L.R. 240, [1984] C.L.Y. 1206 followed, *Hellyer Brothers Ltd v. McLeod* [1987] I.C.R. 526, [1987] C.L.Y. 1354, *Wickens v. Champion Employment* [1984] I.C.R. 365, [1984] C.L.Y. 1220 considered, *Construction Industry Training Board v. Labour Force Ltd* [1970] 3 All E.R. 220, [1970] C.L.Y. 2813 and *Ironmonger v. Movefield Ltd* [1988] I.R.L.R. 461, [1989] C.L.Y. 1410 distinguished on their facts.

McMEECHAN v. SECRETARY OF STATE FOR EMPLOYMENT [1997] I.C.R. 549, Waite, L.J., CA.

2196. Contract of employment–fixed term contracts–letter confirming termination at end of fixed term not unfair dismissal

[Employment Rights Act 1996 s.95(1)(b), s.197(1).]

F commenced employment with L in March 1994 under a fixed term contract of one year's duration. He was employed under a further fixed term contract of one year to run from March 1995 to March 1996. In February 1996 L wrote to F to confirm that his contract would terminate in March 1996. Although the contract contained a clause excluding F's statutory right to claim unfair dismissal, F presented a complaint of unfair dismissal to an industrial tribunal. The tribunal held that it had jurisdiction to consider the complaint on the basis that the contract had not expired by effluxion of time, within the meaning of the Employment Rights Act 1996 s.95(1)(b), but that the letter from L in February 1996 constituted a termination of F's employment. L appealed.

Held, allowing the appeal, that there was a distinction between informing someone that a contract would end through effluxion of time and exercising a power contained in a contract to bring it to an end by notice. The letter in the instant case clearly fell within the former category and F's claim of unfair dismissal was excluded by s.197(1) of the 1996 Act.

LONDON UNDERGROUND LTD v. FITZGERALD [1997] I.C.R. 271, Morison, J., EAT.

2197. Contract of employment–fixed term contracts–unfair dismissal waiver clauses

[Employment Rights Act 1996 s.197.]

C originally commenced employment with H in 1987 under an indefinite contract of employment. In March 1991 he was appointed to a management position on a fixed term contract for a period of twelve months. The contract contained a clause by which C agreed to waive his rights to claim unfair dismissal or redundancy payments. In December 1991 a new fixed term contract for a period of two years was signed, which also contained a waiver clause. Four further extensions of periods varying between three and eight months were agreed. On each occasion C signed the same waiver clause. His employment ended on March 31, 1995, whereupon he presented an application to an industrial tribunal claiming a redundancy payment. H relied on the waiver clause as excluding the jurisdiction of the tribunal. The tribunal upheld C's claim and H appealed.

Held, allowing the appeal, that (1) in the case of unfair dismissal waiver clauses, questions of renewal and re-engagement are irrelevant. If the employment continues for a further fixed term, it must be for a term of one year or more, *Ioannou v. BBC* [1974] I.R.L.R. 77, [1975] C.L.Y. 1091 and *Dixon v. BBC* [1979] I.R.L.R. 114, [1979] C.L.Y. 1019 followed, *Mulrine v. University of Ulster* [1993] I.R.L.R. 545, [1994] C.L.Y. 1919 not followed. The only question is whether the contractual arrangements comply with the provisions of the Employment Rights Act 1996 s.197; (2) in the case of redundancy waiver clauses, the original contract must be for a term of two years or more. If the contract is renewed or the employee is re-engaged on different agreed terms, then if the original fixed term is renewed for a further fixed term, whether for a period of two years or less, and during that extended term the parties enter into a s.197(4) waiver agreement, then dismissal expiring out of the expiry of the original fixed term as extended will not give rise to a claim for a redundancy payment. Under s.197(3) and s.197(5) of the 1996 Act there must be a waiver agreement both in relation to the original fixed term and during the currency of each extension of the fixed term, *Open University v. Triesman* [1978] I.R.L.R. 114, [1978] C.L.Y. 1010 not followed. In the instant case, the tribunal erred in looking only at the final contract term for the purposes of deciding whether there was a valid redundancy payment waiver. On a proper analysis, there was a two year fixed term contract, followed by a succession of renewals, each accompanied by a waiver agreement, resulting in a fixed term contract for a period of two years or more for the purposes of s.197(3) and s.197(5) of the 1996 Act.

HOUSING SERVICES AGENCY v. CRAGG [1997] I.R.L.R. 380, Judge Peter Clark, EAT.

2198. Contract of employment—fixed term contracts—waiver of unfair dismissal rights—renewal of contract constituted extension of term under existing contract

[Employment Rights Act 1996 s.95, s.197.]

For the purposes of applying the Employment Rights Act 1996 s.197 to unfair dismissal claims in the context of a series of fixed term contracts, the court may regard renewal of a fixed term contract as an extension of that contract. In such circumstances, the approach taken by Lord Denning in British Broadcasting Corp v. Ioannou [1975] Q.B. 781 may not be of assistance to the claimant. B had worked for his employers since 1986 under a series of fixed term contracts for periods of between two months and three years, each contract containing a term waiving B's rights to claim unfair dismissal in the event of his contract not being renewed. A three year contract expiring in August 1995 was renewed for a period of three months and renewed again in October 1995 for a further period of three months. When his employers failed to renew that contract, B brought a complaint of unfair dismissal, but the industrial tribunal ruled that it had no jurisdiction to hear the complaint. B appealed, relying on the approach taken by Lord Denning in *BBC v. Ioannou* [1975] Q.B. 781, [1975] C.L.Y. 1091 to argue that the Employment Rights Act 1996 s.197 was not applicable as his final contract was the relevant one to consider in order to ascertain whether his waiver of the right to pursue an unfair dismissal claim was still operative, and this contract was for only three months.

Held, dismissing the appeal, that, in order to determine whether there had been a dismissal within the 1996 Act s.95(1)(b) where there had been a series of fixed term contracts, it had to be established whether the renewal was an extension of the term under the existing contract or a renewal under a new contract. Where the only change was an extension to the fixed term, it would almost certainly amount to an extension under the same contract. Since B's extended contract was for a fixed term of more than one year, his contract fell within s.197(1) and he could not invoke the unfair dismissal provisions of the 1996 Act.

BHATT v. CHELSEA AND WESTMINSTER HEALTH CARE TRUST [1997] I.R.L.R. 660, Kirkwood, J., EAT.

2199. Contract of employment–jurisdiction–relevant considerations for determining employee's place of work

[Brussels Convention on Jurisdiction and Enforcement of Judgments in Civil and Commercial Matters 1968 Art.5(1).]

Held, that under the Brussels Convention 1968 Art.5(1) as amended, which conferred jurisdiction upon national courts in matters relating to individual contracts of employment, the place where an employee habitually carried on his work was to be determined by where he had established the centre of his working activities, notwithstanding that he might perform part of his work outside the jurisdiction. In deciding with which state an employee was most closely linked previous case law had to be taken into account, ensuring that proper protection was afforded to the employee as the weaker contracting party, *Mulox IBC v. Geels (C125/92)* [1993] E.C.R. I-4075 considered.

RUTTEN v. CROSS MEDICAL LTD (C383/95) [1997] All E.R. (EC) 121, Judge not specified, ECJ.

2200. Contract of employment–performers–remuneration–period of "tour"

E sought to restrain T from presenting a petition to wind up E on the basis of a statutory demand in the sum of £5,000. T agreed to perform on a European tour under a contract which included a period of seven days off between European and US tours. E refused to pay T for this period, which it claimed T took as holiday and contended that the term "tour" referred only to individual periods of live concerts.

Held, dismissing the notice of motion, that a stay of 28 days on the petition would be granted. Although a winding up petition should not be abused as a means of debt collection, it was quite clear from the evidence and from construction of the contract that the seven day rest period was part of the "tour" and that payment was therefore due to T.

ELVIS COSTELLO LTD v. THOMAS, Trans. Ref: No.1707 of 97, June 10, 1997, Judge Gilliland Q.C., Ch D (Companies Court).

2201. Contract of employment–retirement–wrongful dismissal–notice–Gambia

C appealed against a decision of the Gambian Court of Appeal. T was employed under a contract with C providing for one month's notice until the retirement age of 55. T claimed that he was then asked to continue working until the age of 60, but when he reached the age of 57, he was asked to retire. T contended that had been wrongfully dismissed from a fixed term contract of five years' employment.

Held, allowing the appeal, that the decision of the Court of Appeal was set aside and the decision of the trial judge restored. The Court of Appeal should be loath to set aside the decision of the trial judge, particularly where it involved his assessment of the credibility of a witness, *Powell v. Streatham Manor Nursing Home* [1935] A.C. 243 followed.

CFAO (GAMBIA) LTD v. TAAL, Trans. Ref: No.50 of 1996, February 6, 1997, Lord Hutton, L.C.J., PC.

2202. Contract of employment–termination–futures trader–oral agreement to forfeit commission contrary to Wages Act

[Wages Act 1986.]

D employed M as a trader on the floor of LIFFE, trading on his own account. M resigned and D sought repayment of commission paid to M alleging that there was an oral contract that if he left his employment before the end of three years he would be entitled to only 50 per cent of commission earned to that date. M counterclaimed claiming a loss of opportunity to work on LIFFE.

Held, dismissing the claim and counterclaim, that the oral agreement was not proved and M was entitled to all the commission earned up to the date of his resignation. Any agreement to reduce the amount owed to M would have been unlawful under the terms of the Wages Act 1986. He was entitled to rely on the terms of the Act as a defence to the claim made by D rather than a basis for seeking any remedy for a breach of the Act. The counterclaim was dismissed because M had failed to mitigate his losses by trading off the floor through brokers.

DEGELD OPTIONS LTD v. MALOOK [1997] 6 Bank. L.R. 1, Popplewell, J., QBD.

2203. Contract of employment–termination–whether claim arose "outstanding on the termination of the employee's employment"

[Industrial Tribunals Extension of Jurisdiction (England and Wales) Order 1994 (SI 1994 1623) Art.3; Employment Protection (Consolidation) Act 1978 s.131.]

S appealed against an industrial tribunal's decision that it did not have jurisdiction to determine her claim for damages for breach of contract under the Employment Protection (Consolidation) Act 1978 s.131 after the trust withdrew its offer of employment before the date on which S was due to start work. Although finding that a valid contract of employment existed, the tribunal held that S's claim did not come within the Industrial Tribunals Extension of Jurisdiction (England and Wales) Order 1994 Art.3(c) in that it was not a claim "outstanding on the termination of the employee's employment". The trust contended that no contract of employment existed, merely a contract for employment, and that there was a distinction between "employment" and "contract of employment".

Held, allowing the appeal, that a contract of employment existed which S would have performed on reporting for work on the agreed start date. Since that contract was terminated, it was difficult to see how there could be no termination of the employee's employment, because, having entered into the contract, S was undoubtedly an employee. Article 3(c) of the Order, the object of which was to enable an industrial tribunal to hear both a claim for unfair dismissal and one for breach of contract arising under the same contract, had to be interpreted purposively. Whilst two years' service was required to bring an unfair dismissal claim unless the claim was founded on an inadmissible reason, eg. trade union membership, there was no reason in principle why someone who had not yet begun work but whose contract had been terminated for such a reason could not bring an unfair dismissal claim before the tribunal. It followed that the phrase "termination of the employee's employment" could be interpreted as "termination of the employee's contract of employment" and the tribunal had erred in concluding that it did not have jurisdiction to hear S's claim.

SARKER v. SOUTH TEES ACUTE HOSPITALS NHS TRUST [1997] I.R.L.R. 328, Keene, J., EAT.

2204. Discrimination–disabled persons–abolition of Committees for the Employment of People with Disabilities

DISABILITY DISCRIMINATION (ABOLITION OF DISTRICT ADVISORY COMMITTEES) ORDER 1997, SI 1997 536; made under the Disability Discrimination Act 1995 s.60, s.67. In force: March 31, 1997; £1.10.

This Order provides for the cessation of effect of the Disabled Persons (Employment) Act 1944 s.17 and Sch.2 so far as concerns district advisory committees known as Committees for the Employment of People with Disabilities.

2205. Dismissal–allegations made against employee leading to dismissal–disclosure of details of allegations and identity of informant

P was employed by T as an operations manager, responsible for putting major contracts out to tender. T's managing director informed P that serious allegations had been made against him by a third party, but refused to give details of the allegations or the name of the informant. At a disciplinary hearing, allegations of gross misconduct concerning P's dealings with external contractors were made, but T once again refused to furnish further particulars about the allegations and P was summarily dismissed without pay. In view of the difficulty he faced in obtaining other employment, P, relying on *Norwich Pharmacal Co v. Customs and Excise Commissioners* [1974] A.C. 133, [1973] C.L.Y. 2643, issued a notice of motion seeking an order obliging T to disclose precise details of the allegations made against him and the identity of the person who had made the allegations, and allowing him to use the information provided to found an action against the unknown informant.

Held, granting the order, that there were limits to the jurisdiction of *Norwich Pharmacal* and the court had to decide whether it should exercise its discretion to allow discovery against T so that P could bring proceedings against a third party in order to clear his name. An action in defamation or malicious falsehood would be appropriate, but without further evidence concerning the allegations it was impossible for P to know whether he had a viable cause of action. In this regard, P was not in the same situation as the plaintiff in *Norwich Pharmacal*, who had known with certainty that a tort had been committed against him by a third party. However, the purpose of a court order was to enable justice to be done and, in the instant case, justice demanded that P be given the assistance he needed to enable him to clear his name.

P v. T LTD; *sub nom.* A v. B LTD; A v. COMPANY B LTD [1997] 1 W.L.R. 1309, Sir Richard Scott, V.C., Ch D.

2206. Dismissal—constructive   dismissal—resignation—employer's   actions effective cause of dismissal

[Employment Rights Act 1996 s.95(1).]

J commenced employment with S in 1964 as a typist and by 1992 had become manageress of S's furnishing company. Partly due to economic difficulties in 1992 and 1993, S made a number of unilateral changes to J's conditions, reducing her pay, hours of work and responsibilities. These changes took place between July and October 1993. In November 1993 J was offered a job by another furnishing company which she accepted. She resigned and claimed constructive dismissal, on the basis that the unilateral changes to her terms and conditions amounted to a series of breaches of contract which had a cumulative effect entitling her to resign and regard herself as constructively dismissed. The tribunal held that although the unilateral changes did amount to breaches of contract, J had not proved that her resignation was a consequence of those breaches. J appealed and S cross appealed.

Held, allowing the appeal, dismissing the cross appeal and remitting the case to the tribunal, that in order to decide whether an employee has left in consequence of fundamental breach, the tribunal must look to see whether the employer's repudiatory breach was the effective cause of the resignation, *Norwest Holst Group Administration Ltd v. Harrison* [1985] I.C.R. 668, [1985] C.L.Y. 1151, *Walker v. Josiah Wedgwood & Sons Ltd* [1978] I.C.R. 744, [1978] C.L.Y. 904 and *O'Grady v. Financial Management Group Services Ltd* (Unreported, 1994) followed. It was important to appreciate that in a situation of potential constructive dismissal there may have been concurrent causes operating on the mind of an employee whose employer had committed fundamental breaches of contract. Where there was more than one cause operating on the mind of an employee it was the task of the tribunal to determine whether the employer's actions were the effective cause of the resignation. In the instant case the tribunal did not ask themselves the right question; having found that J's departure was prompted by the offer of alternative employment the tribunal took the view that it therefore followed that she had not left in consequence of the fundamental breaches of contract. Had the tribunal asked the right question it would have been bound to conclude that the main operative cause of J's resignation was the very serious and fundamental breaches of her contract by S. In the circumstances, the tribunal was amply justified in finding that all the unilateral changes in J's terms and conditions were serious breaches of contract.

JONES v. F SIRL & SON (FURNISHERS) LTD [1997] I.R.L.R. 493, Judge Colin Smith Q.C., EAT.

2207. Dismissal—wrongful dismissal—chief executive of large public company—damages

C was given judgment on liability after being wrongfully dismissed from his position of Chief Executive of BET Plc and Chairman and President of BET Inc in the USA, when Rentokil, R, became its majority shareholder. C had a service contract with a rolling three year notice period and claimed for (1) a deliverable salary of £490,000 per annum for both contracts; (2) salary increases of 10.5 per cent per annum; (3) bonus payments of 60 per cent compared to BET's offer of six per cent; (4) £2.1 million in lost share options; (5) a three per cent discount rate on his pension, which should not be reduced for early retirement, nor because of actual pension income received during the three years; (6) £16,042 per annum for the private use of a car and chauffeur; (7) a lifetime's medical insurance cover; (8) loss of holidays at £4,027 plus interest; (9) £8,000 under an employees' share scheme; (10) unpaid salary and interest to date at four per cent. BET contended that C had failed to mitigate his loss by seeking alternative employment.

Held, assessing the award, that the following amounts were appropriate: (1) £490,000 was agreed; (2) given R's current profitability and increases in excess of 10 per cent awarded to C's successor, a figure of 10 per cent was appropriate; (3) C had exceeded his targets in each of the three years he was employed and had received the maximum of 60 per cent bonus and, on the assumption that he would have been number two in the hierarchy, he should be awarded a sum half way between those of the present two top executives, represented by 50 per cent for each of the three years; (4) it was agreed that C had previously exercised his options up to the ceiling of seven times his basic salary; however the contract was a once only grant of those options and therefore no award was appropriate; (5) the *Auty* calculation producing a figure of £495,000 was correct, *Auty v. National Coal Board* [1985] 1 W.L.R. 784, [1985] C.L.Y. 942 followed; (6) C had claimed to the Inland Revenue, and admitted in cross-examination, that his private use of the car was minimal and therefore £2,000 per annum was appropriate; (7) C, in common with other comparable employees, was entitled to lifetime medical cover with a multiplier of 14 and, taking a three per cent discount rate, at a figure of £3,166 per annum; (8) the figures were agreed; (9) the whole claim was excluded by an exemption clause, and (10) the figures were agreed. With regard to mitigation, C had made proper attempts to obtain alternative employment but was unlikely to be successful considering the narrow range of external appointments in comparable positions and his age of 55.

CLARK v. BET PLC [1997] I.R.L.R. 348, Timothy Walker, J., QBD.

2208. Employment Act 1989 (c.38)—Commencement No.2 Order

EMPLOYMENT ACT 1989 (COMMENCEMENT NO.2) ORDER 1997, SI 1997 134 (C.9); made under the Employment Act 1989 s.30. Commencement details: bringing into force various provisions of the Act on March 3, 1997; £0.65.

This Order brings into force the remaining provisions of the Employment Act 1989.

2209. Employment agencies—client introducing temporary workers to other business—commission

R ran an employment agency which hired various temporary workers for C. It was agreed that if C took the workers on permanently, C would not be liable to pay a placement fee to R. C introduced the workers to another employment agency, who then supplied the same workers back to C. However under cl.6 of the standard terms and conditions, C as "the client" was liable to pay a fee to R, "the employment business", where C introduced a worker to "other employers with resulting engagement from .... provided that the engagement (took) place within six months the termination of any temporary assignment". The term "engagement" included "employment or use, whether under a contract of services or for services".

By cl.3, the fee for such an introduction was to be calculated as a percentage of "the annual commencing gross taxable pay ... by the client to the (worker)".

Held, that C was not liable under the agreement for introducing the workers to another agency because: (1) on a proper construction of cl.6, "other employers" did not include "other employment businesses", and (2) alternatively, the "annual commencing pay" of the temporary workers could not be calculated and the possible range of earnings prevented a term from being implied to remedy the problem. Insofar as cl.3 and cl.6 referred to the calculation of an introduction fee for temporary workers, they were void for uncertainty, but severable from the remainder of the contract.

RENEE MAYER AGENCY v. CRS, February 14, 1997, H.H.J. Morgan, CC (Warrington). [*Ex rel.* Timothy Hanson, Barrister, 7 Fountain Court, Birmingham].

2210.   Employment Appeal Tribunal—jurisdiction to hear appeals from industrial tribunal in breach of contract case

[Employment Protection (Consolidation) Act 1978 s.136; Industrial Tribunals Act 1996 s.21.]

Held, that the EAT did not have jurisdiction to hear appeals arising from decisions of industrial tribunals which involved breach of contract claims after the Industrial Tribunals Act 1996 came into force. Under the Employment Protection (Consolidation) Act 1978 s.136, the EAT had jurisdiction to hear appeals on a point of law which arose from any decision under, or by virtue of, a number of Acts, including "this Act", and the EAT's jurisdiction under s.136 extended to hearing appeals in breach of contract cases which, in 1994, had been brought within the jurisdiction of industrial tribunals. However, s.136 was repealed by the 1996 Act s.21, which made no reference to "this Act" and a literal construction of that section therefore deprived the EAT of the power to hear appeals from decisions of industrial tribunals where their jurisdiction derived from the 1996 Act. It was for Parliament, and not the courts, to correct what appeared to be a lacuna in the legislation.

PENDRAGON PLC v. JACKSON, *The Times*, November 19, 1997, Morison, J., EAT.

2211.   Employment Appeal Tribunal—procedure—review of decision to dismiss appeal—duty to give reasons for rejecting application for review

[Employment Appeal Tribunal Rules 1993 (SI 1993 2854) r.31 (2).]

P appealed against a decision of the EAT refusing his application for review of a decision to dismiss appeals against an industrial tribunal decision and declining to give reasons for that refusal. P contended that the refusal to review the decision amounted to an order finally disposing of the proceedings under the Employment Appeal Tribunal Rules 1993 r.31 (2), and that he was entitled to be given reasons as his application had been made within the prescribed time limit.

Held, dismissing the appeal, that P's interpretation of r.31 was incorrect. He had two appeals from the industrial tribunal decision, one of which was against the original decision and the second concerned a review of that decision. The dismissal of those appeals had been accompanied by a reasoned judgment following an oral hearing and amounted, therefore, to a valid order disposing of the proceedings. Although P was entitled to seek a review of the order, the refusal of his application, without an oral hearing or written reasons, was valid, as the proceedings had already been disposed of under the Rules.

Observed, that whilst the EAT was not obliged to give reasons when rejecting a review application, it would be good practice to state briefly the reasons for doing so.

PERSSON v. MATRA MARCONI SPACE UK LTD, *The Times*, December 10, 1996, Mummery, L.J., CA.

2212. Employment Appeal Tribunal–reporting restrictions–circumstances in which tribunal had power to make an order protecting identity of parties

[Industrial Tribunals Act 1996 s.31 (2).]

N sought to challenge a restricted reporting order made by the President of the EAT in an appeal from a decision of an industrial tribunal upholding a complaint of sexual harassment by A, a transsexual, against her employers, B. N contended that the appeal tribunal did not have jurisdiction to make the order in the circumstances of the case.

Held, discharging the order, that if the press wanted to make representations about a restricted reporting order, it should apply to be joined as a party, although joinder would not automatically be granted and the applicant would have to make out a good case. The Industrial Tribunals Act 1996 s.31 (2) appeared to set out the circumstances in which a restricted reporting order could be made by the appeal tribunal, namely on appeals from an industrial tribunal's grant or refusal of a restricted reporting order or appeals from interlocutory decisions of the tribunal where the tribunal had made such an order. Neither situation applied here and, as Parliament had considered the circumstances in which an order should be made, no inherent power to make an order could be implied. A decision of the industrial tribunal as to liability could not be interpreted as an interlocutory decision simply because no determination as to remedy had been made, and in any case, without evidence, it could not be said that the fact that a person was a transsexual was grounds for protecting their identity.

A v. B, *ex p.* NEWS GROUP NEWSPAPERS LTD, *The Times,* July 4, 1997, Morison, J., Cons Ct.

2213. Engineering Construction Board–levy on employers

INDUSTRIAL TRAINING LEVY (ENGINEERING CONSTRUCTION BOARD) ORDER 1997, SI 1997 408; made under the Industrial Training Act 1982 s.11, s.12. In force: February 19, 1997; £1.95.

This Order gives effect to proposals of the Engineering Construction Industry Training Board for the imposition of a levy on employers in the construction industry for the purpose of raising money towards meeting the expenses of the Board.

2214. Equal opportunities–part time workers–pension schemes–limitation of effects in time did not apply to right to join scheme–European Union

[Council Directive 86/378 on equal treatment for men and women in occupational social security schemes.]

D commenced employment with S in 1972 as a part time helper with the aged. She worked seven hours a week until she took voluntary early retirement in November 1990. Part time workers working less than 40 per cent of the normal working week were excluded from S's pension scheme until January 1991, when the restriction was lifted to bring the scheme into line with the requirements of Council Directive 86/378. Transitional arrangements were introduced to attribute notional insurance periods to those employees previously excluded from the scheme. Affiliation to the pension scheme was compulsory for S's employees under Dutch law. D commenced proceedings claiming that when she agreed to take voluntary early retirement she should have been made aware of the forthcoming changes to the pension scheme, and that had she been made aware she would have delayed her retirement to take advantage of the transitional arrangements. She claimed that under the Treaty of Rome 1957 Art.119 she should be entitled to a pension based on her period of service after April 8, 1976, the date of the judgment in *Defrenne v. Societe Anonyme Belge de Navigation Aerienne (SABENA) (C43/75)* [1976] E.C.R. 455, [1976] C.L.Y. 1164, or alternatively in respect of her period of service since May 17, 1990, the date of the judgment in *Barber v. Guardian Royal Exchange Assurance Group* (C262/88) [1990] I.R.L.R. 240, [1987] C.L.Y. 1633. The court at first instance stayed the proceedings and referred to the Court a number of questions including, inter alia, whether the right to join an occupational pension scheme falls within the scope of Art.119 of the Treaty and is covered by the prohibition on discrimination, and if so, whether the limitation of the effects in time of the judgment in the *Barber* case applies to the right to join an occupational pension scheme and to the right to payment of a retirement pension where the employee was excluded from the membership of such a scheme in breach of Art.119.

Held, answering the first question in the affirmative and the second question in the negative, that (1) as held in *Fisscher v. Voorhuis Hengelo BV (C128/93)* [1994] I.R.L.R. 662, [1995] 1 C.L.Y. 1999, the right to join an occupational pension scheme falls within the scope of Art.119 of the Treaty. That interpretation does not depend on the purpose of the national legislation enabling membership to be made compulsory, nor on the fact that the employer lodged an objection to the decision to make such membership compulsory; (2) as held in *Vroege v. NCIV Instituut voor Volkshuisvesting BV* (C57/93) [1994] I.R.L.R. 651, [1995] 1 C.L.Y. 2000 and *Fisscher v. Voorhuis Hengelo BV*, the limitation of the effects in time of the judgment in *Barber* do not apply to the right to join an occupational pension scheme. It has been clear since the judgment in *Bilka-Kaufhaus GmbH v. Karin Weber von Hartz (C170/84)* [1986] I.R.L.R. 317, [1987] C.L.Y. 1633 that Art.119 prohibits discrimination in the award of benefits by an occupational pension scheme which results from discrimination as regards the right to join such a scheme, and so the reasons which led the Court to limit the effects in time of the *Barber* judgment do not apply in the instant case. Since the judgment in *Bilka* imposed no time limit, the direct effect of Art.119 may be relied upon retroactively from April 8, 1976, and (3) administrators of an occupational pension scheme must, like the employer, comply with Art.119 and workers who are discriminated against may assert their rights directly against those administrators.

DIETZ v. STICHTIING THUISZORG ROTTERDAM (C435/93) [1996] I.R.L.R. 692, GF Mancini (President), ECJ.

2215. Equal pay–codes of practice

CODE OF PRACTICE ON EQUAL PAY (APPOINTED DAY) ORDER 1997, SI 1997 131 (C.6); made under the Sex Discrimination Act 1975 s.56A. Commencement details: bringing into force various provisions of the code on March 26, 1997; £1.10.

The Sex Discrimination Act 1975 provides for the Equal Opportunities Commission to issue codes of practice for the elimination in the field of employment of discrimination within the meaning of that Act. Under this Order a Code of Practice on Equal Pay came into effect on March 26, 1997.

2216. Equal pay–pregnant employee–appropriate comparators–maternity pay

See Northern Ireland: EMPLOYMENT: Gillespie v. Northern Health and Social Services Board (No.2). §5227

2217. Equal treatment–promotion–civil servants working part time–national rule governing calculation of length of service not contrary to Equal Treatment Directive–European Union

[Council Directive 76/207 on equal treatment for men and women as regards access to employment Art.3; Council Directive 75/117 on the application of the principle of equal pay for men and women; Treaty of Rome 1957 Art.119.]

G, an employee of the Bavarian state civil service who worked one half of normal working hours, applied for promotion. Under Bavarian civil service rules, promotion was to be based on, inter alia, length of service, and periods of employment during which the hours worked were between one half and two thirds of normal working hours were to be treated as equivalent to two thirds. G asked that her employment be treated as full time employment for the purposes of calculating her length of service, but her application was refused. G brought proceedings against the state on the ground that the rejection of her candidature was contrary to the Treaty of Rome 1957 Art.119, Council Directive 75/117 and Council Directive 76/

207 Art.3, contending that, as her case concerned a system for the classification of salaries, it fell within the scope of the term "pay" as used in Art.119, and, further, that, since the majority of part time employees in G's department were women, the selection process for promotion resulted in indirect discrimination.

Held, that, while the principle of equal pay for men and women enshrined in Art.119 applied to employment in the public service, Art.119 did not extend to aspects of employment other than those expressly referred to, *Defrenne v. Sabena (C149/77)* [1978] E.C.R. 1365, [1978] C.L.Y. 1291 followed. Since the Bavarian rule relating to promotion concerned access to career advancement and was only indirectly linked to pay, it did not fall within the ambit of Art.119 or Council Directive 75/117. However, Council Directive 76/207 Art.3 precluded such a rule unless it was justified by objective criteria unrelated to any sex discrimination and it was for the national court to determine whether the measure in question could be objectively justified or not.

GERSTER v. FREISTAAT BAYERN (C1/95) [1997] I.R.L.R. 699, JL Murray (President), ECJ.

2218. Equal treatment–recruitment–German law limiting compensation for discrimination by employer to three months prospective salary did not breach Equal Treatment Directive–European Union

[Council Directive 76/207 on equal treatment for men and women as regards access to employment.]

Upon a reference from a German court, the ECJ was asked to determine whether Council Directive 76/207 precluded provisions of national law which set a limit of three months' prospective salary on the amount of compensation payable to an unsuccessful job applicant who had been subjected to discrimination.

Held, that, where compensation was awarded to penalise breaches of the prohibition of discrimination, such compensation had to be more than nominal so as to guarantee effective protection and to provide a deterrent to employers, *Van Colson v. Land Nordrhein-Westfalen (C14/83)* [1984] E.C.R. 1891, [1986] C.L.Y. 1455 followed. It was also necessary that provisions circumscribing compensation payable for discrimination were analagous to the limits set down in other areas of domestic civil and labour law. Council Directive 76/207 precluded domestic law provisions which required fault to be established before discrimination compensation could be awarded, *Dekker v. Stichting Vormingscentrum voor Jonge Volwassenen Plus (C177/88)* [1990] E.C.R. I-3941, [1991] C.L.Y. 4081 followed. Provided that the employer could prove that the unsuccessful job applicant would not have been recruited even if he had not been discriminated against, a ceiling of three months' salary was lawful. However, where the applicant would have been successful but for the discrimination the same limit could not be applied. Neither could a limit of six months' earnings be imposed on an aggregate amount of compensation where claims were made by several applicants.

DRAEHMPAEHL v. URANIA IMMOBILIENSERVICE OHG (C180/95), *The Times*, May 2, 1997, GC Rodriguez Iglesias (President), ECJ.

2219. Freedom of movement–employment rights–spouse not EU national–no exercise of right to freedom of movement–spouse not entitled to rely on EU law–European Union

[Council Regulation 1612/68 on freedom of movement for workers within the Community Art.11; Treaty of Rome 1957 Art.48.]

Held, that a national of a non-Member State who was married to a national of a Member State was not entitled to rely on Council Regulation 1612/68 Art.11 to challenge the validity of a law of that country which placed limitations on the length of an employment contract where the worker had never exercised the right to freedom of movement within the Community. Free movement rights under Art.11 were not intended to apply to wholly internal situations where there was no link with EC law, and in such circumstances it was irrelevant that the national law was incompatible with the Treaty of Rome 1957 Art.48(2).

LAND NORDRHEIN-WESTFALEN v. UECKER (C64/96); JACQUET v. LAND NORDRHEIN-WESTFALEN (C65/96), *The Times*, August 11, 1997, JC Moitinho de Almeida (President), ECJ.

2220. Freedom of movement—Turkish workers—right to reside in Member State whilst seeking new employment—European Union

[Treaty of Rome 1957 Art.6, Art.48, Art.49, Art.50; Agreement of 12 September 1963 establishing an Association between the European Community and Turkey.]

Under the Treaty of Rome 1957 and subsequent agreements a Turkish national has a right of abode in a Member State whilst seeking employment. T, a Turkish national, had been legally employed on German ships and had been granted a series of fixed term residence permits, the last of which stated that it would expire when T ceased to be employed in German shipping. When T left his job as a seaman, he applied to the German authorities for an unlimited residence permit to enable him to seek employment on land. His application was refused and, on appeal, the matter was referred to the ECJ for a ruling on the interpretation and effect on the Council of the EC/Turkey Association Decision No.1/80 Art.6.

Held, under the Agreement of 12 September 1963 establishing an Association between the European Community and Turkey, the contracting parties were to be guided by the Treaty of Rome 1957 Art.48, Art.49 and Art.50 in order to progressively secure freedom of movement for workers between them. Whilst Decision No.1/80 did not confer full freedom of movement on Turkish workers, it did give them certain rights in a Member State they had lawfully entered and been employed in for a certain period and, under Art.6, this included a right of residence. T had been legally employed in Germany for almost eight years and therefore enjoyed free access to any paid employment he chose in that state under Art.6. Article 48 of the EC Treaty entitled workers of a Member State to reside in another Member State for the purpose of seeking employment there and, in accordance with the EC/Turkey Agreement and Decision No.1/80, Member States must treat Turkish nationals with rights in accordance with Treaty principles, so far as possible. In order to give full effect to Art.6, a Turkish national who had legally worked in a Member State for more than four years had to be entitled to reside there for a reasonable period while seeking new employment, if his right of free access to any paid employment of his choice was not to be deprived of any substance. It was for the Member State to decide how long that reasonable period should be, but it had to be long enough not to endanger T's prospects of finding new employment.

TETIK v. LAND BERLIN (C171/95) [1997] All E.R. (EC) 464, Judge not specified, ECJ.

2221. Industrial tribunals—discretion—extension of time limit for serving notice of appearance by respondent—balance of risk of prejudice to be considered as between parties

[Industrial Tribunals (Constitution and Rules of Procedure) Regulations 1993 (SI 1993 2687) Sch.1.]

KS appealed against an industrial tribunal decision refusing a time extension for the serving of a notice of appearance after the expiry of the time limit provided by the Industrial Tribunals (Constitution and Rules of Procedure) Regulations 1993 Sch.1 r.3(1). The tribunal chair refused the extension on the ground that KS had disregarded its responsibilities and failed to give valid explanations for the delay.

Held, allowing the appeal and remitting the matter to a different tribunal chair, that it was the respondent's duty when seeking a time extension for serving a notice of appearance prior to a full hearing on the merits to put before the tribunal all relevant documents and factual material to explain both non-compliance with the time limit and the basis of the respondent's case. The tribunal had to take all such material and other relevant factors into account in deciding whether to exercise the discretion to permit a time extension. In so doing, the possible prejudice to either party had to be weighed in the balance. The tribunal had erred in its failure to take into account the merits of KS's defence or the prejudice KS could suffer if the extension were refused. Such factors also had to be balanced against the prejudice S would suffer if the extension was granted.

KWIK SAVE STORES LTD v. SWAIN [1997] I.C.R. 49, Mummery, J., EAT.

2222. Industrial tribunals–EAT not permitted to interfere with decision where no error of law and decision not perverse

PO appealed against the EAT's decision to allow an appeal by L, a postman who had been dismissed for wilfully delaying delivery of the mail. An industrial tribunal found that, although PO's investigation of the incident which led to L's dismissal was inadequate and the dismissal unfair in this respect, no compensation or order for reinstatement should be made because L's conduct was blameworthy. It concluded that PO would probably have dismissed L, and acted fairly in so doing, even if a more thorough investigation had been undertaken and that on the balance of probabilities L had wilfully delayed delivery. The EAT allowed L's appeal on the ground that the tribunal had failed to deal with the main part of L's defence and remitted the matter for a rehearing.

Held, allowing the appeal, that it was not for the EAT to interfere in a decision of an industrial tribunal where the tribunal had neither erred in law nor reached a decision which was perverse. Having weighed the evidence, the tribunal had decided that it was unnecessary to deal with the main part of L's defence and, as the tribunal of fact, it was quite entitled to reach such a conclusion.

POST OFFICE v. LEWIS, *The Times*, April 25, 1997, Henry, L.J., CA.

2223. Industrial tribunals–jurisdiction–claim arising where contract of employment terminated before work commenced

See EMPLOYMENT: Sarker v. South Tees Acute Hospitals NHS Trust. §2203

2224. Industrial tribunals–jurisdiction–compensation for injury to feelings

See EMPLOYMENT: Cleveland Ambulance NHS Trust v. Blane. §2190

2225. Industrial tribunals–no case to answer–reliance upon earlier county court decision based on similar facts did not amount to error on part of tribunal

MG appealed against an EAT decision ([1997] I.C.R. 417) that the industrial tribunal hearing an unfair dismissal claim arising from similar facts of a pension dispute, which was the subject of an earlier county court decision, had made references to the binding nature of the court decision that were fatal to the validity of its own findings. The EAT held that the tribunal erred in accepting MG's submission of no case to answer on the conclusion of R's evidence, based on an erroneous finding of issue estoppel and that there was insufficient identity between the issues before the court and tribunal with the result that the tribunal was not entitled to find itself bound by the former, *Sheffield v. Oxford Controls Co Ltd* [1979] I.C.R. 396, [1979] C.L.Y. 1012 considered. MG contended that the EAT had misconstrued the tribunal decision, in that there was sufficient material before the tribunal for it to base the finding of no case to answer, with the county court decision merely providing support for the tribunal decision, not dictating the final conclusion.

Held, allowing the appeal and upholding the tribunal decision, that taking the decision as a whole the misuse of language occasioned by the use of the word "binding" was an attempt to show that the tribunal was looking to the antecedent finding of the court as evidence for the existence of exceptional circumstances to support a departure from normal practice of not entertaining a no case submission. The tribunal had correctly directed itself in law on the limitations of issue estoppel and been aware of the issues raised in both the pensions dispute and unfair dismissal claim. The tribunal reached its own conclusions on the oral and documentary evidence and it was unrealistic to believe that, in the absence of the county court proceedings, the tribunal would have decided the matter in any other way.

JONES v. MID GLAMORGAN CC (NO.2),Trans. Ref: EATRF 97/0005/B, May 13, 1997,Waite, L.J., CA.

2226. Industrial tribunals-power to regulate own procedure-order concerning exchange of witness statements within powers

[Industrial Tribunals (Constitution and Rules of Procedure) Regulations 1993 (SI 1993 2687) Sch.1 r.9, Sch.1 r.13.1.]

Held, that an industrial tribunal acted within its powers under the Rules of Procedure r.9 and r.13(1) set out in the Industrial Tribunals (Constitution and Rules of Procedure) Regulations 1993 Sch.1 in making an order that there should be simultaneous exchange of statements of witnesses on whom the parties intended to rely and that no further witnesses should be called without the tribunal's leave. Notwithstanding a direction issued by the President of Industrial Tribunals to the effect that the preparation of witness statements prior to the hearing was a matter for the parties' discretion, r.9 and r.13, properly construed, gave an industrial tribunal the power to regulate its own procedure in the interests of achieving a fair and efficient hearing of cases.

EUROBELL (HOLDINGS) PLC v. BARKER, *The Times,* November 12, 1997, Morison, J., EAT.

2227. Industrial tribunals-pre hearing review-service of order-determination when order "sent"-time ran from date of receipt

[Industrial Tribunals (Constitution and Rules of Procedure) Regulations 1993 (SI 1993 2687) Sch.1; Interpretation Act 1978 s.7.]

On November 20, 1996 O was ordered by a chairman at a pre hearing review to pay a deposit as a condition of continuing his claims of race discrimination and unfair dismissal against his employers, I. The order was posted on November 22 and received by O's representatives on November 25. O paid the deposit in cash on December 13. On December 17, the chairman struck out the case after being mistakenly informed that the deposit had not been paid. Upon an application for a review of that decision by O a full tribunal revoked the original striking out order. It held that the 21 day period for payment of the deposit, under the Industrial Tribunals (Constitution and Rules of Procedure) Regulations 1993 Sch.1 r.7(7), ran from the date when the order was posted, not when it was received by the applicant and had therefore expired, but granted O an extension of time for the payment of the deposit to December 13. I appealed on the basis that the power to extend time under the 1993 Regulations, r.15 did not extend to r.7(7), and O cross appealed on the ground that time ran from the date of receipt or delivery of the order and not when it was posted, by virtue of the Interpretation Act 1978 s.7.

Held, dismissing the appeal and allowing the cross appeal, that r.7(7) was to be interpreted in accordance with the Interpretation Act 1978 s.7, and the period of 21 days began with date of deemed service in the ordinary course of post unless the contrary was proved, *R. v. County of London Quarter Sessions Appeals Committee, ex p. Rossi* [1956] 1 Q.B. 682, [1956] C.L.Y. 5264 distinguished, *R. v. Secretary of State for the Home Department, ex p. Yeboah* [1987] 1 W.L.R. 1586, [1988] C.L.Y. 1858 and *Derrybaa Ltd v. Castro-Blanco* [1986] I.C.R. 546, [1986] C.L.Y. 1199 considered. In the instant case, it was proved that the order was delivered on November 25 and the consequence was that payment of the deposit on December 13 was within the period of 21 days.

Observed, that the power to extend time under r.15 could apply to cases falling within r.7.

IMMIGRATION ADVISORY SERVICE v. OOMMEN [1997] I.C.R. 683, Keene, J., EAT.

2228. Industrial tribunals—reporting restrictions—identification of parties—public interest considerations

[Industrial Tribunals (Constitution and Rules of Procedure) Regulations 1993 (SI 1993 2687) Sch.1 r.14.]

Held, that, where an industrial tribunal was hearing a case of alleged sexual misconduct, it should not accede automatically to a request by one or both parties that a direction be made under the Industrial Tribunals (Constitution and Rules of Procedure) Regulations 1993 Sch.1 r.14 to prohibit identification of the parties involved, but should give careful consideration to whether it was in the public interest to prevent the press making such information public.

X v. Z LTD, *The Times*, April 18, 1997, Staughton, L.J., CA.

2229. Industrial tribunals—sitting "in private"—national security—applicant's husband excluded from hearing

[Employment Protection (Consolidation) Act 1978 Sch.9.]

F, a former employee of the FCO, brought proceedings against the FCO in October 1995 claiming unfair dismissal and sex discrimination. In March 1996 the tribunal made an order that the hearings should take place in private on the grounds of national security, acting pursuant to a ministerial direction issued under the Employment Protection (Consolidation) Act 1978 Sch.9 para.1 (4A). The tribunal further ordered that F's husband should be excluded from the hearing. F appealed.

Held, allowing the appeal, that the expression "in private" is not absolute in effect. F wished to have her husband present, not only to support her but also to assist her representative in the presentation of the case. No specific or personal objection had been taken by the FCO to the presence of F's husband. Moreover, the purpose of the ministerial direction is to protect national security, and there was no suggestion that those interests were prejudiced by the presence of F's husband. The meaning of "in private" is a question of fact and degree, and in the instant case the tribunal would still be sitting "in private" notwithstanding the attendance of F's husband.

FRY v. FOREIGN AND COMMONWEALTH OFFICE [1997] I.C.R. 512, Mummery, J., EAT.

2230. Industrial tribunals—unfair dismissal claim—chairman in minority—lay members not given opportunity to approve written reasons for decision—claim remitted for rehearing

Where the written reasons given by an industrial tribunal had not been approved, the case should be remitted for a rehearing. M's complaint that he had been unfairly selected for redundancy by his employers, MD, was upheld by the two lay members of the industrial tribunal, but not by its chairman. MD wished to appeal against the decision, but, before the appeal was heard, it became apparent that the two lay members of the tribunal felt that, in producing the extended written reasons for the decision, the chairman had not given them sufficient opportunity to check or approve the final draft of the decision before signing it and promulgating it. As this created doubt over the accuracy and completeness of the written reasons for the decision which was the subject of the appeal, the EAT held that the only way of doing justice to both M and MD was to remit the claim for rehearing by a differently constituted tribunal. M appealed, contending that the proper course was to invite the original tribunal to confirm and clarify the reasons for their decision before proceeding with MD's appeal.

Held, dismissing the appeal, that the role of the Court of Appeal was limited to ensuring that the EAT had exercised its discretion lawfully and properly in deciding how best to resolve this difficult situation. Given that the arguments put forward by M and MD were equally persuasive, the court could not say that, in deciding to remit the claim for rehearing, the EAT had used an approach or produced a result that was clearly wrong.

MAURE v. MacMILLAN DISTRIBUTION LTD, *The Independent*, February 4, 1997,Waite, L.J., CA.

2231. Insolvency–employee claims–DTI liability for compensation–partnership not insolvent unless all partners bankrupt

[Employment Protection (Consolidation) Act 1978 s.122(1), s.127.]

F, who was employed by a partnership comprising C and H, was dismissed when the firm ceased trading. She brought a claim for unfair dismissal and arrears of wages against C and H. Given the likelihood that neither C nor H could meet any order for compensation the Secretary of State forTrade and Industry was joined as a party to the proceedings. In the case of payments other than a redundancy payment it was necessary for F to show, for the purposes of the Employment Protection (Consolidation) Act 1978 s.122(1)(a) that her employer "had become insolvent". At the tribunal hearing it was found that only C had been adjudicated bankrupt and the tribunal concluded that H was not insolvent for the purposes of s.127 of the 1978 Act. There being no express provision in s.127 concerning the determination of when a partnership was insolvent, the tribunal held that F was entitled to elect which of the partners she wished to proceed against and since C was clearly insolvent F could also proceed against the Secretary of State. The Secretary of State appealed.

Held, allowing the appeal, that for the purposes of s.122(1)(a) of the 1978 Act the Secretary of State would not be liable to meet the claims of a former employee against a partnership unless and until every partner had been adjudged bankrupt and was therefore "insolvent" under s.127 of the 1978 Act.

SECRETARY OF STATE FOR TRADE AND INDUSTRY v. FORDE [1997] I.C.R. 231, Judge Hicks Q.C., EAT.

2232. Insolvency–employee claims–guarantee institution responsible for payment of claims where employee resides and works in Member State other than that in which employer established–European Union

[Council Directive 80/987 relating to the protection of employees in the event of the insolvency of their employer Art.3.]

Where an employee lives and works in a different member state to their employer, the state institution responsible under Council Directive 80/987 Art.3 for guaranteeing the employee's payment on the employer's insolvency will normally be the state in which the employer was established.

Held, that, where an employer was established in a Member State other than the one in which an employee lived and worked, the guarantee institution responsible under Council Directive 80/987 Art.3 for guaranteeing payment of an employee's claims on the employer's insolvency was the institution of the state in which either it had been decided to open proceedings for the collective satisfaction of creditors' claims, or it had been established that the employer's business had closed down, which would normally be the state in which the employer was established.

DANMARKS AKTIVE HANDELSREJSENDE v. LONMODTAGERNES GARANTIFOND (C117/96), *The Times*, November 20, 1997, JC Moitinho de Almeida (President), ECJ.

2233. Insolvency–employee claims–unfair dismissal–determination of employer's insolvency

[Employment Protection (Consolidation) Act 1978 s.106(5), s.122, s.127(1); Council Directive 80/987 relating to the protection of employees in the event of the insolvency of their employer.]

M was unfairly dismissed by A, which ceased trading and was struck off the register. The industrial tribunal determined that A was "insolvent" within the meaning of the Employment Protection (Consolidation) Act 1978 s.106(5) and ordered that the Secretary of State should pay the compensation out of the National Insurance Fund under the 1978 Act. The Secretary of State appealed on the basis that the tribunal should have used s.127(1)(c) of the Act to determine whether the company was insolvent.

Held, allowing the appeal, that (1) the relevant section for determining insolvency for the purposes of s.122 was s.127(1) which provided an exhaustive list of criteria; (2) it was not enough for s.127(1)(c) that the company could not pay its debts and the tribunal had made no other findings of fact which brought the case within the correct definition; (3) there was no tension between that definition and Council Directive 80/987 relating to the protection of employees in the event of the insolvency of their employer from compensation from the National Insurance Fund as the latter was not intended to apply to a complaint to an industrial tribunal.

SECRETARY OF STATE FOR EMPLOYMENT v. McGLONE [1997] B.C.C. 101, Judge Peter Clark, E.A.T.

2234. Licensed premises—persons under 18—deregulation

DEREGULATION (EMPLOYMENT IN BARS) ORDER 1997, SI 1997 957; made under the Deregulation and Contracting Out Act 1994 s.1. In force: March 7, 1997; £1.10.

This Order amends the Licensing Act 1964 to disapply the prohibition on employing persons under 18 in bars from the employment of persons of or over 16 pursuant to a training scheme approved for the purpose by the Secretary of State.

2235. Maternity pay—compensation of employers

STATUTORY MATERNITY PAY (COMPENSATION OF EMPLOYERS) AMENDMENT REGULATIONS 1997, SI 1997 574; made under the Social Security Contributions and Benefits Act 1992 s.167, s.171, s.175. In force: April 6, 1997; £0.65.

These Regulations amend the Statutory Maternity Pay (Compensation of Employers) and Miscellaneous Amendment Regulations 1994 (SI 1994 1882) which enable an employer to recover payments of statutory maternity pay, and, if he is a small employer, an additional amount in respect of such pay. These Regulations increase the additional amount from 5.5 per cent to 6.5 per cent of the payment of statutory maternity pay.

2236. Maternity rights—notification of intention to return—illness prevented return on due date

[Employment Protection (Consolidation) Act 1978 s.45(1), s.47(3), s.47(4), s.47(5), s.55.]

G, a long serving employee with K, became pregnant in late 1993 and went on maternity leave on April 8, 1994. She gave birth on May 20, 1994 and in July 1994 gave statutory notice of her intention to return to work on August 12, 1994. On that date G obtained a doctor's certificate stating that she was unfit to return to work and personally handed it to her supervisor the same day. She obtained further sickness certificates covering the period to November 7, 1994. On November 3, 1994 K informed G that since she had failed to exercise her statutory right to return to work her contract of employment had terminated. G applied to an industrial tribunal, claiming unfair dismissal. The tribunal found that G had failed under s.47(3) of the Employment Protection (Consolidation) Act 1978 to postpone validly her proposed date of return, but the proper construction of the events of August 12, 1994 was that G exercised her right to return to work on that day and that, having done so, she handed in a medical certificate and went on sick leave. The tribunal then found that K's actions on November 3, 1994 amounted to an unfair dismissal. K appealed, arguing that the tribunal erred in law in construing G's actions on August 12, 1994 as an exercise of her right to return to work.

Held, allowing the appeal and remitting the matter to the same tribunal, that (1) the combination of s.45(1), s.56 and s.47(5), together with s.47(3) and s.47(4) of the Employment Protection (Consolidation) Act 1978, led to the conclusion that as a matter of statutory construction something more was required of an employee to complete the statutory process than simply to acquire the right to return by a valid s.33 notice and to exercise it by a valid s.47 notice. What was required was an actual physical return to work, regardless of the unfairness which it might impose in particular cases. The conclusion was not altered by consideration of the relevant authorities, *Lavery v. Plessey Telecommunications Ltd* [1983] I.R.L.R. 202, [1983] C.L.Y. 1252 and *Dowuona v. John Lewis Plc* [1987] I.R.L.R. 310, [1988] C.L.Y. 1288 followed, and *Institute of the Motor Industry v. Harvey* [1992] I.R.L.R. 343, [1992] C.L.Y. 1952 considered. An actual return to work involved more than sending, or calling in for the sole purpose of delivering, a medical certificate, and (2) the fact that G's claim for a deemed unfair dismissal under s.56 of the Employment Protection (Consolidation) Act 1978 failed was no objection to a claim under s.55 of the 1978 Act if she established as a fact that there was a contract of employment between her and K Ltd in existence on November 3, 1994, and that she was then dismissed.

KWIK SAVE STORES LTD v. GREAVES [1997] I.R.L.R. 268, Judge Hicks Q.C., EAT.

2237. Maternity rights—notification of intention to return—illness preventing return by notified date—whether dismissal for failure to return unfair

C commenced employment with L in July 1989. In October 1994 she informed the Chief Executive, W, that she was pregnant and would be commencing maternity leave on April 17, 1995 and returning to work on August 21. On August 15 C confirmed that she would be returning to work on August 21 but on August 18 she wrote stating that she was ill and enclosing a two week sickness certificate from her doctor. C requested that L provide her with a form to claim SSP which was forwarded on August 27. On August 25 W wrote to C explaining what her responsibilities would be when she returned to work. On September 1 C provided another two week sick note and obtained a further note for six weeks on September 15. On September 18 W wrote to C stating that because she had not returned to work within the statutory four week period beyond her original notified date of return her employment had been terminated "by effect of the provisions of the legislation and your illness combined". C presented a complaint of unfair dismissal and sex discrimination, which was upheld by the industrial tribunal. L appealed.

Held, dismissing the appeal, that (1) on the facts of the present case, the tribunal was entitled to conclude that C's letter of August 18 was not a notification of the postponement of the date of return, but was an assertion that she remained an employee who would be absent from work through sickness and claiming SSP as an employee, *Kelly v. Liverpool Maritime Terminals* [1988] I.R.L.R. 310, [1989] C.L.Y. 1478, distinguished. The actions of L demonstrated an intention to continue the contract and not to treat it as being at an end at the expiry of four weeks after the notified day of return. There was no agreement under the contract that it would terminate on expiry of the statutory right to return, *Crees v. Royal London Insurance* [1997] I.R.L.R. 85, [1997] C.L.Y. 2239 distinguished. The tribunal did not err in treating W's letter of September 18 as a dismissal, and (2) the tribunal did not err in holding that C had been discriminated against on the ground of her sex. C was dismissed because of the breakdown in relations between herself and W. Comparing her case with that of a man whose relationship has similarly broken down, in C's case L used as an excuse for dismissing her a fact which applied only to a woman, namely the expiry of the four week period following maternity leave, *Brown v. Rentokil Ltd*

[1995] I.R.L.R. 211 distinguished, *Webb v. EMO Air Cargo (UK) Ltd (No.2)* [1995] I.R.L.R. 645, [1995] 1 C.L.Y. 2041 considered.

LEWIS WOOLF GRIPTIGHT LTD v. CORFIELD [1997] I.R.L.R. 432, Judge Peter Clark, EAT.

2238. **Maternity rights–notification of intention to return–illness preventing return by notified date–whether dismissal for failure to return unfair**

[Employment Protection (Consolidation) Act 1978 s.39, s.42(1), s.140.]

C, who had more than two years' continuous employment with RLI, commenced her maternity leave on October 1, 1994. The provisions in her contract of employment dealing with maternity rights included a clause to the effect that if she did not return to work by the end of the 29 week period beginning with the week of the child's birth, or at the end of a single further permissible extension of four weeks, then her contract terminated with immediate effect. C gave notice in January 1995 that she intended to return to work at the end of her period of maternity leave. However in March 1995 she indicated that, due to illness, she wished to postpone her date of return to work for four weeks. RLI replied that she could do so but that the last possible day on which she could return was May 12, 1995 and that she must give three weeks' notice prior to that date. C gave the required notice but did not in fact return to work due to her prolonged illness, and was informed by RLI that her contract had accordingly terminated. Her complaint of unfair dismissal was rejected by an industrial tribunal on the basis that she had not been dismissed. C appealed, arguing that the effect of the Employment Protection (Consolidation) Act 1978 s.42(1) was that by the simple act of giving notice of her intention to return C had indeed returned to work and it was immaterial that she was at the relevant time unfit to return to work.

Held, dismissing the appeal, that the return to work referred to in s.39 and s.42 of the 1978 Act was a phyiscal return to work in the ordinary sense of language. An employee was to exercise her right to return under s.42(1) by giving notice and then by returning to work, *Kelly v. Liverpool Maritime Terminals* [1988] I.R.L.R. 310, [1989] C.L.Y. 1478, and *Hilton International Hotels (UK) Ltd v. Kaissi* [1994] I.R.L.R. 270 considered. If C's arguments were correct then s.42(5) and s.42(6), which dealt with a return to work during a period of industrial action, would largely be otiose; (2) the clause in C's contract which stated that a failure to return to work within the period of maternity leave or to give proper notice of an intention to do so would result in the immediate termination of the contract did not exclude or limit any provision of the 1978 Act and accordingly was not avoided by s.140. The clause did no more than repeat the effect of the statute as interpreted in *Kelly v. Liverpool Maritime Terminals*.

CREES v. ROYAL LONDON INSURANCE [1997] I.R.L.R. 85, J Hull Q.C., EAT.

2239. **Maternity rights–refusal of alternative post–seagoing stewardess requesting shore based post**

[Sex Discrimination Act 1975 s.1(1), s.6(2), s.50(1).]

I was employed by P&O as a seagoing stewardess. She became pregnant in July 1994 and informed the personnel manager that she wished to work on shore after the 28th week of her pregnancy. On the facts found by the industrial tribunal, the personnel manager said, "We don't do that any more", and took no further steps to find her alternative work. Evidence was presented to the tribunal that suitable temporary work was available for I on shore. I's baby was born on April 28, 1995. Between February 1 and March 14 she received higher rate maternity pay, at 90 per cent of her salary; from March 15 to June 6 she received lower rate maternity pay of £52.50 per week and after June 7 she was on income support. She returned to work on November 1, 1995. I claimed that she had suffered unlawful sex discrimination contrary to the Sex Discrimination Act 1975 s.1(1)(a) and s.6(2)(a) in that she had been refused access to opportunities of transfer on the grounds of pregnancy. The tribunal rejected her claim and I appealed, contending in addition to her main claim of discrimination that the tribunal failed to consider I's claim that the statutory maternity pay and other benefits received by I did not constitute an "adequate allowance" as defined in *Gillespie v. Northern Health and Social Services Board (C342/93)* [1996] I.R.L.R. 214, [1996] 1 C.L.Y. 2570.

Held, finding that I had suffered unlawful discrimination and remitting the case for determination of remedies, that (1) the tribunal erred in basing its decision that no discrimination occured on a comparison between a pregnant woman and a sick man. It is well established that no comparison is necessary because pregnancy is a female only condition, *Webb v. EMO Air Cargo (UK) Ltd (C32/93)* [1994] I.R.L.R. 482, [1994] C.L.Y. 4825, and *Dekker v. Stichting Vormingscentrum voor Jonge Volwassenen (VJV-Centrum) Plus (C177/88)* [1991] I.R.L.R. 27, [1991] C.L.Y. 4081 applied. The correct inference from the facts was that it was the policy of P&O that no women seafarers were offered shore based work after the 28th week of pregnancy, *King v. Great Britain China Centre Ltd* [1991] I.R.L.R. 513, [1992] C.L.Y. 1959 applied. Further, an employer cannot avoid the effect of s.6(2)(a) of the 1975 Act by contracting out a job to which the employee could be transferred. Section 50(1) of the 1975 Act was inserted for the avoidance of doubt where access to benefits, facilities or services are provided indirectly by the employer through a third party and it follows that the same principle applies to access to opportunities for promotion, transfer or training, *O'Shea v. Royle Publications Ltd* (Unreported, 1995) followed, and (2) it was not appropriate to extend the principle of adequate pay referred to in *Gillespie* either to a claim brought against an employer which is not an emanation of the state, or in respect of a period outside the statutory maternity leave period, or in circumstances where the maternity pay paid to I was not adequate.

ISKE v. P&O EUROPEAN FERRIES (DOVER) LTD [1997] I.R.L.R 401, Judge Peter Clark, EAT.

2240. **Mentally disabled—employer's insurance policy—discrimination between mentally and physically disabled—Canada**

[Saskatchewan Human Rights Code 1979 s.16(1).]

G, an employee of B, became disabled as a result of a mental disorder and was unable to perform her duties. Under the terms of her employment she was on sick leave for 90 days and was then paid benefits under an insurance policy for a further two years. Under the terms of the insurance policy any employee, regardless of status, who had incurred a disability rendering him unable to work would receive an income replacement benefit. Employees who sustained physical disabilities would continue to receive the benefit until they reached the retirement age of 65; employees who had a mental disability were only entitled to receive the benefit for two years except where the individual remained in an institution. G filed a complaint that the operation of the scheme, in differentiating between physical and mental disability, constituted unlawful discrimination contrary to the Saskatchewan Human Rights Code 1979 s.16(1). G's complaint was upheld at first instance and by the Court of Appeal. B appealed.

Held, dismissing the appeal, that (1) while the insurance plan gave each employee similar protection before the insured risk of disability materialised, the plan also provided a significant benefit to employees after the risk of disability materialised and this benefit was not distributed equally. The fact that it was initially unclear who would later be treated distinctively does not lessen the conclusion that the plan discriminated against those with a mental disability, *University of British Columbia v. Berg* [1993] 2 S.C.R. 353 applied; (2) in determining whether there was discrimination in the instant case the correct comparison is between the treatment afforded to those with mental disabilities and those with physical disabilities, not between the disabled and the able bodied. In order to find discrimination on the basis of disability, it was not necessary that all disabled persons be mistreated equally, *Janzen v. Platy Enterprises Ltd* [1989] 1 S.C.R. 1252 and *Brooks v. Canada Safeway Ltd* [1989] 1 S.C.R. 1219 applied. Discrimination against a subset of the relevant group may be considered discrimination against the relevant group generally for the purposes of human rights legislation. It was appropriate in the circumstances to compare the benefits received by the mentally disabled with those received by the physically disabled. That such a comparison was appropriate was confirmed by the fact that the purpose of the benefits payable to both groups was the same, namely to insure against the income related consequences of becoming disabled, *Brooks v. Canada Safeway Ltd* [1989] 1 S.C.R. 1219 applied. The result of such a comparison was that less favourable benefits are provided to the mentally disabled and that the plan was therefore discriminatory and contravened s.16 of the Human Rights Code.

BATTLEFORDS AND DISTRICT COOPERATIVE LTD v. GIBBS (1997) 2 B.H.R.C. 92, Lamer, C.J., Sup Ct (Can).

2241. Part time employment—legislation removing minimum hours requirement not retrospective—claims for unfair dismissal and redundancy incompetent

[European Communities Act 1972 s.2(2); Employment Protection (Part-time Employees) Regulations 1995 (SI 1995 31) Reg.4; Council Directive 76/207 Art.1; Treaty of Rome 1957 Art.119; Council Directive 75/117 on equal pay.]

J commenced employment with HLBC in November 1990 under a part time contract working less than 16 hours per week. He was dismissed in July 1993 and in October 1993 presented a complaint of unlawful race discrimination, not having sufficient qualifying service to present a complaint of unfair dismissal. The Employment Protection (Part-time Employees) Regulations 1995, which removed the requirement for minimum weekly working hours in order to qualify for the right not to be unfairly dismissed, commenced on February 6, 1995. J brought an application to amend his originating application in April 1995 to include claims for unfair dismissal and redundancy. The tribunal allowed the application to amend, holding that the 1995 Regulations were retrospective in effect. HLBC appealed.

Held, allowing the appeal, that (1) there was nothing in the Regulations to displace the general presumption that they did not have retrospective effect. If they did purport to have retrospective effect they would be ultra vires the power contained in the European Communities Act 1972 s.2(2) by reason of para.1 (1)(b) of the Act, *Plewa v. Chief Adjudication Officer* [1995] 1 A.C. 249, [1994] C.L.Y. 4179, applied, *Harvey v. Institute of the Motor Industry (No.2)* [1996] I.C.R. 981, [1995] 1 C.L.Y. 2038, distinguished. The fact that the employer was an emanation of the state was immaterial and the tribunal erred in holding otherwise, and (2) the time limits laid down by domestic UK law applied to claims for unfair dismissal based on Community law in the form of the Treaty of Rome 1957 Art.119 and the Equal Pay Directive 75/117. There was no discretion to extend such time limits and accordingly J's claims for unfair dismissal and redundancy were out of time insofar as they sought to rely on either Art.119 or the Equal Pay Directive. Claims for redundancy pay could not be brought under the Equal Treatment Directive 76/207 since statutory redundancy payments were "pay" within Art.119 of the Treaty of Rome 1957. J might be able to bring a claim for unfair dismissal based on the Equal Treatment Directive if compensation for unfair dismissal was held not to be "pay", *Biggs v. Somerset CC* [1996] I.C.R. 364, [1995] 1 C.L.Y. 2112, *Barber v. Staffordshire CC* [1996] I.C.R. 379, [1996] 1 C.L.Y. 2578, *Gillespie v. Northern Health and Social Services Board (C342/93)* [1996] I.C.R. 498, [1996] 1 C.L.Y. 2570, applied.

HAMMERSMITH AND FULHAM LBC v. JESUTHASAN [1996] I.C.R. 991, Butterfield, J., EAT.

2242. Race discrimination—compensation—prison officers—industrial tribunal entitled to make separate awards against employer and employees

Held, that an industrial tribunal acted within its discretion when, in awarding compensation to a prison officer who had suffered a sustained campaign of racial discrimination by fellow officers, it made separate awards against the Prison Service and against each of the prison officers who were guilty of discrimination, *Deane v. Ealing LBC* [1993] I.C.R. 329, [1993] C.L.Y. 1768 distinguished. The award of £21,000 for injury to feelings was not unduly excessive given the circumstances of the case.

HM PRISON SERVICE v. JOHNSON; ARMITAGE v. JOHNSON; MARSDEN v. JOHNSON; JOHNSON v. HM PRISON SERVICE [1997] I.C.R. 275, Smith, J., EAT.

2243. Race discrimination–concessionaires at department store–liability of principal under race relations legislation

[Race Relations Act 1976 s.7.]

H operated a system whereby it granted licences under which the licensee was given responsibility for a particular department in H's store in which the licensee's goods would be sold. The licensee provided the workforce, but each employee had to be approved by H and had to adhere to H's standards of dress, deportment and behaviour, and approval could be withdrawn at any time. The contract between H and the licensee meant that at the moment of sale a worker would be an employee of the licensee, but would be selling goods that belonged to H, not the licensee. The three respondents had each either lost or failed to gain approval from H, for what they claimed were reasons which amounted to unlawful racial discrimination. H appealed against an EAT decision that it could be liable for racial discrimination under the Race Relations Act 1976 s.7.

Held, dismissing the appeal, that in view of the contractual arrangements between H and its licensees, the work done by the licensees' employees was also work done for H, as the principal, within the meaning of s.7. The alternative construction would leave persons in the situation of the respondents without a personal remedy in the event of discriminatory acts by the principal. The court had to interpret s.7 in a way which was not only consistent with the words used, but which gave effect to the statutory purpose of providing a victim of unlawful discrimination with a remedy, where otherwise she would not have one. That principle also applied to the question of whether the respondents were persons whom their employer "supplies under a contract made with" H under s.7, which had to be answered in the affirmative, even though the supply of workers might not be the primary purpose of the contract between H and the licensee.

HARRODS LTD v. REMICK; HARRODS LTD v. SEELEY; ELMI v. HARRODS LTD, *The Times*, July 22, 1997, Sir Richard Scott V.C., CA.

2244. Race discrimination–disciplinary procedures–supplying information to fellow employee who had been subjected to race discrimination by employers

[Race Relations Act 1976 s.2.]

Y was employed as an assistant catering manager by C. His place of employment was Carmel College, a leading Jewish boarding school. An Egyptian chef was employed by C at the school. The chef was transferred from the school to another school by C because of his racial origin. Y was aware of the reason for the transfer of the chef, who had commenced proceedings in the industrial tribunal. Y provided the chef with information which led to a settlement of the chef's claim. Shortly after the settlement of the chef's claim, Y was continuously subjected to disciplinary action and as a result was forced to resign from his job.

Held, that Y had been victimised within the meaning of the Race Relations Act 1976 s.2. Y was awarded as compensation: Loss of earnings: £2,280. Future loss of earnings: £8,250. Loss of pension rights: £1,800. Injury to feelings: £2,500. Total award: £14,830.

YOUNG v. COMPASS GROUP, April 16, 1996, Judge not specified, IT. [*Ex rel.* Edmund Cofie, Barrister].

2245. Race discrimination–effective date of termination–internal disciplinary appeal

[Race Relations Act 1976 s.4(1); Sex Discrimination Act 1975 s.6.]

A appealed against an EAT decision that an industrial tribunal had no jurisdiction to hear her complaint of racial discrimination, because A did not come within the Race Relations Act 1976 s.4(1), because she was not seeking employment, nor within s.4(2) because she was not an employee at the time of the appeal hearing. A, an employee for less than two years, was summarily dismissed for misconduct. The case was originally dismissed by the industrial tribunal because it was out of time, but the EAT allowed her appeal on the basis that an internal appeal decision which was itself tainted by discrimination was the effective date of termination and was within the time limits. However, the subsequent appeal by P was allowed. A contended that the 1976 Act should be construed widely enough to include a dismissed employee seeking reinstatement in line with the parallel provisions of the Sex Discrimination Act 1975 s.6, or alternatively, that the dismissal was conditional on the outcome of the appeal procedure.

Held, dismissing the appeal, that although it was unsatisfactory, it was clear that the 1976 Act did not cover a complaint of racial discrimination by a past employee at an internal appeal hearing. The appeal procedure did not create a conditional dismissal, *J Sainsbury v. Savage* [1981] I.C.R. 1, [1981] C.L.Y. 968 and *Nagarajan v. Agnew* [1995] I.C.R. 520, [1994] C.L.Y. 1969 followed.

ADEKEYE v. POST OFFICE (NO.2); *sub nom.* POST OFFICE v. ADEKEYE [1997] I.C.R. 110, Peter Gibson, L.J., CA.

2246. Race discrimination–employer's liability for acts of racial harassment by employees

[Race Relations Act 1976 s.32.]

Employers are liable for offences committed under the Race Relations Act 1976 by their employees regardless of the common law principles of vicarious liability. J suffered racial harassment at the hands of his co-workers whilst employed by T and subsequently handed in his notice. He brought an action against T for racial discrimination. Pursuant to the Race Relations Act 1976 s.32(1) an employer was liable for acts done by an employee "in the course of his employment... whether or not it was done with the employer's knowledge or approval". The industrial tribunal found that the harassment J suffered fell within s.32(1), but the EAT held that "in the course of his employment" under s.32(1) had to be construed in accordance with the common law principles governing an employer's vicarious liability, such that an act was not done in the course of employment where it could not be said to be either an act authorised by the employer or an improper method of carrying out an authorised act, and the incidents of racial harassment described could not be considered to be in any way connected to an authorised act. J appealed.

Held, allowing the appeal, that in order to give effect to the legislative purpose of the Act, it was necessary to give s.32(1) a wide interpretation and not restrict the concept of "in the course of his employment" any more than the natural meaning of the words required. Vicarious liability under the common law and liability under the Act were not sufficiently similar to justify applying the common law principles to the interpretation of s.32(1) and to do so would create the anomaly that the more serious the act of racial harassment, the more likely it was to be considered unauthorised and therefore unactionable. The purpose of the Act was to deter racial harassment in the workplace by making employers liable for the acts of their employees, unless they could show themselves to have taken reasonable steps to prevent the discrimination. It would be wrong and contrary to the purpose of the Act to allow an employer to escape liability for serious harassment by seeking to apply to it principles drawn from a completely separate area of law.

JONES v. TOWER BOOT CO LTD; *sub nom.* TOWER BOOT CO LTD v. JONES [1997] 2 All E.R. 406, McCowan, L.J., CA.

2247. Race discrimination—unfair dismissal—no discrimination if less favourable treatment not proved

[Race Relations Act 1976.]

E appealed against a decision of the Employment Appeal Tribunal allowing the appeal of the PO against an industrial tribunal award to him of £1,250 for injured feelings and £10,000 in total for financial losses caused by unfair dismissal on the grounds of race.

Held, dismissing the appeal, that E had failed to provide evidence that he had been treated any differently from other staff and the tribunal had erred by making an inference that the lack of satisfactory explanations for comments by a manager on E's performance was therefore evidence of racial discrimination, *King v. Great Britain China Centre Ltd* [1991] I.R.L.R. 513, [1992] C.L.Y. 1959 followed.

ESSIEN v. POST OFFICE, Trans. Ref: CCRTF 96/0436/C, October 18, 1996, Saville, L.J., CA.

2248. Race discrimination—unlawful discrimination—refusal to promote—measure of damages

[Race Relations Act 1976 s.1.]

CC was a cash and carry retail company wholly owned by N. D was employed by CC as a checkout assistant. In response to a notice advertised internally, she applied for a post in the company's cash office in which she had already worked on occasion as a relief operator. Work in the office was divided into two shifts: a morning and early afternoon shift staffed by white employees; and an afternoon and evening shift on which the employees were black or asian. The post advertised was on the morning shift, and five employees applied. Of these, D and three others were Asian and one, L, was white european. No interviews were held, and L was chosen for the position. D was upset and disappointed with this decision, and asked the company manager, who made the selection, why she had not been chosen. He informed her that she lacked experience and ability but, thinking that she was possibly considering an industrial tribunal claim, refused to provide reasons in writing. From this point until the end of the tribunal hearing, D received a further five reasons for her non-appointment. As a result of the company's treatment of her and her perception that she had been discriminated against on the grounds of her race, D was made acutely unhappy and suffered actual injury to her health in the form of clinical depression. She became unable to work and received psychiatric treatment for six months, including the prescription of anti-depressants. During this period D's ability to cope with life was markedly impaired and considerable strain was placed on her relationship with her family. By the end of her treatment in March 1995, although she was recovering, it was clear she was still depressed. By the hearing of her case in March and April 1996, D had largely recovered, but was still deeply distressed when recalling details in the course of giving evidence.

Held, finding in favour of D's application, that (1) following the guidance set out in *King v. Great Britain China Centre Ltd* [1992] I.C.R. 516, [1992] C.L.Y. 1959, D had been discriminated against on the grounds of her race, contrary to the Race Relations Act, 1976 s.1 (a). In rejecting the company's explanation of primary facts indicative of racial discrimination, the tribunal made particular reference to (i) the subjective nature of L's selection, (ii) the lack of safeguards such as interviews or marking, (iii) the failure to appoint the candidate with the best paper qualifications, (iv) suggestions that D did not "fit in" with other employees in the cashroom, despite having regularly worked there in the past without complaint and (v) the various different reasons or combinations of reasons given by the company for D's non-appointment, which appeared to be an attempt to cover up what was subsequently recognised as race discrimination. It was also noted that this was a good example of a failure by an employer to follow good procedure as recommended by the Race Relations Code of Practice and of the difficulties to which such a failure may bring an employer and (2) this was a bad case of unlawful discrimination leading to moderately severe psychiatric damage. Damages would be awarded as if for tort, compensating for all loss reasonably foreseeable as the result of the unlawful discrimination. Such loss could include injury to health. An award could also include compensation for injury to feelings, although this did not exhaust the general damages which could be awarded. It was therefore appropriate to award damages as follows: £5,000 for psychiatric damage; £6,000 for injury to feelings caused by the unlawful discrimination; interest of £695.80. Total award: £11,695.

D'SILVA v. HAMBLETON AND NURDIN & PEACOCK PLC, TJ Mason (Chairman), IT.

2249. Redundancy – management restructuring

[Employment Protection (Consolidation) Act 1978 s.81 (2); .]

B commenced employment with S in 1990 as a petrol station manager. In 1995 S decided that its management structure was too top heavy and so a reorganisation took place, one of the aims of which was to achieve a delayering of management. Under the reorganisation the post of petrol station manager would disappear and a new post of petrol filling station controller was to be created. B was told that his position had been made redundant and he decided not to apply for the new post because it entailed a substantial drop in salary. He found employment elsewhere and presented a complaint of unfair dismissal in July 1995, on the grounds that his previous position had not been made redundant. The tribunal upheld his claim by a majority, applying the so-called "function test" to conclude that the requirements of S's business for B to carry out work of the kind which he was required to do and was in fact doing had not ceased or diminished and accordingly B was not redundant. S appealed, arguing that the tribunal had erred in law by applying the wrong test.

Held, allowing the appeal, that (1) while there might be a number of underlying causes leading to a true redundancy situation, including a reorganisation in the interests of efficiency or a reduction in production requirements, the only question to be asked under the Employment Protection (Consolidation) Act 1978 s.81 (2) (b) was whether there was a diminution or cessation in the employer's requirement for employees to carry out work of a particular kind, or an expectation or such cessation or diminution in the future; (2) if the answer to that question was "yes", s.81 (2) of the Act required that the tribunal must then determine the issue of causation, namely whether the dismissal of the employee was wholly or mainly attributable to the statutory redundancy situation. Even if a redundancy situation arose the employee would not have been dismissed for that reason if that situation did not cause the dismissal, *Nelson v. BBC (No.1)* [1977] I.R.L.R. 148, [1977] C.L.Y. 1123, *Nelson v. BBC (No.2)* [1979] I.R.L.R. 346, [1980] C.L.Y. 1018, considered. If the requirement for employees to perform the work of two separate positions diminished so that one employee could do both jobs, then the dismissed employee would be dismissed by reason of redundancy, *Cowen v. Haden Carrier Ltd* [1982] I.R.L.R. 225, [1983] C.L.Y. 1276, considered. But if the requirement for employees to do work of a particular kind remained the same, there can be no dismissal by reason of redundancy, notwithstanding any unilateral variation of contracts of employment; (3) both the "contract" and "function" tests were based on a misconceived reading of the words of s.81 (2) (b), *Haden Carrier* considered, *Pink v. White* [1985] I.R.L.R. 489, [1985] C.L.Y. 1198, not followed, and (4) in the instant case the tribunal erred in failing to ask itself whether there was a true redundancy situation, looking at the overall requirement of S for employees to carry out work of a particular kind and whether that situation caused B's dismissal.

SAFEWAY STORES PLC v. BURRELL [1997] I.C.R. 523, Judge Peter Clark, EAT.

2250. Redundancy–mobility clause in contract of employment–determination of place of employment

[Employment Protection (Consolidation) Act 1978 s.81 (2).]

H and others, W, were employed as waitresses by HT, who supplied catering services to a number of companies. W had all worked for several years at one company, HS, but each had a mobility clause in their contracts of employment obliging them to work at other companies if required. When HS's need for HT's catering services diminished, HT purported to dismiss W pursuant to redundancy notices, but W contended that they had been unfairly dismissed or unfairly selected for redundancy as they worked for HT, not HS, and HT had made no efforts to find work for them at any of the other companies it had contracts with, although waitresses with shorter service records had been retained. HT appealed against an EAT decision allowing W's appeal against an industrial tribunal's determination that they had been dismissed for redundancy.

Held, allowing the appeal, that an employee's place of work for redundancy purposes under the Employment Protection (Consolidation) Act 1978 s.81 (2) had to be determined primarily by reference to the factual situation existing prior to the dismissal and not by reference to the contract of employment alone. The fact that an employee had a mobility clause in her contract should not be regarded as widening the location of her employment for the purposes of the business, when she had in fact worked in only one place. To do so could have the effect of encouraging the use of mobility clauses to defeat genuine redundancy claims. The question of where an employee worked was one for the industrial tribunal and, in the instant case, W had clearly been employed by HT at HS and it was a redundancy situation which led to their dismissal.

HIGH TABLE LTD v. HORST, *The Times*, July 9, 1997, Peter Gibson, L.J., CA.

2251. Redundancy–non eligibility of director employed under contract of service–controlling beneficial interest defined employment status

[Employment Protection (Consolidation) Act 1978 s.106.]

B was a 50 per cent shareholder of C Ltd and worked full-time for the company as a scanner operator and in a sales capacity, drawing a salary subject to PAYE and national insurance deductions. In 1993 his co-director left the business. Administrative receivers were appointed in October 1994 and B was informed that he should regard his contract as terminated. His application to the Secretary of State for a redundancy payment pursuant to the Employment Protection (Consolidation) Act 1978 s.106 was refused on the grounds that he was not an employee. I, who had been a sole trader for several years, formed a company in 1984 to take over his business. He held 99 per cent of the shares and worked for the company under a contract which provided for the payment of a salary and pension contributions. In January 1995 the company went into receivership and I's claim for a redundancy payment was also rejected by the Secretary of State on the basis that he was not an employee. Both B and I complained unsuccessfully to industrial tribunals. Their appeals were heard together.

Held, dismissing both appeals, that (1) the issue of whether a particular individual is an employee is always coloured by the context in which the question of the claimant's work status has arisen; (2) the answers to the several tests used to determine employment status will highlight conflicting factors operating in any given situation, some pointing to an employment relationship, and some away from it. What the decision making body must do is consider the relevance of all the factors, decide what weight should be given to each of them, evaluate them and balance one against the other to arrive at a conclusion; (3) although a director, managing director or a shareholder of a company may enter into and work under a contract of service with the company, if an individual is able, by reason of his controlling beneficial interest in the shares of the company, to prevent his dismissal from his position in the company, he is outside the class of persons intended to be protected by the provisions of the 1978 Act and is not an employee within the meaning of that Act, *Lee v. Lee's Air Farming Ltd* [1961] A.C. 12 distinguished; (4) the tribunal made no error of law in B's case. As a 50 per cent shareholder, B was entitled to block any decision to dismiss him, and if he did agree to a decision to dismiss himself, then that would not be a "dismissal" within the meaning of the Act, and (5) for the same reasons, the tribunal made no error of law in holding that I was not an employee.

BUCHAN v. SECRETARY OF STATE FOR EMPLOYMENT; IVEY v. SECRETARY OF STATE FOR EMPLOYMENT [1997] I.R.L.R. 80, Mummery, J., EAT.

2252. Redundancy–point based agreed selection criteria–individual scores kept from employees–selection system rendered a sham–unfair application of accepted criteria

The respondents were selected for redundancy following the application of redundancy selection criteria by J, the criteria having previously been agreed with representatives of the respondents' trade union. The criteria resulted in individual scores being allotted to each employee. The redundancy procedure provided for an appeals process. At all times J withheld from the respondents both their own individual scores and those of comparators and did not engage in any consultation with the respondents about the selection process. The respondents' complaints of unfair dismissal were upheld by the industrial tribunal, on the basis that the redundancy procedure was unfair due to the absence of consultation or the provision of information. J appealed, arguing that the need for individual consultation could be dispensed with once fair selection criteria had been agreed.

Held, dismissing the appeal, that in each case of redundancy what is required is a fair process, where an opportunity to contest the selection of each individual is available to the individual employee. This does not suggest that individual consultation is essential in every case, and in some cases an individual's opportunity to contest his selection can be achieved through his trade union, *R. v. British Coal Corp and Secretary of State for Trade and Industry, ex p. Price* [1994] I.R.L.R. 72, applied. A policy decision to withhold all markings in a particular selection process may result in individual unfairness if no opportunity is thereafter given to the individual to know how he has been assessed. In the instant case, the tribunal was entitled to conclude that the withholding of the actual marks from each employee once the assessment had taken place did render the appeal system a sham, and as such, constituted unfairness in the manner in which the agreed and acceptable criteria were being applied.

JOHN BROWN ENGINEERING LTD v. BROWN [1997] I.R.L.R. 90, Lord Johnston, EAT.

2253. Redundancy–selection criteria–agreed procedure–suitable alternative employment

[Employment Protection (Consolidation) Act 1978 s.59, s.81 (2).]

B commenced employment with BK in 1970 as a payroll clerk. In April 1993 a reorganisation of the business took place resulting in two divisions being split into separate sections and formation of a separate company. As a consequence fewer employees were required to carry out payroll and accounting functions and the tribunal found that BK were required to select two from four employees to carry out the new accounting jobs, with the result that B and another employee were made redundant. B contended that he had been unfairly selected for redundancy contrary to BK's agreed redundancy procedure made some years earlier. The tribunal dismissed B's complaint, holding that there was no customary arrangement or agreed procedure in operation at the time. In the alternative, the tribunal held that if there was an agreed procedure, the vast majority of the applicable criteria had been taken into account so that B suffered no prejudice, and to the extent that the procedure had not been followed there were special reasons for departing from the criteria within the meaning of the Employment Protection (Consolidation) Act 1978 s.59(b). B appealed, arguing, inter alia, that the tribunal erred in holding that the question whether the agreed procedure was in operation was a question of fact rather than law.

Held, dismissing the appeal, that (1) whether an agreement remained in operation so as to be an agreed procedure within s.59 turned on a consideration of all the relevant evidence as to whether the agreement was in fact regarded and treated by the parties at the time as governing the redundancy situation which had arisen. It was a question of fact for the tribunal and in the instant case there was sufficient evidence for the tribunal to conclude that there was no agreed procedure in existence at the relevant time. Before it could be shown that there was an agreed procedure within s.59 evidence had to be adduced that the employers and the employee's representatives were in fact purporting to operate such an agreed procedure. It was not enough to point to the existence of a procedure in writing which was apt to cover the redundancy situation, and (2) in the alternative, the common sense view on the facts was that BK were not selecting for redundancy at all. A position had been reached as a result of the reorganisation whereby, on application of the 1978 Act s.81(2)(b) all five employees in the accounts department were made redundant and in reality no selection process was carried out. BK were then embarking on consideration of suitable alternative employment and the touchstone of such a situation was reasonableness rather than the application of agreed selection criteria or the application of objective criteria, *Akzo Coatings Plc v. Thompson* (Unreported, 1996) applied.

BALL v. BALFOUR KILPATRICK LTD [1997] I.C.R. 740, Judge Colin Smith Q.C., EAT.

2254. Redundancy–selection criteria–health and safety representative not entitled to additional protection

[Employment Protection (Consolidation) Act 1978 s.57(3), s.57A.]

R commenced employment with S as a setter/operator in 1974. In 1991 he was elected to the position of health and safety representative and subsequently became chairman of the health and safety committee. He took his safety duties seriously and spent about one third of his working time on these duties. In 1994 S identified a need for redundancies which affected R's department. The selection method used was a points scoring system involving seven criteria based entirely on performance in the department. R was selected for redundancy after the assessment. He appealed, arguing that his health and safety duties operated to his detriment when the selection criteria were applied. His score was increased following the appeal to reflect his safety knowledge, but there was no reflection in the scoring of his duties as a safety representative. R was dismissed and complained that he had been unfairly dismissed for an inadmissible reason, namely the performance of his duties as a health and safety representative, and that his dismissal was automatically unfair by reason of the Employment Protection (Consolidation) Act 1978 s.57A(1)(a) or (b). The industrial tribunal found that although R's health and safety activities did not contribute to his dismissal and that the dismissal was therefore not automatically unfair, S's refusal to take into account R's performance as a health and safety representative was unreasonable, and the dismissal was accordingly unfair under s.57(3) of the 1978 Act. R appealed against the finding in respect of s.57A, and S appealed against the finding of unfair dismissal.

Held, dismissing R's appeal, allowing S's appeal and substituting a finding of fair dismissal, that (1) although the important role of health and safety representatives cannot be underestimated, the protection afforded to such representatives in a redundancy situation is neutral. They are not entitled to additional protection over their fellow employees in a redundancy selection pool; (2) having found as a fact that R's insistence on complying with his health and safety duties did not cause his supervisor to be biased against him, it was not open to the tribunal to find that R's dismissal was for an inadmissible reason under s.57A; (3) contrary to the tribunal's finding, health and safety representative duties are not carried out as a second job and such duties do not form part of the employees' duties performed under his contract of employment, and (4) in holding that it was unreasonable for the employer not to have regard to the performance by R of those duties the tribunal fell into the error of rewriting the employer's selection procedure, contrary to the principle stated in *British Leyland Cars v. Lewis* [1983] I.R.L.R. 58 and *British Aerospace v. Green* [1995] I.R.L.R. 433, [1995] 1 C.L.Y. 2103.

SMITHS INDUSTRIES AEROSPACE AND DEFENCE SYSTEMS v. RAWLINGS [1996] I.R.L.R. 656, Judge Peter Clarke, EAT.

2255. Redundancy–selection criteria–trade union consulted–absence of individual consultation

M, a manager of one of the branches of MB, received notice of redundancy in April 1995, to expire on September 30, 1995. M had previously been informed of the nature of the proposed restructuring exercise and the selection criteria which would be applied in determining candidates for redundancy. On the basis of performance reviews and scores in an executive development forum, EDF, M was selected for redundancy following an assessment the results of which were not made known to him. The results of the EDF paperwork were shown to him on June 23 and M appealed unsuccessfully against his dismissal. He applied to a tribunal claiming that he had been unfairly selected for redundancy on the grounds that there had not been proper individual consultation. The tribunal held that the dismissal was fair, holding that the consultation undertaken with M and his union was adequate. M appealed.

Held, dismissing the appeal, that (1) where no consultation had taken place with either the trade union or the employee the dismissal would normally be unfair, unless the tribunal found that a reasonable employer would have concluded that consultation would be an utterly futile exercise in the circumstances of the case; (2) consultation with the trade union over selection criteria did not of itself release the employer from consulting with the employee individually his being identified for redundancy; (3) it was a question of fact and degree for the tribunal to consider whether consultation with the individual and/or his union was so inadequate as to render the dismissal unfair. A lack of consultation in any particular respect would not automatically lead to that result. The overall picture must be viewed by the tribunal up to the date of termination to ascertain whether the employer had or had not acted reasonably in dismissing the employee on grounds of redundancy, and (4) in the instant case the tribunal addressed itself to the question of the adequacy of consultation and concluded that such consultation as did take place with the union and with M was adequate in the overall context of fairness, taking into account the other factors which weighed in favour of a finding of a fair dismissal, namely the reasonableness of the selection criteria, their reasonable application and attempts to find alternative employment for M. In the circumstances individual consultation with M prior to the decision to identify him for redundancy was not essential in order for the dismissal to be fair.

MUGFORD v. MIDLAND BANK PLC [1997] I.C.R. 399, Judge Peter Clark, EAT.

2256. Restrictive covenants–extent and enforceability

S applied for an injunction to restrain L from breaching contractual restraint of trade clauses after L resigned and took up a position with an alleged competitor, Veeder Root Inc (VR). Both S and VR were involved in the retail distribution of petroleum products by road and in delivery systems controlled by tanker drivers, although S specialised in fail safe devices to prevent overfilling, and VR specialised in gauges and the measurement of tank contents. The relevant clauses restrained L from: (1) employment or association within the UK with any firm connected with overfill prevention or tank gauging equipment, or in the advertising thereof, for 12 months, and (2) soliciting orders from S's suppliers or customers for a period of 24 months. S contended that L had detailed technical knowledge of systems that would be of great value to a competitor. L offered an undertaking not to use specified confidential information and contended that the covenants were unreasonable because the business of his new employer, VR, was substantially different from that of S, especially as his new sales area was predominantly Europe rather than the UK. L argued that, in any event, the injunction should be refused on discretionary grounds because he was married with two children and his damages from loss of employment would outweigh any potential damage to S's business.

Held, allowing the application, that (1) S was entitled to the protection of an injunction against a real risk of loss of its trade secrets and other confidential information; (2) the clause was a minimum necessary to protect S's legitimate concerns; however the restrictions against holding shares and against working in the advertising of similar products were unduly restrictive and were severed, and (3) there was no need for a geographical limitation to the covenant, but a non solicitation clause was unenforceable because it was in restraint of trade. Although L would lose his job, he would not be restrained from other employment outside this narrow field, *Clarke v. Newland* [1991] 1 All E.R. 397, [1991] C.L.Y. 2685 followed and *Littlewoods Organisation Ltd v. Harris* [1977] 1 W.L.R. 1472, [1978] C.L.Y. 2941, *Lansing Linde Ltd v. Kerr* [1991] 1 W.L.R. 251, [1991] C.L.Y. 446 and *Mason v. Provident Clothing & Supply Co Ltd* [1913] A.C. 724 considered.

SCULLY UK LTD v. LEE, Trans. Ref: 1997-S-No.711, August 11, 1997, Judge Havery Q.C., QBD.

2257. Restrictive covenants–joint ventures–non solicitation covenants enforceable against parties to joint venture agreement–protection of legitimate business interest

DD sought to enforce contractual undertakings given by DB and other European bond broking managers not to compete with DD's business or to solicit DD's clients or employees for a period of one year from the date their employment with the joint venture company ceased. Evidence showed that both DD and the brokers had taken legal advice prior to entering into the covenants, which in turn formed part of a joint venture agreement between the parties and under which shares in the joint venture company were held by DD and the managers, with DD supplying premises and equipment. At trial of preliminary issues, the undertakings were held to be valid and enforceable and the managers appealed, contending that DD had no lawful interest in enforcing the covenants, as it was merely an investor and creditor of the joint venture company, and that the covenants themselves went beyond what was necessary to protect DD's business and were void for uncertainty.

Held, dismissing the appeal, that the authorities showed that the categories of enforceability for such covenants were not restricted to employee/employer relationships or to a sale of business situation and could apply between joint venturers, where the terms accorded with the requirement of reasonableness, *Stenhouse Ltd v. Phillips* [1974] A.C. 391, [1974] C.L.Y. 1272, *Allied Dunbar (Frank Weisinger) Ltd v. Weisinger* [1988] I.R.L.R. 60, [1987] C.L.Y. 455 and *Office Angels Ltd v. Rainer-Thomas* [1991] I.R.L.R. 214, [1991] C.L.Y. 447 considered. DD had a legitimate interest of a proprietary nature to protect and it was entirely reasonable to do so by way of restrictive covenants. Although the restriction against broking carried on from "time to time" by DD in the one year period after the managers left could be deemed unreasonably wide in certain circumstances, the facts showed that the managers had knowledge of planned moves into new business areas which were in an advanced stage of preparation. The restriction against soliciting DD's present staff was also reasonable, given that certain employees would have knowledge that fell within the category of specific confidential information.

DAWNAY DAY & CO LTD v. DE BRACONIER D'ALPHEN [1997] I.R.L.R. 442, Evans, L.J., CA.

2258. Restrictive covenants–non solicitation clause–dent repair business–injunction against former employee

D, a car dent repair company, appealed against the refusal to grant an interlocutory injunction against K, its former employee, to enforce a non-solicitation restrictive covenant which was to last for 12 months following termination of employment. The 12 months was then reduced to six months by a memorandum circulated through the company, on the basis that new legislation rendered the change necessary. The dent repair technicians, trained by the company, were allocated specified geographical areas in which to operate. When K left D's employment D suspected that he was trading in breach of the covenant and on further investigation found he had been repairing dents in cars at a garage within K's last allocated area. K refused to make any undertakings, claiming that the business he was involved in was legitimate and that the restrictive covenant was not valid as being an unreasonable restraint of trade. In refusing the injunction the judge held that a clause restraining K from soliciting recent customers, whether or not they were within his area, who he had had dealings with in the past but not recently, was not arguably reasonable. D argued that such a restraint was reasonable on the basis of authority, *Business Seating (Renovations) v. Broad* [1989] I.C.R. 729, [1990] C.L.Y. 1933 and *Office Angels Ltd v. Rainer-Thomas* [1991] I.R.L.R. 214, [1991] C.L.Y. 447. K objected to the fact that the covenant placed a prohibition on use of "his knowledge of the business requirements" of customers and on him exerting "any influence over" such customers, claiming that they would prevent any business being done at all and that the latter was too uncertain to be given effect.

Held, allowing the appeal and granting the injunction, that the judge's conclusion that D was bound to lose in the full hearing was not justified. The restraint period was six months and was limited to any person or business that had been a customer of D within the previous six months which was not unreasonable. It did not matter that there was no backward temporal limit on K's dealings with those customers. K's objections to the wording in the covenants could not be upheld as the phrases were not interpreted as he contended.

DENTMASTER (UK) LTD v. KENT, Trans. Ref: LTA 97/5858/J, May 2, 1997, Waite, L.J., CA.

2259. **Safety representatives–disciplinary action–representative not subjected to detrimental treatment–acted outside agreed procedures**

[Employment Protection (Consolidation) Act 1978 s.22A(1).]

S was employed by V as a forklift driver at their Hull factory. At the relevant times he was also the senior union shop steward and the appointed union safety representative. On May 2, 1995 complaints were made by employees concerning odours emitted by one of the chemicals used by V in its production process, and a production line was shut down as a result. The next day production resumed on that line and two employees complained to the line safety representative. The line was again shut down and the line representative discussed the matter with S, who, after seeking advice from a union researcher, insisted that the men affected be seen by the company doctor or be sent to the hospital. The first aider acceded to S's demand and two other employees also went to hospital. S was then charged with misconduct in that he did not follow agreed procedures for raising a union concern with management. On June 8, S received a written warning and two weeks' suspension without pay. S complained to an industrial tribunal that he had been subjected to a detriment by his employer, contrary to the Employment Protection (Consolidation) Act 1978 s.22A(1), on the ground that he had performed functions as an acknowledged health and safety representative. The tribunal dismissed the complaint, holding that S had gone outside his duties as a safety representative and was in fact acting as a shop steward and trying to use health and safety issues to embarrass the company. S appealed, arguing that the tribunal erred in importing questions of S's reasonableness and motive into their considerations.

Held, dismissing the appeal, that the legislative provisions affording protection to appointed safety representatives was wider than that afforded to ordinary employees, in that the latter must act reasonably in order to secure the statutory protection against detrimental treatment and dismissal. That did not mean that appointed safety representatives could behave in an outrageous manner and still have the statutory protection, *Bass Taverns Ltd v. Burgess* [1995] I.R.L.R. 596, [1996] 1 C.L.Y. 2669 applied. The question for the tribunal in the instant case was whether or not the reason for S being disciplined was that he was performing his functions as a safety representative. On the facts of the case the tribunal were entitled to conclude that S was being disciplined not because of his performing his safety representative functions but because, inter alia, he acted in bad faith, out of a personal agenda to embarrass the company.

SHILLITO v. VAN LEER (UK) LTD [1997] I.R.L.R. 495, Judge Peter Clark, EAT.

2260. Sex discrimination–armed forces–termination of pregnancy–compensation award

See ARMED FORCES: Ministry of Defence v. O'Hare (No.2). §308

2261. Sex discrimination–genuine occupational qualification–defence operated at time of prima facie discrimination

[Sex Discrimination Act 1975 s.1 (1), s.6(1), s.7.]

L operated a number of women only health clubs in various parts of England and Scotland. In March 1996, L advertised vacancies for sales people/trainee managers. W, an experienced male sales representative, rang to enquire about the positions but was told he could not apply because the posts were for "ladies only". W complained to an industrial tribunal that the refusal to allow him to apply for the posts constituted an unlawful act of discrimination contrary to the Sex Discrimination Act 1975 s.1 (1) (a) and s.6(1) (c). L sought to rely on a defence of genuine occupational qualification, in that the post needed to be held by a woman to preserve decency or privacy because women might reasonably object to the prescence of a man in that they are in a state of undress, within the 1975 Act s.7(2) (b) (ii). The tribunal upheld W's complaint, on the basis that s.7(2) (b) (ii) did not apply by virtue of s.7(4); L already had female employees who were capable of carrying out the duties referred to in s.7(2) (b) (ii), whom it would be reasonable to employ on those duties without undue inconvenience. L appealed, arguing, inter alia, that since the health club in question had not yet been opened the tribunal erred in holding that L had female employees who were capable of carrying out the duties which the tribunal held it would be improper for a man to perform by reason of s.7(2) (b) (ii).

Held, allowing the appeal and dismissing the complaint, that (1) s.7(4) looked to the time at which the prima facie discrimination took place, when a complainant was refused an offer of employment. The question was a factual, not a hypothetical one, and in the circumstances there were no employees at the club in question when W was refused employment on the ground of his sex, *Etam v. Rowan* [1989] I.R.L.R. 150, [1990] C.L.Y. 2568 and *Wylie v. Dee & Co (Menswear) Ltd* [1978] I.R.L.R. 103, [1978] C.L.Y. 1038 distinguished, and (2) alternatively, the tribunal erred in failing to direct itself in accordance with s.7(3), and instead took into account an irrelevant factor, namely the extent to which the s.7(2) duties formed a part of the overall working hours under the contract.

LASERTOP LTD v. WEBSTER [1997] I.C.R. 828, Judge Peter Clark, EAT.

2262. Sex discrimination–indirect discrimination–female employee with child care needs–comparison of numbers of male and female employees and females with child care needs–failure to justify discriminatory requirements

[Sex Discrimination Act 1975 s.1 (1) (b); Council Directive 76/207 on equal treatment for men and women as regards access to employment.]

E commenced employment with L in September 1983. In 1987 she became a train operator and also had a child. In order to accommodate her child care needs E organised a shift pattern which involved her working from 8 am to 4 pm on weekdays and one shift on alternate Sundays. In the 1990s L decided to improve efficiency by altering the shift patterns and reducing manning levels through voluntary severances. The new shift arrangements made it impossible for E to continue in employment and look after her child, and she accepted voluntary severance in December 1992. E applied to an industrial tribunal, complaining that she had been indirectly discriminated against on the ground of her sex, contrary to the Sex Discrimination Act 1975 s.1 (1) (b), in that the application of the new rostering arrangement constituted a requirement or condition with which she could not comply, which could not be justifiable irrespective of sex and which was to E's detriment. E's complaint was upheld by the tribunal and L appealed.

Held, dismissing the appeal, that on the facts the tribunal was entitled to conclude that the proportion of female train operators who could comply with the new rostering arrangements was "considerably smaller" than the proportion of men who could do so. Under the Equal Treatment Directive 76/207, equality of treatment is the paramount consideration, *R. v. Secretary of State, ex p. Seymour Smith* [1995] I.R.L.R. 464, [1995] 1 C.L.Y. 2052 applied. As a matter of principle, when weighing the extent of the disproportionate impact that a condition has upon men and women in the relevant pool, the tribunal can properly have regard to the number of women train operators as against the number of male train operators. In assessing the extent of the disproportionate impact, the tribunal is entitled to take account of a wider perspective, including statistics showing the percentage of women who have primary care responsibility for a child, in contrast to the percentage of men in that position. There was evidence to justify the tribunal's conclusion that L could and should have accommodated E's personal requirements, namely that they could have made arrangements which would not have been damaging to their business plans but which could have accommodated the reasonable demands of their employees. Accordingly the tribunal did not err in finding that L had failed to justify the discriminatory requirement.

LONDON UNDERGROUND LTD v. EDWARDS (NO.2) [1997] I.R.L.R. 157, Morison, J., EAT.

2263. Sex discrimination—membership—whether National Federation of Self Employed and Small Businesses Ltd constituted an "employers'organisation"

[Sex Discrimination Act 1975 s.12(1), s.12(3).]

An organisation of the self employed and small businesses was an organisation of employers within the Sex Discrimination 1975 Act s.12 and was therefore required to entertain a member's complaint that renewal of membership had been refused contrary to s.12(3). N appealed against an industrial tribunal decision that it had jurisdiction to entertain a complaint by P that, by refusing to renew her membership, N had discriminated against her unlawfully on grounds of sex or marital status contrary to the Sex Discrimination Act 1975 s.12(3). N argued that the tribunal was not entitled to hear the complaint because it was not an organisation which fell within s.12. It contended that, as it was made up partly of self-employed people, it could not be classed as an "organisation of employers"and also that, as it was mainly concerned with members' interests as business people rather than as employers, the purpose test in s.12(1) was not fulfilled. P argued that N's involvement in putting forward members' names for the employers' panel from which industrial tribunal members were selected meant that it was representative of employers and must necessarily be considered an employers'organisation.

Held, dismissing the appeal, that it was appropriate to examine N's characteristics as a whole rather than rely on the narrow "membership" and "purpose" tests advanced in argument. It was clear that N represented the interests of its members who were employers and as such was an organisation of employers within s.12.

NATIONAL FEDERATION OF SELF EMPLOYED AND SMALL BUSINESSES LTD v. PHILPOTT [1997] I.C.R. 518, Kirkwood, J., EAT.

2264. Sex discrimination—repeated refusal of request for part time work or job sharing amounted to single not continuing act

[Sex Discrimination Act 1975 s.1, s.76(1).]

The appellant employed by the respondent employer, became pregnant and took maternity leave from July 1992. In March 1992 she made a request for her terms of employment to be changed so that she could return to work after her leave on a part-time or job share basis. This request was refused on March 26, 1992. She returned to work in March 1993 and renewed her request for part-time work. This was again refused and the appellant resigned. In August 1993 she presented a complaint to an industrial tribunal, alleging that the refusal to allow her to work part-time constituted unlawful direct or indirect discrimination on the grounds of her sex. The tribunal found that the act of discrimination, if there was one, occurred on March 26, 1992 and that what happened thereafter was a repetition of the original request and refusal. There was no rule operated by the employer and so no continuing act of discrimination had occurred. The tribunal refused to exercise discretion to extend the time limit and dismissed the appellant's complaint. The appellant contended that the refusal on March 26, 1992 did not provide a full cause of action because in an indirect discrimination case time only began to run when an applicant could not comply with a requirement, which in this case was when she could not carry on working full-time.

Held, dismissing the appeal, that (1) the issue of when time started to run had to be determined by reference to the words of the Sex Discrimination Act 1975 s.76(1). According to that section, time started to run when "the act complained of was done" and in this case the act complained of was the refusal on March 26, 1992. The argument that time began to run in an indirect discrimination case only when the cause of action was complete had to be rejected since it would lead to the bizarre conclusion that all the requirements of proportionality, justification and detriment under s.1 (1) (b) of the 1975 Act would need to be complied with. This meant that there would have to be a full argument on the merits before the jurisdictional issue could be determined and, as held in *Hutchinson v. Westward Television Ltd* [1977] I.R.L.R. 69, [1977] C.L.Y. 1073, that could not have been Parliament's intention; (2) the appellant's argument that the alleged unfair constructive dismissal constituted an act of direct discrimination and that time ran from the date of dismissal could not be sustained since she could not demonstrate that she had been treated less favourably than a man would have been treated, and (3) the tribunal did not err in finding that the refusal to allow part-time work was not a continuing act. The mere repetition of a request could not convert a single managerial decision into a policy, practice or rule, *Owusu v. London Fire & Civil Defence Authority* [1995] I.R.L.R. 574, [1996] C.L.Y. 2583 considered.

CAST v. CROYDON COLLEGE [1997] I.R.L.R. 14, B Hargrove Q.C., EAT.

2265. Sex discrimination—unfair dismissal—declaration that qualifying period for protection had been indirectly discriminatory and incompatible with EC law

[Unfair Dismissal (Variation of Qualifying Period) Order 1985 (SI 1985 782); Council Directive 76/207 on equal treatment for men and women as regards access to employment; Treaty of Rome 1957 Art.119.]

A declaration that the Unfair Dismissal (Variation of Qualifying Period) Order 1985 was incompatible with the principle of equal treatment in Council Directive 76/207 did not enable an employee to pursue an action for unfair dismissal in the industrial tribunal as a Directive only affected the rights of citizens as against the state. The Secretary of State appealed against a decision allowing S's appeal against the dismissal of her application for judicial review and a ruling that she was entitled to a declaration that the Unfair Dismissal (Variation of Qualifying Period) Order 1985, which required an employee to have been continuously employed for two years in order to qualify for protection against unfair dismissal, indirectly discriminated against women between 1985 and 1991 and was incompatible with the principle of equal treatment in Council Directive 76/207.

Held, allowing the appeal, that it was clear from the jurisprudence of the ECJ that a Directive only affected the rights and duties of citizens as against the state or an organ of the state and could have no effect on the rights of S or her employers, and thus the declaration would not enable S to pursue an action for unfair dismissal in the industrial tribunal. Since the discriminatory effect of the Order was only in evidence between 1985 and 1991, any declaration would not have the effect of informing the government that new legislation was needed to remedy the situation. Further, it would not be appropriate to issue a declaration in order to enable S or others to bring a *Francovich* action, *Francovich v. Italy*

(C6/90) [1992] I.R.L.R. 84, [1992] C.L.Y. 4815 for damages against the state, *R. v. Secretary of State for Employment, ex p. Equal Opportunities Commission* [1995] 1 A.C. 1, [1994] C.L.Y. 1981 applied. However, it was not necessary for S to resume her action for unfair dismissal in the industrial tribunal and the court would request a preliminary ruling from the ECJ on certain issues regarding the construction of the Treaty of Rome 1957 Art.119 in order to allow it to give judgment.

R. v. SECRETARY OF STATE FOR EMPLOYMENT, *ex p.* SEYMOUR-SMITH [1997] 1 W.L.R. 473, Lord Hoffmann, HL.

2266. **Sex discrimination–voluntary redundancy scheme–claims out of time–just and equitable to hear claims**

[Sex Discrimination Act 1975 s.76(5); Limitation Act 1980 s.33; Employment Protection (Consolidation) Act 1978 s.67(2).]

K and W volunteered for redundancy in August 1989, under the scheme operated by their employer, BCC. Neither K nor W was told that, as women over 55, the payments would be abated; for men, the abatements applied only after the age of 60. When K and W discovered this they sought advice from their union, the NUM, and were advised that nothing could be done. After the publication of the decision of the European Court of Justice in *Barber v. Guardian Royal Exchange Assurance Group (C262/88)* in June 1990 the NUM realised that it might be possible for K and W to bring a claim under the Sex Discrimination Act 1975. Counsel's advice was sought and K lodged a claim of unlawful sex discrimination in July 1991. W lodged her application in February 1992. BCC took the preliminary point that the applications had been lodged out of time. The tribunal extended time on the ground that it was just and equitable to do so, and BCC appealed. The EAT remitted the matters to the tribunal, advising that in determining whether time should be extended the tribunal should use as a checklist the factors mentioned in the Limitation Act 1980 s.33, including, inter alia, the length and reasons for the delay and the extent to which the cogency of evidence was affected by the delay. When the matters returned to the tribunal they considered that it would be just and equitable for the claims to proceed, referring inter alia to *Biggs v. Somerset CC* [1996] I.R.L.R. 203, [1996] 1 C.L.Y. 2577. BCC appealed, arguing that the effect of the decision in *Biggs* was that a tribunal, when exercising its discretion on just and equitable grounds, must leave out of account an applicant's excuse that the delay was due to a misunderstanding of the true position under European law.

Held, dismissing the appeal, that the discretion conferred by the Sex Discrimination Act 1975 s.76(5) to extend time on just and equitable grounds was very much wider than that conferred by the Employment Protection (Consolidation) Act 1978 s.67(2) and equally as wide as the discretion conferred by s.33 of the 1980 Act. If BCC's argument were correct, it would have the effect that the many reported cases in which a mistake of law or inaccurate advice by a lawyer was taken into account in the exercise of the discretion to disapply the limitation period would have to be overruled. It would also result in a judicial amendment of the words of s.76(5) of the 1975 Act, so that the court could not take into account all the circumstances of the case, but all the circumstances bar one. Accordingly, the ruling in *Biggs v. Somerset CC* applied only in the context of s.67(2) of the 1978 Act and the consideration under that section of whether it was "reasonably practicable" for the applicant to present her complaint in time.

BRITISH COAL CORP v. KEEBLE [1997] I.R.L.R. 336, Smith, J., EAT.

2267. **Transfer of undertakings–compromise agreement between transferor and employees–right to claim against transferee not excluded**

[Transfer of Undertakings (Protection of Employment) Regulations 1981 (SI 1981 1794).]

In December 1994 BRS lost a distribution contract to W in a tendering process. BRS's contract expired on January 27, 1995 and prior to that date it negotiated severance agreements with a number of its employees. The terms of the agreement were that in return for accepting voluntary redundancy the employees would forgo any claims they might have against BRS. Independent legal advice was not obtained in relation to the agreements prior to January 27, 1995, but on February 1, compromise agreements were signed under the auspices of ACAS and the employees collected their cheques on February 6. On February 8, they commenced proceedings against W claiming that their employment had been transferred to W under the Transfer of Undertakings (Protection of Employment) Regulations 1981 and that they had been constructively dismissed as their terms and conditions of employment were not acceptable to the new employer. At a preliminary hearing the tribunal accepted W's submission that the compromise agreements inured for the benefit of W and that the tribunal did not have jurisdiction. The 1981 Regulations were assumed to apply. The employees appealed.

Held, allowing the appeal and remitting the case, that after a transfer of an undertaking there is no continuing joint liability between transferor and transferee. After the date of the transfer, the transferor is discharged from all obligations arising under a contract of employment or the employment relationship, *Stirling DC v. Allan* [1995] I.R.L.R. 301 [1995] C.L.Y. 5991 applied. At the date of the transfer, the rights, obligations and liabilities of BRS were transferred to W. Accordingly, the compromise agreements eventually reached between BRS and the employees could not benefit W. There was no privity of contract between BRS and W nor any evidence supporting agency so as to justify an argument that W might be regarded as notional participants to the compromise agreements. Nor was there any scope for arguing that agreements made after a transfer might validate what was agreed before.

THOMPSON v. WALON CAR DELIVERY [1997] I.R.L.R. 343, Byrt, J., EAT.

2268. Transfer of undertakings–constructive dismissal–implied term of trust and confidence–employee's fears in relation to terms and conditions on transfer

[Transfer of Undertakings (Protection of Employment) Regulations 1981 (SI 1981 1794).]

S appealed against an industrial tribunal decision allowing B's claim that his belief as to the nature of changes to his terms and conditions of employment arising from a transfer from local government employment to S struck at the condition of trust and confidence between B and his former employer, amounting to constructive dismissal.

Held, allowing the appeal, that although such a term was present in a contract of employment in either express or implied form, it could only be breached by third party acts in very rare cases. On the facts, B's resignation had taken place after extensive pre-transfer negotiations but before the transfer to S occurred. At common law, therefore, S, as transferee, was not responsible for any breach between B and his former employer. Whilst a transfer could present such dire consequences that the condition of trust and confidence could be undermined, this could not arise when what was actually at risk was the post-transfer preservation of an employee's current terms and conditions, as these were protected under the Transfer of Undertakings (Protection of Employment) Regulations 1981. An employer's conduct, therefore, could not be so drastic, as regards the obligations of trust and goodwill, to change the remedies available under the 1981 Regulations and the term itself properly related to those situations where an employee was forced to resign to protect his interests in the absence of such a remedy.

SITA (GB) LTD v. BURTON, *The Times*, December 5, 1996, Lord Johnston, EAT.

2269. Transfer of undertakings–early retirement–pension enhancement payments–liability between college and council

[Further and Higher Education Act 1992 s.26; Transfer of Undertakings (Protection of Employment) Regulations 1981 (SI 1981 1794) Reg.5; Teachers

(Compensation for Redundancy and Premature Retirement) Regulations 1989 (SI 1989 298).]

Birmingham College of Food, Tourism and Creative Studies, BCF, appealed against a decision on appeal that C's claim against B be dismissed for showing no cause of action and giving C liberty to enter summary judgment against BCF with damages to be assessed. C was employed by BCC for over six years as a teacher at BCF and agreed with BCF to take early retirement on March 31, 1993 on the basis that she would receive an enhancement to her years of service for pension purposes, to be met as to five years by B and the remainder by BCF. This was contrary to the Teachers (Compensation for Redundancy and Premature Retirement) Regulations 1988 which prohibited enhancement greater than the number of years of actual service. On April 1, 1993, pursuant to the Further and Higher Education Act 1992, responsibility for higher education, including all liabilities in respect of staff employed immediately before the takeover, was transferred to BCF, who contended: (1) that C's employment had ended when she stopped work on March 31 so that she was not employed at the relevant time and (2) that s.26 of the 1992 Act should be construed in accordance with the Transfer of Undertakings (Protection of Employment) Regulations 1981 Reg.5 so as to apply only to current employees.

Held, allowing the appeal and striking out the claim against BCF on the ground that it disclosed no cause of action, that (1) the judge below had been correct to hold that there was a difference between employment per se and the period when an employee was not working, and, therefore, that C's employment had lasted until midnight on March 31, and (2) however, s.26 of the 1992 Act was clearly intended to benefit only employees whose employment commenced before the date of transfer and continued afterwards, *Secretary of State for Employment v. Spence* [1987] 1 Q.B. 179, [1986] C.L.Y. 1237 and *Merton LBC v. Haycroft* (Unreported) considered, *Litster v. Forth Dry Dock and Engineering Co Ltd* [1970] 1 A.C. 546, [1989] C.L.Y. 1508 followed. Thus, there could be no transfer of the liability to pay any enhancement by virtue of s.26 of the 1992 Act.

COOKE v. BIRMINGHAM CITY COUNCIL, Trans. Ref: QBENI 96/0021/E, November 14, 1996, Peter Gibson, L.J., CA.

2270. Transfer of undertakings–helicopter service contract awarded to another company–majority of assets retained–undertaking not effectively transferred

[Transfer of Undertakings (Protection of Employment) Regulations 1981 (SI 1981 1794) Reg.3(1).]

BH had contracted with S to provide helicopter services, but later part of the contract was awarded to KLM, who moved its operations from Beccles to Norwich, but did not take over staff or equipment from BH. KLM appealed against a decision granting declarations to B and others, who had been employed by BH at the Beccles site, that when BH's contract ended and KLM had commenced its contract in Norwich, there had been a transfer of undertakings within the meaning of the Transfer of Undertakings (Protection of Employment) Regulations 1981, so that their employment had been transferred to KLM. KLM argued, relying on *Suzen v. Zehnacker Gebaudereinigung GmbH Krankenhausservice (C13/95)* [1997] All E.R. (EC) 289, [1997] C.L.Y. 2278, that the fact that an activity which had been contracted to BH had now been contracted to KLM was not by itself enough to effect a transfer of undertakings. In general an undertaking would also consist of property, staff and other assets, and as KLM had not purchased assets from BH or employed any of its staff, the Regulations did not apply.

Held, allowing the appeal, that it was necessary to determine whether BH's operation at Beccles had been an undertaking or part of an undertaking within the meaning of Reg.3(1), and if so, whether the undertaking was transferred so that it retained its identity in KLM's hands. Applying *Suzen*, the Beccles operation was an undertaking under Reg.3(1) which consisted of assets which included not only staff, but also infrastructure, buildings and contracts, but as the vast majority of BH's assets had been retained by BH, there was no transfer of the undertaking so that BH could be said to have retained its identity with KLM.

BETTS v. BRINTEL HELICOPTERS LTD (T/A BRITISH INTERNATIONAL HELICOPTERS) [1997] 2 All E.R. 840, Kennedy, L.J., CA.

2271. **Transfer of undertakings—identity of transferee not disclosed to employee—validity of transfer**

[Transfer of Undertakings (Protection of Employment) Regulations 1981 Reg.3, Reg.5 (SI 1981 1794); Employment Protection (Consolidation) Act 1978 s.122.]

It is not necessary for an employee to know the identity of the buyer of a business for obligations under a contract of employment to be effectively transferred. S appealed against an industrial tribunal decision that he was liable to pay debts owed by an insolvent company, G, to three of its former employees pursuant to the Employment Protection (Consolidation) Act 1978 s.122. The industrial tribunal found that when G sold its business to I, there was a transfer within the meaning of the Transfer of Undertakings (Protection of Employment) Regulations 1981 Reg.3, but, following *Photostatic Copiers (Southern) Ltd v. Okuda and Japan Office Equipment* [1995] I.R.L.R. 11, [1995] 1 C.L.Y. 2063, the fact that the employees did not know the identity of the buyer until after the transfer took place meant that G's obligations to the employees under their contracts of employment had not been successfully transferred to I by Reg.5 of the Regulations, leaving S liable to pay the outstanding sums.

Held, allowing the appeal, that it was not necessary for an employee to have notice of the transfer and know the identity of the purchaser in order for the obligations under his contract of employment to be effectively transferred by Reg.5. The decision to the contrary in *Photostatic Copiers (Southern) Ltd* did not accord with the object of Reg.5 as amended and should no longer be followed.

SECRETARY OF STATE FOR TRADE AND INDUSTRY v. COOK [1997] I.C.R. 288, Morison, J., EAT.

2272. **Transfer of undertakings—identity of transferee not disclosed to employee—validity of transfer**

[Transfer of Undertakings (Protection of Employment) Regulations 1981 (SI 1981 1794) Reg.5, Reg.8(1).]

A transfer of undertakings was effective regardless of whether the parties consented to the transfer or had notice of the identity of the transferee. MRS appealed against a decision that upon losing its local authority contract to M, the contract of employment of one of its employees, D, had not been successfully transferred to M under the Transfer of Undertakings (Protection of Employment) Regulations 1981 Reg.5, because D had not had notice of the identity of the transferee. D claimed he had been unfairly dismissed in the course of the transfer and MRS contended that liability for the claim had been transferred to M.

Held, allowing the appeal, that Reg.5 introduced a statutory novation which took effect regardless of whether the parties consented to the transfer or had notice of one another's identity, *Secretary of State for Employment v. Spence* [1987] Q.B. 179, [1986] C.L.Y. 1237 applied, *Photostatic Copiers (Southern) Ltd v. Okuda* [1995] I.R.L.R. 11, [1995] 1 C.L.Y. 2063 not followed. Thus D's contract of employment had been transferred to M, pursuant to Reg.5, and by virtue of Reg.8(1) D's contract was deemed to have been terminated by unfair dismissal. MRS's obligations towards D had been brought to an end by the transfer and liability for D's dismissal now rested with M.

MRS ENVIRONMENTAL SERVICES LTD v. DYKE, *The Times*, March 25, 1997, Judge Byrt, Q.C., EAT.

2273. Transfer of undertakings—no employment protection where reorganisation of administrative functions between authorities—European Union

[Council Directive 77/187 relating to the safeguarding of employees' rights in the event of transfers of undertakings Art.1 (1).]

H commenced employment as a secretary to the mayor's office of the municipality of Schierke in May 1992. In July 1994, pursuant to a public law agreement under the applicable local government law, the municipality of Schierke, together with other municipalities, formed an administrative collectivity, G, to which they transferred administrative functions. The municipality then terminated H's contract of employment. H commenced proceedings claiming that under German law her contract of employment had been transferred to the new administrative collectivity and could not therefore be terminated. The Labour Court referred to the European Court of Justice two questions for interpretation under Council Directive 77/187, Art.1 (1), (1) whether Art.1 (1) must be interpreted as meaning that the concept of "a transfer of an undertaking, business or part of a business" applies to the transfer of administrative functions from a municipality to an administrative collectivity, and (2) if the first question is answered in the affirmative, whether Art.1 (1) must be interpreted as meaning that the concept of a "legal transfer" applies to a transfer of an undertaking which is effectuated by a public law agreement.

Held, answering the first question in the negative, that the purpose of the Directive was to protect workers against the potentially unfavourable consequences for them of changes in the structure of undertakings resulting from economic trends at national and community level, through, inter alia, transfers of undertakings, business or parts of businesses to other employers as a result of transfers or mergers. Consequently, reorganisation of structures of the public administration or the transfer of administrative functions between public administrative authorities does not constitute a "transfer of an undertaking" within the meaning of the Directive. In the instant case the transfer carried out between the municipality and the administrative collectivity related only to activities involving the exercise of public authority. Even if those activities were assumed to have aspects of an economic nature, they could only be ancillary. Accordingly, the first question had to be answered in the negative and so the second question did not arise.

HENKE v. GEMEINDE SCHIERKE (C298/94) [1997] All E.R. (EC) 173, GC Rodriguez Iglesias (President), ECJ.

2274. Transfer of undertakings—occupational pensions—acceptance of new contract of employment following tender—employer under no obligation to continue paying pensions contributions—European Union

[Council Directive 77/187 relating to the safeguarding of employees' rights in the event of transfers of undertakings Art.3.]

E worked as a catering service worker offshore in the North Sea, on terms which included payment of contributions by his employer to an occupational pension scheme. In 1994, when the relevant catering contract was put out to tender, S won the contract and E accepted a new contract of employment with them. S refused to continue to pay pension contributions, and E brought a claim that such refusal was contrary to Norwegian law implementing Council Directive 77/187. His claim was dismissed at first instance, and the appeal court referred to the Court a number of questions for an advisory opinion including, inter alia, whether the catering contract was covered by the provisions of Council Directive 77/187, and whether Art.3(3) of the Directive included the right to uphold insurance schemes.

Held, that the catering contract was covered by the Directive but no obligation to pay pension contributions was transferred, that (1) having regard to the wide scope of the transfer concept as established through ECJ jurisprudence, it can be concluded that a succession of two independent service contracts does not as such fall outside the scope of the Directive; (2) the decisive criterion for establishing whether there is a transfer for the purposes of the Directive is, as held in *Spijkers v. Gebroeders Benedik Abbatoir CV (C24/ 85)* [1986] 3 E.C.R. 1119, [1986] C.L.Y. 1362, whether the business in question is transferred and retains its identity following the transfer. In determining this question regard must be had to all the facts and circumstances surrounding the transaction. The termination of a catering contract with one company and the signing of a new contract with another company does not of itself fall outside the scope of the Directive, but other factors, such as the fact that supply of goods or services to one among several customers would not normally qualify as a distinct part of the supplier's business, and (3) the wording of Art.3(3) of the Directive read in conjunction with the general principle in Art.3(1) points to the conclusion that all rights and obligations pertaining to old age, invalidity and survivors' benefits have been excluded from the general transfer of rights and obligations to the transferee.

EIDESUND v. STAVANGER CATERING AS (E2/95) [1996] I.R.L.R. 684, B Haug (President), EFTA.

2275. Transfer of undertakings–occupational pensions–interpretation of Acquired Rights Directive in relation to future pension rights

[Council Directive 77/187 relating to the safeguarding of employees' rights in the event of transfers of undertakings Art.3(3).]

A and other school dinner ladies appealed against the dismissal of their originating summons against LCC, their former employer, and BET Catering Services Ltd, who had taken over their work after a competitive tendering exercise, arguing that Council Directive 77/187 Art.3(3) should have been construed so as to include protection of pension rights arising after the date of transfer, so that their right to belong to an occupational scheme carried over into their new employment.

Held, dismissing the appeal, that Council Directive 77/187, which protected employees' rights upon the transfer of undertakings, made an exception for pension rights under Art.3(3). The wording of Art.3(3) para.2, which provided that Member States should adopt measures to protect employees' rights in relation to certain benefits under company pension schemes and treated both present employees and ex-employees alike, clearly referred to accrued rights in respect of periods of service occurring prior to the transfer, and there was no provision for protection of pension rights arising after that date.

ADAMS v. LANCASHIRE CC [1997] I.R.L.R. 436, Morritt, L.J., CA.

2276. Transfer of undertakings–seamen stationed on continental shelf–whether encompassed by protection legislation

[Council Directive 77/187 relating to the safeguarding of employees rights in the event of transfers of undertakings Art.3(1); Transfer of Undertakings (Protection of Employment) Regulations 1981 (SI 1981 1794) Reg.2(2) Reg. 3(1); Employment Protection (Consolidation) Act 1978.]

The appellants were 145 Swedish crew members of North Sea accommodation vessels for oil and gas workers, known as flotels. The flotels were owned by, SRAB. The appellants were employed by SSAB, who were contracted by SRAB to provide crews for the flotels. In October 1994 SRAB gave notice of termination of the manning agreements to SSAB, who in turn gave notice of termination of employment to the appellants. The flotels were situated within the UK sector of the Continental Shelf of the North Sea. The manning agreement was transferred to DSM. The appellants brought claims of, inter alia, unfair dismissal, relying on the Transfer of Undertakings (Protection of Employment) Regulations 1981 and the Employment Protection (Consolidation) Act 1978. At a preliminary hearing on jurisdiction an industrial tribunal substantially upheld the appellants' claims, apart from a ruling that since the flotels were not situated within the UK as defined by Reg.3(1) of the 1981 Regulations, the Regulations did not apply. The appellants appealed and DSM cross-appealed on the grounds, inter alia, that the appellants did not ordinarily work in the UK and so the tribunal did not have jursidiction to consider their claims.

Held, dismissing the appeal and allowing the cross-appeal in part, that (1) the industrial tribunal correctly decided that the UK sector of the Continental Shelf of the North Sea was not part of the UK for the purposes of Reg.3(1) of the 1981 Regulations. There was no basis for any suggestion that a principle extends EU law to all economic activities being undertaken by a Member State wherever located, simply because, as such, they may be subject to that state's jurisdiction. It was illogical to extend the legislation, even assuming that the flotels were not ships, to vessels situated in an area not exclusively UK territory but merely accessible for limited reasons on a sovereign basis by reason of maritime convention; (2) whether the flotels were ships, was an issue of status or categorisation as a matter of statutory construction, and was a question of law. The tribunal misdirected itself on this issue by placing too much emphasis on the apparent distinction between a hull and a pontoon. The real question was whether the vessel was used, or capable of being used, for navigation. For the purposes of Council Directive 77/187 Art.3(1) the flotels were obviously to be regarded as seagoing vessels; (3) the purpose of the Directive was to regulate the rights of employees in undertakings and accordingly to remove seagoing vessels from the scope of the Directive, the crews of those vessels must be included in the exclusion from the Directive. Reg.2(2) of the 1981 Regulations must be interpreted accordingly; (4) in determining the location of the undertaking for the purposes of the Regulations, the proper approach requires the tribunal to conclude that in the instant case there is only one location for the undertaking so long as it subsists, namely the operational base of the employer. Such location could change physically but would always be ascertainable; (5) the question of whether the employees were "ordinarily working" in the UK would be remitted to the tribunal to determine what was the operational base of SSAB at the relevant time, and (6) with regard to general protection of UK employment law, assuming jurisdiction is given to the tribunal in appropriate cases for the correct reasons, ancillary workers in the North Sea are within the umbrella and scope of the employment protection law.

ADDISON v. DENHOLM SHIP MANAGEMENT (UK) LTD [1997] I.R.L.R. 389, Lord Johnston, EAT.

2277. Transfer of undertakings–teachers–governors of voluntary aided school an emanation of the state–European Union

[Council Directive 77/187 relating to the safeguarding of employees' rights in the event of transfers of undertakings; Transfer of Undertakings (Protection of Employment) Regulations 1981 (SI 1981 1794).]

Three teachers were dismissed for redundancy after the voluntary aided school at which they taught was closed down and replaced by a new school with a temporary governing body. The teachers claimed unfair dismissal on the grounds that they had been dismissed as a result of the transfer of an undertaking. A legislative error prevented them claiming under the Transfer of Undertakings (Protection of Employment) Regulations 1981, and they sought instead to rely directly on Council Directive 77/187. The industrial tribunal and the EAT both found that the teachers were unable to invoke the doctrine of vertical direct effect as the governors of the voluntary aided school were not an emanation of the state as required under EC law. The teachers appealed.

Held, allowing the appeal, that in *Foster v. British Gas Plc* [1991] 2 A.C. 306, [1991] C.L.Y. 1673 it was held that an emanation of the state could be defined as a body who had been made responsible, pursuant to a measure adopted by the state, for providing a public service that was under the control of the state and which exercised special powers for the purpose, beyond those which operated between individuals. Once a voluntary school had decided to enter the state system and had been granted voluntary aided status, it could be considered to have been made responsible for the provision of education, which was a public service. The statutory instrument made by the local authority could be regarded as the measure adopted by the state making the school governors so responsible. The powers of the local authority and the Secretary of State for Education meant that education was a public service under the control of the state. Whilst the spending of public money did not amount to the exercise of a special power for these purposes, it was not necessary to treat the test as being exhaustive. Therefore, the school governors could be considered an emanation of the state for the purposes of vertical direct effect.

NATIONAL UNION OF TEACHERS v. GOVERNING BODY OF ST MARY'S CHURCH OF ENGLAND (AIDED) JUNIOR SCHOOL [1997] I.C.R. 334, Schiemann, L.J., CA.

2278. **Transfer of undertakings–termination of service contract–contract awarded to another company–no assets transferred–applicability of Acquired Rights Directive–European Union**

[Council Directive 77/187 relating to the safeguarding of employees' rights in the event of transfers of undertakings Art.1.]

S, a school cleaner employed by Z, was dismissed after Z's cleaning contract was terminated and awarded to another company. She claimed that the notice of dismissal served upon her had not terminated her relationship with Z. The German court referred to the ECJ the question of whether Council Directive 77/187 Art.1 (1) applied.

Held, that Art.1 (1) did not apply where services were entrusted under a new contract with a second undertaking in the absence of a concomitant transfer from the first undertaking to the second of significant tangible or intangible assets, or the taking over of a major part of the first undertaking's workforce. In determining whether transfer conditions were met, it was necessary to consider the facts involved in the transaction, and in particular those given in *Spijkers v. Gebroeders Benedik Abattoir CV (C24/85)* [1986] E.C.R. 1119, with those circumstances forming singular factors in the overall assessment which could not be considered in isolation. Although an asset transfer was one of the relevant criteria, the absence of assets did not necessarily preclude a transfer. The degree of importance attaching to each criterion varied according to the activity concerned, as in certain sectors an entity could function without significant tangible or intangible assets. In labour intensive sectors a group of workers could retain their identity following a transfer where a new employer not only pursued the same activity but retained numbers and skills in a major part and formed a body of assets enabling the transferor to carry on those activities on a regular basis.

SUZEN v. ZEHNACKER GEBAUDEREINIGUNG GmbH KRANKENHAUSSERVICE (C13/95) [1997] All E.R. (EC) 289, GC Rodriguez Iglesias (President), ECJ.

2279. **Transfer of undertakings–transfer of community home between local authorities–employees dismissed and then re-employed on less favourable terms–contracts of employment did not continue under new employer**

[Transfer of Undertakings (Protection of Employment) Regulations 1981 (SI 1981 1794) Reg.5, Reg.8; Council Directive 77/187 relating to the safeguarding of employees rights in the event of transfers of undertakings Art.4 (1).]

L, suffering financial constraints, arranged with S to take over the management of a community home, but the number of staff employed at the home was to be reduced from 162 to 72 and the job descriptions of the 72 new jobs were to be different, with some staff suffering a substantial reduction in earnings. L gave notice terminating on the grounds of redundancy the employment of the 72 staff who had accepted the new posts offered by S. After taking up their new employment, the employees brought an action before the industrial tribunal contending that the transfer of the home attracted the provisions of the Transfer of Undertakings (Protection of Employment) Regulations 1981 and that, under Reg.5, they were still employed under the terms and conditions of their contracts with L. The IT, finding for S, held that, in terms of Reg.8, the reason for the employees' dismissal was economic or organisational, but the EAT allowing the employees' appeal, substituted a finding that the reason for their dismissal was the transfer. S appealed.

Held, allowing the appeal, that Reg.8 clearly applied to dismissals effected both before and after a transfer, although only the transferor could effect a dismissal prior to the transfer taking place. Reg.8 distinguished between dismissals which were unfair because the main reason for the dismissal was the transfer and dismissals which were considered not unfair because the main reason for them was economic, organisational or technical, as provided for in Council Directive 77/187 Art.4(1). If a contract of employment was terminated for one of the latter reasons, it would not be regarded as having been terminated by the transfer even though the dismissal took place at the time of the transfer. The IT had determined that the reason for the dismissal was economic or organisational and, as the Regulations had to be construed in a way that was consistent with Art.4(1) of the Directive, Reg.5 did not operate to continue the contracts of employment with S.

WILSON v. ST HELENS BC; SANDERS v. ST HELENS BC; MEADE v. BRITISH FUELS LTD; BAXENDALE v. BRITISH FUELS LTD, *The Times*, July 18, 1997, Beldam, L.J., CA.

2280. **Transfer of undertakings–unfair dismissal–disputed employment with transferor**

[Transfer of Undertakings (Protection of Employment) Regulations 1981 (SI 1981 1794) Reg.5(1).]

C appealed a decision by the EAT dismissing his appeal against rejection of his claim of unfair dismissal on the grounds of redundancy. C was appointed as managing director of EGP and Arenascene, A, its wholly owned subsidiary. EGP was then taken over by IRH, and C was appointed as a director of IRH in addition to his previous position. IRH went into receivership and in May 1992 one of the administrative receivers of IRH wrote to C terminating his employment with immediate effect. C continued to work for EGP and, he argued, A. On June 20, 1992 A sold its assets and the respondent company, Sellers Arenascene Ltd, SA, was formed. On June 22, 1992 a letter from the administrative receivers of EGP was sent to C terminating his employment forthwith. C argued that his dismissal was unfair because he had been dismissed allegedly on the grounds of redundancy, but SA continued to trade, and that he had been employed by SA in succession to A. SA argued that there was no contract of employment between C and A and therefore none between C and itself. C argued that under the Transfer of Undertakings (Protection of Employment) Regulations 1981 Reg.5(1) he was entitled to consider himself as an employee of SA following the transfer of A.

Held, allowing the appeal and remitting the case for a further hearing, that the industrial tribunal did not properly direct its attention to the issue of whether C was employed by A at the time of the transfer to SA. The tribunal should consider C's employment position after the letter of May 1992 and before he was dismissed in June 1992, and if he was employed, by which company.

CONNOLLY v. SELLERS ARENASCENE LTD, Sir Brian Neill, CA.

2281. **Transfer of undertakings–unfair dismissal–jurisdiction of industrial tribunal to hear claims against transferor employee**

[Transfer of Undertakings (Protection of Employment) Regulations 1981 (SI 1981 1974) Reg.5.]

A and others were employed by P&O until August 1, 1994. In April and May 1994 they were told that there would be a transfer of their employment to an outside contractor, and that the transferee, Opus, would offering substantially inferior terms and conditions than they enjoyed with P&O. They were further told that if they resigned before the transfer they would receive a generous severance package from P&O, but if they did not resign in writing then they would be deemed to have resigned and would not receive their cheques. As a result, A and others tendered resignation letters in July 1994. The transfer to Opus took effect on August 1, 1994. In October 1994 A and others lodged claims for unfair dismissal against P&O,

claiming that they had been constructively dismissed by P&O. P&O took a preliminary point that, by virtue of the Transfer of Undertakings (Protection of Employment) Regulations 1981 Reg.5(2) and Reg.5(4B), the tribunal did not have jurisdiction to hear the claims since all the liabilities of P&O in respect of anything done before the transfer and in relation to the transfer had been transferred to Opus. The tribunal decided that it did have jurisdiction and P&O appealed.

Held, allowing the appeal and dismissing the claims against P&O, that the combined effect of Reg.5(2) and Reg.5(3) of the 1981 Regulations, as interpreted in *Litster v. Forth Dry Dock Engineering Co. Ltd* [1989] I.C.R. 341, [1989] C.L.Y. 1508, is that if P&O, as transferor, is liable in connection with A's contracts of employment then that liability is transferred to Opus, as transferee. Acts done on behalf of P&O before the transfer are deemed to have been done by Opus. Nothing in the other parts of Reg.5 stand in the way of such a conclusion, *Merckx v. Ford Motors Co (Belgium) SA (C171/94)* [1977] I.C.R. 352, [1996] 1 C.L.Y. 2650 considered.

P&O PROPERTY HOLDINGS LTD v. ALLEN [1997] I.C.R. 436, Lindsay, J., EAT.

2282. Unfair dismissal – bank nurses – whether applicant an employee in terms of Employment Rights Act 1996 s.230(1)

[Employment Rights Act 1996 s.230(1).]

A, was a bank nurse owned, controlled and used by R to work at their hospital. R contested that A was an employee within the meaning of the Employment Rights Act 1996 s.230(1) and therefore unable to bring a claim of unfair dismissal.

Held, that A was an employee under the s.230(1) of the 1996 Act, the tribunal indicated the following as factors consistent with a contract of employment: (1) the mutuality of obligation in that A remained available for work at the end of her shift in consideration of payment for that work; (2) she was paid weekly in arrears and was entitled to annual increments; (3) she was subject to a medical examination on appointment and could be called for another thereafter; (4) she was entitled to join the pension scheme, required to wear a uniform and was subject to the health and safety policy, and (5) she owed a duty of confidentiality and could avail herself of the disciplinary and grievance procedure and was in fact suspended, dismissed and offered a review hearing. However, factors weighing against the finding were; (1) no notice was required to terminate employment; (2) there was no guarantee of regular employment; (3) she was not entitled to sick or holiday pay, and (4) there was no obligation on R to provide work for A and it was solely for A to decide whether she worked or not, *Clark v. Oxfordshire HA* (Unreported, 1995) considered.

AMARASINGHE v. CHASE FARM HOSPITALS NHS TRUST, June 12, 1997, AM Lewzey, IT (Stratford). [*Ex rel.* Edward Grieves, Barrister, 10-11 Gray's Inn Square, Gray's Inn].

2283. Unfair   dismissal – compensation – deductions – severance   payments – sequence of deductions when calculating award

[Employment Protection (Consolidation) Act 1978 s.74.]

C sought review of a decision by a differently constituted EAT that an industrial tribunal had erred when calculating a compensatory award for unfair dismissal under the Employment Protection (Consolidation) Act 1978 s.74. C, who had received a contractual severance payment which exceeded his statutory redundancy payment by £20,500, contended that the tribunal was right to deduct that excess amount from his gross loss, calculated as £43,000, before applying the percentage deduction, in accordance with *Polkey v. AE Dayton Services Ltd* [1988] A.C. 344, [1988] C.L.Y. 1353, to reflect the chance that C would not have been selected for redundancy if a fair procedure had been followed. He argued, inter alia, that the EAT's decision, that the *Polkey* deduction should be applied to the amount representing C's gross loss before credit was given for the contractual severance payment, had been reached in ignorance of the decision in *Cox v. Camden LBC* [1996] I.C.R. 815, [1996] C.L.Y. 2655.

Held, dismissing the original appeal and affirming the industrial tribunal's decision, that under s.74(1) of the Act the first task for an industrial tribunal was to determine the loss sustained "in consequence of the dismissal in so far as that loss is attributable to action taken by the employer". In the instant case, C's loss amounted to £22,500, being £43,000 less the amount of compensation received. The tribunal had then to consider what proportion of C's loss could be attributed to the wrongful action of DE. On the facts, the tribunal decided that C would have had a 50 per cent chance of being retained if the employer had followed a fair procedure, and the tribunal was right to apply this percentage deduction to the amount representing C's net loss after taking account of the termination payment. The decisions in *Derwent Coachworks v. Kirby* [1995] I.C.R. 48, [1995] 1 C.L.Y. 2080 and *Clement-Clarke International Ltd v. Manley* [1979] I.C.R. 74, [1979] C.L.Y. 968 could not be regarded as good law and should not be followed.

DIGITAL EQUIPMENT CO LTD v. CLEMENTS (NO.2) [1997] I.C.R. 237, Morison, J., EAT.

2284. Unfair dismissal—employee dismissed after refusing to accept contract variation—mere threat of deduction of wages insufficient to confer jurisdiction on industrial tribunal

[Employment Protection (Consolidation) Act 1978 s.60A; Wages Act 1986 s.5(1).]

M, employed as a lorry driver by NW, was dismissed from his job after objecting to a provision in a draft employment contract requiring him to repay any costs of training if he resigned before expiry of the contract. M brought a complaint of unfair dismissal before an industrial tribunal under the Employment Protection (Consolidation) Act 1978 s.60A, alleging dismissal for asserting the right of protection against unlawful deductions from pay contrary to the Wages Act 1986. The tribunal held that they lacked jurisdiction to hear M's complaint since he had not been continuously employed for two years at the time of dismissal and no statutory right could come into effect until a deduction had actually taken place. The EAT, allowing M's appeal, held that it was irrelevant for the purposes of s.60A(1)(b) that there was no actual infringement of a statutory right by an employer, and the provision applied where an employee alleged in good faith that there had been infringement. Where an employer sought to impose a variation of a contract which negated a statutory right without an employee's consent, with the sanction of dismissal in the event of refusal to accept the variation, that could constitute infringement of a statutory right at the time the threat was made. NW appealed.

Held, allowing the appeal, that an employee had no general right not to be unfairly dismissed where he had not been continuously employed for two years. Although a complaint could be presented under the 1986 Act even where an employee had not been employed for two years, an industrial tribunal had no jurisdiction to deal with a threatened deduction of wages since s.5(1) stated that a tribunal could only hear complaints where an employer had actually made a deduction. To bring s.60A of the 1978 Act into play, it was sufficient that an employee alleged that his employer had infringed his statutory right and that his allegation was the reason he was dismissed. However, M was unable to establish the circumstances which could lead to such a conclusion.

MENNELL v. NEWELL & WRIGHT (TRANSPORT CONTRACTORS) LTD, *The Times*, July 18, 1997, Mummery, L.J., CA.

2285. Unfair dismissal–employer selectively re-engaged employees dismissed for taking industrial action–compensation payable to those not re-engaged could not be reduced to take account of contributory fault

[Employment Protection (Consolidation) Act 1978 s.62.]

Compensation payable to employees who are dismissed for participating in collective industrial action and subsequently unfairly rejected for re-engagement under the Employment Protection (Consolidation) Act 1978 s.62 cannot be reduced to take account of their contributory fault. CW dismissed 119 bus drivers who had taken part in industrial action, but subsequently re-employed 22 of them. T and 72 other drivers brought claims for unfair dismissal pursuant to the Employment Protection (Consolidation) Act 1978 s.62 and it was found that CW's selective failure to offer re-engagement was unfair. CW appealed against a Court of Appeal ruling ([1996] I.C.R. 237, [1995] 1 C.L.Y. 2091) allowing the employees' appeal against an EAT decision that the amount of compensation payable to them fell to be reduced by such amount as the industrial tribunal considered just and equitable to reflect the fact that the employees' conduct had contributed to their dismissal.

Held, dismissing the appeal, that it could not have been Parliament's intention that the amount of compensation payable in such circumstances should be reduced on the ground of contributory fault. Where employees took part in collective industrial action, it was impossible to attribute blame to any individual complainant, particularly as that blame was shared by those who had been re-employed, *Courtaulds Northern Spinning Ltd v. Moosa* [1984] I.C.R. 218, [1984] C.L.Y. 1301 and *TNT Express (UK) Ltd v. Downes* [1994] I.C.R. 1, [1994] C.L.Y. 1946 considered.

CROSVILLE WALES LTD v. TRACEY; *sub nom.* TRACEY v. CROSVILLE WALES LTD [1997] 3 W.L.R. 800, Lord Nolan, HL.

2286. Unfair dismissal–misapplication of burden of proof–incorrect to stop case after hearing only employer's evidence

[Employment Protection (Consolidation) Act 1978 s.57(3).]

U commenced employment with H in 1970, and in 1974 was appointed manager in charge of one of H's homes for children in care. In July 1992 he was suspended from that post as a result of allegations of sexual abuse made against him by a former resident at the home. H initiated police investigations into the allegations and subsequently charged U. Before the criminal case was heard, H instituted disciplinary proceedings against U. U's representative asked for the disciplinary proceedings to be postponed pending the outcome of the criminal proceedings but H declined this request. U was dismissed at the conclusion of the disciplinary proceedings in May 1993. On September 6, 1993 U was acquitted of three counts of buggery. On September 28, H dismissed U's internal appeal against his dismissal. U presented a complaint to a tribunal that he had been unfairly dismissed. The tribunal upheld U's complaint, after hearing only the evidence presented by H, ruling that H had not shown that it had acted reasonably or fairly in treating U's conduct as a reason for dismissal in the circumstances of the case. H appealed, arguing that the tribunal erred in holding that the onus lay on H to establish the reasonableness of the dismissal.

Held, allowing the appeal and remitting the case to a different tribunal, that (1) the tribunal had erred in placing a burden on H to prove reasonableness, *British Home Stores Ltd v. Burchell* [1980] I.C.R. 303, [1980] C.L.Y. 1004. They had done this by stating that H's witnesses had not shown that H had acted reasonably or fairly in treating U's conduct as a reason for dismissal, and that H had not made out a prima facie case, and (2) the tribunal had been wrong to terminate the proceedings at the end of the employer's evidence; without hearing U's evidence they had not heard sufficient evidence to decide the issue of reasonableness. Although it was open to a tribunal to stop a case at half time where the party going first, and upon whom the onus lay, had clearly failed to establish what he set out to establish, where there was no burden of proof it was even more difficult to envisage arguable cases where it would be appropriate to take such a course.

HACKNEY LBC v. USHER [1997] I.C.R. 705, Judge Peter Clark, EAT.

2287. Unfair dismissal–pleadings–failure to specify nature of alleged misconduct–Antigua and Barbuda

[Industrial Court Act 1976 (Antigua and Barbuda); Labour Code (Antigua and Barbuda).]

Notice of summary dismissal was given to B by her employer stating that the reason for the dismissal was that B and another employee had committed an indecent act during working hours on the employer's premises. The Labour Code (Antigua and Barbuda) required an employer to provide a written statement of the precise reason for the dismissal on request but B's employer failed to do so when requested to provide a statement by B's solicitor. Under the terms of the Industrial Court Act 1976 (Antigua and Barbuda) the case was referred to the Industrial Court. The employer, in asserting that the dismissal had been fair, provided a memorandum giving further details of the indecent act. B argued that the employer was estopped from raising such assertions by reason of the failure to provide the written statement. The Industrial Court upheld the submission but that decision was overturned by the Eastern Caribbean Court of Appeal. B appealed to the Privy Council.

Held, allowing the appeal, that the Code required reasons for a dismissal to be given as formal statutory reasons which could be used in any proceedings to test the fairness of the dismissal. Those reasons were akin to an unamendable pleading and subsequent informal reasons could not replace them. If a statement was not provided then the employer was estopped from adducing evidence of facts that could have been set out in the statement, *Marchant v. Earley Town Council* [1979] I.C.R. 891, [1980] C.L.Y. 1053 distinguished.

BERRIDGE v. BENJIES BUSINESS CENTRE [1997] 1 W.L.R. 53, Lord Hoffmann P.C., PC.

2288. Unfair dismissal–reason for dismissal–reasonableness of employer's response in light of established facts

B appealed against a decision of an Employment Appeal Tribunal that the industrial tribunal erred in upholding her claim of unfair dismissal. B was dismissed from her post as assistant director of education on the grounds of gross misconduct and complained to an industrial tribunal that she had been the victim of sexual and racial discrimination. The tribunal unanimously rejected the claims of racial and sexual discrimination, but upheld her claim of unfair dismissal. B argued that the Employment Appeal Tribunal should not have interfered with what were essentially findings of fact and the tribunal was entitled to find that it was capability rather than conduct which was the reason for her dismissal.

Held, dismissing the appeal, that the industrial tribunal erred in failing to consider adequately whether the dismissal of B was within the range of reasonable responses of a reasonable employer in the light of the established facts. The industrial tribunal wrongly substituted their view of the underlying facts and their response to those facts instead of considering how those facts might have been viewed by a reasonable employer, *Abernethy v. Mott, Hay & Anderson* [1974] I.C.R. 323, [1974] C.L.Y. 1285 considered, *Iceland Frozen Foods v. Jones* [1983] I.C.R. 17, [1983] C.L.Y. 1325 applied.

HACKNEY LBC v. BENN, Trans. Ref: EATRF 95/0262/B, July 31, 1996, Neill, L.J., CA.

2289. Unfair dismissal–reason for dismissal–reasonableness test

[Employment Protection (Consolidation) Act 1978 s.57 (3).]

M was employed as a residential social worker at a residential children's home run by B. On June 26, 1993 M spat in the face of one of the teenage boy residents and caught the same boy in the face with his hand. Taking into account a previous disciplinary warning M received in 1992, M was dismissed following a disciplinary hearing. The panel conducting the hearing did not take evidence directly from the boy involved but referred to a statement prepared by a key worker. M's internal appeal was dismissed and he presented a complaint to a tribunal that he had been unfairly dismissed. The tribunal upheld his complaint on the basis that the investigation conducted by B, and in particular the failure to interview the boy directly, was not an investigation which any reasonable employer would have conducted. B appealed, arguing, inter alia, that the tribunal had incorrectly placed the burden of proof on B and had slavishly applied the test of reasonableness stated in *British Home Stores Ltd v. Burchell* [1980] I.C.R. 303, [1980] C.L.Y. 1004.

Held, allowing the appeal and remitting the matter to a different tribunal, that although the test as stated in *British Home Stores Ltd v. Burchell* was undoubtedly important, an over-simplistic application of that test in each and every conduct case raised the danger of tribunals falling into error in a number of respects, including a failure to appreciate that the burden of demonstrating the reasonableness of the dismissal was neutral and did not lie upon the employer, *Post Office (Counters) Ltd v. Heavey* [1990] I.C.R. 1, [1991] C.L.Y. 1697 followed. Further, while an application of the threefold *Burchell* test might be appropriate where the employer has to decide a factual contest, the position might be otherwise where an employee admitted all or part of the alleged offences, *Royal Society for the Protection of Birds v. Croucher* [1984] I.C.R. 604, [1984] C.L.Y. 1304 applied. Even where an employer did not show that it had fulfilled all the elements of the *Burchell* test, that did not mean that the dismissal would be unfair because dismissal might still fall within the range of reasonable responses open to the reasonable employer, *British Leyland UK Ltd v. Swift* [1981] I.R.L.R. 91, [1981] C.L.Y. 945, *Iceland Frozen Foods Ltd v. Jones* [1983] I.C.R. 17, [1983] C.L.Y. 1325 and *Conlin v. United Distillers* [1994] I.R.L.R. 169 applied. In the instant case, the tribunal applied an incorrect burden of proof by stating that they were not satisfied as to two of the matters in the *Burchell* test. The decision of B was based on M's own admission of misconduct and so this was not a case which called for a full investigation by the employer, *Royal Society for the Protection of Birds v. Croucher* applied. Further, the tribunal substituted its own view for that of management in stating that a reasonable employer would have considered that M had suffered extreme provocation, and the tribunal did not ask itself whether dismissal fell within the range of reasonable responses.

BOYS AND GIRLS WELFARE SOCIETY v. McDONALD [1997] I.C.R. 693, Clark, J., EAT.

2290. **Unfair dismissal–reason for dismissal–tribunal must consider reason used when notice was given and not when employment terminated**

[Employment Protection (Consolidation) Act 1978 s.57; Employment Rights Act 1996 s.98.]

An EAT decided that P's dismissal was unfair because he had not been consulted about the reorganisation of M's financial department which led to the loss of the position he formerly occupied as financial controller and company secretary. However, it was held that the defect was merely procedural and consequently no compensation award was made. P contended that an employer could not rely on a reason established only at the date when the employment terminated, but must abide by the reason for dismissal set out in the notice required by the Employment Protection (Consolidation) Act 1978 s.57 replaced by the Employment Rights Act 1996 s.98.

Held, dismissing the appeal, that, unless it was a case of summary dismissal, an employer's reasons for dismissal given at the date of notice were both relevant and admissible for the purposes of s.57(1) of the 1978 Act; however the employer could rely on a different reason arising by the time the employment actually terminated, *Abernethy v. Mott, Hay & Anderson* [1974] I.C.R. 323 distinguished as relating to summary dismissal in which timing was not considered relevant, *W Devis & Sons Ltd v. Atkins* [1977] A.C. 931, [1977] C.L.Y. 1160 and *Stacey v. Babcock Power Ltd (Construction Division)* [1986] Q.B. 308, [1986] C.L.Y. 1280 considered.

PARKINSON v. MARCH CONSULTING LTD [1997] I.R.L.R. 308, Evans, L.J., CA.

2291. Unfair dismissal—redundancy—alternative employment—change of mind by employee before commencing new contract

[Employment Protection (Consolidation) Act 1978 s.83(2).]

P worked at a hospital located at B, which was run by E. In 1994 E decided to close the hospital at B and transfer its activities to a new hospital at A. There was a surplus of employees and vacancies were to be allocated on open competition between all staff. P successfully applied for a position at the new hospital, and accepted a contract beginning in June 1994. However, in April 1994 she suffered a stress-related illness and on May 25, 1994 advised E that she could not take up the new position. Her claim for a redundancy payment succeeded before an industrial tribunal, which held that she was entitled to withdraw her acceptance of the new post and apply for redundancy as she would have been entitled to do had she not applied for and accepted a new contract. E appealed, arguing that since P had accepted an offer of a new contract that superseded the redundancy and her subsequent letter of resignation amounted to a termination by mutual consent.

Held, allowing the appeal and remitting the case to a different industrial tribunal, that it would be open to a tribunal, considering all the circumstances of the case, to conclude that P had been constructively dismissed under the Employment Protection (Consolidation) Act 1978 s.83(2) and that she had not forfeited her right to a redundancy payment because she had a period of time in which to make up her mind, *Birch v. University of Liverpool* [1985] I.C.R. 470, [1985] C.L.Y. 1150 distinguished, *Turvey v. CW Cheney & Son Ltd* [1979] I.C.R. 341, [1979] C.L.Y. 932 and *Sheet Metal Components Ltd v. Plumridge* [1974] I.C.R. 373, [1974] C.L.Y. 1263 considered. Since the industrial tribunal assumed a dismissal rather than determined and identified it, the case must be remitted for a tribunal to make the necessary findings of fact to enable it to reach a decision on whether there was a dismissal or a constructive dismissal.

EAST SUFFOLK LOCAL HEALTH SERVICES NHS TRUST v. PALMER [1997] I.C.R. 425, Pugsley, J., EAT.

2292. Unfair dismissal—redundancy—alternative employment—immediate re-engagement—unfair dismissal claim after end of trial period—dismissal not to be disregarded

[Employment Protection (Consolidation) Act 1978 s.84(1), s.84(4).]

Until May 1994 J was employed as school keeper of BCS. In 1994 his employers decided to make economies in relation to school services and contracted out the cleaning arrangements. They also decided that the position of school keeper should be replaced with that of site manager, at a lower salary. J was offered the new position and told that if did not accept it he would be made redundant. In the event J accepted the post of site manager, but in September 1994 brought proceedings for unfair dismissal and redundancy. The tribunal found that although there was a significant reduction in J's duties on the introduction of the new position and that J had been dismissed, he was not to be regarded as having been dismissed by reason of the Employment Protection (Consolidation) Act 1978 s.84(1), since he was immediately re-engaged under a new contract and worked for longer than the four week trial period provided for under s.84(4). J appealed, contending that the effect of s.84(1) affected only the claim for redundancy and did not prevent J from bringing a claim for ordinary unfair dismissal.

Held, allowing the appeal and remitting the case to the industrial tribunal, that the provisions of s.84 are limited to Part VI of the Act only, and do not apply to the general right to claim unfair dismissal in Part V, *Hempell v. WH Smith & Sons Ltd* [1986] I.C.R. 365, [1986] C.L.Y. 1273 followed, *Ebac Ltd v. Wymer* [1995] I.C.R. 466, [1995] 1 C.L.Y. 2033 considered. It is in the highest degree unlikely that Parliament should, in this or any other way, have intended that an employer who drives his employee into a constructive dismissal be able to escape the statutory sanctions provided in Part V if the employer could drive that employee into accepting a re-engagement, however inferior, and secondly, keep the employee in that job for at least four weeks. In order to support so improbable a conclusion the clearest language would be needed and such language cannot be found.

JONES v. GOVERNING BODY OF BURDETT COUTTS SCHOOL [1997] I.C.R. 390, Lindsay, J., EAT.

2293. Unfair dismissal–removal of assistant curate in Church of England from diocesan payroll–curate not an employee under employment protection legislation

[Employment Protection (Consolidation) Act 1978 s.54(1).]

C, an assistant curate in the Church of England, carrying out his duties at two churches in the Diocese of Southwark until his removal from the diocesan payroll in May 1994, appealed against an EAT ruling allowing an appeal by the Diocese, its Bishop and the Diocesan Board of Finance from a decision of the industrial tribunal that C was an employee for the purposes of the Employment Protection (Consolidation) Act 1978 and therefore could bring an action for unfair dismissal before the tribunal pursuant to s.54(1).

Held, dismissing the appeal, that the critical question was whether C had a contract, and the industrial tribunal had erred in its approach when concluding that there was a contractually enforceable agreement. No contract could exist unless there was sufficient evidence of an intention to create legal relations. An assistant curate was ordained and called to an office recognised by law, making it unnecessary to enter into a contract, and it was still good law that a curate in the Church of England was not an employee, *National Insurance Act 1911, Re* [1912] 2 Ch. 563 approved. The right not to be unfairly dismissed under s.54(1) could not apply to C because he had no employer. The Diocese, which was not a legal person, was not his employer; the Board of Finance, which paid his stipend, did not appoint him or remove him; and whilst the Bishop had legal responsibility for licensing assistant curates, that relationship arose from canonical obedience and there was no private law contract.

DIOCESE OF SOUTHWARK v. COKER, *The Times*, July 17, 1997, Mummery, L.J., CA.

2294. Wages–unlawful deductions–time limit for claim

[Wages Act 1986 s.5(3).]

G was employed by G4 on terms which provided for payment of a monthly salary plus quarterly commission. G's contract provided that commission could be paid at any time up until the end of the month immediately following the previous quarter. In practice G was paid commission together with his monthly salary, which was paid on the Monday after the third Friday of each month. G claimed that G4 had paid him reduced commission on a number of contracts. The alleged reductions were in respect of the quarters ending September and December 1994. G received his commission payment for the December 1994 quarter, together with his salary for January 1995, on January 20, 1995. He presented a complaint of unlawful deduction from wages to an industrial tribunal on April 20, 1995. G4 contended that the last day for presenting a complaint was three months from January 20, 1995, namely April 19, 1995, and that G's complaint was accordingly out of time. The tribunal held that G's complaint was presented out of time but that it was not reasonably practicable for G to have presented his complaint in time and that accordingly the tribunal had jurisdiction to hear the matter. The tribunal found that G4 had made the unlawful deductions from G's wages as alleged. G4 appealed.

Held, dismissing the appeal, that (1) the tribunal erred in finding that the payment date for the commission was January 20, 1995. Since the payment of commission could have been lawfully made at any time up to January 31, 1995, it was only once that date had passed that an unlawful deduction had been made, *Delaney v. Staples (t/a De Montfort Recruitment)* [1991] I.R.L.R. 112, [1992] C.L.Y. 2028 applied. Accordingly there was no unlawful deduction until February 1, 1995 and G's complaint had been presented in time; (2) in the alternative, the tribunal were entitled to find on the facts that it was not reasonably practicable for the complaint to have been presented in time. G and his advisers reasonably believed that time did not expire until April 30, 1995 and an impediment which can reasonably prevent a complaint being presented in time can include a mistaken belief with regard to essential matters, *Walls Meat Co v. Khan* [1978] I.R.L.R. 499, [1979] C.L.Y. 979; (3) the tribunal was mistaken in finding that the claim in respect of the commission was not a claim made as part of a claim in respect of a series of deductions within the meaning of the Wages Act 1986 s.5(3). They were all similar claims made under the same contract relating to similar payments and accordingly were claims in respect of a series of deductions within the ordinary meaning of the word "series", *Taylorplan Services Ltd v. Jackson* [1996] I.R.L.R. 184, [1996] 1 C.L.Y. 2674 applied.

GROUP 4 NIGHTSPEED LTD v. GILBERT [1997] I.R.L.R. 398, Colin Smith Q.C., EAT.

2295. Articles

Age discrimination *(Mike Stock)*: Adviser 1997, 60, 34. (Extent to which age related dismissals and age bars can be challenged using unfair dismissal, indirect sex discrimination and disability discrimination provisions in absence of express prohibition on age discrimination).

Commercial secrets and the employer/employee relationship *(Paul Lavery)*: I.H.L. 1997, 48(Mar), 93-94. (Duty of confidence and restraint of trade clauses in contracts of employment).

Directors' contracts *(Joyce Cullen)*: T.E.L. & P. 1997, 2(12), 89-91. (Drafting considerations, including restrictions, job description, duration, remuneration, share options, restrictive covenants, solicitation clauses, dismissal and notice).

Disablity discrimination: warnings for your clients *(Rhiain Lewis)*: S.J. 1997, 141(41), 1026. (First cases brought under employment provisions of Disability Discrimination Act 1995).

Disloyalty dismissals: IDS Brief 1997, 593, 7-11. (Dismissals for activities in conflict with employer's interests, with reference to spare time working, disclosure of confidential information and setting up in competition).

Do women have a "right" to work part time? *(Camilla Palmer* and *Joanna Wade)*: Legal Action 1997, Jun, 11-13. (Legal framework governing direct and indirect sex discrimination and issues arising, including interpretation of requirement or condition, proportionate comparison and justifiability).

Double jeopardy for employers *(Lesley Kemp)*: C.L. 1997, 15, Supp Cor 20-21. (Employers' criminal liability in force January 27, 1997 for employing foreign nationals not authorised to work in UK and continuing obligation to refrain from racial discrimination in recruitment).

Employing illegal workers: IDS Brief 1997, 592, 7-10.

Equal pay - the material factor defence: IDS Brief 1997, 589, 7-11. (What amounts under Equal Pay Act 1970 s.1 (3) to genuine reason for unequal pay due to material factor which is not difference of sex and objective justification for cases of disproportionate impact).

Flexible working *(Michael Ryley)*: S.J. 1997, 141(30), 748-750. (Employment law implications, including employer's right to introduce change, employment status, geographical factors, continuity of service, homeworking and health and safety).

Gross misconduct: IDS Brief 1997, 594, 7-11. (Definition and how concept is applied in relation to wrongful and unfair dismissal).

Home working and the law: IT L.T. 1997, 5(1), 4-8. (Issues to be considered in employing teleworkers with particular employment status).

Job sharing after maternity *(Nigel Baker)*: T.E.L. & P. 1997, 3(3), 22-23. (Courts' approach to refusal of job share requests and need for employers to reconsider policies in relation to employees returning from maternity leave).

Liability, compensation and justice in unfair dismissal *(Barry Hough* and *Ann Spowart-Taylor)*: I.L.J. 1996, 25(4), 308-319. (Remedial force of non-compensation aspects of unfair dismissal regime, particularly liability, and whether tribunals have erred in their interpretation of s.74 of 1978 Act in awarding compensation).

Maternity leave - returning part time: IDS Brief 1997, 590, 7-11. (Circumstances in which employer's refusal to allow women to return from maternity leave on more flexible basis amounts to sex discrimination, indirect discrimination claims and issue of justification).

Misconduct dismissals: Burchell revisited: I.R.L.B. 1997, 570, 2-6. (Whether EAT guidelines establishing threefold text for determining fairness of dismissal continue to be relevant in light of subsequent statutory and case law developments).

No laughing matter *(Karon Monaghan* and *Makbool Javaid)*: N.L.J. 1997, 147(6782), 350-352. (Vicarious liability of employers for racial harassment of employees by other employees or third parties over whom employers have control).

Part-time workers: IDS Brief 1996, 578, 7-11. (Statutory employment rights and the circumstances in which equal pay and sex discrimination claims may be brought).

Posting employees abroad *(Janet Gaymer* and *Hilary Belchak)*: T.E.L. & P. 1997, 2(7), 49-51. (Advice to employers on contractual issues, implications of Posted Workers Directive, statutory rights and special considerations including immigration issues).

Public sector employment: I.R.L.B. 1997, 574, 2-9. (Employment law considerations applying to Crown workers, Houses of Parliament, police force, armed services, National Health Service, local government and education services, availability of judicial review and direct effect of EU law).

Recognising new kinds of direct sex discrimination: transsexualism, sexual orientation and dress codes *(Robert Wintemute)*: M.L.R. 1997, 60(3), 334-359. (Comparison of recent cases on employment discrimination).

Redundancy and the transfer of undertakings *(Colin Bourn)*: N.L.J. 1997, 147(6800), 1040-1041. (Developments during 1997 including definition of redundancy, application of Acquired Rights Directive to contracting out, variation of contract terms by transferee and transfer of compromise agreements with transferee).

References and the law *(David McAdam)*: L. Ex. 1997, Jan, 34-35. (Employer's duty of care when preparing reference on behalf of employee).

Resignations: IDS Brief 1997, 600, 7-11. (Legal issues surrounding resignations, with reference to timing and effect of resignations, ambiguous resignations, enforced resignations and payments on termination of employment).

Sexual and racial harassment at work: policy implementation *(Gary Henderson)*: P.L.C. 1997, 8(4), 39-46. (Features of sexual and racial harassment, direct and vicarious liability of employer and introduction of harassment policy by employer).

Smoking policies *(Jason Butwick)*: T.E.L. & P. 1997, 3(4), 30-31. (Extent of employer's duty to provide smoke-free environment for employees and relevant considerations for employers introducing and implementing smoking policies, with reference to case law on rights of smokers and non-smokers).

Sunday trading - employment rights: IDS Brief 1997, 591, 7-10. (Statutory provisions protecting shop workers and betting workers who have opted out of Sunday working).

Suzen and transferring an activity *(Oliver Hyams)*: S.J. 1997, 141(16), 378-379. (Effect on continuity of employment and the right to redundancy payments of ECJ decision limiting meaning of transfer of economic entity).

TUPE and outsourcing: recent developments *(John McMullen)*: P.L.C. 1997, 8(10), 47-53. (Cases on application of TUPE to outsourcing in light of ECJ decision in Suzen, and to reorganisations and variation of employment terms on transfer).

Teleworking and homeworking *(Charles Wynn-Evans)*: T.E.L. & P. 1997, 2(9), 65-67. (Legal issues, including employment status and discrimination protection, and technical considerations for employers).

The Working Time Directive: I.R.L.B. 1996, 558, 2-10. (Purpose and scope of Directive, requirements in relation to maximum weekly working time, paid annual leave, rest periods and breaks, night and shift work, derogations and prospects for implementation in UK).

The cost of getting it wrong *(Charles Wynn-Evans)*: T.E.L. & P. 1997, 3(2), 9-11. (Principles governing awards of compensation against employers in cases of unfair dismissal, wrongful dismissal, discrimination and failure to comply with TUPE and redundancy consultation obligations).

Time off for public duties: IDS Brief 1997, 586, 7-11. (Employees' statutory right to reasonable time off for performance of duties, remedies available to employee dismissed for taking time off and provisions governing jury service).

Time-limits in unfair dismissal cases: practice and procedure *(Martin Edwards)*: Lit. 1997, 16(4), 139-148. (Cases illustrating
difficulties arising on when time begins to run, presentation of claim and applications for extension of time; does not include EEC law considerations).

Unfair dismissal: how much will the industrial tribunal award? *(Robin White)*: S.J. 1997, 141(16), 386-388. (Heads of damage, tribunal's discretion in awarding damages and statistical analysis of awards made, based on decisions from 1995 and 1996).

Vicarious liability and employment discrimination *(Lucy-Ann Buckley)*: I.L.J. 1997, 26(2), 158-166. (Effect of applying Irving test, that employer is not liable for unauthorised act of employee unless act constituted improper mode of doing authorised task, to situations involving race or sex discrimination in employment context).

2296. Books

Bowers, John—Bowers on Employment Law. Paperback: £29.95. ISBN 1-85431-289-8. Blackstone Press.

Bowers, John; Brown, Damian; Mead, Geoffrey—Industrial Tribunal Practice and Procedure: Fourth Set-third Supplement. Hardback: £79.00. ISBN 0-7520-0494-8. FT Law & Tax.

Brearley, Kate; Bloch, Selwyn—Employment Covenants and Confidential Information. Hardback: £65.00. ISBN 0-406-00220-7. Butterworth Law.

Decker, Kurt H.—Drafting and Revising Employment Contracts. Employment Law Library. Paperback: £75.00. ISBN 0-471-19661-4. Wiley.

Duggan, Michael; Mann, Jayne; Ingle, Michael—Directors: Termination of Employment. Special Reports. Hardback: £125.00. ISBN 0-7520-0311-9. FT Law & Tax.

McMullen, John—Business Transfers and Employee Rights. Hardback: £55.00. ISBN 0-406-04467-8. Butterworth Law.

Pitt, G.—Employment Law. 3rd Ed. Paperback: £21.95. ISBN 0-421-60450-6. Sweet & Maxwell.

Spicer, Robert—Industrial Tribunals: Awards and Remedies. Hardback: £160.00. ISBN 1-85811-151-X. CLT Professional Publishing.

Suter, Erich; Benson, Edward—Employment Law Service. Unbound/looseleaf: £100.00. ISBN 0-85308-288-X. Jordan.

Upex, Robert—Law of Termination of Employment. 2nd Ed. Hardback: £90.00. ISBN 0-421-58940-X. Sweet & Maxwell.

Upex, Robert; Shrubshall, Vivian—Contracts of Employment Law. Practitioner Series. Hardback: £50.00. ISBN 0-7520-0066-7. FT Law & Tax.

Wallington, Peter—Butterworths Employment Law Handbook. Paperback: £53.50. ISBN 0-406-04471-6. Butterworth Law.

Younson, Fraser; Jeffreys, Simon; Bowers, John; Napier, Brian—Transfer of Undertakings. Unbound/looseleaf: £195.00. ISBN 0-7520-0476-X. FT Law & Tax.

ENERGY

2297. Energy conservation–electrical equipment

ENERGY EFFICIENCY (REFRIGERATORS AND FREEZERS) REGULATIONS 1997, SI 1997 1941; made under the European Communities Act 1972 s.2. In force: September 3, 1999; £3.20.

These Regulations implement European Parliament and Council Directive 96/57 ([1996] OJ L236/36) on energy efficiency requirements for household electric refrigerators, freezers and their combinations. The Directive specifies minimum standards of energy efficiency to be met by such appliances placed on the Community market. The Regulations prohibit the placing on the Community market of new appliances which exceed maximum allowable electricity consumption values; make provision for the affixing of an EC mark; lay down the rules relating to the compulsory EC declaration of conformity of an appliance; require suppliers to establish and maintain technical documentation to enable assessment of whether the EC mark has been properly affixed to an appliance; and prohibit the affixing to an appliance of misleading markings. They also oblige manufacturers to bring non-conforming appliances on the market into conformity and to achieve a manufacturing process which ensures that appliances comply with their technical documentation and with the requirements of the Regulations.

2298. Energy conservation–electrical equipment–labelling

ENERGY INFORMATION (COMBINED WASHER-DRIERS) REGULATIONS 1997, SI 1997 1624; made under the European Communities Act 1972 s.2. In force: August 1, 1997; £3.70.

These Regulations implement Commission Directive 96/60 ([1996] OJ L266/1) and Council Directive 92/75 ([1992] OJ L297/16) relating to information about energy consumption of mains electric household combined washer-driers. They provide that suppliers must provide labels and tables of information with information about the energy consumption of appliances, consent to the information in labels and information notices being published, be responsible for the accuracy of the information and establish technical documentation to enable it to be assessed. They provide that dealers must attach the label to an appliance displayed to end-users or, where the appliance is not displayed, make the information notice available to potential purchasers before a sale is concluded. Neither requirement applies in distance-sales cases but similar information is to be given where sales are by means of printed communications such as mail order catalogues.

2299. Energy conservation–electrical equipment–labelling

ENERGY INFORMATION (WASHING MACHINES) (AMENDMENT) REGULATIONS 1997, SI 1997 803; made under the European Communities Act 1972 s.2. In force: May 15, 1997; £0.65.

These Regulations exclude washing machines with no internal means to heat water from the provisions of the Energy Information (Washing Machines) Regulations 1996 (SI 1996 600) to implement Commission Directive 96/89 ([1996] OJ L338/85). The earlier Regulations implemented Council Directive 92/75 ([1992] OJ L297/16) and Commission Directive 95/12 ([1995] L136/1). The 1996 Directive added these machines to Art.1 of the 1995 Directive, which excluded other machines from its scope. These Regulations also add a definition of "enforcement action" to the earlier Regulations.

2300. Energy Conservation Act 1996 (c.38)–Commencement No.3 Order

ENERGY CONSERVATION ACT 1996 (COMMENCEMENT NO.3 AND ADAPTATIONS) ORDER 1997, SI 1997 47 (C.4); made under the Energy

Conservation Act 1996 s.2. Commencement details: bringing into force various provisions of the Act on January 14, 1997 and April 1, 1997; £1.10.

This Order brings into force, for energy conservation authorities whose areas are in England or Wales, various provisions of the Energy Conservation Act 1996.

2301. Articles

Bibliography *(Katherine Christie)*: J.E.R.L. 1997, 15(2), 171-180. (Secondary material relating to energy, natural resources and environmental law and policy).

Implications of privatisation, liberalisation and integration of network bound energy systems *(Martha M. Roggenkamp)*: J.E.R.L. 1997, 15(1), 51-61. (Overlap between privatisation and liberalisation policies in European Union and possibility of more integration of sectors of energy industry as result).

Privatisation and environmental regulation: some general observations *(Catherine J. Redgwell)*: J.E.R.L. 1997, 15(1), 33-40. (Effect of increasing privatisation in energy sector on government's protection of environment).

The way forward for the nuclear industry *(Malcolm C. Grimston)*: Env. Liability 1997, 5(2), 50-55. (Impact of deregulation of energy industries on prospects for nuclear investment and need to develop export markets and extend lifespan of existing facilities).

Trans-European networks: an energy progress report *(Debra Johnson)*: U.L.R. 1997, 8(3), 96-103. (EU's methodology for achieving objectives of energy TENs, key problem areas and assessment of progress; includes table of projects).

ENVIRONMENT

2302. Air pollution–blood and animal by product processing plant–odour nuisance–authorisation excluded agreed condition as to odour emissions–inappropriate to include an unenforceable condition within an authorisation

[Environmental Protection (Prescribed Processes and Substances) Regulations 1991 (SI 1991 472) Sch.1; Environmental Protection Act 1990 s.7(1)(c), s.15(1), Part I.]

T sought judicial review of a decision by the Secretary of State, S, allowing P's appeal against the refusal of authorisation to carry on its blood and animal by product processing activities at its premises in Devon and failing to make such authorisation subject to an agreed condition that air emissions be free of offensive odour outside the process boundary. By the Environmental Protection (Prescribed Processes and Substances) Regulations 1991 Sch.1 s.6.9, P required authorisation under the Environmental Protection Act 1990 Part I and, when it was refused, P appealed to S under s.15(1) of the 1990 Act. There was a history of odour nuisance, with complaints from local inhabitants despite substantial modifications that had been made to the plant. T opposed P's application because it did not believe P would be able to prevent offensive odours. S considered that the agreed condition regarding the emissions was unenforceable and under, s.6(4) of the 1990 Act, inappropriate.

Held, allowing the application for judicial review and granting an order of certiorari, that it was inappropriate to include an unenforceable condition within an authorisation. However, S did not have regard to all the factors material to whether the condition was appropriate under s.7(1)(c) of the 1990 Act: the height of emission, the prevailing wind, the lie of the land, the extent of population affected, how offensive the smell was or its frequency. He referred only to the lack of close proximity of the plant to local residents when concluding that the circumstances were not sufficiently exceptional for the condition to be included.

R. v. SECRETARY OF STATE FOR THE ENVIRONMENT, *ex p.* TORRIDGE DC [1997] E.G.C.S. 61, McCullough, J., QBD.

2303. Air pollution–emissions–local authorities powers and duties

AIR QUALITY REGULATIONS 1997, SI 1997 3043; made under the Environment Act 1995 s.87, s.91. In force: December 23, 1997; £1.10.

These Regulations prescribe December 23, 1997 to December 31, 2005, as the relevant period during which local authorities must review the air quality within their area. They also set out relevant air quality objectives to be achieved during that period.

2304. Amenity protection–National Trust empowered to erect fences to preserve Trust common land

[National Trust Act 1907 s.29(A); National Trust Act 1971 s.23(1).]

NT brought an originating summons against A and others, who were members of both NT and the Open Spaces Society, for declaratory relief, seeking to resolve the issue of whether NT could fence common land which it held. Under the National Trust Act 1971 s.23(1), NT had the power to do anything which appeared desirable to provide or improve opportunities for public enjoyment of Trust land, including the erection of buildings and the carrying out of works. A opposed any fencing of NT's common land, regardless of whether the proposed scheme had been approved by Trust officers and members, and sought to rely on the National Trust Act 1907 s.29(A) which imposed a duty on NT to keep common land unenclosed and unbuilt upon as open spaces for public recreation and enjoyment.

Held, granting declaratory relief to NT, that the case turned upon the true construction of the relevant statutes. Notwithstanding NT's broad duty under s.29(A) to maintain common land as open spaces, the words of s.23(1), which were plainly directed towards the improvement of opportunities for public enjoyment of Trust common land, were transparent and unambiguous. The word "works" in s.23(1) was to be defined widely, extending beyond the erection of a building, and gave NT the power to erect fences in appropriate cases.

NATIONAL TRUST FOR PLACES OF HISTORIC INTEREST OR NATURAL BEAUTY v. ASHBROOK, *The Times*, July 3, 1997, Lindsay, J., Ch D.

2305. Ancient monuments–public access–Stonehenge

STONEHENGE REGULATIONS 1997, SI 1997 2038; made under the Ancient Monuments and Archaeological Areas Act 1979 s.19. In force: September 8, 1997; £0.65.

These Regulations regulate public access to Stonehenge, near Amesbury in Wiltshire.

2306. Antarctic Act 1994 (c.15)–Commencement No.1 Order

ANTARCTIC ACT 1994 (COMMENCEMENT) ORDER 1997, SI 1997 1411 (C.51); made under the Antarctic Act 1994 s.35. Commencement details: bringing into force various provisions of the Act on June 1, 1997; £0.65.

This Order brings into force the Antarctic Act 1994 s.5 which makes provision for permits for British vessels and aircraft entering Antarctica.

2307. Antarctic Act 1994 (c.15)–Commencement No.2 Order

ANTARCTIC ACT 1994 (COMMENCEMENT) (NO.2) ORDER 1997, SI 1997 2298 (C.91); made under the Antarctic Act 1994 s.35. Commencement details: bringing into force various provisions of the Act on October 1, 1997; £0.65.

This Order brings into force on October 1, 1997 the Antarctic Act 1994 s.6 which prohibits mineral resource activities in Antarctica by United Kingdom nationals except for certain limited purposes.

2308. Antarctic Act 1994 (c.15)–Commencement No.3 Order

ANTARCTIC ACT 1994 (COMMENCEMENT) (NO.3) ORDER 1997, SI 1997 3068 (C.113); made under the Antarctic Act 1994 s.35. Commencement details: bringing into force various provisions of the Act on January 14, 1998; £0.65.

This Order brings into force the Antarctic Act 1994 s.3, which requires permits for Antarctic expeditions organised in or departing from the United Kingdom, and s.4, which requires permits for manned British stations in Antarctica.

2309. Conservation–endangered species–trade controls

CONTROL OF TRADE IN ENDANGERED SPECIES (ENFORCEMENT) REGULATIONS 1997, SI 1997 1372; made under the European Communities Act 1972 s.2. In force: June 1, 1997; £1.95.

These Regulations make provision for the enforcement of Council Regulation 338/97 ([1997] OJ L61/1) (the principal Regulation) on the protection of species of wild flora and fauna by regulating trade therein and of Commission Regulation 939/97 ([1997] OJ L140/9) (the implementing Regulation). They revoke the Control of Trade in Endangered Species (Enforcement) Regulations 1985 (SI 1985 1155) which made provision for the enforcement of Council Regulation 3626/82 ([1982] OJ L384/1) and Commission Regulation 3418/83 ([1983] OJ L344/1) which are revoked by the Principal Regulation.

2310. Conservation–endangered species–trade controls–fees

CONTROL OF TRADE IN ENDANGERED SPECIES (FEES) REGULATIONS 1997, SI 1997 1421; made under the Finance Act 1973 s.56. In force: July 1, 1997; £1.10.

These Regulations prescribe fees to be paid to the Department of the Environment in connection with the evaluation and processing of applications for import, export and re-export certificates in pursuance of community obligations under Council Regulation 338/97 ([1997] OJ L61/1) on the protection of species of wild fauna and flora by regulating trade therein.

2311. Conservation–habitats

CONSERVATION (NATURAL HABITATS, &C.) (AMENDMENT) REGULATIONS 1997, SI 1997 3055; made under the European Communities Act 1972 s.2. In force: January 30, 1998; £0.65.

These Regulations amend the Conservation (Natural Habitats etc.) Regulations 1994 (SI 1994 2716) which make provision for implementing Council Directive 92/43 ([1992] OJ L206/7) on the conservation of natural habitats and of wild fauna and flora, by providing a new definition of the Habitats Directive so as to give effect to amendments made to the directive to the Act of Accession to the European Union of Austria, Finland and Sweden and by Council Directive 97/62 ([1997] OJ L305/42).

2312. Conservation–habitats–Newbury bypass–judicial review–transport policy–not role of court to supervise choice between incompatible policy objectives

Dense populations of terrestrial pulmonate snails were found on land allocated for the construction of the Newbury bypass. The Secretary of State for the Environment accepted recommendations that the habitat be included for consideration as a designated Special Area of Conservation but elected to go out to public consultation before deciding whether to place it on the candidate list for approval by the European Commission. The Secretary of State for Transport allocated the clearance contract for the land. B sought leave to bring judicial review proceedings arguing that the decision to let the clearance contract placed a fetter on the exercise of the government's discretion in deciding whether to place the site on the candidate list.

Held, dismissing the application, that the applicants had no foundation in law or reasonable expectation in policy to support their claim. The application would require the court to assume a supervisory role over ministerial powers which went beyond the scope of judicial review. The Crown was required to balance two bare and incompatible policy choices. As the relevant matters had been considered and there was no evidence of improper motive or irrationality the decision could not be challenged.

R. v. SECRETARY OF STATE FOR THE ENVIRONMENT, ex p. BERKSHIRE, BUCKINGHAMSHIRE AND OXFORDSHIRE NATURALISTS TRUST [1997] Env. L.R. 80, Sedley, J., QBD.

2313. Conservation–habitats–Newbury   bypass–snails–Special   Area   of Conservation–Crown's EC obligations no defence for squatters in possession proceedings

[Council Directive 92/43 on the conservation of natural habitats and of wild fauna and flora; Conservation (Natural Habitats) Regulations 1994.]

The Secretary of State held a compulsory purchase order for land required for the Newbury bypass. F was one of a group of protestors who had occupied the land without permission. In answer to the DoT's claim for possession F argued that re-taking the land would damage the population of the terrestrial pulmonate snail which justified the designation of the land as a Special Area of Conservation under Council Directive 92/43 on the conservation of natural habitats and of wild fauna and flora. The only way to ensure the protection of the habitat was by occupation and the public interest in the preservation of the habitat should outweigh the DoT's private rights.

Held, granting an order of possession, that there was no breach of the Habitats Directive nor of the regulations by which the Directive was implemented, the Conservation (Natural Habitats) Regulations 1994. Even if there had been a breach, the DoT's title to the land would not have been undermined. F's environmental obligations were not a defence to possession proceedings against those in possession without consent or authority. The court would not balance the Crown's public law duties against its private law rights in such circumstances.

SECRETARY OF STATE FOR TRANSPORT v. FILLINGHAM [1997] Env. L.R. 73, Sedley, J., QBD.

2314. Conservation–hedgerows

HEDGEROWS REGULATIONS 1997, SI 1997 1160; made under the Environment Act 1995 s.97. In force: June 1, 1997; £3.20.

These Regulations make provision for the protection of important hedgerows in England and Wales. To facilitate the protection of those hedgerows, the Regulations apply to a wider class of hedgerows. Before removing any hedgerow, including a stretch of hedgerow, to which these Regulations apply the owner must notify the local planning authority. The hedgerow may then not be removed if the local planning authority serves a hedgerow retention notice, which may be done only if the hedgerow is important according to the specified criteria. They make provision for criminal offences, replacement of hedgerows removed in contravention of the Regulations, appeals against hedgerows retention and other notices, record-keeping by the local planning authority, enforcement by injunction and rights of entry. Further provisions are made for hedgerows owned by the local planning authority and ecclesiastical property.

2315. Contaminated   land–acquisition   by   development   corporation–compensation–valuation as if compulsory purchase

Held, that vacant but contaminated land in London's docklands was valued at £250,000 per acre less deductions for remedial works in connection with the contamination, finance costs, securing access rights, repairs, and allowing for deferral for the works to be carried out. On the basis that capital value comparables were preferred the overall net sum payable by way of compensation was £1,820,000 for 21 useable acres.

BROMLEY LBC v. LONDON DOCKLANDS DEVELOPMENT CORP [1997] 37 R.V.R. 173, Marder Q.C. (President), LandsTr.

2316. Environment Act 1995 (c.25)–Commencement No.9 Order

ENVIRONMENT ACT 1995 (COMMENCEMENT NO.9 AND TRANSITIONAL PROVISIONS) ORDER 1997, SI 1997 1626 (C.68); made under the Environment Act 1995 s.125. Commencement details: bringing into force various provisions of the Act on July 1, 1997; £1.10.

This Order brings into force the Environment Act 1995 s.60(3)(4)(5)(a)(7), which amends the Water Resources Act 1991 s.161 relating to anti-pollution works and operations. The Environment Act 1995 s.16, in so far as it relates to Crown application of the Water Resources Act 1991, except Part II of the 1991 Act, is also brought into operation.

2317. Environment Act 1995 (c.25)–Commencement No.10 Order

ENVIRONMENT ACT 1995 (COMMENCEMENT NO.10) ORDER 1997, SI 1997 3044 (C.112); made under the Environment Act 1995 s.125. Commencement details: bringing into force various provisions of the Act on December 23, 1997; £1.10.

This Order brings into force the remainder of the Environment Act 1995 Part IV, which makes provision for local authorities to contribute to the management of air quality within their areas. It also brings into force the Environmental Protection Act 1990 s.4(4A), which requires local authorities to have regard to the National Air Quality Strategy published under s.80 of the 1995 Act when exercising their powers under Part I of the 1990 Act to prevent or minimise air pollution released from processes prescribed for local control.

2318. Environmental impact–construction work–electricity and pipelines

ELECTRICITY AND PIPE-LINE WORKS (ASSESSMENT OF ENVIRONMENTAL EFFECTS) (AMENDMENT) REGULATIONS 1997, SI 1997 629; made under the European Communities Act 1972 s.2. In force: April 1, 1997; £0.65.

These Regulations amend the Electricity and Pipe-line Works (Assessment of Environmental Effects) Regulations 1990 (SI 1990 442). The amendments are not relevant to Scotland.

2319. Environmental impact–Member States' discretion–criteria for establishing need for Environmental Impact Assessment–European Union

[Council Directive 85/337 on the amendment of the effects of certain public and private projects on the environment.]

A Dutch local authority adopted a zoning plan to carry out the reinforcement of certain dykes. The plans were approved without any consideration being given to the environmental effects of the construction work covered by the plan. The proposed modifications covered land owned by K on which it operated its business and would have the effect of depriving K of access to vital waterways. K's appeal against the approval of the plans was stayed and a reference made to the ECJ to determine a number of questions, including, inter alia, whether Council Directive 85/337 Art.2(1) and Art.4(2) should be interpreted as meaning that where a Member State in its national implementing legislation has laid down specifications, criteria or thresholds for a particular project covered by Annex II of the Directive but those criteria, specifications or thresholds are incorrect, Art.2(1) of the Directive requires that an environmental impact assessment be made if the project is likely to have "significant effects on the environment by virtue of its nature, size or location" and if so, whether those provisions had direct effect.

Held, answering the questions in the affirmative, that (1) although Art.4(2) of the Directive confers on Member States a discretion to specify certain types of projects which will be subject to an assessment or to establish the criteria or thresholds applicable, that discretion is limited by the obligation in Art.2(1) that certain projects likely by virtue of their nature, size or location to have significant effects on the environment are to be subject to an impact assessment. The question whether, in laying down criteria to establish whether a particular project had to undergo an assessment, a Member State had exceeded the limits of the discretions cannot be determined in relation to the characteristics only of that project. It depends on an overall assessment of the characteristics of projects of that nature which could be envisaged in the Member State. A Member State which established criteria or set thresholds at a level such that, in practice, all relevant projects would be exempted in advance from the requirement of an impact assessment would exceed the limits of its discretion under Art.2(1) and Art.4(2) of the Directive unless all projects could, when viewed as a whole, be regarded as not being likely to have significant effects on the environment, *Commission of the European Communities v. Belgium (C133/94)* (Unreported, 1996) applied, and (2) where, pursuant to national law, a court must or may raise of its own motion pleas in law based on a binding national rule which were not put forward by the parties, it must, for matters within its jurisdiction, examine of its own motion whether the legislative or administrative authorities of the Member State remained within the limits of their discretion under Art.2(1) and Art.4(2) of the Directive, and take account thereof when examining the action for annulment. If that discretion has been exceeded and the national provisions must be set aside in that respect, it is for the authorities of the Member State to take all the general or particular measures necessary to ensure that projects are examined in order to determine whether they are likely to have significant effects on the environment and if so, to ensure that they are subject to an impact assessment.

AANNEMERSBEDRIJF PK KRAAIJEVELD BV v. GEDEPUTEERDE STATEN VAM ZUID-HOLLAND (C72/95) [1997] All E.R. (EC) 134, GC Rodriguez Iglesias (President), ECJ.

2320. Environmental management—financial assistance

FINANCIAL ASSISTANCE FOR ENVIRONMENTAL PURPOSES ORDER 1997, SI 1997 651; made under the Environmental Protection Act 1990 s.153. In force: April 1, 1997; £0.65.

This Order varies the Environmental Protection Act 1990 s.153(1) to enable the Secretary of State, with the consent of the Treasury, to give financial assistance to, or for the purposes of, The Tidy Britain Group, a company limited by guarantee whose main objective is to promote the prevention and control of litter.

2321. Environmental protection—Antarctica—Guernsey

ANTARCTIC (GUERNSEY) REGULATIONS 1997, SI 1997 2966; made under the Antarctic Act 1994 s.9, s.10, s.11, s.14, s.25, s.29, s.32. In force: in accordance with Reg.1 (2); £1.10.

These Regulations provide for certain provisions of the Antarctic Regulations 1995 (SI 1995 490) to have effect in the Bailiwick of Guernsey.

2322. Environmental protection—Antarctica—Isle of Man

ANTARCTIC (ISLE OF MAN) REGULATIONS 1997, SI 1997 2968; made under the Antarctic Act 1994 s.9, s.10, s.11, s.14, s.25, s.29, s.32. In force: January 5, 1998; £1.10.

These Regulations provide for certain provisions of the Antarctic Regulations 1995 (SI 1995 490) to have effect in the Isle of Man.

2323. Environmental protection–Antarctica–Jersey

ANTARCTIC (JERSEY) REGULATIONS 1997, SI 1997 2967; made under the Antarctic Act 1994 s.9, s.10, s.11, s.14, s.25, s.29, s.32. In force: in accordance with Reg.1 (2); £1.10.

These Regulations provide for certain provisions of the Antarctic Regulations 1995 (SI 1995 490) to have effect in the Bailiwick of Jersey.

2324. Environmental protection–authorisation for piggery and allied business–management inadequacies

[Environmental Protection Act 1990 s.6(4).]

W applied for judicial review of the decision to grant authorisation to N to run a piggery and allied businesses. The ground of appeal was that the Secretary of State misdirected himself as to the meaning of the Environmental Protection Act 1990 s.6(4) and did not consider whether N had demonstrated how past management failures and design shortcomings would be overcome. An inspector's report concluded that N was unlikely to be able to carry out the process as required.

Held, allowing the application, that the Secretary of State, although not misconstruing s.6(4) of the 1990 Act did not apply the section properly, and should have considered whether N was able to carry out the process so as to comply with conditions of authorisation, rather than whether N was likely to comply. The decision to grant authorisation was quashed.

R. v. SECRETARY OF STATE FOR THE ENVIRONMENT, *ex p.* WEST WILTSHIRE DC [1996] Env. L.R. 312, Malcolm Spence Q.C., QBD.

2325. Environmental protection–coasts–excluded waters

COAST PROTECTION (VARIATION OF EXCLUDED WATERS) REGULATIONS 1997, SI 1997 2675; made under the Coast Protection Act 1949 Sch.4 para.113. In force: December 12, 1997; £0.65.

These Regulations amend the Coast Protection Act 1949 Sch.4 by extending the part of the River Esk in Yorkshire which is not included in the expressions "sea" and "seashore" for the purposes of Part I of the Act which relates to coastal protection.

2326. Environmental protection–extension to Guernsey

FOOD AND ENVIRONMENT PROTECTION ACT 1985 (GUERNSEY) (AMENDMENT) ORDER 1997, SI 1997 1770; made under the Food and Environment Protection Act 1985 s.26. In force: August 22, 1997; £1.10.

This Order provides that the Food and Environment Protection Act 1985 s.14, as substituted by the Environmental Protection Act 1990 s.21, s.147 and Sch.2 para.3, as amended by s.146, shall extend to the Bailiwick of Guernsey with amendments to the Schedule to the Food and Environment Protection Act 1985 (Guernsey) Order 1987 (SI 1987 665) provided for.

2327. Environmental protection–extension to Jersey

FOOD AND ENVIRONMENT PROTECTION ACT 1985 (JERSEY) (AMENDMENT) ORDER 1997, SI 1997 1771; made under the Food and Environment Protection Act 1985 s.26. In force: August 22, 1997; £0.65.

This Order provides that the Food and Environment Protection Act 1985 s.14, as substituted by the Environmental Protection Act 1990 s.147 and Sch.2 para.3, as amended by s.146, shall extend to the Bailiwick of Jersey with amendments to the Schedule to the Food and Environment Protection Act 1985 (Jersey) Order 1987 (SI 1987 667) provided for.

2328. Environmental protection–litter–control areas

LITTER CONTROL AREAS (AMENDMENT) ORDER 1997, SI 1997 633; made under the Environmental Protection Act 1990 s.90; and the Environment Act 1995 s.63, s.75. In force: March 28, 1997; £1.10.

This Order amends two of the prescribed descriptions of land (retail shopping developments, and business or office parks or industrial or trading estates) which may be designated as litter control areas under the Environmental Protection Act 1990 s.90(3). It also substitutes a reference to the new National Park Authorities created under the Environment Act 1995 for the existing reference to joint or special planning boards, and makes consequential revocations.

2329. Environmental protection–litter–control notices

STREET LITTER CONTROL NOTICES (AMENDMENT) ORDER 1997, SI 1997 632; made under the Environmental Protection Act 1990 s.94. In force: March 28, 1997; £0.65.

This Order prescribes further descriptions of commercial or retail premises in respect of which a street litter control notice may be issued by a principal litter authority under the Environmental Protection Act 1990 s.93.

2330. Environmental protection–litter–road cleaning

HIGHWAY LITTER CLEARANCE AND CLEANING (TRANSFER OF RESPONSIBILITY) ORDER 1997, SI 1997 2960; made under the Environmental Protection Act 1990 s.86. In force: April 1, 1998; £1.10.

The Environmental Protection Act 1990 s.89 places a duty on local authorities to ensure that land comprised in the highways maintainable at the public expense within its area are so far as practicable kept clean and clear of litter and refuse. Section 86(11) empowers the Secretary of State to transfer responsibility for the discharge of these duties as respects all or any part of such a highway to the relevant highway authority. This Order transfers responsibility in respect of certain highways from the councils who would otherwise be responsible to the Secretary of State for Transport, who is the highway authority for them.

2331. Environmental protection–waste–packaging

PRODUCER RESPONSIBILITY OBLIGATIONS (PACKAGING WASTE) REGULATIONS 1997, SI 1997 648; made under the Environment Act 1995 s.93, s.94, s.95. In force: March 6, 1997; £6.10.

These Regulations impose on producers obligations to recover and recycle packaging waste, and related obligations, in order to attain the targets specified in European Parliament and Council Directive 94/62 ([1994] OJ L365/10) on Packaging Waste Art.6(1).

2332. Flood control–committees–Anglia

ANGLIAN REGIONAL FLOOD DEFENCE COMMITTEE ORDER 1997, SI 1997 1359; made under the Environment Act 1995 s.16. In force: June 1, 1997; £1.10.

This Order specifies the number of members of the regional flood defence committee known as the Anglian Regional Flood Defence Committee who are to be appointed by each constituent council or group of councils. The Order takes account of changes in local government responsibilities which took effect on April 1, 1997. The Anglian Regional Flood Defence Committee Order 1996 (SI 1996 1618) is revoked.

2333. Flood control–committees–Northumbria

NORTHUMBRIA REGIONAL FLOOD DEFENCE COMMITTEE ORDER 1997, SI 1997 1360; made under the Environment Act 1995 s.16. In force: June 1, 1997; £1.10.

This Order specifies the number of members of the regional flood defence committee known as the Northumbria Regional Flood Defence Committee who are to be appointed by each constituent council or group of councils. It takes account of changes in local government responsibilities which took effect on April 1, 1997. The Northumbria Regional Flood Defence Committee Order 1996 (SI 1996 1617) is revoked.

2334. Flood control–committees–Severn Trent

SEVERN TRENT REGIONAL FLOOD DEFENCE COMMITTEE ORDER 1997, SI 1997 1361; made under the Environment Act 1995 s.16. In force: June 1, 1997; £1.10.

This Order specifies the number of members of the regional flood defence committee known as the Severn Trent Regional Flood Defence Committee who are to be appointed by each constituent council or group of councils. It takes account of changes in local government responsibilities which took effect on April 1, 1997. The Severn Trent Regional Flood Defence Committee Order 1996 (SI 1996 1616) is revoked.

2335. Flood control–committees–Southern Region

SOUTHERN REGIONAL FLOOD DEFENCE COMMITTEE ORDER 1997, SI 1997 1362; made under the Environment Act 1995 s.16. In force: June 1, 1997; £0.65.

This Order specifies the number of members of the regional flood defence committee known as the Southern Regional Flood Defence Committee who are to be appointed by each constituent council or group of councils. It takes account of changes in local government responsibilities which took effect on April 1, 1997. The Southern Water Authority (Regional Land Drainage Committee) Order 1973 (SI 1973 1923) is partly revoked.

2336. Flood control–committees–Thames

THAMES REGIONAL FLOOD DEFENCE COMMITTEE ORDER 1997, SI 1997 1363; made under the Environment Act 1995 s.16. In force: June 1, 1997; £1.10.

This Order specifies the number of members of the regional flood defence committee known as the Thames Regional Flood Defence Committee who are to be appointed by each constituent council or group of councils. It takes account of changes in local government responsibilities which took effect on April 1, 1997. The Thames Regional Flood Defence Committee Order 1990 (SI 1990 1712) is partly revoked.

2337. Flood control–committees–Wessex

WESSEX REGIONAL FLOOD DEFENCE COMMITTEE ORDER 1997, SI 1997 1364; made under the Environment Act 1995 s.16. In force: June 1, 1997; £0.65.

This Order specifies the number of members of the regional flood defence committee known as the Wessex Regional Flood Defence Committee who are to be appointed by each constituent council or group of councils. It takes account of changes in local government responsibilities which took effect on April 1, 1997. The Wessex Regional Flood Defence Committee Order 1996 (SI 1996 1615) is revoked.

2338. Footpaths–intention of owner not to dedicate path to public

[Highways Act 1980 s.31; Wildlife and Countryside Act 1981 Sch.15.]

C, the owner of a wood, appealed against the dismissal of his application that a definitive map should not be modified to show the existence of a public right of way. C claimed that the inspector had erred by finding that there was insufficient evidence of the intention of P, a previous owner, not to dedicate a path through the wood as a public right of way. The issue concerned the proper interpretation of the Highways Act 1980 s.31.

Held, dismissing the appeal, that the inspector had been entitled to find that P failed to make clear by notice or by lodging a statutory declaration that he had no intention to dedicate the path and the judge below had been correct to uphold the inspector's decision, *Fairey v. Southampton CC* [1956] 2 Q.B. 439, [1956] C.L.Y. 3869, *R. v. Secretary of State for the Environment, ex p. Cowell* [1993] J.P.L. 851, [1994] C.L.Y. 4372 and *Jaques v. Secretary of State for the Environment* [1995] J.P.L. 1031, [1994] C.L.Y. 1781 considered. The terms of s.31 required the landowner to do an overt act which showed there was no intention to dedicate. That the public failed to understand that intention was irrelevant.

COTTON v. SECRETARY OF STATE FOR THE ENVIRONMENT, Trans. Ref: QBCOF 96/0299/D, March 10, 1997, Schiemann, L.J., CA.

2339.   Footpaths–modification order to include disputed footpath in definitive map and statement–validity of confirmation of order

[National Parks and Access to the Countryside Act 1949 s.27(4).]

I made a modification order to include a disputed public footpath running over land owned by O in its definitive map and statement. O applied for judicial review, but, as the court could not hear the application until the order had been confirmed, O withdrew his objection. Consequent to this withdrawal, a planned local inquiry was not held and the Secretary of State's inspector confirmed the order. O appealed against the dismissal of his application for judicial review of the confirmed order, contending that (1) the Secretary of State was wrong to confirm the order in the absence of a local inquiry; (2) survey cards of footpaths completed by district and parish councils on I's behalf did not meet the requirements of a statement under the National Parks and Access to the Countryside Act 1949 s.27(4), and (3) I was not empowered to make the modification order without a prior judicial determination of the facts and the law.

Held, dismissing the appeal, that (1) the Secretary of State was not required to continue a local inquiry into a disputed right of way once the only objection had been withdrawn; (2) s.27(4) did not require a statement to be in any particular form or to be attached to the local authority's definitive map of rights of way, and therefore the survey cards did comply with the statutory requirements, and (3) the statutory scheme concerned with rights of way should be interpreted as providing a local authority with the power to consider evidence and make appropriate orders in relation to the existence of disputed rights of way.

R. v. SECRETARY OF STATE FOR THE ENVIRONMENT, *ex p.* O'KEEFE, *The Times*, August 5, 1997, Mummery, L.J., CA.

2340.   Noise Act 1996 (c.37)–Commencement No.2 Order

NOISE ACT 1996 (COMMENCEMENT NO.2) ORDER 1997, SI 1997 1695 (C.70); made under the Noise Act 1996 s.14. Commencement details: bringing into force various provisions of the Act on July 23, 1997; £0.65.

This Order brings into force on July 23, 1997 the provisions of the Noise Act 1996 which relate to the summary procedure for dealing with noise at night and supplementary matters (including powers of entry and seizure).

2341.   Open spaces–parks–conduct of users

ROYAL PARKS AND OTHER OPEN SPACES REGULATIONS 1997, SI 1997 1639; made under the Parks Regulation (Amendment) Act 1926 s.2; and the Crown Estate Act 1961 s.7. In force: October 1, 1997; £1.55.

These Regulations regulate the conduct of persons using specified parks, gardens and other land under the control or management of the Secretary of State for National Heritage. They revoke and re-enact, with minor and drafting amendments, the Trafalgar Square Regulations 1952 (SI 1952 776) and the Royal and other Parks and Gardens Regulations 1977 (SI 1977 217).

2342. Pollution control–agricultural nitrates–designation of nitrate vulnerable zones–construction of Nitrates Directive

[Council Directive 91/676 concerning the protection of waters against pollution caused by nitrates from agricultural sources.]

In two sets of proceedings applicants sought judicial review of decisions by the Secretary of State on the application of the Nitrates Directive to the rivers Waveney, Blackwater and Chelmer and the designation of certain areas of land as nitrate vulnerable zones. The matter concerned the true construction of the Nitrates Directive and the potential invalidity of the Directive in the event of the Secretary of State's construction being held to be incorrect. The Directive concerns the protection of waters against pollution caused by nitrates from agricultural sources. The applicants submitted that the approach adopted by the Secretary of State was wrong and contended that he misdirected himself as to the proper meaning of "waters affected by pollution" within Art.3(1). Alternatively, the applicants submitted that the Directive was unlawful and contrary to Community law because it breached the "polluter pays" principle. The applicants submitted that if there was uncertainty about the interpretation of Art.3(1) then a referral to the ECJ should be made for a preliminary ruling.

Held, that the case should be referred to the ECJ as there was a need for a uniform interpretation of the Directive and a serious and important point of Community law was involved.

R. v. SECRETARY OF STATE FOR THE ENVIRONMENT, *ex p.* STANDLEY; *sub nom.* R. v. SECRETARY OF STATE FOR THE ENVIRONMENT, *ex p.* METSON, Trans. Ref: CO/2057/96, CO/2064/96, May 7, 1997, Potts, J., QBD.

2343. Pollution control–motor vehicle noise and exhaust emissions–fixed penalties

ROAD TRAFFIC (VEHICLE EMISSIONS) (FIXED PENALTY) REGULATIONS 1997, SI 1997 3058; made under the Environment Act 1995 s.87, Sch.11 para.5. In force: December 26, 1997; £1.55.

These Regulations make provision for specified local authorities to issue fixed penalty notices to users of vehicles within their area who contravene, or fail to comply with, the Road Vehicles (Construction and Use) Regulations 1986 (SI 1986 1078) Reg.61 which concerns emissions of smoke and other substances from vehicles and to drivers of vehicles within their area who contravene, or fail to comply with, Reg.98 which concerns the stopping of engines and stationary vehicles to avoid noise and exhaust emissions.

2344. Pollution control–sea pollution–extension of provisions

ENVIRONMENT PROTECTION (OVERSEAS TERRITORIES) (AMENDMENT) ORDER 1997, SI 1997 1748; made under the Food and Environment Protection Act 1985 s.26. In force: August 21, 1997; £0.65.

This Order extends to the Falkland Islands and to South Georgia and the South Sandwich Islands the provisions of the Food and Environment Protection Act 1985 which control the deposit of substances and articles in the sea and under the sea bed.

2345. Pollution control–sea pollution–ports–waste management

MERCHANT SHIPPING (PORT WASTE RECEPTION FACILITIES) REGULATIONS 1997, SI 1997 3018; made under the Merchant Shipping (Prevention of Pollution by Garbage) Order 1988 Art.2; and the Merchant Shipping Act 1995 s.130A, s.130B, s.130D, s.302. In force: January 27, 1998; £1.55.

These Regulations, which revoke and replace the Prevention of Pollution (Reception Facilities) Order 1984 (SI 1984 862) and the Merchant Shipping (Reception Facilities for Garbage) Regulations 1988 (SI 1988 2293) and amend the Merchant Shipping (Fees) Regulations 1996 (SI 1996 3243), require harbour authorities to prepare a waste management plan and introduce a power whereby the Secretary of State may direct a terminal operator to prepare such a plan.

Penalties are also provided for failure to comply with certain requirements of the Regulations or any direction issued.

2346. Pollution control—water pollution—causation—interfering trespassers—statutory interpretation—circumstances in which defendant can be found guilty of causing an event

[Water Resources Act 1991 s.85(1).]

Prior to 1995 E installed a large diesel tank on its premises containing red diesel. The outlet of the tank was governed by a simple tap which was not locked. In March 1995 some unknown person opened the tap and a significant amount of diesel escaped, flowing into a storm drain and from there to a nearby river. The identity of the person responsible for opening the tap could not be established, although there was some suggestion that trespassers might have been involved, in connection with local opposition to E's business. E was convicted under the Water Resources Act 1991 s.85(1) for causing polluting matter to enter controlled waters. E appealed, arguing that the meaning of the word "cause" in s.85(1) of the 1991 Act required that it had to be shown beyond reasonable doubt that a trespasser did not turn on the tap.

Held, dismissing the appeal, that (1) to be found guilty of causing an event, E need not be shown to be the sole cause of that event, nor to know or foresee the consequences of his acts, omissions or role; (2) where there were a number of possible causes the question which the court ought to ask itself was whether the intervening cause, competing cause or other cause was of such a powerful nature that the conduct of E could not amount to a cause at all in the circumstances; (3) whether the conduct of E amounted to causing was a matter of common sense for the adjudicating tribunal on the facts of the particular case, and (4) in the instant case, having regard to the facts that E collected large quantities of diesel on its premises, that the tap controlling the outlet was not locked and was accessible to the public and that the procedures for controlling any overflow were quite inadequate, it was open to the court to find E guilty of causing the pollution, *Alphacell Ltd v. Woodward* [1972] A.C. 824, [1972] C.L.Y. 3549, *National Rivers Authority v. Yorkshire Water Services Ltd* [1995] 1 A.C. 444, [1995] 2 C.L.Y. 5137 and *R. v. CPC (UK) Ltd* [1994] C.L.Y. 2072 applied; *Impress (Worcester) Ltd v. Rees* [1971] 2 All E.R. 357, [1971] C.L.Y. 11974, *Wychavon DC v. National Rivers Authority* [1993] 1 W.L.R. 125, [1993] C.L.Y. 4126 and *Price v. Cromack* [1975] 1 W.L.R. 988, [1975] C.L.Y. 2750 considered.

EMPRESS CAR CO (ABERTILLERY) LTD v. NATIONAL RIVERS AUTHORITY [1997] Env. L.R. 227, Schiemann, L.J., QBD.

2347. Pollution control—water pollution—fuel

CONTROL OF POLLUTION (SILAGE, SLURRY AND AGRICULTURAL FUEL OIL) (AMENDMENT) REGULATIONS 1997, SI 1997 547; made under the Water Resources Act 1991 s.92, s.219. In force: April 1, 1997; £1.10.

These Regulations amend the Control of Pollution (Silage, Slurry and Agricultural Fuel Oil) Regulations 1991 (SI 1991 324). They extend Reg.3 of the 1991 Regulations to the storage and making of field silage; remove the exemption in relation to the making of field silage; extend the Environment Agency's power to serve an anti-pollution notice to anyone with custody or control of certain substances or silage; extend period for compliance with an anti-pollution notice; and permit the Agency to relax the requirements for slurry storage systems in relation to the minimum capacity and distance.

2348. Rights of way–amendment to map to show public footpath–approach where conflicting evidence as to existence of public right of way

[Highways Act 1980 s.31; Wildlife and Countryside Act 1981 s.53(3)(c)(i), Sch.15.]

E applied for judicial review of a decision of the Secretary of State upholding the local authority's refusal to exercise its powers under the Wildlife and Countryside Act 1981 s.53(2) to amend a definitive survey map to show an alleged public footpath. E submitted statements to prove that the footpath had been enjoyed as a public right of way for more than 20 years, as required by the Highways Act 1980 s.31, but there was conflicting evidence from the landowners, who claimed that general access had always been refused. E's application was granted and the Secretary of State appealed.

Held, dismissing the appeal, that under s.53(3)(c)(i), the local authority was required to make amendments to a map where evidence supporting the existence of a right of way was reasonably alleged to subsist. Difficulties arose where there was conflicting evidence as to whether a public right of way in fact existed under s.31 of the 1980 Act. However, in dealing with such cases, the authorities should bear in mind that parties had a right to appeal under Sch.15 of the 1981 Act when those issues could be determined by public inquiry. Where an applicant produced credible evidence of enjoyment as a public right of way for 20 years, but there was conflicting evidence about one of the matters arising under s.31 of the 1981 Act, then the application should be granted unless there was incontrovertible documentary evidence to defeat the claim, *R. v. Secretary of State for the Environment, ex p. Bagshaw* (1994) 68 P. & C.R. 402, [1995] 2 C.L.Y. 4809 approved. In the instant case, it was unreasonable for the Secretary of State to conclude that E's evidence was inadequate to indicate that a right of way was reasonably alleged to subsist.

R. v. SECRETARY OF STATE FOR WALES, *ex p.* EMERY, *The Times*, July 22, 1997, Roch, L.J., CA.

2349. Smoke control–authorisation of fuel

SMOKE CONTROL AREAS (AUTHORISED FUELS) (AMENDMENT) REGULATIONS 1997, SI 1997 2658; made under the Clean Air Act 1993 s.20, s.63. In force: December 3, 1997; £1.10.

These Regulations amend the Smoke Control (Authorised Fuels) Regulations 1991 (SI 1991 1282) in order to authorise Island Lump, Island Nuts and Taybrite briquettes.

2350. Smoke control–exemptions–fireplaces

SMOKE CONTROL AREAS (EXEMPTED FIREPLACES) ORDER 1997, SI 1997 3009; made under the Clean Air Act 1993 s.21. In force: January 9, 1998; £1.10.

This Order exempts certain classes of fireplace from the prohibition contained in the Clean Air Act 1993 s.20 from the emission of smoke in smoke control areas.

2351. Waste–imports–mixture of waste could fall into least harmful category where all constituent parts could be identified as "least harmful"–European Union

[Council Regulation 259/93 on the supervision and control of shipments of waste within, into and out of the European Community Art.10.]

D imported specific types of waste for the purposes of metal recovery, the shipments being governed by Council Regulation 259/93, which divided waste into three assigned categories of green, amber and red. Green waste was considered the least harmful and therefore attracted the least regulation, whilst red waste and amber waste were subject to more stringent regulation under Art.10. EA informed D that a mixture of waste it imported was not included in the annexes which listed which materials fell within the specified categories and therefore should have been treated as unassigned waste falling within the red list procedure, when in fact D had been importing the waste under the green procedure. D applied for judicial review of EA's policy and the decision to take enforcement action against it, arguing that the waste fell within the green list because each constituent part of the mixture could be identified as one listed in the green annexe.

Held, allowing the application, that nothing in Art.10 suggested that wastes could not be mixed. If the words of Art.10 were applied to the instant case, the individual ingredients of the mixture were all listed in the green annexe and therefore could not be considered to be unassigned, although this would be different if the mixture itself were listed as a separate item in an annexe. It was for a criminal court entertaining a prosecution to determine whether the regulations had been properly complied with, but it was appropriate for EA, as principal prosecutor in such cases, to have its own policy and the court was likely to be guided by its view. However, there was more flexibility within the regulatory regime than EA's policy permitted, particularly in relation to the degree of accuracy required when specifying the quantities of individual substances, at least in cases concerning green waste.

R. v. ENVIRONMENT AGENCY, *ex p.* DOCKGRANGE LTD, *The Times*, June 21, 1997, Carnwath, J., QBD.

2352. Waste disposal–contravention of special waste regulations–company not a carrier for purposes of regulations where it had taken waste to its own disposal site

[Control of Pollution (Special Waste) Regulations 1980 (SI 1980 1709) Reg.4; Environmental Protection Act 1990 s.33, s.34(1).]

UOL had engaged SM to collect and dispose of certain waste, but failed to inform them that the material concerned was special waste and did not prepare a consignment note for SM and the local regulatory authority as required by the Control of Pollution (Special Waste) Regulations 1980 Reg.4(1). SM took the waste to their own disposal site, but, when it was discovered that the consignment contained special waste, SM sent it to a properly licensed site and informed the regulatory authority. SM now appealed by way of case stated against convictions of (1) unlawful failure as carriers of special waste to complete their part of the consignment note pursuant to Reg.4(5), and (2) unlawful failure under the Environmental Protection Act 1990 s.34(1)(a) to take reasonable measures as carriers to prevent contravention by another of s.33 of the Act, which prohibited the unlicensed disposal of waste.

Held, allowing the appeal, that (1) SM were not carriers for the purposes of the Regulations as Reg.4(5) defined a carrier as "any person who transfers special waste from the premises at which it is produced to another person for disposal" and SM had delivered the waste to their own disposal site and not to another person, and (2) no offence had actually been committed under s.33, as SM had transferred the waste to a licensed site and therefore it was difficult to see how they could have unlawfully failed to take all reasonable measures to prevent contravention by any other person of s.33, making a conviction under s.34(1)(a) unsustainable.

SHANKS & McEWAN (SOUTHERN WASTE SERVICES) LTD v. ENVIRONMENT AGENCY, *The Independent*, October 17, 1997, Brian Smedley, J., QBD.

2353. Waste disposal–deposit of controlled waste in breach of waste management licence–knowledge required to establish offence

[Environmental Protection Act 1990 s.33(1).]

SM appealed by way of case stated from its conviction of an offence under the Environmental Protection Act 1990 s.33(1) after a tanker had deposited controlled waste in breach of the conditions of SM's waste management licence, the site supervisor having failed to complete a new waste disposal form when the receiving tank was altered. SM contended, inter alia, that s.33(1) required someone who constituted part of the directing mind and will of the company to know both that the waste was being deposited and that the deposit was in breach of the waste management licence conditions.

Held, dismissing the appeal, that knowledge of the breach of the waste management licence conditions was not necessary to establish an offence under s.33(1), the word "knowingly" in that section related only to causing or permitting the controlled waste to be deposited.

SHANKS & McEWAN (TEESSIDE) LTD v. ENVIRONMENT AGENCY [1997] 2 All E.R. 332, Kennedy, L.J., QBD.

2354. Waste disposal—harmful disposal of waste—sentencing discount for guilty plea

[Environmental Protection Act 1990 s.33(1).]

G appealed against a sentence of 18 months' imprisonment concurrent on two counts of unauthorised or harmful disposal of waste under the Environmental Protection Act 1990 s.33(1)(c) and a sentence of nine months' imprisonment concurrent for a third count of unauthorised or harmful waste deposit under s.33(1)(b) of the 1990 Act. The first two counts referred to the disposal of dangerous chemicals in a skip and the taking of another consignment to an incinerator which did not deal with chemical waste. G stated that the load contained paper and cardboard, but the load exploded prior to being placed in the incinerator. Count three referred to leaking containers emitting noxious fumes stored at premises rented by G. G submitted that remarks by the trial judge as to the disregard for human safety involved in the offences were not made out in the evidence and that the sentence was excessive given both his previous good character and the maximum term of two years for offences of this nature.

Held, allowing the appeal in part by quashing the 18 month term and substituting a sentence of 12 months' imprisonment, that although a custodial term was inevitable, insufficient regard had been paid to G's guilty plea, his previous good conduct and the fact that this was not the worst type of case of its kind.

R. v. GARRETT (TERENCE WILLIAM) [1997] 1 Cr. App. R. (S.) 109, Longmore, J., CA (Crim Div).

2355. Waste disposal—licences—canal waste deposited on waste management site—not controlled waste for purposes of licence restriction

[Environmental Protection Act 1990 s.33(6), s.34; Waste Management Licensing Regulations 1994 (SI 1994 1056) Reg.17, Sch.3.]

L appealed by way of case stated against the dismissal of two informations against D under the Environmental Protection Act 1990 s.33(6). D operated a waste management site under a licence granted by L, subject to a daily input restriction of 600 cubic metres. However, L submitted that this had been contravened by the reception of 980.20 cubic metres and amounted to a breach of the site licence amounting to a criminal offence under s.33(6) of the 1990 Act. D argued that part of the waste deposited was canal dredging material, which, by virtue of the Waste Management Licensing Regulations 1994 Reg.17 and Sch.3, was exempt from the conditions of the licence.

Held, dismissing the appeal, that a waste management site licence was only required for the deposit of controlled waste under s.33(1) and did not apply to exempt activities provided under Sch.3 of the 1994 Regulations. Regulation 17 disapplied s.33(1) in regard to exempt activities, a situation which was clearly provided for by virtue of s.34 of the 1990 Act. Criminal proceedings under s.33(6), therefore, only pertained to the deposit of controlled waste covered by the conditions of the licence and not to the deposit of exempt material falling beyond the scope of the licence.

LONDON WASTE REGULATION AUTHORITY v. DRINKWATER SABEY LTD; LONDON WASTE REGULATION AUTHORITY v. MACK [1997] Env. L.R. 137, Smith, J., QBD.

2356. Waste disposal–licences–deposit of controlled waste–waste not properly covered–meaning of "deposit"

[Control of Pollution Act 1974 s.5; Environmental Protection Act 1990 s.33(1)(a), s.33(6); Magistrates Courts Act 1980 s.123; Magistrates Courts Rules 1981 r.100.]

T appealed against a conviction of unlawfully depositing controlled waste in contravention of its licence issued under the Control of Pollution Act 1974 s.5 by failure to cover the waste in accordance with the Environmental Protection Act 1990 s.33(1)(a). The issue was whether T was properly charged with an offence under s.33(1)(a) and, if not, was the prosecution saved by the Magistrates Courts Act 1980 s.123 or the Magistrates Courts Rules 1981 r.100. It was conceded that the waste had not been properly covered, but argued that improper covering did not give rise to unlawful deposit.

Held, dismissing the appeal, that (1) whilst no offence was committed where the deposit itself was lawful, a deposit might be rendered unlawful where it failed to comply with licence conditions. Section 33(6) of the 1990 Act contemplated offences arising from conduct outlined in s.33(1) and breaches of licence conditions. The justices were entitled to find, on the evidence before them, that a charge was justified in terms of s.33(1)(a) and s.33(6) of the 1990 Act. "Deposit" must be construed broadly, *Scott v. Westminster City Council* [1996] 1 C.L.Y. 5145 applied, and did not have to mean only the final resting place, *Leigh Land Reclamation Ltd v. Walsall MBC* (1991) J.P.L. 867, [1991] C.L.Y. 3005 distinguished, and (2) T was properly aware of the charges it faced and the facts justified the conclusion that covering the waste was part of the act of deposit.

THAMES WASTE MANAGEMENT LTD v. SURREY CC [1997] Env. L.R. 148, Rose, L.J., QBD.

2357. Waste disposal–licences–judicial review

[Waste Management Licensing Regulations 1994 (SI 1994 1056) Reg.15.2, Reg.15.4.]

V granted a waste disposal licence to Associated British Ports to dump waste in certain docks, in Barry. J, a concerned citizen and neighbour to the docks, renewed his application for judicial review. It had been contended that V had failed to consider the Waste Management Licensing Regulations 1994 Reg.15.2 and Reg.15.4.

Held, dismissing the application, that the judge had given clear reasons for his conclusions, following the principles in *Westminster City Council v. Great Portland Estates Plc* [1985] A.C. 661, [1984] C.L.Y. 3413, and it would be wrong to interfere with those findings of fact. There had also been undue delay in the application for judicial review and it had been within the judge's discretion to find that the grant of leave would be contrary to good administration.

R. v. VALE OF GLAMORGAN BC, *ex p.* JAMES [1997] Env. L.R. 195, Hirst, L.J., CA.

2358. Waste disposal–offences–power to obtain evidence for investigation in criminal proceedings–risk of self incrimination was not reasonable excuse for failure to comply with requisition

[Environmental Protection Act 1990 s.69, s.71(2); Police and Criminal Evidence Act 1984 s.78.]

The protection against self-incrimination offered by the environmental Protection Act 1990 s.69(8) is limited to situations specified in s.69(3) and does not provide grounds for refusal to disclose information in other circumstances. H, a waste regulation authority, suspected that G had been carrying and disposing of controlled clinical waste without a licence and wrote to G stating that they were investigating the matter with a view to possible criminal proceedings. H then sent a requisition under the Environmental Protection Act 1990 s.71(2) asking G to provide information about their waste operation. G indicated that they were reluctant to comply with the requisition without an assurance that their replies would not be used to incriminate them. H brought criminal proceedings against G for failing without reasonable excuse to comply with the requisition. G made an application for judicial review, contending that H could not lawfully use its powers under s.71 of the 1990 Act for the purpose of investigating alleged criminal conduct. The application was dismissed and G appealed.

Held, dismissing the appeal, that the fact that information provided pursuant to a requisition under s.71 (2) of the 1990 Act might incriminate its provider was not a reasonable excuse for failing to comply with it. The protection against self incrimination afforded by s.69(8) only extended to an individual giving oral answers to an inspector on company premises pursuant to s.69(3) and would not protect the company or other individuals. Information provided in circumstances other than those outlined in s.69(3) was not subject to the protection of s.69(8). It was clear that Parliament intended that a waste regulation authority should be able to use its powers under s.71 to obtain evidence which could then be used in criminal proceedings, subject only to the court's power to exclude evidence under the Police and Criminal Evidence Act 1984 s.78.

R. v. HERTFORDSHIRE CC, *ex p.* GREEN ENVIRONMENTAL INDUSTRIES LTD; *sub nom.* GREEN ENVIRONMENTAL INDUSTRIES LTD, *Re, The Times*, October 9, 1997, Waller, L.J., CA.

2359. Waste disposal–storage of controlled waste on skip site without licence– storage incidental and within statutory exemptions

[Environmental Protection Act 1990 s.33(1); Waste Management Licensing Regulations 1994 (SI 1994 1056) Reg.17, Reg.40.]

N brought an appeal by way of case stated from decisions to dismiss both informations brought against B under the Environmental Protection Act 1990 s.33(1)(b). The issue was whether there was sufficient evidence to conclude that B came within the exemptions set out in the Waste Management Licensing Regulations 1994 Reg.40 thereby discharging the need for a waste management licence. B operated a skip hire business and did at times have controlled waste on his site for which he did not have a waste management licence. N submitted that B had not discharged the burden of establishing that waste stored on site was in a secure container according to the meaning of the word "secure" in Reg.17(5) of the 1994 Regulations and that it was perverse to hold that there had not been adaptation of the premises for the reception of waste by the building of an embankment around B's site.

Held, dismissing the appeal, that the justices were entitled to hold that the requirements of the 1994 Regulations Reg.40 were satisfied even though there had been adaptation of the premises for the reception of waste. In this case the storage of waste was incidental to the collection or transport of it. As no note of the evidence relied on by the justices was put before the court, the word "secure" could not be determined.

NORTH YORKSHIRE CC v. BOYNE [1997] Env. L.R. 91, Pill, L.J., QBD.

2360. Waste management–guidance on concept of waste–European Union

[Council Directive 75/442 on waste Art.3; Council Regulation 259/93 on the supervision and control of shipments of waste within, into and out of the Community Art.2.]

T and others were charged with transporting, discharging, disposing of, or incinerating urban and special waste produced by third parties without obtaining prior authorisation by the competent region. The criminal court made a reference to the ECJ concerning the interpretation of Council Directive 75/442 and Council Regulation 259/93.

Held, that Council Directive 75/442 Art.3(1) required Member States to adopt measures which encouraged the prevention or reduction of waste production, together with waste recovery aimed at extracting secondary raw materials or using the waste as an energy source. Council Regulation 259/93 Art.2(a) set down a common definition of the concept of waste which was directly applicable, even to shipments within a Member State. National legislation which excluded substances and objects capable of economic re-utilisation from their definition of waste was incompatible with the relevant EC law. The system of supervision, which included the requirement for authorisation and registration of undertakings concerned with waste collection, disposal or recovery, was intended to include all objects or substances discarded by their owners, even where they had a commercial value and were collected on a commercial basis for the purpose of recycling, reclamation or re-use.

CRIMINAL PROCEEDINGS AGAINST TOMBESI (C304/94), *Re* [1997] All E.R. (EC) 639, GF Mancini (President), ECJ.

2361. Waste management—judicial review—application delay

See ADMINISTRATIVE LAW: R. v. Environment Agency, *ex p.* Leam. §68

2362. Waste management—licensing—certificates of technical competence

WASTE MANAGEMENT LICENSING (AMENDMENT) REGULATIONS 1997, SI 1997 2203; made under the Environmental Protection Act 1990 s.74. In force: October 9, 1997; £1.10.

The Waste Management Licensing Regulations 1994 (SI 1994 1056) provide that persons are technically competent to manage activities under a waste management licence in relation to certain facilities if they had a relevant certificate of technical competence awarded by the Waste Management Industry Training and Advisory Board. These Regulations amend the 1994 Regulations by replacing Table 1 which classifies types of facility and relevant certificates of technical competence relating to each facility.

2363. Waste management—miscellaneous provisions

WASTE MANAGEMENT (MISCELLANEOUS PROVISIONS) REGULATIONS 1997, SI 1997 351; made under the Environmental Protection Act 1990 s.52, s.74. In force: Reg.2: March 14, 1997; remainder: April 1, 1997; £1.10.

These Regulations make miscellaneous amendments to waste management legislation.

2364. Waste management—technical competence under 1990 Act

SPECIAL WASTE (AMENDMENT) REGULATIONS 1997, SI 1997 251; made under the Environmental Protection Act 1990 s.74. In force: February 28, 1997; £0.65.

These Regulations amend the Special Waste Regulations 1996 (SI 1996 972) Reg.20 and insert a new Reg.20A. Those provisions relate to the qualifications and experience required in order for a person to be treated as technically competent within the meaning of the Environmental Protection Act 1990 s.74.

2365. Water supply—surface water—fishlife—classification of quality

SURFACE WATERS (FISHLIFE) (CLASSIFICATION) REGULATIONS 1997, SI 1997 1331; made under the Water Resources Act 1991 s.82, s.102, s.219. In force: June 12, 1997; £1.95.

The Regulations, together with the Surface Waters (Fishlife) Directions 1997, transpose Council Directive 78/659 ([1978] OJ L222/1) in relation to England and Wales. They prescribe a system for classifying the quality of inland freshwaters which need protection or improvement in order to support fish life.

2366. Water supply–surface water–shellfish–classification of quality

SURFACE WATERS (SHELLFISH) (CLASSIFICATION) REGULATIONS 1997, SI 1997 1332; made under the Water Resources Act 1991 s.82, s.102, s.219. In force: June 12, 1997; £1.55.

The Regulations, together with the Surface Waters (Shellfish) Directions 1997, transpose Council Directive 79/923 ([1979] OJ L281/47) in relation to England and Wales. They prescribe a system for classifying the quality of controlled waters which are coastal or brackish waters and which need protection or improvement in order to support shellfish life and growth.

2367. Water supply–surface waters–classification of dangerous substances

SURFACE WATERS (DANGEROUS SUBSTANCES) (CLASSIFICATION) REGULATIONS 1997, SI 1997 2560; made under the Water Resources Act 1991 s.82, s.102, s.219. In force: November 26, 1997; £1.55.

These Regulations prescribe a system for classifying the quality of inland freshwaters, coastal waters and relevant territorial waters with a view to reducing the pollution of those waters by certain dangerous substances.

2368. Articles

Contaminated land liability *(Ian Doolittle)*: S.J. 1997, 141 (10), 238-239. (Tabular guide to risk of incurring liability for contaminated land for landowners, developers, occupiers, public authorities and agencies, funders, directors, professionals and contractors).

Dumping of wastes at sea: adoption of the 1996 Protocol to the London Convention 1972 *(Rene Coenen)*: R.E.C.I.E.L. 1997, 6(1), 54-61. (Main features, scope and purpose of 1996 Protocol).

Economic instruments as tools for the protection of the international environment *(Paolo Galizzi)*: E.E.L.R. 1997, 6(5), 155-157. (Introduction of market based mechanisms as complement to "command and control" legislation in international environmental protection should recognise developmental differences between states).

Employer's liability: environmental pollution and the ambit of the common law duty of care *(Geoffrey H. Holgate)*: Lit. 1997, 16(3), 103-121. (Analysis on asbestos processing factory owner's liability to local residents for diseases caused by emissions of asbestos dust in 1930s and its significance for neighbour principle in law of tort).

Impact of the contaminated land regime on commercial transactions *(Valerie M. Fogleman)*: Env. Law 1997, 11(3), 8-10. (Considerations regarding potential environmental liability in transactions involving sale or lease of land).

Liability and regulation–some legal challenges faced by operators of United Kingdom nuclear installations *(W.J. Leigh)*: Env. Liability 1997, 5(2), 43-49. (Civil liability for damage to property or personal injuries, regulatory issues concerning design and operation of nuclear installations and impact of EC law on operators' obligations).

Property and the environmental dilemma *(Gary J. Bardill)* and *(Deborah E. Bardill)*: P.V. 1997, 16(3), 4-8. (Implications for property developers and valuers of contaminated land and UK legal framework for apportioning liability for pollution and clean up costs).

Role of law and lawyers in protection of the global environment *(Russell S. Frye)*: I.B.L. 1997, 25(3), 100-101, 104. (Increased awareness of environmental issues by banks, trade and industry and individuals).

Self-monitoring, self-policing, self-incrimination and pollution law *(William Howarth)*: M.L.R. 1997, 60(2), 200-229. (Practical implications of self-regulation of water polluters, role of Environment Agency and admissibility of self-monitored evidence).

Statutory nuisance and contaminated land: a private right extinguished? *(Anthony Hobley)*: Mck. Env. L.B. 1997, Apr, 10-11. (Whether new contaminated land provisions remove individual's right of redress where contamination is prejudicial to health or nuisance).

The trade in wild-collected plants *(Barry A. Thomas* and *Mike Read)*: I.J.B.L.
1996, 1 (2), 161-186. (National and international regulation with examples of
the application to trade in orchids, bulbs and cylads).

2369. **Books**

Bates, John–UK Waste Law. 2nd Ed. Property and Conveyancing Library.
Hardback: £65.00. ISBN 0-421-56950-6. Sweet & Maxwell.

Battersby, Stephen–Dictionary of Environmental Law. Environmental Law.
Hardback: £75.00. ISBN 0-471-96918-4. John Wiley and Sons.

Blackhurst, John; Payne, Michael–Agricultural Pollution. Hardback: £80.00. ISBN
0-421-52610-6. Sweet & Maxwell.

Burton,Tim; Ball, Simon–Water Law. Environmental Law. Hardback: £45.00. ISBN
0-471-96577-4. Chancery Wiley Law Publications.

Fry, Michael–Manual of Environmental Protection Law. Hardback: £70.00. ISBN
0-19-826230-2. Clarendon Press.

Garner, J.F.; Jones, B.L.–Countryside Law. Paperback: £19.95. ISBN 0-7219-
1062-9. Shaw & Sons.

Gauci, Gotthard–Oil Pollution At Sea. Commercial Law. Hardback: £75.00. ISBN
0-471-97066-2. Chancery Wiley Law Publications.

Greenwood, Brian; Marshall, Anna–Environmental Law in CorporateTransactions.
Paperback: £55.00. ISBN 0-406-02294-1. Butterworth Law.

Holder, Jane–Impact of EC Environmental Law in the United Kingdom. European
Law. Hardback: £55.00. ISBN 0-471-97535-4. John Wiley and Sons.

Jones, Professor–Environmental Liability Practice Manual. Paperback: £29.95.
ISBN 0-471-95554-X. Chancery Wiley Law Publications.

Kiss, Alexandre; Shelton, Dinah–Manual of European Environmental Law.
Hardback: £90.00. ISBN 0-521-59122-8. Paperback: £34.95. ISBN 0-521-
59888-5. Cambridge University Press.

Moran, T.–Legal Competence in Environmental Health. Hardback: £39.95. ISBN
0-419-23000-9. E & FN Spon.

Pocklington, David–Law of Waste Management. Paperback: £45.00. ISBN 0-
7219-1520-5. Shaw & Sons.

Tromans, Stephen; Fitzgerald, James–Law of Nuclear Installations and
Radioactive Substances. Hardback: £95.00. ISBN 0-421-53880-5. Sweet &
Maxwell.

Tromans, Stephen; Turrall-Clarke, Robert–Contaminated Land: Supplement 1.
Paperback: £27.00. ISBN 0-421-56240-4. Sweet & Maxwell.

Waite, Andrew–Butterworth's Environmental Law Handbook. Paperback:
£65.00. ISBN 0-406-99154-5. Butterworth Law.

ENVIRONMENTAL HEALTH

2370. **Abatement notices–defences–reasonable excuse–burden of proof on
prosecution to prove excuse was not reasonable**

[Environmental Protection Act 1990 s.80(4).]

Held, that, where a defendant, charged under the Environmental Protection
Act 1990 s.80(4) with failing to comply with an abatement notice relating to the
burning of materials in the open air, contended that he had a reasonable excuse
for not complying with the notice, it was for the prosecution to demonstrate, to
the criminal standard of proof, that the excuse was not reasonable.

POLYCHRONAKIS v. RICHARDS AND JERROM LTD, *The Times*, November 19,
1997, Brooke, L.J., QBD.

2371. Abatement notices–failure to comply–two offences–calculation of fine–date of conviction being date of first offence

[Environmental Protection Act 1990 s.82.]

W pleaded guilty to an offence under the Environmental Protection Act 1990 s.82(8) on October 15, 1996. No financial penalty was imposed and no sentence advanced though the magistrates ordered W to complete the original order under s.82(2) within 21 days. W did not comply and eventually pleaded guilty to a second offence as a new complaint alleging a further default. The case was adjourned for consideration of quantifying the number of days the offence had continued after "conviction". It was an agreed fact that the order had been complied with on February 4, 1997. The prosecution argued that the two fines under s.82(8) were fundamentally different in nature. The first was discretionary both as to imposition and amount. The latter was mandatory in both respects. The defence argued all parts were discretionary. The prosecution further argued that from "conviction" meant from the first conviction in October 1996 whereas the defence argued this fine could only be calculated from January 29, 1997.

Held, that the decision of the court was that the "daily fine" was a mandatory order and at a fixed amount and that it should be calculated from the date of conviction which in this case was October 15, 1996 subject to the 21 day order. W was fined £45,000 for the default, with costs agreed.

PARRY v. WALSALL MBC, March 12, 1997, Magistrates Court (Aldridge and Brownhills). [*Ex rel.* Richard Powell, Barrister, Victoria Chambers, Birmingham].

2372. Abatement notices–failure to comply;–failure to appeal within 21 days–ill health–defence of reasonable excuse–defence not restricted to non receipt of notice

[Environmental Protection Act 1990 s.80(4), s.80(5).]

B appealed by way of case stated against a conviction of contravening the requirements of a noise abatement notice without reasonable excuse contrary to the Environmental Protection Act 1990 s.80(4) and s.80(5), arising from a neighbour's complaint about loud music coming from B's flat. A noise abatement notice was served personally on B. B did not appeal the notice within the stated 21 days, and there was no provision for appealing out of time. B allegedly did not comply with the abatement notice. B was diagnosed as HIV positive and one of her three children suffered from lymphatic cancer, from which he died two days after the notice was served. B sought to raise the defence that the abatement notice was not justified and that due to her and her son's illnesses she had a reasonable excuse for not appealing within 21 days. H argued that B could only raise the defence sought by way of appeal and could not rely on it as a reasonable excuse when no appeal had been made. The case stated was whether the special reason submitted by B in order to raise the defence of reasonable excuse to the prosecution under s.80 of the 1990 Act, had to amount to non-receipt of the notice. Consideration was given to what constituted a reasonable excuse for failing to appeal within 21 days.

Held, allowing the appeal and quashing the conviction, that the view taken by the magistrate as to what constituted a reasonable excuse was too restrictive. The circumstances did not have to amount to non-receipt of the notice for there to be a reasonable excuse. Account should have been taken of the personal circumstances of B at the time of service of the notice, being her illness and the death of her son, so as to constitute a defence of reasonable excuse, *Lambert Flat Management Ltd v. Lomas* [1981] 2 All E.R. 280, [1981] C.L.Y. 1998 considered.

BUTUYUYU v. HAMMERSMITH AND FULHAM LBC (1997) 29 H.L.R. 584, Gage, J., QBD.

2373. Abatement notices—noise caused by poultry—no need to state nature of nuisance alleged

[Environmental Protection Act 1990 s.79(1), s.80(1), s.80(3).]

S served an abatement notice on L under the Environmental Protection Act 1990 s.79(1)(g) requiring them to take specific measures so as to prevent noise from the cockerels and wildfowl that they kept. L appealed against the notice to a magistrates court under the 1990 Act s.80(3). The court dismissed the appeal and L appealed to the High Court on the basis that the abatement notice should have specified the nature of the nuisance alleged, whether one injurious to health or a common law nuisance, and that procedural unfairness had been demonstrated in the case, as L was unaware, until the close of evidence, which of these types of nuisance were being alleged and that in giving their judgment the magistrates did not make clear which type of nuisance they found.

Held, refusing the appeal, that (1) what was required of the contents of an abatement notice was contained in the 1990 Act s.80(1) and a series of regulations pursuant to it. Nowhere was there any mention of the need to specify precisely the nature of the nuisance alleged; (2) from the conduct of the case, during which no submission was made relating to procedural unfairness and no request for an adjournment was made by L, it could not be said that the procedure was unfair, and (3) the judgment of the magistrates could not give rise to any doubt as to the type of nuisance they found.

LOWE v. SOUTH SOMERSET DC, *The Times*, November 18, 1997, Gage, J., QBD.

2374. Abatement notices—notice should specify works required to abate nuisance

[Environmental Protection Act 1990 s.80.]

K appealed by way of case stated against a Crown Court decision allowing F's appeal against the magistrates' determination that abatement notices served on her pursuant to the Environmental Protection Act 1990 s.80 were valid. The notices had stated that F must abate the nuisance caused by a wall which was at risk of collapsing, but failed to specify what steps F had to take to achieve that.

Held, dismissing the appeal, that an abatement notice had to ensure that its recipient knew what nuisance was at issue and what works were required to abate the nuisance, *Sterling Homes (Midlands) Ltd v. Birmingham City Council* [1996] Env. L.R. 121, [1996] 1 C.L.Y. 2689 followed. Where an abatement notice required its recipient to take positive action to abate the nuisance, rather than simply to cease the offending behaviour, it might be necessary to specify exactly what steps were required, in the interests of avoiding doubt. As the notices served upon F had failed to specify any such steps, they could not be regarded as valid.

KIRKLEES MBC v. FIELD, *The Times*, November 26, 1997, Owen, J., QBD.

2375. Abatement notices—prosecutions—sufficiency of evidence—reasonableness of decision to prosecute

[Environmental Protection Act 1990 s.80.]

H was convicted of contravening an abatement notice contrary to the Environmental Protection Act 1990 s.80, which related to noise from a compressor. On appeal to the Crown Court, H claimed the noise came from a washing machine. Several people gave evidence that the noise they had heard was that of a compressor, not a washing machine, the noise of which was recorded and played back to them. One of the witnesses had experience of working in a compressor house, and H's appeal was dismissed. H appealed by way of case stated, arguing that the court's decision that there was a case to answer, and that there was sufficient evidence to convict the appellant, was *Wednesbury* unreasonable.

Held, dismissing the appeal, that the evidence was not so tenuous as to require the Court to accept the submission of no case to answer and it was sufficient to justify a finding that the case was proved to the necessary standard.

HESTER DUTCH v. COVENTRY CITY COUNCIL [1996] Env. L.R. D27, Rose, L.J., QBD.

2376. Fire precautions–shopping centre–construction site–readily inflammable partition–managing agents liable–statutory interpretation

[Fire Precautions Act 1971 s.24.]

D appealed by way of case stated against their conviction of breaching the requirements of the fire certificate under the Fire Precautions Act 1971 s.24. D were agents responsible for running a shopping centre owned by U, a pension fund. The shopping centre, subject to construction work, was separated from the building site by a partition which was covered by the fire certificate. D were convicted of breaching the certificate after replacing the partition with readily inflammable rather than flame resistant material. D contended that (1) compromising the fire resistant qualities of the partition did not constitute a breach of the certificate as the partition was only a temporary measure not a permanent feature; (2) the partition was properly maintained; (3) they were not guilty of an "act" or "default" within the meaning of s.24, and (4) the court was wrong to find that the requisite connection between the commission of the offence and relevant default had been established as D had no power to stop the work, the contractors being in a contractual relationship with U alone.

Held, dismissing the appeal, that (1) the partition was covered by the fire certificate as partitions are, by their very nature, temporary constructions; (2) the partition was not properly maintained as it was replaced by non flame resistant material; (3) D were in default by the failure to perform their contractual duty to ensure that U complied with its obligations, and (4) D, as agents for U, had the power to stop the work of the contractors so as to avoid a breach of the fire certificate.

DTZ DEBENHAM THORPE LTD v. SHROPSHIRE CC, Trans. Ref: CO-712/97, July 10, 1997, Henry, L.J., QBD.

2377. Statutory nuisance–objective test to determine whether condition of premises prejudicial to health

[Environmental Protection Act 1990 s.79(1)(a).]

Held, that an objective test was to be applied in considering whether the condition of premises was prejudicial to health under the Environmental Protection Act 1990 s.79(1)(a), and there was no duty to consider an occupier's individual health requirements.

CUNNINGHAM v. BIRMINGHAM CITY COUNCIL, *The Times*, June 9, 1997, Pill, L.J., QBD.

EQUITY

2378. Limitations–distribution of trust monies–action for damages against solicitor–statutory limitation period applicable to common law claim in negligence did not bar claim in equity

[Limitation Act 1980.]

K, who was severely disabled, sought damages for breach of duty of care, negligence or alternatively breach of fiduciary duty against W, the solicitor representing his stepmother in relation to his father's estate. K argued that W had improperly influenced the distribution of trust monies by sending a letter to the trustees giving false information about his circumstances and suggesting that K's stepmother should benefit instead of him.

Held, that although the common law claim in negligence was statute-barred under the Limitation Act 1980, the claim for breach of fiduciary duty survived through the application of equitable principles as that cause of action was not analogous to the claims to which the time limit applied. The fact that there had been a lengthy delay, due initially to W's concealment of the letter, had to be weighed against the possible injustice which K had suffered as a result of W's conduct. On balance, K's action should be allowed to proceed, *Nelson v. Rye* [1996] 1 W.L.R. 1378, [1996] 1 C.L.Y. 1236 and *Bulli Coal Mining v. Osborne* [1899] A.C. 351 considered.

KERSHAW v. WHELAN (NO.2), *The Times*, February 10, 1997, Ebsworth, J., QBD.

2379. Unjust enrichment–corporate personality–amendment of writ after expiry of limitation period–restitutionary remedy

B, who wished to develop a tennis centre on land used by a squash club, entered into negotiations with BC, owners of the land, and it was agreed that a lease for 31 years would be forthcoming. BC insisted that B should personally control the operation through the medium of the club, to be formed into a company, and B acceded. Substantial sums were invested by B in development work, and BC provided a contractual guarantee. After the development work had been substantially completed, BC, breaching the contract with B, refused to grant the lease, took possession of the centre following a winding up order, and then opened it for business. It was claimed that BC had acquired the centre for about half its estimated value and B issued a writ claiming damages for fraudulent misrepresentation, which he subsequently sought to amend, after the limitation period had expired, to claim that BC had been unjustly enriched and the interests of justice required restitution. B's application for leave to amend was dismissed and his statement of claim was struck out as disclosing no reasonable cause of action. B appealed.

Held, dismissing the appeal, that, whilst the decision not to allow amendment of the writ after expiry of the limitation period could not be faulted, it was not necessarily obvious that B had no arguable case in restitution so that striking out was merited. Although, following *Salomon v. Salomon & Co Ltd* [1897] A.C. 22, B's claim would seem to involve subversion of the doctrine of privity of contract, given that the club was a separate legal entity, in view of the relationship between B, the club and BC, it was not certain that, in all the circumstances, a court would have ruled out a restitutionary remedy.

BRENNAN v. BRIGHTON BC (NO.2), *The Times*, May 15, 1997, Pill, L.J., CA.

2380. Unjust enrichment–subrogation of rights under a debenture–no unjust enrichment despite "technical" enrichment

O, a member of the same group of companies as P, appealed against a declaration that B was entitled to the entire benefit of a charge over P's property, arising from a right of subrogation under a debenture between B's successor, R, and P. Under the terms of an agreement by letter between O and P's parent holding company and R, rights accruing to O under a second charge on P's property, had purportedly been postponed in favour of R. Following assignment of the first charge to B, P defaulted on the terms of a deep discount security issued by P to H, the general manager of its Swiss holding company, and B sought payment of both principal and interest due under the security pursuant to an agreement between H and B.

Held, allowing the appeal, that (1) the terms of the agreement contained within the postponement letter between H and B did not blur the distinction between the holding company and the other group members, with only the former being bound by it, and (2) the right of subrogation as a remedy for unjust enrichment is given in line with settled principles, *Orakpo v. Manson Investments Ltd* [1978] A.C. 95, [1977] C.L.Y. 1977 and *Boscawen v. Bajwa* [1996] 1 W.L.R. 328, [1995] 2 C.L.Y. 3601 considered. On the facts, O had technically been enriched at B's expense, on the basis of the partial repayment of the debt between P and B and consequent on the value of the property being greater than the debt owed to B, but less than the total due by P to B and O combined. However, as P's loan was not actually secured by a charge on P's property, but took effect as a security on a pledge issued by P to H, which was subsequently assigned by him to B, liability remained with H regardless of the outcome of the loan from H to P. To permit subrogation in the circumstances would place B in a better position than if the agreement had bound P and O. However, given that B had opted for a type of negative pledge, instead of a binding agreement, if it obtained subrogation of the benefit of the debenture, the resulting security would exceed the benefit of the pledge.

BANQUE FINANCIERE DE LA CITE v. PARC (BATTERSEA) LTD, Trans. Ref: CHANF 95/0221/B, November 29, 1996, Morritt, L.J., CA.

2381. Articles

A retreat from equitable mutuality? *(Andrew Harper)*: Conv. 1997, May/Jun, 182-198. (Whether apparent shift in boundary between common law and equity towards exclusive recognition of only contractually based obligations is having undesirable consequences, examining cases on subrogation, mutual wills and part performance).

Developments in the law of equitable compensation *(Paul Matthews)*: T. & T. 1997, 3(6), 6-10. (Divergence between common law damages and equitable compensation for breach of trust in terms of quantum, tax treatment, causation and remoteness).

Economic duress: recent difficulties and possible alternatives *(Andrew Phang)*: R.L.R. 1997, 5, 53-65. (Links between doctrines of economic duress and restitution and reasons for significant decline of doctrine of duress in commercial context).

Equity's role in the twentieth century *(Anthony Mason)*: K.C.L.J. 1997/98, 8, 1-22. (Role of equity in commerce, fiduciary relationship and contract, equitable compensation for breach of duty, and third parties and notice).

Financial institutions and misdirected funds *(Sukhninder Panesar)*: J.I.B.L. 1997, 12(5), 175-181. (Financial institutions' equitable liability for assisting in misdirected funds transfers and when receiving benefits of fraud).

Focus: the classes you missed–the law of restitution *(Ian W. Hutton)*: Litigator 1997, Jan, 25-32. (Basic guide to law of restitution, highlighting uncertainties as to its details, boundaries and scope).

General average as restitution *(F.D. Rose)*: L.Q.R. 1997, 113(Oct), 569-574. (Tests for measuring unjust enrichment in general average situations).

Illegality limited *(F.D. Rose)*: K.C.L.J. 1997/98, 8, 69-85. (Extent to which illegality can be used as defence in restitutionary claims).

Is equity efficient? *(Anthony J. Duggan)*: L.Q.R. 1997, 113(Oct), 601-636. (Consideration of various equitable doctrines from point of view of law and economics movement which holds that common law tends towards efficient outcome).

Proprietary estoppel and s.70(1)(g) *(Mark Pawlowski)*: S.J. 1997, 141(3), 64-65. (Whether equity arising out of proprietary estoppel coupled with actual occupation of land can bind third parties as overriding interest and application of modified doctrine of notice based on constructive trust).

Proprietary estoppel–satisfying the equity *(Mark Pawlowski)*: L.Q.R. 1997, 113(Apr), 232-237. (Extent to which court can consider claimant's equity arising from proprietary estoppel to be fully extinguished by date of hearing in view of supervening events and means by which estoppel equity can bind third party).

Restitution and the Rome Convention *(Robert Stevens)*: L.Q.R. 1997, 113(Apr), 249-253. (Possible approaches to determining law governing restitution of benefits conferred under void contract, including treatment of contract that is nullity under Rome Convention).

Restitution, coercion by a third party and the proper role of notice *(Eoin O'Dell)*: C.L.J. 1997, 56(1), 71-79. (Basis for restitutionary action where plaintiff makes payment to defendant under coercion of third party).

Set-off or counterclaim? *(Louis G. Doyle)*: S.J. 1997, 141(14), 326-327. (Distinction between counterclaim and set-off, legal set-off, equitable set-off, exclusion of set-off and practical and procedural differences between defences).

The O'Brien principle and substantive unfairness *(Mindy Chen-Wishart)*: C.L.J. 1997, 56(1), 60-70. (Application of principle on setting aside transactions for undue influence to situation where employee guaranteed employer's debts by mortgaging flat).

The availability of proprietary remedies *(A.J. Oakley)*: Conv. 1997, Jan/Feb, 1-5. (Whether equitable proprietary claim is available to transferor of property under transaction which is void ab initio and use of subrogation to reverse unjust enrichment).

Tracing through the back door? the doctrine of proprietary subrogation *(Paul Matthews)*: T. & T. 1997, 3(5), 18-22. (Application of equitable subrogation where plaintiff's money has been used to discharge defendant's secured debt to bona fide third party without notice of defective title).

2382. Books

Burrows, Andrew; McKendrick, Ewan—Cases and Materials on the Law of Restitution. Hardback: £55.00. ISBN 0-19-876290-9. Oxford University Press.

Ho, Lusina—Equitable Remedies. Paperback: £60.00. ISBN 0-421-58520-X. Sweet & Maxwell.

Martin, Jill—Hanbury and Martin: Modern Equity. 15th Ed. Paperback: £30.00. ISBN 0-421-57860-2. Sweet & Maxwell.

Pettit, Philip H.—Equity and the Law of Trusts. Paperback: £29.95. ISBN 0-406-07277-9. Butterworth Law.

EUROPEAN UNION

2383. Direct effect—EC law without direct effect did not provide for elimination of conflicting national provisions—criminal liability could not be based on unimplemented Directive—European Union

[Council Directive 76/464 on pollution caused by certain dangerous substances discharged into the aquatic environment of the Community.]

A was prosecuted under Italian national provisions on the unauthorised discharge of cadmium into surface waters. He argued that his undertaking was "existing plant" and, in the absence of ministerial decrees limiting cadmium discharge, was not obliged to apply for authorisation. The Pretore found that the national provisions did exclude existing plant from the system of authorisation, but doubted whether those provisions conformed with Council Directive 76/464 on pollution caused by certain dangerous substances discharged into the aquatic environment of the Community, the authorisation regime did not distinguish between new and existing plant. The Pretore therefore stayed proceedings pending a preliminary ruling on whether there was a procedure whereby domestic provisions conflicting with a Directive could be eliminated from national legislation when the Directive had not been fully transposed.

Held, that the obligation on a national court to interpret a Community Directive in the light of the wording and purpose of the Directive did not extend to interpreting it so as to impose on an individual an obligation which had not been transposed, especially where it determined or aggravated that individual's criminal liability. It followed that a national court could not eliminate national provisions contrary to a Directive provision not transposed, where that provision could not be relied upon before the national court, *Marleasing SA v. La Comercial Internacional de Alimentacion SA (C106/89)* [1990] E.C.R. I-4135 applied.

CRIMINAL PROCEEDINGS AGAINST ARCARO (C168/95) [1997] All E.R. (EC) 82, CN Kakouris (President), ECJ.

2384. Equal treatment–application of fundamental principles to national measures–discrimination in administration of beef stocks transfer scheme providing financial aid to beef exporters

[Treaty of Rome 1957 Art.7, Art.40.]

FCT and others were frozen meat exporters who applied for judicial review of the beef stocks transfer scheme, administered by MAFF, which provided financial assistance to meat exporters with slaughtering and cutting facilities following a CEC decision prohibiting the export of beef slaughtered in the UK. FCT contended that the scheme discriminated unfairly against meat exporters without their own slaughtering and cutting facilities and that this breached the fundamental principles of EC law on equal treatment and non discrimination. FCT argued that the fundamental principles of EC law had to be applied where a scheme was a domestic measure falling within the context of EC law, that they had the same scope as the Treaty of Rome 1957 Art.7(1), which prohibited discrimination on grounds of nationality, and that the scheme involved discrimination between producers in the common organisation of agricultural markets, prohibited by Art.40(3) of the Treaty.

Held, dismissing the application, that the fundamental principles were not provided for in the Treaty, but had been developed by the ECJ and it was not obvious that they should have the same scope as Treaty provisions dealing with discrimination and equal treatment. Where a Member State took a measure that was neither required nor permitted by EC law, but might be said to affect the operation of the Single Market, it was not made pursuant to EC law, even though its legality might be affected by it. The ECJ's jurisdiction was limited to areas authorised by the Treaty and the fundamental principles did not apply where the measure was not made pursuant to Treaty rights and obligations. However, where a measure was made pursuant to EC law, the jurisprudence of the ECJ would be applied by the domestic court. Despite the fact that the beef stocks transfer scheme was made in response to a CEC decision and referred to elements of EC law, it was not a measure demanded by EC law or one that required permission from the EU. It did not fall within Art.40(3), and therefore the fundamental principles of non-discrimination and equal treatment did not apply.

R. v. MINISTRY OF AGRICULTURE FISHERIES AND FOOD, *ex p.* FIRST CITY TRADING [1997] Eu L.R. 195, Laws, J., QBD.

2385. European Bank for Reconstruction and Development–capital stock–subscription payments

EUROPEAN BANK FOR RECONSTRUCTION AND DEVELOPMENT (FURTHER PAYMENTS TO CAPITAL STOCK) ORDER 1997, SI 1997 1991; made under the Overseas Development and Co-operation Act 1980 s.4. In force: July 31, 1997; £0.65.

This Order provides for the payment on behalf of the Government of the United Kingdom to the European Bank for Reconstruction and Development of a further subscription not exceeding ECU 851,750,000 to the increased authorised capital stock of the Bank pursuant to arrangements made with the Bank in accordance with Resolution No.59 adopted by the Board of Governors of the Bank on April 15, 1996. It further provides for the redemption of non-interest bearing and non-negotiable notes issued by the Secretary of State in payment of the subscription. It also provides that any sums which may be received by the Government of the United Kingdom in pursuance of the arrangements relating to the further subscription shall be paid into the Consolidated Fund.

2386. European Commission–access to documents–reasons for refusing access to documents relating to possible infringement proceedings–European Union

[Treaty of Rome 1957 Art.169, Art.190; Commission Decision 94/90 on public access to Commission documents Art.1.]

WWF challenged a CEC decision refusing access to documents relating to the building of a visitors' centre in the Burren National Park in Ireland, in respect of which, after investigation, CEC had decided not to initiate infringement proceedings under the Treaty of Rome 1957 Art.169.

Held, annulling the decision, that it had failed to strike a genuine balance between the citizen's interest in obtaining access to the documents and CEC's interest in protecting the confidentiality of its deliberations. CEC had given no indication by reference to document category of its reasons for considering that the documents related to possible infringement proceedings and had failed to state adequately the reasons for its decision, as required under Art.190 of the EC Treaty. The code of conduct on public access to Commission and Council documents, adopted under Commission Decision 94/90 Art.1, contained two categories of documents within the exception to the general principle of citizens' access to documents, the first category being mandatory and the second discretionary in nature. Although not obliged to provide reasons justifying the application of the public interest exception for the mandatory category, CEC was required to indicate the subject matter of documents and particularly whether they involved inspections or investigations relating to possible infringements of EU law.

WORLD WIDE FUND FOR NATURE (WWF UK) v. COMMISSION OF THE EUROPEAN COMMUNITIES (T105/95); *sub nom.* WWF UK v. COMMISSION OF THE EUROPEAN COMMUNITIES (T105/95) [1997] All E.R. (EC) 300, K Lenaerts (President), CFI.

2387. European Commission–communication imposing legal obligations–communication incompetent–European Union

A proposal was submitted by the European Commission to the EC Council regarding the freedom of management and investment of funds for retirement provision. No agreement was reached by the Council, and the Commission withdrew the proposal, subsequently publishing a communication in the Official Journal of the European Communities, the provisions of which were very similar to the terms of the original proposal. The French government challenged the publication on the grounds that its terms were intended to impose new obligations which the Commission did not have power to create. The Commission argued that the publication was merely interpretative of existing Treaty principles.

Held, annulling the communication, that the wording of the communication was imperative and it was intended to constitute an act with legal effect of its own. The Commission had no power to adopt such an act which could only be done by the Council.

FRANCE v. COMMISSION OF THE EUROPEAN COMMUNITIES (C57/95) [1997] All E.R. (EC) 411, GC Rodriguez Iglesias (President), ECJ.

2388. European Commission–decisions–exemptions from levy denied–addressees' right to challenge–European Union

[Treaty of Rome 1957 Art.173; Council Regulation 1101/89 on structural improvements in inland waterway transport.]

The European Council of Ministers adopted Council Regulation 1101/89 on structural improvements in inland waterway transport, which was intended to achieve a substantial reduction of structural overcapacity. The Regulation introduced scrapping schemes which required several Member States to set up a scrapping fund, into which the owner of every vessel covered by the Regulation had to pay a contribution. Art.8(1)(a) established the "old-for-new" rule under which the bringing into service of newly constructed vessels was to be conditional on the owner of the new vessel scrapping a tonnage of equivalent capacity to the new vessel without receiving a scrapping premium, or, if no vessel was scrapped, paying a special premium into the scrapping fund. Art.8(3)(c) allowed the Commission, on application by the owner, to exempt "specialised vessels" from the "old-for-new" requirement. W, a Belgian undertaking, applied for an exemption under Art.8(3)(c) for the bringing into service of a bunkering vessel. On May 6, 1993 the Commission informed W that the request for the exemption had been refused. In implementation of that decision the Belgian authorities demanded from W a special contribution to the scrapping fund. Rather than challenge the validity of the Commission's decision under the Treaty of Rome 1957 Art.173, W brought an action in April 1995 against the decision of the Belgian authorities. The national court referred to the European Court of Justice five questions including whether the Commission's decision was compatible with the aims and objectives of the Regulation of 1989.

Held, that the Commission's decision was binding on the national court. In order to ensure legal certainty, a decision adopted by a Community institution which had not been challenged by its addressee within the time limit laid down by Art.173 became definitive against him. A recipient of aid could not plead the invalidity of a decision, addressed by the Commission to a Member State, notified by that State to the recipient, in proceedings brought before the national courts against the implementing decision taken by the authorities of that State where the recipient of the aid had failed to apply under Art.173 for annulment of the Commission's decision and where undoubtedly he could have done so, *TWD Textilewerke Deggendorf GmbH v. Germany (C188/92)* [1994] E.C.R. I-833, [1994] C.L.Y. 4850, applied. In the instant case all the questions referred by the national court related exclusively to the validity of the Commission's decision of May 6, 1993, by which the court was bound.

WILJO NV v. BELGIUM (C178/95) [1997] All E.R. (EC) 226, C Gulmann (Acting for the President), ECJ.

2389. European Commission—disclosure—secret information used in administrative process—use also permitted in national legal proceedings—opportunity to oppose permitted use wrongly denied—European Union

[Council Regulation 17/62 implementing Art.85 and Art.86 of the Treaty Art.4, Art.20; Treaty of Rome 1957 Art.5.]

P was party to an agreement by a number of Netherlands banks establishing a common procedure for processing payment and transfer orders on pre-printed forms. The banks notified the agreement to the CEC in accordance with Council Regulation 17/62 Art.4. CEC obtained information from a number of parties, including P and sent out a statement of objections. CEC authorised two public utilities which had used the forms provided to attend a hearing in the administrative procedure and, to enable them to prepare for the hearing, CEC sent the utilities copies of the statement of objections. CEC granted the utilities permission to use the information contained within the statement in national legal proceedings. P sought to reverse that decision submitting that the statement of objections was based on secret information which could be disclosed to third parties only for the purposes of the administrative procedure and could not be used in national legal proceedings. P also argued that it should have been given an opportunity to oppose the decision.

Held, that CEC had not erred in allowing the utilities to use the information in national legal proceedings but had erred in not allowing P the opportunity to oppose the decision. The principle of sincere cooperation inherent in the Treaty of Rome 1957 Art.5 required Community institutions to assist any national judicial authority in dealing with an infringement of the rules and that principle entitled a national court to seek information from the Commission relating to any procedure that may have been set in motion. Such cooperation fell outside Art.20(1) of Council Regulation 17/62. It followed that CEC could not be prevented from allowing undertakings to produce documents from the administrative procedure in national legal proceedings. CEC should however give those who had provided the information an opportunity to state their views and identify documents or passages that might be damaging.

POSTBANK NV v. COMMISSION OF THE EUROPEAN COMMUNITIES (T353/94) [1996] All E.R. (EC) 817, Saggio (President), CFI.

2390. European Court of Justice—matter could not be referred after final judgment given in national court

[Treaty of Rome 1957 Art.177.]

M's application for judicial review of a planning decision was dismissed and leave to appeal was refused. M sought to refer the matter to the European Court pursuant to the Treaty of Rome 1957 Art.177.

Held, dismissing the application, that where the national court had already reached a decision on the issues it was too late to seek a reference to the European Court.

McNAMARA v. AN BORD PLEANALA [1997] Eu L.R. 112, Barr, J., HC (Ire).

2391. European police service—immunities and privileges

EUROPEAN COMMUNITIES (IMMUNITIES AND PRIVILEGES OF THE EUROPEAN POLICE OFFICE) ORDER 1997, SI 1997 2973; made under the European Communities Act 1972 s.2. In force: in accordance with Art.1; £1.10.

This Order confers privileges and immunities on the European Police Office "Europol" in accordance with the Protocol on the Privileges and Immunities on Europol, the Members of its Organs, the Deputy Directors and Employees of Europol (Cm.3767). The European Police Office (Legal Capacities) Order 1996 (SI 1996 3157) is revoked.

2392. European police service—treaties

EUROPEAN COMMUNITIES (DEFINITION OF TREATIES) (EUROPEAN POLICE OFFICE) ORDER 1997, SI 1997 2972; made under the European Communities Act 1972 s.1. In force: in accordance with Art.1; £0.65.

This Order declares the Protocol on the Privileges and Immunities of Europol to be a Community Treaty for the purposes of the European Communities Act 1972 s.1 (2).

2393. Fisheries policy—criteria limiting ability of foreign vessels to fish in UK waters breached EC law—compensatory but not exemplary damages recoverable

[Merchant Shipping Act 1988.]

The applicants, owners and managers of Spanish trawlers, had established before the ECJ that the Merchant Shipping Act 1988, which precluded those not meeting criteria relating to nationality, domicile and residence from registering to fish in UK waters, had breached EC law. The issue before the court was whether the breaches were sufficiently serious for the applicants to pursue a claim in damages and whether exemplary damages were available.

Held, that the breaches of EC law comprised in the conditions of nationality, residence and domicile were each sufficiently serious to give rise to liability for any damage which the applicants could prove they had suffered in consequence of the Act. There had been a manifest and grave disregard of the limits of the UK's discretion, in that (1) discrimination on the ground of nationality was the intended effect of the criteria; (2) the government was aware that those criteria would necessarily injure the applicants who would be unable to fish against the British quota; (3) the Act was constructed to ensure it would not be delayed by legal challenges and this made it impossible for the applicants to obtain interim relief without the ECJ's intervention, and (4) the Commission had been consistently hostile to the proposed legislation. The question of whether exemplary damages would also be payable to the applicants depended on whether a similar claim under English law would succeed. Liability for a breach of EC law could best be compared with breach of statutory duty, as it was not possible to compare the UK's actions with the tort of misfeasance. Under English law, a breach of statutory duty only gave rise to exemplary damages if there was express statutory provision for them and no such provision existed in this case.

R. v. SECRETARY OF STATE FOR TRANSPORT, ex p. FACTORTAME LTD (NO.5), The Times, September 11, 1997, Hobhouse, L.J., QBD.

2394. Ministers—designated powers—Designation No.1 Order

EUROPEAN COMMUNITIES (DESIGNATION) ORDER 1997, SI 1997 1174; made under the European Communities Act 1972 s.2. In force: June 4, 1997; £0.65.

This Order designates further Ministers who, and departments which, may exercise powers to make Regulations conferred by the European Communities Act 1972 s.2(2) and specifies matters in relation to which those powers may be exercised.

2395. Ministers—designated powers—Designation No.2 Order

EUROPEAN COMMUNITIES (DESIGNATION) (NO.2) ORDER 1997, SI 1997 1742; made under the European Communities Act 1972 s.2. In force: August 22, 1997; £0.65.

This Order designates Ministers who, and departments which, may exercise powers to make Regulations conferred by the European Communities Act 1972 s.2(2) and specifies matters in relation to which those powers may be exercised.

2396. Ministers—designated powers—Designation No.3 Order

EUROPEAN COMMUNITIES (DESIGNATION) (NO.3) ORDER 1997, SI 1997 2563; made under the European Communities Act 1972 s.2. In force: December 2, 1997; £1.10.

This Order designates Ministers who, and departments which, may exercise powers to make regulations conferred by the European Communities Act 1972 s.2(2) and specifies the matters in relation to which those powers may be exercised. It partly revokes the European Communities (Designation) (No.3) Order 1993 (SI 1993 2661).

2397. Practice direction—European Court of Justice—references by national courts—practice directions

The European Court of Justice has issued a Practice Direction entitled "Note for Guidance on References by National Courts for Preliminary Rulings". Interested parties are reminded that: (1) any court or tribunal may ask the ECJ to interpret a rule of Community law if necessary to give judgment in a case before it, reference of questions of interpretation being compulsory unless already decided or obvious, *CILFIT Srl v. Ministry of Health (C283/81)* [1982] E.C.R. 3415, [1983] C.L.Y. 1472; (2) the ECJ has jurisdiction to rule on the validity of acts of the Community institutions; any national court intending to question the validity of a Community act must refer that question, although it may exceptionally suspend the application of the measure and grant interim relief before referring; (3) questions for a preliminary ruling must be limited to interpretation or validity of a provision of Community, not national, law; (4) the form of the order referring a question, and whether a stay should be granted pending the answer, are matters for national law; (5) the order was to be translated and therefore should be drafted as clearly and precisely as possible; (6) the order should include a statement of reasons sufficient to give those to which it must be notified a clear understanding of the factual and legal context of the main proceedings, *Telemarsicabruzzo SpA v. Circostel (C320/90)* [1993] E.C.R. I-393, [1993] C.L.Y. 4252; (7) as the ECJ cannot decide issues of fact or domestic law, it was preferable for references to be made after the domestic court could, if only as a working hypothesis, define the factual and legal context; (8) the national court should send the order for reference and relevant documents direct to the Court, and (9) proceedings for a preliminary ruling were free of charge.

PRACTICE DIRECTION (EUROPEAN COURT OF JUSTICE: ARTICLE 177 PROCEDURE) [1997] All E.R. (EC) 1, ECJ.

2398. State aids–annulment–CEC refusal to propose "appropriate measures" under Art.93(1)–European Union

[Treaty of Rome 1957 Art.92(3)(c), Art.93(1), Art.173.]

The Netherlands government notified a general regional aid scheme to the Commission which considered it to be compatible with the Treaty of Rome 1957 Art.92(3)(c). S, a UK salt producer became aware that a Netherlands company had applied for aid to construct a salt plant, and requested the Commission to review the scheme and propose "appropriate measures" pursuant to the Treaty of Rome 1957 Art.93(1). The Commission refused and S applied under Art.173 to have the decision annulled.

Held, dismissing the application, that an annulment could be granted only if a Decision or measure produced binding legal effects. A refusal to adopt a measure could be reviewed only if it would have had binding legal effect if taken. The state to which any "appropriate measures" were addressed pursuant to Art.93(1) was not bound to adopt them and the refusal to suggest them was therefore not amenable to action under Art.173.

SALT UNION LTD (VEREIN DEUTSHE SALZINDUSTRIE EV INTERVENING) v. COMMISSION OF THE EUROPEAN COMMUNITIES (FRIMA BV INTERVENING) (T330/94) [1997] All E.R. (EC) 73, CP Briet, CFI.

2399. State aids–French government's assistance to undertakings making employees redundant–classification as state aid–European Union

[Treaty of Rome 1957 Art.92(1).]

French legislation provides that in the event of a redundancy situation in undertakings with more than 50 employees where the number of redundancies was 10 or more within a single period of 30 days, a social plan must be drawn up and implemented. Every such social plan must, inter alia, allow for re-deployment of employees who lose their jobs and incorporate alternatives to training leave agreements. Social plans may be co-financed by the State, up to a specified maximum. By a decision of June 27, 1994, the European Commission classified such co-financing as "state aid" within the meaning of the Treaty of Rome 1957 Art.92(1). The effect of such a classification was that the State assistance was regarded as incompatible with the common market on the basis that it distorted competition by favouring certain undertakings. The French Government brought an application seeking to annul the decision, on the ground that the financial assistance did not benefit undertakings but constituted a general measure for the benefit of employees facing unemployment.

Held, dismissing the application, that (1) Art.92(1) does not distinguish between measures of state intervention by reference to their causes or aims but defines them in relation to their effects, *Italy v. Commission of the European Communities (C387/92)* [1974] E.C.R. 709 applied. The social character of the assistance was not therefore sufficient to exclude it outright from being categorised as aid for the purposes of Art.92(1). Since the French Government has administrative discretion as to the amount of assistance received by different undertakings, it must be held that by virtue of its aim and general scheme that the financial assistance was liable to place certain undertakings in a more favourable situation than others and it thus meets the conditions for classification as state aid under Art.92(1), and (2) the concept of aid encompasses advantages granted by public authorities which normally mitigate the charges included in the budget of an undertaking, *Banco Exterior de Espana SA v. Ayuntamiento de Valencia (C387/92)* [1994] E.C.R. I-877, [1994] C.L.Y. 4949 applied. Since the French Government stated that no minimum social plan existed for which a figure could easily be arrived at the Commission was entitled to conclude that, in drawing up a social plan in collaboration with the State, an undertaking received state aid within the meaning of Art.92(1).

FRANCE v. COMMISSION OF THE EUROPEAN COMMUNITIES (C241/94) [1997] I.R.L.R. 415, GC Rodriguez Iglesias (President), ECJ.

2400. State aids—repayment—recovery of aid unlawfully paid where inconsistent with national law—European Union

[Treaty of Rome 1957 Art.93.]

A had decided to close its plant when it was granted DM 8m in state aid by the Rheinland-Pfalz government. The Commission decided that the aid had been paid illegally and ordered its recovery. The German government did not attempt to recover the aid payments because German administrative law and the principles of certainty and legitimate expectation prevented recovery. The Court of Justice ruled that Germany had failed to fulfil its obligations and the German government then set about recovering the payments. A challenged the attempted recovery in the German courts and the action was adjourned pending determination by the Court of Justice of the question whether an authority was required to reclaim such payments where it was barred from doing so by national law.

Held, ordering the recovery of the sums paid, that an undertaking that had been granted state aid could not entertain a legitimate expectation that the aid was lawful unless it had been granted in compliance with Art.93 of the Treaty. Once it was decided that the aid had been unlawfully paid, the authorities had no option but to recover the payments. At that point the recipient of the aid ceased to be in a state of uncertainty.

LAND RHEINLAND-PFALZ v. ALCAN DEUTSCHLAND GmbH (C24/95) [1997] All E.R. (EC) 427, GC Rodriguez Iglesias (President), ECJ.

2401. Taxation—levy introduced by Denmark incompatible with EC law—European Union

[Sixth Council Directive 77/388 on a common system for VAT Art.33.]

The Danish Government introduced a levy called the labour market contribution. It was based on the VAT calculation in the case of businesses fully subject to VAT and on the aggregate wages and salaries paid in other cases. CEC sought a declaration that the labour market contribution infringed EC law.

Held, granting the declaration, that the levy infringed the Sixth Council Directive 77/388 Art.33 since it was generally charged on the same basis of assessment as VAT, but without complying with the Community rules applying to VAT.

COMMISSION OF THE EUROPEAN COMMUNITIES v. DENMARK (C234/91) [1997] S.T.C. 721, O Due (President), ECJ.

2402. Treaties—Chile

EUROPEAN COMMUNITIES (DEFINITION OF TREATIES) (FRAMEWORK COOPERATION AGREEMENT BETWEEN THE EUROPEAN COMMUNITY AND ITS MEMBER STATES AND THE REPUBLIC OF CHILE) ORDER 1997, SI 1997 2576; made under the European Communities Act 1972 s.1. In force: in accordance with Art.1; £0.65.

This Order declares the Framework Co-operation Agreement between the European Community and its Member States and the Republic of Chile, done at Florence on June 21, 1996, to be a Community Treaty as defined in the European Communities Act 1972 s.1 (2). The objectives of the Agreement are to strengthen existing relations between the parties on the basis of reciprocity and mutual interest, paving the way for the progressive and reciprocal liberalisation of trade, leading ultimately to the establishment of a political and economic association between the EU and Chile.

2403. Treaties–Estonia

EUROPEAN COMMUNITIES (DEFINITION OF TREATIES) (EUROPE AGREEMENT ESTABLISHING AN ASSOCIATION BETWEEN THE EUROPEAN COMMUNITIES AND THEIR MEMBER STATES AND THE REPUBLIC OF ESTONIA) ORDER 1997, SI 1997 269; made under the European Communities Act 1972 s.1. In force: in accordance with Art.1; £1.10.

The Order declares the Europe Agreement establishing an Association between the European Communities and their Member States and the Republic of Estonia, signed on June 12, 1995, to be a Community Treaty as defined in the European Communities Act 1972.

2404. Treaties–European Economic Area–Council Regulation imposing import duty–Regulation adopted prior to entry into force of EEA Agreement–Regulation having direct effect operating in breach of legitimate expectation–European Union

[Treaty of Rome 1957 Art.10; Free Trade Agreement between the Commission of the European Communities and Austria; Council Regulation 3697/93 withdrawing tariff concessions in accordance with Art.23(2) and Art.27(3)(a) of the Free Trade Agreement between the Community and Austria (General Motors Austria); Agreement on a European Economic Area 1992 Art.10; Treaty establishing the European Coal and Steel Community (ECSC) 1951.]

Following negotiations as to the availability of grant aid between O's parent company and the Austrian Government, O commenced the manufacture of gear boxes in Austria with the assistance of grant aid. The Commission's Competition Directorate took the view that the aid was contrary to the Free Trade Agreement between the Community and Austria with the result that the Council adopted Council Regulation 3967/93 withdrawing tariff concessions in accordance with Art.23(2) and Art.27(3) of the Free Trade Agreement between the Commission and Austria, from General Motors Austria, which imposed a duty on gear boxes exported by O to the Community. Following the entry into force of the EEA Agreement, O applied for the annulment of Council Regulation 3697/93 contending, inter alia, that it infringed the public law obligation not to defeat the object and purpose of a treaty before its entry into force, as provided under Art.10 of the EEA Agreement.

Held, annulling Council Regulation 3697/93, that (1) the principle of good faith was the public international law corollary of the principle of legitimate expectation. This was part of the Community legal order and could be relied upon by an economic operator given justified hope by a Community institution. As the Agreement had a known entry into force date, the legitimate expectation principle could be relied upon to challenge the adoption of any measure capable of direct effect contrary to the Agreement, *O'Dwyer v. Council of the European Union (T466/93, T469/93, T473/93, T474/93, T477/93)* [1995] E.C.R II 2071 and *Topfer & Co GmbH v. Commission of the European Communities (C112/77)* [1978] E.C.R. 1019 applied, and (2) where a provision of Art.6 of the EEA Agreement was identical to a corresponding rule of either the Treaty of Rome 1957 and the ECSC Treaty 1951, interpretation was to be in conformity with the relevant ECJ and CFI rulings given prior to the signature date of the EEA Agreement. Under Art.10 of the Treaty of Rome the unilateral charge imposed under Regulation 3967/93 was a charge having equivalent effect within the meaning of Art.10 and its adoption in the period preceding the entry into force of the EEA Agreement infringed O's legitimate expectations. Adoption of the contested Regulation, at a time when the Council knew with certainty of the entry into force of the EEA Agreement, created a situation whereby two contradictory legal rules would exist, a situation which breached the principle of legal certainty. The contested Regulation could not be regarded as certain in application and its application was not foreseeable by those subject to its provisions, *Tagaras v. European Court of Justice (T18/89 and T24/89)* [1991] E.C.R. II 53 applied.

OPEL AUSTRIA GmbH (AUSTRIA INTERVENING) v. EUROPEAN COUNCIL (EUROPEAN COMMISSION INTERVENING) (T115/94) [1997] All E.R. (EC) 97, Lenaerts (President), CFI.

2405. Treaties—Israel

EUROPEAN COMMUNITIES (DEFINITION OF TREATIES) (EURO-MEDITERRANEAN AGREEMENT ESTABLISHING AN ASSOCIATION BETWEEN THE EUROPEAN COMMUNITIES AND THEIR MEMBER STATES AND THE STATE OF ISRAEL) ORDER 1997, SI 1997 863; made under the European Communities Act 1972 s.1. In force: in accordance with Art.1; £0.65.

The Order declares the Euro-Mediterranean Agreement establishing an Association between the European Communities and their Member States and the State of Israel, signed on November 20, 1995, to be a Community Treaty as defined in the European Communities Act 1972 s.1 (2). The Agreement establishes an association with the objectives of providing an appropriate framework for political dialogue, of the harmonious development of economic relations between the Community and Israel through the expansion of trade in goods and services, the liberalisation of the right of establishment and of public procurement, the free movement of capital and the intensification of co-operation in science and technology; of encouraging regional co-operation; and of promoting co-operation in other areas of reciprocal interest. The principal effect of declaring this Agreement to be a Community Treaty as so defined is to bring into play, in relation to it, the provisions of the European Communities Act 1972 s.2 which provides for the implementation of treaties so specified.

2406. Treaties—Latvia

EUROPEAN COMMUNITIES (DEFINITION OF TREATIES) (EUROPE AGREEMENT ESTABLISHING AN ASSOCIATION BETWEEN THE EUROPEAN COMMUNITIES AND THEIR MEMBER STATES AND THE REPUBLIC OF LATVIA) ORDER 1997, SI 1997 270; made under the European Communities Act 1972 s.1. In force: in accordance with Art.1; £1.10.

The Order declares the European Agreement establishing an Association between the European Communities and their Member States and the Republic of Latvia, signed on June 12, 1995, to be a Community Treaty as defined in the European Communities Act 1972.

2407. Treaties—Lithuania

EUROPEAN COMMUNITIES (DEFINITION OF TREATIES) (EUROPE AGREEMENT ESTABLISHING AN ASSOCIATION BETWEEN THE EUROPEAN COMMUNITIES AND THEIR MEMBER STATES AND THE REPUBLIC OF LITHUANIA) ORDER 1997, SI 1997 271; made under the European Communities Act 1972 s.1. In force: in accordance with Art.1; £0.65.

The Order declares the Europe Agreement establishing an Association between the European Communities and their Member States and the Republic of Lithuania, signed on June 12, 1995, to be a Community Treaty. The Agreement establishes an association with the objectives of providing an appropriate framework for political dialogue, gradually establishing a free trade area between the Community and Lithuania, promoting trade and harmonious economic relations, providing a basis for economic, financial, cultural and social co-operation and co-operation in the prevention of illegal activities, as well as Community assistance, supporting Lithuania's efforts to develop its economy and complete the transition into a market economy, providing an appropriate framework for Lithuania's gradual integration into the European Union, and setting up institutions to make the association effective.

2408. Treaties—Morocco

EUROPEAN COMMUNITIES (DEFINITION OF TREATIES) (EURO-MEDITERRANEAN AGREEMENT ESTABLISHING AN ASSOCIATION BETWEEN THE EUROPEAN COMMUNITIES AND THEIR MEMBER STATES AND THE KINGDOM OF MOROCCO) ORDER 1997, SI 1997 2577; made under the European Communities Act 1972 s.1. In force: in accordance with Art.1; £0.65.

This Order declares the Euro-Mediterranean Agreement Establishing an Association between the European Communities and their Member States and the Kingdom of Morocco, done at Brussels on February 26, 1996, to be a Community Treaty as defined by the European Communities Act 1972 s.1 (2).

2409. Treaties—Southern Common Market

EUROPEAN COMMUNITIES (DEFINITION OF TREATIES) (INTER-REGIONAL FRAMEWORK CO-OPERATION AGREEMENT BETWEEN THE EUROPEAN COMMUNITY AND ITS MEMBER STATES AND THE SOUTHERN COMMON MARKET AND ITS PARTY STATES) ORDER 1997, SI 1997 2603; made under the European Communities Act 1972 s.1. In force: in accordance with Art.1; £1.10.

This Order declares the Inter-regional Framework Co-operation Agreement between the European Community and its Member States and the Southern Common Market and its Party States, done at Madrid on December 15, 1995, to be a Community Treaty as defined by the European Communities Act 1972 s.1 (2). The objectives of the Agreement are to strengthen existing relations between the parties and to prepare the conditions enabling an Inter-regional Association to be created.

2410. Articles

A European constitution for citizens: reflections on the rethinking of Union and Community law *(Norbert Reich)*: E.L.J. 1997, 3(2), 131-164. (Development of rights of European citizens as individuals and groups including consumers, social, environmental and human rights).

A comment on the "Manifesto for Social Europe" *(Allan Larsson)*: E.L.J. 1997, 3(3), 304-307. (Concentrating on key areas of employment, working conditions, equality, citizenship and fundamental human rights).

A message for the sceptics - the Sicco L. Mansholt Lecture 1997 presented before the Association of European Journalists in the Netherlands, Amsterdam, April 21, 1997 *(Jacques Santer)*: Eur. Access 1997, 3, 8-11. (Future of European Union).

Agenda 2000-the enlargement perspective *(Hans Van den Broek)*: Eur. Access 1997, 5, 9-10. (Extracts from speech by EU Commissioner to European Parliament about enlargement of EU, conditions for membership and consideration of Cyprus' and Turkey's applications).

An evaluation of medicines regulation *(S.J. Treece)*: Med. L. Int. 1997, 2(4), 315-336. (Comparison of UK's "future system" with systems operating in Europe and US).

Bibliographic snapshot: the Single Market *(Ian Thomson)*: Eur. Access 1997, 2, 34-47. (Key primary and secondary information sources since 1985).

Brussels—myths & realities: Bus. L.R. 1997, 18(7), 180-184. (Structure of CEC and other EU institutions).

Constitutional aspects *(Sophie Boyron)*: I.C.L.Q. 1997, 46(3), 701-703. (EU inter-institutional agreements in 1995, establishment of European Ombudsman and Committee of Inquiry and EU human rights developments).

Court in a political conundrum *(Richard Plender)*: Lawyer 1997, 11(14), 9. (Whether allegations of political bias against ECJ and CFI are unjustified and whether political objections need to be overcome to appoint more judges, reduce number of languages used and tackle problem of delay).

Court of Justice guidance on Article 177 references: I.L.T. 1997, 15(7), 151-152. (Text of ECJ guidance note on improving transfer of cases between national courts and ECJ).

Democracy and rule-making within the EC: an empirical and normative assessment *(P.P. Craig)*: E.L.J. 1997, 3(2), 105-130. (Whether law making machinery of European Communities is democratic and how it could be made more so).

Judicial preferences and the Community legal order *(Damian Chalmers)*: M.L.R. 1997, 60(2), 164-199. (Effectiveness of ECJ and its acceptance by national legal systems, illustrated by cases on state liability).

Reason-giving in English and European Community administrative law *(Robert Thomas)*: E.P.L. 1997, 3(2), 213-222. (Comparison of approach to whether reasons are required for administrative decisions in English courts with that of ECJ).

Reassessing regimes: the international regime aspects of the European Union *(Robert E. Breckinridge)*: J. Com. Mar. St. 1997, 35(2), 173-187. (Distinction between international organisations and regimes, and whether "regime analysis" can be applied when describing organisational and institutional dynamics of EU).

The European Ombudsman—citizen's protector in EU administration *(Jacob Soderman)*: I.L.T. 1997, 15(4), 91-92. (Role of European Ombudsman and complaints procedure).

The European Ombudsman: I.P.E.L.J. 1997, 4(3), 101-102. (Powers of European Ombudsman to investigate complaints of maladministration in EC institutions and complaints procedure).

The European Parliament and comitology: on the road to nowhere? *(Kieran St. Clair Bradley)*: E.L.J. 1997, 3(3), 230-254. (European Parliament's animosity towards growth of supervisory committees, particularly in role of adopting legislation, has resulted in proposals for reform of comitology through political, budgetary and legal means).

The European Parliament: laying the foundations for awareness and support *(Mark Shephard)*: Parl. Aff. 1997, 50(3), 438-452. (Extent to which increased public awareness, including media coverage, lobbyist and constituency activity, has failed to contribute to popular support for European Parliament, and proposals for improvement).

The indemnification of costs in proceedings before the European courts *(Andre Fiebig)*: C.M.L. Rev. 1997, 34(1), 89-134. (Implications of the uncertainties surrounding application of the cost indemnification rules of European courts on litigants and potential litigants).

The rise of committees *(Ellen Vos)*: E.L.J. 1997, 3(3), 210-229. (Increased reliance on committees within EU institutions highlights need for clearly defined rules of procedure, looking at balance of powers, principle of subsidiarity and conflicts encountered within structure of EU).

Transparency in the European Union—an open and shut case *(Janet Mather)*: Eur. Access 1997, 1, 9-11. (Whether EU's policy on public access to its documentation enhances democratic deficit).

What's the damage? *(Richard Pincher)*: Revenue 1997, 3, 3-5. (Circumstances in which a Member State may be liable in damages to individuals for failure to implement EC law correctly).

EXTRADITION

2411. Brazil

BRAZIL (EXTRADITION) ORDER 1997, SI 1997 1176; made under the Extradition Act 1989 s.4. In force: on a date to be notified in the London, Edinburgh and Belfast Gazettes; £1.95.

This Order applies the Extradition Act 1989 Part III, as amended, in the case of Brazil in accordance with the Treaty between Her Majesty's Government and the Government of the Federative Republic of Brazil which was concluded on July 18, 1995.

2412. Committals–locus of crime–warrant failed to specify place of offence–certification of law by court clerk

[Penal Code Art.228 (Portugal); Extradition Act 1989 s.9(8), s.26; European Convention on Extradition Order 1990 (SI 1990 1507).]

D applied for habeas corpus to challenge his committal to prison to await extradition proceedings to Portugal. D had allegedly forged British driving licences and sold them in Portugal and an international warrant had been issued on the basis of 14 crimes of document falsification contrary to the Portuguese Penal Code Art.228 para.1 (a) and 2. D contended that (1) the warrant failed to specify where the offences had been committed and therefore under the Extradition Act 1989 s.9(8) the essential precondition of committal had not been provided; and (2) by reason of being certified only by a court clerk, the extracts from the Portuguese Criminal Code contained in the warrant were not sufficiently authenticated, as required by s.26 of the 1989 Act.

Held, allowing the application, that (1) the European Convention on Extradition Order 1990 Art.12(2)(b) required the requesting government to provide details of the time and place where the offences were allegedly committed. The magistrate below had erred in his decision that it was possible to assume that the offences had taken place in Portugal. There was nothing in *Schmidt* to suggest that the powers of the High Court to grant relief were limited where the conditions of s.9(8) of the 1989 Act had not been satisfied, *Schmidt, Re* [1995] 1 A.C. 339, [1994] C.L.Y. 2137 distinguished, and (2) a court clerk was an officer of the court and his office was sufficient for the purposes of the 1989 Act, *R. v. Superintendent at HM Prison Fox Hill, ex p. Bain* [1989] 1 L.R.B. 156 disapproved and *Schmidt* considered.

DE CANHA, *Re*; *sub nom.* DE CANHA v. PORTUGAL, Trans. Ref: CO/0769/97, July 7, 1997, Lord Bingham of Cornhill, L.C.J., QBD.

2413. Committals–no requirement for charge to state statutory basis

[Magistrates Courts Rules 1981 r.100.]

Held, that where committal proceedings related to a request for extradition, as distinct from "proceedings for an offence" under the Magistrates Courts Rules 1981 r.100, no requirement was imposed that the committal charge should state the statutory basis upon which it was founded.

AL-SALAAM, *Re, The Independent*, April 21, 1997 (C.S.), Auld, L.J., QBD.

2414. Conspiracy–South Africa–status as "designated commonwealth country"–application to crimes committed before 1989

[Extradition Act 1989 s.27.]

An indictment was lodged by the South African government against H in 1991 charging him with various common law offences arising out of conduct in 1986 and 1987. H had already left the country at the time. In 1996 South Africa became a "designated Commonwealth country" under the terms of the Extradition Act 1989. South Africa then sought the return of H and the Department of Justice submitted an extradition request. The Secretary of State considered that H's conduct, had it occurred in Britain, would have constituted conspiracy to defraud, although the South African government did not seek his return on charges of conspiracy. The magistrate committed H to custody to await the Secretary of State's decision as to extradition and H applied for a writ of habeas corpus contending that the 1989 Act did not apply to crimes committed before the Act come into force, that the documents submitted had not been properly authenticated and that the committal on charges of conspiracy should be quashed.

Held, dismissing the application, that (1) the 1989 Act did apply to crimes committed before it came into force as it was a consolidating statute which did not change the law; (2) with regard to the issue of authentication, it was enough if the South African Department of Justice seal was affixed to the papers rather than that of the Justice Minister himself. The words of s.27 "by the official seal of a Minister of the designated Commonwealth country" allowed for authentication by the Department of State of which the appropriate Minister was head, and (3) in deciding to proceed the Secretary of State was entitled to include in the authority any offences which were disclosed by the documents and was not limited to those listed in the indictment. The magistrate had therefore been entitled to commit H on the conspiracy charges even if the South African authorities had not charged him with conspiracy.

R. v. SECRETARY OF STATE FOR THE HOME DEPARTMENT, *ex p.* HILL [1997] 2 All E.R. 638, Hooper, J., QBD.

2415. Conventions—parties to European Convention—Estonia and Latvia

EUROPEAN CONVENTION ON EXTRADITION ORDER 1990 (AMENDMENT) (NO.2) ORDER 1997, SI 1997 2596; made under the Extradition Act 1989 s.4, s.37. In force: December 1, 1997; £1.10.

This Order amends the European Convention on Extradition Order 1990 (SI 1990 1507) by adding Estonia and Latvia to the States parties to the European Convention on Extradition. It also adds the declarations made by Estonia and Latvia and has the effect of revoking the Orders in Council embodying the extradition treaties between the United Kingdom and Estonia and between the United Kingdom and Latvia to the extent that they applied to the United Kingdom, the Channel Islands and the Isle of Man.

2416. Conventions—parties to European Convention—Malta

EUROPEAN CONVENTION ON EXTRADITION ORDER 1990 (AMENDMENT) ORDER 1997, SI 1997 1759; made under the Extradition Act 1989 s.4. In force: September 1, 1997; £1.10.

This Order amends the European Convention on Extradition Order 1990 (SI 1990 1507) by adding Malta to the States parties to the European Convention listed in Sch.2 and adding the reservations made by Malta to the reservations set out in Sch.3.

2417. Conventions—parties to European Convention—Malta

EXTRADITION (DESIGNATED COMMONWEALTH COUNTRIES) ORDER 1991 (AMENDMENT) ORDER 1997, SI 1997 1761; made under the Extradition Act 1989 s.5. In force: September 1, 1997; £0.65.

This Order removes Malta from the list of Commonwealth countries designated for the purposes of the Extradition Act 1989. Section 3(2) provides that, for the purposes for Part III of that Act, a State which is a party to the European Convention on Extradition may be treated as a foreign State. Malta has become a party to the Convention and as a result has been added to the list of States which are party to that Convention.

2418. Criminal evidence—admissibility of computer printouts—hearsay evidence—extradition proceedings were criminal proceedings and normal rules of evidence and procedure applied

[Police and Criminal Evidence Act 1984 s.69; Extradition Act 1989 s.9(2), Sch.1.]

L appealed against the dismissal of his application for a writ of habeas corpus after the stipendiary magistrate ordered he be detained pending his extradition to the US to face charges arising out of his alleged use of a computer in Russia to access the computer of a US bank to transfer funds into his own bank accounts. Computer printouts which recorded the various transfers were admitted in evidence before the magistrate under the Police and Criminal Evidence Act 1984 s.69. L contended that the evidence should not have been admitted under s.69 on the grounds that it was hearsay and s.69 did not apply to extradition proceedings as they were not criminal proceedings.

Held, dismissing the appeal, that the printouts provided a record of the transfers, created by the interaction of the person requesting the transfer and the computer, and had the same evidential status as a photocopy of a forged cheque. If the printouts were hearsay, s.69 would not make them admissible where they would not be otherwise, as the purpose of s.69 was simply to create an additional requirement for the admission of computer evidence. The refusal of an application for habeas corpus by a person committed to prison awaiting extradition was a decision in a criminal cause or matter and therefore extradition proceedings were themselves criminal proceedings, *Amand v. Secretary of State for Home Affairs* [1943] A.C. 147 applied. Further, the Extradition Act 1989 s.9(2) and Sch.1 para.6(1) required extradition proceedings to be conducted "as nearly as may be" as if they were committal proceedings. Committal proceedings were criminal proceedings and thus it would be strange if the magistrate in an extradition matter could not apply the ordinary rules of criminal evidence.

R. v. GOVERNOR OF BRIXTON PRISON, *ex p.* LEVIN; *sub nom.* LEVIN (APPLICATION FOR A WRIT OF HABEAS CORPUS), *Re* [1997] 3 W.L.R. 117, Lord Hoffmann, HL.

2419. Drug offences—failure to provide schedules listing heroin as a prohibited drug—authority to proceed

Held, that, in deciding whether to make an order for committal in respect of an extradition request, the magistrate was not prevented from finding that the authority to proceed related to an extradition crime by the mere omission of the Italian schedules confirming that heroin was a prohibited drug. He could instead rely on, for example, a sworn statement that heroin was included in the schedules, although the Home Secretary would be justified in staying extradition proceedings until the schedules were provided.

AGKURT, *Re, The Independent*, December 9, 1996 (C.S.), Schiemann, L.J., QBD.

2420. Evidence—order for obtaining evidence to support habeas corpus application—a criminal cause—appellate jurisdiction of Court of Appeal Civil Division

[European Convention on Mutual Assistance in Criminal Matters 1959; Supreme Court Act 1981 s.18(1); Extradition Act 1989 s.11(3); Criminal Justice (International Co-operation) Act 1990 s.3.]

C, committed to custody pending his extradition to Switzerland to face fraud charges, sought to appeal against a decision setting aside an order for the issue of letters of request under the Criminal Justice (International Co-operation) Act 1990 s.3 for evidence in support of his application for habeas corpus pursuant to the Extradition Act 1989 s.11(3)(c). The Civil Division of the Court of Appeal was asked to rule on the preliminary issue of whether it had jurisdiction to hear C's appeal under the Supreme Court Act 1981 s.18(1)(a), which precluded the court hearing an appeal from the High Court in "any criminal cause or matter".

Held, dismissing the appeal, that extradition proceedings clearly fell within the expression "criminal cause or matter", as did an application for habeas corpus made in such proceedings. It followed that an order for the obtaining of evidence to support a habeas corpus application in extradition proceedings was also a criminal cause or matter, as where the main proceedings in question were criminal, ancillary or incidental proceedings also fell to be treated as criminal. Orders for the production of evidence for foreign criminal proceedings were treated as criminal and it would be anomalous if a similar order for the purposes of English criminal proceedings were not treated as such. Further, the European Convention on Mutual Assistance in Criminal Matters 1959 clearly related to international cooperation between states in the prosecution of crime and had no civil purpose. The wording of s.3 of the 1990 Act showed a close relationship between an application under that section and the foreign criminal proceedings, suggesting that an order under s.3 was a criminal matter. In the light of those considerations, the court had no jurisdiction to entertain C's appeal.

CUOGHI v. GOVERNOR OF BRIXTON PRISON, *The Times*, July 24, 1997, Lord Bingham of Cornhill, L.C.J., CA.

2421. Extraditable offences – aviation security

EXTRADITION (AVIATION SECURITY) ORDER 1997, SI 1997 1760; made under the Extradition Act 1989 s.4, s.22, s.37. In force: September 1, 1997; £3.20.

This Order applies the Extradition Act 1989 so as to make extraditable, offences described in the Aviation Security Act 1982 s.2 and s.3 and the Aviation and Maritime Security Act 1990 s.1, attempts to commit such offences and participation in the commission of such offences. It applies to certain States, Parties to the Convention for the Suppression of Unlawful Acts against the Safety of Civil Aviation, signed at Montreal on September 23, 1971, and to the Protocol for the Suppression of Unlawful Acts of Violence at Airports Serving International Civil Aviation, signed at Montreal on February 24, 1988.

2422. Extraditable offences – drug trafficking

EXTRADITION (DRUG TRAFFICKING) ORDER 1997, SI 1997 1762; made under the Extradition Act 1989 s.4, s.22, s.37. In force: September 1, 1997; £4.70.

This Order applies the Extradition Act 1989 so as to make extraditable, offences within the meaning of the Drug Trafficking Offences Act 1994 and the Proceeds of Crime (Scotland) Act 1995, attempts to commit such offences and participation in the commission of such offences. It applies to certain States, Parties to the Convention against Illicit Traffic in Narcotic Drugs and Psychotropic Substances, signed at Vienna on December 20, 1988.

2423. Extraditable offences – hijacking

EXTRADITION (HIJACKING) ORDER 1997, SI 1997 1763; made under the Extradition Act 1989 s.4, s.22, s.37. In force: September 1, 1997; £2.40.

This Order applies the Extradition Act 1989 so as to make extraditable, offences under the Aviation Security Act 1982 s.1, attempts to commit such offences and participation in the commission of such offences. It applies to certain States, Parties to the Convention for the Suppression of Unlawful Seizure of Aircraft, signed at The Hague on December 16, 1970.

2424. Extraditable offences – hostage taking

EXTRADITION (TAKING OF HOSTAGES) ORDER 1997, SI 1997 1767; made under the Extradition Act 1989 s.4, s.22, s.37. In force: September 1, 1997; £2.80.

This Order applies the Extradition Act 1989 so as to make extraditable, offences under the Taking of Hostages Act 1982 s.1, attempts to commit such offences and participation in the commission of such offences. It applies to certain States, Parties to the Convention against the Taking of Hostages, signed at New York on December 18, 1979.

2425. Extraditable offences – internationally protected persons

EXTRADITION (INTERNATIONALLY PROTECTED PERSONS) ORDER 1997, SI 1997 1764; made under the Extradition Act 1989 s.4, s.22, s.37. In force: September 1, 1997; £2.80.

This Order applies the Extradition Act 1989 so as to make extraditable offences within the meaning of the Internationally Protected Persons Act 1978, attempts to commit such offences and participation in such offences. It applies to certain States, Parties to the Convention on the Prevention of Crimes Against Internationally Protected Persons, including Diplomatic Agents, signed at New York on December 14, 1973.

2426. Extraditable offences – offences committed on board aircraft

EXTRADITION (TOKYO CONVENTION) ORDER 1997, SI 1997 1768; made under the Extradition Act 1989 s.4, s.22, s.37. In force: September 1, 1997; £2.80.

This Order applies the Extradition Act 1989 so as to make extraditable, offences under the Tokyo Convention Act 1967 s.1, attempts to commit such offences and participation in the commission of such offences. It applies to certain States, Parties to the Convention for the Suppression of Unlawful Seizure of Aircraft, signed at The Hague on December 16, 1970.

2427. Extraditable offences – protection of nuclear material

EXTRADITION (PROTECTION OF NUCLEAR MATERIAL) ORDER 1997, SI 1997 1765; made under the Nuclear Material (Offences) Act 1983 s.7; and the Extradition Act 1989 s.4, s.22, s.37. In force: September 1, 1997; £2.80.

This Order applies the Extradition Act 1989 so as to make extraditable, offences described in the Nuclear Material (Offences) Act 1983, attempts to commit such offences and participation in the commission of such offences. It applies to States Parties to the Convention on the Physical Protection of Nuclear Material, opened for signature at New York and Vienna on March 3, 1980.

2428. Extraditable offences – safety of maritime navigation

EXTRADITION (SAFETY OF MARITIME NAVIGATION) ORDER 1997, SI 1997 1766; made under the Extradition Act 1989 s.4, s.22, s.37. In force: September 1, 1997; £3.20.

This Order applies the Extradition Act 1989 so as to make extraditable, offences described in the Aviation and Maritime Security Act 1990 s.9, s.10, s.11, s.12 and s.13, attempts to commit such offences and participation in the commission of such offences. It applies to certain States Parties to the Convention for the Suppression of Unlawful Acts against the Safety of Maritime Navigation, signed at Rome on March 10, 1988 and to the Protocol for the Suppression of Unlawful Acts against the Safety of Fixed Platforms

2429. Extraditable offences – Theft Act offences – conspiracy to commit offences not extradition crimes

[Extradition Act 1870; Extradition Act 1989 Sch.1; Theft Act 1968; Larceny Act 1861; United Kingdom-United States Extradition Treaty 1972.]

G and O sought judicial review of Orders to Proceed made by the Secretary of State under the Extradition Act 1989 Sch.1 para.4 (2), contending that conspiracy offences were not extradition crimes. Their extraditions had been sought by the United States' government on charges of conspiracy to defraud, steal, handle stolen goods and to obtain property by deception. The Secretary of State conceded that such offences had not been included in Orders to Proceed in fraud cases previously, but that the decision in *R. v. Preddy (John Crawford)* [1996] 3 W.L.R 255, [1996] 1 C.L.Y. 1530 had led to a policy change and that conspiracy to commit offences under the Theft Act 1968 and the earlier Larceny Act 1861 had always been extradition crimes by virtue of the Extradition Act 1870, which listed 19 generic descriptions of offences amounting to extradition crimes.

Held, allowing the applications and quashing the Orders to Proceed, that the list of extradition crimes, as amended, was intended to cover conduct falling within the given generic descriptions and did not require conduct to be matched with a listed offence, *Neilson, Re* [1984] 1 A.C. 606 considered. Considering the history of the list, it could not be concluded that where a specific description of a listed offence was given a conspiracy to commit that offence could be included by implication, *USA v. Bowe* [1990] 1 A.C. 500, [1990] C.L.Y. 2266 followed, and the use of the words "an offence under the Act" was not to be construed as including conspiracy to commit an offence under the 1968 Act, and the absence of any explanation for the exclusion of conspiracy could not justify extending the statutory definition to it. The provisions of the United Kingdom-United States Extradition Treaty 1972 were to be read in conjunction with the 1870 Act, and although treaty provisions could limit the list in the Act they could not extend it.

R. v. SECRETARY OF STATE FOR THE HOME DEPARTMENT, *ex p.* GILMORE, *The Times*, July 4, 1997, Pill, L.J., QBD.

2430. Extraditable offences—torture

EXTRADITION (TORTURE) ORDER 1997, SI 1997 1769; made under the Extradition Act 1989 s.4, s.22, s.37. In force: September 1, 1997; £3.20.

This Order applies the Extradition Act 1989 so as to make extraditable, the offence of torture described in the Criminal Justice Act 1988 s.134, attempts to commit such an offence and participation in such offences, in the case of certain States, Parties to the Convention Against Torture and other Cruel, Inhuman or Degrading Treatment or Punishment adopted by the General Assembly of the United Nations on December 10, 1984.

2431. Fraud—conviction in absentia—whether conviction unfair—Finland

[Extradition Act 1989 s.6(2), s.9(8).]

K applied for habeas corpus ad subjiciendum on the grounds that there was insufficient evidence that he was unlawfully at large, and that, pursuant to the Extradition Act 1989 s.6(2), it was not in the interest of justice that he be returned to Finland, because he had effectively served his sentence during two months served on remand there and while in custody in Britain. K had been convicted in Finland in 1991 of the fraudulent use of a Diner's card to obtain credit in excess of £100,000 and was released pending appeal, whereupon he had moved to Egypt before being arrested in London in 1995.

Held, refusing the application, that (1) the Government of Finland had proved its case to the criminal standard pursuant to the Extradition Act 1989 s.9(8), *R. v. Governor of Brixton Prison, ex p. Evans* [1994] 1 W.L.R. 1006, [1994] C.L.Y. 2132 and *R. v. Governor of Brixton Prison, ex p. Shuter* [1960] 2 Q.B. 89, [1959] C.L.Y. 1274 considered and (2) it was common ground that K had been convicted in his absence in the Court of Appeal in Helsinki and the purpose of s.6(2) was protection from an unfair conviction obtained in absentia, not to allow a fugitive to escape extradition by the numerical calculation of parole possibilities.

KIRIAKOS, *Re*, Trans. Ref: CO/744/96, November 7, 1996, Maurice Kay, J., QBD.

2432. Hong Kong

HONG KONG (EXTRADITION) ORDER 1997, SI 1997 1178; made under the Hong Kong Act 1985 Sch. para.3. In force: July 1, 1997; £1.55.

This Order amends the Extradition Act 1989 so that it applies in relation to the Hong Kong Special Administrative Region from July 1, 1997, the date from which Hong Kong ceases to be a colony.

2433. Hong Kong—right to fair trial—transfer of sovereignty to People's Republic of China

[Extradition Act 1989 s.12(1); Joint Declaration on the Question of Hong Kong 1984.]

The Secretary of State appealed against the decision to quash an extradition warrant issued under the Extradition Act 1989 s.12(1) ordering the return of L to face trial in Hong Kong on the grounds that the Secretary of State had not properly directed himself on his responsibilities to ensure that L would receive a fair trial. L argued that the past conduct of the People's Republic of China was such as to give rise to a serious risk that L would be subjected to injustice or oppression if he returned to Hong Kong.

Held, allowing the appeal, that the decision as to whether it was unjust to order L's return was one for the Secretary of State alone. The court's role, in its supervisory jurisdiction, was one of review, the issue being whether the Secretary of State had addressed the right question in reaching his decision. It was clear on the evidence that the Secretary of State had not fettered his discretion by relying on the Cabinet's view of whether China would comply with its obligations under the Sino-British Joint Declaration on the Question of Hong Kong 1984, but had taken his own decision after considering all of L's representations, including the risk of interference with L's human rights. The Secretary of State had not acted irrationally, on the material available to him, by taking the view that there was every reason for Hong Kong to maintain its existing criminal justice system after the transfer of sovereignty and that no grave risk of injustice or oppression arose in L's case.

R. v. SECRETARY OF STATE FOR THE HOME DEPARTMENT, *ex p.* LAUNDER (NO.2) [1997] 1 W.L.R. 839, Lord Hope of Craighead, HL.

2434. Murder—attempts—extradition to Croatia—return not oppressive where delay of applicant's making—fear of persecution

[Extradition Act 1989 s.6(1), s.11.]

M applied for habeas corpus contesting an order for his extradition to Croatia to serve a sentence of 13 months' imprisonment for attempted murder imposed in June 1991. He had been detained for seven months awaiting extradition. M claimed that he was stateless as his Croatian citizenship had been revoked once it had been discovered that he was by origin Serbian and that he would suffer persecution if he were extradited to Croatia.

Held, refusing the application, that (1) the argument under the Extradition Act 1989 s.11, that it would be oppressive to return him to serve his sentence given the delay that had occurred since his sentence, could not be relied upon because the delay was brought about by his own actions in leaving Croatia, *Kakis v. Cyprus* [1978] 1 W.L.R. 779, [1978] C.L.Y. 1451 considered. The fact that M had committed a serious offence in the UK, ie. facilitating the entry of illegal immigrants, for which a deportation recommendation was made in addition to a sentence of three years, made his situation considerably worse. There was no certainty that he would receive remission in Croatia, but it was not for the court to make a decision in that regard. It was reasonable, in all the circumstances, that M be extradited to Croatia to serve his sentence, and (2) there was a lack of evidence to support M's argument under s.6(1)(d) of the 1989 Act, that he would be persecuted or restricted in his personal liberty on return to Croatia. The matter in any case was going to be raised before the Secretary of State as there had been an application for asylum in relation to the recommendation for M's deportation.

MIJATOVIC, *Re*, Trans. Ref: CO/2400/96, December 17, 1996, Collins, J., QBD.

2435. Terrorism—France—risk of prejudice in French terrorism trial groundless

[Extradition Act 1989 s.6(1).]

R, an Algerian national suspected of involvement in a 1995 bombing campaign in France, sought a writ of habeas corpus following an extradition request by the French government. R contended that his trial by a special assize court would be prejudiced by reason of race, religion, nationality or political opinion under the Extradition Act 1989 s.6(1)(d) and submitted that comments by the Minister of Justice, along with press reports demonstrating widespread intolerance and racism in France towards Algerian Muslims, showed that he would not receive a fair trial under the procedure operated by the assize court.

Held, refusing the application, that it was inconceivable that the media campaign created a risk of prejudice to the trial on the grounds stated in s.6. Despite the statement by the Minister of Justice, the special court judges were sufficiently experienced and capable so as to ensure a fair trial regardless of press comment or the personal views held by the Minister.

RAMDA, *Re*; BOUTARFA, *Re*, *The Independent*, June 27, 1997, Pill, L.J., QBD.

2436. Time limits—Belgium—time limit on enforcement of criminal conviction passed

W applied for a writ of habeas corpus after his committal to await the outcome of extradition proceedings to return him to Belgium. W had been convicted of obtaining money by deception for which he received a custodial term of three years. W relied on expert evidence that, under the Belgian Code of Criminal Procedure Art.92, a criminal judgment could not be enforced more than five years after it became final, and contended that he should be released because his extradition could no longer serve any purpose.

Held, allowing the application, that there was no extant basis for W's extradition and no purpose in his remaining in custody to await the decision of the Secretary of State.

R. v. WORTH, Trans. Ref: CO 1400-96, March 3, 1997, Laws, J., QBD.

2437. **Time limits–German authorities no longer seeking accused's return– immunity from extradition by lapse of time–return unjust and oppressive**

[Extradition Act 1989 s.9, s.11 (3); European Convention on Extradition 1957 Art.10.]

N applied for habeas corpus following committal under the Extradition Act 1989 s.9 for return to face punishment pending a decision by the Secretary of State for the Home Department to return N to Germany. The European Convention on Extradition 1957 Art.10 provides for immunity from prosecution or punishment by virtue of lapse of time. Under German law a 10 year limitation period in respect of immunity from punishment in respect of N's previous convictions for drug trafficking and theft applied. However, in committing N the stipendiary magistrate had found that the definition of an "extradition crime" was not subject to matters of limitation under s.9, even though the German authorities were no longer concerned with pursuing matters against N.

Held, allowing the application, that, irrespective of the correctness of the magistrate's decision regarding the limitation issue, it would be unjust and oppressive under s.11 (3) (a) and s.11 (3) (b) of the 1989 Act for N to be returned given the passage of time since the alleged offences and the decision of the German authorities.

NEUMANN, *Re*, Trans. Ref: CO 2732/96, January 14, 1997, Mance, J., QBD.

2438. **Time limits–two months for surrender and conveyance out of UK– insufficient cause to detain**

[Extradition Act 1989 Sch.1; European Convention on Extradition 1957 Art.12, Art.14.]

A, a fugitive criminal, made an application to be discharged from custody under the Extradition Act 1989 Sch.1 para.10, by which the court must order his discharge within two months after committal unless sufficient cause is shown to the contrary. The issue was whether the Secretary of State had shown sufficient cause to continue to detain. A had absconded to France in breach of a parole licence in September 1991. His return as a fugitive offender was sought in terms of the European Convention on Extradition 1957 Art.12. However, in the meantime a warrant for false accounting was issued by the English authorities, and the USA Government also sought his extradition in relation to alleged drug money laundering. In January 1993 A was returned to England where he was convicted and sentenced to six years' imprisonment. The French authorities also consented to his re-extradition to the USA. On his release, following a requisition from the USA Government. A's extradition to the USA was sought from the UK in October 1995, and an order was made to proceed under the 1989 Act Sch.1 para.4 in November, for the offence of blackmail. However, the Home Office had been under a misapprehension that the offence was covered by the original consent to A's re-extradition to the USA, whereas it was later confirmed that a fresh consent from France would be necessary. A was granted leave to challenge the November order by judicial review on February 8, 1996. It was then made known to the Home Office that the prosecution for the blackmail offence may be time-barred under French law, and the French would not waive the rule of speciality for extradition under the European Convention on Extradition 1957 Art.14. Further delays followed.

Held, allowing the application, that sufficient cause had not been shown. The November order had been made on an incorrect construction of the French order, and clarification was not sought from France until A had already been in custody for five months which should have been unnecessary. After A's arrest on September 1, 1995, it was incumbent on the Home Office to take reasonably expeditious steps to surrender and convey him out of the UK. It was unacceptable that A had been detained in custody for a total of 14 months, and during part of that time, from May to July, nothing had been done by the Home Office to clarify the matter or bring it to an end.

AKBAR, *Re*, Trans. Ref: CO 3690/96, October 29, 1996, Rose, L.J., QBD.

2439. Treaties – Germany – reservation of treaty obligation

[European Convention on Extradition 1957 Art.6, Art.26; Vienna Convention on the Law of Treaties 1969 Art.2.1.]

M, a citizen of the United Kingdom, applied for a writ of habeas corpus following her arrest, after the German government issued a warrant in relation to a mortar attack on British Army barracks in Osnabruk. M was in custody and Germany sought her extradition to Germany. M argued that she should not be extradited to Germany, because of the reservation made by the German government to Art.6 of the European Convention on Extradition 1957, to which both the United Kingdom and the Federal Republic of Germany were parties, stating that extradition of Germans to a foreign country was not permitted by the German Constitution and so would be refused in every case. Under the provisions of Art.26 para.3 of the Convention, M argued that Germany could not require the performance by the United Kingdom of a provision of the Convention which Germany itself would not fulfil.

Held, dismissing the application, that treaties should be interpreted liberally, not strictly as are domestic statutes, *R. v. Governor of Ashford Remand Centre, ex p. Postlethwaite* [1988] 1 A.C. 924, [1987] C.L.Y. 1703 followed. A reservation, under the Vienna Convention on the Law of Treaties 1969 Art.2.1 (d), purported to modify or exclude the legal effect of certain provisions of a treaty. The "reservation" made by the German government did not exclude or modify the legal effect of the Convention. It was instead a statement explaining the position of Germany's domestic law in relation to extradition and Germany did not need to make a reservation to put into effect its Constitution.

McALISKEY, *Re*, Trans. Ref: CO 156/97, January 22, 1997, Kennedy, L.J., QBD.

2440. Warrants – authentication of arrest warrant of foreign state

[Extradition Act 1989; United Kingdom-United States Extradition Treaty 1972 Sch.1 Art.VII.]

B applied for a writ of habeas corpus in respect of his committal to prison pending a warrant for his extradition to the United States to face criminal charges for heroin possession. He argued that the warrant in issue was not authentic as it was a copy of a copy and that the applicable test for authentication of a foreign arrest warrant was contained in the Extradition Act 1989 Sch.1 para.7 and the United Kingdom-United States Extradition Treaty 1972 Sch.1 Art.VII, which required a certified copy of an original document.

Held, dismissing the application, that the authentication of the warrant was governed by s.26 of the Act which permitted verification by the signature of a foreign official in the issuing state or the oath of a witness. The provisions of s.26 applied to cases under s.1 (3) of the Act and were not excluded by Art.VII of the Treaty.

R. v. GOVERNOR OF BRIXTON PRISON, *ex p.* BEKAR, *The Times*, June 10, 1997, Auld, L.J., QBD.

2441. Warrants–locus of crime–jurisdiction of German courts–meaning of "proceeding for an offence" and "prosecution of an offence"

[Extradition Act 1989 s.1 (1), s.2 (1); European Convention on Extradition Order 1990 (SI 1990 1507) Art.1.]

I, detained pending German extradition proceedings, applied for a habeas corpus writ challenging his committal by a stipendiary magistrate. I was the subject of a German warrant of arrest issued in relation to alleged fraud offences committed in Germany against German citizens, the proceeds of which were received in Germany before being transferred to companies controlled by I in Switzerland. I argued that the committal charges were fatally flawed on the ground that his case raised matters of extraterritoriality contrary to the Extradition Act 1989 s.2 (1). In addition, I contended that he was neither a person accused in a foreign state within the meaning of s.1 (1) nor a person against whom competent authorities of the party seeking extradition were proceeding for an offence within the meaning of the European Convention on Extradition Order 1990 Art.1.

Held, dismissing the application, that the German court did have jurisdiction as the offences were committed in Germany and the proceeds of the fraud were received in Germany, it being irrelevant that further offences might have been committed outside Germany, *Treacy v. DPP* [1971] A.C. 537, [1971] C.L.Y. 2188 and *Liangsiriprasert (Somchai) v. United States* [1991] 1 A.C. 225, [1991] C.L.Y. 1743 considered. In addition, competent authorities were proceeding with an offence in Germany such as to satisfy the tests laid down in *Evans, Re* [1994] 1 W.L.R. 1006, [1994] C.L.Y. 2132 and *Kainhofer v. DPP* 132 A.L.R. 483. The argument that the authorities in Germany were merely at an investigative stage failed as they had issued a warrant of arrest on the basis that there was evidence that I had committed the offences. There was no distinction to be drawn between "proceeding for an offence" under the Convention and "prosecution for an offence" under s.1 (1). Accordingly, I was an "accused" person for the purposes of the Act.

ISMAIL, *Re*, Trans. Ref: CO/2905/96, July 2, 1997, Garland, J., QBD.

2442. Warrants–no need for applicant to give notice of intention to make application to court under the Extradition Act 1989 s.16

[Extradition Act 1989 s.12, s.16.]

Held, that, where a person in respect of whom a warrant for return had been issued under the Extradition Act 1989 s.12 wished to apply to the court under s.16, there was no need to give notice of that intention to the Secretary of State before the relevant period of one month had expired. A s.16 application did not amount to a challenge to the lawfulness of the decision and an applicant was not entitled to treat it as an application for a writ of habeas corpus.

CHETTA (NO.2), *Re, The Independent*, May 5, 1997 (C.S.), Pill, L.J., QBD.

2443. Warrants–reasons for issue sufficient and in good faith–mala fides to be proved by applicant

[Extradition Act 1989 s.12; Theft Act 1968.]

JC and CC applied for judicial review of decisions, pursuant to the Extradition Act 1989 s.12, to issue warrants for their extradition to Canada to face charges of dishonestly obtaining mortgage advances and goods and services from builders and suppliers. JC submitted that S had failed to give specific reasons for his decisions and those he did give were provided so long after the decision that they amounted to ex post facto rationalisations. CC claimed that the issue of bad faith had not been considered by S and that he had been subject to such delay that the accurate reminiscence of oral evidence would be prejudiced.

Held, dismissing the applications, that the reasons for the decisions were given accurately and in good faith. It was for the party asserting bad faith to prove the allegations and S's acceptance of the explanations of the Canadian authorities was unimpeachable. It was acceptable that part of the delay had been caused by a lacuna in the Canadian equivalent of the Theft Act 1968 and much of the rest of the delay could be attributed to the applicants leaving Canada, *R. v. Secretary of State for the Home Department, ex p. Doody* (1994) 1 A.C. 531, [1993] C.L.Y. 1213 considered.

R. v. SECRETARY OF STATE FOR THE HOME DEPARTMENT, *ex p.* CHETTA, Trans. Ref: CO 2325-95, November 8, 1996, Rose, L.J., QBD.

2444. Warrants—test for urgency when issuing provisional warrant

[Extradition Act 1989 Sch.1; United States of America (Extradition) Order 1976 (SI 1976 2144) Art.VIII.]

A applied for judicial review of a stipendiary magistrate's decision to issue a provisional warrant for his arrest under the Extradition Act 1989 Sch.1 para.5(1)(b), contending that the warrant could have been sought earlier by the United States Government and they should not be permitted to rely on an urgency of their own making.

Held, dismissing the application, that, under the United States of America (Extradition) Order 1976 Art.VIII(1), a provisional warrant could only be issued in urgent cases and "urgent" in that connection meant urgent at the time of issue, based on the facts existing at that time. There were no grounds for excluding from the category of urgent cases those where the urgency would not have arisen if the requesting state had taken more expeditious action. The magistrate was only entitled to look at the situation in existence at the time the warrant was issued and was under no duty to investigate the factual background as to the cause of the urgency.

R. v. BOW STREET MAGISTRATES COURT, *ex p.* ALLISON; *sub nom.* R. v. GOVERNMENT OF THE UNITED STATES, *ex p.* ALLISON, *The Times*, June 5, 1997, Pill, L.J., QBD.

2445. Articles

Extraditing war criminals: the Eichmann affair *(Therese O'Donnell)*: Pol. J. 1997, 70(4), 351-356. (Issues relating to extradition, jurisdiction, retrospectivity and defence of superior orders which arose during Israeli trial of Adolph Eichmann in 1961).

Extradition and the European Union *(Mark Mackarel* and *Susan Nash)*: I.C.L.Q. 1997, 46(4), 948-957. (Alterations to established extradition procedures brought about by two EU Conventions and implications for legal protection afforded to fugitive offenders).

The concept of double criminality in the context of extraterritorial crimes *(Grainne Mullan)*: Crim. L.R. 1997, Jan, 17-29. (Doctrine of double criminality examined in context of extradition cases and whether extraterritoriality in English law could be developed to improve balance between protection and cooperation).

The scope of Bennett *(Emma Dixon)*: J.R. 1997, 2(2), 86-93. (Power of High Court to review circumstances in which defendant had been extradited as sui generis ground for judicial review of magistrates court which held not to have power to consider that question).

FAMILY LAW

2446. Artificial insemination—HFEA requirement that fertility services be provided by licence holder did not infringe EC rules on freedom to provide services

[Human Fertilisation and Embryology Act 1990 s.28(3); Treaty of Rome 1957 Art.59.]

M, the mother of twin sons by artificial insemination, applied for declarations of paternity under the Human Fertilisation and Embryology Act 1990 s.28(3), which conferred paternity on the unmarried partner of the recipient of donor sperm where treatment was sought as a couple. M and her partner, F, had separated after obtaining fertility treatment together in Rome and F contended that s.28(3) was not satisfied as the treatment was not administered by a licence holder. M argued that s.28(3) should be disapplied as the requirement for a licence constituted a restriction on the freedom to provide services under theTreaty of Rome1957 Art.59.

Held, dismissing the application, that s.28(3) did restrict the freedom to provide services as, due to the practical effect of requiring a licence, most couples would choose to seek treatment in the UK, *R. v. Human Fertilisation and Embryology Authority, ex p. Blood* [1997] 2 W.L.R. 807, [1997] C.L.Y. 3599 considered. However, the application of Art.59 could be limited by reasons of public policy, such as the public interest of protecting those receiving the services, provided that those reasons were objectively valid and justifiable, *Sager v. Dennemeyer & Co Ltd (C76/90)* [1991] E.C.R. I-4221 followed.

U v. W (ATTORNEY GENERAL INTERVENING) [1997] 2 F.L.R. 282, Wilson, J., Fam Div.

2447. Committal orders–breach of non molestation order–procedural irregularities–requirements of justice–no prejudice to contemnor–order not set aside

H appealed against a committal order for breach of a suspended committal order, for which he was sentenced to consecutive sentences of two months and 14 days' imprisonment. The committal proceedings arose from an acrimonious divorce during which W applied for a non molestation injunction against H and an injunction preventing H from disposing of matrimonial assets. H gave undertakings. W made further applications for H's committal for several alleged breaches of the undertakings, and a suspended committal order was made on some of the allegations being found proven. Following further breaches, W applied for a committal order for breach of the undertaking made, and for the suspended committal order to be activated. On his imprisonment H made an application to purge his contempt, expressing regret at his behaviour. H argued that the suspended committal order and therefore the committal order were defective. An amicus was appointed to assist the court.

Held, that, notwithstanding that there had been technical defects in a committal order, it was not in the interests of justice to set aside the order where the contemnor had not suffered any prejudice or injustice by the irregularities. For future guidance: (1) the serious nature of committal orders required that the relevant rules be complied with and the order be properly drawn, which were the responsibility of the judge signing the committal order; (2) a committal order should only be set aside on the basis of a technical defect where to do so was in the interests of justice. Provided that the contemnor was fairly tried and the order had been made on valid grounds, it would not be set aside; (3) where the contemnor was not prejudiced by any technical errors, justice did not require that the order be set aside. If necessary the order could be amended; (4) the court should have regard to the interests of any other party and the credibility of the justice system when considering whether an order should be set aside, and (5) if an injustice had occurred as a result of a defect, the court would consider ordering a new trial, unless if to do so would be unjust.

NICHOLLS v. NICHOLLS [1997] 1 W.L.R. 314, Lord Woolf, M.R., CA.

2448. Committal orders–breach of undertakings–criminal proceedings arising from same facts

H had given an undertaking not to use violence or enter the matrimonial home. W contended that he had breached his undertaking many times and on one occasion had entered the house and tried to rape her. H was arrested and bailed on condition that he lived in a bail hostel, was subject to a curfew and did not contact W. W applied to commit H for breach of his earlier undertaking. At first instance the judge imposed a stay of the committal proceedings pending the outcome of the criminal trial and W appealed.

Held, dismissing the appeal, that the court had to consider the possibility of prejudice to H's criminal defence as well as the principle that breaches of court orders should be dealt with swiftly and decisively. The judge below had correctly concluded that the risk of prejudice to H outweighed the principle of dealing with committal proceedings expeditiously, if allegations, already the subject of contested civil proceedings, were relied upon in the criminal trial.

M v. M (CONTEMPT: COMMITTAL) [1997] 1 F.L.R. 762, Lord Bingham of Cornhill, L.C.J., CA.

2449. Committal orders–non molestation orders–order failed to specify whether consecutive or concurrent with previous order–error of record–whether judge could amend order when dealing with subsequent contempt

[County Court Rules 1981 Ord.29 r.1.]

J was subject to an order which, on its face, committed him to 24 weeks' imprisonment. Subsequently, a different county court judge varied the order so that the sentence should be consecutive to a term of 30 weeks under an earlier committal order. J sought extensions of time in which to appeal. The question was whether the second judge had jurisdiction to amend the order and whether he should have exercised it in the way he did. A had obtained non-molestation orders of which J had been in breach on a number of occasions having been subject to three previous committal orders.

Held, allowing the applications and dismissing the appeals, that as the case concerned the liberty of the subject it was appropriate to consider the merits. There had been a breach of the County Court Rules 1981 because the first application order was silent as to whether it was to be concurrent or consecutive; it failed to identify the order of which J had been in breach; and was in breach of Ord.29 r.1 (5), not having been served until 23 days after it had been made. It was after J had threatened to kill A, on having received the first order, that the matter came before the second judge who heard evidence that it had been intended that the order should run consecutively. The judge told J the total term he would have to serve but the court failed to record the fact. Although technical irregularities would often result in such an order being quashed, there would be substantial injustice to the victim if the court was powerless to correct an error of record. J could consider himself fortunate that the second judge felt constrained to impose only a concurrent sentence for the latest breach, when he amended the first judge's order. J had suffered no injustice.

ABDI v. JAMA [1996] 1 F.L.R. 407, Wall, J., CA.

2450. Divorce–application to set aside decree absolute granted to peer of realm–resident in Philippines–court deceived by peer

[Judicial Proceedings (Regulation of Reports) Act 1926 s.1.]

In 1970 Lord M left the UK to avoid serious fraud charges and settled in the Philippines where he became a hotel proprietor and acquired several massage parlours. He married E but the marriage had broken down by 1989 and he was anxious to marry J who was expecting his child. With the help of his brother-in-law he presented a petition for divorce stating that he was domiciled in England. When asked about the arrangements for the child of the family, he sent a death certificate stating that the child had recently died of pneumonia. In fact the child had not died and E later stated that she had no knowledge of the petition. In December 1990 J and Lord M went through a ceremony of marriage in the Philippines and in January 1991 J gave birth to a son. In November 1991, Lord M died leaving an estate worth £1.5 million. The Queen's Proctor applied to set aside the decree on the grounds that it had been obtained by fraud.

Held, that (1) divorce proceedings were not concluded until the resolution of any application to determine the validity of a decree or order. Therefore the Judicial Proceedings (Regulation of Reports) Act 1926 applied and the evidence given during the hearing could not be reported in accordance with the terms of s.1; (2) the evidence demonstrated that Lord M had acquired a domicile of choice in the Philippines: he indicated that he had no intention of returning to England which he felt had changed since 1970; he had built up a large business in the Philippines; he had acquired a large house and furnished it with his paintings and some of his ancestral furniture, and he had married twice and had two children in the Philippines, and (3) the decree would be set aside on the grounds that there had been a deliberate and sustained deception of the court by Lord M.

MOYNIHAN v. MOYNIHAN (NOS.1 AND 2); *sub nom.* MOYNIHAN, *Re* [1997] 1 F.L.R. 59, Sir Stephen Brown (President), Fam Div.

2451. Divorce–behaviour–insufficient particulars–oral evidence heard–decree nisi granted–no fair hearing

[Matrimonial Causes Act 1973 s.1 (2).]

H appealed against a decree nisi of divorce founded on the Matrimonial Causes Act 1973 s.1 (2) (b) where the recorder had found that the petition gave insufficient details of the behaviour relied upon by W and oral evidence was given. W made allegations that H was a heavy drinker, violent and jealous, which H contested. Having heard evidence the recorder concluded there was an "accumulation of behaviour" which contributed to the marriage breakdown.

Held, allowing the appeal and setting aside the decree nisi, that the allegations had been brief, particularly in relation to H's alleged violence. H had a right to oppose the petition and to have the allegations properly proved against him on a balance of probabilities, there were matters raised in evidence which might have led the court to conclude that H was being unreasonable but no such specific findings were made. The recorder had failed to deal justly with H in granting decree nisi on information which was not properly pleaded and which H had been unable to meet.

BUTTERWORTH v. BUTTERWORTH [1997] 2 F.L.R. 336, Butler-Sloss, L.J., CA.

2452. Divorce–choice of forum–competing petitions issued in two jurisdictions– balance of fairness test to be applied

[Domicile and Matrimonial Proceedings Act 1973 s.5 (6), Sch.1.]

H and W brought divorce petitions in England and Florida respectively. W's application for a stay of proceedings in respect of H's petition was refused in the High Court and W appealed, arguing that Florida was the more appropriate forum.

Held, allowing the appeal and staying the English proceedings, that the appropriate test for determining whether the proceedings should be stayed was the balance of fairness and convenience test in the Domicile and Matrimonial Proceedings Act 1973 s.5 (6) and Sch.1 para.9 (1). A trial judge's discretion could only be set aside if he had clearly erred, but in the instant case the judge had wrongly concluded, relying on *Chatelard v. Chatelard* (Unreported), that W had not shown that Florida was clearly the more appropriate jurisdiction, and he had taken into account aspects of Florida law which were immaterial. It was apparent that H and W's married life together was based in Florida and the case for allowing the proceedings to be conducted there was overwhelming.

BUTLER v. BUTLER [1997] 2 All E.R. 822, Sir Stephen Brown, CA.

2453. Divorce–choice of forum–prenuptial agreement stipulating New York– fairness test for choosing forum of competing petitions

[Domicile and Matrimonial Proceedings Act 1973 s.25, Sch.1.]

H sought a stay of divorce proceedings commenced in England by W contending that, under the terms of a prenuptial agreement negotiated and executed in New York, the parties' rights were to be governed and enforced under New York law.

Held, allowing the application, that although the authorities showed that such agreements were of only limited significance in English law, nothing in the Domicile and Matrimonial Proceedings Act 1973 s.25 led to the conclusion that escape from solemn bargains struck by informed adults was to be readily available in the UK. As held in *De Dampierre v. De Dampierre* [1988] 1 A.C. 92, [1987] C.L.Y. 399, the inquiry into the "balance of fairness" required by Sch.1

para.9(1)(b) to the Act was to be conducted by reference to the principles now deployed in the exercise of the court's inherent jurisdiction to stay matrimonial proceedings where England was forum non conveniens, with a party needing to then establish that another forum was "clearly or distinctly more appropriate", *Spiliada Maritime Corp v. Cansulex* [1987] 1 A.C. 460, [1987] C.L.Y. 3135 followed. Although *Butler v. Butler* [1997] 2 All E.R. 822, [1997] C.L.Y. 2452 had considered that the *Spiliada* requirement ran the risk of replacing the Sch.1 "balance of fairness" criterion, *Chatelard v. Chatelard* (Unreported) suggested that it was the connection between the litigation and the foreign court that mattered, as opposed to that between the family and the foreign state. The facts showed that the forum provisions in the prenuptial agreement formed an exclusive and categorical connection between W's intended litigation and New York, and, satisfied that substantial justice would be done in that forum, the balance of fairness made it appropriate to stay the English proceedings

S v. S (MATRIMONIAL PROCEEDINGS: APPROPRIATE FORUM); *sub nom.* S v. S (DIVORCE: STAYING PROCEEDINGS) [1997] 2 F.L.R. 100, Wilson, J., Fam Div.

2454. **Divorce–foreign judgments–ancillary relief order made in England for payment of capital sum–enforcement of maintenance order in the Netherlands–European Union**

[Brussels Convention on Jurisdiction and Enforcement of Judgments in Civil and Commercial Matters 1968 Art.1, Art.5.]

The parties were married in the Netherlands and later agreed by marriage contract to alter the matrimonial arrangement of community of property to one based on separation of goods. The marriage was later dissolved in London and ancillary relief was awarded to the wife in the form of a capital sum in place of periodic maintenance payments, which included transfer of property to the wife and payment of a lump sum. The court stated that it did not consider the separation of goods agreement to be relevant to its decision. The wife applied to have the order enforced in the Netherlands, relying on the Brussels Convention 1968, and a preliminary reference to the ECJ was made to determine whether the order was excluded by Art.1 of the Convention as relating to "rights in property arising out of a matrimonial relationship", or whether the order fell within Art.5(2) which stated that "matters relating to maintenance" were covered by the Convention.

Held, that it was necessary for the court to distinguish between parts of the order relating to "rights in property arising out of a matrimonial relationship" and "matters relating to maintenance", as an order made in England could relate to both, but only the latter was covered by the Convention. Where the aim of the decision was to provide for one of the spouses, having taken into account the needs and resources of both parties, then it was an order for maintenance and it was irrelevant that payment was as a lump sum, or that the property was to be transferred between spouses. The fact that the court making the order had chosen to disregard the marriage contract was also irrelevant in defining the nature of the order made and an order could be partially enforced if it could be clearly shown that part of it fell within Art.5(2).

VAN DEN BOOGAARD v. LAUMEN (C220/95) [1997] All E.R. (EC) 517, JC Moitinho de Almeida (President), ECJ.

2455. **Divorce–jurisdiction–stay of proceedings pending Scottish petition**

See CHILDREN: M (Minors) (Jurisdiction: Habitual Residence), *Re.* §395

2456. **Divorce–pension rights–financial provision**

DIVORCE ETC. (PENSIONS) (AMENDMENT) REGULATIONS 1997, SI 1997 636; made under the Matrimonial Causes Act 1973 s.25D. In force: immediately after the coming into force of the Pensions Act 1995 s.152, s.153 and s.154; £1.10.

These Regulations amend the Divorce etc (Pensions) Regulations 1996 (SI 1996 1676), which make provision in relation to orders made for ancillary relief in proceedings for divorce, judicial separation or nullity of marriage, so far as those orders relate to the pension rights of a party to the marriage. In particular, they provide for: the updating of references to other Regulations, which have been replaced since the principal Regulations were made; salary related occupational pension schemes, as governed by the amendments to the Pension Schemes Act 1993 effected by the Pensions Act 1995 s.152 to s.154, which come into force at the same time as these Regulations; retirement annuity contracts excluded from the scope of the Pension Schemes Act 1993 Part IV Ch.IV; information provided to the trustees or managers of a pension scheme by the party without pension rights after all the rights of the party with pension rights have been transferred to another scheme; and limitation of the recovery by pension schemes of the costs of providing information for the purpose of the principal Regulations.

2457. **Divorce—refusal of decree nisi—insufficient proof of unreasonable behaviour**

L appealed against the refusal of a decree nisi, despite a decision that his marriage had broken down irretrievably, because his claim that his wife had behaved unreasonably had not been satisfactorily proved. L claimed that his wife, C, had hit him with a metal rack during an argument. C admitted the attack but argued that it was because, shortly after having sexual intercourse, L had told her he was having an affair with another woman.

Held, dismissing the appeal, that the judge below had clearly preferred the evidence of the wife having scrupulously considered all the circumstances including the fact that L had returned to live with his wife shortly after the event, *O'Neill v. O'Neill* [1975] 3 All E.R. 289, [1975] C.L.Y. 1006 and *Buffery v. Buffery* [1988] 2 F.L.R. 365, [1989] C.L.Y. 1731 considered.

HONG THANH LUONG v. CHI TUYET LOUNG (SHIT CHI PHOUNG), Trans. Ref: CCFMF 96/1407/F, April 15, 1997, Bennett, J., CA.

2458. **Family Law Act 1996 (c.27)—Commencement No.1 Order**

FAMILY LAW ACT 1996 (COMMENCEMENT NO.1) ORDER 1997, SI 1997 1077 (C.38); made under the Family Law Act 1996 s.67. Commencement details: bringing into force various provisions of the Act on March 21, 1997; £0.65.

This Order brings into force certain sections of the Family Law Act 1996. These are Part I (general principles underlying Parts II and III of the Act), s.22 (funding for marriage support services), Part III (legal aid for mediation) and Sch.8 Part II (consequential amendments to the Legal Aid Act 1988 c.34).

2459. **Family Law Act 1996 (c.27)—Commencement No.2 Order**

FAMILY LAW ACT 1996 (COMMENCEMENT NO.2) ORDER 1997, SI 1997 1892 (C.76); made under the Family Law Act 1996 s.65, s.67. Commencement details: bringing into force various provisions of the Act on October 1, 1997; £1.10.

This Order brings various provisions of the Family Law Act 1996 into force on July 28, 1997 and October 1, 1997.

2460. **Family proceedings—allocation of proceedings between courts**

FAMILY LAW ACT 1996 (PART IV) (ALLOCATION OF PROCEEDINGS) ORDER 1997, SI 1997 1896 (L.32); made under the Family Law Act 1996 s.57. In force: October 1, 1997; £1.55.

This Order provides for the allocation of proceedings under the Family Law Act 1996 Part IV which relates to family homes and domestic violence, between the High Court, the county courts and the magistrates' courts. It prescribes those proceedings which must be commenced in the High Court; prescribes the courts in which applications to vary, extend or discharge orders are to be brought; regulates transfers between different courts and categories of courts; provides for the Principal Registry of the Family Division to be treated as a county court; provides for proceedings to be taken in Lambeth, Shoreditch and

Woolwich County Courts; and makes provision in relation to proceedings which are commenced or transferred in contravention of this Order.

2461. Family proceedings–Amendment No.1–forms–consent orders–statement of information

FAMILY PROCEEDINGS (AMENDMENT) RULES 1997, SI 1997 637; made under the Matrimonial and Family Proceedings Act 1984 s.40. In force: immediately after the coming into force of the Pensions Act 1995 s.152, s.153 and s.154; £1.10.

These Rules amend the Family Proceedings Rules (SI 1991 1247) so as to update a reference to Regulations in r.2.70 and to amend Form M1 (statement of information for a consent order) to take account of the Pensions Act 1995.

2462. Family proceedings–Amendment No.2–Civil Evidence Act 1995–consequential amendments

FAMILY PROCEEDINGS (AMENDMENT NO.2) RULES 1997, SI 1997 1056 (L.24); made under the Matrimonial and Family Proceedings Act 1984 s.40. In force: April 21, 1997; £6.10.

These Rules amend the Family Proceedings Rules so as to make consequential amendments following the enactment of the Civil Evidence Act 1995. They introduce (in exercise of the powers conferred by the Civil Procedure Act 1997 Sch.2 para.3) a new procedure for applications for ancillary relief brought in certain specified courts; reflect the change in name of chief clerk; and relax for specified purposes the requirements for confidentiality in respect of the report of a guardian ad litem.

2463. Family proceedings–Amendment No.3–applications under Family Law Act 1996 Part IV

FAMILY PROCEEDINGS (AMENDMENT NO.3) RULES 1997, SI 1997 1893 (L.29); made under the Matrimonial and Family Proceedings Act 1984 s.40. In force: October 1, 1997; £7.05.

These Rules amend the Family Proceedings Rules 1991 (SI 1991 1247) so as to provide for the making of applications under the Family Law Act 1996 Part IV and for bringing appeals against orders made on such applications; make provision where the court includes an exclusion requirement in an interim care order or an emergency protection order; require a petitioner to produce the written consent of the respondent to the grant of a divorce decree before the court will direct that, on the absence of an acknowledgement of service, the respondent has been duly served; prevent the statement of arrangements for the children being available for inspection; define the period for which a cause is to be treated as pending for the purposes of r.2.40(1) which requires applications relating to children to be made in the cause where a cause is pending; require applications under the Hague Convention and the European Convention to be issued out of the principal registry of the Family Division in London; make some minor amendments to r.7.2 in its application to proceedings in the Principal Registry of the Family Division; and enable the court to direct a next friend or guardian ad litem to take part in proceedings where the court is considering whether to allow a minor to proceed without such a person.

2464. Family proceedings–enforcement of orders under Family Law Act 1996 Part IV

FAMILY LAW ACT 1996 (MODIFICATIONS OF ENACTMENTS) ORDER 1997, SI 1997 1898 (L.34); made under the Family Law Act 1996 Sch.9 para.3. In force: October 1, 1997; £0.65.

This Order amends the Magistrates' Courts Act 1980 s.65(2) so as to enable proceedings to enforce an order made in proceedings under the Family Law Act 1996 Part IV to be treated as family proceedings. It also amends s.125 to bring a cross-reference up to date.

2465. Family proceedings–fees–Amendment No.1–exemptions

FAMILY PROCEEDINGS FEES (AMENDMENT) ORDER 1997, SI 1997 788 (L.18); made under the Matrimonial and Family Proceedings Act 1984 s.41. In force: March 13, 1997; £0.65.

This Order amends the Family Proceedings Fees Order 1991 (SI 1991 2114) by restoring the provisions governing exemption and remission from court fees to their wording immediately prior to the coming into force of the Family Proceedings Fees (Amendment) Order 1996 (SI 1996 3190). It also revokes the relevant articles of the 1996 Order.

2466. Family proceedings–fees–Amendment No.2–exemptions–recipients of family credit

FAMILY PROCEEDINGS FEES (AMENDMENT) (NO.2) ORDER 1997, SI 1997 1080 (L.25); made under the Matrimonial and Family Proceedings Act 1984 s.41. In force: March 27, 1997; £0.65.

This Order amends the Family Proceedings Order 1991 (SI 1991 2114) by restoring the exemption from court fees for those in receipt of family credit.

2467. Family proceedings–fees–Amendment No.3–non molestation orders– occupation orders

FAMILY PROCEEDINGS FEES (AMENDMENT) (NO.3) ORDER 1997, SI 1997 1899 (L.35); made under the Matrimonial and Family Proceedings Act 1984 s.41. In force: October 1, 1997; £0.65.

This Order amends the Family Proceedings Fees Order 1991 (SI 1991 2114 as amended) to provide a fee of £30 for making an application for a non-molestation order or an occupation order under the Family Law Act 1996 Part IV.

2468. Family proceedings–fees–Amendment No.4–exemptions

FAMILY PROCEEDINGS FEES (AMENDMENT) (NO.4) ORDER 1997, SI 1997 2671 (L.40); made under the Matrimonial and Family Proceedings Act 1984 s.41. In force: December 1, 1997; £0.65.

This Order amends the Family Proceedings Fees Order 1991 (SI 1991 2114) by extending the exemption from payment of court fees to those receiving disability working allowance or income based jobseeker's allowance.

2469. Family proceedings–rights of audience–lay representatives

See ADMINISTRATION OF JUSTICE: D v. S (Rights of Audience). §49, and G (A Minor) (Rights of Audience), *Re*. §50

2470. Financial provision–breach of maintenance order–committal–change in circumstances–judicial review–damages against magistrates inappropriate

[Maintenance Orders Act 1958 s.18.]

M applied for an order of certiorari quashing a decision committing him to prison for 42 days for wilful refusal to pay arrears of maintenance due under a previous order and an order for the magistrates who had committed him to prison to pay him damages. M also appealed by way of case stated against the refusal to cancel the warrant of commitment. In November 1989 an order in full and final settlement of all financial claims was made, inter alia requiring M to pay nominal maintenance in the sum of five pence per annum for each of his three children until they attained the age of 18 years or further order. In October 1994 that order was varied to £240 per month but M failed to pay. In December 1995 the order was further varied to £24 per week and M was required to pay £26 per week towards the arrears. In addition a suspended committal order was made for 42 days, conditional on payment of the total of £50 per week, on the basis that M had wilfully refused to pay the arrears. M's application to remit the arrears was rejected. In October 1994 M had received a redundancy payment of approximately £5,600. In March 1995 a bankruptcy order was made against him. After a notice under the Maintenance Orders Act 1958 s.18 was made the maintenance order was reduced to 80 pence per annum per child due to M being made redundant in January 1996.

Held, allowing the application for judicial review and the appeal by case stated, that (1) the justices should have considered M's ability to pay in the period after the order of December 1995, as his reason then for not making the payments required was not wilful refusal but genuine inability given that he had been made redundant and was living on state benefits. As he was unable to pay, they should have concluded that he ought not to continue to be detained under the warrant; (2) the application for judicial review was allowed on the basis that the court was exercising its residual discretion despite there having been an appellate process which M failed to follow. The 21 days given for appealing against the decision to commit M expired on the same day M's application to set aside the warrant for commitment was dismissed. His actions were perfectly proper and in these exceptional circumstances judicial review was appropriate, and (3) this was not a case where damages should be awarded against magistrates. Their decision, although flawed, was not tainted by malice or perversity.

R. v. WELLINGBOROUGH MAGISTRATES COURT, *ex p.* MONK; MONK v. HIGGINS, Trans. Ref: CO-2683-96, April 18, 1997, Connell, J., QBD.

2471. Financial provision–children's welfare–division of capital sums to enable parties to rehouse themselves

[Matrimonial Causes Act 1973 s.25.]

Held, that, when making financial provision pursuant to the Matrimonial Causes Act 1973 s.25, a court should endeavour to divide the capital sums available so as to enable both parties to rehouse themselves. This was an extremely important consideration where young children were involved, not only for the parent with care but also for the other parent who needed a home in which to enjoy contact time with the children.

MARSHALL v. BECKETT; *sub nom.* M v. B (ANCILLARY PROCEEDINGS: LUMP SUM), *The Times,* October 15, 1997, Thorpe, L.J., CA.

2472. Financial provision–choice of forum–Canadian employee seconded to UK–distribution of matrimonial property

H and W, both Canadian nationals, married in Alberta in 1971 and lived there until 1992, when H was posted to England by his employers. The parties moved to rented accommodation and the matrimonial home in Alberta was sold. In 1995 the parties separated and W returned to Canada where she issued proceedings for the distribution of the proceeds and obtained orders preserving the parties' property there. She was unable to sue for divorce in Alberta until June 1996. In October 1995 H issued divorce proceedings in England and a decree absolute was made in May 1996. H entered a defence to the Alberta proceedings, challenging the jurisdiction of the Alberta court to entertain W's claim. In January 1996 W applied in England for all forms of ancillary relief and obtained an interim maintenance order. H applied to the English court for an injunction restraining W from pursuing her action in Alberta and requiring her to take all necessary steps to have the Albertan restraining order lifted and also made a cross application for ancillary relief. W later made an application to stay the English ancillary relief proceedings.

Held, staying the English proceedings, that it was a matter for the Alberta court to decide whether it had jurisdiction. W's application to stay would be considered first, because if granted then H's applications for injunctions must fail. W satisfied the court that Alberta was plainly the more natural forum, since the parties' entire background and upbringing had been in Canada and they had lived the majority of their lives there. They had never bought a property in England, their assets were in Canada and W had returned to Canada when the marriage broke down. Whilst the jurisdiction of the Alberta courts was limited to the distribution of property and did not extend to maintenance, it was inconceivable that capital issues should be dealt with in Canada while income issues were dealt with in England, so the stay would include the maintenance order obtained by W in England. Although H had argued that since the divorce and ancillary relief were substantially the same thing W should not be entitled to apply for a stay after decree absolute had been made, divorce was discrete from financial issues and any injustice caused to H could be remedied by appropriate orders in costs.

W v. W (FINANCIAL RELIEF: APPROPRIATE FORUM) [1997] 1 F.L.R. 257, Holman, J., Fam Div.

2473. Financial provision—choice of forum—leave to apply for relief where both spouses are foreign nationals

[Matrimonial and Family Proceedings Act 1984 Part III; Matrimonial and Family Proceedings Act 1984 s.16.]

Held, that where husband and wife were Swedish nationals, leave of the court to apply for financial provision under the Matrimonial and Family Proceedings Act 1984 Part III would only be granted where a substantial ground existed, and in deciding whether an appropriate ground did exist, the court could take account of the criteria in s.16 as to the correct forum and whether the applicant had suffered injustice or hardship.

N v. N (OVERSEAS DIVORCE: FINANCIAL RELIEF) [1997] 1 F.L.R. 900, Cazalet, J., Fam Div.

2474. Financial provision—clean break settlement—consent orders—bad legal advice not ground on which order could be put aside

[Matrimonial Causes Act 1973 s.25(1).]

The parties compromised ancillary relief proceedings by a consent order by which W's claim for ancillary relief was dismissed, the matrimonial home to be sold and the proceeds divided. After the consent order was approved by the district judge the prospective purchaser withdrew and, following the slump in the property market, the house was not sold. After mortgage arrears had built up, the building society foreclosed and any sale would not have produced any surplus, leaving W without funds or a home. W sued her solicitors for bad legal advice in advising her to consent to the dismissal of her ancillary relief claim and applied to have the consent order set aside on the grounds that it had been entered into as a result of bad legal advice. The judge dismissed her application and she appealed.

Held, dismissing the appeal, that although the court was to have regard to all the circumstances, including bad legal advice, when considering whether to approve agreed financial arrangements under the Matrimonial Causes Act 1973 s.25(1), once a consent order had been made bad legal advice was not one of the factors which could justify the setting aside of the order. The policy of the law was to encourage a clean break and an end to litigation. It would be unfair on H to set aside the consent order.

HARRIS (FORMERLY MANAHAN) v. MANAHAN [1996] 4 All E.R. 454, Ward, L.J., CA.

2475. Financial provision—clean break settlement—limited liquid assets—substantial costs

The parties married in 1976 and separated in 1993. Their two children lived with M. The net proceeds of sale from the former matrimonial home were used to fund a property for M, while F had bought another property with his new wife and baby. The parties' standard of living had been comfortable but not luxurious. By the time of the hearing they had both incurred costs amounting to 25 per cent of their combined assets. Only £160,000 of F's assets were liquid and M sought a lump sum in that amount on a clean break basis. On the third day of the hearing F offered a lump sum of £140,000 on the basis of no order as to costs.

Held, that the court had to make an order in the light of the evidence irrespective of costs considerations. M required an income of £20,000 which could be provided with the help of a lump sum of £145,000, although that would take up most of F's available capital and it was unclear whether he would be able to meet any costs order made against him. Having regard to the negotiations F would be ordered to pay the costs of the ancillary relief application.

H v. H (FINANCIAL RELIEF: COSTS) [1997] 2 F.L.R. 57, Holman, J., Fam Div.

2476. **Financial provision–clean break settlement–losses from property speculation not amounting to new event justifying leave to appeal out of time**

H sought leave to appeal out of time from an order granting W a clean break divorce with a lump sum payment of £400,000. H contended that the adverse outcome of a property speculation amounted to a new event occurring since the making of an order which invalidated the basis upon which it had been made, *Barder v. Barder* [1988] 1 A.C. 20, [1987] C.L.Y. 1726 considered.

Held, refusing the application, that the shortfall in the valuation occurred due to the non-materialisation of an expected profit and that the transaction itself had not formed a major factor in the case. The impact of the loss fell to be judged against H's financial status and he had shown no evidence of his inability to raise money by disposing of his other business assets or shares. H's affidavit of means submitted for the first instance hearing was itself seriously misleading as it did not reveal the transaction at all and had been subject to criticism by the district judge in that regard.

LLOYD v. LLOYD, Trans. Ref: LTA 96/7742/F, March 12, 1997, Ward, L.J., CA.

2477. **Financial provision–consent orders–periodical payments–extension of term–factors to be taken into account**

[Matrimonial Causes Act 1973 s.28(1A).]

In ancillary relief proceedings W was awarded periodical payments for three years at £8,000 per year, at the end of which her claim for periodical payments would be dismissed. W applied for an extension of the term for the payment of periodical payments. The district judge found that there was jurisdiction to extend the term and fixed the rate of periodical payments at £12,000 per year during the parties' joint lives or further order. A judge on appeal ordered that the periodical payments fixed by the district judge should continue for five years and made an order under the Matrimonial Causes Act 1973 s.28(1A) precluding W from applying for any further extension beyond that date. W appealed.

Held, dismissing the appeal, that formal agreements reached properly and fairly with complete legal advice should not be displaced unless there were good and substantial reasons for concluding that an injustice would be done by holding the parties to the agreement. The judge had made no error in principle or in the exercise of his discretion in arriving at a solution which, on the one hand balanced H's contentions that the consent order was so significant that W's need for continuing periodical payments, however great, should be dismissed and on the other hand W's arguments that her needs and her continuing obligations as far as the parties' children were concerned demanded that she should continue to receive support from H. Although the judge found that the disparity between the parties' means was a result of the success made of his career by H since the marriage had ended and the failure made by W of hers, the single consideration which justified a departure from the principle in *Edgar v. Edgar* [1980] 1 W.L.R. 1410, [1980] C.L.Y. 791 was W's continuing obligations to the children and his order could not be impugned on that ground.

RICHARDSON v. RICHARDSON (NO.2) [1997] 2 F.C.R. 453, Balcombe, L.J., CA.

2478. Financial provision–consent orders–set aside for fraud

[Family Proceedings Rules r.2.42; County Court Rules 1981 Ord.37, r.1.]

The parties separated and commenced ancillary relief negotiations. In April 1987 a consent order was made which provided for a clean break, requiring H to transfer his interest in the former matrimonial home and a life assurance policy to W and pay her a lump sum of £25,000. H owned a private company. In 1986 H's solicitors were informed by the company accountants that there was no market in the company's shares, which information was in turn communicated to W's solicitors. However, in February 1987, unknown to W and her advisers and before the consent order was made, a public limited company made a first formal offer to purchase the shares of H's company. In May 1987 the public limited company concluded a deal to buy the shares for £4.8 million and H eventually received £1.6 million. W learned of the sale a month later but did not inform her solicitor, believing that she had signed away her rights under the terms of the consent order. In 1993 W discovered that the negotiations for the sale of the shares had begun before the consent order was made and applied to set aside the consent order under the Family Proceedings Rules 1991 r.2.42(1).

Held, granting the application, that (1) an application to set aside a consent order made in ancillary relief proceedings on the grounds of material non-disclosure and fraudulent misrepresentation should be brought under the County Court Rules 1981 Ord.37 r.1 and could not be made under r.2.42(1) of the 1991 Rules and the wife would be given leave to amend her application accordingly, and (2) there was a duty in the field of matrimonial litigation to make full and frank disclosure and where fraudulent disclosure was detected no court would be prepared lightly to overlook it. H's conduct in allowing W to remain under a false impression that the shares in his company were worthless was dishonest and fraudulent and the fraud had remained concealed from W until October 1993 when she learned that negotiations had opened before the consent order had been made. In the circumstances leave to bring her application out of time would be granted, the order set aside and an order made for the rehearing of her application for ancillary relief.

T v. T (CONSENT ORDER: PROCEDURE TO SET ASIDE) [1996] 2 F.L.R. 640, Richard Anelay Q.C., Fam Div.

2479. Financial provision–generous provision appropriate after short term marriage

[Matrimonial Causes Act 1973 s.15A(1), s.25A.]

H, aged 59, appealed against ancillary relief, awarded on transfer of the matrimonial home to himself, of a lump sum payment of £195,000 to W, aged 40, and against secured periodical payments of £19,500 per annum to her and of £8,000 per annum to J, the only child, who suffered from bronchial asthma. H also appealed against an award of costs against him on an indemnity basis. H became a client of W, a call girl, and became infatuated with her; however, their subsequent marriage had lasted only nine months. H contended (1) that the lump sum payment should be reduced to £75,000 and settled on J with reversion to himself, and (2) that the periodical payments should be limited to a term of two years and reduced to £10,000 and £4,000 respectively, to be varied on W's application.

Held, dismissing the appeal, that (1) the judge below had made a generous but not unreasonable award, and H had forfeited the sympathy of the court by consistently failing to disclose details of his income and capital; (2) the periodical payments were also generous, but not unreasonable. Although the Matrimonial Causes Act 1973 s.15A(1) and public policy suggested that the payee's self sufficiency was generally desirable, and (3) s.25A was concerned only with the hardship of the payee not the payer. Notwithstanding the brevity of the marriage, it was unnecessary to impose a term for the periodical payments, especially since the strain of the litigation and H's employment of surveillance agents had so exacerbated W's psychiatric problems that she was unlikely to be employed for some time. Early problems with H's payments and his deceptions in court had led to the imposition of a secured order and in the light of his relocation to Athens were not unreasonable, *H v. H (Financial Provision: Short Marriage)* [1981] 2 F.L.R. 392, *Barrett v. Barrett* [1988] 2 F.L.R. 516, [1989] C.L.Y. 1753 considered.

C v. C (FINANCIAL RELIEF: SHORT MARRIAGE) [1997] 2 F.L.R. 26, Ward, L.J., CA.

2480. Financial provision–improvement in husband's financial circumstances– applications for Anton Piller and Mareva injunctions

An ancillary relief order was made on the basis that H would retain an interest in a commercial lease valued at £10,000 from which he would operate his business. W subsequently learned that the property had been sold for £150,000 and applied unsuccessfully for Anton Piller and Mareva relief pending the determination of her application for leave to appeal out of time against the ancillary relief order.

Held, dismissing W's appeal, that the orders sought were draconian and should only be made in exceptional circumstances. While H had concealed information at the ancillary hearing, there was no evidence to suggest that he was in possession of vital material which he might destroy. The court could make an order on the basis that £150,000 had become available to H. The making and enforcing of a Mareva injunction would be an expensive process, the disadvantages of which would outweigh its intended purpose. An injunction preventing H from dealing in the proceeds of sale would be sufficient to protect W's interests.

ARAGHCHINCHI v. ARAGHCHINCHI [1997] 2 F.L.R. 142, Ward, L.J., CA.

2481. Financial provision–lengthy cohabitation following divorce–wife could make fresh application for lump sum order and property adjustment order following separation

[Married Women's Property Act 1882 s.17.]

H and W were divorced in 1968 and H was ordered to pay weekly maintenance for W and their children, a lump sum of £75, and to transfer the ownership of a car to her "in full settlement of any claims the petitioner may have in respect of the matrimonial home" under the Married Women's Property Act 1882 s.17. Soon after the decree absolute, H and W began cohabiting again, but separated once more in 1994. As their financial position had improved during that period, W applied by notice issued in the divorce proceedings for further financial provision and now appealed against a decision refusing to set aside the original lump sum order or to make a property adjustment order.

Held, allowing the appeal, that W's claim should not be regarded as one based on cohabitation, but rather as one based on the divorce decree and held in abeyance during the period of cohabitation. Whilst, in general, a cohabitee should not be treated as having the same rights as a wife or former wife, it was also important to encourage reconciliation wherever possible, particularly where there were children of the marriage. Further, if W's cohabitation with H was treated as cohabitation with a stranger, that would distort the reality of their relationship. If W were not granted leave to make an application for a property adjustment order, she would clearly suffer hardship, and as H had the ability to relieve that hardship, the balance of justice favoured W. The judge was wrong to treat the original order as a disposal of the prayer of petition for a lump sum order and had thus made an error of law in stating that the court had no jurisdiction to hear W's claim. He had also been wrong to find that there had been a comprehensive property settlement at the time of the divorce which precluded the court from entertaining a fresh application for a property adjustment order.

HILL v. HILL, *The Independent*, June 19, 1997, Ward, L.J., CA.

2482. Financial provision–lump sum payments–assessments of wife's financial needs–court's discretion to take into account wife's contribution to marriage

[Matrimonial Causes Act 1973 s.25.]

Held, that a court exercising its discretion in determining a wife's financial needs on an application for a lump sum payment under the Matrimonial Causes Act 1973 s.25 could take into consideration the non-financial aspects of her contribution to the marriage. Where a wife had special talents, both as a housewife and mother and as an active participant in her husband's successful business, it was appropriate for a court, after assessing her reasonable requirements, to make an adjustment to the award to reflect the significant contribution she had made to the welfare of the family, *Dart v. Dart* [1996] 2 F.L.R. 286, [1996] 1 C.L.Y. 2858 considered.

CONRAN v. CONRAN, *The Times*, July 14, 1997, Wilson, J., Fam Div.

2483. Financial provision–lump sum payments–order against bankrupt

Held, that there was no reason in principle why a lump sum order could not be made against an undischarged bankrupt so long as the court had a clear picture of the assets and liabilities of the bankrupt and could decide that it was likely that there would be assets in the future to pay the sum ordered. The fact that payment could not be made within the time fixed by the court for payment did not matter, although interest would accrue until the date of actual payment.

HELLYER v. HELLYER [1996] 2 F.L.R. 579, Aldous, L.J., CA.

2484. Financial provision–lump sum unpaid–application to reduce periodical payments

The parties were married in 1985 and separated in 1992. At the hearing of W's application for ancillary relief, the judge concluded that H had been guilty of material non-disclosure and made an order for the payment of a lump sum and periodical payments on the basis that H had assets which he had not disclosed. H never accepted the finding of non-disclosure but his appeal to the Court of Appeal was unsuccessful. He never paid the lump sum and later applied to reduce the periodical payments order in view of his present assets and the fact that he had a new wife and children. W contended that as long as H remained in contempt by his failure to pay the lump sum, he should not be entitled to proceed with his variation application. The judge found that as long as the lump sum remained unpaid and H gave no explanation for his default, the principle in *Hadkinson v. Hadkinson* [1952] P.285, [1952] C.L.Y. 2648 applied and in the exercise of his discretion he would refuse to allow H to proceed with his variation application. H appealed.

Held, dismissing the appeal, that it was a matter for the discretion of the court to decide whether the contempt had been wilful and impeded the course of justice within the criteria set out in *Hadkinson*. Since there was no other way in which W would be able to secure compliance with the original order and it was intolerable for H to continue to assert that the original order, made by the judge and confirmed by the Court of Appeal, had not been justified, the judge had been right to refuse to proceed further with H's variation application.

BAKER v. BAKER (NO.2) [1997] 1 F.L.R. 148, Sir John Balcombe, CA.

2485. Financial provision–matrimonial home–alleged negligence of valuer–immunity of valuer from suit against public policy to allow relitigation of issues tried in Family Division

An ancillary relief order made in 1982, following N's divorce, required the wife to execute a charge in N's favour on the property she purchased with her share of the proceeds of the former matrimonial home. The charge was for one fifth of the net proceeds of sale of the property to take effect on the youngest child attaining 21 years. The wife could redeem N's charge on an agreed valuation of the property and, in the absence of agreement, the property was to be valued by a surveyor and valuer appointed by the President of the RICS. At the relevant time the wife contended the value was £110,000 whilst N argued it was £120,000 and no agreement was reached. Accordingly the mechanism provided for in the order came into operation and C, the appointed valuer, estimated a value at £70,000. N issued proceedings seeking a ruling as to the fair value to be attributed to the property. N gave notice that he alleged professional negligence in undervaluing the property. C's application to strike out N's particulars of claim on the basis of having no reasonable cause of action was dismissed. C appealed against that dismissal, arguing that he was entitled to immunity either as an arbitrator or as a witness, and that N's claim was a manifest attempt to relitigate issues that had been finalised in the Family Division.

Held, allowing the appeal and striking out the action, that C was not an arbitrator as defined in *Sutcliffe v. Thackrah* [1974] A.C. 727, [1974] C.L.Y. 2552 and *Arenson v. Casson Beckman Rutley & Co* [1977] A.C. 405 and could not claim immunity as such. Also C had submitted his valuation in writing and it was never intended that he would be a witness and therefore witness immunity did not arise. However N's claim was an attempt to plead matters which had already been refused admission in the lower court and it would be against public policy to allow the relitigation of issues already decided in the Family Division, *Walpole v. Partridge & Wilson* [1994] Q.B. 106, [1994] C.L.Y. 3517 and *Smith v. Linskills* [1996] 1 W.L.R. 763, [1996] 2 C.L.Y. 4496 applied.

N v. C, Trans. Ref: CCRT1 96/0511/G, February 21, 1997, Thorpe, L.J., CA.

2486. **Financial provision–periodical payment arrears–order made for payments in near future–special circumstances justifying departure from "one year" starting point**

A was ordered to make periodical payments to his two children. He was adjudicated bankrupt and had irregular employment. He fell into arrears with the payments but there were delays in taking enforcement proceedings. M applied for enforcement of the arrears and F for remission. The justices found that F's work prospects were good and that he was likely to find work within two months with earnings at a similar level to when he had last worked. Following that finding, an analysis of his current expenditure and receipt of child benefit, the justices decided to remit only part of the arrears. They found that there were special circumstances which justified the enforcement of the arrears notwithstanding that they were more than 12 months old. F appealed by way of case stated.

Held, dismissing the appeal, that although caution should be exercised when making orders based on anticipated changes in circumstances, the justices had been justified on the evidence in reaching their decision that the father would find good work within a short period. Special circumstances existed because it was reasonable for M to refrain from potentially expensive enforcement proceedings until substantial arrears built up and it was not practicable to take enforcement action with a pending application to remit the arrears.

C v. S (MAINTENANCE ORDER: ENFORCEMENT) [1997] 1 F.L.R. 298, Wilson, J., Fam Div.

2487. **Financial provision–periodical payments–arrears remitted contrary to Magistrates Courts Rules–availability of other remedies–decision susceptible to judicial review due to procedure followed**

[Magistrates Courts Rules 1981 r.44 (1).]

The remittance of periodical payment arrears without notification to the recipient was a breach of the Magistrates Courts Rules 1981. H and R were divorced parents, and the county court ordered R to make periodical payments to their children. Arrears accrued and H applied for enforcement permission on a form stating "the whole or part of the arrears under the order may be remitted by the justices". There followed court hearings which H did not attend, and correspondence about the disputed amount outstanding in which the court clerk made no further reference to remission of the arrears, and H set out her contentions of the balance to be paid. In

February 1995 the clerk wrote that the court had remitted part of the arrears and ordered R to pay the remainder at a weekly rate. There was some continuing default, and in June 1995 H issued a further complaint for arrears; the justices then remitted the whole of the arrears. H applied for judicial review of the two orders, contending she had had no notice of the intention to remit arrears or any opportunity to make representations concerning the same. The question arose as to the correct procedure for such a review.

Held, allowing the application and quashing the justices orders, that (1) the justices were in breach of the Magistrates Courts Rules 1981 r. 44(1) in remitting any of the arrears without first notifying H that it was their intention to do so; the form H signed contained only a statement of the justices' powers and not a notice of intention. Further, R had raised matters of conduct at the hearing on which it would have been appropriate to have H's comments, and (2) H could have sought a case stated on whether, by their enforcement notice, the justices had given adequate notice of their intention to remit the arrears, but was out of time for this and the court could not extend the time limit. H could only, therefore, now challenge by way of judicial review. The court would not normally exercise its discretion to grant judicial review where other available remedies had not been used, but here H had followed the course stated in the textbooks, and the application for leave was within time for the second order and in the circumstances it was appropriate for the court to grant the review.

R. v. BRISTOL JUSTICES, *ex p.* HODGE; *sub nom.* R. v. BRISTOL MAGISTRATES COURT, *ex p.* HODGE [1997] 2 W.L.R. 756, Cazalet, J., QBD.

2488. **Financial provision–periodical payments–deferred clean break–variation of order**

[Matrimonial Causes Act 1973 s.31 (1).]

The parties divorced after 18 years of marriage. The district judge made an order providing for the sale of the former matrimonial home and ordered H to make periodical payments to W at the rate of £450 per month for two years. H subsequently sought a direction that W should not be entitled to apply to extend the term, which the district judge refused to make. W applied to vary the order for periodical payments, which the district judge did, extending for a further six months. W appealed and the judge deleted the limitation on the term, but reduced the amount of periodical payments to £250 per month. H appealed.

Held, dismissing the appeal, that the power to vary orders in the Matrimonial Causes Act 1973 s.31 (1) was unrestricted and not dependent on exceptional circumstances or material change, which were merely matters which could affect the exercise of the court's discretion. The court should look at the matter de novo. The 1973 Act imposed no more than an aspiration that the parties should be self sufficient and the power to terminate dependency should be exercised only if the adjustment could be made without undue hardship. It was not usually appropriate to terminate periodical payments for a wife in her mid-50s unless she had substantial capital or a significant earning capacity. The risk of ill health and loss of employment were real factors to be taken into account. The judge's finding that the optimism of the district judge at the time of the original order that W could become self sufficient had not been borne out and was wholly unacceptable on the facts, so that it was inappropriate to impose any terms on the payment of periodical payments.

FLAVELL v. FLAVELL [1997] 1 F.L.R. 353, Ward, L.J., CA.

2489. **Financial provision–periodical payments–term of order–variation of term**

[Matrimonial Causes Act 1973 s.28(1A).]

W cross appealed against the dismissal of her claim for periodical payments and H cross appealed the order made in respect of his daughter and the order for costs. A deferred clean break agreed in 1989 after the 20 year marriage ended included the agreement that W had conveyed to her the matrimonial home, a lump sum payment of £5,000 and H undertook to pay the two children £2,500 each per annum until they reached 18 or ceased full time education, whichever was later. The periodical payments order provided for the payment by H of £14,000 per annum until W remarried, cohabited with a man for six months or until the younger child of the marriage attained 18, or until further order. The issue was whether it was appropriate to limit W's entitlement to periodical payments for five years, ie. the period before the younger child attained 18, as the order did not provide to stand dismissed upon the happening of the event and did not provide whether the parties intended the Matrimonial Causes Act 1973 s.28(1A) to apply. H put W on notice that he was not prepared to support her beyond November 1994 and the order was then varied so that H would pay W £17,000 per annum from November 1, 1995 to July 31, 1996 and £12,000 the following year reducing to £7,248 the next year and thereafter nominal payments of 5p per annum. The claim for periodical payments for the daughter was dismissed. W contended that the order under which H was liable to pay for the daughter remained extant, but in suspense pending the making of a further order in the absence of provision for its dismissal. Regarding the cross-appeal against the order made in respect of the daughter, H argued that it was wrong to require an undertaking to be given regarding periodical payments as well as ordering periodical payments to be made to W for the benefit of the child.

Held, dismissing the appeal and cross appeal, that the power to make a periodical payment in respect of the child could be exercised from time to time, but only one periodical payments order could be made in favour of a party to the marriage. The words of the order must be taken as having their usual meaning and it was not possible that the obligation to pay came to an end, but the order was capable of being revived at a later date by an application to vary. Unless there was a specific direction in the order under the Matrimonial Causes Act 1973 s.28(1A) the order could only be extended beyond the agreed term if the application was made before expiry of the term, *Minton v. Minton* [1979] A.C. 593, [1979] C.L.Y. 766 considered, *T v. T (Financial Provision)* [1988] 1 F.L.R. 480 followed. There was power to make an order to the child as well as to the parent for the child. It was within the bounds of proper exercise of discretion to make an order for costs in W's favour though they should be taxed on a standard, not an indemnity, basis.

G v. G (PERIODICAL PAYMENTS: JURISDICTION TO VARY) [1997] 2 W.L.R. 614, Ward, L.J., CA.

2490. **Financial provision–property adjustment orders–transfer of tenancy–adjournment of possession proceedings**

H and W were joint tenants of property owned by NHT. W gave NHT notice to quit which, following *Hammersmith and Fulham LBC v. Monk* [1992] 1 A.C. 478, [1992] C.L.Y. 2684, was effective to determine the tenancy and NHT began possession proceedings. H then made an application under the Matrimonial Causes Act 1973 s.37 to prevent disposition of a matrimonial asset intended to defeat his claim for financial relief, but the judge refused to order an adjournment of the possession proceedings and made a possession order in favour of NHT. H appealed.

Held, allowing the appeal, that the judge should have considered the merits of H's claim under s.37. A tenancy owned jointly by a husband and wife was a joint matrimonial asset capable of being transferred into the sole name of one of them by an order of the court under s.24(1)(a) of the Act. The possession action by the landlord should have been adjourned pending the outcome of the property adjustment application. It was safe to assume that the notice to quit by W was a disposition which was not made for valuable consideration. It was probable that the court would set aside the notice to quit if H could establish that W had given the notice with the intention of defeating his claim for financial relief, and that the tenancy would be transferred to him if there were no notice to quit.

NEWLON HOUSING TRUST v. AL-SULAIMEN [1997] 1 F.L.R. 914, Nourse, L.J., CA.

2491. Financial provision–property adjustment orders–whether the Law of Property Act 1925 s.30 applied

[Law of Property Act 1925 s.30; Trusts of Land and Appointment of Trustees Act 1996 s.6; Matrimonial Causes Act 1973 s.28(3).]

W applied to have H's action under the Law of Property Act 1925 s.30 struck out on the ground that s.30 had been repealed by the Trusts of Land and Appointment of Trustees Act 1996 of which s.6(6) and s.6(8), when integrated with the Matrimonial Causes Act 1973 s.28(3), combined to bar the application. The parties were divorced by decree absolute on April 7, 1986. H left the matrimonial home on July 12, 1990 before remarrying on September 25, 1990. H then applied for a property adjustment order which the court granted. Court orders were subsequently made forcing the sale of the property, allowing H to have conduct of the sale and dispensing with W's signature. W applied, successfully, for a stay of execution pending appeal on the ground that the Matrimonial Causes Act 1973 s.28(3) precluded H from obtaining a property adjustment order against her due to the fact that he had remarried. Following the appeal, which was allowed, H issued the action which was now in contention.

Held, allowing the application, that H could not rely on the Law of Property Act 1925 s.30 as s.30 no longer exists. Accordingly, H's application was struck out for want of jurisdiction.

FISHER v. FISHER, June 10, 1997, Assistant Recorder Maidment, CC (Bromley). [*Ex rel.* Jean Fisher, litigant in person assisted by Laurence Bothwell].

2492. Financial provision–unquantified school fees–enforcement by judgment summons

[Debtors Act 1869 s.5.]

H was ordered to pay his daughter's termly school fees. The amount of fees was not quantifed. He defaulted and W issued a judgment summons for the arrears. The judge found that there had been default within the meaning of the Debtors Act 1869 s.5 and issued a suspended committal order. H appealed.

Held, dismissing the appeal, that, although the amount was not specified in the order, the payment of school fees could be enforced by judgment summons.

L v. L (SCHOOL FEES: MAINTENANCE: ENFORCEMENT) [1997] 2 F.L.R. 252, Ward, L.J., CA.

2493. Marriage–formalities–void for failure to fulfil requirements of 1949 Act

[Marriage Act 1949 s.49(a).]

The parties were Coptic Orthodox Christians who were married in England in 1993, according to the rites of their church without any of the civil formalities required under the Marriage Act 1949. The church was not registered for marriages, the priest was not authorised by English law to solemnise a marriage, no notice of the marriage had been given to the superintendent registrar, no certificate or licence to marry had been issued and no civil ceremony took place in the register office. The parties, and those attending the ceremony, had assumed this was an ordinary marriage. After the ceremony, the parties cohabited and consummated the marriage prior to their eventual separation. W petitioned for nullity under s.49(a) of the 1949 Act. H denied that there was any marriage at all recognisable to English law.

Held, granting the petition, that the marriage had all the hallmarks of a marriage recognisable to English law, *R. v. Bham* [1966] 1 Q.B. 159, [1965] C.L.Y. 849 considered. The marriage was void for lack of due notice to the registrar.

GEREIS v. YAGOUB [1997] 1 F.L.R. 854, H.H.J. Aglionby, Fam Div.

2494. Marriage-notice to registrar-deregulation

DEREGULATION (VALIDITY OF CIVIL PRELIMINARIES TO MARRIAGE) ORDER 1997, SI 1997 986; made under the Deregulation and Contracting Out Act 1994 s.1, s.2. In force: October 1, 1997; £1.10.

This Order amends the Marriage Act 1949 so that a marriage may be solemnized up to 12 months after entry of notice given to a superintendent registrar in the marriage notice book. The relevant period was previously three months. The extended period of validity of civil preliminaries to marriage does not apply to the marriage of a person who is housebound or detained, or to marriages where one of the parties is resident in Scotland or Northern Ireland. The Order also makes consequential amendments to the provisions on offences relating to solemnization of marriages and transitional provision for notices entered in the marriage notice book prior to the date on which it comes into force.

2495. Matrimonial proceedings

FAMILY PROCEEDINGS COURTS (MATRIMONIAL PROCEEDINGS ETC) (AMENDMENT) RULES 1997, SI 1997 1894 (L.30); made under the Magistrates' Courts Act 1980 s.144. In force: October 1, 1997; £7.35.

These Rules amend the Family Proceedings Courts (Matrimonial Proceedings etc) Rules 1991 (SI 1991 1991), so as to provide for the making of applications under the Family Law Act 1996 Part IV, which relates to family homes and domestic violence, and for the enforcement of orders made under that Part. They also enable magistrates to set an order aside where there has been failure of service.

2496. Non molestation orders-protection of privacy did not justify making of non molestation order

[Family Law Act 1996 s.42.]

An article published after divorce about H's misconduct did not amount to "molestation" meriting the granting of a non molestation order. After the publication in a national newspaper of an article relating to his conduct while married to his former wife, W, the applicant, H, was granted an ex parte order forbidding W from harassing him, in particular by procuring or seeking to procure the publication of any information relating to events occurring during the marriage or any information which might affect the determination of financial issues between the parties. When the matter came before the court inter partes, W argued that the facts of the case did not justify the making of a non molestation order under the Family Law Act 1996 s.42.

Held, refusing H's application for a non molestation order and discharging the ex parte injunction, that the term "molestation" referred to conduct which resulted in a high degree of harassment of the other party, thus meriting the court's intervention. Section 42 came within the part of the Act concerned with domestic violence and the facts of the instant case, involving an article published after the parties' divorce revealing details of H's alleged misconduct and his consequent concern to protect his privacy, did not come within the scope of s.42.

C v. C (NON-MOLESTATATION ORDER: JURISDICTION), *The Times*, December 16, 1997, Sir Stephen Brown, Fam Div.

2497. Practice directions-financial provision-financial dispute resolution in family proceedings

[Family Proceedings Rules 1991 (SI 1991 1247); Family Proceedings (Amendment No.2) Rules 1997 (SI 1997 1056).]

This Practice Direction applies to all ancillary relief applications made under the Family Proceedings Rules 1991 r.2.70 to r.2.77: (1) the new procedure, incorporated into the 1991 Rules by the Family Proceedings (Amendment No.2) Rules 1997, was intended to reduce delay and costs, facilitate settlements and increase the court's control over the conduct of proceedings; (2) an important part of the procedure was the financial dispute resolution appointment, which under r.2.75(1) was to be regarded as a meeting for the purposes of conciliation, the content of which was to be kept confidential. Following *D (Minors) (Conciliation: Disclosure of Information), Re* [1993] Fam. 231, [1993] C.L.Y. 2865, any evidence obtained was inadmissible in any other proceedings except a criminal trial for an offence committed at the appointment or, exceptionally, where an admission related to possible harm to a child's well being; (3) parties would be expected to make offers and proposals, which should be given proper consideration by the recipient; (4) legal representatives attending meetings should be aware of the facts of the case, and (5) *Practice Direction (Ancillary Relief Procedure: Pilot Scheme)* [1996] 2 F.L.R. 368, [1996] 1 C.L.Y. 2894 was now withdrawn.

PRACTICE DIRECTION (FAMILY PROCEEDINGS: FINANCIAL DISPUTE RESOLUTION) [1997] 1 W.L.R. 1069, Sir Stephen Brown, Fam Div.

2498. Registrar General–contracting out of functions–re-registration of birth to add father's name

CONTRACTING OUT (FUNCTIONS OF THE REGISTRAR GENERAL IN RELATION TO AUTHORISING RE-REGISTRATION OF BIRTHS) ORDER 1997, SI 1997 962; made under the Deregulation and Contracting Out Act 1994 s.69, s.77. In force: March 18, 1997; £1.10.

This Order makes provision to enable the Registrar General for England and Wales to authorise another person to exercise his functions in relation to authorising the re-registration of births to add the name of a child's father where the parents are not married, or on legitimation of a child.

2499. Articles

Clean break and term orders: when should the "cut off" apply? *(William Massey)*: S.J. 1997, 141 (9), 204-206. (Circumstances where it is appropriate to order that periodical payments to former spouse be terminated after fixed period and power to restrain recipient from applying for extension to term).

Conran-just des(s)erts? *(Glenn Brasse)*: Fam. Law 1997, 27 (Oct), 684-686. (Courts' approach to treatment of wife's contribution to marriage where parties have substantial wealth).

Divorce, separation and mediation–the Family Law Act 1996 *(Philip Brown)*: L. Ex. 1997, Feb, 18-19. (Provisions on divorce and separation, legal aid for mediation and occupation orders regarding matrimonial home).

Family Law Act 1996: domestic violence provisions *(Victoria Teggin* and *Tracey Payne)*: Legal Action 1997, Aug, 10-12. (Non molestation provisions in Part IV including definition of "molestation", court's discretion in making orders, power of arrest and who may apply for order).

Family Law Act 1996: occupation orders *(Victoria Teggin)* and *(Tracey Payne)*: Legal Action 1997, Sep, 9-11. (Criteria for making orders for occupation of family home or transfer of tenancies following relationship breakdown).

Family partnerships and divorce *(Alastair S. Murrie* and *Edward Magrin)*: N.L.J. 1997, 147 (6778), 176. (Settlement problems on divorce where spouses are also business partners or were declared so for tax purposes and IR procedure for investigating tax evasion allegations).

Harassment and domestic violence *(Timothy Lawson-Cruttenden* and *Neil Addison)*: Fam. Law 1997, 27 (Jun), 429-431. (Main provisions of the Protection from Harassment Act 1997, areas in which it is likely to have greatest impact for practitioners, and its in context of existing domestic violence legislation).

In vitro fertilisation: the moral and legal status of the human pre-embryo *(Deirdre Madden)*: M.L.J.I. 1997, 3 (1), 12-20.

Inequality and family values *(Roger Holmes)*: N.L.J. 1997, 147 (6789), 608-609. (Criticism of changes introduced by the Family Law Act 1996 which give cohabitees, single parents and their children less rights than married persons regarding domestic violence and loss of property on separation).

Life after Dart *(Margaret Bennett)*: Fam. Law 1997, 27(Feb), 79. (Recent cases illustrating court's approach to ancillary relief under the Matrimonial Causes Act 1973 s.25 in big money cases).

Ordering a welfare report *(Ivor E. Weintroub)*: N.L.J. 1997, 147(6796), 880-882. (In family proceedings reports from probation officers, procedures for service and national standards for court officers).

Pre-nuptial agreements *(James Harcus)*: Fam. Law 1997, 27(Oct), 669-672. (History of English courts' approach to marriage settlements, discretionary powers in relation to financial awards under Matrimonial Causes Act 1973 s.25 and cases).

Procedures in family proceedings courts: changes made by the subordinate legislation of 1997-a chronological journey through the new rules of procedure *(Robert Stevens)*: J.P. 1997, 161(38), 891-897. (Applications for non molestation or occupation orders).

Spousal maintenance without loss of income support *(Rory Miln)*: Fam. Law 1997, 27(May), 354-355. Use of Matrimonial Homes Act 1983 s.1(3)(c) to require husband to make payments directly into mortgage account so that wife's income support claim is not affected.

Surrogacy - Warnock and after *(Lynne Foxcroft)*: Med. L. Int. 1997, 2(4), 337-355. (Implementation of Warnock Committee's proposals and growing acceptance by judiciary, Parliament and medical profession of Committee's minority view that commercial surrogacy should be allowed in certain circumstances).

The case for fairer sentencing *(Roger Pearson)*: Lawyer 1997, 11(35), 12. (CA rulings on sentencing for contempt of court in matrimonial proceedings show need for guidelines on sentence length).

The case for split hearings *(Iain M. Hamilton)*: Fam. Law 1997, 27(Jan), 22-25. (Advantages of two-stage hearing approach in care proceedings, where preliminary issues of fact relating to threshold criteria are determined at early stage before court determines what order may be appropriate).

The impasse-an insurmountable obstacle for mediation? *(Christopher Richards)*: Fam. Law 1997, 27(Oct), 689-690. (Options for mediators seeking to resolve impasse between separated couples, with case study of couple unable to resolve question of division of equity in matrimonial home).

The uneven scales of justice: private law contact applications in divorce and adoption *(Murray Ryburn)*: Ad. & Fos. 1997, 21(3), 23-34. (Contrasts exclusive approach adopted by courts on applications for post-adoption contact with inclusive approach adopted in contact applications in divorce and separation, with reference to principles applied).

The wife, the donor husband, fertilisation and the law *(Peter De Cruz)*: P.C.L.B. 1997, 10(3), 31-33. (Background to, and key issues of, High Court and CA judgments on whether widow could receive treatment to enable her to have baby using dead husband's sperm).

Valuing pension rights on divorce *(George Sim)*: S.J. 1997, 141(7), 164-165. (How to assess current capital value of divorcing spouse's income upon retirement, considering basic state pension, SERPS, defined benefit schemes and personal pensions, including role of forensic accountant).

2500. Books

Bracewell, Hon Mrs Justice–Family Court Practice: 1997. Hardback: £99.00. ISBN 0-85308-402-5. Family Law.

Bromley, P.M.–Butterworths Family Law Service. Unbound/looseleaf: £295.00. ISBN 0-406-99260-6. Butterworth Law.

Cretney, S.M.–Family Law. 3rd Ed. Textbooks. Paperback: £18.95. ISBN 0-421-58720-2. Sweet & Maxwell.

De Haas, Margaret; Bispham, Christine–Domestic Injunctions. 2nd Ed. Family Practice. Paperback: £39.00. ISBN 0-421-49860-9. Sweet & Maxwell.

Jackson, Jacqui–Splitting Up Precedents. £75.00. ISBN 0-421-58360-6. Sweet & Maxwell.

Jones, Peter; Hussey, Ann–Advocacy in Family Law Proceedings. Family Practice. Paperback: £39.00. ISBN 0-421-60060-8. Sweet & Maxwell.

Oughton, R.D.; Tyler, E.L.G.–Tyler's Family Provision. Hardback: £65.00. ISBN 0-406-02127-9. Butterworth Law.

Young, James–International Law of the Family. Family Law Library. Hardback: £75.00. ISBN 0-421-48910-3. Sweet & Maxwell.

FINANCE

2501. Building societies–mortgages–discharge of constructive notice of undue influence

See REAL PROPERTY: Bradford and Bingley Building Society v. Chandock. §4240

2502. Debentures–management buyout–settlement agreement–guarantee of overdraft–indemnity–meaning of "future indebtedness"

B appealed against the dismissal of its declaration that W was not entitled to enforce a debenture securing £2.322 million. B totally owned W through a subsidiary company and guaranteed W's indebtedness to its bank. After a management buyout, disputes arose and, in accordance with a settlement agreement, a debenture was granted providing that W would be liable for any monies outstanding up to a maximum of £1 million. When W went into receivership, B was obliged to repay £2.322 million to the bank under its guarantee. W relied on *Johnson v. Diamond* (1855) 11 Ex. 73 to contend that, since it had repaid all sums due under the settlement agreement, there was no "indebtedness" secured by the debenture but merely an indemnity. B contended that W was in breach of two clauses of the settlement agreement and also that, in an action under common law, B could recover money it had paid as a surety from W, the principal debtor.

Held, dismissing the appeal, that the debenture expressly included "future indebtedness", which could include cases where there was an obligation to pay an unliquidated sum in the future, or on the arising of a contingency, and cases where an obligation only arose in the future. In addition the indebtedness was clearly included under the terms of the settlement agreement, *Johnson v. Diamond* distinguished, as referring to a contract to pay an unascertained sum to a third party, and *Flint v. Barnard* (1888) 22 Q.B.D. 90 followed.

BANNER LANE REALISATIONS LTD (IN LIQUIDATION) v. BERISFORD PLC [1997] 1 B.C.L.C. 380, Morritt, L.J., CA.

2503. Financial futures–assets–insolvency of Barings–intercompany claims remain property of administrators

ING appealed against an order that, on the true construction of an agreement, the intercompany claims of its subsidiaries against Barings Futures (Singapore) Pte Ltd, BFS, for losses caused by the unauthorised business transactions of its General Manager, Mr Leeson, were excluded from the assets that ING had acquired. ING contended that "claims" referred only to claims against third parties which had remained with the administrators, and not to intercompany claims which had been transferred to ING because, were it otherwise, the acquisition of the share capital of BFS for nominal consideration by one of ING's subsidiaries would have made no commercial sense. ING further argued that funds had been provided to BFS by its subsidiaries in the "ordinary course of business".

Held, dismissing the appeal, that it was clear that the claims were excluded assets under the agreement and remained the property of the administrators of the subsidiaries. ING may well have wished to acquire BFS despite its hopeless insolvency. The activities conducted by Mr Leeson that had led to the claims were outside the course of business, whether ordinary or otherwise, and the term "claims" should not be subject to such limits, *Newtons of Wembley v. Williams* [1965] 1 Q.B. 560, [1964] C.L.Y. 3288 distinguished as referring to the fraudulent actions of an agent not a principal.

HAMILTON v. INTERNATIONALE NEDERLANDEN GROEP NV, Trans. Ref: CHANF 96/1192/B, November 21, 1996, Leggatt, L.J., CA.

2504. Government securities

GOVERNMENT STOCK (AMENDMENT) REGULATIONS 1997, SI 1997 1709; made under the Finance Act 1942 s.47. In force: September 1, 1997; £1.10.

These Regulations amend the Government Stock Regulations 1965 (SI 1965 1420) in relation to strips of Government stock or bonds and to take into account recent changes in Scottish law relating to legal capacity and age.

2505. Guarantees–submission that letter of guarantee failed to specify interest rate payable–guarantee enforceable as letter contained all the terms

[Statute of Frauds 1677 s.4.]

In 1989, L formed a company known as Brunswick Holdings Ltd, BH, to develop a piece of land. M advanced £105,000 and L was required to provide a guarantee as the beneficial owner of BH. After 1990, no further repayments were made. In 1994, L was called on to discharge the outstanding balance, BH being in no position to pay either capital or interest. Subsequently, M issued a writ, no payments having been made. L was given unconditional leave to defend and pleaded that the guarantee letter did not constitute a sufficient agreement. Judgment was entered for M, in the sum of £133,295 with costs, and leave to appeal refused. L appealed with leave of the Court of Appeal. The question was whether a guarantee was unenforceable because of failure to comply with the Statute of Frauds 1677 s.4. It was submitted that the letter did not specify the rate of interest payable. L had deposed that he had been unaware of the true interest rate until 1994.

Held, dismissing the appeal, that all the terms of the contract of guarantee were to be found in the letter. The words "together with interest thereon" referred to the interest due from BH to M. As a result, L had agreed to guarantee both repayment of the loan and the interest due at the contractual rate payable by BH. The further words "other obligations relating to the said loan" put the matter beyond doubt.

MP SERVICES LTD v. LAWYER (1996) 72 P. & C.R. D49, Nourse, L.J., CA.

2506. Letters of credit–expiry date under UCP 500–automatic time extension

A letter of credit was issued by the defendant bank, NBP, to cover the price of cotton to be shipped and sold. The letter of credit was covered by the terms of UCP 500. The shipping documents were presented to the plaintiffs, BV, who accepted, negotiated and remitted them. The documents were passed to NBP who did not take them up. BV disposed of their interest in the cotton at a price much lower than that of the original contract. BV sought damages from NBP as issuing bank. NBP contended that BV had not provided a statement that the documents had been presented in time further to Art.44 of the Uniform Customs and Practice for Documentary Credits 1993 and that the weight certificates were not in the correct form. BV contended that Art.14 of the UCP 500 precluded NBP from relying on this argument.

Held, awarding BV the damages claimed, that Art.44(a) provided an automatic extension of time where the letter of credit expired on a day when the banks were closed. While Art.44(c) required a statement to be presented to the issuing bank, failure to do so could not be intended to override the automatic extension in Art.44(a). Article 44(c) could not be intended to establish a condition precedent to a confirming bank's reimbursement from the issuing bank. If the issuing bank suffered loss as a result of the failure to comply with Art.44(c), it would be entitled to recover damages. It was unlikely that the issuing bank would refrain from examining documents further to Art.14 because of a failure to deliver a statement for the purposes of Art.44(c). In any event, a failure to make such a statement could not constitute a repudiatory breach. Therefore, NBP were precluded under Art.14 from claiming that the documents were not in compliance with the terms of the credit. BV were entitled to damages on the basis that they had disposed of the goods at a suitable price.

BAYERISCHE VEREINSBANK AG v. NATIONAL BANK OF PAKISTAN [1997] 1 Lloyd's Rep. 59, Mance, J., QBD (Comm Ct).

2507. Loans—contractual exclusion of set off of claim in damages against claim for debt reasonable

[Misrepresentation Act 1967 s.3.]

S lent money to EN under a loan agreement. EN failed to pay four instalments and as a result S was entitled to demand payment of the whole outstanding loan. EN argued that the loan was induced by misrepresentation by S and claimed to be entitled to rescission or damages extinguishing the debt. S applied for summary judgment. It was accepted that if there was an arguable claim for rescission the action would have to go to trial. If EN's claim was limited to one for damages for misrepresentation S argued that EN could not say that it had been induced to enter the loan by the misrepresentation and that the terms of the loan agreement prevented S from setting off any claim that it might have. EN argued that the clause was unreasonable and fell within the terms of the Misrepresentation Act 1967 s.3.

Held, granting summary judgment, that (1) although there was an arguable case that there had been a negligent misrepresentation it could not be said that EN had relied upon the misrepresentation when entering the loan agreement. Even if there had been reliance there was no arguable case for rescission. It was impossible to put the parties back in the position they would have been in if there had been no loan; (2) the clause relating to the set off in the agreement did fall within the 1967 Act s.3. For there to be a set off the plaintiff would have to be under some correlative liability and the clause preventing a set off was a clause that restricted or excluded that liability, *Stewart Gill Ltd v. Horatio Myer & Co Ltd* [1992] 1 Q.B. 600, [1992] C.L.Y. 510 applied, *Society of Lloyd's v. Wilkinson (No.2)* [1997] C.L.C. 1,012, [1997] C.L.Y. 3150 not followed, and (3) the clause was, however, reasonable even though it might have had the effect of preventing a set off where there had been a fraudulent misrepresentation, *Continental Illinois National Bank & Trust Co of Chicago v. Papanicolaou* [1986] 2 Lloyd's Rep. 441, [1987] C.L.Y. 2911 and *Society of Lloyd's v. Wilkinson* supra considered.

SKIPSKREDITTFORENINGEN v. EMPEROR NAVIGATION [1997] 2 B.C.L.C. 398, Mance, J., QBD (Comm Ct).

2508. Loans—remortgage—loan exceeding original mortgage discharge figure— agreement not regulated agreement for purposes of Consumer Credit Act 1974

[Consumer Credit Act 1974 s.11 (3), s.18(1) (a).]

H's home was mortgaged to F and he obtained a remortgage from N in 1989. N advanced the funds to H's solicitor who discharged the mortgage to F and paid the balance to H. The remortgage involved only part payment of the interest in the first three years, the rest being capitalised. H soon got into financial difficulties and switched to a "stabilised rate facility" in 1990 which also involved capitalising interest. N sought to enforce the 1990 agreement. H argued that as part of the 1989 loan was over and above that necessary to discharge his existing mortgage, and was cash for his use, the 1989 agreement was a multiple agreement within the meaning of the Consumer Credit Act 1974 s.18, that the 1989 agreement or part of it was therefore a regulated agreement and unenforceable for want of documentation required under the 1974 Act and that the 1990 agreement was no more than a variation of the 1989 agreement which did not entitle N to overcome the unenforceability of the latter.

Held, giving judgment for N, that (1) the 1990 agreement was not a multiple agreement, the stabilised rate facility, like the agreement as a whole, being a debtor-creditor, restricted use agreement; (2) if not, it was not a multiple agreement because it was unitary and therefore not within s.18(1)(a) of the 1974 Act, and it was not within s.18(1)(b) as if it fell into separate categories one being outside the Act and the other within it; (3) the 1990 agreement was not tainted with any illegality of the 1989 agreement, there being no calculated attempt to cure any illegality, *Spector v. Ageda* [1973] 1 Ch. 30 distinguished; (4) the 1989 agreement was not a multiple agreement as it was a single unrestricted use agreement, and s.11(3) of the 1974 Act therefore applied, and (5) if not, the re-financing element of the 1989 agreement was restricted-use credit under s.11(1)(c), and the remainder was unrestricted-use credit, but the 1989 agreement was still not a multiple agreement because it did not fall within s.18(1)(a) as it was incapable of being split up without altering its essential character, nor within s.18(1)(b) as its terms did not place it within two or more categories of agreement mentioned in the Act. The 1989 agreement was therefore not a regulated agreement.

NATIONAL HOME LOANS CORP PLC v. HANNAH [1997] C.C.L.R. 7, H.H.J. Mellor, CC (Norwich).

2509. Loans–remortgage–solicitors–duty of care to mortgagee–breach of contract

See NEGLIGENCE: National Home Loans Corp Plc v. Giffen Couch & Archer. §3829

2510. Lotteries–winding up–unlawful snowball scheme

See INSOLVENCY: Guardearly Ltd, *Re.* §3098

2511. Articles

A commentary on the recent report by the Financial Law Panel on the secondary debt market *(Martin Hughes)*: B.J.I.B. & F.L. 1997, 12(2), 75-78. (Report entitled *Legal Uncertainties in the Secondary Debt Market*, published January 1997, which reviews market practices and identifies relevant legal issues affecting trading of distressed debt).

A question of standards *(Robert S.K. Bell)*: C.M. 1997, 9(11), 149-150. (European developments including capital adequacy reform, Stability Pact for EMU, CEC roundtable conference for small and medium sized enterprises and banks, and harmonisation of accounting standards).

Action on non status lending: Cons. L. Today 1997, 20(9), 5-6. (Guidelines issued by Office of Fair Trading for lenders and brokers offering secured loans to people with poor credit ratings, including practice on dual interest rates and rebates for early settlement of loans).

Corporate debt–the rules for loss relief *(John Lindsay)*: F.I.T.A.R. 1997, 2(4), 66-68.

Critical issues in project finance documentation in the context of syndicated lending in Central and Eastern Europe *(Marjena Fidalgo-Sokalski)*: O.G.L.T.R. 1997, 15(7), 256-263. (Czech Republic, Hungary and Poland).

Cross-default confusion *(Ebo A. Coleman)*: I.F.L. Rev. 1997, 16(4), 49-52. (Disadvantages of the use of standard cross default clause amendments in derivative contracts and the suggested alternative).

FLP interim report: F.S.B.1997, 8, 1-2. (Summary of Financial Law Panel's report on developments in major projects, including guidance on regulation of credit derivatives and single currency and involvement in progress of Bills developing private finance initiative).

Financing satellite projects–the next generation *(John Worthy)*: I.B.F.L. 1997, 15(9), 101-103. (Different financing options available at various stages of project and ways to manage risks effectively).

Flying when grounded *(Stephen Cirell* and *John Bennett)*: L.G.C. Law & Admin. 1997, 7(May), 8-9. (First in series: statutory base needed to regulate

Private Finance Initiative schemes and prevent problems of rules being established by case law).

Official guides to PFI contract terms *(Michael Matheou)*: C.L. 1997, 15, 62. (Private Finance Panel and Treasury booklets giving contract precedents and discussing how to deal with difficult issues in PFI contracts).

PFI and EC procurement rule—a marriage made in hell?: D.I. Bank. & F.N.1997,19,4-5. (How Public Finance Initiative is impeded by need to comply with EU public procurement rules).

Recent developments in the secondary trading of loans *(Matthew Burgess)*: E.F.S.L. 1997, 4(7/8), 183-188. (Establishment of Loan Market Association, Financial Law Panel paper on uncertainties in secondary debt market and relevant recent cases).

The private finance initiative in the United Kingdom: "Treasury guidance on EC procurement procedure" *(Brian Clark)*: P.P.L.R. 1997, 1, CS28-29. (Guidance on application of procurement regime to PFI projects and practical advice to contracting authorities).

Unlocking capital: factoring and invoice discounting *(John Verrill)*: P.L.C. 1997, 8(2), 31-37. (Two means of receivables financing to generate short term working capital from anticipated future sales receipts and debtor assets, including case on priorities between financier and retention of title holder).

2512. Books

Afterman, Allan B.—US Securities Regulation of Foreign Issuers. Hardback: £148.00. ISBN 90-411-0610-3. Kluwer Law International.

Cirell, Stephen; Bennett, John; Hann, Robert—Private Finance Initiative. Unbound/looseleaf: £215.00. ISBN 0-7520-0474-3. FT Law & Tax.

Cuthbert, Neil—Asset and Project Finance. Unbound/looseleaf: £350.00. ISBN 0-7520-0439-5. FT Law & Tax.

Donohue, Jennifer—Derivatives. Unbound/looseleaf: £350.00. ISBN 0-7520-0259-7. FT Law & Tax.

Edwards, Burt—Credit Management Handbook. Hardback: £55.00. ISBN 0-566-07904-6. Gower Publishing Group.

Hudson, Alastair—Law on Financial Derivatives. 2nd Ed. Hardback: £85.00. ISBN 0-421-61770-5. Sweet & Maxwell.

Newton, Alan—Law and Regulation of Derivatives. Hardback: £85.00. ISBN 0-406-04965-3. Butterworth Law.

Rosenthal, Dennis—Financial Advertising and Marketing Law. Paperback: £75.00. ISBN 0-7520-0331-3. FT Law & Tax.

Suratgar, D.; MacDonald, G.—International Project Finance: Law and Practice. Hardback: £85.00. ISBN 0-85121-836-9. FT Law & Tax.

Tyson-Quah, Kathleen—Cross-border Securities. Special Reports. Hardback: £147.00. ISBN 0-7520-0450-6. FT Law & Tax.

Vinter, Graham—Project Finance. Hardback: £85.00. ISBN 0-421-57530-1. Sweet & Maxwell.

FINANCIAL SERVICES

2513. Building societies—equitable interest in land

BUILDING SOCIETIES (PRESCRIBED EQUITABLE INTERESTS) ORDER 1997, SI 1997 2693; made under the Building Societies Act 1986 s.6A. In force: December 5, 1997; £1.10.

This Order prescribes three types of equitable interest in land for the purposes of the Building Societies Act 1986 s.6A(2): firstly, a leaseholder's right to buy the freehold or a greater leasehold interest; secondly, an easement, profit or similar right which belongs with land; and finally, an interest arising under a contract for the development, primarily for residential purposes, of land which includes a right for the developer to call for the legal estate to be transferred to him or to a third party.

2514. Building societies–members resolutions

BUILDING SOCIETIES (MEMBERS' RESOLUTIONS) ORDER 1997, SI 1997 2840; made under the Building Societies Act 1986 Sch.2 para.32. In force: January 1, 1998; £1.10.

This Order amends the provisions of the Building Societies Act 1986 governing the right of members to propose and circulate resolutions at annual general meetings consequent upon the amendments to that Act made by the Building Societies Act 1997.

2515. Building societies–mortgages–form of receipt

BUILDING SOCIETIES (PRESCRIBED FORM OF RECEIPT) RULES 1997, SI 1997 2869; made under the Building Societies Act 1986 Sch.2A para.3. In force: December 1, 1997; £0.65.

These Rules prescribe the form of receipt to be endorsed on or annexed to a building society mortgage.

2516. Building societies–regulatory authorities–designation

BUILDING SOCIETIES (DESIGNATION OF PRESCRIBED REGULATORY AUTHORITIES) ORDER 1997, SI 1997 2302; made under the Building Societies Act 1986 s.53. In force: November 1, 1997; £0.65.

This Order designates the Occupational Pensions Regulatory Authority as a prescribed regulatory authority to which confidential information may be disclosed under the Building Societies Act 1986 s.53(8). The functions for which, and the circumstances in which, such information and further information may be disclosed are set out and consequential amendments are made to the Building Societies (Designation of Prescribed Regulatory Authorities) Order 1988 (SI 1988 630).

2517. Building societies–subsidiary companies–statutory obligation only applied to liabilities due by date association was severed

[Building Societies Act 1986 s.22; Deregulation (Building Societies) Order 1995 (SI 1995 3233) Art.5.]

Held, that the obligation under the Building Societies Act 1986 s.22 only applied to liabilities which were due by the date on which a company ceased to be a subsidiary of the building society, and not to any existing or future liabilities which could be identified at that date, even where they fell to be discharged after the association had ended. Although s.22 had been repealed by the Deregulation (Building Societies) Order 1995, its effect was retained by Art.5 with regard to any liability arising from an obligation entered into before that date.

GYOURY v. NORTHERN ROCK BUILDING SOCIETY [1997] E.G.C.S. 56, Carnwath, J., Ch D.

2518. Building societies–transfer resolutions–voting rights

BUILDING SOCIETIES (TRANSFER RESOLUTIONS) ORDER 1997, SI 1997 2714; made under the Building Societies Act 1986 s.30, Sch.2. In force: December 5, 1997; £0.65.

This Order amends the Building Societies Act 1986 Sch.2 para.30(2)(b) by increasing the percentage of building society members qualified to vote on a shareholding members' resolution who must have voted on such a resolution for it to be effective in transferring the business of the society to a specially formed company if it is passed, from 20 per cent to 50 per cent.

2519. Building Societies Act 1997 (c.32)

This Act amends the Building Societies Act 1986 in relation to the principal purpose and powers of building societies and accountability to members when acquiring or establishing a business. Provision is also made in relation to the lending limit, the funding limit, raising funds and borrowing, powers to trade in certain investments and powers to create floating charges. Amendments are made to the powers of the Building Societies Commission to direct restructuring of a building society's business, make prohibition orders, petition for winding up, direct transfers of engagements or business and revoke or confirm supplementary directions. Provision is made for amalgamating the Building Societies Investor Protection Board and the Deposit Protection Board into a single board and the Deposit Protection Fund into a single fund.

This Act received Royal Assent on March 21, 1997.

2520. Building Societies Act 1997 (c.32)–Commencement No.1 Order

BUILDING SOCIETIES ACT 1997 (COMMENCEMENT NO.1) ORDER 1997, SI 1997 1307 (C.45); made under the Building Societies Act 1997 s.47. Commencement details: bringing into force various provisions of the Act on May 21, 1997; £0.65.

This Order brings into force on May 21, 1997 the Building Societies Act 1997 Sch.8 para.1 (which contain transitional provisions relating to the alteration of societies' purpose, powers and rules) along with related provisions in s.46.

2521. Building Societies Act 1997 (c.32)–Commencement No.2 Order

BUILDING SOCIETIES ACT 1997 (COMMENCEMENT NO.2) ORDER 1997, SI 1997 1427 (C.53); made under the Building Societies Act 1997 s.47. Commencement details: bringing into force various provisions of the Act on June 9, 1997; £1.10.

This Order brings into force various provisions of the Building Societies Act 1997.

2522. Building Societies Act 1997 (c.32)–Commencement No.3 Order

BUILDING SOCIETIES ACT 1997 (COMMENCEMENT NO.3) ORDER 1997, SI 1997 2668 (C.99); made under the Building Societies Act 1997 s.47. Commencement details: bringing into force various provisions of the Act on December 1, 1997; £2.40.

This Order brings into force those provisions of the Building Societies Act 1997 not already in force.

2523. Building Societies Commission–fees

BUILDING SOCIETIES (GENERAL CHARGE AND FEES) REGULATIONS 1997, SI 1997 740; made under the Building Societies Act 1986 s.2, s.116. In force: April 1, 1997; £1.55.

These Regulations, which revoke and replace the Building Societies (General Charge and Fees) Regulations 1996 (SI 1996 609), provide for a general charge to be paid by authorised building societies towards the expenses of the Building Societies Commission.

2524. Building Societies (Distributions) Act 1997 (c.41)

This Act amends the law in respect of the distribution of assets on the take over or conversion of a building society to protect the interests of beneficiaries in the case of trustee account holders.

This Act received Royal Assent on March 21, 1997 and comes into force on March 21, 1997.

2525. Companies–debt instruments–exemptions from Financial Services Act

FINANCIAL SERVICES ACT 1986 (CORPORATE DEBT EXEMPTION) ORDER 1997, SI 1997 816; made under the Financial Services Act 1986 s.46. In force: April 3, 1997; £0.65.

This Order extends the range of corporate debt instruments which can be the subject of transactions which fall within the Financial Services Act 1986 Sch.5 and therefore benefit from the exemption granted in s.43 of that Act.

2526. Confidential information–financial intermediaries–receipt of confidential information did not create fiduciary relationship between finance house and intermediary–misuse of information caused breach of confidence– damages assessed on contractual not tortious basis

I, an independent financial intermediary, approached A, a provider of financial services, through its parent company to arrange finance for a client, AST. A, having received confidential information relating to the profit margin of I, approached AST directly, offering finance at a reduced rate. I contended that the passing of confidential information created a fiduciary relationship between them and A giving rise to fiduciary obligations. In addition, it was argued that A unlawfully breached the duty of confidentiality owed to I and the court awarded I damages. A appealed.

Held, dismissing the appeal, that while the receipt of confidential information by A did not create a fiduciary relationship between the parties, there was a cause of action in breach of confidence as A misused information provided by I for its own benefit, *Lac Minerals Ltd v. International Corona Resources Ltd* [1990] F.S.R. 441, [1991] C.L.Y. 2189 applied. The breach of confidence, combined with A's conduct, amounted to unlawful means so as to constitute the tort of unlawful interference in the business of I. However, the court was wrong to assess the measure of damages on a contractual rather than tortious basis. Accordingly, a reduction in damages was ordered.

INDATA EQUIPMENT SUPPLIES LTD (T/A AUTOFLEET) v. ACL LTD, *The Times*, August 14, 1997, Otton, L.J., CA.

2527. Data protection–exemptions–Pensions Act consequential amendments

DATA PROTECTION (REGULATION OF FINANCIAL SERVICES ETC) (SUBJECT ACCESS EXEMPTION) (AMENDMENT) ORDER 1997, SI 1997 1060; made under the Data Protection Act 1984 s.30. In force: April 6, 1997; £1.10.

This Order makes amendments to the Data Protection (Regulation of Financial Services etc.) (Subject Access Exemption) Order 1987 (SI 1987 1905) Sch.1 which are consequential upon the implementation of the Pensions Act 1995.

2528. Exemptions–investments

FINANCIAL SERVICES ACT 1986 (MISCELLANEOUS EXEMPTIONS) ORDER 1997, SI 1997 3024; made under the Financial Services Act 1986 s.46. In force: January 19, 1998; £0.65.

This Order provides for certain exemptions from the provisions of the Financial Services Act 1986 which are additional to the exemptions specified in Part I Ch.IV of that Act. It widens the current exemption from the need to be authorised on investment exchanges which have been recognised in accordance with s.36 of the 1986 Act.

2529. Financial Services Act 1986–extension of scope–use of computer based systems

FINANCIAL SERVICES ACT 1986 (EXTENSION OF SCOPE OF ACT) ORDER 1997, SI 1997 2543; made under the Financial Services Act 1986 s.2, s.205A. In force: November 10, 1997; £1.10.

The Order extends the activities that constitute the carrying on of investment business for the purposes of the Financial Services Act 1986 to include certain activities carried on in order to communicate through the computer-based system established under the Stock Transfer Act 1982.

2530. Financial Services Act 1986–restriction of scope

FINANCIAL SERVICES ACT 1986 (RESTRICTION OF SCOPE OF ACT AND MEANING OF COLLECTIVE INVESTMENT SCHEME) ORDER 1997, SI 1997 32; made under the Financial Services Act 1986 s.2, s.75. In force: February 6, 1997; £0.65.

This Order amends references to collective investment scheme in the Financial Services Act 1986.

2531. Friendly societies–insurance business

See INSURANCE. §3116

2532. Gilts–strip securities

GILT STRIPS (CONSEQUENTIAL AMENDMENTS) REGULATIONS 1997, SI 1997 2646; made under the Finance Act 1996 s.202. In force: December 1, 1997; £1.10.

These Regulations modify statutory provisions in consequence of a new type of Government security called a "strip", thus enabling holders of Government securities declared strippable to exchange such securities for a number of different "strip" securities representing different payments remaining to be made under the original security. Such exchanges, and the terms on which strips are issued, will be contractual.

2533. Gilts–transfer of strips

STOCK TRANSFER (GILT-EDGED SECURITIES) (CGO SERVICE) (AMENDMENT) REGULATIONS 1997, SI 1997 1329; made under the Stock Transfer Act 1982 s.3. In force: September 1, 1997; £1.10.

These Regulations amend the Stock Transfer (Gilt-Edged Securities) (CGO Service) Regulations 1985 (SI 1985 1144) to make provision in connection with strips of Government stock or bonds. The amendments enable the Bank of England to effect a transfer of strips through the CGO Service notwithstanding that the registered holder's membership of that Service has been suspended or terminated. In such circumstances, the amendments enable the Bank to effect such a transfer on the instructions of any person whose instructions the Bank would be entitled to accept as sufficient authority to effect a transfer by instrument in writing of the strips (or, if strips are not transferable by instrument in writing, any stock held by the relevant person which would be so transferable).

2534. Investments–advertisements–exemptions

FINANCIAL SERVICES ACT 1986 (INVESTMENT ADVERTISEMENTS) (EXEMPTIONS) ORDER 1997, SI 1997 963; made under the Financial Services Act 1986 s.58, s.205A. In force: June 1, 1997; £1.10.

This Order amends certain provisions of the Financial Services (Investment Advertisements) (Exemptions) Order 1996 (SI 1996 1586) which set out various exemptions from the restrictions on advertising imposed by the Financial Services Act 1986 s.57.

2535. Investments–time sharing–PIA ombudsman–extent of jurisdiction–meaning of "predominant purpose"–court not deciding if it should be interpreted objectively or subjectively

[Financial Services Act 1986 s.75(6)(g).]

B reapplied for judicial review of a decision of the PIAO that he had jurisdiction to consider certain complaints under the Financial Services Act 1986. B sold time shares in Spanish holiday villas and contended that, pursuant to s.75(6)(g), the "predominant purpose" of those contracts was that of holidays and any alternative options to take rental income were subsidiary so that they were not brought under the remit of the 1986 Act. B argued that the decision of the PIAO was not provisional as claimed and that the "predominant purpose" of the scheme under the 1986 Act should have been determined objectively and not on the subjective basis of the participants' understanding.

Held, dismissing the application on the grounds that it was premature, that the PIAO had indeed taken a provisional view of his jurisdiction and moreover had invited B to make submissions, which it had so far declined to do. It was inappropriate in judicial review proceedings for the court to establish whether s.75(6)(g) should be interpreted objectively or subjectively, *Duffield v. Pensions Ombudsman* [1996] Pen. L.R. 286, [1996] 2 C.L.Y. 4652 and *Seifert v. Pensions Ombudsman* [1997] 1 All E.R. 214, [1996] 2 C.L.Y. 4661 distinguished because in those cases an unfavourable view of one of the parties was taken in a provisional opinion which may have tainted the ultimate decision.

R. v. PERSONAL INVESTMENT AUTHORITY OMBUDSMAN, *ex p.* BURNS-ANDERSON INDEPENDENT NETWORK PLC, Trans. Ref: FC3 96/7149/D, January 21, 1997, Auld, L.J., CA.

2536. Investor protection—securities—scheme to sell properties with provision for buy back on cessation of occupation—New Zealand

[Securities Act 1978 (New Zealand).]

C operated a retirement village where houses were offered for sale under an agreement whereby the buyer was obliged to sell back the house on cessation of occupation and C was obliged to buy the house at the original price adjusted by an agreed formula. The Securities Act 1978 (New Zealand) imposed restrictions on the offer of securities to the public and the Registrar of Companies sought to exercise his powers under the Act to inspect C's documents. C refused and in an action by the Registrar the judge held that C was an issuer of debt securities to the public and bound by the Act. The Court of Appeal of New Zealand upheld the decision and C appealed to the Privy Council.

Held, dismissing the appeal, that the Act applied to offers of interests and rights which were securities and the transactions entered into by C were a grant of a right to occupy the property in return for paying the purchase price together with a right to repayment when occupation ceased. The right to repayment was not merely ancillary to the purchase of the interest in land but was fundamental to the agreement. Accordingly C was bound by the Act.

CULVERDEN RETIREMENT VILLAGE LTD v. REGISTRAR OF COMPANIES [1997] A.C. 303, Lord Nicholls of Birkenhead, PC.

2537. Investors Compensation Scheme—home income plans—investors had validly assigned right to sue building society in damages but retained right to seek rescission of mortgage

On the advice of financial advisers, a number of home owners entered into home income plans involving the mortgaging of their homes with W, which caused the investors severe loss when economic conditions deteriorated. The investors claimed compensation from ICS by completing a claim form and ICS brought proceedings against W and numerous law firms involved in the mortgages, whilst some of the investors commenced separate actions against W for rescission of the mortgages and damages. The claim form stated that the investors had assigned absolutely to ICS all third party claims except "any claim (whether sounding in rescission for undue influence or otherwise) that you have against the...society in which you claim an abatement of sums which you would otherwise have to repay to the society...". ICS appealed against a Court of Appeal decision that the investors had not validly assigned their right to sue W in damages to ICS.

Held, allowing the appeal, that on the proper construction of the claim form, particularly in the light of the accompanying explanatory note, it was clear that all claims for damages and compensation by the investors had been validly assigned to ICS, such that the investors were not entitled to maintain their claims against W, but ICS could validly maintain them. The investors retained the right to seek rescission of their mortgages on whatever terms the court saw fit, as the right to seek rescission was not assignable as a chose in action, but was a right which attached to the mortgaged property and could only be enforced by the owner of the property. Similarly, the possibility of an abatement of the debt as part of the process of rescission was not an assignable chose in action, and so did not reduce the scope of the chose in action which had been assigned to ICS. The fact that the quantum of damages recovered by ICS might be affected by whether or not the investors managed to secure rescission of their mortgages did not mean that the investors had tried to assign different remedies in respect of the same chose in action.

INVESTORS COMPENSATION SCHEME LTD v. WEST BROMWICH BUILDING SOCIETY, *The Times*, June 24, 1997, Lord Hoffmann, HL.

2538. Investors Compensation Scheme – liability limited according to date incurred

[Financial Services (Compensation of Investors) Rules 1990 r.1.02; Financial Services Act 1986 s.54.]

In April 1986 T entrusted money to B, an employee of an insurance brokers, who absconded with it. When the misconduct was discovered in 1992, T sought to recover compensation from ICS who dismissed his claim, declaring their liability was limited by the Financial Services (Compensation of Investors) Rules 1990 r.1.02(3). T applied for judicial review of their decision.

Held, dismissing the application, that T was not eligible for compensation as the liability was incurred before December 18, 1986 and there was no duty on the ICS to compensate him. A correct interpretation of the 1990 Rules, as amended in 1991, gave that date as the limit for "civil liability" claims brought under the Financial Services Act 1986 s.54 for compensation payments for misconduct by investment brokers, *Securities and Investments Board v. FIMBRA* [1992] Ch. 268, [1992] C.L.Y. 3737 applied.

R. v. INVESTORS COMPENSATION SCHEME LTD, *ex p.* TAYLOR, *The Times*, December 27, 1996, Staughton, L.J., QBD.

2539. National savings – children's bonus bonds – disclosure of information

SAVINGS CERTIFICATES (CHILDREN'S BONUS BONDS) (AMENDMENT) REGULATIONS 1997, SI 1997 1860; made under the National Debt Act 1972 s.11. In force: August 21, 1997; £0.65.

These Regulations amend the Savings Certificates (Children's Bonus Bonds) Regulations 1991 (SI 1991 1407) to permit the Director of Savings to make arrangements under which information about individual holdings of children's bonus bonds may be disclosed to a person for the purpose of enabling him to provide information about the various investment opportunities, services and facilities available from or through the Director of Savings. The amendment also provides for a person receiving such information to be subject to obligation of secrecy imposed by the Regulations.

2540. National savings – guaranteed income bonds – provisions governing calculation of daily interest rate had to be interpreted so as to give effect to promised annual interest rate

The prospectus and newspaper announcement governing W's guaranteed income bond stated that the interest rate for the first five years would be fixed and guaranteed at seven per cent a year. Under cl.4 of the prospectus, interest was to accumulate on a daily basis at 1/365 of the annual interest rate or at 1/366 in a leap year. The director contended that the reference to a leap year referred solely to a calendar year, which would have resulted in bonds yielding £6,996 if bought on March 5, 1996, when W bought the bond, or £7,003 if bought on March 5, 1995. The adjudicator of national savings held that a leap year under cl.4 meant any period of 12 consecutive months including a leap day, but not necessarily starting on January 1, which would yield £7,000 regardless of whether the bond was bought in 1995 or 1996, amounting to an interest rate of seven per cent per annum. The director appealed.

Held, dismissing the appeal, that where there were two possible constructions of a clause governing the daily interest rate, both producing slightly different yields, the construction producing the promised annual rate was to be preferred. In some circumstances the court could look beyond the ordinary meaning of a word in determining the appropriate construction and examine the meaning in the context of the contract. On that basis, the investment year approach advocated by W was the only construction which yielded an interest rate of seven per cent a year, and was to be preferred to the director's calendar year approach which did not.

DIRECTOR OF SAVINGS v. WOOLF; DIRECTOR OF SAVINGS v. KEAR, *The Times*, July 9, 1997, Cresswell, J., QBD (Comm Ct).

2541. **National savings–savings bonds–disclosure of information**

PREMIUM SAVINGS BONDS (AMENDMENT) REGULATIONS 1997, SI 1997 1862; made under the National Debt Act 1972 s.11. In force: August 21, 1997; £0.65.

These Regulations amend the Premium Savings Bonds Regulations 1972 (SI 1972 765) to permit the Director of Savings to make arrangements under which information about individual holdings of premium savings bonds may be disclosed to a person for the purpose of enabling him to provide information about the various investment opportunities, services or facilities available from or through the Director of Savings. The amendment also provides for a person receiving such information to be subject to the obligation of secrecy imposed by the Regulations.

2542. **National savings–savings certificates–disclosure of information**

SAVINGS CERTIFICATES (AMENDMENT) REGULATIONS 1997, SI 1997 1859; made under the National Debt Act 1972 s.11. In force: August 21, 1997; £0.65.

These Regulations amend the Savings Certificates Regulations 1991 (SI 1991 1031) to permit the Director of Savings to make arrangements under which information about individual holdings of savings certificates may be disclosed to a person for the purpose of enabling him to provide information about the various investment opportunities, services and facilities available from or through the Director of Savings. The amendment also provides for a person receiving such information to be subject to the obligation of secrecy imposed by the Regulations.

2543. **National savings–savings certificates–disclosure of information**

SAVINGS CERTIFICATES (YEARLY PLAN) (AMENDMENT) REGULATIONS 1997, SI 1997 1863; made under the National Debt Act 1972 s.11. In force: August 21, 1997; £0.65.

These Regulations amend the Savings Certificates (Yearly Plan) Regulations 1984 (SI 1984 779) to permit the Director of Savings to make arrangements under which information about individual agreements to purchase yearly plan national savings certificates, or about individual holdings of such certificates, may be disclosed to a person for the purpose of enabling him to provide information about the various investment opportunities, services and facilities available from or through the Director of Savings. The amendment also provides for a person receiving such information to be subject to the obligation of secrecy imposed by the Regulations.

2544. **National savings–savings contracts–disclosure of information**

SAVINGS CONTRACTS (AMENDMENT) REGULATIONS 1997, SI 1997 1858; made under the National Debt Act 1972 s.11. In force: August 21, 1997; £0.65.

These Regulations amend the Savings Contracts Regulations 1969 (SI 1969 1342) to permit the Director of Savings to make arrangements under which information about individual savings contracts may be disclosed to a person for the purpose of enabling him to provide information about the various investment opportunities, services and facilities available from or through the Director of Savings. The amendment also provides for a person receiving such information to be subject to the obligation of secrecy imposed by the Regulations.

2545. National savings–stock register–disclosure of information

NATIONAL SAVINGS STOCK REGISTER (AMENDMENT) REGULATIONS 1997, SI 1997 1864; made under the National Debt Act 1972 s.3. In force: August 21, 1997; £0.65.

These Regulations amend the National Savings Stock Register Regulations 1976 (SI 1976 2012) to permit the Director of Savings to make arrangements under which information about individual holdings of stock held on the register may be disclosed to a person for the purpose of enabling him to provide information about the various investment opportunities, services and facilities available from or through the Director of Savings. The amendment also provides for a person receiving such information to be subject to the obligation of secrecy imposed by the Regulations.

2546. Personal equity plans–Amendment No.1–share transfers

PERSONAL EQUITY PLAN (AMENDMENT) REGULATIONS 1997, SI 1997 511; made under the Income and Corporation Taxes Act 1988 s.333; and the Taxation of Chargeable Gains Act 1992 s.151. In force: March 20, 1997; £1.10.

These Regulations further amend the Personal Equity Plan Regulations 1989 (SI 1989 469 as amended by SI 1990 678, SI 1991 733, SI 1991 2774, SI 1992 623, SI 1993 756, SI 1995 1539, SI 1995 3287, SI 1996 846 and SI 1996 1355). The main effect of the amendments is that members and employees of mutual insurance companies and their wholly-owned subsidiaries, who are entitled to acquire shares on advantageous terms in successor companies, will be able to subscribe to a plan by transferring to it shares which they are entitled to acquire in this way. These Regulations also amend the similar provisions relating to shares in the successor companies of building societies so that former employees of societies and their wholly-owned subsidiaries and their dependents who are pensioners may transfer such shares which they are entitled to acquire on advantageous terms to a plan.

2547. Personal equity plans–Amendment No.2–qualifying investments

PERSONAL EQUITY PLAN (AMENDMENT NO.2) REGULATIONS 1997, SI 1997 1716; made under the Income and Corporation Taxes Act 1988 s.333; and the Taxation of Chargeable Gains Act 1992 s.151. In force: August 8, 1997; £1.95.

These Regulations further amend the Personal Equity Plan Regulations 1989 (SI 1989 469 as amended by SI 1990 678, SI 1991 733, SI 1991 2774, SI 1992 623, SI 1993 756, SI 1995 1539, SI 1995 3287, SI 1996 846, SI 1996 1355, SI 1997 511). The main effect of the amendments is that, on the coming into force of these Regulations, investments in open-ended investment companies (and parts of umbrella companies) will become qualifying investments for general plans under similar conditions as apply to investments in authorised unit trusts. Those conditions have themselves been revised in two main respects. The definitions of "securities fund" and "fund of funds" have been brought more closely in line with those used by the Securities and Investments Board and the investment rules have been changed so that investments may be made in sub-funds of umbrella schemes. The amendments also make a number of minor changes to the principal Regulations mainly to reflect market developments.

2548. Articles

A major disability with money *(Claire Gilham)*: L.G.C. Law & Admin. 1997, 10(Oct), 6-7. (Treatment of disabled people during building society share outs, position of local authority care staff as personal trustees of such accounts and discrimination implications for financial services).

Bad investment advice: the options for elderly victims *(Andrew Pickin)*: E.C.A. 1997, 2(5), 12-14. (Guidance for professional advisers assisting investors to recover losses suffered as result of collapse of financial services business, with reference to Investors Compensation Scheme and Ombudsman procedures).

Building society conversions and mergers *(Charles Maggs)*: L.S.G. 1997, 94(11), 39. (Explanation of statutory provisions in s.97-s.102 regulating building societies' conversion to limited companies and distribution of free shares to account holders, following complaints on operation of "per member" approach).

Claims against financial advisers, accountants and regulators *(John L. Powell)*: E.F.S.L. 1997, 4(2), 41-49. (Civil liability for acts by professionals in financial services industry, standard of care, liability to third parties, damages and importance of common law in regulatory framework).

Conflicts of duty and financial services *(Alistair Alcock)*: E.F.S.L. 1997, 4(4), 123-127. (Whether there is conflict between obligations imposed on financial services firms by regulators and their common law fiduciary duties).

Controlling the quality of financial advice: the use of regulatory form to satisfy fiduciary obligations *(Monica Sah* and *Gordon Cameron)*: J.B.L. 1997, Mar, 143-157. (Interaction between information and standards regulation illustrated by controls on selling of packaged investment products).

Elephants and officers: problems of definition *(Anthony Hofler)*: Co. Law. 1996, 17(9), 258-262. (Defining official persons such as officers, secretaries, managers, directors, auditors, administrators and liquidators for purposes of Companies, Insolvency and Financial Services Acts).

Extension of scope of Financial Services Act 1986 *(William Yonge)*: E.F.S.L. 1997, 4(2), 69-70. (FSA authorisation requirements extended to intermediaries holding custody of other persons' assets including FSA regulated instruments, in force June 1, 1997).

Finance from Europe *(Nicholas Lansman)*: C.S.R. 1997, 20(20), 153-154. (Advice on cross border provision of financial services).

Financial regulatory reform in the UK *(Robert Finney)*: I.B.F.L. 1997, 16(5), 47-50. (Function and organisation of NewRO that will be established as single financial services regulator).

Financial services *(Bryan Wordsworth)*: L.S.G. 1997, 94(6), 30. (Advantages for clients of seeking financial advice from solicitors and qualifications for discrete investment business).

IMRO and SFA: investment business on the Internet *(Denton Hall)*: I.H.L. 1997, 52(Jul/Aug), 44-45. (Guidance to regulated firms on advertising business investment services on Internet and procedures for limiting access).

IMRO's micro-scheme and its macro-philosophy: C.M. 1997, 10(3), 236-237. (Pilot study by IMRO involving continuous assessment of compliance of low risk investment firms which is reflected in bonus payments for individuals).

Identifying the true costs of compliance: a financial institution's perspective *(Richard Collins)*: J.F.R. & C. 1997, 5(1), 11-13. (Minimising direct and indirect costs of complying with financial services regulation).

Is compliance enough? *(Alistair Alcock)*: C.M. 1997, 9(12), 169-171. (Significance for compliance officers of recommendations in *Law Commission's Consultation Paper No.236* on financial services regulation in light of PC decision regarding extent of fiduciary duty).

Looking at customer agreements *(Peter Bibby* and *Adrian Butterworth)*: C.M. 1997, 9(11), 151-152. (General regulatory requirement that a firm issues prescribed customer agreement before providing investment services and specific requirements of agreements issued by firms regulated by IMRO, SFA and PIA).

Making the case for legal compliance audits *(Marcia MacHarg)*: I.F.L. Rev. 1997, 16(4), 9-14. (Use of audits to evaluate investment advisers' practices to ensure adherence to regulatory requirements and avoid misconduct in light of recent compliance failures at established investment management organisations).

New controls for the City *(Noel Branton)*: Co. Acc. 1997, 139, 18-20. (Defects in regulatory framework governing financial services since deregulation and prospects for reform, including expansion of Securities and Investments Board).

NewRO: getting it right *(Dermot Turing* and *Monica Sah)*: B.J.I.B. & F.L. 1997, 12(9), 411-415. (Issues arising from proposed establishment of new regulatory authority governing financial services, banks and insurance market including retail/wholesale divide, legislative structure and harmonisation of rulebooks).

Regulatory requirements for investment ads *(Richard Garmon-Jones)*: C.M. 1997, 9(9), 118. (Financial institutions must issue advertisements in compliance with their particular regulator's conduct of business rules and SIB rules).

Research reports: a disaster waiting to happen?: P.L.C.1997, 8(2), 6-7. (Liability of financial advisers and issuing companies where investors rely on overly optimistic research reports distributed close to new issues by brokers and ways to restrict exposure).

SFA: rule waiver and guidance notices: F.S.B.1997, 3, 5-6. (Board Notices 396 on transfer of registered staff between firms, 397 on auditor's report on verification of interim profits, 399 on future demutualisation of certain institutions and 409 waiving requirements for managing Lloyd's accounts).

SIB guidelines on custody *(Freshfields)*: P.L.C. 1997, 8(4), 73-74. (To help firms involved in the custody of investments to decide if authorisation is needed under 1986 Act which makes custody authorisable activity from June 1, 1997).

Surf's up: compliance and the Internet *(Peter G. Cowap)*: E.F.S.L. 1997, 4(1), 25-26. (Problems of regulating investment opportunities placed online).

The Investment Services Directive—an overview *(Emer Cashin)*: J.I.B.L. 1997, 12(4), 148-152. (Directive giving firms "passports" to do cross border business between Member States, implementing provisions of the Investment Services Regulations 1995, in force January 1, 1996 and impact on UK's financial markets).

The UK model of securities regulation *(Eva Z. Lomnicka* and *Jane Welch)*: E.B.L.R. 1997, 8(2), 35-44. (Regime introduced by 1986 Act, including scope of regulatory system, judicial control of regulators, regulatory methods used, and monitoring, sanctions and enforcement).

The liability of financial advisers in the wake of the pension mis-selling scandal *(Gerard McMeel)*: P.N. 1997, 13(3), 97-102. (Including liability under codes of conduct and at common law).

2549. Books

Fisher; Bewsey—Law of Investor Protection. Hardback: £79.00. ISBN 0-421-54630-1. Sweet & Maxwell.

Rider, B.A.K.; Ashe, Michael—Financial Services Law. Paperback: £21.95. ISBN 0-406-04996-3. Butterworth Law.

Sabalot, Deborah—Butterworths Financial Services Law Guide. Paperback: £65.00. ISBN 0-406-89533-3. Butterworth Law.

Whittaker, Andrew; Mitchell, Philip, L.R.—Financial Services: Law and Practice. Unbound/looseleaf: £475.00. ISBN 0-406-99866-3. Butterworth Law.

Wynne, Geoffrey—Butterworth's Banking Law Guide. Butterworths Guide. Paperback: £60.00. ISBN 0-406-04935-1. Butterworth Law.

FOOD AND DRUGS

2550. Advertising—quantitative restrictions—campaign to promote sale of red meat—"British Meat" logo not influencing consumers to buy British meat

[Treaty of Rome 1957 Art.30.]

MLC was a statutory body with the responsibility of promoting livestock products. It arranged an advertising campaign to promote red meat. The advertisements contained a "British Meat" logo. M was a contract slaughterer liable to pay levies to the MLC. MLC issued proceedings to obtain unpaid levies from M and M disclaimed liability arguing that the campaign was in breach of the Treaty of Rome 1957 Art.30. A preliminary issue was ordered to determine whether the campaign contravened the provisions of Art.30 by effecting quantitative restrictions on imports of meat from other member states.

Held, that there was no breach of Art.30, that the courts would not adopt a more liberal approach to Art.30 when considering agricultural produce than other products. The appropriate test was whether the campaign was designed to emphasise the domestic origin of the meat and persuade buyers to buy it because it was British. The references to "British Meat" were simply a logo to give the campaign cohesion and were insignificant in relation to the references to the qualities of the meat. The advertisements did not influence customers to buy British meat at the expense of meat from other member states.

MEAT AND LIVESTOCK COMMISSION v. MANCHESTER WHOLESALE MEAT & POULTRY MARKET LTD [1997] Eu L.R. 136, Moses, J., QBD.

2551. Food composition—baby foods

PROCESSED CEREAL-BASED FOODS AND BABY FOODS FOR INFANTS AND YOUNG CHILDREN REGULATIONS 1997, SI 1997 2042; made under the Food Safety Act 1990 s.6, s.16, s.17, s.26, s.48. In force: March 31, 1999; £3.20.

These Regulations implement Commission Directive 96/5 ([1996] OJ L49/17) on processed cereal-based foods and baby foods for infants and young children. They exempt from their application any baby food which is a milk intended for young children; prohibit the sale of any processed cereal-based food or baby food unless it complies with the labelling, manufacturing and compositional requirements; provide a defence in relation to exports in accordance with Council Directive 89/397 ([1989] OJ L186/23) on the official control of foodstuffs; and apply various sections of the Food Safety Act 1990 including those relating to enforcement and defences.

2552. Food composition—energy restricted diets—weight loss

FOODS INTENDED FOR USE IN ENERGY RESTRICTED DIETS FOR WEIGHT REDUCTION REGULATIONS 1997, SI 1997 2182; made under the Food Safety Act 1990 s.6, s.16, s.17, s.26, s.48. In force: March 31, 1999; £1.95.

These Regulations implement Commission Directive 96/8 ([1996] OJ L55/22) on foods intended for use in energy-restricted diets for weight reduction.

2553. Food composition—formula baby milk

INFANT FORMULA AND FOLLOW-ON FORMULA (AMENDMENT) REGULATIONS 1997, SI 1997 451; made under the Food Safety Act 1990 s.6, s.16, s.17, s.48. In force: March 31, 1997; £1.55.

These Regulations amend the Infant Formula and Follow-on Formula Regulations 1995 (SI 1995 77) which implemented, inter alia, Commission Directive 91/321 ([1991] OJ L175/35) on infant formulae and follow-on formulae, so as to take account of amendments made to that Directive by Commission Directive 96/4 ([1996] OJ L49/12). The amendments now being made relate to the labelling of infant and follow-on formulae and to compositional criteria. A new Sch.8 relating to reference values for nutrition labelling for foods intended for infants and young children is added.

2554. Food composition-novel food-assessment

NOVEL FOODS AND NOVEL FOOD INGREDIENTS REGULATIONS 1997, SI 1997 1335; made under the Food Safety Act 1990 s.6, s.16, s.17, s.18, s.26, s.48. In force: June 16, 1997; £1.55.

These Regulations provide for the enforcement and execution of certain specified provisions of Council Regulation 258/97 ([1997] OJ L43/1) concerning novel foods and novel food ingredients. In particular they designate the Minister of Agriculture, Fisheries and Food and the Secretary of State for Health to act jointly as the food assessment body in Great Britain for the purposes of the Regulation, appoint food authorities to enforce and execute the provisions of the Regulation and establish penalties for contravening certain provisions.

2555. Food composition-novel food-assessment-fees

NOVEL FOODS AND NOVEL FOOD INGREDIENTS (FEES) REGULATIONS 1997, SI 1997 1336; made under the Finance Act 1973 s.56. In force: June 16, 1997; £1.10.

The Regulations establish a scale of fees to be paid to the Minister of Agriculture, Fisheries and Food when, in accordance with his duties under Council Regulation 258/97 ([1997] OJ L43/1) and the Novel Foods and Novel Food Ingredients Regulations 1997 (SI 1997 1335), he processes requests to assess novel foods and novel food ingredients.

2556. Food safety-additives

MISCELLANEOUS FOOD ADDITIVES (AMENDMENT) REGULATIONS 1997, SI 1997 1413; made under the Food Safety Act 1990 s.6, s.16, s.17, s.26, s.48, Sch.1 para.1. In force: July 1, 1997; £1.55.

These Regulations amend the Miscellaneous Food Additives Regulations 1995 (SI 1995 3187). They implement European Parliament and Council Directive 96/85 ([1996] OJ L86/4) amending Directive 95/2 ([1995] OJ L61/1) on food additives other than colours and sweeteners; implement Commission Directive 96/77 ([1996] OJ L339/1) laying down specific purity criteria on food additives other than colours and sweeteners and make a consequential amendment; clarify the provisions in the 1995 Regulations relating to the use of miscellaneous additives in or on compound foods; add to the list of permitted uses for propane, butane and iso-butane on a temporary basis in accordance with Article 5 of Directive 89/107 ([1989] OJ L40/27); make a few corrections to the 1995 Regulations to reflect provisions in Directive 95/2 ([1995] OJ L61/1); apply specified provisions of the Food Safety Act 1990 for the purposes of the 1995 Regulations; and make a correction to the Fruit Juices and Fruit Nectars Regulations 1977 (SI 1977 927) and the Fruit Juices and Fruit Nectars (Scotland) Regulations 1977 to reflect Article 4(3) of Council Directive 93/77 ([1993] OJ L244/23).

2557. Food safety-additives-sweeteners

SWEETENERS IN FOOD (AMENDMENT) REGULATIONS 1997, SI 1997 814; made under the Food Safety Act 1990 s.6, s.16, s.17, s.26, s.48. In force: April 14, 1997; £3.20.

These Regulations, which implement European Parliament and Council Directive 96/83 ([1997] OJ L48/16) amending Council Directive 94/35 ([1994] OJ L237/3) on sweeteners for use in foodstuffs, amend the Sweeteners in Food Regulations 1995 (SI 1995 3123). They insert a new Reg.5A which relates to compound foods, amend Reg.3(4) so that it applies to food for infants and young children not in good health, amend Reg.11 in relation to sweeteners and food from other Member States and amend Sch.1 by adding a list of permitted sweeteners and the foods in or on which they may be used.

2558. Food safety–animal products–beef bones

BEEF BONES REGULATIONS 1997, SI 1997 2959; made under the Food Safety Act 1990 s.6, s.16, s.26, s.48, Sch.1 para.2, Sch.1 para.3, Sch.1 para.5, Sch.1 para.6. In force: December 16, 1997; £1.55.

These Regulations make provision in relation to bones, bone-in beef and other food and ingredients for human consumption derived from bovine animals aged over six months at slaughter.

2559. Food safety–contaminants–maximum levels

CONTAMINANTS IN FOOD REGULATIONS 1997, SI 1997 1499; made under the Food Safety Act 1990 s.6, s.16, s.17, s.26, s.48. In force: July 4, 1997; £1.10.

These Regulations, which apply to Great Britain, make provision for the enforcement and execution of Commission Regulation 194/97 ([1997] OJ L31/48) setting maximum levels for certain contaminants in foodstuffs.

2560. Food safety–delegation of power to prosecute

See FOOD AND DRUGS: Hilliers Ltd v. Sefton MBC. §2566

2561. Food safety–fish and plants

See AGRICULTURE §175, §176, §177

2562. Food safety–fish and seafood

See AGRICULTURE. §178

2563. Food safety–fish

See AGRICULTURE. §174

2564. Food safety–genetically modified organisms–risk assessment

GENETICALLY MODIFIED ORGANISMS (DELIBERATE RELEASE AND RISK ASSESSMENT -AMENDMENT) REGULATIONS 1997, SI 1997 1900; made under the European Communities Act 1972 s.2; and the Environmental Protection Act 1990 s.108, s.111, s.126. In force: August 25, 1997; £1.10.

These Regulations implement Commission Directive 97/35 ([1997] OJ L169/72) adapting to technical progress for the second time Council Directive 90/220 ([1990] OJ L117/15) on the deliberate release into the environment of genetically modified organisms. They amend the Genetically Modified Organisms (Deliberate Release) Regulations 1992 (SI 1992 3280) by substituting a new Sch.2 regarding information for inclusion in an application for consent to market genetically modified organisms and to take account of Council Regulation 258/97 ([1997] OJ L43/1) concerning novel foods and novel food ingredients with regard to cases and circumstances in which a marketing consent is required. They also amend the Genetically Modified Organisms (Risk Assessment) (Records and Exemptions) Regulations 1996 (SI 1996 1106) to take account of the Novel Foods Regulations with regard to exemptions from the requirement to carry out risk assessment.

2565. Food safety–inspections–fees–EC law

CHARGES FOR INSPECTIONS AND CONTROLS REGULATIONS 1997, SI 1997 2893; made under the European Communities Act 1972 s.2; the Finance Act 1973 s.56; and the Food Safety Act 1990 s.17, s.45, s.48. In force: January 1, 1998; £1.95.

These Regulations give effect to Council Directive 85/73 ([1985] OJ L32/14) Art.2 on the financing of health inspections and controls of fresh meat and poultry meat which requires Member States to ensure that fees are collected to cover the costs of inspections and controls provided for by Council Directive 96/23 ([1996]

OJ L125/10) on measures to monitor certain substances and residues thereof in live animals and animal products. Provisions of the Meat (Hygiene, Inspection and Examinations for Residues) (Charges) Regulations 1995 (SI 1995 361) which relate to the subject matter of these Regulations are revoked.

2566. Food safety–local authority delegation of power to prosecute–due diligence defence

[Local Government Act 1972 s.101; Police and Criminal Evidence Act 1984.]

H appealed by way of case stated against a conviction pursuant to the Food Safety Act 1990 after a customer purchased a steak and kidney pie containing a metal bolt. H contended that (1) S had no authority to prosecute the offence and if they did it was authority only to prosecute the company secretary of H, and (2) that because H had the burden of proving a defence of due diligence, then the normal rule should be modified to allow an indefinite stay of proceedings, since it had been an abuse of process for S to have laid its information on the last day of the six month period allowed.

Held, dismissing the appeal, that (1) S was authorised by the Local Government Act 1972 s.101 to delegate any function to an officer and the Chief Officer had been authorised to delegate duties to another person by the standing orders, and (2) H had failed to apply to exclude the evidence of the presence of the bolt under the Police and Criminal Evidence Act 1984 on the basis that the lack of a wrapper disclosing the use by date had prejudiced its due diligence defence. The submission of abuse of process had no chance of success, *Attorney General's Reference (No.1 of 1990), Re* [1992] 3 All E.R. 169, [1992] C.L.Y. 615 considered.

HILLIERS LTD v. SEFTON MBC, Trans. Ref: CO 2165-96, November 29, 1996, Schiemann, L.J., QBD.

2567. Food safety–paralytic shellfish poisoning

See AGRICULTURE §179, §180

2568. Food safety–premises–registration

FOOD PREMISES (REGISTRATION) AMENDMENT REGULATIONS 1997, SI 1997 723; made under the Food Safety Act 1990 s.19, s.48. In force: April 7, 1997; £1.10.

These Regulations amend the Food Premises (Registration) Regulations 1991 (SI 1991 2825) by inserting into them a new category of domestic premises which need not be registered as food business premises under those Regulations.

2569. Imports

IMPORTED FOOD REGULATIONS 1997, SI 1997 2537; made under the Food Safety Act 1990 s.6, s.16, s.17, s.18, s.26, s.48. In force: November 17, 1997; £2.40.

These Regulations contain measures relating to the control of certain types of food imported into Great Britain which are not in free circulation within the European Community. They replace the general provisions of the Imported Food Regulations 1984 (SI 1984 1918) and the Imported Food (Scotland) Regulations 1985 (SI 1985 913) with a new set of provisions, which apply to the whole of Great Britain, for all food other than specified exempt products of animal origin. They also contain amendments to the Food Safety (General Food Hygiene) Regulations 1995 (SI 1995 1763) which implement Commission Directive 96/3 ([1996] OJ L21/42) which grants a derogation from certain provisions of Council Directive 93/43 ([1993] OJ L175/1) on the hygiene of foodstuffs.

2570. Imports–emergency controls–pistachios from Iran

FOOD (PISTACHIOS FROM IRAN) (EMERGENCY CONTROL) ORDER 1997, SI 1997 2238; made under the Food Safety Act 1990 s.6, s.13, s.48. In force: September 16, 1997; £1.10.

This Order prohibits the importation of pistachios originating in or consigned from Iran and implements Commission Decision 97/613 ([1997] OJ L248/33) on the temporary suspension of imports of pistachios and certain products derived from pistachios in or consigned from Iran.

2571. Imports–emergency controls–pistachios from Iran

FOOD (PISTACHIOS FROM IRAN) (EMERGENCY CONTROL) (AMENDMENT) ORDER 1997, SI 1997 3046; made under the Food Safety Act 1990 s.6, s.13, s.48. In force: December 23, 1997; £0.65.

This Order amends the Food (Pistachios from Iran) (Emergency Control) Order 1997 (SI 1997 2238) by exempting from the prohibition on imports of pistachios, imports in accordance with Commission Decision 97/830 ([1997] OJ L343/30) Art.2 imposing special conditions on the import of pistachios and certain products derived from pistachios originating in or consigned from Iran.

2572. Articles

Codex Alimentarius–in the consumer interest? *(Diane McCrea)*: C.P.R. 1997, 7 (4), 132-138. (Role, structure and procedures of the Codex Alimentarius Commision, which establishes and promotes international food standards, and failure to facilitate full consumer participation).

Evidence required to prove food is unfit for consumption *(Katharine Thompson)*: J.P. 1997, 161 (18), 431-432. (Level of proof required to convict food supplier of offence).

Food law enforcement *(Mike Hanson)*: Adviser 1997, 63, 43-45. (Statutory framework for food safety, enforcement through Trading Standards Service and current concerns of Service).

Food safety fears prompt major Brussels shake-up: N.R. EU Init. 1997, Apr, 6-7. (Plans to separate role of legislator from role of enforcer of food safety law within CEC).

Genetic engineering: public concern outstrips labelling law: B.L.E. 1997, 97 (6), 3-4. (EU Regulations on labelling of products containing genetically modified organisms).

2573. Books

Jukes, David J.–Food Legislation of the UK: a Concise Guide. Paperback: £19.99. ISBN 0-7506-3385-9. Butterworth-Heinemann.

Painter, Anthony A.; Harvey, Brian W.–Butterworths Law of Food and Drugs. Unbound/looseleaf: £635.00. ISBN 0-406-99647-4. Butterworth Law.

Schneid, T.D.; Schumann, B.R.–Food Safety Law. Hardback: £52.50. ISBN 0-442-02216-6. VNR-Sax (Chapman & Hall).

FORESTRY

2574. Grants–farm woodland

FARM WOODLAND PREMIUM SCHEME 1997, SI 1997 829; made under the Farm Land and Rural Development Act 1988 s.2. In force: April 1, 1997; £3.20.

This Scheme, which applies to Great Britain, provides for the payment of annual grants to abate financial losses incurred in consequence of the conversion of agricultural land (including, in Scotland, common grazings) to use for woodlands and complies with Council Regulation 2080/92 ([1992] OJ L215/96) instituting a Community aid scheme for forestry measures in agriculture.

Provision is made for applications for grants in respect of eligible land to be made by occupiers of agricultural land carrying on agricultural businesses, and by grazings constables and grazings committees in respect of common grazings in Scotland. The Scheme also excludes certain categories of land; imposes on Scheme participants maximum and minimum limits in relation to the amount of land which may be converted to woodlands; classifies eligible land types; specifies the duration of payments and rates of grant according to the category of woodlands and the type of land from which they were converted; provides for the imposition of limits on the number of applications or approvals during any specified period of Scheme; permits participants to vary their plans with the consent of the appropriate Minister; provides for the withholding or recovery of grants and termination of participation in cases of false statements, failure to observe requirements or excess of area limits; and requires participants to allow entry onto and inspection of their land by persons duly appointed by the appropriate Minister, for the purposes of verifying accuracy of particulars and ensuring compliance with requirements. The Scheme supersedes and amends the Farm Woodland Premium Scheme 1992 (SI 1992 905).

2575. Grants–farm woodland

FARM WOODLAND (AMENDMENT) SCHEME 1997, SI 1997 828; made under the Farm Land and Rural Development Act 1988 s.2. In force: April 1, 1997; £1.10.

This Scheme applies to Great Britain and amends the Farm Woodland Scheme 1988 (SI 1988 1291) which complies with Council Regulation 2080/92 ([1992] OJ L215/96) instituting a Community aid scheme for forestry measures in agriculture. This Scheme removes the requirement for participants in the scheme to continue to run an agricultural business, and for successors to initial entrants to run an agricultural business as well as amending the rates of grant payable according to the use of the land prior to conversion to woodland.

2576. Plant health–Forestry Commissioners–fees

PLANT HEALTH (FEES) (FORESTRY) (GREAT BRITAIN) (AMENDMENT) REGULATIONS 1997, SI 1997 655; made under the European Communities Act 1972 s.2. In force: April 1, 1997; £1.10.

These Regulations amend the Plant Health (Fees) (Forestry) (Great Britain) Regulations 1996 (SI 1996 2291) by adding a further Schedule of services provided by the Forestry Commissioners for which a prescribed fee shall be payable. The services relate to the inspection of imports of certain forestry material from third countries and to the carrying out or supervision of any remedial work arising from such inspections and are provided in accordance with the requirements of Council Directive 77/93 ([1977] OJ L26/20) on protective measures against the introduction into the Community of organisms harmful to plants or plant products and against their spread within the Community.

GOVERNMENT ADMINISTRATION

2577. Appropriation Act 1997 (c.31)

This Act applies a sum out of the Consolidated Fund for the year ending March 31, 1998 and appropriates the supplies granted in this Parliamentary session.

This Act received Royal Assent on March 21, 1997 and comes into force on March 21, 1997.

2578. Appropriation (No.2) Act 1997 (c.57)

An Act granting the sum of £66,285,000 to be issued out of the Consolidated Fund of the United Kingdom for the service of the year ending on March 31, 1997. This Act received Royal Assent on July 31, 1997 and comes into force on July 31, 1997.

2579. Consolidated Fund Act 1997 (c.15)

This Act applies certain sums out of the Consolidated Fund to the service of the years ending on March 31, 1996 and 1997.
This Act received Royal Assent on March 19, 1997 and comes into force on March 19, 1997.

2580. Consolidated Fund (No.2) Act 1997 (c.67)

This Act applies certain sums out of the Consolidated Fund to the service of the years ending on March 31, 1998 and 1999.
This Act received Royal Assent on December 17, 1997.

2581. Crown agents–successor companies–transfer of assets

CROWN AGENTS ACT 1995 (SUCCESSOR COMPANY) ORDER 1997, SI 1997 1140; made under the Crown Agents Act 1995 s.1. In force: March 20, 1997; £0.65.
The Crown Agents Act 1995 s.1 (1) provides that on such day as the Secretary of State may appoint, all property, rights and liabilities to which the Crown Agents for Overseas Governments and Administrations were entitled or subject immediately before that day shall become property, rights and liabilities of a company nominated for the purposes of the section by the Secretary of State. The Act provides that the Secretary of State may, after consulting the Crown Agents, nominate for the purposes of s.1 of that Act any company formed and registered under the Companies Act 1985, but on the appointed day the company in question must be a company limited by shares and wholly owned by the Crown. The Order nominates as the successor company the Crown Agents for Overseas Governments and Administrations Ltd, a company limited by shares and wholly owned by the Crown.

2582. Crown Agents Act 1995 (c.24)–Appointed Day Order

CROWN AGENTS ACT 1995 (APPOINTED DAY) ORDER 1997, SI 1997 1139 (C.41); made under the Crown Agents Act 1995 s.1. Commencement details: bringing into force various provisions of the Act on March 21, 1997; £0.65.
The Crown Agents Act 1995 s.1 (1) provides for the property, rights and liabilities of the Crown Agents for Overseas Governments and Administrations to be transferred to a nominated company on a day to be appointed. This Order appoints March 21, 1997 as that day.

2583. Government departments–trading funds–Driving Standards Agency

DRIVING STANDARDS AGENCY TRADING FUND ORDER 1997, SI 1997 873; made under the Government Trading Funds Act 1973 s.1, s.2, s.2A, s.2C. In force: in accordance with Art.1; £1.10.
This Order provides for the setting up as from April 1, 1997 of a fund with public money under the Government Trading Funds Act 1973 for the operations of the Driving Standards Agency. It designates the Secretary of State for Transport as the authorised lender to the fund, specifies the assets (estimated at £23,320,000) and liabilities (estimated at £17,254,000) which are to be appropriated to the fund and also provides that the maximum borrowing is not to exceed £30,000,000.

2584. Government departments–trading funds–Hydrographic Office

HYDROGRAPHIC OFFICE TRADING FUND (VARIATION) ORDER 1997, SI 1997 1428; made under the Government Trading Funds Act 1973 s.1, s.2A, s.2AA, s.6. In force: July 1, 1997; £0.65.

The Hydrographic Office Trading Fund was established by the Hydrographic Office Trading Fund Order 1996 (SI 1996 773) with effect from April 1, 1996. At the time of the establishment of the fund a final valuation of the assets and liabilities as at April 1, 1996 appropriated to the Fund by the Order had not been carried out and the amount of the revaluation reserve and the public dividend capital were based on an estimated valuation. As a consequence of the subsequent final valuation this Order varies the 1996 Order by substituting an amount of £264,807 for the revaluation reserve and £13,266,833 for the public dividend capital. These amounts represent 0.97 per cent and 49.5 per cent respectively of the amounts by which the value of the assets exceed the amounts of the liabilities and replace amounts of 5.1 per cent and 47.3 per cent respectively.

2585. Government departments–trading funds–Queen Elizabeth II Conference Centre

QUEEN ELIZABETH II CONFERENCE CENTRE TRADING FUND ORDER 1997, SI 1997 933; made under the Government Trading Funds Act 1973 s.1, s.2, s.2A, s.2B, s.2C, s.6. In force: April 1, 1997; £1.10.

This Order provides for the setting up of a fund with public money under the Government Trading Funds Act 1973 for the Queen Elizabeth II Conference Centre and designates the Secretary of State as the authorised lender to the fund. It also specifies the assets (estimated at £4,200,000) and liabilities (estimated at £1,700,000) which are to be appropriated to the fund, and provides that the maximum borrowing is not to exceed £2,000,000.

2586. Ministerial and Other Salaries Act 1997 (c.62)

This Act provides for the alteration of salaries payable under the Ministerial and Other Salaries Act 1975 by introducing a formula which will increase salaries by the average percentage by which the mid-points of the Senior Civil Service bands are increased from April 1, 1998. In addition, an Order may change the annual amount of a salary or provide that the amount of salary may be calculated by reference to another amount or a replacement formula.

This Act received Royal Assent on November 6, 1997.

2587. Ministerial responsibility–transfer

SECRETARY OF STATE FOR THE ENVIRONMENT, TRANSPORT AND THE REGIONS ORDER 1997, SI 1997 2971; made under the Ministers of the Crown Act 1975 s.1, s.2. In force: January 26, 1998; £2.40.

This Order relates to the incorporation of the Secretary of State for the Environment, Transport and the Regions as a corporation sole and transfers certain functions, property, rights and liabilities of the Secretary of State for the Environment and the Secretary of State for Transport to the new body. Consequential amendments are made to the Transport Act 1962, the Parliamentary Commissioner Act 1967, the Transport Act 1968, the Courts Act 1971, the Fair Trading Act 1973, the Road Traffic Regulation Act 1984, the Airports Act 1986, the Road Traffic Act 1988, the Town and Country Planning Act 1990, the Planning (Listed Buildings and Conservation Areas) Act 1990, the Planning (Hazardous Substances) Act 1990, the Water Resources Act 1991, the Land Drainage Act 1991, the Transport and Works Act 1992, the Goods Vehicles (Licensing of Operators) Act 1995, the Channel Tunnel Rail Link Act 1996 and the Town and Country Planning (Scotland) Act 1997.

2588. Secretaries of State–Secretary of State for International Development– transfer of functions

TRANSFER OF FUNCTIONS (INTERNATIONAL DEVELOPMENT) ORDER 1997, SI 1997 1749; made under the Ministers of the Crown Act 1975 s.1, s.2. In force: August 22, 1997; £1.10.

This Order transfers to the Secretary of State for International Development functions of the Secretary of State for Foreign and Commonwealth Affairs under certain Royal Charters and in relation to certain companies; transfers to the Secretary of State for International Development certain property, rights and liabilities to which the Secretary of State for Foreign and Commonwealth Affairs is entitled or subject at the coming into force of the Order in connection with functions relating to international development; makes provision consequential upon the re-allocation of such functions and the transfer of such property, rights and liabilities; constitutes the Secretary of State for International Development and her successors a corporation sole with a common seal; and amends the Parliamentary Commissioner Act 1967 Sch.2 by adding the Department for International Development.

2589. Secretaries of State–Secretary of State for National Heritage–change of name–Secretary of State for Culture, Media and Sport

SECRETARY OF STATE FOR CULTURE, MEDIA AND SPORT ORDER 1997, SI 1997 1744; made under the Ministers of the Crown Act 1975 s.4. In force: August 22, 1997; £1.10.

This Order makes provision for the change in the title of the Secretary of State for National Heritage, now the Secretary of State for Culture, Media and Sport.

HEALTH

2590. Doctors–delegation of supply of drugs to patient

See MEDICINE: R. v. Family Health Service Appeal Authority, *ex p.* Elmfield Drugs Ltd. §3617

2591. Doctors–supply of drugs to addicts–notification of addicts

MISUSE OF DRUGS (SUPPLY TO ADDICTS) REGULATIONS 1997, SI 1997 1001; made under the Misuse of Drugs Act 1971 s.10, s.22, s.31. In force: May 1, 1997; £1.10.

These Regulations revoke that part of the Misuse of Drugs (Notification of and Supply of Addicts) Regulations 1973 (SI 1973 799) dealing with notification of addicts and re-enact that part of those Regulations dealing with supply to addicts with drafting amendments only. Doctors will no longer be required to send to the Home Office particulars of persons whom they consider to be addicted to the controlled drugs specified in the Schedule. The prohibition on doctors supplying or prescribing cocaine, diamorphine (commonly known as heroin) and dipipanone for such persons except under licence of the Secretary of State or in certain cases for medical treatment is re-enacted.

2592. Health authorities–membership and procedure

HEALTH AUTHORITIES (MEMBERSHIP AND PROCEDURE) AMENDMENT REGULATIONS 1997, SI 1997 2991; made under the National Health Service Act 1977 s.126, s.128, Sch.5 para.12. In force: January 6, 1998; £1.55.

These Regulations make amendments to the Health Authorities (Membership and Procedure) Regulations 1996 (SI 1996 707) concerning the membership and procedure of Health Authorities and certain Special Health Authorities.

2593. Medical treatment–application of non resuscitation policy–cerebral palsy patient–not in best interests of patient to resuscitate if suffered cardiac arrest

R, aged 23, was born with a serious malformation of the brain and cerebral palsy. He suffered from, inter alia, severe epilepsy, profound learning disabilities, and was probably blind and deaf. Since he turned 17 he had lived at a NHS trust residential home. In 1995 R was admitted to hospital on five occasions and after the last of these admissions Dr S, R's consultant psychiatrist, concluded that in her opinion it would be in R's best interests to allow nature to take its course the next time he experienced a life threatening crisis and allow him to die with dignity and comfort. Dr S discussed the situation with R's parents and they agreed that should he suffer a life threatening situation involving a cardiac arrest he should not be subjected to cardiopulmonary resuscitation. A Do Not Resuscitate, DNR, notice was signed to this effect. Members of staff at the residential home became concerned when they learned of the existence of the notice, and subsequently sought leave to apply for judicial review of the decision to apply the DNR policy to R. The trust issued an originating summons seeking a declaration that the application of the policy to R was lawful. The application for judicial review was adjourned pending the disposal of the originating summons.

Held, that the application of the DNR policy to R was lawful. The principle of law to be applied in this case, where the court is concerned with circumstances in which steps should not be taken to prolong life, is that of the "best interests of the patient", *J, Re* [1991] Fam.33 applied. The correct approach is to judge the quality of life which R would have to endure given the treatment and decide whether in all the circumstances such a life would be so afflicted as to be intolerable. The extensive medical evidence in this case was unanimous in concluding that it would not be in the best interests of R to subject him to cardiopulmonary resuscitation in the event of his suffering a cardiac arrest. A declaration would be made in terms which would not require a future further application to the Court, *Airedale NHS Trust v. Bland* [1993] A.C. 789, [1993] C.L.Y. 2712 considered.

SOUTH BUCKINGHAMSHIRE NHS TRUST v. R (A PATIENT) [1996] 7 Med. L.R. 401, Sir Stephen Brown, Fam Div.

2594. Medical treatment–consent–caesarean section–capacity–competent mother could refuse caesarean section even where her own death or death or handicap of baby could result–capacity could be eroded by fear of needles

Following a medical examination, MB, who was pregnant, was informed that a caesarean delivery might be required. She consented to the operation but then refused to be given anaesthesia by injection because she had a phobia of needles. When MB went into labour, the hospital treating her obtained a declaration that it would be lawful for doctors, if they deemed it necessary, to perform a caesarean section upon her, which could include the use of needles to administer anaesthesia, because she was incapable of consenting to or refusing treatment, [1997] 1 F.C.R. 609. MB appealed.

Held, dismissing the appeal, that in general it was an assault, both in criminal law and tort, to perform physically invasive medical treatment where the patient did not give consent. There was a rebuttable presumption that all patients had the capacity to consent to or refuse treatment and a competent woman with such capacity could refuse treatment even where that might lead to the death or serious handicap of the baby or to her own death. A person did not have capacity where an impairment of mental functioning made him unable to decide whether consent should be given, and temporary factors, including panic brought on by fear, could completely erode capacity. Applying those principles, MB temporarily lacked capacity because of her fear of needles and therefore the doctors were entitled to administer the anaesthetic in an emergency if it was in MB's best interests to do so. The best interests of the patient were not limited to medical matters and it was obvious that MB was more likely to suffer significant long-term harm from death or injury to the baby than from the giving of the anaesthetic.

MB (CAESAREAN SECTION), *Re*; *sub nom.* L (PATIENT: NON-CONSENSUAL TREATMENT), *Re* [1997] 2 F.C.R. 541, Butler-Sloss, L.J., CA.

2595. Medical treatment–consent–caesarean section–patient could not evaluate information whilst in throes of labour

C was in labour in hospital. The consultant obstetrician was of the opinion that a caesarean section was necessary, but C refused to give consent, having had a previous caesarean, after which she had suffered from back ache and pain in the scar area, saying that she would rather die than undergo the same procedure again. An urgent application was made to the court to authorise treatment. The patient was fully competent mentally and capable of comprehending and retaining information about the proposed treatment and of believing that information.

Held, authorising treatment, that C was in the throes of labour with all the pain and emotional stress that involved. A patient who in those circumstances appeared able to accept the inevitability of her own death was therefore not capable of giving full consideration to the options available. Applying the reasons given in *Norfolk and Norwich Healthcare NHS Trust v. W* [1997] 1 F.C.R. 269, [1997] C.L.Y. 2596 it would be in the best interests of the patient for the operation to be performed.

ROCHDALE HEALTHCARE NHS TRUST v. C [1997] 1 F.C.R. 274, Johnson, J., Fam Div.

2596. Medical treatment–consent–caesarean section–patient not mentally ill but not capable of understanding

W, who had a history of psychiatric treatment, arrived at hospital ready to deliver her baby but in a state of arrested labour and denying that she was pregnant. The health authority sought to bring the labour to an end either by forceps delivery or by caesarean section, since otherwise the foetus would suffocate inside the patient with life threatening consequences for her, and her old caesarean scars could reopen with consequent risk to the life of the foetus and the health of the patient. In the opinion of a consultant psychiatrist, W was not suffering from any mental disorder. However, he was unable to ascertain whether she was incapable of comprehending and retaining information about the proposed treatment or of believing information about the treatment. He believed that she could not balance the information given to her.

Held, authorising treatment, that W lacked the mental competence to make a decision about the treatment proposed because she was incapable of weighing up the considerations involved. Termination of the labour was in her best interests for the above medical reasons. The situation was one where there was a necessity to act in the manner of a reasonable person, taking into account the best interests of the patient, and the court had power at common law to authorise treatment.

NORFOLK AND NORWICH HEALTHCARE NHS TRUST v. W [1996] 2 F.L.R. 613, Johnson, J., Fam Div.

2597. Medical treatment–consent–mentally handicapped prospective donor unable to give valid consent

Y, an adult mentally and physically handicapped from birth, lived in a community home. She had lived until she was 10 with her parents and sisters in a close-knit family, and had since been regularly visited by them. Her mother's health was precarious and her older sister, P, suffered from pre-leukaemic bone marrow disorder. P's only realistic prospect of recovery was a bone marrow transplant from a healthy compatible donor. By reason of her disabilities, Y was unaware of

P's disabilities and unable to consent to the operations required for a donation. P applied for declarations that they were lawful nonetheless.

Held, granting the declarations, that the operations were in Y's best interests as they would tend to prolong the life of both P and the mother, and Y would receive emotional, psychological and social benefit with minimal detriment, *F (Mental Patient: Sterilisation)*, *Re* [1990] 2 A.C. 1, [1989] C.L.Y. 3044 considered.

Y (MENTAL PATIENT: BONE MARROW DONATION), *Re*; *sub nom.* Y (MENTAL INCAPACITY: BONE MARROW TRANSPLANT), RE; Y (ADULT PATIENT) (TRANSPLANT: BONE MARROW), *Re* [1997] 2 W.L.R. 556, Connell, J., Fam Div.

2598. **Medical treatment–consent–no consent required for injection of anaesthetic where patient had needles phobia**

A declaration was sought on the lawfulness of anaesthetising L by means of injection before her child was delivered by emergency operation. L was unable to consent to the procedure due to an extreme phobia against needles.

Held, making the declaration, that medical treatment could be lawfully administered to save life where a patient was incapable of communicating a decision due to an absence of mental competence, *Tameside and Glossop Acute Services NHS Trust v. CH (A Patient)* [1996] 1 F.L.R. 762, [1996] 1 C.L.Y. 2979 followed. In the instant case, where it was highly inadvisable for anaesthetic to be given in any other way and L's fear put her own life and that of her child at risk, her phobia was such that it deprived her of the mental competence to make a decision on treatment. It was in L's best interests that she should receive the treatment advised by her doctors.

L (PATIENT: NON-CONSENSUAL TREATMENT), *Re*; *sub nom.* L (AN ADULT: NON-CONSENSUAL TREATMENT), RE; MB (CAESAREAN SECTION), *Re* [1997] 1 F.C.R. 609, Kirkwood, J., Fam Div.

2599. **Medical treatment–consent–patient not competent to give consent–young person–child's best interests–use of reasonable force–maternity ward amounting to secure accommodation**

[Children Act 1989 s.25(1).]

DB was a 17 year old pregnant crack cocaine addict. She suffered from pre-eclampsia but refused medical examinations and threatened to discharge herself. A caesarean section was performed after which the local authority applied to the High Court and was granted orders for the patient to undergo such treatment as was necessary to recover from the caesarean, inter alia, whether or not she consented and for leave to transfer her to hospital since she needed further treatment for her pre-eclamptic condition, which could be fatal if left untreated. The local authority applied for leave to place DB in secure accommodation, namely the maternity ward of the hospital and for the order for medical treatment to continue. DB argued that the maternity ward was not secure accommodation and that the order should be amended to delete the provision that reasonable force could be used to administer treatment.

Held, allowing the application, that the patient was not competent to give consent to the medical treatment in that she neither comprehended nor retained information so as to be able to make a balanced choice. The salient feature of secure accommodation was the restriction imposed on liberty. A place did not have to be so designated and each case would turn on its facts, which, in this case, could encompass the maternity ward. DB came within the provisions of the Children Act 1989 s.25(1)(b), because if she left hospital, she would be likely to suffer injury. The local authority had parental responsibility under a case order to take steps to protect DB's child's best interests. These could include the use of reasonable force to impose necessary medical treatment should a life threatening situation arise, or where a serious deterioration of health could occur in the absence of appropriate treatment.

A METROPOLITAN BOROUGH COUNCIL v. DB [1997] 1 F.L.R. 767, Cazalet, J., Fam Div.

2600. Medical treatment–consent–refusal to give consent–compulsory detention as mental patient–issues of public importance

[Mental Health Act 1983 s.2.]

S suffered acute pre-eclampsia in her eighth month of pregnancy which endangered her own life and that of her unborn child, but, having an intense aversion to medical intervention, she refused to be admitted to hospital or to have treatment. S was detained under the Mental Health Act 1983 s.2 by the first respondent, a social worker, and was admitted to hospital and then transferred to another. Treatment, culminating in a caesarean section, was administered without S's consent following the granting of an ex parte application made by the hospital of which she had no knowledge and for which she had no opportunity to obtain legal representation. S's detention was terminated after the child was born and her application for leave to move for judicial review was refused as it came after the expiry of the three-month time limit due to delay in obtaining medical records. S appealed.

Held, granting S leave to move for judicial review, that, where issues of general public importance were raised in a judicial review application, such as the application of s.2 to a pregnant woman refusing medical treatment and the events following S's detention under the Act, leave could exceptionally be granted notwithstanding the delay in bringing proceedings.

S'S APPLICATION FOR JUDICIAL REVIEW, *Re*; *sub nom*. R. v. COLLINS, *ex p.* MS; R. v. COLLINS, *ex p.* S, *The Independent*, July 10, 1997, Butler-Sloss, L.J., CA.

2601. Medical treatment–fees

MEDICAL DEVICES FEES (AMENDMENT) REGULATIONS 1997, SI 1997 694; made under the Finance Act 1973 s.56. In force: April 1, 1997; £0.65.

These Regulations amend the Medical Devices Fees Regulations 1995 (SI 1995 2487) which prescribe the fees payable in connection with the services provided by the Department of Health pursuant to the Secretary of State's functions under Council Directive 90/385 ([1990] OJ L189/17) relating to active implantable medical devices and Council Directive 93/42 ([1993] OJ L169/1) concerning medical devices. They vary the fees payable for clinical investigations and applications from notified bodies.

2602. Medical treatment–refusal to fund multiple sclerosis sufferer's treatment with new drug

See NATIONAL HEALTH SERVICE: R. v. North Derbyshire HA, *ex p.* Fisher. §3683

2603. Articles

AIDS: safety, regulation and the law in procedures using blood and blood products *(B.M. Craven)*: Med. Sci. Law 1997, 37(3), 215-227. (Regulation of market for blood focusing on liability and compensation for transfusions of HIV contaminated blood products).

An introduction to European Union health law *(Johannes Dommers)*: E.J.H.L. 1997, 4(1), 19-41. (EU framework for closer cooperation in prevention and treatment of disease, medical research, public health issues and consumer information and protection).

Assisted suicide and refusing medical treatment: linguistics, morals and legal contortions *(David P.T. Price)*: Med. L. Rev. 1997, 4(3), 270-299. (Legal and ethical problems in defining suicide and difficulties over assessing intention and causation regarding patient refusing consent to treatment and doctor assisting in suicide either by positive acts or by failing to act).

Commentary on recently issued guidelines on treatment decisions for patients in persistent vegetative state *(Jennifer Hyslop* and *Denis A. Cusack)*: M.L.J.I. 1996, 2(2), 57-59. (Includes text of BMA guidelines).

Conjoined twins: the legality and ethics of sacrifice *(Sally Sheldon)* and *(Stephen Wilkinson)*: Med. L. Rev. 1997, 5(2), 149-171. (Whether Siamese twins are two persons, legality of surgery which deliberately brings about death of one in order to save other and whether doctor's knowledge that actions will result in death is sufficient mens rea for murder).

Genetic screening and testing and the child patient *(Jean V. McHale)*: C.F.L.Q. 1997, 9(1), 33-42. (Ethical aspects of consent to screening for genetic disorders and whether disclosure of genetic information is in public interest).

In the name of the father? Ex parte Blood: dealing with novelty and anomaly *(Derek Morgan* and *Robert G. Lee)*: M.L.R. 1997, 60(6), 840-856. (Law's approach to moral dilemmas raised by changing social and cultural values in medicine, shown by case on whether wife could be artificially inseminated with sperm taken from unconscious husband who died without giving consent).

Judicially enforced caesareans and the sanctity of life *(Aurora Plomer)*: Anglo-Am. L.R. 1997, 26(2), 235-271. (Conflict between patient's legal right to refuse treatment and moral principles of right to life, with examination of UK and US cases).

Parental consent and children's medical treatment *(Aurora Plomer)*: Fam. Law 1996, 26(Dec), 739-741. (Effect of 1989 Act on conditions under which medical practitioner may lawfully treat child who is under 16 and does not have mental capacity to understand nature and effects of proposed treatment).

Posthumous conception: blood and gametes *(Pamela R. Ferguson)*: S.L.T. 1997, 8, 61-64. (Full legal implications of wife using her deceased husband's sperm to conceive a child).

Prenatal diagnosis of genetic disease: ethics and moral philosophy *(James Dalrymple)*: P.I. 1997, 4(1), 53-62. (Scientific and ethical justifications for pre natal testing and diagnosis, role of genetic counselling, legal issues of consent and confidentiality and moral basis for treatment, including rights of foetus and society).

Problems with "persons" *(Phillip Cole)*: Res Publica 1997, 3(2), 165-183. (Whether patients in persistent vegetative state can be regarded as non persons to whom no moral wrong can be done or whether they have an interest in continued existence so that is morally wrong to terminate treatment).

Quis custodiet ipsos custodes? Abuses of the declaratory jurisdiction *(Barbara Hewson)*: J.R. 1996, 1(4), 204-207. (Whether hospitals' ex parte applications for Caesarean operations or forced intervention in birth without consent of competent woman are abuse of legal system).

Restoring moral and intellectual shape to the law after Bland *(John Keown)*: L.Q.R. 1997, 113(Jul), 482-503. (Doctrine of sanctity of life was misrepresented and misunderstood in decision on withdrawal of treatment from patient in persistent vegetative state).

Sources of health service law: Health Law 1997, Oct, 1-3. (Including civil, criminal, public and common law, primary, secondary and delegated legislation, codes of practice and Department of Health directives).

The caesarean section debate *(Lord Justice Thorpe)*: Fam. Law 1997, 27(Oct), 663-664. (Legal and ethical difficulties faced by Fam Div judges in deciding whether caesarean section might lawfully be performed despite patient's objection, and need for legislation in this area).

The courts and medical treatment *(Lord Justice Thorpe)*: Fam. Law 1996, 26(Dec), 728-732. (Role of judges in making decisions on treatment, with particular reference to decisions of first instance judges in Fam Div).

The doctor and the teenager—questions of consent *(Andrew Downie)*: Fam. Law 1997, 27(Jul), 499-501. (Whether young person can give valid consent to proposed medical treatment, with reference to test of Gillick competence, and issue of confidentiality).

When and where is it right to die? *(Richard Booth)*: Lawyer 1997, 11 (14), 11. (Reaction to the voluntary euthanasia legislation enacted in Australia's Northern Territory to legalise assisted suicide which was promptly repealed and possibility of UK legislation).

Withholding or withdrawing life-sustaining treatment: Report of the Royal College of Paediatrics and Child Health: Med. L. Mon.1997, 4 (9), 1-2. (Detailed guidance for doctors about withholding or withdrawing medical treatment for children).

2604. Books

Montgomery, Jonathan–Health Care Law. Hardback: £30.00. ISBN 0-19-876260-7. Clarendon Press. Paperback: £16.99. ISBN 0-19-876259-3. Oxford University Press.

Richman, Helene Pines–Disability Law and Practice. Hardback: £45.00. ISBN 0-421-54720-0. Sweet & Maxwell.

HEALTH AND SAFETY AT WORK

2605. Chemicals–packaging–information

CHEMICALS (HAZARD INFORMATION AND PACKAGING FOR SUPPLY) (AMENDMENT) REGULATIONS 1997, SI 1997 1460; made under the European Communities Act 1972 s.2; and the Health and Safety at Work etc. Act 1974 s.15, s.82, Sch.3 para.1. In force: July 7, 1997; £1.55.

These Regulations amend the Chemicals (Hazard Information and Packaging for Supply) Regulations 1994 (SI 1994 3247). They amend the 1994 Regulations in that: they introduce a new edition of the approved classification and labelling guide and supplement to the third edition of the approved supply list (thereby implementing part of Council Directive 96/54 ([1996] OJ L248/1) the 22nd ATP to Council Directive 67/548 ([1996] OJ L196/1) (the Dangerous Substances Directive); they apply Reg.8 to Reg.12 of the 1994 Regulations to liquefied petroleum gas, butane and propane and provide a defence in certain circumstances for an offence arising out of the supply of such substances under the 1994 Regulations (thereby implementing part of the Dangerous Substances Directive); they change certain references in the 1994 Regulations from EEC to EC (thereby implementing Council Directive 96/56 ([1996] OJ L236/35) the 8th Amendment to the Dangerous Substances Directive; they introduce an exemption in certain circumstances for substances and preparations marketed for research and development or analysis purposes (thereby implementing part of Council Directive 76/769 ([1976] OJ L262/201) (the Marketing and Use Directive); they introduce a new labelling phrase "For use in industrial installations only" for use in certain circumstances (thereby implementing Commission Directive 96/55 ([1996] OJ L231/20), the 2nd ATP to the Marketing and Use Directive)); and they introduce a new Risk Phrase for the aspiration hazard (thereby implementing part of Council Directive 96/65 ([1996] OJ L265/15), the 4th ATP to Council Directive 88/379 ([1988] OJ L187/14) (the Dangerous Preparations Directive) and part of Commission Directive 96/54 ([1996] OJ L248/1)).

2606. Contributory negligence–sewing machinist–series of needle in finger injuries

[Factories Act 1961 s.14.]

C, a female employee aged 20, suffered injury to her left index finger when the needle penetrated the finger and nail. The needle did not break. After first aid treatment C was referred to hospital suffering from shock. She remained off work for the remainder of that day and the following day, and then returned to the same work. Eight days later she suffered a similar injury whilst working on the same machine. C presented evidence that she had suffered four similar injuries in a very short period of time and B were able to provide evidence that on each occasion she had been reassessed and retrained in her working practice. The last incident was eight days after the incident to which the proceedings related and C was removed from that task and given non-machining work to do. C gave evidence that the finger was numb for a short period of time, then painful and sensitive for several weeks requiring her to take mild painkillers.

Held, that B, as the employer, were primarily liable under the Factories Act 1961 s.14, as they had allowed C's finger to come into contact with the needle. However, the judge found that as C had been retrained and reassessed after each incident there was contributory negligence on her part. The judge commented that whilst evidence was given that it was not unusual for a sewing machinist to occasionally suffer a needle in finger injury, it was highly unusual to find one individual who had suffered four accidents in such a short period and this was clear evidence that she had not been paying full attention. It was held, therefore, that C was 50 per cent to blame for the accident and she was awarded general damages at full liability of £180 and special damages at £20 for loss of earnings for one day. The total award to C after the deduction for contributory negligence was £100.

COWELL v. BAIRDWEAR, Deputy District Judge Craddock, CC (Swansea).

2607. Contributory negligence–unsafe system of work–forklift truck accident– apportionment of liability between employer, occupier and employee

GM, occupiers of cold store premises on which CCC were contracted to do refrigeration work and who employed C, appealed against the apportionment of 40 per cent contributory negligence to C on the basis that it was too low given that C had driven a forklift truck knowingly without authority and lied when asked if he had a licence. Liability between GM as occupiers and CCC as employers was apportioned one third against GM and two thirds against CCC. C had used the forklift truck when he found one unattended with keys in the ignition and received leg injuries after a collision with swing doors. It was submitted by GM that the incident was not foreseeable merely by leaving keys in the truck, while C contended that he used the truck for the purpose of getting the work done when a qualified driver was not available. GM further maintained that the order for costs between the defendants was wrong in principle because an offer of contribution made by GM equalled the eventual apportionment by the judge.

Held, dismissing the appeal, that although C had acted foolishly he did so in an effort to carry out his employer's orders. That C had behaved in such a manner did not obviate GM's duty to visitors to their premises and, by leaving the keys in the truck, they were in breach of that duty. C's action in driving the vehicle was not a novus actus interveniens. The judge's decision on the level of contribution could not be interfered with. He assessed the evidence that C was acting voluntarily and deliberately, did not refer to a supervisor, lied about his ability to drive the truck and drove it badly with his leg outside the vehicle against evidence that C was young and inexperienced, that he had attempted to get CCC to provide a qualified driver and the keys were available in the truck.

GRAND METROPOLITAN PLC (T/A FLEUR DE LYS) v. CLOSED CIRCUIT COOLING LTD (T/A 3CL); *sub nom.* GRAND METROPOLITAN PLC (T/A FLEUR DE LYS) v. COULDING, Trans. Ref: CCRTF 95/0587/C, October 17, 1996, Judge, L.J., CA.

2608. Divers

DIVING AT WORK REGULATIONS 1997, SI 1997 2776; made under the Health and Safety at Work etc. Act 1974 s.15, s.82, Sch.3 para.1, Sch.3 para.5, Sch.3 para.6, Sch.3 para.14, Sch.3 para.15, Sch.3 para.16, Sch.3 para.21. In force: April 1, 1998; £2.80.

These Regulations impose requirements and prohibitions relating to health and safety upon persons who work as divers. The Diving Operations at Work

Regulations 1981 (SI 1981 399 as amended by SI 1990 996 and SI 1992 608) are revoked.

2609. Electricity—noise—extension of jurisdiction of regulations

OFFSHORE ELECTRICITY AND NOISE REGULATIONS 1997, SI 1997 1993; made under the Health and Safety at Work etc. Act 1974 s.15, s.82. In force: February 21, 1998; £1.10.

These Regulations amend the Electricity at Work Regulations 1989 (SI 1989 635) and the Noise at Work Regulations 1989 (SI 1989 1790) so that they now apply outside Great Britain as the Health and Safety at Work etc. Act 1974 applies, as well as applying in Great Britain.

2610. Employers liabilities—duty of care—fatal accidents—changes to procedure—contract labourer not informed

[Health and Safety at Work etc Act 1974 s.3(1).]

Held, that BS were fined £50,000 and ordered to pay costs after pleading guilty to failing to ensure, insofar as was reasonably practicable, that persons not in its employment were not exposed to risks to their health and safety, contrary to the Health and Safety at Work etc Act 1974 s.3(1). B was a contract labourer whose duties included cleaning coke spillage at the coke ovens at Port Talbot. Modifications had been made to the area at the head of the bunker requiring changes in procedure about which B was not informed. The trap door at the head of the bunker was not secured and no relevant instructions preventing its use were given. In accordance with the former practice B opened an unsecured trap door in order to brush the coke spillage into the coke bunker. He fell a distance of about 10 metres into the bunker and suffered fatal injuries.

HEALTH AND SAFETY EXECUTIVE v. BRITISH STEEL PLC, Date not specified, H.H.J. Prosser Q.C., CC (Cardiff). [*Ex rel.* Bryan Thomas, Barrister, Gower Chambers, Swansea].

2611. Employers liabilities—duty of care—fatal accidents—company's liability where failure to ensure employees' safety occurred at store management level

[Health and Safety at Work etc Act 1974 s.2(1), s.3(1).]

G appealed against conviction of failing to ensure, so far as reasonably practicable, the health and safety of an employee contrary to the Health and Safety at Work etc Act 1974 s.2(1) following the death of a duty manager at a supermarket who fell through a trap door in the lift control room. He had entered the room to free the lift, which had become jammed, by hand, a regular though unauthorised practice of which head office was unaware, but failed to notice that the trap door had been left open by contractors. The judge ruled that s.2(1) established strict liability for breaches of duty by the company's servants. G pleaded guilty in response to the ruling, but argued that the head office was remote from the local store and that the company's "directing mind" was not responsible.

Held, dismissing the appeal, that under s.2(1) the company was responsible for a failure at store management level to ensure safety, *R. v. Associated Octel Co Ltd* [1996] 4 All E.R. 846, [1996] 1 C.L.Y. 3019 considered. Section 3(1) of the Act dealt with liability for the health and safety of those who were not employees. Both sections contained the wording "the duty of every employer", and both were to be interpreted so as to impose liability in the event of a failure to ensure safety unless all reasonable precautions had been taken, not only by the company itself but by servants and agents on its behalf. The prosecution did not have to establish that the company's "directing mind", ie. the senior employees who embodied the company, had failed to take all reasonable precautions.

R. v. GATEWAY FOODMARKETS LTD [1997] 3 All E.R. 78, Evans, L.J., CA (Crim Div).

2612. Employers liabilities–duty of care–fatal accidents–lack of supervision

[Health and Safety at Work etc Act 1974 s.2(1).]

BL, who fabricated quarry plant and stone crushing machinery, pleaded guilty to failing to ensure, so far as was reasonably practicable, the health, safety and welfare at work of its employees contrary to the Health and Safety at Work etc Act 1974 s.2(1). A cab crane transporting a lifting beam weighing approximately one tonne broke down. This beam was lowered by releasing the brake on the cab crane and left resting on a stone crushing machine in the process of fabrication. The following day J and D, dressers who cleaned the fabrication, began to work on the stone crushing machine. As they were doing so the beam slid trapping D's head and causing him to suffer fatal injuries.

Held, that the offence involved a lack of supervision and a general failure to take reasonable steps when handling and storing the beam so as to avoid the risk of injury to those employees working in the vicinity of the beam. BL were fined £100,000 and ordered to pay the prosecution costs.

HEALTH AND SAFETY EXECUTIVE v. BROWN LENOX & CO LTD, June 26, 1997, H.H.J. D Roderick Evans Q.C., CC (Merthyr Tydfil). [*Ex rel.* Bryan Thomas, Barrister, Gower Chambers, Swansea].

2613. Employers liabilities–personal injuries–contributory negligence–failure to heed training or request assistance

M, who was employed by C as a chargehand/supervisor, allegedly suffered a straining injury to his stomach as a result of being required to manually handle several rolls of pulp weighing approximately 400 kilograms each. M alleged that he was required to manually handle the rolls of pulp as he was unable to use the forklift truck which was normally provided for this task, as there was a pool of water on the floor. C did not dispute that there was a pool of water on the floor. C's case was that M had received extensive manual handling training and should have known not to attempt to lift such a load, and also that he could have called for assistance either to lift the load, or to have the water cleared up. M's medical evidence confirmed that he had suffered a straining injury to his stomach and that the pain from this injury lasted for a period of two weeks, after which time M gradually returned to his pre-accident position.

Held, that C were primarily liable for the fact that there was a large pool of water on the floor. There was a finding of contributory negligence on the basis that M had moved three or four rolls of pulp on that particular day, and had felt a twinge when he moved the first roll, however, he continued to move the remaining rolls. The judge found that there was no evidence that anyone, including M, had taken steps to bring to the management's attention the fact that there was a large pool of water on the floor. The judge placed reliance upon the fact that (1) M had received manual handling training, and that he knew that it was dangerous and risky to attempt to lift such a large roll and (2) M could have asked a fellow employee for assistance. An award of £125 was made after a 75 per cent reduction for contributory negligence.

MEE-BISHOP v. COURTAULDS CHEMICALS, District Judge Herbert, CC (Nottingham).

2614. Employers liabilities–personal injuries–contributory negligence–misuse of chiropodist's chair–employee using chair unsafely

I appealed against an order for damages for personal injuries against B which assessed contributory negligence at 85 per cent, arguing that this assessment was wrong. The damages were assessed in total at £45,000 for pain and suffering and loss of amenities. B contended that I should have been held wholly to blame for the accident. I was employed by B as a chiropodist. She carried out some of her work whilst sitting on a swivel chair, the height of which could be adjusted. I had the chair at a high level as that was the best way she could reach the patient's foot given her stature. On one occasion the chair came apart and I fell to the ground hurting her back. There was evidence from a supervisor who had criticised I's use of the chair some months after the accident and had directed that she should change the position to conform with training recommendations and hygiene. However, one month later I fell from her chair whilst attending a patient after the chair had collapsed. There was no defect in the chair, but it had been raised too high and had become disengaged from the spindle.

Held, dismissing the appeal and allowing B's appeal against the finding of liability, that there was no basis for the finding that a reasonably prudent employer would have foreseen that I would continue to misuse the chair after she had been told not to. The chair was not inherently dangerous, but had been used unsafely. B had provided satisfactory equipment which could be safely used and had advised I, in emphatic terms, of the possible dangers in misusing the chair.

ISMAIL v. BEXLEY HA, Trans. Ref: CCRTF 96/1181/C, March 13, 1997, Kennedy, L.J., CA.

2615. Employers liabilities-psychiatric harm-death of work colleague not actually witnessed-no claim as neither primary nor secondary victim

[Mines and Quarries Act 1954 s.36(1), s.83(1).]

H brought a claim for damages for psychiatric harm suffered as the result of a accident whilst working at one of B's mines. H was employed as a free steered vehicle, FSV, driver and on the day of the accident he was required to move girders within the mine by way of the FSV. Whilst doing so part of the load fouled a high pressure water hydrant which was protruding into the roadway. As a result the hydrant began to leak. H and a colleague unsuccessfully attempted to stop the leak. H went to seek assistance and as he was returning the hydrant exploded and H's colleague was struck and killed by either the hydrant or the force of the water. Upon learning of the death, H suffered psychiatric harm and injury to his mental health. H alleged that the injuries were caused by the negligence and/or breach of their statutory duty by B, in failing to maintain sufficient clearance on the road and allowing the hydrant to protrude into the roadway. Both matters were relied on as acts of negligence and breaches of the Mines and Quarries Act 1954 s.36(1) and s.83(1). It was also alleged that B failed to heed a previous accident in the mine and reduce the water pressure accordingly. B denied the allegations and submitted in their defence that the matters complained of were caused or contributed to by H's negligence.

Held, that a breach of s.83 had occurred and that breach was causative of the fatal accident. The failure to maintain the minimum clearance and to lessen the projection of the hydrant into the road could have been dealt with by the mine officials if they had seen fit. Despite the breach of duty, H's claim would fail as he did not satisfy the criteria necessary to succeed in a claim of psychiatric harm. As H was never put in fear of his own safety and did not witness the death of the deceased he did not fall within either of the categories laid down in *Alcock v. Chief Constable of South Yorkshire Police* [1992] A.C. 310, [1992] C.L.Y. 3250 as H was neither a primary nor secondary victim, *Duncan v. British Coal Corp* [1997] 1 All E.R. 540, [1996] 12 C.L. 416 considered.

HUNTER v. BRITISH COAL CORP, H.H.J. Bentley, CC (Sheffield).

2616. Employers liabilities-psychiatric harm-employee's electrocution-liability to witness suffering psychiatric injury-breach of statutory duty

[Construction (General Provisions) Regulations 1961 (SI 1961 1580) Reg.44(2).]

Y was working as a labourer for a construction company on CC's land when a workmate was electrocuted and killed. As a result of witnessing the accident, Y suffered grave psychiatric illness and now appealed against the dismissal of his claim against CC for damages for negligence and breach of statutory duty. Whilst CC admitted that they were in breach of the Construction (General Provisions) Regulations 1961 Reg.44(2) with regard to the deceased, they denied any liability to Y on the ground that he was merely a bystander who had not been injured by electrocution, and the harm he suffered was not covered by the Regulations.

Held, allowing the appeal, that CC were liable to Y both for negligence at common law and for breach of statutory duty. Regulation 44(2) was not restricted to physical electrocution, but extended to injury which could have been foreseen as likely to occur as a result of breach. Psychiatric harm suffered by an employee witnessing the event, and working close by so that he was lucky not to have been electrocuted himself, came within the terms of protection afforded by the Regulations.

YOUNG v. CHARLES CHURCH (SOUTHERN) LTD, *The Times*, May 1, 1997, Evans, L.J., CA.

2617. Employers liabilities–safe work–employee suffering pain from own physical condition–no duty to move

W appealed against a judgment awarding damages of £17,559 for personal injuries sustained by H while pressing garments. H suffered from cervical spondylosis, which appeared to be the main cause of her discomfort, but the judge below concluded that W had been notified and had failed to alter H's work situation by providing a higher ironing board, a lighter iron, or job rotation.

Held, allowing the appeal, that the judge below had established that the work conditions and the pattern of work were entirely safe and acceptable. An employer had no duty to offer a wholly different job to, or to dismiss or remove, an employee because she suffered pain when she wished to continue in safe work, *Withers v. Perry Chain Co Ltd* [1961] 1 W.L.R. 1314, [1961] C.L.Y. 5938 followed.

HENDERSON v. WAKEFIELD SHIRT CO LTD, Trans. Ref: CCRTF 96/1252/C, May 12, 1997, Kennedy, L.J., CA.

2618. Fees

HEALTH AND SAFETY (FEES) REGULATIONS 1997, SI 1997 2505; made under the Health and Safety at Work etc. Act 1974 s.43, s.82. In force: November 18, 1997; £4.15.

These Regulations revoke and replace the Health and Safety (Fees) Regulations 1996 (SI 1996 2791). They fix or determine the fees payable by an applicant to the Health and Safety Executive in respect of approvals under health and safety legislation. They also update fees to be paid in respect of medical examinations and which may be charged under the Explosives Act 1875, the Petroleum (Consolidation) Act 1928 and the Petroleum (Transfer of Licences) Act 1936.

2619. Fire precautions

FIRE PRECAUTIONS (WORKPLACE) REGULATIONS 1997, SI 1997 1840; made under the Fire Precautions Act 1971 s.35, s.40, s.43; and the European Communities Act 1972 s.2. In force: December 1, 1997; £3.20.

These Regulations give effect to Council Directive 89/391 ([1989] OJ L183/1) on the introduction of measures to encourage improvements in the safety and health of workers at work and Council Directive 89/654 ([1989] OJ L393/1) Art.6 and para.4 and para.5 of each Annex concerning the minimum safety and health requirements for the workplace in so far as those provisions relate to fire precautions and in so far as more specific legislation does not make appropriate provision.

2620. Hazardous substances–controls

CONTROL OF SUBSTANCES HAZARDOUS TO HEALTH (AMENDMENT) REGULATIONS 1997, SI 1997 11; made under the Health and Safety at Work etc.

Act 1974 s.15, Sch.3 para.1, Sch.3 para.9, Sch.3 para.13. In force: January 9, 1997; £0.65.

These Regulations amend the Control of Substances Hazardous to Health (Amendment) Regulations 1996 (SI 1996 3138) which come into force on January 10, 1997, to correct errors in the entries for Cobalt and Cobalt compounds, Cotton dust and 1,2-Dibromoethane (Ethylene dibromide) in the Schedule to those Regulations.

2621. Industrial injuries—causation—conflicting medical evidence—measure of damages—recorder erred in not addressing and resolving conflict

S brought an action for damages for personal injury against his employer, E, in respect of an accident at work for which E had admitted liability. However, at a trial to determine the measure of damages, E claimed that the serious back problem suffered by S was the result of a pre-existing degenerative condition and had not been caused, as S contended, by the accident. There was conflicting medical evidence from the two consultant orthopaedic surgeons called by S and E, but the judge decided the issue of causation in favour of E. S appealed, arguing that, in reaching his conclusion, the judge had failed to define clearly the issues raised by the medical evidence or make any firm findings of fact and had evaded his responsibility to resolve the issue by wrongly relying on the burden of proof as a test.

Held, allowing the appeal and ordering a new trial, that the recorder had failed in his judgment to address properly and resolve the important issues raised by the conflict of medical opinion. Where a case required a recorder to address and resolve primary issues and any secondary issues which were relevant to the primary issues, it was not open to him to decide the case on the basis of the burden of proof.

SEWELL v. ELECTROLUX LTD, *The Times*, November 7, 1997, Hutchison, L.J., CA.

2622. Industrial injuries—damages—failure to undertake risk assessment—employee damaging back

[Manual Handling Operations Regulations (SI 1992 2793) Reg.4.]

W, aged 60, five feet five inches tall, with a pre-existing back problem, suffered a further injury to her back lifting a bucket of water weighing a total of 21 pounds out of the sink, the height of the lift being 52 inches. The injury took place at some undefined point between removal from the sink, resting on lip of the sink and then a one-handed lift involving twisting and lowering motion to W's right. W claimed damages for the exacerbation of a pre-existing disability.

Held, awarding damages in favour of W, that the operation involved W in a significant degree of risk of being injured. The risk was more than merely minimal or theoretical and called for a risk assessment. Had an assessment been carried out, the necessity of the lift could have been avoided by the simple provision of a hose to fill the bucket via the tap whilst the bucket was on the floor. It was reasonably practical to avoid the need for the lifting operation to be carried out and since H took no steps to avoid the need, they were in breach of their duty under the Manual Handling Operations Regulations Reg.4. W was awarded total damages of £7,920 including £4,000 general damages.

WARREN v. HARLOW DC, January 15, 1997, H.H.J. Diamond Q.C., CC (Central London). [*Ex rel.* Neville B Filar, Solicitor, Thompsons, Ilford].

2623. Industrial injuries—duty of care—safe system of work—experienced worker hurt back by lifting—no duty to supervise all lifting work

R, was injured at work when lifting a box weighing 10.26 kilogrammes to a height of one metre, and twisting slightly. R had worked for the Post Office for 15 years. He had asked earlier to be moved to light work on account of back trouble, but later asked to be moved back to his prior work and was on that work at the time of the accident. The system of work did not give rise to foreseeable injury.

Held, that it was not necessary that the employers should have supervised R closely, because he was experienced and the job was a simple task. The employer's obligation was to take reasonable care to provide a safe system of work and to see that it was followed. In these circumstances, there was no foreseeable risk and the employers were not under a duty to oversee the employee's method of lifting the box.

ROZARIO v. POST OFFICE [1997] P.I.Q.R. P15, Stuart-Smith, L.J., CA.

2624. Industrial injuries–duty of care–safe system of work–repetitive strain injury

The three plaintiffs were employed on a sausage production line at M's factory. Their jobs involved the arrangement of sausages, by hand, in preparation for packaging. The work was performed at speed and was highly repetitive. Following a change in their work routine, associated with the introduction of larger packs of sausages, all three plaintiffs developed symptoms of pain and discomfort in their hands, wrists and forearms. Two of the three plaintiffs had no identifiable pathology to justify their symptoms. The medical consultants called on behalf of the plaintiffs described the condition from which they were suffering as "repetitive strain syndrome" or "over use syndrome", ie. a condition of unknown aetiology but caused by unaccustomed exposure to rapid and repetitive manual work. M's consultant disputed the existence of such a condition and ascribed the plaintiffs' symptoms to constitutional factors.

Held, allowing the claim, that the court preferred the plaintiffs' medical evidence and accepted the existence of a genuine condition, notwithstanding the absence of any identifiable pathology. M was held liable for having failed to warn the plaintiffs regarding the risk of strain injury and having operated a system of work in which production rates were too high and job rotation and rest periods were inadequate.

GANDY, HERRICK AND GERRARD v. MATTESSONS WALL'S LTD, May 8, 1997, Recorder Lewis, CC (Oldham). [*Ex rel.* Sinead Cartwright, Solicitor, Jack Thornley & Partners, Ashton-under-Lyne].

2625. Industrial injuries–duty of care–unguarded saw–unsafe procedure adopted by employee–lack of supervision by employers–breach of statutory duty– contributory negligence

M appealed against a finding dismissing his action against C, his employers, for negligence and breach of statutory duty following an accident in which he suffered a cut across the palm of his left hand resulting in the amputation of his little finger and severe diminution of function of the remaining fingers. M was the only joiner employed by C and he had been in the job for nine weeks when the accident happened. When he was shown the joinery workshop he was not given any instructions by the safety officer as to how to use the circular saw and, although there was a guard available for the saw, there was evidence that the guard had never been used. M's account as to how the accident occurred was rejected and it was found that M had adopted an unsafe procedure for cutting wood, a procedure he knew to be unsafe. It was held that, although C's inadequate supervision was part of the background to the accident, M was solely responsible for the accident.

Held, allowing the appeal and apportioning liability at 75 per cent to M and 25 per cent to C, that, as the judge found that C's lack of supervision was part of the background to the accident, it was not open for him to exonerate C entirely from breach of its statutory duty. The absence of instructions as to how to use the saw safely and the practice of permitting the use of the saw unguarded constituted a wrongful act leading to causation or contribution on the part of C, *Ginty v. Belmont Building Supplies Ltd* [1959] 1 All E.R. 414, [1959] C.L.Y. 2191 applied. In order to exonerate C, it would be necessary to have found that M's adoption of an unsafe procedure was the sole cause of the accident and that the accident would have occurred even if the saw had been guarded which was not the case.

McCREESH v. COURTAULDS PLC, Trans. Ref: QBENF 96/0427/C, April 24, 1997, Thorpe, L.J., CA.

2626. Industrial injuries–vibration white finger in coal industry–date of knowledge of foreseeable risk

B appealed against decisions on preliminary issues that the date from which it had become aware of, and should have taken precautions against, the foreseeable risk of a medical condition, Vibration White Finger, VWF, occurring in its employees was January 1, 1973. B contended that the judge below had erred (1) by finding that an epidemiological survey following the Milne Survey in 1968 of B employees should have been carried out and (2) if such a survey had taken place, that it would have shown an unacceptable level of VWF in the industry.

Held, dismissing the appeal, that there were no grounds to interfere with the findings of the judge below that by January 1, 1973 B had had time to act on the Milne Survey indicating the extent of the condition and that it had failed to institute an epidemiological investigation.

ARMSTRONG v. BRITISH COAL CORP, *The Times*, December 6, 1996, Judge, L.J., CA.

2627. Insect infestation–textile factory–low complaint rate

[Factories Act 1961 s.29(1).]

Four plaintiffs, employed within a textile factory, all claimed to have suffered insect bites at work, on specific days during the period of July to October 1995. They sought to recover damages for personal injury and alleged breach of the Factories Act 1961 s.29(1) and/or negligence. Damages were limited by the particulars of claim to £1,000 and upon the filing of a defence the claims were referred to arbitration. In each case the plaintiffs had not seen the insect that had bitten them and the distribution of bites on their bodies was different. All but one of the plaintiffs had been exposed to household pets prior to the alleged bites. The plaintiffs also sought to rely upon the evidence of previous claimants who had allegedly suffered insect bites. B's accident book recorded a total of 35 reported biting incidents over a 64 month period from 1992 up to the date of the complaints. The plaintiffs sought to suggest that the bites may have been caused by insects living within the textiles on which they were working. B's employees gave evidence that there had been two "fumigations" of the factory but they could not be precise as to who had carried these out nor what had in fact been sprayed. Insect traps had been set after one of the complainants had brought her bites to B's attention but only one insect was caught which was concluded to be of the non-biting variety (having been sent off to D's expert for analysis). At the time of the bites the factory solely supplied Marks & Spencer and no garments produced within the factory had been returned to B.

Held, dismissing the claims and limiting B's experts' fees to £200, that B had adduced expert evidence to show that (1) the biting rate in the case of a minor infestation might be expected at 10 incidents per 100 employees and that in a serious case rates might be as high as 200 per 100 employees but this bite rate was slightly less than 0.25 per 100 employees; (2) the injuries were typical of bites caused by cat fleas, horse fleas or flying insects; (3) due to "sensitisation", the perceived bite was in fact a reaction to a bite which occurred some time beforehand. Evidence was given to the effect that in the "average" adult a reaction time to an insect's bite would ordinarily be between eight and 20 hours, although reaction times of up to five days had been recorded; (4) psychological factors came into play, namely that the plaintiffs felt special as part of a group of people affected by bites; (5) it was most unlikely that an infestation was extant in the factory given that no insects had been seen nor caught, and (6) given that the bites sustained were caused by fleas, the fleas could not have come from the materials with which the plaintiffs had been working because the fleas would have required a host. A new material which had not been exposed to a potential host would therefore not have sustained a flea colony.

DAVIES v. BAIRDWEAR LTD, March 24, 1997, District Judge Schroeder, CC (Telford). [*Ex rel.* Nigel Brockley, Barrister, Bracton Chambes, 95a Chancery Lane].

2628. Lifts

LIFTS REGULATIONS 1997, SI 1997 831; made under the European Communities Act 1972 s.2. In force: July 1, 1997 in accordance with Reg.1; £6.10.

These Regulations, which implement the European Parliament and Council Directive 95/16 ([1995] OJ L213/1) relating to lifts, revoke, with effect from July 1, 1999, the Electrically, Hydraulically and Oil-Electrically Operated Lifts (Components) (EEC Requirements) Regulations 1991 (SI 1991 2748). Part II provides for the application of the Regulations, Part III sets out the general requirements relating to the placing on the market and putting into service of lifts and safety components by a "responsible person", the essential health and safety requirements are set out in Sch.1 and Part IV and Sch.15 relate to the enforcement of the Regulations.

2629. Petrol—exploration—inspections of mines

SECTION 7 OF THE PETROLEUM (PRODUCTION) ACT 1934 AND SECTION 2(1)(A) OF THE PETROLEUM ACT 1987 (MODIFICATION) REGULATIONS 1997, SI 1997 2703; made under the Health and Safety at Work etc. Act 1974 s.80. In force: December 8, 1997; £1.10.

These Regulations make modifications to the Petroleum (Production) Act 1934 s.7 and the Petroleum Act 1987 s.12(1)(a) so as to require the keeping of plans of mines and the inspection of mines by inspectors appointed under that Act who have the powers conferred thereby.

2630. Police—failure to supervise training adequately

H, a woman police constable fractured her leg above her left ankle during a self defence course at the Force Training School in Eperstone, Nottingham. H, who weighed 10 and a half stone and was five feet seven inches in height, was paired with a male officer weighing 13 and a half stone and six feet four inches in height. The accident occurred when H was forced to the ground by the use of a control and restraint technique by the male officer. H had received basic training in self defence but had had no further training for six months prior to the accident and therefore was described as a novice in such techniques. The male officer carried out what was described in the Police Training Manual as a leg trip, a technique held to be clearly risky and dangerous unless carried out expertly by someone who was sufficiently well trained, upon somebody who was sufficiently trained to know what to expect and to receive it, and further it must be practised under the most closely supervised conditions.

Held, awarding damages of £6,000, that the defendants had failed in their duty of care to provide a safe system of training and safe and adequate supervision of H. The defence submissions that there was a lack of resources and they were doing no more and no less than was recommended by the Home Office, did not excuse an inadequate system of training.

HART v. CHIEF CONSTABLE OF NOTTINGHAMSHIRE AND NOTTINGHAMSHIRE POLICE AUTHORITY, October 25, 1996, H.H.J. O'Rourke, CC (Nottingham). [*Ex rel.* Trevor Davies, Barrister, 9 Gough Square, London].

2631. Prosecutions—employers duties—particulars of informations—nature of charge

[Health and Safety at Work etc Act 1974 s.2(1).]

The HSE appealed by case stated against the justices' decision to dismiss an information against SS, a company prosecuted under the Health and Safety at

Work etc Act 1974 s.2(1) for failing to ensure the safety of its employees so far as was reasonably practicable. The information referred specifically to an employee who lost his hand in an accident with a new turning machine. SS argued that the information failed to specify the nature of the charge adequately, and that if the HSE alleged both a failure to guard the machine and to train its operator properly, the information would be duplicitous in that it alleged two different offences.

Held, allowing the appeal, that the HSE had rightly elected to bring a charge under s.2(1) rather than s.2(2) of the Act, as an employer had a comprehensive duty to provide for employees' safety. Section 2(2) did no more than set out examples of the general duty and there was no need for an information to refer to them in specific terms even if applicable. An information would not be bad for duplicity where the employer was accused of contravening more than one aspect of the duty to ensure safety. The justices' decision would be quashed and the case remitted so that the hearing could continue.

HEALTH AND SAFETY EXECUTIVE v. SPINDLE SELECT LTD, *The Times*, December 9, 1996, Tucker, J., QBD.

2632. Safety–confined spaces

CONFINED SPACES REGULATIONS 1997, SI 1997 1713; made under the Health and Safety at Work Act 1974 s.15, s.82, Sch.3 para.1, Sch.3 para.9, Sch.3 para.11, Sch.3 para.18. In force: January 28, 1998; £1.55.

These Regulations, which implement in part Council Directive 92/57 ([1992] OJ L245/6) on the implementation of minimum safety and health requirements at temporary or mobile construction sites, impose requirements and prohibitions with respect to the health and safety of persons carrying out work in confined spaces. The Shipbuilding (Reports on Breathing Apparatus etc.) Order 1961 (SI 1961 114), the Breathing Apparatus etc. (Report on Examination) Order 1961 (SI 1961 1345), the Agriculture (Poisonous Substances) Act 1952 (Repeals and Modifications) Regulations 1975 (SI 1975 45) and the Kiers Regulations 1938 (Metrication) Regulations 1981 (SI 1981 1152) are revoked.

2633. Safety representatives–unauthorised actions

See EMPLOYMENT: Shillito v. Van Leer (UK) Ltd. §2259

2634. Shipping–merchant shipping and fishing vessels

See SHIPPING. §4531

2635. Young persons

HEALTH AND SAFETY (YOUNG PERSONS) REGULATIONS 1997, SI 1997 135; made under the Health and Safety at Work etc Act 1974 s.15, s.82, Sch.3 para.7, Sch.3 para.8, Sch.3 para.14. In force: March 3, 1997; £1.55.

These Regulations amend the Management of Health and Safety at Work Regulations 1992 (SI 1992 2051) so that they give effect to Art.6 and Art.7 of Council Directive 94/33 ([1994] OJ L216/12) on the protection of young people at work, save as permitted by Art.2.2.

2636. Articles

Accidents, incidents and the media: H. & S.M. 1997, 20(4), Supp IF i-ii. (Strategy for dealing with media following workplace accidents, including formulation of plan, appointment of spokespersons and establishment of press office to deal with inquiries).

Alcohol problems at work: H. & S.M. 1997, 20(2), 5-6. (Health and Safety Executive publication providing guidance for employers and advocating introduction of alcohol policy).

At breaking point: I.H.L. 1997, 53(Sep), 20-23. (Requirements and enforcement of the Health and Safety (Display Screen Equipment) Regulations 1992, scope for personal injuries actions against employers, and increasing importance of stress as health and safety issue).

Danger: men at work *(Jeremy Stranks)*: S.J. 1997, 141 (8), 186-187. (Obligation to report incidents with health and safety implications to enforcing authority under RIDDOR 1995, covering notifiable injuries, dangerous occurrences, reportable diseases and record keeping requirements).

Dealing with asbestos: H. & S.M. 1997, 20(2), 10-11. (Health and Safety Executive guidance on employer's legal duties and practical advice on working with asbestos cement and asbestos insulating board).

Demise of the "defence" of delegation in the context of the Health and Safety at Work etc. Act 1974 *(Geoffrey H. Holgate)*: Lit. 1997, 16(7), 281-290. (Strict liability of corporate employers under the Health and Safety at Work Etc Act 1974 s.2(1) and s.3(1) of 1974 Act and unavailability of defence of delegation by management to particular employees).

EC Young Workers Directive and its implementation in the UK *(Michael J. Hibbs)*: Emp. L. Brief. 1997, 4(6), 69-71.

Employer's criminal liability under HSWA 1974 *(Brenda Barrett)*: I.L.J. 1997, 26(2), 149-158. (Scope of employer's duties in relation to protecting workers, with particular reference to interpretation of s.3(1) as to whether contractor's work was within conduct of employer's undertaking).

Fire precautions in the workplace: H. & S.M. 1997, 20(9), 1-2. (Fire Precautions (Workplace) Regulations 1997 in effect December 1, 1997, implement fire safety provisions of Framework Directive 89/391 and Workplace Directive 89/654).

First aid – new ACoP: H.S. 1997, 8(4), 1-4. (Revised Approved Code of Practice on 1981 Regulations, checklist for assessment of first aid needs and requirements for first aid boxes, first aid rooms and staff and information for employees).

Health & safety risk assessment *(Lawrence Waterman* and *Rob Lane)*: C.S.R. 1997, 20(25), 193-194. (Employer's duties in relation to conducting risk assessment for employees and additional requirements under the Health and Safety (Young Persons) Regulations 1997 governing protection of young workers).

Health and safety at work *(Joanna Wade)*: Adviser 1997, 59, 18-20, 29-30. (Rights of pregnant employees and new mothers, including common questions relating to health and safety and remedies available where employers fail to comply with statutory duties).

Health and safety at work: workplace risks and public safety *(James Blaikie)*: S.L.P.Q. 1997, 2(2), 155-161. (Cases showing courts' willingness to extend employers' duties to include health and safety of general public).

Management of Health and Safety at Work Regulations: H.S. 1997, 8(8), 2-3. (Main provisons of amended 1992 Regulations including changes affecting young people and new and expectant mothers).

New workplace fire Regulations in place: H. & S.B. 1997, 262, 2. (Scope of duties imposed on employers and those in control of workplaces under the Fire Precautions (Workplace) Regulations 1997 (SI 1997 1840) and means of enforcement, including list of exempted workplaces).

Out of sight, out of mind? *(Geoffrey H. Holgate)*: S.J. 1997, 141 (32), 790,792. (Liability of public authorities for health and safety of employees of contractors and implications for contracting out process).

Protecting young people at work: H. & S.M. 1997, 20(3), 1-2. (Employers' duties under the Health and Safety (Young Persons) Regulations 1997, in force March 3, 1997, implementing Council Directive 94/33).

Radon in the workplace: H. & S.M. 1997, 20(2), 7-8. (Advice for employers on protecting employees from excessive exposure).

Recording and reporting accidents: H. & S.M. 1997, 20(11), IF i-ii. (Employers' recording and reporting obligations under Reporting of Injuries, Diseases and Dangerous Occurrences Regulations 1995 (SI 1995 3163) and role of safety representatives as detailed in HSE publications L73 and HSE 31).

Risk assessments *(Lawrence Waterman* and *Rob Lane)*: T.E.L. & P. 1997, 2(11), 86-87. (Advice for employers on conducting employee health and safety risk assessments, including action plan).

Roving safety representatives: H. & S.B. 1997, 263, 13-15. (Evaluation of scheme introduced in agricultural industry to increase employee participation in health and safety management including its achievements, longer term potential and application to other industries).

The Working Time Directive and its effect in the UK *(Elspeth Deards)*: Legal Action 1997, Mar, 18-19. (Council Directive 93/104 requiring 48 hour maximum working week, exclusions and derogations, individual workers' rights and ECJ ruling in response to UK challenge to legal basis of Directive under Art.118A).

The decision of the ECJ on the Working Time Directive *(Frank Wooldridge)*: Bus. L.R. 1997, 18(2), 29-32. (Provisions of Directive 93/104, arguments on which UK action for annulment of Directive was based and implications of decision for UK government and workers).

The dismissal or the disciplining of staff for health & safety reasons *(Anthony Arter)*: H. & S.M. 1997, 20(10), IF i-iii. (Protection provided by Employment Rights Act 1996 for employees and health and safety representatives).

The hazards of homework *(Lucinda Ponting)*: H. & S.B. 1997, 259, 8-10. (Health and safety problems associated with homeworking and teleworking and employers' responsibilities to protect employees).

Work-related upper limb disorders: P. Injury 1997, 1 (3), 10-11. (Requirements for successful claim for repetitive strain injury resulting from method of employment under negligence and health and safety at work legislation).

Workers of the Weald unite! *(Bryn Perrins)*: N.L.J. 1997, 147(6789), 596-598. (Influence of EC law on UK Government's policy regarding consultation with trade union representatives culminating in the Health and Safety (Consultation with Employees) Regulations 1996 which oblige employers to consult employees on all health and safety matters).

2637. Books

Bollans, Ian; Preece, Philip—Jordans Health and Safety Management. £150.00. ISBN 0-85308-420-3. Jordan.

Chandler, Peter—A-Z of Health and Safety Law. Hardback: £45.00. ISBN 0-7494-2444-3. Kogan Page.

Curran, Patrick—Injuries At Work. Hardback: £70.00. ISBN 0-421-53020-0. Sweet & Maxwell.

Dewis, Malcolm—Health and Safety At Work Handbook: 1997. Paperback: £59.95. ISBN 1-86012-341-4. Tolley Publishing.

McDonald, Andrew; Georges, Antonis—Industrial Diseases. Tort Law Library. Hardback: £95.00. ISBN 0-421-57000-8. Sweet & Maxwell.

Wright, Frank—Law of Health and Safety At Work. Hardback: £70.00. ISBN 0-421-46060-1. Sweet & Maxwell.

HOUSING

2638. Accommodation—common lodging houses

COMMON LODGING HOUSES (REPEAL) CONSEQUENTIAL PROVISIONS ORDER 1997, SI 1997 221; made under the Housing Act 1996 s.80. In force: March 3, 1997; £0.65.

This Order repeals provisions relating to common lodging houses in four local Acts consequential on the repeal of the Housing Act 1985 Part XII. The Acts are the Poole Corporation Act 1928, the Greater London Council (General Powers) Act 1981, the Greater London Council (General Powers) Act 1984 and the Leicestershire Act 1985.

2639. Children—child in need—local authority duty to assess child in need

[National Health Service and Community Care Act 1990 s.47; Chronically Sick and Disabled Persons Act 1970 s.2; Children Act 1989 s.17; Local Authority Social Services Act 1970 s.7B.]

B applied to be rehoused and requested comprehensive assessments of the family's needs for community care services under the National Health Service and Community Care Act 1990 s.47, the Chronically Sick and Disabled Persons Act 1970 s.2 and the Children Act 1989 s.17. SB, the 11-year-old son, had special educational needs, his mother suffered from severe arthritis and epilepsy and the family were subject to harassment, bullying and taunting. SB's attendance at school was affected by his mother's inability to escort him there, and bullying. At B's application for judicial review of T's failure or refusal to make a service provision decision the judge expressed concern particularly for SB, and opined that urgent relief was required. T gave an undertaking to carry out statutory assessments as soon as practically possible. The criteria for rehousing under s.20 of the 1989 Act were not met; however T accepted that s.17 of the 1989 Act gave it authority and discretion to assess and meet SB's needs, which included the provision of accommodation. B alleged that T had not fulfilled its undertaking as it had not carried out an assessment of SB's needs for rehousing under s.17 and that the court should compel it to honour the undertaking. T argued that (1) the original application for relief was satisfied and the relief sought now was different from that for which leave had been granted; (2) there had been an assessment under s.17 of the 1989 Act, and (3) relief should not be granted because B could use the statutory complaints procedure under the Local Authority Social Services Act 1970 s.7B.

Held, allowing the application for judicial review and ordering T to assess SB for rehousing as a child in need under s.17 of the 1989 Act, that (1) the original application for leave, and subsequent undertaking given by T, included an assessment under s.17, hence the present application was not substantially different from that. The family was entitled to an assessment of SB's needs under s.17 and the court should not prejudge the outcome of any assessment; (2) having regard to the assessment report and correspondence between T and B it was clear that no assessment under s.17 had been carried out and T's undertaking in relation thereto had not been complied with. T approached the assessment with a fundamental misunderstanding of its powers in relation to accommodation under s.17 of the 1989 Act, and (3) T had not complied with the undertaking and it was necessary to ensure this was now done. Had a proper assessment been made, recourse to the statutory complaints procedure would have been considered as sufficient but any further delay in assessment of SB's needs was to be avoided.

R. v. TOWER HAMLETS LBC, *ex p.* BRADFORD, Trans. Ref: CO/4313/95, January 13, 1997, Kay, J., QBD.

2640. Covenants—repairs covenant—notice served on landlord by local authority— provisions of tenancy could not override statutory provision

[Housing Act 1985 s.190(1)(b).]

Following a complaint by the tenant of disrepair to a dwelling house the local authority served a repair notice pursuant to the Housing Act 1985 s.190(1)(b) stating that the dwelling house, although not unfit for human habitation, was in such condition as to interfere materially with the personal comfort of the occupying tenant. The landlord, being the person in control of the premises, appealed against service of the notice in respect of repairs to the fixtures and fittings of the property on the basis that under the tenancy agreement the tenant was subject to a repairing covenant in respect of these repairs and not the landlord.

Held, dismissing the appeal, that the notice had been properly served. The landlord had not denied that the repairs were needed and although it may be that the tenants were in breach of their covenant it was clear from the decision of *Rawlance v. Croydon Corp* [1952] 2 Q.B. 803, [1952] C.L.Y. 1562 that the provisions of the tenancy agreement could not override the statutory regulations.

CONSTANTINOU v. ENFIELD LBC, March 18, 1997, District Judge Silverman, CC (Edmonton). [*Ex rel.* Joanne McCartney, Barrister, Enfield Chambers, Enfield, Middlesex].

2641. Defective premises–breach of repairing covenant–distress and inconvenience and personal injury–measure of damages

P1 was the sole tenant of D's property along with her four children aged between 8 and 17 years at the date of the hearing. P1 had suffered continual difficulties with the boiler within the property. P1 complained to D about the condition of the boiler repeatedly over a period of approximately three years. Eventually in October 1991 the boiler was replaced and the problems abated. P1 by her particulars of claim alleged that it had taken D three weeks to replace the boiler during which time she had been without hot water. As a consequence she and her family had had to visit friends and relatives (occasionally necessitating a taxi journey) in order to bathe. P1 also contended that the bath and toilet had been removed for a period of eight days (in order to eradicate a damp problem) and that she had had to clear up the associated dust and rubble. P1 claimed to have suffered distress and inconvenience caused by the foregoing and further by reason of the coughs, colds and general illnesses that had been suffered by the children during the three year period. The children (although not expressly pleaded as such) sought to recover damages for personal injury. There was a total absence of medical evidence save for a short note from a GP and P1's witness statement.

Held, that the claims should be settled on the following basis: to P1: £1,400. To the children: £100 each.

SEALEY v. HAMMERSMITH AND FULHAM LBC, April 24, 1997, H.H.J. Ryland, CC (Central London). [*Ex rel.* Nigel S Brockley, Barrister, Bracton Chambers, Chancery Lane].

2642. Defective premises–measure of damages

O was a secure tenant of B for over 10 years. She had seven children living with her. There had been extensive rising damp downstairs, and this had worsened problems relating to condensation. There was mould growth throughout much of the property. Attempts by B in 1988-89 had failed to cure the rising damp. Expert evidence for O stated the house was unfit for human habitation. B was on notice for the whole of the limitation period and works had been carried out, but not completed, in a six week period in the year after the issue of proceedings. The floor to the kitchen and downstairs bathroom and toilet had to be replaced and damp proofing reinstalled. A good deal of plaster to walls, and one ceiling had to be removed. The mould required treating. During the execution of works O and her family were severely inconvenienced.

Held, that this was a bad case, but not the very worst. The court awarded general damages of £10,500 (ie. £1,500 per year), and special damages of £5,707. Interest was awarded on the general damages at two per cent from date of issue.

O'CONNOR v. BIRMINGHAM CITY COUNCIL, November 7, 1996, H.H.J. Potter, CC (Birmingham). [*Ex rel.* Anthony Verduyn, Barrister].

2643. Defective premises–measure of damages–failure by local authority to repair property

In March 1985, H became a secure tenant of a one bedroomed flat under a mutual exchange which she vacated on September 18, 1996. The flat suffered from penetrating damp, particularly to the lounge/dining room, caused by defects to the rainwater installations, gutter and roof. The windows could not be opened, and prior to H moving in L had replastered a bedroom wall but had not redecorated. There was also a defective water heater which was replaced but remained defective. To obtain water in the bathroom or kitchen sink H had to turn on the hot water tap at the bath, running back and forth between rooms to keep a hot water supply. During heavy rain H used a bucket to catch the water and put towels around the window sills. H, aged 53, suffered from cervical spondylosis causing pain to her neck, arms and back, and suffered from stress due to the flat's condition and medical evidence corroborated that stress aggravated H's pain. In December 1995 L agreed to works but nothing was done until June 1996 when a consent order was obtained at court. The works caused severe disruption and about one week after commencement H was told by L to vacate in order for internal works to start; she was not offered any temporary accommodation by L. Initially H stayed with a friend, moving some of her possessions herself by taxi. However the situation at the friend's was unsuitable and she then went to stay in an unfurnished flat for four weeks sleeping on a mattress on the floor. On returning to her flat she found the works unfinished and damage to her goods. L later agreed to pay H's rent for the period she was out of occupation.

Held, entering judgment for H in default, that at an assessment of damages hearing L's argument that diminution in value was not an appropriate method of calculation was rejected, and L's submissions that they were only liable to pay the rebated rent for the period that H was out of occupation, on account of her being in receipt of housing benefit, were also rejected. Judgment for H was assessed as follows: (1) diminution in value, based on rent of £40 at 50 per cent for the 16 weeks between May 1995 to September 1995, 30 per cent for the 38 weeks between September 1995 to June 1996, 100 per cent for the four weeks between June 1996 to July 1996, and 50 per cent for the eight weeks between July 1996 to September 1996; (2) special damages of £500, and (3) general damages of £2,000. Interest of £734 was added making a total award of £4,343.

HOLMES v. LAMBETH LBC, February 7, 1997, District Judge Gittens, CC (Wandsworth). [*Ex rel.* Tracey Bloom, Barrister, 1 Pump Court, Temple].

2644. Fire precautions—notice to provide fire escape—undertaking thought to be given confirming premises were not residential—breach of undertaking— nature of consultation with owner

[Housing Act 1985 s.368(1), s.368(2), s.366.]

Justices found that D had contravened an undertaking made under the Housing Act 1985 s.368(2) contrary to s.368(3). A notice had been served, under s.366, requiring a fire escape to be provided in premises owned by D. Following negotiations, the notice was withdrawn on D confirming that the premises were no longer being used for residential purposes. B took this to be an undertaking. When it became apparent that the premises were still occupied and no fire escape had been provided, B prosecuted. D appealed by way of case stated. It was submitted that (1) before a valid undertaking could have been given, under s.368, there had to be consultation; (2) an offer must be made by one party and accepted by the other, and (3) a penal notice should be appended to formal notification of the nature and terms of the undertaking.

Held, dismissing the appeal, that B had been under no general duty to consult D. There was a duty to consult, under s.368(2), where a local authority intended to accept an undertaking rather than secure that part of a property which was not used for human habitation, under s.368(1). The word "consultation" should be given its ordinary meaning and there was no reason to imply contract law into a practical means of dealing with a practical difficulty, *R. v. Secretary of State for Social Services, ex p. AMA* [1986] 1 W.L.R. 1, [1986] C.L.Y. 1635 distinguished. An undertaking had been given within the terms of s.368(2). Had B been obliged to serve a penal notice the legislation would have said so. Justices had been entitled to conclude that consultation had taken place on the face of correspondence between B and D.

Observed, it was unnecessary to resolve the question of undertakings in respect of the whole of a house, as in the instant case, when the terms of s.368 dealt with part of a house used for human habitation.

DESMOND v. BROMLEY LBC (1996) 28 H.L.R. 518, Staughton, L.J., QBD.

2645. Grants—family rehoused on demolition of former home—curtains unsuitable for new house—eligibility for disturbance payment—expense of new curtains a direct consequence of removal

[Land Compensation Act 1973 s.29, s.37, s.38.]

A and his family lived in a private rented house until 1995, when D made a demolition order in respect of the property. Upon taking up residence in the private rented house A had fitted curtains to each of the six windows in the property. Following the demolition D rehoused A and his family in a new council house. The curtains which A had fitted in the old house did not fit the windows in the new house. Upon being rehoused A received a home loss payment of £1,500 under the Land Compensation Act 1973 s.29 and, under s.37 and s.38, a disturbance payment of £183, in respect of van hire and electrical work. From the home loss payment A purchased new curtains at a cost of £300 and claimed this as a disturbance payment from D. D argued that the cost of curtaining the new house was not a natural and direct consequence of the removal.

Held, allowing the claim in full, that the question of whether a particular expense claimed is or is not within the ambit of a disturbance payment will be one of circumstance and degree, *Glasgow Corp v. Anderson* 1976 S.L.T. 225 applied. In the circumstances of the instant case including, inter alia, the fact that A could not re-use the curtains at the new house and that he reasonably required curtains at the new house, it was impossible to avoid the conclusion that the expense of purchasing the new curtains was a direct and natural consequence of the removal.

ALLEN v. DONCASTER MBC (1997) 73 P. & C.R. 98, M St J Hooper, FRICS, Lands Tr.

2646. Grants—improvement grants—refusal of payment—procedure

See CIVIL PROCEDURE: Trustees of the Dennis Rye Pension Fund v. Sheffield City Council. §490

2647. Grants—relocation grants—conditions for payment

RELOCATION GRANTS REGULATIONS 1997, SI 1997 2764; made under the Housing Grants, Construction and Regeneration Act 1996 s.132, s.134. In force: December 16, 1997; £1.10.

These Regulations prescribe conditions for payment of relocation grants and set the maximum amount payable at £20,000.

2648. Grants—relocation grants—form of application

RELOCATION GRANTS (FORM OF APPLICATION) REGULATIONS 1997, SI 1997 2847; made under the Housing Grants, Construction and Regeneration Act 1996 s.132, s.133. In force: December 16, 1997; £5.60.

These Regulations prescribe the form of an application for a relocation grant payable under the Housing Grants, Construction and Regeneration Act 1996 s.134.

2649. Grants—renewal grants

HOUSING RENEWAL GRANTS (AMENDMENT) REGULATIONS 1997, SI 1997 977; made under the Housing Grants, Construction and Regeneration Act 1996 s.3, s.30, s.31, s.146. In force: April 14, 1997; £1.55.

These Regulations amend the Housing Renewal Grants Regulations 1996 (SI 1996 2890) which provide for housing renewal grants generally and for the amount of renovation grant and disabled facilities grant which may be paid by local housing authorities in respect of applications by owner-occupiers and tenants under the Housing Grants, Construction and Regeneration Act 1996 Part II. The amendments reflect changes to housing benefit rules.

2650. Grants–renewal grants–forms

HOUSING RENEWAL GRANTS (PRESCRIBED FORM AND PARTICULARS) (AMENDMENT) REGULATIONS 1997, SI 1997 978; made under the Housing Grants, Construction and Regeneration Act 1996 s.2, s.101, s.146. In force: April 14, 1997; £1.10.

These Regulations amend the form set out in the Schedule to the Housing Renewal Grants (Prescribed Form and Particulars) Regulations 1996 (SI 1996 2891) to be used by owner-occupiers and tenants when applying for housing renewal grants under the Housing Grants, Construction and Regeneration Act 1996 Part I. Most of the amendments are consequential to amendments being made by the Housing Renewal Grants (Amendment) Regulations 1997 (SI 1997 977) to the Housing Renewal Grants Regulations 1996 (SI 1996 2890 amended by SI 1996 3119).

2651. Homelessness–asylum seekers

HOMELESSNESS (PERSONS SUBJECT TO IMMIGRATION CONTROL) (AMENDMENT) ORDER 1997, SI 1997 628; made under the Asylum and Immigration Act 1996 s.9. In force: March 28, 1997; £0.65.

This Order amends the Housing Accommodation and Homelessness (Persons subject to Immigration Control) Order 1996 (SI 1996 1982) Art.4 by introducing a requirement that, for an asylum seeker who has had an appeal outstanding to fall within Class F in Art.4, his original claim must have been determined on or before February 4, 1996.

2652. Homelessness–asylum seekers–asylum not claimed on arrival–relevant date for determining eligibility for housing

[Asylum and Immigration Act 1996 s.9(2); Housing Act 1985 s.6, s.64; Housing Act 1985 Part III; Interpretation Act 1978 s.16(1).]

B and another applied for judicial review of decisions by local authorities that they were no longer eligible for help under the Housing Act 1985 Part III. B entered the UK after February 5, 1996, the date on which, according to the provisions of the Asylum and Immigration Act 1996 s.9(2), asylum seekers like B, who did not claim asylum on arrival, ceased to be eligible for such help, but applied for housing before August 19, 1996, the date on which the 1996 Act came into force. S carried out investigations in accordance with its statutory duties under the 1985 Act but indicated on August 19, 1996 that B was no longer eligible for help. B contended that the relevant date for determining eligibility was the date of the initial application for housing and that s.9(2) could not affect applications made before it came into force. B argued, further, that if it did have such effect, then it would impliedly partially repeal Part III of the 1985 Act, in which case the Interpretation Act 1978 s.16(1) could be invoked to preserve pre-existing rights.

Held, dismissing the application, that, in view of the fact that duties imposed on a housing authority under s.62 to s.64 of the 1985 Act were in different stages, it was appropriate to consider matters at each stage and not take the date of application as the material date. As for the effect on pre-existing rights, B's only right was to have the housing authority make inquiries and provide accommodation pending the conclusion of those inquiries. The coming into force of s.9(2) would inevitably lead the authority to conclude that B was no longer eligible, *R. v. Secretary of State for the Environment, ex p. Shelter and the Refugee Council* [1997] C.O.D. 49, [1997] C.L.Y. 3654 followed.

R. v. SOUTHWARK LBC, *ex p.* BEDIAKO; R. v. WESTMINSTER CITY COUNCIL, *ex p.* ZAFRU, *The Times*, March 17, 1997, Stephen Richards, QBD.

2653. Homelessness–asylum seekers–local authorities–duty to provide suitable accommodation

[Asylum and Immigration Appeals Act 1993; Housing Act 1985 Part III s.62, s.63, s.65, s.69.]

K appealed against the dismissal of her application for judicial review of the decision of K that it had no duty to provide her with suitable accommodation because she was an asylum seeker. K argued that the Asylum and Immigration Appeals Act 1993 had limited the duty of a local housing authority under the Housing Act 1985 Part III s.65 and s.69, in respect of asylum seekers. K contended that (1) it no longer had a statutory duty to provide suitable accommodation for an asylum seeker who was unintentionally homeless and in priority need, but need only discharge the interim duty under s.63 to provide temporary accommodation and (2) para.3 of the 1993 Act meant that, in respect of an asylum seeker only, it had no duty to consider intentionality and need never make enquiries under s.62 of the 1985 Act.

Held, allowing the appeal, that (1) there was no difference between the duty owed to an asylum seeker and that to any other applicant; (2) the purpose of s.4(3) of the 1993 Act was to exclude a duty to provide settled and not merely temporary accommodation to asylum seekers. However, following *R. v. Brent LBC, ex p. Awua* [1996] 1 A.C. 55, [1995] 1 C.L.Y. 2569, and contrary to previous opinion, it was now clear that the s.65 duty could be discharged by the provision of temporary housing to any applicant, which brought the position of other applicants into line with asylum seekers. However, there was no reason why temporary accommodation should ipso facto be suitable, *R. v. Brent LBC, ex p. Awua* [1996] 1 A.C. 55, [1995] 1 C.L.Y. 2569 followed, and (3) the 1993 Act did not support K's contention that they were relieved of the need to undertake s.62 enquiries to determine if a duty was owed under s.65(2) before giving notice under para.3(1) of the 1993 Act.

R. v. KENSINGTON AND CHELSEA RLBC, *ex p.* KORNEVA, *The Times,* January 1, 1997, Simon Brown, L.J., CA.

2654. Homelessness–asylum seekers–local authorities–duty to provide suitable accommodation–extent of provision for those subject to immigration control

[Supreme Court Act 1981 s.31 (2); Asylum and Immigration Act 1996 s.9, s.10, s.11; Housing Act 1985 Part III.]

S sought a declaration under the Supreme Court Act 1981 s.31 (2) as to the extent that the Asylum and Immigration Act 1996 s.9 affected local authority obligations to provide accommodation for persons subject to immigration control under the Housing Act 1985 Part III, with effect from August 19, 1996, the date on which s.9 of the 1996 came into effect. S contended that s.9 should not be interpreted as affecting rights acquired prior to that date.

Held, refusing the declaration, that the effect of s.9(2) of the 1996 Act was to remove those subject to immigration control from the provisions of the 1985 Act unless they belonged to a class of persons covered by orders that the Secretary of State made under s.9(1). Duties were imposed in three stages under the 1985 Act: interim duties, which applied to the homeless in priority need where no decision had been reached as to their status; temporary duties, which applied to the intentionally homeless with priority need and full duties, where unintentional homelessness with priority need had been established. After August 19, s.9 did not remove rights previously acquired, but affected the way they would be dealt with. The 1996 Act fundamentally affected the way such applications were considered in accordance with the principles given in *R. v. Wandsworth LBC, ex p. Mansoor* [1996] 3 W.L.R. 282, [1996] 1 C.L.Y. 3059 and *R. v. Brent LBC, ex p. Awua* [1996] 1 A.C. 55, [1995] 1 C.L.Y. 2569. The ending of benefits under s.10 and s.11 of the 1996 Act also required local authorities to consider financial provision, where assistance could become needed given the absence of other forms of finance. Those with a pre-existing full duty were secure in private accommodation until they become homeless;

however, those caught at the interim stage at the point s.9 became effective were in a precarious situation, as there was nothing for the authority to inquire into, so that non-eligibility occurred on August 19, although authorities were under a public law duty to act reasonably in terminating accommodation provision, *Minister of Health v. Bellotti* [1944] K.B. 298 considered. Given the lack of guidance, the declaratory relief sought was inappropriate.

R. v. SECRETARY OF STATE FOR THE ENVIRONMENT, *ex p.* SHELTER AND THE REFUGEE COUNCIL [1997] C.O.D. 49, Carnwath, J., QBD.

2655. Homelessness–asylum seekers–local housing authority was not entitled to apply legislation retrospectively to remove right to accommodation

[Asylum and Immigration Act 1996 s.9; Housing Act 1985 s.65(2).]

K, an asylum seeker, applied to the local housing authority, H, for accommodation which was granted after H concluded that it owed K a duty under the Housing Act 1985 s.65(2) as he was in priority need and not intentionally homeless. When the Asylum and Immigration Act 1996 s.9 came into force, certain categories of asylum seekers were made ineligible for housing benefits and HLBC, concluding that s.9 removed its obligation to house K, gave him notice to quit. K renewed his application for leave to seek judicial review of the decision, arguing that the 1996 Act s.9 did not affect his right to occupy the accommodation, since to hold otherwise would be contrary to well established principles against the retrospective application of legislation.

Held, allowing the application and granting judicial review after a full hearing, that H was not entitled to serve notice to quit on K, and his right to occupy the accommodation provided had therefore been terminated unlawfully. Section 9 of the 1996 Act did not have retrospective effect and meant only that a person in K's position would no longer be regarded as eligible once the Act was in force. Accordingly, the coming into force of the 1996 Act was not a fresh circumstance which H could regard as a reasonable ground for reconsidering its earlier decision that it owed K a duty under s.65(2) of the 1985 Act, *R. v. Secretary of State for the Environment, ex p. Shelter and the Refugee Council* [1997] C.O.D. 49, [1997] C.L.Y 2654 disapproved.

R. v. HACKNEY LBC, *ex p.* K, *The Times*, November 17, 1997, Lord Woolf, M.R., CA.

2656. Homelessness–eligibility for assistance–Scilly Isles

HOMELESSNESS (ISLES OF SCILLY) ORDER 1997, SI 1997 797; made under the Housing Act 1996 s.225. In force: April 3, 1997; £0.65.

This Order modifies the Housing Act 1996 Part VII as it relates to the Isles of Scilly. It provides that a person is not eligible for assistance in the Isles of Scilly if he has not been resident there for a period of two years and six months during the period of three years immediately before his application. Where a person is not excluded from assistance under that provision, he will have a local connection with the district of that authority.

2657. Homelessness–immigrants–local authority housing–Amendment No.1

ALLOCATION OF HOUSING AND HOMELESSNESS (AMENDMENT) REGULATIONS 1997, SI 1997 631; made under the Housing Act 1996 s.161, s.165, s.185, s.203. In force: Reg.1, Reg.4, Reg.5, Reg.6(a) (in part): March 28, 1997; Reg.2, Reg.3, Reg.6(a) (in part): April 1, 1997; £1.10.

These Regulations amend the classes of persons subject to immigration control prescribed in the Allocation of Housing Regulations 1996 (SI 1996 2753) who are qualified to be allocated housing accommodation under the Housing Act 1996 Part VI and the classes of persons subject to immigration control prescribed in the Homelessness Regulations 1996 (SI 1996 2754) who are eligible for housing assistance under Part VII of the 1996 Act.

2658. Homelessness–immigrants–local authority housing–Amendment No.2

ALLOCATION OF HOUSING AND HOMELESSNESS (AMENDMENT) (NO.2) REGULATIONS 1997, SI 1997 2046; made under the Housing Act 1996 s.161, s.185. In force: August 27, 1997; £0.65.

These Regulations make amendments to the Allocation of Housing and Homelessness Regulations 1996 (SI 1996 as amended by SI 1997 631) and the Homelessness Regulations 1996 (SI 1996 2754 as amended by SI 1997 631). The effect of the amendments is to change the classes of persons prescribed under the Housing Act 1996 s.161 (3) so as to except from the test of habitual residence in the Common Travel Area a person who left the territory of Montserrat after November 1, 1995 because of the effect on that territory of a volcanic eruption.

2659. Homelessness–intentional homelessness–applicants promising to move out when owners returned but not subject to possession proceedings–whether applicants threatened with homelessness

[Housing Act 1985 s.58; Housing Act 1988 s.7, Sch.2.]

The applicants had rented a property, by an oral agreement, on the understanding that they would move out when the owners returned from abroad. B concluded that the applicants were not threatened with homelessness, not having been the subject of possession proceedings. It was submitted that (1) B had failed to have regard to the promise to vacate the property and that it would be unsatisfactory for two families to occupy it concurrently; thus, a judge would be certain to grant a possession order in favour of the landlord, and (2) as B had not said that they had considered whether continued occupation was reasonable it was not open to them to argue it after the event.

Held, dismissing the application, that B's decision had not been unlawful. They had been entitled to conclude that the landlord would not necessarily succeed in possession proceedings. The decision had addressed the central issue and a subsequent affidavit only amplified the reasoning, *R. v. Westminster City Council, ex p. Ermakov* [1996] 2 All E.R. 302, [1995] 1 C.L.Y. 2568 distinguished and *Poyser and Mills' Arbitration, Re* [1964] 2 Q.B. 467, [1963] C.L.Y. 43 applied. In possession proceedings under the Housing Act 1988 s.7 a judge would be likely to follow *Bradshaw v. Baldwin-Wiseman* (1985) 17 H.L.R. 260, [1985] C.L.Y. 1942, as to the consequences of the failure of the landlord to give notice in writing, so that B's decision was not vitiated by a failure to consider Sch.2 Ground 1 of the 1988 Act.

R. v. BRADFORD CITY COUNCIL, *ex p.* PARVEEN (1996) 28 H.L.R. 681, Roger Toulson Q.C., QBD.

2660. Homelessness–intentional homelessness–burden of proof–local authority's duty to consider all information before them

D applied to W for housing as a homeless person. W chose to treat D as being intentionally homeless following a series of interviews. In a decision letter from W, D was informed that, as much of the information she had given had been contradictory, they had chosen to rely upon the events related to them by D in the most recent interview. The letter also stated that some of the aspects of the information given by D had failed to convince them that she was not intentionally homeless. D sought judicial review of that decision.

Held, allowing the application and quashing the decision, that (1) W had a duty to consider all the information placed before them rather than arbitrarily selecting just one version of events, and (2) it lay with W to show that D was intentionally homeless and not with D to prove to the contrary.

R. v. WANDSWORTH LBC, *ex p.* DODIA, Trans. Ref: CO-1157/97, July 18, 1997, Jowitt, J., QBD.

2661. Homelessness–intentional homelessness–Colombian applicant with property abroad–no attempt to realise share in equity–no affect on issue of intentional homelessness

[Housing Act 1985 s.60, s.65.]

A, who had joint British and Colombian nationality, had received a grant of £20,000 to surrender a tenancy from C. The money was used as a contribution to the purchase of a house in Colombia. A's marriage broke down and, having no income, she was unable to keep up mortgage repayments. The house was let and A returned to the UK. When she applied to be housed, under the Housing Act 1985 s.65, C concluded that she was intentionally homeless. A sought judicial review.

Held, allowing the application, that C had misdirected itself under s.60(1). The flaw in C's reasoning was that the only asset that A possessed was a share in the equity of the Colombian house. She could not dispose of the asset and live in it at the same time and, in any event, lacked the means to keep up repayments having been deserted by her husband. That she had made no attempt to realise her share in the equity did not affect the issue of whether she was intentionally homeless, *Galoo v. Bright Grahame Murray* [1994] 1 W.L.R. 1360, [1995] 2 C.L.Y. 3691, *R. v. Hillingdon LBC, ex p. Tinn* (1988) 20 H.L.R. 305, [1988] C.L.Y. 1762, *R. v. Hillingdon LBC, ex p. Puhlhofer* [1986] A.C. 484, [1986] C.L.Y. 1618 and *R. v. Brent LBC, ex p. Awua* (1995) 27 H.L.R. 453, [1995] 1 C.L.Y. 2569 considered. C would be granted leave to appeal.

R. v. CAMDEN LBC, *ex p.* ARANDA (1996) 28 H.L.R. 672, Roger Toulson Q.C., QBD.

2662. Homelessness–intentional homelessness–failure to pay rent–tenant's priorities in spending–housing authority to decide necessities of life and tenant's ability to pay

[Housing Act 1985 s.60(1).]

BLBC appealed against a ruling quashing their decision that B, who was served with a notice to quit after failing to pay rent, was intentionally homeless within the Housing Act 1985 s.60(1) on the grounds that BLBC had failed to make adequate inquiries into B's finances and had drawn unjustified conclusions about B's lifestyle. BLBC, in determining whether B was intentionally homeless, had taken into account the fact that B had chosen to spend her available resources on a university course, the maintenance of her car and nursery fees for her children.

Held, allowing the appeal, that, when assessing whether an applicant was intentionally homeless, a housing authority was obliged to consider whether failure to pay rent was deliberate and whether it was due to the inadequacy of resources to cover the necessities of life, *R. v. Hillingdon LBC, ex p. Tinn* (1988) 20 H.L.R. 305, [1989] C.L.Y. 1882 and *R. v. Wandsworth, ex p. Hawthorne* (1994) 27 H.L.R. 59, [1994] C.L.Y. 2326 considered. Whilst it was important to recognise that what were considered the necessities of life might vary in different families, it was for the housing authority to determine what were necessities in any given case. The court could only quash a decision on normal judicial review principles. In the instant case, BLBC had addressed the right question and there were no grounds for interfering with their decision.

R. v. BRENT LBC, *ex p.* BARUWA, *The Independent*, February 27, 1997, Schiemann, L.J., CA.

2663. Homelessness–intentional homelessness–mortgage met by DSS–sale of property–continued occupation reasonable

A bought a flat with a mortgage and a loan from his family. His income was £1,000 per month of which £650 was paid under the mortgage. A became unemployed and the interest payments on the mortgage were paid by the DSS. A then moved out of the flat, sold the flat and moved to Bangladesh. On his return from Bangaladesh six months later A applied to WCC for accommodation as a homeless person. WCC decided that A was intentionally homeless as he had left the flat when it was reasonable for him to continue to occupy it. A sought judicial review.

Held, dismissing the application, that there was no evidence that there was any threat of possession proceedings or that the family required repayment of the loan. A's actions indicated that he had decided to realise the value of the flat and render himself intentionally homeless.

R. v. WESTMINSTER CITY COUNCIL, *ex p.* ALI (1997) 29 H.L.R. 580, Judge Rich Q.C., QBD.

2664. Homelessness–intentional   homelessness–reasonable   likelihood   of cessation of occupation due to conduct test

[Housing Act 1985 s.60(1).]

R applied for judicial review of HLBC's decision that he was intentionally homeless in terms of the Housing Act 1985 s.60(1). R gave up his tenancy on receiving a seven year sentence for indecently assaulting children and HLBC argued that his offending amounted to deliberate conduct in consequence of which he ceased to occupy his accommodation.

Held, dismissing the application, that the appropriate test for a housing authority considering the question of causation when determining whether an applicant for housing was intentionally homeless was the objective test of whether the applicant's ceasing to occupy his accommodation would reasonably have been regarded at the time as a likely result of his deliberate conduct. It was apparent that HLBC had applied such a test in making its decision.

R. v. HOUNSLOW LBC, *ex p.* R, *The Times,* February 25, 1997, Stephen Richards, QBD.

2665. Homelessness–intentional homelessness–rent withheld due to disrepair– temporary accommodation–guest house accommodation–whether chain of causation of homelessness broken

[Housing Act 1985 Part II; Housing Act 1985 s.62.]

H appealed against a ruling that quashed its decision that F was intentionally homeless and that it owed no duty to rehouse F and her six children. F, a Somalian national, an assured shorthold tenant, withheld a month's rent because of disrepair, was subsequently evicted from her flat and was given temporary accommodation for 42 days in a guest house at a cost of £514 per week while H considered their duty under the Housing Act 1985 Part II. H decided that F was in priority need but was intentionally homeless because she had failed to make payment to her landlord. F later discovered that she would have had a full defence to the possession proceedings on technical grounds. H subsequently reduced F's housing benefit payments to £250, which was the average rent for a five bedroomed property, whereupon F was given notice and re-applied to H as homeless. H claimed it had no duty to rehouse because F had not had any intervening settled accommodation since the original intentional homelessness. F applied to review that decision on the grounds that (1) H should have taken into account the fresh information showing that the order for possession had been made wrongly made, and (2) her stay at the guest house had been settled accommodation since it exceeded the 42 days and the reason for her homelessness was the cut in housing benefit, thus breaking the original intentionality.

Held, dismissing the appeal, quashing the decision and remitting the matter to H, that (1) the trial judge had been correct to decide that H had not been under any duty to review its finding of intentionality in the light of the fresh evidence, particularly since the order for possession had not been appealed or set aside, and (2) a finding of intentionality disqualified a further application under s.62 of the 1985 Act; however if such an application were made, then the local authority had a duty to enquire whether the original intentionality survived or whether it had been superseded either by the acquisition of "a settled residence" or by another supervening event that was a new material cause of homelessness, *R. v. Brent LBC, ex p. Awua* [1996] 1 A.C. 55, [1995] 1

C.L.Y. 2569, *R. v. Basingstoke and Deane BC, ex p. Bassett* (1983) 10 H.L.R. 125, [1984] C.L.Y. 1631 and *Din (Taj) v. Wandsworth LBC* [1983] 1 A.C. 657, [1981] C.L.Y. 1296 followed, and *R. v. Westminster City Council, ex p. Chambers* (1983) 81 L.G.R. 401 distinguished on its facts.

R. v. HARROW LBC, *ex p.* FAHIA (1997) 29 H.L.R. 974, Roch, L.J., CA.

2666. Homelessness–intentional   homelessness–temporary   or   precarious accommodation–pregnancy not cause of homelessness

[Housing Act 1985 s.64.]

A applied for judicial review of the decision that she was intentionally homeless under the Housing Act 1985 s.64. A, a British citizen, married a Nigerian and moved to Nigeria where she lived for six years. Subsequently, she returned to the UK, originally staying with a friend for 19 months and later with another friend for 10 months. Both properties were overcrowded and when A's third child was born she was asked to leave her accommodation and she applied for housing assistance. A contended that H had (1) wrongly identified "temporary" with "precarious" accommodation, and (2) reached an unreasonable conclusion with regard to the immediate cause of A's homelessness, which it asserted was the temporary nature of her accommodation rather than her pregnancy.

Held, refusing the application, that (1) H had been justified in using the term "temporary" in the sense of "precarious" in relation to A's accommodation and had taken into account all material considerations; (2) it was clear from *Awua* and other recent decisions that the obtaining of settled accommodation and certain other events could break the chain of causation, and (3) H had been entitled to consider in a common sense manner that the effective cause of A's homelessness was not her pregnancy but her own action in leaving the flat in Nigeria, which was still occupied by her husband and two other children, *Din v. Wandsworth LBC* [1983] 1 A.C. 657, [1981] C.L.Y. 1296 and *R. v. Brent LBC, ex p. Awua* [1996] 1 A.C. 55, [1995] 1 C.L.Y. 2569 approved, *R. v. Croydon LBC, ex p. Graham* (1994) 26 H.L.R. 286, [1995] 1 C.L.Y. 2572 distinguished on its facts, and *R. v. Harrow LBC, ex p. Fahia* (1997) 29 H.L.R. 94, [1997] C.L.Y. 2665 considered.

R. v. HACKNEY LBC, *ex p.* AJAYI, Trans. Ref: C0/3195/96, May 20, 1997, Dyson, J., QBD.

2667. Homelessness–intentional homelessness–unawareness of prospects of obtaining employment did not constitute unawareness of relevant fact

[Housing Act 1985 s.60(3).]

Held, that it was open to a local authority to conclude that an applicant for housing who had given up rented accommodation in France to come to England in search of employment, but had encountered difficulties in finding work, firstly because she was pregnant and later because of problems with child care, was intentionally homeless. In order for an applicant to establish unawareness of a relevant fact within the Housing Act 1985 s.60(3), the fact relied on had to be sufficiently clear and exact for its existence to be determined objectively. In the instant case, lack of foresight on the part of the applicant as to her true prospects of employment did not constitute unawareness of a relevant fact existing at the time she gave up her accommodation in France.

R. v. WESTMINSTER CITY COUNCIL, *ex p.* N'DORMADINGAR, *The Times*, November 20, 1997, Lightman, J., QBD.

2668. Homelessness–local authority duty to determine housing application–immigration status of applicant uncertain

M was given leave to enter the United Kingdom from Tanzania. He went to live in his son's house, but the son subsequently asked him to leave. M applied to BLBC for accommodation but BLBC indicated its preliminary view that, by leaving Tanzania, M had made himself intentionally homeless. In subsequent decision letters BLBC indicated that M's entry to the country had been sponsored by his son who had guaranteed to provide accommodation and so BLBC had no duty to house M. A further letter indicated that M was in breach of the conditions of entry and accordingly an illegal immigrant. M sought judicial review of the decisions. BLBC invited M's solicitors to withdraw the application whilst a new decision was made, but no action was taken and no decision was reached. At the hearing of M's application for an order of mandamus BLBC resisted the order and sought more time within which to reach a decision as they were awaiting information from the Secretary of State relating to M's status as an immigrant, and they had encountered difficulties in obtaining access to the son's property.

Held, allowing the application, that BLBC would be given 28 days within which to make a decision and three days thereafter to notify M of that decision. BLBC had already had sufficient time within which to make a decision.

R. v. BRENT LBC, *ex p.* MIYANGER (1997) 29 H.L.R. 628, Harrison, J., QBD.

2669. **Homelessness–possession proceedings–tenant obtaining several council houses as a direct result of deliberate deception**

[Housing Act 1985 s.84(2)(a).]

From 1987 to 1993 E lived with her husband in a property (MFH) purchased by them with a mortgage. In May 1988 and October 1989 E applied to S for public authority housing, stating in her application that she and her four children were living with E's mother, together with five other adults. The second application was successful, and E obtained the secure tenancy of a council house (SW) in January 1991. In May 1992 E's mortgagees issued proceedings claiming possession of MFH, and in June 1992 E made a further application for public authority housing, this time to N, for herself and her four children. In December 1992 N granted E a tenancy of a council house (WG). N was then alerted by an anonymous phone call that E already had another council house, and they began possession proceedings to recover WG. S then learnt that E had obtained another council property and began possession proceedings against her in respect of SW. In resisting the action E refused to give discovery, and an order was made prohibiting her from defending the proceedings. Her only defence consisted of a letter from her solicitor, which referred, inter alia, to the obligation of S to provide E with temporary accommodation if they succeeded in obtaining a possession order and the unsuitability of such accommodation for a woman with four children and a baby. A housing officer of S gave evidence to the effect that three of E's children had special educational needs and that these would continue to be met if E were housed in temporary accommodation. A possession order was made in reliance on the Housing Act 1985 s.84(2)(a) on the ground that S had been induced to grant E a tenancy by a false statement made by her. E appealed, contending, inter alia, that the judge did not pay sufficient regard to the risk of E being found to be intentionally homeless and matters concerning the children.

Held, dismissing the appeal, that the words of s.84 of the 1985 Act that the court should not make an order for possession unless it considered it reasonable to make the order were unqualified and of the widest import, *Cumming v. Danson* [1942] 2 All E.R. 653 and *Rushcliffe BC v. Watson* (1991) 24 H.L.R. 124, [1992] C.L.Y. 2323 considered. In a case such as this, where there had been deliberate lying to obtain public housing, only in exceptional cases would the court consider the effect of the homelessness legislation, *Bristol City Council v. Mousah*, (Unreported, 1997) and *Darlington BC v. Sterling* (1997) 29 H.L.R. 309, [1997] C.L.Y. 2717 applied. It was the function of the local authority not the court to decide whether or not a person was intentionally homeless. In deciding questions of reasonableness in a case such as the instant one a court could in exceptional circumstances take into account the nature and degree of the untrue statements and the circumstances in which they were made. In this case E lied deliberately and flagrantly and compounded her lies when her deception was discovered. Apart from merely recognising that E had placed herself in a position in which S would have to consider whether E was intentionally homeless the judge did not need to consider how E would be rehoused. The judge's decision could not be impugned.

SHREWSBURY AND ATCHAM BC v. EVANS, Trans. Ref: CCRTF 96/0218/H, April 22, 1997, Beldam, L.J., CA.

2670. Homelessness–priority need–joint residence of four dependent children

D, aged 55, had joint residence of his four dependent children, aged between seven and 13, from Thursday to Monday each week, but was given only temporary accommodation in a single room after he left the former matrimonial home. D contended that O had applied the wrong test and had considered irrelevant matters, such as whether D would be able to take the children to school while he was in full time employment, and the shortages of its housing stock. D claimed that the residence of the children was not a matter of decision for the housing authority. D applied for judicial review of a decision that he was homeless but not in priority need and a subsequent confirmatory appeal decision.

Held, dismissing the application, that, although certain parts of the report appeared to suggest that the appeal panel had erred, the correct tests had been applied in making its decision that, given D's circumstances, the children could not reasonably be expected to reside with D.

R. v. OXFORD CC, *ex p.* DOYLE, Trans. Ref: CO 683-97, June 20, 1997, Tucker, J., QBD.

2671. Homelessness–priority need–mental illness–assessment of vulnerability of mentally ill applicant

[Housing Act 1985 s.59.]

D sought judicial review of a decision by G, that he was not vulnerable by reason of his mental illness and therefore not in priority housing need, and relief from a subsequent decision to commence possession proceedings against him. D had been charged with theft and his defence was that, as a member of the Yugoslav Royal family, he had a particular kind of credit card which registered transactions automatically without the necessity of producing the card. Whilst D had been remanded in prison, a medical report concluded that he suffered from a psychotic illness in the form of delusions of grandeur. He was acquitted of theft by reason of his mental condition and was subsequently treated in hospital. G construed a hospital medical report to mean that D was able to find and maintain accommodation for himself. The same doctor, when asked for more information, gave a further opinion that D's condition made him "vulnerable" within the meaning of the Housing Act 1985 s.59. G's district medical officer concluded otherwise. G drew attention to D's time in a bail hostel where it appeared he could manage his financial affairs.

Held, allowing the application and quashing the decisions, that whilst in temporary accommodation D had accumulated £196 rent arrears. It was clear that G's officer had been unaware of this and, accordingly, could not have taken it into account. The district medical officer had not examined D nor sought clarification from the hospital consultant psychiatrist with whose view he differed. The second report had specifically addressed the question of whether D was capable of looking after himself. It was a matter of common sense that someone with D's delusions was unlikely to be able to manage his own financial affairs, a view borne out by the medical reports and the rent arrears, *R. v. Waveney DC, ex p. Bowers* [1983] Q.B. 238, [1982] C.L.Y. 1467 and *Ortis v. Westminster City Council* (1995) 27 H.L.R. 364, [1995] 1 C.L.Y. 2576 applied.

R. v. GREENWICH LBC, *ex p.* DUKIC (1997) 29 H.L.R. 87, Roger Toulson Q.C., QBD.

2672. Homelessness–re-offer of accommodation after racist slogans removed

O, a Nigerian, and her dependent son, who were homeless, refused the re-offer of a property because of their fears of racial attack when they found that the doors and windows of the property had been painted with racist slogans and racist threats had been posted inside. O applied to review an appeal decision that it was reasonable, in discharge of its statutory duty, for I to re-offer the same property to her after the offensive material had been removed, claiming that it was merely a cosmetic exercise.

Held, allowing the application and quashing the decision, that the re-offer of the accommodation was not *Wednesbury* unreasonable, but the failure to give reasons for it, in such circumstances, was both unfair and unreasonable, *R. v. Secretary of State for the Home Department, ex p. Doody* [1994] 1 A.C. 531, [1993] C.L.Y. 1213 and *R. v. Kensington and Chelsea RLBC, ex p. Grillo* (1996) 28 H.L.R. 94, [1996] 1 C.L.Y. 3072 followed.

R. v. ISLINGTON LBC, *ex p.* OKOCHA, Trans. Ref: CO/2891/96, January 29, 1997, Judge Richards Q.C., QBD.

2673. Homelessness–suitable accommodation

HOMELESSNESS (SUITABILITY OF ACCOMMODATION) (AMENDMENT) ORDER 1997, SI 1997 1741; made under the Housing Act 1996 s.210, s.215. In force: September 1, 1997; £0.65.

This Order provides that, for the purposes of the Housing Act 1996 s.197(1), duty where other suitable accommodation available, accommodation shall not be regarded as suitable unless the local housing authority is satisfied that it will be available for occupation by the applicant for at least two years beginning with the date on which he secures it.

2674. Homelessness–temporary accommodation–breach of statutory duty to provide temporary accommodation not actionable in tort

[Housing Act 1985 Part III; Housing Act 1985 s.63(1).]

C appealed against a Court of Appeal decision reinstating O's claim for damages for breach of a statutory duty owed to him under the Housing Act 1985 Part III, which had been struck out in the county court as disclosing no cause of action. When O applied to C claiming to be homeless and in priority need, C agreed to make inquiries to determine whether he was homeless and provided him with temporary accommodation pursuant to s.63(1) of the 1985 Act. O contended that, by their actions, C had acknowledged a duty to him under s.63(1) to provide temporary accommodation and had breached that duty by wrongfully evicting him and failing to provide him with alternative accommodation. C argued that its duty under s.63(1) was only enforceable in public law and did not create a private law right which was actionable in tort.

Held, allowing the appeal, that the Act was a social welfare programme intended to confer benefits at public expense pursuant to public policy, which suggested that Parliament did not intend to confer private law rights in relation to it. Further, the duties under Part III had been made largely dependent on the judgment of the local authority, which made it unlikely that Parliament had intended errors of judgment to give rise to an award of damages. Following the ruling in *Cocks v. Thanet DC* [1983] 2 A.C. 286, [1982] C.L.Y. 1465, the duties under Part III which depended upon the local authority being satisfied as to various matters did not give rise to a private law cause of action, and there was nothing to suggest that Parliament had intended the duty to provide temporary accommodation under s.63(1) to be treated differently.

O'ROURKE v. CAMDEN LBC [1997] 3 W.L.R. 86, Lord Hoffmann, HL.

2675. Homelessness–temporary accommodation–extent of statutory duty under Housing Act 1985 s.65(2) where temporary accommodation provided–medical report not supplied

[Housing Act 1985 s.65(2), Sch.1 para.6.]

N accepted that they owed H a duty under the Housing Act 1985 s.65(2) and provided her with temporary accommodation, which had been let to N by the owner for the use of homeless persons, and was thus not a secure tenancy within Sch.1 para.6 of the 1985 Act. N then offered H a secure tenancy of a maisonette on the first and second floors of a property without a lift, which H refused claiming she suffered from joint pains precluding the use of stairs. N wrote that, given they had requested but not received a medical report on her condition, her tenancy would be terminated, and commenced possession proceedings for arrears and by reason of the offer of permanent accommodation. H sought judicial review of N's decision that they had discharged their duty to her under s.65(2). At the hearing N conceded that in the light of the medical evidence produced by H, the maisonette was not suitable accommodation, but argued that it had discharged its duty by provision of the "temporary" accommodation.

Held, dismissing the application, that the provision of temporary accommodation on a non-secure tenancy discharged N's obligations under s.65 of the Act, *R. v. Brent LBC, ex p. Awua* [1996] 1 A.C. 55, [1995] 1 C.L.Y. 2569 applied. If and when H lost that accommodation, N would be under a duty to consider a new application under the homelessness provisions.

R. v. NEWHAM LBC, *ex p.* HASSAN (1997) 29 H.L.R. 378, Judge Stephen Richards, QBD.

2676. Homelessness–temporary accommodation–policy not to provide interim accommodation pending review–lawfulness of policy

[Housing Act 1996 s.202.]

M, who had applied to C for housing, sought a review under the Housing Act 1996 s.202 of the council's decision that she was not homeless and applied for temporary accommodation pending the outcome of that review. The council's policy on interim accommodation, however, was that it could only be provided where there were exceptional reasons. M applied for judicial review of C's decision not to provide her with temporary housing, arguing that it could not have been the intention of the Act that a person seeking review of, or appealing against, a council's decision should be in a worse position than before the Act came into force.

Held, allowing the application and quashing the decision, that, given that there was no restriction on an applicant's right to apply for a review, it could not be the case that a local authority had to exercise its discretionary power to provide temporary accommodation as a matter of course. C's policy of providing interim housing only where there were "exceptional reasons" was not, therefore, unlawful. However, in deciding whether exceptional reasons existed, C was obliged to take into account material considerations such as the merits of the case, whether there was any new evidence which could affect the decision under review, the individual circumstances of the applicant and likely consequences of an adverse decision. C's decision in the instant case was flawed because they had drawn adverse conclusions about M's circumstances based on alleged discrepancies without giving M an opportunity to explain them.

R. v. CAMDEN LBC, *ex p.* MOHAMMED, *The Times*, June 20, 1997, Latham, J., QBD.

2677. Homelessness–temporary accommodation–suitability–local authority not on notice to investigate–applicant suffering multiple chemical sensitivity disorder

[Housing Act 1985 s.62, s.64.]

M suffered from multiple chemical sensitivity disorder. She had applied to join the S housing waiting list. Having received hospital treatment, she moved to a holiday let in Dorset in what was considered environmentally suitable accommodation. M applied for accommodation, under the Housing Act 1985 s.62, as being threatened with homelessness. S, in its decision under s.64, concluded that there was no immediate threat. M sought judicial review on the basis that S had not considered whether the temporary accommodation was suitable.

Held, dismissing the application, that S had made appropriate enquiries, under s.62, before concluding that the holiday let was available for the foreseeable future. S had no reason to suppose that there was an issue of suitability and had not been on notice to investigate it. The point not having been raised it was unnecessary for the decision letter to have considered it, *R. v. Woodspring DC, ex p. Walters* (1984) 16 H.L.R. 73, [1985] C.L.Y. 1616 and *R. v. Hillingdon LBC, ex p. Tinn* (1988) 20 H.L.R. 305, [1988] C.L.Y. 1762 considered and *Poyser and Mills' Arbitration, Re* [1964] 2 Q.B. 467, [1963] C.L.Y. 43 applied.

Observed, it was unfortunate that the application had ever been made since S had said that they would reconsider the matter were M's circumstances to change. Any fresh application to them would have to be considered on its merits.

R. v. SEDGEMOOR DC, *ex p.* MCCARTHY (1996) 28 H.L.R. 607, Roger Toulson Q.C., QBD.

2678. **Homelessness–threats of violence–property's safety–local authority requiring couple to move in before being able to appeal–undue fetter on discretion**

[Housing Act 1985 s.65(2).]

L applied for judicial review of decisions of N that (1) it had discharged its duties under the Housing Act 1985 s.65(2) by making L an offer of accommodation; (2) it was appropriate for N to require that L sign a tenancy and move into the rejected accommodation as a condition of being allowed to appeal against its suitability, and (3) it was appropriate to cancel provision of temporary bed and breakfast accommodation to L. It was accepted that the lives of L and her husband were in danger after a newspaper article alleged that he was a child molester and that L had requested housing outside the borough, but none had been available.

Held, allowing the application, that (1) it appeared that N had correctly decided that L had unreasonably refused the accommodation, not solely because it was unsafe, but because she wanted a two bedroom property with a garden for her dog; (2) however, N had unduly fettered its discretion by adopting a paternalistic and overly inflexible policy that required occupation of the disputed property before an appeal could be mounted, and (3) in the light of N's undertaking to continue to provide temporary accommodation, it was unnecessary to consider the third decision, *R. v. Newham LBC, ex p. Dada* (1995) 27 H.L.R. 502, [1995] 1 C.L.Y. 2580, *R. v. Newham LBC, ex p. Gentle* (1994) 26 H.L.R. 466, [1995] 1 C.L.Y. 2582, *R. v. Secretary of State for the Home Department, ex p. Doody* [1993] 3 W.L.R. 154, [1993] C.L.Y. 1213 followed.

R. v. NEWHAM LBC, *ex p.* LARWOOD, Trans. Ref: CO 1291-96, October 17, 1996, Judge Rich, QBD.

2679. **Housing–introductory tenancies–Amendment No.1**

HOUSING ACT 1996 (CONSEQUENTIAL AMENDMENTS) ORDER 1997, SI 1997 74; made under the Housing Act 1996 s.141, s.142, s.231. In force: February 12, 1997; £1.95.

This Order amends legislation in consequence of the provisions on introductory tenancies in the Housing Act 1996 Part V Ch.I. Most of the amendments are to housing legislation and add references to introductory tenancies where there are already references to secure tenancies.

2680. **Housing–introductory tenancies–possession of land**

INTRODUCTORY TENANTS (REVIEW) REGULATIONS 1997, SI 1997 72; made under the Housing Act 1996 s.129, s.142. In force: February 12, 1997; £1.10.

The Housing Act 1996 Part V Ch.1 established a regime of introductory tenancies. If the landlord is to end such a tenancy he must provide the tenant with a notice stating that the landlord is applying to the court for an order for possession, setting out the reasons for this decision and informing the tenant of his right to request a review of this decision. These Regulations make provision for the procedure to be followed in this review.

2681. Housing Act 1996–Amendment No.2–registered social landlords

HOUSING ACT 1996 (CONSEQUENTIAL AMENDMENTS) (NO.2) ORDER 1997, SI 1997 627; made under the Housing Act 1996 s.52, s.55, s.231. In force: April 1, 1997; £1.10.

This Order amends the Industrial and Provident Societies Act 1965, the Consumer Credit Act 1974, the Housing Act 1985, the Landlord and Tenant Acts 1985 and 1987, the Housing Act 1988 and the Leasehold Reform, Housing and Urban Development Act 1993 in consequence of provisions of the Housing Act 1996 which relate to registered social landlords.

2682. Housing Act 1996 (c.52)–Commencement No.6 Order

HOUSING ACT 1996 (COMMENCEMENT NO.6 AND SAVINGS) ORDER 1997, SI 1997 66 (C.5); made under the Housing Act 1996 s.232. Commencement details: bringing into force various provisions of the Act on February 12, 1997; £1.55.

This Order brings various provisions of the Housing Act 1996 into force.

2683. Housing Act 1996 (c.52)–Commencement No.7 Order

HOUSING ACT 1996 (COMMENCEMENT NO.7 AND SAVINGS) ORDER 1997, SI 1997 225 (C.12); made under the Housing Act 1996 s.232. Commencement details: bringing into force various provisions of the Act on February 28, 1997; £1.55.

This Order brings into force several provisions of the Housing Act 1996 relating to assured tenancies.

2684. Housing Act 1996 (c.52)–Commencement No.8 Order

HOUSING ACT 1996 (COMMENCEMENT NO.8) ORDER 1997, SI 1997 350 (C.16); made under the Housing Act 1996 s.232. Commencement details: bringing into force various provisions of the Act on March 3, 1997; £1.10.

This Order brings into force the Housing Act 1996 Part II so far as it is not already in force, other than s.73. Part II deals with the control of houses in multiple occupation, and the repeal of the Housing Act 1985 Part XII which concerns common lodging houses.

2685. Housing Act 1996 (c.52)–Commencement No.9 Order

HOUSING ACT 1996 (COMMENCEMENT NO.9) ORDER 1997, SI 1997 596 (C.21); made under the Housing Act 1996 s.232. Commencement details: bringing into force various provisions of the Act on March 3, 1997; £1.10.

This Order brings into force the repeals to the Housing Act 1996 Sch.19 Part II relating to the control of houses in multiple occupation.

2686. Housing Act 1996 (c.52)–Commencement No.10 Order

HOUSING ACT 1996 (COMMENCEMENT NO.10 AND TRANSITIONAL PROVISIONS) ORDER 1997, SI 1997 618 (C.22); made under the Housing Act 1996 s.232. Commencement details: bringing into force various provisions of the Act on April 1, 1997 and April 1, 1998; £1.95.

Subject to transitional provisions and savings this Order brings into force the remaining provisions of the Housing Act 1996 Part I (social rented sector), s.106 (low rent test for leasehold enfranchisement: extension of rights), s.118 (estate management schemes in connection with enfranchisement by virtue of s.106), Part IV (housing benefit and related matters) (other than s.120), and s.227 in so far as it relates to specified repeals.

2687. Housing Act 1996 (c.52)–Commencement No.11 Order

HOUSING ACT 1996 (COMMENCEMENT NO.11 AND SAVINGS) ORDER 1997, SI 1997 1851 (C.75); made under the Housing Act 1996 s.232. Commencement details: bringing into force various provisions of the Act on September 1, 1997; £1.55.

This Order brings into force the Housing Act 1996 s.83 which relates to the determination of reasonableness of service charges; s.86 which relates to the appointment of managers and the transfer of jurisdiction to the leasehold valuation tribunal; s.152 to s.154 which deal with anti-social behaviour, the power to grant injunctions and the power of arrest; part of s.155 relating to arrest and remand; s.157 and s.158 dealing with supplementary provisions on power of arrest and interpretation; and consequential repeals in Sch.19 Part III.

2688. Housing benefit–bed and breakfast accommodation–powers of Housing Benefit Review Board–comparators to be other guest houses not advertised rented properties

[Housing Benefit (General) Regulations 1987 (SI 1987 1971) Reg.83.]

The applicants sought review of a Housing Benefit Review Board decision upholding L's decision. The applicants, who were living in guest house accommodation, claimed that the Review Board had failed to determine that the rent was unreasonably high, had unreasonably found that the accommodation was not "bed and breakfast", but was a house in multiple occupation, and had made no finding on their personal circumstances.

Held, allowing the application and remitting the case to a fresh Review Board, that the Housing Benefit (General) Regulations 1987 Reg.83 made it clear that the Review Board must reach its own independent decision. It was unacceptable for the Board to reject undisputed matters of fact, which counsel for the applicants had not been asked to address. Although the cost of breakfast could not be covered by housing benefit, the fact that breakfast and bed linen were provided was relevant in the assessment of the rent, which should be by comparison with other guest houses, rather than with advertised rented properties, *R. v. East Yorkshire Borough of Beverley Housing Benefits Review Board, ex p. Hare* (1995) 27 H.L.R. 637, [1995] 1 C.L.Y. 2594 and *R. v. Housing Benefit Review Board of East Devon DC, ex p. Gibson* (1993) 25 H.L.R. 487, [1994] C.L.Y. 2354 followed.

R. v. LAMBETH LBC HOUSING BENEFIT REVIEW BOARD, *ex p.* HARRINGTON, *The Times*, December 10, 1996, Collins, J., QBD.

2689. Housing benefit–commercial premises occupied as dwelling–eligibility for benefit

[Social Security Contributions and Benefits Act 1992 s.130.]

W sought to review a decision of the Housing Benefit Review Board that he was ineligible for benefit in respect of rented commercial premises which, in breach of a condition of the lease, he used as a dwelling. W claimed that he had been permitted to stay overnight as a nightwatchman by an oral agreement and contended that (1) the Board had misdirected itself in law by finding that a rent book was necessary in a domestic letting, and (2) the landlord could not rely on an ongoing breach of which he was aware while he continued to receive rent, and that therefore the letting was for a combination of residential and commercial accommodation.

Held, dismissing the appeal, that the letting was entirely commercial and (1) the error made by the Board was irrelevant because it was not determinative, and (2) such a waiver did not alter the commercial nature of the tenancy, *Wolfe v. Hogan* [1949] 2 K.B. 194, [1949] C.L.Y. 8608 considered.

R. v. WARRINGTON BC, *ex p.* WILLIAMS, Trans. Ref: CO 3941/95, January 28, 1997, Hidden, J., QBD.

2690. **Housing benefit–Housing Benefit Review Board–assessment of comparators–adequate reasoning**

[Housing Benefit (General) Regulations 1987 (SI 1987 1971) Reg.11; Housing Benefit (General) Regulations 1987 (SI 1987 1971) Reg.83; Rent Officers (Additional Functions) Order 1990 (SI 1990 428).]

MS and AS applied for judicial review of a decision of a Housing Benefit Review Board, HBRB, upholding the levels of housing benefit K awarded to them, which were significantly less than the contractual rent paid for two properties they rented consecutively. MS, AS, and granddaughter, LS, had been burgled in their previous accommodation in Redbridge and LS had suffered racist attacks at school. Subsequently they moved to premises with security cameras and a porter, which were let on a three year assured tenancy with a rent of £498 per week. A rent officer valued the property at £380 per week and, because it was an exceptionally high rental, determined an appropriate rental of £295. MS and AS applied for review, but then moved to an assured shorthold tenancy with a rent of £300 per week, for which the rent officer set an appropriate rent at £240 per week. MS and AS contended that: (1) HBRB had failed to give adequate reasons as required by the Housing Benefit (General) Regulations 1987 Reg.83; (2) HBRB had not compared the accommodation with suitable alternative accommodation as required by Reg.11 and the Rent Officers (Additional Functions) Order 1990 para.1, and (3) HBRB had erred in comparing the rent of the second property with that of a two bedroomed property.

Held, quashing the first decision and remitting the second decision, that HBRB had provided adequate reasons and had used suitable alternative property for comparison, except that the board had unreasonably used a two bedroomed property for comparison in the second application, *R. v. Solihull MBC Housing Benefits Review Board, ex p. Simpson* (1995) 27 H.L.R. 41, [1995] 1 C.L.Y. 2598 followed.

R. v. KENSINGTON AND CHELSEA RLBC HOUSING BENEFITS REVIEW BOARD, *ex p.* SHEIKH, Trans. Ref: CO 1582/96, January 14, 1996, Latham, J., QBD.

2691. **Housing benefit–overpayments–landlord's appeal based on breach of statutory duty–determination by housing authority was public law matter susceptible only to judicial review or statutory review procedure**

[Housing Benefit (General) Regulations 1987 (SI 1987 1971) Reg.79.]

G, a landlord, appealed against a decision ordering the repayment of housing benefit paid direct to G as landlord in respect of a tenant who left without giving the required notice and claimed benefit for the same period at his new accommodation. P contended that its decisions under the Housing Benefit (General) Regulations 1987 were public law matters and were only challengeable by way of either the review procedure under Reg.79 or by way of judicial review.

Held, dismissing the appeal, that where a local authority sought to recover overpaid housing benefit a landlord could not raise a defence based on a breach of statutory duty as the determination was only susceptible to challenge under Reg.79 or on judicial review grounds, *Haringey LBC v. Cotter* [1997] C.L.Y. 2692 and *Warwick DC v. Freeman* (1995) 27 H.L.R. 616, [1996] 1 C.L.Y. 3087 applied. As stated in *Cotter*, the Regulations provided a "detailed, self contained and exhaustive procedure" for determining housing benefit overpayment issues and G was precluded from relying on the principle established in *Wandsworth LBC v. Winder* [1985] A.C. 461, [1985] C.L.Y. 9 because that case was distinguishable by the absence of a statutory procedure.

PLYMOUTH CITY COUNCIL v. GIGG, Trans. Ref: CCRTF 96/1420/E, May 16, 1997, Otton, L.J., CA.

2692. Housing benefit—overpayments—underpayments—set off and counterclaim—exhaustive statutory determination and review procedure precluded private law remedy

[County Court Rules Ord.13 r.5; Housing Benefit (General) Regulations 1987 (SI 1987 1971) Reg.93, Reg.94.]

H claimed the recovery of overpaid housing benefit of £27,250 from C, a landlord. While admitting H's claim to the value of £25,790, C served a defence and counterclaim seeking set off for rent allowance underpayments of £15,835. At first instance, H applied for the counterclaim to be struck out under the County Court Rules 1981 Ord.13 r.5, on the ground that it disclosed no cause of action. The judge refused to strike out the counterclaim in its entirety, finding that whereas the Housing Benefit (General) Regulations 1987 Reg.93 conferred a statutory duty on H to make such payments, and was such that a private law counterclaim could be founded, Reg.94 of the 1987 Regulations merely created discretionary powers, which did not form the basis for any private law right. H appealed and C cross-appealed.

Held, allowing the appeal and dismissing the cross-appeal, that C could not succeed in a claim for breach of statutory duty in the absence of any intention to confer such private law rights on a landlord under the 1987 Regulations, *X (Minors) v. Bedfordshire CC* [1995] 2 A.C. 633, [1995] 2 C.L.Y. 3452 considered, as payments under the Regulations were made to the tenant and not the landlord, with the authority acting as the tenant's agent, *R. v. Haringey LBC, ex p. Ayub* (1993) 25 H.L.R. 566, [1994] C.L.Y. 2356 followed. Given the nature of the exhaustive and self contained duties for claim determination and review provided by the 1987 Regulations, the remedies available to a landlord lay either in using the review procedure contained in Part XI of the Regulations or by way of judicial review. C's counterclaim under Reg.93 should have been struck out at first instance, as it failed to disclose a breach of duty in either public or private law.

HARINGEY LBC v. COTTER, *The Times*, December 9, 1996, Mummery, L.J., CA.

2693. Housing benefit—suspension—judicial review—validity of application—exploration of all other remedies first

O received housing benefit payments from L, having applied under a false name. Some time later she began using her own name again, and informed the council of the change. On the basis that her identity was uncertain, O's benefit was stopped by L, who indicated in letters to O that a review of the decision would be held. No review was forthcoming, and O applied for judicial review to quash L's decision to stop benefit payments.

Held, allowing the application in part, that it was a firmly established principle that all other remedies must be exhausted before an applicant could seek judicial review. However, in the instant case, although the letters did not specifically mention a conclusive word like "review", they clearly evidenced a commitment by L that a review would be held. In such circumstances it was unnecessary for O's application to be barred until every other remedy had been explored. In respect of the three periods under consideration, O was not entitled to benefit for the first period, nor for the second period when she failed to fulfil her obligations under the regulations, but she was entitled to benefit for the third period at issue.

R. v. LAMBETH LBC, *ex p.* OGUNMUYIWA, *The Times*, April 17, 1997, Popplewell, J., QBD.

2694. Housing Grants, Construction and Regeneration Act 1996 (c.53)—Commencement No.3 Order

HOUSING GRANTS, CONSTRUCTION AND REGENERATION ACT 1996 (COMMENCEMENT NO.3) ORDER 1997, SI 1997 2846 (C.108); made under the Housing Grants, Construction and Regeneration Act 1996 s.150. Commencement details: bringing into force various provisions of the Act on December 16, 1997; £1.10.

This Order brings into force the Housing Grants, Construction and Regeneration Act 1996 s.131 to s.140 which relate to relocation grants other than the provisions conferring powers to make subordinate legislation and to give guidance which have already been commenced.

2695. Housing policy–housing transfer–inflexible rent arrears policy

M applied for judicial review of S's decision to refuse her a housing transfer on the basis of a policy decision that tenants in arrears of rent would not qualify. M was a secure tenant repaying arrears of rent regularly by deductions from income support and applied for a transfer because of medical problems. M claimed that S had fettered their discretion by operating a blanket policy and asked for a declaration that the policy was unlawful.

Held, allowing the application in part and quashing the decisions, that, although the policy was not unlawful per se, it was clear that S had applied an inflexible policy, *R. v. Canterbury City Council, ex p. Gillespie* (1986) 19 H.L.R. 7, [1987] C.L.Y. 1907 followed.

R. v. SOUTHWARK LBC, *ex p.* MELAK (1997) 29 H.L.R. 223, Sir Louis Blom-Cooper Q.C., QBD.

2696. Housing policy–overcrowding–rent arrears precluding entitlement to be admitted to waiting list–requisite balancing act of all factors had been carried out

[Housing Act 1985 s.22.]

W appealed against dismissal of her application for judicial review of the decision by WMBC not to admit her to the council's housing waiting list. There was statutory overcrowding at the address at which W lived with her family. W had previously been evicted from a council house because of rent arrears. W's application to be admitted to the housing list was rejected because of previous rent arrears. W argued that WMBC's policy not to allow anyone on the housing list who was in arrears of more than two weeks' rent was unlawful and in breach of the Housing Act 1985 s.22. Further that if no reasonable preference was given at all to those falling within the categories provided in terms then WMBC had not fulfilled its statutory duty. WMBC argued that if a policy to take into account rent arrears was not unlawful, then it was up to each local authority to select its own procedure for determining preferences. The obligation to give reasonable preference had been fulfilled by the council's appeal panel considering W's case.

Held, dismissing the appeal, that the requirement to give reasonable preference did not equate with giving preference to anyone coming within the criteria of s.22 of the 1985 Act so as to give automatic entitlement to council housing, but involved balancing all relevant factors. There was no indication that the appeals panel had not fairly carried out the requisite balancing exercise of all factors relating to W's case, and W's circumstances were not exceptional so as to justify reasonable preference under s.22. W had made no attempt to reduce the arrears still due, which was another factor to be considered.

R. v. WOLVERHAMPTON MBC, *ex p.* WATTERS, *The Times*, March 4, 1997, Leggatt, L.J., CA.

2697. Housing policy–priority needs–health of child at risk–top priority level reserved for violence cases–accommodation unfit for human habitation–inflexible application of priorities policy

[Housing Act 1985 s.604.]

N, a tenant of I and mother of three, obtained in June 1995 a report by an environmental health consultant, H, which stated that her accommodation was affected by damp to such an extent as to make it prejudicial to the health of N and her children and was unfit for human habitation. N supplied the report to I in July 1995. In May 1995 I's Housing Needs Officer, F, had made a report of the state of N's accommodation in the context of her application to be rehoused. F's report referred to N's belief that her son's hospitalisation with pneumonia and blood poisoning was due to the location of her son's bedroom directly above a rubbish chute. In July 1995 the Social Needs Panel or Housing Appeals subcommittee decided that N's application for a transfer be deferred and remedial works carried out. Such works did not remedy the bridging of the damp proof course. A report from environmental consultants in August 1995 concluded that I could reasonably form the opinion for the purposes of the Housing Act 1985 s.604 that the accommodation was unfit for human habitation. On October 11, 1995 the Housing Appeals subcommittee decided to classify N as Social Needs B and Priority 3 under the rehousing policy, Priority 1 being the top priority. In November 1995 N supplied two further health reports from independent bodies, but at a further meeting in January 1996 I rejected a request to reconsider the matter. N applied for judicial review, contending, inter alia, that I had an unlawfully inflexible rehousing policy or applied the policy as to priorities in an inflexible manner such that N was unable to attain Priority 1 notwithstanding the grave ill-health of her son, because that priority was reserved exclusively for cases involving violence.

Held, granting the application and ordering that N's application be considered afresh, that the rehousing policy was applied too inflexibly and the refusal to review the decision of October 11, 1995 was tainted with the same inflexibility. The decision making was tainted by the inevitable exclusion of persons from Priority 1 who, although deserving of the highest priority, had not suffered violence or the threat of violence. Since N had not suffered violence, I decided that she automatically fell outside the highest priority. This conclusion was reinforced by the nature of the correspondence emanating from I.

R. v. ISLINGTON LBC, *ex p.* NELSON, Trans. Ref: C0/1151/96, April 15, 1997, Henderson Q.C., QBD.

2698. **Housing policy–priority needs–housing transfer–authority policy on room sharing by children of opposite sex Wednesbury unreasonable–failure to take account of number involved**

[Housing Act 1985 s.22.]

A applied to her housing authority, L, for a transfer from the two bedroomed flat where she lived with her four children, who all shared one bedroom. L operated a points system for determining priority between applicants, under which the condition of the applicant's accommodation was only taken into account if L's medical officer had made specific recommendations or L's environmental health department had deemed a room to be uninhabitable. Where a person over three years old had to share a room with a person over eight years old who was of the opposite sex but not the partner of the first, a maximum of 20 points would be awarded irrespective of the number of sharers. A sought judicial review on the grounds that L's policy was unlawfully rigid.

Held, allowing the application and directing L to reconsider the application that L's scheme excluded consideration of the condition of an applicant's housing save in two limited circumstances, which was an undue fetter on the scope of the Housing Act 1985 s.22 which envisaged that condition should be an important factor. The limitations of points for room sharers was illogical and irrational in a *Wednesbury* sense in that it failed to take account of the numbers involved.

R. v. LAMBETH LBC, *ex p.* ASHLEY (1997) 29 H.L.R. 385, Tucker, J., QBD.

2699. **Housing policy–priority needs–housing transfer–medical status of tenant–classification of tenant changed after refusal of suitable alternative accommodation–downgrade not provided for in scheme**

W operated a housing transfer scheme under which council tenants could apply for a housing transfer for medical reasons, amongst others. Applications for transfer were dealt with according to their classification priority, with "essential" medical assessments being the highest priority, followed by "most advisable" assessments.

In December 1993 L, who had applied for a transfer, was awarded essential medical status. In January 1996 W offered her a transfer to Kirtley House, which she refused. In February 1996 W informed L that because she had refused suitable alternative accommodation her essential medical status was withdrawn and downgraded to most advisable medical status. At no stage during the relevant period did L's medical condition alter. She applied for judicial review, arguing that, as the housing transfer scheme did not provide for any sanction of downgrading the medical status of an applicant who had refused a transfer, W had acted unlawfully.

Held, granting the application and quashing the decision of W to downgrade L's medical status, that while it was appropriate for a local authority to provide a form of sanction against an unreasonable refusal of suitable alternative accommodation and it was not of itself unlawful to downgrade a person who refused such an alternative, no such sanction was provided for in W's scheme. According to their scheme, they were not entitled to say that if a tenant failed properly to take alternative accommodation that might, or would, indicate that it was no longer essential for him or her to be moved. It would be lawful and proper for them to have a different scheme which enabled them to treat L in the way that they had done but they could not do so under the present scheme.

R. v. WANDSWORTH LBC, *ex p.* LAWRIE; R. v. WANDSWORTH LBC, *ex p.* HESHMATI, Trans. Ref: CO/4402/96; CO/4115/96, May 1, 1997, Popplewell, J., QBD.

2700. **Housing policy–transfer into private sector–nominal consideration–no requirement to set aside true value of disposals where consideration was not money but redevelopment of site**

[Local Government and Housing Act 1989 s.61.]

B, wishing to redevelop two housing estates, entered into a framework agreement with N, a company owned by a property consortium, concerning a scheme of redevelopment. B would transfer the freehold in one estate for nominal monetary consideration and N would develop part of the land as private property and the remainder as social housing. B would transfer the second estate to N on condition that N contracted with its parent, M, to acquire the freehold of the property. M would then lease back some of the dwellings to B and refurbish the entire site with the aid of a council subsidy. The scheme was expected to create a cumulative deficit of £8.929 million for B and O applied for judicial review of the scheme, on the basis that B's decision not to set aside any of the proceeds of sale under the scheme to meet credit liabilities contravened the Local Government and Housing Act 1989 s.61. O contended that B was under a duty to calculate what the consideration for each individual disposal would have been if the sale had been made solely in money, and that the amount was to be treated as a capital receipt, 75 per cent of which had to be set aside. O's application was dismissed and he appealed.

Held, dismissing the appeal, that if O's contentions were accepted, provisions which were designed to prevent local authorities from extravagantly dissipating their assets would have the effect of inhibiting schemes regarded as advantageous by local authorities. For the purposes of s.61, the consideration for the scheme involved an evaluation of the framework agreement as a whole, including the significant benefits to be derived from the scheme, and not just the value of any individual disposals made by virtue of it.

R. v. BRENT LBC, *ex p.* O'MALLEY, *The Times*, September 2, 1997, Judge, L.J., CA.

2701. **Housing policy–transfer of housing estate into private sector–judicial review could be refused despite flaws in consultation process**

W, a council tenant on a housing estate, applied for judicial review of a local authority scheme for the sale, redevelopment and leaseback of the estate on the ground that the consultation process had been flawed. The judge accepted that the statutory consultation process had indeed been flawed because the consultation had originally been undertaken on the basis that only those properties owned by tenants voting in favour of the scheme would be affected and because the consultation had not addressed the question of the leaseback to the council. The judge, however, taking into consideration the approval of the vast majority of residents, the benefit which would be brought about by the scheme and the minimal effect on W's legal rights, refused to grant relief. W appealed.

Held, dismissing the appeal, that, despite finding that the consultation process had been flawed, the judge was fully entitled to exercise his discretion so as to refuse the application and the court would not interfere with his decision.

R. v. SECRETARY OF STATE FOR THE ENVIRONMENT, *ex p.* WALTERS, *The Times,* September 2, 1997, Judge, L.J., CA.

2702. Housing revenue account–calculation of subsidy on change of accounting practice

[Local Government and Housing Act 1989.]

C appealed against the dismissal of its application for relief by way of a declaration that it was entitled to Housing Revenue Account subsidy for the years 1990/91 to 1994/95 calculated by reference to a consolidated rate of interest, to be calculated by reference to interest payable on an accruals basis including a prior year adjustment. To determine the Housing Revenue Account subsidy the Secretary of State issued guidelines by way of subordinate legislation which laid down the formula for calculation, a component of which was the "consolidated rate of interest". The Secretary of State defined part of the formula for calculating interest in two different ways for the period at issue between the parties. It is against that background that the parties disputed whether in calculating the consolidated rate of interest in the 1994/95 financial year when C changed its accounting practice from a "cash basis" to an "accruals basis", with the result that a previous year adjustment arose for interest on housing loans, the adjustment figure should be included. At first instance it was held that the method of calculation properly formulated by the Secretary of State, on a literal construction, resulted in the prior year adjustment being left out of account.

Held, allowing the appeal and granting the declaration sought, that on a proper construction of the provisions of the Local Government and Housing Act 1989 and the Code of Practice on Local Authority Accounting in Great Britain in 1994 and 1995, proper accounting practices required that in a changeover year the prior year adjustment had to be taken into account notwithstanding the Secretary of State's contrary intention. If such a sum was left out of account a local authority would not be complying with proper accounting practices and a fair statement of that local authority's financial status would not be given. The words "during the year" in the amended 1994/95 formula were intended to clarify how to ascertain the borrowing figures; they did not qualify the interest figure.

R. v. SECRETARY OF STATE FOR THE ENVIRONMENT, *ex p.* CAMDEN LBC, Trans. Ref: QBCOF 96/1361/D, March 4, 1997, Roch, L.J., CA.

2703. Joint tenancies–marriage breakdown–injunction preventing husband's exclusion–wife giving notice to terminate joint tenancy–possession proceedings by council were not an abuse of process

[Domestic Violence and Matrimonial Proceedings Act 1976.]

HLBC appealed against a decision upholding the dismissal of its claim for possession against H. Following the breakdown of H and W's marriage, W left the family home, a council property of which they were joint tenants, and H gained an injunction under the Domestic Violence and Matrimonial Proceedings Act 1976 which prohibited W, inter alia, from excluding or attempting to exclude H from the property. After applying to be rehoused, W served notice to terminate the joint tenancy at HLBC's instigation, as it was contrary to council policy to provide accommodation to an existing council tenant. H, however, remained in the home and HLBC brought possession proceedings against him. H contended that W was in breach of the order and in contempt of court and that HLBC had aided and abetted her actions by bringing possession proceedings against him when aware of the terms of the order.

Held, allowing the appeal, that, following the principles in *Hammersmith and Fulham LBC v. Monk* [1992] 1 A.C. 478, [1992] C.L.Y. 2684, W's notice to terminate the joint tenancy was effective and HLBC was entitled to possession. Whilst H's injunction was a prohibition against excluding him, it was not intended to be a mandatory order requiring W to maintain rights in force created by the joint tenancy pending the outcome of any future proceedings dealing with matrimonial property. The injunction was concerned only with the exercise of rights under the tenancy, not their continued existence, and it could not be concluded that HLBC, in carrying out its statutory housing duties, was guilty of an abuse of process of the court.

HARROW LBC v. JOHNSTONE [1997] 1 W.L.R. 459, Lord Mustill, HL.

2704. Local authority housing—allocation scheme—determination of priorities

ALLOCATION OF HOUSING (PROCEDURE) REGULATIONS 1997, SI 1997 483; made under the Housing Act 1996 s.167, s.172. In force: April 1, 1997; £0.65.

The Housing Act 1996 s.167 requires local housing authorities to have an allocation scheme for determining priorities, and as to the procedures to be followed, in allocating housing accommodation. These Regulations prescribe, as regards procedure, the principle that a member shall not, at the time the allocation decision is made, be included in the decision-making body where the housing accommodation in question is in his electoral division or ward, or the person to whom the housing may be allocated resides in that division or ward.

2705. Local authority housing—allocation scheme—determination of priorities— Wales

LOCAL HOUSING AUTHORITIES (PRESCRIBED PRINCIPLES FOR ALLOCATION SCHEMES) (WALES) REGULATIONS 1997, SI 1997 45; made under the Housing Act 1996 s.167, s.172. In force: February 7, 1997; £1.10.

These Regulations apply to local housing authorities in Wales. They prescribe two principles of procedure to be followed in framing housing authority schemes for determining priorities. The first is the principle that no member shall be included in the persons taking an allocation decision on housing accommodation in his electoral division, or involving a resident in his electoral division. The second principle is that local housing authority officers shall be included in the persons by whom allocation decisions can be taken, except where the local housing authority has determined otherwise.

2706. Local authority housing—allocation scheme—reasonable preference to certain categories of persons

ALLOCATION OF HOUSING (REASONABLE AND ADDITIONAL PREFERENCE) REGULATIONS 1997, SI 1997 1902; made under the Housing Act 1996 s.167. In force: November 1, 1997; £1.10.

The Housing Act 1996 Part VI is concerned with the allocation of housing accommodation by a local housing authority in England and Wales and s.167 requires that an authority's scheme for determining priorities in allocating housing gives reasonable preference to a range of persons and additional preference to certain of those persons. These Regulations provide that reasonable preference is also to be given to certain categories of persons who have been homeless, and they widen the category of persons to whom additional preference is to be given.

2707. Local authority housing—forms—Amendment No.1—multiple occupation

HOUSING (PRESCRIBED FORMS) (AMENDMENT) REGULATIONS 1997, SI 1997 872; made under the Housing Act 1985 s.614. In force: April 8, 1997; £1.55.

These Regulations provide for the amendment of prescribed forms relating to houses in multiple occupation following the coming into force of the provisions of the Housing Act 1996 Part II relating to such houses.

2708. Local authority housing—forms—Amendment No.2—deferred action notices

HOUSING (PRESCRIBED FORMS) (AMENDMENT) (NO.2) REGULATIONS 1997, SI 1997 1903; made under the Housing Act 1985 s.614. In force: July 28, 1997; £1.10.

These Regulations amend the forms prescribed by the Housing (Prescribed Forms) (No.2) Regulations 1990 (SI 1990 1730) following the coming into force of the Housing, Grants, Construction and Regeneration Act 1996 Part I Ch.IV which relates to deferred action notices. Such a notice is to be served by a local housing authority if it is satisfied that a dwelling house or house in multiple occupation is unfit for human habitation and are satisfied that serving such a notice is the most satisfactory course of action.

2709. Multiple occupation—execution of works notices—opportunity for representations

HOUSING (ENFORCEMENT PROCEDURES FOR HOUSES IN MULTIPLE OCCUPATION) ORDER 1997, SI 1997 227; made under the Housing Act 1985 s.377A. In force: March 3, 1997; £0.65.

This Order provides that before serving a works notice (a notice requiring the execution of works either to render houses in multiple occupation fit for the number of occupants or to remedy neglect in management), a local authority shall serve a notice and give an opportunity for representations to be made unless it appears to the authority necessary to take action immediately.

2710. Multiple occupation—execution of works notices—recovery of expenses

HOUSING (RECOVERY OF EXPENSES FOR SECTION 352 NOTICES) ORDER 1997, SI 1997 228; made under the Housing Act 1985 s.352A. In force: March 3, 1997; £0.65.

Under the Housing Act 1985 s.352A, a local housing authority may make a reasonable charge to recover certain administrative and other expenses incurred by them in serving a notice requiring the execution of works under s.352 of the Act. The expenses recoverable are set out in s.352A(2) of the Act. This Order specifies £300 as the maximum amount of such a charge.

2711. Multiple occupation—fire precautions

HOUSING (FIRE SAFETY IN HOUSES IN MULTIPLE OCCUPATION) ORDER 1997, SI 1997 230; made under the Housing Act 1985 s.365. In force: in accordance with Art.1; £1.10.

Under the Housing Act 1985 s.365 the local housing authority has powers to require houses in multiple occupation to be provided with means of escape from fire and other adequate fire precautions. Before exercising those powers in relation to certain houses, authorities are required to consult fire authorities. This Order adds specified descriptions of houses to those where this obligation applies and specifies a description of houses in relation to which authorities have a duty to act when they have a power to do so.

2712. Multiple occupation–registration schemes–fees

HOUSES IN MULTIPLE OCCUPATION (FEES FOR REGISTRATION SCHEMES) ORDER 1997, SI 1997 229; made under the Housing Act 1985 s.346A. In force: March 3, 1997; £0.65.

This Order specifies the maximum permissible fees that may be charged by a local housing authority under the Housing Act 1985 s.346A(4) for the first registration of a house in multiple occupation under a registration scheme. Fees under the Houses in Multiple Occupation (Charges for Registration Schemes) Regulations 1991 (SI 1991 982) continue to apply to fees for reorganisation under schemes made before the date this order comes into force. There are transitional provisions for houses registered under an existing scheme which is revoked by a new registration scheme. A registration fee paid within five years of the date the new scheme comes into force shall be deducted from the fee payable to a local housing authority under the new scheme.

2713. Notice to quit–notice delivered to last known address–validity of service

[Law of Property Act 1925 s.196; Local Government Act 1972 s.233.]

E purported to terminate D's tenancy of a council flat by leaving a written notice to quit at the flat addressed to D. E knew that D was no longer resident at the flat, which was occupied by S, the second defendant. S appealed against the grant of a possession order to E on the ground that the notice to quit had not been properly served. E, who at common law was required to show that the notice had either been personally served on the tenant or, if left at the property, had come to his attention, relied on the Law of Property Act 1925 s.196 or the Local Government Act 1972 s.233 to argue that service at D's last known address was valid, even though those conditions were not fulfilled.

Held, allowing the appeal, that (1) s.196 of the 1925 Act only applied where notices to quit were required to be served by an instrument, and in the instant case the tenancy agreement contained no express provision for service, and (2) E's argument that a power to give notice was incidental to its housing authority function and authorised under s.233 of the 1972 Act could not be sustained, as s.233 only allowed service at the tenant's last known address where a notice to quit was "required or authorised by or under any enactment", which was not the case here, and could not have been intended to have such wide effect. On the facts, E and S had created a new tenancy determinable at common law by the personal service of written notice on the tenant, *Wandsworth LBC v. Atwell* (1995) 27 H.L.R. 536, [1995] 1 C.L.Y. 3032 and *Burrows v. Brent LBC* [1996] 1 W.L.R. 1448, [1996] 2 C.L.Y. 3829 considered.

ENFIELD LBC v. DEVONISH, *The Times*, December 12, 1996, Kennedy, L.J., CA.

2714. Possession orders–execution suspended–no new tenancy arose where payments made under terms of order

[Housing Act 1985 s.85.]

H granted P and his partner a secure tenancy of a flat. P fell into arrears and in October 1993 H obtained a possession order suspended on terms that P paid a £10 weekly contribution to the arrears in addition to the current rent; the order referred to P having a right to apply to the judge to suspend the order if he fell behind. P did fall behind, H issued a warrant for possession, P obtained a stay of its execution so long as he paid £15 per week towards the arrears in addition to the current rent. P again fell into arrears, H applied for the warrant to be re-issued and P applied for further time to pay. At first instance the judge held that P's tenancy had determined in October 1993, and that thereafter P had made payments which H accepted as rent, so that P was entitled to re-enter the flat. H appealed.

Held, allowing the appeal, that the payments made by P after October 1993 were apparently tendered under the terms of the order, and where the order drew the tenant's attention to the court's discretion to suspend the execution of the possession under the Housing Act 1985 s.85, it could not reasonably be inferred from subsequent payment that a new tenancy had come into existence,

Greenwich LBC v. Regan (1996) 28 H.L.R. 469, [1996] 2 C.L.Y. 3834 distinguished.
HACKNEY LBC v. PORTER (1997) 29 H.L.R. 401, Beldam, L.J., CA.

2715. **Possession orders—grounds for possession—rent arrears—council adding allegations of nuisance to application for possession—whether court entitled to hear those other allegations**

[Housing Act 1985 s.85(2).]
I obtained an order for possession against R on March 13, 1990, suspended on terms that R pay the current weekly rent plus £2 per week to discharge arrears which stood at £316. R did not comply with the order. As a result, I issued a warrant for possession to be executed on October 6, 1992. R made an application to suspend the warrant for possession and that application was adjourned on January 13, 1993. On August 26, 1994 I restored the application as the arrears had increased to £3,000. The restored application was heard on March 28, 1995 and R's application was dismissed. R made a further application on April 28, 1995 which was finally heard on December 5, 1995 when it was ordered that the possession order be suspended on the payment of current rent plus £3 per week to discharge the arrears which stood at £4,529. R again failed to comply with the order and I applied for a further warrant. R again applied to suspend the warrant. At the application to suspend the warrant heard on November 19, 1996, R relied principally on the fact that she suffered from depression and was suffering dire financial circumstances. I relied on R's poor payment record and allegations of very serious nuisance occurring from the beginning of June 1996, caused principally by one of R's sons who remained at the property. I alleged that they had received numerous complaints of youths gathering both outside and inside R's premises, the youths caused serious nuisance by fighting, chanting, using threatening and abusive behaviour and language towards the other adjoining occupiers, discarding refuse in the communal areas, destroying I's property and playing loud and amplified music during the day and into the early hours of the morning. Further, there had been 15 visits by police officers to the premises between June and October 1996. Those allegations were exhibited to I's affidavit. Although I's claim for possession was based on rent arrears only, I relied on *Cumming v. Danson* [1942] 2 All E.R. 653 and argued that in addition to the tenant's poor payment history, the court was bound to take into consideration the serious allegations of nuisance when it came to exercising his discretion pursuant to the Housing Act 1985 s.85(2).

Held, dismissing R's application on the ground of the poor history of payments shown by the evidence, that insofar as the allegations of nuisance were concerned, there was no finding of fact on the allegations, but it would be quite wrong to ignore the allegations in light of *Cumming v. Danson* and the court was bound to take into account all relevant circumstances as they existed at the date of the hearing.

Observed, there are no reported decisions on whether the courts can consider grounds for possession other than those upon which an order for possession was initially obtained, in the exercise of the discretion under s.85(2) of the 1985 Act. The decision in the instant case was significant in that it showed that the courts could consider different, but relevant grounds for possession in deciding whether or not it was reasonable for the tenancy to come to an end.

ISLINGTON LBC v. REEVES, November 19, 1996, District Judge Southcombe, CC (Clerkenwell). [*Ex rel.* Abimbola Badejo, Barrister].

2716. **Possession orders—nuisance—antisocial behaviour on housing estate—"neighbours" not limited to "adjoining occupiers"**

[Housing Act 1985 Sch.2.]
Conduct which constitutes a nuisance under the Housing Act 1985 Sch.2 need not affect the occupants of immediately adjoining premises, or emanate from the demised property, to constitute a ground for possession of a secure tenancy. L, a

council tenant, appealed against an order for possession obtained by N on the ground that three of L's seven children had behaved in a criminal and anti-social manner so as to create a nuisance or annoyance to their neighbours in terms of the Housing Act 1985 Sch.2 Ground 2. Members of the family had been convicted of numerous offences committed against people and property on the estate where they lived. L contended that the judge had been wrong in law to find that conduct occurring away from the immediate vicinity of the property was a relevant nuisance or annoyance for the purposes of Sch.2, as the victims of such behaviour were not "neighbours" in the statutory sense.

Held, dismissing the appeal (Pill, L.J. dissenting), that "neighbours" was not limited to "adjoining occupiers", but covered those people sufficiently close to the behaviour to be adversely affected by it. However, whilst the conduct complained of did not have to emanate from the demised property, there had to be a link between the behaviour which constituted a nuisance and the fact that the perpetrators lived in the area. In the instant case, the offences committed by the family against the neighbourhood had damaged the quality of life on the estate and prevented residents from enjoying quiet possession of their homes.

NORTHAMPTON BC v. LOVATT, *The Independent*, November 14, 1997, Henry, L.J., CA.

2717. Possession orders—nuisance—no suitable alternative accommodation need be available where order made on ground of nuisance

[Housing Act 1985.]

D appealed against the setting aside of a possession order, made under the Housing Act 1985 Part I Sch.2 Ground 2, after acts of nuisance committed by S's teenage son. The judge below found that it was unreasonable to grant a possession order until suitable alternative accommodation had been provided by D. He found that the trial judge had erred by granting possession to D, despite stressing that S should not be considered as intentionally homeless for the purposes of rehousing under the 1985 Act.

Held, allowing the appeal, that although it would be relevant to consider the effect of a possession order on the tenant and others, it was clear that Part I grounds, unlike Part II and Part III grounds, expressly excluded any requirement for the court to be satisfied that suitable accommodation would be available for a dispossessed tenant. It was therefore not permissible to refuse a possession order on that basis.

DARLINGTON BC v. STERLING (1997) 29 H.L.R. 309, Mummery, L.J., CA.

2718. Possession orders—right to buy—notice seeking possession served before right to buy exercised—tenant entitled to grant of lease

[Housing Act 1985 s.125D; Leasehold Reform, Housing and Urban Development Act 1993.]

S succeeded to the tenancy of a four-bedroomed flat on her mother's death, and served notice claiming a right to buy. C admitted the right to buy and served a s.125 notice specifying price with a draft lease attached. C also served notice seeking possession on ground 16 under occupation. On August 10, 1995, S served a notice under the Housing Act 1985 s.125D, a new section added by the Leasehold Reform, Housing and Urban Development Act 1993, stating her intention to pursue her claim to the right to buy, and on October 11, 1995 served a solicitor's letter agreeing to the proposed price and all terms of the draft lease and giving C seven days to complete. On October 16, 1995, C issued possession proceedings based on ground 16. S defended and claimed a mandatory injunction under s.138 requiring C to grant her a long lease of the flat. C defended the counterclaim on the basis that S was precluded from exercising the right to buy by reason of service of the notice seeking possession before agreement was reached.

Held, dismissing C's claim for possession and granting the injunction, that it was irrelevant when the notice seeking possession was served. Section 121 which excluded the right to buy in certain circumstances, including when a possession order had been made, made no reference to a notice seeking possession. A tenant's notice under s.125D did not constitute the agreement necessary to invoke s.138, as it did not connote agreement of all terms, that is, it did not amount to "an event" referred to in *Dance v. Welwyn Hatfield DC* [1990] 1 W.L.R. 1097, [1990] C.L.Y. 2519. However, there was no doubt that the letter of October 11, 1995 did amount to the necessary agreement and therefore S was entitled to the grant of her lease and the possession claim must be dismissed.

CAMDEN LBC v. SALE, April 24, 1996, H.H.J. Green Q.C., CC (Central London). [*Ex rel.* Philip Rainey, Barrister].

2719. Possession orders—suspended possession order automatically revoked—notice of application for enforcement issued before revocation date—enforcement not possible after revocation

[County Court Rules 1981 Ord.9 r.10.]

V sought possession of the property of which G was the secure tenant under the Housing Act 1985, on the ground that she had caused a nuisance or annoyance to her neighbours. When the case came up for trial on December 20, 1994, G gave detailed undertakings not to cause a nuisance or annoyance, and to be bound by her promises until December 20, 1995. The recorder ordered, inter alia, that "V be granted possession of the property such Order to be suspended upon G complying with her undertakings until 20th December 1995 after which time the possession order be automatically revoked. . . The said suspended possession order be not enforced without the leave of the Court". On October 26, 1995 (before the automatic revocation date) V applied for an order that the suspended possession order take effect. On March 13, 1996, G cross-applied to strike out V's application, on the basis that the suspended possession order had been automatically revoked on December 20, 1995, such that no possession order existed which the Court could enforce. G argued by analogy with CCR Ord.9 r.10, as interpreted by *Webster v. Ellison Circlips Group* [1995] 1 W.L.R. 1447, [1995] 2 C.L.Y. 4092, that the court had to look at the situation which existed on or immediately after December 20, 1995, at which point, it was argued, no breach of undertakings had been proved, so that automatic revocation took place. G further relied by analogy on *Welsh Development Agency v. Redpath Dorman Long* [1994] 1 W.L.R. 1409, [1995] 2 C.L.Y. 4191, where the Court held that leave to amend could not be given if the limitation period had expired at the time when the court was considering the matter, even if it had not expired at the date of the application.

Held, indicating that whilst *Welsh Development Agency v. Redpath* was not binding, its guidelines were useful in the instant case, the possession order had been automatically revoked on December 20, 1995, and leave could not be given to enforce it, notwithstanding that the notice of application was issued prior to the automatic revocation date. V's application was accordingly struck out.

VALE OF GLAMORGAN BC v. GRECH, March 13, 1996, H.H.J. Francis, CC (Cardiff). [*Ex rel.* Robert O'Leary, Barrister].

2720. Possession proceedings—grounds for possession—secure tenancies—local authority seeking to add further grounds to notice and particulars of claim

[Housing Act 1985 s.83, s.84(3).]

C sought the possession of premises let under a secure tenancy. A notice of seeking possession, NOSP, was served pursuant to the provisions of the Housing Act 1985 s.83 for possession under Sch.2 claiming that (1) rent lawfully due from the tenant had not been paid or an obligation of the tenancy had been broken or not performed, and (2) the tenant or a person residing in the dwelling house had been guilty of conduct which is a nuisance or annoyance to neighbours, or has been convicted of using the dwelling house or allowing it to be used for immoral or illegal purposes. The particulars contained in the NOSP dealt with acts of nuisance and waste, on the basis that the same were alleged breaches of the conditions of the tenancy agreement. The particulars of claim also sought possession pursuant to Ground 1 and Ground 2 of Sch.2 of the 1985 Act. During the trial it became apparent that C was in potential difficulties in establishing the conditions of the tenancy agreement. C sought leave to add Ground 3 of Sch.2 (the condition of the dwelling house or of any of the common parts had deteriorated owing to acts of waste by, or the neglect or default of, the tenant or a person residing in the dwelling house) to the NOSP and also to amend the particulars of claim to include Ground 3.

Held, refusing leave to amend the NOSP and the particulars of claim, that s.84(3) does not give the court jurisdiction to grant leave to add a further ground to a NOSP but merely to alter or add to the grounds already specified. It would be inconsistent to allow a landlord to add an entirely new ground to a NOSP, once it had been served, as all the other provisions of the 1985 Act require a landlord to be specific regarding the grounds on which they seek possession. It is not difficult for a landlord, particularly a local authority landlord, to ensure that they have complied with the provisions of the Act and included in the NOSP all the grounds under Sch.2 that they intend to rely on. In the instant case even if the court did have jurisdiction to allow a ground to be added to the NOSP under s.84(3), the court would not have exercised its discretion in favour of C.

CROYDON LBC v. NANA, February 12, 1997, H.H.J. Coningsby Q.C., CC (Croydon). [*Ex rel.* Karen Walden-Smith, Barrister, Lamb Chambers, Temple].

2721. Possession proceedings–possession adjourned on undertaking by tenant–breach of undertaking–landlord released from undertaking

K appealed against a refusal to release it from an undertaking to rehouse O. O was a secure tenant of one of K's flats, who had repeatedly caused neighbours below to suffer flooding. K sought possession and, as terms of a consent order giving K possession of the flat, O undertook not to cause further flooding and K gave an undertaking to offer O suitable alternative ground floor accommodation before enforcement of the order. K offered a suitable property but subsequently withdrew the offer on discovering that O had caused further flooding in breach of her undertaking. K applied to be released from its undertaking to rehouse O, but although the judge below found for K on the merits he determined that he had no jurisdiction to release or vary an undertaking given as part of a consent order in final proceedings.

Held, allowing the appeal, that K was released from the undertaking. An undertaking accepted by the court could be discharged by the court if it was just to do so, whether or not it was incorporated in a consent order. In the instant case there had been no attempt to explain the flooding, which had been found as a fact by the judge below despite denial by O, *Hudson, Re* [1966] 1 Ch. 207, [1966] C.L.Y. 9978 considered and *Russell v. Russell* [1956] P. 283, [1956] C.L.Y. 2748 followed, *Chanel Ltd v. FW Woolworth & Co Ltd* [1981] 1 W.L.R. 485, [1981] C.L.Y. 2126 distinguished because it was primarily contractual.

KENSINGTON HOUSING TRUST v. OLIVER, Trans. Ref: CCRTI 97/0389/H, July 24, 1997, Butler-Sloss, L.J., CA.

2722. Public sector tenancies–leak from adjoining property causing damage–council failing to act promptly–costs

S, a senior citizen, was the tenant of a one bedroomed flat. In January 1995, water penetration made the bedroom uninhabitable by virtue of smell. Approximately six weeks later part of the bathroom ceiling fell in making the bath unusable. There was extensive water penetration to the hall between the bedroom and bathroom. H arranged for two inspections but did not locate the cause of the damage. S had to sleep in the sitting room on a sofa. S suffered from osteoporosis and pre-existing depression. H's workmen happened to be working on a neighbouring property in April 1995 and S asked them to investigate the flat above hers for leaks etc. The workmen discovered a broken bath waste pipe and H authorised immediate repairs. S effected the necessary redecorating works to the bedroom, hall and bathroom of her flat after H's refusal to fund the whole cost.

Held, awarding general damages for the period January to May 1995 of £750. H's liability arose from the breach of the common law duty in negligence to ensure that S's enjoyment of her flat was not interfered with by H's use of its adjoining or neighbouring property. S was also awarded costs on the grounds of H's unreasonable conduct in the handling of S's complaint and the litigation thereof. S was also awarded special damages of £750.

SHAWYER v. HACKNEY LBC, February 14, 1997, Deputy District Judge Navqi, CC (Shoreditch). [*Ex rel.* Lisa Sinclair, Barrister, Chambers of Nicholas Storey, Lincoln's Inn].

2723. Rent officers—housing renewal grants—provision of information

RENT OFFICERS (HOUSING RENEWAL GRANTS FUNCTIONS) ORDER 1997, SI 1997 778; made under the Housing Act 1988 s.121. In force: April 7, 1997; £0.65.

This Order requires rent officers to provide written advice to local housing authorities within 45 working days of receipt of the request for advice or a soon as practicable thereafter. It also makes provision for rent officers to seek further information from local housing authorities.

2724. Rent officers—single room determination

RENT OFFICERS (ADDITIONAL FUNCTIONS) (AMENDMENT) ORDER 1997, SI 1997 1000; made under the Housing Act 1988 s.121. In force: Art.2(a), Art.3(1): October 6, 1997; remainder: April 14, 1997; £1.10.

This Order amends the Rent Officers (Additional Functions) Order 1995 (SI 1995 1642) which conferred functions on rent officers in connection with housing benefit and rent allowance subsidy and requires them to make determinations and re-determinations in respect of tenancies and licences of dwellings. It amends the circumstances in which a single room rent determination may be made to cases where the housing benefit claimant is, or may be, a young individual or single claimant as defined in that provision. Before this amendment, such determinations could only be made in relation to claimants who were young individuals.

2725. Rent officers—single room determination

RENT OFFICERS (HOUSING BENEFIT FUNCTIONS) ORDER 1997, SI 1997 1984; made under the Housing Act 1996 s.122. In force: Art.1, Art.8, Art.10(1): August 18, 1997; remainder: September 3, 1997; £2.80.

This Order, which revokes and re-enacts with modifications the Rent Officers (Additional Functions) Order 1995 (SI 1995 1642) and revokes the Orders which amended it, confers functions on rent officers in connection with housing benefit and rent allowance subsidy and requires rent officers to make determinations and redeterminations relating to a tenancy or licence of a dwelling. The main modifications relate to single room rent determinations.

2726. Repairs—lift repairs—foreseeability—landlord not liable for tenant's injury due to broken lift

B, a tenant of an 18-storey block of flats, injured her back climbing up four flights of steps when the lift was out of order. The county court awarded damages of £24,374 for injury and consequential loss against H, the landlord, for breach of duty to ensure the lift worked. H appealed.

Held, allowing the appeal, that B was not entitled to damages as the possibility of a person stumbling on the stairs due to the lift being unavailable was not sufficiently foreseeable to create a duty of care on the landlord to ensure that it always worked. Further, the lift not working was not a breach of contract as it was not unsafe, just immobile.

BERRYMAN v. HOUNSLOW LBC [1997] P.I.Q.R. P83, Henry, L.J., CA.

2727. Repairs notices–expert evidence–fitness of dwelling for human habitation– test to be applied–no special rules governing receipt of expert evidence

[Housing Act 1985 s.604.]

D appealed against a county court decision to quash the repairs notice served on S and raised the issue of whether the judge should have relied on the evidence of an expert witness in deciding whether the property concerned was fit for habitation.

Held, dismissing the appeal, that it was for the judge to decide a case on the evidence presented to him and he could not substitute his own opinion for an expert's opinion without justification. However, he was not bound to follow expert opinion if other evidence refuted it or if he remained unconvinced. The test to be used in assessing whether a house was fit for human habitation within the Housing Act 1985 s. 604, as amended, remained the "ordinary user" test laid down in *Morgan v. Liverpool Corp* [1927] 2 K.B. 131.

DOVER DC v. SHERRED, *The Times*, February 11, 1997, Evans, L.J., CA.

2728. Right to buy

HOUSING (RIGHT TO ACQUIRE) REGULATIONS 1997, SI 1997 619; made under the Housing Act 1996 s.17. In force: April 1, 1997; £6.10.

These Regulations modify the Housing Act 1985 Part V (the right to buy) for cases where a tenant has the right to acquire the dwelling-house under the Housing Act 1996 s.16. Schedule 1 specifies the modifications and Sch.2 sets out Part V of the 1985 Act as so modified. In particular, the Regulations exclude the right to buy on rent to mortgage terms and the preserved right to buy; remove the exceptions to the right to buy in Sch.5 para.1, Sch.5 para.3 and Sch.5 para.11 of the 1985 Act (charities; certain housing associations; certain dwelling-houses for the elderly); add exceptions to the right to acquire in Sch.5 para.1A, Sch.5 para.9A and Sch.5 para.13 (dwelling-houses in designated rural areas; dwelling-house for persons with special needs; dwelling-houses charged with debts equal to or greater than the purchase price plus discount); provide for the tenant to acquire the dwelling-house at a discount as specified in an order made by the Secretary of State under the Housing Act 1996 s.17; disapply the restrictions on the disposals in National Parks etc in s.157 and s.158 of the 1985 Act and the powers of the Secretary of State to intervene etc. under s.164 to s.170 of that Act; and add provisions in Sch.6 para.22 and Sch.6 para.23 on the discharge or release of charges on landlord's interest in the dwelling-house.

2729. Right to buy–approved lending institutions–No.1 Order

HOUSING (RIGHT TO BUY) (PRIORITY OF CHARGES) ORDER 1997, SI 1997 945; made under the Housing Act 1985 s.156. In force: April 7, 1997; £0.65.

This Order specifies nine bodies as approved lending institutions for the purposes of the Housing Act 1985 s.156. It revokes the Housing (Right to Buy) (Priority of Charges) Order 1996 (SI 1996 2479), but Leek United Home Loans Ltd retains its status as an approved lending institution.

2730. Right to buy–approved lending institutions–No.2 Order

HOUSING (RIGHT TO BUY) (PRIORITY OF CHARGES) (NO.2) ORDER 1997, SI 1997 2327; made under the Housing Act 1985 s.156. In force: October 20, 1997; £0.65.

This Order specifies a further eight bodies as approved lending institutions for the purposes of the Housing Act 1985 s.156 which relates to the priority of charges on disposals under the right to buy. Such bodies are also approved lending institutions for the purposes of s.36, which relates to priority of charges on voluntary disposals by local authorities, and s.171A, which relates to cases in which the tenant's right to buy is preserved. They are also approved lending institutions for the purposes of the Housing Act 1996 s.12, which relates to priority of charges on voluntary disposals by registered social landlords, and s.16, which relates to tenant's right to acquire dwelling.

2731. Right to buy—breach of covenant—possession proceedings—injunction to enforce sale not affected by breach

[Housing Act 1985 Part V; Housing Act 1985 s.121, s.138(3).]

B appealed against a decision granting L, a secure tenant of B, an injunction to enforce his right to buy under the Housing Act 1985 Part V. B contended that allegations of drug dealing from the property, which formed the subject of pending criminal proceedings, along with unauthorised alterations carried out to the property, were flagrant breaches of his secure tenancy, vitiating L's entitlement to an enforcement injunction under s.138 of the 1985 Act.

Held, dismissing the appeal, that the right to buy conferred on a secure tenant under Part V of the 1985 Act can only be extinguished if the tenant is obliged to give up possession under a court order by virtue of s.121 prior to seeking an injunction enforcing the right to buy under s.138(3). On the facts, L had applied to exercise his right prior to B seeking possession of the property, even though that right only became enforceable after possession proceedings were commenced, but the right continued as long as he remained a secure tenant, *Dance v. Welwyn Hatfield DC* [1990] 1 W.L.R. 1097, [1990] C.L.Y. 2519 and *Taylor v. Newham LBC* [1993] 1 W.L.R. 444, [1993] C.L.Y. 2106 followed. Where such conflicting claims occur, the order of hearing is critical because a successful possession application removed the tenant's right to seek an injunction under s.138(3). A distinction exists between the statutory right to buy and the making of the grant under s.138(1) and it is inappropriate to see the right to buy as crystallising when it becomes enforceable under s.138 and cannot be taken as being analogous with an equitable interest in land, *Muir Group Housing Association Ltd v. Thornley* (1992) 25 H.L.R. 89, [1992] C.L.Y. 2315 considered. Neither the breach of covenant by the tenant, nor the commencement of enforcement proceedings, operated to deprive L of his secure status given Parliament's clear intention not to accommodate a reluctant landlord, and, as shown in *Dance* and *Taylor,* once the conditions in s.138(1) had been fulfilled, there was no discretion available to refuse an enforcement injunction under s.138(3) on the grounds of the hardship which L's conduct allegedly caused to other tenants living in the same locality.

BRISTOL CITY COUNCIL v. LOVELL (1997) 29 H.L.R. 528, Lord Woolf, M.R., CA.

2732. Right to buy—duty to disclose structural defects when serving notice of purchase price on tenant

[Housing Act 1985 s.125.]

B served a notice of purchase price under the Housing Act 1985 s.125 on P, who wished to buy a leasehold interest in their flat from B. Following the notice, P was granted a 125 year lease but later brought an action for damages against B alleging that the council had failed to fulfil its duty to inform P of structural defects pursuant to s.125(4A).

Held, allowing the appeal for other reasons, that under the statutory scheme a landlord owed a duty to inform a tenant of any relevant structural defects known to him when serving a notice of purchase price, as well as informing the tenant about service charges, improvements and ordinary external repairs. The statutory scheme was such that it was inappropriate to impose wider common law obligations of disclosure on landlords, and tenants wishing to exercise their right to buy must undertake their own searches and inquiries in the same way as other purchasers of land.

PAYNE v. BARNET LBC, *The Times,* June 24, 1997, Brooke, L.J., CA.

2733. Right to buy—rate of discount

HOUSING (RIGHT TO ACQUIRE) (DISCOUNT) ORDER 1997, SI 1997 626; made under the Housing Act 1996 s.17. In force: April 1, 1997; £3.20.

This Order specifies the amount of discount for the purposes of the Housing Act 1996 s.17 (the right to acquire). Tenants of registered social landlords who have a right to acquire their homes under s.16 and s.17 of the 1996 Act will be able to do so with a discount from the purchase price. The amount of the discount will vary according to the area in which the dwelling is situated.

2734. Right to buy–rate of discount–Wales

HOUSING (RIGHT TO ACQUIRE) (DISCOUNT) (WALES) ORDER 1997, SI 1997 569; made under the Housing Act 1996 s.17. In force: April 1, 1997; £0.65.

This Order specifies the rate of discount under the Housing Act 1996 s.17 for the purposes of the exercise of the right conferred by s.16 of that Act. Tenants of registered social landlords who have a right to acquire their homes pursuant to s.16 and s.17 of that Act will be able to do so with a discount from the open market value.

2735. Right to buy–right to enfranchise–designation of rural areas where rights do not apply

HOUSING (RIGHT TO ACQUIRE OR ENFRANCHISE) (DESIGNATED RURAL AREAS IN THE EAST) ORDER 1997, SI 1997 623; made under the Leasehold Reform Act 1967 s.1AA; and the Housing Act 1996 s.17. In force: April 1, 1997; £3.70.

This Order designates rural areas for the purposes of the Housing Act 1996 s.17 and the Leasehold Reform Act 1967 s.1AA(3)(a). The right of tenants of registered social landlords to acquire their homes under s.16 and s.17 of the 1996 Act and the right of tenants with long leases to enfranchise under s.1AA of the 1967 Act do not apply in respect of properties in areas which have been designated as rural areas. In the case of tenants with long leases, the additional conditions in s.1AA(3)(b) and (c) of the 1967 Act must be fulfilled before the right to enfranchise is excluded.

2736. Right to buy–right to enfranchise–designation of rural areas where rights do not apply

HOUSING (RIGHT TO ACQUIRE OR ENFRANCHISE) (DESIGNATED RURAL AREAS IN THE NORTH EAST) ORDER 1997, SI 1997 624; made under the Leasehold Reform Act 1967 s.1AA; and the Housing Act 1996 s.17. In force: April 1, 1997; £2.80.

This Order designates the areas in the specified districts as rural areas for the purposes of the Housing Act 1996 s.17 (the right to acquire) and the Leasehold Reform Act 1967 s.1AA(3)(a) (additional right to enfranchise). The right of tenants of registered social landlords to acquire their homes under s.16 and s.17 of the 1996 Act and the right of tenants with long leases to enfranchise under s.1AA of the 1967 Act do not apply in respect of properties in areas which have been designated as rural areas. In the case of tenants with long leases, the additional conditions in s.1AA(3)(b) and (c) of the 1967 Act must be fulfilled before the right to enfranchise is excluded. Those parishes in Sch.1 are exempt in their entirety from the right to acquire and the additional right to enfranchise. Those parishes and the unparished areas in Sch.2 contain areas which are exempt from the rights. The maps indicate which areas are excluded. The parish mentioned in Art.2(c) contains one area which is not exempt from the rights, while the remainder of the parish is a designated rural area.

2737. Right to buy–right to enfranchise–designation of rural areas where rights do not apply

HOUSING (RIGHT TO ACQUIRE OR ENFRANCHISE) (DESIGNATED RURAL AREAS IN THE NORTH WEST) ORDER 1997, SI 1997 622; made under the Leasehold Reform Act 1967 s.1AA; and the Housing Act 1996 s.17. In force: April 1, 1997; £1.95.

This Order designates rural areas for the purposes of the Housing Act 1996 s.17 (right to acquire) and the Leasehold Reform Act 1967 s.1AA(3)(a) (additional right to enfranchise). The right of tenants of registered social landlords to acquire their homes under s.16 and s.17 of the 1996 Act and the right of tenants with long leases to enfranchise under s.1AA of the 1967 Act do not apply in respect of properties in areas which have been designated as rural areas. In the case of tenants with long leases, the additional conditions in s.1AA(3)(b) and (c) of the 1967 Act must be fulfilled before the right to enfranchise is excluded. Those parishes in Sch.1 are exempt in their entirety from the right to acquire and the additional right to enfranchise. Those parishes and the unparished areas in Sch.2 contain areas which are exempt from the rights. The maps (included in the order) indicate which areas are excluded. The areas listed in Art.2(c) are designated rural areas with the exception of the non-cross-hatched areas shown on the maps.

2738. **Right to buy – right to enfranchise – designation of rural areas where rights do not apply**

HOUSING (RIGHT TO ACQUIRE OR ENFRANCHISE) (DESIGNATED RURAL AREAS IN THE SOUTH EAST) ORDER 1997, SI 1997 625; made under the Leasehold Reform Act 1967 s.1AA; and the Housing Act 1996 s.17. In force: April 1, 1997; £2.40.

This Order designates specified areas as rural areas for the purposes of the Housing Act 1996 s.17 (the right to acquire) and the Leasehold Reform Act 1967 s.1AA(3)(a) (additional right to enfranchise). The right of tenants of registered social landlords to acquire their homes under s.16 and s.17 of the 1996 Act and the right of tenants with long leases to enfranchise under s.1AA of the 1967 Act do not apply in respect of properties in areas which have been designated as rural areas. In the case of tenants with long leases, the additional conditions in s.1AA(3)(b)(c) of the 1967 Act must be fulfilled before the right to enfranchise is excluded. Those parishes and the unparished area in Sch.1 are exempt in their entirety from the right to acquire and the additional right to enfranchise and those parishes and the unparished areas in Sch.2 contain areas which are exempt from the rights, maps indicate which areas are excluded.

2739. **Right to buy – right to enfranchise – designation of rural areas where rights do not apply**

HOUSING (RIGHT TO ACQUIRE OR ENFRANCHISE) (DESIGNATED RURAL AREAS IN THE SOUTH WEST) ORDER 1997, SI 1997 621; made under the Leasehold Reform Act 1967 s.1AA; and the Housing Act 1996 s.17. In force: April 1, 1997; £2.80.

This Order designates the areas in specified districts and counties as rural areas for the purposes of the Housing Act 1996 s.17 (the right to acquire) and the Leasehold Reform Act 1967 s.1AA(3)(a) (additional right to enfranchise). The right of tenants of registered social landlords to acquire their homes under s.16 and s.17 of the 1996 Act and the right of tenants with long leases to enfranchise under s.1AA of the 1967 Act do not apply in respect of properties in areas which have been designated as rural areas. In the case of tenants with long leases, the additional conditions in s.1AA(3)(b) and (c) of the 1967 Act must be fulfilled before the right to enfranchise is excluded. Those parishes in Sch.1 are exempt in their entirety from the right to acquire and the additional right to enfranchise. Those parishes and the unparished areas in Sch.2 contain areas which are exempt from the rights. Maps, included in the Order, indicate which areas are excluded.

2740. **Right to buy – right to enfranchise – designation of rural areas where rights do not apply**

HOUSING (RIGHT TO ACQUIRE OR ENFRANCHISE) (DESIGNATED RURAL AREAS IN THE WEST MIDLANDS) ORDER 1997, SI 1997 620; made under the Leasehold Reform Act 1967 s.1AA; and the Housing Act 1996 s.17. In force: April 1, 1997; £1.95.

This Order designates specified areas as rural areas for the purposes of the Housing Act 1996 s.17 (the right to acquire) and the Leasehold Reform Act 1967 s.1AA(3)(a) (additional right to enfranchise). The right of tenants of registered social landlords to acquire their homes under s.16 and s.17 of the 1996 Act and the right of tenants with long leases to enfranchise under s.1AA of the 1967 Act do not apply in respect of properties in areas which have been designated as rural areas. In the case of tenants with long leases, the additional conditions in s.1AA(3)(b) and (c) of the 1967 Act must be fulfilled before the right to enfranchise is excluded. Those parishes in Sch.1 are exempt in their entirety from the right to acquire and the additional right to enfranchise. Those parishes and the unparished areas in Sch.1 contain areas which are exempt from the rights. Maps, included in the Order, indicate which areas are excluded.

2741. Right to buy–right to enfranchise–designation of rural areas where rights do not apply–Wales

LEASEHOLD REFORM AND HOUSING (EXCLUDED TENANCIES) (DESIGNATED RURAL AREAS) (WALES) ORDER 1997, SI 1997 685; made under the Leasehold Reform Act 1967 s.1AA; and the Housing Act 1996 s.17. In force: April 1, 1997; £1.55.

In this Order, which applies to Wales, the Secretary of State designates rural areas under the Leasehold Reform Act 1967 s.1AA, and the Housing Act 1996 s.17. Section 1AA of the 1967 Act provides for an additional right to enfranchisement for houses above the applicable "low rent" limit under s.4 of that Act. This Order designates rural areas where this additional right does not apply. Section 16 of the Act provides for a tenant of a registered social landlord to acquire his dwelling. This Order designates rural areas where this right does not apply.

2742. Secure tenancies–change of landlord–disposal costs–interest rate– Amendment No.1

HOUSING (CHANGE OF LANDLORD) (PAYMENT OF DISPOSAL COST BY INSTALMENTS) (AMENDMENT) REGULATIONS 1997, SI 1997 328; made under the Housing Act 1988 s.104, s.111, s.112, s.114. In force: March 11, 1997; £0.65.

These Regulations amend the Housing (Change of Landlord) (Payment of Disposal Cost by Instalments) Regulations 1990 (SI 1990 1019) by increasing, from 6.87 per cent to 7.18 per cent, the rate of interest on outstanding disposal costs which are payable by instalments under the Housing Act 1988 Part IV (change of landlord: secure tenants).

2743. Secure tenancies–change of landlord–disposal costs–interest rate– Amendment No.2

HOUSING (CHANGE OF LANDLORD) (PAYMENT OF DISPOSAL COST BY INSTALMENTS) (AMENDMENT) (NO.2) REGULATIONS 1997, SI 1997 1621; made under the Housing Act 1988 s.104, s.111, s.112, s.114. In force: July 29, 1997; £0.65.

These Regulations amend the Housing (Change of Landlord) (Payment of Disposal Cost by Instalments) Regulations 1990 (SI 1990 1019) by increasing, from 7.18 per cent, to 7.35 per cent, the rate of interest on outstanding disposal costs which are payable by instalments under the Housing Act 1988 Part IV which relates to secure tenants and changes in landlords.

2744. Secure tenancies–change of landlord–disposal costs–interest rate– Amendment No.3

HOUSING (CHANGE OF LANDLORD) (PAYMENT OF DISPOSAL COST BY INSTALMENTS) (AMENDMENT) (NO.3) REGULATIONS 1997, SI 1997 2001; made under the Housing Act 1988 s.104, s.111, s.112, s.114. In force: September 12, 1997; £0.65.

These Regulations amend the Housing (Change of Landlord) (Payment of Disposal Cost By Instalments) Regulations 1990 (SI 1990 1019) by increasing the rate of interest on outstanding disposal costs payable by instalments under the Housing Act 1988 Part IV to 7.78 per cent. The Housing (Change of

Landlord) (Payment of Disposal Cost By Instalments) (Amendment) (No.2) Regulations 1997 (SI 1997 1621) is revoked.

2745. **Secure tenancies—notice to quit—validity of amendments to defective notice**

[Housing Act 1985 s.83(2)(a); Housing Act 1985 Part IV.]

D applied for an extension of time and leave to appeal against an order giving possession of his flat to C, his landlord, and ordering him to pay £4,584 arrears of rent and mesne profits. D was a secure periodic tenant under the Housing Act 1985 Part IV when C served a s.83 notice. Erroneously believing it was defective, C served another notice eight months later. The recorder granted C leave to amend and issue proceedings based on the earlier notice, abridged all time limits and consolidated the actions before giving C possession. D claimed that (1) the second notice was defective in that the Director of Housing had not signed it; (2) even if it was effective, the order should not have been made since it put D out of his home earlier than would otherwise have happened; (3) proceedings had been begun before the date specified in the second notice, and (4) because the Recorder had found C guilty of maladministration, he had erred in finding no breach of duty towards D.

Held, dismissing the application, that (1) the typescript "Director of Housing", coupled with a covering letter from C's estate officer, was substantially within s.83(2)(a) of the 1985 Act and not defective; (2) D's defence on the merits had not been affected by the procedural orders. The court had no regard to the fact that the action had been accelerated, since that was a common consequence of amendments; (3) there was no reason why a landlord might not rely on more than one s.83 notice and the relevant date was the date the first proceedings were begun, not the date of amendment, and (4) the Recorder's reference to maladministration referred to C's slow handling of D's application for housing benefit, for which they had agreed to write off £800 of arrears, not to D's counterclaim, *Stidolph v. American School in London Educational Trust Ltd* (1969) 20 P. & C.R. 802, [1969] C.L.Y. 2033 followed.

CITY OF LONDON CORP v. DEVLIN (1997) 29 H.L.R. 58, Auld, L.J., CA.

2746. **Secure tenancies—notices—Amendment No.1**

SECURE TENANCIES (NOTICES) (AMENDMENT) REGULATIONS 1997, SI 1997 71; made under the Housing Act 1985 s.83. In force: February 12, 1997; £1.10.

These Regulations amend the prescribed form of notice which has to be served on a secure tenant under the Housing Act 1985 before the court can entertain proceedings for possession of a dwelling-house let under a secure tenancy or for the termination of a secure tenancy, unless the court considers it just and equitable to dispense with the requirement of such a notice. The amendments are in consequence of the Housing Act 1985 s.83 and s.83A being substituted by the Housing Act 1996.

2747. **Secure tenancies—notices—Amendment No.2—form of notice seeking possession**

SECURE TENANCIES (NOTICES) (AMENDMENT NO.2) REGULATIONS 1997, SI 1997 377; made under the Housing Act 1985 s.83. In force: February 12, 1997; £0.65.

These Regulations amend the Secure Tenancies (Notices) Regulations 1987 (SI 1987 755) to rectify an error in an amendment made to those Regulations by the Secure Tenancies (Notices) (Amendment) Regulations 1997 (SI 1997 71). The amendment is to the form of notice seeking possession to be given by a landlord to a secure tenant with a periodic tenancy.

2748. Secure tenancies—repairs

SECURE TENANTS OF LOCAL HOUSING AUTHORITIES (RIGHT TO REPAIR) (AMENDMENT) REGULATIONS 1997, SI 1997 73; made under the Housing Act 1985 s.96; and the Housing Act 1996 s.135. In force: February 12, 1997; £0.65.

These Regulations apply the SecureTenants of Local Housing Authorities (Right to Repair) Regulations (SI 1994 133) to introductory tenants of such authorities.

2749. Secure tenancies—succession—agreement that one sister should succeed to secure tenancy—both sisters signed official successor form—no joint tenancy created

[Housing Act 1980 s.30.]

The signing of an official successor form by two people meeting the criteria for successor tenants under the Housing Act 1980 s.30 does not automatically create a joint tenancy where a prior agreement exists that only one of them would succeed to the tenancy. An agreement was reached between two sisters, B and J, that, whilst they both met the criteria under the Housing Act 1980 s.30 to succeed their mother as secure tenant of a property after her death, the successor should be J. An official form to be signed by the successor tenant under s.30 was signed by both sisters and countersigned by a housing officer. J did not object to B's name being put on the rent book provided that this did not affect her status as successor tenant. After the relationship between the sisters broke down, B asked to be rehoused and, on N's advice, served a notice to quit on J to terminate the tenancy. When N sought possession of the property, the judge held that the notice to quit was invalid on the ground that J had succeeded to the secure tenancy as sole tenant, and N appealed. Whilst accepting that J had become the successor tenant as a result of the sisters' agreement, N argued that J had surrendered the tenancy by operation of law on signing the official form or, alternatively, that she was estopped by her actions from denying that she and her sister were joint tenants.

Held, dismissing the appeal, that the statutory provisions did not permit joint succession and the agreement between the sisters vested the tenancy in J alone. By simply signing the official form, J could not be regarded as having unequivocally surrendered her tenancy and replaced it with a joint tenancy. Nothing in J's conduct at the time she signed the form or afterwards gave rise to an estoppel preventing her from denying that the sisters were joint tenants, nor did J's conduct support a conclusion that she had made an unequivocal representation that she and B were joint tenants.

NEWHAM LBC v. PHILLIPS, *The Times*, November 12, 1997, Hutchison, L.J., CA.

2750. Water charges—collection by council on behalf of water company—obligation of tenancy

[Water Act 1973 s.32A; Housing Act 1985 s.84, Sch.2.]

L appealed against a decision refusing to grant a possession order against its tenant, T, which it had sought on the grounds of non payment of water charges which L collected from tenants on behalf of the water company.

Held, dismissing the appeal, that a local authority was legally entitled to agree with a water company to collect water rates from tenants on its behalf and, having negotiated a discounted payment with the water company, to use any surplus for the benefit of its tenants. Such an arrangement with a tenant was possible following the repeal of the Water Act 1973 s.32A. It was not necessary to decide whether the water charges constituted "rent" since they were definitely "an obligation of the tenancy" for the purposes of the Housing Act 1985 Sch.2 ground 1, and T was therefore obliged to pay the charges to L and could be held to account for non-payment. The judge was thus entitled to exercise his discretion as to whether or not to grant a possession order under s.84(2) of the 1985 Act, but should have approached the case on the basis that T was in breach of her tenancy agreement by failing to make the payments and

L and its other tenants had suffered as a result. However, since L and T had reached an agreement over payment of the arrears, there was no reason to consider making a suspended order.

LAMBETH LBC v. THOMAS, *The Times*, March 31, 1997, Mance, J., CA.

2751. Articles

Challenging homelessness decisions under the Housing Act 1996 *(Jon Holbrook and Jan Luba)*: Legal Action 1997, Jan, 21-23. (Statutory right to require local authority to review certain decisions made under Part VII of Act, statutory right of appeal if review is unsuccessful and residual role of judicial review).

Children under the Housing Act *(Geoff Gilbert)*: Childright 1997, 137, 7-8. (Provisions of 1996 Act, with particular reference to impact on children of Part V on introductory tenancies and local authorities' powers of eviction and Part VII on homelessness).

Defending notices seeking possession *(Andrew Dymond)*: Legal Action 1997, Feb, 10-11. (Requirements of form and contents of notice, court's power to dispense with notice requirements and changes under 1996 Act).

Eligibility of persons from abroad under the new homelessness provisions *(Caroline Hunter)*: Legal Action 1997, Mar, 16-18.

Fire precautions – legal controls in houses in multiple occupation: safe havens... or... any port in a storm? *(Ann R. Everton)*: J. Soc. Wel. & Fam. L. 1997, 19(1), 61-71. (Cases concerning fire hazards in such housing, proposals for reform and provisions in 1996 Act).

Getting in on the Act *(Gary Murphy)*: E.G. 1997, 9735, 44-45. (Housing Act 1996 procedure for landlords to sell blocks of flats by auction as alternative to private treaty sale under Landlord and Tenant Act 1987).

Housing Act 1996: what does it mean for houses in multiple occupation? *(Nicholas J. Smith)*: Conv. 1997, May/Jun, 206-215. (Deficiencies of overhaul of safety provisions in Part II of Act, particularly introduction of only discretionary registration scheme for HMOs).

Housing JR: essential respondent cases *(Andrew Arden)* and *(Jonathan Manning)*: J.R. 1997, 2(3), 181-185. (Compilation of 20 judicial review cases where housing authorities were found not to be in breach of statutory duties).

Implementation of Housing Act 1996 *(Nic Madge)*: Legal Action 1997, Feb, 18-19. (Provisions on homelessness, including regulations and Code of Guidance, and introductory tenancies, with dates for implementation of other provisions).

Implementation of the Housing Act 1996 *(Nic Madge)*: Legal Action 1997, Jun, 10-11. (Implementation of provisions on homelessness and allocation, registered social landlords, injunctions to restrain anti social behaviour and houses in multiple occupation).

Introductory tenancies: a nuisance too far? *(Nicholas J. Smith)* and *(Gavin A. George)*: J. Soc. Wel. & Fam. L. 1997, 19(3), 307-320. (Whether problem of neighbour nuisance, with reference to current remedies and effect on security of tenure).

Rent to mortgage explained *(Michael Olaseinde)*: L. Ex. 1997, Oct, 11. (Right to buy procedure and practicalities).

Repair grants: caravans and houseboats *(Rachel Morris)*: Legal Action 1997, Aug, 22. (Relevant provisions of 1996 Act which extend minor works assistance to houseboats and static mobile homes but creates direct discrimination against gypsy travellers).

Residential accommodation: provision and charging *(Alan Maclean)*: S.J. 1997, 141(13), 302-304. (Local authorities' powers and duties under the National Assistance Act 1948 Part III, including arrangements with private and voluntary sector and charging for accommodation).

Restricted access *(John Gallagher)*: Adviser 1997, 59, 10-13. (Provisions to restrict local authorities' duties towards homeless applicants and system for allocation of social housing).

The impact of JR on homelessness decisions *(Derek Ade Obadina)*: J.R. 1996, 1(4), 244-245. (Research into decision making in 20 local authorities' homeless persons units).

The unsettling of settled law on "settled accommodation": the House of Lords and the homelessness legislation old and new *(Caroline Hunter)* and *(Joanna Miles)*: J. Soc. Wel. & Fam. L. 1997, 19(3), 267-289. (Development and application by courts of concept of settled accommodation and its relationship with provisions of Housing Act 1985, impact of HL decision in Awua and changes to homelessness legislation made by Housing Act 1996).

Unauthorised travellers' halting sites *(Garrett Simons)*: I.P.E.L.J. 1997, 4(2), 53-56. (Conflict between local authority's duty to provide halting sites for homeless travellers, planning powers and liability for nuisance to neighbouring landowners).

What is the future for social housing: reflections on the public sector provisions of the Housing Act 1996 *(James Driscoll)*: M.L.R. 1997, 60(6), 823-839. (Background to legislation, provisions governing housing associations, revisions to local authority responsibilities over houses in multiple occupation, powers to combat nuisance behaviour and allocation of public sector tenancies).

2752. Books

Arden, Andrew; Hunter, Caroline—Housing Law Manual. 6th Ed. Paperback: £30.00. ISBN 0-421-55390-1. Sweet & Maxwell.

HUMAN RIGHTS

2753. Adoption—sex discrimination—dispensation with putative father's consent unconstitutional—South Africa

[Child Care Act 1983 s.18(4) (South Africa); Constitution of the Republic of South Africa Act 200 of 1993 s.8(1), s.8(2).]

During the period 1994 to 1995, F became involved with M in an intimate relationship and they lived together as man and wife. On December 12, 1995, M gave birth to a boy, T, and F was the father. In April 1995, after she had discovered she was pregnant, M decided it would be in the best interests of the unborn child that he be put up for adoption, a decision that F resisted. Extensive litigation between the parties commenced early December 1995. Following T's birth, F sought to intervene in the adoption proceedings on the grounds that he was an interested party and wished to be considered a prospective adoptive parent. F sought a stay of the adoption proceedings pending an application to the Constitutional Court challenging the constitutionality of the Child Care Act 1983 s.18(4)(d) insofar as it dispensed with the father's consent in the adoption of an illegitimate child. The Children's Court subsequently made an order sanctioning the child's adoption. F sought a review of the decision, seeking, inter alia, an order declaring that the 1983 Act s.18(4)(d) was inconsistent with the provisions of the Constitution of the Republic of South Africa Act 200 of 1993 s.8(1) and s.8(2), ie. the right to equality and the right not to be unfairly discriminated against. The court set aside the order sanctioning the adoption and referred the 1983 Act s.18(4)(d) issue to the Constitutional Court for determination.

Held, that (1) insofar as the 1983 Act s.18(4)(d) dispensed with a father's consent for the adoption of an illegitimate child, it discriminated not only between the rights of a father in unions recognised as valid marriages and in other unions not so recognised, but also against fathers on the basis of their gender or their marital status; (2) it therefore violated the rights guaranteed by Act 200 of 1993 s.8(1) and s.8(2) which violation was neither reasonable nor justifiable in an open and democratic society based on freedom and equality, and (4) it followed that the 1983 Act s.18(4)(d) was inconsistent with the Constitution and was accordingly invalid to the extent that it dispensed with the father's consent for adoption of an illegitimate child in all circumstances. Consent to an adoption should be given by both parents, irrespective of whether they were married, or whether the child was illegitimate.

FRASER v. CHILDREN'S COURT, PRETORIA NORTH (1997) 1 B.H.R.C. 607, Chaskalson (President), Const Ct (SA).

2754. Assault–assaults by police–constitutional damages–South Africa

[Constitution of the Republic of South Africa 1993 s.7 (4).]

F sued D for damages arising out of a series of assaults allegedly perpetrated on him by members of the South African Police Force acting within the course and scope of their employment with D. F claimed damages, inter alia, for pain and suffering, loss of enjoyment of life and shock, contumelia and medical expenses. He also claimed damages in the sum of R 200,000 on the basis that the alleged assaults infringed his constitutionally guaranteed rights to human dignity, freedom of the person, privacy, and not to be arrested and detained except in accordance with the provisions of the Constitution of the Republic of South Africa 1993. The sum of R 200,000 was stated to include an element of punitive damages in reliance on the entitlement conferred by the Interim Constitution s.7 (4) (a) to "appropriate relief" for an infringement of constitutional rights. D took an exception to the claim on the basis that s.7 (4) (a) did not confer any right to damages. The exception was upheld at first instance and on appeal. F applied for leave to appeal to the Constitutional Court.

Held, dismissing the application for leave to appeal, that, by analogy with awards of damages for breaches of statutory rights, there was no reason in principle why "appropriate relief" in s.7 (4) should not include an award of damages where such an award was necessary to protect and enforce constitutionally enshrined rights, *Callinicos v. Burman* 1963 (1) S.A. 489 (A), *Da Silva v. Coutinho* 1971 (3) S.A. 123 (A) and *Goldberg v. Minister of Prisons* 1979 (1) S.A. 14 (A) applied; (2) in the instant case, there could be no place for further constitutional damages in order to vindicate the rights in question. If F succeeded in proving his allegations, he would be awarded substantial damages which will be sufficient vindication of his constitutional rights. In particular, there was no place for any award of punitive constitutional damages. No evidence had been produced which demonstrated that punitive damages against the government would serve as a significant deterrent against individual or systemic repetition of the infringement of the right not to be beaten and tortured. For an award to have any deterrent effect they would have to be very substantial, and the more substantial they were, the greater the anomaly that a single plaintiff received a windfall of such magnitude, *Rookes v. Barnard* [1964] A.C. 1129, [1964] C.L.Y. 3703 and *Broome v. Cassell & Co* [1972] A.C. 1027, [1972] C.L.Y. 2745 considered.

FOSE v. MINISTER OF SAFETY AND SECURITY (1997) 2 B.H.R.C. 434, Ackermann, J., Const Ct (SA).

2755. Asylum seekers–deportation–right not to be deported to a state where deportee would be subjected to torture–deportation by Switzerland to Turkey of Turkish Kurd

[Convention against Torture and Other Cruel, Inhuman or Degrading Treatment or Punishment 1984 Art.3.]

A, a Turkish citizen of Kurdish background, was a sympathiser of an outlawed Kurdish communist organisation, KAWA. In 1983 and 1984 he was arrested by the Turkish police, whom he claimed tortured him, and subsequently served a term of imprisonment and internal exile for being an active member of KAWA. This was subsequently quashed and replaced with two and a half years' imprisonment and 10 months' internal exile in Izmir for having assisted KAWA militants. Following his release, A claimed he was arrested and tortured several times during 1988 and 1989 and that he had come under the scrutiny of the Turkish military. A had accordingly left Turkey using a falsified identity card, and sought asylum in Switzerland. His application for asylum was rejected on the grounds that his earlier imprisonment was too remote in time to constitute a ground for fear of persecution and that his claims were inconsistent. The Appeal Commission dismissed his appeal against the decision on the grounds that, given the general situation in Turkey and A's background and origin, there was no special, individual and concrete risk shown to preclude his return. A then submitted a communication to the UN Committee against Torture claiming deportation to Turkey would violate Switzerland's obligation under the Convention against Torture and Other Cruel, Inhuman or Degrading Treatment or Punishment 1984 Art. 3 not to expel or return a person to another state where there was substantial grounds for believing that he would be in danger of being subjected to torture. A produced evidence that although Turkey had ratified the Convention, torture was systematically practised there, and that his background and record of involvement with the KAWA indicated he belonged to several target groups of Turkish repression and stood at risk of being arrested and tortured.

Held, that (1) the existence of a consistent pattern of gross, flagrant or mass violations of human rights in a country was not in itself a sufficient ground for determining whether a person would be in danger of being subjected to torture on his return there. There had to be specific grounds indicating that the individual concerned would personally be at risk; (2) the mere fact that a country was a party to the Convention and recognised the Committee's competence did not constitute sufficient guarantee for a person's security; (3) A's ethnic background, political affiliation and history of detention and internal exile, combined with the Turkish security forces' activities and the fact that torture was still systematic in Turkey, constituted substantial grounds for believing he would be in danger of torture if returned there, and the deportation of A would violate Switzerland's obligations under the Convention.

ALAN v. SWITZERLAND (1997) 1 B.H.R.C. 598, Judge not applicable, UNCAT.

2756. **Building societies–income tax–retrospective legislation validating void tax regulations defeated claims to restitution–no breach of property rights or right to fair trial**

[European Convention on Human Rights 1950 Art.6(1); European Convention on Human Rights 1950 Protocol No.1 Art.1; Finance Act 1991 s.53; Income Tax (Building Societies) Regulations 1986 (SI 1986 482).]

The Income Tax (Building Societies) Regulations 1986 introduced transitional provisions relating to a change in the method of calculating the income tax payable by building societies in respect of the interest paid on investors' accounts. W, a building society, obtained a House of Lords ruling in judicial review proceedings commenced on June 18, 1986 that the Regulations were void and later obtained a declaration that it was entitled to repayment of the sums charged. In 1991, L and N commenced proceedings for restitution of sums paid by them under the Regulations, but the Finance Act 1991 s.53 then came into effect, giving retrospective validity to the Regulations, except in relation to building societies who had challenged the Regulations before July 18, 1986, which only applied to W. In the meantime, L, N and Y applied for judicial review of the Treasury Orders setting the relevant tax rate for 1986-87 on technical grounds and brought further actions for restitution. Before those proceedings were resolved, primary legislation was enacted giving retrospective effect to the Treasury Orders. L, N and Y applied to the ECHR, contending that the stifling of their actions constituted a breach of the European Convention of Human Rights 1950 Protocol No.1 Art.1 and also violated Art.6(1) of the Convention.

Held, refusing the applications, that (1) there was no evidence to support the applicants' contention that the Regulations resulted in the interest being taxed twice and a successful claim to restitution would have amounted to a windfall for L, N and Y. Even if the applicants did have "possessions" in the form of vested rights to restitution, the interference with those rights in the form of the primary legislation which stifled their respective legal actions was justified by the public interest in securing payment of taxes, and accordingly there was no breach of Art.1 of Protocol No.1; (2) there had been no breach of Art.1 of Protocol 1 when taken in conjunction with the discrimination provisions in Art.14 of the

Convention, as the applicants could not be regarded as being in an analogous position to W, and, in any case, the decision to exclude W from the effects of the retrospective legislation could be objectively justified, and (3) the applicants could not justifiably claim that they had been denied access to a court in breach of Art.6(1), given that they must have realised that the government would not permit technical defects to defeat Parliament's intention that the interest be taxed.

NATIONAL & PROVINCIAL BUILDING SOCIETY v. UNITED KINGDOM; LEEDS PERMANENT BUILDING SOCIETY v. UNITED KINGDOM; YORKSHIRE BUILDING SOCIETY v. UNITED KINGDOM [1997] B.T.C. 624, R Ryssdal (President), ECHR.

2757. **Children–constitutional prohibition of child labour–compensation for statutory violation–obligation of state governments–India**

[Constitution of India Art.24; Child Labour (Prohibition and Regulation) Act 1986 (India).]

By 1995 child labour in India had become a social problem of epidemic proportions, with some estimates placing the total number of children employed in official and unofficial industries as high as 100 million. M, a public-spirited lawyer, brought a petition against the State of Tamilnadu for violation of the constitutional prohibition on the employment of children in factories or mines or other hazardous employment, set out in the Constitution of India Art.24 and reinforced by the Child Labour (Prohibition and Regulation) Act 1986. A committee was established to investigate the problem and make recommendations. On receiving its report, the Court dealt with the issue on a national basis.

Held, in order to fulfil the constitutional prohibition on the employment of children, the constitutional guarantee of free and universal education, and the legislative intent behind the Child Labour (Prohibition and Regulation) Act 1986, every offending employer must be required to pay compensation of Rs 20,000 for each child employed in contravention of the 1986 Act, and inspectors must be appointed to secure compliance with this aim. The various state governments must also discharge their obligations to dissuade parents and guardians from seeking employment of their children. In cases where it would not be possible for the state to provide employment for adults from the same family to replace the children working in that family, the appropriate government should fund a sum of Rs 25,000 for each child employed in a factory or mine or other hazardous employment. If no adult from the same family secured a job in place of the child, the monthly sum of Rs 25,000 would obviate the need for the child to work since an alternative source of income would have become available to him. The payment must be used for the purposes of educating the child otherwise it would cease. The Secretary to the Minister of Labour of the Government of India should report back to the court within one year about the compliance with the court's directions.

MEHTA v. STATE OF TAMILNADU (1997) 2 B.H.R.C. 258, Singh, J., Sup Ct (India).

2758. **Children–corporal punishment–competence of complaint to ECHR**

See CHILDREN: A and B v. United Kingdom. §427

2759. **Children–wardship–leave of wardship court not required to petition European Court of Human Rights**

[European Commission and Court of Human Rights (Immunities and Privileges) Order 1970 (SI 1970 1941) para.5; European Convention on Human Rights 1950 Art.25.]

Leave of the wardship court is not required to petition the European Court of Human Rights. A Zulu child had been cared for by a white South African woman who brought the child to England. The child's parents objected and sought the child's return to South Africa. The Court of Appeal ordered the child's immediate return. Leave to appeal to the House of Lords was refused. In the wardship proceedings, the applicant sought directions as to whether or not leave was required to petition the European Court of Human Rights on behalf of a ward under the European Convention on Human Rights 1950 Art.25.

Held, that the European Commission and Court of Human Rights (Immunities and Privileges) Order 1970 para.5, had abrogated the ability of the court to fetter the right to petition the European Court of Human Rights on behalf of a ward under Art.25 of the European Convention. The demands of public policy, and not necessarily the requirements of the child's upbringing, required that a petition be capable of being brought on behalf of the ward.

M (PETITION TO EUROPEAN COMMISSION OF HUMAN RIGHTS), *Re* [1997] 1 F.L.R. 755, Johnson, J., Fam Div.

2760. Death penalty—detention on death row for 10 years not cruel, degrading or inhuman treatment—delayed appeal a violation of the International Covenant—Jamaica

[International Covenant on Civil and Political Rights 1966.]

J, a Jamaican citizen, was convicted of murder and sentenced to death, on December 15, 1983. He applied for leave to appeal, but his application was dismissed by the Court of Appeal on February 29, 1988. A reasoned appeal judgment was issued on March 14, 1988. J's petition for special leave to appeal was dismissed by the Judicial Committee of the Privy Council on July 9, 1992. On January 11, 1994, having exhausted domestic remedies, J made an initial submission to the UN Human Rights Committee. In 1995 the offence of which J was convicted was classified as non capital murder and his death sentence was commuted to life imprisonment on March 16, 1995. It was argued, inter alia, that J's detention on death row for 10 years amounted to cruel and degrading treatment and/or punishment in violation of the International Covenant on Civil and Political Rights 1966 Art.7. or to inhuman treatment in violation of the International Covenant Art.10(1). It was also claimed that the delay of 51 months between J's trial and the dismissal of the appeal, partly due to a delay in making the trial transcript available, violated his right to be tried without undue delay and to have his conviction and sentence reviewed by a higher tribunal under the International Covenant Arts.14(3)(c), (5). As a result, the imposition of the capital sentence on completion of a trial conducted without respect to the provisions of the covenant had been a violation of the International Covenant Art.6(2).

Held, by a majority, that (1) the length of time a condemned person spent confined to death row did not in itself amount to cruel and degrading treatment and/or punishment that constituted a violation of the International Covenant by a state party, in the absence of further compelling circumstances; (2) to make the length of detention on death row determinative of such a violation would have been to expedite executions, and inconsistent with the International Covenant's object of reducing the use of the death penalty; (3) the delay of over four years in hearing an appeal in a capital case, without there being exceptional circumstances, was unreasonably long, and therefore a violation of the International Covenant Art.14(3)(c) and Art.14(5); (4) it followed that the imposition of a final sentence of death had been imposed contrary to the provisions of the International Covenant and so violated Art.6; (5) J was therefore entitled to further clemency in addition to the commutation of his death sentence, and (6) the state party would therefore be required to furnish the Committee with information about the measures to be taken to give effect thereto.

JOHNSON v. JAMAICA (1996) 1 B.H.R.C. 37, Judge not applicable, UNHRC.

2761. Debtors—imprisonment of judgment debtors neither unlawful deprivation of liberty nor degrading treatment—Zimbabwe

[Declaration of Rights s.13(1), s.15(1) (Zimbabwe); Magistrates Court (Civil) Rules (Zimbabwe); Magistrates Court Act (Zimbabwe).]

On March 22, 1993 AF obtained a default judgment in the magistrates court against C in an amount of Z$2,839.31. The debt was incurred through the purchase of goods between November 1989 and January 1990. On the day of the judgment a warrant of execution against property was granted. By that stage C had divested himself of all his property, so a messenger of court was unable to effect an attachment to satisfy the judgment debt and costs. The creditors then took out a summons in the magistrates court calling upon C to show cause on October 5, 1993 why a decree of civil imprisonment should not be made against him. C was served with the summons, but failed to appear at the court on the day of the hearing. Consequent upon his default, an order of civil imprisonment for 90 days was made, the maximum sentence permissible. A warrant for C's arrest and detention was made, but despite being in gainful employment, C assiduously avoided all attempts to serve the warrant upon him. In early 1994 he departed to South Africa, returning to Zimbabwe on February 28, 1995. On April 10, 1995, following his return, C lodged an application in the magistrates court that the warrant of arrest be suspended until he was able to find employment. The application was dismissed with costs on October 5, 1995, but the imprisonment order was suspended on the condition that C, then employed, paid off his debts in monthly instalments. In the meantime, the day after his application to the magistrates court, C had applied to the Supreme Court of Zimbabwe for an order declaring that the procedure of civil imprisonment under the Magistrates Court Act and Magistrates Court (Civil) Rules 1980 to be in contravention of the Declaration of Rights s.13(1), s.15(1) and s.18(1). These provided, inter alia, that no one should be deprived of their liberty other than in execution of a court order made in order to secure fulfilment of a legal obligation, or be subjected to degrading punishment, and that everyone was entitled to the protection of the law.

Held, dismissing application, that (1) under the Declaration of Rights s.13(2) a person could be deprived of his liberty in execution of an order made by a court to secure the fulfilment of an obligation imposed by law; (2) magistrates were empowered to issue a decree of civil imprisonment against a judgment debtor Magistrates Court Act s.27; (3) the debtor's obligation was an obligation imposed by law, both a contractual obligation to the creditor and an obligation under the court's direction that the debt be paid; (4) the requirement of s.27 was therefore satisfied; (5) the procedure did not fail adequately to distinguish between debtors unable to pay, and those unwilling, and so did not violate the Declaration s.13(1); (6) imprisonment of a recalcitrant debtor was not "degrading" treatment, because it was remedial in nature, the debtor being able to end it by paying his debt, accordingly civil imprisonment did not contravene the Declaration s.15(1), and (7) s.18(1) was not contravened, it guaranteed protection of the law subject to the provisions of the Constitution and was subordinate to the derogation sanctioned by the Declaration s.13(2)(c), which permitted imprisonment of judgment debtors.

CHINAMORA v. ANGWA FURNISHERS (PRIVATE) LTD (1997) 1 B.H.R.C. 460, Gubbay, C.J., Sup Ct (Zim).

2762. Deportation—British citizen permanently residing in Canada—prohibition on re-entry—alleged violation of civil and political rights

[International Covenant on Civil and Political Rights 1966 Art.12(4).]

S, a British citizen born in 1960, resided in Canada from the age of seven. At no stage had he applied for Canadian citizenship, or his parents on his behalf. Between 1978 and 1991 he was convicted of 42 offences, most of them petty. In 1990 an immigration inquiry was initiated against S and he was ordered to be deported from Canada on account of his criminal convictions. If deported he would be unable to return to Canada without the express consent of the Canadian Minister of Employment and Immigration. He exhausted all domestic appeals, unsuccessfully, and applied to the UN Human Rights Committee alleging, inter alia, a violation of the International Covenant on Civil and Political Rights 1966 Art.12(4) in that the prohibition on him re-entering Canada would constitute an arbitrary bar on him exercising his right to enter "his own country" within the meaning of Art.12(4).

Held, dismissing S's complaint, that the scope of the phrase "his own country" in Art.12.(4) of the Convention was broader than the concept "country of his nationality", and embraced an individual who, because of his special ties to or claims in relation to a given country, could not be considered as a mere alien. But, in a case where an immigrant continued to retain the nationality of his country of origin, and where the country of immigration facilitated acquiring its nationality and the immigrant refrained from doing so, either by choice or by committing acts that would disqualify him from acquiring that nationality, the country of immigration did not become "his own country" within the meaning of Art.12.(4) of the Covenant. There had accordingly been no violation of Art.12(4) by Canada.

STEWART v. CANADA (1997) 2 B.H.R.C. 235, Judge not applicable, UNHRC.

2763. Deportation—convicted drugs courier in advanced stages of AIDS—removal and withdrawal of care and medical treatment would amount to inhuman treatment

[European Convention on Human Rights 1950 Art.3.]

D, a national of St Kitts, was found in possession of a substantial amount of cocaine upon his arrival in the UK and was convicted of illegally importing a controlled drug and sentenced to six years' imprisonment. By the time he was released, D was in the advanced stages of AIDS and was provided with accommodation and care by a UK charity, as well as receiving medical treatment for his condition. The immigration authorities ordered D's removal to St Kitts and his application for judicial review of that decision and subsequent appeal were dismissed. D applied to the ECHR, contending that his removal would breach the European Convention on Human Rights 1950 Art.3, as he would not receive adequate medical treatment and had no family in St Kitts who could care for him.

Held, allowing the application, that whilst contracting states had the right to control the entry and residence of aliens and to impose severe sanctions, including expulsion, for the commission of drug trafficking offences, the prohibition against torture or inhuman or degrading treatment or punishment in Art.3 was an absolute one, which applied regardless of the conduct of the individual concerned and had to be respected when a state was considering an expulsion. Although Art.3 had so far only been applied to the acts or omissions of public authorities in the receiving state, Art.3 could apply to a situation which did not directly or indirectly concern the responsibilities of the public authorities. Withdrawal of the care, support and treatment D was currently receiving in the UK would have serious consequences for him, and, whilst the conditions in St Kitts did not themselves breach the standards demanded by Art.3, D's removal there would expose him to a real risk that he would die in distressing circumstances, which would amount to inhuman treatment contrary to Art.3. Although released alien prisoners did not normally have the right to remain so as to continue to receive medical or welfare services, D's case was exceptional and involved compelling humanitarian factors.

D v. UNITED KINGDOM (1997) 2 B.H.R.C. 273, R Ryssdal (President), ECHR.

2764. Deportation—forfeiture of refugee status—real risk of torture or degrading treatment—no grounds to expel in those circumstances

[European Convention on Human Rights 1950 Art.3, Art.50.]

A, a Somalia national, left Somalia in 1990 and sought refugee status in Austria in November 1990. His application was based on the fact that his father and brother had been executed for assisting his uncle, a member of the opposition United Somali Congress, USC, and that he and his family had been assaulted on suspicion of belonging to the USC. The Styria Public Security Authority rejected his application in April 1991, but that decision was reversed on appeal by the Minister of the Interior. In July 1994 the Federal Refugee Office ordered the forfeiture of A's refugee status, following A's conviction in August 1993 of attempted robbery and two and a half years' prison sentence. In September 1994 the Minister of the Interior dismissed A's appeal against the decision to forfeit his refugee status, on the basis that A had committed a "particularly serious crime", one punishable by up to 10 years' imprisonment. That decision was set aside by the Administrative Court in February 1995 but in April 1995 the Minister concluded, referring to A's previous behaviour and convictions, that he constituted a danger to Austrian society and should have his refugee status forfeited. The Administrative Court upheld this decision in November 1995. Deportation proceedings had been commenced against A in November 1994 but A challenged those on the basis that if he returned to Somalia he would be risking his life. The deportation order was upheld in April 1995 on the ground that A had revealed a tendency towards aggressive behaviour and constituted a danger to Austrian society. In December 1994 A applied to the Commission alleging that his expulsion to Somalia would violate the European Convention on Human Rights 1950 Art.3 in that it would expose him to a real risk of torture or degrading treatment in that country.

Held, allowing the application, that the deportation order constituted a breach of Art.3 which implied the obligation not to expel a person to a country where substantial grounds had been shown that if the person were expelled he would face a real risk of being subjected to torture or degrading treatment, *Soering v. United Kingdom (A/161)* (1989) 11 E.H.R.R. 439, [1989] C.L.Y. 1712, *Cruz Varas v. Sweden (A/201)* (1992) 14 E.H.R.R. 1, [1992] C.L.Y. 2339, *Vilvarajah v. United Kingdom (A/215)* (1992) 14 E.H.R.R. 248, [1992] C.L.Y. 2333, *Chahal v. United Kingdom* (1997) 23 E.H.R.R. 413, [1996] 1 C.L.Y. 3130 applied. Article 3 prohibited, in absolute terms, torture or inhuman or degrading treatment or punishment, irrespective of the victim's conduct. It made no provision for exceptions and no derogation was permissible from it even in the event of a public emergency threatening the life of the nation, *Ireland v. United Kingdom (A/25)* (1978) 2 E.H.R.R. 25, [1979] C.L.Y. 1175, *Tomasi v. France (A/241-A)* (1993) 15 E.H.R.R. 1, [1993] C.L.Y. 2131, *Chahal v. United Kingdom* applied. The principle was equally valid in expulsion cases, and the activities of the individual, however undesirable or dangerous, could not be a material consideration. Although refugee status was granted to A in 1992, the conditions in Somalia at the time of the application were decisive. Since there had been no observable improvement in conditions since 1992, A's deportation to Somalia would breach the Convention Art.3 for as long as he faced a serious risk of being subjected to torture or inhuman or degrading treatment in that country.

AHMED v. AUSTRIA (1997) 24 E.H.R.R. 278, R Bernhardt (President), ECHR.

2765. Detention–arrest of Bulgarian parliamentarian–suspicion of misappropriating public funds–detention's compatibility with ECHR

[European Convention on Human Rights 1950 Art.5(1), Art.18, Art.50.]

L was a Bulgarian citizen and a member of the Bulgarian Government who became Prime Minister in 1990. From 1986 to 1990, as Deputy Prime Minister, L participated in decisions to grant loans and assistance worth nearly $34.6 million and lei 27.1 million to various developing countries. In March 1992, when attempting to leave Sofia for Moscow, L was informed by border police that an order had been made for the withdrawal of his diplomatic passport. As he was not shown the order L refused to hand over the passport. On July 7, 1992 the National Assembly waived L's parliamentary immunity and authorised criminal proceedings against him. On July 9, 1992 L was charged under the Bulgarian Criminal Code with having misappropriated funds allocated to developing countries in order to obtain an advantage for a third party. L was arrested and held in remand on the same day and his lawyer lodged an appeal with the Bulgarian Supreme Court requesting his release. The appeal was dismissed on July 13, 1992. L's health deteriorated and his lawyer made further requests for his release which were also dismissed. L was eventually released on bail and was awarded compensation for non pecuniary damage suffered as a result of the attempts to withdraw his passport in the absence of a lawful order to this effect. In the meantime, he had lodged an application to the Commission, complaining inter alia, that his arrest and detention on remand had been incompatible with the European Convention on

Human Rights 1950 Art.5(1)(c) in that there was no reasonable suspicion of him having committed a crime.

Held, upholding the complaint and awarding L compensation and costs, that the Convention Art.5(1) contained an exhaustive list of permissible grounds for deprivation of liberty which must be strictly interpreted, *Ciulla v. Italy* (A/148) (1991) 13 E.H.R.R. 346 applied. The lawfulness of the detention must be assessed not only by reference to whether it was effected in accordance with domestic law but also whether it was compatible with the purpose of Art.5, namely to protect the individual from arbitrariness, *Bozano v. France* (A/111) (1987) 9 E.H.R.R. 297, [1987] C.L.Y. 1911 and *Benham v. United Kingdom* (1996) 22 E.H.R.R. 293, [1996] 1 C.L.Y. 3155 applied. In the circumstances the Court was not satisfied that the collective decisions for which L was prosecuted constituted a criminal offence under Bulgarian law at the relevant time. No evidence was presented that L sought to obtain an advantage for himself or a third party. Accordingly the deprivation of L's liberty was not "lawful detention" effected "on reasonable suspicion of [his] having committed an offence", and was therefore contrary to Art.5(1) of the Convention.

LOUKANOV v. BULGARIA (1997) 24 E.H.R.R. 121, R Ryssdal (President), ECHR.

2766. **Detention–confinement of asylum seekers at airport hotel–seekers were "victims" and deprived of liberty under ECHR**

[European Convention on Human Rights 1950 Art.5, Art.25.]

The four applicants, all Somali nationals, arrived in France on March 9, 1992 from Syria. The applicants claimed that they were fleeing persecution in Somalia and that their lives were in danger. However the border police refused to admit them to French territory on the ground that their passports had been falsified. They were confined at an hotel and made an unsuccessful application for asylum. They were granted legal aid on March 24 and put in contact with a lawyer. On March 26 they applied to an urgent applications judge seeking an order for their release from confinement at the hotel which they asserted was unlawful. On March 29 they were deported to Syria. On March 31 the judge had ruled that their detention was unlawful and directed that they be released. On March 30 the applicants had appealed to the Refugee Appeals Board seeking a ruling that the Minister of Interior's decision refusing them leave to enter French territory and sending them back to Syria was unlawful. This appeal was rejected in April 1992. Meanwhile, on March 27 the applicants had lodged an application with the Commission, complaining, inter alia, that the French authorities had infringed their right to liberty secured by the European Convention on Human Rights 1950 Art.5(1). The Commission rejected the complaint, holding that the degree of physical restraint necessary for the "deprivation of liberty" under Art.5(1) was lacking. Before the Court and the Commission, the French Government took as a preliminary point the argument that the applicants were not "victims" of a violation of the Convention within the meaning of Art.25, since the urgent applications judge had made an order in their favour

Held, upholding the complaint, that (1) the word "victim" in the context of Art.25 denotes the person directly affected by the act or omission in issue. Consequently a decision or measure favourable to the applicant is not in principle sufficient to deprive him of his status as a "victim" unless the national authorities have acknowledged, either expressly or in substance, and then afforded redress for the breach of the Convention, as held in *Ludi v. Switzerland* (1993) 15 E.H.R.R. 173, [1993] C.L.Y. 2139. In the instant case, although the applicants had obtained a ruling in their favour, that decision was not made until the applicants had been deported to Syria and the date on which they were granted legal aid made it impossible for them to apply any earlier, and (2) while contracting states have the undeniable right to control aliens' entry and residence into their territory, this right must be exercised in accordance with the provisions of Art.5(1). In order to determine whether someone has been "deprived of his liberty" within the meaning of Art.5, account must be taken of a range of criteria such as the type, duration, effects and manner of implementation of the measure in question. As held in *Guzzardi v. Italy* (1981) 3

E.H.R.R. 333, the difference between deprivation of and restriction upon liberty is merely one of degree or intensity, and not one of nature or substance. Confinement of aliens in detention centres pending deportation must not be prolonged excessively, otherwise there would be a risk of turning an inevitable restriction on liberty into a deprivation of liberty. In the instant case, having regard to the restriction suffered by the applicants in terms of surveillance, and the delay in gaining access to a lawyer or review by the courts, the holding of the applicants in transit was the equivalent in practice of a deprivation of liberty.

AMUUR v. FRANCE (1996) 22 E.H.R.R. 533, Bernhardt (President), ECHR.

2767. Detention—pretrial detention in Hungary—public prosecutor an "officer authorised to exercise judicial power"—continuing obligation on judicial authorities to act promptly

[International Covenant on Civil and Political Rights 1966 Art.9(3); Vienna Convention on the Law of Treaties 1969 Art.28; Optional Protocol to the International Covenant on Civil and Political Rights for Hungary 1988.]

V, a Russian citizen, was arrested in Budapest on August 18, 1988 and was charged with murder. After three days in custody he was given a form to sign. Allegedly he was told that it was intended for the Soviet consul, but it was in fact intended for an extension of his provisional custody by 30 days. He remained in custody in the police station for five months. He was then transferred to a prison. On February 8, 1990 V was found guilty of homicide committed with cruelty and was sentenced to 10 years' imprisonment, with subsequent expulsion from Hungary. V appealed to the Supreme Court of Hungary. The appeal was heard, and on October 30, 1990 the Supreme Court sentenced V to a further four years, qualifying the act for which V was convicted as having been committed with the object of financial gain. V's application to the President of Supreme Court for review was dismissed on December 12, 1991. V submitted a communication to the UN Human Rights Committee on May 6, 1992, claiming that Hungary had violated, inter alia, the International Covenant on Civil and Political Rights 1966 Art.9(3). His extended pre trial detention had violated his right to be brought promptly before an authorised judicial officer and to be tried within a reasonable time. It was contended that the Committee was precluded ratione temporis from considering V's complaint: (1) by operation of the Vienna Convention on the Law of Treaties 1969 Art.28 it had no competence to consider complaints that occurred prior to the date of entry into force of the Optional Protocol to the Covenant for Hungary on December 7, 1988, (2) the Art.9(3) obligation was limited in time to the first few days in detention following arrest, which was in August 1988, and did not have continuing effect. The question as to whether V was promptly brought before a judge or authorised officer after his arrest was therefore inadmissible ratione temporis.

Held, by a majority, that (1) the Committee was not precluded ratione temporis from considering whether the detention of V had been contrary to the International Covenant Art.9(3), since the purpose of Art.9(3) was to bring the detention of a person charged with a criminal offence under judicial control, a failure to do so would lead to a continuing violation of Art.9(3) until cured; (2) V's pretrial detention continued until May 1989 and his claims were admissible in their relation to alleged events that occurred after the date of entry into force of the Optional Protocol; (3) it was inherent to the proper exercise of judicial power that it be exercised by an independent, impartial and objective authority; (4) the public prosecutors who ordered and subsequently extended V's pre trial detention could not be so characterised, since they were subordinate to the Chief Public Prosecutor who was elected by and responsible to Parliament; (5) they could not be considered officers "authorised by law to exercise judicial power" within the meaning of Art.9(3); (6) it followed that V's pre trial detention had violated Art.9(3), and (7) it was not for the Committee to assess a person's guilt or innocence in a criminal case, unless the information before it manifestly showed that the courts' decisions were arbitrary or amounted to a denial of justice.

KULOMIN v. HUNGARY (1996) 1 B.H.R.C. 217, Judge not applicable, UNHRC.

2768. Disabled persons–Canada–employee disability pension discrimination

See EMPLOYMENT: Battlefords and District Cooperative Ltd v. Gibbs. §2240

2769. European Commission on Human Rights–admissibility of application–extraterritorial jurisdiction of ECHR contracting state–repetition of former application–alternative international remedies

[European Convention on Human Rights 1950 Art.1, Art.24, Art.26, Art.62.]

Cyprus presented an application to the Commission alleging various violations of the European Convention on Human Rights 1950 including unlawful detention of missing Greek-Cypriots, inhuman treatment of Greek-Cypriots living in Turkish-controlled Cyprus and forced displacement of Greek-Cypriots from their homes in Turkish Cyprus. Turkey submitted that the complaints were inadmissible, on the basis that the facts alleged did not fall within Turkey's jurisdiction within the meaning of the Convention Art.1, that the instant application was a repetition of previous applications and that the alleged victims had failed to exhaust all domestic remedies and comply with the six month rule as required under the Convention Art.26.

Held, admitting the application, that (1) whether Turkey had jurisdiction in Northern Cyprus under Art.1 should be determined at the merits stage, not the admissibility stage. The Commission's examination would be limited to whether its competence was excluded because the matters concerned could not fall within Turkey's jurisdiction, and investigate whether Turkey was actually responsible under the Convention. Jurisdiction was not necessarily limited to a Member State's own national territory, *Loizidou v. Turkey* (1995) 20 E.H.R.R. 99, [1995] 1 C.L.Y. 2655 followed; (2) at the admissibility stage the Commission was not required to determine whether an inter-State application under Art.24 of the Convention was a repetition of a previous application. Examination of the merits would necessarily be involved and the matter would be determined at the merits stage. The previous decisions did not render the issue res judicata and the application was not an abuse of the right to petition; (3) only in exceptional circumstances could an issue be withdrawn from ECHR jurisdiction on the grounds of a special agreement between contracting states. Art.62 established a monopoly for Convention institutions to decide Convention disputes. Only exceptionally could alternative remedies be sought and the obligations on Turkey and Cyprus to participate in intercommunal talks and the Committee on Missing Persons did not amount to a special agreement. Involvement by other international bodies did not exclude investigation by Convention institutions, and (4) in the situation no practicable domestic remedies existed for Greek Cypriots.

CYPRUS v. TURKEY (1997) 23 E.H.R.R. 244, Trechsel (President), Eur Comm HR.

2770. European Court of Human Rights–abuse of process–applications to court before domestic remedies exhausted–allegations not based on untrue facts–special circumstances obviating exhaustion of domestic remedies

[European Convention on Human Rights 1950 Art.26.]

A and others were Turkish citizens who alleged that their homes had been destroyed and the evacuation of their village had been ordered by the Turkish Government, during the course of the conflict between the security forces and the PKK. The applicants complained that the actions were a violation of the European Convention on Human Rights 1950 and the Turkish Government lodged preliminary objections to the complaints, contending, inter alia, that under Art.26 the complaints were an abuse of process and that the applicants had not exhausted the relevant domestic remedies.

Held, allowing the complaints in part, that the Turkish Government's contention that the applications were an abuse of process and had been made for political purposes were rejected. This could only have occurred if the applications had been based on untrue facts, whereas the findings of both the Commission and the Court substantially upheld the allegations as to the destruction of the applicants' property. The requirement for the exhaustion of domestic remedies under Art.26 obliged applicants to first use the remedies provided by the national legal system. However, no obligation arose to use such remedies where these were inadequate or ineffective in nature and special circumstances were recognised in international law which absolved the applicant from this obligation to exhaust domestic remedies where an administrative practice was incompatible with the Convention. In the absence of convincing explanations from the Government, the applicants had demonstrated the existence of special circumstances dispensing with the need to exhaust domestic remedies.

AKDIVAR v. TURKEY (1997) 23 E.H.R.R. 143, R Ryssdal (President), ECHR.

2771. European Court of Human Rights—declaration by Turkey recognising compulsory jurisdiction of Court—allegation pre-dating declaration—court lacked jurisdiction

[European Convention on Human Rights 1950 Art.3, Art.46.]

In 1989 Y was arrested in connection with the abduction of a child from a Turkish hospital. She was held in police custody for several days during which time she was subjected to ill-treatment. On her release she lodged a complaint as a result of which the Public Prosecutor brought proceedings under the Turkish Criminal Code against the police officers involved. The police officers were acquitted due to lack of evidence and an appeal was unsuccessful. In a declaration dated January 22, 1990 the Turkish Government recognised the compulsory jurisdiction of the European Court of Human Rights. Y was not charged in relation to the abduction and in 1991 she brought proceedings under the European Convention on Human Rights 1950 Art.3 complaining of torture. Her complaint was upheld by the Commission but before the Court the Turkish Government maintained that since the facts alleged by Y took place prior to the recognition of the Court's jurisdiction the case fell outside their jurisdiction.

Held, that the Court could not deal with the merits of Y's case, as the moment at which recognition of the Court's compulsory jurisdiction took effect was the date when the declaration was notified to the Secretary General. The very terms of the declaration made under Art.46 of the Convention precluded all argument, as held in *Loizidou v. Turkey (A/310)* (1995) 20 E.H.R.R. 99, [1995] 1 C.L.Y. 2655, *Yagci and Sargin v. Turkey (A/319-A)* (1995) 20 E.H.R.R. 505, [1996] 1 C.L.Y. 3134, *Mansur v. Turkey (A/319-B)* (1995) 20 E.H.R.R. 535, [1996] 1 C.L.Y. 3133 and *Mitap and Muftuoglu v. Turkey (1996)* 22 E.H.R.R. 209 [1996] 1 C.L.Y. 3166.

YAGIZ v. TURKEY (1996) 22 E.H.R.R. 573, R Ryssdal (President), ECHR.

2772. European Court of Human Rights—jurisdiction—request for interpretation of judgment awarding compensation—invitation to interpret Convention in a general way was outside court's jurisdiction

[European Convention on Human Rights 1950 Art.50.]

In February 1995 the European Court of Human Rights gave judgment in favour of A in respect of breaches of the European Convention on Human Rights 1950 by France. The Court found A's claim for compensation for pecuniary damage to be justified in part, and awarded him FF 2 million, plus FF100,000 for costs. Following the judgment A's creditors secured an attachment to the order for compensation and the sum of FF 2 million was paid to them. At A's request, the President of the Commission lodged with the Court a request for interpretation of the 1995 judgment seeking, inter alia, an answer to the question of whether the European Convention on Human Rights 1950 Art.50 meant that any sum awarded under the head of just satisfaction must be paid personally to the applicant and be exempt from attachment.

Held, rejecting the Commission's request for interpretation, that when considering a request for interpretation, the Court is exercising its inherent jurisdiction to clarify the meaning and scope of a previous decision, as stated in *Ringeisen v. Austria (No.3)* (1979-80) 1 E.H.R.R. 513. The question put by the

Commission was an invitation to interpret Art.50 of the Convention in a general abstract way. As held in *Lawless v. Ireland* (No.1) (1979-80) 1 E.H.R.R. 1, [1979] C.L.Y. 1170, such an approach goes outside the bounds laid down not only by the Rules of Court A r.57 but also those of the Court's contentious jurisdiction. In any event, the Court did not in the present case rule that the sum awarded should be free from attachment.

ALLENET DE RIBEMONT v. FRANCE (1996) (1996) 22 E.H.R.R. 582, R Ryssdal (President), ECHR.

2773. European Court of Justice–jurisdiction–national legislation outwith scope of EC law–ECJ could not give guidance on conformity with European Convention on Human Rights–European Union

[European Convention on Human Rights 1950 Art.6; Treaty of Rome 1957 Art.177.]

K, an Austrian national convicted of murder, was sentenced to 20 years' imprisonment in an institution for mentally ill criminals. On appeal the sentence was changed to life imprisonment in an ordinary prison. K did not attend the appeal and had not requested to do so. The ECHR held that in light of the seriousness of the matter K should have had the opportunity to defend himself in person before the court in accordance with the European Convention on Human Rights 1950 Art.6. K then raised an action in Austria seeking a reduction of his sentence and an award of damages under Art.5 of the Convention. He also requested that a preliminary reference to the ECJ be made under the Treaty of Rome 1957 Art.177 as to whether the national court was bound by the decision of the ECHR.

Held, that (1) fundamental rights were part of the general principles of EC law and, in making a preliminary ruling on the interpretation of national law, the court would give guidance as to the compatibility of that legislation with fundamental rights; (2) in the instant case the national legislation lay outwith the scope of EC law and consequently outwith the jurisdiction of the ECJ, and (3) the hypothetical possibility of exercising a right to free movement did not establish a connection with EC law sufficient to ensure the application of Community provisions to the case.

KREMZOW v. AUSTRIA (C299/95), *The Times*, August 11, 1997, JC Moitinho de Almeida (President), ECJ.

2774. Freedom of association–employer refused to be bound by collective agreement–trade union boycott of premises–no violation of employer's rights

[European Convention on Human Rights 1950 Art.11; European Convention on Human Rights 1950 Protocol No.1 Art.1.]

G, a Swedish national, ran a restaurant and youth hostel. He employed less than 10 employees and was not bound by any collective agreement with the relevant trade union, H. In 1987 H requested that G be bound by a collective agreement, either by joining an employers' association or by signing a substitute agreement. G refused to do either, on the grounds that he was politically opposed to collective bargaining. H then declared a boycott against G's premises and two other unions took sympathy action in support. The following year a club in Sweden, S, terminated membership of G's youth hostel. G took proceedings against both the Swedish Government, demanding that they intervene to prohibit H and other unions from continuing action, and against S, claiming that their action against him was unreasonable. Both claims were unsuccessful before the Swedish courts, and G commenced proceedings under the Convention, claiming, inter alia, that the lack of state protection against the industrial action taken by H gave rise to a violation of his right to freedom of association under the European Convention on Human Rights Art.11 and a violation of his right to a peaceful enjoyment of possessions under Protocol No.1 Art.1 in conjunction with Art.17 of the Convention.

Held, dismissing G's application by a majority, that (1) Art.11 was applicable because the industrial action undertaken by H entailed considerable pressure on

G to meet the union's demand and to that extent the enjoyment of his freedom of association was affected; (2) as held in *Sibson v. United Kingdom* (1994) 17 E.H.R.R. 193, [1994] C.L.Y. 2413, although compulsion to join a trade union was not always contrary to the Convention, a form of such compulsion which strikes at the very substance of freedom of association would constitute an interference with that freedom. National authorities may in certain circumstances be obliged to intervene in relationships between private individuals by taking reasonable and appropriate measures to secure the effective enjoyment of the negative right to freedom of association, as discussed in *Platform "Artzte Fur Das Leben" v. Austria* (1991) 13 E.H.R.R. 204. However, in view of the sensitive political and social issues involved in achieving a proper balance between competing interests and in particular, in assessing the appropriateness of state intervention to restrict union action aimed at extending a system of collective bargaining, the contracting states should enjoy a wide measure of appreciation in their choice of the means to be employed. Article 11 did not guarantee a right not to enter into a collective agreement, as stated in *Swedish Engine Drivers' Union v. Sweden* (1979-80) 1 E.H.R.R. 617. Since G did not substantiate his claim that he provided conditions of employment more favourable than those required under a collective agreement, there was no reason to doubt that H pursued legitimate interests consistent with Art.11 of the Convention, and having regard to the special nature of industrial relations in Sweden, there is accordingly no violation of Art.11 (3) as there was no violation of Protocol No.1 Art.1 of the Convention because the facts complained of were not the product of an exercise of government authority, but exclusively concerned relationships of a contractual nature between private individuals.

GUSTAFSSON v. SWEDEN (1996) 22 E.H.R.R. 409, R Ryssdal (President), ECHR.

2775. **Freedom of expression–defamation–material regarding politician–defence of qualified privilege–legitimate public interest–Australia**

[Constitution of Australia s.7, s.24.]

L, a former Prime Minister of New Zealand, commenced proceedings for defamation in the New South Wales Supreme Court against A in respect of a television programme in which certain affairs of L were discussed. A filed a defence in which they stated, inter alia, that the matter complained of was published pursuant to a constitutional freedom to publish material in the course of discussion of government and political matters. That defence was based on two previous decisions of the High Court of Australia in *Stephens v. West Australian Newspapers Ltd* (1994) 182 C.L.R. 211 and *Theophanous v. Herald & Weekly Times Ltd* (1994) 182 C.L.R. 104. A also relied upon a defence of qualified privilege, in that the matters complained of related to subjects of public interest and political matters and that A had a duty to publish the material. L alleged that the defences were bad in law and further that the decisions in *Stephens* and *Theophanous* were wrongly decided.

Held, remitting the matter to the New South Wales Supreme Court, that (1) the Constitution of Australia s.7 and s.24 protected the freedom of communication between the people concerning political or government matters which enabled the people to exercise a free and informed choice as electors. Those sections did not confer rights on individuals but rather precluded the curtailment of the protected freedom by the exercise of legislative or executive power, *Cunliffe v. Commonwealth, The* (1994) 182 C.L.R. 272 applied. The freedom of communication protected by the Constitution was limited to what was necessary for the effective operation of the system of government provided for by the Constitution. Insofar as A's defence rested on a claimed constitutional freedom, it therefore failed; (2) in Australia the common law rules of defamation conformed to the requirements of the Constitution, and freedom of communication precluded an unqualified application in Australia of the English common law of defamation insofar as it continued to provide no defence for the mistaken publication of defamatory matter concerning government and political matters to a wide audience, *Stephens v. West Australian Newspapers Ltd* and *Theophanous v. Herald & Weekly Times Ltd* considered, *McGinty v. Western Australia* (1996) 186 C.L.R. 140 applied. The categories of the defence of qualified privilege extended to protect a communication made to the public on a government or political matter. Reasonableness of conduct was the appropriate criterion to apply in that the publisher must establish that it did not act recklessly and was unaware of the falsity of the matter when the extended category of qualified privilege was invoked to protect a publication that would otherwise be held to have been made to too wide an audience, *Stephens v. West Australian Newspapers Ltd* and *Theophanus v. Herald & Weekly Times* considered.

LANGE v. AUSTRALIAN BROADCASTING CORP (1997) 2 B.H.R.C. 513, Brennan, C.J., HC (Aus).

2776. Freedom of expression–educational radio programmes including listener participation–suspension of service–right to freedom of speech and expression did not include right to receive information simpliciter–Sri Lanka

[Constitution of Sri Lanka Art.10, Art.14(1).]

F complained that the sudden stoppage by SLB of a series of radio programmes, the Non-Formal Education Programmes, NFEP, infringed his right as a participatory listener to freedom of speech under the Constitution of Sri Lanka Art.14(1)(a). The NFEP were launched in June 1994 and were planned to cover a long period with regular educational programmes for those outside the formal school system. Participation was extended to listeners. On February 6, 1995, NFEP broadcast a programme which included a telephone interview with a minister and some workers on strike. The programme was stopped suddenly and there were no more NFEP broadcasts until the morning. F complained that thereafter the NFEP virtually came to an end. It was submitted on behalf of F that the NFEP had been stopped without reason and that F's fundamental right to freedom of speech had been infringed. It was argued that freedom of speech was the right of one person to communicate views and other types of information to others, and necessarily postulated a recipient and included the right of the recipient to receive such communication. It was also submitted that since F had been a participatory listener, stopping the NFEP had infringed his freedom of speech by depriving him of one means of active communication. It was submitted in response that the NFEP had been stopped for valid reasons on February 6, 1995, and that in any case it had been later resumed, although no evidence was submitted to prove the resumption.

Held, that (1) the Constitution Art.14(1)(a) was not to be interpreted narrowly, it encompassed every form of expression including the right to obtain and record information, and might arguably extend to a privilege not to be compelled to disclose sources of information should that privilege be necessary to make the right to information fully meaningful; (2) the right to freedom of speech did not include the right to receive information simpliciter, that right was a corollary to the right to freedom of thought guaranteed by the Constitution Art.10; (3) the sudden and arbitrary stoppage of the NFEP was not justified, and had infringed F's fundamental right to freedom of speech, because it prevented him from further participation in the NFEP as a participatory listener, and (4) SLB and its chairman were responsible for the infringement and were directed to pay F Rs 15,000 in damages and Rs 5,000 as costs.

FERNANDO v. SRI LANKA BROADCASTING CORP (1996) 1 B.H.R.C. 104, Fernando, J., Sup Ct (SrL).

2777. Freedom of expression–exercise of discretionary power to exclude press and public from criminal proceedings–infringement of charter–Canada

[Criminal Code s.486(1) (Canada); Canadian Charter of Rights and Freedoms s.1, s.2.]

C pleaded guilty to charges of sexual assault and sexual interference with young girls. The trial judge made an order under the Criminal Code s.486(1), excluding members of the public and the media from those parts of the sentencing proceedings dealing with the specific acts committed by C. CBC sought an order quashing the exclusion order made by the judge on the basis that it infringed the guarantee of the freedom of expression of the press as set out in the Canadian Charter of Rights and Freedoms s.2(b) and could not be justified under s.1 of the Charter. CBC's application was unsuccessful at first instance and on appeal to the Court of Appeal.

Held, allowing the appeal, that (1) s.486(1) of the Code infringed s.2(b) of the Charter because it had as its purpose the restriction of the free flow of ideas and information, *Irwin Toy Ltd v. Attorney General of Quebec* [1989] 1 S.C.R. 927 applied; (2) s.486(1) of the Code was reasonable and demonstrably justified in a free and democratic society for the purposes of s.1 of the Charter. Section 486(1) aimed at preserving the general principle of openness in criminal proceedings to the extent that openness was consistent with and advances the proper administration of justice. There was proportionality between that aim and the effect of s.486(1), *Dagenais v. Canadian Broadcasting Corp* [1994] 3 S.C.R. 835. First, the grant of judicial discretion in s.486(1) necessarily ensured that any order made would be rationally connected to the legislative objective. Secondly, s.486(1) impaired the rights under s.2(b) of the Charter as little as reasonably possible by providing the judiciary with the standard of the proper administration of justice by which to exercise the statutory discretion. Thirdly, the deleterious effects of s.486(1) in providing for the exclusion of the press and the public from judicial proceedings did not outweigh the salutary effects of such exclusion where it was in the proper interests of the administration of justice. However, in the instant case the discretion was improperly exercised because there was insufficient evidence to support a concern for undue hardship either to the accused or the complainants.

CANADIAN BROADCASTING CORP v. ATTORNEY GENERAL FOR NEW BRUNSWICK (1997) 2 B.H.R.C. 210, Lamer, C.J., Sup Ct (Can).

2778. **Freedom of expression–freedom of association–criminalisation of public gatherings without permits–breach of constitutional guarantees of freedom of speech and association–Zambia**

[Public Order Act s.5(4), s.7 (Zambia); Constitution of Zambia Art.20, Art.21.]

M and seven others were arrested while taking part in a public gathering for which a permit had not been issued under Public Order Act s.5(4). This provided that a permit to convene an assembly or public meeting, or to form a procession in public, would be issued only if the regulating officer was satisfied that the proposed gathering was unlikely to cause or lead to a breach of the peace. They were arrested under Public Order Act s.7 which stated that a gathering that took place without the necessary permit was an unauthorised gathering and that persons taking part in convening, calling or directing the gathering could be arrested and fined and/or imprisoned. The constitutionality of s.5(4) and s.7 were challenged on the grounds that those provisions contravened Constitution of Zambia Art.20 and Art.21, which guaranteed freedom of expression and freedom of assembly. The High Court upheld the impugned provisions as justifiable in a democratic society. M appealed to the Supreme Court. It was noted that the Public Order Act dated from nine years before independence and the Constitution, and that in its original form, Public Order Ordinance No 38 of 1955 was concerned only with prohibiting the wearing of uniforms concerned with political objects and prohibiting quasi military organisations. It was common cause that there was nothing wrong with regulatory provisions in the interests of public order. It was submitted that the freedoms under the Constitution were not absolute, but should only be regulated, not abridged, diminished or denied. The subsection could not be justified in a democratic society, since it reduced fundamental freedoms to the level of a license that could be granted or not on the subjective satisfaction of a regulating officer. The lack of procedural guidelines or controls for such regulation meant it could not be held to be reasonable.

Held, allowing the appeal, that (1) the right to organise and participate in public gatherings was inherent in the freedom to express and receive ideas and information without interference; (2) the requirement of prior permission with the possibility that such permission might be refused on improper, arbitrary, or even unknown grounds was an obvious hindrance to those freedoms and rendered Public Order Act s.5(4) objectionable; (3) in particular, it left an unfettered and uncontrolled subjective discretion to a regulating officer, there were no guidelines for the exercise of the discretion, and no procedural provision for an aggrieved unsuccessful applicant; (4) the drafting of the provision itself was a recipe for arbitrariness and abuse; (5) the cumulative effect was that the provision was not reasonably justifiable in a democratic society; (6) it followed that Public Order Act s.5(4) contravened the Constitution Art.20 and Art.21, was unconstitutional, and therefore null and void and invalid; (7) accordingly prosecution of persons and the criminalisation of gatherings under the provision, and therefore a prosecution under Public Order Act s.7 was unconstitutional and invalid, and (8) *Pumbun v. Attorney General* [1993] 2 L.R.C. 317 and *Munhumeso, Re* [1994] 1 L.R.C. 282 applied.

MULUNDIKA v. ZAMBIA (1996) 1 B.H.R.C. 199, Ngulube, C.J., Sup Ct (Zambia).

2779. Freedom of expression–holocaust denial–permitted restrictions on free speech–France

[International Covenant on Civil and Political Rights 1966 Art.19.]

In July 1990 the French legislature passed the so-called Gayssot Act, which made it an offence to contest the existence of the category of crimes against humanity as defined in the London Charter of August 8, 1945 and on the basis of which the Nazi leaders were tried and convicted at the Nuremberg trials. F, a French academic who had consistently questioned the existence of Nazi gas chambers for extermination purposes, was interviewed by the magazine Le Choc du Mois shortly after the enactment of the Gayssot Act. An article was published in which F reiterated his views that the "myth of the gas chambers is a dishonest fabrication". Both F and the editor of the magazine were charged and convicted of offences under the Gayssot Act and their convictions were upheld on appeal. F presented a communication to the United Nations Human Rights Committee claiming that the Gayssot Act infringed his human rights under the International Covenant on Civil and Political Rights 1966 Art.19 by curtailing his right to freedom of expression and academic freedom in general.

Held, dismissing the complaint, that (1) any restriction of the right to freedom of expression must cumulatively meet three conditions; (a) it must be provided by law, (b) it must address one of the aims set out in Art.19(3)(a) and (b) of the Covenant of 1966, and (c) it must be necessary to achieve a legitimate purpose. The Gayssot Act, as interpreted and applied by the French Courts to F's case, complied with the provisions of the Covenant because his conviction did not encroach on his right to hold and express an opinion in general, but rather related to his violation of the rights and reputation of others. Rights for the protection of which restrictions on the freedom of expression were permitted by Art.19(3) of the Covenant of 1966 may relate to the interests of other persons or those of the community as a whole, and (2) since F's statements were of a nature to raise or strengthen anti-Semitic feeling the restriction of his freedom of expression was permissible under Art.19(3)(a) of the Covenant of 1966. Having regard to the statement by the French Minister of Justice that the denial of the existence of the Holocaust was the principal vehicle for anti-Semitism the Committee was satisfied that the restriction of F's freedom of expression was necessary within the meaning of Art.19(3) of the Covenant of 1966.

FAURISSON v. FRANCE (1997) 2 B.H.R.C. 1, Judge not applicable, UNHRC.

2780. Freedom of expression–journalists–disclosure of source

[Contempt of Court Act 1981 s.10; European Convention on Human Rights 1950 Art.10.]

An unknown person passed a copy of CG's unaudited draft accounts to a journalist employed by CC, who wrote an article which CC published. CG obtained an ex parte order restraining CC from using or publishing any confidential information, particularly CG's unaudited accounts. CC was also ordered to deliver up the accounts plus any copies, but the order was stayed at an inter partes hearing on condition that CC deliver up all the relevant material to its solicitors pending a further order. CG, who wanted to use the information held by CC to help identify who had leaked the accounts, applied to remove the stay, contending that under the Contempt of Court Act 1981 s.10, as applied in *X Ltd v. Morgan Grampian (Publishers) Ltd* [1991] 1 A.C. 1, [1990] C.L.Y. 3581, the interests of justice required disclosure. CC argued that *X Ltd* now had to be read in the light of the ECHR judgment in *Goodwin v. United Kingdom* (1996) 22 E.H.R.R. 123, [1996] 1 C.L.Y. 3145, where it was held that obliging the applicant to disclose his source of information was a breach of the European Convention on Human Rights 1950 Art.10.

Held, allowing the application, that whilst in principle there was little difference between s.10 as applied in *X Ltd* and Art.10 as applied in *Goodwin,* English law was clear and unambiguous and did not involve the exercise of discretion, so that it was unnecessary to apply the Convention. In any case, it was unlikely that reference to Art.10 and *Goodwin* would have any impact on the outcome, as English law involved a similar balancing exercise to that undertaken by the ECHR, embracing the concept of proportionality. Applying English law, the evidence had established that it was necessary in the interests of justice to override the great public importance given to the protection of sources.

CAMELOT GROUP PLC v. CENTAUR COMMUNICATIONS LTD, *The Times,* July 15, 1997, Maurice Kay, J., QBD.

2781. Freedom of expression–Parliamentary privilege–Zimbabwe

See CONSTITUTIONAL LAW: Mutasa v. Makombe. §917

2782. Freedom of expression–prisoners–ban on visits by journalists unless undertakings given not to use material

[Prison Act 1952 s.47; Prison Rules 1964 r.33 (SI 1964 388).]

O applied for judicial review of the Secretary of State's decision not to allow journalists to visit prisoners unless they undertook not to use material acquired during the visit for professional purposes. O contended that the standing orders requiring such undertakings went beyond what was required under the Prison Act 1952 s.47, which gave the Secretary of State power to make rules relating to the regulation and management of prisons, and were therefore ultra vires.

Held, allowing the application, that the restriction in question was a restriction on O's right to free speech which would only be justified if essential for the proper control of prisoners, *R. v. Secretary of State for the Home Department, ex p. Leech* [1994] Q.B. 198, [1994] C.L.Y. 3849 and *R. v. Secretary of State for the Home Department, ex p. Bamber* [1996] 1 C.L.Y. 3148 considered. Interference in the civil rights of an inmate under s.47(1) of the 1952 Act could be justified only to the extent that was absolutely necessary to achieve the statutory objectives. It was reasonable to consider the "interests of any persons" under the Prison Rules 1964 r.33(1) when restricting prisoners' communications. Since a prisoner was allowed to write to the media to make representations about his conviction, sentence or the criminal justice system, there could be no justification for not allowing oral communication to make the same points. A blanket ban on journalists' use of material was not justified.

R. v. SECRETARY OF STATE FOR THE HOME DEPARTMENT, *ex p.* SIMMS; R. v. SECRETARY OF STATE FOR THE HOME DEPARTMENT, *ex p.* O'BRIEN [1997] E.M.L.R. 261, Latham, J., QBD.

2783. Freedom of expression–prisoners' rights–removal of horse racing supplement to newspaper justified in law–Hong Kong

[Prison Rules r.56 (Hong Kong); Bill of Rights Art.9 (Hong Kong), Art.16(2) (Hong Kong).]

C was a convicted prisoner serving a long sentence in Stanley Prison. On May 19, 1995 by order of the Commissioner of Correctional Services, the horse racing supplement of C's copy of the Tin Tin Daily News was removed before the paper was delivered to him. C said that this was a violation of his civil rights. C brought judicial review proceedings of that exercise of administrative discretion. The judge, in an order dated November 2, 1995 declared the act to be unlawful on three grounds; (1) legality: the removal of the horse racing supplement was not authorised under the Prison Rules, (2) rationality: the removal of the supplement had been "wholly irrational", and that even if the Commissioner was allowed under the Prison Rules to determine the conditions for the supply of newspapers, the removal had been *Wednesbury* unreasonable, and (3) the act had been a breach of the Bill of Rights Art.16 which guaranteed freedom of opinion and expression, including the right to receive information. The Commissioner of Correctional Services appealed.

Held, allowing the appeal, that (1) the Prison Rules r.56 provided that the prisoners could receive books and periodicals from outside the prison under conditions determined by the Commissioner; (2) since a newspaper was unquestionably a periodical publication, there was no reason to construe r.56 in an unusual sense; (3) accordingly the removal of the racing supplement from C's newspaper was authorised by law; (4) the removal of the supplement did not violate C's right to receive information under Bill of Rights Art.16, because Art.9 provided that such guaranteed rights could be restricted in the case of prisoners provided the restriction was authorised by law; (5) gambling in prisons was an acknowledged problem and the policy of removing the racing supplement from newspapers was an attempt to alleviate that problem; (6) it could not therefore be said that the Commissioner had acted unreasonably in ordering their removal, nor had irrationally exercised the powers conferred on him by Prison Rules r. 56, and (7) per Liu J: to uphold a Commissioner concern's in prison discipline over the right of a prisoner's right to more up to date advice on horse racing was clearly justified.

CHIM SHING CHUNG v. COMMISSIONER OF CORRECTIONAL SERVICES (1997) 1 B.H.R.C. 394, Litton, L.J.,V.P., CA (HK).

2784. Freedom of expression–right to privacy–possession of indecent or obscene material prohibited by statute–prohibition inconsistent with the right to privacy–prohibition inconsistent with freedom of expression guarantee–South Africa

[Indecent or Obscene Photographic Matter Act 1967 s.2(1) (South Africa); Constitution of the Republic of South Africa Act 200 of 1993 s.13, s.15.]

C and others were charged with possessing video cassettes containing sexually explicit matter in contravention of the Indecent or Obscene Photographic Matter Act 1967 s.2. After making several appearances in the magistrates court, C applied for the proceedings to be postponed pending an application to the Supreme Court regarding the constitutional status of the 1967 Act s.2(1). The application was granted without hearing any evidence, proceedings in the magistrates court being suspended. Before the Supreme Court, C applied to have the matter referred to the Constitutional Court, alleging that the 1967 Act s.2(1) was inconsistent with several sections of the Constitution of the Republic of South Africa Act 200 of 1993. The question referred was whether s.2(1), which prohibited the possession of "indecent or obscene photographic matter", was inconsistent with the provisions of, inter alia, Act 200 of 1993 s.13, which guaranteed the right to personal privacy, and Act 200 of 1993 s.15, which guaranteed freedom of speech, expression and artistic creativity.

Held, that the 1967 Act s.2 was inconsistent with the interim Constitution and invalid because; (1) the combined effect of s.2(1) and s.1 (which defined "indecent and obscene photographic matter" by means of an open ended list of categories), was to sanction unwarranted and unjustifiable invasions of the right to personal privacy regardless of the nature of the material possessed; (2) s.2(1) infringed the right to personal privacy guaranteed by the Act 200 of 1993,s.13; (3) the intrusion was neither reasonable nor justified, and the limitation clause in Act 200 of 1993 s.33(1) could not save it; (4) it was not self evident that the right to freedom of expression in the Constitution extended to sexually explicit materials, that right should be defined widely, and only then to impose any constitutionally justifiable limitations, such as that by s.33(1); (5) the protection afforded by Act 200 of 1993 s.15 extended to sexually explicit material; (6) although possession of material was not an expressive activity, the freedom to receive, hold and consume expressions of others was a necessary corollary of freedom of expression; (7) the 1967 Act s.2(1) read together with the definition of "indecent and obscene photographic material" in s.1, was too broad to constitute a "reasonable" or "justifiable" limitation of Act 200 of 1993 s.15 within the meaning of s.33(1) of the same Act. It therefore followed that sexually explicit material was a category of speech and expression protected by s.15, so that protection necessarily extended to the possession of that material, and (8) the 1967 Act s.2(1) unreasonably and unjustifiable violated that right to freedom of expression.

CASE v. MINISTER OF SAFETY AND SECURITY; CURTIS v. MINISTER OF SAFETY AND SECURITY (1997) 1 B.H.R.C. 541, Chaskalson (President), Const Ct (SA).

2785. **Freedom of religion–ban on publications–compatibility with Constitution–national security–Singapore**

[Constitution of Singapore s.15; Undesirable Publications Act s.3 (Singapore).]

The International Bible Students Association, IBSA, is an organisation under the ambit of the Jehovah's Witnesses. By Order 405/94 made under the Undesirable Publications Act s.3 the Singaporean Minister for Information and Arts prohibited the importation, sale or distribution of publications of the IBSA. The Government made it clear that the sole reason for Order 405/94 was because of the Jehovah's Witnesses' refusal to do national service, and that in the Government's view such refusal accordingly constituted a serious threat to national security. C sought leave for judicial review to obtain an order for certiorari quashing Order 405/94 and a declaration that the Order was invalid, on the grounds that banned publications were essential for Jehovah's Witnesses to "profess, practice and propagate their religion" in accordance with the Constitution of Singapore Art.15 and that Order 405/94 violated their constitutional rights. Application for leave was refused at first instance and C appealed.

Held, dismissing the appeal, that (1) C, as Singaporean citizens, had sufficient locus standi to apply for judicial review to challenge Order 405/94, because they alleged that that Order infringed their constitutional right as citizens to profess, practice and propagate their religion; (2) at the application for leave stage an applicant must only show a prima facie case of reasonable suspicion, *Inland Revenue Commissioners v. National Federation of Self-Employed* [1982] A.C. 617, [1981] C.L.Y. 1433 considered, (3) issues of national security were not justiciable. The court's function was only to see that there was evidence that the decision was based on considerations of national security, *Council of Civil Service Unions v. Minister for the Civil Service* [1985] A.C. 374, [1985] C.L.Y. 12, and *Chung Suan Tze v. Minister of Home Affairs* [1989] 1 M.L.J. 69 applied. It was self evident that issues of national security were involved, as IBSA publications were necessary for the profession, practice and propagation of the Jehovah's Witnesses' faith, a central principle of which was refusal to take part in national service.

CHAN HIANG LENG COLIN v. MINISTER FOR INFORMATION AND THE ARTS (1997) 2 B.H.R.C. 129, Karthigesu, J.A., CA (Singapore).

2786. Freedom of religion–conviction for unauthorised use of religious premises

[European Convention of Human Rights 1950 Art.9.]

In 1983 M, Jehovah's witnesses, rented a room in Crete in order to use it for the purposes of meetings, weddings and worship. M did not obtain authorisation to use the premises for those purposes, although they did apply for such permission. Following complaints made by the local Orthodox parish church they were charged in 1986 of having used the premises as a place of worship without having obtained the necessary authorisation from the recognised ecclesiastical authorities and the Minister of Education. M was acquitted at first instance but on appeal was found guilty and sentenced to three months' imprisonment and fines. In 1991 M applied to the Commission complaining, inter alia, of violations of the European Convention of Human Rights 1950 Art.9 in that their convictions represented an unacceptable constraint on their freedom to practise their religion.

Held, allowing the application, that M's convictions did constitute a violation of the right under Art.9. The requirement to have obtained prior authorisation before using the premises as a place of worship interfered with the freedom to practise religion as it could not be justified as being prescribed by law.

MANOUSSAKIS v. GREECE (1997) 23 E.H.R.R. 387, R Bernhardt (President), ECHR.

2787. Freedom of religion–Jehovah's Witnesses–refusal to allow child to take part in school parade–no breach of right to education or freedom of religion

[European Convention on Human Rights 1950 Art.3, Art.9, Art.13; European Convention on Human Rights 1950 Protocol No.1 Art.2.]

V's parents, as Jehovah's Witnesses, were forbidden from any association with war or violence. In September 1992 V's parents wrote to her school to exempt V from attending school religious education lessons, Orthodox mass and any other event that was contrary to her religious beliefs, including national holiday celebrations and public processions. V was asked in October 1992 to celebrate National Day in which parades took place commemorating the outbreak of war between Greece and Italy. V's request to be excused attendance was refused but she did not take part in the school parade. V was suspended for one day. V applied to the Commission in April 1993 alleging, inter alia, breaches of the right to education in conformity with her religious convictions, and the right to freedom of religion, contrary to the European Convention on Human Rights Art.9 and Protocol No.1 Art.2. V also alleged that she had been denied an effective remedy, contrary to Art.13 of the Convention.

Held, allowing the application, that (1) the word "convictions", as contained in Protocol No.1 Art.2, was, taken on its own, not synonymous with "opinions" and "ideas". It denoted views that attained a certain level of cogency, seriousness, cohesion and importance, *Kjeldsen, Busk Madsen and Pedersen v. Denmark (A/23)* (1979) 1 E.H.R.R. 711 followed. Jehovah's Witnesses had the status of a "known religion" and the observance advantages which flowed from that, *Kokkinakis v. Greece (A/260-A)* (1994) 17 E.H.R.R. 397, [1994] C.L.Y. 2419 followed. V was entitled to rely on the right to respect for her religious convictions. There was a broad duty on the State under Protocol No.1 Art.2 to respect parents' religious convictions which applied to the performance of all the "functions" assumed by the State. The word "respect" implied some positive obligation on the part of the State, *Campbell and Cosans v. United Kingdom (A/ 48)* (1982) 4 E.H.R.R. 293 applied. Nothing in either the purpose of the school parade or in the arrangements for it could offend V's pacifist convictions to an extent prohibited by Protocol No.1 Art.2; (2) since V had already been exempted from religious education and the Orthodox mass as requested, and since the obligation to take part in the school parade did not offend her parents' religious convictions, there was no breach of Art.9, and (3) Art.13 secured to anyone claiming on arguable grounds to be the victim of a violation of his rights and freedoms as protected in the Convention, an effective remedy before a national authority in order both to have his claim decided and, if appropriate, to obtain redress, *Klass v. Germany (A/28)* (1979) 2 E.H.R.R. 214, [1980] C.L.Y. 1388, *Plattform Arzte fur das Leben v. Austria (A/139)* (1991) 13 E.H.R.R. 204,

[1988] C.L.Y. 1807 and *Vilvarajah v. United Kingdom (A/215)* (1992) 14 E.H.R.R. 248, [1992] C.L.Y. 2333 applied. The alleged breaches in the instant case were arguable. No application for judicial review lay against the disciplinary decision of the education authorities, and without a decision on judicial review no compensation could be claimed. Accordingly, there had been a violation of Art.13.

VALSAMIS v. GREECE (1997) 24 E.H.R.R. 294, R Ryssdal (President), ECHR.

2788. **International humanitarian law—ethnic cleansing—genocide—genocidal intention inferred from political doctrine**

[Statute of the International Tribunal Art.4(2), Art.7(1), Art.7(3).]

Indictments were issued against K, as President of the self proclaimed Serbian Republic of Bosnia and Herzegovina, and M, as Commander of the Bosnian Serb army, charging them to be individually responsible for a series of serious violations of international humanitarian law. These included grave breaches of the Geneva Conventions 1949, violations of the law or customs of war, genocide and crimes against humanity. The offences were alleged to have been committed by the forces of the Bosnian Serb administration in the territory of Bosnia and Herzegovina. The first indictment concerned offences allegedly committed between April 1992 and July 1995, the second, during the take over of the "safe area" of Srebenica, in July 1995. Warrants of arrest were issued against K and M, on July 25 and November 16, 1995 respectively. The warrants were not executed. The Tribunal had recourse to a public hearing, in order to enable it to issue international warrants against K and M, and to deal with the failure or refusal of states to co-operate. Responsibility was considered in the light of both (1) the Statute of the International Tribunal Art.7(1) which provided that a person who planned or ordered an offence was individually responsible, and (2) the Statute Art.7(3) which provided that a person who failed to prevent or punish the commission of an offence was responsible for it. Evidence of the context of the offences was advanced to support the inference that; (1) they had been committed in accordance with a political programme, (2) the accused had held authority in the administration, and (3) the accused had been aware of, and had endorsed and participated in, the actions of their subordinates. K and M's offences were examined to determine whether they revealed genocidal intent under the Statute Art.4(2). The question arose whether such intent could be inferred from a political programme or from the nature of certain means used to effect "ethnic cleansing", such as selection of persons for deportation because of their membership of a targeted group.

Held, that (1) there were reasonable grounds for believing K and M had committed the offences as charged; (2) they were unquestionably responsible under the Statute Art. 7(3); (3) their responsibility should be characterised under the Statute Art.7(1) as governmental or military command responsibility; (4) the offences committed by K and M fell within the competence of the Tribunal as acts of genocide within the meaning of Art.4(2); (5) intention could be inferred from a number of factors such as general political doctrine or the repetition of destructive and discriminatory acts. It did not have to be clearly expressed, and (6) since there were reasonable grounds for believing that K and M had committed the offences as charged, the Tribunal (a) confirmed the counts of the indictments, (b) issued international warrants of arrest for K and M, and (c) noted that the failure to effect personal service of the indictments could be ascribed to the refusal of co-operation by the Federal Republic of Yugoslavia (Serbia and Montenegro) and by the Bosnian administration in Pale (Republika Srpska).

PROSECUTOR v. KARADZIC; PROSECUTOR v. MLADIC (1996) 1 B.H.R.C. 1, Jorda (President), Int Trib (Former Yug).

2789. **International humanitarian law–Geneva Conventions–violations–Bosnian Croat forces in Bosnia under Croat control–jurisdiction of International Tribunal–war in Bosnia constituted an "international conflict"**

[Geneva Convention IV 1949; Statute of the International Tribunal Art.2, Art.3.]

R was accused of ordering the attack on October 23, 1993 against the village of Stupni Do, located in the Republic of Bosnia-Herzegovina. The attack was allegedly carried out by the Croatian Defence Council, the HVO, which were identified as the armed forces of the self proclaimed Croatian Community of Herceg-Bosna, acting under R's control. Numerous witnesses testified that R commanded the HVO forces and was the operational commander there. In the attack the villagers were terrorised, shot, stabbed and raped by HVO soldiers; 37 villagers were killed, and nearly all the homes destroyed. The action was not justified by any military objective. There was also evidence, acknowledged by the Republic of Croatia, that the Croatian army had a significant presence in Bosnia during the period and exerted political and military control and influence over the Bosnian Croats, to whom they provided financial and logistical support. R was charged with; (1) grave breaches of the Geneva Convention IV 1949, as recognised by the Statute of the International Tribunal Art.2(a) and (d), wilful killing and destruction of property (counts I and II), (2) violations of the laws and customs of war as recognised by the Statute of the International Tribunal Art.3, deliberate attack on a civilian population and wanton destruction of a village (count III), (3) in the alternative, command responsibility for the Art.2 breaches of the Geneva Convention IV 1949 (count IV and V) and for the Art.3 violations of the laws and customs of war (count VI). The Tribunal had to consider whether it had subject matter jurisdiction over the offences allegedly committed by R, and whether the Prosecutor had established reasonable grounds to believe that R had committed the crimes as charged in the indictment. The prerequisites to establish subject matter jurisdiction were an international armed conflict, in the sense of the Geneva Convention IV 1949, and the victims of the crime had protection under the provisions of the Convention.

Held, that (1) on the evidence that the Croatian army maintained significant and continuous military intervention in support of the Bosnian Croats against the Bosnian government, the conflict could be regarded as "international" within the meaning of the Geneva Convention IV 1949 Art.2; (2) the residents of Stupni Do were protected for the purposes of the Convention Art.4, since Bosnian Croat control of the territory surrounding Stupni Do was an extension of Croatian control, the villagers were constructively in the hands of Croatia, a country of which they were not nationals; (3) the property was protected under the Convention Art.53, it came under the control of an occupying power, Croatia when HVO forces overran the village; (4) the Tribunal had subject matter jurisdiction under the Statute Art.2 in respect of counts I, II, IV and V of the indictment; (5) the Tribunal had jurisdiction to prosecute violations of the laws and customs of war, because (a) the wanton destruction of a village was specified in the Statute Art.3, and (b) an attack on civilian populations was prohibited under Convention and customary law. Therefore subject matter jurisdiction was established in respect of counts III and VI, *Prosecutor v. Martic* (Case IT-95-11-R61) (Unreported, 1996) followed; (6) the Prosecutor had established reasonable grounds that R had committed the crimes as charged, the evidence supported the indictment's characterisation of the attack on Stupni Do and there was proof that R knew about it and actually ordered it, and (7) the Tribunal issued an international arrest warrant for R and noted that failure to effect personal service could be ascribed to refusal by the Republic of Croatia and the Federation of Bosnia and Herzegovina to co-operate with the Tribunal.

PROSECUTOR v. RAJIC (1997) 1 B.H.R.C. 479, Macdonald, J., Int Trib (Former Yug).

2790. Legal aid–availability for UN Human Rights Committee–written submissions to UNHCR a "judicial authority"–New Zealand

[Legal Services Act 1991 s.19 (New Zealand); Treaty of Waitangi (Fisheries Claim) Settlement Act 1992 (New Zealand); International Covenant on Civil and Political Rights 1966.]

T was among 19 representatives of Maori iwi or whanau who lodged a communication with the UN Human Rights Committee. The communication alleged that the Treaty of Waitangi (Fisheries Claim) Settlement Act 1992 violated their rights under various provisions of the International Covenant on Civil and Political Rights 1966 ratified by New Zealand in 1978 and in force by protocol in 1989. The Committee decided on October 13, 1995 that the communication's claim was admissible and requested the New Zealand government to make written submissions relating to the communication. The decision indicated that T would have the opportunity to respond to the government's submissions, and T applied for legal aid to enable her to engage counsel. WDLSC refused to grant legal aid on the ground that it had no jurisdiction under the Legal Services Act 1991 to approve the payment of costs incurred in proceedings issued in courts outside New Zealand. T then sought a review of that decision contending that the UN Human Rights Committee constituted a "judicial authority" within the meaning of the 1991 Act s.19(1)(e)(v) and that WDLSC had jurisdiction to grant legal aid.

Held, allowing the application, that (1) the Committee's main function of considering alleged human rights violations was sufficiently analogous to a dispute between a citizen and a state to be of a judicial nature and its procedures were those of a judicial authority, allowing both sides of a case to be submitted before making decisions, which were then communicated to the parties according to accepted processes; (2) differences of kind and context between the Committee and the bodies enumerated in the 1991 Act s.19 did not prevent it from being a judicial authority, and (4) in ratifying the International Covenant and acceding to the protocol, the Crown had chosen to confer jurisdiction on the Committee to receive and consider communications from New Zealand, so that it had become part of New Zealand's judicial structure, and so it followed that the Committee was a judicial authority for the purposes of the 1991 Act s.19(1)(e).

TANGIORA v. WELLINGTON DISTRICT LEGAL SERVICES COMMITTEE (1997) 1 B.H.R.C. 582, Gallen, J., HC (NZ).

2791. Legal rights–constitutional right to fair hearing–executive committee of private voluntary organisation–Zimbabwe

[Private Voluntary Organisations Act s.21(1) (Zimbabwe); Constitution of Zimbabwe s.18(9).]

H and others were members of the executive committee of the AWC, a registered private voluntary organisation whose purpose was to advance the education of Zimbabwean women. Purporting to act under the Private Voluntary Organisations Act s.21, in November 1995 R issued a notice published in the Government Gazette suspending the applicants as members of the executive committee of the AWC, on the grounds, inter alia, that they were responsible for its maladministration. H and the other applicants applied to the Supreme Court contending that the Private Voluntary Organisations Act s.21 was unconstitutional in that, inter alia, it empowered M to determine their civil rights as members of a private voluntary organisation without affording them a fair hearing as required by the Constitution of Zimbabwe s.18(9).

Held, giving judgment for H, that (1) the rights and obligations performed by the applicants as members of the executive committee of the AWC were "civil rights and obligations" within the meaning of s.18(9), *Konig v. Federal Republic of Germany* (A/27) (1979) 2 E.H.R.R. 170, [1980] C.L.Y. 1382 and *Marumahoko v. Chairman, Public Service Commission* 1991 (1) Z.L.R. 27 (H) considered, and (2) the requirement for a "fair hearing" includes three fundamental requirements of natural justice. Firstly, the right to have notice of the charge or complaint. Secondly, the right to be given the opportunity to adequately state a case in answer to that charge or complaint. Thirdly, the right to an impartial hearing, *Russell v. Duke of Norfolk* [1949] 1 All E.R. 109, [1949] C.L.Y. 744 applied. Section 21(1) which gave the Minister the power to suspend members of the executive committee of a registered private voluntary organisation, excluded by necessary implication the principle of the right to be heard. The Minister could act on the basis of information supplied to him and did not depend on any inquiry into the facts; the discretion was untrammelled and the Minister was not obliged to disclose the reasons for his decision; and the power of the Minister to take urgent action to suspend a large number of persons pointed strongly in the direction of excluding the grant of hearings to those persons. Accordingly, s.21(1) was ultra vires s.18(9) and the whole provision had to be struck down.

HOLLAND v. MINISTER OF THE PUBLIC SERVICE, LABOUR AND SOCIAL WELFARE (1997) 2 B.H.R.C. 478, Gubbay, C.J., Sup Ct (Zim).

2792. Parental rights—deprivation of access—interference aimed at protecting child's health—permanent deprivation amounting to violation of right of family life where mother able to care adequately for child

[European Convention on Human Rights 1950 Art.6, Art.8.]

J complained of violations of her right of respect for her personal and family life under the European Convention on Human Rights 1950 Art.8 following a decision to place her second child, S, with foster parents and so deprive J of parental access. Although initially provisional in nature, the decision had later been taken to permanently deprive access with a view to adoption. J had a history of physical and mental problems and there had been considerable friction between J and the social welfare authorities who had attempted to assist her with problems encountered in the upbringing of her first child. The Commission decided that her complaints were admissible in that her rights under Art.8 had been violated as regards the deprivation of parental rights and access, but found no breach of Art.8 had occurred as a result of the decision to take S into care and in maintaining the care order.

Held, that the provisional taking into care and maintenance of the care order was not a breach of Art.8 in that the domestic legislation involved was clearly intended to protect the child's health and rights and freedoms and were legitimate aims under Art.8(2). Owing to the wide margin of appreciation in such matters, the court's task is not to substitute its view for those of the domestic authorities in the exercise of their responsibilities for the public care of children. However, strict legal scrutiny was required regarding permanent restrictions, such as limits placed on parental rights and access and legal safeguards designed for the effective protection of the rights of parent and child and the respect for family life. Permanent deprivation of rights and access could only be "necessary" under Art.8(2) if supported by particularly strong reasons. The facts showed, however that J's health was not such that she could not care for C and the measures were not justifiable in view of the irreversible effects permanent deprivation would have on J's enjoyment of family life with her daughter. No breach of Art.6(1) had occurred as the proceedings had progressed with exceptional diligence given the complexity of the matters involved.

JOHANSEN v. NORWAY (1997) 23 E.H.R.R. 33, Bernhardt (President), ECHR.

2793. Presumption of innocence—liability for forest fires—presumption of negligence confined to certain landowners—South Africa

[Forest Act 122 of 1984 s.84 (South Africa); Constitution of the Republic of South Africa Act 200 of 1993 s.8, s.25(3)(c).]

South Africa's Forest Act 122 of 1984 established a scheme for the prevention and control of veld, forest and mountain fires, including the establishment of fire control areas. Section 84 of the 1984 Act provided that where a question of negligence arose in respect of a veld, forest or mountain fire which occurred outside of a fire control area, the owner of the land on which the fire occurred should be presumed to have been negligent unless he could prove the contrary. In reliance on this provision P, whose land had been damaged by a fire originating on D's property, sued D in negligence. D challenged s.84 of the 1984 Act as unconstitutional, in that it infringed the presumption of innocence contained in s.25(3)(c) of the Constitution of the Republic of South Africa Act 200 of 1993 and the right to equality before the law contained in s.8 of the Constitution.

Held, dismissing the application, that (1) the word "action" in s.84 of the 1984 Act was capable of being construed as limited to civil proceedings only and so did not infringe the presumption of innocence contained in s.25(3)(c) of the Constitution; (2) s.8 of the Constitution dealt with differentiation in two ways, that which does not involve unfair discrimination and that which does involve unfair discrimination. The right to equality meant the right to be treated as equals, which did not always mean the right to receive equal treatment. One of the objects of s.8 of the Constitution was to ensure that the Government acted in a rational and not an arbitrary manner. Before it can be said that mere differentiation infringes s.8 it must be established that there was no rational relationship between the differentiation in question and the governmental purpose which was proffered to validate it. In the instant case, there could be no doubt that the state has a strong interest in preventing veld and other fires. A rational relationship could be demonstrated between the purpose sought to be achieved by s.84 of the 1984 Act and the means chosen, *Quathlamba (Pty) Ltd v. Minister of Forestry* 1972 (2) SA 783 (N) considered. Similarly there was no unfair discrimination between those who are owners and occupiers of land in fire control areas and those who were not.

PRINSLOO v. VAN DER LINDE (1997) 2 B.H.R.C. 334, Chaskalson (President), Const Ct (SA).

2794. Privacy—assault—consensual sadomasochistic practices—state interference in private life necessary for protection of health

[Offences against the Person Act 1861 s.20, s.47; European Convention on Human Rights 1950 Art.8.]

Interference by a public authority in the consensual activities of a sado-masochistic group was not a violation of the European Convention on Human Rights 1950 Art.8, but was necessary in a democratic society for the protection of health. L and others were members of an organised group of homosexual men who took part in sado-masochistic practices to which they consented. Videos of the activities were seen by police and the men were charged under the Offences Against the Person Act 1861 s.20 and s.47 with wounding and causing bodily harm. They were convicted after the trial judge ruled that consent to assault was no defence. The Court of Appeal dismissed their appeals against conviction, but reduced their sentences, and this decision was upheld in the House of Lords, which ruled that consent was no defence to charges under the 1861 Act and that it was against the public interest for an exception to be made for cases of sado-masochism. L applied to the ECHR alleging a violation of the right to respect for private life, contrary to the European Convention on Human Rights 1950 Art.8.

Held, dismissing the application, unanimously, that there had been no violation of Art.8. The central issue was whether the actions taken by the state authorities were "necessary in a democratic society", since the criminal proceedings clearly amounted to interference by a public authority with the right to respect for private life which had been carried out "in accordance with the law" and pursued the legitimate aim of "the protection of health or morals". The state authorities were entitled to rely on the criminal law in regulating the infliction of physical harm, and could consider the potential for serious harm that could have resulted from the extreme activities of the men, which could not be viewed as purely a matter of their own private morality. The justification for the interference with private life given by the authorities was relevant and sufficient. Furthermore, the reduction in the sentences on appeal and the degree of organisation involved in the group meant that the interference could not be viewed as disproportionate. The interference was necessary in a democratic society for the protection of health.

LASKEY v. UNITED KINGDOM; JAGGARD v. UNITED KINGDOM; BROWN v. UNITED KINGDOM (1997) 24 E.H.R.R. 39, R Bernhardt (President), ECHR.

2795. Privacy–telephone tapping–police officers–interception of calls made from policewoman's office breached right to privacy

[European Convention on Human Rights 1950 Art.8, Art.13; Interception of Communications Act 1985.]

H, who had brought sex discrimination proceedings against the Merseyside Police Authority in respect of her failure to secure promotion beyond the rank of assistant chief constable, alleged that, as part of a campaign against her, the Police Authority had intercepted telephone calls both at her office and her home. When H complained to the Interception of Communications Tribunal, she was informed that it was reasonably satisfied that there had been no contravention of the Interception of Communications Act 1985 in relation to her home, but, under the Act, it could not tell her whether that was because there had been no interception or because it had been carried out lawfully, pursuant to a warrant. The Home Office also informed H that any interception by the Police Authority of calls made through their own internal telephone system fell outside the scope of the Act and did not require a warrant. H petitioned the ECHR, contending that her treatment infringed her right to privacy under the European Convention on Human Rights 1950 Art.8 and her right to an effective remedy for breach of Convention obligations under Art.13.

Held, allowing the application, that there had been a breach of both Art.8 and Art.13. Article 8 could apply to telephone calls made from business premises as well as from the home and H would have a reasonable expectation of privacy in relation to such calls, as she had not been warned that they might be intercepted. There was a reasonable likelihood that calls made by H from her office had been intercepted and this amounted to an interference by a public authority within the meaning of Art.8(2). This interference could not be said to be in accordance with the law under Art.8 as the 1985 Act did not apply to such calls and there was no other provision to regulate their interception. However, H had not established a reasonable likelihood that calls from her home had been intercepted. Article 13 had been violated in that the 1985 Act did not apply to calls made through Merseyside Police's internal telephone system and H had no other means of redress under UK law.

HALFORD v. UNITED KINGDOM [1997] I.R.L.R. 471, R Bernhardt (President), ECHR.

2796. Property rights–delays in eviction proceedings

[European Convention on Human Rights 1950 Art.6; European Convention on Human Rights 1950 Protocol No.1 Art.1.]

In 1983 S applied for and obtained a notice to quit in respect of a tenant who was occupying the flat he had purchased in Rome. In 1984 he began enforcement proceedings. Due to government legislative policy, enforcement of the eviction order was delayed and suspended on several occasions. In 1987 S filed a "declaration of necessity", stating that he needed the flat to live in because he was 71 per cent disabled and had no job. S finally recovered possession of his property in January 1995. In 1991 he had lodged an application with the Commission, complaining of an interference with his right to the peaceful enjoyment of his possessions, as secured by European Convention on Human Rights 1950 Protocol No.1 Art.1, and that his case had not been heard within a reasonable time contrary to Art.6(1) of the Convention. The Commission declared his complaint admissible, and held that the Convention had been violated as alleged.

Held, upholding S's complaint, that (1) the second paragraph in Protocol No.1 Art.1 of the Convention reserved to Member State the right to enact such laws as they deemed necessary to control the use of property in accordance with the general interest. In order to implement social and economic measures with regard to housing, the legislature must have a wide margin of appreciation both as to the existence of a problem warranting public concern and the measures chosen to deal with such a problem. As held in *Mellacher v. Austria (A/169)* (1990) 12 E.H.R.R. 391, [1990] C.L.Y. 2549, the Court would respect the legislature's judgment unless it was manifestly without reasonable foundation. An interference must strike a fair balance between the demands of the general interest of the community and the protection of the individual's fundamental rights, as held in *Sporrong and Lonnroth v. Sweden (A/52)* (1983) 5 E.H.R.R. 35. As held in *James v. UK (A/98)* (1986) 8 E.H.R.R. 123, [1986] C.L.Y. 1650, there must be a reasonable relationship of proportionality between the means employed and the aim pursued. In the instant case, the emergency legislative measures employed by the Italian Government to deal with housing shortages, while having a legitimate aim in the general interest, should have been applied in S's situation to give him priority to enforce eviction. The failure to do so resulted in a breach of the Convention; (2) having regard to the purpose of the proceedings commenced by S in 1983 to secure possession of his flat, Art.6(1) of the Convention was applicable. The inertia of the competent administrative authorities to assist S to secure possession of his flat was the responsibility of the Italian State under Art.6(1) and there had accordingly been a breach of that provision, and (3) S should be awarded the full amount of his claim for pecuniary and non-pecuniary damages and for costs and expenses.

SCOLLO v. ITALY (1996) 22 E.H.R.R. 514, R Ryssdal (President), ECHR.

2797. Property rights-expropriation of property-entitlement to compensation and restitution predicated by citizenship in breach of International Covenant-Czech Republic

[International Covenant on Civil and Political Rights 1966 Art.26; Act 87/91 (Czech Republic).]

A's father was a Czech citizen whose property and business were confiscated by the Czechoslovak government in 1949; after that he fled Czechoslovakia and settled in Australia, where his three sons were born. A's father died in 1985 and in his will he left his Czech property to his sons. In 1991 A and his brothers submitted a claim for the restitution of their property, which was rejected on the grounds that they did not fulfil the requirement of Act 87/91 (which was then in force) that applicants for restitution should have Czech citizenship and be permanent residents in the Czech Republic. After several unsuccessful attempts to pursue his claim with the Czech authorities, A submitted a communication to the UN Human Rights Committee claiming that the application of the requirement in the Act 87/91 violated his rights and those of his brothers to equality before the law and equal protection of the law under the International Covenant on Civil and Political Rights 1966 Art.26.

Held, that (1) although the right to property was not protected under the Covenant, a confiscation of private property, or a state party's failure to pay compensation for such confiscation, could entail a violation of Art.26 if the relevant act or omission was based on discriminatory grounds. In examining whether the conditions for restitution or compensation set out in national legislation were compatible with the Covenant, the Committee should consider all relevant factors, including the original entitlement to the property and the nature of the confiscation, and would not deem a differentiation in treatment to be discriminatory under Art.26 where such differentiation was compatible with provisions of the Covenant and based on reasonable grounds; (2) in the instant case, the continued practice of non restitution to non citizens of the Czech Republic set out in Act 87/91 was discriminatory: in particular A's original entitlement to his property by virtue of inheritance was not predicated on citizenship, and since the state party itself had been responsible for the parents' departure in 1949, it would have been incompatible with the Covenant to require their sons to obtain Czech citizenship as a prerequisite for the restitution of their property or the payment of appropriate compensation, and (3) the fact that the Czech and Slovak legislators had no discriminatory intent in framing Act 87/91 did not prevent the citizenship requirement from violating Art.26, because it was not the intent of the legislature which was dispositive in determining a breach of that article, but rather the consequences of the enacted legislation. It followed that the denial of restitution or compensation to the complainant and his brothers on the grounds that they were not citizens of the Czech Republic constituted a violation of their rights under Art.26 of the Covenant.

ADAM v. CZECH REPUBLIC (1997) 1 B.H.R.C. 451, Judge not applicable, UNHRC.

2798.   Property rights–mining leases–government revocation order invalid–unlawful encroachment on statutorily protected rights–Lesotho

[Human Rights Act 1983 s.2 (Lesotho), s.3 (Lesotho), s.9 (Lesotho).]

SDM and others were registered holders of mining leases concluded with the Basotho Nation, (represented by the government of Lesotho) on August 4, 1988. The 10 year leases conferred wide ranging mining and associated rights on the leaseholders in the lease area. The Lesotho Highlands Development Authority, LHDA, responsible for the Lesotho Highlands water project had certain statutory rights of access and possession over the areas. Conflicts developed in the early 1990s between the leaseholders and LHDA with respect to rights in the lease areas. On July 18, 1991, SDM obtained an ex parte order interdicting LHDA from carrying out work in one of the disputed lease areas. Following opposition, an agreement was later concluded and the interdict was lifted pending final resolution of the conflict. On November 20, 1991, after the Commissioner of Mines had issued notices purporting to cancel the disputed leases, SDM applied to the High Court for review of the cancellation and again an interim agreement was reached. On March 20, 1992, the then government of Lesotho issued an order purporting to revoke the mining leases, thereby expelling the leaseholders without compensation or any legal remedy. SDM sought and obtained a court order setting aside the revocation order on the principal ground that it contravened the Human Rights Act 1983 s.2 and s.9: inter alia, the rights to an effective remedy and a fair and public hearing, and the right to property. The Attorney General and LHDA appealed. It was argued that the 1983 Act was simply a statute of Parliament and could therefore be amended, modified or repealed in any way that pleased a subsequent ruler lawfully in authority. Such amendment need not be express, but implied by its inconsistency with the statute.

Held, dismissing the appeal, that (1) the revocation order was inconsistent with specific rights guaranteed by the 1983 Act s.2 and s.9; (2) the state could only have lawfully revoked the leases had it confined itself to the grounds and procedures established by law for that purpose, in terms of s.3; (3) no such grounds were set out in the revocation order, no satisfactory grounds for departing from the authorised grounds were established, and it was clear that lawful procedures had not been followed; (4) the purported revocation was therefore in conflict with the 1983 Act; (5) it could not be inferred that the revocation order amended the 1983 Act by necessary implication, although s.4 of the revocation order provided that it took effect, "notwithstanding any provision of law to the contrary", it did not follow that that constituted amendment, and (6) it followed that the purported revocation of the leases could not be upheld.

ATTORNEY GENERAL OF LESOTHO v. SWISSBOURGH DIAMOND MINES (PTY) LTD (1997) 1 B.H.R.C. 383, Mahomed (President), CA (Lesotho).

2799.   Property rights–quiet enjoyment–North Cyprus

[European Convention on Human Rights 1950 Protocol No.1 Art.1.]

L, a Greek Cypriot, alleged that following the Turkish occupation of northern Cyprus in 1974 she had been prevented from returning to northern Cyprus and peacefully enjoying her property. In 1989 L presented a complaint to the Commission, alleging interference with her right to the peaceful enjoyment of her possessions under the European Convention on Human Rights 1950 Protocol 1 Art.1. Turkey took as a preliminary objection that the court lacked jurisdiction ratione temporis to examine the allegation, on the basis that in its acceptance of the court's jurisdiction in January 1990 Turkey limited such acceptance to facts occurring subsequent to the time of deposit.

Held, dismissing Turkey's objections, that (1) the Court's jurisdiction extended only to an allegation of continuing violation of property rights after 1990. The establishment of the Turkish Republic of Northern Cyprus did not take effect to extinguish Greek Cypriots' property rights; (2) Turkey was responsible for the policies and actions of the Turkish Republic of North Cyprus, as it was obvious that the Turkish army exercised control. The denial of access for Greek Cypriots was imputable to Turkey, and (3) L was right to complain that not only her right to freedom of movement but also her right to the peaceful enjoyment of her property had suffered interference. Since she was refused access to her property, she was effectively denied all control over her property and the opportunity to use and enjoy it. the compensation issue was reserved.

LOIZIDOU v. TURKEY (1996) (1997) 23 E.H.R.R. 513, R Ryssdal (President), ECHR.

2800. **Right to fair trial—16 year' delay excessive—bias—legitimate justified fear—Italy**

[European Convention on Human Rights 1950 Art.6.]

F and S were arrested in February 1976 and charged with the murder of two police officers. After three trials they were finally convicted of the murders in February 1992. Following their convictions they applied to the European Court of Human Rights, claiming that there had been a violation of European Convention on Human Rights 1950 Art.6(1) in that the hearing had not been concluded within a reasonable time, and also that there had been a violation of Art.6(3)(d) of the Convention in that their convictions had been obtained under duress, including physical pressure resulting in injuries, and that they had not been able to examine a key prosecution witness, V, before his death. They also complained that the tribunal had not been impartial. The Commission upheld these complaints.

Held, allowing the applications, that Art.6(1) was violated by the 16 years' delay and by the lack of the appearance of impartiality but their rights to a fair hearing were not violated; (1) the reasonableness of the length of proceedings would depend on overall assessment of all the circumstances. The case was complex by the nature of the charges and jurisdictional problems because minors were alleged to have acted in concert with adults. Considered separately the periods of delay were reasonable but, taken together, 16 years to convict the defendants of acts occurring when they were minors was too long; (2) insufficient evidence had been adduced to support the assertion that they were convicted on the basis of confessions obtained by physical and psychological duress in police custody; (3) in the circumstances, the admission of incriminating statements by a co-accused who could not be challenged because he died prior to trial did not render the trial unfair. Court of Appeal findings of corroborating evidence which upheld conviction were supported, and (4) judicial impartiality depended on both a subjective and an objective test. Even if a judge's personal impartiality were not questioned, appearances could render a trial unfair. If a legitimate reason to fear impartiality existed and could be objectively justified Art.6(1) would be violated. In the instant case the judgments on other accused referred to F and S as guilty and were cited in the judgment subsequently on F and S, which amounted to a violation.

FERRANTELLI AND SANTANGELO v. ITALY (1997) 23 E.H.R.R. 288, R Ryssdal (President), ECHR.

2801. **Right to fair trial—acquittals—no right to compensation**

[European Convention on Human Rights 1950 Art.6.]

M and Z were charged with forgery and corruption in 1984, and subsequently held in detention for eight months. They were then released on condition they report to the local police every day, in the case of M, and to the investigating judge every week, in the case of Z. After numerous hearings and adjournments, both M and Z were acquitted of all charges by the Dutch Court of Appeal in 1988. M and Z then brought proceedings for financial compensation under the Dutch Criminal Code. These proceedings were dismissed by the Dutch Court of Appeal on the grounds that there were no reasons in equity to award compensation to M and Z. M and Z then lodged applications with the Commission complaining, inter alia, that the European Convention on Human Rights 1950 had been breached in respect of their claims for compensation under the Criminal Code, in that there had not been a fair hearing carried out by an impartial tribunal in the determination of their "civil rights", within the meaning of the Convention Art.6(1). The Commission upheld their complaints.

Held, rejecting M and Z's complaint, that the Convention does not grant to a person charged with a criminal offence but subsequently acquitted, a right either to reimbursement of costs or compensation. In deciding whether a "right", civil or otherwise, could arguably be said to be recognised by Netherlands law the Court must have regard to the wording of the relevant legal provisions and the interpretation given to those words by domestic courts. Although the Dutch Criminal Code provides that certain expenses "shall" be refunded to a former suspect, the Code also states that a competent court "may" award compensation. Any award of compensation was, therefore, contingent on the competent court being of the opinion that "reasons in equity" exist. The grant to a public authority of such a discretion indicates that no right is recognised in law.

MASSON AND VON ZON v. NETHERLANDS (1996) 22 E.H.R.R. 491, R Ryssdal (President), ECHR.

2802. Right to fair trial—allegations of racial bias in jury—jury redirection sufficient to counter bias

[European Convention on Human Rights 1950 Art.6(1).]

G, a black defendant convicted of robbery upon a majority verdict, applied to the European Court of Human Rights on the grounds that his right to fair trial, guaranteed by the European Convention on Human Rights 1950 Art.6(1), had been infringed. During the trial the jury had handed the judge a note asking that one member be excused because of racial bias, but instead the judge had issued a redirection to the jury to consider the case on the evidence alone. G contended that the jury ought to have been discharged.

Held, dismissing the application by a majority, that, as bias among members of the jury could not be proven, an objective test had to be applied. The direction by the judge had been issued after consulting both counsel in the absence of the jury, and his warning to rule out thoughts of prejudice had been clear and carefully worded. He had undoubtedly been aware of the option to discharge the jury but was entitled to issue a redirection which in the circumstances was sufficient to dispel concerns about impartiality.

GREGORY v. UNITED KINGDOM, *The Times*, February 27, 1997, R Ryssdal (President), ECHR.

2803. Right to fair trial—appellate court sitting in private—appellant denied opportunity to comment on evidence—role of Attorney General's department in recommending dismissal

[European Convention on Human Rights Art.6.]

M, a Portugese national who worked for a nationalised engineering company, retired in 1980 after 25 years' service. At the time of his retirement he was classified as a "director" grade. In 1986 he brought proceedings against his employer claiming that he should have been classified in the "director-general" grade at his retirement which would have meant enhanced retirement benefits for him. M claimed the amounts which he would have received since 1980 under the "director-general" grade. His claim was dismissed by an industrial tribunal and that decision was upheld by the Lisbon Court of Appeal. M's appeal to the Supreme Court was dismissed following a sitting in private at which the parties had not been asked to attend and a recommendation by the Attorney General's department at the Supreme Court that the appeal be dismissed. M complained to the Commission, alleging a violation of the European Convention on Human Rights 1950 Art.6(1) in that, inter alia, there had been no fresh assessment by the Supreme Court of the evidence relating to the facts, no public hearing and the role of the Attorney General's department infringed his right to a fair trial by an independent and impartial tribunal. The Commission declared his complaint admissible and found that there had been a violation of Art.6(1) of the Convention.

Held, upholding M's complaint, that (1) since the dispute in question related to social rights and was between two clearly defined parties, the duty of the Attorney General's department was mainly to assist the court and help ensure that its case law is consistent. There was an additional public interest justification for the department's intervention where the proceedings were social in nature; (2) great importance had to be attached to the part actually played by the Attorney General's department, and more particularly to the content and effects of his observations, *Borgers v. Belgium* (1993) 15 E.H.R.R. 204, [1993] C.L.Y. 2128, applied, particularly as the Opinion was intended to advise and therefore influence the Court, and (3) regard being had to what was at stake for M and to the nature of the Attorney General's Opinion, the fact that it was impossible for M to obtain a copy of it and reply to it before judgment was given infringed his right to adversarial proceedings. That right meant in principle the opportunity for parties to a criminal or civil trial to have knowledge of and comment on all evidence adduced and observations filed, even by an independent member of the national legal service, with a view to influencing the Court's decision, *McMichael v. United Kingdom* (1995) 20 E.H.R.R. 205 applied. This in itself amounted to a breach of Art.6(1) of the Convention.

LOBO MACHADO v. PORTUGAL (1997) 23 E.H.R.R. 79, R Ryssdal (President), ECHR.

2804. Right to fair trial–charter right to answer charges and defend oneself–destruction of documents relevant to defence–stay of proceedings–Canada

[Canadian Charter of Rights and Freedoms s.7, s.24(1).]

The complainant visited a sexual assault crisis centre in 1992. When she was interviewed the complainant was informed that what she said could be subpoenaed to court and she consented to this. In March 1993 C was charged with sexual offences against the complainant alleged to have taken place between 1964 and 1966. At a preliminary hearing the trial judge ordered the crisis centre to produce a copy of its file concerning the complainant. When produced the file did not contain notes of the interview with the complainant. At a voir dire hearing the centre's director explained that, as a result of a policy adopted to prevent further victimisation of victims of sexual assaults, the contents of the file had been shredded prior to the order for production. The judge found that the notes of the interview were relevant and material and that the destruction of the notes deprived C of his rights under the Canadian Charter of Rights and Freedoms s.7 to make answer and defence of the charges. He therefore ordered a stay of the proceedings. This decision was reversed by the Court of Appeal, and C appealed.

Held, allowing the appeal, that the entitlement of an accused person to production of material which might affect the conduct of the defence either from the Crown or third parties was a constitutional right, *R v. Stinchcombe* [1991] 3 S.C.R. 326 applied. Breach of that right entitled the accused person to a remedy under s.24(1) of the Charter. The degree of prejudice suffered by an accused was not a consideration to be addressed in determining whether a substantive Charter right had been breached, *R v. Tran* [1994] 2 S.C.R. 951, *R v. Bartle* [1994] 3 S.C.R. 173 applied. A denial of access to a relevant document was a denial to make full answer and defence. The threshold test of the relevance of a document in the possession of a Crown was its usefulness to the defence; if the trial judge determines that it can reasonably be used by the accused either in meeting the case for the Crown, advancing a defence or in making a decision which may affect the conduct of the defence then it is relevant, *R v. Stinchcombe* and *R v. Egger* [1993] 2 S.C.R. 451 followed. Where documents were in the hands of third parties the judge must be satisfied that there was a reasonable possibility that the information was logically probative to an issue at trial or the competence of a witness to testify, *R v. O'Connor* [1995] 4 S.C.R. 411 followed. An accused did not have to demonstrate additional prejudice. In the instant case the judge was entitled to conclude that the notes were relevant and material, and that they were logically probative. While a stay of proceedings should only be granted in the clearest of cases, the judge was right in the instant case to order a stay. There was no alternative remedy which would cure the prejudice to C and there would be irreparable prejudice to the integrity of the judicial system if the prosecution continued.

CAROSELLA v. R (1997) 2 B.H.R.C. 23, Lamer, C.J., Sup Ct (Can).

2805. Right to fair trial—costs—entitlement under ECHR to counsel's fees following acquittal for tax evasion—discretionary nature of award

[European Convention on Human Rights 1950 Art.6(1), Art.6(2), Art.6(3).]

L, a Netherlands national residing outside the Netherlands since the end of 1974, was the subject of a tax investigation by the Netherlands tax authorities in 1977. On January 22, 1980 the authorities sent L additional assessments of his income tax for 1974 and his property tax for 1975 to reflect allegedly incorrect statements returned by L. The Director of State Taxes made a request to the public prosecutor to prosecute L, but a preliminary judicial investigation was not opened until September 3, 1982. L was tried and convicted by the Amsterdam Regional Court in absentia. The judgment of the Regional Court was quashed on appeal and the prosecution declared time barred. The additional tax assessments for the years 1974 and 1975 were quashed in 1988. In 1990 L was awarded reimbursement of certain costs and expenses but he was not awarded his claim for counsel's fees. In June 1990 L complained to the Commission that he had not had a fair hearing before the Amsterdam Court of Appeal in relation to reimbursement of his counsel's fees, contrary to the European Convention on Human Rights 1950 Art.6(1), and secondly that this refusal to reimburse, together with the court's statement that the file of the criminal investigation gave no reason to doubt that his conviction at first instance was correct, contravened the Art.6(2) presumption of innocence.

Held, dismissing the application, that (1) L's request for reimbursement of his counsel's fees was based on the Netherlands Code of Criminal Procedure. It was clear that the Code did not confer any right on L to have the fees reimbursed, even if the conditions specified were met. Proceedings of that nature under the Code were accordingly not covered by Art.6(1), *Masson and Von Zon v. Netherlands* (1996) 22 E.H.R.R. 491, [1997] C.L.Y 2801 followed; (2) in itself the refusal to order the reimbursement to a former accused of necessary costs and expenses following the discontinuation of criminal proceedings did not amount to a penalty or a measure that could be equated with a penalty. But such a decision might raise an issue under Art.6(2) if supporting reasoning, which could not be dissociated from the operative provisions, amounted in substance to a determination of the guilt of the former accused without his having previously been proved guilty according to law and without having had an opportunity to exercise the rights of the defence. In the circumstances L was in a position to exercise the rights of the defence since he had the benefit of appeal proceedings which were in the nature of a complete rehearing. In exercising its discretion under the Criminal Code whether to award L's costs in full the Court of Appeal was entitled to take into account the suspicion which still weighed against L because his conviction had only been quashed as a result of the fact that the original prosecution was time barred. The Court of Appeal was not called upon to reassess L's guilt and accordingly there has been no violation of Art.6(2) of the Convention.

LEUTSCHER v. NETHERLANDS (1997) 24 E.H.R.R. 181, R Ryssdal (President), ECHR.

2806. Right to fair trial–costs proceedings–unreasonable delay by state authorities in costs proceedings following litigation

[European Convention on Human Rights 1950 Art.6.]

Judgment was given against R, a married couple, in 1991 in a dispute with their neighbours, but hearings to determine R's liability for costs were adjourned to establish R's entitlement to legal aid. There was subsequently a delay of 10 months caused by social security officials' mistaken belief that R had separated. R then appealed against an order that they make a contribution of £10,599 towards their neighbours' costs and there was a further delay of 16 months during which the court authorities took no action regarding the appeal. In due course, R were asked to submit documentary evidence, and there was a further period of nine months' delay owing to difficulties experienced by R in obtaining documents from the courts. In 1995, the decision on costs was confirmed and R applied to the ECHR, contending that the delay in resolving the costs issue violated the right to a fair trial under the European Convention on Human Rights 1950 Art.6(1).

Held, allowing the application, that Art.6(1) applied to all stages of legal proceedings for the "determination of... civil rights and obligations" and this included costs proceedings, which had to be regarded as a continuation of the substantive litigation. There had been a delay of over four years in determining a relatively straightforward dispute over costs and, whilst the state authorities could not be blamed for all the time lost, they were responsible for the periods of 10 and 16 months' delay. On the basis of those two periods, viewed in the context of the overall length of the proceedings, there had been an unreasonable delay in dealing with R's case which constituted a violation of Art.6(1).

ROBINS v. UNITED KINGDOM, *The Times*, October 24, 1997, R Bernhardt (President), ECHR.

2807. Right to fair trial–courts martial–army procedure did not establish impartial and independent tribunal

[Army Act 1955; European Convention on Human Rights 1950 Art.6(1).]

The procedure of a court martial, whereby the same person acting as the convening officer also acted as the confirming officer, was not an independent and impartial tribunal and contravened the ECHR 1950 Art.6. F, a member of the British Army, was charged with civilian and military offences following an incident in which he held fellow unit members at gunpoint and threatened to kill some of them and himself. Psychiatric reports into F's behaviour concluded that he had been suffering from post traumatic stress disorder as a result of serving in the Falklands conflict. A decision to charge F with a number of offences was taken by a major general, acting as the convening officer, with responsibility for selecting a prosecuting officer and members of the court martial. The court martial, which was governed by the Army Act 1955, consisted of a president, who was a member of the convening officer's staff and four officers, who all held lower ranks than the convening officer and were members of units commanded by him. At the court martial, F pleaded guilty to most of the charges and was demoted, dismissed from the Army and sentenced to two years' imprisonment. Petitions for a reduction in sentence presented to the confirming officer, who had also acted as the convening officer, and to the reviewing authorities, were dismissed, as was an application for judicial review of the court martial's decision. F applied to the ECHR, contending that the court martial had violated his right to a fair trial under the European Convention on Human Rights 1950 Art.6(1).

Held, allowing the application, that the role of the convening officer was central to the prosecution of F and was closely connected with the prosecuting authorities, in that it was his responsibility to bring the charges, select the members of the court martial and the officers for the prosecution and defence, and to ensure that witnesses attended. In his second role as confirming officer, the convening officer was also responsible for ratifying the court martial's decision and could vary the sentence imposed, which offended the fundamental principle that a tribunal should have the power to make a binding decision which was not subject to amendment by a non-judicial authority. Therefore the court martial could not be considered an independent and impartial tribunal and there had accordingly been a breach of Art.6(1).

FINDLAY v. UNITED KINGDOM, *The Times*, February 27, 1997, R Ryssdal (President), ECHR.

2808. **Right to fair trial—courts martial—Royal Air Force procedure did not meet requirements of independence and impartiality**

[Air Force Act 1955; European Convention on Human Rights 1950 Art.6(1), Art.50.]

A court martial at which a commanding air officer is convening officer as well as fulfilling a prosecution role (by virtue of the Air Force Act 1955) breaches the requirement of independence and impartiality guaranteed under the European Convention on Human Rights 1950 Art.6(1). C, a non commissioned officer in the Royal Air Force, was charged with forgery and deception, to be tried by court martial. The convening officer for the court martial was a commanding Air Officer, who, under the Air Force Act 1955, was to perform a number of duties linked to the prosecution, such as deciding what charges were to be brought, whether a plea to a lesser charge would be accepted and appointing serving members. All the members of the court martial were subordinate to the Air Officer and under his chain of command. C was found guilty, sentenced to imprisonment and dismissed from the Air Force, and his appeals to the confirming officer, the Defence Council and the Courts Martial Appeal Court proved unsuccessful. C applied to the ECHR, alleging that the court martial violated his right to a fair trial under the European Convention on Human Rights 1950 Art.6(1) and seeking compensation under Art.50 for the alleged violation and for the reduction in income which had resulted since his conviction.

Held, allowing the application, that (1) the court martial had violated Art.6(1) in failing to meet the requirements of independence and impartiality, particularly because of the role played by the convening officer, *Findlay v. United Kingdom* [1997] 3 C.L. 342, [1997] 24 E.H.R.R. 221 applied, and (2) C's claim for compensation could not be granted, since the court could not speculate on the outcome of the case if the trial had been carried out in accordance with Art.6(1).

COYNE v. UNITED KINGDOM, *The Times*, October 24, 1997, R Ryssdal (President), ECHR.

2809. **Right to fair trial—criminal procedure—applicant joining proceedings as civil party—human rights not violated following termination of trial**

[European Convention on Human Rights 1950 Art.6.]

H's brother died in a shooting incident off the coast of Corsica in 1978. V was charged with criminal offences in connection with the death. V admitted civil liability for H's injuries and paid FF 500,000 to H's family in September 1978. In 1979 H made an application to be joined as a civil party to the criminal prosecution, as she was entitled to do under French law. However she did not at any stage during the proceedings claim damages nor make a separate application in the civil courts for compensation. Following lengthy preliminary stages V was committed for trial in October 1989. He was eventually tried in November 1991 and acquitted of the charges of fatal wounding and unintentional homicide. No hearing was held on the civil issues and H claimed that the termination of the trial prevented her from filing the submissions she had prepared on the award of damages. H applied to the European Commission in March 1992, alleging a breach of the European Convention on Human Rights 1950 Art.6(1) in that her case had not been heard within a reasonable time. The Commission declared the complaint admissible and found in favour of H.

Held, the complaint was not admissible, that (1) according to the principles laid down in the case law the Court must ascertain whether there was a dispute over a "civil right" which can arguably be said to be recognised under domestic law. The dispute must be genuine and serious; it may relate not only to the existence of the right but also to its scope and the manner of its exercise; and the outcome of the proceedings must be directly decisive for the right in question, *Acquaviva v. France* (Unreported, 1995), applied; (2) French law draws a distinction between a civil party application only and civil party proceedings in which it is sought to obtain compensation for damage sustained as a result of an offence. The admissibility of a civil party application does not absolve the person who makes it from the obligation to lodge a claim for financial reparation if that is what they want, and (3) at no stage did H ever claim damages or make known her intention to do so, despite having the opportunity on numerous occasions. Since V had been committed to trial the outcome of the criminal proceedings was not decisive of H's right to bring a civil action, unlike other cases where there had been a finding of no case to answer, *Tomasi v. France* (1993) 15 E.H.R.R. 1, [1993] C.L.Y. 2131, *Acquaviva v. France* (Unreported, 1995) distinguished.

HAMER v. FRANCE, August 7, 1996, Bernhardt (President), ECHR.

2810. **Right to fair trial–English language school in Greece–permission to open refused on grounds of nationality–right to effective determination by court denied**

[European Convention on Human Rights 1950 Art.6(1); Treaty of Rome 1957.]
H and his wife, UK nationals and graduate teachers of English, were residents of Greece. In 1984 they applied for authorisation to establish a school for English teaching. They were refused permission on the ground that only Greek nationals could be granted such authorisation. H applied to the European Commission alleging that by making nationality a condition for authorisation to establish such a school G was in breach of the Treaty of Rome. The case was referred to the European Court of Justice which in 1988 upheld H's claim. H again applied for authorisation and was again refused, on the grounds of nationality. H brought proceedings in the Supreme Administrative Court asking for the decision to refuse to grant authorisation to be set aside. In May 1989 the Supreme Administrative Court ordered that the decision be set aside. This decision was upheld on appeal. H lodged further applications for authorisation with the competent authorities, but received no reply. In January 1990 they applied to the Commission alleging a violation of the European Convention on Human Rights 1950 Art.6(1), on account of the authorities' refusal to comply with the judgment of the Supreme Administrative Court. G contended, inter alia, that the applications did not comply with the six month time limit and did not fall within the scope of Art.6(1).

Held, dismissing the preliminary objections and holding that Art.6(1) was applicable and had been breached, that (1) since the situation complained of began with the refusal of the relevant authorities to grant H the authorisation they sought and continued after they had lodged their application to the Commission, the objection as to time limits must be dismissed; (2) the application could not be dismissed on the ground of failure to exhaust domestic remedies since the available remedies were not sufficient, and (3) Art.6(1) of the Convention secured to everyone the right to have any claim relating to his civil rights and obligations brought before a court or tribunal, *Philis v. Greece (No.1) (A/209)* (1991) 13 E.H.R.R. 741 considered. That right would be illusory if a Contracting State's domestic legal system allowed a final, binding judicial decision to remain inoperative to the detriment of one party. Execution of a judgment given by any court must be regarded as an integral part of the "trial" for the purposes of Art.6, *Di Pede v. Italy* (Unreported, 1996) and *Zappia v. Italy* (Unreported, 1996) applied. The effective protection of a party to administrative proceedings presupposed an obligation on the part of the administrative authorities to comply with a judgment of the administrative court. Where the administrative authorities failed to comply or delayed doing so the guarantees under Art.6 were rendered devoid of purpose. In the instant case G deprived Art.6 of all useful effect by refraining, for more than five years, from taking the necessary measures to comply with a final, enforceable judicial decision.

HORNSBY v. GREECE (1997) 24 E.H.R.R. 250, R Bernhardt (President), ECHR.

2811. Right to fair trial–judge sitting in both pre trial and trial–whether nullity

[European Convention on Human Rights 1950 Art.6, Art.50.]

B, an Austrian national and resident, was charged and convicted of bribery in 1990. One of the members of the court which heard the case had also taken part in the questioning of witnesses during the investigation. B's lawyer was informed of this fact and given the opportunity to challenge the judge on that basis, but did not do so. The record of the trial indicated that the parties had waived the right to raise this point as a ground of nullity. Following his conviction B appealed on grounds of nullity. His appeal was dismissed on the basis that the waiver was valid and that Austrian law required a ground of nullity to have been first raised during the trial. B's sentence was increased on appeal. B complained to the European Commission that there had been a breach of his right to a fair trial under the European Convention on Human Rights 1950 Art.6(1) on the grounds, inter alia, that the trial court had included a judge disqualified from sitting by law and that after he had lodged his appeal with the Supreme Court the Attorney General submitted observations which were not served on the defence.

Held, upholding the complaint in part, that (1) the court saw no reason to call into question the finding by the Austrian courts that the waiver was validly made, *Casado Coca v. Spain* (1994) 18 E.H.R.R. 1, [1994] C.L.Y. 2415 applied. The offer of waiver was accepted by experienced legal counsel in an unequivocal manner, *Pfeifer and Plankl v. Austria* (1992) 14 E.H.R.R. 692, [1992] C.L.Y. 2341 distinguished. In the absence of any suggestion of prejudice or bias on the part of the judge in question, the Court could not but presume his personal impartiality, *Le Compte, Van Leuven and De Meyere v. Belgium* (1983) 5 E.H.R.R. 169 applied. The mere fact that a trial judge has also dealt with the case at the pre trial stage could not be held as in itself justifying fears as to his impartiality. In the instant case, it had not been established that the judge in question had to take any procedural decisions at all or make any assessment of the evidence or reach any kind of conclusion as to B's involvement. In those circumstances B's fear that the trial court lacked impartiality could not be regarded as objectively justified, *Hauschildt v. Denmark* (1990) 12 E.H.R.R. 266 distinguished; *Nortier v. Netherlands* (1994) 17 E.H.R.R. 273, [1994] C.L.Y. 2399 applied, and (2) under the principle of equality of arms, each party must be afforded a reasonable opportunity to present his case under conditions that do not place him at a disadvantage vis a vis his opponent. Since it was for the defence to assess whether a submission deserves a reaction, it was accordingly unfair for the prosecution to make submissions to a court without the knowledge of the defence, *Lobo Machado v. Portugal* (1997) 23 E.H.R.R. 79, [1997] C.L.Y. 2803 and *Dombo Beheer BV v. Netherlands* (1994) 18 E.H.R.R. 213, [1995] 1 C.L.Y. 2621 applied. Accordingly there had been a breach of Art.6(1) of the Convention.

BULUT v. AUSTRIA (1997) 24 E.H.R.R. 84, Judge Ryssdal (President), ECHR.

2812. Right to fair trial–request for revision of judgment following new documentary evidence

[European Convention on Human Rights 1950 Art.6(1).]

P commenced proceedings complaining of a breach of his right to a fair trial under the European Convention on Human Rights 1950 Art.6(1). At a hearing in 1993 the Court requested that the French Government provide certain documents, which the Government stated that it was unable to do because of the domestic rules of civil procedure and because some of the documents had been destroyed. In its judgment delivered in September 1993 the Court held that there had been no violation of the Convention Art.6. Subsequently, P obtained some of the documents originally requested by the Court and persuaded the Commission to lodge with the Court a request for revision of its judgment in accordance with the Rules of Court A r.58, on the grounds that the discovery of the documents "might by [their] nature have a decisive influence".

Held, the request for revision was admissible and should be referred to the Chamber which gave the original judgment. The possibility of revision which called into question the final character of judgments given by the Court was exceptional, and any request for revision would be subject to strict scrutiny. A request to those appearing before the Court for documents to be produced was not in itself sufficient to warrant the conclusion that the documents in question "might by [their] nature have a decisive influence" within the meaning of the Rules of Court A r.58. Such a request for documents showed no more than that the Court attached some interest to them. However, in the instant case the documents produced had a significant bearing on a matter in direct dispute between the parties, so that the Court could not exclude the possibility that the documents "might by [their] nature have a decisive influence". Whether they cast doubt on the original judgment was for the Chamber which gave that judgment to decide.

PARDO v. FRANCE (1996) 22 E.H.R.R. 563, R Ryssdal (President), ECHR.

2813. Right to fair trial—right to be informed of nature of charges—embezzlement

[European Convention on Human Rights 1950 Art.6(3).]

T, administrator of a public hospital, made an arrangement in 1966 with a bank that interest on deposits would be paid at a higher rate than the legally applicable rate. The difference was paid into his personal bank account. In 1983 T was charged with the embezzlement of public funds and corruption. At his trial the local court held that the sums were not "public funds" but found T guilty of the offence of simple embezzlement and sentenced him to 18 months' imprisonment. On appeal by the hospital, the Supreme Court quashed the original judgment and convicted T of simple embezzlement with the aggravating circumstance that he had taken advantage of the public nature of his position in performing the duties entrusted to him. A sentence of five years' imprisonment was substituted. T lodged a complaint to the Commission, contending that his right to a fair trial under European Convention on Human Rights 1950 Art.6(3) had been violated because he had not been informed of all the components of the charges against him.

Held, dismissing the complaint, that the public nature of T's position was an element intrinsic to the original accusation of embezzlement of public funds and hence known to T from the very outset of the proceedings. Accordingly, he must be considered to have been aware of the possibility that the courts would find that this underlying factual element could constitute an aggravating circumstance for the purpose of determining the sentence. There was no infringement of T's right under Art.6(3)(a) of the Convention to be informed of the nature and cause of the accusation against him.

DE SALVADOR TORRES v. SPAIN (1997) 23 E.H.R.R. 601, R Ryssdal (President), ECHR.

2814. Right to fair trial—right to be tried in reasonable time—seven year delay in bringing accused to trial—balancing of right against public interest— Trinidad and Tobago

[Constitution of Trinidad and Tobago s.4, s.5.]

S was charged on December 16, 1985 with murdering his wife. S was committed to stand trial for manslaughter on November 26, 1986, by the inquiring magistrate, who presumably did not think that the evidence established prima facie the intent to murder. No complaint was made about this first delay. S was granted bail. The DPP then indicted S for murder on September 2, 1993, and subsequently he was arrested on a warrant obtained on the grounds of the indictment. His trial was first scheduled for March 15, 1994. S complained that to try him after such a long time, just over seven years, would be a breach of his constitutional rights. The first trial was adjourned on S's application, and he filed a notice of motion on May 11, 1994 to try to stay the proceedings. This was superseded by S's constitutional motion filed on May 22, 1995 in which S sought a permanent stay on the basis that his right to a trial in reasonable time had been breached and claimed primary relief in a declaration that his further prosecution was contrary to the Constitution of Trinidad and Tobago s.4(a) and s.4(b). These guaranteed, inter alia, the rights to liberty and security of the person, due process, and equality before the law. S also relied on the Constitution s.5(2)(e) and s.5(2)(h), which particularly guaranteed the right to a fair hearing and such procedural provisions needed to effect and protect "the aforementioned rights and freedoms". The judge refused to stay the prosecution but declared S had been arrested and detained unlawfully, and not in accordance with due process of law. S appealed against the refusal to stay the prosecution.

Held, dismissing the appeal, that (1) S's right to be tried within reasonable time had to be balanced against the public interest in having S tried, and the court was entitled to take into account the nature of the prevailing legal administrative system and economic, social and cultural conditions, including to a limited extent, scarcity of funds; (2) criminal proceedings would only be stayed in exceptional circumstances, and there was heavy burden of proof on a defendant who sought a stay on the grounds of delay to show that he would suffer prejudice in such a case to the extent that a fair trial could not be held; (3) in the instant case the seven-year delay was average (though inexcusable) in Trinidad and Tobago and no actual prejudice to S had been shown as a result of it, and (4) the interest of society in requiring S to stand trial therefore outweighed any injury to his defence the delay might have caused, and (5) Opinion per de la Bastide CJ, that the fact that the express right to be tried within reasonable time was omitted from the Constitution suggested that the framers did not wish to create such a right, or endorse it, that this entitled the court to greater flexibility in deciding if a right has been breached, especially when the alleged breach resulted from systemic or institutional delay.

SOOKERMANY v. DPP OF TRINIDAD AND TOBAGO (1997) 1 B.H.R.C. 348, De La Bastide, C.J., CA (Trinidad and Tobago).

2815. Right to fair trial—right to examine witnesses—anonymity of police witnesses—statements insufficient proof of criminal act

[European Convention on Human Rights 1950 Art.6(1), Art.6(3).]

V and others were convicted of attempted manslaughter and robbery with the threat of violence. Evidence proffered by the prosecution included a number of statements made to a named police officer by police officers identified only by a number. V argued that as the police officers identified by a number were anonymous witnesses their statements did not constitute sufficient proof, in the absence of corroborating evidence, to support a conviction. The Regional Court rejected this argument holding that since the police officers had investigative competence, the evidential value of their statements was not affected by their anonymity. On appeal V's lawyers requested that several named and anonymous witnesses be heard. The Court of Appeal referred the case to the investigating judge, who set up a procedure whereby he, the witnesses and a registrar were in one room and the defendants and their lawyers were in another. The defendants could hear the questions put to the witnesses through a sound link and their lawyers were given the opportunity to question the witnesses. The Court of Appeal dismissed the appeal, holding that the reasons for anonymity, including personal safety, were sufficient for anonymity to be continued, and that the statements of the anonymous police officers were corroborated by each other and by evidence available from non anonymous sources. Appeals to the Supreme Court were dismissed for the same reasons, and V applied to the European Court of Human Rights, claiming that there had been a breach of the European Convention on Human Rights 1950 Art.6(1) and Art.6(3)(d), in that the convictions had been based to a decisive extent on the evidence of anonymous witnesses, in respect of whom the rights of the defence had been unacceptably restricted.

Held, that there had been a violation of Art.6(1) taken together with Art.6(3)(d), that all the evidence must normally be produced at a public hearing, in the presence of the accused, with a view to adversarial argument. The use of statements made by anonymous witnesses to found a conviction was not under all circumstances incompatible with the Convention, for example where the life, liberty or security of a witness might be at stake, *Doorson v. Netherlands* (1996) 22 E.H.R.R. 330, [1996] 1 C.L.Y. 3124 applied. In such cases, Art.6(1) taken together with Art.6(3)(d) required that the handicaps under which the defence laboured were sufficiently counterbalanced by the procedures followed by the judicial authorities. In the instant case, the defendants and their lawyers were prevented from observing the demeanour of the police officers under direct questioning and thus from testing their reliability. No sufficient explanation was provided as to why it was necessary to resort to such extreme limitations on the rights of the accused to have the evidence against them given in their presence, or why less far reaching measures were not considered. A civilian witness who identified the accused was not given the protection of anonymity, and there was not sufficient proof of the threat of violence against the police officers. The handicaps under which the defence laboured were not sufficiently counterbalanced by the procedures adopted.

VAN MECHELEN v. NETHERLANDS (1997) 2 B.H.R.C. 486, R Bernhardt (President), ECHR.

2816. Right to fair trial—self incrimination—statements obtained under legal compulsion during DTI investigations

[European Convention on Human Rights 1950 Art.6.]

S was interviewed by DTI inspectors as part of a statutory inquiry into allegations that, while S was chief executive officer of Guinness Plc, the company had taken part in an illegal share support operation to gain advantage in a takeover battle. S was obliged to answer the questions put to him by the inspectors or face contempt of court proceedings. Transcripts of the interviews were passed to the CPS and subsequently to the police who, following an investigation, charged S with theft, false accounting and conspiracy. During S's trial, evidence obtained by the inspectors was admitted and transcripts of the interviews were read to the jury, despite objections by S. S was convicted on 12 counts and was initially sentenced to five years' imprisonment, subsequently reduced to two and a half years on appeal. Following numerous appeals in the UK courts, S applied to the European Commission of Human Rights, alleging violation of his right to a fair hearing under the European Convention on Human Rights 1950 Art.6.1 because the disclosure in criminal proceedings of statements obtained under legal compulsion in non-judicial proceedings infringed his right not to incriminate himself.

Held, allowing the application by 16 votes to four, that the right not to incriminate oneself by remaining silent during interviews was an internationally recognised standard central to the concept of a fair hearing under Art.6. Whether S's right had been infringed depended on the use made by the prosecution during the trial of statements S had been obliged to make. It was irrelevant that the statements were not in themselves incriminating, in the sense of making admissions of guilt, as even neutral evidence could be used in a manner that aided the prosecution. Here the prosecution had used the statements in an incriminating way to prove S's involvement in the unlawful operations and to suggest that S was dishonest. The reading out of the statements during the trial could not be justified by the need to combat fraud and, accordingly, there had been a violation of Art.6.1. The court declined to award compensation, but did award costs.

SAUNDERS v. UNITED KINGDOM (1997) 23 E.H.R.R. 313, R Bernhardt (President), ECHR.

2817. Right to fair trial—tax evasion—access to documents held by Revenue authorities—assessment of fairness of proceedings

[European Convention on Human Rights 1950 Art.6, Art.8.]

M held dual Philippine and French nationality and resided in France. From 1960 to May 1983 he was honorary consul of the Philippines in Bordeaux and Toulouse. In the course of a tax evasion investigation French customs officers seized, in January 1983, 15,000 documents belonging to M which related to businesses operated by him. The proceedings were later discontinued and M brought proceedings for the unlawful interference with his private and family life, contrary to the European Convention on Human Rights 1950 Art.8. The European Court of Human Rights found that there had been a breach of Art.8 and awarded M damages for non-pecuniary loss. After a further investigation the French tax authorities prosecuted M in 1988 for tax evasion and relied, in part, on the documents seized by the customs authorities in contravention of Art.8. M sought to raise this as a preliminary objection to the prosecution, but this argument was dismissed, and M was convicted and sentenced to three years' imprisonment. M's appeals against his conviction were dismissed and he applied to the Commission in September 1991, complaining that the use, in the prosecution, of the documents seized by the customs authorities breached his right under Art.6(1) of the Convention to a fair trial.

Held, dismissing M's complaint, that (1) while it was not for the Court to substitute its view for that of the national courts which were primarily competent to determine the admissibility of evidence, *Schenk v. Switzerland (A/140)* (1991) 13 E.H.R.R. 242 followed, it must still satisfy itself that the proceedings as a whole were fair, having regard to any possible irregularities before the case was brought to trial and before the appeal courts, and ensuring that any remedies to any irregularities had been properly made, *Imbrioscia v. Switzerland (A/275)* (1994) 17 E.H.R.R. 441, [1994] C.L.Y. 2407 followed. In the instant case the courts considered M's objections and dismissed them. Their rulings were based on the documents in the case-file, on which the parties had presented arguments at the hearings, thereby ensuring a fair trial. The failure to produce certain documents therefore did not infringe M's rights to a fair trial, *Bendenoun v. France (A/284)* (1994) 18 E.H.R.R. 54, [1994] C.L.Y. 2397 applied.

MIAILHE v. FRANCE (NO.2) (1997) 23 E.H.R.R. 491, Judge Bernhardt, ECHR.

2818. **Right to fair trial–use of DTI investigation evidence in criminal proceedings– ECHR judgment could not be enforced in precedence over UK law**

[Company Securities (Insider Dealing) Act 1985 s.1 (8); Financial Services Act 1986 s.177.]

Information provided by persons required to cooperate with a DTI investigation could be used in evidence against them notwithstanding that it may result in self incrimination. M and another appealed against conviction of counselling or procuring another to deal in securities contrary to the Company Securities (Insider Dealing) Act 1985 s.1 (8) on the ground that, following the ECHR ruling in *Saunders v. United Kingdom* (1997) 23 E.H.R.R. 313, [1997] C.L.Y. 2816, the requirement contained in the Financial Services Act 1986 s.177 to give assistance in connection with any DTI investigation, the evidence from which could then be used in criminal proceedings, would result in self incrimination and thereby make those proceedings unfair.

Held, dismissing the appeals, that s.177 imposed a duty on requested persons to cooperate in an investigation and provided that their statements might be used in evidence against them. It carried the presumption that evidence so obtained was to be treated as fair. If such evidence was excluded in the present case it would also have to be excluded in every similar case, which would undermine the operation of the 1986 Act and amount to its partial repeal. Although the position was unsatisfactory, an English court had no power to enforce a judgment of the ECHR which would render an English statute ineffective.

R. v. MORRISEY (IAN PATRICK); R. v. STAINES (LORELIE MARION), *The Times*, May 1, 1997, Lord Bingham of Cornhill, L.C.J., CA (Crim Div).

2819. **Right to family life–change of name–rejection by Finnish authorities– compatibility with ECHR's respect for private life**

[European Convention on Human Rights 1950 Art.8.]

S, a Finnish national, applied to the County Administrative Board for permission to change his name, on the grounds that his ancestors had always used the proposed name and that his existing name caused practical difficulties with spelling and pronunciation, and had also given rise to a pejorative nickname. The

Board rejected S's request for permission to change his name because, inter alia, it was not satisfied that the proposed name had been used by his ancestors in such a way as to become "established" as required by the relevant domestic legislation. When L's appeal to the Supreme Administrative Court was dismissed he brought an application to the Commission, complaining, inter alia, that the refusal violated a right to respect for his private life contrary to the European Convention on Human Rights 1950 Art.8.

Held, dismissing the application, that (1) while Art.8 does not contain any explicit reference to names, since it constitutes a means of personal identification and a link to a family, an individual's name does concern his or her private or family life, *Burghartz v. Switzerland* (A/280-B) (1994) 18 E.H.R.R. 101, [1994] C.L.Y. 2427 applied. Accordingly the subject matter of the complaint fell within Art.8; (2) although the boundaries between the State's positive and negative obligations under Art.8 were not capable of precise definition, in both contexts regard had to be given to the fair balance that had to be struck between the competing interests of the individual and of the community as a whole, *Keegan v. Ireland* (A/290) (1994) 18 E.H.R.R. 342, [1995] 1 C.L.Y. 2659 applied. Since there was little common ground between the domestic systems of the Convention countries as to the conditions on which a change of name may be legally effected, the Court deduced that the Contracting States enjoyed a wide margin of appreciation. In the circumstances, the sources of inconvenience complained of by S were sufficient to raise an issue of failure to respect private life under Art.8(1) of the Convention. Furthermore the ancestor of S who last bore the proposed name died more than 200 years ago and no significant weight could be given to those links for the purposes of Art.8.

STJERNA v. FINLAND (1997) 24 E.H.R.R. 195, R Ryssdal (President), ECHR.

2820. Right to family life—cohabitation and subsequent marriage—deportation of overstayer

See IMMIGRATION: Tong v. Secretary of State for the Home Department. §2905

2821. Right to family life—Moroccan child attempting to join father in Netherlands—deprivation of residence rights

[European Convention on Human Rights 1950 Art.8.]

A, a Moroccan national who had held Netherlands nationality since 1990, and his former wife, F, had a son, S, who was born in Morocco in 1980. The marriage was dissolved in 1984 and S remained living in Morocco with F and siblings while A moved to the Netherlands and married K, a Netherlands national. F died in a car accident in 1987. A's marriage with K was dissolved in 1990 and in 1991 A married Y, a Moroccan national living in the Netherlands. S and one of his sisters arrived in the Netherlands in March 1990 without a provisional residence visa. In June 1990 the Deputy Minister refused their applications for a residence permit and ordered their expulsion from the Netherlands. S and A lodged requests for revisions of the Minister's decision and subsequently lodged an appeal with the Council of State. Their appeals were dismissed on reasoning which included an opinion that there was no contravention of the European Convention on Human Rights 1950 Art.8, on the ground that it could not be said that there was an interference with family life as S was not being deprived of residence rights which he had previously enjoyed. S and A applied to the Commission complaining of an interference with their family life contrary to Art.8.

Held, rejecting the complaint, that (1) it followed from the concept of family on which Art.8 was based that a child born of a marital union was ipso iure part of that relationship and from the moment of the child's birth and by the very fact of it there existed between him and his parents a bond amounting to "family life" which subsequent events could not break save in exceptional circumstances, *Gul v. Switzerland* (1996) 22 E.H.R.R. 93, [1996] 1 C.L.Y. 3296 applied; (2) the essential object of Art.8 was to protect the individual against arbitrary action by the public authorities. Regard must be had to the fair balance that has to be struck between the competing interests of the individual and of the community as a whole, and in both contexts the State enjoys a certain margin of appreciation. The extent of a State's obligation to admit to its territory relatives of settled immigrants would vary according to the particular circumstances of the persons involved and the general interest, *Gul* applied. In the instant case the fact of A and S living apart was the result of A's conscious decision to settle in the Netherlands rather than remain in Morocco. Accordingly A was not prevented from maintaining the degree of family life which he had opted for when moving to the Netherlands in the first place, nor was there any obstacle to him returning to Morocco. Article 8 did not guarantee a right to choose the most suitable place to develop family life. In the circumstances the Netherlands government could not be said to have failed to strike a fair balance between A and S's interests on one hand and its own interest in controlling immigration on the other.

AHMUT v. NETHERLANDS (1997) 24 E.H.R.R. 62, Judge Bernhardt (President), ECHR.

2822. **Right to family life–transsexualism–birth certificates–refusal to register transsexual as father of child conceived by artificial insemination by donor did not violate right to family life**

[European Convention on Human Rights 1950 Art.8, Art.14.]

X, a female to male transsexual, had lived with a woman, Y, since 1979 and in 1992 Y gave birth to Z, who had been conceived through artificial insemination by donor. X was refused permission to be registered as the father of Z, although Z was given X's surname, and X, Y and Z applied to the ECHR, claiming that the refusal to register X as Z's father was an infringement of their right to respect for family life under the European Convention on Human Rights 1950 Art.8 and was discriminatory, being in breach of Art.14 taken in conjunction with Art.8.

Held, dismissing the application, that there had been no violation of Art.8, and that it was not necessary to examine separately the complaint under Art.14. "Family life" under Art.8 did not relate solely to families created by marriage and it was clear that X, Y and Z were linked by de facto family ties. This case differed from others concerning transsexuals which had come before the court in that it related to the granting of parental rights and the way the relationship between a child conceived by artificial insemination by donor and the person who fulfilled the paternal role should be treated in law. There was little agreement between the contracting states on these issues and the law appeared to be in a state of transition, so that the UK would be afforded a wide margin of appreciation. It was permissible for the UK to take a cautious approach to changing the law as, whilst the amendments sought might not be harmful to children in Z's position, they might not necessarily be to the children's advantage, as there could be unforeseen implications and the changes might impact on other areas of family law. Further, the applicants could take practical steps to counteract many of the disadvantages suffered as a result of the refusal to register X as Z's father. As transsexuality raised difficult scientific, moral, legal and social issues, the UK was not in breach of Art.8 by failing to formally recognise X as Z's father.

X, Y AND Z v. UNITED KINGDOM (1997) 24 E.H.R.R. 143, R Ryssdal (President), ECHR.

2823. **Social security–benefits–emergency assistance–different treatment of Austrians and non-Austrians in breach of ECHR**

[European Convention of Human Rights 1950 Art.14; European Convention of Human Rights 1950 Protocol No.1 Art.1.]

G, a Turkish national, lived and worked in Austria from 1973 until 1987. From July 1986 to March 1987 he received an advance on his retirement pension in the form of unemployment benefit. When his entitlement to this benefit expired he applied for a further advance in the form of emergency assistance. This request was refused by the national authorities on the grounds that he was not an Austrian national, which was one of the statutory conditions for eligibility to the benefit in question. In May

1990 G applied to the Commission, complaining, inter alia, of a violation of the European Convention of Human Rights 1950 Art.14 and Art.1 of Protocol 1, in that G had been discriminated against in his enjoyment of the rights and freedoms provided for by the Convention on the basis of national origin.

Held, allowing the application that (1) Art.14 had no independent existence as it only had effect in relation to the "enjoyment of the rights and freedoms" safeguarded by the other provisions of the Convention, *Schmidt v. Germany (A291/B)* (1994) 18 E.H.R.R. 513, [1995] 1 C.L.Y. 2666 applied. In the instant case, the right to emergency assistance was a pecuniary right for the purposes of Protocol 1 Art.1. As G was denied emergency assistance on a ground of distinction covered by Art.14 that provision was also applicable, and (2) a difference of treatment was discriminatory for the purposes of Art.14 if it "has no objective and reasonable justification", that is if it did not pursue a "legitimate aim" or if there was not a "reasonable relationship of proportionality between the means employed and the aim sought to be realised". G was legally resident in Austria and worked there at certain times, paying contributions to the unemployment insurance fund in the same capacity and on the same basis as Austrian nationals. He satisfied the other statutory conditions for the award of the benefit in question and the refusal to grant him emergency assistance was based exclusively on the fact that he did not have Austrian nationality. The difference in treatment between Austrians and non-Austrians was not based on any "objective and reasonable justification" and accordingly there had been a breach of Art.14 taken in conjunction with Art.1 of Protocol No.1.

GAYGUSUZ v. AUSTRIA (1997) 23 E.H.R.R. 364, R Ryssdal (President), ECHR.

2824. Torture—failure to exhaust domestic remedies

[European Convention on Human Rights 1950 Art.3, Art.5, Art.15, Art.26.]

A, a Turkish citizen, lived in a south eastern province of Turkey which had been subject to emergency rule since 1987. A alleged that he was taken into custody in November 1992 and was tortured by electrocution and by the "Palestinian hanging", such that he lost the movement in his hands and arms. He was diagnosed as suffering from bilateral radial paralysis. The Public Prosecutor decided that there were no grounds to institute criminal proceedings against A. A brought no proceedings in Turkey in relation to his alleged ill treatment by the police, but in May 1993 lodged a complaint to the Commission alleging that his torture constituted a violation of European Convention on Human Rights 1950 Art.3. A was shot dead in April 1994, and his representatives alleged that he had received death threats in relation to his application to the Commission. Turkey took a preliminary objection that, contrary to Art.26 of the Convention, A had failed to exhaust the domestic remedies available to him.

Held, awarding A's family damages, that (1) Art.26 had to be interpreted flexibly and without excessive formalism. When the Public Prosecutor saw A, he must have been aware that A was paralysed and failed to conduct an inquiry. Special circumstances existed for A, after his period of 14 days in custody, not to exhaust domestic remedies; (2) the "Palestinian hanging" which caused paralysis amounted to torture and contravened Art.3; (3) 14 days' detention without being brought before a judge amounted to delay which contravened Art.5(3); (4) terrorist activity in South East Turkey by the PKK Kurdish Party was such as to create a "public emergency threatening the life of the nation" within the meaning of Art.15 but did not justify 14 days' detention without being brought before the judge; (5) the attitude of the Public Prosecutor who ignored clear evidence of torture was tantamount to undermining the effectiveness of any other remedies that may have been open to A, and (6) although there was no evidence that A was killed for applying to the Commission, compensation was awarded for the extremely serious violations.

AKSOY v. TURKEY (1997) 23 E.H.R.R. 553, R Ryssdal (President), ECHR.

2825. Articles

About LIBERTY: the National Council for Civil Liberties *(John Wadham)*: J.R. 1997, 2(3), 178-180. (Human rights organisation's work regarding test cases and lobbying, and its services for lawyers).

Human rights law update: significant cases *(Susan Nash* and *Mark Furse)*: N.L.J. 1997, 147(6785), 467-468. (Case law developments concerning breach of ECHR Art.6 in UK, where defendants were denied fair or unbiased trials).

Indigenous peoples and international human rights: towards a guarantee for the territorial connection *(Matthew Chapman)*: Anglo-Am. L.R. 1997, 26(3), 357-395. (Use of international law as means to secure recognition of rights of indigenous peoples, identification of rights-holding class and concepts of collective rights and self determination).

Judicial review of discretion in human rights cases *(Nicholas Blake)*: E.H.R.L.R. 1997, 4, 391-403. (Relationship between ECHR and UK judicial review of executive discretion, particularly with regard to cases involving deportation or expulsion).

Law and the other Europeans *(Ian Ward)*: J. Com. Mar. St. 1997, 35(1), 79-96. (Whether national immigration controls breach EC free movement principles and international human rights).

Marital rape and retrospectivity–the human rights dimensions at Strasbourg *(P.R. Ghandhi* and *Jennifer A. James)*: C.F.L.Q. 1997, 9(1), 17-31. (Whether HL judgments that immunity from prosecution for rape no longer applied to husbands contravened ECHR right to fair treatment in criminal trials).

More power to their elbows *(Martin Bowley)*: N.L.J. 1997, 147(6807), 1320-1321. (Developments in judicial tolerance to homosexuality compared to reluctance of government to change policy and case law showing current attitudes to age of consent, employment rights and military).

Pornography and freedom of speech *(Nadine Gourgey)*: Ent. L.R. 1997, 8(3), 89-93. (Whether pornography produced for profit can be characterised as speech and, if so, whether human rights protection should nevertheless be excluded on grounds of harm caused, feminist arguments or offensiveness).

Prisoners and fundamental rights *(Tim Owen)*: J.R. 1997, 2(2), 81-85. (Whether court should apply more rigorous standard of judicial review where executive interferes with fundamental right, focusing on prisoners' right of access to courts and their freedom of speech).

Religious tolerance and freedom in continental Europe *(Ivan C. Iban)*: Ratio Juris 1997, 10(1), 90-107. (Problems posed for European legal systems by emergence of new religious movements and need to focus on the rights of individuals rather than on particular religious groups).

State of ratifications of human rights instruments *(Robin C.A. White)*: E.L.R. 1997, 22, Supp HRS 82-97. (Series of tables showing extent of ratification of various European Conventions, Protocols and Agreements pertaining to human rights).

The European Convention in an international law setting *(Louis Blom-Cooper)*: E.H.R.L.R. 1997, 5, 508-512. (Extent to which UK courts have taken account of ECHR and international human rights law, focusing on application of principle of natural justice in judicial reviews of administrative decisions).

Trespassory assemblies: a judicial perspective *(Neil J. Parpworth)*: J.P. 1997, 161(20), 478-481. (Whether peaceful assembly on road verge exceeded public's right of access so as to constitute trespassory assembly and status of right to assemble under UK law and ECHR).

United Kingdom case law on the "internal flight alternative" *(Hugo Storey)*: I. & N.L. & P. 1997, 11 (2), 57-65. (Judicial interpretation of test for refugee status under Art.1A(2) of Convention).

2826. Books

Blackburn, Robert–European Convention on Human Rights. Hardback: £50.00. ISBN 0-7201-2229-5. Mansell.

Lord Lester of Herne Hill–Butterworths Human Rights Cases. Unbound/looseleaf: £250.00. ISBN 0-406-89081-1. Butterworth Law.

IMMIGRATION

2827. Adoption—breach of immigration controls—genuine relationship between parties

See CHILDREN: J (A Minor) (Adoption: Non Patrial), *Re*. §349

2828. Applications—variation of leave—changes to immigration rules—ultra vires—definition of a valid application

[Immigration Act 1971 s.3(2).]

ILPA applied for leave to move for judicial review of the Secretary of State's proposed changes to the immigration rules. The matters in question were changes to HC 395 Rule 32. The intended changes were (1) a requirement that applications for variations of leave, bar specified exceptions, were to be submitted using a form prescribed for the purpose, in a manner required by the form and including all documents and photographs specified in the form, (2) and further that "an application for such a variation made in any other way is not valid". It was submitted that the Variation of Leave Order, contained reference to an application which had been defined by various judicial decisions as effectively meaning no more than that there must be a clear and unambiguous application for an extension of the leave required. No specific form was needed and there was no question that failure to follow a particular form would lead to a lack of validity of any application. The Secretary of State could make rules pursuant to the power in Immigration Act 1971 s.3(2). It was argued that he sought, in so changing the rule, to change the law which had been set out in a statutory instrument. It was argued that the statutory instrument in question was the Variation of Leave Order, and that under this Order an application for variation of leave meant merely a clear and unambiguous request for the particular leave.

Held, dismissing the application, that (1) the Variation of Leave Order did not define what constituted an application or determine how an application was to be made, (2) it was the Immigration Rules that dealt with the question of whether or not an application had been made and validly made, and (3) the proposed change in the rules was not ultra vires under the powers laid down in Immigration Act 1971 s.3(2).

R. v. SECRETARY OF STATE FOR THE HOME DEPARTMENT, *ex p.* IMMIGRATION LAW PRACTITIONERS ASSOCIATION [1997] Imm. A.R. 189, Collins, J., QBD.

2829. Asylum—adjournment—request for adjournment on ground of ill health—medical certificate did not show applicant could not attend—adjudicator not obliged to accept certificate—decision to proceed in appellant's absence not unreasonable

[Immigration Appeals (Procedure) Rules 1984 (SI 1984 2041) r.34, .]

D appealed against a refusal to grant her asylum. D received notice of the hearing date of July 30, 1996. On July 26, her professional advisers sent a letter to the appellate authorities enclosing a medical certificate and a copy of a referral letter. It was accepted that this letter did not contain any material to indicate that D was unable to attend the coming hearing for medical reasons. On July 29 the appellate authorities telephoned D's advisers to tell them that the adjudicator had refused the application for an adjournment on the ground that the medical certificate received did not state that D could not attend court. On the morning of the hearing the advisers contacted the appellate authorities to say that a further medical certificate, dated July 29, had been obtained and would be faxed to the authority. A medical certificate accompanied by a written application for an adjournment duly arrived. The medical certificate stated that D was suffering from palpitations and also acute something illegible that might have been lumbar fibrositis, and that she was unable to attend court for two weeks. The adjudicator considered the new certificate but proceeded with the hearing and gave his reasons for refusing the claim. He stated that the certificate "did not appear to be satisfactory as a justification for an adjournment which I therefore refused". D applied for leave to appeal which was refused. D then applied for leave to move for judicial review. This was refused, then the appeal was renewed. It was submitted that (1) the adjudicator had erred in law, having failed to refer to Immigration Appeals (Procedure) Rules 1984 r.34(3) as well as r.34(2); (2) there was no evidence to reject the medical certificate, and the adjudicator was bound to accept it as prima facie evidence that D could not attend court, and (3) he had been *Wednesbury* unreasonable in deciding to proceed with the case.

Held, refusing the renewed application for leave to move for judicial review, that (1) it was clear that the adjudicator had had the Immigration Appeals (Procedure) Rules r.34(2) in mind, (2) there was no law which obliged the adjudicator in the circumstances to accept the medical certificate, which was received at the last minute without any explanation as to why D could not attend, and (3) the adjudicator had not been *Wednesbury* unreasonable in deciding to proceed with the hearing.

R. v. IMMIGRATION APPEAL TRIBUNAL, *ex p.* DEEN-KOROMA; *sub nom.* DEEN-KOROMA v. IMMIGRATION APPEAL TRIBUNAL [1997] Imm. A.R. 242, Saville, L.J., CA.

2830. Asylum—adjournment—request for adjournment on ground of ill health caused by pregnancy

O, a Nigerian citizen, who arrived in the United Kingdom on July 29, 1995 from Nigeria, attempted to enter on a false South African passport and was in possession of forged and stolen currency. When this was discovered she claimed asylum on the grounds that it was not safe for her to return to Nigeria. Her application was rejected and her appeal was heard by a special adjudicator on December 5, 1995. O attended, four months pregnant. At the start of the hearing her representative asked for an adjournment because O was feeling unwell as a result of her pregnancy. The adjudicator, who had no medical evidence before him, asked O some preliminary questions to see how fit she was to give evidence. On the grounds of her replies he was satisfied that O was fit to do so, and refused her application saying that if at any time she felt discomfort O was to tell him and he would grant an appropriate adjournment. O gave evidence at some length without any signs of discomfort and without asking for a break. It was submitted that the adjudicator had not given the consideration required in the context of an asylum case as to whether there were grounds for an adjournment and this had been unreasonable and unfair.

Held, in refusing leave to move for judicial review, that (1) the adjudicator's approach had been fair and sensible, and (2) he had no medical evidence in front of him and was obliged to use his own common sense and judgement to assess the request for an adjournment, and his decision had been vindicated.

R. v. SECRETARY OF STATE FOR THE HOME DEPARTMENT, *ex p.* ODUBANJO [1996] Imm. A.R. 504, Tuckey, J., QBD.

2831. Asylum—adjudication—analysis of documentary evidence—adjudicator entitled to take an overview of the evidence

T, a Nigerian citizen from Lagos, arrived in the United Kingdom on September 11, 1994 with false papers. He sought asylum on September 14. His claim was refused on October 19, and T lodged an appeal which was heard by a special adjudicator on November 7, 1995 at which he was present and represented. T submitted documents which he stated had been produced by an organisation in Lagos to which he stated he belonged and submitted documents that seemed to suggest that the club had been involved in considerable anti-government political activity. The adjudicator found it strange that the authors of such anti-government documents would provide their names, addresses and telephone numbers. There was no evidence except T's that he had been arrested, or beaten in custody. The adjudicator was not satisfied with the authenticity of the documents or that the club had more than a social purpose. He dismissed T's appeal and refused leave to move to the tribunal, on the grounds that T had failed to discharge the burden of proof and that he was not satisfied that T had a well founded fear of persecution for a Convention reason. It was argued that the adjudicator's findings were not properly analysed findings of fact applying proper standards of proof to each piece of evidence.

Held, dismissing the application for leave to move for judicial review, that (1) the adjudicator was not obliged to record an assessment of the evidential value of each document put to him, and (2) he was entitled to review the documentary evidence and to record his general conclusion as to its authenticity.

R. v. SECRETARY OF STATE FOR THE HOME DEPARTMENT, *ex p.* OGUNSHAKIN [1997] Imm. A.R. 159, Macpherson of Cluny, J., QBD.

2832. Asylum–adjudication–appeal to special adjudicator–procedure where adjudicator relies on unreported decision

[Immigration Act 1971 s.21.]

S, a citizen of China, was found in the UK on May 3, 1995, walking along the M20. On her arrest she claimed asylum, saying she had fled China after assaulting one of the police who had come to take her mother to a clinic for an abortion, she being pregnant for the fourth time. She was taken into custody and interviewed on May 29, 1995. Her application was refused by the Secretary of State on July 14, 1995. The indication was that the Secretary of State had not accepted S's account, and that in any case he considered flight to another part of China as a viable option in the circumstances S described. S appealed to an adjudicator. The adjudicator accepted S's story, but considered that on the facts S could have moved to another part of China. He dismissed the appeal on October 10, 1995, relying inter alia on an unreported decision of the Tribunal. S applied for leave to appeal to the Tribunal, but the application contained only brief grounds of a general nature and the Tribunal refused leave on November 10, 1995. S applied for judicial review. On behalf of S, detailed matters were relied on which would not have been evidence as issues to the Tribunal. It was complained that the adjudicator had relied on a case that had not been referred to by the parties before him, *Dupovac* (Unreported), that he had drawn adverse inferences from S's asylum interview which had not been properly conducted because S was a minor. The adjudicator had erred in his approach to the question of whether it was reasonable to expect S to have gone to another part of China.

Held, dismissing the application, that (1) the adjudicator had been entitled to give weight to the interview even if it had been improperly conducted; (2) the adjudicator had considered the question of reasonableness in relation to internal flight; (3) where an adjudicator considered a case to be determinative when it had not been referred to in the proceedings before him, he could either reconvene the hearing or give the parties an opportunity to submit written representations but in the instant case he had gone no further than to mention it as supportive of his own conclusions; (4) there had been no error by the Tribunal in refusing leave, on the face of the determination the matters complained of were not evident, nor were they apparent from the grounds submitted to it, and (5) had the adjudicator fallen into error of law, in the circumstances and on the facts there could have been no successful challenge to the Tribunal's decision. Opinion, that if a case arose where the Tribunal's decision could not be challenged but the adjudicator's determination contained deficiencies, the court might consider making a declaration to that effect, inviting the Secretary of State to consider referring the case back to the appellate authorities, pursuant to Immigration Act 1971 s.21.

R. v. IMMIGRATION APPEAL TRIBUNAL, *ex p.* SUI RONG SUEN [1997] Imm. A.R. 355, Collins, J., QBD.

2833. Asylum–appeals–attendance by asylum seeker not necessary to assess credibility

[Asylum and Immigration Appeals Act 1993 s.8(1); Immigration Act 1971 s.21.]

B, a Turkish national of Kurdish ethnic origin, arrived in the United Kingdom on April 20, 1994 and applied for asylum immediately. He was interviewed that day, and again on the April 29, and was refused asylum by a letter of August 18, 1994, on the grounds that his story was not credible. He was refused entry, and on August 30 appealed against the refusal under the Asylum and Immigration Appeals Act 1993 s.8(1). B's representatives wrote to him telling him that his appeal was to be heard by the special adjudicator on August 3, 1995. B intended to appear at the hearing, unrepresented because he could not afford the fees. Around July 26, 1995, as a result of an error in his solicitor's office, B received a letter from them that led him to suppose that the date for the hearing was after August 31. The hearing took place on August 3 without him, and his appeal was dismissed by the adjudicator in a written determination sent to B on August 16, on grounds of credibility. On August 25 B telephoned his solicitors and was given an appointment after his time limit for appeal expired. B went to new solicitors and they asked S to exercise his powers under the Immigration Act 1971 s.21, and refer the case back to the adjudicator so that B might attend the hearing. In a letter of October 24 this application was rejected on the grounds that it was "unlikely in the extreme" that B had any credible explanation of his earlier inconsistencies. It was submitted on behalf of B that (1) the case turned on B's credibility; (2) S had effectively agreed to deal with a situation turning entirely on credibility on the basis of paper and (3) credibility must always be judged by seeing the person in question, and that it was unreasonable to deny B this opportunity.

Held, dismissing a renewed application for judicial review, that (1) it was not necessary always to see an appellant in order to assess their credibility, as had been argued; (2) written submission from two firms of experienced solicitors had not mitigated the damage to his credibility that B had caused by telling different stories at different interviews; (3) if the submission were upheld it would apply to every case of political asylum in which the applicant did not turn up before the adjudicator and then asserted he had more evidence that might be credible, and (4) in light of this S's decision was not unreasonable.

R. v. SECRETARY OF STATE FOR THE HOME DEPARTMENT, *ex p.* BAKIS [1996] Imm. A.R. 487, Schiemann, L.J., CA.

2834. Asylum–appeals–certified claim–statutory procedure

[Asylum and Immigration Appeals Act 1993 Sch.2 para.5; Asylum and Immigration Act 1996 s.1.]

Z, a citizen of Algeria, arrived in the UK on an unknown date, and applied for asylum on November 26, 1996. He was served illegal entry papers at the same time. His application was refused and certified on December 23, 1996. Z appealed under the accelerated procedure, on the grounds that his removal would be contrary to the UK's Convention obligations. The adjudicator found that the Secretary of State had not specifically stated the Asylum and Immigration Appeals Act 1993 Sch.2 para.5(5) did not apply to the claim, accordingly he did not uphold the certificate and referred the case back to the Secretary of State. At the hearing the presenting officer had sought to amend the certificate to include the necessary reference to para.5(5) of the amended Act, but the adjudicator had refused to accept an amendment at that stage. The Secretary of State appealed to the Tribunal, which considered the general approach to be adopted by special adjudicators in determining appeals in certified cases.

Held, remitting the matter for hearing de novo, that (1) in certifying a case under para.5 of the amended Sch.2, the Secretary of State was obliged to refer specifically to one of the subparas. 2, 3 or 4 and also to 5; (2) a failure to refer to para.5(5) in the certificate could not be amended at the hearing before the adjudicator; (3) in an appeal the adjudicator should decide at the outset whether the Secretary of State had fully complied with the statutory procedure, and decide preferably early in the proceedings, or separately, whether to uphold the certificate; (4) the standard of proof in relation to subparas. 2, 3 and 4 of para.5

was the balance of probabilities; (5) in relation to para.5(5) the standard of proof was that of reasonable likelihood; (6) in cases where the adjudicator found that the statutory procedure for a certified claim had not been followed, or that the certificate could not be upheld, he had no power to remit the case to the Secretary of State; (7) the adjudicator in such cases remained seized of the case which then fell to be determined as a non certified case, and should consider if it was necessary to adjourn the hearing to allow full preparation of the appellant's case, and (8) the amendments to the Asylum and Immigration Appeals At 1993 Sch.2 applied to all asylum claims whether lodged before or after the coming into force of Asylum and Immigration Act 1996.

SECRETARY OF STATE FOR THE HOME DEPARTMENT v. ZIAR [1997] Imm. A.R. 456, DC Jackson (Chairman), IAT.

2835. Asylum–appeals–exceptional leave to remain–Secretary of State's refusal to follow recommendation of adjudicator reasonable

K arrived in the UK on September 9, 1994, aged 29, and immediately claimed political asylum. He was interviewed and on October 24, 1994 the Secretary of State set out K's claim in a letter and his reasons for refusing it. K appealed. The claim before the adjudicator was that K had been forced by Gambian rebels to join them. He was then detained as a prisoner in September 1993, and was identified as a Sierra Leone citizen and released about six months later. He was moved to a Red Cross camp and remained there until June 1994, when he managed to get to Freetown and from there to the UK. He was in Freetown about three months. The Secretary of State had concluded that K was not liable to persecution for Convention reasons if he returned. The adjudicator accepted that K had been tortured, but did not accept his entire story. He concluded, on December 28, 1995, that K could be returned to Freetown, but recommended that the Secretary of State exercise discretion outside the rules and grant K exceptional leave to remain for a year, pending a review of progress of the civil war in Sierra Leone. In a letter of May 7, 1996 the Secretary of State set out reasons for declining to do so, having by that time information as to developments between December 1995 and May 1996. K appealed against the tribunal's decision on January 16, 1996, to refuse leave to appeal against the adjudicator's decision, and against the Secretary of State's decision not to exercise his powers outside the rules. It was argued that (1) the decision by the adjudicator that K had no well founded fear of persecution in Freetown and that it would be reasonable for K to go there was at odds with the subsequent recommendation that he should remain in the UK for one year, and (2) that it was unreasonable of the Secretary of State to refuse to follow the recommendation.

Held, dismissing the renewed judicial review application, that (1) there was no conflict in the adjudicator's decision, he had recognised that K would suffer "considerable trauma" if he were in Freetown while the situation was unstable, in view of his past experiences, but that did not undermine his conclusion on the asylum claim; (2) the tribunal's refusal of leave to appeal could not therefore be criticised, and (3) the Secretary of State was entitled to take account of information before him suggesting that conditions in Freetown had improved since the adjudicator's decision, so that it was not appropriate to follow the adjudicator's recommendation.

R. v. SECRETARY OF STATE FOR THE HOME DEPARTMENT, *ex p.* KAMARA; *sub nom.* KAMARA v. SECRETARY OF STATE FOR THE HOME DEPARTMENT [1997] Imm. A.R. 105, Kennedy, L.J., CA.

2836. Asylum–appeals–extent of IAT's jurisdiction in examining adjudicator's findings

N, a citizen of Zaire, arrived in 1994. He was refused asylum and directions were given to remove him on January 9, 1995. His appeal was rejected by a special adjudicator on grounds of credibility, and that he did not have a well founded fear of returning to Zaire. N sought to appeal to the Immigration Appeal Tribunal. The application to the tribunal was supported on very brief grounds, of no substance, and leave to appeal was refused. It was submitted that (1) the decision had been irrational because it gave insufficient weight to complaints about the adjudicator's decision; (2) the adjudicator's decision amounted to an error in law because he did not indicate whether or not he accepted the central evidence of N's case, he did not deal specifically with substantial points put forward on behalf of N, and (3) the adverse decision as to credibility was unreasonable, since there was evidence to suggest that he might not have appreciated the point of N's case. Those submissions included matters not raised in the application to the tribunal, and not evident from the determination.

Held, refusing leave to move for judicial review, that (1) it was difficult to conclude that the tribunal had been irrational in not giving sufficient weight to matters that had not been put before him; (2) the court in any case would be unlikely to review a decision by the tribunal on grounds not apparent from the determination; (3) it was not incumbent on the adjudicator to review specifically every detail of an applicant's case to reject it, there was a limit to the extent of reasoning required where the adjudicator was uniquely placed to determine primary facts, and (4) it was not the role of the court even in asylum cases to submit the adjudicator's findings to the detailed criticisms raised by the application in respect of some of the adjudicator's factual conclusions.

R. v. IMMIGRATION APPEAL TRIBUNAL, *ex p.* NDONGALA [1996] Imm. A.R. 626, Buxton, J., QBD.

2837. **Asylum–appeals–factual error by adjudicator–tribunal had no obligation to search papers for such an error**

B, an Algerian national, was refused asylum by the Secretary of State on April 11, 1996. The adjudicator dismissed the subsequent appeal and leave to appeal was refused by the tribunal. It was submitted that (1) the adjudicator had failed to identify or indicate the basis of B's claim to refugee status, namely that he was a member of a social group, ie. his family, and he feared persecution because of that fact, (2) the tribunal should grant leave with this omission borne in mind, and (3) the adjudicator made a factual error in asserting that B had not been "arrested or charged at any time in the past", which was directly contradicted by evidence before him in interview notes.

Held, refusing application for leave to move for judicial review, that (1) the adjudicator had not referred specifically to a social group, but he had dealt fully with the case on its merits; (2) the error of fact on the part of the adjudicator had not been brought to the attention of the tribunal in grounds put to it, it was not *Wednesbury* unreasonable of them not to have scrutinised both the determination and the interview notes, and (3) it was very important that in appealing to the tribunal appellants should identify the basis for their assertions of error on the part of the adjudicator, and if it were an error of fact it was particularly important that the point be identified.

R. v. IMMIGRATION APPEAL TRIBUNAL, *ex p.* BOUKHELAL [1997] Imm. A.R. 116, Laws, J., QBD.

2838. **Asylum–appeals–failure of legal advisers to comply with procedural rules– impact on legal aid taxation**

[Asylum Appeals (Procedure) Rules 1996 (SI 1996 2070) r.33.]

A applied for leave to move for judicial review of a decision dismissing his appeal against rejection of his asylum claim. He had not attended the hearing of his appeal and it had been heard and dismissed in his absence, with the special adjudicator ordering that he be removed to Pakistan on April 15, 1997, the date of the application. Approximately one week before the date set for the appeal hearing a formal notice of hearing was sent to A's solicitor, who wrote to the appellate authority informing it that they did not anticipate being ready for the hearing. However, they did not submit the certificate of readiness as required.

Held, refusing the application, that A could have obtained an adjournment of the appeal hearing if he had completed and returned the certificate of readiness in the appropriate form. The response A's solicitors gave for their failure to comply with the procedural rules of the court was inadequate. The notice specifically stated that failure to attend the hearing or to submit the certificate of readiness would result in the hearing either proceeding in the appellant's absence or being treated as abandoned. The Asylum Appeals (Procedure) Rules 1996 r.33 had been complied with and the consequences of not attending were made clear. There was no sufficient reason for the fact that the present application was made on the day fixed for A's deportation since that date had been fixed since February.

Observed, that the same solicitors had been instructed throughout and A had a legal aid certificate. The transcript containing criticism of the solicitors' actions was to be made available to the legal aid authorities.

R. v. SPECIAL ADJUDICATOR, *ex p.* ARSHAD, Trans. Ref: CO 1145/97, April 15, 1997, Sedley, J., QBD.

2839. **Asylum–appeals–grounds in application for judicial review neither put to adjudicator nor to tribunal–limit of tribunal's obligation in considering applications for leave to appeal**

P, a Sri Lankan citizen, arrived in the UK on September 12, 1992 and applied for asylum on September 30. He had been pressurised into providing support for the LTTE whilst living in Jaffna. He moved to Colombo in 1990 and was detained and interrogated by government authorities about his connections with the Tamil Tigers and his reason for leaving. The adjudicator found there was a serious possibility he had been ill-treated and beaten in detention. He then worked in Kuwait from July 1990 to July 1991, then returned to Colombo and was again detained and physically ill-treated. The Secretary of State refused asylum by letter on July 15, 1994. P appealed. The adjudicator dismissed the appeal on July 31, 1995. P then applied for leave to appeal, and this was refused by the tribunal on August 14, 1995. This was followed by a judicial review application, refused on May 13, 1996. P made a renewed application. The adjudicator had concluded that it would be safe to return P to Colombo, but not to an area under LTTE control. It was argued that the adjudicator did not have before him up to date material, demonstrating that conditions in Colombo had deteriorated. This had not been raised before the adjudicator, nor in extensive professionally drafted grounds of appeal put to the tribunal.

Held, dismissing the renewed judicial review application, that (1) it was arguable that judicial review could not be sought on the basis of grounds not put to inferior tribunals; (2) assuming that such grounds could be raised, the fact that they had not been raised earlier was a relevant point in determining the reasonableness of the contested decision, and (3) it would place too heavy a burden on the appellate system to expect the tribunal to search the adjudicator's determination for points not brought to its attention nor raised before the adjudicator.

R. v. SECRETARY OF STATE FOR THE HOME DEPARTMENT, *ex p.* PACKEER; *sub nom.* PACKEER v. SECRETARY OF STATE FOR THE HOME DEPARTMENT [1997] Imm. A.R. 110, Waite, L.J., CA.

2840. **Asylum–appeals–issue raised in appeal application not put to the tribunal–scope of tribunal's duty in assessing validity of adjudicator's decision**

A, a Turkish Kurd, arrived in the UK in August 1994, and claimed political asylum. He was given the conventional political asylum questionnaire and later interviewed. The Secretary of State refused asylum on November 17, 1994 and subsequently refused to grant entry. A appealed. The special adjudicator dismissed the appeal in May 1996 and in June the tribunal refused leave. In the interview and in a subsequent letter of clarification to the Home Office, A gave as grounds for claiming asylum his fear of being required to do military service in Turkey, which he feared would entail both harassment and possibly being asked to fight other Kurds. It was argued that the adjudicator had not given adequate reasons for the dismissal, in not explaining what view she had of the possibility of A being asked to fight other Kurds, nor of the extent to which Turkey's military actions had been the subject of international criticism. In professionally drafted grounds in support of the application for leave to appeal given to the tribunal there was no mention of the question of A being forced to do military service in Turkey. The question for the court was whether, even if there were an error of reasoning in the adjudicator's decision, there was a reviewable error of law on the part of the tribunal in failing to identify an issue not brought to its attention in the grounds of appeal submitted.

Held, dismissing the application for judicial review, that (1) the court was restricted to considering whether the tribunal had erred in law on *Wednesbury* principles alone; (2) the relevant question was not whether it was not an abuse of process for the court to entertain an issue not raised in the grounds of appeal, *R. v. Secretary of State for the Home Department, ex p. Zahir Chugtai* [1995] Imm. A.R. 559; (3) nor was the relevant question whether it was a matter of discretion for the court to entertain such a ground, *R. v. Immigration Appeal Tribunal, ex p. Cami Akkulak* (Unreported, 1994), *R. v. Immigration Appeal Tribunal, ex p. Khatiza Begum* (Unreported, 1991); (4) the obligation of the tribunal in general was to scrutinise the adjudicator's determination to see whether on the face of it and in the context of the grounds of appeal put to the tribunal, the determination was a proper one; (5) the tribunal would also have the duty to ensure, irrespective of grounds, that the determination contained no plain errors of construction of statute or immigration rules, that there had been no obvious unfairness or improper procedures and that there were no obvious factual contradictions in the determination; (6) the tribunal's duty would be more extensive where grounds had not been professionally drafted, and (7) in the instant case the tribunal had not acted unreasonably.

R. v. IMMIGRATION APPEAL TRIBUNAL, *ex p.* ARSLAN [1997] Imm. A.R. 63, Laws, J., QBD.

2841. Asylum–appeals–no duty on IAT to enquire into appellant's circumstances

M, a citizen of Kenya, arrived in the UK on September 15, 1995 and applied for leave to enter as a student. The application was refused by the Secretary of State. On September 16, 1995, M applied for asylum, and she was interviewed on the two following days. On September 19, her application was refused by the Secretary of State, who concluded that M had not established a well founded fear of persecution in Kenya for a Convention reason. In October 1995, M discovered she was pregnant. On October 25, 1995, directions were given for her removal, but on November 2 M gave notice of appeal against the Secretary of State's decision to refuse her refugee status. The date initially set for the appeal hearing was January 25, 1996. M had been granted temporary admission because of her pregnancy, on November 13, 1995. In early 1996 she was admitted to hospital because of complications relating to her pregnancy. The hearing was adjourned, and a new date set, for June 18, 1996. On May 18, 1996 M gave birth to a son, and on June 13 she told her then representative that she was not well enough to attend the hearing. The letter sent to inform the appellate authorities of that fact did not arrive. M did not appear at the hearing, and the adjudicator decided to proceed in her absence, and went on to dismiss the appeal. On July 9, 1996, M lodged an application for leave to appeal to the Tribunal, which included a bare assertion that M had been unfit to attend the hearing, without any supporting evidence. The Tribunal refused leave on July 12, 1996. On application for judicial review it was argued that in the circumstances the Tribunal should have called for further medical evidence or arranged an oral hearing of the application, or remitted the case for hearing de novo.

Held, dismissing the application, that (1) to require the appellate authorities to carry out further enquiries as suggested, on bare assertions in the grounds of appeal, would be an intolerable burden; (2) M had been represented and the representatives had not put any supporting evidence to the Tribunal, and (3) in the circumstances there had been nothing procedurally unfair in the Tribunal's approach.

R. v. IMMIGRATION APPEAL TRIBUNAL, *ex p.* MWANIA [1997] Imm. A.R. 413, Forbes, J., QBD.

2842. Asylum–appeals–no duty on Secretary of State to inform adjudicator of previous decisions

[Asylum and Immigration Appeals Act 1993; Convention relating to the Status of Refugees 1951 (United Nations).]

S claimed asylum upon arrival in the UK from India via Portugal. The special adjudicator ordered his removal to Portugal on the basis that there was no reason to believe the Portuguese authorities would not treat G in accordance with the Convention relating to the Status of Refugees 1951. S's application for judicial review of this decision was refused, and he applied for leave to appeal on the grounds that there had been contrary decisions by other adjudicators which the Secretary of State's representative had a duty to produce at the hearing.

Held, dismissing the application, that despite the fact that it was of benefit to special adjudicators to be kept up to date with asylum decisions under the Asylum and Immigration Appeals Act 1993 and any changes with regard to particular countries, it would be too great a burden and too time consuming to require the Secretary of State's representative to refer the special adjudicator to a large number of previous decisions in every case. The facts of the present case did not warrant further investigation as there was no indication that the Portuguese authorities would not comply with their Convention obligations and the decision was in line with previous decisions regarding Portugal.

R. v. SPECIAL ADJUDICATOR, *ex p.* SINGH (GURPREET), *The Times*, December 12, 1996, Brooke, L.J., CA.

2843. Asylum–appeals–non attendance–no explanation–medical certificate submitted considered unsatisfactory.

[Asylum Appeals (Procedure) Rules 1993 (SI 1993 1661) r.10, r.13.]

J, a citizen of Sierra Leone, arrived in the UK on July 30, 1994. On August 8, 1994 he applied for asylum. This was refused by the Secretary of State in December 1994. J appealed. He was due to appear at a hearing before the special adjudicator on November 27, 1995. He did not attend, gave no explanation to his representatives, nor did he make any contact with them. The solicitor therefore had no explanation to give the adjudicator for J's absence. He applied for an adjournment. This was considered under the Asylum Appeals (Procedure) Rules 1993 r.10(1) and refused on the grounds that there was no good cause. The adjudicator then dealt with the appeal in J's absence and on January 4, 1996, dismissed it. J applied for leave to appeal to the tribunal. He asserted that his solicitors had written a letter to the appellate authorities dated November 29, 1995, enclosing a medical certificate, dated November 28, which stated that J was unable to attend work for a week due to influenza. There was no trace of the certificate in the papers. The appeal was made on the basis that the adjudicator's decision was unfair in that J had not had an opportunity to be heard, and that the medical certificate should have been considered by the adjudicator, but was not. A document was received from a medical practitioner stating that he had given J a certificate diagnosing him as suffering from influenza and unable to work for a week, a day after the hearing. This was before the tribunal. The tribunal considered this unsatisfactory and refused the appeal. J appealed against this decision. It was submitted that (1) the material before the tribunal justified the conclusion that J was indeed ill at the time of the hearing, and that leave should therefore have been granted for appeal; (2) alternatively there should at least have been a hearing under the Asylum Appeals (Procedure) Rules 1993 r.13(5) empowering the tribunal to order a hearing of an application of leave under exceptional circumstances that make it desirable or necessary, and (3) on receipt of the information before the tribunal, it was desirable to have a hearing even were it not necessary, *R. v. Immigration Appeal Tribunal, ex p. Mehta (Rashila Prataprai)* [1976] Imm. A.R. 38, [1977] C.L.Y. 13 referred to.

Held, dismissing the application, that (1) no special circumstances had been identified in the application for leave to appeal, no oral hearing had been requested, the tribunal was not expected to determine of its own motion whether one was appropriate; (2) clear material that would entitle the tribunal to conclude that such a hearing would have substantial value, and the identification of that value, were required for the tribunal to be obliged to consider an oral hearing of the application; (3) it had to be appreciated that applications for adjournments would be viewed with great caution, given the tight control needed over the listing of appeals; (4) representatives should therefore inform applicants of the importance of appearing at the hearing at the time fixed if they wanted to give evidence, and (5) the adjudicator or the tribunal had to be provided with information that would properly justify an adjournment, were one sought.

R. v. SECRETARY OF STATE FOR THE HOME DEPARTMENT, *ex p.* JANNEH [1997] Imm. A.R. 154, Latham, J., QBD.

2844. Asylum–appeals–non attendance–notice of hearing sent to applicant but not to representative–applicant asserting did not receive it–adjudicator determined appeal in the applicant's absence

[Immigration Appeals (Procedure) Rules 1984 (SI 1984 2041) r.34; Immigration Appeals (Procedure) Rules 1984 (SI 1984 2041) r.44; Asylum Appeals (Procedure) Rules 1993 (SI 1993 1661) r.25; Asylum Appeals (Procedure) Rules 1993 (SI 1993 1661) r.32.]

S, a Sri Lankan of Tamil origin, arrived in the UK on October 6, 1994, and claimed political asylum. He was interviewed twice. The Secretary of State refused the application in a letter of February 3, 1995. S appealed on March 14, 1995. All relevant documentation was sent to L at his stated address and to his solicitors. A notice for hearing was sent by recorded delivery to his last known address on March 27, 1995, but not to his representatives. S did not appear at the hearing on September 19, 1995. Finally, the Home Office presenting officer concluded that the case could be determined in S's absence, and requested that the adjudicator apply the Asylum Appeals (Procedure) Rules 1993 r.25. The adjudicator found against S on grounds of credibility and concurred with the decision of the Secretary of State. Leave to appeal to the Immigration Appeal Tribunal was refused. In an application for judicial review it was argued that the adjudicator had misdirected himself in presuming that the notice of hearing was deemed to have been delivered to S, that the Immigration Appeals (Procedure) Rules 1984 r.34(5)(a) was omitted from r.25 of the 1993 Rules, so that there was no longer a presumption that if a notice of hearing was sent by post in accordance with r.44 of the 1984 Rules it was deemed to have been delivered to the applicant unless the contrary were shown.

Held, dismissing the application for judicial review, that (1) Immigration Appeals (Procedure) Rules 1993 r.32 laid down that any notice sent by post under the Rules should be deemed delivered on the second day after it was sent; (2) following *R. v. Secretary of State for the Home Department, ex p. Sivanantharajah* [1995] Imm. A.R. 202, [1995] 1 C.L.Y. 2679 the deeming provision applied to all cases even when there was evidence that the notice was received at the wrong time, or not at all, *Secretary of State for the Home Department v. Monic* [1996] 1 C.L.Y 3190 had been wrongly decided, and (3) in recording the decision to proceed, the adjudicator was not bound to state the precise law under which he acted, merely to set out the relevant facts.

R. v. SECRETARY OF STATE FOR THE HOME DEPARTMENT, *ex p.* SASISKATH [1997] Imm. A.R. 83, Hidden, J., QBD.

2845. Asylum–appeals–posting of adjudicator's decision–deemed receipt

[Asylum Appeals (Procedure) Rules 1996 (SI 1996 2070) r.42(1).]

B claimed asylum in the UK but the Immigration Appellate Authority decided that it had no jurisdiction to entertain an appeal by B from a decision of the special adjudicator. The determination of the special adjudicator was deemed to have been received by B on October 10, 1996. This was derived from the fact that the adjudicator's decision had been posted on October 8, 1996 and by the operation of the Asylum Appeals (Procedure) Rules 1996 r.42(1) whereby a letter was deemed received two days after the posting regardless or when it was actually received. Given the deemed received date was October 10, 1996 then the appeal had to be made within five working days thereafter. B asserted that he actually received the adjudicator's decision on October 11, 1996 and therefore had until October 18, 1996 to submit his application

Held, granting leave to apply to judicial review, that the consequences for an applicant could be so dire that the merits of such a draconian rule seemed to be questionable indeed.

R. v. IMMIGRATION APPEAL TRIBUNAL, *ex p.* BELLACHE, April 24, 1997, Evans, L.J., CA. [*Ex rel.* S Field, Barrister, 10-11 Gray's Inn Square, Gray's Inn].

2846. Asylum–appeals–time limits

[Immigration Appeals (Procedure) Rules 1984 (SI 1984 2041; Asylum Appeals (Procedure) Rules 1993 (SI 1993 1661).]

T applied for judicial review of the refusal to grant him political asylum. T served his grounds of appeal to the Immigration Appeal Tribunal in time, but later submitted further grounds which were ignored. T argued that the further grounds should have been taken into account under the Asylum Appeals (Procedure) Rules 1993 as they were received before his application was considered.

Held, dismissing the application, that the submission of further grounds after the expiry of the five day period in which leave to appeal could be submitted was not permissible under the Immigration Appeals (Procedure) Rules 1984.

R. v. IMMIGRATION APPEAL TRIBUNAL, *ex p.* TOPRAK [1996] Imm. A.R. 332, McCullough, J., QBD.

2847. Asylum–appeals–time limits–application for leave to appeal filed one day after five day time limit

[Asylum Appeals (Procedure) Rules 1996 (SI 1996 2070) r.42, para.13; Interpretation Act 1978 s.7.]

B applied for leave to move for judicial review of a decision by the Immigration Appeal Tribunal closing his case on the basis that his application for leave to appeal against the refusal of political asylum was received one day after the five day limit stipulated in the Asylum Appeals (Procedure) Rules 1996 para.13. B stated that he had received the determination on October 11, 1996 and that the five days should have been calculated from that date rather than October 10, when the notice was deemed to have arrived. The IAT submitted that that proposition would be contrary to r.42(1) of the 1996 Rules under which the notice would be deemed to have been received on the second day after sending whether or not it was received, because the notice had been posted on October 8. However, there was no evidence available to confirm the date on which it was sent. B contended that r.42 of the 1996 Rules should be read subject to the Interpretation Act 1978 s.7.

Held, adjourning the application, that an adjournment would allow the parties the opportunity to place before the court any evidence as to the date on which the notice was sent, such as the postmark on the envelope in which it was sent, or the tribunal's records. If it was shown that it may not have been posted until October 9 then the court would give leave to move for judicial review, but if there was proof that it was sent on October 8, B would have to concede that his application could not be pursued. Section 7 of the 1978 Act did not apply as r.42 clearly stated a contrary intention.

R. v. IMMIGRATION APPELLATE AUTHORITIES, *ex p.* BELLACHE, Trans. Ref: CO 922/92, April 8, 1997, McCullough, J., QBD.

2848. Asylum–appeals–tribunal remitting case for de novo hearing–second adjudicator read determination of the first–desirable for previous determination to be removed from file

[Convention Relating to the Status of Refugees 1951 (United Nations).]

A, an Algerian national, arrived in the UK as a stowaway and applied for asylum which was refused. It was noted that A feared persecution by FIS militants but that it would be reasonable to expect him to seek and receive protection from the national authorities, as a result he was not a refugee under the terms of the Convention relating to the Status of Refugees 1951. A stated he did not expect to be killed by militants as his brother had been, nor that he had been threatened indirectly through his brother or family. A's appeal was dismissed. A applied for leave to appeal to the tribunal, which was allowed, and the tribunal directed that there be a de novo hearing before a fresh adjudicator on the grounds that there were two errors in the adjudicator's decision and it could not be shown for certain that these factual errors had been irrelevant. The second adjudicator dismissed the appeal. The tribunal refused an application for leave to appeal. In the course of his determination the second adjudicator referred to the earlier decision, noting that he had had "the advantage of perusing it". It was argued that he should not have taken this advantage and that his means of expressing this suggested that he had been or may have been influenced by it. It was suggested that the adjudicator had failed to have regard to the Amnesty International report, in that he gave no indication of his attitude towards its contents, nor whether they had influenced his decision.

Held, dismissing A's application for leave to move for judicial review, that (1) there was no reason why the second adjudicator should not read the determination of the previous one, when a case was remitted de novo, provided he did not allow it to influence his decision, and there was no evidence that he had, although his choice of phrasing had been unfortunate, and (2) it would, however, be desirable for a previous determination to be removed from the file.

R. v. SECRETARY OF STATE FOR THE HOME DEPARTMENT, *ex p.* AISSAOUI (AHMED) [1997] Imm. A.R. 184, Collins, J., QBD.

2849. Asylum–conscientious objection–Afghan war

B appealed against a decision of the Immigration Appeal Tribunal allowing the appeal of the Secretary of State against a decision of the special adjudicator allowing B's appeal against refusal of asylum. B contended that (1) the IAT had exceeded its jurisdiction by adopting a different view of the facts from that of the adjudicator, in circumstances not included in *R. v. Immigration Appeal Tribunal, ex p. Dauda No.2* [1995] Imm. A.R. 600, and (2) it had perversely ignored the adjudicator's finding that B was a conscientious objector.

Held, dismissing the application, that (1) the list of criteria in *Dauda* was not exhaustive, as evidenced by, *Assah v. Immigration Appeal Tribunal* [1994] Imm. A.R. 519, [1995] 1 C.L.Y. 2676 where the adjudicator's findings of fact were reversed on appeal. There was no evidence to support the adjudicator's decision that the authorities in Russia would now persecute B for his opposition, 10 years earlier, to the Afghan war, *Assah* and *Dauda* considered, and (2) the adjudicator had determined, in common with the IAT, that B was not a conscientious objector, but was politically opposed to the Afghan war.

BORISSOV v. SECRETARY OF STATE FOR THE HOME DEPARTMENT [1996] Imm. A.R. 524, Hirst, L.J., CA.

2850. Asylum–conscientious objection–likelihood of conscription on return giving rise to fear of persecution

T, an Algerian, appealed against a decision of the Immigration Appeal Tribunal upholding the Secretary of State's refusal of his asylum application. T had refused the military call up in Algeria on the ground that he refused to take part in a civil war and contended that the special adjudicator's findings that he would be liable to conscription if returned to Algeria but a refusal to accept that T had previously received a call up were at variance with one another.

Held, allowing the appeal and remitting the matter to the same special adjudicator, that the special adjudicator's findings as to whether T's refusal could amount to a well founded fear of persecution were unclear. The same special adjudicator could make findings of fact as to whether T would be subject to call up and whether his conscription would immediately follow a return to Algeria, it being necessary at each stage of the process for the basis of any fear of persecution to be determined.

TICHERAFI v. SECRETARY OF STATE FOR THE HOME DEPARTMENT, Trans. Ref: LTA 96/7288/D, April 18, 1997, Leggatt, L.J., CA.

2851. Asylum–domestic violence–women in fear of domestic violence not a "social group" for Convention purposes

[Convention relating to the Status of Refugees 1951 (United Nations).]

A Pakistani woman accused of adultery is not part of a "particular social group" for the purposes of claiming refugee status under the Convention relating to the Status of Refugees 1951 Art.1A(2) although her fear of severe penalties (under Sharia law) may be considered compassionate grounds for granting special leave to remain in Britain. The Secretary of State appealed against a decision in judicial review proceedings that S, a Pakistani woman, was a member of a particular social group for the purposes of the United Nations Convention relating to the Status of Refugees 1951, by reason of being liable to persecution under Sharia law as an adulteress. I appealed against a decision refusing her asylum on similar grounds. Both S and I had applied for asylum after escaping from their respective violent husbands, who had each made false allegations of adultery against them. They anticipated ostracism, isolation and violence at the hands of their husbands and lack of protection by the authorities if they returned to Pakistan.

Held, allowing the appeal by the Secretary of State and dismissing that of I, that neither of the two women showed a common uniting attribute or characteristic, separate from the persecution itself, that marked them as members of a group and, therefore, even though the persecution they feared might be real, it was not persecution for a Convention reason, *Attorney General of Canada v. Ward* [1993] 2 S.C.R. 689, *Chan v. Canada* [1996] 28 D.L.R. 213 considered and *A v. Minister for Immigration and Ethnic Affairs* (1997) 2 B.H.R.C. 143, [1997] C.L.Y 2934 and *Secretary of State for the Home Department v. Savchenkov* [1996] Imm. A.R. 28, [1996] 1 C.L.Y. 3205 approved.

R. v. IMMIGRATION APPEAL TRIBUNAL, *ex p.* SHAH; ISLAM v. SECRETARY OF STATE FOR THE HOME DEPARTMENT (1997) 2 B.H.R.C. 590, Waite, L.J., CA.

2852. Asylum–exceptional leave to remain–interests of children were not paramount–immigration history relevant

[Children Act 1989.]

B, a citizen of Bangladesh, entered a polygamous marriage with a British citizen on January 31, 1976. Four children were born, between 1978 and 1984. The husband died in 1986. Three of the children were placed in a Bangladeshi orphanage. On April 21, 1992 she was refused a certificate of right of abode in the United Kingdom because her marriage had been polygamous. In June 1992 she applied for passports for the children, together with one for a fictitious child. The four children were granted passports by reason of their late father's nationality. In August 1992 B sent the children to the United Kingdom and they were placed in care. On January 4, 1995 B arrived under a false name, claiming to be the mother of four children who were not hers. She had forged American visas and claimed to be travelling on to the United States. She was refused leave to enter, but was given temporary admission after she claimed asylum. She contacted her children and on March 28, 1995 she applied for exceptional leave to enter to be with them, using her real name. In July 1995 the children went to live with her. She was refused leave to enter on September 14, 1995. Representations were made, including a psychologist's report concerning emotional problems of two of the children. In a letter of April 30, 1996 S wrote a letter to an MP who had taken up B's case, explaining his reasons for refusing B leave to remain. These included B's immigration history and consideration of the children's circumstances; he also concluded that the children would be able to re-adapt to life in Bangladesh. After reconsideration the decision was reiterated in a letter of June 10, 1996. It was submitted that (1) B could and should have been treated as an illegal immigrant; (2) guidance policy DP/2/93 governed the case, and S was wrong to have taken B's immigration history into account; (3) S failed to give sufficient weight to the interests of the children, and (4) the interests of the children were paramount.

Held, dismissing the application, that (1) the applicant had not been treated as an illegal entrant, it was irrelevant that she could have been; (2) guidance policy DP/2/93 did not apply; (3) S had been entitled to take the immigration history into account; (4) S in the exercise of his discretion in such matters was not obliged to treat the interests of the children as paramount, and (5) although they were a factor to be taken into account the position was not the same as in courts exercising their judgment under the Children Act 1989.

R. v. SECRETARY OF STATE FOR THE HOME DEPARTMENT, *ex p.* BEGUM [1996] Imm. A.R. 582, Dyson, J., QBD.

2853. Asylum—exceptional leave to remain—no legitimate expectation that Secretary of State accept recommendation

E, a Kurdish Alevi and a Tukish citizen, was refused asylum in March 1994. E appealed to the adjudicator. The adjudicator, in a decision of January 19, 1995 concluded that E had not demonstrated the reasonable likelihood of being persecuted in Turkey for a Convention reason; with reference to an Amnesty Interntional report of February 7, 1994 and the general position of Kurds in Turkey, he concluded that there was "the risk of danger to any Kurd" which meant that E should not be returned to Turkey. He recommended that E should be granted exceptional leave to remain. The Secretary of State considered the recommendation but declined to follow it. In a letter of February 16, 1995 he indicated that he was not satisfied that "all Kurds" everywhere in Turkey had a fear of persecution, and concluded that there were parts of Turkey where people such as E could live safely. Following an application for judicial review, granted in April 1995, the Secretary of State reconsidered the recommendation but declined to follow it. On reapplication for judicial review, it was submitted that the Secretary of State was bound by findings of fact made by an adjudicator as grounds for a recommendation, and that an applicant had a legitimate expectation that the Secretary of State would be so bound.

Held, dismissing the application, that (1) an applicant had no legitimate expectation that the Secretary of State would accept an adjudicator's recommendation, only that it would be given serious consideration; (2) assessing the recommendation, the Secretary of State was not restricted to considering the material that had been before an adjudicator; (3) if he disagreed with the recommendation he was obliged to appeal against it to the Tribunal, and (4) the principle of issue estoppel had no application to such cases, *R. v. Secretary of State for the Home Department Ex p Alakesan* [1997] Imm. A.R. 315, [1996] 1 C.L.Y. 3225 followed.

R. v. SECRETARY OF STATE FOR THE HOME DEPARTMENT, *ex p.* ELHASOGLU; *sub nom.* ELHASOGLU v. SECRETARY OF STATE FOR THE HOME DEPARTMENT [1997] Imm. A.R. 380, Henry, L.J., CA.

2854. Asylum—exceptional leave to remain—refusal to renew leave—administrative decision making

[Rules of the Supreme Court Ord.53 r.4(1).]

In 1995, the Secretary of State confirmed a decision refusing to renew A's exceptional leave to remain. An application to seek judicial review out of time had been refused and A renewed his application. The judge found that there had been no adequate explanation for the delay, greatly in excess of the time limit under the Rules of the Supreme Court Ord.53 r.4(1). A, a Sri Lankan national fearing persecution, had been allowed exceptional leave from 1992 to 1994 when the Secretary of State had rejected a claim for asylum. It was argued that the

Secretary of State's reasons were absent or deficient and the decision was perverse.

Held, dismissing the application, that no adequate reason had been given for the delay and the decision made it clear that refusal had been based on the failure to establish personal or compassionate circumstances justifying exceptional leave. There were no grounds, moreover, upon which to make good the assertion of perversity. The Secretary of State was not under an obligation to give reasons for a change of view, notwithstanding no change in material circumstances, when refusing to renew exceptional leave. He was required to consider the current circumstances of a case and might or might not look at the circumstances prevailing when the earlier grant of leave had been made. He had a wide discretion. Were reasons to be required, they need only show that an applicant's case had been considered and that the decision had not been motivated by some factor which ought not to have been taken into account, *R. v. Secretary of State for the Home Department, ex p. Erdogan (Resul)* [1995] Imm. A.R. 430, [1996] 1 C.L.Y. 3207 and *Union of Construction and Allied Trades and Technicians v. Brain* [1981] I.R.L.R. 225 considered.

R. v. SECRETARY OF STATE FOR THE HOME DEPARTMENT, *ex p.* ARULANANDAM; *sub nom.* ARULANANDAM v. SECRETARY OF STATE FOR THE HOME DEPARTMENT [1996] Imm. A.R. 587, Potter, L.J., CA.

2855. **Asylum—exceptional leave to remain—Secretary of State not entitled to reject special adjudicator's findings of fact**

D's application for asylum on the grounds that his life was in danger in Iran was refused by the Secretary of State, but on appeal, the special adjudicator found that D's account of the facts pertaining to the application was true, although asylum was still refused. D applied for judicial review of the Secretary of State's refusal to grant exceptional leave to remain in the UK.

Held, allowing the application, that the Secretary of State could not reject the special adjudicator's findings of fact regarding an applicant's credibility unless he was in possession of additional material or could provide evidence that the adjudicator had been deceived, so that in the instant case, the Secretary of State's decision was irrational, *R. v. Secretary of State for the Home Department, ex p. Alakesan* [1997] Imm. A.R. 315, [1996] 1 C.L.Y. 3225 distinguished.

R. v. SECRETARY OF STATE FOR THE HOME DEPARTMENT, *ex p.* DANAEI, *The Times*, March 28, 1997, Collins, J., QBD.

2856. **Asylum—families—family as social group—mere membership did not confer refugee status—threats by drug cartel**

[Convention relating to the Status of Refugees 1951 Art.1A (United Nations); Asylum and Immigration Appeals Act 1993 s.8.]

Q, from Columbia, appealed against a decision of the Immigration Appeal Tribunal that he was not entitled to asylum. The Asylum and Immigration Appeals Act 1993 s.8 provides a right of appeal if in making the decision the UK breached its obligations under the United Nations Convention 1951. Q's stepfather had refused to trade for a drugs cartel, following which his food stall was blown up, Q's brother was persecuted and Q's cousin was shot dead, Q himself being wounded in the same attack. The issues were (1) whether membership of a particular family could constitute membership of a particular social group for the purposes of Art.1A of the Convention, and (2) whether, to qualify for protection under the Convention, Q had to show that the family as a group was persecuted for one of the reasons set out in Art.1A(2), namely relating to race, religion, nationality, or political opinion. The Secretary of State argued that Q's stepfather would have been unable to get asylum himself as his persecution was not for a Convention reason, so it would be wrong to allow Q asylum on the ground of being a member of the same family. There was no causative link between his membership of the family and the persecution. Q argued that he would not be persecuted but for his membership of the family, *R. v. Immigration Appeal Tribunal, ex p. De Melo* [1996] Imm. A.R. 43, [1996] 1 C.L.Y. 3245 relied on. In *Secretary of State for the*

Home Department v. Savchenkov [1996] Imm. A.R. 28, [1996] 1 C.L.Y. 3205, four principles governing the interpretation of the term "social group" were adopted. It was submitted that the third principle, that there should be a civil or political status reflected in the membership of the particular group, was not met. However, Q submitted that the principle was no more than a guide, *R. v. Immigration Appeal Tribunal, ex p. Syeda Shah* [1996] 1 C.L.Y. 3217.

Held, dismissing the appeal, that (1) being a member of a particular family could be membership of a particular social group for the purposes of the Convention, *Savchenkov* approved, and (2) it was necessary to show that the persecution was due to one of the Convention reasons in order to qualify for the protection sought and Q did not qualify because the fear arose from the stepfather's refusal to join the cartel.

QUIJANO v. SECRETARY OF STATE FOR THE HOME DEPARTMENT [1997] Imm. A.R. 227, Thorpe, L.J., CA.

2857. **Asylum—fear of persecution—application by Tamil fleeing Sri Lanka refused— jurisdiction of IAT to consider matters relating to internal flight alternative**

[Convention relating to the Status of Refugees 1951 (United Nations); Asylum and Immigration Appeals Act 1993 s.8.]

R, a Sri Lankan Tamil, sought judicial review of the Immigration Appeal Tribunal's decision to deny him leave to appeal against the dismissal of his appeal by the special adjudicator against the refusal of his application for asylum. The special adjudicator had held that R's past connection with the Tamil Tigers meant that whilst he had a well founded fear of persecution if he returned to the area of Sri Lanka from which he originated, no such fear could be established in relation to Colombo, to which he had travelled prior to arriving in the UK. On applying for leave to appeal, R did not include in his grounds that the special adjudicator should have considered whether it was reasonable for him to return to Colombo.

Held, dismissing the application, that where an asylum seeker had a well founded fear of persecution in relation to one area of a country, the issue of whether he could reasonably be expected to move to an area of the country where he would be safe went directly to the question of whether the applicant could properly be regarded as a refugee under the Convention relating to the Status of Refugees 1951, or whether he might properly be returned to that part of his native country in accordance with the UK's obligations under the Convention. Therefore, under the Asylum and Immigration Appeals Act 1993 s.8, the Immigration Appeal Tribunal had jurisdiction to consider the internal flight alternative when deciding whether the applicant's removal would be in breach of the Convention. While the immigration appellate bodies need not search for grounds not stated by the applicant, if there was a clear and obvious point of Convention law which might assist the applicant, but which was not used on his behalf, the appellate bodies should still apply it, although in the instant case the Immigration Appeal Tribunal had not erred in refusing R leave to appeal.

R. v. SECRETARY OF STATE FOR THE HOME DEPARTMENT, *ex p.* ROBINSON, *The Times*, August 1, 1997, Lord Woolf, M.R., CA.

2858. **Asylum—fear of persecution—claim by Tamil Sri Lankan—adjudicator erred in failing to consider reasonableness of a return to Colombo**

[European Convention on Human Rights 1950.]

P, a Tamil Sri Lankan came to the United Kingdom and claimed asylum. He was refused and appealed. The adjudicator dismissed that appeal, but recommended that P be granted exceptional leave to remain. It was decided that he did not have a well founded fear of persecution as a reason under the European Convention on Human Rights 1950 but that to return P would be "fraught with risk". Leave to appeal to the Immigration Appeal Tribunal was refused. It was submitted that (1) leave should have been granted; (2) the adjudicator should have considered first, that if P returned would he be subject to fear of persecution for a Convention reason, then if he could be returned without fear of such persecution; (3) the adjudicator did not properly consider the reasonableness of returning P, as he should have, under the Immigration Rules (HC 395) para.343 and the handbook on procedures and criteria for determining refugee status para.91, and (4) the risk to P for reasons outside of the Convention made the decision unreasonable.

Held, granting leave to appeal, that (1) it was not normally necessary when considering whether to return an applicant to one part of his country, to determine first if he had a well founded fear of persecution in another part of the country and (2) the adjudicator had failed properly to consider the issue of reasonableness, in the light of other findings, and should have granted leave to appeal.

R. v. IMMIGRATION APPEAL TRIBUNAL, *ex p.* PROBAKARAN [1996] Imm. A.R. 603, Jowitt, J., QBD.

2859. Asylum—fear of persecution—internal flight—meaning of "expect" and "reasonable" in Immigration Rules HC 395 para.343

[Asylum and Immigration Appeals Act 1993 s.8(2).]

S and H, husband wife, were citizens of Pakistan. They lived for a time in Karachi. They said they suffered persecution there and in October 1990 their house was burnt down. They then moved to Rawalpindi, where they had lived previously to arrange their affairs. In June 1991 they obtained visas for a single visit to the UK, and arrived on September 13, 1991. On September 24, 1991 they submitted a claim for asylum. On August 22, 1994, the Secretary of State refused their claim, on the ground that they had the option of internal flight in Pakistan, to Rawalpindi, and had no well founded fear of persecution for a Convention reason. They successfully appealed under the Asylum and Immigration Appeals Act 1993 s. 8(2). The adjudicator's decision was that given their circumstances, especially their medical condition, it would be unreasonable to expect them to return to Rawalpindi. On appeal the Tribunal reversed the decision on July 15, 1996. S and H appealed. It was submitted that the Immigration Rules (HC 395) para.343 was ambiguous as to the meaning of "unreasonable" and "expect". It was argued that the Tribunal had not been entitled to reverse the decision of the adjudicator as to whether the Secretary of State had been reasonable in expecting H and S to return to Rawalpindi.

Held, dismissing the appeal, that (1) para.343 concerning internal flight, "expect" meant "require" and it was the decision maker who had to be reasonable, the question was not whether it was a reasonable course for the appellant to take; (2) there was no ambiguity in para.343, and (3) there was nothing in the medical reports to suggest that the health of H or S would be adversely affected if they returned to Rawalpindi, on the facts the Tribunal was entitled to reverse the decision of the adjudicator.

R. v. SECRETARY OF STATE FOR THE HOME DEPARTMENT, *ex p.* IKHLAQ; *sub nom.* IKHLAQ v. SECRETARY OF STATE FOR THE HOME DEPARTMENT [1997] Imm. A.R. 404, Staughton, L.J., CA.

2860. Asylum—fear of persecution—religious discrimination against Coptic Christians

D, a citizen of the Sudan and a Coptic Christian, appealed against a decision of the Immigration Appeal Tribunal overturning the special adjudicator's decision allowing D political asylum. D arrived in the UK in June 1988 initially on a six months' visitor's visa and applied for political asylum in December 1990. Following the military coup in the Sudan in June 1989, introducing an Islamic military state, there have been systematic human rights abuses particularly against the Christians. D claimed that he had a well founded fear of persecution on the basis that he would face brutal interrogation as a returned political asylum seeker and he produced as evidence a document purporting to be an order to all chief border officers that anyone returning to Sudan after a year or more away should be interrogated. The Secretary of State claimed that document to be a forgery, citing evidence from external security services and the Government of Sudan. It was observed that it was natural for those sources to claim that the document asserting such a policy was a forgery. Despite some discrepancy regarding D's intentions on first arriving in the UK and the delay before his application for political asylum, the special adjudicator found that his evidence regarding treatment of Christians in Sudan was supported by documentary evidence and that D had discharged the burden of proof upon him that he was likely to face persecution if he returned to Sudan. The Secretary of State claimed that whilst D undoubtedly suffered discrimination as a Christian in Sudan there was no evidence that he would suffer persecution. He pointed to the fact that members of D's family continued to reside in Sudan apparently without persecution.

Held, allowing the appeal and restoring the decision of the special adjudicator, that the tribunal's decision was manifestly misdirected in law. There was no significant material available which was not before the special adjudicator necessitating a fresh hearing. The tribunal's conclusion that there was no evidence to suggest that D would face interrogation and persecution on returning to Sudan was not a fair conclusion to draw from the evidence before it. The tribunal gave too much weight to the evidence that the document submitted by D was a forgery and insufficient weight to all contrary evidence.

SECRETARY OF STATE FOR THE HOME DEPARTMENT v. DRRIAS, Trans. Ref: IATRF 96/1776/D, March 6, 1997, Thorpe, L.J., CA.

2861. Asylum–fear of persecution–safe region existed in country from which applicant fled

A, a Tamil, re-applied for leave to judicially review a decision refusing him leave to appeal against the decision of the special adjudicator upholding the refusal of asylum. A had moved to Colombo from Jaffna province before flying to the UK.

Held, dismissing the re-application, that A had failed to satisfy the burden of proof in demonstrating that Colombo was unsafe and that he feared persecution. In accordance with the rules an application for asylum might be refused if the applicant was able to move to a safe part of the country from which he was fleeing, *Imad Ali El Tanoukhi v. Secretary of State for the Home Department* [1993] Imm. A.R. 71, [1993] C.L.Y. 2230 and *R. v. Secretary of State for the Home Department, ex p. David Siril Vigna* [1993] Imm. A.R. 93, [1993] C.L.Y. 2232 followed.

R. v. IMMIGRATION APPEAL TRIBUNAL, *ex p.* ANANDANADARAJAH [1996] Imm. A.R. 514, Hobhouse, L.J., CA.

2862. Asylum–fear of persecution–safety of return–return to restricted area inappropriate

V applied for judicial review of a decision of the Immigration Appeal Tribunal refusing leave to appeal against the decision that V was not a refugee and refusing him asylum. V was a Tamil from Sri Lanka. Although he was not a supporter of any Tamil separatist movement, he and his family had suffered ill treatment and persecution. V claimed asylum on arriving in the UK. The special adjudicator found on the evidence that V's fear of persecution were he to return to Sri Lanka was justified at the time of application, but that the conduct of the government of Sri Lanka meant that now V had no grounds for fear of persecution in the government controlled areas of Sri Lanka. V argued (1) that the special adjudicator had no material on which to base his conclusion of safe return, and (2) that even if the special adjudicator had grounds for concluding as he did, he did not apply the correct test to determine whether it was reasonable to expect V to return to a restricted part of Sri Lanka.

Held, allowing the application and quashing the decision, that (1) the special adjudicator did not adequately deal with the reasons for his conclusion. He relied on the findings in *R v. Secretary of State for the Home Department Ex P. Sandralingham* [1996] Imm. App. R. 97, [1996] 1 C.L.Y. 3241 and information provided by the UNHCR regarding improved human rights in Sri Lanka. That material, however, referred in particular to certain groups of people and not necessarily someone in V's position, so it was inappropriate to transpose those conclusions to V. The special adjudicator was obliged to consider evidence regarding the situation in Sri Lanka at the time of the appeal hearing,

Sandralingham considered, and (2) the special adjudicator had erred in law by not considering adequately whether it was reasonable to expect V to return to an area of Sri Lanka from which he did not come and to which he would be restricted. Paragraph 343 of the Immigration Rules HC 395 set out the appropriate test that should have been considered.

R. v. SECRETARY OF STATE FOR THE HOME DEPARTMENT, *ex p.* VIJENDRANN, Trans. Ref: CO/2503/95, January 15, 1997, Latham, J., QBD.

2863. Asylum–fear of persecution–tribal violence–definition of persecution

[Convention Relating to the Status of Refugees 1951 (United Nations).]

K, a Kenyan citizen, a Kikuyu, arrived in the UK direct from Nairobi on a flight paid for by his uncle on February 26, 1995. He claimed asylum on arrival. By a letter dated July 24, 1995, the Secretary of State informed him that his application had been refused and that he had not established a well-founded fear of persecution under the terms of the United Nations Convention 1951. K's appeal was dismissed by the special adjudicator in a decision of January 31, 1996, for the same reason. K was then granted leave to appeal to the tribunal, which dismissed the appeal on April 29, 1996, for the same reason. K appealed. K had lived in the Rift Valley. There he and his family were attacked by members of the Kalenjin tribe. He and his family were moved to a camp, then finally to another. It was submitted that (1) K had a well founded fear of persecution because he was a Kikuyu; (2) the adjudicator and the tribunal had interpreted the word "persecution" too narrowly, and had therefore erred in law, and (3) the tribunal's conclusion was wrong in law and therefore not one that a reasonable tribunal could have arrived at. It was argued in response that "persecution" was an ordinary English word, *Brutus v. Cozens* [1973] A.C. 85, [1972] C.L.Y. 706 relied on, and it was for the adjudicator to decide whether the facts amounted to persecution for a Convention reason.

Held, dismissing the appeal, that (1) following *Cozens* the meaning of an ordinary English word was a matter of fact, not law; (2) there was no universally accepted meaning of "persecution" and therefore the adjudicator had to give the word its ordinary English meaning, then decide, looking at the matter in the round and taking all relevant circumstances into account, whether a well-founded fear of persecution for Convention reasons existed, *R. v. Secretary of State for the Home Department, ex p. Ravichandran (No.3)* [1996] Imm. A.R. 97, [1997] C.L.Y. 2867 followed; (3) it was not for the court to substitute another meaning for the word persecution: the adjudicator's conclusions were matters of fact and could only be challenged on *Wednesbury* principles, and (4) the adjudicator had to look towards the future, K could return to the camp, there was no evidence of continuing harrassment, the adjudicator's conclusions were therefore not *Wednesbury* unreasonable.

KAGEMA v. SECRETARY OF STATE FOR THE HOME DEPARTMENT [1997] Imm. A.R. 137, Aldous, L.J., CA.

2864. Asylum–fear of persecution–whether fear of persecution had to be current or whether past fear might suffice

[Convention relating to the Status of Refugees 1951 (United Nations) Art.1A.]

A and others, asylum seekers unable to return to their country of origin, appealed against decisions of the Immigration Appeal Tribunal that they were not entitled to refugee status. A argued that under the Convention relating to the Status of Refugees 1951 Art.1A(2) a person seeking to become a refugee need not show a current well founded fear of persecution in his home country, but had only to demonstrate that at some point in the past he had been caused to go abroad or remain abroad due to such fear of persecution. The Secretary of State submitted that the phrase in Art.1A(2) that "owing to a well founded fear of being persecuted [a person] was outside his country of nationality" was to be construed as meaning that the fear had to exist at the time his claim was determined.

Held, allowing A's appeal, that there were a number of distinct advantages in being recognised as a refugee which were not conferred upon asylum seekers, including irremovability, entitlement to travel abroad, to claim statutory benefits and to obtain indefinite leave to remain after four years. Article 1A(2) was not to be interpreted as restrictively as the Secretary of State contended and an asylum seeker who was unable to return to his country of origin might be entitled to refugee status provided that the fear of past persecution that caused him to flee remained effective as a cause of his continued presence in the UK.

ADAN v. SECRETARY OF STATE FOR THE HOME DEPARTMENT; NOOH v. SECRETARY OF STATE FOR THE HOME DEPARTMENT; LAZAREVIC v. SECRETARY OF STATE FOR THE HOME DEPARTMENT; RADIVOJEVIC v. SECRETARY OF STATE FOR THE HOME DEPARTMENT [1997] 1 W.L.R. 1107, Simon Brown, L.J., CA.

2865. Asylum—fresh claim—appropriate test

K, a citizen of Turkey, sought judicial review of the Secretary of State's decision rejecting his suggestion that he had made a fresh application for asylum. K submitted a number of letters and documents to the Secretary of State to support his claim that he conscientiously objected to military service and that he was the subject of a warrant of arrest in Turkey leading to his fear of persecution if he were to be returned. Evidence relating to these matters had previously been rejected by a special adjudicator as not being credible. K contended that had the new evidence been submitted to the special adjudicator for consideration there was a reasonable prospect that his application would have been successful. It was argued that the Secretary of State had erred in concluding that the application for asylum was not fresh and that this error was open to judicial review. K submitted, in reliance upon *Ladd v. Marshall* [1954] 3 All E.R. 745, [1954] C.L.Y. 2507, that in the context of applications for asylum new evidence should be considered by the court.

Held, dismissing the application, that the evidence submitted to the Secretary of State did not constitute new material amounting to a fresh application for asylum. Following *R. v. Secretary of State for the Home Department, ex p. Onibiyo* [1996] Q.B. 768, [1996] 1 C.L.Y. 3242, where a fresh application was dependant on new material it must satisfy tests, analogous to those in *Ladd v. Marshall*, of previous unavailability, significance and credibility. On the facts the new evidence failed to satisfy the test of previous unavailability as it could reasonably have been obtained to support K's previous application for asylum. Had the material amounted to a fresh application the court would have had no power to intervene in the Secretary of State's decision as he had not erred in rejecting K's suggestion that had the application been submitted to a special adjudicator a different view would have been formed of K's credibility.

R. v. SECRETARY OF STATE FOR THE HOME DEPARTMENT, *ex p.* KABALA, Trans. Ref: FC3 97/6014/D, June 12, 1997, Judge, L.J., CA.

2866. Asylum—fresh claim—appropriate test

Y, a Peruvian citizen, came to the UK in December 1992, seeking leave to enter as a visitor. This was refused, but she was given temporary admission for 20 days. She applied for asylum which was refused on the grounds that it had not been accepted that Y was entitled to refugee status. Y gave notice of appeal. In May 1995 Y met a British citizen, who she married in January 1996. In December 1995 Y made a very detailed statement to her advisers with regard to the asylum claim. There was one critical addition to her story, which was her account of having been raped during the three or four days detention in January 1988 she had referred to initially. Between her marriage on January 3 and the appointed date of the hearing, on January 8, Y telephoned to withdraw the asylum appeal. On February 22, the Immigration Advisory Service, acting for Y, wrote to the Home Office seeking leave for her to remain on the basis of the marriage. This application was refused in March 1996. Further representations were then made on Y's behalf on the basis of asylum, including the statement made in December 1995. In a letter of July 29, 1996, the Secretary of State refused Y's renewed claim for asylum, and refused to accept it as constituting a fresh claim giving rise to rights of appeal to an adjudicator should it be refused. It was submitted that it had been this decision which had been

Wednesbury unreasonable. He should have treated the further representations as a fresh claim, and the letter showed he had failed to apply the acid test laid down in *R. v. Secretary of State for the Home Department, ex p. Onibiyo* [1996] Q.B. 768, [1996] 1 C.L.Y. 3242.

Held, refusing the renewed application for leave to move for judicial review, that (1) the acid test to be applied by the Secretary of State in determining if a fresh claim had been made was laid down in *Onibiyo* and refined in *R. v. Secretary of State for the Home Department, ex p. Ravichandran (No. 2)* [1996] Imm. A.R. 418, [1996] 1 C.L.Y. 3241; (2) it was for the Secretary of State to decide if a fresh claim had been made and his decision could only be challenged on *Wednesbury* grounds, and (3) applying those principles there was nothing unreasonable in the Secretary of State's decision.

R. v. SECRETARY OF STATE FOR THE HOME DEPARTMENT, *ex p.* WARD; *sub nom.* WARD v. SECRETARY OF STATE FOR THE HOME DEPARTMENT [1997] Imm. A.R. 236, Simon Brown, L.J., CA.

2867. Asylum–fresh claim–Secretary of State's conclusion that no fresh application made

[European Convention on Human Rights 1950 Art.3.]

R and S were Sri Lankan citizens. They arrived in the UK in July 1993 and unsuccessfully claimed asylum. Appeals were made to the adjudicator, the tribunal, then the Court of Appeal. On February 12, 1996 the House of Lords refused leave to appeal. On March 1, 1996, fresh leave was granted on the basis of a fresh asylum claim that was not being considered by the Secretary of State. The substantive application was heard on April 1, 1996. The judge concluded, following *R. v. Secretary of State for the Home Department, ex p. Onibiyo* [1996] Imm. A.R. 370, [1996] 1 C.L.Y. 3242, that the Secretary of State, in deciding that there had been no fresh claim in either case, had misdirected himself as to the proper test to be applied. The decision was therefore quashed and referred back to the Secretary of State. In a decision of September 19, 1996, expanded in a letter of September 23, the Secretary of State again decided that there was in fact no fresh application, in doing so he relied on the tribunal decision in *Nitsingham* (Unreported). It was argued that he had erred in placing reliance on *Nitsingham*, since 21 decisions by special adjudicators had come to a contrary conclusion, and that he had been therefore *Wednesbury* unreasonable. It was submitted that (1) in any event, whether or not there was a fresh application was for the court to decide on "precedent fact" basis, and (2) to send R and S back to Sri Lanka would be a breach of the European Convention on Human Rights 1950 Art.3.

Held, refusing the judicial review application, that (1) following views expressed in *Onibiyo* and *R. v. Secretary of State for the Home Department, ex p. Ravichandran (No.2)* [1996] Imm. A.R. 418, [1996] 1 C.L.Y. 3241, where the Secretary of State's decision as to whether there had been a fresh claim was challenged, it was not for the court to enquire into the precedent facts; (2) the Secretary of State had been entitled to give the weight he did to the tribunal's decision in *Nitsingham*, to which special adjudicators would give careful regard, his decisions were not *Wednesbury* unreasonable, and (3) the argument relating to the European Convention of Human Rights was an attempt to repeat the persecution point and added nothing.

R. v. SECRETARY OF STATE FOR THE HOME DEPARTMENT, *ex p.* RAVICHANDRAN (NO.3); R. v. SECRETARY OF STATE FOR THE HOME DEPARTMENT, *ex p.* SANDRALINGHAM (NO.3) [1997] Imm. A.R. 74, Jowitt, J., QBD.

2868. Asylum–fresh claim–Secretary of State's decision that second application based on new information did not constitute fresh asylum claim was not appealable

[Asylum and Immigration Appeals Act 1993 s.8.]

Following the refusal of his application for leave to enter the UK on asylum grounds, C made another application for asylum based on new information, but the Secretary of State found that C's representations did not constitute a fresh claim for asylum and refused to treat it as such. C served the Secretary of State with a purported notice of appeal to a special adjudicator from his refusal to allow C's claim to refugee status, but the Secretary of State replied that his decision was not appealable. C then served the notice of appeal on the Immigration Appellate Authority (IAA) and sought leave to apply for judicial review of the decision to remove him notwithstanding his appeal against the refusal of his second asylum claim. The Secretary of State applied for an order of prohibition preventing IAA from hearing C's appeal and for declaratory and ancillary relief.

Held, granting a declaration that the special adjudicator had no jurisdiction to entertain C's purported appeal and that the notice of appeal had no effect, that the Secretary of State had a sole and unappealable right to determine whether further representations by an applicant constituted a fresh asylum application, subject only to challenge by way of judicial review. The special adjudicator only had jurisdiction to hear appeals from decisions of the Secretary of State that fell within the Asylum and Immigration Appeals Act 1993 s.8 and until the Secretary of State accepted that a fresh application had been made, no decision falling within s.8 could arise.

R. v. SPECIAL ADJUDICATOR, *ex p.* SECRETARY OF STATE FOR THE HOME DEPARTMENT; R. v. SECRETARY OF STATE FOR THE HOME DEPARTMENT, *ex p.* CAKABAY; *sub nom.* R. v. IMMIGRATION APPELLATE AUTHORITY, *ex p.* SECRETARY OF STATE FOR THE HOME DEPARTMENT, *The Times*, November 25, 1997, Lightman, J., QBD.

2869. **Asylum–fresh claim–test to determine whether submission of new evidence amounted to fresh claim**

B's application for asylum in the UK was refused when both the Secretary of State and the special adjudicator took the view that an arrest warrant which B, a Turkish Kurd, presented in support of his application was a forgery. B's solicitors subsequently received another warrant for his arrest, purporting to have been issued in Turkey in respect of B's involvement in an illegal organisation, which they then submitted to an immigration officer. B successfully applied for judicial review of the Secretary of State's refusal to consider the new evidence as a fresh claim for asylum and the Secretary of State appealed.

Held, dismissing the appeal, that the Secretary of State had two questions to determine: (1) whether the new claim was a fresh claim, and (2) if so, whether it should be rejected. Given that an applicant had no right of appeal against a decision on the first question, it was important that the two questions were kept separate. Following *R. v. Secretary of State for the Home Department, ex p. Onibiyo* [1996] Q.B. 768, [1996] 1 C.L.Y. 3242, a new claim had to be sufficiently different from the first claim so as to allow a realistic prospect that a favourable view could be taken despite the first unsuccessful claim, and any fresh evidence submitted had to satisfy the test in *Ladd v. Marshall* [1954] 1 W.L.R. 1489, [1954] C.L.Y. 2507 of being significant, credible and not previously available. In the instant case, the evidence satisfied that test and was apparently credible. Any evidence submitted by the Secretary of State to refute its credibility should have been directed to the second question, and was not an answer to the question of whether there was a fresh claim.

R. v. SECRETARY OF STATE FOR THE HOME DEPARTMENT, *ex p.* BOYBEYI, *The Times*, June 5, 1997, Nourse, L.J., CA.

2870. **Asylum–fresh evidence and fresh claim–review of "acid test"**

[Immigration Act 1971 s.21.]

H, a citizen of Iran, arrived in the UK in February 1994. He claimed asylum on the ground that he had a well founded fear of persecution as a member of the banned Mujahidin movement, and that his brother had been imprisoned and then executed for such activity and he himself had been subsequently interrogated and tortured. The claim was rejected in March 1994 and on appeal by a special adjudicator in September 1994. The adjudicator considered that H had not told the truth and had failed to prove a well founded fear of persecution for a Convention reason. From January 1996, fresh representations were made on behalf of H, stating that he conceded that his original story had been false, and that his true reason for fleeing to the UK had been pro monarchist activity in the Iran-Paad party. The Secretary of State was asked to review the case but he declined, and declined to remit it to a special adjudicator under the Immigration Act 1971 s.21. By way of judicial review it was submitted that H had made a fresh claim for asylum and that the Secretary of State had erred in not considering it as such. The court reviewed the authorities relating to the "acid test" for circumstances in which the Secretary of State was obliged to consider such a request based on fresh evidence as a fresh claim for asylum, giving rise in turn to a right of appeal on refusal.

Held, dismissing the application, that (1) the principles to be derived from the authorities were: (a) the Secretary of State was obliged to give genuine consideration to every potentially genuine asylum claim even when an applicant had unsuccessfully made such a claim previously; (b) mere repeat applications were prohibited by the immigration rules; (c) whatever the reasons for rejecting a previous claim, if evidence was advanced of a new, relevant and substantial change in circumstances which could not have been reasonably advanced earlier, the Secretary of State was obliged to entertain the new claim unless the new evidence was not credible or not capable of producing a different outcome even when accepted, and (d) the Secretary of State could not reasonably refuse to entertain an application for asylum to which none of these exceptions applied; (2) in the instant case the fresh evidence could have been advanced earlier, and (3) this was not a case in which the Secretary of State would be unreasonable not to refer the case back to an adjudicator under the 1971 Act, s.21.

R. v. SECRETARY OF THE HOME DEPARTMENT, *ex p.* HABIBI [1997] Imm. A.R. 391, Sedley, J., QBD.

2871. **Asylum–medical treatment–applicant and daughter found to be HIV positive–less adequate medical facilities in own country–no overriding exceptional circumstances**

[European Convention on Human Rights 1950 Art.3.]

L, a Ugandan citizen, came to the UK in July 1993, and sought asylum, claiming a well founded fear of persecution under the Convention. This was based on living with her father who was, unlike her, involved in politics and opposed to the Ugandan government at the time. At the time of her flight she was unaware that she was pregnant. L's application was considered by the Secretary of State and refused. She appealed to the special adjudicator who dismissed her appeal in June 1995 and the tribunal refused leave to appeal. Her daughter had been born, on January 31, 1994, and both mother and baby were found to be HIV positive in May 1994. L renewed her application for asylum, based upon the exceptional grounds that she and her child were HIV positive. The application was considered and finally refused in November 1995. It was clear that the Secretary of State was aware of the details of the case, but had not found sufficient grounds to justify overturning the original decision. The Secretary of State held that "it would not be fair or proper to treat HIV and AIDS sufferers differently from persons suffering from other medical conditions...". An application for leave to move for judicial review was refused. On a renewed application it was argued that the refusal had been *Wednesbury* unreasonable; the medical facilities in Uganda were inferior to those available in the UK and would not be available to L in her circumstances. Both L and her daughter would have a reduced lifespan in Uganda; to return L to Uganda would subject her to inhuman treatment, contrary to European Convention on Human Rights 1950 Art.3.

Held, dismissing renewed application for judicial review, that (1) although inferior to those in the UK, medical facilities were available throughout Uganda; it was not unreasonable for the Secretary of State to require L's return, but the absence of such facilities might cause the court to take a different view; (2) the possible reduction in lifespan was not in itself a reason against returning L and her daughter to Uganda; (3) the position of L and her daughter was shared by many in Uganda and there were therefore no exceptional circumstances in their case, and (4) their return would not contravene the Convention.

R. v. SECRETARY OF STATE FOR THE HOME DEPARTMENT, *ex p.* I [1997] Imm. A.R. 172, Butler-Sloss, L.J., CA.

2872. **Asylum–refugees–employees sharing common employment did not constitute "particular social group" for Convention purposes**

[Convention relating to the Status of Refugees 1951 Art.1A (United Nations).]

A body of people linked only by their employment does not constitute a "particular social group" for the purposes of the Convention Relating to the Status of Refugees 1951 Art.1A(2). The Secretary of State appealed against a determination of the Immigration Appeal Tribunal that O, a citizen of Algeria, was eligible for asylum on the ground that her membership of a particular social group, within the terms of the Convention relating to the Status of Refugees 1951 Art.1A(2), gave rise to a well founded fear of persecution should she be returned to Algeria. O's duties as a midwife employed by the Algerian Ministry of Health included giving advice on contraception, and O claimed that this put her in danger from Islamic fundamentalists, from whom the authorities were unable to provide protection. The Secretary of State contended that employees sharing a common employer or a common employment did not form a "particular social group" for the purposes of the Convention.

Held, allowing the appeal, that a body of people linked only by their employment did not constitute a particular social group for the purposes of Art.1A(2), *Secretary of State for the Home Department v. Savchenkov* [1996] Imm. A.R. 28, [1996] 1 C.L.Y. 3205 considered. The characteristic that defined a "particular social group" was that its members should not be required to change their behaviour or beliefs because they were fundamental to their individual identities or conscience, and a common employment, such as shared duties in midwifery, did not have such an impact.

OUANES v. SECRETARY OF STATE FOR THE HOME DEPARTMENT; *sub nom.* SECRETARY OF STATE FOR THE HOME DEPARTMENT v. OUANES, *The Times,* November 26, 1997, Pill, L.J., CA.

2873. **Asylum–safe third country–France–Secretary of State was entitled to conclude that France was safe country in spite of views of special adjudicators**

[Asylum and Immigration Act 1996 s.2; Convention relating to the Status of Refugees 1951 (United Nations).]

C, a Turkish Kurd who had claimed political asylum upon her arrival in the UK from Paris, appealed against the dismissal of her application for judicial review of the Secretary of State's decision to issue a certificate pursuant to the Asylum and Immigration Act 1996 s.2(2) authorising C's removal to France as a safe country for investigation of the merits of her asylum claim. Before the removal of their jurisdiction by the 1996 Act, special adjudicators had indicated in some appeals that they were not satisfied that France was a safe country in terms of the requirement that it was one which would not return an asylum seeker to a country where he alleged he would suffer persecution other than in accordance with the Convention relating to the Status of Refugees 1951.

Held, dismissing the appeal, that the Secretary of State had to assure himself that there was no real risk that France would return C to another country except in accordance with the Convention. A remote possibility that the relevant law or procedures in France might change or the unpredictability of human behaviour did not constitute a real risk. The court, unlike the special adjudicators, could not make a decision based upon the merits of the case, but could only review whether, on the material before him, the Secretary of State could properly have reached the conclusion he did. On that basis, the Secretary of State was entitled to form the opinion he did and the court could not interfere with his decision.

R. v. SECRETARY OF STATE FOR THE HOME DEPARTMENT, *ex p.* CANBOLAT; *sub nom.* CANBOLAT v. SECRETARY OF STATE FOR THE HOME DEPARTMENT [1997] 1 W.L.R. 1569, Lord Woolf, M.R., CA.

2874. Asylum—safe third country—Germany—decision contrary to other special adjudicators' decisions—decision validly made on basis of material presented—no duty to give reasons for disagreement

K applied for judicial review of a special adjudicator's decision finding that Germany was a safe third country. K submitted that, in view of other special adjudicators' findings to the contrary, the special adjudicator in the instant case should have given reasons for his decision and in particular made reference to his reasons for disagreeing with them.

Held, dismissing the application, that although no specific reference was made by the special adjudicator to previous contrary decisions, it was apparent he was aware of differing conclusions on the point in issue. The adjudicator did not have to specifically state he was aware of contrary views nor that he disagreed with them. The special adjudicator was required to make his decision on the material before him. He must be aware of the decisions, but there was no duty to analyse and justify the previous decision if the material enabled him to reach that particular decision, *R. v. Secretary of State for the Home Department, ex p. Gnanavarathan* [1995] Imm. A.R. 64 [1995] 1 C.L.Y. 2705 considered and *R. v. Special Adjudicator, ex p. Kanapathypillai* [1996] Imm. A.R. 116, [1996] 1 C.L.Y. 3233 followed.

R. v. SECRETARY OF STATE FOR THE HOME DEPARTMENT, *ex p.* KUMAR (SINATHAMBY) [1996] Imm. A.R. 385, Popplewell, J., QBD.

2875. Asylum—safe third country—Ghana

[Immigration Act 1971 Sch.2.]

W applied for judicial review of a decision of the Secretary of State refusing him exceptional leave to remain and refusing leave to appeal against the refusal of asylum. W entered from Ghana claiming to be a Liberian and was granted exceptional leave to remain because of the Liberian civil war in which his parents had allegedly been killed. W contended that Ghana was not a safe third country, because it had no established procedure for asylum seekers and had not cooperated with the UNHCR. W contended that he was likely to be returned to Liberia and that the Secretary of State had acted contrary to policy as stated in the House of Commons.

Held, dismissing the application, that once W's asylum application had been refused, the question of whether or not Ghana was a safe third country became redundant and his position fell to be determined under the Immigration Act 1971 Sch.2 para 8.1. New policy had been introduced on July 24, 1996 which required that only if the Secretary of State had failed to consider exceptional compassionate circumstances which were likely to alter his decision could the special adjudicator's recommendation be acted upon.

R. v. SECRETARY OF STATE FOR THE HOME DEPARTMENT, *ex p.* WILLIAMS, Trans. Ref: CO/294/97, March 12, 1997, Hidden, J., QBD.

2876. Asylum—safe third country—Sweden—adjudicator correct to order return of applicant

G, a native of Somalia, arrived in the UK from Sweden, which she had reached from Kenya about 14 days previously, and claimed asylum. The Secretary of State concluded that the claim was without foundation and fell to be considered by Sweden, and refused the application. G appealed to the special adjudicator, who was to determine whether or not Sweden was a safe third country. In an application for leave to apply for judicial review, G submitted that (1) the question had been one of fact, not of law; (2) the adjudicator had not satisfied himself that Sweden was a safe third country, but only that the Secretary of State was thus satisfied; (3) the adjudicator had failed to approach the matter in the manner required by the judgment of *R. v. Secretary of State for the Home Department, ex p. Mehari* [1994] Q.B. 474, [1994] C.L.Y. 2454, and (4) the adjudicator had failed to give adequate reasons for his findings upon disputed evidence, as suggested by *R. v. Special Adjudicator, ex p. Gnanavarathan* [1995] Imm A.R. 64, [1995] 1 C.L.Y. 2705. With reference to a letter from the Swedish Immigration Board of January 25, 1996, which had been before the Secretary of State, stating that G "will probably be returned to Britain immediately at the Swedish border", it was argued that declining to change the decision to return G to Sweden was *Wednesbury* unreasonable.

Held, refusing the application for leave to apply for judicial review, that (1) the words of an adjudicator's decision should not be taken out of context; (2) the words of such a decision should not be treated as the words of a statute; (3) read as a whole it was clear the adjudicator's decision had considered the matter correctly, and (4) the Secretary of State's decision to return G to Sweden was not *Wednesbury* unreasonable, despite the letter from the Swedish Immigration Board.

R. v. SECRETARY OF STATE FOR THE HOME DEPARTMENT, *ex p.* GUHAD [1997] Imm. A.R. 1, Jowitt, J., QBD.

2877. Asylum–safe third country–USA–asylum seekers as social group

[Asylum and Immigration Act 1996 s.2(2); Convention relating to the Status of Refugees 1951 (United Nations).]

A, a citizen of Ecuador, arrived in the UK on March 9, 1997 from Ecuador. He had had to change planes in Miami and there his passport had been stamped to say he was in transit without a visa. He remained airside and was not granted admission to the US. He allegedly did not come into contact with any immigration official. On arrival in the UK he claimed asylum. The Secretary of State certified his claim under Asylum and Immigration Act 1996 s.2(2), maintaining that A would not be threatened for a Convention reason in the US and would be treated there in accordance with the United Nations Convention 1951. A applied for leave to move for judicial review. It was submitted that the Secretary of State had been in breach of his own policy announced to Parliament during the passing of the 1996 Act, that applicants who had remained airside during a transit period in a third country would not normally be returned to that country. It was argued that A had not been admitted to the US, that the stamp on his passport indicated this and that he would not be able to make an application for asylum on his return. It was argued that if A's claim were entertained he would be detained pending a decision, which would in the circumstances be persecution under the Convention because as an asylum seeker A was a member of a social group within the Convention. The Secretary of State contested A's statement that he had not come into contact with an immigration official in Miami.

Held, dismissing the application, that (1) the Secretary of State had not been *Wednesbury* unreasonable in making his decision, which was not contrary to his policy on passengers who had only been in transit in third safe countries as announced during the passage of the 1996 Act, and A's version of events in Miami was contested; (2) there was no evidence that the US would not observe its obligations under the Convention, and would at worst return A to the UK, and (3) the submission that asylum seekers were a social group within the Convention and that detention in the circumstances was persecution under the Convention could not be sustained.

R. v. SECRETARY OF STATE FOR THE HOME DEPARTMENT, *ex p.* ARIAS [1997] Imm. A.R. 385, Collins, J., QBD.

2878. Asylum seekers–deportation to state where previously tortured

See HUMAN RIGHTS: Alan v. Switzerland. §2755

2879. Asylum seekers–detention–duty of care of immigration officers

W appealed against an order dismissing his claim for damages against the Home Office for negligent detention. W, from Liberia, came to the UK seeking asylum. He was detained pending consideration of his application. A Liberian Nationality Test undertaken by another person was placed on W's file in error causing the Home Office to doubt that he was a national of Liberia. On discovering the error W was released from detention and granted temporary admission. W argued that his detention was caused by the negligence of the Home Office or its servants in failing to ask the right questions, or failing to require him to sit the nationality test, and by placing another person's test on his file. W argued that he had been negligently detained and that a negligent exercise of a statutory power gave rise to a cause of action in negligence.

Held, dismissing the appeal, that immigration officers do not owe a duty of care to immigrants as that would be inconsistent with the proper performance of their statutory duties. It would not be fair and reasonable to impose liability for negligence on an immigration officer performing his public duty. No cause of action in negligence arose from the negligent performance of an act authorised by statute unless there was, in addition, a common law duty of care, *X (Minors) v. Bedfordshire CC* [1995] 2 A.C. 633, [1995] 1 C.L.Y. 3452 considered.

Observed, that if W had established liability, damages would have been recoverable.

W v. HOME OFFICE [1997] Imm. A.R. 302, Lord Woolf, M.R., CA.

2880. Asylum seekers–detention–Polish gypsies–breach of temporary admission conditions

B and G, Polish citizens of gypsy racial origins, sought judicial review of decisions to detain them pending the outcome of their respective asylum applications. B's wife and five children who arrived with him had been granted temporary admission and G had been granted temporary admission on condition that she reside with her father and brother. However, following a magistrates' court appearance on a theft charge, it was discovered that she was residing elsewhere. Both B and G submitted that they had been detained due to their gypsy status, and that the decision to detain was unreasonable, given the published policy on detaining asylum seekers. G also submitted that the decision to detain her revealed an element of retribution for her court appearance.

Held, dismissing the applications, that the decisions to detain B and G were not part of a blanket policy either to detain or refuse asylum applications from Polish gypsies, even though such applications were dealt with under accelerated procedures involving detention for effective immigration control. B's detention had occurred as a result of his stated intention to seek casual work in the UK, in contravention of temporary admission conditions. G's detention occurred due to her breach of residence conditions, which was revealed at her court appearance, and was not due to the dishonesty offence. In both cases, the detention decisions did not reveal unreasonableness on the part of the decision maker, but stemmed from a correct interpretation of the policy requirements that detention was necessary for those failing to comply with temporary entry conditions or showing a blatant disregard for immigration law.

R. v. SECRETARY OF STATE FOR THE HOME DEPARTMENT, *ex p.* BREZINSKI; R. v. SECRETARY OF STATE FOR THE HOME DEPARTMENT, *ex p.* GLOWACKA, Trans. Ref: CO/4251/95, CO/4237/95, July 19, 1996, Kay, J., QBD.

2881. Asylum seekers–employment–policy refusing to permit asylum seekers to obtain employment pending appeal hearing–no entitlement to social security benefits–Secretary of State acted ultra vires in pursuing policy

Held, that the Secretary of State had acted ultra vires in pursuing his policy of refusing to permit asylum seekers to obtain employment pending the hearing of their appeals against the refusal of asylum when they were unable to claim social security benefits. The policy constituted an unjustifiable interference with the appeal rights of those seeking asylum, since, unable to support themselves, applicants might be denied the opportunity to pursue their appeals. Further, a policy that deprived applicants of the right to work during the fixed period between the date of the refusal of the application and the date of the appeal hearing had to be regarded as irrational. Accordingly, the policy fell to be reconsidered by the Secretary of State.

R. v. SECRETARY OF STATE FOR THE HOME DEPARTMENT, *ex p.* JAMMEH; R. v. SECRETARY OF STATE FOR THE HOME DEPARTMENT, *ex p.* BAJRAKTARI; R. v. SECRETARY OF STATE FOR THE HOME DEPARTMENT, *ex p.* RAJARATNUM; R. v. SECRETARY OF STATE FOR THE HOME DEPARTMENT, *ex p.* PATEL, *The Times*, September 11, 1997, Owen, J., QBD.

2882. Asylum seekers–homelessness–local authority duty to provide accommodation

See HOUSING: R. v. Kensington and Chelsea RLBC, *ex p.* Korneva. §2653, and R. v. Secretary of State for the Environment, *ex p.* Shelter and the Refugee Council. §2654

2883. Asylum seekers–homelessness–relevant date for determining eligibility for housing

See HOUSING: R. v. Southwark LBC, *ex p.* Bediako. §2652

2884. Asylum seekers–local authorities–duty to assist–no power to give cash payments for purchase of everyday necessities

[National Assistance Act 1948 s.21 (1).]

H provided bed and breakfast accommodation under the National Assistance Act 1948 s.21 (1) (a) for asylum seekers who had failed to claim asylum upon entry into the UK and were consequently not eligible for state benefits. The council also made cash payments to the asylum seekers intended to allow them to purchase everyday essentials such as food and toiletries, saving H the expense and difficulty of providing such necessities in kind. In recognition of the financial strain imposed on local authorities providing assistance under s.21 following *R. v. Hammersmith and Fulham LBC, ex p. M* [1997] C.L.Y. 2885, Parliament had approved the payment of an Asylum Seekers' Accommodation Special Grant which was intended to cover all relevant expenditure incurred under s.21. H applied for judicial review of the Secretary of State's decision, detailed in Circular LAC(97)6 para.15(c), that cash payments were not to be regarded as relevant expenditure.

Held, dismissing the application, that there was nothing in s.21 which authorised H to provide asylum seekers with cash payments. Local authorities had a duty to make arrangements for providing asylum seekers with accommodation and other necessary amenities. Providing them with cash to purchase everyday essentials required them to make their own arrangements to obtain what they needed and therefore fell outside the statutory provisions.

R. v. SECRETARY OF STATE FOR HEALTH, *ex p.* HAMMERSMITH AND FULHAM LBC, *The Times*, July 31, 1997, Laws, J., QBD.

2885. Asylum seekers–local authorities–duty to provide assistance

[National Assistance Act 1948 s.21 (1) (a); Asylum and Immigration Act 1996.]

Asylum seekers who had not claimed asylum immediately on arrival in the UK were not precluded from assistance under the National Assistance Act 1948 s.21 (1). Three local authorities and the Secretary of State for Health appealed against the granting of applications by asylum seekers for judicial review of the local authorities' refusal to provide assistance under the National Assistance Act 1948 s.21 (1), by which local authorities could provide residential accommodation to those in need of care and attention. Under the Asylum and Immigration Act 1996, asylum seekers who did not claim asylum immediately upon their arrival in the UK were not entitled to claim any social security benefits or public housing, nor to take up employment, with the result that there were large numbers of destitute asylum seekers in need of assistance. The local authorities argued that s.21 (1) (a) was to be construed narrowly and asylum seekers could not rely on it as they required food and accommodation rather than the care and attention provided for in the section.

Held, dismissing the appeals, that although s.21 (1) (a) did not impose a duty upon local authorities, it had to be interpreted with regard to present circumstances. The fact that the applicants were neither old, ill nor disabled did not preclude them from assistance under s.21 (1) (a) as other circumstances could be considered, such as sleeping rough and going without food, which would result in their needing care and attention. Parliament could not have intended that those in need be without recourse to assistance and local authorities had a responsibility to provide help to asylum seekers who fulfilled the relevant criteria. Although s.21 (1) (a) was not a safety net for all those who lacked money or accommodation, the destitution to which asylum seekers could be reduced over time could satisfy the criteria laid down so that assistance would be available.

R. v. HAMMERSMITH AND FULHAM LBC, *ex p.* M; R. v. LAMBETH LBC, *ex p.* P; R. v. WESTMINSTER CITY COUNCIL, *ex p.* A; R. v. LAMBETH LBC, *ex p.* X, *The Times*, February 19, 1997, Lord Woolf, M.R., CA.

2886. Asylum seekers—local authorities—duty to provide meals

P, a Zairean national, arrived in the UK on December 11, 1996 and claimed asylum two days later. Having no friends or family in the UK she was entirely dependent for her survival on local authority assistance. P applied for leave to move for judicial review of a policy, which she claimed was being operated by H, arguing that it was unreasonable or unlawful. The alleged policy was that asylum seekers should be provided with breakfast and only one other meal a day. In P's case, this was the midday meal which she claimed she could not eat because it was unpalatable, with the result that she was suffering malnutrition.

Held, refusing the application for leave, that it was clear from the affidavit of a senior officer that H did have a policy and the policy is to assess each individual according to their needs. While there may have been a misunderstanding or lack of communication in P's case, H's undertaking to adhere to this policy and to provide P with vouchers to enable her to purchase food from the local supermarket if she so chose established that there was a satisfactory policy in place. Accordingly, there was not an arguable case that H acted unlawfully or in any way unreasonably. As a matter of general principle, the normal minimum requirement should be to provide three meals a day for asylum seekers unless they are assessed and indicate that they are happy to survive on breakfast and one other meal only.

R. v. HOUNSLOW LBC, *ex p.* PULULU, Trans. Ref: CO 948-97, March 21, 1997, Tucker, J., QBD.

2887. British Nationality (Hong Kong) Act 1997 (20)

This Act allows British nationals in Hong Kong to acquire British citizenship provided that, immediately before February 4, 1997, they were resident in Hong Kong, were a British Dependent Territories citizen, a British Overseas citizen, a British subject or a British protected person, and would have been stateless if they had not been such a citizen, subject or person.

2888. British Nationality (Hong Kong) Act 1997 (c.20)

This Act allows British nationals in Hong Kong to acquire British citizenship provided that, immediately before February 4, 1997, they were resident in Hong Kong, were a British Dependent Territories citizen, a British Overseas citizen, a

British subject or a British protected person, and would have been stateless if they had not been such a citizen, subject or person.

This Act received Royal Assent on March 19, 1997 and comes into force on March 19, 1997.

2889. Citizenship—applications—fees

BRITISH NATIONALITY (FEES) (AMENDMENT) REGULATIONS 1997, SI 1997 1328; made under the British Nationality Act 1981 s.41; and the British Nationality (Hong Kong) Act 1997 s.2. In force: June 12, 1997; £0.65.

These Regulations amend the British Nationality (Fees) Regulations 1996 (SI 1996 444) to prescribe a fee of £250 for applications for British citizenship made under the British Nationality (Hong Kong) Act 1997 s.1.

2890. Citizenship—burden of proof of British citizenship discharged by producing genuine British passport—no further proof required from entrant

[Immigration Act 1971 s.3(9).]

O appealed against the Secretary of State's determination that he was an illegal entrant. He had entered the UK using a valid six month British passport but, on seeking to renew it, was served with a notice describing him as an illegal entrant. The Secretary of State questioned O's identity and argued that he had to prove he was in fact the person in whose name the passport had been issued before he could establish a right of abode under the Immigration Act 1971 s.3(9).

Held, quashing the Secretary of State's determination, that the key questions of law raised were: (1) whether the burden of proof lay on the Secretary of State to show that O was an illegal entrant or on O to demonstrate that he was not, and (2) exactly what had to be proven? As a matter of statutory interpretation, the onus of proving British citizenship lay on the person seeking to enter the UK under s.3(8) and the production of a valid British passport was sufficient to establish a right of abode under s.3(9). The raising of doubts over the entrant's identity did not place any further burden of proof on the entrant. If, however, it could be shown that the passport was obtained by fraud, then further sanctions could be applied against him.

R. v. SECRETARY OF STATE FOR THE HOME DEPARTMENT, *ex p.* OBI, *The Times*, May 6, 1997, Sedley, J., QBD.

2891. Citizenship—legitimate expectation created as to applicant's treatment—unfairness of Home Secretary's decision that illegal entrant where no hearing offered

[British Nationality Act 1981 s.4(2).]

K entered the UK in 1992 as a British Dependent Territories citizen under the terms of the British Nationality Act 1981. Having been granted temporary admission, the Chief Immigration Officer informed K by letter that, since he was deemed to be a British citizen, he was entitled to apply for a British passport which would define him as such. K applied for registration as a British citizen but was informed that the earlier information was wrong and that under s.4(2) of the Act he was not eligible to apply for registration until he had spent most of the five years prior to his application within the UK. K then applied for a two year Commonwealth visa but was told he was an illegal entrant and should return to Pakistan. K applied for judicial review of the Secretary of State's decision, arguing that, in the light of the first letter, the decision was either unfair in that he was not given an opportunity for a hearing, was a denial of his legitimate expectation, or was *Wednesbury* unreasonable as unconscionably harsh

Held, allowing the application, that the Secretary of State's decision that he was an illegal entrant, made without giving K an opportunity for a hearing should be quashed. Contrary to the Secretary of State's contention, the doctrine of legitimate expectation did not demand that a person acting on the basis of a representation should prove consequential detriment. Rather, the doctrine was grounded on fairness. There was no reason why the principle that an authority, before making a departure from a public policy pronouncement, should provide those affected with an opportunity to make representations, should not be applied in the case of statements made which affected only one individual.

R. v. SECRETARY OF STATE FOR THE HOME DEPARTMENT, *ex p.* KHAN, *The Independent*, May 15, 1997, McCullough, J., QBD.

2892. Controls–exemptions–Amendment No.1

IMMIGRATION (EXEMPTION FROM CONTROL) (AMENDMENT) ORDER 1997, SI 1997 1402; made under the Immigration Act 1971 s.8. In force: July 1, 1997; £0.65.

This Order amends the Immigration (Exemption from Control) Order 1972 (SI 1972 1613) Art.4. The effect is to exempt members of the staff of the Hong Kong Economic and Trade Office, from any provision of the Immigration Act 1971 relating to those who are not British Citizens (except any provision relating to deportation).

2893. Controls–exemptions–Amendment No.2

IMMIGRATION (EXEMPTION FROM CONTROL) (AMENDMENT) (NO.2) ORDER 1997, SI 1997 2207; made under the Immigration Act 1971 s.8. In force: in accordance with Art.1; £0.65.

This Order amends the Immigration (Exemption from Control) Order 1972 (SI 1972 1613) Art.4 to exempt members and servants of the International Commission on Decommissioning from any provision of the Immigration Act 1971 relating to those who are not British Citizens, except any provision relating to deportation.

2894. Deportation–appeals–appeal lodged but withdrawn on bad advice–no application to adjudicator where appeal withdrawn–incompetent legal advice irrelevant

[Immigration Act 1971 s.3 (5), s.15, s.19, s.20, s.21.]

S had been resident in the United Kingdom for more than seven years before he was served a notice of intention to deport him as an overstayer under the Immigration Act 1971 s.3 (5) (a). He had full right of appeal under the Immigration Act 1971 s.15, and lodged an appeal. He then married a United Kingdom settled citizen. His then representatives erroneously advised S to drop his appeal on the grounds that this marriage automatically gave him right to remain. S maintained his original decision. New representatives then asked the Secretary of State to refer the case to an adjudicator under s.21 of the 1971 Act to allow the airing of claimed compassionate circumstances. The Secretary of State declined on the grounds that s.21 did not apply where an appeal had been withdrawn. It was submitted that the Secretary of State (1) had erred in his interpretation of s.21 and should have exercised his discretion and referred the case to the adjudicator, since S had been so badly advised, and (2) was wrong in not exercising his discretion to issue a fresh notice of intention to deport in response to the incompetence of S's original advisors, and give S a second chance.

Held, in dismissing the application for leave to apply for judicial review, that (1) the true interpretation of s.21, read with s.19 and s.20, was that there was no application where an appeal is withdrawn, because there was no determination by the adjudicator to bring s.21 into play, and (2) the Secretary of State was entitled to refuse to issue a new notice of intention to deport, and had overlooked no material in reaching his conclusion.

R. v. SECRETARY OF STATE FOR THE HOME DEPARTMENT, *ex p.* SAUD [1996] Imm. A.R. 612, Ognall, J., QBD.

2895. Deportation—appeals—appellate authorities not advised of change of representative—no breach of natural justice where adjudicator determined appeal in absence of the appellant

[Immigration Act 1971 s.17(1).]

H, a Moroccan citizen, arrived in the UK on January 21, 1995 seeking political asylum. His application was refused and removal directions were issued for his deportation. He filed a notice of appeal, but failed to specify another country to which he should be returned. The adjudicator sent a notice to H's named representative advising her that this failure would be dealt with as a preliminary issue on appeal, and in the absence of appearance at the hearing it was within the adjudicator's discretion to determine the appeal on the evidence available. Neither H nor his representative appeared at the hearing. The adjudicator accepted the Secretary of State's submission based upon Immigration Act 1971 s.17(1)(b) that there were no valid grounds of appeal as no other country had been specified. H sought judicial review on the grounds that as neither he nor his new solicitors had been notified of the hearing date, he had been denied the opportunity of being heard and had therefore suffered a breach of natural justice. The Secretary of State argued that neither he nor the adjudicator had been notified of the change of representative, despite a notice having been sent to the Chief Immigration Officer and therefore a breach of natural justice had not occurred; nor would any injustice have resulted had it done so.

Held, dismissing the application for judicial review, that (1) the appellate authorities had properly notified the only representative of which they were aware; (2) there had been no breach of natural justice; (3) notice of change of representative to the immigration service could not be taken as notice to the appellate authorities, and (4) in any event the appeal could not have succeeded.

R. v. SECRETARY OF STATE FOR THE HOME DEPARTMENT, *ex p.* HANNACH [1997] Imm. A.R. 162, Tuckey, J., QBD.

2896. Deportation—appeals—failure to receive notice or explanatory statement of deportation appeal

[Immigration Act 1971 s.3(5); Immigration (Procedure) Rules 1984 (SI 1984 2041) r.8.]

L, a Nigerian citizen, first came to the United Kingdom in June 1988, and was granted leave to remain with extensions of stay until March 19, 1993, as a visitor, then as the dependent of her husband, K. K wrote to the Home Office on March 13, 1993, sending the family passports without explanation. The Home Office asked for an explanation. K replied, explaining that he wished to request an extension of leave, which had by then expired. The application was refused on August 24, 1993. S took the date of the explanatory letter as the date of the first application and concluded that there was no right of appeal. He then initiated deportation proceedings against the family and L on April 13, 1994, as overstayers and under the Immigration Act 1971 s.3(5)(a). This decision entailed a restricted right of appeal for L. L's appeal was dismissed by the adjudicator after consideration of the papers on February 2, 1995. A deportation order was made against L on February 23, 1996. L complained that she never received a notice of her deportation appeal or an explanatory statement according to the Immigration (Procedure) Rules 1984 r.8, that it had been the responsibility of the adjudicator to ensure she received it. It was submitted that (1) it had been the duty of S to advise L of the change in her representation that had occurred; (2) the original letter containing the passports should have been treated as the application for leave to remain, granting the rights to appeal against the subsequent refusal, and (3) the application for leave to remain had not been properly determined.

Held, refusing leave to apply for judicial review, that (1) the adjudicator did not have a duty to ensure that L received the explanatory statement; (2) the Home Office had no duty to advise of a change in L's representative; (3) S had not erred in taking the date of the later explanatory letter as the date of the application, and (4) he was not obliged to consider the fact that immigrants were often poorly advised.

R. v. SECRETARY OF STATE FOR THE HOME DEPARTMENT, *ex p.* LADIPO [1996] Imm. A.R. 607, Collins, J., QBD.

2897. **Deportation-applications-variation of leave-passports sent in time without explanation to Home Office-explanation and request for variation of leave received out of time on enquiry-despatch of passports not valid as application for variation of leave.**

L, a Nigerian, came to the UK in June 1988 and was given leave to enter as a visitor for six months. Time extensions were granted to her as a dependant of J, whom she married and who had been given leave to stay temporarily as a student. Their leave expired on March 19, 1993. On March 13, J sent the passports of himself, L and their daughter to the Home Office with a covering letter that was not an application in form. The Home Office acknowledged receipt of the passports on March 19, indicating that receipt of the passports did not constitute an application. Explanation was given shortly afterwards, with applications in proper form, asking for extension of leave to remain. They were refused on August 24. As the application was out of time J was informed that there was no right of appeal. The family remained as overstayers. On November 15, 1993 a letter was sent to the Home Office asking on behalf of the family that they be allowed to remain on the grounds of ill health. This was refused and in April 1994, the Secretary of State decided to deport them as overstayers. Their appeal was heard and dismissed on the papers on February 2, 1995, since J and L had not asked for an oral hearing. A deportation order was made three weeks later. The family appealed for leave to seek judicial review against the decision of the adjudicator and the decision to deport. It was submitted that (1) L did not receive notice of the hearing of appeal nor an explanatory statement; (2) the adjudicator's written statement revealed that he had not taken proper steps to ensure L received the explanatory statement and this was a breach of natural justice; (3) the Secretary of State caused a breach of natural justice when he failed to notify the appellate authorities that there had been a change of representation; (4) the refusal to treat the covering letter as an application was unlawful in that, in the context of J's file, the application was clear and unambiguous, and (5) the Secretary of State's conduct in previous years of accepting covering letters as applications in time for leave to remain as student and dependants created a legitimate expectation that he would treat this application in the same way.

Held, dismissing the judicial review application, that (1) the adjudicator had no duty in the circumstances to ensure that L received the explanatory statement; (2) the Home Office had no duty to advise the appellate authorities of a change in representation, and (3) the Secretary of State had not erred in taking the date of the letter of explanation, not the date of receipt of the passports, as the date of application; letters before the court showed that he had not previously treated the receipt of passports as applications for variation of leave.

R. v. SECRETARY OF STATE FOR THE HOME DEPARTMENT, *ex p.* LADIPO; *sub nom.* LADIPO v. SECRETARY OF STATE FOR THE HOME DEPARTMENT [1997] Imm. A.R. 51, Otton, L.J., CA.

2898. **Deportation-children-parental contact-contact order conditional upon leave to remain**

[Immigration Act 1971 s.15; Immigration Act 1988 s.5.]

C sought to review a decision of the Secretary of State for the Home Department to deport him. C arrived from Bangladesh as a visitor, married a resident and was given leave to remain for 12 months. His wife bore him a daughter, after which she denounced him to the Home Office and C was refused indefinite leave to remain. After his divorce C commenced proceedings to obtain contact with his child and an order for contact for two hours every fortnight was made on terms that C obtain indefinite leave to remain. C's solicitors explained the position to the Home Office and enclosed a copy of the order but received no reply for eight months, whereupon enquiries were made of the mother with regard to frequency of contact. C explained that his contact could not commence until his residence position was confirmed but a further eight months' delay ensued before a deportation order was made.

Held, allowing the application and quashing the deportation order, that the decision of the Secretary of State was both irrational and perverse and, contrary to the assertion of the Secretary of State, had C's access rights been allowed, then the guidance of Home Office Guidance Circular DP/2/93 para.5 would have suggested that deportation should be abandoned. In addition, any appeal that C were to make would now be under the Immigration Act 1971 s.15 rather than the Immigration Act 1988 s.5 and C would be able to argue for the discretion of the Secretary of State to be exercised differently.

R. v. SECRETARY OF STATE FOR THE HOME DEPARTMENT, *ex p.* CHOUDHURY, Trans. Ref: CO/4023/95, March 11, 1997, Hidden, J., QBD.

2899. Deportation–children–parental contact–refusal of variation of leave after marriage breakdown–applicant with contact order for child of marriage

[European Convention on Human Rights 1950 Art.8; Children Act 1989 s.8.]

K, a Pakistani national, married a British citizen in Pakistan in September 1989. On May 22, 1990 their daughter was born. K arrived in the UK in December 1990 and was given leave to enter for 12 months on the basis of the marriage. On June 23, 1993 K applied for indefinite leave to remain in reliance upon the marriage. On July 24, 1993, the couple separated, the wife keeping the daughter. As a result of Home Office enquiries into the application, and the fact that his wife no longer supported the claim, K's application was refused. On September 29, 1993, before notification of the decision on October 13, K applied for a contact order with his daughter under the Children Act 1989 s.8. On April 24, 1994, K was granted a contact order of one hour a week. On June 6 K's appeal to the adjudicator against the refusal of leave to remain was dismissed. On July 6, K made a fresh application to the Home Office for indefinite leave on the basis of the contact order. Subsequently further contact orders were made for one hour a week, then one and a half to two hours a week. A further application for indefinite leave to remain was made on January 25, 1995, and was refused on March 24. K was given the opportunity to depart voluntarily under HC 395 r.246, simultaneous with a notice of intent to deport. K's appeal against this was dismissed on July 7. On August 24 the contact order was amended to provide for four hours every two weeks, then varied to two hours every three weeks. On March 28, 1996, the Home Secretary rejected further representations and the deportation order was served. On May 17 a family assistance order was made providing for six contact sessions over a six month's period. It was argued (1) that the guidance policy DP/2/93 acknowledged the European Convention of Human Rights 1950 Art.8, and provided that deportation proceedings should be abandoned where there was frequent and regular access to a child, and (2) the Secretary of State, while acknowledging the relevance of Art.8 had failed unreservedly to apply it.

Held, dismissing the judicial review application, that (1) the Secretary of State was not bound by the provisions of the European Convention although he was obliged to have regard to it; (2) he had been entitled on the facts to conclude that the access granted by the courts was not "frequent and regular contact", and (3) the decision had not been *Wednesbury* unreasonable.

R. v. SECRETARY OF STATE FOR THE HOME DEPARTMENT, *ex p.* KHAN (KHALID MASOOD) [1997] Imm. A.R. 89, Turner, J., QBD.

2900. Deportation–children–parental contact–relationship with son inadequately examined

N, a Nigerian, applied for judicial review of a decision of the Secretary of State to deport him as an illegal immigrant. N contended that his respective relationships with (1) his son, E born to U, and (2) his wife, C, had not been adequately considered. N had used a false identity to enter on a six month visitor's visa and nine months later his son was born to U, herself a Nigerian and illegal entrant. She later married a British citizen and was currently appealing the refusal of asylum to her. N was given notice that he was an illegal entrant and subsequently married C, claiming that he had been cohabiting with her before he was served with the notice.

Held, allowing the application, that the Secretary of State had ample evidence and reason to conclude that the evidence of prior cohabitation before marriage was insubstantial and that the provisions of Home Office Policy Document DP/2/93 did not apply. Furthermore, para.5 of DP/2/93 did not apply to N's relationship with E because U was not settled in the UK. However, despite this the Secretary of State had failed to consider properly affidavit evidence that N had obtained a parental responsibility order in relation to his son and had made regular financial contributions towards his maintenance.

R. v. SECRETARY OF STATE FOR THE HOME DEPARTMENT, *ex p.* NATUFE, Trans. Ref: CO/953/96, January 22, 1997, Harrison, J., QBD.

2901. Deportation–detention–continued detention pending asylum application

[Immigration Act 1971 Sch. III; Asylum and Immigration Appeals Act 1993 s.6.]

A applied for habeas corpus. A was given leave to enter as a foreign spouse, but his marriage subsequently broke down and he was served with a deportation order. The Secretary of State ordered his detention in December 1996 pursuant to the Immigration Act 1971 Sch. III para.2(3) and A later claimed, but was refused, political asylum. A was successful on appeal, which decision was appealed against by the Secretary of State. The appeal was to be heard in July 1997. A contended that the Asylum and Immigration Appeals Act 1993 s.6 implied that the order made under the 1971 Act could not be enforced after a claim for asylum had been made and therefore it was no longer in force.

Held, dismissing the application, that the 1993 Act s.6 did not affect the validity of such a deportation order except to the extent of preventing any step being taken until the outcome of the asylum claim had been established. Only if the delay caused by the asylum claim became unreasonable could the court decide that the purpose of such detention had become unlawful.

R. v. SECRETARY OF STATE FOR THE HOME DEPARTMENT, *ex p.* ASHFAQ, Trans. Ref: CO 0310-97, May 15, 1997, Latham, J., QBD.

2902. Deportation–drug offences–propensity to re-offend not always relevant

[Immigration Act 1971 s.3, s.15; Treaty of Rome 1957 Art.48; Council Directive 64/221 on special measures concerning the movement of foreign nationals Art.3; European Convention on Human Rights 1950 Art.8.]

L, an Italian citizen, had lived in the United Kingdom since 1971. In 1986 he was convicted of conspiracy to import cannabis and heroin and was sentenced to 22 years in prison, later reduced to 18. On June 11, 1990, whilst in prison, L was served with a notice of intention to deport under the Immigration Act 1971 s.3(5)(b). L was informed of his right to appeal under Immigration Act 1971 s.15(7), but did not exercise it. Unsuccessful representations were made on behalf of L, on the grounds of his family ties in the country, his model conduct in prison, the prospect of employment for him in this country and the fact that it was extremely unlikely he would offend again. On June 22, 1995 it was decided that L was to be released on parole on July 18, 1995, but that he would be deported on that day. L applied for judicial review. It was submitted on his behalf that (1) his failure to appeal in 1990 should not deny him a right of review by the court; (2) the decision to deport had been irrational, given the factors in favour of L remaining; (3) as a potential EU worker in the United Kingdom L had the benefit of the Treaty of Rome 1957 Art.48; (4) Council Directive 64/221 Art.3 suggested that L could not be deported on grounds of past offences alone, but propensity to future offences had to be shown, and (5) deportation would be contrary to the European Convention on Human Rights 1950 Art. 8.

Held, dismissing the application for judicial review, that (1) L should have appealed to the Tribunal, and it was not appropriate for the court to consider the application due to his failure to do so; (2) it made no difference that the basis of the application was the decision to maintain the original decision; (3) on the facts, the decision was not *Wednesbury* unreasonable; (4) the decision in *R. v. Bouchereau* [1978] Q.B. 732, [1978] C.L.Y. 629 still held and was not influenced by later judgments, propensity to re-offend did not always have to be shown to justify deportation; (5) it could not be argued that the principle of proportionality precluded deportation, and (6) the European Convention on Human Rights 1950 Art.8 had no direct application to the case; in any event the nature of the offence meant that the decision was not a breach of the article read as a whole.

R. v. SECRETARY OF STATE FOR THE HOME DEPARTMENT, *ex p.* LUCIANI [1996] Imm. A.R. 558, Buxton, J., QBD.

2903. **Deportation–legitimate expectation to remain–passport retained by Home Office–return of passport did not give legitimate expectation**

D, an Indian citizen, first came to the United Kingdom in 1977, at the age of 14. He made visits to India or Pakistan on five occasions between 1981 and 1989. In January 1990 he was convicted of possession of heroin with intent to supply and sentenced to two years' imprisonment. The judge made no recommendation to deport but left it to the discretion of S, who notified D that he was minded to make an order to deport. D made representations against this decision but the order was made. D's appeal was dismissed on November 23, 1990. D claimed he was not notified of that decision as his solicitors had gone out of business and he made no effort to find out the result. He approached S through his MP on April 23, 1993, four days after the signing of the deportation order. The Home Office wrote to the MP to say that the order had been signed. Two days later, D wrote to the Home Office asking for the return of his passport, which had been retained by the Home Office after his arrest. They returned it, since they had no right to retain it any longer. The passport still had the indefinite leave to remain stamp on it, since the deportation order had not yet been served on D. In May, D went to India to attend a funeral. He returned and then left again for India and stayed there for two years, returning in May 1993 just within the two year period, having married in India in June 1992. His wife came to the United Kingdom in April 1994. In June 1994 D came to the attention of the police in relation to another matter; it was discovered that he was an illegal entrant and steps were taken towards deportation. It was submitted that the Home Office had created a legitimate expectation in D's mind that (1) no deportation order had been signed, and (2) if a deportation order had been signed then he would not be served with it. D argued that these legitimate expectations had been created since (1) his passport had been returned and still contained leave to remain, and (2) he had come back to the country subsequently without being stopped or notified that he was subject to a deportation order.

Held, dismissing an application for judicial review, that in order for there to be a legitimate expectation there has to be clear representation on which to rely and the return of the passport had been no such representation.

R. v. SECRETARY OF STATE FOR THE HOME DEPARTMENT, *ex p.* DEY; *sub nom.* DEY v. SECRETARY OF STATE FOR THE HOME DEPARTMENT [1996] Imm. A.R. 521, Stuart-Smith, L.J., CA.

2904. **Deportation–marriage–applicant granted limited leave on basis of marriage–separation due to marital violence–12 months trial period not discriminatory to women**

C married her second husband and settled in the UK in November 1988. She was granted 12 months' leave to remain in February 1989 as a trial period before being granted unconditional leave to remain. The marriage broke down: C's husband beat her and in October 1989 she left him. As a result, at the end of the 12 month period, the extension of leave was refused. C became an overstayer. C sought leave to remain but in September 1993 a notice of intention to deport was served. It was argued that the 12 month trial period was discriminatory against women, and that the court had the power to say the law was furthermore unjust and so ultra vires. It was further argued that C's son from an earlier marriage, P, aged 13, would be expected to leave with C, but did not wish to do so, and in declining to give notice of deportation against P, the Secretary of State had denied P his statutory right to appeal.

Held, dismissing the judicial review application, that (1) the precaution of granting an initial 12 months' leave after marriage was not unjust; (2) the evidence did not show that more men than women had to leave the country because of marital violence; (3) were that the case, the rule would still not be ultra vires, and (4) P had suffered no disadvantage, if he did not leave with C and the Secretary of State decided to issue a notice of intention to deport, he would have a right of appeal.

R. v. SECRETARY OF STATE FOR THE HOME DEPARTMENT, *ex p.* CHAVRIMOOTOO [1997] Imm. A.R. 79, Jowitt, J., QBD.

2905. **Deportation—marriage—common law relationship not akin to marriage—importance of family unity stated in ECHR relevant—all pertinent facts had to be considered**

[European Convention on Human Rights 1950 Art.8.]

T was Hong Kong Chinese, with a British Dependent Territories Citizenship passport. He was granted one month visitor's leave to enter on December 14, 1979. He then disappeared. In 1991 T tried to regularise his situation, and contacted an advisor who corresponded with the Home Office after which T's application to remain was refused. In February 1992 the authorities issued a notice of intention to deport T as an overstayer. T appealed and the appeal was dismissed in July 1992, a fortnight after T's marriage to B, a British citizen. On March 23, 1993 a daughter was born to the couple. On April 6, 1994 an application for leave to remain on the basis of the marriage was made, at which point T and his new advisors became aware that a deportation order had been signed on March 31, 1993. Representations were made to the Home Office but were unsuccessful. T made an application for judicial review, where he sought to show that he and B had been living together as man and wife prior to the marriage. Leave was granted, reference being made to the interests of the child and also the 15 affidavits that had been submitted to show that the relationship between T and B was a very long one. The matter was referred for reconsideration by S, who wrote a decision letter on March 9, 1995, maintaining the earlier decision on the grounds that he was not satisfied that T and B had been living together in "a common law relationship akin to marriage" before their actual marriage or the date of the notice of intent to deport, and he had fully considered the fact that the child involved was a British citizen. It was submitted that S had been *Wednesbury* unreasonable in deciding that there was not conclusive evidence to show that T and B had been in a genuine common law relationship akin to marriage testified to by the affidavits; the European Convention on Human Rights 1950 Art.8 and policy guidance DP/2/93 both stated that in such cases great consideration had to be given to family unity and S in the letter of March 9 had not sufficiently considered the interference with the family life resulting from deportation.

Held, refusing application for judicial review, that (1) on the evidence, S had not been *Wednesbury* unreasonable in deciding that it was not conclusive that there had been a pre-marital common law relationship between the couple requiring that policy guidance DP/2/93 be followed; (2) the decision letter maintaining the earlier decision had not been as explicit as it might have been; (3) in cases where the European Convention on Human Rights 1950 Art.8 was of relevance it would be helpful if all the factors taken into account were set out in detail, and (4) it was clear that all the relevant factors had been considered.

TONG v. SECRETARY OF STATE FOR THE HOME DEPARTMENT [1996] Imm. A.R. 551, Neill, L.J., CA.

2906. Deportation—marriage—engagement not akin to marriage—right to family life

[European Convention on Human Rights 1950 Art.8.]

S applied to review a decision of the Secretary of State directing his removal from the UK. S contended that the Secretary of State had failed to consider (1) that S had been in a situation akin to marriage with his future wife prior to the service of the deportation order; (2) representations from the Christian Fellowship religious group to which he belonged, and (3) the effect on S's wife of the ill health of her mother, which made his removal a violation of the European Convention on Human Rights 1950 Art.8.

Held, dismissing the application, that the decision was appropriate, that (1) S's engagement to be married was not sufficient proof that he had been in a relationship akin to marriage; (2) there was no duty on the Secretary of State to identify each representation nor was there reason to doubt his assertion that he had considered all the representations made on S's behalf, and (3) the Secretary of State's decision was not irrational and had been made weighing S's clear and continued breach of immigration controls against the disruption to his family's life caused by his deportation, *R. v. Secretary of State for the Home Department, ex p. Patel (Bina Rajendra)* [1995] Imm. A. R. 223, [1996] 1 C.L.Y. 3311 followed.

R. v. SECRETARY OF STATE FOR THE HOME DEPARTMENT, *ex p.* SOGBESAN; R. v. SECRETARY OF STATE FOR THE HOME DEPARTMENT, *ex p.* ANDREWS, Trans. Ref: CO/2946/96, February 5, 1997, Ognall, J., QBD.

2907. Deportation—notice—validity of notice—judge should have given reasons when recommending deportation

[Immigration Act 1971 s.6 (2).]

R pleaded guilty to four counts of supplying crack cocaine. He sold rocks of crack cocaine on four occasions to police officers posing as drug users. He was sentenced to four years' imprisonment, a confiscation order in the amount of £440 was made and he was recommended for deportation. He came to the UK in 1991 and his leave had been extended until 1994. He had married while in the UK, and now had one child of his own and two stepchildren; his wife was expecting a further child. R appealed against the recommendation for deportation, on the grounds that (1) the question of deportation should have started with a notice served under the Immigration Act 1971 s.6 (2) seven days before making an order for recommendation for deportation, and there was no evidence of that, in the absence of a copy of the relevant form known as an IM3 document, and no reference to the date on which it was served in the police records, and (2) no recommendation for deportation should have been made as the court had to consider whether the accused's presence in the UK was detrimental and whether the effect of the order would be to impose hardship on innocent people or break up families, principles set out in *R. v. Nazari* [1980] 1 W.L.R. 1366, [1980] C.L.Y. 581.

Held, quashing that recommendation, that (1) on the evidence the court was satisfied that a notice had been served under the 1971 Act and was served seven days or more before the recommendation, the court log referred to the IM3 being served and the then counsel had made no note of the absence of the notice, and (2) R was married and at the time had one child and another one was due, however the case was a serious one, he was young and had not been in the country for a long time, therefore the judge had good reason to make a recommendation. Counsel had addressed the judge on the question of a recommendation, at the judge's invitation and, although the Court had said in *R. v. Compassi* (1987) 9 Cr. App. R. (S.) 270, [1989] C.L.Y. 1108, that judges should give reasons when making a recommendation, in the instant case the judge had not done so even though he had made enquiry about the necessary matters. The Court wished to stress that it was of crucial importance that judges should give their reasons in a little detail when making recommendations for deportation, as no reasons had been given the recommendation would be quashed.

R. v. RODNEY (RADCLIFF) [1996] 2 Cr. App. R. (S.) 230, Blofeld, J., CA (Crim Div).

2908. **Deportation–police informer–deportation of drug dealer–conducive to the public good**

[Immigration Appeals Act 1993 s.9(1).]

C, a citizen of Ghana, arrived in the UK as a visitor in December 1984. His leave to enter was subsequently extended, but he became an overstayer and was arrested in October 1988. He had married a British citizen, and was released and eventually granted indefinite leave to remain on that basis on February 28, 1991. C was arrested in August 1992 for drug dealing. On February 9, 1993 he was convicted of supplying Class A drugs and sentenced to six years' imprisonment. The Home Office then decided to consider C's immigration status. In December 1994 a letter was written by a senior police officer explaining that C was a valuable informant. This was subsequently placed in evidence before the Immigration Appeal Tribunal. On April 4, 1995 a decision to deport C was made and served. C unsuccessfully appealed to the Tribunal. The Tribunal decided that although the police were anxious that C should not be deported because he was a valuable informant, his deportation was conducive to the public good. C appealed under Immigration Appeals Act 1993 s.9(1). It was argued that the Tribunal had erred in the weight it attached to the evidence of the police, which should have decided the appeal in his favour.

Held, dismissing the appeal, that (1) the appeal was misconceived since it raised no issue of law; (2) the Tribunal had dealt with the case correctly and had considered all the evidence before coming to its conclusion; (3) the decision was not one to be made by the police but by the Secretary of State, and on appeal, the Tribunal, and (4) C's submissions had failed to pay regard to the seriousness of his offence, which was "a very serious and antisocial offence which is seriously destructive to the life of this country".

CM v. SECRETARY OF STATE FOR THE HOME DEPARTMENT [1997] Imm. A.R. 336, Sir Stephen Brown, CA.

2909. **Deportation–recommendation for exceptional leave to remain on compassionate grounds–public interest–immigration policy**

K, a Nepalese citizen brought to this country by M, a wealthy British subject as a result of a pledge given by M to K's late father, applied for judicial review of a decision to deport him in spite of a recommendation by the Immigration Appeal Tribunal that he be given exceptional leave to remain outside the Immigration Rules. Following a recommendation of the adjudicator, that K be interviewed, S issued a further decision that, notwithstanding K's genuine connections with M, such interests did not outweigh the general public interest in the application of a firm but fair immigration control and that K's case did not present exceptionally compelling or compassionate circumstances to allow K to remain.

Held, dismissing the application, that the decision reached was based on the application of policy to the facts of the instant case and did not disclose any perversity on the part of the decision maker. Where S was asked to decide a matter beyond the Immigration Rules he was the first judge of what was relevant to the final conclusion and his judgment was only susceptible to review on strict *Wednesbury* grounds. The decision making process required S to determine whether exceptional facts justified the exercise of his discretion in an applicant's favour, with recommendations by the tribunal or the adjudicator being a factor to be considered, but not determinative of the final decision, *R. v. Secretary of State for the Home Department, ex p. Sakala* [1994] Imm. A.R. 227, [1994] C.L.Y. 2444 and *R. v. Secretary of State for the Home Department, ex p. Gardian* [1996] Imm A.R. 6, [1996] 1 C.L.Y. 3175 followed. The decision as to the weight to be accorded to the relevant factors was a matter for S not least since the issue fell outside the Immigration Rules, given his role as people's democratic representative and interference with the decision would amount to a usurpation of that role.

R. v. SECRETARY OF STATE FOR THE HOME DEPARTMENT, *ex p.* KHADKA [1997] Imm. A.R. 124, Laws, J., QBD.

2910. **Deportation–removal directions–spouse expressing intention of settling in Ireland in event of deportation–whether husband's expressed future intentions satisfied the requirement that applicant had shown another country would admit her**

[Immigration Act 1971 s.17(1)(b); Immigration Appeals (Procedure) Rules 1984 (SI 1984 2041) r.6.]

J, a citizen of Trinidad and Tobago, appealed against removal directions. She was married to a British citizen who had stated that in the event of J being deported to Trinidad and Tobago he would settle in Ireland where he said that he would have no difficulty obtaining employment on the basis of his experience. The adjudicator dismissed J's appeal. J sought leave to appeal to the tribunal on the basis that in all the circumstances she was entitled not to be deported to Trinidad and Tobago, but to be required to go instead to Ireland, and that this was consonant with the Immigration Act 1971 s.17(1)(b). In her application J included a letter of February 5, 1996, intended to comply with Immigration Appeals (Procedure) Rules 1984 (SI 1984 2041) r.6(3), which stated that she was married to a British citizen and that he would exercise his right to move to Ireland should J be unsuccessful in her appeal against the deportation order. This was supported by an affidavit dated May 29, 1996 from J's husband, stating that in those circumstances there was "no doubt at all" that they would move to Ireland. The tribunal refused leave on the basis that the conditional nature of this letter "was not such as to comply with the requirement that the applicant must show that another country would be willing to receive her". It was submitted that in refusing leave on that basis the tribunal had fallen into error.

Held, refusing the application, that (1) the assertion by the husband was no more than a contingent proposal which did not satisfy the statutory criteria, and (2) the tribunal had been correct to refuse leave to appeal.

R. v. SECRETARY OF STATE FOR THE HOME DEPARTMENT, *ex p.* WITHANE [1997] Imm. A.R. 246, Ognall, J., QBD.

2911. **Deportation–terrorism–deportation for public good and in interests of national security**

[Immigration Act 1971 s.3(5)(b), s.15(3).]

S, an Indian citizen, had been granted indefinite leave to remain in the United Kingdom as a foreign spouse on April 29, 1982. On March 29, 1995 the Secretary of State decided to deport S as being in the public good, under the Immigration Act 1971 s.3(5)(b), in a letter of that same date. S instructed solicitors, who wrote to the Under Secretary of State, asking for the reasons behind the Secretary of State's decision, notifying S's intention to make representations against it, and applying for asylum. A reply letter was sent dated April 11 saying that asylum was being considered and enclosing a statement from the Secretary of State of his reasons for deporting S. The letter asserted that S was the General Secretary of the International Sikh Youth Federation Northern faction, and that he had been active in organising terrorist attacks in India. As a result the Secretary of State had decided to deport S as "conducive to the public good for reasons of national security and other reasons of a political nature, namely the international fight against terrorism." It was submitted on behalf of S that (1) a decision to deport under s.3(5)(b) of the Act had to be made personally by the Secretary of State, and that it was not apparent from the decision letters that this was the case; (2) the decision was unfair, unlawful, and unsupported by evidence, because the reasons given related only to Indian national security and S's terrorist activities in India, and did not suggest that S was having a similar effect in Britain; (3) the reference to "other reasons of a political nature" was open to examination by the court, and (4) it was not clear from the Secretary of State's decision that he had properly tried to balance S's own interests with the public interest, as stipulated by Immigration Rules (HC 395) para.364 before deciding as he did.

Held, refusing leave to move for judicial review, that (1) a decision under s.3(5)(b) of the Act had to be made by, or on behalf of, the Secretary of State; it was clear from the papers that the decision had been made personally by the Secretary of State; (2) it was inconceivable that the Secretary of State would not properly take into account all the balancing factors when conducting an exercise of his powers under that section; (3) the definition of the "public good" was not to be limited in the way suggested, since s.15(3) of the Act was not exhaustive, and (4) in cases relating to national security the court was not normally entitled to examine the material before the Secretary of State to assess his decision, and that would apply to the "other reasons of a political nature".

SINGH (RAGHBIR) v. SECRETARY OF STATE FOR THE HOME DEPARTMENT [1996] Imm. A.R. 507, Auld, L.J., CA.

2912. **Entry clearances–adjudication–Somali nationals–sponsors not settled–entry clearances for relatives**

[Immigration Act 1971 s.19(1).]

H and others were citizens of Somalia, all relatives of persons refused refugee status but granted exceptional leave to remain in the United Kingdom. Unsuccessful applications were made for entry clearances so that they could join their sponsors. On appeal the cases were reconsidered, and entry clearance again refused. Exceptional leave outside the rules was considered, but deemed inappropriate. In February 1994 notice of appeal was served and in March 1995 the case came before an adjudicator who decided that he had no jurisdiction to consider the case under the Immigration Act 1971 s.19(1)(a)(i), the sponsors were not "settled" and the application could not be "upgraded". He dismissed the appeal, but gave leave to appeal. The appeals came before the Immigration Appeal Tribunal in June 1995. The Tribunal refused to consider any issues of fact, deciding that S had declined to depart from the rules and therefore it had no jurisdiction to consider his application of the policy of Somali Family Reunion. They dismissed the appeal. It was submitted that (1) following *Secretary of State for the Home Department v. Abdi (Dhudi Saleban)* [1996] Imm. A.R. 148, [1996] 1 C.L.Y. 3181 there was jurisdiction to determine if the decisions were "in accordance with the law" under s.19(1)(a)(i) of the 1971 Act; (2) the decisions were inconsistent and not "in accordance with the law" where S had failed to apply practices in existence at that time, even unpublished practices relating to internal guidance; (3) the appellate authorities could re-examine issues of fact and could allow an appeal even when this would lead only to remittance to S for reconsideration, and (4) the letter of May 20, 1993 from the Minister of State to Mildred Gordon MP, showed that the concessionary treatment of Somalis extended to cases where the sponsor only had exceptional leave to remain and not refugee status.

Held, dismissing the applications, that (1) the applications for entry clearance did not come under the Immigration Rules because the sponsors were not settled; (2) the policy of S had never equated those with only exceptional leave with those granted refugee status, *Abdi* did not apply; (3) on the facts the applications fell outside S's policy, and (4) it was inappropriate to try to upgrade the status of the sponsors to that of refugees.

HERSI v. SECRETARY OF STATE FOR THE HOME DEPARTMENT; USLUSOW v. SECRETARY OF STATE FOR THE HOME DEPARTMENT; NUR v. SECRETARY OF STATE FOR THE HOME DEPARTMENT; WARSAME v. SECRETARY OF STATE FOR THE HOME DEPARTMENT; KAHIE v. SECRETARY OF STATE FOR THE HOME DEPARTMENT [1996] Imm. A.R. 569, Otton, L.J., CA.

2913. Entry clearances–appeals–right of entry to another Member State–right of appeal for nationals of other Member States excluded on grounds of public security–European Union

[Council Directive 64/221 on special measures concerning the movement and residence of foreign nationals Art.8, Art.9.]

Following applications for judicial review by two nationals of other Member States of decisions refusing them entry to the UK on the grounds of public security, without a right of appeal, the UK court referred to the ECJ a number of questions concerning the interpretation of Council Directive 64/221. The applicants contended that nationals of other Member States were entitled, under Art.8, to the same right of appeal as nationals of the relevant Member State in respect of any refusal to recognise their right of entry, or, under Art.9, to an examination of their situation.

Held, that (1) in view of the difficulty of comparing a national's right of entry with that of a national of another Member State, where the law of a Member State provided for remedies against acts of the administration generally, but different remedies applied to nationals of the Member State in respect of their right of entry, the provisions of Art.8 were satisfied provided that nationals of other Member States were entitled to the same remedies as those available against acts of the administration generally; (2) the situations referred to in Art.9(1): (a) where no right of appeal lay to a court of law; (b) where the appeal was restricted to the legal validity of the decision, or (c) where the appeal was not suspensory in effect, applied equally to a decision refusing an initial residence permit or a decision ordering expulsion prior to issuing the permit, and (3) nationals of other Member States refused entry on the grounds of public order or public security had a right of appeal under Art.8. Individuals also had the right to obtain an opinion from an independent competent authority under Art.9 where an administrative authority took a fresh decision on an application after a reasonable period of time had elapsed since the last decision prohibiting entry.

R. v. SECRETARY OF STATE FOR THE HOME DEPARTMENT, *ex p.* SHINGARA (C65/95); R. v. SECRETARY OF STATE FOR THE HOME DEPARTMENT, *ex p.* RADIOM (C111/95) [1997] All E.R. (EC) 577, GC Rodriguez Iglesias (President), ECJ.

2914. Entry clearances–appeals–time limits

[Immigration (Variation of Leave) Order 1976 (SI 1976 1572) s.3(1).]

J applied for leave to review a decision of the Secretary of State that she was out of time for an extension of leave to appeal. After entry as a visitor, J was allowed to remain in the UK as a student until December 31, 1995, which fell on a Sunday. J had sent her application for leave to remain, dated December 30, on the next working day, which was January 2, 1996. J contended that the application had been made in time, because her leave had expired on dies non juridicus.

Held, dismissing the application, that the Immigration (Variation of Leave) Order 1976 s.3(1) clearly required an application for an extension of leave to be made while the current leave was extant, *Kaur (Pritam) v. S Russell & Sons Ltd* [1973] 1 Q.B. 336, [1973] C.L.Y. 1964, and *R. v. Bloomsbury and Marylebone County Court, ex p. Villierwest* [1976] 1 W.L.R. 362, [1976] C.L.Y. 387 distinguished on its facts.

R. v. SECRETARY OF STATE FOR THE HOME DEPARTMENT, *ex p.* JECKA, Trans. Ref: CO/4238/96, February 28, 1997, Popplewell, J., QBD.

2915. Entry clearances–employment–work not incidental to entry as visitor

[Immigration Act 1971 s.13(3) (a); Immigration Rules (HC 395).]

C made a renewed application for judicial review of the decision to refuse entry. C submitted that she was a visitor and therefore the Immigration Act 1971 s.13(3) (a) applied and she had no right of appeal other than to seek judicial review. She claimed that the decision in *R. v. Secretary of State for the Home Department, ex p. Swati* [1986] 1 W.L.R. 477, [1986] C.L.Y. 1711 that other remedies must be taken account of did not apply. C was originally given leave to enter for six months as a visitor and later granted leave to remain as a working holiday maker. C took up employment as a care assistant, but had to go back to Zimbabwe for a family funeral. On her return she was refused entry as the immigration officer decided that the employment was not incidental to a holiday and she did not fulfil the requirements of para.95 of the rules.

Held, dismissing the appeal, that although the Immigration Act 1971 s.13(3)(a) was not exhaustive, the appellant was clearly not a visitor under the Immigration Rules (HC 395) as she intended to take employment in the UK and *R. v. Secretary of State for the Home Department, ex p. Swati* [1986] 1 W.L.R. 4771, [1986] C.L.Y. 1711 applied. Further, the period for which C sought re-entry exceeded the six months period allowed to a visitor

R. v. IMMIGRATION OFFICER (HEATHROW AIRPORT), *ex p.* CHIRENJE [1996] Imm. A.R. 321, Beldam, L.J., CA.

2916. Entry clearances–holidays–Secretary of State concluded applicant already "settled down" in his own country–meaning of "before settling down".

L, a Nigerian, came to the UK on July 2, 1992, as a business visitor. It was accepted that he could be regarded as settled down in Nigeria before he came to the UK. On arrival he told the immigration officer that he intended to stay for two weeks to visit a factory and leave to enter for six months as a visitor was granted. On December 10, 1992 applications were made for L to remain as a working holidaymaker. The application was rejected on March 9, 1993 on the grounds that L had already settled down in Nigeria and therefore did not qualify for admission under the Immigration Rules (HC 251) para.107 and para.37. This decision was upheld by the adjudicator and the Immigration Appeal Tribunal; the Tribunal granted leave to appeal since the central ground of the case had been subject to conflicting decisions of the Tribunal and had not been considered in the Court of Appeal. Before the change of wording effective from October 1, 1994, HC 251 para.37 required that applicants in L's age-group, between 17 to 27 inclusive, should be "coming to the UK for an extended holiday before settling down in their own countries", to be granted leave as working holidaymakers. It was submitted that the wording "before settling down" did not require L to have proved that he had not "settled down" prior to coming to the UK but that his holiday be followed by a period of such "settling down". This view was held by a division of the Tribunal in *Sunita Rani* (Unreported), following a decision to the opposite effect by another division of the Tribunal in *Oliatan-Oladfe Adejumoke v. Secretary of State for the Home Department* [1993] Imm. A.R. 265.

Held, dismissing the appeal, that (1) the rule required that the applicant for leave as a working holidaymaker had not settled down in his own country before making his own application, *Adejumoke* applied to that extent, and (2) the rule did not require that the applicant show an intention of settling down in his own country on completion of the working holiday, *Rani* disapproved.

LANA v. SECRETARY OF STATE FOR THE HOME DEPARTMENT [1997] Imm. A.R. 17, Brooke, L.J., CA.

2917. Entry clearances–indefinite leave to remain–evidence of previous entry clearance

[Immigration Act 1971 s.3(4), s.33(1).]

W, re-applied for leave to apply for judicial review of a decision refusing an in country right of appeal against the refusal of entry rights. W had been granted indefinite leave to remain in the UK, but left the UK and was subsequently refused re-entry on the ground, inter alia, that previous leave had been obtained by deception. W contended that the passport stamp giving indefinite leave was an "other document" for the purposes of the Immigration Act 1971 s.33(1) and constituted entry clearance.

Held, dismissing the applications, that pursuant to s.3(4) of the 1971 Act, indefinite leave lapsed when W left the country and therefore the stamps could not provide subsequent evidence of entry clearance, *R. v. Secretary of State for the Home Department, ex p. Katoorah* [1996] Imm. A.R. 595, [1997] C.L.Y. 2923 followed.

WAGNER v. IMMIGRATION OFFICER, Trans. Ref: LTA 96/7692/D, LTA 96/7861/D, June 4, 1997, Pill, L.J., CA.

2918. Entry clearances—marriage—non EC national—common law relationship with EC national long resident in UK—whether common law wife within meaning of "spouse"

[Commission Regulation 1251/70 on the right of workers to remain in the territory of a Member State after having been employed in that State Art.1, Art.2, Art.3; Council Directive 73/0148 on the abolition of restritions on movement and residence within the Community for nationals of Member States with regard to establishment and the provision of services Art.1; European Convention on Human Rights 1950 Art.8.]

M, a Columbian national, came to the UK in 1990 and was granted leave as a visitor. She became an overstayer. During that period she formed a relationship with B, a Portugese national long resident in the UK. A daughter, F, was born to them on February 6, 1993. In December M and F left to go to Columbia. They returned on March 15, 1995 and M sought leave to enter as B's common law spouse. This was refused but temporary admission until May 25, 1995 was granted. After interviews, the immigration officer set out his refusal in a letter of May 7, 1995 maintaining that there were no exceptional or compelling circumstances to justify granting entry outside the Immigration Rules. After further representations leave to seek for judicial review of a letter of May 19 reconfirming the decision was granted, with the ground being whether the Secretary of State had applied his mind to possible breaches of the right to family life in the European Convention on Human Rights 1950 Art.8. As a result the Secretary of State wrote a letter on January 11, 1996 addressing that question. It was submitted that (1) the decision of the Secretary of State constituted a breach of Commission Regulation 1251/70 Art.1, Art.2 and Art.3 and Council Directive 73/0148 Art.1.1 (c), as the meaning of the word "spouse" had been misconstrued; (2) the effect of the decision would deny F her right to family life, and (3) the Secretary of State should not have considered the exercise of discretion only on the question of the existence of compelling or compassionate circumstances, since the relationship was a stable one.

Held, refusing the application for judicial review, that (1) it was clear in EC law that "spouse" did not include a common law wife, *Netherlands v. Reed* [1986] E.C.R. 1283, [1987] C.L.Y. 1568 relied on; (2) the Secretary of State had properly taken into account the provisions regarding the right to family life, despite its not being part of English law, and (3) the Secretary of State had acted properly in considering the exercise of his discretion on the grounds of compelling or compassionate circumstances.

R. v. SECRETARY OF STATE FOR THE HOME DEPARTMENT, *ex p.* MORENO LOPEZ [1997] Imm. A.R. 11, Dyson, J., QBD.

2919. Entry clearances—marriage—vires of primary purpose test of marriage— different treatment of British and EU nationals

[Immigration (European Economic Area) Order 1994 (SI 1994 1895); Immigration Act 1971 s.3(2).]

T and three others applied for judicial review of the refusal of entry to them on primary purpose grounds, claiming that the primary purpose test itself was unlawful and ultra vires. The applicants contended that: (1) that the subsequent introduction of the Immigration (European Economic Area) Order 1994 had given other European nationals greater rights to bring their spouses into the UK than British nationals had, a situation so unreasonable that Parliament could not have intended it, and (2) that too much importance had been attached to the desire of the British spouse to remain in the UK, as opposed to the intentions of the applicant for entry.

Held, allowing two applications and dismissing two others, that (1) although there were patent differences between the way in which British nationals and those of other EU countries were treated, both on initial entry and on return from work in another EU country, the Immigration Act 1971 s.3(2) expressly allowed such non-uniform decisions and a difference between the rights available under European law and domestic rights did not call into question the vires of the rule, and (2) merely because the sponsor wished to remain in the UK and therefore a firm desire to live together would be conditional on the applicant's successful application for entry, did not automatically make the applicant's primary purpose that of obtaining entry to the UK, *Masood (Sumeina) v. Immigration Appeal Tribunal* [1992] Imm. A.R. 69, [1992] C.L.Y. 2434 disapproved, *R v. Immigration Appeal Tribunal, ex p. Secretary of State for the Home Department* [1992] 3 All. E.R. 798 considered, *R. v. Immigration Appeal Tribunal, ex p. Hoque and Singh* [1988] Imm. A.R. 216, [1989] C.L.Y. 1962 and *R. v. Secretary of State for the Home Department, ex p. Phull* [1996] Imm. A. R. 72, [1996] C.L.Y. 3277 followed.

R. v. IMMIGRATION APPEAL TRIBUNAL, *ex p.* TONDA, Trans. Ref: CO/3767/95, CO/3927/95, CO/2080/96, CO/2080/96, November 29, 1996, Keene, J., QBD.

2920. Entry clearances–students–breach of conditions of entry–return after brief absence–college letter produced to immigration officer did not reveal history–material deceptions on re-entry–standard of proof

[Immigration Act 1971 s.26(1).]

K, a Ugandan citizen, was granted leave to stay in the UK as a student for two years, providing he did not take paid employment during the course. Once in the UK he rejected his chosen course for another and obtained paid employment for three months of the intervening period. His father's death occasioned a return to Uganda. Re-entering the UK he produced a letter from the college at which he was to study. This confirmed that a place had been reserved for him on a full time course, that he had returned home due to bereavement and that he would be resuming his college studies. A subsequent investigation revealed his true immigration history, deemed him to be an illegal entrant and steps were taken to remove him. K sought leave to move for judicial review, claiming that he had committed no misrepresentation of the type referred to in the Immigration Act 1971 s.26(1) (c) and that termination of his leave to stay was therefore unreasonable. Further, that misrepresentation was a fraudulent offence which required a higher standard of proof than the one employed.

Held, dismissing R's application, that (1) the Secretary of State had applied the standard of "a high degree of probability", which was correct, *Akinde v. Secretary of State for the Home Department* [1993] Imm. A.R. 512, [1994] C.L.Y. 2490 applied; (2) there had been a silent misrepresentation that K had previously fulfilled the conditions he recorded in his passport, when he presented it, and (3) if the true facts had been known, and particularly when further investigations had revealed the full immigration history of K, the immigration officer would have refused K leave to enter.

R. v. SECRETARY OF STATE FOR THE HOME DEPARTMENT, *ex p.* KUTEESA [1997] Imm. A.R. 194, Harrison, J., QBD.

2921. Entry clearances–students–immigration officer not satisfied applicant would leave at end of leave period–no exceptional circumstances justified grant of leave–no legitimate expectation created by information from the High Commission

C, a Kenyan, arrived in the UK without entry clearance and sought to enter as a student. He was refused leave to enter on October 20, 1995. C's application was refused under the Immigration Rules (HC 395) para.57 (iv) and para.57 (vi) as the immigration officer was not satisfied that C would leave the UK on completion of the course, nor that C would be able to meet the costs of the course and of maintenance without working or recourse to public funds. In a letter of February 1, 1996, the immigration service explained in detail the reasons for the refusal. C applied for judicial review, arguing that (1) it was disputed whether C had stated that on return to Kenya he proposed to set up his own manufacturing facility, which the immigration officer had concluded to be unrealistic given the nature of the course C proposed to follow and the financial situation of C's family with the result that the decision was irrational; (2) the immigration officer had made an error of fact as to C's bank balance when deciding on his financial situation; (3) the circumstances of the case were sufficiently exceptional to justify granting of leave, despite *R. v. Secretary of State for the Home Department, ex p. Swati* [1986] Imm. A.R. 88, [1986] C.L.Y. 1711 and the fact of alternative remedy, *R. v. Secretary of State for the Home Department, ex p. Hindjou* [1989] Imm. A.R. 24, [1991] C.L.Y. 2048a relied upon, and (4) C had legitimate expectation of entry: he was told by the High Commission that he did not need entry clearance to apply for leave to enter, therefore he did not apply for it.

Held, refusing the judicial review application, that (1) the immigration officer had given more than one reason for refusing the application, and even if the court were able to resolve issues of fact, being wrong on one issue did not invalidate the immigration officer's decision; (2) the decision was not irrational; (3) the case could be distinguished from *Hindjou*; (4) if *Swati* were side-stepped in this case "the principle would be so severely undermined that it would rapidly disappear", and (5) the High Commission did not have to tell C how his appeal rights might be affected by the absence of entry clearance, nor could any legitimate expectation arise from information it gave C.

R. v. SECRETARY OF STATE FOR THE HOME DEPARTMENT, *ex p.* CLAY [1997] Imm. A.R. 7, Dyson, J., QBD.

2922. Entry clearances–students–judicial review of refusal unavailable where out of country appeal existed

[Immigration Act 1971 s.13.]

C and her cousin K, from Zimbabwe and aged 18 and 19 respectively, applied for judicial review to quash the refusal of leave to enter to study a computer course. C's aunt had agreed to pay their living expenses and college fees but had been vague about their subsequent return to Zimbabwe.

Held, dismissing the applications, that it was only in exceptional circumstances that judicial review would be available where there was an alternative procedure. The Immigration Act 1971 s.13 allowed a right of appeal but not while the applicant remained in the UK. Although C's circumstances were unfortunate, they were insufficiently exceptional, *R. v. Chief Immigration Officer Gatwick Airport, ex p. Kharrazi* [1980] 3 All E.R. 373, [1980] C.L.Y. 1428 distinguished.

R. v. SECRETARY OF STATE FOR THE HOME DEPARTMENT, *ex p.* CHINODA, Trans. Ref: FC3 97/5311/D, July 4, 1997, Sir Brian Neill, CA.

2923. Entry clearances–students–lapse of leave to remain as student–no legitimate expection of right to enter following holiday abroad

[Immigration Act 1971 s.3(4).]

K, a Mauritian national, came to the United Kingdom on May 17, 1994 and was given leave to enter as a visitor, later changed in September to leave to remain as a student, extended twice, up to September 30, 1996. The leave was subject to the Immigration Rules (HC 395) para.57(v), requiring that the student did not go into employment. In 1995 K did some work and was warned by the Home Office. On April 5, 1996, K went on holiday returning on April 11. On leaving, his leave had lapsed according to the Immigration Act 1971 s.3(4). On his return he was questioned by an immigration officer. As a result of enquiries, it was decided to treat him as a new arrival, leave to enter was refused and removal instructions were issued. The authorities were not convinced he would leave the country on the completion of his studies. It was submitted that (1) K should not have been treated as a new arrival at all; (2) even so, the determination to refuse leave to enter had been *Wednesbury* unreasonable, because the evidence did not justify it; (3) the current leave stamp in K's passport demonstrated eligibility to enter, and (4) K had a legitimate expectation that he would be treated as a person with a right to enter, based on the statement from the Home Secretary to the House of Commons in April 17, 1991.

Held, dismissing the application for leave to move, that (1) on leaving the country, K's leave had lapsed, the immigration officer had to take into account every relevant factor, which he did; (2) the decision to deny entry had not been *Wednesbury* unreasonable; (3) in the light of *Ghassemian and Mizra v. Home Office* [1989] Imm. A.R. 42, [1991] C.L.Y. 2016 and the Immigration Rules (HC 395) para.25 it was impossible to argue that the current stamp of leave in the passport was equivalent to an entry clearance or evidence of eligibility to enter; (4) the ministerial statement referred to gave K no legitimate expectation that he would be treated as a person with a right to enter, or to appeal, and (5) someone who was visa exempt could not be treated as someone with a visa.

R. v. SECRETARY OF STATE FOR THE HOME DEPARTMENT, *ex p.* KATOORAH; *sub nom.* KATOORAH v. SECRETARY OF STATE FOR THE HOME DEPARTMENT [1996] Imm. A.R. 595, Neill, L.J., CA.

2924. European Economic Area–rights of residence

IMMIGRATION (EUROPEAN ECONOMIC AREA) (AMENDMENT) ORDER 1997, SI 1997 2981; made under the European Communities Act 1972 s.2. In force: February 1, 1998; £0.65.

This Order, which amends the Immigration (European Economic Area) Order 1994 (SI 1994 1895), implements certain requirements of Council Directive 93/96 ([1993] OJ L317/59) on the right of residence of students, Council Directive 90/365 ([1990] OJ L180/28) on the right of residence for employees and self employed persons who have ceased their occupational activity and Council Directive 90/364 ([1990] OJ L180/26) on the right of residence.

2925. Freedom of movement–right of abode–Directive giving residence rights to non-EU spouses of EU workers did not apply to husband of British citizen working in UK

[Council Directive 68/360 on the abolition of restrictions on movement and residence within the Community for workers of Member States and their families Art.4.]

An Indian citizen married to a British citizen was not entitled to indefinite leave to remain in the UK as that would give British citizens and spouses an advantage over those from other Member States in exercising their rights to free movement which would be unacceptable in EC law. A was a British citizen with a right of abode in the UK and a citizen of the European Community. Pursuant to her right to free movement under EC law, A went to live in Germany, where she married S, an Indian citizen, and both lawfully resided and worked in Germany. When they returned to the UK, S applied for indefinite leave to remain, but this was refused and he was given a residence document valid until November 1999. The Immigration Appeal Tribunal allowed S's appeal against the refusal to grant indefinite leave and the Secretary of State appealed. S contended that Council Directive 68/360 Art.4.4 entitled him to the same rights of residence in the UK as his wife, as the Directive represented an amalgam of EC and national law. The Secretary of State argued that rights of residence under EC law remained separate from those under domestic law.

Held, allowing the appeal, that every EC citizen had the right to reside and work anywhere within the EC and non-working spouses were entitled to accompany their spouse even if they were not a national of any Member State. The purpose of the Directive was to ensure that the arrangements made for workers from other Member States and their accompanying families were the same as those for nationals in the host state. There was nothing to suggest that the Directive was to apply to workers who were working in the state in which they were nationals. Under domestic law, people in S's position did not upon marriage become automatically entitled to the same rights as their spouse and there was nothing in EC law to suggest that S was entitled to indefinite leave to remain, as such a right would not be immediately available to every EC citizen entering the UK, nor to their spouse. To grant S such a right would have the effect of giving British citizens and their spouses an advantage over those in other Member States in exercising their rights to free movement and such discrimination would be unacceptable in EC law.

SAHOTA v. SECRETARY OF STATE FOR THE HOME DEPARTMENT; ZEGHRABA v. SECRETARY OF STATE FOR THE HOME DEPARTMENT, *The Times*, April 30, 1997, Judge, L.J., CA.

2926. Illegal entrants–deception used to obtain leave to enter–whether knowledge imputed to others

[Immigration Act 1971 s.26 (1).]

P and R were minors and citizens of the Philippines. Their mother, J, was given leave to enter the United Kingdom in 1984. In September 1989 she divorced her then husband and shortly after married a British citizen, B. In April 1990 she was given leave to remain until April 9, 1991 as a spouse. She was issued a passport by the Philippine Embassy, with leave to remain as a spouse endorsed on it until May 9, 1991. On October 8, 1990 she returned to the Philippines where her children were then living. On November 6 a further passport was issued to her there. On November 15 she applied for visas for P and R and herself for a 20 day visit. On the application forms she was described as the wife of an American citizen, living at the American Forces base in the Philippines. On November 17 P and R, then aged 15 and 12, arrived at Gatwick with their mother. They were given leave to enter as visitors, and J was granted indefinite leave to remain as the wife of B. Around the same time J applied for leave for P and R to remain as her dependants. The authorities made enquiries and discovered that despite her first passport being valid, she had applied for a visa on November 15 on her new passport, and she was granted a two day visa for her and her children. They also discovered that the applications had been supported by notes allegedly from the United States Embassy showing J, P and R to be the dependants of a United States airman. They were advised that there was no such person, and later learned that the notes and other documents had been forged, and also that J had not told the visa officer that she already had leave to remain as B's wife, nor did she tell the immigration officer at Gatwick that she had a different concurrent passport. The authorities came to the conclusion on August 19, 1994 that settlement had been J's intention all along and that she had deceived the authorities in order to gain visas and entry for P and R, which made P and R illegal entrants under the Immigration Act 1971 s. 26 (1) (c). It was submitted that there had been no deception practised with the intention of obtaining leave to enter the United Kingdom and if there had been, it had solely on the part of J, and P and R had no knowledge of it and were not parties to it.

Held, dismissing the application for leave, that (1) it was clear that there was deception on the part of the mother and that the complicated scheme used to secure entry made it likely that the children were parties to it; (2) it was sufficient for the determination under section 26 (1) (c) for S to show that the deception had been likely to influence the decision to allow entry rather than actually effective in obtaining leave to enter; (3) in any case the more stringent test was satisfied, and (4) following *R. v. Secretary of State for the Home Department, ex p. Khan* [1977] 1 W.L.R. 1466 even if it had not been shown that the children had been parties to the deception, the deception of the mother was to be imputed to them.

R. v. SECRETARY OF STATE FOR THE HOME DEPARTMENT, *ex p.* CASTRO [1996] Imm. A.R. 540, Dyson, J., QBD.

2927. Illegal entrants–detention–habeas corpus–admissibility of hearsay evidence

R appealed against the decision refusing habeas corpus on the ground that evidence admitted was hearsay and inadmissible. The judge admitted evidence obtained in Bangladesh, including interviews submitted by immigration officers. R obtained a certificate of entitlement to the right of abode in the UK by claiming to be the son of a UK citizen. R's wife later applied to join him in the UK, together with a child she claimed to be theirs. After receiving letters alleging that the child was not theirs and that R was using a false name and was not the son of the British citizen named, entry clearance officers in Bangladesh made enquiries about R in two villages. The Secretary of State concluded that the certificate of entitlement had been obtained by deception and R was detained as an illegal entrant.

Held, dismissing the appeal, that the disputed evidence was admissible, *R v. Secretary of State for the Home Department ex parte Khawaja* [1984] A.C. 74 applied. The court was entitled to take into account all relevant material on which the Secretary of State might have properly relied, even if it did not meet the standard required for admissibility during a trial. Steps could have been taken to present the evidence in a more convincing manner but was nevertheless highly persuasive evidence to which very considerable weight must be attached. The court could attach whatever weight it thought appropriate to such evidence, including that the evidence should be disregarded altogether. The evidence was more than sufficient to prove that R was not who he claimed to be, he had obtained entry to the UK by fraud and was an illegal entrant.

R. v. SECRETARY OF STATE FOR THE HOME DEPARTMENT, *ex p.* RAHMAN; *sub nom.* RAHMAN SAIDUR, *Re* [1997] 1 All E.R. 796, Hutchison, L.J., CA.

2928. Illegal entrants–foreign nationals on boat–entry not necessary to be illegal entrant

[Immigration Act 1971 s.11.]

A appealed against conviction of assisting illegal entry into the United Kingdom on the basis that the foreign nationals found on a boat by customs officers had not disembarked and were not illegal entrants.

Held, dismissing the appeal, that under the Immigration Act 1971 s.11 a person could be an illegal entrant before the entry was affected, *R. v. Naillie* [1993] 2 All E.R. 782, [1993] C.L.Y. 2196 considered.

R. v. ADAMS [1996] Crim. L.R. 593, Roch, L.J., CA (Crim Div).

2929. Illegal entrants–interviews–mistranslation of caution at interview–attempted exclusion of evidence

[Police and Criminal Evidence Act 1984 s.76.]

Y entered the UK on March 27, 1994 with entry clearance obtained in October 1993. He sought to enter for one month to further his business as a jeweller and to make a social visit. In the interim he had gone to Pakistan, and was suspected of murder. He went into hiding for about five months then made his way to the UK. On entry he told the immigration officer that he proposed to stay for two weeks, that the purpose of his visit was business and a holiday, that he proposed to stay in the Hilton Hotel in London. He was granted six months' entry. He then went straight to Manchester and then sought asylum. He was arrested whilst working in a takeaway in Manchester on November 13, 1994. He was then interviewed as a suspected illegal entrant. In the interview, the caution was mistranslated by the interpreter. As a result of the interview the immigration officer concluded that if the entry officer had been aware of the true facts and intentions as admitted at interview, he would have not granted leave to enter as a visitor. On November 13, 1994, the Secretary of State decided to issue Y with a notice of illegal entry and to authorise deportation. Y appealed. Leave to move was refused on July 27, 1995. Y appealed arguing that (1) in considering the judicial review application, the record of the interview should have been set aside in assessing whether, following *R. v. Secretary of State for the Home Department, ex p. Khawaja* [1984] A.C. 74, [1983] C.L.Y. 1908, the Secretary of State had proved to the requisite standard that Y was an illegal entrant, and (2) the mistranslation of the caution amounted to oppression, had it been correctly translated Y claimed he would have said nothing at all, the interview had been investigating a possible criminal offence as well as the possibility of Y being an illegal entrant, therefore under the Police and Criminal Evidence Act 1984 s.76 the evidence should have been set aside.

Held, dismissing the appeal, that (1) the provisions of the Police and Criminal Evidence Act 1984 applied only to criminal proceedings, it was not improper that the interview notes were consulted and given appropriate weight in considering the application for leave to move, and (2) Y could not argue that had he told the truth to the immigration officer on entry, he would still have been granted leave to enter, *Bugdaycay v. Secretary of State for the Home Department* [1987] A.C. 514, [1987] C.L.Y. 1989 followed.

R. v. SECRETARY OF STATE FOR THE HOME DEPARTMENT, *ex p.* YASIN [1997] Imm. A.R. 96, Kennedy, L.J., CA.

2930. Illegal entrants–marriage–application for leave to remain on basis of marriage–visit to Ireland and return did not mean previous enforcement proceedings had lapsed

A, a Nigerian, entered the UK in May 1991, having misled the immigration officer on entry. This was discovered later and in September 1994, having admitted the deception, A was served with a notice of illegal entry. In February 1995, A married a British citizen. A travelled to Ireland for two days between October 21 and 23, 1995. On return to the UK he did not make any steps to obtain leave to enter and was therefore an illegal entrant. Shortly afterwards A applied for leave to remain on the grounds of his marriage. It was argued that, although prior to October 21, 1995 his marriage post-dated enforcement action and he was not entitled to rely on it under policy statement DP/2/93, because of his re-entry to the UK he was liable to be required to leave again, so the marriage had a different status and pre-dated enforcement action.

Held, dismissing a renewed judicial review application, that (1) A was still an illegal entrant after his visit to Ireland; (2) in general terms the marriage A sought to rely on did not pre-date enforcement action, and (3) A was seeking discretionary leave to remain under the terms of a policy document. The application had to be considered on its merits and the Secretary of State had not been unreasonable in his approach or conclusions.

R. v. SECRETARY OF STATE FOR THE HOME DEPARTMENT, *ex p.* ADEBIYI; *sub nom.* ADEBIYI v. SECRETARY OF STATE FOR THE HOME DEPARTMENT [1997] Imm. A.R. 57, Hobhouse, L.J., CA.

2931. Illegal entrants–marriage–marriage after refusal of asylum–rationality of policy DP/2/93

[European Convention on Human Rights 1950 Art.8; .]

K sought judicial review of the decision to refuse him indefinite leave to remain. K, an Indian citizen, entered the UK clandestinely in March 1991. He applied for political asylum in May 1991, and his application was refused in October 1991. The notice of refusal of asylum was with a notice to him as an illegal entrant. K appealed. On February 20. 1993, K married. His appeal was heard and rejected in May 1996. On June 3, 1993 K applied for leave to remain on the basis of marriage. That was refused. The Secretary of State concluded that the marriage post dated the commencement of enforcement action, which had begun with the service of notice to K as an illegal entrant. It was argued that the policy followed by the Secretary of State in making the decision, DP/2/93, was irrational in not distinguishing between a marriage contracted by an illegal entrant and one contracted by an illegal entrant who at the time of the marriage was irremovable from the UK because of an outstanding asylum appeal. K had also had a legitimate expectation that he would be granted leave in the light of the UK's obligation to respect family life under the European Convention on Human Rights 1950 Art.8.

Held, dismissing the application, that (1) K was an illegal entrant and remained so although pending the determination of his asylum appeal he could not be removed from the UK; (2) it could not be said that the marriage predated enforcement action; (3) the Secretary of State had not been irrational in his decision; (4) the provisions of DP/2/93 applied, and (5) following *R. v. Secretary of State for the Home Department, ex p. Brind* [1991] 1 A.C. 696, [1991] C.L.Y. 71 on the facts of the case K had no legitimate expectation that he would be granted leave to remain on the basis of his marriage.

R. v. SECRETARY OF STATE FOR THE HOME DEPARTMENT, *ex p.* SINGH (BALWANT) [1997] Imm. A.R. 331, Sedley, J., QBD.

2932. **Illegal entrants–marriage–previous deportation–return to UK on false passport–earlier removal directions constituted commencement of enforcement action**

Z, an Algerian citizen, was removed from the UK as an illegal entrant on September 29, 1992. He returned in October 1993 using a false Italian passport. He then married a British citizen. On the basis of the marriage Z sought exceptional leave to remain. The Secretary of State concluded he was an illegal entrant and gave removal directions set for November 8, 1996. It was contended that (1) Z's marriage pre-dated the second set of enforcement proceedings; (2) the Secretary of State had misdirected himself in his application of DP/2/93 in taking the enforcement proceedings ending in removal on September 29, 1992 as "enforcement action" within DP/2/93, and (3) there was no "enforcement action" in being when Z married, the Secretary of State was therefore prima facie in violation of his own policy.

Held, dismissing application for judicial review, that (1) following *R. v. Secretary of State for the Home Department, ex p. Resham Singh* (Unreported, 1996), the Secretary of State was entitled to rely on Z's earlier removal as the commencement of enforcement action for the purposes of DP/2/93, and (2) it was not possible to argue, in the light of the wording of DP/2/93, that enforcement action was no more than part of Z's immigration history, *R. v. Secretary of State for the Home Department, ex p. Adebiyi* [1997] Imm. A.R. 57, [1997] C.L.Y. 2930 followed.

R. v. SECRETARY OF STATE FOR THE HOME DEPARTMENT, *ex p.* ZELLOUF [1997] Imm. A.R. 120, Ognall, J., QBD.

2933. **Isle of Man–Immigration Act 1971–extension of provisions**

IMMIGRATION (ISLE OF MAN) ORDER 1997, SI 1997 275; made under the Immigration Act 1971 s.36; and the Asylum and Immigration Appeals Act 1993 s.15. In force: April 1, 1997; £1.55.

Subject to modifications, this Order extends provisions of the Immigration Act 1971 relating to appeals, related provisions in the Asylum and Immigration Appeals Act 1993 and the Immigration (Carriers' Liability) Act 1987 to the Isle of Man.

2934. **Refugees–application for refugee status–interpretation of Convention provisions–Australia**

[Migration Act 1958 s.4 (Australia); Convention Relating to the Status of Refugees 1951 (United Nations) Art.1.]

A, Chinese nationals, arrived in Australia by boat in December 1993. They were detained as illegal entrants and refused entry permits. They then lodged applications for recognition as refugees, on the basis that they were persons who were outside their country of origin "owing to a well-founded fear of being persecuted for reasons of...membership of a particular social group..", within the meaning of the Migration Act 1958 s.4(1) and the United Nations Convention Art.1 (A) (2). A had just had their first child and they had fled fearing forced sterilisation if they remained in China. Their application was refused by the Minister, but that decision was reversed by the Refugee Review Tribunal. The tribunal's decision was upheld by a Federal Court judge but reversed by the full Federal Court. A appealed to the High Court.

Held, dismissing the appeal, that a holistic approach was required in interpreting provisions of the 1951 Convention, *Golder v. UK* (A/18) (1975) 1 E.H.R.R. 524, *Commonwealth v. Tasmania* (1983) 158 C.L.R. 1 applied. Primacy must be given to the written text, but the context, object and purpose of the treaty must also be considered. The meaning of "particular social group" in Art.1 (A) (2) of the Convention must be construed in the light of the definition of "refugee taken as a whole". That definition was directed to the protection of individuals who have been or were likely to be the victims of intentional discrimination of a particular kind. Conduct would not constitute persecution if it was appropriate and adapted to achieving some legitimate object of the country of the refugee, *Yang v. Carroll* (1994) 852 F Supp 460 considered. The phrase "particular social group" was not capable of a single exhaustive definition. However, the concept of persecution could have no place in defining that phrase. To do so would make the other four grounds of persecution superfluous. Persons who sought to fall within the definition of "refugee" must demonstrate that the form of persecution which they fear was not a defining characteristic of the "particular social group" of which they claim membership, *Secretary of State for Home Dept v. Savchenkov* [1996] Imm. A.R. 28, [1996] 1 C.L.Y. 3205 applied. The existence of a particular social group depended on external perceptions of the group, so that it must be identifiable as a social unit. In the instant case, since the particular social group to which A claimed to belong, namely Han people who have one child, who wish to have another and who were subject to forced sterilisation, was defined by reference to the persecutory conduct, then that group was not a "particular social group" for the purposes of the Convention. There was no social attribute or characteristic linking the couples and nothing external that would allow them to be perceived as a particular social group for Convention purposes.

A v. MINISTER FOR IMMIGRATION AND ETHNIC AFFAIRS (1997) 2 B.H.R.C. 143, Brennan, C.J., HC (Aus).

2935. Special Immigration Appeals Commission Act 1997 (c.68)

This Act establishes the Special Immigration Appeals Commission and makes provision with respect to its jurisdiction.

This Act received Royal Assent on December 17, 1997.

2936. Articles

A survey of some recent tribunal determinations in asylum cases *(Richard McKee)*: I. & N.L. & P. 1997, 11 (3), 79-86. (Arranged by country, issue and procedure, including certified asylum claims).

Asylum and Immigration Act 1996: section 8: J.P. 1997, 161 (6), 147. (Home Office Circular 2 of 1997 on provision in force January 27, 1997 on criminal liability for employers who recruit illegal entrants).

Asylum seekers *(Alison Fenney)*: Adviser 1997, 63, 18-20. (Local authorities' duties to provide assistance to asylum seekers with no other means of support under the National Assistance Act 1948 and extent to which authorities are providing services).

Current issues in immigration law *(Richard McKee)*: I. & N.L. & P. 1997, 11 (2), 46-56. (Rights of appeal for refugees, illegal entrants and overstayers against detention and deportation orders, bail applications, includes glossary of terms used in asylum appeals).

Disability discrimination and employment of immigrants *(Susan Singleton)*: P.P.M. 1997, 15(5), 72-74. (Employment implications of 1995 and 1996 Acts for those disabled or subject to immigration control).

Electronic immigration network to be launched in the United Kingdom *(Finn Jensen)*: I.J.R.L. 1997, 9(2), 274-277. (Service will include database with determinations from Immigration Appeals Tribunal in addition to bulletin boards and Internet site).

Employer sanctions: a UK own goal in Europe? *(Elspeth Guild)*: N.L.J. 1997, 147(6793), 773-774. (Whether Asylum and Immigration Act 1996 s.8 prohibition on employers hiring certain European residents is incompatible with EC law).

Employing illegal workers: IDS Brief 1997, 592, 7-10. (Foreign nationals subject to restrictions on working in UK and steps which can be taken by employers to avoid committing offence of employing foreign nationals who are in breach of immigration conditions).

Gaining access: L.S.G. 1997, 94(38), 22-25. (Immigration solicitors' views of restrictions on legal representation for asylum seekers, homosexuals' lack of equal treatment from immigration authorities and continuing difficulties following abolition of primary purpose rule).

Gaps in international protection and the potential for redress through individual complaints procedures *(Oldrich Andrysek)*: I.J.R.L. 1997, 9(3), 392-414. (Extent of refugees' protection against repatriation under various Conventions and Agreements, and practical effectiveness of European and UN mechanisms for enforcement of these rights).

Homelessness, immigration and asylum law *(Simon Halliday)*: S.L.P.Q. 1997, 2(4), 316-327. (History of developing interrelationship between immigration and homelessness law, outline of current position as to who is denied or entitled to assistance under homelessness legislation and implications for housing authorities).

Immigration controls and employers' sanctions *(Declan O'Dempsey* and *Katie Ghose)*: Emp. L. Brief. 1997, 4(3), 28-32. (Offences committable by employers recruiting illegal immigrants, examining corporate and personal liability, defences, requirements for record keeping with list of specified documents, and possibility of race discrimination).

Judicial review of discretion in human rights cases *(Nicholas Blake)*: E.H.R.L.R. 1997, 4, 391-403. (Relationship between ECHR and UK judicial review of executive discretion, particularly with regard to cases involving deportation or expulsion).

Marriage policy: I. & N.L. & P. 1997, 11(1), 23-24. (Text of Home Office policy on removal or deportation of a person who has married person settled in UK).

New law prohibits employment of illegal immigrants: E.I.R.R. 1997, 278, 24-25. (Criminal offence introduced on January 27, 1997 making it illegal for employers to hire any person not having permission to live and work in UK and implications for employers).

Recent developments in immigration law *(Jawaid Luqmani)*: Legal Action 1997, Nov, 21-25. (Legislation and government policy reviews, and cases on asylum seekers and EC law).

Recent developments in immigration law *(Jawaid Luqmani)*: Legal Action 1997, Mar, 21-28. (Changes in Immigration Rules effective since November 1, 1996, restrictions on employment, restricted service at Public Enquiry Office, compulsory application forms, ILPA meeting with Home Office and recent cases).

Restructuring asylum: recent trends in United Kingdom asylum law and policy *(Colin J. Harvey)*: I.J.R.L. 1997, 9(1), 60-73. (Legislative changes have emphasised policy of deterrence and restriction in relation to refugees and asylum seekers).

Schengen II and Dublin: responsibility for asylum applications in Europe *(Kay Hailbronner)* and *(Claus Thiery)*: C.M.L. Rev. 1997, 34(4), 957-989. (Link between Dublin Convention on responsibility for asylum applications and Schengen Implementation Agreement on internal border controls, defining concept of responsibility and looking at German experience of Schengen system).

The process of protection *(Madeline Garlick)*: Legal Action 1997, Aug, 8. (Reforms needed in procedures for dealing with asylum applications including broad criteria for protection and improvements in primary stage decision making, appeals system and quality of legal advice).

UK immigration and asylum: the 1993 and 1996 Acts *(Bernard Andonian)*: I.L.P. 1997, 22(1), 15-19. (Rights of immigrants, asylum seekers and illegal entrants, employers' duty to check immigrants' status and restrictions on availability of welfare benefits).

Undercutting integration: developments in Union policy on third-country nationals *(Steve Peers)*: E.L.R. 1997, 22(1), 76-84. (Establishment of concept of long term residence of non-nationals of EU, and process of integration and right of residence in Member States in which they have been domiciled).

2937. Books

Boeles, Pieter—Fair Immigration Proceedings in Europe. Nijhoff Law Specials. Hardback: £117.00. ISBN 90-411-0324-4. Kluwer Law International.

Phelan, M.—Immigration Law Handbook. Paperback: £35.00. ISBN 1-85431-596-X. Blackstone Press.

INCOME TAX

2938. Additional voluntary contributions—surplus payments returned to employee

INCOME TAX (CHARGE TO TAX) (PAYMENTS OUT OF SURPLUS FUNDS) (RELEVANT RATE) ORDER 1997, SI 1997 369; made under the Income and Corporation Taxes Act 1988 s.599A. In force: April 6, 1997; £0.65.

The Income and Corporation Taxes Act 1988 provides that where a payment of surplus additional voluntary contributions is returned to an employee or to his personal representatives, the administrator of the scheme shall be charged to income tax under Case VI of Sch.D at the relevant rate on such amount as, after deduction of tax at that rate, would equal the amount of the payment. This Order reduces the relevant rate to 33 per cent.

2939. Appeals

Z applied for an extension of time for appealing an order of the High Court ([1994] C.L.Y. 2526) dismissing his application for an adjournment and affirming a determination made by the Special Commissioners.

Held, dismissing the application, that there was no chance of the appeal succeeding if an extension of time was granted, *Norwich and Peterborough Building Society v. Steed* [1991] 1 W.L.R. 449, [1991] C.L.Y. 2778 followed. The Commissioners heard considerable oral evidence over a 15 day period and concluded that Z's evidence was untruthful; they could not be expected to hear further evidence from a surveyor.

ZIELINSKI v. PICKERING (INSPECTOR OF TAXES) 68 T.C. 295, Nourse, L.J., CA.

2940. Appeals—errors and additions in respect of case stated

See TAXATION: Euro Fire Ltd v. Davison (Inspector of Taxes) (Note). §4741

2941. Assessments—payments on account—prescribed proportions

INCOME TAX (PAYMENTS ON ACCOUNT) (AMENDMENT) REGULATIONS 1997, SI 1997 2491; made under the Taxes Management Act 1970 s.59A. In force: November 7, 1997; £0.65.

The Taxes Management Act 1970 s.59A provides for a taxpayer to make payments on account of income tax as regards a year of assessment, if, as regards the immediately preceding year, certain conditions are satisfied. One of the conditions is that the proportion which the relevant amount bears to the assessed amount is not less than such proportion as may be prescribed. The Income Tax (Payments on Account) Regulations 1996 (SI 1996 1654) prescribed the relevant amount, and that proportion, respectively. These Regulations correct an error in the 1996 Regulations, by amending the proportion from one to four to one to five.

2942. Bonds–personal portfolio bonds–purchase whilst transferor was resident outside UK did not give rise to tax liability–bonds purchased in UK were not tax avoidance vehicles

[Income and Corporation Taxes Act 1988 s.739(1), s.739(2), s.741.]

W and his wife had taken out three offshore personal portfolio bonds, one whilst resident outside the UK and the others after becoming resident in the UK. The IRC appealed against a Court of Appeal ruling upholding a decision to discharge assessments to income tax made against W in respect of the bonds. The IRC contended that the first bond purchased fell foul of the Income and Corporation Taxes Act 1988 s.739, which was aimed at preventing tax avoidance by individuals ordinarily resident in the UK by the transfer of assets abroad. The IRC argued that it was wrong to differentiate between individuals who were not resident in the UK at the time of the transfer and those who were, and the critical test was where the individual was resident at the time the income from the bonds was received. The IRC further submitted that the two bonds purchased in the UK also contravened s.739 as they were not the type of bonds which could fall within the exemption in s.741 for transactions that did not have a purpose of tax avoidance.

Held, dismissing the appeal, that (1) s.739 did not apply where a taxpayer was not ordinarily resident in the UK at the time of the transfer. The words in s.739(1) and s.739(2) suggested that liability to tax could only arise with respect to transferors who were ordinarily resident in the UK and the fact that tax avoidance might arise from that interpretation was not enough to justify departing from the natural meaning of the words, and (2) the personal portfolio bonds taken out in the UK were exempt from the provisions of s.739 by virtue of s.741(a) in the same way as ordinary bonds. The fact that they allowed the purchaser to control and manage the investments comprised in the fund to which the bond was linked did not mean that W was using the bond structure to avoid tax on what was effectively income and gains from his own portfolio of investments. The bond holder had no legal or equitable interest in the underlying investments, merely a contractual right to the benefits promised by the policy, and whilst there was a difference between personal portfolio bonds and other types of bonds, the difference had nothing to do with tax or tax avoidance.

INLAND REVENUE COMMISSIONERS v. WILLOUGHBY [1997] 1 W.L.R. 1071, Lord Nolan, HL.

2943. Building societies–taxation of interest–retrospective legislating validating void regulations–right to challenge

See HUMAN RIGHTS: National & Provincial Building Society v. United Kingdom. §2756

2944. Business expansion scheme–eligibility for relief

[Income and Corporation Taxes Act 1988 s.291(1)(c).]

Held, that a taxpayer would not be eligible for business expansion relief where he had been connected with a company at any time during the period of five years since the company's incorporation, being the "relevant period" under the Income and Corporation Taxes Act 1988 s.291(1)(c).

WILD v. CANNAVAN (INSPECTOR OF TAXES) [1997] S.T.C. 966, Beldam, L.J., CA.

2945. Business expenses–legal expenses incurred defending Stock Exchange disciplinary proceedings–deduction allowed where expenses incurred to prevent destruction of business

[Income and Corporation Taxes Act 1970 s.130(a).]

Expenses incurred in defending allegations of misconduct in Stock Exchange Council disciplinary proceedings were deductible when computing profits from a trade for income tax purposes as an adverse ruling would have destroyed the business. S appealed against a ruling that legal expenses incurred by S in defending himself against allegations of misconduct in Stock Exchange Council disciplinary proceedings were deductible when computing profits from a trade for income tax purposes under Sch. D Case I under the Income and Corporation Taxes Act 1970 s.130(a).

Held, allowing the appeal, that the commissioner had found that an adverse ruling by the disciplinary committee would have destroyed S's business and it was solely in an attempt to avoid that result that S had incurred the expenses. Whilst the commissioner had not accepted that S was wholly unconcerned with his personal reputation, he had correctly found that it was not inevitable that the preservation of S's reputation formed a purpose of the expenditure, *Mallalieu v. Drummond* [1983] 2 A.C. 861, [1983] C.L.Y. 371 distinguished. On appeal, however, the judge held that not only had the expenses to be incurred wholly and exclusively for the purposes of S's trade, but that there had to be a sufficient connection between the expenditure and the carrying on of the trade, and this connection could not exist where expenditure was incurred in defending disciplinary proceedings involving rule breaches which fell outside the ordinary course of a trade. The basis of this decision could not stand, as the commissioner had not been asked to determine whether the expenditure had been incurred outside the ordinary course of trade and the judge was not entitled to take a new point not adduced before the tribunal of fact.

McKNIGHT (INSPECTOR OF TAXES) v. SHEPPARD [1997] S.T.C. 846, Nourse, L.J., CA.

2946. Company cars–car benefit–threshold mileage for insubstantial business use–whether apportionment required when more than one car provided in a year

[Income and Corporation Taxes Act 1988 Sch.6.]

C's employer made two cars available to him during the 1993/94 tax year, both of which shared the same basic cash equivalent value under the Income and Corporation Taxes Act 1988 Sch.6, Part I, Table A. C, whose business usage of the cars was insubstantial in terms of Sch.6 para.5(1), challenged the inspector's assessment of the charge for car benefit under s.157, which was based on proportionate mileage, contending that it fell to be ascertained by reference to the aggregate mileage from both cars and that the cash equivalent should not be increased. His argument was accepted on appeal to the general commissioners and the Crown appealed.

Held, allowing the appeal, that, because the basic cash equivalent of a car depended on a number of variable factors, including the car's original market value, its age and its cylinder capacity, the statutory provisions would only work if applied to each car individually. It was quite possible that, in the course of the same tax year, an employee's car would be replaced by one having a different basic cash equivalent, and the charge for car benefit would have to be calculated by reference to proportional mileage for insubstantial business use. It could not have been Parliament's intention that a different approach be adopted where the cars had the same basic cash equivalent.

HENWOOD (INSPECTOR OF TAXES) v. CLARKE [1997] S.T.C. 789, Ferris, J., Ch D.

2947. Company cars–tax payable could not be deducted as travelling expense

[Income and Corporation Taxes Act 1988 s.157, s.198(1).]

C appealed against the dismissal of his appeal against his tax assessment under the Income and Corporation Taxes Act 1988 s.157 in respect of his private use of a car provided by his employer. C contended that the tax assessment should be allowed under s.198(1) as a travelling expense or an expense wholly, exclusively and necessarily defrayed in the course of his duties.

Held, dismissing the appeal, that C's proposition that tax could be an expense for the purpose of calculating tax payable was circuitous, misconceived and obviously wrong.

CLARKv. BYE (INSPECTOR OF TAXES) [1997] S.T.C. 311, Sir Richard ScottV.C., Ch D.

2948. Double taxation–reliefs–Argentina

DOUBLE TAXATION RELIEF (TAXES ON INCOME) (ARGENTINA) ORDER 1997, SI 1997 1777; made under the Income and Corporation Taxes Act 1988 s.788. In force: July 22, 1997; £3.70.

This Order sets out the Convention between the Government of the United Kingdom and the Government of the Republic of Argentina for the avoidance of double taxation and the prevention of fiscal evasion with respect to taxes on income and capital.

2949. Double taxation–reliefs–Falkland Islands

DOUBLE TAXATION RELIEF (TAXES ON INCOME) (FALKLAND ISLANDS) ORDER 1997, SI 1997 2985; made under the Income and Corporation Taxes Act 1988 s.788. In force: in accordance with Sch. Art.29; £3.20.

This Order, which replaces the Arrangement set out in the Schedule to the Double Taxation Relief (Taxes on Income) (Falkland Islands) Order 1984 (SI 1984 363 as amended), sets out the Arrangement between the Government of the United Kingdom of Great Britain and Northern Ireland and the Government of the Falkland Islands for the avoidance of double taxation and the prevention of fiscal evasion with respect to taxes on income and capital gains.

2950. Double taxation–reliefs–Lesotho

DOUBLE TAXATION RELIEF (TAXES ON INCOME) (LESOTHO) ORDER 1997, SI 1997 2986; made under the Income and Corporation Taxes Act 1988 s.788. In force: in accordance with Sch. Art.29; £3.20.

This Order sets out the Convention between the Government of the United Kingdom of Great Britain and Northern Ireland and the Government of the Kingdom of Lesotho for the avoidance of double taxation and the prevention of fiscal evasion with respect to taxes on income and capital gains.

2951. Double taxation–reliefs–Lloyd's underwriters

LLOYD'S UNDERWRITERS (DOUBLE TAXATION RELIEF) REGULATIONS 1997, SI 1997 405; made under the Finance Act 1993 s.182. In force: March 14, 1997; £1.10.

These Regulations make provision for the application of double taxation relief in relation to the income tax liability of an individual who is a member of Lloyd's in respect of the profits or losses of his underwriting business.

2952. Double taxation–reliefs–Malaysia

DOUBLE TAXATION RELIEF (TAXES ON INCOME) (MALAYSIA) ORDER 1997, SI 1997 2987; made under the Income and Corporation Taxes Act 1988 s.788. In force: in accordance with Sch. Art.30; £3.70.

This Order, which replaces the Agreement set out in the Schedule to the Double Taxation Relief (Taxes on Income) (Malaysia) Order 1973 (SI 1973 1330 as amended by SI 1987 2056), sets out the Agreement between the Government of the United Kingdom of Great Britain and Northern Ireland and the Government of Malaysia for the avoidance of double taxation and the prevention of fiscal evasion with respect to taxes on income.

2953. Double taxation—reliefs—Singapore

DOUBLE TAXATION RELIEF (TAXES ON INCOME) (SINGAPORE) ORDER 1997, SI 1997 2988; made under the Income and Corporation Taxes Act 1988 s.788. In force: in accordance with Sch. Art.29; £4.15.

This Order, which replaces the Arrangement set out in the Schedule to the Double Taxation Relief (Taxes on Income) (Singapore) Order 1967 (SI 1967 483 as amended by SI 1978 787), sets out the Arrangement between the Government of the United Kingdom of Great Britain and Northern Ireland and the Government of the Republic of Singapore for the avoidance of double taxation and the prevention of fiscal evasion with respect to taxes on income and capital gains.

2954. Employee benefits—loans—interest rates

TAXES (INTEREST RATE) (AMENDMENT) REGULATIONS 1997, SI 1997 1681; made under the Finance Act 1989 s.178. In force: August 6, 1997; £0.65.

These Regulations amend the Taxes (Interest Rate) Regulations 1989 (SI 1989 1297) Reg.5 by substituting a new official rate of interest of 7.25 per cent for the purposes of the Income and Corporation Taxes Act 1988 s.160 which relates to the taxation of beneficial loans made to employees.

2955. Employment status—catering industry—profits under purported contract of employment were taxable as profits of trade and not as emolument

M provided catering services at a golf club pursuant to a contract under which she was responsible for purchasing and preparing the food and for recruiting and remunerating staff, while the club provided all the necessary equipment. The contract, which was termed a contract of employment, made M alone responsible for providing the catering and for all the proceeds arising therefrom. M appealed against an assessment to income tax on the profits from the catering business as profits arising or accruing from a trade under Case I of Schedule D, contending that she was employed under a contract of employment by which she was obliged to carry on the catering business and therefore the profits were an emolument of her employment, taxable under Schedule E.

Held, dismissing the appeal, that the question of whether M should be taxed under Schedule D or Schedule E was dependent entirely on the construction of the contractual documents and the circumstances in which they were signed and was a question of law alone. Whilst there was some indication M should be regarded as an employee in that her holidays were regulated, the club provided the equipment and premises and the language of employment was used in the documents, the evidence that M should be regarded as self-employed was overwhelming. She was in business on her own account as the club had no control over the menu, prices, staff, or how the business was conducted. The arrangements described in the contractual documents were incompatible with an employer/employee relationship and the profits realised had to be treated as the profits of trade and not as an emolument of employment.

McMANUS v. GRIFFITHS (INSPECTOR OF TAXES) [1997] S.T.C. 1089, Lightman, J., Ch D.

2956. Employment status—increase in earnings for freelance work—no commencement of "new profession" for purposes of Sch.D

Held, that a television producer who terminated his employment and increased his earnings for freelance work from small amounts to large amounts would not be classified as having commenced a new profession for the purposes of Sch.D income tax.

EDMUNDS v. COLEMAN (INSPECTOR OF TAXES) [1997] S.T.C. 1406, Lightman, J., Ch D.

2957. Foreign dividends–payments by agents

INCOME TAX (PAYING AND COLLECTING AGENTS) (AMENDMENT) REGULATIONS 1997, SI 1997 2705; made under the Income and Corporation Taxes Act 1988 s.118A, s.118E, s.118G, s.118H, s.118I, s.118J, s.118K. In force: December 9, 1997; £2.40.

These Regulations amend the Income Tax (Paying and Collecting Agents) Regulations 1996 (SI 1996 1780) by adding a new Reg.2A to Reg.2N relating to payments of foreign dividends by paying agents; a new Reg.3A specifying certain declarations to be made before exemptions from liability to account for tax on manufactured overseas dividends paid to a depository for a recognised clearing system can apply; a new Reg.6A and Reg.6B which provide for declarations by overseas dividend manufacturers in certain circumstances; and a new Reg.8A, Reg.8B and Reg.8C which relate to collecting agents. Further minor amendments are made to existing regulations.

2958. Foreign exchange–gains and losses–open ended investment company shares

EXCHANGE GAINS AND LOSSES (INSURANCE COMPANIES) (AMENDMENT) REGULATIONS 1997, SI 1997 1155; made under the Finance Act 1993 s.167, s.168. In force: April 28, 1997; £0.65.

These Regulations amend the Exchange Gains and Losses (Insurance Companies) Regulations 1994 (SI 1994 3231 as amended by SI 1996 673) Reg.7 by extending assets to which that Regulation applies so as to include shares in open ended investment companies incorporated in the United Kingdom denominated in a currency other than sterling.

2959. Forestry–land used for producing Christmas trees–land use not capable of amounting to woodlands or forestry purposes

[Income and Corporation Taxes Act 1988 s.53(4).]

J owned an area of land on which she grew trees which were sold as Christmas trees. Assessments were raised on her on the income from these activities. She appealed, contending that the income was exempt from tax under Income and Corporation Taxes Act 1988 s.53(4).

Held, dismissing the appeal, that J's activities met neither of the criteria for relief. The trees were being grown as Christmas trees not for timber.

JAGGERS (T/A SHIDE TREES) v. ELLIS (INSPECTOR OF TAXES) [1996] S.T.C. (SCD) 440, THK Everett, Sp Comm.

2960. Friendly societies–exemptions

FRIENDLY SOCIETIES (PROVISIONAL REPAYMENTS FOR EXEMPT BUSINESS) (AMENDMENT) REGULATIONS 1997, SI 1997 474; made under the Finance Act 1993 s.121. In force: March 20, 1997; £1.10.

These Regulations amend the Friendly Societies (Provisional Repayments for Exempt Business) Regulations 1993 (SI 1993 3112).

2961. Friendly societies–gilts–taxation of interest

FRIENDLY SOCIETIES (GILT-EDGED SECURITIES) (PERIODIC ACCOUNTING FOR TAX ON INTEREST) (AMENDMENT) REGULATIONS 1997, SI 1997 475; made under the Income and Corporation Taxes Act 1988 s.51B; and the Finance Act 1993 s.121. In force: March 20, 1997; £1.10.

These Regulations amend the Friendly Societies (Gilt-edged Securities) (Periodic Accounting for Tax on Interest) Regulations 1996 (SI 1996 21).

2962. **Friendly societies–transfer of assets**

FRIENDLY SOCIETIES (TAXATION OF TRANSFERS OF BUSINESS) (AMENDMENT) REGULATIONS 1997, SI 1997 472; made under the Income and Corporation Taxes Act 1988 s.463. In force: March 19, 1997; £1.10.

These Regulations amend the Friendly Societies (Taxation of Transfers of Business) Regulations 1995 (SI 1995 171).

2963. **Insurance companies–pensions business investment income**

INSURANCE COMPANIES (PENSION BUSINESS) (TRANSITIONAL PROVISIONS) (AMENDMENT) REGULATIONS 1997, SI 1997 2865; made under the Income and Corporation Taxes Act 1988 Sch.19AB para.4. In force: December 31, 1997; £0.65.

The Income and Corporation Taxes Act 1988 Sch.19AB provides for insurance companies carrying on investment business to be entitled to provisional repayments of tax on pension business investment income and that the Inland Revenue may make provision for the amount of such provisional payments to be reduced by a prescribed percentage for accounting periods ending within a transitional period. These Regulations further amend the Insurance Companies (Pension Business) (Transitional Provisions) Regulations 1992 (SI 1992 2326) by prescribing 7.5 per cent as the appropriate percentage for any accounting period ending after December 31, 1995, and before January 1, 1997.

2964. **International organisations–exemptions**

INTERNATIONAL ORGANISATIONS (MISCELLANEOUS EXEMPTIONS) ORDER 1997, SI 1997 168; made under the Income and Corporation Taxes Act 1988 s.582A. In force: January 27, 1997; £0.65.

This Order re-enacts the International Organisations (Miscellaneous Exemptions) Order 1991 (SI 1991 1694) and the International Organisations (Miscellaneous Exemptions) Order 1992 (SI 1992 2655) with amendments which are entirely of a drafting nature to take account of the legislative changes made by the Finance Act 1996.

2965. **Life insurance–reliefs–whether policies validly made before withdrawal of relief**

Life insurance premium relief was withdrawn as from March 13, 1984. On that date L&G purported to conclude a large number of policies on which it claimed deficiency payments. IRC sought to recover payments totalling £5.8 million. L&G appealed.

Held, adjourning the proceedings for agreement between the parties, that (1) a unilateral act on the part of L&G was not sufficient to complete the policies, *Rust v. Abbey Life Assurance Co Ltd* [1979] 2 Lloyd's Rep. 334, [1979] C.L.Y. 1345 applied and (2) the mere fact that a delay occurred in the actual receipt of funds by L&G did not of itself delay the making of a policy.

LEGAL & GENERAL ASSURANCE SOCIETY LTD v. INLAND REVENUE COMMISSIONERS; *sub nom.* LEGAL & GENERAL (UNIT ASSURANCE) LTD v. INLAND REVENUE COMMISSIONERS [1996] S.T.C. (SCD) 419, THK Everett, Sp Comm.

2966. **Manufactured dividends**

MANUFACTURED DIVIDENDS (TAX) REGULATIONS 1997, SI 1997 993; made under the Income and Corporation Taxes Act 1988 Sch.23A para.1, para.2, para.8. In force: July 1, 1997; £1.95.

These Regulations make provision for accounting for tax in relation to manufactured dividends on United Kingdom equities other than manufactured dividends paid by companies resident in the United Kingdom.

2967. Manufactured interest

MANUFACTURED INTEREST (TAX) REGULATIONS 1997, SI 1997 992; made under the Income and Corporation Taxes Act 1988 Sch.23A para.1, para.8. In force: July 1, 1997; £1.10.

These Regulations make provision in relation to accounting for tax by certain companies in respect of payments of manufactured interest on United Kingdom securities made to them by interest manufacturers who are not resident in the United Kingdom. The companies in question are those resident in the United Kingdom or companies that are not so resident but receive such payments for the purposes of a trade carried on by them in the United Kingdom through a branch or agency.

2968. Manufactured overseas dividends–Amendment No.1

INCOME TAX (MANUFACTURED OVERSEAS DIVIDENDS) (AMENDMENT) REGULATIONS 1997, SI 1997 988; made under the Income and Corporation Taxes Act 1988 Sch.23A para.1, para.4, para.8. In force: July 1, 1997; £1.10.

These Regulations make miscellaneous amendments to the Income Tax (Manufactured Overseas Dividends) Regulations 1993 (SI 1993 2004 as amended by SI 1995 1324, SI 1996 1229, SI 1996 2643 and SI 1997 987) and add a new Reg.9A which relates to the offsetting of tax by overseas dividend manufacturers who are not United Kingdom intermediaries.

2969. Manufactured overseas dividends–Amendment No.2

INCOME TAX (MANUFACTURED OVERSEAS DIVIDENDS) (AMENDMENT NO.2) REGULATIONS 1997, SI 1997 2706; made under the Income and Corporation Taxes Act 1988 Sch.23A para.1, para.4. In force: December 9, 1997; £0.65.

These Regulations amend the Income Tax (Manufactured Overseas Dividends) Regulations 1993 (SI 1993 2004) by omitting certain provisions of Reg.12 which relate to the tax treatment of manufactured overseas dividends paid to collecting agents that are representatives of foreign companies. The omitted provisions are rendered obsolete by the Income Tax (Paying and Collecting Agents) (Amendment) Regulations 1997 (SI 1997 2705).

2970. Open ended investment companies

OPEN-ENDED INVESTMENT COMPANIES (TAX) REGULATIONS 1997, SI 1997 1154; made under the Finance Act 1995 s.152. In force: April 28, 1997; £3.70.

These Regulations make provision for the tax treatment under the Tax Acts and the Taxation of Chargeable Gains Act 1992 of open-ended investment companies which are incorporated in the United Kingdom. The Regulations secure that the Tax Acts and the 1992 Act have effect in relation to open-ended investment companies in the same manner as the manner in which they have effect in relation to authorised unit trusts. The Regulations achieve this effect principally by making modification to those enactments.

2971. Open ended investment companies

OPEN-ENDED INVESTMENT COMPANIES (TAX) (AMENDMENT) REGULATIONS 1997, SI 1997 1715; made under the Finance Act 1995 s.152. In force: August 8, 1997; £0.65.

These Regulations make correctional and drafting amendments to the Open-ended Investment Companies (Tax) Regulations 1997 (SI 1997 1154).

2972. Partnerships–losses–individual claiming to carry on trade in partnership with companies–investment activity was not trade

[Income and Corporation Taxes Act 1988 s.385.]

R appealed against the dismissal of his claim for relief under the Income and Corporation Taxes Act 1988 s.385 for losses incurred in a trade previously carried on by two companies. The relief was claimed against income from investments.

Held, dismissing the appeal, that there was no evidence that R had been carrying on trade in partnership with the companies or that he was carrying on trade as an investor.

RIGBY v. SAMSON (INSPECTOR OF TAXES) [1997] S.T.C. 524 (Note), Rattee, J., Ch D.

2973. PAYE–reserve and auxiliary forces

INCOME TAX (EMPLOYMENTS) (AMENDMENT) REGULATIONS 1997, SI 1997 214; made under the Income and Corporation Taxes Act 1988 s.203. In force: April 1, 1997; £0.65.

These Regulations amend the Income Tax (Employments) Regulations 1993 (SI 1993 744) which make special provision for emoluments paid to members of the reserve and auxiliary forces. These Regulations amend the PAYE Regulations so as to provide that the reserve and auxiliary forces to which the Regulations apply are those specified in a substituted Regulation. The new paragraph takes account of the changes made by the enactment and implementation of the Reserve Forces Act 1996.

2974. Payments–payment in lieu of notice made under contractual provision was taxable under Sch. E as emolument from employment

[Income and Corporation Taxes Act 1988 s.19(1), s.148.]

For the purposes of the Income and Corporation Taxes Act 1988 s.19(1), there is a distinction to be drawn between payment in lieu of notice pursuant to the terms of an employment contract and redundancy payments. E appealed against a special commissioners' decision that it should have deducted income tax from payments made in lieu of notice to two former senior employees pursuant to the terms of their contracts of employment. The issue for the court was whether the payments fell within the Income and Corporation Taxes Act 1988 s.19(1), which provided that tax under Sch.E "shall be charged in respect of any office or employment on emoluments therefrom", or whether the provisions of s.148 applied. E argued that the payments were not taxable as they did not arise from employment, but rather from the disappearance of employment.

Held, dismissing the appeal, that a review of the authorities revealed that a payment in lieu of notice was an emolument "from" employment and was therefore taxable under Sch.E. A redundancy payment, which was not taxable, had to be treated as compensation for loss of status and could be regarded as a payment to relieve distress, but the same could not be said about a payment in lieu of notice, which was merely part of the agreed mechanism for bringing to an end an employee's contract of employment, although the distinction was a fine one, *Dale v. de Soissons* (1950) 32 T.C. 118, [1947-51] C.L.C. 4784 applied, *Mairs (Inspector of Taxes) v. Haughey* [1994] 1 A.C. 303, [1993] C.L.Y. 2275 distinguished.

EMI GROUP ELECTRONICS LTD v. COLDICOTT (INSPECTOR OF TAXES); *sub nom.* THORN EMI ELECTRONICS LTD v. COLDICOTT (INSPECTOR OF TAXES) [1997] S.T.C. 1372, Neuberger, J., Ch D.

2975. Pension schemes–transfer between schemes for tax avoidance purposes– Inland Revenue entitled to withdraw approval of original scheme

[Income and Corporation Taxes Act 1988 s.591B; Pension Schemes Act 1993.]

RWI applied for judicial review of a decision to withdraw approval of a pension scheme established in 1988 for the benefit of R, who effectively controlled RWI, and his wife. Under arrangements intended to enable R to extract the value accruing to him under the 1988 scheme so as to avoid the restriction on the way pension benefits could be taken, £900,000 was transferred to a new scheme in 1995. When R ceased to be a paid director of RWI, the IRC exercised its discretion under the Income and Corporation Taxes Act 1988 s.591B to withdraw approval of the 1988 scheme on the ground that the old scheme had been used to engineer a transfer of benefits into a scheme which was never intended to be an approved scheme. RWI contended that there was nothing in the administration of the old scheme which could have caused a loss of approval as the transfer had been properly made by the scheme trustees in accordance with their obligations under the Pension Schemes Act 1993.

Held, dismissing the application, that the IRC were entitled to consider the broad facts and not merely the administration of the old scheme. The principles laid down in *WT Ramsay Ltd v. Inland Revenue Commissioners* [1982] A.C. 300, [1981] C.L.Y. 1385 applied, and the legal nature of a transaction to which tax consequences attached fell to be considered by reference to the series or combination of transactions involved, rather than on an individual basis. On the facts, R had used a scheme comprising a series of transactions with the object of avoiding tax and so the IRC and the court were not restricted to considering the genuineness of each step or transaction, but had to look at the whole scheme. Although R's wife's interest was affected by the decision, her interest was minor and did not form a compelling reason for altering the decision.

R. v. INLAND REVENUE COMMISSIONERS, *ex p.* ROUX WATERSIDE INN LTD [1997] S.T.C. 781, Tucker, J., QBD.

2976. Public revenue dividends—interest rates

TAXES (INTEREST RATE) (AMENDMENT NO.2) REGULATIONS 1997, SI 1997 2707; made under the Finance Act 1989 s.178. In force: December 9, 1997; £0.65.

These Regulations, which amend the Taxes (Interest Rate) Regulations 1989 (SI 1989 1297), make provision for the rate of interest applicable for the purposes of the Income and Corporation Taxes Act 1988 s.118F.

2977. Self assessment—transitional relief—prescribed amounts

INCOME TAX (SCHEDULE 22 TO THE FINANCE ACT 1995) (PRESCRIBED AMOUNTS) REGULATIONS 1997, SI 1997 1158; made under the Finance Act 1995 Sch.22 para.1, para.2, para.3, para.5, para.6, para.7, para.9, para.10. In force: April 25, 1997; £1.10.

These Regulations prescribe amounts under various provisions of the Finance Act 1995 Sch.22 which contains rules designed to prevent the exploitation of the transitional relief provisions for self assessment in the Finance Act 1994 Sch.20.

2978. Stock lending—manufactured payments—consequential amendments

STOCK LENDING AND MANUFACTURED PAYMENTS (REVOCATIONS AND AMENDMENTS) REGULATIONS 1997, SI 1997 987; made under the Income and Corporation Taxes Act 1988 s.51B, s.129, s.737, Sch.23A para.1, Sch.23A para.8. In force: July 1, 1997; £1.10.

These Regulations revoke certain Regulations, and amend other Regulations, relating to stock lending arrangements and manufactured payments. The revocations and amendments reflect changes to simplify the tax treatment of stock lending arrangements and manufactured payments made by the Finance Act 1997 Sch.10.

2979. Tax planning—applicability of Ramsay principle to assignment of dividend

[Income and Corporation Taxes Act 1988 s.470.]

M, who was resident in the UK, owned shares in an Irish company. He transferred the shares to a settlement, the trustee of which was a Guernsey company. M was the beneficiary. The consideration for the transfer was met by the payment of a dividend to an assignee of the trustee, a UK company associated with M's tax consultant. The dividend was then paid on, less commission and fees, to the trustee. M was assessed to tax under Income and Corporation Taxes Act 1988 s.470. The Northern Ireland Court of Appeal decided, by a majority, that the principle in *WT Ramsay Ltd v. Inland Revenue Commissioners* [1982] A.C. 300, [1981] C.L.Y. 1385 did not apply, but remitted the case to the Special Commissioner with a direction to uphold the assessment under s.470. The Revenue appealed against the dismissal of its claim based on the *Ramsay* principle. M cross-appealed against the remittal to the Special Commissioner.

Held, allowing the appeal, that (1) the *Ramsay* principle applied; (2) the assignment of the dividend was a step in the composite transaction inserted with no commercial purpose and was to be disregarded *Furniss (Inspector of Taxes) v. Dawson* [1984] 1 A.C. 474, [1984] C.L.Y. 470, and (3) the amount received by the trustee was income and was properly assessed under s.478. The issues raised by the cross-appeal did not fall for decision.

INLAND REVENUE COMMISSIONERS v. McGUCKIAN [1997] 1 W.L.R. 991, Lord Browne-Wilkinson, HL.

2980. Trusts–pension funds–tax planning–dividend on purchase of own shares– determination of "abnormal amount" for purposes of Income and Corporation Taxes Act 1988 s.709(4)

[Income and Corporation Taxes Act 1988 s.703(1), s.704A, s.709(1).]

U was the trustee of an approved pension fund and so was exempt from income tax. It owned shares in TSM, a property development company. TSM bought its own shares from USS for £2.7 million, and U claimed a resulting credit of £0.8 million. The Revenue raised an assessment of £3.4 million on U to counter an alleged tax advantage from the receipt of an abnormal amount by way of dividend under Income and Corporation Taxes Act 1988 s.704A. U's appeal to the special commissioner was allowed. The Revenue appealed.

Held, allowing the appeal, that (1) an exempt body can obtain a relief from tax within s.709(1), *Sheppard (Trustees of the Woodlands Trust) v. Inland Revenue Commissioners* (No.2) [1993] S.T.C. 240, [1993] C.L.Y. 2259 not followed; (2) in deciding whether an abnormal amount by way of dividend had been received pursuant to s.709(4) the gross amount, including tax credits, should be considered, and (3) whether the statutory defence under s.703(1) was applicable was a matter for the tribunal to which the case was remitted.

INLAND REVENUE COMMISSIONERS v. UNIVERSITIES SUPERANNUATION SCHEME LTD [1997] S.T.C. 1, Sir John Vinelott, Ch D.

2981. Unit trusts–distribution of interest

AUTHORISED UNIT TRUSTS (INTEREST DISTRIBUTIONS) (QUALIFYING INVESTMENTS) ORDER 1997, SI 1997 212; made under the Income and Corporation Taxes Act 1988 s.468L. In force: February 25, 1997; £1.10.

This Order amends the Income and Corporation Taxes Act 1988 s.468L (authorised unit trusts: interest distributions) by adding to the list of "qualifying investments" in subsection (9) of that section qualifying shares in an open-ended investment company which is incorporated in the United Kingdom. The Order also inserts additional subsections in s.468L containing definitions of "open-ended investment company" and other relevant terms

2982. Vocational training–reliefs

VOCATIONAL TRAINING (PUBLIC FINANCIAL ASSISTANCE AND DISENTITLEMENT TO TAX RELIEF) (AMENDMENT) REGULATIONS 1997, SI 1997 635; made under the Finance Act 1991 s.32. In force: April 6, 1997; £0.65.

These Regulations amend the Vocational Training (Public Financial Assistance and Disentitlement to Tax Relief) Regulations 1992 (SI 1992 734) by substituting new definitions of the expressions "training payment" and "training provider".

2983. Vocational training–reliefs

VOCATIONAL TRAINING (TAX RELIEF) (AMENDMENT) REGULATIONS 1997, SI 1997 661; made under the Finance Act 1991 s.32, s.33. In force: April 6, 1997; £1.10.

In addition to other minor amendments, a new Regulation making provision with respect to appeals against the Board's decision on an annual claim is added and new provisions are made with respect to the period for which records are to be retained.

2984. Articles

A bad share day? *(Daron H. Gunson)*: Tax. P. 1997, Jan, 10-11. (Circumstances in which losses on shares can be set against income tax liability, including requirement that shares were subscribed for, relevant disposals of shares, rules for making claims and potential difficulties).

A job with a home *(Arthur Sellwood)*: Tax. 1997, 138(3591), 488-490. (Tax treatment of living accommodation provided by employer, Sch.E liability for benefit in kind and exemptions for representative and other specified employees).

A share in the business *(Colin Chamberlain)*: T.P.T. 1997, 18(7), 49-51, 56. (Conditions of approval and tax reliefs associated with savings related share option schemes, profit sharing schemes and company share option schemes which are open to all employees).

Allowable or not? *(John T. Newth)*: Tax. 1997, 139(3624), 653-655. (Tax allowability of legal and accountancy fees, impact of introduction of self assessment, and professional fee protection insurance).

An unkindly benefit? *(Wilma Teviotdale* and *Susan Thompson)*: Tax. 1997, 139(3616), 453-455. (Inequality in taxation of company cars and taxation of private usage of business cars used by self employed).

Changing times for transfers of assets abroad *(Phillip Dearden)*: Tax. P. 1997, May, 14-16. (Provision to stop UK residents avoiding income tax liability by transfers whereby income becomes payable to non residents whilst transferor retains power to enjoy income and retrospective measure affecting expatriates).

Dead or alive? *(David Jeffery)*: Tax. 1997, 138(3597), 686-688. (Income tax liability of non-resident UK visitors and those leaving UK to reside abroad under available accommodation rule, applicable time limits and residence status requirements).

Employed and self employed: the differences *(Emma Chamberlain* and *Judith Freedman)*: Tax. P. 1997, Jun, 23-25. (Dichotomy between income tax treatment under Sch.E and Sch.D, allowable expenses, NI rules and classification issues).

Employee expenses *(Tim Good)*: Tax. P. 1997, May, 27-28. (Tax treatment of expenses reimbursed to employees, responsibilities of employers, employees and third parties and correct completion of form P11D).

From voluntary to statutory *(Philip Fisher)*: Tax. 1997, 138(3597), 678-680, 682. (SI 2631 1996 and SP 5/96 on scope and operation of PAYE Settlement Agreements for tax on employee benefits and expense payments which replace annual voluntary settlements).

Home is where the work is *(John T. Newth)*: T.P.T. 1997, 18(11), 81-84. (Tax implications of working from home, employment status issues, allowable expenses and self assessment record-keeping requirements).

Income tax–the "one-estate election" and divisions of property: Farm T.B. 1997, 12(2), 11-12. (Rules allowing income and expenditure relating to several properties on one estate to be aggregated for income tax purposes, implications for farm property and whether to make further election on change of ownership).

Interest: the new regime *(James Rouse)*: Tax. P. 1997, Mar, 12-14. (Interest on tax paid late under self assessment applying to liabilities for 1996-97 and later years, late payments on account and problems relating to carry back).

Life after profit-related pay *(Marian Gallagher)*: C.S.R. 1997, 21 (14), 110-111. (Effect of phasing out of tax relief on profit-related pay schemes over three year period and options for replacement).

Maximise your trading loss relief *(Stanley Dencher)*: Tax. 1997, 138(3593), 554, 556-557. (Tax treatment of self employed trading losses sustained during transitional period from preceding to current year basis and worked examples showing computation for "old" traders).

Not a finished product yet *(Paul Aplin)*: Tax. 1997, 139(3611), 320-321. (Tax planning options for Business Expansion Scheme shareholders utilising qualifying periods, trading provisions and qualifying share disposals).

Of much greater interest.. *(Tim Bash)*: Tax. 1997, 139(3625), 675-676. (Effects of self assessment provisions repealing charge to interest on tax assessments under the Taxes Management Act 1970 s.88 from April 6, 1998 and replacing it with charge to interest under s.86, with examples).

Payments on account *(Malcolm Gunn)*: Tax. 1997, 138(3588), 394-396. (Payment on account rules for self assessment, whether to claim reduction in payments due, penalties for incorrect returns and 1996-97 transitional arrangements).

Second-class citizens *(Robert W. Maas)*: Accountancy 1997, 120(1248), 82. (Whether taxpayers not subject to self assessment have fewer rights, with particular reference to PAYE enquiries and claims by children and pensioners for tax deducted at source).

Self assessment (SA): residence rulings and domicile: I.R.T.B. 1997, 29(Jun), 425-427. (Inland Revenue guidance for taxpayers required to certify residence status and domicile in tax return).

Self assessment bulletin – March 1997: Tax. P. 1997, Mar, 46-47. (Employers' liability to provide employees with information about fixed profit car schemes and P11D information, availability of dispensations and PAYE settlement agreements, penalties and compliance timetable).

Self assessment: partnerships: transitional issues: I.R.T.B. 1997, 30(Aug), 450-456. (Frequently asked questions and Inland Revenue answers about transition to tax self assessment including allowances and reliefs, returning accounts information, overlap relief and returning details of taxed income, with worked examples).

Self-assessment: employers' responsibilities *(Richard Baron)*: Tax. P. 1997, Oct, 16-17. (Including travel and subsistence expenses, PAYE settlement agreements, employee records and third party benefits).

Self assessment legislation – Finance Act 1996: I.R.T.B. 1997, 27(Feb), Supp Spe 1-14. (Amending provisions in 1996 Act on self assessment, Inland Revenue guidance booklets currently available and corrections to text of SAT1 and SAT2).

Self assessment returns: Tax. P. 1997, Apr, 34. (Considerations when dealing with self-assessment return including quantification of capital losses, employment supplementary page, self-employment supplementary page and notification of chargeability to tax).

Self-employed sub-contractors and the Inland Revenue *(Liz Polding)*: Cons. Law 1997, 8(2), 45-47. (Criteria applied by Inland Revenue and Contributions Agency in assessing whether worker is self employed and methods of avoiding reclassification of self employed subcontractors as employees).

Statement of Practice SP4/85: relief for interest on loans used to buy land occupied for partnership business purposes: I.R.T.B. 1997, 29(Jun), 437-438. (Revised Inland Revenue guidance on treatment of interest paid by trading entity on loan taken out by partner or director to purchase land or property occupied rent free by business).

Surplus to requirements *(Arthur Sellwood)*: Tax. 1997, 139(3608), 241-244. (Development of tax rules on redundancy and termination payments with reference to decided cases, Revenue Statements of Practice and statutes).

Taking commissions and cashbacks *(Anne Redston)*: T.P.T. 1997, 18(13), 97-99. (Inland Revenue Statement of Practice SP5/95 on its approach to commission rebates, cashbacks or discounts offered in respect of financial or other services).

Tax and NI on employee shares *(John Jones)*: Tax J. 1997, 402, 7-8. (PAYE and NI treatment of unapproved share awards to employees following Inland Revenue and Contributions Agency rule changes and share valuation requirements).

Tax nothings: is there a solution? *(Daron Gunson)*: Tax. P. 1997, Oct, 24-25. (Anomalies flowing from disallowance of certain items of loss or expenditure for tax purposes and proposals for
reform).

The income tax treatment of lump-sum termination payments *(Donald Pearce-Crump)*: Co. Acc. 1997, 138, 33-35, 39-40. (Types of payments arising out of termination of employment taxed under ICTA 1988 s.148).

The tribunal matures *(Christopher Wallworth)*: Tax. 1997, 138(3595), 611, 613-614. (General Commissioners' role under self assessment, revised grounds of appeal against automatic penalties and new powers to supervise investigations).

The United Kingdom's non-resident landlord scheme *(Robert W. Maas)*: T.P.I.R. 1997, 24(5), 18-20. (Effect of self assessment on tax treatment of non-residents' income from UK property).

Tradeable assets *(Aparna Nathan)*: Tax J. 1997, 415, 15-17. (Sch.E income tax liability arising under s.144A and s.203 in respect of employee benefits having tradeable asset status).

INDUSTRY

2985. Coal industry–British Coal Corporation–change of quorum

BRITISH COAL CORPORATION (CHANGE OF QUORUM) REGULATIONS 1997, SI 1997 1588; made under the Coal Industry Nationalisation Act 1946 s.2. In force: July 1, 1997; £0.65.

These Regulations amend the Coal Industry Nationalisation (National Coal Board) Regulations 1946 (SR & O 1946 1094) Reg.4 (as amended by The British Coal Corporation (Change of Quorum) Regulations 1995 (SI 1995 1506)) by substituting a quorum of two for the quorum of three required at a meeting of the British Coal Corporation.

2986. Deep sea mining–Guernsey

DEEP SEA MINING (TEMPORARY PROVISIONS) ACT 1981. (GUERNSEY) ORDER 1997, SI 1997 2978; made under the Deep Sea Mining (Temporary Provisions) Act 1981 s.1, s.18. In force: January 19, 1998; £1.10.

This Order applies the Deep Sea Mining (Temporary Provisions) Act 1981 s.1 to bodies incorporated under the laws of the Bailiwick of Guernsey and extends s.1, s.14, s,17 and s.18(1), with certain modifications, to the Bailiwick of Guernsey.

2987. Deep sea mining–Jersey

DEEP SEA MINING (TEMPORARY PROVISIONS) ACT 1981 (JERSEY) ORDER 1997, SI 1997 2979; made under the Deep Sea Mining (Temporary Provisions) Act 1981 s.1, s.18. In force: January 19, 1998; £1.10.

This Order applies the Deep Sea Mining (Temporary Provisions) Act 1981 s.1 to bodies incorporated under the laws of the Bailiwick of Jersey and extends s.1, s.14, s,17 and s.18(1), with certain modifications, to the Bailiwick of Jersey.

2988. Welsh Development Agency Act 1997 (c.37)

This Act increases from £950 million to £1,350 million the financial limit of the Welsh Development Agency in the Welsh Development Agency Act 1975 s.18(3).

This Act received Royal Assent on March 21, 1997 and comes into force on May 21, 1997.

INFORMATION TECHNOLOGY

2989. Articles

Back to basics: forming a contract: IT L.T. 1997, 5(2), 6-8. (Formation of IT contracts, covering problems arising from heads of agreement, verbal arrangements and sending contract after work is completed).

Doing business on the Internet: exploring new markets *(Simon Jones)*: P.L.C. 1997, 8(2), 17-24. (Advantages for businesses in using Internet, how to set up and design web site, establishing domain name, protecting material against copyright infringement, legal issues of defamation, consumer protection and data protection).

Preparing for the millennium timebomb *(Michael Webster)*: P.P.M. 1997, 15(1), 9-11. (Effect of year 2000 on information systems, advice to businesses on preventative measures to minimise effect and legal implications of contractual or fiduciary liabilities).

Protecting your name from the cyber-squatters *(Nick J. Gardner)*: Eur. Counsel 1997, 2(2), 39-45. (Techniques for protecting Internet domain names; includes example contract terms and steps to registration).

Put IT into practice *(John Jenkins)*: L.S.G. 1997, 94(22), 22, 24. (Law Society Research and Policy Planning Unit survey of solicitors' computer use and role Law Society should play in providing IT support).

Recovering overheads and lost production costs in I.T. contracts *(John Warchus)*: C.T.L.R. 1997, 3(5), 250-253. (Relevance to IT industry of decision that aggrieved party prevented from conducting business at full capacity by breach of contract may be compensated for loss of gross profit, including fixed overheads).

Tariff classification: high tech issues *(Andrew Hart)*: De Voil I.T.I. 1997, 13, 16-18. (Problems experienced by European Commission Customs Service in fixing customs tariff headings for new information technology products including computer networking equipment).

The protection of multimedia products through the European Community's Directive on the legal protection of databases *(Stephan Beutler)*: Ent. L.R. 1996, 7(8), 317-328.

The quiet revolutionaries *(David Hall)*: Legal Bus. 1997, 75(Jun), 99-100, 102. (Changes in methods of information provision and role of information staff in law firms brought about by implementation of new technology, with table of leading city firms and products they use).

To regulate or not to regulate: prevalence and impact of a virtual society *(R.W. Van Kralingen* and *J.E.J. Prins)*: EDI L.R. 1997, 4(2), 91-111. (Need for legal system to adapt to changing world brought about by information and communication technology).

Turn on to intranets *(Nigel Young)*: Lawyer 1997, 11(22), 19. (Advantages and economic efficiency of setting up internal networks with Internet standards and tools to communicate within law firms).

2990. Books

Campbell, Dennis–International Information Technology Law. International Property. Hardback: £75.00. ISBN 0-471-96871-4. Chancery Wiley Law Publications.

Powell, Mark; Gaster, Jens–Legal Protection of Databases in Europe. Current EC Legal Developments Series. Paperback: £95.00. ISBN 0-406-03700-0. Butterworth Law.

Smith, Graham J.H.–Internet Law and Regulation. Hardback: £95.00. ISBN 0-7520-0468-9. FT Law & Tax.